A LEXICON OF GREEK PERSONAL NAMES

THE BRITISH ACADEMY

A LEXICON OF GREEK PERSONAL NAMES

EDITED BY
P. M. FRASER
AND
E. MATTHEWS
WITH THE COLLABORATION OF MANY SCHOLARS

VOLUME IV

MACEDONIA
THRACE
NORTHERN REGIONS OF THE BLACK SEA

EDITORS
P. M. FRASER
E. MATTHEWS

ASSISTANT EDITOR
R. W. V. CATLING

CLARENDON PRESS · OXFORD

This book has been printed digitally and produced in a standard specification in order to ensure its continuing availability

OXFORD
UNIVERSITY PRESS

Great Clarendon Street, Oxford OX2 6DP

Oxford University Press is a department of the University of Oxford. It furthers the University's objective of excellence in research, scholarship, and education by publishing worldwide in

Oxford New York

Auckland Cape Town Dar es Salaam Hong Kong Karachi Kuala Lumpur Madrid Melbourne Mexico City Nairobi New Delhi Shanghai Taipei Toronto

With offices in

Argentina Austria Brazil Chile Czech Republic France Greece Guatemala Hungary Italy Japan South Korea Poland Portugal Singapore Switzerland Thailand Turkey Ukraine Vietnam

Oxford is a registered trade mark of Oxford University Press in the UK and in certain other countries

Published in the United States by Oxford University Press Inc., New York

Reprinted 2008

ISBN 978-0-19-927333-1

Acknowledgements

As always, we wish to repeat our debt to the many individuals whose work in the 1970s and 1980s created the large body of material which constitutes the greater part of the project's archive of more than 400,000 records. In the pre-electronic age, their work involved the preparation of a seemingly infinite number of fiches, which line our offices and are still occasionally consulted in moments of uncertainty. For this volume, we think especially of the late J. M. R. Cormack for Greek Macedonia; F. Papazoglu, who undertook to record the material from Macedonia in the former Jugoslavia, with the assistance of L. Jaguš̌t; of D. M. Pippidi and E. Doruţiu Boilă for Rumania; J. Brashinsky for the amphora stamps from Chersonesos.

Transforming the assembled material into an edited volume is, of course, a separate and demanding task, and in this volume we have dealt with regions of such diversity that we have been particularly reliant on the collaboration of scholars specializing in the regions in question. We wish to give especial acknowledgement to the following scholars, who have read and commented on files, or provided assistance and advice on topographical and bibliographical matters, across a whole region.

Macedonia and Thrace

Centre for Greek and Roman Antiquity, National Hellenic Research Foundation, Athens

Director: M. B. Hatzopoulos

A. Tataki (Macedonia Project)

L. D. Loukopoulou (Thrace Project)

M. Ricl, Belgrade University

Scythia Minor

A. Avram, Maine University, Le Mans

Black Sea coast

†J. Vinogradov, Russian Academy of Sciences, Moscow

Numismatics

W. Stancomb

We thank them for their generosity with their scholarship, and their uniquely informed judgments on difficult matters of interpretation. It goes without saying that any remaining errors and omissions are our responsibility.

Macedonia and Thrace

This volume brings to fruition a long and valued collaboration with colleagues at the Centre for Greek and Roman Antiquity (K.E.R.A.), the National Hellenic Research Foundation, under the direction of M. Hatzopoulos, who has generously authorized access to the resources of the Centre. A. Tataki read and commented on all the files covering Greek Macedonia; L. D. Loukopoulou and S. Psoma and their colleagues made available to us an advance version of their forthcoming corpus of Aegean Thrace, at some cost to their own work schedule. For Macedonia within the former Jugoslavia, we have received much needed guidance on topographical and many other matters from M. Ricl, who has also allowed us to draw on her knowledge of unpublished material in Belgrade.

Scythia Minor

A. Avram has collaborated for several years over the material from this region. More recently he has read and commented on our files from the whole Black Sea region.

Black Sea coast

Throughout the 1990s, J. Vinogradov was an active collaborator, examining all the files of the colonial cities on the north Black Sea coast. He drew our attention to new readings of inscriptions proposed by S. Tokhtas'ev (St Petersburg), with whom we have had recent fruitful exchanges. S. Saprykin (Moscow) reviewed our material from Chersonesos, and assisted with local publications.

Numismatics

We have benefited from the collaboration of W. Stancomb, notably on the coins of the Black Sea area.[1] For the dating of the coinage of Abdera we were fortunate to have access to the chronology established in the doctoral study and forthcoming publication of Dr K. Chryssanthaki (Paris) made available, with Dr Chryssanthaki's permission, through colleagues at K.E.R.A.

For enabling us to cite names from unpublished inscriptions from Thrace in Turkey, we thank M. Sayar (Istanbul); and E. Voutyras and K. Sismanidis (Thessaloniki) for permission to cite the names from a new inscription from Dikaia in Macedonia. A. Łajtar (Warsaw) kindly sent us a copy of his prosopography of Byzantion. K. Hallof, Director of *Inscriptiones Graecae*, Berlin-Brandenburgische Akademie der Wissenschaften, has continued to respond generously to appeals for help and advice.

It would be paradoxical to acknowledge debts for access to unpublished material without also acknowledging the huge debt a project such as the Lexicon owes to the publications of others, especially to editors of epigraphical corpora and the teams collaborating on the *Bulletin Épigraphique*, *Supplementum Epigraphicum Graecum* and *L'Année Épigraphique* whose works make our own task so much more manageable.

Of Lexicon staff, Ilias Arnaoutoglou, in his period as an Assistant Editor, worked on updating all files in this volume, and has continued to inform us of new discoveries and publications since moving to a post at the Research Centre for the History of Greek Law, at the Academy of Athens. Jason Zerdin as IT Assistant managed and developed our data and computer programs. Advice on our core database, typesetting and web-based systems has come, as before, from J. C. Moffett of the Ashmolean Museum, S. Rahtz of Oxford University Computing Services and Y. Haralambous of the École Nationale Supérieure des Télécommunications de Bretagne.

In 2003, the British Academy formally ceased, after 30 years, to be the main funding body of the Lexicon, though we continue as a British Academy Research Project. Core funding now comes from the Arts and Humanities Research Council (A.H.R.C.), whose support we take this opportunity to acknowledge, both for this volume and for our ongoing work on the first volume of the onomasticon of Asia Minor, for which we have also received grants from the J. F. Costopoulos Foundation. It is a particular pleasure to record, once more, the support, moral as well as financial, which we have enjoyed for over a decade from the Archaeological Society at Athens and its General Secretary B. Petrakos, through whose good offices we have also received a substantial benefaction from the National Bank of Greece.

[1] Mr Stancomb wishes to acknowledge the assistance he has received from M. Amandry (Bibliothèque Nationale, Paris); Dr D. Draganov (Archaeological Museum, Ruse, Bulgaria); S. Kovalenko (Dept. of Coins, Pushkin Museum, Moscow); Dr U. Peter (Griechisches Münzwerk, Berlin); Dr E. Stolyarik (American Numismatic Society, New York); Dr B. Weisser (Münzkabinett, Staatliche Museen, Berlin)

Although overall the geographical method and chronological framework of this volume remain essentially the same as those of its predecessors, the material has been differently treated in some significant respects, and, in particular, a different chronological upper limit has been applied in the entries relating to Byzantion. These anomalies have been imposed on us by the nature of the evidence, as, we hope, the following pages indicate.*

The contents of the volume

In the vast region covered by the volume, from Mount Olympus through Macedonia, Thrace and the western and northern shores of the Black Sea, the hellenization of the non-Greek element, indicated in the present context by the use of the Greek language for non-Greek names, had been in progress from the classical period onwards. During the Roman period the region passed through numerous fundamental political and social changes, the product of the establishment of Roman provincial rule in the Balkans, which resulted in intermittent alterations of provincial definition and consequent nomenclature: of the area covered by this volume, only the northern shore of the Black Sea, east of Tyras, was largely excepted from this administrative development.

The whole process of Romanization, especially from the time of Trajan's campaigns onwards, and, in due course, the establishment of the new capital at Constantinople, affected every aspect of society; the impact on individuals, their social environment and hence their names, were all part of this universal change, and we have had to modify our procedures to take account of this new world. This wide-ranging metamorphosis is discussed, in so far as it is relevant to the *Lexicon*, under separate headings below.

Provincial divisions and nomenclature

The first region, as the *Lexicon* continues its journey northwards from Thessaly, is Macedonia, understood as extending from the Vale of Tempe in the south to the Scardus range in the north, and to the river Nestos in the east. This region presented two possible topographical patterns for the *Lexicon*. The first, historically the best adapted to the overall growth of Macedonia as a nation-state was by the use of the traditional tribal regions, approximately twenty in all, from the classical period onwards dominated by urban communities, which formed the focal point of social and administrative development, after the whole region had become subject to Roman rule. The alternative was to start at mid-point of our journey, and take as our basic topographical formula the Macedonia which formed the Roman province of that name, divided first into four, and, some twenty years later, into six 'parts', *μερίδες*, each with its own Roman administration and accompanying military units. The decision to adopt the first alternative has enabled us to codify the name-structure of far smaller units than would have been possible by the adoption of the second, though the latter would certainly have been easier to implement and perhaps presented a more readily accessible corpus of material for the user in terms of topography.

In determining how far to extend our boundaries for this volume, we decided to adopt the divide provided by the Scardus range (the modern Stara Planina) and the upper course of the Danube, westwards of Ratiaria and the river Almus (the Lom of today).[1] The Lexicon therefore does not include the Romanized provinces of Dacia, Moesia Superior, Pannonia and Dalmatia (except for the Grecized coastal zone which was included in volume IIIA).

The continental area thus excluded had no single name before the imperial period; it was scantily and variously populated by a large number of tribes, the names of which are known mostly from Strabo,[2] Pliny and Ptolemy, and from Latin inscriptions of the imperial period. The inhabitants were racially predominantly Scythian, Thracian/Getic, Illyrian, Dardanian and Celtic, of whose languages no significant remains survive except for place-names and personal names almost entirely attested in Latin, not Greek, documents. The first two of these, the Scythians and Thracians, were known in general terms to Herodotus and Thucydides, and the area was recognised as tribal, without civic centres, as, in effect, empty of all except such loosely defined tribes and their sub-divisions.[3] And so it remained, on the whole, through the Macedonian and hellenistic periods, until it came within the administrative scope of the imperial system. It will be of assistance here to describe briefly the changes in names and boundaries that the Balkan provinces underwent, since that has affected the names we have used for the regions included in the *Lexicon*, and consequently the local attribution of individuals resident in them.

The Roman authorities found it necessary to alter and subdivide the provinces on both sides of the Danube as military requirements, dictated by tribal movements and

---

* Citations which occur in abbreviated form can be found in the List of Abbreviations.

[1] The significance of this divide is summarised by A. Mócsy in *Pannonia and Upper Moesia* (London, 1974) pp. 63 f. and 260. Of its consequences for the onomastic evidence he writes (63): 'There is only sporadic epigraphic evidence for names, and to make matters more difficult, it is not always clear whether the non-Latin names on the inscriptions are those of native local inhabitants or of natives of some other Balkan area.' We confine ourselves here to quoting the relevant ancient literary sources, and for details refer to Mócsy' s work and to that of J. J. Wilkes, *Dalmatia* (London, 1969). A massive amount of relevant material is already quoted by M. I. Rostovtsev, *Social and Economic History of the Roman Empire*^{2} (Oxford, 1963) pp. 641 f. See also F. Papazoglu, *The Central Balkan Tribes in pre-Roman Times* transl. M. Stansfield-Popović (Amsterdam, 1978).

[2] Strabo 304, speaking of the consequences of the defeat of Boirebistas, says *οἱ δὲ διαδεξάμενοι τὴν ἀρχὴν ἐς πλείω μέρη διέστησαν, καὶ δὴ καὶ νῦν, ἡνίκα ἔπεμψεν ἐπ' αὐτοὺς στρατείαν ὁ Σεβαστὸς Καῖσαρ, εἰς πέντε μερίδας, τότε δὲ εἰς τέσσαρας διεστῶτες ἐτύγχανον· οἱ μὲν οὖν τοιοῦτοι μερισμοὶ πρόσκαιροι καὶ ἄλλοτ' ἄλλοι.*

[3] Hdt. iv 1-144, his *Σκυθικοὶ λόγοι*, especially ch. 93: *οἱ δὲ Γέται πρὸς ἀγνωμοσύνην τραπόμενοι αὐτίκα ἐδουλώθησαν, Θρηίκων ἐόντες ἀνδρηιότατοι καὶ δικαιότατοι*. Cf. Thuc. ii 96. 1, on the campaign of Sitalkes in 429/8.

revolts, demanded, and since boundaries were uncertain and moveable, it was, as Strabo indicates,[4] difficult for ancient geographers to give clearly-cut lines of demarcation. At the western end of the line, Dalmatia, though tribal in structure, was, apart from the Greek colonial area on the coast, entirely Romanized. The region east of the Drina, which was originally (like Illyricum) described only in tribal geographical terms such as 'Dardania', was formed into a large province, originally called simply 'Moesia',[5] which stretched from the eastern frontier of Dalmatia, approximately along the line of the Drina (w. of Belgrade/ Singidunum) to the Black Sea, between the Haemus range and the Danube.[6] In A.D. 86 Domitian divided Moesia into two, Superior and Inferior, roughly along the line of the Kiambros (Cibrica) river,[7] that is east of Ratiaria. As for the Dacians, the full effect of Roman conquest was not felt until the campaigns of Trajan from A.D. 101 to *c.* 105, by which the Romanization of the whole Balkan area was assured, though local rebellions by the native population on both sides of the Danube led to further military intervention by Marcus Aurelius, with demographic consequences. In *c.* 274, Roman legions were withdrawn from Dacia Traiana by Aurelian, who created a new province out of most of Moesia Inferior, which he called Dacia Ripensis, and at the same time Moesia Superior became Moesia Prima.[8]

A good deal of our onomastic evidence belongs to this later phase of Roman settlement and administration. Numerous legions were settled on the land in the whole region, and the legionaries, veterans and their families, whose origins were very varied and included a considerable oriental element, formed a substantial part of the population, residents of *vici* and *canabae*, together with time-expired auxilia etc. and Italian traders, and gave it its essentially Romanized character, with Latin as the *koine*. This sedentary population was early increased by very substantial transferences of population, consisting of Daci-Getae from north to south of the Danube, which fundamentally affected the demographic, and hence the onomastic, pattern. Strabo tells us that as early as A.D. 5 Aelius Cato transferred to Thrace fifty thousand Getai, 'speaking the same language as the Thracians',[9] and fifty-five years later Plautius Silvanus Aelianus transplanted a further hundred thousand from the same area across the river,[10] along with their rulers. Finally, after overcoming further Dacian and associated resistance, which continued for much of his reign, Marcus Aurelius transported twelve thousand 'free Dacians' into the Dobrudja.[11] The main consequence of this changing racial and administrative situation of Dacia was the Latinization of the region, which, in principle places it, and the other Romanized provinces, beyond the express range of the *Lexicon*.

In treating the different regions we have confined ourselves to the use of general terms, such as 'Thrace', 'Scythia Minor' and so on, and within those limits to following the practice of individual current editions of inscriptions. Thus, for Bulgaria, including its coastal colonies, we have used 'Thrace'; and for Romania we have followed the practice prescribed by the titles of the relevant epigraphical series, 'Scythia Minor', a term already used by Strabo to designate the 'marshlands' of the Dobrudja,[12] though its use as a provincial title to cover the hinterland was due to Diocletian. To distinguish this region from the 'historic' Skythia of the northern Black Sea area, with its Greek colonies, we have spelt it in its Latin form 'Scythia', and not in transliteration from the Greek, *Ἡ μικρὰ Σκυθία* in the usage of Strabo.

The onomastic evidence is assigned to a location in a number of ways. That provided by the early Greek colonies and associated settlements, mainly in the coastal zones, is treated as in previous volumes: under the city in question, or with the designation '(nr.)' if attribution to the *χώρα* is uncertain. In the case of the substantial, largely non-Greek, population of the countryside, more especially during the imperial period, the find-spot of many stones (which themselves have often long since disappeared) is unknown, and that of many others is recorded under variant 'modern' names, which may have changed on several occasions from Ottoman times onwards, before reaching a stable modern Greek, Romanian or Slavonic form. In part because of such uncertainties, but also to avoid unnecessary fragmentation

---

[4] Strabo 313 f. gives a detailed account of the whole region from the Adriatic to the Euxine; cf. 629 (n. 5 below). Cf. Wilkes, *Dalmatia* pp. 78 f., 153 f.

[5] Pliny, *NH* iii 149: 'provincia quae appellatur Moesia'. The province was established by Tiberius in A.D. 15. 'Moesia' is the Latinized form of *Μυσία*, and Strabo and Pliny make it quite clear that they regard the tribal name *Μυσοί* (Mysi), which gave its name to the region, as originally the same as that used of *Μυσία* and the *Μυσοί* in Asia Minor, and Ptolemy (writing in ca.110) calls the Danubian province *Μυσία*. It is to be noted that Strabo (628) blamed the Roman administration for the general confusion regarding provincial boundaries and names: speaking of Asian Mysia he says, *τὰ δ' ἑξῆς ἐπὶ τὰ νότια μέρη τοῖς τόποις τούτοις ἐμπλοκὰς ἔχει μέχρι πρὸς τὸν Ταῦρον, ὥστε καὶ τὰ Φρύγια καὶ τὰ Καρικὰ καὶ τὰ Λύδια καὶ ἔτι καὶ τὰ τῶν Μυσῶν δυσδιάκριτα εἶναι, παραπίπτοντα εἰς ἄλληλα· εἰς δὲ τὴν σύγχυσιν ταύτην οὐ μικρὰ συλλαμβάνει τὸ τοὺς Ῥωμαίους μὴ κατὰ φῦλα διελεῖν αὐτούς, ἀλλὰ ἕτερον τρόπον διατάξαι τὰς διοικήσεις, ἐν αἷς τὰς ἀγοραίους ποιοῦνται καὶ τὰς δικαιοδοσίας.*

[6] For the Drina and Drila, see Ptolemy ii. 6–7, with Müller's note ad. loc. In A.D. 57 Moesia was extended beyond the Dobrudja as far as Tyras, but this boundary was later retracted, although the whole of the north shore of the Black Sea as far as the Cimmerian Bosporos remained subject to the governor of Moesia until the time of the Germanic and other conquests.

[7] Ptolemy iii 10.1.

[8] The corpus published by F. Papazoglu and others, *Inscriptions de la Mésie Supérieure* (Belgrade, 1976–), is confined to that province, while the collective corpus of Latin inscriptions found in Jugoslavia between 1902 and 1970, republished by A. and J. Šašel in *Situla* (cited as Šašel, *IL*), comprises parts of Macedonia, Moesia Superior, Dalmatia, Pannonia Inferior and Superior and Noricum.

[9] 303: *μετῴκησεν ἐκ τῆς περαίας τοῦ Ἴστρου πέντε μυριάδας σωμάτων παρὰ τῶν Γετῶν, ὁμογλώττου τοῖς Θραιξὶν ἔθνους, εἰς τὴν Θράικην.* The racial identification of the Dacians and the Getai as 'Scythians' (not Thracians) is stressed by Pliny iv 80: 'ab eo (i.e. from the mouths of the Danube) in plenum quidem omnes Scytharum sunt gentes, variae tamen litori apposita tenuere, alias Getae, Daci Romanis dicti'. The scholiast on Ptolemy iii 8, where the heading is *Δακίας θέσις*, says *Δακίας θέσις. Δάκαι καὶ Γέται οἱ αὐτοί εἰσι.*

[10] *ILS* 986, Silvanus' lengthy funerary monument (ll. 9 f.): legat. pro praet. Moesiae in qua plura quam centum mill. ex numero Transdanuvianor. ad praestanda tributa cum coniugib. ac liberis ac principibus aut regibus suis transduxit. For Silvanus (cos. suff. A.D. 45 and 74) see *PIR*² P 480.

[11] See Cassius Dio books 71–3 for the prolonged preoccupation of Marcus with the Danube frontier from 168 onwards.

[12] 311: *καὶ ἐκαλεῖτο ἡ χώρα πᾶσα αὕτη, σχεδὸν δέ τι καὶ ἡ ἔξω τοῦ ἰσθμοῦ μέχρι Βορυσθένους, μικρὰ Σκυθία· διὰ δὲ τὸ πλῆθος τῶν ἐνθένδε περαιουμένων τόν τε Τύραν καὶ τὸν Ἴστρον καὶ ἐποικούντων τὴν γῆν καὶ ταύτης οὐκ ὀλίγη μικρὰ προσηγορεύθη Σκυθία, τῶν Θραικῶν τὰ μὲν τῆι βίαι συγχωρούντων, τὰ δὲ τῆι κακίαι τῆς χώρας· ἑλώδης γάρ ἐστιν ἡ πολλὴ αὐτῆς.* Cf. his description of the advances made by the Triballoi (318): *ἐπὶ τοσοῦτον δ' ηὐξήθησαν ὥστε μέχρι τῶν Ἰλλυρικῶν καὶ τῶν Παιονικῶν καὶ Θραικίων προῆλθον . . . μετὰ δὲ τὴν Σκορδίσκων χώραν παρὰ μὲν τὸν Ἴστρον ἡ τῶν Τριβαλλῶν καὶ Μυσῶν ἐστιν, ὧν ἐμνήσθημεν πρότερον, καὶ τὰ ἕλη τὰ τῆς μικρᾶς καλουμένης Σκυθίας τῆς ἐντὸς Ἴστρου· καὶ τούτου ἐμνήσθημεν.*

in the presentation of the onomastic material, we have tried to keep the use of 'modern' nomenclature to a minimum, and have preferred, where possible, to designate approximation to an identifiable ancient locality, often by the designation '(area)'.[13]

During the imperial period, when a city acquired the status of 'colonia' (Philippoi is a classic example), a very considerable area may have been included within its 'territorium' (superseding at times the χώρα of one or more older Greek communities), and when that is known to be the case we have added the designation '[territ.]'.[14] If, however, an old Greek coastal settlement was later included in the 'territorium' of a colonia or other Roman urban unit, we have kept the item under its original name. Our practice of denoting a dubious assignation of an individual to a location by a question mark or an asterisk remains unchanged.

Chronological Limits

A major difference of treatment in this volume concerns the chronological limit imposed on the material from Byzantion itself. The foundation of the new Rome in 323, followed in 330 by the naming of the city as Constantinople, superseded the old Megarian colony of Byzantion, and the changes between the two worlds, with the corresponding triumph of Christianity, are marked in every field of activity. The foundation of Constantinople inaugurated a new era, which has its own current scholarly activity in every field of archaeology and history, not least in prosopography and onomastics in general, and also in the field of epigraphy.[15] Like others in this field,[16] we have therefore excluded onomastic material of Byzantine date from Byzantion itself. Nevertheless, since in dealing with individuals whose years of birth and death are unknown, it is not possible to draw the straight line provided by an historical event, we have chosen a middle course, and have included names of persons, Christian and pagan, who can reasonably be supposed to have lived across the divide of the third and fourth Christian centuries, from the reign of Aurelian to that of Constantine; these, unless specifically dated, are given as 'iii–iv A.D.' It does not need emphasizing that the difficulty of dating with any precision inscriptions (especially private inscriptions) of the later imperial period on their letter-forms alone, in the absence of any historical or onomastic link, has as a consequence that many of the dates indicated by such century-spans are themselves frequently far from certain. Names of a later date (up to vi A.D.) attested outside Byzantion and its territory are included. We are conscious that the chronological segregation of Byzantion creates an overall anomaly in the volume, but to cut the whole volume off at the early fourth century did not seem a viable option.

Treatment of non-Greek names

The volume contains a very large number of Thracian and other indigenous names written in Greek, and also, in the north Euxine region, of names in Greek based primarily on Iranian and associated roots. Our treatment of these names does not differ in principle from that of the previous volumes, in which we have included names of foreign etymology which occurred in Greek; but in this volume we have encountered them on a scale and in a degree of complexity which we have not encountered before. The number of such names is large (Bithus, Aulouzenis, Moukatralis rank among the more common names); they occur in contexts where they are by no means certain to be borne by indigenous people; and they also occur outside our region, in Italy, Egypt and elsewhere. We have therefore had to make some difficult decisions about inclusion and exclusion.

One special point of general principle concerns the inclusion of Thracian individuals, and Thracian names, attested in Egypt and elsewhere beyond the Thracian homeland. We are not the first to face this problem, which, on a lesser scale, also arises with regard to Macedonians.[17] Briefly, we may say that where there seems no reason to doubt the genuine Thracian origin of the bearer of the Thracian name we have included the entry under the regular rubric, 'Thrace', but that when the ethnic is possibly or certainly associated with non-Thracian persons, essentially with parents bearing Egyptian names, as is the case from the later second century B.C. onwards, we have usually omitted them, or, in marginal cases, added a question-mark after the ethnic identification, according to the individual circumstances.[18] Thracian and kindred names also occur in Anatolia throughout the hellenistic and imperial periods unaccompanied by ethnics, that is, as borne by the native population, which in the course of centuries had settled in Asia. Though these may be normal Thracian names such as Moukaporis, they are also excluded from this volume, to be included in due course in their own geographical context.

In the context of Thracian and other non-Greek names, three items require particular explanation: accentuation, the treatment of variant spellings of a single name-form, and the treatment of Thracian names in a Latinized form.

---

[13] There are, nevertheless, cases where stones cannot be assigned, however loosely, to a known ancient settlement. A different level of uncertainty may exist, as in, for example, Paionia, where the identification of modern remains with known ancient settlements is the subject of much disagreement. Our debt to F. Papazoglu's *Les Villes de Macédoine à l'époque romaine* is far greater than the number of citations in the volume would suggest.

[14] The model for this practice will be found in G. Mihailov's *Inscriptiones Graecae in Bulgaria Repertae* (*IGB*). Mihailov also made use of the wider denomination 'regio', mainly to cover settlements on the courses of, and between, rivers.

[15] To name but the salient works: the post-Constantinian volumes of the *Prosopography of the Later Roman Empire*, and the *Prosopography of the Byzantine World* (http://www.kcl.ac.uk/humanities/cch/PBE/), in the course of preparation. On the epigraphical side, in addition to D. Feissel's *Recueil des inscriptions chrétiennes de Macédoine du IIIe–VIe siècle*, see the excellent bibliographical summary of the earlier history of Constantinopolitan epigraphical researches by C. Mango, *AJA* 55 (1951) pp. 52–66, and the publication by I. Shevchenko and C. Mango in *Dumbarton Oaks Papers* 32 (1978) pp. 3 f. A corpus of inscriptions is now in preparation by C. Mango and D. Feissel. For the texts in the Theodosian Walls, B. Meyer-Plath and A. M. Schneider, *Die Landmauer von Konstantinopel* (Berlin, 1943); C. Mango, *Le développement urbain de Constantinople (IVe–VIIe siècles)* (Paris, 1985); id. *Studies on Constantinople* (Aldershot, 1993), and the reassessment by W. D. Lebek, *Epigraphica Anatolica* 25 (1995), pp. 107–53.

[16] See, most recently, A. Łajtar, *Inschriften v. Byzantion* (*IByz*) which stops at A.D. 330. Similarly, B. Latyschev's *IOSPE* I², and V. V. Struve et al., *CIRB*, end with the fourth century.

[17] See A. B. Tataki, *Macedonians Abroad*, who places all the Macedonians attested in Egypt with the regional appellation, datable after 150 B.C., in a separate Appendix (I), on pp. 471 f.; cf. pp. 508 f. The number of possibly 'apocryphal' Macedonians in Egypt is much fewer than that of Thracians.

[18] We have made reference throughout to the publication of C. A. La'da, *Foreign Ethnics in Hellenistic Egypt*; V. Velkov and A. Fol, *Les Thraces en Égypte gréco-romaine* pp. 97 f., give the general historical background for Egypt.

Accentuation

This volume brings us back abruptly to the thorny problem of the accentuation of non-Greek names, which are not naturally adapted to the application of the Greek accentual system. The general principles adopted in the *Lexicon* for the accentuation of personal names were set out in *LGPN* I (p. xiv), where the principle upon which we have (in that and succeeding volumes) extended accentuation to non-Greek names is also given. This volume differs only in the quantity of such names, and in the diversity of their linguistic origins, notably, but not only, Thracian.

We have followed the practice of the ancient scribes in placing accents according to Greek rules on Thracian, Iranian and other names which occur in literary texts.[19] We have extended this practice, where a reasoned justification can be found, to the many such names which are not attested in literary sources, and have, therefore, not followed the practice of D. Detschev in his invaluable Thracian onomasticon[20] (and of most scholars before and after him), in which a Thracian name is accented *only* if it occurs in a literary source. We are aware that our decision, more frequent in an earlier generation than now, does not match the practice of many modern corpora, though we note that we are by no means alone in our approach.[21]

Differences of opinion about the accentuation of personal names are not, of course, limited to non-Greek names, and we have faced a number of difficult choices on all fronts. One pivotal principle in accentuation—to be guided by the form of the genitive—has not proved a comprehensive aid in this volume, where we have often encountered different genitives for what is essentially the same name. If the *Lexicon* retained a different accent for the nominative in all cases, there would be a separate entry for each accented name, which would, we believe, not be helpful to users of the volume (or users consulting all volumes together).

Our work would undoubtedly have been much easier if we had refrained from placing accents at all; it is a bruising experience to wrestle with these problems within the constraining framework of a lexicon, where detailed justification is not possible, and presentation within a reasonably consistent framework essential. We have, however, often been assured that readers consult the *Lexicon* for accents—even when it is conceded that we may get it wrong. The first Reverse Index, in *LGPN II*, appeared unaccented, but the accents were, by 'popular' request, restored for succeeding volumes.

Identification of variant forms of non-Greek names

We have tried, where possible, to subsume under a single entry variant spellings of non-Greek names, which may vary by a consonant or a simple or complex vowel-unit, in one or more element of the name. There is no reason to suppose that any variation of genuine linguistic tradition or usage lies behind such different spellings, some of which are purely etacistic, but others of which were surely determined by pronunciation not etymology. Thus, to take but one out of many examples, we have entered the various forms of the Thracian name *Αὐλού/ώ/ό-πορις* under the diphthongal form alone, while recording the variants in the final brackets. We hope that this type of entry, which occurs especially with Thracian names but also (to a lesser degree) with Iranian derivatives in the northern Black Sea region, will not be regarded as an over-simplification. Where the name or its root are not common enough for us to know which is the basic form, we have tended to leave the variant forms free-standing: for example, *Ἐπτά-*, *Ἐπταί-*, *Ἐπτέ-*, *Ἐπτή-τραλις*. Because of the wide variety of name-forms attested in these regions, we have not attempted a cross-reference system in this volume.

Latin forms of non-Greek names

Our general practice is to include single Latin names (i.e. Roman names such as Publius or Gaius, used in the 'Greek manner') if they are attested in Greek. Greek names attested in Latin are also included, listed under the Greek form with the attested Latin form recorded in the final bracket. (In such cases, any relatives will appear in Greek if they themselves secure an entry in the *Lexicon*, and in Latin if they are truly Latin and do not secure an entry of their own.) This system, most plentifully illustrated in the material from southern Italy recorded in *LGPN* IIIA, has the overriding advantage of preserving the attestation of a Greek name.

In this volume, however, the matter is complicated by the presence of large numbers of Thracian and other non-Greek names recorded in Latin, frequently in oblique cases which allow no certainty as to how the nominative would have been spelt in the Greek (and, indeed even in the Latin) form. It may indeed be argued that Thracian names in Latin are not the business of a Lexicon of Greek Personal Names, or alternatively, that Latin forms of names attested in the region should stand *pari passu* with their Greek counterparts. As a compromise, we have included Thracian names attested in Latin for which there is an attested or *easily assimilated* Greek version of the name.

Finally, a brief word about information technology. In the first volume, a section of the Introduction was devoted to an explanation of the technological developments which made it possible for us to produce our volumes and to provide statistics derived from the contents of each volume. Over time, the need for such explanations has receded. This volume has been produced by the same methods which have served us well in the production of its predecessors. For statistical information, and much else concerning the project and its publications, it is now more appropriate to direct the reader to http://www.lgpn.ox.ac.uk.

P.M.F
E.M.

---

[19] As recorded in H. W. Chandler, *A Practical Introduction to Greek Accentuation* (Oxford, 1881²; repr. New Rochelle, N.Y., 1983). Allowance has, of course, to be made for disagreement between ancient grammarians, and also for falsely transmitted forms and scribal errors. Both categories were, as far as was possible for him, listed by Chandler, whose dense notes contain lively and caustic comments, e.g. his remark (p.92), apropos of Stephanos of Byzantion' s accentuation of *Πάραισος*· 'This [proparoxytone accent] is one out of a host of accentual blunders in the same author'.

[20] *Die thrakischen Sprachreste* (Vienna, 1957)

[21] See, for example, M. B. Hatzopoulos and L. D. Loukopoulou, *Recherches sur les marches orientales des Téménides (Anthémonte–Kalindoia)* 2 pp. 209 f.

Abbreviations of sources used

Abbreviations of Greek and Latin authors used are not included in this list, except that editions of fragments (*FGrH, FVS* etc.) have been retained. The conventions followed are those of Liddell and Scott, *A Greek-English Lexicon* (9th edn., and Supplements) and of the *Diccionario griego-español* (Madrid, 1980-).

A΄ Panell. Synedr. Epigr.	*A΄ Πανελλήνιο Συνέδριο Ἐπιγραφικῆς (Πρακτικά). Στὴν μνήμη Δημητρίου Κανατσούλη. Θεσσαλονίκη 22-23 Ὀκτωβρίου 1999*, edd. I. Touloumakos and I. K. Sverkos (*Ἑταιρεία Ἱστορικῶν καὶ Ἐπιγραφικῶν Σπουδῶν* [Thessaloniki, 2001])
AA	*Archäologischer Anzeiger. Beiblatt zum Jahrbuch des (Kaiserlichen) Deutschen Archäologischen Instituts* (Berlin, 1890–1962); from 1963 published separately as *Archäologischer Anzeiger*
AAA	*Ἀρχαιολογικὰ Ἀνάλεκτα ἐξ Ἀθηνῶν, Athens Annals of Archaeology*, 1– (Athens, 1968–)
ACSS	*Ancient Civilizations from Scythia to Siberia. An International Journal of Comparative Studies in History and Archaeology*, 1– (Leiden, 1994–)
Act. IX Ep. Congr.	*Actes du IXe congrès international d'épigraphie grecque et latine, 31.* VIII. – *7.* IX. *1987, Sofia*, vol. 1 (*Acta Centri Historiae 'Terra Antiqua Balcanica'*, 2 [Sofia, 1987])
Act. XI congr. int. arch. chrét.	*Actes du XIe congrès international d'archéologie chrétienne. Lyon, Vienne, Grenoble, Genève et Aoste, 21-28 septembre 1986*, 3 vols. (*Collection de l'École française de Rome*, 123 [Rome, 1989])
Acta Antiqua	*Acta Antiqua Academiae Scientiarum Hungaricae*, 1– (Budapest, 1951–)
AD	*Ἀρχαιολογικὸν Δελτίον*, 1– (Athens, 1915–35; 1960–); from 1960 published in two parts, *Μελέται* and *Χρονικά*
AE	*Ἀρχαιολογικὴ Ἐφημερίς. Περιοδικὸν τῆς ἐν Ἀθήναις Ἀρχαιολογικῆς Ἑταιρείας* (Athens, 1910–) (for earlier vols. see *EA)*
AEMÖ	*Archäologisch-epigraphische Mittheilungen aus Österreich(-Ungarn)*, 1–20 (Vienna, 1877–97)
AEMTh	*Τὸ Ἀρχαιολογικὸ ἔργο στὴ Μακεδονία καὶ Θράκη*, 1– (Thessaloniki, 1987–)
AEp	*L'Année épigraphique* (Paris, 1888–); 1888–1961 published separately and in *Revue Archéologique*; 1962– separately
AEpThess	B. Kallipolitis and D. Lazaridis, *Ἀρχαῖαι ἐπιγραφαὶ Θεσσαλονίκης* (Thessaloniki, 1946) [repr. in '*Θεσσαλονίκην Φιλίππου Βασίλισσαν'. Μελέτες γιὰ τὴν ἀρχαία Θεσσαλονίκη*, ed. P. Adam-Veleni (Thessaloniki, 1985) pp. 819-861]
Ag.	*The Athenian Agora. Results of Excavations conducted by the American School of Classical Studies at Athens*, 1– (Princeton, 1953–)
Ager	S. L. Ager, *Interstate Arbitrations in the Greek World, 337–90 B. C.* (University of California, *Hellenistic Culture and Society*, 18 [Berkeley, Los Angeles and London, 1996])
AGSP	*Antichnye Gosudarstva Severnogo Prichernomor'ia*, edd. G. A. Koshelenko, I. T. Kruglikova et al. (Akademiia Nauk SSSR, Institut arkheologii, *Arkheologiia SSSR*, 9 [Moscow, 1984])
AIU	*Arkheologicheskie issledovaniia na Ukraine*, 1– (Akademiia Nauk Ukrainskoi SSR, Institut arkheologii [Kiev, 1965/66–])
AJA	*American Journal of Archaeology*, 1–11 (Boston, 1885–96); 2nd ser. 1– (1897–)
AJNum	*American Journal of Numismatics*, 1– (second series, American Numismatic Society [New York, 1989–]); continues *The American Numismatic Society Museum Notes*
Akamatis, *Amph. Pellas*	I. M. Akamatis, *Ἐνσφράγιστες λαβὲς ἀμφορέων ἀπὸ τὴν ἀγορὰ τῆς Πέλλας. Ἀνασκαφὴ 1980–1987. Οἱ ὁμάδες Παρμενίσκου καὶ Ῥόδου* (*Βιβλιοθήκη τῆς ἐν Ἀθήναις Ἀρχαιολογικῆς Ἑταιρείας*, 197 [Athens, 2000])
Akamatis, *Pilines mitres*	I. M. Akamatis, *Πήλινες μίτρες ἀγγείων ἀπὸ τὴν Πέλλα. Συμβολὴ στὴ μελέτη τῆς ἑλληνιστικῆς κεραμεικῆς* (*Δημοσιεύματα τοῦ Ἀρχαιολογικοῦ Δελτίου*, 51 [Athens, 1993])
Akarca	A. Akarca, *Les monnaies grecques de Mylasa* (*Bibliothèque archéologique et historique de l'Institut français d'archéologie d'Istanbul*, 1 [Paris, 1959])
Alekseeva, *Gorgippiia*	E. M. Alekseeva, *Antichnyi gorod Gorgippiia* (Rossiiskaia Akademiia Nauk, Institut arkheologii [Moscow, 1997])
Aleshire, *Asklepieion*	S. Aleshire, *The Athenian Asklepieion: the People, their Dedications, and the Inventories* (Amsterdam, 1989)
AM	*Mitteilungen des Deutschen Archäologischen Instituts, Athenische Abteilung*, 1– (Athens, 1876–1939; Berlin, 1951–)
AMGR	*Annuario del Museo Greco-Romano*, ed. A. Adriani, 1 vol.; subsequently *Annuaire du Musée Gréco-Romain*, 3 vols. (Alexandria, 1934–52)
AMNG	*Die antiken Münzen Nord-Griechenlands.* I, *Dacien und Moesien*; fasc. 1 ed. B. Pick, fasc. 2 edd. B. Pick and K. Regling. II, *Thrakien*; fasc. 1 edd. F. Münzer and M. L. Strack. III, *Makedonien und Paionien*, ed. F. Gaebler (Berlin, 1898–1912)
Amphipolis	D. Lazaridis, *Amphipolis* (Athens, 1997)
Anal. Boll.	*Analecta Bollandiana*, 1– (Société général de Librairie Catholique 'Palmé' [Paris, 1882–])
Anali	*Anali. Spisanie za istoriia, klasicheska kultura i izkustvoznanie (Journal of history, Classical culture and art history)*, 1– (Sofia, 1994–)
Anat. Stud.	*Anatolian Studies. Journal of the British Institute of Archaeology at Ankara*, 1– (London, 1951–)

Ancient Macedonia	*Ancient Macedonia* (Ἀρχαία Μακεδονία). *Papers read at the International Symposia held in Thessaloniki, 1968– (Institute for Balkan Studies,* 122, 155, 193, 204, 240, 272 [Thessaloniki, 1970–])
Andronikos, *Vergina*	M. Andronikos, *Vergina. The Royal Tombs and the Ancient City* (Athens, 1984)
Annot. num.	*Annotazioni numismatiche*, 1– (Milan, 1991–)
Anokhin	V. A. Anokhin, *Monetnoe delo Khersonesa (IV v. do n. e.- XII v. n. e.)* (Akademiia Nauk Ukrainskoi SSR, Institut arkheologii [Kiev, 1977]); English translation, *The Coinage of Chersonesus, IV Century B.C. – XII Century A.D.* (*BAR International Series*, 69 [Oxford, 1980])
Ant. Afric.	*Antiquités Africaines*, 1– (Paris, 1967–)
Ant. Kunst	*Antike Kunst*, 1– (Olten, 1958–)
Ant. terakoti Bulg.	T. Dremsizova-Nelchinova and G. Toncheva, *Antichni terakoti ot Bulgariia* (Sofia, 1971)
Anthémonte–Kalindoia	M. B. Hatzopoulos and L. D. Loukopoulou, *Recherches sur les marches orientales des Téménides (Anthémonte - Kalindoia)*, 2 vols. (*Μελετήματα*, 11 [Athens, 1992, 1996])
Antička bronza u Jugoslaviji	Lj. B. Popović et al., *Antička bronza u Jugoslaviji* (Narodni Muzej Beograd [Belgrade, 1969])
AO	*Arkheologicheskie Otkrytiia*, 1– (Akademiia Nauk SSSR, Institut arkheologii [Moscow, 1965–])
Aphieroma Hammond	*Ἀφιέρωμα στὸν N. G. L. Hammond* (*Παράρτημα Μακεδονικῶν*, 7 [Thessaloniki, 1997])
Apoloniia	*Apoloniia. Razkopkite v nekropola na Apoloniia prez 1947-1949 z. (Apollonia. Les fouilles dans la necropole d'Apollonia en 1947-1949)*, ed. I. Venedikov (Bulgarska Akademiia na Naukite, Arkheologicheski Institut [Sofia, 1963])
AR	*Archaeological Reports* (Society for the Promotion of Hellenic Studies/British School at Athens [London, 1955–])
Araşt. Sonuçları Topl.	*Araştırma Sonuçları Toplantısı*, 1– (T.C. Kültür Bakanlığı, Anıtlar ve Müzeler Genel Müdürlüğü [Istanbul and Ankara, 1983–])
Arch. Bulg.	*Archaeologia Bulgarica*, 1– (Sofia, 1997–)
Arch. Class.	*Archeologia Classica*, 1– (Rome, 1949–)
Arch. Iug.	*Archaeologia Iugoslavica*, 1–23 (Belgrade, 1954–1983); 24 (Ljubljana, 1987)
Arch. Karte Kavadarci	N. Vulić, *Archaeologische Karte von Jugoslawien. Kavadarci* (Belgrade, 1938)
Arch. Pap.	*Archiv für Papyrusforschung und verwandte Gebiete*, 1– (Leipzig, 1901–1990; Stuttgart and Leipzig, 1991–)
Archaiognosia	*Ἀρχαιογνωσία*, 1– (Athens, 1980–)
Archeologia (Warsaw)	*Archeologia. Rocznik Panstwowego Muzeum Archeologicznego w Warszawie i Polskiego Towarzystwa Archeologicznego*, 1– (Warsaw and Wroclaw, 1947–)
Archibald, *Odrysian Kingdom*	Z. H. Archibald, *The Odrysian Kingdom of Thrace. Orpheus Unmasked* (Oxford Monographs on Classical Archaeology [Oxford, 1998])
Archives Stamoulis	Unpublished archives of A. K. P. Stamoulis, kept in the Academy of Athens (non vidimus). Names recorded by Loukopoulou, *Thrace Propontique* pp. 228 ff. Table A1
Arheološki Pregled	*Arheološki Pregled*, 1– (Arheološko društvo Jugoslavije [Belgrade, 1959–])
Arheološki Vestnik	*Arheološki Vestnik*, 1– (Slovenska akademija znanosti in umetnosti, sekcija za arheologijo [Ljubljana, 1950–])
Arkheologiia (Kiev)	*Arkheologiia*, 1– (Akademiia Nauk Ukrainskoi RSR, Institut arkheologii [Kiev, 1947–])
Arkheologiia (Sofia)	*Arkheologiia*, 1– (Bulgarska Akademiia na Naukite, Arkheologicheski Institut i Muzei [Sofia, 1959–])
ASAA	*Annuario della (Regia) scuola archeologica di Atene e delle missioni italiane in Oriente*, 1–16 (Bergamo etc., 1914–42); NS 1– (Rome, 1942–)
Athena	*Ἀθηνᾶ. Σύγγραμμα περιοδικὸν τῆς ἐν Ἀθήναις Ἐπιστημονικῆς Ἑταιρείας*, 1– (Athens, 1889–)
Atti XI Congr. Epig.	*XI congresso internazionale di epigrafia greca e latina. Roma, 18-24 settembre 1997. Atti*, 2 vols. (Rome, 1999)
Audollent, *Defix. Tab.*	A. Audollent, *Defixionum Tabellae* (Paris, 1904)
Austin–Bastianini, *Posidipp.*	*Posidippi Pellaei quae supersunt omnia*, edd. C. Austin and G. Bastianini (*Biblioteca classica*, 3 [Milan, 2002])
AWE	*Ancient West & East*, 1– (Leiden, Boston and Cologne, 2002–)
AZ	*Archaeologische Zeitung*, 1–43 (Deutsches Archäologisches Institut [Berlin, 1843–86])
Bakalakis, *Oinos Ismarikos*	G. Bakalakis, *Οἶνος Ἰσμαρικός. Μικρὰ μελετήματα τοῦ καθηγητὴ Γεωργίου Μπακαλάκη. Τιμητικὸς τόμος* (*Ἀριστοτέλειο Πανεπιστήμιο Θεσσαλονίκης* [Thessaloniki, 1990])
Balty–van Rengen, *Apamea*	J. Balty and W. van Rengen, *Apamea in Syria: the Winter quarters of Legio II Parthica. Roman gravestones from the military cemetery* (Brussels, 1993)
Barnea	I. Barnea, *Les monuments paléochrétiens de Roumanie* (Pontificio Istituto di archeologia cristiana, *Sussidi allo studio delle antichità cristiane*, 6 [Vatican City, 1977])
Bataille, *IG Hatshepsout*	A. Bataille, *Les inscriptions grecques du temple de Hatshepsout à Deir el-Bahari* (Publications de la Société Fouad I de papyrologie, *Textes et documents*, 10 (Cairo, 1951)
BCH	*Bulletin de correspondance hellénique*, 1– (Paris, 1877–)
BE	J. and L. Robert, *Bulletin épigraphique* in *Revue des études grecques* 1938–84; Ph. Gauthier et al. from 1987–
Bellinger, *End of Seleucids*	A. R. Bellinger, *The End of the Seleucids* (*Transactions of the Connecticut Academy of Arts and Sciences*, vol. 38, pp. 51-102 [New Haven, 1949])

Beloch, *GG*	J. Beloch, *Griechische Geschichte*, 4 vols., 2nd edn., 1–2 (Strasbourg, 1912–16); 3–4 (Berlin and Leipzig, 1922–7)
Belomorski Pregled	*Belomorski Pregled*, 1–2 (Sofia, 1941–2); vol. 2 not published
Bernand, *De Thèbes*	A. Bernand, *De Thèbes à Syène* (Paris, 1989)
Bernand, *El-Kanaïs*	A. Bernand, *Le Paneion d'El-Kanaïs. Les inscriptions grecques* (Leiden, 1972)
Bernand, *Inscr. métr.*	E. Bernand, *Inscriptions métriques de l'Égypte gréco-romaine* (Paris, 1969)
Bernand, *Pan du Désert*	A. Bernand, *Pan du Désert* (Leiden, 1977)
Berve	H. Berve, *Das Alexanderreich auf prosopographischer Grundlage*, 2 vols. (Munich, 1926)
Beševliev	*Spätgriechische und spätlateinische Inschriften aus Bulgarien*, ed. V. Beševliev (Deutsche Akademie der Wissenschaften zu Berlin, Institut für griechisch-römische Altertumskunde, *Berliner Byzantinistische Arbeiten*, 30 [Berlin, 1964])
Beševliev, *EP*	V. Beševliev, *Epigrafski Prinosi* (Bulgarska Akademiia na Naukite, Arkheologicheski Institut i Muzei [Sofia, 1952])
BIAB	*Bulletin de l'Institut Archéologique Bulgare* (*Izvestiia na Bulgarskiia Arkheologicheski Institut*), 1–37 (Bulgarska Akademiia na Naukite, Arkheologicheski Institut [Sofia, 1921–1987])
Billows, *Antigonos*	R. A. Billows, *Antigonos the One-eyed and the creation of the Hellenistic State* (*Hellenistic Culture and Society*, 4 [Berkeley and London, 1990])
Blavatskii, *Pantikapei*	V. D. Blavatskii, *Pantikapei. Ocherki istorii stolitsy Bospora* (Moscow, 1964)
BMC Tauric Chersonese	R. S. Poole, B. V. Head and P. Gardner, *A Catalogue of the Greek coins in the British Museum. Tauric Chersonese, Sarmatia, Dacia, Moesia, Thrace etc.* (London, 1877)
BMI	*The Collection of Ancient Greek Inscriptions in the British Museum*, edd. E. L. Hicks, C. T. Newton et al., 4 vols. (London, 1874–1916)
BMNBurgas	*Bulletin du Musée National du Bourgas* (*Izvestiia na Narodniia Muzei Burgas*), 1– (Sofia, 1950–)
BMNRuse	*Bulletin du Musée National à Ruse* (*Izvestiia na Narodniia Muzei v Ruse*), 1– (Varna, 1964–)
BMNVarna	*Bulletin du Musée National à Varna* (*Izvestiia na Narodniia Muzei – Varna*), 1– (Varna, 1965–) [continues *Bulletin de la Société archéologique à Varna* (*Izvestiia na Varnenskoto arkheologichesko druzhestvo*), 1–15 (Varna, 1909–1964)]
BMNWB	*Izvestiia na Muzeite v severozapadna Bulgariia* (*Bulletin of the Museums in northwestern Bulgaria*), 1– (Sofia, 1977–)
BO	*Bibliotheca Orientalis*, 1– (Nederlands Instituut voor het Nabije Oosten te Leiden [Leiden, 1944–])
Boardman, *Gems*	J. Boardman, *Greek Gems and Finger Rings, Early Bronze Age to Late Classical* (London, 1970)
Bosporskii fenomen	*Bosporskii fenomen* (St. Petersburg, 1999)
Boston Coins	A. B. Brett, *Catalogue of Greek Coins* (Museum of Fine Arts, Boston [Boston, 1955])
Bosworth, *Commentary*	A. B. Bosworth, *A Historical Commentary on Arrian's History of Alexander*, 2 vols. (Oxford, 1980, 1995)
BPW	*Berliner philologische Wochenschrift*, 1–64 (Berlin, 1881–1944); 41–64 published as *Philologische Wochenschrift* (1921–44)
Braund, *Georgia*	D. Braund, *Georgia in Antiquity. A History of Colchis and Transcaucasian Iberia, 550 BC-AD 562* (Oxford, 1994)
Breccia, *Iscriz.*	E. Breccia, *Catalogue général des antiquités égyptiennes du Musée d'Alexandrie, Nos. 1–568, Iscrizioni greche e latine* (Cairo, 1911)
Britannia	*Britannia*, 1– (Society for the Promotion of Roman Studies [London, 1970–])
Bronzes antiques du Louvre	A. de Ridder, *Les bronzes antiques du Louvre*, 2 vols. (Paris, 1913–15)
Brown, *Ptolemaic Paintings*	B. R. Brown, *Ptolemaic Paintings and Mosaics and the Alexandrian Style* (*Monographs on Archaeology and Fine Arts*, 6 [Cambridge, Mass., 1957])
BSA	*Annual of the British School at Athens*, 1– (London, 1894/5–)
BSAB	*Bulletin de la Société archéologique bulgare* (*Izvestiia na Bulgarskoto arkheologichesko druzhestvo*), 1–7 (Sofia, 1910–1920)
CAF	*Comicorum Atticorum Fragmenta*, ed. T. Kock, 3 vols. (Leipzig, 1880–88)
CAG	*Commentaria in Aristotelem Graeca*, 23 vols. (Berlin, 1882–1909)
Cat. lampes Mus. Istanbul	D. K. Tezgör and T. Sezer, *Catalogue des lampes en terre cuite du Musée Archéologique d'Istanbul*. I, *Époques protohistorique, archaïque, classique et hellénistique* (Institut français d'études anatoliennes d'Istanbul, *Varia Anatolica*, 6 (1) [Istanbul and Paris, 1995])
CCCA	*Corpus cultus Cybelae Attidisque*, ed. M. J. Vermaseren, 7 vols. (*Études préliminaires aux religions orientales dans l'empire romaine*, 50 [Leiden, 1977–1989])
CCET	*Corpus cultus Equitis Thracii*. I, *Monumenta orae Ponti Euxini Bulgariae*; II, *Monumenta inter Danubium et Haemum reperta*; IV, *Moesia Inferior (Romanian section) and Dacia*; V, *Monumenta intra fines Iugoslaviae reperta*, edd. Z. Gočeva, M. Oppermann et al. (*Études préliminaires aux religions orientales dans l'empire romain*, 74 [Leiden, 1972–1984])
CE	*Chronique d'Égypte*, 1– (Brussels, 1925–)
CEG	P. A. Hansen, *Carmina Epigraphica Graeca*. [I], *Saeculorum VIII-V a.Chr.n.*; II, *Saeculi IV a.Chr.n.* (Berlin, 1983, 1989)
Charistirion Orlandos	*Χαριστήριον εἰς Ἀναστάσιον Κ. Ὀρλάνδον*, 4 vols. (*Βιβλιοθήκη τῆς ἐν Ἀθήναις Ἀρχαιολογικῆς Ἑταιρείας*, 54 [Athens, 1965–68])

Chiron	*Chiron. Mitteilungen der Kommission für alte Geschichte und Epigraphik des Deutschen Archäologischen Instituts*, 1– (Munich, 1971–)
Chrysostomou, *Almopia*	A. Chrysostomou, *Ancient Almopia* (Thessaloniki, 1994)
Chuistova, *AIB*	L. I. Chuistova, *Arkheologiia i istoriia Bospora* (Simferopol, 1966)
CIA	*Corpus Inscriptionum Atticarum*, edd. A. Kirchhoff et al. (Berlin, 1873–). III (1–2), *Inscriptiones Atticae aetatis Romanae*, ed. W. Dittenberger (1878–82). *Appendix. Defixionum tabellae in Attica regione repertae*, ed. R. Wuensch (1897)
CID	*Corpus des inscriptions de Delphes*. I, *Lois sacrées et règlements religieux*, ed. G. Rougemont; II, *Les comptes du quatrième et du troisième siècle*, ed. J. Bousquet; III, *Les hymnes à Apollon*, ed. A. Bélis; IV, *Documents amphictioniques*, ed. F. Lefèvre (Paris, 1977–)
CIG	*Corpus Inscriptionum Graecarum*, edd. A. Boeckh, J. Franz et al., 4 vols. (Berlin, 1825–1877)
CIJ	*Corpus Inscriptionum Judaicarum. Recueil des inscriptions juives qui vont du IIIe siècle avant Jésus-Christ au VIIe siècle de notre ère*, ed. J.-B. Frey, 2 vols. (Pontificio Istituto di archeologia cristiana, *Sussidi allo studio della antichità cristiane*, 1, 3 [Vatican City, 1936, 1952]
CIL	*Corpus Inscriptionum Latinarum*, edd. Th. Mommsen et al., 17 vols. with supplements (Berlin, 1863–)
CIRB	*Corpus Inscriptionum Regni Bosporani*, edd. V. V. Struve et al. (Moscow and Leningrad, 1965)
Cl. Rh.	*Clara Rhodos. Studi e materiali pubblicati a cura dell'Istituto storico-archeologico di Rodi*, 10 vols. (Rhodes, 1928–1941)
Claros	L. and J. Robert, *Claros*. I, *Décrets hellénistiques*, fasc. 1 (Paris, 1989)
Clarysse–van der Veken	W. Clarysse and G. van der Veken, with S. P. Vleeming, *The Eponymous Priests of Ptolemaic Egypt (P.L. Bat. 24). Chronological Lists of the Priests of Alexandria and Ptolemais with a Study of the Demotic Transcriptions of their Names* (*Papyrologica Lugduno-Batava*, 24 [Leiden, 1983])
Class. Num. Group	*Classical Numismatic Group*, sale catalogues, 1– (Lancaster, Pennsylvania, and London, 1975–)
Coinage and Administration	*Coinage and Administration in the Athenian and Persian Empires. The ninth Oxford Symposium on Coinage and Monetary History*, ed. I. Carradice (*BAR International Series*, 343 [Oxford, 1987])
Coll. Alex.	J. U. Powell, *Collectanea Alexandrina* (Oxford, 1925)
Coll. McClean	S. W. Grose, *Fitzwilliam Museum. Catalogue of the McClean Collection of Greek Coins*, 3 vols. (Cambridge, 1923–29)
Coll. Waddington	E. Babelon, *Inventaire sommaire de la Collection Waddington* (Département des Médailles et Antiques de la Bibliothèque Nationale [Paris, 1898])
Coll. Winterthur	H. Bloesch, *Griechische Münzen in Winterthur*, 2 vols. (Winterthur, 1987)
Collart, *Philippes*	P. Collart, *Philippes, ville de Macédoine depuis ses origines jusqu'à la fin de l'époque romaine* (École française d'Athènes, *Travaux et Mémoires*, 5 [Paris, 1937])
Corinth	*Corinth. Results of Excavations conducted by the American School of Classical Studies at Athens*, 1– (Cambridge, Mass., 1929–43; Princeton, 1948–)
Courby, *Les vases grecs*	F. Courby, *Les vases grecs à reliefs* (Paris, 1922)
CPh.	*Classical Philology*, 1– (Chicago, 1906–)
CPR	*Corpus Papyrorum Raineri archeducis Austriae*, edd. C. Wessely et al., 1– (Vienna, 1895–)
CQ	*Classical Quarterly*, 1– (London, 1907–38; Oxford, 1939–)
CR	*Classical Review*, 1– (London, 1887–)
CRAI	*Comptes-rendus de l'Académie des inscriptions et belles-lettres*, 4th ser. (Paris, 1874–)
CVA	*Corpus Vasorum Antiquorum*, various places and dates of publication. See T. H. Carpenter and T. Mannack, *Summary Guide to Corpus Vasorum Antiquorum* (2nd edn., Oxford, 2000)
Dacia	*Dacia. Recherches et découvertes archéologiques en Roumanie*, 1–11/12 (Bucharest, 1924–1947); *Revue d'archéologie et d'histoire ancienne*, NS 1– (Bucharest, 1957–)
Dain, *IGLouvre*	A. Dain, *Inscriptions grecques du Musée du Louvre. Les textes inédites* (Paris, 1933)
Davydova, *Bosp. nadgrob.*	L. I. Davydova, *Bosporskie nadgrobnie rel'efy* (Leningrad, 1990)
DCB	*Dictionary of Christian Biography*, edd. W. Smith and H. Wace, 4 vols. (London, 1877–87)
Detschev	D. Detschev, *Die thrakischen Sprachreste* (*Schriften der Balkankommission, linguistische Abteilung*, 14 [Vienna, 1957])
DGVE	*Drevneishie gosudarstva vostochnoi Evropy. Materialy i issledovaniia* (Rossiiskaia Akademiia Nauk, Institut Rossiiskoi istorii [Moscow, 1994–]); continues *Drevneishie gosudarstva na territorii SSSR* (Moscow, 1971–91)
DHA	*Dialogues d'histoire ancienne*, 1– (Université de Besançon, Centre de recherches d'histoire ancienne [Paris, 1974–])
Dimitrov	D. P. Dimitrov, *Nadgrobnite plochi ot rimsko vreme v Severna Bulgariia* (*Otdelna redica trudove na Bulgarskiia Arkheologicheski Institut*, 1 [Sofia, 1942])
Dimitsas	M. G. Dimitsas, *Ἡ Μακεδονία ἐν λίθοις φθεγγομένοις καὶ μνημείοις σωζομένοις* (Athens, 1896); repr. as *Sylloge Inscriptionum Graecarum et Latinarum Macedoniae*, 2 vols. (Chicago, 1980)
Dion	D. Pandermalis, *Δῖον. Ἀρχαιολογικὸς χῶρος καὶ μουσεῖο* (Athens, 1997)
Dodd, *Byz. Stamps*	E. C. Dodd, *Byzantine Silver Stamps* (*Dumbarton Oaks Studies*, 7 [Washington, D.C., 1961])
Dodoni	*Δωδώνη. Ἐπιστημονικὴ ἐπετηρὶς τῆς Φιλοσοφικῆς Σχολῆς τοῦ Πανεπιστημίου Ἰωαννίνων*, 1– (Ioannina, 1972–)
Draganov, *Kabile*	D. Draganov, *Monetosecheneto na Kabile (The Coinage of Cabyle)* (Sofia, 1993)

Drama	*'Η Δράμα καὶ ἡ περιοχή της. Ἱστορία καὶ πολιτισμός. Ἐπιστημονικὴ συνάντηση, Δράμα 24-25 Νοεμβρίου 1989*, ed. Ch. Koukouli-Chrysanthaki (Drama, 1992)
Drev. Bosp.	*Drevnosti Bospora*, 1– (Institut arkheologii Rossiiskoi Akademii Nauk [Moscow, 1998–])
Drev. Prichern.	*Drevnee Prichernomor'e. Chteniia pam'iati professora Petra Osipovicha Karyshkovskogo*, 1–3 (Odessa, 1990–6)
Dritte Reise	J. Keil and A. von Premerstein, *Bericht über eine dritte Reise in Lydien und den angrenzenden Gebieten Ioniens* (*Denkschriften der Kaiserlichen Akademie der Wissenschaften in Wien*, phil.-hist. Kl., 57 (1) [Vienna, 1914])
Dubois, *IGDOlbia*	L. Dubois, *Inscriptions grecques dialectales d'Olbia du Pont* (École Pratique des Hautes Études, Sciences historiques et philologiques, III. *Hautes études du monde gréco-romain*, 22 [Geneva, 1996])
Düll, *Götterkulte*	S. Düll, *Die Götterkulte Nordmakedoniens in römischer Zeit. Eine kultische und typologische Untersuchung anhand epigraphischer, numismatischer und archäologischer Denkmäler* (*Münchener archäologische Studien*, 7 [Munich, 1977])
Düring	I. Düring, *Aristotle in the ancient biographical tradition* (Acta Universitatis Gothoburgensis, *Studia graeca et latina Gothoburgensia*, 5 [Göteborg, 1957])
Dumont–Homolle	A. Dumont, *Mélanges d'archéologie et d'épigraphie (réunis par Th. Homolle)* (Paris, 1892)
EAD	*Exploration archéologique de Délos faite par l'École française d'Athènes*, 1– (Paris, 1909–)
EAM	*Ἐπιγραφὲς Ἄνω Μακεδονίας* (*Ἐλίμεια, Ἐορδαία, Νότια Λυγκηστίς, Ὀρεστίς*). I, *Κατάλογος ἐπιγραφῶν*, edd. Th. Rizakis and G. Touratsoglou (Athens, 1985)
Eastern cults	M. Tacheva, *Eastern cults in Moesia Inferior and Thracia (5th century BC-4th century AD)* (*Études préliminaires aux religions orientales dans l'empire romain*, 95 [Leiden, 1983])
Ebersolt, *Mission*	J. Ebersolt, *Mission archéologique de Constantinople* (Paris, 1921)
Edirne Müzesi Rehberi	*Edirne Müzesi Rehberi* (*Arkeoloji ve Sanat Yayınları. Müze Rehberleri Dizisi*, 2 [Istanbul, 1984])
EEBS	*Ἐπετηρὶς τῆς Ἑταιρείας Βυζαντινῶν Σπουδῶν*, 1– (Athens, 1924–)
Egnatia	*Ἐγνατία. Ἐπιστημονικὴ ἐπετηρίδα τῆς Φιλοσοφικῆς Σχολῆς*, 1– (*Ἀριστοτέλειο Πανεπιστήμιο Θεσσαλονίκης* [Thessaloniki, 1989–])
Eirene	*Eirene. Studia graeca et latina*, 1– (Československá Akademie Věd. Kabinet pro studia recká, rimská a latinská [Prague, 1960–])
Ellinizm	*Ellinizm. Ekonomika, Politika, Kul'tura*, ed. E. S. Golubstova (Moscow, 1992)
Eph. Ep.	*Ephemeris Epigraphica. Corporis Inscriptionum Latinarum Supplementum*, ed. W. Henzen, 1–9 (Rome, 1872–1913)
Epigr. Anat.	*Epigraphica Anatolica. Zeitschrift für Epigraphik und historische Geographie Anatoliens*, 1– (Bonn, 1983–)
Epigr. arch. Mak.	B. Misailidou-Despotidou, *Ἐπιγραφὲς ἀρχαίας Μακεδονίας ἀπὸ τὴ συλλογὴ τῆς ΙΣΤ' Ἐφορείας Προϊστορικῶν καὶ Κλασικῶν Ἀρχαιοτήτων. Κατάλογος τῆς ἔκθεσης, Ὀκτώβριος - Δεκέμβριος 1997, Κρυπτὴ Στοὰ τῆς Ἀρχαίας Ἀγορᾶς* (Thessaloniki, 1997)
Epigr. Makedonias	*Ἐπιγραφὲς τῆς Μακεδονίας. Γ' διεθνὲς συμπόσιο γιὰ τὴ Μακεδονία, Θεσσαλονίκη 8-12 Δεκεμβρίου 1993*, ed. E. Voutyras (Thessaloniki, 1996)
Epigraphica	*Epigraphica. Rivista italiana di epigrafia*, 1– (Milan, 1937–)
Eretria	*Eretria. Fouilles et recherches*, 1–7 (Berne, 1968–85); 8– (Lausanne, 1993–)
Essays Hersh	*Coins of Macedonia and Rome. Essays in honour of Charles Hersh*, edd. A. Hersh, U. Wartenberg and R. Witschonke (London, 1999)
Essays Laourdas	*Μελετήματα στὴ μνήμη Βασιλείου Λαούρδα* (Thessaloniki and Athens, 1975)
Essays Thomas	*Essays and Texts in honor of J. David Thomas*, edd. T. Gagos and R. S. Bagnall (*American Studies in Papyrology*, 42 [Oakville, Connecticut, 2001])
Ét. Balk.	*Études Balkaniques*, 1– (Académie bulgare des sciences, Institut d'études balkaniques [Sofia, 1964–])
Ét. Thas.	*Études thasiennes*, 1– (Paris, 1944–)
Etiudy	*Etiudy po antichnoi istorii i kul'ture Severnogo Prichernomor'ia*, edd. A. K. Gavrilov et al. (Rossiiskaia Akademiia Nauk, Peterburgskii filial Instituta Rossiiskoi istorii [St. Petersburg, 1992])
Eulimeni	*Εὐλιμένη. Μελετες στήν κλασικὴ ἀρχαιολογία, τὴν ἐπιγραφικὴ, τὴ νομισματικὴ καὶ τὴν παπυρολογία*, 1– (*Μεσογειακὴ Ἀρχαιολογικὴ Ἑταιρεία* [Rethymnon, 2000–])
Evraz. drevn.	*Evraziiskie drevnosti. 100 let B. N. Grakvu, arkhivnye, materialy, publikatsii, stat'i*, edd. A. I. Meliukova, M. G. Moshkova and V. A. Bashilov (Institut arkheologii RAN [Moscow, 1999])
FD	*Fouilles de Delphes*, 1– (Paris, 1909–)
Feissel, *RICM*	D. Feissel, *Recueil des inscriptions chrétiennes de Macédoine du IIIe au VIe siècle* (*BCH* Suppl., 8 [Paris, 1983])
FGrH	F. Jacoby, *Die Fragmente der griechischen Historiker*, I–III C (Berlin/Leiden, 1926–58)
Fıratlı, *Sculpture byzantine*	N. Fıratlı, *La sculpture byzantine figurée au musée archéologique d'Istanbul, (Catalogue revu et présenté par C. Metzger, A. Pralong et J.-P. Sodini)* (*Bibliothèque de l'Institut français d'études anatoliennes d'Istanbul*, 30 [Paris, 1990])
Fıratlı–Robert	N. Fıratlı, *Les stèles funéraires de Byzance gréco-romaine avec l'édition et l'index commenté des épitaphes par L. Robert* (*Bibliothèque archéologique et historique de l'Institut français d'archéologie d'Istanbul*, 15 [Paris, 1964])
Filow, *Duvanlij*	B. D. Filow, *Die Grabhügelnekropole bei Duvanlij in Südbulgarien* (Bulgarski Arkheologicheski Institut [Sofia, 1934])

Florina	I. M. Akamatis and M. Lilimbaki-Akamati, *Hellenistic City in Florina* (Thessaloniki, 1996)
Fouilles et Recherches (Sofia)	*Fouilles et Recherches du Musée National de Sofia* (*Razkopki i prouchvania na Narodnia Muzei v Sofia*), 1–2 (Sofia, 1948)
FRA	M. J. Osborne and S. G. Byrne, *The Foreign Residents of Athens. An Annex to The Lexicon of Greek Personal Names: Attica* (*Studia Hellenistica*, 33 [Louvain, 1996])
Fraser, *Cities*	P. M. Fraser, *Cities of Alexander the Great* (Oxford, 1996)
Fraser, *Ptol. Alex.*	P. M. Fraser, *Ptolemaic Alexandria*, 3 vols. (Oxford, 1972)
Frolova, *CKB A.D. 69-238*	N. A. Frolova, *The Coinage of the Kingdom of Bosporos A.D. 69-238* (*BAR International Series*, 56 [Oxford, 1979])
Frolova, *CKB A.D. 242-341/342*	N. A. Frolova, *The Coinage of the Kingdom of Bosporus A.D. 242-341/342* (*BAR International Series*, 166 [Oxford, 1983])
FVS	*Die Fragmente der Vorsokratiker*, ed. H. Diels, 6th revised edn. by W. Kranz, 3 vols. (Berlin, 1951–2)
Gaidukevich, *AGB Mirmekii*	V. F. Gaidukevich, *Antichnye goroda Bospora, Mirmekii* (Akademiia Nauk SSSR, Institut arkheologii [Leningrad, 1987])
Gaidukevich, *Mirmekii*	V. F. Gaidukevich, *Mirmekii. Sovetskie raskopki v 1956 g., 1934-1956* (*Wykopaliska polsko-radzieckie w Mirmeki*, 2 [Warsaw, 1959])
Gaidukevich, *Ol'viia*	*Ol'viia. Temenos i agora*, ed. V. F. Gaidukevich (Moscow and Leningrad, 1964)
Gerasimov	T. D. Gerasimov, *Antichni i srednovekovni moneti v Bulgarii* (Sofia, 1975)
Germania	*Germania*, 1– (Deutsches Archäologisches Institut, Römisch–Germanische Kommission [Frankfurt, 1918–])
Giannini, *Parad. Gr.*	A. Giannini, *Paradoxographorum Graecorum reliquiae* (*Classici greci e latini. Sezione testi e commenti*, 3 [Milan, 1966])
Glossa kai mageia	*Γλῶσσα καὶ μαγεία. Κείμενα ἀπὸ τὴν ἀρχαιότητα*, edd. A.-Ph. Christidis and D. Jordan (Athens, 1997)
God. Dep. Arkh.	*Godishnik na Departament Arkheologia – NBU* (*Annuary of Department of Archaeology – NBU*), 1– (Sofia, 1994–)
Gorny–Mosch sale	Gorny and Mosch, Giessener Münzhandlung, München (formerly Giessener Münzhandlung, Dieter Gorny GMBH, München), sale catalogues
GP	*The Greek Anthology, The Garland of Philip*, edd. A. S. F. Gow and D. L. Page, 2 vols. (Cambridge, 1968)
Gr. Rom. Settlements in Black Sea	*Greek and Roman Settlements on the Black Sea Coast. A workshop held at the 95th annual meeting of the Archaeological Institute of America, Washington, D.C., USA, December 1993*, ed. G. R. Tsetskhladze (*Colloquenda Pontica* [Bradford, 1994])
Graffiti del Palatino	*Graffiti del Palatino*, edd. P. Castrén, H. Lilius, H. Solin and M. Itkonen-Kaila, 2 vols. (*Acta Instituti Romani Finlandiae*, 3-4 [Helsinki, 1966, 1970])
Grainger, *SPG*	J. D. Grainger, *A Seleukid Prosopography and Gazetteer* (*Mnemosyne* Suppl., 172 [Leiden, New York, Cologne, 1997])
Grandjean, *Arétalogie*	Y. Grandjean, *Une nouvelle arétalogie d'Isis à Maronée* (*Études préliminaires aux religions orientales dans l'empire romain*, 49 [Leiden, 1975])
GRBS	*Greek, Roman and Byzantine Studies*, 1– (San Antonio, Texas, 1956; Cambridge, Mass., 1957–9; Durham, N. Carolina, 1960–)
Greek Colonisation	*The Greek Colonisation of the Black Sea Area. Historical Interpretation of Archaeology*, ed. G. R. Tsetskhladze (*Historia Einzelschriften*, 121 [Stuttgart, 1998])
Greifenhagen, *Schmuckarb.*	A. Greifenhagen, *Schmuckarbeiten in Edelmetall*, 2 vols. (Staatliche Museen Preussischer Kulturbesitz, Antikenabteilung, Berlin [Berlin, 1970, 1975])
Guarducci, *Ep. Gr.*	M. Guarducci, *Epigrafia greca*, 4 vols. (Rome, 1967–78)
Güngerich, *Dion. Byz.*	R. Güngerich, *Dionysii Byzantii Anaplus Bospori* (2nd edn., Berlin, 1958)
GVI	W. Peek, *Griechische Vers-Inschriften*. 1, *Grab-Epigramme* (Berlin, 1955)
Hald, *Auf den Trümmern Stobis*	K. Hald, *Auf den Trümmern Stobis. Beiträge zur Geschichte und Geographie Altmazedoniens* (Stuttgart, 1917)
Hatzopoulos, *Actes Amphipolis*	M. B. Hatzopoulos, *Actes de vente d'Amphipolis* (*Μελετήματα*, 14 [Athens, 1991])
Hatzopoulos, *Actes Chalc.*	M. B. Hatzopoulos, *Actes de vente de la Chalcidique centrale* (*Μελετήματα*, 6 [Athens, 1988])
Hatzopoulos, *Donation*	M. B. Hatzopoulos, *Une donation du roi Lysimaque* (*Μελετήματα*, 5 [Athens, 1988])
Hatzopoulos, *MI*	M. B. Hatzopoulos, *Macedonian Institutions under the Kings. A Historical and Epigraphical Study*, 2 vols. (*Μελετήματα*, 22 [Athens, 1996])
Hatzopoulos–Loukopoulou, *Two Studies*	M. B. Hatzopoulos and L. D. Loukopoulou, *Two Studies in ancient Macedonian Topography* (*Μελετήματα*, 3 [Athens, 1987])
HE	*The Greek Anthology, Hellenistic Epigrams*, edd. A. S. F. Gow and D. L. Page, 2 vols. (Cambridge, 1965)
Hellenika	*Ἑλληνικά*, 1–11 (Athens, 1928–39); 12– (*Ἑταιρεία Μακεδονικῶν Σπουδῶν* [Thessaloniki, 1952–])
Hellenismus	*Hellenismus. Beiträge zur Erforschung von Akkulturation und politischer Ordnung in den Staaten des hellenistischen Zeitalters. Akten des internationalen Hellenismus-Kolloquiums, 9.-14. März 1994 in Berlin*, ed. B. Funck (Tübingen, 1996)
Helly, *Gonnoi*	B. Helly, *Gonnoi*, 2 vols. (Amsterdam, 1973)

Helly, *L'État thessalien*	B. Helly, *L'État thessalien. Aleuas le roux, les tétrades et les tagoi* (*Collection de la Maison de l'Orient Méditerranéen*, 25, Série épigraphique, 2 [Lyon, 1995])
Hesp.	*Hesperia*, 1– (American School of Classical Studies [Princeton, 1932–])
Hess–Leu sale	Adolph Hess AG Luzern, Bank Leu & Co. AG Zürich, sale catalogues (1956–1969)
Heuzey, *Le Mont Olympe*	L. Heuzey, *Le Mont Olympe et l'Acarnanie* (Paris, 1860)
Higgins, *GRJ*	R. A. Higgins, *Greek and Roman Jewelry* (London, 1961)
Historia	*Historia. Zeitschrift für Alte Geschichte*, 1– (Wiesbaden, 1950–)
Historia (Milan)	*Historia. Studi storici per l'antichità classica*, 1–9 (Milan, 1927–35)
Histria	*Histria*, edd. E. Conduracchi, D. Pippidi, P. Alexandrescu et al., 1– (Institutul de arheologie al Academiei România [Bucharest and Paris, 1954–])
*HN*²	B. V. Head, *Historia Numorum. A Manual of Greek Numismatics* (2nd edn. Oxford, 1911)
Hoffmann, *Makedonen*	O. Hoffmann, *Die Makedonen, ihre Sprache und ihr Volkstum* (Göttingen, 1906)
Holleaux, *Études*	M. Holleaux, *Études d'épigraphie et d'histoire grecques*, ed. L. Robert, 6 vols. (Paris, 1938–68)
Holwerda	J. H. Holwerda, *Het laat-grieksche en romeinsche Gebruiksaardewerk uit het Middellandsche-Zee-Gebied in het Rijksmuseum van Oudheden te Leiden* (The Hague, 1936)
Horos	*ΗΟΡΟΣ*, 1– (*Ἑλληνικὴ ἐπιγραφικὴ Ἑταιρεία* [Athens, 1983–])
Hyettos	R. Étienne and D. Knoepfler, *Hyettos de Béotie et la chronologie des archontes fédéraux entre 250 et 171 avant J.-C.* (*BCH* Suppl., 3 [Paris, 1976])
Hyperboreus	*Hyperboreus. Studia Classica*, 1– (Bibliotheca Classica Petropolitana [St. Petersburg, 1994–])
IAK	*Izvestiia Imperatorskoi Arkheologicheskoi Kommissii*, 1–65 (St. Petersburg, 1901–1918); subsequently *Izvestiia Gosudarstvennoi Rossiiskoi Arkheologicheskoi Kommissii*, 66 (Petrograd, 1918)
IApameia	*Die Inschriften von Apameia (Bithynien) und Pylai*, ed. T. Corsten (*IGSK*, 32 [Bonn, 1987])
IApoll	*Corpus des inscriptions grecques d'Illyrie méridionale et d'Épire*. I. 2 A, *Inscriptions d'Apollonia d'Illyrie*, edd. P. Cabanes and N. Ceka; B, *Listes des noms de monétaires d'Apollonia et Épidamne-Dyrrhachion*, ed. H. Ceka, M. Beauregard, and O. Masson (*Études Épigraphiques*, 2 [Paris, 1997])
IAskl	*Altertümer von Pergamon*. VIII (3), *Die Inschriften des Asklepieions*, ed. Ch. Habicht (Deutsches Archäologisches Institut [Berlin, 1969])
Iatrus–Krivina	V. Dimova et al., *Iatrus–Krivina. Spätantike Befestigung und frühmittelalterliche Siedlung an der unteren Donau*, 5 vols. (Akademie der Wissenschaften der DDR, Zentralinstitut für Alte Geschichte und Archäologie, *Schriften zur Geschichte und Kultur der Antike*, 17 [Berlin, 1979])
IBer	*Ἐπιγραφὲς Κάτω Μακεδονίας (μεταξὺ τοῦ Βερμίου ὄρους καὶ τοῦ Ἀξιοῦ ποταμοῦ). Α΄, Ἐπιγραφὲς Βέροιας*, edd. L. Gounaropoulou and M. B. Hatzopoulos (Athens, 1998)
IByz	*Die Inschriften von Byzantion*. I, *Die Inschriften*, ed. A. Łajtar (*IGSK*, 58 [Bonn, 2000])
IC	*Inscriptiones Creticae*, ed. M. Guarducci, 4 vols. (Rome, 1935–50)
Iconomu, *Opaite greco-romane*	C. Iconomu, *Opaite greco-romane* (Muzeul de Archeologie Constanţa [Constanza, 1967])
ICos	*Iscrizioni di Cos*, ed. M. Segre (*Monografie della Scuola archeologica di Atene e delle missioni italiane in Oriente*, 6 [Rome, 1993])
ID	*Inscriptions de Délos*, edd. A. Plassart, J. Coupry, F. Durrbach, P. Roussel and M. Launey, 7 vols. (Paris, 1926–1950)
ID Index	J. Tréheux, *Inscriptions de Délos, Index*. I, *Les étrangers, à l'exclusion des Athéniens de la clérouchie et des Romains* (Académie des Inscriptions et Belles-Lettres [Paris, 1992])
IDidyma	*Didyma*. II, *Die Inschriften*, edd. A. Rehm and R. Harder (Berlin, 1958)
IDR	*Inscriptiones Daciae Romanae*, edd. I. I. Russu et al., 3 vols. in 6 (*Inscriptiones Daciae et Scythiae Minoris antiquae*, series prior [Bucharest, 1975–1988])
IDyrrh	*Corpus des inscriptions grecques d'Illyrie méridionale et d'Épire*. I.1, *Inscriptions d'Épidamne-Dyrrhachion*, edd. P. Cabanes and F. Drini (*Études Épigraphiques*, 2 [Paris, 1995])
IEK	*Die Inschriften von Erythrai und Klazomenai*, edd. H. Engelmann and R. Merkelbach, 2 vols. (*IGSK*, 1–2 [Bonn, 1972–3])
IEph	*Die Inschriften von Ephesos*, edd. R. Merkelbach, J. Nollé et al., 7 vols. in 8 (*IGSK*, 11–17 [Bonn, 1979–81])
IFayoum	*Recueil des inscriptions grecques du Fayoum*, ed. E. Bernand, 3 vols. (vol. I, Leiden, 1975; vols. II–III, Institut français d'archéologie orientale du Caire, *Bibliothèque d'étude*, 79–80 [Paris, 1981])
IG	*Inscriptiones Graecae* (Berlin, 1877–); ² (Berlin, 1913–); ³ Vol. I (1–3) (Berlin, 1981–98), various editors
IGAIMK	*Izvestiia Gosudarstvennoi Akademii istorii material'noi kul'tury*, 1–139 (Moscow, 1927–36); continues *Izvestiia Rossiiskoi Akademii istorii material'noi kul'tury*, 1–4 (Moscow, 1921–25)
IGB	*Inscriptiones Graecae in Bulgaria repertae*, ed. G. Mihailov, 5 vols. in 6 (Sofia, 1951–97; I² 1970)
IGerasa	C. B. Welles, 'The Inscriptions', pp. 355-494 in *Gerasa, City of the Decapolis. An account embodying the record of a joint excavation conducted by Yale University and the British School of Archaeology in Jerusalem (1928–1930) and Yale University and the American Schools of Oriental Research (1930–1931, 1933–1934)*, ed. C. H. Kraeling (New Haven, 1938)
IGLMP	M. T. Manni Piraino, *Iscrizioni greche lapidarie del museo di Palermo* (*Σικελικά*, 6 [Palermo, 1973])
IGLNovae	*Inscriptions grecques et latines de Novae (Mésie Inférieure)*, edd. J. Kolendo and V. Božilova (Ausonius, *Mémoires*, 1 [Bordeaux, 1997])

IGR	*Inscriptiones Graecae ad res Romanas pertinentes*, edd. R. Cagnat, G. Lafaye et al., vols. I, II and IV (Paris, 1906–27)
IGUR	L. Moretti, *Inscriptiones Graecae Urbis Romae*, 4 vols. in 5 (*Studi pubblicati dall'Istituto italiano per la storia antica*, 17, 22 (1-2), 28, 47 [Rome, 1968–1990])
IHermoupolis	E. Bernand, *Inscriptions grecques d'Hermoupolis Magna et de sa nécropole* (Institut français d'archéologie orientale, *Bibliothèque d'étude*, 123 [Cairo, 1999])
IIasos	*Die Inschriften von Iasos*, ed. W. Blümel, 2 vols. (*IGSK*, 28 (1–2) [Bonn, 1985])
IIlion	*Die Inschriften von Ilion*, ed. P. Frisch (*IGSK*, 3 [Bonn, 1975])
IKalch	*Die Inschriften von Kalchedon*, ed. R. Merkelbach (*IGSK*, 20 [Bonn, 1980])
IKAM	*Istoriia i kul'tura antichnogo mira*, ed. M. M. Kobylina (Moscow, 1977)
IKnid	*Die Inschriften von Knidos*, ed. W. Blümel, vol. I (*IGSK*, 41 [Bonn, 1992])
IKyz	*Die Inschriften von Kyzikos u. Umgebung*, ed. E. Schwertheim, 2 vols. (*IGSK*, 18, 26 [Bonn, 1980, 1983])
ILAlg	*Inscriptions latines de l'Algérie*, edd. S. Gsell, H.-G. Pflaum and X. Dupuis, 3 vols. (Paris, 1922, 1976, 2003)
ILaodLyk	*Die Inschriften von Laodikeia am Lykos*. I, *Die Inschriften*, ed. T. Corsten (*IGSK*, 49 [Bonn, 1997])
ILB	B. Gerov, *Inscriptiones latinae in Bulgaria repertae. Inscriptiones inter Oescum et Iatrum repertae* (Sofia, 1989)
ILeukopetra	Ph. M. Petsas, M. B. Hatzopoulos, L. Gounaropoulou and P. Paschidis, *Inscriptions du sanctuaire de la Mère des Dieux autochthone de Leukopetra (Macédoine)* (*Μελετήματα*, 28 [Athens, 2000])
ILGR	*Inscriptiones latinae in Graecia repertae. Additamenta ad CIL III*, ed. M. Šašel Kos (*Epigrafia e Antichità. Studi a cura dell'Istituto di storia antica dell'Università di Bologna*, 5 [Faenza, 1979])
ILind	*Lindos. Fouilles et recherches 1902–1914*. II, *Inscriptions*, ed. C. Blinkenberg, 2 vols. (Berlin and Copenhagen, 1941)
ILNovae	*Inscriptions latines de Novae*, edd. V. Božilova, J. Kolendo and L. Mrozewicz (*Seria Archeologia*, 34 [Poznan, 1992])
ILS	*Inscriptiones latinae selectae*, ed. H. Dessau, 3 vols. in 4 (Berlin, 1892–1916)
IMagnSip	*Die Inschriften von Magnesia am Sipylos*, ed. T. Ihnken (*IGSK*, 8 [Bonn, 1978])
Imhoof-Blumer, *MGr*	F. Imhoof-Blumer, *Monnaies grecques* (Paris and Leipzig, 1883)
IMM	*Die Inschriften von Magnesia am Maeander*, ed. O. Kern (Berlin, 1900)
IMS	*Inscriptions de la Mésie Supérieure*, edd. F. Papazoglu, M. Mirković, B. Dragojević-Josifovska et al., 4 vols. (Belgrade, 1976–)
IMylasa	*Die Inschriften von Mylasa*, ed. W. Blümel, 2 vols. (*IGSK*, 34-35 [Bonn, 1987–88])
In. Fil.	*Inozemna Filolohiia*, 1– (L'vivs'kye derzhavnyi universytet im. Iv. Franka Ukraine, Ministerstvo vyshchoï i seredn'oï spetsial'noï osvity [L'vov, 1964–])
Index Hipp.	*Index Hippocraticus*, edd. J.-H. Kühn, U. Fleischer et al. (Göttingen, 1989)
IOlbia	*Nadpisi Ol'vii (1917-1965)*, edd. T. N. Knipovich and E. I. Levi (Akademiia Nauk SSSR, Institut arkheologii [Leningrad, 1968])
IOrop	*Οἱ ἐπιγραφὲς τοῦ Ὠρωποῦ*, ed. B. Ch. Petrakos (*Βιβλιοθήκη τῆς ἐν Ἀθήναις Ἀρχαιολογικῆς Ἑταιρείας*, 170 [Athens 1997])
IOSPE	*Inscriptiones antiquae orae septentrionalis Ponti Euxini graecae et latinae*, ed. B. Latyschev, 4 vols. (St. Petersburg, 1885–1901; I², 1916)
IPerg	*Altertümer von Pergamon*. VIII (1–2), *Die Inschriften von Pergamon*, ed. M. Fraenkel, (Berlin, 1890, 1895)
IPerinth	M. H. Sayar, *Perinthos-Herakleia (Marmara Ereğlisi) und Umgebung. Geschichte, Testimonien, griechische und lateinische Inschriften* (Österreichische Akademie der Wissenschaften, phil.-hist. Kl., *Denkschriften*, 269; *Veröffentlichungen der Kleinasiatischen Kommission*, 9 [Vienna, 1998])
IPrusa	*Die Inschriften von Prusa ad Olympum*, ed. T. Corsten, 2 vols. (*IGSK*, 39–40 [Bonn, 1991, 1993])
IRhamnous	*Ὁ δῆμος τοῦ Ῥαμνοῦντος. Σύνοψη τῶν ἀνασκαφῶν καὶ τῶν ἐρευνῶν (1813-1998)*. II, *Οἱ ἐπιγραφὲς*, ed. B. Ch. Petrakos (*Βιβλιοθήκη τῆς ἐν Ἀθήναις Ἀρχαιολογικῆς Ἑταιρείας*, 182 [Athens, 1999])
IRhodPer	*Die Inschriften der Rhodischen Peraia*, ed. W. Blümel (*IGSK*, 38 [Bonn, 1991])
ISamothrace	*Samothrace*, 2, part 1, *The Inscriptions on Stone*, ed. P. M. Fraser (*Bollingen Series* LX.2, 1 [New York, 1960])
Iscr. Gr. Verona	T. Ritti, *Iscrizioni e rilievi greci del Museo Maffeiano di Verona* (*Collezione e Musei Archeologici del Veneto*, 21 [Rome, 1981])
ISestos	*Die Inschriften von Sestos und der thrakischen Chersones*, ed. J. Krauss (*IGSK*, 19 [Bonn, 1980])
ISM	*Inscriptiones Scythiae Minoris graecae et latinae* (*Inscriptiones Daciae et Scythiae Minoris antiquae*, series altera [Bucharest, 1980–]). I, *Inscriptiones Histriae et viciniae*, ed. D. M. Pippidi (1983); II, *Tomis et territorium*, ed. I. Stoian (1987); III, *Callatis et territorium*, ed. A. Avram (1999); V, *Capidava–Troesmis–Noviodunum*, ed. A. Doruţiu-Boilă (1980)
ISmyrna	*Die Inschriften von Smyrna*, ed. G. Petzl, 3 vols. (*IGSK*, 23 (1), 24 (1-2) [Bonn, 1982–1990])
Istanbul Ark. Müz.	*Istanbul Arkeoloji Müzeleri Yıllığı (Annual of the Archeological Museums of Istanbul)*, 1– (Istanbul, 1949–)
Istorikogeographika	*Ἱστορικογεωγραφικά. Περιοδικὴ ἔκδοση γιὰ τὴν ἱστορία, γεωγραφία καὶ τοπογραφία τοῦ Ἑλλαδικοῦ χώρου κατὰ τοὺς μέσους χρόνους*, 1– (Ioannina and Thessaloniki, 1986–)

IThrakAig	*Ἐπιγραφὲς τῆς Θράκης τοῦ Αἰγαίου*, edd. L. D. Loukopoulou, S. Psoma et al. (Athens, forthcoming)
ITrall	*Die Inschriften von Tralleis und Nysa*. I, *Die Inschriften von Tralleis*, ed. F. B. Poljakov (*IGSK*, 36 (1) [Bonn, 1989])
IvOl	*Olympia*. v, *Die Inschriften von Olympia*, edd. W. Dittenberger and K. Purgold (Berlin, 1896)
James, *ANT*	M. R. James, *The Apocryphal New Testament. A collection of apocryphal Christian literature in an English translation* (revised and newly translated edn. by J. K. Elliot of *The Apocryphal New Testament* translated by M. R. James (1924) [Oxford, 1993])
JDAI	*Jahrbuch des Deutschen Archäologischen Instituts*, 1– (Berlin, 1886–)
JEA	*Journal of Egyptian Archaeology*, 1– (Egypt Exploration Fund [London, 1914–])
JHS	*Journal of Hellenic Studies*, 1– (Society for the Promotion of Hellenic Studies [London, 1881–])
JNG	*Jahrbuch für Numismatik und Geldgeschichte*, 1– (Bayerische Numismatische Gesellschaft [Munich, 1949–51, 1986– ; Kallmünz, 1952–85])
JÖAI	*Jahreshefte des Österreichischen Archäologischen Institutes in Wien*, 1– (Vienna, 1898–)
Kabile	*Kabile*, edd. T. Ivanov and V. Velkov, 2 vols. (Bulgarska Akademiia na Naukite, Arkheologicheski Institut i Muzei [Sofia, 1982, 1991])
Kalinka, *Denkmäler*	E. Kalinka, *Antike Denkmäler in Bulgarien* (Akademie der Wissenschaften in Wien, *Schriften der Balkankommission, Antiquarische Abteilung*, 4 [Vienna, 1906])
Kanatsoulis	D. Kanatsoulis, *Μακεδονικὴ προσωπογραφία (ἀπὸ τοῦ 148 π.Χ. μέχρι τῶν χρόνων τοῦ Μ. Κωνσταντίνου)* (*Ἑλληνικά* Suppl., 8 [Thessaloniki, 1955]); Supplement (*Δημοσιεύματα τῆς Ἑταιρείας Μακεδονικῶν Σπουδῶν* [Thessaloniki, 1967])
Kaphtantzis	G. B. Kaphtantzis, *Ἱστορία τῆς πόλεως Σερρῶν καὶ τῆς περιφερείας της (ἀπὸ τοὺς προϊστορικοὺς χρόνους μέχρι σήμερα)*, 2 vols. (Athens, 1967, 1972)
Karayotov, *Mesambria*	I. Karayotov, *The Coinage of Mesambria*. I, *Silver and gold coins of Mesambria* (*Thracia Pontica* ser. VI, Thracia Maritima. Corpus Numorum [Sozopol, 1994])
Karyshkovskii, *MO*	P. O. Karyshkovskii, *Monety Ol'vii. Ocherk denezhnogo obrashcheniia Severo-Zapadnogo Prichernomor'ia v antichnuiu epokhu* (Akademiia Nauk Ukrainskoi SSR, Odesskii arkheologicheskii Muzei [Kiev, 1988])
Kat. gr. rim. terakota	M. Veličković, *Katalog grčkih i rimskih terakota* (Narodni Muzej Beograd, *Antika*, 3 [Belgrade, 1957])
Kats	V. I. Kats, *Keramicheskie kleima Khersonesa Tavricheskogo: katalog opredelitel' (Ceramic stamps of Tauric Chersonesus: the determinant catalogue)* (Saratov, 1994)
Kazarow	G. I. Kazarow, *Die Denkmäler des thrakischen Reitergottes in Bulgarien* (*Dissertationes Pannonicae*, ser. II, fasc. 14 [Budapest, 1938])
Kazı Sonuçları	*Kazı Sonuçları Toplantısı*, 1– (T.C. Kültür Bakanlığı, Anıtlar ve Müzeler Genel Müdürlüğü [Ankara, 1979–])
KF	R. Herzog, *Koische Forschungen und Funde* (Leipzig, 1899; repr. Hildesheim and New York, 1983)
KGAM Thess.	G. Despinis, Th. Stephanidou-Tiveriou and E. Voutyras, *Κατάλογος γλυπτῶν τοῦ Ἀρχαιολογικοῦ Μουσείου Θεσσαλονίκης*, 2 vols. (Thessaloniki, 1997, 2003)
Khers. Sbornik	*Khersonesskii Sbornik. Materialy po arkheologii Khersonesa Tavricheskogo*, 1–5 (*Gosudarstvennyi Khersonesskii Muzei* [Sebastopol, 1926–59])
Kindstrand, *Bion of Borysthenes*	J. F. Kindstrand, *Bion of Borysthenes. A collection of the fragments with introduction and commentary* (Acta Universitatis Upsaliensis, *Studia graeca Upsaliensia*, 11 [Stockholm, 1976])
Kings and Colonists	R. A. Billows, *Kings and Colonists. Aspects of Macedonian Imperialism* (*Columbia Studies in the Classical Tradition*, 22 [Leiden, 1994])
Klio	*Klio. Beiträge zur Alten Geschichte*, 1– (Leipzig, 1901–44; Berlin, 1959–)
Kraay-Mørkholm Essays	*Kraay-Mørkholm Essays. Numismatic studies in memory of C. M. Kraay and O. Mørkholm*, edd. G. Le Rider, K. Jenkins, N. Waggoner and U. Westermark (Louvain, 1989)
Krahe, *Altillyr. Personnamen*	H. Krahe, *Lexikon altillyrischer Personennamen* (*Indogermanische Bibliothek, Untersuchungen*, 9 [Heidelberg, 1929])
Kratylos	*Kratylos. Kritisches Berichts- und Rezensionsorgan für indogermanische und allgemeine Sprachwissenschaft*, 1– (Wiesbaden, 1956–)
Kruglikova, *Bospor*	I. T. Kruglikova, *Bospor v pozdneantichnoe vremia (ocherki ekonomicheskoi istorii)* (Moscow, 1966)
KSIA	*Kratkie soobshcheniia o dokladakh i polevych issledovaniiakh Instituta arkheologii*, 1– (Akademiia Nauk SSR, Institut arkheologii [Moscow, 1939–])
KSIIMK	*Kratkie soobshcheniia o dokladakh i polevych issledovaniiakh Instituta istorii material'noi kul'tury* (Akademiia Nauk SSR, Institut istorii material'noi kul'tury [Moscow, 1939–])
KSOGAM	*Kratkie soobshcheniia o polevykh arkheologicheskikh issledovaniiakh Odesskogo Gosudarstvennogo Arkheologicheskogo Muzeia* (Odes'kyi derzhavnyi arkheolohichnyi Muzei [Odessa, 1961–])
Kurgan Solokha	A. P. Mantsevich, *Kurgan Solokha* (Leningrad, 1987)
Kuzmanov, *Antichni lampy*	G. Kuzmanov, *Antichni lampy. Kolektsiia na Natsionaliia Arkheologicheski Muzei* (Bulgarska Akademiia na Naukite, Arkheologicheski Institut i Muzei [Sofia, 1992])
KW	*Griechische Grabreliefs aus Südrussland*, edd. G. von Kieseritzky and C. Watzinger (Berlin, 1909)
La Thessalie	*La Thessalie. Actes de la table-ronde, 21-24 juillet 1975, Lyon* (*Collection de la Maison de l'Orient Méditerranéen*, 6, Série archéologique, 5 [Lyon, 1979])
Labraunda	*Labraunda. Swedish excavations and researches*. III (1-2), *The Greek Inscriptions*, ed. J. Crampa (*Acta Instituti Atheniensis Regni Sueciae*, series in 4°, 5 [Lund, 1969; Stockholm, 1972])

La'da	C. A. La'da, *Foreign ethnics in Hellenistic Egypt* (*Studia Hellenistica*, 38; *Prosopographia Ptolemaica*, 10 [Louvain, 2002])
Lanz sale	Numismatik Lanz, München, sale catalogues
Latomus	*Latomus*, 1– (Brussels, 1937–)
Latreies sten Perifereia	*Λατρείες στὴν 'Περιφέρεια' τοῦ ἀρχαίου Ἑλληνικοῦ κόσμου*, ed. A. A. Avagianou (*Ἐθνικὸ Ἵδρυμα Ἐρευνῶν* [Athens, 2002])
Latyshev, *Menolog. anon.*	*Menologii anonymi byzantini saeculi X quae supersunt: fasciculos duos sumptibus Caesareae Academiae Scientiarum e codice Mosquensi 376 Vlad*, ed. V. V. Latyshev, 2 vols. (Moscow, 1911–12; repr. Leipzig, 1970)
Latyshev, *Sbornik*	V. V. Latyshev, *Sbornik grecheskich nadpisei khristianskich vremen iz yuzhnoi Rossii* (St. Petersburg, 1896)
Launey	M. Launey, *Recherches sur les armées hellénistiques*, 2 vols. (*BEFAR*, 169 [2nd edn. Paris, 1987])
LCM	*Liverpool Classical Monthly*, 1– (Liverpool, 1976–)
Lemerle	P. Lemerle, *Les plus anciens recueils des miracles de saint Démétrius et la pénétration des slaves dans les Balkans*, 2 vols. (Paris, 1979, 1981)
Leroux, *Lagynos*	G. Leroux, *Lagynos. Recherches sur la céramique et l'art ornemental hellénistiques* (Paris, 1913)
Levinskaya	I. Levinskaya, *The Book of Acts in its first century setting*. Vol. 5, *The Books of Acts in its Diaspora setting*. Epigraphical Appendix by I. Levinskaya and S. Tokhtas'ev (Grand Rapids, Michigan and Carlisle, 1996)
LF	*Listy filologické*, 1– (Československá Akademie Věd [Prague, 1946–])
LGPN	*A Lexicon of Greek Personal Names*, edd. P. M. Fraser and E. Matthews. I, *The Aegean Islands, Cyprus, Cyrenaica*; II, *Attica*, edd. M. J. Osborne and S. G. Byrne; III.A, *The Peloponnese, Western Greece, Sicily, and Magna Graecia*; III.B, *Central Greece: from the Megarid to Thessaly* (Oxford, 1987–)
Ling. Balk.	*Balkansko Ezikoznanie (Linguistique balkanique)*, 1– (Bulgarska Akademiia na Naukite [Sofia, 1959–])
Lorber, *Amphipolis*	C. C. Lorber, *Amphipolis. The civic coinage in silver and gold* (Los Angeles, 1990)
Loukopoulou, *Thrace Propontique*	L. D. Loukopoulou, *Contribution à l'histoire de la Thrace Propontique* (*Μελετήματα*, 9 [Athens, 1989])
LSAG^2	L. H. Jeffery, *The Local Scripts of Archaic Greece* (2nd edn. with Supplement by A. W. Johnston [Oxford, 1990])
Lucas	G. Lucas, *Les cités antiques de la haute vallée du Titarèse (Thessalie). Étude de topographie et de géographie historique antique avec corpus des inscriptions* (unpublished diss., Lyon, 1992)
Lucas, *Vall. Titarèse*	G. Lucas, *Les cités antiques de la haute vallée du Titarèse. Étude de topographie et de géographie historique* (*Collection de la Maison de l'Orient Méditerranéen*, 27, Série épigraphique et historique, 4 [Lyon, 1997])
Ma, *Antiochos*	J. Ma, *Antiochos III and the cities of Western Asia Minor* (Oxford, 1999)
Ma, *Teos*	J. Ma, 'A *Horse* from Teos: epigraphical notes on the Ionian-Hellespontine Association of Dionysiac Artists' in *The Epigraphy of the Greek Theatre*, ed. P. Wilson (Oxford, forthcoming)
MAAR	*Memoirs of the American Academy in Rome*, 1– (Bergamo, Rome and Ann Arbor, 1917–)
Macedonia	*A History of Macedonia*. I, N. G. L. Hammond, *Historical Geography* and *Prehistory*; II, N. G. L. Hammond and G. T. Griffith, *550-336 B.C.*; III, N. G. L. Hammond and F. W. Walbank, *336-167 B.C.* (Oxford, 1972–1988)
Maia	*Maia. Rivista di letterature classiche*, 1– (Bologna, 1948–)
Maier, *Mauerbauinschr.*	F. G. Maier, *Griechische Mauerbauinschriften*, 2 vols. (*Vestigia*, 1–2 [Heidelberg, 1959, 1961])
Makedonika	*Μακεδονικά. Σύγγραμμα περιοδικὸν τῆς Ἑταιρείας Μακεδονικῶν Σπουδῶν*, 1– (Thessaloniki, 1940–)
MAMA	*Monumenta Asiae Minoris Antiqua*, 1-8 (*Publications of the American Society for Archaeological Research in Asia Minor* [Manchester, 1928-62]); 9–10 (*JRS* Monographs, 4, 7 [London, 1988; 1993])
Marcadé	J. Marcadé, *Recueil des signatures de sculpteurs grecs*, 2 vols. (Paris, 1953, 1957)
Marsden, *Treatises*	E. W. Marsden, *Greek and Roman Artillery: technical treatises* (Oxford, 1971)
MASP	*Materialy po arkheologii Severnogo Prichernomor'ia*, 1– (Odes'kyi arkheolohichnyi muzei [Odessa, 1957–])
Masson, *OGS*	O. Masson, *Onomastica graeca selecta*, edd. C. Dobias and L. Dubois, I–II (Paris, 1990); III (*Hautes études du monde gréco-romain*, 28 [Geneva, 2000])
May, *Abdera*	J. M. F. May, *The Coinage of Abdera (540-345 B. C.)* (Royal Numismatic Society, *Special Publications*, 3 [London, 1966])
May, *Ainos*	J. M. F. May, *Ainos, its history and coinage, 474-341 B.C.* (Oxford Classical and Philosophical Monographs [Oxford and London, 1950])
MBAH	*Münstersche Beiträge zur antiken Handelsgeschichte*, 1– (Münster, 1982–)
Meïmaris–Bakirtzis	I. Meïmaris and Ch. Bakirtzis, *Ἑλληνικὲς ἐπιγραφὲς ὑστερορρωμαϊκῶν καὶ παλαιοχριστιανικῶν χρόνων ἀπὸ τὴ δυτικὴ Θράκη* (*Παράρτημα Θρακικῆς Ἐπετηρίδας*, 1 [Komotini, 1994])
Mél. arch. hist.	*Mélanges d'archéologie et d'histoire*, 1– (École française de Rome [Paris, 1881–1970])
Mél. Grégoire	*Mélanges Henri Grégoire*, 4 vols. (*Annuaire de l'Institut de philologie et d'histoire orientales et slaves*, 9–12 [Brussels, 1949–53])

Mél. Tisserant — *Mélanges Eugène Tisserant*, 2 vols. (Biblioteca apostolica vaticana, *Studi e testi*, 232 [Vatican City, 1964])

Mello–Voza — M. Mello and G. Voza, *Le iscrizioni latine di Paestum*, 2 vols. (Naples, 1968–9)

Melnik — *Melnik. Gradut v podnozhieto na Slavova krepost*, vol. 1, edd. S. Georgieva and V. Nesheva (Sofia, 1989)

Memnonion — P. Perdrizet and G. Lefebvre, *Les graffites grecs du Memnonion d'Abydos* (Nancy, Paris, and Strasbourg, 1919)

Mendel, *Cat.* — G. Mendel, *Catalogue des sculptures grecques, romaines et byzantines (Musées Impériaux Ottomans)*, 3 vols. (Constantinople, 1912–14)

Mezhd. Kongr. Frakologii V — *V Mezhdunarodnii Kongress po Frakologii, (Mezhdunarodnii simpozium 'Antichnaia Balkanistika 6'), Moskve, 18–22 oktabria 1988 god.*, edd. L. Gindin et al. (*Terra Antiqua Balcanica*, 6 [Sofia, 1991])

MIA — *Materialy i issledovaniia po arkheologii SSSR*, 1– (Akademiia Nauk SSSR [Moscow and Leningrad, 1940–])

Michalowski, *Mirmeki* — K. Michalowski, *Mirmeki. Wykopaliskie odeninka polskiego w.r. 1956* (Warsaw, 1958)

Migeotte, *L'emprunt* — L. Migeotte, *L'emprunt public dans les cités grecques. Recueil des documents et analyse critique* (Quebec and Paris, 1984)

Milet — *Milet. Ergebnisse der Ausgrabungen und Untersuchungen seit dem Jahre 1899*, edd. Th. Wiegand et al., 1– (Berlin, 1906–)

Milliaires — L. Gounaropoulou and M. B. Hatzopoulos, *Les milliaires de la Voie Egnatienne entre Héraclée des Lyncestes et Thessalonique* (*Μελετήματα*, 1 [Athens, 1985])

Minalo — *Minalo*, 1-3 (Bulgaro-makedonsko nauchno spisanie [Sofia, 1909–19])

Minkova, *PNLIB* — M. Minkova, *The Personal Names of the Latin Inscriptions in Bulgaria* (*Studien zur klassischen Philologie*, 118 [Frankfurt, 2000])

Minns, *Scythians* — E. H. Minns, *Scythians and Greeks. A survey of ancient history and archaeology on the north coast of the Euxine from the Danube to the Caucasus* (Cambridge, 1913)

Mitrevski, *Vardarski Rid* — D. Mitrevski, *Staromakedonskiot grad na Vardarski Rid (The ancient Macedonian town at Vardarski Rid)* (Skopje, 2001)

ML — R. Meiggs and D. M. Lewis, *A Selection of Greek Historical Inscriptions to the end of the fifth century B.C.* (Oxford, 1969; revised edn., 1988)

Mnem. — *Mnemosyne. Biblioteca Classica Batava*, 1– (Leiden, 1852–)

Möbius, *Die Ornamente*[2] — H. Möbius, *Die Ornamente der griechischen Grabstelen klassischer und nachklassischer Zeit* (2nd edn. Munich, 1968)

Montana — *Montana*. 1, edd. V. Velkov et al. (Bulgarska Akademiia na Naukite, Arkheologicheski Institut s Muzei [Sofia, 1987]); 2, *Epigrafski pametnitsi ot Montana i raiona*, edd. V. Velkov and G. Aleksandrov (Montana, 1994)

Montreal Exhib. — *Ἑλληνικὸς πολιτισμός, Μακεδονία. Τὸ βασίλειο τοῦ Μεγάλου Ἀλεξάνδρου. Catalogue of the exhibition in the Marché Bonsecours, Montreal, 7 May-19 Sept. 1993*

Moretti, *ISE* — L. Moretti, *Iscrizioni storiche ellenistiche*, 2 vols. (*Biblioteca di studi superiori*, 53, 62 [Florence, 1967, 1976])

Moretti, *Olymp.* — L. Moretti, *Olympionikai, i vincitori negli antichi agoni olimpici* (*Memorie della Accademia Nazionale dei Lincei*, Classe di scienze morali, storiche e filologiche, ser. 8, vol. 8 (2) [Rome, 1957]) [Addenda, *Klio* 52 (1970) pp. 295 ff.; *Miscellanea Greca e Romana* 12 (1987) pp. 67-91; *Proceedings of an International Symposium on the Olympic Games* (Athens, 1992) pp. 119-28]

Moretti, *Tra epigr. e stor.* — L. Moretti, *Tra epigrafia e storia. Scritti scelti e annotati* (*Vetera*, 5 [Rome, 1990])

Mous. Kavalas — D. I. Lazaridis, *Νεάπολις, Χριστούπολις, Καβάλα. Ὁδηγὸς Μουσείου Καβάλας* (Athens, 1969)

Municipium Stobensium — *Municipium Stobensium: West Necropolis 1992. Catalogue of an exhibition held at the Museum of Macedonia, 2 June – 30 August 1994* (Skopje, 1994)

Mus. Arch. di Bari — *Il Museo Archeologico di Bari*, ed. E. M. de Juliis (Bari, 1983)

Mus. Helv. — *Museum Helveticum. Schweizerische Zeitschrift für klassische Altertumswissenschaft*, 1– (Basel, 1944–)

Mushmov — N. A. Mushmov, *Antichnite moneti na Balkanskiia poluostrov i monetitie na Bulgarskitie tsare* (Sofia, 1912)

Musurillo, *Acts Christian Martyrs* — H. Musurillo, *The Acts of the Christian Martyrs: introduction, texts and translations* (Oxford Early Christian Texts [Oxford, 1972])

Myrtos — *Μύρτος. Μνήμη Ἰουλίας Βοκοτοπούλου*, ed. P. Adam-Veleni (Thessaloniki, 2000)

Nachtergael, *Les Galates* — G. Nachtergael, *Les Galates en Grèce et les Sôtéria de Delphes. Recherches d'histoire et d'épigraphie hellénistiques* (*Académie royale de Belgique, Mémoires de la classe des lettres*, 63 (1) [Brussels, 1977]) [Appendix, 'Corpus des actes relatifs aux Sôtéria de Delphes', pp. 391–495]

Nalpantis, *Anaskaphi* — D. Nalpantis, *Ἀνασκαφὴ στὸ οἰκόπεδο τοῦ Μουσείου Βυζαντινοῦ Πολιτισμοῦ στὴ Θεσσαλονίκη. Ταφὲς καὶ εὑρήματα* (*Δημοσιεύματα τοῦ Ἀρχαιολογικοῦ Δελτίου*, 85 [Athens, 2003])

Naville sale — Naville & Cie Genève, sale catalogues 1–14 (Geneva, 1920–9); subsequently *Ars Classica* sale catalogues 15– (1930–)

NE — *Numizmatika i Epigrafika*, 1– (Akademiia Nauk SSSR, Institut arkheologii [Moscow, 1960–])

Nekropol' Nimfeia — N. L. Grach, *Nekropol' Nimfeia* (St. Petersburg, 1999)

Nessebre	*Nessebre*, ed. T. Ivanov, 1–2 (Bulgarska Akademiia na Naukite, Arkheologicheski Institut [Sofia, 1969, 1980])
New Studies on Black Sea	*New Studies on the Black Sea Littoral*, ed. G. R. Tsetskhladze (*Colloquia Pontica*, 1 [Oxford, 1996])
Nicholson Mus.[2]	*Handbook to the Nicholson Museum*, ed. A. D. Trendall (2nd edn., Sydney, 1948)
Nikopolis ad Istrum	T. Ivanov and R. Ivanov, *Nikopolis ad Istrum*, vol. 1 (Sofia, 1994)
Noi monumente	A. Aricescu et al., *Noi monumente epigrafice din Scythia Minor* (Muzeul regional de arheologie Dobrogea [Constanza, 1964])
Nom. Chron.	*Νομισματικὰ Χρονικά*, 1– (*Ἑλληνικὴ Νομισματικὴ Ἑταιρεία* [Athens, 1972–])
North Pontic Archaeology	*North Pontic Archaeology. Recent Discoveries and Studies*, ed. G. R. Tsetskhladze (*Colloquia Pontica*, 6 [Leiden, Boston, Cologne, 2001])
NS	A. Maiuri, *Nuova silloge epigrafica di Rodi e Cos* (Florence, 1925)
NScav	*Notizie degli scavi di antichità* ((Reale) Accademia Nazionale dei Lincei [Rome, 1876–])
Num. Bulg.	*Numismatica Bulgarica*, 1– (Sofia, 2002–)
Num. Sb.	*Numizmaticheskii Sbornik* (Trudy Gosudarstvennogo Istoricheskogo Muzeia [Moscow, 1955–])
Num. Sfrag.	*Numizmatika i Sfragistika* (Sofia, 1993–)
Numismatica	*Numismatica*, 1–18 (Rome, 1935–1952); NS 1–7 (Rome, 1960–1966)
NZ	*Numismatische Zeitschrift*, 1– (Österreichische Numismatische Gesellschaft [Vienna, 1869–])
OAK	*Otchet Imperatorskoi arkheologicheskoi kommissii* (St. Petersburg, 1882–1915)
OGIS	*Orientis Graeci Inscriptiones Selectae. Supplementum Sylloges Inscriptionum Graecarum*, ed. W. Dittenberger, 2 vols. (Leipzig, 1903–5; repr. Hildesheim, 1960)
Oikonomos	G. P. Oikonomos, *Ἐπιγραφαὶ τῆς Μακεδονίας* (*Βιβλιοθήκη τῆς ἐν Ἀθήναις Ἀρχαιολογικῆς Ἑταιρείας* [Athens, 1915])
Olynthus	D. M. Robinson et al., *Excavations at Olynthus*, 14 vols. (Baltimore, 1929–52)
Onomastique latine	*L'Onomastique latine. Actes du colloque international, Paris, 13-15 Octobre, 1975*, edd. N. Duval and H.-G. Pflaum (*Colloques internationaux du Centre National de la Recherche Scientifique*, 564 [Paris, 1977])
Osborne, *Naturalization*	M. J. Osborne, *Naturalization in Athens* (*Verhandelingen van der Koninklijke Academie voor Wetenschappen, Letteren en Schone Kunsten van België, Klasse der Letteren*, 98, 101, 109 [Brussels, 1981–83])
Overbeck	J. Overbeck, *Die antiken Schriftquellen zur Geschichte der bildenden Künste bei den Griechen* (Leipzig, 1868)
PA	*Prosopographia Attica*, ed. J. Kirchner, 2 vols. (Berlin, 1901–3)
PAE	*Πρακτικὰ τῆς ἐν Ἀθήναις Ἀρχαιολογικῆς Ἑταιρείας* (Athens, 1889–)
Page, *FGE*	D. L. Page, *Further Greek Epigrams*, edd. R. D. Dawe and J. Diggle (Cambridge, 1981)
PAmh	*The Amherst Papyri. Being an account of the Greek Papyri in the collection of the Right Hon. Lord Amherst of Hackney, F.S.A. at Didlington Hall Norfolk*, edd. B. P. Grenfell and A. S. Hunt, 2 vols. (London, 1900–1)
Pandermalis, *Dion*	D. Pandermalis, *Δῖον. Ἡ ἀνακάλυψη* (Athens, 1999)
Papazoglou, *Villes*	F. Papazoglou, *Les villes de Macédoine à l'époque romaine* (*BCH* Suppl., 16 [Athens, 1988])
Paroem. Gr.	*Corpus Paroemiographorum Graecorum*, edd. E. L. von Leutsch and F. G. Schneidewin, 2 vols. (Göttingen, 1839, 1851; repr. Hildesheim, 1965)
PAthen	*Papyri Societatis Archaeologicae Atheniensis*, ed. G. A. Petropoulos (*Πραγματεῖαι τῆς Ἀκαδημίας Ἀθηνῶν*, 10 [Athens, 1939])
PBad	*Veröffentlichungen aus den badischen Papyrus-Sammlungen*, edd. W. Spiegelberg, F. Bilabel and G. A. Gerhard, 6 vols. (Heidelberg, 1923–38)
PBerlZill	*Vierzehn Berliner griechische Papyri*, ed. M. Zilliacus (Societas Scientiarum Fennica, *Commentationes Humanarum Litterarum*, 11 (4) [Helsingfors, 1941])
PBingen	*Papyri in honorem Johannis Bingen octogenarii*, ed. H. Melaerts (*Studia varia Bruxellensia ad orbem graeco-latinum pertinentia*, 5 [Louvain, 2000])
PCG	*Poetae Comici Graeci*, edd. R. Kassel and C. Austin, vols. 1, 2, 3(2), 4, 5, 6(2), 7, 8 (Berlin and New York, 1983–)
PCollYoutie	*Collectanea Papyrologica. Texts published in honor of H. C. Youtie*, ed. A. E. Hanson et al. (*Papyrologische Texte und Abhandlungen*, 19-20 [Bonn, 1976])
PColZen	*Zenon Papyri. Business papers of the third century B.C. dealing with Palestine and Egypt*, ed. W. L. Westermann, E. S. Hasenoehrl et al., 2 vols. (*Columbia papyri, Greek series*, 3–4 [New York, 1934, 1940])
PCZ	*Zenon Papyri*, edd. C. C. Edgar et al., 5 vols. (Catalogue général des antiquités égyptiennes du Musée du Caire. Publications de la Société Fouad I de papyrologie, *Textes et documents*, 5 [Cairo, 1925–51])
PDion	*Les archives privées de Dionysios, fils de Kephalas (P.L.Bat. 22). Textes grecs et demotiques*, edd. E. Boswinkel and P. W. Pestman (*Papyrologica Lugduno-Batava*, 22 A-B [Leiden, 1982])
Peek, *AG*	W. Peek, *Attische Grabschriften*, 2 vols. (*AbhBerlAk*, Kl. Spr., Lit., Kunst, 1953 (4); 1956 (3) [Berlin, 1954, 1957])
Peek, *IAEpid*	W. Peek, *Inschriften aus dem Asklepieion von Epidauros* (*Abh. Akad. Leipzig*, 60 (2) [Berlin, 1969])
Peek, *NIEpid*	W. Peek, *Neue Inschriften aus Epidauros* (*Abh. Akad. Leipzig*, 63 (5) [Berlin, 1972])

Pelekidis, *Thessaloniki* — E. Pelekidis, *Ἀπὸ τὴν πολιτεία καὶ τὴν κοινωνία τῆς ἀρχαίας Θεσσαλονίκης (ἐπιγραφικὴ μελέτη)* (Thessaloniki, 1934)

PEleph — *Elephantine-Papyri*, ed. O. Rubensohn (*Ägyptische Urkunden aus den Königlichen Museen zu Berlin, Griechische Urkunden Sonderheft* [Berlin, 1907])

Pella — D. Papakonstantinou-Diamantourou, *Πέλλα*. I, *Ἱστορικὴ ἐπισκόπησις καὶ μαρτυρίαι* (*Βιβλιοθήκη τῆς ἐν Ἀθήναις Ἀρχαιολογικῆς Ἑταιρείας*, 70 [Athens, 1971])

PEnt — *Ἐντεύξεις. Requêtes et plaintes addressées au roi d'Égypte au III*[e] *siècle avant J.-C.*, ed. O. Guéraud (Publications de la Société Royale Égyptienne de papyrologie, *Textes et documents*, I [Cairo, 1931])

PErasm — *Papyri in the Collection of the Erasmus University*, edd. P. J. Sijpesteijn and P. A. Verdult, 2 vols. (*Papyrologica Bruxellensia*, 21 [Brussels, 1986, 1991])

Perlman, *City and Sanctuary* — P. Perlman, *City and Sanctuary in Ancient Greece. The Theorodokia in the Peloponnese* (*Hypomnemata*, 121 [Göttingen, 2000])

Pernik — *Pernik*, edd. T. Ivanov, D. Ovcharov and I. Changova, 3 vols. (Bulgarska Akademiia na Naukite, Arkheologicheski Institut i Muzei [Sofia, 1981–1992])

Peter, *MTD* — U. Peter, *Die Münzen der thrakischen Dynasten (5.-3. Jahrhundert v. Chr.). Hintergründe ihrer Prägung* (Berlin, 1997)

PFrankf — *Griechische Papyri aus dem Besitz des rechtswissenschaftlichen Seminars der Universität Frankfurt*, ed. H. Lewald (*SBHeidAk*, phil.-hist. Kl., 1920 (14) [Heidelberg, 1920])

PFreib — *Mitteilungen aus der Freiburger Papyrussammlung*, edd. J. Partsch et al., 4 vols. (I = *SBHeidAk*, phil.-hist. Kl., 1914 (2); II = *SBHeidAk*, phil.-hist. Kl., 1916 (10); III = *AbhHeidAk*, phil.-hist. Kl., 1927 (7); IV = *Papyrologische Texte und Abhandlungen*, 38 [Bonn, 1986])

PGen — *Les Papyrus de Genève*. I, ed. J. Nicole (Geneva, 1896-1906); I², edd. P. Schubert and I. Jornot (Geneva, 2002); II, ed. C. Wehrli (Geneva, 1986); III, ed. P. Schubert (Geneva, 1996)

PGiss — *Griechische Papyri im Museum des oberhessischen Geschichtsvereins zu Giessen*, I, edd. E. Kornemann and P. M. Meyer (Leipzig and Berlin, 1910–12)

PGissUniv — *Mitteilungen aus der Papyrussammlung der Giessener Universitätsbibliothek*, edd. H. Kling et al., 6 vols. (*Schriften der Justus Liebig-Universität Giessen* [Giessen, 1924–1939])

PGrad — *Griechische Papyri der Sammlung Gradenwitz*, ed. G. Plaumann (*SBHeidAk*, phil.-hist. Kl., 1914 (15) [Heidelberg, 1914])

PGurob — *Greek Papyri from Gurob*, ed. J. G. Smyly (Royal Irish Academy, *Cunningham Memoirs*, 12 [Dublin and London, 1921])

PH — W. R. Paton and E. L. Hicks, *The Inscriptions of Cos* (Oxford, 1891)

PHamb — *Griechische Papyrusurkunden der Hamburger Staats- und Universitätsbibliothek*, ed. P. M. Meyer (Leipzig, 1911–24); *Griechische Papyri der Hamburger Staats- und Universitätsbibliothek*, I, ed. B. Snell (Hamburg, 1954); II, edd. B. Kramer and D. Hagedorn (*Papyrologische Texte und Abhandlungen*, 31 [Bonn, 1984])

PHaun — *Papyri Graecae Haunienses*. I, *Literarische Texte und ptolemäische Urkunden*, ed. T. Larsen (Copenhagen, 1942); II, *Letters and mummy labels from Roman Egypt*, ed. A. Bülow-Jacobsen (*Papyrologische Texte und Abhandlungen*, 29 [Bonn, 1981])

PHeid VIII — *Dokumentarische Papyri des 2. Jh. v. Chr. aus dem Herakleopolites*, ed. D. Kaltsas (*Veröffentlichungen aus der Heidelberger Papyrussammlung*, 8 [Heidelberg, 2001])

PHels — *Papyri Helsigienses*. I, *Ptolemäische Urkunden*, ed. J. Frosen (Societas Scientiarum Fennica, *Commentationes humanarum litterarum*, 80 [Helsinki, 1986])

PHib — *The Hibeh Papyri*. Part I, edd. B. P. Grenfell and A. S. Hunt; Part 2, edd. E. G. Turner and M.-Th. Lenger (*Graeco-Roman Memoirs*, 7, 32 [London, 1906, 1955])

Philippes — P. Collart and P. Ducrey, *Philippes*. I, *Les reliefs rupestres* (*BCH* Suppl., 2 [Paris, 1975])

Philippi — Ch. Koukouli-Chrysanthaki and Ch. Bakirtzis, *Philippi* (Athens, 1995)

Pikoulas, *Chora* — G. A. Pikoulas, *Ἡ χώρα τῶν Πιερῶν. Συμβολὴ στὴν τοπογραφία της* (Athens, 2001)

Pilhofer — P. Pilhofer, *Philippi*. I, *Die erste christliche Gemeinde Europas*; II, *Katalog der Inschriften von Philippi* (*Wissenschaftliche Untersuchungen zum Neuen Testament*, 87, 119 [Tübingen, 1995, 2000])

*PIR*² — *Prosopographia Imperii Romani saec. I. II. III*, edd. E. Groag, A. Stein, L. Petersen et al., I–VII (1) (A–R) (2nd edn. Berlin and Leipzig/Berlin and New York, 1933–1999); [*PIR*¹ vol. III, edd. E. Klebs, H. Dessau, P. von Rohden (Berlin, 1897)]

PKöln — *Kölner Papyri*, edd. B. Kramer, M. Gronewald et al., I– (*Abhandlungen der Rheinisch-Westfälischen Akademie der Wissenschaften, Papyrologica Coloniensia*, 7 [Opladen, Wiesbaden, Paderborn, 1976–])

PLF — *Poetarum Lesbiorum Fragmenta*, edd. E. Lobel and D. L. Page (Oxford, 1955)

PLond — *Greek Papyri in the British Museum*, edd. F. G. Kenyon, H. I. Bell, and T. C. Skeat, 6 vols. (London, 1893–1917, 1974)

PLRE — *Prosopography of the Later Roman Empire*. I, A.D. 260–395, edd. A. H. M. Jones, J. R. Martindale and J. Morris (Cambridge, 1971); II, A.D. 395–527, ed. J. R. Martindale (1980); IIIA-B, A.D. 527–641, ed. J. R. Martindale (1992)

PM — E. Pfuhl and H. Möbius, *Die ostgriechischen Grabreliefs*, 2 vols. (Deutsches Archäologisches Institut [Mainz, 1977, 1979])

PMagd — *Papyrus de Magdola*, ed. J. Lesquier (Paris, 1912)

PMerton	*A Descriptive Catalogue of the Greek Papyri in the Collection of Wilfred Merton, F.S.A.*, edd. H. I. Bell, C. H. Roberts, J. D. Thomas et al., 3 vols. (London/Dublin, 1948–1967)
PMG	*Poetae Melici Graeci*, ed. D. L. Page (Oxford, 1962)
PMich	*Michigan Papyri*, I– (1-8, *University of Michigan Studies, Humanistic Series*, 24, 28, 40, 42-3, 47-8, 50 [Ann Arbor, 1931–51]; 10-12, 14, 16, *American Studies in Papyrology*, 6, 9, 14, 22, 30 [Toronto/Ann Arbor/Atlanta, 1970–]; 9 [Case Western Reserve University, 1971]; 13, 15 [Zutphen, 1977–])
PMünch	*Die Papyri der Bayerischen Staatsbibliothek München*. I^2, *Byzantinische Papyri der Bayerischen Staatsbibliothek München*, edd. A. Heisenberg and L. Wenger; II, *Papiri litterari greci*, ed. A. Carlini; III, *Griechische Urkundenpapyri der Bayerischen Staatsbibliothek München*, edd. U. and D. Hagedorn, R. Hübner and J. C. Shelton (Stuttgart, 1986)
POElephDAIK	*Les papyrus et les ostraka grecs d'Elephantine (P et O ElephDAIK)*, ed. G. Wagner (Deutsches Archäologisches Institut, Abteilung Kairo, *Archäologische Veröffentlichungen*, 70 [Mainz, 1998])
Poikila	*Ποικίλα*, ed. M. B. Sakellariou (*Μελετήματα*, 10 [Athens, 1990])
Polemon	*Πολέμων. Ἀρχαιολογικὸν περιοδικόν*, 1–8 (Athens, 1929–66)
Pontica	*Pontica*, 1– (Muzeul de istorie naţională şi arheologie Constanţa [Constanza, 1970–])
Popescu, *IGL*	E. Popescu, *Inscripţile greceşti şi latine din secolele iv-xiii descoperite în România* (*Inscriptiones Daciae et Scythiae Minoris antiquae* [Bucharest, 1976])
Pottier–Reinach	E. Pottier and S. Reinach, *La nécropole de Myrina* (Paris, 1887)
Poulter, *Nicopolis*	A. G. Poulter, *Nicopolis ad Istrum. A Roman, Late Roman, and early Byzantine city: excavations 1985–1992* (*JRS Monographs*, 8 [London, 1995])
POxy	*The Oxyrhynchus Papyri*, edd. B. P. Grenfell, A. S. Hunt et al., 1– (Egypt Exploration Society [London, 1898–])
PP	*Prosopographia Ptolemaica*, edd. W. Peremans, E. van 't Dack et al., 9 vols. (*Studia Hellenistica*, 6, 8, 11–13, 17, 20–21, 25 [Louvain, 1950–81])
PPC	I. Michaelidou-Nicolaou, *Prosopography of Ptolemaic Cyprus* (*Studies in Mediterranean Archaeology*, 44 [Göteborg, 1976])
PPetr	*The Flinders Petrie Papyri*, edd. J. P. Mahaffy and J. G. Smyly, 3 vols. (Royal Irish Academy, *Cunningham Memoirs*, 8, 9, 11 [Dublin, 1891–1905])
PPetr^2	*The Petrie Papyri*^{2}. I, *The Wills*, ed. W. Clarysse (*Collectanea Hellenistica*, 2 [Brussels, 1991])
PPhrurDiosk	*Das Archiv des Phrurarchen Dioskurides (154-145 v. Chr.?) (P.Phrur.Diosk.). Papyri aus den Sammlungen von Heidelberg, Köln, München und Wien*, edd. J. M. S. Cowey, K. Maresch and C. Barnes (*Abhandlungen der Nordrhein-Westfälischen Akademie der Wissenschaften, Papyrologica Coloniensia*, 30 [Paderborn, 2003])
PPolitJud	*Urkunden des Politeuma der Juden von Herakleopolis (144/3, 133/2 v. Chr.)*, edd. K. Maresch and J. M. S. Cowey (*Papyrologica Coloniensia*, 29 [Wiesbaden, 2001])
Prakt. VIII Diethn. Synedr. Epigr.	*Πρακτικὰ τοῦ Η΄ διεθνοῦς συνεδρίου ἑλληνικῆς καὶ λατινικῆς ἐπιγραφικῆς, Ἀθήνα 3-9 Ὀκτωβρίου 1982* (Athens, 1984)
Pratiques funéraires	*Pratiques funéraires dans l'Europe des XIIIe - IVe s. av. J.-C. Actes du IIIe colloque international d'archéologie funéraire organisé à Tulcea, 15-20 septembre 1997* (Publications de l'Institut de Recherches Eco-Muséologiques de Tulcea [Tulcea, 2000])
Preda, *MGD*	K. Preda, *Monedele Geto-Dacilor* (Academia de ştiinţe sociale şi politice a Republicii socialiste România, Institutul de arheologie, *Biblioteca de arheologie*, 19 [Bucharest, 1973])
Price, *Alexander*	M. J. Price, *The Coinage in the name of Alexander the Great and Philip Arrhidaeus. A British Museum catalogue*, 2 vols. (Zurich and London, 1991)
Pritchett, *Topography*	W. K. Pritchett, *Studies in Ancient Greek Topography*, 1–6 (*University of California Publications, Classical Studies*, 1, 4, 22, 28, 31, 33 [Berkeley and Los Angeles, 1965–89]); 7– (Amsterdam, 1991–)
Probl. ant. ist. kult.	*Problemy antichnoi istorii i kul'tury. Doklady XIV Mezhdunarodnoi konferentsii antichnikov sotsialistichestikikh stran 'Eirene', 18-23 maia 1976 g.*, edd. B. B. Piotrovskii et al. (Akademiia Nauk Armianskoi SSR [Yerevan, 1979])
PRyl	*Catalogue of Greek (and Latin) Papyri in the John Rylands Library, Manchester*, edd. A. S. Hunt et al., 4 vols. (Manchester, 1911–52)
PSI	*Papiri greci e latini*, edd. P. Vitelli, M. Norsa et al., 15 vols. (*Pubblicazioni della Società italiana per la ricerca dei papiri greci e latini in Egitto* [Florence, 1912–79])
PSorb	*Papyrus de la Sorbonne, nos. 1 à 68*, ed. H. Cadell (*Travaux de l'Institut de papyrologie de Paris*, 4 [Paris, 1966])
PStrassb	*Griechische Papyrus der Kaiserlichen Universitäts- und Landesbibliothek zu Strassburg*, ed. F. Preisigke, 2 vols. (Strassburg and Leipzig, 1912, 1920); *Papyrus grecs de la Bibliothèque Nationale et Universitaire de Strasbourg*, edd. P. Collomp (Paris, 1948), J. Schwartz (*Publications de la Bibliothèque Nationale et Universitaire de Strasbourg*, 3-5, 6(1), 10 [Strasbourg, 1973–])
PTeb	*The Tebtunis Papyri*, edd. B. P. Grenfell, A. S. Hunt, J. G. Smyly et al., 3 vols. in 4 (London, 1902–38); vol. IV, edd. J. G. Keenan and J. C. Shelton (*Graeco-Roman Memoirs*, 64 [London, 1976])
PUG	*Papiri dell'Università di Genova*, I– (vol. I, *Università di Genova, Fondazione Nobile Agostino Poggi*, 10 [Milan, 1974]; vols. II–III, *Papyrologica Florentina*, 6, 20 [Florence, 1980, 1991])

Puteoli — *Puteoli. Studi di storia antica*, 1– (Pozzuoli, 1977–)
PWürzb — *Mitteilungen aus der Würzburger Papyrussammlung*, ed. U. Wilcken (Berlin, 1934)
RA — *Revue archéologique* (Paris, 1844–)
Raymond, *MRC* — D. Raymond, *Macedonian Regal Coinage to 413 B.C.* (*Numismatic Notes and Monographs*, 126 [New York, 1953])
RDAC — *Report of the Department of Antiquities of Cyprus* (Nicosia, 1933–48, 1963–)
RE — *Real-Encyclopädie der classischen Altertumswissenschaft*, edd. A. F. Pauly, G. Wissowa, W. Kroll et al., 66 vols. with 15 supplements (Stuttgart, 1894–1980)
REA — *Revue des études anciennes*, 1– (Bordeaux, 1899–)
Recherches amph. grecques — *Recherches sur les amphores grecques. Actes du colloque international organisé par le Centre National de la Recherche Scientifique, l'Université de Rennes II et l'École française d'Athènes (Athènes, 10-12 septembre 1984)*, edd. J.-Y. Empereur and Y. Garlan (*BCH* Suppl., 13 [Athens and Paris, 1986])
REG — *Revue des études grecques*, 1– (Paris, 1888–)
Rev. Num. — *Revue numismatique*, 1– (Paris, 1836–)
Rev. Suisse num. — *Revue Suisse de numismatique* (*Schweizerische numismatische Rundschau*), 1–23 (Geneva, 1891–1923); 24– (Bern, 1930/3–)
Rh. Mus. — *Rheinisches Museum für Philologie*, 1–9 (Bonn, 1827–39); NS 1– (Frankfurt, 1842–)
Rhodes–Osborne — *Greek Historical Inscriptions, 404–323 BC*, edd. P. J. Rhodes and R. Osborne (Oxford, 2003)
Richter, *Engraved Gems* — G. M. A. Richter, *The Engraved Gems of the Greeks, Etruscans and Romans*, 2 vols. (London, 1968, 1971)
Riv. Fil. — *Rivista di filologia e di istruzione classica*, 1– (Turin, 1873–)
RMD — M. M. Roxan, *Roman Military Diplomas*, 3 vols. (University of London, Institute of Archaeology, *Occasional Publications*, 2, 9, 14 [London, 1978–1994]); M. M. Roxan and P. A. Holder, vol. IV (*BICS* Suppl., 82 [London, 2003])
Robert, *Amyzon* — J. and L. Robert, *Fouilles d'Amyzon en Carie*. I, *Exploration, histoire, monnaies et inscriptions* (Paris, 1983)
Robert, *Coll. Froehner* — L. Robert, *Collection Froehner*. I, *Inscriptions grecques* (Paris, 1936)
Robert, *Documents* — L. Robert, *Documents de l'Asie Mineure méridionale. Inscriptions, monnaies et géographie* (Centre de recherches d'histoire et de philologie de la IVe section de l'École pratique des hautes études, III, *Hautes études du monde gréco-romain*, 2 [Geneva and Paris, 1966])
Robert, *Ét. num. gr.* — L. Robert, *Études de numismatique grecque* (Collège de France, Fondation Schlumberger pour la numismatique, *Publications*, 1 [Paris, 1951])
Robert, *EEP* — L. Robert, *Études épigraphiques et philologiques* (*Bibliothèque de l'École des hautes études*, 272 [Paris, 1938])
Robert, *Gladiateurs* — L. Robert, *Les gladiateurs dans l'Orient grec* (*Bibliothèque de l'École des hautes études*, 278 [Paris, 1940; repr. Amsterdam, 1971])
Robert, *Hell.* — L. Robert, *Hellenica. Recueil d'épigraphie, de numismatique, et d'antiquités grecques*, 13 vols. (vol. 1, Limoges, 1940; vols. 2–13, Paris, 1946–65)
Robert, *Noms indigènes* — L. Robert, *Noms indigènes dans l'Asie Mineure gréco-romaine*, I (*Bibliothèque archéologique et historique de l'Institut français d'archéologie d'Istanbul*, 13 [Paris, 1963])
Robert, *OMS* — L. Robert, *Opera minora selecta. Épigraphie et antiquités grecques*, 7 vols. (Amsterdam, 1969–90)
Robinson Bequest — *The David Moore Robinson Bequest of Classical Art and Antiquities. A Special Exhibition (Fogg Art Museum – Harvard University, May 1 to September 20, 1961)* (Harvard, 1961)
Rogozen Treasure — A. Fol, *The Rogozen Treasure* (Bulgarska Akademiia na Naukite, Institut po Trakologiia [Sofia, 1989])
Roman jewellery — L. Ruseva-Slokoska, *Roman jewellery. A collection of the National Archaeological Museum – Sofia* (Sofia and London, 1991)
Roman Onomastics — *Roman Onomastics in the Greek East: social and political aspects. Proceedings of the International Colloquium on Roman Onomastics, Athens, 7-9 September 1993*, ed. A. D. Rizakis (*Μελετήματα*, 21 [Athens, 1996])
Romanizmăt — B. Gerov, *Romanizmăt mezhdu Dunava i Balkana*. I, *Ot Avgust do Hadrian*. II, *Ot Hadrian do Konstantin* (*Godishnik na Sofiiskiia Universitet, Istoriko-filologicheski fakultet*, 45, 48 [Sofia, 1948–9, 1952–3])
Rostovtsev, *ADZh* — M. I. Rostovtsev, *Antichnaia dekorativnaia zhivopis na iugie Rossii* (St. Petersburg, 1913–14)
Rostovtsev, *SB* — M. I. Rostovtsev, *Skythien und der Bosporus*. I, *Kritische Übersicht der schriftlichen und archäologischen Quellen* (Berlin, 1931); II, *Wiederentdeckte Kapitel und Verwandtes*, edd. V. Iu. Zuev and H. Heinen (*Historia Einzelschriften*, 83 [Stuttgart, 1993])
RPC — A. M. Burnett, M. Amandry and P. Rippolès, *Roman Provincial Coinage*. I, *From the Death of Caesar to the Death of Vitellius (44 BC-AD 69)* (London and Paris, 1992); *Supplement* I (1998); II, *From Vespasian to Domitian (AD 69–96)* (1999)
RPh — *Revue de philologie, de littérature et d'histoire anciennes*, 1– (Paris, 1877–)
RQ — *Römische Quartalschrift für Christliche Alterthumskunde und für Kirchengeschichte*, 1– (Rome, 1887–)
Saprykin, *Farms* — S. Iu. Saprykin, *Ancient farms and land-plots on the khora of Khersonesos Taurike (research in the Herakleian Peninsula – 1974-1990)* (*McGill University Monographs in Classical Archaeology and History*, 16 [Amsterdam, 1994])

Šašel, *IL*	A. and J. Šašel, *Inscriptiones Latinae quae in Iugoslavia inter annos MCMXL et MCMLX, inter annos MCMLX et MCMLXX, et inter annos MCMII et MCMXL repertae et editae sunt*, 3 vols. (*Situla, Dissertationes Musei Nationalis Labacensis*, 5, 19, 25 [Ljubljana, 1963–86])
SB	*Sammelbuch griechischer Urkunden aus Ägypten*, edd. F. Preisigke, F. Bilabel et al., 1– (Strasbourg/Berlin/Leipzig etc., 1915–)
SBBayerAk	*Sitzungsberichte der (Königlichen) Bayerischen Akademie der Wissenschaften zu München* (Munich, 1860–)
SBBerlAk	*Sitzungsberichte der (Preussischen) Deutschen Akademie der Wissenschaften zu Berlin*, phil.-hist. Kl. (Berlin, 1882–1938)
Schönert, *Perinthos*	E. Schönert, *Griechisches Münzwerk. Die Münzprägung von Perinthos* (*Schriften der Sektion für Altertumswissenschaft*, 45 [Berlin, 1965])
Schönert-Geiss, *Byzantion*	E. Schönert-Geiss, *Griechisches Münzwerk. Die Münzprägung von Byzantion*, 2 vols. (*Schriften zur Geschichte und Kultur der Antike*, 2 [Berlin and Amsterdam, 1970, 1972])
Schönert-Geiss, *Maroneia*	E. Schönert-Geiss, *Griechisches Münzwerk. Die Münzprägung von Maroneia* (*Schriften zur Geschichte und Kultur der Antike*, 26 [Berlin and Amsterdam, 1987])
SCIV	*Studii şi Cercetări de Istorie Veche*, 1–24 (Bucharest, 1950–1973); subsequently *Studii şi Cercetări de Istorie Veche şi Arheologie*, 25– (Bucharest, 1974–)
Scrinzi	A. Scrinzi, 'Iscrizioni greche inedite di Rodi', in *Atti del Reale Istituto Veneto di scienze, lettere ed arti*, 57 (1898-9) pp. 251–86 (Venice, 1899)
Scythian Neapolis	Yu. P. Zaytsev, *The Scythian Neapolis (2nd century BC to 3rd century AD). Investigations into the Graeco-Barbarian city on the northern Black Sea coast* (*BAR International Series*, 1219 [Oxford, 2004])
SEG	*Supplementum Epigraphicum Graecum*, edd. J. J. E. Hondius, 1–11; A. G. Woodhead, 12–25 (Leiden, 1923–71); edd. H. W. Pleket, R. S. Stroud, A. Chaniotis and J. H. M. Strubbe, 26–7 (Alphen, 1979–80), 28– (Amsterdam, 1982–)
Sel'skaia Okruga Ol'vii	*Sel'skaia Okruga Ol'vii*, edd. S. D. Kryzhitskii et al. (Akademiia Nauk Ukrainskoi SSR, Institut arkheologii [Kiev, 1989])
Sevtopolis	D. P. Dimitrov et al., *Sevtopolis*, 2 vols. (Sofia, 1984)
SGAIMK	*Soobshcheniia Gosudarstvennoi Akademii istorii material'noi kul'tury* (Leningrad, 1931–2)
SGDI	*Sammlung der griechischen Dialekt-Inschriften*, edd. H. Collitz, F. Bechtel et al., 4 vols. (Göttingen, 1884–1915)
SGE	*Soobshcheniia Gosudarstvennogo Ermitazha* (*Bulletin du Musée de l'Hermitage)*, 1– (Leningrad, 1940–)
SGMII	*Soobshcheniia Gosudarstvennogo Muzeia izobrazitelnykh iskusstv imeni A. S. Pushkina*, 1– (Moscow, 1960–)
Shelov, *CB*	D. B. Shelov, *Coinage of the Bosporus VI-II centuries B.C.* (*BAR International Series*, 46 [Oxford, 1978])
Sherk	R. K. Sherk, *Roman Documents from the Greek East. Senatus Consulta and Epistulae to the Age of Augustus* (Baltimore, 1969)
SIRIS	L. Vidman, *Sylloge inscriptionum religionis Isiacae et Sarapiacae* (*Religionsgeschichtliche Versuche und Vorarbeiten*, 28 [Berlin, 1969])
SKhM	*Soobshcheniia Khersonesskogo Muzeia* (Khersones'kyi derzhavnyi istoriko-arkheolohichnyi muzei [Simferopol, 1960–])
Small Obj. from the Pnyx	G. R. Davidson and D. B. Thompson, *Small Objects from the Pnyx*, I (*Hesperia* Suppl., 7 [Princeton, 1943])
SNG Berry	*Sylloge Nummorum Graecorum. The Burton Y. Berry Collection*, ed. M. Thompson (New York, 1961–2)
SNG BM Black Sea	*Sylloge Nummorum Graecorum* IX. *The British Museum*. Part 1, *The Black Sea*, ed. M. J. Price (London, 1993)
SNG Cop. Thrace	*Sylloge Nummorum Graecorum. The Royal Collection of Coins and Medals, Danish National Museum. Thrace*, ed. N. Breitenstein (Copenhagen, 1942)
SNG Stancomb	*Sylloge Nummorum Graecorum* XI. *The William Stancomb Collection of Coins of the Black Sea Region*, ed. W. M. Stancomb (Oxford, 2000)
Sokolovska, *Isar-Marvinci*	V. Sokolovska, *Isar-Marvinci. I Povardarjeto vo antichko vreme (Isar-Marvinci and the Vardar valley in ancient times)* (Skopje, 1986)
Sokolowski	F. Sokolowski, (I) *Lois sacrées de l'Asie Mineure*; (II) *Lois sacrées des cités grecques, Supplément*; (III) *Lois sacrées des cités grecques* (École française d'Athènes, *Travaux et Mémoires*, 9, 11, 18 [Paris, 1955–69])
Sokol'skii, *Tamanskii tolos*	N. I. Sokol'skii, *Tamanskii tolos i rezidentsiia Khrisaliska* (Moscow, 1976)
Solomonik, *GAKh*	E. I. Solomonik, *Graffiti antichnogo Khersonesa* (Akademiia Nauk Ukrainskoi SSR, Institut arkheologii [Kiev, 1978])
Solomonik, *GChKh*	E. I. Solomonik, *Graffiti s chori Khersonesa* (Akademiia Nauk Ukrainskoi SSR, Institut arkheologii [Kiev, 1984])
Solomonik, *LNKhT*	E. I. Solomonik, *Latinskie nadpisi Khersonesa Tavricheskogo* (Akademiia Nauk SSSR, Institut istorii SSSR [Moscow, 1983])

Solomonik, *NEPKh*	E. I. Solomonik, *Novie epigraficheskie pamiatniki Khersonesa*, 2 vols. (Akademiia Nauk Ukrainskoi SSR, Institut arkheologii [Kiev, 1964, 1973])
Sotheby sale	Sotheby & Co. London, sale catalogues
Sov. Arkh.	*Sovetskaia Arkheologiia*, 1–36 (Akademiia Nauk SSSR, Institut istorii material'noi kul'tury [Moscow, 1957–1992])
Sp.	*Spomenik*, 1– (Srpska Kraljevska Akademija [Belgrade, 1888–1948]; Srpska Akademija Nauka (i Umetnosti) [1950–])
Speidel, *Denkmäler*	M. P. Speidel, *Die Denkmäler der Kaiserreiter. Equites Singulares Augusti* (*Beihefte der Bonner Jahrbücher*, 50 [Cologne and Bonn, 1994])
Spiliopoulou-Donderer, *KGN*	I. Spiliopoulou-Donderer, *Kaiserzeitliche Grabaltäre Niedermakedoniens. Untersuchungen zur Sepulkralskulptur einer Kunstlandschaft im Spannungsfeld zwischen Ost und West* (*Peleus*, 15 [Mannheim, 2002])
Spink Num. Circular	*Spink & Son's (Monthly) Numismatic Circular* (London, 1893–)
St. Clas.	*Studii Clasice*, 1– (Societatea de Studii Clasice din Republica Populara (Socialista) România [Bucharest, 1959–])
Starinar	*Starinar*, NS 1– (Srpsko Arheolosko Drustvo, Arheoloski Institut (Beograd) [Belgrade, 1950–])
Steinepigramme	*Steinepigramme aus dem griechischen Osten*, edd. R. Merkelbach and J. Stauber, 5 vols. (Tübingen, Munich and Leipzig, 1998–2004)
Stephanis	I. E. Stephanis, *Διονυσιακοὶ Τεχνῖται. Συμβολὲς στὴν προσωπογραφία τοῦ θεάτρου καὶ τῆς μουσικῆς τῶν ἀρχαίων Ἑλλήνων* (Herakleion, 1988)
Stephanos nomismatikos	*Stephanos nomismatikos. Edith Schönert-Geiss zum 65. Geburtstag*, ed. U. Peter (Berlin, 1998)
Stobi Hell. Rom. Pottery	V. R. Anderson-Stojanović, *Stobi. The Hellenistic and Roman Pottery* (Princeton, 1992)
Stud. Alexandrescu	*Civilisation grecque et cultures antiques périphériques. Hommage à Petre Alexandrescu à son 70e anniversaire*, edd. A. Avram and M. Babeş (Bucharest, 2000)
Stud. Beševliev	*Studia in honorem Veselini Beševliev*, edd. V. Georgiev, B. Gerov, V. Tăpkova-Zaimova, N. Todorov and V. Velkov (Sofia, 1978)
Stud. Blavatskii	*Kul'tura antichnogo mira (K sorokaletiiu nauchnoi deiatel'nosti Vladimira Dmitrievicha Blavatskogo)*, ed. A. I. Boltunova (Akademiia Nauk SSSR, Institut arkheologii [Moscow, 1966])
Stud. Edson	*Ancient Macedonian Studies in honor of Charles F. Edson* (Institute of Balkan Studies [Thessaloniki, 1981])
Stud. Fischer	*In memoriam I. Fischer. Omagiul foştilor colegi şi discipoli*, edd. L. Wald and T. Georgescu (Bucharest, 2004)
Stud. Fol	*Thracia* 11. *Studia in honorem Alexandri Fol*, edd. K. Jordanov, D. Popov and K. Porozhanov (Bulgarska Akademiia na Naukite, Institut po Trakologiia [Sofia, 1995])
Stud. Gerov	*Studia in honorem Borisi Gerov*, edd. M. Tačeva and D. Bojadžiev (Sofia, 1990)
Stud. Orbeli	*Issledovaniia po istorii kul'tury narodov vostoka. Sbornik v chest' Akademika I. A. Orbeli*, ed. V. V. Struve (Moscow and Leningrad, 1960)
Stud. Ščeglov	*The Cauldron of Ariantas. Studies presented to A. N. Ščeglov on the occasion of his 70th birthday*, edd. P. G. Bilde, J. M. Hojte and V. F. Stolba (Aarhus, 2003)
Stud. Siganidou	*Μνείας Χάριν. Τόμος στὴ μνήμη Μαίρης Σιγανίδου*, edd. M. Lilimbaki-Akamati and K. Tsakalou-Tzanavari (Thessaloniki, 1998)
Stud. Tacheva	*Sbornik v chest na Prof. Margarita Tacheva*, edd. K. Boshnakov and D. Boteva (*Jubilaeus*, 5 [Sofia, 2002])
Stud. Zhebelev	*Antichnaia istoriia i kul'tura Sredizemnomor'ia i Prichernomor'ia. Sbornik statei. K stoletiiu so dnia rozhdeniia akademika Sergeia Aleksandrovitsa Zhebeleva, 1867-1967*, ed. V. F. Gaidukevich (Akademiia Nauk SSSR, Institut arkheologii [Leningrad, 1968])
Studies Stobi	*Studies in the Antiquities of Stobi*, ed. J. Wiseman, 3 vols. (Belgrade, 1973, 1975; Titov Veles, 1981)
Studii Cercetări Numismatică	*Studii şi Cercetări de Numismatică*, 1– (Academia Română, Institutul de arheologie 'Vasile Pârvan' [Bucharest, 1957–])
Suppl. Hell.	*Supplementum Hellenisticum*, edd. H. J. Lloyd-Jones and P. J. Parsons (Berlin and New York, 1983)
Suppl. Rod.	G. Pugliese Carratelli, 'Supplemento epigrafico rodio', *ASAA* NS 14–16 (1952–4) pp. 247–316; 'Nuovo supplemento epigrafico rodio', ib. NS 17–18 (1957) pp. 157-181
SVF	*Stoicorum veterum fragmenta*, ed. J. von Arnim, 4 vols. (Leipzig, 1903–24)
Syll^3	*Sylloge Inscriptionum Graecarum*, ed. W. Dittenberger, 4 vols. (3rd edn., ed. F. Hiller von Gaertringen [Leipzig, 1915–24])
Syllogos	*Ἑλληνικὸς φιλολογικὸς σύλλογος. Σύγγραμμα περιοδικόν*, 1–33 (Constantinople, 1863–1911)
Syringes	J. Baillet, *Inscriptions grecques et latines des Tombeaux des Rois ou Syringes*, 3 vols. (*Mémoires de l'Institut français d'archéologie orientale de Caire*, 42 [Cairo, 1920–26])
TAM	*Tituli Asiae Minoris*. I, *Tituli Lyciae lingua lycia conscripti*, ed. E. Kalinka (Vienna, 1901); II (1-3), *Tituli Lyciae*, ed. E. Kalinka (1920–44); III (1), *Tituli Pisidiae*, ed. R. Heberdey (1941); IV (1), *Tituli Bithyniae*, ed. F. K. Dörner (1978); V (1-2), *Tituli Lydiae septentrionalis*, edd. P. Herrmann and J. Keil (1981, 1989)
Tanais I	*Tanais*. I, edd. T. Arsen'eva, B. Böttger, Ju. G. Vinogradov (*Pontus Septentrionalis*, I [Moscow, 1998])

TAPA	*Transactions of the American Philological Association*, 1– (Hartford etc., 1869–)
Tarn, *Alexander*	W. W. Tarn, *Alexander the Great*, 2 vols. (Cambridge, 1948)
Taşlıklıoğlu	Z. Taşlıklıoğlu, *Trakya'da epigrafya araştırmaları (Recherches épigraphiques en Thrace et en Chersonèse)*, 2 vols. (*Istanbul Üniversitesi Edebiyat Fakültesi Yayınları*, 886, 1654 [Istanbul, 1961, 1971])
Tataki	A. B. Tataki, *Ancient Beroea. Prosopography and Society* (*Μελετήματα*, 8 [Athens, 1988])
Tataki, *Edessa*	A. B. Tataki, *Macedonian Edessa. Prosopography and Onomasticon* (*Μελετήματα*, 18 [Athens, 1994])
Tataki, *Macedonians*	A. B. Tataki, *Macedonians Abroad. A Contribution to the prosopography of ancient Macedonia* (*Μελετήματα*, 26 [Athens, 1998])
TCal	M. Segre, 'Tituli Calymnii', *ASAA* NS 6–7 (1944–5, publ. 1952) pp. 1–249
TCam	M. Segre and I. Pugliese Carratelli, 'Tituli Camirenses', *ASAA* NS 11–13 (1947–51) pp. 141–318; 'Tituli Camirenses, Supplementum', ib. NS 14–16 (1952–4) pp. 211–46
Tekmeria	*Τεκμήρια. Beiträge zur Geschichte der griechischen und römischen Welt*, 1– (Thessaloniki, 1995–)
TGE	*Trudy Gosudarstvennogo (ordena Lenina) Ermitazha*, 1– (Leningrad, 1956–)
Thess. Mnem.	A. S. Arvanitopoullos, *Θεσσαλικὰ Μνημεῖα. Περιγραφὴ τῶν ἐν τῷ Ἀθανασακείῳ Μουσείῳ Βόλου γραπτῶν στηλῶν τῶν Παγασῶν* (Athens, 1909)
Thessalonike	*Thessalonike*, 1– (Thessaloniki, 1985–)
Thompson, *Memphis*	D. J. Thompson, *Memphis under the Ptolemies* (Princeton, 1988)
Thracia	*Thracia*, edd. A. N. Fol et al., 1– (Bulgarska Akademiia na Naukite, Institut po Trakologiia [Sofia, 1972–])
Thracia Pontica	*Thracia Pontica* (Acts of International Symposia held at Sozopol in 1979, 1982, 1985, 1988, 1994), 1– (Sozopol, Yambol, Sofia and Varna, 1982–)
Thrak. Epet.	*Θρακικὴ Ἐπετηρίς*, 1–2 (*Ἐτήσιον δημοσίευμα τῆς ἐν Ἀθήναις Θρακικῆς Ἀδελφότητος* [Athens, 1897])
Thrakika	*Θρακικά*, 1–47; NS 1– (*Περιοδικὸν τοῦ ἐν Ἀθήναις Θρακικοῦ Κέντρου* [Athens, 1924–1974; 1980–])
Threatte, *Grammar*	L. Threatte, *The Grammar of Attic inscriptions*. I, *Phonology*; II, *Morphology* (Berlin, 1980, 1996)
Tod, *GHI*	M. N. Tod, *Greek Historical Inscriptions*, 2 vols. (Oxford, 1933, 1948; I^2 1946)
Tolstoi	I. I. Tolstoi, *Grecheskie graffiti drevnikh gorodov Severnogo Prichernomor'ia* (Akademiia Nauk SSSR, Institut istorii material'noi kul'tury, Institut Iazykoznaniia [Moscow and Leningrad, 1953])
Topoi	*ΤΟΠΟΙ. Orient-Occident*, 1– (Association des amis de la bibliothèque Salomon Reinach [Lyon, 1991–])
Torone	*Torone*. I, *The Excavations of 1975, 1976, and 1978*, edd. A. Cambitoglou, J. K. Papadopoulos, and O. Tudor Jones, 3 vols. (*Βιβλιοθήκη τῆς ἐν Ἀθήναις Ἀρχαιολογικῆς Ἑταιρείας*, 206 [Athens, 2001])
Touratsoglou, *Macedonia*	I. Touratsoglou, *Macedonia. History, Monuments, Museums* (Athens, 1995)
TrGF	*Tragicorum Graecorum Fragmenta*, edd. B. Snell, R. Kannicht and S. Radt, 4 vols. (Göttingen, 1971–86)
Türk Tarih Kongresi XI	*Türk Tarih Kongresi XI. Ankara, 5-9 Eylül 1990. Kongreye sunulan bildiriler*, 6 vols. (Ankara, 1994)
Tyana	D. Berges and J. Nollé, *Tyana. Archäologisch-historische Untersuchungen zum südwestlichen Kappadokien*, 2 vols. (*IGSK*, 55 [Bonn, 2000])
Tyche	*Tyche. Beiträge zur alten Geschichte, Papyrologie und Epigraphik*, 1– (Vienna, 1986–)
Uebel, *Kleruchen*	F. Uebel, *Die Kleruchen im ptolemäischen Ägypten bis um die Mitte des 2. Jahrhunderts v.Chr.: nach den griechischen Quellen zusammengestellte Liste mit Anmerkungen* (diss. Jena, 1959); revised as *Die Kleruchen Ägyptens unter den ersten sechs Ptolemäern* (*AbhBerlAk*, Kl. Spr., Lit., Kunst, 1968 (3) [Berlin, 1968])
Unp.	Unpublished material. [Cited with an indication of source in the following brackets]
Unp. (Sayar)	Names in inscriptions to be published by M. H. Sayar
Unp. (Voutyras–Sismanidis)	Inscription from Macedonian Dikaia, to be published by E. Voutyras and K. Sismanidis
UPZ	*Urkunden der Ptolemäerzeit*, ed. U. Wilcken, 2 vols. (Berlin 1927, 1957)
Vaulina–Wąsowicz	M. Vaulina and A. Wąsowicz, *Bois grecs et romains de l'Hermitage* (Académie Polonaise des Sciences, Institut d'histoire de la culture matérielle [Wroclaw, Warsaw, Krakow and Gdansk, 1974])
VDI	*Vestnik drevnei istorii*, 1– (Akademiia Nauk SSSR, Institut istorii [Moscow, 1937–])
Velkov	V. Velkov and A. Fol, *Les Thraces en Égypte gréco-romaine* (*Studia Thracica*, 4 [Sofia, 1977])
Vinogradov, *Pont. Stud.*	J. G. Vinogradov, *Pontische Studien. Kleine Schriften zur Geschichte und Epigraphik des Schwarzmeerraumes* (Mainz, 1997)
Vinogradov–Kryžickij	J. G. Vinogradov and S. D. Kryžickij, *Olbia. Eine altgriechische Stadt im nordwestlichen Schwarzmeerraum* (*Mnemosyne* Suppl., 149 [Leiden, New York and Cologne, 1995])
Vokotopoulou, *Guide*	I. Vokotopoulou, *Guide to the Archaeological Museum of Thessaloniki* (Athens, 1996)
Vollenweider, *Camées*	M.-L. Vollenweider, *Camées et intailles, catalogue raisonné*, vol. 1 (Bibliothèque nationale de France, Département des médailles et antiques [Paris, 1995])
Walbank	F. W. Walbank, *A Historical Commentary on Polybius*, 3 vols. (Oxford, 1957–79)
WChr	L. Mitteis and U. Wilcken, *Grundzüge und Chrestomathie der Papyruskunde*. I, *Historischer Teil*, ed. U. Wilcken, 2 vols. (Leipzig and Berlin, 1912)
Wehrli, *Schule Arist.*	F. Wehrli, *Die Schule des Aristoteles, Texte und Kommentar*, 10 fasc. and supplement (Basel and Stuttgart, 1944–59; 2nd edns. of vols. 2 and 4, 1967–8)

Welles, *RC*	C. B. Welles, *Royal Correspondence in the Hellenistic Period. A Study in Greek Epigraphy* (New Haven, 1934)
Wessel	*Inscriptiones Graecae Christianae Veteres Occidentis*, ed. C. Wessel (*Inscriptiones Christianae Italiae, Subsidia*, 1 [Bari, 1989])
Wilhelm, *Beitr.*	A. Wilhelm, *Beiträge zur griechischen Inschriftenkunde* (*Sonderschriften des Österreichischen Archäologischen Institutes in Wien*, 7 [Vienna, 1909])
Winter, *Typen*	F. Winter, *Die Typen der figürlichen Terrakotten*, 2 vols. (*Die antiken Terrakotten* III (2) [Berlin and Stuttgart, 1903])
Xenia antiqua	*Xenia antiqua*, 1– (Rome, 1992–)
Youroukova	Y. Youroukova, *Coins of the ancient Thracians* (*BAR Supplementary Series*, 4 [Oxford, 1976])
ZA	*Živa antika (Antiquité vivante)*, 1– (Skopje, 1951–)
ZÄS	*Zeitschrift für Ägyptische Sprache und Altertumskunde*, 1– (Berlin and Leipzig, 1866–)
ZfN	*Zeitschrift für Numismatik*, 1–42 (Berlin, 1874–1935)
Zgusta, *KP*	L. Zgusta, *Kleinasiatische Personennamen* (Československá Akademie Věd, *Monografie Orientálního ústavu ČSAV*, 19 [Prague, 1964])
Zgusta, *PNS*	L. Zgusta, *Die Personennamen griechischer Städte der nördlichen Schwarzmeerküste* (Československá Akademie Věd, Sekce jazyka a literatury, *Monografie Orientálního ústavu*, 16 [Prague, 1955])
ZOOID	*Zapiski (Imperatorskogo) Odesskogo obshchestva istorii i drevnostei*, 1– (Odessa, 1878–)
ZPE	*Zeitschrift für Papyrologie und Epigraphik*, 1– (Bonn, 1967–)

A

Ἀβα
SCYTHIA MINOR:
—ISTROS: (1) ii AD *ISM* I 57, 4, [50] (*Eastern cults* pp. 102-3 no. 65) (d. Ἑκαταῖος)
—KALLATIS: (2) iv/iii BC *ISM* III 153 (d. Τιμοκλῆς)

Ἄβαβος
SKYTHIA:
—OLBIA-BORYSTHENES: (1) f. i AD *IOSPE* I^2 79, 3, 25 (*IByz* 3 with comm.); *IOSPE* I^2 181, 5; 182; Zgusta, *PNS* 591 (s. Καλλισθένης, f. Ὀρόντης)

Ἀβαζίων
CIMMERIAN BOSPOROS:
—PANTIKAPAION: (1) imp. *CIRB* 774; Zgusta, *PNS* 38 (s. Πόθος, Χρύσιον)

Ἀβας
CIMMERIAN BOSPOROS:
—NYMPHAION (NR.): (1) iii AD *CIRB* 941 (Ἄβανι (dat.): s. Φάννης)

Ἀβάσκαντος
MACEDONIA (BOTTIAIA):
—BEROIA: (1) ii/iii AD *IBer* 27 A, 10 (slave?)
MACEDONIA (MYGDONIA):
—THESSALONIKE: (2) ii-iii AD *IG* X (2) (1) 464 A; 464 B, 3 (*GVI* 1865) (f. Αἴλ. Νέπως)
MACEDONIA (PIERIA):
—DION: (3) ii-iii AD Oikonomos 24 + *Essays Laourdas* p. 105 (Αἴλ. Ἀ.)
SCYTHIA MINOR:
—TOMIS: (4) ii-iii AD *ISM* II 294 (s. Σωκράτης)
THRACE:
—NICOPOLIS AD ISTRUM (TERRIT.): (5) ii/iii AD *SEG* XLIV 640, 2, 4 (biling.) (*Atti XI Congr. Epig.* I p. 770) (Φ(λ). Ἀ.: f. Ὀσία)
—NOVAE*: (6) i/ii AD *IGLNovae* 98 (*ILB* 315) (Lat. M. Granius Abascantus: freed.)
—PAUTALIA: (7) iii-iv AD *IGB* V 5773 = *SEG* XLVI 865 (Δομίτιος Ἀ.: f. Λ. Δομίτιος Ἀλέξανδρος) ?= (*8*); (8) s. iii AD *IGB* V 5776 = *SEG* XLVI 867 (Λ. Δομίτιος Ἀ.) ?= (7)

Ἀβαύχας
SKYTHIA:
—SKYTHAI: (1) ii AD Luc., *Tox.* 61 (fict.)

Ἀβάχης
TAURIS:
—KALOS LIMEN: (1) ii-iii AD *SEG* XXVI 802 = XXXVIII 749. 3 (Solomonik, *GChKh* p. 8 no. 7)

Ἀββάγαζα
CIMMERIAN BOSPOROS:
—PANTIKAPAION: (1) v/vi AD *VDI* 1998 (1), p. 240 no. 5a, 6 (d. Φαισφάρτα, ?d. Σανάγας)

Ἀβδάρακος
SKYTHIA:
—TANAIS: (1) 244 AD *CIRB* 1287, 14-15 (f. Ἀλέξανδρος, Ὀρστόμηχος)

Ἀβδηρίων
THRACE:
—ABDERA: (1) iii BC *HE* 1920
—STRYME?: (2) f. iv BC *SEG* XXXVIII 674 (*IThrakAig* E146) (Ἀβδηρίω̣ν: s. Ξενοφῶν)

Ἀβέζελμις
THRACE:
—METODIEVO (MOD.): (1) f. iii AD *IGB* II 771 (*CCET* II (2) 415) (?s. Δορπανας)

Ἀβλούζελμις
THRACE?: (1) ii BC *Memnonion* 82 (Velkov 4) (s. Κότυς); (2) ?ii BC *SB* 3678 (Velkov 3) (Ἐβλούζελμις)

Ἀβλώνακος
SKYTHIA:
—OLBIA-BORYSTHENES: (1) ii AD *IOSPE* I^2 175, 7; Zgusta, *PNS* 265 (s. Ἀρσηούαχος)

Ἄβναγος
SKYTHIA:
—OLBIA-BORYSTHENES: (1) ii AD *IOSPE* I^2 101, 4; Zgusta, *PNS* 266 (f. Ῥαθάγωσος); (2) f. ii AD *Drev. Prichern.* 3 pp. 27-8, 6 ([Ἄβ]ναγος: f. (ad.) Ἀργουάναγος)

Ἄβνακος
SKYTHIA:
—OLBIA-BORYSTHENES: (1) i/ii AD *SEG* XLIII 505, 6; Zgusta, *PNS* 267 (f. Πούρθαις); (2) ii AD *IOSPE* I^2 175, 7 (f. Ἄβνωζος) ?= (*3*); (3) s. ii AD *SEG* XLIII 507, 2 ?= (*2*)

Ἄβνωζος
SKYTHIA:
—OLBIA-BORYSTHENES: (1) ii AD *IOlbia* 88, 4; *IOSPE* I^2 91, 7; Zgusta, *PNS* 268 (Ἀμνωζος—*IOlbia* 88: s. Ῥαθάγωσος); (2) *IOSPE* I^2 175, 6 (s. Ἄβνακος)

Ἄβραγος
SKYTHIA:
—OLBIA-BORYSTHENES: (1) ii AD ib. 80, 15; Zgusta, *PNS* 40 ([Ἄ]βραγος?: s. Σαμβοῦς); (2) *IOSPE* I^2 82, 6 (s. Χουάρσαζος) ?= (*5*); (3) ib. 91, 9 (f. Χαράξηνος, Οὐάρζβαλος); (4) ib. 100, 8 (f. Μάθανος); (5) ib. 686, 5 (*VDI* 1975 (1), p. 69) (s. Χουάρσαζος) ?= (*2*); (6) ii/iii AD *IOlbia* 94 (Ἄβρα[γος]?); (7) iii AD *IOSPE* I^2 98, 9 (s. Δημήτριος)
—OLBIA-BORYSTHENES (BEREZAN (MOD.)): (8) f. ii AD *SEG* XLIX 1028 A, 6 (s. Ἀβρύμηος); (9) ib. l. 8 (f. Κοῦλις)
—TYRAS: (10) ii-iii AD *ISM* II 313 (*SEG* XXIV 1080) (s. Ἄττας)

Ἀβρέμιος
MACEDONIA (MYGDONIA):
—THESSALONIKE: (1) v-vi AD *IG* X (2) (1) 633 (Feissel, *RICM* 173; *CIJ* I 693) (Ἀβράμηος—Feissel: Jew)

Ἀβρέξας
IBERIA:
—TSILKANI (MOD.): (1) iii-iv AD *Archeologia* (Warsaw) 17 (1966) p. 59 (gem) (n. pr.?)

Ἀβροτίς
THRACE:
—MARONEIA: (1) i BC-i AD *AD* 26 (1971) Chron. p. 428 no. α (*IThrakAig* E202) (Μαρκία Ἀ.)

Ἀβρέας
MACEDONIA: (1) 326 BC *RE* (-); Berve 6 (Tataki, *Macedonians* p. 217 no. 3)

Ἀβριτία
SKYTHIA:
—TYRAS: (1) iii AD *IGB* I^2 228 bis, 1 (Αὐρ. Ἀ.: d. Αὐρ. Φωρδίγαλος, Μαδινι)

Ἀβρίσκος
CIMMERIAN BOSPOROS:
—PHANAGOREIA: (1) i-ii AD *CIRB* 999

Ἀβρόαγος
SKYTHIA:
—OLBIA-BORYSTHENES: (1) i/ii AD *IOlbia* 79, 10 (*IOSPE* I^2 116); Zgusta, *PNS* 41 (s. Σουσούλων)

Ἀβροζέλμης
THRACE: (1) 400 BC X., *An.* vii 6. 43

Ἀβρόζεος
SKYTHIA:
—TANAIS: (1) 225 AD *CIRB* 1279, 9 (s. Ἀρίστων)

Ἀβροκόμας
CIMMERIAN BOSPOROS:
—PANTIKAPAION: (1) c. 390-380 BC *SEG* L 710 A (vase) (fict.?)
MACEDONIA (EDONIS):
—PHILIPPOI (NR.): (2) ii AD *CIL* III 14206. 18 (Pilhofer 432) (Lat. Abrocomae (dat.): slave?)
MACEDONIA (ODOMANTIKE):
—SKOTOUSSA?: (3) ii-iii AD *SEG* XLVIII 801 (Ἀβροκόμ(α)ς: s. Ἀντίγονος)
THRACE:
—ODESSOS?: (4) s. ii AD *IGB* I^2 206 quater; *Dacia* 21 (1977) p. 161 (date) (s. Φιλόξενος, f. Νικερωτίς)

Ἅβρος
THRACE:
—KALLIPOLIS (NR.): (1) i-ii AD *ISestos* 67 (f. Γ. Ἰούλ. Ὕμνος)
—SESTOS: (2) 132 AD *IG* II^2 3304, 6 (Κλαύδιος Ἄβιος?—apogr., Ἄβ(ρ)ος?)

Ἀβροσύνη
THRACE: (1) 414 BC ib. I^3 422, 197 (*FRA* 2487) ([Ἀβ]ροσύνε̄: slave)

Ἀβρούπολις
THRACE:
—SAPPAIOI: (1) f. ii BC *RE* s.v. Abrupolis (-) (king) ?= (Αὐλούπορις (*25*))

Ἀβρύμηος
SKYTHIA:
—OLBIA-BORYSTHENES (BEREZAN (MOD.)): (1) f. ii AD *SEG* XLIX 1028 A, 6 (f. Ἄβραγος)

Ἀγάητος
SKYTHIA:
—SKYTHAI: (1) vii BC St. Byz. s.v. Παντικάπαιον (king/fict.?)

Ἀγάθα
MACEDONIA (BOTTIAIA):
—BEROIA: (1) ii-i BC *IBer* 392 (Tataki 7) (d. Πατερῖνος)

Ἀγαθάγγελος
CIMMERIAN BOSPOROS:
—PANTIKAPAION: (1) s. i AD *CIRB* 476 (Ἀγαθάγγελ[ος])
MACEDONIA (MYGDONIA):
—THESSALONIKE: (2) iv AD *AEMTh* 15 (2001) p. 325 (f. Μάξιμα)
THRACE:
—BYZANTION: (3) ?ii-i BC *IByz* 117 B (s. Ἀπολλώνιος)

Ἀγαθάνασσα
THRACE: (1) i BC-i AD *NS* 218 (Ἀγαθάνασ(σ)α)

Ἀγάθανδρος
SCYTHIA MINOR:
—TOMIS: (1) ii AD *ISM* II 189, 2 (*GVI* 1026) (s. Ἰουλιανός, Ῥηγῖνα)

Ἀγαθάνωρ
MACEDONIA (BOTTIAIA):
—BEROIA: (1) s. iii BC *IBer* 16 A, 9 ([Ἀγ]αθάνωρ: s. Θαρσυ—)

MACEDONIA (MYGDONIA):
—KALINDOIA: (2) c. 329-326 BC Hatzopoulos, *MI* 2 pp. 84-5 no. 62, 1, 16 (s. Ἀγάθων)
THRACE:
—ASENOVGRAD (MOD.): (3) iv BC *Fouilles et Recherches* (Sofia) 1 (1948) p. 106 (bronze) (*BE* 1950, no. 137)

Ἀγάθαρχος
SKYTHIA:
—OLBIA-BORYSTHENES: (1) m. iv BC Dubois, *IGDOlbia* 25 b, 2 (-κος); (2) iii BC *Arkheologiia* (Kiev) 39 (1982) p. 35 (vase)
THRACE:
—APOLLONIA-SOZOPOLIS: (3) iv BC *BMNBurgas* 4 (2002) p. 121 no. 6 (f. Δίφιλος)

Ἀγαθᾶς
CIMMERIAN BOSPOROS:
—NYMPHAION: (1) f. iii BC *SEG* XXXIX 701. 3
MACEDONIA (PAIONIA):
—ARGOS (NR.): (2) ii-iii AD ib. XVI 401, 3 (s. Εὔτροπος, Ἀγάθη)

Ἀγαθέα
MACEDONIA (MYGDONIA):
—THESSALONIKE: (1) ii/iii AD *IG* X (2) (1) 522 (Ἰουλ. Ἀ.)
—THESSALONIKE?: (2) ?i AD ib. 845 + *SEG* XXX 627 (Ἀγαθέανι (dat.), Ἀγαθέας?)
MACEDONIA (PIERIA):
—DION: (3) ii AD Dimitsas 166 (Οὐλπ. Ἀ.)

Ἀγάθη
MACEDONIA (EDONIS):
—PHILIPPOI: (1) ?v AD *AAA* 13 (1980) p. 95 (Pilhofer 115)
—PHILIPPOI (NR.): (2) imp. *CIL* III 7350 (Pilhofer 448) (Lat. Agathe)
MACEDONIA (MYGDONIA):
—THESSALONIKE?: (3) ?f. iii AD *SEG* XLIV 553, 3 (Αὐρ. Ἀ.: freed.?)
MACEDONIA (PAIONIA):
—ARGOS (NR.): (4) ii-iii AD ib. XVI 401, 1 (m. Φυλλίς, Ἀγαθᾶς, Ἐλπίς, Εὔτροπος, Ὀνομάστη, Σαμβατίς, Τύχη)
THRACE:
—NOVAE: (5) ii AD *IGLNovae* 104 (*ILB* 316) (Lat. Pullia Agathe: m. Ἀγαθίας, Ἀγαθόδωρος)

Ἀγαθημερίς
MACEDONIA: (1) 233 AD *ILeukopetra* 83, 5 (Ἀγαθημερίδαν (acc.): oikogen. slave/freed.)
MACEDONIA (BOTTIAIA):
—BEROIA: (2) imp. *IBer* 234 (Ποπλικία Ἀ.)
MACEDONIA (MYGDONIA):
—THESSALONIKE: (3) ii AD *IG* X (2) (1) 930; cf. *BCH* 99 (1975) p. 182; (4) 134 AD *IG* X (2) (1) 462 A (d. Διοσκουρίδης); (5) iv AD ib. 777
THRACE:
—ABDERA: (6) ii AD *IThrakAig* E67

Ἀγαθήμερος
MACEDONIA (BOTTIAIA):
—BEROIA: (1) ii/iii AD *IBer* 143 A, 6 (Tataki 10) (s. Ἀλέξανδρος); (2) f. iii AD *IBer* 210, 3 (Tataki 1057) (Πετρωνιανὸς Ἀ.: s. Αὐρ. Ἀμμία)
MACEDONIA (MYGDONIA):
—THESSALONIKE: (3) s. i AD *IG* X (2) (1) 69, 49 (Λ. Κομίνιος Ἀ.)
—THESSALONIKE?: (4) ii-iii AD ib. 720, 1 (f. Σιλβανός)
—THESSALONIKE*: (5) iii AD ib. 583, 1 (Αὐρ. Ἀ.)
SKYTHIA:
—TANAIS: (6) 228 AD *CIRB* 1283, 18 (s. Πόπλιος)
TAURIS:
—CHERSONESOS: (7) iv-vi AD Latyshev, *Sbornik* 25 (-θι-)
THRACE:
—BYZANTION: (8) c. 120 AD *FD* III (4) 85, 1 (f. Λάσιος)
—BYZANTION (TERRIT.): (9) imp. Unp. (Sayar) (s. Νικόστρατος)
—BYZANTION:
——(Rhegion): (10) i-ii AD *IByz* 271 (I f. Ἀγαθήμερος II); (11) ib. (II s. Ἀγαθήμερος I, f. Διότιμος)
—PHILIPPOPOLIS-TRIMONTIUM: (12) iii AD *IGB* III 972
—SERDICA (TERRIT.): (13) iii AD ib. V 5699 (Ἀγαθήμερ[ος])

Ἀγαθήνωρ
SCYTHIA MINOR:
—ISTROS: (1) v BC Unp. (Avram, defixio) 2, 2 (s. Διονυσόδωρος); (2) iii BC *ISM* I 1, 7 (Migeotte, *L'emprunt* 40) (s. Σιμύλος); (3) iii-ii BC Unp. (Avram, defixio) 4, 10; (4) iii/ii BC *ISM* I 46, 3 (Ἀγα[θ]ήνωρ: s. Σι—)
—KALLATIS: (5) i-ii AD ib. III 81 (Ἀγαθήν[ωρ]: f. —πος); (6) f. ii AD ib. 179, 4
—KALLATIS (NR.): (7) ii-iii AD ib. 238 (Τ. Φλ. Ἀ.)
SKYTHIA:
—OLBIA-BORYSTHENES: (8) iii BC *IOSPE* I^{2} 27, 2 (s. Πολυ—)
THRACE:
—ODESSOS: (9) ?ii BC *IGB* I^{2} 87 (s. Ἀριστόνομος); (10) ii-i BC *AMNG* I (2) 2219 (coin) (Ἀγαθή(νωρ)); (11) i BC-i AD *IGB* I^{2} 109 (s. Ἀρτεμίδωρος); (12) ib. 110, 1 (Ἀγαθήν[ωρ]: s. Ἀπολλώνιος, f. Σίμη); (13) ib. l. 5 (f. Νουμήνιος); (14) ib. 156 (I f. Ἀγαθήνωρ II); (15) ib. ([Ἀγ]αθήνωρ: II s. Ἀγαθήνωρ I); (16) ib. V 5061 (f. Ζουμαμα); (17) 19 BC ib. I^{2} 46, 28 (f. Ζῆνις); (18) 18 BC ib. l. 29 (s. Ζῆνις); (19) 4 BC ib. l. 43 (f. Ἡρότιμος); (20) i-ii AD ib. 108, 5 (f. Ἀννώ); (21) ib. 143 b, 1, 7 (s. Ἀρτεμίδωρος, f. Ἕλλην); (22) ib. 144 bis, 4 (f. Ἄπφη); (23) ib. 147 (PM 208) (Ἀ. νεώτ.: s. Ἀχιλλᾶς); (24) *IGB* I^{2} 188 (f. Νουμήνιος); (25) ii AD ib. 161 (*CCET* I 59; PM 1408) (s. Ἀπατούριος); (26) *IGB* I^{2} 178 bis (I s. Ἀπολλώνιος, f. Ἀγαθήνωρ II, Ζουδιεγιπτους); (27) ib. (II s. Ἀγαθήνωρ I, ?s. Βοών, Τουτάς); (28) ib. V 5063 (Ἀγαθή[νωρ]: f. Βαθεις); (29) ii-iii AD ib. I^{2} 143 a (Ἀγα[θ]ήνωρ: s. Ἀρτεμίδωρος); (30) ib. 173 (PM 1731); *Dacia* 21 (1977) p. 161 (date) (f. Ἀμύντωρ); (31) f. ii AD *IGB* I^{2} 78 ter, 4 (*CCET* I 30) (s. Μητρόδωρος); (32) *IGB* I^{2} 78 ter, 12 (*CCET* I 30) (f. Ἀντίφιλος); (33) *IGB* I^{2} 78 ter, 14 (*CCET* I 30) (s. Ἀντίφιλος); (34) s. ii AD *IGB* I^{2} 78 (*CCET* I 40) (s. Ἑστιαῖος); (35) ii/iii AD *IGB* I^{2} 165 (PM 1702); *Dacia* 21 (1977) p. 161 (date) (s. Διονύσιος); (36) 215 AD *IGB* I^{2} 47, 7 (Αὐρ. Ἀ.: s. Ἰουλιανός); (37) ib. 47 a, 16 (Αὐρ. Ἀ.: s. Ἡφαιστίων); (38) ib. 47 b, 16 (Αὐρ. Ἀ.: s. Ζωπυρίων); (39) ib. l. 20 (Αὐρ. Φλ. Ἀ.); (40) ib. 47 c, 11 (Αὐρ. Ἀ.: s. Δάδας); (41) 221 AD ib. 47 bis a, 26 (s. Ἑστιαῖος, f. Αὐρ. Νουμήνιος); (42) ib. l. 38 (f. Αὐρ. Ἀπολλόδωρος); (43) ib. 47 bis c, 11 (f. Αὐρ. Ἀπολλόδωρος); (44) ib. l. 21 (f. Αὐρ. Μέντης)
—ODESSOS (NR.): (45) i-ii AD ib. 286 (*CCET* I 83) (Ἀ. ὁ καὶ Δάδας: s. Πόσσις); (46) ii AD *IGB* I^{2} 261, 2 (*CCET* I 77) (s. Ξένανδρος, f. Ξένανδρος); (47) *IGB* I^{2} 292 (PM 1413; *CCET* I 102) (s. Κλεάνωρ); (48) s. ii AD *IGB* I^{2} 254 (PM 1723); *Dacia* 21 (1977) p. 161 (date) (f. Ἀπφία); (49) *IGB* I^{2} 281 (*CCET* I 25) (s. Ἀπολλώνιος); (50) *IGB* I^{2} 288 (*CCET* I 85) (f. Ἑστιαῖος); (51) *IGB* I^{2} 291 (*CCET* I 95) (s. Ζῆνις, f. Ζῆνις)
—ODESSOS?: (52) ii AD *IGB* I^{2} 51 bis b, 4 (I f. Ἀγαθήνωρ II); (53) ib. l. 4 (II s. Ἀγαθήνωρ I)

Ἀγαθητύχη
CIMMERIAN BOSPOROS:
—PANTIKAPAION: (1) iii AD *CIRB* 833; cf. KW pl. 54 no. 732 (n. pr.?)

Ἀγαθία
MACEDONIA (BOTTIAIA):
—BEROIA: (1) 277 AD *ILeukopetra* 112, 2 (Ἀγαθία Στρατονίκη)

Ἀγαθίας
MACEDONIA (MYGDONIA):
—THESSALONIKE: (1) f. iii AD *IG* X (2) (1) 193, 6 (Γ. Κορνήλιος Ἀ.)
—THESSALONIKE?: (2) iii AD ib. 841 (?s. Βαιβία Διονυσία); (3) a. 212 AD ib. 768, 2 + *SEG* XXVII 308 (f. Αὐρ. Ἀγησᾶς)
MACEDONIA (ODOMANTIKE):
—SIRRHA (TERRIT.): (4) ii-iii AD ib. XXX 593 (Pilhofer 713) (Ἀγαθί[ας]: f. Ἡρακλῆς)
THRACE:
—NOVAE: (5) ii AD *IGLNovae* 104 (*ILB* 316) (Lat. Q. Pullius Agathia: I f. Ἀγαθίας II, Ἀγαθόδωρος); (6) *IGLNovae* 104 (*ILB* 316) (Lat. Pullius Agathia: II s. Ἀγαθίας I, Ἀγάθη)
—ODESSOS: (7) ii-iii AD *IGB* I^{2} 141 (f. Ἐλπίς)
—PAUTALIA: (8) ii AD ib. IV 2074, 8
—PERINTHOS-HERAKLEIA: (9) i BC-i AD? *IPerinth* 57, 6 (f. Ἀρριανός)

Ἀγαθῖνος
MACEDONIA: (1) m. ii BC *BGU* 1939 A, 5 (Tataki, *Macedonians* p. 471 no. 1); cf. La'da E1668 ([Ἀ]γαθ[ῖ]νος)
MACEDONIA (CHALKIDIKE):
—POTIDAIA-KASSANDREIA: (2) iii BC *TAPA* 69 (1938) p. 64 n. 45 + *Ancient Macedonia* 1 p. 133 n. 24 (f. —νιος)
SCYTHIA MINOR:
—TOMIS: (3) ii-iii AD *ISM* II 104, 10 ([Ἀγα]θεῖνος?, [Σκυ]θεῖνος?)
SKYTHIA:
—OLBIA-BORYSTHENES: (4) iii BC *IOSPE* I^{2} 201 I, 30 (s. Ἀντιμήστωρ); (5) ib. l. 61 (f. Ἀντιμήστωρ); (6) ib. 201 II, 8 (s. Δημοκῶν); (7) f. iii BC ib. l. 12; *SEG* XXXIX 702, 29 (s. Δήϊμαχος)

Ἀγαθόβουλος
MACEDONIA (BOTTIAIA):
—BEROIA*: (1) ii/iii AD *IBer* 144 B, 14 (Tataki 274) (Αὐρ. Ἀ.: freed.)

Ἀγαθόδωρος
SKYTHIA:
—TANAIS: (1) ii AD *CIRB* 1262, 24 (f. Δημήτριος)
THRACE:
—NOVAE: (2) ii AD *IGLNovae* 104 (*ILB* 316) (Lat. Pullius Agathodorus: s. Ἀγαθίας, Ἀγάθη)
—PERINTHOS-HERAKLEIA: (3) i-ii AD *IPerinth* 93 (f. Χρῆστος); (4) ib. 94 (f. Χρῆστος)

Ἀγαθοκλέα
MACEDONIA (ELIMEIA):
—AIANE: (1) s. ii AD *EAM* 56 (Ἀγαθοκλέ[α]?, Ἀγαθοκλῆς?: d. Κάστωρ, Δημοκρατέα)
MACEDONIA (MYGDONIA):
—CHARAKOMA?: (2) ?ii AD *SEG* XL 536 ([Ἀγ]αθοκλέα)
MACEDONIA (PIERIA):
—DION: (3) i-ii AD Oikonomos 45 (d. Παρδαλίς)

Ἀγαθόκλεια
CIMMERIAN BOSPOROS:
—PANTIKAPAION: (1) ?i AD *CIRB* 536 (-κλια); (2) f. i AD ib. 143, 2; cf. KW pl. 21 no. 315; (3) f. ii AD *CIRB* 654
MACEDONIA (BOTTIAIA):
—EDESSA: (4) v-vi AD Feissel, *RICM* 20 (-κληα); (5) ib. 21 (-θώκλια)
THRACE: (6) ii BC *SBBerlAk* 1936, p. 360 no. 1, 5 (-κληα: slave/freed.)

Ἀγαθοκλείη
TAURIS:
—CHERSONESOS: (1) ii-iii AD *AGSP* p. 351 pl. 160 no. 32 (ring)

'Αγαθοκλῆς

CIMMERIAN BOSPOROS:
—GORGIPPIA: **(1)** f. iii BC *CIRB* 1137 B I, 29 ([Ἀγ]αθοκλῆς: s. Ἄτταλος); **(2)** ib. 1137 B II, 50 (Ἀγαθοκλ[ῆς]: f. Καλλικράτης)
—HERMONASSA: **(3)** iv BC ib. 1056 I, 22; **(4)** ib. 1056 II, 9 (Ἀγα[θο]κλῆ[ς]: f. Ἀγνίων)
—PANTIKAPAION: **(5)** f. ii AD ib. 84, 9; cf. KW pl. 45 no. 648 (f. Ἀχαιμένης)
MACEDONIA: **(6)** m. iii BC *FGrH* 156 F 31 (Tataki, *Macedonians* p. 217 no. 4); **(7)** ?216 BC *IG* VII 313, 1 (*IOrop* 90; Tataki, *Macedonians* p. 217 no. 5) (s. Περιγένης); **(8)** 190 or 189 BC *PHeid* VIII 417, 37; cf. La'da E1783 (f. Ῥόδων); **(9)** c. 148 BC *PTeb* 79, 29 (Tataki, *Macedonians* p. 471 no. 2); cf. La'da E1455 ([Ἀγα]θοκλῆς: f. Δημήτριος)
MACEDONIA (BOTTIAIA):
—BEROIA: **(10)** ii BC *IBer* 196 (Tataki 11) (s. Φίλιππος)
—PELLA: **(11)** m. iv BC *RE* (17) (Tataki, *Macedonians* p. 148 no. 3) (or Thessaly (Pelasgiotis) Krannon: f. Λυσίμαχος, Ἀλκίμαχος, Αὐτόδικος, Φίλιππος); **(12)** iv/iii BC *Pella* p. 139 no. 213 (f. Ποτάμων); **(13)** m. iii BC *SEG* XXXVIII 652 (f. Ἀντιπατρίδης); **(14)** 117 BC *FD* III (2) 70 b, 7 (Tataki, *Macedonians* p. 148 no. 4) (f. Σιμίας)
—PELLA?: **(15)** c. 320-284 BC *RE* (18); *SEG* XXXVIII 619, 9 (Tataki, *Macedonians* p. 148 no. 2) (s. Λυσίμαχος, ?s. Νικαία)
MACEDONIA (CHALKIDIKE):
—GIGONOS?: **(16)** ii AD *SEG* XLVIII 799 (—ΑΘΟΚΛΕΝΙ——ed., [Ἀγ]αθοκλε(ι)? (dat.): f. Ἀλέξανδρος, —μέων)
—TORONE: **(17)** ?353 BC ib. XXIV 574, 20; Hatzopoulos, *Actes Chalc.* p. 80 (date) (f. Κλεόνικος)
MACEDONIA (EDONIS):
—AMPHIPOLIS: **(18)** b. 213 BC Hatzopoulos, *MI* 2 p. 83 no. 61, 11 (*SEG* XLVI 715) ([Ἀγα]θοκλῆς?, [Πυ]θοκλῆς?, —οκράτης—ed. per err.)
MACEDONIA (MYGDONIA):
—DIKAIA: **(19)** c. 365-359 BC Unp. (Voutyras–Sismanidis) l. 64 (f. Κηφισόδωρος)
—THESSALONIKE: **(20)** iii AD *IG* X (2) (1) 500, 3 (Αὐρ. Ἀ.)
—THESSALONIKE?: **(21)** i AD ib. 901; *SEG* XLVII 972 (date) (Μ. Ἐρέννιος Ἀ.: s. Ἐρεννία Συρίσκα)
—ZANKLIVERI (MOD.): **(22)** ii-i BC *Makedonika* 2 (1951) p. 620 no. 43 (s. Στησιμένης, f. Παυσανίας)
MACEDONIA (PAIONIA):
—DEMIR KAPIJA (MOD.): **(23)** iii BC *BCH* 98 (1974) p. 279 (f. Μητρόβιος)
—STOBOI: **(24)** ?ii AD *Studies Stobi* 1 p. 167 n. 59 (Κουιντίλι. Κορν. Ἀ.); **(25)** s. iii AD *JÖAI* 32 (1940) Beibl. col. 16 no. 2. 3 (Παυλι(—) Ἀγαθοκλέους (gen.))
MACEDONIA (PIERIA):
—DION: **(26)** c. 230-200 BC *BCH* 45 (1921) p. 17 III, 54; cf. *IBer* p. 33 n. 12 (Tataki, *Macedonians* p. 100 no. 1) (Ἀγασικλῆς—Hatzopoulos: f. Μέντωρ)
MACEDONIA (PIERIS):
—GALEPSOS: **(27)** 65 or 181 AD *SEG* XXVII 284 (-το-: f. Ζιπύρων)
SCYTHIA MINOR:
—ISTROS: **(28)** iii BC *ISM* I 7, 3 (Ἀγαθ[ο]κλῆ[ς]); **(29)** c. 255 BC ib. 4, 1 + *Pontica* 33-4 (2000-1) pp. 339-44 no. 2 ([Ἀ]γαθοκλῆς); **(30)** s. iii BC *ISM* I 15, 3 (s. Ἀντίφιλος); **(31)** ii AD ib. 212, 11 (s. Ἡρόδωρος)
SKYTHIA:
—OLBIA-BORYSTHENES: **(32)** i AD *AA* 1909, p. 174 (Chuistova, *AIB* p. 84 no. 36 (date) (weight)); **(33)** ii AD *IOlbia* 80, 3 (s. Δαδα—); **(34)** *IOSPE* I² 96, 3 ([Ἀγα]θοκλῆς: s. Στράτων); **(35)** ii-iii AD ib. 136, 6 (II s. Ἀγαθοκλῆς I); **(36)** ib. l. 7 (I f. Ἀγαθοκλῆς II)
—TANAIS: **(37)** f. ii AD *CIRB* 1266, 14 (f. —δρος)
TAURIS:
—CHERSONESOS: **(38)** c. 250-230 BC Anokhin p. 141 no. 103 (coin)
THRACE: **(39)** iii-ii BC *Memnonion* 53; cf. La'da E780 (f. Πέταλος)
—ABDERA: **(40)** s. ii BC *IG* XII (8) 170 d, 54 (Ἀγαθοκλείους (gen.): f. Ἑρμογένης)
—BISANTHE-PANION: **(41)** hell.? Dumont–Homolle 83f (f. Ἑλλάς)
—BYZANTION: **(42)** iv BC *IG* II² 8434 (*FRA* 1381); **(43)** hell. *AD* 18 (1963) Mel. p. 22 no. 37 ?= (*44*); **(44)** *Suppl. Rod.* 29; *SEG* XXXI 734 (ident.) ([Ἀγαθ]οκλῆς) ?= (*43*); **(45)** s. iii BC Schönert-Geiss, *Byzantion* 1233 (coin); **(46)** ii/i BC *IByz* 128 (f. Μοῦσα)
—DUROSTORUM (TERRIT.)?: **(47)** imp. *IGB* II 870 (f. Εὐρυφῶν)
—EMPORION THOUIDAI: **(48)** ii-iii AD ib. III 1768; cf. V 5634 (locn.) ([Ἀγ]αθοκλῆς: f. Σάνκτος)
—LYSIMACHEIA: **(49)** m. ii BC *ISestos* 38 a, 1 (Ἀγαθοκλείου (gen.): f. Κλεογένης)
—MARONEIA: **(50)** 167 BC *SEG* XXXV 823, 5 (*IThrakAig* E168); cf. *SEG* XXXVII 611 (Ἀγαθοκ[λῆς]?—*SEG* XXXV, Ἀγαθομ[ένης]—*SEG* XXXVII)
—MONTANA*: **(51)** 155 AD *CIL* III 7449, 27 (*Montana* II 1) (Lat. Aur. Agathocles)
—PERINTHOS-HERAKLEIA: **(52)** iv-v AD *IPerinth* 197, 1 (*AD* 51-2 (1996-7) Mel. p. 363 no. 182) (Ἀγαθοκλῆδος (gen.))
——(Podargoi): **(53)** iii-ii BC *IPerinth* 61, 18 (s. Ἀπολλώνιος)
—VICUS TRULLENSIUM: **(54)** ii AD *IGB* II 503, 6 (*ILB* 183) (sculptor)

'Αγαθόμορος?

MACEDONIA (PIERIA):
—DION: **(1)** ii AD *GVI* 456 a; cf. Heuzey, *Le Mont Olympe* p. 481 no. 35? (Dimitsas 171) = Dimitsas 184 (Οὔλπιος Ἀ.—apogr., Ἀγαθ(ή)μ(ε)ρος?)

'Αγαθον

CIMMERIAN BOSPOROS:
—PANTIKAPAION: **(1)** i AD *CIRB* 326

'Αγαθονίκη

THRACE:
—BEROE-AUGUSTA TRAIANA: **(1)** c. 320-324 AD *Anal. Boll.* 31 (1912) p. 198; p. 208
—PERINTHOS-HERAKLEIA: **(2)** iii AD *IPerinth* 155 (Αὐρ. Ἀ.)
—SALYMBRIA: **(3)** v-vi AD ib. 224 (*AD* 53 (1998) Mel. p. 471 no. 209) (-νή-: d. Ἀλεξάνδρα)

'Αγαθόνικος

THRACE:
—SEXAGINTA PRISTA: **(1)** 230 AD *CIL* III 7473 (*Romanizmăt* II 115) (Lat. Septimius Agathonicus)

'Αγαθόπους

CIMMERIAN BOSPOROS:
—PANTIKAPAION: **(1)** 204 AD *CIRB* 96, 6 (*SEG* II 485)
MACEDONIA (EDONIS):
—PHILIPPOI: **(2)** ii/iii AD *CIL* III 633 II a, 17 (Pilhofer 163) (Lat. C. Abellius Agathopus)
MACEDONIA (MYGDONIA):
—THESSALONIKE: **(3)** i AD *IG* X (2) (1) 259, 21 (Γ. Ἰούλ. Ἀ.); **(4)** s. i AD ib. 68, 21, 46; 69, 34 (Τ. Κλ. Ἀ., Ἀγαθώπους—l. 46); **(5)** ii AD ib. 1039, 5 (Tataki, *Macedonians* p. 178 no. 1)
—THESSALONIKE?: **(6)** ii-iii AD *IG* X (2) (1) 726 (Δομίτιο[ς] Ἀγαθόπ[ους])
MACEDONIA (PIERIA):
—DION: **(7)** iv AD *SEG* XXXV 736
—DION (TERRIT.): **(8)** ?iii AD *ILGR* 192 (Lat. Domitius [A]gathopus)
THRACE:
—BEROE-AUGUSTA TRAIANA: **(9)** i-ii AD *IGB* III 1599 bis ([Ἀ]γαθόπους)
—BYZANTION: **(10)** ii AD *SEG* L 667 VII (s. Θεόδωρος, f. Λούκις, Εὔθετος)
—MELTA: **(11)** iii AD *ILB* 254 (Lat. Agathupus)
—OESCUS: **(12)** i AD ib. 77, 5 (Lat. Marius Agathopus: f. Μαρυλλῖνα, Marius Iustus)
—PHILIPPOPOLIS-TRIMONTIUM (TERRIT.): **(13)** ii AD *IGB* V 5472, 2 = *SEG* III 538 (*Eastern cults* pp. 199-200 no. 15) (Γ. Μαίλιος Ἀ.: freed.)

'Αγαθος

THRACE:
—PHILIPPOPOLIS-TRIMONTIUM: **(1)** c. 303 AD *Anal. Boll.* 31 (1912) p. 192

'Αγαθούας

CIMMERIAN BOSPOROS:
—GORGIPPIA: **(1)** ii/iii AD *CIRB* 1179, 49 (Ἀγαθοῦ<α>ς?: s. Ἀγαθοῦς)

'Αγαθοῦς

CIMMERIAN BOSPOROS:
—ACHILLEION: **(1)** s. ii AD ib. 1033 (f. Μάσας)
—GORGIPPIA: **(2)** i-ii AD *SEG* XXVII 432 (s. Πρωτογένης); **(3)** i/ii AD *CIRB* 1197 B; **(4)** ii AD ib. 1140, 10 (I f. Ἀγαθοῦς II); **(5)** ib. l. 10 (II s. Ἀγαθοῦς I); **(6)** ib. 1143, 5 (<Γ>αγαθοῦς—Vinogradov, Ἀγαθοῦ? (gen.): ?f. Ἄττας); **(7)** ib. 1151, 7 (s. Χρηστοῦς); **(8)** ib. 1157 A, 4 (s. Μασ—); **(9)** s. ii AD ib. 1129 B, 11 ([Ἀ]γαθοῦς); **(10)** ib. 1145, 3; **(11)** ib. l. 7 (f. Ψυχαρίων); **(12)** 173-210 AD ib. 1134, 24 ((Ἀ)γαθοῦς: f. Σπαρτοκίων); **(13)** ii/iii AD ib. 1179, 30 (s. Κέφθος, f. Γάστεις); **(14)** ib. l. 32 (s. Χρηστίων); **(15)** ib. l. 42 (s. Γοργίας, f. Φαρνακίων, —υς); **(16)** ib. l. 48 (f. —οκλῆς); **(17)** ib. l. 49 (s. Φαρ—, f. Ἀγαθούας); **(18)** ib. l. 54 (f. Γλύκων); **(19)** ib. l. 56 (f. —ος); **(20)** ib. l. 59 (f. Ποθίσκος); **(21)** ib. 1183 ([Ἀγ]αθοῦς); **(22)** *VDI* 1970 (4), p. 149, 6 ([Ἀγα]θοῦς: s. Βόχορος); **(23)** ib. l. 7 ([Ἀγα]θοῦς: s. Ζήνων)
—GORGIPPIA?: **(24)** s. ii AD *CIRB* 1231 B, 12 (f. Σαμβατίων)
—HERMONASSA: **(25)** 123-132 AD ib. 1054, 13 (s. Πολεμοκράτης); **(26)** ib. l. 19 (f. Ἀρισταγόρας)
—KOROKONDAME: **(27)** i BC ib. 1105 (I f. Ἀγαθοῦς II); **(28)** ib. (II s. Ἀγαθοῦς I)
—PANTIKAPAION: **(29)** ii-i BC ib. 704; cf. KW pl. 25 no. 371 ([Ἀγ]αθοῦς); **(30)** i BC-i AD *CIRB* 299 (d. Πόθων, m. Ἔρως); **(31)** i AD ib. 327; cf. KW pl. 29 no. 422 (I f. Ἀγαθοῦς II, Φιλοκλῆς); **(32)** *CIRB* 327; cf. KW pl. 29 no. 422 (II s. Ἀγαθοῦς I, Νικάριον); **(33)** *CIRB* 328 (s. Ἡζοῦς); **(34)** ib. 329 (I f. Ἀγαθοῦς II); **(35)** ib. (II s. Ἀγαθοῦς I); **(36)** ib. 376 (Ἀγαθ(ο)ῦς: f. Γάστεις); **(37)** ib. 499 (I f. Πρόμηθος, Ἀγαθοῦς II); **(38)** ib. (II s. Ἀγαθοῦς I); **(39)** f. ii AD ib. 91, 3; cf. KW pl. 39 no. 574 (f. Ἡρακλείδης); **(40)** 275-278 AD *CIRB* 36, 17 (f. Φάννης); **(41)** ib. l. 58 (Ἀγαθ(οῦς): f. —ος); **(42)** f. iv AD *IAK* 45 (1912) p. 19 no. 9 (Ἀγαθ[οῦς]?: f. Τρύφων)
—PHANAGOREIA: **(43)** s. i BC *CIRB* 992, 1 (f. Γόκων); **(44)** ib. l. 2, 5 (s. Γόκων); **(45)** i AD ib. 987, 2; **(46)** ib. 995 (f. Ἀπολλώνιος); **(47)** 179 AD ib. 1000, 2 (I s. Σακλῆς, f. Ἀγαθοῦς II); **(48)** ib. l. 8 (II s. Ἀγαθοῦς I); **(49)** v AD *SEG* XXXIX 704 + XLVIII 1025 (f. Χίμιρις)
—THEODOSIA: **(50)** iii AD *CIRB* 947 B, 2 ([Ἀγ]αθοῦς: s. Αὐτόνομος)
SKYTHIA:
—TANAIS: **(51)** 228 AD ib. 1282, 26; 1283, 18 (f. Φούρτας)

Ἀγαθοφόρος
Macedonia (Bottiaia):
—Beroia: **(1)** ii ad *IBer* 336 (Tataki 12); **(2)** f. ii ad *IBer* 36, 4 (Tataki 335) (*Λ. Βρούττιος Ἀ.*: f. *Μιλησία*)
Macedonia (Paionia): **(3)** ii-iii ad *Sp.* 77 (1934) p. 57 no. 61
Macedonia (Pieria):
—Pydna (territ.): **(4)** imp. *SEG* xxxviii 629 (*Ἀγαθοφό[ρος]*)

Ἀγαθώ
Macedonia (Mygdonia):
—Thessalonike: **(1)** ii-iii ad *IG* x (2) (1) 857/8; Robert, *OMS* 5 p. 316 (locn.)
Thrace:
—Augustae*: **(2)** i ad *Romanizmăt* i 35 (Dimitrov p. 29 no. 27) (Lat. Agatho: freed.)

Ἀγάθων
Cimmerian Bosporos:
—Bosporos: **(1)** ii bc *IG* ii^2 8424 (*FRA* 1365)
—Kytaia: **(2)** iv bc *SEG* xl 629. 2 (vase)
—Pantikapaion: **(3)** iii bc *CIRB* 244 (s. *Κόλλις*, f. *Εὐπορία*); **(4)** i ad ib. 331, 1 (f. *Γοργίας*)
Macedonia: **(5)** ?417-413 bc *IG* i^3 89, 78 (Tataki, *Macedonians* p. 218 no. 6) (-*θõν*); **(6)** 334-325 bc *RE* (7); Berve 8 (Tataki, *Macedonians* p. 218 no. 7) (s. *Τυρίμμας*)
Macedonia (Bottiaia):
—Aigai: **(7)** s. iv bc *SEG* xxxv 800 (*Ἀγάθων*)
—Beroia: **(8)** iv bc Tataki, *Macedonians* pp. 73-4 no. 3 (I f. *Ἄσανδρος*, *Ἀγάθων* II); **(9)** 313 bc D.S. xix 75. 2 (Tataki, *Macedonians* p. 73 no. 2) (II s. *Ἀγάθων* I); **(10)** 223 bc *IBer* 4, 16 (s. *Λυγκεύς*); **(11)** i-ii ad ib. 339 (*Γ. Σκίρτιος Ἀγάθω[ν]*: s. *Σκιρτία Ζωσίμη*, ?s. *Εὔπορος*); **(12)** f. ii ad ib. 190 (Tataki 1309) (*Φλ. Ἀ.*); **(13)** 192 ad *ILeukopetra* 33, 1 (Tataki 16) (I f. *Ἀγάθων* II); **(14)** *ILeukopetra* 33, 1 (Tataki 15) (II s. *Ἀγάθων* I); **(15)** iii ad *IBer* 208 (Tataki 14); **(16)** 219 ad *ILeukopetra* 69, 8 (Tataki 707) (*Κλ. Ἀ.*)
—Pella: **(17)** imp. *ILGR* 203 (Lat. Agathonis (gen.))
—Pella*: **(18)** ?iii bc *AD* 18 (1963) Chron. p. 200 n. 5 (amph.)
Macedonia (Chalkidike):
—Akanthos: **(19)** v bc *SEG* xlviii 712 (vase) (*Ἀγά[θω]ν*)
Macedonia (Derriopos):
—Stuberra: **(20)** 74 ad *IG* x (2) (2) 325, 46 (f. *Φίλων*)
Macedonia (Derriopos)?: **(21)** iii ad ib. 43 (f. *Νίκη*)
Macedonia (Eordaia):
—Exochi (mod.): **(22)** 265 ad *EAM* 116, 20
Macedonia (Lower Paionia):
—Europos: **(23)** c. 240-220 bc *IG* vii 356, 2 (*IOrop* 98; Tataki, *Macedonians* p. 108 no. 1) (s. *Βουτᾶς*)
Macedonia (Mygdonia):
—Kalindoia: **(24)** c. 329-326 bc Hatzopoulos, *MI* 2 pp. 84-5 no. 62, 1, 16 (f. *Ἀγαθάνωρ*)
—Lete: **(25)** ii ad *Makedonika* 2 (1951) p. 619 no. 42 *θ*, 15 (s. *Νάρις*)
—Thessalonike: **(26)** c. 303 ad Musurillo, *Acts Christian Martyrs* pp. 281 ff.
—Thessalonike?: **(27)** i ad *IG* x (2) (1) 846 (f. *Μάντα*); **(28)** ib. (s. *Διοσκουρίδης*, *Μάντα*); **(29)** i-ii ad ib. 56 (s. *Διονύσιος*)
Macedonia (Pieria):
—Pydna: **(30)** 331 bc *RE* (8); Berve 9 (Tataki, *Macedonians* p. 169 no. 1) (?f. *Ἄσανδρος*)
Macedonia (Sintike):
—Parthikopolis (territ.): **(31)** 146 ad *IGB* iv 2303 (f. *Πύρρος*)
Sarmatia:
—Maiotai: **(32)** 182 bc *SGDI* 1992, 8, 12 (slave/freed.)
Scythia Minor:
—Istros: **(33)** ii/iii ad *ISM* i 225, 11 (s. *Ἀ—*)
—Tomis: **(34)** ii ad ib. ii 125, 7 (f. *Θάλλος*)
Tauris:
—Chersonesos: **(35)** c. 285-272 bc Kats p. 83 no. 1 (amph., tile) (s. *Γνάθων*); **(36)** i bc *IOSPE* i^2 465 (f. *Ἀπολλώνιος*); **(37)** i-ii ad ib. 478 (f. *Θεογένης*)
—Kerkinitis (nr.): **(38)** iii bc Solomonik, *GChKh* 218 (vase) (*[Ἀ]γάθ[ων]?*)
Thrace: **(39)** iv bc *IG* ii^2 8896 (*FRA* 2489); **(40)** s. iv bc *IG* ii^2 8897 (*FRA* 2488)
—Abdera: **(41)** ?vi bc Page, *FGE* 484; **(42)** c. 275-250 bc *IG* xii (9) 218, 2; cf. *Eretria* xi pp. 268-9 no. XXIV (f. *Σωσικράτης*)
—Apollonia-Sozopolis: **(43)** hell.-imp. *AEMÖ* 10 (1886) p. 165 (vase)
—Odessos?: **(44)** ii ad *IGB* i^2 51 bis a, 8 (s. *Δάδας*)
—Oescus*: **(45)** i ad *BSAB* 3 (1912) p. 3 no. 1 (Lat. Agato: freed.)
—Pautalia: **(46)** ii-iii ad *IGB* v 5780 (*Ἀγάθονι* (dat.): s. *Τιμόθεος*)
—Philippopolis-Trimontium (territ.): **(47)** ii-iii ad ib. iii 1216
Thrace?: **(48)** iv-iii bc *SEG* xvii 337. 2 (bullet)

Ἀγαθωνᾶς
Macedonia (Bottiaia):
—Beroia*: **(1)** ii/iii ad *IBer* 144 B, 13 (Tataki 1097) (*Πο. Ἀ.*: freed.)

Ἀγαῖς
Macedonia (Bottiaia):
—Beroia: **(1)** 119 ad *IBer* 25 (Tataki 17) (*Ἀγ(λ)αΐς*?—Cormack: slave?)

Ἀγακλῆς
Macedonia (Bottiaia):
—Pella: **(1)** 263 bc *IG* ix (1)^2 (1) 17, 71 (Tataki, *Macedonians* p. 148 no. 5) (s. *Σίμμιχος*)

Ἀγάλλης
Thrace:
—Byzantion: **(1)** ii bc *IByz* 100 (Fıratlı-Robert p. 94 no. 130) (*Ἀγάλλεος* (gen.)); **(2)** *SEG* l 667 I

Ἀγάνωρ
Macedonia (Bottiaia):
—Beroia: **(1)** 223 bc *IBer* 4, 16 (f. *Ἡλιόδωρος*)

Ἀγάπη
Macedonia (Mygdonia):
—Thessalonike: **(1)** c. 303 ad Musurillo, *Acts Christian Martyrs* pp. 281 ff.; **(2)** v ad *IG* x (2) (1) 1025 (*SEG* xxxiii 218; Tataki, *Macedonians* p. 189 no. 1; *FRA* 2378) (d. *Θεόδουλος*)

Ἀγάπημα
Cimmerian Bosporos:
—Pantikapaion: **(1)** i ad *CIRB* 337 (d. *Ἄμμα*)

Ἀγαπήνωρ
Thrace:
—Bizone: **(1)** iii ad *IGB* i^2 7 (*Ἀγαπή[νωρ]?*)

Ἀγαπητός
Cimmerian Bosporos:
—Pantikapaion?: **(1)** v-vi ad *SEG* xxxix 699 (-*πε*-: f. *Φιλόξενος*)
Macedonia (Edonis):
—Philippoi: **(2)** ii/iii ad *CIL* iii 633 IV b, 7 (Pilhofer 166) (Lat. C. Agapetus: s. *Ἡράκλειτος*)
Macedonia (Mygdonia):
—Thessalonike: **(3)** ii ad *IG* x (2) (1) 241 A II, 18 (*[Π]ινάριος Ἀ.*)

Thrace:
—Perinthos-Herakleia: **(4)** v-vi ad *IPerinth* 226 (*AD* 51-2 (1996-7) Mel. p. 369 no. 187) (-*πι*-: f. *Ἄννα*)

Ἄγαρος
Skythia:
—Skythai: **(1)** 310 bc D.S. xx 24. 3 (king)

Ἀγασίας
Macedonia: **(1)** 194-156 bc *SB* 15240, 9, 12-13, 27, 30, 33, 42 (La'da E1387) (f. *Διόφαντος*)

Ἀγασίκλεια
Macedonia (Elimeia)?: **(1)** m. iii ad *EAM* 63
Thrace:
—Mesambria: **(2)** f. iii bc *IGB* i^2 335 bis (PM 378); cf. *IGB* v 5108 (d. *Νοῖος*)

Ἀγασικλῆς
Macedonia (Mygdonia):
—Apollonia: **(1)** m. iii bc *SEG* xlviii 783, 2; *Horos* 14-16 (2000-3) p. 216, 2?; pp. 217-19 (locn.) (*Ἀ[γασικλῆς]*—*Horos*)
Macedonia (Pieria):
—Dion: **(2)** iv/iii bc *AE* 1910, p. 342 no. 2, 3 (Tataki, *Macedonians* p. 100 no. 2) (s. *Μέντωρ*)
Skythia:
—Olbia-Borysthenes: **(3)** s. iv bc Dubois, *IGDOlbia* 107, 1
Tauris:
—Chersonesos: **(4)** iv/iii bc Kats p. 103 no. 75 (amph.) (f. *Μᾶτρις*); **(5)** c. 300-285 bc ib. p. 83 no. 2 (amph.) ?= (7); **(6)** f. iii bc *IOSPE* i^2 418 (s. *Κτησίας*) ?= (7); **(7)** c. 290-280 bc Anokhin p. 139 no. 84 (coin) ?= (5) (6); **(8)** c. 200-190 bc ib. p. 144 nos. 154-6 (coins) (*Ἀγασ(ικλῆς)*—154-5, *Ἀγασικλ(ῆς)*—156)
Thrace:
—Byzantion: **(9)** m. iii bc *IG* xi (4) 530, 4, 8, 13 (s. *Λεοντίσκος*)

Ἀγγελῆς
Thrace:
—Apollonia-Sozopolis: **(1)** iv bc *BMNBurgas* 4 (2002) p. 120 no. 3 (*Ἀγγέλεω* (gen.): f. *Ἀλπάλη*)

Ἀγγελίς
Scythia Minor:
—Kallatis: **(1)** iii/ii bc *IG* xi (4) 1238; *ID* 1416 A I, 48; 1417 B I, 49; 1452 A, 36 (m. *Παράμονος*)

Ἀγείδας
Scythia Minor:
—Kallatis: **(1)** iv/iii bc *ISM* iii 125, 5 (s. *Ἐχ—*)

Ἀγέλαος
Macedonia: **(1)** ?417-413 bc *IG* i^3 89, 61 (Tataki, *Macedonians* p. 218 no. 8) (s. *Ἀλκέτας*); **(2)** 190 or 189 bc *PHeid* viii 417, 12, 32; cf. La'da E1740 (I f. *Ἀγέλαος* II); **(3)** *PHeid* viii 417, 12, 35, 37 (La'da E1740) (II s. *Ἀγέλαος* I: t.e.)
Macedonia (Bottiaia):
—Beroia: **(4)** 121 bc *IBer* 134, 13 (s. *Δημήτριος*)
Macedonia (Pieria):
—Phila?: **(5)** ?iii bc *RPh* 1911, pp. 133-4 no. 36, 118; cf. Helly, *L'État thessalien* pp. 319-20 (locn.) (s. *Φίλιππος*)
Tauris:
—Chersonesos: **(6)** s. iv bc Solomonik, *GAKh* 148 (vase)

Ἀγέλας
Tauris:
—Chersonesos: **(1)** c. 120-88 bc *IOSPE* i^2 352, 56; 353, [7] (s. *Λαγορῖνος*)

Ἀγέλοχος
Macedonia (Bottiaia):
—Aigai: **(1)** c. 315-280 bc *FD* iii (1) 112, 1; *BCH* 68-9 (1944-5) p. 100 (date) (Tataki,

Macedonians p. 39 no. 1) ([Ἀ]γέλοχος: s. Φίλιππος)

Ἀγέμαχος
Thrace:
—PERINTHOS-HERAKLEIA:
——(Akarnanes): (1) iii-ii BC *IPerinth* 61, 12 (s. Εὔδαμος)

Ἀγέπολις
Tauris:
—CHERSONESOS: (1) f. ii AD Solomonik, *NEPKh* 113, 11 ([Ἀ]γέπολις); (2) c. 114-130 AD *IOSPE* I^2 359, 25; 360, 8; *VDI* 1960 (3), pp. 154-5, 20; *SEG* XLVIII 999, 36 (*T. Φλ. Ἀ.*: s. *T. Φλ. Ἀρίστων*) ?= (*3*); (3) c. 120-130 AD Solomonik, *NEPKh* 112, 5?, 22 (*T. Φλ. Ἀγέπολ[ις]*) ?= (*2*); (4) 129-130 AD *IOSPE* I^2 357, 24; 358, [12]; 359, 22; *VDI* 1960 (3), pp. 154-5, [5]?, 22 (*Φλ. Ἀ.*: f. *T. Φλ. Ἀρίστων*) ?= (*5*); (5) *IOSPE* I^2 359, 24; 701, 2 (*T. Φλ. Ἀ.*: f. *T. Φλ. Πυθόδοτος*) ?= (*4*)

Ἄγερρος
Macedonia: (1) ?417-413 BC *IG* I^3 89, 62 (Tataki, *Macedonians* p. 219 no. 10) (s. Φίλιππος); (2) *IG* I^3 89, 77 (Tataki, *Macedonians* p. 218 no. 9) ([Ἄ]γερρος); (3) iv BC Arr., *An.* iii 23. 9 (Tataki, *Macedonians* p. 129 no. 1) (f. Ἀνδρόνικος)

Ἀγέστρατος
Macedonia (Mygdonia):
—LETE: (1) s. iv BC Hatzopoulos, *MI* 2 pp. 93-4 no. 79, 17

Ἀγήμων
Scythia Minor:
—KALLATIS: (1) s. iii BC *ISM* III 35, 3; 35 B, 34 (s. Πυθίων)
Tauris:
—CHERSONESOS: (2) f. iii BC *SEG* XL 615 B, 25 (f. —ωρος)
Thrace:
—BYZANTION: (3) 378 BC *IG* II^2 41, 24 (Ἡγή-)

Ἀγηνορίδης
Cimmerian Bosporos:
—NYMPHAION: (1) iii BC *CIRB* 912 I, 2 (Ἀ̣γηνορίδης)

Ἀγήνωρ
Macedonia: (1) iv BC Arr., *An.* vi 17. 1; *FGrH* 156 F 9. 36; D.S. xviii 39. 6 (Tataki, *Macedonians* p. 219 no. 12) (f. Πείθων); (2) 221-205 BC *BGU* 1964, 13 (Tataki, *Macedonians* p. 219 no. 11; La'da E1741) (s. Δαΐμαχος: t.e.)
Macedonia (Chalkidike):
—AKANTHOS: (3) v BC Vokotopoulou, *Guide* p. 24 (*BE* 1993, no. 369)

Ἄγης
Thrace:
—BYZANTION: (1) ii-i BC *IByz* 222 (Fıratlı–Robert p. 79 no. 91) (Ἄγη (gen.): s. Φώκριτος, f. Μάμα)

Ἀγήσανδρος
Thrace:
—BEROE-AUGUSTA TRAIANA:
——Emporion Diskodouraterai: (1) ii-iii AD *IGB* II 729 ?= (*2*); (2) 197 AD ib. 728, 7 (*Οὔλπ. Ἀ.*) ?= (*1*)

Ἀγησᾶς
Macedonia (Mygdonia):
—THESSALONIKE?: (1) a. 212 AD *IG* X (2) (1) 768, 1 (*Αὐρ. Ἀ.*: s. Ἀγαθίας)

Ἀγησίας
Macedonia (Pieria):
—PYDNA: (1) iv BC *GRBS* 47 (2002-3) p. 116 no. 4, 8 ([Ἀ]γησίας)

Ἀγησίδαμος
Thrace:
—MESAMBRIA: (1) hell. *IGB* I^2 316, 2 (f. Διονύσιος)

Ἀγησίλα
Thrace:
—MESAMBRIA: (1) iv BC ib. 333 bis (d. Δαμέας); (2) hell.? ib. 342 (d. Πλουτίων)

Ἀγησίλαος
Macedonia (Sintike):
—HERAKLEIA: (1) iii AD *ISamothrace* 58, 2 (Tataki, *Macedonians* p. 111 no. 3) (*M. Ὀρφίδιος Ἀ.*)
Thrace:
—PERINTHOS-HERAKLEIA:
——(Podargoi): (2) iii-ii BC *IPerinth* 61, 20 (s. Ἀπολλόδωρος)

Ἀγησίλας
Cimmerian Bosporos:
—GORGIPPIA: (1) f. iii BC *CIRB* 1137 A II, 7 (s. Διονύσιος); (2) ib. 1137 B I, 35 ([Ἀ]γησίλας: s. Εὔφρων); (3) ib. l. 54 (s. Χαρικλῆς)

Ἄγησις
Thrace:
—LYSIMACHEIA?: (1) iii BC *IG* XII Suppl. p. 39 no 127 C, 56 (*SEG* XXVI 919) (?s. Φιλώτας)

Ἀγησίστρατος
Macedonia (Bottiaia):
—BEROIA: (1) 223 BC *IBer* 4, 18-19 (Ἀγ[ησί]στρατος: f. Παράμονος)

Ἁγία
Macedonia (Mygdonia):
—THESSALONIKE?: (1) i-ii AD *IG* X (2) (1) 689 (d. Ἅγις, Σμαράγδιν)

Ἀγίας
Cimmerian Bosporos:
—GORGIPPIA: (1) ii/iii AD *CIRB* 1179, 40 (f. Δαμόστρατος)
—PHANAGOREIA: (2) iv BC ib. 973 (s. Σ—)
Thrace: (3) 236-221 BC Brown, *Ptolemaic Paintings* p. 19 (Velkov 8; La'da E699) (Ἀγνᾶς—Velkov: s. Ἡρακλεόδωρος)
—LYSIMACHEIA: (4) m. ii BC *ISestos* 38 a, 5 (f. Σώστρατος)

Ἀγίλλας
Skythia:
—OLBIA-BORYSTHENES: (1) iii AD *IOSPE* I^2 103. 7; Zgusta, *PNS* 881 (s. Ῥαδαμψῶν)

Ἄγιλλος
Thrace:
—PERINTHOS-HERAKLEIA: (1) iv-iii BC *IPerinth* 4, 2 (Ἄγιλ(λ)ος)

Ἁγιότης?
Macedonia (Mygdonia):
—THESSALONIKE: (1) ii AD *IG* X (2) (1) 241 A I, 35 (—τάκιος Ἁγιότης)

Ἄγιππος
Macedonia: (1) 326-325 BC *CID* II 32, 43; 72, 5?; 96, [4]?; 99 B, 14; 100 I, [3]; 100 II, 10 (Tataki, *Macedonians* p. 219 no. 13)

Ἆγις
Cimmerian Bosporos:
—GORGIPPIA: (1) f. iii BC *CIRB* 1137 A I, 34 (s. Λύσανδρος); (2) ib. 1137 A II, 16 (s. Ἡρακλείδης)
Macedonia (Mygdonia):
—THESSALONIKE?: (3) i-ii AD *IG* X (2) (1) 689 (f. Ἁγία)
Macedonia (Odomantike):
—SIRRHA: (4) 155 AD Dimitsas 821, 16 (Kaphtantzis 1) (s. Πολύκαρπος)

Macedonia (Paionia): (5) b. 359 BC D.S. xvi 4. 2 (Tataki, *Macedonians* p. 207 no. 1) (king)
Thrace:
—LYSIMACHEIA: (6) s. iii BC *SEG* XXVII 973 bis, 19

Ἀγλάης
Skythia:
—OLBIA-BORYSTHENES (LEUKE)*: (1) imp. ib. XLIII 502. 5 (amph.)

Ἀγλαΐας
Thrace:
—BYZANTION: (1) i AD *RE* (-) (doctor)

Ἀγλαΐδας
Thrace:
—BYZANTION: (1) ii/i BC *IByz* 219 (Fıratlı–Robert p. 78 no. 88) (f. Ἔλεγχος)

Ἀγλάϊνος
Macedonia (Edonis):
—AMPHIPOLIS: (1) b. 357 BC Hatzopoulos, *Actes Amphipolis* p. 20 no. 2, 8 (*SEG* XLI 556) (Ἀγλάϊ<αι>νος)

Ἀγλαΐς
Scythia Minor:
—TROESMIS: (1) ii AD *ISM* V 181 (Lat. Claudia Aglais: m. Ἡδίστη)
Thrace:
—SEXAGINTA PRISTA: (2) s. iii AD *Romanizmăt* II 762 (Lat. Aglais)
Thrace?: (3) iii AD Beševliev, *EP* 62, 8 (Lat. Aglais)

Ἄγλαος
Cimmerian Bosporos:
—PANTIKAPAION: (1) c. 245-240 BC *CIRB* 24 ([Ἄ]γλα[ο]ς: s. Ἡρακλείδης)
Thrace:
—BYZANTION:
——(Delkos): (2) imp. *IByz* 22, 2 (I f. Ἄγλαος II); (3) ib. l. 2 (II s. Ἄγλαος I)

Ἄγλαρχος
Thrace:
—APOLLONIA-SOZOPOLIS: (1) iv BC *IGB* I^2 450 (f. Τίβειος)

Ἀγλώκριτος
Macedonia (Chalkidike):
—TORONE: (1) f. iv BC *IG* II^2 10453 (Tataki, *Macedonians* p. 190 no. 1; *FRA* 7138) (Ἀγλώκρ[ιτος])

Ἄγλων
Cimmerian Bosporos:
—PANTIKAPAION: (1) f. iv BC *CIRB* 160 (f. Ἀπατούριος)

Ἀγλωνίκης
Macedonia (Chalkidike):
—AKANTHOS: (1) f. iv BC Vokotopoulou, *Guide* p. 24

Ἅγνη
Macedonia (Bottiaia):
—BEROIA: (1) ii AD *IBer* 331, 2 (Tataki 1092) (*Ποπιλλία Ἁ.*); (2) v-vi AD *IBer* 435
Macedonia (Mygdonia):
—GERAKAROU (MOD.): (3) iii AD *SEG* XLII 576 (m. Λυσίμαχος)

Ἁγνίας
Tauris:
—CHERSONESOS: (1) iv/iii BC Solomonik, *NEPKh* 135 (f. Ἀπήμαντος); (2) iii BC ib. 136 (Ἀγ<αγ>νίας: f. Στράτων)

'Αγνίων
CIMMERIAN BOSPOROS:
—HERMONASSA: (1) iv BC *CIRB* 1056 II, 9 (s. *'Αγαθοκλῆς*)

'Αγνόθεμις
MACEDONIA: (1) 323 BC Plu., *Alex.* 77 (fict.?)

'Αγνόθεος
MACEDONIA (CHALKIDIKE):
—POTIDAIA-KASSANDREIA: (1) f. iii BC *SEG* XLVI 799

'Αγνόκριτος
TAURIS:
—CHERSONESOS: (1) f. iii BC Solomonik, *NEPKh* 139 (f. *'Αριστώ*)

Ἄγνον
CIMMERIAN BOSPOROS:
—PANTIKAPAION: (1) i AD *CIRB* 486 + *Hyperboreus* 2000, p. 138; cf. KW pl. 37 no. 537 (*'Αγν(ω)ν—CIRB*)

Ἄγνωστος
THRACE:
—DRYS: (1) ?iv BC *IG* XII (9) 1177 + XII Suppl. p. 196 (*'Αγνωστος*)

'Αγοραῖος
MACEDONIA (BOTTIAIA):
—BEROIA: (1) ii/iii AD *IBer* 143 B, 18 (Tataki 19) (f. *Διονύσιος*)
MACEDONIA (DERRIOPOS):
—STUBERRA: (2) 74 AD *IG* X (2) (2) 325, 35 (f. *Ποσείδιππος*)
MACEDONIA (ELIMEIA):
—SIATISTA (MOD.): (3) hell.-imp. *EAM* 32 (s. *'Αντίγονος*)
—VELVENDOS (MOD.): (4) ii AD *SEG* XLVII 1001, 1 (f. *Κάσσανδρος*)

'Αγοράστη
MACEDONIA (BOTTIAIA):
—EDESSA: (1) v-vi AD Feissel, *RICM* 13, 1 (m. *Θεόδωρος*)

'Αγόραστος
CIMMERIAN BOSPOROS:
—PANTIKAPAION: (1) iv AD *ZOOID* 21 (1898) p. 209 no. 19 (s. *Λοῦος*)

'Αγόρεις
CIMMERIAN BOSPOROS:
—GORGIPPIA: (1) iii AD *NE* 9 (1971) p. 10 no. 6 B, 13 (s. *Θαχαμφλίας*)

'Αγρίππας
MACEDONIA (DERRIOPOS):
—STUBERRA: (1) 74 AD *IG* X (2) (2) 325, 56 (s. *'Απολλόδωρος*)
MACEDONIA (ELIMEIA):
—KOZANI (MOD.): (2) ii AD *EAM* 34, 5 (*'Αγρίπ[πας]*)
MACEDONIA (PELAGONIA):
—KOLOBAISA*: (3) ii AD *IG* X (2) (2) 232 (*Γ. Πούμμιος 'Α.*) ?= (*4*)
MACEDONIA (PELAGONIA)?: (4) ii AD ib. 186, 4 (f. (nat.) *Κρατεύας*) ?= (*3*)
SCYTHIA MINOR:
—TOMIS: (5) ii AD *ISM* II 156 (-*ίπας*)

'Αγριππῖνα
MACEDONIA (MYGDONIA):
—THESSALONIKE: (1) ?iii AD *IG* X (2) (1) 496 (-*πεῖ*-: m. *'Αντίνοος*)
SCYTHIA MINOR:
—TOMIS: (2) ii-iii AD *ISM* II 369, 12 (*'Αγριπ(π)εῖνα*: d. *Διονυσόδωρος, 'Ιουλία*)

'Αγροίκιος
MACEDONIA (BOTTIAIA):
—EDESSA: (1) iii AD Feissel, *RICM* 6, 5 (Tataki, *Edessa* 1) (s. *'Επαφρόδιτος, 'Ροδόπη*)
MACEDONIA (EDONIS):
—PHILIPPOI: (2) iv-v AD Feissel, *RICM* 246 (Pilhofer 268) (-*ρύ*-)
MACEDONIA (LYNKESTIS):
—HERAKLEIA*: (3) ii AD *IG* X (2) (2) 124 (s. *Αὐ. Λουκία*)

'Αγροῖκος
SCYTHIA MINOR:
—TOMIS*: (1) ii-iii AD *ISM* II 288 (glad.)

'Αγρότας
SKYTHIA:
—OLBIA-BORYSTHENES: (1) iii BC *IOSPE* I² 189; *IOlbia* 68; 70; Zgusta, *PNS* 882 (s. *Διονύσιος*); (2) *IOSPE* I² 201 II, 27 (f. *Διονύσιος*)

'Αγροτέριον
MACEDONIA (BOTTIAIA):
—BEROIA: (1) iv-v AD *IBer* 445, 5 (Feissel, *RICM* 62) (d. *'Αριστείδης ὁ κὲ Οὐάλ—, Αὐρ. 'Αριανή*)

Ἄγροτος
SKYTHIA:
—OLBIA-BORYSTHENES (TERRIT.): (1) s. vi BC Dubois, *IGDOlbia* 51 b (vase)

Ἄγρων
CIMMERIAN BOSPOROS:
—GORGIPPIA: (1) ii/iii AD *CIRB* 1179, 33 (s. *Γάστεις*)
—PANTIKAPAION: (2) f. iv BC ib. 217 (s. *Ζώπυρος*)
MACEDONIA: (3) ?219 BC *PUG* III 103, 14 (Tataki, *Macedonians* p. 219 no. 14; La'da E1388) (s. *Θεόδωρος*)
MACEDONIA (CHALKIDIKE):
—OLYNTHOS: (4) s. iv BC *IG* II² 10023 (Tataki, *Macedonians* p. 129 no. 2; *FRA* 5880) (f. *Κρατιστώ*)
SKYTHIA:
—OLBIA-BORYSTHENES: (5) iv BC *MIA* 50 (1956) p. 63 (vase-stamp); (6) f. iv BC Dubois, *IGDOlbia* 105 (s. *Τελεσικράτης*)

'Αγυαῖος
CIMMERIAN BOSPOROS:
—HERMONASSA: (1) iv BC *CIRB* 1056 I, 21 (f. —*τος*); (2) ib. 1056 II, 11 (f. *Δημήτριος*) ?= (*3*); (3) ib. l. 16 (f. *Διονύσιος*) ?= (*2*)

'Αγχία
MACEDONIA (EORDAIA):
—ARNISSA (MOD.): (1) iii AD *EAM* 138 (*[Μ]αρκελ(λ)ιανὴ 'Ανχεία*)

'Αγχιαλίς
CIMMERIAN BOSPOROS:
—PANTIKAPAION: (1) imp. *CIRB* 784 (*'Ανχια[λ]ίς*)

'Αγχίαλος
CIMMERIAN BOSPOROS:
—PANTIKAPAION: (1) ii-i BC ib. 127, 1, 6 (*GVI* 1263); cf. KW pl. 37 no. 542 (II s. *'Αγχίαλος* I); (2) *CIRB* 127, 2 (*GVI* 1263); cf. KW pl. 37 no. 542 (I f. *Νικίας, 'Αγχίαλος* II)
THRACE:
—PHILIPPOPOLIS-TRIMONTIUM: (3) ii AD *IGB* III 993 (*'Ανχ*-: f. *Πρόκλα ἡ καὶ Δι*—)

'Αγχίς
MACEDONIA (MYGDONIA):
—THESSALONIKE: (1) ii AD *IG* X (2) (1) 59; *BCH* 97 (1973) p. 586 + Robert, *OMS* 5 p. 285 (name) (*'Αγ(κ)ίς—IG*)

'Αγώ
SCYTHIA MINOR:
—ISTROS: (1) iii BC *ISM* I 266 + *SEG* XXXVI 683 (d. *'Ηγη*—)

Ἄδα
CIMMERIAN BOSPOROS:
—PANTIKAPAION: (1) ii AD *CIRB* 650 (d. *'Ηλιόδωρος*)
THRACE:
—APOLLONIA-SOZOPOLIS: (2) v/iv BC *IGB* I² 415
—MESAMBRIA*: (3) iv BC ib. 334 novies a (freed.)
—ZONE: (4) f. iv BC *SEG* XXXII 675 (*IThrakAig* E411) (d. *Βοστᾶς*)

'Αδαής
MACEDONIA (LYNKESTIS):
—SITARIA (MOD.): (1) f. iii AD *EAM* 167 b (*Π. Τερεντιανὸς 'Α.*)

'Αδαῖος
MACEDONIA: (1) 353 BC *RE* (1) (Tataki, *Macedonians* p. 220 no. 15) (*'Α. ὁ ἐπικαλ. 'Αλεκτρύων*); (2) 334 BC *RE* s.v. Addaios (1); Berve 22 (Tataki, *Macedonians* p. 220 no. 18); (3) iv/iii BC *ISamothrace* 9 with n. 23 (Tataki, *Macedonians* p. 220 no. 20) (*'Αδαῖος*: s. *Κόρραγος*); (4) ?243 BC *PPetr* III 82, 8 (Tataki, *Macedonians* p. 221 no. 22); cf. La'da E1523 (f. *Κεφάλων*); (5) i AD *RE* (8); *GP* 1-46 (Tataki, *Macedonians* p. 220 no. 19)
MACEDONIA (BOTTIAIA):
—ALOROS: (6) i/ii AD *SEG* XXXVIII 631 (Tataki 21); cf. *BE* 1990, no. 457 (f. *'Οδέτα*)
—BEROIA: (7) iii-ii BC *IBer* 154 (*'Αδαῖος*); (8) 223 BC ib. 4, 16 (f. *'Αρμεννος*); (9) ib. l. 25 (*[Ἀ]δαῖος*: s. *'Αριστος*); (10) ib. l. 30 (*'Α(δ)αῖος*: s. *Βετταλός*); (11) ib. l. 33 (*'Α(δ)αῖος*: f. *Νικάνωρ*); (12) ii BC ib. 197 (Tataki 23-4) (s. *Φίλιππος*, f. *'Αδυμος*); (13) 169 BC *RE* (5) (Tataki, *Macedonians* p. 74 no. 4); (14) i BC-i AD *IBer* 142, 14 (Tataki 25) (f. *Μακεδών*); (15) *ILeukopetra* p. 205 (*'Αδαῖ[ος]*: f. *Παρμενίων*); (16) i-ii AD *IBer* 167 (s. *'Ηρακλείδης*); (17) f. i AD ib. 103, 5 (Tataki 22) (s. *Διόδωρος*)
—KYRRHOS: (18) m. iii AD *SEG* XXXV 750, 12 (*Αὐρ. 'Αδέου* (gen.), *'Αδέας* (nom.)—*SEG*)
MACEDONIA (DERRIOPOS):
—STUBERRA: (19) 74 AD *IG* X (2) (2) 326, 32 (f. *'Αντᾶς*)
MACEDONIA (EDONIS):
—AMPHIPOLIS: (20) ?ii/i BC *PAE* 1984, p. 38 no. 2 with pl. 45, 2 (*SEG* XLIII 371) (s. *Φίλαγρος*); (21) 24 BC ib. XL 522 j (s. *Εὐήμερος*)
MACEDONIA (ELIMEIA):
—AIANE: (22) f. iii AD *EAM* 25 (-*δέ*-: f. *Κρισπιανός*)
MACEDONIA (LYNKESTIS):
—HERAKLEIA (NR.): (23) 160 AD *IG* X (2) (2) 9 (*'Ανχαριηνὸς 'Α[δα]ῖος*)
MACEDONIA (MYGDONIA):
—LETE: (24) s. iv BC Hatzopoulos, *MI* 2 pp. 93-4 no. 79, 18 (*[Ἀ]δαῖος*); (25) 117 BC *Syll*³ 700, 51 (I f. *'Αδαῖος* II); (26) ib. l. 51 (II s. *'Αδαῖος* I); (27) ii AD *Makedonika* 2 (1951) p. 619 no. 42 θ, 14 (I f. *'Αδαῖος* II, *Παυσανίας*); (28) ib. l. 14 (II s. *'Αδαῖος* I)
MACEDONIA (ORESTIS):
—LYKE*: (29) hell. *EAM* 179 α; 179 ζ; 179 ια (tile); cf. *AD* 17 (1961-2) Chron. pl. 269; *SEG* XLIX 739 (*'Αδ(α)ῖος—a*)
MACEDONIA (PAIONIA): (30) imp. *Sp.* 98 (1941-8) p. 203 no. 406
MACEDONIA?: (31) c. 205 BC *RE* (3) (*PP* 638; Tataki, *Macedonians* p. 220 no. 17)
SKYTHIA:
—OLBIA-BORYSTHENES: (32) i BC *IOSPE* I² 222 (s. *Δᾶος*)

THRACE: (**33**) m. iii BC Peter, *MTD* pp. 236-49 (coin) (dynast) ?= (*34*)
—KYPSELA: (**34**) ?f. iii BC *CAF* 3 p. 348 fr. 1; cf. Tataki, *Macedonians* p. 220 no. 16; Beloch, *GG* IV (2) p. 346 ?= (*33*)

Ἀδάμας
MACEDONIA (ELIMEIA):
—AIANE*: (**1**) hell. *SEG* XXXIX 567 (bronze) (XLII 554)
THRACE: (**2**) c. 380-360 BC Arist., *Pol.* 1311 b 22
—ZONE: (**3**) m. v BC *SEG* XXVII 346 a (*IThrakAig* E404) (s. *Βοστᾶς*)

Ἀδάνα
MACEDONIA (BOTTIAIA):
—PELLA: (**1**) s. iii BC *SEG* XXIV 551 b (d. *Δαζαῖος*)

Ἄδας
CIMMERIAN BOSPOROS:
—NYMPHAION: (**1**) f. iii BC ib. XXXIX 701. 2 (XLV 997. 2); Zgusta, *PNS* 592 ?= (*2*); (**2**) *SEG* XXXIX 701. 5 (XLV 997. 1) ?= (*1*)
—PANTIKAPAION: (**3**) i AD *CIRB* 373 ([Ἄ]δατος (gen.): f. *Γάϊος*); (**4**) s. ii AD ib. 688 (f. *Κάλλων, Μαστοῦς*); (**5**) 343 or 353 AD ib. 744, 2 (s. *Πάπας*, f. *—λαζικος*)

Ἀδέα
MACEDONIA: (**1**) c. 340-317 BC *RE* s.v. Eurydike (13); Berve 23 (Tataki, *Macedonians* p. 221 no. 23); cf. Beloch, *GG* III (2) pp. 67-9 (*Ἀ. ὕστερον Εὐρυδίκα*: d. *Ἀμύντας, Κυννάνη*)
MACEDONIA (BOTTIAIA):
—BEROIA: (**2**) iii BC *IBer* 391 (Tataki 26) (d. *Κάσσανδρος, Κυννάνα*)
MACEDONIA (ELIMEIA):
—AIANE (TERRIT.): (**3**) 125 AD *EAM* 49 b (m. *Πα—*)

Ἀδεῖα
MACEDONIA (BOTTIAIA):
—EDESSA: (**1**) ii BC Dimitsas 557 = *SEG* XLIX 827; cf. *ZPE* 132 (2000) pp. 161-2 (locn.) (Tataki, *Edessa* 4) (or Macedonia (Mygdonia) Thessalonike: -δῆ-: d. *Ἀρχέλαος*); (**2**) Dimitsas 557 = *SEG* XLIX 827; cf. *ZPE* 132 (2000) pp. 161-2 (locn.) (Tataki, *Edessa* 5) (or Macedonia (Mygdonia) Thessalonike: -δῆ-: d. *Σάμος*)
MACEDONIA (EDONIS):
—AMPHIPOLIS?: (**3**) iii BC Dimitsas 897 (*Aphieroma Hammond* p. 271) (d. *Φίλιππος*)
MACEDONIA?: (**4**) iv/iii BC *IG* VII 279; *RE* Supplbd. 4 (-) (Tataki, *Macedonians* p. 221 no. 24)
TAURIS:
—CHERSONESOS: (**5**) iv BC *IOSPE* I² 712 (d. *Δαμάτριος*)
THRACE:
—BYZANTION?: (**6**) ii-i BC *IByz* 349 (-δῆ-)

Ἀδείμαντος
SKYTHIA:
—OLBIA-BORYSTHENES: (**1**) iii BC *SEG* XXX 958 (vase) (*Ἀδεί(μαντος)*); (**2**) s. iii BC *IOSPE* I² 76, 7 (Sokolowski II 88; Dubois, *IGDOlbia* 88) (s. *Ἀπατούριος*)
THRACE:
—BYZANTION: (**3**) c. 325-300 BC *IG* XI (4) 510, 3, 7

Ἀδέλφιος
MACEDONIA (BOTTIAIA):
—EDESSA: (**1**) iii AD Feissel, *RICM* 6, 6 (Tataki, *Edessa* 3) (s. *Ἐπαφρόδιτος, Ῥοδόπη*)

Ἀδευδᾶτος
MACEDONIA (BOTTIAIA):
—EDESSA: (**1**) v-vi AD Feissel, *RICM* 44 (*Ἀδευδᾶτ[ος]*)

Ἀδίαγος
SKYTHIA:
—TYRAS: (**1**) ii-iii AD *ISM* II 313 (*SEG* XXIV 1080) (s. *Ἄττας*)

Ἄδιμος
MACEDONIA: (**1**) ?417-413 BC *IG* I³ 89, 63 (Tataki, *Macedonians* p. 221 no. 25)

Ἀδίστα
MACEDONIA (BOTTIAIA):
—BEROIA: (**1**) ii BC *IBer* 198 (Tataki 27) (d. *Εὔλανδρος*)
MACEDONIA (ODOMANTIKE):
—TOUMBA (MOD.): (**2**) s. iv BC *SEG* XXXVIII 688 (vase); cf. XLVI 810
THRACE:
—MESAMBRIA: (**3**) ii BC *IGB* I² 339 quater (*Ἀδίστα*)

Ἄδιστος
MACEDONIA (EDONIS):
—AMPHIPOLIS: (**1**) ii BC *IG* II² 8076 (Tataki, *Macedonians* p. 45 no. 1; *FRA* 510)

Ἄδμητος
MACEDONIA: (**1**) 332 BC *RE* (4); Berve 24 (Tataki, *Macedonians* p. 221 no. 26); (**2**) 263 BC *IG* IX (1)² (1) 17, 19 (Tataki, *Macedonians* p. 222 no. 28) (f. *Φίλιππος*); (**3**) 183 BC Plb. xxiii 10. 9 (Tataki, *Macedonians* p. 221 no. 27)
MACEDONIA (BOTTIAIA):
—BEROIA: (**4**) ii BC *IBer* 141, 11 ([Ἄ]δμητος)
MACEDONIA (EDONIS):
—AMPHIPOLIS: (**5**) hell. Dimitsas 852 (s. *Διονύσιος*)
MACEDONIA (ELIMEIA):
—ARKYNIA: (**6**) s. iii BC Plb. ii 66. 5; Helly, *Gonnoi* 12, 2; *SEG* XLIII 706, 1 (Tataki, *Macedonians* p. 70 no. 1); cf. *Chiron* 13 (1983) pp. 26-9 (ident.) (*Ἄκμητος*—Plb: f. *Ἀλέξανδρος*)
MACEDONIA (MYGDONIA):
—APOLLONIA: (**7**) f. ii BC *SEG* XLIV 508 (Hatzopoulos, *MI* 2 p. 87 no. 66) (s. *Παρμενίων*)
—THESSALONIKE: (**8**) c. 230 BC *IG* XI (4) 664, 2, 13; 665, 2, 10, 14, 22; 1053, 5, 15 = X (2) (1) 1028; XI (4) 1076 (Tataki, *Macedonians* p. 178 no. 2) (s. *Βόκρος*); (**9**) i BC *IG* X (2) (1) 1029 (*EAD* XXX 338; Tataki, *Macedonians* p. 178 no. 3) (f. *Φιλήμων*)

Ἀδόης
SKYTHIA:
—OLBIA-BORYSTHENES: (**1**) ii AD *IOSPE* I² 82, 8; Zgusta, *PNS* 43 (*Ἀδόης*: s. *Μάθανος*); (**2**) *IOSPE* I² 130, 9, 19 (f. *Εὐρησίβιος*); (**3**) ib. 156, 1; 202 (s. *Δελφός*)

Ἀδόλιος
MACEDONIA (MYGDONIA):
—THESSALONIKE: (**1**) iii AD *IG* X (2) (1) 555, 2 + *SEG* XXXVIII 695 (*Βίθυς ὁ κὲ Ἀ.*)

Ἀδόλις
MACEDONIA (MYGDONIA):
—THESSALONIKE: (**1**) iii AD *IG* X (2) (1) 561, 2 (*Αἰλ. Πετρωνιανὸς Λύκος Ἀ.*: ?s. *Πετρώνιος Λύκος, Πετιλία Βικτωρία*)

Ἄδοσθος
SKYTHIA:
—OLBIA-BORYSTHENES: (**1**) ?ii AD *IOSPE* I² 204; Zgusta, *PNS* 269 (s. *Ἀρσάκης*)

Ἄδραστος
MACEDONIA (EDONIS):
—PHILIPPOI: (**1**) hell. *RE* (8) (Tataki, *Macedonians* p. 163 no. 1)

MACEDONIA (PIERIA):
—KASTANIA (MOD.): (**2**) imp. *SEG* L 594
SKYTHIA:
—OLBIA-BORYSTHENES: (**3**) ?331 BC ib. XLII 711 (f. *Νικοφάνας*); (**4**) iii BC *IOSPE* I² 201 I, 6 (f. *Ἐπίκουρος*)

Ἄδρηστος
THRACE:
—APOLLONIA-SOZOPOLIS: (**1**) v/iv BC *Boston Coins* 797 (coin); (**2**) iv BC *BMNBurgas* 4 (2002) p. 121 no. 7 (s. *Ἑκαταῖος*)

Ἀδριανός
MACEDONIA (LYNKESTIS):
—HERAKLEIA: (**1**) i AD *IG* X (2) (2) 75, 13 (*Γ. Τιτίνιος Ἀ.*); (**2**) ib. l. 14 (*Γ. Ἀ.*: f. *Σεκοῦνδος*)
SCYTHIA MINOR:
—ISTROS: (**3**) ii AD *ISM* I 211, 9 (*Φλ. Ἀ.*)
—TOMIS: (**4**) ii-iii AD ib. II 28, 6 (I f. *Ἀδριανός* II); (**5**) ib. l. 6 ([Ἀ]δριανός: II s. *Ἀδριανός* I)

Ἀδύλος
MACEDONIA (BOTTIAIA):
—BEROIA: (**1**) 122 BC *IBer* 134, 10

Ἄδυμος
MACEDONIA: (**1**) iii BC *ITrall* 33 B, 25; *BE* 1991, no. 524 (ethn.) (Tataki, *Macedonians* p. 223 no. 33) (f. *Βάκχιος*); (**2**) 267 BC *SEG* XXVII 1114, 18 b (Tataki, *Macedonians* p. 223 no. 34); cf. La'da E1591 (f. *Πτολεμαῖος*); (**3**) 246 BC *PPetr* II 39 e (7), 13 (Tataki, *Macedonians* p. 222 no. 31; La'da E1390) (s. *Διόφαντος*); (**4**) 183 BC *PTeb* 793 I, 20 (Tataki, *Macedonians* p. 223 no. 32); cf. La'da E1389 (I f. *Ἄδυμος* II); (**5**) *PTeb* 793 I, 20, 23 (Tataki, *Macedonians* p. 222 no. 30; La'da E1389) (II s. *Ἄδυμος* I); (**6**) 108 BC *PDion* 23, 3, [13], 21, 23, 32 (Tataki, *Macedonians* p. 471 no. 3; La'da E1391) (s. *Πτολεμαῖος*)
MACEDONIA (BOTTIAIA):
—AIGAI: (**7**) s. iv BC *SEG* XXXV 787 (s. *Κλεώνυμος*, f. *Πευκόλαος, Κρινώ*)
—BEROIA: (**8**) iii-ii BC *IBer* 153 (Tataki 30) (s. *Νικάνωρ*); (**9**) ii BC *IBer* 141, 6; (**10**) ib. l. 41; (**11**) ib. 197 (Tataki 31) (s. *Ἀδαῖος*); (**12**) *IBer* 197 (Tataki 36) (f. *Φίλιννα*); (**13**) i BC *SEG* XVIII 272 (Tataki 32; Tataki, *Macedonians* p. 74 no. 5) (s. *Εὔανδρος*: sculptor); (**14**) i AD *IBer* 125, 5 (Tataki 37) (f. *Φίλιος*); (**15**) *IBer* 344 (Tataki 35) (f. *Μένανδρος*); (**16**) ii-iii AD *ILeukopetra* 154 (f. *—νίδης*); (**17**) ii/iii AD ib. 54, 1 (f. *Λύκα*)
—EDESSA: (**18**) 51 AD *SEG* XLVI 744, 11 (Tataki, *Edessa* 6) (f. *Σεκοῦνδος*)
—MIEZA: (**19**) iii BC *SEG* XXIV 524 I, 17; 524 II, 6, 25 (Hatzopoulos, *MI* 2 p. 106 no. 92) (f. *Τόλων*)
MACEDONIA (CHALKIDIKE):
—NEOS MARMARAS (MOD.): (**20**) ii-i BC *SEG* XXXVIII 600 (f. *Σταπόλεμος*)
MACEDONIA (EDONIS):
—PHILIPPOI (TERRIT.): (**21**) 162 AD Pikoulas, *Chora* p. 120 no. 11 (s. *Ἀπολλόδωρος*)
MACEDONIA (EORDAIA):
—SPILIA (MOD.): (**22**) ii-iii AD *EAM* 101, 4 (f. *Σεδάνη*)
MACEDONIA (KRESTONIA):
—MORRYLOS: (**23**) c. 230-200 BC *BCH* 45 (1921) p. 18 III, 84; cf. *SEG* XXXIX 468 (Tataki, *Macedonians* p. 124 no. 1) (s. *Ἀργαῖος*)
MACEDONIA (LYNKESTIS):
—HERAKLEIA (AREA): (**24**) ii AD *IG* X (2) (2) 20 (s. *Πόντιος*)
MACEDONIA (MYGDONIA):
—HERAKLEIA: (**25**) hell. Hatzopoulos, *MI* 1 p. 211 (f. *Νικόλαος*); (**26**) ib. (s. *Νικόλαος*)
—KALINDOIA: (**27**) 68-98 AD *SEG* XLII 580, 80 (f. *Ἡροῦς*)

—THESSALONIKE: **(28)** 42-32 BC *IG* X (2) (1) 124, 8 (s. *Φίλιππος*); **(29)** i-ii AD ib. 243 I, 3 (*Ἰούλ. Ἀ.*)
MACEDONIA (PELAGONIA):
—DOSTONEIS?: **(30)** ii-iii AD ib. X (2) (2) 181 (s. *Οὐέττιος*)
—KOLOBAISA*: **(31)** ii AD ib. 232
MACEDONIA (PIERIA):
—DION?: **(32)** ii/iii AD Spiliopoulou-Donderer, *KGN* p. 199 no. D17 (s. *Λύκος, Αἰλ. Ὑμνίς*)
—PHYLAKAI?: **(33)** ?i BC Oikonomos 58 = *IG* IX (2) 230 (f. *Ἀμμαδίς*)
MACEDONIA (PIERIS):
—GALEPSOS: **(34)** hell. Dimitsas 918; Hatzopoulos, *MI* I p. 187 n. 3 (locn.) (s. *Ἐπικράτης*)

Ἀδύρα
MACEDONIA (KRESTONIA):
—MORRYLOS: **(1)** iii BC *SEG* XXXVIII 627 (d. *Ἀντίγονος*)

Ἀδύρμαχος
SARMATIA:
—MAIOTAI (MACHLYES): **(1)** ii AD Luc., *Tox.* 44-6; 51-5 (king/fict.)

Ἄδυς
THRACE:
—BYZANTION: **(1)** i-ii AD *IByz* 269 (Fıratlı-Robert pp. 84-5 no. 104) (s. *Ποσειδώνιος*, f. *Διονύσις*)

Ἀδύτιον
THRACE:
—BYZANTION: **(1)** ii BC *Türk Tarih Kongresi XI* (6) p. 2704 with pl. 498. 11 (d. *Βοσπόριχος*)

Ἀδώ
MACEDONIA: **(1)** 303 BC *IG* XI (2) 137, 13, 15; 145, 51-2; 154 B, 7, 35-6; cf. *ID Index* s.v. (Tataki, *Macedonians* p. 223 no. 35)

Ἄδωλος
SKYTHIA:
—OLBIA-BORYSTHENES: **(1)** i/ii AD *IOlbia* 90, 9 (f. *Βάταγος*)

Ἅδων
MACEDONIA (CHALKIDIKE):
—STOLOS?: **(1)** ?350 BC *SEG* XXXVIII 670, 7 (*Ἄδων*—ed.: f. *Ἀρχέστρατος*)
TAURIS:
—CHERSONESOS: **(2)** c. 290-280 BC Anokhin p. 139 no. 83; *Hellenismus* p. 441 no. 2 (coin)

Ἀέλις
SCYTHIA MINOR: **(1)** ii/i BC *Thracia* 4 pp. 105-21 (king)

Ἀέροπος
MACEDONIA: **(1)** m. vi BC *RE* (4); *POxy* 2465 fr. 1 col. ii, 23 (Tataki, *Macedonians* p. 223 no. 37) (*Ἀ.* I: s. *Φίλιππος* I, *Νικονόα*, f. *Ἀλκέτας*: king); **(2)** c. 425-394 BC *RE* (5); *HN*^{2} p. 221; *Kraay-Mørkholm Essays* pp. 304-5; 310-11 (coin); *Macedonia* 2 pp. 168-71 (Tataki, *Macedonians* p. 200 no. 1); cf. *RE* s.v. Archelaos (8); *Historia* 44 (1995) pp. 264; 278-9 (*Ἀ.* II: *Ἀρχέλαος*—Euseb. Arm.: ?s. *Περδίκκας* II, f. *Παυσανίας*: king); **(3)** 338 BC *RE* (6) (Tataki, *Macedonians* p. 223 no. 38); **(4)** f. iii BC *IMM* 5, 12 (Tataki, *Macedonians* p. 225 no. 49) (*Αἰ-*: f. *Ἀρχέλαος*); **(5)** c. 208 BC Liv. xxvii 32. 9 (Tataki, *Macedonians* p. 223 no. 39) (Lat. Aeropus)
MACEDONIA (BOTTIAIA):
—BEROIA: **(6)** i/ii AD *IBer* 40, 4 (*Κλ. Ἀέρο[π]ος*: s. *Κλ. Ἀμμία*)
MACEDONIA (LYNKESTIS): **(7)** iv BC Arr., *An.* i 7. 6; i 17. 8; i 25. 1; Plu., *Mor.* 327 C; *Ancient Macedonia* 2 pp. 512-13 (ident.) (Tataki, *Macedonians* p. 200 no. 1) (s. *Ἀρραβαῖος*, f. *Ἀλέξανδρος, Ἀρραβαῖος, Ἡρομένης*)
—HERAKLEIA (NR.): **(8)** ii-iii AD *IG* X (2) (2) 5 (*Ααί-*: I f. *Ἀέροπος* II); **(9)** ib. (*Ααί-*: II s. *Ἀέροπος* I)
MACEDONIA?: **(10)** iii BC *RE* Supplbd. 1 (7) (Tataki, *Macedonians* p. 224 no. 40) (f. *Πτολεμαῖος*)

Ἀέτιος
THRACE:
—DUROSTORUM: **(1)** c. 390-454 AD *PLRE* II (7) (*Φλ. Ἀ.*: s. Gaudentius, f. Carpilio, Gaudentius)

Ἀζαῖος
MACEDONIA (MYGDONIA):
—THESSALONIKE: **(1)** c. 250-230 BC *IG* VII 320, 2 (*IOrop* 141; Tataki, *Macedonians* p. 179 no. 4) (f. *Δάμων*)

Ἀζάμηος
SKYTHIA:
—OLBIA-BORYSTHENES: **(1)** ?ii AD *IOSPE* I^2 133, 5; Zgusta, *PNS* 608

Ἀζαρίων
SKYTHIA:
—TANAIS: **(1)** 244 AD *CIRB* 1287, 23 (s. *Δημήτριος*)

Ἀζίαγος
SKYTHIA:
—OLBIA-BORYSTHENES: **(1)** ii AD *IOSPE* I^2 86, 10; Zgusta, *PNS* 45 (*Ἀζία(ι)ος*?: s. *Οὐαχώζακος*)

Ἀζιαῖος
SKYTHIA:
—OLBIA-BORYSTHENES: **(1)** c. 150-175 AD *IOSPE* I^2 142, 4; *VDI* 1953 (4), p. 130, 13; cf. *SEG* XLII 713; Zgusta, *PNS* 883 a (f. *Σκάρτανος*)

Ἀζίας
CIMMERIAN BOSPOROS:
—GORGIPPIA: **(1)** ii/iii AD *CIRB* 1179, 56 (f. *Πάπας*)
SKYTHIA:
—TANAIS: **(2)** f. ii AD ib. 1295 (?s. *Σ*—)

Ἄζος
SKYTHIA:
—TANAIS: **(1)** 225 AD ib. 1280, 13 (s. *Ὀχωδίακος*)

Ἀθάμας
MACEDONIA (EDONIS):
—AMPHIPOLIS: **(1)** f. iii BC *IG* XI (4) 1349, 2, 7, 11 (Tataki, *Macedonians* p. 45 no. 2) (f. *Θερσαγόρας*)

Ἀθαναγόρας
TAURIS:
—CHERSONESOS*: **(1)** ii-i BC *IOSPE* I^2 709 (threptos)

Ἀθάναιος
SCYTHIA MINOR:
—TOMIS: **(1)** s. i AD *RPC* II 408-9 (coin) (*Ἀθάν(αιος)*?)
TAURIS:
—CHERSONESOS: **(2)** c. 325-300 BC *IOSPE* I^2 345, 1 + *SEG* XLII 692 ([*Ἀ*]*θάναιος*); **(3)** c. 300-275 BC ib. XLVII 1168, 4 (f. *Βάβων*); **(4)** c. 285-275 BC ib. XLIII 1320 (amph.); **(5)** c. 280-270 BC Kats p. 84 no. 3 (amph.); **(6)** c. 120-88 BC *IOSPE* I^2 352, 58 (f. *Δαμασικλῆς*); **(7)** m. i BC ib. 347, 3; 691, 3 (*Ἀθά[ναιος]*—691: s. *Στρατόνικος*); **(8)** ii AD Solomonik, *NEPKh* 184 (s. *Ἀπολλωνίδης*)

Ἀθαναΐς
THRACE:
—BYZANTION: **(1)** m. iv BC *IG* II^2 8435 (*FRA* 1382) (*Ἀθη-*); **(2)** iii-ii BC *IG* II^2 8436 (*FRA* 1383) (*Ἀθηναΐς*)
—MESAMBRIA: **(3)** iv/iii BC *IGB* I^2 334 quater ([*Ἀθ*]*αναΐς*: ?d. —*ων*)
—SESTOS: **(4)** f. iv BC *IG* II^2 10262 (*FRA* 6635) (*Ἀθη-*)

Ἀθαναίων
SCYTHIA MINOR:
—KALLATIS: **(1)** iii BC *ISM* III 158; **(2)** f. iii BC ib. 6, 3 (f. *Λεοντίσκος*); **(3)** 172 AD ib. 99, 5; 100, [6] ([*T.*] [*Αἰλ.*] [*Μι*]*νίκιος Ἀ.*: f. *T. Αἰλ. Μινίκιος Μοσχίων*); **(4)** 241-244 AD ib. 74, 11 (*Μινίκιος Ἀθανέων*); **(5)** ib. 74 A, 29 (*-νέ-*: s. *Βούκκης*)
THRACE:
—BYZANTION: **(6)** iv BC *IByz* 9; **(7)** m. iii BC *IG* XII (5) 802, 10 ([*Ἀ*]*θηναίων*: f. *Νυμφαῖος*); **(8)** c. 250-220 BC Schönert-Geiss, *Byzantion* 1001-2; 1179-89 (coin)
—BYZANTION (TERRIT.): **(9)** imp. Unp. (Sayar) (*-νέ-*: f. *Δάδας*)
—BYZANTION?: **(10)** ii-i BC *IByz* 355 (*IG* II^2 11325); cf. Robert, *OMS* 7 pp. 638-40 (f. *Ἑρμίας*)
—MESAMBRIA: **(11)** iii BC *IGB* I^2 334 sexies ([*Ἀθα*]*ναίων*?: f. —*ρ(α)στος*); **(12)** ib. 335 (PM 842); cf. *IGB* V 5107 (f. *Μῆνις*); **(13)** ib. I^2 339 ([*Ἀ*]*θαναίων*: s. *Κράτων*); **(14)** i BC ib. 315, 6, 11 (f. *Γλαυκίας*); **(15)** ib. 324 (f. *Κόνων*); **(16)** ib. (s. *Βοσπόριχος*); **(17)** ib. 326, 5 (s. *Ματρόδωρος*)

Ἀθανάσιος
MACEDONIA (BOTTIAIA):
—EDESSA: **(1)** v-vi AD Feissel, *RICM* 35 (*Ἀθαν[άσιος]*)

Ἀθανικῶν
THRACE:
—BYZANTION: **(1)** i BC-i AD *IByz* 39; cf. *BCH* 120 (1996) p. 293 (*-χῶν*: f. [...]*δος* (gen.))

Ἀθανίων
CIMMERIAN BOSPOROS:
—GORGIPPIA: **(1)** f. iii BC *CIRB* 1137 A I, 42 (s. *Στρατόνικος*)

Ἀθανόδωρος
TAURIS:
—CHERSONESOS: **(1)** f. iii BC Kats p. 93 no. 38 (amph.) (f. *Διονύσιος*); **(2)** c. 285-272 BC ib. p. 117 no. 2 (amph.); **(3)** ib. pp. 84-5 no. 6 (amph.) (s. *Νικέας*); **(4)** c. 230-215 BC ib. p. 84 no. 4 (amph.) (s. *Διονύσιος*); **(5)** c. 200-185 BC ib. p. 84 no. 5 (amph.) (s. *Εὐρύδαμος*)

Ἀθανώ
SARMATIA:
—SARMATAI: **(1)** f. ii BC *IG* XII (1) 525 (slave?)

Ἀθαφοῖος
CIMMERIAN BOSPOROS:
—MYRMEKION: **(1)** iv BC *CIRB* 871; Zgusta, *PNS* 609 (*Ἀθαφοίω* (gen.): f. *Ἀκκᾶς*)

Ἀθηνᾶ
MACEDONIA (EDONIS):
—PHILIPPOI: **(1)** ?ii AD *Philippes* I p. 157 no. 135 (Pilhofer 184) (Lat. Aelia Atena)

Ἀθηναγόρας
MACEDONIA: **(1)** 200-197 BC *RE* (4) (Tataki, *Macedonians* p. 224 no. 41)
MACEDONIA (ALMOPIA):
—APSALOS (MOD.): **(2)** iii AD *SEG* XLVII 884 (s. *Τρεβάτιος*)
MACEDONIA (EDONIS):
—AMPHIPOLIS?: **(3)** hell. Dimitsas 898 (f. *Δίων*)
MACEDONIA (LOWER PAIONIA):
—EUROPOS: **(4)** i BC-i AD? *SEG* XXXVIII 609 (s. *Νικόπολις*)

MACEDONIA (LYNKESTIS):
—HERAKLEIA (AREA): **(5)** imp. *IG* X (2) (2) 3 ([Ἀθ]ηναγό[ρα]ς: s. *Τρεβάτιος*)
MACEDONIA (MYGDONIA):
—THESSALONIKE: **(6)** ii-i BC ib. X (2) (1) 953 (s. *K*—); **(7)** 95 BC ib. 4, 2 (s. *Ἀπολλόδωρος*); **(8)** m. iii AD ib. 197, 12 (*Μάρκιος Ἀ.*: II s. *Μάρκιος Ἀθηναγόρας* I, *Ἰουν. Βωτιανή*); **(9)** 246 AD ib. 162, 14; 197, 5 (*Μάρκιος Ἀ.*: I f. *Μάρκιος Διοσκουρίδης*, *Μάρκιος Ἀθηναγόρας* II, *Μαρκία Ἰουν. Παῦλα*)
MACEDONIA?: **(10)** 168 BC Liv. xliv 32. 6 (Tataki, *Macedonians* p. 224 no. 42) (Lat. Athenagoras)
SCYTHIA MINOR:
—ISTROS: **(11)** iii BC *ISM* I 113 (s. *Θεόδοτος*)
THRACE:
—ODESSOS: **(12)** ii-i BC *IGB* I^{2} 153 (f. *Ὑψα*)
—PERINTHOS-HERAKLEIA: **(13)** c. 288-250 BC *IG* VII 3473, 1 (s. *Γλαυκίας*)

'Αθηναγόρης
THRACE:
—APOLLONIA-SOZOPOLIS: **(1)** iv BC *BMNBurgas* 4 (2002) p. 123 no. 16 (Ἀθην[α]γόρεο (gen.): f. *Κωλώτης*); **(2)** iii BC ib. p. 127 no. 27 (Ἀ̣θηνα[γόρης]?: f. *Ἡδίστη*)
—PISTIROS: **(3)** v/iv BC *BSA* 97 (2002) p. 326 (vase)

'Αθηνάδης
CIMMERIAN BOSPOROS:
—PANTIKAPAION: **(1)** v/iv BC Boardman, *Gems* pp. 220; 297 pl. 681 (gem) ([Ἀ]θηνάδης)
SCYTHIA MINOR:
—ISTROS: **(2)** iii/ii BC *ISM* I 120 (Ἀθηνά[δης]?: f. —*γετος*); **(3)** i BC ib. 54, 2 (s. *Ἀπολλόδωρος*); **(4)** i AD ib. 200, 3 (s. *Αἰσχρίων*); **(5)** ii AD ib. 198, 3 (I f. *Ἀθηνάδης* II); **(6)** ib. l. 3 (II s. *Ἀθηνάδης* I, f. *Διογένης*); **(7)** ib. 211, 7 (s. *Μόνιμος*); **(8)** ib. 212, 19 (f. *Μενίσκος*); **(9)** ib. l. 28 (I f. *Ἀθηνάδης* II); **(10)** ib. l. 28 (II s. *Ἀθηνάδης* I); **(11)** ii-iii AD ib. 198, 9 (f. *Διονύσιος*); **(12)** 138 AD ib. 193 I, 90 (Ἀθηνάδους (gen.): f. *Δημόφιλος*); **(13)** ib. l. 107 (f. *Αἰσχρίων*); **(14)** 222-225 AD ib. 100 A, 18 ([Ἀ]θηνάδης: s. *Δαμάτριος*)
THRACE:
—BEROE-AUGUSTA TRAIANA: **(15)** iii AD *IGB* III 1584

'Αθήναιος
CIMMERIAN BOSPOROS:
—GORGIPPIA: **(1)** ?68 AD *CIRB* 1126, 10; cf. *SEG* XLIX 1032 (Ἀθ[ήν]α[ιος]?: f. *Ἀθηνόδωρος*)
—HERMONASSA: **(2)** ii AD *CIRB* 1086, 1 (Ἀθήναι[ος]: f. —*φη*)
—PANTIKAPAION: **(3)** iv BC ib. 164; cf. KW p. 50 fig. 6; **(4)** i AD *CIRB* 357; cf. KW pl. 16 no. 232; **(5)** 82 AD *CIRB* 76, 18 (*SEG* XVIII 310) (f. *Καλοῦς*); **(6)** *CIRB* 76, 23 (*SEG* XVIII 310) (I f. *Ἀθήναιος* II); **(7)** *CIRB* 76, 23 (*SEG* XVIII 310) ([Ἀθ]ήναιος: II s. *Ἀθήναιος* I); **(8)** iii AD *CIRB* 102, 5 (Ἀθήν[ιος]—ed., Ἀθήν[αιος]?)
MACEDONIA (BOTTIAIA):
—PELLA: **(9)** 365 BC *SEG* XXXIV 355, 4; Arr., *Ind.* xviii 3 (Tataki, *Macedonians* p. 148 no. 6) (Ἀ̣θ[άνησ]ς—*SEG*: s. *Δημόνικος*, f. *Δημόνικος*)
MACEDONIA (MYGDONIA):
—THESSALONIKE: **(10)** c. 239-229 BC *IG* XI (4) 666, 3, 24 (Tataki, *Macedonians* p. 179 no. 5) (f. *Ἀριστόβουλος*)
MACEDONIA?: **(11)** 312 BC D.S. xix 94-96 (Tataki, *Macedonians* p. 224 no. 43)
SCYTHIA MINOR:
—ISTROS: **(12)** i BC-i AD *ISM* I 190, 2 (s. *M*—)
—TOMIS: **(13)** iii AD ib. II 22, 3 (Ἀθήνα[ι]ος, Ἀθηνά[δ]ης—*ISM*: f. *Αὐρ. Ἀκύλας*)
SKYTHIA:
—OLBIA-BORYSTHENES: **(14)** f. iv BC Dubois, *IGDOlbia* 102 (*SEG* XLIV 670 (lead)); **(15)** Dubois, *IGDOlbia* 103, 4 (lead); **(16)** iii BC *Arkheologiia* (Kiev) 39 (1982) p. 35 (Vinogradov–Kryžickij pl. 91. 3a (vase)) (Ἀθήναι(ος)) ?= (*20*); **(17)** *IOlbia* 72, 2 (s. *Κόνων*); **(18)** *IOSPE* I^{2} 129, 6 (f. *Κουνοῦς*); **(19)** ib. 201 I, 48 (s. *Πολύξενος*); **(20)** Vinogradov–Kryžickij pl. 91. 7 (stamp) ?= (*16*); **(21)** ?ii-i BC Dubois, *IGDOlbia* 110, 2
TAURIS:
—CHERSONESOS: **(22)** ii AD Solomonik, *NEPKh* 183 (f. *Βασσιανός*); **(23)** 129-130 AD *IOSPE* I^{2} 359, 26; *VDI* 1960 (3), pp. 154-5, 22 (s. *Διογένης*)
—CHERSONESOS?: **(24)** iii-ii BC *IAK* 20 (1906) p. 65 (vase)
THRACE:
—ABDERA: **(25)** c. 415-395 BC May, *Abdera* p. 166 no. 216 (coin); **(26)** c. 395-360 BC Lorber, *Amphipolis* p. 177 (coin); **(27)** c. 336-311 BC Unp. (Chryssanthaki diss.) p. 224 (coin); **(28)** 311-306 BC Maier, *Mauerbauinschr.* 69 II, 142 (f. *Νικηφόρος*)
—APOLLONIA-SOZOPOLIS: **(29)** v/iv BC *IGB* I^{2} 409 (f. *Εἰρηναῖος*); **(30)** ib. 422 bis (s. *Ἀλπάλης*); **(31)** iv BC ib. 463 bis, 2 (s. *Νεάνθης*); **(32)** m. iv BC *SNG BM Black Sea* 164 (coin) (Ἀθήνα̣ι[ος], Ἀθηναγ(όρης)—*SNG*); **(33)** iii/ii BC *IGB* I^{2} 395 bis (s. *Νεάνθης*)
—BYZANTION: **(34)** c. 267 AD *PLRE* I (-)
—MARONEIA: **(35)** ii-i BC *IThrakAig* E212, 39 (s. *Ζωΐλος*)
—ODESSOS: **(36)** 22 BC *IGB* I^{2} 46, 25 (*Μ. Ἀντώνιος Ἀ.*); **(37)** ?ii AD ib. 231 (Ἀθήνα̣ι[ος])

'Αθηναΐς
CIMMERIAN BOSPOROS:
—PANTIKAPAION: **(1)** i AD *CIRB* 573; cf. KW pl. 26 no. 389; **(2)** i-ii AD *CIRB* 572; cf. KW pl. 12 no. 171; **(3)** *SEG* XLV 1013; **(4)** i/ii AD *CIRB* 579
MACEDONIA: **(5)** 154 BC *SGDI* 1925, 2-3, 6, 9-10 (Tataki, *Macedonians* p. 224 no. 44) (-*ναΐς*: slave/freed.)
MACEDONIA (EDONIS):
—AMPHIPOLIS: **(6)** ii BC *IG* II^{2} 8077 (Tataki, *Macedonians* p. 45 no. 3; *FRA* 496)
MACEDONIA (MYGDONIA):
—THESSALONIKE: **(7)** ii AD *IG* X (2) (1) 298 (-*ναείς*: d. *Μωμώ*); **(8)** ib. 545 (*Φλ. Ἀ.*: d. *Ἀννία Κούαρτα*); **(9)** *SEG* XXXVIII 706 (threpte)
MACEDONIA (PIERIA):
—PYDNA (TERRIT.): **(10)** imp. ib. 629
SCYTHIA MINOR:
—ISTROS: **(11)** i AD ib. XXXIX 830 (Ἀ[θ]η[ν]αΐς)
TAURIS:
—CHERSONESOS: **(12)** ?v BC Solomonik, *GAKh* 925 (vase) (*SEG* XXVI 811) (date—A.W.J.)
THRACE:
—APOLLONIA-SOZOPOLIS: **(13)** iv BC *BMNBurgas* 4 (2002) p. 126 no. 23 (d. *Ὀρθαγόρης*); **(14)** s. i BC *IGB* I^{2} 395 quater, 4 (d. *Γύκων*)
—PERINTHOS-HERAKLEIA: **(15)** ii AD *IPerinth* 132
—SALYMBRIA: **(16)** imp. *IByz* S 44 ([Ἀ]θηναείς: d. *Δάαις*)
—STRYME?: **(17)** c. 400-375 BC *Pratiques funéraires* p. 88 no. 4 (*SEG* XLIX 991; *IThrakAig* E135) (d. *Προκλῆς*)
THRACE?: **(18)** ii-iii AD *SEG* XXXVIII 1916 (-*ναε̣ί̣ς*)

'Αθήνη
MACEDONIA (BOTTIAIA):
—PELLA: **(1)** iv BC ib. XXIV 555 (terracotta) (d. *Λυσιμαχίδης*)

'Αθηνῆς
CIMMERIAN BOSPOROS:
—GORGIPPIA: **(1)** m. ii AD *Eirene* 7 (1968) p. 67, 12 (Ἀθήνου (gen.): f. —*ωρος*)

THRACE:
—ABDERA: **(2)** c. 360-350 BC May, *Abdera* pp. 261-2 nos. 452-7 (coin); Masson, *OGS* p. 428
—MARONEIA: **(3)** c. 432-423 BC Schönert-Geiss, *Maroneia* 152 (coin) (Ἀθηνέω (gen.)); **(4)** c. 365-336 BC ib. 405-6; 410-13; 509-10 (coin) (Ἀθηνέω (gen.)); **(5)** 167 BC *SEG* XXXV 823, 5 (*IThrakAig* E168) (Ἀθηνέω (gen.))

'Αθήνιος
CIMMERIAN BOSPOROS:
—PANTIKAPAION: **(1)** i AD *CIRB* 332; cf. KW pl. 46 no. 650 (s. *Μηνᾶς*, f. *Θεόφιλος*, *Μήνιος*)
SKYTHIA:
—TANAIS: **(2)** f. ii AD *CIRB* 1264 A, 14 (I f. *Ἀθήνιος* II); **(3)** ib. l. 14 ([Ἀ]θήνιος: II s. *Ἀθήνιος* I); **(4)** c. 200-210 AD ib. 1277, 18 (f. *Καλοῦς*)
THRACE:
—BYZANTION (TERRIT.): **(5)** imp. Unp. (Sayar) (Ἀθην(ί)ου? (gen.): f. *Διοσκουρίδης*)

'Αθήνιππος
CIMMERIAN BOSPOROS:
—GORGIPPIA: **(1)** f. iii BC *CIRB* 1137 A II, 10; 1137 B II, 11 (f. *Κόνων*); **(2)** ib. l. 34 (s. *Ἡροφάνης*)

'Αθηνίων
MACEDONIA: **(1)** c. 200-175 BC *IG* XI (4) 1273, 3 (Tataki, *Macedonians* p. 225 no. 45; La'da E1392) (s. *Ἡφαιστίων*)
MACEDONIA (CHALKIDIKE):
—OLYNTHOS: **(2)** ?352 BC *TAPA* 65 (1934) p. 128 no. 4, 6, 11; Hatzopoulos, *Actes Chalc.* p. 80 (date) (f. *Ἀντίβιος*, *Νίκανδρος*)
MACEDONIA (EDONIS):
—AMPHIPOLIS: **(3)** s. iv BC *AD* 24 (1969) Chron. p. 355 no. 3 (f. *Ἀρραβαῖος*); **(4)** 37 BC Robert, *Coll. Froehner* 44, 17 (Tataki, *Macedonians* p. 45 no. 4) (s. *Βίθυς*)
MACEDONIA (MYGDONIA):
—KALINDOIA: **(5)** a. 98 AD *SEG* XLII 583, 22 (f. *Ζώπυρος*)
THRACE: **(6)** imp. *IG* II^{2} 8915 (*FRA* 2491) (Ἀθηνί[ων]: f. *Μηνοφίλα*)
—MARONEIA: **(7)** ?iv BC *RE* (10); Overbeck 1975 (Lat. Athenio: painter)

'Αθηνόβιος
THRACE:
—ABDERA: **(1)** c. 336-311 BC Unp. (Chryssanthaki diss.) p. 225 (coin)

'Αθηνογένης
MACEDONIA (MYGDONIA):
—THESSALONIKE: **(1)** f. i AD *IG* X (2) (1) 133, 11; Robert, *OMS* 5 pp. 295-302 (date) (s. *Πλουσία*)

'Αθηνόδοτος
THRACE:
—PERINTHOS-HERAKLEIA: **(1)** ?iv BC *IPerinth* 259, 2

'Αθηνοδώρα
MACEDONIA (PAIONIA):
—KAVADARCI (MOD.): **(1)** ii-iii AD *Sp.* 71 (1931) p. 73 no. 171 (*Αὐρ.? Ἀ.*)

'Αθηνόδωρος
CIMMERIAN BOSPOROS:
—GORGIPPIA: **(1)** ?68 AD *CIRB* 1126, 6, 10; cf. *SEG* XLIX 1032 (s. *Ἀθήναιος*, f. *Νεοκλῆς*); **(2)** ii AD *CIRB* 1140, 8 (Ἀθηνό[δωρος]); **(3)** ib. l. 10; **(4)** ib. 1141, 10 (Ἀθηνόδω̣[ρος]); **(5)** ib. 1151, 4 (Ἀθηνόδω̣ρ[ος]: f. —*θεος*); **(6)** ib. 1159 A, 3 (Ἀθηνόδω[ρος]); **(7)** ib. 1160, 6 ([Ἀ]θηνόδ[ωρος]); **(8)** m. ii AD *Eirene* 7 (1968) p. 67, 4 (s. *Φαρνακίων*) ?= (*24*); **(9)** ib. l. 7 (f. *Πανταλέων*); **(10)** ib. l. 9 ([Ἀ]θηνόδωρος: s. *Πόθος*) ?= (*23*); **(11)** ib. l. 17 (f. *Μοιρόδωρος*); **(12)** ib. l. 23 (f. —*ος*); **(13)** ib. l. 23 (Ἀθηνό[δωρος]?: f. *Νεοκλῆς*); **(14)** s. ii AD *CIRB*

1129 A, 4 ([Ἀ]θηνόδωρος: s. Πανταλέων); **(15)** ib. 1129 B, 6 ([Ἀθη]νόδωρος: s. Χρηστοῦς); **(16)** ?s. ii AD ib. 1147, 2 ([Ἀθ]ηνόδω[ρος]); **(17)** s. ii AD ib. 1150 ([Ἀ]θηνόδω[ρος]); **(18)** 173-210 AD ib. 1134, 10 (s. Σέλευκος); **(19)** ib. l. 19 (Ἀθηνόδω[ρος]); **(20)** ib. l. 22 (s. Νε—); **(21)** ib. 1134 E, 8 (s. Γάϊος); **(22)** ib. 1135, 14 ([Ἀθ]ηνόδωρος—Tokhtas'ev: s. Διο—); **(23)** ii/iii AD ib. 1179, 27 (s. Πόθος) ?= *(10)*; **(24)** ib. l. 30 (s. Φαρνακίων) ?= *(8)*; **(25)** ib. l. 37 (s. Μυρίσκος); **(26)** ib. l. 38 (s. Νεοκλῆς); **(27)** ib. l. 40 (s. Βάγης); **(28)** *SEG* XLIX 1033 B, 4 (*CIRB* 1182 B, 2) ([Ἀθη]νόδωρος?—Tokhtas'ev)
—GORGIPPIA?: **(29)** s. ii AD ib. 1231 B, 11 ([Ἀ]θηνόδωρος)
—MYRMEKION: **(30)** ii AD ib. 886 (Ἀθην(ό)δ(ω)ρος: s. Φιλοκράτης)
—PANTIKAPAION: **(31)** i/ii AD ib. 641 (f. Φαρνάκης)
—THEODOSIA: **(32)** iii AD ib. 947 B, 19 (f. Εὐμ—)
MACEDONIA: **(33)** iii-ii BC *IG* IX (2) 1185 (Tataki, *Macedonians* p. 225 no. 46) (f. Στράτων)
MACEDONIA (CHALKIDIKE):
—ANTHEMOUS: **(34)** iii AD *SEG* XLII 571 (Αὐρ. Ἀ.: s. Αὐρ. Πρόκλος, Αὐρ. Διονυσία)
—OLYNTHOS: **(35)** ?354 BC *TAPA* 69 (1938) pp. 52-3 no. 6, 12 + 70 (1939) p. 62; Hatzopoulos, *Actes Chalc.* p. 80 (date) (s. Ἀριστόδημος)
MACEDONIA (EDONIS):
—PHILIPPOI: **(36)** iii AD *AE* 1950-1, p. 53 no. 1, 1 (Pilhofer 716) (Lat. [M.] Aur. Athenodorus)
MACEDONIA (MYGDONIA):
—THESSALONIKE: **(37)** ii AD *IG* X (2) (1) 326, 3 (s. Σεραπιακός, Λύκα)
SCYTHIA MINOR:
—ISTROS: **(38)** iii BC *St. Clas.* 7 (1965) p. 280 no. 13 (vase) (Ἀθηνόδ[ωρος]?); **(39)** i BC-i AD *ISM* I 191 I, 53 (f. Ἀπολλώνιος); **(40)** ib. 191 II, 3-4 (f. Ἀριστόνικος, Σαραπίων)
SKYTHIA:
—OLBIA-BORYSTHENES: **(41)** iv BC *SEG* XXX 958 (vase); **(42)** f. iv BC Dubois, *IGDOlbia* 103, 3 (lead); **(43)** iii BC *IOlbia* 72, 3 (s. Δημαγόρης); **(44)** *IOSPE* I² 201 I, 57-8 (s. Μόσχος, f. Ἀμύντωρ)
—TANAIS: **(45)** f. ii AD *CIRB* 1266, 10 (Ἀθηνόδω[ρος]); **(46)** 155 AD ib. 1260, 19 (s. Μη—λος); **(47)** 210-226 AD ib. 1281, 18 ([Ἀ]θηνό[δ](ω)ρος: s. Φ—μος) ?= *(49)*; **(48)** 225-228 AD ib. 1279, 27; 1282, 26-7 (Ἀ[θην]όδωρος: f. Ἑρμῆς, Χόμιος); **(49)** 228 AD ib. l. 9 (s. Φαδίναμος) ?= *(47)*
TAURIS:
—CHERSONESOS: **(50)** f. ii AD *SEG* XXXIII 591 A, 5 (Ἀθηνό[δωρος]?: f. —ιδης)
THRACE:
—AINOS: **(51)** i-ii AD Taşlıklıoğlu 2 p. 3 no. 1, 3 (*SEG* XLIX 865); *BE* 1972, no. 275 (locn.) (s. Ἀπολλωνίδας); **(52)** s. ii AD *RE* (22)
—BISANTHE-PANION: **(53)** 160-138 BC *Tekmeria* 6 (2001) p. 156 no. 2 (*SEG* XLIX 876) (s. Ἡράκλειτος)
—BYZANTION?: **(54)** ii BC *IByz* 156 (slave?)
—DIONYSOPOLIS: **(55)** iii AD *IGB* I² 14 b, 20 (Αὐρ. Ἀ.: s. Οὐαλέριος)
—ODESSOS: **(56)** s. iii BC ib. 35, 8
—PHILIPPOPOLIS-TRIMONTIUM: **(57)** imp. ib. III 992 (f. Κλεοπάτρα); **(58)** c. 303 AD *Anal. Boll.* 31 (1912) p. 192

Ἀθηνόκλεια
CIMMERIAN BOSPOROS:
—PANTIKAPAION: **(1)** i AD *CIRB* 333

Ἀθηνοκλῆς
CIMMERIAN BOSPOROS:
—PANTIKAPAION: **(1)** i BC ib. 268 A (s. Τιμόθεος, Εὔκλεια)
MACEDONIA (CHALKIDIKE):
—OLYNTHOS: **(2)** m. iv BC *IG* II² 10024 (Tataki, *Macedonians* p. 129 no. 3; *FRA* 5881) (f. Μελιτώ)
SKYTHIA:
—OLBIA-BORYSTHENES*: **(3)** 106-115 AD *SEG* XL 634 (I f. Ἀθηνοκλῆς II); **(4)** ib. (II s. Ἀθηνοκλῆς I)
THRACE:
—MARONEIA: **(5)** iii BC *IThrakAig* E234 (Ἀθηνοκλῆς: f. Μητρώνασσα)

Ἀθηνόκριτος
THRACE:
—ABDERA: **(1)** v BC D.L. ix 34 (?f. Δημόκριτος, Δάμασος, Ἡρόδοτος: fict.?)

Ἀθηνόμανδρος
SKYTHIA:
—OLBIA-BORYSTHENES (BEREZAN (MOD.)): **(1)** vi BC Dubois, *IGDOlbia* 74 (vase)

Ἀθηνώ
CIMMERIAN BOSPOROS:
—PANTIKAPAION: **(1)** imp. *CIRB* 778 (Ἀ(θ)ηνώ: ?d. Ἀπολλο—)
MACEDONIA (BOTTIAIA):
—BEROIA: **(2)** ii-i BC *IBer* 204 (Tataki 39) (m. Ἀμμία); **(3)** iii AD *IBer* 209 (Tataki 38)
MACEDONIA (MYGDONIA):
—THESSALONIKE?: **(4)** ii-iii AD *IG* X (2) (1) 721
MACEDONIA (PIERIA):
—PYDNA: **(5)** 250 AD *SEG* XLVI 800 A, 41 (Αὐρ. Ἀ.)

Ἀθήνων
THRACE:
—TIRIZIS AKRA*: **(1)** iii/ii BC *IGB* V 5004 bis (Ἀθηνίων?)

Ἄθης
CIMMERIAN BOSPOROS:
—ZENONOS CHERSONESOS*: **(1)** v/iv BC *SEG* XL 643 (Ἀθη.ς, Ἄθη[ν]ις?—Tokhtas'ev)

Ἀθιάγας
SKYTHIA:
—TANAIS: **(1)** 225 AD *CIRB* 1279, 11 (s. Βαλώδιος)

Ἀθλίων
TAURIS:
—CHERSONESOS: **(1)** i BC-i AD *IOSPE* I² 589 (Ἀθλί[ων]: f. Εὐρύδαμος)

Ἄθυς
THRACE:
—BEROE-AUGUSTA TRAIANA (TERRIT.): **(1)** ii-iii AD *IGB* III 1735 (f. —άτραλις)
—DEIZENOI?: **(2)** ii-iii AD ib. 1204 (s. Σπάρτοκος)
—GLAVA PANEGA (MOD.): **(3)** ii-iii AD ib. II 560 (Ἄθυο[ς] (gen.): f. Δίζας)
—MARKIANOPOLIS (TERRIT.): **(4)** iii AD ib. 845 (*CCET* II (1) 376) (f. —ήπορις)
—SKEDABRIA: **(5)** 202 AD *IGB* III 1690 b, 18 (and Thrace Pizos: f. Μουκάτραλις)

Ἄθως
MACEDONIA (EDONIS):
—AMPHIPOLIS: **(1)** ii-iii AD Kazarow 420; cf. *BE* 1949, no. 97 (Ἄθου (gen.): f. Βίθυς)

Αἶα
THRACE:
—APOLLONIA-SOZOPOLIS: **(1)** iv BC *IGB* V 5148 (d. Κλέαρχος)

Αἰάκων
THRACE:
—PLOTINOPOLIS: **(1)** 160 AD *SEG* XXXVII 970, 4 (s. Βιτάλιος)

Αἰαντίδης
CIMMERIAN BOSPOROS:
—KEPOI: **(1)** ?f. iv BC *CIRB* 188 (f. Θεόπομπος)
THRACE:
—MARONEIA: **(2)** f. ii BC *BCH* 66-7 (1942-3) p. 197 no. 1 + *IThrakAig* E258 (Αἰαν[τίδης]?: f. Ἀπολλόδωρος); **(3)** *BCH* 66-7 (1942-3) p. 197 no. 1 (*IThrakAig* E258) (s. Ἀπολλόδωρος, Κλεοπάτρα)
—ODESSOS: **(4)** i BC-i AD *IGB* I² 107, 4, 7, 10 (s. Μένανδρος, f. Ἀρτεμίδωρος); **(5)** 32 BC ib. 46, 15 (f. Ἀμύντωρ); **(6)** 30 BC ib. l. 17 (s. Ἀπολλᾶς); **(7)** i-ii AD ib. 123 (Αἰαντίδης); **(8)** ii AD ib. 50 a, 6 (I s. Ἀπολλώνιος, f. Αἰαντίδης II); **(9)** ib. l. 6 (II s. Αἰαντίδης I); **(10)** f. ii AD ib. 78 ter, 5 (*CCET* I 30) (s. Ἀρτεμίδωρος); **(11)** *IGB* I² 78 ter, 9 (*CCET* I 30) (s. Μένανδρος) ?= *(13)*; **(12)** s. ii AD *IGB* I² 166 (PM 1404); *Dacia* 21 (1977) p. 161 (date) (f. Παρμενίων)
—ODESSOS (NR.): **(13)** i-ii AD *IGB* I² 284 (s. Μένανδρος) ?= *(11)*

Αἶαξ
MACEDONIA (EDONIS):
—AMPHIPOLIS: **(1)** iii AD *Mous. Kavalas* p. 84 no. Λ. 128

Αἰγιαλεύς
THRACE:
—ABDERA: **(1)** c. 336-311 BC May, *Abdera* p. 291 nos. 529-30 (coin); Masson, *OGS* p. 429

Αἰγίνομος
TAURIS:
—CHERSONESOS: **(1)** c. 425-400 BC *SEG* XL 612. 19 (ostrakon)

Αἴγλη
MACEDONIA (BOTTIAIA):
—BEROIA: **(1)** ii-iii AD *IBer* 295 ([Αἴ]γλη: m. Ἐπαφρόδιτος)

Αἰγύπτιος
SCYTHIA MINOR:
—ISTROS: **(1)** s. iv BC *Histria* 4 p. 89 no. 576 (vase)

Αἴγυπτος
MACEDONIA (EDONIS):
—AMPHIPOLIS: **(1)** hell.? *SEG* L 564
MACEDONIA (MYGDONIA):
—THESSALONIKE: **(2)** s. i AD *IG* X (2) (1) 68, 29 (Τ. Κλ. Αἴγ<ι>υπτος)

Αἰδεζυρίς
THRACE: **(1)** i AD *IGB* IV 2338, 16; cf. V 5928 (d. Φλ. Διζάλας, Ῥεπτάτερκος)

Αἰδέσιος
MACEDONIA (SINTIKE):
—PARTHIKOPOLIS: **(1)** ?ii AD *FGrH* 257 F 37, 51 (Tataki, *Macedonians* p. 147 no. 1) (s. Δίζας)

Αἰδήμων
MACEDONIA (MYGDONIA):
—THESSALONIKE: **(1)** 221 AD *IG* X (2) (1) 492, 5 (Μ. Ἐρέννιος Ἀ.: f. Κλ. Ἑόρτη)

Αἰζειός
TAURIS:
—KALOS LIMEN: **(1)** ii-iii AD *SEG* XXVI 802 = XXXVIII 749. 2 (Solomonik, *GChKh* p. 8 no. 7)

Αἰήτης
KOLCHIS:
—PHASIS: **(1)** v BC X., *An.* v 6. 37 (king)

Αἰθαζίη
THRACE:
—PHILIPPOPOLIS-TRIMONTIUM: **(1)** ii-iii AD *IGB* III 974 (d. Ἐπταίτραλις)

Αἰθάλη
Thrace:
—Serdica: (1) 261-268 AD ib. iv 1912 (*Φλ. Ἀ.*)

Αἰθάλης
Macedonia (Mygdonia):
—Thessalonike: (1) ii AD *IG* x (2) (1) 294

Αἰθερία
Macedonia (Derriopos):
—Stuberra?: (1) ii-iii AD *AEMTh* 12 (1998) p. 104
Macedonia (Mygdonia):
—Thessalonike*: (2) iv-v AD Feissel, *RICM* 146; cf. *BE* 2001, no. 293

Αἰθέριος
Macedonia (Bottiaia):
—Edessa: (1) v-vi AD Feissel, *RICM* 4 (Ἐθ-)

Αἴκκυρος?
Macedonia (Bottiaia):
—Beroia: (1) 223 BC *IBer* 4, 22 (*Ạἴκκυρος*?, *Ḍίκκυρος*?: f. *Νικάνωρ*)

Αἰλία
Cimmerian Bosporos:
—Bosporos: (1) 275-278 AD *CIRB* 36, 8; *PIR*^{2} A 284 (queen)
Thrace:
—Odessos: (2) i-ii AD *IGB* I^2 232

Αἰλιανή
Macedonia (Lynkestis):
—Herakleia: (1) ii-iii AD *IG* x (2) (2) 86

Αἰλιανός
Macedonia (Bottiaia):
—Beroia: (1) ii AD *IBer* 363, 3 (Tataki 64) (*Αἴ[λ]ịανός*: f. *Μητρόδωρος*)
Macedonia (Paionia):
—Neapolis? (Izvor (mod.): (2) ii-iii AD Dimitsas 300, 1-2 (s. *Ζωΐλος*, *Οὐαλία*)
Penestai?: (3) c. 200 AD *SEG* xxxix 593, 7 (s. *Ἄνθιμος*)
Scythia Minor:
—Istros: (4) ii AD *ISM* i 197 II, 4 (f. *Αἰμίλιος*); (5) s. ii AD ib. 167, 13 (s. *Ἧλις*)

Αἴλιος
Macedonia (Edonis):
—Philippoi (territ.): (1) ii-iii AD Pikoulas, *Chora* p. 127 no. 21 (Pilhofer 622) (*Αἔ-*)
Macedonia (Elimeia):
—Aiane (territ.): (2) ii-iii AD *EAM* 16 (-λειος)
Skythia: (3) imp. Leroux, *Lagynos* p. 67 no. 134 (vase)
—Olbia-Borysthenes: (4) ii AD *IOSPE* I^2 89, 6 (s. *Ναύτιμος*)
Thrace:
—Serdica (territ.): (5) ii-iii AD *IGB* v 5702 (f. *Δόκιμος*); (6) ib. 5734 (f. *Κάστωρ*)

Αἶλις
Scythia Minor: (1) ii BC *SCIV* 1.1 (1950) pp. 248-9 nos. 33-5; *SNG BM Black Sea* 356-7; *SNG Stancomb* 320-1 (coin) (*Αἴλιος* (gen.): king)

Αἰμιλιανή
Thrace:
—Pautalia: (1) ii-iii AD *IGB* iv 2092 (*[Α]ἰμιλιανή*)

Αἰμιλιανός
Scythia Minor:
—Kallatis: (1) 241-244 AD *ISM* iii 74, 14 (f. *Αἰμίλιος*)
Tauris:
—Chersonesos: (2) f. ii AD Solomonik, *NEPKh* 111, 10 (*[Αἰ]μιλιανός*: s. *Σαβῖνος*) ?= (*3*); (3) ib. 112, 17; 113, 12; *IOSPE* I^2 385 (*Γ. Ἰούλ. Ἀ.*) ?= (*2*)

Thrace:
—Durostorum?: (4) b. 363 AD *Chron. Pasch.* p. 549

Αἰμίλιος
Macedonia (Derriopos):
—Stuberra: (1) 50 AD *IG* x (2) (2) 324, 22 (s. *Λούκιος*); (2) 74 AD ib. 325, 56 (I f. *Αἰμίλιος* II); (3) ib. l. 56 (II s. *Αἰμίλιος* I); (4) 116 AD ib. 327, 38 (f. *Παράμονος*)
Scythia Minor:
—Istros: (5) ii AD *ISM* i 197 II, 4 (s. *Αἰλιανός*)
—Kallatis: (6) 241-244 AD ib. iii 74, 14 (*Αἰμί-λι(ος)*: s. *Αἰμιλιανός*)
Thrace:
—Beroe-Augusta Traiana: (7) i-ii AD *IGB* iii 1609 (*GVI* 91)

Αἰμόνιος
Scythia Minor:
—Tomis: (1) iii AD *ISM* ii 276, 6 (*Αὐρ. Διονύσιος ὁ καὶ Ἀ.*)

Αἶμος
Thrace: (1) ii AD Apul., *Met.* vii 5 (Lat. Haemus: s. *Θήρων*: fict.)

Αἰνείας
Cimmerian Bosporos:
—Pantikapaion: (1) i BC *CIRB* 122, 3, 5 (*Αἰνέας*—l.5: s. *Ἐμμεύς*)
Macedonia (Bottiaia):
—Beroia: (2) i BC *IBer* 195 (Tataki 89) (s. *Ὄκκος*, f. *Ὄκκος*)
Macedonia (Derriopos):
—Stuberra: (3) 74 AD *IG* x (2) (2) 325, 41 (-νή-: f. *Μελάνιππος*)
Macedonia (Edonis):
—Amphipolis?: (4) hell. Dimitsas 904 (f. *Νικόστρατος*); (5) ?222-221 BC *SEG* xlviii 812; cf. Hatzopoulos, *MI* 2 p. 92 no. 77 (s. *Δημήτριος*)
Thrace:
—Byzantion:
——(Athyras): (6) ii-i BC *IByz* 96 (Firatlı-Robert p. 93 no. 126) (*Αἰνήου* (gen.): f. *Πρωτίων*)

Αἴνετος
Macedonia (Chalkidike):
—Olynthos: (1) ?350 BC *TAPA* 65 (1934) p. 125 no. 3, 2; Hatzopoulos, *Actes Chalc.* p. 80 (cate) (s. *Ἄνδρων*)

Αἰντζις
Thrace: (1) 267 BC *SEG* xxvii 1114, 14a (La'da E700) (s. *Πατάμουσος*)

Αἰνησίδαμος
Thrace:
—Bizye: (1) imp.? PM 1950 (-νε-: f. *Δορζίνθης*)
—Byzantion: (2) ?262-254 BC Nachtergael, *Les Galates* 5, [27]; 7, 27 (Stephanis 88); *CID* iv 45; 47 (date) (*[Α]ἰνησίδ[αμος]*: s. *Ἀρίστων*)

Αἰνησίδημος
Macedonia (Chalkidike):
—Olynthos: (1) s. iii BC *SEG* xv 279, 1 + *IOrop* 208 (Tataki, *Macedonians* p. 129 no. 4) (f. *Ἱέρων*)

Αἴνητος
Macedonia?: (1) 287 BC *RE* (4) (Tataki, *Macedonians* p. 225 no. 47)

Αἰνιάδης
Thrace:
—Bizone: (1) ii-iii AD *IGB* I^2 7 bis, 3

Αἶνις
Macedonia (Chalkidike):
—Akanthos: (1) iv/iii BC *SEG* xlvii 871 B, 2, 5

Αἰνώ
Thrace:
—Byzantion?: (1) hell. *IByz* 331 (*Αἰνοῦς* (gen.?): d. *Πάπας*)

Αἴολος
Macedonia: (1) i BC *IGUR* 1497 (Tataki, *Macedonians* p. 225 no. 48 (date))
Macedonia (Bottiaia):
—Pella: (2) iii-ii BC *SEG* l 611 (n. pr.?: ?f. *Γραίη*)
Macedonia (Pieria):
—Pydna: (3) iv BC *GRBS* 43 (2002-3) p. 119 no. 5, 2
Thrace:
—Odessos: (4) iii/ii BC *IGB* I^2 88 bis (f. *Ἀριστομένης*)

Αἰσίας
Scythia Minor:
—Kallatis: (1) c. 250-225 BC Price, *Alexander* 945 (coin) (*Αἰσί(ας)*); (2) iii/ii BC *IGB* I^2 391, 6; (3) *ISM* iii 161 (s. *Ἐπίστρατος*)

Αἰσίλας
Macedonia: (1) 93 BC *Montreal Exhib.* p. 103 no. 52 (coin) (Lat. Aesilas)

Αἰσιμίδης
Cimmerian Bosporos:
—Gorgippia: (1) f. iii BC *CIRB* 1137 A I, 41 (s. *Πάταικος*)

Αἴσυμνος
Macedonia: (1) c. 322-313 BC *IG* vii 4256, 8 (*IOrop* 4); cf. Tataki, *Macedonians* p. 226 no. 50 (s. *Ὀξυμένης*)

Αἰσυμώης
Thrace:
—Sportela: (1) ii-iii AD *IGB* iv 2233, 2 (*Eastern cults* p. 170 no. 16) (*Αἰσυμώους* (gen.): f. *Πιεισειοος*)

Αἰσχίνας
Macedonia (Pieria):
—Phila?: (1) ?iii BC *RPh* 1911, pp. 133-4 no. 36, 127; cf. Helly, *L'État thessalien* pp. 319-20 (locn.) (s. *Αὐτοκράτης*)
Scythia Minor:
—Kallatis: (2) iv/iii BC *ISM* iii 125, 12; (3) hell. *Studii Cercetări Numismatică* 1 (1957) p. 270 no. 20 (weight) (*Αἰσχί(νας)*)
Tauris:
—Chersonesos: (4) c. 325-300 BC Solomonik, *GAKh* 189 (vase) (*Αἰσχί(νας)*); (5) iv/iii BC Kats p. 114 no. 122 (amph.) (f. *Φορμίων*); (6) c. 320-310 BC Anokhin p. 138 no. 68 (coin) (*Αἰσχί(νας)*); (7) c. 315-300 BC Kats p. 85 no. 7 (amph.); (8) iii BC Solomonik, *NEPKh* 161 (s. *Γέρων*); (9) f. iii BC *SEG* xl 615 B, 22 (f. *Τελαμών*); (10) c. 290-280 BC Anokhin p. 140 no. 90 (coin); (11) c. 200-185 BC Kats p. 85 no. 8 (amph.) (s. *Ξενοκλῆς*)
Thrace:
—Mesambria?: (12) hell. *IGB* v 5096 (f. *Βύριχος*)

Αἰσχίνης
Cimmerian Bosporos:
—Myrmekion: (1) hell. Michalowski, *Mirmeki* p. 114 no. 37 (tile)
—Nymphaion: (2) i BC *CIRB* 927 (*Αἰσχί[ν]ης*: s. *Ἀντίοχος*)
—Pantikapaion: (3) i AD ib. 408; cf. KW pl. 49 no. 680; cf. Zgusta, *PNS* 988 (Ἐσκί-: s. *Σαββίων*)
Macedonia (Chalkidike):
—Potidaia-Kassandreia: (4) m. iv BC *IG* II^2 10109 (Tataki, *Macedonians* p. 168 no. 2; *FRA* 6159) (s. *Διονυσόδωρος*)

Macedonia (Derriopos):
—stuberra: (5) 74 ad *IG* x (2) (2) 325, 28 (f. Ἀπολλόδωρος)
Skythia:
—tyras: (6) ii bc *IOSPE* I^2 8; cf. KW pl. 50 no. 687 (f. Ἄρεστος)
Tauris:
—chersonesos: (7) f. ii ad *SEG* xxviii 631, 6 ([Αἰσ]χίνης)
Thrace:
—perinthos-herakleia:
——(Makedones): (8) iii-ii bc *IPerinth* 61, 6 (f. Ἡρακλείδης)

Αἴσχρα
Thrace:
—byzantion: (1) ii-i bc *IByz* 87 (Fıratlı–Robert p. 51 no. 22) (d. Ἐπίνικος)

Αἰσχρίων
Cimmerian Bosporos:
—pantikapaion: (1) iv bc *CIRB* 206 (f. Μητροδώρη)
Macedonia (Bottiaia):
—aigai: (2) f. iii bc *IMM* 10, 11 (Tataki, *Macedonians* p. 39 no. 2) (s. Ἀμύντας)
Macedonia (Chalkidike):
—potidaia-kassandreia: (3) c. 166-156 bc *ID* 1417 A II, 113 (Tataki, *Macedonians* p. 85 no. 1) (f. Θεόξενος)
Scythia Minor:
—istros: (4) i bc-i ad *ISM* i 190, 3 ([Αἰ]σχρίων: s. Χα—); (5) i ad ib. 200, 1 (I s. Τελέστης, f. Αἰσχρίων II); (6) ib. l. 1 (II s. Αἰσχρίων I); (7) ib. l. 3 (f. Ἀθηνάδης); (8) c. 48-52 ad ib. 67, 52; 68, 52 (Ἐσ-); (9) ii ad ib. 196, 5 (s. Κόρινθος); (10) ib. 198, 6 (f. Ἡρόφαντος); (11) ib. 211, 11 (f. Διονύσιος); (12) ib. 212, 15 (I f. Αἰσχρίων II); (13) ib. l. 15 (II s. Αἰσχρίων I); (14) ib. 214, 7 + 226, 5; (15) 138 ad ib. 193 I, 54 (s. Ἀριστόνικος); (16) ib. l. 107-8 (s. Ἀθηνάδης, f. Σατυρίων); (17) ib. 193 II, 55 (f. Διονύσιος); (18) iii ad ib. 222, 6 (Αἰσχρί[ων]?); (19) ib. 291, 10 (s. Ἀρισταγόρας); (20) f. iii ad *Stud. Fischer* p. 32 no. 4, 1 (s. Ἀμ—)
—istros?: (21) ii bc *ISM* i 49, 9 (Αἰσχρί[ων]: f. —τος)
—tomis: (22) iii-ii bc *AMNG* i (2) 2407 (coin) (Αἰσχρί(ων))
Thrace: (23) ?ii bc *SB* 8562 (Velkov 12; La'da E701) (s. Διόδοτος)
—apollonia-sozopolis: (24) ii/i bc *IGB* I^2 390, 3 (s. Ποσείδιππος)
—odessos: (25) 20 bc ib. 46, 27 (f. Ἀριστείδης); (26) f. ii ad ib. 78 ter, 12 (*CCET* i 30) (s. Ξένανδρος)

Αἰσχρόδωρος
Macedonia?: (1) b. 348 bc *Olynthus* 10 p. 421 no. 2176 (bullet) (Guarducci, *Ep. Gr.* 2 p. 522); *BE* 1948, no. 7 (name)

Αἶσχρος
Cimmerian Bosporos:
—gorgippia: (1) f. iii bc *CIRB* 1137 B II, 37 (s. Ὀρθαγόρας)
—pantikapaion: (2) ?v bc *IAK* 47 (1913) p. 55 no. 36 (vase) (Αἴσχρō (gen.))

Αἴσχρων
Tauris:
—chersonesos:
——(Echedamis): (1) s. v bc *DGVE* 1996-7, p. 111 fig. 2, 6 (*SEG* xlix 1031. 3 (ostrakon)) (s. Διονύσιος)
Thrace:
—mesambria: (2) iv/iii bc *IGB* I^2 334

Αἰσχυλῖνος
Macedonia (Bottiaia):
—beroia: (1) 239-229 bc *IBer* 45, 31 (Tataki 90) (s. Ἀριστοκλείδης)

Macedonia (Lower Paionia):
—europos: (2) f. ii bc Helly, *Gonnoi* 31, 4 (Tataki, *Macedonians* p. 108 no. 2) (s. Σωσίδημος)

Αἰσχύλος
Cimmerian Bosporos:
—pantikapaion: (1) iii bc *MIA* 56 (1957) p. 224 (tile) (*Sov. Arkh.* 28 (1958) p. 129 no. 1)
Macedonia (Bisaltia):
—argilos?: (2) 364-357 bc Hatzopoulos, *Actes Amphipolis* p. 15 no. 1, 14; pp. 73-4 (locn., date) (or Macedonia (Edonis) Amphipolis)
Macedonia (Chalkidike):
—potidaia-kassandreia:
——(Hippotadeis): (3) c. 305-297 bc *SEG* xlvii 940, 4 (f. Χαιρεφάνης)
Macedonia (Edonis):
—amphipolis: (4) b. 357 bc Hatzopoulos, *Actes Amphipolis* p. 25 no. 3, 17 (*SEG* xli 557) (Αἰσχύ[λος]: s. Ὀπωρις); (5) m. iii bc Hatzopoulos, *Actes Amphipolis* p. 52 no 12, 1; *SEG* xli 566 (date)
—amphipolis (nr.): (6) a. 357 bc Hatzopoulos, *Actes Amphipolis* p. 43 no. 8, 8 (*SEG* xli 562)
Macedonia (Mygdonia):
—thessalonike: (7) i-ii ad *IG* x (2) (1) 243 I, 1 ([Αἰ]σχύλος: s. Εὐέλπιστος)
Thrace:
—byzantion: (8) s. i ad *IByz* 33, 7 (f. Κρισπῖνα)

Αἴσωπος
Thrace:
—byzantion (territ.): (1) imp. Unp. (Sayar) (Ἐσο-: f. Διοκλῆς); (2) ib. (Ἐ-: f. Διογένης)
—lysimacheia: (3) m. ii bc *ISestos* 38 b, 3 (s. Θεογένης)

Αἰτερνιανή
Thrace:
—perinthos-herakleia: (1) i-ii ad *IPerinth* 89 (threpte)

Αἰφνίδιος
Cimmerian Bosporos:
—myrmekion (nr.): (1) ii ad *CIRB* 894 (Οὐεργίλιος Ἀ.)

Ἀκακία
Sarmatia:
—maiotai: (1) i bc *ILind* 683

Ἀκάκιος
Macedonia (Mygdonia):
—thessalonike: (1) iii ad *IG* x (2) (1) 546, 2 (Φλ. Πάκτωλος ὁ καὶ Ἀ.: f. Αὐρ. Ἀκάκις ὁ καὶ Εὐτύχις, Αὐρ. Λεόντις); (2) m. iii ad ib. 199, 1
Thrace:
—perinthos-herakleia:
——(φυλ. ἑβδομ.): (3) iv-v ad *IPerinth* 176 (*AD* 51-2 (1996-7) Mel. p. 353 no. 177) (Αὐ(ρ.) Ἀ.)

Ἀκάκις
Macedonia (Bottiaia):
—beroia*: (1) iii ad *Makedonika* 14 (1974) p. 173 (ring)
Macedonia (Mygdonia):
—thessalonike: (2) iii ad *IG* x (2) (1) 546, 1 (Αὐρ. Ἀ. ὁ καὶ Εὐτύχις: s. Φλ. Πάκτωλος ὁ καὶ Ἀκάκιος)

Ἀκάμας
Thrace:
—odessos: (1) v/iv bc *IGB* I^2 101 (f. Πρωταγόρης)

Ἄκανθος
Macedonia (Bottiaia):
—beroia: (1) ii/iii ad *IBer* 27 B, 2 (slave?)

Ἀκάσας
Cimmerian Bosporos:
—gorgippia: (1) s. ii ad *CIRB* 1142, 12-13; Zgusta, *PNS* 46 (f. Γοσήτλεις, —ας)

Ἄκαστος
Macedonia (Eordaia):
—pyrgoi (mod.): (1) ii-iii ad *EAM* 130 (Φλ. Ἀ.)
Thrace:
—oescus: (2) imp. *ILB* 27 (Lat. Acastus)

Ἀκέραιος
Macedonia (Mygdonia):
—thessalonike: (1) 161 ad *IG* x (2) (1) 573 bis

Ἀκέρσης
Macedonia (Paionia):
—stoboi*: (1) ii ad *Municipium Stobensium* p. 44 no. 187 (lamp) (Ἀκέρσου (gen.))

Ἀκεσαῖος
Thrace:
—apollonia-sozopolis: (1) s. v bc *IGB* I^2 425 (f. Ἀναξαγόρη)

Ἀκέσανδρος
Macedonia: (1) 246 bc *BGU* 1463, 1, 3-4, 7, etc. (Tataki, *Macedonians* p. 226 no. 51; La'da E1393) (s. Νικάνωρ)
Thrace:
—perinthos-herakleia:
——(Aigikoreis): (2) iii-ii bc *IPerinth* 61, 52 (s. Ἀρτεμίδωρος)

Ἄκεσις
Scythia Minor:
—tomis: (1) hell. Unp. (Avram) (Ἀκέσεως (gen.): f. Ποσειδώνιος)

Ἀκεστορίδης
Macedonia (Pieria):
—dion: (1) iii bc *SEG* xxxi 629 note (Ἀκεστορ[ίδης]?, Ἀκέστορ[ος]? (gen.))

Ἄκεστος
Thrace:
—maroneia: (1) c. 230-200 bc *BCH* 45 (1921) p. 18 III, 91 (Ἀκεστο[ς]: s. Διονυσάς)

Ἀκέστωρ
Scythia Minor:
—istros: (1) iii-ii bc Unp. (Avram, defixio) 4, 9
Thrace:
—maroneia: (2) ii-i bc *IThrakAig* E212, 30 (s. Σωτήριχος); (3) ib. E331 (Ἀκέστ[ωρ]); (4) i bc *SEG* xlvii 1070 (*IThrakAig* E200) (s. Ἀθ—)

Ἀκή
Macedonia (Bottiaia):
—beroia: (1) ii ad *IBer* 489 (Tataki 91)

Ἄκης
Kolchis:
—kolchis: (1) iii/ii bc *VDI* 1948 (2), pp. 135-41 (coins); Braund, *Georgia* p. 145 (Ἄκου (gen.): king)

Ἀκίνδυνος
Thrace:
—markianopolis (territ.): (1) ii-iii ad *IGB* ii 857 (Ἀκίνδυν[ος]: f. Φλ. Στίλας)

Ἀκίς
Cimmerian Bosporos:
—bosporos?: (1) inc. *Ellinizm* p. 289
—hermonassa: (2) 389-349 bc *CIRB* 1037; (3) s. iv bc ib. 1041 ([Ἀ]κίς: d. Παιρισάδης)
Tauris:
—chersonesos: (4) iv/iii bc *IOSPE* I^2 504 (d. Γέρων)

Ἀκίτιος
THRACE:
—PAUTALIA: (1) ii-iii AD *IGB* IV 2089, 1

Ἄκκα
THRACE:
—BYZANTION: (1) f. iii AD *IByz* 308 (d. *Εὔτυχος*)
——(Rhegion): (2) ?ii BC ib. 17 (d. *Ἀπολλώνιος*)

Ἀκκᾶς
CIMMERIAN BOSPOROS:
—MYRMEKION: (1) iv BC *CIRB* 871; Zgusta, *PNS* 46 (s. *Ἀθαφοῖος*)
—NYMPHAION: (2) iii BC *CIRB* 912 I, 11 (s. *Θάβων*)
—PANTIKAPAION: (3) i AD ib. 347 (f. *Ἀπολλώνιος*, *Παιρίσαλος*); (4) i/ii AD ib. 608 (f. *Ἥσυχος*)
SCYTHIA MINOR:
—ISTROS: (5) f. iii AD *Stud. Fischer* p. 32 no. 4, 9 (*Ἀκ⟨κ⟩ᾶ*? (gen.): f. *Χρύσανθος*)

Ἄκκης
MACEDONIA (MYGDONIA):
—APOLLONIA: (1) s. iii BC *AEMTh* 14 (2000) p. 276 (s. *Παρμενίσκος*)

Ἀκκόλεια
MACEDONIA (EDONIS):
—AMPHIPOLIS?: (1) imp. *SEG* XXIV 608 (-λη*α*: d. *Μᾶρκος*)

Ἀκλάνιος
THRACE:
—PAUTALIA: (1) 135 AD *IGB* IV 2057, 9 (*Ἀκλάν[ι]ος*: s. *Φίρμος*)

Ἀκμαῖος
MACEDONIA (EDONIS):
—PHILIPPOI (TERRIT.): (1) ?iii AD *SEG* XXX 594 A, 4 (Pilhofer 580)
—PHILIPPOI (NR.): (2) ?ii AD *CIL* III 14206. 13 (*BCH* 47 (1923) p. 77 no. 36; Pilhofer 451) (Lat. Atiar[i]us Acmeus)

Ἀκοίνιος
MACEDONIA (PAIONIA):
—STOBOI: (1) imp. *Robinson Bequest* 408 (*Φίλος Ἀ.*: s. *Γάϊος*)

Ἀκονία
THRACE:
—MARONEIA: (1) i BC-i AD *BCH* 37 (1913) p. 144 no. 49, 4 (*IThrakAig* E286) (d. *Πλουτογένης*, m. *Ἱέρων*, *Νικίας*, *Διονύσιος*)

Ἀκορνίων
SCYTHIA MINOR:
—TOMIS: (1) ii AD *ISM* II 125, 14 (s. *Λυσίμαχος*)
THRACE:
—DIONYSOPOLIS: (2) hell. *Spink Num. Circular* 105 (1997) p. 372 no. 16; p. 374 no. 30 (coin) (*Ἀκορν(ίων)*?); (3) c. 48 BC *IGB* I² 13, 44 (s. *Διονύσιος*)

Ἀκουσίλαος
MACEDONIA: (1) 74 BC *SB* 7532, 24, 37 (Tataki, *Macedonians* p. 471 no. 6; La'da E1395) (s. *Στράτων*); (2) 51-20 BC *PTeb* 382, 36; *PSI* 1098, 39 (Tataki, *Macedonians* p. 471 no. 5; La'da E1394) (s. *Μάρων*); (3) s. i BC *PTeb* 382, 2, 17, 19 (*PP* 9073; Tataki, *Macedonians* p. 471 no. 7) (I f. *Ἀκουσίλαος* II, *Ἡρακλῆς*); (4) *PTeb* 382, 3, 8, 10, etc. (*PP* 9074; Tataki, *Macedonians* p. 471 no. 4) (II s. *Ἀκουσίλαος* I); (5) 46 AD *PMich* 273, 1; *PSI* 906, 1 (f. *Μυσθᾶς*)
MACEDONIA (MYGDONIA):
—THESSALONIKE: (6) ii-iii AD *IG* X (2) (1) 627 (*Ἰούλ. Μάρκιος Ἀ.*)
MACEDONIA?: (7) 4 BC *SB* 11274, 3 (Tataki, *Macedonians* p. 472 no. 8) (*Ἀ̣κ̣ο̣υ̣σ̣ί̣λ̣α̣ο̣ς̣*?: f. *Πατερμουθίων*)

Ἀκουσίλας
CIMMERIAN BOSPOROS:
—PANTIKAPAION: (1) iii BC *CIRB* 110, 2

Ἀκουσίλεως
CIMMERIAN BOSPOROS:
—NYMPHAION: (1) iii BC ib. 912 II, 9 (f. *Πάραλος*); (2) ib. 912 III, 10 (*Ἀκουσίλ[εως]*)
THRACE:
—APOLLONIA-SOZOPOLIS: (3) iv BC *Apoloniia* p. 336 no. 1209; Imhoof-Blümer, *MGr* p. 237 (coin)

Ἀκουτας
THRACE:
—NICOPOLIS AD NESTUM: (1) ii-iii AD *IGB* IV 2347 (*Ἀκούτα*? (fem.): ?s. *Πύρρος*)

Ἀκοῖτος
MACEDONIA (ODOMANTIKE):
—SIRRHA?: (1) 136 AD *SEG* XXX 598, 5 (?s. *Ἀνίκητος*)
THRACE:
—MARONEIA: (2) ii-i BC *IThrakAig* E212, 50 (s. *Ἐπίγονος*)

Ἄκρατος
CIMMERIAN BOSPOROS:
—PANTIKAPAION: (1) 133 AD *CIRB* 675, 3 (*Ἄκρ[α]τ[ος]*: f. *Διογένεια*)
MACEDONIA (MYGDONIA):
—THESSALONIKE: (2) ii/iii AD *IG* X (2) (1) 262 I, 8

Ἀκρόπολις
MACEDONIA (BOTTIAIA):
—PELLA: (1) imp. *ILGR* 201 (Lat. Fulvia Acropolis)

Ἀκροσας
SCYTHIA MINOR: (1) ii BC *SCIV* 1.1 (1950) pp. 245-7 nos. 27-32; *SNG Stancomb* 317-19 (coin) (*Ἄκροσα* (gen.): king)

Ἀκροτίμη
CIMMERIAN BOSPOROS:
—NYMPHAION: (1) iv BC *CIRB* 917 (*Ἀ[κρ]οτίμη*?: d. *Ἀνδρομήδης*)

Ἀκρωθίς
CIMMERIAN BOSPOROS:
—PANTIKAPAION: (1) f. iv BC ib. 227 (d. *Ἴξις*)

Ἀκτή
MACEDONIA (BOTTIAIA):
—BEROIA: (1) f. ii AD *IBer* 348 (Tataki 93) (d. *Σύνετος*, *Φωτίς*)
MACEDONIA (EDONIS):
—PHILIPPOI (TERRIT.): (2) imp. *CIL* III 706 (Pilhofer 523); Collart, *Philippes* pl. 84. 1 (Lat. Atiaria Acte)

Ἀκτιαῖος
CIMMERIAN BOSPOROS:
—PANTIKAPAION: (1) ii-i BC Tolstoi 156 (vase)

Ἀκτιγαῖος
SKYTHIA:
—OLBIA-BORYSTHENES*: (1) c. 425-400 BC Dubois, *IGDOlbia* 30 (vase)

Ἄκτιος
THRACE:
—ODESSOS: (1) 215 AD *IGB* I² 47 a, 15 (*Αὐρ. Ἀ.*: s. *Εὐέλπιστος*)
—PHILIPPOPOLIS-TRIMONTIUM:
——(Artemisias): (2) c. 163-164 AD ib. III 903; V 5433 (s. *Μάξιμος*)

Ἄκυλα
MACEDONIA (MYGDONIA):
—THESSALONIKE: (1) iii AD *IG* X (2) (1) 476 C (*Ἀ. ἡ καὶ Πωριανή*: d. *Ἀσκληπιάδης*)

Ἀκύλας
MACEDONIA (BOTTIAIA):
—AIGAI: (1) s. iv BC *SEG* XXXV 787 (f. *Κλεώνυμος*)
—EDESSA: (2) 180 AD ib. XXIV 531, 16 (Tataki, *Edessa* 13) (s. *Ἰούλιος*)
MACEDONIA (MYGDONIA):
—THESSALONIKE?: (3) ?ii AD *IG* X (2) (1) 935
SCYTHIA MINOR:
—KALLATIS (NR.): (4) ii-iii AD *ISM* III 243, 7 (*IGB* I² 2) (s. *Σαβῖνα*)
—TOMIS: (5) i-ii AD *ISM* II 174 (*GVI* 1813)
TAURIS:
—CHERSONESOS: (6) c. 120-130 AD Solomonik, *NEPKh* 112, 21 (f. *Ἰουλιανός*)
THRACE:
—ANCHIALOS (TERRIT.)?: (7) iii AD *Arkheologiia* (Sofia) 1988 (3), p. 44 fig. 10 (s. *Ἐπταίκενθος*)
—KELLAI: (8) ii-iii AD *IGB* III 1527 (*Eastern cults* p. 235 no. 26)
—NICOPOLIS AD ISTRUM: (9) ii-iii AD *IGB* II 672 (f. *Πείσων*)
—PIZOS: (10) 202 AD ib. III 1690 e, 12 (f. *Ἀρχέλαος*); (11) ib. l. 16 (f. *Μουκιανός*)

Ἀκυλῖνα
MACEDONIA (BOTTIAIA):
—EDESSA: (1) v-vi AD Feissel, *RICM* 23
THRACE:
—BEROE-AUGUSTA TRAIANA: (2) c. 320-324 AD *Anal. Boll.* 31 (1912) p. 198; p. 208

Ἀκυλῖνος
MACEDONIA (MYGDONIA):
—THESSALONIKE: (1) m. iii AD *IG* X (2) (1) 210, 10; 211, 10 (-λεῖ-)
SCYTHIA MINOR:
—TOMIS: (2) ii-iii AD *ISM* II 121 (-λεῖ-: s. *Ἀρτεμίδωρος*)
THRACE:
—NICOPOLIS AD ISTRUM (TERRIT.): (3) s. ii AD *IGB* II 722 (*Eastern cults* p. 75 no. 6) (-λεῖ-: s. *Πόπλιος*)

Ἀκύλλης
SCYTHIA MINOR:
—KALLATIS: (1) iv BC *ISM* III 154 (s. *Σάτυρος*)
SKYTHIA:
—OLBIA-BORYSTHENES: (2) iv BC *SEG* XXX 958 (vase) (*Ἀκύλ(λης)*?)

Ἀλβούτιος
MACEDONIA (EDONIS):
—PHILIPPOI: (1) ?ii AD *FGrH* 257 F 37. 49 (Tataki, *Macedonians* p. 163 no. 2) (f. *Φρόντων*)

Ἀλγεμας?
THRACE:
—SALYMBRIA: (1) imp. *Archives Stamoulis* d. 35 (Loukopoulou, *Thrace Propontique* p. 230)

Ἄλδις
CIMMERIAN BOSPOROS:
—PANTIKAPAION: (1) iv BC *CIRB* 229; Zgusta, *PNS* 47 (?f. *Φιάτακος*)

Ἀλεκτρύων
MACEDONIA: (1) 353 BC *RE* s.v. Adaios (1) (*Ἀδαῖος ὁ ἐπικαλ. Ἀ.*)

Ἀλεξάνδρα
MACEDONIA: (1) 309 or 311 AD *ILeukopetra* 116, 6 (m. *Αὐρηλία*: slave)
MACEDONIA (BOTTIAIA):
—BEROIA: (2) ?ii AD *IBer* 48, 1 (Tataki 96) (*[Ἀλε]ξάνδρα*); (3) ii-iii AD *IBer* 319 (*Κλ. Ἀ.*); (4) 113 AD *ISamothrace* 47, 6 (Tataki, *Macedonians* p. 81 no. 42) (*Οὐλπ. Ἀ.*); (5) s. ii AD *IBer* 497 C (Tataki 101a); (6) f. iii AD *IBer* 78,

12 (Tataki 776) (Κυϊντιανὴ Ἀ.: d. Π. Μεμ. Κυϊντιανὸς Καπίτων, Ἰουλ. Λυσιμάχη); (7) IBer 354 (Tataki 97); (8) 238 AD ILeukopetra 90, 1 (Ὠλία Ἀ.); (9) a. 249 AD IBer 109, 6 (Tataki 270) (Λ. Αὐρηλιανὴ Ἀ.: d. Λ. Αὐρηλιανὸς Σωτήριχος)
——Blaganoi*: (10) 189 AD SEG XXXVII 590, 4 (Tataki 102) (d. Φοῦσκος)
—BEROIA*: (11) ii AD IBer 380 (Tataki 98)
—EDESSA: (12) ii-iii AD Robert, Gladiateurs p. 84 no. 20 (Tataki, Edessa 16); (13) iii AD Arch. Pap. 22 (1973) p. 204 no. 3 (Tataki, Edessa 14); (14) v-vi AD Feissel, RICM 38 (d. Ἀλέξανδρος, Σαμβάτα)
—ICHNAI?: (15) 172 AD Dimitsas 147, 1 (Κορνηλία Ἀ.: m. Φάβιος Κορνήλιος Δημήτριος, Φάβιος Κορνήλιος Ἄπερ)
—PELLA*: (16) ?iii AD Sp. 98 (1941-8) p. 170 no. 354, 5-6 (Pella 262) (Ἀ[λε]ξάνδρα: d. Ζ—, Κασσάνδρα)
MACEDONIA (CHALKIDIKE):
—GIGONOS?: (17) ii AD SEG XLVIII 799 (Ἀλεξάνδρ[α]: m. Ἀλέξανδρος, —μέων)
MACEDONIA (EDONIS):
—PHILIPPOI: (18) v-vi AD Feissel, RICM 244 (Pilhofer 275) (Ἀλεξά(ν)δρα)
—PHILIPPOI?: (19) v-vi AD Feissel, RICM 181 (Pilhofer 743a)
MACEDONIA (ELIMEIA):
—OBLOSTAI: (20) 200 AD EAM 37, 2
MACEDONIA (LYNKESTIS):
—HERAKLEIA?: (21) i-ii AD IG X (2) (2) 122 ([Π]ουλία Ἀ.: d. Ἀλέξανδρος, m. Γ. Ἰούλ. Ἀλέξανδρος)
MACEDONIA (MYGDONIA):
—KALINDOIA: (22) 254 AD SEG XLII 604, 3; cf. Anthémonte–Kalindoia 2 p. 372 (?d. Αὐρ. Τρόπος, Πολυκαρπία)
—LETE: (23) ii BC SEG XLIV 536 (d. Ἀργαῖος)
—THESSALONIKE: (24) ii AD IG X (2) (1) 588 (d. Νικάνωρ); (25) iii AD ib. 518 bis (Αὐρ. Ἀ.); (26) f. iii AD ib. 201, 2; 202, 2; 203, 2; IBer 69, 8 (Tataki 43) (or Macedonia (Bottiaia) Beroia?: Αἰλ. Ἀ.: d. Αἰλ. Κατίνιος Λέων); (27) SEG XLVIII 854 (m. Σαβῖνα); (28) a. 212 AD IG X (2) (1) 609, 2 (Αὐρ. Ἀ.: d. Αὐρ. Ματρώνα); (29) m. iii AD ib. 210, 8; 211, 9 (Τυλλία Ἀ.); (30) 253 AD ib. 167, 14; p. 88 (stemma) (Στατειλία Ἀ.: d. Αὐρ. Ἰσιδώρα, m. Δομίτιος Στατίλιος Διονύσιος); (31) 261 AD ib. 200, 8, 11 (Οὐαλερία Ἀ.: m. Ποντία Ζωσίμη); (32) f. iv AD ib. 551 (Feissel, RICM 116) (Αἰλ. Ἀ.); (33) v-vi AD ib. 181, 4 (SEG XLVII 1011) (?m. Φλαβία); (34) IG X (2) (1) 404 (Feissel, RICM 169) (Ἀλεξά(ν)δρα: m. Ἀνδρέας)
MACEDONIA (ODOMANTIKE):
—SKOTOUSSA?: (35) ii-iii AD Dimitsas 843 (d. Ἀλέξανδρος, Σελήνη)
MACEDONIA (PAIONIA):
—KAVADARCI (MOD.): (36) ii-iii AD Sp. 71 (1931) p. 67 no. 150 (d. Ἀλέξανδρος); (37) ib. 98 (1941-8) p. 63 no. 132
—NEGOTINO (MOD.): (38) ii-iii AD ib. p. 56 no. 114, 15
—STOBOI: (39) f. iii AD AJA 88 (1984) pp. 567 ff.; cf. SEG XXXIV 678 I, 1; 678 II, 5-6; IG X (2) (2) 333 (stemma) (Γρανία Ἀ.: m. Π. Σέντιος Νικόλαος Σεπτίμιος)
MACEDONIA (PELAGONIA): (40) iii AD ib. 188, 5 (d. Ζωΐλος, Κασσάνδρα)
—DOSTONEIS?: (41) iii AD ib. 206 (m. Αὐρ. Κλαύδιος)
—KERAMIAI (NR.): (42) ii AD ib. 217, 2 (Ἀλ[εξά]νδρα: d. Παράμονος, m. —νος, —κη, —μάχη)
MACEDONIA (PIERIA):
—DION: (43) i-ii AD SEG XXXIV 633 (Ἰουλ. Φρουγιανὴ Ἀ.); (44) ii-iii AD Oikonomos 24 + Essays Laourdas p. 105 ([Κ]λαυδία Ἀλε[ξά]νδρα); (45) ?ii-iii AD Oikonomos 26; (46) ii/iii AD SEG XXXIX 582 (Κλωδία Ἀ.: m. Ποστούμιος Ἀμμιανός)
—DION?: (47) s. ii AD Spiliopoulou-Donderer, KGN pp. 200-1 no. D18
SCYTHIA MINOR:
—KALLATIS?: (48) ii AD ISM V 280, 2 (I 275); cf. ISM III p. 140 (locn.)
—NOVIODUNUM*: (49) ii-iii AD ib. V 276, 3 (Lat. Fl. Alexandra)
THRACE:
—ABDERA: (50) iii AD SEG XXIV 628 (IThrakAig E71) (Αὐρ. Ἀ.: m. Λούκιλλα)
—APPIARIA: (51) f. iii AD CIL III 12452 (Romanizmŭt II 87; Dimitrov p. 23 no. 4) (Lat. Corne. Alex(a)ndra)
—BURDIPTA?: (52) ii-iii AD IGB III 1889 (-άδρα: d. Μυστικός, Σωσάνδρα)
—BYZANTION: (53) c. 238-244 AD Schönert-Geiss, Byzantion 1797-1805 (coin) (Π. Ἀ.)
—DUROSTORUM: (54) imp. AEp 1936, no. 13 (Lat. Alexan[dr]a)
—MARONEIA: (55) v-vi AD SEG XLIX 892, 5 (IThrakAig E357)
—SALYMBRIA: (56) v-vi AD IPerinth 224 (AD 53 (1998) Mel. p. 471 no. 209) (m. Ἀγαθονίκη, Ἰσίδωρος, Ἰωάννης)

Ἀλεξάνδρεια
CIMMERIAN BOSPOROS:
—PANTIKAPAION: (1) ii/i BC CIRB 265; cf. KW pl. 29 no. 417 (-δρια: d. Ὀρόντης); (2) i BC CIRB 269 (-δρεα: d. Ἥδυν, m. Ἀπολλώνιος)
SCYTHIA MINOR:
—TOMIS: (3) v-vi AD Barnea 22 (Popescu, IGL 43) (Lat. Alaxandria)
—ULMETUM: (4) ?v AD Barnea 73, 7 (Popescu, IGL 210) (-δρία: d. Ἀσκληπιάδης, Ἀμμιάς)
THRACE:
—BYZANTION: (5) m. iii AD IByz 307 (Fıratlı-Robert p. 118 no. 198) (d. Ἀλέξανδρος, m. Ἀλέξανδρος)

Ἀλεξανδρία
MACEDONIA (PAIONIA):
—KAVADARCI (MOD.): (1) iii AD Dimitsas 285 (Αὐρηλία Ἀ.: m. Δαλτιανή)

Ἀλέξανδρος
CIMMERIAN BOSPOROS:
—ACHILLEION: (1) f. ii AD CIRB 1028 (s. Ἀπολλόδωρος)
—GORGIPPIA: (2) imp. ib. 1187, 3 ([Ἀλέ]ξανδρος: s. Κ—); (3) ii/iii AD ib. 1179, 16 ([Ἀλέ]ξανδρος); (4) ib. l. 19 (f. —ος)
—GORGIPPIA?: (5) 227-233 AD ib. 1230, 1 ([Ἀλ]έξανδρος: s. Νουμήνιος)
—MYRMEKION: (6) m. i AD ib. 881
—NYMPHAION: (7) f. v BC SEG XLIX 1038 (Bosporskii fenomen p. 187 no. 2) (f. Μολπόθεμις)
—PANTIKAPAION: (8) imp. CIRB 779 (s. Ἔρως); (9) ib. 780 (s. Ἔρως); (10) ibc/iad ib. 141, 2 (GVI 949); cf. KW pl. 14 no. 201 (f. Χρήστη); (11) i BC/i AD CIRB 316 (s. Στέφανος); (12) ib. 325; cf. KW pl. 38 no. 551 (s. Ἔρως); (13) i AD CIRB 474; (14) i/ii AD ib. 591 (f. Γάϊος); (15) ib. 615; cf. KW pl. 29 no. 423 (f. Κόναρος, Κοσσᾶς); (16) CIRB 649; cf. KW pl. 19 no. 276 (f. Πρώτη); (17) 275-278 AD CIRB 36, 28 (I f. Ἀλέξανδρος II); (18) ib. l. 28 (II s. Ἀλέξανδρος I); (19) ib. l. 40 (Ἀλέξαν(δρος): f. Ἀντισθένης)
—PHANAGOREIA: (20) 151 AD ib. 976, 10 (s. Μυρῖνος)
—THEODOSIA: (21) iv AD ib. 951 (s. Φαρνάκης)
MACEDONIA: (22) c. 525-452 BC RE (8); IG I³ 89, 60-1; Raymond, MRC pp. 78-85; 100-7; 126-9 (coin) (Tataki, Macedonians p. 227 no. 55) (Ἀ. I: s. Ἀμύντας I, f. Φίλιππος, Ἀλκέτας, Περδίκκας II, Μενέλαος, Ἀμύντας, Στρατονίκη: king); (23) ?417-413 BC IG I³ 89, 62 (Tataki, Macedonians p. 230 no. 73) ([Ἀλέ]χσανδρος: s. Παντάπονος); (24) c. 413 BC Pl., Gorg. 471 b (s. Ἀλκέτας); (25) iv BC IEph 1419 (Tataki, Macedonians p. 229 no. 68) (s. Ἀμύντας) ?= (115); (26) c. 392-368 BC RE (9); Tod, GHI II 129, [2], 21; Kraay-Mørkholm Essays pp. 308; 313 (coin) (Tataki, Macedonians p. 229 no. 67); cf. Macedonia 2 pp. 180-2 (Ἀ. II: s. Ἀμύντας III, Εὐρυδίκα: king); (27) 356-323 BC RE (10) (Tataki, Macedonians p. 227 no. 56) (Ἀ. III Μέγας: s. Φίλιππος II, Ὀλυμπιάς (Molossoi), f. Ἡρακλῆς, Ἀλέξανδρος: king); (28) 327 BC RE Supplbd. 4 (34e); Berve 40 (Tataki, Macedonians p. 228 no. 63) (Lat. Alexander: fict.?); (29) 323-311 BC RE (11) (Tataki, Macedonians p. 227 no. 57) (s. Ἀλέξανδρος III Μέγας, Ῥωξάνη (Baktria)); (30) hell. IG IX (2) 1186 (Tataki, Macedonians p. 231 no. 77) (f. Ματερώ); (31) c. 315-294 BC RE (14) (Tataki, Macedonians p. 229 no. 71) (s. Κάσσανδρος, Θεσσαλονίκη); (32) 304 BC RE (21); FGrH 533 F 2, 35, 47 (Tataki, Macedonians p. 227 no. 60); (33) iii-ii BC SEG XXVI 1770 (Tataki, Macedonians p. 230 no. 74; La'da E1396) (s. Περιγένης); (34) f. iii BC FGrH 260 F 32. 8; IMagnSip 1, 101; ITrall 25, 4; IIasos 608, 47; Grainger, SPG p. 75 (s. Ἀχαιός); (35) Plu., Demetr. 53 (Tataki, Macedonians p. 227 no. 59) (s. Δημήτριος I Πολιορκητής, Δηϊδάμεια (Molossoi)); (36) IG XII (6) 119, 2 (Tataki, Macedonians p. 231 no. 78) (f. Πέλοψ); (37) c. 295-244 BC RE (15); Eretria XI p. 344 no. XXV, 4 (Tataki, Macedonians p. 230 no. 72) (s. Κράτερος: king); (38) 281 BC Robert, Documents p. 53, 7 (Tataki, Macedonians p. 231 no. 79) (Ἀλέξα[νδρο]ς: f. Φίλιππος); (39) c. 278-276 BC D.S. xxii 4 (Tataki, Macedonians p. 229 no. 69); (40) c. 250 BC IG XII (9) 212, 2; cf. SEG XLIII 591; Ancient Macedonia 6 pp. 609-10 (date) (Tataki, Macedonians p. 231 no. 76) (f. Ἀρριδαῖος); (41) s. iii BC RE (18); (42) c. 245-223 BC ib. s.v. Seleukos (5); Grainger, SPG p. 63 (Ἀ. (ὕστερον) Σέλευκος III Σωτήρ: s. Σέλευκος II Καλλίνικος, Λαοδίκη: king); (43) ?238 BC IG IX (1)² (1) 56 g (PP 14479); cf. ZPE 138 (2001) p. 145 (date) (Ἀλέ[ξαν]δρος: s. Πτολεμαῖος III Εὐεργέτης, Βερενίκη); (44) 232 or 207 BC CPR XVIII 15, 319, 325 (Tataki, Macedonians p. 228 no. 64; La'da E1398); (45) iii/ii BC RE (34); IG XI (4) 750, 3 (Tataki, Macedonians p. 228 no. 62) (and Arkadia Megalopolis: I s. Φίλιππος, f. Φίλιππος, Ἀλέξανδρος II, Ἀπάμα); (46) m. ii BC RE (16); SEG XLVI 829, [1] (Tataki, Macedonians p. 227 no. 58); cf. Beloch, GG IV (2) pp. 141-2 (s. Περσεύς, Λαοδίκη); (47) ?161 BC SGDI 1720, 3-4, 7, 9 (Tataki, Macedonians p. 228 no. 66) (slave/freed.); (48) 148 BC PTeb 99, 45 (Tataki, Macedonians p. 472 no. 12); cf. La'da E1478 (f. Διοσκουρίδης); (49) c. 140-88 BC RE s.v. Ptolemaios (31) (Πτολεμαῖος X Ἀ.: s. Πτολεμαῖος VIII Εὐεργέτης, Κλεοπάτρα III, f. Πτολεμαῖος XI Ἀλέξανδρος); (50) c. 105-80 BC ib. s.v. Ptolemaios (32) (Πτολεμαῖος XI Ἀ.: s. Πτολεμαῖος X Ἀλέξανδρος); (51) c. 100-75 BC SB 8974 fr. 3, 44 (Tataki, Macedonians p. 472 no. 10; La'da E1397) (s. Πτολεμαῖος); (52) c. 40-30 BC RE (28) (PP 14482) (Ἀ. Ἥλιος: s. M. Antonius (Rome), Κλεοπάτρα VII Φιλοπάτωρ); (53) 19 BC POxy 277, 1 (Tataki, Macedonians p. 472 no. 11) (f. Διονύσιος); (54) 16-12 BC BGU 1132, 2, 4; 1151 I, 4-5, 7-8, 13, 16, 19 (Tataki, Macedonians p. 472 no. 9) (s. Νικόδημος); (55) ii AD CIL III 6592 (ILS 2345); Breccia, Iscriz. 480 (Lat. Aurel. Alexandrus); (56) ii-iii AD IGB I² 319, 6 (Tataki, Macedonians p. 226 no. 54) (Ἀλέξανδ[ρος]); (57) 138 AD SEG XXXVII 593, 16 (Ἀττιανὸς Ἀ.)
—ERKEIA?: (58) c. 220-200 BC Helly, Gonnoi 93 B, 27; cf. Lucas, Vall. Titarèse pp. 83-4 no. 36 (Tataki, Macedonians p. 112 no. 1) (resid.

Thessaly (Perrhaibia) Azoros: s. *Δράκων*)
MACEDONIA?:
—RESEN (MOD.): **(59)** s. iii AD *IG* X (2) (2) 50 (or Illyria Dassaretioi?: s. *Ἀπολλόδωρος*, f. *Οὐαλέριος*)
MACEDONIA (ALMOPIA):
—NEROMYLOI (MOD.): **(60)** imp. *SEG* XLVII 918 (f. *Κασσάνδρα*)
MACEDONIA (BISALTIA):
—EUPORIA: **(61)** s. i AD *IBer* 121, 8; 299, 2 (Tataki, *Macedonians* p. 107 no. 1) (s. *Ἀπολλόδωρος*)
—TERPNI (MOD.): **(62)** ii-iii AD *SEG* XXXI 639 (*Π. Αἴλ. Κλαρανὸς Ἀ.*)
MACEDONIA (BOTTIAIA):
—AIGAI: **(63)** m. vi AD ib. XXXIX 639 = XLIV 564 (mosaic)
—AIGAI?: **(64)** i AD *RE* (92) (Tataki, *Macedonians* p. 39 no. 3)
—BEROIA: **(65)** hell. *AD* 32 (1977) Chron. p. 227 (vase) (Tataki 104) ([*Ἀλ*]*έξανδ*[*ρος*]); **(66)** c. 288-262 BC *IG* II² 710, 6 (Osborne, *Naturalization* D81; Tataki 119; Tataki, *Macedonians* p. 74 no. 7) (s. *Μυλλέας*); **(67)** 223 BC *IBer* 4, 13 (f. *Νικάνωρ*); **(68)** ib. l. 15 (f. *Εὐθύνους*); **(69)** ib. l. 18 (f. *Ζωΐλος*); **(70)** ii BC ib. 141, 45; **(71)** ib. 159 (Tataki 125) + Tataki 128 (f. *Ζωΐλος*, *Γλυκιννώ*); **(72)** *IBer* 178 (f. *Κλήτα*); **(73)** ii-i BC ib. 204 (Tataki 129) (f. *Ἱππόστρατος*); **(74)** 180 BC Liv. xl 24. 7 (Tataki 103; Tataki, *Macedonians* p. 74 no. 6) (Lat. Alexander); **(75)** f. i BC *IBer* 162; **(76)** imp. *ILeukopetra* 165 (*Γ. Ἰούλ. Ἀλέξαν*[*δρος*]); **(77)** i AD *IBer* 125, 6 (Tataki 132)(f. *Τύραννος*); **(78)** *IBer* 189 (*Ἀ*(*λ*)*έξανδρος*: f. *Φιλωτέρα*); **(79)** f. i AD ib. 103, 4 (Tataki 117) (s. *Θεόφιλος*); **(80)** *IBer* 103, 4 (Tataki 122) (s. *Φιλοκράτης*); **(81)** *IBer* 103, 8 (Tataki 127) (*Ἀλέ*(*ξ*)*ανδρος*: f. *Δίων*); **(82)** s. i AD *IBer* 117, 26 (Tataki 126) (f. *Διοσκουρίδης*); **(83)** ii-iii AD *IBer* 28; **(84)** ib. (Tataki 120) (s. *Νικόλαος*); **(85)** f. ii AD *IBer* 119, 2 (*Πλαυτ*[*ι*]*ανὸς Ἀλέ*[*ξανδρος*]?); **(86)** ii/iii AD ib. 27 A, 8 (slave?); **(87)** ib. 143 A, 5 (Tataki 118) (s. *Λεύκων*); **(88)** *IBer* 143 A, 6 (Tataki 123) (f. *Ἀγαθήμερος*); **(89)** *IBer* 143 A, 7 (Tataki 121) (s. *Τράλιος*); **(90)** *IBer* 143 B, 30 (Tataki 130) (f. *Λυκολέων*); **(91)** *IBer* 144 B, 10 (Tataki 1150) (*Ῥεφριανὸς Ἀ.*); **(92)** 177 AD *IBer* 81, 4 (Tataki 1227) (*Τερεντιανὸς Ἀ.*); **(93)** 187-194 AD *ILeukopetra* 41, 2 (Tataki 275) (*Μ. Αὐρ. Ἀλέξαδρος*); **(94)** 191 AD *ILeukopetra* 25, 1 (Tataki 116) ([*Ἀ*]*λέξανδρος*: s. *Ἡρακλείδης*); **(95)** 193 AD *ILeukopetra* 38, 1 (Tataki 131) (f. *Τιτιανή*); **(96)** a. 212 AD *IBer* 136, 19 (Tataki 1063) (*Πετρ. Ἀ.*); **(97)** 248 AD *IBer* 54, 2 (*Αὐρ. Ἀ.*: s. *Λυσίμαχος*); **(98)** iv-v AD ib. 455, 6 (Feissel, *RICM* 295); **(99)** 309 or 311 AD *ILeukopetra* 116, 2 (Tataki 124) (*Ἀλέξανδρος*: f. *Αὐρ. Διονυσία*); **(100)** m. iv AD *SEG* XXXV 734 (*Ἀλέξαν*[*δρ*]*ος*)
—BEROIA (TERRIT.): **(101)** ii-iii AD *IBer* 511 (Tataki 107)
—BEROIA (TERRIT.)?: **(102)** ii AD ib. 108
—EDESSA: **(103)** c. 265-260 BC *FD* III (3) 207, 2 (Tataki, *Macedonians* p. 102 no. 2) (s. *Ἀ...ος*); **(104)** f. i BC *SEG* XL 537 (Tataki, *Edessa* 21) (f. *Ζωΐλος*); **(105)** f. i AD Dimitsas 38 (Tataki, *Edessa* 22) (f. *Χάρης*); **(106)** 180 AD *SEG* XXIV 531, 8 (Tataki, *Edessa* 19) (s. *Μαρκία*); **(107)** *SEG* XXIV 531, 11 (Tataki, *Edessa* 20) (s. *Πάπας*); **(108)** iii AD *AD* 24 (1969) Chron. p. 306 (Tataki, *Edessa* 17); **(109)** 229 AD ib. 49 (*Αὐρ. Ἀ.*); **(110)** 234 AD *SEG* XXIV 534, 2 (Tataki, *Edessa* 48) (*Αὐρ. Ἀ.*); **(111)** v-vi AD Feissel, *RICM* 38 (f. *Ἰωάννης*, *Ἀλεξάνδρα*); **(112)** ib. 45
—GENDERRHOS? (MANDALON (MOD.)): **(113)** ii-iii AD *SEG* XLIII 396 (f. *Ἀμμιανός*)
—KYRRHOS?: **(114)** 199 AD *ILeukopetra* 45, 14 (s. *Πυρρούλας*)
—MIEZA: **(115)** m. iv BC *RE* Supplbd. 4 (34 f) (Tataki, *Macedonians* p. 123 no. 1) (f. *Πευκέστας*, *Ἀμύντας*) ?= (*25*)
—PELLA: **(116)** s. iv BC *Α´ Panell. Synedr. Epigr.* p. 190 no. 11 (*SEG* XXX 581) (f. *Ἀντίγονος*); **(117)** iii-ii BC Dimitsas 131 (f. *Δημοκράτεια*); **(118)** v AD *Eulimeni* 3 (2002) p. 102 no. 2 (doctor)
—PELLA?: **(119)** iv/iii BC *RE* (17); Supplbd. 7 (-) (Tataki, *Macedonians* p. 148 no. 7) (s. *Λυσίμαχος*)
MACEDONIA (CHALKIDIKE):
—AKANTHOS: **(120)** c. 230-200 BC *BCH* 45 (1921) p. 18 III, 86 (Tataki, *Macedonians* p. 42 no. 2) (I f. *Ἀλέξανδρος* II); **(121)** *BCH* 45 (1921) p. 18 III, 86 (Tataki, *Macedonians* p. 41 no. 1) (II s. *Ἀλέξανδρος* I)
—GIGONOS?: **(122)** ii AD *SEG* XLVIII 799 (*Ἀ*[*λέξα*]*νδρος*: s. *Ἀγαθοκλῆς*, *Ἀλεξάνδρα*)
—KOMBREIA: **(123)** 87 AD *IG* X (2) (2) 325, 78 (Tataki, *Macedonians* p. 115 no. 1) (s. *Νικόλαος*)
MACEDONIA (DERRIOPOS):
—STUBERRA: **(124)** 74 AD *IG* X (2) (2) 325, 23 (s. *Ζωΐλος*); **(125)** ib. 326, 33 (f. *Γάϊος*); **(126)** ib. l. 47 (f. *Παράμονος*); **(127)** ib. l. 58 (s. *Ἄνδρων*); **(128)** ib. l. 45-6 (s. *Ἄνδρων*); **(129)** ib. l. 61-2 (f. *Παράμονος*); **(130)** 87 AD ib. 325, 73 (s. *Ζωΐλος*); **(131)** ib. l. 75 (f. *Λύκος*); **(132)** 107 AD ib. l. 96 (s. *Ἀντίγονος*); **(133)** 116 AD ib. 327, 14 (s. *Ὀρέστης*); **(134)** ib. l. 18 (s. *Ἐπιγένης*); **(135)** ib. l. 28 (f. *Νικόλας*)
MACEDONIA (EDONIS):
—AMPHIPOLIS: **(136)** 90 BC *SEG* XLVIII 716 ter, 5 (*Μ. Ἄμπιος Ἀ.*); **(137)** ii-iii AD ib. XXXIX 572 (f. *Θεοδότη*); **(138)** v-vi AD Feissel, *RICM* 216
—AMPHIPOLIS?: **(139)** hell. *SEG* L 562, 7-10 (f. *Σιμωνίδης*, *Μήτριχος*, *Θεσσάλαρχος*, *Μανδρογένης*)
—PHILIPPOI: **(140)** imp. *BCH* 47 (1923) p. 94 no. 30 (Pilhofer 89) (Lat. Alexander: f. Longus); **(141)** i-ii AD *BCH* 58 (1934) p. 474 no. 12 (Pilhofer 313) (Lat. M. Antonius Alexander); **(142)** ?ii AD *BCH* 47 (1923) p. 71 no. 26 (Pilhofer 502) (Lat. T. Flavius Alexander: f. *Μακεδονικός*); **(143)** ?iv-v AD *SEG* XXXIV 670 (Pilhofer 124); **(144)** v-vi AD Feissel, *RICM* 248 (Pilhofer 116)
MACEDONIA (ELIMEIA):
—AIANE (TERRIT.): **(145)** c. 225-200 BC *SEG* XL 526, 3 (f. *Νικάνωρ*)
—ARKYNIA: **(146)** s. iii BC Plb. ii 66. 5; Helly, *Gonnoi* 12, 2, 7; *SEG* XLIII 706, 1, 11, 14 (Tataki, *Macedonians* p. 71 no. 2); cf. *Chiron* 13 (1983) pp. 26-9 (ident.) (s. *Ἄδμητος*)
—OBLOSTAI?: **(147)** ?iii AD *EAM* 65 I b
—PALAIOKASTRO (MOD.): **(148)** ii-iii AD ib. 20, 7 (f. *Ἀντίπατρος*)
—SIATISTA (MOD.): **(149)** ii-iii AD ib. 26, 11 (f. *Πρόκλος*)
—XEROLIMNI (MOD.): **(150)** ii AD *Α´ Panell. Synedr. Epigr.* p. 66 no. 13 (*SEG* XLIX 852)
MACEDONIA (ELIMEIA)?: **(151)** f. ii AD *EAM* 10 (*Ἀ. ὁ καὶ Ῥῆγλος*: s. *Ῥοιμητάλκης*)
MACEDONIA (EORDAIA?):
—EUIA: **(152)** 181 BC ib. 87, 14 (Hatzopoulos, *MI* 2 pp. 41-2 no. 17) (*Ἀλέξαν*[*δρος*]: s. *Προΐτος*); **(153)** *EAM* 87, 15 (Hatzopoulos, *MI* 2 pp. 41-2 no. 17) (*Ἀ*[*λέξαν*]*δρος*: f. *Ἀντίγονος*)
MACEDONIA (EORDAIA):
—AGIOS CHRISTOPHOROS (MOD.): **(154)** ii BC *SEG* XXXIX 594 (s. *Πάτης*)
—ARNISA?: **(155)** 202 AD *EAM* 131; Hatzopoulos, *MI* 1 p. 94 n. 4 (locn.) (f. *Κοπρία*)
—ARNISSA (MOD.): **(156)** iii AD *EAM* 138 (*Σ*[*λι*]*ος Ἀ.*)
—DROSIA (MOD.): **(157)** iv BC ib. 86 (sherd) ([*Ἀλ*]*έξανδρος*)
—KORMESTAI: **(158)** ii BC ib. 88 (f. *Ἡδίστη*)
MACEDONIA (KRESTONIA):
—ELEUTHEROCHORI (MOD.): **(159)** inc. *Makedonika* 15 (1975) p. 220
—IORON: **(160)** iii AD *SEG* XLVIII 815
—IORON?: **(161)** i AD ib. XXVII 287 d (s. *Πάτραος*)
MACEDONIA (LOWER PAIONIA):
—EUROPOS: **(162)** ?ii AD ib. XXXVIII 608 = XLV 759 (f. *Φίλιππος*)
MACEDONIA (LYNKESTIS): **(163)** c. 365-330 BC *RE* (12); Berve 37 (Tataki, *Macedonians* p. 201 no. 2) (s. *Ἀέροπος*); **(164)** iii AD *EAM* 163 (*Αὐρ. Ἀ.*)
—HERAKLEIA: **(165)** ii-iii AD *IG* X (2) (2) 61 (s. *Λύσων*)
—HERAKLEIA (AREA): **(166)** imp. ib. 29 ([*Ἀλέξ*]*ανδρος*?); **(167)** ii-iii AD ib. 26; **(168)** ?ii-iii AD ib. 40 (s. *Διονύσιος*)
—HERAKLEIA?: **(169)** i-ii AD ib. 122 (s. *Ἀντίγονος*, f. *Ἰουλ. Ἀλεξάνδρα*); **(170)** ib. (*Γ. Ἰούλ*[*ιος*] *Ἀ.*: s. *Ἰουλ. Ἀλεξάνδρα*); **(171)** 235 AD ib. 136, 5 (s. *Αὐρ. Διογένης*, *Αὐρ. Φίλα*); **(172)** ib. l. 7
—NIKAIA?: **(173)** iii AD ib. 46 (*Φούλβιος Ἀ.*: s. *Αὐρηλία Ἰοῦστα*)
MACEDONIA (MYGDONIA):
—CHALASTRA: **(174)** ii-iii AD ib. X (2) (1) 815, 6 (s. *Τελεσφόρος*, *Συμφορίς*)
—KALINDOIA: **(175)** 68-98 AD *SEG* XLII 580, 30 (s. *Λυσίπονος*); **(176)** ib. l. 33 (s. *Δίζας*); **(177)** ib. l. 44 (s. *Σώστρατος*); **(178)** ib. l. 59 (s. *Στράττος*); **(179)** a. 98 AD ib. 583, 26 (s. *Λυσίπονος*); **(180)** ii-iii AD ib. 599 (s. *Ἀλέξιος*, *Μακεδονία*)
—LETE: **(181)** iv/iii BC *AD* 26 (1971) Chron. p. 395 (s. *Σιμίας*)
—THESSALONIKE: **(182)** iii/ii BC *IG* X (2) (1) 107; *KGAM Thess.* I 67 (date) (s. *Δημήτριος*, f. *Δημήτριος*); **(183)** i AD *IG* X (2) (1) 242, 1; *CPh.* 70 (1975) p. 54 (s. *Δορζίνθης*); **(184)** i-ii AD *IG* X (2) (1) 243 II, 10 (s. *Διοσκουρίδης*); **(185)** ii AD *Makedonika* 14 (1974) pl. 77 ([*Ἀ*]*λέξανδρος*); **(186)** *IG* X (2) (1) 224; 241 B, 4 (*Τ. Κλ. Ἀλέξανδρος*); **(187)** ib. 241 A I, 7 (*—νιανὸς Ἀλέξανδρος*); **(188)** ib. l. 8 ([*Ἐρ*]*έννιος Ἀλέξανδρος*); **(189)** ib. l. 10 ([*Σέρ*]*γιος Ἀλέξανδρος*); **(190)** ib. 241 B, 4 ([*Τι.*] *Κλ. Ἀλέξανδρο*[*ς*]); **(191)** ib. 396, 2 (s. *Σύμφορος*); **(192)** ib. 416, 2 (f. *Ἀντίγονος*); **(193)** ?ii AD ib. 452, 7 + *BCH* 98 (1974) pp. 536-8 (*Κάσσιος Ἀ.*: ?s. *Μ. Κάσσιος Σεουῆρος Παπίας*); **(194)** ii-iii AD *IG* X (2) (1) 309, 6 (*Π. Αἴλ. Ἀ.*); **(195)** ib. 347; **(196)** ib. 505, 2 (s. *Οὐαρινία Ὑγίνη*); **(197)** ib. 641, 2 (*Λ. Βενουλέϊος Ἀ.*: f. *Βενουλεΐα Ἡγησώ*); **(198)** 137-161 AD *Makedonika* 9 (1969) pp. 143-4 (s. *Ἀπολλινάριος*); **(199)** s. ii AD *IG* X (2) (1) 244 I, 15 (s. *Διονύσιος*); **(200)** ib. l. 16 (I f. *Ἀλέξανδρος* II); **(201)** ib. l. 16 (II s. *Ἀλέξανδρος* I); **(202)** 160 AD *SEG* L 646 (*—ιος Αἰλιανὸς Ἀλέξανδρος*: I f. *Αἴλιος Ἀλέξανδρος* II); **(203)** ib. (*Αἴλιος Ἀ.*: II s. *—ιος Αἰλιανὸς Ἀλέξανδρος* I); **(204)** ii/iii AD ib. XLIX 814 I, 2; **(205)** iii AD *PRyl* 93, 22; **(206)** *IG* X (2) (1) 247, 12 (*Ἀβιβιανὸς Ἀλέσαν*[*δρος*]); **(207)** ib. 476 A; **(208)** m. iii AD ib. 206, 2 (*Κλ. Τύλλιος Ἀ. ὁ καὶ Εὐγένιος*: s. *Ἰουλ. Ὀλυμπιάς*); **(209)** c. 240 AD ib. 203, 5; 230?; *IBer* 69, 8 (Tataki 1170S) (or Macedonia (Bottiaia) Beroia?: *Λ. Σεπτίμιος Ἰνστειανὸς Ἀ.*); **(210)** s. iii AD *Hellenika* 29 (1976) pp. 267-77; **(211)** 273 AD *IG* X (2) (1) 529 (*Αἴλ. Ἡλιόδωρος ὁ καὶ Ἀ.*); **(212)** iii/iv AD ib. 591 C, 5 (*Οὐαλέριος Ἀ.*); **(213)** vi AD Feissel, *RICM* 164 A (*SEG* XLVII 979 A) ([*Ἀλέ*]*ξανδρος*)
—THESSALONIKE?: **(214)** iii BC *IG* X (2) (1) 26, 4; cf. *Tyche* 10 (1995) pl. 4 no. 2 (f. *Ἀνδρόνικος*); **(215)** f. i AD *IG* X (2) (1) 263, 2 (*Ἀλέξανδ*[*ρος*]); **(216)** ii-iii AD ib. 856, 1 (s. *Μέστριος*, *Φίλα*); **(217)** iii AD ib. 888 (*Αὐρ. Ἀ.*: s. *Αὐρ. Αἰούτωρ*); **(218)** v-vi AD ib. 782 (Feissel, *RICM* 163)

—THESSALONIKE*: (219) ii AD IG X (2) (1) 284, 15 (Ἀλέξανδ[ρος]: ?s. Πύρος); (220) SEG XLVI 823-4 (terracotta); (221) f. iii AD ib. XLIV 555 (Α΄ Panell. Synedr. Epigr. p. 27 no. 6) (Σεπτίμιος Ἀ.)

MACEDONIA (ODOMANTIKE):

—SIRRHA: (222) 155 AD Dimitsas 821, 27 (Kaphtantzis 1) (s. Διοσκουρίδης); (223) f. iii AD SEG XXX 590, 7 (Αὐρ. Ἀ.: s. Διοσκοῦς); (224) ib. l. 13 (Αὐρ. Ἀ.: s. Γάϊος)

—SIRRHA (NR.): (225) ii/iii AD ib. 602 (s. Μούκασος, Μωμώ)

—SKOTOUSSA?: (226) hell.? Dimitsas 844 (f. Σιμίας); (227) ii-iii AD ib. 843 (s. Διονύσιος, f. Τόρκος, Ἰσιγένης, Ἀλεξάνδρα); (228) 156 AD SEG XXIV 612, 5 (Γν. Τερέντιος Λουκειλιανὸς Ἀ.)

MACEDONIA (ORESTIS): (229) iv BC RE Supplbd. 4 (34g); CEG II 878 (Tataki, Macedonians p. 203 no. 1) (f. Κράτερος, Ἀμφοτερός); (230) 41-54 AD EAM 188, 4 (f. Δράκας); (231) ib. l. 6

—BATTYNAIOI: (232) 192 AD ib. 186, 2, 42 (s. Λεωνίδας); (233) ib. 186 II, 46 (I f. Ἀλέξανδρος II); (234) ib. l. 46 (Ἀλέξανδρος: II s. Ἀλέξανδρος I); (235) ib. 186 III, 44 (ΑΛΕΞΙΩΡΟΨ—lap.: f. Μενέφιλος); (236) ib. l. 56 (f. Γάϊος); (237) ib. l. 57 (s. Παρμενίων)

—KORESSOS (MOD.): (238) s. ii AD ib. 197 (Ἀλέξανδρος)

—LIKNADES (MOD.): (239) hell. ib. 211 (pithos)

—LYKE: (240) ?i-ii AD ib. 147, 3 (s. Δράκας)

—SISANI (MOD.): (241) 146 AD ib. 187, 13 (f. Θεόφιλος); (242) ib. l. 21 (f. Γέμελλος)

MACEDONIA (PAIONIA): (243) iii BC PLond inv. 573 (1) verso, 1 ?= (244); (244) 240 BC PP 9077 (Tataki, Macedonians p. 207 no. 2) ?= (243)

—ARGOS (AREA): (245) ii-iii AD Sp. 71 (1931) p. 33 no. 66 (Οὐιένιος Ἀ.: s. Οὐ. Φρόντων, Αὐρ. Διοφάνεια)

—ASTREA: (246) i/ii AD IBer 102 A, 4; 102 B, 5 (Τι. Κλ. Αἰλιανὸς Ἀ.: s. Παρμενίων)

—BYLAZORA: (247) imp. Sp. 77 (1934) p. 39 no. 15; (248) ib. 98 (1941-8) p. 33 no. 80; (249) ii-iii AD ib. 71 (1931) p. 25 no. 49 (f. Σύρος); (250) ib. 75 (1933) p. 19 no. 37, 1, 8? (f. Λούκιος); (251) iii AD SEG XLVII 896, 2 (f. Αὐρ. Ἰούλιος, Αὐρ. Ἰουλία)

—BYLAZORA (NR.): (252) ii/iii AD ib. XVI 403b (s. Λούκιος); (253) ib. (f. Λούκιος)

—KAVADARCI (MOD.): (254) ii-iii AD Sp. 71 (1931) p. 67 no. 150 (s. Μεστύλης, f. Ἀλεξάνδρα); (255) ib. p. 68 no. 151 (s. Μάντα); (256) ib. p. 237 no. 631 + 75 (1933) p. 41 no. 140 (s. Διοσκουρίδης, Κλεοπάτρα); (257) ib. 98 (1941-8) p. 63 no. 132; (258) SEG XVI 407

—NEAPOLIS (AREA): (259) 83 AD ib. 404, 2 (f. Παράμονος); (260) ib. l. 4 (s. Παράμονος, Νίκη)

—NEAPOLIS? (IZVOR (MOD.): (261) imp. Dimitsas 302; (262) ii-iii AD ib. 300, 1 (s. Ζωΐλος, Οὐαλία); (263) ib. 301, 5 (s. Ἡρακλέων, Παυλῖνα)

—STOBOI: (264) imp. Studies Stobi 3 p. 23 (Ἀλέξα(ν)δρος); (265) s. iii AD JÖAI 32 (1940) Beibl. col. 17 no. 12. 41 (Ἀλεξά(νδρου?) (gen.))

MACEDONIA (PELAGONIA): (266) ii-iii AD IG X (2) (2) 175 (f. Νίκανδρος); (267) iii AD ib. 244 (s. Αὐρ. Ἰουλιανός, Αὐρ. Μαρκελλίνη)

—DOSTONEIS: (268) ii AD ib. 196, 6-7 ([Ἀλέ]ξανδρος: s. Διονύσιος); (269) ib. 197 ([Ἰού]λιος Ἀ.)

—DOSTONEIS?: (270) iii AD ib. 206 (f. Αὐρ. Κλαύδιος)

—KOLOBAISA?: (271) ii AD ib. 234, 7 (s. Παράμονος, Μεμμία)

—MOJNO (MOD.): (272) iii AD ib. 174 (Αὐρήλιος Ἀ.: s. Αὐρ. Φίλιππος)

MACEDONIA (PIERIA):

—DION: (273) ?ii-iii AD Oikonomos 32 (Ἀ[λέ]ξανδρο[ς]: s. Νίκαρχος); (274) v-vi AD SEG XLVIII 790. 2

—PYDNA: (275) iii AD Hellenika 29 (1976) pp. 267-77; (276) 250 AD SEG XLVI 800 A, 36 (Αὐρ. Ἀ.)

MACEDONIA (SINTIKE):

—HERAKLEIA: (277) 230 AD IGB V 5922, 6 (s. Φίλιππος)

—PARTHIKOPOLIS: (278) ii AD ib. IV 2278 (s. Πυρούλας, Ἀρτεμιδώρα); (279) iii AD ib. V 5896, 3 (Μ. Αὐρ. Καπιτωνιανὸς Ἀ.); (280) 210 AD ib. IV 2265, 5 (f. Ἰουλιανός)

—PARTHIKOPOLIS (TERRIT.): (281) ii AD Arkheologiia (Sofia) 1987 (1), p. 24 no. 1, 4 (s. Πύρρος, Κλεοπάτρα)

MACEDONIA (TYMPHAIA): (282) c. 350-314 BC RE (13); Berve 39; IG II^2 1473, 7; FD III (4) 464 (Tataki, Macedonians p. 211 no. 1) (s. Πολυπέρχων)

MACEDONIA?: (283) iii BC PLond 2052, 16; (284) 168 BC Plu., Aem. 18 (Tataki, Macedonians p. 228 no. 65)

PENESTAI:

—USCANA (AREA): (285) imp. Sp. 98 (1941-8) p. 46 no. 96

SCYTHIA MINOR:

—ISTROS: (286) f. iv BC ISM I 232 (f. Ἡγήσανδρος); (287) ii-i BC ib. 126 (Eastern cults p. 105 no. 68) (s. Ἡγησαγόρας); (288) ii AD ISM I 196, 7 (f. Θεόφιλος); (289) ib. l. 9 (f. Ἰουλιανός, Μακρῖνος); (290) ib. l. 23; (291) ib. 197 I, 12 (s. Λούκιος); (292) f. ii AD ib. 353; cf. Ling. Balk. 27 (1984) p. 88 (Ἀλέξαν[δρος]?, Ἰουλ. Ἀλεξάν[δρα]?—Mihailov: ?f. Ἰουλία); (293) 138 AD ISM I 193 II, 69 (f. Κάστος); (294) ii/iii AD ib. 225, 4 (s. Ἀρχιδ—); (295) iii AD ib. 229, 2; (296) ib. l. 4; (297) 222-225 AD ib. 100 A, 16 ([Αὐ]ρ. Ἀ.: s. Ἧλις)

—KALLATIS: (298) ii/i BC IGB II 867 a, 2 = ISM I 219 (V 87); cf. ISM III p. 140 (locn.) (Ἀλέξα[νδρος]); (299) 241-244 AD ib. 74 A, 25 (s. Μάξιμος)

—KALLATIS?: (300) ii AD ib. V 280, 3 (I 275); cf. ISM III p. 140 (locn.) (s. Ἡρακλέων)

—NOVIODUNUM: (301) 178 AD ib. V 233, 9 (Lat. Caius [Al]exander)

—NOVIODUNUM*: (302) ii-iii AD ib. 276, 4 (Lat. P. Alexan[der])

—TOMIS: (303) ii AD ib. II 17, 14 (s. Ἡρακλείδης); (304) ib. 125 II, 21 (f. Ποντικός); (305) ii-iii AD ib. 13, 1 ([Ἀ]λέξα[νδρος]); (306) ib. l. 3 (Ἀλέξαν[δρος]); (307) ib. 23, 5 (Ἀλέξανδρος: s. Ρ—); (308) ib. 58, 4; (309) ib. 282 (f. Ἄφφος); (310) ib. 292 (f. Ἰουλιανός); (311) ib. 396 (Ἀλέξανδρ[ος]); (312) ib. 467 (Ἀλέξανδρ(ο)ς: s. Θεόδοτος); (313) ib. 468, 7 (f. Διογένης); (314) ib. l. 15 (f. Ἰουλιανός); (315) ib. l. 16; (316) ib. l. 18 (s. Μενε—); (317) ib. l. 21; (318) iii AD ib. 24, 6 (Αὐρ. [Ἀλέ]ξανδρος); (319) 201 AD ib. 83 I, 17 (s. Ἧλις); (320) ib. l. 18 (I f. Ἀλέξανδρος II); (321) ib. l. 18 (II s. Ἀλέξανδρος I); (322) ib. l. 37 (Αὐρ. Ἀλέξανδρο[ς]); (323) ib. 83 II, 20 (f. Βασιλικός); (324) ?iv AD AEMÖ 8 (1884) p. 13 no. 33 (Πεδα. Ἀλέξα[νδ]ρος); (325) iv-v AD Barnea 6 (Popescu, IGL 29) (Ἀλέξ(α)νδρος); (326) vi AD Barnea 27 (Popescu, IGL 9) (Ἀλέξα[νδρος])

——(Oinopes): (327) ii-iii AD ISM II 255, 2 (s. Σμάραγδος)

—TOMIS (NR.): (328) ?ii AD ib. 224 (Lat. [Alexa]nder?)

—TOMIS*: (329) ii AD ib. 327, 4

—TROESMIS?: (330) 151-154 AD ib. V 155, 13 (Lat. Fl. Alexander: II s. Ἀλέξανδρος I (Ankyra), Iulia Florentina)

—TROESMIS*: (331) 134 AD ib. 137 I, 24 (Lat. Attius Alex(ander)?); (332) ib. 137 IV, 4 (Lat. Alexande[r]); (333) ib. 137 VII, 5 (Lat. Iul. Alexa[nder])

—ULMETUM: (334) ?v AD Barnea 73, 3 (Popescu, IGL 210) (s. Ἀππᾶς, Δόμνη)

SKYTHIA:

—OLBIA-BORYSTHENES: (335) hell. Arkheologiia (Kiev) 39 (1982) p. 39 (stamp); (336) i/ii AD IOlbia 90, 5 (f. Διονύσιος); (337) ii AD ib. 80, 5 ((Ἀ)λέξανδρος: s. Ἀρσήαχος); (338) IOSPE I^2 129, 7 (f. Μουκούναγος); (339) ?ii-iii AD ib. 111, 4 (Ἀλέξαν[δρος]: s. Ποσίδηος); (340) s. ii AD IOlbia 170, 6 (f. Δημήτριος); (341) 222-235 AD IOSPE I^2 184, 8 (f. Αὐρ. Ἰουλιανός)

—TANAIS: (342) 104 AD CIRB 1259, 13 (f. Μητροφάνης); (343) 225 AD ib. 1279, 24 ([Ἀ]λέξανδρος); (344) c. 225-250 AD ib. 1287, 10; 1288, 13 (s. Σόγος); (345) 244 AD ib. 1287, 14 (Ἀλέξα[νδρος]: s. Ἀβδάρακος)

TAURIS:

—CHERSONESOS: (346) c. 315-300 BC Kats pp. 85-6 no. 9 (amph., tile); (347) imp. IOSPE I^2 435, 6 ([Ἀλ]έξανδρος); (348) ii AD Solomonik, NEPKh 56 (s. Χρηστίων); (349) SEG XXXIII 597 (Ἀλέξ[ανδρος]?); (350) f. ii AD ib. 591 A, 4 ([Ἀλέ]ξανδρος: s. Φ—); (351) m. ii AD ib. XXXVIII 748 (Ἀλέξ[ανδρος]?); (352) 185 AD IOSPE I^2 404, 50; SEG XLVI 931, [2]? (Μ. Αὐρ. Βασιλειδιανὸς Ἀ.)

THRACE: (353) iii BC IG II^2 8907 (FRA 2492) (f. Δουτιον); (354) 231 or 206 BC CPR XVIII 17, 348; cf. La'da E825 (f. Ἀντίγονος); (355) ii-i BC IG II^2 8914 (FRA 2493) (f. Λόγος)

—ABDERA: (356) f. iii BC AMNG II (1) 238 (coin)

—APOLLONIA-SOZOPOLIS: (357) i-ii AD IGB I^2 401, 5 (s. Ἀρισταίνετος); (358) ib. l. 10; (359) ib. l. 12 (f. Κάρπος); (360) v-vi AD Beševliev 177; (361) ib. 180

—BISANTHE-PANION: (362) i AD PM 1876 (s. Σέξτος)

—BYZANTION: (363) i BC Türk Tarih Kongresi XI (6) pp. 2704-5 with pl. 499. 13 (s. Φιλέταιρος); (364) i-ii AD IByz 278 (s. Ἡρακλείδης, f. Νικώ, Τύχη); (365) ii-iii AD IGB I^2 147 bis (f. Χρυσέρως); (366) 117-138 AD IByz 37, 5 (Ἀλέξανδρ[ος]: f. Μήνιος); (367) m. iii AD ib. 307 (Fıratlı–Robert p. 118 no. 198) (s. Δίων, f. Ἀλεξάνδρεια); (368) IByz 307 (Fıratlı–Robert p. 118 no. 198) (s. Ἀλεξάνδρεια); (369) 342 AD RE (72); PLRE I (3) (f. Φοῖβος)

—DIONYSOPOLIS: (370) iii AD IGB I^2 14 b, 23 (Αὐρ. Ἀ.: s. Ζήνων)

—GLAVA PANEGA (MOD.): (371) ii-iii AD ib. II 513 (f. Σεβαζιανός)

—HADRIANOPOLIS (TERRIT.): (372) ii AD ib. III 1797 (Τ. Φλ. Ἀλέ[ξ]αν[δρ]ος)

—KABYLE: (373) ii AD ib. 1776, 2 (s. Διλάης: doctor)

—KALLIPOLIS (NR.): (374) imp. Dumont–Homolle 100g (s. Κάλλιστος)

—KELLAI: (375) 241-244 AD IGB III 1517, 47 (I f. Αὐρ. Ἀλέξανδρος II); (376) ib. l. 47 (Αὐρ. Ἀ.: II s. Ἀλέξανδρος I); (377) ib. l. 55 (f. Ἡλιόδωρος)

—LYSIMACHEIA: (378) 246-205 BC PEnt 51, 1 (La'da E1366); (379) m. ii BC ISestos 38 b, 2 (f. Ἱππόνικος)

—MADYTOS: (380) hell. ib. 60 (s. Σάτοκος)

—MARKIANOPOLIS: (381) ii AD IGB II 798 b, 6 ([Ἀλέ]ξανδρος); (382) ii-iii AD ib. 800 (s. Διλι—); (383) ib. 819 (biling.) (Γ. Οὐαλέριος Ἀ.); (384) iii AD ib. 802 (Αὐρ. Ἀ.: s. Ἴβουβας); (385) ib. 815, 1 (s. Μαρκία)

—MARKIANOPOLIS (TERRIT.): (386) ii-iii AD ib. V 5382 (CCET II (1) 303) (f. Ἡρακλείδης)

—MARONEIA (TERRIT.): (387) iii AD Bakalakis, Oinos Ismarikos p. 555 (IThrakAig E379) (Ἀ. ὁ καὶ Βέβιος: s. Ταρούλας)

—MONTANA*: (388) 155 AD CIL III 7449, 5 (Montana II 1) (Lat. Ulp. Alexander); (389) CIL III 7449, 24 (Montana II 1) (Lat.

Fl. Alexander); (**390**) *CIL* III 7449, 27 (*Montana* II 1) (Lat. Iul. Alexander)

—NICOPOLIS AD ISTRUM (TERRIT.): (**391**) 227 AD *ILB* 438 I, 25 (Lat. Ael. Alex(ander) qui et Pud(ens)); (**392**) ib. l. 53 (Lat. Aur. Alexand(er)); (**393**) ib. 438 II, 15 (Lat. Alexander: f. Sabinus); (**394**) ib. l. 25 (Lat. Valerius Alexand(er))

—NICOPOLIS AD ISTRUM (NR.): (**395**) f. iii AD *IGB* II 703 (*CCET* II (2) 649) (f. *Χρῆστος*)

—NICOPOLIS AD NESTUM: (**396**) ii AD *IGB* IV 2336, 9 (f. *Φίλιππος*); (**397**) ib. l. 13 (*[Ἀλ]έξανδρος*: s. *Ζιπᾶς*)

—NOVAE: (**398**) ii-iii AD *IGLNovae* 9 (Lat. Ael. Alexander)

—ODESSOS: (**399**) imp. *BIAB* 17 (1950) p. 293 no. 18 (*Romanizmăt* II 589) (Lat. C. Rabiriu[s] Alexan[der]); (**400**) i-ii AD *IGB* I² 114 (*Ἀλέξα[νδ]ρος*: f. *Μέμνων*); (**401**) ii AD ib. 146 (PM 206) (s. *Ἑστιαῖος*); (**402**) 215 AD *IGB* I² 47 a, 8 (f. *Αὐρ. Φίρμος*); (**403**) ib. l. 12 (f. *Αὐρ. Ξένων*); (**404**) 221 AD ib. 47 bis b, 25 (I f. *Αὐρ. Ἀλέξανδρος* II); (**405**) ib. l. 25 (*Αὐρ. Ἀ.*: II s. *Ἀλέξανδρος* I); (**406**) ib. 47 bis c, 12 (f. *Αὐρ. Βουβᾶς*); (**407**) ib. l. 16 (I f. *Αὐρ. Ἀλέξανδρος* II); (**408**) ib. l. 16 (*Αὐρ. Ἀ.*: II s. *Ἀλέξανδρος* I)

—OESCUS: (**409**) iii AD *CIL* VI 32624 c, 32 (Lat. Alexander); (**410**) iii/iv AD *ZPE* 112 (1996) p. 103

—PAUTALIA: (**411**) ii-iii AD *IGB* IV 2090, 8 (biling.) (Lat. Alexander); (**412**) iii-iv AD ib. V 5773 = *SEG* XLVI 865 (*Λ. Δομίτιος Ἀ.*: s. *Λ. Δομίτιος Ἀβάσκαντος*)

—PAUTALIA (TERRIT.): (**413**) ii AD *IGB* IV 2214, 11 (I f. *Ἀλέξανδρος* II); (**414**) ib. l. 11 (II s. *Ἀλέξανδρος* I); (**415**) ii-iii AD ib. V 5787; (**416**) ib. 5821 (*Ἀλέξαν[δρος]*: ?f. *Μουκάπορις*); (**417**) ib. 5822 (*Ἀλέξαν[δρος]*: f. *Λούππος*)

—PERINTHOS-HERAKLEIA: (**418**) c. 223-218 BC *PPetr* III 77, 4 (La'da E1959) (s. *Ἐλπίνης*); (**419**) i BC-i AD? *IPerinth* 57, 3 (f. *Ἡρακλείδης*); (**420**) ib. l. 5; (**421**) i-ii AD ib. 94 (f. *Μοσχίς*); (**422**) ii AD ib. 132 (s. *Διότιμος*); (**423**) ii-iii AD ib. 111 (*[Ἀ]λέξανδρο[ς]*); (**424**) ii/iii AD ib. 104 (*Μ. Αὐρ. Ἀ.*: s. *Εὐτύχης*); (**425**) f. iii AD ib. 148-9 (*Αὐρ. Ἀ.*: s. *Αὐρ. Γενουκία*)

—PERINTHOS-HERAKLEIA (NR.): (**426**) i-ii AD ib. 282 (f. *Γαμικός, Ζώσιμος*); (**427**) ii-iii AD ib. 296 (*Ἀλέξαν[δρος]*)

—PERINTHOS-HERAKLEIA*: (**428**) 161 AD ib. 19, 10 (*CIL* III 7394) (Lat. Gaius Alexander)

—PHILIPPOPOLIS-TRIMONTIUM: (**429**) imp. *IGB* III 999, 1 (*Ἀ(λ)έξανδρος*); (**430**) ii-iii AD ib. V 5438 (f. *Μούκας*); (**431**) m. iii AD ib. III 884 b, 17; cf. V 5400 (*Φλ. Ἀ.*); (**432**) ib. III 884 b, 23; cf. V 5400 (*Αὐρ. Ἀ.*); (**433**) vi AD Beševliev 211 = *SEG* XV 432 (*[Ἀλέ]ξανδ[ρος]*)

—PHILIPPOPOLIS-TRIMONTIUM (TERRIT.): (**434**) ii-iii AD *IGB* III 1189; (**435**) ib. 1409

—PHILIPPOPOLIS-TRIMONTIUM (NR.): (**436**) ii-iii AD ib. 1416 (s. *Φίλιππος*)

—PHILIPPOPOLIS-TRIMONTIUM*: (**437**) imp. *AEMÖ* 9 (1895) p. 114 (Lat. Aemilius Alexander)

—RHAIDESTOS: (**438**) ii-i BC PM 384 (f. *Γλυκέρα*)

—SALYMBRIA: (**439**) v-vi AD *AD* 53 (1998) Mel. p. 473 no. 212 (*Ἀλέ[ξαν]δρος*: s. *Ἀρδαβούριος*)

—SERDICA (TERRIT.): (**440**) ii-iii AD *AEMÖ* 10 (1886) p. 238-9 no. 2, 8; (**441**) ib. l. 13 (s. *Ἀσκληπιάδης*)

—TRAIANOPOLIS (NR.): (**442**) byz. *Thrakika* 3 (1932) p. 176 (*Ἀλέ(ξ)[αν]δρος*)

—TYROLOE: (**443**) imp. ib. 15 (1941) p. 107 (*Ἀλέξαν[δρος]*)

—VICUS TRULLENSIUM: (**444**) iii AD *IGB* II 506, 7 (s. *Μοῦσα, Αὐρ. Ν—*)

Ἀλέξαρθος

CIMMERIAN BOSPOROS:

—HERMONASSA*: (**1**) 307 AD *CIRB* 1051 (s. *Μ. Αὐρ. Ἀνδρόνικος*)

Ἀλέξαρχος

MACEDONIA: (**1**) s. iv BC Berve 41 (Tataki, *Macedonians* p. 231 no. 80); cf. Hoffmann, *Makedonen* pp. 266-8; Tarn, *Alexander* pp. 430 ff. (s. *Ἀντίπατρος*)

MACEDONIA (ELIMEIA):

—AIANE (TERRIT.): (**2**) c. 225-200 BC *SEG* XL 526, 4 (*Ἀλέ(ξ)αρχος*: s. *Λεωνίδας*)

Ἀλεξᾶς

CIMMERIAN BOSPOROS:

—PANTIKAPAION: (**1**) i AD *CIRB* 334 (*Ἀλι-*: s. *Ἀντίμαχος*)

Ἀλεξίας

THRACE:

—LYSIMACHEIA: (**1**) ii-i BC *ISestos* 42 (f. *Διονύσιος*)

Ἀλεξίδημος

MACEDONIA (BISALTIA):

—TRAGILOS: (**1**) iv BC *AD* 26 (1971) Chron. p. 413 (s. *Νίκων*)

Ἀλεξίμαχος

MACEDONIA (BOTTIAIA):

—PELLA: (**1**) iii BC ib. 16 (1960) Mel. p. 82; 19 (1964) Chron. p. 339; *SEG* XXXIX 623 (tiles)

THRACE:

—ABDERA: (**2**) c. 415-395 BC May, *Abdera* pp. 162-3 nos. 202-3 (coin)

—ODESSOS: (**3**) 7 BC *IGB* I² 46, 40 (f. *Φιλῖνος*); (**4**) 215 AD ib. 47 c, 10 (f. *Αὐρ. Ἀπελλᾶς*)

Ἀλεξιμένης

MACEDONIA: (**1**) iii BC *HE* 1624

Ἀλέξιος

MACEDONIA (BOTTIAIA):

—BEROIA:

——Kyneoi: (**1**) c. 190 AD *ILeukopetra* 53, 1 (Tataki 134) (*Ἀλεξίου* (gen.), *Ἄλεξις*?: f. *Ἄλεξις*)

MACEDONIA (MYGDONIA):

—KALINDOIA: (**2**) ii-iii AD *SEG* XLII 599 (s. *Δάλης* f. *Ἀλέξανδρος, Στράτων*)

Ἀλέξιππος

MACEDONIA: (**1**) 252 BC *PColZen* 49, 7, 20 (Tataki, *Macedonians* p. 231 no. 82; La'da E1599)

MACEDONIA (BOTTIAIA):

—BEROIA: (**2**) i BC-i AD *IBer* 166 (Tataki 907) (*Π. Μουνάτιος Ἀ.*: s. *Π. Μουνάτιος*)

MACEDONIA (PIERIA):

—DION: (**3**) ii AD *Essays Laourdas* p. 108 no. 7 (s. *Διοσκουρίδης*)

Ἄλεξις

MACEDONIA (BOTTIAIA):

—BEROIA: (**1**) ii-iii AD *IBer* 329 (*Ἀλεξ[ις]*)

——Kyneoi: (**2**) c. 190 AD *ILeukopetra* 53, 1 (Tataki 133) (s. *Ἀλέξιος*)

MACEDONIA (CHALKIDIKE):

—AKANTHOS: (**3**) f. iv BC *AMNG* III (2) 29; *AR* 1981-2, pp. 38 f. (coin); (**4**) iv/iii BC *SEG* XLVII 870, 5 (*Ἄλεξ[ι]ς*: ?s. *Ἀρχέλαος*)

MACEDONIA (DERRIOPOS):

—STUBERRA: (**5**) c. 41-48 AD *IG* X (2) (2) 323, 29 (s. *Δημᾶς*)

MACEDONIA (MYGDONIA):

—THESSALONIKE: (**6**) c. 266 BC ib. XII (9) 1187, 38; Robert, *Ét. Num. Gr.* pp. 179 ff. (date) (Tataki, *Macedonians* p. 188 no. 71) (*[Ἀλ]έξεως*? (gen.))

Ἀλεξίων

SKYTHIA:

—TANAIS: (**1**) 228 AD *CIRB* 1283, 10 (s. *Πάτροκλος*)

Ἀλεξομενός

MACEDONIA (PIERIA):

—PHILA?: (**1**) ?iii BC *RPh* 1911, pp. 133-4 no. 36, 50; cf. Helly, *L'État thessalien* pp. 319-20 (locn.) (*Ἀλεξομε[νός]*: s. *—ρης*)

Ἀλθαιμένης

MACEDONIA: (**1**) iv BC Arr., *An.* iii 11. 8 (Tataki, *Macedonians* p. 231 no. 83) (f. *Δημήτριος*)

Ἀλίαρχος

THRACE:

—MARONEIA: (**1**) ii BC *IG* XII (8) 161, 14 (f. *Ἐπικράτης*)

Ἄλιμος

MACEDONIA (MYGDONIA):

—THESSALONIKE: (**1**) s. i AD ib. X (2) (1) 68, 17 (*Λ. Φήσιος Ἀ.*)

Ἀλιούλας

MACEDONIA (EDONIS):

—PHILIPPOI (TERRIT.): (**1**) ?ii AD *BIAB* 16 (1950) pp. 14-15 no. 11, 3 (Pilhofer 649) (Lat. Aliula: s. *Ζιπᾶς, Καιγενώ*); (**2**) *BCH* 47 (1923) p. 69 no. 25 (Pilhofer 514) (Lat. Aliulas: s. *Ζιπαίβης*, f. *Ζέκη*)

Ἀλιουπαίβης

MACEDONIA (EDONIS):

—PHILIPPOI (NR.): (**1**) ii-iii AD *BCH* 54 (1930) p. 376 (Pilhofer 48); Collart, *Philippes* pl. 36. 3 (*-βες*: s. *Ζιπάλας*)

Ἀλκαῖος

MACEDONIA (BOTTIAIA):

—BEROIA: (**1**) 251 AD *IBer* 137, 9 (Tataki 680) (*Κάσσιος Σαλλούστιος Ἀ.*: II s. *Κάσσιος Σαλλούστιος Ἀλκαῖος* I); (**2**) 251-264 AD *IBer* 56, 2; 137, 9 (Tataki 679) (*Κάσσιος Σαλλούστιος Ἀ.*: I f. *Κάσσιος Σαλλούστιος Ἀλκαῖος* II)

MACEDONIA (EDONIS):

—AMPHIPOLIS: (**3**) iii/ii BC Hatzopoulos, *MI* 2 pp. 91-2 no. 75 (s. *Ἡρακλείδης*)

THRACE:

—AINOS: (**4**) iv/iii BC *IG* II² 495, 10, 21; IV (1)² 58, 7 (s. *Ἡραῖος*)

—APOLLONIA-SOZOPOLIS: (**5**) v/iv BC *Rev. Num.* 1911, p. 295; Mushmov 3152 (coin)

—PERINTHOS-HERAKLEIA:

——(Boreis): (**6**) iii-ii BC *IPerinth* 61, 41 (f. *Μικίων*)

Ἀλκαμένης

MACEDONIA (MYGDONIA):

—THESSALONIKE: (**1**) 167 AD *IG* X (2) (1) 528 (*Κ. Ἐρέννιος Ἀ.*)

Ἄλκανδρος

THRACE:

—APOLLONIA-SOZOPOLIS: (**1**) v/iv BC *IGB* I² 435 (f. *Μεγιστῆς*)

Ἀλκάνωρ

MACEDONIA: (**1**) c. 322-313 BC *IG* VII 4257, 9 (*IOrop* 5; Tataki, *Macedonians* p. 232 no. 84) (s. *Ἀρκεσίλαος*)

MACEDONIA (BOTTIAIA):

—PELLA*: (**2**) iii BC *AEMTh* 3 (1989) p. 82 n. 35 (amph.) (*[Ἀ]λκά[ν]ωρ*)

Ἀλκεβιάδης

THRACE:

—ZONE: (**1**) m. v BC *SEG* XXVII 346 b (*IThrakAig* E405-6) (*Ἀλκεβιάδō* (gen.): f. *Μυρσίνη*)

Ἀλκείδης

MACEDONIA (BOTTIAIA):

—MIEZA: (**1**) hell. *AM* 27 (1902) p. 314 no. 28, 8

Macedonia (Edonis):
—philippoi: (2) s. iii ad *SEG* l 619. 2 (mosaic)
Thrace:
—byzantion: (3) ii ad *IByz* 321 (*Τ. Ἀβούλλιος Ἀ.*)

Ἀλκενίς
Thrace:
—philippopolis-trimontium (territ.): (1) ii ad *IGB* iii 1302, 5; cf. v 5492 (*Αἰλ. Ἀλκενίς*: d. *Ἐπτάκενθος*)

Ἀλκέτας
Macedonia: (1) s. vi bc *RE* (1) (Tataki, *Macedonians* p. 232 no. 85) (s. *Ἀέροπος* I, f. *Ἀμύντας* I: king); (2) c. 480-413 bc *IG* I^3 89, 60-1; Pl., *Gorg.* 471 a (Tataki, *Macedonians* p. 232 nos. 88-89) (*Ἀλκέτε͂ς*—*IG*: s. *Ἀλέξανδρος* I, f. *Ἀλέξανδρος*, *Ἀγέλαος*, *—υρος*); (3) iv bc *FGrH* 143 F 3 (Tataki, *Macedonians* p. 232 no. 86)
Macedonia (Bottiaia):
—aigai: (4) c. 300-275 bc *SEG* xxxv 788 (s. *Φιλώτας*)
—beroia: (5) s. iii bc *IBer* 46, 20 (s. *Φίλιππος*); (6) 239-229 bc ib. 45, 5 (Tataki 136) (f. *Ἀττίνας*); (7) *IBer* 45, 32 (s. *Μ—οικος*); (8) ib. l. 14-15 (Tataki 135) (?s. *Ἀττίνας*)
—ichnai: (9) c. 230-200 bc *BCH* 45 (1921) p. 17 III, 63 (Tataki, *Macedonians* p. 113 no. 1) (f. *Διῆς*)
Macedonia (Krestonia):
—morrylos: (10) ?205 bc *SEG* xxxix 605, 13, 20
Macedonia (Mygdonia):
—lete: (11) s. iv bc Hatzopoulos, *MI* 2 pp. 93-4 no. 79, 13
Macedonia (Orestis): (12) c. 355-319 bc *RE* (5); Berve 45 (Tataki, *Macedonians* p. 204 no. 2) (s. *Ὀρόντης*)
Thrace:
—perni (mod.): (13) hell. *SEG* xxiv 624 (f. *Κρατεύα*)

Ἀλκέτης
Macedonia (Bottiaia):
—beroia: (1) ii ad *IBer* 355 (Tataki 137) (I f. *Ἀλκέτης* II); (2) *IBer* 355 (Tataki 138) (II s. *Ἀλκέτης* I, *Ἄρτεμις*)

Ἄλκη
Macedonia (Mygdonia):
—thessalonike: (1) c. 165 ad *IG* x (2) (1) 484, 2 (*Κουσωνία Ἀ.* (*ἡ*) *καὶ Τροφίμη*: m. *Κουσωνία Τιβερῖνα*)

Ἄλκης
Macedonia (Edonis):
—amphipolis: (1) ii-iii ad *Thracia* 2 p. 277 (*AD* 27 (1972) Mel. p. 142); cf. *Epigraphica* 37 (1975) pp. 30-1 (*Ἄλκου* (gen.): f. *Δίζας*)

Ἄλκηστις
Macedonia (Bottiaia):
—beroia: (1) iii ad *IBer* 127 (Tataki 139) (m. *Τέρπνος*); (2) f. iii ad *IBer* 122, 1 (Tataki 691) (*Κλ. Ἀ.*: d. *Κλ. Τέρπνος*, *Ἰουλιανὴ Ἀμμία*); (3) *IBer* 122, 5 (Tataki 1079) (*Πλωτιανὴ Ἀ.*)

Ἀλκίας
Cimmerian Bosporos:
—pantikapaion: (1) 14 ad *CIRB* 335, 3 (f. *Φιλοπάτρα*)

Ἀλκιβιάδης
Thrace:
—byzantion: (1) i-ii ad *IG* xii (2) 443 (Stephanis 135)
—philippopolis-trimontium (territ.): (2) ii-iii ad *IGB* iii 1094 (*Eastern cults* p. 122 no. 105) (*-κιπι-*)
—zone: (3) s. v bc *SEG* xxxviii 732 (*IThrakAig* E407) (*Ἀλκιβιάδο͂* (gen.): f. *Ἡγησίλαος*)

Ἀλκιδάμας
Macedonia (Mygdonia):
—thessalonike: (1) f. iii ad *IG* x (2) (1) 441 (*Αὐρ. Ἀ.*: f. *Αὐρ. Πυρούλας*, *Αὐρ. Δούλης*); (2) ib. 564, 1; *BCH* 97 (1973) pp. 242-5 (name) (*Πύρρος Ἀ.*: I f. *Αὐρ. Ἀλκιδάμας* II, *Αὐρ. Πυρούλας*, *Αὐρ. Δούλης*); (3) *IG* x (2) (1) 564, 1 (*Αὐρ. Ἀ.*: s. *Πύρρος Ἀλκιδάμας*); (4) ib. l. 5 (*Αὐρ. Ἀ.*: s. *Ζετιτίς*)
Macedonia (Pieris):
—phagres: (5) inc. *AEMTh* 10 (1996) pp. 835 ff.
Thrace:
—pautalia: (6) ii-iii ad *IGB* iv 2078 a, 1

Ἀλκιμάχη
Macedonia (Eordaia):
—kelle?: (1) s. ii ad *EAM* 125, 4 (d. *Κρισπῖνα*)

Ἀλκίμαχος
Macedonia: (1) s. iv bc *IG* xii (5) 1001, 8, 10 (Tataki, *Macedonians* p. 233 no. 91) (f. *Λύσιππος*) ?= (*3*)
Macedonia (Bottiaia):
—beroia: (2) 223 bc *IBer* 4, 38 (s. *Μαχάτας*)
—pella?: (3) 338-334 bc *RE* (5); Berve 47 (Tataki, *Macedonians* p. 148 no. 8) (s. *Ἀγαθοκλῆς*) ?= (*1*)
Macedonia (Chalkidike):
—mende: (4) ?v bc *SEG* xliii 428 (vase)
Macedonia (Mygdonia):
—apollonia: (5) 321-318 bc *IG* ii^2 391, 3, 7 (Tataki, *Macedonians* p. 67 no. 3) (*Ἀλ[κίμ]αχος*: I f. *Ἀλκίμαχος* II); (6) *IG* ii^2 391, 3, 7 (Tataki, *Macedonians* p. 66 no. 2) (II s. *Ἀλκίμαχος* I)
—thessalonike?: (7) ii ad *IG* x (2) (1) 249, 3 (*[Ἀ]λκίμαχος*)
Macedonia (Pieria):
—pydna: (8) c. 230-200 bc *BCH* 45 (1921) p. 17 III, 56; *IG* vii 316, 2, 5 (*IOrop* 132); cf. Tataki, *Macedonians* p. 169 no. 2 (f. *Ἀρχίας*, *Φίλιππος*, *Διονυσογένης*); (9) i bc *GVI* 1063 (s. *Νεοπτόλεμος*)
Macedonia (Pieris):
—oisyme-emathia?: (10) s. iv bc *PAE* 1938, p. 92 no. 1, 4
Skythia:
—olbia-borysthenes: (11) v bc *SEG* xxx 958 (vase) (*[Ἀλ]κίμαχος*)
Thrace:
—perinthos-herakleia:
——(Boreis): (12) iii-ii bc *IPerinth* 61, 43 (s. *Ξεινόθεμις*)

Ἀλκιμέδων
Cimmerian Bosporos:
—pantikapaion: (1) iv bc *SEG* xl 637 = *BE* 1961, no. 429 (vase) (*[Ἀλ]κιμέδων*)
Skythia:
—olbia-borysthenes: (2) m. iv bc Dubois, *IGDOlbia* 13, 6 (*[Ἀ]λκιμέδων*: s. *Πρόμαχος*)

Ἀλκιμένης
Macedonia (Bottiaia):
—pella: (1) 263 bc *IG* ix (1)^2 (1) 17, 69 (Tataki, *Macedonians* p. 149 no. 9) (s. *Ἐπικράτης*)
Thrace:
—ainos: (2) a. 316 bc *IG* iv (1)^2 94 b, 50 (Perlman, *City and Sanctuary* E.1 with pp. 78-9 (date)); cf. Tataki, *Macedonians* p. 172 no. 1 (*Ἀλκιμένευς* (gen.): f. *Ἐπιθέρσης*)

Ἄλκιμος
Cimmerian Bosporos:
—nymphaion: (1) iii bc *TGE* 17 (1976) p. 186 (weight)
—pantikapaion: (2) iii-ii bc *MIA* 56 (1957) p. 101 (tile) (*Sov. Arkh.* 28 (1958) p. 129 no. 2) (*Ἀλκιμ(ος)*?); (3) 14 ad *CIRB* 335, 1 (s. *Ἀσκλᾶς*); (4) i/ii ad ib. 574 (s. *Ἡγήσιππος*); (5) ii-iii ad ib. 718 (f. *Ἀρτίπους*); (6) 275-278 ad ib. 36, 51 (*Ἀλκιμ(ος)*); (7) ib. l. 60 (s. *Ἀντω—*)
Macedonia (Bisaltia):
—tragilos: (8) ii-iii ad *SEG* xxiv 610 (*Ἀλκ(ι)μος*: s. *Γ. Ἰούλ. Ἑρμασίων*)
Macedonia (Bottiaia):
—aigai: (9) s. iv bc ib. xxxv 802 (s. *Κατάνικος*)
—beroia: (10) 223 bc *IBer* 4, 19 (s. *Παράμονος*); (11) 41-44 ad ib. 60, 10 (Tataki 140) (f. *Τασούτας*)
Macedonia (Edonis):
—philippoi (nr.): (12) i ad *BIAB* 16 (1950) pp. 8-9 no. 1, 7 (Pilhofer 440) (Lat. Furius Alcimus)
Macedonia (Odomantike):
—gazoros: (13) 118-119 ad *SEG* xxiv 615, 2, 6 (Pilhofer 548) (s. *Πρωτέας*, f. *Πρωτέας*)
—gazoros?: (14) 158 ad *SEG* xxiv 614, 10 (Pilhofer 544); cf. Hatzopoulos, *MI* 1 pp. 84-6 (s. *Ταράλας*)
Macedonia (Pelagonia): (15) ii-iii ad *IG* x (2) (2) 271 (s. *Δημητριοῦς*)
Macedonia (Pieria):
—pydna: (16) iv bc *GRBS* 43 (2002-3) p. 119 no. 5, 7
Macedonia?: (17) 340 bc *RE* (12) (Tataki, *Macedonians* p. 233 no. 92)
Scythia Minor:
—istros: (18) iii-ii bc Unp. (Avram, defixio) 4, 9
Skythia:
—olbia-borysthenes: (19) ii ad *IOSPE* i^2 131, 14 (f. *Παπάδων*); (20) f. ii ad *SEG* xliii 506, 7 (s. *Παπίας*)
—tanais: (21) 220 ad *CIRB* 1278, 11 (f. *Πάτεις*)
Tauris:
—chersonesos: (22) iv/iii bc Solomonik, *NEPKh* 162; (23) iii bc ib. 159 (f. *Ἑρμόδωρος*); (24) i bc-i ad ib. 41 (*[Ἄ]λκιμος*)
Thrace:
—beroe-augusta traiana (territ.): (25) ii-iii ad *IGB* iii 1718 (f. *Λουκιανός*)
—philippopolis-trimontium: (26) m. iii ad ib. 884 a, 22; cf. v 5400 (*[Ο]ὐαλ. Ἀ.*)

Ἀλκῖνος
Macedonia (Pieria):
—phila?: (1) ?iii bc *RPh* 1911, pp. 133-4 no. 36, 35; cf. Helly, *L'État thessalien* pp. 319-20 (locn.); (2) *RPh* 1911, pp. 133-4 no. 36, 106 + *Polemon* 2 (1934-40) Parart. p. 13 no. 17; cf. Helly, *L'État thessalien* pp. 319-20 (locn.) (*Ἀλκίνου* (gen.)—*Polemon*, *Ἀλκίο[υ]*—*RPh*: f. *Χίονις*)
Tauris:
—chersonesos: (3) f. iii bc Kats p. 99 no. 59 (amph.) (f. *Ἡρόξενος*); (4) c. 170-140 bc Anokhin p. 145 nos. 165; 170 (coin)

Ἀλκίνους
Tauris:
—chersonesos: (1) iii bc *IOSPE* i^2 342, 2 (s. *Ἡρακλείδας*)

Ἀλκιππίδης
Thrace:
—kallipolis: (1) ?ii bc *ISestos* 25 (f. *—ια*)

Ἄλκιππος
Macedonia (Bottiaia):
—beroia: (1) ii-iii ad *IBer* 28 (Tataki 141) (*Ἄλκιππος*)
Thrace:
—perinthos-herakleia?: (2) iv bc Hp., *Epid.* iv 58

Ἀλκισθένης
MACEDONIA (CHALKIDIKE):
—APHYTIS: (1) ?351 BC *A´ Panell. Synedr. Epigr.* pp. 80-1, 22 (s. *Πολύστρατος*)

Ἀλκίφρων
CIMMERIAN BOSPOROS:
—PANTIKAPAION: (1) iv BC *CIRB* 156 (s. *Κόνων*)
THRACE:
—ABDERA: (2) ii/i BC *Syll*³ 656, 50 (Ager 169) (*Ἀλκ[ίφρων]*?: s. *Δημήτριος*); (3) *Syll*³ 656, 50 (Ager 169) (f. *Ἡρακλείδης*)

Ἀλκμέων
THRACE:
—APOLLONIA-SOZOPOLIS: (1) iii BC *BMNBurgas* 4 (2002) p. 126 no. 24 (s. *Φιλήμων*)

Ἀλκυάνα
MACEDONIA (MYGDONIA):
—KALINDOIA: (1) ii/i BC *SEG* XLII 594 (d. *Φίλιππος*, *Ἀριστίππα*)

Ἀλκυονεύς
MACEDONIA: (1) f. iii BC *RE* (1); *FGrH* 161 F 4; D.L. iv 41; vii 36 (Tataki, *Macedonians* p. 233 no. 93) (s. *Ἀντίγονος* II *Γονατᾶς*, *Δημώ*)

Ἄλκων
MACEDONIA?: (1) i BC *GP* 2 (fict.?)

Ἀλλάξαρθος
CIMMERIAN BOSPOROS:
—NYMPHAION: (1) i/ii AD *CIRB* 931 (*Ἀλλάξαρθος*: s. *Θεοφάνης*)

Ἀλλούπορις
MACEDONIA (EDONIS):
—PHILIPPOI (DRAMA (MOD.)): (1) i BC-i AD *GVI* 429 (Pilhofer 509) (s. *Κέτρηζις*)
MACEDONIA?: (2) f. i BC *Xenia antiqua* 10 (2001) p. 19 nos. A-B (or Thrace: *Ἀλλώ-*, *Δαλώπορις*—A: s. *Βαστικίλας*, *Ζαικίς*)
THRACE?: (3) m. iii BC *SEG* XLI 963, 5 (*Ἀλλώ-*: s. *Βακκης*); (4) ib. l. 10 (*Ἀλλώ-*: s. *Ἔρος*)

Ἀλούθαγος
SKYTHIA:
—OLBIA-BORYSTHENES: (1) ii AD *IOSPE* I² 89, 5; Zgusta, *PNS* 270 (*Ἀλούθα(γ)ος*: s. *Ἀντέρως*)

Ἀλπάλη
SCYTHIA MINOR:
—ISTROS: (1) iii-ii BC Unp. (Avram, defixio) 4, 8
THRACE:
—APOLLONIA-SOZOPOLIS: (2) v/iv BC *IGB* I² 422 (d. *Ἀνθεστήριος*); (3) iv BC *BMNBurgas* 4 (2002) p. 120 no. 3 (d. *Ἀγγελῆς*)

Ἀλπάλης
THRACE:
—APOLLONIA-SOZOPOLIS: (1) v/iv BC *IGB* I² 422 bis (*Ἀλπάλεο[ς]* (gen.): f. *Ἀθήναιος*); (2) iv BC *BMNBurgas* 4 (2002) p. 120 no. 2 (*Ἀλπάλε*——ed.: s. *Λητόδωρος*)

Ἀλύπη
MACEDONIA (MYGDONIA):
—THESSALONIKE: (1) ii AD *IG* X (2) (1) 552 (-*λοί*-)

Ἀλύπητος
THRACE:
—BYZANTION: (1) s. ii BC *BMI* 1154a B, 30; *BE* 1972, no. 37 (date) (I f. *Ἀλύπητος* II); (2) *BMI* 1154a B, 30; *BE* 1972, no. 37 (date) (*[Ἀ]λύπητος*: II s. *Ἀλύπητος* I)

Ἀλυπιανή
THRACE:
—BYZANTION: (1) c. 235 AD Schönert-Geiss, *Byzantion* 1792-5 (coin) (*Αὐρ. Ἀ.*)

Ἀλυπιανός
THRACE:
—PERINTHOS-HERAKLEIA: (1) s. ii AD *Corinth* VIII (1) 15, 26 (Stephanis 144) (*Π. Αἴλ. Ἀ.*)

Ἀλυπίων
THRACE:
—GLAVA PANEGA (MOD.): (1) ii-iii AD *IGB* II 559

Ἄλυπος
CIMMERIAN BOSPOROS:
—PANTIKAPAION: (1) i BC/i AD *CIRB* 303; cf. KW pl. 30 no. 436 (f. *Ἀπολλώνιος*)
MACEDONIA (BOTTIAIA):
—BEROIA: (2) ii-iii AD *IBer* 281 (Tataki 142) (-*λοι*-)
—BEROIA?: (3) 38 BC Robert, *Coll. Froehner* 44, 21 (*IG* XII Suppl. p. 149); cf. Tataki, *Macedonians* p. 75 no. 8 (s. *Λέων*)
—EDESSA: (4) 51 AD *SEG* XLVI 744, 10 (Tataki, *Edessa* 310) (*Γ. Φλ. Ἀ.*)
MACEDONIA (CHALKIDIKE):
—POTIDAIA-KASSANDREIA (NR.): (5) iv/iii BC *SEG* XXXVII 559. 2 (*AD* 22 (1967) Chron. p 377 with pl. 284 *β*)
MACEDONIA (DERRIOPOS):
—STUBERRA: (6) 74 AD *IG* X (2) (2) 325, 52 (f. *Στράτων*)
THRACE:
—MARONEIA: (7) ii AD *IThrakAig* E308 (*Φλ. Ἀ.*)
—PAUTALIA (TERRIT.): (8) ii AD *IGB* IV 2214, 5 (f. *Διογένης*)

Ἄλυς
MACEDONIA (BOTTIAIA):
—BEROIA: (1) 181 AD *IBer* 49, 31 (Tataki 1310) (*Φλ. Ἀ.*—*IBer*, *Φλ. Ἀ[ρ]δυς*—Tataki)
MACEDONIA (DERRIOPOS):
—STUBERRA: (2) 121 AD *IG* X (2) (2) 328, 20 (I f. *Ἄλυς* II); (3) ib. l. 20 (II s. *Ἄλυς* I)
THRACE: (4) 46-54 AD *SEG* XVI 415 II, 24 (*IThrakAig* E84) (*Γ. Ἰούλ. Ἀ.*)

Ἀλφίδιος
MACEDONIA (LYNKESTIS):
—HERAKLEIA: (1) i AD *IG* X (2) (2) 75, 22 (s. *Κρίσπος*)

Ἀλφῖνος
SCYTHIA MINOR:
—KALLATIS: (1) iii BC *IOrop* 543 (f. *Ἀπολλώνιος*)
SKYTHIA:
—OLBIA-BORYSTHENES: (2) iii BC *IOSPE* I² 201 I, 15 (*Ἀλφῖ[ν]ος*: s. *Ποσειδώνιος*)

Ἄλφιος
THRACE:
—MESAMBRIA: (1) i BC *IGB* I² 326, 6 (f. *Ἡραίων*)
—SERDICA (TERRIT.): (2) ii-iii AD ib. IV 2006, 1 (f. *Ἀρέθουσα*)

Ἀλφοκράτης
CIMMERIAN BOSPOROS:
—GORGIPPIA: (1) i-ii AD *CIRB* 1138, 2 (*Ἀλφ[οκ]ράτης*: s. *Ἄττας*); (2) ii AD ib. 1141, 14 (-*φα*-); (3) ii-iii AD *NE* 9 (1971) p. 9 no. 6 A, 6 (*Ἀλφοκ[ράτης]*); (4) s. ii AD *CIRB* 1143, 3 (*[Ἀ]λφοκράτης*); (5) ib. 1165, 2 (*Ἀλδοκ[ράτης]*—Vinogradov); (6) ii/iii AD ib. 1179, 60 (*Ἀλφο[κράτ]ης*: f. *Ἀ*—*ας*)

Ἀλφοῦς
SKYTHIA:
—TANAIS: (1) f. ii AD ib. 1266, 12 (s. *Π*—)

Ἀμα
THRACE:
—BEROE-AUGUSTA TRAIANA:
——Emporion Diskodouraterai: (1) iii AD *IGB* II 737, 9 (*[Ἀ]μα*)
—ODESSOS: (2) ii AD ib. I² 187 (d. *Ξένανδρος*)

Ἀμάγη
SARMATIA:
—SARMATAI: (1) ?iii BC Polyaen. viii 56 (*Ἀμόργη*?—Roth: queen)

Ἀμαδίκα
MACEDONIA (BOTTIAIA):
—PELLA: (1) v/iv BC *SEG* XXXII 642 (m. *Ξάνθος*)

Ἀμάδοκος
THRACE: (1) 267 BC ib. XXVII 1114, 4, 6b, 10a, 12b, 18a, 22b; cf. La'da E719; E787; E806 (f. *Χρύσερμος*, *Πτολεμαῖος*, *Βαστακίλας*); (2) *SEG* XXVII 1114, 14b (La'da E702) (s. *Σάτοκος*); (3) 184 BC Liv. xxxix 35, 4 (Lat. Amadocus: king?); (4) 157 BC *UPZ* 123, 3 (Velkov 19); cf. La'da E786 (f. *Πτολεμαῖος*)
THRACE?: (5) ?iii BC *PPetr* II 43, 33 (Velkov 17); cf. *PP* 11346 (f. *Δωσίθεος*); (6) 224 BC *PCollYoutie* 7, 1; 7 verso, 2

Ἀμάδωκος
MACEDONIA (BOTTIAIA):
—AIGAI: (1) s. iv BC *SEG* XXXV 789 (f. *Λυσανίας*, *Παράμονος*, *Νικόστρατος*)
MACEDONIA (PIERIA):
—PYDNA: (2) iv BC *GRBS* 47 (2002-3) p. 122 no. 6, 3 (*Ἀμ(ά)δωκος*?)

Ἀμάζενις
THRACE:
—KABYLE: (1) ii AD *Kabile* 2 p. 29 no. 38 (Lat. Amazeni (gen.): f. Damanoreus)

Ἀμαζονίη
MACEDONIA (MYGDONIA):
—THESSALONIKE: (1) imp.? *IG* X (2) (1) 673 (*GVI* 1196)

Ἀμαίακος
SKYTHIA:
—TANAIS: (1) 225 AD *CIRB* 1279, 19 (f. *Ὀσμάρακος*); (2) 225-244 AD ib. l. 26; 1287, 21 (*Ἀμαείακος*—1279: f. *Σιαύασκος*); (3) 244 AD ib. l. 28 (*Ἀμαία[κος]*—Tokhtas'ev: f. *Αὔασκις*)

Ἀμαίστας
THRACE:
—SEUTHOPOLIS: (1) iii BC *IGB* III 1732 (s. *Μηδίστας*)

Ἀμαντις?
THRACE:
—PERINTHOS-HERAKLEIA:
——(Kastaleis): (1) iii-ii BC *IPerinth* 61, 60 (*Ἀμαντιος* (gen.)—apogr.: f. *Ἀστύνομος*)

Ἀμαρακίς
MACEDONIA (BOTTIAIA):
—BEROIA: (1) 193 AD *ILeukopetra* 42, 1 (*Κλ. Ἀ.*)

Ἀμαραντίς
MACEDONIA (MYGDONIA):
—THESSALONIKE?: (1) ii-iii AD *IG* X (2) (1) 862, 1, 3 (*Δομιτία Ἀ.*)

Ἀμάραντος
SCYTHIA MINOR:
—TOMIS*: (1) ii-iii AD *ISM* II 342 (*GVI* 304); Robert, *Gladiateurs* p. 300 (name) (glad.)

Ἀμαρδίακος
SKYTHIA:
—TANAIS: (1) 225 AD *CIRB* 1279, 23 (s. *Μενέστρατος*)

Ἀμάρθαστος
SKYTHIA:
—TANAIS: (1) 155 AD ib. 1260, 15 (f. —*ων*) ?= (*2*); (2) ib. l. 17 (I f. *Ἀμάρθαστος* II) ?= (*1*);

(3) ib. l. 17 ([Ἀμ]αρθαστος: II s. Ἀμάρθαστος I)

'Αμάς
Thrace:
—ODESSOS: (1) f. ii AD *IGB* I² 178 (PM 1722); *Dacia* 21 (1977) p. 161 (date) (d. Ἀσκληπιάδης, m. Ἀμασιακίς)

'Αμᾶς
Thrace:
—PHILIPPOPOLIS-TRIMONTIUM (TERRIT.): (1) ii-iii AD *IGB* III 1506 (Ἀμᾶτος (gen.): f. —οκος)

'Αμασία
Cimmerian Bosporos:
—PANTIKAPAION: (1) i AD *CIRB* 336

'Αμασιακίς
Thrace:
—ODESSOS: (1) f. ii AD *IGB* I² 178 (PM 1722); *Dacia* 21 (1977) p. 161 (date) (d. Σωκράτης, Ἀμάς)

'Αμαστρις
Macedonia (Edonis):
—PHILIPPOI (NR.): (1) ?ii AD *BCH* 47 (1923) p. 78 no. 38 (Pilhofer 402) (Lat. Valeria A[ma]stris: m. Εὐκαρπία)

'Αμάτοκος
Macedonia (Bottiaia):
—BEROIA: (1) 188 AD *ILeukopetra* 21, 3 (Tataki 68) (Π. Αἴλ. Ἀ.)
Thrace: (2) 160 BC *BGU* 2390, 4, 14; cf. La'da E730 (f. Διζάολος); (3) *BGU* 2390, 37 (La'da E703); (4) c. 85 BC *REG* 32 (1919) pp. 321-2, 2, 22, [24], 30 (s. Τήρης); (5) i AD *IGB* IV 2338, 2; cf. V 5928 (f. Ἔζβενις); (6) 46-54 AD *SEG* XVI 415 III, 35 (*IThrakAig* E84) (f. Ἐσβενις)
—BRANIČEVO (MOD.): (7) iv BC *Rogozen Treasure* p. 47 no. 23; *Arkheologiia* (Sofia) 1987 (3), pp. 26-37 (f. Τήρης)
—BYZANTION?: (8) ii BC *IByz* 325 (Ἀμάτοκ[ος]: f. Ἑρμίας)
—GLAVA PANEGA (MOD.): (9) ii-iii AD *IGB* II 532-3 (I f. Τ. Φλ. Ἀμάτοκος II) ?= (*12*); (10) ib. 532-4 (Τ. Φλ. Ἀ.: II s. Ἀμάτοκος I) ?= (*13*)
—ODRYSAI: (11) f. iv BC *RE* s.v. Amadokos (3); Rhodes–Osborne 47, [5], [8], [10], 14, etc.: *Rogozen Treasure* p. 48 no. 23; Peter, *MTD* pp. 132-40 (coin) (Ἀμάδοκος—lit. test. and Rhodes–Osborne: s. Μήτοκος: king)
—PAUTALIA (TERRIT.): (12) ii-iii AD *IGB* IV 2217; [2218] (Τ. Φλ. Ἀ.: I f. Τ. Φλ. Ἀμάτοκος II) ?= (*9*); (13) ib. 2217-18 (Τ. Φλ. Ἀ.: II s. Τ. Φλ. Ἀμάτοκος I) ?= (*10*)
Thrace?: (14) ii BC *Memnonion* 601 (Velkov 22); (15) f. ii BC *PTeb* 1058, 3 (*PP* 8582; Velkov 21)

'Αμβατία
Tauris:
—KERKINITIS: (1) iv BC *IOSPE* I² 339 (d. Ἡρόδοτος)

'Αμβίκατος
Macedonia (Bottiaia):
—KYRRHOS: (1) iii-ii BC *SEG* XXVII 258 (f. Ξένανθος)

'Αμβούας
Macedonia (Bottiaia):
—EDESSA: (1) 51 AD ib. XLVI 744, 3 (Tataki, *Edessa* 236) (Μ. Οὐίβιος Ἀ.)

'Αμβουστος
Skythia:
—TANAIS: (1) 220 AD *CIRB* 1278, 25; Zgusta, *PNS* 274 (f. —κος)

'Αμβροσία
Macedonia (Edonis):
—AMPHIPOLIS: (1) hell. *SEG* XXIV 597 (d. Ἡρακλείδης)
Thrace:
—PERINTHOS-HERAKLEIA: (2) iii AD *IPerinth* 153 (Αὐρηλιανὶ Ἀ. (dat.): d. Αὐρ. Ἀμβρόσις, Αὐρ. Ἡσυχίς)

'Αμβρόσις
Macedonia (Pieria):
—PYDNA: (1) 250 AD *SEG* XLVI 800 A, 34 (Κλ. Ἀ.)
Thrace:
—PERINTHOS-HERAKLEIA: (2) iii AD *IPerinth* 153 (Αὐρ. Ἀ.: f. Αὐρηλιανὴ Ἀμβροσία)

'Αμείνανδρος
Macedonia (Bottiaia):
—AIGAI: (1) c. 300-275 BC *SEG* XXXV 804 (Ἀμε(ί)νανδρος, Ἀμ(ύ)νανδρος?: s. Κέββας)

'Αμεινίας
Cimmerian Bosporos:
—BOSPOROS: (1) ?17 BC *IOSPE* I² 354 A, 2 (Ἀμιν[ίας])
—PANTIKAPAION?: (2) 129 AD *CIRB* 705, 4 (f. Μέμνων)
Macedonia: (3) iii BC *Milet* VI (2) 793, 4; cf. Stephanis 1423; Tataki, *Macedonians* p. 342 no. 46 (s. Ποσειδώνιος); (4) *IG* XII (6) 120, 6 (Tataki, *Macedonians* p. 233 no. 96); cf. La'da E1433 (f. Ἀριστόλαος)

'Αμεινόνικος
Macedonia (Bottiaia):
—PELLA: (1) iii BC Akamatis, *Amph. Pellas* p. 31 no. PAR1 (amph.) (*SEG* L 613)

'Αμειψίας
Macedonia (Pieris):
—NEAPOLIS: (1) 356 BC *IG* II² 128, 4 (Tataki, *Macedonians* p. 125 no. 2) (Ἀμειψ[ίας]: f. Διοσκουρίδης)

'Αμερίας
Macedonia: (1) iii BC *RE* (-); Hoffmann, *Makedonen* pp. 2-17 (*PP* 16816; Tataki, *Macedonians* p. 234 no. 97)
Macedonia (Mygdonia):
—KALINDOIA: (2) c. 319 BC Hatzopoulos, *MI* 2 pp. 84-5 no. 62, 27 (Ἀμερίας—Hatzopoulos: s. Κυδίας)

'Αμέριμνος
Macedonia: (1) f. i BC *BGU* 1740, 18 (*PP* 2592; Tataki, *Macedonians* p. 472 no. 13) (Ἀμέριμ[νος]: katoikos)
Macedonia (Bottiaia):
—BEROIA: (2) ii-iii AD *IBer* 305 (Ἀ. ὁ καὶ Λυχνᾶς)
Skythia:
—OLBIA-BORYSTHENES (ACHILLEIOS DR.): (3) ii-iii AD *IOSPE* I² 330

'Αμετέρα
Macedonia (Bottiaia):
—SKYDRA: (1) iii AD *SEG* XLIX 793, 4 (Ἀμ(φο)τέρα—edd.)

'Αμηρύγκας
Macedonia (Pieria):
—PYDNA: (1) iv BC *GRBS* 43 (2002-3) p. 119 no. 5, 3

'Αμία
Macedonia (Lynkestis):
—HERAKLEIA (AREA): (1) iii AD *IG* X (2) (2) 34 (Αὐ(ρ). Ἀ.)
Macedonia (Mygdonia):
—HERAKLEIA: (2) m. iii AD *SEG* XLVIII 710
—THESSALONIKE: (3) ii-iii AD *IG* X (2) (1) 408 (-μεί-: m. Βάλης)

'Αμιανή
Macedonia (Paionia):
—KAVADARCI (MOD.): (1) iii/iv AD Unp. (Papazoglu archive)

'Αμιζώκης
Skythia:
—SKYTHAI: (1) ii AD Luc., *Tox.* 38-43 (fict.)

'Αμιλλα
Macedonia (Bottiaia):
—BEROIA: (1) c. 180-219 AD *ILeukopetra* 15, 1 (Tataki 1055) (Πετρωνία Ἀ.)
Macedonia (Mygdonia):
—THESSALONIKE: (2) 134 AD *IG* X (2) (1) 462 B (d. Διοσκουρίδης)

'Αμιλλος
Penestai?: (1) ii-iii AD *SEG* XXXIX 618; cf. *BE* 1991, no. 378 (name) (-μειλο-: s. Ἀπολλόδωρος)

'Αμιν
Cimmerian Bosporos:
—PANTIKAPAION: (1) ii-i BC *CIRB* 266

'Αμινος
Thrace:
—PERINTHOS-HERAKLEIA: (1) v-vi AD *IPerinth* 225

'Αμισήτιος
Macedonia (Mygdonia):
—THESSALONIKE: (1) iii AD *IG* X (2) (1) 606

'Αμμα
Cimmerian Bosporos:
—PANTIKAPAION: (1) i AD *CIRB* 337; Zgusta, *PNS* 593 (m. Ἀγάπημα)

'Αμμάδα
Macedonia (Bottiaia):
—PELLA: (1) ?iii BC *SEG* L 610 (Ἀμμά[δ]α)

'Αμμάδας
Macedonia (Eordaia):
—MAVROPIGI (MOD.): (1) ii/i BC ib. XXXVIII 665 (f. Διομήδης)

'Αμμαδίκα
Macedonia (Bottiaia):
—PELLA: (1) ?iv BC ib. XLIII 440 (Ἀμμαδίκα)
Macedonia (Mygdonia):
—THESSALONIKE: (2) ?i AD ib. XXXVIII 701 + XLIII 469 (Ἀτερία Ἀμμαδείκ[α])

'Αμμάδικος
Macedonia (Bottiaia):
—BEROIA: (1) f. i BC *IBer* 163 (Tataki 145) (f. Νικάδας)
Macedonia (Mygdonia):
—KALINDOIA: (2) c. 314 BC Hatzopoulos, *MI* 2 pp. 84-5 no. 62, 32 (Ἀμμά[δικος]?, Ἀμμά[δας]?: f. Περδίκκας)

'Αμμαδίς
Macedonia (Pieria):
—PHYLAKAI?: (1) ?i BC Oikonomos 58 = *IG* IX (2) 230 (d. Ἄδυμος)

'Αμμαδίσκος
Macedonia: (1) hell. *Memnonion* 102 (Tataki, *Macedonians* p. 234 no. 98; La'da E1401) (Ἀμμάδοκος?—*SB* 1076, Ἀμμάδικος?: s. Γλαῦκος)

'Αμμακώ
Macedonia (Paionia):
—BYLAZORA (NR.): (1) ii-iii AD *SEG* XXXVIII 713 n. b (d. Ζώσιμος)
—NEGOTINO (MOD.): (2) ii-iii AD ib. 713 n. a (d. Ποσειδώνιος, m. Ποσειδώνιος); (3) iii AD ib. 713 (d. Δάδης)

Ἀμμαλίνη
Macedonia (Lynkestis):
—sitaria (mod.): **(1)** f. iii ad *EAM* 167 b (-λεί-)

Ἀμμαλῖνος
Macedonia (Elimeia):
—kozani (mod.): **(1)** ii ad ib. 34, 3 + *SEG* xlvi 759 ([Ἀ]μμαλεῖ[νος]?)

Ἀμμένα
Macedonia (Pieria):
—pydna (territ.): **(1)** iii bc *Klio* 52 (1970) p. 61 no. 13 (d. *Εὐρείας*, m. *Κλεονίκη*)

Ἀμμία
Cimmerian Bosporos:
—pantikapaion: **(1)** i bc/i ad *CIRB* 300 (d. *Ψυχαρίων*); **(2)** i ad ib. 338
Macedonia: **(3)** ii ad *IBer* 74, 5 (Tataki 1090) (*Ποντία Ἀ.*)
Macedonia (Bisaltia):
—euporia?: **(4)** ii-iii ad *SEG* xxx 615 (xxxix 591) (*Ἀ. ἡ καὶ Ποπιλλία*)
Macedonia (Bottiaia):
—aigai: **(5)** f. iii bc ib. xxxv 783 (*Ἀμμ[ία]*)
—beroia: **(6)** ii-i bc *IBer* 204 (Tataki 153) (d. *Ἀθηνώ*); **(7)** i-ii ad *IBer* 339 (m. *Εὔπορος*); **(8)** i/ii ad ib. 40, 2 (Tataki 692) (*Κλ. Ἀ.*: d. *Τι. Κλ. Πιερίων*, m. *Κλ. Λουκία*, *Κλ. Πιερίων*, *Κλ. Ἀμύντας*, *Κλ. Ἀέροπος*); **(9)** ii ad *IBer* 169, 1 (Tataki 147); **(10)** *IBer* 420, 6 (Lat. Domitia Ammia: d. *Γν. Δομίτιος Μενέλαος*); **(11)** ii-iii ad *ILeukopetra* 144; **(12)** *IBer* 371, 1 (Tataki 149) (m. *Κοναρτίων*); **(13)** s. ii ad *IBer* 310, 3 (d. —μος, ?d. *Φίλα*, *Πιθάνη*); **(14)** ii/iii ad ib. 211, 1 (Tataki 154) (d. *Παράμονος*) ?= (*16*); **(15)** f. iii ad *IBer* 122, 1 (Tataki 582) (*Ἰουλιανὴ Ἀ.*: m. *Κλ. Ἄλκηστις*); **(16)** *IBer* 210, 2 (Tataki 258) (*Αὐρ. Ἀ.*: m. *Πετρωνιανὸς Ἀγαθήμερος*) ?= (*14*); **(17)** 212 ad *ILeukopetra* 62, 4 (*Ποπιλλία Ἀ.*); **(18)** 216 ad ib. 68, 2 (m. *Αὐρ. Φίλα*); **(19)** 229 ad *IBer* 68, 11 (Tataki 983) (*Οὐαλεριανὴ Ἀ.*)
—beroia?: **(20)** f. iii ad *IBer* 386, 5 (Tataki 148) (*Ἀμμ[ία]*)
—mieza: **(21)** iii bc *SEG* xxiv 526
Macedonia (Edonis):
—amphipolis: **(22)** 157 ad Dimitsas 863 (d. *Τόρκος*, *Ἡρώ*)
Macedonia (Elimeia):
—diporo (mod.): **(23)** ii bc *EAM* 44 (d. *Πελειγένης*)
Macedonia (Eordaia):
—agios panteleimonas (mod.): **(24)** s. ii ad ib. 126 (d. *Παράμονος*)
—mavropigi (mod.): **(25)** iii/ii bc ib. 120; cf. *SEG* xli 578 b
—ryaki (mod.): **(26)** ii-i bc *EAM* 121 (d. *Κρατεύας*)
Macedonia (Krestonia):
—ioron?: **(27)** i ad *SEG* xxvii 287 a (d. *Μένανδρος*)
Macedonia (Lynkestis):
—ano vevi (mod.): **(28)** ii ad *EAM* 164 (d. *Ἀντίγονος*, m. *Ἀντίπατρος*)
—florina (mod.): **(29)** hell. *Florina* p. 22 (pithos)
—herakleia: **(30)** imp. *IG* x (2) (2) 100
Macedonia (Lynkestis)?: **(31)** s. ii ad *EAM* 156 (d. *Ἐπιγένης*)
Macedonia (Mygdonia):
—arethousa?: **(32)** f. i bc *EAD* xxx 185 (Tataki, *Macedonians* p. 68 no. 1) (or Syria Arethousa: d. *Ἀνδρομαχίδης*)
—kalindoia: **(33)** iii bc *SEG* xlii 592
—thessalonike: **(34)** f. i ad *IG* x (2) (1) 126, 6; Robert, *OMS* 5 pp. 295-302 (date) (m. *Ταῦρος ὁ καὶ Ῥῆγλος*); **(35)** f. iii ad *IG* x (2) (1) 188, 10; 189, 7 (*Αὐρ. Ἀπολλοδωριανὴ Ἀ.*)
Macedonia (Odomantike):
—sirrha?: **(36)** ii-iii ad Kaphtantzis 21 (*Ἀμμία*)
Macedonia (Paionia):
—antigoneia? (budur čiflik (mod.)): **(37)** imp. *SEG* xiii 405 ([*Ἀμ*]*μία*: m. *Νουμήνιος ὁ καὶ Τίτος*)
—argos (nr.): **(38)** ii-iii ad *Sp.* 71 (1931) p. 38 no. 83, 2 (m. *Γαΐα*)
—astrea: **(39)** i/ii ad *IBer* 102 B, 2-3 (*Ἀουιδία Ἀ.*: d. *Φίλων*)
—bylazora: **(40)** ii ad *Sp.* 98 (1941-8) p. 29 no. 73 (d. *Μέστριος*, *Σεμέλη*)
—kavadarci (mod.): **(41)** ii ad ib. p. 67 no. 140 (?d. *Ποσειδώνιος*); **(42)** ii/iii ad Unp. (Kavadarci Mus.) inv. 6/II (d. *Γάϊος*, m. *Γάϊος*)
—neapolis? (izvor (mod.): **(43)** ii-iii ad *Sp.* 98 (1941-8) p. 28 no. 68 (d. *Ποσειδώνιος*, *Γαΐα*)
—neapolis? (smilovci (mod.)): **(44)** ii ad ib. p. 31 no. 76 (m. *Γάϊος*, *Ζωΐλος*)
—neapolis? (vladilovci (mod.)): **(45)** ii-iii ad ib. 71 (1931) p. 31 no. 62, 4
Macedonia (Pelagonia): **(46)** 81 ad *IG* x (2) (2) 276 (d. *Εὔβουλος*, *Νανοῦς*); **(47)** ii ad ib. 260; cf. 261 (?m. *Ἀσκληπιόδωρος*); **(48)** ii-iii ad ib. 260
—keramiai (nr.): **(49)** ii-iii ad ib. 210 (m. *Κάσσανδρος*, *Γάϊος*)
Macedonia (Pieria):
—phylakai?: **(50)** ?i bc Oikonomos 58 = *IG* ix (2) 230 (d. *Οὐαδύρα*)

Ἀμμιανός
Macedonia (Bottiaia):
—beroia: **(1)** ii-iii ad *IBer* 226 (Tataki 156); **(2)** iii ad *IBer* 220 (Tataki 157); **(3)** f. iii ad *IBer* 212 (Tataki 158) (*Ἀνμι-*: I f. *Ἀμμιανός* II); **(4)** *IBer* 212 (Tataki 159) (*Ἀνμι-*: II s. *Ἀμμιανός* I, *Μελίτα*)
—edessa: **(5)** 229 ad *Ancient Macedonia* 1 p. 200 no. 12, 33 (Tataki, *Edessa* 50) (*Αὐρ. Ἀμ(μ)ιανός*)
—genderrhos? (mandalon (mod.)): **(6)** ii-iii ad *SEG* xliii 396 (*Ἀμ(μ)ιανός*: s. *Ἀλέξανδρος*)
Macedonia (Chalkidike):
—anthemous: **(7)** ii-iii ad ib. xlii 570 (*Οὐεντουληνὸς Ἀ.*: s. *Οὐεντουληνὸς Σμέρτις*, *Αὐρ. Κλεοπάτρα*)
Macedonia (Mygdonia):
—thessalonike: **(8)** ii ad *IG* x (2) (1) 241 A I, 12 (*Ἀμμι[α]ṿ[ός]*)
—thessalonike?: **(9)** ii ad ib. 248 II, 4 (*Ἀμμι[ανός]*?: f. *Νουμήνιος*)
Macedonia (Pieria):
—dion: **(10)** ii/iii ad *SEG* xxxix 582 (*Ποστούμιος Ἀ.*: s. *Κλωδία Ἀλεξάνδρα*)

Ἀμμιάς
Scythia Minor:
—ulmetum: **(1)** ?v ad Barnea 73, 11 (Popescu, *IGL* 210) (*Ἀμμιάδος* (gen.): m. *Ἀλεξάνδρεια*)

Ἄμμιλα
Macedonia (Bottiaia):
—beroia: **(1)** 191-192 ad *ILeukopetra* 27, 5; 28, 5; 29, 5 (Tataki 44) (*Αἰλ. Ἀ.*, *Ἐλία Ἀμίλα*—27)

Ἄμμιν
Macedonia (Bottiaia):
—beroia: **(1)** ii ad *IBer* 296 (Tataki 161)

Ἄμμιον
Cimmerian Bosporos:
—pantikapaion: **(1)** ii/i bc *CIRB* 265; cf. KW pl. 29 no. 417 (d. *Ὀρόντης*)
Macedonia (Bottiaia):
—pella: **(2)** m. iv bc *SEG* xxxviii 648 (d. *Ἡρακλείδης*)

Ἀμμιώ
Macedonia (Edonis):
—amphipolis: **(1)** 165 ad ib. xlix 676 (*Ἀμμιοῦνι* (dat.): d. *Διονύσιος*)

Ἄμμων
Thrace:
—beroe-augusta traiana: **(1)** c. 320-324 ad *Anal. Boll.* 31 (1912) pp. 197 ff.; p. 207

Ἀμμώνιος
Macedonia: **(1)** m. ii bc *BGU* 2423, 37 (Tataki, *Macedonians* p. 473 no. 18; La'da E1405) (s. *Τρύφων*); **(2)** b. 112 bc *PDion* 40, 2 (Tataki, *Macedonians* p. 473 no. 21); cf. La'da E1672 (f. ...ῳνιος); **(3)** 145 bc *PPhrurDiosk* 18, 44; **(4)** 135-131 bc Bernand, *De Thèbes* 243, 9 (Tataki, *Macedonians* p. 473 no. 19); cf. La'da E1445 (f. *Ἀσκληπιάδης*); **(5)** 113 bc *PDion* 21, 28, 42 (Tataki, *Macedonians* p. 472 no. 16; La'da E1403) (s. *Δημήτριος*: katoikos); **(6)** 111 bc *PDion* 22, 12 (Tataki, *Macedonians* p. 473 no. 20); cf. La'da E1567 (f. *Ὀνίας*); **(7)** 107 bc *SB* 11410 B, 11 (Tataki, *Macedonians* p. 472 no. 14); **(8)** 60 bc *BGU* 1816, 2 (Tataki, *Macedonians* p. 473 no. 17; La'da E1404) (s. *Ἡρακλείδης*)
Macedonia (Edonis):
—amphipolis: **(9)** 214 bc *BGU* 2397, 20 (Tataki, *Macedonians* p. 46 no. 7; La'da E131)
Macedonia (Mygdonia):
—thessalonike: **(10)** ii-iii ad *IG* x (2) (1) 541, 3
Tauris:
—chersonesos*: **(11)** i-ii ad *IAK* 16 (1905) p. 107 (lamp)
Thrace:
—byzantion: **(12)** c. 225-200 bc *PMich* 781 II, 19 (La'da E339) (s. *Φίλων*)

Ἀμμώνις
Macedonia (Chalkidike):
—kombreia: **(1)** 87 ad *IG* x (2) (2) 325, 79 (Tataki, *Macedonians* p. 115 no. 2) (*Ἀμμώνεος* (gen.): f. *Νικόλαος*)

Ἄμναγος
Skythia:
—olbia-borysthenes: **(1)** ii ad *IOSPE* I² 162, 9; Zgusta, *PNS* 275 (s. *Ῥα*—)

Ἀμπέλιν
Macedonia (Mygdonia):
—thessalonike: **(1)** ii ad *IG* x (2) (1) 712 (*Ῥεία Ἀμπέλιν*)

Ἀμπελίνη
Macedonia (Lynkestis):
—herakleia?: **(1)** i-ii ad *SEG* xv 380 (*Ἀμπέλιν ἡ*?—Robert)

Ἀμπελίων
Thrace:
—maroneia: **(1)** i bc *IG* II² 8793 (*FRA* 3530)

Ἀμπέλοργος
Thrace:
—apollonia-sozopolis: **(1)** iv bc *IGB* I² 433 (f. *Ποσίδειος*)

Ἀμπελοχία
Macedonia (Mygdonia):
—thessalonike: **(1)** v-vi ad *IG* x (2) (1) 337 (Feissel, *RICM* 176)

Ἀμπλιάνη
Thrace:
—beroe-augusta traiana: **(1)** c. 320-324 ad *Anal. Boll.* 31 (1912) p. 198; p. 208

Ἄμυκος
Macedonia (Pieria):
—dion (territ.): **(1)** ii ad Oikonomos 48 (f. *Αὐρ. Λυκιδίων*)

Ἀμύνανδρος

Macedonia (Mygdonia):

—thessalonike: **(1)** ii ad *IG* x (2) (1) 429; cf. *BCH* 99 (1975) p. 175-7 (f. *Μακεδόνιος*)

Thrace:

—maroneia: **(2)** ii-i bc *IThrakAig* E212, 8 (s. *Θεόξενος*); **(3)** imp. ib. E289 (s. *Διοσκουρίδης*); **(4)** i-ii ad Bakalakis, *Oinos Ismarikos* p. 1015 with fig. 17 + *IThrakAig* E288, 2 (*Ἀμύν[αν]δρος*: f. *Ἡρακλείδης*); **(5)** Bakalakis, *Oinos Ismarikos* p. 1015 with fig. 17 + *IThrakAig* E288, 5 (s. *Ἡρακλείδης*); **(6)** iii ad *Thrak. Epet.* 4 (1983) p. 425 n. 24 + *IThrakAig* E192 (*[Ἀ]μύνα[νδ]ρος*: s. *Θεόδωρος*)

Ἀμύντας

Cimmerian Bosporos:

—pantikapaion: **(1)** iii ad *CIRB* 109, 2

Macedonia: **(2)** c. 565-495 bc *RE* (10) (Tataki, *Macedonians* p. 234 no. 99) (*Ἀ.* I: s. *Ἀλκέτας*, f. *Ἀλέξανδρος* I, *Γυγαία*: king); **(3)** v bc *RE* (11) (Tataki, *Macedonians* p. 234 no. 100); cf. Beloch, *GG* iii (2) pp. 65-6 (s. *Ἀλέξανδρος* I, f. *Ἀρριδαῖος*); **(4)** f. v bc *RE* Supplbd. 4 (20a) (and Caria Alabanda: *Ἀμύντης*—Hdt.: s. *Βουβάρης* (Persia), *Γυγαία*); **(5)** c. 435-369 bc ib. (14); *HN*² pp. 221-2; *Kraay-Mørkholm Essays* pp. 307-8; 312-13 (coin) (Tataki, *Macedonians* p. 236 no. 110); cf. Beloch, *GG* iii (2) pp. 65-7; *Historia* 44 (1995) pp. 265 ff. (*Ἀ.* III: s. *Ἀρριδαῖος*, f. *Ἀλέξανδρος* II, *Περδίκκας* III, *Φίλιππος* II, *Εὐρυνόα*, *Ἀρχέλαος*, *Ἀρριδαῖος*, *Μενέλαος*: king); **(6)** 429 bc *RE* (12) (Tataki, *Macedonians* p. 237 no. 118) (s. *Φίλιππος*); **(7)** v/iv bc Ael., *VH* xii 43 (s. *Μενέλαος*) ?= (*14*); **(8)** 413-399 bc Arist., *Pol.* 1311 b, 14 (s. *Ἀρχέλαος*); **(9)** iv bc *IEph* 1419 (Tataki, *Macedonians* p. 237 no. 119) (f. *Ἀλέξανδρος*); **(10)** Arr., *An.* i 14. 2 (Tataki, *Macedonians* p. 238 no. 126) (f. *Φίλιππος*); **(11)** Arr., *An.* i 29. 3; iii 5. 5 (Tataki, *Macedonians* p. 238 no. 120) (f. *Βάλακρος*); **(12)** Arr., *An.* iv 13. 3 (Tataki, *Macedonians* p. 238 no. 125) (f. *Σώστρατος*); **(13)** f. iv bc Did., *in D.* col. 13. 2 (Tataki, *Macedonians* p. 238 no. 121) (f. *Ἱππόστρατος*); **(14)** ?394 bc *RE* (13); *Kraay-Mørkholm Essays* pp. 305-6; 311 (coin); cf. *Macedonia* 2 pp. 168-70 (Tataki, *Macedonians* p. 234 no. 101); *Historia* 44 (1995) p. 279 (*Ἀ.* II *ὁ μικρός*: king) ?= (7); **(15)** c. 365-336 bc *RE* (15); Berve 61; *IG* vii 3055, 7 (*SEG* xliv 414); Rhodes–Osborne 75 A, 4 (*IOrop* 1); cf. *Eretria* xi pp. 367-87 (Tataki, *Macedonians* p. 237 no. 117) (s. *Περδίκκας* III, f. *Ἀδέα ὕστερον Εὐρυδίκα*) ?= (*19*); **(16)** c. 365-333 bc *RE* (16); Berve 58; Rhodes–Osborne 75 B, 4 (*IOrop* 2); cf. *Eretria* xi pp. 367-87 (Tataki, *Macedonians* p. 236 no. 109) (s. *Ἀντίοχος*); **(17)** ?359-357 bc *SEG* xxxviii 662, 11; cf. Hatzopoulos, *Donation* pp. 55-61 (f. *Ξενόκριτος*); **(18)** s. iv bc *RE* (22); *FGrH* 122 (Tataki, *Macedonians* p. 235 no. 103); **(19)** 338-336 bc *FGrH* 135-6 F 20; Just. ix 5. 8 (Tataki, *Macedonians* p. 234 no. 102); cf. *RE* (19) ?= (*15*); **(20)** 335 bc ib. Supplbd. 4 (5a); Berve 62 (Tataki, *Macedonians* p. 235 no. 104); **(21)** 334 bc *RE* (5); Berve 59 (Tataki, *Macedonians* p. 201 no. 4) (s. *Ἀρραβαῖος*); **(22)** 331 bc Curt. v 2. 5 (Tataki, *Macedonians* p. 235 no. 107) (Lat. Amyntas); **(23)** 330 bc Berve 64 (Tataki, *Macedonians* p. 235 no. 105) (Lat. Amyntas); **(24)** Berve 65 (Tataki, *Macedonians* p. 235 no. 106) (Lat. Amyntas); **(25)** hell.? *CIA* iii 3623 (fals.?); cf. *Mus. Helv.* 1993, p. 52 (Tataki, *Macedonians* p. 238 no. 122) (f. *Κάσσανδρος*); **(26)** ?313 bc *IG* xi (2) 135, 38; 145, 47; 154 B, 24-5 (Tataki, *Macedonians* p. 235 no. 108); **(27)** 301 bc *RE* (6); **(28)** iii bc *ISmyrna* 183 (Tataki, *Macedonians* p. 237 no. 116) (s. *Ὀλύμπιχος*); **(29)** 256 bc *PCZ* 59127, 2, 6 (Tataki, *Macedonians* p. 238 no. 127); cf. La'da E1487 (f. *Ἐργεύς*); **(30)** 243 bc *PSI* 389, 9 (Tataki, *Macedonians* p. 237 no. 115; La'da E1742) (*[Ἀμύ]ντας*: s. *Μενέλαος*: t.e.); **(31)** iii/ii bc ib. E1406 (*[Ἀμ]ύντας*); **(32)** *IG* xii Suppl. p. 190 no. 634 (Tataki, *Macedonians* p. 236 no. 111) (s. *Ἀρτεμίδωρος*: date—Knoepfler); **(33)** c. 223 bc *PTeb* 815 fr. 2 recto II, 24 (Tataki, *Macedonians* p. 238 no. 123); cf. La'da E1810 (f. *Νικαία*); **(34)** ?219 bc *PUG* iii 104, 21 (II s. *Ἀμύντας* I); **(35)** ib. l. 22 (I f. *Ἀμύντας* II); **(36)** 192 bc *PTeb* 816, 44 (Tataki, *Macedonians* p. 238 no. 124); cf. La'da E1592 (f. *Πτολεμαῖος*); **(37)** m. i bc *AD* 11 (1927-8) pp. 58-9 no. 5, 4-5; cf. *SEG* xxxi 582 (Tataki, *Macedonians* p. 236 no. 113) (s. *Γλαῦκος*)

Macedonia (Bottiaia):

—aigai: **(38)** f. iii bc *IMM* 10, 11 (Tataki, *Macedonians* p. 39 no. 5) (f. *Αἰσχρίων*); **(39)** c. 266 bc *IG* xii (9) 1187, 30; Robert, *Ét. Num. Gr.* pp. 179 ff. (date) (Tataki, *Macedonians* p. 39 no. 4) (s. *Μένων*); **(40)** ?ii bc *SEG* xxxviii 721 (f. *Νόστιμος*: locn.—Tataki)

—aloros: **(41)** 328-325 bc *RE* (18); Berve 60 (Tataki, *Macedonians* p. 44 no. 1) (s. *Νικόλαος*) ?= (*99*)

—beroia: **(42)** m. iii bc *Thess. Mnem.* 82 (Tataki 165; Tataki, *Macedonians* p. 75 no. 9) (f. *Ἀντίγονος*); **(43)** 223 bc *IBer* 4, 30 (f. *Σταπόλεμος*); **(44)** ib. l. 31 (*Ἀμύν[τ]ας*: f. *Ὀρέστης*); **(45)** b. 167 bc ib. 1 A, 3, 17 (Tataki 167) (f. *Ζώπυρος*) ?= (*49*); **(46)** ii bc *IBer* 141, 18; **(47)** ib. 158 (s. *Πευκόλαος*) ?= (*48*); **(48)** ib. (f. *Ἀρτεμίδωρος*) ?= (*47*); **(49)** f. ii bc ib. 155 (f. *Ζώπυρος*) ?= (*45*); **(50)** 122 bc ib. 134, 6 (*[Ἀμ]ύντας*: f. *Καλλιμέδων*); **(51)** ib. l. 10 (*[Ἀμ]ύντας*); **(52)** f. i ad ib. 103, 9 (Tataki 166) (f. *Διογένης*); **(53)** 69-84 ad *IBer* 61, 3 (Tataki 169); **(54)** i/ii ad *IBer* 40, 3-4 (Tataki 709) (*Κλ. Ἀ.*: s. *Κλ. Ἀμμία*); **(55)** f. ii ad *IBer* 119, 3 (f. *Τ. Φλαούϊος Παράμονος*); **(56)** ib. 243 (Tataki 1064) (*Πετρώνιος Ἀ.*: f. *Ζώσιμος*); **(57)** 203 ad *ILeukopetra* 47, 3 (Tataki 168) (f. *Λαδόμα*)

—beroia (territ.): **(58)** ?iv bc *IBer* 498 (Tataki 164) (s. *Στράτων*)

—beroia?: **(59)** 178 bc *SGDI* 2071, 8 (s. *Λᾶτος*)

—beroia (territ.)?: **(60)** iv bc *IBer* 510 (Tataki 162) (*[Ἀ]μύντας*)

—mieza: **(61)** 321 bc *RE* (20); Berve 56 (Tataki, *Macedonians* p. 123 no. 2) (s. *Ἀλέξανδρος*); **(62)** i ad Dimitsas 18 (291; Tataki 1000) (*Λ. Οὐολκάκιος Ἀ.*)

—pella: **(63)** iv bc *IG* iv (1) 103 (Tataki, *Macedonians* p. 149 no. 11) (f. *Δ*—); **(64)** iii bc *AD* 16 (1960) Mel. p. 82 (tile); **(65)** 263 bc *IG* ix (1)² (1) 17, 69 (Tataki, *Macedonians* p. 149 no. 10) (s. *Ἀ*—)

—tyrissa?: **(66)** s. iv bc *SEG* xliii 446 (*Ἀμύντας*)

Macedonia (Chalkidike):

—antigoneia?: **(67)** hell.? Hatzopoulos, *MI* 1 p. 203 n. 8 (f. *Κλέαρχος*)

Macedonia (Derriopos):

—stuberra: **(68)** 74 ad *IG* x (2) (2) 326, 41 (*Ἀ.*: s. *Πρῖμος*); **(69)** 87 ad ib. 325, 73 (s. *Ἀπολλόδωρος*)

Macedonia (Edonis):

—amphipolis: **(70)** iv-iii bc *PAE* 1956, p. 142 pl. 47c; **(71)** iv/iii bc *SEG* xxxv 708 (*CEG* ii 724; *Amphipolis* p. 111 fig. 80) (s. *Μονούνιος*); **(72)** hell. Dimitsas 851 (*Ἀμυνία* (gen.)—Dimitsas, *Ἀμύντα*: f. *Ἀριστοκλῆς*)

—amphipolis?: **(73)** iii bc *SEG* xxiv 609 = xliii 372 (f. *Ὀλώϊχος*)

Macedonia (Elimeia):

—aiane (territ.): **(74)** ?iii ad *EAM* 24 b (I f. *Ἀμύντας* II *ὁ καὶ Κρίσπος*); **(75)** ib. (*Ἀ. ὁ καὶ Κρίσπος*: II s. *Ἀμύντας* I)

—kozani (mod.): **(76)** imp. ib. 21

—petrana (mod.): **(77)** ii-iii ad ib. 72 (I f. *Ἀμύντας* II); **(78)** ib. (*Ἀ. νεώτ.*: II s. *Ἀμύντας* I)

—velvendos (mod.): **(79)** i-ii ad ib. 78, 4 (*Τιβ. Κ[λ]. [Ἀ]μύ[ν]τας*: s. *Ἀπολλόδωρος*)

—xerolimni (mod.): **(80)** ii bc *Α΄ Panell. Synedr. Epigr.* p. 61 no. 7 (*SEG* xlix 846) (s. *Σαβύττιος*)

Macedonia (Eordaia):

—exochi (mod.): **(81)** 223 ad ib. xlvi 745, 9 (f. *Αὐρ. Ἰουλία*)

—kormestai: **(82)** ii bc *EAM* 88 (f. *Ἰόλλας*)

—ryaki (mod.): **(83)** ii-i bc ib. 121 (*Ἀμύ[ντας]*: f. *Νε*—); **(84)** i-ii ad ib. 96 (?f. *Ἡδόνη*)

Macedonia (Lynkestis): **(85)** 331 bc Berve 63 (Tataki, *Macedonians* p. 201 no. 3) (Lat. Amyntas)

—herakleia (area): **(86)** ii-iii ad *IG* x (2) (2) 25 (*Ἀ. Κελε*—)

Macedonia (Mygdonia):

—apollonia: **(87)** f. ii bc *SEG* xliv 508 (Hatzopoulos, *MI* 2 p. 87 no. 66) (f. *Ἀντίγονος*)

—lete: **(88)** s. iv bc ib. 79, 2 (f. *Λύσανδρος*); **(89)** f. ii bc *SEG* xlvi 764, 6 (f. *Ἀντιφῶν*); **(90)** 117 bc *Syll*³ 700, 51 (s. *Διῆς*)

—thessalonike: **(91)** imp. *SEG* xlvii 963 (s. *Ζωΐλος*); **(92)** i ad *IG* x (2) (1) 316; cf. *Tyche* 10 (1995) pl. 6 (f. *Ἀπολλώνιος*); **(93)** i-ii ad *IG* x (2) (1) 243 II, 11 (s. *Διονύσιος*); **(94)** s. i ad ib. 68, 6, 10; 69, 5, 10 (*Τ. Φλ. Ἀ.*: s. *Εὐκτίμενος*)

Macedonia (Orestis):

—battynaioi: **(95)** 192 ad *EAM* 186 I, 49 (s. *Νικόλαος*)

Macedonia (Pieria):

—pydna: **(96)** iv bc *GRBS* 43 (2002-3) p. 119 no. 5, 7

Macedonia (Sintike):

—parthikopolis (nr.): **(97)** ii-iii ad *IGB* iv 2291, 1, 6 (s. *Τήρης*)

Macedonia (Tymphaia): **(98)** c. 365-330 bc *RE* (17); Berve 57 (Tataki, *Macedonians* p. 211 no. 2) (s. *Ἀνδρομένης*)

Macedonia?: **(99)** 330 bc Berve 65 (Tataki, *Macedonians* p. 235 no. 106) ?= (*41*); **(100)** iii bc *PPetr* ii 30 b, 20; Uebel, *Kleruchen* 828 (Tataki, *Macedonians* p. 236 no. 114) (s. *Κόρραγος*)

Ἀμύντης

Thrace:

—perinthos-herakleia?: **(1)** iv bc Hp., *Epid.* iv 50 (*Ἀμυντέω* (gen.))

Ἀμυντιανή

Macedonia (Bottiaia):

—beroia: **(1)** ii-iii ad *IBer* 284 (Tataki 170) (d. *Τιτιανός*)

Scythia Minor:

—kallatis: **(2)** iii ad *ISM* iii 142

Ἀμυντιανός

Macedonia (Bottiaia):

—beroia: **(1)** 192 ad *ILeukopetra* 29, 1 (*Σεμπρώνιος Ἀμυντιανὸς Φλῶρος*); **(2)** 210-212 ad ib. 57, 9; 59, 11; 60, 14; 61, [16]; 62, 17; 64, 4 (Tataki 276) (*Αὐρ. Ἀ.*, *Αὐρηλιανὸς Ἀ.*—59-60 and 62)

—mieza: **(3)** ii-iii ad ib. 171

Macedonia?: **(4)** m. ii ad *RE* (1); *FGrH* 150

Ἀμύντιχος

Macedonia (Bottiaia):

—beroia: **(1)** hell. *SEG* xxiv 522 (vase) (Tataki 172)

Macedonia (Pieria):

—pydna: **(2)** iv bc *GRBS* 47 (2002-3) p. 122 no. 6, 6

Ἀμύντωρ
MACEDONIA: (1) 311-306 BC Maier, *Mauerbauinschr.* 69 II, 139 (Tataki, *Macedonians* p. 238 no. 128) (s. Γέρων)
MACEDONIA (BOTTIAIA):
—PELLA: (2) iv BC Arr., *An.* iii 27. 4; *Ind.* xviii 3 (Tataki, *Macedonians* p. 149 no. 12) (f. Ἡφαιστίων)
MACEDONIA (EDONIS):
—AMPHIPOLIS: (3) b. 213 BC Hatzopoulos, *MI* 2 p. 83 no. 61, 9 (*SEG* XLVI 715) ([Ἀμύ]ντωρ—ed., [Μέ]ντωρ?)
MACEDONIA (PIERIA):
—PYDNA: (4) iv BC *GRBS* 47 (2002-3) p. 116 no. 4, 5
MACEDONIA?: (5) ?s. iv BC *HE* 746 (Tataki, *Macedonians* p. 239 no. 130) (s. Φίλιππος); (6) 334-333 BC *IG* II² 405, 12, 15; cf. Osborne, *Naturalization* D21 (*PA* 750; Tataki, *Macedonians* pp. 238-9 no. 129) (s. Δημήτριος)
SKYTHIA:
—OLBIA-BORYSTHENES: (7) iii BC *IOSPE* I² 201 I, 58 (s. Ἀθηνόδωρος)
THRACE:
—BYZANTION: (8) 208 BC *FD* III (3) 183, 2 (s. Ἀριστείδας)
—ODESSOS: (9) 38 BC *IGB* I² 46, 9 (s. Ἕλλην); (10) 32 BC ib. l. 15 (s. Αἰαντίδης); (11) i-ii AD ib. 108, 1, 7 (s. Νουμήνιος, f. Μακού); (12) ii-iii AD ib. 127 (s. Ἱερώνυμος, f. Μακού); (13) ib. 173 (PM 1731); *Dacia* 21 (1977) p. 161 (date) (s. Ἀγαθήνωρ); (14) s. ii AD *IGB* I² 79, 3 (*CCET* I 33) (s. Μεν—)
—ODESSOS (TERRIT.): (15) iii AD *IGB* I² 279 (*CCET* I 26)
—ODESSOS (NR.): (16) i BC-i AD *IGB* I² 283 bis (*CCET* I 97) (f. Μένανδρος)

Ἀμυώ?
THRACE:
—SALYMBRIA: (1) vi AD *BCH* 36 (1912) pp. 635-6 no. 92 (*AD* 53 (1998) Mel. p. 477 no. 219) (gen.: m. Μαρκελλῖνος)

Ἀμφήριτος
MACEDONIA (CHALKIDIKE):
—AKANTHOS: (1) inc. Polyaen. vi 54 (Ἀμφίρητος—ms., Ἀμφάρητος?)

Ἀμφίας
TAURIS:
—CHERSONESOS: (1) iv BC Solomonik, *NEPKh* 166 (s. Μᾶτρις)
THRACE: (2) 263-227 BC *PCZ* 59473, 5 (Velkov 24; La'da E704)
—APOLLONIA-SOZOPOLIS: (3) v/iv BC Unp. (Sofia, Nat. Mus. of Hist.) inv. 3210 (coin)

Ἀμφικλέα
THRACE:
—BYZANTION: (1) iii BC *IByz* 64 (d. Φιλίσκος)

Ἀμφικτύων
MACEDONIA: (1) ?273 BC *FD* III (1) 108, 2 + *BCH* 68/9 (1944/5) p. 100 no. 10 (Tataki, *Macedonians* p. 239 no. 131) (Ἀν[φ]ικ[τ]ύων: s. Βάκχιος)

Ἀμφίλοχος
CIMMERIAN BOSPOROS:
—PANTIKAPAION: (1) f. iv BC *CIRB* 167
MACEDONIA: (2) 338 BC *RE* (4); *SEG* XXX 163 (Tataki, *Macedonians* p. 239 no. 132)
THRACE:
—APOLLONIA-SOZOPOLIS: (3) iv BC *Rev. Num.* 1900, p. 41 no. 4 ([Ἀμ]φίλοχος); (4) *IGB* I² 443 (s. Εὔγνωτος)
—PERINTHOS-HERAKLEIA:
——(Podargoi): (5) iii-ii BC *IPerinth* 61, 24 (s. Ὑπερείδης)
—PERINTHOS-HERAKLEIA?: (6) iv BC Hp., *Epid.* iv 45

Ἀμφίμαχος
MACEDONIA?: (1) 321-316 BC *RE* (9); Berve 66 (Tataki, *Macedonians* p. 239 no. 133) (?s. Φίλιννα (Larisa))

Ἀμφιονίδης
SCYTHIA MINOR:
—TOMIS: (1) 201 AD *ISM* II 83 I, 19 (f. Δημήτρις)

Ἀμφίπολις
MACEDONIA (BOTTIAIA):
—PELLA: (1) f. ii BC *SEG* XLIV 546 ([Ἀ]μφίπολις)
MACEDONIA (EDONIS):
—AMPHIPOLIS: (2) iii AD ib. XXIV 598; cf. XXXVII 580 (?m. Παράμονος)
MACEDONIA (MYGDONIA):
—THESSALONIKE: (3) ii AD *IG* X (2) (1) 428 (*GVI* 428)

Ἀμφιτίων?
CIMMERIAN BOSPOROS:
—PANTIKAPAION: (1) i BC-i AD *CIRB* 301; cf. KW pl. 32 no. 452 (Ἀμφιτ̣ίων—*CIRB*, Ἀμφείων—KW)

Ἀμφίτριτος
MACEDONIA (CHALKIDIKE):
—AKANTHOS: (1) iv/iii BC *SEG* XLVII 871 A, 1 (Ἀν-: f. Σίμη)

Ἀμφίων
MACEDONIA (MYGDONIA):
—THESSALONIKE: (1) m. i BC ib. 970 (biling.) (*ILGR* 220); *KGAM Thess.* 1 61 (date) (Π. Τετρήνιος Ἀ.)
MACEDONIA (PIERIA):
—DION*: (2) s. ii AD *ILGR* 180; *Prakt. VIII Diethn. Synedr. Epigr.* 1 p. 276 (Lat. P. Anthestius Amphio: freed.)
TAURIS:
—CHERSONESOS: (3) iv BC Solomonik, *GAKh* 215 (sherd) (*SEG* XXVI 806) (Ἀμφίω[ν]: s. —οχος)
THRACE:
—BYZANTION: (4) ii AD *Türk Tarih Kongresi XI* (6) p. 2703 with pl. 495. 5 (Ἀνφεί-: s. Εὐτυχία)
—MESAMBRIA: (5) ii BC *IGB* I² 314 b, 1, 11 (Ἀμφίονος (gen.): f. Γλαυκίας)
—PAUTALIA (TERRIT.): (6) ii-iii AD ib. V 5813 (-φεί-: s. Φλ. Πρόκλος)

Ἀμφοτερός
MACEDONIA: (1) m. iv BC Plu., *Mor.* 177 F (Tataki, *Macedonians* p. 239 no. 134) (fict.?)
MACEDONIA (ORESTIS): (2) 334-331 BC *RE* (4); Berve 68 (Tataki, *Macedonians* p. 204 no. 3) (s. Ἀλέξανδρος)

Ἀμώρθαστος
SKYTHIA:
—OLBIA-BORYSTHENES: (1) ii AD *IOSPE* I² 80, 5; Zgusta, *PNS* 273 (Ἀμώ[ρ]θαστος: f. Ἀμωρόμαρος)

Ἀμωρόμαρος
SKYTHIA:
—OLBIA-BORYSTHENES: (1) ii AD *IOSPE* I² 80, 4; Zgusta, *PNS* 276 (Ἀμω[ρό]μαρος: s. Ἀμώρθαστος); (2) *IOSPE* I² 84, 9 (f. Βάγαος); (3) ib. 101, 6 (f. Εὐρησίβιος); (4) ib. 130, 9-10; 155 (Ἀ[μω]ρόμαρος: s. Εὐρησίβιος)

Ἀμώσπαδος
SKYTHIA:
—OLBIA-BORYSTHENES: (1) m. ii AD ib. 105, 4; *VDI* 1953 (4), p. 130, 7; Zgusta, *PNS* 50 (Ἀμώσσπαδος—*VDI* err.: s. Ἀχιλλεύς)

Ἀνα
SCYTHIA MINOR:
—ISTROS: (1) i BC-i AD *ISM* I 191 II, 12

Ἀναγόρης
SKYTHIA:
—OLBIA-BORYSTHENES: (1) v BC Tolstoi 13 (*LSAG*² p. 372 no. 58; *SEG* XXX 946 (vase)) (Ἀναγόρη—*SEG*)

Ἀναθεμενός
CIMMERIAN BOSPOROS:
—NYMPHAION: (1) iv BC *CIRB* 921 (Ἀνα(θ)εμενός: f. Λεωκράτης)

Ἀναίη
CIMMERIAN BOSPOROS:
—PANTIKAPAION: (1) f. iii BC ib. 245 (d. Μιτραβάτης)

Ἀνακούβαρος
THRACE:
—BISANTHE-PANION: (1) iv-vi AD *AD* 49-50 (1994-5) Mel. p. 314 no. 139 (Παῦλος ὁ καὶ Ἀ.)

Ἀνάκριτος
MACEDONIA (CHALKIDIKE):
—AKANTHOS: (1) f. v BC *SEG* XLI 553 (amph.)

Ἀνακτόριος
MACEDONIA (BOTTIAIA):
—BEROIA: (1) ii-iii AD *IBer* 91, 6 (Tataki 628) (Ἰούν. Ἀντίγονος ὁ καὶ Ἀ.: s. Ἰουν. Κάλη)

Ἀνάληψις
MACEDONIA (PELAGONIA): (1) iii AD *IG* X (2) (2) 178 (-λημψ-: m. Ἀρίστη, Ἀφροδιτώ)

Ἀναξαγόρας
MACEDONIA: (1) ii/i BC *IvOl* 317, 3 (Tataki, *Macedonians* p. 240 no. 135) (f. Ἡροφῶν)
SKYTHIA:
—OLBIA-BORYSTHENES: (2) s. iv BC *IOSPE* I² 195, 4 (*CEG* II 883; Dubois, *IGDOlbia* 47) (s. Δημαγόρης); (3) c. 70 BC *IOSPE* I² 35, 1, 4 (f. Ποσίδεος)

Ἀναξαγόρη
THRACE:
—APOLLONIA-SOZOPOLIS: (1) s. v BC *IGB* I² 425 (d. Ἀκεσαῖος)

Ἀναξαγόρης
SKYTHIA:
—OLBIA-BORYSTHENES: (1) s. vi BC Dubois, *IGDOlbia* 23, verso, 3-5, 9-10
—OLBIA-BORYSTHENES (LEUKE): (2) ?v-iv BC *SEG* XLIII 502. 4 (vase) ([Ἀνα]ξαγόρ[ης])
THRACE:
—APOLLONIA-SOZOPOLIS: (3) v/iv BC *IGB* I² 421 bis (Ἀναξαγορέω (gen.): f. Θεόμνηστος)

Ἀνάξανδρος
MACEDONIA?: (1) b. 348 BC *Olynthus* 10 p. 422 no. 2177 (bullet)
THRACE:
—APOLLONIA-SOZOPOLIS: (2) f. v BC *IGB* I² 405 (*CEG* I 172) ([Ἀ]νάξανδρος: f. Δεινῆς)

Ἀνάξαρχος
THRACE:
—ABDERA: (1) c. 380-320 BC *RE* (1); *FVS* 72; Berve 70; (2) s. iv BC *Ét. Thas.* 5 p. 235 no. 411 (f. Ἑρμόθεστος)

Ἀναξήνωρ
THRACE:
—ABDERA: (1) c. 415-395 BC May, *Abdera* p. 163 nos. 204-5 (coin); (2) iv BC Hp., *Epid.* vii 114

Ἀναξιάδης
CIMMERIAN BOSPOROS:
—GORGIPPIA: (1) f. iii BC *CIRB* 1137 B I, 18 ([Ἀνα]ξιάδης: s. Σίνδος)

Ἀναξίβιος
THRACE:
—PERINTHOS-HERAKLEIA:
——(Podargoi): **(1)** iii-ii BC *IPerinth* 61, 27 ((*Ἀ*)*ναξίβιος*)

Ἀναξίδικος
THRACE:
—ABDERA: **(1)** c. 500-475 BC *Horos* 14-16 (2000-2003) p. 253 no. 3 (*IThrakAig* E31) (s. *Νύμφις*); **(2)** c. 439-411 BC May, *Abdera* pp. 169-70 no. 226 (coin) ?= (*3*); **(3)** c. 415-395 BC ib. pp. 163-5 nos. 206-14 (coin) ?= (*2*); **(4)** m. iv BC *Ét. Thas.* 3 p. 317 no. 110 (f. *Θαρσύνων*)

Ἀναξίδοτος
MACEDONIA: **(1)** ?308-304 BC *Eretria* XI p. 109 no. 5, 2, 7 (*IG* XII (9) 205) + *IG* XII (9) 226 (Tataki, *Macedonians* p. 240 no. 137); *Eretria* XI pp. 111-17 (date) (f. *Ἀπολλόδωρος*); **(2)** *IG* XII (9) 206, 2, 8, 20; cf. *Eretria* XI pp. 210-11 no. XI (Tataki, *Macedonians* p. 240 no. 136); *Eretria* XI pp. 111-17 (date) (s. *Ἀπολλόδωρος*)
MACEDONIA (BOTTIAIA):
—PELLA: **(3)** iv BC Arr., *Ind.* xviii 3; xxvii 8 (Tataki, *Macedonians* p. 149 no. 13) (f. *Ἀρχίας*); **(4)** iv/iii BC *SEG* XXIV 538 (XXXIX 619); **(5)** 117 BC *FD* III (2) 70 b, 6 with Add. p. 294 (Tataki, *Macedonians* p. 149 no. 14) (f. —*ανωρ*)

Ἀναξίδωρος
MACEDONIA (MYGDONIA):
—THESSALONIKE?: **(1)** s. ii AD *IG* X (2) (1) 252, 5 (*Ἀναξίδ*[*ω*]*ρος*: s. *Εὔβουλος*)

Ἀναξικράτης
CIMMERIAN BOSPOROS:
—GORGIPPIA: **(1)** f. iii BC *CIRB* 1137 A I, 7 (f. *Νικόστρατος*); **(2)** ib. 1137 A II, 3 (f. *Ἡρόδωρος*); **(3)** ib. 1137 B I, 28 (f. —*φ.λος*) ?= (*4*); **(4)** ib. l. 32 (f. —*στρατος*) ?= (*3*)
THRACE:
—BYZANTION: **(5)** 409 BC X., *HG* i 3. 18 (*FRA* 1384)

Ἀναξίλα
THRACE:
—BYZANTION: **(1)** ii-i BC *IByz* 210 (Fıratlı–Robert p. 69 no. 68) (d. *Τιμογένης*)

Ἀναξίλαος
THRACE:
—BYZANTION: **(1)** 409 BC X., *HG* i 3. 18 (*FRA* 1385)

Ἀναξίλας
MACEDONIA (CHALKIDIKE):
—POTIDAIA-KASSANDREIA: **(1)** ?254 BC Nachtergael, *Les Galates* 9, 55; cf. Stephanis 1733 (Tataki, *Macedonians* p. 85 no. 2) (f. *Μοιραγένης*)

Ἀναξίλεως
CIMMERIAN BOSPOROS:
—HERMONASSA: **(1)** iv BC *CIRB* 1056 I, 10 (f. —*ς*); **(2)** ib. l. 15 (f. —*πος*); **(3)** ib. 1056 II, 10 (*Ἀ*[*ν*]*αξί*[*λεως*]: f. *Ἀρτέμων*)

Ἀναξιμένης
SCYTHIA MINOR:
—ISTROS: **(1)** ii AD *ISM* I 212, 25 (s. *Κλειτοφῶν*)
SKYTHIA:
—OLBIA-BORYSTHENES: **(2)** s. iv BC *SEG* L 702 III, 2 (s. *Ἡρόφιλος*); **(3)** iii BC *IOlbia* 30; cf. *SEG* XXXIV 759 ([*Ἀνα*]*ξιμένης*?); **(4)** f. i AD *IOlbia* 42, 2-3; cf. Vinogradov–Kryžickij p. 144 (date) (f. *Ἀντιφῶν*) ?= (*6*); **(5)** i/ii AD *IOlbia* 90, 2 (f. *Εὐρησίβιος*); **(6)** ii AD *IOSPE* I^2 40, 7 (f. *Ἀντιφῶν*) ?= (*4*); **(7)** ib. 130, 3 (*Ἀναξιμ*[*έ*]*νης*: s. *Σωκράτης*); **(8)** ib. 131, 8 (s. *Εὐρησίβιος*); **(9)** ib. 132, 7; *IOlbia* 79, 5; cf. *SEG* XLII 713 (I f. *Ἀναξιμένης* II); **(10)** *IOSPE* I^2 183, 5 (s. *Ποσίδηος*); **(11)** c. 150-175 AD ib. 132, 6; *IOlbia* 79, 5; cf. *SEG* XLII 713 (II s. *Ἀναξιμένης* I)

Ἀναξιπόλη
CIMMERIAN BOSPOROS:
—NYMPHAION: **(1)** iv BC *CIRB* 918; cf. *Hyperboreus* 2000, pp. 137-8 (*Ἀναξιπόλης* (masc.)—ed.: d. *Φάνις*)

Ἀναξίπολις
THRACE:
—ABDERA: **(1)** c. 415-395 BC May, *Abdera* pp. 161-2 no. 200 (coin) ?= (*2*); **(2)** ib. pp. 168-9 nos. 220-3 (coin) ?= (*1*); **(3)** c. 395-360 BC ib. pp. 212-13 nos. 283-6 (coin); **(4)** 346 BC *IG* II^2 218, 16, 30 (*FRA* 1) (*Ἀναξιπόλιδι* (dat.): s. *Διονυσόδωρος*); **(5)** c. 336-311 BC May, *Abdera* p. 291 nos. 531-2 (coin)

Ἀνάξιππος
MACEDONIA: **(1)** b. 330 BC *RE* (2); Berve 72 (Tataki, *Macedonians* p. 240 no. 138)
MACEDONIA (CHALKIDIKE):
—MENDE: **(2)** ?v-iv BC Paus. v 25. 7
THRACE:
—MARONEIA: **(3)** ii-i BC *IThrakAig* E212, 15 (s. *Φιλόξενος*); **(4)** i BC ib. E213, 6 (f. *Τιμοξενίδης*)

Ἀναξίστρατος
CIMMERIAN BOSPOROS:
—PANTIKAPAION: **(1)** iv BC *CIRB* 157 (*Ἀναξίστρατ*[*ος*]: s. *Ἱστιαῖος*)

Ἀναξίων
CIMMERIAN BOSPOROS:
—PANTIKAPAION: **(1)** iv BC ib. 224 (f. *Σωσίκα*)
THRACE:
—ABDERA: **(2)** iv BC Hp., *Epid.* iii 17. 8; *CMG* V (10) ii 1 p. 178

Ἀναξώ
THRACE:
—BYZANTION: **(1)** ii-i BC *IByz* 148 (d. *Λυκοῦργος*)

Ἄνασσα
THRACE:
—PERINTHOS-HERAKLEIA: **(1)** iii AD *IPerinth* 150 (*Αὐρ. Ἄννασα*)

Ἀναστάσιος
MACEDONIA (MYGDONIA):
—THESSALONIKE: **(1)** ?v-vi AD *AD* 4 (1918) Parart. p. 31
MACEDONIA (ODOMANTIKE):
—SIRRHA: **(2)** v-vi AD Feissel, *RICM* 210
THRACE:
—MARONEIA: **(3)** v-vi AD Meïmaris–Bakirtzis 12 (*IThrakAig* E356)
—PERINTHOS-HERAKLEIA: **(4)** iv-vi AD *Araşt. Sonuçları Topl.* 2000 (1), p. 290

Ἀνατολή
CIMMERIAN BOSPOROS:
—PANTIKAPAION: **(1)** i AD *CIRB* 339
MACEDONIA (MYGDONIA):
—THESSALONIKE: **(2)** ii-iii AD *IG* X (2) (1) 642, 6 (*Μεττία Ἀν*<*ι*>*ατολή*: d. *Μᾶρκος, Οὐαριανὴ Παυλῖνα*)

Ἀνατολῖνος
THRACE:
—BYZANTION: **(1)** c. 303 AD *Anal. Boll.* 31 (1912) p. 192 (-*τυ*-)

Ἀνατόλιος
MACEDONIA (BOTTIAIA):
—BEROIA: **(1)** vi AD *IBer* 429, 2 ([*Ἀνα*]*τόλιος*?, [*Ἀποσ*]*τόλιος*—*IBer*)

SCYTHIA MINOR:
—SALSOVIA: **(2)** iv AD Popescu, *IGL* 272 c, 8 (Lat. Anatoli[us])

Ἀνάχαρσις
SKYTHIA:
—SKYTHAI: **(1)** m. vi BC *RE* (-); cf. Vinogradov, *Pont. Stud.* pp. 626-31 (?s. *Γνοῦρος, Δαυκέτης*: king)

Ἀνάψυξις
THRACE:
—MARONEIA: **(1)** 360 BC *IG* IV $(I)^2$ 94 b, 29 (Perlman, *City and Sanctuary* E.1 with pp. 69-70 (date))

Ἀνδοκίς
SKYTHIA:
—OLBIA-BORYSTHENES: **(1)** m. v BC Dubois, *IGDOlbia* 99 a (vase) (*Ἀνδοκίδος* (fem. gen.)—Dubois, *Ἀνδόκιδος* (masc. nom.)—edd. pr.)

Ἀνδράβυς
THRACE:
—MARONEIA: **(1)** i BC-i AD *IG* II^2 9288 (*FRA* 3531) (*Ἀνδράβυδος* (gen.): f. *Θρᾶιττα*)

Ἀνδράγαθος
MACEDONIA: **(1)** 242 BC *PSI* 394, 8 (Tataki, *Macedonians* p. 240 no. 140); cf. La'da E1416 (f. *Ἀπολλόδωρος*)
MACEDONIA (EDONIS):
—AMPHIPOLIS?: **(2)** 288 BC Polyaen. iv 12. 2
MACEDONIA (ELIMEIA):
—AIANE (TERRIT.): **(3)** 161-180 AD *EAM* 36, 6 (*Αἴλ. Ἀ.*: s. *Ἀντίγονος*)

Ἀνδραλέων
CIMMERIAN BOSPOROS:
—GORGIPPIA: **(1)** ii/iii AD *CIRB* 1179, 52 (*Ἀνδραλέ*[*ω*]*ν*: s. *Πόσις*)

Ἀνδρέας
MACEDONIA (EDONIS):
—PHILIPPOI: **(1)** iv/v AD *SEG* XLV 796, 1 (mosaic) = XXXVI 629 (Pilhofer 42); cf. *SEG* XLVI 789; **(2)** ?v AD Feissel, *RICM* 247 (Pilhofer 104; *PLRE* II (7)) (*Ἀ. οὗ τὸ ἐπίκλην Κομιτᾶ*); **(3)** v-vi AD Feissel, *RICM* 225 (Pilhofer 353)
—PHILIPPOI (NR.): **(4)** iv-v AD *AE* 1973, Chron. p. 39 (pithos) (Pilhofer 421)
MACEDONIA (LYNKESTIS):
—HERAKLEIA: **(5)** iii AD *IG* X (2) (2) 97 (*Αὐρ. Ἀ.*: f. *Λυσίμαχος*)
MACEDONIA (MYGDONIA):
—OSBE: **(6)** f. iv BC *IBer* 147 (Tataki, *Macedonians* p. 145 no. 1) (s. *Ἄνδρων*)
—THESSALONIKE: **(7)** iv-vi AD *Tekmeria* 7 (2002) p. 101 no. 6; **(8)** v AD Feissel, *RICM* 102 B ([*Ἀ*]*νδρέας*); **(9)** v-vi AD *IG* X (2) (1) 404 (Feissel, *RICM* 169) (s. *Πέτρος, Ἀλεξάνδρα*); **(10)** 532 AD ib. 133
—THESSALONIKE?: **(11)** v-vi AD ib. 165 (*SEG* XLVII 1008) (f. *Δημήτριος*); **(12)** ?vi AD *IG* X (2) (1) 793 (Feissel, *RICM* 142) (s. *Ἀρε*—)
MACEDONIA (PIERIA):
—DION: **(13)** iv-v AD *Dion* p. 44
MACEDONIA (SINTIKE):
—PARTHIKOPOLIS: **(14)** vi AD Beševliev 243, 2
SCYTHIA MINOR: **(15)** ii BC *SCIV* 1.1 (1950) pp. 246-7 nos. 29-32; *SNG Stancomb* 317 (coin) (*Ἀνδρέ*(*ας*))
THRACE:
—BYZANTION: **(16)** f. iii AD *IByz* 308 (-*δρή*-)
—BYZANTION (NR.): **(17)** v-vi AD *AD* 53 (1998) Mel. p. 503 no. 239. 2 (brick)
—PERINTHOS-HERAKLEIA: **(18)** iv BC *IG* II^2 10069 (*FRA* 6030) (*Ἀνδρέ*[*ας*])

Ἀνδρείας
MACEDONIA (EDONIS):
—AMPHIPOLIS: **(1)** 192 BC *SEG* XLVI 716 B, 4

Ἀνδριανή
MACEDONIA (MYGDONIA):
—THESSALONIKE: (1) ii-iii AD *IG* X (2) (1) 599 (m. *M. Ἀονιάνιος Ἰσίδωρος*)

Ἀνδρίας
THRACE: (1) iii/ii BC ib. V (1) 811, 4 (*Ἀνδρίας*)

Ἀνδρικός
CIMMERIAN BOSPOROS:
—BOSPOROS: (1) iii BC ib. II² 8426 (*FRA* 1366) (f. *Εὐπορία*)
THRACE:
—AINOS: (2) ii BC *IG* II² 7969/70 (*FRA* 231) (*Ἀν(δ)ρικός*: s. *Ἀνδρόνικος*)

Ἀνδρίσκα
MACEDONIA: (1) 244 AD *ILeukopetra* 100, 7 (oikogen. slave/freed.)

Ἀνδρίσκος
MACEDONIA (BOTTIAIA):
—PELLA?: (1) iv/iii BC *Arch. Pap.* 22 (1973) p. 203 no. 1 (f. *Παυσανίας*)
—TYRISSA? (ASVESTARI (MOD.)): (2) f. ii BC *SEG* XLVII 999, 10
MACEDONIA (EDONIS):
—AMPHIPOLIS: (3) s. iv BC Hatzopoulos, *Actes Amphipolis* p. 50 no. 11, 6 (*SEG* XLI 565) (*[Ἀν]δρίσκος*)
MACEDONIA (ORESTIS):
—BATTYNAIOI: (4) 192 AD *EAM* 186 II, 50 (*Ἀνδρίσκος*: f. *Νίκανδρος*); (5) ib. l. 56 (s. *Νικόλαος*)
MACEDONIA?: (6) c. 151-146 BC *RE* (4); cf. Walbank 3 pp. 668-9 (*ὁ Ψευδοφίλιππος*)

Ἀνδροκλείδης
MACEDONIA (BOTTIAIA):
—BEROIA: (1) s. iii BC *IBer* 16 B, 24 (s. *Φίλιππος*)

Ἀνδροκλῆς
MACEDONIA (MYGDONIA):
—THESSALONIKE: (1) 95 BC *IG* X (2) (1) 4, 4 (f. *Νικήρατος*)
—THESSALONIKE?: (2) i AD ib. 844 (f. *Μόσχιον*)
MACEDONIA?: (3) 168 BC *RE* Supplbd. 4 (13a) (Tataki, *Macedonians* p. 241 no. 143) (Lat. Androcles)
TAURIS:
—CHERSONESOS: (4) iv/iii BC *IOSPE* I² 463 (s. *Προμαθίων*)
THRACE:
—APOLLONIA-SOZOPOLIS: (5) iv BC *BMNBurgas* 4 (2002) p. 122 no. 9 (*Ἀνδροκ[λ]ῆς*: s. *Ἀστυάναξ*)

Ἄνδροκλος
MACEDONIA: (1) iv BC Arr., *An.* iii 29. 1 (Tataki, *Macedonians* p. 241 no. 144) (f. *Ἀρχέλαος*)
THRACE:
—APOLLONIA-SOZOPOLIS: (2) v/iv BC *IGB* I² 420 (f. *Πάρμις*)

Ἀνδρομάχα
MACEDONIA (EDONIS):
—AMPHIPOLIS: (1) iii BC *SEG* XXIV 591

Ἀνδρομαχίδης
MACEDONIA (MYGDONIA):
—ARETHOUSA?: (1) f. i BC *EAD* XXX 185 (Tataki, *Macedonians* p. 68 no. 2) (or Syria Arethousa: f. *Ἀμμία*)

Ἀνδρόμαχος
MACEDONIA: (1) 331-329 BC *RE* (6); Berve 75 (Tataki, *Macedonians* p. 242 no. 149) (s. *Ἱέρων*); (2) m. iii BC *RE* (9); Grainger, *SPG* p. 8; cf. Beloch, *GG* IV (2) pp. 205-6 (?s. *Ἀχαιός*, f. *Ἀχαιός*); (3) f. ii BC Bataille, *IG Hatshepsout* 43; 48; 49 (Tataki, *Macedonians* p. 241 no. 147; La'da E1407)
MACEDONIA (BOTTIAIA):
—BEROIA: (4) ii BC *SEG* XXIV 504 b; *IBer* 160 (Tataki 177) (s. *Τύριος*, f. *Τύριος*); (5) *SEG* XXIV 504 d; *IBer* 160 (stemma) (f. *Τύριος*)
MACEDONIA?: (6) 332 BC *RE* (7); Berve 76 (Tataki, *Macedonians* p. 241 no. 146) (Lat. Andromachus); (7) Arr., *An.* ii 20. 10 (Berve 77)
THRACE: (8) 180 BC *Essays Thomas* p. 78, 2 (La'da E705) (II s. *Ἀνδρόμαχος* I); (9) *Essays Thomas* pp. 78, 4; cf. La'da E705; E710; E779 (I f. *Ἀνδρόμαχος* II, *Ἀρισταῖος*, *Παραιβάτης*)
—ABDERA: (10) iv BC Paus. vi 14. 12 (f. *Πυθῆς*)
—BYZANTION: (11) iv/iii BC *Suda M* 1464 (f. *Ὅμηρος*)
THRACE?: (12) 241 BC *PFrankf* 5, 20 (s. *Φιλουμένη*)

Ἀνδρομένης
MACEDONIA (EDONIS):
—AMPHIPOLIS: (1) s. iv BC *PAE* 1981, p. 25 with pl. 43 β, 15 (*Ἀνδρομέν[ης]*)
MACEDONIA (MYGDONIA):
—KALINDOIA: (2) a. 98 AD *SEG* XLII 582, 42 (s. *Φίλαγρος*)
MACEDONIA (TYMPHAIA): (3) iv BC Arr., *An.* iii 27. 1 (Tataki, *Macedonians* p. 212 no. 3) (f. *Ἀμύντας*, *Ἄτταλος*, *Πολέμων*, *Σιμμίας*)
SKYTHIA:
—TANAIS: (4) ii AD *CIRB* 1262, 10 (s. *Τρύφων*); (5) m. ii AD ib. 1238 (f. *Τρύφων*) ?= (6); (6) c. 200-210 AD ib. 1277, 19 (*Ἀνδρομέ[ν]ης*—Tokhtas'ev: f. *Τρύφων*) ?= (5)

Ἀνδρομήδης
CIMMERIAN BOSPOROS:
—NYMPHAION: (1) iv BC ib. 917 (*Ἀν[δ]ρομήδ[η]ς*: f. *Ἀκροτίμη*)

Ἀνδρονίκη
MACEDONIA (MYGDONIA):
—THESSALONIKE?: (1) ii AD *IG* X (2) (1) 249, 6 (*[Ἀ]νδρονίκη*)

Ἀνδρόνικος
CIMMERIAN BOSPOROS:
—HERMONASSA*: (1) 307 AD *CIRB* 1051 (*M. Αὐρ. Ἀνδρ[ό]νεικος*: s. *Πάππος*, f. *Ἀλέξαρθος*)
—PANTIKAPAION: (2) i AD ib. 564; cf. KW pl. 50 no. 702 (*Ἀνδρόνε[ικ]ος*: f. *Δῖος*)
MACEDONIA: (3) iv BC *RE* (10); Berve 78 (Tataki, *Macedonians* p. 129 no. 5); cf. Billows, *Antigonos* p. 277 + 367 (ident.) (s. *Ἀγέρρος*, ?f. *Πρωτέας*, *Θεόδωρος*) ?= (12); (4) Arr., *An.* ii 20. 2 (Tataki, *Macedonians* p. 243 no. 155) (f. *Πρωτέας*); (5) iii BC *IG* XII (5) 571, 15 (Tataki, *Macedonians* p. 243 no. 154) (f. *Παυσανίας*); (6) ?c. 285-260 BC *SEG* XIV 398 a, [1], 4 (Tataki, *Macedonians* p. 242 no. 151) (*Ἀνδρόνι[κος]*); (7) 190 BC *RE* (14); Grainger, *SPG* p. 77 (Lat. Andronicus); (8) 169 BC *RE* (13) (Tataki, *Macedonians* p. 242 no. 152)
MACEDONIA (BOTTIAIA):
—ALLANTE: (9) c. 230-200 BC *BCH* 45 (1921) p. 17 III, 64 (Tataki, *Macedonians* p. 43 no. 1) (s. *Χιωνίδης*)
—KYRRHOS: (10) m. i BC *IG* XII (5) 891, 1 (Tataki, *Macedonians* p. 116 no. 1) (s. *Ἑρμίας*)
—MIEZA: (11) ?ii AD Dimitsas 19 (292; Tataki 178) (-νει-: f. *Τι. Κλ. Ἱλαρίων*)
MACEDONIA (CHALKIDIKE):
—OLYNTHOS: (12) 334-314 BC *RE* (11); Berve 79 (*PP* 10062a; Tataki, *Macedonians* p. 129 no. 5) ?= (3)
MACEDONIA (DERRIOPOS):
—STUBERRA: (13) 107 AD *IG* X (2) (2) 325, 99 (-νει-: f. *Παράμονος*)
MACEDONIA (EDONIS):
—AMPHIPOLIS: (14) m. iii BC Hatzopoulos, *Actes Amphipolis* p. 52 no 12, 3; *SEG* XLI 566 (date) (f. *Σωσικράτης*); (15) Hatzopoulos, *Actes Amphipolis* p. 52 no 12, 7; *SEG* XLI 566 (date) (f. *Μαχάτας*); (16) c. 200-170 BC Hatzopoulos, *MI* 2 no. 65, 2 (*SEG* XLVI 720) (f. *Ἐπιγένης*); (17) imp. Kaphtantzis 657, 1 (-νει-: ?s. *Ἀπολλωνᾶς*)
—PHILIPPOI: (18) ii-iii AD *BCH* 55 (1931) pp. 200-1 no. 14 (Pilhofer 334) (*[Ἀν]δρόνεικο[ς]*)
MACEDONIA (ELIMEIA):
—VELVENDOS (MOD.): (19) ?iii AD *EAM* 80 (*[Μ.] [Οὔ]λπ. Ἀνδ[ρ]όνεικος*)
MACEDONIA (KRESTONIA):
—BRAGYLAI: (20) c. 230-200 BC *BCH* 45 (1921) p. 18 III, 70 (Tataki, *Macedonians* p. 84 no. 1) (s. *Κάσσανδρος*)
MACEDONIA (LOWER PAIONIA):
—GORTYNIA?: (21) imp. *Sp.* 98 (1941-8) p. 48 no. 101 (Sokolovska, *Isar Marvinci* p. 131) (*Ἀνδρόνι[κος]*)
MACEDONIA (MYGDONIA):
—KALINDOIA: (22) 68-98 AD *SEG* XLII 580, 86 (-νει-: I f. *Ἀνδρόνικος* II); (23) ib. l. 86 (-νει-: II s. *Ἀνδρόνικος* I); (24) ib. 581, 2 (*Τ. Φλαούϊος Ἀ.*: s. *Φίλιππος*) ?= (25); (25) a. 98 AD ib. 582, 1 (-νει-: f. *Τ. Φλαούϊος Ἀπολλώνιος*) ?= (24)
—THESSALONIKE: (26) iii AD *IG* X (2) (1) 518 bis (*Φλ. Ἀ.*)
—THESSALONIKE?: (27) iii BC ib. 26, 3; cf. *Tyche* 10 (1995) pl. 4 no. 2 (s. *Ἀλέξανδρος*); (28) ii-iii AD *IG* X (2) (1) 752 (*[Ἀν]δρόνεικος*)
—THESSALONIKE*: (29) 187 BC ib. 3, 1
MACEDONIA (PELAGONIA):
—KERAMIAI (NR.): (30) iii AD ib. X (2) (2) 225 (*Αὐρήλιος Ἀνδρόνεικ[ο]ς*: f. *Παράμονος*)
MACEDONIA (TYMPHAIA):
—SYDENDRO (MOD.): (31) s. ii AD *EAM* 53 (-νει-: s. *Κλεόδημος*)
MACEDONIA?: (32) f. i BC *Xenia antiqua* 10 (2001) p. 19 nos. A-B (or Thrace: f. *Ζαικίς*); (33) ib. (or Thrace: s. *Βαστικίλας*, *Ζαικίς*)
SCYTHIA MINOR:
—ISTROS: (34) 138 AD *ISM* I 193 I, 98 (-νει-: f. *Ῥοῦφος*)
THRACE:
—AINOS: (35) ii BC *IG* II² 7969/70 (*FRA* 232) (f. *Ἀνδρικός*)
—BYZANTION: (36) c. 310-366 AD *PLRE* I (3)
—BYZANTION (NR.): (37) i BC *IByz* 226 (Fıratlı–Robert p. 81 no. 96) (-νει-: s. *Πάπας*, f. *Ἐπίκτησις*)
—KOMOTINI (MOD.): (38) vi AD Meïmaris–Bakirtzis 40 (*SEG* XLIV 573; *IThrakAig* E494) (*[Ἀν]δρόνικος*)
—NICOPOLIS AD ISTRUM: (39) iii AD *IGB* II 682 (*Eastern cults* p. 75 no. 7) (-νει-: f. *Λούκιος*)
—PERINTHOS-HERAKLEIA: (40) iii-iv AD *IPerinth* 188 (*AD* 51-2 (1996-7) Mel. p. 350 no. 175) (*Οὐαλέριος Ἀνδρόνεικος*)

Ἀνδροσθένης
CIMMERIAN BOSPOROS:
—GORGIPPIA: (1) f. iii BC *CIRB* 1137 B I, 10 (*Ἀνδροσ[θ]ένης*: f. *Εὔφρων*)
MACEDONIA: (2) 198-197 BC *RE* (6) (Tataki, *Macedonians* p. 243 no. 156) (Lat. Androsthenes)
MACEDONIA (MYGDONIA):
—CHARAKOMA?: (3) ?ii AD *SEG* XXIX 580 (s. *Φίλων*, *Εὐρυδίκη*); (4) ib. (f. *Εὐρυδίκη*)
—KALINDOIA: (5) i BC/i AD ib. XLII 598; cf. *Anthémonte–Kalindoia* 2 p. 280 (ident.) (s. *Λεόκριτος*); (6) 68-98 AD *SEG* XLII 580, 43 (f. *Κότυς*); (7) a. 98 AD ib. 582, 7; cf. *BE* 1999, no. 362 (s. *Λεόκριτος*); (8) *SEG* XLII 582, 13 (s. *Σιτάλκης*)
SCYTHIA MINOR:
—KALLATIS: (9) s. i BC *ISM* III 38, 3 (f. *Ἡρακλέων*)

Ἀνδρότιμος
MACEDONIA (EDONIS):
—AMPHIPOLIS: (1) iv/iii BC *SEG* XXXI 617

Ἄνδρυς
SCYTHIA MINOR:
—TOMIS: **(1)** ii AD *ISM* II 380, 2 (*GVI* 668)

Ἄνδρων
MACEDONIA (CHALKIDIKE):
—OLYNTHOS: **(1)** ?350 BC *TAPA* 65 (1934) p. 125 no. 3, 2; Hatzopoulos, *Actes Chalc.* p. 80 (date) (f. *Αἴνετος*)
—POTIDAIA-KASSANDREIA: **(2)** ?iv/iii BC *BCH* 17 (1893) p. 633 (Tataki, *Macedonians* p. 85 no. 3) (s. *Καλλίδρομος*)
MACEDONIA (DERRIOPOS):
—STUBERRA: **(3)** 74 AD *IG* X (2) (2) 325, 28 (s. *Σωσίας*); **(4)** ib. 326, 46 (f. *Ἀλέξανδρος*); **(5)** ib. l. 59 (f. *Ἀλέξανδρος*); **(6)** 107 AD ib. 325, 98 (f. *Μενεκράτης*)
MACEDONIA (EDONIS):
—AMPHIPOLIS: **(7)** a. 357 BC Hatzopoulos, *Actes Amphipolis* p. 31 no. 5, 4 (*Ἀνδ[ρω]ν*?)
MACEDONIA (MYGDONIA):
—OSBE: **(8)** f. iv BC *IBer* 147 (Tataki, *Macedonians* p. 145 no. 2) (f. *Ἀνδρέας*)
MACEDONIA (PIERIA):
—PYDNA: **(9)** m. iv BC *SEG* XLV 803 A (coin graffito)
SARMATIA:
—SARMATAI: **(10)** ii-iii AD *IG* X (2) (2) 514 (slave?)
SCYTHIA MINOR:
—ISTROS: **(11)** ii AD *ISM* I 197 II, 6 (s. *Λογγῖνος*); **(12)** ii/iii AD ib. 225, 10 (s. *Λ—*); **(13)** f. iii AD ib. 218, 5 (f. *Αἴλλεις*)
—TOMIS: **(14)** 201 AD ib. II 83 I, 22 (s. *Λογγῖνος*)
THRACE:
—BISANTHE-PANION: **(15)** ii-i BC *IG* XII (9) 1126 (s. *Ἀπολλώνιος*)
—BYZANTION: **(16)** ii-i BC *IByz* 223 (Fıratlı–Robert pp. 79-80 no. 92) (f. *Πάπας*)
—DIONYSOPOLIS: **(17)** ii BC *IGB* I^2 22 II, 3 (f. *Ἐπίκουρος*)
—MARONEIA: **(18)** iv-iii BC *IThrakAig* E227 (s. *Διφιλίδης*)
—PERINTHOS-HERAKLEIA:
——(Akarnanes): **(19)** iii-ii BC *IPerinth* 61, 10 (f. *Εὔανδρος*)

Ἀνέγκλητος
MACEDONIA (MYGDONIA):
—THESSALONIKE: **(1)** i AD *IG* X (2) (1) 317 (*-νκλη-*)
MACEDONIA (PAIONIA):
—KAVADARCI (MOD.): **(2)** i AD Šašel, *IL* 1237 (Lat. Memmius Anecletus: freed.)
SCYTHIA MINOR:
—DINOGETIA (NR.): **(3)** ii/iii AD *ISM* V 302 (Lat. [A]nencletus)

Ἀνθᾶς
SCYTHIA MINOR:
—ISTROS: **(1)** ii AD ib. I 196, 12, 15; 201 I, 21-2 (f. *Παπίας, Τιμοκλῆς*)

Ἀνθέμιος
MACEDONIA (BOTTIAIA):
—EDESSA: **(1)** v-vi AD Feissel, *RICM* 31 (*PLRE* III (1)) (doctor)

Ἀνθεμόκριτος
CIMMERIAN BOSPOROS:
—NYMPHAION: **(1)** iii BC *CIRB* 926 (f. *Ἀπασικ—ς*)

Ἀνθεστήριος
CIMMERIAN BOSPOROS:
—GORGIPPIA: **(1)** f. iii BC ib. 1137 A I, 44 (s. *Εὔφρων*)
—PANTIKAPAION: **(2)** f. i AD ib. 302 (*Α. ὁ καὶ Κτησαμενός*: s. *Ἡγήσιππος*); **(3)** f. ii AD ib. 651 (s. *Μητρόφιλος*, f. *Ἀριστόμαχος*)
SCYTHIA MINOR:
—ISTROS: **(4)** ii BC *ISM* I 60, 4 (f. *—νικος*)
SKYTHIA:
—OLBIA-BORYSTHENES: **(5)** c. 250-225 BC *SEG* XXXIV 758, 2, 46 (s. *Ἀη—*)
—OLBIA-BORYSTHENES*: **(6)** iv BC *ZOOID* 23 (1900) p. 19 no. 3 (vase)
THRACE:
—APOLLONIA-SOZOPOLIS: **(7)** v BC *IGB* I^2 431 (f. *Ἐλευσίς*); **(8)** v/iv BC ib. 407 (s. *Ἀρτεμίδωρος*); **(9)** ib. 422 (f. *Ἀλπάλη*)
—APOLLONIA-SOZOPOLIS?: **(10)** v/iv BC ib. 331 (or Thrace Odessos?)
—MESAMBRIA: **(11)** v/iv BC Karayotov, *Mesambria* I p. 79 no. 1 (coin)
—ODESSOS: **(12)** v/iv BC *IGB* I^2 96 (f. *Παιδάρχη*); **(13)** ii-iii AD ib. 54 (*[Ἀν]θεστήριος*); **(14)** s. ii AD ib. 182 (PM 1611); *Dacia* 21 (1977) p. 161 (date) (s. *Μηνόδωρος*); **(15)** 221 AD *IGB* I^2 47 bis a, 30 (*Αὐρ. Ἀνθιστήριος*: s. *Μηνόδωρος*); **(16)** ib. 47 bis b, 18 (*Αὐρ. Ἀ.*: s. *Σωκράτης*)
—ODESSOS*: **(17)** hell. *SEG* XXX 705 (tile)

Ἀνθεστηρίς
THRACE:
—APOLLONIA-SOZOPOLIS: **(1)** v-iv BC *IGB* I^2 441

Ἀνθέστιος
MACEDONIA (BOTTIAIA):
—BEROIA: **(1)** 208 AD *ILeukopetra* 52, 20
SKYTHIA:
—OLBIA-BORYSTHENES: **(2)** ii AD *IOSPE* I^2 86, 8 (s. *Σαμβίων*) ?= (*3*); **(3)** ib. 129, 8 (s. *Σαμβίων*) ?= (*2*)

Ἀνθεσφόρος
MACEDONIA (MYGDONIA):
—THESSALONIKE?: **(1)** ii AD *IG* X (2) (1) 694 (*Ἄννιος Ἀντεσφόρος*)

Ἀνθηρά
THRACE:
—PERINTHOS-HERAKLEIA: **(1)** s. iv BC ib. II^2 10070 (*FRA* 6031)

Ἄνθηρον
MACEDONIA: **(1)** iii-ii BC *IG* II^2 9258 (Tataki, *Macedonians* p. 243 no. 157; *FRA* 3459)

Ἄνθιμος
PENESTAI?: **(1)** c. 200 AD *SEG* XXXIX 593, 8 (f. *Αἰλιανός*)
THRACE:
—BYZANTION: **(2)** ii-iii AD *IByz* 309 (s. *Ζωΐλος*)
—DEULTUM: **(3)** ii-iii AD *IGB* III 1849, 7

Ἄνθις
MACEDONIA (CHALKIDIKE):
—OLYNTHOS: **(1)** ?c. 355-350 BC *SEG* XXXVIII 640, 3 (s. *Ἡγέστρατος*)
THRACE:
—SALYMBRIA?: **(2)** iv-vi AD Mendel, *Cat.* 789

Ἀνθίς
MACEDONIA (MYGDONIA):
—THESSALONIKE: **(1)** ii AD *IG* X (2) (1) 389; cf. *BCH* 97 (1973) p. 589 (*-θείς*)
—THESSALONIKE*: **(2)** ii-iii AD *IG* X (2) (1) 740 (Lat. Anthis: m. Restituta: imp. slave?)
SCYTHIA MINOR:
—KALLATIS: **(3)** iii BC ib. II^2 8945 (*FRA* 2642)
THRACE:
—BYZANTION: **(4)** imp. *IByz* 238 (d. *Ἀπφοῦς*)

Ἄνθος
MACEDONIA (BOTTIAIA):
—BEROIA: **(1)** ii-iii AD *IBer* 350 (Tataki 181)
SKYTHIA:
—OLBIA-BORYSTHENES: **(2)** iii AD *IOSPE* I^2 98, 8 (s. *Καλλισθένης*)
THRACE:
—BYZANTION: **(3)** c. 164-169 AD Schönert-Geiss, *Byzantion* 1399; 1418-19 (coin) (?s. *Νίκων*)
—PHILIPPOPOLIS-TRIMONTIUM: **(4)** c. 303 AD *Anal. Boll.* 31 (1912) p. 192

Ἀνθοῦσα
SCYTHIA MINOR:
—AXIOPOLIS*: **(1)** v-vi AD Popescu, *IGL* 195, 2 (d. *Γιβάστης*)
THRACE:
—BEROE-AUGUSTA TRAIANA: **(2)** c. 320 AD *Anal. Boll.* 31 (1912) p. 208; cf. p. 198

Ἀνθράκιον
THRACE: **(1)** ?iii BC *IG* II^2 8898 (*FRA* 2494)

Ἀνθρωπίων
SCYTHIA MINOR:
—ISTROS: **(1)** i BC-i AD *ISM* I 191 I, 9; **(2)** ib. 191 II, 44 (s. *Μόσχος*)
THRACE:
—ODESSOS (NR.): **(3)** f. iii AD *IGB* V 5076 (*CCET* I 9) (f. *Σιληνός*)

Ἄνθυλλα
MACEDONIA (BOTTIAIA):
—EDESSA: **(1)** iii AD Feissel, *RICM* 8 (Tataki, *Edessa* 24) (d. *Ξανθίας*)

Ἀνίκατος
THRACE:
—BYZANTION: **(1)** hell.-imp. *IByz* 303
—BYZANTION?: **(2)** i BC/i AD *SEG* XXIX 1706 (*Ἀνείκατ[ος]*: ?f. *Πυθόδωρος*)

Ἀνίκητος
CIMMERIAN BOSPOROS:
—PANTIKAPAION: **(1)** iv-v AD Latyshev, *Sbornik* 91a
MACEDONIA (BOTTIAIA):
—BEROIA*: **(2)** ii/iii AD *IBer* 144 B, 12 (Tataki 710) (*Κλ. Ἀνείκητος*: freed.)
—EDESSA: **(3)** 180 AD *SEG* XXIV 531, 10 (Tataki, *Edessa* 25) (s. *Δρῶβυς*)
MACEDONIA (CHALKIDIKE):
—ANTHEMOUS: **(4)** iii AD *Anthémonte–Kalindoia* I p. 62 no. A17 (*Α(ὐ)ρ. Ἀνείκητος*: s. *Αὐρ. Ἐλπίς*)
—STREPSA?: **(5)** 198 AD *SEG* XXIX 648 (*Ἀνεί-*)
MACEDONIA (LYNKESTIS):
—HERAKLEIA (AREA): **(6)** ii-iii AD *IG* X (2) (2) 17 (*-εί-*)
MACEDONIA (MYGDONIA):
—THESSALONIKE: **(7)** iii AD ib. X (2) (1) 247, 10 (*[Τ]ύλλιος Ἀνείκητος*)
MACEDONIA (ODOMANTIKE):
—SIRRHA?: **(8)** 136 AD *SEG* XXX 598, 1, 6 (*-νεί-*: s. *Ἀπολλόδοτος*, ?f. *Ἀκοῦτος, Ἐπιμελεάς, Ζώη*)
THRACE:
—ANCHIALOS: **(9)** ?iii AD *IGB* I^2 370, 9 (*Τ. Φλ. (Ἀ)νείκητος*: II s. *Μ. Φλ. Ἀνίκητος* I); **(10)** ib. l. 13 (*Μ. Φλ. Ἀ(νε)ίκ[ητ]ος*: I f. *Τ. Φλ. Ἀνίκητος* II)
—BYZANTION: **(11)** ii-iii AD *IByz* 107 (Fıratlı–Robert p. 96 no. 138) (*[Ἀ]νείκητος*: I f. *Ἀνίκητος* II); **(12)** *IByz* 107 (Fıratlı–Robert p. 96 no. 138) (*Ἀνείκητο[ς]*: II s. *Ἀνίκητος* I)
—MONTANA*: **(13)** ii AD *Montana* II 55 (Lat. Anicetus: imp. slave); **(14)** s. ii AD ib. 111 (Lat. A[ure]lius Anicetus: freed.)
—NICOPOLIS AD ISTRUM: **(15)** ii-iii AD *IGB* II 683 (*CCET* II (2) 626) (I f. *Κορνήλιος Ἀνίκητος* II); **(16)** *IGB* II 683 (*CCET* II (2) 626) (*Κορνήλιος Ἀνείκητος*: II s. *Ἀνίκητος* I)
—VOJVODA (MOD.): **(17)** v AD *BIAB* 33 (1972) p. 273 (brick) (Lat. Anicetus)

Ἀνισαλῶ?
CIMMERIAN BOSPOROS:
—TEMRYUK (MOD.): **(1)** iv-v AD *SEG* XVI 440; cf. Vinogradov, *Pont. Stud.* p. 159 (*Ἀνισαλοι* (dat.))

῎Αννα
CIMMERIAN BOSPOROS:
—PANTIKAPAION: (1) i AD *CIRB* 340; Zgusta, *PNS* 594 (d. *Σ—*)
MACEDONIA (MYGDONIA):
—THESSALONIKE: (2) s. iii AD *SEG* XLIV 556, 2 (*Ἀ. ἡ καὶ Ἀσυγκρίτιον*: Jew); (3) 491-518 AD *Mél. Tisserant* 2 p. 302 (Jew)
MACEDONIA (PELAGONIA):
—KOLOBAISA*: (4) ii AD *IG* X (2) (2) 232 ?= (*5*)
MACEDONIA (PELAGONIA)?: (5) ii AD ib. 186, 5 (or Arabia Felix Amara?: m. (nat.) *Κρατεύας*: Jew?) ?= (*4*)
THRACE:
—BEROE-AUGUSTA TRAIANA: (6) c. 320-324 AD *Anal. Boll.* 31 (1912) p. 198; cf. p. 208
—PERINTHOS-HERAKLEIA: (7) v-vi AD *IPerinth* 226 (*AD* 51-2 (1996-7) Mel. p. 369 no. 187) (d. *Ἀγαπητός, Μαρία*)
—SALYMBRIA: (8) iv-v AD *BCH* 36 (1912) p. 637 no. 94 (*AD* 53 (1998) Mel. p. 459 no. 198)

῎Αννη
CIMMERIAN BOSPOROS:
—PANTIKAPAION: (1) iv BC *CIRB* 158; Zgusta, *PNS* 594 (d. *Θεόδοτος*); (2) s. iv BC *CIRB* 209; cf. KW pl. 1 no. 25
THRACE:
—BYZANTION: (3) i BC-i AD *IByz* 207 (Firatlı–Robert p. 67 no. 63); (4) i BC/i AD *SEG* L 667 III (d. *῎Ερως*)

Ἀννι
THRACE:
—ODESSOS: (1) ii AD *IGB* I^2 171 (PM 1453) (d. *῞Ελλην*); (2) *IGB* I^2 183 (PM 1738) (d. *Ξένων*); (3) m. ii AD *IGB* I^2 150 (PM 859) (d. *Νικομήδης*); (4) s. ii AD *IGB* I^2 166 (PM 1404); *Dacia* 21 (1977) p. 161 (date) (*Ἀννει*: d. *Παρμενίων, Μάμα*)

Ἀννιανός
SCYTHIA MINOR:
—TOMIS: (1) ii-iii AD *ISM* II 18, 4 (s. *Πρίσκος*)

Ἀννίκα
MACEDONIA (BOTTIAIA):
—EDESSA: (1) ii BC *BSA* 58 (1963) p. 22 no. 3 + Tataki, *Edessa* 26 (*Ἀννήρα*—*BSA*: d. *Μεθωνάδης*, m. *Μεθωνάδης*)

Ἀννίκας
MACEDONIA (BOTTIAIA):
—BEROIA: (1) 118 BC *IBer* 134, 23 (*Ἀνίκαντος*? (gen.): f. *Ζάνατος*)
MACEDONIA (CHALKIDIKE):
—CHALKIDEIS: (2) c. 355-352 BC *Olynthus* 9 pp. 76-8 nos. 119-25 (coin); *Ancient Macedonia* I p. 254 (date) (*Ἀννίκα* (gen.))
—STOLOS?: (3) ?351 BC *SEG* XXXVIII 673, 6, 8 (*Ἀννίκαντος* (gen.): f. *Διονύσιος*) ?= (*4*); (4) ?350 BC ib. 670, 3 (*Ἀννίκαντος* (gen.): f. *Φίλιππος*) ?= (*3*)

῎Αννιν
CIMMERIAN BOSPOROS:
—MYRMEKION (NR.): (1) i/ii AD *CIRB* 891; cf. KW pl. 13 no. 193 (*Ἀννειν*—Tokhtas'ev); (2) f. ii AD *CIRB* 892; Zgusta, *PNS* 594 (*Ἀνειν*)

῎Αννιον
THRACE:
—MESAMBRIA: (1) i BC-i AD *IGB* I^2 340
—ODESSOS: (2) i AD ib. 227, 2 (-*νει*-: d. *῞Ελλην*)

῎Αννιος
MACEDONIA (LYNKESTIS):
—HERAKLEIA (AREA): (1) ?ii AD *IG* X (2) (2) 15 (f. *Γάϊος*)

Ἀννίων
CIMMERIAN BOSPOROS:
—PANTIKAPAION: (1) i-ii AD *CIRB* 575; cf. KW pl. 36 no. 514 (s. *Χ—*)

Ἀννύθης
MACEDONIA (CHALKIDIKE):
—STREPSA?: (1) 285 BC *SEG* XXXVIII 619, 21 (f. *Γούρας*)

Ἀννώ
THRACE:
—ODESSOS: (1) i-ii AD *IGB* I^2 108, 5 (d. *Ἀγαθήνωρ*, m. *Μακού*)

Ἀνοθήνης
CIMMERIAN BOSPOROS:
—PANTIKAPAION: (1) s. iv BC *CIRB* 170 + *Hyperboreus* 1994 (1), pp. 159-60; cf. KW pl. 6 no. 109 (*Ἀνοθήν*[*ο*]*ς* (gen.): f. *Ἀτότης*)

Ἀνόπτηνις
CIMMERIAN BOSPOROS:
—PANTIKAPAION: (1) s. i BC *CIRB* 282; Zgusta, *PNS* 579 (f. *Μαστοῦς*); (2) imp. *CIRB* 781 (s. *Τιράνης*, f. *῎Ερως*); (3) i AD ib. 348 (-*πτε*-: f. *Ἀπολλώνιος*); (4) ib. 545; cf. KW pl. 12 no. 169; (5) i-ii AD *CIRB* 631 (f. *Πίνυτος*); (6) i/ii AD ib. 620; cf. KW pl. 36 no. 530 (f. *Μάης*)

Ἀνόπτης
CIMMERIAN BOSPOROS:
—PANTIKAPAION: (1) imp. *CIRB* 775 ([*Ἀ*]*νόπτης*)

῎Ανος
CIMMERIAN BOSPOROS:
—PHANAGOREIA: (1) 51 AD *SEG* XLIII 510, 5 (Levinskaya pp. 237-8 no. 6) (s. *Ψυχαρίων*: Jew?)

Ἀνουβίων
SCYTHIA MINOR:
—TOMIS: (1) imp. *ISM* II 314 (*Ἀνουβ*[*ίων*]?)

Ἀνταγόρας
THRACE:
—STRYME?: (1) m. v BC *CEG* II 728 (*IThrakAig* E109) (*Ἀνταγόρō* (gen.): f. *Ἡράïννα*); (2) m. iv BC ib. E149 (*Ἀνταγόρας*: s. *Ἄστος*)

Ἀνταῖος
MACEDONIA (MYGDONIA):
—ARETHOUSA: (1) c. 315-280 BC *FD* III (1) 186, 2 + p. 105 n. 1 (*Syll*^{3} 269 K); Tataki, *Macedonians* p. 68 no. 3 ([*Ἀν*]*ταῖος*: f. *Πουλυδάμας*)
THRACE: (2) ii BC *IG* XII (1) 877
—MESAMBRIA: (3) s. iii BC *IGB* I^2 308 ter, 7 (*Ἀνταῖος*: s. *Θεσσαλός*)

Ἀντάλκης
CIMMERIAN BOSPOROS:
—GORGIPPIA: (1) f. iii BC *CIRB* 1137 A II, 40; 1137 B II, 41 (s. *Σίνδοκος*)

Ἀντανδρίς
SKYTHIA:
—OLBIA-BORYSTHENES (BEREZAN (MOD.)): (1) v BC *ZOOID* 27 (1907) Prot. p. 60 (vase)

῎Αντανδρος
MACEDONIA (MYGDONIA):
—THESSALONIKE: (1) ii AD *IG* X (2) (1) 622 ([*Ἄ*]*ντανδρος*: s. *Ἀντώνιος*)
THRACE:
—PERINTHOS-HERAKLEIA: (2) iv-iii BC *IPerinth* 4, 14

Ἀντάνωρ
MACEDONIA: (1) c. 375-373 BC *IG* II^2 102, 7 (Tod, *GHI* II 129; Tataki, *Macedonians* p. 243 no. 159) (-*τή*-)

MACEDONIA (BOTTIAIA):
—BEROIA: (2) c. 230-200 BC *BCH* 45 (1921) p. 17 III, 57 (Tataki, *Macedonians* p. 75 no. 10) (s. *Νεοπτόλεμος*)

Ἀντᾶς
CIMMERIAN BOSPOROS:
—PANTIKAPAION: (1) 275-278 AD *CIRB* 36, 67 (s. *Παπίας*)
MACEDONIA (DERRIOPOS):
—STUBERRA: (2) 74 AD *IG* X (2) (2) 326, 32 (s. *Ἀδαῖος*)

Ἀντέας
MACEDONIA: (1) iv BC Arr., *An.* iii 5. 5; vi 28. 4; *Ind.* xviii 3; *FGrH* 156 F 1 (*Ὄνασος*—Arr. *An.* iii, *Εὔνους*—Arr. *Ind.*, *Ἀνθης*—*FGrH*: f. *Λεόννατος*)

Ἀντέρως
CIMMERIAN BOSPOROS:
—PANTIKAPAION: (1) i AD *CIRB* 333
MACEDONIA (BOTTIAIA):
—BEROIA: (2) ii-iii AD *IBer* 297, 1, 6 (*Κλ. Ἀ.*: f. *Χρήσιμος, Χρησίμα, Ἐρωτίς, Παράμονος, Νίκων*)
MACEDONIA (EDONIS):
—PHILIPPOI: (3) ?ii AD *AD* 17 (1961-2) Chron. p. 240 with pl. 287 γ (Pilhofer 154) (Lat. M. Poblicius Ante[ros]); (4) ii/iii AD *CIL* III 633 II a, 6 (Pilhofer 163); *CRAI* 1923, p. 277 (date); Collart, *Philippes* pls. 64-5 (Lat. C. Abellius Anteros)
MACEDONIA (MYGDONIA):
—THESSALONIKE: (5) i-ii AD *IG* X (2) (1) 115 (*Ἀντ*[*έρ*]*ως*: f. *Νικίας*)
—THESSALONIKE?: (6) i BC ib. 912
SKYTHIA:
—OLBIA-BORYSTHENES: (7) ii AD *IOSPE* I^2 89, 6 (f. *Ἀλούθαγος*)
THRACE:
—TYRODIZA-TIRISTASIS: (8) imp. *CIL* III 7385 (Lat. L. Tutilius Anteros)

Ἀντήνωρ
MACEDONIA: (1) 172-168 BC *RE* (6) + Supplbd. 4 (Tataki, *Macedonians* p. 243 no. 160)
MACEDONIA (BOTTIAIA):
—BEROIA: (2) 223 BC *IBer* 4, 12 (s. *Σωσιμένης*)
THRACE:
—APOLLONIA-SOZOPOLIS: (3) ?iv BC *IGB* I^2 455 ([*Ἀ*]*ντήνωρ*: s. *Ἀριστομήδης*, f. *Δημῶναξ*)

Ἀντηρίς
MACEDONIA (BOTTIAIA):
—ALOROS? (KLEIDI (MOD.)): (1) iii BC *AD* 25 (1970) Chron. p. 388 (d. *Ἀρχέμαχος*)

Ἀντιάδας
THRACE:
—AINOS: (1) c. 453-451 BC May, *Ainos* pp. 66-8 nos. 85-91 (coin)

Ἀντιάδης
CIMMERIAN BOSPOROS:
—GORGIPPIA: (1) f. iii BC *CIRB* 1137 A II, 19; 1137 B II, 18 (s. *Ἡρόδωρος*); (2) ib. 1137 B I, 11 (*Ἀντι*[*ά*]*δης*: f. *—δωρος*)

Ἀντιαλκίδας
THRACE:
—SALYMBRIA: (1) i BC-i AD *IByz* S 24, 3 (f. *Ἡρόδωρος*)

Ἀντιάναξ
SCYTHIA MINOR:
—ISTROS (NR.): (1) hell.? *ISM* I 109 (f. *Ἱέρων*)
SKYTHIA:
—OLBIA-BORYSTHENES: (2) s. iv BC *SEG* L 702 II, 3

Ἀντίανδρος
THRACE:
—MESAMBRIA: (1) i BC *IGB* I^2 324 (s. *Πυθόδωρος*)

Ἀντίβιος

MACEDONIA (CHALKIDIKE):
—OLYNTHOS: **(1)** ?f. iv BC *TAPA* 65 (1934) p. 133 no. 9 (Ἀντίβ[ιος]); **(2)** ?352 BC ib. p. 128 no. 4, 11; Hatzopoulos, *Actes Chalc.* p. 80 (date) (s. Ἀθηνίων)
THRACE:
—ABDERA (TERRIT.)?: **(3)** iv BC *SEG* XXVII 350 + *IThrakAig* E80 (Ἀντίβι[ος], Ἀντιγέν[ης]—*SEG*: f. Παρμένων)

Ἀντιβίων

CIMMERIAN BOSPOROS:
—NYMPHAION: **(1)** iii BC *CIRB* 912 I, 10 (s. Παρμένων)
TAURIS:
—CHERSONESOS: **(2)** c. 325-315 BC Kats p. 86 no. 10 (amph.); **(3)** iv/iii BC *IOSPE* I² 410 (s. Βίων)

Ἀντιγένης

CIMMERIAN BOSPOROS:
—PANTIKAPAION: **(1)** ii-iii AD *CIRB* 783, 1 (s. Εὐτυχίδης, f. Εὐτυχίδης)
MACEDONIA: **(2)** ?417-413 BC *IG* I³ 89, 63 (Tataki, *Macedonians* p. 244 no. 161) (-νε̄ς); **(3)** iv BC Arr., *Ind.* XV 10 (Tataki, *Macedonians* p. 244 no. 164) (f. Πείθων); **(4)** 254-238 BC *PMich* 34, 4, 13; *PPetr*² 1, 93 (Tataki, *Macedonians* p. 244 nos. 162-3; La'da E1408)
MACEDONIA (BOTTIAIA):
—BEROIA: **(5)** 177 AD *IBer* 135 B, 28 (Tataki 185) (f. Λεοντίσκος)
—PELLA?: **(6)** c. 380-316 BC *RE* (9); Berve 83 (Tataki, *Macedonians* p. 149 no. 15)
MACEDONIA (EDONIS):
—AMPHIPOLIS: **(7)** hell.? *BCH* 18 (1894) p. 423 no. 4 (55 (1931) pp. 176-7 no. 6) (f. Ἀρτεμίδωρος); **(8)** ib. p. 423 no. 4 (55 (1931) pp. 176-7 no. 6) (s. Ἀρτεμίδωρος); **(9)** ?iii BC *PAE* 1982, p. 47 (s. Διογένης); **(10)** ii BC *SEG* XXIV 594, 2 (f. Ἐμπεδοκλῆς); **(11)** ib. l. 3 (s. Ἐμπεδοκλῆς); **(12)** hell.-imp. ib. XL 522 a
—PHILIPPOI: **(13)** hell.-imp. ib. XXVI 731 (Pilhofer 325) (Ἀντιγέν[ης])
MACEDONIA (ELIMEIA):
—OBLOSTAI?: **(14)** ?iii AD *EAM* 65 I b
MACEDONIA (PIERIA):
—DION: **(15)** s. iv BC *SEG* XXXIII 511 A = XXXVI 611 (f. Νίκανδρος)
—PYDNA: **(16)** ii BC ib. L 626 ([Ἀν]τ[ι]γένη[ς]?: f. Σωκράτις)
SCYTHIA MINOR:
—ISTROS: **(17)** ii AD *ISM* I 211, 13 (f. Ἀρτεμίδωρος); **(18)** 138 AD ib. 193 I, 59 (s. Φίλιππος); **(19)** ib. 193 II, 75 (f. Δημήτριος)
THRACE: **(20)** 414 BC *IG* I³ 427, 3 (*FRA* 2495) ([Ἀν]τιγένε̄ς: slave)
—PAUTALIA: **(21)** ii-iii AD *IGB* IV 2070 (Ἀντιγέ[ν]ο[υ]ς (gen.))
—PERINTHOS-HERAKLEIA: **(22)** iv BC Hp., *Epid.* ii 2. 19; ii 3. 11?; iv 20h?; iv 21; vi 4. 2? (Ἀρτιγένης—iv 20h)
—SAPAI: **(23)** c. 230-200 BC *BCH* 45 (1921) p. 18 III, 83 (s. Κλέων)
—ZONE?: **(24)** iv/iii BC *IG* XII (8) 267, 8; cf. *IThrakAig* E400 (locn.) (s. Ἱστιαῖος)

Ἀντιγόνα

MACEDONIA: **(1)** iii BC Tataki, *Macedonians* p. 245 no. 167 (Ἀντ[ιγόνα]: d. Δημήτριος); **(2)** i BC-i AD *SEG* XXIX 231 (Tataki, *Macedonians* p. 244 no. 166; *FRA* 3460) (d. Ἀντίγονος)
MACEDONIA?:
—RESEN (MOD.): **(3)** s. iii AD *IG* X (2) (2) 50 (or Illyria Dassaretioi?: m. Οὐαλέριος)
MACEDONIA (BOTTIAIA):
—BEROIA: **(4)** iv-iii BC *IBer* 148 (Tataki 188) (d. Δαβρείας); **(5)** ii BC *IBer* 178 (d. Οὐένετος, ?m. Κλήτα); **(6)** ii-iii AD ib. 129, 1 (d. Διοσκουρίδης, ?m. Κώνωψ); **(7)** ii/iii AD ib. 394, 2 (Tataki 186); **(8)** ?iii AD *IBer* 213 (Tataki 187) (d. Ἀντίγονος, Ἀπολλωνία)
—PELLA: **(9)** s. iii BC *SEG* XXIV 551 b (d. Φίλιππος)
MACEDONIA (CHALKIDIKE):
—ANTHEMOUS: **(10)** s. ii AD *ZPE* 140 (2002) p. 127
—POTIDAIA-KASSANDREIA (NR.): **(11)** hell. *SEG* XXIX 631 (d. Εὐφάνης)
MACEDONIA (EDONIS):
—AMPHIPOLIS: **(12)** iii-ii BC *RA* 1935 (2), p. 66 no. 1 (Kaphtantzis 604) (Ἀ[ν]τιγόνα); **(13)** iii-iv AD *SEG* XXVII 253, 2 (m. Φιλόκαλος)
—AMPHIPOLIS?: **(14)** ii-i BC *BCH* 55 (1931) p. 191 no. 12 (d. Μενέλαος)
MACEDONIA (EORDAIA):
—MAVROPIGI (MOD.): **(15)** imp. *AD* 39 (1984) Chron. p. 257 (loomweight) ([Ἀν]τιγόνα)
MACEDONIA (LOWER PAIONIA):
—EUROPOS: **(16)** ?ii AD *SEG* XXXVIII 612 (m. Μᾶρκος)
MACEDONIA (MYGDONIA):
—THESSALONIKE: **(17)** ii BC *IG* X (2) (1) 327, 2 (I d. Σωτήριχος, ?m. Κράτερος, Ἀντιγόνα II); **(18)** ib. l. 3 (II d. Εὐφράνωρ, ?d. Ἀντιγόνα I); **(19)** 71 or 188 AD *SEG* XXXI 644 = XLV 818 (Ποντία Ἀ.: d. Πόντιος Βίταλος, Ποντία Εὐτυχίς); **(20)** ii-iii AD *IG* X (2) (1) 480, 5 (Κασσία Ἀ.); **(21)** *SEG* XXX 645; **(22)** iii AD *IG* II² 10683 = X (2) (1) 434; *SEG* XXXVI 647 (date)
—THESSALONIKE?: **(23)** ii AD *IG* X (2) (1) 885 (m. Γερμανά)
MACEDONIA (ODOMANTIKE):
—SIRRHA: **(24)** ii-iii AD Kaphtantzis 45 ([Ἀν]τιγόνα); **(25)** ?157 AD ib. 11, 1 (*Dodoni* 18 (1989) p. 245 no. 53) (Διδιανὴ Ἀ.: d. Διδιανός, Ἐπιδία Μάγνα)
MACEDONIA (PELAGONIA):
—MOJNO (MOD.): **(26)** iii AD *IG* X (2) (2) 174 (Αὐρη[λία] [Ἀν]τιγόνα)
MACEDONIA (PIERIA):
—DION: **(27)** ii-iii AD *Klio* 52 (1970) p. 64 no. 18 (Κομινία Ἀ.)
—KOLINDROS (MOD.): **(28)** imp. Dimitsas 204 (m. Ἱππόστρατος)
THRACE: **(29)** ?161 BC *SGDI* 2052, 3, 6 (slave/freed.); **(30)** 138 BC *FD* III (2) 237, 4-5, 7, 9, 12 (slave/freed.)

Ἀντιγόνεια

MACEDONIA (MYGDONIA):
—THESSALONIKE: **(1)** iii AD *SEG* XXXVII 587 (Αὐρ. Ἀ.)

Ἀντιγόνη

MACEDONIA: **(1)** iv BC *RE* (5) (Tataki, *Macedonians* p. 245 no. 168) (d. Κάσσανδρος, m. Βερενίκη); **(2)** iv/iii BC *RE* (6) (*PP* 14483) (d. Φίλιππος, Βερενίκη, m. Πτολεμαῖος (Molossoi))
MACEDONIA (BOTTIAIA):
—BEROIA: **(3)** ii-iii AD *IBer* 315 (Tataki 189) (—ορια Ἀντιγ[όνη]?)
—EDESSA: **(4)** iii AD Feissel, *RICM* 5 (Tataki, *Edessa* 27)
MACEDONIA (ELIMEIA):
—DETELA: **(5)** f. iii BC *SEG* XLIII 937, 5; cf. *BE* 1996, no. 241 (Tataki, *Macedonians* p. 193 no. 1) (m. Φίλιππος)
MACEDONIA (PELAGONIA):
—KERAMIAI (NR.): **(6)** ii-iii AD *IG* X (2) (2) 222; **(7)** 193-211 AD ib. 218, 8 (Αὐρηλία Ἀ. ἡ καὶ Σαραπιάς)
MACEDONIA (PIERIA):
—PYDNA?: **(8)** s. iv BC *RE* (7); Berve 86 (Tataki, *Macedonians* p. 150 no. 16) (or Macedonia (Bottiaia) Pella)
SCYTHIA MINOR:
—TOMIS: **(9)** i-ii AD *ISM* II 165 (PM 1735); cf. *IByz* 370 A; *BE* 2001, no. 308 (Ἀ.: ?d. Αὐλόσανις)

Ἀντιγονίων

MACEDONIA (ELIMEIA):
—OBLOSTAI?: **(1)** ?iii AD *EAM* 65 I a
MACEDONIA (PIERIA):
—DION: **(2)** ii AD *Essays Laourdas* p. 109 no. 10 (s. Νικαρέτη)

Ἀντίγονος

MACEDONIA: **(1)** 382-301 BC *RE* (3); Berve 87 (Tataki, *Macedonians* p. 245 no. 169) (Ἀ. I Μονόφθαλμος: s. Φίλιππος, f. Δημήτριος I Πολιορκητής, Φίλιππος, Φοῖνιξ: king); **(2)** c. 319-240 BC *RE* (4) (Tataki, *Macedonians* p. 245 no. 170) (Ἀ. II Γονατᾶς: s. Δημήτριος I Πολιορκητής, Φίλα, f. Δημήτριος II, Ἀλκυονεύς: king); **(3)** 304 BC *RE* (10) (*PP* 15178; Tataki, *Macedonians* p. 245 no. 172); **(4)** 292-288 BC Moretti, *Olymp.* 527; 533; *RE* (11) (Tataki, *Macedonians* p. 245 no. 173); **(5)** c. 263-221 BC *RE* (5); Supplbd. 1 (-) (Tataki, *Macedonians* p. 245 no. 171); cf. Beloch, *GG* IV (2) p. 139 (Ἀ. III Δώσων: s. Δημήτριος ὁ Καλός, Ὀλυμπιάς (Thessaly, Larisa): king); **(6)** c. 245-205 BC *IG* VII 506, 3 (Tataki, *Macedonians* p. 246 no. 178) (s. Ἀσκληπιάδης); **(7)** 236 BC *PPetr*² 16, 4 (Tataki, *Macedonians* p. 248 no. 185); cf. La'da E1770 (f. Κίλλης); **(8)** b. 183 BC *IG* XI (4) 1307, 2; *ID* 1417 A II, 92; cf. 1403 Bb II, 67 (Tataki, *Macedonians* p. 248 no. 183) (f. Ἄξιος); **(9)** 221 BC *SB* 13841, 2 (Tataki, *Macedonians* p. 247 no. 182); cf. La'da E1409 (f. Ἀντίλοχος); **(10)** 179 BC *RE* (6) (Tataki, *Macedonians* p. 246 no. 179) (Lat. Antigonus: s. Ἐχεκράτης); **(11)** c. 179 BC Liv. xl 57. 3; 58. 1 ?= (*12*) (*53*); **(12)** c. 169 BC ib. xliv 26-7; Tataki, *Macedonians* p. 246 no. 176 ?= (*11*); **(13)** c. 160-150 BC Grainger, *SPG* p. 8; cf. *ZPE* 131 (2000) pp. 107-8 (Lat. Antigonus: s. Δημήτριος I Σωτήρ, Λαοδίκη); **(14)** i BC-i AD *SEG* XXIX 231 (Tataki, *Macedonians* p. 247 no. 181; *FRA* 3461) (f. Ἀντιγόνα); **(15)** f. iii AD *RE* Supplbd. 11 (16); *PIR*² A 736; *GVI* 882; *CIL* III 14429; *AEp* 1964, no. 180; 1965, no. 242; *Arkheologiia* (Sofia) 1976, p. 61 no. 3; D.C. lxxvii 8. 1-2 (Tataki, *Macedonians* p. 247 no. 180) (Lat. Domitius Antigonus—*AEp* 1964: s. Φίλιππος)
—BONTHITAI: **(16)** m. i BC *AD* 11 (1927-8) pp. 58-9 no. 5, 19 (Tataki, *Macedonians* p. 83 no. 1) (s. Δήμακος)
MACEDONIA (ALMOPIA):
—MARGARITA (MOD.): **(17)** iii AD *SEG* II 405 (Chrysostomou, *Almopia* p. 82)
MACEDONIA (BOTTIAIA):
—AIGAI: **(18)** s. iv BC *SEG* XXXV 777 (Ἀντίγον[ος]: s. —τέλης); **(19)** ib. 779 (s. Κλε—); **(20)** c. 340-330 BC ib. 772, 6
—BEROIA: **(21)** m. iii BC *Thess. Mnem.* 82 (Tataki 194; Tataki, *Macedonians* p. 75 no. 11) (s. Ἀμύντας); **(22)** 223 BC *IBer* 4, 15 (s. Φοινικίδης); **(23)** ib. l. 20 (f. Μένανδρος); **(24)** ib. l. 22 (f. Νικάνωρ); **(25)** ib. l. 36 (s. Μενεκράτης); **(26)** ii BC ib. 141, 13; **(27)** ib. 201 (f. Μαχάτας); **(28)** ii-i BC ib. 182 (Tataki 196) (s. Μένων); **(29)** *IBer* 392 (Tataki 200) (f. Πατερῖνος); **(30)** 115 BC *IBer* 134, 31 (s. Παράμονος); **(31)** 112 BC ib. l. 43 (f. Κάσσανδρος); **(32)** i BC ib. 164 (Tataki 201) (Ἀντίγον[ος]: f. —ένηα); **(33)** ii AD *IBer* 79, 3 (Tataki 199) (f. Μενέλαος); **(34)** *IBer* 395 (Tataki 192); **(35)** ii-iii AD *IBer* 91, 4 (Tataki 628) (Ἰούν. Ἀ. ὁ καὶ Ἀνακτόριος: s. Ἰουν. Κάλη); **(36)** s. ii AD *IBer* 75, 7 (Tataki 190); **(37)** ii/iii AD *IBer* 143 A, 3 (Tataki 195) (s. Γάϊος); **(38)** 177 AD *IBer* 135, 3 (Tataki 1196) (Στάτιος Ἀ.); **(39)** ?iii AD *IBer* 213 (Tataki 191) (f. Ἀντιγόνα); **(40)** 210 AD *ILeukopetra* 57, 1 (Tataki 197) (s. Παράμονος); **(41)** a. 212 AD *IBer* 136, 8 (Tataki 1197) (Στάτ. Ἀντί[γο]νος); **(42)** ?254 AD *ILeukopetra* 108, 1 (Ποπίλλιος Ἀ.: s. Καρπ—)
—EDESSA: **(43)** ii-iii AD *SEG* II 403 (Tataki, *Edessa* 28) ([Ἀ]ντίγο[νος])

—ICHNAI: **(44)** c. 265-260 BC *FD* III (3) 207, 2 (Tataki, *Macedonians* p. 113 no. 2) (s. Ἀσάνδρος)
—MIEZA: **(45)** hell. *AM* 27 (1902) p. 314 no. 28, 9 ([Ἀν]τίγονος)
—PELLA: **(46)** s. iv BC *A´ Panell. Synedr. Epigr.* p. 190 no. 11 (*SEG* XXX 581) (s. Ἀλέξανδρος); **(47)** ib. XLVIII 823 B (Ἀντίγον[ος]: f. Μνασινίκα); **(48)** iii BC *AD* 16 (1960) Mel. p. 82 (tile)
—TYRISSA? (ASVESTARI (MOD.)): **(49)** f. ii BC *SEG* XLVII 999, 11
MACEDONIA (CHALKIDIKE):
—NEOS MARMARAS (MOD.): **(50)** ii-i BC ib. XXXVIII 600 (Ἀντ[ί]γον[ος]: f. Βιλίστα)
—OLYNTHOS: **(51)** f. iii BC *IG* XI (4) 531, 4, 11 (Tataki, *Macedonians* p. 129 no. 6) (s. Νικόδημος)
MACEDONIA (DERRIOPOS): **(52)** imp. *IG* X (2) (2) 311 (s. Ζώπυρος)
—STUBERRA: **(53)** a. 179 BC *IGB* V 5003; cf. Tataki, *Macedonians* p. 177 no. 1 (s. Ἡράκλειτος) ?= (*11*); **(54)** c. 41-48 AD *IG* X (2) (2) 323, 14 (f. Νέρων); **(55)** ib. l. 21 (s. Φίλιππος); **(56)** 74 AD ib. 325, 21 (f. Ἀπολλόδωρος); **(57)** ib. l. 39 (s. Διοσκουρίδης); **(58)** ib. l. 48 (f. Κάσσανδρος); **(59)** ib. l. 51 (s. Κάσσανδρος); **(60)** ib. 326, 21 (Ἀ.: s. Στράτων); **(61)** ib. l. 22 (s. Παρμενίων); **(62)** ib. l. 29 (s. Ὀλυμπιάδης); **(63)** ib. l. 35 (s. Ἀπολλόδωρος); **(64)** ib. l. 37 (s. Λυσίμαχος); **(65)** ib. l. 52 (f. Εὔλαιος); **(66)** ib. l. 64 (s. Μένανδρος); **(67)** ib. l. 53-4 (s. Παράμονος); **(68)** 107 AD ib. 325, 95 (f. Νικόλαος, Κόρραγος); **(69)** ib. l. 97 (f. Ἀλέξανδρος); **(70)** ib. l. 103 (f. Μένανδρος)
MACEDONIA (EDONIS):
—AMPHIPOLIS: **(71)** a. 357 BC Hatzopoulos, *Actes Amphipolis* p. 31 no. 5, 6; **(72)** a. 332 BC *CEG* II 879 (*SEG* XLVIII 716 bis) (s. Κάλλας); **(73)** m. iii BC Hatzopoulos, *Actes Amphipolis* p. 52 no 12, 5; *SEG* XLI 566 (date) (s. Μαχάτας); **(74)** c. 223 BC *PTeb* 815 fr. 8 II, 3-4 (Tataki, *Macedonians* p. 46 no. 9); cf. La'da E136 (f. Πέρσης)
—PHILIPPOI: **(75)** imp. *BCH* 61 (1937) p. 415 no. 8 (Pilhofer 344) (Lat. Antigonus: ?f. Bassus)
—PHILIPPOI (DRAMA (MOD.)): **(76)** ?ii-i BC *SEG* XLVIII 794 (Pilhofer 501b) (f. Διοσκουρίδης)
MACEDONIA (ELIMEIA):
—AGALAIA (MOD.): **(77)** s. ii AD *EAM* 55 (f. Κλεοπάτρα)
—AIANE: **(78)** ii BC ib. 41 (f. Φειδίστη); **(79)** ib. 43; cf. *SEG* XXXIX 565 (Ἀντιγόν[ο]υ (gen.)—edd., Ἀντιγόν[α]ι (dat.)—*SEG*: s. Πρασαίδης)
—AIANE (TERRIT.): **(80)** 161-180 AD *EAM* 36, 7 (Ἀντίγο[νος]: f. Αἰλ. Ἀνδράγαθος); **(81)** ?iii AD ib. 24 a (Ἀ. [ὁ] [καὶ] Ἰούλις: s. Καλλιναῖος)
—OBLOSTAI?: **(82)** ?iii AD ib. 65 II a
—SIATISTA (MOD.): **(83)** hell.-imp. ib. 32 (f. Ἀγοραῖος)
MACEDONIA (EORDAIA?):
—EUIA: **(84)** 181 BC ib. 87, 15 (Hatzopoulos, *MI* 2 pp. 41-2 no. 17) (s. Ἀλέξανδρος); **(85)** *EAM* 87, 18 (Hatzopoulos, *MI* 2 pp. 41-2 no. 17)
MACEDONIA (EORDAIA):
—ANATOLIKO (MOD.): **(86)** ii-iii AD *SEG* XLVII 882, 5
—ASVESTOPETRA (MOD.): **(87)** i BC-i AD? ib. XLV 735 (s. Φίλιππος)
—EUIA? (POLYMYLOS (MOD.)): **(88)** ii BC *A´ Panell. Synedr. Epigr.* p. 56 no. 3 (*SEG* XLIX 773) (f. Δίφιλος)
—KELLE?: **(89)** m. ii BC ib. XLVII 903 (s. Δικαῖος)
—KOMANOS (MOD.): **(90)** s. ii AD *EAM* 100 (f. Λέων)
MACEDONIA (KRESTONIA):
—IORON?: **(91)** s. ii AD *IBer* 87, 4 (Tataki 198) (or Macedonia (Bottiaia) Beroia: f. Ἰσιδώρα)
—MORRYLOS: **(92)** iii BC *SEG* XXXVIII 627 (f. Ἀδύρα); **(93)** ii BC ib. XXXIX 612 (s. Νίκανδρος)
MACEDONIA (LOWER PAIONIA): **(94)** imp. *Sp.* 77 (1934) p. 42 no. 23; cf. 98 (1941-8) no. 98
MACEDONIA (LYNKESTIS):
—ANO VEVI (MOD.): **(95)** ii AD *EAM* 164 (f. Ἀμμία)
—HERAKLEIA: **(96)** i AD *IG* X (2) (2) 75, 54 (f. Λυσίμαχος); **(97)** ib. 76
—HERAKLEIA (AREA): **(98)** ii AD ib. 21 (s. Διονύσιος)
—HERAKLEIA (NR.): **(99)** ii-iii AD ib. 10 (s. Νουμήνιος)
—HERAKLEIA*: **(100)** i-ii AD ib. 122 (f. Ἀλέξανδρος)
—VEVI (MOD.): **(101)** imp. *EAM* 182
MACEDONIA (MYGDONIA):
—APOLLONIA: **(102)** f. ii BC *SEG* XLIV 508 (Hatzopoulos, *MI* 2 p. 87 no. 66) (Ἀντ[ίγον]ος: s. Ἀμύντας)
—KALINDOIA: **(103)** c. 334 BC ib. 62, 11 (f. Τρωΐλος); **(104)** c. 327 BC ib. l. 18 (s. Μένανδρος); **(105)** 68-98 AD *SEG* XLII 580, 10 (s. Δημήτριος)
—LETE: **(106)** s. iv BC Hatzopoulos, *MI* 2 pp. 93-4 no. 79, 9; **(107)** ib. l. 10; **(108)** ib. l. 12; **(109)** ib. l. 13; **(110)** ib. l. 15; **(111)** c. 325-300 BC *SEG* XLIV 535; *KGAM Thess.* I 30 (date) (f. Λυσιδίκα); **(112)** s. i BC *SEG* XLVII 905, 1 (s. Εὔλανδρος); **(113)** ib. l. 3 (s. Εὔλανδρος); **(114)** imp. *AD* 52 (1997) Chron. p. 645 (mosaic)
—THESSALONIKE: **(115)** ii-i BC *IG* X (2) (1) 77, 7 (f. Φιλωτέρα); **(116)** 95 BC ib. 4, 6 (f. Παράμονος); **(117)** ?39 BC ib. 30, 4; 50, 5; 109, 10 (f. Δημήτριος); **(118)** i AD ib. 259, 30 (s. Νικηφόρος); **(119)** i-ii AD ib. 421, 1; cf. *Myrtos* p. 275 (f. Ἑλλανίχα); **(120)** *IG* X (2) (1) 421, 2; cf. *Myrtos* p. 275 (s. Ἑλλανίχα); **(121)** f. i AD *IG* X (2) (1) 133, 13; Robert, *OMS* 5 pp. 295-302 (date) (f. Μενέλαος); **(122)** ii AD *IG* X (2) (1) 241 A II, 3 (Ἐβού[τιος] Ἀντίγον[ος]); **(123)** ib. 320, 1 (Διγίτιος Ἀ.); **(124)** ib. 416, 1 (s. Ἀλέξανδρος, f. Θεόφιλος); **(125)** 219 AD ib. 153, 17 (Φλαβιανὸς Ἀ.: s. Φλαβιανὸς Μάγνος)
—THESSALONIKE?: **(126)** i AD ib. 682 ([Ἀ]ντίγον[ος]); **(127)** 181 AD ib. 693
MACEDONIA (ODOMANTIKE):
—SIRRHA: **(128)** 155 AD Dimitsas 821, 2 (Kaphtantzis 1) (s. Διοσκουρίδης)
—SKOTOUSSA?: **(129)** ii-iii AD *SEG* XLVIII 801 (f. Ἀβροκόμας)
MACEDONIA (ORESTIS):
—BATTYNAIOI: **(130)** 192 AD *EAM* 186 I, 51 (s. Κάσσανδρος); **(131)** ib. l. 56 (s. Εὐχίδης); **(132)** ib. 186 III, 48 (s. Γέλων); **(133)** ib. 186 IV, 47 (s. Κλεῖτος) ?= (*134*); **(134)** ib. l. 48 (f. Κλεῖτος) ?= (*133*)
MACEDONIA (PAIONIA):
—ASTREA: **(135)** c. 230-200 BC *BCH* 45 (1921) p. 17 III, 69 (Tataki, *Macedonians* p. 71 no. 1) (s. Ἀριστοκράτης)
—DOBEROS: **(136)** ii AD *ISmyrna* 373 (Tataki, *Macedonians* p. 101 no. 2) (Φλαούϊος Ἀ.)
MACEDONIA (PELAGONIA):
—DOSTONEIS: **(137)** f. ii AD *IG* X (2) (2) 195 (f. Π. Αἴλ. Διονύσιος)
—KERAMIAI (NR.): **(138)** ii AD ib. 220 (Τ. Αἴλιος Ἀ.); **(139)** 193-211 AD ib. 218, 6 (Αὐρήλιος Ἀ. ὁ καὶ Πολέμων); **(140)** ib. l. 10, 12 (Αὐρ. Ἀ.)
—KOLOBAISA*: **(141)** ?f. ii AD ib. 231 (f. Τ. Φλ. Ἀπολλόδωρος)
MACEDONIA (PIERIA):
—HERAKLEION: **(142)** c. 230-200 BC *BCH* 45 (1921) p. 17 III, 51 (Tataki, *Macedonians* p. 111 no. 1) (s. Ποσειδώνιος)
—LIVADI (MOD.): **(143)** imp. *SEG* XXXVIII 630 (?s. Παράμονος)
—PYDNA: **(144)** imp. ib. XLVII 907 (f. Καλλικράτης); **(145)** i-ii AD ib. XXXVIII 666 (f. Αὐρηλία)
MACEDONIA?: **(146)** 331 BC Curt. V 2. 5 (Tataki, *Macedonians* p. 246 no. 175) (Lat. Antigonus)
SCYTHIA MINOR:
—TOMIS: **(147)** ii AD *ISM* II 17, 1 (s. Ῥοῦφος); **(148)** ii-iii AD ib. 19 b, 2 (Ἀντίγον[ος])
TAURIS:
—CHERSONESOS: **(149)** iii BC *IOSPE* I² 340, 3 ([Ἀντί]γονος: s. Πρόνους); **(150)** ii BC ib. 524 ([Ἀντ]ίγονος?); **(151)** ii AD ib. 565 (Solomonik, *LNKhT* 25) (Lat. L. Aur. Antigonus: f. L. Aur. Severus)
THRACE: **(152)** 231 or 206 BC *CPR* XVIII 17, 348, 353, 360 (La'da E825) (s. Ἀλέξανδρος: t.e.)
—ABDERA: **(153)** c. 311-280 BC *AMNG* II (1) 215 (coin) (Ἀντίγο(νος))
—BYZANTION*: **(154)** i-ii AD *IByz* 242 (slave)
—STORGOSIA*: **(155)** ?ii-iii AD *ILB* 231 (Lat. L. Val. Antigonus: freed.)
—VICUS TRULLENSIUM: **(156)** 161-169 or 198-209 AD ib. 180, 3 (Lat. Antigonus: f. Firmus)

Ἀντίδοτος
MACEDONIA (CHALKIDIKE):
—CHALKIDEIS: **(1)** ?350 BC *TAPA* 59 (1928) p. 226, 9; 62 (1931) p. 43 no. 2, 1; 65 (1934) p. 125 no. 3, 7; 69 (1938) p. 50 no. 4, 2; *SEG* XXXVII 570, 2; XXXVIII 670, 1; 671, 3; XXXIX 617; XLVII 922 (s. Πολυκλῆς)
—OLYNTHOS: **(2)** f. iv BC *Olynthus* 10 p. 479 no. 2526; **(3)** ?350 BC *TAPA* 62 (1931) p. 43 no. 2, 7; Hatzopoulos, *Actes Chalc.* p. 80 (date) (s. Θεόδωρος)
MACEDONIA (EDONIS):
—AMPHIPOLIS: **(4)** m. iii BC Hatzopoulos, *Actes Amphipolis* p. 52 no 12, 10; *SEG* XLI 566 (date) (f. Ἀστιάδης)
MACEDONIA (MYGDONIA):
—THESSALONIKE: **(5)** s. i AD *IG* X (2) (1) 32, 7 (Ἀντ̣ίδοτο[ς])

Ἀντίδωρος
CIMMERIAN BOSPOROS:
—GORGIPPIA: **(1)** f. iii BC *CIRB* 1137 A I, 18 (s. Ἡρόδωρος)
MACEDONIA (BOTTIAIA):
—PELLA: **(2)** iii BC Akamatis, *Amph. Pellas* p. 31 no. PAR2 (amph.) (*SEG* L 613) (Ἀντ[ί]δωρος)
MACEDONIA (CHALKIDIKE):
—OLYNTHOS: **(3)** f. iii BC *IG* XI (4) 531, 3, [10] (Tataki, *Macedonians* p. 130 no. 7) (s. Νικόδημος)
MACEDONIA (EDONIS):
—AMPHIPOLIS: **(4)** iv/iii BC *AEMTh* 15 (2001) p. 118 (f. Ἀρχεβούλη)

Ἀντίθεος
THRACE:
—ODESSOS: **(1)** c. 45-42 BC *IGB* I² 43, 2 (f. Διογένης)

Ἀντικλῆς
MACEDONIA: **(1)** 327 BC *RE* Supplbd. 4 (8); Berve 88 (Tataki, *Macedonians* p. 248 no. 186) (s. Θεόκριτος)
THRACE:
—KALLIPOLIS: **(2)** i BC-i AD *ISestos* 15 (f. Βίτα)

Ἀντικράτης
MACEDONIA (PIERIA):
—PYDNA: **(1)** c. 169 BC *SEG* XLIII 451, 8 (f. Κλεόβουλος)
MACEDONIA (PIERIS):
—NEAPOLIS: **(2)** s. iv BC ib. 430 (Pilhofer 6) (f. Διεύς, Φίλτων)
SCYTHIA MINOR:
—ISTROS: **(3)** iv/iii BC *ISM* I 246, 3 (f. —νης)
—TOMIS: **(4)** i BC ib. II 2 A, 53 (s. Εὔδοξος)
THRACE:
—LYSIMACHEIA: **(5)** ?c. 214-210 BC *IOrop* 125, 4, 8 (s. Τίμων)
—STRYME?: **(6)** m. v BC *CEG* II 728 (*IThrakAig* E109) (s. Ἑκαταῖος)

'Αντικρατίδης
SKYTHIA:
—OLBIA-BORYSTHENES: **(1)** s. iv BC Dubois, *IGDOlbia* 107, 5

'Αντιλέων
MACEDONIA (CHALKIDIKE):
—POTIDAIA-KASSANDREIA: **(1)** c. 245-239 BC *SEG* XXXIX 595, 1; 596, 1 ?= (*2*); **(2)** c. 240-220 BC ib. XXXVII 558, 4; *Poikila* p. 141 (date) (Ἀντιλέ[ω]ν) ?= (*1*)

'Αντίλοχος
MACEDONIA: **(1)** 221 BC *SB* 13841, 2 (Tataki, *Macedonians* p. 248 no. 187; La'da E1409) ([Ἀν]τίλοχος: s. Ἀντίγονος)
TAURIS:
—CHERSONESOS: **(2)** s. v BC *SEG* XL 612. 16 (ostrakon) (Ἀντίλοχ(ος)); **(3)** imp. *IOSPE* I^2 434, 4, 8; **(4)** i AD *SEG* XLVI 927, 4 (s. Ἐ—); **(5)** ?114 AD ib. XLVIII 999, 43 (s. Χρηστίων); **(6)** 129-130 AD *IOSPE* I^2 359, 29; *VDI* 1960 (3), pp. 154-5, 27 (f. Ἀρίστων); **(7)** 130 AD ib. l. 25 (I f. Ἀντίλοχος II); **(8)** ib. l. 25 (II s. Ἀντίλοχος I)
THRACE:
—PERINTHOS-HERAKLEIA: **(9)** ii AD *IPerinth* 102, 8 (s. Ἐπίγονος)

'Αντίμαχος
CIMMERIAN BOSPOROS:
—NYMPHAION: **(1)** inc. *CIRB* 938
—PANTIKAPAION: **(2)** i AD ib. 334 (f. Ἀλεξᾶς); **(3)** ib. 541; **(4)** i/ii AD ib. 32, 7; **(5)** ib. 644; **(6)** 82 AD ib. 76, 10 (*SEG* XVIII 310) (Ἀντίμαχος—*CIRB*); **(7)** 106 AD *CIRB* 697 (Οὔλπ. Ἀντ[ί]μαχος: s. Μαστοῦς); **(8)** iii AD ib. 103, 7 (Ἀν[τ]ί[μ]αχος: f. Δάδας); **(9)** ib. 725 (Ἀντίμα[χος]); **(10)** 216 AD ib. 53, 11 (f. Οὔλπ. Ἀντισθένης); **(11)** 221 AD ib. 99, 9 (f. Μαστοῦς)
MACEDONIA: **(12)** 142 BC *SB* 12720, 2, 9, 17, 23 (Tataki, *Macedonians* p. 473 no. 23; La'da E1411) (s. Ἀριστομήδης); **(13)** 132 BC *PGissUniv* 5, 2 (Tataki, *Macedonians* p. 473 no. 24); cf. La'da E1410 (I f. Ἀντίμαχος II); **(14)** *PGissUniv* 5, 2 and verso (Tataki, *Macedonians* p. 473 no. 22; La'da E1410) (II s. Ἀντίμαχος I)
MACEDONIA (BOTTIAIA):
—BEROIA: **(15)** 121 BC *IBer* 134, 14 (Ἀν[τ]ί-μαχος: f. Νικάνωρ)
—PELLA?: **(16)** iv/iii BC *Arch. Pap.* 22 (1973) p. 203 no. 1 (s. Παυσανίας, Φιλοπάτρα)
MACEDONIA (EDONIS):
—HILL 133 (MOD.): **(17)** s. vi BC *PAE* 1964, p. 38 with pl. 23 β (vase) (Ἀντίμα[χος])
MACEDONIA (MYGDONIA):
—THESSALONIKE: **(18)** ii BC *IG* X (2) (1) 28, 5 (s. Ἀριστόξενος)
MACEDONIA?: **(19)** 171 BC *RE* Supplbd. 4 (12a) (Tataki, *Macedonians* p. 248 no. 189) (Lat. Antimachus); **(20)** 169 BC *RE* Supplbd. 1 (22a) (Tataki, *Macedonians* p. 248 no. 188)
SKYTHIA:
—TANAIS: **(21)** ii AD *CIRB* 1262, 12 (I f. Ἀντίμαχος II); **(22)** ib. l. 12 (II s. Ἀντίμαχος I); **(23)** ib. 1263, 12 (f. —ος); **(24)** 154-170 AD ib. 1239, 8 (s. Χαρίτων); **(25)** 220-225 AD ib. 1278, 8; 1279, 5 (s. Πασίων); **(26)** 225 AD ib. l. 11; **(27)** ib. l. 28 (f. Ξιαμφώκανος); **(28)** 225-228 AD ib. l. 12; 1283, 15 (f. Εὐτύχης); **(29)** 225-236 AD ib. 1250, 12; 1280, 28 (s. Κίμβρος)
—TANAIS*: **(30)** ii-iii AD *Tanais* 1 p. 103 (amph.) (Ἀντίμα(χος))
THRACE:
—BYZANTION: **(31)** m. iv BC *IG* II^2 8437 (*FRA* 1386) (s. Ἀπολλώνιος)

'Αντιμένης
MACEDONIA (MYGDONIA):
—LETE: **(1)** f. ii BC *SEG* XLVI 764, 13 (f. Φίλιππος)

THRACE:
—APOLLONIA-SOZOPOLIS: **(2)** iv BC *IGB* I^2 463 bis, 2 (s. Μήτρων)

'Αντιμένων
MACEDONIA (MYGDONIA):
—KALINDOIA: **(1)** c. 326 BC Hatzopoulos, *MI* 2 pp. 84-5 no. 62, 19 (s. Μένανδρος)
—LETE: **(2)** ii AD *Makedonika* 2 (1951) p. 619 no. 42 θ, 7 (s. Νικάνωρ)

'Αντιμήστωρ
SKYTHIA:
—OLBIA-BORYSTHENES: **(1)** iii BC *IOSPE* I^2 201 I, 30 (f. Ἀγαθῖνος); **(2)** ib. l. 61 (s. Ἀγαθῖνος)

'Αντίμοιρος
MACEDONIA (CHALKIDIKE):
—MENDE: **(1)** v/iv BC *RE* (-) (Tataki, *Macedonians* p. 120 no. 3)

'Αντινικίδης
MACEDONIA (EDONIS):
—PHILIPPOI: **(1)** c. 230-200 BC *BCH* 45 (1921) p. 18 III, 80 (Tataki, *Macedonians* p. 163 no. 3) (s. Ἐπικράτης)

'Αντίνοος
MACEDONIA (MYGDONIA):
—THESSALONIKE: **(1)** ?iii AD *IG* X (2) (1) 496 (s. Ζώσιμος, Ἀγριππῖνα)
THRACE:
—KOILA: **(2)** imp. *BCH* 36 (1912) p. 288 n.2 (Αἰλ. Ἀ.)

'Αντιόχεια
THRACE:
—ODESSOS: **(1)** v-vi AD Beševliev 115, 5 (-χια)

'Αντιοχιανός
THRACE:
—EMPORIUM PIRETENSIUM: **(1)** iii AD *CIL* III 14427 (*ILB* 399; *Eastern cults* p. 219 no. 2) (Lat. [A]urel. An[t]iochia[n]us)

'Αντιοχίδης
MACEDONIA (MYGDONIA):
—KALINDOIA: **(1)** a. 98 AD *SEG* XLII 583, 9 (Ἀντιοχίδευς (gen.))

'Αντιοχίς
MACEDONIA: **(1)** s. iii BC *RE* (4); Grainger, *SPG* p. 8 (d. Σέλευκος II Καλλίνικος, Λαοδίκη); **(2)** iii/ii BC *RE* (5); Grainger, *SPG* p. 8 (d. Ἀντίοχος III Μέγας, Λαοδίκη (Pontos), m. Ἀριαράθης, Ὀροφέρνης, Μιθριδάτης (all Kappadokia))
MACEDONIA (EDONIS):
—AMPHIPOLIS: **(3)** ii-i BC *SEG* XXXV 709 (—νία Ἀ.)
MACEDONIA (MYGDONIA):
—THESSALONIKE: **(4)** f. iii AD *IG* X (2) (1) 628 A, 1 (Αἰκουανὴ Ἀ.: m. Γεμινία Ὀλυμπιάς)
THRACE:
—PERINTHOS-HERAKLEIA: **(5)** hell.? ib. II^2 10071 (*FRA* 6032) (d. Ἀντίοχος)

'Αντίοχος
CIMMERIAN BOSPOROS:
—NYMPHAION: **(1)** i BC *CIRB* 927 (f. Αἰσχίνης)
—PANTIKAPAION: **(2)** imp. ib. 785 (f. —φέρ[ν]ης)
MACEDONIA: **(3)** 417-413 BC *IG* I^3 89, 69 ?= (*33*); **(4)** iv BC Rhodes–Osborne 75 B (*IOrop* 2, 4); cf. *Eretria* XI pp. 367-87; Arr., *An.* i 17. 9; ii 6. 3 (Tataki, *Macedonians* p. 251 no. 212) (f. Ἀμύντας); **(5)** 333 BC *RE* (13); Berve 91 (Tataki, *Macedonians* p. 249 no. 195); **(6)** 327 BC Berve 90 (Tataki, *Macedonians* p. 249 no. 194); **(7)** 323-261 BC *RE* (21); Grainger, *SPG* pp. 9-13; cf. Beloch, *GG* IV (2) pp. 198-9 (Ἀ. I Σωτήρ: s. Σέλευκος I Νικάτωρ (Europos), Ἀπάμη (Sogdiane), f. Ἀντίοχος II Θεός, Σέλευκος, Ἀπάμη, Στρατονίκη: king); **(8)** c. 286-246 BC *RE* (22); Grainger, *SPG* pp. 13-15; cf. Beloch, *GG* IV (2) pp. 200-1 (Ἀ. II Θεός: s. Ἀντίοχος I Σωτήρ, Στρατονίκη, f. Ἀντίοχος Ἱέραξ, Σέλευκος II Καλλίνικος, Στρατονίκη, Λαοδίκη, Ἀπάμη: king); **(9)** c. 265-226 BC *RE* (23); Grainger, *SPG* pp. 35-6; cf. Beloch, *GG* IV (2) pp. 202-4 (Ἀ. Ἱέραξ: s. Ἀντίοχος II Θεός, Λαοδίκη, ?f. Λαοδίκη); **(10)** c. 243-187 BC *RE* (25); Grainger, *SPG* pp. 15-22; Ma, *Antiochos* (Ἀ. III Μέγας: s. Σέλευκος II Καλλίνικος, Λαοδίκη, f. Ἀντίοχος, Ἀντίοχος IV Ἐπιφάνης, Σέλευκος IV Φιλοπάτωρ, Ἀντιοχίς, Λαοδίκη, Κλεοπάτρα I: king); **(11)** 221-193 BC *RE* (26); Grainger, *SPG* pp. 36-7 (s. Ἀντίοχος III Μέγας, Λαοδίκη (Pontos)); **(12)** c. 218-164 BC *RE* (27); Grainger, *SPG* pp. 22-7; Ma, *Antiochos* p. 340 no. 31 A I, 3; *Chiron* 18 (1988) pp. 451-4 (name) (Ἀ. IV Ἐπιφάνης (ὁ πρὶν) Μιθριδάτης: s. Ἀντίοχος III Μέγας, Λαοδίκη (Pontos), f. Ἀντίοχος V Εὐπάτωρ, Νῦσα: king); **(13)** c. 190-170 BC Grainger, *SPG* p. 37 (s. Σέλευκος IV Φιλοπάτωρ, Λαοδίκη); **(14)** c. 173-162 BC *RE* (28); Grainger, *SPG* pp. 27-8 (Ἀ. V Εὐπάτωρ: s. Ἀντίοχος IV Ἐπιφάνης, Λαοδίκη: king); **(15)** c. 158-129 BC *RE* (30); Grainger, *SPG* pp. 29-31; cf. *ZPE* 131 (2000) pp. 107-8 (Ἀ. VII Σιδήτης: s. Δημήτριος I Σωτήρ, Λαοδίκη, f. Ἀντίοχος IX Κυζικηνός, Ἀντίοχος, Λαοδίκη, Λαοδίκη, Σέλευκος: king); **(16)** s. ii BC *FGrH* 260 F 32. 20; Grainger, *SPG* p. 37 (s. Ἀντίοχος VII Σιδήτης, Κλεοπάτρα Θεά); **(17)** c. 148-142 BC *RE* (29); Grainger, *SPG* pp. 28-9 (Ἀ. VI Ἐπιφάνης: s. Ἀλέξανδρος Βάλας (Smyrna), Κλεοπάτρα Θεά: king); **(18)** c. 142-96 BC *RE* (31); Grainger, *SPG* pp. 31-2 (Ἀ. VIII Γρυπός: s. Δημήτριος II Νικάτωρ, Κλεοπάτρα Θεά, f. Ἀντίοχος XI Φιλάδελφος, Φίλιππος I Φιλάδελφος, Ἀντίοχος XII Διόνυσος, Δημήτριος III Φιλοπάτωρ, Σέλευκος VI, Λαοδίκη Θεά: king); **(19)** c. 135-95 BC *RE* (32); Grainger, *SPG* pp. 32-3 (Ἀ. IX Κυζικηνός: s. Ἀντίοχος VII Σιδήτης, Κλεοπάτρα Θεά, f. Ἀντίοχος X Εὐσεβής: king); **(20)** c. 115-93 BC *RE* (34); Grainger, *SPG* p. 34 (Ἀ. XI Φιλάδελφος: s. Ἀντίοχος VIII Γρυπός, Τρύφαινα: king); **(21)** c. 115-84 BC *RE* (35); Grainger, *SPG* p. 34 (Ἀ. XII Διόνυσος: s. Ἀντίοχος VIII Γρυπός, Τρύφαινα: king); **(22)** c. 115-83 BC *RE* (33); Grainger, *SPG* pp. 33-4 (Ἀ. X Εὐσεβής: s. Ἀντίοχος IX Κυζικηνός, f. Ἀντίοχος XIII Ἀσιατικός: king); **(23)** c. 90-64 BC *RE* (36); Grainger, *SPG* pp. 34-5; cf. Bellinger, *End of Seleucids* p. 83 (Ἀ. XIII Ἀσιατικός: s. Ἀντίοχος X Εὐσεβής, ?s. Κλεοπάτρα Σελήνη: king); **(24)** 73 BC *POxy* 3482, 3, 29 (Tataki, *Macedonians* p. 473 no. 25); cf. La'da E1510 (f. Θέων)
MACEDONIA (BOTTIAIA): **(25)** iv BC Arr., *An.* iii 11. 8 (Tataki, *Macedonians* p. 193 no. 1) (f. Ἡρακλείδης)
MACEDONIA (CHALKIDIKE):
—POTIDAIA-KASSANDREIA?: **(26)** iv BC *TAPA* 69 (1938) p. 59 no. 12 (or Macedonia (Chalkidike) Olynthos: [Ἀντί]οχος: f. Ἐπιχάρης)
MACEDONIA (EDONIS):
—AMPHIPOLIS: **(27)** b. 213 BC Hatzopoulos, *MI* 2 p. 83 no. 61, 9 (*SEG* XLVI 715) (s. Διονύσιος)
MACEDONIA (KRESTONIA):
—BRAGYLAI: **(28)** c. 230-200 BC *BCH* 45 (1921) p. 18 III, 71 (Tataki, *Macedonians* p. 84 no. 2) (f. Κεφάλων)
MACEDONIA (LOWER PAIONIA):
—EUROPOS: **(29)** m. iv BC *RE* Supplbd. 3 (-) (Tataki, *Macedonians* p. 108 no. 3) (f. Σέλευκος I Νικάτωρ, Λαοδίκη, ?f. Διδύμεια)

MACEDONIA (MYGDONIA):
—THESSALONIKE: **(30)** i AD *IG* X (2) (1) 310, 5 (*M. Μονδίκιος Ἀ.*); **(31)** i-ii AD ib. 373 (*Τυρέλλιος Ἀ.*); **(32)** ii AD ib. 241 A II, 20 ([*Ἀντ*]*ίοχος*: s. *Βήρυλλος*)
MACEDONIA (ORESTIS): **(33)** 429 BC Th. ii 80. 6 (Tataki, *Macedonians* p. 204 no. 4) (king) ?= (*3*)
MACEDONIA (PELAGONIA):
—KOLOBAISA (NR.): **(34)** ii AD *IG* X (2) (2) 235
SCYTHIA MINOR:
—ISTROS: **(35)** ii AD *ISM* I 197 II, 9 (s. *Ἀσκληπιόδωρος*)
—TOMIS: **(36)** ii-iii AD ib. II 468, 12 (I f. *Ἀντίοχος* II); **(37)** ib. l. 12 (II s. *Ἀντίοχος* I)
SKYTHIA?: **(38)** hell. Tolstoi 255 (vase)
THRACE:
—AGATHOPOLIS: **(39)** iv/iii BC *Thracia Pontica* 5 p. 112 no. 2, 10 ([*Ἀντί*]*οχος*?: s. *Ἀριστόδημος*)
—BYZANTION: **(40)** ii AD Firatlı–Robert p. 92 no. 124 (PM 780)
—DIONYSOPOLIS: **(41)** ?ii/iii AD *IGB* I² 15 bis, 10 ((*Ἀ*)*ντίοχ*(*ος*): f. *M. Αὐ*[*ρ*.] *—κωρος*)
—KRASALOPARA: **(42)** 202 AD ib. III 1690 b, 52 (and Thrace Pizos: f. *Μουκάπορις*)
—PAUTALIA: **(43)** ii-iii AD ib. IV 2059 ([*Αἴ*]*λ*. *Ἀντίοχ*[*ος*])
—PERINTHOS-HERAKLEIA: **(44)** hell.? *IG* II² 10071 (*FRA* 6033) (f. *Ἀντιοχίς*)
—PHILIPPOPOLIS-TRIMONTIUM (TERRIT.): **(45)** ii-iii AD *IGB* III 1111 (f. *Τήρης*)
—RHAIDESTOS: **(46)** ?ii-i BC PM 1405 (s. *Σαραπίων*)
—STRYME?: **(47)** m. iv BC *BCH* 79 (1955) p. 283 = Bakalakis, *Oinos Ismarikos* p. 553 (*IThrakAig* E150) (s. *Ἀρίγνωτος*)

Ἀντιπᾶς
MACEDONIA (ORESTIS):
—SISANI (MOD.): **(1)** 146 AD *EAM* 187, 20 (f. *Γάϊος*)

Ἀντιπάτρα
THRACE:
—PHILIPPOPOLIS-TRIMONTIUM: **(1)** 293 AD *Cod. Just.* iv 49. 9; cf. *Klio* 58 (1976) p. 79 (Lat. Aur. Zania Antipatra)

Ἀντιπατρίδης
MACEDONIA (BOTTIAIA):
—PELLA: **(1)** m. iii BC *SEG* XXXVIII 652 (s. *Ἀγαθοκλῆς*)
MACEDONIA (CHALKIDIKE):
—APHYTIS: **(2)** ?351 BC *A΄ Panell. Synedr. Epigr.* pp. 80-1, 6, 13, 20 (s. *Κατάστασις*)
—OLYNTHOS: **(3)** ?355 BC *TAPA* 69 (1938) p. 51 no. 5, 14; Hatzopoulos, *Actes Chalc.* p. 80 (date) ([*Ἀντι*]*πατρίδης*?, [*Εὐ*]*πατρίδης*—ed.: s. *Κλε—ης*)
MACEDONIA?: **(4)** s. iv BC Berve 92 (Tataki, *Macedonians* p. 252 no. 213)
THRACE:
—STRYME?: **(5)** m. iv BC *IThrakAig* E161 (f. *Γλαῦκος*, *Κρίτων*)

Ἀντιπατρίς
CIMMERIAN BOSPOROS:
—PANTIKAPAION: **(1)** i AD *CIRB* 341

Ἀντίπατρος
CIMMERIAN BOSPOROS:
—GORGIPPIA: **(1)** i BC/i AD *Hyperboreus* 2002 (1), p. 185 (s. *Πανταλέων*); **(2)** ii AD *CIRB* 1176, 2 ([*Ἀ*]*ντίπατρος*); **(3)** s. ii AD ib. 1142, 5 (*Ἀντίπα*[*τρος*]); **(4)** ib. l. 6 (*Ἀντίπα*[*τρος*])
—PANTIKAPAION: **(5)** i AD ib. 132, 8 (*GVI* 679) (s. *Ἀργόναις*, *Μᾶ*)
MACEDONIA: **(6)** 327 BC *RE* (15); Berve 93 (Tataki, *Macedonians* p. 252 no. 216) (s. *Ἀσκληπιόδωρος*); **(7)** c. 322-313 BC *IG* VII 4256, 9 (*IOrop* 4; Tataki, *Macedonians* p. 253 no. 219) (s. *Σῶσις*); **(8)** c. 315-287 BC *RE* (13) (Tataki, *Macedonians* p. 253 no. 218) (s. *Κάσσανδρος*, *Θεσσαλονίκη*); **(9)** f. iii BC *RE* (14) (Tataki, *Macedonians* p. 253 no. 220); cf. Beloch, *GG* IV (2) p. 128 (*Ἀ. Ἐτησίας*: s. *Φίλιππος*) ?= (*10*); **(10)** 278 BC *RE* Supplbd. 3 (20a) ?= (*9*); **(11)** c. 140-130 BC *PBingen* 36, 7 (La'da E1412); **(12)** 238 AD *ILeukopetra* 89, 8 (oikogen. slave/freed.)
—PALIOURA: **(13)** 398-319 BC *RE* (12); Berve 94 (Tataki, *Macedonians* p. 146 no. 1) (s. *Ἰόλαος*, f. *Κάσσανδρος*, *Ἰόλαος*, *Νικάνωρ*, *Πλείσταρχος*, *Φίλιππος*, *Ἀλέξαρχος*, *Φίλα*, *Νικαία*, *Εὐρυδίκα*, ?f. *Περίλαος*, *Ἀρχίας*)
MACEDONIA (BOTTIAIA):
—AIGAI: **(14)** iv BC Arr., *Ind.* xviii 6 (Tataki, *Macedonians* p. 40 no. 6) (f. *Λεόννατος*)
—BEROIA: **(15)** 223 BC *IBer* 4, 14 (s. *Δημόφιλος*); **(16)** ii BC ib. 141, 10 ([*Ἀν*]*τίπατρος*)
—TYRISSA?: **(17)** s. iv BC *SEG* XLIII 446 (s. *Ἡγησικράτης*); **(18)** ib. ([*Ἀ*]*ντίπατρο*[*ς*])
MACEDONIA (CHALKIDIKE):
—AKANTHOS: **(19)** inc. *RE* (31); Supplbd. 1 (24a) (Tataki, *Macedonians* p. 42 no. 3) (fict.?)
—OLYNTHOS: **(20)** iv BC *TAPA* 62 (1931) p. 54 no. 5 (s. *Σωσικράτης*); **(21)** ?352 BC ib. 69 (1938) p. 48 no. 3, 6; *SEG* XXXVIII 637, 3; Hatzopoulos, *Actes Chalc.* p. 80 (date) (f. *Διοπείθης*)
MACEDONIA (EDONIS):
—AMPHIPOLIS: **(22)** a. 357 BC Hatzopoulos, *Actes Amphipolis* pp. 38-9 no. 7, 3 (*Ἀντίπ*(*α*)*τ*(*ρ*)*ος*: s. *Κλεινίας*); **(23)** hell. *SEG* XXXII 290 (Tataki, *Macedonians* p. 46 no. 10; *FRA* 497) (s. *Θεόδωρος*); **(24)** c. 60 BC *IG* VII 420, 12 (*IOrop* 528); cf. Stephanis 1488 (Tataki, *Macedonians* p. 46 no. 11); cf. *LGPN* II s.v. (13) (f. *Κράτερος*)
—PHILIPPOI: **(25)** ii-i BC *BCH* 59 (1935) p. 158 no. 54 (Pilhofer 303) (s. *Τιμόδημος*)
MACEDONIA (ELIMEIA):
—PALAIOKASTRO (MOD.): **(26)** ii-iii AD *EAM* 20, 3, 6 (s. *Ἀλέξανδρος*)
MACEDONIA (LYNKESTIS):
—ANO VEVI (MOD.): **(27)** ii AD ib. 164 (s. *Ῥοιμητάλκης*, *Ἀμμία*)
—HERAKLEIA: **(28)** i AD *IG* X (2) (2) 75, 24 (f. *Θεόφιλος*); **(29)** ib. l. 43 (s. *Θεόφιλος*)
MACEDONIA (MYGDONIA):
—APOLLONIA: **(30)** f. ii BC *SEG* XLIV 508 (Hatzopoulos, *MI* 2 p. 87 no. 66) (s. *Παράμονος*)
—THESSALONIKE: **(31)** i BC/i AD *RE* (23); *GP* 75-724 (Tataki, *Macedonians* p. 179 no. 6)
MACEDONIA (ORESTIS):
—LYKE: **(32)** ii-iii AD *SEG* XLVII 910, 3 (*Λ. Φλαούϊος Φαβρικιανὸς* [*Ἀντ*]*ίπατρος*: s. *Λ. Φλαούϊος Φαβρικιανός*)
—PLATANIA (MOD.): **(33)** imp.? *EAM* 204 (f. *Ἡρακλέας*)
MACEDONIA (PIERIA):
—DION: **(34)** hell. *SEG* L 589 (f. *Νικαρίστη*)
—SYKIA (MOD.): **(35)** i BC-i AD ib. XXV 709 (f. *Μελανίων*)
MACEDONIA?: **(36)** c. 319-317 BC D.S. xix 16. 1 (Tataki, *Macedonians* p. 252 no. 214); **(37)** c. 265-257 BC *Cl. Rh.* 9 (1938) p. 183, 8; Robert, *Documents* p. 55 n. 4 (ethn.) (Tataki, *Macedonians* p. 253 no. 221) (or Thasos?: f. *Λείμων*); **(38)** f. ii BC *PHamb* 28, 2 (*PP* 2192 with Add.); **(39)** c. 185 BC *ID* 427, [15]; 442 B, 95; cf. *ID Index* p. 11 s.v. (?s. *Ἐπίγονος*); **(40)** 171 BC Liv. xlii 66. 9 (Lat. Antipater); **(41)** ?ii AD *PFreib* 2 a II, 6 (fict.)
SCYTHIA MINOR:
—ISTROS: **(42)** 138 AD *ISM* I 193 I, 84 (I f. *Ἀντίπατρος* II); **(43)** ib. l. 84 (II s. *Ἀντίπατρος* I)
—TROESMIS: **(44)** 218-222 AD ib. V 151, 8 (Lat. M. Ulp. Antipater)
TAURIS:
—CHERSONESOS: **(45)** iii BC *IOSPE* I² 511; **(46)** 174 AD *SEG* XLV 985 A, 36 (I f. *Ἀντίπατρος* II); **(47)** ib. l. 36 (II s. *Ἀντίπατρος* I)
THRACE:
—BEROE-AUGUSTA TRAIANA: **(48)** 187 AD *IGB* III 1552, 13 (s. *Ἀπολλώνιος*)
—BYZANTION: **(49)** c. 250-220 BC Schönert-Geiss, *Byzantion* 1026-36 (coin); **(50)** i BC-i AD *IByz* 178 (Firatlı–Robert p. 111 no. 183) (f. *Ἀρτεμίδωρος*, *Φυλλίς*)
—DIONYSOPOLIS: **(51)** iii AD *IGB* I² 14 a, 3 (*M. Αὐρ. Ἀ.*: s. *Πάπας*); **(52)** ib. l. 5 (f. *Αὐρ. Ἄττας*); **(53)** ib. 14 c, 14 (*Φλ. Ἀ.*); **(54)** ib. l. 16 (*Αὐρ. Ἀ.*: s. *Σουπερίων*)
—LYSIMACHEIA: **(55)** m. ii BC *ISestos* 38 b, 3 (s. *Φιλώτας*)
—ODESSOS: **(56)** i-ii AD *IGB* I² 51 b, 9 ([*Ἀντί*]*πατρος*: s. *Ἀπολλώνιος*); **(57)** ii AD ib. 50 a, 9 (f. *Διονύσιος*); **(58)** f. ii AD ib. 78 ter, 9 (*CCET* I 30) (*Ἀ*[*ν*]*τίπατρος*: f. *Ζωπυρίων*); **(59)** s. ii AD *IGB* I² 166 (PM 1404); *Dacia* 21 (1977) p. 161 (date) (f. *Μάμα*); **(60)** 215 AD *IGB* I² 47 b, 18 (*Αὐρ. Ἀ.*: s. *Δάδας*); **(61)** 221 AD ib. 47 bis a, 39 (f. *Αὐρ. Μοσχίων*); **(62)** ib. 47 bis b, 24 (f. *Αὐρ. Διονύσιος*); **(63)** ib. 47 bis c, 37 (*Αὐρ. Ἀ.*: s. *Ἀττῆς*)
—PERINTHOS-HERAKLEIA: **(64)** i-ii AD *IPerinth* 134 (s. *Στρατόνικος*)
—ZONE: **(65)** s. iv BC *SEG* XLIII 480 (*IThrakAig* E421) (f. *Μένανδρος*)

Ἀντισθένης
CIMMERIAN BOSPOROS:
—MYRMEKION: **(1)** s. i AD *CIRB* 883 (*Ἀντισθ*(*έ*)*νης*)
—PANTIKAPAION: **(2)** i BC ib. 270 (s. *Πατάσιος*); **(3)** f. ii AD ib. 83, 4 (f. *Ἔρως*); **(4)** 204 AD ib. 96, 4 (*SEG* II 485) (s. *Ἡρακλείδης*); **(5)** 216 AD *CIRB* 53, 10 (*Οὔλπ. Ἀ.*: s. *Ἀντίμαχος*); **(6)** 275-278 AD ib. 36, 30 (*Ἀντισ*[*θένης*]: s. *Ποσείδεος*); **(7)** ib. l. 40 (*Ἀντισθ*(*ένης*): s. *Ἀλέξανδρος*)
SKYTHIA:
—SOLOKHA (MOD.): **(8)** v BC *Kurgan Solokha* p. 80 no. 55
—TANAIS: **(9)** ii AD *CIRB* 1263, 11; **(10)** 220 AD ib. 1278, 6 (f. *Θιάγαρος*); **(11)** 225 AD ib. 1279, 16 (f. *Φορίανος*); **(12)** ib. 1280, 14 (s. *Μεύακος*)

Ἀντίστασις
CIMMERIAN BOSPOROS:
—PANTIKAPAION: **(1)** 344-310 BC ib. 113, 1 (*CEG* II 885) (*-σστα-*: s. *Φανόμαχος*)

Ἀντιφάνης
CIMMERIAN BOSPOROS:
—NYMPHAION: **(1)** iii BC *CIRB* 912 I, 5 (f. *—υς*) ?= (*2*); **(2)** ib. l. 9 (f. *Μένων*) ?= (*1*); **(3)** ib. 912 II, 19 (s. *Προμαθίων*); **(4)** ib. 912 III, 9 (*Ἀντιφάν*[*ης*])
MACEDONIA: **(5)** 241 BC *PPetr* III 54 B c, 5 (Tataki, *Macedonians* p. 253 no. 223; La'da E1413); **(6)** f. i AD *RE* (17); *GP* 725-82 (Tataki, *Macedonians* p. 254 no. 224)
MACEDONIA (BISALTIA):
—TRAGILOS: **(7)** hell.? Dimitsas 907 (f. *Μέγων*)
MACEDONIA (CHALKIDIKE):
—APHYTIS: **(8)** ?351 BC *A΄ Panell. Synedr. Epigr.* pp. 80-1, 16, 24 (f. *Ἀριστοτέλης*)
—STOLOS?: **(9)** ?351 BC *SEG* XXXVIII 673, 10 (f. *Πολέμαρχος*)
MACEDONIA (DERRIOPOS):
—STUBERRA: **(10)** i BC/i AD *IG* XII (8) 206, 11 (Tataki, *Macedonians* p. 177 no. 2) (s. *Διοσκουρίδης*); **(11)** 74 AD *IG* X (2) (2) 325, 47 (f. *Ἐπιγένης*)
MACEDONIA (MYGDONIA):
—KALINDOIA: **(12)** c. 310 BC Hatzopoulos, *MI* 2 pp. 84-5 no. 62, 36 (s. *Σωσ—*)
—THESSALONIKE: **(13)** s. i AD *IG* X (2) (1) 68, 30 (s. *Ἐπικράτης*)

MACEDONIA (ODOMANTIKE):
—BERGE: (14) iv-iii BC *RE* (19) ?= (*15*); (15) 360 BC *IG* IV (1)² 94 b, 19 (Perlman, *City and Sanctuary* E.1 with p. 69 f. (date); Tataki, *Macedonians* p. 73 no. 1) ?= (*14*)
MACEDONIA (PIERIA):
—PHYLAKAI?: (16) ?i BC Oikonomos 58 = *IG* IX (2) 230 (*Ἀντιφίνης*—lap. & Oikonomos, *Ἀντιφ(ά)νης*—*IG*: s. *Παρμενίσκος*)
MACEDONIA?: (17) 330 BC *RE* Supplbd. 4 (12a); Berve 95 (Tataki, *Macedonians* p. 253 no. 222) (Lat. Antiphanes)
THRACE:
—PĂRVENEC (MOD.): (18) v-iv BC *SEG* XLIII 483 (s. *Ἥρανδρος*)
—PERINTHOS-HERAKLEIA: (19) c. 230-200 BC *BCH* 45 (1921) p. 19 III, 97 (s. *Δορ—*)
—SALYMBRIA?: (20) ?v/iv BC *POxy* 2538 ii, 16
—SAPAI: (21) c. 230-200 BC *BCH* 45 (1921) p. 18 III, 83 (s. *Κλέων*)
—STRYME?: (22) v/iv BC *SEG* XXIV 632 (*IThrakAig* E126) (f. *Ἀπολλόδωρος*)

Ἀντιφίλα
MACEDONIA (PIERIA):
—PYDNA: (1) iv BC *GRBS* 43 (2002-3) p. 111 no. 2, 11

Ἀντιφίλη
SCYTHIA MINOR:
—ISTROS: (1) iii-ii BC Unp. (Avram, defixio) 4, 7

Ἀντιφιλίδης
THRACE:
—BYZANTION?: (1) iii BC *SEG* XIII 539 + Firatlı–Robert p. 154 (*Ἀντιφιλ[ίδο]υ* (gen.): I f. *Ἀντιφιλίδης* II); (2) *SEG* XIII 539 + Firatlı–Robert p. 154 (*Ἀν[τι]φι[λ]ί[δης]*?: II s. *Ἀντιφιλίδης* I)

Ἀντίφιλος
MACEDONIA (BISALTIA):
—TRAGILOS: (1) ?iv BC Kaphtantzis 532 (f. *Ἐπιχάρης*)
MACEDONIA (BOTTIAIA):
—EDESSA: (2) 171 BC Liv. xlii 51. 5 (Tataki, *Edessa* 30; Tataki, *Macedonians* p. 102 no. 3) (Lat. Antiphilus)
MACEDONIA (CHALKIDIKE):
—OLYNTHOS: (3) s. v BC *IG* II² 10017 (Tataki, *Macedonians* p. 130 no. 8; *FRA* 5882)
MACEDONIA (EDONIS):
—AMPHIPOLIS: (4) iii/ii BC *Ét. Thas.* 3 p. 318 no. 113 (Tataki, *Macedonians* p. 46 no. 12)
MACEDONIA (MYGDONIA):
—LETE: (5) s. iv BC Hatzopoulos, *MI* 2 pp. 93-4 no. 79, 6
SCYTHIA MINOR:
—ISTROS: (6) s. iii BC *ISM* I 15, 3 (f. *Ἀγαθοκλῆς*)
—KALLATIS: (7) iii BC ib. III 159 (f. *Τούσα*)
TAURIS:
—CHERSONESOS: (8) iv BC Solomonik, *NEPKh* 177 (f. *Κάμμις*); (9) imp. *IOSPE* I² 426
THRACE:
—ANCHIALOS: (10) ii BC *IGB* V 5133 (f. *Πασίξενος*)
—BYZANTION: (11) hell. Unp. (Sayar); (12) i BC-i AD *IByz* 171 (Firatlı–Robert p. 110 no. 178) (s. *Σωσίβιος*); (13) i BC/i AD *IG* XII (8) 206, 5 (I f. *Ἀντίφιλος* II); (14) ib. l. 5 (II s. *Ἀντίφιλος* I); (15) i AD *RE* (4); *GP* 783-1100
—BYZANTION?: (16) i BC *IByz* 361 (PM 1686) ([*Ἀ*]*ντίφιλος*)
—MESAMBRIA: (17) ii/i BC *IGB* V 5104 (f. *Ἐχέστρατος*); (18) i BC ib. I² 324 (*Ἀντ[ίφ]ιλος*: f. *Βοσπόριχος*); (19) ib. (s. *Καλλιγείτων*)
—ODESSOS: (20) i BC-i AD ib. 117, 3 (f. *Ἀριστοκλῆς νεώτ.*); (21) i-ii AD ib. 128, 1 (s. *Ἀρτεμίδωρος*); (22) f. ii AD ib. 78 ter, 7 (*CCET* I 30) (s. *Ζωπυρίων*); (23) *IGB* I² 78 ter, 12, 14 (*CCET* I 30) (s. *Ἀγαθήνωρ*, f. *Ἀγαθήνωρ*); (24) *IGB* I² 178 (PM 1722); *Dacia* 21 (1977) p. 161 (date) (f. *Ζωπυρίων*); (25) s. ii AD *IGB* I² 164 (*CCET* I 54; PM 1416) (f. *Διονύσιος ὁ καὶ Σκῶρις*); (26) iii AD *IGB* I² 176 bis; *Dacia* 21 (1977) p. 161 (date) (s. *Διονύσιος*); (27) 221 AD *IGB* I² 47 bis, 6 (*M. Αὐρ. Ἀ.*: s. *Ἀσκληπιάδης*)
—PHILIPPOPOLIS-TRIMONTIUM (TERRIT.): (28) ii/iii AD ib. III 1452, 9 (*Eastern cults* p. 121 no. 104) (*Ἀντ(ίφ)ιλος*: s. *Χρύσιππος*)
—SALYMBRIA: (29) ?iv-iii BC *IByz* S 22 (*SGDI* 3071) (s. *Σαμύλος*)

Ἀντιφῶν
MACEDONIA (CHALKIDIKE):
—TORONE: (1) ?353 BC *SEG* XXIV 574, 5; Hatzopoulos, *Actes Chalc.* p. 80 (date) (f. *Φιλώνιχος*) ?= (*2*); (2) *SEG* XXIV 574, 10; Hatzopoulos, *Actes Chalc.* p. 80 (date) (f. *Διονύσιος*) ?= (*1*)
MACEDONIA (MYGDONIA):
—LETE: (3) f. ii BC *SEG* XLVI 764, 6 ([*Ἀ*]*ν̣τ̣ιφῶν*: s. *Ἀμύντας*)
SKYTHIA:
—OLBIA-BORYSTHENES: (4) i-ii AD *IOSPE* I² 155, 7 (f. *Σάλλιος*); (5) f. i AD *IOlbia* 42, 1, 3; cf. Vinogradov–Kryžickij p. 144 (date) (s. *Ἀναξιμένης*) ?= (7); (6) s. i AD *IOlbia* 85, 4 (*IOSPE* I² 104) (f. *Σπωτάγανος*); (7) ii AD ib. 40, 7 (s. *Ἀναξιμένης*) ?= (*5*); (8) ib. 134, 6 (f. *Σωκράτης*); (9) ?ii-iii AD ib. 108 ([*Ἀν*]*τιφῶν*)
THRACE:
—AINOS: (10) i-ii AD *IG* XII (8) 218, 7 ([*Ἀ*]*ντιφῶν*)

Ἀντιχάρης
MACEDONIA (PELAGONIA):
—KERAMIAI (NR.): (1) ii-iii AD ib. X (2) (2) 210 (f. *Λυσᾶς*)
THRACE:
—DIONYSOPOLIS: (2) ii-iii AD *IGB* I² 31, 2 (f. *—ν*)

Ἀντύαλος
MACEDONIA (PAIONIA):
—STOBOI*: (1) i BC-i AD *AJA* 76 (1972) p. 417 (terracotta) (*Ἀντ̣ύαλο(ς)*)

Ἄντυλλα
THRACE:
—MADYTOS: (1) imp. *ISestos* 61 (Lat. Servilia Antylla: m. Q. Cornelius Crispus)

Ἄντων
MACEDONIA (CHALKIDIKE):
—CHALKIDEIS: (1) viii/vii BC Plu., *Mor.* 761 B (fict.?)
MACEDONIA (SINTIKE):
—PARTHIKOPOLIS: (2) ii-iii AD *IGB* V 5898 (I f. *Ἄντων* II); (3) ib. (II s. *Ἄντων* I)

Ἀντωνία
CIMMERIAN BOSPOROS:
—PANTIKAPAION: (1) i/ii AD *CIRB* 576
MACEDONIA (MYGDONIA):
—THESSALONIKE: (2) v-vi AD *IG* X (2) (1) 406 (Feissel, *RICM* 191) (*Ἀντωνῖνα*—Feissel)
—THESSALONIKE?: (3) ii AD *IG* X (2) (1) 706 (d. *Ἰούλιττα*)
MACEDONIA (PELAGONIA):
—DOSTONEIS: (4) iii AD ib. X (2) (2) 201, 8-9
MACEDONIA (SINTIKE):
—HERAKLEIA: (5) ii-iii AD *IGB* IV 2327

Ἀντωνιάς
THRACE:
—PERINTHOS-HERAKLEIA: (1) f. iii AD *IPerinth* 163 (*Οὐαλερία Ἀ.*)

Ἀντωνῖνα
MACEDONIA (MYGDONIA):
—THESSALONIKE: (1) imp. *SEG* XXXV 769
—THESSALONIKE?: (2) v-vi AD *IG* X (2) (1) 782 (Feissel, *RICM* 163) (*Ἀ(ν)τονῆνα*)
THRACE:
—PHILIPPOPOLIS-TRIMONTIUM: (3) iii AD *IGB* III 949

Ἀντωνῖνος
MACEDONIA (EORDAIA):
—KELLE?: (1) s. ii AD *EAM* 125, 6 (-*νεῖ*-: s. *Κρισπῖνα*)
MACEDONIA (MYGDONIA):
—THESSALONIKE?: (2) 535 AD *IG* X (2) (1) 804, 11 (Feissel, *RICM* 134)
SKYTHIA:
—TANAIS: (3) 228 AD *CIRB* 1282, 32 (I f. *Ἀντωνῖνος* II); (4) ib. l. 32 (*Ἀντωνεῖ[νος]*: II s. *Ἀντωνῖνος* I)
THRACE:
—OESCUS: (5) 368 AD *ILB* 9 with pl. 3; cf. *SEG* XLIV 644
—PERINTHOS-HERAKLEIA: (6) c. 100-115 AD ib. XXVI 1288, 12 (-*νεῖ*-: s. *Σύμμαχος*)
—PHILIPPOPOLIS-TRIMONTIUM: (7) ii AD *IGB* III 997, 4 (*Ἀντωνεῖ[νος]*)

Ἀντώνιος
MACEDONIA (MYGDONIA):
—THESSALONIKE: (1) i-ii AD *IG* X (2) (1) 243 II, 6 (s. *Κλεοπάτρα*); (2) iii AD ib. 622 (f. *Ἄντανδρος*)
SCYTHIA MINOR:
—TOMIS: (3) ii AD *ISM* II 125 I, 20 (f. *Πάπας*)
SKYTHIA:
—OLBIA-BORYSTHENES: (4) ii AD *IOSPE* I² 106, 4 (f. *Σωχούβαζος*); (5) ib. 131, 11 (*Ἀντώ(ν)ιο(ς)*: f. *Πιστοῦς*); (6) s. ii AD *IOlbia* 170, 9
TAURIS:
—CHERSONESOS: (7) ?114 AD *SEG* XLVIII 999, 39 (*Ἀντώνι[ος]*: s. *Ἡρακλείδας*)
THRACE:
—BEROE-AUGUSTA TRAIANA: (8) ii-iii AD *IGB* III 1604 (*Ἀντων(ί)ου* (gen.))
—PHILIPPOPOLIS-TRIMONTIUM (TERRIT.): (9) i-ii AD ib. 1098
—PIZOS: (10) 202 AD ib. 1690 e, 13 (I f. *Ἀντώνιος* II); (11) ib. l. 13 (II s. *Ἀντώνιος* I)

Ἀντώνις
THRACE:
—PERINTHOS-HERAKLEIA: (1) ii-iii AD *IPerinth* 222

Ἀνχαρηνός
MACEDONIA (LYNKESTIS):
—HERAKLEIA (NR.): (1) 160 AD *IG* X (2) (2) 9 (*Ἀ. Ἀδαῖος*)

Ἀνώ
THRACE:
—ODESSOS: (1) i BC-i AD *IGB* I² 206 bis (PM 1682) (-*νών*: d. *Ζωπυρίων*)

Ἄνων
SKYTHIA:
—OLBIA-BORYSTHENES: (1) ii AD *IOSPE* I² 685, 4 + *VDI* 1975 (1), p. 71 (f. *—χηος*)

Ἀξία
CIMMERIAN BOSPOROS:
—PANTIKAPAION: (1) 93-123 AD *CIRB* p. 936 no. 1, 5 (d. *Παυλ—*)

Ἀξιδάρης
MACEDONIA (CHALKIDIKE):
—POTIDAIA-KASSANDREIA (NR.): (1) ii AD *TAPA* 69 (1938) pp. 61-2 no. 15, 9

Ἀξιοθέα
THRACE: (1) 225 BC *PPetr*² 24, 26 (Velkov 26; La'da E856) (d. *Διζούλας*)
—ABDERA: (2) ii BC *IG* XII (1) 386

Ἄξιος
MACEDONIA: (1) b. 183 BC ib. XI (4) 1307, [2]; *ID* 1417 A II, 92; cf. 1403 Bb II, 67; cf.

ID Index s.v. (Tataki, *Macedonians* p. 254 no. 225) (*Θάσιος*—1403: s. *Ἀντίγονος*)

Ἀξίωμα
MACEDONIA (MYGDONIA):
—THESSALONIKE: **(1)** s. i AD *IG* X (2) (1) 68, 40; 69, 26 (m. *Κάσσανδρος*)

Ἀόσας
CIMMERIAN BOSPOROS:
—GORGIPPIA: **(1)** m. ii AD *Eirene* 7 (1968) p. 67, 17 (s. *Σαμβατίων*)

Ἀοταῖος
SCYTHIA MINOR:
—TOMIS: **(1)** ii AD *ISM* II 125, 15 (f. *Δῖος*) ?= *(2)*; **(2)** ib. 125 II, 19 (f. *Μαγνίων*) ?= *(1)*

Αὐτοκλῆς
CIMMERIAN BOSPOROS:
—PANTIKAPAION: **(1)** iv BC *CIRB* 174 (f. *Γῆρος*)

Ἄπακος
MACEDONIA (ELIMEIA):
—AIANE: **(1)** v BC *Α΄ Panell. Synedr. Epigr.* p. 68 no. 14 (bronze) (*SEG* XLIX 671) (-*ρος*)

Ἀπάμη
MACEDONIA: **(1)** iv/iii BC Jo. Mal. p. 198; cf. Beloch, *GG* IV (2) p. 198 (d. *Σέλευκος* I *Νικάτωρ*, *Ἀπάμη* (Sogdiane)); **(2)** c. 290-250 BC *RE* (3); Grainger, *SPG* p. 38 (d. *Ἀντίοχος* I *Σωτήρ*, *Στρατονίκη*, m. *Βερενίκη*); **(3)** m. iii BC ib. (d. *Ἀντίοχος* II *Θεός*)
MACEDONIA?: **(4)** f. ii BC *RE* (4); *IG* II^2 3172 (Tataki, *Macedonians* p. 254 no. 227); cf. Beloch, *GG* IV (2) p. 137; *RE* s.v. Prusias (1) cols. 1086-7 (?d. *Δημήτριος* II, *Στρατονίκη*, m. *Νικομήδης* II *Ἐπιφανής* (Bithynia): queen)

Ἀπαντία
MACEDONIA (BOTTIAIA):
—EDESSA: **(1)** v-vi AD Feissel, *RICM* 23

Ἀπατούρη
CIMMERIAN BOSPOROS:
—PANTIKAPAION: **(1)** iv BC *CIRB* 159; cf. KW pl. 5 no. 94 ([*Ἀ*]*πατούρη*, [*Ἀ*]*πατουρίς*—Latyshev)
SKYTHIA:
—OLBIA-BORYSTHENES (BEREZAN (MOD.)): **(2)** v BC Dubois, *IGDOlbia* 75 (vase) (*Ἀπατόρης* (gen.)—n. pr.?)

Ἀπατούριος
CIMMERIAN BOSPOROS:
—NYMPHAION: **(1)** iii BC *CIRB* 912 I, 4 ?= *(2)*; **(2)** ib. l. 8 (f. *Ἀπολλᾶς*) ?= *(1)*
—PANTIKAPAION: **(3)** s. v BC ib. 153 (*Ἀπ*[*ατ*]*όρ̣ι̣ο̣ς*: f. *.ορ..της*); **(4)** f. iv BC ib. 160 (s. *Ἀγλων*); **(5)** s. iv BC ib. 116 (*CEG* II 735) (s. *Ζήνων*); **(6)** 195 BC *Syll*^{3} 585, 22 (s. *Νίκων*); **(7)** ii AD *CIRB* 652 (f. *Ἀπολλωνίδης*, *Φαρνάκης*); **(8)** iii AD ib. 109, 3 (*Ἀπατούρι̣*[*ος*])
MACEDONIA (EDONIS):
—PHILIPPOI: **(9)** hell. Hatzopoulos, *MI* I p. 188 n. 1
SCYTHIA MINOR:
—ISTROS: **(10)** iii-ii BC *ISM* I 18, 23 (s. *Θ*—) ?= *(11)*; **(11)** ii BC ib. 71 (*Ἀπατούρι̣*[*ος*]: s. *Θεόπομπος*) ?= *(10)*; **(12)** f. ii BC ib. 20, 2 ([*Ἀπατο*]*ύριος*?: s. *Παρμενίσκος*); **(13)** i BC ib. 54, 1, 4, 53 (f. *Ἀρισταγόρας*); **(14)** i BC-i AD *IG* II^2 8941 (*FRA* 2627) (f. *Σίμη*); **(15)** *ISM* I 191 II, 50 (f. *Δημήτριος*); **(16)** 138 AD ib. 193 I, 20 (s. *Δημήτριος*)
—TOMIS:
——(Hopletes): **(17)** ii AD ib. II 123 (s. *Εὐέλπιστος*)
SKYTHIA:
—OLBIA-BORYSTHENES: **(18)** vi/v BC *SEG* XLVIII 1012 (-*τό*-); **(19)** v BC Dubois, *IGDOlbia* 101 (-*τό*-: s. *Ὑπάνιχος*); **(20)** v/iv BC *IOSPE* I^2 208 a; cf. KW pl. 1 no. 19 (-*τό*-: s. *Θεόδοτος*); **(21)** iv BC *MIA* 50 (1956) p. 63 (vase-stamp) (Vinogradov–Kryžickij pl. 91. 2); **(22)** s. iv BC *SEG* L 702 II, 1, 5 (*Ἀπατούρις*—l.1); **(23)** iii BC ib. XXX 943 (vase) ([*Ἀπ*]*ατούριος*); **(24)** s. iii BC *IOSPE* I^2 76, 7 (Sokolowski II 88; Dubois, *IGDOlbia* 88) (f. *Ἀδείμαντος*)
—OLBIA-BORYSTHENES*: **(25)** iv BC *ZOOID* 23 (1900) p. 19 no. 3 (vase) (-*τό*-)
—TANAIS: **(26)** ii AD *CIRB* 1262, 20 (f. *Δημήτριος*) ?= *(27)*; **(27)** ib. l. 28 (f. *Ἀρνάκης*) ?= *(26)*
TAURIS:
—KERKINITIS: **(28)** s. v BC *SEG* XXXVII 665, 1 (sherd) (-*τό*-)
THRACE:
—APOLLONIA-SOZOPOLIS: **(29)** v BC *IGB* I^2 432 (-*ό*-: s. *Λύδος*); **(30)** v/iv BC ib. 434 (-*τό*-: f. *Πίπων*)
—BYZANTION: **(31)** m. iv BC D. xxiii passim
—ODESSOS: **(32)** i BC-i AD *IGB* I^2 44, 7 (f. *Ξένανδρος*); **(33)** ib. 51 c, 8 (I f. *Ἀπατούριος* II); **(34)** ib. l. 8 (II s. *Ἀπατούριος* I); **(35)** ib. l. 11 ([*Ἀ*]*π̣α̣τούριος*); **(36)** 40 BC ib. 46, 7 (I f. *Ἀπατούριος* I); **(37)** ib. l. 7 (II s. *Ἀπατούριος* I); **(38)** I AD ib. l. 47 (f. *Διονύσιος*); **(39)** f. i AD ib. 224 ([*Ἀπ*]*ατούριος*); **(40)** ii AD ib. 161 (*CCET* I 59; PM 1408) (f. *Ἀγαθήνωρ*); **(41)** s. ii AD *IGB* I^2 163 bis (*CCET* I 55; PM 1537) (s. *Ποσειδώνιος*)

Ἄπαυλος?
MACEDONIA (PIERIS):
—OISYME-EMATHIA?: **(1)** iv BC *PAE* 1938, p. 95 no. 2 (*Ἄπαυλ*[*ος*]?)

Ἀπελλαῖος
MACEDONIA (EDONIS):
—AMPHIPOLIS: **(1)** imp. *BCH* 22 (1898) pp. 349-50 n. 2 (Dimitsas 858) (*Γ. Οὐελλ*[*έιος*] *Ἀπελλαῖος*: s. *Δημήτριος*); **(2)** iii AD *AEMTh* 15 (2001) p. 115 (f. *Ἀλφία Τ*—)

Ἀπελλᾶς
CIMMERIAN BOSPOROS:
—GORGIPPIA: **(1)** m. ii AD *Eirene* 7 (1968) p. 67, 8 (*Ἀπελ*[*λᾶς*]?: f. *Ψυχαρίων*) ?= *(2)*; **(2)** ib. l. 25 (f. *Θεόκριτος*) ?= *(1)*
MACEDONIA: **(3)** 69-84 AD *IBer* 61, 4 (*Ἀπελ*[*λᾶς*]?)
MACEDONIA (BOTTIAIA):
—BEROIA: **(4)** c. 230-200 BC *BCH* 45 (1921) p. 17 III, 58 (Tataki 210; Tataki, *Macedonians* p. 75 no. 12) (s. *Φιλώτας*)
MACEDONIA (EDONIS):
—AMPHIPOLIS: **(5)** a. 357 BC Hatzopoulos, *Actes Amphipolis* p. 34 no. 6, 10; **(6)** 4 or 120 AD *SEG* XL 522 g (s. *Διογένης*)
MACEDONIA (MYGDONIA):
—KALINDOIA: **(7)** 68-98 AD ib. XLII 580, 61 (s. *Νικάνωρ*); **(8)** a. 98 AD ib. 583, 8 (f. —*ν*)
—THESSALONIKE: **(9)** ?i AD *IG* X (2) (1) 128, 1 and Add.; **(10)** s. i AD ib. 69, 31 (s. *Ἀπολλώνιος*); **(11)** ii AD ib. 226, 11; cf. Robert, *OMS* 5 p. 298 n. 193 (*Γ. Ἰούλ. Ἀπε*[*λλᾶς*]?)
SCYTHIA MINOR:
—ISTROS: **(12)** i BC-i AD *ISM* I 191 II, 28 (s. *Λυσίμαχος*); **(13)** ib. 209, 2 = 185 (*Ἀπελ*[*λᾶς*]: f. —*ωρος*); **(14)** ii AD ib. 196, 3; **(15)** ib. 286 (I f. *Ἀπελλᾶς* II); **(16)** ib. (II s. *Ἀπελλᾶς* I)
—KALLATIS: **(17)** s. i AD ib. III 67, 3 (*Ἀπελ*[*λᾶς*]?: ?s. —*σκος*)
TAURIS:
—CHERSONESOS: **(18)** ii AD *IOSPE* I^2 455 (s. *Κιράθων*, f. *Κυράθων*); **(19)** ib. 513 (I f. *Ἀπελλᾶς* II *ὁ κὲ Προμαθίων*); **(20)** ib. (*Ἀ. ὁ κὲ Προμαθίων*: II s. *Ἀπελλᾶς* I, f. *Ἡμέρα*); **(21)** ib. 582, 3; **(22)** f. ii AD *KSIIMK* 15 (1947) p. 59, 10 (Solomonik, *NEPKh* 112 d); cf. *VDI* 1993 (4), p. 63 (*Ἀπελλᾶ*[*ς*])
THRACE:
—BYZANTION: **(23)** i BC-i AD *Türk Tarih Kongresi XI* (6) p. 2703 with pl. 493. 2 (s. *Ἄτταλος*); **(24)** ii AD *IByz* 357 (threptos)
—MESAMBRIA: **(25)** iii-ii BC *IGB* I^2 335 octies (*Ἀπελλ̣ᾶ̣ς*)
—ODESSOS: **(26)** i BC-i AD ib. V 5061 (s. *Κλεάνωρ*); **(27)** i-ii AD ib. I^2 51 c, 6 (s. *Γλαυκίας*); **(28)** ib. 193 (f. —*πα*); **(29)** ii AD ib. 132 b (f. *Ἑστιαῖος*); **(30)** ib. 185 (*Ἀπελλᾶδος* (gen.): f. *Θιαθιοῦς*); **(31)** ib. 186 ter (PM 1641) (f. *Παρθενία*); **(32)** ii-iii AD *IGB* I^2 191 (s. *Ζωΐλος*); **(33)** f. ii AD ib. 78 ter, 3 (*CCET* I 30) (s. *Μένανδρος*); **(34)** m. ii AD *IGB* I^2 150 (PM 859) (s. *Δημήτριος*, f. *Ἀσκληπιάδης*); **(35)** s. ii AD *IGB* I^2 181 (PM 1605); *Dacia* 21 (1977) p. 161 (date) (s. *Ξένων*); **(36)** 215 AD *IGB* I^2 47 a, 23 (*Αὐρ. Ἀπελᾶς*: s. *Μᾶρκος*); **(37)** ib. 47 b, 8 (*Αὐρ. Ἀπελᾶς*: s. *Σωτήρ*); **(38)** ib. l. 25-6 (-*πελᾶς*: f. *Αὐρ. Ἐπαμείνων*, *Αὐρ. Μᾶρκος*); **(39)** ib. 47 c, 9 (-*πελᾶς*: f. *Αὐρ. Ἀτανδρίων*); **(40)** ib. l. 10 (*Αὐρ. Ἀπελᾶς*: s. *Ἀλεξίμαχος*); **(41)** 221 AD ib. 47 bis b, 13 (f. *Αὐρ. Μάρκελλος*); **(42)** ib. 47 bis c, 11 (f. *Αὐρ. Μακεδών*); **(43)** ib. l. 14 (f. *Αὐρ. Βαλέριος*); **(44)** ib. l. 30 (I f. *Αὐρ. Ἀπελλᾶς* II); **(45)** ib. l. 30 (*Αὐρ. Ἀ.*: II s. *Ἀπελλᾶς* I); **(46)** ib. l. 38 (f. *Αὐρ. Διονύσιος*); **(47)** ib. l. 39 (f. *Αὐρ. Θουθους*)
—ODESSOS (NR.): **(48)** i BC-i AD ib. 294 ([*Ἀπ*]*ε̣λλᾶς*: s. *Παρμενίων*); **(49)** s. ii AD ib. 287 (*CCET* I 87) (s. *Ξένανδρος*)
—TRAIANOPOLIS (TERRIT.): **(50)** iii AD *SEG* XXXIII 565 (*IThrakAig* E457) (s. *Δορζίνθης*)

Ἀπελλέας
MACEDONIA (EDONIS):
—AMPHIPOLIS: **(1)** iv/iii BC *SEG* XXXI 618 (s. *Ἀπολλωνίδας*)

Ἀπελλῆς
MACEDONIA: **(1)** 221-218 BC *RE* (6) (Tataki, *Macedonians* p. 255 no. 228); **(2)** 185-179 BC *RE* (7) (Tataki, *Macedonians* p. 255 no. 229)
MACEDONIA (MYGDONIA):
—THESSALONIKE: **(3)** ?ii AD *IG* X (2) (1) 127, 7 (f. *Διογένης*)
THRACE:
—APOLLONIA-SOZOPOLIS: **(4)** i-ii AD *IGB* I^2 401, 21 (*Ἀ(π)ελλῆς*: s. *Κορνοῦτος*)
—BYZANTION: **(5)** 340 BC *IG* II^2 235, 8, [15] (s. *Ζώπυρος*); **(6)** iii BC *RE* Supplbd. 5 (5a) (f. *Ἀριστοφάνης*)
—MARONEIA: **(7)** c. 365-336 BC Schönert-Geiss, *Maroneia* 427-9 (coin) (*Ἀπέλλεω* (gen.))
—MONTANA*: **(8)** 155 AD *CIL* III 7449, 24 (*Montana* II 1) (Lat. Ael. Apelles)
—STRYME?: **(9)** c. 400-375 BC *BCH* 83 (1959) p. 719 (*IThrakAig* E136) (*Ἀπέλλ̣ε̣ω̣* (gen.): f. *Ἐχέδημος*)

Ἀπελλικῶν
CIMMERIAN BOSPOROS:
—GORGIPPIA: **(1)** f. iii BC *CIRB* 1137 A I, 11 (s. *Βάβας*); **(2)** ib. 1137 B I, 16 (f. *Βάκχιος*)

Ἄπελλις
MACEDONIA (EDONIS):
—PHILIPPOI: **(1)** iii BC *Ét. Thas.* 3 p. 319 no. 113 bis (Tataki, *Macedonians* p. 163 no. 6) (s. *Μενεκλῆς*)

Ἄπερ
MACEDONIA (DERRIOPOS):
—STUBERRA: **(1)** c. 41-48 AD *IG* X (2) (2) 323, 8 (f. *Ἐπιγένης*); **(2)** ib. l. 23 (?s. *Λέων*)

Ἀπήμαντος
CIMMERIAN BOSPOROS:
—GORGIPPIA: **(1)** f. iii BC *CIRB* 1137 A II, 11; 1137 B I, 34 (s. *Γοργίας*); **(2)** ib. 1137 B II, 24 (s. *Παγουρίων*)

Macedonia (Edonis):
—Philippoi: **(3)** s. iii bc *IG* vii 2433 II, 11 (Tataki, *Macedonians* p. 163 no. 5) ([Ἀ]πείμα[ντος]?: f. Νικόμαχος)
Macedonia (Pieris):
—Neapolis: **(4)** c. 412-408 bc *IG* xii (8) 263, 13 + xii Suppl. p. 151; cf. *Ét. Thas.* 3 p. 145 n. 3 (Tataki, *Macedonians* p. 125 no. 3)
Tauris:
—Chersonesos: **(5)** s. iv bc *IOSPE* I^2 710 (Solomonik, *NEPKh* 172) (f. Θεόφαντος); **(6)** iv/iii bc ib. 135 (s. Ἁγνίας)

Ἀπήμων
Thrace:
—Dionysopolis: **(1)** ii bc *IGB* I^2 22 II, 4 (s. Νικίας); **(2)** c. 170 ad *JÖAI* 15 (1912) p. 50 no. 15, 10 (f. Θεόδωρος)

Ἀπῆς
Thrace:
—Odessos: **(1)** 215 ad *IGB* I^2 47 c, 24 (Ἀπῆ (gen.): f. Αὐρ. Ἡφαιστίων)

Ἀπίντας
Cimmerian Bosporos:
—Nymphaion: **(1)** iii bc *CIRB* 912 II, 16; Zgusta, *PNS* 907 (s. Γύλλος)

Ἀποβαλλίς
Cimmerian Bosporos:
—Nymphaion: **(1)** iv bc *CIRB* 919; Zgusta, *PNS* 908 (d. Ὀνήσιμος)

Ἀποδήμιος
Macedonia (Mygdonia):
—Thessalonike?: **(1)** ii-iii ad *IG* x (2) (1) 903
Thrace:
—Philippopolis-Trimontium (territ.)?: **(2)** iv ad *BIAB* 12 (1938) p. 298 no. 23 (ring) (Μηδοπαιου (gen.), Ἀποδημίου? (retrors.?))

Ἀπολαύστη
Scythia Minor:
—Tomis: **(1)** ii ad *ISM* ii 97, 14 (Ἰουλ. Ἀ.)

Ἀπόλλα
Scythia Minor:
—Istros: **(1)** iv/iii bc ib. i 245 (d. Ἐλπίας)

Ἀπολλάθεος
Tauris:
—Chersonesos: **(1)** c. 325-315 bc Kats p. 87 no. 12 (amph.)

Ἀπολλᾶς
Cimmerian Bosporos:
—Gorgippia: **(1)** f. iii bc *CIRB* 1137 B I, 6 ([Ἀπ]ολλᾶς: s. Σάτυρος)
—Hermonassa: **(2)** iv bc ib. 1056 II, 2 (s. Τ—)
—Nymphaion: **(3)** iii bc ib. 912 I, 8 ([Ἀπ]ολλᾶς: s. Ἀπατούριος)
Macedonia (Bisaltia):
—Terpni (mod.): **(4)** i-ii ad *SEG* i 283 (f. Ἰσίδωρος)
Macedonia (Edonis):
—Amphipolis: **(5)** iii bc ib. xxiii 616; *PP* 15317a (Tataki, *Macedonians* p. 47 no. 13) (s. Φιλώτας)
Macedonia (Paionia):
—Bylazora: **(6)** ii-iii ad *JÖAI* 6 (1903) Beibl. col. 2 no. 1
Skythia:
—Olbia-Borysthenes: **(7)** s. iv bc Dubois, *IGDOlbia* 107, 4
—Tyras: **(8)** c. 300-275 bc *SEG* xlix 1051 B, 1 (s. Ἡρόδοτος)
Tauris:
—Chersonesos: **(9)** iv/iii bc Kats pp. 114-15 no. 123 (amph., tile) (f. Φορμίων); **(10)** iii bc Solomonik, *NEPKh* 30; **(11)** ib. 153 (f. Ἡρόδοτος); **(12)** ib. 154 (f. Ἡρόφιλος); **(13)** Kats p. 107 no. 89 (amph.) (f. Ξενοκλῆς); **(14)** f. iii bc ib. p. 93 no. 41 (amph.) (f. Διοσκουρίδας); **(15)** c. 285-272 bc ib. p. 86 no. 11 (amph.) (s. Χορειός); **(16)** c. 250-230 bc Anokhin pp. 140-1 nos. 98; 111 (coins); **(17)** ii bc *IOSPE* I^2 487 (f. Πασίων); **(18)** ii-i bc ib. 411 (f. Δήλιος)
Thrace:
—Abdera: **(19)** c. 395-360 bc May, *Abdera* p. 227 nos. 349-50 (coin); cf. Masson, *OGS* p. 429 (Ἀπολλᾶδος (gen.))
—Apollonia-Sozopolis: **(20)** v/iv bc *IGB* I^2 409 ter (Ἀπολλᾶν (acc.)); **(21)** f. iv bc ib. 433 bis (s. Ἡφαίστιος); **(22)** iii bc ib. v 5153, 2
—Byzantion: **(23)** s. iii bc *IByz* 305 (s. Μήνιος); **(24)** ii-i bc ib. 79 (Fıratlı–Robert p. 48 no. 8) (I f. Ἀπολλᾶς II); **(25)** *IByz* 79 (Fıratlı–Robert p. 48 no. 8) (II s. Ἀπολλᾶς I); **(26)** s. ii bc *BMI* 1154a B, 31; *BE* 1972, no. 37 (date) (f. Βάτακος)
—Byzantion (nr.): **(27)** i bc *IByz* 252 (Fıratlı–Robert pp. 63-4 no. 55)
—Byzantion?: **(28)** ii bc *IByz* 338 (Fıratlı–Robert p. 127 no. 214); cf. *IKalch* 44 (s. Διονύσιος)
—Mesambria: **(29)** ii/i bc *IGB* v 5104; **(30)** c. 100-71 bc Karayotov, *Mesambria* i p. 110 nos. 775-8; Price, *Alexander* 1120 (coin) (Ἀπολλᾶ (gen.))
—Odessos: **(31)** 37 bc *IGB* I^2 46, 10 (s. Ἑκαταῖος); **(32)** 34 bc ib. l. 13 (s. Διονύσιος); **(33)** 33 bc ib. l. 14 (s. Ἀπολλώνιος); **(34)** 30 bc ib. l. 17 (f. Αἰαντίδης); **(35)** 27 bc ib. l. 20 (f. Ποσείδηος)
—Sestos: **(36)** a. 129 bc *ISestos* 1, 2 (f. Μένανδρος)

Ἀπολλινάριος
Macedonia (Mygdonia):
—Thessalonike: **(1)** 137-161 ad *Makedonika* 9 (1969) pp. 143-4 (-λλει-: f. Ἀλέξανδρος)
Thrace:
—Beroe-Augusta Traiana (territ.): **(2)** ii-iii ad *IGB* iii 1713 ter ([Ἀπ]ολλινάριος: s. Δο—); **(3)** ib. v 5596 (Φλ. [Ἀπ]ολινάριο[ς])
—Diospolis: **(4)** imp. ib. iii 1788 (-πολι-); **(5)** ii-iii ad ib. 1789 (Ἀ[π]ολινάριος)
—Kabyle: **(6)** ii-iii ad ib. 1774, 2 ([Μ.] Οὔλπ. Ἀπολινάριος)
—Maroneia: **(7)** iv-v ad Meïmaris–Bakirtzis 5 (*IThrakAig* E346) ([Ἀ]πολινάριος)
—Montana: **(8)** ii ad *Montana* ii 13 (Lat. Claudius Apollinarius: s. Tib. Cl. Vitulus)
—Pautalia: **(9)** ii ad *IGB* iv 2074, 18 (s. Αὐλούτραλις); **(10)** ii-iii ad ib. 2065 (Φλ. Ἀ.)
—Pautalia (territ.): **(11)** ii ad ib. 2214, 8 (Φλ. Ἀπολινάριος)
—Perinthos-Herakleia?: **(12)** iii ad *IPerinth* 309 (Αὐρ. Ἀπελινάριος: s. Αὐρ. Ζωΐλος, Αὐρ. Πίση)
—Philippopolis-Trimontium: **(13)** imp. *IGB* iii 1026, 4; **(14)** c. 195 ad ib. 882, 9 ([Β]αίβιος Ἀπολινάριος)
—Philippopolis-Trimontium (territ.): **(15)** ii-iii ad ib. 1215 (-πολι-: f. —νος)
—Philippopolis-Trimontium:
——Parembole: **(16)** ii-iii ad ib. 1512, 3 (Ἰούλ. Ἀπολινάριος)
Thrace?: **(17)** ii ad *SEG* xxxiv 775 (bronze); cf. *IGB* v 5645 (-πολι-: s. Πρίσκος)

Ἀπολλινάρις
Scythia Minor:
—Istros: **(1)** iii ad *ISM* i 283 (*Eastern cults* p. 231 no. 21) (Ἀ. Δολιχηνάρις)
—Kallatis*: **(2)** 241-244 ad *ISM* iii 74, 4 (Ἐρέννιος Ἀπολινάρ(ις))
Thrace:
—Beroe-Augusta Traiana (territ.): **(3)** ii-iii ad *IGB* iii 1656 (-πολι-: s. Διο—)
—Draganovec (mod.): **(4)** iii ad ib. v 5307 (*CCET* ii (2) 490) ([Ἀ]πολινάρις)
—Hadrianopolis (territ.)?: **(5)** ii-iii ad *IGB* v 5612 (Ἰούλ. Ἀπολλινά[ρις])
—Iatrus: **(6)** f. iii ad *Arkheologiia* (Sofia) 1984 (1), p. 42 no. 4 (Lat. Ulp. Apolin[aris])
—Nicopolis ad Istrum: **(7)** ii-iii ad *IGB* ii 663 (Αἴλ. Ἀπολινάρις)
—Nicopolis ad Istrum (territ.): **(8)** iii ad ib. v 5251 (-πολι-); **(9)** 227 ad *ILB* 438 I, 41 (Lat. Aur. Apolinar(is) qui et Pistus)
—Pautalia: **(10)** ii-iii ad *IGB* iv 2072, 12 (Ἀπολλινά[ρις]: s. —κυρος)
—Philippopolis-Trimontium (territ.): **(11)** ii-iii ad ib. iii 1192 (-πολι-: s. Χρήστος); **(12)** ib. 1279 (-πολι-: I f. Ἀπολλινάρις II); **(13)** ib. (-πολι-: II s. Ἀπολλινάρις I)
—Serdica (territ.): **(14)** ii-iii ad *AEMÖ* 10 (1886) pp. 238-9 no. 2, 11 (-πολι-)
—Serdica (territ.)?: **(15)** ii-iii ad *BIAB* 11 (1937) p. 307 (terracotta) (-πολι-)

Ἀπολλόδοτος
Macedonia: **(1)** 214 bc *BGU* 2397, [4], 10-11, 19, etc. (Tataki, *Macedonians* p. 255 no. 231; La'da E1415) (s. Κότυς)
Macedonia (Odomantike):
—Sirrha?: **(2)** 136 ad *SEG* xxx 598, 1, 3, 7 (f. Ἀνίκητος)
Scythia Minor:
—Istros: **(3)** iii bc *ISM* i 184 (Ἀπολλόδοτ[ος])
—Kallatis: **(4)** s. iii bc ib. iii 35 A, 35 (f. Ἀσκλαπιόδωρος); **(5)** ib. 35 B, 30
Thrace:
—Maroneia: **(6)** ii-i bc *IThrakAig* E212, 10 (I f. Ἀπολλόδοτος II); **(7)** ib. l. 10 (II s. Ἀπολλόδοτος I); **(8)** ib. l. 26 (I f. Ἀπολλόδοτος II); **(9)** ib. l. 26 (II s. Ἀπολλόδοτος I); **(10)** ib. l. 42 (s. Σ—)
—Philippopolis-Trimontium: **(11)** c. 235-238 ad *IGB* iii 1515, 12; cf. v 5548 (Ἀπαλοδωτος—lap.: f. Αὐρ. Ἀπολλωνίδης)

Ἀπολλοδώρα
Cimmerian Bosporos:
—Pantikapaion: **(1)** s. i ad *CIRB* 342; cf. KW pl. 19 no. 274
Tauris:
—Chersonesos: **(2)** ii-iii ad *IOSPE* I^2 452 (d. Ἀπολλόδωρος)
Thrace:
—Beroe-Augusta Traiana: **(3)** c. 320-324 ad *Anal. Boll.* 31 (1912) p. 198; p. 208 (Ἀπλόδωρα—ms., Ἀπ(ο)λ(λ)όδωρα?)
—Bisanthe-Panion: **(4)** iii bc *CEG* ii 729 (Ἀπολλοδώρης (gen.))

Ἀπολλοδωριανή
Macedonia (Mygdonia):
—Thessalonike: **(1)** f. iii ad *IG* x (2) (1) 188, 10; 189, 6 (Αὐρ. Ἀπολλοδωριανὴ Ἀμμία)

Ἀπολλόδωρος
Cimmerian Bosporos:
—Achilleion: **(1)** f. ii ad *CIRB* 1028 (Ἀπολ(λό)δωρ(ο)ς: f. Ἀλέξανδρος); **(2)** ib. 1029 (Ἀπολλόδω[ρος]: s. Ἀσκληπιός)
—Gorgippia: **(3)** f. iii bc ib. 1137 B I, 7 (f. —ιππος); **(4)** ib. 1137 B II, 32 (s. Ἐπικράτης)
—Pantikapaion: **(5)** f. v bc *MIA* 103 (1962) p. 170 (vase) (-δδ-); **(6)** f. iv bc *CIRB* 207; cf. KW pl. 1 no. 4 (f. Μητρόδωρος); **(7)** imp. *CIRB* 800 (Ἀπ(ο)λ(λό)δωρος: f. Μυρῖνος); **(8)** f. ii ad ib. 653; cf. KW pl. 49 no. 686 (Ἀπ(ο)λ(λό)δωρος: s. Ἀπολλώνιος)
—Phanagoreia: **(9)** 344-311 bc *CIRB* 971 (Ἀπ[ολλ]όδω[ρ]ος: s. Φαναγόρης)
Macedonia: **(10)** ?308-304 bc *Eretria* xi p. 109 no. 5, 2, 7, 17 (*IG* xii (9) 205) + *IG* xii (9) 226; 206, 2, 8; cf. *Eretria* xi pp. 210-11 no. XI (Tataki, *Macedonians* p. 256 no. 233); *Eretria* xi pp. 111-17 (ident., date) (s. Ἀναξίδοτος, f. Ἀναξίδοτος); **(11)** 242 bc *PSI* 394, 7

(Tataki, *Macedonians* p. 256 no. 234; La'da E1416) (s. *'Ανδράγαθος*); **(12)** 197 BC *RE* (45) (Tataki, *Macedonians* p. 256 no. 232); **(13)** m. ii BC Helly, *Gonnoi* 49, 7 (Tataki, *Macedonians* p. 215 no. 1); **(14)** ?150 BC *PBad* II 11, 5 (Tataki, *Macedonians* p. 256 no. 236); cf. La'da E1517 (f. *Καλλίας*); **(15)** *PBad* II 11, 8 (Tataki, *Macedonians* p. 256 no. 235); cf. La'da E1517 (s. *Καλλίας*)

MACEDONIA?:

—RESEN (MOD.): **(16)** s. iii AD *IG* X (2) (2) 50 (or Illyria Dassaretioi?: f. *'Αλέξανδρος*)

MACEDONIA (BISALTIA):

—EUPORIA: **(17)** s. i AD *IBer* 121, 9; 299, [1], 2 (Tataki, *Macedonians* p. 107 no. 3) (I f. *'Αλέξανδρος, Βάστος, Τάρυς, 'Απολλόδωρος* II); **(18)** *IBer* 299, 3 (Tataki, *Macedonians* p. 107 no. 2) (II s. *'Απολλόδωρος* I)

—TERPNI (MOD.): **(19)** iii BC *SEG* XXV 719 (XLVIII 846) (f. *Διοσκουρίδης, 'Ιππῶναξ*)

MACEDONIA (BOTTIAIA):

—BEROIA: **(20)** i BC-i AD *IBer* 142, 11 (Tataki 214) (s. *Μάντα*); **(21)** ii-iii AD *IBer* 28 (Tataki 212) (*[Άπο]λλόδωρος*); **(22)** f. iii AD *IBer* 494 (Tataki 211); **(23)** 216-232 AD *ILeukopetra* 67, 2; 78, 7 + *Tyche* 16 (2001) pp. 151-2 (Tataki 745) (*Κλεωνυμιανὸς 'Α.*)

—BEROIA?: **(24)** i BC/i AD *GP* 408

—EDESSA: **(25)** 51 AD *SEG* XLVI 744, 12 (Tataki, *Edessa* 33) (f. *Μελέτη*); **(26)** iii AD Feissel, *RICM* 11 (Tataki, *Edessa* 32) (f. *Βραγάντις*)

MACEDONIA (CHALKIDIKE):

—MENDE: **(27)** ?iv/iii BC *FD* III (1) 438; *BCH* 105 (1981) pp. 433-408 (*FRA* 3678) (*[Διον]ύσιος*: s. *'Ασκληπιάδης*)

—OLYNTHOS: **(28)** ?355 BC *TAPA* 69 (1938) p. 51 no. 5, 9; Hatzopoulos, *Actes Chalc.* p. 80 (date) (f. *Εὐβουλίδης*); **(29)** ?352 BC *TAPA* 69 (1938) p. 48 no. 3, 11; Hatzopoulos, *Actes Chalc.* p. 80 (date); **(30)** ?350 BC *TAPA* 65 (1934) p. 125 no. 3, 2; Hatzopoulos, *Actes Chalc.* p. 80 (date) (-λλώ-: s. *Χάλκων*)

—POTIDAIA-KASSANDREIA: **(31)** iv/iii BC *RE* (43) (Tataki, *Macedonians* p. 85 no. 4) (tyrant)

—STOLOS?: **(32)** ?350 BC *SEG* XXXVIII 671, 4 (s. *Πόρις*)

MACEDONIA (DERRIOPOS):

—STUBERRA: **(33)** i AD *IG* X (2) (2) 330 (f. *'Αρχέπολις*); **(34)** c. 41-48 AD ib. 323, 10 (s. *Διοκλῆς*); **(35)** ib. l. 11 (f. *Ροῦφος*); **(36)** 50 AD ib. 324, 18 (s. *Τιμέας*); **(37)** ib. l. 24 (f. —ων); **(38)** 74 AD ib. 325, 2; 326, 2 (f. *Νικόλαος*); **(39)** ib. 325, 19 (s. *Κλέαρχος*); **(40)** ib. l. 21 (s. *'Αντίγονος*); **(41)** ib. l. 27 (s. *Αἰσχίνης*); **(42)** ib. l. 57 (f. *'Αγρίππας, 'Επίκαδος*); **(43)** ib. 326, 35 (f. *'Αντίγονος*); **(44)** ib. l. 26-7 (s. *Φίλιππος*); **(45)** 87 AD ib. 325, 73 (f. *'Αμύντας*)

MACEDONIA (EDONIS):

—AMPHIPOLIS: **(46)** 331-323 BC *RE* (42); Berve 101 (Tataki, *Macedonians* p. 47 no. 14); **(47)** hell.? *AD* 22 (1967) Chron. p. 427 (f. *Γοργίας*); **(48)** hell. ib. 24 (1969) Chron. p. 355 no. 5 (*[Άπο]λλόδω[ρος]*); **(49)** *SEG* XXIV 588 (*'Απολλόδω[ρος]*: f. *'Απολλοφάνης*); **(50)** iii BC *RA* 1935 (2), p. 67 no. 2 (Kaphtantzis 605) (f. *Φιλωτέρα*); **(51)** c. 265-255 BC *SGDI* 2588, 2 (Tataki, *Macedonians* p. 47 no. 15) (s. *'Ελλάνικος*); **(52)** i BC-i AD *SEG* XXVII 247; cf. *PAE* 1977, p. 52 fig. 3 (f. *Λυσίστρατος*); **(53)** 67 BC *SEG* XXXVI 583, 2; **(54)** 37 BC Robert, *Coll. Froehner* 44, 10 (Tataki, *Macedonians* p. 47 no. 16) (f. *Γλαυκίας*)

—PHILIPPOI (TERRIT.): **(55)** 162 AD Pikoulas, *Chora* p. 120 no. 11 (f. *'Άδυμος*)

MACEDONIA (ELIMEIA):

—OBLOSTAI: **(56)** 200 AD *EAM* 37, 5 (*'Απ[ολ]λόδωρος*: s. *Λούκιος*); **(57)** ib. l. 7 (s. *Μᾶρκος*)

—VELVENDOS (MOD.): **(58)** i-ii AD ib. 78, 5 (*[Ά]πολλ[όδ]ωρ[ος]*: f. *Τιβ. Κλ. 'Αμύντας*); **(59)** s. ii AD ib. 57 (f. *Λεύκιππος*)

MACEDONIA (EORDAIA):

—KELLE?: **(60)** s. ii BC ib. 118; Hatzopoulos, *MI* 1 p. 94 n. 4 (locn.) (f. *Νικαία*)

MACEDONIA (KRESTONIA):

—MORRYLOS: **(61)** ii-iii AD *SEG* XXXIX 613, 1 (s. *'Ήλιος, 'Άρτεμις*)

MACEDONIA (LYNKESTIS):

—MELITI (MOD.): **(62)** f. iii AD *EAM* 166, 2 (s. *Πρωτᾶς, Μέστα*)

MACEDONIA (MYGDONIA):

—THESSALONIKE: **(63)** i BC-i AD *IG* X (2) (1) 86, 6 (*[Ά]πολλόδωρος*); **(64)** 95 BC ib. 4, 2 (*'Απολλόδωρος*: f. *'Αθηναγόρας*); **(65)** ii AD ib. 241 A I, 2 (*[Άπο]λλόδωρος*); **(66)** 141 AD ib. 137, 11; cf. *BCH* 97 (1973) p. 587

MACEDONIA (ODOMANTIKE):

—GAZOROS: **(67)** 215 or 174 BC *SEG* XXX 1892, 27 (Hatzopoulos, *MI* 2 pp. 57-8 no. 39) (*'Απολ(λ)όδ(ω)ρος*: f. *Διονύσιος*)

—GAZOROS (NR.): **(68)** i AD *SEG* XXXVIII 2038 (Pilhofer 539b) (*'Απολ(λ)όδωρος*: s. *Βίθυς*)

—SIRRHA: **(69)** hell. *SEG* XXX 616 (s. *Λυσίας*)

MACEDONIA (PAIONIA):

—ARGOS: **(70)** ii AD *ZA* 15 (1965) p. 117; cf. Papazoglou, *Villes* p. 311 (locn.) (*Μαίκιος 'Α.*)

—NEGOTINO (MOD.): **(71)** iii AD *Sp.* 98 (1941-8) p. 60 no. 123 (*'Απωλώδωρ(ο)ς*: f. *Διονύσιος*)

MACEDONIA (PELAGONIA):

—KOLOBAISA*: **(72)** ?f. ii AD *IG* X (2) (2) 231 (*Τ. Φλαούϊος 'Α.*: s. *'Αντίγονος*)

MACEDONIA (PIERIA):

—PHILA?: **(73)** ?iii BC *RPh* 1911, pp. 133-4 no. 36, 125; cf. Helly, *L'État thessalien* pp. 319-20 (locn.) (*'Απο[λλόδω]ρος*: I f. *'Απολλόδωρος* II); **(74)** *RPh* 1911, pp. 133-4 no. 36, 125; cf. Helly, *L'État thessalien* pp. 319-20 (locn.) (II s. *'Απολλόδωρος* I)

MACEDONIA (PIERIS):

—GALEPSOS: **(75)** hell.? Dimitsas 913; Hatzopoulos, *MI* 1 p. 187 n. 3 (locn.) (*'Απολλ(ό)δωρος*: s. *Θήρων*)

PENESTAI:

—USCANA?: **(76)** ii-iii AD *SEG* XXXIX 618 (-πολώ-: f. *'Άσανδρος, 'Άμιλλος*)

SCYTHIA MINOR:

—ISTROS: **(77)** iv BC *ISM* I 243 (*[Άπο]λλόδωρος*); **(78)** ii BC *Histria* 9 pp. 143-4 no. 204 (f. *Καλλικράτης*); **(79)** i BC *ISM* I 54, 3 (f. *'Αθηνάδης*); **(80)** i BC-i AD ib. 191 I, 36 (*[Άπολ]λόδωρος*: s. *Διονύσιος*); **(81)** ib. 191 II, 9 (s. *Κλειτοφῶν*); **(82)** ib. l. 16 (f. *'Αρτεμίδωρος*); **(83)** 138 AD ib. 193 I, 55 (f. *'Ηγησαγόρας*); **(84)** ib. l. 106 (s. *'Ηρόφαντος*); **(85)** c. 138-160 AD ib. 137, 12-13; 193 II, 34 (f. *Κάρπος, Καλλίστρατος*) ?= (*86*); **(86)** c. 140-160 AD ib. 207, 11 (*[Άπο]λλόδωρος*: f. *Κάρπος*) ?= (*85*)

—KALLATIS: **(87)** hell. *Studii Cercetări Numismatică* 1 (1957) pp. 260-3 nos. 2-3 (weight) (*NZ* 10 (1917) p. 75 no. 3) (*'Απολλόδω(ρος)*); **(88)** *ISM* III 164 (*[Άπο]λλόδω[ρος]*); **(89)** c. 265-260 BC *FD* III (3) 207, 4 (f. *'Ιέρων*); **(90)** iii/ii BC *ISM* III 161 (s. *Διονύσιος*)

—KALLATIS?: **(91)** hell.? *Dacia* 13 (1969) p. 258 no. 1082 (amph.)

—TOMIS: **(92)** i BC *ISM* II 2 A, 58 (f. *Μῆνις*); **(93)** ib. l. 64 (s. *'Ηραίων*)

SKYTHIA:

—OLBIA-BORYSTHENES: **(94)** v BC *SEG* XXX 958 (vase); **(95)** iii BC *IOSPE* I^2 201 I, 60 (s. *Διόδωρος*); **(96)** ?ii-i BC Dubois, *IGDOlbia* 110, 2

TAURIS:

—CHERSONESOS: **(97)** v/iv BC Solomonik, *GAKh* 295 (vase); **(98)** f. iv BC ib. 296 (vase) (*'Απο(λ)λόδω[ρος]*); **(99)** iii BC Kats p. 111 no. 103 (amph.) (f. *Σιμαῖος*); **(100)** f. iii BC *SEG* XL 615 A, 1 (*[Ά]πολλό[δωρος]?*); **(101)** c. 285-272 BC Kats p. 118 no. 5 (amph.) (*'Απολλόδ[ωρος]*); **(102)** f. ii BC *IOSPE* I^2 351, 4; 402, 8 (s. *'Ηρόγειτος*); **(103)** c. 180-170 BC Anokhin p. 145 no. 159 (coin); **(104)** ii-iii AD *IOSPE* I^2 452 (f. *'Απολλοδώρα*)

THRACE: **(105)** ?v/iv BC *Syllogos* 27 (1900) p. 389 no. 1 (*'Απολλοδώρō* (gen.): f. *'Αρισταγόρη*); **(106)** 221 BC *PTeb* 815 fr. 5, 37 (Velkov 27; La'da E707) (s. *Νεοπτόλεμος*); **(107)** 156 BC *SGDI* 1895, 4-5, 9 (s. *Δωρίς*: endogen. slave/freed.)

—ABDERA: **(108)** iv/iii BC *IThrakAig* E46 (f. *Γλύκιννα*); **(109)** s. iii BC *ISamothrace* 22, 47 (s. *Πυθόδ—*)

—APOLLONIA-SOZOPOLIS: **(110)** iv BC *IGB* I^2 456 (*'Απολλόδ[ωρος]?*: f. *Πλεισ—*)

—APOLLONIA-SOZOPOLIS?: **(111)** f. iv BC ib. 479 bis (f. *'Εκαταίη*)

—BEROE-AUGUSTA TRAIANA: **(112)** ii-iii AD *SEG* XXXIX 649, 9 (f. *Τρόφιμος ὁ καὶ 'Ασβόλις*); **(113)** iii AD *IGB* III 1571, 6 (*Μ. Αὐρ. 'Α.*: s. *Δημοσθένης*); **(114)** 210-213 AD ib. 1555, 9 (*Τ. Φλ. [Ά]πολλόδωρος*)

—BEROE-AUGUSTA TRAIANA (TERRIT.): **(115)** ii-iii AD ib. 1667 (*'Απολ(λ)όδωρος*); **(116)** ib. 1683, 3; **(117)** ib. 1772 (s. *Οὔρσουλος*)

—BOSAGYRA: **(118)** iii AD ib. 1829 (s. *Ρησκούπορις*)

—BYZANTION: **(119)** s. iv BC *IByz* 124 (Fıratlı–Robert p. 100 no. 151) (s. *Νικάνωρ*); **(120)** *IG* II^2 8438 (*FRA* 1387) (s. *Θράσων*); **(121)** ii-i BC *Türk Tarih Kongresi XI* (6) p. 2703 with pl. 498. 12 (s. *Διονύσιος*); **(122)** *IByz* 94 (Fıratlı–Robert p. 92 no. 122) (f. *Ζώπυρος*); **(123)** *IByz* 256 (Fıratlı–Robert p. 71 no. 74) (*'Απολ[λόδωρ]ος?*: s. *Μήνιος*); **(124)** i BC *IByz* 231 (Fıratlı–Robert p. 84 no. 103) (f. *Διονύσιος*); **(125)** i BC-i AD *IByz* 227 (Fıratlı–Robert pp. 81-2 no. 97) (s. *Διονύσιος*, f. *Λυσιδίκη*)

—BYZANTION (TERRIT.): **(126)** i BC *IByz* 203 (Fıratlı–Robert pp. 62-3 no. 52) (s. *'Απολλώνιος*)

—BYZANTION:

—(Krateinea): **(127)** i-ii AD *IByz* 319 b (Fıratlı–Robert p. 123 no. 206) (f. *Πείσων*)

—DADOPARA: **(128)** f. iii AD *SEG* XLII 651, 3 (*Αὐρ. 'Απολλώδωρος*: s. *Αὐλούπορις*)

—DODOPARON: **(129)** ii-iii AD *IGB* III 1795 (*'Απ[ολλό]δωρος*: s. *Πρόκλος*)

—HADRIANOPOLIS (TERRIT.): **(130)** ii-iii AD ib. 1828 (f. *Βενδίς*); **(131)** ib. (s. *Βενδίς*); **(132)** iii AD ib. 1813 (*[Α]ὐρ. 'Α.*: ?s. *Πίνκισος*)

—KARDIA: **(133)** 129-121 BC *PRyl* 261 (La'da E980)

—MARKIANOPOLIS (NR.): **(134)** f. iii AD *IGB* II 830 (*CCET* II (1) 229) (*'Α. ὁ καὶ Δισάτραλις*: s. *Αὐλούζενις*)

—MARONEIA: **(135)** iii BC *SEG* XXIV 1181 a (vase) (La'da E1821) (s. *Λυσίας*); **(136)** ii-i BC *IThrakAig* E212, 48 (f. *'Ηρακλείδης*); **(137)** f. ii BC *BCH* 66-7 (1942-3) p. 197 no. 1 (*IThrakAig* E258) (s. *Αἰαντίδης*, f. *Αἰαντίδης, Διονυσία*); **(138)** i-ii AD *SEG* XLVII 1072 (*IThrakAig* E272) (*'Απολλόδ(ω)ρ(ο)ς*: f. *'Ηρακλᾶς*); **(139)** ii AD *IG* XII (8) 220, 12; **(140)** ii-iii AD *IThrakAig* E191 (I f. *'Απολλόδωρος* II); **(141)** ib. (*'Απολλόδ[ωρ]ος*: II s. *'Απολλόδωρος* I)

—MESAMBRIA: **(142)** ii/i BC *IGB* V 5103, 2 (s. *Παυσανίας*)

—MONTANA*: **(143)** 155 AD *CIL* III 7449, 21 (*Montana* II 1) (Lat. Ael. Apollodorus)

—NICOPOLIS AD NESTUM: **(144)** ii AD *IGB* IV 2348 (s. *Πύρρος*)

—NICOPOLIS AD NESTUM (TERRIT.): **(145)** iii AD ib. 2351 (*Αὐρ. 'Α.*)

—ODESSOS: **(146)** v/iv BC ib. I^2 98 (*'Απολλόδωρ[ος]*: f. *Στράτων*); **(147)** ii-i BC ib. 230; **(148)** 26 BC ib. 46, 21 (f. *'Αρτεμίδωρος*); **(149)** ii AD ib. 50 b, 9 (*'Απολλόδ[ωρος]?*); **(150)** ib. 66, 1 (f. *Πία*); **(151)** s. ii AD ib. 167 (PM 1727); *Dacia* 21 (1977) p. 161 (date) (f. *'Αρτεμίδωρος*); **(152)** iii AD *IGB* I^2 176 bis;

Dacia 21 (1977) p. 161 (date) (f. Ἀπφία); **(153)** 215 AD *IGB* I^2 47 a, 28 (Αὐρ. Ἀ.: s. Μέντης); **(154)** 221 AD ib. 47 bis a, 38 (Αὐρ. Ἀ.: s. Ἀγαθήνωρ); **(155)** ib. 47 bis c, 10 (Αὐρ. Ἀ.: s. Ἀγαθήνωρ); **(156)** ib. l. 13 (f. Αὐρ. Διονύσιος); **(157)** ib. l. 18 (Οὐαλέριος Ἀ.: I f. Αὐρ. Ἀπολλόδωρος II); **(158)** ib. l. 18 (Αὐρ. Ἀ.: II s. Οὐαλέριος Ἀπολλόδωρος I); **(159)** ib. l. 35 (f. Αὐρ. Κοσκώνιος)
—ODESSOS?: **(160)** imp. ib. 206 quinquies (s. Νικίας)
—PAUTALIA: **(161)** ii-iii AD ib. IV 2055 (s. Γάϊος); **(162)** ib. 2072, 8 (s. Ἡροῦς)
—PERINTHOS-HERAKLEIA: **(163)** iv/iii BC *IEph* 1464, 2 (?f. Ἀρτεμίδωρος); **(164)** hell.? *IG* II^2 10072 (*FRA* 6034) ([Ἀπολ]λόδωρος: I f. Ἀπολλόδωρος II); **(165)** *IG* II^2 10072 (*FRA* 6035) ([Ἀπολ]λόδωρος: II s. Ἀπολλόδωρος I); **(166)** c. 100-115 AD *SEG* XXVI 1288, 4 (s. Πόπλιος, f. Βάσσος)
——(Podargoi): **(167)** iii-ii BC *IPerinth* 61, 20 (f. Ἀγησίλαος); **(168)** ib. l. 23 (f. Σῶσις)
—PHILIPPOPOLIS-TRIMONTIUM: **(169)** ii-iii AD *IGB* III 912, 5; **(170)** iii AD ib. 1476, 3 (f. Αὐρ. Ἀπολλωνίδης)
——Vicus Pecetum: **(171)** 227 AD *CIL* VI 32543, 18 (Lat. [M.] [Aur.] Apollodorus)
—PIZOS: **(172)** ?172 AD *IGB* III 1691 (—ης ὁ καὶ Ἀ.)
—SALYMBRIA: **(173)** 407 BC *IG* I^3 118, 37, 44-5 (-δō-: s. Ἐμπέδος); **(174)** imp. *IByz* S 12 ([Ἀπ]ολλόδωρ[ο]ς: f. Ματρόδωρος)
—STROUNEILOS: **(175)** 202 AD *IGB* III 1690 d, 66 (and Thrace Pizos: f. Θύλης?)
—STRYME?: **(176)** v/iv BC *SEG* XXIV 632 (*IThrakAig* E126) (Ἀπο[λλ]όδωρος: s. Ἀντιφάνης)
—ZONE: **(177)** f. iv BC ib. E412 (s. Βοστᾶς); **(178)** s. iv BC *PAE* 1969, p. 64 with pl. 75 *a* (*IThrakAig* E423) (f. Μύλλος); **(179)** *SEG* XXXIII 566 (*IThrakAig* E424) (f. Προκλῆς)
THRACE?: **(180)** ?iii BC *IG* II^2 8908; cf. *SEG* XXVIII 288 (*FRA* 2496) (f. Δριαλλία)

Ἀπολλόθεμις
THRACE: (1) ii BC *ILAlg* II 824 (s. Ἀσκληπιόδωρος)
—BYZANTION: (2) c. 240-220 BC *IOrop* 83 (s. Πρασίδας)
—PERINTHOS-HERAKLEIA:
——(Kastaleis): (3) iii-ii BC *IPerinth* 61, 58 (f. Ζηνόδοτος)

Ἀπολλοκλῆς
SCYTHIA MINOR:
—KALLATIS: (1) iv/iii BC *ISM* III 125, 9

Ἀπολλοῦς
MACEDONIA (MYGDONIA):
—THESSALONIKE*: (1) f. iii AD *SEG* XLVI 825 (terracotta) (Ἀπολλοῦνος (gen.))
SCYTHIA MINOR:
—TOMIS: (2) i BC *ISM* II 2, 26, 29; 2 A, 46 (s. Νικήρατος)
SKYTHIA:
—OLBIA-BORYSTHENES: (3) i/ii AD *IOlbia* 79, 9 (*IOSPE* I^2 116) (f. Σαβῖνος)

Ἀπολλοφάνης
CIMMERIAN BOSPOROS:
—GORGIPPIA: (1) f. iii BC *CIRB* 1137 B II, 27
—PANTIKAPAION: (2) iv BC ib. 161 (s. Ἀπολλώνιος)
MACEDONIA (EDONIS):
—AMPHIPOLIS: (3) hell. *SEG* XXIV 588 ([Ἀπολ]λοφάνης: s. Ἀπολλόδωρος)
—PHILIPPOI: (4) ?i AD Acta Apocr. Paul., *3 Cor.* 2. 2 (James, *ANT* p. 289) (fict.)
MACEDONIA (MYGDONIA):
—LETE: (5) 22 or 139 AD Dimitsas 678, 11 (f. Ἰόλαος)
MACEDONIA (ODOMANTIKE):
—SIRRHA: (6) 155 AD ib. 821, 13 (Kaphtantzis 1) (s. Τορκούλας)
MACEDONIA (PIERIA):
—PYDNA: (7) 368 BC D. xix 194-5 (Tataki, *Macedonians* p. 170 no. 3)
MACEDONIA (PIERIS):
—NEAPOLIS: (8) ?ii BC Dumont–Homolle 110b 29 = *AE* 1936, p. 32 no. 1 (Pilhofer 5); (9) f. ii BC Dumont–Homolle 110b 29 = *AE* 1936, p. 32 no. 1; Collart, *Philippes* pl. 22. 3
MACEDONIA?: (10) 325 BC *RE* (8); Berve 105 (Tataki, *Macedonians* p. 256 no. 237)
SCYTHIA MINOR:
—KALLATIS: (11) iv/iii BC *ISM* III 125, 8; (12) s. i AD ib. 67, 2 (Ἀπολλοφά[νης]: ?s. Σάτυρος)
SKYTHIA:
—OLBIA-BORYSTHENES (BEREZAN (MOD.)): (13) f. v BC *SEG* XXXII 772 (vase)
TAURIS:
—CHERSONESOS: (14) ?f. iv BC *CIRB* 173 (f. Βίων); (15) iii BC *IOSPE* I^2 521 (f. Τιμοξένα); (16) c. 200-185 BC Kats p. 87 no. 13 (amph.) (s. Ἡρωΐδας)
THRACE:
—AINOS: (17) ii BC *SEG* XXVII 251 (s. Ἰσόδημος)
—BEROE-AUGUSTA TRAIANA (TERRIT.): (18) iii AD *IGB* V 5609 (Αὐρ. Ἀπολλοφάνη[ς])
—BYZANTION: (19) i BC-i AD *IByz* 270 (Fıratlı–Robert pp. 86-7 no. 108a) (s. Μενεκράτης)
—HADRIANOPOLIS: (20) imp. *Syllogos* 27 (1900) p. 389 no. 5 ([Ἀπ]ολλοφάνης)
—ODESSOS?: (21) ii-iii AD *IGB* I^2 144, 4 (f. Φαίνιππος)
—PERINTHOS-HERAKLEIA:
——(Geleuntes): (22) iii-ii BC *IPerinth* 61, 36 (Ἀπολλοφάνευς (gen.): f. Θεόνομος)
—SALYMBRIA: (23) hell. *IByz* S 48 (Ἀπολλοφάνηος (gen.))

Ἀπολλοφάνιον
THRACE:
—MESAMBRIA: (1) hell. *IGB* I^2 327

Ἀπολλοφανίων
THRACE:
—BYZANTION (TERRIT.): (1) i-ii AD *IByz* 111 (I f. Ἀπολλοφανίων II); (2) ib. (II s. Ἀπολλοφανίων I)

Ἀπόλλων
CIMMERIAN BOSPOROS:
—MYRMEKION: (1) i AD *CIRB* 877 (Ἀπολλωνο—?: s. Γάστεις)

Ἀπολλωνᾶς
MACEDONIA (EDONIS):
—AMPHIPOLIS: (1) imp. Kaphtantzis 657, 6 (Ἀπολλωνᾶνι (dat.): ?f. Ἀνδρόνικος, Μάξιμος)

Ἀπολλωνία
CIMMERIAN BOSPOROS:
—PANTIKAPAION: (1) i BC *CIRB* 271 (Ἀπολλω[νί]α); (2) i AD ib. 331, 2 (m. Γοργίας); (3) ib. 343; cf. KW pl. 51 no. 691 (Ἀπ[ο]λλων[ία]: m. Ἄττας, Ἔρως); (4) *CIRB* 344 (m. Ἡλιοδώρα)
MACEDONIA (BOTTIAIA):
—BEROIA: (5) ?iii AD *IBer* 213 (Tataki 215) (d. Μέστυς, m. Ἀντιγόνα)
—EDESSA: (6) iii AD *Arch. Pap.* 22 (1973) p. 209 no. 17 (Tataki, *Edessa* 34)
—PELLA: (7) iii-ii BC Dimitsas 134
MACEDONIA (EDONIS):
—AMPHIPOLIS: (8) ii-iii AD ib. 865
—AMPHIPOLIS (TERRIT.): (9) ii-iii AD ib. 867 (d. Ἀπολλώνιος, m. Ζωσίμη)
MACEDONIA (MYGDONIA):
—THESSALONIKE: (10) ii AD *IG* X (2) (1) 393 (m. Ὀνήσιμος); (11) 159 AD ib. 322, 1 (-πολω-: d. Διαδουμενός); (12) 165 AD ib. 461, 5 (Ἀ. Νίκα: m. Ἀπολλώνιος)
—THESSALONIKE?: (13) ii AD ib. 907; (14) 152 AD ib. 923, 4 (m. Ἀρτέμιν, Διοσκουρίδης)
TAURIS:
—CHERSONESOS: (15) iv-iii BC *IOSPE* I^2 505 ([Ἀπο]λλωνία: d. Πάσιχος); (16) iv/iii BC Solomonik, *NEPKh* 151 (d. Ἡρόδοτος)
THRACE:
—DODOPARON: (17) ii AD *IGB* III 1796, 4 ([Ἀπολ]λωνία: d. Οὐλπ. Πούτη, M. Οὔλπ. —)
—MARONEIA: (18) ii-iii AD Dumont–Homolle 110b 18 (*IThrakAig* E280) (Φλ. Ἀ.)

Ἀπολλωνιανός
THRACE:
—OESCUS: (1) iii AD *ILB* 28 (Lat. Apollonianus)

Ἀπολλωνίδας
MACEDONIA (EDONIS):
—AMPHIPOLIS: (1) iv/iii BC *SEG* XXXI 618 (Ἀπολλων[ί]δας: f. Ἀπελλέας)
TAURIS:
—CHERSONESOS: (2) c. 325-315 BC Kats pp. 87-8 no. 15 (amph.) ?= (*3*); (3) iv/iii BC ib. p. 99 no. 61 (amph.) (f. Θεογένης) ?= (*2*); (4) ib. p. 100 no. 64 (amph.) (f. Ἴστρων); (5) c. 300-285 BC ib. p. 88 no. 16 (amph.); (6) iii BC ib. p. 104 no. 76 (amph.) (f. Μᾶτρις); (7) c. 262-237 BC ib. p. 88 no. 18 (amph.) (s. Ἴστρων); (8) c. 230-215 BC ib. p. 88 no. 17 (amph.) (s. Ἀπολλώνιος); (9) c. 215-200 BC ib. p. 89 no. 19 (amph.) (s. Σιμαῖος); (10) ii BC *ID* Index I s.v. (-δης: s. Ἀπολλώνιος); (11) c. 120-110 BC Anokhin p. 146 no. 180 (coin); (12) ii AD *IOSPE* I^2 464; cf. KW pl. 33 no. 468 (s. Μένανδρος)
THRACE:
—AINOS: (13) i-ii AD Taşlıklıoğlu 2 p. 3 no. 1, 4 (*SEG* XLIX 865); *BE* 1972, no. 275 (locn.) (f. Ἀθηνόδωρος)
—BYZANTION: (14) c. 230-200 BC *BCH* 45 (1921) p. 19 III, 99 (f. Σκύμνος)
——(Rhegion): (15) ii BC *IByz* 99 (Fıratlı–Robert p. 94 no. 129) (s. Μήνιος)
—LYSIMACHEIA: (16) i BC *SGDI* 4108, 22

Ἀπολλωνίδης
CIMMERIAN BOSPOROS:
—GORGIPPIA: (1) s. iv BC *SEG* XLVII 1175, 1 (sherd) (Ἀπολλων(ί)δ[ης]?)
—HERMONASSA: (2) imp. *CIRB* 1095; cf. KW 611 with fig. 14 (Ἀπολλ[ωνί]δης: f. Ἡζοῦς)
—MYRMEKION (NR.): (3) imp. *CIRB* 895 (Ἀπ<π>ολ(λω)νίδης: f. Πρώτη)
—NYMPHAION: (4) i/ii AD ib. 935 (I f. Ἀπολλωνίδης II); (5) ib. (II s. Ἀπολλωνίδης I)
—PANTIKAPAION: (6) i BC-i AD ib. 511; cf. KW pl. 54 no. 739 (f. Σαραπίων); (7) hell.-imp. *CIG* 8556 c (lead) (Ἀπολλων[ί]δης); (8) i AD *CIRB* 345 (s. Διογένης); (9) ib. 509; cf. KW pl. 27 no. 404 (s. Σαβίων, Χρήστη); (10) i-ii AD *CIRB* 577; cf. KW pl. 33 no. 475; (11) ii AD *CIRB* 652 ([Ἀ]πολλωνίδη[ς]: s. Ἀπατούριος); (12) f. ii AD ib. 84, 4; cf. KW pl. 45 no. 648 (f. Κοσσοῦς)
MACEDONIA (BOTTIAIA):
—BEROIA: (13) m. iii BC *IBer* 19 (Tataki 217) (s. Δεξίλαος); (14) 239-229 BC *IBer* 45, 3 (Tataki 216) (s. Γλαυκίας); (15) 178 BC *Syll*^{3} 636, 6 (Tataki 218; Tataki, *Macedonians* p. 75 no. 13) (f. Σιμωνίδης)
—EDESSA: (16) 51 AD *SEG* XLVI 744, 13 (Tataki, *Edessa* 35) (s. Θευδᾶς)
—PELLA: (17) c. 230-200 BC *BCH* 45 (1921) p. 17 III, 61 (Tataki, *Macedonians* p. 150 no. 17)
MACEDONIA (CHALKIDIKE):
—OLYNTHOS: (18) 349 BC *RE* (14) (Tataki, *Macedonians* p. 130 no. 9; *FRA* 5883)
MACEDONIA (EDONIS):
—AMPHIPOLIS: (19) iii BC *AD* 23 (1968) Chron. p. 358 with pl. 305 *a*

Macedonia (Pieris):
—Neapolis: **(20)** c. 230-200 BC *BCH* 45 (1921) p. 18 III, 82 (Tataki, *Macedonians* p. 125 no. 4) (s. *Φίλτων* I)
Macedonia?: **(21)** 320 BC *RE* (10); Berve 103; **(22)** 286 BC *RE* (11) (Tataki, *Macedonians* p. 257 no. 239)
Scythia Minor:
—Istros: **(23)** iii BC *ISM* I 124 ([Ἀπολ]λω-νίδης?); **(24)** i BC-i AD ib. 191 II, 23 (s. *Λυσί-μαχος*); **(25)** ii AD ib. 204, 9 (s. *Μενέχαρμος*); **(26)** iii AD ib. 181, 7 (Ἀ[πολλω]νίδης: f. *Αὐρ. Βασιλεύς*, *Αὐρ. —μων*, *Αὐρ. Πο—*)
Skythia:
—Olbia-Borysthenes: **(27)** v BC Dubois, *IGDOlbia* 101 (s. *Τιμόθεος*)
Tauris:
—Chersonesos: **(28)** ?v-iv BC *SEG* XLIV 657 (weight) (Ἀπολλονίδō (gen.)); **(29)** c. 290-280 BC Anokhin p. 139 no. 82 (coin); **(30)** c. 250-230 BC ib. pp. 140-1 nos. 99; 112 (coins); **(31)** c. 47-44 BC ib. p. 148 no. 201 (coin); **(32)** ii AD Solomonik, *NEPKh* 184 (f. *Ἀθάναιος*); **(33)** 129 AD *IOSPE* I² 359, 31 (f. *Ἀρίστων*); **(34)** 129-130 AD ib. l. 28; *VDI* 1960 (3), pp. 154-5, 23 (f. *Φιλόμουσος*); **(35)** 130 AD *IOSPE* I² 357, 25 (s. *Ἰδ—*); **(36)** 174 AD *SEG* XLV 985 A, 34 ([Ἀ]πολλων[ίδ]ης: s. *Ἱέρων*)
Thrace: **(37)** 414 BC *IG* I³ 427, 12 (*FRA* 2497) (Ἀπ̣ολλō[νί]δε̄ς: slave)
—Aigos Potamoi?: **(38)** hell. *ISestos* 72 (f. *Δη-μᾶς*)
—Ainos: **(39)** c. 223 BC *PTeb* 815 fr. 2 II, 9 (La'da E85) (s. *Ἀπολλώνιος*)
—Apollonia-Sozopolis: **(40)** v/iv BC *IGB* I² 412 (f. *Φιλτάτη*); **(41)** iv BC ib. 451 (f. *Λαμ-πιτώ*)
—Bourdapa: **(42)** ii-iii AD ib. III 1340 (f. *Ἀπολ-λώνις ὁ καὶ Λογγῖνος*)
—Byzantion: **(43)** i BC-i AD *IByz* 19, 12
—Byzantion (territ.): **(44)** imp. Unp. (Sayar) (f. *Ῥοῦφος*)
—Chersonesos: **(45)** iv BC *IG* II² 10505 (*FRA* 7301) (s. *Διονυσόδωρος*)
—Hadrianopolis (territ.): **(46)** imp. *IGB* III 1832, 5 (Ἀπολ[λω]νίδης: s. *Αὐλούζενις*)
—Kardia: **(47)** i-ii AD *IKyz* I 494 (*Steinepi-gramme* 2 p. 46)
—Koila: **(48)** ii-iii AD *ISestos* 30 (*Αἰλ. Ἀ.*: s. *Αἰλ. Ζωσίμη*)
—Lysimacheia: **(49)** m. ii BC ib. 38 a, 4 (f. *Μενέστρατος*)
—Odessos: **(50)** v/iv BC *IGB* I² 99 (f. *Ἡρακλεί-δης*)
—Pautalia:
——Karistoron: **(51)** ii-iii AD ib. IV 2155 (f. *—βιος*)
—Philippopolis-Trimontium: **(52)** iii AD ib. III 1476, 3 (*Αὐρ. Ἀ.*: s. *Ἀπολλόδωρος*); **(53)** c. 235-238 AD ib. 1515, 12; cf. V 5548 (*Αὐρ. Ἀ.*: s. *Ἀπολλόδοτος*)
—Philippopolis-Trimontium (territ.): **(54)** ii-iii AD ib. III 1507 (*CCCA* VI 359)
—Serdica: **(55)** iii AD *IGB* IV 1906 (*Αὐρ. Ἀ.*: s. *Μαρκιανός*)
—Stryme?: **(56)** m. iv BC *IThrakAig* E152 (Ἀπ̣ολλ̣ω̣νίδης: f. *Δημήτριος*)

Ἀπολλωνικέτης
Macedonia (Pieris):
—Galepsos: **(1)** hell. *SEG* XXXII 297 (Tataki, *Macedonians* p. 110 no. 1; *FRA* 1434) (Ἀπολ-λωνικέτ(η)ς: s. *Κώδων*)

Ἀπολλώνιος
Cimmerian Bosporos:
—Achilleion: **(1)** ii AD *CIRB* 1030 (s. *Νικ-άνωρ*)
—Achilleion (nr.): **(2)** 105 AD ib. 1021, 5 (I f. *Δάδας*, ?f. *Μαίσωος*, *Ταυρίσκος*, *Ἀπολλώνιος* II); **(3)** ib. l. 11-12 (II ?s. *Ἀπολλώνιος* I, *Γλυκαρία*)
—Bosporos: **(4)** 346 BC Rhodes–Osborne 64, 2, 67 (s. *Λεύκων*)
—Gorgippia: **(5)** f. iii BC *CIRB* 1137 A I, 9 (s *Δημήτριος*); **(6)** ib. l. 20 (f. *Διονύσιος*); **(7)** ib. l. 24; 1137 B I, 46 (f. *Δαναός*); **(8)** ib. 1137 A I, 39 (s. *Γλαῦκος*); **(9)** ib. l. 43 (s. *Στρατόνικος*) ?= (*13*); **(10)** ib. 1137 A II, 15 (s. *Ποσίδεος*); **(11)** ib. l. 39 (s. *Ἐπι-κράτης*); **(12)** ib. 1137 B I, 12 ([Ἀπ]ολλώνιος: s. *Διονύσιος*); **(13)** ib. l. 62 (s. *Στρατόνικος*) ?= (*9*); **(14)** i BC/i AD *Hyperboreus* 2002 (1), p. 185 (s. *Πανταλέων*); **(15)** ii AD *CIRB* 1143, 4 (Ἀπολλώ[νιος]: f. *—σμος*); **(16)** f. ii AD *SGE* 35 (1972) p. 51, 2 (*CIRB* 1132) + *CIRB* 1162 (Ἀπ[ο]λλ[ώνιος]?); **(17)** s. ii AD ib. 1145, 10
—Gorgippia?: **(18)** s. ii AD ib. 1231 B, 10 (Ἀπολλών[ιος]?: f. *Ζαζζοῦς*)
—Hermonassa: **(19)** iv BC ib. 1056 II, 1 (Ἀπολ-λών̣ι[ος]); **(20)** i AD ib. 1075 ([Ἀπολ]λώνιος: f. *Βοῦδας*); **(21)** i-ii AD ib. 1081 (s. *Νικομήδης*); **(22)** 123-132 AD ib. 1054, 11 (s. *Χρυσαλίσκος*); **(23)** ib. l. 20 (f. *Δάδας*)
—Korokondame: **(24)** imp.? ib. 1110 (f. *Ὀστρακίων*)
—Nymphaion: **(25)** iii BC ib. 912 II, 18 (s. *Πρό-μηθος*); **(26)** f. iii BC *SEG* XXXIX 701. 2 (XLV 997. 2) ?= (*27*); **(27)** ib. XXXIX 701. 5 (XLV 997. 1) ?= (*28*) (*26*); **(28)** ib. 997. 7; cf. L 696 ?= (*27*); **(29)** ib. XLV 997. 7; **(30)** 105 BC *ID* 2128 (Ἀπολ[λ]ών(ι)ος: f. *Εὔτυχος*)
—Pantikapaion: **(31)** iv BC *CIRB* 161 (f. *Ἀπολλοφάνης*); **(32)** ib. 162 (KW 22) (Ἀπολ-λών[ιος]?, Ἀπόλλων—*CIRB*: s. *Κυλίανις*); **(33)** *CIRB* 191 (f. *Ἱστιαῖος*); **(34)** s. iv BC ib. 163; cf. KW pl. 1 no. 21 (s. *Νεομήνιος*); **(35)** iii-ii BC *CIRB* 256, 3 ([Ἀπολ]λώνιος: s. *Πολύ-γνωτος*); **(36)** ii-i BC ib. 261 (s. *Δημήτριος*); **(37)** ib. 264; cf. KW pl. 37 no. 550 (f. *Πολυ-σθένης*); **(38)** i BC *CIRB* 269 (I f. *Ἀπολλώνιος* II); **(39)** ib. (II s. *Ἀπολλώνιος* I, *Ἀλεξάνδρεια*); **(40)** ib. 270 (f. *Πτολεμαῖος*); **(41)** s. i BC ib. 119, 1 (*GVI* 1471); cf. KW pl. 34 no. 485 (I f. *Ἀπολλώνιος* II); **(42)** *CIRB* 119, 1, 13 (*GVI* 1471); cf. KW pl. 34 no. 485 (II s. *Ἀπολ-λώνιος* I); **(43)** imp. *CIRB* 773 (f. *Χρηστίων*); **(44)** ib. 801 (f. *Ματρόδωρος*); **(45)** i BC/i AD ib. 303; cf. KW pl. 30 no. 436 (s. *Ἄλυπος*); **(46)** *CIRB* 304; **(47)** ib. 477; cf. KW pl. 12 no. 157; **(48)** i AD *CIRB* 336; **(49)** ib. 347 (s. *Ἀκκᾶς*); **(50)** ib. 348 (s. *Ἀνόπτηνις*); **(51)** ib. 349; cf. KW pl. 39 no. 570 (s. *Ἰχω—*); **(52)** *CIRB* 352; cf. KW pl. 47 no. 666 (Ἀπολ(λ)ώνιος: s. *Πογάσιος*); **(53)** *CIRB* 353 (s. *Ἡζοῦς*); **(54)** ib. 354 (Ἀπ(ο)λ(λ)ώνιος: s. *Πόθος*); **(55)** ib. 383 (f. *Δημήτριος*); **(56)** ib. 440 (f. *Καλοῦς*); **(57)** ib. 458 (f. *Μακά-ριος*); **(58)** ib. 469 (f. *Μέναιχμος*); **(59)** ib. 578; cf. KW pl. 46 no. 657 (s. *Δαλάσιος*); **(60)** i-ii AD *CIRB* 600 (f. *Ἔρως*); **(61)** f. i AD ib. 346 (I f. *Ἀπολλώνιος* II); **(62)** ib. (II s. *Ἀπολλώ-νιος* I); **(63)** ib. 350 (s. *Καλλιγένης*); **(64)** ib. 494 (I f. *Ἀπολλώνιος* II, *Ποθοῦσα*); **(65)** ib. (II s. *Ἀπολλώνιος* I); **(66)** i/ii AD ib. 579 (s. *Κο-σοῦς*) **(67)** ib. 580; cf. KW pl. 18 no. 258 (s. *Μηνᾶς*); **(68)** ?ii AD *CIRB* 676 ([Ἀπ]ολλώνιος: f. *Ἀσκληπιάδης*); **(69)** f. ii AD ib. 653; cf. KW pl. 49 no. 686 (Ἀπ(ο)λ(λ)ώνιος: f. *Ἀπολλόδωρος*); **(70)** *CIRB* 714; cf. KW pl. 17 no. 257 (f. *Στρατόνικος*); **(71)** 123 AD *CIRB* 33, 6 (f. *Τρύ-φων*); **(72)** iii AD ib. 109, 5
—Phanagoreia: **(73)** s. i BC ib. 992, 7 (s. *Γό-κων*); **(74)** i AD ib. 995 (s. *Ἀγαθοῦς*, f. *Χρησ-τοῦς*); **(75)** ib. 996 (f. *Ἀσκληπιάδης*); **(76)** 123 AD ib. 975, 3 (Ἀπολλώ[νι]ο[ς]: f. *Φαρνάκης*)
—Taman Peninsula: **(77)** ii AD ib. 1222 (Ἀπολ-λών(ιος)); **(78)** f. ii AD ib. 1223; cf. KW pl. 44 no. 620 (Ἀπολ(λ)ών[ιος])
—Theodosia: **(79)** iii AD *CIRB* 947 B, 5 ([Ἀ]πολλώνιο[ς]: f. *Ψυχαρίων*)
—Tyritake: **(80)** i AD ib. 904; **(81)** f. ii AD ib. 908 (Ἀπολλώ[νιος]: f. *Κράτιππος*)
Macedonia: **(82)** s. iii BC La'da E1428; **(83)** ?219 BC *PUG* III 103, 13 (Tataki, *Macedo-nians* p. 259 no. 250); cf. La'da E1642 (f. *Φίλιππος*); **(84)** *PUG* III 104, 16 (s. *Ἡρα-κλείδης*); **(85)** 213 BC *PFrankf* 1, 6, 14, 16, 20 etc. (Tataki, *Macedonians* p. 257 no. 243; La'da 1427); **(86)** ii BC *SEG* XLI 1635, 7 (Tataki, *Macedonians* p. 259 no. 248); cf. La'da E1418 (I f. *Ἀπολλώνιος* II); **(87)** *SEG* XLI 1635, 7 (Tataki, *Macedonians* p. 258 no. 244; La'da E1418) (II s. *Ἀπολλώνιος* I); **(88)** 186-182 BC *IFayoum* 150, 7 (Tataki, *Macedo-nians* p. 258 no. 246; La'da 1424) (s. *Μαχά-τας*); **(89)** 182 BC *PRyl* 585, 2, 42 (Tataki, *Macedonians* p. 259 no. 249); cf. La'da E1496 (f. *Ἡρακλείδης*); **(90)** m. ii BC *PTeb* 1075 fr. 2, 20 (Tataki, *Macedonians* p. 475 no. 40); cf. La'da E1545 (f. *Νεῖλος*); **(91)** *BGU* 1938 B, 5 (Tataki, *Macedonians* p. 474 no. 33); cf. La'da E1673; **(92)** 173 BC *PGiss* 2 II, 1 (Tataki, *Macedonians* p. 257 no. 241; La'da E1429); **(93)** 164-152 BC *UPZ* 9; 12-16; 64-71; 73-4; 90-3; 104 + pp. 113-16 and Index s.v.; Thompson, *Memphis* pp. 245 ff. (La'da E1419) (s. *Γλαυκίας*); **(94)** 145 BC *PPhrur-Diosk* 18, 43; **(95)** 144-141 BC *PBingen* 35, 3 (La'da E1421) (Ἀπ[ολλ]ώνιος: s. *Ἑρμόφιλος*); **(96)** a. 142 BC *PWürzb* 4, 3 (La'da E1425) (s. ...ά̣του (gen.)); **(97)** c. 132 BC *PGissUniv* 6, 2 (Tataki, *Macedonians* p. 475 no. 37); cf. La'da E1484 (f. *Εἰρηναῖος*); **(98)** *PGissUniv* 7, 4 (Tataki, *Macedonians* p. 475 no. 38); cf. La'da E1485 (f. *Ἑξάκων*); **(99)** 115 BC *PTeb* 30, 3, 10, 15, 23 (Tataki, *Macedonians* p. 475 no. 35); cf. La'da E1461 (f. *Διδύμαρχος*); **(100)** 111 BC *PDion* 22, 26 (Tataki, *Macedonians* p. 474 no. 34); cf. La'da E1402 (f. *—ώνιος*); **(101)** 108-105 BC *PDion* 17, 32; 19, 28; cf. La'da E1468 (Ἀπο[λλώνιος]: f. *Διονύσιος*); **(102)** 107 BC *SB* 11410 B, 12 (Tataki, *Macedo-nians* p. 474 no. 26); **(103)** 103 BC *PTeb* 105, 1, 11 (Tataki, *Macedonians* p. 475 no. 43); cf. La'da E1657 (f. *Ὡρίων*); **(104)** 102 BC *PWürzb* 6, 29, 31, 42 (Tataki, *Macedonians* p. 474 no. 30; La'da E1422) (s. *Ἰσχυρίων*); **(105)** 78 BC *BGU* 1736, 8, 20; *PBingen* 48, 9 (Tataki, *Macedonians* p. 474 no. 31; La'da 1423) (s. *Κάλλις*: katoikos); **(106)** 74 BC *SB* 7532, 26, 37 (Tataki, *Macedonians* p. 474 no. 27; La'da E1417) (s. *Ἀμ.συστος*); **(107)** 73 BC *POxy* 1628, 5 (Tataki, *Macedonians* p. 475 no. 42); cf. La'da E1619 (f. *Σαραπίων*); **(108)** *POxy* 3482, 3, 30 (Tataki, *Macedonians* p. 475 no. 36); cf. La'da E1469 (f. *Διονύσιος*); **(109)** 68 BC *BGU* 1731, 3 (Tataki, *Macedo-nians* p. 475 no. 39); cf. La'da E1509 (f. *Θέρα-ανδρος*); **(110)** 63 BC *POxy* 1644, 5 (Tataki, *Macedonians* p. 474 no. 28; La'da E1420) (s. *Διονύσιος*, *Ἀρσινόη*: katoikos); **(111)** 51 BC *PSI* 1098, 40 (Tataki, *Macedonians* p. 475 no. 41); cf. La'da E1558 (f. *Νικίας*); **(112)** i AD *PMich* 303, 4 (s. *Μάρων*); **(113)** 12 AD *PKöln* 227 B, 7-8 (s. *Πάπος*, f. *Πάπος*)
Macedonia (Bisaltia):
—Argilos?: **(114)** 364-357 BC Hatzopoulos, *Actes Amphipolis* p. 15 no. 1, 5, 9; pp. 73-4 (locn., date) (or Macedonia (Edonis) Amphi-polis)
Macedonia (Bottiaia):
—Aigai: **(115)** ?ii BC *BSA* 39 (1938-9) p. 95 no. 5 = *SEG* XLVI 828; cf. *Myrtos* pp. 441-51 (f. *Φίλιππος*: locn.—Hatzopoulos)
—Edessa: **(116)** 169 AD *Arch. Pap.* 22 (1973) p. 208 no. 12 (Tataki, *Edessa* 239) (*Οὔλπ. Ἀπολ-λώνειος*: f. *Λυκῖνος*)
—Pella: **(117)** iii BC Akamatis, *Amph. Pellas* p. 31 no. PAR3 (amph.) (*SEG* L 613); **(118)** *Α΄ Panell. Synedr. Epigr.* p. 181 no. 6 (*Pella*

p. 197 no. 65) (f. Νικοστράτη); **(119)** ii/i BC *SEG* XLVIII 830 (vase)

MACEDONIA (CHALKIDIKE):

—MENDE: **(120)** 127 BC *PP* 3823 (Tataki, *Macedonians* p. 120 no. 5) (s. Ἀ—ιος)

—POTIDAIA-KASSANDREIA: **(121)** iii BC *IG* II² 9000 (Tataki, *Macedonians* p. 85 no. 7; *FRA* 2774) (f. Θάλλος); **(122)** ii BC *IG* II² 8998 (Tataki, *Macedonians* p. 85 no. 6; *FRA* 2775) (f. Διονυσόδωρος)

—POTIDAIA-KASSANDREIA?: **(123)** hell.-imp. *IG* II² 8996 (Tataki, *Macedonians* p. 85 no. 5; *FRA* 2776) (s. Ἀριστοφάνης)

MACEDONIA (DERRIOPOS):

—STUBERRA: **(124)** 74 AD *IG* X (2) (2) 325, 64; 326, 67 (f. Ποσείδιππος); **(125)** 90 AD ib. l. 79 (s. Εὐβουλίδης)

MACEDONIA (EDONIS):

—AMPHIPOLIS: **(126)** hell.? Kaphtantzis 645 (f. Κράτων); **(127)** ii BC *Iscr. Gr. Verona* p. 115 no. 56 (Tataki, *Macedonians* p. 47 no. 20) (f. Ἀσκληπιάδης); **(128)** ii-i BC *IG* II² 8078 (Tataki, *Macedonians* p. 47 no. 19; *FRA* 498) (s. Σιτάλκης); **(129)** i BC *IG* XII (1) 127, 37 (Tataki, *Macedonians* p. 47 no. 17); **(130)** 37 BC Robert, *Coll. Froehner* 44, 15 (Tataki, *Macedonians* p. 47 no. 18) (s. Γλαυκίας, ?s. Κλεοπάτρα); **(131)** ii/iii AD *SEG* XXXV 713, 1 (f. Διονυσοφάνης)

—AMPHIPOLIS (TERRIT.): **(132)** ii-iii AD Dimitsas 867 (f. Ἀπολλωνία)

—PHILIPPOI: **(133)** hell. Hatzopoulos, *MI* 1 p. 188 n. 1

—PHILIPPOI (NR.): **(134)** i-ii AD Dimitsas 1090 (fals.?) (Pilhofer 671) (Κλ. Ἀ.)

MACEDONIA (MYGDONIA):

—APOLLONIA?: **(135)** ?s. i BC *AE* 1983, p. 75 (I f. Ἀπολλώνιος II); **(136)** ib. (II s. Ἀπολλώνιος I)

—KALINDOIA: **(137)** c. 333 BC Hatzopoulos, *MI* 2 pp. 84-5 no. 62, 12 (f. Καλλίας); **(138)** i BC *SEG* XLII 589 (f. Μητρόδωρος); **(139)** I AD ib. XXXV 744, 5, 49 (II s. Ἀπολλώνιος I, Στρaττώ); **(140)** ib. l. 6, 43 (I s. Κερτίμμας, f. Ἀπολλώνιος II); **(141)** 68-98 AD ib. XLII 580, 13 + *BE* 1999, no. 362 (Ἀπολ(λ)ώνιος: s. Λεόκριτος); **(142)** *SEG* XLII 580, 18 (f. Ἡράκων); **(143)** ib. l. 47 (s. Φίλαγρος); **(144)** 70 AD ib. 587, 3; **(145)** a. 98 AD ib. 582, 2 (Τ. Φλαούϊος Ἀ.: s. Ἀνδρόνικος); **(146)** ib. l. 12 (f. Δημήτριος); **(147)** ib. l. 27 (I f. Ἀπολλώνιος II); **(148)** ib. l. 27 (II s. Ἀπολλώνιος I); **(149)** ib. l. 28 (f. Διοσκουρίδης); **(150)** ib. 583, 16 (f. Νίκων)

—LETE: **(151)** c. 230-200 BC *BCH* 45 (1921) p. 18 III, 74 (Tataki, *Macedonians* p. 117 no. 1) (s. Διονυ—)

—PERDYLOS: **(152)** ?i-ii AD *SEG* XXIX 581 (f. Ἐπιγόνη)

—THESSALONIKE: **(153)** ii-i BC *IG* X (2) (1) 78, 4 (s. Δωσίθεος); **(154)** i BC/i AD ib. 58, 9; 318, 1; *KGAM Thess.* 1 111 (date) (f. Πρίαμος); **(155)** *IG* X (2) (1) 318, 3 (s. Πρίαμος); **(156)** i AD ib. 316; cf. *Tyche* 10 (1995) pl. 6 (s. Ἀμύντας); **(157)** i-ii AD *IG* X (2) (1) 243 I, 13 (s. Λυσίμαχος); **(158)** ib. 243 II, 9 (s. Βρύζος); **(159)** s. i AD ib. 69, 31 (-πολό-: f. Ἀπελλᾶς); **(160)** ii-iii AD ib. 431 (Feissel, *RICM* 113) (I f. Ἀπολλώνιος II); **(161)** *IG* X (2) (1) 431 (Feissel, *RICM* 113) (II s. Ἀπολλώνιος I); **(162)** 132 AD *IG* X (2) (1) 503, 1 (Ἀ. ὁ καὶ Μάξιμος: s. Ἀρτεμᾶς); **(163)** 165 AD ib. 461, 1, 13 (s. Ἀπολλωνία Νίκα)

—THESSALONIKE?: **(164)** imp. *Mél. arch. hist.* 32 (1912) p. 352 no. 5 (Ἀπολλούν(ι)ος); **(165)** ii-iii AD *IG* X (2) (1) 261, 13; **(166)** s. ii AD ib. 904; *JDAI* 84 (1969) p. 154 no. R20 (date) (s. Εὔπορος, f. Μύστα)

MACEDONIA (ODOMANTIKE):

—SIRRHA: **(167)** 155 AD Dimitsas 821, 24 (Kaphtantzis 1) (s. Τιμόθεος, f. Φίλητος)

MACEDONIA (PELAGONIA):

—DOSTONEIS?: **(168)** 232 AD *IG* X (2) (2) 191 (f. Νίκη)

MACEDONIA (PIERIA):

—DION: **(169)** ii AD *Klio* 52 (1970) p. 52 no. 3 (f. Σώσανδρος); **(170)** ib. (s. Σώσανδρος)

—PYDNA (LOULOUDIES (MOD.)): **(171)** s. vi AD *SEG* XLVIII 809. 12 (brick)

MACEDONIA (SINTIKE):

—PARTHIKOPOLIS: **(172)** ii-iii AD *IGB* V 5899 (f. Πιερίων)

MACEDONIA?: **(173)** 105 BC *PDion* 19, 28 (La'da 1426) (Ἀπολλώ[νιος]); **(174)** 72 BC *BGU* 1738, 1, 13 and verso (Tataki, *Macedonians* p. 474 no. 29; La'da E2638) (s. Εὔβουλος: katoikos)

SARMATIA:

—MAIOTAI: **(175)** i BC *IG* II² 9256 (*FRA* 3449) (f. Παρμένων)

SCYTHIA MINOR:

—DINOGETIA (NR.): **(176)** ii-iii AD *ISM* V 301 (Lat. Apollonius: freed.)

—ISTROS: **(177)** iv BC Unp. (Avram, defixio) 1, 11 ([Ἀπο]λλώνιος); **(178)** *ISM* I 110 ([Ἀπ]ολλώνιο[ς]: s. Δημοτέλης); **(179)** iii BC ib. 119 (?f. Ἡφαιστόδωρος); **(180)** iii-ii BC Unp. (Avram, defixio) 4, 1 (Ἀπολλώνι(ο)ς); **(181)** f. iii BC *ISM* I 145 (f. Ξενοχάρης); **(182)** s. iii BC ib. 15, 2 (s. Κλεόμβροτος); **(183)** ii BC ib. 173 (s. Μητρόβιος); **(184)** i BC-i AD ib. 191 I, 18 ([Ἀ]πολ[λ]ώνιος); **(185)** ib. l. 53 ([Ἀπολ]λώνιος: s. Ἀθηνόδωρος); **(186)** ib. 191 II, 45 (s. Πολυαίνετος); **(187)** i AD ib. 200, 8 (s. Ἀρτεμίδωρος); **(188)** ?ii AD ib. 285 (s. Δατειζεις); **(189)** 138 AD ib. 193 I, 29 (I f. Ἀπολλώνιος II); **(190)** ib. l. 29 (II s. Ἀπολλώνιος I); **(191)** ib. l. 94 (f. Ποσειδώνιος); **(192)** iii AD ib. 229, 3

—KALLATIS: **(193)** iii BC *IOrop* 543 (s. Ἀλφῖνος); **(194)** iii-ii BC *ISM* III 162 (s. Λάμπις); **(195)** s. iii BC ib. 35 A, 23 (I f. Ἀπολλώνιος II) ?= (*197*); **(196)** ib. l. 23 ([Ἀπ]ολλώνιος: II s. Ἀπολλώνιος I); **(197)** ib. l. 24 (f. Φίλιππος) ?= (*195*); **(198)** ib. 35 B, 41 (s. Σῖμος); **(199)** ii BC ib. 165 (s. Ἐπίστρατος); **(200)** ii-i BC ib. 135, 5, 9 (II s. Ἀπολλώνιος I); **(201)** ib. l. 10 (I s. Μενεκράτης, f. Ἀπολλώνιος II, Μενεκράτης); **(202)** m. i AD ib. 31, 11, 16; **(203)** s. i AD ib. 69, 4 (Ἀπολλώνι[ος]?); **(204)** ib. 80, 2; **(205)** f. iii AD ib. 105, 6 (Ἀπολλώ[νιος])

—KALLATIS?: **(206)** ii/i BC *IGB* II 867 a, 7 = *ISM* I 219 (V 87); cf. *ISM* III p. 140 (locn.) (s. Ἄτταλος)

—TOMIS: **(207)** i BC ib. II 2 B, 52 (s. Ὑγιαίνων); **(208)** f. i AD *RPC* I 1819 (coin) (Ἀπολ(λ)ώ(νιος)?); **(209)** ii AD *ISM* II 17, 4 (f. Ἴλαρος); **(210)** ii-iii AD ib. 137 (Lat. [Ap]olloniu[s]); **(211)** ib. 295 (Lat. Apollonius: s. Δάδας, Μάμα); **(212)** ii/iii AD ib. 127; cf. *SEG* XLV 953 bis (Σηδάτιος [Ἀ]πολλώνιος)

SKYTHIA:

—OLBIA-BORYSTHENES: **(213)** iv-iii BC *IOSPE* I² 196 ([Ἀπ]ολλώνιος)

—TANAIS: **(214)** 104 AD *CIRB* 1259, 19 (f. Βοΐδας); **(215)** c. 200-210 AD ib. 1277, 17 (f. —δα—νος) ?= (*219*); **(216)** c. 200-228 AD ib. l. 8; 1282, 3 ([Ἀπο]λλώνιος—1277: f. Δημήτριος); **(217)** 220 AD ib. 1278, 12 (I f. Ἀπολλώνιος II); **(218)** ib. l. 12 (II s. Ἀπολλώνιος I); **(219)** 220-229 AD ib. 1245, 16; 1278, 18; *Stud. Zhebelev* p. 47, 17 (f. Φαλδάρανος) ?= (*215*)

—TYRAS: **(220)** s. iii BC *VDI* 1966 (2), p. 152, 6 (s. Χρ—)

TAURIS:

—CHERSONESOS: **(221)** iv BC Solomonik, *GAKh* 1709 (vase) ([Ἀπ]ολ(λ)ώνιος); **(222)** iv/iii BC Solomonik, *NEPKh* 141 (s. Πυρρῖνος); **(223)** ib. 168; **(224)** *IOSPE* I² 467 (s. Πολύαρχος); **(225)** ib. 474 (f. Ἡράκλειος); **(226)** Kats p. 94 no. 45 (amph.) (f. Εὔμηλος); **(227)** ib. p. 102 no. 71 (amph.) (f. Λύκων); **(228)** c. 315-300 BC ib. p. 89 no. 20 (amph.); **(229)** iii BC *IAK* 65 (1918) p. 12 no. 2; **(230)** Solomonik, *NEPKh* 149 (s. Σαννίων); **(231)** *IOSPE* I² 341, 1 (Ἀπολλών[ιος]?); **(232)** ib. 466 (s. Ἡρακλεόδωρος); **(233)** ib. 521; **(234)** Kats p. 88 no. 17 (amph.) (f. Ἀπολλωνίδας); **(235)** iii-ii BC *Sov. Arkh.* 24 (1955) p. 263 (vase) (*VDI* 1956 (3), p. 149; *TGE* 7 (1962) p. 153 fig. 19); **(236)** f. iii BC Kats p. 89 no. 21 (amph.) ([Ἀπολ]λώνιος: I f. Ἀπολλώνιος II); **(237)** *ISM* III 12, 5, [11] (s. Παρ—); **(238)** *SEG* XXXIX 702, 1, 13, 23 (I s. Εὐφρόνης, f. Ἀπολλώνιος II, Εὐφρόνης, ?f. Ἀπ—); **(239)** ib. l. 5 (II s. Ἀπολλώνιος I); **(240)** c. 285-272 BC Kats p. 90 no. 25 (amph., tile) (s. Πασιάδας); **(241)** c. 262-237 BC ib. p. 89 no. 21 (amph.) ([Ἀπολλ]ώνιος: II s. Ἀπολλώνιος I); **(242)** ib. p. 89 no. 23 (amph.) (s. Θεοφάνης); **(243)** ib. p. 90 no. 26 (amph.) (s. Σώπολις); **(244)** ib. p. 90 no. 27 (amph.); **(245)** 250-230 BC Anokhin pp. 141-2 nos. 104; 117 (coins); **(246)** c. 237-230 BC Kats p. 89 no. 22 (amph.) (s. Εὔμηλος); **(247)** c. 230-215 BC ib. p. 89 no. 24 (amph.) (s. Πάρμις); **(248)** ii BC *ID* Index I s.v. Ἀπολλωνίδης (f. Ἀπολλωνίδας) ?= (*250*); **(249)** f. ii BC *IOSPE* I² 351, 2 (s. Παρθενοκλῆς); **(250)** *IG* XI (4) 844, 3 ([Ἀπ]ολλώνιος) ?= (*248*); **(251)** i BC *IOSPE* I² 465 (s. Ἀγάθων); **(252)** m. i BC ib. 347, 2; 691, 2 (s. Ζῆθος); **(253)** imp. ib. 384, 4 ([Ἀπολ]λώνιος); **(254)** i AD *SEG* XLVI 927, 7 ([Ἀπο]λλώνιος); **(255)** ii AD Solomonik, *NEPKh* 56 (f. Χρηστίων); **(256)** *IOSPE* I² 432, 2 (Τ. Φλ. Ἀ.: s. Τ. Φλ. Ἀρίστων, f. Τ. Φλ. Ἀρίστων, Τ. Φλ. Ἀττίνας, Λαοδίκη); **(257)** ib. 455 (f. Κιλία); **(258)** ib. 701, 4; **(259)** f. ii AD *KSIIMK* 15 (1947) p. 59, 3 (Solomonik, *NEPKh* 112 d); cf. *VDI* 1993 (4), p. 63 (Ἀπολλών[ιος]: f. —ης) ?= (*261*); **(260)** *KSIIMK* 15 (1947) p. 59, 9 (Solomonik, *NEPKh* 112 d); cf. *VDI* 1993 (4), p. 63 (Φλ. Ἀ.); **(261)** *IOSPE* I² 359, 27; Solomonik, *NEPKh* 111, 6; *VDI* 1960 (3), pp. 154-5, 22 (f. Ἑρμοκλῆς) ?= (*259*); **(262)** ?114 AD *SEG* XLVIII 999, 35 (Ἀπολλώνιος: s. Παρθενοκλῆς); **(263)** ib. l. 40 ([Ἀ]πολλών[ιος]: s. Ἡρόγειτος); **(264)** c. 120-130 AD Solomonik, *NEPKh* 112, 12 (s. Ζῆθος); **(265)** ib. l. 14; **(266)** ib. l. 15 ([Ἀπολ]λώνιος: s. Ἀρίστων); **(267)** 129 AD *IOSPE* I² 359, 32 (f. Ζῆθος); **(268)** 130 AD *VDI* 1960 (3), pp. 154-5, 25 (f. Ἀρίστων); **(269)** 174 AD *SEG* XLV 985 A, 37 (I f. Ἀπολλώνιος II); **(270)** ib. l. 37 (II s. Ἀπολλώνιος I)

—KERKINITIS: **(271)** 118 BC *IG* II² 1008, 114 (*FRA* 2829) (Ἀπο[λ]λώνιος: f. —ωρος)

THRACE: **(272)** 231 or 206 BC *CPR* XVIII 18, 370; cf. La'da E840 ([Ἀ]πολλώνιος: f. Πύθων); **(273)** c. 223 BC *PTeb* 815 fr. 6 II, 34 (Velkov 28; La'da E826) (s. Ἐπι....κος: t.e.); **(274)** 46-54 AD *SEG* XVI 415 I, 13 (*IThrakAig* E84) (f. Τιβ. Κλ. Ῥοιμητάλκας)

—ABDERA: **(275)** iv BC Hp., *Epid.* iii 17. 13; *CMG* V (10) ii 1 p. 183; **(276)** iii BC *SEG* XXXIX 647 (*IThrakAig* E51) (s. Τεῖσις)

—AGATHOPOLIS: **(277)** f. iii AD *IGB* I² 475 (*CCET* I 171) (Ἀπολλώνι[ος])

—AINOS: **(278)** c. 223 BC *PTeb* 815 fr. 2 II, 9; cf. La'da E85 (f. Ἀπολλωνίδης) ?= (*279*); **(279)** 222 BC *PPetr* II 47, 30 (III 55b; La'da E86) ?= (*278*); **(280)** 194 BC *Milet* I (3) 54, 5 (and Caria Miletos: s. Δημήτριος)

—APOLLONIA-SOZOPOLIS: **(281)** i-ii AD *IGB* I² 401, 8 (f. Πολύξενος, Π—ων); **(282)** ib. l. 19 (f. Λουκίσανδρος)

—BEROE-AUGUSTA TRAIANA: **(283)** 187 AD ib. III 1552, 13 (f. Ἀντίπατρος)

—BISANTHE-PANION: **(284)** ii-i BC *IG* XII (9) 1126 (f. Ἄνδρων)

—BIZONE: **(285)** iii/ii BC *IIasos* 408, 11 (f. Κτησίας); **(286)** i-ii AD *IGB* I² 6, 12 ([Ἀ]πολ(λ)ώνιος: f. Μιν—)

—BIZYE: **(287)** f. i AD ib. 378, 4; II 743, 5; *BSA* 12 (1905-6) p. 175 no. 1 (s. *'Επταίκενθος*)
—BOURDAPA: **(288)** ii-iii AD *IGB* V 5506 (*[Ἀ]πολλώ[νιος]?*)
—BYZANTION: **(289)** m. iv BC *IG* II^2 8437 (*FRA* 1388) (f. *'Αντίμαχος*); **(290)** iii BC *IG* II^2 8446 = 8445; cf. *AM* 67 (1942) p. 106 no. 200 (*FRA* 1389) (f. *Σταφύλος*); **(291)** iii/ii BC *IByz* 163 (Fıratlı–Robert p. 50 no. 17) (f. *Παρμενίσκα*); **(292)** ii BC *IByz* 86 (s. *Γέρων*); **(293)** ib. 95 (Fıratlı–Robert p. 93 no. 125) (f. *.απρες*); **(294)** *IByz* 125 (Fıratlı–Robert p. 101 no. 153) (I f. *Μάτρων, 'Απολλώνιος* II); **(295)** *IByz* 125 (Fıratlı–Robert p. 101 no. 153) (II s. *'Απολλώνιος* I); **(296)** *IByz* 154 (Fıratlı–Robert p. 105 no. 165) (f. *Βόσπων*); **(297)** *IByz* 358 (Fıratlı–Robert p. 60 no. 45) (*'Απολ(λ)ώνιος*: f. *'Απφη*); **(298)** ii-i BC *Istanbul Ark. Müz.* 7 (1956) p. 55 with fig. 3 (f. *Φιλίσκος*); **(299)** ?ii-i BC *IByz* 117 B (f. *'Αγαθάγγελος*); **(300)** ii-i BC ib. 148 (f. *'Ολυμπιάς*); **(301)** ib. 200 (Fıratlı–Robert p. 61 no. 47) (s. *Φίλων*); **(302)** *IByz* 213 (Fıratlı–Robert p. 72 no. 75) (s. *Μίκκος*); **(303)** *IByz* 220 (Fıratlı–Robert pp. 78-9 no. 89) (*'Απολλώ[νιος]*: f. *'Ιάσων*); **(304)** *IByz* 221 (Fıratlı–Robert p. 79 no. 90) (f. *Τρυφῶσα*); **(305)** i BC-i AD? *IByz* 117 A (f. *'Ισίδωρος*); **(306)** i BC-i AD ib. 234 (f. *Δάδας*); **(307)** ii AD ib. 321, 1 (s. *Μηνόφιλος*, f. *Νέα*)
—BYZANTION (TERRIT.): **(308)** ii BC ib. 193 (s. *Σίμων*); **(309)** i BC ib. 203 (Fıratlı–Robert pp. 62-3 no. 52) (f. *'Απολλόδωρος*); **(310)** imp. Unp. (Sayar) (f. *Φιλίσκος ὁ καὶ Κτῆτος*)
—BYZANTION:
——(Delkos): **(311)** i BC *IByz* 201 (Fıratlı–Robert p. 62 no. 50) (f. *Διόδωρος*); **(312)** imp. *IByz* 22, 4 (f. *Φίλων*)
——(Philokterea): **(313)** i-ii AD ib. 319 a (Fıratlı–Robert p. 123 no. 206) (f. *'Ροῦφος*)
——(Rhegion): **(314)** ?ii BC *IByz* 17 (f. *'Ακκα*); **(315)** i BC-i AD ib. 244 (-λό-: f. *'Αφία, 'Απολλώνις*)
——(Rhegion?): **(316)** i BC ib. 151 (f. *Κρίτων*)
—BYZANTION?: **(317)** hell.-imp. ib. 342 (f. *Θίθα*)
—DIONYSOPOLIS: **(318)** iii/ii BC *IGB* I^2 20 (s. *Δημοφῶν*); **(319)** ii-i BC *SNG Stancomb* 122 (coin)
—GANOS: **(320)** imp. Dumont–Homolle 88a (s. *Σεύθης*)
—KORPILOI: **(321)** imp. *IG* XII (8) 126
—LYSIMACHEIA: **(322)** ?ii AD *CIL* III 14406 f; cf. Robert, *Hell.* 5 p. 52 (Lat. Aelius Apollinius)
—MARKIANOPOLIS: **(323)** ii AD *IGB* II 798 b, 7 (*[Ἀπο]λλώνιος*)
—MARKIANOPOLIS (NR.): **(324)** iii AD *SEG* XL 596 (*'Απολλών(ι)ο(ς)*: s. *'Ιουλιανός*)
—MARKIANOPOLIS?: **(325)** ii-iii AD *IGB* V 5394 (or Thrace Pautalia?: s. *'Ροιμητάλκης*)
—MARONEIA: **(326)** ii-i BC *IThrakAig* E212, 23 (f. *Σιτάλκας*); **(327)** ib. l. 36 (f. *'Ηρακλείδης*); **(328)** ib. l. 41 (f. *Διονύσιος*); **(329)** ib. l. 49 (s. *Σώπατρος*); **(330)** ib. l. 55 (s. *'Επάλκης*); **(331)** i BC ib. E243 (*'Απολ(λ)ών[ιος]*: f. *Διονύσιος*); **(332)** imp. ib. E289 (s. *Διοσκουρίδης*); **(333)** *IG* XII (8) 134 (*'Απολ(λ)ώνιος*: f. *Θεόξενος*); **(334)** ii/iii AD Grandjean, *Arétalogie* p. 120 = *SEG* XLVIII 903 (*IThrakAig* E203) (I f. *'Απολλώνιος* II); **(335)** Grandjean, *Arétalogie* p. 120 = *SEG* XLVIII 903 (*IThrakAig* E203) (II s. *'Απολλώνιος* I); **(336)** iii AD ib. E316
—MESAMBRIA: **(337)** iii BC *IGB* V 5121 (f. *'Ηρίχα*); **(338)** ii BC ib. I^2 329, 7 (*[Ἀπο]λλώνιος*: ?s. *Βύριχος*); **(339)** ii/i BC ib. V 5104 IV (*'Απολλώνιο[ς]*: f. *Διονύσιος*); **(340)** ib. 5104 VI (s. *Διονύσιος*)
—NICOPOLIS AD ISTRUM: **(341)** ii-iii AD ib. II 663 (f. *Κλαύδις*)
—NICOPOLIS AD ISTRUM (TERRIT.): **(342)** 227 AD *ILB* 438, 8 (Lat. Apol(l)oni(u)s)
—ODESSOS: **(343)** v/iv BC *IGB* I^2 97; **(344)** s. iii BC ib. 36, 5 (s. *Σίμων*); **(345)** i BC-i AD ib. 110, 2 (f. *'Αγαθήνωρ*); **(346)** 33 BC ib. 46, 14 (f. *'Απολλᾶς*); **(347)** 25 BC ib. l. 22 (f. *Νουμήνιος*); **(348)** 23 BC ib. l. 24 (s. *Προμαθίων*) ?= (*353*); **(349)** 6 BC ib. l. 41 (f. *Προμαθίων*); **(350)** i-ii AD ib. 51 b, 9 (f. *'Αντίπατρος*); **(351)** ib. 190 (f. *Μακού*); **(352)** 14-37 AD ib. 57, 5 (II s. *'Απολλώνιος* I); **(353)** ib. l. 6 (*'Απολ(λ)ών(ι)ος*: I s. *Προμαθίων*, f. *'Απολλώνιος* II) ?= (*348*); **(354)** ii AD ib. 50 a, 6 (f. *Αἰαντίδης*); **(355)** ib. l. 8 (f. *Ποσείδιππος*); **(356)** ib. 133 (f. *'Ιααθιθις?*); **(357)** ib. 178 bis (f. *'Αγαθήνωρ*); **(358)** ib. V 5067, 1 (II s. *'Απολλώνιος* I, f. *Βλωστι*); **(359)** ib. l. 2 (I f. *'Απολλώνιος* II); **(360)** f. ii AD ib. I^2 78 ter, 13 (*CCET* I 30) (I f. *'Απολλώνιος* II); **(361)** *IGB* I^2 78 ter, 13 (*CCET* I 30) (II s. *'Απολλώνιος* I); **(362)** m. ii AD *IGB* I^2 169 (PM 1725); *Dacia* 21 (1977) p. 161 (date) (s. *'Αρτεμίδωρος*); **(363)** s. ii AD *IGB* I^2 79 bis, 3 (*CCET* I 34) (f. *Μένανδρος*); **(364)** *IGB* I^2 175 (PM 1739); *Dacia* 21 (1977) p. 161 (date) (f. (nat.) *Γάϊος*); **(365)** 221 AD *IGB* I^2 47 bis a, 11 (I f. *M. Αὐρ. 'Απολλώνιος* II *νεώτ.*); **(366)** ib. l. 11 (*M. Αὐρ. 'Α. νεώτ.*: II s. *'Απολλώνιος* I); **(367)** ib. 47 bis c, 31 (f. *Αὐρ. 'Ιερώνυμος*)
—ODESSOS (NR.): **(368)** i BC-i AD ib. 265 (s. *Σίμων*); **(369)** ib. 293, 3; **(370)** i-ii AD ib. 285 (I f. *'Απολλώνιος* II); **(371)** ib. (II f. *'Απολλώνιος* I); **(372)** s. ii AD ib. 281 (*CCET* I 25) (f. *Προμαθίων, 'Αγαθήνωρ, Διονύσιος*)
—PAUTALIA: **(373)** ii AD *IGB* IV 2074, 17 (-λλό-: f. *Διογένης*); **(374)** ii-iii AD ib. V 5780 (s. *Τιμόθεος*)
——(Herakleis): **(375)** ?ii AD ib. IV 2077, 14 (*Αἰλ. 'Απολλό[νιος]*)
—PERINTHOS-HERAKLEIA: **(376)** i BC/i AD *Ag.* XVII 642 (*[Ἀ]πολλ[ώνιος]*: s. *Εὐα—*); **(377)** i-ii AD *IPerinth* 93 (f. *Κοσμία*); **(378)** i/ii AD ib. 64, 3 (*Φλ. 'Απο[λλ]ώνιος*); **(379)** ii AD ib. 100 (f. *'Αφροδίτη*); **(380)** ii-iii AD ib. 103 (I f. *'Απολλώνιος* II); **(381)** ib. (-πολώ-: II s. *'Απολλώνιος* I)
——(Makedones): **(382)** iii-ii BC ib. 61, 5 (s. *Σωσιμένης*)
——(Podargoi): **(383)** iii-ii BC ib. l. 18 (f. *'Αγαθοκλῆς*); **(384)** ib. l. 26 (*'Απολλών(ι)ος*: f. *Καλλιμέδων*)
—PHILIPPOPOLIS-TRIMONTIUM (TERRIT.): **(385)** ii-iii AD *IGB* III 1212 (*'Απ[ολ]λών[ιος]*)
—RHAIDESTOS: **(386)** imp. PM 1896; cf. *JÖAI* 23 (1926) Beibl. col. 136 no. 33 (f. *'Απολ—*)
—SALYMBRIA: **(387)** hell. *IByz* S 42 (f. ..όσιον)
—SERDICA (TERRIT.): **(388)** ii-iii AD *IGB* V 5697 (*'Απ[ολ]λώνιος*: f. *Παρηγόρις*)
—TYRODIZA-TIRISTASIS: **(389)** imp. Dumont–Homolle 89b (s. *Δόλης, 'Ηρυλλα*)
THRACE?: **(390)** ii-iii AD *SEG* XXXVIII 1916

'Απολλώνις
MACEDONIA (BOTTIAIA):
—BEROIA: **(1)** iii AD *IBer* 214; 356 (Tataki 711) (*Κλ. 'Α.*: ?f. *Ζωσίμη*)
MACEDONIA (MYGDONIA):
—THESSALONIKE: **(2)** ii-iii AD *IG* X (2) (1) 300; cf. *BCH* 98 (1974) p. 549
THRACE:
—APOLLONIA-SOZOPOLIS: **(3)** i-ii AD *IGB* I^2 401, 18 (s. *'Αρτεμίδωρος*)
—BOURDAPA: **(4)** ii-iii AD ib. III 1340 (*'Α. ὁ καὶ Λογγῖνος*: s. *'Απολλωνίδης*)
—BYZANTION:
——(Rhegion): **(5)** i BC-i AD *IByz* 244 (-λό-: s. *'Απολλώνιος*)
—BYZANTION?: **(6)** i BC-i AD ib. 375 (Fıratlı–Robert p. 126 no. 211) (s. *'Ολυμπᾶς*, f. *Νικώ, Καλλιγόνα*)
—DODOPARON: **(7)** ii AD *IGB* III 1794 (s. *Αὐλούζενις*)
—PAUTALIA (TERRIT.): **(8)** ii AD ib. IV 2214, 15
THRACE?: **(9)** f. iii AD *AE* 1984, pp. 173-4 no. 3136

'Απολλωνίς
MACEDONIA (CHALKIDIKE):
—AKANTHOS: **(1)** iv/iii BC *SEG* XLVII 871 B, 1; cf. XLIX 672 (*'Απολλωνίδος* (gen.): m. *Μέλισσα*)
SCYTHIA MINOR:
—ISTROS: **(2)** iii/ii BC *ISM* I 120 (*[Ἀπο]λλωνίς*: d. *Διογένης*)
THRACE:
—APOLLONIA-SOZOPOLIS: **(3)** v/iv BC *IGB* I^2 438 (d. *Δισκοῦς*); **(4)** ib. 448

'Απολλωνοφάνης
MACEDONIA (MYGDONIA):
—LETE: **(1)** iv/iii BC *IMM* 2, 10 (Tataki, *Macedonians* p. 118 no. 2) (s. *Λυσανίας*)
THRACE:
—MARONEIA: **(2)** 311-306 BC Maier, *Mauerbauinschr.* 69 II, 145 (*'Απολλωνοφάνευς* (gen.): f. *Καλλίας*)

'Απολλώνυμος
SCYTHIA MINOR:
—KALLATIS: **(1)** s. iii BC *ISM* III 35 A, 22 (*[Ἀπ]ολλώνυμος*: s. *Σάτυρος*)

'Απολλῶς
CIMMERIAN BOSPOROS:
—PANTIKAPAION: **(1)** f. ii AD *CIRB* 703 (s. *Πόλλα*)

'Αποστολία
MACEDONIA (MYGDONIA):
—THESSALONIKE: **(1)** v-vi AD *IG* X (2) (1) 334 (Feissel, *RICM* 167)

'Απουλλος
SCYTHIA MINOR:
—ISTROS: **(1)** 138 AD *ISM* I 193 I, 21 (f. *Χαιρέας*)

'Αππας
TAURIS:
—CHERSONESOS: **(1)** f. ii AD Solomonik, *NEPKh* 111, 7 (s. *Χρ—*); **(2)** ?114 AD *SEG* XLVIII 999, 39 (f. *Εὔμαχος, Χρηστίων*); **(3)** c. 120-130 AD Solomonik, *NEPKh* 112, 21; cf. *VDI* 1993 (4), p. 63

'Αππᾶς
SCYTHIA MINOR:
—ULMETUM: **(1)** ?v AD Barnea 73, 4 (Popescu, *IGL* 210) (*'Αππᾶδος* (gen.): f. *'Αλέξανδρος*)

'Αππατίων
THRACE:
—PERINTHOS-HERAKLEIA: **(1)** c. 100-115 AD *SEG* XXVI 1288, 14 (Stephanis 289); cf. Robert, *OMS* 6 pp. 296 f. (*Κόϊντος 'Α.*)

'Αππιανός
THRACE:
—PAUTALIA (TERRIT.): **(1)** ii-iii AD *IGB* V 5789 (*[Ἀ]ππιανός*)

'Αππιος
MACEDONIA (LYNKESTIS):
—HERAKLEIA (AREA): **(1)** ii AD *IG* X (2) (2) 23 (f. *'Επίνικος*)
MACEDONIA (MYGDONIA):
—THESSALONIKE: **(2)** i-ii AD ib. X (2) (1) 243 I, 10 (f. *Μᾶρκος*)

'Απριάτη
THRACE:
—BYZANTION: **(1)** ii-i BC *SEG* L 667 II (*'Απριάτης* (gen.): d. *'Ηρόθεμις*)

'Απρίων
MACEDONIA (BOTTIAIA):
—BEROIA: **(1)** ii/iii AD *IBer* 27 A, 10 (slave?)

Ἀπρουσία
MACEDONIA (CHALKIDIKE):
—POTIDAIA-KASSANDREIA (TERRIT.): (1) imp. Dimitsas 771 (d. Φιλουμένη)

Ἀπρωνία
THRACE:
—ODESSOS: (1) ii-iii AD *IGB* I² 228, 8

Ἀπρωνιανός
SCYTHIA MINOR:
—ISTROS: (1) ii AD *ISM* I 197 I, 10 (f. Σεραπίων)

Ἀπτέκενθος
THRACE:
—ODESSOS (NR.): (1) i-ii AD *IGB* I² 281 bis (f. —επιερις)

Ἀπτηλᾶς
SCYTHIA MINOR:
—ISTROS: (1) i BC-i AD *ISM* I 191 II, 52 (s. Μενίσκος)

Ἄπτος
MACEDONIA (SINTIKE):
—HERAKLEIA: (1) ii-iii AD *SEG* XXXI 630 (Tataki, *Macedonians* pp. 110-11 no. 1) (and Macedonia (Pieria) Dion: doctor)
THRACE:
—KALYVIA (MOD.): (2) imp. *SEG* XLI 596 (vase) (f. Τραλλις)

Ἄπφη
CIMMERIAN BOSPOROS:
—PANTIKAPAION: (1) iv BC *CIRB* 164; cf. KW p. 50 fig. 6; Zgusta, *PNS* 595
SCYTHIA MINOR:
—TOMIS: (2) ii-iii AD *ISM* II 238, 4
THRACE:
—BYZANTION: (3) ii BC *IByz* 358 (Fıratlı–Robert p. 60 no. 45) (d. Ἀπολλώνιος); (4) ii AD *Türk Tarih Kongresi XI* (6) p. 2703 with pl. 495. 5 (d. Κόϊντος)
—ODESSOS: (5) i-ii AD *IGB* I² 144 bis, 4 (d. Ἀγαθήνωρ)

Ἀπφία
CIMMERIAN BOSPOROS:
—ACHILLEION (NR.): (1) i/ii AD *CIRB* 1022
SCYTHIA MINOR:
—ISTROS: (2) iii AD *ISM* I 291, 3 (d. Φίλιππος)
—KALLATIS: (3) ii/iii AD ib. III 180 (Ἀ. Ἰουλία)
SKYTHIA:
—OLBIA-BORYSTHENES: (4) iii BC *SEG* XXX 958 (vase)
THRACE:
—BISANTHE-PANION: (5) iii-iv AD *AD* 49-50 (1994-5) Mel. p. 306 no. 130 (d. Χαρίτιος); (6) ib. p. 307 no. 131
—DIONYSOPOLIS?: (7) ?ii AD *IGB* I² 28 (PM 1246) ([Ἀ]πφία: ?d. Φαρ—)
—ODESSOS: (8) i BC-i AD *IGB* I² 107, 1 (d. Ἀρτεμίδωρος, m. Ἀρτεμίδωρος); (9) iii AD ib. 176 bis; *Dacia* 21 (1977) p. 161 (date) (d. Ἀπολλόδωρος)
—ODESSOS (TERRIT.): (10) ?i AD *IGB* I² 276
—ODESSOS (NR.): (11) s. ii AD ib. 254 (PM 1723); *Dacia* 21 (1977) p. 161 (date) (d. Ἀγαθήνωρ)

Ἀπφοῦς
CIMMERIAN BOSPOROS:
—PANTIKAPAION: (1) i BC-i AD *CIRB* 537; cf. KW pl. 40 no. 591 (f. Χαρίξενος); (2) i AD *CIRB* 370; Zgusta, *PNS* 595 (f. Βίων)
SCYTHIA MINOR:
—ISTROS: (3) ii AD *ISM* I 196, 18 (I f. Ἀπφοῦς II); (4) ib. l. 18 (II s. Ἀπφοῦς I); (5) ib. 211, 4 (f. Διογένης); (6) ib. 296; cf. *Riv. Fil.* 111 (1983) pp. 54-5 (Ἀπφοῦτι (dat.): ?f. Κουτιλίη)
THRACE:
—BEROE-AUGUSTA TRAIANA: (7) 196-217 AD *IGB* III 1556, 7; 1557, 7; 1558 (f. Αὐρ. Δημήτριος)
—BYZANTION: (8) ii-i BC *IByz* 93 (Fıratlı–Robert p. 91 no. 121) (f. Ἀπφουτίων); (9) i BC-i AD *Türk Tarih Kongresi XI* (6) pp. 2704-5 with pl. 499. 14 (s. Πάπας); (10) *IByz* 240 (s. Εὐφρόνιος, f. Μάμα); (11) imp. ib. 238 (f. Ἀνθίς)
—BYZANTION (TERRIT.): (12) ii-i BC ib. 110 (s. Μηνᾶς)
—BYZANTION:
——(Nikatea?): (13) imp. ib. 248 ([Ἀπ]φοῦς: s. Χαιρέας)

Ἀπφουτίων
THRACE:
—BYZANTION: (1) ii-i BC ib. 93 (Fıratlı–Robert p. 91 no. 121) (s. Ἀπφοῦς)
—BYZANTION (TERRIT.): (2) imp. Unp. (Sayar) (Ἀπφο(υ)τίων: f. Τρωάδας)

Ἀπώ
THRACE:
—ODESSOS: (1) i AD *IGB* V 5062 (-πών: d. Γλαυκίας); (2) ii AD ib. I² 179 bis; cf. *Dacia* 21 (1977) p. 161 + *AE* 1984, p. 177 no. 1278 (date) (d. Ζώπυρος); (3) ii-iii AD *IGB* I² 107 bis (d. Ἡράκων)

Ἀραβιανός
SCYTHIA MINOR:
—ISTROS: (1) ii AD *ISM* I 197 I, 5 (I f. Ἀραβιανός II); (2) ib. l. 5 (II s. Ἀραβιανός I)

Ἀραβωνία
MACEDONIA (BOTTIAIA):
—EDESSA: (1) ii-iii AD *SEG* L 601 (ring)

Ἀράθης
CIMMERIAN BOSPOROS:
—PANTIKAPAION: (1) 210 AD *CIRB* 97, 7 (s. Πάππος)
SKYTHIA:
—TANAIS: (2) 220 AD ib. 1278, 10 (s. Φιδανους); (3) 228 AD ib. 1282, 7 (f. Νικόστρατος)

Ἀρακήβιος
SCYTHIA MINOR:
—TOMIS: (1) ii-iii AD *ISM* II 20, 2 (Αὐρ. Ἀρακήβι[ος]?)

Ἀραμάθης
CIMMERIAN BOSPOROS:
—PORTHMION: (1) iv BC *SEG* XXXVII 678 (Ἀραμαθεῦ (gen.))

Ἀραμίων
CIMMERIAN BOSPOROS:
—PANTIKAPAION: (1) iv AD *CIRB* 739 (Ἀραμί[ω]ν)

Ἀραούηβος
SKYTHIA:
—TANAIS: (1) 225 AD ib. 1279, 24 (Ἀραούηβος)

Ἀρατίδης
MACEDONIA (EDONIS):
—AMPHIPOLIS: (1) s. iv BC *PAE* 1981, p. 25 with pl. 43 β, 5 (f. —οκλῆς)

Ἄρατος
CIMMERIAN BOSPOROS:
—PANTIKAPAION: (1) ii AD *CIRB* 93, 3 ([Ἄ]ρατος)
MACEDONIA (EDONIS):
—AMPHIPOLIS: (2) a. 357 BC Hatzopoulos, *Actes Amphipolis* pp. 38-9 no. 7, 1 (Ἄρατος)
MACEDONIA (MYGDONIA):
—LETE: (3) f. ii BC *SEG* XLVI 764, 9 ([Ἄ]ρατος: s. Μένανδρος)

Ἀργαῖος
CIMMERIAN BOSPOROS:
—NYMPHAION: (1) v/iv BC *CIRB* 916 (f. Βοσπόριχος)
MACEDONIA: (2) s. vii BC *RE* (5) (Tataki, *Macedonians* p. 259 no. 251) (s. Περδίκκας I, Κλεοπάτρα, f. Φίλιππος I: king); (3) ?388-359 BC *RE* (6); *Macedonia* 2 pp. 175-6; *Historia* 44 (1995) pp. 280-2 (Tataki, *Macedonians* p. 259 no. 252) (?s. Ἀρχέλαος: king); (4) iv/iii BC Paus. i 7. 1 (*PP* 14489) (s. Πτολεμαῖος I Σωτήρ (Eordaia): fict.?); (5) 159 BC *PHamb* 238, 2; cf. La'da E1814 (f. Φίλινα)
MACEDONIA (EDONIS):
—AMPHIPOLIS: (6) ii BC *SEG* XXV 716; cf. *AD* 26 (1971) Chron. pl. 412 β (s. Πολύστρατος)
MACEDONIA (KRESTONIA):
—MORRYLOS: (7) c. 230-200 BC *BCH* 45 (1921) p. 18 III, 84 + *SEG* XXXIX 468 (Tataki, *Macedonians* p. 125 no. 2) (Ἀργαῖος: f. Ἄδυμος, Σέλευκος)
MACEDONIA (LOWER PAIONIA):
—EUROPOS: (8) c. 324 BC *RE* Supplbd. 1 (7b); Berve 107 (Tataki, *Macedonians* p. 108 no. 4); (9) ?iii BC *SEG* XXXVIII 616 (f. Βηδέτας)
—GORTYNIA?: (10) ?iii-ii BC Mitrevski, *Vardarski Rid* p. 46 fig. 53 (stamp)
MACEDONIA (MYGDONIA):
—DIKAIA: (11) c. 365-359 BC Unp. (Voutyras–Sismanidis) l. 46
—LETE: (12) ii BC *SEG* XLIV 536 (Ἀ[ργ]αῖος?: f. Ἀλεξάνδρα)
MACEDONIA?: (13) iv BC Arr., *An.* vii 16. 1 (Tataki, *Macedonians* p. 260 no. 255) (f. Ἡρακλείδης)
THRACE: (14) c. 175 BC *PTeb* 779, 2 (Velkov 29; La'da E709)

Ἀργαμηνός
SKYTHIA:
—OLBIA-BORYSTHENES: (1) ii AD *IOSPE* I² 96, 6; Zgusta, *PNS* 53; cf. *SEG* XXXIII 574 (Π. Αἴλ. Ἀ.)

Ἀργανθώνιος
MACEDONIA (MYGDONIA):
—CHALASTRA?: (1) m. v BC ib. XLIII 453 (vase) (-θό-: fict.?)

Ἀργεῖος
MACEDONIA (BOTTIAIA):
—MIEZA: (1) iii/ii BC ib. 424 (f. Στρατονίκη); (2) m. ii BC ib. 419 (s. Ἀριστοφάνης, Θεσσαλονίκη)
MACEDONIA (MYGDONIA):
—LETE: (3) c. 230-200 BC *BCH* 45 (1921) p. 18 III, 73 (Tataki, *Macedonians* p. 118 no. 3) (s. Μελάνθιος)

Ἀργόδας
CIMMERIAN BOSPOROS:
—PANTIKAPAION: (1) i AD *CIRB* 510; Zgusta, *PNS* 772 (f. Παιριφάνης)

Ἀργόναις
CIMMERIAN BOSPOROS:
—PANTIKAPAION: (1) i AD *CIRB* 132, 4 (*GVI* 679) (f. Ἀντίπατρος)

Ἀργότας
SKYTHIA:
—SKYTHAI: (1) f. v BC Dubois, *IGDOlbia* 4 (ring); cf. Vinogradov, *Pont. Stud.* pp. 616 ff.; (2) c. 180-150 BC *CIRB* 75, 1, 7; *Arkheologiia* (Kiev) 2003 (1), pp. 46-9 = *Scythian Neapolis* p. 51; Zgusta, *PNS* 773 (s. Ἰδ..θου (gen.) — Vinogradov: king)

Ἀργουάναγος
SKYTHIA:
—OLBIA-BORYSTHENES: (1) ii AD *IOlbia* 86, 10; Zgusta, *PNS* 54 (f. Νεῖλος); (2) *IOSPE* I² 91, 4 (f. Καινάξαρθος); (3) ib. 686, 2 (*VDI* 1975 (1), p. 69) (s. Κάραξτος) ?= (6); (4) f. ii AD *Drev. Prichern.* 3 pp. 27-8, 6 (s. (nat.)

Σάος, s. (ad.) *'Άβναγος*); **(5)** ii-iii AD *IOSPE* I^2 138, 6 (f. *Κάραξτος*); **(6)** c. 150-175 AD ib. 82, 3; 132, 10; cf. *SEG* XLII 713 (s. *Κάραξτος*) ?= (*3*); **(7)** s. ii AD *IOlbia* 81, 4 (*IOSPE* I^2 94) (f. *Ναύτιμος*); **(8)** ii/iii AD *IOlbia* 52, 3; *IOSPE* I^2 103, 3 (f. *Σίανος*)

'Αργοῦτος
SCYTHIA MINOR:
—TOMIS*: **(1)** ii-iii AD *ISM* II 343 (Robert, *Gladiateurs* p. 105 no. 45) (glad.)

'Αργυραῖος
MACEDONIA (MYGDONIA):
—THESSALONIKE: **(1)** iii AD *IG* X (2) (1) 247, 9 (*'Αργυρδος*—apogr., *'Αργυρ(αῖ)ος*?)

'Αρδαβούριος
THRACE:
—SALYMBRIA: **(1)** v-vi AD *AD* 53 (1998) Mel. p. 473 no. 212 ([*'Αρδ*]*αβούριος*?: f. *'Αλέξανδρος*)

'Αρδάγδακος
SKYTHIA:
—TANAIS: **(1)** 225 AD *CIRB* 1279, 14; Zgusta, *PNS* 55 (s. *Πόπλιος*)

'Αρδάρακος
CIMMERIAN BOSPOROS:
—PANTIKAPAION: **(1)** iii AD *CIRB* 103, 2; Zgusta, *PNS* 56 ([*'Αρ*]*δάρακο*[*ς*]: f. *Πάππος*); **(2)** 275-278 AD *CIRB* 36, 45 (*'Αρδάρακ*(*ος*): s. *Σαμβίων*); **(3)** ib. l. 60 (*'Αρδάρακ*(*ος*))
—PHANAGOREIA: **(4)** iii AD Greifenhagen, *Schmuckarb.* 2 p. 81 (ring)
—PHANAGOREIA (NR.): **(5)** iii AD *CIRB* 1016, 3 (f. *Μενέστρατος*)
SKYTHIA:
—TANAIS: **(6)** 188 AD ib. 1242, 17 (s. *Τρύφων*) ?= (*9*); **(7)** c. 200-210 AD ib. 1277, 5 (*'Αρδά*[*ρα*]*κος*: s. *Συνέκδημος*); **(8)** ib. l. 10; **(9)** 220 AD ib. 1278, 15 (s. *Τρύφων*) ?= (*6*); **(10)** 225 AD ib. 1280, 30 (*'Αρδάρακος*: f. *Λόγωζις*)

'Αρδαρίσκος
SKYTHIA:
—TANAIS: **(1)** f. ii AD ib. 1264 A, 10; Zgusta, *PNS* 56 ([*'Α*]*ρδαρίσκος*: s. *Ψυχαρίων*)

'Άρδαρος
CIMMERIAN BOSPOROS:
—GORGIPPIA: **(1)** ii AD *CIRB* 1141, 12; Zgusta, *PNS* 56 (s. *Ζαζζοῦς*); **(2)** f. ii AD *CIRB* 1172, 3 (*'Άρδαρ*[*ος*]); **(3)** s. ii AD ib. 1145, 10 (f. —*ρος*); **(4)** ib. 1146, 3 ([*'Αρ*]*δαρος*)
—GORGIPPIA?: **(5)** s. ii AD ib. 1231 A, 6 (s. *Πο*—); **(6)** ii/iii AD ib. 1232, 11 ([*'Α*]*ρδαρος*: s. *Νεοκλῆς*)
—PANTIKAPAION: **(7)** 221 AD ib. 99, 14 (s. *Θεόφιλος*); **(8)** 275-278 AD ib. 36, 27 (*'Αρδαρ*(*ος*)—Vinogradov: f. *Φαδίναμος*); **(9)** iv-v AD *SEG* XLV 1015 e (amph.) (*'Αρδαρ*(*ος*)?)
—THEODOSIA: **(10)** iii AD *CIRB* 947 A, 15 (f. —*μίων*)
SKYTHIA:
—TANAIS: **(11)** ii AD ib. 1263, 4; **(12)** f. ii AD ib. 1266, 5 (s. *Νικίας*); **(13)** ib. l. 6 (s. *Πάππος*); **(14)** 123 AD ib. 1265, 5 ([*'Α*]*ρδαρος*: s. *'Αρισ*—); **(15)** 155 AD ib. 1260, 18 (s. *Μύρων*); **(16)** 225 AD ib. 1279, 16 (f. *Μίδαχος*); **(17)** ib. 1280, 13 (s. *Μαστοῦς*)

'Αρδινδιανός
SKYTHIA:
—TANAIS: **(1)** 210-226 AD ib. l. 17; 1285, 12; Zgusta, *PNS* 280 (*'Αρδινδια*[*νός*]—1280, *'Αρδινζιανός*—1285: s. *Χρύσιππος*)

'Αρδονάγαρος
SKYTHIA:
—TANAIS: **(1)** 244 AD *CIRB* 1287, 24; Zgusta, *PNS* 278 (f. *'Ηθιόχακος*)

'Αρδόναστος
SKYTHIA:
—TANAIS: **(1)** 225 AD *CIRB* 1279, 25; Zgusta, *PNS* 279 ([*'Α*]*ρδόναστος*: s. *Σώφρων*)

'Αρδρίνη
MACEDONIA (BISALTIA):
—TRAGILOS: **(1)** v/iv BC *AD* 26 (1971) Chron. p. 418 (*Ancient Macedonia* 3 p. 144 with pl. 34)

'Αρέθουσα
THRACE:
—SERDICA (TERRIT.): **(1)** ii-iii AD *IGB* IV 2006, 4 (d. *'Άλφιος*)

'Αρείβαλις
SKYTHIA:
—OLBIA-BORYSTHENES: **(1)** ii AD *IOSPE* I^2 80, 13; Zgusta, *PNS* 555 ((*'Α*)*ρείβαλις*?, .*δρείβαλις*?: s. *Ραπάκης*)

'Αρείβαλος
THRACE:
—PAUTALIA: **(1)** ii AD *IGB* IV 2074, 11

'Αρείμων
CIMMERIAN BOSPOROS:
—PANTIKAPAION: **(1)** ?i AD *CIRB* 415

'Άρειος
MACEDONIA: **(1)** 74 BC *SB* 7532, 25, 36 (Tataki, *Macedonians* p. 475 no. 44; La'da E1431) (s. *'Ηρακλᾶς*); **(2)** 5 AD *CPR* I 224, 4 (s. *'Ηρωΐδης*: t.e.)

'Αρεῖφιλος
CIMMERIAN BOSPOROS:
—PANTIKAPAION: **(1)** i AD *CIRB* 355 (s. *Δημήτριος*, f. *Θεοφίλη*)

'Αρεσίας
CIMMERIAN BOSPOROS:
—THEODOSIA: **(1)** iv BC ib. 948 (s. *Καλλίγειτος*)
MACEDONIA (EDONIS):
—PHILIPPOI: **(2)** v-vi AD Feissel, *RICM* 242 (Pilhofer 292) (*'Αρεσίου* (gen.))

'Αρεσίδημος
MACEDONIA (CHALKIDIKE):
—OLYNTHOS: **(1)** ?350 BC *TAPA* 65 (1934) p. 125 no. 3, 7; Hatzopoulos, *Actes Chalc.* p. 80 (date) (f. *Φιλοκράτης*)

'Άρεσκος
THRACE:
—BYZANTION: **(1)** ii/i BC *IByz* 233 (f. *'Αττυληνή*)

'Αρέσκουσα
CIMMERIAN BOSPOROS:
—NYMPHAION: **(1)** imp. *CIRB* 937 (d. *Μοκκάπορις*)
—PANTIKAPAION: **(2)** i AD ib. 356; cf. KW pl. 43 no. 630
MACEDONIA (MYGDONIA):
—AGIOS VASILEIOS (MOD.): **(3)** ii AD *SEG* I 279
—THESSALONIKE: **(4)** ii AD *IG* X (2) (1) 114, 6 (*Φλωρία 'Α.*: m. *Οὖηρος*); **(5)** ib. 315, 3 (*Πακωνία 'Α.*); **(6)** ii-iii AD ib. 347; **(7)** c. 175-200 AD *SEG* XXXVI 646 + XLVII 973; cf. XLIII 468; *KGAM Thess.* I 140 (date) (*Οὐαρε*[*ι*]*νία 'Α.*: m. *Μ. Οὐαρίνιος 'Αρέσκων*)
MACEDONIA (PAIONIA):
—STOBOI: **(8)** i-ii AD *Sp.* 71 (1931) p. 227 no. 600 (*Αἴβουτ. 'Α.*: m. *Αἴβουτ. Κεικι*—, *Αἴβουτ. Φίλη*)
MACEDONIA (PIERIA):
—DION?: **(9)** 180 or 181 AD *AEMTh* 15 (2001) p. 343 (*Οὐλπ. 'Α.*: m. *Οὐλπ. Σεκουνδίων*)
THRACE:
—BYZANTION: **(10)** i BC-i AD *IByz* 131 (Fıratlı–Robert p. 98 no. 144) (d. *Γοργίας*)

'Αρέσκων
CIMMERIAN BOSPOROS:
—PANTIKAPAION: **(1)** i AD *CIRB* 386 (*'Αρέσκω*[*ν*])
MACEDONIA (MYGDONIA):
—THESSALONIKE: **(2)** c. 175-200 AD *SEG* XXXVI 646 + XLVII 973; cf. XLIII 468; *KGAM Thess.* I 140 (date) (*Μ. Οὐαρ*[*ί*]*νιος 'Α.*: s. *Λ. Σηνάτιος Οἴκιος*, *Οὐαρινία 'Αρέσκουσα*)

'Άρεστος
SKYTHIA:
—TYRAS: **(1)** ii BC *IOSPE* I^2 8; cf. KW pl. 50 no. 687; Zgusta, *PNS* 914 (*'Α*[*ρ*]*εστος*: s. *Αἰσχίνης*)

'Αρεταινέας
MACEDONIA (PIERIA):
—METHONE: **(1)** 333 BC *Hesp.* 9 (1940) p. 62 no. 8 I, 35 (Tataki, *Macedonians* p. 122 no. 1; *FRA* 3667) (*'Αρ*[*ετ*]*αινέ*[*ας*]?)

'Αρέτη
CIMMERIAN BOSPOROS:
—PANTIKAPAION: **(1)** i BC-i AD *CIRB* 581; cf. KW pl. 13 no. 185 (d. *Σαραπίων*); **(2)** i AD *CIRB* 332; cf. KW pl. 46 no. 650 (m. *Θεόφιλος*, *Μήνιος*); **(3)** *CIRB* 357; cf. KW pl. 16 no. 232; **(4)** *CIRB* 358; **(5)** i/ii AD ib. 583; cf. KW pl. 23 no. 320 (-*ρί*-: d. *'Ήρων*); **(6)** ?iii AD *KSIA* 116 (1969) p. 54 no. 6
MACEDONIA (BOTTIAIA):
—BEROIA: **(7)** ii-iii AD *IBer* 277 (d. *Πύρρος*)
MACEDONIA (MYGDONIA):
—THESSALONIKE: **(8)** i BC-i AD *A' Panell. Synedr. Epigr.* p. 14 no. 1 (*Καμερία 'Α.*); **(9)** ii AD *IG* X (2) (1) 392 (m. *Μάρκελλος*, *Μαρκίων*)
—THESSALONIKE?: **(10)** i BC ib. 912 ([*'Α*]*ρέτη*); **(11)** ii-iii AD ib. 208, 6 (*Οὐαρεινία 'Α.*)
—THESSALONIKE*: **(12)** ii-iii AD ib. 443 (slave?)
SKYTHIA:
—OLBIA-BORYSTHENES: **(13)** i BC-i AD *IOSPE* I^2 221; *SEG* XXXVI 720 (d. *Παπίας*); **(14)** i AD *IOlbia* 100 = *IOSPE* I^2 309; cf. *Hyperboreus* 1996 (2), pp. 127-37; **(15)** *SEG* XLVI 948
THRACE: **(16)** 414 BC *IG* I^3 422, 195 (*FRA* 2498) ([*'Α*]*ρέτε̄*: slave)
—BYZANTION (TERRIT.): **(17)** ii BC *IByz* 129 (Fıratlı–Robert p. 97 no. 142) (*'Αρέτης* (fem. gen.)—*IByz*, *'Αρέτης* (masc. nom.)—Robert: d. *Φιλήμων*)
—ODESSOS: **(18)** i-ii AD *IGB* I^2 143 b, 4 (d. *'Έλλην*, m. *'Έλλην*)

'Αρέτης
MACEDONIA: **(1)** 333-331 BC Berve 109; Hoffmann, *Makedonen* p. 179 (name) (Tataki, *Macedonians* p. 260 no. 258) ?= (*'Άρετις* (*1*))

'Άρετις
MACEDONIA: **(1)** 334 BC *RE* Supplbd. 4 (-); Berve 110 (Tataki, *Macedonians* p. 260 no. 259) ?= (*'Αρέτης* (*1*))

'Αρεύς
CIMMERIAN BOSPOROS:
—PANTIKAPAION: **(1)** iii-ii BC *CIRB* 257; cf. KW pl. 23 no. 334 (*'Αρεως* (gen.): f. —*γένης*)

'Αρηΐφιλος
CIMMERIAN BOSPOROS:
—PANTIKAPAION: **(1)** f. i AD *CIRB* 466 (f. *Μαστοῦς*)

'Αρήτα
THRACE:
—PERINTHOS-HERAKLEIA: **(1)** iii-iv AD *IPerinth* 151 (*AD* 51-2 (1996-7) Mel. p. 345 no. 173) (*Αὐρ. 'Αρήτη*)

Ἀρήτη
MACEDONIA (BOTTIAIA):
—PELLA: (1) iv/iii BC *A´ Panell. Synedr. Epigr.* p. 187 no. 9; cf. *Makedonika* 15 (1975) p. 193 pl. 102 a (d. *Εὐαίνετος*)
THRACE:
—APOLLONIA-SOZOPOLIS?: (2) iv BC *IGB* I^2 479 (d. *Διονῦς*)

Ἄρητος
SCYTHIA MINOR:
—ISTROS: (1) v BC Unp. (Avram, defixio) 2, 3 (s. *Λυκῆς*)

Ἀρθάμμανος
SKYTHIA:
—OLBIA-BORYSTHENES: (1) ii AD *IOSPE* I^2 82, 7; Zgusta, *PNS* 57 (Ἀρθάμμ[α]νος: s. *Πίνμαζος*); (2) iii AD *IOSPE* I^2 135, 8 (-θιέμ-: f. *Διονύσιος*)

Ἀρθέων
THRACE:
—MARONEIA (NR.): (1) iv BC *SEG* XIII 409 (*IThrakAig* E222) (s. *Θεοξενίδης*)

Ἄρθμιος
MACEDONIA (BISALTIA):
—ARGILOS?: (1) f. iv BC *SEG* XXX 548 (s. *Λακ—*)

Ἀριάγνη
MACEDONIA (BOTTIAIA):
—BEROIA: (1) 181 AD *IBer* 49, 1, 12 (Tataki 221) (d. *Βάστος*)
—BEROIA*: (2) s. ii AD *ILeukopetra* 151, 1 (Tataki 220) (m. *Παράμονος*: freed.)

Ἀριάδνη
THRACE:
—BESSOI: (1) c. 455-515 AD *PLRE* II (-) (*Αἰλ. Ἀ.*: d. *Λέων*)

Ἀριανή
MACEDONIA (BOTTIAIA):
—BEROIA: (1) iv-v AD *IBer* 445, 1 (Feissel, *RICM* 62) (*Αὐρ. Ἀριανή*: m. *Ἀγροτέριον*)

Ἀριάντας
SKYTHIA:
—SKYTHAI: (1) vi BC Hdt. iv 81 (king)

Ἀριαπείθης
SKYTHIA:
—SKYTHAI: (1) vi/v BC ib. 76; 78 (f. *Σκύλης*, *Ὀκταμασάδης*: king)

Ἀριαράθη
CIMMERIAN BOSPOROS:
—PANTIKAPAION: (1) i/ii AD *CIRB* 582 + KW pp. 34-5 no. 195 with pl. 13 (d. *Φιλόμηλος*, m. *Μακαρία*)

Ἀριαράθης
CIMMERIAN BOSPOROS:
—PANTIKAPAION: (1) i AD *CIRB* 344; (2) ib. 359 (f. *Ἀριαράμνης*); (3) i/ii AD ib. 638; cf. KW pl. 53 no. 724 (s. *Τιράνιος*)
SKYTHIA:
—OLBIA-BORYSTHENES: (4) f. ii AD *IOSPE* I^2 95, 8; Zgusta, *PNS* 541 (s. *Διονύσιος*)

Ἀριαράμνης
CIMMERIAN BOSPOROS:
—PANTIKAPAION: (1) i AD *CIRB* 359 (s. *Ἀριαράθης*); (2) i/ii AD ib. 597 (f. *Δαΐσκος*)

Ἀρίβαλος
SCYTHIA MINOR:
—TOMIS: (1) ii AD *ISM* II 125 II, 22 (-ρεί-: s. *Γάϊος*)

Ἀρίγνωτος
SCYTHIA MINOR:
—ISTROS: (1) iii-ii BC Unp. (Avram, defixio) 4, 7
THRACE:
—STRYME?: (2) m. iv BC *BCH* 79 (1955) p. 283 = Bakalakis, *Oinos Ismarikos* p. 553 (*IThrakAig* E150) (f. *Ἀντίοχος*)

Ἀρίδηλος
MACEDONIA (CHALKIDIKE):
—SANE-OURANOUPOLIS: (1) iv/iii BC *SEG* XLIII 432 (f. *Τιμόστρατος*)

Ἀριεύς
CIMMERIAN BOSPOROS:
—PANTIKAPAION: (1) i AD *CIRB* 444 (Ἀριέους (gen.): f. *Κοσοῦς*)

Ἀρίζηλος
SKYTHIA:
—OLBIA-BORYSTHENES: (1) f. iv BC Dubois, *IGDOlbia* 102 (*SEG* XLIV 670 (lead))

Ἀριμνήστη
MACEDONIA (CHALKIDIKE):
—STAGEIROS: (1) iv BC *RE* s.v. Arimnestos (7) (d. *Νικόμαχος*, *Φαιστίς*)

Ἀρίμνηστος
MACEDONIA (CHALKIDIKE):
—STAGEIROS: (1) iv BC ib. (7) (s. *Νικόμαχος*, *Φαιστίς*)
THRACE:
—NICOPOLIS AD NESTUM (TERRIT.): (2) ii AD *IG* II^2 10770; *Tekmeria* 6 (2001) pp. 149 ff. (locn.); cf. *LGPN* II s.v. (12) (f. *Ἀριστοβούλη*)

Ἀρίννας
THRACE:
—MARONEIA?: (1) v-iv BC *IThrakAig* E487 (s. *Παρμένων*)

Ἀρισταγόρας
CIMMERIAN BOSPOROS:
—GORGIPPIA: (1) f. iii BC *CIRB* 1137 A II, 50 (s. *Δημήτριος*)
—HERMONASSA: (2) 123-132 AD ib. 1054, 19 (s. *Ἀγαθοῦς*)
—PANTIKAPAION: (3) i BC/i AD ib. 310; cf. KW pl. 25 no. 368 (-σστα-: s. *Κυρίαινα*)
MACEDONIA (PIERIA):
—PYDNA?: (4) iii BC *TCal* 25, 5 (Tataki, *Macedonians* p. 170 no. 4) (Ἀ[ρισ]ταγόρ[ας])
SCYTHIA MINOR:
—ISTROS: (5) ii-i BC *SNG Stancomb* 215 (coin) (Ἀριστα(γόρας)?); (6) i BC *ISM* I 54, 1, 3, 53 (s. *Ἀπατούριος*); (7) i BC-i AD ib. 191 I, 51 (f. *—λας*); (8) ib. 191 II, 18 (s. *Πυθόδωρος*); (9) ib. l. 34 (s. *Νικήρατος*); (10) c. 48-52 AD ib. 67, 53; 68, 53; (11) 138 AD ib. 193 I, 13 (f. *Ἀρτεμᾶς*); (12) ib. l. 19 (f. *Χαιρέας*); (13) ib. l. 56 (f. *Δημοχάρης*); (14) ib. l. 63 (f. *Ἀρτεμᾶς*); (15) ib. 193 II, 66 (f. *Θεοκλῆς*); (16) iii AD ib. 291, 10 (f. *Αἰσχρίων*)
THRACE:
—BYZANTION?: (17) i BC-i AD *IByz* 356 (f. *Φιλώτας*)

Ἀρισταγόρη
THRACE: (1) ?v/iv BC *Syllogos* 27 (1900) p. 389 no. 1 (d. *Ἀπολλόδωρος*)

Ἀρισταγόρης
CIMMERIAN BOSPOROS:
—HERMONASSA: (1) iv BC *CIRB* 1056 I, 18 (f. *—νιδης*)
—PANTIKAPAION: (2) ?s. iv BC ib. 165 (s. *Νυμφαγόρης*)
THRACE:
—ABDERA: (3) c. 395-360 BC May, *Abdera* p. 236 no. 398 (coin) (Ἀρισταγόρεω (gen.))

Ἀρισταινέτη
THRACE:
—BEROE-AUGUSTA TRAIANA: (1) c. 320-324 AD *Anal. Boll.* 31 (1912) p. 198; p. 207
—PERINTHOS-HERAKLEIA: (2) ii AD *IPerinth* 102, 1 (d. *Ἑρμογένης*)

Ἀρισταίνετος
THRACE:
—APOLLONIA-SOZOPOLIS: (1) i-ii AD *IGB* I^2 401, 5 (f. *Ἀλέξανδρος*)
—BYZANTION: (2) ii/iii AD Philostr., *VS* 591; *ILS* 1511-12; Schönert-Geiss, *Byzantion* 1462-63; 1510; 1521-2; 1600-5 (coin); cf. *RE* s.v. Sallius cols. 1908-10; *IByz* s.v. 308 (ident.) (*Γ. Σάλλιος Ἀ.*)
—KELLAI: (3) 241-244 AD *IGB* III 1517, 18; 1518 (*Αὐρ. Ἀριστένετος*)
—PAUTALIA: (4) ii AD ib. IV 2074, 10; (5) ii-iii AD ib. V 5778 (s. *Δημήτριος*)
—PERINTHOS-HERAKLEIA: (6) i-ii AD *IPerinth* 135 (I f. *Ἀρισταίνετος* II); (7) ib. (II s. *Ἀρισταίνετος* I); (8) i/ii AD ib. 64, 2 (*Τ. Φλ. Ἀρισταίνετο[ς]*)
—PHILIPPOPOLIS-TRIMONTIUM (TERRIT.): (9) iii AD *IGB* III 1311 (-στέ-)

Ἀρισταῖος
SCYTHIA MINOR:
—ISTROS: (1) i BC *ISM* I 267, 1 (*GVI* 1519) (f. *Μειδίας*)
THRACE: (2) 180 BC *Essays Thomas* pp. 78, 3 (La'da E710) (Ἀρι(σ)ταῖος: s. *Ἀνδρόμαχος*)

Ἀρίστανδρος
MACEDONIA (CHALKIDIKE):
—OLYNTHOS: (1) m. iv BC *IG* II^2 10020a (Tataki, *Macedonians* p. 130 no. 10; *FRA* 5884) (f. *Θεοτίμη*)
MACEDONIA (MYGDONIA):
—THESSALONIKE: (2) ii BC *IG* X (2) (1) 28, 4 (s. *Ἀριστόνους*)
MACEDONIA (ORESTIS):
—LYKE*: (3) hell. *EAM* 179 β (tile); *SEG* XLIX 739; cf. *AD* 17 (1961-2) Chron. pl. 269 β
THRACE:
—PERINTHOS-HERAKLEIA:
——(Kastaleis): (4) iii-ii BC *IPerinth* 61, 59 (Ἀρ(ί)σντανδρος: s. *Εὐρύμαχος*)

Ἀρίσταρχος
CIMMERIAN BOSPOROS:
—PANTIKAPAION: (1) hell. *AA* 1907, p. 127 Aa, 4 (lead)
KOLCHIS:
—KOLCHIS: (2) f. i BC App., *Mith* 114; *SNG BM Black Sea* 1020 (coin)
MACEDONIA: (3) s. iii BC La'da E1432
MACEDONIA (BOTTIAIA):
—BEROIA: (4) 223 BC *IBer* 4, 34 ([Ἀ]ρίσταρχος: f. *Σωγένης*)
MACEDONIA (CHALKIDIKE):
—NEAPOLIS?: (5) c. 470-460 BC *SEG* XL 549 (vase) (Ἀρί[σταρχος]?)
—STOLOS?: (6) c. 350 BC ib. 553, 5 (s. *Α—*)
MACEDONIA (EDONIS):
—AMPHIPOLIS: (7) 192 BC ib. XLVI 716 B, 3 ([Ἀρί]σταρχο[ς]?)
MACEDONIA (MYGDONIA):
—THESSALONIKE: (8) ?39 BC *IG* X (2) (1) 30, 1; 50, 2; 109, 8 (I f. *Ἀρίσταρχος* II); (9) ib. 30, 1; 50, 2; 109, 8 (II s. *Ἀρίσταρχος* I); (10) m. i AD *Act. Ap.* 19. 29; 20. 4; 27. 2; *Ep.Col.* 4. 10 (Tataki, *Macedonians* p. 179 no. 7)
—THESSALONIKE?: (11) i AD *IG* X (2) (1) 848 + *SEG* XXX 628 (*GVI* 365) ([Ἀρ]ίσταρχος)
MACEDONIA (ORESTIS):
—LYKE (NR.): (12) f. iii AD *EAM* 170, 3 (?s. *Γλαῦκος*)
SKYTHIA:
—OLBIA-BORYSTHENES: (13) s. iv BC Dubois, *IGDOlbia* 46 (f. *Παρθενίς*)
THRACE:
—PERINTHOS-HERAKLEIA:

—(Podargoi): **(14)** iii-ii BC *IPerinth* 61, 19 (f. *Ἀριστόδημος*)
—SESTOS: **(15)** f. iv BC *IG* II^2 10262 (*FRA* 6636)
—STRYME? (NR.): **(16)** c. 450-425 BC *SEG* XXXIII 564 (*IThrakAig* E111) (*Ἀρίστα(ρ)χος*: s. *Πυθώνυμος*)

Ἀρίστας
Thrace:
—STRYME?: **(1)** c. 425-400 BC *AD* 52 (1997) Chron. p. 880 (*IThrakAig* E119) (s. *Ἡρόβουλος*); **(2)** f. iv BC ib. E134 (s. *Κωμαῖος*)

Ἀριστᾶς
Thrace:
—MARONEIA: **(1)** ii AD *SEG* XXX 700, 2 + *IThrakAig* E256 A ([*Ἀρ*]*ιστᾶς*)

Ἀριστέας
Cimmerian Bosporos:
—GORGIPPIA: **(1)** i-ii AD *CIRB* 1138, 7 (f. *—λης*)
Macedonia: **(2)** c. 225-200 BC *ICos* ED 56, 5, 13 (Tataki, *Macedonians* p. 261 no. 262) (s. *Κλέανδρος*)
Macedonia (Bottiaia):
—MIEZA: **(3)** iii/ii BC *SEG* XLIII 412 (f. *Φίλα*); **(4)** f. ii BC ib. 416 (*Ἀρ*[*ιστέα*]*ς*?, *Ἀρ*[*γεῖο*]*ς*?: s. *Καλλικλῆς*, *Φίλα*)
Macedonia (Chalkidike):
—STRATONIKEIA?: **(5)** i-ii AD ib. XXIV 576 (-*σστέ*-: f. *Ἀφθόνητος*)
Macedonia (Edonis):
—AMPHIPOLIS: **(6)** s. iv BC *PAE* 1981, p. 25 with pl. 43 *β*, 17 ([*Ἀρ*]*ιστέας*?)
Macedonia (Mygdonia):
—THESSALONIKE: **(7)** i-ii AD *IG* X (2) (1) 243 II, 12 (s. *Σεύθης*); **(8)** m. iii AD ib. 206, 5 (*Γ. Ἰούλ. Ἀ.*: f. *Γ. Ἰουλ. Ὀλυμπιάς*); **(9)** vi AD ib. 1030 (*IC* 4 p. 406 no. 481; Feissel, *RICM* 287); cf. *LGPN* I s.v. (15) (and Crete Gortyn)
Tauris:
—CHERSONESOS: **(10)** m. iv BC Solomonik, *GAKh* 297 (vase) (*Ἀριστέα* (gen.?))
Thrace:
—ABDERA: **(11)** c. 311-280 BC *AMNG* II (1) 216 (coin)
—LYSIMACHEIA: **(12)** f. ii BC *IIasos* 184, 9 (f. *Ἐπίνικος*)

Ἀριστέης
Thrace:
—PERINTHOS-HERAKLEIA?: **(1)** iv BC Hp., *Epid.* iv 45

Ἀρίστεια
Macedonia (Mygdonia):
—THESSALONIKE?: **(1)** ?i AD *IG* X (2) (1) 55 (-*τια*: d. *Αὖλος*, m. *Μ. Ἐρέννιος Πωλλίων*)

Ἀριστείδας
Thrace:
—BYZANTION: **(1)** 208 BC *FD* III (3) 183, 2 (f. *Ἀμύντωρ*)

Ἀριστείδης
Cimmerian Bosporos:
—PANTIKAPAION: **(1)** ii AD *CIRB* 667 B (-*στη*-: s. *Διονύσιος*); **(2)** 130 AD ib. 656, 1; cf. KW pl. 18 no. 272 (s. *Ἀφφοῦς*, *Λανδίκη*)
Macedonia (Bottiaia):
—BEROIA: **(3)** iv-v AD *IBer* 445, 3 (Feissel, *RICM* 62) (*Ἀρεστίδης ὁ κὲ Οὐαλ—*: f. *Ἀγροτέριν*)
Macedonia (Eordaia):
—BOKERIA: **(4)** i BC/i AD *GP* 441; *AAA* 4 (1971) pp. 115-17 (locn.) (Tataki, *Macedonians* p. 83 no. 1)
Macedonia (Mygdonia):
—THESSALONIKE: **(5)** 491-518 AD *Mél. Tisserant* 2 p. 301

Scythia Minor:
—ISTROS: **(6)** ii BC *ISM* I 31, [3], 14 + *SEG* XLIX 1007 ([*Ἀρ*]*ιστίδης*: s. .*αντ—μος*); **(7)** 218 AD *ISM* I 99, 11 (-*στί*-)
—TOMIS: **(8)** i BC ib. II 2 B, 53 (f. *Ἑστιαῖος*)
Skythia:
—OLBIA-BORYSTHENES: **(9)** iv-iii BC *Arkheologiia* (Kiev) 39 (1982) p. 32 (vase) (*Ἀριστεί*(*δης*)); **(10)** iv/iii BC ib. p. 35 (vase) (*Ἀριστεί*(*δης*)); **(11)** iii BC *IOSPE* I^2 201 I, 2 (*Ἀριστείδ*[*ης*]: f. *Διονύσιος*)
Thrace:
—BYZANTION: **(12)** hell.-imp. *IByz* 304 (f. *Λυκῖνος*)
—ODESSOS: **(13)** 20 BC *IGB* I^2 46, 27 (s. *Αἰσχρίων*)

Ἀριστεύς
Macedonia (Chalkidike):
—POTIDAIA-KASSANDREIA: **(1)** ii BC *Tekmeria* 6 (2001) pp. 54-5 no. 1, 1 (I f. *Ἀριστεύς* II); **(2)** ib. l. 1 (II s. *Ἀριστεύς* I, *Πολυξένη*)

Ἀρίστη
Macedonia (Bottiaia):
—EDESSA: **(1)** 234 AD *SEG* XXIV 534, 3 (Tataki, *Edessa* 42) (*Αὐρ. Ἀ.*)
Macedonia (Paionia):
—STOBOI (AREA): **(2)** ii-iii AD Unp. (Stobi) (*Κομεινία Ἀρίστη*: m. *Μάνιοι Γάϊος*, *Λουκιδία*, *Γαιανός*, *Λουκιανός*)
Macedonia (Pelagonia): **(3)** iii AD *IG* X (2) (2) 178 (d. *Ἀνάληψις*)

Ἀριστῆς
Thrace:
—MARONEIA: **(1)** iii-ii BC *AD* 26 (1971) Chron. p. 428 no. *ε* + *IThrakAig* E241 (*Ἀριστῆος* (gen.))
—PERINTHOS-HERAKLEIA?: **(2)** iv BC Hp., *Epid.* iv 33 (*Ἀριστῆος* (gen.), *Ἀριστείδου*—var. lect.)

Ἀριστίππα
Macedonia (Mygdonia):
—KALINDOIA: **(1)** ii/i BC *SEG* XLII 594 (-*σστί*-: d. *Μενέλαος*, m. *Ἀλκυάνα*, *Μενέλαος*, *Ἄτταλος*)

Ἀρίστιππος
Macedonia (Chalkidike):
—OLYNTHOS: **(1)** s. iv BC Berve 12 (Tataki, *Macedonians* p. 130 no. 11)
Macedonia (Orestis):
—BATTYNAIOI: **(2)** 192 AD *EAM* 186 IV, 46
Thrace:
—PERINTHOS-HERAKLEIA: **(3)** ii-iii AD *IPerinth* 65, 10 (*Ἀρί*[*σ*]*τιππος*)

Ἀριστιώ
Macedonia (Pieria):
—DION: **(1)** iii BC *SEG* XXXIV 629 (d. *Μέντωρ*)

Ἀριστίων
Cimmerian Bosporos:
—PANTIKAPAION: **(1)** iv BC *CIRB* 13 (s. *Ἀριστοφῶν*); **(2)** i/ii AD ib. 585 (f. *Ἀρτέμων*); **(3)** ib. 599 (f. *Ἐπίκαιρος*); **(4)** 275-278 AD ib. 36, 38 ([*Ἀ*]*ρι*[*σ*]*τ*[*ίω*]*ν*?: s. *Παγκλῆς*)
Macedonia (Bottiaia):
—PELLA?: **(5)** 117 BC *FD* III (2) 70 b, 6 (Tataki, *Macedonians* p. 150 no. 18) (s. *Πυθ—*)
Macedonia (Edonis):
—PHILIPPOI: **(6)** 242 BC *SEG* XII 373, 55 (Tataki, *Macedonians* p. 163 no. 7) (f. *Ἡρακλεόδωρος*)
Macedonia (Pieria):
—PYDNA: **(7)** iv BC *GRBS* 47 (2002-3) p. 122 no. 6, 4 (-*σστί*-)
Thrace:
—APOLLONIA-SOZOPOLIS: **(8)** iv/iii BC *IGB* I^2 308, 3 ([*Ἀρι*]*στίων*: s. *Σωσίας*)
—PERINTHOS-HERAKLEIA:

—(Akarnanes): **(9)** iii-ii BC *IPerinth* 61, 13 (s. *Σῶσος*)

Ἀριστοβούλα
Thrace:
—BYZANTION: **(1)** ii BC *IByz* 287 (Fıratlı–Robert pp. 55-6 no. 35) (d. *Προμαθίων*, m. *Βακίων*); **(2)** ii AD *IByz* 312 (Fıratlı–Robert p. 120 no. 202)

Ἀριστοβούλη
Macedonia:
—DEGME: **(1)** iii/ii BC *Thess. Mnem.* 57 (Tataki, *Macedonians* p. 99 no. 1) (d. *Εὐκράτης*)
Macedonia (Bottiaia):
—PELLA: **(2)** f. v BC *SEG* XXXVIII 647; *BE* 1990, no. 464 (date) (-*βό*-)
Macedonia (Chalkidike):
—TORONE: **(3)** iv/iii BC *Ét. Thas.* 3 p. 318 no. 111 (Tataki, *Macedonians* p. 190 no. 2) (d. *Βιακράτης*)
Macedonia (Lower Paionia):
—EUROPOS: **(4)** iii BC *SEG* XLIII 399 A
Thrace:
—NICOPOLIS AD NESTUM (TERRIT.): **(5)** ii AD *IG* II^2 10770; *Tekmeria* 6 (2001) pp. 149 ff. (locn.); cf. *LGPN* II s.v. (11) (d. *Ἀρίμνηστος*)

Ἀριστόβουλος
Cimmerian Bosporos:
—PANTIKAPAION: **(1)** i BC/i AD *CIRB* 304; **(2)** v-vi AD *IAK* 10 (1904) p. 88 no. 103 (f. *Φῆλιξ*)
Macedonia (Chalkidike):
—CHALKIDEIS: **(3)** ?352 BC *TAPA* 65 (1934) p. 128 no. 4, 3; *SEG* XXXVIII 637, 6; XLVI 804, 1 (s. *Καλλικράτης*)
—OLYNTHOS: **(4)** ?352 BC *TAPA* 62 (1931) p. 50 no. 3, 11; **(5)** c. 350 BC *SEG* XLVII 922 (s. *Εὐφάνης*)
—POTIDAIA-KASSANDREIA: **(6)** iv BC *RE* (14); Berve 121; *FGrH* 139 (Tataki, *Macedonians* p. 86 no. 9) (II s. *Ἀριστόβουλος* I)
—POTIDAIA-KASSANDREIA*: **(7)** f. iv BC *SEG* XLV 801 (vase) (s. *Εὐβουλίδης*)
Macedonia (Derriopos):
—STUBERRA: **(8)** 224 AD *IG* X (2) (2) 331, 5 (*Λικίνιος Ἀ.*)
Macedonia (Edonis):
—PHILIPPOI: **(9)** ii/iii AD *CIL* III 633 II b, 21 (Pilhofer 163); *CRAI* 1923, p. 277 (date); Collart, *Philippes* pls. 64-5 (Lat. P. Vettius Aristobulus)
Macedonia (Mygdonia):
—THESSALONIKE: **(10)** c. 239-229 BC *IG* XI (4) 666, 3, 24 (Tataki, *Macedonians* p. 179 no. 8) ([*Ἀρ*]*ιστόβουλος*: s. *Ἀθήναιος*)
Macedonia (Pieria):
—PHILA?: **(11)** ?iii BC *RPh* 1911, pp. 133-4 no. 36, 59; cf. Helly, *L'État thessalien* pp. 319-20 (locn.) (f. *—νις*); **(12)** *RPh* 1911, pp. 133-4 no. 36, 71; cf. Helly, *L'État thessalien* pp. 319-20 (locn.) (*Ἀριστόβου*(*λος*)—ed., *Ἀριστόβ*(*ι*)*ος*?: s. *—λαος*)
Scythia Minor:
—ISTROS: **(13)** v BC Unp. (Avram, defixio) 2, 5 (*Ἀρι*(*σ*)*τόβόλος*)
Thrace:
—BYZANTION: **(14)** i BC *IByz* 212 (Fıratlı–Robert pp. 70-1 no. 71) (s. *Ἀριστοκράτης*, f. *Ἀριστοδίκη*)
—BYZANTION (TERRIT.): **(15)** ii-iii AD *IByz* 28 (*IGB* I^2 474) (s. *Μῆνις*)
—LYSIMACHEIA: **(16)** c. 208 BC *FD* III (4) 135, 2-3, 7, 15 (s. *Θεογένης*)
—MARONEIA: **(17)** m. iii BC *IThrakAig* E231 ([*Ἀ*]*ριστόβο*[*υλος*]: s. *Ἡγίας*); **(18)** ii BC *IG* XII (8) 161, 14 (s. *Ἀριστ—*); **(19)** ii-i BC *IThrakAig* E212, 47 (s. *Ξένων*)
—STRYME? (NR.): **(20)** c. 425-400 BC Bakalakis, *Oinos Ismarikos* p. 553 (*IThrakAig* E120) (s. *Νουμήνιος*)

'Αριστογένης
Macedonia (Bottiaia):
—BEROIA: **(1)** 223 BC *IBer* 4, 17 (Ἀριστογέν[ης]: s. Ἕρμων)
Macedonia (Edonis):
—AMPHIPOLIS (NR.): **(2)** a. 357 BC Hatzopoulos, *Actes Amphipolis* p. 43 no. 8, 6 (*SEG* XLI 562) (s. Ἀστῖνος)
Tauris:
—CHERSONESOS: **(3)** f. iii BC ib. XL 615 A, 15 (Ἀριστογέν[ης]: f. Παρθένιος); **(4)** ii AD *IOSPE* I^2 425, 2 (f. Δημοκράτης)

'Αριστόδημος
Cimmerian Bosporos:
—BOSPOROS: **(1)** imp. *TAM* IV (1) 239, 1 (s. Ταυρέας) ?= (*2*); **(2)** ib. l. 2, 5 (f. Λύκος, Σαμβίων) ?= (*1*)
—GORGIPPIA: **(3)** f. iii BC *CIRB* 1137 A II, 13 (f. Σκύθας); **(4)** ib. 1137 B II, 51 (s. Σκύθας)
—PANTIKAPAION: **(5)** i BC/i AD ib. 323, 1; **(6)** ib. l. 3; **(7)** 82 AD ib. 76, 22 (*SEG* XVIII 310) ([Ἀρ]ιστόδημος: s. Καλλισθένης); **(8)** ii AD *CIRB* 690
Macedonia: **(9)** 278 BC *RE* (15) (Tataki, *Macedonians* p. 262 no. 264); **(10)** ii BC *IG* II^2 9270 (Tataki, *Macedonians* p. 262 no. 265; *FRA* 3463) (f. Σκίρτος)
Macedonia (Chalkidike):
—MENDE?: **(11)** hell.? Dimitsas 772 (s. Γέρων)
—OLYNTHOS: **(12)** ?354 BC *TAPA* 69 (1938) pp. 52-3 no. 6, 13 + 70 (1939) p. 62; Hatzopoulos, *Actes Chalc.* p. 80 (date) (f. Ἀθηνόδωρος)
—POTIDAIA-KASSANDREIA: **(13)** m. iii BC *Thess. Mnem.* 167 (Tataki, *Macedonians* p. 86 no. 11) (s. Ἀρτέμων)
Macedonia (Derriopos):
—STUBERRA: **(14)** c. 41-48 AD *IG* X (2) (2) 323, 27 (f. Διονυσοφάνης)
Macedonia (Mygdonia):
—CHARAKOMA?: **(15)** 149 AD Papazoglou, *Villes* pp. 215-16 (Tataki, *Macedonians* p. 98 no. 2) (I f. Ἀριστόδημος II ὁ καὶ Πρόκλος); **(16)** Papazoglou, *Villes* pp. 215-16 (Tataki, *Macedonians* p. 98 no. 1) (Ἀ. ὁ καὶ Πρόκλος: II s. Ἀριστόδημος I)
Macedonia (Orestis):
—BATTYNAIOI: **(17)** 192 AD *EAM* 186 I, 55 (Ἀριστόδημο[ς]: f. Φίλων); **(18)** ib. 186 II, 57 (s. Φίλων)
Skythia:
—OLBIA-BORYSTHENES: **(19)** iii BC *IOSPE* I^2 201 II, 18 (f. Δαϊκράτης)
—TANAIS: **(20)** ii AD *CIRB* 1262, 23 ([Ἀ]ριστόδημος: s. Ἐρωνᾶς); **(21)** 188 AD ib. 1242, 12 (f. Συνέκδημος); **(22)** 228 AD ib. 1282, 17 (s. Δάδας)
Thrace: **(23)** 160 BC *BGU* 2390, 40-1; cf. La'da E788 (f. Πτολεμαῖος)
—AGATHOPOLIS: **(24)** iv/iii BC *Thracia Pontica* 5 p. 112 no. 2, 12 with fig. 2 (Ἀρισστόδη[μος]: f. Ἀντίοχος)
—PERINTHOS-HERAKLEIA:
——(Podargoi): **(25)** iii-ii BC *IPerinth* 61, 19 (s. Ἀρίσταρχος)
—PERINTHOS-HERAKLEIA?: **(26)** iv BC Hp., *Epid.* iv 4 (s. Φίλις)

'Αριστοδίκη
Thrace:
—BYZANTION: **(1)** i BC *IByz* 212 (Fıratlı-Robert pp. 70-1 no. 71) (d. Ἀριστόβουλος)
—SESTOS: **(2)** f. iv BC *IG* II^2 10262 (*FRA* 6637)

'Αριστόδικος
Scythia Minor:
—KALLATIS?: **(1)** hell.? *Dacia* 13 (1969) p. 257 no. 1063 (amph.)

'Αριστοκλέα
Macedonia (Pieria):
—DION: **(1)** 213 AD *Essays Laourdas* p. 108 no. 6; *Stud. Edson* p. 294 (date)

'Αριστόκλεια
Macedonia (Chalkidike):
—TORONE (NR.): **(1)** i BC/i AD *SEG* III 496 + XXIX 592 (d. Νέστωρ)
Macedonia (Pieris):
—GALEPSOS: **(2)** hell.? Dimitsas 914; Hatzopoulos, *MI* 1 p. 187 n. 3 (locn.) (-κληα: d. Πολύδωρος)

'Αριστοκλείδης
Macedonia (Bottiaia):
—BEROIA: **(1)** 239-229 BC *IBer* 45, 31 (Tataki 222) (f. Αἰσχυλῖνος)
—EDESSA: **(2)** f. ii BC *SEG* XLIII 388, 1 (Tataki, *Edessa* 36) (f. Εὐρυνόα)
Macedonia (Pieria):
—PYDNA: **(3)** c. 330 BC *IG* II^2 339 b, 2 (Tataki, *Macedonians* p. 170 no. 5) ([Ἀριστοκ]λείδης?: f. Λύκος)

'Αριστοκλῆς
Cimmerian Bosporos:
—GORGIPPIA: **(1)** f. iii BC *CIRB* 1137 A I, 10 (s. Σκύθας) ?= (*4*); **(2)** ib. l. 50 (f. Πασίων); **(3)** ib. 1137 A II, 46 (f. Θεόμνηστος); **(4)** ib. 1137 B I, 24 ([Ἀρ]ιστοκλῆς: s. Σκύθας) ?= (*1*)
—NYMPHAION: **(5)** f. iii BC *SEG* XLV 997. 9
—PANTIKAPAION: **(6)** i AD *CIRB* 338; **(7)** 275-278 AD ib. 36, 63 (Ἀριστοκλ(ῆς)—Vinogradov)
Macedonia: **(8)** f. iii BC *Dritte Reise* 47, 1, 4 (Tataki, *Macedonians* p. 262 no. 266) (s. Εἰκάδιος, f. Μηνογένης)
Macedonia (Bottiaia):
—BEROIA: **(9)** 223 BC *IBer* 4, 34 (s. Μικίων)
Macedonia (Chalkidike):
—OLYNTHOS: **(10)** c. 244-242 BC *PPetr* II 35 a, 15 (III 54 b; *PP* 2539; Tataki, *Macedonians* p. 130 no. 12; La'da E1923)
—POTIDAIA-KASSANDREIA: **(11)** c. 300 BC *IG* II^2 1956, 114 (Tataki, *Macedonians* p. 86 no. 12; *FRA* 2777)
—TORONE: **(12)** ?353 BC *SEG* XXIV 574, 5; Hatzopoulos, *Actes Chalc.* p. 80 (date) (s. Παρμένων) ?= (*13*); **(13)** *SEG* XXIV 574, 15; Hatzopoulos, *Actes Chalc.* p. 80 (date) (f. Καλλιτέλης) ?= (*12*)
Macedonia (Edonis):
—AMPHIPOLIS: **(14)** s. iv BC *PAE* 1981, p. 25 with pl. 43 β, 2-3 (f. Θεαίνετος, ...ạ...); **(15)** *IGB* I^2 459, 4 (Tataki, *Macedonians* p. 47 no. 21) (Ἀριστοκλείους (gen.): f. Δήμη); **(16)** hell. Dimitsas 851 ([Ἀρι]στοκλῆς: s. Ἀμύντας); **(17)** hell.? *SEG* L 564
Macedonia (Mygdonia):
—LETE: **(18)** f. ii BC ib. XLVI 764, 17 (Ἀριστοκλ[ῆς]: f. Διοσκουρίδης)
Macedonia (Paionia):
—ANTIGONEIA? (TREMNIK (MOD.)): **(19)** c. 200 AD ib. XL 559
Macedonia (Pieria):
—PHILA?: **(20)** ?iii BC *RPh* 1911, pp. 133-4 no. 36, 114; cf. Helly, *L'État thessalien* pp. 319-20 (locn.) (s. Ἀγ—)
Scythia Minor:
—ISTROS?: **(21)** iii/ii BC *Stud. Tacheva* pp. 280-1, 2 (Ἀρ[ι]στοκλῆ[ς]: f. Διοσκουρίδης)
—KALLATIS: **(22)** s. iii BC *ISM* III 35 B, 37 (f. Δίων)
Skythia:
—OLBIA-BORYSTHENES: **(23)** iii BC *IOSPE* I^2 201 I, 59 (s. Εὑρήμων)
—OLBIA-BORYSTHENES (NR.): **(24)** iv/iii BC *VDI* 1985 (1), p. 41 (vase)
Tauris:
—CHERSONESOS: **(25)** iii BC Solomonik, *NEPKh* 30 (f. Μαρκώ)
Thrace:
—ABDERA: **(26)** ii-i BC *SEG* XXIV 627 (*IThrakAig* E62) (Ἀριστοκλήους (gen.): f. Μηνόδωρος)
—LYSIMACHEIA: **(27)** c. 208 BC *FD* III (4) 135 I, 24 (s. Μητρόδωρος); **(28)** ib. 135 III, 18 (s. Κάλλων)
—ODESSOS: **(29)** i BC *IGB* I^2 154 (PM 922) (s. Ζῆνις) ?= (*31*); **(30)** i BC-i AD *IGB* I^2 117, 2 (Ἀ. νεώτ.: s. Ἀντίφιλος); **(31)** 8 BC ib. 46, 39 (s. Ζῆνις) ?= (*29*); **(32)** s. ii AD ib. 220 (*CCET* I 57; PM 1418) (s. Ἕλλην); **(33)** c. 170 AD *JÖAI* 15 (1912) p. 51 no. 16, 10 (f. —άνης)
—PERINTHOS-HERAKLEIA:
——(Geleuntes): **(34)** iii-ii BC *IPerinth* 61, 34 (Ἀρ(ι)στοκλεῦς (gen.): f. Λεοντιάδης)

'Αριστοκράτεια
Macedonia (Bottiaia):
—PELLA: **(1)** iv BC Tataki, *Macedonians* p. 150 no. 19 (d. Δαμασίας)

'Αριστοκράτης
Cimmerian Bosporos:
—GORGIPPIA: **(1)** f. iii BC *CIRB* 1137 B II, 56 (s. Δημήτριος)
—PANTIKAPAION: **(2)** ii-i BC ib. 263; cf. KW pl. 32 no. 446 (f. Γαττίων)
Macedonia (Bottiaia):
—PELLA: **(3)** f. v BC *SEG* XXXVIII 647; *BE* 1990, no. 464 (date) (f. Πυθαγόρης); **(4)** iv/iii BC *AD* 16 (1960) Mel. p. 82; *SEG* XXXIX 623; XLIII 444 (tiles)
Macedonia (Chalkidike):
—AKANTHOS: **(5)** v/iv BC ib. XLI 554 (vase)
Macedonia (Derriopos):
—STUBERRA: **(6)** 74 AD *IG* X (2) (2) 325, 25 (f. Ποσείδιππος)
Macedonia (Edonis):
—AMPHIPOLIS: **(7)** hell.? *SEG* XXX 549 (f. Φιλοξενίς)
Macedonia (Paionia):
—ASTREA: **(8)** c. 230-200 BC *BCH* 45 (1921) p. 17 III, 69 (Tataki, *Macedonians* p. 72 no. 3) (f. Ἀντίγονος)
Scythia Minor:
—ISTROS: **(9)** i BC-i AD *ISM* I 191 I, 13 ([Ἀ]ριστοκράτης); **(10)** ib. 191 II, 43 (s. Κλύτος); **(11)** ib. l. 46 (s. Πολυαίνετος); **(12)** ib. 270, 1, 3; **(13)** ii AD ib. 212, 26 (s. Ἀρτεμίδωρος); **(14)** 138 AD ib. 193 I, 33 (s. Ἡρόδωρος); **(15)** 222-225 AD ib. 100 B, 16, 19 (Ἀριστοκράτ(ης): I f. Αὐρ. Ἀρτεμίδωρος, Αὐρ. Ἀριστοκράτης II); **(16)** ib. l. 18 (Αὐρ. Ἀριστοκράτ[ης]: II s. Ἀριστοκράτης I)
Skythia:
—OLBIA-BORYSTHENES: **(17)** iii BC Dubois, *IGDOlbia* 109, 3 (*SEG* XXXVII 673); **(18)** *IOSPE* I^2 32 A, 91 (Maier, *Mauerbauinschr.* 82); **(19)** *IOSPE* I^2 201 I, 13 (s. Ἀρίστων); **(20)** ib. l. 46 (s. Θεοκλῆς); **(21)** ib. l. 52 (f. Ἀρίστων); **(22)** ib. l. 64 (f. Δάμασος)
—OLBIA-BORYSTHENES*: **(23)** iv BC *ZOOID* 23 (1900) p. 24 no. 19 (vase) (Ἀριστοκρατέω (gen.))
Thrace: **(24)** 218 BC *PEnt* 48, 1, 6, 8, verso (Velkov 30; La'da E711)
—APOLLONIA-SOZOPOLIS: **(25)** iv BC *BMN-Burgas* 4 (2002) p. 125 no. 21 ([Ἀρισ]τοκράτης?, [Αὐ]τοκράτης?: f. —ντα)
—BYZANTION: **(26)** i BC *IByz* 212 (Fıratlı-Robert pp. 70-1 no. 71) (Ἀριστοκράτηος (gen.): f. Ἀριστόβουλος)
—LYSIMACHEIA: **(27)** 309-307 or 301-296 BC *IG* II^2 1957, 19 + *ZPE* 146 (2004) p. 85 (*FRA* 3385)

'Αριστόκριτος
Cimmerian Bosporos:
—NYMPHAION: **(1)** iii BC *CIRB* 912 II, 7 (s. Θράσυλλος)
Macedonia (Edonis):
—PHILIPPOI (TERRIT.)?: **(2)** imp. *CIL* III 7379 (Lat. Aristocritus: s. Κλεοπάτρα: locn.—Loukopoulou)

SKYTHIA:

—OLBIA-BORYSTHENES: (3) iii BC *IOSPE* I^2 201 I, 11 (s. Ποσειδώνιος); (4) ib. l. 36 (f. Ποσειδώνιος)

Ἀριστολάϊος

SCYTHIA MINOR:

—ISTROS: (1) 138 AD *ISM* I 193 I, 15 (Ἀριστο[λ]άϊος: s. Θεόφιλος); (2) ib. l. 91 (s. Θεόφιλος)

Ἀριστόλαος

MACEDONIA: (1) c. 280-246 BC *IG* XII (6) 120, 6, 30; Paus. vi 17. 3 (Tataki, *Macedonians* p. 263 no. 267; La'da E1433) (s. Ἀμεινίας)

MACEDONIA (BOTTIAIA):

—BEROIA: (2) 223 BC *IBer* 4, 14 (f. Εὔφρων)

MACEDONIA (ELIMEIA):

—AIANE (TERRIT.): (3) ii AD *EAM* 49 a (f. Λύκος)

MACEDONIA (ORESTIS):

—BATTYNAIOI: (4) 192 AD ib. 186 I, 48 (f. Ὀρέστης)

SCYTHIA MINOR:

—ISTROS: (5) i BC-i AD *ISM* I 191 II, 20 (s. Θεόφιλος); (6) 138 AD ib. 193 II, 72 (s. Σατυρίων)

Ἀριστόλεως

MACEDONIA (MYGDONIA):

—ARETHOUSA: (1) c. 360 BC *IG* II^2 1176, 23 (Tataki, *Macedonians* p. 69 no. 4) (f. Πήληξ)

THRACE:

—MARONEIA: (2) c. 365-336 BC Schönert-Geiss, *Maroneia* 536-64 (coin)

Ἀριστόλοχος

TAURIS:

—CHERSONESOS: (1) f. iii BC *SEG* XL 615 A, 6 (Ἀριστόλ[οχος]: f. Ἡρόστρατος); (2) ii/iii AD Solomonik, *NEPKh* 57 ([Ἀ]ριστό[λο]χος: s. Θρασύλοχος)

THRACE: (3) 218-214 BC *SB* 11061, 7; *PHamb* 26, 11, verso; 188, 7, 10-11, 14; 189, 6, 12-13, 15, etc.; *BGU* 1265, 7; 1944, 5, [8], [10], etc.; 1958, 6, 12-13, 15 etc.; 1959, 10; 1960, 6 (Velkov 31; La'da E827) (s. Στράτιος: t.e.); (4) 160 BC *BGU* 2390, 39 (La'da E712) (Ἀριστ[ό]λ[ο]χος)

Ἀριστόλυκος

MACEDONIA (MYGDONIA):

—THESSALONIKE?: (1) ii AD *IG* X (2) (1) 709 (s. Νικησώ)

Ἀριστόμαχος

CIMMERIAN BOSPOROS:

—MYRMEKION: (1) f. iv BC *CIRB* 874 (f. Καλλίμαχος)

—PANTIKAPAION: (2) f. ii AD ib. 651 (s. Ἀνθεστήριος)

MACEDONIA: (3) 221 BC *PEnt* 8, 1 and verso (Tataki, *Macedonians* p. 263 no. 270; La'da E1436); (4) ?219 BC *PUG* III 105, 7 (Tataki, *Macedonians* p. 263 no. 269; La'da E1435); (5) *PUG* III 105, 12 (Tataki, *Macedonians* p. 263 no. 271; La'da E1434) (s. Ἡρ—); (6) a. 188 BC *IPrusa ad Olympum* 1001, 2 (Tataki, *Macedonians* p. 263 no. 272) (f. Κόρραγος)

MACEDONIA (BOTTIAIA):

—BEROIA: (7) 41-44 AD *IBer* 60, 7 (Tataki 223)

MACEDONIA (CHALKIDIKE):

—OLYNTHOS: (8) m. iv BC *IG* II^2 10018 (Tataki, *Macedonians* p. 130 no. 13; *FRA* 5885) (s. Χαιρεφάνης)

MACEDONIA (MYGDONIA):

—KALINDOIA: (9) a. 98 AD *SEG* XLII 582, 50 (f. Δημήτριος)

SCYTHIA MINOR:

—ISTROS: (10) iii BC *ISM* I 8, 5 (f. Κλέαρχος); (11) ii AD ib. 57, 5 (*Eastern cults* pp. 102-3 no. 65); *ISM* I 198, 7 (f. Ἡράκων) ?= (*12*); (12) 138 AD ib. 193 I, 45 (s. Ἡράκων) ?= (*11*)

—TOMIS: (13) i BC ib. II 2 A, 54 (f. Τιμοκλῆς)

THRACE:

—APOLLONIA-SOZOPOLIS: (14) v/iv BC *IGB* I^2 436 (s. Ἑκαταῖος)

—BYZANTION: (15) ii AD X. Eph. ii. 5 etc. (fict.)

—PERINTHOS-HERAKLEIA:

——(Akarnanes): (16) iii-ii BC *IPerinth* 61, 8 (f. Δέλφων)

—PERINTHOS-HERAKLEIA*: (17) c. 304 AD *Act. Sanct.* Oct. IX p. 545 (Lat. Aristemacus, Aristemachus—var. lect.)

—STRYME?: (18) c. 375-350 BC *IThrakAig* E142 ([Ἀρι]στόμαχος: f. Εὐβούλη)

—ZONE: (19) iii BC *IG* XII (8) 155, 5

THRACE?: (20) 316-309 BC ib. II^2 1956, 32; *Ancient Macedonia* 5 p. 445 with n. 10 (date) (*FRA* 2499)

Ἀριστομένης

MACEDONIA (MYGDONIA):

—KALINDOIA: (1) ii-i BC *SEG* XXVIII 541, 4; *Anthémonte–Kalindoia* 1 pp. 100-1 (locn.) (f. Φιλώτας); (2) *SEG* XXVIII 541, 5; *Anthémonte–Kalindoia* 1 pp. 100-1 (locn.) (s. Φιλώτας, f. Φιλώτας)

—SOCHOS (MOD.): (3) s. ii AD *SEG* XLVIII 839

SCYTHIA MINOR:

—ISTROS: (4) ii BC *ISM* I 31, 1; (5) i BC-i AD ib. 191 II, 48 (s. Μήνιος); (6) ii AD ib. 198, 10 (s. Ἀρτεμᾶς); (7) 138 AD ib. 193 I, 83 (s. Ἑστιαῖος)

—KALLATIS: (8) iii BC *IGB* I^2 307 bis, 4 (Ἀριστομένειος (gen.): f. Γλαυκίας)

SKYTHIA:

—OLBIA-BORYSTHENES: (9) s. iv BC Dubois, *IGDOlbia* 107, 3 (Ἀριστομένιος (nom.)); (10) *SEG* L 702 IV, 2 (Ἀριστ(ο)μένης); (11) ib. l. 9

THRACE:

—HERAION TEICHOS: (12) c. 265-260 BC *FD* III (3) 207, 3 (?f. Μελεσικράτης)

—LYSIMACHEIA: (13) m. ii BC *ISestos* 38 b, 9 (f. Ἡγησίδημος)

—ODESSOS: (14) iv/iii BC *IGB* I^2 13 bis, 2 (s. Διονύσιος); (15) iii/ii BC ib. 88 bis (s. Αἴολος)

—STRYME?: (16) s. v BC *SEG* XLVII 1103 (*IThrakAig* E112) (f. Βιτίων)

THRACE?: (17) i BC/i AD *RE* s.v. Aristomachos (22); *GP* 122; cf. *LGPN* I s.v. (108) (or Thasos?: Ἀριστόμαχος—Pl.: painter)

Ἀριστομήδης

MACEDONIA: (1) 142 BC *SB* 12720, 2, 23 (Tataki, *Macedonians* p. 476 no. 45); cf. La'da E1411 (Ἀριστόδημος—La'da per err.: f. Ἀντίμαχος)

THRACE:

—APOLLONIA-SOZOPOLIS: (2) ?iv BC *IGB* I^2 455 ([Ἀρ]ιστομήδης: f. Ἀντήνωρ)

Ἀριστόνα

MACEDONIA (PIERIA):

—KOLINDROS (MOD.): (1) 122 AD *SEG* XXXI 632

Ἀριστονίκα

MACEDONIA: (1) 177 BC *SGDI* 1872, 3, 6 (Tataki, *Macedonians* p. 264 no. 273) (slave/freed.)

Ἀριστονίκη

CIMMERIAN BOSPOROS:

—GORGIPPIA: (1) s. iv BC *CIRB* 14 (d. Ξενόκριτος, m. Δημητρίη: locn.—Vinogradov)

—PANTIKAPAION: (2) ii AD ib. 657 (Ἀρ(ι)στονείκη: d. Ὅπλων)

MACEDONIA (DERRIOPOS):

—STUBERRA: (3) iv/iii BC *IG* X (2) (2) 318 (d. Θεόδωρος)

Ἀριστόνικος

CIMMERIAN BOSPOROS:

—PANTIKAPAION: (1) i BC-i AD *CIRB* 299 (f. Ἔρως)

—PANTIKAPAION*: (2) f. i AD ib. 360; cf. KW pl. 34 no. 486 (freed.)

MACEDONIA (CHALKIDIKE):

—OLYNTHOS: (3) ?iv BC *SEG* XXXVIII 642; cf. XLVII 923 (s. Πολεμοκράτης); (4) m. iv BC *RE* (4); Berve 132 (Stephanis 367; Tataki, *Macedonians* p. 131 no. 15); (5) s. iv BC *SEG* XIX 595 (Tataki, *Macedonians* p. 131 no. 16) (f. Ἡρακλεόδωρος)

MACEDONIA (EDONIS):

—AMPHIPOLIS: (6) hell. *SEG* XXIV 596 (f. Πολέμαρχος)

SCYTHIA MINOR:

—ISTROS: (7) i BC-i AD *ISM* I 191 II, 3 (-νει-: s. Ἀθηνόδωρος); (8) ib. l. 47 (-νει-: s. Ὄσπος); (9) 138 AD ib. 193 I, 54 (-νει-: f. Αἰσχρίων); (10) ib. l. 92 (-νει-: s. Θεότιμος); (11) ib. 193 II, 71 (-νει-: f. Διογένης)

SKYTHIA:

—OLBIA-BORYSTHENES: (12) ii AD *IOSPE* I^2 89, 7 (Α. ὁ καὶ Βασιλεύς: s. Διονύσιος)

—TANAIS: (13) f. ii AD *CIRB* 1266, 7 (Ἀριστ[ό]νεικος: f. Μάσταρος)

TAURIS:

—CHERSONESOS?: (14) 115 AD *IOSPE* I^2 543

THRACE:

—MESAMBRIA: (15) ii/i BC *IGB* V 5103, 3 (-νει-: f. Κράτων)

Ἀριστονόη

MACEDONIA (EDONIS):

—AMPHIPOLIS (TERRIT.): (1) f. iii BC *BCH* 55 (1931) p. 172 no. 1

Ἀριστόνομος

THRACE:

—ODESSOS: (1) ?ii BC *IGB* I^2 87 (f. Ἀγαθήνωρ)

Ἀριστόνους

MACEDONIA (BOTTIAIA):

—BEROIA: (1) s. ii BC *IBer* 24, 3 (Tataki 224) (s. Διονύσιος); (2) 122 BC *IBer* 134, 8

—PELLA: (3) c. 360-316 BC *RE* (8); Berve 133; *IG* XII (9) 221, 2, 7; *SEG* XXXVI 331 B, 24 = Perlman, *City and Sanctuary* N.1 II, 17 (Tataki, *Macedonians* p. 150 no. 20); cf. *Eretria* XI pp. 188-90 (ident., date) (or Macedonia (Eordaia): s. Πεισαῖος); (4) f. iii BC *AD* 16 (1960) Mel. p. 82; *SEG* XXXIX 623; XLIII 444 (tiles)

MACEDONIA (CHALKIDIKE):

—TORONE: (5) c. 440-420 BC *IG* I^3 1379 (Tataki, *Macedonians* p. 191 no. 3; *FRA* 7139) (s. Ἑρμοτέλης)

MACEDONIA (MYGDONIA):

—THESSALONIKE: (6) ii BC *IG* X (2) (1) 28, 4 (f. Ἀρίστανδρος); (7) i AD ib. 242, 3 (Ἀριστόνου(ς): s. Πόπλιος)

THRACE:

—ABDERA: (8) ii BC ib. XII (8) 161, 16 (f. Ἀρχαγόρας)

Ἀριστόξενος

MACEDONIA (BOTTIAIA):

—BEROIA: (1) iii-ii BC *IBer* 154 ([Ἀρισ]τόξενος)

MACEDONIA (MYGDONIA):

—THESSALONIKE: (2) ii BC *IG* X (2) (1) 28, 5 (f. Ἀντίμαχος)

SKYTHIA:

—NIKONION: (3) v-iv BC *MASP* 5 (1966) p. 80 n. 22 (vase)

—OLBIA-BORYSTHENES: (4) c. 340-320 BC *Num. Sb.* 1977 (1), pp. 110-20 (weight) (Ἀριστόξ(ενος))

Ἀριστοπάτρα

MACEDONIA (ORESTIS): (1) iv BC Str. 702 a (Tataki, *Macedonians* p. 204 no. 5); cf. Fraser, *Cities* pp. 224-6 (m. Κράτερος, Ἀμφοτερός: fict.?)

Ἄριστος

MACEDONIA (BOTTIAIA):
—BEROIA: **(1)** 223 BC *IBer* 4, 25 (Ἄ(ρ)ιστος: f. Ἀδαῖος)
MACEDONIA (LYNKESTIS):
—HERAKLEIA?: **(2)** ii-iii AD *IG* X (2) (2) 131 (f. Σέμνος)

Ἀριστοτέλης

MACEDONIA (CHALKIDIKE):
—APHYTIS: **(1)** ?351 BC *A΄ Panell. Synedr. Epigr.* pp. 80-1, 11, 26 (s. Θέωρος); **(2)** ib. l. 15, 24 (s. Ἀντιφάνης)
—OLYNTHOS: **(3)** ?352 BC *SEG* XXXVIII 637, 8 (s. Κτησίας)
—STAGEIROS: **(4)** 384-322 BC *RE* (18); Supplbd. 11 (-); Berve 135; *FD* III (1) 400, [3], 7; *IEph* 2011, 1; *CR* 8 (1958) p. 108 (date); cf. *SEG* XXXVIII 410 (Tataki, *Macedonians* p. 175 no. 2) (s. Νικόμαχος, Φαιστίς, f. (nat.) Νικόμαχος, Πυθιάς, ?f. (ad.) Νικάνωρ)
SKYTHIA:
—OLBIA-BORYSTHENES: **(5)** V BC Dubois, *IGDOlbia* 97 (vase) (*SEG* XLVI 953)

Ἀριστοτίμα

MACEDONIA (PIERIA):
—DION: **(1)** v/iv BC ib. XXV 705 (d. Σώσος)

Ἀριστότιμος

MACEDONIA (CHALKIDIKE):
—CHALKIDEIS: **(1)** ?353 BC ib. XXIV 574, 3; XXXVII 576, 4; Hatzopoulos, *Actes Chalc.* p. 80 (date) (f. Εὐφραντίδης)

Ἀριστοφάνης

CIMMERIAN BOSPOROS:
—PANTIKAPAION: **(1)** iv BC *CIRB* 166 (s. Ἡραῖος)
MACEDONIA: **(2)** 327 BC *RE* Supplbd. 4 (8a); Berve 136 (Tataki, *Macedonians* p. 264 no. 274)
MACEDONIA (BOTTIAIA):
—MIEZA: **(3)** hell. *AM* 27 (1902) p. 314 no. 28, 1; **(4)** iii/ii BC *SEG* XLIII 406; 407; 409; 411, [1] (f. Εὔιππος, Λύσων, Καλλικλῆς); **(5)** ib. 423; 424 (s. Λύσων, Δημαρέτη); **(6)** f. ii BC ib. 413; 414; 419; 421; 422 (s. Καλλικλῆς, Φίλα, f. Ἀργεῖος, Λύσων)
—PELLA: **(7)** iii BC Akamatis, *Amph. Pellas* p. 31 no. PAR4 (amph.) (*SEG* L 613)
MACEDONIA (CHALKIDIKE):
—OLYNTHOS: **(8)** 343 BC Aeschin. ii 154-5; 158 (Tataki, *Macedonians* p. 131 no. 17; *FRA* 5886)
—POTIDAIA-KASSANDREIA?: **(9)** hell.-imp. *IG* II² 8996 (Tataki, *Macedonians* p. 86 no. 13; *FRA* 2778) (f. Ἀπολλώνιος)
SCYTHIA MINOR:
—TOMIS: **(10)** i BC *ISM* II 2, 25
THRACE:
—BYZANTION: **(11)** c. 265-187 BC *RE* (14); *PP* 16513; Fraser, *Ptol. Alex.* 2 pp. 662-3 nn. 96 ff. (s. Ἀπελλῆς)

Ἀριστόφιλος

MACEDONIA (MYGDONIA):
—THESSALONIKE: **(1)** ?105 BC *IG* X (2) (1) 135, 4

Ἀριστοφῶν

CIMMERIAN BOSPOROS:
—PANTIKAPAION: **(1)** iv BC *CIRB* 13 (f. Ἀριστίων); **(2)** iii BC ib. 241; cf. KW pl. 55 no. 738 (s. Φορμίων)
MACEDONIA (PAIONIA):
—KAVADARCI (MOD.): **(3)** ?ii AD *Sp.* 75 (1933) p. 39 no. 128 (f. Μακεδών); **(4)** ib. (s. Μακεδών)
THRACE:
—BYZANTION?: **(5)** ii-i BC *IByz* 349 (Ἀριστο[φ]ῶν)

Ἀρίστυλλα

MACEDONIA (BOTTIAIA):
—BEROIA: **(1)** iii BC *IBer* 150 (Tataki 225) (m. Παρμένεια)

Ἀριστώ

CIMMERIAN BOSPOROS:
—PANTIKAPAION: **(1)** f. iv BC *CIRB* 167
MACEDONIA (EDONIS):
—AMPHIPOLIS: **(2)** hell. *AD* 24 (1969) Chron. p. 355 no. 4 (d. Διονύσιος); **(3)** ii BC *IG* II² 8079 (Tataki, *Macedonians* p. 48 no. 23; *FRA* 499) (-σστώ)
—AMPHIPOLIS?: **(4)** iii BC *SEG* XXIV 609 = XLIII 372 (d. Νουμήνιος)
TAURIS:
—CHERSONESOS: **(5)** ?iv-iii BC ib. XLIV 657 (weight) (Ἀριστοῦς (gen.)); **(6)** f. iii BC Solomonik, *NEPKh* 139 (d. Ἀγνόκριτος)

Ἀρίστων

CIMMERIAN BOSPOROS:
—GORGIPPIA: **(1)** f. iii BC *CIRB* 1137 B II, 23 (s. Πάτρων); **(2)** ii AD ib. 1151, 3 (s. Πόθος) ?= (5); **(3)** s. ii AD ib. 1148, 4 (Ἀρίσ(τ)ων); **(4)** 173-210 AD ib. 1134 E, 4 (Ἀρίστων—Tokhtas'ev); **(5)** ii/iii AD ib. 1179, 26 (s. Πο—) ?= (2); **(6)** ib. l. 34 (s. Βάγιος); **(7)** ib. l. 37 (Ἀ[ρί]στων: s. Χρηστίων); **(8)** ib. l. 59 (f. Πόθις)
—NYMPHAION: **(9)** i/ii AD ib. 935 (Ἀρ[ί]στων: f. Φάννης)
—PANTIKAPAION: **(10)** i AD ib. 133, 1 (I f. Ἀρίστων II); **(11)** ib. l. 1, 3 (II s. Ἀρίστων I); **(12)** m. i AD ib. 501, 4 (s. Πτολλᾶς, Εὐκράτεια); **(13)** ib. l. 4 (s. Πτολλᾶς, Εὐκράτεια); **(14)** i/ii AD ib. 79 A, 4 ([Ἀρ]ίστων); **(15)** 82 AD ib. 76, 14 (*SEG* XVIII 310) (s. Καλοῦς); **(16)** *CIRB* 76, 23 (*SEG* XVIII 310) (s. Θεότιμος); **(17)** ?s. ii AD *CIRB* 90, 4 (s. Πτολλᾶς); **(18)** 478 AD *SEG* XLVIII 995 (f. Σανάγας)
—THEODOSIA: **(19)** iii AD *CIRB* 947 B, 4 ([Ἀ]ρίστων: s. Δαμᾶς)
MACEDONIA: **(20)** 331 BC *RE* (28); Berve 137 (Tataki, *Macedonians* p. 264 no. 275); **(21)** s. iii BC *Milet* I (3) 67 I, 8 (Tataki, *Macedonians* p. 265 no. 277) (f. Ταυρέας); **(22)** ?219 BC *PUG* III 105, 8 (Tataki, *Macedonians* p. 265 no. 276; La'da E1437) (s. Θεωτ—)
MACEDONIA (BOTTIAIA):
—BEROIA: **(23)** ii-iii AD *IBer* 317, 2 (Tataki 226) ([Ἀ]ρίστων: f. Γαλέστης); **(24)** ?ii/iii AD *ILeukopetra* 153, 2 (?f. (nat.) Ἀρτεμισία)
MACEDONIA (CHALKIDIKE):
—CHALKIDEIS: **(25)** c. 373-370 BC *Olynthus* 9 pp. 78-82 nos. 126-36 (coin); *Ancient Macedonia* 1 p. 254 (date)
—OLYNTHOS: **(26)** ?c. 355-349 BC *TAPA* 69 (1938) p. 56 no. 9, 6
MACEDONIA (EORDAIA):
—EUIA? (POLYMYLOS (MOD.)): **(27)** ii/iii AD *A΄ Panell. Synedr. Epigr.* p. 57 no. 4 (*SEG* XLIX 774); **(28)** iv-vi AD *AD* 32 (1977) Chron. p. 228 (mosaic); *BE* 1999, no. 325 (locn.) (s. Νικόλαος)
MACEDONIA (MYGDONIA):
—KALINDOIA: **(29)** 68-98 AD *SEG* XLII 580, 65 (s. Ἀρριδαῖος)
—THESSALONIKE: **(30)** iii AD *IG* X (2) (1) 445, 2 (Λ. Ἀ.: f. Φουσκιανὴ Διονυσία)
—THESSALONIKE?: **(31)** ii-iii AD ib. 731
MACEDONIA (PAIONIA): **(32)** s. iv BC *RE* (32); **(33)** f. iii BC Polyaen. iv 12. 3; cf. *RE* (32) (s. Αὐδωλέων)
MACEDONIA*: **(34)** ii-iii AD *EAM* 18; 101 (sculptor)
SCYTHIA MINOR:
—ISTROS: **(35)** iv/iii BC *ISM* I 248 (s. Πανσανίας); **(36)** 138 AD ib. 193 I, 86 (s. Φιλόδημος); **(37)** iii AD ib. 303, 5 (f. Πώμη); **(38)** ib. l. 6 (s. Χρύσιππος, Πώμη)
——Chora Dagei: **(39)** c. 159-161 AD ib. 378 C, 23 (f. Ἀρτεμίδωρος)
—KALLATIS: **(40)** iv/iii BC ib. III 125, 4 (s. Ἐχ—); **(41)** f. iii BC ib. 66, 8 (Ἀρίστω[ν]); **(42)** i BC/i AD ib. 40, 4; 41, 13; 42, 10 (I f. Ἀρίστων II); **(43)** ib. 40, 4; 41, 12; 42, 10; 44, 4, 32; 45, 5 (II s. Ἀρίστων I, f. Ἀρίστων III); **(44)** f. i AD ib. 44, 4, 32; 45, 1, 4 (III s. Ἀρίστων II); **(45)** ii-iii AD ib. 89 (*CCET* IV 101) (s. Ἀν—); **(46)** 241-244 AD *ISM* III 74 A, 26 (s. Εὐπρέπης)
—TOMIS: **(47)** i AD ib. II 126 (f. Διοσκουρίδης)
SKYTHIA:
—OLBIA-BORYSTHENES: **(48)** m. iv BC Dubois, *IGDOlbia* 13, 4 (f. Θεοκλῆς); **(49)** iii BC *IOSPE* I² 191 (f. Εὐβίοτος); **(50)** ib. 201 I, 24 (f. Θρασυδάμας); **(51)** ib. l. 26 (f. Ἱκέσιος); **(52)** ib. l. 42 (s. Θεοκλῆς); **(53)** ib. l. 52 (s. Ἀριστοκράτης); **(54)** ib. l. 13-14 (f. Ἀριστοκράτης, Θεοκλῆς); **(55)** ib. 201 II, 9 (s. Νικήρατος); **(56)** ii BC *ISM* III 166 (s. —πολις); **(57)** ii-i BC *SEG* XXX 950 (vase) (s. Καλλίνικος); **(58)** imp. *IOSPE* I² 147, 8 (f. Παππίας); **(59)** ii AD ib. 93, 10 (s. Οὐαργάδακος)
—TANAIS: **(60)** ii AD *CIRB* 1262, 30 (Ἀρίστω[ν]); **(61)** f. ii AD ib. 1264 A, 6 (s. Θεότιμος); **(62)** ib. 1266, 11 (s. Π—); **(63)** 104 AD ib. 1259, 22 (s. Δῖος); **(64)** 225 AD ib. 1279, 10 (f. Ἀβρόζεος); **(65)** ib. l. 19 ([Ἀ]ρίστων—Tokhtas'ev: s. —στρατος); **(66)** ib. 1280, 14; 1281, 17 (s. Φαζίναμος); **(67)** ib. 1280, 24 (Ἀρίστω[ν]: f. —ιος); **(68)** 228 AD ib. 1283, 9 (s. Μενέστρατος)
TAURIS:
—CHERSONESOS: **(69)** iv/iii BC Kats p. 101 no. 67 (amph., tile) (f. Κοτυτίων); **(70)** ib. pp. 109-10 no. 99 (amph., tile) (f. Πρύτανις); **(71)** iii BC *IOSPE* I² 346, 3 (f. —νος); **(72)** c. 200-185 BC Kats p. 90 no. 28 (amph.) (s. Χορειός); **(73)** ii BC Vinogradov, *Pont. Stud.* p. 370; **(74)** i AD *SEG* XLVI 927, 1; **(75)** ii AD *VDI* 1938 (3), p. 77 no. 6 (Ἀρίσ[τω]ν: f. Ἑρμῆς); **(76)** *IOSPE* I² 385, 3 (f. —ων); **(77)** ib. 396; **(78)** ib. 432, 2 (*Τ. Φλ. Ἀ.*: f. *Τ. Φλ. Ἀπολλώνιος*) ?= *(81) (85)*; **(79)** ib. l. 3 (*Τ. Φλ. Ἀ.*: s. *Τ. Φλ. Ἀπολλώνιος*); **(80)** f. ii AD *KSIIMK* 15 (1947) p. 59, 5 (Solomonik, *NEPKh* 112 d); cf. *VDI* 1993 (4), p. 63 (s. Ἀπολλων—) ?= *(91)*; **(81)** Solomonik, *NEPKh* 113, 10 (*Φλ. Ἀ.*: f. —ων) ?= *(82) (78)*; **(82)** ib. l. 13 (*Φλ. Ἀ.*) ?= *(81)*; **(83)** *IOSPE* I² 359, 19, 35; 423; *SEG* XLVIII 999, 38 (s. Ἀττίνας) ?= *(94)*; **(84)** *IOSPE* I² 391 (Solomonik, *NEPKh* 112 c) ([Ἀρ]ίστων: s. Ζῆθος); **(85)** c. 114-130 AD *IOSPE* I² 357, [24]; 358, 11; 359, 21, 25; Solomonik, *NEPKh* 112, 7; *VDI* 1960 (3), pp. 154-5, 20-1; *SEG* XLVIII 999, 36, 42 (*Τ. Φλ. Ἀ.*: I s. *Φλ. Ἀγέπολις*, f. *Τ. Φλ. Ἀρίστων* II, *Τ. Φλ. Ἀγέπολις*) ?= *(78)*; **(86)** *IOSPE* I² 359, 21; *VDI* 1960 (3), pp. 154-5, 21; *SEG* XLVIII 999, 42 (*Τ. Φλ. Ἀ.*: II s. *Τ. Φλ. Ἀρίστων* I); **(87)** c. 120-130 AD Solomonik, *NEPKh* 112, 15 (f. Ἀπολλώνιος); **(88)** 129 AD *IOSPE* I² 359, 30 (s. Ἀπολλωνίδης); **(89)** 129-130 AD ib. l. 23; *VDI* 1960 (3), pp. 154-5, 21 (f. Ζῆθος); **(90)** *IOSPE* I² 359, 29; *VDI* 1960 (3), pp. 154-5, 27 (s. Ἀντίλοχος); **(91)** 130 AD ib. l. 24 (s. Ἀπολλώνιος) ?= *(80)*; **(92)** 174 AD *SEG* XLV 985 A, 34 (s. Θεαγένης); **(93)** ib. l. 36 (*Τ. Φλ. Ἀ.*) ?= *(95)*; **(94)** ib. l. 39 ([Ἀρίσ]των?: f. Ἀττίνας) ?= *(83)*; **(95)** 185 AD *IOSPE* I² 404, 51 ([*Τ.*] *Φλ. Ἀ.*) ?= *(93)*; **(96)** iii AD *NE* 11 (1974) p. 41 no. 6 (Ἀρίστ[ων]?)
THRACE: **(97)** 178 BC *PFreib* 23, 9; cf. La'da E816 ([Ἀρ]ίστων); **(98)** 142 BC *SB* 12720, 3; cf. La'da E749 (f. Ἡρακλείδης)
—BYZANTION: **(99)** s. vi BC Hdt. iv 138 (*RE* (18)); **(100)** 409 BC X., *HG* i 3. 18 (*FRA* 1390); **(101)** ?262-254 BC Nachtergael, *Les Galates* 5, 27; 7, [27]; cf. Stephanis 88; *CID* IV 45; 47 (date) (f. Αἰνησίδαμος); **(102)** i BC *IByz* 155 (Fıratlı–Robert pp. 105-6 no. 166)

(s. *Ἀσκλαπιάδας*); **(103)** s. i AD *IByz* 32, 5 (f. *Σωτήριχος*)
—LYSIMACHEIA: **(104)** iii BC *IThrakAig* E265; **(105)** *IG* XII (9) 792
—MESAMBRIA: **(106)** iii BC *IGB* I² 335 ter (PM 1014); **(107)** i BC *IGB* I² 344, 3
—NICOPOLIS AD ISTRUM (TERRIT.): **(108)** 227 AD *ILB* 438 I, 14 (Lat. Aristo: s. Atron. Severus)
—ODESSOS: **(109)** v/iv BC *IGB* I² 101 bis (*[Ἀ]ρίστω[ν]?*: f. *Ἱππῶναξ*); **(110)** iv BC ib. 101 ter (tile); cf. V 5042 (f. *Νικίας*)
—PHILIPPOPOLIS-TRIMONTIUM (TERRIT.): **(111)** iii AD ib. III 1095
—SALYMBRIA: **(112)** ii-iii AD *IByz* S 66 (f. *Θεόμνηστος*)
—SKAPTOPARA: **(113)** 238-244 AD *IGB* V 5872 (f. *Ἀρτεμίδωρος*)

Ἀριστῶναξ
THRACE:
—ABDERA: **(1)** c. 395-360 BC Lorber, *Amphipolis* p. 178 (coin)

Ἀριστωνᾶς
SCYTHIA MINOR:
—ISTROS: **(1)** iii-ii BC Unp. (Avram, defixio) 4, 3

Ἀριστώνυμος
SKYTHIA:
—OLBIA-BORYSTHENES (BEREZAN (MOD.)): **(1)** m. vi BC Dubois, *IGDOlbia* 43

Ἄριχος
SKYTHIA:
—OLBIA-BORYSTHENES: **(1)** c. 475-450 BC Karyshkovskii, *MO* pp. 34 ff.; *SNG BM Black Sea* 374-6; 379-80; 385-9; Dubois, *IGDOlbia* pp. 8-9 (coin); Masson, *OGS* 3 p. 138 (name); cf. Vinogradov, *Pont. Stud.* p. 156 no. 8; *SEG* XLVIII 1004 (n. pr.?)
THRACE:
—BYZANTION:
——(Athyras): **(2)** i BC *IByz* 224 (Fıratlı–Robert p. 80 no. 94)

Ἄρκαπος?
MACEDONIA (ELIMEIA):
—AIANE: **(1)** m. v BC *SEG* XLIII 363 E; cf. *BE* 1994, no. 385 (n. pr.?)

Ἀρκαρία
MACEDONIA (BOTTIAIA):
—BEROIA: **(1)** f. iii AD *IBer* 98, 9 (Tataki 1087) (*Πομπωνία Ἀ. ἡ καὶ Ἡγήσιλλα*: m. *Σεπτίμιος Πομπώνιος Προκλιανὸς Ὀρέστης*)

Ἀρκέσας
THRACE:
—LYSIMACHEIA: **(1)** m. ii BC *ISestos* 38 b, 1 (s. *Διονυσόδωρος*); **(2)** ib. l. 4 (s. *Νικόμαχος*)

Ἀρκεσίλαος
MACEDONIA: **(1)** c. 323 BC *RE* (14); Berve 142 (Tataki, *Macedonians* p. 265 no. 278) ?= *(2)*; **(2)** c. 322-313 BC *IG* VII 4257, 9 (*IOrop* 5; Tataki, *Macedonians* p. 265 no. 279) (f. *Ἀλκάνωρ*) ?= *(1)*
THRACE:
—LYSIMACHEIA: **(3)** c. 208 BC *FD* III (4) 134 I, 22 (f. *—λαος*)
—PERINTHOS-HERAKLEIA?: **(4)** v/iv BC Hp., *Epid.* vi 3.5; vi 3. 14

Ἀρκεσίλας
THRACE:
—BYZANTION: **(1)** iv/iii BC *IByz* 59 (Fıratlı–Robert p. 49 no. 12) (s. *Ἡρώϊχος*)

Ἀρκεσίλεως
THRACE:
—APOLLONIA-SOZOPOLIS: **(1)** v/iv BC *IGB* I² 410 (s. *Μνησῖνος*)

Ἀρκεσίλη
THRACE:
—STRYME?: **(1)** c. 375-350 BC *SEG* XXVII 335 (*IThrakAig* E139) (d. *Ἡράκλειος*)

Ἀρκεσῖνος
MACEDONIA (MYGDONIA):
—THESSALONIKE: **(1)** 223 BC *IG* X (2) (1) 2, 4 (*Ἀρκε[σί]νος*: f. *Πάνταυχος*)

Ἀρκεσώ
TAURIS:
—CHERSONESOS: **(1)** iii BC Solomonik, *NEPKh* 125 (*Ἀρ[κ]εσώ?*: d. *Ἱπ......ος* (gen.))

Ἁρμαγένης
SCYTHIA MINOR:
—KALLATIS: **(1)** s. iii BC *ISM* III 35 A, 33 (*Ἀ.*—lap., *(Ἑ)ρμαγένης?*: s. *Δαμοφῶν*)

Ἀρμάδης
CIMMERIAN BOSPOROS:
—PANTIKAPAION: **(1)** iv BC *CIRB* 168; Zgusta, *FNS* 616 (f. *Γόρδις, Ἀρτεμιδώρη*)

Ἀρμένα
MACEDONIA (EDONIS):
—PHILIPPOI: **(1)** ii-i BC *BCH* 59 (1935) p. 158 no. 54 (Pilhofer 303) (d. *Σωτᾶς*)

Ἄρμεννος
MACEDONIA (BOTTIAIA):
—BEROIA: **(1)** 223 BC *IBer* 4, 16 (s. *Ἀδαῖος*)
—TYRISSA? (ASVESTARI (MOD.)): **(2)** f. ii BC *SEG* XLVII 999, 24 (*Ἄρμε[νν]ος*)
MACEDONIA (EORDAIA?):
—EUIA: **(3)** 181 BC *EAM* 87, 16 (Hatzopoulos, *MI* 2 pp. 41-2 no. 17) (*Ἄρμεν[νος]*: f. *Νικάνωρ*)

Ἄρμηος
SKYTHIA:
—OLBIA-BORYSTHENES: **(1)** f. ii AD *Drev. Prichern.* 3 pp. 27-8, 12 (s. *Μουρ—*)

Ἁρμοδία
MACEDONIA (BOTTIAIA):
—PELLA: **(1)** iii-ii BC Dimitsas 132 (d. *Εὔνομος*)

Ἁρμόδιος
MACEDONIA: **(1)** 69 BC *IFayoum* 135, 31 (Tataki, *Macedonians* p. 476 no. 46; La'da E1438) (s. *Ἀσκληπιάδης*: katoikos)
MACEDONIA (PAIONIA):
—STOBOI: **(2)** ii-iii AD *AJA* 88 (1984) p. 581 (*Σεπτ. Ἁρμόδ[ιος]?*); **(3)** ib. (*Σεπτ. Ἁρμόδις*)
MACEDONIA (PIERIA):
—DION: **(4)** ii-iii AD Oikonomos 42
SCYTHIA MINOR:
—ISTROS: **(5)** iii BC *ISM* I 1, 2 (Migeotte, *L'emprunt* 40) (*Ἁρμ[ό]δ[ι]ος*: f. *—δωρος*)
THRACE:
—APOLLONIA-SOZOPOLIS: **(6)** v/iv BC *IGB* I² 409 bis (f. *Βαλαίκων*)
—MARONEIA: **(7)** iii BC *AD* 52 (1997) Chron. p. 880; **(8)** *IThrakAig* E233
—ODESSOS: **(9)** ?s. iv BC *Memnonion* 382 (La'da E1915)

Ἁρμονία
MACEDONIA (ELIMEIA):
—VELVENDOS (MOD.): **(1)** s. ii AD *EAM* 57 (*Ἁρμον[ία]*: d. *Κασσάνδρα*, m. *Λεύκιππος*)
TAURIS:
—CHERSONESOS: **(2)** iii BC *IOSPE* I² 506 (*[Ἁ]ρμονία*)

Ἁρμόνιος
THRACE:
—NICOPOLIS AD NESTUM*: **(1)** v-vi AD Beševliev 235

Ἁρμοννώ
MACEDONIA (EDONIS):
—PHILIPPOI (TERRIT.): **(1)** f. ii AD Pikoulas, *Chora* pp. 125-6 no. 18 (Pilhofer 619) (*Οὐλπ. Ἁ.*: freed.?)

Ἀρνάκης
SKYTHIA:
—TANAIS: **(1)** ii AD *CIRB* 1262, 28 (s. *Ἀπατούριος*)

Ἀρνίας
MACEDONIA (CHALKIDIKE):
—STREPSA?: **(1)** b. 348 BC *SEG* XXXVII 583, 4 (s. *Νεμήνιος*)
MACEDONIA (MYGDONIA):
—THESSALONIKE: **(2)** c. 208 BC *FD* III (4) 134, 10 (Tataki, *Macedonians* p. 179 no. 9) (f. *Ζω...*)
TAURIS:
—CHERSONESOS: **(3)** f. ii BC *IGB* I² 39, 6 (*[Ἀ]ρνίου?* (gen.)—ed., *[Ἀπολλ]ωνίου?*: f. *Χρῆστος*)

Ἀρνίς
MACEDONIA (MYGDONIA): **(1)** imp. Dimitsas 685 (*Οὐλπ. Ἀ.*)

Ἀροάστιρος?
SKYTHIA:
—TANAIS: **(1)** 244 AD *CIRB* 1287, 29 (*Ἀροάστ[ιρος]?*, *Ἀροάσι[ρος]*—Latyshev: f. *Γοδόσαυος*)

Ἀρπαλεύς
THRACE:
—APOLLONIA-SOZOPOLIS: **(1)** iv BC *IGB* I² 463 bis, 2 (s. *Ζώπυρος*)

Ἀρπάλη
THRACE:
—BYZANTION: **(1)** hell. Unp. (Sayar) (d. *Καλλίστρατος*)

Ἁρπάλης
MACEDONIA (CHALKIDIKE):
—OLYNTHOS: **(1)** ?350 BC *TAPA* 59 (1928) p. 226, 4; Hatzopoulos, *Actes Chalc.* p. 80 (date) (*Ἁρπάλεος* (gen.): f. *Εὐβουλίδης*)
THRACE:
—ODESSOS: **(2)** f. ii AD *IGB* I² 78 ter, 5 (*CCET* I 30) (*Ἁρπάλεος* (gen.): f. *Ἕλλην*)

Ἁρπαλίς
THRACE:
—PAUTALIA: **(1)** ii-iii AD *IGB* IV 2053, 9 (*Οὐλπ. Ἁρπαλίς*)

Ἅρπαλος
MACEDONIA: **(1)** iv BC Arr., *An.* i 14. 3; D.S. xvii 17. 4 (f. *Κάλας*) ?= *(3)*; **(2)** c. 360-324 BC *RE* (2); Berve 143 (Tataki, *Macedonians* p. 194 no. 3) (s. *Μαχάτας*); **(3)** c. 357 BC *RE* (1) (Tataki, *Macedonians* p. 194 no. 2) ?= *(1)*; **(4)** c. 285 BC *SEG* XXXVIII 619, 4 (f. *Λιμναῖος*)
MACEDONIA (BOTTIAIA):
—AIGAI: **(5)** s. iv BC ib. XXVI 781 = XXXV 781 (s. *Πευκόλαος*)
—BEROIA: **(6)** 248 BC *IBer* 3, 4, 9, 14 (Tataki 228); cf. *RE* Supplbd. 4 (3a) ?= *(7)*; **(7)** 223 BC *IBer* 4, 11 (f. *Πολεμαῖος*) ?= *(6)*; **(8)** 178-172 BC *RE* (3); *Syll*³ 636, 5; *BCH* 63 (1939) p. 159 inv. 5575, 7 (Tataki 230; Tataki, *Macedonians* p. 76 no. 14) (*[Ἅρπ]α[λος]*—*BCH*: s. *Πολεμαῖος*); **(9)** s. ii BC *IBer* 202 (s. *Πύθων*); **(10)** ii/i BC ib. 2, 35, 40; **(11)** 41-44 AD ib. 60, 3 (Tataki 231) (I f. *Ἅρπαλος* II); **(12)** *IBer* 60, 3 (Tataki 229) (II s. *Ἅρπαλος* I)
—PELLA (NR.): **(13)** iii BC *Α´ Panell. Synedr. Epigr.* p. 183 no. 7 (*SEG* XXX 582) (s. *Διονυσογένης*); **(14)** iii/ii BC *Α´ Panell. Synedr. Epigr.* p. 183 no. 7 (*SEG* XXX 582) (f. *Ζώπυρος*)

Macedonia (Chalkidike):
—olynthos: (15) iii/ii bc *IG* xii (3) 41-2 (Tataki, *Macedonians* p. 131 no. 18) (f. *Σῖμος*)
Macedonia (Edonis):
—amphipolis: (16) ?c. 167 bc *SEG* xxiv 580, 8; cf. Hatzopoulos, *MI* 1 p. 136 (f. *Ἑρμοίτας*)
Macedonia (Mygdonia):
—kalindoia: (17) c. 307 bc ib. 62, 39 (f. *Φα—*)
Macedonia (Pieria):
—pydna: (18) iv bc *GRBS* 43 (2002-3) p. 110 no. 1 a, 9
Thrace: (19) 190 or 189 bc *PHeid* viii 417, 13, 33, [41] (La'da E713)

Ἁρπαλοσκύτα?
Macedonia (Bottiaia):
—aigai: (1) s. iv bc *SEG* xxxv 790 + xlviii 872; cf. *BE* 1999, no. 336

Ἁρποκράτης
Thrace:
—apollonia-sozopolis: (1) i-ii ad *IGB* 1^2 401, 15 (f. *Πῖος*)

Ἁρποκρατίων
Thrace:
—perinthos-herakleia: (1) ii ad *IPerinth* 27-8 (*Π. Αἰλ. Ἁ. ὁ καὶ Πρόκλος*)

Ἀρραβαῖος
Macedonia: (1) ?417-413 bc *IG* 1^3 89, 67; (2) 406 bc *Suda E* 3695 (*Ἀρριβαῖος—Suda*, *Ἀρρι-(δ)αῖος?*); (3) c. 334 bc Arr., *An.* i 12. 7; 1. 20. 10 (f. *Ἀμύντας, Νεοπτόλεμος*) ?= (*11*); (4) c. 260-240 bc *IG* iv $(1)^2$ 96, 67 (Perlman, *City and Sanctuary* E.3) (f. *Κάσσανδρος*) ?= (*12*) (*16*); (5) 179 bc *PFreib* 35, 6 (Tataki, *Macedonians* p. 310 no. 29); cf. La'da E1755 ([*Ἐρρε*]*βαῖος*: I f. *Ἀρραβαῖος* II); (6) *PFreib* 35, [6], [9], 13, [15], 16 (*PP* 9743; Tataki, *Macedonians* p. 310 no. 28; La'da E1755) (*Ἐρρεβ*[*αῖος*]: II s. *Ἀρραβαῖος* I)
Macedonia (Edonis):
—amphipolis: (7) s. iv bc *AD* 24 (1969) Chron. p. 355 no. 3 (s. *Ἀθηνίων*)
Macedonia (Elimeia):
—kalamitsi (mod.): (8) m. ii ad *EAM* 51 (*Ἀρά-*: f. *—βιλας*)
Macedonia (Lynkestis): (9) s. v bc Th. iv 79. 2; *IG* 1^3 89, 10, 56-58 (Tataki, *Macedonians* p. 202 no. 7) (I s. *Βρομερός*, ?f. *Ἀρραβαῖος* II: king); (10) f. iv bc Arist., *Pol.* 1311 b, 13; cf. *Ancient Macedonia* 2 pp. 511-16 (stemma); Tataki, *Macedonians* p. 201 no. 5 (II ?s. *Ἀρραβαῖος* I, f. *Ἀέροπος*: king) ?= (*17*); (11) c. 370-336 bc Berve 144 (Tataki, *Macedonians* p. 201 no. 6) (s. *Ἀέροπος*) ?= (*3*); (12) 315 bc *IG* xii (2) 645, 25; *Ancient Macedonia* 2 pp. 514-16 (ident., stemma) (Tataki, *Macedonians* p. 202 no. 8) ?= (*4*)
Macedonia (Mygdonia):
—lete: (13) s. iv bc Hatzopoulos, *MI* 2 pp. 93-4 no. 79, 7 (*Ἀρραβαῖος*)
Macedonia (Orestis):
—battynaioi: (14) 192 ad *EAM* 186 III, 53 (*Ἀραβέος*: s. *Νίκανδρος*)
—nestorion (mod.): (15) ii ad ib. 198 (*Ἀρρα-β*[*αῖος*]: ?f. *—γόνη*)
—pentavryso (mod.): (16) ?f. iii bc ib. 190 with comm. (f. *Κάσσανδρος*) ?= (*4*)
Macedonia (Pelagonia): (17) c. 359 bc Tod, *GHI* ii 148; cf. Papazoglou, *Villes* p. 278 (ident.) (f. *Μενέλαος*) ?= (*10*)

Ἀρρενείδης
Skythia:
—olbia-borysthenes: (1) iv/iii bc *IOlbia* 71 II, 5 (Dubois, *IGDOlbia* 11)

Ἀρριανός
Tauris:
—chersonesos: (1) ?ii ad *IOSPE* 1^2 451, 3

Thrace:
—perinthos-herakleia: (2) i bc-i ad? *IPerinth* 57, 6 (s. *Ἀγαθίας*); (3) iii ad *IGB* iii 884, 23 ([*Αὐ*]*ρ. Ἀ.*)
—philippopolis-trimontium: (4) m. iii ad ib. 884 c, 13; cf. v 5400 (*Αὐρ. Ἀ.*)

Ἀρριδαῖος
Macedonia: (1) s. v bc *RE* (2); Hatzopoulos, *MI* 2 pp. 19-20 no. 1 A, 1-2; Tod, *GHI* ii 129, 20 (Tataki, *Macedonians* p. 266 no. 283) (*Ἐρριδαῖος—MI*: s. *Ἀμύντας*, f. *Ἀμύντας* III); (2) c. 400-348 bc *RE* (3); *Macedonia* 2 pp. 699-701; cf. Beloch, *GG* iii (2) pp. 66-7 (Lat. Arridaeus: s. *Ἀμύντας* III, *Γυγαία*); (3) c. 358-317 bc *RE* (4); Berve 781 (*Φίλιππος* III *Ἀ.*: s. *Φίλιππος* II, *Φίλιννα* (Larisa): king); (4) 323-318 bc *RE* (5); Berve 145 (Tataki, *Macedonians* p. 266 no. 282); (5) c. 278-276 bc *RE* (6); *FGrH* 260 F 3. 11 (Armenian); (6) c. 250 bc *IG* xii (9) 212, 2; cf. *SEG* xliii 591; *Ancient Macedonia* 6 pp. 609-10 (date) (s. *Ἀλέξανδρος*); (7) 238 bc *PPetr*^{2} 1, 80 (Tataki, *Macedonians* p. 266 no. 281; La'da E1439); (8) c. 230-200 bc *SEG* xli 89, 2 (*FRA* 3462; Tataki, *Macedonians* p. 261 no. 260) (*Ἀριδ*[*αῖος*]?)
Macedonia (Chalkidike):
—antigoneia?: (9) hell.? Robert, *OMS* 2 pp. 1296-7 (Tataki, *Macedonians* p. 64 no. 1) (s. *Ἀρχίδαμος*)
Macedonia (Derriopos):
—stuberra: (10) 74 ad *IG* x (2) (2) 325, 45 (f. *Ῥοτίλιος*); (11) ib. 326, 34 (f. *Δημήτριος*)
Macedonia (Edonis):
—amphipolis?: (12) 359-336 bc Procl., *in R.* ii 116 (fict.?)
Macedonia (Elimeia):
—aiane (territ.): (13) f. ii ad *EAM* 9 (f. *Φιλωτέρα*)
—velvendos (mod.): (14) hell.? *SEG* xlviii 872 (loomweight)
Macedonia (Elimeia)?: (15) v bc *RE* (1); *Macedonia* 2 p. 18 (Tataki, *Macedonians* p. 194 no. 4) (f. *Δέρδας*, ?f. *Πανσανίας*)
Macedonia (Mygdonia):
—kalindoia: (16) ii bc *AEMTh* 6 (1992) p. 399 (*Ἀρι-*: f. *Στραττώ*); (17) 68-98 ad *SEG* xlii 580, 65 (f. *Ἀρίστων*)
Macedonia?: (18) ?m. iii bc *IEph* 1451, 2; cf. *Eretria* xi p. 335 (ident.) ([*Ἀρ*]*ριδαῖος*) ?= (*19*); (19) 254 bc *IDidyma* 492, 24 (Welles, *RC* 18) ?= (*18*)
Thrace:
—bisanthe-panion: (20) 188-159 bc *JÖAI* 23 (1926) Beibl. col. 151 no. 87, 9 (*OGIS* 301); cf. Tataki, *Macedonians* p. 266 no. 284 (f. *Διόδωρος*)

Ἀρρωκότης?
Thrace:
—pautalia (territ.): (1) ii-iii ad *IGB* v 5854 (*Ἀρρ*(*ω*)*κότης*)

Ἀρσαῖος
Macedonia: (1) iv bc Arr., *An.* iv 13. 4, 7; cf. Hoffmann, *Makedonen* p. 180 (Tataki, *Macedonians* p. 267 no. 287) (*Ἀ.*—mss., *Ἀρσέας*—Hoffmann: f. *Ἐπιμένης, Εὐρύλοχος*)

Ἀρσάκης
Macedonia: (1) 190 or 189 bc *PHeid* viii 417, 19, 25-6, 36, 39 (La'da E1440)
Skythia:
—olbia-borysthenes: (2) ii ad *IOSPE* 1^2 93, 7; Zgusta, *PNS* 544 (f. *Ζωΐλος*); (3) *IOSPE* 1^2 204 (f. *Ἄδοσθος*)

Ἀρσάκις
Cimmerian Bosporos:
—pantikapaion: (1) iv-v ad *IAK* 10 (1904) p. 86 no. 100

Ἀρσακόμας
Skythia:
—skythai: (1) ii ad Luc., *Tox.* 44-55 (s. *Μαριάντας*: fict.)

Ἀρσαλίων
Skythia:
—olbia-borysthenes: (1) imp. *IOSPE* 1^2 148, 4; Zgusta, *PNS* 60 (f. *Κούκαις*)

Ἀρσάνας
Kolchis:
—vani (mod.): (1) ii-i bc Vinogradov, *Pont. Stud.* p. 577; cf. Braund, *Georgia* p. 146

Ἀρσενία
Thrace:
—perinthos-herakleia: (1) iii-iv ad *IPerinth* 312 (*Αὐρ. Ἀρσεν*[*ία*])

Ἀρσένιος
Macedonia (Bottiaia):
—beroia: (1) 214 ad *ILeukopetra* 65, 18 (Tataki 232)
Macedonia (Mygdonia):
—thessalonike?: (2) iii ad *IG* x (2) (1) 839, 1 (*Αὐρ. Ἀ.*: ?f. *Αὐρήλιος*)

Ἀρσένις
Cimmerian Bosporos:
—pantikapaion: (1) v-vi ad *ZOOID* 31 (1913) p. 71 no. 164

Ἀρσηούαχος
Skythia:
—olbia-borysthenes: (1) i/ii ad *IOSPE* 1^2 200, 3; Zgusta, *PNS* 61 (*-σηόαχος*: f. *Ζαλσίς*); (2) ii ad *IOlbia* 80, 5 (*-σήαχος*: f. *Ἀλέξανδρος*); (3) *IOSPE* 1^2 82, 9; Zgusta, *PNS* 61 (s. *Κάσαγος*); (4) *IOSPE* 1^2 83, 3 (s. *Εὐρησίβιος*); (5) ib. 93, 4; 129, 3 (*Ἀρσήοχος*—129: f. *Μ. Οὔλπ. Πύρρος*); (6) ib. 175, 8 (f. *Ἀβλώνακος*)

Ἀρσινόη
Cimmerian Bosporos:
—pantikapaion: (1) ii ad *CIRB* 658 ([*Ἀρ*]*σινόη*)
Macedonia: (2) c. 316-270 bc *RE* (26) (*PP* 14491) (d. *Πτολεμαῖος* I *Σωτήρ* (Eordaia), *Βερενίκη*, m. *Πτολεμαῖος, Λυσίμαχος, Φίλιππος*: queen); (3) c. 245-204 bc *RE* (27) (*PP* 14492); *IG* ix $(1)^2$ (1) 56 d; cf. *ZPE* 138 (2002) p. 145 (d. *Πτολεμαῖος* III *Εὐεργέτης*, *Βερενίκη*, m. *Πτολεμαῖος* V *Ἐπιφάνης*: queen); (4) c. 65-41 bc *RE* (28) (*PP* 14493) (d. *Πτολεμαῖος* XII *Αὐλητής*)
Macedonia (Bottiaia):
—pella?: (5) iv/iii bc *RE* (25) (*PP* 14490) (d. *Λυσίμαχος*, ?d. *Νικαία*, m. *Πτολεμαῖος* III *Εὐεργέτης, Λυσίμαχος, Βερενίκη*: queen)
Macedonia (Eordaia): (6) iv bc *RE* (24); cf. *FGrH* 631 F 1 (Tataki, *Macedonians* p. 267 no. 288) (?d. *Μελέαγρος*, m. *Πτολεμαῖος* I *Σωτήρ, Μενέλαος*)
Macedonia?: (7) 63 bc *POxy* 1644, 12, 20 (d. *Πτολεμαῖος*, m. *Πασίων, Πτολεμαῖος, Ἀπολλώνιος, Βερενίκη*)

Ἀρσίφρων
Scythia Minor:
—istros (nr.): (1) hell.? *ISM* i 109

Ἀρταβάζης
Macedonia: (1) 232 or 207 bc *CPR* xviii 19, [392], 397, 404 (Tataki, *Macedonians* p. 267 no. 290; La'da E1441)

Ἀρτεμᾶς
Cimmerian Bosporos:
—gorgippia: (1) ii ad *CIRB* 1166, 3 ([*Ἀρ*]*τεμᾶς*)

Macedonia (Bisaltia):
—euporia?: **(2)** ii-iii ad *RA* 1945, p. 38 (f. *Διοσκουρίδης*)
Macedonia (Derriopos):
—stuberra: **(3)** 74 ad *IG* x (2) (2) 326, 49 (s. *Λυσίμαχος*)
Macedonia (Eordaia):
—akrini (mod.): **(4)** ii bc *EAM* 90, 2 with pl. 32 (*Ἀρτεμ[ᾶ]ς*: s. *Νικάνωρ*)
Macedonia (Mygdonia):
—lete?: **(5)** ii-iii ad *SEG* i 277 (*Ἀρτεμᾶνει* (dat.))
—thessalonike: **(6)** i ad *IG* x (2) (1) 418, 1 (*Γν. Ἰούλ. Ἀ.*: s. *Φιλόμουσος*, *Θυμέλη*); **(7)** 132 ad ib. 503, 2 (f. *Ἀπολλώνιος ὁ καὶ Μάξιμος*)
Scythia Minor:
—istros: **(8)** ii ad *ISM* i 198, 11 (f. *Ἀριστομένης*); **(9)** 138 ad ib. 193 I, 13 (s. *Ἀρισταγόρας*); **(10)** ib. l. 38 (*Ἀρτεμᾶ* (gen.): f. *M. Οὔλπ. Δημήτριος*); **(11)** ib. l. 63 (s. *Ἀρισταγόρας*); **(12)** ib. l. 101 (s. *Φίλων*); **(13)** ib. 193 II, 73 (f. *Φίλων*)
—istros [nr.]:
——Vicus Secundini: **(14)** 202 ad ib. 344, 9 (Lat. Artema (abl.): s. *Διοσκουρίδης*)

Ἀρτεμῆς
Skythia:
—olbia-borysthenes: **(1)** iv/iii bc *VDI* 1977 (2), p. 152 (vase) (1985 (1), p. 41) (*Ἀρτεμέω* (gen.))
—olbia-borysthenes (berezan (mod.)): **(2)** v bc *SEG* xxxii 754 (vase) (*Ἀρτεμέω* (gen.))

Ἀρτεμία
Macedonia (Lynkestis):
—herakleia: **(1)** v-vi ad ib. xxxiii 508 (mosaic)

Ἀρτεμιδώρα
Macedonia (Bottiaia):
—beroia: **(1)** 184 ad *ILeukopetra* 17, 2 (Tataki 233); **(2)** iii ad *IBer* 362, 3 (Tataki 234) (?d. *Παρασκευή*)
Macedonia (Mygdonia):
—thessalonike: **(3)** i/ii ad *SEG* xxxviii 710; **(4)** ii/iii ad ib. xlix 814 II, 8 (*Ῥουπιλλία Ἀ.*); **(5)** m. iii ad *IG* x (2) (1) 204, 15 (*Γ. Ἰουλ. Ἀ.*: d. *Γ. Ἰούλ. Ἀρτεμίδωρος*, *Αὐρ. Γαϊανή*, m. *Γ. Ἰούλ. Ῥουφινιανὸς Ἀρτεμίδωρος*, *Π. Αἴλ. Ῥουφινιανὸς Νικόστρατος*, *Π. Αἴλ. Νεβία Ἀρτεμιδώρα*); **(6)** ib. 205, 10; 558, 2 (*Π. Αἴλ. Νεβία Ἀ.*: d. *Π. Αἴλ. Ῥουφινιανὸς Πρόκλος*, *Γ. Ἰουλ. Ἀρτεμιδώρα*, m. *Τ. Ἰούλ. Λυσίμαχος*); **(7)** ib. l. 3 (d. *Φιλωτέρα*); **(8)** 240-249 ad ib. 159, 14; 164, 15 (*Φλ. Αἰλιανὴ Σεμπρωνία Ἀ.*: m. *Φλ. Αἰλιανὸς Σεμπρώνιος Δράκων*, *Φλ. Αἰλιανὸς Σεμπρώνιος Ἀρτεμίδωρος*)
—thessalonike (nr.): **(9)** ii-iii ad ib. 1003, 1; **(10)** iii ad ib. 1006, 4 (*Αὐρ. Ἀρτεμιδώρα*)
—thessalonike?: **(11)** ii ad ib. 703 (?m. *Δανάη*); **(12)** ib. 915; cf. *Tyche* 10 (1995) pl. 14 no. 19b; **(13)** ii-iii ad *IG* x (2) (1) 728, 3
Macedonia (Odomantike):
—sirrha?: **(14)** ii-iii ad Dimitsas 826, 3, 5 (*Dodoni* 18 (1989) p. 248 no. 57) (d. *Βάρβαρος*)
—skotoussa?: **(15)** ii-iii ad *BCH* 18 (1894) p. 439 no. 2 (Dimitsas 845) = Dimitsas 911 (d. *Δημέας*)
Macedonia (Paionia):
—kavadarci (mod.): **(16)** ?ii ad Unp. (Skopje)
—negotino (mod.): **(17)** ii-iii ad *Sp.* 75 (1933) p. 37 no. 114 (d. *Διονύσιος*, *Μάντα*); **(18)** ib. 98 (1941-8) p. 56 no. 114, 6 (*Αὐρ. Ἀ.*)
Macedonia (Pieria):
—dion: **(19)** ?ii-iii ad Dimitsas 180 (*Αὐρ. Ἀ.*)
Macedonia (Sintike):
—herakleia: **(20)** ii ad *IGB* iv 2325 (d. *Πύθιος*)
—neine: **(21)** iii ad ib. 2255 (*[Α]ὐρ. Ἀρτεμι[δ]ώρα*)
—parthikopolis: **(22)** ii ad ib. 2272 (d. *Πύρρος*); **(23)** ib. 2278 (m. *Ἀλέξανδρος*)
—parthikopolis (territ.): **(24)** 235-253 ad ib. 2314; *JDAI* 84 (1969) p. 160 (date) (d. *Μουκάσης*, *Σούρα*)
—parthikopolis (nr.): **(25)** iii ad *IGB* iv 2296 (*Αὐρ. Ἀ.*)
Macedonia?: **(26)** c. 100-75 bc *SB* 8974 fr. 3, 54; cf. La'da E1544 (d. *Ἡρακλείδης*, m. *Νέαρχος*, *Ἀσκληπιάδης*)
Scythia Minor:
—halmyris (nr.): **(27)** iv ad Popescu, *IGL* 168, 1 (Lat. Artemidora: m. *Ἡράκλειος*, Victor, Iulina, Vitalis)
Tauris:
—chersonesos: **(28)** iii bc Solomonik, *NEPKh* 181 (*[Ἀρ]τεμιδώρ[α]*: d. *Παρθένιος*)
Thrace:
—kellai: **(29)** 241-244 ad *IGB* iii 1517, 29 (*Αὐρ. Ἀ.*); **(30)** ib. l. 30 (*Αὐρ. Ἀ.*); **(31)** ib. l. 34 (*Ἰουλία Ἀ.*)
—perinthos-herakleia: **(32)** iii-iv ad *IPerinth* 180, 8 (*AD* 51-2 (1996-7) Mel. p. 338 no. 170) (*Αὐρ. Ἀ.*)
—plotinopolis: **(33)** imp. *Thrakika* 2 (1929) p. 89 (*IThrakAig* E468)

Ἀρτεμιδώρη
Cimmerian Bosporos:
—hermonassa: **(1)** iv-iii bc *CIRB* 1069
—pantikapaion: **(2)** iv bc ib. 168 (d. *Ἁρμάδης*, *Δημητρία*)

Ἀρτεμίδωρος
Cimmerian Bosporos:
—gorgippia: **(1)** f. iii bc ib. 1137 A I, 30; 1137 B I, 50 (f. *Διονύσιος*); **(2)** ib. 1137 A II, 52 (s. *Μενεκλῆς*)
—hermonassa: **(3)** iv bc ib. 1056 I, 19 (f. *—ρης*); **(4)** ib. 1056 II, 6 (s. *Ἐ—*)
—pantikapaion: **(5)** i ad ib. 373 (I f. (nat.) *Ἀρτεμίδωρος* II); **(6)** ib. (II s. (nat.) *Ἀρτεμίδωρος* I, ?s. (ad.) *Γάϊος*); **(7)** i/ii ad ib. 584; cf. KW pl. 40 no. 606 (s. *Διογᾶς*)
Macedonia: **(8)** hell. *Memnonion* 180 (Tataki, *Macedonians* p. 267 no. 291; La'da E1442); **(9)** iii/ii bc *IG* xii Suppl. p. 190 no. 634 (Tataki, *Macedonians* p. 268 no. 293) (f. *Ἀμύντας*: date—Knoepfler); **(10)** hell.-imp. *IEph* 3299 (Tataki, *Macedonians* p. 267 no. 292) (s. *Ἄτταλος*); **(11)** 19 bc *POxy* 277, 2 (Tataki, *Macedonians* p. 476 no. 48) (I f. *Ἀρτεμίδωρος* II); **(12)** *POxy* 277, 2, 7, 9, 17 (Tataki, *Macedonians* p. 476 no. 47) (II s. *Ἀρτεμίδωρος* I); **(13)** ii-iii ad *IDR* iii (4) 30 (Lat. P. [Ael.] [Art]emidorus)
Macedonia (Bottiaia):
—aigai: **(14)** s. iv bc *SEG* xxxv 773 (*Ἀρτεμίδωρ[ος]*: s. *Καλλίας*); **(15)** ib. (*[Ἀρτεμί]δωρος*?: f. *Καλλίας*)
—beroia: **(16)** ii bc *IBer* 158 (s. *Ἀμύντας*); **(17)** ib. 179 (s. *Βίλος*); **(18)** f. ii bc ib. 157 (Tataki 237) (*[Ἀρ]τεμίδωρο[ς]*: f. *Χαιρεφάνης*); **(19)** ii-iii ad *IBer* 367 (Tataki 235) (s. *Καικίλις Βηρ—*, *Κεκιλία Τρύφαινα*); **(20)** ii/iii ad *IBer* 145, 7 (Tataki 593) (*Ἰούλ. Ἀ.*)
—edessa: **(21)** 229 ad Tataki, *Edessa* 240 (*Οὔλπ. Ἀ.*)
—mieza: **(22)** hell. *AM* 27 (1902) p. 314 no. 28, 4 (-δο-)
—pella: **(23)** c. 214-200 bc *IOrop* 130, 4 (Tataki, *Macedonians* p. 151 no. 22) (f. *Ἡράκλειτος*)
Macedonia (Chalkidike):
—gigonos?: **(24)** s. ii ad *SEG* xlviii 798
Macedonia (Edonis):
—amphipolis: **(25)** ?iv/iii bc Kaphtantzis 644 (f. *Πολέμων*, *Κράτων*); **(26)** hell.? *BCH* 18 (1894) p. 423 no. 4 (55 (1931) pp. 176-7 no. 6) (s. *Ἀντιγένης*, f. *Ἀντιγένης*); **(27)** ii bc *IG* ii² 8081 (Tataki, *Macedonians* p. 48 no. 26; *FRA* 500) (f. *Δημήτριος*); **(28)** i bc *IG* ii² 8080 (Tataki, *Macedonians* p. 48 no. 25; *FRA* 501) (s. *Ἐπιμένης*)
—philippoi: **(29)** s. iii bc *IG* vii 2433 II, 5 (Tataki, *Macedonians* p. 163 no. 8) (*Ἀρταμίδ[ωρος]*: s. *Μιννίων*); **(30)** ii-i bc *SEG* iii 504 (*SIRIS* 118; Pilhofer 193) (f. *Κάστωρ*)
Macedonia (Krestonia):
—morrylos: **(31)** ii-iii ad *SEG* xxxix 613, 2 (s. *Ἥλιος*, *Ἄρτεμις*)
Macedonia (Lynkestis): **(32)** iii ad *EAM* 163 (*Αὐρ. Ἀ.*)
Macedonia (Mygdonia):
—dikaia (nr.)?: **(33)** s. ii ad *SEG* l 648 (-μεί-: s. *Συρίων*)
—kalindoia: **(34)** ?255 ad ib. xlii 603 b (s. *Διοσκουρίδης*, f. *Διοσκουρίδης*, *Εὐφρόσυνος*)
—thessalonike: **(35)** ii ad *IG* x (2) (1) 241 A I, 5 (f. *Φίλιππος*) ?= (*37*); **(36)** ib. 241 A II, 4 (*Δ. Κατ[ίλιος] Ἀρτεμίδω[ρος]*); **(37)** ib. 507, 2 (f. *Φίλιππος*) ?= (*35*); **(38)** ii-iii ad ib. 346, 1; **(39)** ib. 533 (*Π. Αἴλ. Ἀρτεμίδωρος*: f. *Ἀρτεμισία*); **(40)** iii ad ib. 247, 13 (*Ἀκοριανὸς Ἀρ(τ)εμίδ(ω)[ρος]*); **(41)** *SEG* xxxviii 711 (*Αὐρ. Ἀ.*); **(42)** m. iii ad *Charistirion Orlandos* 2 pp. 375-91 (*Τι. Φλ. Ἀ.*: s. *Νου. Μέστριος Πρίσκος*); **(43)** *IG* x (2) (1) 204, 16 (*Γ. Ἰούλ. Ἀ.*: f. *Γ. Ἰουλ. Ἀρτεμιδώρα*); **(44)** 249 ad ib. 164, 10 (*Φλ. Αἰλιανὸς Σεμπρώνιος Ἀ.*: s. *Φλ. Σεμπρώνιος Αἰλιανός*, *Φλ. Αἰλιανὴ Σεμπρωνία Ἀρτεμιδώρα*)
—thessalonike (nr.): **(45)** ii-iii ad *SEG* xxxviii 708
—thessalonike?: **(46)** ii ad *IG* x (2) (1) 251, 8 (*Τ. Ἰούλ. Πωλλίων [ὁ] [καὶ] [Ἀρ]τεμίδ[ωρος]*); **(47)** ii-iii ad ib. 724 (*KGAM Thess.* i 131) (s. *Διονυσία*); **(48)** *IG* x (2) (1) 725; **(49)** ib. 728, 1 (*Δούλης (ὁ) κὲ Ἀρτεμίδορος*); **(50)** 193 ad ib. 806 (*Ἰούλ. Κο[σκ]ωνιανὸ[ς] [Ἀρ]τεμίδω[ρος]*)
Macedonia (Mygdonia)?:
—herakleia: **(51)** ii ad *GVI* 569; cf. *Milliaires* p. 70 n. 1 (locn.)
Macedonia (Odomantike):
—sirrha (nr.): **(52)** c. 98-117 ad *CIL* iii 14206. 4 (Pilhofer 559) (Lat. Claudianus Artemidorus)
Macedonia (Pieria):
—dion: **(53)** f. ii ad *SEG* xxxiii 513; cf. Spiliopoulou-Donderer, *KGN* p. 198 no. D16 (date) (*Ἰούλ. Ἀ.*)
—pydna: **(54)** 250 ad *SEG* xlvi 800 A, 26 (*Αὐρ. Ἀ.*)
Macedonia (Sintike): **(55)** 158 ad *IGB* v 5926 (s. *Μουκάσης*)
—neine: **(56)** iii ad ib. iv 2254; cf. v 5881 (*Αὐρ. Ἀ.*); **(57)** 222 ad ib. 5886, 2 (*Αὐρ. Ἀ.*: s. *Πυρούσαλα*, *Δημήτριος*)
—parthikopolis: **(58)** ii ad ib. iv 2277 (s. *Πύρσος*); **(59)** ib. 2280 (*[Ἀρτε]μίδωρος*)
—parthikopolis (territ.): **(60)** ii ad ib. 2302, 1 (s. *Οὐίβιος*, f. *Λούκιος*, *Τερεντία*)
Macedonia (Sintike)?: **(61)** 144 ad ib. 2331, 1 (s. *Τευτάμας*, *Βουζάη*)
Scythia Minor:
—istros: **(62)** s. iv bc *ISM* i 239 (s. *Θεοκλῆς*); **(63)** iii bc ib. 266 (*Ἀρτεμ[ίδωρος]*?); **(64)** ii-i bc *SEG* xix 489 b (weight); **(65)** i bc-i ad *ISM* i 189, 7 (*Ἀρτεμ[ίδωρος]*?); **(66)** ib. 191 II, 16 (s. *Ἀπολλόδωρος*); **(67)** ib. l. 17 (s. *Πυθόδωρος*); **(68)** ib. l. 22 (f. *Θεόδωρος*); **(69)** ib. l. 25-7 (f. *Δημόχαρις*, *Διονύσιος*, *Δημήτριος*); **(70)** i bc/i ad ib. 56, 2 (*Ἀρτεμ[ίδωρος]*?); **(71)** i ad ib. 200, 8 (f. *Ἀπολλώνιος*); **(72)** c. 48-52 ad ib. 67, 38; 68, 41 (f. *Μειδίας*); **(73)** ii ad ib. 137, 10 (*[M.] Οὔλπ. Ἀ.*) ?= (*101*); **(74)** ib. 196, 14 (f. *Πολύτιμος*); **(75)** ib. l. 22 (f. *Ἑρμόδωρος*); **(76)** ib. 201 II, 21 (*Οὔλπ. Ἀ.*: f. *Εὐάρεστος*); **(77)** ib. 202, 2; **(78)** ib. 211, 13 (s. *Ἀντιγένης*); **(79)** ib. l. 16 (s. *Φαῖδρος*) ?= (*94*); **(80)** ib. 212, 9 (s. *Καλλίστρατος*); **(81)** ib. l. 16 (f. *Σύμμαχος*); **(82)** ib. l. 20 (s.

Κουραγένης); (83) ib. l. 26 (f. Ἀριστοκράτης); (84) ib. 214, 9 + 226, 7 (Ἀρτεμί[δωρος]?); (85) 138 AD ib. 180, 1; 193 II, 16-17; cf. p. 318 (stemma) (f. Κάρπος) ?= (88); (86) ib. 193, 9 (s. Εὐξενίδης); (87) ib. 193 I, 34 (s. Ἡρόδωρος); (88) ib. l. 40 (f. Κάρπος) ?= (85); (89) ib. l. 74 (Αἰλ. Ἀ.: s. Φαιδρίας); (90) ib. l. 76 (Μ. Οὔλπ. Ἀ.: s. Μ. Οὔλπ. Εὐξενίδης); (91) ib. l. 82 (s. Ἡγήμων); (92) ib. l. 72-3 (f. Μ. Οὔλπ. Εὐξενίδης, Μ. Οὔλπ. Δημήτριος); (93) ib. 193 II, 27 (s. Θεόδωρος); (94) ib. l. 36 (s. Φαῖδρος) ?= (79); (95) ib. l. 59 (s. Εὐξενίδης); (96) ib. l. 64 (s. Νουμήνιος); (97) ib. l. 65 (s. Γρήγορος); (98) ib. l. 2-3, 14, 16, 20 (s. Ἡρόδωρος, f. Κάρπος); (99) c. 138-160 AD ib. 193 I, 41; 207, 10 (Αἰλ. Ἀ.: s. Διοσκουρίδης); (100) ib. 193 II, 60; 207, 8 (s. Κάρπος); (101) c. 140-160 AD ib. l. 3; cf. *ZPE* 120 (1998) p. 107 (Μ. Ο[ὔλπ.] [Ἀρτεμί]δωρος, Μ. Ὀ—λωρος—*ZPE*) ?= (73); (102) s. ii AD *ISM* I 167, 16 (Ἀρτεμίδω(ρος): f. Μ. Διονυτᾶς); (103) ii/iii AD ib. 227, 8 (?s. Ἐ—); (104) ib. l. 10; (105) ib. 363, 4 (*CCET* IV 62) (s. Διονύσιος); (106) iii AD *ISM* I 303, 9 (s. Χρύσιππος, Πώμη); (107) f. iii AD *Stud. Fischer* p. 32 no. 4, 3; (108) *ISM* I 143, 8 (Ἀρτεμίδ[ωρος]: f. Αὐρ. Μαρκιανός); (109) ib. 218, 9 (f. Αὐρ. Ἄμανδος); (110) 222-225 AD ib. 100, 10 (f. Αὐρ. Γρήγορος); (111) ib. 100 B, 16 (Αὐρ. Ἀ.: s. Ἀριστοκράτης)

——Chora Dagei: (112) c. 159-161 AD ib. 378 C, 23 (s. Ἀρίστων)

—ISTROS (NR.): (113) hell.? ib. 109 (f. Θαλωνίς)

—KALLATIS: (114) iii-ii BC ib. III 171 (f. Θεόπομπος); (115) ii BC *IByz* 72 (Fıratlı–Robert pp. 48-9 no. 10) (f. Φαίκων); (116) ii/iii AD *ISM* III 181, 6 (f. Ἡλιόδωρος)

—KALLATIS?: (117) ii/i BC *IGB* II 867 a, 5 = *ISM* I 219 (v 87); cf. *ISM* III p. 140 (locn.) (s. Ὑγιαίνων)

—TOMIS: (118) i BC ib. II 2 A, 48 (f. Ἡραίων); (119) ib. l. 52 (f. Μῆνις); (120) f. i AD *RPC* I 1803-4 (coin) (Ἀρτεμίδω(ρος)); (121) ii AD *ISM* II 125 II, 23 (s. Ἀσκλῆς); (122) ii-iii AD ib. 121 (f. Ἀκυλῖνος)

—TOMIS?: (123) iv BC ib. 456 (f. Νικήρατος)

SKYTHIA:

—OLBIA-BORYSTHENES: (124) f. iv BC Dubois, *IGDOlbia* 104 (s. Διονύσιος); (125) ib. (-ρως: s. Δεινομένης); (126) ib. 105 (s. Τελεσικράτης); (127) m. iv BC ib. 106, 1 (*SEG* XLIV 669) (s. Ἡρόφιλος); (128) iii BC *IOSPE* I^2 201 II, 29 (s. Τ—); (129) c. 150-175 AD ib. 142, 10; 176; cf. *SEG* XLII 713 (f. Σάτυρος); (130) iii AD *IOlbia* 83, 10 (*IOSPE* I^2 97) (s. Ποσ—); (131) ib. 135, 4 (f. Ἡρακλείδης)

—OLBIA-BORYSTHENES (BEREZAN (MOD.)): (132) inc. Vinogradov, *Pont. Stud.* pp. 639-40 (vase)

—OLBIA-BORYSTHENES?: (133) iii BC *SEG* XXXVII 671 (bronze) (s. Πολύχαρμος, f. Μῖκος)

—TANAIS: (134) i BC-i AD? *New Studies on Black Sea* p. 47 fig. 8 (Ἀρτεμίδ[ωρος]?)

—TYRAS: (135) 181 AD *IOSPE* I^2 2, 27 (f. Ἱερώνυμος, Θεοδᾶς) ?= (136); (136) ib. l. 28-9 (f. Νίγερ, Μακάριος) ?= (135); (137) iii AD *IGB* I^2 228 bis, 9 (f. Μαδινι)

TAURIS:

—CHERSONESOS: (138) iv BC *SEG* XXVIII 634 (s. Ξανθίας); (139) iv-iii BC Solomonik, *NEPKh* 29 (f. Καλλιάδας); (140) f. iv BC *SEG* XXVI 803 (Ἀρτεμίδ[ωρος]: f. Πασιάδας); (141) iv/iii BC Solomonik, *NEPKh* 157 ([Ἀρτε]μίδωρος: s. Δαμάτριος); (142) ib. 158; (143) iii BC *MIA* 34 (1953) p. 73 (bronze); cf. Vinogradov, *Pont. Stud.* p. 637 (s. Διοσκουρίδας); (144) *IOSPE* I^2 414 (Ἀρτεμίδ[ωρος]: f. Πασιάδας); (145) f. iii BC Kats p. 112 no. 111 (amph.) (f. Σώκριτος); (146) *SEG* XL 615 A, 7 (s. Ἀρ—); (147) c. 290-280 BC Anokhin p. 139 no. 85 (coin) ?= (148); (148) ib. pp. 139-40 no. 88 (coin) ?= (147); (149) c. 272-262 BC Kats p. 91 no. 29 (amph.) (s. Πασιάδας); (150) c. 250-230 BC Anokhin p. 141 no. 110 (coin) (Ἀρτεμίδω(ρος))

THRACE: (151) 236 BC *PPetr*^{2} 16, 55 (Velkov 32; La'da E714); (152) 46-54 AD *SEG* XVI 415 II, 21 (*IThrakAig* E84) (Γ. Ἰούλ. Ἀ.)

—ABDERA: (153) i BC-i AD *SEG* XLVII 1032 (*IThrakAig* E64) (f. Βεισούλας)

—ANCHIALOS (TERRIT.): (154) iii AD *IGB* V 5648 (Π[ο]ύ(λ). Ἀ.)

—APOLLONIA-SOZOPOLIS: (155) s. v BC ib. I^2 445 (f. Θέστωρ); (156) v/iv BC ib. 407 (f. Ἀνθεστήριος); (157) ib. 418 (f. Σκύλλη); (158) i-ii AD ib. 401, 18 (f. Ἀπολλώνις)

—BYZANTION: (159) ii-i BC *IByz* 190 (Fıratlı–Robert p. 59 no. 41) (f. Ποσειδώνιος); (160) i BC-i AD *IByz* 178 (Fıratlı–Robert p. 111 no. 183) (s. Ἀντίπατρος)

—BYZANTION (TERRIT.): (161) i BC *IByz* 134 (Fıratlı–Robert p. 99 no. 146a) (f. Κράτεια)

—BYZANTION?: (162) i BC *Syllogos* 16 (1885) Parart. p. 5 no. 3 (-ρως); (163) ?14 BC *IByz* 324 (Robert, *Hell.* 11-12 p. 578; *Eastern cults* p. 33 no. 54) (or Thrace Mesambria?: s. Φιλόστρατος); (164) *IByz* 324 (Robert, *Hell.* 11-12 p. 578; *Eastern cults* p. 33 no. 54) (or Thrace Mesambria?: s. Συνίστωρ)

—DIONYSOPOLIS: (165) ii AD *IGB* I^2 28 bis; *Dacia* 21 (1977) p. 161 (date) (s. Φιλ—); (166) *IGB* I^2 28 bis; *Dacia* 21 (1977) p. 161 (date) (f. Φιλ—)

—GABRICA (MOD.): (167) f. iii AD *IGB* II 778 (*CCET* II (2) 408)

—HADRIANOPOLIS (TERRIT.): (168) iii AD *IGB* III 1834 (Αὐρ. Ἀ.)

—LYSIMACHEIA: (169) c. 208 BC *FD* III (4) 134 I, 29; (170) ii-i BC *IG* II^2 9222 (*FRA* 3286) (s. Ἀρτέμων)

—MARONEIA: (171) ii-i BC *IThrakAig* E212, 43 (f. Στέφανος)

—MESAMBRIA: (172) ii BC *IGB* I^2 325, 4 (s. Ἀρτεμ—); (173) ii/i BC ib. V 5104 III (f. Χαιρεφάνης)

—MONTANA: (174) 160 AD *CIL* III 12371 (*Montana* II 51) (Lat. Aelius Artem(i)dorus)

—ODESSOS: (175) v/iv BC *IGB* I^2 100 ([Ἀρ]τεμίδωρος: s. Στρατῖνος); (176) f. iv BC ib. V 5060 (f. Εἶφίς); (177) s. iii BC ib. I^2 36, 11 (f. Θεσσαλός); (178) iii/ii BC ib. 38, 3 ([Ἀρτ]εμίδωρος); (179) i BC-i AD ib. 107, 1 (f. Ἀπφία); (180) ib. l. 9 (s. Αἰαντίδης, Ἀπφία); (181) ib. 109 (f. Ἀγαθήνωρ); (182) ib. (f. Ἀσσει); (183) ib. 206 bis (PM 1682) (f. Νουμήνιος); (184) 35 BC *IGB* I^2 46, 12 (f. Παρμένων); (185) 26 BC ib. l. 21 (s. Ἀπολλόδωρος); (186) 24 BC ib. l. 23 (f. Ἀσκληπιάδης); (187) 15 BC ib. l. 32 (s. Νουμήνιος); (188) 11 BC ib. l. 36 (s. Ἑστιαῖος); (189) i AD ib. 186 bis (PM 1661); *Dacia* 21 (1977) p. 161 (date) (Ἀρτ[εμί]δωρος: f. Δημήτριος); (190) *IGB* I^2 195 ([Ἀρ]τεμίδωρος); (191) i-ii AD ib. 51 b, 4 (I f. Ἀρτεμίδωρος II); (192) ib. l. 4 ([Ἀρτεμ]ίδωρος: II s. Ἀρτεμίδωρος I); (193) ib. 113 (Ἀρ[τε]μίδωρος: f. Ἀφφία); (194) ib. 118 ([Ἀρ]τεμίδω[ρο]ς: f. Δημήτριος); (195) ib. 128, 2, 5 (f. Ἀντίφιλος, Μενεσθεύς); (196) ib. l. 9 (s. Κόνων); (197) ib. 143 b, 1 (f. Ἀγαθήνωρ); (198) ib. 144 bis, 1, 6 (s. Ζωΐλος); (199) ib. 193; (200) ib. 200 (Ἀρτεμίδ[ωρος]: f. Μένανδρος); (201) ib. 204 (Ἀρτεμίδ[ωρος]: f. Ζωΐλος); (202) ib. 206; *Dacia* 21 (1977) p. 161 (date) ([Ἀρτ]εμίδωρος); (203) s. i AD *IGB* I^2 160 (*CCET* I 52; PM 1446) (s. Νουμήνιος); (204) ii AD *IGB* I^2 50 a, 4 (?f. (nat.) Ἡφαιστίων); (205) ib. l. 7 (f. Παρμένων); (206) ib. l. 11 (f. Δάδας); (207) ?ii AD ib. 115, 4 (f. Ἰαδώ); (208) ii AD ib. 203 (Ἀρτεμίδ[ωρος]); (209) ii-iii AD ib. 143 a (f. Ἀγαθήνωρ); (210) f. ii AD ib. 78 ter, 5 (*CCET* I 30) (f. Αἰαντίδης); (211) *IGB* I^2 78 ter, 6 (*CCET* I 30) (s. Ἱερώνυμος); (212) *IGB* I^2 78 ter, 7 (*CCET* I 30) (f. Καλλισθένης); (213) *IGB* I^2 78 ter, 10 (*CCET* I 30) (Ἀρτεμίδω[ρος]: f. Ἡρότιμος); (214) *IGB* I^2 78 ter, 11 (*CCET* I 30) (Ἀρτεμίδω[ρος]: f. Ζωπυρίων); (215) *IGB* I^2 78 ter, 11 (*CCET* I 30) (s. Δημήτριος); (216) m. ii AD *IGB* I^2 169 (PM 1725); *Dacia* 21 (1977) p. 161 (date) (f. Ἀπολλώνιος); (217) *IGB* I^2 176 ter (PM 1693); *IGB* I^2 272 (PM 1676); *Dacia* 21 (1977) p. 161 (date) (s. Ἱππομέδων, f. Ξένων); (218) *IGB* I^2 177; *Dacia* 21 (1977) p. 161 (date) (f. Ξένων); (219) s. ii AD *IGB* I^2 79 bis, 5 (*CCET* I 34) (I f. Ἀρτεμίδωρος II); (220) *IGB* I^2 79 bis, 5 (*CCET* I 34) (II s. Ἀρτεμίδωρος I); (221) *IGB* I^2 167 (PM 1727); *Dacia* 21 (1977) p. 161 (date) (s. Ἀπολλόδωρος); (222) 215 AD *IGB* I^2 47 a, 9 (Αὐρ. Ἀ.: s. Ξένανδρος); (223) ib. l. 19 (Αὐρ. Ἀ.: s. Διονύσιος); (224) 221 AD ib. 47 bis a, 10 (f. Μ. Αὐρ. Μενεκράτης); (225) ib. l. 12 (I f. Μ. Αὐρ. Ἀρτεμίδωρος II); (226) ib. l. 12 (Μ. Αὐρ. Ἀ.: II s. Ἀρτεμίδωρος I); (227) ib. l. 14 (f. Μ. Αὐρ. Ξένανδρος); (228) ib. l. 17 (f. Μ. Αὐρ. Εὐφάνης); (229) ib. 47 bis b, 23 (Αὐρ. Ἀ. νεώτ.: s. Διονύσιος); (230) ib. l. 29 (Αὐρ. Ἀ.: s. Διονύσιος)

—ODESSOS (NR.): (231) iii/ii BC ib. 283 (*CCET* I 96) (s. Θεόξενος); (232) i BC-i AD *IGB* I^2 257 (*CCET* I 68) (s. Σίμων); (233) s. ii AD *IGB* I^2 254 (PM 1723); *Dacia* 21 (1977) p. 161 (date) (f. Μόσχος); (234) iii AD *IGB* I^2 270 (Αὐρ. Ἀ.: s. Ἡφαιστίων)

—OESCUS: (235) imp. *Romanizmăt* II 341 (Lat. Artemidorus); (236) 217 AD *ILB* 19, 5 (Lat. T. Aurel. Art[emido]rus)

—PERINTHOS-HERAKLEIA: (237) iv/iii BC *IEph* 1464, 3 (Ἀρτεμί[δωρος]?: ?s. Ἀπολλόδωρος); (238) iii BC *IPerinth* 42 (*SIRIS* 128; *Eastern cults* p. 27 no. 47 (date)) (s. Ἡραΐσκος); (239) ii-i BC *IPerinth* 50 (s. Μηνόδωρος); (240) ii AD ib. 101 (Ἀ. ὁ καὶ Κυρήνιος: s. Νικόστρατος, f. Νάρκισσος, Παῦλα)

——(Aigikoreis): (241) iii-ii BC ib. 61, 52 (f. Ἀκέσανδρος)

—SALYMBRIA (NR.): (242) hell.-imp. *IByz* S 56

—SERDICA: (243) i AD *IG* II^2 4786; *St. Clas.* 9 (1967) pp. 107-110 (*FRA* 2500)

—SKAPTOPARA: (244) 238-244 AD *IGB* V 5872 (s. Ἀρίστων)

THRACE?: (245) iii BC *CPR* XIII 4 X, 189 (f. Τήρης)

Ἀρτεμίκλεια

MACEDONIA (BOTTIAIA):

—BEROIA: (1) ii BC *IBer* 178 (-κλῃα: d. Οὐένετος)

Ἀρτέμιν

CIMMERIAN BOSPOROS:

—PANTIKAPAION: (1) i AD *CIRB* 361 (-μειν)

MACEDONIA (BOTTIAIA):

—SKYDRA?: (2) imp. Dimitsas 122 (Τερεντία Ἀρτέμειν)

MACEDONIA (MYGDONIA):

—THESSALONIKE: (3) ii-iii AD *IG* X (2) (1) 419 (Ἀρτέμινι (dat.): d. Ῥηγῖνα); (4) ii/iii AD ib. 386; *KGAM Thess.* I 125 (date) (Πεσκεννία Κουΐντα ἡ καὶ Ἀ.); (5) 209 AD *IG* X (2) (1) 506, 1 (-μειν: d. Μᾶρκος, m. Ἰσίδωρος, Ἰουνία)

—THESSALONIKE?: (6) 152 AD ib. 923, 2 (-μειν: d. Διοσκουρίδης, Ἀπολλωνία)

Ἄρτεμις

MACEDONIA (BISALTIA):

—TERPNI (MOD.): (1) ii-iii AD *SEG* XLIX 810

MACEDONIA (BOTTIAIA):

—BEROIA: (2) ii AD *IBer* 355 (Tataki 238) (m. Ἀλκέτης)

MACEDONIA (KRESTONIA):

—MORRYLOS: (3) ii-iii AD *SEG* XXXIX 613, 5 (m. Ἀπολλόδωρος, Ἀρτεμίδωρος)

MACEDONIA (LYNKESTIS):

—NIKAIA?: (4) ii/iii AD *IG* X (2) (2) 45 (biling.) (Οὐαληρία Ἀρτέμειν (dat.): m. Ἰούλιος Ἰουλιανός, Ἰουλία Ἄρτεμις); (5) ib. (biling.) (Ἰουλία

Ἀρτέμεινι (dat.): d. Ἰούλιος Τήρης, Οὐαληρία Ἄρτεμις)
MACEDONIA (MYGDONIA):
—LETE: **(6)** 180 AD *SEG* XLVIII 808 (Ἀρτέμινι (dat.))
—THESSALONIKE?: **(7)** ii AD *IG* X (2) (1) 891 (Ἀρτέμει (dat.))
MACEDONIA (PAIONIA):
—KAVADARCI (MOD.): **(8)** ii/iii AD Unp. (Papazoglu archive) (Ἀρτέμινι (dat.): m. Μουνδίκιος)
MACEDONIA (SINTIKE):
—PARTHIKOPOLIS (NR.): **(9)** ii-iii AD *IGB* IV 2297
SKYTHIA:
—OLBIA-BORYSTHENES*: **(10)** m. vi BC *SEG* XLIV 668 (vase); cf. *BE* 1996, no. 301 (n. pr.?: ?d. Ὑπάσις)

Ἀρτεμισία
MACEDONIA (BOTTIAIA):
—BEROIA: **(1)** ii BC *IBer* 180 (Tataki 239); **(2)** ?ii/iii AD *ILeukopetra* 153, 1 (-μει-: ?d. (nat.) Ἀρίστων, ?d. (ad.) Λυκόφρων, Λαδόμα); **(3)** ?277 AD ib. 111, 2 (Αὐρ. Ἀρτειμισ[ία])
—PELLA: **(4)** ii/iii AD *SEG* XLVIII 826 (-μει-)
MACEDONIA (EDONIS):
—AMPHIPOLIS: **(5)** ii AD Dimitsas 874
MACEDONIA (LYNKESTIS):
—ACHLADA (MOD.): **(6)** f. iii AD *EAM* 169, 1 (Αὐρ. Ἀρτεμεισία: d. Αὐρ. Μέμη)
MACEDONIA (MYGDONIA):
—THESSALONIKE: **(7)** ii-iii AD *IG* X (2) (1) 533 (d. Π. Αἲλ. Ἀρτεμίδωρος); **(8)** ib. 584 (Αἲλ. Ἀ.)
MACEDONIA (PELAGONIA):
—DOSTONEIS?: **(9)** iii AD ib. X (2) (2) 202, 2 (-μει-)
THRACE:
—ABDERA: **(10)** c. 500-475 BC *Horos* 14-16 (2000-2003) p. 250 no. 2 (*IThrakAig* E32) (Ἀρτεμισίης (gen.): d. Νυμφόδωρος)
—ABRYTTOS (TERRIT.): **(11)** ii-iii AD *IGB* I^2 306 = II 758 (or Thrace Naulochos?: -μει-: d. Ἀρτέμων)
—APOLLONIA-SOZOPOLIS?: **(12)** c. 180-150 BC *Milet* I (3) 56 (and Caria Miletos: d. Περίτας)
—MARONEIA: **(13)** hell. *IThrakAig* E254 ([Ἀρ]τεμισία)
—PERINTHOS-HERAKLEIA: **(14)** i-ii AD *ISM* II 365, 14 (*GVI* 1161) (Καικιλία Ἀ.: d. Φλ. Θεοδώρα, m. Πρίσκος, Θεοδώρα, Ἱερωνίς); **(15)** ii-iii AD *IPerinth* 103 (-μει-: d. Σόφος)
—PHILIPPOPOLIS-TRIMONTIUM: **(16)** ii-iii AD *IGB* III 955 (Ἀρτεμ[ι]σία)

Ἀρτεμίσιος
MACEDONIA (MYGDONIA):
—LETE (NR.): **(1)** ii-iii AD *AD* 2 (1916) Parart. p. 12
—THESSALONIKE*: **(2)** c. 303 AD Musurillo, *Acts Christian Martyrs* pp. 281 ff. (-μή-)
SARMATIA:
—MAIOTAI: **(3)** ii BC *IRhamnous* 234 (Ἀρτεμίσ[ιος])
THRACE: **(4)** c. 190-180 BC *Milet* VI (2) 796, 18 (f. Ἑρμίας)
—NOVAE*: **(5)** 368 AD *IGLNovae* 178 (Φλ. Ἀ[ρτε]μίσιος)

Ἀρτεμίσκη
MACEDONIA (BISALTIA):
—TERPNI (MOD.): **(1)** ii-iii AD *SEG* XLIX 810

Ἀρτεμίστη
THRACE:
—ZONE: **(1)** f. iv BC Bakalakis, *Oinos Ismarikos* p. 710 (*IThrakAig* E413) (d. Θράσων)

Ἀρτεμώ
MACEDONIA (MYGDONIA):
—THESSALONIKE: **(1)** ii AD *IG* X (2) (1) 414 (m. Γαληνός, Ἱλαρία)
THRACE:
—ELAIOUS: **(2)** iii BC *AD* 49 (1994) Chron. p. 299 no. β with pl. 96 β (Ἀρτέμων—ed.: d. Κάρος: name—*LGPN*)
—STRYME?: **(3)** m. iv BC *IThrakAig* E151 (d. Ἡγησιππίδης)

Ἀρτέμων
CIMMERIAN BOSPOROS:
—HERMONASSA: **(1)** iv BC *CIRB* 1056 I, 12 (f. —ατος); **(2)** ib. 1056 II, 10 (s. Ἀναξίλεως); **(3)** ib. l. 13 (s. Ἑρμαγόρης)
—PANTIKAPAION: **(4)** iv-iii BC ib. 747 (f. Μητρόδωρος); **(5)** i/ii AD ib. 585 (s. Ἀριστίων); **(6)** f. ii AD ib. 659 (s. Ὄλυμπος); **(7)** ib. 714; cf. KW pl. 17 no. 257
MACEDONIA: **(8)** f. iii BC *Thess. Mnem.* 11 (Tataki, *Macedonians* p. 268 no. 294) (f. Σωσικράτεια); **(9)** 138 AD *SEG* XXXVII 593, 17 (Αἲλ. Ἀ.)
MACEDONIA (BOTTIAIA):
—BEROIA: **(10)** ii/iii AD *IBer* 143 A, 10 (Tataki 240) (f. Ξενο—ς)
MACEDONIA (CHALKIDIKE):
—POTIDAIA-KASSANDREIA: **(11)** iv/iii BC *RE* (18) (Tataki, *Macedonians* p. 86 no. 14); **(12)** m. iii BC *Thess. Mnem.* 167 (Tataki, *Macedonians* p. 86 no. 15) (f. Ἀριστόδημος)
MACEDONIA (MYGDONIA):
—KALINDOIA: **(13)** 68-98 AD *SEG* XLII 580, 57 (I f. Ἀρτέμων II); **(14)** ib. l. 57 (II s. Ἀρτέμων I)
—THESSALONIKE: **(15)** 159 AD *AD* 24 (1969) Chron. p. 300 (*Klio* 65 (1983) p. 164)
SCYTHIA MINOR:
—TOMIS: **(16)** ii-i BC *IGB* I^2 43 bis, 3 (Ἀρ[τέ]μων?: s. Χαιρίων)
SKYTHIA:
—OLBIA-BORYSTHENES: **(17)** iv BC *IOSPE* I^2 209 (s. Εὐρησίβιος)
THRACE:
—ABDERA: **(18)** v BC D.L. ix 50 (?f. Πρωταγόρης); **(19)** c. 450-425 BC May, *Abdera* pp. 139-40 no. 187 (coin)
—ABRYTTOS (TERRIT.): **(20)** ii-iii AD *IGB* I^2 306 = II 758 (or Thrace Naulochos?: Ἀρ[τέμ]ων: f. Ἀρτεμισία)
—LYSIMACHEIA: **(21)** iii BC *ITrall* 33 B, 13 (s. Λέων); **(22)** ii-i BC *IG* II^2 9222 (*FRA* 3387) (f. Ἀρτεμίδωρος)
—MARKIANOPOLIS (TERRIT.): **(23)** iii AD *IGB* V 5372 (*CCET* II (1) 335) (f. Γ—ς)
—MARONEIA: **(24)** ii-i BC *JHS* 16 (1896) p. 319 no. 19 (*IThrakAig* E287) (s. Διογένης)
—MONTANA*: **(25)** 155 AD *CIL* III 7449, 8, 23 (*Montana* II 1) (Lat. Aur. Artemo: doctor)
—NOVAE: **(26)** imp. *IGLNovae* 115 (*ILB* 274) (Lat. Tib. Iul. Ar[t]emo)
—ODESSOS: **(27)** s. iii BC *IGB* I^2 82 bis (I f. Ἀρτέμων II); **(28)** ib. (II s. Ἀρτέμων I); **(29)** i-ii AD ib. 116, 1 (f. Μάμα); **(30)** ii AD ib. 50 a, 5 (s. Πόσσις); **(31)** 215 AD ib. 47 a, 21 (f. Αὐρ. Πρωταγόρας); **(32)** ib. 47 c, 13 (Αὐρ. Ἀ.: s. Διονύσιος); **(33)** 221 AD ib. 47 bis a, 31 (f. Αὐρ. Διόδωρος); **(34)** ib. 47 bis c, 25 (Αὐρ. Ἀρτέμ[ω]ν: s. Διονύσιος)
—PERINTHOS-HERAKLEIA: **(35)** ii-iii AD *IPerinth* 65, 7
—STRYME?: **(36)** c. 400-375 BC *IThrakAig* E164 (s. Μάνδρων, f. Μητρόδοτος)
—STRYME? (NR.): **(37)** v/iv BC Bakalakis, *Oinos Ismarikos* p. 553 (*IThrakAig* E127) (f. Ἡράϊννα)

Ἀρτιδόνης
MACEDONIA (PAIONIA):
—BYLAZORA: **(1)** ii-iii AD *JÖAI* 6 (1903) Beibl. col. 4 no. 4 (Ἀρτιδόνεος (gen.): f. Δούλης)

Ἀρτίδονις
MACEDONIA (EDONIS):
—PHILIPPOI (TERRIT.): **(1)** i-ii AD Pikoulas, *Chora* p. 134 no. 36 (Ἀρτιδόνιος (gen.): f. Συραβίθυς)
THRACE:
—SAPPAIOI: **(2)** iii BC *IG* XII (9) 795 (Ἀρτιδόνιος (gen.), Ἀρτιδῶν—*IG* index: f. Αὐλούζελμις)

Ἀρτικῶν
SKYTHIA:
—OLBIA-BORYSTHENES: **(1)** m. iv BC Dubois, *IGDOlbia* 25 a, 1

Ἀρτιλῶ
MACEDONIA (CHALKIDIKE):
—ANTHEMOUS: **(1)** f. i BC *SEG* XLII 566; cf. *Anthémonte–Kalindoia* 2 p. 227 (name) (d. Βορτᾶς)

Ἀρτίμας
SCYTHIA MINOR:
—KALLATIS: **(1)** iii-ii BC *SNG Stancomb* 82 (coin) (Ἀρτί(μας)?)

Ἀρτινοίη
CIMMERIAN BOSPOROS:
—PANTIKAPAION: **(1)** s. iv BC *CIRB* 169

Ἀρτίπους
CIMMERIAN BOSPOROS:
—PANTIKAPAION: **(1)** ii-iii AD ib. 718 (s. Ἄλκιμος)

Ἀρτίς
SCYTHIA MINOR:
—ISTROS: **(1)** iv BC *ISM* I 237; Robert, *Noms indigènes* p. 345 (name)
—ISTROS?: **(2)** iii BC *IGB* II 877; cf. V 5393 (locn.) (d. Ἰστρόδωρος)

Ἀρτυσίλη
THRACE:
—MARONEIA: **(1)** s. iii BC *IThrakAig* E252 (d. Ἡγήσιππος)

Ἀρύββας
MACEDONIA (PIERIA):
—PYDNA: **(1)** iv BC *GRBS* 43 (2002-3) p. 119 no. 5, 4

Ἀρχαγόρας
THRACE:
—ABDERA: **(1)** ii BC *IG* XII (8) 161, 16 (s. Ἀριστόνους)

Ἀρχαγόρης
THRACE:
—ABDERA: **(1)** c. 415-395 BC May, *Abdera* p. 169 no. 224 (coin)

Ἀρχάθιος
SKYTHIA:
—TANAIS: **(1)** 244 AD *CIRB* 1287, 23; Zgusta, *PNS* 545 a (f. Ἰζια—)

Ἀρχαιάναξ
CIMMERIAN BOSPOROS:
—BOSPOROS: **(1)** v BC *RE* s.v. Archaianaktidai (-) (Ἀρχαιανακτίδαι (n. gent.))

Ἀρχαῖος
SKYTHIA:
—OLBIA-BORYSTHENES: **(1)** s. vi BC Vinogradov–Kryžickij pl. 105. 7 (vase)

Ἄρχανδρος
MACEDONIA (EDONIS):
—AMPHIPOLIS: **(1)** b. 213 BC Hatzopoulos, *MI* 2 p. 83 no. 61, 7 (*SEG* XLVI 715) (f. Νικόστρατος)
SKYTHIA:
—TYRAS: **(2)** iii BC ib. XXX 923 = 970 (amph.); cf. XLV 1026. 4 ([Αὐ]σανδρος?, [Ἀρ]χανδρος?—edd. prr.: s. Φιλοκλῆς)

TAURIS:
—CHERSONESOS: (3) c. 315-300 BC Kats p. 91 no. 30 (amph.)

Ἀρχέβιος
THRACE:
—BYZANTION: (1) c. 389 BC D. xx 60-3; xxiii 189

Ἀρχεβούλη
MACEDONIA (EDONIS):
—AMPHIPOLIS: (1) iv/iii BC *AEMTh* 15 (2001) p. 118 (Ἀρχεβού[λ]η: d. Ἀντίδωρος)

Ἀρχέβουλος
THRACE:
—APOLLONIA-SOZOPOLIS: (1) v/iv BC *IGB* v 5151 with pl. 25 (Ἀρχίβουλος—*IGB* per err.: s. Ἕρμιππος)

Ἀρχέδαμος
MACEDONIA: (1) m. iv BC Ael., *VH* xiv 48 (Tataki, *Macedonians* p. 268 no. 296)

Ἀρχέδημος
CIMMERIAN BOSPOROS:
—GORGIPPIA: (1) f. iii BC *CIRB* 1137 B I, 31 ([Ἀρ]χέδημος: s. Κρατῖνος); (2) ib. l. 36; 1137 B II, 14 (s. Ἑστιαῖος); (3) ib. 1137 B I, 57 (s. Φιλῖνος)
—HERMONASSA: (4) iv BC ib. 1056 I, 11 (f. —ημος); (5) ib. 1056 II, 7 (f. Δῖος)
MACEDONIA (CHALKIDIKE):
—APHYTIS: (6) ?351 BC *A' Panell. Synedr. Epigr.* pp. 80-1, 21 (f. Πίτθις)
MACEDONIA (EDONIS):
—PHILIPPOI (NR.): (7) ii-iii AD *BCH* 24 (1900) pp. 313-14 (Pilhofer 22) (freed.?)
MACEDONIA (MYGDONIA):
—THESSALONIKE: (8) c. 266 BC *IG* XII (9) 1187, 37; Robert, *Ét. Num. Gr.* pp. 179 ff. (date) (Tataki, *Macedonians* p. 180 no. 11) (f. —ος); (9) c. 230-200 BC *BCH* 45 (1921) p. 17 III, 66 (Tataki, *Macedonians* p. 179 no. 10) (s. Τιμόθεος)
MACEDONIA (PIERIA):
—DION: (10) iii/ii BC Oikonomos 3 ([Ἀ]ρχέδημο[ς]: ?f. Πραξίνικος)
THRACE:
—BEROE-AUGUSTA TRAIANA: (11) c. 214 AD *IGB* III 1560, 5 (f. Ἀρχίας)

Ἀρχελάϊος
SCYTHIA MINOR:
—ISTROS: (1) 138 AD *ISM* I 193 II, 30 (s. Ξενοχάρης)

Ἀρχελαΐς
CIMMERIAN BOSPOROS:
—PANTIKAPAION: (1) i AD *CIRB* 362; cf. KW pl. 13 no. 181 (d. Ἀρχέλαος)
MACEDONIA (ORESTIS):
—PORIA (MOD.): (2) imp. *SEG* XLIX 777 ([Ἀρ]χελαΐς?)

Ἀρχέλαος
CIMMERIAN BOSPOROS:
—PANTIKAPAION: (1) ii-i BC *CIRB* 262; cf. KW pl. 37 no. 539 (I f. Ἀρχέλαος II, Θαῦνος); (2) *CIRB* 262; cf. KW pl. 37 no. 539 (II s. Ἀρχέλαος I); (3) *CIRB* 292; cf. KW pl. 32 no. 449 (f. Φάννας); (4) i AD *CIRB* 362; cf. KW pl. 13 no. 181 (f. Ἀρχελαΐς); (5) v-vi AD *IAK* 10 (1904) p. 87 no. 101 (Ἀ[ρ]χέλαος)
MACEDONIA: (6) c. 450-399 BC *RE* (7); *IG* I³ 89, 60; *HN²* pp. 220-1; *Kraay-Mørkholm Essays* p. 304; pp. 309-10 (coin) (Tataki, *Macedonians* p. 270 no. 306) (Ἀρχέλας—*IG*: s. Περδίκκας II, Σιμίχη, f. Ὀρέστης, ?f. Ἀμύντας, Ἀργαῖος, Παυσανίας: king); (7) ?c. 400-359 BC *RE* (9) (Tataki, *Macedonians* p. 268 no. 298); cf. Beloch, *GG* III (2) pp. 66-7 (s. Ἀμύντας III, Γυγαία); (8) 331 BC *RE* (10); Berve 158 (Tataki, *Macedonians* p. 269 no. 305) (s. Θεόδωρος); (9) 329 BC *RE* (11); Berve 157 (Tataki, *Macedonians* p. 269 no. 304) (s. Ἄνδροκλος); (10) 322 BC *RE* (19); Berve 159 (Tataki, *Macedonians* p. 269 no. 299); (11) f. iii BC *IMM* 5, 12, 19 (Tataki, *Macedonians* p. 269 no. 303) (s. Ἀέροπος); (12) 243 BC *RE* (22) (Tataki, *Macedonians* p. 269 no. 301)
MACEDONIA (BOTTIAIA):
—EDESSA: (13) ii BC Dimitsas 557 = *SEG* XLIX 827; cf. *ZPE* 132 (2000) pp. 161-2 (locn.) (Tataki, *Edessa* 37) (or Macedonia (Mygdonia) Thessalonike: f. Ἀδεία, Θράσων)
—PELLA: (14) ii-i BC *A' Panell. Synedr. Epigr.* p. 176 no. 2 ([Ἀρ]χέλαος)
MACEDONIA (CHALKIDIKE):
—AKANTHOS: (15) iv/iii BC *SEG* XLVII 870, 5 (Ἀρχελάō (gen.): ?f. Ἄλεξις)
MACEDONIA (EDONIS):
—AMPHIPOLIS: (16) iv BC ib. XXIV 587
—PHILIPPOI (NR.): (17) imp. ib. II 422 (Pilhofer 413)
MACEDONIA (ELIMEIA):
—AIANE: (18) s. ii AD *EAM* 15 b (Ἀρχέ[λαος]?)
MACEDONIA (EORDAIA):
—AKRINI (MOD.): (19) ii-i BC ib. 89; cf. *BE* 1995, no. 409 (f. Ὀηδέα)
MACEDONIA (MYGDONIA):
—KALINDOIA: (20) 68-98 AD *SEG* XLII 580, 82 (s. Δρούα); (21) ib. l. 87 (s. Λυσανίας); (22) a. 98 AD ib. 582, 40 (f. Κλαρόνικος); (23) ib. l. 41 (s. Ῥοῖμος)
MACEDONIA?: (24) f. iv BC *FGrH* 115 F 307 (f. Ἡρακλείδης)
SCYTHIA MINOR:
—ISTROS: (25) i BC-i AD *ISM* I 191 I, 49 (f. —ων); (26) ib. 191 II, 19 (s. Πυθόδωρος); (27) 138 AD ib. 193 II, 56 (s. Διονύσιος)
—TOMIS: (28) ii-iii AD ib. II 238, 1 (f. Οὐαλέριος)
THRACE:
—ABDERA: (29) c. 346-336 BC May, *Abdera* pp. 284-5 nos. 519-28 (coin)
—APOLLONIA-SOZOPOLIS: (30) hell.-imp. *AEMÖ* 10 (1886) p. 165 (vase) (Ἀρχέλα(ος))
—BISANTHE-PANION: (31) ii-i BC *BCH* 24 (1900) p. 165 no. 7 (s. Δημόφιλος)
—BISANTHE-PANION?: (32) imp. Unp. (Sayar)
—BYZANTION: (33) ii BC *Türk Tarih Kongresi XI* (6) p. 2705 with pl. 500. 15 (s. Μειδίας)
—BYZANTION?: (34) imp. *CIG* 2039 (Τιβ. Κλ. Αὐρηλιανὸς Ἀ.)
—KABYLE: (35) ii-iii AD *IGB* III 1774, 4 (*Μ. Οὔλπ. Ἀ.*)
—PIZOS: (36) 202 AD ib. 1690 e, 12 (s. Ἀκύλας)

Ἀρχέλας
THRACE:
—AINOS: (1) 194 BC *Milet* I (3) 54, 5 (and Caria Miletos: s. Διονύσιος)

Ἀρχέλοχος
SCYTHIA MINOR:
—ISTROS: (1) ?iv-iii BC *ISM* I 249 (f. Μητρόδωρος); (2) iii BC ib. 8, 2 (f. Πυθοτέλης)

Ἀρχέμαχος
MACEDONIA (BOTTIAIA):
—ALOROS? (KLEIDI (MOD.)): (1) iii BC *AD* 25 (1970) Chron. p. 388 (f. Ἀντηρίς)

Ἀρχέμβροτος
THRACE:
—MARONEIA: (1) f. v BC Schönert-Geiss, *Maroneia* 27-30 (coin)

Ἀρχέμορος
MACEDONIA?: (1) 202 BC Sil. xvii 426 with comm. (Lat. Archemorus: fict.?)

Ἀρχένους
THRACE:
—PERINTHOS-HERAKLEIA: (1) iv-iii BC *IPerinth* 4, 1 (f. Χαβρίας)

Ἀρχέπολις
MACEDONIA: (1) 330-325 BC *CID* II 32, 43; 69, 20; 71, 42; 72, [5]; 86, 8 etc. with Index; Berve 160 (Tataki, *Macedonians* p. 270 no. 307)
MACEDONIA (BOTTIAIA):
—BEROIA?: (2) 38 BC Robert, *Coll. Froehner* 44, 19 (*IG* XII Suppl. p. 149); cf. Tataki, *Macedonians* p. 76 no. 15 (Ἀρχεπόλεως (gen.): f. Διονύσιος)
MACEDONIA (DERRIOPOS):
—STUBERRA: (3) i AD *IG* X (2) (2) 330 (s. Ἀπολλόδωρος)
MACEDONIA (MYGDONIA):
—THESSALONIKE: (4) 38 BC Robert, *Coll. Froehner* 44, 8 (Tataki, *Macedonians* p. 180 no. 12) (s. Νικόπολις); (5) i BC/i AD *IG* X (2) (1) 58, 10; *KGAM Thess.* I 111 (date) (f. Πρῖμος)
MACEDONIA?: (6) 330 BC *RE* Supplbd. 4 (-); Berve 161 (Tataki, *Macedonians* p. 270 no. 308) (Lat. Archepolis)
THRACE:
—ZONE: (7) m. iv BC *PAE* 1969, p. 64 with pl. 76 a (*IThrakAig* E418) (s. Σωκλῆς)

Ἀρχεπτόλεμος
MACEDONIA (CHALKIDIKE):
—TORONE: (1) ?353 BC *SEG* XXIV 574, 18; Hatzopoulos, *Actes Chalc.* p. 80 (date) (s. Κλεόμαχος)

Ἀρχεσίς
THRACE: (1) hell.? *IG* II² 8899 (*FRA* 2501)

Ἀρχέστρατος
CIMMERIAN BOSPOROS:
—GORGIPPIA: (1) f. iii BC *CIRB* 1137 B I, 27 (f. —ας)
MACEDONIA: (2) c. 300 BC *IEph* 1452, 1 (*IEK* 505; Tataki, *Macedonians* p. 270 no. 309) (s. Νίκων); (3) ?c. 240-220 BC *IOrop* 64, 3 (Tataki, *Macedonians* p. 270 no. 310) (s. Ξένων)
MACEDONIA (CHALKIDIKE):
—POTIDAIA-KASSANDREIA: (4) ?m. iii BC *FD* III (4) 351, 5 (Tataki, *Macedonians* p. 86 no. 16) (s. Παρμενίσκος)
—STOLOS?: (5) ?350 BC *SEG* XXXVIII 670, 7 (s. Ἄδων)
THRACE:
—ABDERA: (6) s. iv BC *IThrakAig* E41 (s. Εὐπείθης); (7) *SEG* XLVII 1030 + *IThrakAig* E44 (Ἀρ[χέστρ]ατος?: f. Ἀγα.....ος); (8) c. 346-336 BC *AMNG* II (1) 186 (coin)
—ODESSOS: (9) i-ii AD *IGB* I² 51 c, 4 (f. Ἧδυς)

Ἀρχεσώ
TAURIS:
—CHERSONESOS: (1) iii BC *IOSPE* I² 507 (d. Λύσανδρος)

Ἄρχετος
KOLCHIS:
—PICHVNARI (MOD.): (1) v-iv BC *DHA* 20 (1994) p. 138 (vase)

Ἀρχη
TAURIS:
—TAUROI: (1) f. ii BC *AA* 2000, p. 479 no. 2

Ἀρχήνασσα
THRACE:
—ABDERA: (1) c. 325-300 BC *BCH* 66-7 (1942-3) p. 195 no. 4 (*IThrakAig* E45)
—ZONE: (2) s. iv BC *SEG* XXXIV 710 = XLVIII 904 bis = XLIX 894 (*IThrakAig* E402) (d. Κέφαλος)

Ἀρχίας
CIMMERIAN BOSPOROS:
—PANTIKAPAION: (1) i AD *CIRB* 408; cf. KW pl. 49 no. 680 (s. *Σαββίων*)
MACEDONIA: (2) iv BC *FGrH* 156 F 9. 21 (Tataki, *Macedonians* p. 271 no. 311) (?s. *Ἀντίπατρος*)
MACEDONIA (BOTTIAIA):
—PELLA: (3) 326-324 BC *RE* (17); Berve 162 (Tataki, *Macedonians* p. 151 no. 23) (s. *Ἀναξίδοτος*); (4) ?iii BC *SEG* II 401 (s. *Σωσίων*)
MACEDONIA (CHALKIDIKE):
—DION: (5) iii BC *IG* XII (8) 233 (Tataki, *Macedonians* p. 100 no. 3) (or Macedonia (Pieria) Dion: f. *Εὐθύδικος*, *Εὐάρατος*)
—STOLOS?: (6) ?350 BC *SEG* XXXVIII 670, 4 (s. *Ὀπωρις*)
MACEDONIA (PIERIA):
—PYDNA: (7) c. 230-200 BC *BCH* 45 (1921) p. 17 III, 55 (Tataki, *Macedonians* p. 170 no. 6) (s. *Ἀλκίμαχος*)
MACEDONIA?: (8) imp.? *GP* 3588-3795; pp. 432-5 (ident., date)
SCYTHIA MINOR:
—KALLATIS: (9) 241-244 AD *ISM* III 74, 12 (*Αἰλ. Ἀρχ(ίας)* (n. pr.?))
TAURIS:
—CHERSONESOS: (10) iii AD *IOSPE* I² 479 (*M. Ἀ.*: f. *M. Αὐρ. Ἰάσων*)
THRACE: (11) ii BC *Memnonion* 415 (Velkov 33; La'da E715)
—AGRIANES: (12) ii BC *IG* XII Suppl. p. 189 no. 629
—BEROE-AUGUSTA TRAIANA: (13) c. 214 AD *IGB* III 1560, 5 (s. *Ἀρχέδημος*)
—BYZANTION: (14) iii BC *IByz* 68 (Fıratlı–Robert p. 48 no. 6) (f. *Μᾶτρις*)
—LYSIMACHEIA: (15) ii-i BC *ISmyrna* 689 III, 31 (s. *Μηνόφιλος*)

Ἀρχιβιάδας
THRACE:
—BYZANTION: (1) 389-349 BC Polyaen. V 44. 1 (-δης)

Ἀρχίβιος
MACEDONIA: (1) m. ii BC *BGU* 2423, 32 (Tataki, *Macedonians* p. 476 no. 49; La'da E1443) (s. *Πτολεμαῖος*)

Ἀρχιγένης
MACEDONIA (PIERIA):
—DION: (1) iii BC *SEG* XXXI 629, 4 (*Ἀρχιγ[ένης]*?)

Ἀρχίδαμος
MACEDONIA (CHALKIDIKE):
—ANTIGONEIA?: (1) hell.? Robert, *OMS* 2 pp. 1296-7 (Tataki, *Macedonians* p. 64 no. 2) (f. *Ἀρριδαῖος*, *Ἄρχιππος*, *Τιμοκράτης*)
—CHALKIDEIS: (2) c. 376-373 BC *Olynthus* 9 pp. 68-71 nos. 104-12 (coin); *Ancient Macedonia* I p. 254 (date)
—OLYNTHOS: (3) ?350 BC *TAPA* 62 (1931) p. 43 no. 2, 3; Hatzopoulos, *Actes Chalc.* p. 80 (date) (s. *Μήτριχος*)

Ἀρχίδημος
SKYTHIA:
—OLBIA-BORYSTHENES: (1) ii AD *IOSPE* I² 84, 3 (*Ἀρχέδημος*—*IOSPE* per err.: s. *Δάδακος*)

Ἀρχιδία
THRACE:
—PERINTHOS-HERAKLEIA: (1) i-ii AD *IPerinth* 108 (biling.) (*Ἰουλ. Ἀ. Ἰουλιανή*)

Ἀρχίης
MACEDONIA?: (1) b. 348 BC *Olynthus* 10 p. 422 no. 2180 (bullet)

Ἀρχικλῆς
TAURIS:
—CHERSONESOS: (1) c. 210-200 BC Anokhin p. 144 nos. 147; 150 (coins) (*Ἀρχίκλειο(ς)* (gen.)—147)
THRACE:
—ZONE: (2) c. 425-400 BC *IThrakAig* E403 (?s. *Ἐ*—)

Ἀρχίλοχος
THRACE:
—APOLLONIA-SOZOPOLIS: (1) v/iv BC *SNG Berry* 392; *Coll. Waddington* 1027 (coin) (*Ἀρχί̣λοχος*—392, *[Ἀρ]χίλοχος*—1027)

Ἀρχῖνος
MACEDONIA: (1) s. iv BC *Syll*³ 267 C, 1 + *BCH* 70 (1946) p. 38 n.2 (Tataki, *Macedonians* p. 271 no. 312) (*[Ἀρ]χῖνος*?: f. *Εὐδ.....*)
MACEDONIA (PIERIA):
—PHILA?: (2) ?iii BC *RPh* 1911, pp. 133-4 no. 36, 39; cf. Helly, *L'État thessalien* pp. 319-20 (locn.)

Ἄρχιον
MACEDONIA (CHALKIDIKE):
—POTIDAIA-KASSANDREIA: (1) iii BC *IG* II² 8997 (Tataki, *Macedonians* p. 87 no. 17; *FRA* 2779) (d. *Διονύσιος*)

Ἄρχιππος
CIMMERIAN BOSPOROS:
—HERMONASSA: (1) iv BC *CIRB* 1060; cf. KW pl. 6 no. 112 (s. ..*άσιππος*)
—NYMPHAION: (2) iii BC *CIRB* 912 III, 13 (*Ἀρχιπ[πος]*)
MACEDONIA (BOTTIAIA):
—AIGAI: (3) iv BC *SEG* XXXV 806 (*Ἀρχιπ[πο]ς*: f. *Ἡρακλείδης*)
—BEROIA: (4) 239-229 BC *IBer* 45, 29 (Tataki 18)
MACEDONIA (CHALKIDIKE):
—ANTIGONEIA?: (5) hell.? Robert, *OMS* 2 pp. 1296-7 (Tataki, *Macedonians* p. 64 no. 3) (s. *Ἀρχίδαμος*)
MACEDONIA (EDONIS):
—AMPHIPOLIS: (6) b. 357 BC Hatzopoulos, *Actes Amphipolis* p. 20 no. 2, 10 (*SEG* XLI 556)
MACEDONIA (EORDAIA?):
—EUIA?: (7) 181 BC *EAM* 87, 1 (Hatzopoulos, *MI* 2 pp. 41-2 no. 17) (*Ἀρχιπ̣π̣[ος]*)
MACEDONIA (MYGDONIA): (8) m. ii BC *SEG* VIII 370 (Bernand, *Inscr. métr.* 9; Tataki, *Macedonians* p. 203 no. 1) (s. *Ζωΐλος*)
MACEDONIA (PIERIA):
—PHYLAKAI?: (9) ?i BC Oikonomos 60 = *IG* IX (2) 231 (s. *Νικάνωρ*)
TAURIS:
—CHERSONESOS?: (10) imp. *SEG* XLIII 501 (amph.) (*Ἀρχιππ(ος)*)
THRACE:
—AINOS: (11) iii-ii BC *PAE* 1912, p. 187 no. 91 (f. *Ἑρμαγένης*)

Ἄρχος
MACEDONIA (PELAGONIA):
—KERAMIAI (NR.): (1) ii-iii AD *IG* X (2) (2) 223 (s. *Οὐαλέριος*)
THRACE:
—PERINTHOS-HERAKLEIA: (2) iv-iii BC *IPerinth* 4, 5 (*Ἄ[ρ]χος*, *—να[ρ]χος*?)

Ἄρχων
MACEDONIA (BOTTIAIA):
—PELLA: (1) c. 370-321 BC *RE* (5); Berve 163; *CEG* II 877 (Tataki, *Macedonians* p. 151 no. 24) (s. *Κλεῖνος*, *Σύνεσις*)
MACEDONIA (CHALKIDIKE):
—OLYNTHOS: (2) 360 BC *IG* IV (1)² 94 b, 14 (Perlman, *City and Sanctuary* E.1 with p. 69 f. (date); Tataki, *Macedonians* p. 131 no. 19)
—POTIDAIA-KASSANDREIA: (3) c. 240-220 BC *SEG* XXXVII 558, 1; *Poikila* p. 141 (date)
MACEDONIA (MYGDONIA):
—LETE: (4) iv/iii BC *SEG* XXIV 544 (Tataki, *Macedonians* p. 118 no. 4) (s. *Φιλίσκος*)
—THESSALONIKE: (5) i BC/i AD *IG* X (2) (1) 58, 18; cf. *SEG* XLVII 971; *KGAM Thess.* I 111 (date) (*Καλλίστρατος ὁ καὶ Ἀ.*)
THRACE:
—LYSIMACHEIA: (6) c. 208 BC *FD* III (4) 135 II, 7 (s. *Χορειός*)

Ἄρωγος
MACEDONIA (BOTTIAIA):
—BEROIA: (1) ii-iii AD *IBer* 240 (s. *Εὔοδος*, *Ζωσίμη*)

Ἀρωμάτιν
THRACE:
—BYZANTION: (1) imp. *IByz* 24

Ἀρώτης
SKYTHIA:
—OLBIA-BORYSTHENES?: (1) c. 200-175 BC *IG* XI (4) 814, 3, 9; cf. *ID* Index I s.v. *Ἀγρότας* (*Ἀρώτου* (gen.)—lap., *Ἀ(γ)ρ(ό)τας*?—Tréheux: f. *Διόδωρος*)

Ἀσαίη
CIMMERIAN BOSPOROS:
—PANTIKAPAION: (1) iv BC Tolstoi 218 (vase)

Ἀσαμήνης?
SCYTHIA MINOR:
—ISTROS: (1) v-iv BC *St. Clas.* 7 (1965) p. 279 no. 9 (vase) (*Ἀσαμήνεια* (poss. adj.))

Ἄσανδρος
CIMMERIAN BOSPOROS:
—BOSPOROS: (1) c. 90-17 BC *RE* (4); *PIR*² A 1197; *SNG BM Black Sea* 961-8 (coins); Sokol'skii, *Tamanskii tolos* p. 40; cf. *Hyperboreus* 1994-5 (2), pp. 138-9 (*Ἀσόανδρος*—Sokol'skii: king) ?= (*Ἀσάνδροχος* (*1*))
MACEDONIA: (2) c. 380-329 BC *RE* (2); Berve 165 (Tataki, *Macedonians* p. 271 no. 313) (s. *Φιλώτας*); (3) s. iv BC *IG* XII (9) 197, 2 (Tataki, *Macedonians* p. 77 no. 18); cf. *Eretria* XI p. 172 (name) (*Ἄσα̣[νδρ]ος*: f. *Μυλλένας*)
MACEDONIA (BOTTIAIA):
—BEROIA: (4) 323-313 BC *RE* (3); Berve 164; *Kings and Colonists* pp. 91-2 (Tataki, *Macedonians* p. 76 no. 16) (s. *Ἀγάθων*); (5) 239-229 BC *IBer* 45, 33 (f. *Παυσανίας*); (6) 178 BC *SGDI* 2071, 2, 6 (Tataki, *Macedonians* p. 77 no. 17) (s. *Μένανδρος*)
—ICHNAI: (7) c. 265-260 BC *FD* III (3) 207, 2 (Tataki, *Macedonians* p. 113 no. 3) (f. *Ἀντίγονος*)
MACEDONIA (CHALKIDIKE):
—TORONE: (8) ?353 BC *SEG* XXIV 574, 12, 16; Hatzopoulos, *Actes Chalc.* p. 80 (date) (s. *Ἐπικράτης*)
MACEDONIA (EDONIS):
—AMPHIPOLIS: (9) a. 357 BC Hatzopoulos, *Actes Amphipolis* p. 34 no. 6, 2; *SEG* XLI 560 (date) (*Ἄσ̣ανδρος*)
—AMPHIPOLIS (NR.): (10) a. 357 BC Hatzopoulos, *Actes Amphipolis* p. 43 no. 8, 3 (*SEG* XLI 562) (f. *Μεννέας*)
MACEDONIA (ORESTIS):
—LYKE*: (11) hell. *EAM* 179 γ (tile); cf. *AD* 17 (1961-2) Chron. pl. 269 ε
MACEDONIA (PIERIA):
—PHILA?: (12) ?iii BC *RPh* 1911, pp. 133-4 no. 36, 110; cf. Helly, *L'État thessalien* pp. 319-20 (locn.) (s. *Δημέας*)
—PYDNA: (13) iv BC *GRBS* 43 (2002-3) p. 119 no. 5, 5
PENESTAI:
—USCANA?: (14) ii-iii AD *SEG* XXXIX 618 (*[Ἄ]σανδρος*: s. *Ἀπολλόδωρος*)

SKYTHIA:
—TANAIS: (**15**) 220-225 AD *CIRB* 1278, 9; 1280, 12 (s. *Θαύμαστος*)

Ἀσάνδροχος
CIMMERIAN BOSPOROS:
—BOSPOROS: (**1**) i BC ib. 40, 1 (?f. *Ἀσποῦργος*: king) ?= (*Ἄσανδρος* (*1*))

Ἄσανος
SKYTHIA:
—OLBIA-BORYSTHENES: (**1**) iii AD *IOlbia* 83, 11 (*IOSPE* I^2 97); Zgusta, *PNS* 62 (f. *Μουγίσαγος*)

Ἄσαρος
CIMMERIAN BOSPOROS:
—NYMPHAION: (**1**) v BC *CIRB* 914; Zgusta, *PNS* 63 (s. *Ἀτάκης*)

Ἀσβόλις
THRACE:
—BEROE-AUGUSTA TRAIANA: (**1**) ii-iii AD *SEG* XXXIX 649, 10 (*Τρόφιμος ὁ καὶ Ἀ.*: s. *Ἀπολλόδωρος*)
—SPINOPARA: (**2**) ii AD *IGB* IV 2192, 8

Ἀσία
SCYTHIA MINOR:
—ISTROS?: (**1**) iii BC Brown, *Ptolemaic Paintings* p. 25 no. 17 (La'da E2628) (*Ἀ. Ἴστρα*—lap.)
THRACE: (**2**) ?ii BC *ILind* 695

Ἀσιανός
THRACE:
—DIONYSOPOLIS: (**1**) iii AD *IGB* I^2 14 c, 23 (f. *Αὐρ. Εὐτύχης*)

Ἀσιάρχης
SCYTHIA MINOR:
—ISTROS:
——(Rhomaioi): (**1**) iii AD *ISM* I 142, 5 (*Αὐρ. Ἀ.*: s. *Χαρμίδης*)

Ἀσίας
MACEDONIA (MYGDONIA):
—LETE?: (**1**) 22 or 139 AD Dimitsas 678, 9 (*Ἀ.*—lap., *Ἀσ(τ)ίας*?: f. *Ζωπᾶς*)

Ἀσιατικός
CIMMERIAN BOSPOROS:
—PANTIKAPAION: (**1**) i AD *CIRB* 142, 1, 6 (*GVI* 979) (f. *Χρηστίων*)
MACEDONIA (MYGDONIA):
—KALINDOIA: (**2**) a. 98 AD *SEG* XLII 582, 49 (s. *Ἑρμέρως*)
—THESSALONIKE: (**3**) s. i AD *IG* X (2) (1) 68, 24; 69, 18 (s. *Φίλα*); (**4**) ib. l. 32 (f. *Ξανθίων*)
THRACE:
—BEROE-AUGUSTA TRAIANA: (**5**) 180-185 AD *IGB* III 1585, 10 (*Ἀσια[τικός]*: f. *Φίλιππος*); (**6**) f. iii AD *SEG* XLVIII 893. 1 (*M. Αὐρ. Ἀ.*)
—ERGISSENOI: (**7**) ii AD *IGB* III 1593, 20 (s. *Ἰάσων*)
—GLAVA PANEGA (MOD.): (**8**) ii-iii AD ib. II 516 (s. *Θεόδωρος*)
—KELLAI: (**9**) ?ii-iii AD ib. III 1532-3 (f. *Φλ. Σείτη*)
—MARKIANOPOLIS?: (**10**) 117-138 AD *Ant. Afric.* 25 (1989) pp. 209-10 no. 16, 13 (Lat. M. Sextilius Asiaticus)
—MESAMBRIA: (**11**) i-ii AD *IGB* I^2 340 bis (s. *Σεραπίων*)
—NICOPOLIS AD ISTRUM: (**12**) ii-iii AD ib. II 661 (s. *Σωκράτης*)
—ODESSOS: (**13**) f. ii AD ib. I^2 77, 3 (*CCET* I 31) (f. *Ἐπταίκενθος*)
—PERINTHOS-HERAKLEIA: (**14**) 128-136 AD *IPerinth* 37 (*Λάρκιος Ἀ.*: f. *Λαρκία Γηπαιπυρίς*)
—SERDICA: (**15**) f. iii AD *IGB* IV 1910, 9 (*Ἀντωνιανὸς Ἀ.*)
—SERDICA (TERRIT.): (**16**) ii-iii AD ib. 2007 (f. —α)

Ἀσίδημος
MACEDONIA (BISALTIA):
—EUPORIA?: (**1**) imp.? Kaphtantzis 511
MACEDONIA?: (**2**) 221 BC *PPetr* III 112 c, 24; cf. La'da E1444 (or Thessaly: *Ἀσίδ[ημος]*: I f. *Ἀσίδημος* II); (**3**) *PPetr* III 112 c, 24 (La'da E1444) (or Thessaly: II s. *Ἀσίδημος* I)

Ἀσκάνιος
THRACE:
—ABDERA: (**1**) iv/iii BC *RE* (8)
—PHILIPPOPOLIS-TRIMONTIUM (TERRIT.): (**2**) iii AD *IGB* III 1090 (f. —ακετης)

Ἄσκιος
SKYTHIA:
—OLBIA-BORYSTHENES: (**1**) f. iv BC Dubois, *IGDOlbia* 103, 7 (lead) (*Ἄσκιος*)

Ἀσκλαπιάδας
SCYTHIA MINOR:
—KALLATIS: (**1**) s. iii BC *ISM* III 35, 2 (f. *Σῖμος*)
TAURIS:
—CHERSONESOS: (**2**) ii-i BC *IOSPE* I^2 468 (s. *Χάρμιππος*)
THRACE:
—BYZANTION: (**3**) s. iv BC *IByz* 124 (Fıratlı–Robert p. 100 no. 151) (s. *Νικάνωρ*); (**4**) c. 307-304 BC *IG* II^2 555, 1, 17, 23, etc. (*Ἀσκληπιάδης*); (**5**) c. 200 BC ib. 884, 12 (*Ἀσκληπιάδης*: f. *Μηνοφάνης*); (**6**) ii-i BC *Türk Tarih Kongresi XI* (6) p. 2704 with pl. 497. 9 (f. *Δαμοξένα*); (**7**) i BC *IByz* 155 (Fıratlı–Robert pp. 105-6 no. 166) (f. *Ἀρίστων*)
—BYZANTION (TERRIT.): (**8**) i BC *IByz* 186 (Fıratlı–Robert p. 71 no. 72) (f. *Δαμάτριος*)
—SALYMBRIA: (**9**) hell. *IByz* S 41 (s. *Θεογένης*, f. *Μόσχιον*)

Ἀσκλαπιόδωρος
SCYTHIA MINOR:
—KALLATIS: (**1**) iii BC *IG* II^2 8946 (*FRA* 2643) (-κλη-: f. *Εἰκάδιος*); (**2**) s. iii BC *ISM* III 35 A, 35 (s. *Ἀπολλόδοτος*)

Ἀσκλάπων
THRACE:
—MARONEIA: (**1**) iii-ii BC *IG* II^2 2947 (*FRA* 3532) (I f. *Ἀσκλάπων* II); (**2**) *IG* II^2 2947 (*FRA* 3533) (II s. *Ἀσκλάπων* I)

Ἀσκλᾶς
CIMMERIAN BOSPOROS:
—PANTIKAPAION: (**1**) imp. *CIRB* 808 (*[Ἀ]σκλᾶς*); (**2**) 14 AD ib. 335, 1 (f. *Ἄλκιμος*)
MACEDONIA (EDONIS):
—PHILIPPOI?: (**3**) imp. *AE* 1950-1, p. 71 no. 15 (Pilhofer 730) (or Macedonia (Mygdonia) Thessalonike: Lat. Ascla)
SKYTHIA:
—TANAIS: (**4**) 228 AD *CIRB* 1283, 16 (s. *Ἡρακλείδης*)
THRACE:
—ABDERA?: (**5**) ii-iii AD *Belomorski Pregled* I (1942) p. 336 no. 43 (*IThrakAig* E483)
—NICOPOLIS AD ISTRUM: (**6**) ii-iii AD *IGB* II 693 (s. *Χρῆστος*)
—NICOPOLIS AD NESTUM: (**7**) ii AD ib. IV 2336, 5
—PERINTHOS-HERAKLEIA: (**8**) c. 100-115 AD *SEG* XXVI 1288, 11 (s. *Ἰουλιανός*)

Ἀσκληπᾶς
CIMMERIAN BOSPOROS:
—THEODOSIA: (**1**) iii AD *CIRB* 947 A, 11 (*Ἀσκλη[πᾶς]*?: f. *Χωνδίακος*)
MACEDONIA (BOTTIAIA):
—BEROIA: (**2**) ii/iii AD *IBer* 143 C, 17 (Tataki 1065) (*Πε. Ἀ.*)
—EDESSA: (**3**) 180 AD *SEG* XXIV 531, 18 (Tataki, *Edessa* 38) (f. *Ἰουλιανός*)
MACEDONIA (MYGDONIA):
—THESSALONIKE: (**4**) ii AD *IG* X (2) (1) 226, 8; cf. Robert, *OMS* 5 p. 298 n. 193 (s. *Ἐπ—*)
MACEDONIA (SINTIKE):
—HERAKLEIA: (**5**) 230 AD *IGB* V 5922, 5 (*Ἀσκληπῆ* (gen.): f. *Διονύσιος*)
—PARTHIKOPOLIS?: (**6**) ii-iii AD ib. 5925, 2, 9 (s. *Δημήτριος*)
THRACE:
—NICOPOLIS AD NESTUM: (**7**) ii AD ib. IV 2336, 1-2 (f. *Διογενιανός*, *Ἀσκληπιόδωρος*)
—SERDICA: (**8**) ii AD ib. 1957, 5 (s. *Ἀσκληπιάδης*, *Θεοφίλη*)

Ἀσκληπιάδης
CIMMERIAN BOSPOROS:
—PANTIKAPAION: (**1**) ?s. i AD *CIRB* 491; cf. KW pl. 39 no. 559 (f. *Περιγένης*); (**2**) ?ii AD *CIRB* 676 (*[Ἀ]σκληπιάδη[ς]*: s. *Ἀπολλώνιος*, *Ἡδεῖα*); (**3**) ib. (*[Ἀ]σ[κ]ληπιάδης*: f. *Ἡδεῖα*)
—PHANAGOREIA: (**4**) i AD ib. 996 (*Ἀσκ(λ)ηπιάδης*: s. *Ἀπολλώνιος*); (**5**) ii AD ib. 1001 (f. *Δημήτριος*)
MACEDONIA: (**6**) c. 245-205 BC *IG* VII 506, 3 (Tataki, *Macedonians* p. 272 no. 315) (*Ἀσκλαπιάδας*: f. *Ἀντίγονος*); (**7**) 184 BC *PHeid* VIII 414, 45 (La'da E1449); (**8**) 145 BC *PTeb* 32, 17 (Tataki, *Macedonians* p. 477 no. 54; La'da E1448) (s. *Πτολεμαῖος*); (**9**) 135-131 BC Bernand, *De Thèbes* 243, 8 (Tataki, *Macedonians* p. 476 no. 51; La'da E1445) (s. *Ἀμμώνιος*); (**10**) c. 100-75 BC *SB* 8974 fr. 3, 51, 54 (Tataki, *Macedonians* p. 476 no. 52; La'da E1446) (II s. *Ἀσκληπιάδης* I, *Ἀρτεμιδώρα*: katoikos); (**11**) *SB* 8974 fr. 3, [7-8], 10, 34, 47, 51, 55 (Tataki, *Macedonians* p. 477 no. 56); cf. La'da E1446; E1544 (I f. *Νέαρχος*, *Ἀσκληπιάδης* II); (**12**) 69 BC *IFayoum* 135, 31 (Tataki, *Macedonians* p. 477 no. 55); cf. La'da E1438 (f. *Ἁρμόδιος*: katoikos); (**13**) 54 BC *PSI* 1097, 1 (Tataki, *Macedonians* p. 477 no. 53; La'da E1447) (*[Ἀσ]κληπειάδης*: s. *Διονύσιος*)
MACEDONIA (BISALTIA):
—TRAGILOS: (**14**) iv BC *RE* (27); *FGrH* 12 (Tataki, *Macedonians* p. 192 no. 1)
MACEDONIA (BOTTIAIA):
—BEROIA: (**15**) b. 167 BC *IBer* I A, 4, 18 (Tataki 245) (s. *Ἡρᾶς*); (**16**) 118 BC *IBer* 134, 22 (s. *Ὀρέστης*); (**17**) 193-195 AD *ILeukopetra* 42, 8; 43, 5 (Tataki 277) (*Αὐρηλιανὸς Ἀσσκληπιάδης*—42, *Αὐρήλιος Ἀ.*—43)
—PELLA: (**18**) 231 or 206 BC *CPR* XVIII 20, 410; 21, 433, 438; cf. La'da E1944-5 (I f. *Δημήτριος*, *Ἀσκληπιάδης* II, *Διοδώρα*); (**19**) *CPR* XVIII 21, 436; cf. La'da E1943 (II s. *Ἀσκληπιάδης* I, f. *Ἀσκληπιάδης* III); (**20**) *CPR* XVIII 21, 436, 441, 450 (La'da 1943) (III s. *Ἀσκληπιάδης* II: t.e.)
—PELLA? (GIANNITSA (MOD.)): (**21**) ?i AD Dimitsas 128 (f. *Ἡρακλείδης*)
—PELLA*: (**22**) i BC *AD* 18 (1963) Chron. p. 203 n. 8 = *SEG* XLVIII 829 (lamp)
MACEDONIA (CHALKIDIKE):
—POTIDAIA-KASSANDREIA: (**23**) c. 208 BC *FD* III (4) 135, 23 (Tataki, *Macedonians* p. 87 no. 18) (s. *Δημήτριος*)
MACEDONIA (EDONIS):
—AMPHIPOLIS: (**24**) ii BC *Iscr. Gr. Verona* p. 115 no. 56 (Tataki, *Macedonians* p. 48 no. 27) (s. *Ἀπολλώνιος*); (**25**) 179 BC *SEG* XXXI 614, 8 (Hatzopoulos, *MI* 2 pp. 49-50 no. 29) (f. *Τιμωνίδης*)
MACEDONIA (ELIMEIA):
—AIANE*: (**26**) ?iii BC *EAM* 69 (seal)
—KENTRO (MOD.): (**27**) f. iii AD ib. 60 a (*[Ἀσκ]ληπιάδης*)
—XEROLIMNI (MOD.): (**28**) ii AD *Α΄ Panell. Synedr. Epigr.* p. 65 no. 11 (*SEG* XLIX 850) (*[Ἀσκλ]ηπιάδης*)

MACEDONIA (LYNKESTIS):
—HERAKLEIA: **(29)** ii-iii AD *IG* X (2) (2) 58 (Ἀσσκληπιάδ[η]ς)
MACEDONIA (MYGDONIA):
—THESSALONIKE: **(30)** 48 AD ib. X (2) (1) 623 A; **(31)** ?ii AD ib. 935 ([Ἀσ]κληπιά[δης]); **(32)** m. ii AD *SEG* XLIII 462, 2 (*Κάσσιος Ἀ.*: s. *Κ. Ἐρέννιος Σαβῖνος, Καττία Ἐλπίς*); **(33)** s. ii AD *IG* X (2) (1) 244 I, 10 (*Αἰλ. Ἀ.*); **(34)** iii AD ib. 476 C (f. *Ἄκυλα ἡ καὶ Πωριανή*)
MACEDONIA (PELAGONIA): **(35)** ii AD ib. X (2) (2) 260-1 (f. *Ἀσκληπιόδωρος*); **(36)** ii-iii AD ib. 260
—KERAMIAI (AREA): **(37)** ii AD ib. 184 (f. *Ἀβιδία Ζωϊλιανή*)
SCYTHIA MINOR:
—ISTROS: **(38)** ii AD *ISM* I 212, 27 (s. *Κλεινίας*); **(39)** f. iii AD *Stud. Fischer* p. 32 no. 4, 6 (f. *—φιος*); **(40)** *ISM* I 218, 7 (f. *Αὐρ. Ὀλύμπιος*)
—KALLATIS: **(41)** i BC ib. III 173 (Ἀσκληπι[άδης]); **(42)** 241-244 AD ib. 74, 9 (s. *Ὑγιαίνων*); **(43)** ib. 74 A, 24 (s. *Ἱερώνυμος*); **(44)** ib. l. 18-19 (s. *Θεόδωρος*, f. *Θεόδωρος*); **(45)** ib. 74 B, 26
—TOMIS: **(46)** ii BC ib. II 392 ([Ἀσκλ]ηπιάδης: s. *Νικήρατος*); **(47)** ii AD ib. 17, 18 (*Αἰλ. Ἀσκληπ[ιά]δης*); **(48)** ib. 125 II, 24; **(49)** ii-iii AD ib. 13, 4 (Ἀσκλη[πιάδης]?); **(50)** ib. 173 (f. *Φλ. Ἀκυλίνη, Ἰούλ. Αὐγουρῖνος*); **(51)** ib. 245 ([Ἀσκλη]πιάδης); **(52)** ib. 339; **(53)** iii AD ib. 269, 8; cf. *ZPE* 39 (1980) p. 200
—ULMETUM: **(54)** ?v AD Barnea 73, 10 (Popescu, *IGL* 210) (f. *Ἀλεξάνδρεια*)
SKYTHIA:
—OLBIA-BORYSTHENES: **(55)** imp. *IOSPE* I² 113, 5 (s. *Ποσίδηος*); **(56)** ib. 127 ([Ἀσ]κληπιάδ[ης]); **(57)** ib. 153, 2 (s. *Ἐπικράτης*)
—TANAIS: **(58)** c. 200-225 AD *CIRB* 1277, 12; 1280, 6 (s. *Οὐαλέριος*); **(59)** 209 AD ib. 1276, 3; **(60)** 220 AD ib. 1278, 19 ([Ἀ]σκλη[πιά]δης); **(61)** 228 AD ib. 1282, 20 (f. *Σοζίρσανος*); **(62)** 244 AD ib. 1287, 12 (f. *Ξάρθανος*)
TAURIS:
—CHERSONESOS: **(63)** 129 AD *IOSPE* I² 359, 32 (f. *Πατέρων*); **(64)** 130 AD *VDI* 1960 (3), pp. 154-5, 26 (I f. *Ἀσκληπιάδης* II); **(65)** ib. l. 26 (II s. *Ἀσκληπιάδης* I)
—CHERSONESOS*: **(66)** ?i-ii AD *IAK* 25 (1907) p. 134 (lamp)
THRACE: **(67)** hell. *Syringes* 18 (Velkov 34; La'da E716) (s. *Βίθυς*); **(68)** 241 BC *PFrankf* 5, 19 (Ἀσσ-)
—BEROE-AUGUSTA TRAIANA: **(69)** ii-iii AD *IGB* III 1583
—BEROE-AUGUSTA TRAIANA (TERRIT.): **(70)** iii AD ib. 1700 bis, 2 (Ἀσσκ-: f. *Αὐρ. Διvίας*)
—BISANTHE-PANION: **(71)** ?ii AD *CIL* III 7388 (Lat. P. Aelius Asclepiades)
—BYZANTION: **(72)** i BC-i AD *IByz* 19, 7 (*Κορνήλιος Ἀ.*)
—KELLAI: **(73)** 241-244 AD *IGB* III 1517, 20 (*Αὐρ. Ἀσκ(λ)ηπιάδης*: II s. *Ἀσκληπιάδης* I); **(74)** ib. l. 21 (I f. *Αὐρ. Ἀσκληπιάδης* II); **(75)** ib. l. 23 (*Αὐρ. Ἀ.*: s. *Κέλερ*); **(76)** ib. l. 45 (f. *Αὐρ. Ῥουφῖνος*)
—LYSIMACHEIA?: **(77)** c. 208 BC *FD* III (4) 135 I, 17 ([Ἀσκλ]ηπιάδης: s. *Ἀρι—*)
—MADYTOS: **(78)** hell. *ISestos* 60 (f. *Δαλεις*)
—MARKIANOPOLIS: **(79)** ii AD *IGB* V 5339, 5 (Ἀσκληπιάδ[ης])
—MESAMBRIA: **(80)** f. iii AD ib. I² 317, 3 (I f. *Αὐρ. Ἀσκληπιάδης* II); **(81)** ib. l. 3 (*Αὐρ. Ἀ.*: II s. *Ἀσκληπιάδης* I)
—NICOPOLIS AD ISTRUM: **(82)** ii-iii AD ib. II 689 (s. *Δε—*, f. *Ἡρακλιανός, Οὐαλερία*); **(83)** f. iii AD ib. 645, 13 (f. *Ἀσκληπιόδωρος*)
—NICOPOLIS AD ISTRUM (TERRIT.): **(84)** ?iii AD ib. 718 (Ἀ[σ]κλ[η]πειάδης: s. *Ἀσκληπιόδοτος*)
—ODESSOS: **(85)** 24 BC ib. I² 46, 23 (s. *Ἀρτεμίδωρος*); **(86)** f. ii AD ib. 178 (PM 1722); *Dacia* 21 (1977) p. 161 (date) (f. *Ἀμάς*); **(87)** m. ii AD *IGB* I² 150 (PM 859) (s. *Ἀπελλᾶς*: doctor); **(88)** *IGB* I² 169 (PM 1725); *Dacia* 21 (1977) p. 161 (date) (f. *Τόμιον*); **(89)** *IGB* I² 174 (PM 1726); *Dacia* 21 (1977) p. 161 (date) (f. *Θιθίς*); **(90)** 215 AD *IGB* I² 47 b, 27 ((Ἀσ)κληπιάδης: f. *Αὐρ. Διονῦς*); **(91)** ib. 47 c, 23 (f. *Αὐρ. Μητρόδωρος*); **(92)** 221 AD ib. 47 bis, 6 (f. *Μ. Αὐρ. Ἀντίφιλος*); **(93)** ib. 47 bis a, 37 (*Αὐρ. Ἀ.*: s. *Μήνιος*); **(94)** ib. 47 bis c, 39 (I f. *Αὐρ. Ἀσκληπιάδης* II); **(95)** ib. l. 39 (*Αὐρ. Ἀ.*: II s. *Ἀσκληπιάδης* I); **(96)** ib. l. 40 (f. *Αὐρ. Παρμένων*)
—PAUTALIA: **(97)** s. ii AD *SEG* XLVI 864 I, 20
——Karistoron: **(98)** ii-iii AD *IGB* IV 2166 (Ἀσκληπιάδης); **(99)** ib. 2169 (*Μ. Οὔλπ. Ἀ.*)
—PERINTHOS-HERAKLEIA: **(100)** ii-iii AD *IPerinth* 122 (s. *Γαῦρος*)
——(φυλ. πρωτ.): **(101)** iii AD ib. 164 (f. *Αὐρ. Μηνιανός*)
—PHILIPPOPOLIS-TRIMONTIUM: **(102)** ii-iii AD *IGB* III 964
—PHILIPPOPOLIS-TRIMONTIUM (TERRIT.): **(103)** ii AD ib. 1421, 2 + V 5524 (*Ἀδριάνιος Ἀ*[σκλη]πιάδης); **(104)** ib. III 1449 (f. *Εὐστόχιος Κέλερ*)
—SERDICA: **(105)** ii AD ib. IV 1923, 7 ([Ἀσκλη]πιάδης: s. *Στέφανος*); **(106)** ib. 1957, 2 (f. *Νικήτης, Ἀσκληπᾶς, Χρῆστος*); **(107)** ii-iii AD ib. 1922, 3; **(108)** ib. 1936 (s. *Γάϊος*); **(109)** f. iii AD ib. 1910, 10 (*Ἀντωνιανὸς Ἀ.*)
—SERDICA (TERRIT.): **(110)** ii-iii AD ib. 2042 (I f. *Ἀσκληπιάδης* II); **(111)** ib. (II s. *Ἀσκληπιάδης* I, f. *Γάϊος*); **(112)** *AEMÖ* 10 (1886) pp. 238-9 no. 2, 13 (f. *Ἀλέξανδρος*)
—SESTOS: **(113)** imp. *ISestos* 5 ([Ἀσ]κληπιάδης: s. *Νικόμαχος*)

Ἀσκληπιακός
MACEDONIA (MYGDONIA):
—THESSALONIKE: **(1)** 244 AD *IG* X (2) (1) 215, 3; 216 (*Φλ. Τερεντιανὸς Ἀ.*: I f. *Φλ. Αἰλ. Τερεντιανὸς Ἀσκληπιακός* II); **(2)** ib. 215, 9 (*Φλ. Αἰλ. Τερεντιανὸς Ἀ.*: II s. *Φλ. Τερεντιανὸς Ἀσκληπιακός* I)

Ἀσκληπιάς
MACEDONIA (BOTTIAIA):
—EDESSA: **(1)** 204 AD *Arch. Pap.* 22 (1973) p. 206 no. 8 (Tataki, *Edessa* 39); **(2)** 246 AD *SEG* XXXVI 619, 5 (Tataki, *Edessa* 83) (*Δομιτία Ἀ.*)
THRACE:
—BYZANTION (TERRIT.): **(3)** imp. Unp. (Sayar) (?d. *Κάλαμος*)
THRACE?: **(4)** 157 BC *UPZ* 123, 4, 16; cf. La'da E786 (m. *Πτολεμαῖος*)

Ἀσκληπίδης
MACEDONIA (SINTIKE):
—HERAKLEIA: **(1)** 230 AD *IGB* V 5922, 8 (Ἀσκληπίδ[ης]: s. *Διόδωρος*)
THRACE:
—HERAION TEICHOS: **(2)** c. 45-42 BC ib. I² 43, 4, 26 (f. *Μηνογένης*)

Ἀσκληπιοδότη
THRACE:
—ABDERA: **(1)** iii AD *SEG* XXVIII 558, 1 (*IThrakAig* E68) (*Κασσία Ἀ.*)
—BISANTHE-PANION: **(2)** ii-iii AD Dumont–Homolle 83i (d. *Ζωΐλος, Εὐτέρπη*)
—KALLIPOLIS: **(3)** imp. *ISestos* 20 (Ἀσκληπιοδ[ότη]?)
—MARKIANOPOLIS: **(4)** c. 303-305 AD Latyshev, *Menolog. anon.* pp. 106-10; cf. *Anal. Boll.* 31 (1912) p. 244
—PERINTHOS-HERAKLEIA: **(5)** hell.-imp. *IPerinth* 269; **(6)** iii AD ib. 125 (*Αὐρ. Ἀ.*); **(7)** iv AD ib. 219, 14 (*AD* 49-50 (1994-5) Mel. p. 343 no. 165) (m. *Λούκις, Θεόδοτος, Δόμνα, Λουκιανή, Ζώη, Θεοδούλη*); **(8)** iv-v AD *IPerinth* 178, 6 (*AD* 51-2 (1996-7) Mel. p. 361 no. 181)
—PHILIPPOPOLIS-TRIMONTIUM (TERRIT.): **(9)** ii-iii AD *IGB* III 1537, 5 (*Κλ. Ἀντία Ἀ.*)
—SALYMBRIA: **(10)** iii AD *IByz* S 20 (Ἀσκληπιοδ[ότ]η)

Ἀσκληπιοδοτιανός
THRACE:
—PERINTHOS-HERAKLEIA:
——(Theseidai): **(1)** iii AD *IPerinth* 154 (*Αὐρ. Ἀσκληπιοδοτιανὸς Ῥουφῖνος*)
—PHILIPPOPOLIS-TRIMONTIUM: **(2)** m. iii AD *IGB* III 884 b, 19; cf. V 5400 (*Αὐρ. Ἀ.*)

Ἀσκληπιόδοτος
MACEDONIA: **(1)** iii BC *ICos* ED 19, 2 (Tataki, *Macedonians* p. 272 no. 316) ([Ἀσκ]λαπιόδοτος: s. *—ίδας*)
MACEDONIA (SINTIKE):
—HERAKLEIA: **(2)** 171-169 BC Liv. xlii 51. 7; xliv 2. 10 (Tataki, *Macedonians* p. 111 no. 2) (Lat. Asclepiodotus)
SKYTHIA:
—SKYTHAI: **(3)** ii-iii AD *IGR* I 178 d (*Graffiti del Palatino* I 249)
THRACE:
—APOLLONIA-SOZOPOLIS: **(4)** i-ii AD *IGB* I² 401, 11 (s. *Τελεσφόρος*)
—BEROE-AUGUSTA TRAIANA: **(5)** iii AD ib. III 1592, 2 (*Αὐρ. Ἀ. ὁ καὶ Φαλακρίων*); **(6)** ib. 1596
—BYZANTION:
——(Keramea): **(7)** iii AD *IByz* 318 (Fıratlı–Robert pp. 121-2 no. 204) (*Αὐρ. Ἀσκληπι[ό]δοτος*: s. *Γάϊος*)
—BYZANTION (TERRIT.)?: **(8)** iii AD *IByz* 383 ([*Αὐρ.*] *Ἀσκληπιόδοτ[ος]*)
—NICOPOLIS AD ISTRUM (TERRIT.): **(9)** ?iii AD *IGB* II 718 (Ἀσσκ(λ)η[π]ε[ι]όδοτος: f. *Ἀσκληπιάδης*)
—NICOPOLIS AD NESTUM?: **(10)** 221 AD ib. IV 2305, 4 (*Αὐρ. Ἀ.*: s. *Σω—*)
—ODESSOS: **(11)** 238 AD ib. I² 48, 8 (*Γ. Φλ. Ἀ.*)
—PHILIPPOPOLIS-TRIMONTIUM: **(12)** ii-iii AD ib. III 994 (Ἀσκληπιόδο[τος]); **(13)** iii AD ib. V 5463; III 1150 + 1151 (*SEG* XLIX 908) (*Αὐρ. Ἀ.*: s. *Αἰλ. Ἰουλιανός*)
—SERDICA: **(14)** ii AD *IGB* IV 1923, 6 ([Ἀσκλ]ηπιόδοτος: s. *Ἐπιγένης*)

Ἀσκληπιοδώρα
MACEDONIA (BOTTIAIA):
—BEROIA: **(1)** 227 AD *ILeukopetra* 72, 10 (*Αὐρ. Ἀσσκληπιοδώρα*); **(2)** 239 AD ib. 91, 3 ((*Α*)*ὐρ. Ἀσκληπιοδώ(ρα)*)
MACEDONIA (SINTIKE):
—PARTHIKOPOLIS (TERRIT.): **(3)** ii/iii AD *IGB* IV 2313 with pl. 153 (Ἀσκληπιοδώρω (dat.)—ed. per err.)

Ἀσκληπιόδωρος
MACEDONIA: **(1)** m. iv BC *RE* (5); Berve 167 (Tataki, *Macedonians* p. 273 no. 318) (s. *Εὔνικος*, f. *Ἀντίπατρος*); **(2)** 316 BC *RE* (9); cf. Tataki, *Macedonians* p. 152 no. 26; **(3)** m. ii BC *BGU* 2423, 33 (Tataki, *Macedonians* p. 477 no. 57); cf. La'da E1513 (f. *Ἱέρων*)
MACEDONIA (BOTTIAIA):
—BEROIA: **(4)** ii-i BC *IBer* 30 (Tataki 246) (s. *Πλευρᾶτος*); **(5)** 114 BC *IBer* 134, 35 (f. *Λυσίμαχος*); **(6)** 234 AD *ILeukopetra* 85, 6 (Tataki 69) (*Αἰλ. Ἀ.*)
—EDESSA: **(7)** 246 AD *SEG* XXXVI 617, 12; 618, 2; 619, 5; 620, 14; XXXVIII 619 (Tataki, *Edessa* 156) (*Κλ. Ἀ.*)
—MIEZA?: **(8)** iii BC *SEG* XXIV 524 I, 5, 17? (Hatzopoulos, *MI* 2 p. 106 no. 92) (Ἀσσ-)
—PELLA: **(9)** 326 BC *RE* (7); Berve 168 (Tataki, *Macedonians* p. 152 no. 26) (?s. *Τίμανδρος*); **(10)** hell.? *SEG* II 400 (s. *Ξάνθος*); **(11)** 242 BC ib. XII 374, 1 (Tataki, *Macedonians* p. 152 no. 25); **(12)** iii/ii BC *Α΄ Panell. Synedr. Epigr.* p. 189 no. 10 (*SEG* XXX 580) (s. *Μύρμηξ*)

MACEDONIA (CHALKIDIKE):
—ANTHEMOUS: (13) f. ii BC ib. XLII 562 (s. Ἰέρων); (14) 106 BC ib. 561 (f. Ποσειδώνιος)
—APHYTIS: (15) iv-iii BC ib. XXIX 572 (f. Φοῖνιξ)
—CHALKIDEIS: (16) c. 379-376 BC *Olynthus* 9 pp. 56-8 nos. 84-9 (coin); *Ancient Macedonia* 1 p. 254 (date)
—OLYNTHOS: (17) m. iv BC *IG* II² 10019 (Tataki, *Macedonians* p. 131 no. 20; *FRA* 5887) (s. Θράσων, f. Ἐπικύδης)
—OLYNTHOS*: (18) m. v BC *Olynthus* 13 p. 426 (amph.) (Ἀσκληπ(ιόδωρος))
MACEDONIA (DERRIOPOS):
—STUBERRA: (19) c. 41-48 AD *IG* X (2) (2) 323, 16 (f. Ζωΐλος); (20) 87 AD ib. 325, 72 (s. Ζωΐλος); (21) 90 AD ib. 326, 76 (s. Ζωΐλος); (22) ib. l. 81 (f. Φοῦσκος)
MACEDONIA (EORDAIA):
—KELLE?: (23) iii-ii BC *AEMTh* 9 (1995) p. 20 (vase) (s. Νικάνωρ)
MACEDONIA (LOWER PAIONIA):
—EUROPOS: (24) 205 AD *SEG* XXXVIII 615 (Ἀσκληπ[ιόδωρος]?: ?s. Ἰουβέντιος Ἐ—, Ἰουβεντία —α)
MACEDONIA (MYGDONIA):
—KALINDOIA: (25) 68-98 AD ib. XLII 580, 96 (s. Σῶσος)
—THESSALONIKE: (26) ?39 BC *IG* X (2) (1) 50, 7 (f. Διονυσόδωρος); (27) f. i AD ib. 133, 9; Robert, *OMS* 5 pp. 295-302 (date) (II s. Ἀσκληπιόδωρος I); (28) *IG* X (2) (1) 133, 10; Robert, *OMS* 5 pp. 295-302 (date) (I f. Ἀσκληπιόδωρος II); (29) ii-iii AD *IG* X (2) (1) 186, 5 (Λογγινιανὸς Ἀ.: s. Ἀρρία Προκλιανὴ Φιλίστη)
—THESSALONIKE?: (30) ii-iii AD *SEG* XXVII 313
MACEDONIA (ODOMANTIKE):
—SIRRHA: (31) ii-iii AD ib. XXX 606 (Ἀσκληπιόδ[ωρος]?: s. Μάξιμος)
MACEDONIA (PELAGONIA): (32) ii AD *IG* X (2) (2) 261; cf. 260 (s. Ἀσκληπιάδης, ?s. Ἀμμία)
MACEDONIA (SINTIKE):
—HERAKLEIA: (33) ii AD *IGB* IV 2325 (s. Πύθιος)
—PARTHIKOPOLIS (NR.): (34) ii AD ib. 2294 (-πιώ-)
MACEDONIA?: (35) 331 BC *RE* (6); Berve 169 (Tataki, *Macedonians* p. 273 no. 319) (s. Φίλων); (36) 321 BC *RE* (8); Berve 170 (Tataki, *Macedonians* p. 272 no. 317); (37) 226 BC *PPetr*² 24, 4 (La'da E1743) (s. Διονύσιος: t.e.)
SCYTHIA MINOR:
—ISTROS: (38) ii AD *ISM* I 197 II, 9 (f. Ἀντίοχος)
—TOMIS: (39) ii-iii AD ib. II 27, 11 ([Ἀσ]κληπιόδω[ρος]); (40) f. iii AD ib. 122 (Ἀσκληπιώδ[ωρος]?)
THRACE: (41) ii BC *ILAlg* II 824 (f. Ἀπολλόθεμις)
—ABDERA: (42) ii BC *SEG* XLVII 1033 (*IThrakAig* E59) (f. Νικάνωρ)
—AINOS: (43) c. 208 BC *FD* III (4) 134 I, 15 (f. —όδωρος)
—NICOPOLIS AD ISTRUM: (44) f. iii AD *IGB* II 645, 12 (s. Ἀσκληπιάδης)
—NICOPOLIS AD ISTRUM (TERRIT.): (45) ii AD ib. V 5244 b, 8 (Ἀσκληπιόδ[ωρος]?)
—NICOPOLIS AD NESTUM: (46) ii AD ib. IV 2336, 2 ([Ἀσκλ]ηπιόδωρος: s. Ἀσκληπᾶς)
—PAUTALIA: (47) ii-iii AD ib. 2081; (48) s. ii AD *SEG* XLVI 864, 14 (s. Ἡρακλίας)
—PHILTEPARA: (49) 211-222 AD ib. XXVI 824 B (weight) (Αὐρ. Ἀ.)
—TOPEIROS: (50) iii AD ib. XLV 881 (*IThrakAig* E91) ([Ἀσ]κληπιόδ[ωρος]?)
THRACE?: (51) 316-309 BC *IG* II² 1956, 11; *Ancient Macedonia* 5 p. 445 with n. 10 (date) (*FRA* 2502)

Ἀσκληπιός
CIMMERIAN BOSPOROS:
—ACHILLEION: (1) ii AD *CIRB* 1029 (Ἀσκ[λη]πιό[ς]: f. Ἀπολλόδωρος)
MACEDONIA (MYGDONIA):
—THESSALONIKE?: (2) f. iii AD *SEG* XXXVI 649; *KGAM Thess.* I 130 (date) (Αὐρ. Ἀ.)

Ἀσκληπίων
MACEDONIA (MYGDONIA):
—THESSALONIKE: (1) ii AD *IG* X (2) (1) 490

Ἀσκλήπων
MACEDONIA (MYGDONIA):
—THESSALONIKE: (1) ii-iii AD *SEG* XLIII 353

Ἀσκλῆς
SCYTHIA MINOR:
—TOMIS: (1) ii AD *ISM* II 125 II, 23 (Ἀσκλῆ (gen.), Ἀσκλη[πιάδου]—ed.: f. Ἀρτεμίδωρος)

Ἄσκλυς
SCYTHIA MINOR:
—TOMIS: (1) ii AD ib. 156

Ἀσκοσίδης
MACEDONIA (MYGDONIA):
—KALINDOIA: (1) 68-98 AD *SEG* XLII 580, 11; cf. *Anthémonte–Kalindoia* 2 p. 229 (name) (-σεί-: f. Τράλις)

Ἄσος
MACEDONIA (SINTIKE):
—NEINE: (1) 77 AD *IGB* V 5883, 8 (f. Καλδένθης)

Ἄσουπος?
CIMMERIAN BOSPOROS:
—ZENONOS CHERSONESOS*: (1) imp. *SEG* XL 628 (vase) (Ἀσουπου (gen.))

Ἄσπακος
SKYTHIA:
—TANAIS: (1) 220-225 AD *CIRB* 1278, 17; 1279, 24 (f. Γώσακος)

Ἀσπαμιθάρης
CIMMERIAN BOSPOROS:
—PANTIKAPAION: (1) iv BC ib. 211; Zgusta, *PNS* 65 (f. Νεομήνιος); (2) ?iii BC *CIRB* 242 (Ἀσπαμ[ιθάρης]?)

Ἀσπάνδανος
SKYTHIA:
—TANAIS: (1) 225 AD ib. 1279, 14; Zgusta, *PNS* 750 (s. Λειμανός)

Ἄσπαρ
THRACE:
—BEROE-AUGUSTA TRAIANA: (1) iii AD *IGB* III 1580

Ἀσπασία
MACEDONIA (BOTTIAIA):
—BEROIA: (1) ii BC *SEG* XXIV 504 c; *IBer* 160 (stemma) (Tataki 247) (d. Γαλέστης)
THRACE:
—MARONEIA: (2) i AD *IG* XII (8) 215, 17

Ἀσπασίη
THRACE:
—APOLLONIA-SOZOPOLIS: (1) vi BC *IGB* I² 404 (d. Ἐργῖνος); (2) iv BC *BMNBurgas* 4 (2002) p. 124 no. 17 (Ἀσπασί[η]: d. Μανδρόστρατος)

Ἀσπάσιος
MACEDONIA (EDONIS):
—PHILIPPOI: (1) ii/iii AD *CIL* III 633 I, 18 (Pilhofer 164); *CIL* III 633 II c, 3 (Pilhofer 163); *CRAI* 1923, p. 277 (date); Collart, *Philippes* pls. 64-5 (Lat. M. Alfenus Aspasius)
THRACE:
—ABDERA: (2) c. 475-450 BC May, *Abdera* p. 96 no. 60 with pl. 4 (coin); Masson, *OGS* p. 428 n. 8 (name) (Ἀσπά(σιος))

Ἀσπίας
MACEDONIA (CHALKIDIKE):
—OLYNTHOS: (1) ?354 BC *TAPA* 69 (1938) pp. 52-3 no. 6, 4; Hatzopoulos, *Actes Chalc.* p. 80 (date) (f. Στρήνιος)

Ἀσπιλία
MACEDONIA (BOTTIAIA):
—EDESSA: (1) v-vi AD Feissel, *RICM* 20 (-σπη-); (2) ib. 22

Ἀσποῦργος
CIMMERIAN BOSPOROS:
—BOSPOROS: (1) c. 30 BC-38 AD *RE* (-); *PIR*² A 1265; *IOSPE* I² 37, 4; 573 (*SEG* XLII 699); *CIRB* 39; 40; 41; [42]; 958; 985, 2; *SEG* XXXII 790; XLVI 940 I, 1; 940 II, 1; Zgusta, *PNS* 66 (?s. Ἀσάνδροχος, f. Κότυς, Μιθριδάτης: king); (2) i AD *IGUR* 567 b (s. Βιόμασος)
—GORGIPPIA: (3) s. ii AD *CIRB* 1142, 6; (4) 173-210 AD ib. 1134, 18 (Ἀσποῦργ[ος]) ?= (*5*); (5) *SEG* XXXVI 700, 9 ([Ἀσπο]ῦργος?) ?= (*4*)
SKYTHIA:
—OLBIA-BORYSTHENES: (6) ii AD *IOSPE* I² 84, 5 (s. Παρσπάνακος)

Ἀσπώ
THRACE:
—ABDERA: (1) f. iv BC *SEG* XLVII 1029 + *IThrakAig* E39 ([Ἀ]σπώ)
—STRYME?: (2) c. 375-350 BC ib. E140 (d. Μητρόδοτος)

Ἀσσει
THRACE:
—ODESSOS: (1) i BC-i AD *IGB* I² 109 (d. Ἀρτεμίδωρος)

Ἄσσκος?
SCYTHIA MINOR:
—TOMIS: (1) ii-iii AD *ISM* II 468, 6 (f. —γένης)

Ἀστακίδης
THRACE:
—PHILIPPOPOLIS-TRIMONTIUM: (1) ii-iii AD *IGB* III 1021 (*GVI* 614)

Ἀστέας
SCYTHIA MINOR:
—KALLATIS: (1) iii BC *Dacia* 3-4 (1927-32) p. 462 o (vase)
THRACE:
—BYZANTION?: (2) i BC *IByz* 351 (f. Ἀφφη)
—ODESSOS (NR.): (3) f. iii AD *IGB* V 5076 (*CCET* I 9) (s. Ἡρακλείδης)

Ἀστειός
CIMMERIAN BOSPOROS:
—NYMPHAION: (1) iii BC *CIRB* 912 II, 1 (f. —ρος)

Ἄστεος
THRACE:
—BEROE-AUGUSTA TRAIANA: (1) 222-235 AD *IGB* III 1590, 11 (*Eastern cults* pp. 232-3 no. 23); cf. *SEG* XL 568 (Ἀ. ὁ καὶ Ἰούλιος)

Ἀστέρις
THRACE:
—BISANTHE-PANION?:
——Komneoi: (1) iv-vi AD *AD* 49-50 (1994-5) Mel. p. 315 no. 141

Ἀστήρ
MACEDONIA (CHALKIDIKE):
—OLYNTHOS: (1) 353 BC *RE* (4) (Tataki, *Macedonians* p. 132 no. 21) (or Macedonia (Edonis) Amphipolis)
SKYTHIA:
—TANAIS: (2) ii AD *CIRB* 1263, 15; (3) 225 AD ib. 1280, 27 (f. Ἑρμῆς); (4) 229 AD *Stud. Zhebelev* p. 47, 18 (f. Ζήνων); (5) 244 AD *CIRB* 1287, 15 (f. —νακος); (6) ib. l. 27 (f. Εὐ—)

THRACE:
—BYZANTION: (7) ii-i BC *IApameia* 140 (s. *Μενεσθεύς*)

Ἀστιάδης
MACEDONIA (EDONIS):
—AMPHIPOLIS: (1) m. iii BC *SEG* XXIV 584, 10; XLI 566 (date) (Ἀστιάδης?, Ἀστιδίης—ed.: s. Ἀντίδοτος)

Ἀστίας
MACEDONIA (EDONIS):
—AMPHIPOLIS: (1) s. iv BC Hatzopoulos, *Actes Amphipolis* p. 48 no. 10 A, 6 (*SEG* XLI 564) (f. —ρης)

Ἀστικός
THRACE:
—SERDICA: (1) f. iii AD *IGB* IV 1910, 8; 1928 (*Λ. Φούλβιος Ἀ.*)
—SERDICA (TERRIT.): (2) iii AD ib. 1985, 4 (*Eastern cults* p. 167 no. 9) (*Αὐρ. Ἀ.*)

Ἀστικόσης
MACEDONIA (EDONIS):
—PHILIPPOI: (1) ?ii AD *FGrH* 257 F 37. 47 (Tataki, *Macedonians* p. 164 no. 9) (f. *Βαστία*)

Ἀστῖνος
MACEDONIA (EDONIS):
—AMPHIPOLIS (NR.): (1) a. 357 BC Hatzopoulos, *Actes Amphipolis* p. 43 no. 8, 7 (*SEG* XLI 562) (f. Ἀριστογένης)

Ἀστίων
MACEDONIA (MYGDONIA):
—KALINDOIA: (1) c. 311 BC Hatzopoulos, *MI* 2 pp. 84-5 no. 62, 35 (Ἀστί[ων]?, Ἀστί[ας]?: f. *Φαδδῦς*)

Ἄστος
THRACE:
—STRYME?: (1) m. iv BC *IThrakAig* E149 (Ἀ-στου (gen.): f. Ἀνταγόρας)

Ἀστράγαλος
CIMMERIAN BOSPOROS:
—PANTIKAPAION: (1) ii BC *CIRB* 258; cf. KW pl. 35 no. 500 (s. *Διόφαντος*)

Ἀστραπία
THRACE:
—MARKIANOPOLIS: (1) iii AD *IGB* II 814, 1 (*GVI* 1442; PM 2143) (-πεία)

Ἀστυάναξ
MACEDONIA (MYGDONIA):
—THESSALONIKE: (1) f. ii AD *IG* X (2) (1) 267 (her.?)
THRACE:
—APOLLONIA-SOZOPOLIS: (2) iv BC *BMNBurgas* 4 (2002) p. 122 no. 9 (f. Ἀνδροκλῆς)

Ἀστυδάμας
CIMMERIAN BOSPOROS:
—PANTIKAPAION: (1) iv BC *IGAIMK* 104 (1935) p. 301 nos. 11-12 (tile) (Ἀστυδά(μαντος)? (gen.))

Ἀστύδημος
CIMMERIAN BOSPOROS:
—HERMONASSA: (1) iv BC *CIRB* 1056 II, 17 (Ἀστύδη[μος]: f. *Πάταικος*)

Ἀστυκράτης
THRACE:
—SIMEONOVGRAD (MOD.): (1) s. v BC *SEG* XLIX 993 (vase) (Ἀστυκράτ(ης))

Ἀστυμήδης
CIMMERIAN BOSPOROS:
—BOSPOROS: (1) s. iv BC ib. XXI 298, 10 + *ZPE* 136 (2001) p. 67 no. 2 (Osborne, *Naturalization* D25) (Ἀστυμ[ήδης])

Ἀστύνομος
THRACE:
—PERINTHOS-HERAKLEIA:
——(Kastaleis): (1) iii-ii BC *IPerinth* 61, 60 (s. Ἄμαντις)

Ἀσυγκρίτιον
MACEDONIA (MYGDONIA):
—THESSALONIKE: (1) f. iii AD *SEG* XLIV 556, 3 (Ἄννα ἡ καὶ Ἀσυνκρίτιον: Jew)

Ἀσυγκρίτιος
MACEDONIA (BOTTIAIA):
—EDESSA: (1) iii AD ib. XLV 755 (vase) (-συν-)
THRACE:
—BYZANTION: (2) ?iv AD Ebersolt, *Mission* p. 41 no. 3 (Ἀσυνκρίτι[ος])

Ἀσύγκριτος
MACEDONIA (CHALKIDIKE):
—ANTIGONEIA (NR.): (1) imp. *SEG* XXIX 622 (Ἀσύν[κριτος])
—MENDE?: (2) ?ii AD ib. 614 (Ἀσύνκρι[τ]ος)
MACEDONIA (MYGDONIA):
—THESSALONIKE: (3) ii AD *IG* X (2) (1) 478, 1 (*Λούκι[ος] [Ἀ]σύνκριτος, Λούκι[ος] [ἀ]σύνκριτος—IG*)
THRACE:
—NOVAE (NR.): (4) iii AD *IGLNovae* 183 (*SEG* XLVII 1150) (-σύν-: s. *Εὐάγγελος*)

Ἀσφάλιος
THRACE:
—PAUTALIA (TERRIT.): (1) ii-iii AD *IGB* IV 2123

Ἀσφώρουγος
SKYTHIA:
—OLBIA-BORYSTHENES: (1) ii-iii AD *IOlbia* 102, 1; Zgusta, *PNS* 67 (s. *Κάραξτος*)

Ἄσων
THRACE:
—KELLAI: (1) 241-244 AD *IGB* III 1517, 41 (*Αὐρ. Ἀ.*: s. *Αὐρήλιος*); (2) ib. l. 53

Ἀσώπιος
THRACE:
—BYZANTION: (1) m. iii BC Schönert-Geiss, *Byzantion* 1103-30 (coin)

Ἀτάδων
SKYTHIA:
—OLBIA-BORYSTHENES: (1) f. ii AD *IOSPE* I² 85, 3; 106, 10; Zgusta, *PNS* 596 (s. *Μήτακος*)

Ἀτάης
SKYTHIA:
—OLBIA-BORYSTHENES: (1) m. iv BC Dubois, *IGDOlbia* 106, 10 (*SEG* XLIV 669); cf. Vinogradov, *Pont. Stud.* p. 158 no. 12 ter (name)

Ἀταίας
SCYTHIA MINOR: (1) m. iv BC *AJNum* 13 (2001) pp. 22-3 (coin) (king)

Ἀτάκης
CIMMERIAN BOSPOROS:
—NYMPHAION: (1) v BC *CIRB* 914; Zgusta, *PNS* 596 (f. Ἄσαρος)
SKYTHIA:
—OLBIA-BORYSTHENES: (2) m. iv BC Dubois, *IGDOlbia* 25 a, 4; cf. Vinogradov, *Pont. Stud.* p. 156 no. 6 (name) (Ἀτάκους (gen.))

Ἀτακούας
CIMMERIAN BOSPOROS:
—GORGIPPIA: (1) ii AD *CIRB* 1141, 7; Zgusta, *PNS* 596; (2) *CIRB* 1142, 11 (f. —κλῆς); (3) ib. 1143, 2 (Ἀτα[μ]ο[ς]?—ed., Ἀτα[κ]ο[ύας]?—Vinogradov: f. *Ῥόδων*); (4) s. ii AD ib. 1142, 5 ([Ἀτ]ακούας); (5) ii/iii AD ib. 1179, 41 (s. *Πάππος*)

Ἀταλάντη
MACEDONIA (BOTTIAIA):
—BEROIA: (1) iii AD *BE* 1939, no. 11 (Tataki 248) (m. *Εὐφίλητος*)
MACEDONIA (ORESTIS): (2) c. 360-321 BC *RE* (5); Berve 177 (Tataki, *Macedonians* p. 204 no. 6) (d. Ὀρόντης)
THRACE:
—ANCHIALOS: (3) imp. *IGB* I² 372 bis, 4 (*Eastern cults* p. 266 no. 1) (-λάτη)

Ἀταμάζας
CIMMERIAN BOSPOROS:
—GORGIPPIA: (1) imp. *CIRB* 1190, 2; Zgusta, *PNS* 596; (2) ii AD *CIRB* 1167, 3 ([Ἀ]ταμάζ[ας]); (3) s. ii AD ib. 1175 A, 3; (4) ib. 1175 B + *SEG* XLIX 1033 note (Ἀταμάζας); (5) ii/iii AD *CIRB* 1179, 39 (Ἀττα-: s. *Πάπας*); (6) ib. l. 43 (s. *Κάρσας*); (7) *SEG* XLIX 1033 A, 2 (*CIRB* 1182 A, 1) ([Ἀταμ]άζας)
—GORGIPPIA?: (8) s. ii AD ib. 1231 A, 17 (s. *Δάζεις*); (9) ii/iii AD ib. 1232, 4 (Ἀταμάζ[ας])
SKYTHIA:
—TANAIS: (10) c. 225-250 AD ib. 1288, 5

Ἀτανδρίων
THRACE:
—ODESSOS: (1) 215 AD *IGB* I² 47 a, 24 (*Αὐρ. Ἀ.*: s. *Νουμήνιος*); (2) ib. 47 b, 11 (*Αὐρ. Ἀ.*: s. *Ξένων*); (3) ib. 47 c, 9 (*Αὐρ. Ἀ.*: s. Ἀπελλᾶς)

Ἀταρρίας?
MACEDONIA: (1) 341-316 BC *RE* (-); Berve 178 with n. 3 (Tataki, *Macedonians* p. 273 no. 320) (*Ταρρίας*—Plu., Ἀρρίας—Ael. ms.: s. *Δεινομένης*)

Ἀτᾶς
CIMMERIAN BOSPOROS:
—PANTIKAPAION: (1) ii-iii AD *IAK* 9 (1904) pp. 115-16 no. 240 (ring) (Ἀτᾶνος (gen.))

Ἀτάσας
SKYTHIA:
—TANAIS: (1) ii AD *CIRB* 1262, 14; Zgusta, *PNS* 596 (f. *Ἡρακλείδης*)

Ἀταχαίης
CIMMERIAN BOSPOROS:
—HERMONASSA: (1) iv BC *CIRB* 1061; Zgusta, *PNS* 596 (Ἀταχαίω (gen.): f. Ἀτοῦς)

Ἀτέας
SKYTHIA:
—SKYTHAI: (1) c. 375-339 BC *RE* (-) (king)

Ἀτερόνιος
THRACE:
—PHILIPPOPOLIS-TRIMONTIUM*: (1) iv-vi AD *RA* 1940 (1), pp. 208-9 (loomweight)

Ἀτήθυος
CIMMERIAN BOSPOROS:
—THEODOSIA: (1) iii AD *CIRB* 947 A, 17; Zgusta, *PNS* 617 (f. —υσος)

Ἄτης
MACEDONIA (PELAGONIA):
—KERAMIAI (NR.): (1) ii AD *IG* X (2) (2) 209
SCYTHIA?:
—SKIROI: (2) iii/ii BC *Stud. Tacheva* pp. 280-1, 15 (Ἄτη[ς])

Ἀτίας
CIMMERIAN BOSPOROS:
—GORGIPPIA: (1) ii/iii AD *CIRB* 1179, 31 (f. *Φαρνακίων*)
THRACE: (2) 203 BC *BGU* 1266 A, 39, 45; 2386, 5 (Velkov 35; La'da E717) (Ἀττίας—1266 A l. 45)
—SALYMBRIA: (3) imp. *IByz* S 37 (s. *Δαϊμένης*)

Ἀτιλία
MACEDONIA (MYGDONIA):
—THESSALONIKE?: (**1**) i-ii AD *IG* X (2) (1) 874 (d. *Γάϊος*)
THRACE:
—PHILIPPOPOLIS-TRIMONTIUM: (**2**) imp. *IGB* III 1026, 3

Ἀτιλιανός
MACEDONIA (LYNKESTIS):
—HERAKLEIA?: (**1**) iii AD *IG* X (2) (2) 138 (s. *Αὐρ. Κλημεντῖνος, Αἰλ. Ἀτιλία*)
THRACE:
—BEROE-AUGUSTA TRAIANA: (**2**) ii-iii AD *IGB* III 1610 (-τει-)
—PHILIPPOPOLIS-TRIMONTIUM (TERRIT.): (**3**) ii-iii AD ib. 1176 (-τει-)

Ἀτίλιος
MACEDONIA (BOTTIAIA):
—AIGAI: (**1**) 229 AD *ILeukopetra* 73, 5

Ἀτίμητος
MACEDONIA (EDONIS):
—PHILIPPOI*: (**1**) 37 AD *BCH* 58 (1934) p. 450 no. 1 A (Pilhofer 282) (Lat. Atimetus: imp. freed.)
MACEDONIA (MYGDONIA):
—THESSALONIKE: (**2**) ii-iii AD *SEG* L 641 (*Κλ. Ἀτείμητος*)
THRACE:
—PHILIPPOPOLIS-TRIMONTIUM (TERRIT.): (**3**) ii-iii AD *IGB* III 1195 (*Ἀντώνιος Ἀτείμητος*)

Ἀτίνας
CIMMERIAN BOSPOROS:
—GORGIPPIA: (**1**) s. ii AD *CIRB* 1142, 14 (f. *Πόθος*)

Ἀτοτᾶς
SKYTHIA:
—OLBIA-BORYSTHENES: (**1**) ii AD *IOSPE* I^2 685, 6 + *VDI* 1975 (1), p. 71 (*Ἀτοτᾶτος* (gen.): f. *Θαβοῦς*)

Ἀτότης
CIMMERIAN BOSPOROS:
—PANTIKAPAION: (**1**) s. iv BC *CIRB* 170; cf. KW pl. 6 no. 109; Zgusta, *PNS* 596 (s. *Ἀνοθήνης*)

Ἀτοῦς
CIMMERIAN BOSPOROS:
—HERMONASSA: (**1**) iv BC *CIRB* 1061; Zgusta, *PNS* 596 (s. *Ἀταχαίης*)

Ἄτραμις
CIMMERIAN BOSPOROS:
—PANTIKAPAION: (**1**) c. 390-380 BC *SEG* L 710 A (vase) (fict.?)

Ἀτρείδης
MACEDONIA (ELIMEIA):
—AIANE: (**1**) i-ii AD *EAM* 7 (s. *Κάπυλλος*)

Ἄτριος
THRACE:
—ODESSOS: (**1**) ii-iii AD *IGB* I^2 228, 6

Ἀτταεις
CIMMERIAN BOSPOROS:
—HERMONASSA: (**1**) s. v AD *CIRB* 1099, 10 + *SEG* XXXIX 697

Ἀττακῖνος
MACEDONIA: (**1**) ?417-413 BC *IG* I^3 89, 73 (Tataki, *Macedonians* p. 273 no. 321)

Ἀττακόας
CIMMERIAN BOSPOROS:
—GORGIPPIA: (**1**) ii AD *CIRB* 1140, 5; Zgusta, *PNS* 596 (s. *Μυρῖνος*)

Ἄτταλος
CIMMERIAN BOSPOROS:
—GORGIPPIA: (**1**) f. iii BC *CIRB* 1137 A I, 2 (f. *Βλάστος*); (**2**) ib. 1137 B I, 29 (f. *Ἀγαθοκλῆς*)
MACEDONIA: (**3**) c. 390-336 BC *RE* (4); Berve 182 (Tataki, *Macedonians* p. 273 no. 322); (**4**) 333-331 BC *RE* (6); Berve 183 (Tataki, *Macedonians* p. 274 no. 323); (**5**) hell.? *IG* II^2 9264 (Tataki, *Macedonians* p. 275 no. 329; *FRA* 3464) (f. *Μένανδρος*); (**6**) hell. *SEG* XV 878, 1 (Bernand, *Inscr. métr.* 12; Tataki, *Macedonians* p. 275 no. 328); cf. La'da E1505 (f. *Ἡράκλειτος*); (**7**) 321 BC *RE* (7); Berve 184 (Tataki, *Macedonians* p. 274 no. 324); (**8**) hell.-imp. *IEph* 3299 (Tataki, *Macedonians* p. 274 no. 327) (f. *Ἀρτεμίδωρος*)
MACEDONIA (BOTTIAIA):
—PELLA: (**9**) iii BC *AD* 18 (1963) Chron. p. 203; *SEG* XXXIX 623 (tiles)
MACEDONIA (EDONIS):
—AMPHIPOLIS?: (**10**) hell. Dimitsas 896 (f. *Διονυσοφάνης*)
MACEDONIA (ELIMEIA?):
—ERDARRIOI: (**11**) m. ii BC *EAM* 4 (f. *Πολύστρατος*)
MACEDONIA (MYGDONIA):
—KALINDOIA: (**12**) ii/i BC *SEG* XLII 594 (f. *Φίλιππος*); (**13**) ib. (s. *Φίλιππος, Ἀριστίππα*); (**14**) 68-98 AD ib. 580, 4 (f. *Τρυφωνᾶς*)
—LETE: (**15**) s. iv BC Hatzopoulos, *MI* 2 pp. 93-4 no. 79, 11 ([*Ἄ*]*τταλος*)
—THESSALONIKE: (**16**) ii-iii AD *IG* X (2) (1) 63; cf. *Maia* 25 (1973) p. 199 (name) (*Ἄτ*(*τ*)*αλος*); (**17**) iii AD *IG* X (2) (1) 548 (*Αὐρ. Εὐγένις ὁ καὶ Ἀ.*)
MACEDONIA (TYMPHAIA): (**18**) c. 360-317 BC *RE* (5); Berve 181 (Tataki, *Macedonians* p. 212 no. 4) (s. *Ἀνδρομένης*)
SCYTHIA MINOR:
—DINOGETIA (NR.): (**19**) ii/iii AD *ISM* V 298 (Lat. L. Iul. Attalus: I f. *Ἄτταλος* II); (**20**) ib. l. 5-6 (Lat. L. Iul. Attalus iunior: II s. *Ἄτταλος* I, Iulia Saturnina)
—KALLATIS?: (**21**) ii/i BC *IGB* II 867 a, 7 = *ISM* I 219 (V 87); cf. *ISM* III p. 140 (locn.) (f. *Ἀπολλώνιος*)
—NOVIODUNUM (NR.): (**22**) iii-iv AD Barnea 63 b (Popescu, *IGL* 267 b)
—TOMIS: (**23**) iii AD *ISM* II 459, 9 + *SEG* XXVII 1293
—TOMIS*: (**24**) iii AD *ISM* II 340 (*GVI* 406; Robert, *Gladiateurs* p. 107 no. 47) (glad.)
SKYTHIA:
—OLBIA-BORYSTHENES: (**25**) i/ii AD *IOSPE* I^2 39, 3, 35, 40 (f. *Καρζόαζος*)
THRACE: (**26**) c. 244-242 BC *PPetr* II 35 a II, 12 (Velkov 36; La'da E718)
—BYZANTION: (**27**) i BC-i AD *Türk Tarih Kongresi XI* (6) p. 2703 with pl. 493. 2 (f. *Ἀπελλᾶς*)
—BYZANTION (NR.): (**28**) ii BC *SEG* XXIX 667 (s. *Μητρόδωρος*)
—KARDIA: (**29**) m. iii BC *TCal* 34, 3 (f. *Μητρόδωρος*)
—MARONEIA: (**30**) ii BC Grandjean, *Arétalogie* p. 118 (*Eastern cults* p. 29 no. 49; *IThrakAig* E182) (*Ἄ*[*τ*]*ταλος*: f. *Παράμονος*); (**31**) i/ii AD *JHS* 16 (1896) p. 319 no. 18 (*IThrakAig* E370)
—PAUTALIA (TERRIT.): (**32**) ii AD *IGB* IV 2214, 7 (*Κλ. Ἀ.*)
—PHILIPPOPOLIS-TRIMONTIUM: (**33**) m. iii AD ib. III 884 b, 14; cf. V 5400 (*Αὐρ. Ἀ.*)
—VICUS TRULLENSIUM: (**34**) ii AD ib. II 503, 4 (*ILB* 183) (Lat. P. Ael. Attalus)

Ἄττας
CIMMERIAN BOSPOROS:
—GORGIPPIA: (**1**) imp. *CIRB* 1189, 2; Zgusta, *PNS* 596 (s. *No*—); (**2**) *CIRB* 1191, 1; (**3**) i-ii AD *NE* 9 (1971) p. 5 no. 2, 4; (**4**) *CIRB* 1138, 3 (f. *Ἀλφοκράτης*); (**5**) ii AD ib. 1143, 5 (*Ἄττα* (gen.)—ed., *Ἄττα*(*ς*)?: ?s. *Ἀγαθοῦς*); (**6**) m. ii AD *Eirene* 7 (1968) p. 67, 1 (s. *Ἀχαιμένης*); (**7**) s. ii AD *CIRB* 1134, 13; 1140, 21; *Eirene* 7 (1968) p. 67, 8 (s. *Κοσσοῦς*, f. *Κοσσοῦς*); (**8**) *CIRB* 1145, 5 (f. *Ἥδυκος*); (**9**) ib. 1146, 8; (**10**) 173-210 AD ib. 1134, 23 (f. *Κοθίνας*); (**11**) ib. l. 24 (f. *Πόθος*); (**12**) ii/iii AD ib. 1180, 2 (f. *Σανόκας*); (**13**) *VDI* 1970 (4), p. 149, 11 (s. *Νουμήνιος*); (**14**) iii AD *CIRB* 1186, 2
—GORGIPPIA?: (**15**) 227-233 AD ib. 1230, 9 (f. —*ηνιος*)
—PANTIKAPAION: (**16**) i AD ib. 343; cf. KW pl. 51 no. 691 (s. *Ἀπολλωνία, Ἀγα*—); (**17**) *CIRB* p. 937 no. 2 (s. *Δημήτριος*); (**18**) ii AD ib. 660; cf. KW pl. 44 no. 631 (s. *Τρύφων*) ?= (*20*); (**19**) *CIRB* 709, 2 (f. *Τιμόθεος Σίνδαξ*); (**20**) f. ii AD ib. 83, 9 (s. *Τρύφων*) ?= (*18*)
—PATRAEUS: (**21**) i/ii AD ib. 1018 (s. *Καλλισθένης*)
—ZENONOS CHERSONESOS*: (**22**) iii AD ib. 898, 2 (f. —*ακλιος*)
MACEDONIA (BOTTIAIA):
—EDESSA: (**23**) iii AD *SEG* XLV 753 (*Ζώπυρος ὁ κὲ Ἀ.*)
SCYTHIA MINOR:
—ISTROS: (**24**) i BC-i AD *ISM* I 191 II, 53 (s. *Πολυαίνετος*)
—TOMIS: (**25**) ii AD ib. II 17, 15 (s. *Διοσκουρίδης*); (**26**) ib. 125, 6 (s. *Λούκιος*) ?= (*27*); (**27**) ib. 125 II, 18 (*Ἄτα* (gen.): f. *Γαληνός*) ?= (*28*) (*26*); (**28**) ib. l. 20 (*Ἄττα* (gen.): f. *Ἥλιος*) ?= (*27*); (**29**) ii-iii AD ib. 307, 4 (*Ἄττα* (gen.), *Θιθίσαττα*—ed.: ?f. *Θιθίς*); (**30**) ib. l. 6 (*Ἄττα* (gen.), *Κιάττα* (gen.)—ed.: s. *Μενέφιλος, Θιθίς*); (**31**) iii AD ib. 389 (*Ἄττα* (gen.): f. *Ἕρμιππος*)
—TOMIS?: (**32**) ii AD ib. V 78, 1 (*CCET* IV 106); *ISM* V 128, 1 (*CCET* IV 52) (s. *Πόσσης*, f. *Ἰοῦστος*)
SKYTHIA:
—OLBIA-BORYSTHENES: (**33**) ii AD *IOlbia* 86, 7 (s. *Θεοκλῆς*); (**34**) ?ii-iii AD *IOSPE* I^2 107, 4 (f. *Σώμαχος*); (**35**) 198-211 AD ib. 174, 12 (f. *Κονκόρδιος*)
—TANAIS: (**36**) f. ii AD *CIRB* 1266, 8 (f. *Χόφαρνος*); (**37**) 104 AD ib. 1259, 21 (s. *Διόφαντος*); (**38**) c. 192-210 AD ib. 1243, 15; 1277, 9 (s. *Ἡρακλείδης*) ?= (*39*); (**39**) c. 200-236 AD ib. 1250, 11; 1277, 22; 1285, 11 (f. *Ἡρακλείδης*) ?= (*38*)
—TYRAS: (**40**) ii-iii AD *ISM* II 313 (*SEG* XXIV 1080) (f. *Ἄβραγος, Ἀδίαγος, Ἰράσταμος*)
TAURIS:
—CHERSONESOS: (**41**) f. ii AD ib. XXXIII 601 ([*Ἄ*]*ττας*)
THRACE:
—DIONYSOPOLIS: (**42**) iii AD *IGB* I^2 14 a, 5 (*Αὐρ. Ἄττα* (gen.): s. *Ἀντίπατρος*); (**43**) ib. 14 b, 12 (*Ἄττα* (gen.): f. *Αὐρ. Ποσειδώνιος*)
—ODESSOS: (**44**) ii-iii AD *ZPE* 137 (2001) p. 175 (bronze) (f. *Ὀρφεύς*); (**45**) s. ii AD *IGB* I^2 234 (*CCET* I 32)
—SEUTHOPOLIS: (**46**) hell. *SEG* XXXV 833. 2 (vase) (*Ἄττα* (gen.))

Ἄττης
CIMMERIAN BOSPOROS:
—HERMONASSA: (**1**) iv BC *CIRB* 1056 I, 9; Zgusta, *PNS* 596 (f. —*ων*)
—KOROKONDAME: (**2**) v BC *CIRB* 1102 (s. *Ἰκέσιος*)
—MYRMEKION: (**3**) iv BC *SEG* XLVIII 1005 (*Ἄττεω* (gen.): f. *Σωσίβιος, Κυλίανις*)
—PANTIKAPAION: (**4**) f. iv BC *CIRB* 175 (*Ἄττεω* (gen.): f. *Γλαυκίων*); (**5**) s. iv BC ib. 209; cf. KW pl. 1 no. 25 (*Ἄττεω* (gen.): f. *Τάτυς*)
THRACE:
—ODESSOS: (**6**) 13 BC *IGB* I^2 46, 34 (*Ἄττεω* (gen.): f. *Εὐπόλεμος*)

'Αττῆς
THRACE:
—ODESSOS: (1) 221 AD ib. 47 bis, 8 (*M. Αὐρ. 'Α.*: s. *Διονύσιος*); (2) ib. 47 bis b, 30 (*'Αττῆ* (gen.): f. *Αὐρ. Διονύσιος*); (3) ib. 47 bis c, 24 (*'Αττῆ* (gen.): f. *Αὐρ. Φαῦστος*); (4) ib. l. 36-7 (*'Αττῆ* (gen.): f. *Αὐρ. Ἕλλην, Αὐρ. Ἀντίπατρος*)

'Αττιανός
TAURIS:
—CHERSONESOS: (1) 174 AD *SEG* XLV 985 A, 32; 985 B, 27 (*T. Φλ. 'Α.*)

'Αττίας
CIMMERIAN BOSPOROS:
—SEMENOVKA (MOD.): (1) iii AD *KSIA* 89 (1962) p. 99 (amph.) (*MIA* 155 (1970) p. 45) (*'Αττ<η>ας*?—*MIA*, *'Αττίνας*?)
SKYTHIA:
—TANAIS: (2) f. iii AD *CIRB* 1286, 6; Zgusta, *PNS* 596 (s. *Νε—ος*)

'Αττίδως?
MACEDONIA (PELAGONIA): (1) ii-i BC *IG* X (2) (2) 159, 3, 7, 8 (*'Αττιδω* (voc./gen.): s. *Κάλας*)

'Αττική
MACEDONIA (MYGDONIA):
—LETE: (1) s. ii AD *SEG* XXXVIII 633 (m. *Λ. Ἄννιος Μακεδών, Τυλλία Γλύκιννα*)
THRACE:
—BYZANTION: (2) i-ii AD *BMI* 1011; cf. *IByz* p. 263 (d. *Χρυσέρως*)

'Αττίκιλλα
MACEDONIA (BOTTIAIA):
—BEROIA: (1) ?211 AD *ILeukopetra* 60, 2 (d. *Σόφη*)
MACEDONIA (MYGDONIA):
—THESSALONIKE: (2) ?ii AD *IG* X (2) (1) 539 + *BCH* 97 (1973) p. 593 (*Ἀντωνία 'Αττίκιλ[λα]*?, *'Αττική(α)*—ed.: d. *Ἀντώνιος 'Αττικός, Φαβία Σαμβώ*)
THRACE:
—TYRODIZA-TIRISTASIS: (3) ii-iii AD PM 1623 (*Βενουλεῖα 'Αττίκιλλ[α]*: m. *Βενουλέϊος Σκύμνος*)

'Αττικός
MACEDONIA (BOTTIAIA):
—EDESSA: (1) ii AD *BSA* 58 (1963) p. 24 no. 7 (Tataki, *Edessa* 12) (*Π. Αἰλ. Τερεντιανὸς 'Α.*)
MACEDONIA (MYGDONIA):
—THESSALONIKE: (2) i AD *IG* X (2) (1) 259, 31 (*M. Δόλλιος 'Α.*); (3) ?ii AD ib. 539; 540? (*Ἀντώνιος 'Α.*: I f. *Γ. Ἀντώνιος 'Αττικός* II, *Ἀντωνία 'Αττικίς, Ἀντωνία Πίστις*); (4) ib. 540 (*Γ. Ἀντώνιος 'Αττικὸς νέος*: II s. *Ἀντώνιος 'Αττικός* I, *Φαβία Σαμβώ*)
MACEDONIA (PAIONIA):
—KAVADARCI (MOD.): (5) 210 AD *Sp.* 98 (1941-8) p. 57 no. 115 (?f. (nat.) *Χιόνη*)
—STOBOI: (6) ?ii AD *Studies Stobi* 1 p. 162 (*Φ. Αὐφιδηνὸς 'Α.*)
THRACE:
—BAZOPARA: (7) 202 AD *IGB* III 1690 c, 65 (and Thrace Pizos: *'Αττικ<ι>ός*: s. *Δυτούτραλις*)
—MARKIANOPOLIS: (8) ?ii AD ib. V 5346 (*—ς Ἡράνιος 'Α.*)

'Αττίνας
MACEDONIA: (1) c. 329 BC *RE* Supplbd. 4 (2); Berve 185 (Tataki, *Macedonians* p. 275 no. 330); (2) hell. *AMGR* 1935-9, p. 121 no. 4 (Tataki, *Macedonians* p. 275 no. 331; La'da E1451) (s. *Δημήτριος*)
MACEDONIA (BOTTIAIA):
—BEROIA: (3) 239-229 BC *IBer* 45, 5, 12-13, 25-6 (Tataki 252) (s. *Ἀλκέτας*, ?f. *Ἀλκέτας, Λαρέτας*)
—MIEZA: (4) iii BC *SEG* XXIV 524 I, 11 (Hatzopoulos, *MI* 2 p. 106 no. 92)
—TYRISSA? (ASVESTARI (MOD.)): (5) f. ii BC *SEG* XLVII 999, 12 (*'Ατ[τ]ίνας*) ?= (6); (6) ib. l. 18 (*'Ατ[τ]ίνας*) ?= (7) (5); (7) ib. l. 24 ?= (6)
MACEDONIA (MYGDONIA):
—LETE: (8) s. iv BC Hatzopoulos, *MI* 2 pp. 93-4 no. 79, 8
TAURIS:
—CHERSONESOS: (9) ii AD *IOSPE* I² 432, 4; Zgusta, *PNS* 596 (*T. Φλ. 'Α.*: s. *T. Φλ. Ἀπολλώνιος*); (10) *IOSPE* I² 620 (*'Αττίν[ας]*); (11) ib. 699, 4 (*'Αττίν[ας]*); (12) f. ii AD ib. 359, 20, 35; 423; *SEG* XLVIII 999, 38 (f. *Ἀρίστων*); (13) c. 120-130 AD Solomonik, *NEPKh* 112, 15; cf. *VDI* 1993 (4), p. 63; (14) 174 AD *SEG* XLV 985 A, 36 (*'Α[τ]τ[ί]να[ς]*: s. *Πάτρος*); (15) ib. l. 38 (s. *Εὐρύδαμος*); (16) ib. l. 39 (s. *Ἀρίστων*)
THRACE:
—AINOS: (17) 236-232 or 206 BC *PPetr*² 16, 90; *CPR* XVIII 30, 130 (La'da E90) (s. *Καλλιφάνης*: t.e.)
—ALOPEKONNESOS: (18) i BC *IG* XII (8) 190 a, 14 (s. *Διογένης*)
—CHERSONESOS: (19) 183 BC ib. II² 2332 II, 163 (*FRA* 7302)

Ἄττιος
THRACE:
—BIZYE (TERRIT.): (1) ii-iii AD *IGB* V 5660 (f. *Διονύσιος*)

Ἄττυα
MACEDONIA (ELIMEIA):
—AIANE: (1) hell.? *SEG* XLIII 363 C (*'Αττύα(ς)*?)

'Αττυληνή
THRACE:
—BYZANTION: (1) ii/i BC *IByz* 233 (d. *Ἄρεσκος*)

'Αττύλος
MACEDONIA (BOTTIAIA):
—BEROIA: (1) iv-iii BC *IBer* 148 (Tataki 253) (s. *Μένανδρος*); (2) 248 BC *IBer* 3, 2 (Tataki 254) (s. *Νικάνωρ*)

Ἄττων
THRACE:
—ODESSOS: (1) 221 AD *IGB* I² 47 bis a, 21 (f. *M. Αὐρ. Ἑκατόδωρος*)

'Ατώτας
TAURIS:
—CHERSONESOS: (1) iv BC *IOSPE* I² 712; Zgusta, *PNS* 596

'Ατώτης
CIMMERIAN BOSPOROS:
—PANTIKAPAION: (1) s. iv BC *CIRB* 189; Zgusta, *PNS* 596 (f. *Θῦς*); (2) i AD *CIRB* 401 (f. *Ἔρως*)

Αὐάρθακος
SKYTHIA:
—TANAIS: (1) 225 AD ib. 1279, 17 (s. *Ζεύακος*)

Αὔασις
CIMMERIAN BOSPOROS:
—PANTIKAPAION: (1) f. iv BC ib. 193, 1, 3; cf. KW pl. 5 no. 104; Zgusta, *PNS* 68 (f. *Βόλας, Σῖμος*)

Αὔασκις
SKYTHIA:
—TANAIS: (1) 244 AD *CIRB* 1287, 28 (s. *Ἀμαίακος*)

Αὐβάδαγος
SKYTHIA:
—TANAIS: (1) 225 AD ib. 1279, 28 (*Αὐβάδαγ[ος]*: s. *—ναειστος*)

Αὐγάζων
THRACE:
—PHILIPPOPOLIS-TRIMONTIUM (TERRIT.): (1) ii-iii AD *IGB* III 1319

Αὔγη
KOLCHIS:
—VANI (MOD.): (1) i BC Braund, *Georgia* p. 147 n. 110 (vases)
MACEDONIA (MYGDONIA):
—THESSALONIKE: (2) ii AD *SEG* XXXVI 644 (*KGAM Thess.* I 58)
MACEDONIA (ODOMANTIKE):
—DRABESKOS?: (3) iv/iii BC *SEG* XXIV 578 (*CEG* II 726; Pilhofer 570)
MACEDONIA (PIERIA):
—DION: (4) imp. *CIL* III 594 (Dimitsas 189); cf. *Klio* 52 (1970) p. 64 (Lat. Iulia Auge)
THRACE:
—APOLLONIA-SOZOPOLIS: (5) iv BC *IGB* I² 430

Αὐγούστα
MACEDONIA (BOTTIAIA):
—BEROIA*: (1) iii AD *SEG* L 580

Αὐγουστάλιος
THRACE:
—NICOPOLIS AD ISTRUM (TERRIT.): (1) ii AD *IGB* V 5244 a, 12 (f. *Ἰανουαρία*)

Αὐγουστιανός
THRACE:
—SERDICA (TERRIT.): (1) ii-iii AD *AEMÖ* 10 (1886) pp. 238-9 no. 2, 7

Αὐγουστῖνος
THRACE:
—BISANTHE-PANION (NR.): (1) iii AD *AD* 49-50 (1994-5) Mel. p. 328 no. 153 (*Ἀγωστεῖ-*: f. *Καπιτωλῖνα*)

Αὔδωκος?
SCYTHIA MINOR:
—TOMIS: (1) ii-iii AD *ISM* II 468, 20 (*Αὐδώκου* (gen.))

Αὐδωλέων
MACEDONIA (PAIONIA): (1) c. 315-285 BC *RE* (-); *IG* II² 654, 12, 37 (*Syll*³ 371); *SEG* XII 263, 2; *AMNG* III (2) pp. 203-5 nos. 1-13 (coin) (*Αὐτολέων*—Polyaen. and Plu.: s. *Πάτραος*, f. *Ἀρίστων*: king)
—STOBOI*: (2) s. iii AD Šašel, *IL* 1248 (Lat. Sex. Cornelius Audoleo: freed.)

Αὐζάκενθος
THRACE:
—PHILIPPOPOLIS-TRIMONTIUM (TERRIT.): (1) imp. *IGB* III 1393

Αὐλείνη
CIMMERIAN BOSPOROS:
—PANTIKAPAION: (1) iv-iii BC Richter, *Engraved Gems* I p. 124 no. 486 (ring)

Αὐλενις
THRACE:
—ERGISSENOI: (1) ii AD *IGB* III 1593, 18 (f. *Σεύθης*)

Αὖλος
MACEDONIA (MYGDONIA):
—THESSALONIKE?: (1) ?i AD *IG* X (2) (1) 55 (f. *Ἀρίστεια*)
THRACE:
—BYZANTION: (2) i BC-i AD *IByz* 215 (Fıratlı–Robert p. 73 no. 78) (s. *Λύδιος*)
—PERINTHOS-HERAKLEIA: (3) f. iii AD *IPerinth* 157 (f. *Αὐρ. Σεβῆρα*)

Αὐλόσανις
SCYTHIA MINOR:
—TOMIS: (1) i-ii AD *ISM* II 165 (PM 1735); cf. *IByz* 370 A; *BE* 2001, no. 308 (?f. *Ἀντιγόνη*)

Αὐλουδέα

THRACE:

—RHAIDESTOS: (1) ii-iii AD *JÖAI* 23 (1926) Beibl. col. 137 no. 36

Αὐλουδένθης

THRACE:

—KELLAI: (1) ii-iii AD *IGB* III 1524 (*Αὐλου-δέν[θης]*)

Αὔλουζεις

THRACE:

—HERAION TEICHOS?: (1) ii-i BC Taşlıklıoğlu 2 p. 93 no. 1 (*Αὐλούζειδος* (gen.): s. *Ταρούλας*, f. (nat.) *Αὐλούπορις*)

—MARONEIA: (2) ii-i BC *IThrakAig* E212, 57 (*Αὐλούζειδος* (gen.): f. *—νίδης*)

Αὐλούζελμις

CIMMERIAN BOSPOROS:

—PANTIKAPAION: (1) i/ii AD *CIRB* 586; cf. KW pl. 39 no. 572 (s. *Δαλάζελμος*); (2) *CIRB* 587; cf. KW pl. 23 no. 337; Zgusta, *PNS* 556 (-λύ-: s. *Δαλάζελμος*)

THRACE:

—SAPPAIOI: (3) iii BC *IG* XII (9) 795 + *BE* 1951, no. 57 (*Διλ[ί]ζελμις*—*IG*, *Αὐλόζελμις*—Russu: s. *Ἀρτίδουις*)

THRACE?: (4) hell. *SEG* XL 1169 (f. *Δολήζελμις*)

Αὐλούζενις

MACEDONIA (EDONIS):

—SKIAZERENOI: (1) i-ii AD ib. XLVII 936 (Pilhofer 509a) (f. *Μεστυπαίβης*)

TAURIS:

—CHERSONESOS: (2) ii AD Solomonik, *LNKhT* 26 (Lat. Auluzenus)

THRACE: (3) 46-54 AD *SEG* XVI 415 I, 5 (*IThrakAig* E84) (*Τιβ. Κλ. Ἀ.*); (4) ii-iii AD Dain, *IGLouvre* 25; (5) *IGB* V 5394 bis (s. *Μουκάπορις*)

—ANCHIALOS: (6) imp. *CIL* XIII 11941, 1 (Lat. Aulusan[us]: f. *Αὐλούπορις*); (7) i-ii AD *IGB* I^2 374 (I f. *Αὐλούζενις* II); (8) ib. (-νης: II s. *Αὐλούζενις* I)

—ANCHIALOS (TERRIT.): (9) ii/iii AD ib. III 1846, 2 (s. *Κουίζερις*, *Δεντουσυκος*)

—BAZOPARA: (10) 202 AD ib. 1690 d, 23 (and Thrace Pizos: f. *Κάστωρ*); (11) ib. 1690 c, 63-4 (and Thrace Pizos: s. *Μουκάπορις*, f. *Μουκάτραλις*)

—BEROE-AUGUSTA TRAIANA: (12) ii AD ib. 1598 (s. *Διόσπορις*); (13) ii-iii AD ib. 1599 (s. *Βρίζενις*); (14) f. ii AD *CIL* VIII 3198 + 18312 (Lat. Auluzenis: f. *Μουκάτραλις*)

—BEROE-AUGUSTA TRAIANA (TERRIT.): (15) ii-iii AD *IGB* III 1670 (*Αὐλού[ζε]νις*: f. *Μουκάπορις*); (16) ib. 1703 (f. *Ἑρμογένης*); (17) ib. 1713 b, 5 (f. *Αὐλου—*); (18) ib. 1743 (*Αὐλούζεν[ις]*); (19) ib. 1760 (s. *Κακοῦς*)

—BIZYE?: (20) f. i AD ib. I^2 402, 4 (f. *Λεοντώι*)

—BIZYE (TERRIT.)?: (21) ii-iii AD ib. III 1852, 6

—DODOPARON: (22) ii AD ib. 1794 (f. *Ἀπολλώνις*)

—DRAGANOVEC (MOD.): (23) f. iii AD ib. V 5300 (*CCET* II (2) 459) (f. *Μουκάπορις*)

—GABARE (MOD.): (24) iii AD *Romanizmăt* II 261 (Lat. Aulozene(m) (acc.))

—GELOUPARA: (25) 202 AD *IGB* III 1690 c, 21 (and Thrace Pizos: I f. *Αὐλούζενις* II); (26) ib. l. 21 (and Thrace Pizos: II s. *Αὐλούζενις* I); (27) ib. l. 27 (and Thrace Pizos: *(Α)ὐλούζενις*: f. *Μουκάτραλις*)

—GLAVA PANEGA (MOD.): (28) ii-iii AD ib. II 542 (*Αὐλουζένε[ος]* (gen.): f. *Μοκιανός*)

—HADRIANOPOLIS (TERRIT.): (29) imp. ib. III 1832, 6 (*Αὐλ[ού]ζενις*: f. *Ἀπολλωνίδης*); (30) ii-iii AD ib. 1806 (f. *Μουκάπορις*)

—HADRIANOPOLIS (TERRIT.)?: (31) ii-iii AD *Thrakika* 9 (1938) p. 407 (*IThrakAig* E478) (*Αὐλου[ζ]ένεος* (gen.): I f. *Αὐλούζενις* II); (32) *Thrakika* 9 (1938) p. 407 (*IThrakAig* E478) (II s. *Αὐλούζενις* I)

—KABYLE: (33) ii AD *Kabile* 2 p. 24 no. 19 (Lat. [Au]luzeni (gen.))

—KELLAI: (34) ii-iii AD *IGB* III 1529

—KRASALOPARA: (35) 202 AD ib. 1690 b, 48 (and Thrace Pizos: s. *Βρίζενις*); (36) ib. l. 49 (and Thrace Pizos: s. *Δίβιθυς*); (37) ib. l. 50 (and Thrace Pizos: s. *Μουκάπορις*); (38) ib. l. 56 (and Thrace Pizos: f. *Βρινκαζεις*); (39) ib. l. 68 (and Thrace Pizos: f. *Σοῦρις*)

—MARKIANOPOLIS: (40) iii AD ib. V 5360 (*CCET* II (1) 200) (f. *Ζένις*); (41) f. iii AD *IGB* V 5343 (*CCET* II (1) 197) + *CCET* II 208 (-ζη-: s. *Μουκάπορις*)

—MARKIANOPOLIS (TERRIT.): (42) imp. *SEG* XXXIX 676 (-ξε-: f. *Βίθυς*); (43) ii-iii AD *IGB* II 846 (*Αὐλο[ύ]ζεν[ις]*: s. *Μουκάπορις*); (44) f. iii AD ib. V 5381 = *CCET* II (1) 302 (f. *—ιος*)

—MARKIANOPOLIS (NR.): (45) ii-iii AD *IGB* V 5368 (s. *Πῖος*); (46) iii AD ib. II 839 (*[Αὐ]λούζεν[ις]*); (47) f. iii AD ib. 830 (*CCET* II (1) 229) (f. *Ἀπολλόδωρος ὁ καὶ Δισάτραλις*); (48) *IGB* V 5365 (*CCET* II (1) 226) (f. *Κερζετραυς*); (49) *IGB* V 5380 (*CCET* II (1) 244) (f. *Διζάπορις*)

—MUSENOI: (50) ii-iii AD *IGB* V 5652 (s. *Ἑρμόδωρος*)

—NICOPOLIS AD ISTRUM: (51) ?iii AD *ILB* 375 (Lat. [Au]luzeni (gen.))

—NICOPOLIS AD ISTRUM (TERRIT.): (52) 227 AD ib. 438 II, 13 (Lat. Auluzeni (gen.): f. Berilo)

—ODESSOS (NR.): (53) i-ii AD *IGB* I^2 281 bis; (54) ii-iii AD ib. 275 (*CCET* I 18) (*Αὐλούζαν[ος]*)

—PAUTALIA (TERRIT.): (55) ii-iii AD *IGB* V 5824 (s. *Δίζας*)

—PHILIPPOPOLIS-TRIMONTIUM: (56) iii AD *CIL* VI 2601 (Lat. Val. Aulusanus)

—PHILIPPOPOLIS-TRIMONTIUM (TERRIT.): (57) ii-iii AD *IGB* III 1112 (*[Α]ὐλουζένε[ος]* (gen.)); (58) ib. 1169 (I f. *Αὐλούζενις* II); (59) ib. (*[Α]ὐλούζενις*: II s. *Αὐλούζενις* I); (60) ib. 1218 (*Αὐλουζένε[ος]* (gen.)); (61) ib. 1404 (s. *Διουζής*); (62) ib. (s. *Λογγῖνος*); (63) iii AD ib. 1090 (f. *Βίθυς*)

—SALYMBRIA: (64) imp. *IByz* S 18 (*Αὐλούζεν[ις]*: f. *Αὐλούπορις*)

—SKEDABRIA: (65) 202 AD *IGB* III 1690 b, 22 (and Thrace Pizos: s. *Τάρσας*)

—SPORTELA: (66) ii-iii AD ib. IV 2234, 4 (*[Αὐλ]ούζενις*)

—STRATOPARA: (67) 202 AD ib. III 1690 b, 26 (and Thrace Pizos: f. *Ζουραζεις*); (68) ib. l. 31 (and Thrace Pizos: f. *Ἐπτήτραλις*)

—XANTHI (MOD.): (69) iii AD *IThrakAig* E104 (s. *Διασενις*)

THRACE?: (70) ii-iii AD Beševliev, *EP* 25 (*SEG* XV 472) (-νεις: s. *Κῶκος*); (71) f. iii AD *AE* 1984, pp. 173-4 no. 3136 (*Αὐλό(ζ)ενις*)

Αὐλούκενθος

THRACE:

—BEROE-AUGUSTA TRAIANA (TERRIT.): (1) ii AD *IGB* III 1734 (s. *Τάρσας*)

—BESSOI: (2) ii AD *CIL* III 4378 + *Stud. Beševliev* pp. 202-7 (Lat. Ulp. Aulucentus)

—BIZYE: (3) c. 153 AD Taşlıklıoğlu 2 p. 67 no. 1, 13 + *BE* 1972, no. 292 (s. *Δυτούκενθος*)

—NICOPOLIS AD ISTRUM: (4) ii-iii AD *IGB* II 677 (*Eastern cults* p. 163 no. 3) (f. *Μουκάζενις*)

—PHILIPPOPOLIS-TRIMONTIUM: (5) ii-iii AD *IGB* V 5467 (*Κλ. Ἀ.*: f. *Κλ. Γάϊος*, *Κλ. Κοδρᾶτος*)

Αὐλούκενις

THRACE:

—ODESSOS (TERRIT.): (1) iii AD ib. I^2 278

Αὐλουμένης

THRACE:

—BEROE-AUGUSTA TRAIANA:

——Karasoura: (1) ii-iii AD ib. III 1627, 2 + *SEG* XLI 589 (*[Αὐλ]ουμένης*: s. *Βίθυς*)

—PHILIPPOPOLIS-TRIMONTIUM (TERRIT.): (2) ii-iii AD *IGB* III 1316; cf. V 5493 bis (*[Αὐ]λουμένης Σέρδων*)

Αὐλούπορις

CIMMERIAN BOSPOROS:

—MYRMEKION: (1) i AD *CIRB* 878 (f. *Βασιλείδης*)

MACEDONIA (EDONIS):

—PHILIPPOI: (2) ii-iii AD *BIAB* 16 (1950) p. 9 no. 2 (Pilhofer 50); Collart, *Philippes* pl. 36. 1 (f. *Καρώσης ὁ καὶ Ἀ—λας*)

SCYTHIA MINOR:

—ISTROS [NR.]:

——Vicus Quintionis: (3) 139-161 AD *ISM* I 324, 13 (Lat. Auluporis: f. *Δέρζενις*)

THRACE: (4) i-ii AD *IGB* III 1880 (f. *—ων*); (5) 46-54 AD *SEG* XVI 415 I, 6 (*IThrakAig* E84) (*Τιβ. Κλ. Ἀ.*); (6) *SEG* XVI 415 III, 30 (*IThrakAig* E84) (f. *Καρώσης*)

—ANCHIALOS: (7) imp. *CIL* XIII 11941, 1 (Lat. Aulupor(is): s. *Αὐλούζενις*)

—BEROE-AUGUSTA TRAIANA (TERRIT.): (8) ii-iii AD ib. III 1659 (*Αὐλ[ούπ]ορις*: f. *—νης*)

—BIZYE: (9) ii-iii AD *JÖAI* 23 (1926) Beibl. col. 123 no. 9 (*Αὐλω[π]όρεος* (gen.)); (10) c. 153 AD Taşlıklıoğlu 2 p. 67 no. 1, 12 + *BE* 1972, no. 292 (f. *Φίρμος*)

—BIZYE (TERRIT.)?: (11) ii-iii AD *IGB* III 1853 (f. *Μαρτιάλης*)

—DADOPARA: (12) f. iii AD *SEG* XLII 651, 4 (f. *Αὐρ. Ἀπολλόδωρος*)

—DUROSTORUM (TERRIT.)?: (13) iii AD *IGB* II 868, 7 (*CCET* II (1) 186) (f. *Λαπέπωρ*, *Προκίλιος*)

—HADRIANOPOLIS (TERRIT.): (14) ii-iii AD *IGB* III 1806 (s. *Μουκάτραλις*)

—HERAION TEICHOS?: (15) ii-i BC Taşlıklıoğlu 2 p. 93 no. 1 (s. (nat.) *Αὔλουζεις*, s. (ad.) *Θρασέας*)

—KELLAI*: (16) iii AD *IGB* III 1516 b, 13 (f. *Πουριζ—*); (17) ib. l. 27 (s. *Και—*)

—MARKIANOPOLIS: (18) 161 AD ib. V 5334, 4 (*Π. Αἰλ. Ἀ.*)

—MARKIANOPOLIS (TERRIT.): (19) iii AD ib. II 841, 3 (II s. *Αὐλούπορις* I); (20) ib. l. 4 (I f. *Αὐλούπορις* II); (21) ib. V 5329, 2 (s. *Μουκάσης*)

—MARKIANOPOLIS (NR.): (22) iii AD ib. II 838 (f. *Αὐ—*)

—PHILIPPOPOLIS-TRIMONTIUM: (23) iii AD ib. III 963 (*Αὐλούπορ[ις]*: f. *Σοῦρις*)

—SALYMBRIA: (24) imp. *IByz* S 18 (s. *Αὐλούζενις*, f. *Ἀ—*)

—SAPPAIOI: (25) ii/i BC *Ét. Thas.* 5 p. 45 no. 175, 24 (king?) ?= (*Ἀβρούπολις* (*1*))

—SERDICA (TERRIT.): (26) ii-iii AD *Sp.* 98 (1941-48) p. 127 no. 280, 7 (f. *Σαικέλης*)

—SEUTHOPOLIS (NR.): (27) f. iii AD *IGB* V 5613 (*Αὐλούπ[ορις]*)

—STRATOPARA: (28) 202 AD ib. III 1690 b, 25 (and Thrace Pizos: I f. *Αὐλούπορις* II); (29) ib. l. 25 (and Thrace Pizos: II s. *Αὐλούπορις* I); (30) ib. l. 29 (and Thrace Pizos: f. *Μουκάτραλις*)

THRACE?: (31) ii BC *SEG* XI 12 (-πορες); (32) ii/iii AD *CIL* VI 32625 a II, 8 (Lat. Aur. Aulupor)

Αὐλουσουκος

THRACE:

—MARKIANOPOLIS (TERRIT.): (1) ii-iii AD *IGB* II 844 (*Αὐλουσουκο(ς)*: d. *Βίθυς*)

Αὐλούτραλις

THRACE:

—BAZOPARA: (1) 202 AD ib. III 1690 d, 12 (and Thrace Pizos: f. *Γενικείλας*); (2) ib. l. 19 (and Thrace Pizos: f. *Δόλης*)

—HADRIANOPOLIS (TERRIT.): (3) ii-iii AD ib. 1814 (s. *Βρίζενις*)

—PAUTALIA: (4) ii AD ib. IV 2074, 19 (f. Ἀπολλινάριος); (5) ii-iii AD ib. 2079, 1 (T. Αὐρ. Ἀουλ[ούτ]ρα(λ)ης: s. Χρῆστος)
—PHILIPPOPOLIS-TRIMONTIUM: (6) ii-iii AD ib. III 977 (f. Ἡραΐς)
—PHILIPPOPOLIS-TRIMONTIUM (TERRIT.): (7) ii-iii AD ib. 1446 (Αὐλούτρα(λ)ις?); (8) iii AD ib. V 5475, 1 (Αὐλο[ύ]τραλις: s. Ἐ—ις)
—PHILIPPOPOLIS-TRIMONTIUM?: (9) ii-iii AD ib. 5436 (s. Σιγος)
—SERDICA: (10) ii-iii AD ib. IV 1947 (f. Σέρκις)
THRACE?: (11) ?ii BC *SB* 3672 (Velkov 37) (Α[ὐλ]ο[ύτ]ραλης?)

Αὔναμος
SKYTHIA:
—TANAIS: (1) 228 AD *CIRB* 1282, 5 (Ἡρακλείδης ὁ καὶ Α.: s. Ἡρακλείδης)

Αὐξάνιος
MACEDONIA (MYGDONIA):
—THESSALONIKE: (1) ii AD *IG* X (2) (1) 391 (Αἰλ. Ἀχιλλεὺς ὁ κὲ Α.: s. Αἰλ. Ἀχιλλεύς)

Αὐξάνουσα
MACEDONIA (MYGDONIA):
—THESSALONIKE: (1) iv-vi AD Feissel, *RICM* 112 (mosaic)

Αὐξάνων
SCYTHIA MINOR:
—TOMIS: (1) ii-iii AD *ISM* II 34, 6 (Αὐξά[νων]?)

Αὐξησιλεώ
SCYTHIA MINOR:
—ISTROS: (1) f. iv BC ib. I 240 (d. Ἡφαιστοκλῆς)

Αὔξιμος
MACEDONIA (MYGDONIA):
—THESSALONIKE: (1) ii-iii AD *IG* X (2) (1) 345 (—νιος Α.); (2) iii AD ib. 220, 3 (Κλ. Α. ὁ καὶ Πιέρις: s. Κλ. Γάϊος)

Αὔξων
MACEDONIA (MYGDONIA):
—THESSALONIKE: (1) ii-iii AD ib. 439

Αὐράζακος
SKYTHIA:
—TANAIS: (1) c. 225-250 AD *CIRB* 1288, 15 ([Αὐ]ράζακος: s. Ἀρι—); (2) 244 AD ib. 1287, 12 (s. Ῥόδων)

Αὐρηλία
MACEDONIA: (1) 309 or 311 AD *ILeukopetra* 116, 4 (d. Ἀλεξάνδρα: oikogen. slave/freed.)
MACEDONIA (BOTTIAIA):
—BEROIA: (2) iii AD *IBer* 50 (Tataki 256); (3) *IBer* 215 (Tataki 255)
MACEDONIA (CHALKIDIKE):
—POTIDAIA-KASSANDREIA (NR.): (4) ?iii AD Dimitsas 746, 4 (d. Σεουῆρος Σώσανδρος, Ὀλυμπιάς)
MACEDONIA (MYGDONIA):
—THESSALONIKE: (5) ii-iii AD *IG* X (2) (1) 518
MACEDONIA (PELAGONIA):
—DOSTONEIS: (6) iii AD ib. X (2) (2) 201, 1 (m. Ὄρεινος, Διομήδης, Νικομήδης, Ὀρείνη)
MACEDONIA (PIERIA):
—PYDNA: (7) i-ii AD *SEG* XXXVIII 666 (Αὐρ(ηλία): d. Ἀντίγονος, m. Φιλίππα)
THRACE:
—PERINTHOS-HERAKLEIA: (8) iii AD *IPerinth* 160 (Αὐρ(ηλία))

Αὐρηλιανή
MACEDONIA (DERRIOPOS)?: (1) ii-iii AD *IG* X (2) (2) 44 ([Α]ὐρηλιανή: m. Λυσίμαχος ὁ καὶ Κάτων)

Αὐρηλιανός
MACEDONIA (PAIONIA):
—STOBOI: (1) iv/v AD Feissel, *RICM* 279 (mosaic) (-ρηλλι-)
THRACE:
—KELLAI: (2) 241-244 AD *IGB* III 1517, 10 (f. Κλ. Μάσχλος)

Αὐρήλιος
MACEDONIA (BOTTIAIA):
—BEROIA: (1) iii AD *IBer* 215 (Tataki 273)
—EDESSA: (2) iii AD Tataki, *Macedonians* p. 102 no. 4 (s. Λυσίμαχος); (3) 229 AD Tataki, *Edessa* 47 (f. Αὐρ. Εὐδ—)
MACEDONIA (EDONIS):
—AMPHIPOLIS (TERRIT.)?: (4) iii AD *SEG* XXXIII 544
MACEDONIA (LYNKESTIS):
—HERAKLEIA: (5) i AD *IG* X (2) (2) 75, 8 (s. Σεκοῦνδος)
MACEDONIA (MYGDONIA):
—THESSALONIKE: (6) ?iv AD *AEMTh* 15 (2001) p. 325
—THESSALONIKE?: (7) iii AD *IG* X (2) (1) 839, 2 (?s. Αὐρ. Ἀρσένιος)
MACEDONIA (ODOMANTIKE):
—SKOTOUSSA?: (8) ii-iii AD Dimitsas 910
MACEDONIA (PIERIA):
—DION (TERRIT.): (9) ?iii AD *SEG* XXVI 728
SCYTHIA MINOR:
—TOMIS: (10) iii AD *SBBayerAk* 1875, p. 84 no. 9 (Αὐρίδιος—apogr.: s. Ἡρακλείδης)
THRACE:
—AINOS: (11) ii-iii AD Dumont–Homolle 103
—BAZOPARA: (12) 202 AD *IGB* III 1690 c, 62 (and Thrace Pizos: s. Μουκάτραλις)
—GOLJAMA BRESTNICA (MOD.): (13) iii AD ib. II 589 (-ρήλις: s. Μεστόης)
—KELLAI: (14) 241-244 AD ib. III 1517, 41 (f. Αὐρ. Ἄσων)
—ROSICA (MOD.): (15) ii-iii AD ib. V 5284
—SERDICA (TERRIT.): (16) ii-iii AD *AEMÖ* 10 (1886) pp. 238-9 no. 2, 8 (-ρήλις); (17) *IGB* V 5743

Αὐτάνδρος
MACEDONIA: (1) ?417-413 BC *IG* I^3 89, 68 (Tataki, *Macedonians* p. 275 no. 332)

Αὐτέας
TAURIS:
—CHERSONESOS: (1) iii BC *IOSPE* I^2 340, 3 (f. Πρόνους)

Αὐτόδαμος
THRACE:
—BYZANTION: (1) ?464 BC *IG* I^3 1144, 120 ([Αὐ]τόδε̄μος?)

Αὐτόδικος
MACEDONIA (BOTTIAIA):
—PELLA: (1) c. 350-280 BC *RE* (7) + Supplbd. 4 (-); Berve 187 (Tataki, *Macedonians* p. 152 no. 27); *IG* VII 279 (*IOrop* 383) (s. Ἀγαθοκλῆς)

Αὐτοκλῆς
SCYTHIA MINOR:
—ISTROS: (1) iii BC *ISM* I 156 (Αὐτοκλ[ῆς]?)
SKYTHIA:
—TYRAS: (2) c. 300-275 BC *SEG* XLIX 1051 B, 1 (Αὐτοκ(λ)ῆς: s. Οἰνιάδης); (3) s. iii BC *VDI* 1966 (2), p. 152, 5 (s. Ἀπ—)
TAURIS:
—CHERSONESOS: (4) f. iii BC *SEG* XL 615 A, 13 (s. Αὐτο—)

Αὐτοκράτης
MACEDONIA (PIERIA):
—PHILA?: (1) ?iii BC *RPh* 1911, pp. 133-4 no. 36, 127; cf. Helly, *L'État thessalien* pp. 319-20 (locn.) (f. Αἰσχίνας)

THRACE:
—ODESSOS: (2) ii AD *IGB* I^2 183 (PM 1738) (f. Ξένων); (3) m. ii AD *IGB* I^2 177 ter; *Dacia* 21 (1977) p. 161 (date) (s. Καλλικράτης)
—ODESSOS (NR.): (4) iii BC *IGB* I^2 253

Αὐτόλυκος
MACEDONIA (PIERIA):
—PYDNA (TERRIT.): (1) imp. *SEG* XXXVIII 629
THRACE:
—ABDERA: (2) iii AD ib. XXVIII 558, 4 (*IThrakAig* E71) (*M.* Οὔλπ. Α.)
—BEROE-AUGUSTA TRAIANA (TERRIT.): (3) iii AD *IGB* V 5629 (Αὐρ. Α.)
—PERINTHOS-HERAKLEIA:
——(Aigikoreis): (4) iii-ii BC *IPerinth* 61, 53 (s. Δημόδοτος)
—SERDICA: (5) ii-iii AD *IGB* IV 1922, 1

Αὐτομένης
MACEDONIA: (1) 160 BC *PHels* 31, 3 (Tataki, *Macedonians* p. 275 no. 333); cf. La'da E1465 (f. Διόδοτος)

Αὐτονόα
MACEDONIA (BOTTIAIA):
—EDESSA: (1) imp. Dimitsas 41 (47; Tataki, *Edessa* 65)

Αὐτόνομος
CIMMERIAN BOSPOROS:
—THEODOSIA: (1) iii AD *CIRB* 947 B, 2 ([Αὐ]τόνομος: f. Ἀγαθοῦς)

Αὐτοφῶν
TAURIS:
—CHERSONESOS: (1) iii BC Solomonik, *NEPKh* 173 (Αὐτοφ[ῶν]?: ?f. Εὐφρονίς)

Αὐχένιος
THRACE:
—PHRYGIA*: (1) v AD *SEG* XXXIX 665, 7 (*AD* 53 (1998) Mel. p. 468 no. 207) (estate)

Ἀφαίστιος
TAURIS:
—CHERSONESOS: (1) hell. Solomonik, *GAKh* 383 (vase) (Ἀφαίστιο[ς]? (n. pr.?))

Ἀφαιστίων
SCYTHIA MINOR:
—KALLATIS: (1) s. iii BC *ISM* III 35 B, 38 (s. Σκύθας)

Ἀφαιστόδωρος
TAURIS:
—CHERSONESOS: (1) f. iii BC *SEG* XL 615 B, 2-4

Ἀφαρεύς
MACEDONIA (MYGDONIA):
—THESSALONIKE: (1) 166 AD *IG* X (2) (1) 472 A (Κλ. Α.: s. Κλ. Λέων)

Ἄφδαλος
MACEDONIA (BOTTIAIA):
—BEROIA?: (1) 210 AD *ILeukopetra* 55, 1 (s. Διονύσιος)

Ἀφθείμακος
SKYTHIA:
—TANAIS: (1) 220 AD *CIRB* 1278, 22; Zgusta, *PNS* 72 (s. Διο—); (2) 220-236 AD *CIRB* 1250, 15; 1278, 28 (Ἀφθαίμακος—1250: s. Ἄψαχος)

Ἀφθόνητος
MACEDONIA: (1) m. iv BC Ael., *VH* xiv 48 (Tataki, *Macedonians* p. 276 no. 334); (2) 327 BC Curt. viii 6. 9; Berve 296 (Tataki, *Macedonians* p. 306 no. 11) (Lat. Elapthonius, et Aphthonius—Hedicke)
MACEDONIA (BOTTIAIA):
—ALLANTE: (3) 323 BC *SEG* XXXVI 331 B, 22 (Tataki, *Macedonians* p. 44 no. 2) (s. Πυθόδωρος)
MACEDONIA (CHALKIDIKE):
—STRATONIKEIA?: (4) i-ii AD *SEG* XXIV 576 (s. Ἀριστέας)

Ἀφία
THRACE:
—BYZANTION:
——(Rhegion): (1) i BC-i AD *IByz* 244 (d. Ἀπολλώνιος)

Ἀφίον
SCYTHIA MINOR:
—KALLATIS: (1) iii AD *ISM* III 91 (*CCET* IV 95) ([Ἀ]φίον: d. —ωρος)

Ἀφόβητος
MACEDONIA: (1) 330 BC *RE* Supplbd. 4 (-); Berve 190 (Tataki, *Macedonians* p. 276 no. 335) (Lat. Aphobetus)
MACEDONIA (BOTTIAIA):
—BEROIA: (2) f. ii AD *IBer* 216 (Εἰούλ. [Ἀφό]βητος: I f. Ἰούλ. Ἀφόβητος II); (3) ib. (Ἰούλ. Ἀ[φό]βητος νέος: II s. Ἰούλ. Ἀφόβητος I)

Ἀφράνιος
CIMMERIAN BOSPOROS:
—PANTIKAPAION: (1) i BC/i AD *CIRB* 319 (f. Φαρνάκης); (2) i/ii AD ib. 640 (s. Φαρνάκης)

Ἀφροδεσά
THRACE:
—BIZYE: (1) imp.? PM 1950 (d. Δορζίνθης)

Ἀφροδισία
CIMMERIAN BOSPOROS:
—BOSPOROS: (1) i-ii AD *IG* II² 8425 (*FRA* 1367) (d. Δημήτριος)
MACEDONIA (EDONIS):
—AMPHIPOLIS: (2) imp. Kaphtantzis 663 (-δεισεία)
MACEDONIA (MYGDONIA):
—THESSALONIKE: (3) ?ii-iii AD *SEG* XXX 639
—THESSALONIKE?: (4) ii AD *IG* X (2) (1) 883, 1 (-δει-: m. Γ. Ἰούλ. Καλλίστρατος); (5) ii-iii AD ib. 869 (-δει-: threpte); (6) s. iii AD *AEpThess* p. 10 no. 8 B (-δει-: m. Ἡρακλέων, Ἀφρόδισις)
MACEDONIA (PIERIS):
—GALEPSOS: (7) ii-iii AD *BCH* 55 (1931) pp. 193-4 no. 13 ([Ἀφρο]δεισία)
SARMATIA:
—SARMATAI: (8) 153-144 BC *SGDI* 2274, 3, 6, 10 etc. (slave/freed.); (9) *FD* III (3) 24, 4, 6, 9 etc. (slave/freed.)
SCYTHIA MINOR:
—ISTROS: (10) imp. PH 364
THRACE: (11) m. ii BC *IG* IX (1)² (3) 624 c, 6 (?m. Σωστράτα (Other): slave/freed.); (12) imp. ib. II² 8900 (*FRA* 2503) (Ἀφροδ[ισία]: d. Σαδάλας)
—BYZANTION: (13) i BC *IG* II² 8439 (*FRA* 1391)
—MARONEIA: (14) iii-ii BC *IThrakAig* E240 (-δει-: d. Δημόκριτος)

Ἀφροδισιάς
MACEDONIA (PIERIA):
—DION: (1) f. ii AD *SEG* XXXIII 513; cf. Spiliopoulou-Donderer, *KGN* p. 198 no. D16 (date) (Ἰουλ. Ἀ.)

Ἀφροδισίη
CIMMERIAN BOSPOROS:
—PANTIKAPAION: (1) v BC *SEG* XL 637 (vase) ([Ἀ]φροδισίη)

Ἀφροδίσιος
CIMMERIAN BOSPOROS:
—PANTIKAPAION: (1) 275-278 AD *CIRB* 36, 12 (-δεί-: f. Ἰούλ. Χόφαρνος)
MACEDONIA: (2) 12 AD *PKöln* 227 B, 23 (f. Ἰσχυρίων)
MACEDONIA (BOTTIAIA):
—BEROIA: (3) i AD *IBer* 188 (Tataki 309) (-δεί-: f. Βαδήα); (4) f. ii AD *IBer* 337 (Tataki 308) (-δεί-); (5) ii/iii AD *IBer* 145, 15 (Tataki 869) (Μαρωνιανὸς Ἀφροδείσιος); (6) 177 AD *IBer* 135 B, 25 (Tataki 1228) (Τερεντιανὸς Ἀφροδείσιος)
MACEDONIA (MYGDONIA):
—THESSALONIKE: (7) iii AD *IG* X (2) (1) 247, 7 ([Τύ]λλιος Ἀφροδείσ[ιος])
—THESSALONIKE?: (8) iii AD ib. 771, 1 (Φλ. Ἀφροδίσ[ιο]ς: s. Φλ. Σεκούνδιλλα)
MACEDONIA (PIERIA):
—PYDNA (TERRIT.): (9) m. iii AD *SEG* XXXI 636 (s. Κλεονίκη)
SKYTHIA:
—SKYTHAI: (10) hell.-imp. *NS* 233 (-δεί-)
—TANAIS: (11) ii AD *CIRB* 1262, 15 ([Ἀφρ]οδείσιος: s. Αἰσ—); (12) c. 200-210 AD ib. 1277, 16 (Ἀ[φ]ροδείσιος: s. Χρυσέρως)
THRACE: (13) 142 or 141 BC *SGDI* 2175, 9 (slave/freed.)
—ABDERA (TERRIT.)?: (14) ii-iii AD Kazarow 283 (*IThrakAig* E82) (-δεί-)
—BIZYE (TERRIT.): (15) ii AD *IGB* III 1863, 2, 9 (*GVI* 262) (-δεί-)
—BYZANTION: (16) ii/i BC *IByz* 119 (Fıratlı-Robert pp. 115-16 no. 192) (f. Μένανδρος)
—MARONEIA: (17) hell.-imp. *FRA* 3534 (s. Σεύθης)
—NOVAE*: (18) 368 AD *IGLNovae* 178 (Φλ. Ἀφροδείσι[ος])

Ἀφρόδισις
MACEDONIA (BOTTIAIA):
—BEROIA: (1) i AD *IBer* 188 (-δεί-: s. Λιμναῖος, ?s. Βαδήα)
MACEDONIA (MYGDONIA):
—THESSALONIKE?: (2) s. iii AD *AEpThess* p. 10 no. 8 B (-δεί-: s. Ἀφροδισία); (3) iii/iv AD *IG* X (2) (1) 366 (Feissel, *RICM* 121) (Αὐρ. Ἀφροδείσις)

Ἀφροδίτη
MACEDONIA (PIERIA):
—DION (TERRIT.): (1) i-ii AD Oikonomos 47 (-δεί-: threpte)
THRACE:
—PERINTHOS-HERAKLEIA: (2) ii AD *IPerinth* 100 (-δεί-: d. Ἀπολλώνιος)

Ἀφρόδιτος
MACEDONIA (MYGDONIA):
—THESSALONIKE: (1) 132 AD *IG* X (2) (1) 35, 4 (-δει-)

Ἀφροδιτώ
MACEDONIA (BOTTIAIA):
—BEROIA: (1) f. iii AD *IBer* 217 (Tataki 311)
—BEROIA*: (2) s. ii AD *IBer* 374 (Tataki 310)
MACEDONIA (LYNKESTIS):
—HERAKLEIA (AREA): (3) iii AD *IG* X (2) (2) 37
MACEDONIA (MYGDONIA):
—THESSALONIKE: (4) ii-iii AD ib. X (2) (1) 498 (-δει-); (5) ib. 590 (-δει-: m. Θεόδωρος); (6) s. ii AD *SEG* XLVIII 850; (7) 252 AD *IG* X (2) (1) 166, 5 (Πετρωνία Ἀφροδειτώ)
MACEDONIA (ORESTIS):
—SISANI (MOD.): (8) 146 AD *EAM* 187, 16 (-δει-: m. Μάξιμος)
MACEDONIA (PELAGONIA): (9) iii AD *IG* X (2) (2) 178 (d. Ἀνάληψις)
MACEDONIA (PIERIA):
—DION: (10) ii AD *Klio* 52 (1970) p. 59 no. 12 (-δει-)

Ἀφυκτολις
THRACE:
—PAUTALIA: (1) s. ii AD *SEG* XLVI 864, 19 (s. Εὔφημος)

Ἄφφη
THRACE:
—BYZANTION?: (1) i BC *IByz* 351 (d. Ἀστέας)
—PHILIPPOPOLIS-TRIMONTIUM (TERRIT.): (2) ii-iii AD *IGB* III 1320, 1 (d. Κοκκήϊος)

Ἀφφία
THRACE:
—BYZANTION: (1) i-ii AD *IByz* 266 (Fıratlı-Robert p. 85 no. 105) (d. Τρόφιμος)
—ODESSOS: (2) i-ii AD *IGB* I² 113 (Ἀφφία: d. Ἀρτεμίδωρος)

Ἄφφος
SCYTHIA MINOR:
—TOMIS: (1) ii-iii AD *ISM* II 282 (s. Ἀλέξανδρος)
THRACE:
—PHILIPPOPOLIS-TRIMONTIUM (TERRIT.): (2) ii-iii AD *IGB* III 1315 (*CCCA* VI 351) (Ἄφος: f. Χρῆστος)

Ἀφφοῦς
CIMMERIAN BOSPOROS:
—PANTIKAPAION: (1) 130 AD *CIRB* 656, 2; cf. KW pl. 18 no. 272 (Ἀφφοῦτος (gen.): f. Ἀριστείδης, Παντόνικος)
MACEDONIA (PIERIA):
—DION*: (2) f. iii AD Oikonomos 35; cf. Spiliopoulou-Donderer, *KGN* p. 195 no. D12 (date) (Ἀφφοῦ (dat.): freed.)
THRACE:
—SALYMBRIA: (3) iii AD *IByz* S 20 (Αὐρ. Ἀφοῦς)

Ἀχαΐκαρος
CIMMERIAN BOSPOROS:
—BOSPOROS: (1) her.? *RE* (-); Str. 762 (mantis)

Ἀχαιμένης
CIMMERIAN BOSPOROS:
—BOSPOROS: (1) ii AD *IOSPE* I² 202; Zgusta, *PNS* 546 (I f. Τ. Φλ. Ἀχαιμένης II); (2) *IOSPE* I² 202 (Τ. Φλ. Ἀ.: II s. Ἀχαιμένης I)
—GORGIPPIA: (3) m. ii AD *Eirene* 7 (1968) p. 67, 1 (f. Ἄττας); (4) iii AD *NE* 9 (1971) p. 10 no. 6 B, 7 ([Ἀ]χαιμένης)
—PANTIKAPAION: (5) i AD *CIRB* 331, 4; (6) i/ii AD ib. 622 (f. Μάμιος); (7) 82 AD ib. 76, 16 (*SEG* XVIII 310) (s. Γάϊος); (8) ii AD *CIRB* 709, 6 (or Cimmerian Bosporos Pantikapaion?: f. Καλλιστράτεια); (9) f. ii AD ib. 84, 8; cf. KW pl. 45 no. 648 (s. Ἀγαθοκλῆς)
—THEODOSIA: (10) iii AD *CIRB* 947 A, 1 ([Ἀ]χαιμ[έ]νης: s. Ὀμψάλακος)
SKYTHIA:
—TANAIS: (11) 155 AD ib. 1260, 20 ([Ἀ]χαιμένης: s. Θ—λος); (12) 220 AD ib. 1278, 14 (f. Ξ—) ?= (*13*); (13) c. 225-250 AD ib. 1288, 14 (Ἀχαιμέν[ης]: f. Ξηγόδις) ?= (*12*); (14) 228 AD ib. 1282, 31 (Ἀχαιμένης: f. Μακάριος)

Ἀχαιός
MACEDONIA: (1) c. 320-260 BC *RE* (3); *ILaodLyk* 1, 7, 9, 15, 24 (Tataki, *Macedonians* p. 276 no. 336); cf. Beloch, *GG* IV (2) pp. 204-5 (?s. Σέλευκος I Νικάτωρ, Ἀπάμη (Sogdiane), f. Ἀλέξανδρος, Λαοδίκη, Ἀντιοχίς, ?f. Ἀνδρόμαχος); (2) c. 255-213 BC *RE* (4); Grainger, *SPG* p. 5; cf. Beloch, *GG* IV (2) pp. 205-6 (s. Ἀνδρόμαχος)

Ἀχαξης
CIMMERIAN BOSPOROS:
—PANTIKAPAION: (1) f. v BC *CVA* Oxford 1 p. 39 no. 2 (vase)

Ἀχέλης
THRACE:
—PERINTHOS-HERAKLEIA: (1) ?iv BC *IPerinth* 259, 12 (Ἀχελέω (gen.))

Ἀχελώϊος
THRACE:
—PERINTHOS-HERAKLEIA:
——(Aigikoreis): (1) iii-ii BC ib. 61, 50
——(Boreis): (2) iii-ii BC ib. l. 38 (s. Πυθαγόρης)
—PERINTHOS-HERAKLEIA?: (3) iv BC Hp., *Epid.* iv 6 (Ἀχελώ(ι)ος)

'Αχιλλαῖος
SKYTHIA:
—TYRAS: (1) 181 AD *IOSPE* I² 2, 29 (f. *Διονυσόδωρος*)

'Αχιλλᾶς
MACEDONIA (BOTTIAIA):
—BEROIA: (1) iii AD *IBer* 218 (Tataki 314)
MACEDONIA (MYGDONIA):
—THESSALONIKE?: (2) ii-iii AD *IG* X (2) (1) 822 (I f. *'Αχιλλᾶς* II); (3) ib. (II s. *'Αχιλλᾶς* I, f. *'Αχιλλᾶς* III); (4) ib.; *ZPE* 10 (1973) pp. 71-2 (*Κλ. 'Α.*: III s. *'Αχιλλᾶς* II)
SCYTHIA MINOR:
—ISTROS: (5) 218-225 AD *ISM* I 99, 9; 100, 11 (f. *'Αχιλλεύς*)
—TOMIS: (6) 201 AD ib. II 83 I, 16 (f. *'Αχιλλεύς*); (7) ib. l. 32 (f. (ad.) *Χρυσάων*)
THRACE:
—ODESSOS: (8) i-ii AD *IGB* I² 147 (PM 208) (f. *'Αγαθήνωρ*); (9) 221 AD *IGB* I² 47 bis b, 31 (f. *Αὐρ. Κρατίδημος*)
—PERINTHOS-HERAKLEIA: (10) iii AD *IPerinth* 152 (*M. Αὐρ. ὁ καὶ 'Α.*)

'Αχιλλεύς
CIMMERIAN BOSPOROS:
—PANTIKAPAION: (1) i AD *CIRB* 363; cf. KW pl. 33 no. 460 (s. *Πόθος*); (2) s. i AD *CIRB* 518 (s. *Κούλιος*)
MACEDONIA: (3) 113 BC *PDion* 21, 29, 43 (Tataki, *Macedonians* p. 477 no. 59; La'da E1452) (s. *Πανίσκος*); (4) 111 BC *PDion* 22, 26 (Tataki, *Macedonians* p. 477 no. 60); cf. La'da E1497 (*-ιλεύς*: f. *'Ηρακλείδης*)
—MEGARA: (5) s. iv BC Plu., *Pyrrh.* 2 (or Epiros)
MACEDONIA (BOTTIAIA):
—BEROIA: (6) ii AD *IBer* 222 (Tataki 315) (*'Αχχιλῖ* (dat.)); (7) *IBer* 404, 26 (*GVI* 1594; Tataki 316) (f. *Παρθενόπη*); (8) ii-iii AD *IBer* 290 (Tataki 317); (9) *IBer* 361; (10) iii AD ib. 218 (Tataki 313); (11) a. 212 AD *IBer* 136, 26 (Tataki 70) (*Αἰλ. 'Α.*)
MACEDONIA (MYGDONIA):
—THESSALONIKE: (12) ii AD *IG* X (2) (1) 391 (I f. *Αἰλ. 'Αχιλλεὺς* II *ὁ καὶ Αὐξάνιος*); (13) ib. (*Αἰλ. 'Α. ὁ κὲ Αὐξάνιος*: II s. *Αἰλ. 'Αχιλλεύς* I); (14) ii/iii AD ib. 262, 3 (*Γ. Οὐίβιος Λέπιδος 'Α.*)
SCYTHIA MINOR:
—ISTROS: (15) ii/iii AD *ISM* I 225, 3; (16) 218-225 AD ib. 99, 9; 100, 10 (s. *'Αχιλλᾶς*)
—TOMIS: (17) 201 AD ib. II 83 I, 16 (s. *'Αχιλλᾶς*)
SKYTHIA:
—OLBIA-BORYSTHENES: (18) imp. *IOSPE* I² 265 ([*'Αχι*]*λλεύς*); (19) ii AD *IOlbia* 80, 4 (f. *Ζωΐλος*); (20) *IOSPE* I² 80, 7; 86, 3; 176, 4 (s. *Δημήτριος*); (21) ib. 86, 5 (f. *Παπίας*); (22) ?ii AD ib. 99, 5 (f. *Μᾶρκος*); (23) ii AD ib. 102, 8 (s. *Ποσείδηος*); (24) ib. 105, 8 (s. *Ζῆθος*); (25) ib. 130, 8 (f. *Δημήτριος*); (26) ib. 144, 4 (f. *Φάρναγος*); (27) ib. 206, 5 (s. *Ποσειδώνιος, Κρέουσα*); (28) f. ii AD *Drev. Prichern.* 3 pp. 27-8, 3 (*'Α*[*χιλ*]*λεύς*: s. *Καλανδίων*); (29) ii-iii AD *IOlbia* 102, 4 (s. *Καλλικλῆς*); (30) *IOSPE* I² 137, 8 (s. *Σύντροφος*); (31) ib. 138, 3, 13 (f. *Λεωνίδης*); (32) ib. l. 8 (*Π. Αἰλ. 'Α.*); (33) m. ii AD ib. 105, 5; *VDI* 1953 (4), p. 130, 8 (f. *'Αμώσπαδος*) ?= (*35*); (34) ii/iii AD *IOlbia* 52, 2 (s. *Κάδδινος*)
—OLBIA-BORYSTHENES (NR.): (35) m. ii AD *VDI* 1953 (4), p. 130, 9 (f. *Στράτων*) ?= (*33*)
THRACE:
—KELLAI (NR.): (36) ii-iii AD *IGB* III 1543
—PHILIPPOPOLIS-TRIMONTIUM: (37) c. 303 AD *Anal. Boll.* 31 (1912) p. 192
—SERDICA (TERRIT.): (38) ii-iii AD *AEMÖ* 10 (1886) pp. 238-9 no. 2, 8

'Αχίλλητος
SKYTHIA:
—OLBIA-BORYSTHENES: (1) ii AD *IOSPE* I² 84, 4 (s. *Νικήρατος*)

'Αχίλλιος
MACEDONIA (MYGDONIA):
—THESSALONIKE: (1) v-vi AD Feissel, *RICM* 136 (*SEG* XLVII 980)

'Αχιλλόδωρος
SCYTHIA MINOR:
—ISTROS: (1) i BC-i AD *ISM* I 191 II, 10 (s. *Κλειτοφῶν*)
SKYTHIA:
—OLBIA-BORYSTHENES: (2) s. vi BC Dubois, *IGDOlbia* 23 verso (f. *Πρωταγόρης*); (3) f. iv BC ib. 105 (s. *Τελεσικράτης*)

'Αχολίς
MACEDONIA (MYGDONIA):
—THESSALONIKE?: (1) ii-iii AD *IG* X (2) (1) 722 (*Αἰλ. 'Α.*)

'Αχύριος
MACEDONIA (PAIONIA):
—STOBOI: (1) 281 AD *Sp.* 71 (1931) p. 238 no. 636, 3-4 (*CIJ* I 694) (*Κλ. Τιβ. Πολύχαρμος ὁ καὶ 'Α.*: Jew)

'Αψαχος
SKYTHIA:
—TANAIS: (1) 220-236 AD *CIRB* 1250, 16; 1278, 28; Zgusta, *PNS* 73 ([*'Α*]*ψα*[*χος*]—1278: f. *'Αφθείμακος*)

'Αψιμάχις
MACEDONIA (MYGDONIA):
—THESSALONIKE: (1) m. iii AD *IG* X (2) (1) 207, 3 (*Αὐρ. Στατίλιος Θεόδωρος ὁ καὶ 'Α.*: s. *Αὐρ. 'Ισιδώρα*)

'Αψίνθιος
THRACE:
—APOLLONIA-SOZOPOLIS: (1) v/iv BC *IGB* I² 426 (f. *Θεμισταγόρη*)

B

Βάβας
CIMMERIAN BOSPOROS:
—GORGIPPIA: (1) f. iii BC *CIRB* 1137 A I, 11; Zgusta, *PNS* 597; *Hellenismus* p. 443 no. 5 (name) (f. *'Απελλικῶν*)
THRACE: (2) 550-556 AD *PLRE* III (-); *RE* (2)

Βάβος
SKYTHIA:
—TANAIS: (1) 193 AD *CIRB* 1237, 17; Zgusta, *PNS* 597 ((*Β*)*άβος*: f. *Βόρασπος*); (2) 220 AD *CIRB* 1245, 6 (s. *Βαιόρασπος*)
THRACE:
—BARGALA: (3) ii-iii AD *SEG* XLIV 513 (*Β*[*άβος*]: f. *Δίζης*) ?= (*4*); (4) ib. 514 (f. *Μούκας*) ?= (*3*)

Βαβύλος
MACEDONIA (PAIONIA):
—BYLAZORA: (1) ii-iii AD ib. XVI 402, 1, 3 (f. *Λούκασος, Σεκοῦνδος*); (2) ib. l. 4

Βαβυλών
MACEDONIA (EORDAIA):
—AGIOS CHRISTOPHOROS (MOD.): (1) f. iii AD *EAM* 136

Βάβων
TAURIS:
—CHERSONESOS: (1) c. 300-275 BC *SEG* XLVII 1168, 3; *Hellenismus* p. 443 no. 5a; Zgusta, *PNS* 597 (s. *'Αθάναιος*); (2) iii BC Kats p. 91 no. 31 (amph.) (I f. *Βάβων* II); (3) f. iii BC ib. pp. 102-3 no. 73 (amph.) (f. *Μάρων*); (4) c. 215-200 BC ib. p. 91 no. 31 (amph.) (II s. *Βάβων* I)

Βαγδόσαυος
SKYTHIA:
—TANAIS: (1) 228 AD *CIRB* 1282, 18 (s. *Σιναίωσος*)

Βάγδοχος
SKYTHIA:
—TANAIS: (1) 225 AD ib. 1279, 26 (s. *Σύμφορος*)

Βάγης
CIMMERIAN BOSPOROS:
—GORGIPPIA: (1) m. ii AD *Eirene* 7 (1968) p. 67, 12 (s. *Κοσσοῦς*) ?= (*3*); (2) 173-210 AD *CIRB* 1134 E, 6 (*Βάγη*(*ς*)); (3) ii/iii AD ib. 1179, 40 (f. *Κοσσοῦς, 'Αθηνόδωρος*) ?= (*1*)
—GORGIPPIA?: (4) s. ii AD ib. 1231 A, 12 (f. —*ωρος*)
—HERMONASSA: (5) 123-132 AD ib. 1054, 8; Zgusta, *PNS* 76 (s. *Σωσίπατρος*)
—PANTIKAPAION: (6) f. i AD *CIRB* 364; cf. KW pl. 38 no. 541 (f. *Βάκχιος*)

Βάγιος
CIMMERIAN BOSPOROS:
—GORGIPPIA: (1) ii AD *CIRB* 1140, 21; Zgusta, *PNS* 76; (2) ii/iii AD *CIRB* 1179, 34 (f. *'Αρίστων*)

Βάδαγος
SKYTHIA:
—OLBIA-BORYSTHENES: (1) ii-iii AD *IOSPE* I² 137, 9; Zgusta, *PNS* 77 (s. *'Ιέζδραδος*)

Βαδάκης
CIMMERIAN BOSPOROS:
—PANTIKAPAION: (1) 275-278 AD *CIRB* 36, 26 (*Βαδά*[*κ*]*ης*: s. *Μενέστρατος*)
SKYTHIA:
—OLBIA-BORYSTHENES: (2) ii AD *IOSPE* I² 93, 7; Zgusta, *PNS* 77 (s. *Ραδαμψῶν*)

Βαδᾶς
SKYTHIA:
—OLBIA-BORYSTHENES: (1) ii AD *IOSPE* I² 685, 8 + *VDI* 1975 (1), p. 71; Zgusta, *PNS* 78 (*Βαδᾶτος* (gen.): f. *Εἰρηναῖος*)

Βαδήα
MACEDONIA (BOTTIAIA):
—BEROIA: (1) i AD *IBer* 188; cf. 184 note (name) (*Βαδήα*: d. *'Αφροδίσιος*, ?m. *'Αφροδίσις*)

Βαδίσκος
Scythia Minor:
—kallatis: **(1)** v/iv bc *ISM* iii 254 (vase); cf. *SEG* xxxiv 736

Βαδοῦς
Macedonia (Pelagonia): **(1)** ii-i bc *IG* x (2) (2) 158 (*Βαδοῦνος* (gen.): f. *Λόλα*)

Βάζης
Macedonia (Mygdonia):
—kalindoia: **(1)** a. 98 ad *SEG* xlii 583, 20; cf. *Anthémonte–Kalindoia* 2 p. 230

Βαζοβαλίς
Thrace:
—pautalia:
——Karistoron: **(1)** ii-iii ad *IGB* iv 2173 (*Αἰλ. B.*)

Βαθεις
Thrace:
—odessos: **(1)** ii ad ib. v 5063 (d. *Ἀγαθήνωρ*); **(2)** f. ii ad ib. i² 187 bis (PM 1728); *Dacia* 21 (1977) p. 161 (date) (d. *Νουμήνιος*, m. *Νουμήνιος*)

Βαθυλλίων
Cimmerian Bosporos:
—pantikapaion: **(1)** i ad *CIRB* 341

Βάθυλλος
Cimmerian Bosporos:
—pantikapaion: **(1)** iii bc ib. 22 (s. *Δέρκις*); **(2)** 214 ad ib. 98, 14 (*Βάθυλλ(ος)*: f. *Κάλλιστος*)
Tauris:
—chersonesos: **(3)** s. v bc *SEG* xxvi 805 (ostraka); xlvi 922 note (date) (s. *Νικαγόρας*); **(4)** c. 325-315 bc Kats p. 91 no. 32 (amph.) ?= (*5*); **(5)** c. 320-310 bc Anokhin p. 138 no. 72 (coin); cf. *SEG* xlvi 922 (ident.) ?= (*4*); **(6)** c. 280-270 bc Anokhin p. 140 no. 91 (coin)

Βαιόρασπος
Skythia:
—tanais: **(1)** 220 ad *CIRB* 1245, 6 (f. *Βάβος*) ?= (*Βόρασπος* (*1*))

Βαιορμαῖος
Skythia:
—olbia-borysthenes: **(1)** iii ad *IOlbia* 83, 8 (*IOSPE* i² 97); Zgusta, *PNS* 80 (s. *Παπίας*)

Βαῖος
Cimmerian Bosporos:
—zenonos chersonesos*: **(1)** iii ad *CIRB* 898, 1 (f. *—ακος*)

Βάκις
Cimmerian Bosporos:
—pantikapaion: **(1)** iv bc *IGAIMK* 104 (1935) p. 301 no. 13 (tile) (*Βάκιδ(ος)* (gen.))
Tauris:
—chersonesos: **(2)** f. iii bc *SEG* xl 615 A, 18 (s. *Ῥινίας*)

Βακίων
Cimmerian Bosporos:
—pantikapaion: **(1)** iii-ii bc Audollent, *Defix. Tab.* 92, 2; **(2)** ~ ib. l. 6
Thrace:
—byzantion: **(3)** ii bc *IByz* 287 (Fıratlı–Robert pp. 55-6 no. 35) (s. *Μενίσκος*, *Ἀριστοβούλα*); **(4)** ~ *IByz* 287 (Fıratlı–Robert pp. 55-6 no. 35) (f. *Μενίσκος*); **(5)** ii-i bc *IByz* 90 (Fıratlı–Robert pp. 90-1 no. 118) (f. *Ὀλύμπιχος*)

Βακκης?
Thrace?: **(1)** m. iii bc *SEG* xli 963, 5 (*Βάκκειος* (gen.): f. *Ἀλλούπορις*)

Βάκος
Tauris:
—chersonesos: **(1)** iv bc Solomonik, *NEPKh* 138 (s. *Ζευξίδαμος*)

Βακυλίων
Cimmerian Bosporos:
—hermonassa: **(1)** iii bc *CIRB* 1071 (*Βακυαίων*—*CIRB*, *Βακυ(λ)ίων*—Shkorpil: s. *Μοσχίων*)

Βακχᾶς
Macedonia (Paionia):
—kavadarci (mod.): **(1)** ii ad *Sp.* 71 (1931) p. 74 no. 174, 4 (*Βακχᾶ* (gen.): f. *Τίτος*)

Βακχίδης
Macedonia (Bottiaia):
—beroia: **(1)** 114 bc *IBer* 134, 36 (f. *Κλεῖτος*)

Βάκχιος
Cimmerian Bosporos:
—achilleion: **(1)** i ad *CIRB* 1023 (-χχι-: s. *Ὑγιαίνων*)
—gorgippia: **(2)** f. iii bc ib. 1137 B I, 16 ([*Βάκ*]*χιος*?: s. *Ἀπελλικῶν*); **(3)** ~ ib. 1137 B II, 38 (I f. *Βάκχιος* II); **(4)** ~ ib. l. 38 (II s. *Βάκχιος* I)
—pantikapaion: **(5)** iii bc Chuistova, *AIB* p. 51 n. 7 (weight); **(6)** ii-i bc *CIRB* 272; cf. KW pl. 25 no. 361; **(7)** ?i ad *CIRB* 381 (f. *Γλυκαρίων*); **(8)** i ad ib. 394 (f. *Δῖος*); **(9)** f. i ad ib. 364; cf. KW pl. 38 no. 541 (I s. *Βάγης*, f. *Βάκχιος* II); **(10)** ~ *CIRB* 364; cf. KW pl. 38 no. 541 (II s. *Βάκχιος* I); **(11)** m. i ad *CIRB* 365; cf. KW pl. 52 no. 712 (s. *Πάπας*); **(12)** i/ii ad *CIRB* 79 A, 4 (f. *Κέστιος*); **(13)** ~ ib. 588; cf. KW pl. 51 no. 713 (s. *Βασιλίσκος*); **(14)** ii ad *CIRB* 680, 2 (-χχι-: f. *Μοίριππος*)
Macedonia: **(15)** iii bc *ITrall* 33 B, 25; *BE* 1991, no. 524 (ethn.) (Tataki, *Macedonians* p. 277 no. 3) (s. *Ἄδυμος*); **(16)** ?273 bc *FD* iii (1) 108, 2; cf. *BCH* 68/9 (1944/5) p. 100 no. 10 (Tataki, *Macedonians* p. 277 no. 4) (f. *Ἀμφικτύων*)
Macedonia (Bottiaia):
—beroia: **(17)** 120 bc *IBer* 134, 16 (s. *Ὀ—*)
Macedonia (Chalkidike):
—potidaia-kassandreia: **(18)** iii/ii bc *AA* 1932, p. 155 no. 4 (Tataki, *Macedonians* p. 87 no. 19) (*Βακχ*[*ίας*]?—Tataki: s. *Διονύσιος*)
Macedonia (Mygdonia):
—kalindoia: **(19)** i bc/i ad *SEG* xlii 597; **(20)** 68-98 ad ib. 580, 45 (-χχι-: f. *Μένανδρος*)
—thessalonike: **(21)** i bc/i ad *IG* x (2) (1) 58, 11; *KGAM Thess.* i 111 (date) (*Δοσένιος B.*)
—thessalonike?: **(22)** ii-iii ad *IG* x (2) (1) 261, 14 (*—ανὸς Βάκ*[*χ*]*ιος*)
Macedonia (Sintike):
—herakleia: **(23)** ii ad *IGB* v 5923 (*Τιβ. Κλ. B.*)
Skythia:
—olbia-borysthenes: **(24)** ?ii-i bc Dubois, *IGDOlbia* 110, 2
Tauris:
—chersonesos: **(25)** 174 ad *SEG* xlv 985 A, 32-3; 985 B, 25 (*Οὔλπ. B.*)
Thrace:
—byzantion: **(26)** ii bc *IByz* 104 (Fıratlı–Robert pp. 95-6 no. 135) (s. *Κοννίων*)
—byzantion?: **(27)** imp. Robert, *OMS* 7 p. 652 (f. *Κοάρτα*, *Διογένης*)
—lysimacheia: **(28)** c. 208 bc *FD* iii (4) 135 II, 15 (f. *Σωσίλεως*)
—maroneia: **(29)** iv bc *IGB* i² 104 (f. *Μητροφάνης*)
—perinthos-herakleia: **(30)** iii bc *ITrall* 33 B, 3 (s. *Πολέμων*)
——(Kastaleis): **(31)** iii-ii bc *IPerinth* 61, 57 (*B.*—apogr., *Βάκχις*? (nom.): f. *Πausανίας*)
—traianopolis: **(32)** ii ad *SEG* xxiv 643, 4 (*IThrakAig* E438) (*Βά(κ)χιος*: f. *Διογένεια*)
Thrace?: **(33)** 316-309 bc *IG* ii² 1956, 5 (*FRA* 2504); *Ancient Macedonia* 5 p. 445 with n. 10 (date)

Βακχίς
Macedonia (Bottiaia):
—beroia: **(1)** ii-iii ad *IBer* 219 (Tataki 693) (*Κλ. B.*: m. *Κλ. Τύραννα*)
—pella: **(2)** imp. *IG* ii² 10055 (Tataki, *Macedonians* p. 152 no. 28; *FRA* 5981) (d. *Γλαυκίας*)
Thrace:
—apollonia-sozopolis: **(3)** i-ii ad *IGB* i² 401, 16 (*Βακ(χ)ίς*: d. *Μύρων*)

Βακχις
Thrace:
—nicopolis ad istrum (territ.): **(1)** ii ad ib. v 5244 a, 21 (*Βακχι*[*ς*]: s./d. *Ἡλιόδωρος*)

Βάκχος
Scythia Minor:
—kallatis: **(1)** iii/ii bc *ISM* iii 161 (f. *Σάτυρος*)

Βακχύλος
Macedonia (Bottiaia):
—beroia: **(1)** 239-229 bc *IBer* 45, 29 (Tataki 319)
Macedonia (Derriopos):
—stuberra: **(2)** 74 ad *IG* x (2) (2) 325, 44 (f. *Τιμόθεος*)
Macedonia (Mygdonia):
—thessalonike: **(3)** s. i ad *SEG* xxxviii 702 (*Π. Ἔλβιος B.*: f. *Τρύφαινα*); **(4)** 125 ad *Klio* 65 (1983) p. 163 (s. *Θεοδῆς*)

Βάκχων
Macedonia (Chalkidike):
—olynthos: **(1)** ?355 bc *TAPA* 69 (1938) p. 51 no. 5, 4; Hatzopoulos, *Actes Chalc.* p. 80 (date) (s. *Πόλυς*)

Βάκων
Thrace:
—koila: **(1)** imp. *ISestos* 35 (s. *Πριβᾶτος*)

Βάλαγρος
Macedonia: **(1)** m. iii bc *IG* xi (4) 585, 3 (f. *Θρασέας*) ?= (*Βάλακρος* (*1*))
Macedonia?: **(2)** 296 bc ib. xi (2) 154 A, 41 (Tataki, *Macedonians* p. 277 no. 6); **(3)** ?b. 168 bc *RE* (-); *FGrH* 773 (Tataki, *Macedonians* p. 277 no. 5) ?= (*Βάλακρος* (*12*))

Βαλαίκων
Thrace:
—apollonia-sozopolis: **(1)** v/iv bc *IGB* i² 409 bis (s. *Ἁρμόδιος*)

Βάλακρος
Macedonia: **(1)** ?c. 380-322 bc *RE* (1); Berve 200; *JNG* 14 (1964) pp. 79-82 (coin) (Tataki, *Macedonians* p. 279 nos. 20 and 24) (s. *Νικάνωρ*, f. *Φίλιππος*, ?f. *Νικάνωρ*) ?= (*Βάλαγρος* (*1*)); **(2)** 333-332 bc *RE* (2); Berve 199 (Tataki, *Macedonians* p. 279 no. 15) (s. *Ἀμύντας*); **(3)** ?332 bc Berve 203 (Tataki, *Macedonians* p. 278 no. 14) (Lat. Balacrus); **(4)** 331-329 bc *RE* (3); Berve 202 (Tataki, *Macedonians* p. 278 no. 13) ?= (*5*); **(5)** 327 bc *RE* (4); Berve 201 (Tataki, *Macedonians* p. 278 no. 12) ?= (*4*); **(6)** 257 bc *PLond* 1953, 12, 28 (Tataki, *Macedonians* p. 280 no. 23); cf. La'da E1560 (f. *Νικόμαχος*)
Macedonia (Bottiaia):
—beroia: **(7)** s. iii bc Plb. xxvii 8. 5 (Tataki, *Macedonians* p. 77 no. 20) (f. *Πάνταυχος*); **(8)** 223 bc *IBer* 4, 37 (s. *Λαμέδων*); **(9)** 168 bc Plb. xxix 4. 6 (Tataki 320; Tataki, *Macedonians* p. 77 no. 19) (s. *Πάνταυχος*)
—tyrissa? (asvestari (mod.)): **(10)** f. ii bc *SEG* xlvii 999, 23

MACEDONIA (CHALKIDIKE):
—TORONE?: (11) iv/iii BC *Epigr. Anat.* 21 (1993) p. 15 no. 1 + *BE* 1995, no. 521 (locn.) (*Βάλ[ακρος]*: f. *Στέφανος*)
MACEDONIA?: (12) ?iii-ii BC *IPerg* 201 (Tataki, *Macedonians* p. 279 no. 18) (s. *Μελέαγρος*) ?= (*Βάλαγρος* (*3*)); (13) c. 280 BC D.H. xx 9. 1 (Tataki, *Macedonians* p. 279 no. 19); cf. *Suda* *Π* 3232 (s. *Νίκανδρος*); (14) f. ii BC *SEG* XXV 540 (Tataki, *Macedonians* p. 280 no. 22) (or Athens: I f. *Βάλακρος* II); (15) ~ *SEG* XXV 540 (Tataki, *Macedonians* p. 279 no. 16) (or Athens: II s. *Βάλακρος* I)

Βάλας
MACEDONIA (MYGDONIA):
—THESSALONIKE: (1) ii AD *IG* X (2) (1) 1027 (*Νίκανδρος ὁ καὶ Β.*); (2) ~ ib. 371-2 (*Νέος Νουμίσιος Φῆλιξ ὁ καὶ Β.*: f. *Ἱέραξ*, *Ἑρμῆς*, *Χρήστη*)

Βαλεντῖνος
MACEDONIA (BOTTIAIA):
—BEROIA*: (1) 545 AD *IBer* 438, 1 (-λλε-)
SCYTHIA MINOR:
—ISTROS: (2) ii AD *ISM* I 197 I, 1 (-τεῖ-: s. *Κάστος*)

Βαλερία
MACEDONIA (LYNKESTIS):
—HERAKLEIA?: (1) iii AD *IG* X (2) (2) 138 (d. *Αὐρ. Κλημεντῖνος*, *Αἰλ. Ἀτιλία*)
THRACE:
—MESAMBRIA (TERRIT.): (2) iv AD *IGB* V 5129, 25 (d. *Φλ. Ζῆνις*, *Αὐρ. Μαρτῖνα*)

Βαλεριανός
SCYTHIA MINOR:
—TOMIS: (1) ii-iii AD *ISM* II 26, 3 (s. *Βαλέριος*)
THRACE: (2) 533-559 AD *PLRE* III (1)
—DIONYSOPOLIS: (3) iii AD *IGB* I^2 14 c, 13 (f. *Αὐρ. Βίκτωρ*)

Βαλέριος
MACEDONIA (MYGDONIA):
—THESSALONIKE: (1) iv-vi AD Feissel, *RICM* 290 (Tataki, *Macedonians* p. 190 no. 4)
SCYTHIA MINOR:
—ISTROS: (2) ii AD *ISM* I 197 II, 5 (s. *Ἥλιος*); (3) f. iii AD *Stud. Fischer* p. 32 no. 4, 8 (f. *Μαίωρ*)
—TOMIS: (4) ii-iii AD *ISM* II 26, 3 (f. *Βαλεριανός*); (5) ~ ib. l. 8 (f. *Ποσειδώνις*)
THRACE:
—MARKIANOPOLIS: (6) ii AD *IGB* V 5340, 5 ([*Βα*]*λέριος*?)
—NICOPOLIS AD ISTRUM: (7) ii-iii AD ib. II 662 (f. *Ἡρακλιανός*)

Βαλέρις
SCYTHIA MINOR:
—TOMIS: (1) ii-iii AD *ISM* II 468, 22
THRACE:
—KABYLE*: (2) ii-iii AD *SEG* XLII 648
—PHILIPPOPOLIS-TRIMONTIUM (TERRIT.): (3) ii-iii AD *IGB* III 1434 (s. *Βε—*)

Βάλης
MACEDONIA (MYGDONIA):
—THESSALONIKE: (1) ii-iii AD *IG* X (2) (1) 408 (*Βάλεντι* (dat.): s. *Ἀμία*)
SCYTHIA MINOR:
—KALLATIS: (2) 241-244 AD *ISM* III 74 B, 24
THRACE:
—BOURDAPA: (3) ii-iii AD *IGB* III 1354 (f. *Μουκαπουιους*)
—NICOPOLIS AD ISTRUM: (4) ii-iii AD ib. II 657 (*Βάλη*[*ντ*]*α* (acc.))
—ODESSOS: (5) iii AD ib. I^2 134, 1; (6) 215 AD ib. 47 c, 17 (f. *Αὐρ. Ἰούλιος*); (7) 221 AD ib. 47 bis b, 11 (f. *Αὐρ. Νουμήνιος*); (8) ~ ib. l. 33 (f. *Αὐρ. Βαλέρις*)
—ODESSOS (NR.): (9) ii-iii AD ib. 260

Βαλώδιος
SKYTHIA:
—TANAIS: (1) 209 AD *CIRB* 1276, 6 (-δις: s. *Δ—*) ?= (*2*); (2) 211-226 AD ib. 1279, 7; 1281, 9 (-δις: s. *Δημήτριος*) ?= (*1*); (3) 225 AD ib. 1279, 12 (f. *Ἀθιάγας*)

Βανας
CIMMERIAN BOSPOROS:
—PANTIKAPAION: (1) 275-278 AD ib. 36, 31 (s. *Δημήτριος*)

Βάξαγος
SKYTHIA:
—OLBIA-BORYSTHENES: (1) ii AD *IOSPE* I^2 84, 8; Zgusta, *PNS* 82 (s. *Ἀμωρόμαρος*)

Βαρβάρα
THRACE:
—BEROE-AUGUSTA TRAIANA: (1) c. 320-324 AD *Aral. Boll.* 31 (1912) p. 198; p. 208

Βαρβαριανός
THRACE:
—SOSTRA: (1) iii AD *ILB* 263 (Lat. C. Iulius Barbarianus)

Βαρβαρίων
CIMMERIAN BOSPOROS:
—PANTIKAPAION: (1) 275-278 AD *CIRB* 36, 27 (s. *M..ακ(—)*)
SCYTHIA MINOR:
—ISTROS: (2) 138 AD *ISM* I 193 I, 95 (*Β. Τιτθᾶς*: ?s. *Τιτθᾶς*)

Βάρβαρος
CIMMERIAN BOSPOROS:
—PANTIKAPAION: (1) 275-278 AD *CIRB* 36, 33 (*Βάρβα*[*ρ*]*ος*—Vinogradov: s. *Θεόφιλος*)
MACEDONIA (DERRIOPOS): (2) 95 AD *IG* X (2) (2) 300, 5 (s. *Φίλιππος*)
MACEDONIA (EDONIS):
—AMPHIPOLIS: (3) imp. *SEG* XXIV 602 (f. *Ἑαρίνη*)
MACEDONIA (LYNKESTIS):
—HERAKLEIA: (4) i AD *IG* X (2) (2) 75, 31 (*K. Ἰούλ. Β.*)
MACEDONIA (MYGDONIA):
—THESSALONIKE?: (5) ii/iii AD *AEpThess* p. 35 no. 13, 7 (f. *Ἕσπερος*, *Δείδας*)
MACEDONIA (ODOMANTIKE):
—SIRRHA?: (6) ii-iii AD Dimitsas 826, 4 (*Dodoni* 18 (1989) p. 248 no. 57) (f. *Ἀρτεμιδώρα*)
MACEDONIA (SINTIKE):
—PARTHIKOPOLIS: (7) 230 AD *IGB* V 5902 (*Αὐρ. Β.*)
SCYTHIA MINOR:
—ISTROS: (8) ii AD *ISM* I 211, 5 ([*Β*]*άρβαρος*: s. *Τιμύλος*)
—ULMETUM: (9) iii AD ib. V 81, 6 (Lat. Barbarus: s. Aemilius, *Θεοδότη*)
THRACE:
—PERINTHOS-HERAKLEIA: (10) 196-198 AD *IPerinth* 56, 14 (*Στατίλιος Β.*)
—SERDICA: (11) ii AD *IGB* IV 1923, 13 (*Βάρβα*[*ρος*])

Βαρβατίων
MACEDONIA (MYGDONIA):
—THESSALONIKE: (1) v/vi AD *CIL* III 14203. 39; *PLRE* II (-) (Lat. Ba(r)bation)
SCYTHIA MINOR:
—SALSOVIA: (2) iv AD Popescu, *IGL* 272 e, 3 (Lat. Barbatio)
THRACE: (3) 545-547 AD *PLRE* III (-)

Βάργος
THRACE:
—PAUTALIA:
——(Herakleis): (1) ?ii AD *IGB* IV 2077, 16 (*Βεργος*: f. *Διονύσις*)

Βαρδάνης
CIMMERIAN BOSPOROS:
—PANTIKAPAION: (1) 275-278 AD *CIRB* 36, 35; Zgusta, *PNS* 773a (f. *Ἰώδας*)

Βαρδίας
MACEDONIA (BOTTIAIA):
—BEROIA: (1) i BC-i AD *IBer* 165 (Tataki 322) (s. *Ἡρακλείδης*)
—MIEZA: (2) hell. *AM* 27 (1902) p. 314 no. 28, 12

Βαρδίων
MACEDONIA (MYGDONIA):
—THESSALONIKE*: (1) v-vi AD *IG* X (2) (1) 781 (Feissel, *RICM* 151)

Βαρκέτις
CIMMERIAN BOSPOROS:
—BOSPOROS: (1) ii AD Luc., *Tox.* 50 (d. *Λευκάνωρ*: fict.)

Βαρναβᾶς
THRACE:
—MARONEIA (NR.): (1) iv-vi AD *SEG* XLIX 887 (mosaic)

Βαρναῖος
MACEDONIA (BOTTIAIA):
—BEROIA: (1) ii BC *IBer* 181 (Tataki 323) (f. *Διογένης*)

Βαρσαβᾶς
THRACE: (1) c. 149 BC D.S. xxxii 15. 7 (king)

Βάσα
MACEDONIA (BOTTIAIA):
—EDESSA: (1) v-vi AD *SEG* XXVIII 544 (Feissel, *RICM* 51) (m. *Ἡσύχιος*)
MACEDONIA (CHALKIDIKE):
—POTIDAIA-KASSANDREIA (NR.): (2) imp. Dimitsas 750 (m. *Μάξιμος*)
MACEDONIA (LYNKESTIS):
—SITARIA (MOD.): (3) f. iii AD *EAM* 167 b (*Τερεντιανὴ Β.*)

Βάσης
MACEDONIA (CHALKIDIKE):
—SPARTOLOS?: (1) ?352 BC *SEG* XLVI 804, 7 (*Β*[*ά*]*σης*: f. *Πείσων*)

Βάσθης
SKYTHIA:
—SKYTHAI: (1) ii AD Luc., *Tox.* 43 (fict.)

Βασία
SCYTHIA MINOR:
—KALLATIS (NR.): (1) ii-iii AD *ISM* III 243, 5 (*IGB* I^2 2) (d. *Σαβῖνα*)

Βασιέλας
MACEDONIA (EDONIS):
—PHILIPPOI: (1) i-ii AD Dimitsas 973 (Pilhofer 86) (s. *Βίθυς*, f. *Ποσειδώνιος*)

Βασίλεια
MACEDONIA (EDONIS):
—PHILIPPOI: (1) ii-iii AD *BCH* 59 (1935) p. 156 no. 52 (Pilhofer 266) (-λια: m. *Οὐαρίνιος Καρποφόρος*)
MACEDONIA (MYGDONIA):
—THESSALONIKE: (2) ii-iii AD *IG* X (2) (1) 665, 3 (*SEG* XLIII 460) (-λεα: m. *M. Κάσσιος Εὔπορος*); (3) 156 AD *IG* X (2) (1) 460 (*Ἀκκτία Βασίλῃα*: d. *Ἰουλ. Σεβήρα*)
—THESSALONIKE?: (4) i AD ib. 848 (*GVI* 365) (*Β. Λεώκιν*)

Βασιλείδας
SCYTHIA MINOR:
—KALLATIS: (1) ii/i BC *ISM* III 108 (I f. *Βασιλείδας* II); (2) ~ ib. (II s. *Βασιλείδας* I)

Βασιλείδης
Cimmerian Bosporos:
—Myrmekion: (1) i ad *CIRB* 878 (s. *Αὐλούπορις*)
—Pantikapaion: (2) i bc ib. 284; cf. KW pl. 24 no. 347 (f. *Μοκκοῦς*); (3) f. i ad *CIRB* 366 (s. *Μήνιος*); (4) f. ii ad ib. 81, 6; cf. KW pl. 33 no. 455; (5) ~ *CIRB* 661 (s. *Χόνδεις*, f. *Μακαρία*); (6) ~ ib. 662; cf. KW pl. 35 no. 494 (I f. *Βασιλείδης* II); (7) ~ *CIRB* 662; cf. KW pl. 35 no. 494 (II s. *Βασιλείδης* I); (8) 127 ad *CIRB* 61, 5 (f. *Μαστοῦς*); (9) 227 ad ib. 147, 7 (f. *Καλλιότερος*); (10) iv-v ad *SEG* xlv 1015 f (amph.) (*Βασιλ(είδης)*?) ?= (*19*)
Macedonia (Mygdonia):
—Thessalonike: (11) iv-v ad *AEp* 1900, no. 161 (Lat. Fl. Basilides); (12) 491-518 ad *Mél. Tisserant* 2 pp. 301-2 (*Βασιλίδης*—p. 301)
Skythia:
—Tanais: (13) f. ii ad *CIRB* 1266, 13 (s. *Δορύλαος*); (14) 155 ad ib. 1260, 22 ([*Βα*]*σιλεί-δη*[*ς*]—Tokhtas'ev); (15) c. 200-220 ad ib. 1245, 10; 1246, 9; 1248, 9; 1277, 8 (s. *Θεόνικος*); (16) c. 220-230 ad ib. 1278, 11; 1286, 11 (f. *Ἡρόξενος*)
—Tanais*: (17) ii-iii ad *NE* 12 (1978) p. 48 (amph.) (*Βασιλί(δης)*?)
Tauris:
—Chersonesos: (18) ii ad Solomonik, *NEPKh* 126 (s. *Καλοῦς*)
—Chersonesos (territ.): (19) m. iv ad *VDI* 1998 (1), p. 212 (amph.) (*Βασιλ(είδης)*?) ?= (*10*)
Thrace:
—Maroneia: (20) ii bc *IThrakAig* E364 ([*Β*]*ασιλίδης*)

Βασιλειδιανός
Tauris:
—Chersonesos: (1) 185 ad *IOSPE* I^2 404, 50; *SEG* xlvi 931, 2? (*Μ. Αὐρ. Βασιλειδιανὸς Ἀλέξανδρος*)

Βασίλειος
Macedonia (Edonis):
—Philippoi (territ.): (1) f. vi ad Pikoulas, *Chora* pp. 129-30 no. 29 (Pilhofer 630) (-λι-)
Macedonia (Lynkestis):
—Herakleia: (2) v-vi ad *IG* x (2) (2) 151 (-λησς)
Macedonia (Paionia):
—Stoboi*: (3) v-vi ad Unp. (Stobi excav.) inv. I-88-2 (-λιος)
Thrace:
—Ainos: (4) v ad *SEG* xxxvi 662 (-σείλεος)
—Plotinopolis: (5) imp. *Thrakika* 2 (1929) p. 89 (*IThrakAig* E468)

Βασιλεύς
Scythia Minor:
—Istros: (1) iii ad *ISM* i 181, 7 (*Αὐρ. Β.*: s. *Ἀπολλωνίδης*)
—Tomis: (2) iii ad ib. ii 22, 4 (*Αὐρ. Β.*)
Skythia:
—Olbia-Borysthenes: (3) ii ad *IOSPE* I^2 89, 9 (*Ἀριστόνικος ὁ καὶ Β.* (n. pr.?): s. *Διονύσιος*); (4) f. iii ad ib. 185, 3 ([*Α*]*ὐρ. Β.*: s. *Καλλισθένης*)
Thrace:
—Novae: (5) ii/iii ad *IGB* v 5262, 3 (biling.) (*SEG* xlvii 1153) (s. *Κυζίκιος*)
—Odessos: (6) 215 ad *IGB* I^2 47 c, 21 (*Αὐρ. Β.*: s. *Μένανδρος*)

Βασίλη
Cimmerian Bosporos:
—Pantikapaion: (1) imp. *CIRB* 749; (2) i ad ib. 375; cf. KW pl. 26 no. 374 (*Βασιλι*[..]*ινα*—Newton, *Βασίλειν*—KW, *Βασιλι*[*κ*]*ή*?: m. *Γάϊος*); (3) ~ *CIRB* 413; cf. KW pl. 48 no. 665 (?m. *Ἔρως*); (4) ii ad *CIRB* 751
—Pantikapaion (nr.): (5) i-ii ad ib. 962
—Zenonos Chersonesos*: (6) f. i ad ib. 899 (d. *Ἡρακλείδης*, *Γάστιον*)

Βασιλιανός
Skythia:
—Olbia-Borysthenes: (1) ii bc *SEG* xxx 958 (vase) (*Βασιλι(α)νός*—ed., *Βασιλί(δ)ης*?)
Thrace:
—Nicopolis ad Istrum: (2) iv ad *IGB* ii 656, 6; cf. v 5212 (*Βασιλια*[*ν*]*ὸς Μακεδόνιος*)
—Spinopara: (3) ii ad ib. iv 2192, 8

Βασιλική
Macedonia (Bottiaia):
—Beroia*: (1) iii ad *SEG* l 579
Scythia Minor:
—Kallatis: (2) iii ad *ISM* iii 187, 9
Tauris:
—Chersonesos: (3) iii ad *VDI* 1938 (3), p. 80 no. 10. I (d. *Ἰουλιανός*)

Βασιλικός
Scythia Minor:
—Tomis: (1) 201 ad *ISM* ii 83 II, 19 (*Β.*—apogr., *Βασιλίσκος*—*ISM*: s. *Ἀλέξανδρος*)

Βασίλιν
Cimmerian Bosporos:
—Hermonassa: (1) imp. *CIRB* 1092

Βασιλίνη
Cimmerian Bosporos:
—Pantikapaion: (1) i ad ib. 367

Βασιλιόδωρος
Macedonia (Mygdonia):
—Thessalonike?: (1) ii-iii ad *IG* x (2) (1) 897; cf. *Tyche* 10 (1995) pl. 13 (*Αἴλ. Β.*)

Βασιλίσκος
Cimmerian Bosporos:
—Pantikapaion: (1) i ad *CIRB* 418 (f. *Ἡλίς*); (2) ~ ib. 489; cf. KW pl. 46 no. 652 (s. *Χρῆστος*); (3) i/ii ad *CIRB* 588; cf. KW pl. 51 no. 713 (f. *Βάκχιος*); (4) ii ad *CIRB* 694 (f. *Πάσων*); (5) 275-278 ad ib. 36, 54 (*Βασιλίσκ(ος)*: s. *Φίλιππος*)
—Phanagoreia: (6) i ad ib. 987, 3

Βασίλισσα
Macedonia (Bottiaia):
—Edessa (nr.): (1) v-vi ad *Makedonika* 15 (1975) p. 206
Scythia Minor:
—Troesmis: (2) f. ii ad *ISM* v 184, 7 (Lat. Marcia Basilissa); (3) 165-170 ad ib. 160, 13 (*Eastern cults* p. 78 no. 13) (Lat. Marcia Basiliss(a))
Thrace:
—Byzantion: (4) 294 ad *Cod. Just.* iv 29.14; cf. *Klio* 58 (1976) p. 79 (Lat. Basilissa)
—Philippopolis-Trimontium: (5) 293 ad *Cod. Just.* v 12. 14; cf. *Klio* 58 (1976) p. 80 (Lat. Basilissa)

Βασίλος
Thrace:
—Byzantion: (1) ii/i bc *IByz* 233 (*Ἀ. Ἀττυληνὸς Β.*)

Βασκίλας
Macedonia (Edonis):
—Philippoi: (1) i-ii ad *BCH* 47 (1923) p. 86 no. 4 (Pilhofer 87) (Lat. Manli Ba[sci]la? (gen.))
—Philippoi (territ.): (2) ?ii ad *BCH* 24 (1900) p. 307 (Pilhofer 517) (Lat. Bascila? (gen.), Rascila—ed.: f. *Βίθυς*); (3) ~ *BCH* 47 (1923) pp. 64-5 no. 24, 7 (Pilhofer 519) (Lat. Bascilas: s. *Βίθυς*)

Βάσσα
Macedonia (Chalkidike):
—Potidaia-Kassandreia (nr.): (1) ?iii ad *SEG* xlv 774 (*Βάσσῃ* (dat.), *Βάσσης* (nom.)—*SEG* index per err.: d. *Δομέτιος*, *Κοσμία*)
Thrace:
—Beroe-Augusta Traiana: (2) c. 320-324 ad *Anal. Boll.* 31 (1912) p. 198; p. 208
—Odessos: (3) v ad Beševliev 113, 5

Βάσσαρος
Cimmerian Bosporos:
—Pantikapaion: (1) iii-iv ad *CIRB* 737 (f. *Κάρπος*)

Βασσιανός
Macedonia (Eordaia):
—Krannestai: (1) ii-iii ad *IG* x (2) (2) 36, 4 (*Βασσια*[*νός*]: s. *Νίκανδρος*, *Ἰουλία*)
Macedonia (Sintike):
—Parthikopolis: (2) 121 ad *IGB* iv 2270, 10 (*Ἐρέννιος Β.*: s. *Μ. Ἐρέννιος Παυλῖνος*)
Scythia Minor:
—Tomis: (3) iii-iv ad *ISM* ii 384, 14 (Barnea 1; Popescu, *IGL* 18); cf. *SEG* xlviii 980 (f. *Λιλλᾶς*)
Skythia:
—Tyras: (4) 181 ad *IOSPE* I^2 2, 27 (f. —*ιος*)
Tauris:
—Chersonesos: (5) ii ad Solomonik, *NEPKh* 183 (s. *Ἀθήναιος*)
Thrace:
—Serdica: (6) ii-iii ad *IGB* iv 1922, 5

Βάσσιλα
Macedonia (Bottiaia):
—Beroia?: (1) ii ad *IBer* 396, 1 (Tataki 324)

Βάσσος
Macedonia (Bottiaia):
—Beroia: (1) ii/iii ad *IBer* 27 B, 3 (slave?)
Macedonia (Edonis):
—Philippoi (nr.): (2) ii-iii ad Dimitsas 1087 (fals.?) (Pilhofer 668)
Macedonia (Elimeia)*: (3) ii-iii ad *EAM* 20, 3 (freed.)
Macedonia (Mygdonia):
—Thessalonike: (4) ii-iii ad *IG* x (2) (1) 665, 7 (*SEG* xliii 460); (5) 206 ad *IG* x (2) (1) 236, 8 ([*Β*]*άσσος*)
—Thessalonike?: (6) i ad ib. 681 (I ?f. —*ος Βάσσος* II); (7) i-ii ad ib. 825; (8) i-iii ad ib. 977
Macedonia (Pelagonia):
—Dostoneis: (9) ii ad ib. x (2) (2) 199 (f. *Δημάρχη*); (10) ~ ib. (s. *Δημάρχη*)
Scythia Minor:
—Istros: (11) ii ad *ISM* i 212, 24 (s. *Νίννος*)
—Tomis: (12) ii ad ib. ii 77, 6 (s. *Μενεκράτης*); (13) vi ad Barnea 27 (Popescu, *IGL* 9) (*Βάσος*)
Skythia:
—Tanais: (14) 220 ad *CIRB* 1278, 15 (s. *Β*—)
Tauris:
—Chersonesos: (15) iii ad *VDI* 1938 (3), p. 77 no. 8 (s. *Πατερίων*)
Thrace: (16) ii-iii ad *IGB* iii 1170; (17) iii ad Beševliev, *EP* 24
—Byzantion: (18) i bc *IByz* 137 (Fıratlı-Robert p. 100 no. 149) (*Δ*—*ος ὁ καὶ Β.*)
—Glava Panega (mod.): (19) ii-iii ad *IGB* ii 566 (I f. *Οὔλπιος Βάσσος* II)
—Hadrianopolis: (20) ?iii ad *Edirne Müzesi Rehberi* p. 26 (Unp. (Sayar)) (s. *Θεόδουλος*); (21) ?iv ad Taşlıklıoğlu 2 p. 34 no. 3 (*AD* 49-50 (1994-5) Mel. p. 280 no. 111); cf. *SEG* xxxiv 696 (*Βαεσου* (gen.)—lap., *Βά(σ)σου*—*SEG*, *Ῥαεγου*—*AD*)
—Kellai: (22) 241-244 ad *IGB* iii 1517, 48 (f. *Αὐρ. Εὐτύχης*)
—Pautalia (territ.): (23) ii-iii ad ib. v 5836
—Perinthos-Herakleia: (24) c. 100-115 ad *SEG* xxvi 1288, 12 (s. *Ἀπολλόδωρος*)

—PHILIPPOPOLIS-TRIMONTIUM: **(25)** ii-iii AD *IGB* III 956 (f. *Βένδιος*)
—PHILIPPOPOLIS-TRIMONTIUM (TERRIT.): **(26)** iii AD ib. 1318 (f. *Αὐρ. Ῥοιμητάλκης, Αὐρ. Σκαυριανός, Αὐρ. Δημήτρις*)
—SERDICA: **(27)** m. ii AD ib. IV 1953, 2 (s. *Μοκα—*); **(28)** iii AD ib. 1934, 7 (I f. *Βάσσος* II); **(29)** ~ ib. l. 7 (II s. *Βάσσος* I, f. *Αὐρ. Τάρσας*)
—TODORIČENE (MOD.): **(30)** ii-iii AD ib. II 590 (f. *Φλάβις*)
—TYRODIZA-TIRISTASIS: **(31)** imp. Dumont–Homolle 89d (f. *Βρουτία*)

Βασσοῦς
THRACE:
—ODESSOS: **(1)** i BC-i AD *IGB* I² 51 c, 9 (s. *Ἐπαμείνων*); **(2)** ii AD ib. 133 (s. *Σκάβης*)

Βαστάκας
CIMMERIAN BOSPOROS:
—PANTIKAPAION: **(1)** iv BC *CIRB* 171; Zgusta, *PNS* 83 (s. *Σμόρδος*); **(2)** ii AD *CIRB* 753 (*Β[ασ]τάκου* (gen.): f. *Δημόστρατος*)
SKYTHIA:
—TANAIS: **(3)** ii AD ib. 1262, 11 (*Βαστάκου* (gen.): f. *Μακάριος*)

Βαστακίλας
THRACE: **(1)** 267 BC *SEG* XXVII 1114, 12b (La'da E719) (s. *Ἀμάδοκος*); **(2)** 172-169 BC *OGIS* 734, 3 (Velkov 39); cf. La'da E770 (f. *Λυσίμαχος*); **(3)** ~ *OGIS* 734, 4 (Velkov 40) (s. *Λυσίμαχος*)
—NICOPOLIS AD NESTUM (TERRIT.): **(4)** ii AD *IGB* IV 2350 (-*κεί*-: f. *Μεστίκενθος*)
THRACE?: **(5)** 282 BC *PP* 2196 Add. (s. *Σωσίπατρος*); **(6)** ii-i BC *BGU* 1223, 2

Βαστακίλης
THRACE:
—APOLLONIA-SOZOPOLIS: **(1)** iv BC *IGB* I² 440 (*Βασστακίλεω* (gen.): f. *Διοσκορίδη*)

Βασταρεύς
MACEDONIA (PAIONIA):
—DEMIR KAPIJA (MOD.): **(1)** hell. *SEG* XLV 807 D (sherd) (*Βασταρεύς*: s. *Πάτραος*)
—LAIAIOI: **(2)** m. v BC *AMNG* III (2) p. 147 no. 16 (coin) (*Βαστάρεος* (gen.))

Βάστας
CIMMERIAN BOSPOROS:
—PANTIKAPAION: **(1)** m. i AD *CIRB* 437; cf. KW pl. 17 no. 249

Βαστεκίλας
MACEDONIA (ODOMANTIKE):
—GAZOROS (TERRIT.): **(1)** ii AD *SEG* L 568 (s. *Κρούσπις*)

Βαστία
MACEDONIA (EDONIS):
—PHILIPPOI: **(1)** ?ii AD *FGrH* 257 F 37. 47 (Tataki, *Macedonians* p. 164 no. 10) (s. *Ἀστικόσης*)

Βαστικίλας
MACEDONIA (MYGDONIA):
—LETE: **(1)** ii AD *Makedonika* 2 (1951) p. 619 no. 42 *θ*, 16 (-*κεί*-: f. *Ζιπᾶς*)
MACEDONIA (ODOMANTIKE):
—GAZOROS: **(2)** 215 or 174 BC *SEG* XXX 1892, 26 (Hatzopoulos, *MI* 2 pp. 57-8 no. 39) (f. *Κοζισίοτος*)
MACEDONIA?: **(3)** f. i BC *Xenia antiqua* 10 (2001) p. 19 nos. A-B (or Thrace: -*κεί*-: f. *Ἀνδρόνικος, Ἀλλούπορις, Μήτοκος*)

Βαστοκίλας
THRACE:
—BAZOPARA: **(1)** 202 AD *IGB* III 1690 c, 42 (and Thrace Pizos: -*στοκεί*-: s. *Βίθυς*)
—PHILIPPOPOLIS-TRIMONTIUM (TERRIT.): **(2)** ii-iii AD ib. 1488 (or Thrace Diokletianopolis: -*στοκεί*-)

Βάστος
MACEDONIA (BISALTIA):
—EUPORIA: **(1)** s. i AD *IBer* 121, 7; 299, 1 (Tataki, *Macedonians* p. 107 no. 4) (s. *Ἀπολλόδωρος*)
MACEDONIA (BOTTIAIA):
—BEROIA: **(2)** 181 AD *IBer* 49, 1, 11-13 (Tataki 326) (f. *Ἀριάγνη, Ἡρακλείδης, Σύρος*)
MACEDONIA (MYGDONIA):
—KALINDOIA: **(3)** 68-98 AD *SEG* XLII 580, 38 (f. *Πολεμοκράτης*); **(4)** ~ ib. l. 64 (f. *Σύρος*); **(5)** a. 98 AD ib. 582, 48 (I f. *Βάστος* II); **(6)** ~ ib. l. 48 (II s. *Βάστος* I)
THRACE?: **(7)** f. i BC Lucas Pythion 4 B, 6 (slave/freed.)

Βάσυλλος
SCYTHIA MINOR:
—ISTROS: **(1)** 138 AD *ISM* I 193 II, 57; cf. *Ling. Balk.* 27 (1984) p. 87 (*Βά(θ)υλλος*?: s. *Φίλιππος*)

Βάταγος
SKYTHIA:
—OLBIA-BORYSTHENES: **(1)** i/ii AD *IOlbia* 90, 9 (s. *Ἄδωλος*)

Βατάκης
CIMMERIAN BOSPOROS:
—PANTIKAPAION: **(1)** ii AD *CIRB* 750 (s. *Μάης*)

Βάτακος
SKYTHIA:
—OLBIA-BORYSTHENES: **(1)** iii BC *IOSPE* I² 201 I, 44; cf. Vinogradov, *Pont. Stud.* p. 159 no. 15 (name) (s. *Τιμόθεος*)
THRACE:
—APOLLONIA-SOZOPOLIS: **(2)** v/iv BC Mushmov 3141 (coin) (*Βάτακ[ος]*?)
—BYZANTION: **(3)** s. ii BC *BMI* 1154a B, 31; *BE* 1972, no. 37 (date) (*[Β]άτακος*: s. *Ἀπολλᾶς*)

Βατακῶν
TAURIS:
—KALOS LIMEN (NR.): **(1)** iv/iii BC *Hellenismus* p. 444 no. 7 (vase) (*Βατακῶντος* (gen.))

Βατᾶς
TAURIS:
—CHERSONESOS: **(1)** iii BC Solomonik, *GAKh* 442 (vase); *Hellenismus* p. 445 no. 7a (*Βατα* (gen.?)—ed., *Βατα(—)*?)
THRACE:
—PERINTHOS-HERAKLEIA:
——(Geleuntes): **(2)** iii-ii BC *IPerinth* 61, 31 (*Βατᾶδος* (gen.): f. *Θεόδοτος*)

Βατίκων
SKYTHIA:
—OLBIA-BORYSTHENES: **(1)** s. iv BC *SEG* L 702 II, 1, 6

Βάτος
SKYTHIA:
—OLBIA-BORYSTHENES: **(1)** f. ii AD *IOSPE* I² 85, 9 (f. —ος)

Βατουδεις
THRACE:
—MARKIANOPOLIS (TERRIT.): **(1)** iii-iv AD *IGB* V 5328, 2 (*CCET* II (1) 365) (s. *Δάζις*)

Βάττας
CIMMERIAN BOSPOROS:
—GORGIPPIA: **(1)** f. iii BC *CIRB* 1137 B II, 16 (*[Β]άττα* (gen.): f. *Μένιππος*)
—PANTIKAPAION: **(2)** iv BC ib. 172; *Hellenismus* p. 445 no. 7b (name) (s. *Ποσειδεώνιος*)
TAURIS:
—CHERSONESOS: **(3)** f. iii BC *CIRB* 243; cf. KW pl. 4 no. 84 (s. *Πολύδοξος*)

Βαττίων
SKYTHIA:
—OLBIA-BORYSTHENES: **(1)** f. iv BC *IOlbia* 97

Βάτων
CIMMERIAN BOSPOROS:
—HERMONASSA: **(1)** iv BC *CIRB* 1056 I, 3 (f. —ος)
MACEDONIA (EDONIS):
—AMPHIPOLIS: **(2)** s. iv BC *AD* 24 (1969) Chron. p. 355 no. 6 (f. *Νικησώ*)
MACEDONIA (MYGDONIA):
—KALINDOIA: **(3)** a. 98 AD *SEG* XLII 582, 16 (f. *Πατουμάσης*)
SKYTHIA:
—OLBIA-BORYSTHENES*: **(4)** v-iv BC ib. XXX 920 (vase) (*Βάτω[ν]*, *Βάτο[ς]*?)

Βαῦδος
THRACE:
—PERINTHOS-HERAKLEIA*: **(1)** c. 320-324 AD *Anal. Boll.* 31 (1912) pp. 194 ff.

Βέβαιος
MACEDONIA:
—KELLION: **(1)** imp. *Athena* 25 (1913) p. 410 no. 54 (*SEG* XLIX 772); Kanatsoulis 491 (*Φ(λ). Εὔπορος Β.*: sculptor)

Βέβιος
THRACE:
—MARONEIA (TERRIT.): **(1)** iii AD Bakalakis, *Oinos Ismarikos* p. 555 (*IThrakAig* E379) (*Ἀλέξανδρος ὁ καὶ Β.*: s. *Ταρούλας*)

Βειβους
THRACE:
—KELLAI*: **(1)** iii AD *IGB* III 1516 b, 25 (s. *Βιάρτας, Δαρουβυρ—*)

Βεισούλας
THRACE:
—ABDERA: **(1)** i BC-i AD *SEG* XLVII 1032 (*IThrakAig* E64) (s. *Ἀρτεμίδωρος*)

Βεισταβάκης
THRACE:
—TYRODIZA-TIRISTASIS?: **(1)** ii-i BC *Stephanos nomismatikos* p. 586; cf. *RA* 1878, p. 293; Firatlı–Robert p. 145 (f. *Σάλμος, Γέτας*)

Βειτύριγος
THRACE:
—ODESSOS (NR.): **(1)** ii AD *IGB* I² 271 (PM 1730); *Dacia* 21 (1977) p. 161 (date) (f. *Ἡράκων*)

Βελισάριος
MACEDONIA (BOTTIAIA):
—BEROIA: **(1)** vi AD *IBer* 452 (Feissel, *RICM* 75; *PLRE* III (2)) (Lat. Belesario (gen.))

Βελίττας
SKYTHIA:
—SKYTHAI: **(1)** ii AD Luc., *Tox.* 43 (fict.)

Βελλικός
SKYTHIA:
—TANAIS: **(1)** 225 AD *CIRB* 1280, 16 (s. *Ζωρθίνης*)

Βενδιδώρα
THRACE: **(1)** hell.? *CIA* III (2) 3619 (fals.?); cf. *Mus. Helv.* 1993, pp. 51-2
—LYSIMACHEIA: **(2)** iii BC *IG* II² 9223 (*FRA* 3388) (d. *Βηρισάδης*)

Βενδίδωρος
THRACE:
—BYZANTION?: **(1)** hell. *ISamothrace* 27, 5; cf. Robert, *OMS* 6 pp. 603-5 (*[Βε]νδίδωρος*)

Βενδιζητα
THRACE:
—BOURDAPA: **(1)** ii-iii AD *IGB* III 1344; cf. V 5501 (*Βενδι(ς) Ζητα*?—Dobruski)

Βενδικός
THRACE:
—MARKIANOPOLIS (TERRIT.): **(1)** f. iii AD ib. II 861 (PM 1295; *CCET* II (1) 275) (f. *Βίοδης Ἀντώνις*)

Βενδῖνα
THRACE:
—BRESTE (MOD.): **(1)** ?iii AD *ILB* 176; *Onomastique latine* p. 348 (name) (Lat. Bendina: d. *Βιθύας*, m. *Ταρσάνιος*)

Βένδιον
THRACE:
—MARONEIA (TERRIT.): **(1)** iii AD Bakalakis, *Oinos Ismarikos* p. 555 (*IThrakAig* E379) (d. *Ῥοῦφος*)

Βένδιος
THRACE:
—PHILIPPOPOLIS-TRIMONTIUM: **(1)** ii-iii AD *IGB* III 956 (s. *Βάσσος*)

Βενδίς
MACEDONIA (EDONIS):
—PHILIPPOI: **(1)** imp. *BCH* 61 (1937) p. 416 no. 10 (Pilhofer 134) (Lat. Be[n]dis: m. *Μουκιανός*); **(2)** ~ Collart, *Philippes* p. 442 n. 1 (Lat. – qua et Bendis: d. Valeria)
—PHILIPPOI (TERRIT.): **(3)** ?ii AD *BIAB* 16 (1950) pp. 14-15 no. 11, 6 (Pilhofer 649) (Lat. Bendi (dat.): d. *Παίβης*); **(4)** ~ Pikoulas, *Chora* p. 115-16 no. 4, 3 (Pilhofer 638) (Lat. Bendis: d. Sauciles, ?d. Prima, m. *Ζιπύρων*)
THRACE:
—ASOMATOI (MOD.): **(5)** ?iii AD *SEG* XVI 414 + *Epigraphica* 37 (1975) p. 33 (*IThrakAig* E386) (d. *Βίζος*)
—BOURDAPA: **(6)** ii-iii AD *IGB* III 1347; cf. V 5502 (*Ὀεν*-: d. *Δρωδήγης*)
—HADRIANOPOLIS (TERRIT.): **(7)** ii AD ib. III 1801 (*Φλ. Β.*); **(8)** ii-iii AD ib. 1828 ([*Βε*]*νδίς*: d. *Ἀπολλόδωρος*, m. *Ἀπολλόδωρος*)
—MARONEIA: **(9)** ii-i BC *SEG* XLIV 601 + *IThrakAig* E268 (*Β̣ενδ*[*ίς*]: d. *Μητροφάνης*); **(10)** ii AD Masson, *OGS* p. 608 (*IThrakAig* E279) (d. *Διουκίλας*)

Βενδιφάνης
THRACE:
—AINOS: **(1)** iii/ii BC *AD* 26 (1971) Chron. p. 260 with pl. 231 γ (f. *Διοσκουρίδης*)

Βενενᾶτος
MACEDONIA (LYNKESTIS):
—HERAKLEIA*: **(1)** v-vi AD *IG* X (2) (2) 152 (*Β*[*ε*]*νενᾶτος*)

Βενέρης
SCYTHIA MINOR:
—TOMIS: **(1)** ?v AD Barnea 33 (Popescu, *IGL* 35)

Βενερία
MACEDONIA (BOTTIAIA):
—EDESSA: **(1)** iii AD *BSA* 58 (1963) p. 23 no. 4 (Tataki, *Edessa* 43) (*Αὐρ. Β.*: m. *Οὐαλέριος*)
MACEDONIA (PELAGONIA):
— (NR.)?: **(2)** iii AD *IG* X (2) (2) 190

Βενζείς
CIMMERIAN BOSPOROS:
—PANTIKAPAION: **(1)** i-ii AD *CIRB* 663; cf. KW pl. 13 no. 183 (d. *Μοκάπορις*)

Βένζης
MACEDONIA (MYGDONIA):
—KALINDOIA: **(1)** 68-98 AD *SEG* XLII 580, 78; cf. *Anthémonte–Kalindoia* 2 p. 233 (name) (s. *Διοσκουρίδης*)

Βενιαμῆς
MACEDONIA (MYGDONIA):
—THESSALONIKE: **(1)** iv-vi AD Feissel, *RICM* 293 (*Β. ὁ καὶ Δομέτιος*: Jew)

Βενῖλος
THRACE: **(1)** 550-551 AD *PLRE* III (-)

Βενοῦστα
MACEDONIA (BOTTIAIA):
—BEROIA: **(1)** ii-iii AD *IBer* 235 (-*σστα*)

Βέρβος
MACEDONIA (EDONIS):
—IOLLITAI: **(1)** ii-iii AD *BCH* 24 (1900) p. 317, 2 (Pilhofer 417) (f. *Βίθυς*)

Βεργαῖος
MACEDONIA (ODOMANTIKE)?: **(1)** c. 375-350 BC Peter, *MTD* pp. 104-6 (coin); *BCH* 126 (2002) pp. 210-29 (n. pr.?: king?)

Βερενίκα
MACEDONIA (MYGDONIA):
—LETE: **(1)** c. 325-300 BC *SEG* XLIV 535; *KGAM Thess.* I 30 (date)

Βερενίκη
CIMMERIAN BOSPOROS:
—PANTIKAPAION: **(1)** i AD *CIRB* 368; cf. KW pl. 22 no. 313 (*Βε*[*ρ*]*ενί*[*κ*]*η*); **(2)** ~ *CIRB* 369 (-*ρνί*-: d. *Λύσανδρος*); **(3)** ii AD ib. 707 (*Βερνεί*-: m. *Στρατονίκη*)
MACEDONIA: **(4)** c. 340-278 BC *RE* (9); Berve 211 (*PP* 14497); cf. Beloch, *GG* III (2) pp. 180-1 (d. *Μάγας*, *Ἀντιγόνη*, m. *Μάγας*, *Ἀντιγόνη*, *Πτολεμαῖος* II *Φιλάδελφος*, *Ἀρσινόη*, *Φιλωτέρα*, ?m. *Θεοξένα*); **(5)** c. 275-246 BC *RE* (10) (*PP* 14498); cf. Grainger, *SPG* p. 39 (d. *Πτολεμαῖος* II *Φιλάδελφος*, *Ἀρσινόη*); **(6)** c. 273-220 BC *RE* (11) (*PP* 14499); *IG* IX (1)² (1) 56 c; cf. *LGPN* I s.v. (3) (I d. *Μάγας*, *Ἀπάμη*, m. *Πτολεμαῖος* IV *Φιλοπάτωρ*, *Ἀλέξανδρος*, *Μάγας*, *Ἀρσινόη*, *Βερενίκη* II: queen); **(7)** ?239-238 BC *RE* (12) (*PP* 14500); *IG* IX (1)² (1) 56 e; cf. *ZPE* 138 (2002) p. 145 (II d. *Πτολεμαῖος* III *Εὐεργέτης*, *Βερενίκη* I); **(8)** 193 BC Robert, *Hell.* 7 pp. 9-10, 4, 30 (Tataki, *Macedonians* p. 281 no. 30) (and Lycia Telmessos: d. *Πτολεμαῖος*); **(9)** c. 120-80 BC *RE* (13) + s.v. Kleopatra (21) (*PP* 14522) (*Κλεοπάτρα Β.*: d. *Πτολεμαῖος* IX *Λάθυρος*, ?d. *Κλεοπάτρα*); **(10)** c. 80-55 BC *RE* (14) (*PP* 14502) (d. *Πτολεμαῖος* XII *Αὐλητής*, *Κλεοπάτρα* V *Τρύφαινα*: queen); **(11)** 63 BC *POxy* 1644, 6 (Tataki, *Macedonians* p. 478 no. 61); cf. La'da E1543 (d. *Διονύσιος*, *Ἀρσινόη*, m. *Μοσχίων*)
MACEDONIA (MYGDONIA):
—THESSALONIKE*: **(12)** m. i BC *IG* X (2) (1) 378; *KGAM Thess.* I 65 (date) (Lat. Attia Berenice: freed.)
MACEDONIA (PIERIA):
—DION: **(13)** iv-iii BC *SEG* XLVIII 787 (d. *Κόρραγος*)
THRACE:
—BYZANTION: **(14)** 369 AD *Chron. Pasch.* P302a
—MARONEIA: **(15)** ii BC *IThrakAig* E242 A (d. *Ἡρακλείδης*)
—SEUTHOPOLIS*: **(16)** c. 300-280 BC *SEG* XLII 661, 2, 7, 17, 36; cf. XLVI 877 (m. *Ἐβρύζελμις*, *Τήρης*, *Σάτοκος*, *Σαδάλας*: queen?)

Βερεννώ
MACEDONIA (BOTTIAIA):
—AIGAI: **(1)** m. iv BC ib. XXXV 775 (d. *Φίλιστος*)

Βέρνας
MACEDONIA (EDONIS):
—PHILIPPOI: **(1)** ii-iii AD *Philippes* I p. 51 no. 20 (*AD* 22 (1967) Chron. p. 422; Pilhofer 167) (sculptor?)

Βερνίκα
MACEDONIA (BOTTIAIA):
—AIGAI: **(1)** iv/iii BC *SEG* XXXV 798 (?d. *Στρωφακίδης*)

Βερόη
MACEDONIA (MYGDONIA):
—THESSALONIKE?: **(1)** v-vi AD Feissel, *RICM* 165 (*SEG* XLVII 1008) (m. *Δημήτριος*)

Βερονίκη
MACEDONIA (BOTTIAIA):
—BEROIA: **(1)** iii AD *IBer* 356 (Tataki 327)
MACEDONIA (MYGDONIA):
—THESSALONIKE: **(2)** ii AD *IG* X (2) (1) 424 (*Ἐρεννία Β.*)
THRACE:
—BEROE-AUGUSTA TRAIANA: **(3)** c. 320-324 AD *Anal. Boll.* 31 (1912) p. 198; p. 207
—BYZANTION: **(4)** c. 252-253 AD Schönert-Geiss, *Byzantion* 1836-9; 1850 (coin) (-*νεί*-)
—MARONEIA: **(5)** i BC-i AD *IThrakAig* E303 (-*νεί*-: d. *Φιλέρως*); **(6)** i AD *BCH* 66-7 (1942-3) p. 198 no. 2 (*IThrakAig* E297) (d. *Γάϊος*)

Βερονικιανός
THRACE:
—PERINTHOS-HERAKLEIA: **(1)** ii AD *IPerinth* 67 I, 6 (*CIL* III 7398) (Lat. Aelius Beronicianus)

Βέσουλα
THRACE:
—DYME (MOD.): **(1)** i AD *AD* 26 (1971) Chron. pl. 422 γ (*Belomorski Pregled* I (1941) p. 335 no. 40; *IThrakAig* E387); cf. Bakalakis, *Oinos Ismarikos* p. 1015 (d. *Μοκάπορις*)

Βεσπρης
MACEDONIA (EDONIS):
—AMPHIPOLIS: **(1)** ii-iii AD *Thrakika* 13 (1940) p. 28 P (*Βεσπρη* (gen.?))

Βεσσοδένθης
THRACE:
—BAZOPARA: **(1)** 202 AD *IGB* III 1690 d, 52 (and Thrace Pizos: *Βεσ*(*σ*)*οδένθης*: f. *Τήρης*)
—SKEPTA: **(2)** 202 AD ib. 1690 c, 17 (and Thrace Pizos: f. *Δυτούπορις*)

Βεσσός
MACEDONIA (PAIONIA): **(1)** hell. Plu., *Mor.* 553 D-F

Βετος
MACEDONIA (EDONIS):
—AMPHIPOLIS: **(1)** imp. Kaphtantzis 662 (terracotta) (?f. *Μᾶρκος*)

Βετταλός
MACEDONIA (BOTTIAIA):
—BEROIA: **(1)** 223 BC *IBer* 4, 30 (f. *Ἀδαῖος*)

Βηδέτας
MACEDONIA (LOWER PAIONIA):
—EUROPOS: **(1)** ?iii BC *SEG* XXXVIII 616 (s. *Ἀργαῖος*)

Βῆλος
MACEDONIA (EDONIS):
—AMPHIPOLIS: **(1)** hell.-imp. Kaphtantzis 738 (?f. *Ῥόδη*)

Βηρανός
THRACE:
—DRAGANOVEC (MOD.)*: **(1)** iii AD *IGB* V 5293 (*CCET* II (2) 458) (*Αἴλ. Β.*)

Βήριμος
MACEDONIA (BOTTIAIA):
—EDESSA: **(1)** f. ii AD *SEG* XXXIX 589; cf. XLIII 391 (Tataki, *Edessa* 67) (s. *Ζωΐλος*, f. *Μάγνα*)

Βηρισάδης
THRACE: **(1)** 359-356 BC *RE* (-); Rhodes–Osborne 47, 5, 8, [9], etc. (?s. *Κότυς*, ?f. *Κετρίπορις*: king)
—LYSIMACHEIA: **(2)** iii BC *IG* II^2 9223 (*FRA* 3389) (-ρει-: f. *Βενδιδώρα*)

Βῆρος
MACEDONIA (ODOMANTIKE):
—SIRRHA?: **(1)** iii AD *IGB* V 5932 (s. *Γάϊος ὁ καὶ Κερδώλας*)

Βήρυλλος
MACEDONIA (MYGDONIA):
—THESSALONIKE: **(1)** ii AD *IG* X (2) (1) 241 A II, 20 (f. *Ἀντίοχος*)

Βησαντίς
MACEDONIA (PAIONIA): **(1)** c. 400 BC Overbeck 926; cf. *RE* s.v. Deinomenes (7) (queen/fict.?)

Βησάρτης
MACEDONIA (MYGDONIA):
—THESSALONIKE: **(1)** i AD *IG* X (2) (1) 259, 3 + *SEG* XXX 622 (*Γ. Ἰούλ. Β.*)

Βησέλων
MACEDONIA (EDONIS):
—PHILIPPOI (DRAMA (MOD.)): **(1)** ii-iii AD *AD* 52 (1997) Chron. p. 847, 8 with pl. 314 β

Βία
MACEDONIA (MYGDONIA):
—THESSALONIKE: **(1)** ii AD *SEG* XXXVIII 706 (*Αἰλ. Βεία*)

Βιαῖος
MACEDONIA (BOTTIAIA):
—PELLA: **(1)** s. iv BC ib. XLVIII 823 A (s. *Πίθων*)
MACEDONIA (PAIONIA):
—EUDARISTOS: **(2)** ?f. ii BC *AD* 23 (1968) Mel. p. 111 no. 77; Papazoglou, *Villes* p. 327 (ethn.); Tataki, *Macedonians* p. 208 no. 7 (f. *Νικάνωρ*)

Βιακράτης
MACEDONIA (CHALKIDIKE):
—TORONE: **(1)** iv/iii BC *Ét. Thas.* 3 p. 318 no. 111 (Tataki, *Macedonians* p. 191 no. 4) (f. *Ἀριστοβούλη*)

Βιάνωρ
CIMMERIAN BOSPOROS:
—NYMPHAION: **(1)** iii BC *CIRB* 912 III, 6
SCYTHIA MINOR:
—ISTROS: **(2)** s. iii BC *ISM* I 15, 2 (f. *Διονύσιος*); **(3)** i BC-i AD ib. 186 (*Βιάν[ωρ]*: f. *Μηνόδωρος*); **(4)** ii AD ib. 131 (*CCET* IV 63) (s. *Κλεογένης*); **(5)** ~ *ISM* I 212, 10 (I f. *Βιάνωρ* II); **(6)** ~ ib. l. 10 (II s. *Βιάνωρ* I); **(7)** 138 AD ib. 193 II, 38 (s. *Ἑκαταῖος*)
THRACE: **(8)** c. 359 BC *RE* (4); Osborne, *Naturalization* T58 (and Athens)
—MESAMBRIA: **(9)** ii BC *IGB* I^2 314 b, 7 (*Βιάνωρ*: s. *Διονύσιος*)
THRACE?: **(10)** ii BC *ISM* I 36, 6 + *Pontica* 33-4 (2000-1) pp. 346-7 no. 3 (s. *Κλειτοφῶν*)

Βιάρτας
THRACE:
—BESSOI: **(1)** imp. *CIL* XIII 8312 (Lat. Longinus Biarta: s. Bises)
—KELLAI*: **(2)** iii AD *IGB* III 1516 b, 22 (s. *Δυτούπορις*, f. *Βίθυς*, *Βειβους*)
—SKEDABRIA: **(3)** 202 AD ib. 1690 b, 15 (and Thrace Pizos: f. *Βίθης*)

Βίας
MACEDONIA (CHALKIDIKE):
—STOLOS?: **(1)** c. 350 BC *SEG* XL 553, 5 (s. *Ναύτων*)
SKYTHIA:
—TYRAS: **(2)** v-iv BC ib. XLV 1026. 18 (vase)

Βιάτωρ
MACEDONIA (BOTTIAIA):
—EDESSA: **(1)** iii AD ib. XXXVIII 605, 4 (Tataki, *Edessa* 68)
THRACE:
—DIONYSOPOLIS: **(2)** iii AD *IGB* I^2 14 b, 17 (*Αὐρ. Β.*: s. *Μακεδών*)
—NICOPOLIS AD ISTRUM (TERRIT.): **(3)** ii-iii AD ib. II 720
—ODESSOS: **(4)** 215 AD ib. I^2 47 c, 29 (f. *Αὐρ. Ζιέρις*); **(5)** 221 AD ib. 47 bis b, 10 (f. *Αὐρ. Ἑστιαῖος*); **(6)** ~ ib. 47 bis c, 29 (f. *Αὐρ. Νουμήνιος*); **(7)** ~ ib. l. 34 (f. *Αὐρ. Διονύσιος*)

Βιβώ
MACEDONIA (BOTTIAIA):
—BEROIA: **(1)** hell. *SEG* XXXVI 609 (vase) (Tataki 331)

Βιγιλέντιος
MACEDONIA (BOTTIAIA):
—EDESSA: **(1)** v-vi AD Feissel, *RICM* 39

Βιζῆς
MACEDONIA (ODOMANTIKE):
—DRABESKOS?: **(1)** ii-iii AD *SEG* XXX 619, 4 (Pilhofer 572) (*Βιζῆ* (gen.): f. *Τόρκος*)

Βίζος
THRACE:
—ASOMATOI (MOD.): **(1)** ?iii AD *SEG* XVI 414 + *Epigraphica* 37 (1975) p. 33 (*IThrakAig* E386) (f. *Βενδίς*)

Βιζώνης
SCYTHIA MINOR: **(1)** ii BC *SCIV* I.1 (1950) pp. 235-6 nos. 10-11; *SNG Stancomb* 313 (coin) (*Βιζώ(νης)*?, *Βιζω(—)*—*SCIV*, *Βιζω(—)*—*SNG*)
THRACE: **(2)** c. 223 BC *PTeb* 815 fr. 2 II, 36 (Velkov 43); cf. La'da E852

Βιήσιος
MACEDONIA (MYGDONIA):
—LETE: **(1)** 121 AD *SEG* I 276, 20 (*Περίτας ὁ καὶ Β.*: s. *Φίλα*)

Βίθας
MACEDONIA (MYGDONIA):
—THESSALONIKE: **(1)** m. ii AD *IG* X (2) (1) 219, 4 (*Βείθαν* (acc.): s. *Βίθυς*)
THRACE:
—SKEDABRIA: **(2)** 202 AD *IGB* III 1690 b, 17 (and Thrace Pizos: *Βεί-*: s. *Τάρσας*)
—SPORTELA: **(3)** ii-iii AD ib. IV 2234, 6 (*Βεί-*: f. *Ἐπτέκενθος*)

Βίθης
THRACE:
—HADRIANOPOLIS (TERRIT.): **(1)** iii AD ib. III 1833 (*Βειθήους* (gen.): f. *Κόρινθος*)
—SKEDABRIA: **(2)** 202 AD ib. 1690 b, 15 (and Thrace Pizos: *Βεί-*: s. *Βιάρτας*); **(3)** ~ ib. l. 19 (and Thrace Pizos: *Βειθήους* (gen.): f. *Μουκάτραλις*)

Βιθίπης
THRACE:
—BOURDAPA: **(1)** ii-iii AD ib. 1338 (*Βειθιπήους* (gen.): f. *Δεντουσυκος*)

Βιθύας
THRACE:
—BRESTE (MOD.): **(1)** ?iii AD *ILB* 176; *Onomastique latine* p. 348 (name) (Lat. Bitua: f. *Βενδῖνα*)

Βιθυκεῖλας
THRACE:
—BAZOPARA: **(1)** 202 AD *IGB* III 1690 d, 21 (and Thrace Pizos: *Βει-*: f. *Ἐπτήτραλις*)

Βιθύκενθος
MACEDONIA (EDONIS):
—PHILIPPOI (TERRIT.): **(1)** ?ii AD *CIL* III 703, 4 (Pilhofer 524); Collart, *Philippes* pl. 84. 2 (Lat. Bithicenthus: s. *Κερζούλας*)
THRACE: **(2)** 46-54 AD *SEG* XVI 415 I, 11 (*IThrakAig* E84) (*Βει-*: f. *Τιβ. Κλ. Ῥοιμητάλκας*)
—BEROE-AUGUSTA TRAIANA (TERRIT.): **(3)** ii AD *IGB* III 1714 (*Τ. Φλ. Βειθύκενθος*: s. *Ἔζβενις*)
—BESSOI: **(4)** 133 AD *CIL* II 2984 (Lat. Biticentus: f. *Δόλης*)
—GLAVA PANEGA (MOD.): **(5)** ii-iii AD *IGB* II 512 (*Αἰλ. Βειθύκενθος*)
—MARKIANOPOLIS (TERRIT.): **(6)** iii AD ib. V 5329, 2 (*Βιθίκην(θος)*?: s. *Δέζαλος*)

Βιθυνία
MACEDONIA (CHALKIDIKE): **(1)** 223 AD *SEG* XLVIII 879; *BE* 1999, no. 365 (locn.) (*Βει-θ[υ]νία*)
MACEDONIA (MYGDONIA):
—THESSALONIKE: **(2)** iii AD *IG* X (2) (1) 565, 4, 7 (*Ἰουλ. Βειθυνία*: m. *Μαρῖνος*)
THRACE:
—SERDICA: **(3)** ii-iii AD *IGB* IV 1961 (*Βειθυν[ία]*: d. *Βιθύνιος*)

Βιθυνικός
MACEDONIA (MYGDONIA):
—THESSALONIKE?: **(1)** ii-iii AD *IG* X (2) (1) 810 (*Δέκμιος Βιθυν(ι)κός*: s. *Δεκμία Διοσκόρη*)
THRACE:
—BEROE-AUGUSTA TRAIANA: **(2)** iii AD *IGB* V 5566 (*Βει-*: f. *Αὐρ. Μάρκελλα*)
—BYZANTION (TERRIT.): **(3)** imp. Unp. (Sayar) (-νει-: f. *Ἰουλιανός*)
—PHILIPPOPOLIS-TRIMONTIUM: **(4)** ii-iii AD *IGB* V 5440 (*Οὐλπ. Βειθυνικός*)
—PHILIPPOPOLIS-TRIMONTIUM (TERRIT.): **(5)** ii-iii AD ib. III 1143 (*Βειθυνικό[ς]*)
—PHILIPPOPOLIS-TRIMONTIUM:
——(Hebreis): **(6)** 222-235 AD ib. 1473, 11 (*Βει-*: f. *Αὐρ. Καρδένθης*)

Βιθύνιος
THRACE:
—SERDICA: **(1)** ii-iii AD ib. IV 1961 (*Βειθύνι[ος]*—ed., *Βειθυνι[κός]*?: f. *Βιθυνία*)

Βίθυς
CIMMERIAN BOSPOROS:
—PANTIKAPAION: **(1)** iii AD *CIRB* 109, 4 (I f. *Βίθυς* II); **(2)** ~ ib. l. 4 (II s. *Βίθυς* I)
—PANTIKAPAION*: **(3)** ii AD ib. 666, 1; cf. KW pl. 15 no. 208 (*Βεί-*: f. *Δίζας*)
MACEDONIA (ALMOPIA):
—MONASTIRAKI (MOD.): **(4)** iii AD *SEG* XXVIII 546 (*Βεί-*: f. *Λιμναῖος*)
MACEDONIA (BOTTIAIA):
—BEROIA: **(5)** ?171 AD *ILeukopetra* 9, 2 (*Βεί-*: f. *Εὐρυδίκη*)
MACEDONIA (DERRIOPOS):
—STUBERRA: **(6)** 74 AD *IG* X (2) (2) 325, 62 (*Βεί[θυς]*: f. *Μέστυς*)
MACEDONIA (EDONIS):
—AMPHIPOLIS: **(7)** 37 BC Robert, *Coll. Froehner* 44, 14, 16-17 (Tataki, *Macedonians* p. 49 no. 29) (s. *Γλαυκίας*, ?s. *Κλεοπάτρα*, f. *Μητρόδωρος*, *Ἀθηνίων*, *Φιλέρως*); **(8)** ii-iii AD Kazarow 420; cf. *BE* 1949, no. 97 (*Βεί-*: s. *Ἄθως*); **(9)** ~ *Thracia* 2 p. 276 + *Epigraphica* 37 (1935) p. 30
—IOLLITAI: **(10)** ii-iii AD *BCH* 24 (1900) p. 317, 2 (Pilhofer 417) (*[Βί]θυς*: s. *Βέρβος*); **(11)** ~ *BCH* 24 (1900) p. 317, 4 (Pilhofer 417) (s. *Ζιπαίβης*)
—PHILIPPOI: **(12)** i-ii AD Dimitsas 973 + *BSA* 23 (1918-19) p. 81 (Pilhofer 86) (f. *Βασιέλας*); **(13)** iii AD *AE* 1950-1, p. 72 no. 16 (Pilhofer 731) (Lat. M. Aur. Bitys)
—PHILIPPOI (TERRIT.): **(14)** imp. *BCH* 21 (1897) p. 528 no. 3 (Pilhofer 462) (*[Β]είθυς*);

(**15**) ~ *CIL* III 14206. 20 (Pilhofer 526) (Lat. Bitus: s. Ῥηβούκενθος); (**16**) ?ii AD *BCH* 24 (1900) p. 307 (Pilhofer 517) (Lat. [B]ithus qui et Crispus: s. Βασκίλας); (**17**) ~ *BCH* 47 (1923) pp. 64-5 no. 24, 7 (Pilhofer 519) (Lat. Bithus: f. Βασκίλας); (**18**) ~ *CIL* III 703, 1 (Pilhofer 524) (Lat. Bithus qui et Macer: s. Tauzix); (**19**) ~ *CIL* III 703, 2 (Pilhofer 524) (Lat. Bithus: f. Tauzix); (**20**) ~ *CIL* III 703, 3 (Pilhofer 524) (Lat. Bithus: s. Tauzix); (**21**) ?iii AD *SEG* XXX 594 A, 5 (Pilhofer 580) (Βεί-); (**22**) ~ *SEG* XXX 594 A, 7 (Pilhofer 580) (Βεί-: s. Ση(—)); (**23**) iii-iv AD Pikoulas, *Chora* p. 118 no. 9a (*SEG* XLIX 706) (f. Σκαρούσης)

—PHILIPPOI (DRAMA (MOD.)): (**24**) ii-iii AD *AD* 52 (1997) Chron. p. 847, 1 with pl. 314 β ([Β]ίθυς); (**25**) ~ ib. l. 11 with pl. 314 β

—PROUPTOSOURENOI: (**26**) ii-iii AD Dimitsas 1051, 4 = 1082 (Pilhofer 456); cf. *BCH* 47 (1923) p. 75 no. 34 (Βεί-: s. Τάρσας, Μελγίς)

—SKAPORENOI: (**27**) ?ii AD ib. 24 (1900) p. 310 no. 3 (Pilhofer 512) (Lat. Bithus: f. Σεκούς)

MACEDONIA (MYGDONIA):

—ARDROLOS: (**28**) i/ii AD *SEG* XLII 590 (f. Μουκάσης, Ἡρακλείδης, Διοκλῆς, Σεύθης, Ἱεροκλῆς)

—KALINDOIA: (**29**) 68-98 AD ib. 580, 32 (Βεί-: f. Τράλις); (**30**) ~ ib. l. 76 (Βεί-: s. Πάμφιλος); (**31**) a. 98 AD ib. 582, 26 (Βεί-: s. Κλαρόνικος); (**32**) ~ ib. l. 33 (Βεί-: f. Βίλσης); (**33**) ~ ib. l. 66 (Βεί-: f. Κήζεβις)

—LETE: (**34**) ii AD *Makedonika* 2 (1951) p. 619 no. 42 θ, 17 (Βεί-: f. Ἐπικράτης); (**35**) 121 AD *SEG* I 276, 20 (Βεί-: f. Ἡρωΐδης)

—THESSALONIKE: (**36**) c. 208 BC *FD* III (4) 134, 25 (Tataki, *Macedonians* p. 180 no. 16) (f. —τας); (**37**) m. ii AD *IG* X (2) (1) 219, 4 (Βεί-: f. Βίθας); (**38**) iii AD ib. 555, 2 + *SEG* XXXVIII 695 ([Βί]θυς ὁ κὲ Ἀδόλιος)

—THESSALONIKE?: (**39**) i AD *IG* X (2) (1) 679; (**40**) f. ii AD *JDAI* 84 (1969) p. 151 no. R13 (Βεί-: s. Διζάλας)

MACEDONIA (ODOMANTIKE):

—GAZOROS (NR.): (**41**) i AD *SEG* XXXVIII 2038 (Pilhofer 539b) (Βεί-: f. Ἀπολλόδωρος)

—GAZOROS?: (**42**) 158 AD *SEG* XXIV 614, 3 (Pilhofer 544); cf. Hatzopoulos, *MI* I pp. 84-6 (Βεί-: f. Δούλης)

—SIRRHA: (**43**) ii-iii AD *SEG* XXX 613, 1 (Βεί-: f. Τορκουᾶτος); (**44**) 155 AD Dimitsas 821, 1 (Kaphtantzis 1) (Βεί-: f. Τορκουᾶτος); (**45**) f. iii AD *SEG* XXX 590, 25 (Βίθ[υ]ς: f. Αὐρ. Διονύσιος); (**46**) ~ ib. l. 27 (f. Αὐρ. Διοσκοῦς)

—SIRRHA?: (**47**) ii-iii AD Dimitsas 826, 2 (*Dodoni* 18 (1989) p. 248 no. 57) (Βεί-: f. Κόϊντος); (**48**) 157 AD *Belomorski Pregled* 1 (1942) p. 318 no. 1 (Kaphtantzis 10) (Βείθ[υς]: I f. Βίθυς II); (**49**) ~ *Belomorski Pregled* 1 (1942) p. 318 no. 1 (Kaphtantzis 10) ([Βε]ίθυς: II s. Βίθυς I)

MACEDONIA (PELAGONIA):

—DOSTONEIS: (**50**) ?ii AD *IG* X (2) (2) 200 (Βεί-: f. Δούλης)

MACEDONIA (SINTIKE):

—NEINE: (**51**) 77 AD *IGB* V 5883, 6 (Βεί-: f. Κίμβρος); (**52**) ii AD ib. IV 2253 (Βεί-: s. Κειλαίβιθυς)

—NEINE (NR.): (**53**) ii-iii AD ib. 2261 (Βεί-)

—PARTHIKOPOLIS: (**54**) ?ii AD *FGrH* 257 F 37, 52 (Tataki, *Macedonians* p. 147 no. 2) (s. Διζάστης); (**55**) 150 AD *IGB* IV 2274 ([Βί]θυς: s. Τήρης)

—PARTHIKOPOLIS (TERRIT.): (**56**) 198 AD ib. 2311, 1 (Βεί-: s. Παράμονος, f. Πυρούσαλα); (**57**) ?242 AD ib. 2322 (s. Δίζας)

SCYTHIA MINOR:

—CAPIDAVA: (**58**) 168 AD *ISM* V 15, 7 (Lat. Bitus: f. Ἐπτάκενθος)

—IBIDA: (**59**) ii AD ib. 228, 6 (Lat. Bitus: f. Βιθιδία)

—ISTROS: (**60**) ii/i BC *EAD* XXX 418, 2 (slave)

—ISTROS [NR.]:

——Vicus Quintionis: (**61**) 149 AD *ISM* I 326, 9 (Lat. Bithus: f. Δουρίζης); (**62**) 177 AD ib. 332, 8 (Lat. Bit(us): f. Δέρζενις)

—TOMIS: (**63**) ii-iii AD ib. II 303 (Lat. Bitus: f. Saturninus)

SKYTHIA:

—OLBIA-BORYSTHENES*: (**64**) 248 AD *IOSPE* I^2 167, 8 (Lat. Pyrrus Bithus)

TAURIS:

—CHERSONESOS: (**65**) iii-ii BC ib. 523

THRACE: (**66**) iv BC *IG* II^2 8927 (*FRA* 2505) (f. Φιλόνικος); (**67**) hell. *Syringes* 18 (Velkov 49); cf. La'da E716 (f. Ἀσκληπιάδης); (**68**) 274 BC *PCZ* 59001, 23-4, [48], 51, verso (Velkov 50; La'da E721) (f. Ζώπυρος); (**69**) 257 BC *PSorb* 17a, 7; 17b, 7, 21; cf. La'da E842 (f. Σπόκης); (**70**) s. iii BC *SEG* XXVII 973 bis, 23; (**71**) 226 BC *PPetr* III 21 a, 3, 10 (Velkov 56); cf. La'da E851 (f. Φοῖνιξ); (**72**) ?217-186 BC *PHeid* VIII 412, 19, 24 (La'da E2621); (**73**) ?211-186 BC *PHeid* VIII 412, 21, 27 (La'da E722); (**74**) ii-i BC *Ag.* XVII 505 (*FRA* 2506); (**75**) f. ii BC *IC* 2 p. 30 no. 15 (s. Κελήκενθος); (**76**) 183 BC *SGDI* 2009, 5, 7 (slave/freed.); (**77**) c. 181 BC *PTeb* 1002, 91 (Velkov 55) (f. Στράτων); (**78**) 180-145 BC *BGU* 1271, 12 (Velkov 58); cf. La'da E849 (f. —κράτης); (**79**) i AD *IG* II^2 8901 (*FRA* 2507); (**80**) ?i AD *CIL* VIII 25364 (Lat. C. Iulius Bitus); (**81**) 46-54 AD *SEG* XVI 415 I, 14 (*IThrakAig* E84) (Τιβ. Κλ. Βείθυς); (**82**) ?i/ii AD *CIL* VIII 2251 (Lat. T. Flavius Bitus: I f. Βίθυς II); (**83**) ~ ib. (Lat. Bitus: II s. Βίθυς I); (**84**) 80 AD ib. XVI 158; *AEp* 1972, no. 537 (Lat. Bithus: f. Δουρίζης); (**85**) 88 AD *ZPE* 117 (1997) p. 231 no. 2 (Lat. Bithus); (**86**) ii-iii AD *IMS* I 96 (Lat. B(i)ti (gen.): f. Βιτίων); (**87**) s. ii AD *CIL* VI 34619 (Lat. T. Aur. Bithus); (**88**) iii AD ib. 3195, 2 (Speidel, *Denkmäler* 598) (Lat. M. Aurel. Bithus); (**89**) ~ *CIL* XIII 1843 (Lat. [A]urel. Bitus)

—AINOS: (**90**) hell.-imp. *FRA* 233 (f. Εὐφροσύνη)

—BAZOPARA: (**91**) 202 AD *IGB* III 1690 d, 42 (and Thrace Pizos: Β[ε]ίθυς: f. Μουκάτραλις); (**92**) ~ ib. l. 46 (and Thrace Pizos: Βεί-: f. Ῥουστικός); (**93**) ~ ib. 1690 e, 93 (and Thrace Pizos: Βεί-: f. Ἐπτήπορις); (**94**) ~ ib. 1690 c, 41 (and Thrace Pizos: Βεί-: s. Τήρης) ?= (*95*); (**95**) ~ ib. l. 42 (and Thrace Pizos: Βεί-: f. Βαστοκείλας) ?= (*94*); (**96**) ~ ib. l. 66 (and Thrace Pizos: Βείθυ[ς]: s. Βε—λος); (**97**) ~ ib. l. 67 (and Thrace Pizos: Βεί-: s. Βρινκάζερις); (**98**) ~ ib. l. 69 (and Thrace Pizos: Βεί-: f. Βουργειλος); (**99**) ~ ib. l. 70 (and Thrace Pizos: Βεί-: s. Βιθύτραλις)

—BEROE-AUGUSTA TRAIANA (TERRIT.): (**100**) ii-iii AD ib. 1649 (f. Ῥοδόπη); (**101**) 222-230 AD ib. 1666, 4 (Βεί-: s. Κέλσος, f. Θεαγένης); (**102**) ~ ib. l. 6 (Βεί-: f. —νις)

—BEROE-AUGUSTA TRAIANA:

——Emporion Diskodouraterai: (**103**) ii-iii AD ib. II 738, 3 (s. Διμης, Δωρουτελμίς)

——Karasoura: (**104**) ii-iii AD ib. III 1627, 3 + *SEG* XLI 589 (Βεί-: f. Αὐλουμένης, Τήρης); (**105**) iii AD *IGB* III 1626, 15 (Βεί(θ)υς: f. Δόλης)

—BESSOI: (**106**) 88 AD *CIL* XVI 35 (*AEp* 1927, no. 44; 1928, no. 155; 1933, no. 1; 1955, no. 90) (Lat. Bithus: s. Σεύθης); (**107**) ii AD *Puteoli* 11 (1987) pp. 139-40 no. 6 (Lat. L. Flavius Bithus: I f. Ποτάμιλλα (Misenum), Βίθυς II (Misenum)); (**108**) 118-133 AD *CIL* III 104 (Lat. L. Valerius Bitus); (**109**) 140 AD *RMD* 39 (*IDR* I p. 108 no. 13) (Lat. Bithus: s. Solas); (**110**) ii/iii AD *Puteoli* 12-13 (1988-9) pp. 224-5 no. 10 (Lat. Naevius Bithus)

—BESSOI?: (**111**) 120-130 AD *NScav* 1928, p. 196 (Lat. Flavi. Bithus: s. L. Flavius Silius)

—BESSOPARA: (**112**) ii-iii AD *IGB* III 1332 (Βεί-: f. Σεβαζιανός); (**113**) iii AD ib. 947, 9 (Βεί-: s. Δίζας)

—BISANTHE-PANION: (**114**) c. 208 BC *FD* III (4) 133 II, 28 (Βίθυς: s. Κλέων)

—BOURDAPA: (**115**) i-ii AD *IGB* III 1350 (Βεί-: f. Ῥυμησυκις); (**116**) ii-iii AD ib. 1342 (f. Ἐπτέκενθος); (**117**) 227 AD *CIL* VI 32543, 12 (Lat. M. Aur. Bitus)

—BYZANTION (TERRIT.): (**118**) i-ii AD *IByz* 189 ([Β]είθυς: s. Σφοδρίας)

—ČOMAKOVCI (MOD.): (**119**) ?iii AD *ILB* 165 (Lat. Bitus: f. –telas); (**120**) ~ ib. 166 (Lat. Bitus: ?s. Ep–)

—DIOSOURA: (**121**) ii AD *IGB* V 5589, 3 (Βεί-: ?f. Νέπως, Διονύσιος, Ἐπτηπυρίς)

—DIOSPOLIS: (**122**) ii-iii AD ib. III 1784 (Βεί-: s. Διζάζελμις)

—GABARE (MOD.): (**123**) ii-iii AD ib. II 509 (Βείθ[υς]: f. —βανος)

—GELOUPARA: (**124**) 202 AD ib. III 1690 c, 22 (and Thrace Pizos: Βεί-: f. Δυτούτραλις); (**125**) ~ ib. l. 25 (and Thrace Pizos: Βεί-: f. Μουκάτραλις)

—GLAVA PANEGA (MOD.): (**126**) iii AD ib. II 555 (Βεί-: s. Διέρνης)

—HADRIANOPOLIS (TERRIT.): (**127**) ii-iii AD ib. III 1802 (f. Πιστοῦς); (**128**) ~ ib. 1803, 3 (Βείθ[υ]ς: f. Ἐπτηπυρίς); (**129**) iii AD ib. 1804 (Βεί-: f. Πόσσης)

—KARAŠ (MOD.): (**130**) ii-iii AD ib. II 498-9 (I f. Βίθυς II); (**131**) ~ ib. (Βεί-: II s. Βίθυς I, f. Μαρτιάλης)

—KELLAI (NR.): (**132**) iii AD ib. III 1542 (Β(ε)ίθυς: s. Θάλλος)

—KELLAI*: (**133**) iii AD ib. 1516 a, 26 (Βεί-: s. —πιος); (**134**) ~ ib. 1516 b, 24 (s. Βιάρτας, Δαρουβυρ—)

—KOMOTINI (MOD.): (**135**) imp. *Belomorski Pregled* 1 (1942) p. 336 no. 41 (*BE* 1948, no. 148; *IThrakAig* E482) (Βεί-: f. Μακέσαλα); (**136**) ~ *Belomorski Pregled* 1 (1942) p. 336 no. 41 (*BE* 1948, no. 148; *IThrakAig* E482) (Βεί-: f. Σουσᾶς)

—KOURPISOS: (**137**) 202 AD *IGB* III 1690 c, 35 (and Thrace Pizos: Βεί-: f. Μουκάπορις); (**138**) ~ ib. l. 38 (and Thrace Pizos: Βεί-: f. Μουκάτραλις)

—KRASALOPARA: (**139**) 202 AD ib. 1690 b, 57 (and Thrace Pizos: Βεί-: f. Βρίζενις); (**140**) ~ ib. l. 61 (and Thrace Pizos: Βεί-: s. Δίβιθυς); (**141**) ~ ib. l. 65 (and Thrace Pizos: Βεί-: f. Μουκάπορις)

—LYSIMACHEIA: (**142**) iv/iii BC *RE* (6); *IG* II^2 808, 15; *SEG* XXXVIII 619, 10; XLVIII [817]?; *FGrH* 81 F 12; cf. Hatzopoulos, *Donation* pp. 38-9 (ident.) (s. Κλέων) ?= (*143*)

—LYSIMACHEIA?: (**143**) iii BC *IG* XI (4) 1242 (Βίθ[υς]) ?= (*142*)

—MARKIANOPOLIS: (**144**) 230 AD *ZPE* 137 (2001) p. 246 (Lat. M. Aurelius Bithus)

—MARKIANOPOLIS (TERRIT.): (**145**) imp. *SEG* XXXIX 676 (Βεί-: s. Αὐλούζενις); (**146**) ii-iii AD *IGB* II 843, 3 (Βεί-: f. Ζοιθα); (**147**) ~ ib. 844 (f. Αὐλουσυκος)

—MESAMBRIA: (**148**) ii BC ib. I^2 322 ter, 4 (*Eastern cults* p. 25 no. 42) ([Βί]θυς?, [Ἄ]θυς—ed.)

—MESAMBRIA (TERRIT.): (**149**) f. ii AD *IGB* I^2 354 quater (*CCET* I 111) (Βεί-: f. Ταρούλας ὁ καὶ Σκῶρις)

—MONTANA (TERRIT.): (**150**) iii AD *Montana* II 67 (Lat. Bithus: f. Zimius)

—NICOPOLIS AD ISTRUM: (**151**) ?iii AD *ILB* 375 (Lat. Bi[t]us: f. Ἐπτάπορις); (**152**) f. iii AD *IGB* II 694 (*CCET* II (2) 629) (Βεί-: f. Μουκάτραλις)

—NICOPOLIS AD ISTRUM (TERRIT.): (**153**) iii AD *IGB* II 719 (f. Ζιαμήτραλις)

—NICOPOLIS AD NESTUM: (**154**) ii AD ib. IV 2341 (Βεί-: f. Διζάλας); (**155**) ~ ib. 2346 (Βεί-:

f. *Σεύθης*); **(156)** ii-iii AD ib. 2337, 14 ([*Βί*]*θυς*: s. *Πλύσος*)
—NOVAE*: **(157)** f. iii AD *IGLNovae* 49 (Lat. T. Aur. Bithus)
—ODRYSAI: **(158)** c. 171-167 BC *RE* (3) (s. *Κότυς*)
—OMURTAG (MOD.): **(159)** f. iii AD *IGB* II 769 (*CCET* II (2) 531) (f. *Μουκάκενθος*)
—PAUTALIA: **(160)** 196 AD *IMS* II 53 I B b, 53 (*CIL* III 14507); cf. *ZPE* 146 (2004) pp. 216-20; *AEp* 1901, no. 126 (Lat. M. Aur. Bithus); **(161)** v AD *Arch. Bulg.* 2001 (3), p. 29 (Lat. Bitus)
—PAUTALIA (TERRIT.): **(162)** ii-iii AD *IGB* IV 2134 (*Βεί-*: s. *Διζαζενις*); **(163)** ~ ib. 2225 (*Βεί-*: f. *Πολιτικός*); **(164)** ~ ib. v 5861 (*Βεί-*)
—PHILIPPOPOLIS-TRIMONTIUM: **(165)** ii AD ib. III 918 (*Eastern cults* p. 264 no. 2) (*Βεί-*: s. *Κότυς*); **(166)** ~ *IGB* III 1005 (s. *Δόλης*, f. *Δόλης*); **(167)** ii-iii AD ib. 951 (*Βεί-*: f. *Σκέλης*); **(168)** 160 AD *RMD* 105 (Mello–Voza 66) (Lat. C. Iul. Bithus: I s. *Σεύθης*, f. *Βενδίς* (Poseidonia-Paestum), *Βίθυς* II (Poseidonia-Paestum), Longinus, Iulia); **(169)** c. 186 AD *IGB* III 881, 8 (*Βεί-*: f. —*δωρος*); **(170)** iii AD ib. 1474, 11 (*Αἰμίλιος Βείθυς*); **(171)** ~ *CIL* VI 2601 (Lat. Aur. Bithus); **(172)** 222 AD *ZPE* 127 (1999) p. 245 no. 1 (Lat. Bith[us]: f. M. Aurelius –)
—PHILIPPOPOLIS-TRIMONTIUM (TERRIT.): **(173)** imp. *IGB* III 1283 (s. *Δείσορος*); **(174)** ii-iii AD ib. 1057 (f. *Ἐπτέπυρις*); **(175)** ~ ib. 1199 (f. *Μουκάκενθος*); **(176)** ~ ib. 1307 (*Β̣εί-*); **(177)** ~ ib. 1398 (s. *Δίνις*); **(178)** ~ ib. 1402 (*CCCA* VI 352) (*Βεί-*); **(179)** ~ *IGB* III 1405 (*Βεί-*: s. *Μουκάτραλις*); **(180)** ~ ib. 1439 (*Βεί*[*θυς*]: ?s. *Σάλας*) ?= *(181)*; **(181)** ~ ib. 1440 (*Βεί-*: f. *Διώστραλις*) ?= *(182)* *(180)*; **(182)** ~ ib. 1441 (*Βεί-*: f. *Σάλας*) ?= *(181)*; **(183)** ~ ib. 1465 (*Βεί-*: f. *Κερκῆς*); **(184)** ~ ib. 1496 (*Βεί-*: f. *Ἡρόφιλος*); **(185)** ii/iii AD ib. 1452, 7 (*Eastern cults* p. 121 no. 104) (*Βείθυ*(*ς*)); **(186)** iii AD *IGB* III 1090 (*Βεί-*: s. *Αὐλούζενις*); **(187)** ~ ib. 1419 + v 5522 ([*Αὐρ.*] *Β.*: s. *Ἐπικράτης*); **(188)** ~ ib. III 1430 (*Βεί-*: s. *Λοῦππος*); **(189)** iv/v AD *God. Dep. Arkh.* 1 (1994) p. 133
—PHILIPPOPOLIS-TRIMONTIUM:
——Vicus Diiesure: **(190)** 227 AD *CIL* VI 32543, 36 (Lat. [M.] [Aur.] Bithus)
—PLATANIA (MOD.): **(191)** iii AD *SEG* XXXII 676 (Pilhofer 510) (*Βεί-*: f. *Δεντούπης*)
—SEKINENOI: **(192)** ii-iii AD *IGB* IV 2230 (*Βεί-*: s. *Πυρούλας*)
—SERDICA: **(193)** ii-iii AD ib. 2010, 2 (*Βείθυ*[*ς*]: f. *Ἡρακλείδης*); **(194)** iii AD *CIL* VI 2570 (Lat. Aur. Vitus)
—SERDICA (TERRIT.): **(195)** imp. *IGB* IV 2051 (*Β̣ίθυς*); **(196)** ii-iii AD *Sp.* 98 (1941-48) p. 127 no. 280, 5 (s. *Μούκκος*); **(197)** ~ *IGB* IV 1984; cf. v 5690 (*Βεί-*: f. *Δημοσθένης*)
—SERDICA:
——Vicus Potolense: **(198)** 266 AD *CIL* VI 2819 + 32567 (Lat. Aur. Bitus)
—SKEDABRIA: **(199)** 202 AD *IGB* III 1690 b, 20 (and Thrace Pizos: *Βεί-*: f. *Μουκάτραλις*)
—SPORTELA: **(200)** ii-iii AD ib. IV 2232, 3 (*Β̣ε̣ί̣θ̣*[*υς*]: f. *Δίζας*); **(201)** ~ ib. 2233, 4 (*Eastern cults* p. 170 no. 16) (*Βεί-*: s. *Μουκάτραλις*); **(202)** ~ *IGB* IV 2234, 5 (*Βεί-*: s. *Μουκα*—)
—STORGOSIA (NR.): **(203)** iii AD *Roman jewellery* p. 163 no. 177 (ring) (Lat. Aurelius Bitus)
—STRATOPARA: **(204)** 202 AD *IGB* III 1690 b, 32 (and Thrace Pizos: *Βεί-*: s. *Μουκάτραλις*); **(205)** ~ ib. l. 34 (and Thrace Pizos: *Βεί-*: s. *Ἐπτήτραλις*)
—TĂMNO CAVE (MOD.): **(206)** ii-iii AD ib. II 751 b (Lat. Bitus)
—TIRIZIS AKRA*: **(207)** c. 16 BC-14 AD ib. I² 12, 1 (f. *Φάρσαλος*)
—VICUS TRULLENSIUM: **(208)** ?iii AD *ILB* 181 (Lat. Bithus)
THRACE?: **(209)** iii-ii BC *BGU* 1251, 3 (Velkov 53) (f. *Νικαγόρας*); **(210)** m. iii BC *SB* 12221, 13; **(211)** 243 BC *PEnt* 12, 1 (*PP* 3855; Velkov 46)

Βιθύτραλις
THRACE:
—BAZOPARA: **(1)** 202 AD *IGB* III 1690 c, 43 (and Thrace Pizos: *Βει-*: f. *Δυτούτραλις*); **(2)** ~ ib. l. 70 (and Thrace Pizos: *Βει-*: f. *Βίθυς*)
—PHILIPPOPOLIS-TRIMONTIUM: **(3)** ii-iii AD ib. v 5462 (*Βει-*: s. *Τασης*, f. *Αἰλ. Πολέμων*)

Βίκτωρ
MACEDONIA (MYGDONIA):
—THESSALONIKE: **(1)** ii-iii AD *IG* x (2) (1) 1035, 1 (*IGB* III 1019; Tataki, *Macedonians* p. 180 no. 17) (glad.)
MACEDONIA (PIERIA):
—PYDNA*: **(2)** s. iii AD *Hellenika* 29 (1976) p. 274
SARMATIA:
—SARMATAI: **(3)** iv AD *RE* s.v. Victor (9); *PLRE* I (4)
SCYTHIA MINOR:
—KALLATIS (NR.)?: **(4)** ?iii AD *IGB* I² 12 ter, 6 (*CCET* I 1) (f. *Ἑρμογένης*)

Βικ-ωρία
MACEDONIA (PAIONIA):
—STOBOI: **(1)** v-vi AD Unp. (Stobi excav.) inv. I-78-13)

Βικτωρῖνος
MACEDONIA (BOTTIAIA):
—BEROIA*: **(1)** ii AD *IBer* 260, 2 (Tataki 333) (-*ρεί-*)
SCYTHIA MINOR:
—KALLATIS (NR.): **(2)** ii-iii AD *ISM* III 243, 7 (*IGB* I² 2) (s. *Σαβῖνα*)
THRACE:
—MARKIANOPOLIS?: **(3)** iii AD ib. II 814, 10 (*GVI* 1442; PM 2143) (*Βεικτορῖν*<*ιν*>*ος*)
—PHILIPPOPOLIS-TRIMONTIUM: **(4)** c. 303 AD *Anal. Boll.* 31 (1912) p. 192 (*Βίκτωρ Ῥῆνος*—ms., *Βικτωρ*<*ρ*>(*ῖ*)*νος*?)

Βίκων
SCYTHIA MINOR:
—KALLATIS: **(1)** iv/iii BC *ISM* III 125, 2 (s. *Αἰγε*—); **(2)** iii/ii BC ib. 36, 1 (s. *Διοσκουρίδας*)

Βιλάρρα?
MACEDONIA (BOTTIAIA):
—AIGAI: **(1)** s. iv BC *SEG* XXXV 784 + *ZPE* 72 (1988) pp. 111-12; cf. *SEG* XLVIII 874 + *BE* 1999, no. 336 (*Βίλα*?—Hatzopoulos: d. *Τέλλος*)

Βίλθης
MACEDONIA (CHALKIDIKE):
—STREPSA?: **(1)** b. 348 BC *SEG* XXXVII 583, 3 (*Βίλθεος* (gen.): f. —*ιος*)

Βιλίστα
MACEDONIA (CHALKIDIKE):
—NEOS MARMARAS (MOD.): **(1)** ii-i BC ib. XXXVIII 600 (d. *Ἀντίγονος*)

Βιλιστίχη
MACEDONIA: **(1)** c. 268-250 BC Moretti, *Olymp.* 549; 552 (*PP* 5066); *PP* 14717; cf. Masson, *OGS* pp. 467-70 (Tataki, *Macedonians* p. 281 no. 32) (d. *Φίλων*)

Βίλιστος
MACEDONIA (DERRIOPOS):
—STUBERRA: **(1)** 90 AD *IG* x (2) (2) 326, 73 (f. *Σίμων*) ?= *(2)*; **(2)** ~ ib. l. 77 (f. *Ζωΐλος*) ?= *(1)*
MACEDONIA (PIERIA):
—PYDNA: **(3)** 250 AD *SEG* XLVI 800 A, 10 (*Οὐρβανιανὸς Β.*)

Βιλκεύς
MACEDONIA (MYGDONIA):
—THESSALONIKE: **(1)** i AD *IG* x (2) (1) 402 (*Βίλκεως* (gen.): f. *Μελίς*)

Βιλλέας
MACEDONIA: **(1)** s. iv BC *IEph* 1431 (Tataki, *Macedonians* p. 281 no. 33) (f. *Νεοπτόλεμος*)

Βιλοίτας
MACEDONIA (BOTTIAIA):
—BEROIA: **(1)** ii-i BC *IBer* 182 (Tataki 332) (*Βι*(*λ*)*οίτας*: f. *Εὐρυδίκη*)

Βιλόκκα
MACEDONIA (BOTTIAIA):
—AIGAI?: **(1)** hell. Unp. (Vergina Exhib.) 43 (vase)

Βίλος
MACEDONIA (BOTTIAIA):
—BEROIA: **(1)** ii BC *IBer* 179 (*Βίλ*[*ος*]: f. *Ἀρτεμίδωρος*)
MACEDONIA (EORDAIA?):
—EUIA: **(2)** 181 BC *EAM* 87, 12 (Hatzopoulos, *MI* 2 pp. 41-2 no. 17) (s. *Νικάνωρ*)
MACEDONIA (ORESTIS):
—LYKE*: **(3)** hell. *EAM* 179 δ (tile); cf. *AD* 17 (1961-2) Chron. pl. 270 *γ*

Βίλσης
MACEDONIA (MYGDONIA):
—KALINDOIA: **(1)** a. 98 AD *SEG* XLII 582, 33; cf. *Anthémonte–Kalindoia* 2 p. 234 (name) (s. *Βίθυς*)

Βιλταλώ
MACEDONIA (CHALKIDIKE):
—STOLOS?: **(1)** ?350 BC *SEG* XXXVIII 670, 2 (d. *Διονυσιφάνης*)

Βινδέμιος
MACEDONIA (MYGDONIA):
—THESSALONIKE: **(1)** ?vi AD Feissel, *RICM* 92 (?f. *Δημήτριος*)

Βινκέντιος
MACEDONIA (CHALKIDIKE):
—POTIDAIA-KASSANDREIA (TERRIT.): **(1)** v-vi AD *SEG* XXIX 589 (Feissel, *RICM* 207)

Βιόμασος
CIMMERIAN BOSPOROS:
—BOSPOROS: **(1)** i AD *IGUR* 567 b (f. *Ἀσποῦργος*)
—ZENONOS CHERSONESOS*: **(2)** f. i AD *CIRB* 900 (*Βιόμα*[*σ*]*ος*: f. *Ζοτουμᾶς*)

Βίος
MACEDONIA (ODOMANTIKE):
—SIRRHA: **(1)** f. iii AD *SEG* XXX 590, 28 (*Αὐρ. Β.*, *Βί*(*θυ*)*ς*—Mihailov: s. *Ἑρμῆς*)

Βίσδης
THRACE:
—MARKIANOPOLIS (TERRIT.): **(1)** f. iii AD *IGB* II 861 (PM 1295; *CCET* II (1) 275) (*Β. Ἀντόνις*: s. *Βενδικός*)

Βισθᾶς
TAURIS:
—CHERSONESOS: **(1)** iv BC Solomonik, *NEPKh* 165; *Hellenismus* p. 445 no. 9 (s. *Φίλων*); **(2)** iii BC *SEG* XXXIII 599; *Hellenismus* p. 445 no. 9 (s. *Διονύσιος*); **(3)** 192 BC *Syll*³ 585, 57; *Hellenismus* p. 445 no. 9 (f. *Ἡρακλείδας*)

Βισίζης?
MACEDONIA (EDONIS):
—AMPHIPOLIS: **(1)** ii-iii AD *Thrakika* 13 (1940) pp. 22-5 *E* + *Epigraphica* 37 (1975) p. 27 (*Βισιζε* (gen.): f. *Δούλης*)

Βίστης
Cimmerian Bosporos:
—pantikapaion: (1) i bc *CIRB* 298; cf. *Etiudy* p. 193 no. 17 (*Βίστε[ιος]*? (gen.)); (2) imp. *CIRB* 760; Zgusta, *PNS* 85 (s. *Ποσειδώνιος, Μύρτιν*); (3) i bc/i ad *CIRB* 320; cf. KW pl. 30 no. 427 (*Βί[στ]ους*? (gen.), *Βι[έ]ους*—KW: f. *Φάννας*)

Βίτα
Thrace:
—kallipolis: (1) i bc-i ad *ISestos* 15 (d. *Ἀντικλῆς*)

Βιταλιανός
Macedonia (Mygdonia):
—thessalonike: (1) v-vi ad *IG* x (2) (1) 66 (Feissel, *RICM* 93)

Βιτάλιος
Scythia Minor:
—tomis: (1) iii ad *ISM* ii 100 (*Βει-*)
Thrace:
—plotinopolis: (2) 160 ad *SEG* xxxvii 970, 4 (*Βει-*: f. *Αἰάκων*)

Βιτάλις
Macedonia (Edonis):
—philippoi (territ.): (1) ii-iii ad Pikoulas, *Chora* p. 127 no. 21 (Pilhofer 622) (*Βειτάλες*)
Thrace:
—bizye: (2) imp. Dumont–Homolle 62a 1 (*Βει-*: s. *Στλάκκιος*)

Βιταλίων
Scythia Minor:
—tomis: (1) 200-201 ad *ISM* ii 82 B, 20 (*Βειταλίω[ν]*)

Βίταλος
Macedonia (Mygdonia):
—thessalonike: (1) 71 or 188 ad *SEG* xxxi 644 = xlv 818 (*Πόντιος Βείταλος*: f. *Πόντιος Πρόκλος, Ποντία Ἀντιγόνα*)
Macedonia (Paionia):
—kavadarci (mod.): (2) ii-iii ad *Sp.* 71 (1931) p. 70 no. 159

Βιτελλιανός
Macedonia (Bottiaia):
—beroia: (1) v-vi ad *IBer* 422 (Feissel, *RICM* 69) (*-τιλι-*)

Βιτέλλιος
Macedonia (Mygdonia):
—thessalonike?: (1) iii ad *IG* x (2) (1) 479 + *SEG* xxxviii 693

Βίτθις
Macedonia (Edonis):
—amphipolis: (1) ii-iii ad *Thrakika* 13 (1940) p. 27 *Λ* + *Epigraphica* 37 (1975) pp. 28-9 (s. *Τόκης*)

Βιτιδανός
Macedonia (Bottiaia):
—edessa: (1) v-vi ad Feissel, *RICM* 46

Βιτίων
Thrace: (1) ii-iii ad *IMS* i 96 (Lat. Bitio: s. *Βίθυς*)
—stryme: (2) s. v bc *SEG* xlvii 1103 + *IThrakAig* E112 (*[Β]ιτίων*: s. *Ἀριστομένης*)

Βίτος
Tauris:
—chersonesos*: (1) 383-395 ad *IOSPE* i² 450, 6 (*Φλ. Β.*)

Βιτούλουσος
Macedonia (Sintike):
—neine: (1) 77 ad *IGB* v 5883, 10 (s. *Μόκασος*)

Βιτράσις
Scythia Minor:
—kallatis: (1) c. 199 ad *ISM* iii 73 B, 2 (*Βει-*: s. *Πάρις*)

Βίτταλος
Cimmerian Bosporos:
—pantikapaion: (1) iii-ii bc Audollent, *Defix. Tab.* 92, 1

Βίττας
Macedonia (Paionia):
—neapolis (area): (1) 83 ad *SEG* xvi 404, 4 (*Βίτ[τα]ς, Βίττος*?, *Βιτίας*?: s. *Παράμονος, Νίκη*)

Βίττων
Macedonia (Chalkidike):
—olynthos: (1) ?c. 355-349 bc *TAPA* 69 (1938) p. 55 no. 7, 1 (f. *—ων*)

Βίτων
Cimmerian Bosporos:
—myrmekion: (1) i/ii ad *CIRB* 879; *Topoi* 3 (1993) p. 198 (date) (s. *Ἥλιος*)
Macedonia (Edonis):
—amphipolis: (2) ?iii bc *HE* 2695 (Tataki, *Macedonians* p. 49 no. 30) (s. *Νικαγόρας*)

Βιώ
Macedonia (Chalkidike):
—potidaia-kassandreia: (1) iv/iii bc *Ancient Macedonia* 1 p. 132 n. 20 (d. *Εὐγείτων*)

Βίων
Cimmerian Bosporos:
—pantikapaion: (1) i ad *CIRB* 370 (s. *Ἀπφοῦς*); (2) ~ ib. 378 (f. *Γάστεις*); (3) f. i ad ib. 431 (f. *Θεόφιλος*); (4) 275-278 ad ib. 36, 75 (I f. *Βίων* II); (5) ~ ib. l. 75 (II s. *Βίων* I)
Macedonia (Bisaltia):
—tragilos: (6) hell.? *SEG* xxx 617 (f. *Κράτιστος*)
Macedonia (Bottiaia):
—beroia: (7) ii/iii ad *IBer* 144 B, 8 (Tataki 669) (*Καπρείλιος Β.*)
—mieza: (8) iii bc *SEG* xxiv 524 I, 21 (Hatzopoulos, *MI* 2 p. 106 no. 92)
—pella: (9) iii bc Akamatis, *Amph. Pellas* p. 32 no. PAR5 (amph.) (*SEG* l 613)
Macedonia (Mygdonia):
—thessalonike: (10) iii ad *IG* x (2) (1) 247, 10 (*Ἰούλ. Β.*)
Macedonia (Paionia):
—stoboi: (11) s. i ad *Arheološki Vestnik* 41 (1990) p. 579 (*AEp* 1990, no. 884) (Lat. A. Pontii Vionis (gen.))
Skythia:
—olbia-borysthenes: (12) c. 325-255 bc *RE* (10); Kindstrand, *Bion of Borysthenes*
Tauris:
—chersonesos: (13) ?f. iv bc *CIRB* 173 (s. *Ἀπολλοφάνης*); (14) 359 bc *CID* ii 5 I, 9 (f. *Θρασυδαῖος*); (15) iv/iii bc *IOSPE* i² 410 (s. *Σιμίας*, f. *Ἀντιβίων*)
Thrace:
—abdera: (16) v/iv bc *RE* (11); *FVS* 77
—maroneia: (17) ii-i bc *IThrakAig* E212, 58 (s. *Παρμενίων*)

Βλάστη
Macedonia (Eordaia):
—arnisa?: (1) m. ii ad *EAM* 122; Hatzopoulos, *MI* 1 p. 94 n. 4 (locn.) (*[Βλ]άστη*?: m. *Κασσία, Ἡρωΐδης, Λ—α*)

Βλάστος
Cimmerian Bosporos:
—gorgippia: (1) f. iii bc *CIRB* 1137 A I, 2 (s. *Ἄτταλος*); (2) ~ ib. 1137 A II, 30 (s. *Κοτυτίων*)
—pantikapaion: (3) f. iv bc ib. 185 (s. *Δαμέας*)
Macedonia (Mygdonia):
—thessalonike: (4) 249 ad *IG* x (2) (1) 542

Macedonia (Odomantike):
—serres (mod.) (area): (5) 76 ad *Tekmeria* 6 (2001) p. 14 (*Γ. Ἰούλ. Β.*)
Skythia:
—olbia-borysthenes*: (6) i bc-i ad *Arkheologiia* (Kiev) 8 (1973) p. 93 (terracotta)
Thrace:
—oescus: (7) s. ii ad *ILB* 87 (Lat. Ve[ll]ius Blastus)

Βλέψος
Cimmerian Bosporos:
—gorgippia: (1) f. iii bc *CIRB* 1137 A I, 12 (s. *Ἡρακλείδης*); (2) ~ ib. l. 21 (*[Β]λέψος*: s. *Γοργίας*)

Βλίτων
Skythia:
—olbia-borysthenes: (1) iii-ii bc *SEG* xxx 958 (vase)

Βλόσυς
Thrace:
—abdera: (1) c. 450-425 bc May, *Abdera* pp. 138-9 nos. 184-5 (coin); Masson, *OGS* p. 429 (*Βλόσυος* (gen.))

Βλώστα
Thrace:
—kellai*: (1) iii ad *IGB* iii 1516 b, 21 (d. *Σάλας, Ζείλη*)

Βλωστι
Thrace:
—odessos: (1) i-ii ad ib. i² 188 (d. *Ζῆνις*); (2) ii ad ib. 185 bis (PM 1729) (*Βλωστε[ι]ν*: d. *Ξένανδρος*); (3) ~ *IGB* v 5067, 7 (d. *Ἀπολλώνιος, Ζουκαιβλωστι*); (4) m. ii ad ib. i² 177 ter; *Dacia* 21 (1977) p. 161 (date) (*Βλώστι[ν]*: d. *Ποτάμων*)

Βοδύλος
Macedonia (Mygdonia):
—kalindoia: (1) a. 98 ad *SEG* xlii 582, 43; cf. *Anthémonte–Kalindoia* 2 p. 234 (name) (s. *Καρβερένθης*)

Βόηθος
Macedonia: (1) m. ii bc *BGU* 1938 B, 12 (Tataki, *Macedonians* p. 478 no. 62); cf. La'da E1674 (*Βόηθος*)
Macedonia (Mygdonia):
—arethousa?: (2) f. i bc *EAD* xxx 185 (Tataki, *Macedonians* p. 69 no. 5) (or Syria Arethousa: s. *Σάμος*)
Macedonia (Pieria):
—pydna: (3) 250 ad *SEG* xlvi 800 A, 20 (*Αὐρ. Β.*)
Skythia:
—tyras: (4) 181 ad *IOSPE* i² 2, 22 (f. *Θεόδωρος*)
Thrace:
—ainos: (5) 194 bc *Milet* i (3) 54, 4 (f. *Δημήτριος*)

Βοθύλις
Cimmerian Bosporos:
—hermonassa: (1) f. i ad *CIRB* 1076 (*Βοθύλιος*—Index: s. *Ὠνίας*)

Βοΐδας
Cimmerian Bosporos:
—hermonassa: (1) i ad ib. 1075 (s. *Ἀπολλώνιος*)
Skythia:
—tanais: (2) 104 ad ib. 1259, 19 (s. *Ἀπολλώνιος*)

Βοΐδιον
Macedonia (Bottiaia):
—pella: (1) iv bc *SEG* xxxv 755 + xxxviii 650 (*Βοιδ[ίων]*—755, *Βοΐδ[ιον]*—650)
Skythia:
—olbia-borysthenes: (2) iv bc ib. xxx 958 (vase)

Βοΐσκος
MACEDONIA (BOTTIAIA):
—BEROIA: (1) 112 BC *IBer* 134, 42 (s. *Εὐκλῆς*)
TAURIS:
—CHERSONESOS: (2) iii BC *IOSPE* I^2 470 (s. *Νεομήνιος*); (3) ii AD ib. 390, 2 (f. *—ης*) ?= (*10*); (4) f. ii AD *KSIIMK* 15 (1947) p. 59, 6 (Solomonik, *NEPKh* 112 d); cf. *VDI* 1993 (4), p. 63 (s. *Ζῆθος*); (5) ~ Solomonik, *NEPKh* 111, 3; *SEG* XLVIII 999, 37 (s. *Ἡρόξενος*) ?= (*10*); (6) ~ Solomonik, *NEPKh* 111, 5 (s. *Χρηστίων*); (7) ~ ib. l. 10; *SEG* XLVIII 999, 38 ([*Βοΐσ*]*κος*—*SEG*: s. *Φιλόμουσος*); (8) c. 120-130 AD Solomonik, *NEPKh* 112, 19; cf. *VDI* 1993 (4), p. 63 (*Βοΐσ*[*κος*]); (9) 129 AD *IOSPE* I^2 359, 18 (f. *Χρηστίων*); (10) 129-130 AD ib. l. 28-9; 701, 3; *VDI* 1960 (3), pp. 154-5, 24 (f. *Δημοκράτης*, *Ἡρόξενος*) ?= (*3*) (*5*); (11) 130 AD ib. l. 29 (s. *Διοσκουρίδης*); (12) 154 AD *SEG* XLVI 928, 6 (*Βοΐσ*[*κος*])

Βοιωτός
MACEDONIA (ODOMANTIKE):
—SIRRHA: (1) i BC/i AD *IG* XII (8) 206, 8; cf. Robert, *OMS* 6 p. 604 n. 7 (Tataki, *Macedonians* p. 172 no. 1) (s. *Βριαρεύς*); (2) f. iii AD *SEG* XXX 590, 9 (f. *Αὐρ. Τόρκος*)
MACEDONIA?: (3) 312 BC *RE* (8) (Tataki, *Macedonians* p. 282 no. 39)
THRACE:
—MESAMBRIA: (4) iii/ii BC *IGB* I^2 322 bis (f. *Λάϊος*)

Βόκρος
MACEDONIA: (1) v BC *FGrH* 631 F 1 + Hoffmann, *Makedonen* p. 270 (Tataki, *Macedonians* p. 282 no. 40) (?s. *Ἀμύντας*, ?f. *Μελέαγρος*: fict.?)
MACEDONIA (MYGDONIA):
—THESSALONIKE: (2) c. 230 BC *IG* XI (4) 664, 13; 665, 14; 1053, 5, 15 = X (2) (1) 1028; XI (4) 1076 (Tataki, *Macedonians* p. 180 no. 18) (f. *Ἄδμητος*)

Βόλας
CIMMERIAN BOSPOROS:
—PANTIKAPAION: (1) f. iv BC *CIRB* 193, 2; cf. KW pl. 5 no. 104 (*Βό-*?, *Βōλᾶς*?: s. *Αὔασις*, *Ἰτίη*)

Βολλίων
TAURIS:
—CHERSONESOS: (1) m. iv BC Solomonik, *GAKh* 447 (vase) (*Βολλ*[*ίων*]?); (2) c. 230-215 BC Kats p. 91 no. 33 (amph.) (s. *Νικέας*) ?= (*3*); (3) c. 210-200 BC Anokhin p. 144 nos. 148; 151 (coins) ?= (*2*)

Βόλων
MACEDONIA (MYGDONIA):
—ARETHOUSA: (1) 360 BC *IG* IV (1)^2 94 b, 16 (Perlman, *City and Sanctuary* E.1 with p. 69 f. (date); Tataki, *Macedonians* p. 69 no. 6)
MACEDONIA?: (2) 330 BC *RE* Supplbd. 4 (2); Berve 218 (Tataki, *Macedonians* p. 283 no. 41) (Lat. Bolon)
SKYTHIA:
—TANAIS*: (3) ii-iii AD *Tanais* 1 p. 103 (amph.)

Βόνδις
THRACE:
—BOURDAPA: (1) hell. *SEG* XXXIX 660 = XLI 608. 2 = XLVII 1094. 2

Βόνζης
MACEDONIA (SINTIKE):
—PARTHIKOPOLIS: (1) ?ii AD *FGrH* 257 F 37, 48 (Tataki, *Macedonians* p. 147 no. 3) (s. *Τόνος*)

Βονιφάτιος
MACEDONIA (MYGDONIA):
—THESSALONIKE?: (1) v-vi AD *IG* X (2) (1) 338, 7 (Feissel, *RICM* 160) (*Βονο-*)
THRACE: (2) 413-432 AD *PLRE* II (3); *RE* (1)

Βονωλας
THRACE:
—PAUTALIA (TERRIT.): (1) ii-iii AD *IGB* IV 2110 (*Μᾶρκος ὁ καὶ Β.*: s. *Ἐπιγένης*)

Βορεΐδης
THRACE:
—BESSOI: (1) 561 AD *POxy* 1903, 9; 2046, [20], 48
—HADRIANOPOLIS: (2) v-vi AD Ebersolt, *Mission* p. 52 no. 9 (s. *Παῦλος*)

Βόρασπος
SKYTHIA:
—TANAIS: (1) 193 AD *CIRB* 1237, 16 (s. *Βάβος*) ?= (*Βαιόρασπος* (*1*))

Βορδίνος
MACEDONIA: (1) ?417-413 BC *IG* I^3 89, 72 (Tataki, *Macedonians* p. 283 no. 42); cf. Masson, *OGS* 2 p. 293

Βορέας
MACEDONIA (MYGDONIA):
—THESSALONIKE*: (1) f. iii AD *IG* X (2) (1) 187, 12 (*Γεμείνιος Ζώσιμος ὁ καὶ Β.*: freed.?)

Βορτᾶς
MACEDONIA (CHALKIDIKE):
—ANTHEMOUS: (1) f. i BC *SEG* XLII 566; cf. *Anthémonte–Kalindoia* 2 pp. 234-6 (name) (f. *Ἀρτιλώ*)

Βόρυς
MACEDONIA (MYGDONIA):
—CHALASTRA?: (1) vi/v BC *SEG* XLVI 724 (vase)

Βοσβᾶς
THRACE:
—BYZANTION: (1) c. 303 AD *Anal. Boll.* 31 (1912) p. 192

Βοσις
THRACE:
—SKEDABRIA: (1) 202 AD *IGB* III 1690 b, 19 (and Thrace Pizos: *Μουκάτραλις Β.*: s. *Βείθης*)
—SKEPTA: (2) 202 AD ib. 1690 c, 14 (and Thrace Pizos: f. *Μουκάτραλις*)

Βοσπορεύς
SCYTHIA MINOR:
—TOMIS: (1) ii-iii AD *ISM* II 21, 8 ([*Β*]*οσπορεύς*)

Βοσπόριος
THRACE:
—PERINTHOS-HERAKLEIA:
——(Kastaleis): (1) iii-ii BC *IPerinth* 61, 61

Βοσποριχη
CIMMERIAN BOSPOROS:
—PANTIKAPAION: (1) i AD *CIRB* 473 ([*Βο*]*σπορ*[*ίχ*]*η*?)

Βοσπόριχος
CIMMERIAN BOSPOROS:
—NYMPHAION: (1) v/iv BC ib. 916 (s. *Ἀργαῖος*)
—THEODOSIA: (2) v/iv BC *Arch. Class.* 25-6 (1973-4) p. 350 no. 18 (vase) (s. *Τίμωρις*)
SKYTHIA:
—OLBIA-BORYSTHENES: (3) iii BC *IOSPE* I^2 201 II, 10 (f. *Μῦς*)
—OLBIA-BORYSTHENES (TERRIT.): (4) f. v BC Dubois, *IGDOlbia* 52 (vase)
THRACE:
—BYZANTION: (5) iv BC *ICos* ED 40, 5 ([*Β*]*οσπόριχο*[*ς*]: s. *—ν*); (6) c. 340 BC D. xviii 90; (7) ii BC *Türk Tarih Kongresi XI* (6) p. 2704 with pl. 498. 11 (f. *Ἀδύτιον*); (8) ~ *IByz* 235 (f. *Ἡρόφαντος*)
—BYZANTION?: (9) ii BC *ISamothrace* 28 c, 15; Robert, *OMS* 6 pp. 605-6 (locn.) ([*Βο*]*σπόριχο*[*ς*]: f. *Κλέων*); (10) ~ *IByz* 376 (I f. *Βοσπόριχος* II); (11) ~ ib. (II s. *Βοσπόριχος* I, f. *Βοσπόριχος* III, *Βοσπόριχος* IV); (12) ~ ib. (III s. *Βοσπόριχος* II)
—MESAMBRIA: (13) iii/ii BC *IGB* I^2 330 ter (PM 1098) (s. *Ματρόδωρος*, f. *Πολυαίνετος*, *Ματρόδωρος*); (14) i BC *IGB* I^2 324 (s. *Ἀντίφιλος*); (15) ~ ib. (f. *Ἀθαναίων*)
—SALYMBRIA: (16) i BC-i AD Unp. (Sayar) (f. *Λαγόρας*)

Βόσπορος
THRACE:
—LYSIMACHEIA: (1) ?ii AD *CIL* III 14406 f; cf. Robert, *Hell.* 5 p. 52 (Lat. Pa[ul]us Antoniu[s] Bosp[o]rus)

Βόσπων
THRACE:
—BYZANTION: (1) s. iii BC Schönert-Geiss, *Byzantion* 1148-53 (coin); (2) ii BC *IByz* 154 (Firatlı–Robert p. 105 no. 165) (s. *Ἀπολλώνιος*)

Βοστάγων
CIMMERIAN BOSPOROS:
—PANTIKAPAION: (1) i/ii AD *CIRB* 638; cf. KW pl. 53 no. 724; Zgusta, *PNS* 282

Βοστακίων
CIMMERIAN BOSPOROS:
—NYMPHAION: (1) f. iii BC *SEG* XXXIX 701. 3

Βόστακος
CIMMERIAN BOSPOROS:
—NYMPHAION: (1) i AD *CIRB* 929 (s. *Εὖνος*); (2) s. ii AD ib. 934 (*Βό*(*σ*)*τακος*)

Βοστάκων
CIMMERIAN BOSPOROS:
—PANTIKAPAION: (1) i/ii AD ib. 645 (f. *Δαμοφίλα*, *Κάχιον*, *Εἰκόνιν*)

Βοστᾶς
THRACE:
—BYZANTION: (1) hell. *BCH* 102 (1978) p. 530 (s. *Διοκλῆς*)
—BYZANTION (TERRIT.): (2) ?ii AD Unp. (Sayar) (s. *Διοκλῆς*)
—ZONE: (3) m. v BC *SEG* XXVII 346 a (*IThrakAig* E404) (f. *Ἀδάμας*); (4) ?iv BC *PAE* 1984, p. 29 (sherd) (*Βοστᾶ* (gen.)); (5) f. iv BC *IThrakAig* E412 ([*Β*]*οστᾶς*: f. *Ἀπολλόδωρος*); (6) ~ *SEG* XXXII 675 (*IThrakAig* E411) (f. *Ἄδα*)

Βοτῆς
CIMMERIAN BOSPOROS:
—PANTIKAPAION: (1) i AD *CIRB* 371; cf. Robert, *Noms indigènes* p. 418 n. 4 (*Βότει* (voc.): f. *Φιλόμηλος*)

Βότρης
MACEDONIA: (1) ?417-413 BC *IG* I^3 89, 77 (Tataki, *Macedonians* p. 283 no. 43) (*-τρε̄ς*)

Βότριχος
MACEDONIA (BOTTIAIA):
—BEROIA: (1) 223 BC *IBer* 4, 17 (s. *Νίκαιχμος*)

Βότρυς
MACEDONIA (BOTTIAIA):
—BEROIA: (1) ii-iii AD ib. 357 (Tataki 334) (s. *Κλεαγόρα*)
MACEDONIA (MYGDONIA):
—THESSALONIKE: (2) ii AD *IG* X (2) (1) 401
THRACE:
—BYZANTION: (3) ii-i BC *IByz* 82 (Firatlı–Robert p. 51 no. 25) (f. *Ἐπίκτησις*)
—MESAMBRIA: (4) iii BC *IGB* I^2 337 bis (PM 2262) (s. *Πυθόδωρος*, f. *Πυθόδωρος*)

Βόττακος
MACEDONIA (LOWER PAIONIA):
—EUROPOS (NR.): (1) iv BC *SEG* XLV 762; cf. *BE* 1996, no. 261 (locn.)

Βοττύλος
SKYTHIA:
—OLBIA-BORYSTHENES: (1) iii BC *IOSPE* I² 201 II, 20; Zgusta, *PNS* 935 (f. *Διονύσιος*)

Βότυς
MACEDONIA (PELAGONIA):
—MARIOVO (MOD.): (1) imp. *IG* X (2) (2) 167 (f. *Ταρουσίνας*)

Βούβαλος
MACEDONIA (CHALKIDIKE):
—POTIDAIA-KASSANDREIA: (1) ?304 BC ib. V (2) 550, 29 (Tataki, *Macedonians* p. 87 no. 20)
THRACE:
—PHILIPPOPOLIS-TRIMONTIUM: (2) c. 183 AD *CIL* VI 37184, 10 (Lat. M. Aurel. Bubalus)

Βούβαρος
MACEDONIA: (1) 267 BC *SEG* XXVII 1114, 16 a; cf. *BE* 1977, no. 566 (Tataki, *Macedonians* p. 283 no. 46); cf. La'da E1593 (*Βουβάρου* (gen.): f. *Πτολεμαῖος*)

Βουβᾶς
THRACE:
—ODESSOS: (1) 221 AD *IGB* I² 47 bis c, 12 (*Αὐρ. Β.*: s. *Ἀλέξανδρος*)

Βούδεις
SKYTHIA:
—OLBIA-BORYSTHENES: (1) i/ii AD *IOlbia* 90, 13 (f. *Διονυσόδωρος*)

Βουζάη
MACEDONIA (SINTIKE)?: (1) 144 AD *IGB* IV 2331, 6 (m. *Ἀρτεμίδωρος, Τηρέτιθος*)

Βούζης
THRACE: (1) 528-556 AD *PLRE* III (-); *RE* (1)

Βουθειθερίς
THRACE:
—ODESSOS: (1) ii-iii AD *IGB* V 5074. 5a (*Ἡλιοδώρα Β.*)

Βουκάρτας
MACEDONIA (BOTTIAIA):
—TYRISSA? (ASVESTARI (MOD.)): (1) f. ii BC *SEG* XLVII 999, 2, 4 (?s. *Φίλαγρος*)

Βουκέντιος
THRACE:
—BESSOI: (1) f. vi AD Procop. vi 26. 3, 15 f

Βούκκαλος
MACEDONIA (PAIONIA):
—KAVADARCI (MOD.): (1) ii AD *Sp.* 71 (1931) p. 237 no. 632 = 75 (1933) p. 41 no. 136 (s. *Γ. Κορνηλιανὸς Οὐάλης ὁ καὶ Σωσίπατρος*)

Βούκκης
SCYTHIA MINOR:
—KALLATIS: (1) 241-244 AD *ISM* III 74 A, 29; cf. *SEG* XLVII 1129 (*Βούκκη* (gen.): f. *Ἀθαναίων*)

Βουκόλις
MACEDONIA (EDONIS):
—PHILIPPOI: (1) s. iii AD ib. L 618. 1 (mosaic)

Βουκούθης
MACEDONIA (EDONIS):
—AMPHIPOLIS: (1) 158 or 274 AD ib. XV 415, 3

Βούκουλος
MACEDONIA (LYNKESTIS):
—SKOPOS (MOD.): (1) ii-iii AD *EAM* 158 (*[Β]ούκουλος*)

Βοῦκρος
MACEDONIA: (1) ?417-413 BC *IG* I³ 89, 68 (Tataki, *Macedonians* p. 283 no. 47) (*Βοῦκ[ρο]ς*?, *Βοῦκ[ρι]ς*?)

Βούλα
MACEDONIA (ODOMANTIKE):
—SIRRHA: (1) ?i AD *ILGR* 228; Detschev p. 79 (name) (Lat. Bula)

Βουλαγόρης
THRACE:
—PERINTHOS-HERAKLEIA?: (1) iv BC Hp., *Epid.* iv 35 (*Βουλαγόρεω* (gen.))

Βούλαρχος
MACEDONIA (CHALKIDIKE):
—STOLOS?: (1) ?350 BC *SEG* XXXVIII 671, 9 (s. *Πεδίων*)

Βουλάστης
CIMMERIAN BOSPOROS:
—MYRMEKION: (1) iv BC *CIRB* 872; cf. KW p. 2 no. 5 (*[Β]ουλάστης*: s. *Διονυσόδωρος*)

Βούλιος
CIMMERIAN BOSPOROS:
—PANTIKAPAION: (1) iv BC *CIRB* 205 (f. *Μητρόβιος*)

Βοῦλις
SKYTHIA:
—TYRAS?: (1) hell.? *SEG* III 580 (tile) (*Βούλιος* (gen.))
THRACE:
—SALYMBRIA: (2) i BC-i AD *Archives Stamoulis* d. 35 (Loukopoulou, *Thrace Propontique* p. 244) (s. *Ἡρότιμος*)

Βουλόνα
MACEDONIA (PIERIA):
—PYDNA: (1) iv BC *GRBS* 43 (2002-3) p. 111 no. 2, 8

Βούπλαγος
MACEDONIA: (1) iii BC *IG* IX (2) 174 (Tataki, *Macedonians* p. 284 no. 50) (*[Β]ούπλα(γ)ος*: s. *Μεννείας*)

Βουράδις
THRACE:
—HADRIANOPOLIS: (1) iv-v AD *SEG* VIII 45, 1, 3, 7 (*Βουραειδεις*—l.1, *Βοραειδεις*—l.7: s. *Ζουράζιος*)

Βουργειλος
THRACE:
—BAZOPARA: (1) 202 AD *IGB* III 1690 c, 69 (and Thrace Pizos: s. *Βίθυς*)

Βουρείλας
MACEDONIA (ODOMANTIKE):
—SIRRHA: (1) 155 AD Dimitsas 821, 8 (Kaphtantzis 1) (f. *Διοσκουρίδης*); (2) ~ Dimitsas 821, 11 (Kaphtantzis 1) (f. *Ἰουλιανός*)

Βοῦρις
MACEDONIA (MYGDONIA):
—KALINDOIA: (1) a. 98 AD *SEG* XLII 582, 37; cf. *Anthémonte–Kalindoia* 2 pp. 236-7 (name) (I f. *Βοῦρις* II); (2) ~ *SEG* XLII 582, 37 (II s. *Βοῦρις* I)

Βουτᾶς
MACEDONIA (LOWER PAIONIA):
—EUROPOS: (1) c. 240-220 BC *IG* VII 356, 2 (*IOrop* 98; Tataki, *Macedonians* p. 108 no. 5) (f. *Ἀγάθων*)
THRACE:
—MARONEIA: (2) c. 365-336 BC Schönert-Geiss, *Maroneia* 502-3 (coin); Masson, *OGS* p. 437 (*Βουτᾶ* (gen.))

Βουτίς
SCYTHIA MINOR:
—TOMIS: (1) ii AD *ISM* II 125, 12 (*Βουτείν* (acc.): d. *Ἡρόξενος*)

Βουτουνᾶς
SKYTHIA:
—OLBIA-BORYSTHENES: (1) ii-iii AD *IOSPE* I² 136, 12; Zgusta, *PNS* 624 (*Βουτουνᾶτος* (gen.): f. *Σιρδούχανσος*)

Βόχορος
CIMMERIAN BOSPOROS:
—GORGIPPIA: (1) ii/iii AD *VDI* 1970 (4), p. 149, 7 (f. *Ἀγαθοῦς*)

Βοών
THRACE:
—ODESSOS: (1) ii AD *IGB* I² 178 bis (d. *Ζώπυρος*, ?m. *Ἀγαθήνωρ, Ζουδιεγιπτους*)

Βραβεύς
THRACE:
—MARONEIA: (1) c. 400-378 BC Schönert-Geiss, *Maroneia* 161 (coin); Masson, *OGS* p. 438 (*Βραβέως* (gen.)—Masson)

Βραγάντις
MACEDONIA (BOTTIAIA):
—EDESSA: (1) iii AD Feissel, *RICM* 11 (Tataki, *Edessa* 69) (s. *Ἀπολλόδωρος, Εὐσέβιον*)

Βράδακος
CIMMERIAN BOSPOROS:
—PANTIKAPAION: (1) i BC/i AD *CIRB* 324; cf. KW pl. 13 no. 186; (2) 82 AD *CIRB* 76, 9 (*SEG* XVIII 310) (f. *Μήνιος*)

Βραίαδος
SKYTHIA:
—OLBIA-BORYSTHENES: (1) ii AD *IOSPE* I² 100, 7; Zgusta, *PNS* 623 (f. *Χάνωσος*)

Βράκη
THRACE:
—ODESSOS: (1) iii AD *IGB* I² 141 bis (*Βράκη*: d. *Γύλων*)

Βράματις?
MACEDONIA (ODOMANTIKE):
—DRABESKOS?: (1) iv BC Kaphtantzis 568, 12 (Pilhofer 575) (*Βραμάτιδος* (gen.): f. *Δούλης*)

Βράμης
MACEDONIA (EDONIS):
—AMPHIPOLIS: (1) ii-iii AD *Thrakika* 13 (1940) p. 28 *Φ*; *Thracia* 2 p. 277 (*Βράμη* (gen.?))

Βράσιος
MACEDONIA (EDONIS):
—AMPHIPOLIS: (1) vi AD *SEG* XLVIII 730

Βράσις
MACEDONIA (ODOMANTIKE):
—SIRRHA: (1) f. iii AD ib. XXX 590, 32 (*Αὐρ. Β.*: s. *Δίζας*); (2) ~ ib. l. 33 (*Αὐρ. Β.*)

Βρασίτραλις
THRACE:
—BEROE-AUGUSTA TRAIANA:
——Karasoura: (1) ii-iii AD *IGB* III 1631, 4 (s. *Μουκάτραλις*)
—KOURPISOS: (2) 202 AD ib. 1690 c, 36 (and Thrace Pizos: -*σή*-: s. *Μουκάτραλις*)

Βράσος
MACEDONIA (ODOMANTIKE):
—SIRRHA: (1) f. iii AD *SEG* XXX 590, 8 (f. *Αὐρ. Ἰούλιος*); (2) ~ ib. l. 15 (f. *Αὐρ. Διονύσιος*)
THRACE:
—NICOPOLIS AD NESTUM: (3) ii-iii AD *IGB* IV 2347 (f. *Πύρρος*)

Βραυρώ
MACEDONIA (EDONIS):
—EDONOI: (1) 424 BC Th. iv 107 (queen)

Βρεῦκος
MACEDONIA (DERRIOPOS):
—STUBERRA: (1) c. 41-48 AD *IG* x (2) (2) 323, 19 (s. Ἐπίκαδος)

Βριαρεύς
MACEDONIA (ODOMANTIKE):
—SIRRHA: (1) i BC/i AD ib. XII (8) 206, 8; cf. Robert, *OMS* 6 p. 604 n. 7 (Tataki, *Macedonians* p. 172 no. 2) (Βριάρεως (gen.): f. Βοιωτός)

Βρίζενις
THRACE:
—BAZOPARA: (1) 202 AD *IGB* III 1690 d, 33 (and Thrace Pizos: Βρεί-: f. Μουκάτραλις); (2) ~ ib. 1690 c, 52 (and Thrace Pizos: Βρεί-: f. Μουκάτραλις)
—BEROE-AUGUSTA TRAIANA: (3) ii-iii AD ib. 1599 (Βρεί-: f. Αὐλούζενις)
—BOURDAPA: (4) ii-iii AD ib. 1366 (Βρίζεν[ι]ς)
—HADRIANOPOLIS (TERRIT.): (5) ii-iii AD ib. 1807, 7 (Βρεί-: f. Σεβαστιανός); (6) ~ ib. 1814 (Βριζέν[ε]ος (gen.): f. Αὐλούτραλις)
—KELLAI*: (7) iii AD ib. 1516 b, 18 (Βρεί-: s. Σάλας, Ζείλη)
—KOURPISOS: (8) 202 AD ib. 1690 c, 37 (and Thrace Pizos: Βρεί-: f. Μουκάτραλις)
—KRASALOPARA: (9) 202 AD ib. 1690 b, 48 (and Thrace Pizos: Βρεί-: f. Αὐλούζενις); (10) ~ ib. l. 57 (and Thrace Pizos: Βρεί-: s. Βίθυς); (11) ~ ib. l. 59-60 (and Thrace Pizos: Βρεί-: f. Σεθείλας, Διασκούπορις)
—PHILIPPOPOLIS-TRIMONTIUM: (12) iii AD ib. 976 (s. Ζιακάτραλις)

Βριζῖνος
MACEDONIA (BOTTIAIA):
—BEROIA: (1) 225 AD *ILeukopetra* 71, 13 (Ἰουλ. Δημήτριος ὁ Βριζεῖνος)

Βριθαγόρη
THRACE:
—APOLLONIA-SOZOPOLIS: (1) v/iv BC *IGB* I² 413 (d. Πυθαγόρης)

Βρικέσης
THRACE:
—HADRIANOPOLIS (TERRIT.): (1) iii AD ib. III 1815

Βρῖλος
THRACE:
—BOURDAPA: (1) ii-iii AD ib. 1343 (f. Σεύθης)
—PHILIPPOPOLIS-TRIMONTIUM (TERRIT.): (2) ii-iii AD ib. 1194 (Βρεῖ-: f. Κάσιος)

Βρινκαζεις
THRACE:
—ANCHIALOS (TERRIT.): (1) ii/iii AD ib. 1846, 2 (s. Κουίζερις, Δεντουσυκος)
—BAZOPARA: (2) 202 AD ib. 1690 c, 68 (and Thrace Pizos: s. Δόλης)
—KRASALOPARA: (3) 202 AD ib. 1690 b, 55 (and Thrace Pizos: s. Ἐπταίκενθος); (4) ~ ib. l. 56 (and Thrace Pizos: s. Αὐλούζενις)

Βρινκάζενις
THRACE:
—PHILIPPOPOLIS-TRIMONTIUM: (1) iii AD ib. 917, 6 (Βρινκαζ(έ)νεος (gen.): f. Δίζας ὁ καὶ Ἑρμόδωρος)

Βρινκάζερις
THRACE:
—BAZOPARA: (1) 202 AD ib. 1690 d, 28 (and Thrace Pizos: f. Μουκάτραλις); (2) ~ ib. l. 51 (and Thrace Pizos: Βριγκάζερις: f. Τάρσας); (3) ~ ib. 1690 e, 94 (and Thrace Pizos: f. Δριγγίστας); (4) ~ ib. 1690 c, 47 (and Thrace Pizos: Βρινκάζερις: f. Δριγγίστας Ἑρμογένης); (5) ~ ib. l. 67 (and Thrace Pizos: f. Βίθυς)
—ERGISSENOI: (6) ii AD ib. 1593, 1, 5 (f. Διvίκενθος, Τήρης)
—GELOUPARA: (7) 202 AD ib. 1690 c, 29 (and Thrace Pizos: f. Διασκούπορις)
—KRASALOPARA: (8) 202 AD ib. 1690 b, 70 (and Thrace Pizos: f. Σοῦρις)

Βρινκαζις
THRACE:
—BEROE-AUGUSTA TRAIANA:
——Karasoura: (1) ii-iii AD ib. 1631, 7 (s. Μουκάτραλις)
—BOURDAPA: (2) ii-iii AD ib. 1355 (Βρινκοζι(ς): s Τήραλος)

Βρίνκαινος
THRACE:
—PHILIPPOPOLIS-TRIMONTIUM: (1) ii-iii AD ib. 969

Βρισαΐς
SKYTHIA:
—OLBIA-BORYSTHENES: (1) imp. *IOSPE* I² 237, 9 (Lat. Olbia Brisais)
THRACE:
—BYZANTION?: (2) s. i BC PM 433 (Κορνηλία Βρησαεῖς: d. Λεύκιος)

Βρισηΐς
MACEDONIA (MYGDONIA):
—THESSALONIKE: (1) s. iii AD *IG* x (2) (1) 566, 1 (Ἰουλ. Βρησεΐς)

Βρισούλας
MACEDONIA (SINTIKE)?:
—PETRADENOI: (1) ii AD *IGB* IV 2251; cf. v 5879

Βρίσων
MACEDONIA: (1) 331 BC *RE* (1); Berve 223 (Tataki, *Macedonians* p. 284 no. 53)

Βριταγόρης
THRACE:
—APOLLONIA-SOZOPOLIS: (1) iv BC *BMNBurgas* 4 (2002) p. 123 no. 15 ((Κ)ριταγόρης?: f. Ἡγεάνασσα)

Βρομερός
MACEDONIA (LYNKESTIS): (1) c. 423 BC Th. iv 83. 1 (Tataki, *Macedonians* p. 202 no. 9); cf. Masson, *OGS* 2 p. 323 (f. Ἀρραβαῖος)
THRACE: (2) 231 or 206 BC *CPR* XVIII 5, 91; cf. La'da E828 (I f. Βρομερός II); (3) ~ *CPR* XVIII 5, 91, 95, 100, 103 (La'da E828) (II s. Βρομερός I: t.e.)

Βρόμις
CIMMERIAN BOSPOROS:
—NYMPHAION: (1) f. iii BC *SEG* XLV 997. 10

Βρόταχος
CIMMERIAN BOSPOROS:
—PANTIKAPAION: (1) s. iv BC *CIRB* 232 (f. Φορμίων)

Βρούθενις
THRACE:
—PHILIPPOPOLIS-TRIMONTIUM (TERRIT.): (1) iii AD *IGB* III 1430 (s. Σάτοκος)

Βρουτία
THRACE:
—TYRODIZA-TIRISTASIS: (1) imp. Dumont-Homolle 89d (d. Βάσσος)

Βρύζος
MACEDONIA (MYGDONIA):
—THESSALONIKE: (1) i-ii AD *IG* x (2) (1) 243 II, 9 (f. Ἀπολλώνιος)
THRACE:
—PHILIPPOPOLIS-TRIMONTIUM (TERRIT.): (2) iii AD *IGB* III 1430 (s. Μουκάτραλις)

Βρυκατος?
MACEDONIA (LYNKESTIS): (1) m. iv BC *IG* x (2) (2) 2 (n. pr.?)

Βρυκκαῖος
MACEDONIA (BOTTIAIA):
—TYRISSA? (ASVESTARI (MOD.)): (1) f. ii BC *SEG* XLVII 999, 9

Βρυλουζίης
THRACE:
—SERDICA (NR.): (1) imp. *IGB* v 5687 (Βρυλουζίης)

Βύβλος
MACEDONIA (MYGDONIA):
—THESSALONIKE: (1) s. i AD *IG* x (2) (1) 68, 38; 69, 25 (Λ. Μεινάτιος Β.)

Βυζαντία
MACEDONIA (BOTTIAIA):
—BEROIA: (1) ii-iii AD *IBer* 307 (Tataki 694) (Κλ. Β.)
THRACE: (2) vi AD Beševliev 246, 2-3 (Lat. Bizantia: d. Alziola)

Βύζης
THRACE: (1) c. 149 BC *RE* Supplbd. 1 (1a) (king?)
—SKEDABRIA: (2) 202 AD *IGB* III 1690 b, 13 (and Thrace Pizos: [Β]ύζης: s. Μουκάτραλις)
—STRATOPARA: (3) 202 AD ib. l. 40 (and Thrace Pizos: f. Μουκάτραλις); (4) ~ ib. l. 45 (and Thrace Pizos: f. Σιδμοῦς)

Βύζος
MACEDONIA (EDONIS):
—PROUPTOSOURENOI: (1) ii-iii AD Dimitsas 1051, 1 = 1082 (Pilhofer 456); cf. *BCH* 47 (1923) p. 75 no. 34 (f. Τάρσας); (2) ~ Dimitsas 1051, 4 = 1082 (Pilhofer 456); cf. *BCH* 47 (1923) p. 75 no. 34 (s. Τάρσας, Μελγίς)

Βύθυς
MACEDONIA (EDONIS):
—AMPHIPOLIS: (1) iii BC *SEG* XXIV 591 (Β(ί)θυς?)

Βυλλίς
THRACE:
—MADYTOS: (1) imp. *Sp.* 71 (1931) p. 243 no. 649 (Lat. Venusta Byllis)

Βυργῖνος
MACEDONIA: (1) ?417-413 BC *IG* I³ 89, 61 (Tataki, *Macedonians* p. 284 no. 55) (s. Κράστων)

Βυρδίων
MACEDONIA (PAIONIA):
—KAVADARCI (MOD.): (1) ii AD *Sp.* 71 (1931) p. 74 no. 174, 1 (s. Σιτᾶς)

Βύριχος
THRACE:
—MESAMBRIA: (1) iii BC *IGB* I² 308 quinquies, 3; cf. v 5090; (2) ii BC ib. I² 329, 7 (Β.: ?f. Ἀπολλώνιος)
—MESAMBRIA?: (3) hell. ib. v 5096 (s. Αἰσχίνας, f. Μᾶτρις)

Βύσειλος
MACEDONIA (EDONIS):
—AMPHIPOLIS: (1) ii-iii AD *SEG* XV 416, 1 (Βυσείλου (gen.): f. Ζιπύρων)

Βύσκος
TAURIS:
—CHERSONESOS: (1) f. iv AD Const. Porph., *De admin. imp.* 53, 168 (s. Σουπόλιχος)

Βύτιος
MACEDONIA (ODOMANTIKE):
—SIRRHA: (1) ii-iii AD *SEG* XXX 605 (f. *Μαντώ*)

Βύττακος
MACEDONIA: (1) 217 BC Plb. V 79. 3; *OGIS* 254; Grainger, *SPG* p. 85 (f. *Δημοκράτης*)

Βῶνος
THRACE:
—ODESSOS: (1) vi AD Beševliev 109, 2 (s. *Πέτρος*)

Βώρακος
CIMMERIAN BOSPOROS:
—GORGIPPIA: (1) ii/iii AD *CIRB* 1179, 41; Zgusta, *PNS* 88 (f. *Μηνόδωρος*)

Βώρνων
SKYTHIA:
—OLBIA-BORYSTHENES: (1) ii AD *IOSPE* I² 105, 5; Zgusta, *PNS* 89 (s. *Ῥαδαμψῶν*)

Βωροβάρακος
SKYTHIA:
—TANAIS: (1) 244 AD *CIRB* 1287, 31 (f. *Σίμικος*)

Βωρόψαζος
SKYTHIA:
—OLBIA-BORYSTHENES: (1) ii AD *IOSPE* I² 101, 9; Zgusta, *PNS* 90 (f. *Κάρζεις*)

Βῶσις
THRACE: (1) 46-54 AD *SEG* XVI 415 III, 37 (*IThrakAig* E84) (*Βώσεος* (gen.): f. *Δορζίνθης*)

Βωσκείλας
THRACE:
—PHILIPPOPOLIS-TRIMONTIUM: (1) ii AD *IGB* III 978 (I f. *Βωσκείλας* II); (2) ~ ib. (II s. *Βωσκείλας* I)

Βωτῆνις?
MACEDONIA: (1) iii AD *SEG* XLVII 1006 (*Βωτήνι* (dat.), *Βωτην(η)ι*—ed. pr.)

Βωτιανή
MACEDONIA (MYGDONIA):
—THESSALONIKE: (1) 246 AD *IG* X (2) (1) 162, 16; 197, 9 (*Ἰουν. Β.*: m. *Μάρκιος Διοσκουρίδης, Μάρκιος Ἀθηναγόρας, Μαρκία Ἰουν. Παῦλα*)

Γ

Γαγανος?
CIMMERIAN BOSPOROS:
—GORGIPPIA: (1) 173-210 AD *CIRB* 1134, 17 (*Γάγανο̣[ς]*)
—TYRITAKE: (2) i/ii AD ib. 907 (*[Π]αγανος* (gen.), *Παγαν?* (nom.)—ed., *[Γ]άγανος?*: f. *Σόαιστος, Μασταρίων, Νικηφόρος*)

Γαγγαῖος
SKYTHIA:
—OLBIA-BORYSTHENES: (1) ?ii AD *IOSPE* I² 99, 7; Zgusta, *PNS* 774 (f. *Σαμβίων*)

Γάγιος
THRACE:
—APOLLONIA-SOZOPOLIS: (1) iv BC *BMNBurgas* 4 (2002) p. 124 no. 18 (*ΓΑΓΙΩ* (gen.)—ed., *Γαγίης?*: f. *Δᾶος*)

Γάδας
CIMMERIAN BOSPOROS:
—PANTIKAPAION: (1) f. i AD *CIRB* 372; cf. KW pl. 29 no. 412; Zgusta, *PNS* 91

Γάδεις
CIMMERIAN BOSPOROS:
—GORGIPPIA: (1) 59 AD *CIRB* 1124, 4 (Levinskaya pp. 240-1 no. 8) (f. *—ειμος*)
SKYTHIA:
—OLBIA-BORYSTHENES: (2) i/ii AD *IOlbia* 88, 5 (*Γάδει* (gen.): f. *Πολύδωρος*)

Γαδίκιος
CIMMERIAN BOSPOROS:
—GORGIPPIA: (1) i AD *CIRB* 1196; Zgusta, *PNS* 92 (*-κει-*: f. *Παντακλῆς*); (2) ii AD *CIRB* 1140, 12 (*Γαδίκι[ος]*); (3) ~ ib. l. 20 (f. *Διόφαντος*); (4) ~ ib. 1151, 9 (*Γαδίκι[ος]*); (5) ~ ib. 1154, 5 (*Γαδί[κιος]*); (6) ii-iii AD *NE* 9 (1971) p. 9 no. 6 A, 13; (7) ~ ib. l. 14 (*Γαδί[κιος]*: f. *Σαμβατίων*); (8) m. ii AD *Eirene* 7 (1968) p. 67, 24; (9) s. ii AD *CIRB* 1145, 9 (s. *Ἀθην—*) ?= (*12*); (10) ~ ib. 1148, 5 (*Γαδίκ̣[ιος]*); (11) ~ ib. 1165, 2 (*Γ̣αδίκιος*—Vinogradov); (12) 168 AD ib. 1144, 1 (s. *Ἀ—*) ?= (*9*); (13) 173-210 AD ib. 1135, 17

Γάδις
TAURIS:
—CHERSONESOS: (1) imp. *SEG* XXXVII 659 (lead) (*Γάδιτος* (gen.))

Γαειν
THRACE:
—ODESSOS: (1) f. iii AD *IGB* V 5070, 5 (*Αὐρ. Γ̣α̣ειν?, Ζ̣α̣ειν?*—ed.: d. *Μευαος*)

Γάζα
CIMMERIAN BOSPOROS:
—PANTIKAPAION?: (1) f. i BC *SEG* XXVII 436, [1], 11 + L 709; cf. *IKAM* p. 25 (*[Γά]ζα*—l. 1, *Γαζα* (n. pr.?)—l. 11)

Γαζούριος
TAURIS:
—CHERSONESOS: (1) imp. *IOSPE* I² 412; Zgusta, *PNS* 284 (*[Γα]ζούριος?*); (2) i AD *SEG* XLVI 927, 3 (s. *Ν—*); (3) i-ii AD *IOSPE* I² 471 (s. *Μητρόδωρος*); (4) f. ii AD *SEG* XXXV 859; *KSIIMK* 15 (1947) p. 59, 7 (Solomonik, *NEPKh* 112 d); cf. *VDI* 1993 (4), p. 63 (s. *Μητρόδωρος*)

Γαῖα
MACEDONIA (PAIONIA):
—ARGOS (NR.): (1) ii-iii AD *Sp.* 71 (1931) p. 38 no. 83, 5-6 (*Γ]α̣ί̣[α]*: d. *Γάϊος, Ἀμμία*)
—BYLAZORA: (2) ii-iii AD ib. 75 (1933) p. 17 no. 31, 1 (m. *Ἐπιγόνη*)
—KAVADARCI (MOD.): (3) ii AD ib. 71 (1931) p. 74 no. 174, 1 (d. *Τίτος*); (4) ii-iii AD *Minalo* 2 (1911) pp. 54 f. (m. *Διονύσιος*); (5) ii/iii AD Unp. (Papazoglu archive) (m. *Λούκιος*); (6) ~ Unp. (Kavadarci Mus.) inv. 10/II (*Ὀβουλκία Γ.*)
—NEAPOLIS? (IZVOR (MOD.): (7) ii-iii AD *Sp.* 98 (1941-8) p. 28 no. 68 (m. *Ποσειδώνιος, Ἀμμία*)
—NEGOTINO (MOD.): (8) imp. ib. p. 58 no. 118; (9) ii-iii AD ib. p. 56 no. 114, 8 (*Αὐρ. Γ.*)
THRACE:
—MEZDRA (MOD.): (10) iii AD *IGB* II 493 (d. *Οὐάλης*)

Γαϊανή
MACEDONIA (MYGDONIA):
—THESSALONIKE: (1) ii-iii AD *IG* X (2) (1) 516; *Ancient Macedonia* 2 pp. 328-30 (d. *Τιτινία Τριβούλα*); (2) iii AD *IG* X (2) (1) 597, 1 (*Γαϊ̣α̣ν̣ή*); (3) m. iii AD ib. 204, 18 (*Αὐρ. Γ.*: m. *Γ. Ἰουλ. Ἀρτεμιδώρα*)
MACEDONIA (PAIONIA):
—KAVADARCI (MOD.): (4) ii-iii AD *Sp.* 71 (1931) p. 71 no. 163
—STOBOI (AREA): (5) ii-iii AD Unp. (Stobi) (threpte)

MACEDONIA (PELAGONIA): (6) iii AD *IG* X (2) (2) 240 (*Σεπτιμία Γ.*); (7) ~ ib. 273 (*Αὐρ. Γ.*: d. *Αὐρ. Γαϊανός, Αὐρ. Ἰουλιανή*)
MACEDONIA (PIERIA):
—DION?: (8) f. ii AD Spiliopoulou-Donderer, *KGN* p. 202 no. D19 (*Γαϊαν(ή)?*: d. *Σεμπρωνία Ἠλιόνη*)
THRACE:
—PHILIPPOPOLIS-TRIMONTIUM?: (9) ?ii AD *IGB* III 1018, 3

Γαϊανός
MACEDONIA (BOTTIAIA):
—BEROIA: (1) 177 AD *IBer* 135 B, 30 (*Ἀ̣γ̣χαριηνός Γ.*); (2) 181 AD ib. 82, 6 (s. *Τ. Ἰουουέντιος Γάϊος*)
—PELLA: (3) ii AD *SEG* XLVII 926; XLVIII 827 (*Λ. Καλπούρνιος Γ.*)
MACEDONIA (DERRIOPOS): (4) ii-iii AD *IG* X (2) (2) 317 (s. *Διονύσιος*)
MACEDONIA (MYGDONIA):
—THESSALONIKE: (5) f. iii AD ib. X (2) (1) 182, 10 (*Ἰούλ. Γ.*: s. *Ἰούλ. Κάστωρ, Αἰλ. Γεμινία Ὀλυμπιάς*)
MACEDONIA (PAIONIA):
—BYLAZORA: (6) ii-iii AD *Sp.* 71 (1931) p. 40 no. 89 = 71 (1931) p. 153 no. 384 (*Αὐρ. Γάϊ(α)ος*: f. *Διοσκουρίδης*)
—KAVADARCI (MOD.): (7) ii AD Unp. (Kavadarci Mus.) inv. 65/II (*Π. Αἴλιος Γ.*); (8) ii-iii AD *Sp.* 71 (1931) p. 61 no. 132 (*[Γ]αϊανός*); (9) 219 AD ib. 98 (1941-8) p. 55 no. 110 (*Λ. Μούστιος Γ.*: f. *Λ. Μ. Οὐιταλός*); (10) 325 AD *SEG* XLIV 561 (*Γρανώνιος Γ.*: s. *Οὐάλης*)
—STOBOI (AREA): (11) ii-iii AD Unp. (Stobi) (*Μάνιος Γαϊανός*: s. *Κομεινία Ἀρίστη, Μάνιος Γάϊος*)
MACEDONIA (PELAGONIA): (12) iii AD *IG* X (2) (2) 243 (*-ει-*: s. *Αὐρ. Ἰούλιος*); (13) ~ ib. 249 (s. *Αὐρ. Μαρκιανός, Αἰλ. Βικτωρίνη*); (14) ~ ib. 273 (*Αὐρ. Γ.*: f. *Αὐρ. Νικόστρατος, Αὐρ. Φίλιππος, Αὐρ. Γαϊανή*)
—MOJNO (MOD.): (15) 253-259 AD ib. 173 (sculptor)
THRACE:
—PAUTALIA (TERRIT.): (16) ii-iii AD *IGB* IV 2137 (s. *Γάϊος*)
—PHILIPPOPOLIS-TRIMONTIUM: (17) ii AD ib. V 5411 (s. *Γάϊος*)

Γαιδρῆς
MACEDONIA (EDONIS):
—AMPHIPOLIS: **(1)** ii-iii AD *SEG* XV 416, 2 (*Γαιδρέους* (gen.): f. *Δαντώ*)

Γάϊος
CIMMERIAN BOSPOROS:
—ACHILLEION (NR.): **(1)** i/ii AD ib. XLV 979
—GORGIPPIA: **(2)** m. ii AD *Eirene* 7 (1968) p. 67, 19 (s. *Φαρ—*); **(3)** 173-210 AD *CIRB* 1134 E, 8 (f. *Ἀθηνόδωρος*)
—HERMONASSA: **(4)** iii AD ib. 1090
—PANTIKAPAION: **(5)** imp. ib. 112, 4; **(6)** i AD ib. 373 (s. *Ἄδας*, ?f. (ad.) *Ἀρτεμίδωρος*); **(7)** ~ ib. 375; cf. KW pl. 26 no. 374 (I f. *Γάϊος* II); **(8)** ~ *CIRB* 375; cf. KW pl. 26 no. 374 (II s. *Γάϊος* I, *Βασιλική*); **(9)** i-ii AD *CIRB* 590; cf. KW pl. 54 no. 730 (s. *Νικίας*); **(10)** s. i AD *CIRB* 374 (s. *Μηνόδωρος*); **(11)** i/ii AD ib. 591 (s. *Ἀλέξανδρος*); **(12)** 82 AD ib. 76, 16 (*SEG* XVIII 310) (f. *Ἀχαιμένης*); **(13)** ii AD *CIRB* 751 (s. *Διογένης*); **(14)** iii AD ib. 101, 3 (s. *Φούρτας*)
—PANTIKAPAION*: **(15)** m. i AD ib. 382; cf. KW pl. 42 no. 613 (f. *Δαμᾶς*)
MACEDONIA (BOTTIAIA):
—BEROIA: **(16)** ii/iii AD *IBer* 27 A, 4; **(17)** ~ ib. 143 A, 3-4 (Tataki 337-8) (f. *Ἀντίγονος*, *Διονύσιος*)
—EDESSA: **(18)** 180 AD *SEG* XXIV 531, 17 (Tataki, *Edessa* 71) (I f. *Γάϊος* II, *Παράμονος*); **(19)** ~ *SEG* XXIV 531, 17 (Tataki, *Edessa* 70) (II s. *Γάϊος* I)
MACEDONIA (CHALKIDIKE):
—POTIDAIA-KASSANDREIA (TERRIT.)?: **(20)** imp. *SEG* XXIX 575
—SPARTOLOS (NR.)?: **(21)** imp. ib. 598, 4
MACEDONIA (DERRIOPOS):
—STUBERRA: **(22)** c. 41-48 AD *IG* X (2) (2) 323, 18 (f. *Λούκιος*); **(23)** ~ ib. l. 23 (?s. *Λέων*); **(24)** 74 AD ib. 325, 37 (s. *Διονύσιος*); **(25)** ~ ib. 326, 33 (s. *Ἀλέξανδρος*); **(26)** 116 AD ib. 327, 40-1 (f. *Κλέαρχος*, *Πρόκλος*)
MACEDONIA (EDONIS):
—AMPHIPOLIS (TERRIT.): **(27)** ii-iii AD Dimitsas 867 (f. *Ζώσιμος*)
—PHILIPPOI (TERRIT.): **(28)** i-ii AD Pikoulas, *Chora* p. 163 no. 72, 4 (Pilhofer 606) (s. *Ἡρόδοτος*, *Δομιτία*); **(29)** ii-iii AD Pikoulas, *Chora* p. 135 no. 38 (Pilhofer 614); Collart, *Philippes* pl. 37. 2 (*Γάϊου[ς]* (nom.): s. *Μᾶρκος*)
MACEDONIA (LYNKESTIS):
—HERAKLEIA: **(30)** i AD *IG* X (2) (2) 75, 19 (s. *Σεκοῦνδος*) ?= (*31*); **(31)** ~ ib. l. 44 (f. *Σεκοῦνδος*) ?= (*30*); **(32)** ~ ib. l. 50 (s. *Μάξιμος*); **(33)** ~ ib. l. 52 (s. *Παῦλος*)
—HERAKLEIA (AREA): **(34)** ?ii AD ib. 15 (*Γ(άϊος)*: s. *Θάλλος*); **(35)** ~ ib. (*Γ(άϊος)*: s. *Ἄννιος*); **(36)** ii AD ib. 22 (*Γέ-*: s. *Διονύσιος*)
MACEDONIA (MYGDONIA):
—ARETHOUSA: **(37)** imp.? *FGrH* 81 F 73 (Tataki, *Macedonians* p. 69 no. 7)
—KALINDOIA*: **(38)** ii-i BC *SEG* XLII 585 (f. *Λεύκιος Φερράνιος*)
—THESSALONIKE: **(39)** ii AD ib. XLIII 463 (f. *Νικέρως*); **(40)** ii-iii AD *IG* X (2) (1) 516; *Ancient Macedonia* 2 pp. 328-30 (s. *Τιτινία Τριβούλα*)
—THESSALONIKE?: **(41)** i-ii AD *IG* X (2) (1) 874 (f. *Ἀτιλία*)
MACEDONIA (ODOMANTIKE):
—GAZOROS?: **(42)** 144 AD *SEG* XXX 599, 4 (Pilhofer 552); cf. *SEG* XXXVII 579 (s. *Τορκᾶτος*, ?f. *Οὐενερία*)
—SIRRHA: **(43)** ii-iii AD ib. XXX 603; **(44)** 155 AD Dimitsas 821, 6 (Kaphtantzis 1) (s. *Μᾶρκος*); **(45)** ~ Dimitsas 821, 15 (Kaphtantzis 1) (f. *Ἰσίδωρος*); **(46)** f. iii AD *SEG* XXX 590, 13 (f. *Αὐρ. Ἀλέξανδρος*); **(47)** ~ ib. l. 31 (f. *Αὐρ. Ἰσίδοτος*)
—SIRRHA?: **(48)** iii AD *IGB* V 5932 (*Γ. ὁ καὶ Κερδώλας*: f. *Βῆρος*)
MACEDONIA (ORESTIS):
—BATTYNAIOI: **(49)** 192 AD *EAM* 186 III, 56 (s. *Ἀλέξανδρος*)
—SISANI (MOD.): **(50)** 146 AD ib. 187, 20 (s. *Ἀντιπᾶς*)
MACEDONIA (PAIONIA): **(51)** imp. *Sp.* 75 (1933) p. 77 no. 217 (ring)
—ARGOS (NR.): **(52)** ii-iii AD ib. 71 (1931) p. 38 no. 83, 1 (s. *Παράμονος*, f. *Γαΐα*)
—EUDARISTOS?: **(53)** imp. ib. 98 (1941-8) p. 61 no. 127 (?f. *Ἑλένη*)
—KAVADARCI (MOD.): **(54)** imp. ib. p. 76 no. 162 (s. *Διονῦς*, *Ἰουλία*); **(55)** ?ii AD ib. 71 (1931) p. 75 no. 176, 7; cf. Düll, *Götterkulte* p. 340 no. 131 (s. *Μελέαγρος*); **(56)** ii-iii AD *Sp.* 75 (1933) p. 35 no. 104; **(57)** ii/iii AD Unp. (Kavadarci Mus.) inv. 10/II (f. *Ζώσιμος*); **(58)** ~ ib. (s. *Κούαρτος*); **(59)** ~ ib. inv. 6/II (s. *Παράμονος*, *Ἀμμία*); **(60)** ~ ib. (f. *Ἀμμία*)
—NEAPOLIS? (IZVOR (MOD.): **(61)** ii-iii AD *Sp.* 98 (1941-8) p. 28 no. 68 (s. *Διονύσιος*)
—NEAPOLIS? (SMILOVCI (MOD.)): **(62)** ii AD ib. p. 31 no. 76 (s. *Διονύσιος*, *Ἀμμία*)
—NEAPOLIS? (VLADILOVCI (MOD.)): **(63)** ii-iii AD ib. 71 (1931) p. 31 no. 62 (f. *Λούκιος*)
—STOBOI: **(64)** imp. *Robinson Bequest* 408 (f. *Φίλος Ἀκοίνιος*)
MACEDONIA (PELAGONIA): **(65)** imp. *IG* X (2) (2) 272 (f. *Μᾶρκος*); **(66)** ii AD ib. 248 (s. *Διονῦς*, f. *Π. Αἴλ. Μαρκελλῖνος*)
—KERAMIAI (NR.): **(67)** ii-iii AD ib. 210 (s. *Λυσᾶς*, *Ἀμμία*)
MACEDONIA (PIERIA):
—DION: **(68)** i BC-i AD *SEG* XXXVIII 618 = XLVIII 789 (s. *Δ. Σέργιος Μᾶρκος*, *Σεξτία Μάξιμα*); **(69)** ii-iii AD Dimitsas 165, 1
MACEDONIA (SINTIKE):
—NEINE: **(70)** 173 AD *IGB* IV 2240 (f. *Πύρρος*)
—PARTHIKOPOLIS (NR.): **(71)** 159 AD ib. 2286, 2; **(72)** ~ ib. l. 3 (s. *Διοσκοῦς*)
SCYTHIA MINOR:
—ISTROS:
——Chora Dagei: **(73)** c. 159-161 AD *ISM* I 378 C, 24 (f. *Μίκκος*)
—KALLATIS: **(74)** ii/iii AD ib. III 182 (s. *Φιλοδέσποτος*)
—TOMIS: **(75)** ii AD ib. II 125 II, 22 (f. *Ἀρίβαλος*); **(76)** ii-iii AD ib. 185 (s. *Διογένης*, *Εἶα*); **(77)** ~ ib. 321 (f. *Δημοσθένης*)
SKYTHIA:
—OLBIA-BORYSTHENES: **(78)** f. ii AD *IOSPE* I^2 85, 8 (*Γάϊος*: s. *Κάσαγος*)
—TANAIS: **(79)** f. ii AD *CIRB* 1266, 9 (*Γάϊ[ος]*: f. *Κοσσοῦς*); **(80)** 104 AD ib. 1259, 8 (s. *Χαρίτων*)
TAURIS:
—CHERSONESOS: **(81)** i BC-i AD *IOSPE* I^2 454 (f. *Καλλέας*); **(82)** 174 AD *SEG* XLV 985 A, 35 (f. *Πείσων*)
THRACE:
—APOLLONIA-SOZOPOLIS: **(83)** i-ii AD *IGB* I^2 401, 14 (s. *Νέανδρος*)
—BEROE-AUGUSTA TRAIANA (TERRIT.): **(84)** ii-iii AD ib. III 1742 (f. *Φίλιππος*); **(85)** ~ ib. V 5625 (s. *Φίλιππος*)
—BIZYE (TERRIT.): **(86)** ii AD ib. III 1861, 3 (s. *Μέννης*)
—BYZANTION: **(87)** i BC-i AD *Türk Tarih Kongresi XI* (6) p. 2703 with pl. 493. 2 (*Γάϊος*); **(88)** ii AD *IByz* 317 b (Fıratlı–Robert p. 120 no. 201) (*Γαῦρος ὁ καὶ Γ.*: s. *Φιλώτας*)
——(Keramea): **(89)** iii AD *IByz* 318 (Fıratlı–Robert pp. 121-2 no. 204) (f. *Αὐρ. Ἀσκληπιόδοτος*)
—LIPNICA (MOD.): **(90)** iii AD *IGB* II 501 (s. *Μακος ὁ καὶ Γόλης*)
—MARKIANOPOLIS: **(91)** ii AD ib. V 5339, 2
—MARONEIA: **(92)** ii-i BC *IThrakAig* E212, 44 (s. *Λοκρίων*); **(93)** i AD *BCH* 66-7 (1942-3) p. 198 no. 2 (*IThrakAig* E297) (f. *Βερονίκη*); **(94)** ii/iii AD *AD* 26 (1971) Chron. pp. 428-9 no. η (*IThrakAig* E295) (f. *Καρτοῦς*)
—ODESSOS: **(95)** s. ii AD *IGB* I^2 175 (PM 1739); *Dacia* 21 (1977) p. 161 (date) (s. (nat.) *Ἀπολλώνιος*, s. (ad.) *Σουσᾶς*)
—PAUTALIA: **(96)** ii-iii AD *IGB* IV 2055 (f. *Ἀπολλόδωρος*); **(97)** s. ii AD *SEG* XLVI 864, 7; **(98)** ~ ib. l. 10 (s. *Φαέσαξ*); **(99)** iv AD Beševliev 36
—PAUTALIA (TERRIT.): **(100)** ii-iii AD *IGB* IV 2136 (f. *Μᾶρκος*); **(101)** ~ ib. 2137 (f. *Γαϊανός*)
—PERINTHOS-HERAKLEIA (NR.): **(102)** ii AD *IPerinth* 281 (f. *Γάϊς*)
—PHILIPPOPOLIS-TRIMONTIUM: **(103)** ii AD *IGB* III 1014 (f. *Θεοδόσιος*); **(104)** ~ ib. V 5411 (f. *Γαϊανός*); **(105)** c. 303 AD *Anal. Boll.* 31 (1912) p. 192
—PHILIPPOPOLIS-TRIMONTIUM (TERRIT.): **(106)** ii-iii AD *IGB* III 1458-9 (f. *Λουκιανός*)
—PHILIPPOPOLIS-TRIMONTIUM:
——(Artemisias): **(107)** 163-164 AD ib. 902, 5 (s. *Μᾶρκος*)
—SERDICA: **(108)** ii-iii AD ib. IV 1936 (f. *Ἀσκληπιάδης*)
—SERDICA (TERRIT.): **(109)** ii-iii AD *Starinar* 15-16 (1964-5) p. 250 no. 6 (s. *Πρόκλος*); **(110)** ~ *IGB* IV 2042 (s. *Ἀσκληπιάδης*)
—SKAPTOPARA: **(111)** 238-244 AD ib. V 5872 (f. *Μίκκος*)

Γαιπες
THRACE:
—SERDICA: **(1)** iii AD ib. IV 1954, 4 (gen.: s. *Ἑρμαδίων*)

Γάϊς
CIMMERIAN BOSPOROS:
—ACHILLEION: **(1)** ii AD *CIRB* 1034 (*[Γ]άεις*—Shkorpil, *[Τ]άεις*—*CIRB*: s. *Πόθων*)
MACEDONIA (DERRIOPOS):
—STUBERRA: **(2)** 116 AD *IG* X (2) (2) 327, 17 (s. *Ἐπιγένης*)
THRACE:
—GLAVA PANEGA (MOD.): **(3)** ii-iii AD *IGB* II 554 (s. *Γόλης*)
—PERINTHOS-HERAKLEIA (NR.): **(4)** ii AD *IPerinth* 281 (s. *Γάϊος*)

Γαιτέας
MACEDONIA: **(1)** ?417-413 BC *IG* I^3 89, 65 (Tataki, *Macedonians* p. 285 no. 1)
MACEDONIA (BOTTIAIA):
—BEROIA: **(2)** 239-229 BC *IBer* 45, 31 (s. *Χαιρεκράτης*)
MACEDONIA (EDONIS):
—AMPHIPOLIS?: **(3)** hell. *SEG* XLIII 373; Hatzopoulos, *MI* 1 p. 192 n. 9 (name) (*[Γ]αιτέας*: s. *Λάγος*)
MACEDONIA (MYGDONIA):
—THESSALONIKE: **(4)** 223 BC *IG* X (2) (1) 2, 5 (s. *Παΐλλος*)

Γαλάτεια
MACEDONIA (EDONIS):
—PHILIPPOI (NR.): **(1)** imp. Pilhofer 445 (Lat. Tatinia Galatia)

Γαλάτη
MACEDONIA (BOTTIAIA):
—PELLA? (GIANNITSA (MOD.)): **(1)** imp. Dimitsas 130

Γαλάτης
MACEDONIA (MYGDONIA):
—THESSALONIKE: **(1)** f. iii AD *IG* X (2) (1) 564, 5 (*Αὐρ. Γ.*: s. *Ζετιτίς*)
—THESSALONIKE?: **(2)** iii AD ib. 896 (f. *Αὐρ. Πύρος*)
MACEDONIA (ODOMANTIKE):
—SIRRHA: **(3)** f. iii AD *SEG* XXX 590, 14 (*Αὐρ. Γ.*: s. *Ἰσίδωρος*)

Γαλέστας
Macedonia (Pieria):
—Pydna: **(1)** iv BC *GRBS* 43 (2002-3) p. 111 no. 2, 12

Γαλέστης
Macedonia (Bottiaia):
—Aigai: **(1)** ii BC *SEG* L 655 (vase)
—Beroia: **(2)** ii BC ib. XXIV 504 a; 504 c; *IBer* 160 (stemma) (Tataki 342) (s. *Τύριος*, f. *Ἀσπασία*); **(3)** i BC-i AD *IBer* 142, 8 (Tataki 343) (I f. *Γαλέστης* II); **(4)** ~ *IBer* 142, 8 (Tataki 341) (II s. *Γαλέστης* I); **(5)** ii-iii AD *IBer* 317, 1 (Tataki 340) (s. *Ἀρίστων*)

Γαληνιανός
Macedonia (Mygdonia):
—Thessalonike: **(1)** f. iii AD *Tekmeria* 5 (2000) p. 18 no. 5 (*Γ. Ἰούλ. Γ.*)

Γαληνός
Macedonia (Mygdonia):
—Thessalonike: **(1)** i-ii AD *IG* X (2) (1) 243 II, 4 (*Τ. Σεουρεῖνος Γ.*); **(2)** ii AD ib. 414 (s. *Κ. Ποπίλλιος Ἵλαρος, Ἀρτεμώ*)
Scythia Minor:
—Tomis: **(3)** ii AD *ISM* II 125 II, 18 (*Γαλη[ν]ός*: s. *Ἄττας*)

Γάλλος
Macedonia (Paionia):
—Stoboi: **(1)** 232 AD *AJA* 75 (1971) p. 401; *BE* 1972, no. 256 a (slave?)

Γαμέτη
Macedonia (Sintike):
—Parthikopolis: **(1)** ii AD *IGB* IV 2279, 2 (d. *Ἡρακλεόδωρος*)

Γαμικός
Macedonia (Odomantike):
—Sirrha (territ.)*: **(1)** i AD *Klio* 67 (1985) pp. 458-61 (Pilhofer 558) (Lat. Gamicus: freed.)
Thrace:
—Perinthos-Herakleia (nr.): **(2)** i-ii AD *IPerinth* 282 (s. *Ἀλέξανδρος*)

Γάμος
Macedonia (Lynkestis):
—Herakleia: **(1)** imp. *IG* X (2) (2) 99 (s. *Πελήνα*)
Macedonia (Mygdonia):
—Thessalonike?: **(2)** ii AD ib. X (2) (1) 852

Γανύων
Thrace:
—Apollonia-Sozopolis: **(1)** iv BC *IGB* I² 457 (s. *Θαρσαγόρης*)

Γάος
Skythia:
—Tanais: **(1)** 210-226 AD *CIRB* 1281, 11 (*Γαος*—Tokhtas'ev: f. *Ζῆθος*) ?= (*2*); **(2)** 225 AD ib. 1279, 18; Zgusta, *PNS* 93 ?= (*1*)

Γαρούλας?
Thrace:
—Philippopolis-Trimontium (territ.): **(1)** ii-iii AD *IGB* III 1408 + V 5519 (*Γαρούλου* (gen.), (*Τ*)*αρούλου*?: f. *Κέρζα*)

Γαρρήσκιος
Macedonia (Edonis):
—Amphipolis: **(1)** a. 357 BC Hatzopoulos, *Actes Amphipolis* pp. 38-9 no. 7, 20

Γάστειν
Cimmerian Bosporos:
—Pantikapaion: **(1)** i-ii AD *CIRB* 592; Zgusta, *PNS* 94 (d. *Καλοῦς*); **(2)** i/ii AD *KSIA* 116 (1969) pp. 51-2 no. 3 (*Γάσστ[ειν]*?)

Γάστεις
Cimmerian Bosporos:
—Gorgippia: **(1)** i AD *CIRB* 1192, 1 (*GVI* 1022); Zgusta, *PNS* 94 (s. *Χορηγίων*); **(2)** ii AD *NE* 9 (1971) p. 6. no. 3, 1 (*Γάσ[τεις]*); **(3)** ~ *CIRB* 1140, 17 (f. —*κης*) ?= (*6*); **(4)** ~ ib. 1154, 3; **(5)** ~ ib. 1161, 5 (*Γάστε[ις]*); **(6)** 173-210 AD ib. 1135, 8 (f. —*κης*) ?= (*3*); **(7)** ii/iii AD ib. 1179, 30 (s. *Ἀγαθοῦς*); **(8)** ~ ib. l. 33 (*Γάσ[τεις]*: f. *Ἄγρων*); **(9)** iii AD *NE* 9 (1971) p. 10 no. 6 B, 16 (*Γάστ[εις]*: f. *Πόθος*)
—Korokondame: **(10)** i-ii AD *CIRB* 1106 (-*σθεις*: f. —*τερ*); **(11)** ii/iii AD ib. 1108 (*Γάστη* (dat.): f. *Μοι*—)
—Myrmekion: **(12)** i AD ib. 877 (f. *Ἀπόλλων*)
—Pantikapaion: **(13)** i AD ib. 137, 2 (*GVI* 1316) (f. *Λυσίμαχος*); **(14)** ~ *CIRB* 376 (*Γάστ<ι>εις*: s. *Ἀγαθοῦς*: reading—Yailenko); **(15)** ~ ib. 377 (s. *Μοιραγένης*); **(16)** ~ ib. 378 (*[Γά]στεις*: s. *Βίων*); **(17)** ~ ib. 379 (*Γ[ά]στεις*: s. *Πα*—); **(18)** ~ ib. 400 A; cf. KW pl. 50 no. 693 (*Γάστη* (gen.): f. *Ἑρμῆς*); **(19)** i-ii AD *CIRB* 607; cf. KW pl. 37 no. 536 (f. *Ἡρακλείδης*); **(20)** f. i AD *CIRB* 561 (-*στης*: s. *Καλλισθένης*, *Ψύχη*); **(21)** m. i AD ib. 380 (s. *Νάνεις*); **(22)** ~ ib. 556; **(23)** s. i AD ib. 558 (f. *Ψυχαρίων*); **(24)** f. ii AD ib. 715; cf. KW pl. 14 no. 210
Skythia:
—Tanais: **(25)** 104 AD *CIRB* 1259, 17 (f. *Θώραξ*)

Γάστιον
Cimmerian Bosporos:
—Zenonos Chersonesos*: **(1)** f. i AD ib. 899 (*[Γ]άστιον*: m. *Βασίλη*)

Γάστρων
Thrace:
—Lysimacheia: **(1)** m. ii BC *ISestos* 38 b, 2 (f. *Περδίκκας*)

Γάταλος
Sarmatia:
—Sarmatai: **(1)** 179 BC Plb. XXV 2. 12 (king)

Γαττίων
Cimmerian Bosporos:
—Pantikapaion: **(1)** ii-i BC *CIRB* 263; cf. KW pl. 32 no. 446; Zgusta, *PNS* 625 (s. *Ἀριστοκράτης*)

Γαυάνης
Macedonia (Bottiaia):
—Beroia: **(1)** f. i BC *IBer* 205 (Tataki 345) (I f. *Γαυάνης* II, *Παλάμανδρος*); **(2)** ~ *IBer* 205 (Tataki 344) (II s. *Γαυάνης* I)

Γαυδίων
Macedonia (Mygdonia):
—Kalindoia: **(1)** a. 98 AD *SEG* XLII 582, 64 (f. *Διοσκουρίδης*)

Γαυκίας
Macedonia (Lynkestis):
—Herakleia (nr.): **(1)** imp. *IG* X (2) (2) 11 (f. *Ἡρᾶς*)

Γαύκιον
Thrace:
—Byzantion: **(1)** ii BC *IByz* 77 (Firatlı–Robert p. 51 no. 24) (d. *Μενίσκος*)

Γαῦκος
Cimmerian Bosporos:
—Achilleion?: **(1)** s. i AD *CIRB* 1026 (*Γ*(*λ*)*αῦκος*—ed.)
Scythia Minor:
—Istros: **(2)** ii AD *ISM* I 196, 7 (*Γα[ῦκος]*: s. *Πρόκλος*); **(3)** ~ ib. 197 I, 7; 201 I, 16 (f. *Μακρῖνος*); **(4)** ~ ib. 197 I, 16 (I f. *Γαῦκος* II); **(5)** ~ ib. l. 16 (II s. *Γαῦκος* I); **(6)** 138 AD ib. 193 II, 48 (*Π. Αἴλ. Γ.*)
—Kallatis: **(7)** iii-ii BC *ZfN* 30 (1913) p. 300 no. 251a (coin) (*Γαῦ*(*κος*)?); **(8)** iii/ii BC *IG* XI (4) 1238; cf. *St. Clas.* 7 (1965) p. 305 (*Γ*(*λ*)*αῦκος*—*IG*: s. *Γοῦρος*, f. *Παράμονος*)
—Tomis: **(9)** 201 AD *ISM* II 83 I, 33; cf. *St. Clas.* 7 (1965) p. 305 (f. *Χρυσάων*)

Γαῦρος
Scythia Minor:
—Kallatis: **(1)** f. iii AD *ISM* III 188 (s. *Μα*—)
Thrace:
—Byzantion: **(2)** i-ii AD *IByz* 106 (Firatlı–Robert p. 96 no. 137) (f. *Μηνόφιλος*); **(3)** ii AD *IByz* 317 b (Firatlı–Robert p. 120 no. 201) (*Γ. ὁ καὶ Γάϊος*: s. *Φιλώτας*)
—Deultum: **(4)** ii-iii AD *IGB* III 1849, 4 (I f. *Παπιανός*, *Γαῦρος* II); **(5)** ~ ib. l. 4 (II s. *Γαῦρος* I)
—Oescus*: **(6)** a. 195 AD *ILB* 76, 4 (Lat. Aurel. Gaurus)
—Perinthos-Herakleia: **(7)** i-ii AD *IPerinth* 96 (f. *Τερτία*); **(8)** ii-iii AD ib. 122 (f. *Ἀσκληπιάδης*)

Γελασῖνος
Macedonia (Sintike):
—Parthikopolis (territ.): **(1)** 162 AD *IGB* IV 2304, 8 (-*σεί*-: sculptor)

Γελάσιος
Macedonia (Mygdonia):
—Thessalonike: **(1)** m. iii AD *SEG* XXXV 767

Γέλων
Macedonia: **(1)** c. 238 BC *IG* II² 1299, 97; *ZPE* 78 (1989) p. 241 (date) (Tataki, *Macedonians* p. 285 no. 3)
Macedonia (Orestis):
—Battynaioi: **(2)** 192 AD *EAM* 186 II, 53 (s. *Παράμονος*); **(3)** ~ ib. l. 55 (f. *Παρμενίων*); **(4)** ~ ib. 186 III, 48 (f. *Ἀντίγονος*); **(5)** ~ ib. 186 IV, 44 (s. *Ὀ*—)
Thrace:
—Apollonia-Sozopolis: **(6)** v/iv BC *IGB* I² 444 (*[Γ]έλωνο*(*ς*)? (gen.), *[Τ]έλωνο*(*ς*)?: f. *Ξένων*)

Γέλως
Macedonia (Bottiaia):
—Beroia: **(1)** 177 AD *IBer* 135 A, 16 (Tataki 1311) (*Φλαύϊος Γ.*)
Macedonia (Edonis):
—Philippoi: **(2)** ii/iii AD *CIL* III 633 II b, 7 (Pilhofer 163); *CRAI* 1923, p. 277 (date); Collart, *Philippes* pls. 64-5 (Lat. M. Plotius Gelos)

Γέμελλος
Macedonia (Bottiaia):
—Beroia: **(1)** ii-iii AD *IBer* 371, 3 (Tataki 348) (f. *Κουαρτίων*)
Macedonia (Chalkidike):
—Potidaia-Kassandreia (territ.): **(2)** ?iii AD *TAPA* 69 (1938) p. 68 no. 22 (*SEG* XXIX 605)
—Singos (nr.): **(3)** 180 AD ib. 593, 4 (f. *Ζώπυρος*, *Ὀλυμπιάς*)
Macedonia (Derriopos):
—Stuberra: **(4)** 74 AD *IG* X (2) (2) 325, 30 (s. *Εὐβουλίδης*)
Macedonia (Mygdonia):
—Charakoma?: **(5)** 69-79 AD *SEG* XXIX 579
—Thessalonike: **(6)** 131 AD *IG* X (2) (1) 553 (*[Γέ]μελλος*)
Macedonia (Orestis):
—Sisani (mod.): **(7)** 146 AD *EAM* 187, 21 (s. *Ἀλέξανδρος*)
Thrace:
—Philippopolis-Trimontium (territ.): **(8)** ii-iii AD *IGB* III 1123 (I f. *Γέμελλος* II); **(9)** ~ ib. (*[Γέ]μελλος*: II s. *Γέμελλος* I)

Γέμινος
Macedonia (Mygdonia):
—THESSALONIKE: (**1**) s. i AD *IG* x (2) (1) 68, 23 (*Διονύσιος ὁ καὶ Γ.*: s. *Κλεοπάτρα*)

Γενέθλιος
Thrace:
—PHILIPPOPOLIS-TRIMONTIUM: (**1**) c. 303 AD *Anal. Boll.* 31 (1912) p. 192

Γενήμανος?
Macedonia (Mygdonia):
—THESSALONIKE?: (**1**) 152 AD *IG* x (2) (1) 923, 5 (*Γε(ρ)μανός?*: f. *Διοσκουρίδης*)

Γενθήνα
Macedonia (Bottiaia):
—PELLA: (**1**) iii/ii BC *SEG* XXXVIII 653 (d. *Μαγεάτης*)

Γένθιος
Macedonia (Bottiaia):
—EDESSA: (**1**) iii AD *Arch. Pap.* 22 (1973) p. 209 no. 17 (Tataki, *Edessa* 72) (*Γέν[τ]ιος*—ed., *Γέν[θ]ιος*—Tataki)

Γενικείλας
Thrace:
—BAZOPARA: (**1**) 202 AD *IGB* III 1690 d, 12 (and Thrace Pizos: s. *Αὐλούτραλις*)
—GEUPASA: (**2**) ii-iii AD ib. 1811 (*-κέλ-*: f. *Σουντους*)

Γεννάδιος
Scythia Minor:
—TOMIS: (**1**) v-vi AD Barnea 30 (Popescu, *IGL* 13)

Γεόκας
Cimmerian Bosporos:
—PANTIKAPAION: (**1**) iii AD *CIRB* 727

Γερμανά
Macedonia (Mygdonia):
—THESSALONIKE?: (**1**) ii AD *IG* x (2) (1) 885 (*Γερμανάνη* (dat.): d. *Ἀντιγόνα*)

Γερμανός
Macedonia (Bottiaia):
—BEROIA: (**1**) ii/iii AD *IBer* 27 A, 1 (slave?)
Macedonia (Chalkidike):
—MONI VATOPEDIOU (MOD.)?: (**2**) 203 AD Dimitsas 781, 1 (s. *Ἡρακλᾶς*)
Macedonia (Lower Paionia):
—IDOMENE?: (**3**) ii/iii AD Sokolovska, *Isar-Marvinci* p. 130
Macedonia (Mygdonia):
—THESSALONIKE: (**4**) ii AD *IG* x (2) (1) 559; (**5**) s. ii AD *SEG* L 640 (*Γερ[μα]νός*: threptos)
—THESSALONIKE?: (**6**) f. ii AD *JDAI* 84 (1969) p. 151 no. R13 (f. *Διζάλας*)
Scythia Minor:
—ISTROS: (**7**) c. 140-160 AD *ISM* I 207, 20 (*Γερμαν[ός]*: f. *—νος*)
Skythia:
—OLBIA-BORYSTHENES: (**8**) ii AD *IOSPE* I^2 105, 7 (s. *Δάδος*)
Thrace:
—BEROE-AUGUSTA TRAIANA:
——Karasoura: (**9**) iii AD *IGB* III 1626, 4 (I f. *Γερμανός* II); (**10**) ~ ib. l. 4 (II s. *Γερμανός* I)
—DIONYSOPOLIS: (**11**) iii AD ib. I^2 14 c, 22 (f. *Αὐρ. Κλαύδιος*)
—MADYTOS: (**12**) imp. *ISestos* 59 (*Γερμαν[ός]*: s. *Ὑγῖνος, Νίκη*)
—PAUTALIA: (**13**) 135 AD *IGB* IV 2057, 8

Γερμᾶς?
Macedonia (Pieria):
—PYDNA: (**1**) iv BC *GRBS* 43 (2002-3) p. 119 no. 5, 3 (*Γε[ρ]μᾶς?*)

Γεροντία
Macedonia (Bottiaia):
—BEROIA: (**1**) vi AD *IBer* 452 (Feissel, *RICM* 75) (Lat. Gerontia)

Γεροντίδας
Scythia Minor:
—KALLATIS: (**1**) 12-19 AD *IGB* v 5011, 13 (s. *Σῖμος*)

Γερόντιν
Macedonia (Bottiaia):
—BEROIA: (**1**) iv-v AD *IBer* 445, 6 (Feissel, *RICM* 62) (threpte)

Γερόντιος
Macedonia (Chalkidike):
—POLICHNE?: (**1**) ?353 BC *SEG* XXXVII 576, 6 (?s. *Στράτων*)
Macedonia (Mygdonia):
—THESSALONIKE: (**2**) 507 AD Feissel, *RICM* 131, 1 (*Αὐρ. Γ.*: f. *Φίλιππος*)

Γέρων
Macedonia: (**1**) s. iv BC *IEph* 1432 (Tataki, *Macedonians* p. 285 no. 5) (f. *Νίκαρχος*); (**2**) 311-306 BC Maier, *Mauerbauinschr.* 69 II, 139 (Tataki, *Macedonians* p. 285 no. 4) (f. *Ἀμύντωρ*)
Macedonia (Chalkidike):
—MENDE?: (**3**) hell.? Dimitsas 772 (f. *Ἀριστόδημος, Νικοκράτης*)
Macedonia (Mygdonia):
—ARETHOUSA?: (**4**) f. iv BC *SEG* XXXI 643 (s. *Ἐπικύδης*)
Scythia Minor:
—TOMIS: (**5**) i BC *ISM* II 2, 26, 30; 2 A, 47 (f. *Ποσειδώνιος*) ?= (*6*); (**6**) ~ ib. l. 51 (f. *Δημήτριος*) ?= (*5*)
Tauris:
—CHERSONESOS: (**7**) iv/iii BC *IOSPE* I^2 504 (f. *Ἀκίς*); (**8**) iii BC Solomonik, *NEPKh* 161 (f. *Αἰσχίνας*); (**9**) f. iii BC *SEG* XL 615 A, 7 (f. *Πολύαρχος*); (**10**) c. 220-210 BC Anokhin p. 143 no. 131 (coin)
Thrace:
—BYZANTION: (**11**) ?253 BC Nachtergael, *Les Galates* 10, 13; cf. Stephanis 2616 (f. *Χαρῖνος*); (**12**) ii BC *IByz* 86 (f. *Ἀπολλώνιος*)
—DIONYSOPOLIS: (**13**) iii AD *IGB* I^2 14 b, 11 (*Αὐρ. Γ.*: s. *Οὐαλέριος*); (**14**) ~ ib. l. 16 (*Αὐρ. Γ.*: s. *Ἡρακλείδης*)
—LYSIMACHEIA: (**15**) m. ii BC *ISestos* 38 b, 7 (s. *Μένανδρος*)

Γεσείλας
Thrace:
—BOURDAPA: (**1**) hell.? *SEG* XXXIX 658

Γέτας
Macedonia (Edonis):
—EDONOI: (**1**) c. 480-460 BC *AMNG* III (2) p. 144 no. 1; *BCH* 35 (1911) p. 126 (coin); *Coinage and Administration* pp. 44-5 (date) (king)
Thrace:
—MARONEIA: (**2**) iii BC *IG* II^2 9287 (*FRA* 3535) (f. *Θρᾶιξ*)
—TYRODIZA-TIRISTASIS?: (**3**) ii-i BC *Stephanos nomismatikos* p. 586 (s. *Βεισταβάκης*)

Γετόμουσος
Skythia:
—OLBIA-BORYSTHENES: (**1**) ii AD *IOSPE* I^2 84, 7; Zgusta, *PNS* 760 (f. *Ζουρόζις*)

Γετούλας
Macedonia (Odomantike):
—GAZOROS (TERRIT.): (**1**) 132 AD *SEG* XXX 597, 5 (Pilhofer 539) (s. *Διούλας*)

Γεωργία
Thrace:
—MARONEIA: (**1**) v-vi AD Meïmaris–Bakirtzis 11 (*SEG* XXX 699; *IThrakAig* E347)
—ODESSOS: (**2**) vi AD Beševliev 118, 2-3

Γεώργιος
Macedonia (Mygdonia):
—HERAKLEIA: (**1**) m. iii AD *SEG* XLVIII 710 (*Γεό-*)
—THESSALONIKE: (**2**) iv-vi AD *Tekmeria* 7 (2002) p. 102 no. 7; (**3**) v-vi AD *IG* x (2) (1) 653 (Feissel, *RICM* 139) (*-όρ-*)
Macedonia (Pieria):
—PYDNA (LOULOUDIES (MOD.)): (**4**) iv-vi AD *AEMTh* 2 (1988) p. 197 (*Γεόργηος*)
Scythia Minor:
—TOMIS: (**5**) vi AD Popescu, *IGL* 49 (Lat. Georgius)
Thrace:
—BISANTHE-PANION: (**6**) iv-vi AD *AD* 49-50 (1994-5) Mel. p. 316 no. 142 (*Γεόργιο[ς]*: f. *Μαρία*)
—RHAIDESTOS: (**7**) iv-vi AD Taşlıklıoğlu I p. 25 no. 2 (*AD* 49-50 (1994-5) Mel. p. 299 no. 125 b) (f. *Θεόπεμπτος*)
—SALYMBRIA: (**8**) iv-vi AD *Thrak. Epet.* 1 (1897) p. 307 no. 28 (*AD* 53 (1998) Mel. p. 464 no. 204) (*Γεό-*)
—SERDICA: (**9**) v-vi AD Beševliev 5 (Lat. Georgius: f. *Ἰωάννης*)

Γηπαιπυρίς
Thrace:
—PERINTHOS-HERAKLEIA: (**1**) 128-136 AD *IPerinth* 37 (*Λαρκία Γ.*: d. *Λάρκιος Ἀσιατικός*)

Γηπαίπυρος
Thrace:
—AINOS: (**1**) i-ii AD *IG* XII (8) 218, 4 with Index (*Γηπ[αι]πυρον* (gen.)—lap., *Γηπ[αι]πύρο(υ)*—ed.: f. *Ἰουλία*)

Γηπεπυρίς
Thrace:
—BOURDAPA: (**1**) ii-iii AD *IGB* III 1346 (d. *Μοντανός*)
—NICOPOLIS AD NESTUM: (**2**) iii AD ib. IV 2343 (Kaphtantzis 480); cf. Pilhofer 527 (*Αὐρ. Γ.*: d. *Ἔζβενις*)

Γήρης
Thrace:
—PAUTALIA: (**1**) s. ii AD *SEG* XLVI 864, 17 (*Τήρης?*)

Γῆρος
Cimmerian Bosporos:
—PANTIKAPAION: (**1**) iv BC *CIRB* 174 (s. *Αὐτοκλῆς*)

Γῆρυς
Tauris:
—KALOS LIMEN: (**1**) ii BC Solomonik, *GChKh* 457 (vase) (*SEG* XXXVIII 749. 10) (*Γήρυ(ος)?* (gen.))

Γησενίδης
Macedonia (Edonis):
—AMPHIPOLIS: (**1**) imp. ib. XXXIX 571 (f. *Ματτία*)

Γιβάστης
Scythia Minor:
—AXIOPOLIS*: (**1**) v-vi AD Popescu, *IGL* 195, 4 (f. *Ἀνθοῦσα*)

Γίλος
Tauris:
—CHERSONESOS: (**1**) c. 475-450 BC *SEG* XL 612. 21 (ostrakon) (*Γίλο[ς]*)

Γίλπυρις
Thrace:
—KRASALOPARA: (**1**) 202 AD *IGB* III 1690 b, 58 (and Thrace Pizos: s. *Δυτούτραλις*)

Γιργαῖος
Macedonia (Edonis):
—amphipolis: **(1)** c. 200-170 bc Hatzopoulos, *MI* 2 p. 87 no. 65, 6 (*SEG* xlvi 720) (*Γιργαῖ[ος]*: f. ..λος)

Γίς
Cimmerian Bosporos:
—hermonassa: **(1)** i bc *CIRB* 1074

Γιτις
Thrace:
—serdica (territ.): **(1)** ii-iii ad *IGB* iv 1983 (gen.?)

Γλαοκίας
Thrace:
—apollonia-sozopolis: **(1)** iv bc *SNG BM Black Sea* 169; *SNG Stancomb* 46 (coin) (*Γλαο(κίας)*?, *[Ἀ]γλαο[ς]—SNG*) ?= (*Γλαυκίας* (*38*))

Γλαύκα
Macedonia (Eordaia): **(1)** s. ii ad *ILeukopetra* 134, 1 (Tataki, *Macedonians* p. 198 no. 1) (d. *Λούκιος*, m. *Μαρκία*)

Γλαυκία
Cimmerian Bosporos:
—pantikapaion: **(1)** i/ii ad *CIRB* 593 (d. *Τιμοκράτης*)
Macedonia (Edonis):
—amphipolis (territ.)?: **(2)** ii-iii ad Pikoulas, *Chora* p. 163 no. 71 (*[Γ]λαυκί[α]*?: d. *—ρων*)

Γλαυκίας
Cimmerian Bosporos:
—gorgippia: **(1)** f. iii bc *CIRB* 1137 A I, 32 (I f. *Γλαυκίας* II); **(2)** ~ ib. l. 32 (II s. *Γλαυκίας* I)
—pantikapaion: **(3)** ?ii bc ib. 260; cf. KW pl. 32 no. 450 (f. *Σταφύλος*); **(4)** imp. *CIRB* 770 (f. *Φάννας*)
Macedonia: **(5)** 331 bc *RE* (3); Berve 226 (Tataki, *Macedonians* p. 286 no. 6); **(6)** b. 164 bc *UPZ* 3; 5; 6-8; 10, 3; 11, 3; 12-16; 18; 20; 45 + p. 105 and Index s.v.; cf. La'da E1419 (f. *Πτολεμαῖος*, *Σαραπίων*, *Ἵππαλος*, *Ἀπολλώνιος*: katoikos); **(7)** 169 bc *RE* Supplbd. 4 (1a) (Tataki, *Macedonians* p. 286 no. 8)
Macedonia (Bottiaia):
—beroia: **(8)** s. iii bc *IBer* 16 B, 36 (f. *Δημήτριος*) ?= (*9*); **(9)** 239-229 bc ib. 45, 4 (Tataki 356) (f. *Ἀπολλωνίδης*) ?= (*8*); **(10)** 223 bc *IBer* 4, 25 (*(Γ)λαυκίας*: s. *Εὐβίοτος*)
—pella: **(11)** iii bc Akamatis, *Amph. Pellas* p. 32 nos. PAR6 (amph.) (*SEG* l 613); **(12)** imp. *IG* II^2 10055 (Tataki, *Macedonians* p. 153 no. 29; *FRA* 5982) (f. *Βακχίς*)
—pella?: **(13)** iv/iii bc *IG* x (2) (1) 676 (*Pella* p. 143 no. 242); cf. Robert, *OMS* 5 p. 310 (f. *Κλεώ*)
Macedonia (Chalkidike):
—olynthos: **(14)** ?350 bc *TAPA* 65 (1934) p. 125 no. 3, 5; cf. *SEG* xxxviii 639 (name); Hatzopoulos, *Actes Chalc.* p. 80 (date) (*Γλα(υ)κίας*: f. *Σιληνός*)
—stolos?: **(15)** ?350 bc *SEG* xxxviii 671, 5 (s. *Στράτων*)
Macedonia (Edonis):
—amphipolis: **(16)** 37 bc Robert, *Coll. Froehner* 44, 10, 12 (Tataki, *Macedonians* p. 49 nos. 31-2) (I s. *Ἀπολλόδωρος*, f. *Γλαυκίας* II) ?= (*18*); **(17)** ~ Robert, *Coll. Froehner* 44, 12 (Tataki, *Macedonians* p. 49 no. 32) (II s. *Γλαυκίας* I, ?s. *Κλεοπάτρα*); **(18)** ~ Robert, *Coll. Froehner* 44, 14-15 (Tataki, *Macedonians* p. 49 nos. 33-34) (f. *Βίθυς*, *Κότυς*, *Ἀπολλώνιος*) ?= (*16*)
Macedonia (Lynkestis):
—ethniko (mod.): **(19)** s. ii ad *EAM* 154 (f. *Ἰουλία*)
—herakleia (area): **(20)** ii-iii ad *IG* x (2) (2) 41 (f. *Νίκαρχος*)
—herakleia (nr.): **(21)** 160 ad ib. 9 (freed.?)
Macedonia (Mygdonia):
—kalindoia: **(22)** c. 308 bc Hatzopoulos, *MI* 2 p. 84 no. 62, 38 (s. *Δαβρείας*); **(23)** ii/iii ad *Tekmeria* 6 (2001) p. 63 no. 2
—lete: **(24)** ii ad *Makedonika* 2 (1951) p. 619 no. 42 θ, 5 (f. *Ἰσίδωρος*)
—thessalonike: **(25)** i-ii ad *IG* x (2) (1) 939 (*Πρ. Γ.*)
Macedonia (Paionia):
—bylazora: **(26)** ii-iii ad *Sp.* 75 (1933) p. 17 no. 31, 2 (f. *Φιλόμουσος*)
Macedonia (Pieria):
—herakleion: **(27)** c. 230-200 bc *BCH* 45 (1921) p. 17 III, 51 (Tataki, *Macedonians* p. 111 no. 2) (s. *Ποσειδώνιος*)
—phylakai: **(28)** f. ii bc *IBer* 140, 5 (Tataki, *Macedonians* p. 167 no. 1) (s. *Παρμενίων*)
Macedonia?: **(29)** c. 220-200 bc Helly, *Gonnoi* 100, 5 (or Thessaly?)
Scythia Minor:
—istros: **(30)** iii bc *ISM* i 1, 16 (Migeotte, *L'emprunt* 40) (f. *Διογένης*); **(31)** ~ *ISM* i 12, 2 (s. *Πολύφημος*)
—kallatis: **(32)** iii bc *IGB* I^2 307 bis, 3 (*(Γ)λ(α)υκίας*: s. *Ἀριστομένης*)
—tomis: **(33)** i bc *ISM* ii 2 A, 61 (s. *Στράτων*)
Tauris:
—chersonesos: **(34)** ii-iii ad *IOSPE* I^2 519, 1 (*GVI* 1684); cf. KW pl. 23 no. 319 (f. *Οἰνάνθη*)
Thrace: **(35)** hell. *Syringes* 487 (Velkov 68; La'da E723); **(36)** f. iii bc *SEG* xlvii 1868
—ainos?: **(37)** iii-ii bc ib. xviii 378 (s. *Θεόδωρος*)
—apollonia-sozopolis: **(38)** iv bc *SNG BM Black Sea* 171; *Coll. Winterthur* 1160 (coin) (*Γλαυ(κίας)*?) ?= (*Γλαοκίας* (*1*))
—bisanthe-panion: **(39)** c. 133-86 bc Moretti, *ISE* 116 (*SEG* xxxvii 602) (s. *Ζωτᾶς*)
—byzantion: **(40)** ii-i bc *IByz* 145 (f. *Δαμοκρατία*); **(41)** i bc/i ad *SEG* l 667 III (f. *Ἔρως*)
—byzantion?: **(42)** ii bc *ISamothrace* 28 c, 16; Robert, *OMS* 6 pp. 605-6 (locn.) (*[Γλα]υκίας*: s. *Λέων*)
—dionysopolis: **(43)** iii ad *IGB* I^2 14 a, 4 (*Αὐρ. Γ.*: s. *Διογένης*)
—markianopolis: **(44)** ii ad ib. v 5340, 6 (*[Γλα]υκίας*?)
—maroneia: **(45)** imp. *IG* II^2 9286 (*FRA* 3536) (s. *Τάλουλος*)
—mesambria: **(46)** ii bc *IGB* I^2 314 b, 1, 11 (*Γ(λ)αυκίας*—l.1: s. *Ἀμφίων*); **(47)** i bc ib. 315, 5, 11 (s. *Ἀθαναίων*: doctor)
—odessos: **(48)** i ad ib. v 5062 (f. *Ἀπώ*); **(49)** i-ii ad ib. I^2 51 c, 6 (f. *Ἀπελλᾶς*); **(50)** f. ii ad ib. 187; 187 bis (PM 1728); *Dacia* 21 (1977) p. 161 (date) (f. *Διονύσιος*); **(51)** 221 ad *IGB* I^2 47 bis a, 24 (*Γλαυκία* (gen.): f. *Αὐρ. Νουμήνιος*)
—pautalia: **(52)** ii-iii ad ib. v 5779 (s. *Στράτων*)
—perinthos-herakleia: **(53)** c. 288-250 bc *IG* vii 3473, 1 (f. *Ἀθηναγόρας*)
—sestos: **(54)** a. 129 bc *ISestos* 1, 1 (s. *Κιλλαῖος*)
Thrace?: **(55)** 316-309 bc *IG* II^2 1956, 4 (*FRA* 2508); *Ancient Macedonia* 5 p. 445 with n. 10 (date); **(56)** ~ *IG* II^2 1956, 45; *Ancient Macedonia* 5 p. 445 with n. 10 (date) (*FRA* 2509)

Γλαυκιννώ
Macedonia (Bottiaia):
—beroia: **(1)** ii bc *IBer* 159 (Tataki 358) (*Γλαυκιννω*—apogr., *Γλ<α>υκιννώ*?—*IBer*: d. *Ἱπποκράτης*)

Γλαύκιππος
Thrace:
—lysimacheia: **(1)** iii-ii bc *ISestos* 46 (*[Γ]λαύκιππο[ς]*: s. *Εὔβουλος*)

Γλαυκίων
Cimmerian Bosporos:
—pantikapaion: **(1)** v/iv bc *CIRB* 115 (*CEG* i 176) (f. *Σάνων*); **(2)** f. iv bc *CIRB* 175 (s. *Ἄττης*)

Γλαῦκον
Thrace:
—lysimacheia: **(1)** iii bc *IG* II^2 9224 (*FRA* 3390) (d. *Πάρις*)

Γλαῦκος
Cimmerian Bosporos:
—gorgippia: **(1)** f. iii bc *CIRB* 1137 A I, 39 (f. *Ἀπολλώνιος*); **(2)** ~ ib. 1137 B I, 17 (*[Γ]λαῦ[κ]ος*: s. *Δημοφῶν*)
—pantikapaion: **(3)** i ad ib. 445 (f. *Κοσσᾶς*)
Macedonia: **(4)** hell. *Memnonion* 102 (Tataki, *Macedonians* p. 287 no. 10); cf. La'da E1401 (*Κλαῦκος*: f. *Ἀμμαδίσκος*); **(5)** s. iii bc ib. E1453 (*[Γ]λαῦκος*); **(6)** m. i bc *AD* 11 (1927-8) pp. 58-9 no. 5, 5; cf. *SEG* xxxi 582 (Tataki, *Macedonians* p. 287 no. 11) (f. *Ἀμύντας*)
Macedonia (Bottiaia):
—edessa: **(7)** v-vi ad Feissel, *RICM* 43 (?s. *Παραμονίων*)
—pella: **(8)** iii bc Akamatis, *Amph. Pellas* p. 32 no. PAR7 (amph.) (*SEG* l 613)
Macedonia (Edonis):
—philippoi: **(9)** imp. *BCH* 61 (1937) p. 419 no. 15 (Pilhofer 381) (Lat. C. Acutius Glaucus)
Macedonia (Eordaia):
—pontokomi (mod.): **(10)** iii-iv ad *SEG* l 620; cf. *AEMTh* 14 (2000) p. 622 (vase)
Macedonia (Lynkestis):
—herakleia?: **(11)** ii-iii ad *IG* x (2) (2) 129 (Lat. M. Domitius Glaucus)
Macedonia (Mygdonia):
—thessalonike: **(12)** ii ad ib. x (2) (1) 241 A II, 30 (s. *Ἀπολω—*); **(13)** ?ii ad ib. 458 (*Τ. Οὐεττήδιος Γ.*)
Macedonia (Orestis):
—lyke (nr.): **(14)** f. iii ad *EAM* 170, 4 (?f. *Ὀρέστης*, *Ἀρίσταρχος*)
Skythia:
—olbia-borysthenes (leuke)*: **(15)** f. v bc Dubois, *IGDOlbia* 48 (vase) (s. *Ποσίδηος*)
Thrace:
—anchialos: **(16)** iii ad *IGB* I^2 373, 4
—anchialos (territ.): **(17)** ii-iii ad ib. iii 1843 (*Φλ. Γ.*)
—byzantion: **(18)** c. 200 bc *IG* II^2 884, 13 (s. *Λυσίας*)
—dionysopolis: **(19)** iii ad *IGB* I^2 14 bis, 6 (*[Γ]λαῦκος*)
—maroneia: **(20)** ii-i bc *IThrakAig* E212, 16 (f. *Διονύσιος*)
—pautalia: **(21)** s. ii ad *SEG* xlvi 864, 13 (f. *Ἡρωΐδης*)
——(Herakleis): **(22)** ?ii ad *IGB* iv 2077, 13 (s. *—ων*)
—philippopolis-trimontium: **(23)** ii-iii ad ib. iii 885, 5 (*Γλα(ῦ)κος*: s. *Θάλλος*); **(24)** iii ad ib. v 5468, 15 (f. *Αὐρ. Χρῆστος*)
—stryme: **(25)** m. iv bc *IThrakAig* E161 (s. *Ἀντιπατρίδης*)

Γλαυκώπιος
Thrace:
—odessos?: **(1)** vi ad Beševliev 100, 3 (or Thrace Hadrianopolis?: -κό-: f. *Εὐσταθία*)

Γλάφυρος
Thrace:
—novae: **(1)** ii ad *IGLNovae* 92 (*ILB* 319) (Lat. T. Aelius Glaphyrus)

Γλύκαινα
Scythia Minor:
—istros*: (1) iii ad *ISM* i 292, 2 (*Ἰουλ. Γλύκενα*: d. *Ἰουλ. Καλλιοτέρα*)

Γλυκαρία
Cimmerian Bosporos:
—achilleion (nr.): (1) 105 ad *CIRB* 1021, 5 (m. *Δάδας*, ?m. *Μαίσωος*, *Ταυρίσκος*, *Ἀπολλώνιος*)
—nymphaion: (2) s. i bc ib. 913 (-*ρεία*)

Γλυκάριν
Cimmerian Bosporos:
—pantikapaion: (1) i/ii ad ib. 594

Γλυκάριον
Cimmerian Bosporos:
—pantikapaion: (1) i bc/i ad ib. 305; cf. KW pl. 20 no. 286

Γλυκαρίων
Cimmerian Bosporos:
—gorgippia: (1) f. i ad *CIRB* 1197 A (s. *Ποθίσκος*); (2) s. ii ad ib. 1145, 2 ([*Γ*]*λυκαρίων*); (3) 173-210 ad ib. 1134, 26 (*Γλυκαρί*[*ων*]: f. *Εὔμαχος*)
—pantikapaion: (4) ii-i bc ib. 264; cf. KW pl. 37 no. 550 (s. *Μενεκλῆς*); (5) ?i ad *CIRB* 381 (s. *Βάκχιος*); (6) i ad ib. 838 (*SEG* xxvi 846); *Topoi* 3 (1993) p. 182 (date); (7) f. i ad *VDI* 1968 (2), p. 131, 1 (I f. *Γλυκαρίων* II); (8) ~ ib. l. 1 (II s. *Γλυκαρίων* I); (9) i/ii ad *CIRB* 596 (s. *Ψυχαρίων*)

Γλυκεῖα
Scythia Minor:
—kallatis: (1) iii/ii bc *IKyz* i 510, 4 (*Steinepigramme* 2 p. 55) (-*κέα*: m. *Ἡδεῖα*)
Thrace:
—byzantion: (2) ?ii-i bc *IByz* 139 (-*κέα*: d. *Ἡράκων*); (3) ii/i bc ib. 192 (Fıratlı–Robert p. 57 no. 37) (*Πῶλλα Πακωνία Γλυκῆα*: d. *Σπόριος*); (4) i bc-i ad *IByz* 270 (Fıratlı–Robert pp. 86-7 no. 108a) (-*κέα*: d. *Μενεκράτης*)
——(Rhegion?): (5) hell.? *SGDI* 3074 (*IByz* 297) ([*Γ*]*λυκέα*: d. *Μᾶτρις*)
—salymbria (nr.): (6) hell. ib. S 54 (d. *Μηνακῶν*)

Γλυκέρα
Thrace:
—maroneia: (1) hell. *EEBS* 42 (1975-6) p. 226 (*IThrakAig* E251) (d. *Προκλῆς*)
—rhaidestos: (2) ii-i bc PM 384 (d. *Ἀλέξανδρος*)

Γλυκερία
Macedonia (Mygdonia):
—thessalonike?: (1) v-vi ad *IG* x (2) (1) 785 + Feissel, *RICM* 168 (*Γλυκερίᾳ*: d. *Δημήτριος*, *Σαββατίς*)
Thrace:
—maroneia: (2) iv-v ad *IThrakAig* E344 (-*ρῆα*)
—traianopolis: (3) m. ii ad *DCB* (-)

Γλυκέριος
Macedonia (Edonis):
—philippoi: (1) v-vi ad Feissel, *RICM* 244 (Pilhofer 275) (*Γλ*[*υ*]*κέρ*[*ιος*]?—Feissel)
Thrace:
—bisanthe-panion: (2) iv-vi ad *AD* 49-50 (1994-5) Mel. p. 329 no. 154

Γλύκερον
Thrace:
—bizye?: (1) ?ii ad Unp. (Sayar)

Γλύκερος
Macedonia (Bottiaia):
—beroia: (1) ii bc *IBer* 179 (*Γλύκερ*[*ος*]: f. *Ματερώ*)
Thrace*: (2) ii-iii ad Kuzmanov, *Antichni lampy* 282 (lamp)

Γλύκιννα
Macedonia (Mygdonia):
—lete: (1) s. ii ad *SEG* xxxviii 633 (*Τυλλία Γ.*: d. *Ἀττική*)
Thrace:
—abdera: (2) iv/iii bc *IThrakAig* E46 ([*Γλ*]*ύκιννα*: d. *Ἀπολλόδωρος*)
—heraion teichos?: (3) ii bc Taşlıklıoğlu i p. 7 no. 2 (d. *Μοκάπορις*, *Διονυσία*)

Γλυκιννώ
Macedonia (Bottiaia):
—beroia: (1) ii bc *IBer* 159 (Tataki 357) (d. *Ἀλέξανδρος*)

Γλυκίων
Thrace:
—byzantion (territ.): (1) imp. Unp. (Sayar) (f. *Πυθᾶς*)

Γλυκυτής
Thrace:
—odessos: (1) s. ii ad *IGB* i² 181 (PM 1605); *Dacia* 21 (1977) p. 161 (date) (d. *Χαιρέας*)

Γλύκων
Cimmerian Bosporos:
—bosporos?: (1) ii ad *SEG* xvi 441 + *BCH* 103 (1979) p. 522 n. 2 (s. *Φιλάδελφος*)
—gorgippia: (2) ii ad *CIRB* 1157 A, 5; (3) m. ii ad *Eirene* 7 (1968) p. 67, 15 (s. *Χρηστίων*); (4) ii/iii ad *CIRB* 1179, 22 (*Γ*[*λ*]*ύκων*: s. *Σωσίας*); (5) ~ ib. l. 54 (s. *Ἀγαθοῦς*)
—gorgippia?: (6) ii/iii ad ib. 1232, 12 (s. *Πάβας*)
—pantikapaion: (7) i ad ib. 139, 4 (f. *Μοῦσα*); (8) ii ad ib. 664; cf. KW pl. 33 no. 459 (I f. *Γλύκων* II); (9) ~ *CIRB* 664; cf. KW pl. 33 no. 459 (II s. *Γλύκων* I)
Macedonia (Edonis):
—philippoi (territ.): (10) hell.? Dimitsas 1081 (fals.?) (Pilhofer 664)
—philippoi?: (11) ?i-ii ad *AE* 1950-1, p. 67 no. 10 (Pilhofer 725) (or Macedonia (Mygdonia) Thessalonike: Lat. M. Capinius Glyco: f. M. Capinius Priscus)
Macedonia (Mygdonia):
—thessalonike: (12) 90 ad *SEG* xlii 625, 5 (*Γ. Αὐτρώνιος Λίβερ ὁ καὶ Γ.*)
—thessalonike?: (13) iii ad *IG* x (2) (1) 893 (*Αὐρ. Γ.*)
Macedonia (Odomantike):
—sirrha: (14) 155 ad Dimitsas 821, 25 (Kaphtantzis i) (f. *Διογένης*)
Scythia Minor:
—istros: (15) ii ad *ISM* i 196, 3; 201 I, 4 (I f. *Γλύκων* II); (16) ~ ib. 196, 3; 201 I, 4 (II s. *Γλύκων* I); (17) ~ ib. 196, 6; 201 I, 7 (s. *Πίστος*); (18) ~ ib. 196, 7 (II s. *Γλύκων* I); (19) ~ ib. l. 8 (I f. *Γλύκων* II); (20) ~ ib. 197 II, 3 (f. *Καλανδίων*); (21) c. 140-160 ad ib. 207, 19 (*Γλύκ*[*ω*]*ν*: f. —*ος*)
Skythia:
—tanais: (22) ii ad *CIRB* 1263, 9 (*Γλ*(*ύ*)*κων*)
Thrace:
—anchialos (territ.): (23) ii-iii ad *IGB* iii 1842 (s. *Χρύσιππος*)
—byzantion: (24) ii-i bc *IByz* 103 (Fıratlı–Robert p. 95 no. 134) (s. *Μουκάπορις*); (25) ~ *IByz* 116 (f. *Ζωΐλος*)
—dionysopolis: (26) iii ad *IGB* i² 14 b, 18 (*Αὐρ. Γ.*: s. *Θειπης*)
—madytos: (27) imp. *ISestos* 63
—odessos: (28) 215 ad *IGB* i² 47 b, 21 (*Αὐρ. Γ.*: s. *Μαρτιάλης*); (29) ~ ib. 47 c, 16 (f. *Αὐρ. Μᾶρκος*)
—odessos?: (30) ii ad ib. 51 bis b, 3 (f. *Ἡρακλείδης*)
—philippopolis-trimontium:
——Parembole: (31) ii-iii ad ib. iii 1513 ([*Γλ*]*ύκων*: s. *Εὔας*)
—salymbria: (32) imp. *IByz* S 17 (f. *Ποσειδώνις*)

Γνάθιος
Thrace:
—apollonia-sozopolis: (1) v bc *BMNBurgas* 2 (1965) p. 38 fig. 45 no. 240 (vase)

Γνάθων
Tauris:
—chersonesos: (1) iv/iii bc Kats p. 83 no. 1 (amph., tile) (f. *Ἀγάθων*)

Γναῖος
Macedonia (Tymphaia):
—agios georgios (mod.): (1) 153 ad *EAM* 12, 6 (*Νεοπτόλεμος ὁ καὶ Γ.*: s. *Δημήτριος*)
Thrace:
—mesambria: (2) c. 41-54 ad *IGB* i² 322; cf. v 5098 (I f. *Γναῖος* II); (3) ~ ib. i² 322; cf. v 5098 (II s. *Γναῖος* I)

Γναφίσκος
Cimmerian Bosporos:
—gorgippia: (1) ii/iii ad *CIRB* 1179, 43 (f. *Ποθεινός*)

Γνησία
Thrace:
—nicopolis ad istrum: (1) ii/iii ad *Nikopolis ad Istrum* i p. 154 no. 13 with fig. 144 (Lat. [Ant]onia Gnesia)

Γνοῦρος
Skythia:
—skythai: (1) f. vi bc Hdt. iv 76 (s. *Λύκος*, f. *Ἀνάχαρσις*, *Σαύλιος*: king)

Γνώμα
Thrace:
—mesambria*: (1) v bc *IGB* i² 334 octies (freed.)

Γνῶσις
Macedonia (Bottiaia):
—pella: (1) s. iv bc *SEG* xxiv 558 a (mosaic); Guarducci, *Ep. Gr.* 3 p. 441 (date)

Γοαζείρα
Macedonia (Sintike):
—neine: (1) ii ad *IGB* iv 2251

Γόαξις
Macedonia (Edonis):
—edonoi: (1) 424 bc Th. iv 107. 3 (*RE* Supplbd. 7 (-))

Γοδόσαυος
Skythia:
—tanais: (1) 244 ad *CIRB* 1287, 29 (s. *Ἀροάστιρος*)

Γοζίνης
Cimmerian Bosporos:
—gorgippia: (1) ii/iii ad ib. 1179, 57 (*Γοζίνου* (gen.): f. *Πάππος*)

Γοζιοῦς
Cimmerian Bosporos:
—myrmekion: (1) f. ii ad ib. 885 (s. *Σώστρατος*, f. *Λυσίμαχος*)

Γοΐσκος
Cimmerian Bosporos:
—pantikapaion: (1) ii ad ib. 679 B; Zgusta, *PNS* 629 (s. *Μυρῖνος*)

Γοκους
Thrace:
—byzantion (territ.): (1) imp. Unp. (Sayar) (*Γόκουσ*[*α*]?)

Γόκουσα
THRACE:
—BYZANTION: **(1)** ii-i BC *Istanbul Ark. Müz.* 7 (1956) p. 55 with fig. 3; cf. Fıratlı–Robert p. 146; **(2)** ~ *IByz* 160 (Fıratlı–Robert p. 106 no. 168) (d. *Εὐφίλητος*); **(3)** i BC-i AD *IByz* 149 (Fıratlı–Robert pp. 102-3 no. 157) (*Γού-*: d. *Μένανδρος*)
—SALYMBRIA (NR.): **(4)** ii BC *IByz* S 51 (or Thrace Byzantion: *Γούκο[υσα]*)

Γόκων
CIMMERIAN BOSPOROS:
—KEPOI: **(1)** i-ii AD *CIRB* 1012 (s. *Παπίας*)
—MYRMEKION: **(2)** i AD ib. 868; Zgusta, *PNS* 586 (s. *Ἥλιος*)
—PANTIKAPAION: **(3)** i AD *CIRB* 384 A (*Γό-[κ]ων*: f. *Θεμιστοκλῆς*, *—μη—*); **(4)** iii AD ib. 728
—PHANAGOREIA: **(5)** s. i BC ib. 992, 1-2, 4; cf. *Etiudy* pp. 190-2 no. 12 (s. *Ἀγαθοῦς*, f. *Ἀγαθοῦς*, *Τρύφων*, *Ἀπολλώνιος*)
SKYTHIA:
—TANAIS: **(6)** f. ii AD *CIRB* 1266, 3 (f. *Πατεροῦς*)
THRACE:
—BYZANTION?: **(7)** ii-i BC *IByz* 329 (s. *Μηνακῶν*)
—RHAIDESTOS: **(8)** i BC-i AD PM 182 a (II s. *Γόκων* I); **(9)** ~ ib. 182 a-b (I f. *Γόκων* II, *Πυθίς*)

Γολαῖος
SKYTHIA:
—OLBIA-BORYSTHENES: **(1)** s. ii AD *SEG* XLIII 507, 5 (f. *—υς*)

Γόλας
SKYTHIA:
—OLBIA-BORYSTHENES: **(1)** ii AD *IOSPE* I^2 83, 9; 99, 4; Zgusta, *PNS* 285 (f. *Δωτοῦς*)

Γόλης
THRACE:
—GLAVA PANEGA (MOD.): **(1)** ii-iii AD *IGB* II 554 (*Γολήους* (gen.): f. *Γάϊς*)
—LIPNICA (MOD.): **(2)** iii AD ib. 501 (*Μακου τοῦ καὶ Γολείους* (gen.): f. *Γάϊος*)

Γόλυς
MACEDONIA:
—PRASSIOI: **(1)** s. iv BC *IG* II^2 9269 (Tataki, *Macedonians* p. 169 no. 1; *FRA* 3467) (*(Π)όλυς*?: f. *Σάτυρος*)

Γομαρία
CIMMERIAN BOSPOROS:
—PANTIKAPAION: **(1)** ii-i BC *CIRB* 292; cf. KW pl. 32 no. 449; Zgusta, *PNS* 630

Γοργάτας
MACEDONIA: **(1)** 334-330 BC *RE* Supplbd. 4 (-); Berve 232 (Tataki, *Macedonians* p. 287 no. 13) (Lat. Gorgatas)

Γοργία
CIMMERIAN BOSPOROS:
—PANTIKAPAION: **(1)** imp. *CIRB* 786 (d. *Ἑρμα—*)

Γοργίας
CIMMERIAN BOSPOROS:
—GORGIPPIA: **(1)** f. iii BC ib. 1137 A I, 21 (f. *Βλέψος*); **(2)** ~ ib. l. 25, 58; 1137 B II, 55 (I f. *Γοργίας* II); **(3)** ~ ib. 1137 A I, 25, 58; 1137 B II, 55 (II s. *Γοργίας* I); **(4)** ~ ib. 1137 A I, 51 (f. *Παγουρίων*) ?= (*5*); **(5)** ~ ib. l. 53 (f. *Στρατόνικος*) ?= (*6*) (*4*); **(6)** ~ ib. l. 55 (f. *Εὔβουλος*) ?= (*5*); **(7)** ~ ib. 1137 A II, 11; 1137 B I, 34 (f. *Ἀπήμαντος*); **(8)** ~ ib. l. 52 (s. *Παγουρίων*); **(9)** ii AD *NE* 9 (1971) p. 6 no. 3, 7 (*Γοργία[s]*); **(10)** ~ *CIRB* 1166, 2 (*Γοργί[ας]*); **(11)** m. ii AD *Eirene* 7 (1968) p. 67, 5 (f. *Φαρνακίων*); **(12)** s. ii AD *SEG* XXXVI 707, 3 (*Γοργία[s]*); **(13)** ii/iii AD *CIRB* 1179, 22 (f. *Σωσίας*); **(14)** ~ ib. l. 42-3 (f. *Ἀγαθοῦς*)
—GORGIPPIA?: **(15)** s. ii AD ib. 1231 A, 12 (*Γοργία[s]*)
—PANTIKAPAION: **(16)** iii-ii BC *Sov. Arkh.* 28 (1958) pp. 132-3 (tile); **(17)** i AD *CIRB* 331, 3 (s. *Ἀγάθων*, *Ἀπολλωνία*)
MACEDONIA: **(18)** c. 380-324 BC *RE* (3); Berve 233 (Tataki, *Macedonians* p. 287 no. 14); **(19)** 334-330 BC *RE* Supplbd. 4 (3a); Berve 234 (Tataki, *Macedonians* p. 287 no. 15) (Lat. Gorgias)
MACEDONIA (BOTTIAIA):
—MIEZA: **(20)** iii BC *SEG* XXIV 524 II, 7, 14, 20, 27, 34 (Hatzopoulos, *MI* 2 p. 106 no. 92) (f. *Ζώπυρος*)
MACEDONIA (CHALKIDIKE):
—OLYNTHOS: **(21)** s. iv BC *IG* II^2 10020 (Tataki, *Macedonians* p. 132 no. 22; *FRA* 5888) (s. *Διοκλῆς*); **(22)** 216 BC *Milet* I (3) 181, 9 (Tataki, *Macedonians* p. 132 no. 23) (f. *Χειρικράτης*)
MACEDONIA (EDONIS):
—AMPHIPOLIS: **(23)** hell.? *AD* 22 (1967) Chron. p. 427 (s. *Ἀπολλόδωρος*)
MACEDONIA (MYGDONIA):
—KALINDOIA: **(24)** 68-98 AD *SEG* XLII 580, 29 (s. *Φιλώτας*)
MACEDONIA (PELAGONIA): **(25)** ii-i BC *IG* X (2) (2) 159, 8 (s. *Ἐπιγένης*)
MACEDONIA (PIERIA):
—DION: **(26)** iii BC *SEG* XXXI 629, 3 (s. *Φερεκλῆς*)
SCYTHIA MINOR:
—KALLATIS: **(27)** iii-ii BC *ZfN* 30 (1913) p. 300 no. 253b (coin) (*Γοργ(ίας)*?, *Γόργ(υθος)*?); **(28)** iii/ii BC *CIRB* 252 (f. *Δαμοφῶν*)
SKYTHIA:
—OLBIA-BORYSTHENES: **(29)** f. iv BC Dubois, *IGDOlbia* 104 (s. *Ἡροκράτης*); **(30)** iii BC *IOSPE* I^2 201 I, 23 (s. *Εὐβίοτος*)
—TANAIS: **(31)** 220 AD *CIRB* 1278, 8 (*Γ[ο]ργίας*—Tokhtas'ev: s. *Φαρνακίων*); **(32)** ~ ib. l. 16 (*Γοργί[ας]*: f. *Σαμβατίων*); **(33)** 228 AD ib. 1283, 13 (f. *Εὐτυχιανός*)
THRACE:
—BEROE-AUGUSTA TRAIANA (TERRIT.): **(34)** iii AD *IGB* III 1677 (*GVI* 193)
—BYZANTION: **(35)** i BC-i AD *IByz* 102 (Fıratlı–Robert p. 95 no. 133) (f. *Τύραννος*); **(36)** ~ *IByz* 131 (Fıratlı–Robert p. 98 no. 144) (*Γωρ-*: f. *Ἀρέσκουσα*)
—SPINOPARA: **(37)** ii AD *IGB* IV 2192, 13

Γοργίππα
TAURIS:
—CHERSONESOS: **(1)** iv BC Solomonik, *NEPKh* 166 (d. *Μᾶτρις*)

Γόργιππος
CIMMERIAN BOSPOROS:
—BOSPOROS: **(1)** ?iv BC *CIG* 8566 b (ring) (f. *Ὄρχαμος*); **(2)** iv BC Polyaen. viii 55; *CIRB* 1015 (Rhodes–Osborne 65 D); cf. *SEG* XLV 1016; *IGAIMK* 104 (1935) p. 302 no. 14 (tile); *Hyperboreus* 1994-5 (2), p. 136 n. 16 (s. *Σάτυρος*, f. *Κομοσαρύη*)

Γοργόνεια
THRACE:
—ODESSOS: **(1)** ii-iii AD *IGB* V 5074. 4b

Γοργόνιος
THRACE:
—BISANTHE-PANION: **(1)** byz.? *JÖAI* 23 (1926) Beibl. col. 157 no. 94g, 2

Γοργόνις
MACEDONIA (BOTTIAIA):
—BEROIA: **(1)** iv AD *SEG* XLIX 688 (*Γογώρνι* (gen.?/n. pr.?): ?f. *Ἰουστῖνος*: Jew)

Γόργος
CIMMERIAN BOSPOROS:
—GORGIPPIA: **(1)** f. iii BC *CIRB* 1137 B II, 57 (f. *Θράσυλλος*)
THRACE:
—VICUS TRULLENSIUM: **(2)** 161-169 or 198-209 AD *ILB* 180, 5 (Lat. Gorgus: f. *Ζωΐλος*)

Γοργόσας
CIMMERIAN BOSPOROS:
—GORGIPPIA: **(1)** ii/iii AD *CIRB* 1179, 44 (f. *Χαχας*)

Γόργυθος
MACEDONIA (MYGDONIA):
—DIKAIA: **(1)** c. 365-359 BC Unp. (Voutyras–Sismanidis) ll. 28-9, 38, 51
SCYTHIA MINOR:
—KALLATIS: **(2)** iii BC *ISM* III 126, 3 (f. *...ρατος*)

Γόρδιος
TAURIS:
—CHERSONESOS: **(1)** f. i AD *SGE* 25 (1964) p. 63 (vase)

Γόρδις
CIMMERIAN BOSPOROS:
—PANTIKAPAION: **(1)** iv BC *CIRB* 168 (s. *Ἀρμάδης*, *Δημητρία*); **(2)** s. iv BC ib. 184 (f. *Ἥδικα*)

Γορτας
THRACE:
—PAUTALIA: **(1)** s. ii AD *SEG* XLVI 864 I, 25

Γόσα
TAURIS:
—CHERSONESOS: **(1)** iii BC *IAK* 65 (1918) p. 12 no. 2; *Hellenismus* p. 447 no. 10a (name) (d. *Φίλιππος*)

Γοσαμφλίας
CIMMERIAN BOSPOROS:
—PANTIKAPAION: **(1)** 275-278 AD *CIRB* 36, 14 (*Γ[ο]σ[α]μφλί[α]ς*?—Vinogradov, *Γ[ο]σ[ε]μφλί[ας]*—*CIRB*: f. *Μενέστρατος*)

Γοσήτλεις
CIMMERIAN BOSPOROS:
—GORGIPPIA: **(1)** s. ii AD ib. 1142, 13 (s. *Ἀκάσας*)

Γόσων
TAURIS:
—CHERSONESOS: **(1)** iv BC Solomonik, *NEPKh* 28; *Hellenismus* p. 446 no. 10 (*Γόσω[ν]*—ed., *Πόσω[ν]*?: s. *Παπίας*) ?= (*2*); **(2)** f. iv BC *IOSPE* I^2 512; *Hellenismus* p. 446 no. 10 (date) ?= (*1*)

Γότος
CIMMERIAN BOSPOROS:
—PANTIKAPAION: **(1)** s. iv BC *CIRB* 226; cf. *SEG* XXX 982 (f. *Κοιράνης*)

Γουβάζης
KOLCHIS:
—LAZOI: **(1)** m. v AD *PLRE* II (-) (king); **(2)** 541-555 AD ib. III (-); *RE* (-) (king)

Γούρας
MACEDONIA (CHALKIDIKE):
—SPARTOLOS?: **(1)** ?352 BC *SEG* XLVI 804, 8 (s. *Πείσων*)
—STREPSA?: **(2)** 285 BC ib. XXXVIII 619, 20 (s. *Ἀννύθης*)
MACEDONIA (MYGDONIA):
—THESSALONIKE: **(3)** s. iii BC *IG* X (2) (1) 94 (f. *Ἱερομνήμων*); **(4)** ii-iii AD *SEG* L 644 (*Γούρα* (dat.))

Macedonia (Odomantike):
—berge: (5) iv bc *AE* 1936, Chron. p. 17 no. 9 (Pilhofer 567) (s. *Σκόρος*)

Γουράσιος
Macedonia (Edonis):
—philippoi: (1) iv-vi ad Feissel, *RICM* 236 (Pilhofer 102)

Γουρθειθος
Thrace:
—abryttos: (1) iii ad *IGB* ii 744, 9 + v 5264 ([*Γ*]*ουρθειθος*: f. *Δρει—ούζερις*)

Γουρθιθις
Thrace:
—dionysopolis: (1) iii ad ib. I^{2} 14 c, 17 (*Αὐρ. Γ.*: s. *Πάπας*)

Γοῦρος
Scythia Minor:
—kallatis: (1) iii/ii bc *IG* xi (4) 1238 (f. *Γαῦκος*)

Γραίη
Macedonia (Bottiaia):
—pella: (1) iii-ii bc *SEG* l 611 (?d. *Αἴολος*)

Γράνιος
Macedonia (Paionia):
—stoboi: (1) s. iii ad *JÖAI* 32 (1940) Beibl. col. 19 no. 13. 138 (*ΓΡΑΝΟΥ*—lap.)
Thrace:
—philippopolis-trimontium: (2) iii ad *IGB* iii 917, 5 (f. *Ἡρακλείδης*)

Γράπτη
Macedonia (Bottiaia):
—beroia: (1) ii ad *IBer* 309, 2
—edessa: (2) iii-iv ad *GVI* 2036, 13 (*IDyrrh* 527 bis; Tataki, *Edessa* 149) (*Κλ. Γ.*)
Macedonia (Mygdonia):
—thessalonike?: (3) ii-iii ad *IG* x (2) (1) 921

Γράπτος
Macedonia (Lynkestis):
—herakleia?: (1) ii ad ib. x (2) (2) 125 (f. *Ἱστορία*)
Macedonia (Mygdonia):
—thessalonike*: (2) imp. *SEG* xlvii 994 (terracotta)

Γρατίσημα?
Macedonia (Bottiaia):
—beroia*: (1) v-vi ad *IBer* 447, 4 (Feissel, *RICM* 60) (Lat. Gratissima?)

Γρᾶτος
Macedonia (Derriopos):
—stuberra: (1) 74 ad *IG* x (2) (2) 326, 62 (s. *Ἐπίκαδος*)
Thrace:
—beroe-augusta traiana:
——Karasoura: (2) ii-iii ad *IGB* iii 1630 (f. *Μουκάτραλις*)

Γράφη
Thrace: (1) i bc-i ad *NS* 217

Γραφικός
Macedonia (Bottiaia):
—edessa: (1) iii ad Dimitsas 4, 1, 7 (*GVI* 1772; Tataki, *Edessa* 74); (2) 243 ad *Athena* 12 (1900) p. 72 no. 9, 1 (Tataki, *Edessa* 297) (*Φαβ. Γ.*)
Scythia Minor:
—tomis: (3) s. ii ad *ISM* ii 131 (*IGB* iii 1874; *CCET* iv 26 (locn., date)) (f. *Μᾶρκος*)
Thrace:
—philippopolis-trimontium (territ.): (4) ii-iii ad *IGB* iii 1480 (or Thrace Diokletianopolis: [*Γρ*]*αφικός*)

Γρεφίς
Macedonia (Bottiaia):
—beroia: (1) f. iii ad *IBer* 342, 2 (Tataki 361) ([*Αὐρ.*] *Γ.*: m. *Λεοντίσκος*, *Φιλίππα*)

Γρηγορία
Thrace:
—beroe-augusta traiana: (1) c. 320-324 ad *Anal. Boll.* 31 (1912) p. 198; p. 208

Γρηγόριος
Macedonia (Bottiaia):
—beroia: (1) ii-iii ad *IBer* 329 (threptos)
Macedonia (Mygdonia):
—thessalonike: (2) ?vi ad Feissel, *RICM* 94 (monogram) (*SEG* xlvii 995)

Γρήγορος
Scythia Minor:
—istros: (1) i ad *ISM* i 200, 4 (f. *Δημοχάρης*); (2) ~ ib. l. 12 (f. *Πολυαίνετος*); (3) 138 ad ib. 193 I, 28 (s. *Κάρπος*); (4) ~ ib. 193 II, 65 (f. *Ἀρτεμίδωρος*); (5) 222-225 ad ib. 100, 9 (*Αὐρ. Γ.*: s. *Ἀρτεμίδωρος*)

Γρυλίων
Thrace: (1) 414 bc *IG* I^{3} 422, 196 (*FRA* 2510) ([*Γρ*]*υλίōν*: slave)

Γυγαία
Macedonia: (1) vi/v bc *RE* Supplbd. 4 (-) (Tataki, *Macedonians* p. 288 no. 18) (*Γυγαίη*—Hdt.: d. *Ἀμύντας* I, m. *Ἀμύντας*); (2) v/iv bc Just. vii 4. 5 (Tataki, *Macedonians* p. 288 no. 19); cf. Beloch, *GG* iii (2) pp. 66-7 (Lat. Gygaia: m. *Ἀρχέλαος*, *Ἀρριδαῖος*, *Μενέλαος*)

Γύγης
Cimmerian Bosporos:
—pantikapaion: (1) iv bc Blavatskii, *Pantikapei* p. 93 (vase) (*Γύγηντος* (gen.))
Macedonia (Chalkidike):
—torone: (2) a. 322 bc *IG* xii (6) 46, 1, 5 (Tataki, *Macedonians* p. 191 no. 5) (s. *Μενεσθεύς*)

Γυδίας
Macedonia (Mygdonia):
—kalindoia: (1) c. 316 bc Hatzopoulos, *MI* 2 p. 84 no. 62, 30; cf. *Anthémonte–Kalindoia* 2 p. 238 (name) (s. *Κρίθων*)

Γύζη
Thrace:
—kellai*: (1) iii ad *IGB* iii 1516 b, 20 (d. *Σελας*, *Ζείλη*)

Γυκεῖα
Scythia Minor:
—istros: (1) iii bc *ISM* i 114 (d. *Διονύσιος*)

Thrace:
—byzantion: (2) i bc-i ad *IByz* 153 (Fıratlı-Robert pp. 103-4 no. 160) (-*κέα*: d. *Φιλόξενος*)
——(Rhegion): (3) f. i bc *IByz* 197 (Fıratlı-Robert p. 59 no. 42) ([*Γυ*]*κῆα*?: d. *Ζωτᾶς*)

Γύκεις
Scythia Minor:
—tomis: (1) ii-iii ad *ISM* ii 468, 3 (?s. *Κο*—)

Γυκέρα
Thrace:
—dionysopolis: (1) iii/ii bc *IGB* I^{2} 21 (*Γ*(*λ*)*υκέρα*—ed.: m. *Καλλικράτης*)

Γυκία
Tauris:
—chersonesos: (1) s. i bc Const. Porph., *De admin. imp.* 53, 239 ff. (d. *Λάμαχος*)

Γύκων
Thrace:
—apollonia-sozopolis: (1) s. i bc *IGB* I^{2} 395 quater, 4 (*Γ*(*λ*)*ύκων*?: f. *Ἀθηναΐς*)

Γῦλις
Macedonia (Mygdonia):
—kalindoia: (1) c. 324 bc Hatzopoulos, *MI* 2 p. 84 no. 62, 21 (s. *Εὐρύτιος*)

Γύλλος
Cimmerian Bosporos:
—nymphaion: (1) iii bc *CIRB* 912 II, 16; Zgusta, *PNS* 942 (f. *Ἀπίντας*)

Γύλων
Thrace:
—odessos: (1) iii ad *IGB* I^{2} 141 bis (*Γύ*[*λ*]*ων*?—ed., *Γύ*[*κ*]*ων*?: f. *Βράκη*)

Γυμνάσιον
Macedonia (Bottiaia):
—pella: (1) hell. Tataki, *Macedonians* p. 153 no. 30 (d. *Δημήτριος*)
Thrace: (2) ii bc *IG* II^{2} 8902a (*FRA* 2511)

Γυναῖς
Cimmerian Bosporos:
—korokondame: (1) ii-iii ad *CIRB* 1109 A (*Γύναι* (voc.)—n. pr.?: d. *Στέφανος*)

Γυνδάνης
Skythia:
—skythai: (1) ii ad Luc., *Tox.* 61 (fict.)

Γύρτος
Macedonia (Mygdonia):
—kalindoia: (1) c. 332 bc Hatzopoulos, *MI* 2 p. 84 no. 62, 13; cf. *Anthémonte–Kalindoia* 2 p. 238 (name) (f. *Ἰκκότας*)

Γώσακος
Skythia:
—tanais: (1) 220-225 ad *CIRB* 1278, 17; 1279, 24 (s. *Ἄσπακος*)

Δ

Δα
Tauris:
—kalos limen*: **(1)** ii bc Solomonik, *GChKh* 456 (vase); cf. *SEG* xxxviii 749. 9; *Hellenismus* p. 448 no. 12 (or Pontos Sinope)

Δάαις
Thrace:
—salymbria: **(1)** imp. *IByz* S 44 (s. *Κότυς*, f. *Ἀθηναΐς*)

Δαβεις
Thrace:
—gorsko ablanovo (mod.): **(1)** iii ad *IGB* ii 752 (*CCET* ii (2) 582)

Δαβρέας
Macedonia: **(1)** c. 235-200 bc La'da E1744 (s. *Εὐρύλοχος*: t.e.); **(2)** 145 bc *PPhrurDiosk* 18, 43, 54 (*Δαβρ̣έ̣α̣ς*)

Δαβρείας
Macedonia (Bottiaia):
—beroia: **(1)** iv-iii bc *IBer* 148 (Tataki 362) (*Δαβρ[είας]*: f. *Ἀντιγόνα*)
Macedonia (Eordaia):
—kelle?: **(2)** ii-i bc *EAM* 93; Hatzopoulos, *MI* i p. 94 n. 4 (locn.) (s. *Ὀνόμαστος*) ?= (*4*); **(3)** ~ *SEG* xlviii 804; **(4)** s. ii bc *EAM* 118 (s. *Ὀνόμαστος*, f. *Πραξινόη*) ?= (*2*)
Macedonia (Mygdonia):
—kalindoia: **(5)** c. 308 bc Hatzopoulos, *MI* 2 p. 84 no. 62, 38 (*Δαβρ[είας]*: f. *Γλαυκίας*)

Δαγδας
Macedonia (Pelagonia): **(1)** ii ad *IG* x (2) (2) 242 (s. *Οὐάλης*)

Δάγουζις
Macedonia (Mygdonia):
—kalindoia: **(1)** a. 98 ad *SEG* xlii 582, 70; cf. *Anthémonte–Kalindoia* 2 p. 239 (name) (*Δαγούζιος* (gen.): f. *Τηρήπης*)

Δάγουσις
Macedonia (Edonis):
—philippoi (territ.): **(1)** 167 ad Pikoulas, *Chora* p. 159 no. 66 (Pilhofer 599) (*Δαγούσιδος* (gen.): f. *Μάντα*)

Δάδα
Macedonia (Bottiaia):
—beroia: **(1)** ii bc *IBer* 181 (Tataki 363)

Δάδαγος
Skythia:
—olbia-borysthenes: **(1)** f. i ad *IOlbia* 42, 4; cf. Vinogradov–Kryžickij p. 144 (date); Zgusta, *PNS* 99 (s. *Πάδαγος*); **(2)** c. 81-96 ad *IOSPE* i² 139, 4; *SEG* xliv 666 (date) (*Δάδα[γ]ος*: f. *Πεισίστρατος*); **(3)** ii-iii ad *IOSPE* i² 137, 10 (s. *Κουζαῖος*)

Δαδαῖος
Cimmerian Bosporos:
—pantikapaion: **(1)** iv bc *CIRB* 179; Zgusta, *PNS* 598 (f. *Δροβολους*)
—theodosia: **(2)** iii ad *CIRB* 947 B, 11 (*Δα̣δ̣α̣ῖ̣ος*: f. *Τρύφων*)

Δάδακος
Skythia:
—olbia-borysthenes: **(1)** imp. *IOlbia* 87, 3; Zgusta, *PNS* 99 (s. *Ἱεροσῶν*); **(2)** ii ad *IOSPE* i² 84, 3 (f. *Ἀρχίδημος*)

Δάδας
Cimmerian Bosporos:
—achilleion (nr.): **(1)** 105 ad *CIRB* 1021, 9 (s. *Ἀπολλώνιος*, *Γλυκαρία*)
—gorgippia: **(2)** imp. ib. 1187, 2; Zgusta, *PNS* 598; **(3)** s. ii ad *CIRB* 1145, 9 (s. *Ταυρέας*); **(4)** ii/iii ad *SEG* xlix 1033 A, 4 (*CIRB* 1182 A, 3); **(5)** 244 ad ib. 1287, 11 (f. *Σάρακος*)
—hermonassa: **(6)** 123-132 ad ib. 1054, 18 (f. *Δημοκράτης*); **(7)** ~ ib. l. 20 (s. *Ἀπολλώνιος*)
—pantikapaion: **(8)** i/ii ad ib. 595; **(9)** iii ad ib. 103, 5; **(10)** ~ ib. l. 7 (s. *Ἀντίμαχος*); **(11)** ~ ib. 727 (f. *Χόδιος*); **(12)** 221 ad ib. 100, 7
—phanagoreia: **(13)** i ad ib. 998
—phanagoreia (nr.): **(14)** iii ad ib. 1016, 4 (s. *Νουμήνιος*)
—theodosia: **(15)** iii ad ib. 947 A, 10 (s. *Εὐχάριστος*); **(16)** ~ ib. 947 B, 13 (f. *Εὔδαμος*)
Macedonia (Bottiaia):
—ichnai: **(17)** hell.? *IG* ii² 8944 (Tataki, *Macedonians* p. 113 no. 4; *FRA* 2638) (*Δάδου* (gen.): f. *Εὐρυδίκη*)
Macedonia (Edonis):
—amphipolis: **(18)** m. iii bc Hatzopoulos, *Actes Amphipolis* p. 52 no 12, 8; *SEG* xli 566 (date) (*Δάδου* (gen.): f. *Καλλίστρατος*)
—philippoi: **(19)** imp. *CIL* iii 676 (Pilhofer 346) (Lat. Gaius Dada)
Macedonia (Sintike)?: **(20)** ii ad *IGB* iv 2332
Scythia Minor:
—istros: **(21)** i bc-i ad *ISM* i 187; **(22)** 138 ad ib. 193 II, 26 (s. *Μήνιος*)
—kallatis: **(23)** s. i ad ib. iii 67, 4
—tomis: **(24)** ii ad ib. ii 17, 12 (s. *Ἑστιαῖος*); **(25)** ~ ib. l. 17 (f. *Σεραπίων*); **(26)** ii-iii ad ib. 18, 1; **(27)** ~ ib. 26, 5 (s. *Διονύσιος*); **(28)** ~ ib. 295 (Lat. Dada: f. *Ἀπολλώνιος*)
—ulmetum: **(29)** ii ad ib. v 79, 2 (*CCET* iv 108) (Lat. Dada (gen.): f. Ithazis)
Skythia:
—olbia-borysthenes (nr.): **(30)** m. ii ad *VDI* 1953 (4), p. 130, 4 (s. *Πεισίστρατος*)
—tanais: **(31)** ii ad *CIRB* 1263, 12; **(32)** f. ii ad ib. 1264 A, 7; **(33)** 104 ad ib. 1259, 16 (s. *Θεόνικος*); **(34)** 154-170 ad ib. 1260a, 16; **(35)** 155 ad ib. 1260, 18 (*[Δ]άδας*: s. *Θεάγγελος*); **(36)** 192 ad ib. 1243, 16 (s. *Ζήνων*, f. *Εὖϊος*); **(37)** 193 ad ib. 1237, 9, 12 (s. *ΕΚΙΣ* (lap.), f. *Ζήνων*); **(38)** 220 ad ib. 1278, 10 (f. *Φάννης*); **(39)** ~ ib. l. 12 (s. *Πάππος*); **(40)** 225 ad ib. 1280, 12 (f. *Φαρνάκης*); **(41)** 228 ad ib. 1282, 13 (s. *Οὐαλέριος*); **(42)** ~ ib. l. 17 (f. *Ἀριστόδημος*); **(43)** ~ ib. 1283, 13 (f. *Καρδίους*); **(44)** ~ ib. l. 15 (s. *Χοδιάκιος*); **(45)** 230 ad ib. 1284, 10 (f. *—ς*); **(46)** 244 ad ib. 1287, 20 (f. *[Ἀ]ρσοα—ος*)
Thrace: **(47)** ?ii-i bc *Syringes* 693; 698 (Velkov 69; La'da E724) (s. *Ζίπυρος*)
—byzantion: **(48)** i bc *IByz* 198 (Fıratlı–Robert pp. 59-60 no. 43) (*Μ. Ἀντώνιος Δ.*); **(49)** i bc-i ad *IByz* 234 (s. *Ἀπολλώνιος*, f. *Χρήστη*)
—byzantion (territ.): **(50)** imp. Unp. (Sayar) (s. *Ἀθαναίων*)
—markianopolis (territ.): **(51)** iii ad *IGB* ii 853 (*CCET* ii (1) 258) (s. *Δαλήπορις*)
—odessos: **(52)** i-ii ad *IGB* i² 51 c, 5 (f. *Διονύσιος*); **(53)** ii ad ib. 50 a, 11 (s. *Ἀρτεμίδωρος*); **(54)** 215 ad ib. 47 b, 18 (f. *Αὐρ. Ἀντίπατρος*); **(55)** ~ ib. 47 c, 11 (f. *Αὐρ. Ἀγαθήνωρ*)
—odessos (nr.): **(56)** i-ii ad ib. 286 (*CCET* i 83) (*Ἀγαθήνωρ ὁ καὶ Δ.*: s. *Πόσσις*)
—odessos?: **(57)** ii ad *IGB* i² 51 bis a, 8 (f. *Ἀγάθων*)
—perinthos-herakleia: **(58)** i bc-i ad? Dumont–Homolle 72d, 8; cf. *IPerinth* 57 (om. per err.) (f. *Σωτήριχος*)
—stryme: **(59)** m. iv bc *SEG* xlvii 1104 + *IThrakAig* E153 (*Δάδου* (gen.): f. *Δημήτριος*)

Δάδης
Macedonia (Paionia):
—negotino (mod.): **(1)** iii ad *SEG* xxxviii 713 (*Δάδεος* (gen.): f. *Ἀμμακώ*)

Δαδῖνος
Macedonia: **(1)** ?417-413 bc *IG* i³ 89, 66 (Tataki, *Macedonians* p. 289 no. 3) (*Δαδ[ῖ]νος*)

Δάδος
Cimmerian Bosporos:
—gorgippia: **(1)** ii/iii ad *CIRB* 1179, 53 (f. *Κατόκας*)
—pantikapaion: **(2)** 275-278 ad ib. 36, 67 (s. *Στράτων*)
Skythia:
—olbia-borysthenes: **(3)** inc. *IOSPE* i² 281 (s. *Σατυ—*); **(4)** imp. ib. 149, 2; Zgusta, *PNS* 598; **(5)** i/ii ad *IOlbia* 88, 3 (I f. *Δάδος* II) ?= (*10*); **(6)** ~ ib. l. 3 (II s. *Δάδος* I) ?= (*9*); **(7)** ~ *IOSPE* i² 200, 2; 203, 5 (s. *Σωσίβιος*); **(8)** ii ad *IOlbia* 86, 7 (f. *Ποσείδηος*); **(9)** ~ *IOSPE* i² 91, 5 (II s. *Δάδος* I) ?= (*6*); **(10)** ~ ib. l. 6 (I f. *Δάδος* II) ?= (*5*); **(11)** ~ ib. 105, 7 (f. *Γερμανός*); **(12)** ii-iii ad ib. 52, [1], 16 (s. *Τούμβαγος*); **(13)** c. 193-211 ad ib. 42, 3; 43, 6; 174, 10 (f. *Καλλισθένης*); **(14)** iii ad ib. 135, 4 (f. *Δανδάξαρθος*)

Δαδοῦς
Cimmerian Bosporos:
—theodosia: **(1)** iii ad *CIRB* 947 A, 13; Zgusta, *PNS* 598 (*[Δ]αδοῦς*: s. *Τιμοκράτης*)

Δαδοῦχος
Macedonia (Mygdonia):
—thessalonike*: **(1)** ii-iii ad *IG* x (2) (1) 811 (*Κ. Φούριος Δ.*: freed.)
Thrace:
—byzantion?: **(2)** i-ii ad *GVI* 1083 with n. (*Φλ. Δ.*: f. *Μαρκιανή*)

Δαέζερις
Thrace:
—gorna bešovica (mod.): **(1)** iii ad *IGB* v 5180, 1 (f. *Αὐρ. Μάξιμος*, *Αὐρ. Οὐαλεριανός*)

Δαζαῖος
Macedonia (Bottiaia):
—pella: **(1)** s. iii bc *SEG* xxiv 551 b (f. *Ἀδάνα*)

Δάζεις
Cimmerian Bosporos:
—gorgippia?: **(1)** s. ii ad *CIRB* 1231 A, 17; Zgusta, *PNS* 599 (*Δάζει* (gen.): f. *Αταμάζας*)

Δάζις
Thrace:
—markianopolis (territ.): **(1)** iii-iv ad *IGB* v 5328, 2 (*CCET* ii (1) 365) (*Δαζι* (gen.): f. *Βατουδεις*)

Δάης
Scythia Minor:
—tomis: **(1)** ii ad *ISM* ii 125 I, 19 (*Δάη* (gen.): f. *Ποσειδώνιος*)

Δαιδάλις
Macedonia (Mygdonia):
—thessalonike: **(1)** iii ad *IG* x (2) (1) 561, 1 (*Αἴλ. Πετρωνιανὸς Εὔτυχος Δ.*: ?s. *Πετρώνιος Λύκος*, *Πετιλία Βικτωρία*)

Δαϊκράτης
Skythia:
—olbia-borysthenes: **(1)** hell. *Arkheologiia* (Kiev) 39 (1982) p. 39 (stamp); **(2)** iii bc *IOSPE* i² 201 II, 18 (s. *Ἀριστόδημος*)

Δαικώσης
THRACE: (1) iii AD Speidel, *Denkmäler* 608, 2 (Lat. Aurel. Daicosi (dat.))
—HADRIANOPOLIS (TERRIT.): (2) ii-iii AD *IGB* III 1803, 2 (f. *Μουκάκενθος*)

Δαΐμαχος
MACEDONIA: (1) 221-205 BC *BGU* 1964, 2, 4-5, etc. (Tataki, *Macedonians* p. 289 no. 4); cf. La'da E1741 (f. *Ἀγήνωρ*)

Δαϊμένης
THRACE:
—SALYMBRIA: (1) imp. *IByz* S 37 (f. *Ἀτίας*)

Δάϊππος
THRACE:
—TYRODIZA-TIRISTASIS: (1) hell.? Dumont–Homolle 91b (f. *Κρίτα*)

Δαίσης
THRACE:
—PHILIPPOPOLIS-TRIMONTIUM (TERRIT.): (1) i-ii AD *IGB* III 1188 (*Δαισήους* (gen.): f. *Διvιζήτης*)

Δαίσιος
THRACE?: (1) 228-221 BC *PTeb* 815 fr. 2, v I, 20; Velkov 71

Δαΐσκος
CIMMERIAN BOSPOROS:
—PANTIKAPAION: (1) i/ii AD *CIRB* 597 (s. *Ἀριαράμνης*)
SKYTHIA:
—TANAIS: (2) f. ii AD ib. 1266, 11 (*Δ[αΐ]σκος*: f. *Πάππος*)
TAURIS:
—CHERSONESOS: (3) ii AD *MIA* 34 (1952) p. 190 ?= (*4*); (4) m. ii AD *SEG* XXXV 859 (s. *Μητρόδωρος*) ?= (*3*)

Δακίσκος
SCYTHIA MINOR:
—TOMIS: (1) iii AD *ISM* II 352 (Lat. Daciscus)

Δάκος
CIMMERIAN BOSPOROS:
—PANTIKAPAION: (1) v/iv BC Tolstoi 147 (vase)

Δαλάζελμος
CIMMERIAN BOSPOROS:
—PANTIKAPAION: (1) i/ii AD *CIRB* 586; cf. KW pl. 39 no. 572 (f. *Αὐλούζελμις*); (2) ~ *CIRB* 587; cf. KW pl. 23 no. 337 (*Δαλάζ(ε)λμος*: f. *Αὐλούζελμις*)

Δαλᾶς
CIMMERIAN BOSPOROS:
—PANTIKAPAION: (1) iv BC *CIRB* 181; cf. *Etiudy* p. 184 no. 5; Zgusta, *PNS* 559 (*Δαλᾶτος* (gen.): f. *Δώρων*)

Δαλάσιος
CIMMERIAN BOSPOROS:
—PANTIKAPAION: (1) i AD *CIRB* 578; cf. KW pl. 46 no. 657; Zgusta, *PNS* 559 (f. *Ἀπολλώνιος*)

Δαλεις
THRACE:
—MADYTOS: (1) hell. *ISestos* 60 (d. *Ἀσκληπιάδης*)

Δαλήζαλις
THRACE:
—BAZOPARA: (1) 202 AD *IGB* III 1690 c, 54 (and Thrace Pizos: f. *Μουκάτραλις*)

Δαληζένθης
MACEDONIA (MYGDONIA):
—KALINDOIA: (1) 68-98 AD *SEG* XLII 580, 79; cf. *Anthémonte–Kalindoia* 2 p. 240 (name) (*Δαληζενθέου* (gen.): f. *Παράμονος*)

Δαλήπορις
THRACE:
—MARKIANOPOLIS (TERRIT.): (1) iii AD *IGB* II 853 (*CCET* II (1) 258) (*Δαλε-*: f. *Δάδας*)
—SKEPTA: (2) 202 AD *IGB* III 1690 c, 13 (and Thrace Pizos: f. *Κέλσος*)

Δάλης
MACEDONIA (MYGDONIA):
—KALINDOIA: (1) 68-98 AD *SEG* XLII 580, 73; cf. *Anthémonte–Kalindoia* 2 pp. 240-1 (name) (s. *Διοσκουρίδης*); (2) ~ *SEG* XLII 580, 84 (f. *Διοσκουρίδης*); (3) a. 98 AD ib. 582, 9 (s. *Ταρουσίτας*); (4) ~ ib. l. 30 (s. *Ζίγρας*); (5) ~ ib. l. 67 (f. *Νουμήνιος*); (6) ~ ib. l. 68 (s. *Κότυς*); (7) ii-iii AD ib. 599 (f. *Ἀλέξιος*)

Δαλήτραλις
THRACE: (1) ?ii-iii AD Moretti, *Tra epigr. e stor.* p. 209 (Lat. Valerius Dalat[ralis]?)
—BAZOPARA: (2) 202 AD *IGB* III 1690 d, 30 (and Thrace Pizos: *Δα(λ)ήτραλις*: f. *Μουκάτραλις*); (3) ~ ib. l. 50 (and Thrace Pizos: f. *Σεύθης*)
—BIZYE (TERRIT.)?: (4) ii-iii AD ib. 1852, 3 (-λαί-: s. *Ἐυ—*)
—DRAGANOVEC (MOD.): (5) ii-iii AD ib. V 5288 (*Δαλέ-*: f. *Τουριδάτης*)
—MARKIANOPOLIS (TERRIT.): (6) iii AD ib. 5329, 3 (*Δαλέ-*: s. *Κελέπυρις*) ?= (*7*); (7) ~ ib. l. 4 (*Δαλέ-*: f. *Δερνάης*) ?= (*6*)
—STROUNEILOS: (8) 202 AD ib. III 1690 d, 63 (and Thrace Pizos: *Δαλ<τ>ήτραλις*: f. *Ἰούλις*)

Δάλις
TAURIS:
—CHERSONESOS: (1) iii BC Solomonik, *NEPKh* 167; *Hellenismus* p. 448 no. 13 (s. *Κλεῖτος*) ?= (*2*); (2) ~ Solomonik, *NEPKh* 173; *Hellenismus* p. 448 no. 13 (*Δάλι[ς]*?, *Δαλί[ων]*?) ?= (*1*); (3) ~ Solomonik, *NEPKh* 173 (*Δάλι[ς]*?)
THRACE:
—SESTIS (MOD.): (4) iii AD *IThrakAig* E394 (*Δάλιος* (gen.): f. *Διονύσιος*)

Δαλμάτις
THRACE:
—SPINOPARA: (1) ii AD *IGB* IV 2192, 12

Δαλόσακος
CIMMERIAN BOSPOROS:
—PANTIKAPAION: (1) 285 AD *CIRB* 734; Zgusta, *PNS* 560 (f. *Φίλων*)
SKYTHIA:
—TANAIS: (2) 225-228 AD *CIRB* 1279, 25; 1283, 13 (s. *Σύμφορος*)

Δαλτιανή
MACEDONIA (PAIONIA):
—KAVADARCI (MOD.): (1) iii AD Dimitsas 285; cf. Detschev 115 (name) (d. *Αὐρ. Ἀλεξανδρία*)

Δάλων
MACEDONIA (EDONIS):
—AMPHIPOLIS: (1) iii/ii BC *SEG* XXXI 616 (f. *Παντάρετος*)

Δαμάγης
THRACE:
—BYZANTION: (1) hell.? *IByz* 299 (*SGDI* 3063) (*Δαμά(γ)ης*—Robert, *Δαμά(ρ)ης*—Bechtel: f. *—οφάνης*)

Δαμάγητος
THRACE:
—BYZANTION: (1) c. 340 BC D. xviii 90

Δαμαῖος
MACEDONIA (MYGDONIA):
—THESSALONIKE: (1) s. ii BC *IG* X (2) (1) 108, 11 + *BCH* 19 (1895) p. 335 no. 10, 8 (Tataki, *Macedonians* p. 181 no. 19; Stephanis 146) (s. *Ἡγήσανδρος*)

Δαμαλίς
MACEDONIA (EDONIS):
—PHILIPPOI (NR.): (1) imp. *CIL* III 655 = 14206. 16 (Pilhofer 455) (Lat. [M]arronia Damalis)
MACEDONIA (MYGDONIA):
—THESSALONIKE: (2) ?ii AD *IG* X (2) (1) 452, 8 + *BCH* 98 (1974) pp. 536-8 (*Κασσία Δ.*: ?d. *M. Κάσσιος Σεουῆρος Παπίας*)

Δάμαλσος
THRACE:
—BOURDAPA: (1) hell. *SEG* XXXIX 660 = XLI 608. 2 = XLVII 1094. 2

Δαμάρετος
TAURIS:
—CHERSONESOS: (1) c. 330-320 BC Anokhin p. 138 no. 67 (coin) (*Δαμάρε(τος)*?)

Δαμαρίων
THRACE:
—NICOPOLIS AD NESTUM: (1) ii-iii AD *IGB* IV 2347 (?s. *Πύρρος*)

Δαμᾶς
CIMMERIAN BOSPOROS:
—PANTIKAPAION: (1) i BC/i AD *CIRB* 319 (f. *Στρατονίκη*); (2) f. i AD ib. 360; cf. KW pl. 34 no. 486; (3) ii-iii AD *CIRB* 720; cf. KW pl. 56 no. 761 (I f. *Δαμᾶς* II); (4) ~ *CIRB* 720; cf. KW pl. 56 no. 761 (II s. *Δαμᾶς* I); (5) f. ii AD *CIRB* 665 (f. *Δαμόφιλος*)
—PANTIKAPAION*: (6) m. i AD ib. 382; cf. KW pl. 42 no. 613 (s. *Γάϊος*)
—THEODOSIA: (7) iii AD *CIRB* 947 B, 4 (f. *Ἀρίστων*)
MACEDONIA (MYGDONIA):
—THESSALONIKE: (8) 42-32 BC *IG* X (2) (1) 124, 9 (s. *Μενέδημος*)
SARMATIA:
—MAIOTAI: (9) ii/i BC *EAD* XXX 418, 1 (slave)
SCYTHIA MINOR:
—ISTROS: (10) ii/i BC ib. l. 19 (slave)
—NOVIODUNUM (NR.): (11) 218-235 AD *ISM* V 245, 7 (*Eastern cults* p. 225 no. 10) (Lat. Fl. Damas)
—TOMIS: (12) ii AD *ISM* II 125 I, 22 (s. *Λυσίμαχος*)
THRACE:
—BISANTHE-PANION: (13) ii-iii AD Dumont–Homolle 83i (s. *Ζωΐλος*, *Εὐτέρπη*)
—BYZANTION: (14) ii BC *IByz* 75 (Firatlı–Robert p. 50 no. 19) (f. *Μήνιος*)
—BYZANTION (TERRIT.): (15) i-ii AD *IByz* 245 (s. *Χρηστακῶν*, f. *Τίτθα*)
—BYZANTION:
——(Bathonea): (16) i-ii AD ib. 315 c (Firatlı–Robert pp. 122-3 no. 205) (s. *Ῥοῦφος*)
—BYZANTION?: (17) ii AD *IByz* 360 = *ISestos* 6 (s. *Μήνιος*)
—PERINTHOS-HERAKLEIA: (18) ii-iii AD *IPerinth* 92 (I f. *Δαμᾶς* II); (19) ~ ib. (II s. *Δαμᾶς* I)
—PHILIPPOPOLIS-TRIMONTIUM (NR.): (20) ii-iii AD *IGB* III 1412 + V 5521

Δαμασίας
MACEDONIA (BOTTIAIA):
—PELLA: (1) iv BC Tataki, *Macedonians* p. 153 no. 32 (f. *Ἀριστοκράτεια*)
MACEDONIA (EDONIS):
—AMPHIPOLIS: (2) 320 BC Moretti, *Olymp.* 473; *FGrH* 255. 10, 3 (Tataki, *Macedonians* p. 50 no. 36)

Δαμασικλῆς
TAURIS:
—CHERSONESOS: (1) c. 120-88 BC *IOSPE* I² 352, 57 (*Δαμ[ασικλ]ῆς*: s. *Ἀθάναιος*)

Δαμασίλεως
MACEDONIA (EDONIS):
—AMPHIPOLIS: (1) s. iv BC Hatzopoulos, *Actes Amphipolis* p. 45 no. 9, 3 (*SEG* XLI 563); cf. *SEG* XLIV 504 (s. *Εὔδημος*)

Δαμάσιππος
MACEDONIA: (1) ?338 BC Polyaen. iv 2. 3 (Tataki, *Macedonians* p. 289 no. 6); (2) 162 BC *RE* Supplbd. 1 (3a) (*PP* 16103)
THRACE:
—ABDERA: (3) v BC *RE* (4); *FVS* 68 A 1 (?f. *Δημόκριτος, Δάμασος, Ἡρόδοτος*)

Δάμασος
SKYTHIA:
—OLBIA-BORYSTHENES: (1) iii BC *IOSPE* I² 201 I, 64 (s. *Ἀριστοκράτης*)
THRACE:
—ABDERA: (2) v BC *RE* (6); cf. *FVS* 68 A 1-2; 18 (*Δαμάστης—Suda Δ* 447: ?s. *Ἡγησίστρατος, Ἀθηνόκριτος, Δαμάσιππος*)

Δαματρία
TAURIS:
—CHERSONESOS: (1) iii BC *IOSPE* I² 510 (d. *Θεοφάνης*); (2) ~ ib. 511 (d. *Τίμων*)

Δαμάτριος
SCYTHIA MINOR:
—ISTROS: (1) 222-225 AD *ISM* I 100 A, 18 (f. *Ἀθηνάδης*); (2) ~ ib. l. 21 (*Δα(μά)τριος*: f. *—τρις*)
—KALLATIS: (3) s. iii BC ib. III 35 A, 28 (I f. *Δαμάτριος* II); (4) ~ ib. l. 28 (II s. *Δαμάτριος* I); (5) iii/ii BC ib. 161 (s. *Κρηθεύς*); (6) 12-15 AD ib. 44, 3 (f. *Διόδωρος*); (7) s. ii AD ib. 70, 3
—KALLATIS (NR.): (8) ii-iii AD ib. 236 (*[Δ]αμάτριος*: ?f. *—ινος*)
TAURIS:
—CHERSONESOS: (9) iv BC Solomonik, *NEPKh* 155 (s. *Εὐάνθης*); (10) ~ *IOSPE* I² 712 (f. *Ἀδεία*); (11) ~ *SEG* XXVIII 635 (*Δ[αμά]τρ[ιος]*?: f. *Ματρόδωρος*); (12) iv/iii BC Solomonik, *NEPKh* 156; (13) ~ ib. 157 (*[Δα]μάτριος*: f. *Ἀρτεμίδωρος*); (14) ~ Kats p. 111 no. 106 (amph.) (f. *Σῖμος*); (15) iii BC *IOSPE* I² 708 (s. *Στέφανος*, f. *Στέφανος*); (16) ii-i BC ib. 475 (f. *Ἡράκλειος*); (17) ~ ib. 492 (f. *Σιμαῖος*); (18) m. i BC ib. 347, [2]? with Add. p. 519; 691, 2 (*[Δαμ]άτριος*: f. *Λάμαχος*)
THRACE:
—BYZANTION: (19) c. 230-200 BC *BCH* 45 (1921) p. 19 III, 98 (s. *Φίλων*); (20) i BC-i AD *IByz* 286 (Fıratlı–Robert pp. 74-5 no. 82)
—BYZANTION (TERRIT.): (21) i BC *IByz* 186 (Fıratlı–Robert p. 71 no. 72) (s. *Ἀσκλαπιάδας*)
—BYZANTION?: (22) ?iii BC *IByz* 347 (PM 844; *IKalch* 52) (or Bithynia Kalchedon: s. *Μήνιος*); (23) ii AD *IByz* 357 (f. *Τιμοκράτης*)
—MESAMBRIA: (24) iii BC *Milet* I (3) 70, 11 (*[Δημή]τριος*); (25) s. iii BC *IGB* I² 339 ter (*[Δ]αμάτριος*: s. *Ἡρώνυμος*); (26) ii BC ib. 314 b, 3 (f. *Θεόδωρος*); (27) ii/i BC ib. V 5104 I (*[Δα]μάτριος*: f. *Ἰσίων*)
—ODESSOS: (28) ?ii AD ib. I² 89 (I f. *Δαμάτριος* II); (29) ~ ib. (*[Δ]αμάτριος*: II s. *Δαμάτριος* I)

Δάμαχος
MACEDONIA (EORDAIA):
—ARNISA?: (1) 202 AD *EAM* 131; Hatzopoulos, *MI* 1 p. 94 n. 4 (locn.)

Δαμέας
CIMMERIAN BOSPOROS:
—PANTIKAPAION: (1) f. iv BC *CIRB* 185 (f. *Βλάστος*)
THRACE:
—AINOS?: (2) s. iv BC Peek, *NIEpid* 16, 28 + Perlman, *City and Sanctuary* E.6 (or Korinthia Korinth?: s. *Σαμοκλῆς*)

—MESAMBRIA: (3) iv BC *IGB* I² 333 bis (f. *Ἀγησίλα*); (4) c. 55 BC ib. 323, 3 (s. *Διονύσιος*)
—MESAMBRIA?: (5) iii/ii BC ib. 102 (PM 923); cf. Robert, *OMS* 5 p. 259 (locn.)

Δαμῆς
MACEDONIA (CHALKIDIKE):
—ANTHEMOUS: (1) ii BC *SEG* XLII 560; cf. *Anthémonte–Kalindoia* 2 p. 242 (name) (*Δαμέους* (gen.): f. *Σωσιγένης*)

Δαμιανή
THRACE:
—ODESSOS: (1) vi AD Beševliev 106, 4

Δάμιππος
MACEDONIA (EDONIS):
—AMPHIPOLIS: (1) c. 353 BC *FGrH* 115 F 248 (Tataki, *Macedonians* p. 50 no. 37) (s. *Ἐπίλυκος*)

Δαμναγόρας
THRACE:
—PERINTHOS-HERAKLEIA?: (1) iv BC Hp., *Epid.* vi 3. 5; vi 3. 14

Δαμνάζης
KOLCHIS:
—LAZOI: (1) c. 475-522 AD *RE* s.v. Zammaxes (-); *PLRE* II (-) (*Ζαμμάξης—Chron. Pasch.*: f. *Ζτάθιος*: king)

Δαμόγνητος
MACEDONIA (BOTTIAIA):
—BEROIA: (1) 239-229 BC *IBer* 45, 30

Δαμοθάρης
MACEDONIA (BOTTIAIA):
—EDESSA: (1) 51 AD *SEG* XLVI 744, 15 (Tataki, *Edessa* 75) (f. *Ἐπαφρᾶς*)

Δαμοκάδης
THRACE:
—BYZANTION: (1) s. iv BC *IByz* 124 (Fıratlı–Robert p. 100 no. 151) (s. *Νικάνωρ*)

Δαμοκλῆς
MACEDONIA (PIERIA):
—DION: (1) iii BC *SEG* XXXI 629, 4
TAURIS:
—CHERSONESOS: (2) iv BC *IOSPE* I² 406, 2 (f. *Κανθάρα*); (3) iv/iii BC Kats p. 104 no. 79 (amph., tile) (f. *Μῆνις*) ?= (*4*); (4) c. 300-285 BC ib. p. 92 no. 34 (amph.) ?= (*3*); (5) c. 300-275 BC *SEG* XLVII 1168, 3 (*Δαμόκλειος* (gen.): f. *—ς*); (6) iii BC Kats p. 127 no. 40 (amph.) (f. *Πυθόδοτος*) ?= (*8*); (7) iii-ii BC *IOSPE* I² 713 (*Δ[αμοκ]λῆς*: f. *Νάνα*); (8) s. iii BC Kats p. 110 no. 101 (amph.) (f. *Πυθόδοτος*) ?= (*6*); (9) ii-iii AD *IOSPE* I² 452 (f. *Λαγορῖνος*); (10) ~ *SEG* XXXVII 658 (f. *Εὐρύδαμος*); (11) 129 AD *IOSPE* I² 359, 33; *SEG* XXVIII 631, [3]? (s. *Λαγορῖνος*)
—KERKINITIS (NR.): (12) ii/i BC ib. XLVI 919 (vase) (potter)

Δαμοκράτης
THRACE:
—BYZANTION: (1) ii-i BC *IByz* 362 (Fıratlı–Robert p. 66 no. 61) (*Δαμοκράτη* (gen.): f. *Μίκη*)

Δαμοκρατία
THRACE:
—BYZANTION: (1) ii-i BC *IByz* 145 (d. *Γλαυκίας*)
—PAUTALIA: (2) m. iii AD *IG* X (2) (1) 572 = *AA* 1970, pp. 93-8 (*Πο. Ἀντία Δ.*)

Δαμόκριτος
MACEDONIA (MYGDONIA):
—THESSALONIKE?: (1) i AD *IG* X (2) (1) 913

THRACE:
—AINOS: (2) a. 316 BC ib. IV (1)² 94 b, 48 (Perlman, *City and Sanctuary* E.1 with pp. 78-9 (date); Tataki, *Macedonians* p. 176 no. 1) (s. *Πεισίστρατος*)

Δαμονίκα
MACEDONIA (MYGDONIA):
—THESSALONIKE: (1) ii-iii AD *AD* 26 (1971) Chron. p. 377 no. 2 (*-νεί-*)

Δαμόνικος
MACEDONIA (BOTTIAIA):
—BEROIA: (1) hell. *SEG* XXXVI 609 (vase) = XXXIV 618 note (Tataki 365)
MACEDONIA (PAIONIA):
—ANTIGONEIA? (TREMNIK (MOD.)): (2) ii-iii AD *Sp.* 71 (1931) p. 98 no. 231 (*Σέξτ. Δαμόνεικος*)

Δαμοξένα
THRACE:
—BYZANTION: (1) ii-i BC *Türk Tarih Kongresi XI* (6) p. 2704 with pl. 497. 9 (d. *Ἀσκλαπιάδας*)

Δαμοσθένης
SCYTHIA MINOR:
—KALLATIS: (1) s. iii BC *ISM* III 35 A, 38 (s. *Διονύσιος*)

Δαμόστρατος
CIMMERIAN BOSPOROS:
—GORGIPPIA: (1) ii/iii AD *CIRB* 1179, 40 (s. *Ἀγίας*)
MACEDONIA (PIERIA):
—DION: (2) iii BC *SEG* XXXI 629, 2 (*Δαμόστρ[ατος]*)
THRACE:
—VRACA (MOD.): (3) ii-iii AD *IGB* II 487 (f. *Ἰουλιανός*)

Δαμοτέλης
MACEDONIA (CHALKIDIKE):
—OLYNTHOS: (1) ?325 BC *CID* II 101 I, 12 (Tataki, *Macedonians* p. 132 no. 24)
SKYTHIA:
—TYRAS: (2) iii BC *SEG* XLV 1026. 14 (vase) (*Δαμοτ[έλ]ης*—Vinogradov)
TAURIS:
—CHERSONESOS: (3) c. 300-285 BC Kats p. 92 no. 35 (amph.); (4) c. 237-230 BC ib. p. 92 no. 36 (amph.) (s. *Διαγόρας*)

Δαμότιμος
MACEDONIA (CHALKIDIKE):
—OLYNTHOS: (1) c. 370-327 BC *FD* III (1) 400, [4]; *CR* 8 (1958) p. 108 (date) (Tataki, *Macedonians* p. 132 no. 25) (f. *Καλλισθένης*)

Δαμοφίλα
CIMMERIAN BOSPOROS:
—PANTIKAPAION: (1) i/ii AD *CIRB* 645 (d. *Βοστάκων, Χοίδρα*)

Δαμόφιλος
CIMMERIAN BOSPOROS:
—PANTIKAPAION: (1) i-ii AD ib. 592; (2) f. ii AD ib. 665 (s. *Δαμᾶς*)
—PANTIKAPAION?: (3) i AD *SEG* XLV 1011 (f. *Καλοῦς*)
THRACE:
—BYZANTION: (4) i BC *IByz* 150 (I f. *Δαμόφιλος* II, *Σωστράτα*); (5) ~ ib. (II s. *Δαμόφιλος* I)

Δαμοφῶν
SCYTHIA MINOR:
—KALLATIS: (1) s. iii BC *ISM* III 35 A, 33 (f. *Ἑρμαγένης*); (2) ~ ib. 35 B, 24 (*Δαμ[οφ]ῶν*: f. *Ἡρέας*); (3) iii/ii BC *CIRB* 252 (*Δη-*: s. *Γοργίας*)
THRACE:
—BYZANTION: (4) s. iv BC *IByz* 57 (Fıratlı–Robert p. 47 no. 1) (s. *Μένων*)

Δαμοχάρης
THRACE:
—LYSIMACHEIA: **(1)** c. 208 BC *FD* III (4) 134 II, 11 (f. *Διονύσιος*)

Δαμώ
MACEDONIA (CHALKIDIKE):
—OLYNTHOS: **(1)** ii BC *NS* 536 + *AM* 51 (1926) p. 6 (Tataki, *Macedonians* p. 132 no. 26) ([*Δ*]*αμ*[*ώ*]: name—Wilhelm)
THRACE:
—AINOS: **(2)** ii-i BC *IG* XII (1) 389
—BYZANTION: **(3)** ii/i BC *IByz* 166 (Firatlı–Robert p. 108 no. 173) (d. *Νικώ*)

Δάμων
CIMMERIAN BOSPOROS:
—PANTIKAPAION: **(1)** ?iv/iii BC *CIRB* 238
—THEODOSIA: **(2)** iii-ii BC ib. 950 (f. *Καλλίαρος*)
MACEDONIA: **(3)** 333 BC *RE* Supplbd. 4 (15a); Berve 241 (Tataki, *Macedonians* p. 290 no. 9)
MACEDONIA (BOTTIAIA):
—GENDERRHOS? (MANDALON (MOD.)): **(4)** s. iv BC *SEG* XLIII 395 (*Δά*[*μ*]*ων*: f. *Θήρων*)
MACEDONIA (EDONIS):
—AMPHIPOLIS: **(5)** a. 357 BC Hatzopoulos, *Actes Amphipolis* pp. 38-9 no. 7, 7
MACEDONIA (MYGDONIA):
—THESSALONIKE: **(6)** c. 250-230 BC *IG* VII 320, 2 (*IOrop* 141; Tataki, *Macedonians* p. 181 no. 20) (s. *Ἀζαῖος*); **(7)** c. 143 BC *IG* X (2) (1) 1031, 1 (*IvOl* 325; Tataki, *Macedonians* p. 181 no. 21) (s. *Νικάνωρ*)
MACEDONIA (PIERIA):
—PHILA?: **(8)** ?iii BC *RPh* 1911, pp. 133-4 no. 36, 4; cf. Helly, *L'État thessalien* pp. 319-20 (locn.) ([*Δ*]*άμων*: s. *Ἐχένικος*)
SCYTHIA MINOR:
—KALLATIS: **(9)** f. iii BC *ISM* III 78 (f. *Διονύσιος*)
THRACE: **(10)** 274 BC *PCZ* 59001, 18, 45; cf. La'da E726 (f. *Δημήτριος*)
—ABDERA: **(11)** hell.? Hp., *Ep.* 17 (f. *Φιλοποίμην*: fict.)
—BYZANTION: **(12)** s. iii BC Schönert-Geiss, *Byzantion* 1235-9 (coin)
—BYZANTION?: **(13)** hell.? *RE* (16); *FGrH* 389

Δανάη
MACEDONIA (BOTTIAIA):
—BEROIA: **(1)** ii AD *IBer* 346, 3 (Tataki 366) (m. *Πάνταυχος*)
MACEDONIA (MYGDONIA):
—THESSALONIKE?: **(2)** ii AD *IG* X (2) (1) 703 (?d. *Πύρρος*, *Ἀρτεμιδώρα*)

Δαναός
CIMMERIAN BOSPOROS:
—GORGIPPIA: **(1)** f. iii BC *CIRB* 1137 A I, 24; 1137 B I, 46 (s. *Ἀπολλώνιος*)
THRACE:
—ZONE: **(2)** s. v BC *SEG* XIII 412 (*IThrakAig* E408) (f. *Κλεόστρατος*)

Δαναράζμακος
SKYTHIA:
—TANAIS: **(1)** 220 AD *CIRB* 1278, 18; cf. Zgusta, *PNS* 100 (*Ἀρδ*[*αρ*]*ακος*—*CIRB*, [*Δαν*]*αρά*[*ζμ*]*ακος*?—Latyshev and Tokhtas'ev: s. *Ὀδίαρδος*); **(2)** 225-230 AD *CIRB* 1280, 31; 1284, 19 (*Δαναράσμακος*—no. 1284: s. *Μήνιος*)

Δάνδαμις
SKYTHIA:
—SKYTHAI: **(1)** ii AD Luc., *Tox.* 38-42 (fict.)

Δανδάξαρθος
SKYTHIA:
—OLBIA-BORYSTHENES: **(1)** iii AD *IOSPE* I² 135, 3; Zgusta, *PNS* 101 (s. *Δάδος*)

Δανήπη
THRACE:
—HERAION TEICHOS?: **(1)** ii-i BC Taşlıklıoğlu 2 p. 93 no. 1 (d. *Ἐπτήκησος*)

Δανιήλ
MACEDONIA (EDONIS):
—PHILIPPOI: **(1)** v-vi AD *Act. XI congr. int. arch. chrét.* 3 p. 2701
THRACE:
—ODESSOS: **(2)** vi AD Beševliev 107, 3 ([*Δα*]*νιήλ*)

Δάντης
MACEDONIA (EDONIS):
—AMPHIPOLIS: **(1)** ii/iii AD *SEG* XXXV 713, 3 + *BE* 1999, no. 377; cf. *SEG* XLVIII 722 (*Δάντος* (gen.): f. *Φιλού*)

Δαντοῦς
MACEDONIA (EDONIS):
—PHILIPPOI (TERRIT.): **(1)** ?ii AD *BIAB* 16 (1950) pp. 14-15 no. 11, 3 (Pilhofer 649); *Ét. Balk.* 1987, p. 109 (name) (Lat. Dantus: s./d. *Ζιπᾶς*, Caigeno)
MACEDONIA (MYGDONIA):
—AINEIA?: **(2)** ii-iii AD *SEG* XXXVIII 707; cf. *BE* 1990, no. 476 (*Δαντοῦ* (dat.): m. *Κόρραγος*, *Μελίτων*, *Νικώ*)

Δαντώ
MACEDONIA (EDONIS):
—AMPHIPOLIS: **(1)** ii-iii AD *SEG* XV 416, 2 (d. *Γαιδρῆς*); **(2)** 158 or 274 AD ib. 415, 5 (d. *Ζειβούρης*)

Δᾶος
CIMMERIAN BOSPOROS:
—PANTIKAPAION: **(1)** i AD *CIRB* 547 (f. *Χρηστίων*)
MACEDONIA (CHALKIDIKE):
—OLYNTHOS: **(2)** f. iv BC *Olynthus* 5 p. 262 no. 1110 (vase)
MACEDONIA (PAIONIA):
—KAVADARCI (MOD.): **(3)** iii/iv AD Unp. (Kavadarci Mus.) inv. 11/II
SKYTHIA:
—OLBIA-BORYSTHENES: **(4)** i BC *IOSPE* I² 222; Zgusta, *PNS* 761 (f. *Ἀδαῖος*)
THRACE:
—APOLLONIA-SOZOPOLIS: **(5)** iv BC *BMNBurgas* 4 (2002) p. 124 no. 18 (s. *Γάγιος*); **(6)** ~ ib. p. 126 no. 25 (f. *Διοσκουρίδης*)

Δαππαεις
CIMMERIAN BOSPOROS:
—HERMONASSA: **(1)** s. v AD *CIRB* 1099, 7 + *SEG* XXXIX 697

Δάπυξ
THRACE:
—GETAI: **(1)** 29 BC *RE* (-); D.C. li 26 (king)

Δάρδανος
MACEDONIA (BOTTIAIA):
—SKYDRA?: **(1)** 105 AD *SEG* XVII 317, 13 (*Κλ. Δ.*: freed.?)
THRACE:
—SERDICA: **(2)** c. 180 AD *CIL* VI 32628, 13 (Lat. M. Aurel. Dardanus)

Δαρέας
MACEDONIA (KRESTONIA): **(1)** ii AD *SEG* XXXVII 561 + *BE* 1989, no. 450 (s. *Σώπατρος*, f. *Νικάνωρ*)

Δαρεῖος
CIMMERIAN BOSPOROS:
—PANTIKAPAION: **(1)** c. 390-380 BC *SEG* L 710 A (vase) (fict.?)
MACEDONIA (TYMPHAIA):
—AGIOS GEORGIOS (MOD.): **(2)** iii-ii BC *EAM* 74 (*Δαρείας*?)

Δαρίκιος
THRACE: **(1)** 361 AD *PLRE* I (-)

Δάροκος
MACEDONIA (EDONIS):
—AMPHIPOLIS: **(1)** ii-iii AD *Thrakika* 13 (1940) p. 25 *Z*; *Epigraphica* 37 (1975) p. 26

Δαρος?
THRACE:
—PHILIPPOPOLIS-TRIMONTIUM (TERRIT.): **(1)** ii-iii AD *IGB* III 1108 (s. *—τραλις*)

Δαρουτούρμη
THRACE:
—DYME (MOD.): **(1)** i AD *AD* 26 (1971) pl. 422 c (*Belomorski Pregled* 1 (1941) p. 335 no. 40; *IThrakAig* E387); cf. Bakalakis, *Oinos Ismarikos* p. 1015

Δάρσης
THRACE?: **(1)** m. iii BC *SEG* XLI 963, 4 (s. *Κάρος*)

Δασείλας
MACEDONIA (MYGDONIA):
—KALINDOIA: **(1)** 68-98 AD ib. XLII 580, 6, 28; cf. *Anthémonte–Kalindoia* 2 p. 242 (name) (*Δασείλου* (gen.): f. *Νίκων*)

Δάσεις
CIMMERIAN BOSPOROS:
—GORGIPPIA: **(1)** s. ii AD *CIRB* 1145, 7 (*-σσεις*: f. *Φαρνάκης*)
—HERMONASSA: **(2)** i/ii AD ib. 1057 (*GVI* 1477) (f. *Τιμόθεος*)

Δάσιος
SCYTHIA MINOR:
—AXIOPOLIS*: **(1)** f. iv AD Barnea 71 (Popescu, *IGL* 194); *Anal. Boll.* 31 (1912) p. 259 (*Τά-*)
THRACE:
—DUROSTORUM: **(2)** 303 AD ib. 16 (1897) pp. 5-16; Wessel 455

Δαστίδιος
MACEDONIA (PAIONIA):
—KAVADARCI (MOD.): **(1)** iii AD *Sp.* 71 (1931) p. 64 no. 138 (*Αὐρ. Δ.*)

Δασχάς
CIMMERIAN BOSPOROS:
—PANTIKAPAION: **(1)** ii BC *CIRB* 273; cf. KW pl. 14 no. 217; Zgusta, *PNS* 632 (m. *Θεόμνηστος*); **(2)** i BC/i AD *CIRB* 306; cf. KW pl. 20 no. 297 (*Δασχαῖ* (voc.): d. *Κίνωλις*)

Δατειζεις
SCYTHIA MINOR:
—ISTROS: **(1)** i BC-i AD *ISM* I 191 I, 50 (*Δατειζει* (gen.): f. *—μος*) ?= (*2*); **(2)** ~ ib. 191 II, 51 (*Δατιζει* (gen.): f. *Δωτοῦς*) ?= (*1*); **(3)** ?ii AD ib. 285 (*Δατειζει* (gen.): f. *Ἀπολλώνιος*)

Δατείτας
MACEDONIA (MYGDONIA):
—KALINDOIA: **(1)** 68-98 AD *SEG* XLII 580, 15; cf. *Anthémonte–Kalindoia* 2 p. 242 (name) (*Δατείτου* (gen.): f. *Ῥοιμητάλκης*)

Δαυκέτης
SKYTHIA:
—SKYTHAI: **(1)** ii AD Luc., *Scyth* 4 (?f. *Ἀνάχαρσις*: fict.)

Δαῦνις
THRACE:
—PERINTHOS-HERAKLEIA:
——(Geleuntes): **(1)** iii-ii BC *IPerinth* 61, 33 (f. *Νίκανδρος*)

Δαφναῖος
MACEDONIA (MYGDONIA):
—THESSALONIKE?: **(1)** i BC-i AD *IG* X (2) (1) 909 (f. *Τιμόφιλος*)

Δάφνη
MACEDONIA (BOTTIAIA):
—BEROIA: (1) ii AD *IBer* 304, 2 with fig. 304 (Tataki 368) (*Δάφν(η)*, *Δάφνι*—ed.: m. *Πο. Ἥλιος*); (2) ~ *IBer* 316 (Tataki 367)

Δαφνίδιος
THRACE:
—SERDICA: (1) iv-v AD Beševliev 17, 4 (Lat. Iul. Dafnidius: s. Laurentius, Maximilla)

Δαφνικός
MACEDONIA (MYGDONIA):
—THESSALONIKE: (1) 10 BC *AD* 23 (1968) Chron. p. 332 (*Φλ. Δ.*: f. *Φλ. Κούαρτα*)

Δάφνις
MACEDONIA (MYGDONIA):
—THESSALONIKE: (1) iv AD *IG* X (2) (1) 777 (*Δομε. Δ.*)

Δαφνίς
MACEDONIA (EDONIS):
—PHILIPPOI (NR.): (1) i-ii AD *BCH* 47 (1923) p. 93 no. 26 (Pilhofer 454) (Lat. [V]ergilia Daphnis: m. *Ὑγῖνος*, Oppius Macrianus)
MACEDONIA (PAIONIA):
—KAVADARCI (MOD.): (2) iii AD Unp. (Kavadarci Mus.) inv. 117/II (*Δάφνηδι* (dat.): d. *Σωζομένη*)

Δάφνος
CIMMERIAN BOSPOROS:
—PANTIKAPAION: (1) ?s. i AD *CIRB* 78; cf. KW pl. 42 no. 627 (s. *Ψυχαρίων*)
MACEDONIA (EDONIS):
—PHILIPPOI: (2) imp. *CIL* III 659 (*ILS* 7189; Pilhofer 493) (Lat. C. Vibius Daphnus: s. C. Vibius Florus)
MACEDONIA (MYGDONIA):
—THESSALONIKE: (3) i AD *IG* X (2) (1) 388 (*T. Τεσσίδιος Δ.*); (4) ii AD *AD* 26 (1971) Chron. p. 377 no. 3 (s. *Πέργαμος*, *Νόημα*); (5) s. ii AD *SEG* XLVIII 851
SKYTHIA:
—TANAIS: (6) 193 AD *CIRB* 1237, 10 (*Ἰούλ. Δ[ά]φνος?*, *Δ[ί]ον(ν)ος?*—Vinogradov)
THRACE:
—PERINTHOS-HERAKLEIA: (7) i-ii AD *IPerinth* 223 (*GVI* 1303) (*Δ[ά]φνος*)

Δάφνων
MACEDONIA (MYGDONIA):
—DIKAIA: (1) c. 365-359 BC Unp. (Voutyras–Sismanidis) l. 63 (s. *Πολύζηλος*)

Δεβαβενζίς
MACEDONIA (SINTIKE):
—PARTHIKOPOLIS (NR.): (1) s. ii AD *IGB* IV 2292

Δεβας?
MACEDONIA (EDONIS):
—AMPHIPOLIS: (1) ii-iii AD *Thracia* 2 p. 279 + *Epigraphica* 37 (1975) p. 32 (*Δεβα* (gen.?), *Τουκουδεβα*—Mihailov: f. *Τουκος*)

Δέγμος
MACEDONIA (ORESTIS):
—BATTYNAIOI: (1) 192 AD *EAM* 186 II, 51 (s. *Φίλιππος*)

Δεδατος
KOLCHIS:
—VANI (MOD.): (1) s. iv BC Braund, *Georgia* p. 136 fig. 7 (ring) (nom./gen.?)

Δέζαλος
THRACE:
—MARKIANOPOLIS (TERRIT.): (1) iii AD *IGB* V 5329, 3 (f. *Βιθύκενθος*)

Δειγηπις?
MACEDONIA (ODOMANTIKE):
—GAZOROS (TERRIT.)?: (1) hell. *BCH* 24 (1900) p. 306 (*Δειγηπ[ις]*: s. *Παίβης*)

Δείδας
MACEDONIA (MYGDONIA):
—THESSALONIKE?: (1) ii/iii AD *AEpThess* p. 35 no. 13, 4 (s. *Βάρβαρος*, *Οὐαδέα*)
THRACE:
—TYRODIZA-TIRISTASIS: (2) imp. Dumont–Homolle 89b (f. *Δόλης*)

Δείδης
THRACE:
—BESSOPARA: (1) iii AD *IGB* III 947, 7 (s. *Λείλοος*)

Δειδίκυρος
MACEDONIA (SINTIKE):
—PARTHIKOPOLIS (NR.): (1) s. ii AD ib. IV 2292

Δεῖδις
THRACE:
—SERDICA: (1) ii-iii AD ib. 1938 (*CCCA* VI 340) (s. *Δίζας*)

Δεῖδος
MACEDONIA (SINTIKE):
—PARTHIKOPOLIS (NR.): (1) ii-iii AD *IGB* V 5918 (s. *Πυρούλας*, f. *Πυρούλας*, *Πυρούλας ὁ μικρός*); (2) 165 AD ib. IV 2288 (*Δείδου* (gen.): f. *Κοῖντα*)

Δειζέζενις
THRACE:
—BEROE-AUGUSTA TRAIANA:
——Karasoura: (1) iii AD ib. III 1626, 10 (*Δειζεζένε(ος)* (gen.): f. *Δόλης*)

Δειζεζες
THRACE:
—PALAMARCA (MOD.): (1) f. iii AD ib. II 761 (*CCET* II (2) 548) (s. *Δερ—*)

Δεϊκράτης
MACEDONIA (CHALKIDIKE):
—OLYNTHOS: (1) iv BC *Small Obj. from the Pnyx* p. 6 no. 9 (Tataki, *Macedonians* p. 132 no. 27) (f. *Εὐβούλη*)

Δείναρχος
CIMMERIAN BOSPOROS:
—GORGIPPIA: (1) f. iii BC *CIRB* 1137 B I, 26 ([*Δεί*]*ναρχος*: s. *Κτησίας*)

Δεινῆς
THRACE:
—APOLLONIA-SOZOPOLIS: (1) f. v BC *IGB* I^2 405 (*CEG* I 172) (*Δ̣ε̣ινῆ[ς]*: s. *Ἀνάξανδρος*)

Δεινίας
CIMMERIAN BOSPOROS:
—NYMPHAION: (1) iv BC *Nekropol' Nimfeia* p. 67 with pl. 72. 3 (s. *Εὔφραῖος*)
MACEDONIA (BISALTIA):
—TRAGILOS (NR.): (2) ii-iii AD *SEG* XXX 611 (*Δεινεία* (gen.): f. *Πυρούλας*)
MACEDONIA (BOTTIAIA):
—BEROIA: (3) 223 BC *IBer* 4, 31 (f. *Τιμοκράτης*)
THRACE:
—ABDERA: (4) iv BC Hp., *Epid.* vii 117
—BEROE-AUGUSTA TRAIANA (TERRIT.): (5) ii-iii AD *IGB* III 1683, 4
—GLAVA PANEGA (MOD.): (6) ii-iii AD ib. II 517 (s. *Ποτάμων*); (7) ~ ib. 521
—MARONEIA: (8) iii AD *IThrakAig* E218 (s. *Εὐρύνομος*)
—PHILIPPOPOLIS-TRIMONTIUM (TERRIT.): (9) ii AD *IGB* III 1117 (*Οὔλπ. Δ.*: f. *Οὔλπ. Διογενιανός*)

Δεινοκλῆς
THRACE:
—AINOS: (1) a. 316 BC *IG* IV $(1)^2$ 94 b, 46 (Perlman, *City and Sanctuary* E.1 with pp. 78-9 (date)) (s. *Φιλόξενος*)

Δεινόμαχος
MACEDONIA (CHALKIDIKE):
—OLYNTHOS: (1) ?277 or 276 BC *FD* III (1) 105, 2 (Tataki, *Macedonians* p. 132 no. 28) (s. *Ἡρακλείδας*)

Δεινομένης
MACEDONIA: (1) iv BC Plu., *Mor.* 339 B (Tataki, *Macedonians* p. 291 no. 14) (f. *Ἀταρρίας?*)
SKYTHIA:
—OLBIA-BORYSTHENES: (2) f. iv BC Dubois, *IGDOlbia* 104 (*Δεινομένευς* (gen.): f. *Ἀρτεμίδωρος*)
THRACE:
—MESAMBRIA: (3) ii/i BC *IGB* V 5103, 1, [2] (s. *Ἡρότιμος*); (4) i BC ib. I^2 326, 2 (s. *Νουμήνιος*)

Δεινόστρατος
CIMMERIAN BOSPOROS:
—PANTIKAPAION: (1) 389-349 BC *CIRB* 6, 2 (f. *Στρατοκλῆς*)

Δείνων
SKYTHIA:
—OLBIA-BORYSTHENES: (1) v-iv BC *SEG* XLIV 670 n. (sherd) (*Δένω[ν]*: ?s. *Ἐπικράτης*); (2) f. iv BC Dubois, *IGDOlbia* 102; cf. *SEG* XLIV 670 (lead) (*Δέ̣-*)

Δειοκοῦς
MACEDONIA (CHALKIDIKE):
—ANTIGONEIA: (1) i/ii AD ib. XXXVIII 598; *BE* 1989, no. 454 (name) (*Δειο(σ)κοῦς?*—*BE*)

Δείσορος
THRACE:
—PHILIPPOPOLIS-TRIMONTIUM (TERRIT.): (1) imp. *IGB* III 1283 (f. *Βίθυς*)

Δεκάμνιχος
MACEDONIA: (1) s. v BC Arist., *Pol.* 1311 b, 30 (Tataki, *Macedonians* p. 291 no. 15)

Δεκέβαλος
SCYTHIA MINOR:
—TOMIS (NR.): (1) ii/iii AD *SEG* XL 605 = XLIII 493 (*Δεκέβα[λ]ος*: f. *Ναιέτων*)
THRACE:
—DUROSTORUM: (2) ii-iii AD *CIL* III 7477 (Lat. Valerius Decibal(u)s: s. Valerius Marcus)
—NICOPOLIS AD ISTRUM (TERRIT.): (3) 227 AD *ILB* 438 I, 52 (Lat. Deceb(alus): s. Crescens)
—NOVAE*: (4) 222-235 AD *IGLNovae* 82, 4 (Lat. Fl. Decebalus)
THRACE?: (5) 203 AD Speidel, *Denkmäler* 58 I, 8 (Lat. Silvin. Decibal(us))

Δέκεντος
THRACE:
—PAUTALIA (TERRIT.): (1) ii-iii AD *IGB* IV 2231 (s. *Ποτάμων*, f. *Φλ. Μόδεστα*)

Δεκιμία
MACEDONIA (PAIONIA):
—BYLAZORA: (1) ii-iii AD *SEG* XVI 402, 2 (*-κυ-*)

Δεκίμιος
MACEDONIA (LYNKESTIS):
—HERAKLEIA (AREA): (1) imp. *IG* X (2) (2) 3 (f. *Τρεβάτιος*)

Δέκιμος
MACEDONIA (ODOMANTIKE):
—SIRRHA (TERRIT.): (1) ii-iii AD *SEG* XXX 593 + Kaphtantzis 478 (f. *Καπίτων*)

Δεκμιανός
THRACE:
—MEZDRA (MOD.): (1) ii-iii AD *IGB* II 489 (s. *Ταρούλας*)

Δέκμος
THRACE:
—APOLLONIA-SOZOPOLIS: (1) i-ii AD ib. I² 400 (f. (nat.) *Μήτοκος*)

Δεκουρᾶτος
MACEDONIA (MYGDONIA):
—THESSALONIKE*: (1) iii AD *SEG* XLIV 557

Δέκρυμνος
THRACE:
—DRAGANOVEC (MOD.): (1) f. iii AD *IGB* V 5294 (*CCET* II (2) 484) (f. *Ζουλγήσης*)

Δελοῦς
MACEDONIA (MYGDONIA):
—THESSALONIKE?: (1) ii-iii AD *IG* X (2) (1) 856, 2; cf. *Maia* 25 (1973) p. 200 (*Δελουση*—*IG*, *Λελοῦς ἤ*—*Maia*: d. *Μέστριος*, *Φίλα*)

Δελτίς
MACEDONIA (MYGDONIA):
—THESSALONIKE?: (1) ii AD *IG* X (2) (1) 916 (*Δελτι* (dat.): d. *Δίων*, *Κούθιν*)

Δελφικός
SCYTHIA MINOR:
—ISTROS: (1) ii/iii AD *ISM* I 225, 5 (s. *M*—)

Δελφίνιος
CIMMERIAN BOSPOROS:
—GORGIPPIA: (1) f. iii BC *CIRB* 1137 B II, 7 (*Δελφ[ί]νιος*: s. *Στρατόνικος*)

Δελφίς
MACEDONIA (PIERIA):
—DION: (1) ii-iii AD *SEG* XXXVI 613 (d. *Δῶρος*)

Δελφός
SKYTHIA:
—OLBIA-BORYSTHENES: (1) ii AD *IOlbia* 80, 6 (*Δε[λ]φός*: f. *Διονύσιος*); (2) ~ *IOSPE* I² 156, 2; 202 (f. *Ἀδόης*)
—TYRAS: (3) 181 AD ib. 2, 31 (I f. *Δελφός* II); (4) ~ ib. l. 31 (II s. *Δελφός* I)
TAURIS:
—CHERSONESOS: (5) iii BC Solomonik, *NEPKh* 144 (s. *Εὐκλείδας*); (6) ~ ib. 145 (*SEG* XXX 964); (7) c. 237-230 BC Kats p. 92 no. 37 (amph.) (s. *Ἴστρων*) ?= (*9*); (8) c. 210-200 BC Anokhin p. 144 no. 153 (coin) ?= (*9*); (9) c. 190-180 BC ib. p. 145 no. 158 (coin) ?= (7) (*8*); (10) imp. Solomonik, *NEPKh* 46 (f. *Δουλίων*); (11) ii AD *VDI* 1938 (3), p. 80 no. 10. II (*Δε[λ]φός*: s. *Στρατόνικος*)
—CHERSONESOS (NR.): (12) iv/iii BC *NE* II (1974) p. 40 no. 5 (*Δελ[φός]*?)

Δέλφων
THRACE:
—PERINTHOS-HERAKLEIA:
——(Akarnanes): (1) iii-ii BC *IPerinth* 61, 8 (s. *Ἀριστόμαχος*)

Δένβερ
MACEDONIA (BOTTIAIA):
—BEROIA*: (1) ii AD *IBer* 260, 1 (Tataki 371)

Δενδύζελμις
THRACE?: (1) c. 220 BC *PPetr* III 112 f, 17 (*PP* 2877; Velkov 79)

Δενθαιβαρις
MACEDONIA (SINTIKE):
—PARTHIKOPOLIS (TERRIT.): (1) 125 AD *IGB* IV 2321 (*[Δε]νθαιβαρι?* (dat.))

Δενθηβαρις
THRACE:
—PAUTALIA (TERRIT.): (1) ii-iii AD ib. 2119

Δέντης
MACEDONIA (LYNKESTIS):
—HERAKLEIA (NR.): (1) ii-iii AD *IG* X (2) (2) 10 (s. *Νουμήνιος*, f. *Νουμήνιος*)
MACEDONIA (ODOMANTIKE):
—BERGE: (2) ii-iii AD *BCH* 81 (1957) p. 606 (Pilhofer 568a) (f. *Δίζας*)

Δεντοζίλης
THRACE?: (1) s. iv BC Vollenweider, *Camées* 26 (ring) (*Δεντοζίλη* (gen.?))

Δέντος
THRACE:
—BARGALA: (1) ii-iii AD *SEG* XLIV 518 (s. *Ἔπτηλος*)

Δεντούζελμις
THRACE?: (1) 140-116 BC ib. XLI 1634, 4

Δεντούπης
THRACE:
—PLATANIA (MOD.): (1) iii AD ib. XXXII 676 (Pilhofer 510) (*[Δ]εντούπης*: s. *Βίθυς*, f. *Οὐάλης*)

Δεντουρμής
MACEDONIA (MYGDONIA):
—THESSALONIKE?: (1) ?ii AD *IG* X (2) (1) 1020 (*Δεντουρμης* (fem. nom.)—lap., *Δεντούρμη?*)

Δεντοῦς
MACEDONIA (BOTTIAIA):
—BEROIA: (1) ii AD Dimitsas 212 + *SEG* XXVIII 551 (Tataki 372) (m. *Ζιπᾶς*, *Σεκοῦνδα*)
MACEDONIA (PIERIS):
—AKONTISMA (NR.): (2) ii-iii AD *Thrakika* 13 (1940) p. 25 (*Δεντο[ῦς]?*: d. *Δόλης*)

Δεντούσκαιλα
MACEDONIA (SINTIKE):
—PARTHIKOPOLIS (TERRIT.): (1) ii/iii AD *IGB* IV 2312 (d. *Πυρούσαλα*)

Δεντούσταινα
THRACE:
—NICOPOLIS AD ISTRUM: (1) ii AD *ILB* 406 (Lat. Annia D[en]tustaina)

Δεντουσυκος
THRACE:
—ANCHIALOS (TERRIT.): (1) ii/iii AD *IGB* III 1846, 5 (*Δεντυ-*: d. *Δύτενις*, m. *Βρινκαζεις*, *Αὐλούζενις*, *Μουκάτραλις*)
—BOURDAPA: (2) ii-iii AD ib. 1338 (d. *Βιθίπης*)
—NICOPOLIS AD ISTRUM (TERRIT.): (3) ii AD *ILB* 378 (Lat. Dentusucus: d. Gerulonis (gen.), m. Silvanus, Marcus)

Δέντων
THRACE:
—BESSOI: (1) imp. *CIL* XI 82 (Lat. T. Mucius Dento)

Δεξίθεος
THRACE:
—LYSIMACHEIA?: (1) ?255 BC Nachtergael, *Les Galates* 8, 48; cf. Stephanis 1574 (f. *Λύσανδρος*)

Δεξικράτης
THRACE:
—SALYMBRIA: (1) imp. *IByz* S 7 (f. *Δι*—)

Δεξίλαος
MACEDONIA (BOTTIAIA):
—BEROIA: (1) m. iii BC *IBer* 19 (Tataki 373) (f. *Ἀπολλωνίδης*)

Δέξιος
MACEDONIA (MYGDONIA)?:
—HERAKLEIA: (1) f. iv BC *SEG* XXVII 299; *Milliaires* p. 70 n. 1 (locn.)
THRACE:
—BYZANTION: (2) ii/i BC *IByz* 187 (Fıratlı–Robert pp. 53-4 no. 32) (s. *Μένανδρος*)

Δέξτερ
THRACE:
—SERDICA: (1) ii-iii AD *IGB* IV 1963, 6 (*GVI* 386) (*Δέσκτερ*: s. *Σάλας*, *Ἐπτησυκος*)

Δεονῦς
THRACE:
—ABDERA: (1) c. 475-450 BC May, *Abdera* pp. 105-8 nos. 87-97 (coin) (*Δεο(νῦς)*?) ?= (*2*); (2) c. 450-425 BC ib. pp. 136-7 nos. 175-6 (coin); Masson, *OGS* pp. 429-30 (*Δεονῦδος* (gen.)) ?= (*1*)
—MARONEIA: (3) c. 432-423 BC Schönert-Geiss, *Maroneia* 85-91 (coin); Masson, *OGS* p. 438 with n. 88 (*Δεονῦτος* (gen.)—91, *Δεουνῦς*—Masson); (4) c. 400-378 BC Schönert-Geiss, *Maroneia* 155-8 (coin) (*Δεονῦος* (gen.)—155-7)

Δεουνσᾶς
THRACE:
—ABDERA: (1) c. 450-425 BC May, *Abdera* p. 139 no. 186 (coin); cf. Masson, *OGS* p. 430

Δέος
MACEDONIA (BOTTIAIA):
—BEROIA?: (1) imp. *IG* II² 8406 (Tataki 374; Tataki, *Macedonians* p. 77 no. 21; *FRA* 1313) (s. *Δημήτριος*)

Δεπανήτης
THRACE:
—BOURDAPA: (1) ii-iii AD *IGB* III 1353 (s. *Κότυς*)

Δέρδας
MACEDONIA: (1) ?417-413 BC *IG* I³ 89, 69 (*[Δέ]ρδας*) ?= (*10*); (2) ?394 BC Arist., *Pol.* 1311 b, 4 (Tataki, *Macedonians* p. 195 no. 8); (3) s. iv BC *SEG* XXXVIII 641 (f. *Λεωνίδας*); (4) 329-328 BC *RE* Supplbd. 4 (4); Berve 250 (Tataki, *Macedonians* p. 195 no. 9) (Lat. Derdam—Hedicke, pendam/berdes—mss.); (5) 153 BC *TAM* V (2) 1190, 4 (Tataki, *Macedonians* p. 469 no. 2) (s. *Δερκυλίδης*)
MACEDONIA (BOTTIAIA):
—BEROIA: (6) i BC-i AD *IBer* 142, 11 (Tataki 369) (f. *Λυσίμαχος*)
MACEDONIA (EDONIS):
—AMPHIPOLIS: (7) s. iv BC Hatzopoulos, *Actes Amphipolis* p. 48 no. 10 B, 1 (*SEG* XLI 564) (*Δωρδα*—lap., *Δ(έ)ρδας*)
MACEDONIA (ELIMEIA): (8) f. iv BC *RE* (2); *Essays Hersh* pp. 5-11 (coin); *Macedonia* 2 pp. 18-19 (Tataki, *Macedonians* p. 194 no. 6); (9) 348 BC *RE* (3); *Macedonia* 2 p. 19 (Tataki, *Macedonians* p. 194 no. 7)
MACEDONIA (ELIMEIA)?: (10) s. v BC *RE* (1); *Macedonia* 2 p. 18 (Tataki, *Macedonians* p. 194 no. 5) (s. *Ἀρριδαῖος*) ?= (*1*)

Δέρζενις
SCYTHIA MINOR:
—ISTROS [NR.]:
——Vicus Quintionis: (1) 139-161 AD *ISM* I 324, 13 (Lat. Derzenus: s. *Αὐλούπορις*); (2) 177 AD ib. 332, 7 (Lat. Derz(enus)?: s. *Βίθυς*)

Δερζίζενις
THRACE:
—BEROE-AUGUSTA TRAIANA (TERRIT.): (1) iii AD *SEG* XLV 847 (*Αὐ. Δερζείζενις*)
—BESSOI: (2) 138 AD *CIL* XVI 83 (Lat. Derzizenus: s. Clagissa)

Δερζίτραλις
THRACE:
—ODESSOS (NR.): (1) iii AD *BMNVarna* 10 (1955) p. 133 no. 19 (Lat. Derzitralus: s. *Μουκάπορις*)

Δέρζων
SCYTHIA MINOR?: (1) imp. *CCET* IV 189 (s. *Θιούθιος*)

Δερης?
MACEDONIA (EDONIS):
—AMPHIPOLIS: (1) ii-iii AD *Thracia* 2 p. 278 + *Epigraphica* 37 (1935) p. 31 (*Δερη* (gen.): f. *Ζιπᾶς*)

Δέρκις
CIMMERIAN BOSPOROS:
—PANTIKAPAION: (1) iii BC *CIRB* 22 (f. *Βάθυλλος*)

Δερκυλίδης
MACEDONIA: (1) 153 BC *TAM* V (2) 1190, 4 (Tataki, *Macedonians* p. 469 no. 3) (*Δερκ[υλί]δης*: f. *Δέρδας*)
MACEDONIA (BOTTIAIA):
—BEROIA: (2) 223 BC *IBer* 4, 24 (*Δερ[κ]υλίδης*: f. *Διονύσιος*)
MACEDONIA (CHALKIDIKE):
—POTIDAIA-KASSANDREIA: (3) c. 240-220 BC *SEG* XXXVII 558, 3; *Poikila* p. 141 (date) (s. *Στράτων*)

Δερκύλος
MACEDONIA (CHALKIDIKE):
—OLYNTHOS: (1) ?350 BC *TAPA* 65 (1934) p. 125 no. 3, 4, 8; Hatzopoulos, *Actes Chalc.* p. 80 (date) (s. *Στράτιος*)

Δερνάης
THRACE:
—MARKIANOPOLIS (TERRIT.): (1) iii AD *IGB* V 5329, 4 (s. *Δαλήτραλις*)

Δερναῖος
THRACE:
—ODESSOS: (1) 42 BC ib. I[2] 46, 5 (f. *Κότυς*)

Δεσάκενθος
THRACE:
—BOURDAPA: (1) ii-iii AD ib. III 1358 (f. *Θεαθώ*)

Δεσπίνη
THRACE:
—MESAMBRIA: (1) iv-vi AD *SEG* XL 576 (*[Δε]σπίνη*)

Δέσχας
CIMMERIAN BOSPOROS:
—PANTIKAPAION: (1) i AD *CIRB* 452; Zgusta, *PNS* 633 (f. *Λύσανδρος*)

Δηδηγνος?
THRACE:
—BOURDAPA: (1) hell. *SEG* XXXIX 661 = XLI 608. 1 = XLVII 1094. 1 (*Δηδημιου* (gen.)—1094: f. *Λαῖσμος*)

Δῆζος
THRACE:
—ASTAI: (1) ii BC *IGB* I[2] 312, 3 (f. *Δε—της*)
—KABYLE: (2) 218-200 BC Draganov, *Kabile* 901-2 (coin)

Δηΐμαχος
SKYTHIA:
—OLBIA-BORYSTHENES: (1) iii BC *IOSPE* I[2] 201 I, 50 (s. *Ὀρθόβουλος*); (2) f. iii BC ib. 201 II, 12; *SEG* XXXIX 702, 29 (f. *Ἀγαθῖνος*)
THRACE:
—SESTOS: (3) i AD *GP* 219

Δήλιος
TAURIS:
—CHERSONESOS: (1) iv BC Solomonik, *GAKh* 577 (vase) (*Δήλι(ος)*? (n. pr.?)); (2) ii-i BC *IOSPE* I[2] 411 (s. *Ἀπολλᾶς*)
THRACE:
—PISTIROS: (3) inc. Archibald, *Odrysian Kingdom* p. 230 (vase)

Δηλόπτιχος
SCYTHIA MINOR:
—KALLATIS: (1) iii-ii BC *NZ* 10 (1917) p. 88 no. 229a (coin) (*Δηλό(πτιχος)*?)
THRACE:
—BYZANTION: (2) ?354 BC Rhodes–Osborne 57, 13 (f. *Ἀγ—*); (3) c. 350-325 BC *IOlbia* 9, 3 (Dubois, *IGDOlbia* 18) (s. *Μενίσκος*) ?= (*4*); (4) iv/iii BC *CIRB* 17 (f. *Τεισίας, Φρασίδαμος*) ?= (*3*)
—HERAION TEICHOS?: (5) f. iv BC Taşlıklıoğlu I p. 10 no. 3 (*Δηλόπτιχ[ος]*)

Δημαγόρης
SKYTHIA:
—OLBIA-BORYSTHENES: (1) s. iv BC *IOSPE* I[2] 195, 5 (*CEG* II 883; Dubois, *IGDOlbia* 47) (f. *Ἀναξαγόρας*); (2) iii BC *IOlbia* 72, 3 (f. *Ἀθηνόδωρος*)

Δημαίνετος
MACEDONIA (BOTTIAIA):
—AIGAI: (1) f. iv BC *SEG* XXXV 771 (s. *Δημήτριος*)
MACEDONIA (MYGDONIA):
—LETE: (2) f. ii BC ib. XLVI 764, 11 (*Δημαίν[ετος]*: f. *Σίμαλος*)

Δήμακος
MACEDONIA:
—BONTHITAI: (1) m. i BC *AD* 11 (1927-8) pp. 58-9 no. 5, 19 (Tataki, *Macedonians* p. 84 no. 2) (f. *Ἀντίγονος*)

Δημάλκας
SCYTHIA MINOR:
—KALLATIS: (1) i BC *ISM* III 39, 9 (*Δ[η]μά[λ]κας*: s. *Μορφίων*)

Δημάνθης
CIMMERIAN BOSPOROS:
—GORGIPPIA: (1) f. iii BC *CIRB* 1137 A I, 47 (s. *Δημόχαρις*)

Δημάρατος
THRACE:
—MARONEIA: (1) f. iii BC *IThrakAig* E228
—PERINTHOS-HERAKLEIA?: (2) iv BC Hp., *Epid.* iv 54

Δημαρέτη
MACEDONIA (BOTTIAIA):
—MIEZA: (1) iii/ii BC *SEG* XLIII 410 (d. *Ζωΐλος*, m. *Σπάρτη*)
THRACE:
—LYSIMACHEIA: (2) hell. *ISestos* 40

Δημάρετος
SCYTHIA MINOR:
—TOMIS: (1) ii BC *ISM* II 167 (*Δημάρε̣[τος]*)
THRACE:
—PERINTHOS-HERAKLEIA:
——(Podargoi): (2) iii-ii BC *IPerinth* 61, 21 (s. *Ζηνόδοτος*)

Δημάρχη
MACEDONIA (MYGDONIA):
—THESSALONIKE: (1) ii AD *IG* X (2) (1) 459 A (d. *Νικάνωρ*, m. *Θεανώ*)
MACEDONIA (PAIONIA):
—BYLAZORA (NR.): (2) ii-iii AD *SEG* XVI 403b (*[Δημ]άρχη*: m. *Λούκιος*)

MACEDONIA (PELAGONIA):
—DOSTONEIS: (3) ii AD *IG* X (2) (2) 194 (*Αἰλ. Δ.*); (4) ~ ib. 199 (d. *Βάσσος*, m. *Βάσσος, Μέστα*)

Δημαρχίδης
MACEDONIA (PIERIA):
—PHILA?: (1) ?iii BC *RPh* 1911, pp. 133-4 no. 36, 48 + *Polemon* 2 (1934-40) Parart. p. 12 no. 17; cf. Helly, *L'État thessalien* pp. 319-20 (locn.) (*[Δη]μαρχίδης*: f. *Δήμαρχος*)

Δήμαρχος
CIMMERIAN BOSPOROS:
—GORGIPPIA: (1) f. iii BC *CIRB* 1137 A I, 49 (s. *Νουμήνιος*)
—PANTIKAPAION: (2) hell. *AA* 1907, p. 127 Aa, 2 (lead)
—PHANAGOREIA?: (3) 389-349 BC *CIRB* 1111 (s. *Σκύθης*)
MACEDONIA: (4) s. iii BC *SB* 4307 (Tataki, *Macedonians* p. 292 no. 18; La'da E1745) (t.e.)
MACEDONIA (BOTTIAIA):
—BEROIA: (5) 223 BC *IBer* 4, 33 (*(Δ)ήμαρχος*: s. *Διαγόρας*)
MACEDONIA (CHALKIDIKE):
—OLYNTHOS: (6) ?352 BC *TAPA* 65 (1934) p. 128 no. 4, 7, 12; *SEG* XLVII 922; Hatzopoulos, *Actes Chalc.* p. 80 (date) (s. *Φανόλεως*); (7) s. iv BC *IG* XII (8) 435 (Tataki, *Macedonians* p. 133 no. 29) (s. *Ἰσχόμαχος*)
MACEDONIA (MYGDONIA):
—DIKAIA: (8) c. 365-359 BC Unp. (Voutyras–Sismanidis) l. 36
MACEDONIA (PIERIA):
—PHILA?: (9) ?iii BC *RPh* 1911, pp. 133-4 no. 36, 48 + *Polemon* 2 (1934-40) Parart. p. 12 no. 17; cf. Helly, *L'État thessalien* pp. 319-20 (locn.) (*Δή[μαρχος]*?: s. *Δημαρχίδης*)
MACEDONIA?: (10) 327-323 BC *RE* (5); Berve 255 (Tataki, *Macedonians* p. 292 no. 17)

Δημᾶς
MACEDONIA (DERRIOPOS):
—STUBERRA: (1) c. 41-48 AD *IG* X (2) (2) 323, 29 (f. *Ἄλεξις*) ?= (*2*); (2) 50 AD ib. 324, 23 (f. *Παρᾶς*) ?= (*1*)
MACEDONIA (MYGDONIA):
—THESSALONIKE: (3) 154 AD ib. X (2) (1) 288, 7 (*M. Κάσσ[ι]ος Ἕρμων ὁ καὶ Δ̣ημᾶς*)
TAURIS:
—CHERSONESOS: (4) iii AD Solomonik, *NEPKh* 63 (Solomonik, *LNKhT* 30) (Lat. Aurel[ius] Demas)
THRACE:
—AIGOS POTAMOI?: (5) hell. *ISestos* 72 (*Δημᾶ[ς]*: s. *Ἀπολλωνίδης*)

Δημέας
MACEDONIA: (1) ?219 BC *PUG* III 103, 8 (Tataki, *Macedonians* p. 292 no. 19); cf. La'da E1594 (f. *Πτολεμαῖος*)
MACEDONIA (BOTTIAIA):
—EDESSA: (2) ii/i BC *Ancient Macedonia* I p. 202 no. 16 (Tataki, *Edessa* 76) (*Δ..έας*—ed., *Δ[ημ]έας*—Tataki: s. *Ἐπικράτης*)
MACEDONIA (ODOMANTIKE):
—SKOTOUSSA?: (3) ii-iii AD *BCH* 18 (1894) p. 439 no. 2 (Dimitsas 845) = Dimitsas 911 (f. *Ἀρτεμιδώρα*)
MACEDONIA (PIERIA):
—PHILA?: (4) ?iii BC *RPh* 1911, pp. 133-4 no. 36, 53; cf. Helly, *L'État thessalien* pp. 319-20 (locn.) (f. *—ος*) ?= (*5*); (5) ~ *RPh* 1911, pp. 133-4 no. 36, 110; cf. Helly, *L'État thessalien* pp. 319-20 (locn.) (f. *Ἄσανδρος*) ?= (*4*)
MACEDONIA (SINTIKE):
—NEINE: (6) ii-iii AD *IGB* IV 2260
—PARTHIKOPOLIS: (7) 158 AD ib. 2263, 15 (s. *Παράμονος*); (8) 219 AD ib. V 5901 (f. *Παράμονος*)

THRACE:
—RHAIDESTOS: **(9)** ii AD *JÖAI* 23 (1926) Beibl. col. 137 no. 34 = *IG* x (2) (1) 711; cf. *CPh.* 70 (1975) pp. 50-1 (name) (*Δ.*, *Δημέα*?)

Δημειός
THRACE:
—APOLLONIA-SOZOPOLIS: **(1)** v/iv BC *IGB* I² 448 (*Δημειδ* (gen.))

Δήμη
MACEDONIA (EDONIS):
—AMPHIPOLIS: **(1)** s. iv BC ib. 459, 3 (Tataki, *Macedonians* p. 50 no. 38) (d. *Ἀριστοκλῆς*)

Δημῆς
THRACE:
—APOLLONIA-SOZOPOLIS?: **(1)** iv BC *IGB* I² 476 (s. *Θαρσύνων*)

Δήμητρα
MACEDONIA (EDONIS):
—AMPHIPOLIS: **(1)** hell. *SEG* XXIV 595 (d. *Τεισαμενός*)

Δημητρία
CIMMERIAN BOSPOROS:
—PANTIKAPAION: **(1)** iv BC *CIRB* 168 (*Δη[μ]η-τρ[ία]*: m. *Γόρδις*, *Ἀρτεμιδώρη*)
MACEDONIA?:
—HERAKLEIA: **(2)** m. iv BC *Philippi* p. 74 fig. 58 (Pilhofer 379a) (d. *Διονύσιος*)
MACEDONIA (BOTTIAIA):
—AIGAI: **(3)** s. iv BC *SEG* XXXV 773 (*Δημη[τ]ρία*: d. *Καλλίας*)
—BEROIA: **(4)** iii AD *IBer* 220 (Tataki 375)
—BEROIA*: **(5)** v-vi AD *IBer* 432 (Feissel, *RICM* 70)
—EDESSA: **(6)** v-vi AD ib. 30
MACEDONIA (MYGDONIA):
—THESSALONIKE: **(7)** ii-iii AD *IG* x (2) (1) 438 (m. *Δημήτριος*, *Μάξιμα*); **(8)** ~ ib. 611, 1 (*Οὐλπ. Δ.*)
—THESSALONIKE?: **(9)** v-vi AD ib. 794 (Feissel, *RICM* 178; *SEG* XLVII 988) (m. *Ἀ—ιος*)
MACEDONIA?: **(10)** 236 BC *PPetr²* 16, 79 (?d. *Κάλας*)
THRACE: **(11)** iii BC *CPR* XIII 14 a III, 47 (La'da E857); **(12)** ?164 BC *SGDI* 1849, 3, 5, 7 (*Δαματρία*—ll. 5 and 7: slave/freed.); **(13)** i BC *IG* II² 8903 (*FRA* 2512) (d. *Σεργίων*)
—ČOMAKOVCI (MOD.): **(14)** ?iii AD *ILB* 167 (Lat. [D]emetria)
—DUROSTORUM: **(15)** ii-iii AD *CIL* III 14434 (Lat. Marina Demetria)
—MARONEIA: **(16)** iii AD Dumont–Homolle 110b 9 (*IThrakAig* E311) (*Βρουττία Δ.*)
—SALYMBRIA?: **(17)** iii AD *AEMÖ* 17 (1894) p. 57 no. 3, 1 (or Thrace Perinthos-Herakleia: *Αὐρ. Δ.*: d. *Χρηστῖνος*, m. *Αὐρ. Μηνόδωρος*)

Δημητριανή
MACEDONIA (MYGDONIA):
—THESSALONIKE: **(1)** iii AD *IG* x (2) (1) 547 (*Αὐρ. Δημητριανὴ ἡ καὶ Ματρώνα*)

Δημητριανός
MACEDONIA (KRESTONIA):
—IORON: (1) iii AD *SEG* XLVIII 815
THRACE:
—NICOPOLIS AD ISTRUM: **(2)** imp. *ILB* 368 (Lat. Demetrianus)
—NICOPOLIS AD ISTRUM (TERRIT.): **(3)** ii AD *IGB* v 5244 a, 3 (s. *Σουσίων*) ?= (*4*); **(4)** ~ ib. l. 5-6 (f. *Ἡρακλιανός*, *—είνος*) ?= (*3*)
—PHILIPPOPOLIS-TRIMONTIUM (TERRIT.): **(5)** ii AD ib. III 1421, 1; cf. v 5524 (*Ἀδριάνιος Δημ[η]τριανός*)

Δημητριάς
MACEDONIA (BOTTIAIA):
—BEROIA: **(1)** 239 AD *ILeukopetra* 92, 2 (*Αὐρ. Δ.*)

Δημητρίη
CIMMERIAN BOSPOROS:
—GORGIPPIA: **(1)** s. iv BC *CIRB* 14 (d. *Ἀριστονίκη*: locn.—Vinogradov)
—PANTIKAPAION: **(2)** iv BC ib. 176 (*[Δημ]ητρίη*: d. *Ποσείδιππος*)

Δημήτριος
CIMMERIAN BOSPOROS:
—BOSPOROS: **(1)** i-ii AD *IG* II² 8425 (*FRA* 1368) (f. *Ἀφροδισία*)
—BOSPOROS?: **(2)** ?ii/i BC *JDAI* 23 (1908) p. 73; Courby, *Les vases grecs* p. 412; Blavatskii, *Pantikapei* p. 122 with fig. 31; *MIA* 103 (1962) p. 205 (vase) (potter)
—GORGIPPIA: **(3)** f. iii BC *CIRB* 1137 A I, 5 (f. *Σίνδος*); **(4)** ~ ib. l. 9 (f. *Ἀπολλώνιος*); **(5)** ~ ib. l. 38; 1137 B I, 51 (s. *Στρατόνικος*); **(6)** ~ ib. 1137 A II, 5 (II s. *Δημήτριος* I); **(7)** ~ ib. l. 29 (s. *Σίνδοκος*); **(8)** ~ ib. l. 50-1 (f. *Ἀρισταγόρας*, *Μεγάνωρ*); **(9)** ~ ib. l. 5-6 (I f. *Δημήτριος* II, *Ἱπποκράτης*); **(10)** ~ ib. 1137 B I, 2 (*[Δημ]ήτριος*: s. *Τιμέας*); **(11)** ~ ib. l. 20; 1137 B II, 4 (f. *Παπύλος*); **(12)** ~ ib. l. 8 (*Δημή[τριος]*: I f. *Δημήτριος* II); **(13)** ~ ib. l. 8 (II s. *Δημήτριος* I); **(14)** ~ ib. l. 56 (f. *Ἀριστοκράτης*); **(15)** ii AD ib. 1153 (*[Δ]ημήτ[ριος]*); **(16)** m. ii AD *Eirene* 7 (1968) p. 67, 22 (s. *Θεόκριτος*); **(17)** s. ii AD *CIRB* 1208, 4 (*Δημήτ[ριος]*); **(18)** ii/iii AD ib. 1179, 45 (*Δημήτρι[ος]*)
—GORGIPPIA?: **(19)** s. ii AD ib. 1231 B, 5 (I f. *Δημήτριος* II); **(20)** ~ ib. l. 5 (*[Δημή]τριος*: II s. *Δημήτριος* I)
—HERMONASSA: **(21)** iv BC ib. 1056 II, 8 (*Δημή[τριος]*: f. *Ἱπποκράτης*); **(22)** ~ ib. l. 11 (s. *Ἀγυαῖος*); **(23)** ~ ib. 1062 (s. *Σῶσις*); **(24)** ~ ib. 1068 (f. *Σῶσις*)
—KYTAIA: **(25)** iv BC ib. 943 (f. *Χανάκης*)
—MYRMEKION: **(26)** iv BC *MIA* 4 (1941) p. 193 no. 189 (vase); **(27)** ~ *CIRB* 873 (*[Δημ]ήτριος*: s. *—λλω—*); **(28)** ii BC Gaidukevich, *AGB Mirmekii* p. 78
—NYMPHAION: **(29)** ii-iii AD *CIRB* 936 (f. *Χρήστη*, *Παρρησία*)
—PANTIKAPAION: **(30)** s. iv BC ib. 192, 2; cf. KW pl. 5 no. 88 (f. *Ἱστιαῖος*) ?= (*32*); **(31)** ~ *CIRB* 192, 4; cf. KW pl. 5 no. 88 (s. *Ἐπιχάρης*); **(32)** ~ *CIRB* 192, 7; cf. KW pl. 5 no. 88 (f. *Παρμένων*) ?= (*30*); **(33)** ii-i BC *CIRB* 261 (f. *Ἀπολλώνιος*); **(34)** c. 180-150 BC ib. 75, 9, 13 (*Δημή[τριος]*: f. *Θεόκριτος*); **(35)** i AD ib. 355 (f. *Ἀρείφιλος*); **(36)** ~ ib. 383 (s. *Ἀπολλώνιος*); **(37)** ~ ib. 553; cf. KW pl. 22 no. 318 (f. *Χρύσιον*); **(38)** ~ *CIRB* p. 937 no. 2 (s. *Πατίας*, f. *Ἄττας*) ?= (*45*); **(39)** f. i AD ib. 442; cf. KW pl. 29 no. 418 (s. *Κολιδίων*, *Χανίκα*); **(40)** m. i AD *CIRB* 501, 1 (f. *Πτολλᾶς*); **(41)** ~ ib. 568; **(42)** s. i AD ib. 424; **(43)** i/ii AD ib. 82, 4; **(44)** ~ ib. l. 8 (s. *Μονόχορδος*, f. *Πάπας*); **(45)** ~ ib. 612; cf. KW pl. 41 no. 575 (f. *Ἰούλ. Πατίας*) ?= (*38*); **(46)** ~ *CIRB* 644 (*Δημήτρι[ος]*: s. *Ἀρισ—*); **(47)** ii AD ib. 706 (*Ἰο[ύ]λ. Δ.*: f. *Σόγαμος*); **(48)** f. ii AD ib. 89, 5; **(49)** 275-278 AD ib. 36, 31 (*Δημήτ(ριος)*: f. *Βανας*); **(50)** ~ ib. l. 58 (*Δημ[ή]τρ[ιος]*); **(51)** ~ ib. l. 63 (*Δημήτρ(ιος)*: f. *—κρατ(ης)*); **(52)** ~ ib. l. 73 (*Δημή[τριος]*?); **(53)** ~ ib. l. 74 (*Δημή[ριος]*: f. *—ατης*)
—PHANAGOREIA: **(54)** v/iv BC *SEG* XXVII 448 (f. *Μικκαλίων*, *Πατίκα*); **(55)** i AD *CIRB* 997 (f. *Ἠλίς*); **(56)** ii AD ib. 1001 (s. *Ἀσκληπιάδης*)
—THEODOSIA: **(57)** iii AD ib. 947 A, 5 (s. *Καρδίους*); **(58)** ~ ib. l. 7 (s. *Ψυχαρίων*); **(59)** ~ ib. 947 B, 7 (*Δημήτριος*: f. *Εὔοδος*); **(60)** ~ ib. l. 16 (*Δημή[τριος]*); **(61)** ~ ib. l. 18 (*[Δ]ημήτριο[ς]*: f. *Ἔρως*)
—ZENONOS CHERSONESOS*: **(62)** iii AD ib. 898, 3 (s. *Θάμφλας*); **(63)** ~ ib. l. 4 (*Δημήτ[ριος]*: f. *Ἡρακλείδης*)
MACEDONIA: **(64)** iv BC Plu., *Demetr.* 2 (Tataki, *Macedonians* p. 294 no. 36) (s. *Φίλιππος*); **(65)** c. 336-283 BC *RE* (33); Berve 257; *Macedonia* 3 p. 637 Index s.v.; cf. Beloch, *GG* IV (2) pp. 134-5 (*Δ.* I *Πολιορκητής*: s. *Ἀντίγονος* I *Μονόφθαλμος*, *Στρατονίκη*, f. *Ἀντίγονος* II *Γονατᾶς*, *Ἀλέξανδρος*, *Δημήτριος ὁ Καλός*, *Δημήτριος ὁ Λεπτός*, *Κόρραγος*, *Στρατονίκη*, *Φίλα*: king); **(66)** 331-326 BC *RE* (25); Berve 256 (Tataki, *Macedonians* p. 293 no. 30) (s. *Ἀλθαιμένης*); **(67)** 330 BC *RE* (24); Berve 260 (Tataki, *Macedonians* p. 293 no. 26); **(68)** hell. *AMGR* 1935-9, p. 121 no. 4 (Tataki, *Macedonians* p. 295 no. 39); cf. La'da E1451 (f. *Ἀττίνας*); **(69)** iii BC *PGurob* 18, 4 (*PP* 8881; Tataki, *Macedonians* p. 294 no. 35) (s. *Πυρρίας*); **(70)** ~ ib. p. 295 no. 38 (f. *Ἀντιγόνα*); **(71)** f. iii BC *RE* (35) (Tataki, *Macedonians* p. 292 no. 21) (*Δ. ὁ Καλός*: s. *Δημήτριος* I *Πολιορκητής*, *Πτολεμαΐς*, f. *Ἀντίγονος* III *Δώσων*, ?f. *Ἐχεκράτης*); **(72)** ~ *RE* (36) (Tataki, *Macedonians* p. 292 no. 23) (*Δ. ὁ Λεπτός*: s. *Δημήτριος* I *Πολιορκητής*); **(73)** c. 276-229 BC *RE* (34); *Macedonia* 3 pp. 322-336; cf. Beloch, *GG* IV (2) pp. 136-9 (*Δ.* II: s. *Ἀντίγονος* II *Γονατᾶς*, *Φίλα*, f. *Φίλιππος* V, ?f. *Ἀπάμη*: king); **(74)** ?275 or 266 BC *FD* III (4) 408, 26 (Tataki, *Macedonians* p. 215 no. 2) (*Δημή[τρ]ιος*: f. *—νιος*); **(75)** s. iii BC *Memnonion* 589 (Tataki, *Macedonians* p. 295 no. 40); cf. La'da E1460 (f. *Δῆς*); **(76)** ~ *Syringes* 611 (Tataki, *Macedonians* p. 295 no. 41); cf. La'da E1549 (f. *Νικάδας*); **(77)** c. 225-200 BC *PMich* 781, 50; cf. La'da E1456 (I f. *Δημήτριος* II); **(78)** ~ *PMich* 781, 50 (La'da E1456) (II s. *Δημήτριος* I); **(79)** ?219 BC *PUG* III 104, 2, 4; La'da E1537; E1643 (f. *Μένανδρος*, *Φίλιππος*); **(80)** c. 208-181 BC *RE* (37) (Tataki, *Macedonians* p. 293 no. 24) (s. *Φίλιππος* V); **(81)** ii BC *IG* II² 9259 (Tataki, *Macedonians* p. 294 no. 31; *FRA* 3468) (s. *Νικίας*); **(82)** 186-150 BC *RE* (40); Grainger, *SPG* pp. 39-42; cf. *ZPE* 131 (2000) pp. 106-8 (*Δ.* I *Σωτήρ*: s. *Σέλευκος* IV *Φιλοπάτωρ*, *Λαοδίκη*, f. *Ἀντίοχος* VII *Σιδήτης*, *Δημήτριος* II *Νικάτωρ*, *Ἀντίγονος*: king); **(83)** c. 185-180 BC *SEG* XXXIX 606, 4 (s. *Σώπατρος*); **(84)** m. ii BC *PTeb* 1075 fr. 2, 17 (Tataki, *Macedonians* p. 478 no. 66); cf. La'da E1620 (f. *Σαραπίων*); **(85)** 159 BC *SB* 11893, 2 (Tataki, *Macedonians* p. 294 no. 32; La'da E1458) (*Δημήτριος*: s. *Πτολεμαῖος*); **(86)** c. 159-125 BC *RE* (41); Grainger, *SPG* pp. 42-4; cf. *ZPE* 131 (2000) pp. 107-8 (*Δ.* II *Νικάτωρ*: s. *Δημήτριος* I *Σωτήρ*, f. *Σέλευκος* V, *Ἀντίοχος* VIII *Γρυπός*, *Λαοδίκη*: king); **(87)** c. 148 BC *PTeb* 79, 29 (Tataki, *Macedonians* p. 478 no. 64; La'da E1455) (*Δημή[τριος]*: s. *Ἀγαθοκλῆς*); **(88)** a. 132 BC *PKöln* 366, 1, 10, 14, 19 (La'da E1457) (s. *Διονύσιος*); **(89)** c. 115-88 BC *RE* (42); Grainger, *SPG* p. 44 (*Δ.* III *Φιλοπάτωρ*: s. *Ἀντίοχος* VIII *Γρυπός*, *Τρύφαινα*: king); **(90)** 113 BC *PDion* 21, 28 (Tataki, *Macedonians* p. 478 no. 65); cf. La'da E1403 (f. *Ἀμμώνιος*); **(91)** v-vi AD Feissel, *RICM* 285 (*[Δη]μήτρ(ιος)*)
MACEDONIA (BOTTIAIA):
—AIGAI: **(92)** f. iv BC *SEG* XXXV 771 (f. *Δημαίνετος*)
—BEROIA: **(93)** s. iii BC *IBer* 16 B, 35 (s. *Γλαυκίας*); **(94)** ii BC ib. 141, 44; **(95)** s. ii BC ib. 18, 2; 24, 1 (Tataki 383) (f. *Μαρσύας*); **(96)** ii/i BC *IBer* 161 (s. *Ἡρόδοτος*); **(97)** 121 BC ib. 134, 13 (*Δημ[ήτρ]ιος*: f. *Ἀγέλαος*); **(98)** 113 BC ib. l. 39 (s. *Κλέων*); **(99)** i BC-i AD ib. 142, 4 (Tataki 381) (s. *Νικόλαος*); **(100)** f. i AD *IBer* 103, 7 (Tataki 380) (s. *Διονύσιος*); **(101)** ii AD *IBer* 492 (Tataki 378); **(102)** ii-iii AD *IBer* 90, 3 (Tataki 987) (*Οὐαριανὸς Δειδιανὸς Δ.*: s. *Οὐαριανὸς Διοσκουρίδης*, *Διδιανὴ Μαντώ*); **(103)** ~ *IBer* 263, 2 (*[Δ]ημήτρι[ος]*: f. *Μεγέθιος*); **(104)** ?171-208 AD *ILeukopetra* 130, 1 (s. *Διονύσιος*); **(105)** ?ii/iii AD ib. 131, 1 (*Δημήτ[ρ]ιος*: f. *Διοσκοῦς*); **(106)** ii/iii AD *IBer* 143 B, 14 (Tataki 1175) (*Σέργιος Δ.*); **(107)** f. iii AD

IBer 221 (Tataki 65) ((*Α*)ἰλιανὸς *Δ*.); **(108)** 210 AD *ILeukopetra* 55, 10; 56, 8; 57, 7 (Ἰουλιανὸς *Δ*.); **(109)** 225 AD ib. 71, 13 (Ἰούλ. *Δ*. ὁ Βριζῖνος) ?= (*110*); **(110)** 229 AD ib. 74, 14 (Ἰουλιανὸς *Δ*.) ?= (*109*); **(111)** 238-239 AD ib. 87, 14; 88, 3; 89, 16; 90, 11; 91, 24; 92, 13; 93, 30; 94, 7 (Ἰουλιανὸς *Δ*., Εἰου(λ)ιαν(ν)ὸς *Δ*.) ?= (*112*); **(112)** 248 AD *IBer* 53, 14; 54, 10 (Tataki 587) (Ἰουλιανὸς *Δ*.) ?= (*111*)
—BEROIA?: **(113)** imp. *IG* II^2 8406 (Tataki 382; Tataki, *Macedonians* p. 77 no. 22; *FRA* 1314) (f. *Δέος*)
—EDESSA: **(114)** f. i AD Dimitsas 38 (Tataki, *Edessa* 77) (s. *Χάρης*); **(115)** ?ii AD *SEG* XII 346 (Tataki, *Edessa* 78) (f. *Μᾶρκος ὁ καὶ Κυρήνιος*); **(116)** v-vi AD Feissel, *RICM* 13, 5 (s. *Θεόδωρος*); **(117)** ~ ib. 17
—EDESSA*: **(118)** v-vi AD ib. 26
—ICHNAI?: **(119)** 172 AD Dimitsas 147, 2 (*Φάβιος Αἰλ. Δ.*: I f. *Φάβιος Κορνήλιος Δημήτριος* II, *Φάβιος Κορνήλιος Ἄπερ*); **(120)** ~ ib. l. 5 (*Φάβιος Κορνήλιος Δ.*: II s. *Φάβιος Αἰλ. Δημήτριος* I, *Κορνηλία Ἀλεξάνδρα*)
—MIEZA: **(121)** f. ii BC *SEG* XLIII 422 (f. *Καλλιστώ*)
—PELLA: **(122)** v/iv BC ib. XXXII 642 (f. *Ξάνθος*); **(123)** iv BC Tataki, *Macedonians* p. 153 no. 34 (f. *Εὔφημος*); **(124)** s. iv BC *SEG* XLI 575, 1 (f. *Καλλίας*); **(125)** hell. Tataki, *Macedonians* p. 153 no. 33 (f. *Γυμνάσιον*); **(126)** iii BC Akamatis, *Amph. Pellas* pp. 32-3 nos. PAR8-10 (amph.) (*SEG* L 613); **(127)** f. iii BC ib. XLI 575, 2-3 (s. *Καλλίας*, f. *Ὀαδίστη*); **(128)** 231 or 206 BC *CPR* XVIII 21, 437, 451 (La'da E1944) (s. *Ἀσκληπιάδης*: t.e.)
MACEDONIA (CHALKIDIKE):
—OLYNTHOS: **(129)** 300 BC *IG* II^2 1263, 5, 21, 41, 48 (Tataki, *Macedonians* p. 133 no. 32; *FRA* 5889) (s. *Σώσανδρος*); **(130)** c. 240-230 BC *IG* VII 265, 1, 3 (*IOrop* 56; Tataki, *Macedonians* p. 133 no. 31) (s. *Ζωΐλος*); **(131)** f. i BC *BGU* 1732, 1, 2, 5, etc. (*SB* 7420; *PP* 2626; Tataki, *Macedonians* p. 133 no. 30; La'da E1924)
—POTIDAIA-KASSANDREIA: **(132)** iv/iii BC *Tekmeria* 6 (2001) p. 43 no. 1 (s. *Ἑρμῶναξ*); **(133)** c. 208 BC *FD* III (4) 135, 23 (Tataki, *Macedonians* p. 87 no. 21) (f. *Ἀσκληπιάδης*)
—POTIDAIA-KASSANDREIA?: **(134)** iv BC *TAPA* 69 (1938) p. 60 no. 13 (or Macedonia (Chalkidike) Olynthos: f. *Μειδίας*)
—SKIONE: **(135)** iv BC *IG* II^2 10365 (Tataki, *Macedonians* p. 173 no. 2; *FRA* 6903)
—STREPSA?: **(136)** 285 BC *SEG* XXXVIII 619, 22 (f. *Εὐάλκης*, ?f. *Χιωνίδης*)
MACEDONIA (DERRIOPOS): **(137)** ii-iii AD *IG* X (2) (2) 314 ([*Δ*]*ημή*]*τριος*)
—STUBERRA: **(138)** 74 AD ib. 325, 54 (I f. *Δημήτριος* II); **(139)** ~ ib. l. 54 (II s. *Δημήτριος* I); **(140)** ~ ib. 326, 33 (s. *Ἀρριδαῖος*)
MACEDONIA (EDONIS):
—AMPHIPOLIS: **(141)** iv BC *RE* (93) (Tataki, *Macedonians* p. 50 no. 39); **(142)** b. 213 BC Hatzopoulos, *MI* 2 p. 83 no. 61, 10 (*SEG* XLVI 715) (*Δημήτρι*[*ος*]); **(143)** ii BC *IG* II^2 8081 (Tataki, *Macedonians* p. 50 no. 40; *FRA* 502) (s. *Ἀρτεμίδωρος*); **(144)** imp. *BCH* 22 (1898) pp. 349-50 n. 2 (Dimitsas 858) (s. *Δίβρης*, f. *Γ. Οὐελλέϊος Ἀπελλαῖος*); **(145)** ~ Unp. (Amphipolis) (*Δε-*: f. *Τρύφων*)
—AMPHIPOLIS?: **(146)** ?222-221 BC *SEG* XLVIII 812; cf. Hatzopoulos, *MI* 2 p. 92 no. 77 (f. *Αἰνείας*)
—EDONOI: **(147)** c. 450 BC *AMNG* III (2) p. 146 no. 14 (coin) (*Δημητρίō* (gen.): king?)
—PHILIPPOI (DRAMA (MOD.)): **(148)** i-ii AD *AD* 51 (1996) Chron. p. 577, 21 (Lat. Demetrius: I f. *Δημήτριος* II); **(149)** ~ ib. l. 21 (Lat. Demetrius: II s. *Δημήτριος* I)
—PHILIPPOI*: **(150)** 533-536 AD *DCB* (13) (bp.)

MACEDONIA (ELIMEIA):
—AIANE (TERRIT.): **(151)** 125 AD *EAM* 49 b (f. *Πα—*)
MACEDONIA (MYGDONIA):
—BORMISKOS?: **(152)** f. iii BC *SEG* XLIX 844. 3-15 (tiles); *BE* 1996, no. 270 (locn.)
—KALINDOIA: **(153)** iii/ii BC *SEG* XXXI 623 (XLII 591); *KGAM Thess.* I 52 (date) (f. *Φίλα*); **(154)** f. ii BC Hatzopoulos, *MI* 2 p. 88 no. 67 Index; **(155)** ii/i BC *SEG* XLII 595 (f. *Μεννίδας*); **(156)** 68-98 AD ib. 580, 10 (f. *Ἀντίγονος*); **(157)** ~ ib. l. 16 (s. *Φίλων*); **(158)** ~ ib. l. 34 (s. *Δίζας*); **(159)** ~ ib. l. 37 (I f. *Δημήτριος* II); **(160)** ~ ib. l. 37 (II s. *Δημήτριος* I); **(161)** ~ ib. l. 46 (f. *Μένυλλος*); **(162)** ~ ib. l. 58 (I f. *Δημήτριος* II); **(163)** ~ ib. l. 58 (II s. *Δημήτριος* I); **(164)** a. 98 AD ib. 582, 12 (s. *Ἀπολλώνιος*); **(165)** ~ ib. l. 50 (s. *Ἀριστόμαχος*); **(166)** ~ ib. l. 55 (f. *Ἱππίας*)
—LETE: **(167)** s. iv BC Hatzopoulos, *MI* 2 pp. 93-4 no. 79, 12; **(168)** ii AD *Makedonika* 2 (1951) p. 619 no. 42 *θ*, 1 (*BCH* 68-9 (1944-5) p. 431) (s. *Περίτας*)
—LETE?: **(169)** 22 or 139 AD Dimitsas 678, 4 (f. *Μεννίδας*)
—THESSALONIKE: **(170)** iii/ii BC *IG* X (2) (1) 107; *KGAM Thess.* I 67 (date) (f. *Ἀλέξανδρος*); **(171)** ~ *IG* X (2) (1) 107; *KGAM Thess.* I 67 (date) (s. *Ἀλέξανδρος*, *Νικαία*); **(172)** ii-i BC *IG* X (2) (1) 80 (*Μάνιος Κόρτιος Σίγνιος ὁ ἐπικαλ. Δ.*: s. *Μάνιος*); **(173)** s. ii BC ib. 27, 4 (I f. *Δημήτριος* II); **(174)** ~ ib. l. 4 (II s. *Δημήτριος* I); **(175)** c. 39 BC ib. 30, [4]; 50, 4; 109, 10 (s. *Ἀντίγονος*); **(176)** 27 BC-14 AD *SEG* XLVI 812, 5 (f. *Νικόλαος ὁ καὶ Κλειτόμαχος*); **(177)** f. i AD *IG* X (2) (1) 126, 3; Robert, *OMS* 5 pp. 295-302 (date) (*Δ.*: s. *Φαῦστος*); **(178)** ~ *IG* X (2) (1) 126, 4; Robert, *OMS* 5 pp. 295-302 (date) (s. *Νικόπολις*); **(179)** s. i AD *IG* X (2) (1) 69, 30 (f. *Περίτας*); **(180)** ~ ib. l. 35 (s. *Διονύσιος*); **(181)** ii AD ib. 226, 13; cf. Robert, *OMS* 5 p. 298 n. 193; **(182)** ii-iii AD *IG* X (2) (1) 438 (s. *Δημητρία*); **(183)** iii AD ib. 411, 7 (*Αὐρ. Δημή*[*τριος*]); **(184)** v-vi AD Feissel, *RICM* 188 (*SEG* XLVII 989) ([*Δη*]*μήτ*[*ριος*]?); **(185)** ~ *IG* X (2) (1) 335 (Feissel, *RICM* 149); **(186)** ?vi AD ib. 92 (?s. *Βιδέμιος*)
—THESSALONIKE?: **(187)** 46 AD Dimitsas 366, 10 (*Epigr. arch. Mak.* 36); cf. *Essays Laourdas* pp. 98-100; *Tekmeria* 6 (2001) p. 126 n. 2 (locn.) (f. *Ἡρακλείδης*); **(188)** ii-iii AD *IG* X (2) (1) 747 (*Δημή*[*τ*]*ριος*); **(189)** ?v AD ib. 784, 10 (Feissel, *RICM* 159); **(190)** v-vi AD ib. 165 (*SEG* XLVII 1008) (s. *Ἀνδρέας*, *Βερόη*); **(191)** ~ *IG* X (2) (1) 780 (Feissel, *RICM* 130); **(192)** ~ *IG* X (2) (1) 785 (Feissel, *RICM* 168) (f. *Γλυκερία*); **(193)** vi AD *IG* X (2) (1) 281 (Feissel, *RICM* 98)
—THESSALONIKE*: **(194)** b. 305 AD *DCB* (6); **(195)** 519 AD *IG* X (2) (1) 674, 2 (Feissel, *RICM* 132); cf. *Tyche* 10 (1995) pl. 12 no. 17
MACEDONIA (ODOMANTIKE):
—SIRRHA: **(196)** f. iii AD *SEG* XXX 590, 22 ([*Δη*]*μήτρ*[*ιος*]?)
—SKOTOUSSA?: **(197)** ii-iii AD *BCH* 18 (1894) p. 439 no. 2 (Dimitsas 845) = Dimitsas 911
MACEDONIA (ORESTIS):
—BATTYNAIOI: **(198)** 192 AD *EAM* 186 IV, 50 (f. *Δημήτρης*)
—LIKNADES (MOD.): **(199)** hell. ib. 210 (pithos)
—LYKE: **(200)** s. ii AD ib. 149, 6 (f. *Νίκαρχος*)
MACEDONIA (PAIONIA):
—DEMIR KAPIJA (MOD.): **(201)** hell. *SEG* XLV 807 E (sherd) (f. *Νικάνωρ*)
—KAVADARCI (MOD.): **(202)** ?ii AD Unp. (Skopje); **(203)** ~ ib. (f. *Διονύσιος*)
—NEGOTINO (MOD.): **(204)** ii-iii AD *Sp.* 75 (1933) p. 37 no. 114 (f. *Διονύσιος*); **(205)** iii AD *SEG* XXXVIII 714 (s. *Διονυσία*)
—STOBOI*: **(206)** v/vi AD ib. XL 552

MACEDONIA (PELAGONIA): **(207)** 94 or 211 AD *IG* X (2) (2) 278 (*Δ. ὁ καὶ Καπίτων*: s. *Φίλιππος*)
MACEDONIA (PIERIA): **(208)** ?ii BC ib. XII Suppl. p. 25 no. 80 (Tataki, *Macedonians* p. 168 no. 1) (f. *Θεοκρίτα*)
—DION: **(209)** ?ii-iii AD Dimitsas 180
—PYDNA: **(210)** 360 BC *IG* IV (1)^2 94 b, 7 (Perlman, *City and Sanctuary* E.1 with p. 69 (date); Tataki, *Macedonians* p. 170 no. 7) (*Δαμά-*)
MACEDONIA (SINTIKE):
—PARTHIKOPOLIS?: **(211)** ii-iii AD *IGB* V 5925, 2, 9 (f. *Ἀσκληπᾶς*)
—PARTHIKOPOLIS*: **(212)** vi AD Beševliev 241, 3
MACEDONIA (TYMPHAIA): **(213)** 188 AD *EAM* 71 ([*Δ*]*ημήτριο*[*ς*]: f. *Νίκανδρος*)
—AGIOS GEORGIOS (MOD.): **(214)** 153 AD ib. 12, 5 (f. *Νεοπτόλεμος ὁ καὶ Γναῖος*)
MACEDONIA?: **(215)** 334-333 BC *IG* II^2 405, 15; cf. Osborne, *Naturalization* D21 (*PA* 750; Tataki, *Macedonians* p. 295 no. 37) (*Δ*[*ημ*]*ήτριο*[*ς*]: f. *Ἀμύντωρ*); **(216)** 327 BC *RE* Supplbd. 4 (48 a); Berve 258 (Tataki, *Macedonians* p. 294 no. 34) (*Δ. ὁ προσονομαζόμενος Φείδων*: s. *Πυθῶναξ*); **(217)** 263 BC *PHib* 209, 6 (Tataki, *Macedonians* p. 294 no. 33; La'da E2652) (*Δημή*[*τριος*]: s. *Πτολεμαῖος*: t.e.); **(218)** c. 220-200 BC Helly, *Gonnoi* 99, 3 (or Thessaly?: *Δημήτρ*[*ιος*])
SCYTHIA MINOR:
—CARSIUM: **(219)** ii-iii AD *ISM* V 102, 3 (Lat. Ulp. Demetrius)
—ISTROS: **(220)** i BC-i AD ib. I 186 ([*Δ*]*ημήτριος*: s. *Κρατε—*); **(221)** ~ ib. 191 I, 32; **(222)** ~ ib. 191 II, 27 (s. *Ἀρτεμίδωρος*); **(223)** ~ ib. l. 49 (I f. *Δημήτριος* II); **(224)** ~ ib. l. 49 (II s. *Δημήτριος* I, f. *Δημήτριος* III); **(225)** ~ ib. l. 49 (III s. *Δημήτριος* II); **(226)** ~ ib. l. 50 (s. *Ἀπατούριος*); **(227)** ~ ib. l. 11-12 (I f. *Δημήτριος* II); **(228)** ~ ib. l. 11-12 (II s. *Δημήτριος* I); **(229)** i-ii AD ib. 290, 2 (I ?f. *Δημήτριος* II); **(230)** ~ ib. l. 3 (II ?s. *Δημήτριος* I); **(231)** c. 48-52 AD ib. 67, 38; 68, 41 (f. *Καλλίστρατος*); **(232)** ~ ib. 67, 52; 68, 52; **(233)** ii AD ib. 57, 2 (*Eastern cults* pp. 102-3 no. 65) (*Οὔλπ. Δ.*); **(234)** ~ *ISM* I 212, 18 (f. *Ποντικός*); **(235)** 138 AD ib. 193, 8 (f. *Καλλίστρατος*); **(236)** ~ ib. 193 I, 20 (f. *Ἀπατούριος*); **(237)** ~ ib. l. 24 (f. *Μενίσκος*); **(238)** ~ ib. l. 73 (*Μ. Οὔλπ. Δ.*: s. *Ἀρτεμίδωρος*); **(239)** ~ ib. 193 II, 75 (s. *Ἀντιγένης*); **(240)** 138-160 AD ib. 193 I, 38; 207, 8 (*Μ. Οὔλπ. Δ.*: s. *Ἀρτεμᾶς*); **(241)** 222-225 AD ib. 100, 13 (s. *Δομετιανός*)
—KALLATIS: **(242)** iii/ii BC *RE* (77) (*FGrH* 85)
—PEUKE: **(243)** iv-iii BC *IG* II^2 10077 (*FRA* 6051) (f. *Θεόδωρος*)
—TOMIS: **(244)** i BC *ISM* II 2 A, 51 (s. *Γέρων*); **(245)** ~ ib. l. 57 (f. *Διονύσιος*); **(246)** ~ ib. l. 60 (s. *Ἑκαταῖος*); **(247)** ii AD ib. 125, 11 (f. *Σεκοῦνδος*); **(248)** ~ ib. 125 I, 24 (s. *Δημῶναξ*); **(249)** ii-iii AD ib. 27, 10 ([*Οὐαλέ*]*ριος Δημήτ*[*ριος*]); **(250)** ~ ib. 394, 3 ([*Δη*]*μήτριο*[*ς*]); **(251)** s. ii AD ib. 131 (*IGB* III 1874; *CCET* IV 26 (locn., date)) (s. *Μᾶρκος*); **(252)** iii AD *ISM* II 24, 4 (*Αὐρ. Δ.*)
SKYTHIA:
—OLBIA-BORYSTHENES: **(253)** f. iv BC Dubois, *IGDOlbia* 103, 6 (lead); **(254)** ~ ib. 104 (f. *Μητρόδωρος*); **(255)** iv/iii BC ib. 95 (vase) (s. *Σωκράτης*); **(256)** ~ *SNG BM Black Sea* 552 (coin) (*Δημή*(*τριος*)?); **(257)** iii BC *Arkheologiia* (Kiev) 39 (1982) p. 35 (Vinogradov–Kryžickij pl. 91. 3a (vase)) (*Δημή*(*τριος*)); **(258)** ~ *IOlbia* 72, 1 (s. *Φώκριτος*); **(259)** iii-ii BC *Arkheologiia* (Kiev) 39 (1982) p. 34 (vase); **(260)** ~ ib. (vase) (*Δη*[*μήτ*]*ριος*); **(261)** iii/ii BC *IOSPE* I^2 187 (f. *Εὐρησίβιος*); **(262)** ii BC ib. 220 b; cf. KW pl. 26 no. 381 (s. *Δημοκῶν*, *Μητροβία*); **(263)** ~ *IOSPE* I^2 220 c; cf. KW pl. 26 no. 381 (f. *Δημοκῶν*); **(264)** ii-i BC *IG* II^2 8423 (*FRA* 1363) (f. *Πόθος*); **(265)** ii AD *IOSPE* I^2

80, 8; 86, 4; 176, 4 (f. Ἀχιλλεύς); **(266)** ~ ib. 89, 3 (s. Πραξιάναξ); **(267)** ~ ib. 93, 5 (s. Ξησσάγαρος); **(268)** ~ ib. 100, 5 (f. Μενέστρατος); **(269)** ~ ib. 130, 7 (Δημήτρ[ιος]: s. Ἀχιλλεύς); **(270)** ~ ib. 686, 3 (*VDI* 1975 (1), p. 69) (s. Μενέστρατος); **(271)** s. ii AD *IOlbia* 170, 5 (s. Ἀλέξανδρος); **(272)** iii AD *IOSPE* I² 98, 10 (f. Ἄβραγος)

—OLBIA-BORYSTHENES (NR.): **(273)** iv/iii BC *VDI* 1985 (1), p. 41 (vase) (Δη[μ]ήτριος)

—OLBIA-BORYSTHENES*: **(274)** iii-ii BC *ZOOID* 23 (1900) p. 30 no. 40 (vase)

—TANAIS: **(275)** ii AD *CIRB* 1262, 20 (s. Ἀπατούριος); **(276)** ~ ib. l. 24 (s. Ἀγαθόδωρος); **(277)** 154-170 AD ib. 1260a, 15 ([Δη]μήτριος); **(278)** 155 AD ib. 1260, 16 (I f. Δημήτριος II); **(279)** ~ ib. l. 16 ([Δ]ημήτριος: II s. Δημήτριος I); **(280)** c. 200-210 AD ib. 1277, 11 (Δη[μήτ]ριος); **(281)** ~ ib. l. 16 ([Δ]ημήτριος: ?f. Ἰαρδο—); **(282)** c. 200-228 AD ib. l. 8; 1282, 3 (Δημήτ[ριος]—1277: s. Ἀπολλώνιος); **(283)** f. iii AD ib. 1251 a, 6 (Δημ(ή)τριος: s. Φαζίναμος) ?= (*292*); **(284)** 209 AD ib. 1276, 1 (Δημή[τρι]ος: s. Χ—); **(285)** 210-226 AD ib. 1246, [14]; 1248, 13 ([Δημή]τριος: s. Ἀπολ—) ?= (*296*); **(286)** 211-226 AD ib. 1279, 7; 1281, 9 (f. Βαλώδιος); **(287)** 220 AD ib. 1278, 4 (Δημήτριος: s. Ἡρακλείδης); **(288)** ~ ib. l. 15 (s. —μαχος); **(289)** 220-225 AD ib. l. 16; 1279, 20 (Δημή[τριος]: f. Ὀδίαρδος); **(290)** 225 AD ib. l. 6 (f. Σύμφορος); **(291)** ~ ib. l. 13 (f. Δυνάτων, Ἰραύαδις); **(292)** 225-229 AD ib. 1280, 10; *Stud. Zhebelev* p. 47, 14 (s. Φαζίναμος) ?= (*283*); **(293)** 228 AD *CIRB* 1282, 11 (f. Πόπλιος); **(294)** ~ ib. l. 23 (Δημήτρι[ος]: f. Ὀχωδίακος); **(295)** 229 AD *Stud. Zhebelev* p. 47, 20 (s. Ἡρζῆς); **(296)** 236 AD *CIRB* 1249, 6 ([Δημή]τριος: s. Ἀπολλ—) ?= (*285*); **(297)** 244 AD ib. 1287, 20 (Δημή[τριος]?: f. Χαρίτων); **(298)** ~ ib. l. 23 (Δημήτριος: f. Ἀζαρίων)

TAURIS:

—CHERSONESOS: **(299)** c. 100-90 BC Anokhin p. 147 no. 191 (coin); **(300)** i BC-i AD *IOSPE* I² 454 (f. Ἡδυτέα)

THRACE: **(301)** 274 BC *PCZ* 59001, 18, 45, verso (La'da E726) (s. Δάμων); **(302)** c. 223 BC *PTeb* 815 fr. 1 II, 36; cf. La'da E838 (f. Νίκων); **(303)** 221 BC *PPetr* III 112 a I, 4 (Velkov 81; La'da E725) (Δημητου (gen.)—pap., Δημητ(ρί)ου—edd.); **(304)** 218 BC *PEnt* 22, 7 (Velkov 83; La'da E727); **(305)** 160 BC *BGU* 2390, 39 (La'da E728); **(306)** c. 125-100 BC *PTeb* 86, 2, 6, 8, etc. (Velkov 84; La'da E729)

—ABDERA: **(307)** f. iv BC *SEG* XLVII 1031 (*IThrakAig* E40) (s. Πυθόδωρος); **(308)** c. 336-311 BC May, *Abdera* p. 291 nos. 533-4 (coin); **(309)** ii/i BC *Syll*³ 656, 50 (Ager 169) ([Δη]μήτριος: f. Ἀλκίφρων)

—AINOS: **(310)** c. 208 BC *FD* III (4) 135 II, 17 (s. Θράσων); **(311)** 194 BC *Milet* I (3) 54, 4-5 (and Caria Miletos: s. Βόηθος, f. Ἀπολλώνιος); **(312)** i BC *IG* II² 5423 (*AM* 67 (1942) p. 172 no. 362; *FRA* 234) (f. Εὐημερίς); **(313)** ~ *IG* II² 7975 (*FRA* 236) (f. Ἐπίτευγμα); **(314)** ?i BC *Ag.* XVII 397 (*FRA* 235) ([Δη]μήτριος); **(315)** imp. Dimitsas 1007 (Pilhofer 68) (s. Σωτήριχος); **(316)** i AD *ISamothrace* 42, 5

—ANCHIALOS (TERRIT.): **(317)** ii-iii AD *IGB* I² 385, 2 (s. Δημ—)

—APOLLONIA-SOZOPOLIS: **(318)** v BC ib. 447 (s. Ἑκατώνυμος)

—BEROE-AUGUSTA TRAIANA: **(319)** 196-217 AD ib. III 1556, [6]; 1557, 7; 1558 (Αὐρ. Δ.: s. Ἀπφοῦς)

—BISANTHE-PANION: **(320)** 188-159 BC *OGIS* 302 (*Tekmeria* 6 (2001) p. 156 no. 1) (s. Ποσειδώνιος) ?= (*322*); **(321)** 158-138 BC *OGIS* 303 (f. Ζωτᾶς) ?= (*321*) (*323*); **(322)** ~ *SEG* XLIX 877 (f. Φίλων) ?= (*322*)

—BIZONE: **(323)** iii AD *IGB* I² 10, 4 (Δημήτρ[ιος]: f. —ης)

—BYZANTION: **(324)** iii BC *RE* (76); *FGrH* 162 (*PP* 5082); **(325)** i BC *RE* (87); **(326)** i BC-i AD *IByz* 177 (Fıratlı–Robert p. 111 no. 182) (s. Μητρόδωρος); **(327)** i-ii AD *IByz* 311 (Fıratlı–Robert pp. 119-20 no. 200) (I f. Δημήτριος II, Φο—); **(328)** ~ *IByz* 311 (Fıratlı–Robert pp. 119-20 no. 200) (II s. Δημήτριος I); **(329)** ii-iii AD *IByz* 310 a-b (Fıratlı–Robert pp. 118-19 no. 199) (I f. Σωκράτης, Δημήτριος II); **(330)** ~ *IByz* 310 b (Fıratlı–Robert pp. 118-19 no. 199) (II s. Δημήτριος I)

—BYZANTION?: **(331)** i-ii AD *IByz* 354 (Fıratlı–Robert p. 126 no. 212) (f. Ὀνήσιμος)

—DIONYSOPOLIS: **(332)** ii BC *IGB* I² 22 I, 5; **(333)** ii-iii AD ib. 31, 5 (Δη(μ)ήτ[ριος]: f. Διονύσιος); **(334)** a. 217 AD ib. 16, 10 (Μ. Α[ὐρ.] Δ.: s. Διογένης); **(335)** 218-222 AD ib. 17 (f. Θεόδωρος)

—HADRIANOPOLIS?: **(336)** imp. Unp. (Sayar) (Lat. Demetrius)

—HERAION TEICHOS?: **(337)** ii BC Taşlıklıoğlu I p. 4 no. 1 (Δημήτρ(ι)ος: f. Διονυσία)

—KALLIPOLIS: **(338)** imp. *ISestos* 19 (s. Ἰσίων)

—LYSIMACHEIA: **(339)** hell. *SEG* XLIII 774 (f. Μητρόδωρος); **(340)** iii BC *IG* II² 9225 (*FRA* 3391) (s. Τεισικλῆς); **(341)** ii BC Robert, *Coll. Froehner* 58 (I f. Δημήτριος II); **(342)** ~ ib. (II s. Δημήτριος I); **(343)** m. ii BC *ISestos* 38 a, 5 (f. Ζώτιχος); **(344)** ~ ib. l. 6 (f. Θέογνις); **(345)** ~ ib. l. 6 (s. Μένης)

—MARKIANOPOLIS: **(346)** iii-iv AD *IGB* II 820, 1 ([Δ]ημήτριο[ς]: f. Πρεν—)

—MARKIANOPOLIS (TERRIT.): **(347)** 153 AD *Romanizmăt* II 568 (Lat. Demetrius)

—MARONEIA: **(348)** ii-i BC *IThrakAig* E212, 2, 5 (f. Ξενόκριτος)

—NICOPOLIS AD ISTRUM (TERRIT.): **(349)** ii AD *IGB* V 5244 a, 14 (Δημήτρι[ος])

—NOVAE: **(350)** ii AD *IGLNovae* 48 (Lat. Demetrius: f. Νέστωρ)

—ODESSOS: **(351)** i BC-i AD *IGB* V 5066 (s. Τηρίβασις); **(352)** i AD ib. I² 186 bis (PM 1661); *Dacia* 21 (1977) p. 161 (date) (s. Ἀρτεμίδωρος); **(353)** i-ii AD *IGB* I² 116, 4 (f. Σεραπίων); **(354)** ~ ib. 118 ([Δ]ημήτριο[ς]: s. Ἀρτεμίδωρος); **(355)** i/ii AD ib. 177 bis (PM 1736); *Dacia* 21 (1977) p. 161 (date) (f. Πρῖμα); **(356)** f. ii AD *IGB* I² 78 ter, 11 (*CCET* I 30) (f. Ἀρτεμίδωρος); **(357)** m. ii AD *IGB* I² 150 (PM 859) (f. Ἀπελλᾶς); **(358)** iii AD *IGB* I² 155 (PM 941) (Δημ[ήτ]ριος)

—PAUTALIA: **(359)** ii-iii AD *IGB* V 5778 (I f. Δημήτριος II); **(360)** ~ ib. (II s. Δημήτριος I, f. Ἀρισταίνετος)

—PHILIPPOPOLIS-TRIMONTIUM: **(361)** ii-iii AD ib. III 1303, 4 (Δ. ὁ κὲ Μουκινος: s. Διο—)

—SERDICA: **(362)** v-vi AD Beševliev 13 (Lat. Demetrius); **(363)** vi AD ib. 25 (-μί-)

—STRYME: **(364)** m. iv BC *IThrakAig* E152 (s. Ἀπολλωνίδης); **(365)** ~ *SEG* XLVII 1104 (*IThrakAig* E153) (Δημήτριο[ς]: s. Δάδας)

—PHILIPPOPOLIS-TRIMONTIUM (TERRIT.): **(9)** iii AD ib. III 1318 (Αὐρ. Δ.: s. Βάσσος)

Δημητριοῦς

MACEDONIA (PELAGONIA): **(1)** ii-iii AD *IG* X (2) (2) 271 (Δημητριοῦτος (gen.): m. Ἄλκιμος)

Δημήτρις

MACEDONIA (BOTTIAIA):

—BEROIA: **(1)** ii/iii AD *IBer* 27 A, 3 (s. Σάτυρος)

MACEDONIA (ORESTIS):

—BATTYNAIOI: **(2)** 192 AD *EAM* 186 IV, 50 (Δημητρης—lap.: s. Δημήτριος)

SCYTHIA MINOR:

—ISTROS: **(3)** ii/iii AD *ISM* I 225, 7 (s. Ἀμ—); **(4)** f. iii AD ib. 218, 10 (Κλ. Δ.: s. Σέξτος)

—TOMIS: **(5)** ii-iii AD ib. II 26, 7 (s. Πάπας); **(6)** 201 AD ib. 83 I, 19 (s. Ἀμφιονίδης); **(7)** ~ ib. l. 25 (Δημήτ[ρις]: s. —ίων)

THRACE:

—APOLLONIA-SOZOPOLIS: **(8)** i-ii AD *IGB* I² 401, 9 (s. Πρότιμος)

Δῆμις

THRACE:

—PERINTHOS-HERAKLEIA: **(1)** c. 580-570 BC *IG* XII (6) 577, 2 (Δῆμι[ς]: s. Πυθοκλῆς)

Δημόδικος

MACEDONIA (EDONIS):

—AMPHIPOLIS: **(1)** iv/iii BC *SEG* XXXI 617 (Δημόδι[κος])

Δημόδοτος

THRACE:

—PERINTHOS-HERAKLEIA:

——(Aigikoreis): **(1)** iii-ii BC *IPerinth* 61, 53 (f. Αὐτόλυκος)

Δημοκάδης

THRACE:

—ABDERA?: **(1)** iii-ii BC *IThrakAig* E61 ([Δ]ημοκάδης)

Δημοκλῆς

MACEDONIA (PIERIA):

—PYDNA: **(1)** iii BC *SEG* L 625 (f. Κλεονίκη)

Δήμοκλος

SKYTHIA:

—OLBIA-BORYSTHENES: **(1)** vi/v BC Dubois, *IGDOlbia* 92 (bronze) (f. Λήναιος)

Δημοκρατέα

MACEDONIA (ELIMEIA):

—AIANE: **(1)** s. ii AD *EAM* 56 (m. Ἔρως, Προκόπη, Ἀγαθοκλέα, Δημοκράτης)

Δημοκράτεια

MACEDONIA (BOTTIAIA):

—PELLA: **(1)** iii-ii BC Dimitsas 131 (d. Ἀλέξανδρος)

MACEDONIA (MYGDONIA):

—THESSALONIKE: **(2)** f. iii AD *IG* X (2) (1) 189, 13 (Ἰουλ. Δ.)

Δημοκράτης

CIMMERIAN BOSPOROS:

—HERMONASSA: **(1)** 123-132 AD *CIRB* 1054, 18 (s. Δάδας)

—PHANAGOREIA: **(2)** 123 AD ib. 975, 2 (s. Ἀ—)

MACEDONIA: **(3)** 236 BC *PPetr*² 16, 57 (Tataki, *Macedonians* p. 296 no. 44; La'da E1459); **(4)** 201 BC *RE* (8) (Tataki, *Macedonians* p. 296 no. 45); **(5)** c. 175-164 BC *OGIS* 254; Grainger, *SPG* p. 86 (s. Βύττακος)

MACEDONIA (ELIMEIA):

—AIANE: **(6)** s. ii AD *EAM* 56 (s. Κάστωρ, Δημοκρατέα)

MACEDONIA (LOWER PAIONIA):

—IDOMENE?: **(7)** 161 AD Sokolovska, *Isar-Marvinci* p. 131 (Μ. Αὐρ. Δ.); **(8)** ~ ib. (s. Νίκων)

MACEDONIA (MYGDONIA):

—THESSALONIKE: **(9)** i BC-i AD *IG* X (2) (1) 129, 5; **(10)** ?i AD ib. 53 (s. Μένανδρος); **(11)** i-ii AD ib. 115 (f. Ἀμ—)

—THESSALONIKE?: **(12)** iii AD ib. 859, 6 (s. Θράσων, Διονυσία)

MACEDONIA (PAIONIA):

—KAVADARCI (MOD.): **(13)** ?ii AD Unp. (Skopje)

SCYTHIA MINOR:

—ISTROS: **(14)** ii AD *ISM* I 137, 14 (f. Αἴλ. Διονύσιος); **(15)** ~ ib. 201 II, 17 ([Δημ]οκράτης?: s. Θεαγένης); **(16)** 138 AD ib. 193 I, 102 (Αἴλ. Δ.)

SKYTHIA:

—OLBIA-BORYSTHENES (NR.): **(17)** m. iv BC *Hyperboreus* 2002 (1), p. 73 (sherd) (Δημοκρα(της)?)

TAURIS:

—CHERSONESOS: **(18)** iv BC Solomonik, *GAKh* 578 (vase); **(19)** ii AD *IOSPE* I² 425, 2 (s. Ἀριστογένης); **(20)** ~ *SEG* XLVI 932 (Δημοκράτ[ης]: f. —της); **(21)** 129-130 AD *IOSPE*

I² 359, 28; *VDI* 1960 (3), pp. 154-5, 24 (s. *Βοΐσκος*); (**22**) 130 AD ib. l. 23 (f. *Νικαγόρας*)

Δημοκρατία
THRACE:
—BYZANTION: (**1**) i-ii AD *IByz* 265 (Firatlı–Robert p. 86 no. 108) (*Δ. ἡ καὶ Παρθενική*: d. *Δίων*)

Δημοκρατιανός
MACEDONIA (MYGDONIA):
—THESSALONIKE: (**1**) f. iii AD *IG* X (2) (1) 188, 5; 189, 10 (*Αὐρ. Δημοκρατιανὸς Κόρραγος*)

Δημόκριτος
MACEDONIA (BOTTIAIA):
—PELLA: (**1**) s. iv BC *A΄ Panell. Synedr. Epigr.* p. 185 no. 8 ([*Δη*]*μόκριτος*: s. ...*ων*); (**2**) f. iii BC *SEG* XXIV 550 (s. *Χαιρίων*)
MACEDONIA (EDONIS):
—AMPHIPOLIS: (**3**) inc. *PAE* 1971, p. 45 (*Δημόκρ*[*ιτος*]?, *Δημοκρ*[*άτης*]?)
MACEDONIA (MYGDONIA):
—CHARAKOMA?: (**4**) c. 230-200 BC *BCH* 45 (1921) p. 18 III, 72 (Tataki, *Macedonians* p. 98 no. 3) (s. *Εὔδημος*)
—LETE: (**5**) ii AD *Makedonika* 2 (1951) p. 619 no. 42 *θ*, 6 (s. *Διογένης*)
—THESSALONIKE: (**6**) ii AD *IG* X (2) (1) 390, 6
MACEDONIA (ODOMANTIKE):
—SIRRHA (TERRIT.): (**7**) s. ii AD *Tekmeria* 6 (2001) p. 49 (s. *Διοσκουρίδης*)
THRACE:
—ABDERA: (**8**) c. 465-380 BC *RE* Supplbd. 12 (6); *FVS* 68 (?s. *Ἡγησίστρατος, Ἀθηνόκριτος, Δαμάσιππος*); (**9**) c. 415-395 BC May, *Abdera* pp. 172-3 nos. 234-7 (coin); (**10**) iv-iii BC *Recherches amph. grecques* p. 493 no. 3 (amph.) ([*Δ*]*ημόκριτος*)
—ABDERA?: (**11**) ii-iii AD *Belomorski Pregled* 1 (1942) p. 336 no. 43 (*IThrakAig* E483)
—APOLLONIA-SOZOPOLIS: (**12**) iv BC *Anali* 5 (1-4), p. no. 2.3 (coin)
—MARONEIA: (**13**) hell.? *SEG* XXVI 822 (*IThrakAig* E247); (**14**) iii-ii BC ib. E240 (f. *Ἀφροδισία*)

Δημοκῶν
SKYTHIA:
—OLBIA-BORYSTHENES: (**1**) m. iv BC Dubois, *IGDOlbia* 106, 10 (*SEG* XLIV 669); (**2**) s. iv BC ib. L 702 III, 4; (**3**) iii BC *IOSPE* I² 32 A, 19 (Maier, *Mauerbauinschr.* 82); (**4**) ~ *IOSPE* I² 201 I, 8 (s. *Εὐβίοτος*); (**5**) ~ ib. 201 II, 8 (f. *Ἀγαθῖνος*); (**6**) ~ ib. l. 33; (**7**) ii BC ib. 220 b-c; cf. KW pl. 26 no. 381 (s. *Δημήτριος*, f. *Δημήτριος*)

Δημονίκη
MACEDONIA (PELAGONIA): (**1**) i AD *IG* X (2) (2) 236, 9 (*Κλαυδία Δ.*: d. *Τι. Κλαύδιος Φόρτιος, Αἰλία Πρόκλα*)

Δημόνικος
MACEDONIA (BISALTIA):
—AROLOS: (**1**) hell.? Kaphtantzis 520 (Papazoglou, *Villes* p. 363 (terracotta) (fals.?))
MACEDONIA (BOTTIAIA):
—PELLA: (**2**) 365 BC *SEG* XXXIV 355, 5 (Tataki, *Macedonians* p. 153 no. 35) (*Δαμόνι*[*κο*]*ς*: f. *Ἀθήναιος*); (**3**) 326 BC *RE* Supplbd. 4 (2a); Berve 262 (Tataki, *Macedonians* p. 153 no. 36) (s. *Ἀθήναιος*)
MACEDONIA (EDONIS):
—AMPHIPOLIS (NR.): (**4**) a. 357 BC Hatzopoulos, *Actes Amphipolis* p. 43 no. 8, 5 (*SEG* XLI 562) (s. *Ῥίχνος*)
MACEDONIA (ODOMANTIKE):
—SIRRHA: (**5**) hell. ib. XXX 616 (*Δημόνι*[*κ*]*ο*[*ς*])
THRACE:
—ODESSOS: (**6**) i BC-i AD *IGB* I² 151 (PM 713) (f. *Τούτα*)

Δημόπολις
SKYTHIA:
—OLBIA-BORYSTHENES: (**1**) iii BC Dubois, *IGDOlbia* 109, 4 (*SEG* XXXVII 673); (**2**) ?ii-i BC Dubois, *IGDOlbia* 110, 4

Δημοσθένης
CIMMERIAN BOSPOROS:
—AKRA: (**1**) imp. *ZOOID* 31 (1913) Prot. p. 36 no. 2
MACEDONIA: (**2**) 198-197 BC *RE* Supplbd. 4 (3a) (Tataki, *Macedonians* p. 296 no. 47)
MACEDONIA (EDONIS):
—AMPHIPOLIS: (**3**) ii-iii AD *SEG* XXXIX 572 (s. *Ἴσος*)
—PHILIPPOI: (**4**) ii AD *BCH* 56 (1932) pp. 230-1 no. 21 (Pilhofer 355) (*Δημοσθέν*[*ης*]: s. *Φλ. Μέστα*)
MACEDONIA (ODOMANTIKE):
—SIRRHA: (**5**) 155 AD Dimitsas 821, 5 (Kaphtantzis 1) (f. *Θεόπομπος*)
MACEDONIA (PIERIS):
—NEAPOLIS: (**6**) 356 BC *IG* II² 128, 3, 9 (Tataki, *Macedonians* p. 125 no. 6) (s. *Θεόξενος*)
SCYTHIA MINOR:
—ISTROS: (**7**) ii AD *ISM* I 201 I, 9; (**8**) ii-iii AD ib. 195, 15 (*Δημοσθ*[*ένης*]); (**9**) 138 AD ib. 193 II, 31 (*Αἰλ. Δ.*)
—NOVIODUNUM: (**10**) ii/iii AD ib. V 272, 3 ([*Δ*]*ημοσθ*[*ένης*]: s. —*ιππος*)
—TOMIS: (**11**) ii-iii AD ib. II 278 (I f. *Αὐρ. Δημοσθένης* II); (**12**) ~ ib. (*Αὐρ. Δ.*: II s. *Δημοσθένης* I); (**13**) ~ ib. 282 (f. *Χρύσιον*); (**14**) ~ ib. 321 (s. *Γάϊος*); (**15**) ~ ib. 468, 10 (f. *Θρασυμήδης*); (**16**) s. ii AD ib. 131 (*IGB* III 1874; *CCET* IV 26 (locn., date)) (s. *Μᾶρκος*)
—TOMIS?: (**17**) ii/iii AD *ISM* V 272, 3; cf. III p. 140 (locn.) ([*Δ*]*ημοσθ*[*ένης*]: s. —*ιππος*)
THRACE: (**18**) hell.-imp. *RE* (10)
—ABDERA: (**19**) ii AD *AD* 24 (1969) Chron. p. 356 (*IThrakAig* E103) (s. —*λος*)
—ANCHIALOS (TERRIT.): (**20**) ii-iii AD *IGB* III 1847, 2 (*Δημοσθέ*[*νη*]*ς*: f. —*ενις*)
—BAZOPARA: (**21**) 202 AD ib. 1690 c, 46 (and Thrace Pizos: s. *Τήρης*)
—BEROE-AUGUSTA TRAIANA: (**22**) iii AD ib. 1571, 7 (f. *M. Αὐρ. Ἀπολλόδωρος*); (**23**) ~ ib. 1616 b (I f. *Αὐρ. Δημοσθένης* II); (**24**) ~ ib. (*Αὐρ. Δ.*: II s. *Δημοσθένης* I)
—BYZANTION: (**25**) c. 176-177 AD Schönert-Geiss, *Byzantion* 1408-9; 1442-3 (coin)
—ERGISSENOI: (**26**) ii AD *IGB* III 1593, 7 (*Φλ. Δ.*)
—LYSIMACHEIA: (**27**) m. ii BC *ISestos* 38 a, 2 (s. *Λυσικράτης*)
—MESAMBRIA: (**28**) f. iii AD *IGB* I² 317, 4 (*Αὐρ. Δ.*: s. *Τάτας*)
—NICOPOLIS AD NESTUM: (**29**) iii AD ib. V 5930, 11 (-*σθί*-: s. *Ἑρμογένης, Ματρώνα*)
—PAUTALIA: (**30**) iii AD ib. 5867, 10 (f. *Αὐρ. Ἡραΐς*)
—PERINTHOS-HERAKLEIA: (**31**) ii-iii AD *IPerinth* 65, 9
—SERDICA (TERRIT.): (**32**) ii-iii AD *IGB* IV 1984; cf. V 5690 (s. *Βίθυς*)
—VICUS TRULLENSIUM: (**33**) 161-169 or 198-209 AD *ILB* 180, 4 (Lat. Demosteni (gen.): f. *Νικόστρατος*)

Δημοστράτεια
CIMMERIAN BOSPOROS:
—PANTIKAPAION: (**1**) i BC *CIRB* 285 (-*τηα*: ?d. *Νάνα*)

Δημόστρατος
CIMMERIAN BOSPOROS:
—PANTIKAPAION: (**1**) i BC/i AD ib. 313; cf. KW pl. 40 no. 593 (*Δημόστ*(*ρ*)*ατος*: f. *Μηνόφιλος*); (**2**) ii AD *CIRB* 753 (s. *Βαστάκας*); (**3**) ~ ib. (s. *Θεαγένης*)
MACEDONIA (EDONIS):
—AMPHIPOLIS: (**4**) 359-336 BC *FGrH* 257 F 36. 1; Procl., *in R.* ii 116 (f. *Φιλίννιον*: fict.?)
SKYTHIA:
—OLBIA-BORYSTHENES: (**5**) iv BC *IOSPE* I² 326 (Dubois, *IGDOlbia* 49) ([*Δη*]*μόστρατος*)
THRACE:
—MARONEIA: (**6**) i BC *IThrakAig* E204, 6 (s. *Ἰσι*—); (**7**) i BC-i AD *SEG* XXVII 341 + *IThrakAig* E201 ([*Δη*]*μόστρατος*); (**8**) i-ii AD Bakalakis, *Oinos Ismarikos* p. 1015 with fig. 17 + *IThrakAig* E288, 4, 7 (s. *Ἡρακλείδης*, f. *Σάτριος*)

Δημοσῶν
CIMMERIAN BOSPOROS:
—GORGIPPIA: (**1**) f. iii BC *CIRB* 1137 B I, 14 (s. *Σίμων*)

Δημοτέλης
SCYTHIA MINOR:
—ISTROS: (**1**) iv BC *ISM* I 110; cf. *Ling. Balk.* 27 (1984) p. 85 (*Δημο*[*τέλ*]*ης*?—Avram, *Δημο*-[*κλ*]*ῆς*?—Mihailov: s. *Θεόγνητος*, f. *Ἀπολλώνιος*)
TAURIS:
—CHERSONESOS: (**2**) ii AD *IOSPE* I² 436, 6 (s. *Θεόφιλος*); (**3**) 174 AD *SEG* XLV 985 A, 38 (I f. *Δημοτέλης* II); (**4**) ~ ib. l. 38 (II s. *Δημοτέλης* I)

Δημότιμος
MACEDONIA (BOTTIAIA):
—PELLA: (**1**) iii BC Akamatis, *Amph. Pellas* p. 34 no. PAR14 (amph.) (*SEG* L 613)

Δημοῦχος
THRACE:
—APOLLONIA-SOZOPOLIS: (**1**) iv BC *IGB* I² 463 bis, 1 (f. *Ὀρσίλεως*); (**2**) f. iv BC *Class. Num. Group* 58, 347 (coin)

Δημόφιλος
MACEDONIA (BOTTIAIA):
—BEROIA: (**1**) 223 BC *IBer* 4, 14 ((*Δ*)*ημόφιλος*: f. *Ἀντίπατρος*)
MACEDONIA (MYGDONIA):
—THESSALONIKE: (**2**) iv AD *DCB* (-) (bp.)
SCYTHIA MINOR:
—ISTROS: (**3**) 138 AD *ISM* I 193 I, 90 (s. *Ἀθηνάδης*); (**4**) iii AD ib. 192, 5 ([*Δη*]*μόφιλ*[*ος*]?)
THRACE:
—BEROE-AUGUSTA TRAIANA: (**5**) ii/iii AD *SEG* XLVIII 894 (*Αὐρ. Δ.*: s. *Χρῆστος*)
—BISANTHE-PANION: (**6**) ii-i BC *BCH* 24 (1900) p. 165 no. 7 ([*Δη*]*μόφιλος*?: f. *Ἀρχέλαος, Κλεόστρατος*)
—DIONYSOPOLIS: (**7**) iii/ii BC *IGB* I² 20 (f. *Ἐράτων*)
—MEZDRA (MOD.): (**8**) ii-iii AD ib. II 492 (I f. *Δημόφιλος* II); (**9**) ~ ib. (II s. *Δημόφιλος* I, f. *Ἡρακλιανός*)

Δημοφῶν
CIMMERIAN BOSPOROS:
—GORGIPPIA: (**1**) f. iii BC *CIRB* 1137 B I, 17 (f. *Γλαῦκος*)
—HERMONASSA: (**2**) 389-349 BC ib. 1037 (s. *Ἐργῖνος*)
—PANTIKAPAION: (**3**) iv BC ib. 177 (s. *Διονύσιος*); (**4**) ?f. ii AD ib. 85, 4 (*Δημοφῶ*[*ν*]: s. —*ρανος*)
—TEMRYUK (MOD.): (**5**) iv-v AD *SEG* XVI 440
THRACE:
—APOLLONIA-SOZOPOLIS: (**6**) ?iii BC *IGB* I² 458 bis, 1, 5 (f. *Νικοῦς*)
—DIONYSOPOLIS: (**7**) iii-ii BC *SNG BM Black Sea* 217; *SNG Stancomb* 123-5 (coin); (**8**) iii/ii BC *IGB* I² 20 (f. *Ἀπολλώνιος*); (**9**) iii AD ib. 14 a, 4 (*Αὐρ. Δ.*: s. *Νουμήνιος*)

Δημοχάρης
Scythia Minor:
—istros: (1) i ad *ISM* i 200, 4 (s. *Γρήγορος*); (2) ii ad ib. 212, 23 (s. *Δε—ος*); (3) 138 ad ib. 193 I, 56 (s. *Ἀρισταγόρας*)
Thrace:
—dionysopolis: (4) iii-ii bc *IGB* I^2 27 (f. *Ῥοδόκλεια*)
—maroneia: (5) iii-ii bc *SEG* xxvii 344 (*IThrakAig* E246) (*[Δ]ημοχάρεως?* (gen.), *[Τ]ιμοχάρεως?*); (6) ii-i bc ib. E212, 39 (*Δημοχάρ[ης]*)

Δημόχαρις
Cimmerian Bosporos:
—gorgippia: (1) f. iii bc *CIRB* 1137 A I, 33 (s. *Ὄρχαμος*); (2) ~ ib. l. 47 (f. *Δημάνθης*)
—korokondame: (3) ii ad ib. 1107 (*Δημόχα[ρις]* (fem.)—ed.: d. *Ῥόδων*)
Scythia Minor:
—istros: (4) i bc-i ad *ISM* i 191 II, 25 (s. *Ἀρτεμίδωρος*); (5) ~ ib. l. 41 (s. *Ποσειδώνιος*)

Δημύλος
Thrace:
—odessos: (1) i/ii ad *IGB* I^2 177 bis (PM 1736); *Dacia* 21 (1977) p. 161 (date) (f. *Ἡρακλέων*)

Δημώ
Macedonia (Bottiaia):
—pella: (1) f. iii bc *Thess. Mnem.* 16 (Tataki, *Macedonians* p. 153 no. 37) (d. *Ξενόφαντος*)
Macedonia (Mygdonia):
—thessalonike: (2) ii ad *IG* x (2) (1) 507, 3 (d. *Ζωΐλος*)
Scythia Minor:
—istros: (3) iii bc *ISM* i 250

Δήμων
Thrace:
—apollonia-sozopolis: (1) v/iv bc *IGB* I^2 448 bis (*Δήμων*: f. *Ἐπικ—*)

Δημῶναξ
Cimmerian Bosporos:
—gorgippia: (1) f. iii bc *CIRB* 1137 A II, 27 (f. *Μυστίας*)
Scythia Minor:
—tomis: (2) ii ad *ISM* ii 125, 10 (*Δημωνάκτου* (gen.): I f. *Δημῶναξ* II) ?= (4); (3) ~ ib. l. 10 (II s. *Δημῶναξ* I); (4) ~ ib. 125 I, 24 (*Δημωνάκτου* (gen.): f. *Δημήτριος*) ?= (2)
Thrace:
—apollonia-sozopolis: (5) ?iv bc *IGB* I^2 455 with apogr. (*[Δη]μῶναξ?*—ed., *[Τι]μῶναξ?*, *[Ἑρ]μῶναξ?*: s. *Ἀντήνωρ*)

Δημώνασσα
Cimmerian Bosporos:
—myrmekion: (1) s. v bc *SEG* xlviii 1007 (vase)
Skythia:
—olbia-borysthenes: (2) vi/v bc Dubois, *IGDOlbia* 92 (bronze) (d. *Λήναιος*)

Δημωφέλης
Macedonia (Mygdonia):
—dikaia: (1) c. 365-359 bc Unp. (Voutyras-Sismanidis) l. 53 (*Δημωφέ(λ)ης*)

Δητούβιθυς
Macedonia (Edonis):
—amphipolis: (1) ii-iii ad Kaphtantzis 699; *Epigraphica* 37 (1975) p. 34 (name) (*Δητούβιθ[υς]?*: f. *Ζίπερ*)

Δῖα
Cimmerian Bosporos:
—nymphaion: (1) v bc *CIRB* 915
Macedonia (Derriopos): (2) ii-iii ad *IG* x (2) (2) 303 (*Δεῖα*)

Macedonia (Mygdonia):
—thessalonike: (3) ii-iii ad ib. x (2) (1) 582, 1 (*Κλωδία Δ.*)
—thessalonike?: (4) i-ii ad ib. 686; cf. *BCH* 98 (1974) p. 544 fig. 15; p. 550 (*Δεῖα*: m. *Μέλανδρος*)
Macedonia (Pieria):
—dion: (5) ?iii ad Dimitsas 178 (*Δεῖα*: d. *Αὐρ. Λύκος*)

Διαγόρας
Cimmerian Bosporos:
—pantikapaion: (1) 275-278 ad *CIRB* 36, 37 (*Διαγ(όρας)*: s. *Μακάριος*)
Macedonia (Bottiaia):
—beroia: (2) 223 bc *IBer* 4, 33 (*(Δ)ιαγόρας*: f. *Δήμαρχος*)
Macedonia (Edonis):
—amphipolis: (3) iv bc *AD* 22 (1967) Chron. p. 426 (f. *Ἡράκλειτος*)
Scythia Minor:
—istros: (4) s. iv bc *ISM* i 238 (f. *Ἡρώνυμος*)
—tomis: (5) s. ii bc ib. ii 1 a, 15
Tauris:
—chersonesos: (6) c. 300-290 bc Anokhin p. 139 no. 78 (coin) ?= (7); (7) f. iii bc Kats p. 92 no. 36 (amph.) (f. *Δαμοτέλης*) ?= (6)
Thrace:
—abdera: (8) iii bc *SEG* xxx 662 (bronze)

Διαδουμενός
Macedonia (Mygdonia):
—thessalonike: (1) s. ii ad *IG* x (2) (1) 245 I, 4 (*[Δι]αδουμενός*); (2) 159 ad ib. 322, 2 (f. *Ἀπολλωνία*); (3) ii/iii ad ib. 262 II, 8
Macedonia (Paionia):
—stoboi*: (4) iii ad *SEG* xxiv 496 (slave?)
Sarmatia*: (5) i-ii ad *BPW* 1930, cols. 1006-7 (bronze) (*Φλ. Δ.*)
Thrace:
—aquae calidae*: (6) imp. *CIL* iii 7408 = Kazarow 971 (Lat. L. Titovius Diadumenus: freed.)
—byzantion (territ.): (7) imp. Unp. (Sayar) (s. *Θεόκριτος*)

Διαζεῖπα
Macedonia (Bisaltia):
—euporia?: (1) 154 or 271 ad *SEG* xxx 591 + *AD* 23 (1968) Chron. pl. 273 στ.; *BE* 1992, no. 305 (locn.) (*διὰ Ζειπα*—*SEG*: d. *Δυτούλας*)

Διάζελμις
Thrace?: (1) 31 bc *SEG* xxviii 1492

Διάζενις
Thrace:
—philippopolis-trimontium (territ.): (1) ii-iii ad *IGB* iii 1457 (f. *Μουκάβεσος*)

Δίαιτος
Macedonia (Mygdonia):
—lete: (1) f. ii bc *SEG* xlvi 764, 14 (*Δίαιτ[ος]*: f. *Φιλουμενός*)

Διάλτυρις
Thrace:
—nicopolis ad istrum?: (1) 159 ad *Chiron* 29 (1999) p. 149 no. 1 (Lat. Dialpuri (gen.): f. *Σοῦρις*)

Διαρζις
Thrace:
—odessos (nr.): (1) ii-iii ad *IGB* I^2 258 (*Διαρζιω* (gen.): f. *Κοωκοῦς*)

Δίας
Cimmerian Bosporos:
—nymphaion: (1) v bc *CIRB* 915 (*Δία* (gen.))
—pantikapaion: (2) m. vi bc Tolstoi 185 (*LSAG*² p. 373 no. 68 (vase))

Thrace:
—maroneia: (3) ii ad *IThrakAig* E268 (s. *Μούπορις*)

Διάσενις
Thrace:
—dyme (mod.): (1) i ad *AD* 26 (1971) Chron. pl. 422 γ (*Belomorski Pregled* 1 (1941) p. 335 no. 40; *IThrakAig* E387); cf. Bakalakis, *Oinos Ismarikos* p. 1015 (*Διασένεως* (gen.): f. *Ῥοιμητάλκης*)
—kellai*: (2) iii ad *IGB* iii 1516 b, 26 (s. *Μουκα—*)
—xanthi (mod.): (3) iii ad *IThrakAig* E104 (f. *Αὐλούζενις*)

Διάσιος
Cimmerian Bosporos:
—hermonassa: (1) iv bc *CIRB* 1056 I, 17

Διάσκενθος
Thrace:
—bazopara: (1) 202 ad *IGB* iii 1690 d, 48 (and Thrace Pizos: f. *Σκέλης*)
—kellai*: (2) iii ad ib. 1516 b, 30 (s. *Δόλης*)

Διασκούπορις
Thrace:
—bazopara: (1) 202 ad ib. 1690 d, 13 (and Thrace Pizos: f. *Δυτούτραλις*); (2) ~ ib. l. 32 (and Thrace Pizos: f. *Μουκάτραλις*); (3) ~ ib. 1690 c, 44 (and Thrace Pizos: s. *Μουκάπορις*); (4) ~ ib. l. 53 (and Thrace Pizos: f. *Μουκάτραλις*)
—geloupara: (5) 202 ad ib. l. 26 (and Thrace Pizos: f. *Μουκάτραλις*); (6) ~ ib. l. 29 (and Thrace Pizos: *Δ. Χαράκων*: s. *Βρινκάζερις*)
—krasalopara: (7) 202 ad ib. 1690 b, 60 (and Thrace Pizos: s. *Βρίζενις*)

Διάτραλις
Thrace:
—beroe-augusta traiana:
——Karasoura: (1) ii-iii ad ib. 1631, 10 (*[Δ]ιατρα[λις]?*: s. *Μουκάτραλις*)

Διαφάνης
Thrace:
—byzantion: (1) ii bc *IByz* 101 (Fıratlı-Robert pp. 94-5 no. 132) (*Διαφάνη* (gen.): f. *Διονύσιος*)

Δίβιθυς
Thrace:
—krasalopara: (1) 202 ad *IGB* iii 1690 b, 49 (and Thrace Pizos: -βει-: f. *Αὐλούζενις*); (2) ~ ib. l. 61 (and Thrace Pizos: -βει-: f. *Βίθυς*)

Δίβρης
Macedonia (Edonis):
—amphipolis: (1) imp. *BCH* 22 (1898) pp. 349-50 n. 2 (Dimitsas 858) (*Διβρέους* (gen.): f. *Δημήτριος*)

Δίβυθος
Thrace?: (1) 316-309 bc *IG* II^2 1956, 22; *Ancient Macedonia* 5 p. 445 with n. 10 (date) (*FRA* 2513)

Διδᾶς
Macedonia (Paionia): (1) iii/ii bc Liv. xl 21 9-11 etc.; *RE* Supplbd. 4 (2) (Tataki, *Macedonians* p. 208 no. 8) (Lat. Didas)
Macedonia (Pieris):
—phagres (territ.)?: (2) ii-iii ad Pikoulas, *Chora* p. 168 no. 78 (*Διδᾶ* (gen.): f. *Λυσανίας*)

Δίδαυος
Skythia:
—olbia-borysthenes: (1) f. iii bc Vinogradov, *Pont. Stud.* p. 159 no. 13 (sherd)

Διδιανός
Macedonia (Odomantike):
—sirrha: (1) ?157 ad Kaphtantzis 11, 5 (*Dodoni* 18 (1989) p. 245 no. 53) (*Διδιανὸς*

Πρείσκος—Cousinery: s. Πρίσκος, f. Διδιανὴ Ἀντιγόνα)

Διδύκαιμος
THRACE:
—ROGOZEN (MOD.): (1) f. iv BC *Rogozen Treasure* p. 47 no. 2; *Arkheologiia* (Sofia) 1987 (3), p. 26-37

Διδύμαρχος
CIMMERIAN BOSPOROS:
—PANTIKAPAION: (1) iv BC *CIRB* 182 (Διδύμαρ[χος]: f. Ἐντρέχης)
MACEDONIA: (2) 115 BC *PTeb* 30, 3, 7, 10, 15, 23, 28 (Tataki, *Macedonians* p. 475 no. 35; La'da E1461) (s. Ἀπολλώνιος)

Διδύμεια
MACEDONIA: (1) iv BC Berve 268 (Tataki, *Macedonians* p. 297 no. 50) (?d. Ἀντίοχος, Λαοδίκη, m. Νικάνωρ, Νικομήδης)

Διδύμη
MACEDONIA (BOTTIAIA):
—BEROIA: (1) ii-iii AD *IBer* 247 (Tataki 384); (2) 211 AD *ILeukopetra* 59, 5 (Tataki 385) (m. Φλ. Σύμφορος)
MACEDONIA (MYGDONIA):
—THESSALONIKE: (3) ii-iii AD *IG* x (2) (1) 745, 2 (Δ̣ι̣δ̣[ύμη])
MACEDONIA (PIERIA):
—DION: (4) ii AD Oikonomos 33

Διδύμιος
THRACE:
—PAUTALIA: (1) s. ii AD *SEG* XLVI 864, 15 (s. Ἡρωΐδης)
—SERDICA (NR.): (2) f. ii AD ib. III 552 (ring); cf. XLVIII 957 (Διδύμι(ο)ς?)

Διδυμόξαρθος
SKYTHIA:
—TANAIS: (1) 188 AD *CIRB* 1242, 5 (s. Χόδαινος)

Δίδυμος
MACEDONIA: (1) iii/ii BC *Arch. Pap.* 48 (2002) pp. 78-9 col. II, 16 (f. Ἡρακλείδης); (2) 132 BC ib. p. 78; cf. La'da 1497a (f. Ἡρακλείδης); (3) 92 BC *PTeb* 104, 35, 46 (Tataki, *Macedonians* p. 478 no. 69; La'da E1746) (s. Πτολεμαῖος: t.e.)
MACEDONIA?: (4) 99 BC *SB* 9255, 7 (Tataki, *Macedonians* p. 478 no. 68; La'da E1462) (Δ̣ί̣δ̣υμ[ος])
THRACE: (5) 183 BC *PTeb* 793 XI, 5; cf. La'da E752 ([Δίδ]υμ[ο]ς: f. Ἡσίοδος)
—SPINOPARA: (6) ii AD *IGB* IV 2192, 11

Διέρνης
THRACE:
—GLAVA PANEGA (MOD.): (1) iii AD ib. II 555 (Διέρνεος (gen.): f. Βίθυς)

Διεύς
MACEDONIA (PIERIS):
—NEAPOLIS: (1) s. iv BC *SEG* XLIII 430 (Pilhofer 6) (s. Ἀντικράτης)

Διζάζελμις
MACEDONIA (EDONIS):
—PHILIPPOI (TERRIT.): (1) i BC-i AD Pikoulas, *Chora* p. 132 no. 35 (Pilhofer 615) (Διζάζελμ[ις]: ?f. Γηνηβρυ—)
SKYTHIA:
—OLBIA-BORYSTHENES*: (2) ii-iii AD *IOSPE* I² 223 (-ζηλ-: s. Σεύθης)
THRACE: (3) i BC *SNG BM Black Sea* 320-1; *HN*² p. 286; *REA* 16 (1914) p. 401 (coin)
—DIOSPOLIS: (4) ii-iii AD *IGB* III 1784 (Διζάζ̣ε̣[λμις]?, Διζαζ̣ε̣[νις]?: f. Βίθυς)
—DIZUROI: (5) ii-iii AD *IOSPE* I² 223; *RE* (-) (-ζη-: s. Σεύθης)

THRACE?: (6) ii BC *Memnonion* 7 (Velkov 87)

Διζάζενις
THRACE:
—PAUTALIA (TERRIT.): (1) ii-iii AD *IGB* IV 2134 (Διζάζεν[ις]: f. Βίθυς); (2) ~ ib. 2226 ([Δι]ζάζενις)

Διζάκενθος
THRACE:
—PAUTALIA (TERRIT.): (1) ii-iii AD ib. 2116 (Διζ[ά]κενθος: f. Ἐπτάκενθος)

Διζάλας
MACEDONIA (EDONIS):
—PHILIPPOI (TERRIT.): (1) ?ii AD *BCH* 47 (1923) pp. 64-5 no. 24, 6 (Pilhofer 519) (Lat. Dizala: s. Brassis)
MACEDONIA (MYGDONIA):
—THESSALONIKE: (2) ii AD *SEG* XXXIX 634; cf. XLIII 466
—THESSALONIKE?: (3) f. ii AD *JDAI* 84 (1969) p. 151 no. R13 (I s. Γερμανός, f. Δουλαρίων, Διζάλας II, Βίθυς); (4) ~ ib. (II s. Διζάλας I)
MACEDONIA (SINTIKE):
—HERAKLEIA: (5) ?i AD *CIL* VI 2645 (Dimitsas 846) (Lat. Dizalas: f. C. Iulius Gemellus)
THRACE: (6) i AD *IGB* IV 2338, 2, 14; cf. V 5928 (Φλ. Δ.: s. Ἐζβενις, f. Αἰδεζυρίς)
—BOURDAPA: (7) ii-iii AD ib. III 1351 (f. Μουκάκενθος)
—LJUBLEN (MOD.): (8) s. ii AD ib. II 753 (*CCET* II (2) 562) (I f. Διζάλας II); (9) ~ *IGB* II 753 (*CCET* II (2) 562) (II s. Διζάλας I)
—MONTANA (NR.): (10) iii AD *IGB* II 483 (*Montana* II 102) (f. Ἡραΐς)
—NICOPOLIS AD NESTUM: (11) ii AD *IGB* IV 2341 (s. Βίθυς)
—PAUTALIA (TERRIT.): (12) ii-iii AD ib. V 5826 (f. Πύρος)
—PHILIPPOPOLIS-TRIMONTIUM (TERRIT.): (13) 98-117 AD ib. III 1116; cf. V 5479 (date) (s. Κότυς)

Διζάλης
MACEDONIA (CHALKIDIKE):
—POTIDAIA-KASSANDREIA (NR.): (1) ii-iii AD *BE* 1970, no. 371 (*Makedonika* 15 (1975) p. 234 no. 123 with pl. 150 β) (s. Ζιπύρων)

Διζάολος
THRACE: (1) 160 BC *BGU* 2390, 4-5, [8], 14, etc. (La'da E730) (s. Ἀμάτοκος)

Διζάπης
MACEDONIA (ODOMANTIKE):
—DRABESKOS?: (1) ii-iii AD *SEG* XXX 619, 1 (Pilhofer 572) (s. Διοσκουρίδης)
THRACE: (2) 221 BC *PPetr* III 112 b, 4 (Velkov 88; La'da E731)

Διζάπολις
THRACE: (1) ii BC *SEG* I 556 (Velkov 89); cf. La'da E778 (f. Παῖσις)

Διζάπορις
THRACE: (1) 222 BC *PEnt* 14, 1 (Velkov 90; La'da E732)
—MARKIANOPOLIS (NR.): (2) f. iii AD *IGB* V 5380 (*CCET* II (1) 244) (s. Αὐλούζενις)
THRACE?: (3) m. iii BC *SB* 12221, 26 (f. Σάτοκος)

Δίζας
CIMMERIAN BOSPOROS:
—PANTIKAPAION*: (1) ii AD *CIRB* 666, 1; cf. KW pl. 15 no. 208 (s. Βίθυς)
MACEDONIA (EDONIS):
—AMPHIPOLIS: (2) ii-iii AD *Thrakika* 13 (1940) p. 26 *K*; cf. *Epigraphica* 37 (1975) p. 28; (3) ~ *Thracia* 2 p. 277 (*AD* 27 (1972) Mel. p. 142); cf. *Epigraphica* 37 (1975) pp. 30-1 (s. Ἄλκης)

—PHILIPPOI: (4) iii AD *BCH* 60 (1936) p. 337, 13 (Pilhofer 133) (Διζανος (gen.): f. Αὐρ. Ζιπύρων)
—PHILIPPOI (TERRIT.): (5) ?iii AD *SEG* XXX 594 A, 3 (Pilhofer 580) (s. Καλ(—)); (6) ~ *SEG* XXX 594 A, 8 (Pilhofer 580) (s. Σηβ(—)); (7) ~ *SEG* XXX 594 A, 9 (Pilhofer 580) (s. Δυδι(—))
—PHILIPPOI (DRAMA (MOD.)): (8) ii-iii AD *AD* 52 (1997) Chron. p. 847, 4 with pl. 314 β
MACEDONIA (MYGDONIA):
—KALINDOIA: (9) 68-98 AD *SEG* XLII 580, 33-4; cf. *Anthémonte–Kalindoia* 2 pp. 243-4 (name) (f. Ἀλέξανδρος, Δημήτριος)
MACEDONIA (ODOMANTIKE):
—BERGE: (10) ii-iii AD *BCH* 81 (1957) p. 606 (Pilhofer 568a) (s. Δέντις)
—DRABESKOS?: (11) ii-iii AD *SEG* XXX 619, 5 (Pilhofer 572) (f. Σάνβος)
—SIRRHA: (12) f. iii AD *SEG* XXX 590, 32 (s. Αὐρ. Βράσις)
—SIRRHA?: (13) ii-iii AD Kaphtantzis 39 (Δίζ[α]? (gen.): f. Φιλίσκος)
MACEDONIA (PAIONIA):
—STOBOI: (14) ii AD Šašel, *IL* 457 (Lat. Dizas: f. Μουκάκενθος)
MACEDONIA (SINTIKE):
—PARTHIKOPOLIS: (15) ?ii AD *FGrH* 257 F 37, 51 (Tataki, *Macedonians* p. 147 no. 4) (f. Αἰδέσιος)
—PARTHIKOPOLIS (TERRIT.): (16) ?242 AD *IGB* IV 2322 (f. Βίθυς)
THRACE: (17) iii AD *CIL* XIV 3623, 2 (Speidel, *Denkmäler* 674) (Lat. Aur. Disza)
—BESSOPARA: (18) iii AD *IGB* III 947, 9 (Δεί-: f. Βίθυς); (19) ~ ib. l. 11 (Δεί-: s. Σάλας)
—BOURDAPA: (20) ii AD ib. 1348 (Διζαδος (gen.): f. Τιούτα)
—DIOSPOLIS?: (21) ii-iii AD ib. 1782, 2; cf. IV 2028 (or Thrace Serdica: Δ̣ίζ̣α̣ (dat.): s. Μουκάτραλις)
—GLAVA PANEGA (MOD.): (22) ii-iii AD ib. II 523 (s. Κούλιος); (23) ~ ib. 560 (s. Ἄθυς); (24) ?iii AD *ILB* 195 (Lat. Diszas: s. Taesus)
—MEZDRA (MOD.): (25) imp. *SEG* XLIX 896 (Δίζζας)
—NICOPOLIS AD ISTRUM:
——Vicus Saprisara: (26) ?iii AD *CIL* VI 2933 (Lat. Aur. Diza)
—PAUTALIA: (27) ii AD *IGB* II 511 (s. Μουκάσης); (28) ~ ib. IV 2067 (s. Δίλζης); (29) ii-iii AD ib. 2104, 3 + V 5781 (Δίδιος Δ.); (30) iii AD *CIL* VI 32624 d, 1 (Lat. M. Aur. Diza); (31) ~ ib. 32624 c, 12 (Lat. M. Aur. Dizas)
—PAUTALIA (TERRIT.): (32) ii-iii AD *IGB* IV 2130 (Αὐρ. Δ.); (33) ~ ib. V 5824 (f. Αὐλούζενις); (34) s. ii AD ib. 5858 ([Δ]ί̣ζας: s. Διουζίης)
—PHILIPPOPOLIS-TRIMONTIUM: (35) iii AD ib. III 917, 6 (Δ. ὁ καὶ Ἑρμόδωρος: s. Βρινκάζενις)
—PHILIPPOPOLIS-TRIMONTIUM (TERRIT.): (36) ii-iii AD ib. 1106 (Δίζ(α)ς: s. Μουκάπορις); (37) ~ ib. 1166 (s. Ἐπτήτραλις); (38) ~ ib. 1175 (Δίζ[ας]: s. Ἡρακλείδης); (39) ~ ib. 1201 (s. Ζεισισος); (40) ~ ib. 1395; (41) ~ ib. 1466 ([Δί]ζας) ?= (44); (42) ii/iii AD ib. 1452, 7 (*Eastern cults* p. 121 no. 104) (Δε(ιζ)ηου? (gen.): f. Χρῆστος); (43) iii AD *IGB* III 1305 (Αὐρ. Δ.) ?= (44); (44) ~ ib. 1310 (Αὐρ. Δίζ̣[ας]) ?= (41) (43)
—PHILIPPOPOLIS-TRIMONTIUM:
——Vicus Ardicenum: (45) 227 AD *CIL* VI 32543, 27 (Lat. M. Aur. Diza)
——Vicus Cuntiegerum: (46) 227 AD ib. l. 6 (Lat. M. Aur. Diza)
——Vicus Pupeses: (47) 227 AD ib. l. 29 (Lat. M. Aur. Diza)
——Vicus Verocasenum: (48) 227 AD ib. l. 8 (Lat. M. Aur. Diza)
—SERDICA: (49) ii-iii AD *IGB* IV 1922, 8; (50) ~ ib. 1938 (*CCCA* VI 340) (f. Δεΐδις); (51) iii AD

IGB IV 1927 (*Eastern cults* p. 166 no. 8) (*Αὐρ. Δ.*: s. *Λούκιος*)
—SERDICA (TERRIT.): **(52)** ii-iii AD *Sp.* 98 (1941-48) p. 127 no. 280, 2; p. 277 (name) (*Δίζα* (gen.), *Διζαεκενθος*?: ?s. *Ἔκενθος*); **(53)** ~ ib. p. 127 no. 280, 4 (f. *Τήρης*); **(54)** ~ *IGB* IV 2004 (s. *Θίντος*); **(55)** ~ ib. 2011 (s. *Σευθείλας*, f. *Ἡρακλείδης*); **(56)** ~ ib. 2015 a (*Eastern cults* p. 167 no. 10) (f. *Μοκᾶς*); **(57)** ~ *IGB* IV 2027 (f. *Ὦιτα*)
—SPORTELA: **(58)** ii-iii AD ib. 2232, 3 (s. *Βίθυς*)
—TYRODIZA-TIRISTASIS: **(59)** imp. Dumont–Homolle 89b (s. *Δόλης*, *Ἡρυλλα*)
THRACE?: **(60)** ii AD *IG* X (2) (1) 910, 5 (Lat. Diza: f. *Μάντα*); **(61)** 230 AD *ZPE* 137 (2001) p. 246 (Lat. M. Aureli Dizaes (gen.))

Δίζασσκος
THRACE?: **(1)** f. i BC *ISamothrace* 33 I, 12

Διζάστης
MACEDONIA (SINTIKE):
—PARTHIKOPOLIS: **(1)** ?ii AD *FGrH* 257 F 37, 52 (Tataki, *Macedonians* p. 147 no. 5) (f. *Βίθυς*)
—PARTHIKOPOLIS (TERRIT.): **(2)** ii-iii AD *SEG* L 631 + *Istorikogeographika* 6 (1998) p. 90 fig. 3 (*Διζαετος*—ed.: f. *Δούλης*)

Διζάτραλις
THRACE:
—PAUTALIA (TERRIT.): **(1)** ii-iii AD *IGB* V 5825 (f. *Μουκάζενις*)

Δίζδων
THRACE:
—DIONYSOPOLIS: **(1)** ii AD ib. I² 27 bis (f. *Λεστόρμη*)

Δίζης
THRACE:
—BARGALA: **(1)** ii-iii AD *SEG* XLIV 513 (*Δίζες*: s. *Βάβος*)
—ČOMAKOVCI (MOD.): **(2)** ?iii AD *ILB* 165 (Lat. Dize (gen.): f. *Μουκαπουιους*)
—MASHOV (MOD.): **(3)** 230-245 AD *BMNWB* 24 (1996) pp. 17 ff. (Minkova, *PNLIB* p. 153) (Lat. M. Aurelius Dize)
—NICOPOLIS AD ISTRUM (TERRIT.): **(4)** ii/iii AD *ILB* 430 (Lat. Aurel. Dizze (dat.))
THRACE?: **(5)** 236 AD *RMD* 77, 27 (Lat. M. Aureli. Dizes)

Διζίας
THRACE:
—ČOMAKOVCI (MOD.): **(1)** iii AD *ILB* 163, 2 (Lat. Dizias: ?s. Bitipel)

Δίζος
THRACE:
—ČOMAKOVCI (MOD.): **(1)** ?iii AD ib. 167 (Lat. Dizus)

Δίζουζος
THRACE:
—GLAVA PANEGA (MOD.): **(1)** ii-iii AD *IGB* II 541

Διζούλας
THRACE: **(1)** 225 BC *PPetr²* 24, 26 (Velkov 92); cf. La'da E856 (*Διζούλου* (gen.): f. *Ἀξιοθέα*)
THRACE?: **(2)** hell.? *PPetr²* 24, 26 n. (*Διζούλου* (gen.)); **(3)** iii BC *CPR* XIII 4 VII, 110; *PPetr²* 24, 26 n. ([.].ρζουλας—ed., [*Δ*]ιζούλας?—Clarysse); **(4)** 165 BC *PHels* 5, 13 (*Διζούλου* (gen.): s. *Καθι*—)

Δίζων
THRACE:
—PHILIPPOPOLIS-TRIMONTIUM: **(1)** 196 AD *IMS* II 53 I b, 12 (*CIL* III 14507); cf. *ZPE* 146 (2004) pp. 216-20; *AEp* 1901, no. 126 (Lat. T. Ael. Dizo)

Διήγησις
MACEDONIA (MYGDONIA):
—THESSALONIKE: **(1)** ii AD *IG* X (2) (1) 615 (*Φλ. Δ.*)

Διήγυλις
THRACE: **(1)** m. ii BC *RE* (-) (king)
—KAINOI: **(2)** m. ii BC ib. (f. *Ζιβέλμιος*: king)

Διῆς
MACEDONIA: **(1)** s. iii BC *Memnonion* 589 (Tataki, *Macedonians* p. 297 no. 49; La'da E1460) (*Δι*(*γ*)*ῆς*?: s. *Δημήτριος*)
MACEDONIA (BOTTIAIA):
—ICHNAI: **(2)** c. 230-200 BC *BCH* 45 (1921) p. 17 III, 63 (Tataki, *Macedonians* p. 113 no. 5) (s. *Ἀλκέτας*)
MACEDONIA (MYGDONIA):
—LETE: **(3)** 117 BC *Syll³* 700, 51 (f. *Ἀμύντας*)
THRACE:
—PERINTHOS-HERAKLEIA (NR.): **(4)** v BC *IPerinth* 288 (*Δίω* (gen.): s. *Ἵππων*)

Διήων
THRACE: **(1)** 362 BC *IG* II² 115, 2 + Add. p. 658

Διιστέφης
SKYTHIA:
—OLBIA-BORYSTHENES: **(1)** iii BC *IOSPE* I² 201 I, 32 (s. *Ἑστιαῖος*)

Δικαιόνικος
MACEDONIA (BOTTIAIA):
—PELLA: **(1)** iii-ii BC *AJA* 77 (1973) p. 69 no. 1 (f. *—ιων*?)

Δικαῖος
MACEDONIA: **(1)** 223 BC *PTeb* 815 fr. 3 verso, 37 (Tataki, *Macedonians* p. 297 no. 51; La'da E1463)
MACEDONIA (BOTTIAIA):
—ALLANTE: **(2)** c. 230-200 BC *BCH* 45 (1921) p. 17 III, 64 (Tataki, *Macedonians* p. 44 no. 3) (s. *Χιωνίδης*)
—BEROIA: **(3)** f. ii AD *IBer* 348 (Tataki 386) (s. *Σύνετος*, *Φωτίς*)
MACEDONIA (CHALKIDIKE):
—CHALKIDEIS: **(4)** c. 350-348 BC *Olynthus* 9 pp. 85-6 nos. 138-9 (coin); *Ancient Macedonia* 1 p. 254 (date)
MACEDONIA (DERRIOPOS):
—STUBERRA: **(5)** 74 AD *IG* X (2) (2) 325, 15, 28; 326, 14 (*Δ. ὁ καὶ Ῥοῦφος*: s. *Πετίκιος*); **(6)** ~ ib. l. 24-5 ([*Δι*]*καῖος*: s. *Παράμονος*)
MACEDONIA (EORDAIA):
—KELLE?: **(7)** m. ii BC *SEG* XLVII 903 (f. *Ἀντίγονος*)
MACEDONIA (MYGDONIA):
—THESSALONIKE?: **(8)** ii AD *IG* X (2) (1) 225, 3 (*Π. Μέμμιος Δ.*)
MACEDONIA (PIERIA):
—DION: **(9)** iii BC *SEG* XXXIV 628 (s. *Δωριεύς*)
THRACE:
—BYZANTION:
——(Rhegion): **(10)** i BC-i AD *IByz* 249 (Fıratlı–Robert p. 80 no. 93) (f. *Διννσις*)
—MARONEIA: **(11)** iii BC *IThrakAig* E257, 3 (f. *Ἑρμόφαντος*) ?= *(13)*; **(12)** ~ ib. l. 4 (s. *Διογένης*) ?= *(13)*; **(13)** ~ ib. l. 7 (f. *Διόφαντος*) ?= *(12)* *(11)*

Δικαιόφρων
SCYTHIA MINOR:
—KALLATIS: **(1)** iii AD *ISM* III 142

Δικέβαλος
SCYTHIA MINOR:
—SALSOVIA: **(1)** iv AD Popescu, *IGL* 272 e, 6 (Lat. Dicebalus)

THRACE:
—MARKIANOPOLIS (TERRIT.): **(2)** iii-iv AD *IGB* V 5328, 3 (*CCET* II (1) 365) (*Δικεβαλι* (gen.): f. *Εἰθία*)
—NICOPOLIS AD ISTRUM (TERRIT.): **(3)** ii-iii AD *IGB* II 709 (s. *Δίκεδος*)

Δίκεδος
THRACE:
—NICOPOLIS AD ISTRUM (TERRIT.): **(1)** ii-iii AD ib. (*Δικέδου* (gen.): f. *Δικέβαλος*)

Δικηναις
THRACE:
—STRAŽA (MOD.): **(1)** ii AD ib. V 5281 (*CCET* II (2) 534) (s. *Διουρπος*)

Διλάης
THRACE:
—KABYLE: **(1)** ii AD *IGB* III 1776, 2 (f. *Ἀλέξανδρος*)

Δίλζης
THRACE:
—PAUTALIA: **(1)** ii AD ib. IV 2067 (*Δίλζενος* (gen.): f. *Δίζας*)

Διλίπορις
THRACE:
—BYZANTION: **(1)** i BC *IByz* 195 (Fıratlı–Robert p. 53 no. 30) (*Διλί*[*πορις*]: f. *Ἐπίκτησις*)
—BYZANTION?: **(2)** i BC *IByz* 369 (PM 1663) (*Διλιπόρηος* (gen.): f. *Μήνιος*)

Δίλιππος
THRACE?: **(1)** ii BC *ILAlg* II 510 (*Μοκάζελμος Δ.*)

Διλόπολις
THRACE?: **(1)** ii BC *Hellenika* 10 (1937-8) pp. 200-4; cf. Masson, *OGS* p. 339 (or Bithynia: f. *Ἐπιγένης*)

Διμης?
THRACE:
—BEROE-AUGUSTA TRAIANA:
——Emporion Diskodouraterai: **(1)** ii-iii AD *IGB* II 738, 1 (*Διμη*[*ς*]—apogr., *Διλλης*?—Mihailov: s. *Ἐπτέθισις*, f. *Βίθυς*, *Ζουροτελμίς*)

Δίμνος
MACEDONIA (BOTTIAIA):
—EDESSA: **(1)** ii BC Dimitsas 557 = *SEG* XLIX 827; cf. *ZPE* 132 (2000) pp. 161-2 (locn.) (Tataki, *Edessa* 79) (or Macedonia (Mygdonia) Thessalonike: f. *Θράσων*)
MACEDONIA (MYGDONIA):
—CHALASTRA: **(2)** 330 BC *RE* (-); Berve 269 (Tataki, *Macedonians* p. 98 no. 1) (*Λίμνος*—Plu.)

Δίνδας
THRACE:
—BEROE-AUGUSTA TRAIANA:
——Emporion Diskodouraterai: **(1)** iii AD *IGB* II 737, 2 (*Αὐρ. Δίνδας*: s. *Τυρέλσης*, f. *Σαβῖνος*)

Δίνδος
CIMMERIAN BOSPOROS:
—GORGIPPIA: **(1)** f. iii BC *CIRB* 1137 B I, 23; cf. *Etiudy* pp. 192-3 no. 14 (*Δίνδος*: f. *Περδίκκας*)

Δινέδινις
THRACE:
—BEROE-AUGUSTA TRAIANA:
——Emporion Diskodouraterai: **(1)** 218-235 AD *IGB* II 730, 10 (*Αὐρ. Δ.*)

Δινείλας
MACEDONIA (MYGDONIA):
—KALINDOIA: **(1)** a. 98 AD *SEG* XLII 583, 25; cf. *Anthémonte–Kalindoia* 2 p. 244 (name) (s. *Κοσιδέλθης*)

THRACE:
—PAUTALIA (TERRIT.): **(2)** ii-iii AD *IGB* IV 2121 (*Δινείλου* (gen.): f. *Μοντανός*)

Δινίας
SCYTHIA MINOR:
—TOMIS: **(1)** iv-v AD Barnea 5 (Popescu, *IGL* 25)
THRACE:
—BEROE-AUGUSTA TRAIANA (TERRIT.): **(2)** iii AD *IGB* III 1700 bis, 2 (*Αὐρ. Δ.*: s. *Ἀσκληπιάδης*)
—DIOSPOLIS?: **(3)** ii-iii AD ib. 1782, 4; cf. IV 2028 (or Thrace Serdica: *Διν[ί]ας*)
—PAUTALIA (TERRIT.): **(4)** ii AD ib. 2214, 12 (f. *Δῖος*)
—PHILIPPOPOLIS-TRIMONTIUM (TERRIT.): **(5)** imp. ib. III 1392 (*Δινίο[υ]* (gen.): f. *Σοῦρις*); **(6)** iii AD ib. 1291 (*Αὐρ. Δινία[ς]*)

Διvιζήτης
THRACE:
—PHILIPPOPOLIS-TRIMONTIUM (TERRIT.): **(1)** i-ii AD ib. 1188 + V 5486 (s. *Δαίσης*)

Δινίκενθος
MACEDONIA (EDONIS):
—PHILIPPOI (TERRIT.): **(1)** i-ii AD *AD* 52 (1997) Chron. p. 847 with pl. 314 *α* (Lat. Dinicenthus)
THRACE: **(2)** 46-54 AD *SEG* XVI 415 I, 8 (*IThrakAig* E84) (*Τιβ. Κλ. Δ.*)
—ERGISSENOI: **(3)** ii AD *IGB* III 1593, 1 (s. *Βρινκάζερις*)
—PAUTALIA (TERRIT.): **(4)** iii AD ib. IV 2221 (*Αὐρ. Δινίκενθος*)
—ROSICA (MOD.): **(5)** ii-iii AD ib. V 5283 (*-νεί-*: f. *Ἱέρων*)

Δίνις
MACEDONIA (EDONIS):
—PHILIPPOI (DRAMA (MOD.)): **(1)** i-ii AD *Drama* p. 75 (Pilhofer 501c) (Lat. Dinis: s. *Κετρίλας*)
—PHILIPPOI*: **(2)** i-ii AD *BCH* 62 (1938) p. 476 (Pilhofer 388) (Lat. Dinis Defcila)
THRACE: **(3)** 26 AD *RE* (-); Tac., *Ann.* iv 50 (Lat. Dinis); **(4)** 46-54 AD *SEG* XVI 415 I, 4 (*IThrakAig* E85); *Thrakika* 8 (1937) p. 15 no. 1 (*IThrakAig* E85) (*Τιβ. Κλ. Δ.*); **(5)** ~ *SEG* XVI 415 I, 7 (*IThrakAig* E84) (*Μ. Οὐέττιος Δ.*); **(6)** ii-iii AD *IMS* I 91 (Lat. Dines: s. Celsus)
—BEROE-AUGUSTA TRAIANA: **(7)** iii AD *IGB* V 5634 (f. *Αὐρ. Θεόπομπος*); **(8)** f. iii AD ib. 5577, 5 (*Φλ. Δ.*: s. *Λογγῖνος*) ?= *(9)*; **(9)** ~ ib. 5578, 4 (f. *Τ. Φλ. Νέπως*) ?= *(8)*
—BEROE-AUGUSTA TRAIANA (TERRIT.): **(10)** ii AD ib. 5592 (*Eastern cults* p. 174 no. 20) (*Τ. Φλ. Δ.*: s. *Σκέλης*)
—BESSOI: **(11)** i-ii AD *CIL* X 3590 (Lat. C. Iulius Pudens qui Dines: s. Sautis)
——Diniscorta: **(12)** f. ii AD *Stud. Gerov* p. 253 (Lat. Dini (gen.): f. *Τάρσας*)
—BIZYE (NR.): **(13)** imp. *JÖAI* 23 (1926) Beibl. col. 130 no. 24 (*Δίνεως* (gen.))
—BYZANTION?: **(14)** s. iii BC *IByz* 340 (Fıratlı–Robert p. 97 no. 140) (*Δίνεως* (gen.): f. *Μοκαζοίρη*)
—DRAGANOVEC (MOD.): **(15)** f. iii AD *IGB* V 5309 (*CCET* II (2) 498) (*Δίνεω[ς]* (gen.): f. —ọς)
—KELLAI: **(16)** ii-iii AD *IGB* III 1520 (f. *Αὐρ. Μουκιανός*)
—MARKIANOPOLIS (TERRIT.): **(17)** ii-iii AD ib. II 843, 1 (s. *Μουκάτραλις*); **(18)** iii AD ib. 796, 1 (s. *Ῥησκούπορις*)
—ODESSOS: **(19)** ii AD ib. I^2 50 b, 19 (f. —*δωρος*)
—PHILIPPOPOLIS-TRIMONTIUM: **(20)** s. ii AD ib. III 965-6; IV 2014 (*Eastern cults* p. 196 no. 10); cf. *IGB* V 5427 (date) (f. *Δορζένθης*); **(21)** 196 AD *IMS* II 53 I b, 38 (*CIL* III 14507); cf. *ZPE* 146 (2004) pp. 216-20 (Lat. M. Aur. Dines)
—PHILIPPOPOLIS-TRIMONTIUM (TERRIT.): **(22)** ii-iii AD *IGB* III 1073 (f. *Μουκάκενθος*); **(23)** ~ ib. 1190 (s. *Σύρος*); **(24)** ~ ib. 1197 (*Δινε[ος]* (gen.): f. *Μουκάπορις*); **(25)** ~ ib. 1371 (*Φλ. Δ. ὁ καὶ Ἑρμῆς*); **(26)** ~ ib. 1398 (f. *Βίθυς*)
—SKEDABRIA: **(27)** 202 AD ib. 1690 b, 21 (and Thrace Pizos: f. *Μουκάτραλις*)

Δίννυς
MACEDONIA (CHALKIDIKE):
—STOLOS?: **(1)** ?351 BC *SEG* XXXVIII 672, 3, 10 (s. *Πόττης*)

Δίντας
THRACE:
—BIZYE: **(1)** 12-19 AD *IGB* V 5011, 7 (*Δίντα* (gen.): f. *Μόσχος*)

Δινύσις
THRACE:
—BYZANTION:
——(Rhegion): **(1)** i BC-i AD *IByz* 249 (Fıratlı–Robert p. 80 no. 93); Masson, *OGS* 3 p. 209 (name) (*Δινυσις*, *Δινυξις*?—Robert: s. *Δικαῖος*)

Διογᾶς
CIMMERIAN BOSPOROS:
—PANTIKAPAION: **(1)** i/ii AD *CIRB* 584; cf. KW pl. 40 no. 606 (f. *Ἀρτεμίδωρος*)

Διογείτων
THRACE:
—HADRIANOPOLIS: **(1)** imp.? *Thrakika* 16 (1941) p. 85 (*Διογείτ[ων]*?)
—STRYME?: **(2)** v-iv BC *IThrakAig* E131 (*[Δ]ịογείτων*: s. *Ἑκαταῖος*)

Διογένεια
CIMMERIAN BOSPOROS:
—PANTIKAPAION: **(1)** 133 AD *CIRB* 675, 2 (*[Δι]ογένηα*: d. *Ἄκρατος*)
MACEDONIA (MYGDONIA):
—KALINDOIA: **(2)** ?255 AD *SEG* XLII 603 b (*Διογενιᾶνι* (dat.): ?m. *Εὐφρόσυνος*)
MACEDONIA (PIERIA):
—PYDNA: **(3)** ?i AD Dimitsas 157
SCYTHIA MINOR:
—TOMIS: **(4)** v-vi AD Barnea 19, 6 (Popescu, *IGL* 40) (Lat. Diogeni[a]: m. Nazarin–)
THRACE:
—DEULTUM: **(5)** 294 AD *Cod. Just.* viii 50. 17; cf. *Klio* 58 (1976) p. 84 (Lat. Diogenia)
—HADRIANOPOLIS: **(6)** 293 AD *Cod. Just.* vii 16.16; cf. *Klio* 58 (1976) p. 82 (Lat. Diogenia)
—MARONEIA: **(7)** iii AD *IThrakAig* E396, 10 (*-νια*: ?m. *Ῥόδη*, *Σαβῖνα*)
—PAUTALIA: **(8)** ii-iii AD *IGB* IV 2090, 5 (biling.)
—TRAIANOPOLIS: **(9)** ii AD *SEG* XXIV 643, 4 (*IThrakAig* E438) (d. *Βάκχιος*)

Διογένης
CIMMERIAN BOSPOROS:
—HERMONASSA: **(1)** iv BC *CIRB* 1063 (*Διογέ[νης]*: s. *Ἡρακλε—*)
—PANTIKAPAION: **(2)** iii BC ib. 110, 3 (s. *Ἰε—*); **(3)** i BC/i AD ib. 311 (s. *Ἰσιγόνη*); **(4)** i AD ib. 345 (*Διωγένης* (gen.?)—lap.: f. *Ἀπολλωνίδης*); **(5)** ~ ib. 385 (s. *Διόδοτος*); **(6)** ~ ib. 386 (*Διọγένης*: f. *Ἀπε—*); **(7)** ~ ib. 387 (*Διογέ[νης]*: s. —*γο*—); **(8)** i-ii AD Vaulina–Wąsowicz pl. 124 no. 63 B, 10 (reading—Tokhtas'ev); **(9)** ii AD *CIRB* 751 (f. *Γάϊος*); **(10)** f. ii AD ib. 756
—TYRITAKE: **(11)** i AD ib. 903 (s. *Παιρίσαλος*)
MACEDONIA: **(12)** iii BC *GVI* 1537, 1, 3; Robert, *Hell.* 11-12 p. 276 f. (locn.) (Tataki, *Macedonians* p. 298 no. 55) (s. *Ἡρακλείδης*); **(13)** s. iii BC *RE* (12); Osborne, *Naturalization* T100 (Tataki, *Macedonians* p. 298 no. 53; *FRA* 3469) (and Athens Kolonos?: ?f. *Πausίμαχος* (Athens Kolonos?)); **(14)** 226 BC $PPetr^2$ 27, 8 (Tataki, *Macedonians* p. 297 no. 52; La'da E1464); **(15)** m. ii BC *BGU* 1939 A, 12 (Tataki, *Macedonians* p. 479 no. 70); cf. La'da E1808 (f. *Κλεοπάτρα*); **(16)** 102 BC *IG* II^2 1335, 22 (Tataki, *Macedonians* p. 298 no. 54; *FRA* 3470)
MACEDONIA (BOTTIAIA):
—BEROIA: **(17)** ii BC *IBer* 181 (Tataki 388) (s. *Βαρναῖος*); **(18)** f. i AD *IBer* 103, 9 (Tataki 387) (s. *Ἀμύντας*)
—EDESSA: **(19)** v-vi AD Feissel, *RICM* 36
—MIEZA?: **(20)** iii BC *SEG* XXIV 524 I, 6 (Hatzopoulos, *MI* 2 p. 106 no. 92) (s. *Πυθογένης*)
—PELLA: **(21)** c. 325-300 BC *SEG* XL 547; *KGAM Thess.* I 23 (date)
MACEDONIA (EDONIS):
—AMPHIPOLIS: **(22)** ?iii BC *PAE* 1982, p. 47 (f. *Ἀντιγένης*); **(23)** 4 or 120 AD *SEG* XL 522 g (f. *Ἀπελλᾶς*)
MACEDONIA (LYNKESTIS):
—HERAKLEIA?: **(24)** 235 AD *IG* X (2) (2) 136, 1 (*Αὐρήλιος Διογέν[ης]*: f. *Παῖτος*, *Ἀλέξανδρος*); **(25)** ~ ib. l. 6
MACEDONIA (MYGDONIA):
—KALINDOIA: **(26)** 68-98 AD *SEG* XLII 580, 49 (s. *Τρυφωνᾶς*)
—LETE: **(27)** ii AD *Makedonika* 2 (1951) p. 619 no. 42 *θ*, 6-7 (f. *Δημόκριτος*, *Ἡρωΐδης*)
—ORAIOKASTRO (MOD.): **(28)** v-iv BC *SEG* XLIX 750 (s. *Ἕσπερος*)
—THESSALONIKE: **(29)** i BC-i AD *IG* X (2) (1) 129, 9 (s. *Δ*—); **(30)** 95 BC ib. 4, 3 (s. *Ἐπιγένης*); **(31)** 27 BC-14 AD ib. 31, 14; **(32)** c. 23 BC ib. 97, 3; 113, 2 (s. *Λυσίμαχος*); **(33)** 90 AD *SEG* XLII 625, 9 (f. *Ἑρμογένης*); **(34)** ?ii AD *IG* X (2) (1) 127, 5 (*Γ. Λάππιος Δ.*); **(35)** ~ ib. l. 6 (f. *Θεότιμος*); **(36)** ~ ib. l. 7 (s. *Ἀπελλῆς*); **(37)** ii AD ib. 424 (f. *Κρητικός*)
—THESSALONIKE?: **(38)** ii AD ib. 922 (*Δει-*: f. *Ἡρακλείδης*)
—THESSALONIKE*: **(39)** i-ii AD ib. 688, 2 (Lat. T. Minucius Diogenes: freed.)
MACEDONIA (ODOMANTIKE):
—SIRRHA: **(40)** ii AD Dimitsas 811, 9 (Kaphtantzis 15) (I f. *Τιβ. Κλ. Διογένης* II); **(41)** ~ Dimitsas 811, 10 (Kaphtantzis 15); Dimitsas 812, 6 (Kaphtantzis 16) (*Τι(β). Κλ. Δ.*: II s. *Διογένης* I, f. *Τιβ. Κλ. Φλαουϊανὸς Λυσίμαχος*); **(42)** 155 AD Dimitsas 821, 25 (Kaphtantzis 1) (s. *Γλύκων*); **(43)** f. iii AD *SEG* XXX 590, 4 (*Αὐρ. Δ.*: s. *Διονυσόδωρος*)
MACEDONIA (ORESTIS):
—LYKE: **(44)** ?i-ii AD *EAM* 147, 2 (*[Δ]ιογέ[νης]*: f. *Λυσίμαχος*)
MACEDONIA (SINTIKE):
—HERAKLEIA: **(45)** ii-iii AD *IGB* IV 2327 (*[Δι]ογένης*)
SCYTHIA MINOR:
—ISTROS: **(46)** v BC Unp. (Avram, defixio) 2, 1, 4 (s. *Ὀνόμαστος*); **(47)** iii BC *ISM* I 1, 3, [11], 15 (Migeotte, *L'emprunt* 40); *ISM* I 2, [2] + *Pontica* 33-4 (2000-1) pp. 337-9 no. 1 (I s. *Γλαυκίας*, f. *Διογένης* II); **(48)** ~ *ISM* I 1, 3, 10 (Migeotte, *L'emprunt* 40); *ISM* I 2, 2 + *Pontica* 33-4 (2000-1) pp. 337-9 no. 1 (II s. *Διογένης* I); **(49)** iii/ii BC *ISM* I 120 (*Διογέ[νης]*: f. *Ἀπολλωνίς*); **(50)** i BC-i AD ib. 29 (*Διογέ[νης]*: f. *Μόσχιον*); **(51)** ~ ib. 191 I, 23; **(52)** ~ ib. l. 25; **(53)** ~ ib. l. 44 (*[Δ]ιογένης*); **(54)** ~ ib. l. 19-20; **(55)** ~ ib. 191 II, 7 (s. *Παπίας*); **(56)** ~ ib. l. 24 (f. *Ζωΐλος*); **(57)** ~ ib. l. 29 (f. *Παπίας*); **(58)** ~ ib. l. 37 (s. *Ζωΐλος*); **(59)** ~ ib. l. 54 (s. *Θεόφιλος*); **(60)** ii AD ib. 57, 3 (*Eastern cults* pp. 102-3 no. 65) (s. *Θεόδωρος*); **(61)** ~ *ISM* I 198, 2 (s. *Ἀθηνάδης*); **(62)** ~ ib. 203 (*Διο[γέν]ης*?); **(63)** ~ ib. 211, 4 (s. *Ἀπφοῦς*); **(64)** 138 AD ib. 193 I, 78 (s. *Διονύσιος*); **(65)** ~ ib. 193 II, 53 (s. *Χαιρέας*); **(66)** ~ ib. l. 71 (s. *Ἀριστόνικος*); **(67)** c. 138-160 AD ib. 193 I, 77;

207, 8 (s. Κάρπος); (68) s. ii AD ib. 167, 17; (69) iii AD ib. 223 ([Δι]ογένης?); (70) ~ ib. 309 (s. Ζωΐλος, f. Ζωΐλων); (71) f. iii AD ib. 143, 7 ([Α]ὐρ. Δ.: s. Τρύφων); (72) 222-225 AD ib. 100, 6 (Φλ. Δ.)
—KALLATIS: (73) f. ii BC IIasos 197, 7 (resid. Caria Iasos: s. Τανύβοτος: metic); (74) ii AD ISM III 139, 8
—TOMIS: (75) i BC ib. II 2 A, 56 (f. Διονύσιος); (76) f. i AD RPC I 1810 (coin) (Διογ(ένης)?); (77) ii-iii AD ISM II 185 (I f. Γάϊος, Διογένης II); (78) ~ ib. (II s. Διογένης I, Εἷα); (79) ~ ib. 468, 7 (s. Ἀλέξανδρος); (80) iii AD ib. 22, 2 (?f. Αὐρ. Θεόδωρος); (81) ~ ib. l. 8 (Αὐρ. Διογ[ένης]); (82) f. iii AD ib. 273, 2 (f. Αὐρ. Εὐτυχιανός)
SCYTHIA MINOR?: (83) ii AD CCET IV 120 (Αὐρ. Δ.)
SKYTHIA:
—OLBIA-BORYSTHENES: (84) s. vi BC KSIA 156 (1978) p. 44 (vase) (Διογέ[νης]); (85) iii BC IOlbia 26, 3 (f. Ἡφαιστόδωρος); (86) ii AD IOSPE I^2 128, 4 (s. Μακεδών)
TAURIS:
—CHERSONESOS: (87) imp.? ib. 625 (Διογένες (voc.?)—n. pr.?); (88) f. ii AD KSIIMK 15 (1947) p. 59, 6 (Solomonik, NEPKh 112 d); cf. VDI 1993 (4), p. 63 (Διο[γ]ένης); (89) ~ Solomonik, NEPKh 129, 2 (f. —νης) ?= (91); (90) c. 120-130 AD ib. 112, 9 (Διο(γ)ένης: f. —ρος); (91) ~ IOSPE I^2 359, 30; 386, 2; Solomonik, NEPKh 112, 10 (f. Θεαγένης) ?= (89); (92) 129-130 AD IOSPE I^2 359, 27; VDI 1960 (3), pp. 154-5, 22 (f. Ἀθήναιος); (93) 174 AD SEG XLV 985 A, 39 (f. Εὐρύδαμος); (94) iii AD Solomonik, NEPKh 186, 3 (Διογέν[ης]); (95) f. iv AD Const. Porph., De admin. imp. 53. 131, 131 (I f. Διογένης II); (96) ~ ib. l. 131 (II s. Διογένης I)
—CHERSONESOS*: (97) 488 AD Latyshev, Sbornik 7, 15
THRACE: (98) 241 BC PFrankf 5, 22 (s. Πτολεμαῖος)
—AINOS?: (99) 208-211 AD AEp 1986, no. 628 (Lat. Diogenen (acc.): s. Θεόχαρις)
—ALOPEKONNESOS: (100) i BC IG XII (8) 190 a, 15 (f. Ἀττίνας)
—ANCHIALOS: (101) imp. RA 1912 (2), p. 262 no. 48 (s. Κλήμης)
—APOLLONIA-SOZOPOLIS: (102) iii BC BMN-Burgas 4 (2002) p. 127 no. 27
—BIZYE (TERRIT.): (103) ii-iii AD IGB III 1864 ([Δ]ιογένης)
—BYZANTION: (104) ii-i BC IByz 80 (Fıratlı–Robert p. 50 no. 20) (Διογένηος (gen.): I f. Διογένης II); (105) ~ IByz 80 (Fıratlı–Robert p. 50 no. 20) (II s. Διογένης I); (106) i BC IByz 243 (f. Θεοδώρα); (107) ~ ib. 345 (Fıratlı–Robert p. 103 no. 158) (M. Ὤλιος Δ.)
—BYZANTION (TERRIT.): (108) imp. Unp. (Sayar) (I f. Διογένης II); (109) ~ ib. (II s. Διογένης I); (110) ~ ib. (s. Αἴσωπος)
—BYZANTION:
——(Kallichoritis): (111) iii AD IByz 320; cf. Fıratlı–Robert p. 165 (f. Αὐρ. Θεόφιλος)
—BYZANTION?: (112) imp. Robert, OMS 7 p. 652 (s. Βάκχιος)
—DIONYSOPOLIS: (113) iii AD IGB I^2 14 a, 4 (f. Αὐρ. Γλαυκίας); (114) a. 217 AD ib. 16, 10 (f. M. Αὐρ. Δημήτριος)
—DRAGANOVEC (MOD.): (115) f. iii AD ib. V 5296 (CCET II (2) 445)
—GLAVA PANEGA (MOD.): (116) ii-iii AD IGB II 525 (s. Μᾶρκος); (117) iii AD ib. 535 (Αὐρ. Δ.)
—KELLAI: (118) 241-244 AD ib. III 1517, 27 (Αὐρ. Δ.: s. Διονύσιος)
—LYSIMACHEIA: (119) iii BC ITrall 33 B, 15 (s. Λέων)
—MARONEIA: (120) hell. EEBS 42 (1975-6) p. 226 (IThrakAig E251) (s. (nat.) Ἡγήσιππος, s. (ad.) Προκλῆς); (121) ~ ib. E259, 1, 8 (s. Σωτήριχος, f. —ος); (122) iii BC ib. E257, 1 ([Διο]γένης) ?= (123); (123) ~ ib. l. 5 (f. Δικαῖος) ?= (122); (124) ii-i BC JHS 16 (1896) p. 319 no. 19 (IThrakAig E287) (Δι[ογ]ένης: f. Ἀρτέμων); (125) ~ ib. E212, 22 (f. Ἡγήσιππος); (126) ~ ib. l. 24 (s. Ποσειδώνιος); (127) i-ii AD ib. E314 (Λ. Διογέ[νης])
—NICOPOLIS AD ISTRUM (TERRIT.): (128) 227 AD ILB 438 I, 48 (Lat. Aur. Diogenes)
—NICOPOLIS AD ISTRUM (NR.): (129) f. iii AD IGB II 706 (CCET II (2) 655) (Διογέ[νης]: f. Τιμοκράτης)
—ODESSOS: (130) ii BC IGB I^2 206 ter (PM 1795) (s. Μένανδρος, f. Μένανδρος); (131) c. 45-42 BC IGB I^2 43, 2 (s. Ἀντίθεος); (132) 3 BC ib. 46, 44 (f. Πόσσις); (133) i-ii AD ib. 106 bis (f. Νουμήνιος); (134) m. ii AD ib. 174 (PM 1726); Dacia 21 (1977) p. 161 (date) (s. Ζωπυρίων); (135) 215 AD IGB I^2 47 b, 22 (f. Αὐρ. Παρμένων)
—ODESSOS (NR.): (136) i-ii AD ib. 259 (f. —ενίδης)
—PAUTALIA: (137) ii AD ib. IV 2074, 16 (s. Ἀπολλώνιος); (138) s. ii AD SEG XLVI 864, 2 ((Διο)γένης: I f. Διογένης II); (139) ~ ib. l. 2 (II s. Διογένης I); (140) ~ ib. l. 8 (I f. Διογένης II); (141) ~ ib. l. 8 (II s. Διογένης I); (142) ~ ib. l. 18 (s. Ζείγεθος)
—PAUTALIA (TERRIT.): (143) ii AD IGB IV 2214, 5 (s. Ἄλυπος); (144) ii-iii AD ib. 2148 ([Δι]ογένης); (145) ~ ib. 2210 (s. Μουκιανός)
—PAUTALIA*: (146) 312-316 AD Beševliev 34, 4; AEp 1978, no. 720 (date) (Lat. Sallustius Diogenes)
—PERINTHOS-HERAKLEIA: (147) c. 100-115 AD SEG XXVI 1288, 11 (f. Μίκκαλος); (148) iii-iv AD IPerinth 185 (AD 51-2 (1996-7) Mel. p. 347 no. 174) (Φλ. Δειωγένης); (149) f. iii AD IPerinth 157 (Αὐρ. Δ.)
——(φυλ. ἑκτ.): (150) iii-iv AD ib. 180, 1 (AD 51-2 (1996-7) Mel. p. 338 no. 170) (f. Αὐρ. Μάρκελλος)
—PHILIPPOPOLIS-TRIMONTIUM: (151) ?iii AD CIL VI 32563 fr. 10, 6 (Lat. Aur. Diogen(es))
——Vicus C–menos: (152) 227 AD ib. 32543, 25 (Lat. M. Aur. Diogenes)
—PLASTINA (MOD.): (153) iii AD IGB II 770 (CCET II (2) 444) (Αἰλ. Δ.)
—PLOTINOPOLIS: (154) 499 AD Meïmaris–Bakirtzis 23 (SEG XLIV 607; IThrakAig E474); cf. PLRE II (5 + 7)
—SALYMBRIA: (155) imp. Archives Stamoulis d. 35 (Loukopoulou, Thrace Propontique p. 250) (s. Βυ—)
—SERDICA: (156) ii-iii AD IGB IV 1960, 3 (Α— Διογένης); (157) ~ ib. V 5700 (f. Φίλιος); (158) iii AD CIL VI 2742 (Lat. Diogenes Gaius); (159) 261-268 AD IGB IV 1912 (Φλ. Δ.)
—SERDICA (TERRIT.): (160) ii-iii AD ib. V 5707
—TOPEIROS: (161) imp. Thrakika 8 (1937) p. 21 no. 4 (IThrakAig E95)
—TRAIANOPOLIS: (162) iii AD SEG XXIV 642 (ZPE 10 (1973) p. 99; IThrakAig E436)
—TRAIANOPOLIS (TERRIT.): (163) f. ii AD ib. E446 (I f. Διογένης II); (164) ~ ib. (Δι[ογέν]ης: II s. Διογένης I)

Διογενιανός
SCYTHIA MINOR:
—SALSOVIA: (1) iv AD Popescu, IGL 272 c, 4 (Lat. Diogenianus)
—TOMIS: (2) 200-201 AD ISM II 82 B, 17 (Γ. Διογενια[νός])
THRACE:
—KALLIPOLIS: (3) ii AD ISestos 11, 35 (Τ. Φλ. Δ.)
—NICOPOLIS AD NESTUM: (4) ii AD IGB IV 2336, 1 ([Διογ]ενιανός: s. Ἀσκληπᾶς)
—NIKOPOL (MOD.): (5) 211-217 AD ILB 143, 8 (Lat. Arius Diogenianus)
—PAUTALIA: (6) ii-iii AD IGB IV 2066 (Διογ[ε]νιανός); (7) s. ii AD SEG XLVI 864, 10 (s. Φαέσαξ)
——(Herakleis): (8) ?ii AD IGB IV 2077, 17 (f. Ἰουλιανός)
—PHILIPPOPOLIS-TRIMONTIUM (TERRIT.): (9) ii AD ib. III 1117 (Οὔλπ. Δ.: s. Οὔλπ. Δεινίας)

Διόγνητος
CIMMERIAN BOSPOROS:
—PANTIKAPAION: (1) v-iv BC Tolstoi 204 (vase) (Διόγνη(τος))
MACEDONIA (CHALKIDIKE):
—APHYTIS: (2) 360 BC IG IV (1)^2 94 b, 24 (Perlman, City and Sanctuary E.1 with p. 69 f. (date); Tataki, Macedonians p. 66 no. 1)
MACEDONIA (EDONIS):
—PHILIPPOI (DRAMA (MOD.)): (3) ii-i BC SEG XLVIII 793 (Pilhofer 501) (f. Δορζίλας)
MACEDONIA (PIERIA):
—PYDNA: (4) iv BC GRBS 43 (2002-3) p. 115 no. 3, 1 (Δι[ό]γνητος)
TAURIS:
—CHERSONESOS: (5) f. iii BC SEG XL 616 A, 4 (Διόγν[ητος])
THRACE:
—BYZANTION?: (6) iii AD IByz 323 (Σεκουνδῖνος Διόγν[ητος]: f. Αὐρ. Εὐφημία)

Διοδότη
CIMMERIAN BOSPOROS:
—PANTIKAPAION: (1) i AD CIRB 388 (d. Πρέπων)

Διόδοτος
CIMMERIAN BOSPOROS:
—PANTIKAPAION: (1) i AD ib. 385 (f. Διογένης)
MACEDONIA: (2) c. 275-250 BC Thess. Mnem. 6 = Möbius, Die Ornamente^2 pl. 53a; cf. La Thessalie p. 99 pl. 12 (Tataki, Macedonians p. 298 no. 57) (s. Τιμόθεος); (3) 160 BC PHels 31, 3 (Tataki, Macedonians p. 299 no. 63; La'da E1465) (s. Αὐτομένης)
MACEDONIA (CHALKIDIKE):
—POTIDAIA-KASSANDREIA: (4) c. 300 BC IG II^2 1956, 112 (Tataki, Macedonians p. 87 no. 22; FRA 2780)
MACEDONIA (EDONIS):
—PHILIPPOI: (5) iv/iii BC SEG XXIV 620 (Pilhofer 246) (s. Ἐπιγένης)
SCYTHIA MINOR:
—ISTROS: (6) ii AD ISM I 196, 17; 201 II, 5 (f. Πολύστρατος)
THRACE: (7) ?ii BC SB 8562; cf. La'da E701 ([Διό]δοτος?: f. Αἰσχρίων); (8) c. 175 BC PTeb 779, 2, 8 (Velkov 95; La'da E733) (Δ[ιό]δοτος)
—DUROSTORUM: (9) ii AD IGB II 864 (—εὺς ὁ [καὶ] [Δ]ιόδοτ[ος])
—MARONEIA: (10) s. ii BC IG XII (8) 170 c, 40 (s. Ζήνων)
—PERINTHOS-HERAKLEIA: (11) i/ii AD IPerinth 64, 5 (s. Παπίας)
——(Kastaleis): (12) iii-ii BC ib. 61, 56 (f. Τιμόθεος)

Διοδώρα
MACEDONIA (BOTTIAIA):
—BEROIA: (1) ii AD IBer 232, 5 (Tataki 389) (d. Μάξιμα)
—PELLA: (2) 231 or 206 BC CPR XVIII 20, [410], [414-15], 425; 21, 433, 441, 445 (La'da E1945) (d. Ἀσκληπιάδης)
MACEDONIA (CHALKIDIKE):
—POTIDAIA-KASSANDREIA (TERRIT.): (3) imp. SEG XXIX 588, 4 (m. Λικινία Νικόπολις)
MACEDONIA (MYGDONIA):
—THESSALONIKE: (4) ii-iii AD Nalpantis, Anaskaphi p. 111 no. BE 118 (d. Διονύσις, Κοπρία)
THRACE:
—SALYMBRIA (NR.): (5) hell. IByz S 53 (d. Μηνόδωρος)

Διόδωρος
Cimmerian Bosporos:
—nymphaion: **(1)** iii bc *CIRB* 912 II, 11 (f. *Ἱππόμαχος*)
—pantikapaion: **(2)** i bc ib. 123, 1, 3 (*GVI* 1467) (f. *Καλοῦς*); **(3)** f. i ad *CIRB* 389 (s. *Ἔρως*)
Macedonia: **(4)** 221 bc *PHib* 90, 6, 9, 12-14, 16-17, 19 (*PP* 2278 with Add.; Tataki, *Macedonians* p. 299 no. 60); **(5)** 159 bc *SB* 7632, 18; 7632 verso, 2 (Tataki, *Macedonians* p. 299 nos. 61 and 64; La'da E1466)
Macedonia (Almopia):
—milia (mod.): **(6)** ii-i bc *SEG* xii 347 (f. *Φιλητίων*)
Macedonia (Bottiaia):
—beroia: **(7)** ii bc *IBer* 173 (f. *Στράτων*); **(8)** f. i ad ib. 103, 5 (Tataki 390) (f. *Ἀδαῖος*)
—edessa: **(9)** hell. *IG* ii^2 8481 (*FRA* 1497; Tataki, *Macedonians* p. 102 no. 5) (f. *Εἰρήνη*)
—pella: **(10)** iii bc *SEG* xliii 437
Macedonia (Chalkidike):
—olynthos: **(11)** ?350 bc *TAPA* 62 (1931) p. 43 no. 2, 6, 10; Hatzopoulos, *Actes Chalc.* p. 80 (date) (f. *Πυθίων*); **(12)** c. 100 bc *GP* 253 (Tataki, *Macedonians* p. 133 no. 33) (s. *Καλλιγένης*: fict.?)
—torone: **(13)** ?353 bc *SEG* xxiv 574, 9; Hatzopoulos, *Actes Chalc.* p. 80 (date) (f. *Ποσείδιππος*)
Macedonia (Edonis):
—amphipolis: **(14)** 168 bc Liv. xliv 44. 4 (Lat. Diodorus)
Macedonia (Mygdonia):
—thessalonike: **(15)** ii ad *IG* iv (1) 591, 3 + *Mnem.* NS 47 (1919) pp. 259-60 (Tataki, *Macedonians* p. 181 no. 22) (f. *M. Οὔλπ. Ἡλιόδωρος, M. Οὔλπ. Θεόδωρος*); **(16)** ?ii ad *IG* x (2) (1) 568 (*T. Φλ. Δ.*)
Macedonia (Paionia): **(17)** ?ii ad *AM* 27 (1902) p. 318 no. 45 (f. *Φιλήμων*)
Macedonia (Sintike):
—herakleia: **(18)** 230 ad *IGB* v 5922, 9 (-δο-: f. *Ἀσκληπίδης*)
Scythia Minor:
—istros: **(19)** iii bc *ISM* i 8, 3 (s. *Θρασυκλῆς*)
—kallatis: **(20)** s. iii bc ib. iii 10, 2 (s. *Ἡ—*); **(21)** 12-15 ad ib. 44, 3 (s. *Δαμάτριος*); **(22)** 241-244 ad ib. 74 B, 29 (f. *Ῥόνοικος*)
Skythia:
—nikonion: **(23)** hell. *MASP* 5 (1966) p. 80 no. 24 (*Διόδω(ρος)*)
—olbia-borysthenes: **(24)** v bc Tolstoi 14 (*LSAG*^{2} p. 372 no. 58 (vase)) (f. *Διονύσιος*); **(25)** iv/iii bc *IOSPE* i^2 210 (s. *Διονύσιος*); **(26)** iii bc ib. 201 I, 60 (f. *Ἀπολλόδωρος*)
—olbia-borysthenes?: **(27)** c. 200-175 bc *IG* xi (4) 814, [2], 9 (s. *Ἀρώτης*)
—tanais: **(28)** ii ad *CIRB* 1262, 25 (f. *Εὔϊος*)
Tauris:
—chersonesos: **(29)** ii bc Solomonik, *GAKh* 623 (vase) (*Διόδω(ρος)*)
—kerkinitis: **(30)** v-iv bc Solomonik, *GChKh* 119 (vase) (*SEG* xxxiii 611) (*Διόδωρ(ος)*)
Thrace:
—abdera: **(31)** s. ii bc *IG* xii (8) 170 d, 53 (f. *Νικομήδης*)
—anchialos (territ.): **(32)** ii-iii ad *IGB* i^2 385, 4 (s. *Π—*)
—beroe-augusta traiana: **(33)** ii-iii ad ib. iii 1606 (s. *—μπος*)
—beroe-augusta traiana (territ.): **(34)** ii-iii ad ib. 1653, 6 (II s. *Αὐρ. Διόδωρος* I, *Φλ. Τιούτα*); **(35)** iii ad ib. l. 1 (*Αὐρ. Δ.*: I s. *Ἰνγένους*, f. *Διόδωρος* II)
—bisanthe-panion: **(36)** 188-159 bc *JÖAI* 23 (1926) Beibl. col. 151 no. 87, 8 (*OGIS* 301); cf. Tataki, *Macedonians* p. 299 no. 62 (s. *Ἀρριδαῖος*)
—bizone: **(37)** iii ad *IGB* i^2 10, 8 (*Διόδω[ρος]*: f. *Δίων*)
—byzantion: **(38)** ii-i bc *IByz* 229 (Firatlı–Robert pp. 82-3 no. 100) (f. *Θεοβούλα*); **(39)** i bc *IByz* 105 (Firatlı–Robert p. 96 no. 136) (f. *Ἐπαφρόδιτος*); **(40)** i-ii ad *IByz* 281 (Firatlı–Robert pp. 87-8 no. 110) (*Δ. ὁ καὶ Καλλίστρατος*: I f. *Τατίς, Πῶλλα, Παῦλα, Διόδωρος* II); **(41)** ~ *IByz* 281 (Firatlı–Robert pp. 87-8 no. 110) (II s. *Διόδωρος* I *ὁ καὶ Καλλίστρατος*); **(42)** s. i ad *IByz* 35, 4 (s. *Κόϊντος*)
—byzantion (territ.): **(43)** i bc-i ad ib. 264 (Firatlı–Robert p. 86 no. 107) (f. *Φίλων*); **(44)** imp. Unp. (Sayar) (f. *Ἑκατόδωρος*)
—byzantion:
——(Delkos): **(45)** i bc *IByz* 201 (Firatlı–Robert p. 62 no. 50) (s. *Ἀπολλώνιος*)
——(Philokterea): **(46)** 85-96 ad *IByz* 30, 10 (f. *Ῥοῦφος*)
—byzantion (nr.): **(47)** imp. Unp. (Sayar) (f. *Θεοβούλα*)
—hadrianopolis: **(48)** a. 132 ad *FD* iii (4) 102, 3 (*Διόδωρ[ος]*)
—hadrianopolis (territ.): **(49)** iii ad *IGB* iii 1834 (*Αὐρ. Δ.*)
—kellai: **(50)** 241-244 ad ib. 1517, 56 (f. *Αὐρ. Μουκιανός*)
—maroneia: **(51)** ii-i bc *IThrakAig* E212, 32 (s. *Διονύσιος*)
—mesambria: **(52)** ii bc *IGB* i^2 325, 6 (s. *Ἡ—*); **(53)** i bc ib. 315, 15 (s. *Διοσκουρίδας*); **(54)** i-ii ad ib. 343 quater
—novae: **(55)** iii ad ib. v 5259 (*Αὐρ. Διό[δω]ρος*)
—odessos: **(56)** 221 ad ib. i^2 47 bis a, 19 (f. *M. Αὐρ. Δομετιανός*); **(57)** ~ ib. l. 31 (*Αὐρ. Δ.*: s. *Ἀρτέμων*)
—pautalia: **(58)** ii-iii ad ib. iv 2073, 4 (*Διόδω[ρος]*); **(59)** 225 ad *RMD* 309 (Lat. M. Aurelius Diodorus)
——(Herakleis): **(60)** ?ii ad *IGB* iv 2077, 10 (-δο-)
—perinthos-herakleia: **(61)** hell.? *IPerinth* 63, 1 (*[Δι]όδωρος?*: s. *Λάμψις*); **(62)** i-ii ad ib. 139; **(63)** ii ad ib. 67 II, 7 (*CIL* iii 7398) (Lat. Aelius Diodorus)
—philippopolis-trimontium (territ.): **(64)** ii-iii ad *IGB* iii 1278 (*M. Αὐρ. Δ.*)
—salymbria (nr.): **(65)** ?i bc *IByz* S 47 (PM 1737) (f. *Μενίσκος*)

Διόκλεια
Thrace: **(1)** c. 125-100 bc *IG* ii^2 8904 (*FRA* 2514)

Διοκλείδας
Thrace:
—byzantion: **(1)** ii bc Schönert-Geiss, *Byzantion* 1251 (coin) (*Διοκλεί(δας)?*)

Διοκλείδης
Cimmerian Bosporos:
—pantikapaion: **(1)** i ad *CIRB* 498 (*Διο[κ]λεί[δ]ης*: f. *Πρῖμος*); **(2)** ~ ib. 508 (*Διο[κλ]είδης*)
Macedonia (Pieria):
—dion: **(3)** hell.? *AD* 26 (1971) Chron. p. 401 (*Διοκλε[ίδου], Διοκλέ[ους]?* (gen.))
Thrace:
—abdera: **(4)** iii bc Ath. 206 D; *RE* (3)

Διοκλῆς
Cimmerian Bosporos:
—gorgippia: **(1)** f. iii bc *CIRB* 1137 A I, 46; 1137 A II, 42 (s. *Ζήνων*)
Macedonia: **(2)** ?219 bc *PUG* iii 103, 11 (Tataki, *Macedonians* p. 300 no. 65; La'da E1467) (s. *Μόσχος*); **(3)** 92 bc *PTeb* 104, 35 (Tataki, *Macedonians* p. 479 no. 71); cf. La'da E1759 (*Διοκλ[ῆς]*: f. *Ἡράκλειος*)
Macedonia (Chalkidike):
—akanthos?: **(4)** imp. Robert, *OMS* 2 p. 1286 (s. *Δα—ος*)
—olynthos: **(5)** ?352 bc *TAPA* 69 (1938) p. 48 no. 3, 9, 15; Hatzopoulos, *Actes Chalc.* p. 80 (date) (s. *Χάρων*); **(6)** s. iv bc *IG* ii^2 10020 (Tataki, *Macedonians* p. 133 no. 34; *FRA* 5890) (f. *Γοργίας*)
Macedonia (Derriopos):
—stuberra: **(7)** c. 41-48 ad *IG* x (2) (2) 323, 11 (f. *Ἀπολλόδωρος*)
Macedonia (Edonis):
—amphipolis: **(8)** ?ii ad Dimitsas 905
Macedonia (Mygdonia):
—ardrolos: **(9)** i/ii ad *SEG* xlii 590 (s. *Βίθυς*)
Scythia Minor:
—istros: **(10)** iv bc Unp. (Avram, defixio) 1, 10; **(11)** i bc-i ad *ISM* i 191 I, 37 (f. *—ν*); **(12)** ~ ib. 191 II, 13 (f. *Νουμήνιος*); **(13)** s. ii ad ib. 167, 5 (f. *Ζιπᾶς*)
Skythia:
—olbia-borysthenes: **(14)** s. iv bc *SEG* l 702 III, 4
Tauris:
—chersonesos: **(15)** imp. *IOSPE* i^2 434, 2-3
Thrace:
—byzantion: **(16)** hell. *BCH* 102 (1978) p. 530 (f. *Βοστᾶς*)
—byzantion (territ.): **(17)** imp. Unp. (Sayar) (s. *Αἴσωπος*); **(18)** ?ii ad ib. (f. *Βοστᾶς*)
—byzantion?: **(19)** ?ii-i bc *IByz* 365 (*Διοκλῆος* (gen.): f. *Εὐθάκων*)
—odessos: **(20)** 215 ad *IGB* i^2 47 a, 22 (*Αὐρ. Δ.*: s. *Ἧλις*); **(21)** ~ ib. l. 26 (*Αὐρ. Δ.*: s. *Ἐπαμείνων*); **(22)** ~ ib. 47 b, 14 (*Αὐρ. Δ.*: s. *Μοσχίων*); **(23)** ~ ib. 47 c, 14 (*Αὐρ. Δ.*: s. *Μᾶρκος*)
—perinthos-herakleia: **(24)** i-ii ad *IPerinth* 214, 11 (*GVI* 1969); cf. *Tekmeria* 5 (2000) pp. 148-50 (*Διόκλειος* (gen.): f. *Δωρᾶς*)
——(Akarnanes): **(25)** iii-ii bc *IPerinth* 61, 14 (s. *Σωτηρίδης*)

Διόμανδρος
Thrace:
—apollonia-sozopolis: **(1)** s. v bc *IGB* i^2 417 (f. *Μητροβίη*)

Διομβρίων
Thrace:
—perinthos-herakleia?: **(1)** iii ad *IPerinth* 310 (*Αὐρ. Δ.*)

Διομήδης
Cimmerian Bosporos:
—myrmekion (nr.): **(1)** f. ii ad *CIRB* 892
—pantikapaion: **(2)** i ad ib. 484 (f. *Πάμφιλος, Ψυχάριον*); **(3)** ~ ib. 508 (*Διομή[δης]*); **(4)** ii ad ib. 761 (f. *Οἰνάνθη*)
—pantikapaion*: **(5)** i-ii ad ib. 598 (*[Δ]ιομήδης*: threptos)
Macedonia: **(6)** m. ii bc *BGU* 1938 B, 3 (Tataki, *Macedonians* p. 479 no. 72); cf. La'da E1675
Macedonia (Bottiaia):
—beroia: **(7)** 177 ad *IBer* 135 A, 21 (Tataki 1068) (*Πετρώνιος Δ.*)
—edessa: **(8)** iii ad *SEG* xxxix 588 (Tataki, *Edessa* 81)
Macedonia (Elimeia):
—kozani (mod.): **(9)** ii-i bc *EAM* 5 (s. *Διονύσιος*)
Macedonia (Eordaia):
—mavropigi (mod.): **(10)** ii/i bc *SEG* xxxviii 665 (s. *Ἀμμάδας*)
Macedonia (Mygdonia):
—thessalonike: **(11)** ii-iii ad *IG* x (2) (1) 381; **(12)** 141 ad ib. 137, 12; cf. *BCH* 97 (1973) p. 587 (f. *Μᾶρκος*)
—thessalonike?: **(13)** ii ad *IG* x (2) (1) 250 I, 8 (*—ϛικιανὸς Δ.*)
Macedonia (Pelagonia):
—dostoneis: **(14)** iii ad ib. x (2) (2) 201, 3 (s. *Αὐρ. Λυσίμαχος, Αὐρηλία*)
Skythia:
—olbia-borysthenes: **(15)** i ad *IOSPE* i^2 182

Thrace:
—Apollonia-Sozopolis: **(16)** v/iv BC *IGB* I² 446 ([Διο]μήδης?, [Εὐ]μήδης?: f. Ἑκαταῖος)
—Geloupara: **(17)** 202 AD ib. III 1690 c, 31 (and Thrace Pizos: I f. Διομήδης II); **(18)** ~ ib. l. 31 (and Thrace Pizos: II s. Διομήδης I)
—Montana: **(19)** ii/iii AD *CIL* III 7445 (*Montana* II 31) (Lat. Diomedes: f. Apoll–)
—Montana (territ.): **(20)** ii/iii AD *Romanizmăt* II 247 (Lat. Diomedes)
—Nicopolis ad Istrum: **(21)** iii AD *IGB* II 691 (f. Αὐρ. Ὀνησίων)

Δίοννος
Tauris:
—Chersonesos (territ.): **(1)** iv-iii BC Solomonik, *GChKh* p. 7 no. 4

Διονύννης
Thrace:
—Perinthos-Herakleia: **(1)** v/iv BC *IPerinth* 140 (Διονυννέω (gen.): f. Ἡρογείτων)

Διονυος?
Macedonia (Lynkestis):
—Herakleia (area): **(1)** 286 AD *IG* X (2) (2) 18 C (Διονύ(σι)ος?, Διονῦ<ο>ς?: f. Φίλητος)

Διονῦς
Macedonia (Derriopos):
—Stuberra: **(1)** 74 AD ib. 326, 36 (s. Νάσων)
Macedonia (Paionia):
—Kavadarci (mod.): **(2)** imp. *Sp.* 98 (1941-8) p. 76 no. 162 (f. Γάϊος)
Macedonia (Pelagonia): **(3)** ii AD *IG* X (2) (2) 248 (I f. Διονῦς II); **(4)** ~ ib. (II s. Διονῦς I, f. Διονῦς III); **(5)** ~ ib. (III s. Διονῦς II, f. Διονῦς IV); **(6)** ~ ib. (IV s. Διονῦς III, f. Γάϊος)
Scythia Minor:
—Tomis: **(7)** ii-iii AD *ISM* II 160 (Lat. Dionus, Dionus(ius)—ed.)
—Tomis [nr.]:
——Vicus Clementiani: **(8)** ii/iii AD ib. (*CCCA* VI 454; *Eastern cults* p. 79 no. 14) (Lat. Aur. Dionus)
Thrace:
—Apollonia-Sozopolis?: **(9)** iv BC *IGB* I² 479 (f. Ἀρήτη)
—Odessos: **(10)** 215 AD ib. 47 b, 27 (Αὐρ. Δ.: s. Ἀσκληπιάδης)

Διονυσᾶς
Macedonia (Bottiaia):
—Beroia: **(1)** i-ii AD *IBer* 335, 3 (Κορνήλιος Δ.)
——Blaganoi*: **(2)** 189 AD *SEG* XXXVII 590, 8 (Tataki 391) (f. Κλεοπάτρα)
Macedonia (Pieria):
—Dion: **(3)** ii-iii AD Dimitsas 174 (Ἐρέννιος Δ.: f. Διονυσόδωρος)
Tauris:
—Chersonesos: **(4)** iv BC Solomonik, *GAKh* 624 (*SEG* XXXVIII 749. 15 (vase)) (Διονυ(σ)ᾶς)
Thrace:
—Abdera: **(5)** c. 395-360 BC May, *Abdera* pp. 213-14 nos. 287-92 (coin); **(6)** c. 336-311 BC ib. p. 292 nos. 535-8 (coin) (Διονυσᾶδος (gen.)); **(7)** iii BC *AMNG* II (1) 230 (coin); **(8)** c. 230-200 BC *BCH* 45 (1921) p. 18 III, 88, 90 (s. Διονυσόδωρος, f. Εὔφαντος: locn.—Oulhen)
——(Eurysthenidai): **(9)** s. iv BC *SEG* XLVI 841 (*IThrakAig* E16) (Διονυσᾶδος (gen.): f. Ἑρμῶναξ)
—Abdera?: **(10)** s. iv BC ib. E42 (Διονυσᾶδος (gen.))
—Maroneia: **(11)** c. 230-200 BC *BCH* 45 (1921) p. 18 III, 92 (f. Ἄκεστος, Καλλικρατίδης, Ἐπίγονος)

Διονύσερμος
Skythia:
—Olbia-Borysthenes: **(1)** iv BC *IOSPE* I² 216 (Διονύσερμ[ος]?)

Διονυσία
Macedonia (Bottiaia):
—Beroia: **(1)** ii AD *IBer* 222 (Tataki 392); **(2)** ~ *IBer* 223 (Tataki 818) (Λονγιν[ία] Δ.); **(3)** 240 AD *IBer* 51, 2 (Tataki 762) (Κορνηλία Δ.); **(4)** 309 or 311 AD *ILeukopetra* 116, 2 (Tataki 259) (Αὐρ. Δ.: d. Ἀλέξανδρος)
—Beroia*: **(5)** s. ii AD *IBer* 334 (Tataki 1136) (Ποειμιλλιανὴ Δ.: freed.)
Macedonia (Chalkidike):
—Anthemous: **(6)** iii AD *SEG* XLII 571 (Αὐρ. Δ.: m. Αὐρ. Διονύσιος, Αὐρ. Ἀθηνόδωρος, Αὐρ. Νικόβουλος)
—Moni Vatopediou (mod.): **(7)** 203 AD Dimitsas 781, 1 (d. Διονύσιος)
—Potidaia-Kassandreia (nr.): **(8)** 253 AD *SEG* XXXVIII 599, 3 (Αὐρ. Δ.: d. Αὐρ. Πέρινθος, Αὐρ. Διονυσοδώρα)
—Singos (nr.): **(9)** 180 AD ib. XXIX 593, 4 (m. Ζώπυρος, Ὀλυμπιάς)
Macedonia (Edonis):
—Amphipolis: **(10)** v-vi AD Feissel, *RICM* 216 ([Δ]ονυσία)
Macedonia (Mygdonia):
—Lete (nr.): **(11)** ii-iii AD *AD* 2 (1916) Parart. p. 12
—Thessalonike: **(12)** ii-i BC *IG* X (2) (1) 77, 8 (d. Φιλωτέρα); **(13)** s. i AD ib. 73 (Ἀντωνία Δ.); **(14)** ?ii AD ib. 568 (Φλ. Δ.); **(15)** ii/iii AD *SEG* XLIX 814 II, 9 (Τερεντία Δ.); **(16)** iii AD *IG* X (2) (1) 445, 7 (Φουσκιανὴ Δ.: d. Λ. Ἀρίστων, Φουσκιανὴ Ἐλευθέριν); **(17)** ?iv AD *AEMTh* 15 (2001) p. 326
—Thessalonike?: **(18)** ii AD *IG* X (2) (1) 269 (—ία Δ.); **(19)** ii-iii AD ib. 724 (*KGAM Thess.* I 131) (m. Ἀρτεμίδωρος); **(20)** iii AD *IG* X (2) (1) 771, 4 (d. Φλ. Σεκούνδιλλα); **(21)** ~ ib. 841 (Βαιβία Δ.: ?m. Ἀγαθίας, Ὀνήσιμος); **(22)** ~ ib. 859, 4 (m. Μέμμιος, Δημοκράτης); **(23)** ~ ib. l. 8 (Διον(υ)σία)
Macedonia (Paionia):
—Bylazora: **(24)** iii AD *JÖAI* 6 (1903) Beibl. col. 3 no. 2 (*Sp.* 71 (1931) p. 25 no. 48, 5-6) (Αὐρ. Δ.: ?d. Μ. Αὐρ. Διονύσιος, Ποβλ. Μακεδονία)
—Negotino (mod.): **(25)** iii AD *SEG* XXXVIII 714 (Διον[υσία]: m. Μακεδών, Δημήτριος, —δης)
Scythia Minor:
—Istros (nr.): **(26)** ii AD *ISM* I 371, 2 (*CIL* III 7528) (Lat. Ael. Dionysia)
Skythia:
—Tyras: **(27)** ii AD *IOSPE* I² 11 (Δ. Πία)
Thrace:
—Byzantion: **(28)** ii/i BC *IByz* 255 (Fıratlı–Robert p. 71 no. 73) (d. Νεμέριος); **(29)** i BC *IByz* 204 (Fıratlı–Robert p. 63 no. 53) (d. Μᾶτρις)
—Heraion Teichos?: **(30)** ii BC Taşlıklıoğlu I p. 4 no. 1 (d. Δημήτριος, m. Γλύκιννα)
—Maroneia: **(31)** f. ii BC *BCH* 66-7 (1942-3) p. 197 no. 1 (*IThrakAig* E258) ([Διο]νυσία: d. Ἀπολλόδωρος, Κλεοπάτρα); **(32)** i AD *SEG* XXVII 343, 3 (*IThrakAig* E302) (d. Μελανιππίδης)
—Novae: **(33)** s. ii AD *IGLNovae* 91 (*ILB* 317) (Lat. Aelia Dionysia: m. Aelia Publia)
—Perinthos-Herakleia (nr.): **(34)** iii AD *IPerinth* 283 (Αὐρ. Δ.)
—Philippopolis-Trimontium: **(35)** 294 AD *Cod. Just.* V 16. 19; cf. *Klio* 58 (1976) p. 80 (Lat. Dionysia)

Διονυσιανός
Macedonia (Bottiaia):
—Beroia: **(1)** f. iii AD *IBer* 95, 2; 96, 2 (Tataki 279) (Αὐρ. Διονυσιανὸς Μαρκελλιανὸς Βάσσος: II s. Αὐρ. Διονυσιανὸς I Μάρκελλος, Ἀκουτία Ῥαβωνία); **(2)** ~ *IBer* 95, 4; 96, 5 (Tataki 281) (Αὐρ. Διονυσιανὸς Μάρκελλος: I f. Αὐρ. Διονυσιανὸς II Μαρκελλιανὸς Βάσσος, Αὐρ. Διονυσιανὸς III Μαρκελλιανὸς Μάρκελλος); **(3)** ~ *IBer* 96, 10 (Tataki 280) (Αὐρ. Διονυσιανὸς Μαρκελλιανὸς Μάρκελλος: III s. Αὐρ. Διονυσιανὸς I Μάρκελλος, Ἀκουτία Ῥαβωνία)
Macedonia (Edonis):
—Amphipolis: **(4)** ii-iii AD *AEp* 1916, no. 49 (Lat. Aur. Dionysianus)

Διονυσιάς
Macedonia (Mygdonia):
—Thessalonike?: **(1)** ii-iii AD *IG* X (2) (1) 261, 6, 9

Διονυσίδης
Thrace:
—Anchialos (territ.): **(1)** ii-iii AD *IGB* I² 385, 3 (s. Πρ—)

Διονυσίδωρος
Cimmerian Bosporos:
—Pantikapaion (nr.): **(1)** ii AD *CIRB* 963 (s. Μακάριος)
Macedonia (Chalkidike):
—Polichne?: **(2)** ?353 BC *SEG* XXXVII 576, 18 (f. Πόλυς)

Διονυσικλῆς
Thrace:
—Maroneia: **(1)** ii AD *IG* XII (8) 220, 14 (f. Σει—)

Διονυσιόδωρος
Skythia:
—Olbia-Borysthenes: **(1)** c. 150-175 AD *IOSPE* I² 132, 9; 176, 5; *VDI* 1953 (4), p. 130, 10; cf. *SEG* XLII 713 (s. Ἔρως)

Διονύσιος
Cimmerian Bosporos:
—Bosporos: **(1)** imp. *CIRB* 1235 (f. Πολύκαιρος)
—Gorgippia: **(2)** f. iii BC ib. 1137 A I, 4 (f. Δίων); **(3)** ~ ib. l. 13 (s. Εὐπόλεμος); **(4)** ~ ib. l. 20 (s. Ἀπολλώνιος); **(5)** ~ ib. l. 30; 1137 B I, 50 (s. Ἀρτεμίδωρος); **(6)** ~ ib. 1137 A I, 45; 1137 A II, 41 (f. Ἡγησίλοχος); **(7)** ~ ib. l. 7 (f. Ἀγησίλας); **(8)** ~ ib. l. 31 (f. Κόδρος); **(9)** ~ ib. l. 38 (s. Λύσανδρος); **(10)** ~ ib. 1137 B I, 9 (f. —ιδίας); **(11)** ~ ib. l. 12 (f. Ἀπολλώνιος); **(12)** ~ ib. l. 25 (f. —δωρος); **(13)** ~ ib. l. 30 (f. —μαχος); **(14)** ~ ib. l. 41 (I f. Διονύσιος II); **(15)** ~ ib. l. 41 (II s. Διονύσιος I); **(16)** ~ ib. l. 47; 1137 B II, 33 (s. Καλλίμαχος); **(17)** 173-210 AD ib. 1135, 21 (s. Χαδι—); **(18)** ~ ib. l. 22 (s. Ζαζζοῦς); **(19)** ~ ib. l. 26 (Δ[ιονύ]σιος: f. Πόθος)
—Hermonassa: **(20)** iv BC ib. 1056 II, 16 (s. Ἀγυαῖος)
—Myrmekion: **(21)** iii BC ib. 876 (Δι[ο]νύ[σι]ος: f. Ματερίνη)
—Nymphaion: **(22)** iii BC ib. 912 I, 7 (f. Μοσχίων)
—Pantikapaion: **(23)** iv BC ib. 177 (f. Δημοφῶν); **(24)** iii BC ib. 110, 4 (s. Δι—); **(25)** ~ Rostovtsev, *ADZh* p. 143 (vase) (Διονύ(σιος)?); **(26)** i BC/i AD *CIRB* 307; cf. KW pl. 43 no. 622 (Διονύ[σιος]: I f. Διονύσιος II); **(27)** ~ *CIRB* 307; cf. KW pl. 43 no. 622 (Διονύ[σιος]: II s. Διονύσιος I); **(28)** i AD *CIRB* 326; **(29)** ~ ib. 390; cf. KW pl. 24 no. 349 (s. Λάμαχος); **(30)** ~ *CIRB* 391 (s. Νίκανδρος); **(31)** ?i AD ib. 453; cf. KW pl. 46 no. 651 (f. Λυσίμαχος); **(32)** f. i AD *CIRB* 554; cf. KW pl. 20 no. 287; **(33)** ~ *CIRB* 560; **(34)** m. i AD ib. 430 (Διον(ύ)σιος: f. Καλλιγένης); **(35)** s. i AD ib. 393 B; cf. KW pl. 43 no. 624 (s. Διόφαντος); **(36)** ii AD *CIRB* 667 A; 667 B (Δυ-: s. Νίκανδρος, f. Ἀριστείδης); **(37)** ~ ib. 795 (I f. Διονύσιος II) ?= (*40*); **(38)** ~ ib. (II s. Διονύσιος I, Κολία); **(39)** f. ii AD ib. 88, 5 (s. Μύρμηξ); **(40)** ~ ib. 682 (f. Ἰάμβλοχος) ?= (*37*); **(41)** ~ ib. 700 (I f. Διονύσιος II); **(42)** ~ ib. (II s. Διονύσιος

I, f. *Πάτεις*); **(43)** 127 AD ib. 61, 4 (f. *Ἑρμων*); **(44)** 221 AD ib. 100, 3; **(45)** 275-278 AD ib. 36, 66 (*Διονύσ(ιος)*: f. *Μοκκοῦς*); **(46)** ~ ib. l. 71 (*Διονύσ(ιος)*: f. *Παγα.*); **(47)** ~ ib. l. 76 (*Διον[ύ]σ[ιος]*)

—PANTIKAPAION (NR.): **(48)** ii AD ib. 964 (*Διον<ι>ύσ(ιος)*?: f. *Ἀσσα—*)

—PANTIKAPAION*: **(49)** hell.-imp. *IAK* 25 (1907) p. 62 no. 197 (vase) (*Διονύσι[ος]*)

—PHANAGOREIA: **(50)** i AD *CIRB* 987, 5; **(51)** ii AD ib. 990, 3 (*Διονύσ[ιος]*); **(52)** ~ ib. l. 4 (*[Διον]ύσιο[ς]*)

—PHANAGOREIA*: **(53)** 16 AD ib. 985, 7 (Levinskaya pp. 236-7 no. 5) (*Δ. ὁ καὶ Λογγίων*: threptos)

—ZENONOS CHERSONESOS*: **(54)** ii AD *Drev. Bosp.* 2 p. 195 no. 3 (*[Δ]ιονύσιος*)

KOLCHIS:

—PICHVNARI (MOD.): **(55)** f. iv BC *Anat. Stud.* 51 (2001) p. 78 (vase) (s. *Λεωδάμας*)

MACEDONIA: **(56)** 314-307 BC *RE* (48) (Tataki, *Macedonians* p. 300 no. 68); **(57)** iii BC *IG* XII (9) 796 (Tataki, *Macedonians* p. 300 no. 67); **(58)** ?s. iii BC *Syringes* 222 (Tataki, *Macedonians* p. 301 no. 72); cf. La'da E1580 (*[Διο]νύσ[ιος]*: f. *Φιλῖνος*); **(59)** c. 244-242 BC *PPetr* III 54 b fr. 3, 4 (unp.) (La'da E1476); **(60)** c. 235-200 BC ib. E1750 (s. *Μενέλαος*: t.e.); **(61)** 232 or 207 BC *CPR* XVIII 25, 54, 58 (Tataki, *Macedonians* p. 301 no. 70; La'da E1749) (s. *Ἀα...τ̣ο̣υ̣* (gen.): t.e.); **(62)** 221 BC *PEnt* 88, 1 (Tataki, *Macedonians* p. 302 no. 73); cf. La'da E1670 (*Διο[ν]ύσ[ι]ος*: f. *—π̣ι̣ε̣..*); **(63)** m. ii BC *BGU* 1938 B, 8 (Tataki, *Macedonians* p. 481 no. 89); cf. La'da E1676 (*[Δι]ονύσιος*); **(64)** ~ *BGU* 1939 A, 6 (Tataki, *Macedonians* p. 480 no. 81; La'da E1474) (s. *Πολυκράτης*); **(65)** 173 BC *PGiss* 2 I, 9-10 (Tataki, *Macedonians* p. 300 no. 66; La'da E1477) (f. *Ὀλυμπιάς*); **(66)** 159-101 BC *PTeb* 106, 6 (Tataki, *Macedonians* p. 481 no. 88); cf. La'da E1534 (*Δ. ὁ καὶ Πετοσῖρις*: f. *Μάρων ὁ καὶ Νέκσαφθις*); **(67)** 137 BC *Arch. Pap.* 47 (2001) p. 61 B, 1; cf. La'da 1503 (f. *Ἡράκλειος*); **(68)** a. 132 BC *PKöln* 366, 1; cf. La'da E1457 (f. *Δημήτριος*); **(69)** 112 BC *PTeb* 31, [3], 9, 11, 16 (Tataki, *Macedonians* p. 480 no. 85); cf. La'da E1470 (I f. *Διονύσιος* II); **(70)** ~ *PTeb* 31, [3], 9-10, 15 (Tataki, *Macedonians* p. 479 no. 75; La'da E1470) (II s. *Διονύσιος* I); **(71)** 110-107 BC *PDion* 14, [30], 42; 15, 29, 41; 18, [29], 49 (Tataki, *Macedonians* p. 480 no. 82; La'da E1475) (s. *Πτολεμαῖος*); **(72)** 108-105 BC *PDion* 17, 32; 19, 28 (La'da E1468) (s. *Ἀπολλώνιος*); **(73)** b. 50 BC *BGU* 1831, 4 (La'da E1471) (II s. *Διονύσιος* I: katoikos) ?= (*78*); **(74)** 92 BC *PTeb* 104, 34, 46 (Tataki, *Macedonians* p. 479 no. 78; La'da E1748) (s. *Ἑρμαΐσκος*: t.e.); **(75)** ~ *PTeb* 104, 34, 46 (Tataki, *Macedonians* p. 480 no. 80; La'da E1751) (s. *Πάτρων*: t.e.); **(76)** ~ *PTeb* 104, 35 (Tataki, *Macedonians* p. 480 no. 86); cf. La'da E1747 (I f. *Διονύσιος* II); **(77)** ~ *PTeb* 104, 35, 47 (Tataki, *Macedonians* p. 479 no. 77; La'da E1747) (II s. *Διονύσιος*: t.e.); **(78)** 80-30 BC *BGU* 1733, 1, 4-5, 9-10, 12, 18, 20, 24 (Tataki, *Macedonians* p. 479 no. 76; La'da E1472) (II s. *Διονύσιος* I: katoikos) ?= (*73*); **(79)** ~ *BGU* 1733, 4-5 (Tataki, *Macedonians* p. 480 no. 87); cf. La'da E1472 (I f. *Διονύσιος* II) ?= (*84*); **(80)** 74 BC *SB* 7532, 26, 36 (Tataki, *Macedonians* p. 480 no. 79; La'da E1473) (s. *Ἰσίδωρος*); **(81)** 73 BC *POxy* 3482, 3, 7-8, 11, 14, 16 etc. (Tataki, *Macedonians* p. 479 no. 74; La'da E1469) (s. *Ἀπολλώνιος*: katoikos); **(82)** 63 BC *POxy* 1644, 5 (Tataki, *Macedonians* p. 480 no. 83); cf. La'da E1420; E1570; E1595 (f. *Πασίων, Πτολεμαῖος, Ἀπολλώνιος, Βερενίκη*); **(83)** 54 BC *PSI* 1097, 1 (Tataki, *Macedonians* p. 480 no. 84); cf. La'da E1447 (f. *Ἀσκληπιάδης*); **(84)** 51 BC *BGU* 1831, 4; cf. La'da E1471 (I f. *Διονύσιος* II) ?= (*79*); **(85)** ?s. i BC *ZPE* 136 (2001) pp. 134-5 no. 16, 3; cf. La'da E1621 (f. *Σεραπίων*); **(86)** 19 BC *POxy* 277, 1, 9-11 (Tataki, *Macedonians* p. 479 no. 73) (s. *Ἀλέξανδρος*); **(87)** 12 AD *PKöln* 227 B, 16, 22 (II s. *Διονύσιος* I, f. *Διονύσιος* III); **(88)** ~ ib. l. 16, 22, 26 (III s. *Διονύσιος* II, *Θάσιον*); **(89)** ~ ib. l. 22 (*Δ̣ιο̣νύσ̣(ιος)*: I s. *Ζωΐλος*, f. *Διονύσιος* II)

—RESEN (MOD.): **(90)** iii AD *IG* X (2) (2) 49 (*Αἴλιος Διονύσι[ος]*)

MACEDONIA?:

—HERAKLEIA: **(91)** m. iv BC *Philippi* p. 74 fig. 58 (Pilhofer 379a) (f. *Δημητρία*)

MACEDONIA (BOTTIAIA):

—AIGAI?: **(92)** i AD *IG* XII (8) 206, 12 (Tataki, *Macedonians* p. 40 no. 7)

—BEROIA: **(93)** 223 BC *IBer* 4, 24 (s. *Δερκυλίδης*); **(94)** f. ii BC ib. 156 (Tataki 406) (f. *Σεύθης*); **(95)** s. ii BC *IBer* 24, 3 (Tataki 402) (f. *Ἀριστόνους*); **(96)** ~ *IBer* 203 (Tataki 401) (s. *Πάνταυχος*); **(97)** ?i BC *IBer* 507 (Tataki 405) (f. *Φίλιννα*); **(98)** f. i AD *IBer* 103, 7 (Tataki 403) (f. *Δημήτριος*); **(99)** ii AD *IBer* 225, 2 (*Διονύσι[ος]*?: f. *Μαρ—*); **(100)** ~ ib. 300 (Tataki 200) (s. *Κάσσανδρος*); **(101)** ~ *IBer* 397, 1 (Tataki 393) (f. *Σ—*); **(102)** ?171-208 AD *ILeukopetra* 130, 1 (f. *Δημήτριος*); **(103)** ii/iii AD *IBer* 143 A, 4 (Tataki 399) (s. *Γάϊος*); **(104)** ~ *IBer* 143 B, 18 (Tataki 397) (s. *Ἀγοραῖος*); **(105)** ~ *IBer* 144 B, 5 (Tataki 404) (f. *Ζωΐλος*); **(106)** ~ *IBer* 145, 3 (Tataki 1098) (*Ποπίλλιος Δ.*); **(107)** 195 AD *ILeukopetra* 43, 16 (Tataki 394); **(108)** f. iii AD *IBer* 267, 3 (Tataki 395) (s. *Εὐκτήμων, Νίκη*)

—BEROIA?: **(109)** 38 BC Robert, *Coll. Froehner* 44, 19 (*IG* XII Suppl. p. 149); cf. Tataki, *Macedonians* p. 78 no. 23 (s. *Ἀρχέπολις*); **(110)** 210 AD *ILeukopetra* 55, 1 (f. *Ἄφδαλος*)

—BEROIA*: **(111)** 254 AD ib. 109, 3 (freed.)

—EDESSA: **(112)** ii AD *BSA* 58 (1963) p. 24 no. 6 (Tataki, *Edessa* 82); **(113)** 229 AD ib. 51 (*Αὐρ. Δ.*); **(114)** v-vi AD Feissel, *RICM* 26

—KYRRHOS: **(115)** ii AD *IG* II² 9140 (Tataki, *Macedonians* p. 116 no. 3; *FRA* 3157) (f. *Ἡδίστη*); **(116)** 199 AD *ILeukopetra* 45, 2 (Tataki, *Macedonians* p. 116 no. 2) (s. *Ἐνθαδίων*, f. *Ἰουλία*)

—PELLA: **(117)** iv BC *BSA* 41 (1940-45) p. 114 no. 26 (s. *Μεγακλῆς*); **(118)** ~ Arr., *An.* ii 12. 2 (Tataki, *Macedonians* p. 154 no. 38) (f. *Μένης*); **(119)** s. iv BC *Α΄ Panell. Synedr. Epigr.* p. 179 no. 4 (*SEG* XXX 583) (f. *Σωστράτη*); **(120)** f. i BC ib. XLVII 933

—SKYDRA: **(121)** iii AD Dimitsas 126, 4 (*Αὐρ. Δ.*)

MACEDONIA (CHALKIDIKE):

—ANTHEMOUS: **(122)** ii BC *SEG* XLII 560 (s. *Τράλις*); **(123)** iii AD ib. 571 (*Αὐρ. Δ.*: s. *Αὐρ. Πρόκλος, Αὐρ. Διονυσία*)

—APHYTIS: **(124)** ?351 BC *Α΄ Panell. Synedr. Epigr.* pp. 80-1, 5, 13, 18 (s. *Κατάστασις*)

—MONI VATOPEDIOU (MOD.): **(125)** 203 AD Dimitsas 781, 1-2 (f. *Διονυσία*)

—OLYNTHOS: **(126)** ?iv BC *FGrH* 70 F 98 (Tataki, *Macedonians* p. 133 no. 36); **(127)** f. iv BC *Olynthus* 5 p. 262 no. 1109 (vase); **(128)** ?352 BC *TAPA* 65 (1934) p. 128 no. 4, 4; Hatzopoulos, *Actes Chalc.* p. 80 (date) (*Διο̣νύσιος*: s. *Ἴθύρας*); **(129)** 350 BC *SEG* XXXIX 617 (s. *Στράτων*); **(130)** ?iv/iii BC *Syringes* 6 (Tataki, *Macedonians* p. 133 no. 35; La'da E1925)

—POLICHNE?: **(131)** ?353 BC *SEG* XXXVII 576, 17 (s. *Ξένων*)

—POTIDAIA-KASSANDREIA: **(132)** inc. *Suda B* 279 (Tataki, *Macedonians* p. 88 no. 24) (tyrant); **(133)** iii BC *IG* II² 8997 (Tataki, *Macedonians* p. 88 no. 26; *FRA* 2782) (f. *Ἄρχιον*); **(134)** ~ *IG* II² 9001 (Tataki, *Macedonians* p. 88 no. 28; *FRA* 2783) (f. *Σωσίβιος*); **(135)** iii/ii BC *AA* 1932, p. 155 no. 4 (Tataki, *Macedonians* p. 88 no. 27) (f. *Βάκχιος*); **(136)** ~ *IG* XI (4) 1216; 1228, 3, 14; 1229, 3, 14 (Tataki, *Macedonians* p. 88 no. 25) (s. *Νουμήνιος*)

—STOLOS?: **(137)** ?351 BC *SEG* XXXVIII 672, 8, 16 (f. *Ἕρμων*); **(138)** ~ ib. l. 9 (s. *Κτήσων*); **(139)** ~ ib. l. 13 (f. *Χορόνικος, Εὐβουλίδης, Θεόδωρος*); **(140)** ~ ib. 673, 5, 8 (s. *Ἀννίκας*)

—TORONE: **(141)** ?353 BC ib. XXIV 574, 9; Hatzopoulos, *Actes Chalc.* p. 80 (date) (s. *Ἀντιφῶν*)

MACEDONIA (DERRIOPOS): **(142)** ii AD *IG* X (2) (2) 304; **(143)** ii-iii AD ib. 317 (f. *Γαϊανός*); **(144)** f. ii AD ib. 305 (*Φ. Δ.*: s. *Τ. Φ. Ὑγῖνος*)

—STUBERRA: **(145)** 74 AD ib. 325, 37 (s. *Γάϊος*); **(146)** ~ ib. l. 50 (s. *Παράμονος*); **(147)** ~ ib. l. 53 (s. *Σώπατρος*); **(148)** ~ ib. l. 60 (f. *Ζωΐλος*); **(149)** ~ ib. 326, 18 (s. *Ὀρέστης*); **(150)** ~ ib. l. 19 (f. *Ὀρέστης*); **(151)** ~ ib. l. 40 (I f. *Διονύσιος* II); **(152)** ~ ib. l. 44 (f. *Καλλέας*); **(153)** ~ ib. l. 51 (s. *Παράμονος*); **(154)** ~ ib. l. 39-40 (II s. *Διονύσιος* I); **(155)** ~ ib. l. 44-5 (f. *Κεφάλων*); **(156)** 74-116 AD ib. 325, 22; 327, 6-7 (s. *Ζώανδρος*, f. *Μάξιμος*); **(157)** 90 AD ib. 326, 75 (f. *Παράμονος*); **(158)** 107 AD ib. 325, 102 (f. *Λογισμός*); **(159)** 116 AD ib. 327, 22 (f. *Ὀρέστης*); **(160)** 119 AD ib. 294 (f. *Φρόντων*); **(161)** ~ ib. (s. *Φρόντων*)

MACEDONIA (EDONIS):

—AMPHIPOLIS: **(162)** a. 357 BC Hatzopoulos, *Actes Amphipolis* p. 34 no. 6, 9; **(163)** ~ ib. pp. 38-9 no. 7, 19 (*Διονύ(σ)ιος*); **(164)** s. iv BC *AD* 24 (1969) Chron. p. 355 no. 1 (s. *Πάπας*); **(165)** hell. *AEMTh* 6 (1992) p. 552 (f. *Ζώπυρος*); **(166)** ~ *AD* 24 (1969) Chron. p. 355 no. 4 (f. *Ἀριστώ*); **(167)** ~ Dimitsas 852 (f. *Ἄδμητος*); **(168)** c. 321-306 BC *IG* XII (6) 19, 2, 12 (Tataki, *Macedonians* p. 50 no. 43) (s. *Λ.......ης*) ?= (*286*); **(169)** iii BC *PAE* 1985, p. 74 (*SEG* XLVIII 719) (f. *Μόσχος*); **(170)** b. 213 BC Hatzopoulos, *MI* 2 p. 83 no. 61, 9 (*SEG* XLVI 715) (f. *Ἀντίοχος*); **(171)** 242 BC ib. XII 373, 33 (Tataki, *Macedonians* p. 50 no. 41) (s. *Ἐπιγένης*); **(172)** f. ii BC *AD* 26 (1971) Chron. p. 417 (f. *Μοιροφάνης*); **(173)** hell.-imp. *RA* 1945, p. 48 no. 2 (*Διο[νύσ]ιος*: f. *Νικώ*); **(174)** 157 AD Dimitsas 863 (f. *Τόρκος*); **(175)** 165 AD *SEG* XLIX 676 (f. *Ἡλιόδωρος, Ἀμμιώ*)

—AMPHIPOLIS?: **(176)** ii BC ib. XLVII 886; cf. *BE* 1998, no. 277 (f. *Ζησώ*)

—AMPHIPOLIS (TERRIT.)?: **(177)** 223 AD *BCH* 24 (1900) p. 308 (Pilhofer 593) (*[Διο]νύσιος*: f. *Μάντας*)

—AMPHIPOLIS*: **(178)** ii/i BC *Kat. gr. rim. terakota* pp. 93; 99 nos. 45-6 (terracotta) (*Διονύ[σι]ος*); **(179)** 37 BC Robert, *Coll. Froehner* 44, 12; *Ancient Macedonia* 5 p. 1471 (name) (Tataki, *Macedonians* p. 50 no. 42) (freed.)

—PHILIPPOI: **(180)** ii AD *BCH* 56 (1932) p. 226 no. 17 (Pilhofer 81) (*Λ. Βάσσιος Διονύσι[ος]*, *Λ. Βάσσιος Διονυσί[ου]*—ed.); **(181)** ii/iii AD *CIL* III 633 IV b, 3 (Pilhofer 166); cf. *AM* 33 (1908) p. 40 (Lat. Dionysi (gen.?), Dionysid(orus)?—Fredrich)

—PHILIPPOI (DRAMA (MOD.)): **(182)** i-ii AD *AD* 51 (1996) Chron. p. 577, 6 (Lat. C. Iunius Dionisius)

—PHILIPPOI (TERRIT.)?: **(183)** hell.? *SEG* XXXV 746 (Pilhofer 577) (s. *Φίλιππος*)

MACEDONIA (ELIMEIA):

—KOZANI (MOD.): **(184)** ii-i BC *EAM* 5 (f. *Διομήδης*)

—VELVENDOS (MOD.): **(185)** ii AD *SEG* XLVII 1001, 5 (s. *Ζω—*)

MACEDONIA (EORDAIA): **(186)** imp. Dimitsas 288 (s. *Μακεδών, Φιλωτέρα*)

MACEDONIA (LYNKESTIS):

—HERAKLEIA: **(187)** imp. *IG* X (2) (2) 100 (*Διονύ[σιος]*?); **(188)** ii-iii AD ib. 83 (*Αὐρήλιος Δ.*)

—HERAKLEIA (AREA): **(189)** ii AD ib. 21 (f. *Ἀντίγονος*); **(190)** ~ ib. 22 (f. *Γάϊος*); **(191)** ?ii-iii AD ib. 40 (f. *Ἀλέξανδρος*)

MACEDONIA (MYGDONIA):

—CHARAKOMA?: **(192)** imp. *SEG* XXIX 582

—KALINDOIA: **(193)** 68-98 AD ib. XLII 580, 36 (f. *Νίκων*); **(194)** ~ ib. l. 48 (f. *Λούκιος*); **(195)** a. 98 AD ib. 582, 10 (s. *Ὀρτᾶς*); **(196)** ~ ib. l. 51 (f. *Μητρᾶς*); **(197)** ~ ib. l. 54 (I f. *Διονύσιος* II); **(198)** ~ ib. l. 54 (II s. *Διονύσιος* I); **(199)** ~ ib. 583, 19 (f. *Ταρούλας*)

—LETE: **(200)** ii AD *Makedonika* 2 (1951) p. 619 no. 42 *θ*, 4 (f. *Λᾶνδρος*)

—SOCHOS (MOD.): **(201)** ii AD Dimitsas 740, 1 (f. *Εὐδαίμων*)

—THESSALONIKE: **(202)** s. iii BC *IG* X (2) (1) 75 (f. *Ἑκαταῖος*); **(203)** 121-108 BC *FD* III (1) 577, 1 (Tataki, *Macedonians* p. 181 no. 24) (I f. *Διονύσιος* II); **(204)** ~ *FD* III (1) 577, 1 (Tataki, *Macedonians* p. 181 no. 23) (II s. *Διονύσιος* I); **(205)** i BC-i AD *IG* X (2) (1) 99 (f. *Παρμενίων*); **(206)** imp. *Tekmeria* 7 (2002) p. 92 no. 3; **(207)** 27 BC-14 AD *IG* X (2) (1) 31, 23; **(208)** ?i AD ib. 128, 6 ([*Διο*]*νύσιος*); **(209)** i AD ib. 259, 33 (f. (nat.) *Στράτων*); **(210)** ?i AD *SEG* XXXVIII 701 (*Ἀτέριος Δ.*); **(211)** i-ii AD *IG* X (2) (1) 243 I, 2 ([*Ρ*]*ουτίλιος Δ.*); **(212)** ~ ib. 243 II, 11 (f. *Ἀμύντας*); **(213)** f. i AD ib. 133, 8; Robert, *OMS* 5 pp. 295-302 (date) (s. *—ων*); **(214)** s. i AD *IG* X (2) (1) 68, 23; 69, 17 (*Δ. ὁ καὶ Γέμινος*: s. *Κλεοπάτρα*); **(215)** ~ ib. l. 9 (*Τ. Φλ. Δ.*); **(216)** ~ ib. l. 35 (-*σει*-: f. *Δημήτριος*); **(217)** ii AD ib. 241 A II, 21 ([*Ιο*]*ύλ. Δ.*); **(218)** ~ ib. 425; **(219)** ~ ib. 426 (s. *Διονύσις*); **(220)** ~ ib. 456, 5 (s. *Εὐτυχία*); **(221)** ~ *SEG* XXXVI 645; *KGAM Thess.* I 59 (date) (I f. *Διονύσιος* II *ὁ καὶ Λογγῖνος*); **(222)** ~ *SEG* XXXVI 645; *KGAM Thess.* I 59 (date) (*Δ. ὁ καὶ Λογγῖνος*: II s. *Διονύσιος* I); **(223)** ii-iii AD *IG* X (2) (1) 348 (f. *Θεοδώρα*); **(224)** ~ *SEG* L 642 (*Φλ. Δ.*: I f. *Φλ. Διονύσιος* II); **(225)** ~ ib. (*Φλ. Δ.*: II s. *Φλ. Διονύσιος* I, *Τυχαροῦς*); **(226)** s. ii AD *IG* X (2) (1) 244 I, 15 (f. *Ἀλέξανδρος*); **(227)** iii AD ib. 662 (*Αἰλ. Δ.*); **(228)** f. iii AD ib. 190, 5; 191, 6 (*Μινίκιος Δ.*); **(229)** m. iii AD ib. 212-13 (*Μ. Αὐρ. Δ.*); **(230)** 253 AD ib. 167, 8; p. 88 (stemma) (*Δομίτιος Στατείλιος Δ.*: II s. *Δομίτιος Διονύσιος* I, *Στατιλία Ἀλεξάνδρα*); **(231)** ~ ib. 167, 12; p. 88 (stemma) (*Δομίτιος Δ.*: I f. *Δομίτιος Στατίλιος Διονύσιος* II)

—THESSALONIKE?: **(232)** i-ii AD ib. 56 (f. *Ἀγάθων*); **(233)** i-iii AD ib. 975 (f. *Νίκανδρος*); **(234)** ii AD ib. 248 I, 6 ([*Δ*]*ιονύσιος*); **(235)** ~ ib. 250 I, 6 (s. *Κόρραγος*, f. *Τελεσφόρος*); **(236)** iii AD ib. 859, 8; **(237)** ~ ib. 896 (s. *Αὐρ. Πύρος*)

MACEDONIA (ODOMANTIKE):

—DRABESKOS?: **(238)** iv/iii BC *SEG* XXIV 578 (*CEG* II 726; Pilhofer 570)

—GAZOROS: **(239)** 215 or 174 BC *SEG* XXX 1892, 26 (Hatzopoulos, *MI* 2 pp. 57-8 no. 39) (*Διονύ*[*σ*]*ιος*: s. *Ἀπολλόδωρος*)

—GAZOROS (TERRIT.): **(240)** 84-106 AD *SEG* XXX 596, 1, 9 (Pilhofer 555) (s. *Διοσκουρίδης*, *Σούρα*)

—SIRRHA: **(241)** 62 or 178 AD *JDAI* 84 (1969) p. 157 no. R27, 1, 5 (f. *Διοσκουρίδης*); **(242)** ii-iii AD *Belomorski Pregled* 1 (1942) pp. 329-30 no. 27 = Kaphtantzis 28 (*Δ*[*ι*]*ονύσιος*: f. *Ζώσιμος*, *Ἐπικτοῦς*); **(243)** ~ Dimitsas 819 (Kaphtantzis 25); **(244)** ~ *SEG* XXXIII 550 (*Διον*[*ύσιος*]: s. *Κουσπίδιος Τιμόξενος*); **(245)** 155 AD Dimitsas 821, 12 (Kaphtantzis 1) (f. *Διοσκουρίδης*); **(246)** f. iii AD *SEG* XXX 590, 15 (*Αὐρ. Δ.*: s. *Βράσος*)

—SIRRHA (TERRIT.): **(247)** ii-iii AD Kaphtantzis 473 (*SEG* XLVIII 883) (s. *Νικόπολις*); **(248)** ~ Kaphtantzis 474 (s. *Ἰσᾶς*)

—SIRRHA (NR.): **(249)** ii-iii AD *Tekmeria* 6 (2001) p. 10; **(250)** ~ *AD* 51 (1996) Chron. p. 576 with pl. 168 *β*

—SIRRHA?: **(251)** ii-iii AD *SEG* XLVIII 884 (f. *Νίκη*)

—SKOTOUSSA?: **(252)** ii-iii AD Dimitsas 843 (f. *Ἀλέξανδρος*)

—SKOTOUSSA (TERRIT.)?: **(253)** 59 or 175 AD *SEG* XXXIV 677

MACEDONIA (ORESTIS):

—AGIA ANNA (MOD.): **(254)** imp.? *EAM* 206

—LYKE: **(255)** s. ii AD ib. 149, 8 (*Τ. Φλ. Δ.*)

MACEDONIA (PAIONIA):

—BYLAZORA: **(256)** iii AD *JÖAI* 6 (1903) Beibl. col. 3 no. 2 (*Sp.* 71 (1931) p. 25 no. 48, 1-2) (*M. Αὐρ. Δ.*: ?f. *Αὐρ. Διονυσία*)

—DEMIR KAPIJA (MOD.): **(257)** hell. *SEG* XLV 807 E (sherd) (s. *Πάπας*)

—EUDARISTOS?: **(258)** 102 AD ib. XXXII 655, 1 (s. *Σεκοῦνδος*, *Σεκοῦνδα*)

—KAVADARCI (MOD.): **(259)** ?ii AD Unp. (Skopje) (s. *Δημήτριος*); **(260)** ii-iii AD *Minalo* 2 (1911) pp. 54 f. (s. *Ἡρακλείδης*); **(261)** ~ *Sp.* 71 (1931) p. 71 no. 163; **(262)** ~ ib. p. 237 no. 631 = 75 (1933) p. 41 no. 140 (s. *Διοσκουρίδης*, *Κλεοπάτρα*); **(263)** ii/iii AD Unp. (Papazoglu archive); **(264)** iii AD *Sp.* 71 (1931) p. 65 no. 142, 1 (*Δ*[*ι*]*ονύ*[*σιος*]: f. *Ζωΐλος*)

—NEAPOLIS (AREA): **(265)** 83 AD *SEG* XVI 404, 6 (s. *Διοσκουρίδης*)

—NEAPOLIS? (IZVOR (MOD.): **(266)** imp. *Sp.* 98 (1941-8) p. 28 no. 67; **(267)** ii-iii AD ib. p. 28 no. 68 (f. *Ζωΐλος*, *Γάϊος*)

—NEAPOLIS? (SMILOVCI (MOD.)): **(268)** ii AD ib. p. 31 no. 76 (f. *Γάϊος*, *Ζωΐλος*)

—NEGOTINO (MOD.): **(269)** ii-iii AD ib. 71 (1931) p. 65 no. 144, 1 (s. *Διοσκουρίδης*, f. *Θεογένης*); **(270)** ~ ib. 75 (1933) p. 37 no. 114 (s. *Δημήτριος*, f. *Ἀρτεμιδώρα*); **(271)** iii AD ib. 98 (1941-8) p. 60 no. 123 (*Διονύσιος*: s. *Ἀπολλόδωρος*: reading—Papazoglu)

—STOBOI: **(272)** s. iii AD *JÖAI* 32 (1940) Beibl. col. 18 no. 15. 57 (*Διον*(*ύσιος*?) *Μα*—); **(273)** ~ ib. (*Διονύ*(*σιος*?) *Ἐ*—*λε*—)

—STOBOI (AREA): **(274)** ii-iii AD Unp. (Kavadarci Mus.) inv. 61/II (f. *Φοῦσκα*)

MACEDONIA (PELAGONIA):

—DOSTONEIS: **(275)** ii AD *IG* X (2) (2) 196, 1 (*Διονύσ*[*ιος*]: s. *Ζώπυρος*, f. *Μέλητος*, *Ἀλέξανδρος*, *Νίκαρχος*); **(276)** f. ii AD ib. 195 (*Π. Αἴλιος Δ.*: s. *Ἀντίγονος*)

MACEDONIA (PIERIA):

—DION*: **(277)** ?iii AD *ILGR* 191 (Lat. Aur. Dionysius)

—LAGORACHI (MOD.): **(278)** imp. *Klio* 52 (1970) p. 64 no. 16 (f. *—βαντα*: freed.)

—PYDNA: **(279)** iv BC *GRBS* 47 (2002-3) p. 122 no. 6, 3

MACEDONIA (PIERIS):

—OISYME-EMATHIA: **(280)** i-ii AD *SEG* XXXII 844 (Tataki, *Macedonians* p. 106 no. 1); cf. Hatzopoulos, *MI* 1 pp. 186-7 (f. *Ἱπποκλέα*)

MACEDONIA (SINTIKE):

—HERAKLEIA: **(281)** 230 AD *IGB* V 5922, 4 (s. *Ἀσκληπᾶς*)

—MEINE: **(282)** ii-iii AD ib. 5887 (s. *Νικοστρατικός*); **(283)** 222 AD ib. 5886, 6 (f. *Αὐρ. Πύρρος*, *Αὐρ. Ἀρτεμίδωρος*)

—PARTHIKOPOLIS (TERRIT.): **(284)** ii AD *Arkheologiia* (Sofia) 1987 (1), p. 25 no. 3 (s. *Ζόνκος*, f. *Πυρούλας*, *Σκάρκεζα*); **(285)** ii/iii AD *IGB* IV 2313 (*Διονύ*[*σιος*])

MACEDONIA?: **(286)** 306-301 BC *IG* II² 560, 6; *RE* Supplbd. 4 (69a) (*Διονύσι*[*ος*]) ?= (*168*); **(287)** ?274 BC *PSI* 321, 4, 9, [14], [16], 18, 20, 28; **(288)** 226 BC *PPetr*² 24, 4; cf. La'da E1743 (f. *Ἀσκληπιόδωρος*)

SCYTHIA MINOR:

—ISTROS: **(289)** iv BC Unp. (Avram, defixio) 1, 2; **(290)** ~ *IOlbia* 7, 3 (Dubois, *IGDOlbia* 19) (*Διον*[*ύ*]*σιος*: f. *Θεόδοτος*); **(291)** iv/iii BC *ISM* I 19, 11 (Migeotte, *L'emprunt* 42); *IOlbia* 15, 3 (s. *Στρουθίων*); **(292)** iii BC *Histria* 9 pp. 142-3 no. 203; **(293)** ~ *ISM* I 114 (f. *Γυκεῖα*); **(294)** iii-ii BC ib. 9, 2 (Migeotte, *L'emprunt* 41) (s. *Ἱέρων*); **(295)** s. iii BC *AMNG* I (1) 476 (coin) (*Διονύ*(*σιος*)); **(296)** ~ *ISM* I 15, 1 (*Δι*[*ον*]*ύσιος*: s. *Βιάνωρ*); **(297)** ii-i BC ib. 125 (*Διονύσιος*: s. *Μενίσκος*, f. *Μοιρώ*); **(298)** i BC-i AD ib. 191 I, 36 (f. *Ἀπολλόδωρος*); **(299)** ~ ib. 191 II, 8 (s. *Κλειτοφῶν*); **(300)** ~ ib. l. 26 (s. *Ἀρτεμίδωρος*); **(301)** ~ ib. l. 31 (I f. *Διονύσιος* II *νεώτερος*); **(302)** ~ ib. l. 31 (*Δ. νεώτερος*: II s. *Διονύσιος* I, f. *Διονύσιος* III); **(303)** ~ ib. l. 31 (III s. *Διονύσιος* II *νεώτερος*); **(304)** ~ ib. l. 36 (s. *Θεοκλῆς*); **(305)** ~ ib. 364 (f. *Σιμάδας*); **(306)** ii AD ib. 137, 14 ([*Α*]*ἰλ. Δ.*: s. *Δημοκράτης*); **(307)** ~ ib. l. 17 (s. *Διονυσόδωρος*); **(308)** ~ ib. 196, 23 (f. *Τέρτις*); **(309)** ~ ib. 198, 8 (s. *Ἀθηνάδης*); **(310)** ~ ib. 202, 4; **(311)** ~ ib. l. 6; **(312)** ~ ib. 211, 11 (s. *Αἰσχρίων*); **(313)** ~ ib. 214, 4 + 226, 2; **(314)** f. ii AD *SEG* L 683 B, 8 (f. *Κλειτοφῶν*); **(315)** 138 AD *ISM* I 193, 10 (f. *Ἡρόδωρος*); **(316)** ~ ib. 193 I, 17 (s. *Κρατήσιππος*); **(317)** ~ ib. l. 22 (f. *Ἡγήμων*); **(318)** ~ ib. l. 23 (s. *Ἡρόδωρος*); **(319)** ~ ib. l. 26 (s. *Μήνιος*); **(320)** ~ ib. l. 35 (II s. *Διονύσιος* I); **(321)** ~ ib. l. 35 (I f. *Διονύσιος* II); **(322)** ~ ib. l. 52 (I f. *Διονύσιος* II); **(323)** ~ ib. l. 52 (II s. *Διονύσιος* I); **(324)** ~ ib. l. 58 (f. *Ἑστιαῖος*); **(325)** ~ ib. l. 67 (f. *Διονυσόδωρος*); **(326)** ~ ib. l. 78 (f. *Διογένης*, *Πίστος*); **(327)** ~ ib. l. 80 (s. *Διονυσόδωρος*); **(328)** ~ ib. l. 88 (f. *Θεόγνητος*); **(329)** ~ ib. l. 96 (f. *Διονυσόδωρος*); **(330)** ~ ib. l. 100 (f. *Μόνιμος*); **(331)** ~ ib. l. 105 (s. *Φίλων*); **(332)** ~ ib. 193 II, 37 (f. *Εὐξενίδης*); **(333)** ~ ib. l. 39 (*Δ. Ὄπληξ, ὁ πλήξ*?: s. *Φίλων*); **(334)** ~ ib. l. 41 (s. *Μόνιμος*); **(335)** ~ ib. l. 55 (s. *Αἰσχρίων*); **(336)** ~ ib. l. 56 (f. *Ἀρχέλαος*); **(337)** ~ ib. l. 78 (s. *Φιλόδημος νεώτ.*); **(338)** c. 140-160 AD ib. 207, 12 (*Διονύ*[*σ*]*ιο*[*ς*]: s. *Μοιρόδωρος*); **(339)** ii/iii AD ib. 363, 1, 5 (*CCET* IV 62) (s. *Σατυρίων*, f. *Ἀρτεμίδωρος*); **(340)** f. iii AD *ISM* I 143, 9 (f. *Αὐρ. —φιλος*); **(341)** 222-225 AD ib. 100, 7 (*Αὐρ. Δ.*: I s. *Ἑστιαῖος*, f. *Αὐρ. Διονύσιος* II); **(342)** ~ ib. l. 7 (*Αὐρ. Δ.*: II s. *Αὐρ. Διονύσιος* I)

—KALLATIS: **(343)** iii BC *IGB* I² 13 ter, 3 (*Διο*[*νύσιος*]: I f. *Διονύσιος* II); **(344)** ~ ib. l. 3 (II s. *Διονύσιος* I); **(345)** iii-ii BC *ISM* III 138, 1, 3 (*GVI* 1279 with Add. p. 693) (s. *Ποσειδώνιος*); **(346)** f. iii BC *ISM* III 78 (s. *Δάμων*, f. *Καθαρά*); **(347)** s. iii BC ib. 11, 1 (s. *Ποτάμων*); **(348)** ~ ib. 35 A, 25 (s. *Καλχάδων*); **(349)** ~ ib. l. 38 (f. *Δαμοσθένης*); **(350)** ~ ib. 35 B, 39; **(351)** iii/ii BC ib. 161 (*Διονύ*[*σιος*]: f. *Ἀπολλόδωρος*); **(352)** ii-i BC ib. 172; **(353)** ii/i BC *SNG Stancomb* 101 (coin) (*Διονύ*(*σιος*)); **(354)** f. iii AD *ISM* III 94 (f. *Αὐρ. Χρυσέα*); **(355)** 241-244 AD ib. 74, 13 (s. *Καλλίστρατος*); **(356)** ~ ib. 74 A, 17 (I f. *Διονύσιος* II); **(357)** ~ ib. l. 17 (II s. *Διονύσιος* I); **(358)** ~ ib. l. 31 (f. *Πάγχαρις*)

—KALLATIS?: **(359)** ii/i BC *IGB* II 867 a, 10 = *ISM* I 219 (v 87); cf. *ISM* III p. 140 (locn.) (s. *Ὀρθόβιος*)

—TOMIS: **(360)** ii-i BC ib. II 36 ([*Διο*]*νύσιος*: s. *Διοσκουρίδης*); **(361)** i BC ib. 2 A, 56 (s. *Διογένης*); **(362)** ~ ib. l. 57 (s. *Δημήτριος*); **(363)** ~ ib. 2 B, 50 (f. *Ἡφαιστίων*); **(364)** i BC-i AD ib. 154, 1 (*Eastern cults* p. 10 no. 14) (s. *Ἡδύλος*); **(365)** ?41-54 AD *RPC* I 1829 (coin); **(366)** ii AD *ISM* II 11, 3; **(367)** ~ ib. 17, 2 (f. *Χρύσης*); **(368)** ~ ib. 125 I, 21 (f. *Φειδίας*); **(369)** ii-iii AD ib. 26, 4 (s. *Μᾶρκος*); **(370)** ~ ib. l. 5 (f. *Δάδας*); **(371)** ~ ib. 31 I, 5 ([*Διον*]*ύσιος*); **(372)** ~ ib. 31 III, 6 (*Μάρκιος Διονύσ*[*ιος*]); **(373)** ~ ib. l. 7 (*Μάρκιος Διονύ*[*σιος*]); **(374)** ~ ib. l. 9 (*Μάρκιος Διον*[*ύσιος*]); **(375)** ~ ib. 104, 13 ([*Δ*]*ιονύσιος*: s. *Δαμ*—); **(376)** ~ ib. 251 (*Διονύσι*[*ος*]); **(377)** ~ ib. 468, 6 (f. *Τάνης*); **(378)** 200-201 AD ib. 82 B, 13; **(379)** ~ ib. l. 16; **(380)** iii AD ib. 276, 4 (*Αὐρ. Δ. ὁ καὶ Αἰμόνιος*); **(381)** 201 AD ib. 83 I, 21 (f. *Τούρβων*); **(382)** ~ ib. l. 27 (*Διονύσ*[*ιος*]: s. *Δώτιος*)

——(Hopletes): **(383)** iii AD ib. 254 (*Διονύσι*[*ος*]:

s. Κρήσκης)

SKYTHIA:

—OLBIA-BORYSTHENES: **(384)** v BC Tolstoi 14 (*LSAG*^{2} p. 372 no. 58 (vase)) (s. Διόδωρος); **(385)** f. iv BC Dubois, *IGDOlbia* 104 (f. Ἀρτεμίδωρος); **(386)** m. iv BC ib. 13, 7 ([Διον]ύσιος: s. Ποσείδιππος); **(387)** s. iv BC *SEG* L 702 IV, 1; **(388)** iv/iii BC *IOSPE* I^2 210 (f. Διόδωρος); **(389)** hell. Winter, *Typen* 2 p. 57 no. 9 (terracotta); **(390)** hell.? *FGrH* 804; **(391)** iii BC Dubois, *IGDOlbia* 109, 2 (*SEG* XXXVII 673); **(392)** ~ *IOSPE* I^2 189; *IOlbia* 68; 70 (f. Ἀγρότας, Ποσίδεος) ?= (*404*) (*403*); **(393)** ~ *IOSPE* I^2 201 I, 2 (s. Ἀριστείδης); **(394)** ~ ib. l. 41 (f. Σύμμαχος); **(395)** ~ ib. l. 54 (f. Φιλόμηλος); **(396)** ~ ib. 201 II, 20 (s. Βοττύλος); **(397)** ~ ib. l. 22 (s. Ὀρθόβουλος); **(398)** ~ ib. l. 27 (s. Ἀγρότας); **(399)** iii-ii BC ib. 186, 1 (f. Νικόδρομος); **(400)** ~ ib. l. 2, 5 (s. Νικόδρομος); **(401)** c. 265-260 BC *FD* III (3) 207, 4 (I f. Διονύσιος II); **(402)** ~ ib. l. 4 (II s. Διονύσιος I); **(403)** c. 200-175 BC *IG* XI (4) 813, 2, 9 (f. Ποσίδεος) ?= (*392*); **(404)** ii BC *SEG* XL 633 (f. Ποσίδεος) ?= (*392*); **(405)** ?ii-i BC Dubois, *IGDOlbia* 110, 4; **(406)** ~ ib. l. 5; **(407)** i/ii AD *IOlbia* 90, 4 (s. Ἀλέξανδρος); **(408)** ii AD ib. 80, 6 (s. Δελφός); **(409)** ~ *IOSPE* I^2 84, 7 (s. Ἑρμογένης); **(410)** ~ ib. 89, 8 (f. Ἀριστόνικος ὁ καὶ Βασιλεύς); **(411)** ?ii-iii AD ib. 111, 6; **(412)** ii-iii AD ib. 192 (f. —ων); **(413)** f. ii AD ib. 95, 9 (f. Ἀριαράθης); **(414)** iii AD ib. 135, 7 (s. Ἀρθάμμανος)

—SKYTHAI: **(415)** 414 BC *IG* I^3 422, 199 (*FRA* 6909) (Δι[ον]ύσιος: slave)

—TANAIS: **(416)** ii AD *CIRB* 1263, 10 ([Διο]νύσι[ος]—Tokhtas'ev); **(417)** 225 AD ib. 1280, 18 ([Δ]ιονύσιος: s. Πάτεις); **(418)** 228 AD ib. 1283, 12 (s. Σόγος); **(419)** ~ ib. l. 14 (f. Διόφαντος)

—TYRAS: **(420)** m. ii BC *IIasos* 408, 13 (f. Ἑρμίας); **(421)** 181 AD *IOSPE* I^2 2, 30 (s. Πίσκας)

SKYTHIA?: **(422)** iii AD Greifenhagen, *Schmuckarb.* 2 p. 81 (ring) (Διω-)

TAURIS:

—CHERSONESOS: **(423)** v-iv BC Solomonik, *GChKh* 5 (vase) (Δι[ο]νύσιο[ς]); **(424)** iv BC Solomonik, *NEPKh* 142; **(425)** iv/iii BC ib. 151; **(426)** ~ *SEG* XXXIII 598; **(427)** ~ ib. XXXVI 696 (s. Παντάγνωτος: doctor); **(428)** iii BC *IOlbia* 26, 5 (s. Θάγων) ?= (*439*); **(429)** ~ Solomonik, *NEPKh* 33 (s. Καλλιάδας); **(430)** ~ ib. 150 (s. Σαννίων); **(431)** ~ *IOSPE* I^2 498 ([Διον]ύσιος: ?s. —οχος, ?f. —δρος); **(432)** ~ ib. 708 (f. Θεαγενίς); **(433)** ~ Kats p. 113 no. 117 (vase) (f. Σωτήριος); **(434)** ~ *SEG* XXXIII 599 (f. Βισθᾶς); **(435)** f. iii BC Kats p. 84 no. 4 (amph.) (f. Ἀθανόδωρος); **(436)** ~ ib. pp. 100-1 no. 65 (amph.) (f. Καλλιάδας); **(437)** ~ *SEG* XL 615 B, 9-11 (f. Προμαθίων); **(438)** c. 262-237 BC Kats p. 93 no. 38 (amph.) (s. Ἀθανόδωρος); **(439)** c. 215-200 BC ib. p. 93 no. 39 (amph.) (s. Θάγων) ?= (*428*); **(440)** f. ii BC *IOSPE* I^2 351, 2 (f. Πλειστῶναξ); **(441)** imp. ib. 522 ([Διο]νύσι[ος]: f. —ρη—); **(442)** ~ ib. 706 (Δι[ο]νύσι[ος]); **(443)** ii AD ib. 443 (Αὐρ. Δ.: s. Πρίσκος); **(444)** ~ ib. 459; **(445)** ii/iii AD *SEG* XXXIII 603 (f. Ἧλις)

——(Echedamis): **(446)** s. v BC *DGVE* 1996-7, p. 111 fig. 2, 6 (*SEG* XLIX 1031. 3 (ostrakon)) (f. Αἴσχρων)

THRACE: **(447)** 274 BC *PCZ* 59001, 24, 51, verso (Velkov 96; La'da E736); **(448)** 237 BC *PPetr*^{2} 6, 39 (Velkov 97; La'da E737) (Διονύσιος); **(449)** 219-217 BC *RE* (68); Plb. v 65, 10 (*PP* 2157); **(450)** c. 170-90 BC *RE* (134) (*PP* 16845); cf. *Suda* Δ 1172; Fraser, *Ptol. Alex.* 2 pp. 678-9 n. 207 (ethn.) (s. Τήρης); **(451)** 154 BC *SGDI* 1902, 3 (slave/freed.); **(452)** ?s. i BC *ZPE* 136 (2001) pp. 134-5 no. 16, 4; cf. La'da E734 ([Διο]νύσιος: I f. Διονύσιος II); **(453)** ~ *ZPE* 136 (2001) pp. 134-5 no. 16, [4], 13 (La'da E734) (II s. Διονύσιος I); **(454)** c. 428-440 AD *PLRE* II (13); *RE* (89) (Φλ. Δ.)

—ABDERA: **(455)** f. iii BC *SEG* XXVII 323 (*IThrakAig* E47); **(456)** ii BC *IG* XII (8) 161, 16 (Διο[ν]ύσιος: I f. Διονύσιος II); **(457)** ~ ib. l. 16 (II s. Διονύσιος I)

—AINOS: **(458)** iii BC ib. II^2 7983 (*FRA* 237) (f. Πυθόδωρος); **(459)** ii BC *IG* II^2 7976 (*FRA* 238) (f. Ἐ—ρος); **(460)** ~ *SEG* XXXIV 1253 ([Διο]νύσιος: s. Μενεκλῆς); **(461)** 194 BC *Milet* I (3) 54, 3 (and Caria Miletos: II s. Διονύσιος I); **(462)** ~ ib. l. 5 (f. Ἀρχέλας); **(463)** ~ ib. l. 3-4 (and Caria Miletos: I s. Σπάρτακος, f. Διονύσιος II, Πυθίων); **(464)** i-ii AD *IG* XII (8) 218, 8 (f. —ιον)

—AINOS?: **(465)** 208-211 AD *AEp* 1986, no. 628 (Lat. [Dio]nysius)

—APROI: **(466)** ii-iii AD *IKyz* I 506, 9 (*Steinepigramme* 2 p. 42)

—BEROE-AUGUSTA TRAIANA (TERRIT.): **(467)** iii AD *SEG* XLI 587 (Αὐρ. Δ.)

—BISANTHE-PANION: **(468)** c. 208 BC *FD* III (4) 133 I, 18 (f. ...ημος)

—BIZONE: **(469)** ii-iii AD *IGB* I^2 7 bis, 2 ([Διο]νύσιος?)

—BIZYE: **(470)** ii-iii AD *SEG* XXXII 660, 8 (f. Μ. Αὐρ. Καλανδίων); **(471)** 212-217 AD *IGB* V 5659, 7 (Αὐρ. [Διο]νύσιος: s. Θεμίσων)

—BIZYE (TERRIT.): **(472)** ii-iii AD ib. 5660 (Διονύσ(ι)ο[ς]: s. Ἄττιος)

—BYZANTION: **(473)** arch. Aesop., *Vita G* 79 (king/fict.); **(474)** ?354 BC Rhodes–Osborne 57, 13 (Διω-: s. Ἡραίων); **(475)** iii BC *IByz* 60 (Fıratlı–Robert p. 47 no. 3) (f. Κλεώ); **(476)** f. iii BC *IG* XI (4) 627, 4, 11 (s. Ἱαρώνυμος); **(477)** iii/ii BC *IByz* 170 (Fıratlı–Robert p. 109 no. 177) (s. Ποσείδιππος); **(478)** c. 220-200 BC Schönert-Geiss, *Byzantion* 1043 (coin); **(479)** ii BC *IByz* 101 (Fıratlı–Robert pp. 94-5 no. 132) (s. Διαφάνης); **(480)** ~ *IByz* 216 (Fıratlı–Robert p. 75 no. 82a) (f. Μενίσκος, Κρατιστώ); **(481)** ii-i BC *Türk Tarih Kongresi XI* (6) p. 2703 with pl. 498. 12 (f. Ἀπολλόδωρος); **(482)** i BC *IByz* 231 (Fıratlı–Robert p. 84 no. 103) (s. Ἀπολλόδωρος, f. Καλλώ); **(483)** i BC-i AD *IByz* 19, 11; **(484)** ~ ib. 227 (Fıratlı–Robert pp. 81-2 no. 97) (f. Ἀπολλόδωρος); **(485)** ~ *IByz* 277 (f. Ἡρόξενος); **(486)** i-ii AD ib. 16 (Fıratlı–Robert p. 59 no. 41) (f. Ἐπικράτη); **(487)** ~ *IByz* 315 a (Fıratlı–Robert pp. 122-3 no. 205) (f. Ἡρακλέων); **(488)** s. i AD *IByz* 32, 2 (II s. Διονύσιος I); **(489)** ~ ib. l. 3 (I f. Διονύσιος II); **(490)** ~ ib. 34, 3 (Τι(β). Κλ. Δ.); **(491)** i/ii AD *SEG* L 667 VI (s. Φλ. Κοσμίων, Παῦλα); **(492)** ii AD *RE* (114); Güngerich, *Dion. Byz.*; **(493)** ii-iii AD *IByz* 140 (f. Μαρκία); **(494)** iii AD *BCH* 27 (1903) p. 297 A, 10 (Stephanis 722) (Μ. Αὐρ. Δ.); **(495)** c. 238-244 AD Schönert-Geiss, *Byzantion* 1797-1805 (coin) (Μ. Αὐρ. Δ.)

—BYZANTION (TERRIT.): **(496)** ii BC *IByz* 92 (Fıratlı–Robert p. 91 no. 120) (f. Ξύστος); **(497)** ii-i BC *IByz* 263 (s. Μεννέας); **(498)** imp. Unp. (Sayar) (f. Φαδος); **(499)** i-ii AD *IByz* 272 (Fıratlı–Robert pp. 88-9 no. 112)

—BYZANTION:

——(Delkos): **(500)** imp. *IByz* 21; cf. *BE* 2001, no. 308 (Δ(ι)ονύσιος—ed., Δονύσιος?—Brixhe: f. Τρόφιμος)

——(Rhegion): **(501)** i BC-i AD *IByz* 249 (Fıratlı–Robert p. 80 no. 93) (f. Μαμμία)

—BYZANTION?: **(502)** ii BC *IByz* 327 (Fıratlı–Robert p. 94 no. 131) (s. Κόλλος); **(503)** ~ *IByz* 338 (Fıratlı–Robert p. 127 no. 214); cf. *IKalch* 44 (f. Ἀπολλᾶς); **(504)** imp. *IByz* 332 (s. Μᾶρκος)

—DIONYSOPOLIS: **(505)** hell. *Spink Num. Circular* 105 (1997) p. 374 nos. 26-7 (coin); **(506)** ii BC *IGB* I^2 22 II, 7 (f. Τρύφων); **(507)** c. 48 BC ib. 13, 45 (Διον[ύ]σιος: f. Ἀκορνίων); **(508)** ii-iii AD *GVI* 520; cf. Robert, *OMS* 5 pp. 226-9 (doctor); **(509)** ~ *IGB* I^2 31, 5 (s. Δημήτριος)

—DIONYSOPOLIS (NR.): **(510)** ii-i BC ib. 33

—DIOSOURA: **(511)** ii AD ib. V 5589, 7 (Διονύ[σιο]ς: ?s. Βίθυς)

—KARDIA: **(512)** f. iv BC *RDAC* 1970, pp. 103-11 (*PPC* Δ 66) (Διον[ύ]σιο[ς])

—KELLAI: **(513)** 241-244 AD *IGB* III 1517, 4 (f. Αὐρ. Κλαυδιανός); **(514)** ~ ib. l. 12 (f. Αὐρ. Μουκιανός); **(515)** ~ ib. l. 27 (f. Αὐρ. Διογένης)

—KOVAČEVEC (MOD.): **(516)** ii-iii AD *Romanizmăt* II 571 (Lat. Dionysius)

—LYSIMACHEIA: **(517)** hell. *SEG* XL 226 (*FRA* 3392) (s. Κλεῖνος); **(518)** ?s. iii BC *FD* III (1) 430, 1 (s. Θευδόσιος); **(519)** s. iii BC Polyaen. iv 17; **(520)** c. 208 BC *FD* III (4) 134 II, 11 (s. Δαμοχάρης); **(521)** ~ ib. 135 II, 14 (s. Πρ[.....]ξ̣ενος); **(522)** ii-i BC *ISestos* 42 (s. Ἀλεξίας)

—MADYTOS: **(523)** imp. ib. 57

—MARKIANOPOLIS: **(524)** iii AD *IGB* II 801 (f. Αὐρ. Μαρτῖνος)

—MARONEIA: **(525)** iii BC *IThrakAig* E232 ([Δι]ονύσ[ιος]: f. —ατα—); **(526)** ii BC *Milet* I (3) 82, 10 (f. Ὀλυμπιάδης); **(527)** ii-i BC *IThrakAig* E212, 14 (f. Διοσκουρίδης); **(528)** ~ ib. l. 16 (s. Γλαῦκος); **(529)** ~ ib. l. 29 (s. Ἱέρων); **(530)** ~ ib. l. 31 (s. Διονυσοφάνης); **(531)** ~ ib. l. 32 (Διονύσ[ιο]ς: f. Διόδωρος); **(532)** ~ ib. l. 41 (s. Ἀπολλώνιος); **(533)** ~ ib. l. 52 (s. Δόλης); **(534)** ~ ib. l. 56 (f. Φιλάργυρος); **(535)** f. ii BC *SEG* XXXIV 709 (*IThrakAig* E278) (Διονύ[σιος]: f. Ἡδεῖα); **(536)** 102 BC *IG* II^2 1028 III, 152 (*FRA* 3537) (Δ[ι]ον[ύ]σιος: I f. Διονύσιος II); **(537)** ~ *IG* II^2 1028 III, 152 (*FRA* 3538) (II s. Διονύσιος I); **(538)** i BC *IThrakAig* E213, 8 (Διονύσ[ιος]: f. —βιος); **(539)** ~ ib. E243 (Διενύσ[ιος]?: s. Ἀπολλώνιος); **(540)** i BC-i AD *BCH* 37 (1913) p. 144 no. 49, 5 + *IThrakAig* E286 (II s. Διονύσιος I, Ἀκονία); **(541)** ~ *BCH* 37 (1913) p. 144 no. 49, 1-3, 5 (*IThrakAig* E286) (I s. Ἱέρων, f. Ἱέρων, Νικίας, Διονύσιος II); **(542)** hell.-imp. *FRA* 3539 (f. Τέχνων); **(543)** ~ Dumont–Homolle 110b 13 (*IThrakAig* E291) (f. Δωρίων); **(544)** ~ ib. E294 (Διονύσ(ι)ος?); **(545)** imp. Dumont–Homolle 110b 16 (*IThrakAig* E293) (s. Κτησίβιος); **(546)** i AD *SEG* XXVII 343, 1, 4 (*IThrakAig* E302) (s. Δωρίων); **(547)** ii AD Dumont–Homolle 110b 11 (*IThrakAig* E276) ([Δι]ονύσιος: f. Ῥουφία Πρίσκα); **(548)** ~ *IG* XII (8) 220, 13 (f. Εὐβούλα); **(549)** ~ *SEG* XXX 700, 1 (*IThrakAig* E256 A) (Δ̣ι̣[ο]νύσιος); **(550)** iii AD ib. E195 (s. Θεόδοτος); **(551)** v-vi AD *SEG* XLVI 854 + *IThrakAig* E348 (Διονύσ(ι)ος)

—MESAMBRIA: **(552)** iv/iii BC *IGB* I^2 334 septies ([Δ]ιονύ[σιος]?); **(553)** hell. ib. 316, [1], 6 ([Δι]ονύσιος: s. Ἁγησίδαμος); **(554)** iii BC *IOSPE* I^2 688 (f. Σάτυρος); **(555)** ii BC *IGB* I^2 314 b, 3 (Διον[ύ]σιος) ?= (*556*); **(556)** ~ ib. l. 7 (f. Βιάνωρ) ?= (*555*); **(557)** c. 150-89 BC *Milet* I (3) 48, 6 (f. Καλλικλέα); **(558)** ii/i BC *IGB* V 5104 IV (Διονύσι[ος]: s. Ἀπολλώνιος); **(559)** ~ ib. 5104 VI (Διονύ[σι]ος: s. Οἰνίας, f. Ἀπολλώνιος); **(560)** c. 55 BC ib. I^2 323, 3 (Διονύσι[ος]: f. Δαμέας); **(561)** i-ii AD ib. 340 bis (f. Τίτθα); **(562)** ii AD ib. V 5124

—NICOPOLIS AD ISTRUM (TERRIT.): **(563)** 227 AD *ILB* 438 I, 6 (Lat. Ulp. Dionysius)

—ODESSOS: **(564)** iv/iii BC *IGB* I^2 13 bis, 3 (f. Ἀριστομένης); **(565)** iii/ii BC ib. 37 bis, 18; **(566)** ii-i BC ib. 45, 34; **(567)** ~ ib. 153; **(568)** i BC-i AD ib. 159 (*CCET* I 50; PM 1312) (s. Πρωταγόρας); **(569)** 34 BC *IGB* I^2 46, 13 (f. Ἀπολλᾶς); **(570)** 21 BC ib. l. 26 (s. Ζωπυρίων); **(571)** 9 BC ib. l. 38 (f. Ἡφαιστίων); **(572)** 5 BC ib. l. 42 (s. Ἑκατόδωρος); **(573)** 1 BC ib. l. 46 (s. Πόσσις); **(574)** i-ii AD ib. 51 b, 7 ([Διο]νύσιος: s. Θεμιστᾶς); **(575)** ~ ib. 51 c, 5 (s. Δάδας); **(576)** ~ ib. 53, 2 ([Διο]νύσιος); **(577)** ~ ib. 138 bis, 4

(*Διονύσι[ος]*); **(578)** ~ ib. 140 bis, 1 (s. *Ῥοῦφος*); **(579)** ~ ib. l. 3 (f. *Τούτα*); **(580)** ~ ib. 142 bis (f. *Ἑλένη*); **(581)** ~ ib. 198 bis (f. —*αιους*); **(582)** ~ ib. 211 (*Δ. Πάπας*: s. *Ἑστιαῖος*); **(583)** ~ ib. v 5064 (*[Διον]ύσιος*); **(584)** I AD ib. I² 46, 47 (s. *Ἀπατούριος*); **(585)** ii AD ib. 50, 27 (f. *Ἑστιαῖος*); **(586)** ~ ib. 50 a, 9 (s. *Ἀντίπατρος*); **(587)** ~ ib. l. 13 (I f. *Διονύσιος* II *ὁ κὲ Θουθύλων*); **(588)** ~ ib. l. 13 (*Δ. ὁ κὲ Θουθύλων*: II s. *Διονύσιος* I); **(589)** ~ ib. l. 14 (*Διον[ύ]σιος*: s. *Μοσχίων*); **(590)** ~ ib. l. 16 (*Διονύσι[ος]*: f. —*νιος*); **(591)** ~ ib. 66, 5 (*[Διο]νύσιος*: s. *Ἀγα—*); **(592)** ~ ib. 115, 1 (I f. *Διονύσιος* II *ὁ καὶ Πίπης*); **(593)** ~ ib. l. 1 (*Δ. ὁ καὶ Πίπης*: II s. *Διονύσιος* I); **(594)** ~ ib. v 5063 (*Διονύ[σιος]*?: f. *Κόνων*); **(595)** ii-iii AD ib. I² 107 bis (f. *Κρίτων*); **(596)** ~ ib. 210 (s. *Θεοτίδης*); **(597)** f. ii AD ib. 78 ter, 3 (*CCET* I 30) (s. *Ἐπικράτης*); **(598)** ~ *IGB* I² 178 (PM 1722); *Dacia* 21 (1977) p. 161 (date) (f. *Σωκράτης*); **(599)** ~ *IGB* I² 187; 187 bis (PM 1728); *Dacia* 21 (1977) p. 161 (date) (s. *Γλαυκίας*, f. *Νουμήνιος*); **(600)** m. ii AD *IGB* I² 174 bis (PM 1703); *Dacia* 21 (1977) p. 161 (date) (f. *Λούκιος*); **(601)** s. ii AD *IGB* I² 164 (*CCET* I 54; PM 1416) (*Δ. ὁ καὶ Σκῶρις*: s. *Ἀντίφιλος*); **(602)** ~ *IGB* I² 170 (PM 1701); *Dacia* 21 (1977) p. 161 (date) (*[Δ]ιονύσ[ιο]ς ὁ καὶ Ἀ...ελων*: s. *Ἡρωΐδης*); **(603)** ii/iii AD *IGB* I² 165 (PM 1702); *Dacia* 21 (1977) p. 161 (date) (f. *Ἀγαθήνωρ*); **(604)** iii AD *IGB* I² 176 bis; *Dacia* 21 (1977) p. 161 (date) (f. *Ἀντίφιλος*); **(605)** 215 AD *IGB* I² 47 a, 17 (*Αὐρ. Δ.*: s. *Μήνιος*); **(606)** ~ ib. l. 19 (f. *Αὐρ. Ἀρτεμίδωρος*); **(607)** ~ ib. l. 20 (I f. *Αὐρ. Διονύσιος* II); **(608)** ~ ib. l. 20 (*Αὐρ. Δ.*: II s. *Διονύσιος* I); **(609)** ~ ib. l. 25 (f. *Αὐρ. Μένιππος*); **(610)** ~ ib. 47 b, 10 (*Αὐρ. Δ.*: s. *Μέντης*); **(611)** ~ ib. l. 15 (*Αὐρ. Δ.*: s. *Ζωπυρίων*); **(612)** ~ ib. 47 c, 13 (f. *Αὐρ. Ἀρτέμων*); **(613)** 221 AD ib. 47 bis, 8 (f. *Μ. Αὐρ. Ἀττῆς*); **(614)** ~ ib. 47 bis a, 13 (I s. *Χρῆστος*, f. *Μ. Αὐρ. Διονύσιος* II); **(615)** ~ ib. l. 13 (*Μ. Αὐρ. Δ.*: II s. *Διονύσιος* I); **(616)** ~ ib. l. 18 (f. *Μ. Αὐρ. Χρῆστος*); **(617)** ~ ib. l. 34 (f. *Αὐρ. Μάρκος*); **(618)** ~ ib. 47 bis b, 16 (*Αὐρ. Δ.*: s. *Μάξιμος*); **(619)** ~ ib. l. 23 (f. *Αὐρ. Ἀρτεμίδωρος νεώτ.*); **(620)** ~ ib. l. 24 (*Αὐρ. Δ.*: s. *Ἀντίπατρος*); **(621)** ~ ib. l. 29 (s. *Φιλῖνος*, f. *Αὐρ. Ἀρτεμίδωρος*); **(622)** ~ ib. l. 30 (*Αὐρ. Δ.*: s. *Ἀττῆς*); **(623)** ~ ib. l. 34 (*Αὐρ. Δ.*: s. *Φιλῖνος*); **(624)** ~ ib. 47 bis c, 13 (*Αὐρ. Δ.*: s. *Ἀπολλόδωρος*); **(625)** ~ ib. l. 25 (f. *Αὐρ. Ἀρτέμων*); **(626)** ~ ib. l. 34 (*Αὐρ. Δ.*: s. *Βιάτωρ*); **(627)** ~ ib. l. 38 (*Αὐρ. Δ.*: s. *Ἀπελλᾶς*)

—ODESSOS (NR.): **(628)** i BC-i AD ib. 293, 2 (I f. *Διονύσιος* II); **(629)** ~ ib. l. 2 (*[Διο]νύσιος*: II s. *Διονύσιος* I); **(630)** 79-81 AD ib. 58 a, 3; 58 b, [2] (f. *Ἡρακλέων*); **(631)** ii-iii AD ib. 256 (PM 1695) (f. *Μένανδρος*); **(632)** s. ii AD *IGB* I² 281 (*CCET* I 25) (s. *Ἀπολλώνιος*); **(633)** ~ *IGB* I² 287 (*CCET* I 87) (f. *Σίμων*); **(634)** f. iii AD *IGB* V 5076 (*CCET* I 9) (*Διονύ(σ)ιος*: s. *Σιωσα—*)

—ODESSOS?: **(635)** iii BC *IGB* I² 479 ter (PM 1732); cf. *IGB* V 5156 (f. *Ναεις*); **(636)** ~ ib. I² 479 ter (PM 1732); cf. *IGB* V 5156 (f. *Ζουλεμης*); **(637)** ii AD ib. I² 51 bis b, 5 (s. *Οὐαλέριος*); **(638)** ~ ib. l. 9 (s. *Ὀρφεύς*)

—PAUTALIA: **(639)** ii-iii AD ib. II 540 (f. *Μαρκιανός*)

—PERINTHOS-HERAKLEIA: **(640)** 316-309 BC *IG* II² 1956, 121 (*FRA* 6037); *Ancient Macedonia* 5 p. 445 with n. 10 (date); **(641)** 249 BC *PCZ* 59325, 48 (La'da E1960); **(642)** ii BC *ISmyrna* 145 (PM 925) (f. *Ἰσιάς*); **(643)** iii AD *IPerinth* 155 (*Αὐρ. Δ.*); **(644)** f. iii AD ib. 22, 9 (f. *M. Αὐρ. Χρῆστος*)

——(Akarnanes): **(645)** iii-ii BC ib. 61, 15 (s. *Φίλων*)

——(Basileidai): **(646)** s. iii BC ib. 62, 3 (f. *Θρασύβουλος*)

——(*φυλ. δευτ.*): **(647)** iii AD ib. 156 (*Αὐρ. Δ.*: f. *Αὐρ. Χρυσόγονος*)

—PISTIROS: **(648)** iv BC *IGB* III 1067 (s. *Διοτρέφης*); **(649)** iv-iii BC *SEG* XLIX 912. 5 (vase) (*Ζιονύσι(ος)*)

—SALYMBRIA: **(650)** c. 460-450 BC *IG* I³ 1154 (*FRA* 6631) (f. *Πυθαγόρας*); **(651)** imp. *AEMÖ* 17 (1894) p. 57 no. 4 (f. *Λυσανίας*)

—SESTOS: **(652)** hell.? *RA* 1912, p. 263 no. 49 (*[Διον]ύσιος*: s. *Σάτυρος*)

—SOSTIS (MOD.): **(653)** iii AD *IThrakAig* E394 (*Διονύσιος*: I s. *Δάλις*, f. *Αὐρ. Διονύσιος* II); **(654)** ~ ib. (*Αὐρ. Διονύσιος*: II s. *Διονύσιος* I, f. *Αὐρ. Μελάμπους*)

—ZONE?: **(655)** i-ii AD ib. E426 (s. *Τελεσφόρος*)

THRACE?: **(656)** 316-309 BC *IG* II² 1956, 3 (*FRA* 2515); *Ancient Macedonia* 5 p. 445 with n. 10 (date); **(657)** ~ *IG* II² 1956, 14; *Ancient Macedonia* 5 p. 445 with n. 10 (date) (*FRA* 2516); **(658)** s. iii BC *Thess. Mnem.* 47 (Velkov 99) (s. *Σεύθης*); **(659)** ii-iii AD *IGUR* 132 (*Αὐρ. Δ.*); **(660)** s. iii AD Dain, *IGLouvre* 27; *Dacia* 19 (1975) p. 200 no. 6 (locn., date) (or Macedonia?: f. *Ἰοῦστος*)

Διονῦσις

CIMMERIAN BOSPOROS:

—NYMPHAION: **(1)** f. iii BC *SEG* XLV 997. 3

MACEDONIA (BOTTIAIA):

—BEROIA: **(2)** ii AD *IBer* 224 (Tataki 407) (s. *Εὐτυχίδης*)

MACEDONIA (CHALKIDIKE):

—STREPSA?: **(3)** 198 AD *SEG* XXIX 648

MACEDONIA (LYNKESTIS):

—ACHLADA (MOD.): **(4)** f. iii AD *EAM* 169, 2 (s. *Αὐρ. Μέμη*)

—HERAKLEIA: **(5)** ii-iii AD *IG* X (2) (2) 60

MACEDONIA (MYGDONIA):

—LETE?: **(6)** ii-iii AD *SEG* I 277 (*Δειο-*)

—THESSALONIKE: **(7)** ii AD *IG* X (2) (1) 426 (f. *Διονύσιος*); **(8)** ii-iii AD Nalpantis, *Anaskaphi* p. 111 no. BE 118 (f. *Διοδώρα*); **(9)** iii AD *IG* X (2) (1) 307 (*Αὐρ. Δ. ὁ καὶ Συνδήρας*); **(10)** v-vi AD Feissel, *RICM* 166 (*SEG* XLVII 978)

MACEDONIA (ODOMANTIKE):

—SIRRHA: **(11)** f. iii AD ib. XXX 590, 25 (*[Αὐρ.] Δ.*: s. *Βίθυς*)

MACEDONIA (SINTIKE):

—HERAKLEIA: **(12)** ii AD *IGB* IV 2325

SCYTHIA MINOR:

—TOMIS: **(13)** ii-iii AD *ISM* II 26, 9 (s. *Ἑστιαῖος*); **(14)** ~ ib. 369, 11 (s. *Διονυσόδωρος*, *Ἰουλία*); **(15)** ~ ib. 468, 5 (s. *Μητρόδωρος*); **(16)** ~ ib. l. 9 (s. *Τιμόθεος*); **(17)** ~ ib. l. 17 (s. *Καλλικράτης*)

THRACE: **(18)** ii-i BC *IG* II² 8905 (*FRA* 2517); **(19)** imp. *Arkheologiia* (Sofia) 1971 (3), pp. 26-7 nos. 14-15; 37; 40 (stamp) (Lat. Dionisis)

—APOLLONIA-SOZOPOLIS: **(20)** i-ii AD *IGB* I² 401, 7 (*Διονύ[σις]*: s. *Κάσιος*)

—BYZANTION: **(21)** i-ii AD *IByz* 269 (Fıratlı–Robert pp. 84-5 no. 104) (s. *Ἄδυς*); **(22)** ii AD *IByz* 312 (Fıratlı–Robert p. 120 no. 202) (*Διιύσις*—*IByz* per err.: s. *Νικίας*)

—BYZANTION (TERRIT.): **(23)** i-ii AD *IByz* 174 (s. *Εἰράνιχος*); **(24)** ii-iii AD ib. 25; cf. Robert, *OMS* 5 p. 225 (s. *Νίκων*)

—BYZANTION?: **(25)** i AD *IByz* 372 (*Δ. ὁ καὶ Πόπλιος*: s. *Μενίσκος*, f. *Πῶλλα*, *Μενεκράτης*); **(26)** ii AD ib. 334 (s. *Ἡρόξενος*)

—MARKIANOPOLIS (NR.): **(27)** f. iii AD *IGB* II 837 (*CCET* II (1) 331) (s. *Μένανδρος*)

—PAUTALIA:

——(Herakleis): **(28)** ?ii AD *IGB* IV 2077, 16 (s. *Βάργος*)

—PHILIPPOPOLIS-TRIMONTIUM: **(29)** imp. ib. III 1004

—PHILIPPOPOLIS-TRIMONTIUM (TERRIT.): **(30)** imp. *Latomus* 19 (1960) p. 124 no. 15 (vase) (*[Διο]νύσις*)

—SALYMBRIA: **(31)** imp. *IByz* S 8 (s. *Ἐπίκτητος*)

—TĂMNO CAVE (MOD.): **(32)** ii-iii AD *IGB* II 751 b

Διονυσιφάνης

MACEDONIA (CHALKIDIKE):

—OLYNTHOS: **(1)** v/iv BC *IG* XII (8) 434 (Tataki, *Macedonians* p. 134 no. 37) (f. *Νικώ*)

—STOLOS?: **(2)** ?350 BC *SEG* XXXVIII 670, 2 (f. *Βιλταλώ*)

MACEDONIA (EDONIS):

—AMPHIPOLIS?: **(3)** iv BC ib. XLVII 887 (*Διονυσιφά[νης]*: s. *Κτησικράτης*)

Διονυσογένης

MACEDONIA (BOTTIAIA):

—PELLA (NR.): **(1)** iii BC *Α΄ Panell. Synedr. Epigr.* p. 183 no. 7 (*SEG* XXX 582) (f. *Ἄρπαλος*)

MACEDONIA (MYGDONIA):

—THESSALONIKE: **(2)** 132 AD *IG* X (2) (1) 35, 4 (f. *Καπίτων*)

—THESSALONIKE?: **(3)** ii AD ib. 715 (?f. *Εὐμένης*)

MACEDONIA (PIERIA):

—PYDNA: **(4)** c. 230-200 BC *BCH* 45 (1921) p. 17 III, 55 (Tataki, *Macedonians* p. 170 no. 8) (s. *Ἀλκίμαχος*)

THRACE:

—ODESSOS: **(5)** iii BC *IGB* I² 105 (s. *Ἑρμάφιλος*); **(6)** ii AD ib. 50 b, 6 (*Δυονυσογ[ένης]*); **(7)** ~ ib. 171 (PM 1453) (f. *Παρμένων*)

Διονυσόδοτος

MACEDONIA (BOTTIAIA):

—MIEZA: **(1)** i AD Mendel, *Cat.* 1036 (Tataki 408) (s. *Τάρης*)

Διονυσοδώρα

MACEDONIA (CHALKIDIKE):

—POTIDAIA-KASSANDREIA (NR.): **(1)** 253 AD *SEG* XXXVIII 599, 1 (*Αὐρ. [Διονυ]σοδώρα*: m. *Αὐρ. Διονυσία*)

Διονυσόδωρος

CIMMERIAN BOSPOROS:

—GORGIPPIA: **(1)** f. iii BC *CIRB* 1137 B I, 37 (f. *Παπίας*); **(2)** ~ ib. 1137 B II, 26 (s. *Ἀπολ—*)

—HERMONASSA: **(3)** iv BC ib. 1056 II, 12 (*Διονυσόδ[ωρος]*: f. *Θεογένης*)

—MYRMEKION: **(4)** iv BC ib. 872 (f. *Βουλάστης*)

—PANTIKAPAION: **(5)** 82 AD ib. 76, 20 (*SEG* XVIII 310) (s. *Σώστρατος*)

MACEDONIA: **(6)** 232 or 207 BC *CPR* XVIII 28, 97 (Tataki, *Macedonians* p. 302 no. 75); cf. La'da E1752 (I f. *Διονυσόδωρος* II); **(7)** ~ *CPR* XVIII 28, [97], 102, 106, 108 (Tataki, *Macedonians* p. 302 no. 74; La'da E1752) (II s. *Διονυσόδωρος* I: t.e.)

MACEDONIA (BOTTIAIA):

—PELLA: **(8)** c. 250-225 BC Akamatis, *Amph. Pellas* p. 34 no. PAR15 (amph.); pp. 19-20 (date) (*SEG* L 613)

MACEDONIA (CHALKIDIKE):

—POTIDAIA-KASSANDREIA: **(9)** m. iv BC *IG* II² 10109 (Tataki, *Macedonians* p. 168 no. 4; *FRA* 6160) (f. *Αἰσχίνης*); **(10)** ii BC *IG* II² 8998 (Tataki, *Macedonians* p. 88 no. 29; *FRA* 2784) (s. *Ἀπολλώνιος*)

—POTIDAIA-KASSANDREIA?:

——(Boutapedieis): **(11)** ?f. iii BC *SEG* XLVI 797; *BE* 1998, no. 267 (locn.)

MACEDONIA (EDONIS):

—AMPHIPOLIS: **(12)** s. iv BC *PAE* 1981, p. 25 with pl. 43 *β*, 1 (*[Διον]υσόδωρος*)

MACEDONIA (MYGDONIA):

—THESSALONIKE: **(13)** ?39 BC *IG* X (2) (1) 50, 7 (s. *Ἀσκληπιόδωρος*); **(14)** ii AD ib. 330

—THESSALONIKE?: **(15)** i-ii AD ib. 687; **(16)** ii AD ib. 704 (s. *Ἐπίκτησις*)

MACEDONIA (ODOMANTIKE):

—SIRRHA: **(17)** 183 AD Dimitsas 816 (Kaphtantzis 12) (— *ὁ καὶ Διονυσόδ[ω]ρος*: s. *Τορκουᾶτος*); **(18)** f. iii AD *SEG* XXX 590, 5 (f. *Αὐρ. Διογένης*)

Macedonia (Pieria):
—dion: **(19)** ii-iii ad Dimitsas 174 (s. *Ἐρέννιος Διονυσᾶς*)
Sarmatia:
—maiotai: **(20)** hell.-imp. *NS* 229
Scythia Minor:
—istros: **(21)** v bc Unp. (Avram, defixio) 2, 2 (f. *Ἀγαθήνωρ*); **(22)** iii-ii bc ib. 4, 5 (*Διον[υσό]δωρος*); **(23)** c. 48-52 ad *ISM* i 67, 53; 68, 53; **(24)** ii ad ib. 137, 17 (*Διονυσό-δ[ωρος]*: f. *Διονύσιος*); **(25)** 138 ad ib. 193 I, 14 (*Διονυσόδωρ[ος]*: f. *Κουσίας*); **(26)** ~ ib. l. 44 (s. *Κουσίας*); **(27)** ~ ib. l. 67 (s. *Διονύσιος*); **(28)** ~ ib. l. 80 (f. *Διονύσιος*); **(29)** ~ ib. l. 96 (s. *Διονύσιος*); **(30)** ~ ib. 193 II, 50 (f. *Ἱερώνυμος*); **(31)** ~ ib. l. 76 (f. *Χαιρήμων*); **(32)** f. iii ad ib. 143, 11 ([*Αὐρ.*] [*Διον*]*υσόδ*[*ωρος*]?)
—kallatis: **(33)** 241-244 ad ib. iii 74 A, 23 (s. *Ἰταλικός*)
—tomis: **(34)** ii-iii ad ib. ii 369, 1 (I f. *Ἰούλις, Διονυσόδωρος* II, *Λεοντιανός, Διονύσις, Ἀγριππῖνα*); **(35)** ~ ib. l. 10 (II s. *Διονυσόδωρος* I, *Ἰουλία*)
Skythia:
—olbia-borysthenes: **(36)** s. v bc *IOlbia* 58, 3 (Dubois, *IGDOlbia* 2) (*Διονυσ[ό]δωρος*: s. *Λήναιος*); **(37)** s. iv bc *SEG* l 702 III, 3 (s. *Ἡραγόρης*); **(38)** i/ii ad *IOlbia* 90, 12 (s. *Βούδεις*)
—tyras: **(39)** 181 ad *IOSPE* I^2 2, 29 (s. *Ἀχιλλαῖος*)
Thrace:
—abdera: **(40)** 346 bc *IG* II^2 218, 2, 16, 30 (*FRA* 2) (f. *Διοσκουρίδης, Χαρμῆς, Ἀναξίπολις*); **(41)** ?253 bc Nachtergael, *Les Galates* 10, 14 (Stephanis 765) (s. *Πάρμις*); **(42)** c. 230-200 bc *BCH* 45 (1921) p. 18 III, 88 (f. *Διονυσᾶς*: reading—Oulhen); **(43)** ~ ib. l. 89 (s. *Νυμφόδωρος*: reading—Oulhen)
—apollonia-sozopolis: **(44)** iv bc *BMN-Burgas* 4 (2002) p. 119 no. 1 (f. *Ζωβίη*); **(45)** i-ii ad *IGB* I^2 401, 12 (*Διονυσό[δω]ρος*: s. *Ἡρακλείδης*)
—chersonesos: **(46)** iv bc *IG* I^2 10505 (*FRA* 7303) (f. *Ἀπολλωνίδης*)
—dionysopolis: **(47)** iii ad *IGB* I^2 14 b, 22 (*Αὐρ. Δ.*: s. *Σιγηρός*); **(48)** 241-244 ad ib. 22 bis, 10 (*Διονυσόδ[ωρος]*)
—limnai: **(49)** ii-i bc *IKyz* i 507, 1, 3 (s. *Πυθέας*)
—lysimacheia: **(50)** m. ii bc *ISestos* 38 b, 1 (f. *Ἀρκέσας*); **(51)** ~ ib. l. 8 (s. *Φίλιππος*)
—mesambria: **(52)** iii bc *IGB* I^2 336 (s. *Τελεσάγορος*, f. *Τελεσάγορος*)
—odessos: **(53)** 215 ad ib. 47, 7 (*Αὐρ. Δ.*: s. *Ἰουλιανός*)
—philippopolis-trimontium: **(54)** m. iii ad ib. iii 884 b, 18; cf. v 5400 (*Αὐρ. Δ.*)
—philippopolis-trimontium (territ.): **(55)** iii ad ib. iii 1126 (*Αὐρ. Δ.*)

Διονυσόμανδρος
Thrace:
—apollonia-sozopolis: **(1)** iv bc ib. I^2 428 (*Διονυσόμαν[δρος]*: f. *Ἐλεοσίνιος*)

Διόνυσος
Thrace:
—byzantion: **(1)** hell.-imp. *IByz* 302 (*Διονύσ(ι)ος*?: s. *Μήνιος*)

Διονυσοφάνης
Macedonia (Chalkidike):
—anthemous: **(1)** i bc/i ad *SEG* xlii 567 (s. *Σέλης*)
Macedonia (Derriopos):
—stuberra: **(2)** c. 41-48 ad *IG* x (2) (2) 323, 27 (s. *Ἀριστόδημος*)
Macedonia (Edonis):
—amphipolis: **(3)** ii/iii ad *SEG* xxxv 713, 1 (s. *Ἀπολλώνιος*, f. *Λᾶγος*)
—amphipolis?: **(4)** hell. Dimitsas 896 (s. *Ἄτταλος*)
Macedonia (Mygdonia):
—thessalonike: **(5)** 223 bc *IG* x (2) (1) 2, 6 (f. *Ἐ—*); **(6)** i bc-i ad ib. 129, 4; **(7)** ?39 bc ib. 30, 6; 50, 6; 109, 11 (f. *Στίλβων*)
Skythia:
—olbia-borysthenes: **(8)** s. iii bc *IOSPE* I^2 76, 5 (Sokolowski ii 88; Dubois, *IGDOlbia* 88) (f. *Ἐπιχάρης*)
Tauris:
—chersonesos: **(9)** ii bc Vinogradov, *Pont. Stud.* p. 370 (*SEG* xxviii 658) ([*Διον*]*υσοφάνη*[*ς*])
Thrace:
—bisanthe-panion: **(10)** iv bc Unp. (Sayar) (s. *Πολύδιγγος*)
—byzantion: **(11)** i-ii ad *IByz* 232 (*-σω-*: s. *Θεόδωρος*)
—maroneia: **(12)** ii-i bc *IThrakAig* E212, 31 (*Διονυ[σοφ]άνης*: f. *Διονύσιος*)
—stryme: **(13)** c. 425-400 bc *SEG* xxxv 765 (*IThrakAig* E121) (s. *Θεοκλῆς*); **(14)** c. 400-375 bc *SEG* xlvii 1106 (*IThrakAig* E137) (f. *Πατροκλῆς*); **(15)** f. iv bc ib. E147 (*Διονυσοφά[νης]*: f. *Λεοντι—*)

Διονυσοφῶν
Macedonia (Bottiaia):
—pella: **(1)** c. 380-350 bc *SEG* xliii 434, 1, 5; cf. xlvi 776
Macedonia (Mygdonia):
—lete: **(2)** m. i bc ib. xvii 318, 1; *KGAM Thess.* i 56 (date) (s. *Ἱππόστρατος*)

Διονυττᾶς
Scythia Minor:
—istros: **(1)** ii ad *ISM* i 196, 11; 211, 15 (s. *Πίστος*); **(2)** s. ii ad ib. 167, 16 + *Ling. Balk.* 27 (1984) p. 87 (*M. Δ.*: s. *Ἀρτεμίδωρος*)

Διόξενος
Macedonia: **(1)** 330 bc Curt. vi 7. 15; *RE* Supplbd. 4 (-); Berve 280 (Tataki, *Macedonians* p. 302 no. 76) (Lat. Dioxenum—Vogel & Berve, Theoxenum—Hedicke)

Διοπείθης
Macedonia (Chalkidike):
—olynthos: **(1)** ?352 bc *TAPA* 69 (1938) p. 48 no. 3, 6; *SEG* xxxviii 637, 2; Hatzopoulos, *Actes Chalc.* p. 80 (date) (s. *Ἀντίπατρος*)
Scythia Minor:
—istros: **(2)** ?iv bc *ISM* i 259 (f. *Ἀπολλ—*); **(3)** iii bc ib. 250

Δῖος
Cimmerian Bosporos:
—hermonassa: **(1)** iv bc *CIRB* 1056 II, 7 (s. *Ἀρχέδημος*)
—nymphaion: **(2)** v bc ib. 911 (s. *Ἁρμα—*)
—pantikapaion: **(3)** i ad ib. 394 (s. *Βάκχιος*); **(4)** ~ ib. 564 + KW pl. 50 no. 701 (s. *Ἀνδρόνικος*)
—pantikapaion?: **(5)** m. i bc *SEG* xxvii 436, 1, 13
Scythia Minor:
—tomis: **(6)** ii ad *ISM* ii 125, 15 (s. *Ἀσταῖος*)
Skythia:
—tanais: **(7)** ii ad *CIRB* 1262, 21 (*Δεῖ-*: f. *Θίμβρος*); **(8)** 104 ad ib. 1259, 22 (*Δεῖ-*: f. *Ἀρίστων*); **(9)** c. 200-210 ad ib. 1277, 14 (*Δεῖ-*: f. *Διόφαντος*)
Thrace:
—abdera: **(10)** iv/iii bc *SEG* xxx 661 + *IThrakAig* E49 ([*Δ*]*ῖος*?: s. *Ἑρμόφιλος*)
—dionysopolis: **(11)** hell. *Spink Num. Circular* 105 (1997) pp. 372-3 nos. 12; 18 (coin) (*Δίου* (gen.))
—pautalia (territ.): **(12)** ii ad *IGB* iv 2214, 12 (*Δεῖ-*: s. *Δινίας*)
—philippopolis-trimontium: **(13)** imp. ib. iii 1004 (*Δεῖ-*: s. *Ζωΐλος*)
—serdica (territ.): **(14)** ii-iii ad *AEMÖ* 10 (1886) pp. 238-9 no. 2, 8 (*Δῖο[ς]*)

Διοσκόρη
Macedonia (Mygdonia):
—lete (nr.): **(1)** c. 220-230 ad *SEG* xlviii 855 (*-σσκό-*: m. *Παράμονος, Στρατονίκη, Παραμόνα, Σωκράτης*)
—thessalonike?: **(2)** ii ad *IG* x (2) (1) 808, 5 (d. *Εὔτυχος, Συμφέρουσα*); **(3)** ii-iii ad ib. 810 (*Δεκμία Δ.*: m. *Δέκμιος Χαρίτων, Δέκμιος Βιθυνικός*)
Macedonia (Paionia):
—kavadarci (mod.): **(4)** ii-iii ad *Sp.* 98 (1941-8) p. 64 no. 134

Διόσκορος
Thrace:
—ainos: **(1)** ii ad *SEG* xxxvi 657, 7 (s. *Φιλαπόδημος, Ἰωνία*)

Διοσκουρίδας
Scythia Minor:
—kallatis: **(1)** iii/ii bc *ISM* iii 36, 2 (f. *Βίκων*); **(2)** a. 15 ad ib. 45, 3 (f. *Φίλων*)
Tauris:
—chersonesos: **(3)** c. 300-285 bc Kats p. 93 no. 40 (amph.); **(4)** iii bc *MIA* 34 (1953) p. 73 (bronze); cf. Vinogradov, *Pont. Stud.* p. 637 (*-σκδρ-*: f. *Ἀρτεμίδωρος*); **(5)** f. iii bc Kats p. 109 no. 96 (amph.) (f. *Ποσειδώνιος*); **(6)** ~ *SEG* xl 615 A, 12 (*Διοσ[κουρίδας]*?: s. *—ιτος*); **(7)** c. 262-237 bc Kats p. 93 no. 41 (amph.) (s. *Ἀπολλᾶς*); **(8)** ~ ib. p. 93 no. 42 (amph.) (s. *Θεόδωρος*); **(9)** c. 215-200 bc ib. pp. 93-4 no. 43 (amph.) (s. *Πυθόδωρος*)
Thrace:
—kypsela: **(10)** hell. *IG* xii (1) 112, 7
—mesambria: **(11)** iii/ii bc Karayotov, *Mesambria* i pp. 89-91 nos. 202-4; 220-31; Price, *Alexander* 1004 (coin); **(12)** ~ *IGB* I^2 335 septies (PM 2268); cf. *IGB* v 5111; **(13)** i bc ib. I^2 315, 15 (f. *Διόδωρος*)

Διοσκουρίδης
Cimmerian Bosporos:
—pantikapaion: **(1)** f. iv bc *CIRB* 178 (*-σκδρ-*: s. *Θάγυς*); **(2)** i ad ib. 446; cf. KW pl. 25 no. 367 (*Δ[ιο]σκουρίδης*)
Macedonia: **(3)** 315-314 bc *RE* (1) (Tataki, *Macedonians* p. 302 no.77) (s. *Πολεμαῖος*); **(4)** m. ii bc *BGU* 1939 A, 10 (Tataki, *Macedonians* p. 481 no. 92; La'da E1479) (s. *Νικο—*); **(5)** 148 bc *PTeb* 99, 45 (*PP* 2203 with Add.; Tataki, *Macedonians* p. 481 no. 91; La'da E1478) (s. *Ἀλέξανδρος*); **(6)** 113 bc *PDion* 27, [2], 8, 11, 17, 20 (Tataki, *Macedonians* p. 481 no. 90; La'da E1480); **(7)** iii-iv ad *IG* II^2 4828; *AM* 67 (1942) p. 59 no. 99 (locn.) (Tataki, *Macedonians* p. 106 no. 2; *FRA* 1650)
Macedonia (Bisaltia):
—arolos? (ambeloi (mod.)): **(8)** 21 ad *SEG* xxiv 613
—euporia?: **(9)** ii-iii ad *RA* 1945, p. 38 (s. *Ἀρτεμᾶς*); **(10)** iii ad ib. p. 39 (s. *Εὐβίοτος*, f. *Εὐβίοτος*)
—terpni (mod.): **(11)** iii bc *SEG* xxv 719 (xlviii 846) (s. *Ἀπολλόδωρος*)
Macedonia (Bottiaia):
—beroia: **(12)** 41-44 ad *IBer* 60, 9 (Tataki 409); **(13)** s. i ad *IBer* 117, 25 (Tataki 410) (s. *Ἀλέξανδρος*); **(14)** ii-iii ad *IBer* 90, 5 (Tataki 988) (*Οὐαριανὸς Δ.*: f. *Οὐαριανὸς Διδιανὸς Δημήτριος*); **(15)** ~ *IBer* 92, 4 (Tataki 629) (*Ἰούν. Δ. ὁ καὶ Δουλκίτιος*: s. *Ἰουν. Κάλη*); **(16)** ~ *IBer* 129, 1 (f. *Ἀντιγόνα*)
—mieza: **(17)** hell. *AM* 27 (1902) p. 314 no. 28, 7 (*Διοσκουρ[ίδης]*)

Macedonia (Chalkidike):
—Anthemous: **(18)** 106 BC *SEG* XLII 561 (s. Κίλας)
—Potidaia-Kassandreia: **(19)** v/iv BC ib. XLV 798 (f. Μελάνθιος)
Macedonia (Derriopos):
—Stuberra: **(20)** i BC/i AD *IG* XII (8) 206, 12 (Tataki, *Macedonians* p. 177 no. 3) (f. Ἀντιφάνης); **(21)** 74 AD *IG* X (2) (2) 325, 39 (f. Ἀντίγονος); **(22)** 116 AD ib. 327, 30 (f. Σωσίας)
Macedonia (Edonis):
—Amphipolis: **(23)** hell.? *SEG* XXXIII 504 (tile) (potter); **(24)** 157 AD Dimitsas 863 (f. Ἡρώ)
—Amphipolis (territ.): **(25)** 20 BC or 96 AD *SEG* XXXV 710 (f. Μάντα); **(26)** 56 or 172 AD ib. XXX 600 (Δι[οσκ]ουρίδης: f. Μαντώ); **(27)** 61 or 177 AD Kaphtantzis 589 (f. ..ματοης?)
—Amphipolis?: **(28)** ii-iii AD Dimitsas 906 (Kaphtantzis 543) (s. Ἡλιζις)
—Amphipolis (territ.)?: **(29)** 22 or 149 AD *SEG* XXXIII 543 (Pilhofer 596); **(30)** 121 AD *BCH* 24 (1900) p. 309 (Pilhofer 585) (f. Σαιδείλας)
—Philippoi: **(31)** imp. *AE* 1950-1, p. 65 no. 8 (Pilhofer 723) (Lat. Dioscuridu (gen.): I f. Διοσκουρίδης II); **(32)** ~ *AE* 1950-1, p. 65 no. 8 (Pilhofer 723) (Lat. Dioscuride (dat.): II s. Διοσκουρίδης I); **(33)** ~ Collart, *Philippes* p. 415 n. 5 (Pilhofer 408) (Lat. Dioscuridis (gen.): f. Care.is)
—Philippoi (territ.): **(34)** ?212 AD Pikoulas, *Chora* p. 164 no. 73, 10 (Pilhofer 607) (Διοσκουρί[δη]ς: f. Λεωνίδης)
—Philippoi (Drama (mod.)): **(35)** ?ii-i BC *SEG* XLVIII 794 (Pilhofer 501b) (s. Ἀντίγονος); **(36)** i-ii AD *AD* 51 (1996) Chron. p. 577, 18 (Lat. Dioscurides: f. Ταρουσίνας)
Macedonia (Mygdonia):
—Kalindoia: **(37)** ?i-ii AD *SEG* XXIX 628, 2 (f. Τερτία); **(38)** 68-98 AD ib. XLII 580, 60 (s. Νικόμαχος); **(39)** ~ ib. l. 72 (s. Ταρουσίνας) ?= (*55*); **(40)** ~ ib. l. 73 (f. Δάλης); **(41)** ~ ib. l. 75 + *BE* 1999, no. 362 (f. Νικύλος); **(42)** ~ *SEG* XLII 580, 78 (Δι(οσ)κουρίδης: f. Βένζης); **(43)** ~ ib. l. 84 (s. Δάλης); **(44)** ~ ib. l. 85 (f. Ζιπύρων); **(45)** ~ ib. l. 88 (s. Ταράλας); **(46)** ~ ib. l. 91 (?s. Μάντα); **(47)** a. 98 AD ib. 582, 18 (f. Ζωΐλος); **(48)** ~ ib. l. 28 (s. Ἀπολλώνιος); **(49)** ~ ib. l. 31 (?s. Κοσουμάσης); **(50)** ~ ib. l. 35 (I f. Διοσκουρίδης II); **(51)** ~ ib. l. 35 (II s. Διοσκουρίδης I); **(52)** ~ ib. l. 39 (s. Μένανδρος); **(53)** ~ ib. l. 44 (I f. Διοσκουρίδης II); **(54)** ~ ib. l. 44 (II s. Διοσκουρίδης I); **(55)** ~ ib. l. 62 (f. Ταρουσίνας, Μιήζεις) ?= (*39*); **(56)** ~ ib. l. 64 (s. Γαυδίων); **(57)** ~ ib. 583, 10 (f. —όλας); **(58)** 254 AD ib. 604, 1 (Αὐρ. Δ.: f. Αὐρ. Τρόπος); **(59)** ~ ib. l. 2 (Αὐρ. Δ.); **(60)** ?255 AD ib. 603 b (s. Ἀρτεμίδωρος); **(61)** ~ ib. (f. Ἀρτεμίδωρος)
—Lete: **(62)** f. ii BC ib. XLVI 764, 17 (-σακου-: s. Ἀριστοκλῆς)
—Lete?: **(63)** 22 or 139 AD Dimitsas 678, 2 (f. Παυσανίας)
—Thessalonike: **(64)** 15 BC *IG* X (2) (1) 85 (f. —ίτας); **(65)** i-ii AD ib. 243 I, 8 (f. Νικόλαος); **(66)** ~ ib. 243 II, 10 (f. Ἀλέξανδρος); **(67)** s. i AD ib. 68, 11 ([Δ]ιοσκουρίδης); **(68)** ~ ib. l. 15 ([Διο]σκουρίδης); **(69)** ii AD ib. 241 A II, 35 (Αἴλ. [Δ]ιοσκ[ουρίδης]); **(70)** ~ ib. 241 B, 2 ([Δι]οσκουρίδ[ης]: s. Εὔπορος); **(71)** ~ ib. 315, 5 (f. Λύσιππος); **(72)** ~ ib. 422 (Διοσ(κ)ορίδης); **(73)** 134 AD ib. 462 A-B (f. Ἀγαθημερίς, Ἀμιλλα); **(74)** s. ii AD *SEG* XLVIII 850; **(75)** 173-182 AD *IG* X (2) (1) 508, 1 (Μ. Ἄππ[ιος] [Διοσ]κουρί[δης]: I ?f. Διοσκουρίδης II); **(76)** ~ ib. l. 6 (Διοσκ[ουρίδης]: II ?s. Μ. Ἄππιος Διοσκουρίδης I); **(77)** 246 AD ib. 162, 9; 197, 10 (Μάρκιος Δ.: s. Μάρκιος Ἀθηναγόρας, Ἰουν. Βωτιανή)
—Thessalonike (nr.): **(78)** ii-iii AD *AD* 31 (1976) p. 238 no. 1 with pl. 192 α (Διεσκουρ[ίδης]); **(79)** ~ *IG* X (2) (1) 1003, 1
—Thessalonike?: **(80)** i AD ib. 846 (s. Δρύλης, f. Ἀγάθων); **(81)** ii AD ib. 879; **(82)** s. ii AD ib. 902 (f. Ἑρμῆς); **(83)** 152 AD ib. 923, 1 (I s. Γενήμανος, f. Διοσκουρίδης II, Ἀρτέμιν); **(84)** ~ ib. l. 3 (II s. Διοσκουρίδης I, Ἀπολλωνία)
Macedonia (Odomantike):
—Drabeskos?: **(85)** ii-iii AD Kaphtantzis 569 (Pilhofer 576) (Δι[οσκο]υρίδης); **(86)** ~ *SEG* XXX 619, 1 (Pilhofer 572) (f. Διζάπης); **(87)** ~ *SEG* XXX 619, 2 (Pilhofer 572) (s. Ζιπύρων); **(88)** ~ *SEG* XXX 619, 6 (Pilhofer 572) ([Διοσ]κουρίδης: f. Μαν—)
—Gazoros (territ.): **(89)** 101-106 AD *SEG* XXX 596, 10 (Pilhofer 555) (s. Τόρκος); **(90)** 106 AD *SEG* XXX 596, 1, 5 (Pilhofer 555) (s. (nat.) Παίβης, s. (ad.) Μούκασος, f. Διονύσιος, Τόρκος)
—Gazoros (territ.)?: **(91)** ?132 AD *RA* 1945 (2), pp. 44-5 (Pilhofer 551) ([Δι]οσκουρίδης: f. Ἀρσ—)
—Oldenoi: **(92)** ii-iii AD *AE* 1936, Chron. p. 17 no. 10, 1, 10 (Pilhofer 568; *SEG* L 605) (s. Σύρος)
—Sirrha: **(93)** 62 or 178 AD *JDAI* 84 (1969) p. 157 no. R27, 1, 5 (s. Διονύσιος, ?f. Μωμώ); **(94)** s. ii AD Dimitsas 812, 13 (Kaphtantzis 16) (s. Ποσείδιππος); **(95)** 155 AD Dimitsas 821, 2 (Kaphtantzis 1) (f. Ἀντίγονος); **(96)** ~ Dimitsas 821, 8 (Kaphtantzis 1) (s. Βουρείλας); **(97)** ~ Dimitsas 821, 12 (Kaphtantzis 1) (s. Διονύσιος); **(98)** ~ Dimitsas 821, 17 (Kaphtantzis 1) (f. Τορκουᾶτος); **(99)** ~ Dimitsas 821, 20, 22 (Kaphtantzis 1) (f. Τορκουπαίβης); **(100)** ~ Dimitsas 821, 27 (Kaphtantzis 1) (f. Ἀλέξανδρος); **(101)** ~ Dimitsas 821, 31 (Kaphtantzis 1) (f. Ζώσιλμος); **(102)** f. iii AD *SEG* XXX 590, 12 (Αὐρ. Δ.: s. Πίστος); **(103)** ~ ib. l. 17 (Διοσκουρίδης: I f. Αὐρ. Διοσκουρίδης II); **(104)** ~ ib. l. 17 (Αὐρ. Διοσκουρί[δης]: II s. Διοσκουρίδης I)
—Sirrha (territ.): **(105)** 55 or 171 AD ib. XXXIV 676 (Διοσκουρίδης: s. Τόρκος, Μαντώ); **(106)** s. ii AD *Tekmeria* 6 (2001) p. 49 (f. Δημόκριτος)
—Sirrha (nr.): **(107)** ii-iii AD *SEG* XXIV 579, 1 (Pilhofer 561) ([Φλ]άβιος Διοσκουρ[ί]δης); **(108)** ~ *SEG* XXIV 579, 5 (Pilhofer 561) (s. Πύλης)
Macedonia (Paionia):
—Astrea: **(109)** 227 AD *ZPE* 121 (1998) pp. 283-86 (Lat. M. Aurelius Dioscorides)
—Bylazora: **(110)** ii-iii AD *Sp.* 71 (1931) p. 40 no 89 = 71 (1931) p. 153 no. 384 (s. Αὐρ. Γαϊανός, Σεμέλη); **(111)** iii AD ib. p. 27 no. 53 (Αὐρ. Δ.)
—Demir Kapija (mod.): **(112)** ii AD *SEG* XXIX 578 (Διοσ[κουρίδ]ης? (n. pr.?))
—Kavadarci (mod.): **(113)** ?ii AD *Sp.* 75 (1933) p. 33 no. 89; cf. Düll, *Götterkulte* p. 396 no. 241 (ΔΙΟΣΚΟΥΡΙΔΙΙΙ (maj.), Διοσκουριδίω? (dat.)—ed.: s. Κόϊντος); **(114)** ii AD *Sp.* 98 (1941-8) p. 67 no. 140 (f. Ζωΐλος); **(115)** ii-iii AD ib. 71 (1931) p. 237 no. 631 = 75 (1933) p. 41 no. 140 (s. Πυθίας, f. Ἀλέξανδρος, Διονύσιος); **(116)** ~ *SEG* XVI 407
—Neapolis (area): **(117)** 83 AD ib. 404, 7 (f. Διονύσιος)
—Negotino (mod.): **(118)** imp. *Sp.* 98 (1941-8) p. 58 no. 118 (Δ. ὁ καὶ Τρεῖλας: I f. Διοσκουρίδης II); **(119)** ~ ib. (II s. Διοσκουρίδης I ὁ καὶ Τρεῖλας); **(120)** ii-iii AD ib. 71 (1931) p. 65 no. 144, 1 (f. Διονύσιος)
—Stoboi: **(121)** ii-iii AD ib. p. 46 no. 104 + *Studies Stobi* 1 p. 181 no. 7 ([Διοσκου]ρίδης?)
Macedonia (Pelagonia): **(122)** ii-iii AD *IG* X (2) (2) 237 (Αἴ(λιος) Δ.); **(123)** ~ ib. 255 (f. Ἰουλιανός); **(124)** ~ ib. 268 (s. Ὀλυμπιάς); **(125)** iii AD ib. 188, 3 (f. Ζωΐλος)
Macedonia (Pieria):
—Dion: **(126)** ii AD *Essays Laourdas* p. 108 no. 7 (f. Ἀλέξιππος)
Macedonia (Pieris):
—Galepsos: **(127)** 63 BC or 53 AD *SEG* XXVII 285 (f. Καζίζης)
—Neapolis: **(128)** c. 412-408 BC *IG* XII (8) 263, 12 + XII Suppl. p. 151; cf. *Ét. Thas.* 3 p. 145 n. 3 (Tataki, *Macedonians* p. 126 no. 7) (Διοσκõρι<ά>δεω (gen.)); **(129)** 356 BC *IG* II^2 128, 4, [9] (Tataki, *Macedonians* p. 126 no. 8) ([Δι]ο[σκ]ουρίδης: s. Ἀμειψίας)
—Oisyme-Emathia?: **(130)** s. iv BC *PAE* 1938, p. 92 no. 1, 2 (Διοσκουρίδ[ης])
Macedonia (Sintike):
—Parthikopolis*: **(131)** ii AD *IGB* IV 2269 (terracotta)
Scythia Minor:
—Istros: **(132)** iii BC *ISM* I 12, 3, 14 (s. Στρουθίων); **(133)** i BC-i AD ib. 191 II, 33 (s. Θεοκλῆς); **(134)** ~ ib. l. 40 (s. Παπίας); **(135)** 138 AD ib. 193 II, 29 (f. Ποσειδώνιος); **(136)** ~ ib. l. 68 (f. Θεόπομπος); **(137)** c. 138-160 AD ib. 193 I, 41; 207, 11 (f. Αἴλ. Ἀρτεμίδωρος)
—Istros (nr.):
——Vicus Secundini: **(138)** 202 AD ib. 344, 10 (Lat. Dioscoridentis (gen.): f. Ἀρτεμᾶς)
—Istros?: **(139)** iii/ii BC *Stud. Tacheva* pp. 280-1, 2 (Διοσ[κο]υρίδης: s. Ἀριστοκλῆς)
—Kallatis: **(140)** ii/iii AD *ISM* III 181, 2 (s. Μάξιμος); **(141)** f. iii AD ib. 105, 3 ([Διο]σκουρίδης)
—Kallatis?: **(142)** ii/i BC *IGB* II 867 a, 4 = *ISM* I 219 (v 87); cf. *ISM* III p. 140 (locn.) (s. Δ—)
—Tomis: **(143)** ii-i BC ib. II 36 (f. Διονύσιος); **(144)** i BC ib. 2, [1], 29 (f. Σαραπίων); **(145)** ~ ib. 2 A, 50 (s. Ἡρώνυμος); **(146)** ~ ib. l. 62 (s. Σωκράτης); **(147)** i AD ib. 126 (s. Ἀρίστων); **(148)** i-ii AD ib. 150, 2 (f. Νουμήνιος); **(149)** f. i AD *RPC* 1 1808-9 (coin) (Διοσκου(ρίδης)); **(150)** ii AD *ISM* II 17, 15 (Διοσκ[ουρ]ίδη[ς]: f. Ἄττας) ?= (*151*); **(151)** ~ ib. l. 16 (Διοσ[κ]ουρί[δης]: I f. Διοσκουρίδης II) ?= (*150*); **(152)** ~ ib. l. 16 (II s. Διοσκουρίδης I); **(153)** ~ ib. 125, 3 (Δ[ιο]σκουρίδης: f. Ἡρόξενος); **(154)** ii-iii AD ib. 394, 4 ([Δι]οσκουρ[ίδης]); **(155)** ~ ib. 468, 14 (f. Χαιρήμων)
Skythia:
—Olbia-Borysthenes: **(156)** m. iv BC Dubois, *IGDOlbia* 106, 4 (*SEG* XLIV 669) (-σκõρ-: s. Φιλογήθης); **(157)** iii BC Dubois, *IGDOlbia* 84 (vase) (s. Ἡφαιστικῶν); **(158)** ii BC *SNG BM Black Sea* 599; 611 (coins) (Διοσ(κουρίδης)?)
Tauris:
—Chersonesos: **(159)** ii AD *IOSPE* I^2 441 (-σσκου-: I f. Διοσκουρίδης II); **(160)** ~ ib. (-σσκου-: II s. Διοσκουρίδης I); **(161)** c. 120-130 AD Solomonik, *NEPKh* 112, 14 (Διοσκου[ρίδης]?); **(162)** 129 AD *IOSPE* I^2 359, 24 (f. Εὐρύδαμος); **(163)** 129-130 AD ib. l. 34; *VDI* 1960 (3), pp. 154-5, 27 (f. Μητρόδωρος); **(164)** 130 AD ib. l. 29 (f. Βοΐσκος)
Thrace:
—Abdera: **(165)** 346 BC *IG* II^2 218, 1, 7, 15, etc. (*FRA* 3) (s. Διονυσόδωρος)
—Ainos: **(166)** iii/ii BC *AD* 26 (1971) Chron. p. 260 with pl. 231 γ (s. Βενδιφάνης); **(167)** ii-i BC *SEG* XXXVI 661 (f. —ίδης)
—Apollonia-Sozopolis: **(168)** s. v BC *IGB* I^2 414 (-σκõρ-: f. Μενάλκης); **(169)** iv BC *BMN-Burgas* 4 (2002) p. 123 no. 13 (Δ(ι)οσκõρίδεω (gen.): f. —ης); **(170)** ~ ib. p. 126 no. 25 (-σκõρ-: s. Δᾶος)
—Byzantion: **(171)** m. iii BC Schönert-Geiss, *Byzantion* 1044-1102 (coin) (Διοσκουρ(ίδης))
—Byzantion (territ.): **(172)** imp. Unp. (Sayar) (Διο-: s. Ἀθήνιος)
—Byzantion:
——(Rhegion): **(173)** i BC-i AD *IByz* 253 A (s. Ζηνόβιος)

—MARONEIA: (**174**) hell.? *IThrakAig* E367 (*Διοσκο[υρί]δης*); (**175**) ii-i BC ib. E212, 9 (I f. *Διοσκουρίδης* II); (**176**) ~ ib. l. 9 (II s. *Διοσκουρίδης* I); (**177**) ~ ib. l. 11 (*Δ. ...βᾶς*); (**178**) ~ ib. l. 14 (s. *Διονύσιος*); (**179**) ~ ib. l. 34 (s. *—υως* (gen.)); (**180**) ~ ib. l. 40 ([*Διοσκ*]*ουρίδης*: s. *Καλλιγένης*); (**181**) ~ ib. l. 53 (f. *Φᾶσις*); (**182**) imp. ib. E289 (f. *Ἀμύνανδρος, Ἀπολλώνιος*)

—ODESSOS: (**183**) i BC *IGB* I^2 148 (PM 165) (*Διοσκουριδίου* (gen.): f. *Ἑστιαῖος*); (**184**) f. ii AD *IGB* I^2 221 (PM 1699); *Dacia* 21 (1977) p. 161 (date) (s. *Ἡρακλείδης*)

—ODESSOS?: (**185**) ii AD *IGB* I^2 51 bis a, 6 (s. *Σατυρίων*)

—PERINTHOS-HERAKLEIA: (**186**) iii BC *IPerinth* 2, 2 (*Διοσ*[*κου*]*ρίδης*: f. *Ποσειδώνιος*)

—PHILIPPOPOLIS-TRIMONTIUM: (**187**) ii-iii AD *IGB* III 893 (*Π. Αἰλ. Διοσκου*[*ρίδης*])

—STRYME: (**188**) v/iv BC *IThrakAig* E129 (*Διοσκ̣ρίδ*[*ης*]); (**189**) c. 375-350 BC *SEG* XXXVIII 722 + *AD* 35 (1980) Chron. pl. 255 *β* (*IThrakAig* E146) ([*Δ*]*ιοσκου*[*ρίδης*], *ΌΣΚΟΥ*—Pleket)

Διοσκοῦς

MACEDONIA (BOTTIAIA):

—BEROIA: (**1**) ?ii/iii AD *ILeukopetra* 131, 1 (s. *Δημήτριος*)

MACEDONIA (EDONIS):

—PHILIPPOI (TERRIT.): (**2**) ?iii AD *SEG* XXX 594 B, 3 (Pilhofer 580) (s. *Δ(—)*); (**3**) ~ *SEG* XXX 594 B, 6 (Pilhofer 580) (s. *Ζι(—)*)

MACEDONIA (ODOMANTIKE):

—SIRRHA: (**4**) 155 AD Dimitsas 821, 32 (Kaphtantzis 1) (s. *Τόρκος*); (**5**) f. iii AD *SEG* XXX 590, 4 (*Αὐρ. Δ(ι)οσκοῦνος* (gen.): s. *Λούκιος*); (**6**) ~ ib. l. 7 (f. *Αὐρ. Ἀλέξανδρος*); (**7**) ~ ib. l. 27 (*Αὐρ. Δ.*: s. *Βίθυς*)

MACEDONIA (PAIONIA):

—KAVADARCI (MOD.): (**8**) ii/iii AD *Sp.* 75 (1933) p. 40 no. 131 (*Διοσκοῦνος* (gen.): f. *Πούπλιος*)

—NEAPOLIS (AREA): (**9**) i AD *SEG* XVI 405

MACEDONIA (SINTIKE):

—PARTHIKOPOLIS (NR.): (**10**) 159 AD *IGB* IV 2286, 3 (*Διοσκοῦνος* (gen.): f. *Γάϊος*)

Διοσκύθης

MACEDONIA (EDONIS):

—PHILIPPOI (TERRIT.): (**1**) ?ii AD *CIL* III 703, 5 (Pilhofer 524); Collart, *Philippes* pl. 84. 2 (Lat. Dioscuthis (gen.): f. Sabinus)

Διόσπορις

THRACE:

—BAZOPARA: (**1**) 202 AD *IGB* III 1690 d, 18 (and Thrace Pizos: *Διόσπ̣[ορ]ις*: s. *Σάλας*)

—BEROE-AUGUSTA TRAIANA: (**2**) ii AD ib. 1598 (*Δεόσπουρ-*: f. *Αὐλούζενις*)

Διότιμος

CIMMERIAN BOSPOROS:

—PANTIKAPAION: (**1**) iv BC *IGAIMK* 104 (1935) p. 302 no. 17 (tile); (**2**) iii/ii BC *CIRB* 253 (f. *Διόφαντος*)

MACEDONIA (CHALKIDIKE):

—POTIDAIA-KASSANDREIA: (**3**) c. 262 BC *IG* IX (1)^2 (1) 18, 12 (Tataki, *Macedonians* p. 88 no. 30) (f. *Ἐπίγονος*)

MACEDONIA (EDONIS):

—AMPHIPOLIS: (**4**) hell. Dimitsas 921 (s. *Ξενοφῶν*)

SKYTHIA:

—OLBIA-BORYSTHENES: (**5**) iv BC Tolstoi 61 (vase) (*Διότι(μ)ος*)

TAURIS:

—CHERSONESOS: (**6**) c. 120-110 BC Anokhin p. 146 nos. 181; 183 (coins)

THRACE:

—BEROE-AUGUSTA TRAIANA (TERRIT.): (**7**) iv BC *IGB* III 1639 (s. *Σῶζις*)

—BYZANTION:

——(Rhegion): (**8**) i-ii AD *IByz* 271 (s. *Ἀγαθήμερος*, ?s. *Πῶλλα*)

—LYSIMACHEIA: (**9**) 213 BC *BGU* 2396, 6 (s. *Ποσειδώνιος*)

—PERINTHOS-HERAKLEIA: (**10**) ii AD *IPerinth* 132 (*-τει-*: f. *Ἀλέξανδρος*)

Διοτρέφης

THRACE:

—PISTIROS: (**1**) iv BC *IGB* III 1067 (f. *Διονύσιος*)

Διούζενις

THRACE:

—BESSOI (DIPSCURTI): (**1**) 52 AD *CIL* XVI 1 (Lat. Diuzeni (gen.): f. Sparticus)

Διουζίης

THRACE:

—PAUTALIA (TERRIT.): (**1**) s. ii AD *IGB* V 5858 (*Διουζ̣[ήου]* (gen.): f. *Δίζας*)

—PHILIPPOPOLIS-TRIMONTIUM (TERRIT.): (**2**) ii-iii AD ib. III 1404 (*Διουζήου* (gen.): f. *Αὐλούζενις*)

—TOPEIROS: (**3**) i AD *Thrakika* 8 (1937) pp. 30-1 no. 9 + *IThrakAig* E87 (*Δι*[*ο*]*υζ*[*ί*]*ου* (gen.))

—TOPEIROS?: (**4**) 46-54 AD *SEG* XVI 415 III, 34 (*IThrakAig* E84) (s. *Ζυκουλήσης*)

Διουκίλας

THRACE:

—BAZOPARA: (**1**) 202 AD *IGB* III 1690 d, 20 (and Thrace Pizos: *-κεί-*: f. *Δρινγίστας*)

—MARONEIA: (**2**) ii AD Masson, *OGS* p. 608 (*IThrakAig* E279) (*Διουκίλου* (gen.): f. *Βενδίς*)

THRACE?: (**3**) ii BC *Memnonion* 372 (Velkov 104) (s. *Κοζίβιθυς*)

Διούλας

MACEDONIA (EDONIS):

—PHILIPPOI (DRAMA (MOD.)): (**1**) i-ii AD *Drama* p. 75 (Pilhofer 501c) (Lat. Diulas: f. *Κετρίλας*); (**2**) ~ *Drama* p. 75 (Pilhofer 501c) (Lat. Diulas: s. *Κετρίλας*)

MACEDONIA (ODOMANTIKE):

—GAZOROS: (**3**) 158 AD *SEG* XXIV 614, 6 (Pilhofer 544); cf. *SEG* XXXII 635 ((*Δ*)*ιούλα*? (dat.), *ΑΙΟΥΛΑ*—lap.: s. *Ἥρων*)

—GAZOROS (TERRIT.): (**4**) 132 AD ib. XXX 597, 4-6 (Pilhofer 539) (s. *Κλεώ*, f. *Γετούλας, Κλεώ*)

—SIRRHA: (**5**) ii-iii AD *SEG* XXX 604 (I f. *Διούλας* II); (**6**) ~ ib. (II s. *Διούλας* I)

Διούπορις

THRACE:

—BAZOPARA: (**1**) 202 AD *IGB* III 1690 d, 44 (and Thrace Pizos: f. *Μουκάτραλις*)

Διουρπος

THRACE:

—STRAŽA (MOD.): (**1**) ii AD ib. V 5281 (*CCET* II (2) 534) (f. *Δικηναις*)

Διοφάνεια

MACEDONIA (PAIONIA):

—ARGOS (AREA): (**1**) ii-iii AD *Sp.* 71 (1931) p. 33 no. 66 (*Αὐρ. Δ(ι)οφάνεια*: m. *Οὐιένιος Ἀλέξανδρος, Οὐιένιος Λούκιος*)

Διοφάνης

MACEDONIA: (**1**) 171 BC *RE* Supplbd. 4 (1) (Tataki, *Macedonians* p. 303 no. 78)

MACEDONIA (CHALKIDIKE):

—POTIDAIA-KASSANDREIA: (**2**) c. 300 BC *IG* II^2 1956, 116 (Tataki, *Macedonians* p. 88 no. 31; *FRA* 2785)

MACEDONIA (MYGDONIA):

—THESSALONIKE*: (**3**) i AD *AD* 22 (1967) Chron. pl. 292 *δ* (vase) (potter)

THRACE:

—APOLLONIA-SOZOPOLIS: (**4**) v/iv BC *IGB* V 5147 (f. *Φιράδμων*)

—BEROE-AUGUSTA TRAIANA: (**5**) ii-iii AD ib. 5580 (s. *Οὐ—*); (**6**) iii AD ib. III 1574, 2 (f. *Αὐρ. Φρόντων*); (**7**) iii-iv AD *SEG* XLVIII 893. 2 (*Φλ. Δ.*)

——Karasoura: (**8**) ii-iii AD *IGB* III 1632, 5 (f. *Οὐαλεντῖνος*)

—BISANTHE-PANION*: (**9**) iii AD Unp. (Sayar) (Lat. Aure[liu]s Diophanes)

—NICOPOLIS AD ISTRUM (TERRIT.): (**10**) 227 AD *ILB* 438 I, 10 (Lat. Aur. Diophanes)

Διόφαντος

CIMMERIAN BOSPOROS:

—GORGIPPIA: (**1**) f. iii BC *CIRB* 1137 A I, 14; 1137 A II, 12 (f. *Πασίων*); (**2**) ii AD ib. 1140, 20 (s. *Γαδίκιος*); (**3**) s. ii AD ib. 1129 A, 9 ([*Δι*]*όφαντο*[*ς*]); (**4**) ~ ib. 1142, 18 (f. *—θος*)

—PANTIKAPAION: (**5**) iii/ii BC ib. 253 (s. *Διότιμος*); (**6**) ii BC ib. 258; cf. KW pl. 35 no. 500 (f. *Ἀστράγαλος*); (**7**) i AD *CIRB* 393 A-B; cf. KW pl. 43 no. 624 (s. *Κοσοῦς*, f. *Διονύσιος*); (**8**) i/ii AD *CIRB* 668 (I f. *Διόφαντος* II); (**9**) ~ ib. (II s. *Διόφαντος* I); (**10**) 82 AD ib. 76, 19 (*SEG* XVIII 310) (I f. *Διόφαντος* II); (**11**) ~ *CIRB* 76, 19 (*SEG* XVIII 310) (II s. *Διόφαντος* I); (**12**) 93-123 AD *CIRB* 1048, 8; (**13**) ii AD ib. 669; cf. KW pl. 53 no. 720 (s. *Ἡρόδωρος*); (**14**) ~ *CIRB* 670; cf. KW pl. 30 no. 426 (*Διόφα(ν)τος*: s. *Τιμόθεος*); (**15**) f. ii AD *CIRB* 671; cf. KW pl. 16 no. 255 (s. *Χρηστίων*)

MACEDONIA: (**16**) 246 BC *PPetr* II 39 e (7), 15 (Tataki, *Macedonians* p. 303 no. 79); cf. La'da E1390 (*Δαΐφαντος*—marginalia: f. *Ἄδυμος*); (**17**) 236 BC *PPetr*^{2} 16, 89 (Tataki, *Macedonians* p. 303 no. 80); cf. La'da E1778 (f. *Πτολεμαῖος*); (**18**) 175-156 BC *SB* 15240, 29, 44 (La'da E1753) (s. *Ἀγασίας*: t.e.); (**19**) m. ii BC D.S. xxxii 10. 2 (resid. Arabia Abai: I f. *Διόφαντος* II, *Ἡραῒς προσαγορευθεῖσα Διόφαντος* II); (**20**) ~ ib. (resid. Arabia Abai: II s. *Διόφαντος* I); (**21**) ~ ib. 10. 8-9 (resid. Arabia Abai: *Ἡραῒς προσαγορευθεῖσα Δ.*: II s./d. *Διόφαντος* I)

MACEDONIA (CHALKIDIKE):

—OLYNTHOS: (**22**) m. iv BC *IG* II^2 10025 (Tataki, *Macedonians* p. 134 no. 38; *FRA* 5891) (f. *Μιννώ*)

SCYTHIA MINOR:

—TOMIS: (**23**) iii-ii BC *AMNG* I (2) 2409 (coin) (*Διόφα(ντος)*?); (**24**) ii AD *ISM* II 11, 4

SKYTHIA:

—TANAIS: (**25**) ii AD *CIRB* 1268, 4; (**26**) 104 AD ib. 1259, 21 (f. *Ἄττας*); (**27**) ii/iii AD ib. 1244, 6 (*Δ*[*ιόφ*]*α̣ντο*[*ς*]?—Tokhtas'ev); (**28**) c. 200-210 AD ib. 1277, 14 (*Δ̣ιόφαντ*[*ος*]: f. *Δῖος*); (**29**) 220 AD ib. 1245, 17 (s. *Νεόπολος*); (**30**) 225 AD ib. 1279, 22 (f. *Κ—*); (**31**) 228 AD ib. 1283, 14 (s. *Διονύσιος*)

TAURIS:

—CHERSONESOS: (**32**) imp. *IOSPE* I^2 489 (f. *Πρῖμος*)

THRACE:

—ABDERA: (**33**) c. 336-311 BC May, *Abdera* p. 292 no. 539 (coin)

—DRYS: (**34**) iv/iii BC *ISM* I 234

—MARONEIA: (**35**) iii BC *IThrakAig* E257, 6 (s. *Δικαῖος*)

—NICOPOLIS AD ISTRUM (TERRIT.): (**36**) 227 AD *ILB* 438 I, 20 (Lat. Diophantus: f. Firm(us))

Διοχάρης

SCYTHIA MINOR:

—ISTROS: (**1**) iii-ii BC *ISM* I 17, 3 (s. *Π—*)

Δίπορις

THRACE:

—PHILIPPOPOLIS-TRIMONTIUM (TERRIT.): (**1**) ii-iii AD *IGB* III 1394 (f. *Ἀπούσιος Κίσσος*)

Διρβέας

MACEDONIA: (**1**) ?417-413 BC *IG* I^3 89, 67 (Tataki, *Macedonians* p. 303 no. 81) (*Διρβέ*[*α*]*ς*)

Δισάτραλις
THRACE:
—MARKIANOPOLIS (NR.): (1) f. iii AD *IGB* II 830 (*CCET* II (1) 229) (Ἀπολλόδωρος [ὁ] [καὶ] [Δι]σάτραλις: s. Αὐλούζενις)

Δισκορίδη
THRACE:
—APOLLONIA-SOZOPOLIS: (1) iv BC *IGB* I^2 440 (Δι(ο)σκōρίδη(ς)?: d. Βαστακίλης)

Δισκοῦς
THRACE:
—APOLLONIA-SOZOPOLIS: (1) v/iv BC ib. 438 (Δισκōτος (gen.): f. Ἀπολλωνίς)

Δισλοιας
THRACE:
—ROGOZEN (MOD.): (1) f. iv BC *Rogozen Treasure* p. 47 no. 10; *Arkheologiia* (Sofia) 1987 (3), pp. 26-37

Δισούπης
THRACE?: (1) 316-309 BC *IG* II^2 1956, 30; *Ancient Macedonia* 5 p. 445 with n. 10 (date) (*FRA* 2518)

Διστιχις?
MACEDONIA (BOTTIAIA):
—BEROIA: (1) ii-iii AD *IBer* 171

Δίσυρος
THRACE:
—KRASALOPARA: (1) 202 AD *IGB* III 1690 b, 54 (and Thrace Pizos: f. Μουκαβίθυρις)

Διτούκενθος
SCYTHIA MINOR:
—ISTROS [NR.]:
——Vicus Quintionis: (1) 167 AD *ISM* I 327, 7 (Lat. Ditugentus: f. Μουκάπορις)

Διτούπαιβις
MACEDONIA (EDONIS):
—AMPHIPOLIS: (1) ii-iii AD *Thrakika* 13 (1940) pp. 20-1 *B* + *Epigraphica* 37 (1975) pp. 26-7

Διφιλίδης
THRACE:
—MARONEIA: (1) iv-iii BC *IThrakAig* E227 (Διφιλίδης?: f. Ἄνδρων)

Δίφιλος
CIMMERIAN BOSPOROS:
—BOSPOROS: (1) iv BC *RE* (13)
MACEDONIA (BOTTIAIA):
—BEROIA: (2) s. iii BC *IBer* 151 (s. Νεοπτόλεμος); (3) 223 BC ib. 4, 35 (s. Ἐπικράτης)
—PELLA: (4) c. 230-200 BC *BCH* 45 (1921) p. 17 III, 61 (Tataki, *Macedonians* p. 154 no. 39)
MACEDONIA (EORDAIA):
—EUIA? (POLYMYLOS (MOD.)): (5) ii BC *A' Panell. Synedr. Epigr.* p. 56 no. 3 (*SEG* XLIX 773) (Δεί-: s. Ἀντίγονος)
MACEDONIA?: (6) 312 BC *RE* (8) (Tataki, *Macedonians* p. 303 no. 82)
SKYTHIA:
—OLBIA-BORYSTHENES: (7) v BC *IOSPE* I^2 215 (Δίφ[ιλος]?: f. Χάρμος)
THRACE: (8) 232 or 207 BC *CPR* XVIII 10, 196, 205 (La'da E739)
—AINOS: (9) 309-307 or 301-296 BC *IG* II^2 1957, 22 + *ZPE* 146 (2004) p. 85 (*FRA* 239)
—APOLLONIA-SOZOPOLIS: (10) iv BC *BMN-Burgas* 4 (2002) p. 121 no. 6 (s. Ἀγάθαρχος)
—MARONEIA: (11) ii-i BC *IThrakAig* E212, 38 (Δεί-: f. Ἡρακλείδης)
—ODESSOS: (12) iv/iii BC *CIRB* 237 (s. Μνησιφῶν)
—PERINTHOS-HERAKLEIA: (13) hell.? *IPerinth* 63, 3 (s. Λεύκιος)
—PHILIPPOPOLIS-TRIMONTIUM: (14) c. 303 AD *Anal. Boll.* 31 (1912) p. 192

Διώ
THRACE:
—MESAMBRIA: (1) iv BC *IGB* I^2 332 (?d. Ξάνθος)

Δίων
CIMMERIAN BOSPOROS:
—GORGIPPIA: (1) f. iii BC *CIRB* 1137 A I, 4 (s. Διονύσιος); (2) ~ ib. 1137 B II, 13 (Δίω[ν]: f. Ἡρογείτων)
—PANTIKAPAION: (3) f. iv BC ib. 178 (f. Θεομνήστη)
MACEDONIA (BOTTIAIA):
—BEROIA: (4) f. i AD *IBer* 103, 8 (Tataki 411) (s. Ἀλέξανδρος)
MACEDONIA (EDONIS):
—AMPHIPOLIS?: (5) hell. Dimitsas 898 (s. Ἀθηναγόρας)
MACEDONIA (MYGDONIA):
—THESSALONIKE: (6) i AD *IG* X (2) (1) 367, 1, 3 (f. Φίλιννα)
—THESSALONIKE?: (7) ii AD ib. 916 (f. Δελτίς)
SCYTHIA MINOR:
—ISTROS: (8) f. ii AD *ISM* I 193 I, 47; *SEG* L 683 B, 6 (f. Ἑστιαῖος)
—KALLATIS: (9) s. iii BC *ISM* III 35 B, 37 (s. Ἀριστοκλῆς); (10) iii AD ib. 187, 7 (f. Αὐρ. Ἡσύχις)
SKYTHIA:
—OLBIA-BORYSTHENES: (11) i/ii AD *SEG* XLIII 505, 11 (f. ΤΥΝΑΟΒΩΝ)
TAURIS:
—CHERSONESOS: (12) iii BC *IOSPE* I^2 509 (Δίω[ν]); (13) c. 250-230 BC Anokhin pp. 140-1 nos. 97; 109 (coins)
THRACE: (14) m. ii BC Phld., *Acad. Ind.* 79, 18 (*PP* 16748)
—BIZONE: (15) iii AD *IGB* I^2 10, 8 (s. Διόδωρος)
—BYZANTION: (16) iii BC *IByz* 62 (Fıratlı–Robert p. 49 no. 13) (f. Εὐπαλῖνος); (17) s. ii BC *BMI* 1154a B, 32 + Robert, *OMS* 2 p. 1093; *BE* 1972, no. 37 (date) ([Δί]ων?: s. Κόθων); (18) i-ii AD *IByz* 265 (Fıratlı–Robert p. 86 no. 108) (f. Δημοκρατία ἡ καὶ Παρθενική); (19) m. iii AD *IByz* 307 (Fıratlı–Robert p. 118 no. 198) (f. Ἀλέξανδρος)
—BYZANTION?: (20) ii-i BC *IByz* 335 (s. Ἑρμάφιλος)
—NICOPOLIS AD ISTRUM: (21) ii-iii AD Poulter, *Nicopolis* p. 322 no. 15.1 (vase) (Δίων)
—ODESSOS: (22) ii-iii AD *IGB* I^2 129; (23) s. ii AD ib. 167 (PM 1727); *Dacia* 21 (1977) p. 161 (date) (f. Κοηΐς)
—PERINTHOS-HERAKLEIA: (24) 316-309 BC *IG* II^2 1956, 124 (*FRA* 6038); *Ancient Macedonia* 5 p. 445 with n. 10 (date); (25) iii-iv AD *IPerinth* 168 (*AD* 51-2 (1996-7) Mel. p. 337 no. 169) (Δίω[ν]: f. Αὐρ. Φιλοκύρις)
—PLOTINOPOLIS: (26) 160 AD *SEG* XXXVII 970, 4 (s. Μουτοῖος)

Διωνᾶς
MACEDONIA (CHALKIDIKE):
—POTIDAIA-KASSANDREIA (NR.): (1) ?ii AD ib. XLV 773 (f. Οὐαλερία)

Διώστραλις
THRACE:
—PHILIPPOPOLIS-TRIMONTIUM (TERRIT.): (1) ii-iii AD *IGB* III 1440 (s. Βίθυς)

Δοκίμη
THRACE:
—TOPEIROS: (1) imp. *Thrakika* 8 (1937) p. 22 no. 5 (*IThrakAig* E94)

Δόκιμος
MACEDONIA: (1) 322-317 BC *RE* (4); Berve 285 (Tataki, *Macedonians* p. 304 no. 84) ?= (*2*); (2) 313-301 BC *RE* (5) ?= (*1*)
MACEDONIA (MYGDONIA):
—THESSALONIKE: (3) 221 AD *IG* X (2) (1) 154, 3 (Μ. Κανίνιος Δ.)
MACEDONIA (TYMPHAIA):
—OROPEDIO (MOD.): (4) f. iii AD *EAM* 61 a ([Δ]όκιμος)
SCYTHIA MINOR:
—TOMIS: (5) i BC *ISM* II 2 B, 51 (f. Τριακάδας)
THRACE: (6) f. v BC *AMNG* III (2) pp. 144-5 nos. 2-7 (Δόκι[μος]?, Δοκί[θεος]—Gaebler: king?)
—SERDICA (TERRIT.): (7) ii-iii AD *IGB* V 5702 (s. Αἴλιος)

Δοκίων
CIMMERIAN BOSPOROS:
—NYMPHAION: (1) i AD *CIRB* 929 (s. Εὔνος)

Δολήζελμις
THRACE?: (1) hell. *SEG* XL 1169 (s. Αὐλούζελμις); (2) 219 BC *PEnt* 30, 6 (*PP* 8677; Velkov 198) (Δ(ο)λήζελμις?—Velkov, δε Λήζελμις—ed.)

Δόλης
MACEDONIA (MYGDONIA):
—KALINDOIA: (1) a. 98 AD *SEG* XLII 582, 14 (I f. Δόλης II); (2) ~ ib. l. 14 (II s. Δόλης I)
MACEDONIA (PIERIS):
—AKONTISMA (NR.): (3) ii-iii AD *Thrakika* 13 (1940) p. 25 (Δολήου (gen.): f. Δεντους)
THRACE: (4) 46-54 AD *SEG* XVI 415 II, 22 (*IThrakAig* E84) (Τιβ. Κλ. Δ.); (5) 252 AD *AEp* 1993, no. 1590 (Lat. Aurel. Dolens); (6) ~ Balty–van Rengen, *Apamea* p. 47 pl. 21 (Lat. Aurel. Dolens)
—APROI: (7) f. ii AD *AEp* 1929, no. 211 (Lat. C. Iul. Doles)
—ASOMATOI (MOD.): (8) ?iii AD *SEG* XVI 414 (*IThrakAig* E386) (Δολέου (gen.): f. Ἰουλιανός)
—BAZOPARA: (9) 202 AD *IGB* III 1690 d, 14 (and Thrace Pizos: s. Σαλ—ασις); (10) ~ ib. l. 16 (and Thrace Pizos); (11) ~ ib. l. 17 (and Thrace Pizos: Δολῆρ[υς]: f. Ἐπτήτραλις); (12) ~ ib. l. 19 (and Thrace Pizos: s. Αὐλούτραλις); (13) ~ ib. l. 29 (and Thrace Pizos: Δολήους (gen.): f. Μουκάτραλις); (14) ~ ib. l. 47 (and Thrace Pizos: f. Σάλας); (15) ~ ib. l. 49 (and Thrace Pizos: f. Σκέλης); (16) ~ ib. l. 57-8 (and Thrace Pizos: s. Δριγυίστας, f. Μουκάτραλις); (17) ~ ib. 1690 c, 68 (and Thrace Pizos: Δολήους (gen.): f. Βρινκαζεις); (18) ~ ib. l. 71 (and Thrace Pizos: Δολήους (gen.): f. Δυτούτραλις Τραζυρέσης)
—BEROE-AUGUSTA TRAIANA (TERRIT.): (19) ii-iii AD ib. 1709 (Δολήους (gen.): f. Τράλις ὁ καὶ Σκοπιάδης); (20) ~ ib. 1741, 1 (s. Μουκάπορις); (21) ~ ib. V 5611 (f. Μουκάπορις)
—BEROE-AUGUSTA TRAIANA:
——Karasoura: (22) iii AD ib. III 1626, 6 (Δολήους (gen.): f. Κότυς); (23) ~ ib. l. 10 (s. Δειζέζενις); (24) ~ ib. l. 15 (s. Βίθυς)
—BESSOI: (25) i-ii AD *MAAR* 9 (1931) p. 94 no. 7 (Lat. Ti(b). Cl. Dolenti (dat.)); (26) 96 AD *RMD* 6 (Lat. Dolenti (dat.): s. Sublusus, f. Valens); (27) 133 AD *CIL* II 2984 (Lat. Iulius Longinus Doles: s. Βιθύκενθος)
—KELLAI: (28) 241-244 AD *IGB* III 1517, 7 (f. Μουκιανός)
—KELLAI*: (29) iii AD ib. 1516 b, 7 (f. Βε—, Δο—, Δια—, Μου—); (30) ~ ib. l. 30 (Δολήους (gen.): f. Διάσκενθος, Μουκάτραλις, Μουκάπορις)
—MARONEIA: (31) ii-i BC *IThrakAig* E212, 51 (s. Ἡρωΐδης); (32) ~ ib. l. 52 (Δολήου (gen.): f. Διονύσιος); (33) ii AD ib. E249 (Δωλέου (gen.): f. ....ς)
—PAUTALIA: (34) imp. *CIL* VI 2616 (Lat. Dolenti (dat.))
—PAUTALIA (TERRIT.): (35) ii AD *IGB* IV 2147, 6 (I s. Καριέλας, f. Δόλης II); (36) ii-iii AD ib. V 5827; (37) iii AD ib. IV 2147, 2 (II s. Δόλης I, f. Χαρίτιος)

—PHILIPPOPOLIS-TRIMONTIUM: (**38**) ii AD ib. III 1005 (*Δο*[*λ*]*ήους* (gen.): f. *Βίθυς*); (**39**) ~ ib. (s. *Βίθυς*)
—PHILIPPOPOLIS-TRIMONTIUM (TERRIT.): (**40**) i-ii AD ib. 1317, 7
—SALYMBRIA: (**41**) imp. *Archives Stamoulis* d. 35 (Loukopoulou, *Thrace Propontique* p. 252) (?f. *Ἀθίνιος Παῦλος*)
—SAPPAIOI: (**42**) 71 AD *CIL* XVI 12 (Lat. Doles: s. *Ἔζβενις*)
—SESTOS: (**43**) i-ii AD *ISestos* 7
—SKEDABRIA: (**44**) 202 AD *IGB* III 1690 b, 14 (and Thrace Pizos: *Δόλης*: s. *Μουκάτραλις*)
—SKEPTA: (**45**) 202 AD ib. 1690 c, 18 (and Thrace Pizos: f. *Σοῦρις Παντᾶς*)
—TYRODIZA-TIRISTASIS: (**46**) imp. Dumont–Homolle 89b (s. *Δείδας*, f. *Ἀπολλώνιος*, *Κάρκος*, *Δίζας*)

Δόλιος
MACEDONIA (ELIMEIA):
—AIANE: (**1**) f. v BC *SEG* XLIII 363 A (vase) (*Δολίō* (gen.)—n. pr.?: ?f. *.αλις*)

Δολιχηνάρις
SCYTHIA MINOR:
—ISTROS: (**1**) iii AD *ISM* I 283 (*Eastern cults* p. 231 no. 21) (*Ἀπολλινάρις Δολιχην*[*άρ*]*ις*)

Δόλιχος
CIMMERIAN BOSPOROS:
—PANTIKAPAION: (**1**) iii AD *CIRB* 109, 6 (s. *Μη—*)
MACEDONIA (BOTTIAIA):
—KYRRHOS: (**2**) ii/iii AD *SEG* XLVI 760 ([*Δ*]*όλιχος*)

Δόλων
SARMATIA:
—MAIOTAI: (**1**) ii BC *IG* II^2 9252 (*FRA* 3450) (slave?)

Δομετία
MACEDONIA:
—RESEN (MOD.): (**1**) iii AD *IG* X (2) (2) 49
MACEDONIA (EORDAIA):
—VOSKOCHORI (MOD.): (**2**) f. vi AD *EAM* 106 (mosaic) (Feissel, *RICM* 77)
MACEDONIA (MYGDONIA):
—THESSALONIKE: (**3**) 170-180 AD *SEG* XXXV 766
—THESSALONIKE?: (**4**) ii-iii AD *IG* X (2) (1) 727 (*Δομετ*[*ία*]: d. *Δομε—*)
MACEDONIA (PAIONIA):
—NEGOTINO (MOD.): (**5**) ii-iii AD *Sp.* 98 (1941-8) p. 53 no. 107
MACEDONIA (PELAGONIA): (**6**) ii-iii AD *IG* X (2) (2) 257, 3 (m. *Φροντῖνος*)
MACEDONIA (PIERIA):
—DION: (**7**) f. ii AD *SEG* XLIX 700; cf. Spiliopoulou-Donderer, *KGN* p. 195 no. D13 (date) (m. *Παῦλος*)
THRACE:
—BISANTHE-PANION: (**8**) iv-v AD *JÖAI* 23 (1926) Beibl. col. 159 no. 95 (*AD* 49-50 (1994-5) Mel. p. 310 no. 135)

Δομετιανός
MACEDONIA (BOTTIAIA):
—BEROIA: (**1**) iv AD *IBer* 442
SCYTHIA MINOR:
—ISTROS: (**2**) 222-225 AD *ISM* I 100, 13 (f. *Δημήτριος*)
THRACE:
—APROI*: (**3**) ii-iii AD Unp. (Sayar) (glad.)

Δομέτιος
MACEDONIA (CHALKIDIKE):
—POTIDAIA-KASSANDREIA (NR.): (**1**) ?iii AD *SEG* XLV 774 (f. *Βάσση*)

MACEDONIA (MYGDONIA):
—THESSALONIKE: (**2**) iv-vi AD Feissel, *RICM* 293 (*Βενιαμῆς ὁ καὶ Δ.*: Jew)
THRACE:
—PERINTHOS-HERAKLEIA*: (**3**) c. 320-324 AD *Anal. Boll.* 31 (1912) p. 208 (bp.)
—PHILIPPOPOLIS-TRIMONTIUM: (**4**) c. 303 AD ib. p. 192

Δομέτις
SCYTHIA MINOR:
—ISTROS: (**1**) ii AD *ISM* I 196, 18 (s. *Λούκιος*) ?= (*Δομίτιος* (*1*))

Δόμης
CIMMERIAN BOSPOROS:
—HERMONASSA: (**1**) iv BC *CIRB* 1056 I, 14 (*Δόμεω* (gen.): f. *—ος*)

Δομῆτις
THRACE:
—SERDICA (TERRIT.): (**1**) ii-iii AD *AEMÖ* 10 (1886) pp. 238-9 no. 2, 10

Δομιτία
MACEDONIA (EDONIS):
—PHILIPPOI (TERRIT.): (**1**) i-ii AD Pikoulas, *Chora* p. 163 no. 72, 3 (Pilhofer 606) (*Δο*[*μι*]*τία*: m. *Γάϊος*, *Μᾶρκος*)

Δομιτιανός
MACEDONIA (LYNKESTIS):
—HERAKLEIA?: (**1**) ii-iii AD *IG* X (2) (2) 132 (s. *Ἰουλία*)

Δομίτιος
SCYTHIA MINOR:
—ISTROS: (**1**) ii AD *ISM* I 201 I, 11 (s. *Λούκιος*) ?= (*Δομέτις* (*1*))

Δόμνα
MACEDONIA (MYGDONIA):
—THESSALONIKE: (**1**) ?iv AD *AEMTh* 15 (2001) p. 326 (*Δώ-*)
—THESSALONIKE?: (**2**) iii AD *IG* X (2) (1) 859, 8 + *CPh.* 70 (1975) p. 51
THRACE:
—PERINTHOS-HERAKLEIA: (**3**) iv AD *IPerinth* 219, 4 (*AD* 49-50 (1994-5) Mel. p. 343 no. 165) (d. *Λούκις*, *Ἀσκληπιοδότη*)
—SALYMBRIA: (**4**) iv-v AD *BCH* 36 (1912) p. 637 no. 95 (*AD* 53 (1998) Mel. p. 460 no. 199) (d. *Κυριακός*)

Δόμνη
SCYTHIA MINOR:
—ULMETUM: (**1**) ?v AD Barnea 73, 5 (Popescu, *IGL* 210) (m. *Ἀλέξανδρος*)
THRACE:
—BEROE-AUGUSTA TRAIANA: (**2**) iii-iv AD *IGB* III 1616 c (d. *Διου—*)

Δομνῖνα
MACEDONIA (BOTTIAIA):
—EDESSA: (**1**) v-vi AD Feissel, *RICM* 25, 9

Δομνῖνος
MACEDONIA (MYGDONIA):
—THESSALONIKE?: (**1**) vi AD *IG* X (2) (1) 795, 3 (Feissel, *RICM* 157) (*Δομνῆνο*[*ς*])
SKYTHIA:
—TYRAS: (**2**) iii AD *IGB* I^2 229, 1 (*-νεῖ-*: s. *Αὐρ. Ἡρακλείδης*, *Μαδαγαύα*)
THRACE:
—ODESSOS: (**3**) vi AD Beševliev 118, 4 (*-μνῆ-*)

Δομνίων
SKYTHIA:
—OLBIA-BORYSTHENES: (**1**) 198-211 AD *IOSPE* I^2 174, 11 (f. *Μαρκιανός*)

Δόμνος
SKYTHIA:
—TANAIS: (**1**) ii AD *CIRB* 1262, 6 (s. *Σέλευκος*)

Δομύνυος
SCYTHIA MINOR:
—TOMIS: (**1**) iii AD *SBBayerAk* 1875, p. 84 no. 9 (s. *Ἡρακλείδης*)

Δόναξ
MACEDONIA (BOTTIAIA):
—BEROIA: (**1**) ii AD *IBer* 301, 1 (Tataki 1099) (*Πο. Δ.*: s. *Παραμόνα*, f. *Εὐτύχα*)

Δονικιανός?
SCYTHIA MINOR:
—TOMIS: (**1**) ii AD *ISM* II 11, 6

Δόρζας
THRACE:
—KELLAI: (**1**) 241-244 AD *IGB* III 1517, 26 (*Αὐρ. Δ.*: s. *Μουκιανός*); (**2**) ~ ib. l. 6-7 (f. *Αὐρ. Μουκιανός*)
—NICOPOLIS AD ISTRUM: (**3**) ii-iii AD ib. II 675
—NICOPOLIS AD ISTRUM (TERRIT.): (**4**) f. iii AD ib. 724 (*CCET* II (2) 639) (*Δόρσο*[*υ*] (gen.): f. *Ζείσκωρις*)

Δορζείσης
THRACE:
—PAUTALIA: (**1**) s. ii AD *SEG* XLVI 864 I, 22 (s. *Δυραῖος*)

Δορζένθης
THRACE:
—ERGISSENOI: (**1**) ii AD *IGB* III 1593, 21 (s. *Ἰάσων*)
—KRASALOPARA: (**2**) 202 AD ib. 1690 b, 66 (and Thrace Pizos: f. *Μουκάπορις*)
—PHILIPPOPOLIS-TRIMONTIUM: (**3**) s. ii AD ib. 965-6; IV 2014 (*Eastern cults* p. 196 no. 10); cf. *IGB* V 5427 (date) (*Δορζίνθης*—2014: s. *Δίνις*)
—PHILIPPOPOLIS-TRIMONTIUM (TERRIT.): (**4**) ii-iii AD ib. III 1209 (s. *Δ—*)

Δορζίζενις
THRACE:
—EMPORION THOUIDAI: (**1**) ii-iii AD ib. 1767; cf. V 5634 (locn.) (*Δορζιζένε*[*ς*] (gen.), *Δορζιζένθο*[*υ*]?: f. *Κλαυδιανός*)

Δορζίλας
MACEDONIA (EDONIS):
—PHILIPPOI (DRAMA (MOD.)): (**1**) ii-i BC *SEG* XLVIII 793 (Pilhofer 501) (s. *Διόγνητος*)

Δορζίνθης
MACEDONIA (MYGDONIA):
—THESSALONIKE: (**1**) i AD *IG* X (2) (1) 242, 2; *CPh.* 70 (1975) p. 54 (f. *Ἀλέξανδρος*)
THRACE: (**2**) 46-54 AD *SEG* XVI 415 III, 29 (*IThrakAig* E84) (f. *Λογγῖνος*); (**3**) ~ *SEG* XVI 415 III, 37 (*IThrakAig* E84) (s. *Βῶσις*)
—BEROE-AUGUSTA TRAIANA (TERRIT.): (**4**) ii-iii AD *IGB* III 1701 (f. *Ἐπτησυκος*)
—BIZYE: (**5**) imp.? PM 1950 (s. *Αἰνησίδαμος*, f. *Πάπας*, *Ἀφροδεσά*)
—MARONEIA: (**6**) ii BC *IThrakAig* E364
—SALYMBRIA: (**7**) hell. *Archives Stamoulis* d. 35 (Loukopoulou, *Thrace Propontique* p. 252) (*-ζήνθις*)
—TRAIANOPOLIS (TERRIT.): (**8**) iii AD *SEG* XXXIII 565 (*IThrakAig* E457) (*Δορζένθης*: f. *Ἀπελλᾶς*)

Δόριζος
CIMMERIAN BOSPOROS:
—NYMPHAION: (**1**) imp. *CIRB* 937; cf. *Kratylos* 2 (1957) p. 167 (name) (f. *Μοκκάπορις*)

Δορίτιος
CIMMERIAN BOSPOROS:
—PANTIKAPAION: (**1**) i/ii AD *CIRB* 456

Δορκάς
THRACE: (**1**) 180 or 179 BC *SGDI* 2062, 4 (slave/freed.)

—LYSIMACHEIA: **(2)** iii BC *IG* II^2 9226 (*FRA* 3393)

Δόρκιον

THRACE: **(1)** iii BC *IG* II^2 8906 (*FRA* 2519)

Δόρκος

THRACE:

—MARONEIA: **(1)** s. ii BC *IG* XII (8) 170 c, 41; cf. XII Suppl. p. 148 (s. *Μητρόδοτος*)

Δόρκων

MACEDONIA (EDONIS):

—AMPHIPOLIS: **(1)** f. iii BC *Mous. Kavalas* pp. 112-13 no. *Λ*. 203 (f. *Νικάσιππος*)

Δορνιας?

MACEDONIA (EDONIS):

—AMPHIPOLIS: **(1)** ii-iii AD *Thrakika* 13 (1940) p. 28 *X* (*Δορνια* (gen.?))

Δορπανας

THRACE:

—METODIEVO (MOD.): **(1)** f. iii AD *IGB* II 771 (*CCET* II (2) 415) (?f. *Ἀβέζελμις*)

Δορύλαος

CIMMERIAN BOSPOROS:

—HERMONASSA: **(1)** i AD *CIRB* 1078 (s. *Θ*—)

SKYTHIA:

—TANAIS: **(2)** f. ii AD ib. 1266, 13 (*Δορύλα[ος]*: f. *Βασιλείδης*)

Δορύμαχος

CIMMERIAN BOSPOROS:

—PANTIKAPAION: **(1)** f. ii AD ib. 677; cf. KW pl. 12 no. 178 (*Δορύμ[αχ]ος*, *Δορύλ[αι]ος*?—KW)

Δορύπολις

THRACE: **(1)** 139-122 BC *FD* III (1) 568, 6, 9, 11, 15 (slave/freed.)

Δορυφόρος

MACEDONIA (PAIONIA):

—STOBOI*: **(1)** i-ii AD Šašel, *IL* 1258 (Lat. A. Pontius Doryphorus: freed.?)

SCYTHIA MINOR:

—ISTROS: **(2)** ii AD *ISM* I 196, 14; 201 I, 14 (f. *Καλλέας*)

Δοσίτραλις

THRACE:

—SEUTHOPOLIS (NR.): **(1)** ii-iii AD *IGB* III 1759

Δοσυμόξαρθος

SKYTHIA:

—TANAIS: **(1)** 220-228 AD *CIRB* 1245, 7; 1251, 7; 1282, 4 (f. *Νιβλόβωρος*)

Δουάραγος

SKYTHIA:

—OLBIA-BORYSTHENES: **(1)** iii AD *IOSPE* I^2 135, 6; Zgusta, *PNS* 287 (s. *Πίδος*)

Δούδης

THRACE:

—DUROSTORUM (TERRIT.)?: **(1)** iii AD *IGB* II 868, 5 (*CCET* II (1) 186) (*Δούδου* (gen.): f. *Ῥοιμητάλκης*)

—ODESSOS*: **(2)** vi AD Beševliev 89, 4

Δουλάζενις

THRACE:

—SAPPAIOI: **(1)** 71 AD *CIL* XVI 12 (Lat. Dulazenus: f. *Ἐζβενις*)

Δούλαιμος

MACEDONIA (PIERIS):

—PHAGRES (TERRIT.)?: **(1)** 215 AD Pikoulas, *Chora* p. 167 no. 76 (*Δουλαίμου* (gen.): f. *Ζηνήκενθος*)

Δουλαῖος

MACEDONIA: **(1)** f. iii AD *SEG* XLVIII 880 (s. *Ὕλλος*, *Ζωσώ*)

Δουλαρίων

MACEDONIA (MYGDONIA):

—THESSALONIKE?: **(1)** f. ii AD *JDAI* 84 (1969) p. 151 no. R13 (s. *Διζάλας*)

Δούλας

SKYTHIA:

—TANAIS: **(1)** 225 AD *CIRB* 1279, 18 (f. *Ὀχωδίακος*); **(2)** 244 AD ib. 1287, 16 (s. *Τρύφων*); **(3)** ~ ib. l. 30 (f. —*ζιους*)

Δουλήζελμις

THRACE?: **(1)** 316-309 BC *IG* II^2 1956, 26; *Ancient Macedonia* 5 p. 445 with n. 10 (date) (*FRA* 2520)

Δούλης

MACEDONIA (BOTTIAIA):

—BEROIA:

——Kyneoi: **(1)** 171 AD *ILeukopetra* 5, 3 (Tataki 420) (f. *Ζωσίμη*)

MACEDONIA (DERRIOPOS):

—ALKOMENA: **(2)** ii-iii AD *IG* X (2) (2) 351 (f. *Μεστύλας*)

—ALKOMENA*: **(3)** 215 or 173 BC ib. 347

—STUBERRA: **(4)** 74 AD ib. 326, 48-9 (s. *Κετρίπορις*)

MACEDONIA (EDONIS):

—AMPHIPOLIS: **(5)** ii-iii AD *Thrakika* 13 (1940) pp. 22-5 *E*; cf. *Epigraphica* 37 (1975) p. 27 (s. *Βειζης*); **(6)** ~ *AD* 26 (1971) Chron. p. 417 = *SEG* XXX 609 (*Δουλέους* (gen.): f. *Μέστος*)

—PHILIPPOI (TERRIT.): **(7)** ?ii AD *BCH* 47 (1923) pp. 64-5 no. 24, 6 (Pilhofer 519) (Lat. Dul[is] (gen.): f. *Ζιπύρων*); **(8)** ~ *BCH* 47 (1923) pp. 64-5 no. 24, 6 (Pilhofer 519) (Lat. Dulis (gen.): f. –ubres)

—PHILIPPOI (DRAMA (MOD.)): **(9)** ?ii AD *BCH* 47 (1923) p. 73 no. 29 (Pilhofer 504) (Lat. Dulis (gen.): f. Erizelmis)

MACEDONIA (MYGDONIA):

—KALINDOIA: **(10)** ii/i BC *SEG* XLII 578, 7 (f. —*ειτ[ο]ς*); **(11)** a. 98 AD ib. 582, 34 (f. *Μέστεις*); **(12)** ~ ib. l. 59 (s. *Ζειδέβης*); **(13)** ~ ib. 583, 23 (?s. *Ζιπύρων*)

—THESSALONIKE: **(14)** f. iii AD *IG* X (2) (1) 441 (*Αὐρ. Δ.*: s. *Αὐρ. Ἀλκιδάμας*, *Αὐρ. Μάντα*); **(15)** ~ ib. 564, 1 (*Αὐρ. Δ.*: s. *Πύρρος Ἀλκιδάμας*); **(16)** ~ ib. l. 5 (*Αὐρ. Δ.*: s. *Ζετιτίς*)

—THESSALONIKE (NR.): **(17)** iii AD ib. 1002 + *Tyche* 10 (1995) pl. 14 no. 20 (f. *Ἡρωΐδης*)

—THESSALONIKE?: **(18)** ii AD *IG* X (2) (1) 249, 9 (*[Δο]υλέους* (gen.)); **(19)** ii-iii AD ib. 728, 1 (*Δ.* (*ὁ*) *κὲ Ἀρτεμίδωρος*)

MACEDONIA (ODOMANTIKE):

—DRABESKOS?: **(20)** iv BC Kaphtantzis 568, 11 (Pilhofer 575) (*Δ[ούλ]ης*?: s. *Βράματις*)

—GAZOROS (TERRIT.): **(21)** ii-iii AD *SEG* XXX 610 (Pilhofer 538) (s. *Μέστος*)

—GAZOROS?: **(22)** 158 AD *SEG* XXIV 614, 3 (Pilhofer 544); cf. Hatzopoulos, *MI* 1 pp. 84-6 (*Δουλέους* (gen.): s. *Βίθυς*)

—SIRRHA: **(23)** f. iii AD *SEG* XXX 590, 6 (*Δουλήους* (gen.): f. *Αὐρ. Τόρκος*); **(24)** ~ ib. l. 19 (*Αὐ[ρ.] [Δο]ύλης*: s. *Τραι*—)

—SIRRHA (TERRIT.): **(25)** ii-iii AD ib. 607 (Pilhofer 556) (*Δουλέου* (gen.): f. *Κλεώ*)

—SIRRHA?: **(26)** ?iii AD Kaphtantzis 40 (s. *Ζιπύρων*)

MACEDONIA (PAIONIA):

—BYLAZORA: **(27)** ii-iii AD *JÖAI* 6 (1903) Beibl. col. 4 no. 4 (*Δ[α]ύλης*—ed.: s. *Ἀρτιδόνης*)

—NEAPOLIS (AREA): **(28)** ii-iii AD *Sp.* 71 (1931) p. 35 no. 75

MACEDONIA (PELAGONIA): **(29)** 55 or 210 AD *IG* X (2) (2) 279 (s. *Κότυς*); **(30)** 67 AD ib. 250 (f. *Μεστικένα*); **(31)** ii AD ib. 277 (s. *Εὔβουλος*)

—DOSTONEIS: **(32)** ?ii AD ib. 200 (s. *Βίθυς*); **(33)** ii-iii AD ib. 198 (f. *Ζωΐλος*)

MACEDONIA (SINTIKE):

—PARTHIKOPOLIS (TERRIT.): **(34)** ii-iii AD *SEG* L 631 (s. *Διζάστης*)

—PARTHIKOPOLIS (NR.): **(35)** 159 AD *IGB* IV 2286, 1 (f. *Νηνας*)

THRACE: **(36)** imp. *Arkheologiia* (Sofia) 1971 (3), pp. 26-7 nos. 13; 17; 34; 36; 39; 46; 48-9 (stamp) (Lat. Dules); **(37)** ii-iii AD *IGB* III 1876 (I f. *Δούλης* II); **(38)** ~ ib. (II s. *Δούλης* I, f. *Δούλης* III); **(39)** ~ ib. (III s. *Δούλης* II)

—BESSOI: **(40)** 70 AD *CIL* XVI 10 (Lat. Dule: s. Datuos)

—BYZANTION?: **(41)** i AD *IByz* 368 (*Δώλειος* (gen.): f. *Λυσάνδρα*)

—PAUTALIA (TERRIT.): **(42)** iii AD *IGB* IV 2202 (f. *Μουκιανός*)

Δουλίων

TAURIS:

—CHERSONESOS: **(1)** imp. Solomonik, *NEPKh* 46 (*Δουλίων*: s. *Δελφός*)

Δοῦλκα

THRACE:

—ODESSOS: **(1)** v-vi AD Beševliev 128

Δουλκίτιος

MACEDONIA (BOTTIAIA):

—BEROIA: **(1)** ii-iii AD *IBer* 92, 6 (Tataki 629) (*Ἰούν. Διοσκουρίδης ὁ καὶ Δ.*: s. *Ἰουν. Κάλη*)

—EDESSA: **(2)** v-vi AD Feissel, *RICM* 25, 4

Δούπτουνος

CIMMERIAN BOSPOROS:

—BOSPOROS: **(1)** 483 AD *CIRB* 67, 2 (*SEG* XLVIII 993) (*Τιβ. Ἰούλ. Δ.*: king)

Δουράζερις

THRACE:

—PHILIPPOPOLIS-TRIMONTIUM (TERRIT.): **(1)** iii AD *IGB* III 1202 (f. *Αὐρ. Ἡλιόδωρος*)

Δοῦρις

MACEDONIA (MYGDONIA):

—KALINDOIA: **(1)** ?i-ii AD *SEG* XXIX 628, 1 (s. *Ταρουσίμας*)

Δούσκελος

MACEDONIA (ODOMANTIKE):

—SIRRHA (NR.): **(1)** 25 or 141 AD ib. XXXII 647 (Pilhofer 560) (*Δούσκελε* (voc.): s. *Πύρος*)

Δουσπιερίς

THRACE:

—ODESSOS: **(1)** f. ii AD *IGB* I^2 168 (PM 1724); *Dacia* 21 (1977) p. 161 (date) (d. *Πόσις*)

Δουτζάγας

CIMMERIAN BOSPOROS:

—HERMONASSA: **(1)** v AD *CIRB* 1099, 6 + *SEG* XXXIX 697

Δούτιον

THRACE: **(1)** iii BC *IG* II^2 8907 (*FRA* 2521) (d. *Ἀλέξανδρος*)

Δράκας

MACEDONIA (BOTTIAIA):

—BEROIA: **(1)** ii/iii AD *IBer* 143 B, 15 (Tataki 1312) (*Φλ. Δ.*)

MACEDONIA (EORDAIA):

—AKRINI (MOD.): **(2)** f. ii BC *EAM* 92, 2; cf. *Ling. Balk.* 30 (1987) p. 61 (name) (s. *Περδίκκας*, f. *Ἐπικράτης*)

MACEDONIA (ORESTIS): **(3)** 41-54 AD *EAM* 188, 4; *Ling. Balk.* 30 (1987) p. 61 (name) (s. *Ἀλέξανδρος*)

—LYKE: **(4)** ?i-ii AD *EAM* 147, 3 (*Δρά[κας]*?, *Δρά[κων]*?: f. *Ἀλέξανδρος*)

Δρακόλας

MACEDONIA (SINTIKE):

—NEINE: **(1)** 77 AD *IGB* V 5883, 7 (f. *Μόκασος*)

Δρακόντις
THRACE:
—NOVAE: (1) iii AD ib. II 741, 2, 6 (s. *Σαβινιανός*, *Κορινθία*)

Δρακοντίς
MACEDONIA (BOTTIAIA):
—BEROIA: (1) 229 AD *ILeukopetra* 75, 1, 13 (Tataki 260) (*Αὐρ. Δ.*)

Δράκων
MACEDONIA:
—ERKEIA?: (1) c. 220-200 BC Helly, *Gonnoi* 93 B, 27; cf. Lucas, *Vall. Titarèse* pp. 83-4 no. 36 (Tataki, *Macedonians* p. 112 no. 2) (*Δρά[κω]ν*: f. *Ἀλέξανδρος*)
MACEDONIA (BOTTIAIA):
—BEROIA: (2) 177 AD *IBer* 135 B, 32 (Tataki 841) (*Λ. Μάγνιος Δ.*)
MACEDONIA (MYGDONIA):
—THESSALONIKE: (3) 240 AD *IG* X (2) (1) 159, 5 (*Φλ. Αἰλιανὸς Σεντρώνιος Δ.*: s. *Φλ. Σεμπρώνιος Αἰλιανός*, *Φλ. Αἰλιανὴ Σεμπρωνία Ἀρτεμιδώρα*)
THRACE: (4) 215 BC *BGU* 1275, 21 (Velkov 108; La'da E741) (t.e.?)
—PAUTALIA: (5) s. ii AD *SEG* XLVI 864, 12 (f. *Μουκιανός*)
—PAUTALIA (TERRIT.): (6) ii AD *IGB* IV 2124 (s. *Καπίτων*)
—SERDICA: (7) 117-138 AD ib. 1925 b, 12 (*Δρά[κ]ων*)

Δραυκενθίη
THRACE:
—PHILIPPOPOLIS-TRIMONTIUM (TERRIT.): (1) ii-iii AD ib. III 1464 (d. *Φίλιππος*)

Δρεβις
MACEDONIA (EDONIS):
—HILL 133 (MOD.): (1) m. v BC Pritchett, *Topography* I pp. 46-7 no. 1, 4 (sherd); cf. *SEG* XLVI 723

Δρένις
THRACE:
—GELOUPARA: (1) 202 AD *IGB* III 1690 c, 32 (and Thrace Pizos: *Δρένεο[ς]* (gen.): f. *Μουκάπορις*)

Δρεπάλας
MACEDONIA (ODOMANTIKE):
—SIRRHA: (1) 155 AD Dimitsas 821, 33 (Kaphtantzis 1) (f. *Ἡρακλέων*)

Δριαζις
THRACE?: (1) 316-309 BC *IG* II² 1956, 29; *Ancient Macedonia* 5 p. 445 with n. 10 (date) (*FRA* 2522)

Δριαλλία?
THRACE?: (1) ?iii BC *IG* II² 8908; cf. *SEG* XXVIII 288 (name, locn.) (*FRA* 2523) (d. *Ἀπολλόδωρος*)

Δρίβαλος
THRACE:
—DIONYSOPOLIS: (1) iii AD *IGB* I² 14 b, 19 (*Δρεί-*: f. *Αὐρ. Οὐΐκτωρ*)

Δρίζενις
THRACE:
—MARKIANOPOLIS (TERRIT.): (1) f. iii AD ib. V 5385 = *CCET* II (1) 359 (f. *Καιγεις*)

Δρίμακος
MACEDONIA (CHALKIDIKE):
—OLYNTHOS: (1) 350 BC *SEG* XXXIX 617 (f. *Φορμίων*)
SKYTHIA:
—SKYTHAI: (2) ?iv-iii BC *IG* XII (9) 1132 (slave?)

Δριμύλος
TAURIS:
—CHERSONESOS: (1) c. 300-285 BC Kats p. 120 no. 12 (amph.) (*Δριμύ(λος)*?)

Δρινγίστας
THRACE: (1) iii AD *SEG* XLVIII 1084 (*Δρον-*: f. *Πανάστης*)
—BAZOPARA: (2) 202 AD *IGB* III 1690 d, 20 (and Thrace Pizos: s. *Διουκίλας*); (3) ~ ib. l. 24 (and Thrace Pizos: *Δρ[ι]νγε[ί]στας*: f. *Κέλσος*); (4) ~ ib. l. 57 (and Thrace Pizos: *Δρινγίστ[ας]*: f. *Δόλης*); (5) ~ ib. 1690 e, 94 (and Thrace Pizos: *-γεί-*: s. *Βρινκάζερις*); (6) ~ ib. 1690 c, 47 (and Thrace Pizos: *Δρινγείστας Ἑρμογένης*: s. *Βρινκάζερις*)
—SECURISCA: (7) iii AD *ILB* 133 (Lat. Aurel. Drigissa: f. Ael. Valentinus, ?f. Ael. Sissa)

Δριωζίγης
MACEDONIA (EDONIS):
—POLGENOI: (1) 43 BC *SEG* XXXIV 665 (Pilhofer 390) (s. *Ῥηβούκενθος*)

Δροβολους
CIMMERIAN BOSPOROS:
—PANTIKAPAION: (1) iv BC *CIRB* 179; cf. *Etiudy* pp. 188-9 no. 10; Zgusta, *PNS* 580 (s. *Δαδαῖος*)

Δρόλης
THRACE:
—MONTANA (TERRIT.): (1) ii-iii AD *IGB* V 5162 (*Δρο(λ)ήους* (gen.): f. *—ζενις*)
—SERDICA: (2) s. ii AD *Sp.* 77 (1934) p. 53 no. 51 (f. *Μάξιμος*)
—SERDICA (TERRIT.): (3) ii-iii AD *IGB* V 5746; (4) iii AD ib. 5736 (*Αὐρ. Δρόλ[ης]*)

Δρομιχαίτης
THRACE?: (1) 316-309 BC *IG* II² 1956, 42; *Ancient Macedonia* 5 p. 445 with n. 10 (date) (*FRA* 2524)

Δροσερία
MACEDONIA (BOTTIAIA):
—EDESSA: (1) v-vi AD Feissel, *RICM* 31; (2) ~ ib. 45

Δροσίς
THRACE:
—PERINTHOS-HERAKLEIA: (1) i-ii AD *IPerinth* 99 (*Βολοσσία Δ.*)

Δρόσος
MACEDONIA (BOTTIAIA):
—BEROIA: (1) ii/iii AD *IBer* 144 A, 9 (Tataki 421); (2) ~ *IBer* 145, 12 (Tataki 597) (*Ἰούλ. Δ.*)
MACEDONIA (MYGDONIA):
—THESSALONIKE: (3) ii AD *IG* X (2) (1) 454 A-B (s. *Μεμμία*)

Δρόσων
THRACE:
—ZONE: (1) f. iv BC Bakalakis, *Oinos Ismarikos* p. 710 (*IThrakAig* E417) (f. *Σχινείση*)

Δρούα
MACEDONIA (MYGDONIA):
—KALINDOIA: (1) 68-98 AD *SEG* XLII 580, 81-2; cf. *Anthémonte-Kalindoia* 2 pp. 250-1 (name) (m. *Κόϊντος*, *Ἀρχέλαος*)

Δρουβιος?
THRACE:
—NICOPOLIS AD ISTRUM:
——Dizerpara: (1) 224 AD *ZPE* 127 (1999) p. 248 + 130 (2000) p. 280 (Lat. M. Aurelius [–] [qui] [et] Drubius?: s. *Σπόρος*, f. Valerius)

Δρουβις
MACEDONIA (EDONIS):
—AMPHIPOLIS: (1) b. 357 BC Hatzopoulos, *Actes Amphipolis* p. 20 no. 2, 5 with p. 22 n. 1 (name) (*SEG* XLI 556)

Δροῦσος
CIMMERIAN BOSPOROS:
—GORGIPPIA: (1) m. ii AD *Eirene* 7 (1968) p. 67, 24 (f. *Μαθιάνης*)
—PANTIKAPAION: (2) i-ii AD *CIRB* 672; cf. KW pl. 44 no. 634 (s. *Μέσσιος*); (3) 81 AD *CIRB* 70, 6 (Levinskaya p. 231 no. 1) (Jew?)
SKYTHIA:
—TANAIS: (4) ii AD *CIRB* 1262, 8 (s. *Πασίων*)
THRACE:
—SERDICA: (5) iii AD *IGB* IV 1975, 5 (f. *Αὐρ. Μᾶρκος*)

Δρύκαλος
MACEDONIA (BOTTIAIA):
—AIGAI: (1) c. 300-275 BC *SEG* XXXV 791 (s. *Πιερίων*)

Δρύλης
MACEDONIA (MYGDONIA):
—THESSALONIKE?: (1) i AD *IG* X (2) (1) 846 (*Δρυλέους* (gen.): f. *Διοσκουρίδης*)

Δρῶβυς
MACEDONIA (BOTTIAIA):
—EDESSA: (1) 180 AD *SEG* XXIV 531, 11 (Tataki, *Edessa* 85) (*Δρώβυος* (gen.): f. *Ἀνίκητος*)

Δρωδήγης
THRACE:
—BOURDAPA: (1) ii-iii AD *IGB* III 1347 (f. *Βενδίς*)

Δρῶλος
MACEDONIA (EDONIS):
—PHILIPPOI (DRAMA (MOD.)): (1) ii-iii AD *AD* 52 (1997) Chron. p. 847, 4 with pl. 314 β; (2) ~ ib. l. 10 with pl. 314 β

Δρωπίδας
MACEDONIA: (1) iv BC Arr., *An.* i 15. 8; iii 11. 8; iii 27. 4; iv 8. 1; iv 9. 3 (Tataki, *Macedonians* p. 304 no. 85) (f. *Κλεῖτος*, *Λανίκα*)

Δρωπίων
MACEDONIA (DERRIOPOS):
—STUBERRA: (1) 74 AD *IG* X (2) (2) 326, 50 (f. *Ποσείδιππος*)
MACEDONIA (EDONIS):
—AMPHIPOLIS: (2) ii BC *SEG* XXIV 605 (f. *Εὐγένεια*)
MACEDONIA (PAIONIA): (3) m. iii BC Paus. x 13. 1; *Syll*³ 394; *SEG* XII 263 (s. *Λέων*: king)

Δύβηζις
MACEDONIA (MYGDONIA):
—KALINDOIA: (1) a. 98 AD ib. XLII 582, 24 (*Δυβήζιος* (gen.): f. *Ἱέρων*)

Δύδης
THRACE:
—HADRIANOPOLIS (TERRIT.): (1) ii-iii AD *IGB* III 1805 (s. *Μουκάτραλις*)
—PHILIPPOPOLIS-TRIMONTIUM: (2) ii-iii AD ib. V 5462 (*Δυδήους* (gen.): f. *Κουήτη*)
—SKEDABRIA: (3) 202 AD ib. III 1690 b, 16 (and Thrace Pizos: s. *Κέλσος*)
—TOPEIROS: (4) iii AD *IThrakAig* E88 (*Δ. ὁ καὶ Εὐάγριος*)

Δύδιος
THRACE:
—NICOPOLIS AD NESTUM: (1) ii AD *IGB* IV 2336, 3-4 (f. *—ας*, *—ος*)

Δυζάτραλις
THRACE:
—MARKIANOPOLIS (TERRIT.): (1) f. iii AD ib. II 856 (*CCET* II (1) 256) (*Δυζάτραλις*: s. *Ἰούλιος*)

Δυλάζενις
THRACE:
—PHILIPPOPOLIS-TRIMONTIUM (TERRIT.): (**1**) ii-iii AD *IGB* III 1210 (*Δυλαζένε[ος]* (gen.): f. *Τήρης*)

Δυμιννώ
MACEDONIA (BOTTIAIA):
—AIGAI: (**1**) s. iv BC *SEG* XXXV 782 (*Δυμινν[ώ]*, *Δύμινν[α]*?: d. *Κλέανδρος*)

Δύναμις
CIMMERIAN BOSPOROS:
—BOSPOROS: (**1**) c. 70-14 BC *RE* (-); *IOSPE* I² 354, 3 (*SEG* XLII 698); *CIRB* 30; 31; 38; 978; 979; 1046; *SEG* XLV 1018; [1022] (d. *Φαρνάκης* (Pontos): queen)
MACEDONIA (MYGDONIA):
—THESSALONIKE: (**2**) i AD *IG* X (2) (1) 418, 2 (*Ἰουλ. Δ.*: d. *Φιλόμουσος*, *Θυμέλη*)
—THESSALONIKE?: (**3**) ii-iii AD ib. 812 (m. *Ἡλιόδωρος*)
MACEDONIA (TYMPHAIA):
—OROPEDIO (MOD.): (**4**) f. iii AD *EAM* 61 b
THRACE:
—BYZANTION: (**5**) i BC-i AD *IByz* 277 (d. *Ἡρόξενος*)

Δυνας
THRACE:
—PAUTALIA (TERRIT.): (**1**) ii AD *IGB* IV 2214, 10 (s. *Ἐπτέκενθος*)

Δυνάτων
CIMMERIAN BOSPOROS:
—GORGIPPIA: (**1**) 173-210 AD *CIRB* 1134, 21 (*[Δ]υνάτων*)
—PANTIKAPAION: (**2**) i-ii AD ib. 637
SKYTHIA:
—TANAIS: (**3**) 225 AD ib. 1279, 12 (s. *Δημήτριος*)

Δυνις
THRACE?: (**1**) 246-221 BC *PPetr* I 29, 9-10 (Velkov 109) (*Δυνεως* (gen.)—l. 10)

Δύννιχος
MACEDONIA (EDONIS):
—AMPHIPOLIS: (**1**) a. 357 BC Hatzopoulos, *Actes Amphipolis* pp. 38-9 no. 7, 7 (*Δύννιχος*)

Δυνούζης
MACEDONIA (EDONIS):
—PHILIPPOI (TERRIT.): (**1**) ii-iii AD Pikoulas, *Chora* p. 158 no. 65, 1 (Pilhofer 598) (*Δυνουζειφος* (gen.)—Salač, *Δυνούζενος*—Edson: f. *Μᾶρκος*)

Δύντος
THRACE:
—KAZANLAK (MOD.): (**1**) f. v BC *SEG* XLVI 850 (*Δύντō* (gen.?): s. *Ζηΐλας*)

Δυραῖος?
THRACE:
—PAUTALIA: (**1**) s. ii AD ib. 864 I, 22 (*Δυραίο* (gen.)—lap.: f. *Δορζείσης*)

Δυρπάναις
SKYTHIA:
—OLBIA-BORYSTHENES: (**1**) ii AD *IOSPE* I² 106, 9; Zgusta, *PNS* 587 (s. *Ὠφελίων*)

Δύσμος
THRACE:
—TRAIANOPOLIS: (**1**) v AD Meïmaris–Bakirtzis 26, 2 (*SEG* XXIV 644; *IThrakAig* E444)

Δύτενις
THRACE:
—ANCHIALOS (TERRIT.): (**1**) ii/iii AD *IGB* III 1846, 5 (f. *Δεντουσυκος*)

Δυτουβορις
THRACE:
—NICOPOLIS AD ISTRUM (TERRIT.): (**1**) f. iii AD *CCET* II (2) 675, 5 (*ILB* 349) (Lat. Dutuborini (dat.): d. *Πόρις*)

Δυτούζελμις
MACEDONIA (EDONIS):
—PHILIPPOI (DRAMA (MOD.)): (**1**) ii-iii AD *AD* 52 (1997) Chron. p. 847, 7 with pl. 314 β

Δυτούκενθος
THRACE:
—BIZYE: (**1**) c. 153 AD Taşlıklıoğlu 2 p. 67 no. 1, 13 + *BE* 1972, no. 292 (f. *Αὐλούκενθος*)

Δυτούλας
MACEDONIA (BISALTIA):
—EUPORIA?: (**1**) 154 or 271 AD *SEG* XXX 591; cf. *AD* 23 (1968) Chron. pl. 273 στ.; *BE* 1992, no. 305 (locn.) (*Δυτούλου* (gen.): f. *Διαζείπα*)
MACEDONIA (ODOMANTIKE):
—SIRRHA: (**2**) f. iii AD *SEG* XXX 590, 30 (*Δυτούλα* (gen.): f. *Αὐρ. Τορκουᾶτος*)

Δυτούπορις
THRACE:
—KELLAI*: (**1**) iii AD *IGB* III 1516 b, 22 (*Δυτούπορ[ις]*: f. *Βιάρτας*)
—SKEPTA: (**2**) 202 AD ib. 1690 c, 17 (and Thrace Pizos: s. *Βεσσοδένθης*)

Δυτούτραλις
THRACE:
—BAZOPARA: (**1**) 202 AD ib. 1690 d, 13 (and Thrace Pizos: s. *Διασκούπορις*); (**2**) ~ ib. l. 43 (and Thrace Pizos: *Δυτ[ο]ύτ[ρ]αλ(ις)*: f. *Μουκάτραλις*); (**3**) ~ ib. l. 61 (and Thrace Pizos: I f. *Δυτούτραλις* II); (**4**) ~ ib. l. 61 (and Thrace Pizos: II s. *Δυτούτραλις* I); (**5**) ~ ib. 1690 c, 43 (and Thrace Pizos: s. *Βιθύτραλις*); (**6**) ~ ib. l. 45 (and Thrace Pizos: I f. *Δυτούτραλις* II); (**7**) ~ ib. l. 45 (and Thrace Pizos: *Δυτο[ύτρ]αλις*: II s. *Δυτούτραλις* I); (**8**) ~ ib. l. 49 (and Thrace Pizos: s. *Σάλας*); (**9**) ~ ib. l. 56 (and Thrace Pizos: *Δυτούτραλις*: f. *Μουκάτραλις*); (**10**) ~ ib. l. 58 (and Thrace Pizos: f. *Ἐπτήπορις*); (**11**) ~ ib. l. 65 (and Thrace Pizos: f. *Ἀττικός*); (**12**) ~ ib. l. 71 (and Thrace Pizos: *Δ. Τραζυρεσης*: s. *Δόλης*)
—GELOUPARA: (**13**) 202 AD ib. l. 22 (and Thrace Pizos: s. *Βίθυς*)
—KRASALOPARA: (**14**) 202 AD ib. 1690 b, 58 (and Thrace Pizos: f. *Γίλπυρις*)
—STROUNEILOS: (**15**) 202 AD ib. 1690 d, 68 (and Thrace Pizos: *Δυτο̣ύ̣[τρ]αλις*: s. *Μουκάτραλις*)

Δυτύλος
MACEDONIA (MYGDONIA):
—KALINDOIA: (**1**) a. 98 AD *SEG* XLII 582, 47; cf. *Anthémonte–Kalindoia* 2 p. 251 (name) (*Δυτύλου* (gen.): f. *Λούκιος*)

Δωλέπορις
THRACE:
—PHILIPPOPOLIS-TRIMONTIUM: (**1**) ii-iii AD *IGB* III 967; cf. V 5428 (s. *Ζορδέγων*)

Δωνᾶτος
MACEDONIA (EDONIS):
—PHILIPPOI: (**1**) s. iv AD Feissel, *RICM* 235 (Pilhofer 101)
SKYTHIA:
—OLBIA-BORYSTHENES: (**2**) imp. *IOSPE* I² 230

Δωρᾶς
CIMMERIAN BOSPOROS:
—PANTIKAPAION: (**1**) ii AD *CIRB* 660; cf. KW pl. 44 no. 631 (s. *Σάσας*)

THRACE:
—PERINTHOS-HERAKLEIA: (**2**) i-ii AD *IPerinth* 214, 11 (*GVI* 1969); cf. *Tekmeria* 5 (2000) pp. 148-50 (s. *Διοκλῆς*)

Δώρημα
THRACE:
—BYZANTION: (**1**) i BC-i AD *IByz* 205 (Fıratlı–Robert p. 65 no. 59) (d. *Ἑρμῆς*)

Δωριάς
MACEDONIA (EDONIS):
—AMPHIPOLIS: (**1**) iii BC *SEG* XLIX 675 (d. *Χαριδάμα*)

Δωριεός
SKYTHIA:
—OLBIA-BORYSTHENES: (**1**) v BC Dubois, *IGDOlbia* 101 (s. *Νυνφόδωρος*)

Δωριεύς
MACEDONIA (PIERIA):
—DION: (**1**) iii BC *SEG* XXXIV 628 (f. *Δικαῖος*, *Πρωτοφάνης*)
SCYTHIA MINOR:
—KALLATIS: (**2**) iv/iii BC *ISM* III 153 (*Δωριέος* (gen.))
SKYTHIA:
—OLBIA-BORYSTHENES: (**3**) ?ii-i BC Dubois, *IGDOlbia* 110, 6
TAURIS:
—CHERSONESOS: (**4**) iii BC Solomonik, *GChKh* 31 (pithos) (*Δωρι[εύς]*?)

Δωρίμα
MACEDONIA (BOTTIAIA):
—PELLA: (**1**) s. iv BC *SEG* XLVI 778 (vase) (*Δώρ(η)μα*? (n. pr.?))

Δωρίς
MACEDONIA (BOTTIAIA):
—BEROIA: (**1**) ii-iii AD *IBer* 38 (Tataki 422); (**2**) f. iii AD *IBer* 494 (Tataki 423)
MACEDONIA (CHALKIDIKE):
—MONI VATOPEDIOU (MOD.): (**3**) ii-iii AD *SEG* XXIX 649
MACEDONIA (EDONIS):
—AMPHIPOLIS: (**4**) ii-iii AD Dimitsas 888 (*Ποπ(ω)νία Π(ώ)λλα ἡ ἐπιλεγ. Δ.*: m. *Π. Ἐβούτιος Ποπωνιανός*, *Ποπωνία Πουπιλία ἡ ἐπιλεγ. Νηνακοῦς*)
SCYTHIA MINOR:
—IBIDA: (**5**) ii AD *ISM* V 227, 4 (Lat. Cocceiae Dorine (dat.))
THRACE: (**6**) 156 BC *SGDI* 1895, 4-5, 9 (m. *Ἀπολλόδωρος*: slave/freed.)
—PHILIPPOPOLIS-TRIMONTIUM: (**7**) ii AD *IGB* III 1005 (d. *Τάρσας*)

Δωρίτσης
THRACE: (**1**) i AD *IGerasa* 201 (Lat. Doritses: s. *Τάρσις*)

Δωρίχα
THRACE: (**1**) vii/vi BC *RE* s.v. *Ῥοδῶπις* (-); *PLF* p. 13 no. 15 b, 11; cf. p. 106 no. 202 (*Δ. ἡ καὶ Ῥοδῶπις*: slave/het.)

Δωρίων
CIMMERIAN BOSPOROS:
—PANTIKAPAION: (**1**) ?ii AD *CIRB* 673; cf. KW pl. 16 no. 235
MACEDONIA: (**2**) m. ii BC *PTeb* 1075 fr. 2, 16 (Tataki, *Macedonians* p. 481 no. 95); cf. La'da E1481 (*Δω[ρίω]ν*: I f. *Δωρίων* II) ?= (*4*); (**3**) ~ *PTeb* 1075 fr. 2, 16 (Tataki, *Macedonians* p. 481 no. 94; La'da E1481) (*[Δω]ρίων*: II s. *Δωρίων* I); (**4**) ~ *PTeb* 1075 fr. 2, 21; cf. La'da E1652 (*Δω[ρ]ίων*: f. *Φ̣......*) ?= (*2*); (**5**) 89 BC *UPZ* 125, 29 (Tataki, *Macedonians* p. 481 no. 93; La'da E1482)
THRACE:
—MARONEIA: (**6**) hell.-imp. Dumont–Homolle 110b 13 (*IThrakAig* E291) (s. *Διονύσιος*); (**7**) i AD *SEG* XXVII 343, 1, 4 (*IThrakAig* E302) (f. *Διονύσιος*)
—MESAMBRIA: (**8**) c. 230 BC *PHib* 267, 4; Uebel, *Kleruchen* 1273 (La'da E1840)

Δωροθέα
MACEDONIA (EDONIS):
—PHILIPPOI: (1) iv-v AD *AAA* 13 (1980) p. 95 (Pilhofer 114)
THRACE:
—BEROE-AUGUSTA TRAIANA: (2) c. 320-324 AD *Anal. Boll.* 31 (1912) p. 198; p. 207
—MARONEIA: (3) iv-v AD Meïmaris–Bakirtzis 5 (*IThrakAig* E346) (*Δο-*)

Δωρόθεος
CIMMERIAN BOSPOROS:
—HERMONASSA: (1) hell.-imp. *CIRB* 1094, 3 (I f. *Δωρόθεος* II); (2) ~ ib. l. 3 (II s. *Δωρόθεος* I)
MACEDONIA (CHALKIDIKE):
—OLYNTHOS: (3) iv/iii BC *RE* (29) (Tataki, *Macedonians* p. 134 no. 39) (s. *Ἡγήσανδρος*: sculptor); (4) ii/i BC *IG* II² 10021 (Tataki, *Macedonians* p. 134 no. 40; *FRA* 5892) (*[Δ]ωρόθε[ος]*: f. *Κεφαλίων*)
MACEDONIA (EDONIS):
—AMPHIPOLIS: (5) s. iv BC *Mous. Kavalas* pp. 117-18 no. *Λ*. 202 (s. *Καλλίας*)
—PHILIPPOI: (6) 262-254 BC Nachtergael, *Les Galates* 5, [26]; 8, 19; 9, [28] (Stephanis 809; Tataki, *Macedonians* p. 164 no. 11) (s. *Καλλίστρατος*)
MACEDONIA (LYNKESTIS):
—KATO KLEINES (MOD.): (7) imp. *EAM* 184
THRACE:
—BYZANTION?: (8) c. 225-200 BC *PMich* 781 II, 25 (La'da E343) (s. *Καλλικράτης*)
—PERINTHOS-HERAKLEIA: (9) iv-v AD *SEG* L 668 bis (*Δωρόθε[ος]*)

Δωρομέδων
CIMMERIAN BOSPOROS:
—PANTIKAPAION: (1) f. i AD *CIRB* 395; cf. KW pl. 25 no. 378 (s. *Ποσείδιππος*)

Δῶρος
MACEDONIA (MYGDONIA):
—THESSALONIKE: (1) 42-32 BC *IG* X (2) (1) 124, 6; (2) ?ii AD ib. 517; (3) 129 AD ib. 311, 1; (4) ii/iii AD ib. 262 III, 7
MACEDONIA (PIERIA):
—DION: (5) ii-iii AD *SEG* XXXVI 613 (f. *Δελφίς*)
SCYTHIA MINOR:
—KALLATIS: (6) ii BC *IG* II² 8947 (*FRA* 2644) (f. *Μένανδρος*)
THRACE:
—MESAMBRIA: (7) iii-ii BC *IGB* I² 349 sexies

Δωροῦς
MACEDONIA (EDONIS):
—AMPHIPOLIS: (1) iii-ii BC *Makedonika* 2 (1941-52) p. 649 (Kaphtantzis 641)

Δωρουτελμίς?
THRACE:
—BEROE-AUGUSTA TRAIANA:
——Emporion Diskodouraterai: (1) ii-iii AD *IGB* II 738, 2; cf. V 5256 (*Δωρουτ[ελμις]*?—ed., *Δωρουτ[ουρμη]*?—Beševliev: m. *Βίθυς*, *Ζουροτελμίς*)

Δωροφόρος
MACEDONIA (LOWER PAIONIA):
—IDOMENE?: (1) iii AD *CCET* V 46

Δώρων
CIMMERIAN BOSPOROS:
—PANTIKAPAION: (1) iv BC *CIRB* 181 (s. *Δαλᾶς*)

Δωρώνδας
TAURIS:
—CHERSONESOS: (1) f. iii BC *SEG* XL 615 A, 19 (*[Δ]ωρώνδας*?)

Δωρώς?
MACEDONIA (PIERIA):
—PYDNA: (1) iv BC *GRBS* 43 (2002-3) p. 110 no. 1 a, 10 (*Δῶρ(ο)ς*?)

Δωσίθεος
MACEDONIA (MYGDONIA):
—THESSALONIKE: (1) ii-i BC *IG* X (2) (1) 78, 5 (f. *Ἀπολλώνιος*); (2) ?105 BC ib. 135, 4 (s. *Ποσειδώνιος*)
—THESSALONIKE?: (3) f. i AD ib. 263, 6; (4) ii AD ib. 890 (f. *Ἡδίστη*)
THRACE: (5) 210-183 BC *PPetr* III 34 a, 2 (Velkov 111; La'da E742)
—BISANTHE-PANION: (6) iii-v AD *AD* 49-50 (1994-5) Mel. p. 308 no. 133 (*-σή-*)
THRACE?: (7) ?iii BC *PPetr* II 43, 33 (*PP* 11346; Velkov 110) (s. *Ἀμάδοκος*)

Δώτιος
SCYTHIA MINOR:
—TOMIS: (1) 201 AD *ISM* II 83 I, 27 (f. *Διονύσιος*)

Δωτοῦς
SCYTHIA MINOR:
—ISTROS: (1) i BC-i AD ib. I 191 II, 51 (s. *Δατειζεις*)
SKYTHIA:
—OLBIA-BORYSTHENES: (2) ii AD *IOSPE* I² 83, 9; 99, 4; Zgusta, *PNS* 967a (s. *Γόλας*); (3) ii-iii AD *IOSPE* I² 138, 5 (*Δωτοῦ* (gen.): f. *Νάβαζος*)

E

Ἐακύτας
MACEDONIA (BOTTIAIA):
—MIEZA: (1) iii BC *SEG* XXIV 524 II, [3], 11, 23 (Hatzopoulos, *MI* 2 p. 106 no. 92)

Ἐαρίνη
MACEDONIA (EDONIS):
—AMPHIPOLIS: (1) imp. *SEG* XXIV 602 (d. *Βάρβαρος*)
MACEDONIA (ELIMEIA):
—KOZANI (MOD.): (2) ii AD *EAM* 52 (*Ἐαρίνη*: d. *Ἡρακλείδης*)
MACEDONIA (MYGDONIA):
—THESSALONIKE: (3) ii-iii AD *IG* X (2) (1) 510 (*Ὑα-*: d. *Ὑγίεια*, m. *Ὑγίεια*)

Ἐάρινος
MACEDONIA (MYGDONIA)?:
—HERAKLEIA: (1) ii AD *GVI* 569; cf. *Milliaires* p. 70 n. 1 (locn.) (*Εἰά-*)

Ἔβενος
SKYTHIA:
—OLBIA-BORYSTHENES: (1) f. ii AD *Drev. Prichern.* 3 pp. 27-8, 8 (s. *Πτούδαγος*); (2) ?ii-iii AD *IOSPE* I² 111, 7; Zgusta, *PNS* 968

Ἔβρενις
SCYTHIA MINOR:
—CAPIDAVA:
——Vicus Scenopesis: (1) 138-161 AD *ISM* V 21, 7 (Lat. Ebrenus)

THRACE: (2) 46-54 AD *SEG* XVI 415 II, 25 (*IThrakAig* E84) (*Τιβ. Κλ. Ἐ.*); (3) ~ *SEG* XVI 415 II, 27 (*IThrakAig* E84) (*Γ. Ἰούλ. Ἐ.*)
—STRATOPARA: (4) 202 AD *IGB* III 1690 b, 41 (and Thrace Pizos: f. *Μουκάτραλις*)

Ἔβρος
MACEDONIA (MYGDONIA):
—THESSALONIKE?: (1) 147 AD *IG* X (2) (1) 691 + *BCH* 98 (1974) p. 550 (*Προκουλέϊος Ἐ.*)

Ἐβρύζελμις
THRACE: (1) iii BC *ZPE* 140 (2002) p. 204, 3; cf. La'da E831 (*Ἐβρύζελ[μις]*: f. *Θεόδωρος*, *Μενέλαος*, *Νουμήνιος*); (2) 274 BC *PCZ* 59001, 21, 49, verso (Velkov 114; La'da E743) ?= (*9*); (3) s. iii BC *CE* 76 (2001) pp. 175-6 II, 8; cf. La'da E795 (f. *Ἐβρύζελμις*)
—ODRYSAI: (4) c. 390-383 BC Tod, *GHI* II 117, 5, 11, 18, 22; Peter, *MTD* pp. 106-12 (coin); *RE* Supplbd. 3 (-) (king)
—PISTIROS: (5) iv-iii BC *SEG* XLIX 912. 6 (vase) (*Ἐβρύζελμι(ς)*)
—PRIANEIS: (6) f. iii BC ib. XXXIX 653; *Tekmeria* 4 (1998-9) pp. 101-9 (date) (s. *Σεύθης*) ?= (7)
—SEUTHOPOLIS: (7) c. 300-280 BC *SEG* XLII 661, 8 (s. *Σεύθης*, *Βερενίκη*) ?= (*6*)
THRACE?: (8) b. 238 BC *PHib* 81, 19 (Velkov 115) (s. *Ζίπυρος*); (9) c. 270-250 BC *PHib* 208, [5], 7, 10 (*PP* 3904a; Velkov 113) ?= (*2*)

Ἐβρύζενις
THRACE:
—GLAVA PANEGA (MOD.): (1) iii AD *IGB* II 538 (s. *Μουκακάκης*)

Ἔβρυλος
THRACE:
—HERAION TEICHOS?: (1) ii BC Taşlıklıoğlu 1 p. 7 no. 2 (f. *Σισομάρκη*)

Ἐγκόλπιος
MACEDONIA (EDONIS):
—PHILIPPOI (NR.)*: (1) imp. Dimitsas 993 (Pilhofer 40) (*Ἐν-*: freed.)

Ἐγκώμιον
MACEDONIA (MYGDONIA):
—THESSALONIKE: (1) ?i-ii AD *SEG* XXVII 310 (*Ἐν-*: threpte)

Ἔζβενις
THRACE: (1) i AD *IGB* IV 2338, 2, 14; cf. V 5928 (s. *Ἀμάτοκος*, f. *Φλ. Διζάλας*); (2) ~ ib. IV 2338, 20; cf. V 5928 (s. *Τήρης*); (3) 46-54 AD *SEG* XVI 415 III, 35 (*IThrakAig* E84) (*Ἐσ-*: s. *Ἀμάτοκος*)
—BEROE-AUGUSTA TRAIANA (TERRIT.): (4) ii AD *IGB* III 1714 (*Ἐσβένειος* (gen.): f. *Τ. Φλ. Βιθύκενθος*)
—BESSOI: (5) imp. *CIL* XIII 7585 (Lat. Esbeni (gen.): f. Dolanus)
—MARONEIA: (6) iii AD *IThrakAig* E396, 2 (s. *Τήρης*, f. *Αὐρ. Κρονίων*)

—NICOPOLIS AD NESTUM: **(7)** iii AD *IGB* IV 2343 (Kaphtantzis 480); cf. Pilhofer 527 (f. *Αὐρ. Γηπεπυρίς, Αὐρ. Μεστίκενθος*)
—PAUTALIA: **(8)** ii-iii AD *IGB* IV 2104, 1 (s. *Σάλος*)
—PAUTALIA (TERRIT.): **(9)** ii-iii AD ib. 2229 (*Φλ. Ἐ.*: f. *Μητρόπολις*)
—SAPPAIOI: **(10)** 71 AD *CIL* XVI 12 (Lat. Hezbenus: s. *Δουλάζενις*, f. *Δόλης*)

'Εζιωπην?
THRACE?: (1) i AD *IGerasa* 200 (biling.) (*Ζιωπην* (gen.)—ed. pr.: f. *Ζιμίκενθις*)

Ἔθαρος
MACEDONIA: **(1)** ?417-413 BC *IG* I^3 89, 74 (Tataki, *Macedonians* p. 305 no. 2)

Ἔθυλλα
TAURIS:
—CHERSONESOS: **(1)** hell. Solomonik, *GAKh* 673 (vase)

Εἶα
SCYTHIA MINOR:
—TOMIS: **(1)** ii-iii AD *ISM* II 185 (m. *Διογένης, Γάϊος*)
THRACE:
—BYZANTION: **(2)** ii AD *IByz* 282 (d. *Παπᾶς*)
—BYZANTION (TERRIT.): **(3)** i-ii AD ib. 268 (Fıratlı–Robert pp. 83-4 no. 102) (m. *Ζώτιχος*); **(4)** ~ *IByz* 275 (Fıratlı–Robert p. 87 no. 109) (d. *Ἡλιάδης*)

Εἰδιανός
THRACE:
—PHILIPPOPOLIS-TRIMONTIUM (TERRIT.): **(1)** i-ii AD *IGB* III 1196 (*Εἰδι[α]νό[ς]*: f. *Ῥοῦφος*)

Εἰθία
THRACE:
—MARKIANOPOLIS (TERRIT.): **(1)** iii-iv AD ib. V 5328, 3 (*CCET* II (1) 365) (d. *Δικέβαλος*)

Εἰθίαλος
THRACE:
—MARKIANOPOLIS (NR.): **(1)** f. iii AD *IGB* V 5380 (*CCET* II (1) 244) (f. *Εἶθις*)

Εἶθις
THRACE:
—MARKIANOPOLIS (NR.): **(1)** f. iii AD *IGB* V 5380 (*CCET* II (1) 244) (s. *Εἰθίαλος*)

Εἰκάδας
THRACE:
—SERDICA: **(1)** ii-iii AD *IGB* IV 1936 (s. *Εὔμηλος*)

Εἰκάδιος
MACEDONIA: **(1)** f. iii BC *Dritte Reise* 47, 2 (Tataki, *Macedonians* p. 305 no. 3) (f. *Ἀριστοκλῆς*)
SCYTHIA MINOR:
—KALLATIS: **(2)** iii BC *IG* II^2 8946 (*FRA* 2646) (s. *Ἀσκλαπιόδωρος*)
THRACE:
—LYSIMACHEIA: **(3)** i BC-i AD *IG* II^2 9230 (*Ag.* XVII 532; *FRA* 3394) (f. *Νίκων*)

Εἰκαδίων
MACEDONIA (BOTTIAIA):
—BEROIA: **(1)** 223 BC *IBer* 4, 32 (*Εἰκα(δ)ίων*: f. *Ἡγήσανδρος*)

Εἰκόνιν
CIMMERIAN BOSPOROS:
—PANTIKAPAION: **(1)** i/ii AD *CIRB* 645 (d. *Βοστάκων, Χοίδρα*)

Εἰράνα
TAURIS:
—CHERSONESOS: **(1)** ?iv-iii BC *SEG* XLIV 657 (weight); **(2)** iv/iii BC ib. XXXIII 598 (d. *Ἡρόνικος*)
THRACE:
—BYZANTION: **(3)** c. 400-375 BC *IG* II^2 8440 (biling.) (*FRA* 1392) (*Ε(ἰ)ρήνη*)

Εἰράνιχος
SCYTHIA MINOR:
—TOMIS: **(1)** i BC *ISM* II 2 A, 59 (f. *Νουμήνιος*)
THRACE:
—BYZANTION (TERRIT.): **(2)** i-ii AD *IByz* 174 (f. *Διονύσις*)

Εἰρηναῖος
MACEDONIA: **(1)** c. 132 BC *PGissUniv* 6, 2 (Tataki, *Macedonians* p. 481 no. 96; La'da E1484) (s. *Ἀπολλώνιος*); **(2)** 12 AD *PKöln* 227 B, 4 (f. *Λεωνίδης*)
MACEDONIA (DERRIOPOS):
—STUBERRA: **(3)** 74 AD *IG* X (2) (2) 326, 59 (s. *Φιλόνικος*)
MACEDONIA (EDONIS):
—AMPHIPOLIS: **(4)** ii-iii AD Kaphtantzis 656 (*Ναίω* (dat.)—ed.)
MACEDONIA (MYGDONIA):
—THESSALONIKE: **(5)** ii AD *IG* X (2) (1) 241 B, 7 (*[Εἰρ]ηναῖος*: s. *Παραμόνα*); **(6)** iii AD ib. 247, 13 (*[Σ]ερβείλι(ο)ς Εἰρη(ν)αῖος*); **(7)** f. iii AD ib. 182, 10 (*Ἰούλ. Ἐ.*: s. *Ἰούλ. Κάστωρ, Αἰλ. Γεμινία Ὀλυμπιάς*)
—THESSALONIKE?: **(8)** ii AD ib. 702 (s. *Τέρτις*)
SKYTHIA:
—OLBIA-BORYSTHENES: **(9)** ii AD *IOSPE* I^2 685, 7; cf. *VDI* 1975 (1), p. 71 (s. *Βαδᾶς*)
THRACE:
—AINOS: **(10)** hell.? *IG* II^2 7971 (*FRA* 240) (f. *Εἰρήνη*)
—APOLLONIA-SOZOPOLIS: **(11)** v/iv BC *IGB* I^2 409 (s. *Ἀθήναιος*)
—BEROE-AUGUSTA TRAIANA:
——Karasoura: **(12)** iii AD ib. III 1629, 2 (*-νέ-*: f. *Αὐρ. Σευουῆρος*)

Εἰρήνη
MACEDONIA: **(1)** iv/iii BC *RE* (3) (*PP* 14507) (d. *Πτολεμαῖος* I *Σωτήρ* (Eordaia), *Θαΐς* (Athens)); **(2)** 182-178 BC *PMich* 182, 8, 16, 33, 41-2 46, 48; 183 verso, 1; 193 I, 1 (Tataki, *Macedonians* p. 305 no. 4; La'da E1802) (d. *Ὀρφεύς*)
MACEDONIA (BOTTIAIA):
—BEROIA: **(3)** f. iii AD *IBer* 359 (Tataki 250) (*Ἀττία Ἐ.*)
—EDESSA: **(4)** hell. *IG* II^2 8481 (*FRA* 1498; Tataki, *Macedonians* p. 102 no. 6) (d. *Διόδωρος*)
MACEDONIA (MYGDONIA):
—THESSALONIKE: **(5)** i AD *IG* X (2) (1) 367, 1 (m. *Φίλιννα*); **(6)** ?ii AD *SEG* XXX 644 (*Λαρκία Ἰρήνη*); **(7)** 154-155 AD *IG* X (2) (1) 288, 5; 289, 5; *SEG* XLIII 462, 3 (m. *Κότυς*); **(8)** c. 303 AD Musurillo, *Acts Christian Martyrs* pp. 281 ff.
MACEDONIA (PIERIS):
—PHAGRES: **(9)** 86 or 202 AD Pikoulas, *Chora* p. 169 no. 82 (*SEG* XXVII 297) (*Ἡρί-*: d. *Νίκαρχος*)
SARMATIA:
—MAIOTAI: **(10)** hell.-imp. *AM* 23 (1898) p. 394 no. 64 (*Εἴ[ρ]ήνα*)
—SARMATAI: **(11)** 142 BC *SGDI* 2142, 6, 9 (*-να*: slave/freed.)
SKYTHIA:
—OLBIA-BORYSTHENES: **(12)** imp. *IOSPE* I^2 234 (Lat. Irene: m. Aelius Saturninus, Aelia Saturnina)
THRACE: **(13)** iv BC *Ag.* XVII 506 (*FRA* 2525)
—AINOS: **(14)** hell.? *IG* II^2 7971 (*FRA* 242) (d. *Εἰρηναῖος*); **(15)** ii BC *IG* II^2 7972 (*FRA* 241) (d. *Σπάρτοκος*)
—BEROE-AUGUSTA TRAIANA: **(16)** c. 320-324 AD *Anal. Boll.* 31 (1912) p. 198; p. 208
—DUROSTORUM: **(17)** imp. *CIL* III 7479 + 12454 (Lat. -ria Irene)
—MARONEIA: **(18)** v-vi AD *SEG* XLIX 892, 4 (*IThrakAig* E357) (*Ἡρί-*)

Εἰρηνικός
MACEDONIA (BOTTIAIA):
—EDESSA (NR.): **(1)** v-vi AD *Makedonika* 15 (1975) p. 206
THRACE:
—PERINTHOS-HERAKLEIA: **(2)** v-vi AD *IPerinth* 227 (*AD* 51-2 (1996-7) Mel. p. 377 no. 192) (*Ἡρι-*)

Εἶσα
CIMMERIAN BOSPOROS:
—PANTIKAPAION: **(1)** imp. *CIRB* 787 (*Εἶσ[α]*)

Εἰσάτραλις
THRACE:
—MARKIANOPOLIS: **(1)** iii AD *IGB* II 804, 3 (*CCET* II (1) 201) (*Ἐ. ὁ καὶ Λούκιος*: s. *Σκάρις*)
—MARKIANOPOLIS (TERRIT.): **(2)** s. ii AD *IGB* II 848 (*CCET* II (1) 285) (f. *Πιεζεις*)

Εἰσγούδιος
CIMMERIAN BOSPOROS:
—PANTIKAPAION*: **(1)** 483 AD *CIRB* 67, 5 (*SEG* XLVIII 993)

Εἰτίζενις
THRACE:
—MARKIANOPOLIS (TERRIT.): **(1)** f. iii AD *IGB* II 858 (*CCET* II (1) 251) (*Εἰτίζ(ε)ν[ις]*?: f. *Ὑγιος*)

Εἰφίς
THRACE:
—ODESSOS: **(1)** f. iv BC *IGB* V 5060 (d. *Ἀρτεμίδωρος*)

Ἐκάγαρχος
MACEDONIA (BOTTIAIA):
—TYRISSA? (ASVESTARI (MOD.)): **(1)** f. ii BC *SEG* XLVII 999, 20

Ἑκαταία
MACEDONIA (MYGDONIA):
—THESSALONIKE?: **(1)** a. 212 AD *IG* X (2) (1) 768, 3 (*-τέα*: d. *Μένανδρος*)

Ἑκαταίη
MACEDONIA (EDONIS):
—AMPHIPOLIS (TERRIT.): **(1)** iv BC *SEG* I 291 (d. *Κώραβος*)
THRACE:
—APOLLONIA-SOZOPOLIS?: **(2)** f. iv BC *IGB* I^2 479 bis (d. *Ἀπολλόδωρος*)

Ἑκαταῖος
CIMMERIAN BOSPOROS:
—GORGIPPIA: **(1)** f. iii BC *CIRB* 1137 B I, 8 (f. *Σῶσις*); **(2)** ~ ib. 1137 B II, 25 (*[Ἑ]καταῖος*: s. *Εὔρυτος*)
—MYRMEKION*: **(3)** iv BC *SEG* XXXVII 666. 7 (tile) (*Ἑκατα[ῖος]*)
—PANTIKAPAION: **(4)** iv/iii BC *CIRB* 117 (*CEG* II 737) (s. *Λήναιος*); **(5)** s. i BC *CIRB* 121 (*GVI* 1812); **(6)** iii AD *CIRB* 103, 4 (*Ἑκατᾶ(ς)*—ed., *Ἑκατα(ῖος)*?)
—SINDOI: **(7)** v/iv BC Polyaen. viii 55; *SEG* XLIII 515, 5 + XLVIII 1027 (f. *Ὀκταμασάδης*: king)
MACEDONIA: **(8)** 336 BC *RE* Supplbd. 4 (1b); Berve 292 (Tataki, *Macedonians* p. 305 no. 7); **(9)** 334-330 BC *RE* Supplbd. 4 (1a); Berve 293 (Tataki, *Macedonians* p. 305 no. 6) (Lat. Hecataeus)
MACEDONIA (CHALKIDIKE):
—POTIDAIA-KASSANDREIA: **(10)** m. iii BC *Thess. Mnem.* 71 (Tataki, *Macedonians* p. 89 no. 32) (s. *Εὐριπίδης*)

MACEDONIA (EDONIS):
—AMPHIPOLIS: **(11)** m. iii BC Hatzopoulos, *Actes Amphipolis* p. 52 no 12, 3; *SEG* XLI 566 (date) (f. *Κίσσος*)
MACEDONIA (MYGDONIA):
—THESSALONIKE: **(12)** s. iii BC *IG* X (2) (1) 75 ([*Ἐκ*]*αταῖος*: s. *Διονύσιος*)
SCYTHIA MINOR:
—ISTROS: **(13)** i BC *ISM* I 54, 3 (f. *Ξενοχάρης*); **(14)** ii AD ib. 214, 6 + 226, 4 (s. *Ἀ—*); **(15)** f. ii AD ib. 57, 4, [50] (*Eastern cults* pp. 102-3 no. 65); *SEG* L 683 B, 5 (s. *Εὐξενίδης*, f. *Ἄβα*); **(16)** 138 AD *ISM* I 193 II, 38 (f. *Βιάνωρ*); **(17)** c. 140-160 AD ib. 207, 14 (*Π. Αἴλ. Ἑ.*)
—KALLATIS: **(18)** ii/iii AD ib. III 183, 3 (II 362) ([*Ἑ*]*κατῆος*)
—TOMIS: **(19)** i BC ib. 2 A, 60 (f. *Δημήτριος*)
SKYTHIA:
—NIKONION: **(20)** ii-i BC *MASP* 5 (1966) p. 80 no. 28 (vase)
—OLBIA-BORYSTHENES (NR.): **(21)** s. vi BC *AIU* 1968 (2), p. 184 (vase) (*Sel'skaia Okruga Ol'vii* p. 85 fig. 32. 16)
THRACE: **(22)** ?ii BC *ZPE* 136 (2001) p. 130 no. 14, 7; cf. La'da E746 (*Ἑκαταῖος*: f. *Ζωΐλος*); **(23)** f. ii BC *Iasos* 191, 12 (resid. Caria Iasos: s. *Ζώνιος*: metic); **(24)** i BC-i AD? *IG* XII (3) 96, 15 (*Ἑκαταῖος*)
—ABDERA: **(25)** c. 415-395 BC May, *Abdera* pp. 173-4 nos. 238-43 (coin); **(26)** s. iv BC *RE* (4); *FGrH* 264 (or Ionia Teos)
—APOLLONIA-SOZOPOLIS: **(27)** v-iv BC *IGB* I² 441; **(28)** v/iv BC ib. 436 (f. *Ἀριστόμαχος*); **(29)** ~ ib. 446 ([*Ἑκ*]*αταῖος*: s. *Διομήδης*); **(30)** ~ ib. 447 bis (f. *Πληιστίδης*); **(31)** ~ ib. V 5149 (s. *Σύμμαχος*); **(32)** iv BC *BMNBurgas* 4 (2002) p. 121 no. 7 (f. *Ἄδρηστος*); **(33)** f. iv BC Gerasimov p. 28 no. 21; *Stud. Fol* p. 398 (coin); **(34)** s. iii BC *ISM* III 11, 3 (f. *Φίλων*); **(35)** ?ii-i BC *BMNBurgas* 4 (2002) pp. 127-8 no. 28; **(36)** ii/i BC *IGB* I² 390, 2 (s. *Ζωπᾶς*)
—BYZANTION: **(37)** c. 200 BC *IG* II² 884, 12, 16 (*RE* (1)) (s. *Κόλχος*)
—BYZANTION?: **(38)** imp. *IByz* 40
—KARDIA: **(39)** s. iv BC *RE* Supplbd. 3 (1a); Berve 294 (tyrant); **(40)** iv/iii BC *IG* IV (1)² 49, 4 (f. *Ἡγησίστρατος*)
—LYSIMACHEIA: **(41)** m. ii BC *ISestos* 38 b, 5 (s. *Κρατῖνος*)
—MESAMBRIA: **(42)** iii BC *IGB* I² 334 quinquies (*Ἑκατα*[*ῖος*]: f. *Ἐπιμένης*); **(43)** 244 BC *SEG* XXXII 118 I, 73 (*FRA* 3684) ?= (*44*); **(44)** ?c. 240-225 BC *IG* VII 281, 1 (*IOrop* 50); *Hyettos* p. 296 (date) (s. *Νουμήνιος*) ?= (*43*); **(45)** i BC *IGB* I² 326, 3 (s. *Μοιραγένης*)
—ODESSOS: **(46)** c. 100-72 BC Price, *Alexander* 1196-9; *SNG Stancomb* 271 (coin) (*Ἑκα*(*ταῖος*)); **(47)** 37 BC *IGB* I² 46, 10 (f. *Ἀπολλᾶς*)
—PISTIROS: **(48)** v/iv BC *BSA* 97 (2002) p. 326 (vase)
—STRYME: **(49)** m. v BC *CEG* II 728 (*IThrakAig* E109) (f. *Ἀντικράτης*)
—STRYME?: **(50)** v-iv BC ib. E131 ([*Ἑκ*]*αταῖος*: f. *Διογείτων*)

Ἑκατερός
MACEDONIA: **(1)** m. iv BC Plu., *Mor.* 177 F (Tataki, *Macedonians* p. 306 no. 8) (fict.?)

Ἑκατέων
SKYTHIA:
—OLBIA-BORYSTHENES: **(1)** c. 400-375 BC *IOSPE* I² 160 (Dubois, *IGDOlbia* 7) ([*Ἑκα*]*τέων*?); **(2)** s. iv BC *SEG* L 702 IV, 5; **(3)** iii BC *IOSPE* I² 201 I, 37 (s. *Παντακλῆς*); **(4)** ~ ib. l. 65 ([*Ἑκ*]*ατέων*: s. *Ἀριστο—*)

Ἑκατεώνυμος
SKYTHIA:
—OLBIA-BORYSTHENES: **(1)** iii BC ib. l. 9 (f. *Νικοκλῆς*)

Ἑκατόδωρος
THRACE:
—APOLLONIA-SOZOPOLIS: **(1)** iv BC *IGB* I² 423 (s. *Μηνόδωρος*)
—BYZANTION: **(2)** c. 250-220 BC Schönert-Geiss, *Byzantion* 1017-25; 1191-9; 1240-1 (coin) ?= (*3*); **(3)** 220 BC Plb. iv 47 ?= (*2*); **(4)** i BC *IByz* 290 (Fıratlı–Robert p. 113 no. 188) (*-τώ-*: f. (nat.) *Βοσ—*)
—BYZANTION (TERRIT.): **(5)** imp. Unp. (Sayar) (s. *Διόδωρος*)
—ODESSOS: **(6)** iii BC *IGB* I² 74 (s. *Ζώπυρος*: sculptor); **(7)** 5 BC ib. 46, 42 (f. *Διονύσιος*); **(8)** f. ii AD ib. 168 (PM 1724); *Dacia* 21 (1977) p. 161 (date) (s. *Ὀνήσιμος*); **(9)** 221 AD *IGB* I² 47 bis a, 21 (*M. Αὐρ. Ἑ.*: s. *Ἄττων*)
—PERINTHOS-HERAKLEIA:
——(Boreis): **(10)** iii-ii BC *IPerinth* 61, 42 (s. *Μητρόπυθος*)

Ἑκατοκλῆς
SKYTHIA:
—OLBIA-BORYSTHENES: **(1)** s. vi BC Dubois, *IGDOlbia* 62 (vase) (f. *Τύχων*); **(2)** v BC ib. 101 (f. *Ἰητρόδωρος*)

Ἑκατόμβιος
THRACE:
—ABDERA: **(1)** f. iv BC *BCH* 37 (1913) p. 118 no. 36; cf. *AM* 51 (1926) p. 19 no. 7 (*IThrakAig* E37) (f. *Πόλυς*)

Ἑκατώνασσα
THRACE:
—APOLLONIA-SOZOPOLIS: **(1)** v/iv BC *IGB* I² 405 bis (*Ἑκατώνα*[*σ*]*α*: d. *Ἡρόδωρος*)

Ἑκατώνυμος
CIMMERIAN BOSPOROS:
—PHANAGOREIA: **(1)** f. v BC *CIRB* 993
SKYTHIA:
—OLBIA-BORYSTHENES: **(2)** iii BC *IOSPE* I² 201 II, 11 (f. *Μένανδρος*)
THRACE:
—ABDERA: **(3)** c. 336-311 BC May, *Abdera* p. 292 no. 540 (coin)
—APOLLONIA-SOZOPOLIS: **(4)** v BC *IGB* I² 447 (f. *Δημήτριος*)

Ἐκενθος?
THRACE:
—SERDICA (TERRIT.): **(1)** ii-iii AD *Sp.* 98 (1941-48) p. 127 no. 280, 2; p. 277 (name) (*Δίζα Ἐκένθο*[*υ*] (gen.), *Διζαέκενθος*?: ?f. *Δίζας*)

Ἕκτωρ
MACEDONIA: **(1)** c. 360-331 BC *RE* Supplbd. 4 (10a); Berve 295 (Tataki, *Macedonians* p. 306 no. 10) (s. *Παρμενίων*)
MACEDONIA (BOTTIAIA):
—SKYDRA: **(2)** iii BC *SEG* XXIV 524 I, 2 (Hatzopoulos, *MI* 2 p. 106 no. 92; Tataki, *Macedonians* p. 174 no. 1) (*Ἑ*<*σ*>*κτωρ*: s. *Μαννίας*)
MACEDONIA (MYGDONIA):
—THESSALONIKE: **(3)** iii AD *IG* X (2) (1) 471 A-B
SCYTHIA MINOR:
—CIUS*: **(4)** ii AD *ISM* V 123, 6-7 (Lat. Ulp. Hector)

Ἔκφαντος
THRACE:
—MARONEIA: **(1)** iii-ii BC Dumont–Homolle 110b 5, 3 (Wilhelm, *Beitr.* p. 199 no. 171; *IThrakAig* E175) (f. *—τος*)

Ἐλασιππίδας
SCYTHIA MINOR:
—KALLATIS: **(1)** iv/iii BC *ISM* III 125, 7

Ἔλβιος
MACEDONIA (DERRIOPOS):
—STUBERRA: **(1)** 74 AD *IG* X (2) (2) 325, 38 (s. *Λυσίμαχος*); **(2)** 87 AD ib. l. 76 (f. *Λούκιος*)

Ἔλεγχος
THRACE:
—BYZANTION: **(1)** ii/i BC *IByz* 219 (Fıratlı–Robert p. 78 no. 88) (s. *Ἀγλαΐδας*)

Ἐλεκῶπις
CIMMERIAN BOSPOROS:
—NYMPHAION: **(1)** v BC Tolstoi 107 (vase)

Ἑλένη
CIMMERIAN BOSPOROS:
—ACHILLEION: **(1)** ii AD *CIRB* 1031
—PANTIKAPAION: **(2)** s. i AD ib. 397 (d. *Ἴναχος*)
—PANTIKAPAION*: **(3)** ii AD ib. 666, 5; cf. KW pl. 15 no. 208
MACEDONIA (BOTTIAIA):
—EDESSA: **(4)** 23 AD *Athena* 12 (1900) p. 70 no. 2, 6-7 (Tataki, *Edessa* 7) (*Αἰλ. Ἑ.*)
MACEDONIA (MYGDONIA):
—THESSALONIKE: **(5)** ?i AD *SEG* XXXVIII 701 (*Ἀτερία Ἑ.*)
—THESSALONIKE?: **(6)** ii AD *IG* X (2) (1) 881
MACEDONIA (PAIONIA):
—EUDARISTOS?: **(7)** imp. *Sp.* 98 (1941-8) p. 61 no. 127 (?d. *Γάϊος*)
THRACE:
—ODESSOS: **(8)** i-ii AD *IGB* I² 142 bis (d. *Διονύσιος*)
—PHILIPPOPOLIS-TRIMONTIUM (TERRIT.): **(9)** ii-iii AD ib. III 1432

Ἕλενος
CIMMERIAN BOSPOROS:
—PANTIKAPAION: **(1)** i AD *CIRB* 396 ([*Ἕ*]*λενος*: s. *Πόθος*); **(2)** ~ ib. 493 (f. *Πόθος*)
MACEDONIA (BOTTIAIA):
—BEROIA: **(3)** ii-iii AD *IBer* 227 (Tataki 433) (f. *Φιλωτέρα*); **(4)** ~ *IBer* 228 (Tataki 432); **(5)** 177 AD *IBer* 327 (Tataki 650) (*Και*[*πια*]*νὸς Ἕ.*: s. *Καιπιανὴ Ὠφελίμα*)
MACEDONIA (EDONIS):
—PHILIPPOI: **(6)** ii/iii AD *CIL* III 633 II b, 1 (Pilhofer 163); *CRAI* 1923, p. 277 (date); Collart, *Philippes* pls. 64-5 (Lat. M. Herennius Helenus)
MACEDONIA (MYGDONIA):
—THESSALONIKE: **(7)** iii AD *IG* X (2) (1) 220, 1 (*Πομπώνιος Ἕ.*); **(8)** 240 AD ib. 178, 5 ([*T.*]? *Φλ.* [*Ἕ*]*λενος*)
—THESSALONIKE?: **(9)** ii-iii AD ib. 698 (f. *Νικέρως*)
THRACE:
—MONTANA*: **(10)** 155 AD *CIL* III 7449, 22 (*Montana* II 1) (Lat. Aur. Helenus)

Ἐλεοσίνιος
THRACE:
—APOLLONIA-SOZOPOLIS: **(1)** iv BC *IGB* I² 428 (*Ἐλεοσίνι*[*ος*]: s. *Διονυσόμανδρος*)

Ἐλευθέριν
MACEDONIA (LOWER PAIONIA):
—EUROPOS: **(1)** i BC *SEG* XLIII 399 B (*Σερουειλία Ἐ.*)
MACEDONIA (MYGDONIA):
—THESSALONIKE: **(2)** iii AD *IG* X (2) (1) 445, 1 ([*Φουσ*]*κιανὴ Ἐ.*: m. *Φουσκιανὴ Διονυσία*)

Ἐλευθέριον
MACEDONIA (BOTTIAIA):
—BEROIA: **(1)** f. ii AD *IBer* 36, 6 (Tataki 434) (m. *Μιλησία*)

Ἐλευθέριος
MACEDONIA (MYGDONIA):
—THESSALONIKE?: **(1)** ?vi AD *IG* X (2) (1) 790, 2 (Feissel, *RICM* 140)

Ἐλευθερίων
Scythia Minor:
—istros: (1) ii ad *ISM* i 197 II, 13 (*Αἴλ. Ἐ.*)

Ἐλεύθερος
Thrace:
—deultum: (1) ii-iii ad *IGB* iii 1849, 8
—pautalia: (2) ii-iii ad ib. iv 2073, 3

Ἐλευσίνιος
Scythia Minor:
—tomis: (1) ii bc *SNG BM Black Sea* 302; *AMNG* i (2) 2410 (coin) (*Ἐλευσί(νιος)?*)
Thrace:
—odessos: (2) f. ii ad *IGB* i^2 78 ter, 8 (*CCET* i 30) (-σεί-: I f. *Ἐλευσίνιος* II); (3) ~ *IGB* i^2 78 ter, 8 (*CCET* i 30) (-σεί-: II s. *Ἐλευσίνιος* I)

Ἐλεύσιος
Thrace:
—bisanthe-panion: (1) v-vi ad *AD* 49-50 (1994-5) Mel. p. 321 no. 147 (*Λεύκιος*—Dumont–Homolle)

Ἐλευσίς
Thrace:
—apollonia-sozopolis: (1) v bc *IGB* i^2 431 (d. *Ἀνθεστήριος*)

Ἑλικών
Scythia Minor:
—dinogetia (nr.): (1) ii/iii ad *ISM* v 303 (*Ἑ̣λ̣ικῶ̣[ν]?*, *Ἑλικω̣[νιος]*—ed.: s. *Ὀλυμπι—*)

Ἑλικωνιάς
Cimmerian Bosporos:
—pantikapaion: (1) m. i ad *CIRB* 425 (d. *Χρῦσος, Θεονίκη*); (2) ~ ib. 433; (3) 81 ad ib. 70, 17 (Levinskaya p. 231 no. 1) (Jew?)

Ἕλιξ
Macedonia (Edonis):
—philippoi: (1) imp. *BCH* 58 (1934) p. 479 no. 22 (Pilhofer 259) (Lat. Helici (dat.))

Ἑλλακόμη
Thrace:
—aproi: (1) iv-v ad Unp. (Sayar) (m. *Ὑπατία*)

Ἕλλαν
Macedonia (Pieria):
—pydna: (1) iv bc *GRBS* 43 (2002-3) p. 110 no. 1 a, 3
Thrace:
—mesambria: (2) i bc *IGB* i^2 324 (f. *Ζώπυρος*)

Ἑλλανίδης
Cimmerian Bosporos:
—gorgippia: (1) f. iii bc *CIRB* 1137 A II, 32; 1137 B II, 36 (f. *Ποσίδεος*); (2) ~ ib. 1137 B I, 4 (f. *Λύσανδρος*)

Ἑλλάνικος
Macedonia: (1) 334-331 bc *RE* (3); Berve 298 (Tataki, *Macedonians* p. 306 no. 12)
Macedonia (Edonis):
—amphipolis: (2) c. 265-255 bc *SGDI* 2588, 2 (Tataki, *Macedonians* p. 51 no. 44) (f. *Ποσειδώνιος, Ἡρακλειόδωρος, Ἀπολλόδωρος, Ξάνθιππος*)

Ἑλλανίχα
Macedonia (Mygdonia):
—thessalonike: (1) i-ii ad *IG* x (2) (1) 421, 1-2 + *BCH* 97 (1973) p. 589; cf. *Myrtos* p. 275 (*Ἑλλανίχα*—apogr., Daux, *Ἑλλανί(κ)α*—ed.: d. *Ἀντίγονος*, m. *Ἀντίγονος, Φίλων*)

Ἑλλανίων
Macedonia (Elimeia): (1) ?257 bc *FD* iii (4) 417, 14 (Tataki, *Macedonians* p. 195 no. 10) (f. *Φίλαρχος*)

Ἑλλάς
Cimmerian Bosporos:
—pantikapaion: (1) i ad *CIRB* 398; cf. KW pl. 13 no. 202
Macedonia (Bottiaia):
—beroia?: (2) f. ii ad *SEG* l 623 (*IBer* p. 33 ζ) (m. *Μένανδρος*)
Macedonia (Mygdonia):
—thessalonike: (3) v-vi ad *SEG* xlv 821 (mosaic) (*Ἑλλὰς ἡ καὶ Κλημεντίνη*)
Thrace: (4) i bc-i ad *ASAA* 2 (1916) p. 176 no. 166
—bisanthe-panion: (5) hell.? Dumont–Homolle 83f (d. *Ἀγαθοκλῆς*)

Ἕλλην
Thrace:
—mesambria: (1) i ad *IGB* i^2 343 (PM 1323; *CCET* i 153); cf. *IGB* v 5115 (I f. *Ἕλλην* II); (2) ~ ib. i^2 343 (PM 1323; *CCET* i 153); cf. *IGB* v 5115 (II s. *Ἕλλην* I)
—odessos: (3) ii-i bc *AMNG* i (2) 2220 (coin) (*Ἕλλη(ν)*); (4) i bc *IGB* i^2 154 (PM 922) (f. *Σαρκοῦς*); (5) i bc-i ad *IGB* i^2 151 (PM 713) (s. *Ἰσόχρυσος*); (6) 43 bc *IGB* i^2 46, 4 (f. *Νουμήνιος*); (7) 38 bc ib. l. 9 (f. *Ἀμύντωρ*); (8) 36 bc ib. l. 11 (s. *Νουμήνιος*); (9) 31 bc ib. l. 16 (f. *Ἑρμάφιλος*); (10) 14 bc ib. l. 33 (s. *Ἐπιμένης*); (11) i ad ib. 158 (s. *Ἑστιαῖος*); (12) ~ ib. 227, 3 (f. *Ἄννιον*); (13) i-ii ad ib. 51 c, 7 (s. *Χαιρέας*); (14) ~ ib. 83 (*Ἕμηνος*—lap., *Ἕ(λλ)ηνος*: f. *—ωρος*); (15) ~ ib. 126 (*Ἕλ[λη]ν*: s. *Νουμήνιος*); (16) ~ ib. 143 b, 4 (f. *Ἀρέτη*); (17) ~ ib. l. 7 (s. *Ἀγαθήνωρ, Ἀρέτη*); (18) ~ ib. 201; (19) ~ ib. 202 (*Ἕλλ[ην]?*: f. *Νουμήνιος*); (20) ii ad ib. 50 a, 15 (f. *Ἀ—δωρος*); (21) ~ ib. 171 (PM 1453) (*[Ἕλλ]ην?*: f. *Ἀννι*); (22) ii-iii ad *IGB* v 5040 (*Ἕλλ[ην]*: f. *Μητρόδωρος*); (23) f. ii ad ib. i^2 78 ter, 4 (*CCET* i 30) (f. *Μένιππος*); (24) ~ *IGB* i^2 78 ter, 5 (*CCET* i 30) (s. *Ἀρπάλης*); (25) ~ *IGB* i^2 78 ter, 10 (*CCET* i 30) (*Ἕλλ(η)ν*: s. *Χαιρέας*); (26) ~ *IGB* i^2 171 bis (PM 1612); *Dacia* 21 (1977) p. 161 (date) (f. *Ζουκηπιστος*); (27) m. ii ad *IGB* i^2 174 (PM 1726); *Dacia* 21 (1977) p. 161 (date) (f. *Νάνα*); (28) s. ii ad *IGB* i^2 220 (*CCET* i 57; PM 1418) (f. *Ἀριστοκλῆς*); (29) ii/iii ad *IGB* i^2 165 (PM 1702); *Dacia* 21 (1977) p. 161 (date) (f. *Θηβαΐς*); (30) 215 ad *IGB* i^2 47 a, 13 (*Αὐρ. Ἕ.*: s. *Ἡφαιστίων*); (31) ~ ib. 47 b, 12 (*Αὐρ. Ἕ.*: s. *Μᾶρκος*); (32) 221 ad ib. 47 bis c, 36 (*Αὐρ. Ἕ.*: s. *Ἀττῆς*)

Ἐλπίας
Cimmerian Bosporos:
—pantikapaion: (1) i ad *CIRB* 71, 3 + Levinskaya pp. 74; 232-3 no. 2; cf. *Rh. Mus.* 111 (1968) pp. 95-6 no. 6 (*Ἐλπία[ς]*)
Scythia Minor:
—istros: (2) iv/iii bc *ISM* i 245 (*Ἐλπίου* (gen.): f. *Ἀπόλλα*)
Tauris:
—chersonesos: (3) s. iv bc Solomonik, *GAKh* 956 (vase)

Ἐλπιδηφόρος
Macedonia (Bottiaia):
—edessa: (1) 180 ad *SEG* xxiv 531, 9 (Tataki, *Edessa* 242) (*Οὔλπ. Δομίτιος Ἐ.*)
Macedonia (Edonis):
—philippoi: (2) ?iv-v ad *SEG* xxxiv 666 (Pilhofer 122)
Macedonia (Lynkestis):
—herakleia (nr.): (3) ii-iii ad *IG* x (2) (2) 8 (-πει-)
Thrace:
—aquae calidae*: (4) iii ad *IGB* i^2 383 (*Ἐλπ̣ιδηφόρος*: f. *Αὐρ. Καλανδίων*)
—byzantion: (5) 218-222 ad *RE* Supplbd. 10 (-) (Stephanis 833); cf. *BE* 1953, no. 205 (threptos)
—maroneia*: (6) ii ad *SEG* xlix 889 + *IThrakAig* E313 (*Αἴλ. Ἐ.*: imp. freed.)
—novae*: (7) f. iii ad *IGLNovae* 82, 11 (Lat. Aur. Elpidephorus)
—perinthos-herakleia: (8) i-ii ad *IPerinth* 96 (*Γ. Ναιμώνιος Ἐ.*)
—philippopolis-trimontium: (9) ?ii ad *IGB* iii 970
—sexaginta prista: (10) s. ii ad *BIAB* 11 (1937) p. 285 (*Romanizmăt* ii 81) (Lat. Aur. Helpideforus)

Ἐλπιδία
Macedonia (Bottiaia):
—beroia: (1) b. 216 ad *SEG* xxxiii 533, 3 (xxxvii 591; Tataki 1093) (*Ποπιλλία Ἐ.*: m. *Φουλκίνιος Σίλων, Φουλκίνιος Τιβερῖνος, Φουλκινία Λαῖτα, Φουλκινία Βάσσα*)
Macedonia (Paionia):
—stoboi: (2) iv-v ad Feissel, *RICM* 280 (mosaic)
Scythia Minor:
—tomis: (3) f. iii ad *ISM* ii 273, 5 (*Στατιλία Ἐ.*: m. *Αὐρ. Μουσίκις*)
Thrace:
—byzantion (territ.)?: (4) iii ad *IByz* 383 (*[Αὐ]ρ. Ἐ.*)

Ἐλπιδιανός
Macedonia (Pieria):
—dion: (1) s. ii ad Oikonomos 11; cf. Spiliopoulou-Donderer, *KGN* p. 203 no. D20 (date) (f. *Ἑρμαδίων*)

Ἐλπίδιος
Macedonia (Chalkidike):
—anthemous: (1) iii ad *SEG* xlii 569 (ii 413) (f. *Πουπλικία*)
Macedonia (Edonis):
—philippoi: (2) 379 ad Feissel, *RICM* 233, 10 (Pilhofer 360) (s. *Αὐρ. Καπίτων, Βεβία Παῦλα*)
Macedonia (Mygdonia):
—thessalonike: (3) iv/v ad *SEG* xxiv 564 b

Ἐλπίδις
Macedonia (Paionia):
—stoboi: (1) iv-v ad Feissel, *RICM* 279 (mosaic)

Ἐλπιδίων
Skythia:
—tanais: (1) 228 ad *CIRB* 1283, 15, 18 (f. *Σαμβίων*)

Ἐλπίνης
Thrace:
—perinthos-herakleia: (1) c. 223-218 bc *PPetr* iii 77, 4; cf. La'da E1959 (f. *Ἀλέξανδρος*)

Ἐλπινίκη
Thrace:
—maroneia: (1) iii ad *SEG* xlix 891, 3 (*IThrakAig* E312) (*Ἐλ[πι]νείκη*: d. *Σμάραγδος, Ἐλπίς*)

Ἐλπίνικος
Macedonia (Pieria):
—pydna: (1) 250 ad *SEG* xlvi 800 A, 28 (*Αὐρ. Ἐλπίνεικος*)
Tauris:
—chersonesos: (2) f. iii bc ib. xl 615 B, 1 (*Ἐλ(π)ίνικος*)

Ἐλπῖνος
Skythia:
—olbia-borysthenes: (1) v bc Dubois, *IGD-Olbia* 34 (vase)

Ἐλπίς
Macedonia (Bottiaia):
—beroia: (1) ii ad *IBer* 232, 4 (Tataki 438) (d. Ἐπίγονος); (2) f. iii ad *IBer* 229, 1 (Tataki 437) (m. Χρυσῆτ̈ς)
—beroia (territ.): (3) f. ii ad *IBer* 502 (Tataki 847) (Μαλεία Ἐλπ[ίς]?: m. Μάλειος Κορν. Θεόδοτος)
—tyrissa? (asvestari (mod.)): (4) f. iii ad *SEG* xlviii 828
Macedonia (Chalkidike):
—anthemous: (5) iii ad *Anthémonte–Kalindoia* 1 p. 62 no. A17 (*SEG* ii 412) (Αὐρ. Ἐ.: m. Αὐρ. Ἀνίκητος)
Macedonia (Edonis):
—philippoi: (6) imp. *BCH* 47 (1923) p. 94 no. 32 (Pilhofer 128) (Lat. Elpis); (7) ~ ib. 756; (8) ~ Collart, *Philippes* p. 415 n. 4 (Pilhofer 342) (Lat. Pisidia Helpis)
—philippoi (nr.): (9) ?ii ad *CIL* iii 14206. 14 (Pilhofer 430) (Lat. Aninia Elpis)
Macedonia (Lynkestis):
—herakleia (nr.): (10) ii-iii ad *IG* x (2) (2) 8
Macedonia (Mygdonia):
—thessalonike: (11) f. i ad ib. x (2) (1) 423 (Τορπιλία Ἐ.); (12) ii ad ib. 425; (13) ~ ib. 427; (14) ~ ib. 600 (Lat. Aemilia Elpis); (15) ~ ib. 708 (Κουσωνία Ἐ.); (16) ii-iii ad Nalpantis, *Anaskaphi* p. 110 no. BE 115; (17) m. ii ad *SEG* xliii 462, 5 (Καττία Ἐ.: m. Κάσσιος Ἀσκληπιάδης)
Macedonia (Paionia):
—argos (nr.): (18) ii-iii ad ib. xvi 401, 3 (d. Εὔτροπος, Ἀγάθη)
Scythia Minor:
—dinogetia (nr.): (19) ii-iii ad *ISM* v 301 (Lat. Helpis: freed.)
Thrace: (20) imp. Unp. (Sayar)
—byzantion: (21) i bc-i ad *IByz* 19, 11
—maroneia: (22) ii ad *IThrakAig* E275 (Ἀτερία Ἐ.); (23) iii ad *SEG* xlix 891, 3 (*IThrakAig* E312) (m. Ἐλπινίκη)
—novae*: (24) i ad *Archeologia* (Warsaw) 50 (1999) p. 26 no. 4 (Lat. Valeria Elphis: freed.)
—odessos: (25) ii-iii ad *IGB* i² 141 (d. Ἀγαθίας)
—perinthos-herakleia: (26) ii-iii ad *IPerinth* 137 (Κλ. Ἐ.: d. Κλ. Ἐρασῖνος, Κλ. Δονᾶτα)
—transmarisca: (27) ii-iii ad *Dacia* 5-6 (1935-6) p. 452 (Lat. Vibia Helpis)

Ἔμη
Thrace:
—odessos: (1) iii-ii bc *IGB* i² 157 (d. Εὐπ—)

Ἐμίνακος
Skythia:
—olbia-borysthenes: (1) m. v bc *SNG BM Black Sea* 358; Dubois, *IGDOlbia* pp. 10-11 (coins); cf. Vinogradov, *Pont. Stud.* p. 155 no. 5 (name)

Ἐμμεῖς
Cimmerian Bosporos:
—pantikapaion: (1) i bc *CIRB* 122, [1], 5 (m. Αἰνείας)

Ἐμμένης
Macedonia (Lynkestis):
—herakleia: (1) i ad *IG* x (2) (2) 75, 46 (s. Ἡραγόρας)

Ἐμπεδοκλῆς
Macedonia (Edonis):
—amphipolis: (1) ii bc *SEG* xxiv 594, 1, 4 (Ἐν-: s. Ἀντιγένης, f. Ἀντιγένης)

Ἔμπεδος
Thrace:
—salymbria: (1) 407 bc *IG* i³ 118, 37 (f. Ἀπολλόδωρος)

Ἐμπεδοτίμη
Thrace:
—perinthos-herakleia?: (1) iv bc Hp., *Epid.* ii 3. 4

Ἐμπειρικός
Cimmerian Bosporos:
—pantikapaion: (1) f. ii ad *CIRB* 655 (Ἀ. Συτέσιος Ἐνπιρικός)

Ἐνδημία
Macedonia (Paionia):
—kavadarci (mod.): (1) 224 ad *SEG* xxxviii 716 (Ἐν(δ)ημία)
Macedonia (Paionia)?: (2) ii-iii ad ib. xl 564

Ἔνδημος
Macedonia (Bottiaia):
—beroia: (1) ii ad *IBer* 241 (Tataki 347) (Γέλλιος Ἰουλιανὸς Ἐ.); (2) ii-iii ad *IBer* 283 (Tataki 440) (f. Τιμόθεος); (3) 234-244 ad *ILeukopetra* 86, 2; 87, 13; 88, 2; 89, 15; 91, 21; 92, 11; 93, 29; 94, 6; 95, 25; 96, [7]; 100, 14 (Tataki 588) (Ἰουλιανὸς Ἐ., Εἰουλιανὸς Ἐ.—89)
Thrace:
—pautalia: (4) ii-iii ad *IGB* iv 2072, 14 (—ενδημος—ed.)

Ἐνθαδίων
Macedonia (Bottiaia):
—kyrrhos: (1) 199 ad *ILeukopetra* 45, 1, 3, 16 (Tataki, *Macedonians* p. 116 no. 4) (f. (nat.) Διονύσιος, f. (ad.) Ἰουλία)

Ἐνόδιος
Macedonia (Bottiaia):
—skydra*: (1) 105 ad *SEG* xvii 317, 16 (slave?)

Ἔντιμος
Thrace:
—maroneia: (1) ii ad *IG* xii (8) 220, 15 (f. Τίθυτα)

Ἐντρέχης
Cimmerian Bosporos:
—pantikapaion: (1) iv bc *CIRB* 182 (s. Διδύμαρχος)

Ἐντρόπη
Macedonia (Mygdonia):
—thessalonike?: (1) ii-iii ad *IG* x (2) (1) 760 (Ἐν[τρ]όπη?)

Ἐξάκεστος
Macedonia: (1) 102 bc *PWürzb* 6, 30 (Tataki, *Macedonians* p. 499 no. 254; La'da E1659) ([Ἐξάκ]εστος?, [Εὐάρ]εστος?)

Ἐξάκων
Macedonia: (1) c. 132 bc *PGissUniv* 7, 3 (Tataki, *Macedonians* p. 482 no. 97; La'da E1485) (s. Ἀπολλώνιος)

Ἐξήκεστος
Macedonia: (1) f. i bc Cic., *in Pis.* 89 (Lat. Execestus) ?= (2); (2) ~ D.S. xxxvii 5a (f. Εὐφάνης) ?= (1)
Macedonia (Bisaltia):
—argilos?: (3) 364-357 bc Hatzopoulos, *Actes Amphipolis* p. 15 no. 1, 3; pp. 73-4 (locn., date) (or Macedonia (Edonis) Amphipolis: Ἐξή[κεσ]τος)
Macedonia (Edonis):
—philippoi: (4) hell. Hatzopoulos, *MI* 1 p. 188 n. 1 (f. —λης); (5) m. iii bc *SEG* xxiv 621 (Pilhofer 327) (f. Εὐηφένης)

Ἔξοχος
Thrace:
—apollonia-sozopolis: (1) i-ii ad *IGB* i² 401, 14 (Ἔξοχ[ο]ς: s. Ἑρμάφιλος)

Εὔβουλος
Skythia:
—olbia-borysthenes: (1) v bc Dubois, *IGD-Olbia* 101 (-βō-: s. Μοιραγόρης)

Εὔδημος
Cimmerian Bosporos:
—pantikapaion: (1) iv bc *CIRB* 220 (f. Ποσειδεώνιος)

Εὔκαρπος
Skythia:
—olbia-borysthenes: (1) m. iv bc Dubois, *IGDOlbia* 106, 5 (*SEG* xliv 669)

Εὐκλείδης
Thrace:
—apollonia-sozopolis: (1) iv bc *IGB* i² 429 (s. Μεγακλῆς)

Εὔξενος
Cimmerian Bosporos:
—patraeus: (1) iv bc *CIRB* 1017 (*GVI* 338; *CEG* ii 738) (f. Σάτυρος)

Εὔπραξις
Skythia:
—olbia-borysthenes*: (1) iv bc *ZOOID* 23 (1900) p. 24 no. 20 (vase)

Ἑορταῖος
Macedonia (Lynkestis):
—herakleia?: (1) iii ad *IG* x (2) (2) 139 (Ἑορτ[αῖος])

Ἑορτάσης
Thrace:
—perinthos-herakleia: (1) iii-iv ad *IPerinth* 151 (*AD* 51-2 (1996-7) Mel. p. 345 no. 173) ([Ἑ]ορτάσης)

Ἑόρτη
Macedonia (Mygdonia):
—thessalonike: (1) 221 ad *IG* x (2) (1) 492, 3 (Κλ. Ἑ.: d. Μ. Ἐρέννιος Αἰδήμων, Κλ. Παραμόνα)
—thessalonike?: (2) 155 ad ib. 805, 2 (Ἐρεννία Ἰόρτη)

Εὐφάνης
Cimmerian Bosporos:
—hermonassa: (1) iv bc *CIRB* 1056 II, 5 (s. Θεόδωρος)

Εὔφημος
Scythia Minor:
—istros: (1) iii-ii bc *ISM* i 261, 1

Εὐφραῖος
Cimmerian Bosporos:
—nymphaion: (1) iv bc *Nekropol' Nimfeia* p. 67 with pl. 72. 3 (Εὐφραῖ[ος]: f. Δεινίας)

Ἐπάγαθος
Cimmerian Bosporos:
—pantikapaion: (1) i ad *CIRB* 548 (f. Χρήστη)
Macedonia (Bottiaia):
—beroia: (2) f. ii ad *IBer* 273 (Tataki 712) (Κλ. Ἐ.); (3) ii/iii ad *IBer* 27 A, 12 (s. Μάξιμος); (4) ~ ib. l. 18 (slave?)
Macedonia (Mygdonia):
—thessalonike: (5) ii ad *IG* x (2) (1) 246, 3 (Μ. [Ἀ]κείλιος Ἐπάγα[θος]); (6) s. ii ad ib. 244 I, 3 (Σερρουίλιος Ἐ.); (7) 250 ad ib. 165, 9 (Κο[ρ]νήλιος Ἐ.: II s. Κορνήλιος Ἐπάγαθος I, Αὐρ. Ζωσίμη); (8) ~ ib. l. 13 + *BCH* 97 (1973) p. 587 (Κωρνήλιος Ἐ.: I f. Κορνήλιος Ἐπάγαθος II)
Macedonia (Odomantike):
—sirrha: (9) 33 or 133 ad *SEG* xvi 411 (f. Τιμαρέτη)

Macedonia (Pieria):
—pydna: **(10)** 250 ad ib. xlvi 800 A, 35 (*Αὐρ. Ἐ.*)
Skythia:
—tanais: **(11)** 244 ad *CIRB* 1287, 13 (s. *Πεισίθεος*)
Thrace:
—nicopolis ad istrum*: **(12)** ii ad *ILB* 391 (Lat. C. Val. Epagathus: f. C. Val. Castus: freed.)
—philippopolis-trimontium: **(13)** ii ad *IGB* iii 1010 (s. *Παυλῖνα*)

Ἐπαίνετος
Macedonia: **(1)** ?308 bc *IG* v (2) 550, 12 (*PP* 17207; Tataki, *Macedonians* p. 307 no. 14) (s. *Σιλανός*) ?= (*3*)
Macedonia (Chalkidike):
—olynthos: **(2)** ?352 bc *TAPA* 65 (1934) p. 128 no. 4, 14; Hatzopoulos, *Actes Chalc.* p. 80 (date) ([*Ἐπ*]*αίνετος*)
Macedonia?: **(3)** 312 bc D.S. xix 79. 2 (*PP* 13763; Tataki, *Macedonians* p. 307 no. 13) ?= (*1*)

Ἔπαινος
Macedonia (Edonis):
—amphipolis: **(1)** hell.? *SEG* xl 522 k (terracotta) (n. pr.?)

Ἐπάλκης
Thrace:
—maroneia: **(1)** ii-i bc *IThrakAig* E212, 55 (f. *Ἀπολλώνιος*)

Ἐπαμείνων
Thrace:
—agathopolis: **(1)** iv/iii bc *Thracia Pontica* 5 p. 112 no. 2, 10 (s. *Δ—*)
—mesambria: **(2)** ii-i bc *IGB* I^2 328 (*Eastern cults* p. 26 no. 43) (*Ἐπα*[*μεί*]*νων*: f. *Εὐφαμίδας*)
—odessos: **(3)** i bc-i ad *IGB* I^2 51 c, 9 (f. *Βασσοῦς*); **(4)** 215 ad ib. 47 a, 26 (-*μί*-: f. *Αὐρ. Διοκλῆς*); **(5)** ~ ib. 47 b, 25 (*Αὐρ. Ἐπαμίνων*: s. *Ἀπελλᾶς*); **(6)** ~ ib. 47 c, 25 (-*μί*-: f. *Αὐρ. Ξένων*); **(7)** 221 ad ib. 47 bis a, 27 (*Αὐρ. Ἐ.*: s. *Εὐτυχίδης*); **(8)** ~ ib. 47 bis b, 15 (I f. *Αὐρ. Ἐπαμείνων* II); **(9)** ~ ib. l. 15 (*Αὐρ. Ἐ.*: II s. *Ἐπαμείνων* I)

Ἔπανδρος
Macedonia (Mygdonia):
—oraiokastro (mod.): **(1)** v-iv bc *SEG* xlix 750 (*Ἐπάναρος*—ed.: s. *Ἕσπερος*)

Ἐπαφρᾶς
Cimmerian Bosporos:
—pantikapaion: **(1)** f. i ad *CIRB* 392 (f. *Καλλικλῆς*, *Διοφ—*); **(2)** ii ad ib. 687 ([*Ἐπα*]*φρᾶς*?: f. *Ἑρμογένεια*)
Macedonia (Bottiaia):
—beroia: **(3)** ii/iii ad *IBer* 143 C, 7 (Tataki 598) (*Ἰού. Ἐ.*); **(4)** 177 ad *IBer* 135 A, 11 (Tataki 779) (*Κυϊντιλιανὸς Ἐ.*)
—edessa: **(5)** 51 ad *SEG* xlvi 744, 15 (Tataki, *Edessa* 89) (s. *Δαμοθάρης*)
Macedonia (Derriopos):
—stuberra: **(6)** 74 ad *IG* x (2) (2) 326, 62 (s. *Πολυκλῆς*)
Macedonia (Edonis):
—philippoi: **(7)** imp. *BCH* 58 (1934) p. 482 no. 36 (Pilhofer 294) (Lat. Epaphran—lap.)
Macedonia (Pieria):
—dion: **(8)** imp. *SEG* xlix 705 (*Ἐπαφρᾶνος* (gen.)); **(9)** ?ii ad Dimitsas 185

Ἐπαφρόδιτος
Cimmerian Bosporos:
—gorgippia: **(1)** ii-iii ad *NE* 9 (1971) p. 9 no. 6 A, 9 ([*Ἐπαφρ*]*όδειτος*: s. *Ὑγ—*); **(2)** s. ii ad *CIRB* 1145, 8 (*Ἐπαφρόδει*[*τος*]); **(3)** ii/iii ad *VDI* 1970 (4), p. 149, 11 ([*Ἐπαφρό*]*δειτος*)
Macedonia: **(4)** 253 ad *ILeukopetra* 103, 11 (slave/freed.)
Macedonia (Bottiaia):
—beroia: **(5)** ii-iii ad *IBer* 295 (*Ἐπαφ*[*ρόδιτ*]*ος*: s. *Αἴγλη*); **(6)** 210 ad *ILeukopetra* 56, 1 ([*Ἐπαφ*]*ρόδιτος*: s. *Φιλώτας*); **(7)** ~ ib. l. 7 (*Κλ. Ἐπαφρόδειτος*)
—edessa: **(8)** 168 ad *SEG* xii 345 (Tataki, *Edessa* 132) (*Λ. Ἰούλ. Ἐπαφρόδειτος*); **(9)** iii ad Feissel, *RICM* 6, 9 (Tataki, *Edessa* 91) (I f. *Ἐπαφρόδιτος* II); **(10)** ~ Feissel, *RICM* 6, 9 (Tataki, *Edessa* 90) (II s. *Ἐπαφρόδιτος* I, f. *Ἀγροίκιος*, *Ἀδέλφιος*, *Πρίσκος*)
Macedonia (Chalkidike):
—potidaia-kassandreia (territ.): **(11)** ii/iii ad *SEG* xlvi 746; *BE* 1997, no. 400 (locn.) (*Λούτειος Ἐπαφρόδειτος*); **(12)** f. iii ad *Tekmeria* 7 (2002) p. 168 (*Λούτειος Ἐπαφρόδειτος*: f. *Αὐφάτιος Θέωρος*)
Macedonia (Edonis):
—amphipolis: **(13)** imp. Kaphtantzis 666 (gem)
—amphipolis (territ.): **(14)** i-ii ad *CIL* iii 14205 (Lat. C. Lucc[eius] Epaphro[ditus])
—philippoi: **(15)** f. i ad *Ep. Philipp.* ii 25; iv 13; cf. Pilhofer 1 p. 225
—philippoi (nr.): **(16)** imp. *BCH* 47 (1923) p. 92 no. 23 (Pilhofer 425) (Lat. [E]paphrodit[us])
Macedonia (Mygdonia):
—thessalonike: **(17)** ii ad *IG* x (2) (1) 370, 2; **(18)** ~ ib. 658, 1 (*Γ. Κλ. Ἐπαφρόδειτος*); **(19)** s. ii ad ib. 245 II, 2 (*Ἐπαφρόδ*[*ιτος*]); **(20)** iii ad ib. 637 (*Κουσώνιος Ἐπαφρόδειτος*)
Scythia Minor:
—istros: **(21)** ii ad *ISM* i 201 II, 3 (-*δει*-)
—tomis: **(22)** imp. ib. ii 297 (Lat. Catonius Ep[aphro]ditus: freed.)
Skythia?: **(23)** ii ad *VDI* 1951 (1), p. 155 no. 4 (locn.) (Lat. M. Rubrius Epaphroditus)
Thrace: **(24)** c. 161-169 ad *ILB* 441; *Romaniznăt* ii 205 (Lat. Iulius Epaphroditus)
—byzantion: **(25)** i bc *IByz* 105 (Firatlı-Robert p. 96 no. 136) (-*δει*-: s. *Διόδωρος*); **(26)** i bc-i ad *IByz* 19, 9 (*Λεύκιος Ἐπαφρόδειτος*)
—byzantion*: **(27)** ii-i bc ib. 313 (Firatlı-Robert p. 159) (*Ἐπαφρόδειτος*—Robert: slave)
—markianopolis (territ.): **(28)** f. iii ad *IGB* v 5381 = *CCET* ii (1) 302 (*Ἐπαφρόδε*[*ι*]*τος*: f. *—δωρος*)
—maroneia: **(29)** ii-i bc *IThrakAig* E212, 50 (-*δει*-: s. *Φᾶσις*); **(30)** i ad Dumont-Homolle 110b 12 (*IThrakAig* E292) (-*δει*-: f. *Φᾶσις*); **(31)** ii ad ib. E307 (*Οὔλπ. Ἐπαφρόδειτος*)
—perinthos-herakleia:
——(*φυλ. δευτ.*): **(32)** ii/iii ad *IPerinth* 104 (-*δει*-: I f. *Ἐπαφρόδιτος* II); **(33)** ~ ib. (-*δει*-: II s. *Ἐπαφρόδιτος* I)
—philippopolis-trimontium: **(34)** c. 303 ad *Anal. Boll.* 31 (1912) p. 192

Ἐπάφρων
Thrace: **(1)** ?ii ad *IG* xii (9) 1196, 10 (*Γ. Κουρ. Ἐ.*)

Ἐπήρατος
Macedonia: **(1)** 340 bc *CID* ii 43, 17 (Tataki, *Macedonians* p. 307 no. 15)

Ἐπιαῖος
Thrace:
—duvanli (mod.): **(1)** vi bc *SEG* xliii 484

Ἐπιγᾶς
Macedonia: **(1)** ?252 ad *ILeukopetra* 105, 3 (slave/freed.)
Macedonia (Derriopos):
—stuberra: **(2)** 50 ad *IG* x (2) (2) 324, 20 (s. *Εὔιος*)

Ἐπιγενᾶς
Thrace:
—apollonia-sozopolis: **(1)** i bc/i ad *Thracia Pontica* 5 p. 172 (unp.)

Ἐπιγένεια
Macedonia (Mygdonia):
—thessalonike: **(1)** i-ii ad *IG* x (2) (1) 286 (-*νηα*: d. *Ἐπιγένης*)

Ἐπιγένης
Macedonia: **(1)** ?179 bc *PFreib* 36/37, 12-13 (Tataki, *Macedonians* p. 307 no. 16; La'da E1486)
Macedonia (Bottiaia):
—beroia: **(2)** iii bc *IBer* 23, 2 (Tataki 444) (f. *Κύνανα*); **(3)** 232-234 ad *ILeukopetra* 80, 3; 81, 13; 82, 7; 84, 18 (Tataki 72) (*Αἴλ. Ἐ.*, *Ἔλιος Ἐ.*—80)
Macedonia (Derriopos):
—stuberra: **(4)** c. 41-48 ad *IG* x (2) (2) 323, 7 (s. *Ἄπερ*); **(5)** 74 ad ib. 325, 47 (s. *Ἀντιφάνης*); **(6)** 87 ad ib. l. 81 (f. *Φίλιππος*); **(7)** 90 ad ib. 326, 80 (s. *Παρμενίων*); **(8)** 116 ad ib. 327, 17-8 (f. *Γάϊς*, *Ἀλέξανδρος*); **(9)** 121 ad ib. 328, 11 (*Ἐπιγώνης*—Dimitsas: s. *Παράμονος*)
Macedonia (Edonis):
—amphipolis: **(10)** 242 bc *SEG* xii 373, 33 (Tataki, *Macedonians* p. 51 no. 45) (f. *Διονύσιος*); **(11)** c. 200-170 bc Hatzopoulos, *MI* 2 p. 87 no. 65, 2 (*SEG* xlvi 720) ([*Ἐπ*]*ιγένης*?, [*Ἀντ*]*ιγένης*?: s. *Ἀνδρόνικος*); **(12)** i bc-i ad ib. xxvii 248, 4 (*Ἐπιγένη*[*ς*])
—philippoi: **(13)** iv/iii bc ib. xxiv 620 (Pilhofer 246) (f. *Διόδοτος*)
Macedonia (Lynkestis)?: **(14)** s. ii ad *EAM* 156 (f. *Ἀμμία*)
Macedonia (Mygdonia):
—thessalonike: **(15)** 95 bc *IG* x (2) (1) 4, 3 (f. *Διογένης*); **(16)** i-ii ad ib. 286 (f. *Ἐπιγένεια*); **(17)** s. i ad ib. 68, 33; 69, 22 (f. *Φίλιππος*)
Macedonia (Paionia):
—neapolis? (smilovci (mod.)): **(18)** iii/iv ad *ZA* 23 (1973) p. 150 no. 4 (f. *Καλπουρνιανός*)
Macedonia (Pelagonia): **(19)** ii-i bc *IG* x (2) (2) 159, 8 (f. *Γοργίας*)
—dostoneis?: **(20)** ii-iii ad ib. 203 (s. *Μεστύλος*)
Macedonia (Pieria):
—dion: **(21)** f. iii bc *SEG* xlix 703
Scythia Minor:
—kallatis: **(22)** s. iii bc *ISM* iii 12, 4 (s. *Ἀριστο—*); **(23)** i-ii ad ib. 136, 2
Thrace:
—antisara: **(24)** s. vi bc *AD* 25 (1970) Chron. p. 398 (vase) (*Ἐπιγέν*[*ης*])
—byzantion: **(25)** ii/i bc *RE* (17) (Lat. Epigenes)
—maroneia: **(26)** c. 432-423 bc Schönert-Geiss, *Maroneia* 92 (coin)
—pautalia (territ.): **(27)** ii-iii ad *IGB* iv 2110 (f. *Μᾶρκος ὁ καὶ Βονωλας*)
—perinthos-herakleia: **(28)** c. 100-115 ad *SEG* xxvi 1288, 3, 11 (s. *Ἧδυς*, f. *Φιλήμων*)
—philippopolis-trimontium: **(29)** iii ad *IGB* v 5439 (s. *Μουκιανός*)
—rhaidestos: **(30)** i bc-i ad PM 182 d (s. *Παπίας*, f. *Παπίας*); **(31)** ~ ib. 182 c (s. *Παπίας*)
—serdica: **(32)** ii ad *IGB* iv 1923, 3 (f. *—ς*) ?= (*33*); **(33)** ~ ib. l. 6 (*Ἐπιγέ*[*ης*]: f. *Ἀσκληπιόδοτος*) ?= (*32*)
Thrace?: **(34)** ii bc *Hellenika* 10 (1937-8) pp. 200-4; cf. Masson, *OGS* p. 339 (or Bithynia: s. *Διλόπολις*)

Ἐπιγήθης
Macedonia (Pieris):
—oisyme-emathia: **(1)** c. 230-200 bc *BCH* 45 (1921) p. 18 III, 81 (Tataki, *Macedonians* p. 128 no. 1) (s. *Τελεσίας*)

Ἐπιγόνη
Macedonia (Bottiaia):
—beroia: **(1)** ii-iii ad *IBer* 332 (Tataki 455) (m. *Παράμονος*); **(2)** 187 ad *ILeukopetra* 20,

10 (Tataki 261) (*Αὐρ. Ἐπ[ι]γόνη*); **(3)** f. iii AD *IBer* 230, 1 (Tataki 182) (*Ἀννία Ἐ.*: m. *Φλαβιανὸς ὁ καὶ Παπποῦς*)
—EDESSA: **(4)** ii-iii AD *Arch. Pap.* 22 (1973) p. 205 no. 5 (Tataki, *Edessa* 170) (*Κοκκεία Ἐ.*: m. *Καλλιγένης*)
MACEDONIA (CHALKIDIKE):
—POTIDAIA-KASSANDREIA (TERRIT.): **(5)** i-ii AD *TAPA* 62 (1931) p. 54 no. 6 + 69 (1938) p. 67 n. 49 (*BCH* 103 (1979) p. 306 no. 50; *ILGR* 226) (Lat. Antonia Epigone: m. *Ζωσίμη*)
MACEDONIA (EDONIS):
—PHILIPPOI: **(6)** ii AD *AD* 42 (1987) Chron. p. 443 (Pilhofer 156) (Lat. Cassia Epigone: m. Q. Cassius Saturninus)
MACEDONIA (MYGDONIA):
—PERDYLOS: **(7)** ?i-ii AD *SEG* XXIX 581 (d. *Ἀπολλώνιος*)
—THESSALONIKE: **(8)** ii AD *KGAM Thess.* 11 318; **(9)** ii-iii AD *IG* X (2) (1) 455, 13 (*GVI* 318) (?m. *Ἐπίγονος*); **(10)** ~ *IG* X (2) (1) 459 B (Feissel, *RICM* 114) (*Μεστρία Ἐ.*)
—THESSALONIKE?: **(11)** ii-iii AD *IG* X (2) (1) 814, 4 (*Αἰλ. Ἐ.*: d. *Μ. Λικίννιος Χαίρων, Οὐλπ. Λεοντώ*)
MACEDONIA (PAIONIA):
—BYLAZORA: **(12)** ii-iii AD *Sp.* 75 (1933) p. 17 no. 31, 1 (d. *Γαΐα*, m. *Φιλόμουσος*)
MACEDONIA (PELAGONIA): **(13)** iii AD *IG* X (2) (2) 295
MACEDONIA?: **(14)** iii AD *AD* 38 (1983) Chron. p. 411

Ἐπιγονής
MACEDONIA (EDONIS):
—AMPHIPOLIS: **(1)** ii-iii AD *SEG* XXXIV 608 (*Ἐπιγονῆνι* (dat.), *Ἐπιγόνη*?)

Ἐπίγονος
MACEDONIA (BOTTIAIA):
—BEROIA: **(1)** imp. *IBer* 233; **(2)** ~ ib. 234 (*Γ. Λάππιος Ἐ.*); **(3)** ii AD ib. 232, [1], 4 (Tataki 447) (f. *Ἐλπίς*); **(4)** ii-iii AD *IBer* 231 (Tataki 446); **(5)** 171 AD *ILeukopetra* 7, 3 (*Ν. Δέλλιος Ἐ.*); **(6)** ii/iii AD *IBer* 143 C, 16 (Tataki 599) (*Ἰού. Ἐ.*)
MACEDONIA (CHALKIDIKE):
—MENDE?: **(7)** iii AD *IG* XII (2) 409 (Tataki, *Macedonians* p. 120 no. 7) (*Αὐρ. Ἐ.*)
—POTIDAIA-KASSANDREIA: **(8)** c. 262 BC *IG* IX (1)² (1) 18, 12 (Tataki, *Macedonians* p. 89 no. 33) (s. *Διότιμος*)
MACEDONIA (LOWER PAIONIA):
—EUROPOS: **(9)** ?ii AD *SEG* XXXVIII 613 (?s. *Πολέμων*); **(10)** 205 AD ib. 615 = XLV 760 (?s. *Ἰουβέντιος Ἐ—*, *Ἰουβεντία —α*)
MACEDONIA (MYGDONIA):
—LETE: **(11)** s. iv BC Hatzopoulos, *MI* 2 pp. 93-4 no. 79, 14
—THESSALONIKE: **(12)** hell.? *RE* (6); *GP* 2196-99 (Tataki, *Macedonians* p. 181 no. 25); **(13)** ?i AD *SEG* XXXVIII 701 (*Μ. Ἀτέριος Ἐ.*); **(14)** ii-iii AD *IG* X (2) (1) 455, 7, 14 (*GVI* 318) (?s. *Κούαρτος, Ἐπιγόνη*); **(15)** ~ *IG* X (2) (1) 857/8; Robert, *OMS* 5 p. 316 (locn.) (*Αἰ-*); **(16)** s. ii AD *SEG* XLV 817 (XLVIII 853) (f. *Παραμόνα*)
—THESSALONIKE?: **(17)** i AD *IG* X (2) (1) 678
MACEDONIA (PIERIA):
—DION: **(18)** hell. *SEG* L 589 (f. *Σικελία*)
MACEDONIA?: **(19)** c. 185 BC *ID* 427, [15]; 442 B, 95; cf. *ID Index* p. 11 s.v. *Ἀντίπατρος* (?f. *Ἀντίπατρος*)
SCYTHIA MINOR:
—NOVIODUNUM: **(20)** ii AD *ISM* V 270, 6 (Lat. C. Iulius Epigonus)
SKYTHIA:
—TANAIS: **(21)** c. 200-210 AD *CIRB* 1277, 15 (f. *Ἡρακλείδης*)
TAURIS:
—CHERSONESOS: **(22)** 174 AD *SEG* XLV 985 A, 36 (s. *Ποντικός*)
THRACE:
—MARONEIA: **(23)** c. 230-200 BC *BCH* 45 (1921) p. 18 III, 92 ([*Ἐ*]*πίγονος*: s. *Διονυσᾶς*); **(24)** ii-i BC *IThrakAig* E212, 50 (f. *Ἀκοῦτος*); **(25)** 167 BC *SEG* XXXV 823, 3 (*IThrakAig* E168)
—PERINTHOS-HERAKLEIA: **(26)** ii AD *IPerinth* 102, 7 (f. *Ἀντίλοχος*)

Ἐπιγώ
MACEDONIA (BOTTIAIA):
—BEROIA: **(1)** ii-iii AD *IBer* 490 (*Ἐπιγοῦς* (nom./gen.?))

Ἐπιθέρσης
MACEDONIA (CHALKIDIKE):
—OLYNTHOS: **(1)** ?352 BC *TAPA* 62 (1931) p. 50 no. 3, 4 ([*Ἐπι*]*θέρσης*: s. *Θρασύλαος*)
THRACE:
—AINOS: **(2)** a. 316 BC *IG* IV (1)² 94 b, 50 (Perlman, *City and Sanctuary* E.1 with pp. 78-9 (date)); cf. Tataki, *Macedonians* p. 173 no. 4 (s. *Ἀλκιμένης*)

Ἐπιθυμήτη
MACEDONIA (PIERIA):
—DION: **(1)** s. ii AD *SEG* XXXVI 614; cf. Spiliopoulou-Donderer, *KGN* p. 185 no. D1 (date)

Ἐπιθύμητος
MACEDONIA (PAIONIA):
—STOBOI: **(1)** s. iii AD *JÖAI* 32 (1940) Beibl. col. 16 no. 3. 7 (?s. *Σαβῖνος*)
THRACE:
—BEROE-AUGUSTA TRAIANA: **(2)** ii-iii AD *IGB* III 1616 a (f. *Ἐπίπολις*)

Ἐπίκαδος
MACEDONIA (DERRIOPOS):
—STUBERRA: **(1)** c. 41-48 AD *IG* X (2) (2) 323, 13 (f. *Εὔβιος*); **(2)** ~ ib. l. 20 (f. *Βρεῦκος*); **(3)** 50 AD ib. 324, 21 (s. *Λυσίμαχος*); **(4)** 74 AD ib. 325, 57 (f. *Ἀπολλόδωρος*); **(5)** ~ ib. 326, 63 (f. *Γρᾶτος, Θεογείτων*)
MACEDONIA (ORESTIS):
—BATTYNAIOI: **(6)** 192 AD *EAM* 186 II, 49 (f. *Στράτων*)

Ἐπίκαιρος
CIMMERIAN BOSPOROS:
—PANTIKAPAION: **(1)** i/ii AD *CIRB* 599 (*Ἐ*[*πί*]*καιρο*[*ς*]?: s. *Ἀριστίων*)

Ἐπικαρπία
MACEDONIA (MYGDONIA):
—THESSALONIKE?: **(1)** i AD *IG* X (2) (1) 845

Ἐπίκουρος
SKYTHIA:
—OLBIA-BORYSTHENES: **(1)** iii BC *IOSPE* I² 201 I, 6 (s. *Ἄδραστος*); **(2)** f. iii BC *Arkheologiia* (Kiev) 39 (1982) p. 32 (vase) (*Ἐπίκου*(*ρος*))
THRACE:
—DIONYSOPOLIS: **(3)** ii BC *IGB* I² 22 II, 3 (s. *Ἄνδρων*)

Ἐπικράτη
THRACE:
—BYZANTION: **(1)** i-ii AD *IByz* 16 (Fıratlı–Robert p. 59 no. 41) (d. *Διονύσιος*)

Ἐπικράτης
CIMMERIAN BOSPOROS:
—GORGIPPIA: **(1)** f. iii BC *CIRB* 1137 A II, 39 (f. *Ἀπολλώνιος*); **(2)** ~ ib. 1137 B I, 13; 1137 B II, 29 ([*Ἐ*]*πικράτης*: s. *Σίνδος*) ?= (*5*); **(3)** ~ ib. l. 35 (*Ἐπικρ*[*ά*]*τη*[*ς*]: I f. *Ἐπικράτης* II); **(4)** ~ ib. l. 35 (II s. *Ἐπικράτης* I); **(5)** ~ ib. l. 31-2 (f. *Ἴτης, Ἀπολλόδωρος*) ?= (*2*)
—MYRMEKION: **(6)** i/ii AD ib. 884 (*Ἐπει-*)
—NYMPHAION: **(7)** iii BC ib. 912 III, 5; **(8)** f. iii BC *TGE* 17 (1976) p. 186 (weight)
—PANTIKAPAION: **(9)** iii BC *MIA* 56 (1957) p. 222 (tile)
—PHANAGOREIA: **(10)** iii AD *CIRB* 1003, 6 (*Ἐπι*[*κρ*]*ά*[*της*]?: f. *Εὔφρων*)
—TEMRYUK (MOD.): **(11)** 284-245 BC ib. 1036, 3 (f. *—άτης*); **(12)** ~ ib. l. 4 ([*Ἐπ*]*ικράτης*)
MACEDONIA: **(13)** iii BC *IG* V (2) 342 (Tataki, *Macedonians* p. 307 no. 17) (*Ἐπικράτη*[*ς*])
MACEDONIA (BOTTIAIA):
—AIGAI: **(14)** iv/iii BC *SEG* XXXV 798 (s. *Στρωφακίδης*)
—BEROIA: **(15)** iii/ii BC *IBer* 39 (Tataki 448); **(16)** 223 BC *IBer* 4, 35 (*Ἐπικρ*[*ά*]*της*: f. *Δίφιλος*); **(17)** 120 BC ib. 134, 17 (s. *Νικόλαος*)
—EDESSA: **(18)** ii/i BC *Ancient Macedonia* 1 p. 202 no. 16 (Tataki, *Edessa* 92) (s. *Μένανδρος*, f. *Μένανδρος, Νικάνωρ, Δημέας, Φίλα*)
—PELLA: **(19)** f. iii BC *SEG* XXIV 549; **(20)** 263 BC *IG* IX (1)² (1) 17, 69 (Tataki, *Macedonians* p. 154 no. 40) (f. *Ἀλκιμένης*)
MACEDONIA (CHALKIDIKE):
—AKANTHOS: **(21)** 360 BC *IG* IV (1)² 94 b, 22 (Perlman, *City and Sanctuary* E.1 with p. 69 f. (date); Tataki, *Macedonians* p. 42 no. 5)
—STOLOS?: **(22)** ?350 BC *SEG* XXXVIII 670, 5 (s. *Ὀπωρίς*)
—TORONE: **(23)** ?353 BC ib. XXIV 574, 17; Hatzopoulos, *Actes Chalc.* p. 80 (date) (f. *Ἀσανδρος*)
MACEDONIA (EDONIS):
—AMPHIPOLIS: **(24)** c. 230-210 BC *BCH* 45 (1921) p. 18 III, 78; Hatzopoulos, *MI* 2 p. 83 no. 61, 5; cf. *BE* 1994, no. 432 (Tataki, *Macedonians* p. 51 no. 46) (f. *Ξενότιμος*); **(25)** ?c. 167 BC *SEG* XXIV 580, 6; cf. Hatzopoulos, *MI* 1 p. 136 ([*Ἐ*]*πικράτης*: s. *Σερ—*)
—AMPHIPOLIS (NR.): **(26)** a. 357 BC Hatzopoulos, *Actes Amphipolis* p. 43 no. 8, 4 (*SEG* XLI 562) (f. *Νικάνωρ*)
—PHILIPPOI: **(27)** c. 230-200 BC *BCH* 45 (1921) p. 18 III, 80 (Tataki, *Macedonians* p. 164 no. 12) (f. *Ἀντινικίδης*)
MACEDONIA (EORDAIA):
—AKRINI (MOD.): **(28)** f. ii BC *EAM* 92, 5 (s. *Δράκας*)
MACEDONIA (MYGDONIA):
—DIKAIA: **(29)** c. 365-359 BC Unp. (Voutyras–Sismanidis) l. 46
—LETE: **(30)** s. iv BC Hatzopoulos, *MI* 2 pp. 93-4 no. 79, 8; **(31)** ii AD *Makedonika* 2 (1951) p. 619 no. 42 θ, 17 (s. *Βίθυς*)
—THESSALONIKE: **(32)** i AD *IG* X (2) (1) 259, 33 (f. (ad.) *Στράτων*); **(33)** s. i AD ib. 68, 30 (f. *Ἀντιφάνης*); **(34)** s. iii AD ib. 566, 1 (*Π. Μέμιος Ἐ.*)
—THESSALONIKE?: **(35)** i AD ib. 679
MACEDONIA (ODOMANTIKE):
—SIRRHA: **(36)** iii BC *Α΄ Panell. Synedr. Epigr.* p. 173 no. 1 (*Pella* p. 140 no. 223; Tataki, *Macedonians* p. 172 no. 3) (f. *Μέλισσα*)
MACEDONIA (PAIONIA):
—KAVADARCI (MOD.): **(37)** ii AD *Sp.* 71 (1931) p. 66 no. 148 (f. *Μακέτη*)
—NEAPOLIS? (SMILOVCI (MOD.)): **(38)** ii-iii AD ib. 98 (1941-8) p. 32 no. 78
MACEDONIA (PIERIA):
—DION: **(39)** ii-iii AD *SEG* XXXVI 613 (f. *Ἑρμόστρατος*)
MACEDONIA (PIERIS):
—GALEPSOS: **(40)** hell. Dimitsas 918; Hatzopoulos, *MI* 1 p. 187 n. 3 (locn.) (s. *Πολεμαρχίδης*) ?= (*41*); **(41)** ~ Dimitsas 918; Hatzopoulos, *MI* 1 p. 187 n. 3 (locn.) (f. *Ἄδυμος*) ?= (*40*)
SCYTHIA MINOR:
—ISTROS: **(42)** iii-ii BC *ISM* I 387 (f. *Εὐκράτης*)
—TOMIS: **(43)** ii AD ib. II 125, 8 (f. *Σεκοῦνδος*); **(44)** ii-iii AD ib. 31 II, 12 (f. *Θεόδωρος*)

SKYTHIA:
—OLBIA-BORYSTHENES: **(45)** v-iv BC *SEG* XLIV 670 n. (sherd) ([Ἐ]πικρ[άτης]?: ?f. *Δείνων*); **(46)** iv BC *KSIA* 156 (1978) p. 52 (bone); **(47)** f. iv BC *CEG* II 734 (Dubois, *IGDOlbia* 45) (s. *Ἰσοκράτης*); **(48)** m. iv BC ib. 106, 3 (*SEG* XLIV 669) (s. *Ἡροσῶν*); **(49)** s. iv BC ib. L 702 IV, 10; **(50)** iv/iii BC Dubois, *IGDOlbia* 108 (vase); **(51)** iii BC ib. 109, 7 (*SEG* XXXVII 673); **(52)** ~ *IOSPE* I^2 190 b; 191 (s. *Νικήρατος*); **(53)** ~ ib. 201 I, 25 (f. *Ποσειδώνιος*); **(54)** imp. ib. 153, 3 (f. *Ἀσκληπιάδης*); **(55)** ii AD ib. 93, 9 (s. *Κόξουρος*); **(56)** ~ ib. 134, 5 (f. *Ἱεροσῶν*); **(57)** f. ii AD *SEG* XLIII 506, 4 (s. *Μαίακος*)
—OLBIA-BORYSTHENES (BEREZAN (MOD.)): **(58)** f. ii AD ib. XLIX 1028 A, 4 (*Αἰλ. Ἐ.*: f. *Κάρπος*)
TAURIS:
—CHERSONESOS: **(59)** iv BC *IOSPE* I^2 520
THRACE: **(60)** 232 or 207 BC *CPR* XVIII 19, 391, 398, 400, 402 (La'da E744)
—AINOS: **(61)** 156 BC *ID* 1416 B I, 107 (s. *Ποσειδώνιος*)
—APOLLONIA-SOZOPOLIS: **(62)** inc. *Stud. Fol* p. 400 (lead)
—BISANTHE-PANION: **(63)** v-iv BC Dumont–Homolle 83a (f. *Κόμψη*)
—BYZANTION: **(64)** iii BC *ISM* I 65, 7, 26 (*Syll*^{3} 707) (s. *Νικόβουλος*)
—MARONEIA: **(65)** s. iii BC *ISamothrace* 2, 4, 12 (s. *Ἀρκεσ—*); **(66)** ii BC *IG* XII (8) 161, 14 (s. *Ἀλίαρχος*)
—MESAMBRIA: **(67)** ii/i BC *IGB* V 5103, 3 (f. *Πυθάγγελος*); **(68)** ~ ib. l. 7 (*Ἐπικρ[ά]της*: s. *Πυθάγγελος*)
—ODESSOS: **(69)** f. ii BC ib. I^2 39, 4 (f. *Σωκράτης ὁ καὶ Παπίας*); **(70)** f. ii AD ib. 78 ter, 3 (*CCET* I 30) (f. *Διονύσιος*)
—PHILIPPOPOLIS-TRIMONTIUM (TERRIT.): **(71)** iii AD *IGB* III 1419 + V 5522 ([*Αὐρ.*] *Ἐ.*: II s. *Ἐπικράτης* I); **(72)** ~ ib. III 1419: cf. *IGB* V 5522 ([Ἐ]πικράτης: I f. *Αὐρ. Βίθυς*, *Αὐρ. Ἐπικράτης* II)

'Επικρατίδας
MACEDONIA (BOTTIAIA):
—PELLA: **(1)** 190 BC *Syll*^{3} 585, 103 (Tataki, *Macedonians* p. 154 no. 41) (f. *Ὀνάσιμος*)

'Επικτᾶς
MACEDONIA (PAIONIA):
—STOBOI: **(1)** s. iii AD *JÖAI* 32 (1940) Beibl. col. 20 no. 14. 147
MACEDONIA (PIERIA):
—DION?: **(2)** ii/iii AD Spiliopoulou-Donderer, *KGN* p. 199 no. D17 (f. *Λύκος*)

'Επίκτησις
MACEDONIA (MYGDONIA):
—THESSALONIKE?: **(1)** ii AD *IG* X (2) (1) 704 (m. *Διονυσόδωρος*); **(2)** ii-iii AD ib. 903
MACEDONIA (PAIONIA):
—STOBOI: **(3)** ii-iii AD *Sp.* 71 (1931) p. 242 no. 644, 2 (?d. *Θυόδοτος*, m. *Νικίας*: freed.?)
MACEDONIA (PELAGONIA):
—KERAMIAI (NR.): **(4)** iii AD *IG* X (2) (2) 214 ([Ἐ]πίκτησις)
SCYTHIA MINOR:
—TOMIS*: **(5)** ii AD *ISM* II 208 (freed.)
THRACE: **(6)** i BC *Ag.* XVII 507 (*FRA* 2526) ([Ἐ]πίκτησις)
—BYZANTION: **(7)** ii-i BC *IByz* 82 (Fıratlı–Robert p. 51 no. 25) (d. *Βότρυς*); **(8)** i BC *IByz* 195 (Fıratlı–Robert p. 53 no. 30) (d. *Διλίπορις*)
—BYZANTION (NR.): **(9)** i BC *IByz* 226 (Fıratlı–Robert p. 81 no. 96) (d. *Ἀνδρόνικος*)
—NICOPOLIS AD ISTRUM: **(10)** ii-iii AD *IGB* II 670, 4 (*Δεκμία Ἐ.*)
—PERINTHOS-HERAKLEIA: **(11)** i-ii AD *IPerinth* 97 (d. *Ἡρόξενος*); **(12)** ii-iii AD ib. 122 (d. *Ἀσκ—*); **(13)** ~ ib. 211, 9

'Επίκτητος
CIMMERIAN BOSPOROS:
—KIMMERIKON: **(1)** iii AD *KSIIMK* 43 (1952) pp. 69-70 (vase)
MACEDONIA (BOTTIAIA):
—BEROIA: **(2)** ii/iii AD *IBer* 27 A, 14 (s. *Μάξιμος*); **(3)** 181 AD ib. 49, 34 (Tataki 73) (*Τ. Αἴλ. Ἐ.*)
—EDESSA*: **(4)** m. ii AD *CIL* III 7316 (Dimitsas 49; Tataki, *Edessa* 95) (Lat. Epictetus: freed.)
—MIEZA (TERRIT.)?: **(5)** m. iii AD *SEG* XXXV 726 (Tataki 449); cf. Hatzopoulos, *MI* 1 p. 116 n. 4 (locn.)
MACEDONIA (MYGDONIA):
—THESSALONIKE: **(6)** ii AD *IG* X (2) (1) 1041, 5 (XII (8) 581 A; Tataki, *Macedonians* p. 182 no. 26); **(7)** ii-iii AD *IG* X (2) (1) 505, 4 (s. *Οὐαρινία Ὑγίνη*); **(8)** ~ ib. 544, 6; cf. *BCH* 98 (1974) p. 549 (*Λ. Ἀτέλλιος Ἐ.*: ?s. *Γορδιανὸς Ἰταμός*, *Κλ. Λούκουλλα Θάλλουσα*); **(9)** ~ *SEG* XXX 642
—THESSALONIKE?: **(10)** ii-iii AD *IG* X (2) (1) 722 (*Αἴλ. Ἐ.*)
MACEDONIA (PAIONIA):
—STOBOI*: **(11)** s. iii AD Šašel, *IL* 1248 (Lat. C. Fulcinius Epictetus: freed.); **(12)** ~ ib. (Lat. L. Mettius Epictetus: freed.)
MACEDONIA (PIERIA):
—DION: **(13)** ii-iii AD Dimitsas 170 (*Οὔλπ. Ἐ.*)
SCYTHIA MINOR:
—TOMIS: **(14)** ii-iii AD *ISM* II 31 II, 24 (*Ἰούλ. Ἐπίκτητ[ος]*: I ?f. *Ἰούλ. Ἐπίκτητος* II); **(15)** ~ ib. l. 25 (*Ἰούλ. Ἐπίκτητ[ος]*: II ?s. *Ἰούλ. Ἐπίκτη-ος* I)
TAURIS:
—CHERSONESOS*: **(16)** ii AD *IOSPE* I^2 562, 8 (Solomonik, *LNKhT* 13) (Lat. [Ci]ncius Epictet[us]: freed.)
THRACE:
—AINOS: **(17)** imp. *IG* II^2 7974 (*FRA* 244)
—BYZANTION: **(18)** i BC-i AD *IByz* 19, 10; **(19)** ii AD ib. 314 (Fıratlı–Robert pp. 120-1 no. 203) (s. *Μόσχος*, f. *Ζωσίμη*)
—MARONEIA: **(20)** f. i AD *IG* II^2 8628 (*FRA* 3540)
—PERINTHOS-HERAKLEIA: **(21)** 196-198 AD *IPerinth* 56, 18 (f. *Εὐτύχης*)
—SALYMBRIA: **(22)** imp. *IByz* S 8 (f. *Διονύσις*)

'Επικτοῦς
MACEDONIA (ODOMANTIKE):
—SIRRHA: **(1)** ii-iii AD *Belomorski Pregled* I (1942) pp. 329-30 no. 27 = Kaphtantzis 28 (d. *Διονύσιος*)

'Επικύδης
MACEDONIA (CHALKIDIKE):
—OLYNTHOS: **(1)** m. iv BC *IG* II^2 10019 (Tataki, *Macedonians* p. 134 no. 42; *FRA* 5893) (s. *Ἀσκληπιόδωρος*); **(2)** 322 BC *RE* (2) (Tataki, *Macedonians* p. 134 no. 41)
MACEDONIA (MYGDONIA):
—ARETHOUSA?: **(3)** f. iv BC *SEG* XXXI 643 (f. *Γέρων*)
SCYTHIA MINOR:
—KALLATIS: **(4)** iv BC *ISM* III 76 (f. *Μεγιστώ*)

'Επίλυκος
MACEDONIA (CHALKIDIKE):
—STRATONIKEIA?: **(1)** i-ii AD *SEG* XXIV 575 (f. *Νικοπτολέμα*)
MACEDONIA (EDONIS):
—AMPHIPOLIS: **(2)** c. 353 BC *FGrH* 115 F 248 (Tataki, *Macedonians* p. 51 no. 47) (f. *Δάμιππος*)
THRACE:
—APOLLONIA-SOZOPOLIS: **(3)** iii BC *IGB* V 5153, 3 ([Ἐ]πίλυκος) ?= (*4*); **(4)** ~ ib. l. 4 ([Ἐ]πίλυκος) ?= (*3*)

'Επίμαχος
MACEDONIA (MYGDONIA):
—THESSALONIKE: **(1)** i AD *IG* X (2) (1) 242, 7, 10 (s. *Φίλιππος*, f. *Φίλιππος*)

'Επιμελεάς
MACEDONIA (ODOMANTIKE):
—SIRRHA?: **(1)** 136 AD *SEG* XXX 598, 5 (*Ἐπιμελεάδι* (dat.): ?d. *Ἀνίκητος*)

'Επιμελής
THRACE: **(1)** 182 BC *SGDI* 2036, 4-5, 9, 11, 13 (*Ἐπιμελέος* (gen.)—l. 13: slave/freed.)

'Επιμένης
MACEDONIA: **(1)** 327 BC *RE* Supplbd. 4 (3); Berve 300 (Tataki, *Macedonians* p. 308 no. 18) (s. *Ἀρσαῖος*)
MACEDONIA (EDONIS):
—AMPHIPOLIS: **(2)** i BC *IG* II^2 8080 (Tataki, *Macedonians* p. 51 no. 48; *FRA* 503) (f. *Ἀρτεμίδωρος*)
MACEDONIA (MYGDONIA):
—LETE: **(3)** s. iv BC Hatzopoulos, *MI* 2 pp. 93-4 no. 79, 16 ([Ἐ]πιμένης)
—THESSALONIKE: **(4)** f. i AD *IG* X (2) (1) 133, 14; Robert, *OMS* 5 pp. 295-302 (date) (f. *Νικόλαος*); **(5)** s. i AD *IG* X (2) (1) 68, 16; 69, 13 (*Ἐπειμένης*—68: f. *Θεόδωρος*)
THRACE:
—MESAMBRIA: **(6)** iii BC *IGB* I^2 334 quinquies (*Ἐπιμέ[νης]*: s. *Ἑκαταῖος*)
—ODESSOS: **(7)** 29 BC ib. 46, 18 (f. *Τιμοκράτης*); **(8)** 14 BC ib. l. 33 (f. *Ἕλλην*); **(9)** i-ii AD ib. 232; **(10)** 221 AD ib. 47 bis b, 32 (*Αὐρ. Ἐ.*: s. *Ἧλις*)
—SEUTHOPOLIS*: **(11)** c. 300-280 BC *SEG* XLII 661, 1, 4, 10, 13, 19; cf. XLVI 877

'Επινίκη
MACEDONIA (CHALKIDIKE):
—MENDE?: **(1)** m. iv BC *AM* 66 (1941) p. 66 no. 14 (Tataki, *Macedonians* p. 121 no. 9) (d. *Φίλτων*, *Θεοτίμη*)
MACEDONIA (LYNKESTIS):
—HERAKLEIA: **(2)** ii-iii AD *IG* X (2) (2) 83 (*Οὐαλερία Ἐπινείκη*)
MACEDONIA (MYGDONIA):
—THESSALONIKE: **(3)** iii AD ib. X (2) (1) 470, 2 (*Αὐρ. Ἐ.*: m. *Μ. Αὐρ. Θεοδᾶς*)

'Επινικίς
MACEDONIA (BOTTIAIA):
—EDESSA: **(1)** iii AD Feissel, *RICM* 9, 5 (Tataki, *Edessa* 96) (d. *Στερκόριος*, *Παραμόνα*)

'Επίνικος
MACEDONIA: **(1)** c. 185-180 BC *SEG* XXXIX 606, 8
MACEDONIA (BOTTIAIA):
—BEROIA: **(2)** 223 BC *IBer* 4, 28 (s. *Νικίας*); **(3)** 116 BC ib. 134, 29 (s. *—ιος*)
MACEDONIA (DERRIOPOS):
—STUBERRA: **(4)** 74 AD *IG* X (2) (2) 326, 45 (-νει-: f. *Φίλιππος*)
MACEDONIA (LYNKESTIS):
—HERAKLEIA (AREA): **(5)** ii AD ib. 23 (-νει-: s. *Ἄππιος*)
THRACE:
—BYZANTION: **(6)** ii-i BC *IByz* 87 (Fıratlı–Robert p. 51 no. 22) (f. *Αἴσχρα*)
—LYSIMACHEIA: **(7)** f. ii BC *Iasos* 184, 8 (s. *Ἀριστέας*)
—MARONEIA: **(8)** iii AD Dumont–Homolle 110b 9 (*IThrakAig* E311) (*Βρούττιος Ἐπίνεικος*)

'Επίνους
MACEDONIA: **(1)** iv/iii BC *Thess. Mnem.* 172 (Tataki, *Macedonians* p. 308 no. 19) (*Ἐπίνου* (gen.)—lap., *Ἐπῖνος*—Arvanitopoulos and Tataki: f. *Νικαία*)

Ἐπίξενος
MACEDONIA (CHALKIDIKE):
—POTIDAIA-KASSANDREIA (NR.): (1) imp. Dimitsas 750 (f. *Μάξιμος*)
MACEDONIA (EDONIS):
—AMPHIPOLIS: (2) hell.? *SEG* XXXIII 504 (tile) (*Ἐπίξενος*: f. *Κέβων*)
MACEDONIA (KRESTONIA):
—IORON: (3) iii AD ib. XLVIII 815
MACEDONIA (MYGDONIA):
—APOLLONIA: (4) 360 BC *IG* IV (1)^2 94 b, 15 (Perlman, *City and Sanctuary* E.1 with p. 69 f. (date); Tataki, *Macedonians* p. 67 no. 5)

Ἐπίπολις
THRACE:
—BEROE-AUGUSTA TRAIANA: (1) ii-iii AD *IGB* III 1616 a (s. *Ἐπιθύμητος*)

Ἐπισᾶς
THRACE:
—ODESSOS?: (1) ii AD ib. I^2 51 bis a, 5 (*Ἐπισᾶ* (gen.): f. *Ἰούλιος*)

Ἐπισθένης
MACEDONIA (CHALKIDIKE):
—OLYNTHOS: (1) c. 400 BC X., *An.* vii 4. 7 (Tataki, *Macedonians* p. 134 no. 43)
MACEDONIA (EDONIS):
—AMPHIPOLIS: (2) 401 BC X., *An.* i 10. 7 (Tataki, *Macedonians* p. 51 no. 49) ?= (*Πλεισθένης* (*1*))

Ἐπίστρατος
SCYTHIA MINOR:
—KALLATIS: (1) iii/ii BC *ISM* III 161 (f. *Αἰσίας*); (2) ii BC ib. 165 (f. *Ἀπολλώνιος*)
—TOMIS: (3) hell. Unp. (Avram); (4) 54-68 AD *RPC* I 1837; 1840-1 (coin); (5) ii AD *ISM* II 17, 7 (f. *Λέων*) ?= (7); (6) ~ ib. l. 11 (II s. *Ἐπίστρατος* I); (7) ~ ib. l. 10-11 (I f. *Νατάλιος*, *Ἐπίστρατος* II) ?= (*5*)

Ἐπιτέλης
MACEDONIA (BOTTIAIA):
—BEROIA: (1) 223 BC *IBer* 4, 26 (*[Ἐ]πιτέ(λ)ης*: s. *Μένανδρος*)
MACEDONIA (CHALKIDIKE):
—POTIDAIA-KASSANDREIA?: (2) 285 BC *SEG* XXXVIII 619, 16 (f. *Πύλων*)
MACEDONIA (DERRIOPOS):
—STUBERRA: (3) 74 AD *IG* X (2) (2) 325, 27 (f. *Κλέαρχος*)

Ἐπίτευγμα
THRACE:
—AINOS: (1) i BC ib. II^2 7975 (*FRA* 245) (*Ἐπίτε(υ)γμα*: d. *Δημήτριος*)

Ἐπιτύγχανος
SCYTHIA MINOR:
—TOMIS: (1) ii-iii AD *ISM* II 104, 14 (*[Ἐπι]τύνχανος*)
THRACE:
—NOVAE: (2) f. ii AD *IGLNovae* 95 (*ILB* 324) (Lat. Sex. Caesernius Epitychanus)
—PERINTHOS-HERAKLEIA: (3) iii AD *IPerinth* 125 (*Αὐρ. Ἐπιτύ(γχ)ανος*)
—PHILIPPOPOLIS-TRIMONTIUM (TERRIT.): (4) ii AD *IGB* III 1122 (*Οὖλπ. [Ἐπιτ]ύγχανος?*)
—SALYMBRIA: (5) imp. *Archives Stamoulis* d. 35 (Loukopoulou, *Thrace Propontique* p. 256)

Ἐπιτυγχάνων
SKYTHIA:
—TANAIS: (1) imp. *CIRB* 1240 (*[Ἐπιτυγ]χάνων?*)
THRACE:
—MARONEIA: (2) ii-i BC *IThrakAig* E212, 54 (*-νχά-*: f. *Ἡρακλείδης*)

Ἐπιφάνεια
MACEDONIA (MYGDONIA):
—THESSALONIKE: (1) v-vi AD Feissel, *RICM* 288 (Tataki, *Macedonians* p. 190 no. 5) (*[Ἐ]πιφαν[ία]*—Feissel, *[Ἐ]πιφάν[ιος]?*)
MACEDONIA (PIERIA):
—DION: (2) ii-iii AD Dimitsas 181; cf. *SEG* XXXIX 584 (*Τιτία Φλαυΐα Ἐ.*)

Ἐπιφάνης
MACEDONIA (EDONIS):
—AMPHIPOLIS: (1) s. iv BC *PAE* 1981, p. 25 with pl. 43 *β*, 4 (s. *Νικοφῶν*)
TAURIS:
—CHERSONESOS: (2) iii BC *IOSPE* I^2 495 (f. *Τελαμών*); (3) ~ *SEG* XLII 700 (f. *Θεόδωρος*)

Ἐπιφάνιος
MACEDONIA (PIERIA)*: (1) s. vi AD ib. XLVIII 809. 1-11; *Istorikogeographika* 2 (1987-8) p. 196 (brick)
THRACE:
—LYSIMACHEIA (NR.): (2) v-vi AD *ISestos* 50 (*AD* 49-50 (1994-5) Mel. p. 332 no. 157) (*-νηος*)

Ἐπιφάνις
THRACE:
—ODESSOS: (1) vi AD Beševliev 105, 4-5

Ἐπιχάρης
CIMMERIAN BOSPOROS:
—PANTIKAPAION: (1) s. iv BC *CIRB* 192, 5; cf. KW pl. 5 no. 88 (f. *Δημήτριος*)
MACEDONIA (BISALTIA):
—TRAGILOS: (2) ?iv BC Kaphtantzis 532 (s. *Ἀντίφιλος*)
MACEDONIA (CHALKIDIKE):
—APHYTIS: (3) ?351 BC *Α΄ Panell. Synedr. Epigr.* pp. 80-1, 25 (f. *Εὐδημίδης*)
—MENDE: (4) vi/v BC *SEG* XLVI 769 D (vase) (*-ρε̄ς*)
—OLYNTHOS: (5) ?350 BC *TAPA* 62 (1931) p. 43 no. 2, 10; *SEG* XLVII 922; Hatzopoulos, *Actes Chalc.* p. 80 (date) (f. *Νίκανδρος*)
—OLYNTHOS?: (6) f. iii BC *IG* XII (8) 116 (Tataki, *Macedonians* p. 135 no. 44) (s. *Εὐκτήμων*, f. *Κτησώ*)
—POTIDAIA-KASSANDREIA?: (7) iv BC *TAPA* 69 (1938) p. 59 no. 12 (or Macedonia (Chalkidike) Olynthos: *[Ἐ]πιχάρης*: s. *Ἀντίοχος*)
MACEDONIA (EDONIS):
—AMPHIPOLIS: (8) a. 357 BC Hatzopoulos, *Actes Amphipolis* p. 34 no. 6, 10
MACEDONIA (MYGDONIA):
—DIKAIA: (9) c. 365-359 BC Unp. (Voutyras–Sismanidis) l. 53
MACEDONIA (ORESTIS):
—BATTYNAIOI: (10) 192 AD *EAM* 186 III, 58 (s. *Κοῖνος*) ?= (*11*); (11) ~ ib. l. 59 (f. *Ὑάκινθος*) ?= (*10*)
SKYTHIA:
—OLBIA-BORYSTHENES: (12) s. iii BC *IOSPE* I^2 76, 5 (Sokolowski II 88; Dubois, *IGDOlbia* 88) (s. *Διονυσοφάνης*)
THRACE:
—LYSIMACHEIA: (13) ?182 BC *Milet* I (3) 47, 3 (and Caria Miletos: *[Ἐ]πιχάρης*: s. *Στράταρχος*)

Ἐπίχαρμος
CIMMERIAN BOSPOROS:
—HERMONASSA: (1) iv BC *CIRB* 1056 II, 4 (s. *Πολ—*)
MACEDONIA (PIERIA):
—PYDNA: (2) iv BC Arr., *Ind.* xviii 5 (Tataki, *Macedonians* p. 170 no. 9) (f. *Μέτρων*)
SCYTHIA MINOR:
—KALLATIS: (3) iii-ii BC Mushmov 223-4 (coin) (*Ἐπίχα(ρμος)?*, *Ἐπιχά(ρης)?*)
THRACE:
—SALYMBRIA: (4) hell. *IByz* S 43 (s. *Πυθογένης*)

Ἐπιχθόνιος?
MACEDONIA (PAIONIA):
—NEGOTINO (MOD.): (1) ii-iii AD *Sp.* 98 (1941-8) p. 56 no. 114, 2 (n. pr.?: s. *Νέανδρος*)

Ἐπόκιλλος
MACEDONIA: (1) 330-327 BC *RE* (-); Berve 301 (Tataki, *Macedonians* p. 308 no. 20) (s. *Πολυείδης*)

Ἔποχος
MACEDONIA (CHALKIDIKE):
—AKANTHOS: (1) v/iv BC *SEG* XLI 554 (vase)

Ἐπτάζενις
THRACE:
—NICOPOLIS AD NESTUM: (1) 142 AD *RMD* 264 (Lat. Eptazenus: f. *Ἐπταίτραλις*)

Ἐπταίκενθος
THRACE: (1) i AD *IGerasa* 199 (biling.) (*Ἐπτάκεντος*: f. *Μουκάσης*); (2) 46-54 AD *SEG* XVI 415 II, 20 (*IThrakAig* E84) (*Τιβ. Κλ. Ἐ.*); (3) 90 AD *CIL* XVI 36 (Lat. Eptacentis (gen.): f. *Μουκάπορις*)
—ANCHIALOS (TERRIT.)?: (4) iii AD *Arkheologiia* (Sofia) 1988 (3), p. 44 fig. 10 (*Ἐπταίκε[νθος]*: f. *Ἀκύλας*)
—BARGALA (AREA): (5) iii AD *Sp.* 98 (1941-8) p. 95 no. 209; cf. Papazoglou, *Villes* p. 88 n. (*Αὐρ. Ἐ.*: s. *Μεστύλος*)
—BIZYE: (6) f. i AD *IGB* I^2 378, 5; II 743, 5; *BSA* 12 (1905-06) p. 175 no. 1 (f. *Ἀπολλώνιος*)
—KELLAI: (7) 241-244 AD *IGB* III 1517, 39 (I f. *Αὐρ. Ἐπταίκενθος* II); (8) ~ ib. l. 39 (*Αὐρ. Ἐ.*: II s. *Ἐπταίκενθος* I)
—KRASALOPARA: (9) 202 AD ib. 1690 b, 55 (and Thrace Pizos: f. *Βρινκαζεις*); (10) ~ ib. l. 62 (and Thrace Pizos: *Ἐπταίκε(ν)θος*: s. *Μουκάτραλις*)
—ODESSOS: (11) f. ii AD ib. I^2 77, 2 (*CCET* I 31) (s. *Ἀσιατικός*)
—PAUTALIA: (12) ii-iii AD *IGB* IV 2069 (f. *Ἡρωΐδης*)
—SERDICA: (13) imp. *AEp* 1928, no. 165 (Lat. Eptaecentus: f. Fuscus Dorilsis)
—SERDICA (TERRIT.): (14) ii-iii AD *Sp.* 98 (1941-48) p. 127 no. 280, 1 (*Ἐπταίκεν[θος]*); (15) ~ ib. l. 3; (16) ~ *IGB* IV 2031
—SPORTELA: (17) ii-iii AD ib. 2232, 6 (s. *Ἐπτηλος*)

Ἐπταίτραλις
THRACE:
—ERGISSENOI: (1) ii AD ib. III 1593, 17 (s. *Ἐνγιϛ.ηνος* (gen.))

Ἐπτάκενθος
SCYTHIA MINOR:
—CAPIDAVA: (1) 168 AD *ISM* V 15, 6 (Lat. Eftacentus: s. *Βίθυς*)
THRACE:
—BEROE-AUGUSTA TRAIANA (TERRIT.): (2) ii-iii AD *IGB* III 1739 (*Ἐπτάκεν[θος]*)
—BESSOI: (3) 138 AD *CIL* XVI 83 (Lat. Eptakent(us): s. Clagissa)
—PAUTALIA (TERRIT.): (4) ii-iii AD *IGB* IV 2116 (*Ἐπτ[ά]κε[ν]θος?*: s. *Διζάκενθος*)
—PHILIPPOPOLIS-TRIMONTIUM (TERRIT.): (5) ii AD ib. III 1302, 5 (f. *Αἰλ. Ἀλκενίς*)

Ἔπταλας
THRACE:
—BOURDAPA: (1) ii-iii AD ib. 1341 (*Ἐπτελου* (gen.): f. *Ταταζια*)
—PHILIPPOPOLIS-TRIMONTIUM (TERRIT.): (2) ii AD ib. 1255; (3) iii AD ib. 1079 (*Ἐπταλ[ου]?* (gen.): f. *Μουκάζενις*)

Ἐπτάπορις
THRACE:
—ABRYTTOS: (1) iii AD ib. II 744, 3 (*[Ἐπ]τάπορις*: f. *Μάξιμος*)

—BESSOI: (2) 138 AD *CIL* XVI 83 (Lat. Eptaperi (dat.): s. Clagissa); (3) 158 AD ib. 108 (*IDR* I p. 118 no. 16) (Lat. Heptapori (dat.): s. Ἴσος)
—NICOPOLIS AD ISTRUM: (4) ?iii AD *ILB* 375 (Lat. Ef[ta]por[i]s: s. Βίθυς)

Ἔπταπυς
MACEDONIA (SINTIKE):
—HERAKLEIA: (1) ii AD *IGB* IV 2325 (Ἐπτ[α]πυς)

Ἐπτάτραλις
THRACE:
—BESSOI: (1) ii AD *CIL* III 4378 + *Stud. Beševliev* pp. 202-7 (Lat. Ulp. Eptatralis)
—MARKIANOPOLIS (TERRIT.): (2) s. ii AD *IGB* II 847 (*CCET* II (1) 282) (f. —ζενις)
—MARKIANOPOLIS (NR.): (3) f. iii AD *IGB* II 836 (*CCET* II (1) 330) (Ἐπ[τάτρα]λις: f. Μουκάτραλις)
—NICOPOLIS AD NESTUM: (4) 142 AD *RMD* 264 (Lat. L. Petronius Eptaetralis: s. Ἐπτάζενις)
—PHILIPPOPOLIS-TRIMONTIUM: (5) ii-iii AD *IGB* III 974 (f. Αἰθαζίη)

Ἑπτάχρυσος
MACEDONIA (BOTTIAIA):
—BEROIA: (1) ii-iii AD *IBer* 235 (Ἑπτάχρυσος); (2) ii/iii AD ib. 143 C, 6 (Tataki 600) (Ἰού. Ἑ.)

Ἐπτέζενις
THRACE:
—BESSOPARA: (1) ii-iii AD *IGB* III 1335 (Ἐπ(τ)ειζε̣[νις])
—MONTANA (TERRIT.): (2) ii/iii AD *Romanizmăt* II 24 (Lat. Eptezenus)
—PAUTALIA (TERRIT.): (3) ii AD *IGB* IV 2214, 17; (4) f. iii AD *Arkheologiia* (Sofia) 1993 (2), p. 15 (*Montana* II 91) (Lat. Ulp. Eptezenus)

Ἐπτέθισις
THRACE:
—BEROE-AUGUSTA TRAIANA:
——Emporion Diskodouraterai: (1) ii-iii AD *IGB* II 738, 1 ([Ἐ]πτέθισι (gen.): f. Διμης)

Ἐπτέκενθος
THRACE:
—BOURDAPA: (1) ii-iii AD ib. III 1342; cf. V 5500 (s. Βίθυς)
—PAUTALIA: (2) ii-iii AD ib. IV 2072, 6 (f. Χρύσιππος)
—PAUTALIA (TERRIT.): (3) ii AD ib. 2214, 10 + V 5868 (Ἐπτέκε(ν)[θ]ος: f. Δυνας)
—SERDICA: (4) ii-iii AD ib. IV 1922, 4 (Ἐ. ὁ Καπίτων)
—SPORTELA: (5) ii-iii AD ib. 2234, 6 (Ἐπ̣τ̣εί-κενθος: s. Βίθας); (6) ~ ib. l. 7 (Ἐπ(τ)είκενθος)
—VICUS LONGINOPARA: (7) ?iii AD *ILB* 209 (Lat. Eftecenthus: s. Cocus)

Ἔπτενις
THRACE:
—MONTANA (TERRIT.): (1) iii AD *Montana* II 67 (Lat. Eptenis (gen.): f. Μούκων)
—STRATOPARA: (2) 202 AD *IGB* III 1690 b, 35 (and Thrace Pizos: s. Κρήσκης); (3) ~ ib. l. 38 (and Thrace Pizos: f. Μουκάτραλις)

Ἐπτέπυρις
THRACE:
—NICOPOLIS AD NESTUM: (1) ii-iii AD ib. IV 2337, 3
—PHILIPPOPOLIS-TRIMONTIUM (TERRIT.): (2) ii-iii AD ib. III 1057 (s. Βίθυς); (3) ~ ib. 1097 (s. Μουκάτραλις)
—SERDICA?: (4) s. ii AD *Sp.* 77 (1934) p. 53 no. 51 (s. Τίτος)

Ἐπτέτραλις
THRACE:
—STRATOPARA: (1) 202 AD *IGB* III 1690 b, 46 (and Thrace Pizos: s. Μουκάτραλις)

Ἐπτήκενθος
THRACE:
—BEROE-AUGUSTA TRAIANA (TERRIT.): (1) ii-iii AD ib. 1733 (Ἐπτήκεν[θ]ο̣ς: f. —α̣ζενις)

Ἐπτήκησος
THRACE:
—HERAION TEICHOS?: (1) ii-i BC Taşlıklıoğlu 2 p. 93 no. 1; cf. *Epigraphica* 37 (1975) p. 59 (name) (f. Δανηπη)

Ἔπτηλος
THRACE:
—BARGALA: (1) ii-iii AD *SEG* XLIV 518 (f. Δέντος)
—SERDICA: (2) ii-iii AD *IGB* IV 1959, 4 ([Ἐπ]τηλος?: f. Ἐπτηπουος)
—SPORTELA: (3) ii-iii AD ib. 2232, 6 (f. Ἐπταίκενθος)

Ἐπτημενηκα
THRACE:
—PAUTALIA:
——Karistoron: (1) ii-iii AD ib. 2153 (d. Ζέρις)

Ἐπτήπορις
THRACE:
—BAZOPARA: (1) 202 AD ib. III 1690 d, 22 (and Thrace Pizos: s. ..καδος); (2) ~ ib. 1690 e, 93 (and Thrace Pizos: s. Βίθυς); (3) ~ ib. 1690 c, 58 (and Thrace Pizos: s. Δυτούτραλις)
—KRASALOPARA: (4) 202 AD ib. 1690 b, 51 (and Thrace Pizos: s. Μουκάτραλις)

Ἐπτηπουος
THRACE:
—SERDICA: (1) ii-iii AD ib. IV 1959, 3 (d. Ἐπτηλος)

Ἐπτηπυρίς
THRACE:
—DIOSOURA: (1) ii AD ib. V 5589, 8 (Ἐπτη[πυ]ρίς: ?d. Βίθυς)
—HADRIANOPOLIS (TERRIT.): (2) ii-iii AD ib. III 1803, 3 (d. Βίθυς, m. Νικήτας)
—KELLAI*: (3) iii AD ib. 1516 a, 31 (Ἐπτ[ηπ]υρίς); (4) ~ ib. 1516 b, 28

Ἐπτησυκος
THRACE:
—BEROE-AUGUSTA TRAIANA (TERRIT.): (1) ii-iii AD ib. 1701 (d. Δορζίνθης, m. Ῥοῦφος Ῥουφιανός)
—HADRIANOPOLIS (TERRIT.): (2) iii AD ib. 1831 (Ἐπτησυχεος (gen.): d. Αὐρ. Μουκάζενις)
—PHILIPPOPOLIS-TRIMONTIUM (TERRIT.): (3) iii AD ib. V 5475, 4 (d. Μουσ—)
—SERDICA: (4) ii-iii AD ib. IV 1963, 5 (*GVI* 386) (Ἐπτε-: d. Θίντος, m. Δέξτερ)

Ἐπτήτραλις
THRACE:
—BAZOPARA: (1) 202 AD *IGB* III 1690 d, 17 (and Thrace Pizos: s. Δόης); (2) ~ ib. l. 21 (and Thrace Pizos: s. Βιθυκεῖλας)
—BEROE-AUGUSTA TRAIANA:
——Karasoura: (3) iii AD ib. 1626, 5 (s. Μουκα(—))
—PHILIPPOPOLIS-TRIMONTIUM (TERRIT.): (4) ii-iii AD ib. 1166 (f. Δίζας)
—STRATOPARA: (5) 202 AD ib. 1690 b, 31 (and Thrace Pizos: s. Αὐλούζενις); (6) ~ ib. l. 34 (and Thrace Pizos: s. Βίθυς)

Ἐράκτωρ
MACEDONIA (BOTTIAIA):
—TYRISSA? (ASVESTARI (MOD.)): (1) f. ii BC *SEG* XLVII 999, 21

Ἐρασῖνος
SCYTHIA MINOR:
—KALLATIS: (1) ii-i BC *AD* 18 (1963) Mel. p. 20 no. 33

THRACE:
—PERINTHOS-HERAKLEIA: (2) ii-iii AD *IPerinth* 137 (Κλ. Ἐρασεῖνος: f. Κλ. Ἐλπίς)
——(φυλ. τεταρτ. Εὐανθίς): (3) iii AD ib. 130, 1 (-σεῖ-: I f. Αὐρ. Ἐρασῖνος II); (4) ~ ib. l. 1 (Αὐρ. Ἐρασεῖνος: II s. Ἐρασῖνος I)

Ἐραστής
THRACE:
—BIZYE (TERRIT.): (1) ii AD *IGB* III 1863, 13; Robert, *Hell.* 11-12 p. 291 with n. 4 (name) (Ἐραστῆδι (dat.))

Ἔραστος
MACEDONIA (MYGDONIA):
—THESSALONIKE: (1) ii AD *IG* X (2) (1) 386 bis (Lat. G. Hostius Erastus: s. C. Hostius Felix, Hostia Prima)
MACEDONIA (PAIONIA):
—STOBOI: (2) ii AD *JÖAI* 6 (1903) Beibl. col. 9 no. 12 (Lat. Erastus)
THRACE:
—SERDICA: (3) ?ii AD *IGB* IV 1935, 2 (II s. Ἔραστος I); (4) ~ ib. l. 3 (I f. Ἔραστος II)

Ἐρατηοῶ
MACEDONIA (EDONIS):
—AMPHIPOLIS: (1) s. iv BC *AD* 24 (1969) Chron. p. 355 no. 2 (d. Νίκανδρος)

Ἐρατίων
CIMMERIAN BOSPOROS:
—PANTIKAPAION: (1) i BC/i AD *CIRB* 315; cf. KW pl. 55 no. 747 (s. Σωσιγένης)

Ἐρατονίκη
MACEDONIA (MYGDONIA):
—THESSALONIKE?: (1) iii AD *IG* X (2) (1) 859, 6 ((Στ)ρατονίκη?)

Ἐράτων
MACEDONIA (CHALKIDIKE):
—AKANTHOS: (1) iv-iii BC *SEG* XXIX 595 (s. Ξενοφῶν, f. Ξενοφῶν)
SCYTHIA MINOR:
—KALLATIS: (2) iv BC *ISM* III 77 ([Ἐ]ράτων—ed., [Κ]ράτων?: f. ΤΩΚΩ)
THRACE:
—DIONYSOPOLIS: (3) iii/ii BC *IGB* I² 20 (s. Δημόφιλος)
—NAULOCHOS?: (4) s. iii BC ib. V 5085 (PM 1104 Add) (or Thrace Mesambria: s. Σίμιχος, f. Μίκκα); (5) ~ *IGB* V 5085 (PM 1104 Add) (or Thrace Mesambria: s. Κήτων, Μίκκα)

Ἐργασίων
SCYTHIA MINOR:
—ISTROS: (1) iii-ii BC *Stud. Fischer* p. 31 no. 3
SKYTHIA:
—OLBIA-BORYSTHENES: (2) s. iv BC *SEG* XLVIII 1016 (sherd)
THRACE:
—APOLLONIA-SOZOPOLIS: (3) ii BC *IG* II² 8350-1; cf. Robert, *Hell.* 11-12 pp. 376-7 (ethn.) (s. Θούλης)

Ἐργεύς
MACEDONIA: (1) 256 BC *PCZ* 59127, 1 (La'da E1487) (Ἐ̣ργεύς: s. Ἀμύντας); (2) 171 BC *PTeb* 819, 43 (Tataki, *Macedonians* p. 309 no. 21); cf. La'da E1663 (Ἐργεῦτος (gen.): f. Λιμναῖος)

Ἐργῖνος
CIMMERIAN BOSPOROS:
—HERMONASSA: (1) 389-349 BC *CIRB* 1037 (f. Δημοφῶν)
MACEDONIA (CHALKIDIKE):
—POTIDAIA-KASSANDREIA: (2) ?c. 265-254 BC Nachtergael, *Les Galates* 2 bis, [3]; 3, 13; 9, 48 (Stephanis 887; Tataki, *Macedonians* p. 89 no. 34) (s. Σιμύλος)

THRACE:
—APOLLONIA-SOZOPOLIS: **(3)** vi BC *IGB* I^2 404 (f. *Ἀσπασίη*)

Ἐρεννιανός
MACEDONIA (PIERIA):
—DION*: **(1)** f. iii AD *SEG* XLIX 696

Ἐρέννιος
MACEDONIA (MYGDONIA):
—KALINDOIA: **(1)** a. 98 AD ib. XLII 582, 17 (s. *Λάκων*)

Ἐρίσκοπος
THRACE:
—SALYMBRIA: **(1)** iii BC *IByz* S 3, 5 (f. *Χίμαρος*)

Ἑρμαγένης
SCYTHIA MINOR:
—TOMIS: **(1)** ii-i BC *ISM* II 120, 5 (sculptor)
THRACE:
—AINOS: **(2)** iii-ii BC *PAE* 1912, p. 187 no. 91 (s. *Ἀρχιππος*)
—BYZANTION?: **(3)** ii-i BC *IByz* 363 (Fıratlı–Robert pp. 124-5 no. 207) (*Ἑρμαγένη* (gen.): f. *Λαυδίκη*)

Ἑρμαγόρας
MACEDONIA (CHALKIDIKE):
—OLYNTHOS: **(1)** ?352 BC *SEG* XXXVIII 637, 2
MACEDONIA (EDONIS):
—AMPHIPOLIS: **(2)** a. 357 BC Hatzopoulos, *Actes Amphipolis* pp. 38-9 no. 7, 14; p. 43 no. 8, 7 (*SEG* XLI 562); **(3)** iii BC *RE* (4) (Tataki, *Macedonians* p. 52 no. 51)
TAURIS:
—KERKINITIS: **(4)** f. iii BC *SNG BM Black Sea* 698; 705 (coins) (*Ἑρμα(γόρας)?*)

Ἑρμαγόρης
CIMMERIAN BOSPOROS:
—HERMONASSA: **(1)** iv BC *CIRB* 1056 II, 13 (f. *Ἀρτέμων*)
SKYTHIA:
—OLBIA-BORYSTHENES: **(2)** v BC *IOSPE* I^2 212 (f. *Ναΐος*)
THRACE:
—ABDERA: **(3)** f. iv BC *SEG* XLVII 1028 (*IThrakAig* E38) (*Ἑρμαγόρεω* (gen.): f. *Ψάμμις*)

Ἑρμαδίων
CIMMERIAN BOSPOROS:
—GORGIPPIA: **(1)** f. ii AD *SGE* 35 (1972) p. 51, 4 (*CIRB* 1132) + *CIRB* 1162; **(2)** ii/iii AD ib. 1179, 41 (f. *Φαρνακίων*); **(3)** ~ ib. l. 60 (s. *Νουμήνιος*)
MACEDONIA (BOTTIAIA):
—BEROIA: **(4)** ?171 AD *ILeukopetra* 11, 1 (Tataki 450) (f. *Ἑρμᾶς*)
MACEDONIA (EDONIS):
—PHILIPPOI: **(5)** ii-iii AD *BCH* 59 (1935) p. 141 no. 40 (*SIRIS* 123; Pilhofer 307); *BCH* 59 (1935) p. 142 no. 41 (*SIRIS* 124; Pilhofer 311) (*Κ. Φλ. Ἑ.*: I f. *Κ. Φλ. Ἑρμαδίων* II); **(6)** ~ *BCH* 59 (1935) p. 142 no. 41 (*SIRIS* 124; Pilhofer 311) (*Κ. Φλ. Ἑ.*: II s. *Κ. Φλ. Ἑρμαδίων* I)
MACEDONIA (MYGDONIA):
—THESSALONIKE: **(7)** ii/iii AD *IG* X (2) (1) 522
MACEDONIA (PIERIA):
—DION: **(8)** s. ii AD Oikonomos 11; cf. Spiliopoulou-Donderer, *KGN* p. 203 no. D20 (date) (s. *Ἐλπιδιανός, Καρπίμη*)
THRACE:
—AINOS: **(9)** imp. *BCH* 24 (1900) p. 169 no. 2 (*SEG* XLIX 868) (*[Ἑρ]μαδίων*)
—NICOPOLIS AD ISTRUM: **(10)** ?iii AD *ILB* 370 (Lat. Hermadion Phrygillio)
—SERDICA: **(11)** iii AD *IGB* IV 1954, 4 (f. *Γαιπες*)

Ἑρμαῖος
CIMMERIAN BOSPOROS:
—PANTIKAPAION: **(1)** f. iv BC *SEG* L 704, 1 (*Ἑρμαῖο[ς]*)
SCYTHIA MINOR:
—TOMIS: **(2)** ii AD *ISM* II 387 (-μέ-)
THRACE:
—APOLLONIA-SOZOPOLIS: **(3)** iv BC *IGB* I^2 430
—MESAMBRIA: **(4)** ii BC ib. 322 ter, 5 (*Eastern cults* p. 25 no. 42)

Ἑρμαΐς
MACEDONIA (BOTTIAIA):
—EDESSA: **(1)** iii AD Feissel, *RICM* 7 (Tataki, *Edessa* 97) (m. *Ξανθίας*)
MACEDONIA (MYGDONIA):
—THESSALONIKE: **(2)** ii AD *SEG* XXXIX 634; cf. XLIII 466
MACEDONIA (ODOMANTIKE):
—SIRRHA: **(3)** ii-iii AD Kaphtantzis 36 (*Κλ. Ἑ.*: m. *Ξάνθιλλα*)
MACEDONIA (PIERIA):
—DION (TERRIT.): **(4)** ii AD *Klio* 52 (1970) p. 50 no. 1 (*Οὐ(λ)π. Ἑ.*)
SCYTHIA MINOR:
—TROESMIS: **(5)** ii AD *ISM* V 190 (Lat. Iulia Hermai[s]: d. C. Iul. Marinus)
THRACE:
—ABDERA: **(6)** hell.? Hp., *Ep.* 17 (fict.)

Ἑρμαΐσκος
MACEDONIA: **(1)** 92 BC *PTeb* 104, 34 (Tataki, *Macedonians* p. 482 no. 98); cf. La'da E1748 (f. *Διονύσιος*)

Ἑρμανούβιος
MACEDONIA (PIERIA):
—DION: **(1)** imp. *SEG* XXXIV 625 (-βει-: f. *Ἰγνατία Ἐρεννία*)

Ἑρμᾶς
CIMMERIAN BOSPOROS:
—PANTIKAPAION: **(1)** imp. *CIRB* 790
MACEDONIA:
—RESEN (MOD.): **(2)** 218 AD *IG* X (2) (2) 48, 35 (*Αὐρήλιος Ἑ. ὁ Κάσσιος*)
MACEDONIA (BOTTIAIA):
—BEROIA: **(3)** ii AD *IBer* 338, 1 (*Γ. Οὐα. Ἑ.*: f. *Μάξιμα, Νίκανδρος*); **(4)** c. 120-140 AD ib. 349 A; 349 B (Tataki 452) (s. *Φαῦστα*); **(5)** ?171 AD *ILeukopetra* 11, 1 (Tataki 453) (s. *Ἑρμαδίων*)
—PELLA: **(6)** ii-iii AD *Tekmeria* 6 (2001) p. 129 no. 2 (*Ἑρμᾶν* (acc.))
MACEDONIA (DERRIOPOS)*: **(7)** 112 AD *IG* X (2) (2) 309, 12 (biling.) (freed.)
MACEDONIA (EDONIS):
—AMPHIPOLIS (TERRIT.)*: **(8)** ?ii-i BC Kaphtantzis 579 (terracotta) (*hερμᾶ* (gen.?))
MACEDONIA (MYGDONIA):
—THESSALONIKE: **(9)** ii-iii AD *AD* 31 (1976) Chron. p. 195 with pl. 125 β (*Τ. Φλ. Κλαυδιανὸς Ἑ.*); **(10)** ~ *IG* X (2) (1) 511 (*Ἑρμᾶνι* (dat.)); **(11)** m. ii AD ib. 400; cf. *JDAI* 84 (1969) pp. 176-7 no. R86; *KGAM Thess.* I 122 (date)
MACEDONIA (PAIONIA):
—STOBOI: **(12)** s. iii AD *JÖAI* 32 (1940) Beibl. col. 18 no. 12. 45 (f. *Ζωΐλος*)
SCYTHIA MINOR:
—NOVIODUNUM: **(13)** ii AD *ISM* V 270, 8 (Lat. C. Iulius Hermas)
TAURIS:
—CHERSONESOS: **(14)** inc. *SEG* XXXVIII 749. 6 (vase)
THRACE:
—ODESSOS*: **(15)** ii-iii AD *IGB* I^2 141 (*Ἑρμᾶνος* (gen.): freed.)

Ἑρμασίων
MACEDONIA (BISALTIA):
—TRAGILOS: **(1)** ii-iii AD *SEG* XXIV 610 (*Γ. Ἰούλ. Ἑ.*: f. *Ἄλκιμος*)

Ἑρμάφιλος
MACEDONIA (MYGDONIA):
—THESSALONIKE: **(1)** ii AD *IG* X (2) (1) 241 A II, 19 (*Πινάριος Ἑρμάφιλος*)
SCYTHIA MINOR:
—TOMIS: **(2)** ii AD *ISM* II 69, 5; 70, 5 (*Τ. Κομίνιος Κλαυδιανὸς Ἑ.*: s. *Εὐμένης*); **(3)** ~ ib. 290, 6, 9 (s. *Ἑρμῆς, Ἀμπλιᾶτα* (Sidon)) ?= (4); **(4)** ~ ib. l. 16 (f. *Ὁμηρικός*) ?= (3)
THRACE:
—APOLLONIA-SOZOPOLIS: **(5)** i-ii AD *IGB* I^2 401, 14 (f. *Ἔξοχος*)
—BIZYE: **(6)** imp. Unp. (Sayar) (*Ἑρμάφιλος*: f. *Πολύϊδος*)
—BYZANTION (TERRIT.): **(7)** hell.-imp. *IByz* 185 (slave?)
—BYZANTION?: **(8)** ii-i BC ib. 335 (f. *Δίων*); **(9)** i BC ib. 364 (*Ἑρμ(ά)φιλος*: f. *Μήνιος*)
—ODESSOS: **(10)** iii BC *IGB* I^2 105 (f. *Διονυσογένης*); **(11)** i BC-i AD ib. 138 (*Ἑρμάφ[ιλος]*: f. —ώνιος); **(12)** 31 BC ib. 46, 16 (s. *Ἕλλην*); **(13)** i-ii AD ib. 200 (f. *Θαθοις*); **(14)** f. ii AD ib. 78 ter, 8 (*CCET* I 30) (f. *Ζωΐλος*); **(15)** f. iii AD *IGB* V 5038 (*Ἑ[ρ]μάφιλος*: s. *Ἡφαιστίων*)

Ἑρμαφρόδιτος?
MACEDONIA (PAIONIA):
—NEGOTINO (MOD.): **(1)** ii-iii AD Hald, *Auf den Trümmern Stobis* p. 60 (maj.) (*Ἑρ[μ]αφρόδιτος?*: reading—Hallof)

Ἑρμείας
MACEDONIA (BOTTIAIA):
—BEROIA: **(1)** ii AD *IBer* 360, 8; 500 (Tataki 1020) (*Ποπλίκιος Ἑ.*: f. *Ποπλίκιος Ῥοῦφος, Ποπλικία Σεμπρωνίλλα*: doctor); **(2)** ii/iii AD *IBer* 143 C, 10 (Tataki 601) (*Ἰού. Ἑ.*)
MACEDONIA (MYGDONIA):
—THESSALONIKE: **(3)** ii-iii AD *IG* X (2) (1) 468 (*Κ. Φούριος Ἑ.*: s. *Κλ. Φούριος Μέστος, Αἰλ. Φίλα*); **(4)** ii/iii AD ib. 355, 1

Ἑρμέρως
MACEDONIA (BOTTIAIA):
—EDESSA: **(1)** 51 AD *SEG* XLVI 744, 14 (Tataki, *Edessa* 237) (*Μ. Οὐίβιος Ἑ.*)
MACEDONIA (EDONIS):
—AMPHIPOLIS: **(2)** ?ii AD *RA* 1945, pp. 47-8 no. 1
—PHILIPPOI: **(3)** ii/iii AD *CIL* III 633 II a, 3 (Pilhofer 163); *CRAI* 1923, p. 277 (date); Collart, *Philippes* pls. 64-5 (Lat. Hermeros: s. *Μητρόδωρος*)
MACEDONIA (MYGDONIA):
—KALINDOIA: **(4)** a. 98 AD *SEG* XLII 582, 49 (f. *Ἀσιατικός*)
—THESSALONIKE: **(5)** s. i AD *IG* X (2) (1) 68, 27; 69, 19 (f. *Μᾶρκος*); **(6)** ii AD ib. 304, 2 (f. *Παλλάς*)
—THESSALONIKE?: **(7)** s. ii AD ib. 902 (s. *Ἑρμῆς, Εὔνοια*)
SCYTHIA MINOR:
—ISTROS: **(8)** 222-225 AD *ISM* I 100 B, 21 (*Π. Αἰλ. Ἑρμέρω[ς]*, *Ἑρμερι[νός]*—ed.)
—TOMIS: **(9)** 201 AD ib. II 83 II, 25 (*Π. Αἰλ. Ἑ.*)

Ἑρμῆς
CIMMERIAN BOSPOROS:
—GORGIPPIA: **(1)** ?s. ii AD *CIRB* 1147, 4; **(2)** s. ii AD ib. 1177, 3; **(3)** ii/iii AD ib. 1179, 32 (s. *Χρηστίων*); **(4)** ~ ib. l. 33, 59 (f. *Χρηστίων*); **(5)** ~ ib. l. 54 (f. *Πάππος*); **(6)** ~ ib. 1180, 3 (f. *Πόθος*)
—PANTIKAPAION: **(7)** imp. ib. 778; **(8)** ~ ib. 788; cf. KW p. 59 fig. 9 (*Ἑρ(μῆ)ς?*: s. *Φάνvας*); **(9)** i AD *CIRB* 367; **(10)** ~ ib. 400 A-B; cf. KW pl. 50 no. 693 (s. *Γάστεις*, f. *Μαστοῦς*); **(11)** ~ *CIRB* 447 (s. *Θεοδᾶς*); **(12)** ~ ib. 500 (f. *Πρωτογένης, Θεονίκη, Ἑρμόδωρος, Φαρνάκης*); **(13)** i-ii AD Vaulina–Wąsowicz pl. 124 no. 63 B, 11 (reading—Tokhtas'ev); **(14)** f. i AD *CIRB* 399 (s. *Ἑρμίας*); **(15)** i/ii AD ib. 619; **(16)** iii AD ib. 102, 6

—PHANAGOREIA: (17) iv AD ib. 988
MACEDONIA (BOTTIAIA):
—BEROIA: (18) ii AD *IBer* 169, 5 (Tataki 455) (s. *Τέρπνη*); (19) ii/iii AD *IBer* 145, 10 (Tataki 460) (f. *Κράτερος*)
MACEDONIA (EDONIS):
—PHILIPPOI (TERRIT.): (20) ?iii AD Pikoulas, *Chora* p. 149 no. 59, 11 (Pilhofer 602; *SEG* L 618); cf. *BE* 1944, no. 129 (Ἑρ[μ]ῆνι? (dat.), Σερωηνί—ed.)
MACEDONIA (ELIMEIA):
—VELVENDOS (MOD.): (21) ii AD *SEG* XLVII 1001, 2
MACEDONIA (MYGDONIA):
—THESSALONIKE: (22) s. i AD *IG* X (2) (1) 68, 26 (*Κλ. Μινούκιος Ῥοῦφος ὁ καὶ Ἑ.*); (23) ii AD ib. 372, 3 (s. *Νέος Νουμίσιος Φῆλιξ ὁ καὶ Βάλας*); (24) ~ ib. 427; (25) ii-iii AD ib. 665, 4 (*SEG* XLIII 460) (f. *Μ. Κάσσιος Εὔπορος*); (26) ~ *IG* X (2) (1) 744, 1 ([*Π.*] *Ἀβούδιος Ἑ.*); (27) ~ ib. l. 3 (*Π. Ἀβούδιος Ἑ.*); (28) 118 AD ib. 524, 4 (*Ἰούλ. Ἑ.*: s. *Πύρρος*, f. *Ἰουλία*); (29) 154 AD ib. 526, 1 (*Μ. Ἰούλ. Ἑ.*: f. *Ἰουλ. Ἑρμιόνη*); (30) ii/iii AD ib. 262 IV, 7; (31) 242 AD ib. 160, 4 (—*τιος* [*Μι*]*νουκκιανὸς Ἑ.*: s. *Αἴλ. Μάξιμος*); (32) 252 AD ib. 166, 4 (*Κλ. Ἑ.*)
—THESSALONIKE?: (33) ii AD ib. 694; cf. *CPh.* 70 (1975) p. 53 (Ἑρμῆνι (dat.)); (34) ii-iii AD *IG* X (2) (1) 741; (35) ~ ib. 897 + *CPh.* 70 (1975) pp. 53 ff.; cf. *Tyche* 10 (1995) pl. 13 (*Κάσσιος Ἑ.*, Ἑρμῆνι (dat.)); (36) s. ii AD *IG* X (2) (1) 902 (s. *Διοσκουρίδης*, f. *Εὔνους*, *Ἑρμέρως*)
—THESSALONIKE*: (37) f. iii AD *SEG* L 643 (freed.)
MACEDONIA (ODOMANTIKE):
—SIRRHA: (38) f. iii AD ib. XXX 590, 28 (Ἑρμῆνος (gen.): f. *Αὐρ. Βίθυς*)
MACEDONIA (PAIONIA):
—ANTIGONEIA? (TREMNIK (MOD.)): (39) ii AD *Sp.* 98 (1941-8) p. 107 no. 231 (*Αἴλιος Ἑ.*)
—KAVADARCI (MOD.): (40) ii-iii AD *Arheološki Pregled* 2 (1960) p. 108 with pl. XVIII.3; cf. *BCH* 112 (1988) p. 459 (name) (Ἑρμῆνι (dat.): s. *Οὐαλερία*)
—STOBOI: (41) ii-iii AD *SEG* XLVII 955 (Ἑρμῆ[ς])
SCYTHIA MINOR:
—CAPIDAVA: (42) ii AD *ISM* V 25, 6 (Lat. C. Iul. Hermes: f. Iulius Valens, Iul. Vitalis); (43) iii AD ib. 42, 2 (Lat. Aur. Hermes)
—ISTROS: (44) ii AD ib. I 201 II, 13 (*Αἴλ. Ἑ.*)
—KALLATIS: (45) 103-116 AD ib. III 83 (Lat. T. Turpilius Hermes: freed.?)
—TOMIS: (46) ii AD ib. II 290, 5, 7 (Ἑρμητι (dat.): s. *Σωκράτης*, f. *Ἑρμάφιλος*); (47) ii-iii AD ib. 20, 5 (s. *Μάξιμος*); (48) iii AD ib. 24, 2 (I f. *Ἑρμῆς* II); (49) ~ ib. l. 2 (—*ος Ἑ.*: II s. *Ἑρμῆς* I)
—TOMIS*: (50) ii AD ib. 261, 8 (biling.) (Ἑρμ[ῆς]: freed.?); (51) ?iii AD ib. 383, 16 (Lat. Hermes)
SKYTHIA:
—OLBIA-BORYSTHENES*: (52) iii AD *ACSS* 8 (2002) p. 205 (Lat. Antonius Hermes)
—TANAIS: (53) f. ii AD *CIRB* 1264 B, 3 (Ἑρμῆς—Tokhtas'ev); (54) 225 AD ib. 1280, 22 (f. —*ιος*); (55) ~ ib. l. 27 (s. *Ἀστήρ*); (56) 228 AD ib. 1282, 27 (s. *Ἀθηνόδωρος*); (57) 244 AD ib. 1287, 9 (f. *Μενέστρατος*)
TAURIS:
—CHERSONESOS: (58) ii AD *VDI* 1938 (3), p. 77 no. 6 (s. *Ἀρίστων*)
THRACE: (59) imp. *CIL* III 7595 (Lat. L. Iunius Ermes); (60) iii AD ib. VI 3217, 5 (Speidel, *Denkmäler* 735) (Lat. Pon. Erm(es): s. M. Aur. Optatus)
—APOLLONIA-SOZOPOLIS: (61) i-ii AD *IGB* I² 401, 15 (f. *Ζώπυρος*)
—BYZANTION: (62) i BC-i AD *IByz* 176 (Firatlı–Robert p. 111 no. 181) (Ἑρμῆτος (gen.): f. —*ητην*); (63) ~ *IByz* 205 (Firatlı–Robert p. 65 no. 59) (Ἑρμᾶ (gen.): s. *Ξενόφαντος*, f. *Δώρημα*)
—NICOPOLIS AD ISTRUM: (64) ii-iii AD *IGB* II 661 (*Κλ. Ἑ.*)
—NOVAE: (65) f. ii AD *IGLNovae* 94, 2 (*ILB* 326) (Lat. M. Atronio Hermeti (dat.): f. M. Atronius Valens)
—ODESSOS (NR.): (66) s. ii AD *IGB* I² 287 (*CCET* I 87) (*Λ. Φαρσουλήϊος Ἑ.*)
—OESCUS*: (67) s. i AD *ILB* 55, 9 (Lat. G. Iulius Hermes: freed.)
—PERINTHOS-HERAKLEIA: (68) i-ii AD *IPerinth* 112 (*Ἰουβέντιος Ἑ.*); (69) ~ ib. 215, 2; (70) c. 304 AD *DCB* (17) (Lat. Hermes)
—PHILIPPOPOLIS-TRIMONTIUM: (71) ii-iii AD *IGB* III 1000
—PHILIPPOPOLIS-TRIMONTIUM (TERRIT.): (72) ii-iii AD ib. 1371 (*Φλ. Δίνις ὁ καὶ Ἑ.*)

Ἑρμιανός
THRACE:
—PAUTALIA (TERRIT.): (1) ii-iii AD ib. IV 2228 (*Τ. Φλ. Ἑ*[*ρμι*]*ανός*?: f. *Μοκασοκος*, *Μοκαζίη*)

Ἑρμίας
CIMMERIAN BOSPOROS:
—PANTIKAPAION: (1) f. i AD *CIRB* 399 (f. *Ἑρμῆς*)
MACEDONIA: (2) 219 BC *PEnt* 15, 1, 8 (Tataki, *Macedonians* p. 309 no. 24) (s. *Ἱππόνικος*: t.e.); (3) 216 BC *Klio* 18 (1925) p. 95; *PGrad* 4 ?= (4); (4) 216-215 BC *PFrankf* 4, 7; *BGU* 1943, 5 (Tataki, *Macedonians* p. 309 no. 23; La'da E1488) ?= (3); (5) 89 BC *UPZ* 125, 29 (Tataki, *Macedonians* p. 482 no. 99; La'da E1489); (6) ~ *UPZ* 125, 29, 35 (Tataki, *Macedonians* p. 482 no. 100); cf. La'da E1498 (f. *Ἡρακλείδης*)
MACEDONIA (BOTTIAIA):
—EDESSA: (7) i-ii AD Touratsoglou, *Macedonia* p. 191 pl. 239
—KYRRHOS: (8) m. i BC *IG* XII (5) 891, 11 (Tataki, *Macedonians* p. 116 no. 5) (f. *Ἀνδρόνικος*)
MACEDONIA (CHALKIDIKE):
—STRATONIKEIA?: (9) i-ii AD *SEG* XXIV 576 (f. *Ἡδίστη*)
MACEDONIA (EDONIS):
—AMPHIPOLIS: (10) ?iii BC *IG* II² 8084 (*FRA* 506) (f. *Μητρόβιος*); (11) ii BC *IG* II² 8084 bis (Tataki, *Macedonians* p. 52 no. 52; *FRA* 504) (f. *Μητρόβιος*); (12) ii-i BC *IG* II² 8085 (Tataki, *Macedonians* p. 52 no. 53; *FRA* 505) (f. *Μητρόβιος*)
MACEDONIA (SINTIKE):
—PARTHIKOPOLIS: (13) f. iii AD *IGB* V 5909
SKYTHIA:
—TYRAS: (14) m. ii BC *IIasos* 408, 12 (s. *Διονύσιος*: metic)
TAURIS:
—CHERSONESOS: (15) i AD *IOSPE* I² 502
THRACE: (16) c. 190-180 BC *Milet* VI (2) 796, 18 (s. *Ἀρτεμίσιος*)
—BARGALA*: (17) v AD Feissel, *RICM* 283 (bp.)
—BYZANTION: (18) i BC *IByz* 91 (Firatlı–Robert p. 91 no. 119) (*Ἑ. Ἐγνάτιος*: slave?)
—BYZANTION?: (19) ii BC *IByz* 325 (s. *Ἀμάτοκος*); (20) ii-i BC ib. 355 (*IG* II² 11325); Robert, *OMS* 7 pp. 638-40 (s. *Ἀθαναίων*)
—LYSIMACHEIA: (21) c. 240-220 BC *IG* VII 357, 2 (*IOrop* 164) (f. *Ὀλυμπος*)
—PHILIPPOPOLIS-TRIMONTIUM (TERRIT.): (22) iii AD *IGB* III 1191 (*Αὐρ. Ἑ.*: s. *Κάλλιστος*)

Ἑρμιόνεις
SCYTHIA MINOR:
—ISTROS: (1) v-vi AD *SEG* XLIV 624 (vase) (Ἑρμιόνει (gen.?))

Ἑρμιόνη
MACEDONIA: (1) 239 AD *ILeukopetra* 90, 10 (-*μη*-: slave)
MACEDONIA (BOTTIAIA):
—AIGAI: (2) i BC *SEG* XLIX 841
—BEROIA: (3) ii-iii AD *IBer* 237 (Tataki 462) ([Ἑρ]μιόνη); (4) ~ *IBer* 361; (5) iii AD ib. 236, 1 (Tataki 461) (m. *Καλανδίων*); (6) ~ *IBer* 405, 9 (Tataki 463)
—BEROIA?: (7) ii-iii AD *IBer* 388, 8 (Tataki 464)
—EDESSA: (8) f. ii AD *SEG* XXXIX 589 (Tataki, *Edessa* 99) (m. *Μάγνα*)
MACEDONIA (LYNKESTIS):
—HERAKLEIA: (9) ii-iii AD *IG* X (2) (2) 89
MACEDONIA (MYGDONIA):
—THESSALONIKE: (10) 120 AD ib. X (2) (1) 525 (Ἑρμιόνη); (11) 154 AD ib. 526, 4 (*Ἰουλ. Ἑ.*: d. *Μ. Ἰούλ. Ἑρμῆς*, *Ἰουλ. Τερτία*); (12) iii AD ib. 415 (*Αὐρ. Ἑ.*: m. *Μ. Ῥω—νιος Σερ—ρώνιος*?)
—THESSALONIKE?: (13) ii-iii AD ib. 818 (m. *Λύκος*)
MACEDONIA (PAIONIA):
—STOBOI: (14) ?s. ii AD *JÖAI* 6 (1903) Beibl. col. 6 no. 6
MACEDONIA (PIERIA):
—DION: (15) v-vi AD Feissel, *RICM* 78
THRACE:
—BEROE-AUGUSTA TRAIANA (TERRIT.): (16) ii-iii AD *IGB* III 1669
—NOVAE: (17) iii AD ib. II 741, 8 (d. *Σαβινιανός*, *Κορινθία*)
—PERINTHOS-HERAKLEIA?: (18) i-ii AD *SEG* L 667 ter (Ἑρμιώ[νη]?, Ἑρμίω[ν]?)

Ἕρμιππος
MACEDONIA (EDONIS):
—PHILIPPOI: (1) s. iv BC ib. XXXVIII 660 (XLIII 450; Pilhofer 387) (f. *Κλεομοιρίς*)
MACEDONIA (MYGDONIA):
—DIKAIA: (2) c. 365-359 BC Unp. (Voutyras–Sismanidis) l. 53
—THESSALONIKE: (3) iii AD *SEG* XXVII 311 (*Κάσσιος Ἑ.*)
SCYTHIA MINOR:
—ISTROS: (4) 222-225 AD *ISM* I 100 A, 20 (f. *Νικήρατος*)
—TOMIS: (5) iii AD ib. II 389 (s. *Ἄττας*)
TAURIS:
—CHERSONESOS (NR.): (6) hell. *AZ* 1857, p. 75 (tile)
THRACE:
—APOLLONIA-SOZOPOLIS: (7) v/iv BC *IGB* V 5151 (f. *Ἀρχέβουλος*); (8) ~ ib. 5152 (I f. *Ἕρμιππος* II); (9) ~ ib. (II s. *Ἕρμιππος* I)

Ἑρμογένα?
MACEDONIA (MYGDONIA):
—THESSALONIKE: (1) b. 268 AD *IG* X (2) (1) 238, 7 (Ἑ(ρ)μογένας (fem. gen.?))

Ἑρμογένεια
CIMMERIAN BOSPOROS:
—PANTIKAPAION: (1) ii AD *CIRB* 687 (-*νια*: d. *Ἐπαφρᾶς*, *Καλλίκλεια*)
MACEDONIA (BOTTIAIA):
—ICHNAI: (2) imp. *AM* 27 (1902) p. 310 no. 16 (*Μιδία Ἑρμογένια*)

Ἑρμογένης
CIMMERIAN BOSPOROS:
—ACHILLEION: (1) i/ii AD *CIRB* 1025; cf. KW pl. 47 no. 669 (f. *Θεαγένης*)
—PANTIKAPAION: (2) f. i AD *CIRB* 494 (f. *Ἔρως*); (3) ii AD ib. 86, 2; (4) f. ii AD ib. 87, 5 (Ἑρ[μογέν]ης?: f. *Μακάριος*)
MACEDONIA (CHALKIDIKE):
—OLYNTHOS: (5) c. 300 BC *IEph* 1454, 2 (Tataki, *Macedonians* p. 135 no. 45) (f. *Λεύκιππος*)
MACEDONIA (LOWER PAIONIA):
—GORTYNIA?: (6) imp. *Sp.* 98 (1941-8) p. 48 no. 100 (Sokolovska, *Isar-Marvinci* p. 130)

MACEDONIA (MYGDONIA):
—APOLLONIA: **(7)** f. ii BC *SEG* XLIV 508 (Hatzopoulos, *MI* 2 p. 87 no. 66) (s. *Μητρόδωρος*)
—CHARAKOMA?: **(8)** 69-79 AD *SEG* XXIX 579
—KALINDOIA: **(9)** 68-98 AD ib. XLII 580, 62 (s. *Ζωΐλος*)
—THESSALONIKE: **(10)** i AD *IG* X (2) (1) 402 (f. *Χαιρέας*); **(11)** ~ ib. (s. *Χαιρέας, Μελίς*); **(12)** i-ii AD ib. 243 I, 11; **(13)** 90 AD *SEG* XLII 625, 9 (s. *Διογένης*); **(14)** 165 AD *IG* X (2) (1) 450 (f. *Νικόλαος*)
MACEDONIA (PAIONIA):
—KAVADARCI (MOD.): **(15)** ?ii AD *Sp.* 71 (1931) p. 75 no. 176, 6; cf. Düll, *Götterkulte* p. 340 no. 131 (s. *Μακεδών*)
MACEDONIA (PIERIA):
—DION: **(16)** ii-iii AD *Chiron* 24 (1994) p. 219 fig. 1 (unp.) (s. *Νουμήνιος, Συμφέρουσα*)
MACEDONIA (SINTIKE):
—NEINE: **(17)** ii AD *IGB* IV 2245 (*Eastern cults* p. 258 no. 12) (s. *Πύρρος*)
SCYTHIA MINOR:
—ISTROS: **(18)** ii AD *ISM* I 196, 12 (*Αἰλ. Ἑ.*)
—KALLATIS (NR.)?: **(19)** ?iii AD *IGB* I^2 12 ter, 2 (*CCET* I 1) (s. *Βίκτωρ, Νωστάτη*)
—TOMIS: **(20)** ?i-ii AD Mushmov 1719 (coin); **(21)** ii-iii AD *ISM* II 26, 1 (s. *Μ—*); **(22)** ~ ib. 366 (*GVI* 1035) (*Ἑ. ὁ καὶ Κυζίκιος*); **(23)** ~ *ISM* II 372 (*GVI* 987; *CCET* IV 32) (s. *Ὕλας, Ματρώνα*); **(24)** s. ii AD *SEG* XXXIII 586 (s. *Κέστιος, Μόσχιον*)
SKYTHIA:
—OLBIA-BORYSTHENES: **(25)** ii AD *IOSPE* I^2 84, 8 (f. *Διονύσιος*)
—SKYTHAI: **(26)** c. 513-535 AD *PLRE* III (1) (f. *Σατορνῖνος*)
THRACE:
—ABDERA: **(27)** s. ii BC *IG* XII (8) 170 d, 54 (s. *Ἀγαθοκλῆς*)
—ANCHIALOS (TERRIT.): **(28)** ii-iii AD *IGB* V 5647, 4 (*Eastern cults* p. 200 no. 17) (f. *Χρήσιμος*)
—BARGALA (AREA): **(29)** iii AD *Sp.* 98 (1941-8) p. 95 no. 209 (f. *Αὐρ. Λυκόφρων*)
—BAZOPARA: **(30)** 202 AD *IGB* III 1690 c, 48 (and Thrace Pizos: *Δριγγίστας Ἑ.*: s. *Βρινκάζερις*)
—BEROE-AUGUSTA TRAIANA (TERRIT.): **(31)** ii-iii AD ib. 1703 (s. *Αὐλούζενις*)
—BYZANTION: **(32)** ii BC *IByz* 71 (Fıratlı–Robert p. 50 no. 16) (*Ἑρμογένη* (gen.): f. *Σύρος*)
—MARKIANOPOLIS: **(33)** ii AD *IGB* II 798 a, 3 (*Ἑρμογ[ένης]*)
—NICOPOLIS AD NESTUM: **(34)** iii AD ib. V 5930, 2 (f. *Θέκλα, Δημοσθένης*)
—PAUTALIA: **(35)** ii-iii AD ib. IV 2072, 7 (f. *Σαβῖνος*); **(36)** ~ ib. l. 18 (*Φλ. Ἑ.*); **(37)** iii AD ib. V 5867, 6 (*Μ. Αὐρ. Ἑ.*: s. *Μοκάζενις*); **(38)** iv AD Beševliev 36
——(Herakleis): **(39)** ?ii AD *IGB* IV 2077, 9 (*Ἑρμογέ(νης)*?: s. *—νος*)
—PERINTHOS-HERAKLEIA: **(40)** i-ii AD *IPerinth* 68 (*Κύντιος Ἑ.*); **(41)** c. 100-115 AD *SEG* XXVI 1288, 12 (s. *Νικίας*); **(42)** ii AD *IPerinth* 102, 1 (II s. *Ἑρμογένης* I, f. *Ἀρισταινέτη*); **(43)** ~ ib. l. 2 (I f. *Ἑρμογένης* II)
—PHILIPPOPOLIS-TRIMONTIUM: **(44)** ii AD *IGB* III 990 (f. *Μ. Οὔλπ. Φίλιππος*)
—SERDICA (TERRIT.): **(45)** ii-iii AD *AEMÖ* 10 (1886) pp. 238-9 no. 2, 6; **(46)** iii AD *IGB* V 5704 (*Α(ὐ)ρ. Ἑ.*)
—SPINOPARA: **(47)** ii AD ib. IV 2193 (*[Ἑρ]μογένης*)
—TIRIZIS AKRA*: **(48)** 337-342 AD ib. V 5002 (*Φλ. Ἑ.*)

Ἑρμόδοτος
THRACE:
—MARONEIA: **(1)** iii BC *IThrakAig* E257, 2 (s. *Δικαῖος*)

—PERINTHOS-HERAKLEIA: **(2)** iv-iii BC *IPerinth* 4, 2 (f. *Προκλῆς*)

Ἑρμοδώρα
THRACE:
—PHILIPPOPOLIS-TRIMONTIUM (NR.): **(1)** ii-iii AD *IGB* V 5518

Ἑρμόδωρος
CIMMERIAN BOSPOROS:
—GORGIPPIA: **(1)** 173-210 AD *CIRB* 1134, 26 (f. *—ος*)
—PANTIKAPAION: **(2)** i AD ib. 500 (s. *Ἑρμῆς*)
MACEDONIA: **(3)** iv BC Arr., *An.* iii 11. 8 (Tataki, *Macedonians* p. 309 no. 25) (f. *Σώπολις*)
MACEDONIA (MYGDONIA):
—THESSALONIKE: **(4)** ii-iii AD *IG* X (2) (1) 665, 7 (*SEG* XLIII 460)
MACEDONIA (SINTIKE):
—HERAKLEIA: **(5)** ii AD *IGB* IV 2323 (*-μώ-*)
SCYTHIA MINOR:
—ISTROS: **(6)** ii AD *ISM* I 196, 21 (s. *Ἀρτεμίδωρος*); **(7)** ~ ib. 197 I, 3 (f. *Ποντικός*); **(8)** 138 AD ib. 193 II, 77 (f. *Κλειτοφῶν*)
—TOMIS: **(9)** 201 AD ib. II 83 I, 29 (s. *Θεόδοτος*); **(10)** ~ ib. l. 31 (f. *Ποντικός*)
SKYTHIA:
—OLBIA-BORYSTHENES: **(11)** 149 AD *SEG* XXX 1334 (s. *Καλλιφάνης*, f. *Εὐμενεανός, Ἰταλικός*)
TAURIS:
—CHERSONESOS: **(12)** c. 490-470 BC ib. XL 612. 15 (ostrakon) (*Ἑρμόδ[ωρος]*: f. *Χαρικλῆς*); **(13)** iii BC Solomonik, *NEPKh* 159; cf. *VDI* 1975 (1), p. 175 (s. *Ἄλκιμος*)
THRACE:
—APOLLONIA-SOZOPOLIS: **(14)** i-ii AD *IGB* I^2 401, 7 (s. *Ἑ—σος*)
—BEROE-AUGUSTA TRAIANA: **(15)** iii AD ib. III 1573, 14 (*Ἑρμόδω[ρος]*: f. *Αὐρ. Πανδίων*)
—BYZANTION: **(16)** i BC-i AD *IByz* 230 (Fıratlı–Robert p. 83 no. 101) (s. *Μηνόφιλος*, f. *Ματρώ*)
—DIONYSOPOLIS: **(17)** iii AD *IGB* I^2 14 c, 21 (*Αὐρ. (Ἑ)ρμόδωρος*: s. *Λούκιος*)
—MESAMBRIA: **(18)** ii BC ib. 325, 5 (s. *Χ—*)
—MUSENOI: **(19)** ii-iii AD ib. V 5652 (f. *Αὐλούζενις*)
—NICOPOLIS AD NESTUM: **(20)** ii AD ib. IV 2336, 11 (*[Ἑ]ρμόδωρος*)
—ODESSOS?: **(21)** ii AD ib. I^2 51 bis b, 6 (*Ἑρμόδωρ(ος)*: f. *Ζώπυρος*)
—PHILIPPOPOLIS-TRIMONTIUM: **(22)** iii AD ib. III 917, 7 (*Δίζας ὁ καὶ Ἑ.*: s. *Βρινκάζενις*)
—SERDICA (TERRIT.): **(23)** ii-iii AD ib. IV 2047 (I f. *Οὔλπ. Ἑρμόδωρος* II); **(24)** ~ ib. (*Οὔλπ. Ἑ.*: II s. *Ἑρμόδωρος* I)
—TYRODIZA-TIRISTASIS: **(25)** iii-ii BC Dumont–Homolle 90 (*[Ἑ]ρμόδωρος*: f. *Φανόδικος*)

Ἑρμόθεστος
THRACE:
—ABDERA: **(1)** s. iv BC *Ét. Thas.* 5 p. 235 no. 411 (s. *Ἀνάξαρχος*)

Ἑρμοίτας
MACEDONIA: **(1)** 232 or 207 BC *CPR* XVIII 12, 237, 250 (Tataki, *Macedonians* p. 309 no. 26; La'da E1490)
MACEDONIA (BOTTIAIA):
—BEROIA: **(2)** s. iii BC *IBer* 16 A, 21 (f. *Ἰόλλας*)
MACEDONIA (EDONIS):
—AMPHIPOLIS: **(3)** ?c. 167 BC *SEG* XXIV 580, 8; cf. Hatzopoulos, *MI* 1 p. 136 (s. *Ἅρπαλος*)

Ἑρμοκάλλης
THRACE:
—ABDERA: **(1)** c. 450-425 BC May, *Abdera* pp. 125-6 nos. 134-8 (coin); Masson, *OGS* p. 430 (name) (*Ἑρμοκάλ(λης)*: f. *Σμόρδος*)

Ἑρμοκλῆς
TAURIS:
—CHERSONESOS: **(1)** f. ii AD *IOSPE* I^2 359, 27; Solomonik, *NEPKh* 111, 6; *VDI* 1960 (3), pp. 154-5, 22 (s. *Ἀπολλώνιος*)
THRACE:
—AINOS: **(2)** v/iv BC *Kazı Sonuçları* 12 (2), p. 283 (s. *Ἡρακλέων*)

Ἑρμοκράτης
CIMMERIAN BOSPOROS:
—PANTIKAPAION: **(1)** iv BC *IGAIMK* 104 (1935) p. 302 nos. 19-20; 308 no. 67 (tile) (*Ἑρμοκρ(άτης)*); **(2)** f. iv BC *CIRB* 213 (f. *Νυμφόδωρος*); **(3)** i AD ib. 368; cf. KW pl. 22 no. 313; **(4)** f. ii AD *CIRB* 754 (s. *Χρηστίων*)
TAURIS:
—CHERSONESOS: **(5)** ii-iii AD *IOSPE* I^2 440 (*[Αὐρ.] Ἑ.*: s. (nat.) *Τιμόθεος*, s. (ad.) *Μύρων*)
THRACE:
—BOURDAPA: **(6)** ii-iii AD *IGB* III 1356-7 (*Ἀδριάνιος Ἑ.*)
—PERINTHOS-HERAKLEIA: **(7)** iv-v AD *IPerinth* 197, 2 (*AD* 51-2 (1996-7) Mel. p. 363 no. 182)

Ἑρμοκρατίδης
THRACE:
—ABDERA: **(1)** c. 450-425 BC May, *Abdera* pp. 134-5 nos. 164-70 (coin) (*Ἑρμοκρατίδεω* (gen.))

Ἑρμόλαος
MACEDONIA: **(1)** 327 BC *RE* (1); Berve 305 (Tataki, *Macedonians* p. 309 no. 27) (s. *Σώπολις*)
MACEDONIA (BOTTIAIA):
—KYRRHOS: **(2)** 150 AD *SEG* XXX 553, 3 (*Αὐρ. Ἑ.*)
MACEDONIA (MYGDONIA):
—LETE?: **(3)** 22 or 139 AD Dimitsas 678, 4 (s. *Μένανδρος*)

Ἑρμόλυκος
MACEDONIA (EDONIS):
—PHILIPPOI: **(1)** 316-309 BC *IG* II^2 1956, 150; *Ancient Macedonia* 5 p. 445 with n. 10 (date) (Tataki, *Macedonians* p. 164 no. 13; *FRA* 7228)

Ἕρμος
MACEDONIA (BOTTIAIA):
—TYRISSA? (ASVESTARI (MOD.)): **(1)** f. ii BC *SEG* XLVII 999, 12

Ἑρμόστρατος
MACEDONIA (PIERIA):
—DION: **(1)** ii-iii AD ib. XXXVI 613 (s. *Ἐπικράτης*)
THRACE:
—ABDERA: **(2)** ?475-450 BC *IG* I^3 1018 (*CEG* I 316) (f. *Πύθων*); **(3)** f. iii BC *AMNG* II (1) 159; 181 (coin)

Ἑρμοτέλης
MACEDONIA (CHALKIDIKE):
—TORONE: **(1)** c. 440-420 BC *IG* I^3 1379 (Tataki, *Macedonians* p. 191 no. 6; *FRA* 7140) (f. *Ἀριστόνους*)

Ἑρμότιμος
THRACE:
—PHILIPPOPOLIS-TRIMONTIUM (TERRIT.): **(1)** iii AD *IGB* III 1207 (*Αὐρ. Ἑρμότ[ιμος]*?)

Ἑρμοῦς
MACEDONIA (ODOMANTIKE):
—SIRRHA: **(1)** f. iii AD *SEG* XXX 590, 10 (*Αὐρ. Ἑ.*: s. *Κέρδων*)

Ἑρμοφαῖος
SKYTHIA:
—OLBIA-BORYSTHENES (LEUKE): **(1)** v-iv BC ib. XLIII 502. 2 (vase) (*ὁρμοφαιõ* (gen.): f. *Σ—*)

Ἑρμόφαντος
THRACE:
—STRYME?: (1) m. iv BC ib. XLIX 1000 (*IThrakAig* E381) (f. Μητρώνασσα, Θεοφάνης)

Ἑρμόφιλος
MACEDONIA: (1) 144-141 BC *PBingen* 35, 3; cf. La'da E1421 (f. Ἀπολλώνιος)
MACEDONIA (BOTTIAIA):
—BEROIA: (2) ii-iii AD *IBer* 252 (Tataki 465) (s. Κίσσος)
THRACE:
—ABDERA: (3) iv/iii BC *SEG* XXX 661 + *IThrakAig* E49 ([Ἑρ]μόφιλος?, [Δη]μόφιλος?: f. Δῖος); (4) c. 311-280 BC Unp. (Chryssanthaki diss.) p. 239 (coin) (Ἑρμόφι(λος))

Ἕρμων
CIMMERIAN BOSPOROS:
—PANTIKAPAION: (1) i AD *CIRB* 402 (f. Ἔρως); (2) ii AD ib. 674 (I f. Ἕρμων II); (3) ~ ib. (II s. Ἕρμων I); (4) 127 AD ib. 61, 3 (s. Διονύσιος)
KOLCHIS: (5) ii BC *IG* II² 9050 (*FRA* 2935) (f. Κέρδων)
—VANI (MOD.): (6) hell. *MBAH* 12 (1993) p. 69 (brick) (Ἕρμω(ν))
MACEDONIA: (7) c. 147-135 BC *BGU* 1256, 3 (Tataki, *Macedonians* p. 482 no. 102; La'da E1491) (s. Θεόκριτος); (8) 103 BC *PTeb* 105, 52, 67 (Tataki, *Macedonians* p. 482 no. 101; La'da E1754) (t.e.)
MACEDONIA (BOTTIAIA):
—AIGAI: (9) s. iv BC *SEG* XXXV 782 (Ἑρμ[ωνος]? (gen.))
—BEROIA: (10) 223 BC *IBer* 4, 18 (f. Ἀριστογένης)
—BEROIA (TERRIT.)?: (11) s. iv BC *A' Panell. Synedr. Epigr.* p. 196 (vase)
MACEDONIA (CHALKIDIKE):
—OLYNTHOS*: (12) f. iv BC *Olynthus* 10 pp. 175-6 no. 526 (bronze) (Ἑρμω[ν])
—STOLOS?: (13) ?351 BC *SEG* XXXVIII 672, 7, 15 (s. Διονύσιος)
MACEDONIA (MYGDONIA):
—THESSALONIKE: (14) 154 AD *IG* X (2) (1) 288, 6 (*M.* Κάσσ[ι]ος Ἕρμων ὁ καὶ Δημᾶς)
SCYTHIA MINOR:
—KALLATIS?: (15) ii/i BC *IGB* II 867 a, 8 = *ISM* I 219 (v 87); cf. *ISM* III p. 140 (locn.) (f. Πολυκράτης)
SKYTHIA:
—SKYTHAI: (16) m. ii BC *Iasos* 408, 16 (f. Κέρδων)
—SOLOKHA (MOD.): (17) v BC *Kurgan Solokha* pp. 80 no. 55 (*hέρ-*)
TAURIS:
—CHERSONESOS: (18) inc. *SEG* XXXVIII 749. 5 (vase) (Ἑρμ[ων]?); (19) iv BC Solomonik, *GAKh* 698 (vase) (Ἑρμω[ν]?)
THRACE:
—ABDERA: (20) c. 311-280 BC Unp. (Chryssanthaki diss.) p. 239 (coin)
—STRYME: (21) c. 375-350 BC *SEG* XXIV 639 (*IThrakAig* E141) (s. Πολυάρητος)

Ἑρμῶναξ
CIMMERIAN BOSPOROS:
—KOROKONDAME: (1) iii BC *North Pontic Archaeology* pp. 350-2 no. 4 with fig. 6 (Ἑρμῆναξ—ed.: s. Φιλίσκος)
MACEDONIA (CHALKIDIKE):
—POTIDAIA-KASSANDREIA: (2) iv/iii BC *Tekmeria* 6 (2001) p. 43 no. 1 (f. Δημήτριος)
THRACE:
—ABDERA: (3) c. 336-311 BC Unp. (Chryssanthaki diss.) p. 287; pp. 330-2 (coin); (4) c. 325-300 BC *BCH* 66-7 (1942-3) p. 195 no. 4 (*IThrakAig* E45)
——(Eurysthenidai): (5) s. iv BC *SEG* XLVI 841 (*IThrakAig* E16) (s. Διονυσᾶς)

Ἕρος?
THRACE?: (1) m. iii BC *SEG* XLI 963, 10 (Ἕρου (gen.): f. Ἀλλούπορις)

Ἐρρεβαῖος
MACEDONIA (BOTTIAIA):
—AIGAI: (1) c. 300-275 BC ib. XXXV 788 (f. Φιλώτας)

Ἐρρένιος
SCYTHIA MINOR:
—ISTROS: (1) ii AD *ISM* I 212, 17 (s. Κλειτοφῶν)

Ἐρύθη?
THRACE:
—BOURDAPA: (1) ii-iii AD *IGB* III 1352 + V 5503 (Συρυθη—lap., (Ἐ)ρύθη—Mihailov, Σ(ε)υθη(ς)?—Russu: d. Οἴρινθος)

Ἐρυμενίδας
THRACE:
—MESAMBRIA: (1) iii/ii BC ib. I² 338 quater (s. Ὀμφαλίων)

Ἐρύων
SCYTHIA MINOR:
—KALLATIS: (1) iii-ii BC *AMNG* I (1) 249 (coin) (Ἐρύων?, Ἐρυωι—ed.)

Ἐρωνᾶς
SKYTHIA:
—TANAIS: (1) ii AD *CIRB* 1262, 23 (f. Ἀριστόδημος)

Ἔρως
CIMMERIAN BOSPOROS:
—GORGIPPIA: (1) m. ii AD *Eirene* 7 (1968) p. 67, 11 (s. Ποθίσκος); (2) s. ii AD *CIRB* 1129 A, 6; *Eirene* 7 (1968) p. 67, 6 (f. Φαρνάκης); (3) ~ *CIRB* 1142, 14 (s. Πόθος); (4) ~ ib. 1145, 8 (s. Μενέστρατος); (5) 173-210 AD ib. 1134 E, 4 ([Ἔ]ρως); (6) ~ ib. 1135, 17 (f. Κοσσοῦς); (7) ii/iii AD ib. 1134, 20; *VDI* 1970 (4), p. 149, 10 (s. Νουμήνιος); (8) ~ *CIRB* 1179, 35 (f. Φαρνάκης) ?= (*9*); (9) ~ ib. l. 36 (f. Φαρνακίων) ?= (*8*); (10) ~ ib. l. 36 (s. Φαρνακίων); (11) ~ ib. l. 51 (s. Χρηστίων, f. Νουμήνιος)
—GORGIPPIA?: (12) s. ii AD ib. 1231 B, 13 (s. Ἀχη—?)
—HERMONASSA: (13) ii AD ib. 1055 (f. —λιος)
—MYRMEKION: (14) i AD ib. 880 (s. Χοσᾶς, f. Κόλλα)
—PANTIKAPAION: (15) i BC ib. 275 (s. Τυλλης); (16) ~ ib. 288 ([Ἔ]ρως: f. Πατροφίλα); (17) i BC-i AD ib. 299 (s. Ἀριστόνικος, Ἀγαθοῦς); (18) imp. ib. 755 (s. Φίλων); (19) ~ ib. 758; (20) ~ ib. 767 (f. Σῶσος); (21) ~ ib. 779 (f. Ἀλέξανδρος); (22) ~ ib. 780 (f. Ἀλέξανδρος); (23) ~ ib. 781 (s. Ἀνόπτηνις); (24) ~ ib. 789 (s. Φίλων); (25) i BC/i AD ib. 305; cf. KW pl. 20 no. 286; (26) ~ *CIRB* 325; cf. KW pl. 38 no. 551 (s. —ο.ίδης, f. Ἀλέξανδρος); (27) i AD *CIRB* 343; cf. KW pl. 51 no. 691 (s. Ἀπολλωνία, Ἀγα—); (28) ~ *CIRB* 401 (s. Ἀτώτης); (29) ~ ib. 402 (s. Ἕρμων); (30) ~ ib. 403 (s. Πανέρως); (31) ~ ib. 405; cf. KW pl. 35 no. 499 (s. Φάννης); (32) ~ *CIRB* 406; cf. KW pl. 24 no. 406 (s. Φιλόμουσος); (33) ~ *CIRB* 413; cf. KW pl. 48 no. 665 (?s. Βασίλη, f. Ἥλιος); (34) ~ *CIRB* 489; cf. KW pl. 46 no. 652 (s. Χρήστος); (35) i-ii AD *CIRB* 600 (s. Ἀπολλώνιος); (36) f. i AD ib. 389 (f. Διόδωρος, Ψύχη); (37) ~ ib. 494 (s. Ἑρμογένης); (38) ~ ib. 570 (f. —ως); (39) i/ii AD *KSIA* 116 (1969) p. 51 no. 3 (Ἔρως: f. Στέφανος); (40) ~ *CIRB* 625; cf. KW pl. 56 no. 762 (Ἐρώτους (gen.): f. Μοῦσα); (41) ~ *CIRB* 627 (f. Ὀνήσιμος); (42) ~ ib. 636 (f. Τιμόθεος); (43) 82 AD ib. 76, 24 (*SEG* XVIII 310) (Ἔρω[ς]: f. Ῥοῦφος); (44) ii AD *CIRB* 683 (f. Ἵλαρος); (45) f. ii AD ib. 83, 4 (s. Ἀντισθένης); (46) ~ ib. 716; cf. KW pl. 26 no. 384 (f. Ψυχαρίων); (47) iii AD *CIRB* 721; cf. KW pl. 56 no. 760 (s. Ζήνων); (48) ~ *CIRB* 729 (f. Ἥδιστος); (49) 275-278 AD ib. 36, 22 (s. Ῥαδάμασις); (50) iv-v AD *SEG* XLV 1015 f (amph.) (Ἔρωτ[ος]? (gen.))
—PANTIKAPAION (NR.): (51) i AD *CIRB* 961; cf. KW pl. 35 no. 511 (s. Κίνωλις); (52) ii AD *CIRB* 965 (f. Σπαρόβαϊς)
—PORTHMION (NR.): (53) 225 AD ib. 897, 5 (Ἰούλ. Ἔ.: s. Κόϊντος)
—THEODOSIA: (54) iii AD ib. 947 B, 18 (s. Δημήτριος)
MACEDONIA (BOTTIAIA):
—BEROIA: (55) i-ii AD *IBer* 419 (Tataki 652) (Lat. T. Caesernius Eros: f. T. Caesernius Apronianus); (56) ii AD *IBer* 238 (Tataki 466); (57) ii-iii AD *IBer* 28 (Tataki 467) (s. Εὐβίοτος)
MACEDONIA (CHALKIDIKE):
—ANTHEMOUS: (58) 62 AD *SEG* XLII 559 (f. Σεραπίων)
MACEDONIA (DERRIOPOS):
—STUBERRA: (59) 74 AD *IG* X (2) (2) 326, 30 (f. Ὕμνος)
MACEDONIA (EDONIS):
—PHILIPPOI (TERRIT.)*: (60) i-ii AD *BCH* 47 (1923) p. 59 no. 17 Pilhofer 582 (Lat. L. Firmius Eros: s. C. Firmius: freed.)
MACEDONIA (ELIMEIA):
—AIANE: (61) s. ii AD *EAM* 56 ([Ἔρ]ωτα (acc.): s. Κάστωρ, Δημοκρατέα)
MACEDONIA (MYGDONIA):
—KALINDOIA: (62) 68-98 AD *SEG* XLII 580, 7, 35 (f. Μένανδρος); (63) ~ ib. l. 77 (s. Εὔπορος)
—THESSALONIKE: (64) i AD *IG* X (2) (1) 87, 4 (*Π.* Ποπίλλιος Ἔ.); (65) ~ ib. 259, 23 + *SEG* XXX 622 (*M.* Ὄμβρειος Ἔ.); (66) ii AD *IG* X (2) (1) 712
MACEDONIA (PIERIA):
—DION: (67) ii-iii AD Dimitsas 175 (?f. Πολύχαρμος); (68) ?iii AD Oikonomos 44; *Klio* 52 (1970) p. 53 no. 4; cf. *SEG* XLIV 526 (f. Θερίνη)
SCYTHIA MINOR:
—TOMIS: (69) ii-iii AD *ISM* II 275, 1 (*GVI* 1942); (70) ~ *ISM* II 284
SKYTHIA:
—OLBIA-BORYSTHENES: (71) ?ii AD *IOSPE* I² 99, 6 (f. Πήρακος); (72) ii-iii AD ib. 138, 5 (s. Εὐρησίβιος); (73) f. ii AD ib. 85, 5 (f. Πανέρως); (74) c. 150-175 AD ib. 132, 10; 176, 5; *VDI* 1953 (4), p. 130, 11; cf. *SEG* XLII 713 (f. Διονυσιόδωρος)
—TANAIS: (75) ii AD *CIRB* 1262, 13 (s. Μηνόφιλος); (76) ~ ib. l. 26 (f. Πάγκαρπος); (77) ~ ib. l. 29; (78) ~ ib. l. 31; (79) ~ ib. 1263, 15; (80) f. ii AD ib. 1266, 13 (s. Φίλων); (81) ~ ib. 1298, 2 (Ἔρω[ς]); (82) 104 AD ib. 1259, 8 (f. Ξένων); (83) ~ ib. l. 18 (s. Ζηνόβιος); (84) 155 AD ib. 1260, 19 (s. Παρθενοκλῆς); (85) 225 AD ib. 1280, 19 (s. Ὀχωδίακος); (86) 236 AD ib. 1250, 13 (s. Μαστοῦς)
—TANAIS?: (87) 133 AD ib. 1315 ([Ἔ]ρως: f. Παρθενοκλῆς)
TAURIS:
—CHERSONESOS: (88) ii BC Solomonik, *GAKh* 699 (vase) (Ἔρω[ς]?); (89) i BC-i AD? *IOSPE* I² 472 (I f. Ἔρως II); (90) ~ ib. (II s. Ἔρως I)
THRACE:
—BERGULA-ARKADIOPOLIS*: (91) i BC-i AD Taşlıklıoğlu 2 p. 6 no. 1 (freed.)
—BYZANTION: (92) ii/i BC *IByz* 260 (Fıratlı–Robert p. 76 no. 84) (*Γ.* Ὀλούσιος Ἔ.); (93) i BC/i AD *SEG* L 667 III (s. Γλαυκίας, f. Ἄννη)
—BYZANTION (NR.): (94) ii-i BC *IByz* 130 (Fıratlı–Robert pp. 97-8 no. 143) (f. —α)
—NICOPOLIS AD ISTRUM: (95) ii-iii AD *Nikopolis ad Istrum* I p. 155 no. 14 (Lat. Q. Grat-Eros)
—NICOPOLIS AD ISTRUM (TERRIT.): (96) 227 AD *ILB* 438 II, 22 (Lat. Herotis (gen.): f. Vales)

—PHILIPPOPOLIS-TRIMONTIUM (TERRIT.): (97) ii-iii AD *IGB* III 1463 (s. *Τήρης*)

Ἐρωτιανός

MACEDONIA (CHALKIDIKE):
—MENDE: (1) imp. *SEG* XXIX 617 (I f. *Ἐρωτιανός* II); (2) ~ ib. (II s. *Ἐρωτιανός* I, *Εὐφροσύνη*)
MACEDONIA (PIERIA):
—PYDNA: (3) 250 AD ib. XLVI 800 A, 19 (*Αὐρ. Ἐ.*)

Ἐρώτιν

SCYTHIA MINOR:
—TOMIS: (1) ii-iii AD *ISM* II 197 (*GVI* 1043a) + *SEG* XXV 760

Ἐρωτίς

CIMMERIAN BOSPOROS:
—PANTIKAPAION*: (1) i AD *CIRB* 407
MACEDONIA (BOTTIAIA):
—BEROIA: (2) ii-iii AD *IBer* 297, 5 (d. *Κλ. Ἀντέρως, Νικέα*)
—EDESSA: (3) m. iii AD *Ancient Macedonia* 4 p. 68 (*Αὐρ. Ἐ.*)

Ἕσπερος

MACEDONIA (BOTTIAIA):
—BEROIA: (1) m. ii AD *IBer* 318 (Tataki 468)
—EDESSA: (2) 180 AD *SEG* XXIV 531, 12 (Tataki, *Edessa* 100) (s. *Σεμέλη*)
MACEDONIA (EDONIS):
—AMPHIPOLIS: (3) s. iv BC *PAE* 1981, p. 25 with pl. 43 *β*, 7; (4) m. iii BC Hatzopoulos, *Actes Amphipolis* p. 50 no. 11, 11 (*SEG* XLI 565) (f. *Ἀ—*)
MACEDONIA (MYGDONIA):
—ORAIOKASTRO (MOD.): (5) v-iv BC ib. XLIX 750 (*Ὥσπερος*—ed.: f. *Διογένης, Κρίτων, Μένων, Ἔπανδρος, ΙΟΒΙΛΗΣ*)
—THESSALONIKE?: (6) ii/iii AD *AEpThess* p. 35 no. 13, 3 (s. *Βάρβαρος, Οὐαδέα*)
MACEDONIA (PAIONIA)?:
—KASARSENOI: (7) ii-iii AD *Sp.* 75 (1933) p. 46 no. 153; Papazoglou, *Villes* p. 343 n. 32 (locn.) (f. *Ἰούλιος*)

Ἑστιαία

CIMMERIAN BOSPOROS:
—PANTIKAPAION: (1) 284-245 BC *CIRB* 21 (d. *Μηνόδωρος*)

Ἑστιαῖος

CIMMERIAN BOSPOROS:
—GORGIPPIA: (1) f. iii BC ib. 1137 A I, 23 (f. *Ἡρόδωρος*) ?= (*4*); (2) ~ ib. 1137 A II, 48 (s. *Ἡρόδωρος*); (3) ~ ib. 1137 B I, 36; 1137 B II, 14 (f. *Ἀρχέδημος*); (4) ~ ib. 1137 B I, 43 (f. *Ἡρόδωρος*) ?= (*1*); (5) ~ ib. l. 45 (s. *Κρατῖνος*)
—HERMONASSA: (6) f. iv BC *SEG* XLIV 659 (vase) ([*Ἑ*]*στιαῖος*)
—KEPOI?: (7) ii BC Guarducci, *Ep. Gr.* 3 pp. 356-7 (ring) (Higgins, *GRJ* p. 174)
—NYMPHAION: (8) iii BC *CIRB* 912 I, 3 ([*Ἑστ*]*ιαῖος*?)
MACEDONIA (CHALKIDIKE):
—POTIDAIA-KASSANDREIA (NR.): (9) ?iii BC *SEG* XXIX 632 ([*Ἑσ*]*τιαῖος*: f. *Πρωτίων*)
SCYTHIA MINOR:
—ISTROS: (10) iii BC *ISM* I 255 (s. *Μοιρόδωρος*); (11) iii/ii BC ib. 263 (f. *Νουμήνιος*); (12) f. ii BC ib. 26, 1 (s. *Μικκαλίων*); (13) f. ii AD ib. 193 I, 47; *SEG* L 683 B, 6 (s. *Δίων*); (14) 138 AD *ISM* I 193 I, 16 (f. *Πολύφημος*); (15) ~ ib. l. 58 (s. *Διονύσιος*); (16) ~ ib. l. 83 (f. *Ἀριστομένης*); (17) 222-225 AD ib. 100, 7 (*Ἑ*[*στ*]*ιαῖος*: f. *Αὐρ. Διονύσιος*)
—TOMIS: (18) i BC ib. II 2 B, 53 (s. *Ἀριστείδης*); (19) 54-68 AD *RPC* I 1836 (coin); (20) ii AD *ISM* II 17, 12 (f. *Δάδας*); (21) ii-iii AD ib. 26, 6 (f. *Οἰκωρσις*) ?= (*22*); (22) ~ ib. l. 9 (f. *Διονύσις*) ?= (*21*); (23) ~ ib. 31 II, 14 (f. *Θεόδωρος*)
SKYTHIA:
—OLBIA-BORYSTHENES: (24) iii BC Dubois, *IGDOlbia* 109, 7 (*SEG* XXXVII 673); (25) ~ *IOSPE* I^2 201 I, 32 (f. *Διστέφης*)
—TANAIS: (26) i BC-i AD? *New Studies on Black Sea* p. 47 fig. 8
TAURIS:
—CHERSONESOS: (27) iii BC Solomonik, *NEPKh* 180 ([*Ἑσ*]*τιαῖος*?: f. *Εὔθυνος*); (28) ii BC *SEG* XLVI 924, 1 ([*Ἑ*]*στιεῖο*[*ς*]?)
THRACE:
—APOLLONIA-SOZOPOLIS: (29) i-ii AD *IGB* I^2 401, 4 (*Ἑστιαῖ*[*ος*]: f. *Ποσειδώνις*)
—BISANTHE-PANION: (30) 158-138 BC *OGIS* 304 (*Tekmeria* 6 (2001) p. 157 no. 3) (s. *Ἰζίμαρτος*)
—BYZANTION: (31) 378 BC *IG* II^2 41, 24; (32) m. ii BC *Milet* I (3) 153, 1 (*IByz* 2)
—DIONYSOPOLIS: (33) iii AD *IGB* I^2 14 b, 13 (f. *Αὐρ. Πυθοκλῆς*); (34) ~ ib. 14 c, 11 (*Αὐρ. Ἑ.*: s. *Θαῆς*)
—KARDIA: (35) 232 or 207 BC *CPR* XVIII 12, 248 (La'da E982) (s. *Μοσχίων*: t.e.)
—ODESSOS: (36) ii-i BC *IGB* I^2 78 bis (*CCET* I 28) (s. *Πόσις*); (37) c. 100-72 BC Price, *Alexander* 1205-7 (coin) (*Ἑστιαί*(*ος*)—1206, *Ἑσστιαί*(*ος*)—1207); (38) i BC *IGB* I^2 148 (PM 165) (s. *Διοσκουρίδης*); (39) ~ *IGB* I^2 149 (PM 201) (I f. *Ἑστιαῖος* II); (40) ~ *IGB* I^2 149 (PM 201) (II s. *Ἑστιαῖος* I); (41) i BC-i AD *IGB* I^2 203 bis ([*Ἑ*]*στιαῖος*: s. *Σιρούων*); (42) 39 BC ib. 46, 8 (*Ἑστιαῖος*: s. *Ἀ......ωρος*); (43) 11 BC ib. l. 36 (f. *Ἀρτεμίδωρος*); (44) i AD ib. 158 (*Ἑστια*[*ῖος*]: f. *Ἕλλην*); (45) i-ii AD ib. 108, 8 (s. *Κουνοῦς*); (46) ~ ib. 111 (f. *Ξένων*); (47) ~ ib. 211 (f. *Διονύσιος Πάπας*); (48) ii AD ib. 50, 27 (s. *Διονύσιος*); (49) ~ ib. 132 a (I f. *Ἑστιαῖος* II); (50) ~ ib. (II s. *Ἑστιαῖος* I); (51) ~ ib. 132 b (s. *Ἀπελλᾶς*); (52) ~ ib. 146 (PM 206) (f. *Ἀλέξανδρος*); (53) ii-iii AD *IGB* I^2 231 (s. *Ζωΐλος*); (54) 117-138 AD ib. 49, 3 (*Ἑστι*[*αῖος*]); (55) s. ii AD ib. 78 (*CCET* I 40) (s. *Νικίας*, f. *Νικίας*, *Ἀγαθήνωρ*); (56) ~ *IGB* I^2 170 (PM 1701); *Dacia* 21 (1977) p. 161 (date) ([*Ἑ*]*στιαῖος*: f. *Φιλίστη*); (57) 221 AD *IGB* I^2 47 bis a, 26 (-*τιέ*-: f. *Ἀγαθήνωρ*); (58) ~ ib. 47 bis b, 10 (*Αὐρ. Ἑ.*: s. *Βιάτωρ*); (59) ~ ib. 47 bis c, 20 (f. *Αὐρ. Θίας*); (60) ~ ib. l. 40 (*Σπούριος Ἑ.*)
—ODESSOS (NR.): (61) s. ii AD ib. 288 (*CCET* I 85) (*Ἑσ*[*τιαῖος*]?: s. *Ἀγαθήνωρ*)
—PERINTHOS-HERAKLEIA: (62) iv BC *RE* (7)

Ἑστίας

SCYTHIA MINOR:
—KALLATIS: (1) s. iii BC *ISM* III 35 A, 37 (*Ἑστίου* (gen.): f. *Ζώπυρος*)

Ἐσχάτιος

THRACE:
—BISANTHE-PANION: (1) c. 230-200 BC *BCH* 45 (1921) p. 19 III, 96

Ἐτεόδωρος

MACEDONIA: (1) ?ii-i BC *IG* IX (2) 175 (Tataki, *Macedonians* p. 310 no. 30) (s. *Στρατοκλῆς*)

Ἐτεωνεύς

MACEDONIA?: (1) s. iii BC *IG* XII (6) 344 (*Ἐτεω*[*νεύς*]: f. *Ὑπερβάσσας*) ?= (*3*); (2) 243-221 BC *PP* 1902 with Add. (f. *Πτολεμαῖος*) ?= (*3*); (3) 211 BC ib. 5122 (I f. *Ἐτεωνεύς* II) ?= (*1*) (*2*)

Ἔτυμος

MACEDONIA (BOTTIAIA):
—BEROIA: (1) s. i AD *IBer* 123, 8 (Tataki 713) (*Τι. Κλ. Ἔ.*)

Εὐάγγελος

MACEDONIA (BOTTIAIA):
—BEROIA: (1) ii/iii AD *IBer* 145, 11 (Tataki 1100) (*Ποπίλλιος Εὐάγγελος*)
MACEDONIA (MYGDONIA):
—THESSALONIKE: (2) 261 AD *IG* X (2) (1) 200, 6 (*Πόντιος Εὐάγγελος*: f. *Ποντία Ζωσίμη*)
—THESSALONIKE?: (3) iv-v AD ib. 788, 3 (Feissel, *RICM* 177) (f. *Θωμᾶς, Λεόντιος*)
MACEDONIA (SINTIKE):
—HERAKLEIA (TERRIT.): (4) ii-iii AD *IGB* V 5924, 3 (*Βάλης Εὐάγγελος*)
THRACE:
—NOVAE (NR.): (5) iii AD *IGLNovae* 183 (*SEG* XLVII 1150) (-*άγε*-: I f. *Ἀσύγκριτος, Εὐάγγελος* II); (6) ~ *IGLNovae* 183 (*SEG* XLVII 1150) (-*άγε*-: II s. *Εὐάγγελος* I)

Εὐαγόρας

THRACE:
—ABDERA: (1) c. 336-311 BC Unp. (Chryssanthaki diss.) p. 225 (coin)

Εὐαγόρης

SCYTHIA MINOR:
—ISTROS: (1) f. iv BC *ISM* I 231, 2 (*Εὐαγόρō* (gen.): f. *Ἡδίστη*)

Εὐάγορος

MACEDONIA (PAIONIA):
—STOBOI: (1) v-vi AD Unp. (Skopje Mus.) (*Εὐαγόρου* (gen.))

Εὐάγριος

THRACE:
—PAUTALIA:
——(Herakleis): (1) ?ii AD *IGB* IV 2077, 5 (s. *Μουκιανός*)
—TOPEIROS: (2) iii AD *IThrakAig* E88 (*Δύδης ὁ καὶ Ἐ.*)

Εὐαγρίων

MACEDONIA: (1) 89 BC *UPZ* 125, 29 (Tataki, *Macedonians* p. 482 no. 103; La'da E1492)

Εὐάγων

THRACE:
—ABDERA: (1) c. 411-386 BC May, *Abdera* pp. 214-15 nos. 293-6 (coin)

Εὐάδεια

MACEDONIA: (1) f. i BC Cic., *in Pis.* 89 (Lat. Euhadia); (2) i AD *IG* II^2 9260 (Tataki, *Macedonians* p. 310 no. 31; *FRA* 3471) (d. *Μηνᾶς*)

Εὐαίνετος

MACEDONIA (BOTTIAIA):
—PELLA: (1) iv/iii BC *Α΄ Panell. Synedr. Epigr.* p. 187 no. 9; cf. *Makedonika* 15 (1975) p. 193 pl. 102 a (f. *Ἀρήτη*)
MACEDONIA (EDONIS):
—AMPHIPOLIS: (2) a. 357 BC Hatzopoulos, *Actes Amphipolis* p. 34 no. 6, 8 ?= (*3*); (3) s. iv BC *FD* III (4) 391, 2 (Tataki, *Macedonians* p. 52 no. 54) (s. ......*ν*) ?= (*2*)

Εὐαίων

THRACE:
—SALYMBRIA: (1) hell. *IByz* S 2

Εὐάκης

THRACE:
—BYZANTION: (1) m. iii BC *IG* XI (4) 570, 4, 8 (s. *Τείσανδρος*)

Εὐάλκης

MACEDONIA (CHALKIDIKE):
—STREPSA?: (1) 285 BC *SEG* XXXVIII 619, 22 (s. *Δημήτριος*)
MACEDONIA (ODOMANTIKE):
—GAZOROS?: (2) 158 AD ib. XXIV 614, 2 (Pilhofer 544); cf. Hatzopoulos, *MI* I pp. 84-6 (f. *Σύρος*)

Εὐαλκίδης
CIMMERIAN BOSPOROS:
—PANTIKAPAION: **(1)** v BC *CIRB* 152 (s. *Λεώδικος*)
MACEDONIA (CHALKIDIKE):
—ANTIGONEIA?: **(2)** m. iii BC *SEG* XXIX 568 (s. *Λυσίστρατος*)

Εὐανδρίδας
TAURIS:
—CHERSONESOS: **(1)** c. 450-425 BC ib. XL 612. 11-12 (ostraka)

Εὔανδρος
MACEDONIA (BOTTIAIA):
—BEROIA: **(1)** i BC ib. XVIII 272 (Tataki 470; Tataki, *Macedonians* p. 78 no. 25) (f. *Ἄδυμος*) ?= (*3*); **(2)** m. i BC *IG* IX (2) 601; *SEG* XVII 318, 5; *KGAM Thess.* I 56 (date) (Tataki 469; Tataki, *Macedonians* p. 78 no. 24) (I f. *Εὔανδρος* II); **(3)** ~ *IG* IX (2) 601; *SEG* XVII 318, 4; *KGAM Thess.* I 56 (date) (Tataki 471; Tataki, *Macedonians* p. 78 no. 26) (II s. *Εὔανδρος* I: sculptor) ?= (*1*)
MACEDONIA (CHALKIDIKE):
—POTIDAIA-KASSANDREIA: **(4)** c. 235-230 BC *IG* VII 247, 26 (*IOrop* 71; Tataki, *Macedonians* p. 89 no. 35) (f. *Ἡράκλειτος*)
THRACE:
—MESAMBRIA: **(5)** ii-i BC *IGB* I^2 327 ter (f. *Μ—*)
—NICOPOLIS AD ISTRUM: **(6)** ii-iii AD ib. II 661 (*Πόρκιος Ἐ.*)
—PERINTHOS-HERAKLEIA:
——(Akarnanes): **(7)** iii-ii BC *IPerinth* 61, 10 (s. *Ἄνδρων*)

Εὐάνθης
CIMMERIAN BOSPOROS:
—GORGIPPIA: **(1)** f. iii BC *CIRB* 1137 B II, 40 (f. *Ὄρχαμος*)
—PANTIKAPAION: **(2)** i AD ib. 470; cf. KW pl. 15 no. 215
—PHANAGOREIA: **(3)** iii BC *CIRB* 994 (*Εὐ[άν]θης*)
TAURIS:
—CHERSONESOS: **(4)** iv BC Solomonik, *NEPKh* 155 (f. *Δαμάτριος*)

Εὐάνιος
MACEDONIA (CHALKIDIKE):
—AKANTHOS: **(1)** v/iv BC *SEG* XLI 554 (vase)

Εὐάρατος
MACEDONIA (CHALKIDIKE):
—DION: **(1)** iii BC *IG* XII (8) 233 (Tataki, *Macedonians* p. 100 no. 4) (or Macedonia (Pieria) Dion: s. *Ἀρχίας*)

Εὐάρεστος
CIMMERIAN BOSPOROS:
—PANTIKAPAION: **(1)** iii AD *CIRB* 103, 11 (f. *Ἡ—ης*)
MACEDONIA (BOTTIAIA):
—BEROIA: **(2)** ii-iii AD *IBer* 28 (Tataki 472) (*Ε̣ὐάρεσ[τος]*); **(3)** 170 AD *ILeukopetra* 3, 3 (s. *Νικολαΐς*)
MACEDONIA (PAIONIA):
—NEAPOLIS (AREA): **(4)** ii-iii AD *Sp.* 71 (1931) p. 37 no. 80; cf. Düll, *Götterkulte* p. 404 no. 259 (f. *Συγκλητική*)
SCYTHIA MINOR:
—ISTROS: **(5)** ii AD *ISM* I 201 II, 21 (s. *Οὐλπ. Ἀρτεμίδωρος*)
THRACE: **(6)** ii/iii AD *Starinar* 43-44 (1992-3) pp. 143-5 (vase-stamp) (Lat. Cl. Domitius Euarestus)

Εὐάρης
SKYTHIA:
—OLBIA-BORYSTHENES: **(1)** v BC *SEG* XLVIII 1017 A (sherd)

Εὐαρίνα
SKYTHIA:
—OLBIA-BORYSTHENES: **(1)** v BC ib. (sherd)

Εὐάριστος
CIMMERIAN BOSPOROS:
—GORGIPPIA?: **(1)** s. ii AD *CIRB* 1231 A, 9 (*Εὐάρι[στος]*)
SCYTHIA MINOR:
—TOMIS: **(2)** ii-iii AD *ISM* II 337 (f. *Λούκιος*)
SKYTHIA:
—TANAIS: **(3)** 228 AD *CIRB* 1282, 25 (f. *Σιαύνανσος*)
THRACE:
—ODESSOS: **(4)** ii-iii AD *IGB* I^2 198 (f. *Λούκιος*)

Εὐαρχίδας
TAURIS:
—CHERSONESOS: **(1)** s. v BC *SEG* XL 612. 5 (ostrakon) (f. *Ζηνόδοτος*)

Εὔαρχος
MACEDONIA (BOTTIAIA):
—PELLA: **(1)** iv-iii BC *AD* 16 (1960) Mel. p. 82; *SEG* XXXIX 623; XLIII 444 (tiles)

Εὔας
THRACE:
—PHILIPPOPOLIS-TRIMONTIUM:
——Parembole: **(1)** ii-iii AD *IGB* III 1513 (*Εὔαδος* (gen.): f. *Γλύκων*)

Εὐβάρνακος
SKYTHIA:
—TANAIS: **(1)** 220 AD *CIRB* 1278, 14 (*Εὐβάρν̣α̣κ̣[ος]*: f. *Ὀξαρδώζις*)

Εὐβία
PENESTAI:
—USCANA?: **(1)** ?ii AD *SEG* XXXIX 578, 3 (?m. *Λύκος*)

Εὔβιος
MACEDONIA (DERRIOPOS):
—STUBERRA: **(1)** c. 41-48 AD *IG* X (2) (2) 323, 13 (s. *Ἐπίκαδος*)
SKYTHIA:
—OLBIA-BORYSTHENES: **(2)** s. iii BC *IOSPE* I^2 76, 10 (Sokolowski II 88; Dubois, *IGDOlbia* 88) (f. *Ἡρακλείδης*)
THRACE:
—BYZANTION: **(3)** ii-i BC *IG* II^2 8442 (*FRA* 1393) (f. *Μένανδρος*); **(4)** i BC *IByz* 147 (Fıratlı–Robert pp. 100-1 no. 152) (f. *Πλατθίς*)
—MARONEIA: **(5)** ii BC *AD* 26 (1971) Chron. p. 428 no. δ (*IThrakAig* E267) (s. *Μητρόδωρος*)

Εὐβίοτος
CIMMERIAN BOSPOROS:
—BOSPOROS: **(1)** ii AD Luc., *Tox.* 51-55 (king/fict.)
MACEDONIA (BISALTIA):
—EUPORIA?: **(2)** iii AD *RA* 1945, p. 39 (f. *Διοσκουρίδης*); **(3)** ~ ib. (*Εὐβίοτος*: s. *Διοσκουρίδης*)
MACEDONIA (BOTTIAIA):
—BEROIA: **(4)** s. iii BC *IBer* 46, 1 ?= (*5*); **(5)** 223 BC ib. 4, 25 (*Εὐβίοτ̣[ος]*: f. *Γλαυκίας*) ?= (*4*); **(6)** ii-iii AD ib. 28 (Tataki 473) (f. *Ἔρως*); **(7)** f. iii AD *IBer* 217
SKYTHIA:
—OLBIA-BORYSTHENES: **(8)** iii BC *Arkheologiia* (Kiev) 39 (1982) p. 35 (vase); **(9)** ~ *IOSPE* I^2 191 (s. *Ἀρίστων*); **(10)** ~ ib. 201 I, 8 (f. *Δημοκῶν*); **(11)** ~ ib. l. 23 (f. *Γοργίας*); **(12)** ~ ib. l. 49 (f. *Ὀρθόβουλος*); **(13)** ~ ib. 201 II, 3; **(14)** ~ ib. l. 19 (s. *Μητρόδωρος*)

Εὔβολος
CIMMERIAN BOSPOROS:
—NYMPHAION: **(1)** 105 BC *ID* 2128 (s. *Εὔτυχος*)

Εὐβούλα
MACEDONIA (BOTTIAIA):
—PELLA: **(1)** f. iii BC *SEG* XXIV 547 (d. *Λύσων*)
MACEDONIA (CHALKIDIKE):
—ANTHEMOUS: **(2)** i BC/i AD ib. XLII 567 (d. *Σέλης*)
MACEDONIA (PIERIA):
—PYDNA: **(3)** iv BC *GRBS* 43 (2002-3) p. 111 no. 2, 6
THRACE:
—MARONEIA: **(4)** ii-i BC *IThrakAig* E212, 7 (d. *Θεόξενος*); **(5)** ii AD *IG* XII (8) 220, 13 (d. *Διονύσιος*)

Εὐβούλη
MACEDONIA: **(1)** 234 AD *ILeukopetra* 84, 8 (slave/freed.)
MACEDONIA (BOTTIAIA):
—BEROIA: **(2)** 214 AD ib. 65, 19; **(3)** 219 AD ib. 69, 2 (Tataki 695) (*Κλ. Ἐ.*)
MACEDONIA (CHALKIDIKE):
—OLYNTHOS: **(4)** iv BC *Small Obj. from the Pnyx* p. 6 no. 9 (Tataki, *Macedonians* p. 135 no. 46) (d. *Δεικράτης*)
MACEDONIA (MYGDONIA):
—THESSALONIKE: **(5)** c. 225 AD *IG* X (2) (1) 183, 7; 184, 7; 185, 7; 209, 3 (*Ῥουφρία Κλ. Ἐ.*: d. *Κλ. Μένων*)
THRACE:
—STRYME: **(6)** c. 375-350 BC *IThrakAig* E142 (d. *Ἀριστόμαχος*)

Εὐβουλίδας
SCYTHIA MINOR:
—KALLATIS: **(1)** f. iii BC *ISM* III 6, 1

Εὐβουλίδης
MACEDONIA: **(1)** ?iv-iii BC *JÖAI* 69 (2000) p. 81 no. 5; **(2)** 174-172 BC *PFreib* 34, 7; *PMich* 190, 14, 35 (Tataki, *Macedonians* p. 311 no. 32); cf. La'da E1761 (f. *Θεοκλῆς*)
MACEDONIA (BOTTIAIA):
—BEROIA: **(3)** 177 AD *IBer* 135 A, 14 (Tataki 1198) (*Στάτιος Ἐ.*)
—PELLA: **(4)** iii BC Akamatis, *Amph. Pellas* p. 34 no. PAR16 (amph.) (*SEG* L 613)
MACEDONIA (CHALKIDIKE):
—OLYNTHOS: **(5)** ?355 BC *TAPA* 69 (1938) p. 51 no. 5, 8; Hatzopoulos, *Actes Chalc.* p. 80 (date) (s. *Ἀπολλόδωρος*); **(6)** ?350 BC *TAPA* 59 (1928) p. 226, 3; Hatzopoulos, *Actes Chalc.* p. 80 (date) (s. *Ἀρπάλης*)
—POTIDAIA-KASSANDREIA*: **(7)** f. iv BC *SEG* XLV 801 (vase) (f. *Ἀριστόβουλος*)
—STOLOS?: **(8)** ?351 BC ib. XXXVIII 672, 12 (s. *Διονύσιος*)
MACEDONIA (DERRIOPOS):
—STUBERRA: **(9)** c. 41-48 AD *IG* X (2) (2) 323, 21 (f. *Σωσίας*); **(10)** ?54 AD ib. 324, 3, 8 (s. *Ζωΐλος*, f. *Ζωΐλος*); **(11)** 74 AD ib. 325, 24 (f. *Κτήσων*); **(12)** ~ ib. l. 30 (f. *Γέμελλος*); **(13)** ~ ib. l. 61 (f. *Παράμονος*); **(14)** ~ ib. 326, 20 (s. *Μενεκράτης*); **(15)** ~ ib. l. 28 (s. *Φίλιππος*); **(16)** 90 AD ib. l. 80 (f. *Ἀπολλώνιος*)
MACEDONIA (MYGDONIA):
—THESSALONIKE: **(17)** s. i AD ib. X (2) (1) 68, 20; 69, 15 (s. *Ὑάκινθος*)
—THESSALONIKE?: **(18)** iii AD ib. 771, 8 (s. *Φλ. Σεκούνδιλλα*)
THRACE:
—ODESSOS: **(19)** i-ii AD *IGB* I^2 194

Εὔβουλος
CIMMERIAN BOSPOROS:
—GORGIPPIA: **(1)** f. iii BC *CIRB* 1137 A I, 55 (s. *Γοργίας*); **(2)** ~ ib. 1137 A II, 23 (f. *Παράμονος*) ?= (*4*); **(3)** ~ ib. l. 24 (s. *Καλλίμαχος*); **(4)** ~ ib. 1137 B I, 61 (f. *Παράμονος*) ?= (*5*) (*2*); **(5)** ~ ib. 1137 B II, 21 (*Εὔ[β]ουλ[ος]*: f. *Παράμονος*) ?= (*4*)
MACEDONIA: **(6)** 231 BC *SB* 9258, 5 (Tataki, *Macedonians* p. 311 no. 33) (f. *Σαραπίων*)

Macedonia (Bottiaia):
—beroia: (7) i bc-i ad *IBer* 142, 9 (Tataki 475) (*Εὔβουλο[ς]*, *Εὐβουλίδης*—Tataki: f. *Ζωΐλος*)
—beroia (territ.)?: (8) 245 ad ib. 282 (*Αὐρ. Ε(ὔ)βουλος*?, *Ἕρβουλος*—apogr., Tataki)
—pella: (9) iii bc Akamatis, *Amph. Pellas* p. 34 nos. PAR17-18 (amph.) (*SEG* l 613)
Macedonia (Edonis):
—philippoi (territ.): (10) ?iii ad Pikoulas, *Chora* p. 149 no. 59, 16 (Pilhofer 602; *SEG* l 618); cf. *BE* 1944, no. 129 (-*που*-)
Macedonia (Mygdonia):
—aineia: (11) 360 bc *IG* iv (1)² 94 b, 10 (Perlman, *City and Sanctuary* E.1 with p. 69 f. (date); Tataki, *Macedonians* p. 41 no. 2)
—thessalonike?: (12) s. ii ad *IG* x (2) (1) 252, 5 (*Εὔβουλ[ο]ς*: f. *Ἀναξίδωρος*)
Macedonia (Pelagonia): (13) 81 ad ib. x (2) (2) 276 (f. *Ἀμμία*, *Νικόλαος*); (14) ii ad ib. 277 (f. *Δούλης*)
Macedonia (Pieria):
—dion: (15) i-ii ad *Dion* p. 48
Macedonia?: (16) 72 bc *BGU* 1738, 13 (Tataki, *Macedonians* p. 482 no. 104); cf. La'da E2638 (f. *Ἀπολλώνιος*)
Scythia Minor:
—tomis: (17) ii ad *ISM* ii 125, 13 (f. *Φιλώτας*)
Tauris:
—chersonesos: (18) iv bc Solomonik, *NEPKh* 137 (-*βο*-: s. *Ξένων*); (19) ~ Solomonik, *GAKh* 732 (vase) (*Εὔβο[υλος]*?)
Thrace: (20) 146 bc *PKöln* 187, 16; cf. La'da E781 (f. *Πλούταρχος*)
—lysimacheia: (21) iii-ii bc *ISestos* 46 (f. *Γλαύκιππος*)

Εὔγαμος
Macedonia (Bottiaia):
—beroia: (1) ii ad *IBer* 223 (Tataki 476)
Thrace:
—odessos (nr.): (2) s. ii ad *IGB* i² 287 (*CCET* i 87) (*Οὐαλέριος Ἐ.*)

Εὐγείτων
Macedonia (Bottiaia):
—pella: (1) iii bc Akamatis, *Amph. Pellas* p. 35 nos. PAR19-21 (amph.) (*SEG* l 613) (*Εὐγεί(των)*?)
Macedonia (Chalkidike):
—potidaia-kassandreia: (2) iv/iii bc *Ancient Macedonia* i p. 132 n. 20 (f. *Βιώ*)

Εὐγένεια
Cimmerian Bosporos:
—myrmekion (nr.): (1) ii ad *CIRB* 893; cf. KW pl. 51 no. 703 (-*νια*: d. *Νεοκλῆς*)
—pantikapaion: (2) i ad *CIRB* 409; cf. KW pl. 21 no. 304 (*Εὐγένεια*); (3) i-ii ad *CIRB* 601 (-*νια*)
Macedonia: (4) ii bc *IG* xii (1) 305 (Tataki, *Macedonians* p. 311 no. 34)
Macedonia (Bottiaia):
—pella: (5) v/iv bc *Egnatia* 5 (1995-2000) p. 261 (*SEG* xlix 755) (d. *Ξένων*)
Macedonia (Edonis):
—amphipolis: (6) ii bc ib. xxiv 605 (*[Ε]ὐγένει[α]*: d. *Δρωπίων*)
Macedonia (Krestonia):
—mandres (mod.): (7) 36 or 153 ad ib. xliii 426 (-*νεα*)
Macedonia (Mygdonia):
—charakoma?: (8) iii/ii bc *AD* 22 (1967) Chron. p. 377 with pl. 284 *a* (-*νηα*: d. *Φυλακίδης*)
—thessalonike: (9) 42-32 bc *IG* x (2) (1) 124, 6 (*Εὐγέν[ε]ια*)
Thrace:
—nicopolis ad nestum (territ.): (10) 538 ad Beševliev 231, 2 (-*νια*)
—perinthos-herakleia: (11) ii-i bc *ISmyrna* 689 III, 36 (d. *Ἱππομέδων*, m. *Διογένης* (Laodikeia on Lykos))

Εὐγένης
Macedonia (Bottiaia):
—edessa: (1) v-vi ad Feissel, *RICM* 53
Macedonia (Chalkidike):
—skione: (2) f. iv bc *IG* ii² 10366 (Tataki, *Macedonians* p. 173 no. 5; *FRA* 6904) (s. *Καλλίας*)

Εὐγενίδης
Macedonia (Bottiaia):
—beroia: (1) 250 ad *ILeukopetra* 101, 4 (*Παπίας Θα[ύμασ]τος ὁ καὶ Εὐ[γε]νείδης*)

Εὐγένιος
Macedonia (Bottiaia):
—aigai: (1) m. vi ad *SEG* xxxix 639 = xliv 564 (mosaic)
—beroia: (2) v-vi ad *IBer* 423 (Feissel, *RICM* 66)
Macedonia (Lynkestis):
—herakleia (area): (3) iii ad *IG* x (2) (2) 27
Macedonia (Mygdonia):
—thessalonike: (4) m. iii ad ib. x (2) (1) 206, 4 (*Κλ. Τύλλιος Ἀλέξανδρος ὁ καὶ Ἐ.*: s. *Ἰουλ. Ὀλυμπιάς*)
Macedonia?: (5) ?iii-iv ad *Tyana* i pp. 195-6 no. 19
Thrace:
—bisanthe-panion: (6) iv-v ad *AD* 49-50 (1994-5) Mel. p. 311 no. 136 (f. *Λεοντία*)
—odessos: (7) vi ad Beševliev 98, 5 (f. *Κωνσταντῖνος*: doctor)

Εὐγένις
Macedonia (Mygdonia):
—thessalonike: (1) iii ad *IG* x (2) (1) 548 (*Αὐρ. Ἐ. ὁ καὶ Ἄτταλος*)
Thrace:
—perinthos-herakleia: (2) iv-v ad *IPerinth* 228 (*AD* 51-2 (1996-7) Mel. p. 366 no. 184) (Jew)

Εὔγνωστος
Macedonia?: (1) 332 bc *RE* Supplbd. 4 (-); Berve 308 (Tataki, *Macedonians* p. 311 no. 35) (s. *Ξενόφαντος*)

Εὔγνωτος
Thrace:
—apollonia-sozopolis: (1) iv bc *IGB* i² 443 (*Εὔ[γ]νωτος*: f. *Ἀμφίλοχος*)

Εὐδαίμων
Macedonia (Mygdonia):
—sochos (mod.): (1) ii ad Dimitsas 740, 1 (s. *Διονύσιος*)
Thrace:
—byzantion: (2) c. 303 ad *Anal. Boll.* 31 (1912) p. 192
—perinthos-herakleia: (3) ii ad *IPerinth* 217 (*GVI* 1631) (f. *Σεκοῦνδα*)
—philippopolis-trimontium: (4) 163-164 ad *IGB* iii 902, 10; 903; v 5433 (*Φλ. Ἐ. ὁ καὶ Φλαουϊανός*)

Εὔδαμος
Cimmerian Bosporos:
—theodosia: (1) iii ad *CIRB* 947 B, 13 (*Εὔδα[μο]ς*: s. *Δάδας*)
Macedonia (Chalkidike):
—potidaia-kassandreia: (2) ii bc *Tekmeria* 6 (2001) pp. 54-5 no. 1, 5 (f. *Πολυξένη*)
Macedonia (Derriopos):
—alkomena: (3) 317 bc Berve 310 (Tataki, *Macedonians* p. 198 no. 2) (s. *Κρατεύας*)
Macedonia?: (4) 326-317 bc *RE* (5); Berve 311 (Tataki, *Macedonians* p. 311 no. 36)
Thrace:
—perinthos-herakleia:
——(Akarnanes): (5) iii-ii bc *IPerinth* 61, 12 (f. *Ἀγέμαχος*)

Εὐδᾶς
Cimmerian Bosporos:
—kimmerikon: (1) iii ad *CIRB* 946 (*Εὐδᾶς*—Tokhtas'ev)
Thrace:
—byzantion: (2) i-ii ad *IByz* 315 d (Fıratlı-Robert pp. 122-3 no. 205) (*Εὐδᾶ* (gen.))

Εὐδημίδης
Macedonia (Bottiaia):
—beroia: (1) 223 bc *IBer* 4, 16 (*Εὐδη[μί](δ)ης*: s. *Μαχάτας*)
Macedonia (Chalkidike):
—aphytis: (2) ?351 bc *Α΄ Panell. Synedr. Epigr.* pp. 80-1, 25 (s. *Ἐπιχάρης*)
—torone: (3) c. 450-420 bc *IG* i³ 1377 (Tataki, *Macedonians* p. 191 no. 7; *FRA* 7141) (f. *Ναύτης*)

Εὔδημος
Macedonia: (1) 311-306 bc Maier, *Mauerbauinschr.* 69 II, 149 (Tataki, *Macedonians* p. 312 no. 38) (s. *Πύρρος*)
Macedonia (Chalkidike):
—mende: (2) f. iv bc *SEG* xv 241, 2 (Tataki, *Macedonians* p. 121 no. 10) (f. *Θεοτιμίδης*)
—potidaia-kassandreia: (3) iii bc *Milet* i (3) 63, 4 (Tataki, *Macedonians* p. 89 no. 36) (f. —*ικράτης*)
Macedonia (Edonis):
—amphipolis: (4) s. iv bc Hatzopoulos, *Actes Amphipolis* p. 45 no. 9, 3 (*SEG* xli 563); cf. *SEG* xliv 504 (f. *Δαμασίλεως*)
—amphipolis?: (5) ?222-221 bc ib. xlviii 812
Macedonia (Elimeia):
—velvendos (mod.): (6) ii ad ib. xlvii 1001, 2 (s. *Ποσειδώνιος*)
Macedonia (Mygdonia):
—charakoma: (7) c. 230-200 bc *BCH* 45 (1921) p. 18 III, 72 (Tataki, *Macedonians* p. 98 no. 4) (f. *Δημόκριτος*)
—thessalonike: (8) ii ad *IG* x (2) (1) 930 + *BCH* 99 (1975) p. 182 (*Μ. Ἐρέννιος Εὔ(μ)η(λ)ος*?—ed., *Εὔ(δ)ημος*—*BCH*)
Thrace:
—kallipolis?: (9) imp. *ISestos* 26
Thrace?: (10) 316-309 bc *IG* ii² 1956, 8 (*FRA* 2527); *Ancient Macedonia* 5 p. 445 with n. 10 (date)

Εὐδήμων
Skythia:
—tanais: (1) 188 ad *CIRB* 1242, 13 (f. *Μάης*)

Εὐδία
Cimmerian Bosporos:
—pantikapaion: (1) i ad ib. 410; cf. KW pl. 56 no. 757

Εὐδίκη
Skythia:
—olbia-borysthenes (berezan (mod.)): (1) f. v bc Dubois, *IGDOlbia* 40 (vase)

Εὔδικος
Macedonia (Bottiaia):
—beroia: (1) 223 bc *IBer* 4, 27 (f. *Νίκανδρος*)
Macedonia (Chalkidike):
—olynthos: (2) f. iii bc *IG* xii (8) 116 (Tataki, *Macedonians* p. 135 no. 47) (f. *Εὐκτήμων*)
Macedonia (Edonis):
—amphipolis: (3) s. iv bc Hatzopoulos, *Actes Amphipolis* p. 45 no. 9, 6 (*SEG* xli 563); cf. *SEG* xliv 504
Macedonia (Eordaia):
—brynaioi: (4) 57-55 bc *EAM* 115, 4 (Tataki, *Macedonians* p. 84 no. 1) (s. *Ταυρίων*)
Macedonia (Mygdonia):
—chalastra?: (5) f. iv bc *SEG* xliv 524 (vase) (s. *Μενεστ*—)

Εὐδίων
THRACE:
—PERINTHOS-HERAKLEIA: (1) ii AD *IPerinth* 49 B (*Ε[ὐ]δίων*: s. *Φίλλυς*)

Εὐδοκία
MACEDONIA (SINTIKE):
—PARTHIKOPOLIS: (1) vi AD Beševliev 243, 6

Εὐδοξία
MACEDONIA (BOTTIAIA):
—EDESSA: (1) v-vi AD Feissel, *RICM* 31
THRACE:
—TRAIANOPOLIS: (2) v AD Meïmaris–Bakirtzis 30 (*SEG* XXX 785; *IThrakAig* E441) (*Εὐδοξί[α]*?)

Εὐδόξιος
MACEDONIA (BOTTIAIA):
—EDESSA: (1) v-vi AD Feissel, *RICM* 16
THRACE:
—PERINTHOS-HERAKLEIA: (2) v-vi AD *IPerinth* 233 (*AD* 51-2 (1996-7) Mel. p. 379 no. 194) (f. *Στεφανάκις*)

Εὔδοξος
SCYTHIA MINOR:
—TOMIS: (1) i BC *ISM* II 2 A, 53 (f. *Ἀντικράτης*)

Εὔδρομος
TAURIS:
—CHERSONESOS: (1) c. 310-290 BC Anokhin pp. 138-9 nos. 75-77 (coins); (2) f. iii BC *SEG* XL 615 A, 9-10 (*Εὔδρο[μος]*: f. *Λυσίστρατος*)

Εὐδωρίδας
MACEDONIA (CHALKIDIKE):
—CHALKIDEIS: (1) c. 352-350 BC *Olynthus* 9 pp. 83-4 no. 137 (coin); *Ancient Macedonia* 1 p. 254 (date)

Εὔδωρος
MACEDONIA (BOTTIAIA):
—MIEZA: (1) f. iii BC *SEG* XLVII 914 (f. *Ῥόδη*)
—PELLA*: (2) iii BC *AEMTh* 3 (1989) p. 82 n. 35 (amph.)
SKYTHIA:
—OLBIA-BORYSTHENES: (3) f. iv BC Dubois, *IGDOlbia* 104 (s. *Πρωτογένης*); (4) iii BC *IOSPE* I^2 201 I, 17 (s. *Πρωτογένης*); (5) ~ ib. l. 33 (f. *Πρωτογένης*); (6) ~ *SEG* XXXIV 773 with n. (vase); (7) s. iii BC ib. XLII 716 (s. *Πρωτογένης*, f. *Εὔνικος*)

Εὐελπίδης
MACEDONIA (MYGDONIA):
—THESSALONIKE: (1) s. ii AD *IG* X (2) (1) 244 I, 8 (*Αἴλ. Ἐ.*)

Εὐέλπιστος
MACEDONIA (EDONIS):
—PHILIPPOI: (1) imp. *BCH* 58 (1934) pp. 474-5 no. 13 (Pilhofer 289) (Lat. Valerius Euhelpi[stus]?, Euhelpi[dius]—edd.)
MACEDONIA (MYGDONIA):
—THESSALONIKE: (2) i-ii AD *IG* X (2) (1) 243 I, 1 (f. *Αἰσχύλος*); (3) ii AD *AD* 21 (1966) Chron. pl. 352 (*Οὐαρείνι[ος] [Ε]ὐέλπιστος*); (4) ?ii AD *IG* X (2) (1) 127, 3 (*Γ. Ἰούλ. Σερουειλιανὸς Ἐ.*); (5) ii AD ib. 239, 8
SCYTHIA MINOR:
—TOMIS: (6) ii-iii AD *ISM* II 404
——(Hopletes): (7) ii AD ib. 123 (s. *Ποσειδώνιος*, f. *Ἀπατούριος*)
THRACE:
—ODESSOS: (8) 215 AD *IGB* I^2 47 a, 15 (f. *Αὐρ. Ἄκτιος*)

Εὐήθης
THRACE:
—ODESSOS*: (1) ii-iii AD ib. 129 (*[Ε]ὐήθης*: freed.)

Εὐῆθις
THRACE:
—PERINTHOS-HERAKLEIA: (1) i BC-i AD? *IPerinth* 57, 1 (*Σπέλλιος Ἐ.*)

Εὐημερία
THRACE:
—KOILA: (1) imp. *ISestos* 31 (*Κλ. Ἐ.*)

Εὐημερίς
THRACE:
—AINOS: (1) i BC *IG* II^2 5423 (*AM* 67 (1942) p. 172 no. 362; *FRA* 246) (d. *Δημήτριος*)

Εὐήμερος
MACEDONIA (DERRIOPOS):
—STUBERRA: (1) 121 AD *IG* X (2) (2) 328, 15 (s. *Ζωΐλος*)
MACEDONIA (EDONIS):
—AMPHIPOLIS: (2) 24 BC *SEG* XL 522 j (f. *Ἀδαῖος*)
—PHILIPPOI: (3) i-ii AD *BCH* 53 (1929) pp. 83-4 no. 7 (*SIRIS* 121; Pilhofer 132); Collart, *Philippes* pl. 81. 1 (Lat. Q. Mofius Euhemer: doctor)
—PHILIPPOI*: (4) i-ii AD *AE* 1950-1, pp. 62-3 no. 6 (Pilhofer 721) (Lat. L. Licinius Euhemer: f. L. Licinius Saturninus: freed.)
MACEDONIA (MYGDONIA):
—KALINDOIA: (5) 68-98 AD *SEG* XLII 580, 52 (s. *Τρυφωνᾶς*)
—THESSALONIKE: (6) s. i AD *IG* X (2) (1) 68, 25 (*Γν. Ὀκταούϊος Ἐ.*)
—THESSALONIKE?: (7) iii AD ib. 931 (Feissel, *RICM* 118)

Εὔηνος
THRACE?: (1) 246 BC *PPetr* II 18 I, 5, 9 (f. *Κότυς*)

Εὐήνωρ
SCYTHIA MINOR:
—ISTROS: (1) iv BC *ISM* I 251 + *BE* 1984, no. 268 (s. *Π—*)
THRACE:
—APOLLONIA-SOZOPOLIS: (2) iv BC Mushmov 3140 (coin) (*Ε(ὐ)ήνωρ*?, *Ἐγήνωρ*—Mushmov)

Εὐηφένης
MACEDONIA (EDONIS):
—PHILIPPOI: (1) m. iii BC *SEG* XXIV 621 (Pilhofer 327) (s. *Ἐξήκεστος*)

Εὐθάκων
THRACE:
—BYZANTION?: (1) ?ii-i BC *IByz* 365 (s. *Διοκλῆς*)

Εὐθεσίων
CIMMERIAN BOSPOROS:
—PANTIKAPAION: (1) ii BC Gaidukevich, *AGB Mirmekii* p. 116; *Sov. Arkh.* 21 (1954) p. 121; 28 (1958) p. 126 (tile)

Εὔθετος
THRACE:
—BYZANTION: (1) ii AD *SEG* L 667 VII (*Εὔθετες*—lap.: s. *Ἀγαθόπους*, *Φῆστα*)

Εὐθήνα
TAURIS:
—CHERSONESOS: (1) f. iv BC *IOSPE* I^2 512 (*Εὐθήνα*: d. *Θεοτέλης*)

Εὐθήριος
MACEDONIA (MYGDONIA):
—THESSALONIKE*: (1) v-vi AD Feissel, *RICM* 147, 7 (*SEG* XLVII 982)
SKYTHIA:
—OLBIA-BORYSTHENES: (2) vi/v BC ib. XLVIII 1012 (f. *Ἡρακλείδης*)
TAURIS:
—CHERSONESOS?: (3) 383-395 AD *IOSPE* I^2 450, 8 (*[Ε]ὐθήριος*)

Εὔθιος
SKYTHIA:
—OLBIA-BORYSTHENES: (1) c. 325-300 BC ib. 345, 2; cf. *SEG* XLII 692 (*[Ε]ὔθ̣ιο̣ς*?)

Εὐθύδαμος
THRACE:
—ABDERA: (1) iii BC ib. XXX 662 (bronze)

Εὐθύδικος
MACEDONIA (CHALKIDIKE):
—DION: (1) iii BC *IG* XII (8) 233 (Tataki, *Macedonians* p. 100 no. 5) (or Macedonia (Pieria) Dion: s. *Ἀρχίας*)
MACEDONIA (PIERIA):
—PYDNA: (2) iv BC *GRBS* 43 (2002-3) p. 110 no. 1 a, 7

Εὐθυκράτης
MACEDONIA: (1) 337-329 BC *CID* II 69, 19; 74 II, 23; 76 I, 18; 79 A II, [8]; 80, [7]; 82, 19; 86, [7]; 89, [7] (Tataki, *Macedonians* p. 312 no. 39); (2) c. 235-200 BC *TCam* 35, 28; *IG* XII (1) 104 c, 7 (Tataki, *Macedonians* p. 312 no. 40) (s. *Καλλίας*: sculptor)
MACEDONIA (CHALKIDIKE):
—OLYNTHOS: (3) 348 BC *RE* (4) (Tataki, *Macedonians* p. 135 no. 48)

Εὐθυμία
THRACE:
—AINOS: (1) hell. PH 271 (d. *Κράτης*)
—BEROE-AUGUSTA TRAIANA: (2) c. 320-324 AD *Anal. Boll.* 31 (1912) p. 198; cf. p. 207 (*Εὐλαλία*—p. 207)

Εὐθυμίδης
MACEDONIA (CHALKIDIKE):
—NEAPOLIS?: (1) c. 470-460 BC *SEG* XL 549 (vase) (*Εὐθυ[μίδης]*)
MACEDONIA (MYGDONIA):
—LETE: (2) s. iv BC Hatzopoulos, *MI* 2 pp. 93-4 no. 79, 14

Εὐθυμίη
CIMMERIAN BOSPOROS:
—NYMPHAION: (1) c. 480-470 BC *SGDI* 5579 (Tolstoi 108; *LSAG*^{2} p. 373 no. 63; *Arch. Class.* 25-6 (1973-4) p. 349 no. 15 (vase))

Εὔθυνος
CIMMERIAN BOSPOROS:
—PANTIKAPAION: (1) ii-i BC *CIRB* 748 (*Εὐθ(υ)νος*: f. *Πασικράτης*)
TAURIS:
—CHERSONESOS: (2) iii BC Solomonik, *NEPKh* 180 (*Εὔθυνος*: s. *Ἑστιαῖος*); (3) ~ *IOSPE* I^2 507

Εὐθύνους
MACEDONIA (BOTTIAIA):
—BEROIA: (1) 223 BC *IBer* 4, 14 (s. *Ἀλέξανδρος*)
MACEDONIA (EDONIS):
—AMPHIPOLIS: (2) iv BC *SEG* XXXV 707 (*Εὐθύνου* (gen.): f. *Φίλιννα*)

Εὐθύφρων
CIMMERIAN BOSPOROS:
—GORGIPPIA: (1) f. iii BC *CIRB* 1137 A I, 26 (f. *Ἡρόδωρος*)

Εὔϊον
THRACE: (1) ii BC *IG* II^2 8909 (*FRA* 2528)

Εὔϊος
CIMMERIAN BOSPOROS:
—PANTIKAPAION: (1) ii-iii AD *CIRB* 783, 2; (2) 275-278 AD ib. 36, 21 (*[Ε]ὔϊος*: s. *Μενέστρατος*); (3) ~ ib. l. 55 (f. *—ων*); (4) ~ ib. l. 65 (f. *—αρος*)
MACEDONIA (DERRIOPOS):
—STUBERRA: (5) 50 AD *IG* X (2) (2) 324, 20 (f. *Ἐπιγᾶς*)

Skythia:
—Tanais: (**6**) ii AD *CIRB* 1262, 25 (s. *Διόδωρος*); (**7**) f. ii AD ib. 1264 A, 14 (s. *Τρύφων*); (**8**) ~ ib. 1266, 6 ([*Ε*]*ὔϊος*); (**9**) 192 AD ib. 1243, 16 (s. *Δάδας*); (**10**) c. 200-220 AD ib. 1277, 21; 1278, 5 (s. *Ῥόδων*); (**11**) 225 AD ib. 1280, 12 (f. *Φορήρανος*)
Tauris:
—Chersonesos: (**12**) iii BC Solomonik, *NEPKh* 163 (s. *Θεοφάνης*)
Thrace: (**13**) 153-144 BC *SGDI* 2263, 4, 6, 10, 15 (slave/freed.)

Εὐίππας
Macedonia (Pieria):
—Pydna: (**1**) iv BC *GRBS* 47 (2002-3) p. 116 no. 4, 1 (?s. *Σιτάλκας*)

Εὔιππος
Macedonia (Bottiaia):
—Mieza: (**1**) iii/ii BC *SEG* XLIII 407; 417? (s. *Ἀριστοφάνης*, ?f. *Σπάρτη*); (**2**) f. ii BC ib. 418 (s. *Καλλικλῆς*, *Φίλα*)

Εὔκαιρος
Cimmerian Bosporos:
—Gorgippia: (**1**) iii AD *NE* 9 (1971) p. 10 no. 6 B, 14
Skythia:
—Olbia-Borysthenes: (**2**) s. i AD *IOlbia* 85, 9 (*IOSPE* I^2 104) (f. *Μικίων*)

Εὐκαμπίδας
Scythia Minor:
—Kallatis: (**1**) iv/iii BC *ISM* III 125, 6

Εὐκαρπία
Macedonia (Edonis):
—Philippoi (nr.): (**1**) ?ii AD *BCH* 47 (1923) p. 78 no. 38 (Pilhofer 402) (Lat. Valeria Eucarpia: d. *Ἄμαστρις*)

Εὔκαρπος
Macedonia (Bottiaia):
—Beroia: (**1**) ii-iii AD *IBer* 38 (Tataki 714) (*Κλ. Εὔκαρπ*[*ος*]); (**2**) ii/iii AD *IBer* 143 B, 13 (Tataki 479) (*Εὐκ*(*α*)*ρπος*: f. *Σύμφορος*); (**3**) 184 AD *ILeukopetra* 17, 1 (Tataki 478)
Macedonia (Mygdonia):
—Thessalonike: (**4**) ii-iii AD *IG* X (2) (1) 669, 2 (*Οὐαλερ*[*ια*]*νὸς Εὔκα*[*ρ*]*πος*)
Thrace:
—Kellai: (**5**) 241-244 AD *IGB* III 1517, 19 (*Αὐρ. Ἐ.*)

Εὐκλάδιος
Thrace:
—Philippopolis-Trimontium (territ.): (**1**) iii AD ib. 1448, 5 (Beševliev 220)

Εὔκλεια
Cimmerian Bosporos:
—Pantikapaion: (**1**) i BC *CIRB* 268 A; 268 B (m. *Ἀθηνοκλῆς*)
Macedonia (Bottiaia):
—Edessa?: (**2**) iii-iv AD *GVI* 2036, 5 (*IDyrrh* 527 bis; Tataki, *Edessa* 101) (m. *Ἡδεῖα ἡ καὶ Μαρία*)
Macedonia (Lynkestis):
—Herakleia: (**3**) ii-iii AD *IG* X (2) (2) 84 (m. *Κλ. Οὖρσος*)
Macedonia (Mygdonia):
—Thessalonike: (**4**) i-ii AD ib. X (2) (1) 1024 (II^2 8841/2; Tataki, *Macedonians* p. 182 no. 27; *FRA* 2379) (d. *Ζώπυρος*); (**5**) ii-iii AD *IG* X (2) (1) 620 (*Κλ. Εὔκλια*: d. *Φλ. Ὀπτάτη*)
Macedonia (Pieria):
—Dion: (**6**) s. iv BC *SEG* XXXVI 612 (d. *Ἡγήσανδρος*)
Thrace:
—Lysimacheia: (**7**) hell. *ISestos* 41

Εὐκλείδας
Tauris:
—Chersonesos: (**1**) c. 325-315 BC Kats p. 94 no. 44 (amph.); (**2**) iii BC Solomonik, *NEPKh* 144 (f. *Δελφός*)

Εὐκλείδης
Macedonia: (**1**) s. iii BC *Milet* I (3) 67 I, 9 (Tataki, *Macedonians* p. 313 no. 41) (f. *Σίμαινα*); (**2**) 98 or 65 BC *SEG* VIII 504 (Tataki, *Macedonians* p. 313 no. 42); cf. La'da E1646 (f. *Φιλόξενος*)
Macedonia (Chalkidike):
—Olynthos: (**3**) s. iv BC *RE* (3) (Tataki, *Macedonians* p. 135 no. 49)
Thrace:
—Byzantion: (**4**) iv AD *PLRE* I (22) (s. *Μάξιμος*)
—Perinthos-Herakleia:
——(Theseidai): (**5**) s. iii BC *IPerinth* 62, 3 (f. *Τληπόλεμος*)

Εὐκλέων
Scythia Minor:
—Istros: (**1**) 138 AD *ISM* I 193 I, 32 (s. *Σέξτος*)
—Kallatis: (**2**) iii BC ib. III 126, 5 (f. *Κρατέας*); (**3**) ii/i BC *SNG Stancomb* 97-8 (coin) (*Εὐκλέ*(*ων*)?)
Thrace:
—Apollonia-Sozopolis: (**4**) ?iii BC *IGB* I^2 458 bis, 4 (f. *Καλλιάνασσα*)
—Byzantion: (**5**) ii BC *IByz* 74 (Fıratlı–Robert p. 50 no. 18) (s. *Μενίσκος*); (**6**) i BC-i AD *IByz* 133 (Fıratlı–Robert pp. 98-9 no. 146) (f. *Ὑγίεια*)
—Byzantion?: (**7**) ii-i BC *IByz* 344 (Fıratlı–Robert p. 128 no. 217) (f. *Ὑγεία*)

Εὐκλῆς
Macedonia (Bottiaia):
—Beroia: (**1**) 112 BC *IBer* 134, 42 (*Ε̣ὐκλῆς*: f. *Βοΐσκος*)
—Pella: (**2**) iii BC Akamatis, *Amph. Pellas* p. 35 nos. PAR22-3 (amph.) (*SEG* L 613)
Macedonia (Chalkidike):
—Olynthos: (**3**) ?350 BC *TAPA* 59 (1928) p. 226, 12; Hatzopoulos, *Actes Chalc.* p. 80 (date) (f. *Φαρνάβαζος*)
Scythia Minor:
—Istros: (**4**) i BC-i AD *ISM* I 191 II, 21 (s. *Θεόφιλος*)
Skythia:
—Tyras: (**5**) s. iii BC *VDI* 1966 (2), p. 152, 2 (*Εὐκλέω*[*ς*] (gen.))
Tauris:
—Chersonesos: (**6**) iv BC Solomonik, *GAKh* 735 (vase) ([*Ε*]*ὐκλ*<*λ*>*ῆς*)
Thrace:
—Dionysopolis: (**7**) hell. *Spink Num. Circular* 105 (1997) pp. 372-4 nos. 14-15; 17; 29 (coin) (*Εὐκλέου*(*ς*) (gen.))

Εὐκολίνα
Thrace: (**1**) c. 155 BC *SGDI* 1711, 3-4, 10 (slave/freed.)

Εὐκολῖνος
Macedonia (Bottiaia):
—Pella: (**1**) iii BC *SEG* XLIII 437 (f. *Μάμαλα*)

Εὐκράτεια
Cimmerian Bosporos:
—Pantikapaion: (**1**) m. i AD *CIRB* 501, 2 (-*τια*: m. *Ἀρίστων*, *Ἀρίστων* (sic))

Εὐκράτης
Cimmerian Bosporos:
—Pantikapaion: (**1**) i-ii AD ib. 602 (I f. *Εὐκράτης* II); (**2**) ~ ib. (II s. *Εὐκράτης* I); (**3**) iii AD Vaulina–Wąsowicz pl. 124 no. 62 (*Εὐκρά*(*της*)?)
—Theodosia: (**4**) iii AD *CIRB* 947 A, 8 ([*Ε*]*ὐκρ*(*ά*)*της*: s. *Πάππος*)
Macedonia:
—Degme: (**5**) iii/ii BC *Thess. Mnem.* 57 (Tataki, *Macedonians* p. 99 no. 2) (f. *Ἀριστοβούλη*) ?= (*6*); (**6**) ~ *Thess. Mnem.* 139 (Tataki, *Macedonians* p. 99 no. 3) (f. *Σωκράτης*) ?= (*5*)
Macedonia (Bottiaia):
—Beroia: (**7**) 189 AD *ILeukopetra* 24, 12 (s. *Φίλιππος*)
Scythia Minor:
—Istros: (**8**) iii-ii BC *ISM* I 387 (s. *Ἐπικράτης*)
—Tomis: (**9**) i BC ib. II 2 B, 48 (f. *Χαιρήμων*)
Skythia:
—Olbia-Borysthenes: (**10**) s. iii BC *IOSPE* I^2 76, 6 (Sokolowski II 88; Dubois, *IGDOlbia* 88) (f. *Ποσειδώνιος*)
Tauris:
—Chersonesos: (**11**) f. ii BC *IOSPE* I^2 351, 1 (s. *Πρύτανις*)
Thrace:
—Abdera: (**12**) s. iii BC *ISamothrace* 22, 46 (s. *Ἡρακλείδης*)
—Beroe-Augusta Traiana: (**13**) iii AD *IGB* III 1575, 2 (f. *Οὐλπ. Πόπλιος*)
—Kardia: (**14**) iii BC *IG* II^2 8960 (*FRA* 2670) (f. *Εὔφρων*)
—Maroneia: (**15**) iii-ii BC *IThrakAig* E363
—Zone: (**16**) f. iv BC *PAE* 1969, p. 67 with pl. 83 α (*IThrakAig* E414) (s. *Πολυχάρης*)

Εὐκρατίδης
Cimmerian Bosporos:
—Gorgippia: (**1**) f. iii BC *CIRB* 1137 A II, 43 (f. *Φιλῖνος*)
Macedonia (Bottiaia):
—Pella: (**2**) s. iv BC *AD* 16 (1960) Mel. p. 82; *SEG* XXXIX 623; XLIII 444 (tiles)

Εὐκράτις
Thrace:
—Hadrianopolis: (**1**) 294 AD *Cod. Just.* viii 42.20; cf. *Klio* 58 (1976) p. 84 (Lat. Eucratidi (dat.))

Εὔκριτος
Tauris:
—Chersonesos: (**1**) s. iv BC *CIRB* 194 (f. *Καλλικράτης*); (**2**) iv/iii BC Solomonik, *NEPKh* 175 (s. *Μενοίτας*)

Εὐκτήμων
Macedonia (Bottiaia):
—Beroia: (**1**) ii-iii AD *IBer* 319 (*Γαλεριανὸς Ἐ.*); (**2**) f. iii AD ib. 267, 2 (Tataki 480) (f. *Κουσπίδιος Ὀνησᾶς*, *Διονύσιος*)
Macedonia (Chalkidike):
—Olynthos: (**3**) f. iii BC *IG* XII (8) 116 (Tataki, *Macedonians* p. 135 no. 50) (s. *Εὔδικος*, f. *Ἐπιχάρης*)
Macedonia (Elimeia):
—Xerolimni (mod.): (**4**) i BC-i AD *Α΄ Panell. Synedr. Epigr.* p. 62 no. 9 (*SEG* XLIX 848) (*Λ*̣*εύκιος Κουσώνιος Ἐ.*)
Macedonia (Pieria):
—Methone: (**5**) s. v BC *IG* II^2 9330 (Tataki, *Macedonians* p. 122 no. 3; *FRA* 3668)
Scythia Minor:
—Tomis*: (**6**) ii AD Iconomu, *Opaite greco-romane* nos. 271-7; 329-32; 374-6; 397-402; 435; *ISM* V 114; 235; *SEG* XXXIV 741; XLVIII 1000 bis. 2 (lamps) (-*μον*)
Thrace:
—Abdera: (**7**) f. iii BC *IMM* 11, 7
—Byzantion: (**8**) i BC-i AD *IByz* 209 (Fıratlı–Robert p. 69 no. 67) (s. *Μένανδρος*)
—Pistiros: (**9**) iv-iii BC *SEG* XLIX 912. 8 (vase) (*Εὐκτή*(*μων*))

Εὐκτίμενος
Macedonia (Mygdonia):
—Lete: (**1**) ii AD *Makedonika* 2 (1951) p. 619 no. 42 θ, 11 (s. *Ζώσιμος*)

—THESSALONIKE: (2) s. i AD *IG* X (2) (1) 68, 5, 10 (f. *T. Φλ. Ἀμύντας*)

Εὔκτος
MACEDONIA (BOTTIAIA):
—PELLA?: (1) c. 179-168 BC *RE* Supplbd. 4 (2) (Tataki, *Macedonians* p. 154 no. 42)

Εὐκύδης
THRACE:
—APOLLONIA-SOZOPOLIS: (1) iii BC *Apoloniia* p. 337 no. 1210; *SNG BM Black Sea* 189 (coin) ([*Ν*]*αυκύδης*—*SNG*)

Εὐκυδίδης
MACEDONIA (MYGDONIA):
—THESSALONIKE: (1) hell.? *IG* X (2) (1) 49

Εὔλαιος
MACEDONIA (BOTTIAIA):
—BEROIA: (1) ii-i BC *IBer* 184 (*Εὔλαι[ος]*: f. *Οὐαδήα*); (2) f. ii AD ib. 7 A, 33; (3) ~ *ISamothrace* 47, 5, 10; *IBer* 105, 9 (Tataki 715; Tataki, *Macedonians* p. 79 no. 30) (*Τι. Κλ. Ἐ.*); (4) ~ *IBer* 105, 5 (Tataki 1319) (*T. Φλ. Καισεννιανὸς Ἐ.*)
—GENDERRHOS? (ANYDRON (MOD.)): (5) 132 or 135 AD *SEG* XLIII 394 (s. *Λαοίτας*)
—MIEZA (TERRIT.)?: (6) i BC ib. XXIV 505 (Tataki 481); cf. Hatzopoulos, *MI* 1 p. 116 (locn.) (or Macedonia (Bottiaia) Beroia: f. *—τίας*)
—PELLA?: (7) c. 179-168 BC *RE* Supplbd. 4 (3) (Tataki, *Macedonians* p. 154 no. 43)
MACEDONIA (DERRIOPOS):
—STUBERRA: (8) 74 AD *IG* X (2) (2) 325, 40 (s. *Πετίκιος*); (9) ~ ib. 326, 52 (s. *Ἀντίγονος*)
MACEDONIA (MYGDONIA):
—THESSALONIKE: (10) i-ii AD ib. X (2) (1) 243 I, 6 ([*Ά*]*βέλλιος Εὔλαιος*)
MACEDONIA (PIERIA):
—PYDNA: (11) f. ii BC *SEG* L 629 (f. *Λαμάγα*)

Εὐλαμπία
THRACE:
—HADRIANOPOLIS:
——Kitoroi: (1) vi AD Beševliev 102, 4 (*-λαυπί-*)

Εὔλανδρος
MACEDONIA: (1) ?417-413 BC *IG* I³ 89, 63 (Tataki, *Macedonians* p. 313 no. 44)
MACEDONIA (BOTTIAIA):
—BEROIA: (2) ii BC *IBer* 198 (Tataki 482) (f. *Ἀδίστα*)
MACEDONIA (EORDAIA):
—KELLE?: (3) ii BC *EAM* 91; Hatzopoulos, *MI* 1 p. 94 n. 4 (locn.) ([*Ε*]*ὔλανδ[ρος]*?: f. *Πρωτογένης*)
MACEDONIA (KRESTONIA):
—MORRYLOS?: (4) hell. *SEG* XXXIX 609, 3
MACEDONIA (MYGDONIA):
—LETE: (5) s. i BC ib. XLVII 905, 1 (f. *Ἀντίγονος*, *—αιος*); (6) ~ ib. l. 4 (f. *Ἀντίγονος*)
—THESSALONIKE: (7) 27 BC-14 AD *IG* X (2) (1) 31, 17

Εὐμάρης
SCYTHIA MINOR:
—ISTROS: (1) iv/iii BC *ISM* I 246, 1 + *SEG* XXXVI 682 ([*Ε*]*ὐμάρης*)
TAURIS:
—CHERSONESOS: (2) iii BC Solomonik, *NEPKh* 160 (*Εὐμάρειος* (gen.): f. *Ἡρώι*)

Εὔμαχος
CIMMERIAN BOSPOROS:
—GORGIPPIA: (1) 173-210 AD *CIRB* 1134, 26 (s. *Γλυκαρίων*)
—PANTIKAPAION: (2) f. ii AD ib. 84, 6; cf. KW pl. 45 no. 648 (I f. *Εὔμαχος* II); (3) ~ *CIRB* 84, 6; cf. KW pl. 45 no. 648 (II s. *Εὔμαχος* I)

SKYTHIA:
—TYRAS: (4) iv/iii BC *SEG* XLV 1026. 7 (vase) (reading—Vinogradov)
TAURIS:
—CHERSONESOS: (5) ?114 AD ib. XLVIII 999, 39 (s. *Ἄππας*)
THRACE:
—MESAMBRIA: (6) ii/i BC *IGB* V 5103, 2 (s. *Μέμνων*)

Εὐμενεανός
SKYTHIA:
—OLBIA-BORYSTHENES: (1) 149 AD *SEG* XXX 1334 (and Bithynia Prousias: s. *Ἑρμόδωρος*)

Εὐμένης
MACEDONIA: (1) c. 244-242 BC *PPetr* III 54 b fr. 1, 5 (unp.) (Tataki, *Macedonians* p. 313 no. 45; La'da E1493); (2) 168 BC *RE* (9) (Tataki, *Macedonians* p. 313 no. 46) (Lat. Eumenes)
MACEDONIA (MYGDONIA):
—KALINDOIA: (3) 68-98 AD *SEG* XLII 580, 51 (s. *Μένανδρος*)
—THESSALONIKE?: (4) ii AD *IG* X (2) (1) 715 (?s. *Διονυσογένης*, *Κλεοπάτρα*); (5) ii-iii AD ib. 887 ([*Ε*]*ὐμένης*)
SCYTHIA MINOR:
—TOMIS: (6) ii AD *ISM* II 70, 4 (f. *T. Κομίνιος Κλαυδιανὸς Ἑρμάφιλος*)
SKYTHIA:
—OLBIA-BORYSTHENES: (7) s. iv BC *SEG* L 702 IV, 6; (8) iv/iii BC *IOlbia* 71 II, 6 (Dubois, *IGDOlbia* 11) (s. *Λεω—*); (9) iii BC *IOSPE* I² 201 II, 26 (s. *Συρίσκος*)
TAURIS:
—NEAPOLIS: (10) iii BC *Sov. Arkh.* 28 (1958) pp. 310-13 no. 2 (*Εὐμέν[ης]*)
THRACE:
—KARDIA: (11) c. 362-317 BC *RE* (4); Berve 317 (s. *Ἱερώνυμος*)
—LYSIMACHEIA: (12) m. iii BC *IG* X (2) (1) 301 (s. *Ζώπυρος*)

Εὐμήδης
MACEDONIA: (1) c. 235-200 BC La'da E1756 (s. *Λυσίμαχος*: t.e.)

Εὐμήειον
MACEDONIA (BOTTIAIA):
—BEROIA: (1) iii AD *IBer* 365 (*-κει-*)

Εὐμηλίδης
CIMMERIAN BOSPOROS:
—PANTIKAPAION: (1) f. iii BC *RPh* 1937, p. 325 no. 6 A, 20 (*Εὐμηλ[ί]δης*: f. *Ἡροφάνης*)

Εὔμηλος
CIMMERIAN BOSPOROS:
—BOSPOROS: (1) c. 340-304 BC *RE* (11); *CIRB* 18; 19; 974; 1043; *IG* II² 653, 33; *SEG* XL 623, 1 (s. *Παιρισάδης*, *Καμασαρύη*, f. *Σπάρτοκος*, *Σέλευκος*)
—GORGIPPIA: (2) f. iii BC *CIRB* 1137 B II, 10 ([*Ε*]*ὔμηλος*: f. *Μᾶτρις*)
MACEDONIA: (3) 72 BC *ZÄS* 93 (1966) pp. 94-5 (Tataki, *Macedonians* p. 482 no. 105); cf. La'da E1581 (f. *Πολέμων*)
MACEDONIA (EDONIS):
—AMPHIPOLIS: (4) 285-246 BC *BCH* 95 (1971) p. 567 (Tataki, *Macedonians* p. 52 no. 55) (f. *Σατυρίων*)
TAURIS:
—CHERSONESOS: (5) f. iii BC Kats p. 89 no. 22 (amph.) (f. *Ἀπολλώνιος*); (6) c. 272-262 BC ib. p. 94 no. 45 (amph.) (s. *Ἀπολλώνιος*)
THRACE:
—SERDICA: (7) ii-iii AD *IGB* IV 1936 (f. *Ἰκάδας*)

Εὔμητις
MACEDONIA (EDONIS):
—AMPHIPOLIS: (1) v/iv BC *SEG* XXIV 586 (*Amphipolis* p. 88 fig. 49) (d. *Ἡγησίστρατος*)

Εὔμολπος
MACEDONIA (CHALKIDIKE):
—OLYNTHOS: (1) iii/ii BC *NS* 520 (Tataki, *Macedonians* p. 135 no. 51) (f. *Μουσαῖος*)
THRACE:
—APOLLONIA-SOZOPOLIS: (2) ?iii BC *IGB* I² 458 bis, 2

Εὔμορφος
MACEDONIA (PIERIA):
—DION: (1) ii-iii AD Oikonomos 20 ([*Κ*]*ορν[ήλ]ιος Εὔ[μ]ορφ[ος]*)

Εὔμουσος
THRACE:
—NICOPOLIS AD ISTRUM (TERRIT.): (1) ii-iii AD *IGB* V 5252 (*Ἔλιος Ἐ.*)

Εὔνη
TAURIS:
—CHERSONESOS: (1) imp. *MIA* 34 (1953) p. 194 (vase)

Εὐνίκη
CIMMERIAN BOSPOROS:
—BOSPOROS?: (1) i AD *CIRB* 1047, [5]; 1118 (*Εὐν[είκη]*?: m. *Τιβ. Ἰούλ. Ῥησκούπορις*: queen)

Εὔνικος
MACEDONIA: (1) iv BC Arr., *An.* iii 5. 1; 6. 8 (Tataki, *Macedonians* p. 314 no. 47) (f. *Ἀσκληπιόδωρος*)
MACEDONIA (CHALKIDIKE):
—OLYNTHOS: (2) c. 425-400 BC *Olynthus* 10 pp. 199-200 no. 626 (lamp)
SCYTHIA MINOR:
—KALLATIS: (3) i AD *IG* II² 10282 (*FRA* 2645)
SKYTHIA:
—OLBIA-BORYSTHENES: (4) iii BC *IOSPE* I² 201 II, 34 (s. *Ἐ—*) ?= (*5*); (5) s. iii BC *SEG* XLII 716 (s. *Εὔδωρος*) ?= (*4*)

Εὔνοια
KOLCHIS: (1) hell.-imp. *BCH* 34 (1910) p. 243 no. 8
MACEDONIA (MYGDONIA):
—THESSALONIKE?: (2) s. ii AD *IG* X (2) (1) 902 (m. *Εὔνους*, *Ἑρμέρως*)
MACEDONIA (PIERIA):
—DION: (3) i-ii AD Oikonomos 31

Εὐνόϊκος
SKYTHIA:
—TANAIS: (1) 154-170 AD *CIRB* 1260a, 18 (f. *—ς*); (2) 209 AD ib. 1276, 4 (s. *.υν—*); (3) 220 AD ib. 1278, 8 (I f. *Εὐνόϊκος* II); (4) ~ ib. l. 8 (II s. *Εὐνόϊκος* I); (5) ~ ib. l. 26 ([*Ε*]*ὐνόϊκο[ς]*); (6) 225 AD ib. 1279, 11 (f. *Ῥαχοίσακος*)

Εὐνομία
THRACE: (1) iii BC *AD* 23 (1968) Mel. pp. 110-11 no. 74 (*Εὐνο[μία]*?)

Εὔνομος
MACEDONIA (BOTTIAIA):
—PELLA: (1) iii-ii BC Dimitsas 132 (f. *Ἁρμοδία*)
MACEDONIA (MYGDONIA):
—THESSALONIKE: (2) s. ii AD *IG* X (2) (1) 244 II, 5 (I f. *Εὔνομος* II); (3) ~ ib. l. 5 (II s. *Εὔνομος* I)

Εὖνος
CIMMERIAN BOSPOROS:
—NYMPHAION: (1) f. iii BC *SEG* XXXIX 701. 5; cf. Masson, *OGS* p. 338 (name); (2) i AD *CIRB* 929 ([*Ε*]*ὖνος*?, [*Θ*]*υνός*—*CIRB*: s. *Μασταροῦς*, f. *Βόστακος*, *Δοκίων*)
—PANTIKAPAION: (3) iv BC ib. 159; cf. *Etiudy* p. 183 no. 3; cf. KW pl. 5 no. 94 ([*Θ*]*υνῶ* (gen.)—*CIRB*, [*Ε*]*ὔνῶ*?)

Εὔνοστος
MACEDONIA (PIERIA):
—LEIBETHRA (NR.): **(1)** iv/iii BC *Essays Laourdas* p. 112 no. 4 (f. *Μάνιχχος*)
SCYTHIA MINOR:
—ISTROS: **(2)** ii AD *ISM* I 211, 8 (*Εὔ[νοσ]τος*?: f. *Κερκᾶς*)

Εὔνους
MACEDONIA (MYGDONIA):
—THESSALONIKE: **(1)** i-ii AD *IG* X (2) (1) 243 I, 7 + *Maia* 25 (1973) p. 200
—THESSALONIKE?: **(2)** s. ii AD *IG* X (2) (1) 902 (s. *Ἑρμῆς, Εὔνοια*)
MACEDONIA (PAIONIA):
—KAVADARCI (MOD.): **(3)** ii-iii AD *Sp.* 98 (1941-8) p. 77 no. 164 (f. *Εὔτυχος*)
SCYTHIA MINOR:
—TOMIS: **(4)** ii-iii AD *ISM* II 32, 8 (*Κάσις Εὔνου[ς]*)
THRACE: **(5)** 153-144 BC *SGDI* 1926, [2], 4, 6 (slave/freed.)

Εὔνυμφος
MACEDONIA (BOTTIAIA):
—PELLA: **(1)** 150 AD *SEG* XLVIII 825 (f. *Εὐπορία*)

Εὔνων
SKYTHIA:
—TANAIS: **(1)** 228 AD *CIRB* 1282, 15 (s. *Συνέκδημος*); **(2)** 230 AD ib. 1284, 18 (s. *Χορφρασμος*); **(3)** ~ ib. l. 21 (I f. *Εὔνων* II); **(4)** ~ ib. l. 21 (II s. *Εὔνων* I)

Εὐνώνας
SARMATIA:
—AORSOI: **(1)** 49 AD Tac., *Ann.* xii 15-20; *RE* (-) (Lat. Eunones)
SKYTHIA:
—TANAIS: **(2)** f. ii AD *CIRB* 1264 A, 3 (s. *Μενέστρατος*); **(3)** 244 AD ib. 1287, 26 (f. *Φηδάνακος*)

Εὐξείνιος
SCYTHIA MINOR:
—ISTROS: **(1)** ii/iii AD *ISM* I 227, 7 (?s. *Α—*)

Εὔξεινος
SCYTHIA MINOR:
—CIUS*: **(1)** 244-246 AD ib. V 124, 12 (Lat. Aur. Euxinus)

Εὐξενίδης
SCYTHIA MINOR:
—ISTROS: **(1)** ii BC ib. I 36, 3; cf. *Pontica* 33-4 (2000-1) pp. 346-7 no. 3 (s. *Μόνιμος*); **(2)** i BC-i AD *ISM* I 186 (s. *Κάρπος*); **(3)** ii AD ib. 212, 21 (s. *Μόνιμος*); **(4)** f. ii AD ib. 57, 4 (*Eastern cults* pp. 102-3 no. 65); *SEG* L 683 B, 5 (f. *Ἑκαταῖος*); **(5)** 138 AD *ISM* I 193, 9 (f. *Ἀρτεμίδωρος*); **(6)** ~ ib. 193 I, 25 (s. *Παγκράτης*); **(7)** ~ ib. l. 27 (II s. *Εὐξενίδης* I); **(8)** ~ ib. l. 27 (I f. *Εὐξενίδης* II); **(9)** ~ ib. l. 57 (s. *Πολυαίνετος*); **(10)** ~ ib. l. 72, 76 (*M. Οὔλπ. Ἐ.*: s. *Ἀρτεμίδωρος*, f. *M. Οὔλπ. Ἀρτεμίδωρος*); **(11)** ~ ib. l. 87 (I f. *Εὐξενίδης* II); **(12)** ~ ib. l. 87 (II s. *Εὐξενίδης* I); **(13)** ~ ib. l. 104 (s. *Νουμήνιος*); **(14)** ~ ib. l. 36-7 (*Φλ. Ἐ.*: f. *Ἱππόλοχος*); **(15)** ~ ib. 193 II, 37 (s. *Διονύσιος*); **(16)** ~ ib. l. 59 (f. *Ἀρτεμίδωρος*); **(17)** ~ ib. l. 80 (f. *Μοιρόδωρος*); **(18)** c. 140-160 AD ib. 207, 7 (*Κομίνιος Ἐ. νεώτ.*); **(19)** ii/iii AD ib. 227, 9 (?s. *Εὐ—*)
THRACE:
—ODESSOS: **(20)** ii AD *IGB* I² 68 (I f. *Εὐξενίδης* II); **(21)** ~ ib. (*Ἐ. νέος*: II s. *Εὐξενίδης* I)
THRACE?: **(22)** ii BC *ISM* I 36, 5 + *Pontica* 33-4 (2000-1) pp. 346-7 no. 3

Εὐξένιππος
MACEDONIA?: **(1)** 329 BC *RE* Supplbd. 4 (4); Berve 318 (Tataki, *Macedonians* p. 314 no. 48) (Lat. Euxenippus—Hedicke)

Εὔξενος
CIMMERIAN BOSPOROS:
—GORGIPPIA: **(1)** f. iii BC *CIRB* 1137 A I, 3 (I f. *Εὔξενος* II); **(2)** ~ ib. l. 3 (II s. *Εὔξενος* I)
MACEDONIA (BOTTIAIA):
—AIGAI: **(3)** s. iv BC *SEG* XXXV 786 (s. *Τελευτίας*, f. *Πρόξενος*)
MACEDONIA (KRESTONIA):
—MORRYLOS: **(4)** c. 185-180 BC ib. XXXIX 606, 1 (s. *Σάμος*)
SKYTHIA:
—OLBIA-BORYSTHENES: **(5)** s. iv BC ib. XXXII 794, [2], 13; cf. Vinogradov, *Pont. Stud.* pp. 276-322 (*Εὔξεν[ος]*: f. *Καλλίνικος*); **(6)** iii BC *IOSPE* I² 201 I, 19 (s. *Καλλίστρατος*)

Εὐξίθεμις
THRACE:
—MARONEIA: **(1)** c. 365-336 BC Schönert-Geiss, *Maroneia* 484-5 (coin) (*Εὐξιθέμιος* (gen.))

Εὐξίθεος
MACEDONIA (CHALKIDIKE):
—OLYNTHOS: **(1)** ?352 BC *TAPA* 69 (1938) p. 48 no. 3, 16; Hatzopoulos, *Actes Chalc.* p. 80 (date) (s. *Ξάνθιππος*)
MACEDONIA (EDONIS):
—AMPHIPOLIS: **(2)** m. iii BC *BCH* 63 (1939) p. 6 (f. *Νικαία*)
TAURIS:
—CHERSONESOS: **(3)** iii BC Solomonik, *NEPKh* 174 (s. *Χαιρομένης*)

Εὐοδία
MACEDONIA (BOTTIAIA):
—BEROIA: **(1)** m. ii AD *IBer* 239 (Tataki 485) (m. *Φορτουνᾶτος*)
MACEDONIA (EDONIS):
—PHILIPPOI: **(2)** f. i AD *Ep. Philipp.* iv 2
MACEDONIA (MYGDONIA):
—THESSALONIKE: **(3)** ii-iii AD *IG* X (2) (1) 466 (*Σκρει[βω]νεία Εὐωδία*: m. *Φ. Σατρονίλα*)

Εὐοδιανή
MACEDONIA (EDONIS):
—PHILIPPOI: **(1)** iv-v AD *AAA* 13 (1980) p. 95 (Pilhofer 114) (*Εὐω-*)

Εὔοδος
CIMMERIAN BOSPOROS:
—PHANAGOREIA: **(1)** i AD *IGUR* 567 a (f. *Ἥδυκος*)
—THEODOSIA: **(2)** iii AD *CIRB* 947 B, 7 (s. *Δημήτριος*)
MACEDONIA (BOTTIAIA):
—BEROIA: **(3)** ii-iii AD *IBer* 240 (f. *Ἄρωγος*)
MACEDONIA (MYGDONIA):
—THESSALONIKE: **(4)** ii AD *IG* X (2) (1) 110; cf. *BCH* 98 (1974) p. 532 (*Ἰούλ. Ἐ.*); **(5)** ~ *IG* X (2) (1) 312 (f. *Σεκοῦνδος, Μυρῶσα*); **(6)** ii/iii AD *SEG* XXXIX 636; cf. XLIII 464 (*M. Οὐαρείνιος Ἐ.*); **(7)** 249 AD *IG* X (2) (1) 542 (*M. Φούριος Ἐ.*: s. *M. Φούριος Νίκων*)
SCYTHIA MINOR:
—ISTROS: **(8)** 138 AD *ISM* I 193 II, 70 (s. *Θεόπομπος*)
—TOMIS: **(9)** ii-iii AD ib. II 468, 2

Εὐπάλαμος
TAURIS:
—CHERSONESOS: **(1)** iii BC Kats p. 114 no. 120 (amph.) (*[Εὐπ]άλαμος*?: f. *Ὕμνος*)

Εὐπαλῖνος
THRACE:
—BYZANTION: **(1)** iii BC *IByz* 62 (Firatlı-Robert p. 49 no. 13) (s. *Δίων*)

Εὐπατρία
MACEDONIA (PAIONIA):
—NEGOTINO (MOD.): **(1)** ii-iii AD *Sp.* 98 (1941-8) p. 56 no. 114, 10 (*Αὐρ. Ἐ.*)

Εὐπάτριος
MACEDONIA (PAIONIA):
—NEGOTINO (MOD.): **(1)** ii-iii AD ib. l. 8

Εὐπάτωρ
CIMMERIAN BOSPOROS:
—BOSPOROS: **(1)** c. 125-173 AD *RE* s.v. Iulius (218); *PIR*² I 300; cf. *SEG* XXXIX 696; Frolova, *CKB A.D. 69-238* pp. 38-9 (*Τιβ. Ἰούλ. Ἐ.*: king)

Εὐπείθης
THRACE:
—ABDERA: **(1)** s. iv BC *IThrakAig* E41 (f. *Ἀρχέστρατος*)

Εὔπλοκος
MACEDONIA (PELAGONIA): **(1)** ii-iii AD *IG* X (2) (2) 257, 1 (*Ὠφελίων Εὔ<συ>πλοκος—IG*)

Εὔπλους
MACEDONIA (DERRIOPOS):
—STUBERRA: **(1)** 116 AD ib. 327, 21 (*Φ. Ἐ.*)
MACEDONIA (MYGDONIA):
—THESSALONIKE: **(2)** s. ii AD ib. X (2) (1) 244 I, 21 (*Κλ. Ἐ.*)
SKYTHIA:
—OLBIA-BORYSTHENES: **(3)** ii AD *IOlbia* 82; *IOSPE* I² 90; 100, 6; 175, 8 (*Εὔ[πλους]*—90: s. *Καλανδίων*); **(4)** ii/iii AD *IOlbia* 52, 6 (I f. *Εὔπλους* II); **(5)** ~ ib. l. 6 (II s. *Εὔπλους* I); **(6)** iii AD *IOSPE* I² 98, 11 (s. *Σώμαχος*)

Εὐπόλεμος
CIMMERIAN BOSPOROS:
—BOSPOROS: **(1)** ii BC *IG* II² 8427 (*FRA* 1369) (f. *Ἡδεῖα*)
—GORGIPPIA: **(2)** f. iii BC *CIRB* 1137 A I, 13 (f. *Διονύσιος*)
MACEDONIA: **(3)** iv/iii BC *RE* (8); Robert, *Coll. Froehner* 52, 10 etc. with comm.; *Iasos* 32, 5; *Labraunda* III (2) 42, 1; Akarca pp. 101-2 (coin) (Tataki, *Macedonians* p. 314 no. 49); cf. *REA* 100 (1998) pp. 167-90 (s. *Πώταλος*); **(4)** 313 BC D.S. xix 77. 6; *SEG* XXX 325. 2, 2
MACEDONIA (BOTTIAIA):
—KYRRHOS: **(5)** hell. *IG* II² 9141 (Tataki, *Macedonians* p. 117 no. 6; *FRA* 3158) (f. *Νουμήνιος*)
—MIEZA: **(6)** iii BC *SEG* XXIV 524 I, 19; 514 II, 5? + Hatzopoulos, *MI* 2 p. 106 no. 92 (*[Εὐ]πόλεμος*?—l.19, *Εὐπόλ[εμος]*?—l.5: s. *Σταρτ—*)
MACEDONIA (DERRIOPOS):
—STUBERRA: **(7)** c. 41-48 AD *IG* X (2) (2) 323, 19 (f. *Θεοδίας*)
MACEDONIA (EDONIS):
—PHILIPPOI: **(8)** s. iii BC ib. VII 2433 II, 14 (Tataki, *Macedonians* p. 164 no. 14) (s. *Μενέδημος*)
SCYTHIA MINOR:
—ISTROS: **(9)** f. ii BC *ISM* I 26, 4 (s. *Κλεομέδων*)
—KALLATIS: **(10)** iii-ii BC ib. III 163 (*Εὐπόλεμ[ος]*: s. *Ἡρόδοτος*)
THRACE:
—ODESSOS: **(11)** 13 BC *IGB* I² 46, 34 (s. *Ἄττης*)
—PERINTHOS-HERAKLEIA: **(12)** iv-iii BC *IPerinth* 4, 1 (*Εὐπόλ[εμος]*: s. *—κλείδης*)

Εὔπολις
CIMMERIAN BOSPOROS:
—GORGIPPIA: **(1)** f. iii BC *CIRB* 1137 A I, 22; 1137 A II, 18 (f. *Σάτυρος*)
SCYTHIA MINOR:
—ISTROS?: **(2)** iii BC *ISM* I 65, 4 (s. *Φιλόμηλος*)
SKYTHIA:
—OLBIA-BORYSTHENES: **(3)** iv BC *MIA* 50 (1956) p. 63 (vase-stamp); **(4)** iii BC Dubois, *IGDOlbia* 109, 2 (*SEG* XXXVII 673) (*Εὔπο[λ]ις*); **(5)** ?ii-i BC Dubois, *IGDOlbia* 110, 1

THRACE:
—MARONEIA: **(6)** c. 365-336 BC Schönert-Geiss, *Maroneia* 460-3; 535 (coin) (*Εὐπόλιος* (gen.), *Εὐμόλιος* (gen.)—535 ed.)

Εὐπορία
CIMMERIAN BOSPOROS:
—BOSPOROS: **(1)** iii BC *IG* II^2 8426 (*FRA* 1370) (d. *Ἀνδρικός*)
—PANTIKAPAION: **(2)** iii BC *CIRB* 244 (d. *Ἀγάθων*, *Ἰωνίη*)
MACEDONIA (BOTTIAIA):
—BEROIA: **(3)** ii AD *IBer* 336 (Tataki 486)
—EDESSA: **(4)** s. ii BC *SEG* XXVIII 678 (Tataki, *Edessa* 103; Tataki, *Macedonians* p. 103 no. 7) (d. *Ῥόδων*); **(5)** iii AD *Makedonika* 15 (1975) p. 203 (Tataki, *Edessa* 102) (d. *Παράμονος*, m. *Κράτων*)
—PELLA: **(6)** 150 AD *SEG* XLVIII 825 (d. *Εὔνυμφος*, *Πίστη*)
—SKYDRA: **(7)** iii AD Dimitsas 126, 3 (*Οὐλπ.* *Ἐ.*)
MACEDONIA (EDONIS):
—AMPHIPOLIS (NR.): **(8)** ii AD *IG* X (2) (1) 864; cf. *BE* 1959, no. 338; Robert, *OMS* 5 p. 269 n. 11 (*Αὐφωνία* *Ἐ.*: m. *Γ. Αὐφούστιος Πριμιγένης*, *Γ. Αὐφούστιος Μαννεῖος*)
MACEDONIA (MYGDONIA):
—THESSALONIKE: **(9)** 141 AD *IG* X (2) (1) 448
—THESSALONIKE*: **(10)** i AD ib. 878 (biling.) (Lat. Agilleia Euporia: freed.)
SCYTHIA MINOR:
—KALLATIS?: **(11)** imp.? *ISmyrna* 147 ([*Ε*]*ὐπορία*)
THRACE: **(12)** i BC *IG* II^2 8910 (*FRA* 2529)

Εὔπορος
MACEDONIA:
—KELLION: **(1)** imp. *Athena* 25 (1913) p. 410 no. 54 (*SEG* XLIX 772); Kanatsoulis 491 (*Φ*(*λ*). *Ἐ. Βέβαιος*: sculptor)
MACEDONIA (BOTTIAIA):
—BEROIA: **(2)** i-ii AD *IBer* 339 ([*Εὔ*]*πορος*: s. *Ἀμμία*, ?f. *Γ. Σκίρτιος Ἀγάθων*); **(3)** s. ii AD ib. 266 (Tataki 488); **(4)** 177 AD *IBer* 135 A, 20 (Tataki 1313) (*Φλαούϊος* *Ἐ.*); **(5)** 216 AD *SEG* XXXVII 540, 2 (*Αὐρ. Εὔπ*[*ορος*]?)
MACEDONIA (EDONIS):
—PHILIPPOI (TERRIT.): **(6)** ?iii AD Pikoulas, *Chora* p. 149 no. 59, 14 (Pilhofer 602; *SEG* L 618); cf. *BE* 1944, no. 129
MACEDONIA (ELIMEIA): **(7)** m. ii AD *EAM* 50 (*Λ. Κάνειος* *Ἐ.*)
MACEDONIA (LOWER PAIONIA):
—EUROPOS: **(8)** ?ii AD *SEG* XXXVIII 613
MACEDONIA (MYGDONIA):
—KALINDOIA: **(9)** 68-98 AD ib. XLII 580, 77 (f. *Ἔρως*)
—THESSALONIKE: **(10)** ii AD *IG* X (2) (1) 241 B, 2-3 (*Εὔπορο*[*ς*]: f. *Διοσκουρίδης*, *Θεόφιλος*); **(11)** ii-iii AD ib. 665, 2 (*SEG* XLIII 460) (*M. Κάσειος Εὔπωρος*: s. *Ἑρμῆς*, *Βασίλεια*); **(12)** ?ii-iii AD ib. XXX 639; **(13)** ii-iii AD ib. XLV 815 (*T. Φλ.* *Ἐ.*); **(14)** s. ii AD *IG* X (2) (1) 245 II, 3; **(15)** ?iv-v AD *Tekmeria* 7 (2002) pp. 86-9 no. 1
—THESSALONIKE?: **(16)** s. ii AD *IG* X (2) (1) 904; *JDAI* 84 (1969) p. 154 no. R20 (date) (f. *Ἀπολλώνιος*)
MACEDONIA (PELAGONIA): **(17)** ii-iii AD *IG* X (2) (2) 258 (threptos)
—DOSTONEIS: **(18)** iii AD ib. 201, 5 (f. *Λυσίμαχος*, *Νεστόριος*)
SKYTHIA:
—TANAIS: **(19)** 104 AD *CIRB* 1259, 11 (s. *Μακάριος*)

Εὐπορώ
MACEDONIA (BOTTIAIA):
—BEROIA: **(1)** ii AD *IBer* 301, 1 (Tataki 262) (*Πο.* *Ἐ.*: m. *Εὐτύχα*)

Εὐποσία
MACEDONIA (MYGDONIA):
—THESSALONIKE?: **(1)** ii-iii AD *AEpThess* p. 6 no. 4 (*Οὐαρινία* *Ἐ.*)

Εὔπραξις
MACEDONIA (EDONIS):
—AMPHIPOLIS: **(1)** iii BC *AD* 23 (1968) Chron. p. 358 with pl. 305 *α*
—AMPHIPOLIS*: **(2)** ?ii AD Dimitsas 905 (freed.)

Εὐπρέπης
MACEDONIA (BOTTIAIA):
—BEROIA: **(1)** ii-iii AD *IBer* 340 (Tataki 489)
MACEDONIA (MYGDONIA):
—THESSALONIKE: **(2)** iv-vi AD Feissel, *RICM* 112 (mosaic) (*Εὐπρέπη* (voc.))
MACEDONIA (PIERIA):
—DION: **(3)** ii-iii AD Oikonomos 41
SCYTHIA MINOR:
—KALLATIS: **(4)** 241-244 AD *ISM* III 74 A, 26 (f. *Ἀρίστων*)
SKYTHIA:
—TANAIS: **(5)** 225 AD *CIRB* 1279, 4 (s. *Σύμφορος*)

Εὐπρέπιος
CIMMERIAN BOSPOROS:
—HERMONASSA: **(1)** i AD ib. 1077; cf. KW pl. 42 no. 609 (*Ε*[*ὐπρ*]*έπιος*?: f. *.ασος*)
—PANTIKAPAION: **(2)** iv AD *ZOOID* 31 (1913) p. 66 no. 142 a

Εὐπρόσοδος
THRACE:
—ODESSOS: **(1)** c. 225-200 BC Price, *Alexander* 1174; *SNG Stancomb* 252 (coin) (*Εὐπρό*(*σοδος*)?); **(2)** 221 AD *IGB* I^2 47 bis c, 32 (*Αὐρ.* *Ἐ.*: s. *Φιλῖνος*)

Εὐπ-οίητος?
MACEDONIA: **(1)** iii BC *HE* 3344 with n. (Tataki, *Macedonians* p. 315 no. 51) (*Αἰπιόρητος*—P and Russu: f. *Νικάνωρ*, *Φίλα*)

Εὐρέας
MACEDONIA (PIERIA):
—PYDNA (TERRIT.): **(1)** iii BC *Klio* 52 (1970) p. 61 no. 13 (f. *Ἀμμένα*)

Εὕρετος
THRACE:
—ANCHIALOS: **(1)** c. 180 AD *CIL* VI 32628, 10 (Lat. M. Aurel. Heuretus)

Εὑρήμων
CIMMERIAN BOSPOROS:
—PANTIKAPAION: **(1)** i/ii AD *CIRB* 80, 5; cf. KW pl. 33 no. 454; **(2)** s. ii AD *CIRB* 79 B; **(3)** iii AD ib. 102, 3 (*Εὑρ*[*ήμων*]?)
SKYTHIA:
—OLBIA-BORYSTHENES: **(4)** iii BC *IOSPE* I^2 201 I, 29 (s. *Τιμησίθεος*); **(5)** ~ ib. l. 59 (f. *Ἀριστοκλῆς*)
—TANAIS: **(6)** f. ii AD *CIRB* 1266, 12 (s. *Κόδρος*); **(7)** 228 AD ib. 1282, 33 (f. *—υς*—Vinogradov)

Εὐρησίβιος
SKYTHIA:
—OLBIA-BORYSTHENES: **(1)** c. 400-375 BC Dubois, *IGDOlbia* 8; 9; [10]? (s. *Συρίσκος*); **(2)** iv BC Tolstoi 50 (vase) ([*Εὑρη*]*σίβιος*); **(3)** ~ *IOSPE* I^2 209 (f. *Ἀρτέμων*); **(4)** f. iv BC Dubois, *IGDOlbia* 12 (vase) (her.?); **(5)** iv/iii BC *IOlbia* 71 I, 4 (Dubois, *IGDOlbia* 11) ([*Εὐ*]*ρησίβιος*: s. *Λεωκράτης*); **(6)** ~ *IOlbia* 71 II, 7 (Dubois, *IGDOlbia* 11) (s. *Ἐ*—); **(7)** iii BC *IOSPE* I^2 201 I, 1 (s. *Λεωκράτης*); **(8)** ~ ib. l. 45 (s. *Πανδίων*); **(9)** ~ ib. 201 II, 30 (*Εὑρη*[*σίβιος*]); **(10)** ~ ib. l. 31 (s. *Δη*—); **(11)** iii/ii BC ib. 187 (s. *Δημήτριος*); **(12)** i BC *SNG BM Black Sea* 685 (coin) (*Εὑρη*(*σίβιος*)?, *Εὑρή*(*μων*)?); **(13)** i BC-i AD *IOSPE* I^2 221; *SEG* XXXVI 720 (s. *Καλλισθένης*); **(14)** imp. *IOSPE* I^2 151, 1 (*Εὑρη*[*σίβιος*]?); **(15)** i/ii AD *IOlbia* 90, 2 (s. *Ἀναξιμένης*); **(16)** ~ *IOSPE* I^2 39, 1; 106, 6; 175, 4 (f. *Ὀμψάλακος*); **(17)** ii AD *IOlbia* 80, 7 (*Εὑρ*(*η*)*σίβιος*: f. *Ζήνων*); **(18)** ~ *IOSPE* I^2 83, 4 (f. *Ἀρσηούαχος*); **(19)** ~ ib. 101, 5 (s. *Ἀμωρόμαρος*); **(20)** ~ ib. 105, 3 (f. *Σωκράτης*) ?= (*26*); **(21)** ~ ib. 130, 8, 18 (*Εὑρησ*[*ίβ*]*ιος*: s. *Ἀδόης*); **(22)** ~ ib. l. 10; 155 (f. *Ἀμωρόμαρος*); **(23)** ~ ib. 131, 4; 134, 7 (s. *Στράτων*); **(24)** ~ ib. 131, 10 (f. *Ἀναξιμένης*); **(25)** ii-iii AD ib. 138, 5 (f. *Ἔρως*); **(26)** s. ii AD *SEG* XLIII 507, 3 (f. *—ατης*) ?= (*20*)
THRACE:
—APOLLONIA-SOZOPOLIS: **(27)** iv BC *BMN-Burgas* 4 (2002) p. 120 no. 4 (f. *Λυκεῖς*)

Εὑρήσιππος
THRACE:
—ABDERA: **(1)** c. 336-311 BC May, *Abdera* p. 292 nos. 541-2 (coin); Masson, *OGS* p. 430

Εὐρίας
MACEDONIA (BOTTIAIA):
—TYRISSA? (ASVESTARI (MOD.)): **(1)** f. ii BC *SEG* XLVII 999, 23 (*Εὐρ*[*ε*]*ίας*—ed.)

Εὐριπίδης
MACEDONIA (CHALKIDIKE):
—POTIDAIA-KASSANDREIA: **(1)** m. iii BC *Thess. Mnem.* 71 (Tataki, *Macedonians* p. 89 no. 37) (-*ρει*-: f. *Ἑκαταῖος*)

Εὐροψάτιος
CIMMERIAN BOSPOROS:
—THEODOSIA: **(1)** iii AD *CIRB* 947 A, 12 (s. *Χαρίτων*)

Εὐρύαλος
CIMMERIAN BOSPOROS:
—PANTIKAPAION: **(1)** c. 390-380 BC *SEG* L 710 A (vase) (fict.?)

Εὐρύδαμος
TAURIS:
—CHERSONESOS: **(1)** iii BC Kats p. 111 no. 104 (amph.) (f. *Σιμαῖος*); **(2)** s. iii BC ib. p. 84 no. 5 (amph.) (f. *Ἀθανόδωρος*); **(3)** c. 210-200 BC Anokhin p. 143 nos. 134-5; 140 (coins); **(4)** i BC-i AD *IOSPE* I^2 589 ([*Εὐ*]*δαμος*—ed., [*Εὐρ*]*ύδαμος*—Saprykin: s. *Ἀθλίων*); **(5)** ii-iii AD *SEG* XXXVII 658 (s. *Δαμοκλῆς*); **(6)** f. ii AD Solomonik, *NEPKh* III, 2, 5 ?= (*7*); **(7)** c. 120-130 AD ib. 112, 11 (*Φλ. Εὐρύδα*[*μος*]) ?= (*6*); **(8)** 129 AD *IOSPE* I^2 359, 24 (s. *Διοσκουρίδης*); **(9)** 174 AD *SEG* XLV 985 A, 38 (f. *Ἀττίνας*); **(10)** ~ ib. l. 39 (s. *Διογένης*)

Εὐρυδίκα
MACEDONIA: **(1)** c. 340-317 BC *RE* (13); Berve 23; cf. Beloch, *GG* III (2) pp. 67-9 (*Ἀδέα ὕστερον* *Ἐ.*: d. *Ἀμύντας*, *Κυννάνη*); **(2)** c. 340-275 BC *RE* (16); Berve 321 (*PP* 14509); cf. Beloch, *GG* IV (2) pp. 178-9 (d. *Ἀντίπατρος*, m. *Πτολεμαῖος Κεραυνός*, *Μελέαγρος*, *Πτολεμαῖς*, *Λυσάνδρα*)
MACEDONIA (LYNKESTIS): **(3)** c. 410-340 BC *RE* (14); *SEG* XXXVI 651; XLIII 471; L 649; *Ancient Macedonia* 5 p. 1356; *Mél. Grégoire* p. 625 f.; cf. *BE* 1984, no. 249; *SEG* XXXVIII 720 (date); *AA* 2000, pp. 392-403 (Tataki, *Macedonians* p. 315 no. 52) (d. *Σίρρας*, m. *Ἀλέξανδρος* II, *Περδίκκας* III, *Φίλιππος* II, *Εὐρυνόα*: queen)

Εὐρυδίκη
MACEDONIA (BOTTIAIA):
—BEROIA: **(1)** ii-i BC *IBer* 182 (Tataki 491) (d. *Βιλοίτας*); **(2)** ?171 AD *ILeukopetra* 9, 2 (-*ρο*-: d. *Βίθυς*); **(3)** 234 AD ib. 82, 1 (*Στατιανὴ* *Ἐ.*); **(4)** 309 or 311 AD ib. 116, 8 (Tataki 490)

——Blaganoi*: **(5)** 216 AD *SEG* XXXVII 592 (Tataki 696) (*Κλ. Εὐριδίκη*: m. *Κλ. Κοπρύλος*)
—ICHNAI: **(6)** hell.? *IG* II^2 8944 (Tataki, *Macedonians* p. 113 no. 6; *FRA* 2639) (d. *Δάδας*)
—PELLA?: **(7)** iv/iii BC *RE* (18) (d. *Λυσίμαχος*, ?d. *Νικαία*)
—SKYDRA: **(8)** ?iii AD *SEG* II 396; cf. Robert, *Hell.* I pp. 70-1 (-*ρο*-: m. *Αὐρ. Φιλιππάριον*)
MACEDONIA (EDONIS):
—AMPHIPOLIS: **(9)** iii-ii BC *PAE* 1984, p. 35 with pl. 40 α ([*Ε*]*ὐρυδίκ*[*η*]?)
MACEDONIA (LOWER PAIONIA):
—IDOMENE?: **(10)** ii/iii AD Sokolovska, *Isar-Marvinci* p. 130 (*Κ. 'Ε.*)
MACEDONIA (MYGDONIA):
—CHARAKOMA?: **(11)** ?ii AD *SEG* XXIX 580 (d. *Ἀνδροσθένης*, m. *Ἀνδροσθένης*)
—THESSALONIKE: **(12)** ii AD *IG* X (2) (1) 501; cf. *BCH* 97 (1973) p. 591
MACEDONIA (PIERIA):
—DION: **(13)** ii AD Oikonomos 43 (*Αὐΐα 'Ε.*: m. *Αὐϊανὸς Ὀπιμιανός*)
—PYDNA: **(14)** ii-iii AD Dimitsas 156 (*Εὐρι-δί*[*κη*]: d. —*οτος*, —*νίκη*)

Εὐρυδικιανός
MACEDONIA (ORESTIS):
—ROKASTRO (MOD.): **(1)** iii AD *SEG* XLIX 791 (*Αὐρ. Εὐρυδικιανὸς Ζώσιμος*)

Εὐρύδικος
MACEDONIA:
—MEGARA: **(1)** hell. ib. XLVI 691 (pithos) (f. *Φίλιππος*)
MACEDONIA (BOTTIAIA):
—BEROIA: **(2)** m. iii AD *IBer* 101, 10; *EAM* 38 (Tataki 415) (*Δομίτιος 'Ε.*)

Εὐρύλοχος
MACEDONIA: **(1)** ?417-413 BC *IG* I^3 89, 62 (Tataki, *Macedonians* p. 316 no. 56) (s. *Bo......* (gen.)); **(2)** 346-336 BC *RE* (6); Berve 323; *CID* II 36 I, 23 (Tataki, *Macedonians* p. 315 no. 54); **(3)** 327 BC *RE* Supplbd. 4 (5a); Berve 322 (Tataki, *Macedonians* p. 316 no. 55) (s. *Ἀρσαῖος*); **(4)** c. 235-200 BC La'da E1744 (f. *Δαβρέας*)
MACEDONIA (BOTTIAIA):
—AIGAI: **(5)** 324 BC Berve 324 (Tataki, *Macedonians* p. 40 no. 8); **(6)** iii BC *SEG* II 394 (s. *Μένανδρος*)
MACEDONIA (CHALKIDIKE):
—POTIDAIA-KASSANDREIA: **(7)** iv/iii BC D.L. ii 127
MACEDONIA (EDONIS):
—AMPHIPOLIS: **(8)** iv BC *SEG* XXIV 587 (s. *Ἰσοκράτης*)
—AMPHIPOLIS?: **(9)** ii-i BC *BCH* 55 (1931) p. 191 no. 12 (f. *Πευκέστης*)
MACEDONIA (PIERIA):
—DION: **(10)** c. 180 BC *SEG* XLVIII 785, 2
THRACE:
—ABDERA: **(11)** 360 BC *IG* IV (1)^2 94 b, 28 (Perlman, *City and Sanctuary* E.1 with pp. 69-70 (date))

Εὐρύμαχος
THRACE:
—PERINTHOS-HERAKLEIA:
——(Kastaleis): **(1)** iii-ii BC *IPerinth* 61, 59 (f. *Ἀρίστανδρος*)

Εὐρυμέδων
MACEDONIA (BOTTIAIA):
—BEROIA: **(1)** ii/iii AD *IBer* 27 A, 21 (f. *Χρήσιμος*)
—MIEZA: **(2)** hell.-imp. *AD* 22 (1967) Chron. p. 412 (f. *Μελάνθιος*)

Εὐρυνόα
MACEDONIA: **(1)** f. iv BC Just. vii 4. 5 + Hoffmann, *Makedonen* p. 218 (Tataki, *Macedonians* p. 316 no. 57) (Lat. Euryone—mss., Eurynoe—edd.: d. *Ἀμύντας* III, *Εὐρυδίκα*)
MACEDONIA (BOTTIAIA):
—EDESSA: **(2)** f. ii BC *SEG* XLIII 388, 1 (Tataki, *Edessa* 105) (d. *Ἀριστοκλείδης*)

Εὐρύνομος
THRACE:
—MARONEIA: **(1)** iii AD *IThrakAig* E218 (*Εὐρύνομ*[*ος*]: f. *Δεινίας*)

Εὐρύστρατος
THRACE:
—APOLLONIA-SOZOPOLIS: **(1)** iii/ii BC *IGB* I^2 469 bis, 1 with pl. ([*Εὐ*]*ρύστρατος*)

Εὐρύτιος
MACEDONIA (MYGDONIA):
—KALINDOIA: **(1)** c. 325-324 BC Hatzopoulos, *MI* 2 p. 84 no. 62, 20-1 (f. *Κράτιππος*, *Γῦλις*)

Εὔρυτος
CIMMERIAN BOSPOROS:
—GORGIPPIA: **(1)** f. iii BC *CIRB* 1137 A I, 56 (s. *Κρατῖνος*); **(2)** ~ ib. 1137 A II, 37 (I f. *Εὔρυτος* II); **(3)** ~ ib. l. 37 (II s. *Εὔρυτος* I); **(4)** ~ ib. 1137 B II, 25 (f. *Ἑκαταῖος*)

Εὐρυφύλη?
MACEDONIA (BOTTIAIA):
—PELLA: **(1)** s. iv BC *SEG* XLIX 756 (d. *Νικάδας*)

Εὐρυφῶν
THRACE:
—DUROSTORUM (TERRIT.)?: **(1)** imp. *IGB* II 870 ([*Εὐ*]*ρυφῶν*: s. *Ἀγαθοκλῆς*)

Εὐρώπη
MACEDONIA: **(1)** 336 BC *RE* Supplbd. 3 (-); Berve 326 (Tataki, *Macedonians* p. 316 no. 58) (d. *Φίλιππος* II, *Κλεοπάτρα*)
MACEDONIA (LYNKESTIS):
—HERAKLEIA?: **(2)** i-ii AD *IG* X (2) (2) 121 (freed.)
MACEDONIA (MYGDONIA):
—THESSALONIKE: **(3)** 167 AD ib. X (2) (1) 527 (*Οὐλπ. 'Ε.*)

Εὐσέβεια
MACEDONIA (MYGDONIA):
—THESSALONIKE: **(1)** iii/iv AD ib. 591 B, 2 (*Εὐσέβει*(*α*)); **(2)** b. 361 AD *PLRE* I (-); *RE* (1) (*Φλ. Εὐσέβια*: ?d. *Φλ. Εὐσέβιος*)
MACEDONIA (PAIONIA):
—STOBOI: **(3)** v-vi AD Unp. (Stobi excav.) inv. I-70-46 (*Εὐ*[*σέ*]*βια*)
THRACE:
—BISANTHE-PANION: **(4)** iv-vi AD *AD* 49-50 (1994-5) Mel. p. 317 no. 143 ([*Εὐ*]*σέβια*)

Εὐσέβης
PENESTAI?: **(1)** c. 200 AD *SEG* XXXIX 593, 1 (f. —*α*)
SCYTHIA MINOR:
—KALLATIS: **(2)** 241-244 AD *ISM* III 74 A, 21 (I f. *Εὐσέβης* II); **(3)** ~ ib. l. 21 (II s. *Εὐσέβης* I)

Εὐσέβιον
MACEDONIA (BOTTIAIA):
—EDESSA: **(1)** iii AD Feissel, *RICM* 11 (Tataki, *Edessa* 106) (m. *Βραγάντις*)

Εὐσέβιος
CIMMERIAN BOSPOROS:
—PANTIKAPAION: **(1)** 438 AD Latyshev, *Sbornik* 86 (*SEG* XLVIII 992)
MACEDONIA (MYGDONIA):
—THESSALONIKE: **(2)** v-vi AD ib. XLV 821 (mosaic)
—THESSALONIKE?: **(3)** f. iv AD *PLRE* I (39); *RE* (2) (*Φλ. 'Ε.*: I ?f. *Φλ. Εὐσέβιος* II, *Φλ. Ὑπάτιος*, *Φλ. Εὐσέβεια*); **(4)** c. 359 AD *PLRE* I (40) (*Φλ. 'Ε.*: II ?s. *Φλ. Εὐσέβιος* I)
TAURIS:
—CHERSONESOS: **(5)** ii AD *IOSPE* I^2 582, 2 (*Εὐσέ*[*βιος*]?: f. *Θεαγένης*)
THRACE:
—MARONEIA: **(6)** iii AD *IThrakAig* E396, 12 (f. *Αὐρ. Εὐχάρεια*)
—ODESSOS: **(7)** ii AD *IGB* I^2 136 ([*Εὐ*]*σέβιο*[*ς*]?)
—ŠUMEN (MOD.): **(8)** iv-vi AD *BIAB* 4 (1926-7) p. 106 (Lat. Eusebius)

Εὐσθένης
SCYTHIA MINOR:
—ISTROS: **(1)** iv BC *ISM* I 171 (*CEG* II 882) (f. *Μενέχαρμος*)
SKYTHIA:
—OLBIA-BORYSTHENES: **(2)** f. iv BC Dubois, *IGDOlbia* 104 (s. *Πρωτογένης*)

Εὐσταθία
MACEDONIA (EDONIS):
—AMPHIPOLIS: **(1)** iii AD *Anal. Boll.* 31 (1912) p. 169 (d. *Λαμπάδιος*, m. *Μώκιος*)
SKYTHIA:
—OLBIA-BORYSTHENES: **(2)** ii-iii AD *IOlbia* 172 ([*Εὐ*]*σταθία*)
THRACE:
—ODESSOS?: **(3)** vi AD Beševliev 100, 2 (or Thrace Hadrianopolis?: d. *Γλαυκώπιος*)

Εὐστάθιος
MACEDONIA (EDONIS):
—PHILIPPOI: **(1)** iv-v AD Feissel, *RICM* 239 (monogram) (Pilhofer 106) (*Εὐστά*(*θιος*)?)
MACEDONIA (MYGDONIA):
—THESSALONIKE: **(2)** ii/iii AD *IG* X (2) (1) 355, 2
MACEDONIA (PAIONIA):
—STOBOI: **(3)** s. iv AD *Arch. Iug.* 22-3 (1982-3) p. 59 no. 8 (mosaic) (bp.); **(4)** vi AD *Antička bronza u Jugoslaviji* p. 158 no. 343 (stamp); cf. *BE* 1972, no. 256 c (Jew)
SCYTHIA MINOR:
—ISTROS: **(5)** v-vi AD *SEG* XLIV 625-626 (vases)
—KALLATIS: **(6)** vi AD Barnea 49 (Popescu, *IGL* 88)
TAURIS:
—CHERSONESOS (TERRIT.): **(7)** m. iv AD *VDI* 1998 (1), p. 212 (amph.) (*Εὐστά*(*θιος*)?)
THRACE:
—BYZANTION: **(8)** c. 303 AD *Anal. Boll.* 31 (1912) p. 192
—LJUTIBROD (MOD.): **(9)** iii-iv AD *IGB* V 5170

Εὔστομος
THRACE:
—SECURISCA: **(1)** s. ii AD *ILB* 135 (Lat. M. Ulpius Eustomus: s. M. Ulpius Fructus)

Εὐστοργία
MACEDONIA (MYGDONIA):
—THESSALONIKE: **(1)** iv AD Feissel, *RICM* 124 ([*Αὐρ*]*ηλ*[*ία*] *'Ε.*)

Εὐστόργιος
MACEDONIA (MYGDONIA):
—THESSALONIKE: **(1)** v-vi AD ib. 181, 3 (*SEG* XLVII 1011) (f. *Φλαβία*)

Εὐστόχιος
THRACE:
—PHILIPPOPOLIS-TRIMONTIUM: **(1)** 225-250 AD ib. III 542 (ring) ?= (*2*)
—PHILIPPOPOLIS-TRIMONTIUM (TERRIT.): **(2)** ii AD *IGB* III 1449; 1537; V 5591 (*'Ε. Κέλερ*: s. *Ἀσκληπιάδης*) ?= (*1*)

Εὐστράτιος
THRACE:
—RHAIDESTOS*: **(1)** iv-vi AD Dumont–Homolle 76z 2 (seal)

Εὐσχήμων
Macedonia (Mygdonia):
—thessalonike: **(1)** ii ad *IG* x (2) (1) 241 A II, 10
Scythia Minor:
—tomis: **(2)** ii-iii ad *ISM* ii 32, 9 (*Εὐσχή[μω]ν*: s. *Φιλουμενός*)
Skythia:
—tanais: **(3)** 209 ad *CIRB* 1276, 2 (*Εὐσχή[μ]ων*: s. *M*—) ?= (*4*); **(4)** c. 220-230 ad ib. 1282, 6; 1286, 6 (s. *Μηνόφιλος*) ?= (*3*)

Εὔτακτος
Macedonia (Mygdonia):
—thessalonike: **(1)** ii-iii ad *IG* x (2) (1) 504 (*Λ. Σέξτιος Ἐ.*: f. *Σεξτία Μάξιμα*)
Macedonia (Orestis):
—sisani (mod.): **(2)** 146 ad *EAM* 187, 17 (f. *Ὑψίγονος*)

Εὐταξία
Sarmatia:
—maiotai: **(1)** 153-144 bc *SGDI* 2165, 5, 8, 13 etc. (m. *Παρνάσσιος*: slave/freed.)
Thrace:
—byzantion: **(2)** ii bc *IByz* 71 (Fıratlı–Robert p. 50 no. 16) (d. *Σύρος*)

Εὐτέρπη
Thrace:
—bisanthe-panion: **(1)** ii-iii ad Dumont–Homolle 83i (m. *Δαμᾶς*, *Ἀσκληπιοδότη*)

Εὔτιμος
Cimmerian Bosporos:
—gorgippia: **(1)** f. iii bc *CIRB* 1137 A I, 16 (f. *Ἱπποκράτης*) ?= (*2*); **(2)** ~ ib. l. 19 (f. *Νυμφόδωρος*) ?= (*1*)

Εὐτόκιος
Thrace: **(1)** iv/v ad Eun., *Hist.* fr. 106 (*Suda E* 3770)

Εὐτράπελος
Macedonia (Bottiaia):
—beroia: **(1)** ?171 ad *ILeukopetra* 12, 1, 17 (Tataki 1314) (or Macedonia (Elimeia) Alaibeoi: *Φλαΰϊος Ἐ.*)

Εὐτροπία
Macedonia (Mygdonia):
—thessalonike: **(1)** v/vi ad *CIL* iii 14203. 39 (Lat. Eutropia)

Εὐτρόπιος
Macedonia (Bottiaia):
—beroia: **(1)** ii/iii ad *IBer* 27 A, 2 (*Εὐτρόπ[ιος]*: slave?); **(2)** v-vi ad ib. 424 (Feissel, *RICM* 65)
Macedonia (Mygdonia):
—thessalonike: **(3)** ?v ad *IG* x (2) (1) 331, 4 (Feissel, *RICM* 203) (Lat. Eutropi (gen.))

Εὐτρόπις
Cimmerian Bosporos:
—pantikapaion: **(1)** 339 ad *CIRB* p. 937 no. 3

Εὔτροπος
Macedonia (Mygdonia):
—thessalonike: **(1)** ?ii ad *IG* x (2) (1) 571, 4
Macedonia (Paionia):
—argos (nr.): **(2)** ii-iii ad *SEG* xvi 401, 1 (I f. *Εὔτροπος* II, *Φυλλίς*, *Ἐλπίς*, *Ὀνομάστη*, *Σαμβατίς*, *Ἀγαθᾶς*, *Τύχη*); **(3)** ~ ib. l. 4 (II s. *Εὔτροπος* I, *Ἀγάθη*)
—stoboi: **(4)** i-ii ad *Sp.* 71 (1931) p. 227 no. 600 (f. *Αἴβουτ. Κεικι*—, *Αἴβουτ. Φίλη*)

Εὐτύχα
Macedonia (Bottiaia):
—beroia: **(1)** ii ad *IBer* 301, 2 (Tataki 492) (d. *Πο. Δόναξ*, *Πο. Εὐπορώ*)

Εὐτυχᾶς
Macedonia: **(1)** 238 ad *ILeukopetra* 89, 9 (slave/freed.)
Macedonia (Bottiaia):
—beroia: **(2)** ii/iii ad *IBer* 145, 1 (Tataki 496) (*Εὐτυχᾶνος* (gen.): I f. *Εὐτυχᾶς* II); **(3)** ~ *IBer* 145, 1 (Tataki 495) (II s. *Εὐτυχᾶς* I)
—beroia?: **(4)** m. ii ad *IBer* 383, 11 (Tataki 494)

Εὐτυχάσα?
Macedonia (Lynkestis):
—herakleia (area): **(1)** ii-iii ad *IG* x (2) (2) 39

Εὐτύχη
Cimmerian Bosporos:
—bosporos?: **(1)** f. iv bc *CVA* Zurich 1 pl. 29, 12 (vase) (*Arch. Class.* 25-6 (1973-4) p. 350 no. 19); cf. *SEG* xxix 715 (*Ἐ.*—n. pr.?: ?d. *Ἰσόδημος*)

Εὐτύχης
Cimmerian Bosporos:
—pantikapaion: **(1)** iv-v ad *OAK* 1894, p. 89
—phanagoreia: **(2)** m. ii ad *SEG* xliii 512, 5 (*[Εὐ]τύχης*)
—phanagoreia?: **(3)** 335 ad *CIRB* 1112, 3
Macedonia (Bottiaia):
—beroia: **(4)** ii/iii ad *IBer* 143 A, 25 (Tataki 602) (*Ἰού. Ἐ.*)
Macedonia (Edonis):
—philippoi: **(5)** ii-iii ad *SEG* ii 425 (Pilhofer 137); **(6)** ii/iii ad *CIL* iii 633 III c, 12 (Pilhofer 165); *CRAI* 1923, p. 277 (date) (Lat. Petronius Eutyches)
—philippoi (nr.): **(7)** ?ii ad *SEG* ii 421 (Pilhofer 410) (*Ἰούλ. Ἐ.*)
Macedonia (Mygdonia):
—peristera (mod.): **(8)** iii ad *SEG* xxix 590 (f. *Ζώσιμος*, *Σύρος*)
—thessalonike: **(9)** ?ii ad *IG* x (2) (1) 534 (*Γ. Ἰούλ. Ἐ.*); **(10)** f. iii ad *SEG* xlviii 854 (f. *Σαβῖνα*)
—thessalonike?: **(11)** s. iii ad *IG* x (2) (1) 809 (*Κλ. Ἐβούδ. Ἐ.*)
Macedonia (Paionia):
—stoboi: **(12)** ?s. ii ad *JÖAI* 6 (1903) Beibl. col. 6 no. 6
Macedonia (Pieria):
—dion: **(13)** 59 ad Dimitsas 186
Scythia Minor:
—aegyssus (nr.): **(14)** ii ad *ISM* v 244, 5 (Lat. [Ul]pius Euty[ches]?)
—carsium: **(15)** f. iii ad ib. 104, 2 (Lat. Iul. Eutyches)
—tomis: **(16)** ii ad ib. ii 119 (*CCCA* vi 438) (Lat. C. Antonius Eutyches); **(17)** ii-iii ad *ISM* ii 468, 15; **(18)** 201 ad ib. 83 I, 26 (*T. Φλ. Εὐ[τύ]χης*); **(19)** ~ ib. l. 39 (*T. Φλ. Εὐτύχη[ς]*)
Skythia:
—tanais: **(20)** 225-228 ad *CIRB* 1279, 12; 1283, 14 (s. *Ἀντίμαχος*); **(21)** 228 ad ib. l. 11 (*Εὐ[τ]ύχης*: s. *Θεαγένης*)
Tauris:
—kalos limen: **(22)** ii-iii ad *SEG* xxvi 802 (Solomonik, *GChKh* p. 8 no. 7) (*Εὐτύ(χ)ης*?)
Thrace:
—dionysopolis: **(23)** iii ad *IGB* I^2 14 c, 23 (*Αὐρ. Ἐ.*: s. *Ἀσιανός*)
—hadrianopolis: **(24)** imp. *Syllogos* 27 (1900) p. 389 no. 3; **(25)** i-ii ad Taşlıklıoğlu 2 p. 44 no. 16
—kellai: **(26)** 241-244 ad *IGB* iii 1517, 48 (*Αὐρ. Ἐ.*: s. *Βάσσος*)
—nicopolis ad istrum: **(27)** iii ad ib. ii 646, 7 (*Ἰούλ. Ἐ.*)
—novae: **(28)** i-ii ad *IGLNovae* 114 (*ILB* 269) (Lat. C. Vibius Eut[y]c[hes]); **(29)** ii-iii ad *IGLNovae* 43 (Lat. Val. Eutyches)
—oescus: **(30)** ii-iii ad *ILB* 43 (Lat. L. Val. Eutyches)
—oescus*: **(31)** ii ad ib. 84 (Lat. Q. Pompeius Eutyches: freed.)
—pautalia: **(32)** ii-iii ad *IGB* iv 2084 (*Πετρώνιος Ε[ὐτύ]χης*: f. *Πετρώνιος*, *Πετρωνία*)
—perinthos-herakleia: **(33)** ii/iii ad *IPerinth* 104 (f. *M. Αὐρ. Ἀλέξανδρος*); **(34)** 196-198 ad ib. 56, 18 (s. *Ἐπίκτητος*); **(35)** iii ad ib. 131, 1 (*Αὐρ. Ἐ.*: s. *Σύμφορος*)
—philippopolis-trimontium: **(36)** ii-iii ad *IGB* iii 912, 4

Εὐτυχία
Cimmerian Bosporos:
—pantikapaion: **(1)** i-ii ad *CIRB* 603
Macedonia (Bottiaia):
—beroia: **(2)** iii ad *IBer* 275 (Tataki 498)
—skydra*: **(3)** 105 ad *SEG* xvii 317, 15 (slave?)
Macedonia (Chalkidike):
—antigoneia?: **(4)** ii-iii ad ib. xxix 571
—potidaia-kassandreia (nr.): **(5)** imp. *CIL* iii 7332 (*BCH* 103 (1979) pp. 300-2 no. 36) (Lat. Eutuchia)
Macedonia (Edonis):
—amphipolis: **(6)** hell.? *AD* 22 (1967) Chron. p. 427 (*Εὐτυχί[α]*—ed., *Εὐτυχί[ς]*?); **(7)** ?ii ad *RA* 1945, pp. 47-8 no. 1; **(8)** ii-iii ad *SEG* xxvii 252, 1 (d. *Νετειλία*)
—philippoi: **(9)** i-ii ad Collart, *Philippes* p. 414 n. 1 with pl. 68. 1 (Pilhofer 338); *CIL* iii 14206. 12, 5 (Pilhofer 407) (Lat. Marronia Eutychia)
—philippoi (territ.): **(10)** ii-iii ad Dimitsas 1054 = 1103 (Pilhofer 459)
—philippoi (drama (mod.)): **(11)** i-ii ad *CIL* iii 14206. 30 (Pilhofer 477) (Lat. –ia Eutyc[hia]?)
—philippoi (nr.): **(12)** ?i-ii ad *BCH* 57 (1933) p. 376 no. 32 (Pilhofer 420) (Lat. –onia Eutichia)
Macedonia (Eordaia):
—pyrgoi (mod.): **(13)** ii-iii ad *EAM* 129 (*[Εὐτυ]χιανῖ* (dat.), *Εὐτυχιανή*?: d. *Λυκαρίων*, *Σελήνη*)
Macedonia (Mygdonia):
—thessalonike: **(14)** ii ad *IG* x (2) (1) 456, 2 (I m. *Λούκιος*, *Διονύσιος*, *Ὑπερήφανος*, *Εὐτυχία* II); **(15)** ~ ib. l. 4 (II d. *Εὐτυχία* I); **(16)** ~ *KGAM Thess.* ii 318; **(17)** ii-iii ad *IG* x (2) (1) 381; **(18)** ii/iii ad *SEG* xl 556; **(19)** c. 303 ad Musurillo, *Acts Christian Martyrs* pp. 281 ff.
—thessalonike?: **(20)** ii ad *IG* x (2) (1) 696 (threpte); **(21)** ~ ib. 922 (m. *Ἡρακλείδης*); **(22)** s. iii ad *AEpThess* p. 10 no. 8 A (*Αὐρ. Ἐ.*: d. *Ἐφηβικός*, m. *Ἐφηβικός*)
Macedonia (Pieria):
—dion: **(23)** ii ad *Essays Laourdas* p. 109 no. 8 (d. *Ἡρακλέα*)
Thrace:
—anchialos: **(24)** 294 ad *Cod. Just.* v 71. 16; cf. *Klio* 58 (1976) p. 81 (Lat. Eutychia)
—byzantion: **(25)** ii ad *Türk Tarih Kongresi XI* (6) p. 2703 with pl. 495. 5 (m. *Ἀμφίων*, *Ζη*—)
—perinthos-herakleia: **(26)** iii ad *IPerinth* 105 (*Αὐρ. Ἐ.*: d. *Κόσμος*)
—philippopolis-trimontium: **(27)** i-ii ad *IGB* iii 989 (*Κασκ[ε]λλί(α) Ἐ.*)

Εὐτυχιανή
Macedonia (Edonis):
—philippoi: **(1)** v-vi ad Feissel, *RICM* 249 (Pilhofer 308)
Macedonia (Pieria):
—dion: **(2)** ii-iii ad Dimitsas 170
Thrace:
—beroe-augusta traiana: **(3)** c. 320-324 ad *Anal. Boll.* 31 (1912) p. 198; p. 207

—PERINTHOS-HERAKLEIA: **(4)** i-ii AD *IPerinth* 107 (*Οὐαληρία Ἐ.*)

Εὐτυχιανός

CIMMERIAN BOSPOROS:

—PANTIKAPAION (NR.): **(1)** V AD *SEG* XXVIII 642

MACEDONIA (CHALKIDIKE):

—ANTIGONEIA?: **(2)** ii-iii AD ib. XXIX 571 (*Εὐ(τ)υχιανός*)

MACEDONIA (EDONIS):

—PHILIPPOI*: **(3)** imp. *BCH* 56 (1932) p. 228 no. 20 (Pilhofer 354) (Lat. [C.] [S]emp[roni]us Fru[ctus] [Eu]tychian[us]: freed.)

MACEDONIA (ELIMEIA):

—OBLOSTAI?: **(4)** ?iii AD *EAM* 65 I b

MACEDONIA (MYGDONIA):

—THESSALONIKE: **(5)** ii AD *IG* X (2) (1) 401; **(6)** ii-iii AD ib. 518 (*Καικίνας Ἐ.*); **(7)** 243 AD ib. 161, 1 (*Ε̣ὐτυχ[ια]νός*: s. *Ἰούλ. Παράμονος*)

—THESSALONIKE (NR.): **(8)** ii-iii AD ib. 1000 (*[Εὐτυ]χιανός*)

—THESSALONIKE?: **(9)** ii AD ib. 695

MACEDONIA (ORESTIS):

—BATTYNAIOI: **(10)** 192 AD *EAM* 186 I, 50 (s. *Φίλανδρος*)

MACEDONIA (PIERIA):

—DION: **(11)** ?ii-iii AD *SEG* XXXIII 515

SCYTHIA MINOR:

—KALLATIS: **(12)** 241-244 AD *ISM* III 74 B, 27 (*Ἰούλ. Ἐ.*)

—TOMIS: **(13)** f. iii AD ib. II 273, 1 (*Αὐρ. Ἐ.*: s. *Διογένης*, f. *Αὐρ. Μουσίκις*)

SKYTHIA:

—TANAIS: **(14)** 228 AD *CIRB* 1283, 10 (s. *M*—); **(15)** ~ ib. l. 12 (s. *Γοργίας*)

THRACE:

—APOLLONIA-SOZOPOLIS: **(16)** v-vi AD Beševliev 180

—AQUAE CALIDAE*: **(17)** vi AD ib. 171, 2-3 (bp.)

—HADRIANOPOLIS (NR.): **(18)** imp. *Thrakika* 16 (1941) p. 85

—KELLAI: **(19)** ii-iii AD *IGB* III 1519; **(20)** 241-244 AD ib. 1517, 16 (*Κλ. Εὐτυχιανὸς ὁ καὶ Σιμπλίκις*)

—MARKIANOPOLIS: **(21)** ii AD ib. II 799 (*[Εὐ]τ̣υχιανός*)

—PAUTALIA: **(22)** ii-iii AD ib. IV 2072, 11 (*Εὐτυχ[ιαν]ός*)

—PAUTALIA (TERRIT.): **(23)** ii-iii AD ib. 2122 (I f. *Εὐτυχιανός* II); **(24)** ~ ib. (*[Εὐτυ]χιανός*: II s. *Εὐτυχιανός* I)

—PERINTHOS-HERAKLEIA: **(25)** iii AD *IPerinth* 174 (*Βεντίδιος Ἐ.*)

—PERINTHOS-HERAKLEIA*: **(26)** f. iii AD ib. 78 (*CIL* III 7326) (Lat. Eutychianus: freed.)

Εὐτυχίδας

MACEDONIA (MYGDONIA):

—THESSALONIKE?: **(1)** i-ii AD Mendel, *Cat.* 971 (s. *Φίλων*)

Εὐτυχίδης

CIMMERIAN BOSPOROS:

—PANTIKAPAION: **(1)** ii-iii AD *CIRB* 783, 3 (-χεί-: f. *Ἀντιγένης*); **(2)** ~ ib. l. 6 (-χεί-: s. *Ἀντιγένης*)

MACEDONIA (BOTTIAIA):

—BEROIA: **(3)** ii-i BC *IBer* 31, 3 (f. *Κρίτων*); **(4)** ii AD ib. 224 (Tataki 497) (-χεί-: f. *Διονύσις*)

—EDESSA: **(5)** v-vi AD Feissel, *RICM* 40

MACEDONIA (MYGDONIA):

—THESSALONIKE: **(6)** ii-iii AD *IG* X (2) (1) 493

MACEDONIA (PIERIA):

—PYDNA: **(7)** ?i AD Dimitsas 157 (*Κορνήλιος Ἐ.*)

THRACE:

—ODESSOS: **(8)** 221 AD *IGB* I^2 47 bis a, 20 (*Γ. Σόσσιος Ἐ.*); **(9)** ~ ib. l. 27 (f. *Αὐρ. Ἐπαμείνων*); **(10)** ~ ib. 47 bis b, 38 (f. *Αὐρ. Ἧλις*)

Εὐτύχιος

MACEDONIA (MYGDONIA):

—THESSALONIKE: **(1)** iii AD *IG* X (2) (1) 547; **(2)** s. iii AD *SEG* XLIV 556, 1 (*M. Αὐρ. Ἰακὼβ ὁ καὶ Ἐ.*: Jew); **(3)** iv AD *IG* X (2) (1) 397 (Feissel, *RICM* 123)

THRACE: **(4)** ii-iii AD *Romanizmăt* II 117 (Lat. Eutychius)

—OESCUS*: **(5)** s. i AD *ILB* 13 (Lat. Eutychius)

Εὐτύχις

MACEDONIA (BOTTIAIA):

—BEROIA: **(1)** a. 212 AD *IBer* 136, 17 (Tataki 989) (*Οὐείβ. Ἐ.*)

MACEDONIA (MYGDONIA):

—THESSALONIKE: **(2)** iii AD *IG* X (2) (1) 546, 1 (*Αὐρ. Ἀκάκις ὁ καὶ Ἐ.*: s. *Φλ. Πάκτωλος ὁ καὶ Ἀκάκιος*)

SCYTHIA MINOR:

—TOMIS*: **(3)** iii AD *ISM* II 276, 2 (*Αὐρ. Ἐ.*: freed.)

THRACE:

—SALYMBRIA: **(4)** imp. *IByz* S 10

Εὐτυχίς

MACEDONIA: **(1)** c. 223 BC *PTeb* 815 fr. 4 recto I, 24 (Tataki, *Macedonians* p. 316 no. 59; La'da E1803) (d. *Ταρρίας*)

MACEDONIA (ALMOPIA):

—NOTIA (MOD.): **(2)** ii/iii AD *SEG* XLIII 367, 8 (d. *Ἰουλία*)

MACEDONIA (BOTTIAIA):

—BEROIA: **(3)** ii-iii AD *ILeukopetra* 133, 1 (*Ἰουλ. Εὐτυ̣[χίς]*?); **(4)** c. 211-232 AD ib. 77, 1 (*Ἰουλ. Εὐτ̣[υχίς]*?)

—BEROIA (TERRIT.): **(5)** ii-iii AD *IBer* 508 (Tataki 47) (*Αἰλ. Ἐ.*)

—EDESSA: **(6)** ii AD Dimitsas 39 (Tataki, *Edessa* 248) (*Παπία Εὐτυχής*)

—MIEZA: **(7)** ?ii AD Dimitsas 19 = 292 (Tataki 499) (m. *Τι. Κλ. Ἱλαρίων*)

MACEDONIA (EDONIS):

—AMPHIPOLIS: **(8)** ?iii AD *SEG* XXVIII 539

MACEDONIA (ELIMEIA):

—KOZANI (MOD.): **(9)** ii-i BC *EAM* 46 (*Εὐτύχις*—edd.: d. *Παρμενέα*)

MACEDONIA (MYGDONIA):

—THESSALONIKE: **(10)** 71 or 188 AD *SEG* XXXI 644 = XLV 818 (*Ποντία Ἐ.*: m. *Πόντιος Πρόκλος*, *Ποντία Ἀντιγόνα*); **(11)** ii AD *IG* X (2) (1) 410, 2 (*[Ε]ὐ̣τυχίς*: m. *Παραμόνα*); **(12)** ii-iii AD ib. 563 (*Ἀννία Ἐ.*)

—THESSALONIKE?: **(13)** ii AD ib. 906 (d. *Φαῦστος*)

SCYTHIA MINOR:

—SACIDAVA*: **(14)** iv AD Popescu, *IGL* 191, 12 (Lat. E[ut]ucis)

THRACE: **(15)** ?162 BC *SGDI* 1824, 3-4 (slave/freed.); **(16)** imp. *IG* II^2 8911 (*FRA* 2530)

—ABDERA: **(17)** ii BC *IThrakAig* E54 (*Εὐτυχί[s]*)

—NICOPOLIS AD ISTRUM: **(18)** ii-iii AD *IGB* II 692 (d. *Καλπούρνιος Γάϊος ὁ καὶ Κάρπος*, *Χρήστη*)

Εὐτυχίων

MACEDONIA (BOTTIAIA):

—BEROIA: **(1)** ii-iii AD *IBer* 286 (Tataki 753) (*Κομίνιος Ἐ.*: s. *Φαῦστος*, *Νόημα*); **(2)** a. 212 AD *IBer* 136, 4 (Tataki 283) (*Αὐρ. Ἐ.*)

—EDESSA: **(3)** 180 AD *SEG* XXIV 531, 10 (Tataki, *Edessa* 110) (s. *Μακεδονικός*)

MACEDONIA (MYGDONIA):

—THESSALONIKE*: **(4)** i-ii AD *AD* 24 (1969) Chron. p. 293 no. 21 (ring)

Εὔτυχος

CIMMERIAN BOSPOROS:

—GORGIPPIA: **(1)** ii AD *CIRB* 1140, 18 (s. *Τιμο*—)

—NYMPHAION: **(2)** 105 BC *ID* 2128 (s. *Ἀπολλώνιος*, f. *Εὔβολος*)

MACEDONIA: **(3)** ?254 AD *ILeukopetra* 108, 2 (slave/freed.)

MACEDONIA (BOTTIAIA):

—BEROIA: **(4)** ii AD *IBer* 302 (Tataki 500); **(5)** ~ *IBer* 303; **(6)** ii/iii AD ib. 143 C, 12 (Tataki 603) (*Ἰού. Ἐ.*); **(7)** 238 AD *ILeukopetra* 87, 3 (*Κεκιλλιανὸς Ἐ.*)

—BEROIA (TERRIT.): **(8)** ii-iii AD *IBer* 512, 1 (Tataki 501)

MACEDONIA (CHALKIDIKE):

—POTIDAIA-KASSANDREIA?: **(9)** ii/iii AD *IG* X (2) (1) 112* (Lat. Eutychus)

MACEDONIA (DERRIOPOS):

—STUBERRA: **(10)** 90 AD ib. X (2) (2) 326, 82 (s. *Κλέαρχος*); **(11)** 116 AD ib. 327, 24 (*Ἰ. Ἐ.*); **(12)** 121 AD ib. 328, 17 (*Τ. Φλαούϊος Ἐ.*)

MACEDONIA (EDONIS):

—AMPHIPOLIS: **(13)** ii-iii AD *TAPA* 69 (1938) p. 75 no. 34

—PHILIPPOI (TERRIT.): **(14)** imp. *CIL* III 706 (Pilhofer 523); Collart, *Philippes* pl. 84. 1 (Lat. Servaeus Eutychus)

MACEDONIA (ELIMEIA):

—VELVENDOS (MOD.): **(15)** ii AD *SEG* XLVII 1001, 4 (f. *Πολεμοκράτης*); **(16)** ~ ib. l. 5 (f. *Περίτας*)

MACEDONIA (LOWER PAIONIA):

—IDOMENE?: **(17)** iii AD Sokolovska, *Isar-Marvinci* p. 130

MACEDONIA (LYNKESTIS):

—HERAKLEIA (AREA): **(18)** imp. *IG* X (2) (2) 28 (s. *Ζώσιμος*, *Κασσάνδρα*)

MACEDONIA (MYGDONIA):

—KALINDOIA: **(19)** a. 98 AD *SEG* XLII 583, 15 (s. *Τρυφωνᾶς*)

—THESSALONIKE: **(20)** ?39 BC *IG* X (2) (1) 30, 3; 50, 4; 109, 10 (f. *Θεόδωρος*); **(21)** ii AD ib. 105 (*Αἰμίλιος Ἐ.*); **(22)** ~ ib. 241 A I, 34 (*Ε̣ὔ̣τυχο̣ς̣*); **(23)** ii-iii AD ib. 112 (Lat. Eutychus); **(24)** ~ ib. 413; **(25)** ~ ib. 466 (*Αἴ(λ). Πετρώνιος Ἐ.*); **(26)** ~ ib. 467; **(27)** ~ *SEG* XLIII 353; **(28)** s. ii AD *IG* X (2) (1) 244 I, 6 (*Κάσσιος Ἐ.*); **(29)** iii AD ib. 561, 1 (*Αἴλ. Πετρωνιανὸς Ἐ. Δαιδάλις*: ?s. *Πετρώνιος Λύκος*, *Πετιλία Βικτωρία*); **(30)** iv/v AD *SEG* XXIV 564 a (n. pr.?)

—THESSALONIKE?: **(31)** ii AD *IG* X (2) (1) 808, 1 (f. *Διοσκόρη*)

—THESSALONIKE*: **(32)** 132 AD ib. 503, 4 (threptos)

MACEDONIA (ODOMANTIKE):

—SIRRHA: **(33)** 155 AD Dimitsas 821, 28 (Kaphtantzis 1) (s. *Μουκιανός*); **(34)** ~ Dimitsas 821, 30 (Kaphtantzis 1) (*Τουρπίλλιος Ἐ.*)

MACEDONIA (PAIONIA):

—KAVADARCI (MOD.): **(35)** ii-iii AD *Sp.* 98 (1941-8) p. 77 no. 164 (-κος: s. *Εὔνους*, *Ζωσίμη*)

—NEGOTINO (MOD.): **(36)** ii-iii AD ib. p. 56 no. 114, 4 (n. pr.?)

—STOBOI: **(37)** s. iii AD *JÖAI* 32 (1940) Beibl. col. 19 no. 12. 132; **(38)** ~ ib. cols. 17-18

MACEDONIA (PIERIS):

—AKONTISMA (NR.): **(39)** 19-45 AD *Thrakika* 6 (1935) p. 305 no. 1 (*Eastern cults* p. 202 no. 21) (freed.?)

SCYTHIA MINOR:

—CAPIDAVA*: **(40)** ii AD *ISM* V 45 (Lat. Euticu[s])

—ISTROS: **(41)** ii AD ib. I 196, 18 (*Αἴλ. Ἐ.*)

—TROESMIS: **(42)** ii AD Unp. (Avram) (Lat. Euticus qui et Opellius); **(43)** ~ *ISM* V 193, 8 (Lat. T. Rascanius Eutychu(s))

THRACE: **(44)** 46-54 AD *SEG* XVI 415 II, 23 (*IThrakAig* E84) (*Γ. Ἰούλ. Ἐ.*)

—BIZONE: **(45)** iii AD *IGB* I^2 10, 6 (*Εὐτύχο[υ]* (gen.): f. *—ιος*)

—BYZANTION: **(46)** f. iii AD *IByz* 308 (s. *Μέμμιος Μᾶρκος*, f. *Ἄκκα*)

—SESTOS?: **(47)** imp. Dumont–Homolle 111c 12

THRACE?: **(48)** i BC-i AD *Eastern cults* p. 177 no. 22

Εὔφαιος
Macedonia (Mygdonia):
—kalindoia: (1) a. 98 ad *SEG* xlii 582, 57; cf. *Anthémonte–Kalindoia* 2 p. 256 (name) (s. *Ζωΐλος*)

Εὐφαμίδας
Thrace:
—mesambria: (1) hell. *SEG* xxx 705 (tile) ?= (*3*); (2) iii/ii bc Karayotov, *Mesambria* 1 p. 90 nos. 212-18; Price, *Alexander* 1035 (coin) (*Εὐφα(μίδας)*?—Karayotov, *Εὐφά(νης)*?); (3) ii-i bc *IGB* i² 328 (*Eastern cults* p. 26 no. 43) (*Εὐφα[μ]ίδας*: s. *Ἐπαμείνων*) ?= (*1*); (4) c. 100-71 bc Karayotov, *Mesambria* 1 p. 113 nos. 842-9; Price, *Alexander* 1125-6 (coin) (*Εὐφα(μίδας)*?—Karayotov, *Εὐφά(νης)*?)

Εὐφάμιος
Macedonia (Orestis):
—battynaioi: (1) 192 ad *EAM* 186 I, 47 (s. *Νικάνωρ*)

Εὔφαμος
Thrace:
—mesambria: (1) iii bc *IGB* i² 308 bis, 11 (s. *Παυσανίας*)
—perinthos-herakleia: (2) iii bc *IG* xii (9) 802 (s. *Ξάνθιππος*)

Εὐφάνης
Macedonia: (1) f. i bc D.S. xxxvii 5a (*Εὐφήνης*—mss. and Loeb, *Ἐ.*—Dind.: s. *Ἐξήκεστος*)
Macedonia (Chalkidike):
—olynthos: (2) c. 350 bc *SEG* xlvii 922; cf. *BE* 1999, no. 369 (*Εὐθάνης*—ed.: f. *Ἀριστόβουλος*)
—potidaia-kassandreia (nr.): (3) hell. *SEG* xxix 631 (f. *Ἀντιγόνα*)
Thrace:
—byzantion: (4) iii bc *IByz* 65 (f. *Ματρώ*)
—odessos: (5) i-ii ad *IGB* i² 131, 1 (s. *Ζωπυρίων*); (6) 221 ad ib. 47 bis a, 17 (*M. Αὐρ. Ἐ.*: s. *Ἀρτεμίδωρος*)

Εὐφάνιος
Macedonia (Pieria):
—pydna: (1) iv bc *GRBS* 43 (2002-3) p. 110 no. 1 a, 4

Εὔφαντος
Macedonia (Bisaltia):
—arolos?: (1) m. i ad Kaphtantzis 509
Macedonia (Chalkidike):
—olynthos: (2) iv/iii bc *RE* (-); *FGrH* 74 (Tataki, *Macedonians* p. 136 no. 52)
Macedonia (Mygdonia):
—thessalonike: (3) i bc/i ad *IG* x (2) (1) 58, 15; *KGAM Thess.* i 111 (date) (f. *Σεκοῦνδος*)
Thrace:
—abdera: (4) c. 230-200 bc *BCH* 45 (1921) p. 18 III, 90 (s. *Διονυσᾶς*: reading—Oulhen)

Εὐφημία
Macedonia (Bottiaia):
—edessa: (1) v-vi ad Feissel, *RICM* 42 (-*φι*-)
Scythia Minor:
—tomis: (2) ?v ad Barnea 33 (Popescu, *IGL* 35)
Thrace:
—beroe-augusta traiana: (3) c. 320-324 ad *Anal. Boll.* 31 (1912) p. 198; p. 207
—byzantion?: (4) iii ad *IByz* 323 (*Αὐρ. Ἐ.*: d. *Σεκουνδῖνος*)
—lysimacheia (nr.): (5) iv-vi ad *ISestos* 49 (*AD* 49-50 (1994-5) Mel. p. 331 no. 156)

Εὔφημος
Macedonia (Bottiaia):
—pella: (1) iv bc Tataki, *Macedonians* p. 154 no. 44 (s. *Δημήτριος*)
Macedonia (Edonis):
—amphipolis: (2) v-vi ad *SEG* xlviii 723 (-*φι*-)
Macedonia (Mygdonia):
—thessalonike: (3) ii ad ib. xxxvi 644 + *KGAM Thess.* i 58 (*Π. Ποπιλλιανὸς Ἐ.*)
Macedonia (Pelagonia): (4) imp. *IG* x (2) (2) 253
Thrace:
—apollonia-sozopolis: (5) iv bc *IGB* i² 424 (f. *Ἴων*)
—markianopolis: (6) ii ad ib. v 5339, 6 (*Εὐφημ[ος]*: f. —*διος*)
—pautalia: (7) s. ii ad *SEG* xlvi 864, 19 (f. *Ἀφυκτολις*)

Εὐφίλητος
Macedonia (Bottiaia):
—beroia: (1) iii ad *BE* 1939, no. 11 (Tataki 502) (-*φή*-: s. *Ἀταλάντη*)
Macedonia (Chalkidike):
—olynthos (nr.): (2) ii-iii ad *SEG* xxix 626 (*Ε̣ὐφίλ[ητος]*)
Thrace:
—byzantion: (3) ii-i bc *IByz* 160 (Fıratlı–Robert p. 106 no. 168) (f. *Γόκουσα*)

Εὐφορβίδης
Macedonia (Pieria):
—phila?: (1) ?iii bc *RPh* 1911, pp. 133-4 no. 36, 97; cf. Helly, *L'État thessalien* pp. 319-20 (locn.) (*Εὐφορβεί[δης]*, *Εὐφόρβο̣υ̣?* (gen.): f. *Φείδις*)

Εὔφορβος
Macedonia: (1) 235-200 bc *PP* 2293a (Tataki, *Macedonians* p. 316 no. 60; La'da E1494)

Εὐφραίνων
Macedonia (Mygdonia):
—thessalonike: (1) ii/iii ad *IG* x (2) (1) 262 I, 7

Εὐφραῖος
Macedonia (Bottiaia):
—pella: (1) iv bc *Pella* p. 138 no. 206 (f. *Μελιννίχη*)
Macedonia (Chalkidike):
—olynthos: (2) 350 bc *SEG* xxxix 617 (f. *Χαιρικλῆς*)
Scythia Minor:
—kallatis: (3) s. iii bc *ISM* iii 35 B, 25 (s. *Σάτυρος*)

Εὐφράντας
Tauris:
—chersonesos: (1) c. 475-450 bc *SEG* xl 612. 9 (ostrakon) (*Εὐφράντα[ς]*—ed., *Εὐφράντα*?)

Εὐφραντίδης
Macedonia (Chalkidike):
—chalkideis: (1) ?353 bc ib. xxiv 574, 3; xxxvii 576, 3; xlvii 922; Hatzopoulos, *Actes Chalc.* p. 80 (date) (*Εὐριαντίδης*—922: s. *Ἀριστότιμος*)

Εὐφραντικός
Macedonia (Mygdonia):
—thessalonike: (1) m. iii ad *IG* x (2) (1) 195, 6; 196, 2 (*Γ. Ἰούλ. Ἐ.*)

Εὐφράνωρ
Macedonia: (1) 174 bc *RE* Supplbd. 4 (3a) (Lat. Euphranor)
Macedonia (Mygdonia):
—thessalonike: (2) ii bc *IG* x (2) (1) 327, 1, 3 (f. *Κράτερος*, *Ἀντιγόνα*); (3) 154 ad ib. 288, 2 (*Εὐφρά[νωρ]*)
Macedonia?: (4) 169 bc *RE* Supplbd. 4 (4a) (Tataki, *Macedonians* p. 317 no. 61) (Lat. Euphranor)
Scythia Minor:
—istros: (5) ii bc *ISM* i 175 (*[Εὐ]φράνωρ*)

Εὐφρᾶς
Cimmerian Bosporos:
—pantikapaion: (1) v-vi ad *IAK* 10 (1904) p. 89 no. 105 (*Εὐφρᾶ* (gen.?), *Εὐφρα*—?)
Macedonia (Bottiaia):
—pella: (2) 229 ad *SEG* xliii 441
Macedonia (Mygdonia):
—thessalonike: (3) m. ii ad ib. 462, 5 (*Βαίβιος Ἐ.*)

Εὔφρασις
Scythia Minor:
—axiopolis*: (1) f. iv ad Barnea 71 (Popescu, *IGL* 194); *Anal. Boll.* 31 (1912) p. 259

Εὐφράτας
Kolchis:
—abasgoi: (1) f. vi ad *PLRE* iii (2)

Εὐφράτης
Macedonia (Edonis):
—amphipolis: (1) iii ad *Anal. Boll.* 31 (1912) p. 169 (f. *Μώκιος*)
Macedonia (Mygdonia):
—thessalonike*: (2) ii-iii ad *IG* x (2) (1) 1019 (*GVI* 1019) (glad.?)
Thrace:
—byzantion: (3) ii ad *IByz* 321 (*Τ. Ἀβούλλιος Ἐ.*)
—philippopolis-trimontium (territ.): (4) ii-iii ad *IGB* iii 1433 (s. *Ὑάκινθος*)

Εὔφριλλος
Macedonia (Bottiaia):
—pella: (1) iv bc *SEG* xxiv 542 (f. *Φανόκριτος*)

Εὐφρόνης
Tauris:
—chersonesos: (1) f. iii bc ib. xxxix 702, 2 (f. *Ἀπολλώνιος*); (2) ~ ib. l. 5 (s. *Ἀπολλώνιος*)

Εὐφρόνιμος
Skythia:
—olbia-borysthenes: (1) iii bc *IOSPE* i² 201 I, 34 (s. *Μητρόδωρος*)

Εὐφρόνιος
Macedonia (Bottiaia):
—beroia?: (1) 178 bc *SGDI* 2071, 8 (f. *Μένανδρος*)
Macedonia (Chalkidike):
—potidaia-kassandreia: (2) hell. *IG* xii (1) 429 (Tataki, *Macedonians* p. 89 no. 38)
Scythia Minor:
—kallatis: (3) iii-ii bc *SNG BM Black Sea* 206 (coin) (*Εὐφρό(νιος)*?)
Tauris:
—chersonesos: (4) c. 262-237 bc Kats p. 94 no. 46 (amph.) (s. *Φιλαθάναιος*)
Thrace:
—byzantion: (5) i bc-i ad *IByz* 240 (f. *Ἀπφοῦς*); (6) ii ad ib. 108 (s. *Νίκων*)

Εὐφρόνις
Cimmerian Bosporos:
—nymphaion: (1) f. iii bc *SEG* xxxix 701. 3

Εὐφρονίς
Macedonia (Pieria):
—dion: (1) hell. ib. l 589
Scythia Minor:
—kallatis: (2) iii-iv ad *ISM* iii 148, 10 (d. *Ἱμέριος*, *Μουσική*)
Tauris:
—chersonesos: (3) iii bc Solomonik, *NEPKh* 173 (*Εὐφρον[ίς]*?: ?d. *Αὐτοφῶν*)

Εὐφροσύνη
Kolchis: (1) i bc *IG* ii² 9049 (*FRA* 2936) (d. *Χαιρήμων*)
Macedonia (Chalkidike):
—mende: (2) imp. *SEG* xxix 617 (m. *Ἐρωτιανός*)

MACEDONIA (EDONIS):
—AMPHIPOLIS: (3) ii BC *IG* II² 8082 (Tataki, *Macedonians* p. 52 no. 56; *FRA* 507)
MACEDONIA (MYGDONIA):
—LETE (NR.)*: (4) c. 160-180 AD *SEG* XLVII 974; *KGAM Thess.* I 123 (date) (m. Ὀνήσιμος: slave?)
—THESSALONIKE: (5) ii AD *IG* X (2) (1) 664, 5 (*SEG* XLIII 459) (m. Ζωΐς); (6) ii/iii AD *Tekmeria* 6 (2001) p. 4 no. 2 (Φλ. Ἐ.: m. Φλ. Ὀλυμπιάς); (7) iii AD *IG* X (2) (1) 260 A (Εὐφρο[σύ]νη: d. Διοσκο—)
MACEDONIA (PAIONIA):
—DEMIR KAPIJA (MOD.): (8) ii-iii AD Hald, *Auf den Trümmern Stobis* p. 59 f.
SCYTHIA MINOR:
—TOMIS*: (9) ii AD *ISM* II 289
THRACE: (10) ?161 BC *SGDI* 1826, 2, 4, 6, 7 (-να: slave/freed.)
—AINOS: (11) hell.? *IG* II² 7977 (*FRA* 248) (d. Ἡλιοφῶν); (12) hell.-imp. ib. 249 (d. Βίθυς)
—MARONEIA: (13) i-ii AD *SEG* XXIV 638 (*IThrakAig* E304)
—NOVAE: (14) ii AD *IGLNovae* 103 (*ILB* 303) (Lat. Paccia Euphro[syne])

Εὐφρόσυνος
CIMMERIAN BOSPOROS:
—HERMONASSA: (1) 345 AD *CIRB* 1091, 2 ([Ε]ὐφρόσυνος ὁ καὶ Πάτειρος: s. Σαμβίων)
MACEDONIA (BOTTIAIA):
—BEROIA: (2) a. 212 AD *IBer* 136, 6 (Tataki 1315) (Φλ. Ἐ.: s. Φλ. Οὐρβανός)
MACEDONIA (DERRIOPOS):
—STUBERRA: (3) 116 AD *IG* X (2) (2) 327, 16 (s. Ζωΐλος)
MACEDONIA (EDONIS):
—AMPHIPOLIS: (4) 90 BC *SEG* XLVIII 716 ter, 4, 7 (s. Νικάνωρ)
MACEDONIA (MYGDONIA):
—KALINDOIA: (5) ?255 AD ib. XLII 603 b (s. Ἀρτεμίδωρος, ?s. Διογένεια)
—THESSALONIKE: (6) ii AD *IG* X (2) (1) 241 A I, 32; (7) ~ ib. 241 A II, 15 (Κ. Ἀστρίκι. [Εὐ]φρόσυν[ος]); (8) ii-iii AD ib. 659 (Lat. [Euph](r)osynus); (9) v-vi AD ib. 337 (Feissel, *RICM* 176)
—THESSALONIKE?: (10) ii-iii AD *IG* X (2) (1) 870 (Κ. Φάβιος Ἐ.: s. Σπένδουσα)
MACEDONIA (ORESTIS):
—SISANI (MOD.): (11) 146 AD *EAM* 187, 12 (Αἰλ. Ἐ.)
MACEDONIA (PAIONIA):
—BYLAZORA: (12) ii-iii AD *Sp.* 71 (1931) p. 26 no. 51 ([Εὐ]φρόσυνος)
—NEGOTINO (MOD.): (13) imp. ib. 98 (1941-8) p. 60 ([Εὐφρόσ]υνος?: I ?f. Εὐφρόσυνος II, Χρυσέρως); (14) ~ ib. p. 60 no. 124 ([Εὐφ]ρόσυνος: II ?s. Εὐφρόσυνος I)
MACEDONIA (PELAGONIA): (15) ii-iii AD *IG* X (2) (2) 256 (s. Νίκη)
MACEDONIA (PIERIA):
—PYDNA (LOULOUDIES (MOD.)): (16) s. vi AD *SEG* XLIX 728 A-B
SCYTHIA MINOR:
—AEGYSSUS (NR.): (17) iii AD *ISM* V 242, 2
THRACE:
—BYZANTION: (18) ii-i BC *IByz* 83 (Fıratlı-Robert p. 51 no. 26) (s. Πρῶτος)
—PHILIPPOPOLIS-TRIMONTIUM*: (19) ii AD *Arkheologiia* (Sofia) 1968 (2), p. 44 no. 1 (Lat. T. Aelius Euphrosynus: imp. freed.)
—SALYMBRIA: (20) imp. *IByz* S 9 ([Ε]ὐφρόσυνος)

Εὐφρώ
MACEDONIA (MYGDONIA):
—THESSALONIKE: (1) ii AD *IG* X (2) (1) 313

Εὔφρων
CIMMERIAN BOSPOROS:
—GORGIPPIA: (1) f. iii BC *CIRB* 1137 A I, 44 (f. Ἀνθεστήριος); (2) ~ ib. 1137 B I, 10 (s. Ἀνδροσθένης); (3) ~ ib. l. 35 (f. Ἀγησίλας); (4) ~ ib. 1137 B II, 53 (f. Φιλέας)
—PHANAGOREIA: (5) iii AD ib. 1003, 5 (Θύφρ(ω)ν—ed., Εὔφρ(ω)ν—Tokhtas'ev, [Εὐ]θύφρ(ω)ν?—Yailenko and Vinogradov: s. Ἐπικράτης)
MACEDONIA (BOTTIAIA):
—BEROIA: (6) 223 BC *IBer* 4, 14 (s. Ἀριστόλαος)
SKYTHIA:
—OLBIA-BORYSTHENES: (7) f. iv BC Tolstoi 7 (vase)
THRACE: (8) 201 BC *PPetr* III 57 a, 1, 7; 57 b, 5a; cf. La'da E754 (f. Θεότιμος)
—KARDIA: (9) iii BC *IG* II² 8960 (*FRA* 2671) (s. Εὐκράτης)

Εὐχάρεια
THRACE:
—MARONEIA: (1) iii AD *IThrakAig* E396, 11 (Αὐρ. Ἐ.: d. Εὐσέβιος, ?m. Ῥόδη, Σαβῖνα)

Εὐχάρης
MACEDONIA?: (1) 244 BC *PSI* 388, 27 (f. Λάαγος)

Εὐχάριον
MACEDONIA (MYGDONIA):
—THESSALONIKE?: (1) ii-iii AD *IG* X (2) (1) 813 (d. Αἰλ. Τελεσφόρος, Αἰλ. Τερτία)

Εὔχαρις
MACEDONIA (MYGDONIA):
—THESSALONIKE?: (1) ii-iii AD ib. 753 ([Εὔ]χαρις)

Εὐχάριστος
CIMMERIAN BOSPOROS:
—GORGIPPIA: (1) ii/iii AD *VDI* 1970 (4), p. 149, 9 (f. —κης)
—THEODOSIA: (2) iii AD *CIRB* 947 A, 10 (Εὐχάρισ[τος]: f. Δάδας)
MACEDONIA (BOTTIAIA):
—EDESSA: (3) 229 AD Tataki, *Edessa* 111 (Εὐχάρισ[το]ς)

Εὐχαρίων
CIMMERIAN BOSPOROS:
—PANTIKAPAION: (1) i/ii AD *CIRB* 643; cf. KW pl. 16 no. 240

Εὐχείας
SCYTHIA MINOR:
—KALLATIS: (1) iii BC *ISM* III 126, 7 (f. Κερκίνος)

Εὐχίδης
MACEDONIA (ORESTIS):
—BATTYNAIOI: (1) 192 AD *EAM* 186 I, 56 (-χεί-: f. Ἀντίγονος)

Εὔχρους
MACEDONIA (EDONIS):
—AMPHIPOLIS*: (1) iii AD Robert, *Hell.* 5 p. 77 no. 314 (*GVI* 732) (glad.)

Εὐχρωτίς
THRACE:
—NOVAE: (1) s. ii AD *IGLNovae* 181 (*SEG* XLVII 1152)

Εὐψύχις
THRACE:
—PERINTHOS-HERAKLEIA (NR.): (1) iii AD *IPerinth* 283 (Αὐρ. Ἐ.)

Ἐφηβικός
MACEDONIA (MYGDONIA):
—THESSALONIKE?: (1) s. iii AD *AEpThess* p. 10 no. 8 A (f. Αὐρ. Εὐτυχία); (2) ~ ib. (s. Εὐτυχία)

Ἐφιάλτης
MACEDONIA?: (1) 333 BC *RE* (6); Berve 330

Ἔφιππος
MACEDONIA (CHALKIDIKE):
—OLYNTHOS: (1) s. iv BC *RE* (4); Berve 331 (Tataki, *Macedonians* p. 136 no. 53)

Ἔφορος
THRACE:
—LYSIMACHEIA: (1) iii BC *IG* XII Suppl. p. 39 no. 127 C, 53 (*SEG* XXVI 919) (I f. Ἔφορος II); (2) ~ *IG* XII Suppl. p. 39 no. 127 C, 53 (*SEG* XXVI 919) (II s. Ἔφορος I)

Ἐχέδημος
THRACE:
—STRYME: (1) c. 400-375 BC *BCH* 83 (1959) p. 719 (*IThrakAig* E136) (s. Ἀπελλῆς)

Ἐχεκράτης
MACEDONIA: (1) iii BC Liv. xl 54. 4 (Lat. Echecrates: ?s. Δημήτριος ὁ Καλός, f. Ἀντίγονος)
TAURIS:
—CHERSONESOS: (2) iii BC Kats p. 109 no. 97 (amph.) (Ἐ(χ)εκράτης?, Ἐσεκράτης—ed.: f. Προμαθίων)
THRACE:
—ABDERA: (3) c. 395-360 BC May, *Abdera* pp. 219-21 nos. 316-23 (coin)
—PERINTHOS-HERAKLEIA:
——(Aigikoreis): (4) iii-ii BC *IPerinth* 61, 45

Ἐχεκρατίδης
MACEDONIA (PIERIA):
—METHONE: (1) s. iv BC *IEph* 1434, 1 (Tataki, *Macedonians* p. 123 no. 4) (s. Ξεννέας)

Ἐχέλεως
SCYTHIA MINOR:
—ISTROS: (1) f. vi BC *ISM* I 101 + *Stud. Alexandrescu* p. 251 (Ἐχέλε[ως]?, Ἐχελέ[ων]?)

Ἐχένικος
MACEDONIA (PIERIA):
—PHILA?: (1) ?iii BC *RPh* 1911, pp. 133-4 no. 36, 4; cf. Helly, *L'État thessalien* pp. 319-20 (locn.) (f. Δάμων); (2) ~ *RPh* 1911, pp. 133-4 no. 36, 55; cf. Helly, *L'État thessalien* pp. 319-20 (locn.) (f. —όστρατος)

Ἐχέπολις
THRACE:
—MESOCHORI (MOD.): (1) f. v BC *CEG* II 727 (Bakalakis, *Oinos Ismarikos* p. 554; *IThrakAig* E388)

Ἐχέστρατος
THRACE:
—MESAMBRIA: (1) ii/i BC *IGB* V 5104 (s. Ἀντίφιλος)

Ἐχετόδωρος
THRACE:
—BYZANTION: (1) 257 BC *PCZ* 59089, 21 (La'da E344)

F

Φαδδῦς
Macedonia (Mygdonia):
—kalindoia: (1) c. 311 bc Hatzopoulos, *MI* 2 p. 84 no. 62, 35; cf. *Anthémonte–Kalindoia* 2 pp. 256-7 (name) (s. Ἀστίων)

Z

Ζαβάγιος
Cimmerian Bosporos:
—gorgippia: (1) ii/iii ad *CIRB* 1179, 27; Zgusta, *PNS* 106

Ζάβαγος
Cimmerian Bosporos:
—kytaia: (1) ii ad *CIRB* 944

Ζάβαργος
Cimmerian Bosporos:
—pantikapaion: (1) iii ad ib. 101, 1; Zgusta, *PNS* 107 (f. —γος)
Skythia:
—tanais: (2) ii ad *CIRB* 1268, 9 (f. —ων); (3) 220 ad ib. 1278, 12 (s. Χαρίτων)

Ζαες
Macedonia (Edonis):
—philippoi (drama (mod.)): (1) ii-iii ad *AD* 52 (1997) Chron. p. 847, 11 with pl. 314 β

Ζαζζοῦς
Cimmerian Bosporos:
—gorgippia: (1) ii ad *CIRB* 1140, 1; Zgusta, *PNS* 289 (f. Μυρίσκος); (2) ~ *CIRB* 1140, 19 (s. Ἀπολλο—); (3) ~ ib. 1141, 12 (f. Ἄρδαρος); (4) ~ ib. 1151, 2 (Ζαζοῦσ-: f. —ης); (5) ~ ib. l. 10 (Ζαζοῦσ-: f. —ωρος); (6) m. ii ad *Eirene* 7 (1968) p. 67, 5 (Ζαζοῦσ-: f. Μάστακος); (7) ~ ib. l. 22 (f. Σπαρ—); (8) ?s. ii ad *CIRB* 1147, 3 ([Ζ]αζζοῦς); (9) 173-210 ad ib. 1135, 16 (f. Σύμμαχος); (10) ~ ib. l. 22 (Ζαζ[ζοῦς]: f. Διονύσιος); (11) ~ ib. l. 26 (Ζαζ[ζοῦς]?); (12) ii/iii ad ib. 1179, 38 (s. Τιμόθεος)
—gorgippia?: (13) s. ii ad ib. 1231 B, 10 (s. Ἀπολλώνιος)

Ζαιβαλώ
Macedonia (Sintike):
—parthikopolis (nr.): (1) ii-iii ad *IGB* v 5918 ((dat.): ?m. Πυρούλας, Πυρούλας ὁ μικρός)

Ζαίδαρος
Cimmerian Bosporos:
—taman peninsula: (1) i bc/i ad *SEG* xlv 1018 (f. Μαθιάνης)

Ζαικα
Macedonia (Pelagonia):
—mariovo (mod.): (1) 132 ad *IG* x (2) (2) 164 (Ζαικα—?: m. Ἰσιάς, —ίνη)
Macedonia (Sintike):
—parthikopolis (territ.): (2) 146 ad *IGB* iv 2303; (3) 198 ad ib. 2311, 2 (m. Πυρούσαλα)

Ζαικένθης
Macedonia (Sintike):
—parthikopolis: (1) ?ii ad *FGrH* 257 F 37, 53 (Tataki, *Macedonians* p. 147 no. 6) (s. Μουκάσης)

Ζαικίς
Macedonia?: (1) f. i bc *Xenia antiqua* 10 (2001) p. 19 nos. A-B (or Thrace: d. Ἀνδρόνικος, m. Ἀνδρόνικος, Ἀλλούπορις, Μήτοκος)

Ζαινειλα
Thrace:
—odessos: (1) ii-iii ad *IGB* i² 130, 4 (Ζαινε<ι>λα?: ?d. Η—)

Ζαιπα
Thrace:
—pautalia (territ.): (1) ii-iii ad ib. iv 2112, 2

Ζαίπυρος
Macedonia (Pieria):
—dion: (1) ii-iii ad Dimitsas 164 (s. Μέστης)

Ζαλίας
Macedonia (Chalkidike):
—potidaia-kassandreia: (1) ?m. iii bc *FD* iii (4) 351, 5 (Tataki, *Macedonians* p. 89 no. 39) (s. Σάτυρος)

Ζάλμοξις
Thrace: (1) vi bc *RE* (-); Detschev s.v. (slave/fict.?)

Ζαλσίς
Skythia:
—olbia-borysthenes: (1) i/ii ad *IOSPE* i² 200, 3; Zgusta, *PNS* 561 (d. Ἀρσηόαχος)

Ζάνατος
Macedonia (Bottiaia):
—beroia: (1) 118 bc *IBer* 134, 23 (s. Ἀννίκας)

Ζάρανδος
Skythia:
—tanais: (1) 228 ad *CIRB* 1282, 15 (f. Μάρδανος)

Ζαύνας
Kolchis:
—lazoi: (1) f. vi ad *PLRE* ii (-); *RE* (-) (s. Φαρασμάνης, f. Ῥουφῖνος, Λεόντιος)

Ζειβούρης
Macedonia (Edonis):
—amphipolis: (1) 158 or 274 ad *SEG* xv 415, 5 (Ζειβούρεος (gen.): f. Δαντώ)

Ζείγεθος
Thrace:
—pautalia: (1) s. ii ad ib. xlvi 864, 18 (f. Διογένης)

Ζειδέβης
Macedonia (Mygdonia):
—kalindoia: (1) a. 98 ad ib. xlii 582, 59; cf. *Anthémonte–Kalindoia* 2 p. 257 (name) (f. Δούλης)

Ζειδυμαρχίς
Macedonia (Bottiaia):
—pella: (1) iv-iii bc *SEG* xxiv 543

Ζείζα
Scythia Minor:
—kallatis: (1) f. ii ad *ISM* iii 175 (d. Σιλανός)

Ζειζεις
Thrace:
—breste (mod.): (1) ?iii ad *ILB* 176 (Lat. Zises: s. Μουκάζενις, f. Ταρσάνιος)
—pautalia:
——Karistoron: (2) ii ad *IGB* iv 2175 ([Πο]ντικὸς ὁ καὶ Ζειζε[ις])
—vicus trullensium: (3) iii ad ib. ii 506, 7 (s. Μοῦσα, Αὐρ. Ν—)

Ζειζοδύνων
Thrace:
—serdica (territ.): (1) ?ii ad ib. iv 2048 (Φλ. Ποντικὸς ὁ κα(ὶ) Ζειζοδύνων)

Ζείλας
Cimmerian Bosporos:
—pantikapaion: (1) i/ii ad *CIRB* 144, 10; cf. *St. Clas.* 8 (1966) p. 337 (s. Τάρσας)

Ζείλη
Scythia Minor:
—tomis: (1) ii-iii ad *ISM* ii 303 (Lat. Ziles: m. Curitthie, Valeria, Sabina)
Thrace:
—kellai*: (2) iii ad *IGB* iii 1516 b, 17 (m. Βρίζενις, Τάρσας, Γύζη, Βλώστα)
—koinare (mod.): (3) ?iii ad *ILB* 154, 7 (Lat. Valeriae Zileni (dat.): m. Maximus)

Ζεινης
Thrace:
—durostorum (territ.)?: (1) iii ad *IGB* ii 872 (s. Ζορδησιοσος)

Ζεισαλβης?
Macedonia (Edonis):
—philippoi (drama (mod.)): (1) ii-iii ad *AD* 52 (1997) Chron. p. 847, 3 with pl. 314 β

Ζεισεις
Thrace:
—vicus trullensium: (1) iii ad *IGB* ii 506, 2 (f. Αὐρ. Ν—)

Ζεισισος
Thrace:
—kellai*: (1) iii ad ib. iii 1516 a, 28
—philippopolis-trimontium (territ.): (2) ii-iii ad ib. 1201 (Ζισει-: f. Δίζας)

Ζεισκεαγις
SCYTHIA MINOR:
—ISTROS: (1) i AD *ISM* I 200, 10 (*Ζεισκεαγι* (gen.): f. *Παγκράτης*)

Ζείσκωρις
THRACE:
—NICOPOLIS AD ISTRUM (TERRIT.): (1) f. iii AD *IGB* II 724 (*CCET* II (2) 639) (s. *Δόρζας*)

Ζείτραλις
THRACE:
—MEDOVINA (MOD.): (1) f. iii AD *IGB* II 763 (*CCET* II (2) 542)
—PHILIPPOPOLIS-TRIMONTIUM (TERRIT.): (2) ii-iii AD *IGB* III 1147 ([*Ζ*]ε̣*ίτραλις*: s. *Τ*—)

Ζεκαιδένθη
MACEDONIA (SINTIKE):
—PARTHIKOPOLIS (TERRIT.): (1) ii AD *Arkheologiia* (Sofia) 1987 (1), p. 25 no. 2 (d. *Πυρούλας*, m. *Τόνος*)

Ζεκαλώη
MACEDONIA (SINTIKE):
—PARTHIKOPOLIS (NR.): (1) ii AD *IGB* IV 2294

Ζέκη
MACEDONIA (EDONIS):
—PHILIPPOI (TERRIT.): (1) ?ii AD *BCH* 47 (1923) p. 69 no. 25 (Pilhofer 514) (Lat. Zeces: d. *Ἀλιούλας*)
MACEDONIA (SINTIKE):
—PARTHIKOPOLIS (NR.): (2) 159 AD *IGB* IV 2286, 4

Ζεκυνθείς
CIMMERIAN BOSPOROS:
—PANTIKAPAION: (1) i-ii AD *CIRB* 634; Zgusta, *PNS* 997 (d. *Σωπᾶς*, *Σάνεια*)

Ζελμούτας
MACEDONIA (EDONIS):
—AMPHIPOLIS?: (1) ii-iii AD Dimitsas 906 (Kaphtantzis 543) (s. *Ἡλιζις*)

Ζένις
THRACE:
—MARKIANOPOLIS: (1) iii AD *IGB* V 5360 (*CCET* II (1) 200) (s. *Αὐλούζενις*)

Ζεράζενις
THRACE:
—PHILIPPOPOLIS-TRIMONTIUM (TERRIT.): (1) ii-iii AD *IGB* III 1325 (*Ζεράζεν̣[ις]*: f. *Μούκα*)

Ζεργέδης
MACEDONIA (EDONIS):
—PHILIPPOI (TERRIT.): (1) ?iii AD *SEG* XXX 594 A, 10 (Pilhofer 580) (s. *Κ*(—))

Ζέρις
THRACE:
—PAUTALIA:
——Karistoron: (1) ii-iii AD *IGB* IV 2153 (f. *Ἐπτημενηκα*)

Ζερκίων
THRACE:
—APOLLONIA-SOZOPOLIS: (1) iv BC ib. I² 421 (s. *Ἡρόδωρος*)

Ζερούλας
THRACE:
—SERDICA: (1) 237 AD *CIL* XVI 146 (Speidel, *Denkmäler* 79) (Lat. M. Aureli Zerula (dat.): s. *Μουκάτραλις*)

Ζετιτίς
MACEDONIA (MYGDONIA):
—THESSALONIKE: (1) f. iii AD *IG* X (2) (1) 564, 2 (m. *Αὐρ. Ἀλκιδάμας*, *Αὐρ. Δούλης*, *Αὐρ. Πυρούλας*, *Αὐρ. Γαλάτης*)

Ζεύακος
SKYTHIA:
—TANAIS: (1) 225 AD *CIRB* 1279, 17 (f. *Αὐάρθακος*)

Ζευξίδαμος
TAURIS:
—CHERSONESOS: (1) iv BC Solomonik, *NEPKh* 138 (f. *Βάκος*)

Ζεύξιππος
THRACE:
—BYZANTION: (1) ?iv AD *RE* (1)

Ζεῦξις
MACEDONIA: (1) iii/ii BC ib. (3); Grainger, *SPG* pp. 122-3; Ma, *Antiochos* pp. 123-30 (s. *Κύναγος*)

Ζέφος
CIMMERIAN BOSPOROS:
—GORGIPPIA: (1) 173-210 AD *SEG* XXXVI 700, 7 (*Ζέφο(ς)*)

Ζῆθος
SKYTHIA:
—OLBIA-BORYSTHENES: (1) ii AD *IOSPE* I² 105, 8 (f. *Ἀχιλλεύς*); (2) ~ ib. 129, 5 (f. *Ποσειδῆς*); (3) f. ii AD *IOlbia* 79, 12 (*IOSPE* I² 116) (f. *Φάρναγος*) ?= (*4*); (4) ~ *SEG* XLIII 506, 16 (f. *Φάρνακος*) ?= (*3*)
—TANAIS: (5) 210-226 AD *CIRB* 1281, 11 (f. *Γαος*) ?= (*6*); (6) 225 AD ib. 1280, 16 (f. —ς) ?= (*5*); (7) 244 AD ib. 1287, 7 (I f. *Ζῆθος* II); (8) ~ ib. l. 7 (II s. *Ζῆθος* I)
TAURIS:
—CHERSONESOS: (9) m. i BC *IOSPE* I² 347, 2; 691, [3] (f. *Ἀπολλώνιος*); (10) s. i BC Const. Porph., *De admin. imp.* 53, 276 (s. *Ζήθων*); (11) imp. *IOSPE* I² 412; (12) ii AD ib. 386, 5 (*Ζ*ῆ̣*θος*); (13) ~ ib. 392, 5; (14) ~ ib. 394 (*Ζῆθο[ς]*); (15) ~ *SEG* XXXIII 592; (16) ~ ib. XXXVII 656 (lead) ([*Ζ*]ῆ*θος*: f. *Αἰλ. Λαοδίκη*); (17) ~ ib. XLVI 932 (*Φλ. Ζ.*); (18) f. ii AD *KSIIMK* 15 (1947) p. 59, 6 (Solomonik, *NEPKh* 112 d); cf. *VDI* 1993 (4), p. 63 (f. *Βοίσκος*); (19) ~ Solomonik, *NEPKh* 111, 4 (I f. *Ζῆθος* II); (20) ~ ib. l. 4 (II s. *Ζῆθος* I); (21) ~ ib. 116, 3 (*Ζῆθο[ς]*); (22) ~ *IOSPE* I² 359, 22; 391 (Solomonik, *NEPKh* 112 c); *VDI* 1960 (3), pp. 154-5, 21 (s. *Ἀρίστων*, f. *Ἀρίστων*); (23) ~ *SEG* XXVIII 631, 2 (*Ζῆ(θ)ος*); (24) c. 120-130 AD Solomonik, *NEPKh* 112, 12 (f. *Ἀπολλώνιος*); (25) m. ii AD *SEG* XLVI 930, 4 (f. —ος); (26) 129 AD *IOSPE* I² 359, 32 (*Ζῆθ<υ>ος*: s. *Ἀπολλώνιος*); (27) 129-130 AD ib. l. 29; *VDI* 1960 (3), pp. 154-5, 26 (s. *Πυθόδοτος*); (28) 130 AD ib. l. 18, 30 (f. *Ἡρωΐδας*)
THRACE:
—PAUTALIA: (29) s. ii AD *SEG* XLVI 864, 9 (f. *Σέξτος*)
—PHILIPPOPOLIS-TRIMONTIUM (TERRIT.): (30) ii-iii AD *IGB* III 1537, 2 (slave?)

Ζήθων
TAURIS:
—CHERSONESOS: (1) s. i BC Const. Porph., *De admin. imp.* 53, 276 (f. *Ζῆθος*)

Ζηΐλας
THRACE:
—KAZANLAK (MOD.): (1) f. v BC *SEG* XLVI 850 (*Ζηΐλα* (gen.): f. *Δύντος*)

Ζηκαλώγη
MACEDONIA (ODOMANTIKE):
—GAZOROS (TERRIT.): (1) hell. ib. XXXIX 569 (Pilhofer 554) (d. *Τραλικείλας*)

Ζήμαρχος
THRACE:
—BESSOI: (1) 561 AD *POxy* 1903, 9; 2046, 47

Ζημοκάρτης
THRACE:
—SALYMBRIA: (1) iv-v AD *BCH* 36 (1912) p. 574 nos. 29-30 (*AD* 53 (1998) Mel. p. 462 no. 202) (*Ζημωκάρτης* (estate)—29)

Ζηνᾶς
THRACE:
—PERINTHOS-HERAKLEIA*: (1) 88 AD *IPerinth* 44, 7 (*Τιβ. Κλ. Ζηνᾶ(ς)*: imp. freed.)

Ζηνδη
THRACE:
—SALYMBRIA: (1) imp. *IByz* S 14; cf. Robert, *Hell.* 7 p. 48 n. 6

Ζηνέας
THRACE:
—ABDERA: (1) a. 316 BC *IG* IV (1)² 94 b, 51 (Perlman, *City and Sanctuary* E.1 with pp. 78-9 (date)) (s. *Πῦθις*)

Ζηνήκενθος
MACEDONIA (PIERIS):
—PHAGRES (TERRIT.)?: (1) 215 AD Pikoulas, *Chora* p. 167 no. 76 (s. *Δούλαιμος*)

Ζηνικέτης
THRACE:
—LYSIMACHEIA: (1) hell. *ISestos* 40 (*Ξηνικέτης*—apogr.)

Ζήνιος
THRACE:
—ODESSOS (NR.): (1) s. ii AD *IGB* I² 269 (*CCET* I 12) (s. *Ἀσ̣*—)

Ζῆνις
THRACE:
—ANCHIALOS: (1) i-ii AD *IGB* I² 375 (PM 883) (*Ζήνιδος* (gen.): f. *Σίμη*)
—MESAMBRIA (TERRIT.): (2) iv AD *IGB* V 5129, 2 (*Φλ. Ζ.*: f. *Νωμινᾶτος*, *Μαρκιανός*, *Βαλερία*)
—ODESSOS: (3) ii-i BC ib. 5024 (*Ζῆνε[ι]* (dat.)) ?= (*5*); (4) i BC ib. I² 154 (PM 922) (*Ζῆνι* (gen.): f. *Ἀριστοκλῆς*) ?= (*6*); (5) 19-18 BC *IGB* I² 46, 28-9 (*Ζῆνι* (gen.): s. *Ἀγαθήνωρ*, f. *Ἀγαθήνωρ*) ?= (*3*); (6) 8 BC ib. l. 39 (*Ζῆνι* (gen.): f. *Ἀριστοκλῆς*) ?= (*4*); (7) i AD ib. 186 bis (PM 1661); *Dacia* 21 (1977) p. 161 (date) (*Ζῆνι* (gen.): f. *Φιλίστη*); (8) i-ii AD *IGB* I² 139 bis (*Ζήνιδος* (gen.): f. *Φιλίστη*); (9) ~ ib. 188 (*Ζήνιδος* (gen.): f. *Βλωστι*); (10) ~ ib. 197 (*Ζήνιδος* (gen.)); (11) f. ii AD ib. 77, 4 (*CCET* I 31) (*Ζῆνι* (gen.): s. *Ποσειδώνιος*); (12) ~ *IGB* I² 78 ter, 2 (*CCET* I 30) (*Ζήνιδος* (gen.): f. *Νουμήνιος*)
—ODESSOS (NR.): (13) s. ii AD *IGB* I² 291 (*CCET* I 95) (*Ζήνει* (gen.): f. *Ἀγαθήνωρ*); (14) ~ *IGB* I² 291 (*CCET* I 95) (s. *Ἀγαθήνωρ*)

Ζηνίς
THRACE:
—SALYMBRIA: (1) ii-i BC *IByz* S 35 (PM 511) (d. *Ζήνων*)

Ζηνίων
THRACE:
—AINOS?: (1) 239 BC *SB* 11376, 7-8

Ζηνοβία
MACEDONIA (MYGDONIA):
—THESSALONIKE: (1) vi AD Feissel, *RICM* 164 B (*SEG* XLVII 979 B)

Ζηνόβιος
CIMMERIAN BOSPOROS:
—GORGIPPIA: (1) ii AD *CIRB* 1153
—PANTIKAPAION: (2) i AD ib. 411 (I f. *Ζηνόβιος* II); (3) ~ ib. (II s. *Ζηνόβιος* I); (4) i/ii AD ib. 630

MACEDONIA (BOTTIAIA):
—BEROIA: (5) v-vi AD *IBer* 439 (Feissel, *RICM* 71; *PLRE* III (1)) (f. Ἰωάννης)
MACEDONIA (EDONIS):
—AMPHIPOLIS: (6) imp. *SEG* XXIV 603 (f. Σιτᾶς)
MACEDONIA (MYGDONIA):
—THESSALONIKE: (7) iii AD *IG* X (2) (1) 247, 5 ([Ζη]νόβιος?)
SKYTHIA:
—TANAIS: (8) 104 AD *CIRB* 1259, 18 (f. Ἔρως)
THRACE:
—BYZANTION:
——(Rhegion): (9) i BC-i AD *IByz* 253 A (f. Διοσκουρίδης)

Ζηνόδοτος
SKYTHIA:
—OLBIA-BORYSTHENES: (1) f. iv BC Dubois, *IGDOlbia* 104 (f. Φορμίων)
TAURIS:
—CHERSONESOS: (2) s. v BC *SEG* XL 612. 5 (ostrakon) (s. Εὐαρχίδας)
THRACE: (3) c. 223 BC *PTeb* 815 fr. 5, 12 (Velkov 120; La'da E829) (s. Χαρίδημος: t.e.)
—IATRUS*: (4) i-ii AD *Arkheologiia* (Sofia) 1984 (1), pp. 41-2 no. 3 (Lat. Ti. Claudios Zhnodotos)
—PERINTHOS-HERAKLEIA:
——(Kastaleis): (5) iii-ii BC *IPerinth* 61, 55 (s. Στησαγόρης); (6) ~ ib. l. 58 (s. Ἀπολλόθεμις)
——(Podargoi): (7) iii-ii BC ib. l. 21 (f. Δημάρετος)

Ζηνοδώρα
THRACE: (1) iii AD *CIL* VI 2734 (Lat. Aurelia Zenodora)

Ζηνόδωρος
CIMMERIAN BOSPOROS:
—PANTIKAPAION: (1) 221 AD *CIRB* 99, 12 (Ἰούλ. Ζ(η)νόδωρος)
THRACE:
—KARDIA?: (2) hell. *Syringes* 606, 3 (La'da E981) (Ζηνόδω[ρος])

Ζηνόθεμις
MACEDONIA (CHALKIDIKE):
—MENDE: (1) s. vi BC *SEG* XLIII 429 (vase)
THRACE:
—LYSIMACHEIA: (2) 238 BC *PPetr*^{2} 3, 95 (La'da E1367) ([Ζη]νόθεμις, [Φα]νόθεμις?, [Ἀγ]νόθεμις—edd., [Μη]νόθεμις?) ?= (3)
—LYSIMACHEIA?: (3) 232-226 BC *PP* 7935; cf. *PPetr*^{2} 3 comm. on l. 95 ?= (2)

Ζήνων
CIMMERIAN BOSPOROS:
—BOSPOROS: (1) ii AD *IOSPE* I^2 204 (s. Στρατόνικος)
—GORGIPPIA: (2) f. iii BC *CIRB* 1137 A I, 46; 1137 A II, 42 (f. Διοκλῆς); (3) ii/iii AD *VDI* 1970 (4), p. 149, 8 (f. Ἀγαθοῦς)
—PANTIKAPAION: (4) s. iv BC *CIRB* 116 (*CEG* II 735) (f. Ἀπατούριος); (5) i/ii AD *CIRB* 145 (*GVI* 1475) (f. Στρατόνικος); (6) iii AD *CIRB* 721; cf. KW pl. 56 no. 760 (f. Ἔρως); (7) 275-278 AD *CIRB* 36, 33 ([Ζ]ήνων: f. Μενέστρατος); (8) ~ ib. l. 44; (9) ~ ib. l. 64 ([Ζ]ήνων: s. Μενέστρατος)
MACEDONIA (BOTTIAIA):
—SKYDRA?: (10) 105 AD *SEG* XVII 317, 12 (Κλ. Ζ.: freed.?)
MACEDONIA (EDONIS):
—PHILIPPOI (TERRIT.): (11) ?iii AD Pikoulas, *Chora* p. 149 no. 59, 20 (Pilhofer 602; *SEG* L 618); cf. *BE* 1944, no. 129 (Ζήνονος (gen.): f. —ιναπος)
MACEDONIA (LYNKESTIS):
—HERAKLEIA: (12) i AD *IG* X (2) (2) 78 (biling.) (Lat. Zenon)
MACEDONIA (MYGDONIA):
—THESSALONIKE: (13) ii AD ib. X (2) (1) 536 + *BCH* 97 (1973) p. 593 (Τι. Κλ. Μαρκιανὸς Ζ.); (14) ii-iii AD *IG* X (2) (1) 473 (Γ. Ἰούλ. Ζ.: f. Ἰσίδωρος)
MACEDONIA (PAIONIA):
—KAVADARCI (MOD.): (15) ii AD *Sp.* 98 (1941-8) p. 77 no. 165; cf. 75 (1933) p. 40 no. 135 (s. Κούτης)
SKYTHIA:
—OLBIA-BORYSTHENES: (16) ii AD *IOlbia* 80, 7 (s. Εὐρησίβιος); (17) ii-iii AD *IOSPE* I^2 136, 3 (s. Στρατόνικος); (18) iii AD ib. 135, 5 (s. Ζωτικός)
—TANAIS: (19) f. ii AD *CIRB* 1295 (Ζήνω[ν]); (20) 192 AD ib. 1243, 16 (f. Δάδας) ?= (21); (21) 193 AD ib. 1237, 8, 12 (I s. Δάδας, f. Ζήνων II) ?= (20); (22) ~ ib. l. 12 (II s. Ζήνων I); (23) 210-226 AD ib. 1245, 4, 14; 1246, [5]; 1248, [7]; 1278, 7 (s. Φάννης); (24) 229 AD *Stud. Zhebelev* p. 47, 17 (s. Ἀστήρ); (25) 244 AD *CIRB* 1287, 17 (f. —νικος)
THRACE:
—ABDERA: (26) c. 360-350 BC May, *Abdera* pp. 259-60 nos. 447-8 (coin)
—AINOS?: (27) 239 BC *SB* 11376, 7-8 (La'da E87)
—ANCHIALOS (TERRIT.): (28) ii-iii AD *IGB* I^2 385, 6 (s. Ζ—)
—BYZANTION?: (29) ii AD *IByz* 330 (f. Ζώτιχος)
—DIONYSOPOLIS: (30) iii AD *IGB* I^2 14 b, 23 (f. Αὐρ. Ἀλέξανδρος)
—HADRIANOPOLIS (TERRIT.): (31) ii-iii AD ib. III 1818 (s. Πολέμων)
—MARONEIA: (32) c. 365-336 BC Schönert-Geiss, *Maroneia* 468-83; 521-34 (coin); (33) s. ii BC *IG* XII (8) 170 c, 40 (f. Διόδοτος)
—PERINTHOS-HERAKLEIA: (34) 144 AD *IGB* V 5636, 16; *SEG* XLII 647 (f. Νάρκισσος)
—SALYMBRIA: (35) ii-i BC *IByz* S 35 (PM 511) (f. Φιλοθέα, Ζηνίς)
—STRYME: (36) s. v BC *IThrakAig* E113 (s. Ποσιδήϊος)

Ζήσιμος
THRACE:
—PAUTALIA: (1) s. ii AD *SEG* XLVI 864 II, 24

Ζησίς
MACEDONIA (ODOMANTIKE):
—SIRRHA: (1) 105 or 221 AD ib. XXX 595 (Ζησῖ (dat.))

Ζησώ
MACEDONIA (EDONIS):
—AMPHIPOLIS?: (1) ii BC ib. XLVII 886; cf. *BE* 1998, no. 277 (name) (d. Διονύσιος)
THRACE:
—ČOMAKOVCI (MOD.): (2) imp. *Arkheologiia* (Sofia) 1975 (3), pp. 38-9 no. 4 (Lat. Zeso)

Ζια
THRACE:
—NICOPOLIS AD ISTRUM (TERRIT.): (1) f. iii AD *CCET* II (2) 675, 8 (*ILB* 349) (Lat. Zia: d. Carcenus)

Ζιακάτραλις
THRACE:
—PHILIPPOPOLIS-TRIMONTIUM: (1) iii AD *IGB* III 976 (f. Βρίζενις)

Ζιαμάρκη
THRACE:
—DIOSPOLIS: (1) iii AD ib. 1787, 6

Ζιαμήτραλις
THRACE:
—NICOPOLIS AD ISTRUM (TERRIT.): (1) iii AD ib. II 719 (s. Βίθυς)

Ζιασάλβη
THRACE:
—BEROE-AUGUSTA TRAIANA: (1) 535 AD *SEG* XLIX 873, 2

Ζιβέλμιος
THRACE:
—KAINOI: (1) s. ii BC *RE* (-) (s. Διήγυλις: king)

Ζιγέθης
THRACE:
—PAUTALIA (TERRIT.): (1) iii AD *IGB* IV 2211

Ζίγρας
MACEDONIA (MYGDONIA):
—KALINDOIA: (1) a. 98 AD *SEG* XLII 582, 30; cf. *Anthémonte–Kalindoia* 2 p. 259 (name) ((Σ)ί(π)ρας?: f. Δάλης)

Ζιέρις
THRACE:
—ODESSOS: (1) 215 AD *IGB* I^2 47 c, 29 (Αὐρ. Ζ.: s. Βιάτωρ)

Ζίλης
MACEDONIA (SINTIKE):
—PARTHIKOPOLIS (NR.): (1) ii-iii AD ib. IV 2289

Ζιμίκενθις
THRACE?: (1) i AD *IGerasa* 200 (biling.) (s. Ἐζιωπην)

Ζινήγορος?
THRACE:
—KOILA: (1) imp. *BCH* 36 (1912) p. 288 n.2 (Αἰλ. Ζινηγόρου(?) (gen.))

Ζινόπορις
THRACE:
—ODESSOS: (1) ii-iii AD *IGB* I^2 184 (Ζεινώπορεις: s. Ζ—)

Ζιουρις
THRACE:
—ABRYTTOS (NR.): (1) f. iii AD ib. V 5269 (*CCET* II (2) 614) (s. Ἀμιαζεν—)

Ζιπαίβης
MACEDONIA (EDONIS):
—IOLLITAI: (1) ii-iii AD *BCH* 24 (1900) p. 317, 4 (Pilhofer 417) (f. Βίθυς)
—PHILIPPOI (TERRIT.): (2) ?ii AD *BCH* 47 (1923) p. 69 no. 25 (Pilhofer 514); *Dacia* 2 (1958) p. 523 (name) (Lat. Zepa[ib]is (gen.): f. Ἀλιούλας); (3) ~ *BCH* 47 (1923) pp. 64-5 no. 24, 5 (Pilhofer 519) (Lat. Zipaibis (gen.))

Ζιπάκενθος
MACEDONIA (EDONIS):
—PHILIPPOI (TERRIT.): (1) ?ii AD *CIL* III 703, 4 (Pilhofer 524); Collart, *Philippes* pl. 84. 2 (Lat. Zipacenthus: s. Tauzix)

Ζιπάλας
MACEDONIA (EDONIS):
—PHILIPPOI (NR.): (1) ii-iii AD *BCH* 54 (1930) p. 376 (Pilhofer 48); Collart, *Philippes* pl. 36. 3 (f. Ἀλιουπαίβης)
MACEDONIA (ODOMANTIKE):
—GAZOROS (TERRIT.): (2) 148 or 264 AD *BCH* 35 (1911) p. 115 (Pilhofer 540; *AD* 52 (1997) Chron. p. 847 with pl. 314 δ; *SEG* L 569) (Ζειπάλα (gen.), Ζειπα λα—ed.: f. Κοζίλας)

Ζίπαρος
MACEDONIA (MYGDONIA):
—THESSALONIKE?: (1) 155 AD *IG* X (2) (1) 805, 4 (Ζεί-)

Ζιπᾶς
MACEDONIA (BOTTIAIA):
—BEROIA: (1) ii AD Dimitsas 212; cf. *SEG* XXVIII 551 (Tataki 503) (Ζει-: s. Δεντοῦς)

Macedonia (Edonis):
—amphipolis: **(2)** ii-iii ad *Thrakika* 13 (1940) pp. 19-20 *A* + *Epigraphica* 37 (1975) p. 26 (s. *Σάνβος*); **(3)** ~ *Thracia* 2 p. 278 + *Epigraphica* 37 (1935) p. 31 (s. *Δερης*); **(4)** 165 ad *SEG* xlix 676; cf. *AEMTh* 12 (1998) p. 78 and p. 82 fig. 4 (*Ζει-*)
—philippoi: **(5)** imp. *BIAB* 16 (1950) p. 9 no. 3 (Pilhofer 51) (Lat. Valerius Z[i]pa: s. *Μάντα*); **(6)** ?ii ad *Philippes* i p. 120 no. 96 (Pilhofer 171) (Lat. Zipas)
—philippoi (territ.): **(7)** imp. Pikoulas, *Chora* p. 159 no. 67 (*Ζειπᾶ* (gen.)); **(8)** ~ *CIL* iii 14206. 10 (*AM* 33 (1908) p. 44 no. 6; Pilhofer 515) (Lat. Zipas Margulas); **(9)** i-ii ad *AD* 52 (1997) Chron. p. 847 with pl. 314 α (Lat. Zipa: s. Trais); **(10)** ?ii ad *BIAB* 16 (1950) pp. 14-15 no. 11, 1, 3 (Pilhofer 649) (Lat. Zipa: I s. *Μάλθας*, f. *Ἀλιούλας*, *Ζιπᾶς* II, *Δαντοῦς*); **(11)** ~ *BIAB* 16 (1950) pp. 14-15 no. 11, 3 (Pilhofer 649) (Lat. Zipa: II s. *Ζιπᾶς* I, Caigeno); **(12)** ~ *BCH* 47 (1923) p. 69 no. 25 (Pilhofer 514) (Lat. Zipas); **(13)** ~ *BCH* 47 (1923) pp. 62-3 no. 21, 6 (Pilhofer 520) (Lat. Zipas); **(14)** ~ Pikoulas, *Chora* p. 115-16 no. 4, 6 (Pilhofer 638) (Lat. Zipae (gen.): f. Prima); **(15)** ii-iii ad *BCH* 24 (1900) p. 317 (Pilhofer 535); cf. Collart, *Philippes* pl. 37. 3 (*Ζει-*: f. *Ροῦφος*); **(16)** s. ii ad Pikoulas, *Chora* p. 158 no. 64 (Pilhofer 597); cf. *Dacia* 19 (1975) p. 198 no. 2 (date); Collart, *Philippes* pl. 38. 2 (*Ζει-*); **(17)** ?iii ad Pikoulas, *Chora* p. 146 no. 59, 18 (Pilhofer 602; *SEG* l 618); cf. *BE* 1944, no. 129 (s. *Ζίποδος*); **(18)** ~ *SEG* xxx 594 A, 2 (Pilhofer 580) (*Ζει-*: s. *Τα(—)*); **(19)** ~ *SEG* xxx 594 A, 11 (Pilhofer 580) (*Ζει-*: s. *Δαν(—)*); **(20)** ~ *SEG* xxx 594 B, 2 (Pilhofer 580) (*Ζει-*: s. *Ζει(—)*); **(21)** ~ *SEG* xxx 594 B, 5 (Pilhofer 580) (*Ζει-*: s. *Δι(—)*); **(22)** ~ *SEG* xxx 594 B, 7 (Pilhofer 580) (*Ζει-*: s. *Μαρ(—)*); **(23)** ~ *SEG* xxx 594 B, 9 (Pilhofer 580) (*Ζει-*: I f. *Ζιπᾶς* II); **(24)** ~ *SEG* xxx 594 B, 9 (Pilhofer 580) (*Ζει-*: II s. *Ζιπᾶς* I); **(25)** ~ *SEG* xxx 594 B, 10 (Pilhofer 580) (*Ζει-*: s. *Ταρ(—)*)
—philippoi (drama (mod.)): **(26)** i-ii ad *AD* 51 (1996) Chron. p. 577, 19 (Lat. Cornelius Zipa); **(27)** ii-iii ad ib. 52 (1997) Chron. p. 847, 2 with pl. 314 *β*
—philippoi (nr.): **(28)** imp. *CIL* iii 6115 a (Pilhofer 35) (Lat. Zipas: f. Secunda)
—philippoi (territ.)?: **(29)** imp. *CIL* iii 7378 (biling.) (*Thrakika* 8 (1937) p. 21 no. 3) (*Ποπίλλιος Ζειπᾶς*)
—skaporenoi?: **(30)** ?ii ad *BCH* 24 (1900) p. 310 no. 3 (Pilhofer 512) (Lat. Zipa: s. *Μέστος*)
Macedonia (Mygdonia):
—lete: **(31)** ii ad *Makedonika* 2 (1951) p. 619 no. 42 *θ*, 16 (*Ζει-*: s. *Βαστικίλας*)
—thessalonike: **(32)** a. 212 ad *SEG* xxix 584
—thessalonike (nr.): **(33)** ?iii ad *IG* x (2) (1) 1004, 7 (*Ἡρωΐδης* (ὁ) κὲ Ζ.)
Macedonia (Odomantike):
—gazoros (territ.): **(34)** 148 or 264 ad *BCH* 35 (1911) p. 115 (Pilhofer 540; *AD* 52 (1997) Chron. p. 847 with pl. 314 *δ*; *SEG* l 569) (*Ζει-*: s. *Κοζείκενθος*)
—sirrha: **(35)** f. iii ad ib. xxx 590, 36 (*Ζει-*)
Macedonia (Pieria):
—dion?: **(36)** s. ii ad ib. xxxv 814 + xlviii 876 (*Ζ̣ει-*)
Scythia Minor:
—istros: **(37)** s. ii ad *ISM* i 167, 5 (s. *Διοκλῆς*)
Thrace:
—nicopolis ad nestum: **(38)** ii ad *IGB* iv 2336, 13 (*Ζ(ε)ιπᾶς*: f. *Ἀλέξανδρος*)
—serdica: **(39)** imp. Minkova, *PNLIB* p. 282 (Lat. Zipas)

Ζίπερ
Macedonia (Edonis):
—amphipolis: **(1)** ii-iii ad *Thrakika* 13 (1940) pp. 20-1 *B* + *Epigraphica* 37 (1975) pp. 26-7; **(2)** ~ Kaphtantzis 699; *Epigraphica* 37 (1975) p. 34 (name) (s. *Δητούβιθυς*)

Ζίποδος?
Macedonia (Edonis):
—philippoi (territ.): **(1)** ?iii ad Pikoulas, *Chora* p. 146 no. 59, 18 (Pilhofer 602; *SEG* l 618); cf. *BE* 1944, no. 129 (*Ζι̣πόδου* (gen.), *Ζιποβου*—ed.: f. *Ζιπᾶς*)

Ζιποίτης
Thrace?: **(1)** iii bc *PMagd* 39, 13 (Velkov 121)

Ζίπυρος
Macedonia (Edonis):
—amphipolis: **(1)** ii-iii ad *Thrakika* 13 (1940) p. 28 *Ψ* (*-πι-*); **(2)** ~ ib. pp. 20-1 *Γ* + *Epigraphica* 37 (1975) p. 27 (*Ζύπηρος ν(εώτ.)*?—Mihailov)
—philippoi (territ.): **(3)** imp.? Pikoulas, *Chora* p. 135 no. 37 (*Ζεί-*: f. *Ἡρόδοτος*)
Thrace: **(4)** 274 bc *PCZ* 59001, 24, [51], verso (La'da E745) (s. *Βίθυς*); **(5)** ?ii-i bc *Syringes* 693; 698 (Velkov 122); cf. La'da E724 (f. *Δάδας*)
—gabare (mod.): **(6)** iii ad *Romanizmăt* ii 261 (Lat. Ziepyr)
Thrace?: **(7)** b. 238 bc *PHib* 81, 18 + *PP* 2279 Add. (name) (f. *Ἐβρύζελμις*)

Ζιπύρων
Macedonia (Chalkidike):
—moni iviron (mod.): **(1)** ii-iii ad Dimitsas 777; cf. Robert, *OMS* 2 p. 1288 n. 1 (*Ζειπύροντος* (gen.): f. *Ζώσιμος*)
—potidaia-kassandreia (nr.): **(2)** ii-iii ad *BE* 1970, no. 310 (*Makedonika* 15 (1975) p. 234 no. 123 with pl. 150 *β*) (*Ζει-*: f. *Διζάλης*)
Macedonia (Edonis):
—amphipolis: **(3)** ii ad *SEG* xxxix 570 (*Ζει-*); **(4)** ii-iii ad ib. xv 416, 1 (*Ζει-*: s. *Βύσειλος*); **(5)** 158 or 274 ad ib. 415, 1 (*Ζει-*: I f. *Ζιπύρων* II); **(6)** ~ ib. l. 1 (*Ζει-*: II s. *Ζιπύρων* I, f. *Βουκούθης*); **(7)** iii-iv ad *AD* 38 (1983) Chron. p. 332 (*Ζει-*)
—amphipolis?: **(8)** ii-iii ad Dimitsas 906 (Kaphtantzis 543) (*Ζει-*: s. *Ἡλιζις*)
—amphipolis (territ.)?: **(9)** imp. *AD* 38 (1983) Chron. p. 332 n. 3 (or Macedonia (Pieris) Phagres); **(10)** 192 ad Pikoulas, *Chora* p. 160 no. 69 (*Ζει-*: s. *—εμος*)
—philippoi: **(11)** f. i ad *AM* 33 (1908) p. 45 no. 11 (fals.?) (Pilhofer 699) (Lat. Ziryronivs—lap.); **(12)** iii ad *BCH* 60 (1936) p. 337, 1, 13 (Pilhofer 133) (*Αὐρ. Ζ.*: s. *Δίζας*)
—philippoi (territ.): **(13)** imp. Pikoulas, *Chora* p. 137 no. 41 (*[Ζ]ιπύρων*); **(14)** ~ ib. p. 152 no. 60 (Pilhofer 603) (*Ζει-*: s. *Πατουμάστης*); **(15)** ?ii ad *BCH* 47 (1923) pp. 64-5 no. 24, 6 (Pilhofer 519) (Lat. Zipyro: s. *Δούλης*); **(16)** ~ Pikoulas, *Chora* p. 115-16 no. 4, 1 (Pilhofer 638) (Lat. Zipyr(o)?: s. Soudilae (gen.), *Βενδίς*); **(17)** ii-iii ad Pikoulas, *Chora* p. 123 no. 13, 5; cf. *BE* 2002, no. 291 (*Ζει-*: s. *Σκάρης*)
—philippoi (drama (mod.)): **(18)** ii-iii ad *AD* 52 (1997) Chron. p. 847, 6 with pl. 314 *β* (*Ζει-*); **(19)** ~ ib. l. 9 with pl. 314 *β* (*Ζει-*)
—sceveni?: **(20)** iii-iv ad Pikoulas, *Chora* p. 119 no. 10 (Pilhofer 644) (Lat. Zipyronis (gen.): f. Dagos)
Macedonia (Mygdonia):
—kalindoia: **(21)** 68-98 ad *SEG* xlii 580, 85; cf. *Anthémonte–Kalindoia* 2 pp. 257-8 (name) (*Ζει-*: s. *Διοσκουρίδης*); **(22)** a. 98 ad *SEG* xlii 583, 24 (*Ζει-*: f. *Ζώπυρος*, ?f. *Δούλης*)

Macedonia (Odomantike):
—drabeskos?: **(23)** ii-iii ad ib. xxx 619, 3 (Pilhofer 572) (*Ζιπύροντος* (gen.): f. *Διοσκουρίδης*)
—sirrha?: **(24)** ?iii ad Kaphtantzis 40 (f. *Δούλης*)
Macedonia (Pieris):
—galepsos: **(25)** 65 or 181 ad *SEG* xxvii 284 (s. *Ἀγαθοκλῆς*)
—phagres (territ.)?: **(26)** ii-iii ad Pikoulas, *Chora* p. 168 no. 77 (*Ζειπύροντος* (gen.): f. *Μάντα*)

Ζίπυς
Thrace:
—nicopolis ad istrum (territ.): **(1)** iii ad *IGB* ii 711 (s. *Μουκατρας*)

Ζισουρας
Thrace:
—nicopolis ad istrum: **(1)** ii-iii ad ib. 673

Ζμάδης
Cimmerian Bosporos:
—nymphaion: **(1)** i ad *CIRB* 928; Zgusta, *PNS* 637 (f. *Ἡδοῦς*)

Ζόβην
Cimmerian Bosporos:
—pantikapaion: **(1)** i bc/i ad *CIRB* 320; cf. KW pl. 30 no. 427; *Etiudy* p. 186 no. 8; Robert, *Noms indigènes* p. 538

Ζοιθα
Thrace:
—markianopolis (territ.): **(1)** ii-iii ad *IGB* ii 843, 2 (d. *Βίθυς*)

Ζόλτης
Thrace: **(1)** s. iii bc *ISM* i 15, [14], [21], 31, 35, 38, 57

Ζορδέγων
Thrace:
—philippopolis-trimontium: **(1)** ii-iii ad *IGB* iii 967 + v 5428 (*Ζορδέγονος* (gen.): f. *Δωλέπορις*)

Ζορδησιοσος
Thrace:
—durostorum (territ.)?: **(1)** iii ad ib. ii 872 (f. *Ζεινης*)

Ζοτομᾶς
Skythia:
—tanais: **(1)** ii ad *CIRB* 1268, 7; Zgusta, *PNS* 638 (f. *—ους*)

Ζοτουμᾶς
Cimmerian Bosporos:
—pantikapaion: **(1)** f. ii ad *CIRB* 89, 2
—zenonos chersonesos*: **(2)** f. i ad ib. 900 (*[Ζο]τουμᾶς*: s. *Βιόμασος*)

Ζουδιεγιπτους
Thrace:
—odessos: **(1)** ii ad *IGB* i² 178 bis (d. *Ἀγαθήνωρ*, ?d. *Βοών*, *Τουτάς*)

Ζούθης
Scythia Minor:
—istros: **(1)** iii ad *ISM* i 303, 7 (*Ζούθει* (dat.): s. *Χρύσιππος*, *Πώμη*)

Ζουκαιβλωστι
Thrace:
—odessos: **(1)** ii ad *IGB* v 5067, 4 (d. *Σκωρισεισος*, m. *Βλωστι*)

Ζουκη
Scythia Minor:
—kallatis: **(1)** iii-iv ad *ISM* iii 193 (d. *Βακ—*)

Ζουκηπιστος
Thrace:
—odessos: **(1)** f. ii ad *IGB* i² 171 bis (PM 1612); cf. *IGB* v 5049; *Dacia* 21 (1977) p. 161 (date) (d. *Ἕλλην*)

Ζουλγήσης
THRACE:
—DRAGANOVEC (MOD.): **(1)** f. iii AD *IGB* v 5294 (*CCET* II (2) 484) (s. *Δέκρυμνος*)

Ζουλεμης
THRACE:
—ODESSOS?: **(1)** iii BC *IGB* I^{2} 479 ter (PM 1732); cf. *IGB* v 5156 (d. *Διονύσιος*)

Ζουμαμα
THRACE:
—ODESSOS: **(1)** i BC-i AD ib. 5061 (d. *Ἀγαθήνωρ*)

Ζουραζεις
THRACE:
—ODESSOS: **(1)** f. iii AD ib. I^{2} 162, 5 (*CCET* I 60; PM 1383); cf. *IGB* v 5046 (*Ζουραζ[εις]*?: s. *M. Αὐρ. Σκόντις*)
—STRATOPARA: **(2)** 202 AD ib. III 1690 b, 26 (and Thrace Pizos: s. *Αὐλούζενις*)

Ζουράζερις
THRACE:
—DRAGANOVEC (MOD.): **(1)** f. iii AD ib. v 5287 (*CCET* II (2) 457) (f. *Μάξιμος*)

Ζουράζιος
THRACE:
—HADRIANOPOLIS: **(1)** iv-v AD *SEG* VIII 45, 2 (*Ζουραζιο* (gen.): f. *Βουράδις*)

Ζούρης
SCYTHIA MINOR:
—ISTROS: **(1)** i AD *ISM* I 200, 5 (*Ζούρηι* (gen.): f. *Χαιρέας*)
SKYTHIA:
—TYRAS: **(2)** 181 AD *IOSPE* I^{2} 2, 23; Zgusta, *PNS* 589 (*Ζούρη* (gen.): f. *Καῖσαρ*)
THRACE:
—APRILOVO (MOD.): **(3)** f. iii AD *IGB* II 765 (*CCET* II (2) 539) (*Ζουρήους* (gen.): f. *Σαικίθης*)

Ζουρόζιος
SKYTHIA:
—OLBIA-BORYSTHENES: **(1)** ii AD *IOSPE* I^{2} 102, 8; Zgusta, *PNS* 588 (f. *Πουρθάκης*)

Ζουρόζις
SKYTHIA:
—OLBIA-BORYSTHENES: **(1)** ii AD *IOSPE* I^{2} 84, 6; Zgusta, *PNS* 588 (s. *Γετόμουσος*)

Ζουροτελμίς
THRACE:
—BEROE-AUGUSTA TRAIANA:
——Emporion Diskodouraterai: **(1)** ii-iii AD *IGB* II 738, 3 (*Ζουροτε[λ]μίς*: d. *Διμης, Δωρουτελμίς*)

Ζτάθιος
KOLCHIS:
—LAZOI: **(1)** f. vi AD *PLRE* II (-); *RE* s.v. Tzath (1) (*Z.*—Jo.Mal., *Τζάθιος*—*Chron. Pasch.*, *Τζάθος*—Zon.: s. *Δαμνάζης*)

Ζυβαρα
THRACE:
—PAUTALIA: **(1)** s. ii AD *SEG* XLVI 864 II, 25

Ζυκουλαίσης
THRACE: **(1)** 46-54 AD ib. XVI 415 I, 15 (*IThrakAig* E84) (*Τιβ. Κλ. Ζυκολαίσης*)
—PHILIPPOPOLIS-TRIMONTIUM (TERRIT.): **(2)** ii AD *IGB* III 1324 (*T. Φλ. Ζυκουδαίσης*—ed.)

Ζυκουλήσης
MACEDONIA (EDONIS):
—AMPHIPOLIS: **(1)** ii-iii AD Kaphtantzis 689; *Epigraphica* 37 (1975) p. 35 (name) (*Τσουκολειζι*)

THRACE:
—TOPEIROS: **(2)** i AD *Thrakika* 8 (1937) pp. 30-1 no. 9 (*IThrakAig* E87) (s. *Τυρέλσης*) ?= (*5*) (*3*); **(3)** ~ *SEG* XXXIII 535 (*IThrakAig* E86) (s. *Τυρέλσης*) ?= (*2*) (*4*)
—TOPEIROS?: **(4)** 46-54 AD *SEG* XVI 415 III, 33 (*IThrakAig* E84) (s. *Τυρέλσης*) ?= (*3*); **(5)** ~ *SEG* XVI 415 III, 34 (*IThrakAig* E84) (f. *Διουζίης*) ?= (*2*)

Ζυρίδης
THRACE:
—BISANTHE-PANION?: **(1)** s. v BC PM 58 (f. *Σημωνίδης*)

Ζώα
THRACE:
—BYZANTION?: **(1)** ii-i BC *IByz* 343 (d. *Μήνιος*)

Ζώανδρος
MACEDONIA (DERRIOPOS):
—STUBERRA: **(1)** 74 AD *IG* X (2) (2) 325, 30-1 (*Ζό-*: s. *Ζωΐλος*); **(2)** ~ ib. 326, 21 (*Ζό-*: s. *Στράτων*); **(3)** 74-116 AD ib. 325, 22; 327, 7 (*Ζόανδρος*—327: f. *Διονύσιος*)

Ζώβεις
SKYTHIA:
—OLBIA-BORYSTHENES: **(1)** ii AD *IOSPE* I^{2} 105, 6; 176, 6; Zgusta, *PNS* 998 (I f. *Ζώβεις* II); **(2)** ~ *IOSPE* I^{2} 105, 6; 176, 6 (II s. *Ζώβεις* I)

Ζωβία
MACEDONIA (BOTTIAIA):
—PELLA: **(1)** v/iv BC *Egnatia* 5 (1995-2000) p. 261 (*SEG* XLIX 754)
MACEDONIA (MYGDONIA):
—THESSALONIKE: **(2)** ?i AD *IG* X (2) (1) 53 (d. *Μένανδρος*)

Ζωβίη
THRACE:
—APOLLONIA-SOZOPOLIS: **(1)** iv BC *BMNBurgas* 4 (2002) p. 119 no. 1 (d. *Διονυσόδωρος*)

Ζωβῖνος
THRACE?: **(1)** iii AD *CIL* X 1754, 8 (Lat. Aur. Zobinus)

Ζωγένης
CIMMERIAN BOSPOROS:
—PANTIKAPAION: **(1)** f. iv BC *CIRB* 217 (s. *Ζώπυρος*)

Ζώη
MACEDONIA (BOTTIAIA):
—BEROIA: **(1)** ii AD *IBer* 241 (Tataki 346) (*Γελλία Ζόη*)
—EDESSA: **(2)** f. iii AD Spiliopoulou-Donderer, *KGN* p. 206 no. E3 (*Ζό-*: d. *Αὐρ. Κλαυδία*)
MACEDONIA (LYNKESTIS):
—ACHLADA (MOD.): **(3)** m. iii AD *EAM* 172 (*Ζό-*)
MACEDONIA (ODOMANTIKE):
—SIRRHA?: **(4)** 136 AD *SEG* XXX 598, 6 (?d. *Ἀνίκητος*)
THRACE:
—MELTA: **(5)** iii AD *ILB* 254 (Lat. Licinia Zue)
—PERINTHOS-HERAKLEIA: **(6)** iv AD *IPerinth* 219, 6 (*AD* 49-50 (1994-5) Mel. p. 343 no. 165) (d. *Λούκις, Ἀσκληπιοδότη*)
—PHILIPPOPOLIS-TRIMONTIUM: **(7)** ii AD *IGB* III 1020, 8 (*GVI* 2088)

Ζωΐλα
MACEDONIA (ORESTIS):
—PLATANIA (MOD.): **(1)** f. ii AD *EAM* 218 (*[Z]ωΐλα*)

Ζωϊλιανή
MACEDONIA (MYGDONIA):
—CHALASTRA: **(1)** ii-iii AD *IG* X (2) (1) 815, 5 (d. *Τελεσφόρος, Συμφορίς*)
MACEDONIA (PELAGONIA):
—KERAMIAI (AREA): **(2)** ii AD ib. X (2) (2) 184 (*Ἀβιδία Z.*: d. *Ἀσκληπιάδης*)

Ζωΐλος
CIMMERIAN BOSPOROS:
—PANTIKAPAION: **(1)** f. iv BC *CIRB* 183
MACEDONIA: **(2)** 12 AD *PKöln* 227 B, 15 (*Ζωΐ[λ]ος*: f. *Θάσιον*); **(3)** ~ ib. l. 22 (*Ζωΐλ(ος)*: f. *Διονύσιος*); **(4)** 237 AD *PSI* 1254, 6, 20, 24 (slave)
MACEDONIA (BISALTIA):
—EUPORIA?: **(5)** ii-iii AD *SEG* XXX 615 (XXXIX 591) (f. *Ἀμμία ἡ καὶ Ποπιλλία*)
MACEDONIA (BOTTIAIA):
—BEROIA: **(6)** iv BC Arr., *Ind.* xviii 6 (Tataki, *Macedonians* p. 78 no. 27) (f. *Μυλλέας*); **(7)** iv/iii BC *SEG* XXXIX 576 (vase) (*Ζωΐ[λος]*?); **(8)** 223 BC *IBer* 4, 18 (s. *Ἀλέξανδρος*); **(9)** ii BC ib. 159 (Tataki 512) (s. *Ἀλέξανδρος*); **(10)** i BC-i AD *IBer* 142, 9 (Tataki 514) (s. *Εὔβουλος*); **(11)** ii/iii AD *IBer* 143 A, 27 (Tataki 604) (*Ἰού. Z.*); **(12)** ~ *IBer* 143 B, 25 (Tataki 516) (f. *Μόσχος*); **(13)** ~ *IBer* 143 C, 20 (Tataki 1044) (*Πατ. Z.*); **(14)** ~ *IBer* 144 B, 5 (Tataki 513) (*[Z]ωΐλος*: s. *Διονύσιος*); **(15)** ~ *IBer* 144 B, 7 (Tataki 515) (f. *Κοΐντος*)
—BEROIA*: **(16)** ii-iii AD *IBer* 376 (Tataki 508) (*Ζο-*)
—EDESSA: **(17)** f. i BC *SEG* XL 537 (Tataki, *Edessa* 112) (s. *Ἀλέξανδρος*); **(18)** f. ii AD *SEG* XXXIX 589 (Tataki, *Edessa* 113) (f. *Βήριμος*)
—MIEZA: **(19)** iii/ii BC *SEG* XLIII 410 (f. *Δημαρέτη*)
MACEDONIA (CHALKIDIKE):
—OLYNTHOS: **(20)** ?352 BC *TAPA* 69 (1938) p. 48 no. 3, 4; Hatzopoulos, *Actes Chalc.* p. 80 (date) (s. *Φιλοκράτης*); **(21)** c. 240-230 BC *IG* VII 265, 3 (*IOrop* 56; Tataki, *Macedonians* p. 136 no. 54) (f. *Δημήτριος*)
—OLYNTHOS?: **(22)** ?350 BC *SEG* XXXVII 570, 5, 7 (s. *Θεογείτων*)
—POLICHNE?: **(23)** ?353 BC ib. 576, 7 (s. *Στράτων*)
—POTIDAIA-KASSANDREIA: **(24)** iii BC *IG* II^{2} 8999 (Tataki, *Macedonians* p. 90 no. 40; *FRA* 2786) (*[Z]ωΐλος*)
—POTIDAIA-KASSANDREIA (TERRIT.): **(25)** iii-iv AD *SEG* XXIX 577 (*Ζο-*)
—STOLOS?: **(26)** ?351 BC ib. XXXVIII 672, 4 ?= (*27*); **(27)** ~ ib. l. 5, 15 (s. *Κράσης*) ?= (*26*); **(28)** ~ ib. l. 14; 673, 9 (f. *Πολυκλῆς*)
MACEDONIA (DERRIOPOS):
—STUBERRA: **(29)** i AD *IG* X (2) (2) 344; **(30)** c. 41-48 AD ib. 323, 16 (s. *Ἀσκληπιόδωρος*); **(31)** ~ ib. l. 22 (-ΐλλ-: f. *Πρῖμος*); **(32)** ~ ib. l. 24 (s. *Φίλιππος*); **(33)** ~ ib. l. 25 (s. *Φίλων*); **(34)** ~ ib. l. 28 (s. *Νικόλαος*); **(35)** ~ ib. l. 29 (f. *Στράτων*); **(36)** 50 AD ib. 324, 22 (s. *Πούβλιος*); **(37)** 53 AD ib. l. 10 (s. *Εὐβουλίδης*); **(38)** ~ ib. l. 12 (s. *Νικόστρατος*); **(39)** ?54 AD ib. l. 3, 8 (f. *Εὐβουλίδης*); **(40)** 74 AD ib. 325, 20 (s. *Φίλων*); **(41)** ~ ib. l. 23 (f. *Ἀλέξανδρος*); **(42)** ~ ib. l. 24 (s. *Πραξίας*); **(43)** ~ ib. l. 31 (f. *Ζώανδρος, Νικόμαχος*); **(44)** ~ ib. l. 33 (f. *Λυσίας*); **(45)** ~ ib. l. 42 (s. *Παράμονος*); **(46)** ~ ib. l. 56 (f. *Πάνταυχος*); **(47)** ~ ib. l. 60 (s. *Διονύσιος*); **(48)** ~ ib. 326, 31 (f. *Μένανδρος*); **(49)** ~ ib. l. 60 (s. *Στρατόνικος*); **(50)** 87 AD ib. 325, 73 (f. *Ἀλέξανδρος*); **(51)** ~ ib. l. 73 (f. *Σωτάδης, Ἀσκληπιόδωρος*); **(52)** ~ ib. l. 76 (s. *Τίτος*); **(53)** ~ ib. l. 81; **(54)** ~ ib. l. 82 (s. *Παρμενίων*); **(55)** 90 AD ib. 326, 76 (f. *Ἀσκληπιόδωρος*); **(56)** ~ ib. l. 77 (s. *Βίλιστος*); **(57)** 116 AD ib. 327, 16 (f. *Εὐφρόσυνος*); **(58)** ~ ib. l. 27 (s. *Λύκαρος*); **(59)** 121 AD ib. 328, 15 (f. *Εὐήμερος*)

MACEDONIA (EDONIS):
—AMPHIPOLIS: **(60)** iv BC *RE* Supplbd. 15 (14); *FGrH* 71 (Tataki, *Macedonians* p. 52 no. 57); **(61)** s. iv BC Hatzopoulos, *Actes Amphipolis* p. 45 no. 9, 7 (*SEG* XLI 563); cf. *SEG* XLIV 504 (f. *Κλέϊππος*); **(62)** i BC *IG* II² 8083 (*FRA* 508) (f. *Ζωΐς*); **(63)** ?ii AD *BCH* 22 (1898) p. 350 (s. *Κάσσανδρος*); **(64)** ii-iii AD Dimitsas 857 (Kaphtantzis 613) (*Ζωΐλο[ς]*: ?s. *Στέφανος*)
—AMPHIPOLIS?: **(65)** imp.? Dimitsas 864 (Kaphtantzis 611) (*Zo-*)
MACEDONIA (ELIMEIA):
—AIANE*: **(66)** hell.-imp. *SEG* XLIII 365 (pithos)
MACEDONIA (KRESTONIA):
—IORON?: **(67)** i AD ib. XXVII 287 c (s. *Πάτραος*)
MACEDONIA (LOWER PAIONIA):
—EUROPOS: **(68)** i BC-i AD? ib. XXXVIII 609 (f. *Νικόπολις*)
—IDOMENE?: **(69)** s. ii BC *BCH* 98 (1974) p. 279 (s. *Ἰσχόλαος*)
MACEDONIA (MYGDONIA): **(70)** m. ii BC *SEG* VIII 370 (Bernand, *Inscr. métr.* 9; Tataki, *Macedonians* p. 203 no. 2) (f. *Ἄρχιππος*)
—ARETHOUSA: **(71)** 104 BC *ID* 2595, 16, 50 (Tataki, *Macedonians* p. 69 no. 8) (or Syria Arethousa: s. *Σάμος*)
—KALINDOIA: **(72)** 68-98 AD *SEG* XLII 580, 39 (f. *Λυσανίας*); **(73)** ~ ib. l. 40 (s. *Λυσανίας*); **(74)** ~ ib. l. 62 (f. *Ἑρμογένης*); **(75)** ~ ib. l. 71 (f. *Σώπατρος*); **(76)** ~ ib. l. 89 (s. *Σῶσος*); **(77)** a. 98 AD ib. 582, 15 (f. *Κλεάνωρ*); **(78)** ~ ib. l. 18 (s. *Διοσκουρίδης*); **(79)** ~ ib. l. 57 (f. *Εὔφαιος*)
—LETE: **(80)** iv-iii BC ib. XXXIX 609, 7 (Tataki, *Macedonians* p. 118 no. 6)
—THESSALONIKE: **(81)** ii-i BC *IG* X (2) (1) 82 (f. *Παρμενίων*); **(82)** 61 BC ib. 221 (f. —σος); **(83)** imp. *SEG* XLVII 963 (f. *Ἀμύντας*); **(84)** f. i AD *IG* X (2) (1) 126, 4; Robert, *OMS* 5 pp. 295-302 (date) (*Z. ὁ καὶ Μενίσκος*: s. *Παρμενίων*); **(85)** ~ *IG* X (2) (1) 133, 10; Robert, *OMS* 5 pp. 295-302 (date) (II s. *Ζωΐλος* I); **(86)** ~ *IG* X (2) (1) 133, 11; Robert, *OMS* 5 pp. 295-302 (date) (I s. *Λυσίπονος*, f. *Ζωΐλος* II); **(87)** s. i AD *IG* X (2) (1) 32, 6 (*[Ζ]ωΐλος*); **(88)** ~ ib. 69, 11 (s. *Σωσιπάτρα*); **(89)** i/ii AD *AD* 24 (1969) Chron. p. 300 (*Ζοεί-*); **(90)** ii AD *IG* X (2) (1) 507, 4 (f. *Δημώ*); **(91)** ~ ib. 1041, 6 (XII (8) 581 A; Tataki, *Macedonians* p. 182 no. 29) ?= (*92*); **(92)** ~ *IG* X (2) (1) 1041, 7 (XII (8) 581 A) ?= (*91*); **(93)** ?iii AD ib. X (2) (1) 477 (f. *Νικήτας*, *Μάγνα*)
MACEDONIA (ODOMANTIKE):
—SIRRHA: **(94)** ii AD *ISamothrace* 46, 9 (Tataki, *Macedonians* p. 172 no. 4) (f. *Παράμονος*); **(95)** 155 AD Dimitsas 821, 29 (Kaphtantzis 1) (f. *Παράμονος*)
MACEDONIA (ORESTIS):
—BATTYNAIOI: **(96)** 192 AD *EAM* 186 III, 46 (*Ζωΐλος*: s. *Φίλων*); **(97)** ~ ib. l. 50 (f. ..νίας); **(98)** ~ ib. l. 55 (f. *Ὀρέστης*)
MACEDONIA (PAIONIA):
—ANTIGONEIA? (TREMNIK (MOD.)): **(99)** ii-iii AD *SEG* II 441
—KAVADARCI (MOD.): **(100)** ii AD *Sp.* 98 (1941-8) p. 67 no. 140 (s. *Διοσκουρίδης*); **(101)** ii-iii AD ib. p. 65 no. 135 (*Ζοΐ-*); **(102)** ~ *SEG* XVI 407; **(103)** iii AD *Sp.* 71 (1931) p. 65 no. 142, 1 (s. *Διονύσιος*)
—NEAPOLIS? (IZVOR (MOD.): **(104)** ii-iii AD ib. 98 (1941-8) p. 28 no. 68 (s. *Διονύσιος*); **(105)** ~ Dimitsas 300, 3 (f. *Ἀλέξανδρος*, *Αἰλιανός*)
—NEAPOLIS? (SMILOVCI (MOD.)): **(106)** ii AD *Sp.* 98 (1941-8) p. 31 no. 76 (s. *Διονύσιος*, *Ἀμμία*)
—NEGOTINO (MOD.): **(107)** ii AD ib. p. 58 no. 120 (f. *Κλεονίκη*)
—STOBOI: **(108)** ii-iii AD ib. 71 (1931) p. 46 no. 104 + *Studies Stobi* 1 p. 181 no. 7; **(109)** s. iii AD *ÖJAI* 32 (1940) Beibl. col. 18 no. 12. 45 (*Ζωεΐ(λος)*: s. *Ἑρμᾶς*); **(110)** ~ ib. col. 20 no. 6. 93 (*Ζωεΐ-*)
MACEDONIA (PELAGONIA): **(111)** ii-i BC *IG* X (2) (2) 158 (f. *Ζώπυρος*); **(112)** ii-iii AD ib. 282 (I f. *Ζωΐλος* II, *Φιλιστῆς*); **(113)** ~ ib. (II s. *Ζωΐλος* I); **(114)** iii AD ib. 188, 2 (*Ζω[ΐλος]*: s. *Διοσκουρίδης*, f. *Ἀλεξάνδρα*)
—DOSTONEIS: **(115)** ii-iii AD ib. 198 (*Ζοΐ-*: s. *Δούλης*)
—KERAMIAI (NR.): **(116)** iii AD ib. 213
MACEDONIA (SINTIKE):
—HERAKLEIA: **(117)** 37-69 AD *CIL* VI 2767 (Kaphtantzis 505) (Lat. Zoilus: f. C. Iulius Montanus)
—PARTHIKOPOLIS: **(118)** f. iii AD *IGB* V 5910 (*Ἰσιδωριανὸς Z.*)
—PARTHIKOPOLIS (TERRIT.): **(119)** f. ii AD ib. IV 2315 (f. *Νίκαρχος*); **(120)** ~ ib. (s. *Νίκαρχος*)
MACEDONIA?: **(121)** 330 BC Berve 339 (Lat. Zoilus)
SCYTHIA MINOR:
—ISTROS: **(122)** i BC-i AD *ISM* I 191 II, 24 (s. *Διογένης*); **(123)** ~ ib. l. 37 (f. *Διογένης*) ?= (*124*); **(124)** ~ ib. l. 39 (f. *Μόσχος*) ?= (*123*); **(125)** ii-iii AD ib. 133 (*CCET* IV 75); **(126)** s. ii AD *ISM* I 167, 18 (*Zo-*); **(127)** iii AD ib. 309 (f. *Διογένης*)
—TOMIS: **(128)** ii AD ib. II 59, 6 (*Π. Αἰλ. [Ἀν]τώνιος Ζωΐ[λο]ς*)
SKYTHIA:
—OLBIA-BORYSTHENES: **(129)** iii BC *Arkheologiia* (Kiev) 39 (1982) p. 34 (Vinogradov–Kryžickij pl. 91. 4 (vase)) (*Ζωΐ(λος)*); **(130)** ~ *IOSPE* I² 201 I, 21 (s. *Πεδιεύς*); **(131)** ii AD *IOlbia* 80, 4 (s. *Ἀχιλλεύς*); **(132)** ~ *IOSPE* I² 93, 6 (s. *Ἀρσάκης*)
TAURIS:
—CHERSONESOS: **(133)** c. 260-250 BC Anokhin p. 140 no. 94 (coin); **(134)** c. 250-230 BC ib. p. 142 no. 120 (coin) ?= (*135*); **(135)** c. 220-210 BC ib. p. 143 no. 129 (coin) ?= (*134*)
THRACE: **(136)** ?ii BC *ZPE* 136 (2001) p. 130 no. 14, 7 (La'da E746) (s. *Ἑκαταῖος*)
—BEROE-AUGUSTA TRAIANA: **(137)** ii-iii AD *SEG* III 551 (stamp)
—BISANTHE-PANION: **(138)** ii-iii AD Dumont–Homolle 83i (*Zo-*: s. *Θαλάβηος*, f. *Δαμᾶς*, *Ἀσκληπιοδότη*)
—BYZANTION: **(139)** c. 250-230 BC *IG* VII 339, 1 (*IOrop* 115) (f. *Μήνιος*); **(140)** ii BC *IByz* 346; cf. Robert, *OMS* 7 p. 643 (f. *Ὀλυμπιάς*); **(141)** ii-i BC *IByz* 116 (s. *Γλύκων*); **(142)** ii-iii AD ib. 309 (f. *Ἄνθιμος*); **(143)** ~ *IGUR* 573 (f. *Ἧρις*)
—ČOMAKOVCI (MOD.): **(144)** ?iii AD *ILB* 167 (Lat. Zoilus: f. Dam–)
—MARONEIA: **(145)** ii-i BC *IThrakAig* E212, 39 (f. *Ἀθήναιος*)
—NICOPOLIS AD ISTRUM:
——(Artemisias): **(146)** ii-iii AD *IGB* V 5234, 4 (f. *Χρῆστος*)
—ODESSOS: **(147)** f. ii BC ib. I² 41, 2 (f. *Κρατισθένης*); **(148)** c. 45-42 BC ib. 43, 2 (s. *Μηνόδωρος*); **(149)** 17 BC ib. 46, 30 (f. *Παρμένων*); **(150)** i-ii AD ib. 144 bis, 1, 7 (f. *Ἀρτεμίδωρος*); **(151)** ~ ib. 204 (*Ζωΐλος*: s. *Ἀρτεμίδωρος*); **(152)** 2 AD ib. 46, 48 (f. *Μοσχίων*); **(153)** ii-iii AD ib. 191 (f. *Ἀπελλᾶς*); **(154)** ~ ib. 231 (*Ζωΐλ[ος]*: f. *Ἑστιαῖος*); **(155)** f. ii AD ib. 78 ter, 8 (*CCET* I 30) (s. *Ἑρμάφιλος*); **(156)** 221 AD *IGB* I² 47 bis a, 25 (*Zo-*: s. *Τιμοκράτης*)
—PAUTALIA: **(157)** ii-iii AD ib. IV 2076 (*Eastern cults* p. 169 no. 13) (f. *Χρῆστος*)
—PERINTHOS-HERAKLEIA: **(158)** 316-309 BC *IG* II² 1956, 123 (*FRA* 6040); *Ancient Macedonia* 5 p. 445 with n. 10 (date) (*Ζ(ω)ΐλος*); **(159)** c. 304 AD *Act. Sanct.* Oct. IX p. 547 (Lat. Zoilus)
——(Aigikoreis): **(160)** iii-ii BC *IPerinth* 61, 48 (*Ζ(ω)ΐλος*)
——(Boreis): **(161)** iii-ii BC ib. l. 39 (f. *Μητρόδωρος*)
—PERINTHOS-HERAKLEIA?: **(162)** iv BC Hp., *Epid.* ii 3. 3; **(163)** iii AD *IPerinth* 309 (*Αὐρ. Z.*: f. *Αὐρ. Ἀπολλινάριος*)
—PHILIPPOPOLIS-TRIMONTIUM: **(164)** imp. *IGB* III 1004 (*Ζωΰ-*: f. *Δῖος*); **(165)** c. 303 AD *Anal. Boll.* 31 (1912) p. 192 (*Ζωή-*)
—PHILIPPOPOLIS-TRIMONTIUM (TERRIT.): **(166)** ii-iii AD *IGB* III 1205 (*Αἰλ. Z.*)
—SERDICA: **(167)** 117-138 AD ib. IV 1925 b, 14 (II s. *Ζωΐλος* I); **(168)** ~ ib. l. 15 (I f. *Ζωΐλος* II)
—VICUS TRULLENSIUM: **(169)** 161-169 or 198-209 AD *ILB* 180, 5 (Lat. Zoilus: s. *Γόργος*)
THRACE?: **(170)** 316-309 BC *IG* II² 1956, 12; *Ancient Macedonia* 5 p. 445 with n. 10 (date) (*FRA* 2531); **(171)** ~ *IG* II² 1956, 15; *Ancient Macedonia* 5 p. 445 with n. 10 (date) (*FRA* 2532)

Ζωΐλων
SCYTHIA MINOR:
—ISTROS: **(1)** 138 AD *ISM* I 193 I, 71 (s. *Νίκανδρος*); **(2)** iii AD ib. 309 (s. *Διογένης*)

Ζωΐς
CIMMERIAN BOSPOROS:
—ACHILLEION: **(1)** ii AD *CIRB* 1030
MACEDONIA (EDONIS):
—AMPHIPOLIS: **(2)** i BC *IG* II² 8083 (Tataki, *Macedonians* p. 52 no. 58; *FRA* 509) (d. *Ζωΐλος*)
MACEDONIA (MYGDONIA):
—THESSALONIKE: **(3)** ii AD *IG* X (2) (1) 664, 2, 6 (*SEG* XLIII 459) (*Zo-*: d. *Εὐφροσύνη*)
THRACE:
—AINOS: **(4)** iii BC *BCH* 91 (1967) p. 43 (d. *Σκύθης*)

Ζωΐχη
MACEDONIA (BOTTIAIA):
—BEROIA: **(1)** ii AD *IBer* 492 (Tataki 509) (*Zo-*)
MACEDONIA (EORDAIA):
—EXOCHI (MOD.): **(2)** 265 AD *EAM* 116, 2 (*Ζοεί-*: d. *Κλεαγόρα*); **(3)** 275 AD ib. 117 a, 3; 117 b, 3 (*Αὐρ. Ζοείχη*—117 a, *Ζοΐχη*—117 b)

Ζωκρέων
TAURIS:
—CHERSONESOS: **(1)** s. iv BC Solomonik, *GAKh* 743 (vase) (*Ζωκρέ(ων)*?)

Ζώνιος
THRACE: **(1)** f. ii BC *Iasos* 191, 12 (*Ζωνίου* (gen.): f. *Ἑκαταῖος*)

Ζωοφόρος
MACEDONIA (BOTTIAIA):
—EDESSA: **(1)** imp. Tataki, *Edessa* 114 (*Ζωοφόρος* (n. pr.?))

Ζωπάκων
THRACE:
—ODESSOS: **(1)** 221 AD *IGB* I² 47 bis a, 33 (*Αὐρ. Z.*: s. *Θεόφιλος*)

Ζωπᾶς
MACEDONIA (MYGDONIA):
—KALINDOIA: **(1)** a. 98 AD *SEG* XLII 582, 53 (f. *Νίκων*)
—LETE?: **(2)** 22 or 139 AD Dimitsas 678, 9 (s. *Ἀσίας*)
—THESSALONIKE: **(3)** 27 BC-14 AD *IG* X (2) (1) 31, 16 (s. *Καλ*—)
THRACE:
—APOLLONIA-SOZOPOLIS: **(4)** ii/i BC *IGB* I² 390, 2 (f. *Ἑκαταῖος*)
—AQUAE CALIDAE*: **(5)** iii AD ib. 380 (s. *Ἰούλιος*)
—BYZANTION (TERRIT.): **(6)** imp. Unp. (Sayar)

Ζωπύρα
MACEDONIA (ELIMEIA):
—AIANE (TERRIT.): **(1)** f. iii AD *A' Panell. Synedr. Epigr.* p. 55 no. 2 (*Ἀβρουλε[ία] Ζωπύρα*)

Macedonia (Lynkestis):
—Herakleia (nr.): **(2)** iii ad *IG* x (2) (2) 33 II (m. *Ζώπυρος*)
Thrace: **(3)** ?161 bc *SGDI* 1715, 3-4 (slave/freed.)

Ζωπυρίων
Cimmerian Bosporos:
—Gorgippia: **(1)** f. iii bc *CIRB* 1137 B I, 5 (I f. *Ζωπυρίων* II); **(2)** ~ ib. l. 5 ([*Ζ*]*ωπυρ*[*ίων*]: II s. *Ζωπυρίων* I)
Macedonia: **(3)** c. 327-325 bc *RE* (1); Berve 340 (Tataki, *Macedonians* p. 318 no. 4) (Lat. Zopyrio); **(4)** 226 bc *PPetr* III 21 b, 4, 11 (Tataki, *Macedonians* p. 318 no. 5; La'da E1757) (s. *Μοσχίων*: t.e.)
Macedonia (Bottiaia):
—Beroia: **(5)** 223 bc *IBer* 4, 34 (f. *Φίλιππος*)
Thrace: **(6)** iii bc *IG* II^2 8917; cf. *SEG* XXVIII 289 (*FRA* 2533) (s. *Μορφή*); **(7)** 216 bc *BGU* 1958, 5, 11, 13, etc. (La'da E747); **(8)** 214 bc *BGU* 1944, 5-6, 26, [27]; cf. La'da E834; E844 (f. *Μενέμαχος, Στράτων*)
—Odessos: **(9)** i bc-i ad *IGB* I^2 206 bis (PM 1682) (f. *Ἀνών*); **(10)** 21 bc *IGB* I^2 46, 26 (f. *Διονύσιος*); **(11)** i-ii ad ib. 121 ([*Ζω*]*πυρίων*: I f. *Ζωπυρ*[*ίων* II); **(12)** ~ ib. (*Ζωπυρ*[*ίων*]: II s. *Ζωπυρίων* I); **(13)** ~ ib. 131, 2 (f. *Εὐφάνης*); **(14)** f. ii ad ib. 78 ter, 7 (*CCET* I 30) (f. *Ἀντίφιλος*); **(15)** ~ *IGB* I^2 78 ter, 9 (*CCET* I 30) (s. *Ἀντίπατρος*); **(16)** ~ *IGB* I^2 78 ter, 11 (*CCET* I 30) (s. *Ἀρτεμίδωρος*); **(17)** ~ *IGB* I^2 178 (PM 1722); *Dacia* 21 (1977) p. 161 (date) (s. *Ἀντίφιλος*); **(18)** m. ii ad *IGB* I^2 174 (PM 1726); *Dacia* 21 (1977) p. 161 (date) (f. *Διογένης*); **(19)** 215 ad *IGB* I^2 47 b, 13 (I f. *Αὐρ. Ζωπυρίων* II); **(20)** ~ ib. l. 13 (*Αὐρ. Ζωποιρίων*: II s. *Ζωπυρίων* I); **(21)** ~ ib. l. 15-16 (-ποι-: f. *Αὐρ. Διονύσιος, Αὐρ. Ἀγαθήνωρ*)

Ζώπυρος
Cimmerian Bosporos:
—Gorgippia: **(1)** f. iii bc *CIRB* 1137 A II, 8 (s. *Ὑψικλῆς*)
—Pantikapaion: **(2)** f. iv bc ib. 217 (f. *Παρμένων, Ἄγρων, Ζωγένης*); **(3)** iii-ii bc *MIA* 56 (1957) p. 101 (tile) (*Ζώ*(*πυρος*)?); **(4)** ii ad *CIRB* 680, 5 (*Ζω<ρ>πυρος*)
—Phanagoreia: **(5)** iv ad ib. 988 (-πη-)
Macedonia (Bottiaia):
—Beroia: **(6)** b. 167 bc *IBer* 1 A, 3, 17 (Tataki 518) (s. *Ἀμύντας*) ?= (7); **(7)** f. ii bc *IBer* 155 (s. *Ἀμύντας*) ?= (6); **(8)** f. i ad ib. 103, 6 (f. *Κλέανδρος*)
—Edessa: **(9)** 180 ad *SEG* XXIV 531, 12 (Tataki, *Edessa* 115) (s. *Οὐαλέριος*); **(10)** iii ad *SEG* XLV 753 (*Ζ. ὁ κὲ Ἄττας*)
—Mieza: **(11)** iii bc ib. XXIV 524 II, 7, 14, 20, 27, 34 (Hatzopoulos, *MI* 2 p. 106 no. 92) (s. *Γοργίας*)
—Pella: **(12)** s. iv bc *SEG* XXXVIII 651 (f. *Λυσιστράτη*)
—Pella (nr.): **(13)** iii/ii bc *Α΄ Panell. Synedr. Epigr.* p. 183 no. 7 (*SEG* XXX 582) (s. *Ἄρπαλος*)
Macedonia (Chalkidike):
—Olynthos: **(14)** ?355 bc *TAPA* 69 (1938) p. 51 no. 5, 6, 10; Hatzopoulos, *Actes Chalc.* p. 80 (date) (s. *Ἵππαρχος*); **(15)** ?352 bc *TAPA* 62 (1931) p. 50 no. 3, 10
—Potidaia-Kassandreia: **(16)** ?iii bc *IG* IX (2) 1180 (Tataki, *Macedonians* p. 90 no. 41) (s. *Μνησιγένης*)
—Singos (nr.): **(17)** 180 ad *SEG* XXIX 593, 6 (s. *Γέμελλος, Διονυσία*)
Macedonia (Derriopos): **(18)** imp. *IG* x (2) (2) 311 (f. *Ἀντίγονος*)
Macedonia (Derriopos)?:
—Dolenestai: **(19)** 87 ad ib. 325, 80; Hatzopoulos, *MI* 1 p. 87 (ethn.) (f. *Κάσσανδρος*)

Macedonia (Edonis):
—Amphipolis: **(20)** hell. *AEMTh* 6 (1992) p. 552 (s. *Διονύσιος*)
Macedonia (Lynkestis):
—Herakleia (nr.): **(21)** iii ad *IG* x (2) (2) 33 II (s. *Μύρων, Ζωπύρα*)
Macedonia (Mygdonia):
—Kalindoia: **(22)** 68-98 ad *SEG* XLII 580, 14 (s. *Μένανδρος*); **(23)** a. 98 ad ib. 583, 22 (s. *Ἀθηνίων*); **(24)** ~ ib. l. 24 (s. *Ζιπύρων*)
—Lete: **(25)** ii ad *Makedonika* 2 (1951) p. 619 no. 42 θ, 13 (s. *Λυσίμαχος*)
—Thessalonike: **(26)** ii-i bc *IG* x (2) (1) 79 (*Λ. Κοίλιο*[*ς*] *Ζ.*); **(27)** i-ii ad ib. 1024 (II^2 8841/2; Tataki, *Macedonians* p. 182 no. 30; *FRA* 2380) (f. *Εὔκλεια*)
Macedonia (Odomantike):
—Sirrha: **(28)** 155 ad Dimitsas 821, 19 (Kaphtantzis 1) (f. *Κόπρυλλος*)
Macedonia (Paionia):
—Negotino (mod.): **(29)** ii-iii ad *Sp.* 77 (1934) p. 43 no. 24
—Stoboi: **(30)** v-vi ad Feissel, *RICM* 281 (f. *Θεόφιλος*); **(31)** ~ ib. 282 (*Ζώπ*(*υ*)*ρος*)
Macedonia (Pelagonia): **(32)** ii-i bc *IG* x (2) (2) 158 (s. *Ζωΐλος*)
—Bostoneis: **(33)** ii ad ib. 196, 2 ([*Ζώ*]*πυρος*, *Πύρος*—ed. pr.: f. *Διονύσιος*)
Macedonia (Pelagonia)?: **(34)** imp. *Sp.* 98 (1941-8) p. 176 no. 367; Papazoglou, *Villes* p. 288 (locn.) (*Ζώ-*)
Scythia Minor:
—Kallatis: **(35)** s. iii bc *ISM* III 35 A, 32 (s. *Πρωτόπολις*); **(36)** ~ ib. l. 37 (s. *Ἑστίας*)
Tauris:
—Chersonesos: **(37)** c. 355 bc Anokhin p. 136 no. 34 (coin); **(38)** ?s. iv bc Solomonik, *NEPKh* 169 (s. *Ἡρόφιλος*)
—Chersonesos?: **(39)** imp. *SEG* XLIII 501 (amph.) (*Ζώπυρ*(*ος*)?)
Thrace: **(40)** v bc *RE* (4) (*FRA* 2534) (slave); **(41)** 190 or 189 bc *PHeid* VIII 417, [13], 33, 40 (La'da E748) (t.e.)
—Apollonia-Sozopolis: **(42)** v/iv bc *SNG Berry* 393; *Coll. Waddington* 1023 (coin) (*Ζώπυ*[*ρος*]—*SNG*) ?= (44); **(43)** iv bc *BMNBurgas* 4 (2002) p. 125 no. 22 (f. *Φύρσων*); **(44)** ~ *SNG Stancomb* 35 (coin) (*Ζώπ*[*υρος*]) ?= (42); **(45)** ~ *IGB* I^2 452 (s. *Ἡγησαγόρας*); **(46)** ~ ib. 463 bis, 2 (f. *Ἀρπαλεύς*); **(47)** ~ ib. l. 3 (s. *Θα—*); **(48)** i-ii ad ib. 401, 15 (s. *Ἑρμῆς*)
—Byzantion: **(49)** ?464 bc *IG* I^3 1144, 125 (*Ζό-*); **(50)** 340 bc ib. II^2 235, 8, 15 (*Ζώ*[*π*]*υρος*: f. *Ἀπελλῆς*); **(51)** ii-i bc *IByz* 94 (Firatlı–Robert p. 92 no. 122) (s. *Ἀπολλόδωρος*)
—Byzantion?:
——(Dionysia): **(52)** ii-i bc *IByz* 378 (f. *Φίλιππος*)
—Lysimacheia: **(53)** m. iii bc *IG* x (2) (1) 301 (f. *Εὐμένης*)
—Mesambria: **(54)** ii bc *IGB* I^2 314 b, 14 (s. *Χαιρέας*); **(55)** i bc ib. 324 (s. *Ἕλλαν*)
—Odessos: **(56)** iii bc ib. 74 (f. *Ἑκατόδωρος*); **(57)** ii ad ib. 178 bis (f. *Βοών, Τουτάς*); **(58)** ~ ib. 179 bis; cf. *Dacia* 21 (1977) p. 161 + *AE* 1984, p. 177 no. 1278 (date) (f. *Ἀπώ*); **(59)** ii-iii ad *IGB* I^2 173 (PM 1731); *Dacia* 21 (1977) p. 161 (date) (f. *Μάμα*)
—Odessos?: **(60)** ii ad *IGB* I^2 51 bis b, 6 (s. *Ἑρμόδωρος*)
—Perinthos-Herakleia:
——(Akarnanes): **(61)** iii-ii bc *IPerinth* 61, 9 (s. *Κρίτων*)

Ζωρθίνης
Skythia:
—Tanais: **(1)** 220 ad *CIRB* 1278, 14 (s. *Φαζ—*) ?= (*Ζώρθινος* (1)); **(2)** 225 ad ib. 1280, 17 (*Ζωρθίνου* (gen.): f. *Βελλικός*)

Ζώρθινος
Skythia:
—Tanais: **(1)** 209 ad ib. 1276, 7 (s. *Φ—*) ?= (*Ζωρθίνης* (1))

Ζώρσανος
Skythia:
—Olbia-Borysthenes: **(1)** i/ii ad *IOSPE* I^2 39, 39; 169, 3; *SEG* XLIII 505, 3; Zgusta, *PNS* 639 (s. *Νικήρατος*)

Ζῶσα
Macedonia (Paionia):
—Kavadarci (mod.): **(1)** iii ad Unp. (Kavadarci Mus.) inv. 32/II (*Ζοῦ-*: d. *Σεκοῦνδα*)

Ζωσάριν
Macedonia (Pieria):
—Dion: **(1)** ii-iii ad Oikonomos 22 (*Αἰλ. Ζ.*)
Thrace:
—Byzantion?: **(2)** imp. *AEMÖ* 19 (1896) p. 59 (PM 1685) (d. *Κοῦνος*)

Ζωσάριον
Macedonia (Mygdonia):
—Thessalonike?: **(1)** iii ad *IG* x (2) (1) 774, 2

Ζωσάρις
Thrace:
—Nicopolis ad Nestum: **(1)** ii-iii ad *IGB* IV 2337, 8 ([*Ζ*]*ωσάρις*)

Ζωσαροῦς
Thrace:
—Komotini (mod.): **(1)** imp. *Belomorski Pregled* 1 (1942) p. 337 no. 44 (*IThrakAig* E488); cf. *BE* 1948, no. 148 (d. *Κέρδων*)

Ζωσᾶς
Macedonia (Bottiaia):
—Beroia: **(1)** ii/iii ad *IBer* 27 A, 2 (s. *Ζώσιμος*); **(2)** ~ ib. l. 7 (s. *Μάξιμος*); **(3)** ?ii/iii ad *ILeukopetra* 132, 1 (?f. *Μελίτα*); **(4)** 177 ad *IBer* 135 A, 10 (Tataki 74) (*Αἰλ. Ζ.*); **(5)** ~ *IBer* 135 A, 12 (Tataki 1316) (*Τ. Φλ. Ζ.*)
Macedonia (Edonis):
—Philippoi (nr.): **(6)** ?ii ad *BCH* 47 (1923) pp. 78-9 no. 40 (Pilhofer 411) (Lat. Varin. Zosas: f. *Σωσίας*)
Macedonia (Eordaia):
—Exochi (mod.): **(7)** iii ad *EAM* 100a (*Ζωσᾶ*(*ς*))
Macedonia (Mygdonia):
—Thessalonike?: **(8)** ii ad *IG* x (2) (1) 710
Macedonia (Odomantike):
—Sirrha: **(9)** 155 ad Dimitsas 821, 31 (Kaphtantzis 1) (f. *Τόρκος*)
—Sirrha?: **(10)** 155 ad *Belomorski Pregled* 1 (1942) p. 321 no. 6 (Kaphtantzis 2)
Macedonia (Pieria):
—Dion: **(11)** imp. *SEG* XLIX 704 (mosaic)

Ζώσιλμος?
Macedonia (Odomantike):
—Sirrha: **(1)** 155 ad Dimitsas 821, 31 (Kaphtantzis 1) (*Ζώσι<λ>μος*?: s. *Διοσκουρίδης*)

Ζωσίμα
Macedonia (Derriopos): **(1)** ii-iii ad *IG* x (2) (2) 317 ([*Ζω*]*σίμα*: m. *Ἰουλιανός, Λυσικλῆς*)

Ζωσιμᾶς
Macedonia (Odomantike):
—Sirrha: **(1)** ii-iii ad Kaphtantzis 36 (*Κλ. Ζ.*: f. *Ξάνθιλλα*)

Ζωσίμη
Macedonia (Bottiaia):
—Beroia: **(1)** i-ii ad *IBer* 339 (*Σκιρτία Ζ.*: m. *Γ. Σκίρτιος Ἀγάθων*); **(2)** ii-iii ad ib. 240 (m. *Ἄρωγος*); **(3)** ~ ib. 242 (Tataki 523); **(4)** iii ad *IBer* 214 (Tataki 522) (?d. *Κλ. Ἀπολλώνις*); **(5)** ~ *IBer* 285 (Tataki 263) (*Αὐρ. Ζ.*); **(6)** f. iii ad *IBer* 236, 4 (Tataki 526) (m. *Φίλητος*)

——Kyneoi: **(7)** 171 AD *ILeukopetra* 5, 3 (Tataki 527) (d. Δούλης)
—EDESSA: **(8)** 253 AD *AD* 24 (1969) Chron. p. 306 (Tataki, *Edessa* 44) (Αὐρ. Ζ.)
—MIEZA (TERRIT.)?: **(9)** m. iii AD *SEG* XXXV 726 (Tataki 524); cf. Hatzopoulos, *MI* I p. 116 n. 4 (locn.)
MACEDONIA (CHALKIDIKE):
—POTIDAIA-KASSANDREIA (TERRIT.): **(10)** i-ii AD *TAPA* 62 (1931) p. 54 no. 6 + 69 (1938) p. 67 n. 49 (*BCH* 103 (1979) p. 306 no. 50; *ILGR* 226) (Lat. Antonia Zosime: d. M. Antonius Primus, Ἐπιγόνη)
MACEDONIA (EDONIS):
—AMPHIPOLIS (TERRIT.): **(11)** ii-iii AD Dimitsas 867 (d. Ζώσιμος, Ἀπολλωνία)
MACEDONIA (LYNKESTIS):
—HERAKLEIA (AREA): **(12)** imp. *IG* X (2) (2) 28 (d. Ζώσιμος, Κασσάνδρα)
MACEDONIA (MYGDONIA):
—THESSALONIKE: **(13)** 48 AD ib. X (2) (1) 623 A; **(14)** ii AD ib. 515 (m. Αἰλ. Μωμώ); **(15)** ii-iii AD Nalpantis, *Anaskaphi* p. 112 no. BE 118; **(16)** ~ *IG* X (2) (1) 602; **(17)** 129 AD ib. 521, 1 (Ῥεία Ζ.: m. Παράμονος, Οὐίβιος, Σεραπᾶς, Μ. Ἀλφῆνος Πρίσκος); **(18)** ii/iii AD *SEG* XXXIX 637; cf. XLIII 465 (Φλ. Ζ.); **(19)** iii AD *IG* X (2) (1) 411, 3 ([Ζω]σίμη); **(20)** ~ ib. 586, 2 (I m. Ζωσίμη II); **(21)** ~ ib. l. 3 ([Ζω]σίμ̣η: II d. Ζωσίμη I, Σω—, m. Αὐρ. Ζώσιμος); **(22)** ~ ib. 605 (Αὐρ. Ζωσί[μη]?); **(23)** 250 AD ib. 165, 14 (Αὐρ. Ζ.: m. Κορνήλιος Ἐπάγαθος); **(24)** c. 260 AD ib. 491; 557 B, 2 (m. Μύλαγος); **(25)** 261 AD ib. 200, 5 (Ποντία Ζ.: d. Πόντιος Εὐάγγελος, Οὐαλερία Ἀλεξάνδρα)
—THESSALONIKE?: **(26)** ii AD ib. 906 (Δωμετιαν[ή] Ζ.); **(27)** ii-iii AD ib. 745, 3; **(28)** ii/iii AD ib. 723, 5 (Lat. Sept. Zosime)
MACEDONIA (ODOMANTIKE):
—BERGE: **(29)** hell. Hatzopoulos, *MI* I p. 215 (Σω-: d. Κοίταρος)
MACEDONIA (PAIONIA):
—KAVADARCI (MOD.): **(30)** ii-iii AD *Sp.* 98 (1941-8) p. 77 no. 164 (m. Εὔτυχος)
MACEDONIA (PIERIA):
—DION: **(31)** ?ii AD Dimitsas 185
SCYTHIA MINOR:
—TOMIS: **(32)** ii-iii AD *ISM* II 294
THRACE:
—BYZANTION: **(33)** ii AD *Türk Tarih Kongresi XI* (6) p. 2703 with pl. 495. 5 (d. Κόϊντος); **(34)** ~ *IByz* 314 (Fıratlı–Robert pp. 120-1 no. 203) (d. Ἐπίκτητος)
—KOILA: **(35)** ii-iii AD *ISestos* 30 (Αἰλ. Ζ.: m. Αἰλ. Ἀπολλωνίδης)
—PERINTHOS-HERAKLEIA: **(36)** iii AD *IPerinth* 131, 6 (Αὐρ. Ζ.)
—PERINTHOS-HERAKLEIA*: **(37)** v-vi AD ib. 236 (*AD* 51-2 (1996-7) Mel. p. 378 no. 193) (Ζο-)

Ζωσιμιανή
MACEDONIA (BOTTIAIA):
—EDESSA: **(1)** v-vi AD Feissel, *RICM* 45 (Ζωσιμιαν(ή))

Ζωσιμίων
THRACE:
—BYZANTION: **(1)** ii AD *Türk Tarih Kongresi XI* (6) p. 2703 with pl. 495. 5 (s. Κόϊντος)

Ζώσιμος
CIMMERIAN BOSPOROS:
—PANTIKAPAION: **(1)** imp. *CIRB* 790; **(2)** ii AD ib. 605; cf. KW pl. 51 no. 708 (I f. Ζώσιμος II); **(3)** ~ *CIRB* 605; cf. KW pl. 51 no. 708 (II s. Ζώσιμος I)
MACEDONIA (BISALTIA):
—TERPNI (MOD.): **(4)** ii-iii AD *SEG* XLIX 810
MACEDONIA (BOTTIAIA):
—BEROIA: **(5)** f. ii AD *IBer* 243 (Tataki 530) (s. Πετρώνιος Ἀμύντας, Νικόπολις); **(6)** s. ii AD *IBer* 244 (Tataki 531) (s. Τριακαδίων); **(7)** ?171-208 AD *ILeukopetra* 130, 2 (f. Πασιθέα); **(8)** ii/iii AD *IBer* 27 A, 2 (f. Ζωσᾶς); **(9)** ~ ib. 143 B, 17 (Tataki 1237) (Τιτιανὸς Ζ.); **(10)** ~ *IBer* 144 B, 4 (Tataki 529) (f. —δης); **(11)** ~ *IBer* 144 B, 6 (Tataki 748) (Κλώδιος Ζ.); **(12)** ~ *IBer* 144 B, 9 (Tataki 1152) (Ῥοπίλιος Ζ.); **(13)** ~ *IBer* 145, 5 (Tataki 644) (Καικίλιος Ζ.); **(14)** 193-217 AD *ILeukopetra* 128, 1 (s. Λυκολέων); **(15)** iii AD Mendel, *Cat.* 936 (*SEG* L 585); *IBer* 280 (Τ. Σεγνοῦννος Ζ.: ?f. Τ. Σεγνοῦννος Ἰουκοῦνδος)
—EDESSA: **(16)** iii AD *BSA* 58 (1963) p. 23 no. 4 (Tataki, *Edessa* 54) (Αὐρ. Ζ.: f. Οὐαλέριος); **(17)** 229 AD *Ancient Macedonia* I p. 200 no. 12, 32 (Tataki, *Edessa* 53) (Αὐρ. Ζ.); **(18)** ~ ib. 320 (—ος Ζ.)
—PELLA: **(19)** 150 AD *SEG* XLVIII 825 (?s. Εὔνυμφος, Πίστη)
MACEDONIA (CHALKIDIKE):
—MONI IVIRON (MOD.): **(20)** ii-iii AD Dimitsas 777; cf. Robert, *OMS* 2 p. 1288 n. 1 (s. Ζιπύρων)
MACEDONIA (EDONIS):
—AMPHIPOLIS: **(21)** m. ii AD *SEG* XXXV 712 (f. Λύκα)
—AMPHIPOLIS (TERRIT.): **(22)** ii-iii AD Dimitsas 867 (s. Γάϊος, f. Ζωσίμη)
—PHILIPPOI: **(23)** imp. *BCH* 47 (1923) pp. 88-9 no. 8 (Pilhofer 373) (Lat. Marron. Zosimus); **(24)** ~ *CIL* III 685 (Pilhofer 63) (Lat. Zosimus); **(25)** ?ii AD *BCH* 61 (1937) p. 419 no. 13 (Pilhofer 386) (Lat. Ulpius Zosimus); **(26)** ii-iii AD *SEG* III 499-501 (Pilhofer 142-4); Collart, *Philippes* pl. 67. 2 (Μ. Βελλέϊος Ζ.); **(27)** f. ii AD Eus., *HE* iii 36. 13; cf. *RE* s.v. Polykarpos (1) col. 1682; Pilhofer I pp. 206 ff.; **(28)** ii/iii AD *CIL* III 633 III c, 13 (Pilhofer 165); *CRAI* 1923, p. 277 (date) (Lat. Petronius Zosimus)
MACEDONIA (ELIMEIA):
—AIANE (TERRIT.): **(29)** 148 AD *EAM* 11, 5 (Γ. Ἰούλ. Ζ.: freed.)
—OBLOSTAI?: **(30)** ?iii AD ib. 65 II a
MACEDONIA (LYNKESTIS):
—HERAKLEIA (AREA): **(31)** imp. *IG* X (2) (2) 28 (f. Εὔτυχος, Ζωσίμη)
—HERAKLEIA?: **(32)** ii-iii AD ib. 133
MACEDONIA (MYGDONIA):
—KALINDOIA: **(33)** 68-98 AD *SEG* XLII 580, 100 (Τ. Κλαύδιος Ζ.); **(34)** a. 98 AD ib. 582, 19 (I s. Κότυς, f. Ζώσιμος II); **(35)** ~ ib. l. 19 (II s. Ζώσιμος I); **(36)** ~ ib. l. 23; cf. *BE* 1999, no. 362 (Ἱέρων ὁ καὶ Ζ.: s. Ἱέρων); **(37)** ~ *SEG* XLII 582, 58 (s. Νικόστρατος)
—LETE: **(38)** ii AD *Makedonika* 2 (1951) p. 619 no. 42 θ, 12 (f. Εὐκτίμενος)
—PERISTERA (MOD.): **(39)** iii AD *SEG* XXIX 590 (s. Εὐτύχης, Μαρκελλῖνα)
—THESSALONIKE: **(40)** imp. *CIL* III 14203. 42 (Lat. Zosimus); **(41)** i AD *IG* X (2) (1) 259, 25 (Γ. Ῥάϊος Ζ.); **(42)** i-ii AD ib. 243 II, 14 (Μ. Καικίλιος Ζ.); **(43)** f. i AD ib. 133, 18; Robert, *OMS* 5 pp. 295-302 (date) (Τ. Μέμμιος Ζ.); **(44)** s. i AD *IG* X (2) (1) 68, 36; 69, 24 (Μ. Ἐρέννιος Ζ.); **(45)** ~ ib. l. 50 (Π. Κερρήνιος Ζ.); **(46)** ii AD ib. 241 A I, 4; **(47)** ii-iii AD ib. 287 (Τ. Φλ. Ζώσιμ[ος]); **(48)** ~ ib. 442 (s. Νίκη); **(49)** ~ ib. 668 (Lat. T. Brotius Sosimus: freed.?); **(50)** 125 AD *Klio* 65 (1983) p. 163 (Τ. Κλ. Ζ.); **(51)** 145 or 261 AD *IG* X (2) (1) 451, 2 (Λ. Κανουλέϊος Ζ.); **(52)** ii/iii AD ib. 262 I, 8; **(53)** ?iii AD ib. 496 (f. Ἀντίνοος); **(54)** iii AD ib. 497, 1 (Λ. Φάβις Ζ.: II ?s. Λ. Φάβιος Ζώσιμος I); **(55)** ~ ib. l. 2 (Λ. Φάβιος Ζ.: I ?f. Λ. Φάβις Ζώσιμος II); **(56)** ~ ib. 586, 1 ([Αὐ]ρ. Ζ.: s. Ζωσίμη); **(57)** m. iii AD ib. 150, 16; **(58)** s. iii AD ib. 556 ([Αὐρ.] Ζ.); **(59)** ?v AD *AD* 4 (1918) Parart. p. 21 (brick)
—THESSALONIKE?: **(60)** ii AD *IG* X (2) (1) 249, 5; **(61)** ~ ib. 898 (Ζοή-); **(62)** ii-iii AD ib. 758 A, 3; 758 B, 10; **(63)** iii AD ib. 774, 1
—THESSALONIKE*: **(64)** ii-iii AD ib. 409; **(65)** ii/iii AD ib. 723, 1, 6 (biling.) (s. Avia Salvia: freed.); **(66)** f. iii AD ib. 187, 11 (Γεμείνιος Ζ. ὁ καὶ Βορέας: freed.?); **(67)** c. 303 AD Musurillo, *Acts Christian Martyrs* pp. 281 ff.
MACEDONIA (ODOMANTIKE):
—SIRRHA: **(68)** ii-iii AD *Belomorski Pregled* I (1942) pp. 329-30 no. 27 = Kaphtantzis 28 (s. Διονύσιος); **(69)** f. iii AD *SEG* XXX 590, 18 (Αὐρ. Ζ.: s. Μ—); **(70)** ~ ib. l. 23 ([Αὐρ.] [Ζ]ώσιμος)
—SIRRHA?: **(71)** ii-iii AD ib. XLVIII 884 (s. Ἡρόδοτος)
MACEDONIA (ORESTIS):
—ROKASTRO (MOD.): **(72)** iii AD ib. XLIX 791 (Αὐρ. Εὐρυδικιανὸς Ζ.)
MACEDONIA (PAIONIA):
—BYLAZORA (NR.): **(73)** ii-iii AD ib. XXXVIII 713 n. b (f. Ἀμμακώ)
—KAVADARCI (MOD.): **(74)** ii/iii AD Unp. (Papazoglu archive) (threptos); **(75)** ~ Unp. (Kavadarci Mus.) inv. 10/II (s. Γάϊος)
MACEDONIA (PELAGONIA):
—DOSTONEIS?: **(76)** iii AD *IG* X (2) (2) 202, 1
MACEDONIA (PIERIA):
—DION: **(77)** i-ii AD Oikonomos 31; **(78)** ii AD ib. 15 (Ζώσ[ιμος]); **(79)** ~ ib. 30; cf. Spiliopoulou-Donderer, *KGN* p. 188 no. D5 (date); **(80)** ii-iii AD Oikonomos 22 (Αἰλ. Ζώσιμ[ος]); **(81)** iii/iv AD *SEG* XXXIX 581 (Ἄννιος Ζ.)
—PYDNA: **(82)** 250 AD ib. XLVI 800 A, 21 (Τ. Ὀκτάβιος Ζ.)
SCYTHIA MINOR:
—KALLATIS: **(83)** 241-244 AD *ISM* III 74 B, 25
—ULMETUM: **(84)** 216 AD ib. V 76, 4 = II 130 (*CCET* IV 202) (Lat. Valerius Zosimus)
THRACE: **(85)** iii AD *RDAC* 2002, p. 372 no. 11 (f. Νικηφόρος)
—AINOS: **(86)** i-ii AD *SEG* XXXVI 660 (f. Ἰόλα)
—BYZANTION: **(87)** i BC-i AD *IByz* 208 (Fıratlı–Robert p. 68 no. 66) (I f. Ζώσιμος II, —λα); **(88)** ~ *IByz* 208 (Fıratlı–Robert p. 68 no. 66) ([Ζώ]σιμος: II s. Ζώσιμος I); **(89)** i-ii AD *IByz* 273 (Fıratlı–Robert p. 85 no. 106) (threptos); **(90)** iii AD *IByz* 295 (Fıratlı–Robert p. 52 no. 28)
——(Rhegion): **(91)** i BC-i AD? *IByz* 172 (s. Κόϊντος)
—BYZANTION*: **(92)** ii BC ib. 100 (Fıratlı–Robert p. 94 no. 130) (freed.); **(93)** ~ *SEG* L 667 I (freed.)
—DIOSPOLIS: **(94)** imp. *IGB* III 1790 (Ζ(ώ)σιμος)
—ERGISSENOI: **(95)** ii AD ib. 1593, 13 (Λ. Λουκρήτιος Ζ.)
—HADRIANOPOLIS: **(96)** imp.? Dumont–Homolle 62 (s. Ὀνησιφῶν, f. Ὀνησιφῶν)
—MARONEIA (TERRIT.): **(97)** iii AD Bakalakis, *Oinos Ismarikos* p. 555 (*IThrakAig* E379) ((Ζ)ώσιμος: s. Ταρούλας)
—NICOPOLIS AD ISTRUM (TERRIT.): **(98)** s. ii AD *CCET* II (2) 674 (*ILB* 350) (Lat. L. Tanicius Zosimus)
—ODESSOS?: **(99)** ii-iii AD *IGB* I^2 303 (Ζώσιμ[ος])
—PERINTHOS-HERAKLEIA (NR.): **(100)** i-ii AD *IPerinth* 282 (s. Ἀλέξανδρος)
—PHILIPPOPOLIS-TRIMONTIUM: **(101)** iv AD Beševliev 207, 4, 16
—SERDICA (NR.): **(102)** imp. Beševliev, *EP* 103 (tile) (Lat. Zosim(us))
—TYRODIZA-TIRISTASIS: **(103)** ii-iii AD PM 1623 (Βενουλέϊος Ζ.: f. Βενουλέϊος Σκύμνος)

Ζωσοῦς
MACEDONIA (LYNKESTIS):
—HERAKLEIA: **(1)** ii-iii AD *IG* X (2) (2) 85 (m. Ἡράκλεια)

MACEDONIA (PAIONIA):
—STOBOI*: (2) i AD Šašel, *IL* 1252 (biling.) (*Σεντία Ζοσοῦνι* (dat.): freed.)

Ζωσώ
MACEDONIA: (1) f. iii AD *SEG* XLVIII 880 (m. *Δουλαῖος*)

Ζώσων
MACEDONIA (MYGDONIA):
—THESSALONIKE: (1) v-vi AD Feissel, *RICM* 166 (*SEG* XLVII 978)

Ζωτᾶς
THRACE:
—BISANTHE-PANION: (1) 158-138 BC *OGIS* 303 (s. *Δημήτριος*) ?= (*2*); (2) c. 133-86 BC Moretti, *ISE* 116 (*SEG* XXXVII 602); Hatzopoulos–Loukopoulou, *Two Studies* pp. 80-1 (ident.) (f. *Γλαυκίας*) ?= (*1*)
—BYZANTION:
——(Rhegion): (3) f. i BC *IByz* 197 (Firatlı–Robert p. 59 no. 42) (f. *Γυκεῖα*)

Ζωτική
THRACE:
—APROI: (1) ?iii AD Taşlıklıoğlu 2 p. 81 no. 9 (*AD* 49-50 (1994-5) Mel. p. 289 no. 118); cf. *SEG* XXXVII 598 (m. *Βειφανία Σεκοῦνδα*)

Ζωτικός
MACEDONIA (EDONIS):
—PHILIPPOI: (1) ii AD *BCH* 57 (1933) pp. 370-2 no. 28, 4 (Pilhofer 91) (Lat. [Here]nnius Zoticus)
SCYTHIA MINOR:
—NOVIODUNUM (NR.): (2) iii-iv AD Barnea 63 b (Popescu, *IGL* 267 b)
—TROESMIS: (3) ii AD *ISM* V 174, 6; 175, 1 (Lat. Antistius Zoticus: s. C. Antistius Valens, Atilia Fortunata)
SKYTHIA:
—OLBIA-BORYSTHENES: (4) iii AD *IOSPE* I² 135, 6 (f. *Ζήνων*)
THRACE:
—BISANTHE-PANION: (5) iv-v AD *JÖAI* 23 (1926) Beibl. col. 159 no. 95 (*AD* 49-50 (1994-5) Mel. p. 310 no. 135)
—LYSIMACHEIA (NR.): (6) iv-vi AD *ISestos* 49 (*AD* 49-50 (1994-5) Mel. p. 331 no. 156) (*Ζωτικ(ός)*)
—NICOPOLIS AD ISTRUM (TERRIT.): (7) ii AD *ILB* 376 (Lat. Tib. Cl. Zoticus: freed.)
—ODESSOS: (8) vi AD *SEG* XL 597, 4 (*[Ζω]τικός*)
—PAISOULAI-MAXIMIANOPOLIS: (9) vi AD Meïmaris–Bakirtzis 32 (*SEG* XLIV 604; *IThrakAig* E390)
—PERINTHOS-HERAKLEIA: (10) iii AD *IPerinth* 147 (s. *ΠΑΦΙΟΜΝΑ*); (11) iv-v AD ib. 178, 2 (*AD* 51-2 (1996-7) Mel. p. 361 no. 181) (f. *Αὐρ. Δόμνος*)
—PHILIPPOPOLIS-TRIMONTIUM: (12) c. 303 AD *Anal. Boll.* 31 (1912) p. 192

Ζώτιχος
THRACE:
—BYZANTION: (1) i BC-i AD *IByz* 228 (Firatlı–Robert p. 82 no. 98) (s. *Συρίσκος*); (2) iii AD *ISM* II 257 (PM 1174) (f. *Αὐρ. Σωζομενός*)
—BYZANTION (TERRIT.): (3) imp. *IByz* 237 (s. *Ποππαῖος*); (4) i-ii AD ib. 268 (Firatlı–Robert pp. 83-4 no. 102) (s. *Μίλων, Εἶα*)
—BYZANTION?: (5) ii AD *IByz* 330 (s. *Ζήνων*)
—LYSIMACHEIA: (6) m. ii BC *ISestos* 38 a, 5 (s. *Δημήτριος*)

H

Ἡβατίων
CIMMERIAN BOSPOROS:
—MYRMEKION (NR.): (1) i-ii AD *VDI* 1965 (2), p. 99 no. 4; cf. *SEG* XXVIII 662; *Topoi* 3 (1993) pp. 198-9 no. 4

Ἡβήσας
THRACE:
—MARONEIA: (1) c. 400-378 BC Schönert-Geiss, *Maroneia* 163 (coin); Masson, *OGS* p. 438

Ἡγεάνασσα
THRACE:
—APOLLONIA-SOZOPOLIS: (1) iv BC *BMNBurgas* 4 (2002) p. 123 no. 15 (d. *Βριταγόρης*)

Ἡγεκράτης
THRACE:
—PERINTHOS-HERAKLEIA: (1) vi/v BC *IPerinth* 70 (f. *Ἡγησιπόλη*)

Ἡγέλοχος
MACEDONIA: (1) 334-331 BC *RE* (1); Berve 341 (Tataki, *Macedonians* p. 319 no. 1) (s. *Ἱππόστρατος*)

Ἡγέμων
THRACE:
—ODESSOS: (1) 44 BC *IGB* I² 46, 3 (s. *Σώστρατος*)

Ἡγέστρατος
MACEDONIA (CHALKIDIKE):
—OLYNTHOS: (1) ?c. 355-350 BC *SEG* XXXVIII 640, 4 (*Ἡγέστρατος*: f. *Ἡγίας, Ἄνθις*)
MACEDONIA?: (2) 182 BC *IG* II² 2314, [3], 7 (f. *Καλλικράτης*)
THRACE:
—HERAION TEICHOS: (3) c. 133-86 BC *SEG* XLII 662 (s. *Ποτάμων*)
—STRYME: (4) v/iv BC *IThrakAig* E130 (*Ἡ(γ)έσστρατος?, Ἡρ(ό)σστρατος?*: f. *Πρωτόφαος*)

Ἡγήμων
MACEDONIA (EDONIS):
—AMPHIPOLIS: (1) f. iii BC *Ant. Kunst* 12 (1969) pp. 68-71; cf. *SEG* XLVII 879 (f. *Φανίς*)
SCYTHIA MINOR:
—ISTROS: (2) 138 AD *ISM* I 193 I, 22 (s. *Διονύσιος*); (3) ~ ib. l. 82 (f. *Ἀρτεμίδωρος*)
SKYTHIA:
—OLBIA-BORYSTHENES: (4) s. iv BC *SEG* L 702 IV, 7 (*Ἡγήμ(ω)ν*)

Ἡγησαγόρας
SCYTHIA MINOR:
—ISTROS: (1) iii-ii BC *ISM* I 17, 4 (*Ἡγησαγόρ[ας]*); (2) iii/ii BC ib. 64, 10, 33, 35 (*IGB* I² 388 bis); cf. *SEG* L 661 (s. *Μόνιμος*); (3) ii-i BC *ISM* I 126 (*Eastern cults* p. 105 no. 68) (f. *Ἀλέξανδρος*); (4) i BC-i AD *ISM* I 188 (*Ἡγησα[γόρας]?*); (5) ~ ib. 209, 5 = 185 (f. *—ης*); (6) i AD ib. 200, 2 (f. *Μοιράδωρος*); (7) c. 48-52 AD ib. 67, 53; 68, 53; (8) 138 AD ib. 193 I, 55 (s. *Ἀπολλόδωρος*); (9) ii/iii AD ib. 227, 13 (*Ἡγησαγό[ρας]*)
THRACE:
—APOLLONIA-SOZOPOLIS: (10) iv BC *IGB* I² 452 (f. *Ζώπυρος*)

Ἡγησαγόρης
SCYTHIA MINOR:
—ISTROS: (1) v/iv BC *ISM* I 144 (*Ἡγησαγόρ[ης]*: f. *Ἱππόλοχος*); (2) ~ ib. (*Ἡγησαγ[όρ]ης*: s. *Θεόδοτος*); (3) iv BC ib. 236 (*Ἡγησαγόρεω* (gen.): f. *Ἱππόλοχος*); (4) ~ ib. 237 (*Ἡγησαγό[ρης]*)
SKYTHIA:
—OLBIA-BORYSTHENES: (5) m. iv BC Dubois, *IGDOlbia* 106, 8 (*SEG* XLIV 669)
THRACE:
—ABDERA: (6) c. 415-395 BC May, *Abdera* pp. 170-1 nos. 228-32 (coin)
—MARONEIA: (7) c. 365-336 BC Schönert-Geiss, *Maroneia* 499-501 (coin) (*Ἡγησαγόρεω* (gen.))

Ἡγησάνδρα
MACEDONIA (ELIMEIA):
—AIANE: (1) ii-i BC *EAM* 42 (*Ἡγησάνδρα*: d. *—ανδρος*)
MACEDONIA (MYGDONIA):
—THESSALONIKE: (2) ii AD *SEG* XXXVI 645; *KGAM Thess.* I 59 (d. *Φιλώτας*)

Ἡγήσανδρος
MACEDONIA: (1) iv BC Arr., *An.* iii 5. 1 (Tataki, *Macedonians* p. 319 no. 3) (f. *Μενοίτας*); (2) 327 BC *CID* II 97, 30; 99 A, [0] (Tataki, *Macedonians* p. 319 no. 2) (f. *Λέων*)
MACEDONIA (BOTTIAIA):
—BEROIA: (3) 223 BC *IBer* 4, 31 (s. *Εἰκαδίων*)
MACEDONIA (CHALKIDIKE):
—OLYNTHOS: (4) iv/iii BC *IG* XII (2) 202 (Tataki, *Macedonians* p. 136 no. 55) (f. *Δωρόθεος*)
MACEDONIA (MYGDONIA):
—THESSALONIKE: (5) s. ii BC *BCH* 19 (1895) p. 335 no. 10, 8 (Tataki, *Macedonians* p. 182 no. 31) (f. *Δαμαῖος*)
MACEDONIA (PIERIA):
—DION: (6) s. iv BC *SEG* XXXVI 612 (f. *Εὔκλεια*)
SCYTHIA MINOR:
—ISTROS: (7) f. iv BC *ISM* I 232 (s. *Ἀλέξανδρος*)
THRACE:
—PERINTHOS-HERAKLEIA: (8) iv-iii BC *IPerinth* 4, 3 (s. *Κλέανδρος*)

Ἡγήσαρχος
MACEDONIA: (1) 250 BC *PColZen* 54, 4, 12, 17, 43, 45 (Tataki, *Macedonians* p. 319 no. 4; La'da E1758) (s. *Θεόπομπος*, f. *Νικόδημος, Θεόπομπος*: t.e.)
MACEDONIA (CHALKIDIKE):
—OLYNTHOS: (2) f. iv BC *SEG* XXXIV 660 bis (f. *Κρατιννώ*)

Ἡγησιάναξ
SCYTHIA MINOR:
—ISTROS: (1) iii-ii BC Unp. (Avram, defixio) 4, 4

Ἡγησίας
MACEDONIA (ELIMEIA):
—AIANE (TERRIT.): **(1)** f. iii AD *A΄ Panell. Synedr. Epigr.* p. 55 no. 2

Ἡγησίδημος
MACEDONIA (EDONIS):
—AMPHIPOLIS: **(1)** iii BC *Polemon* 5 (1952-3) p. 57 no. 3 (Tataki, *Macedonians* p. 52 no. 59) (f. *Μενέλαος*)
THRACE:
—APOLLONIA-SOZOPOLIS: **(2)** v/iv BC Sotheby sale (28th May 1900) 317 (coin); **(3)** ~ *IGB* I^2 410 bis (f. *Ἡγησίλεως*)
—LYSIMACHEIA: **(4)** m. ii BC *ISestos* 38 b, 9 (s. *Ἀριστομένης*)

Ἡγησίδικος
MACEDONIA (EDONIS):
—PHILIPPOI: **(1)** s. iv BC *SEG* XXXVIII 660 (XLIII 450; Pilhofer 387)

Ἡγησικράτης
MACEDONIA (BOTTIAIA):
—TYRISSA?: **(1)** s. iv BC *SEG* XLIII 446 (f. *Ἀντίπατρος*)

Ἡγησίλαος
THRACE:
—ZONE: **(1)** s. v BC ib. XXXVIII 732 (*IThrakAig* E407) (s. *Ἀλκιβιάδης*)

Ἡγησίλεως
THRACE:
—APOLLONIA-SOZOPOLIS: **(1)** v/iv BC *IGB* I^2 410 bis (s. *Ἡγησίδημος*)
—MARONEIA: **(2)** c. 400-378 BC Schönert-Geiss, *Maroneia* 162 (coin)
—PERINTHOS-HERAKLEIA: **(3)** ?iv BC *IPerinth* 259, 4 (*Ἡγησίλ[εως]*)

Ἡγήσιλλα
MACEDONIA (BOTTIAIA):
—BEROIA: **(1)** f. iii AD *IBer* 98, 10 (*Πομπωνία Ἀρκαρία ἡ καὶ Ἡ.*: m. *Σεπτίμιος Πομπώνιος Προκλιανὸς Ὀρέστης*)

Ἡγησίλοχος
CIMMERIAN BOSPOROS:
—GORGIPPIA: **(1)** f. iii BC *CIRB* 1137 A I, 45; 1137 A II, 41 (s. *Διονύσιος*)

Ἡγησίμαχος
MACEDONIA: **(1)** 326 BC Curt. viii 13. 13; cf. Berve 344 (Tataki, *Macedonians* p. 320 no. 6) (Lat. Hegesimachus)
THRACE:
—MARONEIA: **(2)** ii-i BC *IThrakAig* E212, 25 (I f. *Ἡγησίμαχος* II); **(3)** ~ ib. l. 25 (II s. *Ἡγησίμαχος* I)

Ἡγησίμβροτος
MACEDONIA (BOTTIAIA):
—BEROIA: (1) ii/iii AD *IBer* 145, 14 (Tataki 716) (*Κλ. Ἡ.*)

Ἡγησῖνος
MACEDONIA (BOTTIAIA):
—PELLA: **(1)** iii BC Akamatis, *Amph. Pellas* pp. 35-6 nos. PAR24-8 (amph.) (*SEG* L 613)

Ἡγησιπόλη
THRACE:
—PERINTHOS-HERAKLEIA: **(1)** vi/v BC *IPerinth* 70 (d. *Ἡγεκράτης*)

Ἡγησίπολις
MACEDONIA (PIERIS):
—GALEPSOS: **(1)** hell. Dimitsas 918; Hatzopoulos, *MI* I p. 187 n. 3 (locn.) (s. *Πολεμαρχίδης*)

SKYTHIA:
—OLBIA-BORYSTHENES: **(2)** vi-v BC *SEG* XXXII 755 (vase)
THRACE:
—PERINTHOS-HERAKLEIA: **(3)** s. vi BC *IPerinth* 69 (s. *Φαναγόρης*)

Ἡγησιππίδης
THRACE:
—STRYME: **(1)** m. iv BC *IThrakAig* E151 (f. *Ἀρτεμώ*)

Ἡγήσιππος
CIMMERIAN BOSPOROS:
—MYRMEKION: **(1)** ii/iii AD *CIRB* 870, 5 (*[Ἡ]γήσιππος*)
—PANTIKAPAION: **(2)** f. i AD ib. 302 (f. *Ἀνθεστήριος ὁ καὶ Κτησαμενός*); **(3)** i/ii AD ib. 574 (f. *Ἄλκιμος*)
MACEDONIA (BISALTIA):
—ARGILOS?: **(4)** f. iv BC *SEG* XXX 547 (f. *Μνησαγόρης*)
MACEDONIA (CHALKIDIKE):
—MEKYBERNA: **(5)** s. iv BC *RE* (4); *FGrH* 391 (Tataki, *Macedonians* p. 119 no. 1)
MACEDONIA (MYGDONIA):
—KALINDOIA: **(6)** c. 331 BC Hatzopoulos, *MI* 2 p. 84 no. 62, 14 (s. *Νικόξενος*)
SKYTHIA:
—TANAIS: **(7)** ii AD *CIRB* 1268, 9 (*Ἡγ(ή)σιππο[ς]*)
THRACE:
—ABDERA: **(8)** c. 450-425 BC May, *Abdera* pp. 135-6 nos. 171-4 (coin)
—AINOS: **(9)** hell. *SEG* XXXVI 658 (I f. *Ἡγήσιππος* II); **(10)** ~ ib. (II s. *Ἡγήσιππος* I)
—MARONEIA: **(11)** hell. *EEBS* 42 (1975-6) p. 226 (*IThrakAig* E251) (f. (nat.) *Διογένης*); **(12)** s. iii BC ib. E252 (f. *Ἀρτυσίλη*); **(13)** ii-i BC ib. E212, 22 (s. *Διογένης*)
—PERINTHOS-HERAKLEIA?: **(14)** iv BC Hp., *Epid.* iv 40; vi 6. 13

Ἡγησιπύλη
THRACE: **(1)** vi/v BC *RE* (-) (*FRA* 2535) (d. *Ὄλορος*, m. *Κίμων* (Athens), ?m. *Ἐλπινίκη* (Athens))

Ἥγησις
SCYTHIA MINOR:
—ISTROS: **(1)** iii-ii BC Unp. (Avram, defixio) 4, 4 (*Ἡγήσι(ο)ς*?—ed.)

Ἡγησίσκα
MACEDONIA (BOTTIAIA):
—PELLA: **(1)** s. iv BC *AEMTh* 6 (1992) p. 127 (*AD* 47 (1992) Chron. p. 447)

Ἡγησίστρατος
MACEDONIA (EDONIS):
—AMPHIPOLIS: **(1)** v/iv BC *SEG* XXIV 586 (*Amphipolis* p. 88 fig. 49) (f. *Εὔμητις*)
THRACE:
—ABDERA: **(2)** v BC *FVS* 68 A 1-2 (?f. *Δημόκριτος, Δάμασος, Ἡρόδοτος*: fict.?)
—KARDIA: **(3)** iv/iii BC *IG* IV $(1)^2$ 49, 1, 3 (s. *Ἑκαταῖος*)

Ἡγησιφῶν
THRACE:
—LYSIMACHEIA: **(1)** m. ii BC *ISestos* 38 a, 3 (f. *Μελάνθιος*)

Ἡγησώ
MACEDONIA: **(1)** iii BC *HE* 3345 (Tataki, *Macedonians* p. 320 no. 7) (m. *Νικάνωρ, Φίλα*); **(2)** f. iii BC Austin–Bastianini, *Posidipp.* 36, 8
MACEDONIA (BOTTIAIA):
—MIEZA: **(3)** ii BC *SEG* XLIII 415 (d. *Παράμονος*)

MACEDONIA (MYGDONIA):
—THESSALONIKE: **(4)** ii-iii AD *IG* X (2) (1) 641, 4 (*Βενουλεία Ἡ.*: d. *Λ. Βενουλέϊος Ἀλέξανδρος*)

Ἡγητορίδης
SCYTHIA MINOR:
—TOMIS: **(1)** 37-41 AD *RPC* I 1825-7 (coin)

Ἡγήτωρ
CIMMERIAN BOSPOROS:
—NYMPHAION: **(1)** f. iv BC *CIRB* 922 (f. *Μῆτρις*)
MACEDONIA (LYNKESTIS):
—HERAKLEIA: **(2)** i AD *IG* X (2) (2) 75, 16 (*Κ. Φούριος Ἡγήτω(ρ)*)
THRACE:
—BYZANTION: **(3)** iii BC *RE* Supplbd. 6 (2)

Ἡγίας
MACEDONIA (CHALKIDIKE):
—APHYTIS: **(1)** v BC *AAA* 4 (1971) pp. 362-3 (vase) (*SEG* L 571 B)
—OLYNTHOS: **(2)** ?c. 355-350 BC ib. XXXVIII 640, 3 (s. *Ἡγέστρατος*); **(3)** iv/iii BC ib. XXXIX 1156, 2, 6 (s. *Παρμενίσκος*)
SCYTHIA MINOR:
—KALLATIS: **(4)** iii-ii BC *NZ* 10 (1917) p. 89 no. 243a (coin) (*Ἡγία* (gen.))
THRACE:
—MARONEIA: **(5)** m. iii BC *IThrakAig* E231 (*[Ἡ]γίας*?: f. *Ἀριστόβουλος*)

Ἡγῖνος
THRACE:
—PERINTHOS-HERAKLEIA:
——(Podargoi): **(1)** iii-ii BC *IPerinth* 61, 17 (*Ἡγίνου* (gen.): f. *Καλλίστρατος*)

Ἡγουμενός
CIMMERIAN BOSPOROS:
—GORGIPPIA: **(1)** 168 AD *CIRB* 1144, 1 (f. *—νος*); **(2)** ii/iii AD ib. 1179, 39 (f. *Νεοκλῆς*); **(3)** ~ ib. l. 46, 58 (*Ἡγου[μενός]*—l. 46: f. *Φαρνακίων*)
—PANTIKAPAION: **(4)** i AD ib. 450 (*(Ἡ)γουμενός*: f. *Ὑγιαίνων*)

Ἡγοῦς
SKYTHIA:
—OLBIA-BORYSTHENES: **(1)** iv BC Tolstoi 53 + *BE* 1958, no. 348 (vase) (*Ἡγοῦτος* (gen.))
THRACE:
—APOLLONIA-SOZOPOLIS: **(2)** iv/iii BC *IGB* I^2 449 (d. *Κρεσφόντης*)

Ἡδεῖα
CIMMERIAN BOSPOROS:
—BOSPOROS: **(1)** ii BC *IG* II^2 8427 (*FRA* 1371) (d. *Εὐπόλεμος*)
—HERMONASSA: **(2)** iv BC *CIRB* 1064
—PANTIKAPAION: **(3)** i AD ib. 616; cf. KW pl. 52 no. 704 (-δί-); **(4)** f. i AD *CIRB* 412 (-δ̣ί̣-); **(5)** 57 AD ib. 69, 7 (*[Ἡ]δεία*); **(6)** ?ii AD ib. 676 (d. *Ἀσκληπιάδης*, m. *Ἀσκληπιάδης*); **(7)** f. ii AD ib. 756 (-δέα); **(8)** iii AD ib. 728 (-δί-)
MACEDONIA (BOTTIAIA):
—BEROIA: **(9)** 193 AD *ILeukopetra* 37, 1 (Tataki 697) (*Κλ. Ἡδέα*)
—EDESSA: **(10)** 180 AD *SEG* XXIV 531, 14 (Tataki, *Edessa* 119) (-δέα: m. *Σατορνῖλος*)
—EDESSA?: **(11)** iii-iv AD *GVI* 2036, 5 (*IDyrrh* 527 bis; Tataki, *Edessa* 118) (*Ἡδαῖα ἡ καὶ Μαρία*: d. *Εὔκλεια*, m. *Τίτος*)
MACEDONIA (EORDAIA):
—KARYOCHORI (MOD.): **(12)** ?i AD *SEG* XLVII 902 + *AD* 47 (1992) Chron. p. 457 with pl. 125 δ (*Κ̣λ. Ἡδέα*, *[Κ]λ. Ἡδόνα*—ed.)
MACEDONIA (LOWER PAIONIA):
—EUROPOS: **(13)** 194 BC *SGDI* 2082, 3, 5-7 (Tataki, *Macedonians* p. 108 no. 7) (slave/freed.)
MACEDONIA (MYGDONIA):
—THESSALONIKE: **(14)** ii-iii AD *SEG* XLV 815 (*Φλ. Ἡδέα*)
SCYTHIA MINOR:
—KALLATIS: **(15)** iii/ii BC *IKyz* I 510, 3 (*Steinepigramme* 2 p. 55) (*Ἡδέ[α]*: d. *Γλυκεῖα*)

SKYTHIA:
—OLBIA-BORYSTHENES: (16) hell. *NS* 95 (Ἡδε[ῖα]: d. Ἀριστοκ—)
THRACE:
—MARONEIA: (17) f. ii BC *SEG* XXXIV 709 (*IThrakAig* E278) ([Ἡ]δεῖα: d. Διονύσιος); (18) i AD *SEG* XXX 698 (*IThrakAig* E255) (-δέα: ?d. Σεύθης); (19) s. ii AD Dumont–Homolle 110b 22 (*IThrakAig* E298) (d. Τάρσας)

Ἡδείη
CIMMERIAN BOSPOROS:
—PATRAEUS: (1) iv BC *CIRB* 1017 (*GVI* 338; *CEG* II 738) (-δέ-: m. Φιλονοίη)

Ἡδικα
CIMMERIAN BOSPOROS:
—PANTIKAPAION: (1) s. iv BC *CIRB* 184; Zgusta, *PNS* 641 (d. Γόρδις)

Ἡδίστη
MACEDONIA: (1) f. iii BC *IG* II² 9261 (Tataki, *Macedonians* p. 320 no. 8; *FRA* 3472) (d. Βα—); (2) 218 BC *PEnt* 69, 1 and verso (Tataki, *Macedonians* p. 320 no. 9; La'da E1804) (d. Νικάνωρ)
MACEDONIA (BOTTIAIA):
—KYRRHOS: (3) ii AD *IG* II² 9140 (Tataki, *Macedonians* p. 117 no. 7; *FRA* 3159) (d. Διονύσιος)
—PELLA: (4) f. iii BC *SEG* XXIV 549 (d. Νέανδρος)
MACEDONIA (CHALKIDIKE):
—STRATONIKEIA?: (5) i-ii AD ib. 576 (-σστη: d. Ἑρμίας)
MACEDONIA (EDONIS):
—AMPHIPOLIS: (6) hell.? ib. XXX 550 (d. —χίων)
—PHILIPPOI*: (7) i-ii AD *AE* 1950-1, pp. 62-3 no. 6 (Pilhofer 721) (Lat. Licinia Hediste: freed.)
MACEDONIA (EORDAIA):
—KORMESTAI: (8) ii BC *EAM* 88 (d. Ἀλέξανδρος)
MACEDONIA (MYGDONIA):
—THESSALONIKE?: (9) ii AD *IG* X (2) (1) 890 ([Ἡ]δίστη: d. Δωσίθεος)
SCYTHIA MINOR:
—ISTROS: (10) f. iv BC *ISM* I 231, 1, 8 (d. Εὐαγόρης); (11) i BC-i AD ib. 191 II, 29
—TROESMIS: (12) ii AD ib. V 181 (Lat. Claudia Hediste: d. Ἀγλαΐς)
THRACE:
—APOLLONIA-SOZOPOLIS: (13) iii BC *BMN-Burgas* 4 (2002) p. 127 no. 27 (Ἡδίσ[τη]?: d. Ἀθηναγόρης)

Ἥδιστος
CIMMERIAN BOSPOROS:
—PANTIKAPAION: (1) f. ii AD *CIRB* 87, 2; (2) iii AD ib. 729 (s. Ἔρως)
MACEDONIA (MYGDONIA):
—THESSALONIKE: (3) b. 268 AD *IG* X (2) (1) 238, 3 (—χίκιος Ἡ.)

Ἡδόνη
MACEDONIA (EORDAIA):
—RYAKI (MOD.): (1) i-ii AD *EAM* 96 (?d. Ἀμύντας: freed.)
THRACE:
—NOVAE: (2) ii AD *IGLNovae* 48 (Lat. Hedone: d. Νύμφιος)

Ἡδόνιν
CIMMERIAN BOSPOROS:
—PANTIKAPAION: (1) ii-i BC *CIRB* 276; cf. KW pl. 23 no. 276 (-νειν: m. Μαστοῦς, Θεαγένης)

Ἡδοῦς
CIMMERIAN BOSPOROS:
—NYMPHAION: (1) i AD *CIRB* 928; Zgusta, *PNS* 291 (s. Ζμάδης)

Ἡδύβιος
CIMMERIAN BOSPOROS:
—PANTIKAPAION: (1) i AD *CIRB* 326 (I f. Ἡδύβιος II); (2) ~ ib. (II s. Ἡδύβιος I); (3) 82 AD ib. 76, 17 (*SEG* XVIII 310) (s. Λάμαχος)

Ἡδυγένης
CIMMERIAN BOSPOROS:
—PANTIKAPAION: (1) f. ii AD *CIRB* 87, 3 (Ἡ[δυγ]ένης)

Ἥδυκος
CIMMERIAN BOSPOROS:
—GORGIPPIA: (1) s. ii AD ib. 1145, 5 (s. Ἄττας)
—PHANAGOREIA: (2) i AD *IGUR* 567 a (s. Εὔοδος)

Ἡδύκων
SKYTHIA:
—TANAIS: (1) 236 AD *CIRB* 1250, 17 (f. Μύριππος)

Ἡδύλη
MACEDONIA (CHALKIDIKE):
—POTIDAIA-KASSANDREIA: (1) m. iii BC *Thess. Mnem.* 18 (Tataki, *Macedonians* p. 90 no. 42)
THRACE:
—KABYLE: (2) hell. *SEG* XLII 652. 2

Ἡδυλίσκος
CIMMERIAN BOSPOROS:
—PANTIKAPAION: (1) ii AD *CIRB* 712 (f. Φιλώτας)

Ἡδύλος
CIMMERIAN BOSPOROS:
—BOSPOROS: (1) ?257 BC Nachtergael, *Les Galates* 7, 41 (s. Χρυσόλαος)
SCYTHIA MINOR:
—TOMIS: (2) ii BC *AMNG* I (2) 2477 (coin) (Ἡδύ(λος)?); (3) i BC *ISM* II 2 B, 54 (s. Θεόφαντος); (4) i BC-i AD ib. 154, 1 (*Eastern cults* p. 10 no. 14) (f. Διονύσιος)
TAURIS:
—CHERSONESOS: (5) 130 AD *VDI* 1960 (3), pp. 154-5, 28 (f. Καλλικλῆς)
THRACE:
—DIONYSOPOLIS: (6) hell. *Spink Num. Circular* 105 (1997) p. 371 no. 6 (coin) (Ἡδύ(λος?))
—MARONEIA: (7) ii BC *IThrakAig* E253 (Ἡδ[ύλος]?: f. Κρατίστα)

Ἥδυν
CIMMERIAN BOSPOROS:
—GORGIPPIA: (1) i/ii AD *CIRB* 1197 B
—MYRMEKION: (2) i BC-i AD *SEG* XXVIII 643 (d. Τρύφων)
—PANTIKAPAION: (3) i BC *CIRB* 269 (m. Ἀλεξάνδρεια); (4) i AD ib. 440; (5) ~ ib. 451; (6) f. ii AD ib. 677; cf. KW pl. 12 no. 178

Ἡδυς
MACEDONIA (MYGDONIA):
—THESSALONIKE?: (1) i/ii AD *IG* X (2) (1) 271; (2) ii-iii AD ib. 899
THRACE:
—ODESSOS: (3) i-ii AD *IGB* I² 51 c, 4 (s. Ἀρχέστρατος)
—PERINTHOS-HERAKLEIA: (4) c. 100-115 AD *SEG* XXVI 1288, 3 (f. Ἐπιγένης)

Ἡδυτέα
TAURIS:
—CHERSONESOS: (1) i BC-i AD *IOSPE* I² 454 (d. Δημήτριος)

Ἡδύφιλος
CIMMERIAN BOSPOROS:
—PANTIKAPAION: (1) iv AD *CIRB* 739 (s. Σωσίπατρος)

Ἥδων
MACEDONIA (CHALKIDIKE):
—STAGEIROS: (1) v-iv BC *SEG* XLVIII 841 (Ἥδωνος (gen./n. pr.?): ?f. Μελίτων)

Ἡδώνης
MACEDONIA (CHALKIDIKE):
—OLYNTHOS: (1) ?350 BC *TAPA* 62 (1931) p. 43 no. 2, 8; Hatzopoulos, *Actes Chalc.* p. 80 (date) (Ἡδώνεος (gen.): f. Νίκων)

Ἡετίων
MACEDONIA (EDONIS):
—AMPHIPOLIS: (1) f. iii BC *HE* 1317 (Tataki, *Macedonians* p. 46 no. 6)

Ἡζοῦς
CIMMERIAN BOSPOROS:
—HERMONASSA: (1) imp. *CIRB* 1095; cf. KW 611 with fig. 14; Zgusta, *PNS* 291 (s. Ἀπολλωνίδης)
—PANTIKAPAION: (2) i AD *CIRB* 328 (f. Ἀγαθοῦς); (3) ~ ib. 353 (Ἡζ[οῦς]?: f. Ἀπολλώνιος, Παρθενοκλῆς); (4) ii AD ib. 713; cf. KW pl. 21 no. 316; (5) s. ii AD *KSIA* 116 (1969) p. 53 no. 5 (f. Φάννας)

Ἡθιόχακος
SKYTHIA:
—TANAIS: (1) 244 AD *CIRB* 1287, 24 ([Ἡ]θιόχακος: s. Ἀρδονάγαρος)

Ἦθος
MACEDONIA (BOTTIAIA):
—BEROIA: (1) f. ii BC *IBer* 156 (Tataki 534) (s. Σιτάλκης)

Ἡλιάδης
THRACE:
—BYZANTION (TERRIT.): (1) i-ii AD *IByz* 275 (Fıratlı–Robert p. 87 no. 109) (f. Εἶα)

Ἡλιάς
CIMMERIAN BOSPOROS:
—PANTIKAPAION: (1) f. i AD *CIRB* 466; (2) ii AD ib. 762 (Ἡλιά[ς])

Ἡλιογένης
CIMMERIAN BOSPOROS:
—PANTIKAPAION: (1) i/ii AD ib. 606 (s. Ἡρᾶς)

Ἡλιοδώρα
CIMMERIAN BOSPOROS:
—PANTIKAPAION: (1) i BC/i AD ib. 416; cf. KW pl. 52 no. 714; (2) i AD *CIRB* 344 (d. Κούλιος, Ἀπολλωνία); (3) f. ii AD ib. 716; cf. KW pl. 26 no. 384
MACEDONIA (MYGDONIA):
—CHARAKOMA?: (4) ?ii AD *SEG* XL 536
—THESSALONIKE: (5) m. iii AD *IG* X (2) (1) 558, 3 (d. Φιλωτέρα); (6) s. iii AD ib. 180, 6 (Αἰλ. Βαιβία Ἡ.: d. Αἰλ. Βαίβιος Ἡλιόδωρος)
SCYTHIA MINOR:
—TOMIS: (7) iii AD *ISM* II 351 (Lat. Va. Eliodora)
THRACE:
—AINOS: (8) hell. *BCH* 24 (1900) p. 168 no. 1 (*SEG* XLIX 868)
—ODESSOS: (9) ii-iii AD *IGB* V 5074. 5a (Ἡ. Βουθειθερίς)

Ἡλιόδωρος
CIMMERIAN BOSPOROS:
—PANTIKAPAION: (1) s. i BC *CIRB* 125, 2, 5 (*GVI* 710) (II s. Ἡλιόδωρος I); (2) ~ *CIRB* 125, 3 (*GVI* 710) (I f. Μηνόδωρος, Ἡλιόδωρος II); (3) ?i AD *CIRB* 417 (Ἡλιόδω[ρος]: s. Μαστοῦς, Χρύσιον); (4) ii AD ib. 650 (f. Ἄδα)
MACEDONIA: (5) iii BC *IG* II² 9274 + Peek, *AG* I p. 22 no. 70 ([Ἡλ]ιόδωρος?, [Δ]ιόδωρος?: f. ..ομίς); (6) m. ii BC *BGU* 2423, 26 (Tataki, *Macedonians* p. 483 no. 109); cf. La'da E1677; (7) ~ *BGU* 2423, 30 (Tataki, *Macedonians* p. 483 no. 107); cf. La'da E1552 (f. Νίκανδρος); (8) 107-101 BC *SEG* XXXIII 1359, 3 (Tataki, *Macedonians* p. 483 no. 106; La'da E1495) (s. Πτολεμαῖος); (9) 74 BC *SB* 7532,

25 (Tataki, *Macedonians* p. 483 no. 108); cf. La'da E1596 (f. *Πτολεμαῖος*)
MACEDONIA (BOTTIAIA):
—BEROIA: **(10)** 223 BC *IBer* 4, 15 (Ἡλιό(δ)ωρος: s. Ἀγάνωρ)
MACEDONIA (CHALKIDIKE):
—POTIDAIA-KASSANDREIA: **(11)** i BC *SEG* XLII 421, 11 (*IOrop* 608; Tataki, *Macedonians* p. 90 no. 43) (s. *Θεόδοτος*)
MACEDONIA (EDONIS):
—AMPHIPOLIS: **(12)** 165 AD *SEG* XLIX 676 (s. *Διονύσιος*)
—AMPHIPOLIS (TERRIT.): **(13)** i BC-i AD? Kaphtantzis 584 (Ἡλιόδωρος?: s. *Κλεοπάτρα*)
—PHILIPPOI (TERRIT.): **(14)** ?iii AD Pikoulas, *Chora* p. 146 no. 59, 13 (Pilhofer 602; *SEG* L 618); cf. *BE* 1944, no. 129 (Ἡλι[όδ]ωρος)
MACEDONIA (MYGDONIA):
—LETE: **(15)** ii AD *Makedonika* 2 (1951) p. 619 no. 42 *θ*, 10 (s. *Ταρούλας*)
—THESSALONIKE: **(16)** i-ii AD *IG* X (2) (1) 243 I, 14; **(17)** f. i AD ib. 133, 6; Robert, *OMS* 5 pp. 295-302 (date) (I? f. Ἡλιόδωρος II?); **(18)** ~ *IG* X (2) (1) 133, 6; Robert, *OMS* 5 pp. 295-302 (date) ([Ἡλιόδω]ρος: II? s. Ἡλιόδωρος I?); **(19)** ii AD *IG* IV (1) 591, 4 + *Mnem.* NS 47 (1919) pp. 259-60 (Tataki, *Macedonians* p. 185 no. 54; Stephanis 1066) (*Μ. Οὔλπ. Ἡ.*: s. *Διόδωρος*); **(20)** s. iii AD *IG* X (2) (1) 179, 10; 180, 13 (*Αἴλ. Ἡ.*: I f. *Αἴλ. Βαίβιος Ἡλιόδωρος* II); **(21)** ~ ib. l. 9 (*Αἴλ. Βαίβιος Ἡ.*: II s. *Αἴλ. Ἡλιόδωρος* I, f. *Αἴλ. Βαιβία Ἡλιοδώρα*); **(22)** 273 AD ib. 529 (*Αἴλ. Ἡ. ὁ καὶ Ἀλέξανδρος*)
—THESSALONIKE?: **(23)** ii-iii AD ib. 812 (s. *Δύναμις*); **(24)** v-vi AD ib. 787 (Feissel, *RICM* 156) (Ἡλιόδω[ρος])
SCYTHIA MINOR:
—ISTROS: **(25)** ii AD *ISM* I 196, 16 (I f. Ἡλιόδωρος II); **(26)** ~ ib. l. 16 (II s. Ἡλιόδωρος I); **(27)** ~ ib. 201 II, 10 ([Οὔλ]π. Ἡ.)
—KALLATIS: **(28)** ii/iii AD ib. III 181, 5 (s. Ἀρτεμίδωρος); **(29)** 241-244 AD ib. 74 A, 20 (s. *Θεόδωρος*); **(30)** ~ ib. l. 22 (s. *Φαρνάκης*)
—NOVIODUNUM*: **(31)** f. iii AD ib. V 273, 6 (Lat. Q. Iul. Heliodorus)
THRACE:
—BEROE-AUGUSTA TRAIANA: **(32)** 212-217 AD *IGB* V 5600, 7 (*Eastern cults* pp. 233-4 no. 24)
—KELLAI: **(33)** 241-244 AD *IGB* III 1517, 9 (*Αὐρ. Ἡ.*: s. Ἰούλιος); **(34)** ~ ib. l. 55 (s. Ἀλέξανδρος)
—LYSIMACHEIA?: **(35)** i/ii AD *SEG* XXXVIII 735, 11
—NICOPOLIS AD ISTRUM (TERRIT.): **(36)** ii AD *IGB* V 5244 a, 21 ([Ἡ]λιό[δ]ωρος: f. *Βακχις*)
—PAUTALIA:
——(Herakleis): **(37)** ?ii AD ib. IV 2077, 18
—PHILIPPOPOLIS-TRIMONTIUM: **(38)** iv-v AD Beševliev 209, 1, 9 (s. Ἰουλιανός)
—PHILIPPOPOLIS-TRIMONTIUM (TERRIT.): **(39)** iii AD *IGB* III 1202 (*Αὐρ. Ἡ.*: s. *Δουράζερις*)

Ἡλιόνη
MACEDONIA (PIERIA):
—DION?: **(1)** f. ii AD Spiliopoulou-Donderer, *KGN* p. 202 no. D19 (*Σεμπρωνία Ἡ.*: m. *Γαϊανή*)

Ἥλιος
CIMMERIAN BOSPOROS:
—GORGIPPIA: **(1)** s. ii AD *CIRB* 1142, 15 (f. —ης)
—MYRMEKION: **(2)** i AD ib. 868 (Ἡλ[ι]ος: f. *Γόκων*); **(3)** i/ii AD ib. 879; *Topoi* 3 (1993) p. 198 (date) (Ἡλίω (gen.): f. *Βίτων*)
—PANTIKAPAION: **(4)** imp. *CIRB* 792 (s. Ἡλίων); **(5)** ~ ib. 793 (f. *Θράσων*); **(6)** i AD ib. 413; cf. KW pl. 48 no. 665 (s. Ἔρως); **(7)** ~ *CIRB* 549 (f. *Χρηστίων*); **(8)** f. i AD ib. 505; cf. KW pl. 27 no. 400 (f. Ῥόδων); **(9)** m. i AD *CIRB* 414; cf. KW pl. 48 no. 662 (s. *Μοσχίων*); **(10)** i/ii AD *CIRB* 635; cf. KW pl. 35 no. 502 (f. *Στρατόνικος*); **(11)** ii AD *CIRB* 701; **(12)** 221 AD ib. 99, 18 (s. *Παυλῖνος*); **(13)** 275-278 AD ib. 36, 76 (-λει-: f. *Κοτιοῦς*)
—PANTIKAPAION?: **(14)** iii AD *SEG* XLV 1014
—THEODOSIA: **(15)** iii AD *CIRB* 947 A, 3 (s. *Ποσίδεος*)
MACEDONIA (BOTTIAIA):
—BEROIA: **(16)** ii AD *IBer* 304, 1 (Tataki 1101) (*Πο. Ἡ.*: I f. *Πο. Ἥλιος* II); **(17)** ~ *IBer* 304, 3 (Tataki 1102) (*Πο. Ἡ.*: II s. *Πο. Ἥλιος* I, *Δάφνη*)
—PELLA: **(18)** ?iii AD Dimitsas 143 (*Λ. Αἴλ. Ἥλειος*)
MACEDONIA (KRESTONIA):
—MORRYLOS: **(19)** ii-iii AD *SEG* XXXIX 613, 4 (Ἡλιοῦνι (dat.): f. Ἀπολλόδωρος, Ἀρτεμίδωρος)
MACEDONIA (MYGDONIA):
—THESSALONIKE: **(20)** i-ii AD *IG* X (2) (1) 243 I, 7 + *Maia* 25 (1973) p. 200; **(21)** ii/iii AD *IG* X (2) (1) 262 IV, 9
SCYTHIA MINOR:
—CAPIDAVA: **(22)** ii AD *ISM* V 29, 3; 30, 6 (*CCET* IV 9) (Lat. Coc. Elius—29, Coc. Helius—30: s. Cocceius Vitales, Coc. Iulia) ?= *(23)*
—CAPIDAVA (NR.): **(23)** ii AD *ISM* V 6 with pl. (Lat. M. Coc. Hilus) ?= *(22)*
—ISTROS: **(24)** ii AD ib. I 128 (*Eastern cults* p. 104 no. 67); **(25)** ~ *ISM* I 196, 13 (f. Ἡρακλείδης); **(26)** ~ ib. 197 II, 5 (f. *Βαλέριος*)
—TOMIS: **(27)** ii AD ib. II 17, 9 (f. *Χρήστος*); **(28)** ~ ib. 125 II, 20 (s. Ἄττας); **(29)** ii-iii AD ib. 468, 8 (f. *Θεόδοτος*)
—ULMETUM: **(30)** iii AD ib. V 73, 7 (Lat. Cocc. Elius)
SKYTHIA:
—OLBIA-BORYSTHENES: **(31)** ii AD *IOSPE* I^2 128, 9 (f. Ἡλίτας)

Ἡλιοφῶν
MACEDONIA (BOTTIAIA):
—BEROIA: **(1)** ii-iii AD *IBer* 341 (f. *Οὐαλέρις*)
MACEDONIA (PIERIA):
—KOLINDROS (MOD.): **(2)** ii-iii AD *Klio* 52 (1970) p. 64 no. 17
THRACE:
—AINOS: **(3)** hell.? *IG* II^2 7977 (*FRA* 250) (f. *Εὐφροσύνη*)

Ἧλις
CIMMERIAN BOSPOROS:
—PANTIKAPAION: **(1)** imp. *CIRB* 791; Robert, *Noms indigènes* pp. 443 f. (name) (s. *Κοῖδος*?); **(2)** i AD *CIRB* 340; **(3)** i/ii AD ib. 80, 7; cf. KW pl. 33 no. 454; **(4)** 275-278 AD *CIRB* 36, 68 (s. *Δικυλ*—)
SCYTHIA MINOR:
—ISTROS: **(5)** ii AD *ISM* I 196, 8; 201 I, 17 (s. *Νουμήνιος*); **(6)** s. ii AD ib. 167, 13 (Ἡλι (gen.): f. *Αἰλιανός*); **(7)** f. iii AD *Stud. Fischer* p. 32 no. 4, 7 (Ἡλει (gen.): f. *Ποντικός*); **(8)** 222-225 AD *ISM* I 100, 12 (Ἡλει (gen.): I f. *Αὐρ. Ἧλις* II) ?= *(10)*; **(9)** ~ ib. l. 12 (*Αὐρ. Ἡλει* (gen.): II s. Ἧλις I); **(10)** ~ ib. 100 A, 15 (Ἡλει (gen.): f. *Αὐρ. Αἰλιανός*) ?= *(11)* *(8)*; **(11)** ~ ib. l. 16 (Ἡλει (gen.): f. *Αὐρ. Ἀλέξανδρος*) ?= *(12)* *(10)*; **(12)** ~ ib. l. 17 (Ἡλει (gen.): f. *Αὐρ. Σατουρνῖλος*) ?= *(11)*
—TOMIS: **(13)** 201 AD ib. II 83 I, 17 (Ἡλει (gen.): f. Ἀλέξανδρος); **(14)** ~ ib. l. 28 (Ἡλει (gen.): f. *Αὐ—ων*)
TAURIS:
—CHERSONESOS: **(15)** ii AD *IOSPE* I^2 582, 1 (s. *Θάμιχος*); **(16)** ii/iii AD *SEG* XXXIII 603 (Ἡλ<ρ>ις: s. *Διονύσιος*, f. —νοος)
THRACE:
—DIONYSOPOLIS: **(17)** 241-244 AD *IGB* I^2 22 bis, 9
—ODESSOS: **(18)** 215 AD ib. 47 a, 22 (Ἡλι (gen.): f. *Αὐρ. Διοκλῆς*); **(19)** 221 AD ib. 47 bis b, 32 (Ἡλει (gen.): f. *Αὐρ.* Ἐπιμένης); **(20)** ~ ib. l. 38 (*Αὐρ. Ἡλεις*: s. *Εὐτυχίδης*)
—PERINTHOS-HERAKLEIA: **(21)** iv-v AD *IPerinth* 181 (*Αὐρ. Σεπτ. Ἡ.*)

Ἡλίς
CIMMERIAN BOSPOROS:
—GORGIPPIA: **(1)** ?93-123 AD *CIRB* 1125, 10 (d. *Νυμφαγόρας*)
—PANTIKAPAION: **(2)** i BC/i AD ib. 308; cf. KW pl. 49 no. 683 (m. Ἡρακλείδης); **(3)** ?i AD *CIRB* 415; cf. KW p. 29 no. 162; Zgusta, *PNS* 615 (Ἡλί<φ>ς—*CIRB*, Ἡλιφίς—KW); **(4)** i AD *CIRB* 418 (d. *Βασιλίσκος*); **(5)** ~ ib. 419 (d. *Φάννης*)
—PHANAGOREIA: **(6)** i AD ib. 997 (Ἡλί(ς): d. *Δημήτριος*)

Ἡλίτας
CIMMERIAN BOSPOROS:
—PANTIKAPAION: **(1)** imp. ib. 108 (s. *Θευ*—)
SKYTHIA:
—OLBIA-BORYSTHENES: **(2)** ii AD *IOSPE* I^2 128, 9 (s. Ἥλιος)

Ἡλίττας
CIMMERIAN BOSPOROS:
—HERMONASSA: **(1)** 123-132 AD *CIRB* 1054, 21
—PANTIKAPAION: **(2)** i-ii AD ib. 632 (Ἰούλ. Ἡ.) ?= *(3)*; **(3)** s. i AD ib. 434 (Ἰούλ. Ἡ.) ?= *(2)*

Ἡλίων
CIMMERIAN BOSPOROS:
—PANTIKAPAION: **(1)** imp. ib. 792 (f. Ἥλιος)
TAURIS:
—CHERSONESOS: **(2)** imp. *SEG* XXXVII 655 (lead) (s. *Πρω*—); **(3)** i AD Solomonik, *GChKh* nos. 101; 433 (vases) (Ἡλίω(ν))

Ἥλμανος
SKYTHIA:
—OLBIA-BORYSTHENES: **(1)** iii AD *IOSPE* I^2 103, 6; Zgusta, *PNS* 109 (f. Ῥευρόμανος)

Ἡμέρα
CIMMERIAN BOSPOROS:
—PANTIKAPAION: **(1)** ?i AD *CIRB* 475; cf. KW pl. 21 no. 300 (m. *Μοῦσα*)
TAURIS:
—CHERSONESOS: **(2)** ii AD *IOSPE* I^2 513 (d. Ἀπελλᾶς ὁ κὲ *Προμαθίων*)

Ἥμων
MACEDONIA (LYNKESTIS):
—HERAKLEIA (AREA): **(1)** ii-iii AD *IG* X (2) (2) 39

Ἡνλιζις
MACEDONIA (EDONIS):
—AMPHIPOLIS?: **(1)** ii-iii AD Dimitsas 906 (Kaphtantzis 543) (Ἡνλιζει (gen.): f. *Διοσκουρίδης*, *Ζελμούτας*, *Ζιπύρων*, *Καλλιόπη*)

Ἡπατίων
CIMMERIAN BOSPOROS:
—GORGIPPIA: **(1)** i-ii AD *CIRB* 1198 (s. *Πατέρας*)

Ἧπις
MACEDONIA (BOTTIAIA):
—BEROIA: **(1)** ii AD *IBer* 301, 3 (Tataki 535) (s. *Παραμόνα*)

Ἡραγένης
THRACE:
—SERDICA: **(1)** f. iii AD *IGB* V 5785, 4; 5790; 5792; 5803; 5814-15 (*Αὐρ. Ἡ.*: s. Ἥρανος)

Ἡραγόρας
MACEDONIA (LYNKESTIS):
—HERAKLEIA: **(1)** i AD *IG* X (2) (2) 75, 46 (Ἡραγόρου (gen.): f. Ἐμμένης)

Thrace:
—Maroneia: **(2)** 167 BC *SEG* xxxv 823, 6 (*IThrakAig* E168) (f. *Πυθίων*)
—Odessos: **(3)** ii AD *IGB* I^2 50 b, 8 with Index (s. *Στ—*)

Ἡραγόρης
Skythia:
—Olbia-Borysthenes: **(1)** vi/v BC Tolstoi 41 (*LSAG*^{2} p. 372 no. 58 (vase)); **(2)** m. iv BC Dubois, *IGDOlbia* 106, 7 (*SEG* xliv 669) (*Ἡραγόρη(ς)*); **(3)** s. iv BC ib. L 702 III, 3 (f. *Διονυσόδωρος*); **(4)** iv/iii BC *IOlbia* 71 II, 4 (Dubois, *IGDOlbia* 11) (s. *Πρα—*); **(5)** iii BC ib. 109, 5 (*SEG* xxxvii 673)
Thrace:
—Abdera: **(6)** c. 415-395 BC May, *Abdera* p. 162 no. 201 (coin) (*Ἡραγόρεω* (gen.)); **(7)** c. 395-360 BC ib. p. 209 no. 273 (coin); **(8)** f. iii BC Unp. (Chryssanthaki diss.) p. 396 (coin)
—Perinthos-Herakleia?: **(9)** v/iv BC *IGB* v 5155 (or Thrace Apollonia-Sozopolis: s. *Σάτυρος*, f. *Σάτυρος*); **(10)** iv BC Hp., *Epid.* ii 1. 7 (*Ἡραγόρεω* (gen.))

Ἡράϊννα
Thrace:
—Stryme: **(1)** m. v BC *CEG* II 728 (*IThrakAig* E109) (*Ἡραΐνη(ι)* (dat.): d. *Ἀνταγόρας*)
—Stryme? (nr.): **(2)** v/iv BC Bakalakis, *Oinos Ismarikos* p. 553 (*IThrakAig* E127) (d. *Ἀρτέμων*)

Ἡραῖος
Cimmerian Bosporos:
—Gorgippia: **(1)** f. iii BC *CIRB* 1137 B II, 22 (*Ἡραῖος*: s. *Τιμοσθένης*)
—Myrmekion: **(2)** iv/iii BC *Stud. Blavatskii* pp. 70-1 (vase) (f. *Ἡροφάνης*)
—Pantikapaion: **(3)** iv BC Tolstoi 149 (vase); **(4)** ~ *CIRB* 166 (f. *Ἀριστοφάνης*); **(5)** ii AD ib. 692 (s. *Μόνιμος*, *Μᾶ*)
Tauris:
—Chersonesos: **(6)** 129 AD *IOSPE* I^2 359, 31 (s. *Χηματῖνος*)
Thrace:
—Ainos: **(7)** iv/iii BC *IG* II^2 495, 10, [21]; IV (1)^2 58, 7 (f. *Ἀλκαῖος*)

Ἡραΐς
Macedonia: **(1)** m. ii BC D.S. xxxii 10. 2-9 (resid. Arabia Abai: *Ἡραΐς μετανομασθεῖσα Διόφαντος*: d. *Διόφαντος*)
Macedonia (Bottiaia):
—Pella: **(2)** ?iii BC *SEG* II 401 (d. *Σωσίων*)
Macedonia (Mygdonia):
—Thessalonike*: **(3)** iii AD *IG* x (2) (1) 550 (*Αὐρ. Ἡραείς*)
Thrace:
—Beroe-Augusta Traiana: **(4)** ii AD *IGB* v 5585, 5
—Bourdapa: **(5)** ii-iii AD ib. III 1345 (d. *Μουκιανός*)
—Byzantion: **(6)** c. 198 AD Schönert-Geiss, *Byzantion* 1462-3; 1510; 1522 (coin) (*Αἰλ. Ἡ.*)
—Hadrianopolis: **(7)** 293 AD *Cod. Just.* viii 13.16; cf. *Klio* 58 (1976) p. 83 (Lat. Heraidi (dat.))
—Hadrianopolis (territ.): **(8)** ii AD *IGB* III 1798, 4; cf. v 5643 (*Ἡραΐς*)
—Kellai: **(9)** ii-iii AD ib. III 1530 (*Φλ. Ἡ.*); **(10)** 241-244 AD ib. 1517, 36 (*Αὐρ. Ἡ.*); **(11)** ~ ib. l. 44 (m. *Αὐρ. Κενθίαρος*); **(12)** ~ ib. l. 33-4 (*Αὐρ. Ἡ.*)
—Maroneia: **(13)** m. iv BC *AD* 26 (1971) Chron. p. 428 no. στ + *IThrakAig* E223 (d. *Παντακλῆς*); **(14)** iii BC *AD* 52 (1997) Chron. p. 880; **(15)** ~ *IThrakAig* E233; **(16)** iii AD Meïmaris–Bakirtzis 3 (*SEG* xliv 592) + *IThrakAig* E329 B
—Montana (nr.): **(17)** iii AD *IGB* II 483 (*Montana* II 102) (d. *Διζάλας*)
—Nicopolis ad Nestum?: **(18)** 221 AD *IGB* IV 2305, 2 (d. *Λεωνίδης*)
—Pautalia: **(19)** iii AD ib. v 5867, 9 (*Αὐρ. Ἡ.*: d. *Δημοσθένης*); **(20)** iv AD Beševliev 36
—Philippopolis-Trimontium: **(21)** ii-iii AD *IGB* III 952; **(22)** ~ ib. 977 (d. *Αὐλούτραλις*); **(23)** ~ ib. 980
—Stryme: **(24)** c. 375-350 BC *SEG* xxxviii 722 (*IThrakAig* E143)

Ἡραΐσκος
Thrace:
—Perinthos-Herakleia: **(1)** iii BC *IPerinth* 42 (*SIRIS* 128); *Eastern cults* p. 27 no. 47 (date) (*Ἡραϊ-*: f. *Ἀρτεμίδωρος*)

Ἡραίων
Scythia Minor:
—Kallatis: **(1)** s. i BC *ISM* III 38, 6 (s. *Ἱκέσιος*); **(2)** 241-244 AD ib. 74, 9 (*-ρέ-*: f. *Θεόδωρος*) ?= (7); **(3)** ~ ib. l. 10 (*-ρέ-*: s. *Ἰταλικός*); **(4)** ~ ib. l. 14 (*-ρέ-*: s. *Νουμήνιος*); **(5)** ~ ib. l. 15 (*-ρέ-*: I f. *Ἡραίων* II) ?= (7); **(6)** ~ ib. l. 15 (*-ρέ-*: II s. *Ἡραίων* I); **(7)** ~ ib. 74 A, 16 (*-ρέ-*: f. *Ὑγιαίνων*) ?= (5) (2)
—Tomis: **(8)** i BC ib. II 2 A, 48 (s. *Ἀρτεμίδωρος*); **(9)** ~ ib. l. 64 (f. *Ἀπολλόδωρος*)
Thrace:
—Byzantion: **(10)** ?354 BC Rhodes–Osborne 57, 13 (*Ἑι-*: f. *Διονύσιος*)
—Mesambria: **(11)** i BC *IGB* I^2 326, 6 (s. *Ἄλφιος*); **(12)** 71 BC ib. 314 a, 1 (s. *Πασίων*)
—Odessos?: **(13)** ii AD ib. 51 bis b, 1 (*Ἡρέ-*: s. *Θο—*); **(14)** ~ ib. l. 8 (*Ἡρέ-*: s. *Οὐάλης*)

Ἡρακᾶς
Cimmerian Bosporos:
—Hermonassa: **(1)** 208 AD *CIRB* 1053 (s. *Ποντικός*)

Ἡρακλᾶς
Cimmerian Bosporos:
—Gorgippia: **(1)** ii AD ib. 1140, 11; *Eirene* 7 (1968) p. 67, 12 (f. *Χρυσέρως*)
Macedonia: **(2)** 74 BC *SB* 7532, 26 (Tataki, *Macedonians* p. 483 no. 110); cf. La'da E1431; E1584 (f. *Ἄρειος*, *Πολυδεύκης*)
Macedonia (Bottiaia):
—Beroia: **(3)** ii/iii AD *IBer* 27 A, 6 (slave?); **(4)** ~ ib. 143 B, 16 (Tataki 1317) (*Φλ. Ἡ.*); **(5)** ~ *IBer* 144 A, 5 (Tataki 1318) (*Φλ. Ἡ.*)
Macedonia (Chalkidike):
—Moni Vatopediou (mod.): **(6)** 203 AD Dimitsas 781, 1 (f. *Γερμανός*)
Macedonia (Mygdonia):
—Thessalonike: **(7)** 129 AD *IG* x (2) (1) 502 (*Λ. Ἀρούντιος Ἡ.*)
Scythia Minor:
—Istros: **(8)** ii AD *ISM* I 201 II, 18 (*—σσιος Ἡ.*)
—Tomis: **(9)** ii-iii AD ib. II 31 II, 1 (*[Ἡρα]κλᾶς*: s. *Τόμος*); **(10)** ~ ib. l. 2 (I f. *Ἡρακλᾶς* II); **(11)** ~ ib. l. 2 (*[Ἡρ]ακλᾶς*: II s. *Ἡρακλᾶς* I)
Thrace:
—Byzantion (territ.): **(12)** i BC *IByz* 173 (s. *—κλῆς*)
—Maroneia: **(13)** i-ii AD *SEG* xlvii 1072 (*IThrakAig* E272) (s. *Ἀπολλόδωρος*)
—Montana*: **(14)** 155 AD *CIL* III 7449, 11 (*Montana* II 1) (Lat. Fla. Heracla)
—Perinthos-Herakleia: **(15)** iii AD *IPerinth* 29 (*Αὐρ. Ἡρ(α)κλᾶς*)
—Philippopolis-Trimontium (territ.): **(16)** ii-iii AD *IGB* III 1214 (f. *—ος*)

Ἡρακλέα
Macedonia (Bottiaia):
—Beroia: **(1)** ii-iii AD *IBer* 245 (Tataki 536); **(2)** ~ *IBer* 305 (Tataki 537); **(3)** 232 AD *ILeukopetra* 80, 1 (*Ποπιλία Ἡ.*) ?= (*Ἡράκλεια* (1))
Macedonia (Mygdonia):
—Thessalonike: **(4)** ii-iii AD *IG* x (2) (1) 467 (*Ἐρεννία Ἡ.*, *Ἡράκλε(ι)α*—ed.)
Macedonia (Pieria):
—Dion: **(5)** ii AD *Essays Laourdas* p. 109 no. 8 (m. *Εὐτυχία*)
Skythia: **(6)** i-ii AD *VDI* 1951 (1), pp. 150-1 no. 1

Ἡρακλέας
Macedonia (Orestis):
—Platania (mod.): **(1)** imp.? *EAM* 204 (*Ἡρακλεαι*—lap., *Ἡρακλέας*?—ed.: s. *Ἀντίπατρος*)

Ἡράκλεια
Macedonia (Bottiaia):
—Beroia: **(1)** ii-iii AD *IBer* 246 (Tataki 1094) (*Ποπιλλία Ἡ.*) ?= (*Ἡρακλέα* (3))
Macedonia (Lynkestis):
—Herakleia: **(2)** ii-iii AD *IG* x (2) (2) 85 (*-κλια*: d. *Ζωσοῦς*)
—Herakleia?: **(3)** ii-iii AD ib. 134 (*Πολεμωνιανὴ Ἡ.*)
Macedonia (Mygdonia):
—Thessalonike: **(4)** ii AD ib. x (2) (1) 587
Thrace:
—Perinthos-Herakleia: **(5)** ii AD *IPerinth* 123
—Serdica: **(6)** 117-138 AD *IGB* IV 1925 c, 13 (*-κλια*)

Ἡρακλείδας
Cimmerian Bosporos:
—Pantikapaion: **(1)** 275-278 AD *CIRB* 36, 25 (f. *Ψυχαρίων*)
Scythia Minor:
—Kallatis: **(2)** iii BC *ISM* III 126, 6 (s. *Ἱέρων*); **(3)** ~ ib. 131, 2 (*GVI* 1392); *ISM* III 132, 1, [5] (f. *Νικασώ*); **(4)** ~ ib. 170 (*[Ἡρ]ακλείδας*); **(5)** ?264 BC *FD* III (1) 158, 2 (*-δης*: s. *Ἱέρων*); **(6)** s. iii BC *ISM* III 8, 1; **(7)** ~ ib. 35 A, 27 (*Ἡρακλεί[δας]*?: f. *Μενίσκος*)
Tauris:
—Chersonesos: **(8)** inc. Solomonik, *GAKh* 887 (vase) (*-κλί-*); **(9)** v BC ib. 886 (vase) (*-κλέ-*); **(10)** c. 425-400 BC *SEG* XL 612. 7 (ostrakon) (*[Ἡ]ρακλέδας*: ?s. *Θ—*); **(11)** c. 300-275 BC *IOSPE* I^2 344, 1; *SEG* xlvii 1168, 1 (s. *Παρμένων*); **(12)** iii BC *IOSPE* I^2 342, 1 (*Ἡρακλ[είδας]*?); **(13)** ~ ib. l. 2 (*Ἡρακ[λείδας]*?: f. *Ἀλκίνους*); **(14)** ~ ib. l. 3 (f. *—ρος*); **(15)** ~ ib. 344, 2, 15 (f. *Συρίσκος*); **(16)** ~ ib. 581, 7 (*Ἡρ[α]κλείδα[ς]*); **(17)** ~ ib. 689, 7 (*Ἡρακλεί[δας]*?); **(18)** iii-ii BC ib. 350 (*Ἡρακλε[ίδας]*?: f. *Χρύσανθος*); **(19)** f. iii BC *SEG* XL 615 B, 6-7 (s. *Ἀσ—*); **(20)** 192 BC *Syll*^{3} 585, 56; 604, 8, 14, 17 (s. *Βιοθᾶς*); **(21)** ?i AD Solomonik, *NEPKh* 43 (s. *Ξάνθος*); **(22)** ii AD *IOSPE* I^2 390, 3 (*Ἡρακλεί[δας]*); **(23)** ?114 AD *SEG* xlviii 999, 40 (*Ἡρακλείδ(ας)*: f. *Ἀντώνιος*)
—Chersonesos (nr.): **(24)** iii BC Solomonik, *GChKh* 48 (vase) (*SEG* xxxiii 609. 2; Saprykin, *Farms* pl. 32. 2) (*[Ἡρ]ακλείδα[ς]*)
Thrace:
—Ainos: **(25)** c. 360 BC *RE* (2); Osborne, *Naturalization* T53 (and Athens: *-δης*)
—Byzantion: **(26)** 389 BC D. xx 60 (*RE* (11)) (*-δης*); **(27)** s. iv BC *SEG* xviii 180, 2 (*Ἡρακλ[είδ]ας*?, *Ἡράκλ[ειτ]ος*?: f. *Καλλικλῆς*); **(28)** iii BC *IIlion* 62, 6 (*RE* Supplbd. 3 (61a)) (*-δης*: s. *Σατυρίσκος*: sculptor); **(29)** s. iii BC Schönert-Geiss, *Byzantion* 1209-11 (coin) (*Ἡρακλε(ίδας)*?); **(30)** iii/ii BC *IG* XI (4) 778, 3, 11 (*-δης*: s. *Ξείνας*); **(31)** 190 BC *RE* (31) (*-δης*)
—Mashov (mod.): **(32)** 230-245 AD *BMNWB* 24 (1996) pp. 17 ff. (Minkova, *PNLIB* p. 153) (Lat. M. Aurelius Heraclidas)
—Mesambria: **(33)** iv BC *IGB* I^2 333 (f. *Χοιρίνα*); **(34)** ii BC ib. 314 b, 13 (s. *Ἡρόδωρος*); **(35)** ~ ib. 325, 1 (f. *Ἡρότιμος*); **(36)** f. ii BC ib. 343 septies, 2, 8; cf. v 5117 (f. *Ναυσίστρατος*); **(37)** i BC ib. I^2 324 (f. *Θεότιμος*)

Ἡρακλείδης

CIMMERIAN BOSPOROS:

—BOSPOROS: **(1)** c. 265-260 BC *FD* III (3) 207, 5 (f. *Νικίας*)

—GORGIPPIA: **(2)** f. iii BC *CIRB* 1137 A I, 12 (f. *Βλέψος*); **(3)** ~ ib. l. 48 (f. *Σωσίπατρος*); **(4)** ~ ib. 1137 A II, 16 (f. *Ἆγις*)

—HERMONASSA: **(5)** f. iv BC Unp. (Taman Arch. Mus.) (*Ἡρακλείδεω* (gen.): f. *Πυθογείτων*)

—NYMPHAION: **(6)** iii BC *CIRB* 912 II, 8 (s. *Πλοῦσις*)

—PANTIKAPAION: **(7)** f. iv BC ib. 190; cf. KW pl. 6 no. 110 (f. *Ἱπποκράτη*); **(8)** c. 245-240 BC *CIRB* 24 (f. *Ἀγλαος*); **(9)** ii-i BC ib. 266 (f. *Παιρίσαλος*); **(10)** s. ii BC *SEG* XXXVII 674; **(11)** i BC/i AD *CIRB* 308; cf. KW pl. 49 no. 683 (-*κλί*-: I f. *Ἡρακλείδης* II); **(12)** ~ *CIRB* 308; cf. KW pl. 49 no. 683 (II s. *Ἡρακλείδης* I, *Ἡλίς*); **(13)** i AD *CIRB* 502; cf. KW pl. 47 no. 661; **(14)** ~ *CIRB* 516 (-*κλί*-); **(15)** ~ ib. 567; **(16)** i-ii AD ib. 607; cf. KW pl. 37 no. 536 (s. *Γάστεις*); **(17)** f. i AD *CIRB* 554; cf. KW pl. 20 no. 287 (f. *Χρύσιον*); **(18)** ?s. i AD *CIRB* 526; **(19)** i/ii AD ib. 626; **(20)** 81 AD ib. 70, 16 (Levinskaya p. 231 no. 1) (Jew?); **(21)** 82 AD *CIRB* 76, 13 (*SEG* XVIII 310) (f. *Στράτων*) ?= (*22*); **(22)** ~ *CIRB* 76, 14 (*SEG* XVIII 310) (I f. *Ἡρακλείδης* II) ?= (*21*); **(23)** ~ *CIRB* 76, 14 (*SEG* XVIII 310) (II s. *Ἡρακλείδης* I); **(24)** ii AD *CIRB* 757 (s. *Χαρίτων*); **(25)** f. ii AD ib. 91, 3; cf. KW pl. 39 no. 574 (s. *Ἀγαθοῦς*); **(26)** ~ *CIRB* 681 (f. *Θεοφίλη*); **(27)** ~ ib. 684; cf. KW pl. 52 no. 711 (-*κλί*-: I f. *Ἡρακλείδης* II); **(28)** ~ *CIRB* 684; cf. KW pl. 52 no. 711 (II s. *Ἡρακλείδης* I, *Ἰσιγόνη*); **(29)** s. ii AD *CIRB* 79 B; **(30)** 204 AD ib. 96, 5 (*SEG* II 485) (f. *Ἀντισθένης*); **(31)** 275-278 AD *CIRB* 36, 37 (*Ἡρακλ(είδης)*: s. *Χο(—)*)

—ZENONOS CHERSONESOS*: **(32)** f. i AD ib. 899 (f. *Βασίλη*); **(33)** iii AD ib. 898, 4 (*[Ἡ]ρακλείδ(ης)*: s. *Δημήτριος*)

KOLCHIS:

—VANI (MOD.): **(34)** hell. *MBAH* 12 (1993) p. 71 (brick)

MACEDONIA: **(35)** iii BC *GVI* 1537, 1; Robert, *Hell.* 11-12 p. 276 f. (locn.) (Tataki, *Macedonians* p. 321 no. 16) (f. *Διογένης*); **(36)** ?219 BC *PUG* III 104, 17 (f. *Ἀπολλώνιος*); **(37)** c. 205-192 BC *SEG* XLVIII 811 (s. *Φανίας*); **(38)** ii BC *RE* (62) (Overbeck 2147-8; Tataki, *Macedonians* p. 321 no. 13) (Lat. Heraclides: painter); **(39)** c. 197-132 BC *Arch. Pap.* 48 (2002) pp. 78-9 col II, 16 (s. *Δίδυμος*: katoikos); **(40)** 182 BC *PRyl* 585, 1, 42 (Tataki, *Macedonians* p. 321 no. 14; La'da E1496) (s. *Ἀπολλώνιος*); **(41)** m. ii BC *BGU* 1938 B, 6 (Tataki, *Macedonians* p. 484 no. 122); cf. La'da E1678 (*[Ἡ]ρακλείδης*); **(42)** ~ *BGU* 1939 A, 3 (Tataki, *Macedonians* p. 484 no. 120); cf. La'da E1813 (f. *Πτολέμα*); **(43)** ~ *BGU* 2423, 38 (Tataki, *Macedonians* p. 484 no. 116; La'da E1501) (*Ἡρακλείδ[ης]*: s. *Σωσίβιος*); **(44)** c. 150-125 BC *SB* 15369, 5; cf. La'da E1524 (f. *Κεφάλων*); **(45)** 145 BC *PPhrurDiosk* 18, 42, 44 (*Ἡρακλείδ̣ης*: s. *.....α̣..ε̣ίδης*); **(46)** 132 BC *Arch. Pap.* 48 (2002) p. 78 (La'da 1497a) (s. *Δίδυμος*: katoikos); **(47)** 124 BC *SB* 9366, 2, 6 (Tataki, *Macedonians* p. 483 no. 114; La'da E1500) (s. *Θεόδωρος*: katoikos); **(48)** 111 BC *PDion* 22, 26 (Tataki, *Macedonians* p. 483 no. 111; La'da E1497) (s. *Ἀχιλλεύς*); **(49)** f. i BC *BGU* 1733, 17, 20, 25 (*PP* 9284; Tataki, *Macedonians* p. 484 no. 115) (s. *Λύκος*); **(50)** 89 BC *UPZ* 125, 29-30, 35 (Tataki, *Macedonians* p. 483 no. 112; La'da E1498) (s. *Ἑρμίας*); **(51)** 72 BC *BGU* 1738, 11 (Tataki, *Macedonians* p. 484 no. 121); cf. La'da E1654 (f. *Χαιρήμων*); **(52)** ~ *BGU* 1738, 12 (Tataki, *Macedonians* p. 484 no. 117; La'da E1502) (s. *Χαιρήμων*); **(53)** 60 BC *BGU* 1816, 2 (Tataki, *Macedonians* p. 484 no. 118); cf. La'da E1404 (f. *Ἀμμώνιος*); **(54)** 51 BC *BGU* 1832, 3 (Tataki, *Macedonians* p. 484 no. 119); cf. La'da E1499 (I f. *Ἡρακλείδης* II); **(55)** ~ *BGU* 1832, 3 (Tataki, *Macedonians* p. 483 no. 113; La'da E1499) (II s. *Ἡρακλείδης* I: katoikos); **(56)** 5 AD *CPR* I 224, 3 (s. *Πανίσκος*: t.e.)

MACEDONIA (BOTTIAIA): **(57)** 335-331 BC *RE* (17); Berve 347 (Tataki, *Macedonians* p. 193 no. 2) (s. *Ἀντίοχος*)

—AIGAI: **(58)** iv BC *SEG* XXXV 806 (*Ἡρακλε[ίδης]*?: s. *Ἀρχιππος*); **(59)** iv/iii BC ib. 776 (s. *Φίλων*)

—BEROIA: **(60)** 120 BC *IBer* 134, 18 (*Ἡ̣ρ̣α̣κ̣λ[εί]δης*: f. *Παράμονος*); **(61)** i BC-i AD ib. 165 (Tataki 540) (*Ἡρακλεί[δης]*: f. *Βαρδίας*); **(62)** i-ii AD *IBer* 167 (*Ἡρ[ακ]λ̣ε̣[ί]δ[ης]*: f. *Ἀδαῖος*); **(63)** 181 AD ib. 49, 11 (Tataki 538) (s. *Βάστος*); **(64)** 191 AD *ILeukopetra* 25, 1 (Tataki 539) (f. *Ἀλέξανδρος*); **(65)** 264 AD *IBer* 55, 13 (*Μάρκιος Ἡ.*)

—MIEZA: **(66)** hell. *AM* 27 (1902) p. 314 no. 28, 10 (*Ἡ(ρ)ακλε[ίδης]*?)

—PELLA: **(67)** m. iv BC *SEG* XXXVIII 648 (f. *Ἄμμιον*); **(68)** s. iv BC *A' Panell. Synedr. Epigr.* p. 191 no. 12; cf. *BE* 2002, no. 269 (*[Ἡ]ρακλε(ί)δης*—ed., *Ἡρακλέδης*?—Hatzopoulos); **(69)** iii BC *SEG* XXIV 539 (f. *Νίκων*); **(70)** ii/i BC ib. XLVIII 824 (-*κλίδ*-: f. *Φίλαγρος*)

—PELLA? (GIANNITSA (MOD.)): **(71)** ?i AD Dimitsas 128 (-*κλί*-: s. *Ἀσκληπιάδης*)

MACEDONIA (CHALKIDIKE):

—OLYNTHOS: **(72)** iv BC *IG* II² 10027 (Tataki, *Macedonians* p. 136 no. 57; *FRA* 5894) (f. *Στράτων*); **(73)** ?277 or 276 BC *FD* III (1) 105, 2 (Tataki, *Macedonians* p. 136 no. 56) (-*δας*: f. *Δεινόμαχος*)

—POTIDAIA-KASSANDREIA: **(74)** f. iii BC *SEG* XLVI 799

—POTIDAIA-KASSANDREIA?: **(75)** v/iv BC ib. 794 (*Ἡρακ(λ)είδης*: s. *Θευγένης*)

MACEDONIA (EDONIS):

—AMPHIPOLIS: **(76)** hell. ib. XXIV 597 (f. *Ἀμβροσία*); **(77)** iii/ii BC Hatzopoulos, *MI* 2 pp. 91-2 no. 75 (f. *Ἀλκαῖος*)

MACEDONIA (ELIMEIA):

—KOZANI (MOD.): **(78)** ii AD *EAM* 52 (-*κλί*-: f. *Ἐαρίνη*)

MACEDONIA (LYNKESTIS):

—ACHLADA (MOD.): **(79)** m. iii AD ib. 172 (*Αὐρ. Ἡ.*)

—SKOPOS (MOD.): **(80)** iii AD ib. 162 (*Αὐρ. Ἡ.*)

MACEDONIA (MYGDONIA):

—ARDROLOS: **(81)** i/ii AD *SEG* XLII 590 (s. *Βίθυς*)

—HERAKLEIA: **(82)** hell. Hatzopoulos, *MI* 1 p. 211 (f. *Νικάνωρ*)

—KALINDOIA: **(83)** 68-98 AD *SEG* XLII 580, 19 (f. *Μεννίδης*); **(84)** ~ ib. 581, 11 (*[Ἡρα]κλείδης*?: s. *Μένανδρος*); **(85)** ~ ib. l. 12 (f. *Μένανδρος*); **(86)** a. 98 AD ib. 582, 8 (s. *Νικόμαχος*); **(87)** ~ ib. l. 38 (s. *Καπένα*)

—LETE: **(88)** f. ii BC ib. XLVI 764, 1 (*[Ἡρακ]λείδη[ς]*?: s. *Μένανδρος*); **(89)** ~ ib. l. 7 (f. *Μύρων*)

—THESSALONIKE: **(90)** i AD *IG* X (2) (1) 259, 25 (s. *Κόρραγος*); **(91)** i-ii AD ib. 243 II, 1 (I f. *Ἡρακλείδης* II); **(92)** ~ ib. l. 1 (II s. *Ἡρακλείδης* I); **(93)** ~ ib. 243 III, 3; **(94)** 3 AD *SEG* XLIII 353 (f. *Κλέων*); **(95)** ii AD *IG* X (2) (1) 241 A II, 17 (*Ῥέφριος Ἡ.*)

—THESSALONIKE?: **(96)** 46 AD Dimitsas 366, 10 (*Epigr. arch. Mak.* 36); cf. *Essays Laourdas* pp. 98-100; *Tekmeria* 6 (2001) p. 126 n. 2 (locn.) (s. *Δημήτριος*); **(97)** ii AD *IG* X (2) (1) 922 (-*κλί*-: s. *Διογένης*, *Εὐτυχία*); **(98)** ?iii AD ib. 854; cf. *SEG* XXX 632 (-*κλί*-: f. *Ἡράκλειος*)

MACEDONIA (PAIONIA):

—KAVADARCI (MOD.): **(99)** ii-iii AD *Minalo* 2 (1911) pp. 54 f. (s. *Ποσειδώνιος*, f. *Διονύσιος*); **(100)** ~ *Sp.* 71 (1931) p. 71 no. 161 (-*κλί*-)

—NEGOTINO (MOD.): **(101)** ii-iii AD ib. 75 (1933) p. 36 no. 106

MACEDONIA (PIERIA):

—DION: **(102)** ?ii AD Dimitsas 177 (*Σέρβιος Ἡ.*: s. *Νίκη*)

—PYDNA: **(103)** 250 AD *SEG* XLVI 800 A, 42 (*Αὐρ. Ἡ.*)

MACEDONIA (SINTIKE):

—PARTHIKOPOLIS: **(104)** f. iii AD *IGB* V 5905

MACEDONIA?: **(105)** 359 BC *FGrH* 115 F 307 (s. *Ἀρχέλαος*); **(106)** 324 BC *RE* (16); Berve 348 (Tataki, *Macedonians* p. 321 no. 15) (s. *Ἀργαῖος*); **(107)** 286 BC *RE* (33) (Tataki, *Macedonians* p. 321 no. 12); **(108)** f. i BC *SB* 8974 fr. 3, 54 (*Ἡρα[κλείδης]*?: f. *Ἀρτεμιδώρα*)

SARMATIA:

—MAIOTAI: **(109)** ii/i BC *EAD* XXX 418, 11 (slave)

SCYTHIA MINOR:

—ISTROS: **(110)** iii BC *ISM* I 124 (*[Ἡρακ]λείδης*?); **(111)** ii AD ib. 196, 13 (s. *Ἥλιος*); **(112)** ~ ib. 197 I, 14 (f. *Λούκιος*); **(113)** ~ ib. 211, 2 (s. *Α̣—*)

—KALLATIS: **(114)** ii BC *RE* (51) + Fraser, *Ptol. Alex.* 2 pp. 741-2 n. 172 (ident.) (and Egypt Alexandria?: *Ἡ. ὁ ἐπικαλ. ὁ Λέμβος*: s. *Σαραπίων*); **(115)** f. ii AD *ISM* III 111, 6 (*Ἡρακλε[ίδης]*—ed., *Ἡρακλέ[ων]*?: f. *Μόνιμος*); **(116)** 241-244 AD ib. 74 A, 27 (f. *Πομπηϊανός*); **(117)** ~ ib. 74 B, 30

—TOMIS: **(118)** i BC ib. II 166, 7, 13-14 (s. *Φίλων*); **(119)** ii AD ib. 17, 14 (*Ἡρακλε[ίδης]*?: f. *Ἀλέξανδρος*); **(120)** ii-iii AD ib. 23, 9 (*[Ἰο]ύλ. Ἡ.*); **(121)** ~ ib. 31 II, 4 (*[Ἡ]ρακλείδης*: s. *Θεόδοτος*); **(122)** iii AD *SBBayerAk* 1875, p. 84 no. 9 (-*κλί*-: f. *Αὐρήλιος*, *Δομύνυος*); **(123)** 201 AD *ISM* II 83 II, 26 (*Ἰούλ. Ἡ.*); **(124)** v-vi AD Barnea 13, 2 (Popescu, *IGL* 45) (-*κλί*-)

SKYTHIA:

—OLBIA-BORYSTHENES: **(125)** vi/v BC *SEG* XLVIII 1012 (s. *Εὐθήριος*); **(126)** v-iv BC *IOSPE* I² 211 (f. *Λεωδάμας*); **(127)** s. iv BC Dubois, *IGDOlbia* 107, 2 (*Ἡρα(κλ)είδης*); **(128)** iv/iii BC *SEG* XLII 715 (s. *Λέων*); **(129)** ~ ib. (f. *Λέων*); **(130)** s. iii BC *IOSPE* I² 76, 10 (Sokolowski II 88; Dubois, *IGDOlbia* 88) (s. *Εὔβιος*); **(131)** i-ii AD *IOSPE* I² 155, 4 (*Ἡρα[κλ]είδης*: s. *Κρατῖνος*); **(132)** i/ii AD *SEG* XLIII 505, 9 (f. *Καλλίστρατος*) ?= (*135*); **(133)** ii AD *IOSPE* I² 91, 6 (f. *Χούναρος*); **(134)** ~ ib. 100, 4 (f. *Τούμβαγος*) ?= (*136*); **(135)** ~ ib. 140, 4 (f. *Καλλίστρατος*) ?= (*132*); **(136)** f. ii AD ib. 85, 7 (*[Ἡ]ρακλείδης*: s. *Τούμβαγος*) ?= (*134*); **(137)** iii AD ib. 135, 4 (s. *Ἀρτεμίδωρος*)

—OLBIA-BORYSTHENES?: **(138)** iv/iii BC *SEG* XXXVII 681; XLII 728 (locn.) (*Ἡ̣ρ̣α̣κ̣λείδης*)

—TANAIS: **(139)** ii AD *CIRB* 1262, 14 (s. *Ἀτάσας*); **(140)** ~ ib. 1263, 5 (*[Ἡ]ρα[κλ]είδης*: s. *Σευ—*); **(141)** ~ ib. l. 17 (*[Ἡρ]ακλείδης*); **(142)** ~ ib. 1268, 8 (f. *—νος*); **(143)** 104 AD ib. 1259, 14 (s. *Πάβας*); **(144)** c. 192-210 AD ib. 1243, 15; 1277, 9 (f. *Ἄττας*); **(145)** c. 200-210 AD ib. l. 15 (*Ἡρακλείδ[ης]*: s. *Ἐπίγονος*); **(146)** c. 200-236 AD ib. 1250, 11; 1277, 22; 1285, 11 (s. *Ἄττας*); **(147)** f. iii AD ib. 1286, 9 (*Ἡρακλ[είδ]ης*: s. *Πάππος*); **(148)** c. 210-236 AD ib. 1250, 16; 1281, 20 (f. *Κοσσοῦς*); **(149)** 220 AD ib. 1278, 4 (f. *Δημήτριος*); **(150)** ~ ib. l. 10 (f. *.γαλο̣ρασμος*: reading—Tokhtas'ev); **(151)** ~ ib. l. 13 (f. *Φαρνάκης*); **(152)** 225 AD ib. 1279, 17 (s. *Μαρκιανός*); **(153)** ~ ib. 1280, 9 (II s. *Ἡρακλείδης* I); **(154)** ~ ib. l. 9-10 (I f. *Ἡρακλείδης* II); **(155)** 228 AD ib. 1282, 5 (I f. *Ἡρακλείδης* II *ὁ καὶ Αὔναμος*); **(156)** ~ ib. l. 5 (*Ἡ. ὁ καὶ Αὔναμος*: II s. *Ἡρακλείδης* I); **(157)** ~ ib. l. 24 (s. *Μενίδωρος*); **(158)** ~ ib. 1283, 8 (*Ἡρ̣α̣κ̣λ[είδ]ης*: f. *Νιγοσας*); **(159)** ~ ib. l. 16

(f. Ἀσκλᾶς); (160) 244 AD ib. 1287, 17 (Ἡρακλε(ί)δης—Tokhtas'ev)
—TYRAS: (161) iii AD IGB I^2 229, 1, 4 (Αὐρ. Ἡ.: f. Δομνῖνος)
SKYTHIA?: (162) inc. SEG III 613 (f. Μύρων)
TAURIS:
—CHERSONESOS: (163) i BC-i AD IOSPE I^2 460 ([Ἡρ]ακλείδης); (164) imp. ib. 435, 4 ([Ἡρ]ακλείδης: s. Ἡρο—); (165) ~ ib. 540; (166) f. ii AD KSIIMK 15 (1947) p. 59, 9 (Solomonik, NEPKh 112 d); cf. VDI 1993 (4), p. 63 (Ἡρακλε[ίδης]?); (167) ~ Solomonik, NEPKh 111, 8 (f. Στρατόνικος); (168) ~ ib. l. 9 (f. Νῖκος); (169) c. 120-130 AD ib. 112, 19 ([Ἡρακ]λείδης?: s. Θεαγενίων); (170) iii AD ib. 19, 2 ([Ἡρακ]λείδης?: s. Ῥουφῖνος)
THRACE: (171) 323 BC Berve 350; (172) 232 or 206 BC CPR XVIII 4, 68, 79, 84 (La'da E830) (s. Φιλόξενος: t.e.); (173) ?ii BC ZPE 136 (2001) pp. 130-2 no. 14, 4; cf. La'da E759 ([Ἡρα]κλείδης?); (174) 142 BC SB 12720, 3 (La'da E749) (s. Ἀρίστων, Θαΐς); (175) i AD IGB IV 2338, 8, 15; cf. V 5928 (f. Ῥεπτάτερκος)
—ABDERA: (176) s. iii BC ISamothrace 22, 46 (f. Εὐκράτης); (177) ii/i BC Syll^3 656, 49 (Ager 169) (s. Ἀλκίφρων)
—AGIASMA (MOD.): (178) s. iii AD Thrakika 6 (1935) p. 310 no. 2 (IThrakAig E384) (s. Τήρης)
—AGRIANES: (179) 236 BC PPetr^2 16, 47; cf. La'da E2 ([Ἡρακ]λείδης: f. Πτολεμαῖος)
—AINOS: (180) hell. SEG XXXVI 654, 13 ([Ἡρ]ακλείδης); (181) f. i AD ib. XXIX 452, 8 (Stephanis 2831) (-κλί-)
—ANCHIALOS (TERRIT.): (182) ii AD IGB III 1841, 4 (s. Πολύξενος)
—APOLLONIA-SOZOPOLIS: (183) i-ii AD ib. I^2 401, 9 ([Ἡρα]κλείδης: s. Πάπας); (184) ~ ib. l. 13 ((Ἡρ)ακ(λ)είδης: f. Διονυσόδωρος)
—BYZANTION: (185) i BC-i AD IByz 267 (Fıratlı–Robert pp. 72-3 no. 77) (Κ. Ἄττιος Ἡρακλίδης); (186) i-ii AD IByz 278 (f. Ἀλέξανδρος)
—DIONYSOPOLIS: (187) hell. Spink Num. Circular 105 (1997) p. 372 no. 16; p. 374 no. 29 (coin); (188) ii BC IGB I^2 22 I, 4; (189) iii AD ib. 14 b, 16 (f. Αὐρ. Γέρων)
—KALLIPOLIS: (190) imp. ISestos 19 (-κλί-: f. Ἰσίων)
—MARKIANOPOLIS (TERRIT.): (191) ii-iii AD IGB V 5382 (CCET II (1) 303) (s. Ἀλέξανδρος)
—MARONEIA: (192) 400 BC X., An. vii 3. 16; vii 4. 2; vii 5. 5-11; vii 6. 2-7; Ath. 252 a; (193) c. 365-335 BC Schönert-Geiss, Maroneia 464-7; 514-20 (coin) (Ἡρακλείδεω (gen.)—514-20); (194) ii BC IThrakAig E242 A (-κλί-: f. Βερενίκη); (195) ii-i BC ib. E212, 36 (s. Ἀπολλώνιος); (196) ~ ib. l. 38 (s. Δίφιλος); (197) ~ ib. l. 47 (f. Θεόξενος); (198) ~ ib. l. 48 (s. Ἀπολλόδωρος); (199) ~ ib. l. 54 (s. Ἐπιτυγχάνων); (200) i BC ib. E204, 7 (Ἡρα[κλ]ε̣ί̣[δης]); (201) i-ii AD Bakalakis, Oinos Ismarikos p. 1015 with fig. 17 + IThrakAig E288, [1], 6 (s. Ἀμύνανδρος, f. Δημόστρατος, Ἀμύνανδρος); (202) ~ SEG XXIV 634, 3 (IThrakAig E181) ([Κ]ο̣ρνήλιος Ἡ.)
—MESAMBRIA: (203) iii-ii BC IG II^2 9339 (FRA 3685) (f. Πάρμις)
—ODESSOS: (204) inc. RE (50); (205) v/iv BC IGB I^2 99 (s. Ἀπολλωνίδης); (206) ii AD ib. 140, 1, 5 (s. Σωκράτης, f. Σωκράτης); (207) f. ii AD ib. 221 (PM 1699); Dacia 21 (1977) p. 161 (date) (f. Διοσκουρίδης); (208) 221 AD IGB I^2 47 bis a, 29 (f. Αὐρ. Αἰμίλιος); (209) ~ ib. l. 32 (Αὐρ. Ἡ.: s. Τίτος); (210) ~ ib. 47 bis b, 35 (I f. Αὐρ. Ἡρακλείδης II); (211) ~ ib. l. 35 (Αὐρ. Ἡ.: II s. Ἡρακλείδης I)
—ODESSOS (NR.): (212) f. iii AD ib. V 5076 (CCET I 9) (f. Ἀστέας)
—ODESSOS?: (213) ii AD IGB I^2 51 bis b, 3 (s. Γλύκων)
—PAUTALIA: (214) ii-iii AD ib. IV 2072, 15 (-κλί-); (215) s. ii AD SEG XLVI 864, 16 (f. Ἰουλιανός); (216) ~ ib. 864 I, 21
—PAUTALIA (TERRIT.): (217) ii-iii AD IGB IV 2198, 4 (s. Περσεύς)
—PERINTHOS-HERAKLEIA: (218) iv BC Hp., Epid. iv 34 (Ἡρακλείδεω (gen.)); (219) ii-i BC ISmyrna 689 III, 21 (s. Φιλόστρατος); (220) i BC-i AD? IPerinth 57, 3 (s. Ἀλέξανδρος)
——(Makedones): (221) iii-ii BC ib. 61, 6 (s. Αἰσχίνης)
—PHILIPPOPOLIS-TRIMONTIUM: (222) iii AD IGB III 917, 5 (s. Γράνιος)
—PHILIPPOPOLIS-TRIMONTIUM (TERRIT.): (223) ii-iii AD ib. 1175 + V 5484 (-κλί-: f. Δίζας)
—RHAIDESTOS: (224) imp. Unp. (Thessaloniki Mus.) inv. 943b (f. Πολύγνωτος)
—SALYMBRIA: (225) imp. IByz S 39
—SERDICA: (226) ii-iii AD IGB IV 2010, 2 (s. Βίθυς)
—SERDICA (TERRIT.): (227) ii-iii AD ib. 2011 (s. Δίζας); (228) 198-217 AD ib. 2023, 10 (Eastern cults p. 168 no. 11) (Αἰλ. Ἡρακλίδης); (229) f. i AD IGB V 5701 (Αὐρ. Ἡ.: s. Μᾶρκος)
THRACE?: (230) 316-309 BC IG II^2 1956, 16; Ancient Macedonia 5 p. 445 with n. 10 (date) (FRA 2536); (231) ~ IG II^2 1956, 41; Ancient Macedonia 5 p. 445 with n. 10 (date) (FRA 2537); (232) ii BC ISM I 27, 5; cf. SEG XLIX 1007 (f. —κος); (233) ~ ISM I 36, 5 + Pontica 33-4 (2000-1) pp. 346-7 no. 3 ([Ἡρ]α̣κλείδης)

Ἡρακλειόδωρος
MACEDONIA (EDONIS):
—AMPHIPOLIS: (1) c. 265-255 BC SGDI 2588, 2 (Tataki, Macedonians p. 53 no. 60) (s. Ἑλλάνικος)

Ἡράκλειος
MACEDONIA: (1) 137 BC Arch. Pap. 47 (2001) p. 61 B, 1 (La'da E1503) (s. Διονύσιος); (2) 103 BC PTeb 105, 53 (Tataki, Macedonians p. 485 no. 125; La'da E1760) (s. Σαραπίων: t.e.); (3) 92 BC PTeb 104, 35, 47 (Tataki, Macedonians p. 484 no. 123; La'da E1759) (s. Διοκλῆς: t.e.); (4) 78 BC BGU 1736, 8, 21 (Tataki, Macedonians p. 485 no. 124; La'da E1504) (II s. Ἡράκλειος I: katoikos); (5) ~ BGU 1736, 9 (Tataki, Macedonians p. 485 no. 126); cf. La'da E1504 (I f. Ἡράκλειος II)
MACEDONIA (BOTTIAIA):
—EDESSA?: (6) b. 474 AD PLRE II (4); RE (15) (s. Φλῶρος)
MACEDONIA (MYGDONIA):
—THESSALONIKE?: (7) ?iii AD IG X (2) (1) 854; cf. SEG XXX 632 (-κλι-: s. Ἡρακλείδης)
SCYTHIA MINOR:
—HALMYRIS (NR.): (8) iv AD Popescu, IGL 168, 14 (Lat. Heraclius: s. Nepotianus, Ἀρτεμιδώρα)
TAURIS:
—CHERSONESOS: (9) iv/iii BC IOSPE I^2 474 (s. Ἀπολλώνιος); (10) c. 315-300 BC Kats pp. 94-5 nos. 47-48 (amph., tile); (11) iii BC IOSPE I^2 510; (12) ?iii BC ib. 690 ([Ἡρά]κλειος); (13) iii BC Kats p. 95 no. 49 (amph.) (I f. Ἡράκλειος II); (14) iii-ii BC Solomonik, NEPKh 34 ([Ἡρά]κ̣λειος: f. —ε̣ια); (15) f. iii BC Kats p. 106 no. 85 (amph.) (f. Νικέας); (16) c. 215-200 BC ib. p. 95 no. 49 (amph.) (II s. Ἡράκλειος I); (17) ~ ib. p. 95 no. 50 (amph.) (s. Φορμίων); (18) ii BC SEG XLVI 924, 2 (f. —ς); (19) ii-i BC IOSPE I^2 475 (s. Δαμάτριος); (20) c. 180-170 BC Anokhin p. 145 no. 160 (coin); (21) 179 BC IOSPE I^2 402, 11; (22) c. 120-88 BC ib. 352, 57 (f. Μῆνις); (23) c. 110-100 BC Anokhin p. 147 no. 189 (coin) ([Ἡ]ράκλε(ιος)?)
THRACE:
—NOVAE: (24) f. iii AD IGLNovae 104 bis, 6 (Lat. T. Heraclius: s. -erinus)
—STRYME?: (25) c. 375-350 BC SEG XXVII 335 (IThrakAig E139) (f. Ἀρκεσίλη)

Ἡράκλειτος
CIMMERIAN BOSPOROS:
—GORGIPPIA: (1) f. iii BC CIRB 1137 A II, 45; 1137 B II, 49 (f. Μένανδρος)
MACEDONIA: (2) hell. SEG XV 878, 1 (Bernand, Inscr. métr. 12; Tataki, Macedonians p. 322 no. 19; La'da E1505) (s. Ἄτταλος); (3) ?304 BC IG V (2) 550, 17 (Tataki, Macedonians p. 321 no. 17); (4) iii BC ITrall 33 B, 20 (Tataki, Macedonians p. 322 no. 20) (f. Φιλώτας); (5) c. 259-244 BC PHib 110, 61, 70 (Tataki, Macedonians p. 322 no. 21); cf. La'da E1650-1 (f. Φοῖνιξ ὁ πρεσβύτ., Φοῖνιξ ὁ νεώτ.); (6) 61 or 57 BC BGU 1772, 8, 31 (Tataki, Macedonians p. 485 no. 127); cf. La'da E1512 (f. Ἰατροκλῆς)
MACEDONIA (BOTTIAIA):
—PELLA: (7) iii-ii BC Dimitsas 137 (f. Σωπάτρα); (8) c. 214-200 BC IOrop 130, 2, 4 (Tataki, Macedonians p. 154 no. 45) (s. Ἀρτεμίδωρος)
MACEDONIA (CHALKIDIKE):
—POTIDAIA-KASSANDREIA: (9) c. 235-230 BC IG VII 247, 22, 25 (IOrop 71; Tataki, Macedonians p. 90 no. 44) (s. Εὔανδρος)
—POTIDAIA-KASSANDREIA?: (10) ?iv/iii BC IC 3 p. 118 no. 27 (Tataki, Macedonians p. 90 no. 45) (-κλετ-: s. Μεν—)
MACEDONIA (DERRIOPOS):
—STUBERRA: (11) a. 179 BC IGB V 5003; cf. Tataki, Macedonians p. 177 no. 4 (f. Ἀντίγονος); (12) c. 41-48 AD IG X (2) (2) 323, 25 (f. Φίλιππος); (13) 74 AD ib. 326, 65 (s. Παράμονος)
MACEDONIA (EDONIS):
—AMPHIPOLIS: (14) iv BC AD 22 (1967) Chron. p. 426 (s. Διαγόρας)
—PHILIPPOI: (15) ii/iii AD CIL III 633 IV b, 7 (Pilhofer 166) (Lat. Heraclitus: f. Ἀγαπητός)
—PHILIPPOI (DRAMA (MOD.)): (16) ii-i BC SEG XLVIII 792 (Pilhofer 501a) (f. Σκηζις)
SCYTHIA MINOR:
—KALLATIS: (17) 12-19 AD IGB V 5011, 12 (s. Μόνιμος)
—TOMIS: (18) i BC ISM II 166, 3 (?s. (ad.) Φίλων); (19) ii AD ib. 208
TAURIS:
—CHERSONESOS: (20) c. 280-270 BC Anokhin p. 140 no. 92 (coin) ?= (21); (21) c. 250-230 BC ib. pp. 140-1 nos. 96; 108 (coins) ?= (20)
—TAURIS: (22) iii BC IOSPE I^2 684
THRACE:
—BISANTHE-PANION: (23) 160-138 BC Tekmeria 6 (2001) p. 156 no. 2 (SEG XLIX 876) ([Ἡρά]κ̣λειτος: f. Ἀθηνόδωρος)
—CHERSONESOS: (24) ?c. 450-440 BC IG I^3 1301 (FRA 7304) (hερά-: s. Ναυκλῆς)
—PERINTHOS-HERAKLEIA: (25) 316-309 BC IG II^2 1956, 122 (FRA 6041); Ancient Macedonia 5 p. 445 with n. 10 (date)

Ἡρακλεόδωρος
CIMMERIAN BOSPOROS:
—PANTIKAPAION: (1) i BC CIRB 128, 3 (GVI 845) (Ἡρακλε(ό)δωρος: s. Φιλέταιρος, Τρυφωνίς)
MACEDONIA (CHALKIDIKE):
—OLYNTHOS: (2) s. iv BC SEG XIX 595 (Tataki, Macedonians p. 136 no. 58) (s. Ἀριστόνικος)
MACEDONIA (EDONIS):
—AMPHIPOLIS: (3) s. iv BC Hatzopoulos, Actes Amphipolis p. 48 no. 10 B, 4 (SEG XLI 564)
—PHILIPPOI: (4) 242 BC ib. XII 373, 55 (Tataki, Macedonians p. 164 no. 15) (s. Ἀριστίων)
MACEDONIA (SINTIKE):
—PARTHIKOPOLIS: (5) ii AD IGB IV 2279, 4 ((Ἡ)ρακλεό(δ)ωρος: f. Γαμέτη)
TAURIS:
—CHERSONESOS: (6) iii BC IOSPE I^2 466 (f. Ἀπολλώνιος)
THRACE: (7) 236-221 BC Brown, Ptolemaic Paintings p. 19; cf. La'da E699 (f. Ἁγίας); (8)

136 BC *PSI* 1311, [2], 9 etc. (La'da E750) (s. *Λέων*: katoikos)

Ἡράκλεος
TAURIS:
—CHERSONESOS: **(1)** iii-ii BC *IOSPE* I^2 480 (f. *Κτησίας*); **(2)** c. 250-230 BC Anokhin pp. 141-2 nos. 105; 118 (coins) (*Ἡ.*—Saprykin)
THRACE:
—ODESSOS: **(3)** c. 100-72 BC Price, *Alexander* 1208 (coin)

Ἡρακλέων
CIMMERIAN BOSPOROS:
—BOSPOROS: **(1)** imp. *IG* II^2 8428 (*FRA* 1372)
—GORGIPPIA: **(2)** ii/iii AD *CIRB* 1179, 58 (s. *Νεοκλῆς*)
—PANTIKAPAION: **(3)** imp. ib. 796; **(4)** i AD ib. 504 (f. *Πύρρος*); **(5)** i/ii AD ib. 646
MACEDONIA: **(6)** 239 AD *ILeukopetra* 91, 7 (s. *Ἑρμιόνη*: slave/freed.)
MACEDONIA (BOTTIAIA):
—BEROIA: **(7)** ii-iii AD *IBer* 231 (Tataki 541); **(8)** iii AD *IBer* 248, 1 (Tataki 284) (*Αὐρ. Ἡ.*)
—PELLA: **(9)** iii BC *PAE* 1912, p. 188 no. 122 (Tataki, *Macedonians* p. 155 no. 46); **(10)** iii/ii BC *Polemon* 4 (1949-50) p. 3 no. 238 (Tataki, *Macedonians* p. 155 no. 47) (s. *Μοσχίων*); **(11)** imp. *ILGR* 201 (Lat. C. Fictorius Heracleon)
MACEDONIA (CHALKIDIKE):
—ANTIGONEIA: **(12)** c. 230-200 BC *BCH* 45 (1921) p. 18 III, 76 (Tataki, *Macedonians* p. 64 no. 4) (*[Ἡ]ρακλέων*: s. *Ξένων*)
MACEDONIA (DERRIOPOS):
—STUBERRA: **(13)** 74 AD *IG* X (2) (2) 326, 55 (s. *Ροῦφος*)
MACEDONIA (EDONIS):
—AMPHIPOLIS: **(14)** ii-iii AD Kazarow 419 (s. *Στράτων*)
—PHILIPPOI: **(15)** v-vi AD Feissel, *RICM* 250 (Pilhofer 110) (*Ἐρα-*)
MACEDONIA (MYGDONIA):
—THESSALONIKE?: **(16)** ii AD *IG* X (2) (1) 892; **(17)** ii-iii AD ib. 728, 4; **(18)** s. iii AD *AEpThess* p. 10 no. 8 B (s. *Ἀφροδισία*)
MACEDONIA (ODOMANTIKE):
—SIRRHA: **(19)** 155 AD Dimitsas 821, 33 (Kaphtantzis 1) (s. *Δρεπάλας*)
MACEDONIA (PAIONIA): **(20)** ii-iii AD *Sp.* 77 (1934) p. 57 no. 61
—NEAPOLIS? (IZVOR (MOD.): **(21)** ii-iii AD Dimitsas 301, 1 (s. *Φίλιππος*, f. *Λούκιος*, *Ἀλέξανδρος*)
MACEDONIA (PELAGONIA):
—KOLOBAISA (NR.): **(22)** ii AD *IG* X (2) (2) 235
MACEDONIA (SINTIKE):
—PARTHIKOPOLIS?: **(23)** ii-iii AD *IGB* V 5925, 9
SCYTHIA MINOR:
—ISTROS: **(24)** 138 AD *ISM* I 193 I, 53 (s. *Τέρτιος*)
—KALLATIS: **(25)** iii BC ib. III 167 (s. *Νίκων*); **(26)** s. i BC ib. 38, 3 (s. *Ἀνδροσθένης*); **(27)** s. i AD ib. 68 (s. *Πύρσος*); **(28)** iii AD ib. 186 (s. *Ἰσαγόρας*); **(29)** f. iii AD ib. 105, 8 (*Δομίτι[ος] [Ἡρακλ]έων?*); **(30)** 241-244 AD ib. 74 A, 32 (?s. *Κορνήλιος*)
—KALLATIS?: **(31)** ii/i BC *IGB* II 867 a, 11 = *ISM* I 219 (V 87); cf. *ISM* III p. 140 (locn.) (*[Ἡ]ρακλέων*: s. *Ἀριστ—*); **(32)** ii AD ib. V 280, 3 (I 275); cf. *ISM* III p. 140 (locn.) (f. *Ἀλέξανδρος*)
SKYTHIA:
—TYRAS: **(33)** 181 AD *IOSPE* I^2 2, 31 (s. *Σωμᾶς*)
THRACE:
—AINOS: **(34)** v/iv BC *Kazı Sonuçları* 12 (2), p. 283 (f. *Ἑρμοκλῆς*)
—BYZANTION: **(35)** i-ii AD *IByz* 315 a-b (Fıratlı-Robert pp. 122-3 no. 205) (s. *Διονύσιος*, f. *Κάλα*, *Ματροδώρα*); **(36)** ii AD *IByz* 246 (I f. *Ἡρακλέων* II); **(37)** ~ ib. (II s. *Ἡρακλέων* I)
—BYZANTION?: **(38)** imp. ib. 350
—ODESSOS: **(39)** i/ii AD *IGB* I^2 177 bis (PM 1736); *Dacia* 21 (1977) p. 161 (date) (s. *Δημύλος*); **(40)** ii AD *IGB* I^2 186 (PM 1734) (f. *Τερτία*)
—ODESSOS (NR.): **(41)** 79-81 AD *IGB* I^2 58 a, 3; 58 b, 2 (s. *Διονύσιος*)
—ODESSOS?: **(42)** ii AD ib. 51 bis a, 3 (f. *—ίδης*)
—RHAIDESTOS: **(43)** ii-iii AD *IG* X (2) (1) 273 (*Ἡρακλέω[ν]*: f. *Μαίων*: locn.—Loukopoulou)

Ἡρακλῆς
MACEDONIA: **(1)** c. 327-309 BC *RE* Supplbd. 4 (2); Berve 353 (Tataki, *Macedonians* p. 322 no. 22) (s. *Ἀλέξανδρος* III *Μέγας*, *Βαρσίνη* (Persia)); **(2)** 33 AD *PMich* 259, [2], 13-14, 21 (s. *Χαιρήμων ὁ καὶ Μιεύς*: katoikos); **(3)** 229 AD *ILeukopetra* 75, 9 (slave/freed.)
MACEDONIA (ODOMANTIKE):
—SIRRHA (TERRIT.): **(4)** ii-iii AD *SEG* XXX 593 (Pilhofer 713) (*Ἡρακλῆδι* (dat.): s. *Ἀγαθίας*)
THRACE: **(5)** ii-iii AD *CIL* XIII 8067 (Lat. Her[acles]?: I f. *Ἡρακλῆς* II); **(6)** ~ ib. (Lat. M. Aur. Heracle (dat.): II s. *Ἡρακλῆς* I)

Ἡρακλιανός
MACEDONIA (BOTTIAIA):
—BEROIA: **(1)** ii AD *IBer* 247 (Tataki 544)
SCYTHIA MINOR:
—ISTROS: **(2)** 222-225 AD *ISM* I 100 A, 19 (*Ἡρακλιαν[ός]*: f. *Καλλίνικος*)
TAURIS:
—CHERSONESOS: **(3)** ?ii AD *IOSPE* I^2 476 (*Α(ἴλ)ιος Ἡ.*)
THRACE:
—BEROE-AUGUSTA TRAIANA: **(4)** ii-iii AD *SEG* XXXIX 649, 11 (-*κλει*-); **(5)** iii AD *IGB* III 1615 (*Ἡρακλιανὸς ὁ καὶ Βρε—*)
—BEROE-AUGUSTA TRAIANA (TERRIT.): **(6)** ii-iii AD ib. 1761 (*Ἡρακλια[νός]*: f. *—βιος*)
—BESSOPARA: **(7)** ii AD ib. 1329 (*Γ. Αὐφίδιος Ἡ.*)
—DIOSPOLIS: **(8)** iii AD ib. 1787, 1 (*Αὐρ. Ἡρακ<ε>λιανός*)
—KELLAI: **(9)** 241-244 AD ib. 1517, 49 (*Αὐρ. Ἡ.*: s. *Σώσανδρος*); **(10)** ~ ib. l. 50 (*Αὐρ. Ἡ.*: s. *Μουκιανός*)
—MEZDRA (MOD.): **(11)** ii-iii AD ib. II 492 (s. *Δημόφιλος*)
—NICOPOLIS AD ISTRUM: **(12)** ii-iii AD ib. 662 (s. *Βαλέριος*); **(13)** ~ ib. 689 (s. *Ἀσκληπιάδης*); **(14)** iii AD ib. 671 (*Αὐρ. Ἡρακλει[ανός]?*)
—NICOPOLIS AD ISTRUM (TERRIT.): **(15)** ii AD ib. V 5244 a, 5 (s. *Δημητριανός*); **(16)** ~ ib. l. 9 (s. *Σουσίων*) ?= (*17*); **(17)** ~ ib. l. 11 (f. *Φῆστος*) ?= (*16*)
—ODESSOS: **(18)** 215 AD ib. I^2 47 b, 19 (*Αὐρ. Ἡ.*: s. *Ἰούλ. Μέστος*)
—PHILIPPOPOLIS-TRIMONTIUM: **(19)** imp. ib. III 992 (*Ἐρέννιος Ἡ.*); **(20)** ii-iii AD ib. 912, 4; **(21)** m. iii AD ib. 884 a, 18; cf. V 5400
—SERDICA (TERRIT.): **(22)** iii AD ib. IV 2046 (s. *Ἑρμ—*)
THRACE?: **(23)** iii AD *SEG* XXXI 671 (gem)

Ἡρακλίας
THRACE:
—PAUTALIA: **(1)** s. ii AD ib. XLVI 864, 14 (f. *Ἀσκληπιόδωρος*)

Ἧρακος
CIMMERIAN BOSPOROS:
—KEPOI: **(1)** inc. ib. XLV 983 (vase)

Ἡράκων
CIMMERIAN BOSPOROS:
—ACHILLEION: **(1)** ii AD *CIRB* 1032 (s. *Ὀρύγιος*)
MACEDONIA: **(2)** 330-324 BC *RE* (1); Berve 354 (Tataki, *Macedonians* p. 323 no. 23)
MACEDONIA (MYGDONIA):
—KALINDOIA: **(3)** 68-98 AD *SEG* XLII 580, 18 (s. *Ἀπολλώνιος*); **(4)** ~ ib. l. 20 (s. *Κερτίμμας*)
—THESSALONIKE?: **(5)** iii BC *IG* X (2) (1) 26, 7; cf. *Tyche* 10 (1995) pl. 4 no. 2 (s. *Νικόδημος*); **(6)** ii AD *IG* X (2) (1) 248 II, 5 (*Ἡράκω[ν]*: f. *Ξάνθος*)
MACEDONIA (SINTIKE):
—PARTHIKOPOLIS?: **(7)** ii-iii AD *IGB* V 5925, 12, 17
SCYTHIA MINOR:
—ISTROS: **(8)** ii AD *ISM* I 57, 5 (*Eastern cults* pp. 102-3 no. 65); *ISM* I 198, 7 (s. *Ἀριστόμαχος*); **(9)** 138 AD ib. 193 I, 45 (f. *Ἀριστόμαχος*)
THRACE:
—BYZANTION: **(10)** iii BC *IByz* 67 (Fıratlı-Robert p. 48 no. 5) (*Ἡράκωντος* (gen.): f. *Θευφάνης*); **(11)** ?ii-i BC *IByz* 139 (f. *Γλυκεία*)
—BYZANTION (TERRIT.): **(12)** ii BC ib. 88 (f. *Παύσιλλα*)
—ODESSOS: **(13)** ii-iii AD *IGB* I^2 107 bis (f. *Ἀπφώ*); **(14)** f. ii AD ib. 77, 4 (*CCET* I 31) (f. *Θεόδοτος*) ?= (*15*); **(15)** ~ *IGB* I^2 179 bis; cf. *Dacia* 21 (1977) p. 161 + *AE* 1984, p. 177 no. 1278 (date) (f. *Θεόδοτος*) ?= (*14*)
—ODESSOS (NR.): **(16)** ii AD *IGB* I^2 271 (PM 1730); *Dacia* 21 (1977) p. 161 (date) (s. *Βειτύριγος*)

Ἥρανδρος
THRACE:
—PĂRVENEC (MOD.): **(1)** v-iv BC *SEG* XLIII 483 (f. *Ἀντιφάνης*)
—STRYME? (NR.): **(2)** v/iv BC *BCH* 79 (1955) p. 283 = Bakalakis, *Oinos Ismarikos* p. 552 (*IThrakAig* E128) (f. *Μητρόδοτος*)

Ἥρανος
THRACE:
—SERDICA: **(1)** f. iii AD *IGB* V 5785, 4; 5790?; 5792; 5803; 5813-16 (s. *Λούκιος*, f. *Αὐρ. Ἡραγένης*)

Ἡραπίδης
SCYTHIA MINOR:
—ISTROS: **(1)** 138 AD *ISM* I 193 II, 43 (s. *Μόνιμος*)

Ἡρᾶς
CIMMERIAN BOSPOROS:
—PANTIKAPAION: **(1)** i/ii AD *CIRB* 606 (f. *Ἡλιογένης*); **(2)** iii AD ib. 102, 4
MACEDONIA (BOTTIAIA):
—BEROIA: **(3)** b. 167 BC *IBer* 1 A, 4, 18 (Tataki 545) (f. *Ἀσκληπιάδης*)
MACEDONIA (LYNKESTIS):
—HERAKLEIA (NR.): **(4)** imp. *IG* X (2) (2) 11 (*Ἡρα*—ed.: s. *Γαυκίας*)
MACEDONIA (SINTIKE):
—PARTHIKOPOLIS?: **(5)** ii-iii AD *IGB* V 5925, 19
TAURIS:
—CHERSONESOS (TERRIT.): **(6)** iv/iii BC *SEG* XLIX 1026 (amph.)
THRACE:
—BYZANTION (TERRIT.): **(7)** ii BC *IByz* 191 (s. *Ἡρόστρατος*, f. *Κόρρις*)
—MARONEIA: **(8)** f. iii BC *IThrakAig* E230 A (*[Ἡ]ρᾶς*: s. *Σάτυρος*)
—PERINTHOS-HERAKLEIA: **(9)** i-ii AD *IPerinth* 97 (f. *Σωτήριχος*)

Ἡράφιλος
THRACE:
—NICOPOLIS AD ISTRUM (TERRIT.): **(1)** ii AD *IGB* V 5244 b, 7 (*Β. Ἡ.*)

Ἡρέας
SCYTHIA MINOR:
—KALLATIS: **(1)** s. iii BC *ISM* III 35 B, 24 (s. *Δαμοφῶν*)

TAURIS:
—CHERSONESOS: **(2)** iv/iii BC Solomonik, *NEPKh* 168 (f. *Νάνα*); **(3)** c. 300-285 BC Kats p. 121 no. 18 (amph., monogram); **(4)** ~ ib. pp. 95-6 no. 51 (amph.)
THRACE:
—DIONYSOPOLIS: **(5)** ii-i BC *SNG Stancomb* 118 (coin) (*Ἡρέ(ας)*?)

Ἡρζῆς
SKYTHIA:
—TANAIS: **(1)** 229 AD *Stud. Zhebelev* p. 47, 20 (*Ἡρζέως* (gen.): f. *Δημήτριος*)

Ἧρις
CIMMERIAN BOSPOROS:
—MYRMEKION: **(1)** ?v-iv BC *SEG* XXXVII 666. 7 (vase); cf. XLVIII 1007 (*Ἥριο[ς]*? (gen.))
TAURIS:
—CHERSONESOS: **(2)** iv-iii BC *IOSPE* I² 415 (f. *Φορμίων*)
THRACE:
—BYZANTION: **(3)** c. 200 BC *IG* II² 884, 5, [15] (s. *Κόθων*); **(4)** ii BC *IByz* 291 (Fıratlı–Robert pp. 113-14 no. 189) (*Ἥριος* (gen.): s. *Μήνιος*); **(5)** i BC *IByz* 146 (Fıratlı–Robert p. 116 no. 193) (f. *Στρούθιον*); **(6)** i BC-i AD *IByz* 253 (Fıratlı–Robert p. 117 no. 197a) (*Ἥρειδος* (gen.)); **(7)** ii-iii AD *IGUR* 573 (s. *Ζωΐλος*)
—BYZANTION (TERRIT.): **(8)** imp. *IByz* 20 (s. *Μελίφθογγος*)

Ἡρίχα
TAURIS:
—CHERSONESOS: **(1)** m. iv BC Solomonik, *GAKh* 297 + *SEG* XXXVIII 749. 14 (vase)
THRACE:
—MESAMBRIA: **(2)** iii BC *IGB* V 5121 (d. *Ἀπολλώνιος*)

Ἡρόβουλος
THRACE:
—MARONEIA: **(1)** c. 400-378 BC Schönert-Geiss, *Maroneia* 159-60 (coin) (-*βō*-); **(2)** c. 325-300 BC *IThrakAig* E224 (s. *Πόσις*)
—STRYME: **(3)** c. 425-400 BC *AD* 52 (1997) Chron. p. 880 (*IThrakAig* E119) (*Ἡροβόλō* (gen.): f. *Ἀρίστας*)
—STRYME?: **(4)** iv BC ib. E157 (*[Ἡρ]όβōλος*?, *[Θε]όβōλος*?: f. —*ρος*)

Ἡρόγειτος
TAURIS:
—CHERSONESOS: **(1)** iv/iii BC Kats p. 106 no. 86 (amph.) (f. *Νικέας*); **(2)** c. 315-300 BC ib. p. 96 no. 52 (amph.); **(3)** iii BC Solomonik, *NEPKh* 37 (*Ἡρόγε[ιτος]*?); **(4)** ~ Kats p. 87 no. 14 (amph.) (f. *Ἀπολλω*—); **(5)** c. 262-237 BC ib. p. 96 no. 53 (amph.) (s. *Καλλιάδας*); **(6)** f. ii BC *IOSPE* I² 351, 4; 402, 8 (f. *Ἀπολλόδωρος*); **(7)** ii AD ib. 358, 13 (*[Ἡρό]γειτος*?: s. *Τελέδαμος*); **(8)** f. ii AD Solomonik, *NEPKh* 111, 6 (*[Ἡρό]γειτος*?); **(9)** ?114 AD *SEG* XLVIII 999, 40 (*[Ἡρό]γειτος*: f. *Ἀπολλώνιος*)

Ἡρογείτων
CIMMERIAN BOSPOROS:
—GORGIPPIA: **(1)** f. iii BC *CIRB* 1137 A II, 17 (f. *Κρίθων*); **(2)** ~ ib. 1137 B I, 33 (f. ..*ων*); **(3)** ~ ib. 1137 B II, 13 (*Ἡρογ[ε]ίτων*: s. *Δίων*)
MACEDONIA (PIERIS):
—OISYME-EMATHIA?: **(4)** s. iv BC *PAE* 1938, p. 92 no. 1, 5 (*[Ἡ]ρογείτων*)
SKYTHIA:
—OLBIA-BORYSTHENES: **(5)** iii BC *IOlbia* 26, 1
THRACE:
—ABDERA: **(6)** c. 395-360 BC May, *Abdera* pp. 227-8 no. 351 (coin); **(7)** f. iii BC Unp. (Chryssanthaki diss.) p. 399 (coin)
—AINOS: **(8)** iv BC *IG* II² 7978 (*FRA* 251)
—MARONEIA: **(9)** s. iv BC *SEG* XLIX 888 (*IThrakAig* E225) (f. *Μητροφάνης*)

—PERINTHOS-HERAKLEIA: **(10)** v/iv BC *IPerinth* 140 (s. *Διονύννης*)

Ἡρογένης
SKYTHIA:
—OLBIA-BORYSTHENES: **(1)** v BC Dubois, *IGDOlbia* 97 (vase) (*SEG* XLVI 953)

Ἡρόδικος
THRACE:
—PERINTHOS-HERAKLEIA: **(1)** hell.? *Suda* O 654 (name, ethn.); cf. *RE* Supplbd. 4 (-); cf. *LGPN* I s.v. *Πρόδικος* (5) (*Πρόδικος*—K.O. Müller ap. *Suda*)

Ἡροδότη
THRACE:
—ABDERA: **(1)** ii BC *IThrakAig* E55

Ἡρόδοτος
MACEDONIA (BOTTIAIA):
—BEROIA: **(1)** ii/i BC *IBer* 161 (f. *Δημήτριος*)
MACEDONIA (CHALKIDIKE):
—OLYNTHOS: **(2)** iv BC *RE* (14) (Tataki, *Macedonians* p. 137 no. 59) ?= (*Ἡρόδωρος* (15))
MACEDONIA (EDONIS):
—AMPHIPOLIS: **(3)** hell. *IG* XII (8) 438 (Tataki, *Macedonians* p. 53 no. 61) (f. *Μινίων*); **(4)** ii-iii AD *SEG* XXVII 252, 3
—PHILIPPOI: **(5)** s. iv BC ib. XLII 621 (Pilhofer 55) (s. *Σωσίπολις*)
—PHILIPPOI (TERRIT.): **(6)** imp.? Pikoulas, *Chora* p. 135 no. 37 (s. *Ζίπυρος*); **(7)** i-ii AD ib. p. 163 no. 72, 1, 11 (Pilhofer 606) (s. *Ὀ*—*ων*, f. *Γάϊος*, *Μᾶρκος*)
MACEDONIA (ODOMANTIKE):
—SIRRHA: **(8)** 155 AD Dimitsas 821, 10 (Kaphtantzis 1) (s. *Πουπλᾶς*); **(9)** ~ Dimitsas 821, 14 (Kaphtantzis 1) (f. *Φιλόφρων*)
—SIRRHA?: **(10)** ii-iii AD *SEG* XLVIII 884 (f. *Ζώσιμος*)
SCYTHIA MINOR:
—ISTROS: **(11)** v/iv BC *ISM* I 233 (*Ἡρόδο[τος]*: f. *Θόας*); **(12)** s. iii BC *SNG Stancomb* 192 (coin) (*Ἡρόδο(τος)*)
—KALLATIS: **(13)** iii-ii BC Unp. (New York, ANS) 1957.52.69; cf. *NZ* 10 (1917) p. 88 no. 230a (coin) (*Ἡρόδο(τος)*); **(14)** ~ *ISM* III 163 (f. *Εὐπόλεμος*)
SKYTHIA:
—OLBIA-BORYSTHENES: **(15)** s. iv BC *SEG* L 702 III, 1; **(16)** ~ ib. 702 IV, 11; **(17)** iii BC *IOSPE* I² 201 I, 3 (f. *Μητρόδωρος*); **(18)** s. iii BC ib. 76, 4 (Sokolowski II 88; Dubois, *IGDOlbia* 88) (s. *Παντακλῆς*)
—OLBIA-BORYSTHENES?: **(19)** iv/iii BC *SEG* XXXVII 681; XLII 728 (locn.)
—TYRAS: **(20)** c. 300-275 BC ib. XLIX 1051 B, 1 (f. *Ἀπολλᾶς*)
TAURIS:
—CHERSONESOS: **(21)** iv/iii BC Solomonik, *NEPKh* 151 (f. *Ἀπολλωνία*); **(22)** c. 300-285 BC Kats pp. 96-7 no. 54; p. 121 no. 19 (amph., tile); **(23)** iii BC Solomonik, *NEPKh* 153 (s. *Ἀπολλᾶς*); **(24)** ~ *IOSPE* I² 346, 2 (s. *Ἀρτ*—); **(25)** ~ Kats p. 107 no. 91 (amph., tile) (f. *Πασιάδας*) ?= (26); **(26)** s. iii BC *ISM* III 13, 2 (*Ἡρόδο[τος]*: f. *Πασιάδας*) ?= (25); **(27)** 179 BC *IOSPE* I² 402, 9 (I f. *Ἡρόδοτος* II); **(28)** ~ ib. l. 9 (II s. *Ἡρόδοτος* I); **(29)** s. ii BC *SEG* XLVI 934 (s. *Σώπολις*) ?= (30); **(30)** c. 120-110 BC Anokhin p. 147 no. 187 (*Ἡρόδοτ(ος)*) ?= (29); **(31)** imp. Tolstoi 86 (vase) (*Ἡρόδο(τος)*)
—KERKINITIS: **(32)** iv BC *IOSPE* I² 339 (f. *Ἀμβατία*)
THRACE: **(33)** c. 100-75 BC *SB* 8974 fr. 3 II, 42 (Velkov 126; La'da E751) (s. *Καρδ*—: katoikos)
—ABDERA: **(34)** v BC *FVS* 68 A 2 (?s. *Ἡγησίστρατος*, *Ἀθηνόκριτος*, *Δαμάσιππος*: fict.?); **(35)** c. 475-450 BC May, *Abdera* pp. 111-12 no. 112 (coin) ?= (36); **(36)** c. 450-425 BC ib. p. 124 nos. 132-3 (coin) ?= (35); **(37)** f. iii BC Unp. (Chryssanthaki diss.) p. 395 (coin)
—BYZANTION: **(38)** ii BC *IByz* 377 (Fıratlı–Robert pp. 128-9 no. 218) (f. *Παρμενίσκος*)
—MARONEIA: **(39)** ii-i BC *IThrakAig* E199 (f. *Μητροφάνης*); **(40)** i BC ib. E213, 7 (*Ἡρόδο[τος]*)
—PHILIPPOPOLIS-TRIMONTIUM (TERRIT.): **(41)** ii-iii AD *IGB* III 1211 (s. *B*—)

Ἡρόδωρος
CIMMERIAN BOSPOROS:
—GORGIPPIA: **(1)** f. iii BC *CIRB* 1137 A I, 18 (f. *Ἀντίδωρος*); **(2)** ~ ib. l. 23 (s. *Ἑστιαῖος*) ?= (12); **(3)** ~ ib. l. 26 (s. *Εὐθύφρων*); **(4)** ~ ib. l. 54 (f. *Φιλῖνος*); **(5)** ~ ib. 1137 A II, 3 (s. *Ἀναξικράτης*); **(6)** ~ ib. l. 19; 1137 B II, 18 (f. *Ἀντιάδης*) ?= (7); **(7)** ~ ib. 1137 A II, 21 (I f. *Ἡρόδωρος* II) ?= (6); **(8)** ~ ib. l. 21 (II s. *Ἡρόδωρος* I); **(9)** ~ ib. l. 34; 1137 B II, 20 (I f. *Ἡρόδωρος* II); **(10)** ~ ib. 1137 A II, 34; 1137 B II, 20 (II s. *Ἡρόδωρος* I); **(11)** ~ ib. 1137 A II, 48 (f. *Ἑστιαῖος*); **(12)** ~ ib. 1137 B I, 43 (*[Ἡ]ρόδωρος*: s. *Ἑστιαῖος*) ?= (2)
—PANTIKAPAION: **(13)** ii AD ib. 669; cf. KW pl. 53 no. 720 (f. *Διόφαντος*)
MACEDONIA: **(14)** 181 BC *RE* (3); Liv. xl 23. 4, 9 (Tataki, *Macedonians* p. 323 no. 24)
MACEDONIA (CHALKIDIKE):
—OLYNTHOS: **(15)** iv BC *IG* XIV 1149; Osborne, *Naturalization* T64-65 (Tataki, *Macedonians* p. 137 no. 60) (f. *Σθέννις*: sculptor) ?= (*Ἡρόδοτος* (2)); **(16)** ?354 BC *TAPA* 69 (1938) pp. 52-3 no. 6, 12; Hatzopoulos, *Actes Chalc.* p. 80 (date) (I f. *Ἡρόδωρος* II); **(17)** ~ *TAPA* 69 (1938) pp. 52-3 no. 6, 12; Hatzopoulos, *Actes Chalc.* p. 80 (date) (II s. *Ἡρόδωρος* I)
—STRATONIKEIA?: **(18)** i-ii AD *SEG* XXIV 577 (s. *Θεαγένης*)
MACEDONIA (EDONIS):
—AMPHIPOLIS: **(19)** hell. Dimitsas 851 (*[Ἡ]ρόδωρος*: s. *Τιμοκλῆς*)
MACEDONIA (MYGDONIA):
—KALINDOIA: **(20)** c. 335 BC Hatzopoulos, *MI* 2 p. 84 no. 62, 10 (f. *Σίβρας*); **(21)** a. 98 AD *SEG* XLII 583, 13 (s. *Ἱέρων*)
SCYTHIA MINOR:
—ISTROS: **(22)** i BC-i AD *ISM* I 209, 4 = 185 (f. —*ος*); **(23)** ii AD ib. 212, 11 (f. *Ἀγαθοκλῆς*); **(24)** 138 AD ib. 193, 10 (s. *Διονύσιος*); **(25)** ~ ib. 193 I, 23 (f. *Διονύσιος*); **(26)** ~ ib. l. 43 (f. *Ἱπποσθένης*); **(27)** ~ ib. l. 33-4 (f. *Ἀριστοκράτης*, *Ἀρτεμίδωρος*); **(28)** ~ ib. 193 II, 2, 4, 14, 21 (f. *Ἀρτεμίδωρος*); **(29)** c. 138-160 AD ib. l. 44; 207, 9 (s. *Κάρπος*); **(30)** ii/iii AD ib. 363, 1 (*CCET* IV 62) (s. *Σατυρίων*)
SKYTHIA:
—OLBIA-BORYSTHENES: **(31)** vi-v BC *IOlbia* 129 (*Ἡρόδωρ[ος]*); **(32)** s. iv BC Dubois, *IGDOlbia* 107, 6; **(33)** iii BC *IOSPE* I² 32 A, 23 (Maier, *Mauerbauinschr.* 82); **(34)** ~ *IOSPE* I² 201 I, 12 (f. *Φιλίσκος*); **(35)** ~ ib. l. 4-5; 201 II, 15 (f. *Ἡροσῶν*, *Σταφύλος*); **(36)** ~ ib. 201 I, 55-6 (f. *Θεοδέκτης*, *Λήναιος*)
—TANAIS (NR.): **(37)** s. ii AD *CIRB* 1313 (s. *Θεόπροπος*)
THRACE:
—APOLLONIA-SOZOPOLIS: **(38)** v/iv BC *IGB* I² 405 bis (f. *Ἑκατώνασσα*); **(39)** iv BC *BMNBurgas* 4 (2002) pp. 121-2 no. 8 (f. *Χαρμίων*); **(40)** ~ *IGB* I² 421 (f. *Ζερκίων*); **(41)** iii/ii BC *KF* 68 (s. *Ἡρα*—)
—MESAMBRIA: **(42)** iv/iii BC *IGB* I² 334 ter (*[Ἡ]ρόδωρος*: ?s. *Ἡρώνυμος*); **(43)** iii/ii BC ib. 308 sexies, 1 (f. *Μελσέων*); **(44)** ii BC ib. 314 b, 13 (f. *Ἡρακλείδας*)
—ODESSOS: **(45)** i-ii AD ib. 52, 7 (*Ἡρόδω[ρος]*)
—SALYMBRIA: **(46)** i BC-i AD *IByz* S 24, 2 (s. *Ἀντιαλκίδας*)
—STRYME: **(47)** m. v BC *IThrakAig* E163 (s. *Μένης*)

Ἡρόθεμις
THRACE:
—BYZANTION: **(1)** ii-i BC *SEG* L 667 II (f. Ἀπριάτη)

Ἡροκᾶς
TAURIS:
—CHERSONESOS: **(1)** iii BC Solomonik, *GAKh* 893-5 (vase) (Ἡροκ[ᾶς]?); **(2)** f. iii BC Solomonik, *NEPKh* 164 (f. Σώτιμος); **(3)** c. 285-272 BC Kats p. 97 no. 55 (amph.) (s. Ἡρότιμος)

Ἡρόκλειτος
THRACE:
—ABDERA: **(1)** c. 395-360 BC Lorber, *Amphipolis* p. 176 (coin) (name—Chryssanthaki)

Ἡροκράτης
SKYTHIA:
—OLBIA-BORYSTHENES: **(1)** v BC Dubois, *IGDOlbia* p. 170 note; **(2)** f. iv BC ib. 104 (Ἡροκράτευς (gen.): f. Γοργίας); **(3)** s. iv BC *SEG* L 702 III, 1
TAURIS:
—CHERSONESOS: **(4)** c. 285-272 BC Kats pp. 97-8 no. 56 (amph., tile) (s. Νευμήνιος)
THRACE:
—ABDERA: **(5)** c. 475-450 BC May, *Abdera* p. 108 no. 98 (coin) (Ἡροκ(ράτης)?, Ἡρόκ(λειτος)?)

Ἡρομένης
MACEDONIA (LYNKESTIS): **(1)** 336 BC *RE* Supplbd. 4 (-); Berve 355 (Tataki, *Macedonians* p. 202 no. 10) (s. Ἀέροπος)

Ἡρόνεστος
THRACE:
—STRYME: **(1)** c. 425-400 BC *IThrakAig* E118 ([Ἡρ]όνεστος: s. Ἱππόκριτος); **(2)** c. 375-350 BC *BCH* 79 (1955) p. 283 = Bakalakis, *Oinos Ismarikos* p. 552 (*IThrakAig* E133) (f. Πρωτίς)

Ἡρόνικος
TAURIS:
—CHERSONESOS: **(1)** iv BC Solomonik, *NEPKh* 171 (f. Ἡροτίμα); **(2)** c. 325-315 BC Kats p. 98 no. 57 (amph., tile); **(3)** iv/iii BC *SEG* XXXIII 598 (-νει-: f. Εἰράνα)
—KERKINITIS: **(4)** c. 350-340 BC *SNG BM Black Sea* 694-5 (coins) (Ἡρόνι(κος))

Ἡρόξενος
SCYTHIA MINOR:
—TOMIS: **(1)** ii AD *ISM* II 125, 3 (s. Διοσκουρίδης) ?= (*2*); **(2)** ~ ib. l. 12 (f. Βουτίς) ?= (*3*) (*1*); **(3)** ~ ib. l. 15 (f. Πάπας) ?= (*2*)
SKYTHIA:
—OLBIA-BORYSTHENES: **(4)** iii BC *IOlbia* 72, 2 (f. Ναύτιμος); **(5)** iii AD *IOSPE* I^{2} 98, 6 (s. Σώμαχος)
—TANAIS: **(6)** c. 220-230 AD *CIRB* 1278, 11; 1286, 11 (s. Βασιλείδης)
TAURIS:
—CHERSONESOS: **(7)** c. 315-300 BC Kats p. 98 no. 58 (amph.); **(8)** iii BC Solomonik, *GAKh* 896 (vase) (Ἡρόξ[ενος]?, Ἡροξ[ένα]?); **(9)** ~ *IOSPE* I^{2} 581, 3 (Ἡρόξ[ενος]: f. Φανικός); **(10)** ~ Kats p. 104 no. 77 (amph.) (f. Μᾶτρις); **(11)** c. 262-237 BC ib. p. 99 no. 59 (amph.) (s. Ἀλκῖνος); **(12)** c. 120-110 BC Anokhin p. 147 no. 185 (coin) ([Ἡ]ρόξε(νος)?); **(13)** ii AD *IOSPE* I^{2} 431, 2 (f. Λαοδίκη); **(14)** f. ii AD Solomonik, *NEPKh* 111, 3; *SEG* XLVIII 999, 37 (f. Βοΐσκος); **(15)** ?114 AD ib. l. 37 ([Ἡρόξ]ενος?: s. Χρηστίων); **(16)** 129 AD *IOSPE* I^{2} 359, 28 (s. Βοΐσκος)
THRACE:
—BYZANTION: **(17)** i BC-i AD *IByz* 277 (s. Διονύσιος, f. Δύναμις, Μάμα)
—BYZANTION (TERRIT.): **(18)** imp. Unp. (Sayar) (-ξη-); **(19)** ~ ib.; **(20)** ~ ib.; **(21)** ~ ib. (s. Ῥώμων)
—BYZANTION?: **(22)** ii AD *IByz* 334 (-ξη-: f. Διονύσις)
—DIONYSOPOLIS: **(23)** iii BC *ISM* III 14, 2
—PERINTHOS-HERAKLEIA: **(24)** i BC-i AD? *IPerinth* 57, 7 (s. Μάγνος); **(25)** i-ii AD ib. 97 (s. Μενεκράτης, f. Ἐπίκτησις)

Ἡρόπυθος
MACEDONIA (CHALKIDIKE):
—POTIDAIA-KASSANDREIA (NR.): **(1)** iii BC *TAPA* 69 (1938) p. 67 no. 20 (her.?)
THRACE:
—ABDERA: **(2)** iv BC Hp., *Epid.* iii 17. 9; *CMG* V (10) ii 1 p. 179

Ἡρόστρατος
MACEDONIA (CHALKIDIKE):
—STAGEIROS: **(1)** c. 440-420 BC *IG* I^{3} 1370 (Tataki, *Macedonians* p. 175 no. 3; *FRA* 6958)
TAURIS:
—CHERSONESOS: **(2)** iv BC Solomonik, *GAKh* 897 (vase) (Ἡρόστρ(ατος)); **(3)** f. iii BC *SEG* XL 615 A, 6 (s. Ἀριστόλοχος); **(4)** ~ ib. 615 B, 5-6
THRACE:
—BYZANTION (TERRIT.): **(5)** ii BC *IByz* 191 (f. Ἡρᾶς)
—PERINTHOS-HERAKLEIA:
——(Boreis): **(6)** iii-ii BC *IPerinth* 61, 40 (f. Ἵμερος)

Ἡροσῶν
SKYTHIA:
—OLBIA-BORYSTHENES: **(1)** m. iv BC Dubois, *IGDOlbia* 106, 3 (*SEG* XLIV 669) (f. Ἐπικράτης); **(2)** iv/iii BC Dubois, *IGDOlbia* 95 (vase) (s. Φιλόξενος); **(3)** iii BC *IOSPE* I^{2} 32 A, 2 (Maier, *Mauerbauinschr.* 82); *IOSPE* I^{2} 201 I, 63; cf. 179 comm. (ident.) (s. Πρωτογένης, f. Πρωτογένης) ?= (*6*); **(4)** ~ ib. 201 I, 4 (s. Ἡρόδωρος); **(5)** s. iii BC ib. 76, 9 (Sokolowski II 88; Dubois, *IGDOlbia* 88) (f. Λεοντομένης); **(6)** iii/ii BC *BE* 1990, no. 519 (coin) (Ἡρ(οσῶν): f. Πρωτογένης) ?= (*3*)

Ἡροτίμα
TAURIS:
—CHERSONESOS: **(1)** iv BC Solomonik, *NEPKh* 171; cf. *VDI* 1975 (1), p. 175 (Ἡροτίμα[ς]—ed.: d. Ἡρόνικος)

Ἡρότιμος
CIMMERIAN BOSPOROS:
—PANTIKAPAION: **(1)** iv BC Tolstoi 219 (vase)
TAURIS:
—CHERSONESOS: **(2)** iv/iii BC Kats p. 97 no. 55 (amph.) (f. Ἡροκᾶς)
THRACE:
—BYZANTION: **(3)** ?354 BC Rhodes–Osborne 57, 12 (Εἰ-: f. Κερκίνος)
—MESAMBRIA: **(4)** m. iv BC *IG* II^{2} 9338 (*FRA* 3686) (s. Μένανδρος); **(5)** ii BC *IGB* I^{2} 325, 1 ([Ἡ]ρότιμος: s. Ἡρακλείδας); **(6)** ii/i BC ib. V 5103, 1, [3] (-τει-: f. Δεινομένης) ?= (*8*); **(7)** ~ ib. l. 2, 5 ([Ἡ]ρότειμος: II s. Ἡρότιμος I); **(8)** ~ ib. l. 3 ([Ἡρ]ότειμος: I f. Ἡρότιμος II) ?= (*6*)
—ODESSOS: **(9)** 4 BC ib. I^{2} 46, 43 (s. Ἀγαθήνωρ); **(10)** f. ii AD ib. 78 ter, 10 (*CCET* I 30) (-τεί-: s. Ἀρτεμίδωρος)
—SALYMBRIA: **(11)** i BC-i AD *Archives Stamoulis* d. 35 (Loukopoulou, *Thrace Propontique* p. 260) (f. Βοῦλις)

Ἡροῦς
MACEDONIA (MYGDONIA):
—KALINDOIA: **(1)** 68-98 AD *SEG* XLII 580, 80 (s. Ἄδυμος)

THRACE:
—PAUTALIA: **(2)** ii-iii AD *IGB* IV 2072, 8 (f. Ἀπολλόδωρος)

Ἡροφάνης
CIMMERIAN BOSPOROS:
—GORGIPPIA: **(1)** f. iii BC *CIRB* 1137 B II, 34 (f. Ἀθήνιππος)
—MYRMEKION: **(2)** iv/iii BC *Stud. Blavatskii* pp. 70-1 (vase); cf. *VDI* 1980 (2), p. 77 n. 22 (Ἡροφάνηντος (gen.): s. Ἡραῖος)
—PANTIKAPAION: **(3)** iv/iii BC *MIA* 56 (1957) p. 223 (tile) (Ἡροφά(νης)—*MIA*, Ἡρόφ(ι)λ(ο)ς?); **(4)** f. iii BC *RPh* 1937, p. 325 no. 6 A, 20 (s. Εὐμηλίδης)
SKYTHIA:
—OLBIA-BORYSTHENES: **(5)** v BC Dubois, *IGDOlbia* 97 (vase) (*SEG* XLVI 953)
—TANAIS: **(6)** 228 AD *CIRB* 1282, 14 (f. Οὐαράζακος)
—TANAIS*: **(7)** ii-iii AD *Tanais* I p. 103 (amph.) (Ἡρ[ο]φά[νης]?)
TAURIS:
—CHERSONESOS: **(8)** iv BC *IOSPE* I^{2} 488 (f. Πέλανος)
THRACE:
—ABDERA: **(9)** c. 395-360 BC May, *Abdera* pp. 209-11 nos. 275-80 (coin)

Ἡροφάντα
TAURIS:
—CHERSONESOS: **(1)** ?iv-iii BC *SEG* XLIV 657 (weight) (Ἡροφάντας (gen.?))

Ἡρόφαντος
SCYTHIA MINOR:
—ISTROS: **(1)** ii AD *ISM* I 198, 5 (s. Αἰσχρίων); **(2)** 138 AD ib. 193 I, 106 (f. Ἀπολλόδωρος); **(3)** ~ ib. 193 II, 42 (s. Μήνιος)
—ISTROS (NR.): **(4)** imp. ib. 357 ([Ἡ]ρόφαντος)
—TOMIS: **(5)** ii BC *AMNG* I (2) 2478 (coin) (Ἡρόφ(αντος)?)
TAURIS:
—CHERSONESOS: **(6)** iii BC Solomonik, *NEPKh* 32 (s. Θεόφαντος); **(7)** f. iii BC ib. 139
THRACE:
—BYZANTION: **(8)** ii BC *IByz* 235 (s. Βοσπόριχος)

Ἡρόφιλος
SKYTHIA:
—OLBIA-BORYSTHENES: **(1)** m. iv BC Dubois, *IGDOlbia* 106, 1 (*SEG* XLIV 669) (f. Ἀρτεμίδωρος); **(2)** ~ Dubois, *IGDOlbia* 106, 5 (*SEG* XLIV 669); **(3)** s. iv BC ib. L 702 III, 2 (f. Ἀναξιμένης); **(4)** iii BC *IOSPE* I^{2} 201 II, 36; **(5)** s. iii BC *Arkheologiia* (Kiev) 39 (1982) p. 35 (Vinogradov–Kryžickij pl. 91. 5 (vase)) (Ἡρόφι[λος])
TAURIS:
—CHERSONESOS: **(6)** inc. Solomonik, *GAKh* 898 (vase) (Ἡρόφι[λος]); **(7)** ?s. iv BC Solomonik, *NEPKh* 169 (f. Ζώπυρος); **(8)** iii BC ib. 154 (Ἡρό[φ]ιλος: s. Ἀπολλᾶς)
THRACE:
—APOLLONIA-SOZOPOLIS: **(9)** i-ii AD *IGB* I^{2} 401, 10 (Ἡρόφι(λ)ος: f. Κοδρᾶτος); **(10)** ~ ib. l. 20 (f. ΓΕΝΕΜΗΣ)
—MARONEIA: **(11)** c. 365-336 BC Schönert-Geiss, *Maroneia* 394-8 (coin)
—MESAMBRIA: **(12)** s. iii BC *IGB* I^{2} 335 quinquies (PM 816) (s. Πάρμις)
—PHILIPPOPOLIS-TRIMONTIUM (TERRIT.): **(13)** ii-iii AD *IGB* III 1496 (s. Βίθυς)
—STRYME: **(14)** c. 375-350 BC *IThrakAig* E144 (f. Μητροφῶν)

Ἡροφῶν
CIMMERIAN BOSPOROS:
—PANTIKAPAION (NR.): **(1)** iv BC *CIRB* 959 (f. Ὀλυμπιάς)
MACEDONIA: **(2)** ii/i BC *RE* (2); *IvOl* 317, 3 (Tataki, *Macedonians* p. 323 no. 26) (s. Ἀναξαγόρας: sculptor)

MACEDONIA?: (3) 169-168 BC *RE* (1) (Tataki, *Macedonians* p. 323 no. 25)
THRACE:
—MARONEIA: (4) ii-i BC *IThrakAig* E212, 24 (s. Παπύλος)

Ἥρυλλα
THRACE:
—TYRODIZA-TIRISTASIS: (1) imp. Dumont-Homolle 89b (m. Ἀπολλώνιος, Κάρκος, Δίζας)

Ἡρώ
MACEDONIA (CHALKIDIKE):
—AKANTHOS: (1) f. v BC *SEG* XLI 552 (amph.) (hēρō)
—OLYNTHOS: (2) m. iv BC *FGrH* 124 T 2 (Tataki, *Macedonians* p. 137 no. 62) (m. Καλλισθένης)
MACEDONIA (EDONIS):
—AMPHIPOLIS: (3) 157 AD Dimitsas 863 (d. Διοσκουρίδης, m. Ἀμμία)

Ἡρωδιανός
THRACE:
—BEROE-AUGUSTA TRAIANA: (1) ii-iii AD *IGB* III 1578, 2 (s. Νικίας)
—DUROSTORUM: (2) 169-176 AD *SCIV* 11 (1960) p. 145 no. 2 (*Riv. Fil.* NS 2 (1924) p. 318) (Lat. C. Terentius Hero[di]anus)
—MALČIKA (MOD.): (3) iii AD *ILB* 447 (Lat. Geminius Hero[di]a[n]us)
—MARKIANOPOLIS: (4) iii AD *CIL* VI 32624 b, 16 (Lat. M. Aur. Herodian(us))
—SPINOPARA: (5) ii AD *IGB* IV 2192, 15 (Ἡ[ρω]διανός)

Ἡρῶι
SCYTHIA MINOR:
—ISTROS: (1) f. iv BC *ISM* I 262 + *VDI* 1984 (3), p. 180 (Ἡρώι?, Ἡρωΐ[ς]—Vinogradov)
TAURIS:
—CHERSONESOS: (2) iii BC Solomonik, *NEPKh* 160 (d. Εὐμάρης)

Ἡρωΐδας
SKYTHIA:
—TYRAS: (1) s. iii BC *VDI* 1966 (2), p. 152, 7
TAURIS:
—CHERSONESOS: (2) iv BC *IOSPE* I^2 406, 1 (f. —ων); (3) c. 300-275 BC *SEG* XLVII 1168, 3 (Ἡρωΐδ[ας]); (4) iii BC *IOSPE* I^2 525; (5) s. iii BC Kats p. 87 no. 13 (amph.) (f. Ἀπολλοφάνης); (6) c. 220-210 BC Anokhin p. 143 no. 128 (coin); (7) c. 200-190 BC ib. pp. 144-5 no. 157 (coin); (8) i AD *SEG* XLVI 927, 2 (Ἡρο-: s. Δα—); (9) i-ii AD *IOSPE* I^2 458 (Ἡρόδω[ρ]ο[ς]—ed., Ἡροΐδου? (gen.)—maj.: f. —ν); (10) ii AD ib. 701, 5 (Ἡρο-: f. Ματρόδωρος); (11) ~ ib. l. 8 (Ἡροΐ[δας]); (12) f. ii AD *KSIIMK* 15 (1947) p. 59, 11 (Solomonik, *NEPKh* 112 d); cf. *VDI* 1993 (4), p. 63 (Ἡροΐ[δας]); (13) ~ Solomonik, *NEPKh* 111, 7 (Ἡρο-: I f. Ἡρωΐδας II); (14) ~ ib. l. 7 (Ἡρο-: II s. Ἡρωΐδας I); (15) 130 AD *VDI* 1960 (3), pp. 154-5, 28 (Ἡρο-: I f. Ἡρωΐδας II); (16) ~ ib. l. 28 (Ἡρο-: II s. Ἡρωΐδας I); (17) ~ ib. l. 18, 30 (Ἡρο-: s. Ζῆθος)

Ἡρωΐδης
MACEDONIA: (1) ii-i BC *NS* 622 (Tataki, *Macedonians* p. 323 no. 27) (-δας: s. Σωσικράτης); (2) 145 BC *PPhrurDiosk* 18, 43, 52 (-ρῴ-); (3) 5 AD *CPR* I 224, 4 (Ἡρ[ῳ]δης: f. Ἄρειος); (4) 41 AD *PMich* 267-8, 1 (Ἡ. ὁ καὶ Ἰσίδωρος: I f. Ἡρωΐδης II); (5) ~ ib. l. 1 (II s. Ἡρωΐδης I ὁ καὶ Ἰσίδωρος, f. Ἡρωΐδης III ὁ καὶ Ὀρσεύς); (6) ~ ib. l. 1 (Ἡρώδης ὁ καὶ Ὀρσεὺς νεώτ.: III s. Ἡρωΐδης II)
MACEDONIA (BOTTIAIA):
—EDESSA: (7) 229 AD Tataki, *Edessa* 311 (Φλ. Ἡρώδης)
—PELLA? (GIANNITSA (MOD.)): (8) s. ii AD *JDAI* 84 (1969) p. 152 no. R15 (-ρώ-)
MACEDONIA (EORDAIA):
—ARNISA?: (9) m. ii AD *EAM* 122; Hatzopoulos, *MI* 1 p. 94 n. 4 (locn.) (-ρώ-)
MACEDONIA (MYGDONIA):
—LETE: (10) ii AD *Makedonika* 2 (1951) p. 619 no. 42 θ, 6 (-ρο-: s. Διογένης); (11) 121 AD *SEG* I 276, 20 (-ρώ-: s. Βίθυς)
—THESSALONIKE (NR.): (12) iii AD *IG* X (2) (1) 1002; cf. *Tyche* 10 (1995) pl. 14 no. 20 (-ρώ-: s. Δούλης); (13) ?iii AD *IG* X (2) (1) 1004, 6 (Ἡρώδης (ὁ) κὲ Ζιπᾶς)
—THESSALONIKE?: (14) ii-iii AD ib. 929, 4 (-ρώ-: s. T. Λουκίννιος Οὐνίων)
MACEDONIA (PAIONIA):
—STOBOI: (15) s. iii AD *JÖAI* 32 (1940) Beibl. col. 20 no. 14. 145 (Οὐλ(ιος) Ἡρόδης) ?= (16); (16) ~ ib. col. 21 no. 15. 160 (Ἡρώ[δης]) ?= (15)
SCYTHIA MINOR:
—SALSOVIA: (17) iv AD Popescu, *IGL* 272 c, 2 (Lat. Herodes)
THRACE:
—KELLAI: (18) 241-244 AD *IGB* III 1517, 13 (Αὐρ. Ἡρώδης)
—MARONEIA: (19) ii-i BC *IThrakAig* E212, 51 (-ρώ-: f. Δόλης)
—ODESSOS: (20) s. ii AD *IGB* I^2 170 (PM 1701); *Dacia* 21 (1977) p. 161 (date) (-ρώ-: f. Διονύσιος)
—PAUTALIA: (21) ii-iii AD *IGB* IV 2069 (s. Επταίκενθος: sculptor); (22) ~ ib. 2072, 13 (-ρώ-: s. Σκυ—ης); (23) s. ii AD *SEG* XLVI 864, 13 (-ρώ-: s. Γλαῦκος); (24) ~ ib. l. 15 (-ρώ-: f. Διδύμιος); (25) 161-169 or 244-249 AD *IGB* IV 2052 (Αὐρ. Ἡρώδης: s. Ποσειδώνιος)
—PAUTALIA (TERRIT.): (26) ii-iii AD ib. V 5817 (-ρώ-)
—PHILIPPOPOLIS-TRIMONTIUM: (27) m. iii AD ib. III 884 a, 24; cf. V 5400 (—ος Ἡρώδης)
—PHILIPPOPOLIS-TRIMONTIUM (TERRIT.): (28) ii-iii AD ib. III 1447 (-ρώ-); (29) ~ ib. 1500 (-ρώ-: s. Χρυσ—)
—SERDICA: (30) ii-iii AD *AEMÖ* 10 (1886) p. 238 no. 1 (M. Αὐρ. Ἡρώδης καὶ Πρόκλος)
—SERDICA?: (31) iii AD *CIL* VI 2742 (Lat. Aur. Erodes)

Ἡρωΐχος
THRACE:
—BYZANTION: (1) iv/iii BC *IByz* 59 (Fıratlı-Robert p. 49 no. 12) (f. Ἀρκεσίλας)

Ἥρων
CIMMERIAN BOSPOROS:
—PANTIKAPAION: (1) i/ii AD *CIRB* 583; cf. KW pl. 23 no. 320 (f. Ἀρέτη)
MACEDONIA (CHALKIDIKE):
—OLYNTHOS: (2) ?350 BC *TAPA* 59 (1928) p. 226, 9; Hatzopoulos, *Actes Chalc.* p. 80 (date) (f. Φίλαινα)
MACEDONIA (EDONIS):
—PHILIPPOI (TERRIT.): (3) ?iii AD Pikoulas, *Chora* p. 146 no. 59, 12 (Pilhofer 602; *SEG* L 618); cf. *BE* 1944, no. 129 (Ἡ[ρ]ουνι (dat.))
MACEDONIA (MYGDONIA):
—THESSALONIKE: (4) 155 AD *IG* X (2) (1) 321, 1 (s. Πτολεμαῖος)
MACEDONIA (ODOMANTIKE):
—GAZOROS: (5) 158 AD *SEG* XXIV 614, 6 (Pilhofer 544); cf. *SEG* XXXII 636 (Ἥρουνος (gen.): f. Διούλας)
MACEDONIA (PAIONIA):
—STOBOI: (6) v-vi AD Unp. (Stobi excav.) inv. I-73-4

Ἡρώνασσα
MACEDONIA (CHALKIDIKE):
—AKANTHOS: (1) c. 480-470 BC *SEG* XXXVI 580 (vase); cf. XLV 729 (Ἑρό-: het.?)

Ἡρωνιανός
MACEDONIA (EDONIS):
—PHILIPPOI (NEAPOLIS): (1) i/ii AD *ILGR* 210 (Pilhofer 28) (Lat. Veneteius Heronianus: I f. Φοῖβος ὁ καὶ Ἡρωνιανός II); (2) ~ *ILGR* 210 (Pilhofer 28) (Lat. P. Veneteius Phoebus qui et Heronianus: II s. Ἡρωνιανός I, Licinia Valeria)

Ἡρώνυμος
SCYTHIA MINOR:
—ISTROS: (1) s. iv BC *ISM* I 238 (s. Διαγόρας)
—KALLATIS: (2) iii BC ib. III 160 (f. Χελώνα)
—TOMIS: (3) i BC ib. II 2 A, 50 (f. Διοσκουρίδης)
THRACE:
—MESAMBRIA: (4) iv/iii BC *IGB* I^2 334 ter (?f. Ἡρόδωρος); (5) s. iii BC ib. 339 ter ([Ἡρ]ώνυμος?: f. Δαμάτριος, Ματρόδωρος, Πασίων)

Ἡσίοδος
THRACE: (1) 183-175 BC *PTeb* 779, 2; 793 XI, [5], 6, 8-9, 11 (La'da E752) (s. Δίδυμος)

Ἡσυχία
MACEDONIA (MYGDONIA):
—THESSALONIKE: (1) ii AD *SEG* XXXIX 635; cf. XLIII 467 (Φουλκινία Ἡ.: d. T. Φουλκίνιος Σίλων)

Ἡσύχιος
MACEDONIA (BOTTIAIA):
—EDESSA: (1) v-vi AD ib. XXVIII 544 (Feissel, *RICM* 51) (Ἐσύ-: s. Βάσα)
THRACE:
—PERINTHOS-HERAKLEIA: (2) ii-iii AD *IPerinth* 221, 14 (n. pr.?)

Ἡσύχις
MACEDONIA (MYGDONIA):
—THESSALONIKE: (1) ?iv AD Feissel, *RICM* 127 (Ὑσύχι (voc./n. pr.?))
SCYTHIA MINOR:
—KALLATIS: (2) iii AD *ISM* III 187, 1 (Αὐρ. Ἡ.: s. Δίων)

Ἡσυχίς
THRACE:
—PERINTHOS-HERAKLEIA: (1) iii AD *IPerinth* 153 (Αὐρ. Ἡ.: m. Αὐρηλιανὴ Ἀμβροσία)

Ἥσυχος
CIMMERIAN BOSPOROS:
—PANTIKAPAION: (1) i/ii AD *CIRB* 608 (Ἡ(σ)υχος: s. Ἀκκᾶς)
MACEDONIA (MYGDONIA):
—THESSALONIKE: (2) ii AD *SEG* XXXIX 635; cf. XLIII 467 (Φουλκίνιος Ἡ.: s. T. Φουλκίνιος Σίλων)
THRACE:
—PHILIPPOPOLIS-TRIMONTIUM (TERRIT.): (3) ii-iii AD *IGB* III 1145 (s. Αὐ—)

Ἡφαιστικῶν
SKYTHIA:
—OLBIA-BORYSTHENES: (1) iii BC Dubois, *IGDOlbia* 84 (vase) (f. Διοσκουρίδης)

Ἡφαίστιος
CIMMERIAN BOSPOROS:
—HERMONASSA: (1) iv-iii BC *CIRB* 1069
SCYTHIA MINOR:
—ISTROS: (2) iii-ii BC Unp. (Avram, defixio) 4, 2 (Ἡφαίστ(ι)ος?)
SKYTHIA:
—NIKONION: (3) m. iv BC *MASP* 5 (1966) p. 80 no. 26 (weight)
THRACE:
—APOLLONIA-SOZOPOLIS: (4) f. iv BC *IGB* I^2 433 bis (f. Ἀπολλᾶς)

Ἡφαιστίων
CIMMERIAN BOSPOROS:
—NYMPHAION: **(1)** f. iii BC *North Pontic Archaeology* p. 314 with fig. 7.3; cf. *Hyperboreus* 1997 (2), p. 376 (s. *Κοτυτίων*)
MACEDONIA: **(2)** c. 200-175 BC *IG* XI (4) 1273, 3 (Tataki, *Macedonians* p. 324 no. 28); cf. La'da E1392 (f. *Ἀθηνίων*)
MACEDONIA (BOTTIAIA):
—PELLA: **(3)** c. 356-324 BC *RE* (3); Berve 357; *SEG* XL 547 (Tataki, *Macedonians* p. 155 no. 48) (s. *Ἀμύντωρ*)
MACEDONIA (MYGDONIA):
—THESSALONIKE: **(4)** i BC-i AD *IG* X (2) (1) 129, 7
—THESSALONIKE?: **(5)** iii BC ib. 26, 5; *Tyche* 10 (1995) pl. 4 no. 2 ([*Ἡφα*]*ιστίων*?: s. *Θεοδ*—); **(6)** f. i AD *IG* X (2) (1) 263, 4
SCYTHIA MINOR:
—KALLATIS: **(7)** iii BC *ISM* I 9, 4, 18 (Migeotte, *L'emprunt* 41) (s. *Μᾶτρις*); **(8)** 241-244 AD *ISM* III 74 A, 30 (*Φλ. Ἡ.*)
—TOMIS: **(9)** ii BC ib. II 4, 2 (*Ἡφαιστ*[*ίων*]?); **(10)** i BC ib. 2 B, 50 (s. *Διονύσιος*); **(11)** ii-iii AD ib. 31 II, 5 (s. *Ἥρα.*)
THRACE:
—ODESSOS: **(12)** 9 BC *IGB* I^2 46, 38 (s. *Διονύσιος*); **(13)** ii AD ib. 50, 3 (?s. (nat.) *Ἀρτεμίδωρος*, ?s. (ad.) *Κλεάνωρ*); **(14)** m. ii AD ib. 176 ter (PM 1693); *Dacia* 21 (1977) p. 161 (date) (f. *Ἰαδώ*); **(15)** f. iii AD *IGB* I^2 47 bis b, 22; V 5038 (I f. *Αὐρ. Ἡφαιστίων* II, *Ἑρμάφιλος*); **(16)** ~ ib. I^2 47 bis b, 22; V 5038 (*Αὐρ. Ἡ.*: II s. *Ἡφαιστίων* I); **(17)** 215 AD ib. I^2 47 a, 13 (f. *Αὐρ. Ἕλλην*); **(18)** ~ ib. l. 16 (f. *Αὐρ. Ἀγαθήνωρ*); **(19)** ~ ib. 47 c, 24 (*Αὐρ. Ἡ.*: s. *Ἀπῆς*)
—ODESSOS (NR.): **(20)** iii AD ib. 270 (f. *Αὐρ. Ἀρτεμίδωρος*)

Ἡφαιστόδωρος
SCYTHIA MINOR:
—ISTROS: **(1)** iii BC *ISM* I 119 ([*Ἡφαι*]*στόδωρος*: ?s. *Ἀπολλώνιος*); **(2)** iii/ii BC ib. 46, 2 (f. *Πολυαίνετος*); **(3)** ii AD ib. 212, 14 (s. *Θεόδωρος*)
—KALLATIS: **(4)** 241-244 AD ib. III 74, 12 (*Αἴλ. Ἡ.*)
—TOMIS: **(5)** ii-iii AD ib. II 31 II, 3 (I f. *Ἡφαιστόδωρος* II); **(6)** ~ ib. l. 3 ([*Ἡφ*]*αιστόδωρος*: II s. *Ἡφαιστόδωρος* I); **(7)** 200-201 AD ib. 82 B, 12 ([*Ἡφ*]*αιστόδω*[*ρος*])
SKYTHIA:
—OLBIA-BORYSTHENES: **(8)** vi/v BC Dubois, *IGDOlbia* 31 (vase); **(9)** iii BC *IOlbia* 26, 3 (s. *Διογένης*)
THRACE:
—DIONYSOPOLIS: **(10)** 241-244 AD *IGB* I^2 22 bis, 16 (*Ἡφαιστόδω*[*ρος*]: f. *Αὐρ. Μαρκιανός*)

Ἡφαιστοκλῆς
SCYTHIA MINOR:
—ISTROS: **(1)** f. iv BC *ISM* I 240 (f. *Αὐξησιλεώ*)

Θ

Θαβεις
CIMMERIAN BOSPOROS:
—PANTIKAPAION: **(1)** m. ii AD *CIRB* 678; Zgusta, *PNS* 642 (d. *Ἰσιγόνη*)

Θαβοῦς
SKYTHIA:
—OLBIA-BORYSTHENES: **(1)** ii AD *IOSPE* I^2 685, 6 + *VDI* 1975 (1), p. 71; Zgusta, *PNS* 643 (s. *Ἀτοτᾶς*)

Θαβυττίων
CIMMERIAN BOSPOROS:
—NYMPHAION: **(1)** iii BC *CIRB* 912 II, 13; Zgusta, *PNS* 644 (s. *Θάγυς*)

Θάβων
CIMMERIAN BOSPOROS:
—NYMPHAION: **(1)** iii BC *CIRB* 912 I, 11; Zgusta, *PNS* 645 (f. *Ἀκκᾶς*)

Θαγοῦς
CIMMERIAN BOSPOROS:
—PANTIKAPAION: **(1)** f. iv BC *CIRB* 185; *Hellenismus* p. 449 no. 15 (name) (s. *Ματερίνας*)

Θάγυς
CIMMERIAN BOSPOROS:
—NYMPHAION: **(1)** iii BC *CIRB* 912 II, 13; *Hellenismus* p. 449 no. 15 (name) (f. *Θαβυττίων*)
—PANTIKAPAION: **(2)** f. iv BC *CIRB* 178 (f. *Διοσκουρίδης*); **(3)** s. iv BC ib. 186 (s. —*ων*)

Θάγων
TAURIS:
—CHERSONESOS: **(1)** iii BC Kats p. 93 no. 39 (amph.) (f. *Διονύσιος*) ?= (*2*); **(2)** iii-ii BC *IOlbia* 26, 5; *Hellenismus* p. 449 no. 15 (name) (f. *Διονύσιος*) ?= (*1*)

Θαῆς
THRACE:
—DIONYSOPOLIS: **(1)** iii AD *IGB* I^2 14 c, 11 (*Θαῇ* (gen.): f. *Αὐρ. Ἑστιαῖος*)

Θαθοις?
THRACE:
—ODESSOS: **(1)** i-ii AD ib. 200 (*Θαθο*[*ις*]?: d. *Ἑρμάφιλος*)

Θαίβας
CIMMERIAN BOSPOROS:
—PANTIKAPAION: **(1)** 275-278 AD *CIRB* 36, 29 (*Θαίβα*[*ς*]?: s. *Μενέστρατος*)

Θαΐς
CIMMERIAN BOSPOROS:
—PANTIKAPAION: **(1)** s. i AD ib. 421

Θαλάβηος
THRACE:
—BISANTHE-PANION: **(1)** ii-iii AD Dumont–Homolle 83i (f. *Ζωΐλος*)

Θαλαιώ
SKYTHIA:
—OLBIA-BORYSTHENES: **(1)** m. iv BC Dubois, *IGDOlbia* 106, 2 (*SEG* XLIV 669)

Θαλάμη
MACEDONIA (MYGDONIA):
—THESSALONIKE: **(1)** ii-iii AD *IG* X (2) (1) 217, 1 (*Ἐππία Θ.*: d. *Λ. Ἔππιος Θάλλος, Σερουιλία Σαβῖνα*)

Θάλαμος
CIMMERIAN BOSPOROS:
—PHANAGOREIA: **(1)** iii AD *CIRB* 1003, 4 (*Θά*[*λα*]*μο*[*ς*]?)
MACEDONIA (PAIONIA):
—DEMIR KAPIJA (MOD.): **(2)** ii AD *SEG* XXIX 578
SKYTHIA:
—TANAIS: **(3)** 220 AD *CIRB* 1278, 9 (s. *Πιτοφαρνάκης*)

Θαλάσσιος
MACEDONIA (MYGDONIA):
—THESSALONIKE: **(1)** vi AD Feissel, *RICM* 164 B (*SEG* XLVII 979 B) (-*λάσι*-)
THRACE:
—MARONEIA: **(2)** iv-v AD ib. 1073 (*IThrakAig* E354) (-*λάσι*-: s. *Ἰσαάκιος*: doctor)

Θαλῆς
THRACE:
—APOLLONIA-SOZOPOLIS: **(1)** iii BC *SNG BM Black Sea* 188 (coin)

Θαλίαρχος
MACEDONIA (PIERIS):
—OISYME-EMATHIA?: **(1)** s. iv BC *PAE* 1938, p. 92 no. 1, 4

Θαλλιανός
MACEDONIA (MYGDONIA):
—THESSALONIKE: **(1)** ?i-ii AD *AD* 26 (1971) Chron. p. 376 no. 1 (*Τιβ. Κλ. Θ.*)

Θάλλιος
THRACE:
—BYZANTION: **(1)** i BC-i AD *IByz* 19, 15 (*Πλαύτιος Θ.*)

Θάλλις
THRACE:
—BYZANTION?: **(1)** ii AD *SEG* XLI 1706 (s. *Πυθίων*)

Θαλλίων
THRACE:
—BYZANTION*: **(1)** i-ii AD *IByz* 242 (f. *Τερτία*: slave)

Θάλλος
MACEDONIA (BOTTIAIA):
—BEROIA: **(1)** ii AD *IBer* 308 (Tataki 1250) (*Τυριανὸς Θ.*)
MACEDONIA (CHALKIDIKE):
—POTIDAIA-KASSANDREIA: **(2)** iii BC *IG* II^2 9000 (Tataki, *Macedonians* p. 90 no. 46; *FRA* 2787) (s. *Ἀπολλώνιος*)
MACEDONIA (LYNKESTIS):
—HERAKLEIA (AREA): **(3)** ?ii AD *IG* X (2) (2) 15 (f. *Γάϊος, Κούαρτος, Σεκοῦνδα*)
MACEDONIA (MYGDONIA):
—THESSALONIKE: **(4)** ii-iii AD ib. X (2) (1) 217, 3 (*Λ. Ἔππιος Θ.*: f. *Ἐππία Θαλάμη*); **(5)** ~ ib. 544, 6; cf. *BCH* 98 (1974) p. 549 (*Λ. Ἀτέλλιος Θ.*: ?s. *Γορδιανὸς Ἵταμος, Κλ. Λούκουλλα Θάλλουσα*)
—THESSALONIKE?: **(6)** ii AD *IG* X (2) (1) 875; **(7)** ~ ib. 920; cf. *CPh.* 70 (1975) p. 55 (name) (*Ἀμπιανὸς Θ.*)
SCYTHIA MINOR:
—ISTROS: **(8)** ii/iii AD *ISM* I 225, 12 (*Τ. Φλ. Θάλλ*[*ος*]?, *Θαλά*[*σσιος*]—ed.)
—TOMIS: **(9)** ii AD ib. II 125, 7 (s. *Ἀγάθων*)
SKYTHIA?: **(10)** ii AD *SEG* XLVI 936 (?s. *Κλ. Νεῖλος*)
THRACE:
—KELLAI (NR.): **(11)** iii AD *IGB* III 1542 (f. *Βίθυς*)

—PHILIPPOPOLIS-TRIMONTIUM: (12) ii-iii AD ib. 885, 5 (f. *Γλαῦκος*)
—PHILIPPOPOLIS-TRIMONTIUM?: (13) ii-iii AD ib. 1019, 5 (*Κλ. Θ.*)

Θάλλουσα
MACEDONIA (EDONIS):
—PHILIPPOI?: (1) ii-iii AD *BCH* 59 (1935) p. 157 no. 53 (Pilhofer 302)
MACEDONIA (MYGDONIA):
—THESSALONIKE: (2) ii-iii AD *IG* X (2) (1) 544, 1 (*Κλ. Λούκουλλα Θ.*: ?m. *Λ. Ἀτέλλιος Ἐπίκτητος, Λ. Ἀτέλλιος Θάλλος*)
MACEDONIA (PAIONIA): (3) ii-iii AD *Sp.* 77 (1934) p. 57 no. 61
THRACE:
—BARGALA: (4) ii AD *SEG* XLIV 512 (*CCET* V 41) (*Αἰλ. Θ.*)

Θαλωνίς
SCYTHIA MINOR:
—ISTROS (NR.): (1) hell.? *ISM* I 109 (d. *Ἀρτεμίδωρος*)

Θαμεις
TAURIS:
—CHERSONESOS: (1) imp. *SEG* XXXVII 657 (lead) (s./d. *Χηματῖνος*)

Θάμιχος
TAURIS:
—CHERSONESOS: (1) ii AD *IOSPE* I^2 582, 1 (*Θάμιχ[ος]*: f. *Ἧλις*)

Θαμοῦς
SKYTHIA:
—TANAIS: (1) ii AD *CIRB* 1268, 13; Zgusta, *PNS* 648 (f. *—νους*)

Θάμυρος
MACEDONIA (EDONIS):
—PHILIPPOI: (1) ii/iii AD *CIL* III 633 II a, 26 (Pilhofer 163); *CRAI* 1923, p. 277 (date); Collart, *Philippes* pls. 64-5 (Lat. L. Atiarius Thamyrus)

Θάμφλας
CIMMERIAN BOSPOROS:
—GORGIPPIA: (1) imp. *CIRB* 1188, 8; Zgusta, *PNS* 649 (*Θάμφ[λας]?*); (2) s. ii AD *CIRB* 1142, 10
—ZENONOS CHERSONESOS*: (3) iii AD ib. 898, 3 (*Θάμφλ[ας]*: f. *Δημήτριος*)

Θάμων
MACEDONIA (CHALKIDIKE):
—STOLOS?: (1) ?351 BC *SEG* XXXVIII 673, 4 (f. *Μένιππος*); (2) ?350 BC ib. 671, 9 (s. *Περύσης*)

Θαρσαγόρης
THRACE:
—APOLLONIA-SOZOPOLIS: (1) iv BC *IGB* I^2 457 (*Θαρσαγόρεω* (gen.): f. *Γανύων*)

Θαρσῆς
SKYTHIA:
—OLBIA-BORYSTHENES: (1) ?ii-i BC Dubois, *IGDOlbia* 110, 2

Θαρσικλῆς
CIMMERIAN BOSPOROS:
—MYRMEKION (NR.): (1) ?i AD *CIRB* 890 (f. *Θράσων*)

Θαρσύνων
MACEDONIA (BOTTIAIA):
—BEROIA: (1) f. ii AD *IBer* 7 A, 31
MACEDONIA (EDONIS):
—PHILIPPOI: (2) iv/iii BC Collart, *Philippes* pp. 179-80 n. 5 with pl. 27. 3 (Pilhofer 285) (*[Θ]αρσύν[ων]*)

THRACE:
—ABDERA: (3) m. iv BC *Ét. Thas.* 3 p. 317 no. 110 (*Θαρσύνοντος* (gen.): s. *Ἀναξίδικος*)
—APOLLONIA-SOZOPOLIS?: (4) iv BC *IGB* I^2 476 (f. *Δημῆς*)

Θάσιον
MACEDONIA: (1) 12 AD *PKöln* 227 B, 15, 22, 26 (d. *Ζωΐλος*, m. *Διονύσιος*)

Θάσιος
TAURIS:
—CHERSONESOS: (1) f. iii BC Kats p. 109 no. 98 (amph.) (f. *Προμαθίων*)

Θάτης
CIMMERIAN BOSPOROS:
—HERMONASSA: (1) iii BC *CIRB* 1073 (*Θ[ά]της*: f. *Χανάκης*)

Θατόρακος
SKYTHIA:
—OLBIA-BORYSTHENES: (1) m. iv BC Dubois, *IGDOlbia* 106, 6 (*SEG* XLIV 669); cf. Vinogradov, *Pont. Stud.* p. 158 no. 12 bis (name)

Θαυμαρέτα
MACEDONIA (EDONIS):
—AMPHIPOLIS: (1) v/iv BC *PAE* 1978, p. 56 with pl. 50 γ (vase)

Θαύμαστος
CIMMERIAN BOSPOROS:
—PANTIKAPAION: (1) 93-123 AD *CIRB* 45, 3 (*Τιβ. Ἰούλ. Θαύμ[αστος]?*)
MACEDONIA (BOTTIAIA):
—BEROIA: (2) 250 AD *ILeukopetra* 101, 3 (*Παπίας Θα[ύμασ]τος ὁ καὶ Εὐ[γε]νείδης*)
SKYTHIA:
—TANAIS: (3) 188 AD *CIRB* 1242, 14 (s. *Ῥόδων*) ?= (6); (4) 220-225 AD ib. 1278, 9; 1280, 12 (f. *Ἀσενδρος*); (5) 225 AD ib. l. 18 (f. *Σύμμαχος*); (6) 225-229 AD ib. l. 21; *Stud. Zhebelev* p. 47, 19 (f. *Ῥόδων*) ?= (3); (7) 244 AD *CIRB* 1287, 22 (f. *Σιώμαχος*)

Θαῦνις
CIMMERIAN BOSPOROS:
—PANTIKAPAION: (1) ii-i BC ib. 262; cf. KW pl. 37 no. 539 (s. *Ἀρχέλαος*)

Θαχαμφλίας
CIMMERIAN BOSPOROS:
—GORGIPPIA: (1) ii AD *CIRB* 1157 B, 6 (*[Γοσα]μφλία[ς]?*—Vinogradov, *[Θαχα]μφλία[ς]?*); (2) ~ ib. 1170, 7 (*[Γοσα]μφλί[ας]*—Vinogradov, *[Θαχα]μφλί[ας]?*); (3) iii AD *NE* 9 (1971) p. 10 no. 6 B, 13 (*Θαχαμ[φλίας]*: f. *Ἀγόρεις*)
—GORGIPPIA?: (4) ii/iii AD *CIRB* 1232, 7

Θεάγγελος
CIMMERIAN BOSPOROS:
—GORGIPPIA: (1) i-ii AD ib. 1138, 5 (-νγε-); (2) 16 AD *SEG* XLVI 940 I, 2; 940 II, [1] (-νγε-)
—PANTIKAPAION: (3) 275-278 AD *CIRB* 36, 19 (*Θεάγ[γε]λος*: f. *Φιδανους*)
SKYTHIA:
—TANAIS: (4) ii AD ib. 1263, 16 (*(Θ)εάνγελος*: s. *Ἀ—φων*: reading—Tokhtas'ev); (5) 155 AD ib. 1260, 18 (*Θεάγ[γελο]ς*: f. *Δάδας*)

Θεαγένεια
SCYTHIA MINOR:
—ULMETUM: (1) iii AD *ISM* V 80, 5 (Lat. Theagenia: m. *Θεοδωριανός*, Cocceiana, Sergiana)

Θεαγένης
CIMMERIAN BOSPOROS:
—ACHILLEION: (1) i/ii AD *CIRB* 1025; cf. KW pl. 47 no. 669 (s. *Ἑρμογένης*)

—PANTIKAPAION: (2) ii-i BC *CIRB* 276; cf. KW pl. 23 no. 276 (s. *Ἡδόνιν*); (3) i AD *CIRB* 422; cf. KW pl. 32 no. 453 (*Θ[εα]γένης*: s. *—στων*); (4) 82 AD *CIRB* 76, 18 (*SEG* XVIII 310) (s. *—λης*); (5) ii AD *CIRB* 753 (f. *Δημόστρατος*); (6) f. ii AD ib. 83, 6 (s. *Πόθος*)
MACEDONIA (BOTTIAIA):
—BEROIA: (7) ii/iii AD *IBer* 143 A, 8 (Tataki 548) (*Θεαγένους* (gen.): f. *Σόσσιος*)
MACEDONIA (CHALKIDIKE):
—ANTIGONEIA?: (8) ii AD *SEG* XXIX 570, 6 (s. *Κλ. Μένων*, *Κλ. Μάξιμα*)
—OLYNTHOS: (9) ?352 BC ib. XXXVIII 637, 10 (*[Θε]αγένης*: f. *—εος*)
—STRATONIKEIA?: (10) i-ii AD ib. XXIV 577 (f. *Ἡρόδωρος*)
MACEDONIA (EORDAIA):
—ARNISA?: (11) f. iii AD *EAM* 135; Hatzopoulos, *MI* 1 p. 94 n. 4 (locn.) (*Θεαγέ<αγε>νης*: s. *Παράμονος*)
MACEDONIA?: (12) ?m. ii BC *RE* (10); *FGrH* 774 (Tataki, *Macedonians* p. 324 no. 2)
SCYTHIA MINOR:
—ISTROS: (13) ii AD *ISM* I 201 II, 17 (f. *Δημοκράτης*)
—TOMIS: (14) i BC-i AD ib. II 154, 3 with pl. + *Eastern cults* p. 10 no. 14 (*—δωρος ὁ καὶ Θεα[γέ]νης*)
SKYTHIA:
—OLBIA-BORYSTHENES: (15) ii AD *IOSPE* I^2 106, 7 (f. *Φλιμάνακος*)
—TANAIS: (16) ii AD *CIRB* 1262, 4 (s. *Κάσσανδρος*); (17) 104 AD ib. 1259, 24 (*[Θ]εαγένης*: s. *Μητροφάνης*); (18) 228 AD ib. 1282, 16 (s. *Μακάριος*); (19) ~ ib. l. 32 (*[Θ]εαγέ(ν)ης*: f. *Ἐ—*) ?= (20); (20) ~ ib. 1283, 11 (f. *Εὐτύχης*) ?= (19)
TAURIS:
—CHERSONESOS: (21) ii AD *IOSPE* I^2 453; cf. KW pl. 24 no. 355 (s. *Χρηστίων*); (22) ~ *IOSPE* I^2 493 (f. *Σκύθας*); (23) ~ ib. 582, 2 (s. *Εὐσέβιος*); (24) c. 120-130 AD ib. 359, 30; 386, 2; Solomonik, *NEPKh* 112, 10 (*Θε(α)γένης*—112: s. *Διογένης*); (25) 174 AD *SEG* XLV 985 A, 34 (*Θεα[γέ]νης*: f. *Ἀρίστων*); (26) ~ ib. l. 37 (f. *Χρηστίων*)
THRACE:
—BEROE-AUGUSTA TRAIANA (TERRIT.): (27) 222-230 AD *IGB* III 1666, 7 (s. *Βίθυς*, *—νις*)
—BYZANTION?: (28) i BC *IByz* 339 (Fıratlı–Robert p. 129 no. 220) (*Θεαγένειος* (gen.): I f. *Θεαγένης* II); (29) ~ *IByz* 339 (Fıratlı–Robert p. 129 no. 220) (II s. *Θεαγένης* I)
—DIONYSOPOLIS: (30) iii AD *IGB* I^2 14 a, 7 (*Αὐρ. Θ.*: s. *Κάντιος*); (31) ~ ib. 14 c, 9 (f. *Αὐρ. Πρόκλος*)
—KELLAI: (32) 241-244 AD ib. III 1517, 38 (*Αὐρ. Θ.*: s. *Κόσμος*)
—NICOPOLIS AD ISTRUM: (33) ii-iii AD ib. II 666 (Stephanis 1129)
—PAUTALIA (TERRIT.): (34) ii-iii AD *IGB* V 5796 (s. *Τήρης*)
—PERINTHOS-HERAKLEIA: (35) i-ii AD *IPerinth* 90 (*Τ. Τερέντιος Θ.*)

Θεαγενίς
TAURIS:
—CHERSONESOS: (1) iii BC *IOSPE* I^2 708 (d. *Διονύσιος*, m. *Στέφανος*)

Θεαγενίων
TAURIS:
—CHERSONESOS: (1) c. 120-130 AD Solomonik, *NEPKh* 112, 19 (f. *Ἡρακλείδης*)

Θεάγης
THRACE:
—BIZONE: (1) i-ii AD *IGB* I^2 6, 8 (*Θεά[γης]?*: s. *Σκύθης*)

Θεάδων
SCYTHIA MINOR:
—ISTROS: (1) 138 AD *ISM* I 193 II, 49 (s. *Μενίσκος*)

—TOMIS: **(2)** ii AD ib. II 17, 13 (s. *Κουθίας*); **(3)** 201 AD ib. 83 II, 13 (f. *Ναvάς*)

Θεαθώ
THRACE:
—BOURDAPA: **(1)** ii-iii AD *IGB* III 1358 (d. *Δεσάκενθος*)

Θεαίδητος
SKYTHIA:
—OLBIA-BORYSTHENES: **(1)** imp. *IOSPE* I^2 278

Θεαίνετος
MACEDONIA (EDONIS):
—AMPHIPOLIS: **(1)** s. iv BC *PAE* 1981, p. 25 with pl. 43 β, 3 (s. *Ἀριστοκλῆς*)
THRACE:
—NAULOCHOS?: **(2)** s. iii BC *IGB* V 5085 (PM 1104 Add) (or Thrace Mesambria: *Θεαίν[ετο]ς?*: s. *Κήτων, Μίκκα*)

Θεανώ
MACEDONIA (MYGDONIA):
—THESSALONIKE: **(1)** ii AD *IG* X (2) (1) 459 A (d. *Δημάρχη*)

Θεαρίδας
SCYTHIA MINOR:
—KALLATIS: **(1)** ii-i BC *ISM* III 172 (f. *Κοτυτίς*)

Θειπης
THRACE:
—DIONYSOPOLIS: **(1)** iii AD *IGB* I^2 14 b, 18, 21 (*Θειπη* (gen.): f. *Αὐρ. Γλύκων, Αὐρ. Κλαύδιος*)

Θέκας
CIMMERIAN BOSPOROS:
—GORGIPPIA: **(1)** ii/iii AD *CIRB* 1179, 45; Zgusta, *PNS* 652 (f. *Χρηστίων*); **(2)** ~ *CIRB* 1179, 53 (f. *Πάππος*)

Θέκλα
MACEDONIA (BOTTIAIA):
—EDESSA: **(1)** v-vi AD Feissel, *RICM* 32 (*[Θ]έκλα*)
MACEDONIA (MYGDONIA):
—THESSALONIKE?: **(2)** ?v AD ib. 289 bis (Tataki, *Macedonians* p. 190 no. 6)
MACEDONIA (PIERIA):
—DION: **(3)** iv-v AD Feissel, *RICM* 79 (bronze)
SCYTHIA MINOR:
—TOMIS: **(4)** v-vi AD Barnea 11, 4 (Popescu, *IGL* 38) (*[Θ]έκλα*)
THRACE:
—BEROE-AUGUSTA TRAIANA: **(5)** c. 320-324 AD *Anal. Boll.* 31 (1912) p. 198; p. 207
—BIZYE: **(6)** v-vi AD *JÖAI* 23 (1926) Beibl. col. 125 no. 13 (*AD* 49-50 (1994-5) Mel. p. 340 no. 162)
—NICOPOLIS AD NESTUM: **(7)** iii AD *IGB* V 5930, 4 (d. *Ἑρμογένης, Ματρώνα*)

Θεμισταγόρας
THRACE:
—AINOS: **(1)** 360 BC *IG* IV (1)^2 94 b, 30 (Perlman, *City and Sanctuary* E.1 with pp. 69-70 (date))

Θεμισταγόρη
THRACE:
—APOLLONIA-SOZOPOLIS: **(1)** v/iv BC *IGB* I^2 426 (d. *Ἀψίνθιος*); **(2)** iv BC *BMNBurgas* 4 (2002) p. 124 no. 19 (*[Θ]εμισταγόρη*)

Θεμιστᾶς
SKYTHIA:
—OLBIA-BORYSTHENES: **(1)** iv/iii BC Dubois, *IGDOlbia* 108 (vase)
THRACE:
—ODESSOS: **(2)** i-ii AD *IGB* I^2 51 b, 7 (f. *Διονύσιος*); **(3)** s. ii AD ib. 79 bis, 4 (*CCET* I 34) (f. *—ώνιος*)

Θεμιστοκλῆς
CIMMERIAN BOSPOROS:
—PANTIKAPAION: **(1)** i AD *CIRB* 384 A (*[Θ]εμιστο[κ]λῆς*: s. *Γόκων*)

Θέμιστος
SKYTHIA:
—OLBIA-BORYSTHENES: **(1)** vi-v BC *SEG* XXXII 756 (vase); cf. Vinogradov–Kryžickij p. 118 with pl. 112. 4 (n. pr.?)
TAURIS:
—CHERSONESOS: **(2)** inc. Solomonik, *GAKh* 1382 (vase) (*Θέμισ[τος]?, Θέμις?*); **(3)** 174 AD *SEG* XLV 985 A, 33 (s. *Στράτων*) ?= (*4*); **(4)** iii AD *VDI* 1938 (3), p. 80 no. 10. I (s. *Στράτων*) ?= (*3*); **(5)** 284-305 AD Const. Porph., *De admin. imp.* 53. 2 (I f. *Θέμιστος* II); **(6)** ~ ib. (II s. *Θέμιστος* I)

Θεμιστῶναξ
THRACE:
—TIRIZIS AKRA*: **(1)** iii/ii BC *IGB* V 5004 bis

Θεμίσων
MACEDONIA: **(1)** iii/ii BC *RE* (4); Ma, *Antiochos* p. 321 no. 20
MACEDONIA (BOTTIAIA):
—BEROIA: **(2)** ii-i BC *IBer* 183 (Tataki 549) (s. *Καλλίνας*)
THRACE:
—BIZYE: **(3)** 212-217 AD *IGB* V 5659, 7 (*[Θε]μίσων*: f. *Αὐρ. Διονύσιος*)

Θεόβιος
SKYTHIA:
—OLBIA-BORYSTHENES: **(1)** v-iv BC *IOSPE* I^2 213 (f. *Ποσειδεώνιος*)

Θεοβούλα
THRACE:
—BYZANTION: **(1)** ii-i BC *IByz* 229 (Fıratlı–Robert pp. 82-3 no. 100) (d. *Διόδωρος*)
—BYZANTION (NR.): **(2)** imp. Unp. (Sayar) (-*βό*-: d. *Διόδωρος*)

Θεογείτων
MACEDONIA (CHALKIDIKE):
—OLYNTHOS?: **(1)** ?350 BC *SEG* XXXVII 570, 5, 8 (f. *Ζωΐλος*)
MACEDONIA (DERRIOPOS):
—STUBERRA: **(2)** 74 AD *IG* X (2) (2) 326, 63 (s. *Ἐπίκαδος*); **(3)** ~ ib. l. 40-1 (f. *Παράμονος*)
SKYTHIA:
—OLBIA-BORYSTHENES: **(4)** iii BC *IOSPE* I^2 201 II, 28 (-*γί*-: f. *Τιμέας*)

Θεογένης
CIMMERIAN BOSPOROS:
—HERMONASSA: **(1)** iv BC *CIRB* 1056 II, 12 (*Θεογ[έ]νης*: s. *Διονυσόδωρος*)
MACEDONIA (BOTTIAIA):
—BEROIA: **(2)** 239-229 BC *IBer* 45, 28 (f. *Μαχάτας*); **(3)** 7 BC ib. 22, 2, 7 (f. *Παράμονος*); **(4)** f. i AD ib. 103, 2 (*Γ. Ἰούλ. Θεο(γ)ένης*)
MACEDONIA (PAIONIA):
—KAVADARCI (MOD.): **(5)** iii AD *Sp.* 71 (1931) p. 65 no. 142, 5 (f. *Ἰουλία*)
—NEGOTINO (MOD.): **(6)** ii-iii AD ib. p. 65 no. 144, 4 (f. *Κλεονίκη*); **(7)** ~ ib. l. 4 (s. *Διονύσιος, Κλεονίκη*)
MACEDONIA?: **(8)** 168 BC *RE* (6) (Tataki, *Macedonians* p. 324 no. 3) (Lat. Theogenes)
TAURIS:
—CHERSONESOS: **(9)** c. 315-300 BC Kats p. 99 no. 60 (amph.); **(10)** f. iii BC *SEG* XL 615 A, 12 (*Θεογέν[ης]*: f. *Θεοκλῆς*); **(11)** c. 285-272 BC Kats p. 99 no. 61 (amph.) (s. *Ἀπολλωνίδας*); **(12)** a. 46 BC *IOSPE* I^2 691, 5 (*Θε[ο]γ[έ]νης*: f. *Γ. Ἰούλ. Σάτυρος*); **(13)** i-ii AD ib. 478 (s. *Ἀγάθων*); **(14)** ii AD ib. 699, 3
THRACE:
—BIZONE: **(15)** i-ii AD *IGB* I^2 6, 2, 4 (s. *Σκύθης*, f. *Σκύθης*)
—LYSIMACHEIA: **(16)** c. 208 BC *FD* III (4) 135, 3, 7, 15 (f. *Ἀριστόβουλος*); **(17)** m. ii BC *ISestos* 38 a, 2 (s. *Φοῖνιξ*); **(18)** ~ ib. 38 b, 3 (f. *Αἴσωπος*)
—SALYMBRIA: **(19)** hell. *IByz* S 41 (f. *Ἀσκλαπιάδας*)
—ZONE: **(20)** s. v BC *PAE* 1969, p. 67 with pl. 83 β (*IThrakAig* E409) (f. *Πυθόδωρος*)

Θεογενίδης
CIMMERIAN BOSPOROS:
—HERMONASSA: **(1)** iv BC *CIRB* 1056 I, 4 (f. *—ωρος*) ?= (*2*); **(2)** ~ ib. l. 6 ?= (*1*)

Θεόγνητος
CIMMERIAN BOSPOROS:
—HERMONASSA: **(1)** iv BC ib. l. 5
MACEDONIA (CHALKIDIKE):
—MENDE: **(2)** c. 410-400 BC *SEG* XXIX 612; *KGAM Thess.* I 12 (date); cf. *BE* 1999, no. 368 (s. *Πεpαῖος*)
SCYTHIA MINOR:
—ISTROS: **(3)** iv BC *ISM* I 110 (*Θεόγνη[τος]*: f. *Δημοτέλης*); **(4)** iii BC ib. 23, 2; **(5)** c. 255 BC ib. 4, 2 + *Pontica* 33-4 (2000-1) pp. 339-44 no. 2 (*[Θεό]γνητος?*); **(6)** ii BC *ISM* I 31, 2 (f. *—αρις*); **(7)** ~ ib. 59, 13 ?= (*8*); **(8)** ~ *SEG* L 683 A ?= (7); **(9)** i BC-i AD *ISM* I 189, 5 (*Θεόγνη[τος]*); **(10)** ~ ib. 191 II, 38 (s. *Παπίας*); **(11)** 138 AD ib. 193 I, 88 (s. *Διονύσιος*)
TAURIS:
—CHERSONESOS: **(12)** iii BC Solomonik, *GAKh* 926 (vase) (Tolstoi 93)

Θέογνις
THRACE:
—LYSIMACHEIA: **(1)** m. ii BC *ISestos* 38 a, 6 (s. *Δημήτριος*)
—MESAMBRIA: **(2)** iii/ii BC *IGB* I^2 349 quater (*Θέογνι[ς]?*)

Θεοδᾶς
CIMMERIAN BOSPOROS:
—PANTIKAPAION: **(1)** i AD *CIRB* 447 (*Θ[ε]οδᾶς*: I f. *Θεοδᾶς* II, *Ἑρμῆς, Κουλία*); **(2)** ~ ib. (*[Θ]εοδᾶς*: II s. *Θεοδᾶς* I)
MACEDONIA: **(3)** 138 AD *SEG* XXXVII 593, 19 (I f. *Θεοδᾶς* II); **(4)** ~ ib. l. 19 (II s. *Θεοδᾶς* I)
MACEDONIA (EDONIS):
—AMPHIPOLIS: **(5)** ?c. 167 BC ib. XXIV 580, 7; cf. Hatzopoulos, *MI* I p. 136 (*[Θε]οδᾶς*)
MACEDONIA (MYGDONIA):
—THESSALONIKE: **(6)** s. i AD *IG* X (2) (1) 68, 15; 69, 12 (I f. *Θεοδᾶς* II); **(7)** ~ ib. 68, 15; 69, 12 (II s. *Θεοδᾶς* I); **(8)** iii AD ib. 470, 4 (*M. Αὐρ. Θεο<ο>δᾶ* (dat.)—lap., *Θεο<ο>δ(ᾶ)?*—*IG*: s. *Αὐρ. Ἐπινίκη*)
—THESSALONIKE?: **(9)** 46 AD Dimitsas 366, 9 (*Epigr. arch. Mak.* 36); cf. *Essays Laourdas* pp. 98-100; *Tekmeria* 6 (2001) p. 126 n. 2 (locn.) (f. *Νικήρατος*)
SKYTHIA:
—TYRAS: **(10)** 181 AD *IOSPE* I^2 2, 27 (*Θεοδ[ᾶς]?*: s. *Ἀρτεμίδωρος*)
THRACE:
—BYZANTION: **(11)** ?ii-i BC *IByz* 374 (s. *Μηνόφιλος*, f. *Μόσχιν, Μηνόφιλος*)
—BYZANTION?: **(12)** ii-i BC ib. 336 (Fıratlı–Robert p. 127 no. 215) (f. *—ος*)

Θεοδέκτης
SKYTHIA:
—OLBIA-BORYSTHENES: **(1)** iii BC *IOSPE* I^2 201 I, 55 (s. *Ἡρόδωρος*)

Θεοδῆς
MACEDONIA (MYGDONIA):
—THESSALONIKE: **(1)** s. i AD *IG* X (2) (1) 68, 28; 69, 20 (s. *Πρωτᾶς*); **(2)** 125 AD *Klio* 65 (1983) p. 163 (*Θεόδεος*—ed.: f. *Βακχύλος*)

Θεοδίας
Macedonia (Derriopos):
—Stuberra: **(1)** c. 41-48 ad *IG* x (2) (2) 323, 18 (*Θεοδίας*: s. *Εὐπόλεμος*)

Θεοδοσία
Macedonia (Bottiaia):
—Edessa: **(1)** v-vi ad Feissel, *RICM* 20; **(2)** ~ ib. 22

Θεοδόσιος
Cimmerian Bosporos:
—Bosporos: **(1)** 346 bc Rhodes–Osborne 64, 50
—Pantikapaion: **(2)** 275-278 ad *CIRB* 36, 33 (*Θ[ε]οδόσ(ιος)*: s. *Σιạυαρ(—)*)
Macedonia (Bottiaia):
—Beroia: **(3)** ?iv ad *SEG* xlix 685 (Jew)
Tauris:
—Chersonesos: **(4)** imp. *IOSPE* i² 619; cf. *SEG* xxxiii 605 (*[Θεο]δόσιος?*)
Thrace:
—Maroneia: **(5)** v ad Meïmaris–Bakirtzis 6 (*IThrakAig* E355) (-*σηος*)
—Philippopolis-Trimontium: **(6)** ii ad *IGB* iii 1014 (I s. *Γάϊος*, f. *Θεοδόσιος* II); **(7)** ~ ib. (*[Θ]ε̣ο̣δο̣σ̣[ιος]*: II s. *Θεοδόσιος* I)

Θεοδόσις
Cimmerian Bosporos:
—Pantikapaion: **(1)** v-vi ad *ZOOID* 29 (1911) Prot. p. 4 no. 1; **(2)** ~ ib. 31 (1913) Prot. p. 22 fig. 9; p. 68
Tauris:
—Chersonesos: **(3)** imp. *IOSPE* i² 434, 6
Thrace:
—Apollonia-Sozopolis: **(4)** v-vi ad Beševliev 176 (*Μάγνο(ς) Θεωδώσις*)

Θεοδότα
Thrace:
—Salymbria: **(1)** hell.? *IByz* S 46

Θεοδότη
Cimmerian Bosporos:
—Pantikapaion: **(1)** i bc *CIRB* 277; cf. KW p. 31 fig. 5; **(2)** i/ii ad *CIRB* 609
Macedonia: **(3)** 232 or 207 bc *CPR* xviii 13, 260, 263-4, 267 (Tataki, *Macedonians* p. 324 no. 4; La'da E1806)
Macedonia (Bottiaia):
—Beroia: **(4)** 254 ad *ILeukopetra* 107, 11 (*Αὐρ. Θ.*); **(5)** 313 ad ib. 118, 4 (Tataki 554) ?= *(6)*
—Beroia*: **(6)** 311 ad *ILeukopetra* 117, 1 (Tataki 555) (freed.) ?= *(5)*
—Edessa: **(7)** iii ad *Athena* 12 (1900) p. 71 no. 3, 1; *AD* 8 (1923) p. 266 (Tataki, *Edessa* 120)
Macedonia (Chalkidike):
—Skabla?: **(8)** imp. *SEG* xxix 620; cf. Hatzopoulos, *Actes Chalc.* p. 71 (locn.)
Macedonia (Edonis):
—Amphipolis: **(9)** ii-iii ad Kaphtantzis 656 (*Θεοδότ(η)*, *Θεοδοτείρη*—ed.); **(10)** ~ *SEG* xxxix 572 (d. *Ἀλέξανδρος*)
Macedonia (Mygdonia):
—Kalindoia: **(11)** 68-98 ad ib. xlii 580, 31 (m. *Θεόδοτος ὁ καὶ Μάξιμος*)
—Thessalonike: **(12)** ii ad *IG* x (2) (1) 239, 2 (m. *—γνιος*) ?= *(13)*; **(13)** ~ ib. l. 3 (m. *—πος*) ?= *(12)*; **(14)** ii-iii ad ib. 361, 3 (*M. Ἐρενία Θ.*: m. *M. Ἐρένιος Λάκων*); **(15)** v-vi ad ib. 633 (Feissel, *RICM* 173; *CIJ* i 693) (*Θ.*—*IG*, *Θεωδότη*—Feissel: Jew)
Macedonia (Pieria):
—Dion: **(16)** iv ad *SEG* xxxix 586, 11
Scythia Minor:
—Ulmetum: **(17)** iii ad *ISM* v 81, 4 (Lat. Theodote: m. *Βάρβαρος*, *Θεόδωρος*, Iuliana)
Thrace:
—Beroe-Augusta Traiana: **(18)** c. 320-324 ad *Anal. Boll.* 31 (1912) p. 198; p. 208

Θεόδοτος
Cimmerian Bosporos:
—Pantikapaion: **(1)** iv bc *CIRB* 158 (f. *Ἄννη*); **(2)** i/ii ad ib. 619
Macedonia: **(3)** 331 bc Berve 361 (Tataki, *Macedonians* p. 324 no. 5) (Lat. Theodotus)
Macedonia (Bottiaia):
—Beroia: **(4)** 41-44 ad *IBer* 60, 11 (Tataki 558) (f. *Στράτων*)
—Beroia (territ.): **(5)** f. ii ad *IBer* 502 (Tataki 848) (*Μάλειος Κορν[ήλι]ος Θεόδοτ̣[ος]*: s. *Μαλεία Ἐλπίς*)
—Pella: **(6)** iii bc Akamatis, *Amph. Pellas* pp. 36-7 nos. PAR29-30 (amph.) (*SEG* l 613)
Macedonia (Chalkidike):
—Olynthos: **(7)** ?352 bc *TAPA* 69 (1938) p. 48 no. 3, 17; Hatzopoulos, *Actes Chalc.* p. 80 (date) (f. *Φίλων*)
—Potidaia-Kassandreia: **(8)** c. 300-275 bc Polyaen. vi 7. 2 (Tataki, *Macedonians* p. 90 no. 47); **(9)** i bc *SEG* xlii 421, 11 (*IOrop* 608; Tataki, *Macedonians* p. 90 no. 48) (f. *Ἡλιόδωρος*)
Macedonia (Edonis):
—Amphipolis: **(10)** 37 bc Robert, *Coll. Froehner* 44, 11 (Tataki, *Macedonians* p. 53 no. 62) (f. *Κλεοπάτρα*)
Macedonia (Elimeia):
—Velvendos (mod.): **(11)** iii ad *EAM* 23a
Macedonia (Eordaia):
—Kelle?: **(12)** iv-vi ad *SEG* xxxix 624 (vase); Hatzopoulos, *MI* i pp. 94-5 (locn.)
Macedonia (Mygdonia):
—Kalindoia: **(13)** 68-98 ad *SEG* xlii 580, 31 (*Θ. ὁ καὶ Μάξιμος*: s. *Θεοδότη*)
—Thessalonike: **(14)** ii ad *IG* x (2) (1) 241 A I, 36 (*Ἰούλ. Θ̣ε̣ό̣δοτος*)
Macedonia (Orestis):
—Sisani (mod.): **(15)** 146 ad *EAM* 187, 23 (I f. *Θεόδοτος* II); **(16)** ~ ib. l. 23 (II s. *Θεόδοτος* I)
Macedonia (Paionia): **(17)** 201 bc *PP* 3958; Tataki, *Macedonians* p. 209 no. 10 (s. *Κάσσανδρος*)
Macedonia?: **(18)** 315 bc *RE* (8)
Scythia Minor:
—Istros: **(19)** v/iv bc *ISM* i 144 (*Θεόδ[οτος]*: f. *Ἡγησαγόρης*) ?= *(20)*; **(20)** ~ ib. 169; 170 (f. *Ἱππόλοχος*) ?= *(19)*; **(21)** iv bc *IOlbia* 7, 3 (Dubois, *IGDOlbia* 19) (*[Θ]εόδοτος*: s. *Διονύσιος*); **(22)** iii bc *ISM* i 113 (f. *Ἀθηναγόρας*); **(23)** ~ ib. 114 (f. *Θεόφιλος*); **(24)** iii-ii bc ib. 13, 2; **(25)** i bc-i ad ib. 191 I, 21
—Tomis: **(26)** ii-iii ad ib. ii 31 II, 4 (f. *Ἡρακλείδης*); **(27)** ~ ib. l. 8 (*[Θε]όδοτος*: s. *Κάλος*); **(28)** ~ ib. l. 10 (s. *Μάγνος*); **(29)** ~ ib. l. 13 (s. *Ποντιανός*); **(30)** ~ ib. 467 (f. *Ἀλέξανδρος*); **(31)** ~ ib. 468, 8 (s. *Ἥλιος*); **(32)** 201 ad ib. 83 I, 29 (f. *Ἑρμόδωρος*)
Skythia:
—Olbia-Borysthenes: **(33)** v-iv bc *IOSPE* i² 208 a; cf. KW pl. 1 no. 19 (*Θ[εό]δοτος*: f. *Ἀπατούριος*)
Tauris:
—Chersonesos: **(34)** ii ad *VDI* 1996 (4), p. 50 no. 10, 5 (*SEG* xlvi 931 (om. per err.)) (s. *Μητρόδωρος*)
Thrace:
—Apollonia-Sozopolis: **(35)** ii-iii ad *IGB* i² 319, 2 (s. *No—*)
—Aproi: **(36)** iv-vi ad *AD* 49-50 (1994-5) Mel. p. 294 no. 121 (-*δω*-)
—Byzantion: **(37)** ii bc *IByz* 284 (Fıratlı–Robert pp. 54-5 no. 32) (s. *Μενέφρων*); **(38)** ii/iii ad *DCB* (4)
—Kallipolis: **(39)** i bc-i ad *ISestos* 15 (f. *Πάντα*)
—Markianopolis: **(40)** c. 303-305 ad Latyshev, *Menolog. anon.* pp. 108-10; cf. *Anal. Boll.* 31 (1912) p. 244
—Maroneia: **(41)** c. 365-336 bc Schönert-Geiss, *Maroneia* 385-8 (coin); **(42)** imp. *SEG* xlvii 1071; **(43)** iii ad *IThrakAig* E195 (f. *Διονύσιος*)
—Nicopolis ad Istrum: **(44)** ii-iii ad *IGB* ii 662 (*Βαλέριος Θ.*: s. *Ἰουστῖνος*)
—Nicopolis ad Nestum: **(45)** ii-iii ad ib. iv 2342, 4 (*Θεόδο[τος]*: s. *—ος*)
—Odessos: **(46)** f. ii ad ib. i² 77, 3 (*CCET* i 31) (s. *Ἡράκων*) ?= *(47)*; **(47)** ~ *IGB* i² 179 bis; cf. *Dacia* 21 (1977) p. 161 + *AE* 1984, p. 177 no. 1278 (date) (s. *Ἡράκων*) ?= *(46)*; **(48)** 221 ad *IGB* i² 47 bis a, 28 (*Αὐρ. Θ.*: s. *Μαρκιανός*)
—Perinthos-Herakleia: **(49)** iii ad *IPerinth* 161 (f. *Αὐρ. Καλλίστιον*); **(50)** ~ ib. 218, 11 (s. *Σουσίων*); **(51)** iv ad ib. 219, 3 (*AD* 49-50 (1994-5) Mel. p. 343 no. 165) (s. *Λούκις*, *Ἀσκληπιοδότη*)
——(Geleuntes): **(52)** iii-ii bc *IPerinth* 61, 31 (s. *Βατᾶς*)
—Serdica: **(53)** iii ad *IGB* iv 1975, 2 (*Θε(ό)δοτος*: f. *Αὐρ. Μᾶρκος*)
—Tyrodiza-Tiristasis: **(54)** imp. Dumont–Homolle 89

Θεοδούλη
Macedonia (Bottiaia):
—Beroia*: **(1)** 545 ad *IBer* 438, 3 (*[Θ]εοδούλη*)
—Edessa: **(2)** v-vi ad Feissel, *RICM* 24 (*Θεωδού(λ)ις* (gen.))
Scythia Minor:
—Tomis: **(3)** iv-v ad Barnea 7 (Popescu, *IGL* 27) (Lat. [The]odule: d. Patri–)
Thrace:
—Beroe-Augusta Traiana: **(4)** c. 320-324 ad *Anal. Boll.* 31 (1912) p. 198; p. 208

Θεόδουλος
Macedonia (Bottiaia):
—Beroia: **(1)** v-vi ad *IBer* 424 (Feissel, *RICM* 65)
Macedonia (Mygdonia):
—Thessalonike: **(2)** v ad *IG* x (2) (1) 1025 (*SEG* xxxiii 218; Tataki, *Macedonians* p. 190 no. 7; *FRA* 2381) (*[Θε]όδουλος*: f. *Ἀγάπη*); **(3)** v-vi ad *IG* x (2) (1) 364 (Feissel, *RICM* 171)
—Thessalonike?: **(4)** ?vi ad *IG* x (2) (1) 790, 5 (Feissel, *RICM* 140) (*Θεόδου[λος]*)
Macedonia (Pieria):
—Pydna: **(5)** 250 ad *SEG* xlvi 800 A, 45 (*Αὐρ. Θ.*)
Scythia Minor:
—Tomis: **(6)** ii-iii ad *ISM* ii 18, 5 (*[Ἰ]ούλις Θ.*)
Skythia:
—Olbia-Borysthenes: **(7)** s. ii ad *IOlbia* 81, 13 (*IOSPE* i² 94) (s. *Μακαγος*)
Thrace:
—Bjala (mod.): **(8)** vi ad *BMNVarna* 9 (1973) p. 303 no. 2 (*Θεόδο[υλος]*, *Θεόδ[ωρος]*—ed.)
—Hadrianopolis: **(9)** ?iii ad *Edirne Müzesi Rehberi* p. 26 (Unp. (Sayar)) (f. *Βάσσος*)
—Mesambria (territ.): **(10)** f. iii ad *IGB* i² 358 (*CCET* i 123)
—Serdica: **(11)** iii ad *IGB* iv 1941 (*Eastern cults* p. 193 no. 4) (*Πονπώνιος Θ.*: s. *Λοῦππος*)

Θεοδώρα
Cimmerian Bosporos:
—Pantikapaion: **(1)** i ad *CIRB* 432 A; cf. KW pl. 27 no. 401 (m. *Θεόφιλος*); **(2)** iv-vi ad Latyshev, *Sbornik* 91 (-*δό*-)
Macedonia (Bottiaia):
—Beroia*: **(3)** v-vi ad *IBer* 447, 5 (Feissel, *RICM* 60)
—Edessa: **(4)** v-vi ad ib. 13, 5 (d. *Θεόδωρος*)
Macedonia (Edonis):
—Philippoi: **(5)** iv-v ad ib. 246 (Pilhofer 268)
Macedonia (Mygdonia):
—Thessalonike: **(6)** ii-iii ad *IG* x (2) (1) 300; **(7)** ~ ib. 348 (d. *Διονύσιος*); **(8)** ii/iii ad *SEG* xlix 814 II, 11 (*Πλωτιανὴ Θ.*); **(9)** iii ad ib.

L 639 ((*A*)*ἰλία Θ.*: threpte); (**10**) v-vi AD *IG* X (2) (1) 333 (Feissel, *RICM* 172) (*Θεωδό-*)

—THESSALONIKE (NR.): (**11**) ii-iii AD *SEG* XXXVIII 708

MACEDONIA (SINTIKE):

—PARTHIKOPOLIS: (**12**) 98 or 215 AD *IGB* V 5915

SCYTHIA MINOR:

—NOVIODUNUM (NR.): (**13**) iv AD *ISM* V 250, 4 (Lat. Theodora)

—TOMIS: (**14**) ii-iii AD ib. II 274 (*Βαλερία Θ.*)

SKYTHIA:

—OLBIA-BORYSTHENES: (**15**) imp. *IOSPE* I^2 193 (*Ἰουλ. Θ.*)

THRACE:

—BEROE-AUGUSTA TRAIANA: (**16**) c. 320-324 AD *Anal. Boll.* 31 (1912) p. 198; p. 207

—BYZANTION: (**17**) i BC *IByz* 243 ([*Θ*]*εοδώρα*: d. *Διογένης*); (**18**) i BC-i AD ib. 19, 10 (*Λουσία Θ.*)

——(Athyras): (**19**) hell.-imp. ib. 250 (*Θ*(*ε*)*οδώρα*)

—MARONEIA: (**20**) v AD Meïmaris–Bakirtzis 10 (*SEG* XLIV 597) + *IThrakAig* E349 (*Θεο*[*δ*]*όρα*)

—PERINTHOS-HERAKLEIA: (**21**) i-ii AD *ISM* II 365, 19 (*GVI* 1161) (d. *Πέρινθος*, *Καικιλία Ἀρτεμισία*); (**22**) ~ *ISM* II 365, 23 (*GVI* 1161) (*Φλ. Θ.*: m. *Καικιλία Ἀρτεμισία*); (**23**) ii-iii AD *IPerinth* 92 (d. *Παπίας*); (**24**) iii AD ib. 164 (*Αὐρ. Θεοδόρα*: d. *Σεμπρώνιος*)

Θεοδωριανός

SCYTHIA MINOR:

—ULMETUM: (**1**) ii AD *ISM* V 80, 8 (Lat. Theodorianus: s. G. Iul. Sergis, *Θεαγένεια*)

THRACE:

—ODESSOS: (**2**) 221 AD *IGB* I^2 47 bis b, 12 (*Οὐαλέριος Θ.*)

Θεόδωρος

CIMMERIAN BOSPOROS:

—GORGIPPIA: (**1**) f. iii BC *CIRB* 1137 A II, 22 (f. *Σκύθας*); (**2**) ~ ib. l. 28 (f. *Νικαγόρας*); (**3**) ~ ib. 1137 B I, 19 ([*Θ*]*εόδ*[*ω*]*ρος*: s. *Θεότιμος*); (**4**) ~ ib. l. 38 (f. *Σωσίπατρος*); (**5**) ~ ib. l. 49; 1137 B II, 30 (s. *Φιλίσκος*)

—HERMONASSA: (**6**) iv BC ib. 1056 II, 5 (*Θεόδω*[*ρος*]: f. *Εὐφάνης*)

—PANTIKAPAION: (**7**) imp. ib. 794 (f. *Ἱλαρίων*); (**8**) i BC/i AD ib. 314 (s. *Ναΐς*); (**9**) i AD ib. 135, 1-3 (*GVI* 1362); cf. KW pl. 29 no. 406 (s. *Μητρόδωρος*, *Μᾶ*); (**10**) f. i AD *CIRB* 529 (f. *Φιλάρσενος*); (**11**) m. i AD ib. 423 (s. *Στρούνιος*); (**12**) iv-v AD *SEG* XLV 1015 g (amph.) (*Θεόδω*(*ρος*)?); (**13**) v-vi AD *ZOOID* 22 (1900) p. 59 no. 2 (*Θε*(*ό*)*δ*(*ω*)*ρος*); (**14**) ~ ib. 29 (1911) Prot. pp. 6-8 no. 2 (*Θεόδ*(*ω*)*ρος*); (**15**) vi AD *MIA* 103 (1962) p. 36 (*Θ*[*εό*]*δωρος*)

MACEDONIA: (**16**) f. iv BC Arr., *An.* iii 16. 9 (Tataki, *Macedonians* p. 325 no. 11) (f. *Ἀρχέλαος*); (**17**) s. iv BC Berve 362 (Tataki, *Macedonians* p. 325 no. 7) (?s. *Ἀνδρόνικος*, *Λανίκα*); (**18**) 341-337 BC *CID* II 36 II, 36; 43, 42; 44, [6]; 74 I, [32] (Tataki, *Macedonians* p. 325 no. 8); (**19**) 227 BC *SB* 7631, [5], 29 (Tataki, *Macedonians* p. 326 no. 12); cf. La'da E1769 (f. *Κεφάλων*); (**20**) ?219 BC *PUG* III 103, 14 (Tataki, *Macedonians* p. 325 no. 10); cf. La'da E1388 (f. *Ἄγρων*); (**21**) c. 200 BC *SEG* XXXI 572, 11 (*Θιόδου-*); (**22**) m. ii BC *PTeb* 1075 fr. 2, 19 (Tataki, *Macedonians* p. 486 no. 133); cf. La'da E1506 (I f. *Θεόδωρος* II); (**23**) ~ *PTeb* 1075 fr. 2, 19 (Tataki, *Macedonians* p. 485 no. 130; La'da E1506) (II s. *Θεόδωρος* I); (**24**) 173 BC *PAmh* 43, 16 (Tataki, *Macedonians* p. 325 no. 9; La'da E1507); (**25**) 124 BC *SB* 9366, 2 (Tataki, *Macedonians* p. 485 no. 132); cf. La'da E1500 (f. *Ἡρακλείδης*); (**26**) 107 BC *SB* 11410 B, 12 (Tataki, *Macedonians* p. 485 no. 129); (**27**) 16-12 BC *BGU* 1132, 5, 7, 9; 1151 I, 7 (Tataki, *Macedonians* p. 485 no. 131) (s. *Νικόδημος*); (**28**) s. i AD *RE* (45) (Tataki, *Macedonians* p. 325 no. 6) (doctor)

MACEDONIA (BOTTIAIA):

—AIGAI: (**29**) s. iv BC *SEG* XXVI 782 = XXXV 794 (s. *Θευφάνης*)

—BEROIA: (**30**) iv AD *IBer* 433 (*Θε*[*ό*]*δωρος*)

—EDESSA: (**31**) v-vi AD Feissel, *RICM* 13, 2 (s. *Ἀγοράστη*, f. *Δημήτριος*, *Ἰορδάνης*, *Θεοδώρα*)

MACEDONIA (CHALKIDIKE):

—OLYNTHOS: (**32**) ?c. 355-350 BC *SEG* XXXVIII 640, 3; XXXIX 617 (f. *Λυκόφρων*); (**33**) ?350 BC *TAPA* 62 (1931) p. 43 no. 2, 4; Hatzopoulos, *Actes Chalc.* p. 80 (date) (f. *Σώσων*); (**34**) ~ *TAPA* 62 (1931) p. 43 no. 2, 7; Hatzopoulos, *Actes Chalc.* p. 80 (date) (f. *Ἀντίδοτος*); (**35**) ~ *TAPA* 69 (1938) p. 50 no. 4, 4; Hatzopoulos, *Actes Chalc.* p. 80 (date)

—POTIDAIA-KASSANDREIA: (**36**) ?m. iii BC *FD* III (4) 351, 4 (Tataki, *Macedonians* p. 91 no. 49) (s. *Ἀριστο—*)

—STOLOS?: (**37**) ?351 BC *SEG* XXXVIII 672, 13 (s. *Διονύσιος*)

MACEDONIA (DERRIOPOS):

—STUBERRA: (**38**) iv/iii BC *IG* X (2) (2) 318 (*Θε*[*όδω*]*ρος*: f. *Ἀριστονίκη*); (**39**) ~ ib. (s. *Ἐπ—ο—*)

MACEDONIA (EDONIS):

—AMPHIPOLIS: (**40**) b. 357 BC Hatzopoulos, *Actes Amphipolis* p. 30 no. 4, 2 (*SEG* XLI 558) (*Θ̣εόδωρος*—ed., *Ἡ̣ρόδωρος*?); (**41**) hell. ib. XXXII 290 (Tataki, *Macedonians* p. 53 no. 63; *FRA* 511) (f. *Ἀντίπατρος*); (**42**) ii-iii AD *AE* 1932, Chron. p. 1 no. 12 + *Thrakika* 13 (1940) p. 20 *A*; cf. *Epigraphica* 37 (1975) p. 26 (s. *Ξάνθος*); (**43**) ii/iii AD *SEG* XLVI 722

—AMPHIPOLIS (NR.): (**44**) a. 357 BC Hatzopoulos, *Actes Amphipolis* p. 43 no. 8, 2-3 (*SEG* XLI 562) (s. *Πολέμων*)

MACEDONIA (ELIMEIA):

—KROKOS (MOD.): (**45**) ii-iii AD *EAM* 19 (*Θεώ-*)

MACEDONIA (LYNKESTIS):

—HERAKLEIA: (**46**) v-vi AD *SEG* XXXIII 508 (mosaic)

—KATO KLEINES (MOD.): (**47**) ii-iii AD *EAM* 157, 9 (doctor)

MACEDONIA (MYGDONIA):

—ARETHOUSA: (**48**) c. 375-350 BC *FD* III (1) 396; *SEG* XXVIII 485 (date) (Tataki, *Macedonians* p. 69 no. 9) (s. *—δικος*)

—THESSALONIKE: (**49**) ?39 BC *IG* X (2) (1) 30, [2]; 50, 3; 109, 9 (f. *Νικίας*); (**50**) ~ ib. 30, [3]; 50, 4; 109, 9 (s. *Εὔτυχος*); (**51**) s. i AD ib. 68, 16; 69, 13 (s. *Ἐπιμένης*); (**52**) ii AD ib. IV (1) 591, 11 + *Mnem.* NS 47 (1919) pp. 259-60 (Tataki, *Macedonians* p. 186 no. 55; Stephanis 1165) (*M. Οὖλπ. Θ.*: s. *Διόδωρος*); (**53**) ii-iii AD *IG* X (2) (1) 590 (s. *Ἀφροδιτώ*); (**54**) s. ii AD ib. 245 I, 6; (**55**) m. iii AD ib. 158, 3; p. 88 (stemma) (*T. Στατίλιος Θ.*: s. *T. Στατίλιος Οὐαλεντίων ὁ καὶ Ξύστος*, *Αὐρ. Ἰσιδώρα*); (**56**) ~ ib. 207, 2 (*Αὐρ. Στατίλιος Θ. ὁ καὶ Ἀψιμάχις*: s. *Αὐρ. Ἰσιδώρα*); (**57**) v-vi AD Feissel, *RICM* 194 (*Θεώ-*)

—THESSALONIKE?: (**58**) s. iii AD *IG* X (2) (1) 772 (*Αὐρ. Θ.*: s. *Αὐρ. Σίμων*: Jew?)

MACEDONIA (PAIONIA):

—KAVADARCI (MOD.): (**59**) ii AD *Sp.* 75 (1933) p. 39 no. 124

MACEDONIA (PIERIA):

—DION: (**60**) iii BC *SEG* XXVII 280 (f. *Μενεκρίτη*)

—PYDNA: (**61**) ii-i BC ib. XXXIII 541 + *AD* 30 (1975) Chron. pl. 162 α (*Θεόδωρ*[*ος*]: s. *Μένανδρος*)

SCYTHIA MINOR:

—ISTROS: (**62**) ii BC *ISM* I 60, 8; (**63**) i BC-i AD ib. 191 I, 40-1; (**64**) ~ ib. 191 II, 22 (s. *Ἀρτεμίδωρος*); (**65**) ~ ib. l. 35 (f. *Φίλιππος*); (**66**) ii AD ib. 57, 3 (*Eastern cults* pp. 102-3 no. 65) (f. *Διογένης*); (**67**) ~ *ISM* I 196, 4; 201 I, 5 (f. *Νουμήνιος*); (**68**) ~ ib. 196, 9; 201 II, 4 (s. *Νικήρατος*); (**69**) ~ ib. 197 II, 2 (f. *Λυσίμαχος*); (**70**) ~ ib. 212, 14 (f. *Ἡφαιστόδωρος*); (**71**) 138 AD ib. 193 I, 42 (f. *Κρατήσιππος*); (**72**) ~ ib. l. 51 (s. *Κουραγένης*); (**73**) ~ ib. 193 II, 27 (f. *Ἀρτεμίδωρος*); (**74**) ~ ib. l. 52 (s. *Κάρπος*)

—ISTROS?: (**75**) iii/ii BC *Stud. Tacheva* pp. 280-1, 3 (f. *Μενίσκος*)

—KALLATIS: (**76**) s. i AD *ISM* III 67, 6 (f. *—ος*); (**77**) ii-iii AD ib. 184 (*Φλ. Θε*[*ό*]*δωρος*); (**78**) 241-244 AD ib. 74, 9 (s. *Ἡραίων*); (**79**) ~ ib. 74 A, 18 (f. *Ἀσκληπιάδης*) ?= (*81*); (**80**) ~ ib. l. 19 (s. *Ἀσκληπιάδης*); (**81**) ~ ib. l. 20 (f. *Ἡλιόδωρος*) ?= (*79*)

—KALLATIS?: (**82**) ii/i BC *IGB* II 867 a, 6 = *ISM* I 219 (V 87); cf. *ISM* III p. 140 (locn.) (I f. *Θεόδωρος* II); (**83**) ~ *IGB* II 867 a, 6 = *ISM* I 219 (V 87); cf. *ISM* III p. 140 (locn.) (II s. *Θεόδωρος* I)

—PEUKE: (**84**) iv-iii BC *IG* II^2 10077 (*FRA* 6052) (s. *Δημήτριος*)

—TOMIS: (**85**) ii-iii AD *ISM* II 20, 6 (*Θεόδωρ*[*ος*]); (**86**) ~ ib. 23, 3 (f. *—ρος*); (**87**) ~ ib. l. 4 (I f. *Θεόδωρος* II); (**88**) ~ ib. l. 4 (*—ριος Θ*[*εόδ*]*ωρος*: II s. *Θεόδωρος* I); (**89**) ~ ib. 31 II, 9 (s. *Κυρήνιος*); (**90**) ~ ib. l. 11 (s. *Νικόστρατος*); (**91**) ~ ib. l. 12 (s. *Ἐπικράτης*); (**92**) ~ ib. l. 14 (s. *Ἑστιαῖος*); (**93**) ~ ib. l. 15 (s. *Ῥοῦφος*); (**94**) ~ ib. 104, 15 (*Οὐαλ. Θ.*); (**95**) 151-157 AD ib. 55 (*Θεόδω*[*ρος*]); (**96**) 175-179 AD ib. 116 II, 6 (*Π. Φλ. Θεό*[*δ*]*ορος*); (**97**) iii AD ib. 22, 2 (*Αὐρ. Θ.*: ?s. *Διογένης*)

—TOMIS?: (**98**) ii/iii AD ib. V 126 (I f. *Αὐρ. Θεόδωρος* II); (**99**) ~ ib. (*Αὐρ. Θ.*: II s. *Θεόδωρος* I)

—ULMETUM: (**100**) iii AD ib. 81, 7 (Lat. The[od]orus: s. Aemilius, *Θεοδότη*)

SKYTHIA:

—OLBIA-BORYSTHENES: (**101**) ii-iii AD *IOSPE* I^2 282 ([*Θ*]*εόδωρο̣*[*ς*]); (**102**) s. ii AD *IOlbia* 81, 4 (*IOSPE* I^2 94); *IOSPE* I^2 136, 8 (s. *Τούμβαγος*)

—TYRAS: (**103**) 181 AD ib. 2, 22 (s. *Βόηθος*)

TAURIS:

—CHERSONESOS: (**104**) iv BC Solomonik, *GAKh* 927 (vase) (*Θεόδω*(*ρος*)); (**105**) iii BC Kats p. 110 no. 100 (amph.) (*Θεόδ*(*ω*)*ρος*: f. *Πρύτανις*); (**106**) ~ *SEG* XLII 700 (*Θεόδω*[*ρος*]: s. *Ἐπιφάνης*); (**107**) f. iii BC Kats p. 93 no. 42 (amph.) (f. *Διοσκουρίδας*); (**108**) c. 230-215 BC ib. pp. 99-100 no. 62 (amph.) (s. *Πρύτανις*); (**109**) iv-vi AD Latyshev, *Sbornik* 16 ([*Θεό*]*δωρος*?)

THRACE: (**110**) 316-309 BC *IG* II^2 1956, 185 (*FRA* 2538); *Ancient Macedonia* 5 p. 445 with n. 10 (date); (**111**) iii BC *ZPE* 140 (2002) p. 204, 3 (La'da E831) (s. *Ἐβρύζελμις*, *Δα....ς*: t.e.); (**112**) 267 BC *SEG* XXVII 1114, 6a (La'da E753) (s. *Στράτων*); (**113**) 231 or 206 BC *CPR* XVIII 6, 109, 114, 120 (La'da E832) (s. *Ποσειδώνιος*: t.e.); (**114**) iii-iv AD *IG* II^2 4826, 7 (*FRA* 2539; Stephanis 1160) ([*Θε*]*όδωρος*)

—ABDERA: (**115**) ?375 BC *IG* II^2 77, 5, 11 + Add. p. 658 (f. *Κωμαῖος*)

—AINOS?: (**116**) iii-ii BC *SEG* XVIII 378 (*Ἄνιος* (ethn.)—lap.: f. *Γλαυκίας*)

—BEROE-AUGUSTA TRAIANA (TERRIT.): (**117**) iv/v AD *PLRE* II (46); Beševliev 204

—BYZANTION: (**118**) s. v BC *RE* (38); (**119**) i-ii AD *IByz* 232 (*Θεώ-*: f. *Διονυσοφάνης*); (**120**) ii AD *SEG* L 667 VII (f. *Ἀγαθόπους*)

—DIOKLETIANOPOLIS: (**121**) v-vi AD *PLRE* II (39); Beševliev 224, 3 (f. *Ἰωάννης*)

—DIONYSOPOLIS: (**122**) c. 48 BC *IGB* I^2 13, 3; (**123**) c. 170 AD *JÖAI* 15 (1912) p. 50 no. 15, 10 (s. *Ἀπήμων*); (**124**) iii AD *IGB* I^2 14 b, 9 (*Αὐρ. Θ.*: s. *Μοσχίων*); (**125**) ~ ib. l. 15 (*Αὐρ. Θ.*: s. *Οὐαλέριος*); (**126**) 218-222 AD ib. 17 (s. *Δημήτριος*)

—GLAVA PANEGA (MOD.): (**127**) ii-iii AD ib. II 516 (f. *Ἀσιατικός*)

—HERAION TEICHOS: **(128)** hell. Unp. (Sayar) (f. *Λυσίμαχος*)
—IATRUS: **(129)** imp. *Iatrus–Krivina* 4 p. 211 (tile) (*[Θ]εόδ[ω]ρος*)
—LJUBLEN (MOD.): **(130)** f. iii AD *IGB* V 5271 (*CCET* II (2) 571) (*M. Ἀντώνιος Θ.*)
—LYSIMACHEIA: **(131)** c. 208 BC *FD* III (4) 135 I, 16 (*[Θε]όδωρος*: s. *Κάλλων*)
—MARONEIA: **(132)** iii AD *Thrak. Epet.* 4 (1983) p. 425 n. 24 + *IThrakAig* E192 (*Θ[ε]όδω[ρ]ος*: f. *Ἀμύνανδρος*)
—MESAMBRIA: **(133)** hell.? *IGB* V 5123 (*Θό-*: s. *Παυσανίας*); **(134)** ii BC ib. I^2 314 b, 3 (s. *Δαμάτριος*)
—NICOPOLIS AD ISTRUM: **(135)** ?ii AD ib. II 674, 5 (or Bithynia Nikomedeia: f. *Νίκων*)
—ODESSOS: **(136)** s. ii AD ib. I^2 79 bis, 3 (*CCET* I 34) (I f. *Θεόδωρος* II); **(137)** ~ *IGB* I^2 79 bis, 3 (*CCET* I 34) (II s. *Θεόδωρος* I); **(138)** 215 AD *IGB* I^2 47 a, 14 (*Αὐρ. Θ.*: s. *Τάτας*)
—PAUTALIA: **(139)** s. ii AD *SEG* XLVI 864, 6 (I f. *Θεόδωρος* II); **(140)** ~ ib. l. 6 (II s. *Θεόδωρος* I); **(141)** ~ ib. 864 II, 21
—PERINTHOS-HERAKLEIA: **(142)** iii AD *IPerinth* 173 (*Αὐρ. Θ.*)
——(Theseidai): **(143)** s. iii BC ib. 62, 4 (s. *Θεόπομπος*)
—PHILIPPOPOLIS-TRIMONTIUM: **(144)** v-vi AD *SEG* XLII 632, 2 (*Θεόδωρο<ν>ς*)
—SALYMBRIA: **(145)** 242 BC *WChr* 335, 3 (La'da E2413) (s. *Φανοκλῆς*); **(146)** iv-v AD *BCH* 36 (1912) p. 637 no. 95 (*AD* 53 (1998) Mel. p. 460 no. 199) (*Θεώ-*)
—SVETLEN (MOD.): **(147)** v/vi AD Dodd, *Byz. Stamps* p. 61 no. 5
—TÂRGOVIŠTE (MOD.): **(148)** ii-iii AD *IGB* V 5279 (*[Θ]εόδω[ρος]*)

Θεόκλεια
THRACE:
—BEROE-AUGUSTA TRAIANA: **(1)** c. 320-324 AD *Anal. Boll.* 31 (1912) p. 198 (*-κλία*)

Θεοκλείδης
MACEDONIA?: **(1)** c. 260-250 BC *Eretria* XI p. 273 no. 15, 9 (*Θεοκλείδης*: f. *Πρωτέας*)

Θεοκλῆς
MACEDONIA: **(1)** 238 BC *PPetr*^{2} 3, 33 (Tataki, *Macedonians* p. 326 no. 14); cf. La'da E1789 (f. —ς); **(2)** 173-172 BC *PFreib* 34, 7, 11-12, 18, 20 etc.; *PMich* 190, 14, 19, 32 (Tataki, *Macedonians* p. 326 no. 13; La'da E1761) (s. *Εὐβουλίδης*: t.e.)
MACEDONIA (ODOMANTIKE):
—SIRRHA: **(3)** 155 AD Dimitsas 821, 32 (Kaphtantzis 1) (s. *Σώσιππος*)
SCYTHIA MINOR:
—ISTROS: **(4)** s. iv BC *ISM* I 239 (f. *Ἀρτεμίδωρος*); **(5)** i BC-i AD ib. 191 I, 42-3; **(6)** ~ ib. 191 II, 33 (f. *Διοσκουρίδης*) ?= (7); **(7)** ~ ib. l. 36 (f. *Διονύσιος*) ?= (6); **(8)** 138 AD ib. 193 I, 46 (f. *Μειδίας*); **(9)** ~ ib. 193 II, 66 (s. *Ἀρισταγόρας*); **(10)** c. 140-160 AD ib. 207, 13
—TOMIS: **(11)** f. i AD *RPC* I 1811-12 (coin)
SKYTHIA:
—OLBIA-BORYSTHENES: **(12)** m. iv BC Dubois, *IGDOlbia* 13, 4 (s. *Ἀρίστων*); **(13)** iii BC *IOlbia* 72, 1 (s. *Θρασυδάμας*); **(14)** ~ *IOSPE* I^2 201 I, 14 (*[Θεο]κλῆς*?: s. *Ἀρίστων*); **(15)** ~ ib. l. 46 (f. *Ἀριστοκράτης*); **(16)** ~ ib. l. 42-3 (f. *Ἀρίστων, Μενεκράτης*); **(17)** imp. ib. 289; **(18)** ii AD *IOlbia* 86, 8 (f. *Ἄττας*); **(19)** ?ii/iii AD *IOSPE* I^2 40, 1, 5, 8, 35, 37 (s. *Σάτυρος*)
—TYRAS: **(20)** 211-217 AD *SEG* XLVII 1196, 12 (s. *Ἱεροσῶν*)
TAURIS:
—CHERSONESOS: **(21)** f. iii BC ib. XL 615 A, 12 (s. *Θεογένης*)
THRACE:
—BYZANTION: **(22)** arch.? *An. Ox.* iii 204; 208-13; 215 (fict.)
—STRYME: **(23)** c. 425-400 BC *SEG* XXXV 765 (*IThrakAig* E121) (f. *Διονυσοφάνης*)

Θέοκλος
MACEDONIA (CHALKIDIKE):
—CHALKIDEIS: **(1)** arch.? *RE* (2)

Θεοκρίτα
MACEDONIA (PIERIA): **(1)** ?ii BC *IG* XII Suppl. p. 25 no. 80 (Tataki, *Macedonians* p. 168 no. 2) (d. *Δημήτριος*)
THRACE:
—SALYMBRIA: **(2)** imp. *IByz* S 57

Θεόκριτος
CIMMERIAN BOSPOROS:
—GORGIPPIA: **(1)** f. iii BC *CIRB* 1137 A II, 20 (f. *Ἱπποκράτης*); **(2)** ~ ib. 1137 B I, 15 (s. *Ἱπποκράτης*); **(3)** m. ii AD *Eirene* 7 (1968) p. 67, 22 (f. *Δημήτριος*); **(4)** ~ ib. l. 25 (s. *Ἀπελλᾶς*)
—PANTIKAPAION: **(5)** c. 180-150 BC *CIRB* 75, 9, 13 (s. *Δημήτριος*)
MACEDONIA: **(6)** iv BC Arr., *An.* iv 13. 4 (Tataki, *Macedonians* p. 326 no. 15) (f. *Ἀντικλῆς*); **(7)** c. 147-135 BC *BGU* 1256, 3 (Tataki, *Macedonians* p. 486 no. 134); cf. La'da E1491 (f. *Ἕρμων*)
MACEDONIA (CHALKIDIKE):
—OLYNTHOS: **(8)** f. iv BC *SEG* XXIX 625
SCYTHIA MINOR:
—ISTROS: **(9)** iii BC *ISM* I 8, 2
—TOMIS: **(10)** ii AD ib. II 186 (I f. *Θεόκριτος* II); **(11)** ~ ib. (II s. *Θεόκριτος* I, ?s. *Ῥουφῖνα*)
THRACE:
—BYZANTION (TERRIT.): **(12)** imp. Unp. (Sayar) (f. *Κλοιωνις, Διαδουμενός*)

Θεοκτίστη
THRACE:
—BEROE-AUGUSTA TRAIANA: **(1)** c. 320-324 AD *Anal. Boll.* 31 (1912) p. 198; p. 207

Θεόκτιστος
THRACE:
—ODESSOS*: **(1)** vi AD Beševliev 103, 4 (*Θεώκτισ[τος]*: f. *Σοφία*)

Θεοκύδης
SKYTHIA:
—OLBIA-BORYSTHENES: **(1)** iii BC *IOSPE* I^2 201 I, 31 (s. *Παγκράτης*)
TAURIS:
—CHERSONESOS: **(2)** f. iii BC *SEG* XL 615 A, 10-11, 20 (f. *Ξάνθος*)

Θεόμβροτος
SCYTHIA MINOR:
—KALLATIS: **(1)** s. iii BC *ISM* III 12, 3 (*Θεόμβρο[τος]*)

Θεόμναστος
MACEDONIA (CHALKIDIKE):
—OLYNTHOS: **(1)** 316-309 BC *IG* II^2 1956, 160; *Ancient Macedonia* 5 p. 445 (date) (Tataki, *Macedonians* p. 137 no. 63; *FRA* 5896)

Θεομνήστη
CIMMERIAN BOSPOROS:
—PANTIKAPAION: **(1)** f. iv BC *CIRB* 178 (d. *Δίων*)

Θεόμνηστος
CIMMERIAN BOSPOROS:
—GORGIPPIA: **(1)** f. iii BC ib. 1137 A II, 46 (s. *Ἀριστοκλῆς*)
—NYMPHAION: **(2)** f. v BC *SEG* XLIX 1037 (*Bosporskii fenomen* p. 187 no. 1) (f. *Ποσειδεώνιος*)
—PANTIKAPAION: **(3)** ii BC *CIRB* 273; cf. KW pl. 14 no. 217 (s. *Δασχάς*, f. *Καλλίπολις, Χρύσιον, Θηβαΐς*); **(4)** ii AD *CIRB* 93, 6 (*[Θε]όμνησ[τ]ος*)

MACEDONIA (CHALKIDIKE):
—OLYNTHOS?: **(5)** c. 330-320 BC *SEG* XVIII 36 A, 241 (Tataki, *Macedonians* p. 137 no. 64; *FRA* 5895) (*Θεόμ[νηστ](ος)*?: f. *Στρόμβιχος*)
MACEDONIA (PIERIA):
—DION: **(6)** ii AD Oikonomos 33 (*Θεόμ[νη]στος*)
THRACE:
—APOLLONIA-SOZOPOLIS: **(7)** v/iv BC *IGB* I^2 421 bis (s. *Ἀναξαγόρης*)
—DIONYSOPOLIS: **(8)** iii AD ib. 14 a, 6 (*Αὐρ. Θ.*: s. *Πυθοκλῆς*)
—SALYMBRIA: **(9)** ii-iii AD *IByz* S 66 (s. *Ἀρίστων*)

Θεονίκα
CIMMERIAN BOSPOROS:
—PANTIKAPAION: **(1)** ii AD *CIRB* 692 (d. *Μόνιμος, Μᾶ*)

Θεονίκη
CIMMERIAN BOSPOROS:
—MYRMEKION: **(1)** imp. ib. 888 (*-νεί-*)
—MYRMEKION (NR.): **(2)** i-ii AD *VDI* 1965 (2), p. 99 no. 4 with fig. 5; cf. *Topoi* 3 (1993) pp. 198-9 no. 4 (*-ωνήκη*)
—PANTIKAPAION: **(3)** i AD *CIRB* 427 (m. *Λαοδίκη, Μαμία*); **(4)** ~ ib. 500 (*-νεί-*: d. *Ἑρμῆς*); **(5)** ~ ib. 535; **(6)** ~ ib. 549 (*-νεί-*); **(7)** m. i AD ib. 425 (*-νεί-*: m. *Ἑλικωνιάς*); **(8)** s. i AD ib. 424 (*-νεί-*); **(9)** ~ ib. 426; cf. KW pl. 22 no. 322 (d. *Νικίας*); **(10)** ii-iii AD *CIRB* 783, 4 (*-νεί-*: m. *Ἀντιγένης*)

Θεόνικος
CIMMERIAN BOSPOROS:
—PANTIKAPAION: **(1)** i AD ib. 428 (?s. *Καλλιτύχη*); **(2)** i/ii AD ib. 594 (*-νει-*)
—PHANAGOREIA: **(3)** m. ii AD *SEG* XLIII 512, 3 (*[Θε]όνεικος*?)
SKYTHIA:
—TANAIS: **(4)** 104 AD *CIRB* 1259, 15-16 (*-νει-*: f. *Καλλιγένης, Δάδας*); **(5)** c. 200-220 AD ib. 1245, 10; 1246, 10; 1248, 10; 1277, 9 (*-νει-*: f. *Βασιλείδης*)

Θεονόη
MACEDONIA (BOTTIAIA):
—EDESSA: **(1)** ?ii AD *SEG* XII 346 (Tataki, *Edessa* 150) (*Κλ. Θ.*)

Θεόνομος
THRACE:
—PERINTHOS-HERAKLEIA:
——(Geleuntes): **(1)** iii-ii BC *IPerinth* 61, 36 (s. *Ἀπολλοφάνης*)

Θεοξενίδης
THRACE:
—MARONEIA: **(1)** ii BC Grandjean, *Arétalogie* p. 119, 9 = *AD* 26 (1971) Chron. p. 429 no. ι 9 (*Eastern cults* p. 31 no. 51; *IThrakAig* E183) (f. *Σωκλῆς*)
—MARONEIA (NR.): **(2)** iv BC *SEG* XIII 409 + *IThrakAig* E222 (*Θεοξενίδεω* (gen.): f. *Ἀρθέων*)

Θεόξενος
CIMMERIAN BOSPOROS:
—GORGIPPIA: **(1)** f. iii BC *CIRB* 1137 A I, 27 (f. *Τιμέας*)
MACEDONIA (CHALKIDIKE):
—OLYNTHOS: **(2)** ?350 BC *TAPA* 65 (1934) p. 125 no. 3, 9; Hatzopoulos, *Actes Chalc.* p. 80 (date)
—POTIDAIA-KASSANDREIA: **(3)** c. 166-156 BC *ID* 1417 A II, 113 (Tataki, *Macedonians* p. 91 no. 50) (s. *Αἰσχρίων*)
MACEDONIA (EORDAIA?):
—EUIA: **(4)** 181 BC *EAM* 87, 11 (Hatzopoulos, *MI* 2 pp. 41-2 no. 17) (s. *Κλειτῖνος*)
MACEDONIA (PIERIA):
—DION: **(5)** hell. *SEG* L 589 (f. *Σαβύθη*)

MACEDONIA (PIERIS):
—NEAPOLIS: **(6)** 356 BC *IG* II² 128, 3 (Tataki, *Macedonians* p. 126 no. 11) (Θεόξ[ενος]: f. *Δημοσθένης*)
SCYTHIA MINOR:
—ISTROS: **(7)** v/iv BC *ISM* I 144; 169 (s. *Ἱππόλοχος*)
THRACE:
—AINOS: **(8)** ii AD *SEG* XXXVI 657, 6 (s. *Φιλαπόδημος, Ἰωνία*)
—APOLLONIA-SOZOPOLIS: **(9)** hell.-imp. *AEMÖ* 10 (1886) p. 165 (vase) (Θεόξε(νος))
—LYSIMACHEIA: **(10)** ii BC *IG* II² 9227 (*FRA* 3395) (s. *Κλέων*)
—MARONEIA: **(11)** ii-i BC *IThrakAig* E212, 45 (Θεόξενο[ς]: s. *Ἡρακλείδης*); **(12)** ~ ib. l. 6-8 (f. *Μυκηνεύς, Ἀμύνανδρος, Εὐβούλα*); **(13)** imp. *IG* XII (8) 134 (s. *Ἀπολλώνιος*)
—ODESSOS (NR.): **(14)** iii/ii BC *IGB* I² 283 (*CCET* I 96) (f. *Ἀρτεμίδωρος, Πολέμαρχος*)

Θεόπεμπτος
THRACE:
—RHAIDESTOS: **(1)** iv-vi AD Taşlıklıoğlu I p. 25 no. 2 (*AD* 49-50 (1994-5) Mel. p. 299 no. 125 a) (Θεώ-: s. *Γεώργιος*)

Θεόπολις
CIMMERIAN BOSPOROS:
—HERMONASSA: **(1)** m. iv BC *SEG* XLIV 659 (vase) (Θε[ό]πολις?)

Θεόπομπος
CIMMERIAN BOSPOROS:
—KEPOI: **(1)** ?f. iv BC *CIRB* 188 (s. *Αἰαντίδης*)
MACEDONIA: **(2)** 250 BC *PColZen* 54, 4 (Tataki, *Macedonians* p. 327 no. 18); cf. La'da E1758 (f. *Ἡγήσαρχος*); **(3)** ~ *PColZen* 54, 4, 12, 17, 43 (Tataki, *Macedonians* p. 326 no. 17; La'da E1762) (s. *Ἡγήσαρχος*: t.e.)
MACEDONIA (ODOMANTIKE):
—SIRRHA: **(4)** 155 AD Dimitsas 821, 5 (Kaphtantzis 1) (s. *Δημοσθένης*)
SCYTHIA MINOR:
—ISTROS: **(5)** ii BC *ISM* I 71 (Θεόπομ[πος]: f. *Ἀπατούριος*); **(6)** 27 BC-14 AD ib. 146 (f. *Πάπας*); **(7)** i BC/i AD ib. 55, 4 ([Θεό]πομπος?); **(8)** ii AD ib. 204, 8 (f. *Ποσειδώνιος*); **(9)** 138 AD ib. 193 II, 68 (s. *Διοσκουρίδης*); **(10)** ~ ib. l. 70 (f. *Εὔοδος*)
—KALLATIS: **(11)** iii-ii BC ib. III 171 (s. *Ἀρτεμίδωρος*)
TAURIS:
—CHERSONESOS: **(12)** c. 320-310 BC Anokhin p. 138 no. 69 (coin) (Θεόπ(ομπος)?)
THRACE: **(13)** 46-54 AD *SEG* XVI 415 I, 9 (*IThrakAig* E84) (*Τιβ. Κλ. Θ.*)
—AINOS: **(14)** iv BC *IG* II² 7979 (*FRA* 252)
—BEROE-AUGUSTA TRAIANA: **(15)** iii AD *IGB* V 5634 (*Αὐρ. Θ.*: s. *Δίνις*)
—PERINTHOS-HERAKLEIA: **(16)** ?79 AD *CIL* III 7391 (Lat. Ti(b). Cl. Theopompus: f. Ti(b). Claudius Sabinus)
——(Theseidai): **(17)** s. iii BC *IPerinth* 62, 5 (s. *Θεόδωρος*)

Θεοπρεπία
MACEDONIA (PIERIA):
—DION: **(1)** v-vi AD Feissel, *RICM* 78

Θεοπρέπιος
MACEDONIA (BOTTIAIA):
—EDESSA: **(1)** v-vi AD ib. 4 (Θεωπρέπ(ιος))

Θεοπρεπίς
MACEDONIA (MYGDONIA):
—THESSALONIKE: **(1)** 147 AD *IG* X (2) (1) 608, 1 (*Μεινουκία Θ.*: I m. *Κλ. Ῥόδα, Κλ. Θεοπρεπίς* II); **(2)** ~ ib. l. 2 (*Κλ. Θ.*: II d. *Τι. Κλ. Λύκος, Μινουκία Θεοπρεπίς* I)

Θεοπροπίδης
CIMMERIAN BOSPOROS:
—NYMPHAION: **(1)** 389-349 BC *Hyperboreus* 2002 (1), p. 101 (s. *Μεγακλῆς*)

Θεόπροπος
MACEDONIA (PIERIA):
—PYDNA: **(1)** iv BC *GRBS* 43 (2002-3) p. 119 no. 5, 4
SKYTHIA:
—OLBIA-BORYSTHENES: **(2)** imp. *IOSPE* I² 231
—TANAIS (NR.): **(3)** s. ii AD *CIRB* 1313 (f. *Ἡρόδωρος*)
THRACE:
—MARONEIA: **(4)** ii-i BC *IThrakAig* E212, 13 (s. *Θεόφιλος*); **(5)** i BC ib. E213, 10 (Θεόπρ[οπος]: s. *—ν*)

Θεοσεβής
THRACE:
—PHILIPPOPOLIS-TRIMONTIUM: **(1)** c. 303 AD *Anal. Boll.* 31 (1912) p. 192

Θεότεκνος
SCYTHIA MINOR:
—SALSOVIA: **(1)** iv AD Popescu, *IGL* 272 c, 7 (Lat. Theote[cnus])

Θεοτέλης
CIMMERIAN BOSPOROS:
—GORGIPPIA: **(1)** f. iii BC *CIRB* 1137 A I, 17 (f. *Νίκων*)
—PANTIKAPAION: **(2)** imp. ib. 749
MACEDONIA (PIERIA):
—PYDNA: **(3)** v/iv BC *SEG* L 624
TAURIS:
—CHERSONESOS: **(4)** f. iv BC *IOSPE* I² 512 (f. *Εὐθήνα*)

Θεοτίδης
THRACE:
—ODESSOS: **(1)** i BC-i AD *IGB* I² 145 (PM 207) (f. *Σίμων*); **(2)** ii-iii AD *IGB* I² 210 (Θεοτ[ίδ]ης: f. *Διονύσιος*)
—ODESSOS?: **(3)** i BC-i AD ib. 295 (f. *—ης*)

Θεοτίμα
CIMMERIAN BOSPOROS:
—NYMPHAION: **(1)** i/ii AD *CIRB* 932; cf. KW pl. 42 no. 668 ((Θ)εοτείμα)
—PANTIKAPAION: **(2)** ii AD *CIRB* 679 A (-τεί-); **(3)** ~ ib. 680, 1 (m. *Μοίριππος*)
MACEDONIA (MYGDONIA):
—THESSALONIKE: **(4)** 155 AD *IG* X (2) (1) 321, 2 (-τεί-: d. *Πολύδοξος*)
THRACE:
—BYZANTION: **(5)** iii AD *IByz* 318 (Fıratlı-Robert pp. 121-2 no. 204) (*Αὐ[ρ.] Θεοφίλα ἡ καὶ Θεοτείμα*: d. *Αὐρ. Πόπλιος Θεόφιλος*)

Θεοτίμη
MACEDONIA (CHALKIDIKE):
—MENDE?: **(1)** m. iv BC *AM* 66 (1941) p. 66 no. 14 (or Macedonia Megara: m. *Ἐπινίκη*)
—OLYNTHOS: **(2)** m. iv BC *IG* II² 10020a (Tataki, *Macedonians* p. 137 no. 65; *FRA* 5897) (d. *Ἀρίστανδρος*)

Θεοτιμιανός
SKYTHIA:
—OLBIA-BORYSTHENES?: **(1)** 293-305 AD Popescu, *IGL* 169, 5 (Lat. Nevius Palmas Theotimianus)

Θεοτιμίδης
MACEDONIA: **(1)** a. 306 BC *IG* XII (6) 25, 1, 3, 10, 24 (Tataki, *Macedonians* p. 327 no. 19) (s. *Θεόφιλος*)
MACEDONIA (CHALKIDIKE):
—MENDE: **(2)** f. iv BC *SEG* XV 241, 1 (Tataki, *Macedonians* p. 121 no. 11) (s. *Εὔδημος*)

Θεότιμος
CIMMERIAN BOSPOROS:
—ACHILLEION: **(1)** ii AD *CIRB* 1031 (-τει-)
—GORGIPPIA: **(2)** f. iii BC ib. 1137 B I, 19 (f. *Θεόδωρος*); **(3)** ~ ib. l. 59; 1137 B II, 42 (s. *Θόας*); **(4)** ii/iii AD ib. 1179, 31 (-τει-: f. *Πόθος*)
—PANTIKAPAION: **(5)** i AD ib. 471 (Θε(ό)τειμος: f. *Μητρόφιλος*); **(6)** i/ii AD ib. 82, 2 ((Θ)εότειμος); **(7)** 82 AD ib. 76, 23 (*SEG* XVIII 310) (-τει-: f. *Ἀρίστων*)
MACEDONIA: **(8)** f. ii AD *IBer* 73 (Tataki 71) (*Μ. Αἰλ. Βειλιανὸς Κλαυδιανὸς Θεότειμος*)
—RESEN (MOD.): **(9)** 218 AD *IG* X (2) (2) 48, 30 (*Πόντιος Αὐρήλιος Θεότειμος*)
MACEDONIA (CHALKIDIKE):
—PARTHENONAS (MOD.)?: **(10)** s. vi BC *SEG* XLIII 433 b (vase)
MACEDONIA (MYGDONIA):
—THESSALONIKE: **(11)** ?ii AD *IG* X (2) (1) 127, 5 (-τει-: s. *Διογένης*); **(12)** ii AD ib. 241 A II, 8 ([Θ]εότειμος)
MACEDONIA (ORESTIS):
—BATTYNAIOI: **(13)** 192 AD *EAM* 186 I, 43 (-τει-: s. *Νικόλαος*); **(14)** ~ ib. 186 III, 54 (-τει-: s. *Φίλιππος*)
MACEDONIA (PIERIA):
—DION: **(15)** v/iv BC *SEG* XXXIII 511 B (XXXV 735); *BE* 1987, no. 677 (s. *Παρμένων*)
SCYTHIA MINOR:
—ISTROS: **(16)** 138 AD *ISM* I 193 I, 92 (-τει-: f. *Ἀριστόνικος*)
SKYTHIA:
—OLBIA-BORYSTHENES: **(17)** imp. *IOSPE* I² 148, 2 (-τει-: f. *Μαίφαρνος*)
—TANAIS: **(18)** f. ii AD *CIRB* 1264 A, 4 (-τει-: f. *Φαρνάκης*) ?= (*19*); **(19)** ~ ib. l. 6 (-τει-: f. *Ἀρίστων*) ?= (*18*); **(20)** c. 200-210 AD ib. 1277, 20 (-τει-: s. *Ψυχαρίων*)
TAURIS:
—CHERSONESOS: **(21)** iii BC *IOSPE* I² 340, 2
THRACE: **(22)** 201 BC *PPetr* III 57 a, 1, 7; 57b, 5a (Velkov 131; La'da E754) (s. *Εὔφρων*); **(23)** ii/iii AD *Starinar* 43-44 (1992-3) pp. 143-5 (vase-stamp) (Lat. Theotimus: s. *Στέφανος*)
—MESAMBRIA: **(24)** i BC *IGB* I² 324 (s. *Ἡρακλείδας*)
—NAULOCHOS?: **(25)** s. iii BC ib. V 5085 (PM 1104 Add) (or Thrace Mesambria: f. *Κήτων*)

Θεοφάνης
CIMMERIAN BOSPOROS:
—MYRMEKION: **(1)** i BC/i AD *SEG* XLV 992 (s. *Ἰ—*)
—NYMPHAION: **(2)** i/ii AD *CIRB* 931 (f. *Ἀλλάξαρθος*)
TAURIS:
—CHERSONESOS: **(3)** iii BC Solomonik, *NEPKh* 163 (f. *Εὐΐος*); **(4)** ~ *IOSPE* I² 510 (f. *Δαματρία*); **(5)** ~ ib. 581, 4 (s. *Ἡ—*); **(6)** f. iii BC Kats p. 89 no. 23 (amph.) (f. *Ἀπολλώνιος*); **(7)** ii BC *SEG* XLVI 924, 3 (f. *—ς*); **(8)** i BC-i AD Solomonik, *NEPKh* 41 ([Θ]εοφάνη[ς])
THRACE:
—PHILIPPOPOLIS-TRIMONTIUM: **(9)** iii AD *IGB* III 935 ([Θε]οφάνης: s. *Πρωτόμαχος*)
—STRYME?: **(10)** m. iv BC *SEG* XLIX 1000 (*IThrakAig* E381) (s. *Ἑρμόφαντος*)

Θεόφαντος
MACEDONIA (MYGDONIA):
—THESSALONIKE: **(1)** s. ii BC *IG* X (2) (1) 27, 1 (f. *—ς*)
SCYTHIA MINOR:
—TOMIS: **(2)** i BC *ISM* II 2 B, 54 (Θεοφάνιος—ed. per err.: f. *Ἡδύλος*)
TAURIS:
—CHERSONESOS: **(3)** s. iv BC *IOSPE* I² 710 + Solomonik, *NEPKh* 172 (Θεόφα[ν]τος: s. *Ἀπήμαντος*); **(4)** iii BC ib. 32 (f. *Ἡρόφαντος*)
THRACE:
—BYZANTION (TERRIT.): **(5)** ii-iii AD *IByz* 181 (Θεόφαντο[ς]: f. *Μαρκιανός*)

Θεοφίλα

MACEDONIA (BOTTIAIA):
—BEROIA: **(1)** ii-iii AD *IBer* 249 (Tataki 559); **(2)** 212 AD *ILeukopetra* 61, 4 (—ία Θ.)
MACEDONIA (MYGDONIA):
—THESSALONIKE: **(3)** iii AD *IG* X (2) (1) 531, 6 (*Αἰλ. Θ.*)
THRACE:
—BYZANTION: **(4)** i BC *IByz* 164 (Fıratlı–Robert p. 107 no. 171) (d. *Φιλάδελφος*); **(5)** iii AD *IByz* 318 (Fıratlı–Robert pp. 121-2 no. 204) (*Αὐ[ρ.] Θεοφίλα ἡ καὶ Θεοτίμα*: d. *Αὐρ. Πόπλιος Θεόφιλος*)

Θεοφίλη

CIMMERIAN BOSPOROS:
—MYRMEKION: **(1)** m. i AD *CIRB* 881
—NYMPHAION: **(2)** i-ii AD ib. 933; cf. KW pl. 12 no. 160
—PANTIKAPAION: **(3)** i BC *CIRB* 309; cf. KW pl. 15 no. 219 (d. *Μᾶρκος*); **(4)** i AD *CIRB* 355 (d. *Ἀρεΐφιλος*); **(5)** ~ ib. 400 A; cf. KW pl. 50 no. 693 (?m. *Μαστοῦς*); **(6)** m. i AD *CIRB* 433 (m. *Κόλων*); **(7)** f. ii AD ib. 681 (d. *Ἡρακλείδης*)
—TYRITAKE: **(8)** i AD ib. 904
MACEDONIA (CHALKIDIKE):
—MENDE: **(9)** b. 317 BC *IG* II^2 9337 (Tataki, *Macedonians* p. 121 no. 12; *FRA* 3679) (d. *Σύμμαχος*)
THRACE:
—SERDICA: **(10)** ii AD *IGB* IV 1957, 3 (m. *Νικήτης, Ἀσκληπᾶς, Χρῆστος*)

Θεοφίλης

MACEDONIA (BOTTIAIA):
—ICHNAI: **(1)** imp. *AM* 27 (1902) p. 310 no. 16 (*Ὀρέστιος Θ.*)

Θεοφιλίσκος

CIMMERIAN BOSPOROS:
—PANTIKAPAION: **(1)** imp. *CIRB* 768 (f. *Τιμοκράτης*); **(2)** i AD ib. 337; **(3)** ~ ib. 407; **(4)** i/ii AD ib. 611 (s. *Θεόφιλος*)

Θεόφιλος

CIMMERIAN BOSPOROS:
—NYMPHAION: **(1)** f. iv BC ib. 924 (f. *Τελεσίας*)
—PANTIKAPAION: **(2)** i AD ib. 332; cf. KW pl. 46 no. 650 (s. *Ἀθήνιος, Ἀρέτη*); **(3)** ~ *CIRB* 429 (I f. *Θεόφιλος* II); **(4)** ~ ib. (II s. *Θεόφιλος* I); **(5)** ~ ib. 432 A; cf. KW pl. 27 no. 401 (s. *Ὀνήσιμος, Θεοδώρα*); **(6)** f. i AD *CIRB* 431 (s. *Βίων*); **(7)** m. i AD ib. 430 (s. *Καλλιγένης*); **(8)** ?s. i AD ib. 448; **(9)** i/ii AD ib. 611 (f. *Θεοφιλίσκος*); **(10)** ii AD ib. 92, 2; **(11)** 221 AD ib. 99, 15 (f. *Ἄρδαρος*); **(12)** 275-278 AD ib. 36, 34 (f. *Βάρβαρος*); **(13)** ~ ib. l. 68 (s. *Ἐμι—*); **(14)** ~ ib. l. 70 (*Θεόφιλ(ος)*: f. *Πάπ[ω]ν*); **(15)** f. iv AD ib. 65 (*Θεόφ[ιλ]ος*: s. *Πάτεις*: reading—Tokhtas'ev)
—PHANAGOREIA: **(16)** 304-284 BC ib. 974 (*[Θ]εόφιλο[ς]*: s. *Σάνχος*)
—THEODOSIA: **(17)** iii AD ib. 947 B, 6 (f. *Πάτειρος*)
MACEDONIA: **(18)** a. 306 BC *IG* XII (6) 25, 1, 3 (Tataki, *Macedonians* p. 327 no. 22) (f. *Θεοτιμίδης*); **(19)** ?i BC Bernand, *El-Kanaïs* 23 (Tataki, *Macedonians* p. 486 no. 135; La'da E1508) (s. *Ἱππόστρατος*)
MACEDONIA (BOTTIAIA):
—BEROIA: **(20)** f. i AD *IBer* 103, 4 (Tataki 560) (f. *Ἀλέξανδρος*); **(21)** 41-44 AD *IBer* 60, 3 (Tataki 606) (*[Γ.] [Π]ούλ. Θ.*)
—PELLA: **(22)** 15 BC *Pella* p. 79 no. 92 (Lat. M. Antonius Theophilus)
MACEDONIA (CHALKIDIKE):
—MENDE: **(23)** imp. *SEG* XXIX 615 (I f. *Θεόφιλος* II); **(24)** ~ ib. (II s. *Θεόφιλος* I)
MACEDONIA (EDONIS):
—AMPHIPOLIS: **(25)** ii-iii AD *Thrakika* 13 (1940) p. 28 *Ὦα* (*Τεό-*)

MACEDONIA (LYNKESTIS):
—HERAKLEIA: **(26)** i AD *IG* X (2) (2) 75, 24, 43 (s. *Ἀντίπατρος*, f. *Ἀντίπατρος*)
MACEDONIA (MYGDONIA):
—KALINDOIA: **(27)** 68-98 AD *SEG* XLII 581, 9 (s. *Μελάνθιος*)
—THESSALONIKE: **(28)** ?ii AD *IG* X (2) (1) 127, 1; **(29)** ii AD ib. 241 B, 3 (*[Θ]εόφιλ[ος]*: s. *Εὔπορος*); **(30)** ~ ib. 416, 3 (s. *Ἀντίγονος*); **(31)** 174-206 AD ib. 457, 2; **(32)** iii AD ib. 621, 4 (*Γ. Ἰ(ούλ). Θ.*: ?s. *Ἰουλ. Νιγερία*)
MACEDONIA (ORESTIS):
—SISANI (MOD.): **(33)** 146 AD *EAM* 187, 13 (s. *Ἀλέξανδρος*)
MACEDONIA (PAIONIA):
—STOBOI: **(34)** v-vi AD Feissel, *RICM* 281 (s. *Ζώπυρος*)
MACEDONIA (PIERIA):
—PYDNA: **(35)** 250 AD *SEG* XLVI 800 A, 16; 800 B, 5 (*Αὐρ. Θ.*: s. *Πιερίων*)
SARMATIA*: **(36)** i-ii AD *BPW* 1930, cols. 1006-7 (bronze)
SCYTHIA MINOR:
—ISTROS: **(37)** iii BC *ISM* I 114 (s. *Θεόδοτος*); **(38)** i BC-i AD ib. 189, 4 (*[Θ]εόφιλ[ος]*); **(39)** ~ ib. 191 II, 54 (f. *Διογένης*); **(40)** ~ ib. l. 20-1 (f. *Ἀριστόλαος, Εὐκλῆς*); **(41)** ii AD ib. 196, 7 (s. *Ἀλέξανδρος*); **(42)** 138 AD ib. 193 I, 15 (f. *Ἀριστολάϊος*); **(43)** ~ ib. l. 91 (f. *Ἀριστολάϊος*); **(44)** iii AD ib. 229, 7
—NOVIODUNUM (NR.): **(45)** 212-217 AD ib. V 249, 10 (*Eastern cults* p. 224 no. 9) (Lat. Theophilus: f. *Πολυδεύκης*)
—TOMIS: **(46)** iii-ii BC *AMNG* I (2) 2431-2; 2445 (coin) (*Θεόφι(λος)*); **(47)** i BC *ISM* II 2, 27 (s. *Νουμήνιος*) ?= (*48*); **(48)** ~ ib. 2 B, 49 (f. *Νουμήνιος*) ?= (*47*); **(49)** ii-iii AD ib. 468, 4 (I f. *Θεόφιλος* II); **(50)** ~ ib. l. 4 (II s. *Θεόφιλος* I)
SKYTHIA:
—OLBIA-BORYSTHENES: **(51)** ii AD *IOSPE* I^2 86, 6 (I f. *Θεόφιλος* II); **(52)** ~ ib. l. 6 (II s. *Θεόφιλος* I)
—TANAIS: **(53)** ii AD *CIRB* 1262, 27 (f. *Ὀμψάλακος*)
TAURIS:
—CHERSONESOS: **(54)** iv/iii BC Solomonik, *GAKh* 928 (vase); **(55)** iii BC *IOSPE* I^2 581, 2 (s. *Σκύθας*); **(56)** ii AD ib. 436, 5 (f. *Δημοτέλης*)
THRACE: **(57)** 178 BC *PFreib* 25, 6 (La'da E756) (*Θ[εό]φιλος*); **(58)** ~ *PFreib* 31, 7 (Velkov 132; La'da E755); **(59)** 158 BC *PHeid* VIII pp. 194-5 n. 70 (La'da E757)
—BYZANTION: **(60)** i BC-i AD *IByz* 19, 9 (*Καιπίων Θ.*); **(61)** ~ ib. 202 (Fıratlı–Robert p. 62 no. 51) (I f. *Θεόφιλος* II); **(62)** ~ *IByz* 202 (Fıratlı–Robert p. 62 no. 51) (II s. *Θεόφιλος* I); **(63)** i-ii AD *IByz* 29 (f. *—υσοῦς*)
——(Deutera): **(64)** iii AD ib. 318 (Fıratlı–Robert pp. 121-2 no. 204) (*Αὐρ. Πόπλιος Θ.*: f. *Αὐρ. Θεοφίλα ἡ καὶ Θεοτίμα*)
——(Kallichoritis): **(65)** iii AD *IByz* 320; cf. Fıratlı–Robert p. 165 (*[Αὐρ.] Θ.*: s. *Διογένης*)
—KELLAI (NR.): **(66)** ii-iii AD *IGB* III 1543
—MARONEIA: **(67)** ii-i BC *IThrakAig* E212, 13 (f. *Θεόπροπος*)
—MESAMBRIA: **(68)** iv-vi AD *SEG* XL 575 (*[Θ]εόφιλος*)
—NICOPOLIS AD NESTUM: **(69)** ii-iii AD *IGB* IV 2337, 2
—ODESSOS: **(70)** 215 AD ib. I^2 47 c, 12 (*Αὐρ. Θ.*: s. *Μένιππος*); **(71)** 221 AD ib. 47 bis a, 33 (f. *Αὐρ. Ζωπάκων*); **(72)** ~ ib. 47 bis b, 17 (f. *Αὐρ. Στράτων*); **(73)** ~ ib. l. 28 (*Αὐρ. Θ.*: s. *Μαρκιανός*); **(74)** 238 AD ib. 48, 6 (*Γ. Φλ. Θ.*: I ?f. *Γ. Φλ. Θεόφιλος* II); **(75)** ~ ib. l. 7 (*Γ. Φλ. Θ.*: II ?s. *Γ. Φλ. Θεόφιλος* I)
—PHILIPPOPOLIS-TRIMONTIUM (TERRIT.): **(76)** ii-iii AD ib. III 1124 (*[Θε]όφιλος*)

Θεοφόβιος

KOLCHIS:
—LAZOI: **(1)** 551 AD *PLRE* III (-); *RE* (1)

Θεόφραστος

MACEDONIA?: **(1)** 243 BC Plu., *Arat.* 23 (Tataki, *Macedonians* p. 327 no. 23)

Θεόφρων

SCYTHIA MINOR:
—KALLATIS: **(1)** iii BC *ISM* III 133, 3 (f. *Νικομήδης*)

Θεοχάρης

MACEDONIA (EDONIS):
—AMPHIPOLIS (NR.): **(1)** a. 357 BC Hatzopoulos, *Actes Amphipolis* p. 43 no. 8, 1 (*SEG* XLI 562) (*Θει-*: s. *Νικέας*)
TAURIS:
—CHERSONESOS: **(2)** c. 300-290 BC Anokhin p. 139 no. 81 (coin); **(3)** iii BC Solomonik, *NEPKh* 178 (*Θεοχά[ρ]ειος* (gen.): f. *Ξενοκλῆς*)

Θεόχαρις

MACEDONIA (EDONIS):
—AMPHIPOLIS: **(1)** i BC-i AD *SEG* XXVIII 536 (f. *Λαμπρώ*)
THRACE:
—AINOS?: **(2)** 208-211 AD *AEp* 1986, no. 628 (Lat. Theocharis: f. *Διογένης*)

Θεόχρηστος

THRACE: **(1)** 215 BC *BGU* 2383, 3, 8, 13-14 (La'da E758)

Θεράπων

THRACE:
—NOVAE: **(1)** f. ii AD *IGLNovae* 79 (*ILB* 307) (Lat. C. Vibius Therapo)

Θερίζων

MACEDONIA (EDONIS):
—PHILIPPOI: **(1)** ?ii AD *BCH* 61 (1937) p. 419 no. 13 (Pilhofer 386) (Lat. M. Annius Therizon)

Θερίνη

MACEDONIA (PIERIA):
—DION: **(1)** ?iii AD *Klio* 52 (1970) p. 53 no. 4 (d. *Ἔρως, Ῥώμη*)

Θερμόδων

MACEDONIA (MYGDONIA):
—THESSALONIKE (TERRIT.): **(1)** 208 AD *IG* X (2) (1) 1014

Θέρμος

MACEDONIA (BOTTIAIA):
—KYRRHOS: **(1)** m. iii AD *SEG* XXXV 750, 12 (*Αὐρ. Θ.*)

Θερσαγόρας

MACEDONIA (EDONIS):
—AMPHIPOLIS: **(1)** f. iii BC *IG* XI (4) 1349, 1, 7, 11 (Tataki, *Macedonians* p. 53 no. 64) (s. *Ἀθάμας*); **(2)** 192 BC *SEG* XLVI 716 B, 5 (*[Θερ]σαγόρας*?, *[Π]σαγόρας*—ed.)

Θέρσανδρος

MACEDONIA: **(1)** 68 BC *BGU* 1731, 1, 3-4, 8-9, 13-14, 16, 19 (Tataki, *Macedonians* p. 486 no. 136; La'da E1509) (s. *Ἀπολλώνιος*: katoikos)

Θερσίλοχος

MACEDONIA (BOTTIAIA):
—MIEZA: **(1)** hell. *AM* 27 (1902) p. 314 no. 28, 7 (*[Θε]ρσίλοχος*)

Θέρσιππος

CIMMERIAN BOSPOROS:
—NYMPHAION: **(1)** f. iii BC *SEG* XXXIX 701, 6
MACEDONIA?: **(2)** 333 BC Berve 368 ?= (*3*); **(3)** c. 320 BC *IG* XII (2) 645, 6, 12, 34, 49 (*OGIS* 4) ?= (*2*)

THRACE:
—LYSIMACHEIA: (**4**) s. iii BC *IOrop* 30, 3 (f. *Με—*)

Θερσίτης
MACEDONIA (EDONIS):
—AMPHIPOLIS: (**1**) hell.? *SEG* L 565 (f. *—ππος*)

Θεσσάλαρχος
MACEDONIA (EDONIS):
—AMPHIPOLIS?: (**1**) hell. ib. 562, 9 (s. *Ἀλέξ-ανδρος*)

Θεσσαλονίκη
MACEDONIA: (**1**) c. 350-295 BC Berve 370 (Tataki, *Macedonians* p. 327 no. 24); *IG* X (2) (1) 277 (d. *Φίλιππος* II, *Νικασίπολις* (Thessaly, Pherai), m. *Ἀλέξανδρος*, *Φίλιππος* IV, *Ἀντί-πατρος*)
MACEDONIA (BOTTIAIA):
—MIEZA: (**2**) f. ii BC *SEG* XLIII 414 (d. *Ἀ—*)
MACEDONIA (LYNKESTIS)?: (**3**) ii-iii AD *EAM* 159 b, 4 (*-νεί-*)
MACEDONIA (MYGDONIA):
—THESSALONIKE: (**4**) ii-iii AD *IG* X (2) (1) 341 (*Φλ. Θ.*)

Θεσσαλός
MACEDONIA (DERRIOPOS):
—STUBERRA: (**1**) f. iii AD ib. X (2) (2) 335 (f. *Ποσείδιππος*)
THRACE:
—MESAMBRIA: (**2**) s. iii BC *IGB* I² 308 ter, 7 (*Θεσσα[λός]*: f. *Ἀνταῖος*)
—ODESSOS: (**3**) s. iii BC ib. 36, 10 (s. *Ἀρτεμί-δωρος*); (**4**) ii BC ib. 122 (*[Θ]ε̣σσαλός*: f. *—σας*)

Θεστορίδης
SCYTHIA MINOR:
—ISTROS: (**1**) iii-ii BC Unp. (Avram, defixio) 4, 8 (*[Θ]ε̣στορίδη[ς]*?—ed., *[Ν]ε̣στορίδη[ς]*?)

Θέστωρ
THRACE:
—APOLLONIA-SOZOPOLIS: (**1**) s. v BC *IGB* I² 445 (s. *Ἀρτεμίδωρος*)

Θετίμα
MACEDONIA (BOTTIAIA):
—PELLA: (**1**) c. 380-350 BC *SEG* XLIII 434, 1, 2, 7; cf. XLVI 776

Θέτις
MACEDONIA (MYGDONIA):
—THESSALONIKE?: (**1**) i AD *IG* X (2) (1) 683
THRACE:
—RHAIDESTOS*: (**2**) imp. *CIL* III 729 (Lat. Thetis eadem Burgaena: m. *Περίνθιος*: slave?)

Θευγένης
MACEDONIA (CHALKIDIKE):
—POTIDAIA-KASSANDREIA: (**1**) c. 500-475 BC Marcadé I 29; *LSAG*² p. 369 no. 10 (date) (Tataki, *Macedonians* p. 169 no. 5) (*-νε̄ς*: s. *Πυθοκλῆς*)
—POTIDAIA-KASSANDREIA?: (**2**) v/iv BC *SEG* XLVI 794 + *AAA* 23-8 (1990-5) p. 269 no. 6 (*Θεαγένης*—*SEG* per err.: f. *Ἡρακλείδης*)
TAURIS:
—CHERSONESOS: (**3**) iv/iii BC *SEG* XXVIII 636 (f. *—α*)
THRACE:
—BYZANTION: (**4**) f. iii BC ib. XXIII 661 (f. *Νίκων*)

Θευγέτων
MACEDONIA (CHALKIDIKE):
—OLYNTHOS: (**1**) f. iv BC ib. XXIX 624 (f. *Κηφισόδωρος*)

Θευδᾶς
MACEDONIA (BOTTIAIA):
—EDESSA: (**1**) 51 AD ib. XLVI 744, 13 (Tataki, *Edessa* 123) (f. *Ἀπολλωνίδης*)
MACEDONIA (DERRIOPOS):
—STUBERRA: (**2**) 116 AD *IG* X (2) (2) 327, 36 (s. *Σωσίας*)
MACEDONIA (ODOMANTIKE):
—GAZOROS: (**3**) ii-iii AD *SEG* XXX 571 (Pilhofer 545)
—SIRRHA?: (**4**) iii AD *IGB* V 5931 (s. *Κόπρυλλος*)
MACEDONIA (TYMPHAIA):
—AGIOS GEORGIOS (MOD.): (**5**) imp. *EAM* 30 (freed.)

Θευδίας
MACEDONIA (DERRIOPOS):
—STUBERRA: (**1**) 74 AD *IG* X (2) (2) 326, 53 (f. *Ποσείδιππος*)

Θευδόσιος
THRACE:
—LYSIMACHEIA: (**1**) ?s. iii BC *FD* III (1) 430, 1 (f. *Διονύσιος*)

Θευδότη
MACEDONIA (BOTTIAIA):
—PELLA: (**1**) iii BC *SEG* L 611 bis

Θεύδοτος
MACEDONIA: (**1**) hell.? *SGDI* 1345 (Tataki, *Macedonians* p. 328 no. 26) (*Θεύ[δο]τος*)

Θεύδωρος
MACEDONIA (EDONIS):
—AMPHIPOLIS: (**1**) hell. Scrinzi 35; (**2**) iii BC *SGDI* 3062 (Tataki, *Macedonians* p. 53 no. 65)

Θεύκριτος
MACEDONIA (BOTTIAIA):
—AIGAI: (**1**) s. iv BC *SEG* XIV 477 = XXXV 793 (s. *Θευφάνης*)

Θευπρέπιος
THRACE:
—SERDICA*: (**1**) v-vi AD Beševliev 9 (Lat. Theuprepius: bp.)

Θεύτιμος
MACEDONIA (PIERIA):
—PYDNA: (**1**) iv BC *GRBS* 43 (2002-3) p. 115 no. 3, 2

Θευφάνης
MACEDONIA (BOTTIAIA):
—AIGAI: (**1**) s. iv BC *SEG* XIV 477 = XXXV 793 (f. *Θεύκριτος*) ?= (*2*); (**2**) ~ ib. XXVI 782 = XXXV 794 (f. *Θεόδωρος*) ?= (*1*)
THRACE:
—BYZANTION: (**3**) iii BC *IByz* 67 (Fıratlı–Robert p. 48 no. 5) (s. *Ἡράκων*)

Θεύχρηστος
MACEDONIA: (**1**) s. iv BC *IEph* 1433 (Tataki, *Macedonians* p. 328 no. 27) (s. *Φιλόξενος*)

Θέων
MACEDONIA: (**1**) 218 BC *PEnt* 32, 1 verso 2; 67, 1 (Tataki, *Macedonians* p. 328 no. 28; La'da E1764) (s. *Φίλιππος*: t.e.); (**2**) m. ii BC *BGU* 2423, 39 (Tataki, *Macedonians* p. 486 no. 139; La'da E1511) (s. *—ίδης*); (**3**) 145 BC *PPhrur-Diosk* 18, 44; (**4**) 92 BC *PTeb* 104, 34, 47 (Tataki, *Macedonians* p. 486 no. 138; La'da E1763) (s. *Πτολεμαῖος*: t.e.); (**5**) 73 BC *POxy* 3482, 3, 5, 10, 12, 16 etc. (Tataki, *Macedonians* p. 486 no. 137; La'da E1510) (s. *Ἀντί-οχος*: katoikos)
MACEDONIA (BOTTIAIA):
—EDESSA: (**6**) v/iv BC *AD* 24 (1969) Chron. p. 307 (vase)

MACEDONIA (PIERIA):
—PHILA?: (**7**) ?iii BC *RPh* 1911, pp. 133-4 no. 36, 123; cf. Helly, *L'État thessalien* pp. 319-20 (locn.) (s. *Ξεν—*)
SKYTHIA:
—TANAIS: (**8**) 244 AD *CIRB* 1287, 4 (*Θ[έ]ων*: s. *Φαζίναμος*)
THRACE:
—APROI: (**9**) iii AD *CIL* VI 32624 c, 17 (Lat. M. Aur. Theo)
—BYZANTION: (**10**) c. 200-175 BC *IG* XI (4) 779, 8; 780, 3, 7 (s. *Μενίσκος*); (**11**) 144 BC *ID* 2593, 42
—ODESSOS?: (**12**) imp. *IRhodPer* 267 with comm.
THRACE?: (**13**) 316-309 BC *IG* II² 1956, 39; *Ancient Macedonia* 5 p. 445 with n. 10 (date) (*FRA* 2540)

Θεωνίς
THRACE:
—SOSTRA: (**1**) iii AD *ILB* 263 (Lat. Aurelia Theonis)

Θεώνιχος
CIMMERIAN BOSPOROS:
—GORGIPPIA: (**1**) f. iii BC *CIRB* 1137 B II, 6 (s. *Λεύκων*)

Θεώνυμος
CIMMERIAN BOSPOROS:
—THEODOSIA: (**1**) iii AD ib. 947 B, 8 (*Θεών[υ]μος*: f. *Θ—*)

Θέωρος
MACEDONIA (CHALKIDIKE):
—APHYTIS: (**1**) ?351 BC *Α΄ Panell. Synedr. Epigr.* pp. 80-1, 26 (f. *Ἀριστοτέλης*)
—POTIDAIA-KASSANDREIA (TERRIT.): (**2**) f. iii AD *Tekmeria* 7 (2002) p. 168 (*Αὐφάτιος Θ.*: s. *Λούτιος Ἐπαφρόδιτος*)

Θηβαΐς
CIMMERIAN BOSPOROS:
—PANTIKAPAION: (**1**) ii BC *CIRB* 273; cf. KW pl. 14 no. 217 (d. *Θεόμνηστος*)
THRACE:
—ODESSOS: (**2**) ii/iii AD *IGB* I² 165 (PM 1702); *Dacia* 21 (1977) p. 161 (date) (d. *Ἕλλην*)

Θῆλυς
THRACE:
—SERDICA (TERRIT.): (**1**) ii-iii AD *AEMÖ* 10 (1886) pp. 238-9 no. 2, 12 (*.ηλυς*—apogr., *[Σ]ῆλυς*?—ed., *[Θ]ῆλυς*?)

Θηραμένης
MACEDONIA: (**1**) iv BC Arr., *An.* iii 5. 5 (Tataki, *Macedonians* p. 328 no. 30) (f. *Πολέμων*)

Θηρίμαχος
THRACE:
—BURDIPTA (NR.): (**1**) hell.? *BIAB* 11 (1937) p. 121 fig. 112 (sherd)

Θήρων
MACEDONIA (BOTTIAIA):
—GENDERRHOS? (MANDALON (MOD.)): (**1**) s. iv BC *SEG* XLIII 395 (s. *Δάμων*)
MACEDONIA (PAIONIA):
—STOBOI: (**2**) 232 AD *AJA* 75 (1971) p. 401; *BE* 1972, no. 256 a (slave?)
MACEDONIA (PIERIS):
—GALEPSOS: (**3**) hell.? Dimitsas 913; Hatzopoulos, *MI* 1 p. 187 n. 3 (locn.) (*Θ̣ήρων*: f. *Ἀπολλόδωρος*)
THRACE: (**4**) ii AD Apul., *Met.* vii 5 (Lat. Theron: f. *Αἶμος*: fict.)
—PERINTHOS-HERAKLEIA: (**5**) i BC *IG* XII (8) 186 b, 25

Θησεύς
MACEDONIA (BOTTIAIA):
—BEROIA: (**1**) ii/iii AD *IBer* 143 A, 26 (Tataki 607) (*Ἰού. Θ.*); (**2**) ~ *IBer* 211, 4 (Tataki 1058) (*Πετρωνιανὸς Θ.*); (**3**) 255 AD *IBer* 138, 7

(Tataki 1059) (*Πετρωνιανὸς Θησεὺς ὁ καὶ Ὀξύτερπος*)
MACEDONIA (ORESTIS):
—BATTYNAIOI: **(4)** 192 AD *EAM* 186 II, 43 (f. *Νικάνωρ*)
SCYTHIA MINOR:
—TROESMIS*: **(5)** f. ii AD *ISM* V 189, 7 (Lat. G. Iulius Theseus: freed.)
THRACE: **(6)** ?ii AD *IG* XII (9) 1196, 2, 9 ([*Γ.*] *Κουρ. Θ.*)
—PERINTHOS-HERAKLEIA: **(7)** i-ii AD *IPerinth* 208 (Lat. Theseus)

Θήσκεια?
MACEDONIA (PIERIA):
—DION: **(1)** iv AD *SEG* XXXIX 586, 1 (*Θ(ρ)ήσκεια?*, *Θ(ν)ήσκεια?*, *Θήσ<κ>εια?*: m. *Πολυνίκη*)

Θιάβωγος
SKYTHIA:
—TANAIS: **(1)** 244 AD *CIRB* 1287, 21 (s. *Σιώμαχος*)

Θιάγαρος
CIMMERIAN BOSPOROS:
—BOSPOROS: **(1)** imp.? *Probl. ant. ist. kult.* p. 543 n. 17 (vase)
SKYTHIA:
—TANAIS: **(2)** 220 AD *CIRB* 1278, 6; Zgusta, *PNS* 293 (s. *Ἀντισθένης*); **(3)** ~ *CIRB* 1278, 21 (s. *Μίδαχος*)

Θιαθιοῦς
THRACE:
—ODESSOS: **(1)** ii AD *IGB* I^{2} 185 (d. *Ἀπελλᾶς*)

Θιάρμακος
SKYTHIA:
—TANAIS: **(1)** 244 AD *CIRB* 1287, 10 (*Θιάσμακος?*—Tokhtas'ev: s. *Χρύσιππος*)

Θίας
THRACE:
—ODESSOS: **(1)** 221 AD *IGB* I^{2} 47 bis c, 20 (*Αὐρ. Θ.*: s. *Ἑστιαῖος*)

Θίβρων
CIMMERIAN BOSPOROS:
—HERMONASSA: **(1)** iv BC *CIRB* 1056 II, 15 (f. *Νίκων*)

Θίθα
THRACE:
—BYZANTION?: **(1)** hell.-imp. *IByz* 342 (d. *Ἀπολλώνιος*)

Θιθι
THRACE:
—MARKIANOPOLIS (TERRIT.): **(1)** iii-iv AD *IGB* V 5328, 4 (*CCET* II (1) 365) (d. *Τάρας*)

Θιθίς
SCYTHIA MINOR:
—TOMIS: **(1)** ii-iii AD *ISM* II 307, 4 (*Θιθίσαττα*—ed.: ?d. *Ἄττας*, m. *Ὀνεράτμις*, *Ἄττας*, *Σοζίμιος*)
THRACE:
—ODESSOS: **(2)** m. ii AD *IGB* I^{2} 174 (PM 1726); *Dacia* 21 (1977) p. 161 (date) (*Θηθείσ-*: d. *Ἀσκληπιάδης*)

Θίντας
THRACE:
—PAUTALIA (TERRIT.): **(1)** ii-iii AD *IGB* V 5827

Θίντος
THRACE:
—SERDICA: **(1)** ii-iii AD ib. IV 1963, 5 (*GVI* 386) (f. *Ἐπτησυκος*)
—SERDICA (TERRIT.): **(2)** ii-iii AD *IGB* IV 2004 (f. *Δίζας*)

Θιοδιξας
THRACE:
—SERDICA: **(1)** ii-iii AD ib. 1922, 2

Θιούθιος
SCYTHIA MINOR?: **(1)** imp. *CCET* IV 189 (f. *Δέσζων*)

Θιούτη
MACEDONIA (EDONIS):
—PHILIPPOI (TERRIT.): **(1)** ii-iii AD Pikoulas, *Chora* p. 123 no. 13, 7 + *BE* 2002, no. 291 (*Θει-*, *Σκαρουθειου τῇ*—ed.)

Θίρθαγος
SKYTHIA:
—OLBIA-BORYSTHENES: **(1)** ii AD *IOSPE* I^{2} 685, 5, 11 + *VDI* 1975 (1), p. 71 (f. *Σιουάραγος*)

Θόας
CIMMERIAN BOSPOROS:
—GORGIPPIA: **(1)** f. iii BC *CIRB* 1137 A I, 37 (f. *Προμαθίων*); **(2)** ~ ib. 1137 B I, 59; 1137 B II, 42 (f. *Θεότιμος*)
SCYTHIA MINOR:
—ISTROS: **(3)** v/iv BC *ISM* I 233 (s. *Ἡρόδοτος*)
THRACE:
—LYSIMACHEIA: **(4)** ii BC *IG* II^{2} 9228 (*FRA* 3395)
THRACE?: **(5)** 316-309 BC *IG* II^{2} 1956, 13; *Ancient Macedonia* 5 p. 445 with n. 10 (date) (*FRA* 2541)

Θοθόρσης
CIMMERIAN BOSPOROS:
—BOSPOROS: **(1)** 285-308 AD Frolova, *CKB A.D. 242-341/342* pp. 33-50 (coins) (king)

Θουθεus
THRACE:
—ODESSOS: **(1)** 221 AD *IGB* I^{2} 47 bis c, 39 (*Αὐρ. Θ.*: s. *Ἀπελλᾶς*)

Θουθελων
THRACE:
—ODESSOS: **(1)** ii AD ib. 50 a, 13 (*Διονύσιος ὁ κὲ Θ.*: II s. *Διονύσιος* I)

Θούλης
THRACE:
—APOLLONIA-SOZOPOLIS: **(1)** ii BC *IG* II^{2} 8350-1; cf. Robert, *Hell.* 11-12 pp. 376-7 (ethn.) (f. *Ἐργασίων*)

Θούριππος
MACEDONIA (MYGDONIA):
—BORMISKOS?: **(1)** f. iii BC *SEG* XLIX 844. 3-15; *BE* 1996, no. 270 (locn.)

Θραικίδα
MACEDONIA (PAIONIA):
—STOBOI*: **(1)** imp. *JÖAI* 6 (1903) Beibl. col. 9 no. 12; Detschev p. 206 (name) (Lat. –rtilia Thraecida (nom.?): freed.)

Θρᾶιξ
THRACE:
—MARONEIA: **(1)** iii BC *IG* II^{2} 9287 (*FRA* 3541) (s. *Γέτας*)

Θρᾶισσα
THRACE: **(1)** iii BC Herod. i [1], 79 (*Θρέϊσσα* (n. pr.?): slave/fict.); **(2)** 153-144 BC *SGDI* 1694, 3, 5, 7-8, 11-13 + *SEG* XXII 487 (*Θρᾶισα*—ll. 12-13: slave/freed.)

Θρᾶιττα
THRACE: **(1)** m. iv BC D. lix 35; 120; 124 (n. pr.?: slave?)
—MARONEIA: **(2)** i BC-i AD *IG* II^{2} 9288 (*FRA* 3542) (d. *Ἀνδράβυς*)

Θρακίδας
CIMMERIAN BOSPOROS:
—TYRITAKE: **(1)** i BC/i AD *CIRB* 905 (*Θρακί(δ)ας*: I s. *Θρακίδας* II); **(2)** ~ ib. (*Θρακί(δ)ας*: II s. *Θρακίδας* I)

Θρακίδης
CIMMERIAN BOSPOROS:
—PANTIKAPAION: **(1)** f. i AD ib. 435

Θρασέας
MACEDONIA: **(1)** m. iii BC *IG* XI (4) 585, 3; *ZPE* 89 (1991) p. 151 (stemma) (Tataki, *Macedonians* p. 328 no. 31) (s. *Βάλαγρος*)
THRACE:
—HERAION TEICHOS?: **(2)** ii-i BC Taşlıklıoğlu 2 p. 93 no. 1 (f. (ad.) *Αὐλούπορις*)

Θράσιππος
MACEDONIA (EORDAIA?):
—EUIA?: **(1)** 171 BC *RE* Supplbd. 7 (4) (Tataki, *Macedonians* p. 106 no. 1) (Lat. Thrasippus)

Θρασύβουλος
SKYTHIA:
—OLBIA-BORYSTHENES: **(1)** s. iv BC *IOSPE* I^{2} 166; **(2)** ?ii-i BC Dubois, *IGDOlbia* 110, 6; **(3)** imp. *IOSPE* I^{2} 113, 7 (*-σί-*: f. *Θρασύλληος*); **(4)** ii AD ib. 96, 5 (f. *Φλίμναγος*); **(5)** c. 193-211 AD ib. 42, 1; 43, 2 (s. *Φλίμναγος*)
THRACE:
—PERINTHOS-HERAKLEIA:
——(Basileidai): **(6)** s. iii BC *IPerinth* 62, 2 (s. *Διονύσιος*)

Θρασυδαῖος
TAURIS:
—CHERSONESOS: **(1)** 359 BC *CID* II 5 I, 9 (s. *Βίων*)

Θρασυδάμας
SKYTHIA:
—OLBIA-BORYSTHENES: **(1)** f. iv BC *IOSPE* I^{2} 24, 3 (*IKalch* 16; Dubois, *IGDOlbia* 14) (f. *Κάνωβος*); **(2)** iii BC *IOlbia* 72, 1 (f. *Θεοκλῆς*); **(3)** ~ *IOSPE* I^{2} 201 I, 24 (s. *Ἀρίστων*)

Θρασυκλῆς
MACEDONIA (BOTTIAIA):
—BEROIA: **(1)** s. iii BC *IBer* 16 B, 16 (f. *Θράσων*)
SCYTHIA MINOR:
—ISTROS: **(2)** iii BC *ISM* I 8, 3 (f. *Διόδωρος*)

Θρασύλαος
MACEDONIA (CHALKIDIKE):
—OLYNTHOS: **(1)** ?352 BC *TAPA* 62 (1931) p. 50 no. 3, 4 (f. *Ἐπιθέρσης*)
—POTIDAIA-KASSANDREIA (TERRIT.)?: **(2)** ii BC ib. 69 (1938) p. 69 no. 25 (f. *Πολύαρος*)

Θρασύλληος
SKYTHIA:
—OLBIA-BORYSTHENES: **(1)** imp. *IOSPE* I^{2} 113, 7 (*Θρασ(ύ)λληος*: s. *Θρασύβουλος*)

Θράσυλλος
CIMMERIAN BOSPOROS:
—GORGIPPIA: **(1)** f. iii BC *CIRB* 1137 B II, 57 (s. *Γόργος*)
—NYMPHAION: **(2)** iii BC ib. 912 II, 7 (f. *Ἀριστόκριτος*)

Θρασύλοχος
TAURIS:
—CHERSONESOS: **(1)** ii/iii AD Solomonik, *NEPKh* 57 ([*Θρ*]*ασύ*[*λοχο*]*ς*?: f. *Ἀριστόλοχος*)

Θρασύμαχος
THRACE:
—BYZANTION: **(1)** c. 250-220 BC Schönert-Geiss, *Byzantion* 996 (coin) (*Θρασύμμαγ*[*ος*])

Θρασυμήδης
CIMMERIAN BOSPOROS:
—BOSPOROS: **(1)** s. iv BC *IG* II^{2} 8429 (*FRA* 1373) (f. *Καλλίλεως*)

SCYTHIA MINOR:
—TOMIS: (**2**) ii-iii AD *ISM* II 31 II, 6 (I f. *Θρασυμήδης* II); (**3**) ~ ib. l. 6 ([Θ]ρασυμήδης: II s. *Θρασυμήδης* I); (**4**) ~ ib. l. 7 ([Θ]ρασυμήδης: s. *Χρυσωμ.*); (**5**) ~ ib. 468, 10 (*Θρασυμήδης?*, *Κασυμήδης*—ed.: s. *Δημοσθένης*)
THRACE:
—ABDERA?: (**6**) v-iv BC *IThrakAig* E486 (s. *Μήτρων*)

Θράσυς
THRACE:
—ABDERA: (**1**) c. 415-395 BC May, *Abdera* p. 170 no. 227 (coin)

Θράσων
CIMMERIAN BOSPOROS:
—MYRMEKION (NR.): (**1**) ?i AD *CIRB* 890 (s. *Θαρσικλῆς*)
—PANTIKAPAION: (**2**) imp. ib. 793 (*Θρ[ά]σων*: s. *Ἥλιος*)
MACEDONIA (BOTTIAIA):
—BEROIA: (**3**) s. iii BC *IBer* 16 B, 16 (s. *Θρασυκλῆς*)
—EDESSA: (**4**) ii BC Dimitsas 557 = *SEG* XLIX 827; cf. *ZPE* 132 (2000) pp. 161-2 (locn.) (Tataki, *Edessa* 124) (or Macedonia (Mygdonia) Thessalonike: s. *Ἀρχέλαος*); (**5**) ~ Dimitsas 557 = *SEG* XLIX 827; cf. *ZPE* 132 (2000) pp. 161-2 (locn.) (Tataki, *Edessa* 125) (or Macedonia (Mygdonia) Thessalonike: s. *Δίμνος*)
MACEDONIA (CHALKIDIKE):
—MENDE: (**6**) v/iv BC *SEG* XXIX 613
—OLYNTHOS: (**7**) m. iv BC *IG* II^2 10019 (Tataki, *Macedonians* p. 138 no. 67; *FRA* 5898) (f. *Ἀσκληπιόδωρος*)
—POTIDAIA-KASSANDREIA: (**8**) c. 300 BC *IG* II^2 1956, 113 (Tataki, *Macedonians* p. 91 no. 51; *FRA* 2788)
—SKABLA?: (**9**) imp. *SEG* XXIX 619; cf. Hatzopoulos, *Actes Chalc.* p. 71 (locn.) (?f. *Τραλίπορις*)
MACEDONIA (DERRIOPOS):
—STUBERRA: (**10**) 74 AD *IG* X (2) (2) 325, 55 (f. *Ὀρέστης*)
MACEDONIA (LYNKESTIS):
—HERAKLEIA: (**11**) f. ii AD ib. 73 (*Γ. Μάριος Βλοσσιανὸς Θ.*)
MACEDONIA (MYGDONIA):
—THESSALONIKE: (**12**) ii-iii AD Nalpantis, *Anaskaphi* p. 110 no. BE 115; (**13**) 137-161 AD *Makedonika* 9 (1969) pp. 143-4 (*Γν. Δομίτιος Θ.*)
—THESSALONIKE?: (**14**) iii AD *IG* X (2) (1) 859, 2, 5 (f. *Μέμμιος, Δημοκράτης*)
MACEDONIA (PIERIA):
—PYDNA: (**15**) iv BC *GRBS* 43 (2002-3) p. 111 no. 2, 4 (s. *Νίκυλλα*)
THRACE:
—AINOS: (**16**) c. 208 BC *FD* III (4) 135 II, 17 (f. *Δημήτριος*)
—AINOS*: (**17**) imp. *SEG* XXXVIII 728 (terracotta) (*Θράσσονος* (gen.))
—BYZANTION: (**18**) s. iv BC *IG* II^2 8438 (*FRA* 1394) (f. *Ἀπολλόδωρος*); (**19**) c. 325-300 BC *IByz* 89 (Fıratlı–Robert p. 90 no. 117) (s. *Νίκων*); (**20**) iv/iii BC *IByz* 58 (Fıratlı–Robert p. 47 no. 2) (s. *Κεφαλίων*); (**21**) c. 315-280 BC *FD* III (4) 150, 1 (*Θρά[σ]ων*: f. *Σωχάρης*); (**22**) s. iii BC Schönert-Geiss, *Byzantion* 1131-4 (coin)
—BYZANTION (TERRIT.): (**23**) hell.-imp. *IByz* 185
—MARONEIA: (**24**) ii-i BC *IThrakAig* E212, 53 (f. *Μενεκράτης*)
—ZONE: (**25**) f. iv BC Bakalakis, *Oinos Ismarikos* p. 710 (*IThrakAig* E413) (f. *Ἀρτεμίστη*)

Θρεπτίων
MACEDONIA (MYGDONIA):
—THESSALONIKE: (**1**) b. 268 AD *IG* X (2) (1) 238, 4 (*Αὐρ. Θ.*)

Θρέπτος
TAURIS:
—CHERSONESOS*: (**1**) ii AD *IOSPE* I^2 562, 6 (Solomonik, *LNKhT* 13) (Lat. [P.] Vedius [Th]reptus: freed./doctor)

Θρέσσα
MACEDONIA (MYGDONIA):
—KALINDOIA: (**1**) ?255 AD *SEG* XLII 603 b with comm. + *Anthémonte–Kalindoia* 2 p. 371 (n. pr.?)

Θυαίας
CIMMERIAN BOSPOROS:
—PANTIKAPAION: (**1**) ?i AD *CIRB* 536; Zgusta, *PNS* 1026 (*Θυαιου* (gen.): f. *Χαρικλῆς*)

Θυάνης
KOLCHIS:
—MISIMIANOI: (**1**) 556 AD *PLRE* III (-); *RE* (-)

Θυηζάνης
KOLCHIS:
—SUKHUMI (MOD.): (**1**) ii AD *Stud. Orbeli* pp. 99-100 (gem) + Braund, *Georgia* p. 196 fig. 14 (*Οὐηζάνης*—ed. pr.)

Θύλης?
THRACE:
—STROUNEILOS: (**1**) 202 AD *IGB* III 1690 d, 66 (and Thrace Pizos: *Θύλης?*: s. *Ἀπολλόδωρος*)

Θυλόγανος
SKYTHIA:
—TANAIS: (**1**) 225 AD *CIRB* 1280, 5 (*Καλλισθένης ὁ καὶ Θ.*: s. *Πάππος*)

Θυμέλη
MACEDONIA (BOTTIAIA):
—BEROIA: (**1**) ii-iii AD *IBer* 250 (Tataki 563)
MACEDONIA (MYGDONIA):
—THESSALONIKE: (**2**) i AD *IG* X (2) (1) 418, 4 (m. *Γν. Ἰούλ. Ἀρτεμᾶς, Ἰουλ. Δύναμις*)

Θῦμος
MACEDONIA: (**1**) 182 BC *PMich* 182, 4, 15, 30; 183, 2, 10 (Tataki, *Macedonians* p. 329 no. 33; La'da E1765) (s. *Μεγακλῆς*: t.e.)

Θυόδοτος
MACEDONIA (PAIONIA):
—STOBOI: (**1**) ii-iii AD *Sp.* 71 (1931) p. 242 no. 644, 2 (?f. *Ἐπίκτησις*) ?= (*2*); (**2**) ~ ib. l. 5 (s. *Νίκων*, ?f. *Νικίας*) ?= (*1*)

Θύρσις
MACEDONIA (DERRIOPOS):
—STUBERRA: (**1**) c. 180 BC Liv. xl 24. 7 (Lat. Thursis)

Θύρσος
MACEDONIA (MYGDONIA):
—THESSALONIKE: (**1**) s. i AD *IG* X (2) (1) 68, 45; 69, 33 (*Μ. Μουτίλιος Θ.*, *Θ(ύρ)σος*—68); (**2**) s. ii AD ib. 244 I, 12 (*Ἀβούδιος Θ.*)
—THESSALONIKE*: (**3**) ii/iii AD ib. 723, 1, 6 (biling.) (*Λ. Αὔιος Θ.*: freed.)
THRACE:
—HERAION TEICHOS: (**4**) hell.? Peek, *AG* 2 p. 24 no. 60, 1; *BE* 1958, no. 206 (locn.); cf. *LGPN* IIIA (1) (per err.) (*Θύ[ρ]σος*)

Θῦς
CIMMERIAN BOSPOROS:
—PANTIKAPAION: (**1**) s. iv BC *CIRB* 189; Zgusta, *PNS* 746 (s. *Ἀτώτης*)
TAURIS:
—KALOS LIMEN*: (**2**) ii BC Solomonik, *GChKh* 456 (vase); cf. *SEG* XXXVIII 749. 9 (or Pontos Sinope: f. *Μαιδάτης*)

Θχήτλεις
CIMMERIAN BOSPOROS:
—GORGIPPIA?: (**1**) s. ii AD *CIRB* 1231 B, 8; Zgusta, *PNS* 654 (s. *Νίχεκος*); (**2**) ~ *CIRB* 1231 B, 11 (*Θχ(ή)τλεις*: s. *Ἀθην*—)

Θωμᾶς
MACEDONIA (MYGDONIA):
—THESSALONIKE?: (**1**) iv-v AD *IG* X (2) (1) 788, 2 (Feissel, *RICM* 177) (s. *Εὐάγγελος*)
THRACE:
—PAUTALIA: (**2**) v-vi AD Beševliev 37
—SALYMBRIA: (**3**) vi AD *BCH* 36 (1912) pp. 635-6 no. 92 (*AD* 53 (1998) Mel. p. 477 no. 219) (f. *Μαρκελλῖνος*)

Θῶραξ
SKYTHIA:
—TANAIS: (**1**) 104 AD *CIRB* 1259, 17 (s. *Γάστεις*)

I

Ἰα
Macedonia (Chalkidike):
—potidaia-kassandreia (territ.): (1) iii-iv ad *SEG* xxix 577 (Ἰα)

Ἰααθιθις?
Thrace:
—odessos: (1) ii ad *IGB* I^2 133 (d. Ἀπολλώνιος)

Ἰαδαάκης?
Cimmerian Bosporos:
—pantikapaion: (1) v/iv bc *CIRB* 154 (Ἰαδαάκεος (gen.)—lap., Ἰαδα(τ)άκης?—Boltunova, Ἰαδ(ν)άκης?—Vinogradov: f. Μίδας)

Ἰαδώ
Thrace:
—odessos: (1) ?ii ad *IGB* I^2 115, 4 (-αδών: d. Ἀρτεμίδωρος); (2) m. ii ad ib. 176 ter (PM 1693); *Dacia* 21 (1977) p. 161 (date) (d. Ἡφαιστίων)

Ἰαθίς
Thrace:
—odessos (nr.): (1) ii-iii ad *IGB* I^2 256 (PM 1695) (d. Κόνων)

Ἰαιος?
Cimmerian Bosporos:
—gorgippia: (1) m. ii ad *Eirene* 7 (1968) p. 67, 15 ((Γ)άϊος?: f. —δωρος) ?= (*2*); (2) 173-210 ad *CIRB* 1135, 23 ((Γ)άϊος?—edd.: f. Μοιρόδωρος) ?= (*1*)

Ἰακησινάρις
Thrace:
—philippopolis-trimontium (territ.): (1) iii ad *IGB* III 1141 (?s. Αὐρ. Μουκιανός)

Ἴακχος
Macedonia (Mygdonia):
—thessalonike: (1) iii ad *IG* x (2) (1) 486, 7 (Αἴλ. Ἴαχχος)

Ἰακώβ
Macedonia (Mygdonia):
—thessalonike: (1) s. iii ad *SEG* xliv 556, 1 (*M. Αὐρ. Ἰ. ὁ καὶ Εὐτύχιος*: Jew)

Ἰαμάς
Scythia Minor:
—tomis: (1) ii-iii ad *ISM* II 204 (Ἰαμάτι (dat.))

Ἰάμαχος
Tauris:
—chersonesos: (1) inc. *SEG* xxxviii 749. 1 (vase)
—chersonesos (territ.): (2) ii-iii ad *SKhM* 3 (1963) p. 13; cf. Solomonik, *GChKh* p. 7 no. 6 (s. Σώμαχος)

Ἰάμβλιχος
Skythia:
—tyras*: (1) 116 ad *VDI* 1959 (4), p. 117 no. 6 (Lat. Iul. Iamblic(us))

Ἰάμβλοχος
Cimmerian Bosporos:
—pantikapaion: (1) ii ad *CIRB* 795 (f. Νικοξενία, Μάστας) ?= (*2*); (2) f. ii ad ib. 682 (s. Διονύσιος, f. Φάννας) ?= (*1*)

Ἰάμνεια
Macedonia?: (1) 243-195 bc *PP* 5151; cf. Clarysse–van der Veken p. 10 no. 48; p. 20 no. 96 (d. Ὑπερβάσσας)

Ἰάν
Macedonia (Mygdonia):
—chalastra?: (1) v bc *SEG* xlvi 724 (vase) (Ἴανος (gen.))

Ἰάνγελος
Skythia:
—olbia-borysthenes: (1) ?ii-iii ad *IOSPE* I^2 107, 3; Zgusta, *PNS* 295 (f. —ος)

Ἰανουαρία
Macedonia (Bottiaia):
—beroia*: (1) s. ii ad *IBer* 379 (Tataki 573a) (Ἰουανα-: d. Πλάτανος (Other))
Scythia Minor:
—tomis: (2) iii-iv ad *ISM* II 384, 16 (Barnea 1; Popescu, *IGL* 18); cf. *SEG* xlviii 980 (-βα-: m. Λιλλᾶς); (3) v-vi ad Barnea 8 (Ειεν[ουαρία])
Thrace:
—nicopolis ad istrum (territ.): (4) ii ad *IGB* v 5244 a, 12 (Ἰανουα[ρ]ία: d. Αὐγουστάλιος)

Ἰανουάριος
Thrace: (1) 149 ad Dumont–Homolle 110b, 8 (painter)

Ἴαραξ
Tauris:
—chersonesos: (1) iv bc Solomonik, *GAKh* 947 (vase)

Ἰαρώνυμος
Thrace:
—byzantion: (1) f. iii bc *IG* xi (4) 627, 12 ([Ἱε]ρώνυμος: f. Διονύσιος)

Ἰάς
Sarmatia:
—maiotai: (1) iv bc ib. II^2 9253 (*FRA* 3451) (slave?)

Ἰᾶς
Cimmerian Bosporos:
—gorgippia: (1) ii ad *CIRB* 1140, 3 (s. Πόσις); (2) ii/iii ad ib. 1179, 57 (f. —άτης); (3) ~ ib. 1180, 4 (s. Τιμο—)

Ἰασανδάνακος
Skythia:
—tanais: (1) 244 ad ib. 1287, 30 (Ἰασα[ν]δάνακος: s. Ἰαύακος)

Ἰασιεύς?
Scythia Minor:
—kallatis: (1) iv bc *SEG* xxxv 1356, 3 (Ἰασίεος (gen.): f. Σάτυρος)

Ἰασικλῆς
Tauris:
—chersonesos: (1) m. v bc ib. xl 612. 4 (ostrakon) (s. Νεομήνιος)

Ἰασίμαχος
Cimmerian Bosporos:
—gorgippia: (1) f. iii bc *CIRB* 1137 B II, 44 (Ἰασίμαχ[ος]: f. Σωσίπατρος)

Ἰασόνικος
Macedonia (Bottiaia):
—beroia: (1) 239-229 bc *IBer* 45, 30 (-νει-)

Ἰάσων
Macedonia: (1) 218 bc *RE* (4) (Tataki, *Macedonians* p. 329 no. 1)
Macedonia (Mygdonia):
—thessalonike?: (2) m. i ad *Ep. Rom.* 16. 21 ?= (*3*); (3) ~ *Act. Ap.* 17. 5 ff. (Tataki, *Macedonians* p. 183 no. 34) ?= (*2*)
Macedonia (Pieria):
—dion: (4) imp. *SEG* xxxiv 626
Scythia Minor:
—tomis: (5) ii ad *ISM* II 186 (f. Ῥουφῖνα)
Tauris:
—chersonesos: (6) f. ii ad Solomonik, *NEPKh* III, 3 (Ἰά[σ]ων?); (7) iii ad *IOSPE* I^2 479 (*M. Αὐρ. Ἰ.*: s. *M. Ἀρχίας*)
Thrace:
—bjala slatina (mod.): (8) f. iii ad *CIL* III 12388 (*Romanizmăt* II 27) (Lat. M. Aur. Iaso)
—byzantion: (9) ii-i bc *IByz* 220 (Firatlı–Robert pp. 78-9 no. 89) (Εἰ-: s. Ἀπολλώνιος); (10) hell.-imp. *RE* (9); *FGrH* I Add. p. 10
—ergissenoi: (11) ii ad *IGB* III 1593, 10 (Φλ. Ἰ.); (12) ~ ib. l. 20-1 (f. Ἀσιατικός, Δορζένθης)
—galini (mod.): (13) i bc-i ad *SEG* xxxv 740 (*IThrakAig* E385)
—pautalia (territ.): (14) ii-iii ad *IGB* v 5791 (Ἰούλ. Ἰ.)

Ἰατροκλῆς
Macedonia: (1) 61 or 57 bc *BGU* 1772, 8, 31 (Tataki, *Macedonians* p. 486 no. 140; La'da E1512) (s. Ἡράκλειτος: katoikos)
Macedonia (Edonis):
—philippoi: (2) s. iii bc *IG* vii 2433 II, 5 (Tataki, *Macedonians* p. 164 no. 16) (-κλεῖς: s. Μιννίων)
Scythia Minor:
—kallatis: (3) ii/i bc *AMNG* I (1) 262 (coin monogram) (Ἰατρ(οκλῆς)); (4) s. i ad *ISM* III 32, 8 (f. Ἰσαγόρας)

Ἰαύακος
Skythia:
—tanais: (1) 244 ad *CIRB* 1287, 30; Zgusta, *PNS* 114 (Ναύακος?, (Σ)ιαύακος?: f. Ἰασανδάνακος)

Ἰάφαγος
Skythia:
—olbia-borysthenes: (1) iii ad *IOSPE* I^2 98, 12; Zgusta, *PNS* 115 (s. Πίδεις)

Ἰβάδα
Cimmerian Bosporos:
—kytaia (nr.): (1) ii ad *CIRB* 945 (m. Σαγόδας)

Ἴβουβας?
Thrace:
—markianopolis: (1) iii ad *IGB* II 802 (Ἴβουβα (gen.), Βουβᾶς?: f. Αὐρ. Ἀλέξανδρος)

Ἰγδαμπαίης
Skythia:
—olbia-borysthenes: (1) c. 490-470 bc Dubois, *IGDOlbia* 77 (vase); cf. Vinogradov, *Pont. Stud.* p. 154 no. 3 bis (name)

Ἰγνατία
Macedonia (Mygdonia):
—thessalonike?: (1) ii-iii ad *IG* x (2) (1) 729 (Εἰ-: m. Κλ. Οὐάλης)

Ἰδαῖος
Macedonia (Paionia):
—kavadarci (mod.): (1) ?ii-i bc *SEG* xlvii 946 (n. pr.?)
Thrace?: (2) iii-ii bc Breccia, *Iscriz.* 302 (Velkov 157; La'da E760)

Ἰδάνθεμις
Skythia:
—olbia-borysthenes (berezan (mod.)): (1) m. vi bc Dubois, *IGDOlbia* 27 (vase); cf. Vinogradov, *Pont. Stud.* p. 152 no. 1 (name) (Ἰδανθέμι (dat.))

Ἰδάνθυρσος
SKYTHIA:
—SKYTHAI: (**1**) s. vi BC Hdt. iv 76; 120; 126-7 (s. *Σαύλιος*: king)

Ἴδας
MACEDONIA (EDONIS):
—AMPHIPOLIS: (**1**) iii BC *SEG* XXVII 250 (*Ἴδας*?, *[Μ]ίδας*?—Mihailov, *[Κ]ύδας*?: s. *Μιθροδάτης*)

Ἰδάτας
MACEDONIA: (**1**) ?417-413 BC *IG* I³ 89, 66 (Tataki, *Macedonians* p. 330 no. 3)

Ἴδη
MACEDONIA (MYGDONIA):
—THESSALONIKE: (**1**) ii-iii AD *Makedonika* 14 (1974) p. 375 (*Κλ. Εἴδη*)

Ἰδήρατος
MACEDONIA (CHALKIDIKE):
—SKIONE: (**1**) f. iv BC *IG* II² 10366 (Tataki, *Macedonians* p. 173 no. 6; *FRA* 6905) (s. *Καλλίας*)

Ἰδιβλων
THRACE:
—ODESSOS: (**1**) i BC *IGB* I² 148 (PM 165)

Ἴδιος
CIMMERIAN BOSPOROS:
—PANTIKAPAION: (**1**) iv BC *AA* 1893, p. 93 (vase)

Ἰέζδαγος
SKYTHIA:
—OLBIA-BORYSTHENES: (**1**) ?ii-iii AD *IOSPE* I² 111, 8; Zgusta, *PNS* 113 (*Ἰέζδαγ[ος]*: f. *—ος*)

Ἰέζδραδος
SKYTHIA:
—OLBIA-BORYSTHENES: (**1**) ii-iii AD *IOSPE* I² 137, 9; Zgusta, *PNS* 113 (f. *Βάδαγος*)

Ἱεράγων
MACEDONIA (EDONIS):
—AMPHIPOLIS: (**1**) iv BC *SEG* XLII 555 (s. *Φιλόνικος*)

Ἱέραξ
MACEDONIA (BOTTIAIA):
—BEROIA: (**1**) i/ii AD *IBer* 35 (f. *Κόρραγος*)
MACEDONIA (CHALKIDIKE):
—POTIDAIA-KASSANDREIA: (**2**) ii/iii AD *IG* X (2) (1) 262, 4; cf. Stephanis 2264 (Tataki, *Macedonians* p. 91 no. 52) (f. *Σευῆρος*)
MACEDONIA (EDONIS):
—AMPHIPOLIS: (**3**) 360 BC *IG* IV (1)² 94 b, 18 (Perlman, *City and Sanctuary* E.1 with p. 69 f. (date); Tataki, *Macedonians* p. 53 no. 66) (*Ἱά-*) ?= (*4*); (**4**) 357 BC *RE* (2) ?= (*3*)
MACEDONIA (MYGDONIA):
—THESSALONIKE: (**5**) ii AD *IG* X (2) (1) 372, 3 (s. *Νέος Νουμίσιος Φῆλιξ ὁ καὶ Βάλας*)
—THESSALONIKE?: (**6**) ii-iii AD ib. 736
SCYTHIA MINOR:
—TOMIS: (**7**) ii-iii AD *ISM* II 280

Ἱερατική
MACEDONIA (PELAGONIA):
—KOLOBAISA (NR.): (**1**) ii AD *IG* X (2) (2) 235 (?d. *Νίκη*)

Ἱέρηξ
SCYTHIA MINOR:
—ISTROS: (**1**) v BC Unp. (Avram, defixio) 2, 3 (s. *Λυκῆς*)

Ἱέριος
MACEDONIA (EDONIS):
—AMPHIPOLIS: (**1**) ii-iii AD *Thrakika* 13 (1940) p. 28 *Y*

Ἱερόθεμις
MACEDONIA (CHALKIDIKE):
—SANE: (**1**) vi BC *SEG* XLII 624 (vase) (*[Ἱε]ρόθεμις*?, *[hē]ρόθεμις*?, *[Δω]ρόθεμις*?—*SEG*)

Ἱερόκλεια
MACEDONIA (EDONIS):
—PHILIPPOI: (**1**) ?iii AD *BCH* 59 (1935) p. 154 no. 49 (Pilhofer 291) (*[Αὐ]ρ. Ἱερόκλε[ια]*)
THRACE:
—BYZANTION: (**2**) i/ii AD *SEG* L 667 VI (d. *Φλ. Κοσμίων, Παῦλα*)
—PERINTHOS-HERAKLEIA: (**3**) iii AD *IPerinth* 113 (*Αὐρ. Ἱερόκλε[ια]*)

Ἱεροκλῆς
CIMMERIAN BOSPOROS:
—PANTIKAPAION: (**1**) iv BC Audollent, *Defix. Tab.* 90 (*IAK* 58 (1915) p. 50)
MACEDONIA (BOTTIAIA):
—BEROIA: (**2**) ?ii/iii AD *ILeukopetra* 152 (*[Ἱε]ροκλῆς*: I f. *Ἱεροκλῆς* II); (**3**) ~ ib. (II s. *Ἱεροκλῆς* I)
MACEDONIA (MYGDONIA):
—ARDROLOS: (**4**) i/ii AD *SEG* XLII 590 (s. *Βίθυς*)
SCYTHIA MINOR:
—KALLATIS: (**5**) s. iii BC *ISM* III 35 A, 36 (f. *Νοσσίων*)

Ἱερομνήμων
MACEDONIA (MYGDONIA):
—THESSALONIKE: (**1**) s. iii BC *IG* X (2) (1) 94 (s. *Γούρας*)

Ἱεροσῶν
SKYTHIA:
—OLBIA-BORYSTHENES: (**1**) imp. *IOlbia* 87, 3 (f. *Δάδακος*); (**2**) ~ ib. l. 11 (*Ἱεροσ[ῶν]*); (**3**) ii AD *IOSPE* I² 134, 5 (s. *Ἐπικράτης*)
—TYRAS: (**4**) 181 AD ib. 2, 26 (f. *Σεπτούμιος*); (**5**) 211-217 AD *SEG* XLVII 1196, 12 (f. *Θεοκλῆς*)

Ἱερώ
TAURIS:
—CHERSONESOS: (**1**) iv BC Solomonik, *NEPKh* 140 (*[Ἱ]ερώ*?, *Ἐρώ*—ed.); (**2**) iii BC ib. 174 (d. *Κρόνιος*)

Ἱέρων
MACEDONIA: (**1**) iv BC Arr., *An.* iii 12. 5 (Tataki, *Macedonians* p. 330 no. 5) (f. *Ἀνδρόμαχος*); (**2**) m. ii BC *BGU* 2423, 33 (Tataki, *Macedonians* p. 486 no. 141; La'da E1513) (*[Ἱ]έρων*: s. *Ἀσκληπιόδωρος*)
MACEDONIA (BOTTIAIA):
—BEROIA: (**3**) iii BC *IBer* 150 (Tataki 568) (f. *Νίκυλλα*)
MACEDONIA (CHALKIDIKE):
—AKANTHOS: (**4**) f. v BC *SEG* XLI 551 (vase) (*hιέρōν*)
—ANTHEMOUS: (**5**) f. ii BC ib. XLII 562 (f. *Ἀσκληπιόδωρος*)
—OLYNTHOS: (**6**) s. iii BC ib. XV 279, 1 + *IOrop* 208 (Tataki, *Macedonians* p. 138 no. 68) (s. *Αἰνησίδημος*)
MACEDONIA (EORDAIA):
—KELLE?: (**7**) hell. *AEMTh* 9 (1995) p. 21
MACEDONIA (LYNKESTIS):
—HERAKLEIA: (**8**) i AD *IG* X (2) (2) 75, 32 (f. *Κόϊντος*)
MACEDONIA (MYGDONIA):
—DIKAIA: (**9**) c. 365-359 BC Unp. (Voutyras–Sismanidis) l. 45
—KALINDOIA: (**10**) 68-98 AD *SEG* XLII 580, 17 (s. *Ταρουσίνας*); (**11**) ~ ib. 581, 8 (f. *Νίκων*); (**12**) a. 98 AD ib. 582, 23 + *BE* 1999, no. 362 (I f. *Ἱέρων* II *ὁ καὶ Ζώσιμος*); (**13**) ~ *SEG* XLII 582, 23; cf. *BE* 1999, no. 362 (*Ἱ. ὁ καὶ Ζώσιμος*: II s. *Ἱέρων* I); (**14**) ~ *SEG* XLII 582, 24 (s. *Δύβηζις*); (**15**) ~ ib. l. 52 (s. *Κέτρις*); (**16**) ~ ib. 583, 13 (f. *Ἡρόδωρος*)
SCYTHIA MINOR:
—ISTROS: (**17**) iii-ii BC *ISM* I 9, 3 (Migeotte, *L'emprunt* 41) (f. *Διονύσιος*)
—ISTROS (NR.): (**18**) hell.? *ISM* I 109 (*Γέρωνος* (gen.)—apogr., *(Ἱ)έρωνος*—edd.)
—KALLATIS: (**19**) iv BC ib. III 149 (?s. *Χαρώνδας*); (**20**) iii BC ib. 126, 6 (f. *Ἡρακλείδας*); (**21**) ~ ib. 156 (f. *Νῖκις*); (**22**) c. 265-260 BC *FD* III (3) 207, 4 (s. *Ἀπολλόδωρος*) ?= (*23*); (**23**) ?264 BC ib. III (1) 158, 3 + *REG* 108 (1995) p. 16 n. 19 (f. *Ἡρακλείδας, Σώστρατος*) ?= (*22*)
TAURIS:
—CHERSONESOS: (**24**) iv/iii BC Solomonik, *NEPKh* 162 (f. *Σωτηρίς*); (**25**) iii-ii BC Solomonik, *GAKh* 960 (vase) (*Ἱέρω[ν]*?, *Ἱερώ*?); (**26**) f. ii AD Solomonik, *NEPKh* 111, 13 (f. *—της*); (**27**) 174 AD *SEG* XLV 985 A, 34 (f. *Ἀπολλωνίδης*)
THRACE:
—AINOS: (**28**) ii BC *IG* II² 7982 (*FRA* 254) (f. *Παρθένιον*)
—MARONEIA: (**29**) ii-i BC *IThrakAig* E212, 29 (f. *Διονύσιος*); (**30**) ~ ib. l. 37 (f. *Νικίας*); (**31**) i BC-i AD *BCH* 37 (1913) p. 144 no. 49, 1 (*IThrakAig* E286) (f. *Διονύσιος*); (**32**) ~ *BCH* 37 (1913) p. 144 no. 49, 2 (*IThrakAig* E286) (s. *Διονύσιος, Ἀκονία*)
—NICOPOLIS AD ISTRUM: (**33**) ii-iii AD *IGB* II 663 (f. *Νίκων*)
—NOVAE: (**34**) i/ii AD *IGLNovae* 100 (*ILB* 320) (Lat. Iulius Iero)
—PERINTHOS-HERAKLEIA: (**35**) iii-iv AD *IPerinth* 158 (*AD* 51-2 (1996-7) Mel. p. 344 no. 172) (*Αὐρ. Ἱ.*)
—ROSICA (MOD.): (**36**) ii-iii AD *IGB* V 5283 (s. *Δινίκενθος*)

Ἱερωνίς
THRACE:
—PERINTHOS-HERAKLEIA: (**1**) i-ii AD *ISM* II 365, 18 (*GVI* 1161) (d. *Πέρινθος, Καικιλία Ἀρτεμισία*)

Ἱερώνυμος
MACEDONIA (BOTTIAIA):
—BEROIA: (**1**) 187-193 AD *ILeukopetra* 20, 11; 21, 10; 22, 7; 23, 13; 25, 7; 26, 2; 27, 6; 28, 6; 29, 7; 31, 32; 35, 7; 36, 8; 37, 9; 39, 13; 40, 9; 41, 15 (*Κομίνιος Ἱ., Εἰερώνυμος*—20-21 and 35)
SCYTHIA MINOR:
—ISTROS: (**2**) ii-i BC *ISM* I 268 (s. *Μενίσκος*); (**3**) ii AD ib. 201 II, 12 (f. *Φίλιππος*); (**4**) 138 AD ib. 193 II, 50 (s. *Διονυσόδωρος*)
—KALLATIS: (**5**) 241-244 AD ib. III 74 A, 24 (f. *Ἀσκληπιάδης*)
SKYTHIA:
—TYRAS: (**6**) 181 AD *IOSPE* I² 2, 27 (s. *Ἀρτεμίδωρος*)
THRACE:
—KARDIA: (**7**) v/iv BC Arr., *Ind.* xviii 7 (f. *Εὐμένης*); (**8**) c. 360-260 BC *RE* (10); Berve 383; *FGrH* 154
—ODESSOS: (**9**) ii-i BC *IGB* I² 192 (PM 1752) (f. *Πρωταγόρας*); (**10**) i-ii AD *IGB* I² 202 (*Ἱερώνυ[μος]*: f. *Τρυφῶσα*); (**11**) ii AD ib. 133 bis (*[Ἱ]ερώνυ[μος]*); (**12**) ii-iii AD ib. 127 (f. *Ἀμύντωρ*); (**13**) f. ii AD ib. 78 ter, 6 (*CCET* I 30) (f. *Ἀρτεμίδωρος*); (**14**) 221 AD *IGB* I² 47 bis c, 31 (*Αὐρ. Ἱ.*: s. *Ἀπολλώνιος*)

Ἰέσδαγος
SKYTHIA:
—OLBIA-BORYSTHENES: (**1**) f. ii AD *Drev. Prichern.* 3 pp. 27-8, 11 (*[Ἰ]έσδ[αγος]*: I f. *Ἰέσδαγος* II); (**2**) ~ ib. l. 11 (II s. *Ἰέσδαγος* I)

Ἰζίμαρτος
THRACE:
—BISANTHE-PANION: (**1**) 158-138 BC *OGIS* 304 (*Tekmeria* 6 (2001) p. 157 no. 3) (*Ἰζιμάρτου* (gen.): f. *Ἑστιαῖος*)

Ἰητρόδωρος
SCYTHIA MINOR:
—ISTROS: (1) s. vi BC *SEG* XLVI 889 (vase)
SKYTHIA:
—OLBIA-BORYSTHENES: (2) v BC Dubois, *IGD-Olbia* 101 (s. Ἑκατοκλῆς)

Ἴθαρος
MACEDONIA (ODOMANTIKE):
—SIRRHA?: (1) 155 AD *Belomorski Pregled* 1 (1942) p. 321 no. 6 (Kaphtantzis 2) (Οὔλπ. Ἴ.)

Ἰθυκλέας
CIMMERIAN BOSPOROS:
—HERMONASSA: (1) vi/v BC *SEG* XLIV 659 (vase) + XLVIII 1003; cf. *Hyperboreus* 2000, pp. 136-7 (Ἰ(θ)υκλέας (masc. nom.?))

Ἰθύρας
MACEDONIA (CHALKIDIKE):
—OLYNTHOS: (1) ?352 BC *TAPA* 65 (1934) p. 128 no. 4, 5; Hatzopoulos, *Actes Chalc.* p. 80 (date) (Ἰθύρα (gen.): f. Διονύσιος)

Ἰθύστρατος
THRACE:
—ABDERA: (1) c. 395-360 BC May, *Abdera* p. 208 no. 268 (coin)

Ἰκάριλλα
MACEDONIA (BOTTIAIA):
—EDESSA: (1) v-vi AD Feissel, *RICM* 4

Ἰκαρίων
MACEDONIA (EDONIS):
—PHILIPPOI: (1) ii/iii AD *CIL* III 633 II c, 16 (Pilhofer 163); *CIL* III 633 III a, 6 (Pilhofer 165); *CRAI* 1923, p. 277 (date); Collart, *Philippes* pls. 64-5 (Lat. L. Domitius Icario)

Ἴκαρος
MACEDONIA (BOTTIAIA):
—BEROIA: (1) ii/iii AD *IBer* 143 B, 28 (Tataki 285) (Αὐρ. Ἴ.); (2) ~ *IBer* 143 B, 29 (Tataki 425) (Εἰ-: s. Φιλώτας)
MACEDONIA (EDONIS):
—PHILIPPOI: (3) ii/iii AD *CIL* III 633 II a, 15 (Pilhofer 163); *CRAI* 1923, p. 277 (date); Collart, *Philippes* pls. 64-5 (Lat. L. Domitius Ikarus)

Ἴκας
TAURIS:
—CHERSONESOS: (1) m. iv BC Solomonik, *GAKh* 963 (vase) (Ἴκα (gen.)); (2) f. iii BC *SEG* XL 615 A, 14 (s. Ἥρα—)

Ἰκεσία
THRACE:
—MARONEIA: (1) ii-iii AD Dumont–Homolle 110b 18 (*IThrakAig* E280); cf. *BCH* 37 (1913) p. 146 (Ὀρφ. Εἰκαισία?, Ὀρφει. Καισία—Avezou–Picard)

Ἱκέσιος
CIMMERIAN BOSPOROS:
—HERMONASSA: (1) iii BC *CIRB* 1072 (f. Νυμφαγόρας)
—KOROKONDAME: (2) v BC ib. 1102 (f. Ἄττης)
—PANTIKAPAION: (3) v/iv BC Tolstoi 151 (vase); (4) i AD *CIRB* 533
MACEDONIA (EDONIS):
—PHILIPPOI (TERRIT.): (5) i BC-i AD Pikoulas, *Chora* p. 128 no. 24 (Pilhofer 625) (Εἰ-: s. Φοιβίδης)
SCYTHIA MINOR:
—KALLATIS: (6) s. iii BC *ISM* III 35 B, 22 (f. Μῆνις); (7) i BC ib. 173 ([Ἱ]κέσιος); (8) s. i BC ib. 38, 6 (f. Ἡραίων)
SKYTHIA:
—OLBIA-BORYSTHENES: (9) c. 400-375 BC *IOSPE* I^2 160 (Dubois, *IGDOlbia* 7) ([Ἱκ]έσιος); (10) c. 300-260 BC Karyshkovskii, *MO* pp. 77-85; *SNG BM Black Sea* 498 (coin) (Ἱκ(έσιος)?); (11) iii BC *IOSPE* I^2 201 I, 10 (f. Παντακλῆς); (12) ~ ib. l. 18 (Ἱκέ[σιος]: f. Λεοντομένης); (13) ~ ib. l. 26 (s. Ἀρίστων); (14) ~ ib. l. 38 (s. Σωκράτης); (15) ~ ib. l. 51; 201 II, 16 (s. Παντακλῆς); (16) ~ ib. l. 13 (s. Πολύξενος); (17) ~ ib. l. 40 (Ἱκέ[σιος]); (18) ~ ib. l. 24-5 (s. Λεωδάμας, f. Νουμήνιος); (19) iii-ii BC *Arkheologiia* (Kiev) 39 (1982) p. 34 (vase) (Ἱκέσ(ιος)); (20) f. ii BC *SEG* XLII 717 (f. Φιλτῆς); (21) ~ ib. (Ἱκ[έσ]ιος: s. Φιλτῆς); (22) c. 150-175 AD *IOSPE* I^2 132, 3; cf. *SEG* XLII 713 (s. Μαίακος)
TAURIS:
—CHERSONESOS: (23) 130 AD *VDI* 1960 (3), pp. 154-5, 28 (II s. Ἱκέσιος I); (24) ~ ib. l. 29 (I f. Ἱκέσιος II)
THRACE:
—ABDERA: (25) c. 475-450 BC May, *Abdera* p. 99 no. 70 (coin) (Ἱκέσ(ιος)?); (26) c. 346-336 BC ib. p. 274 nos. 463-4 (coin)
—DIONYSOPOLIS: (27) iii AD *IGB* I^2 14 c, 18 (Αὐρ. Ἱ.: s. Καλλικράτης)
—MARONEIA: (28) c. 365-336 BC Schönert-Geiss, *Maroneia* 419-26 (coin)
—MESAMBRIA: (29) iv BC *IGB* I^2 334 novies a; (30) iii/ii BC Karayotov, *Mesambria* 1 p. 87 no. 128 (Price, *Alexander* 1007 (coin)) (Ἱκέ(σιος))

Ἰκκότας
MACEDONIA (MYGDONIA):
—KALINDOIA: (1) c. 332 BC Hatzopoulos, *MI* 2 p. 84 no. 62, 13; cf. *Anthémonte–Kalindoia* 2 pp. 264-5 (name) (s. Γύρτος)

Ἰκκότιμος
MACEDONIA (LOWER PAIONIA):
—IDOMENE: (1) c. 230-200 BC *BCH* 45 (1921) p. 17 III, 68 (Tataki, *Macedonians* p. 113 no. 1)

Ἱλάρα
MACEDONIA (BOTTIAIA):
—MIEZA: (1) ?ii AD Dimitsas 19 = 292 (Tataki 569) (threpte)
MACEDONIA (EDONIS):
—PHILIPPOI: (2) i-ii AD Collart, *Philippes* p. 414 n. 1 with pl. 68. 2 (Pilhofer 339) (Lat. Pomponia Hilara)
—PHILIPPOI*: (3) ii-iii AD *BCH* 61 (1937) pp. 415-16 no. 9 (Pilhofer 345) (Lat. Vivia Hilara: freed.)
MACEDONIA (MYGDONIA):
—THESSALONIKE: (4) iii AD *IG* X (2) (1) 308, 1 (Αὐρ. Εἰλάρα)
—THESSALONIKE?: (5) i AD ib. 928
THRACE?: (6) iii AD *SEG* XXXI 670 (gem) (d. Μουνάτιος)

Ἱλαρία
MACEDONIA (BOTTIAIA):
—BEROIA: (1) ii-iii AD *IBer* 226 (Tataki 426) (Εἰ-)
MACEDONIA (MYGDONIA):
—THESSALONIKE: (2) ii AD *IG* X (2) (1) 414 (d. Κ. Ποπίλλιος Ἵλαρος, Ἀρτεμώ)
THRACE:
—SALYMBRIA: (3) iv-vi AD *Archives Stamoulis* d. 35 (Loukopoulou, *Thrace Propontique* p. 264)

Ἱλάριος
MACEDONIA (MYGDONIA):
—THESSALONIKE: (1) iii/iv AD *Makedonika* 14 (1974) p. 369 ([Ἱ]λάριος, Λάριος—ed.)

Ἱλαρίων
CIMMERIAN BOSPOROS:
—PANTIKAPAION: (1) imp. *CIRB* 794 (s. Θεόδωρος); (2) ii-iii AD ib. 723; cf. KW pl. 36 no. 525 (I f. Ἱλαρίων II); (3) ~ *CIRB* 723; cf. KW pl. 36 no. 525 (II s. Ἱλαρίων I); (4) f. ii AD *CIRB* 87, 3 (Ἱλα[ρίω]ν); (5) ~ ib. 91, 4; cf. KW pl. 39 no. 574 (Ἱλαρίω[ν])
MACEDONIA (BOTTIAIA):
—MIEZA: (6) ?ii AD Dimitsas 19 = 292 (Tataki 717) (Τι. Κλ. Ἱ.: s. Ἀνδρόνικος, Εὐτυχίς)
MACEDONIA (EDONIS):
—PHILIPPOI: (7) imp. *BCH* 57 (1933) p. 327 no. 5 (Pilhofer 220) (Lat. Hilario)
MACEDONIA (MYGDONIA):
—THESSALONIKE?: (8) ii-iii AD *IG* X (2) (1) 730
SCYTHIA MINOR:
—ISTROS: (9) f. iii AD *ISM* I 218, 3 (s. Λούκιος)
—TOMIS: (10) 201 AD ib. II 83 II, 27 (s. Λούκιος)

Ἵλαρος
CIMMERIAN BOSPOROS:
—PANTIKAPAION: (1) ii AD *CIRB* 683 (s. Ἔρως)
MACEDONIA (BOTTIAIA):
—BEROIA: (2) ii-iii AD *IBer* 350 (Tataki 570); (3) ii/iii AD *IBer* 27 A, 4 (slave?)
—PELLA? (GIANNITSA (MOD.)): (4) imp. Dimitsas 130
MACEDONIA (EDONIS):
—PHILIPPOI: (5) ii AD *BCH* 57 (1933) pp. 370-2 no. 28, 10 (Pilhofer 91) (Lat. L. Atiarius Hilarus); (6) ~ *BCH* 57 (1933) pp. 370-2 no. 28, 11 (Pilhofer 91) (Lat. Q. Cossutius Hilarus); (7) s. iii AD *SEG* L 618. 3 (mosaic)
MACEDONIA (MYGDONIA):
—THESSALONIKE: (8) i AD *IG* X (2) (1) 405; (9) ii AD ib. 414 (Κ. Ποπίλλιος Ἵ.: f. Γαληνός, Ἱλαρία)
—THESSALONIKE?: (10) s. iii AD *AEpThess* p. 10 no. 8 A (Εἴ-)
—THESSALONIKE*: (11) i-ii AD *IG* X (2) (1) 688, 6 (Lat. T. Minucius Hilarus: freed.)
MACEDONIA (PIERIA):
—DION*: (12) ?iii AD *ILGR* 191 (Lat. Aur. Hilarus)
SCYTHIA MINOR:
—TOMIS: (13) ii AD *ISM* II 17, 4 (s. Ἀπολλώνιος)
TAURIS:
—CHERSONESOS: (14) 129-130 AD *IOSPE* I^2 359, 29; *VDI* 1960 (3), pp. 154-5, 29 (Ἵ(λ)αρος—359: f. Ποντικός); (15) 130 AD ib. l. 25 (f. Λούκιος)
THRACE:
—BIZYE (TERRIT.): (16) ii-iii AD *IGB* III 1868 (Ἀντώνις Ἵ.: freed.)
—MONTANA: (17) s. ii AD *Montana* II 12 (Lat. Hilarus)
—SPINOPARA: (18) ii AD *IGB* IV 2192, 13

Ἵλβιος
SKYTHIA:
—OLBIA-BORYSTHENES: (1) ii AD *IOSPE* I^2 83, 6; Zgusta, *PNS* 655 (Ξάρταμος ὁ καὶ Ἵ.: s. Καρζόαζος)

Ἰλιάς
MACEDONIA (LYNKESTIS):
—IDROUSSA (MOD.): (1) ii-iii AD *EAM* 161

Ἰλλυρικός
THRACE:
—SERDICA: (1) ii-iii AD *IGB* IV 1930 (s. Σκάρις)

Ἱματυώ?
MACEDONIA (BISALTIA):
—TERPNI (MOD.): (1) ii-iii AD *SEG* XLIX 810

Ἱμέρα
MACEDONIA (MYGDONIA):
—THESSALONIKE?: (1) ii AD *IG* X (2) (1) 884 (Εἰ-: d. Ἵμερος, Ὠφελίμα)

Ἱμέριος
SCYTHIA MINOR:
—KALLATIS: (1) iii-iv AD *ISM* III 148, 12 (Εἰ-: f. Εὐφρονίς)

THRACE: **(2)** 544 AD *PLRE* III (1)
—PERINTHOS-HERAKLEIA: **(3)** a. 212 AD *IPerinth* 190 (Ἐι-)

Ἱμέρις
THRACE:
—HADRIANOPOLIS:
——Zizina: **(1)** v-vi AD *Epigr. Anat.* 24 (1995) p. 145 no. 11 (Εἰ-)

Ἵμερος
CIMMERIAN BOSPOROS:
—PANTIKAPAION: **(1)** iii AD *CIRB* 752 (Γ. Καίλιος Εἵμερος)
MACEDONIA (MYGDONIA):
—THESSALONIKE?: **(2)** ii AD *IG* X (2) (1) 884 (Εἵ-: f. Ἱμέρα); **(3)** ii-iii AD ib. 811 (Κ. Φούριος Εἵμερος)
MACEDONIA (ODOMANTIKE):
—SIRRHA: **(4)** f. iii AD *SEG* XXX 590, 11 (Αὐρ. Εἵμερος)
THRACE:
—PERINTHOS-HERAKLEIA:
——(Boreis): **(5)** iii-ii BC *IPerinth* 61, 40 (s. Ἡρόστρατος)

Ἰνάρμαζος
SKYTHIA:
—OLBIA-BORYSTHENES: **(1)** i/ii AD *IOlbia* 90, 7 (s. Κουκόδων)

Ἰνάχιος
MACEDONIA (BOTTIAIA):
—BEROIA: (1) 309 or 311 AD *ILeukopetra* 116, 9 (Tataki 773) (Κρισπίνιος ὁ καὶ Ἰ.)

Ἴναχος
CIMMERIAN BOSPOROS:
—PANTIKAPAION: **(1)** s. i AD *CIRB* 397 (f. Ἑλένη)

Ἰνγένης
SCYTHIA MINOR:
—ISTROS: **(1)** ii AD *ISM* I 211, 6 (Οὐλπ. Ἰ.)
THRACE:
—ODESSOS: **(2)** 215 AD *IGB* I^2 47 c, 27 (Αὐρ. Ἰ.: s. Κλ. Κάστος)

Ἰνγένουα
MACEDONIA (PAIONIA):
—STOBOI: (1) v-vi AD Unp. (Stobi excav.)
THRACE:
—NICOPOLIS AD ISTRUM (TERRIT.): **(2)** ii AD *IGB* V 5245 (Ἰνγένουαις (gen.): d. Ἀρούντιος Οὐάλης)

Ἰνγένους
SCYTHIA MINOR:
—ISTROS: (1) ii AD *ISM* I 196, 10 (s. Σίννας)
THRACE:
—BEROE-AUGUSTA TRAIANA (TERRIT.): **(2)** ii-iii AD *IGB* III 1698 (s. Σείτη); **(3)** iii AD ib. 1653, 1 (Ἰνγένοος (gen.): f. Αὐρ. Διόδωρος)
—VICUS TRULLENSIUM: **(4)** iii AD ib. II 506, 4 (f. Μοῦσα)

Ἴνδας?
MACEDONIA (ODOMANTIKE):
—DRABESKOS?: **(1)** iv BC Kaphtantzis 568, 3 (Pilhofer 575) ([Δ]ίνδας?); **(2)** ~ Kaphtantzis 568, 9 (Pilhofer 575) (Σ[κ]ίνδα? (gen.): ?f. Φάνων)

Ἰνδίη
CIMMERIAN BOSPOROS:
—KOROKONDAME: **(1)** v BC *CIRB* 1103

Ἰνινθιμαῖος
CIMMERIAN BOSPOROS:
—BOSPOROS: **(1)** c. 200-239 AD *RE* s.v. Iulius (282); PIR^2 I 360; Frolova, *CKB A.D. 69-238* pp. 54-5 (Τιβ. Ἰούλ. Ἰ., Ἰνινθίμεος—coins: king)

Ἰνισμειός
SARMATIA:
—SARMATAI: **(1)** s. i AD Vinogradov–Kryžickij p. 97 (coins) (king)

Ἰνσάζαγος
SKYTHIA:
—OLBIA-BORYSTHENES: **(1)** ii AD *IOSPE* I^2 102, 10; Zgusta, *PNS* 116 (f. Σθάζεις)

Ἴξις
CIMMERIAN BOSPOROS:
—PANTIKAPAION: **(1)** f. iv BC *CIRB* 227 (f. Τυαίης, Ἀκρωθίς)

Ἰξύπορος
TAURIS:
—CHERSONESOS: **(1)** c. 250-230 BC Anokhin p. 142 no. 115 (coin)

Ἰόδα
CIMMERIAN BOSPOROS:
—KYTAIA (NR.): **(1)** ii AD *CIRB* 945

Ἰοκλῆς
MACEDONIA (CHALKIDIKE):
—AKANTHOS: **(1)** iv/iii BC *SEG* XLVII 870, 1 (Ἰοκλῆς)

Ἰόλα
THRACE:
—AINOS: **(1)** i-ii AD ib. XXXVI 660 (d. Ζώσιμος)

Ἰόλαος
MACEDONIA: **(1)** 432 BC *RE* (4) (Tataki, *Macedonians* p. 330 no. 6); **(2)** c. 345-317 BC *RE* (5); Berve 386 (Tataki, *Macedonians* p. 331 no. 9) (s. Ἀντίπατρος); **(3)** 330 BC Berve 387 (Tataki, *Macedonians* p. 330 no. 7) (Lat. Iolaus); **(4)** 307-301 BC *IG* II^2 561, 6 + *SEG* XXXI 80; cf. *RE* Supplbd. 4 (5a) (Tataki, *Macedonians* p. 330 no. 8) (?s. Κ—)
—PALIOURA: **(5)** v/iv BC *Suda A* 2703 (Tataki, *Macedonians* p. 146 no. 2) (f. Ἀντίπατρος)
MACEDONIA (BOTTIAIA):
—BEROIA: **(6)** 120 BC *IBer* 134, 19 (s. Κύτων); **(7)** i BC ib. 185 (Tataki 572) ([Ἰ]όλαος: s. Νικα—, f. Ὀδέτα)
MACEDONIA (MYGDONIA):
—LETE: **(8)** 22 or 139 AD Dimitsas 678, 10 (Ἰόλα[ος]: s. Ἀπολλοφάνης)
THRACE:
—ODRYSAI: **(9)** 356 BC *FD* III (1) 392, 2 (s. Κερσεβλέπτης)

Ἰόλας
MACEDONIA (LOWER PAIONIA):
—EUROPOS: **(1)** i BC-i AD? *SEG* XXXVIII 609 ([Ἰ]όλας: s. Νικόπολις)

Ἰόλη
MACEDONIA (BOTTIAIA):
—BEROIA: **(1)** c. 120-140 AD *IBer* 349 B (Tataki 573)

Ἰόλιος
THRACE:
—PAUTALIA (TERRIT.): **(1)** ii-iii AD *IGB* V 5857

Ἰόλλας
MACEDONIA (BOTTIAIA):
—BEROIA: **(1)** s. iii BC *IBer* 16 A, 18; **(2)** ~ ib. l. 21 ([Ἰό]λλας: s. Ἑρμοίτας); **(3)** 122 BC ib. 134, 9 (Ἰό[λ]λας)
MACEDONIA (ELIMEIA):
—AIANE (TERRIT.): **(4)** i BC *EAM* 6, 4 with pl. 3 (Ἰόλαος—edd.: f. Πορ—)
MACEDONIA (EORDAIA):
—KELLE?: **(5)** hell. *SEG* XLVIII 805. 3 (pithos); Hatzopoulos, *MI* 1 pp. 94-5 (locn.)
—KORMESTAI: **(6)** ii BC *EAM* 88 (s. Ἀμύντας)

MACEDONIA (MYGDONIA):
—LETE: **(7)** s. iv BC Hatzopoulos, *MI* 2 pp. 93-4 no. 79, 11 ([Ἰ]όλλας)
—THESSALONIKE: **(8)** s. ii BC *IG* X (2) (1) 27, 5 (I f. Ἰόλλας II); **(9)** ~ ib. l. 5 (II s. Ἰόλλας I)
MACEDONIA?: **(10)** iii/ii BC *Anthémonte-Kalindoia* 1 p. 40 no. A1 (Tataki, *Macedonians* p. 215 no. 3) (Ἰόλλα[ς]?)

Ἴολος
THRACE:
—PAUTALIA (TERRIT.): **(1)** iii AD *IGB* V 5833 with comm. (Αὐρ. Ἴολος Φίλαγρος)

Ἰοπᾶς
CIMMERIAN BOSPOROS:
—MYRMEKION: **(1)** iv BC *SEG* XXXVII 666. 7 (vase); cf. XLVIII 1007 (Ἰοπᾶτος (gen.)—Tokhtas'ev)

Ἰορδάνης
MACEDONIA (BOTTIAIA):
—EDESSA: **(1)** v-vi AD Feissel, *RICM* 13, 5 (s. Θεόδωρος); **(2)** ~ ib. 30

Ἰουβῖνος
THRACE:
—KABYLE*: **(1)** 270-275 AD *IGB* V 5637, 9
—ODESSOS: **(2)** vi AD *SEG* XL 598
—PERINTHOS-HERAKLEIA: **(3)** iii AD *IPerinth* 160 (Αὐρ. Εἰουβεῖνος)

Ἰούδας
SKYTHIA:
—TANAIS*: **(1)** ii-iii AD *Tanais* I p. 103 (amph.)

Ἰουκοῦνδος
MACEDONIA (BOTTIAIA):
—BEROIA: **(1)** imp. *ILeukopetra* 166
MACEDONIA (MYGDONIA):
—THESSALONIKE: **(2)** i-ii AD *IG* X (2) (1) 243 II, 5 (s. Ποσειδώνιος); **(3)** s. i AD ib. 593 (I s. Λεύκιος, f. Ἰουκοῦνδος II, Κασσάνδρα); **(4)** ~ ib. (II s. Ἰουκοῦνδος I)
THRACE:
—PAUTALIA: **(5)** ii AD *IGB* IV 2074, 7

Ἰουλία
MACEDONIA (ALMOPIA):
—NOTIA (MOD.): **(1)** ii/iii AD *SEG* XLIII 367, 9 (m. Εὐτυχίς)
MACEDONIA (BOTTIAIA):
—BEROIA: **(2)** 184 AD *ILeukopetra* 16, 1 (m. Κοῦντα); **(3)** f. iii AD *IBer* 97, 3 (Tataki 574) (m. Ποσείδιππος)
—EDESSA: **(4)** ii-iii AD *Arch. Pap.* 22 (1973) p. 205 no. 4 (Tataki, *Edessa* 128) (d. Φίλιππος)
—KYRRHOS: **(5)** 199 AD *ILeukopetra* 45, 1, 16 (Tataki, *Macedonians* p. 116 no. 8) (d. (nat.) Διονύσιος, d. (ad.) Ἐνθαδίων)
MACEDONIA (CHALKIDIKE):
—POTIDAIA-KASSANDREIA (TERRIT.)?: **(6)** imp. *SEG* XXIX 575
MACEDONIA (EORDAIA):
—KRANNESTAI: **(7)** ii-iii AD *IG* X (2) (2) 36, 4 (m. Νικάνδρα, Βασσιανός)
MACEDONIA (LYNKESTIS):
—ETHNIKO (MOD.): **(8)** s. ii AD *EAM* 154 (d. Γλαυκίας)
—HERAKLEIA?: **(9)** ii-iii AD *IG* X (2) (2) 132 (m. Δομιτιανός)
MACEDONIA (MYGDONIA):
—THESSALONIKE: **(10)** ii-iii AD ib. X (2) (1) 665, 9 (*SEG* XLIII 460); **(11)** 118 AD *IG* X (2) (1) 524, 5 (d. Ἰούλ. Ἑρμῆς); **(12)** 130 AD ib. 369 (m. Παράμονος)
—THESSALONIKE?: **(13)** ii-iii AD ib. 872 (d. Ἰούλις); **(14)** 181 AD ib. 693
MACEDONIA (PAIONIA): **(15)** imp. *Sp.* 98 (1941-8) p. 202 no. 399
—DEMIR KAPIJA (MOD.): **(16)** ?ii AD Unp. (Skopje)
—KAVADARCI (MOD.): **(17)** imp. *Sp.* 98 (1941-8) p. 76 no. 162 (m. Γάϊος); **(18)** ii AD ib. 71

(1931) p. 69 no. 153 (m. *Τερτία*); **(19)** ii-iii AD Dimitsas 283; **(20)** iii AD *Sp.* 71 (1931) p. 65 no. 142, 4 (d. *Θεογένης*)
—STOBOI: **(21)** ii-iii AD *JÖAI* 6 (1903) Beibl. col. 6 no. 7
MACEDONIA (PELAGONIA): **(22)** ii-iii AD *IG* X (2) (2) 255 (m. *Ἰουλιανός*); **(23)** ~ ib. 290 (*Εἰ*-: m. *Λυσίμαχος*)
—KOLOBAISA (NR.): **(24)** ii AD ib. 235 (d. *Συνέρως*)
MACEDONIA (PIERIA):
—DION: **(25)** s. ii AD Oikonomos 18; cf. Spiliopoulou-Donderer, *KGN* p. 196 no. D14 (date) (m. *Τιβεριανὸς Κοσμιανός*, *Ἰταλία*)
—DION?: **(26)** i-ii AD *AEMTh* 15 (2001) p. 343 (*Ἰ. ἡ καὶ Κλᾶρα*)
MACEDONIA (SINTIKE):
—PARTHIKOPOLIS: **(27)** ii AD *IGB* IV 2275 (d. *Μ. Οὐαλερία Πυρούσαλα*)
SCYTHIA MINOR:
—ISTROS: **(28)** f. ii AD *ISM* I 353; cf. *Ling. Balk.* 27 (1984) p. 88 (*Ἰουλ. Ἀλεξάν[δρα]*?—Mihailov: ?d. *Ἀλέξανδρος*)
—TOMIS: **(29)** ii-iii AD *ISM* II 369, 4 (m. *Ἰούλις*, *Διονυσόδωρος*, *Λεοντιανός*, *Διονύσις*, *Ἀγριππῖνα*)
THRACE:
—AINOS: **(30)** i-ii AD *IG* XII (8) 218, 4 (*[Ἰ]ουλία*: d. *Γηπαίπυρος*)
—MARKIANOPOLIS*: **(31)** iii AD *IGB* II 816, 6
—MESAMBRIA: **(32)** i-ii AD ib. I^{2} 345, 3 (PM 2088) (d. *Νικίας*)

Ἰουλιάδης
SKYTHIA:
—TANAIS: **(1)** f. ii AD *CIRB* 1264 B (*[Ἰο]υλιάδ[ης]*) ?= (*3*); **(2)** 154-170 AD ib. 1260a, 22 (*Ἰουλ[ι]άδης*) ?= (*3*); **(3)** 155 AD ib. 1260, 12 (*[Ἰο]υλιάδ[ης]*: ?s. *—λειδ—*) ?= (*1*) (*2*); **(4)** 225 AD ib. 1280, 25 (*[Ἰ]ουλιάδης*: s. *Σ—*)

Ἰουλιανή
MACEDONIA (BISALTIA):
—EUPORIA?: **(1)** f. i AD Kaphtantzis 513
MACEDONIA (BOTTIAIA):
—BEROIA: **(2)** ii-iii AD *IBer* 504
MACEDONIA (CHALKIDIKE):
—SPARTOLOS (NR.)?: **(3)** imp. *SEG* XXIX 598, 5
MACEDONIA (EDONIS):
—AMPHIPOLIS (TERRIT.)?: **(4)** ii-iii AD ib. II 419 (Pilhofer 590) (*[Ἰο]υλιαν[ή]*?: d. *—νος Σε—*)
MACEDONIA (ELIMEIA):
—OBLOSTAI: **(5)** 200 AD *EAM* 37, 3
MACEDONIA (MYGDONIA):
—THESSALONIKE?: **(6)** ii AD *IG* X (2) (1) 877
MACEDONIA (PELAGONIA): **(7)** ii-iii AD ib. X (2) (2) 175
—KERAMIAI (NR.): **(8)** ii-iii AD ib. 221

Ἰουλιανός
CIMMERIAN BOSPOROS:
—GORGIPPIA: **(1)** s. ii AD *CIRB* 1129 B, 10 (*Ἰουλιανό[ς]*); **(2)** ~ ib. 1142, 16 (s. *Μᾶρκος*)
KOLCHIS:
—APSILAI: **(3)** ii AD Arr., *Peripl.* 11. 3; *PIR*^{2} I 89 (king)
MACEDONIA (BOTTIAIA):
—BEROIA: **(4)** f. ii AD *IBer* 7 A, 18; 7 *Γ*, 3, 33
—EDESSA: **(5)** 180 AD *SEG* XXIV 531, 18 (Tataki, *Edessa* 130) (s. *Ἀσκληπᾶς*)
MACEDONIA (DERRIOPOS): **(6)** ii-iii AD *IG* X (2) (2) 317 (I f. *Ἰουλιανὸς* II, *Λυσικλῆς*); **(7)** ~ ib. (II s. *Ἰουλιανὸς* I, *Ζωσίμα*)
MACEDONIA (LYNKESTIS):
—HERAKLEIA: **(8)** ii-iii AD ib. 86
MACEDONIA (MYGDONIA):
—THESSALONIKE: **(9)** i/ii AD *AD* 22 (1967) Chron. p. 393 (*Εἰουλι[α]νός*)
—THESSALONIKE?: **(10)** ii AD *IG* X (2) (1) 879; **(11)** ii-iii AD ib. 931 (Feissel, *RICM* 118)
MACEDONIA (ODOMANTIKE):
—SIRRHA: **(12)** 155 AD Dimitsas 821, 11 (Kaphtantzis 1) (s. *Βουρείλας*)
MACEDONIA (PAIONIA):
—KAVADARCI (MOD.): **(13)** ii-iii AD *Sp.* 71 (1931) p. 61 no. 132 (*[Ἰ]ου(ε?)λιανός*); **(14)** ~ ib. 98 (1941-8) p. 65 no. 136 (*GVI* 188) (s. *Χρόνιος*)
—STOBOI (AREA): **(15)** ii-iii AD Unp. (Kavadarci Mus.) inv. 61/II (*Εἰοι*-: s. *Φοῦσκα*)
MACEDONIA (PAIONIA)?:
—KASARSENOI: **(16)** ii-iii AD *Sp.* 75 (1933) p. 46 no. 153; Papazoglou, *Villes* p. 343 n. 32 (locn.) (s. *Ἰούλιος*)
MACEDONIA (PELAGONIA): **(17)** ii-iii AD *IG* X (2) (2) 255 (s. *Διοσκουρίδης*, *Ἰουλία*)
MACEDONIA (SINTIKE):
—PARTHIKOPOLIS: **(18)** f. iii AD *IGB* V 5907 (*[Ἰου]λιανό(ς)*?); **(19)** 210 AD ib. IV 2265, 4 (s. *Ἀλέξανδρος*)
SCYTHIA MINOR:
—ISTROS: **(20)** ii AD *ISM* I 196, 9 (s. *Ἀλέξανδρος*); **(21)** ~ ib. 201 I, 12 (*Ἰουλιαν[ός]*)
—TOMIS: **(22)** ii AD ib. II 189, 1 (*GVI* 1026) (f. *Ἀγάθανδρος*); **(23)** ii-iii AD *ISM* II 21, 4; **(24)** ~ ib. 31 II, 18 (s. *Θρασυ.*); **(25)** ~ ib. l. 23 (I f. *Ἰουλιανὸς* II); **(26)** ~ ib. l. 23 (II s. *Ἰουλιανὸς* I); **(27)** ~ ib. 34, 3 (f. *—ος*); **(28)** ~ ib. 292 (s. *Ἀλέξανδρος*); **(29)** ~ ib. 468, 15 (s. *Ἀλέξανδρος*)
SKYTHIA:
—OLBIA-BORYSTHENES: **(30)** imp. *IOSPE* I^{2} 284 (*Εἰ*-); **(31)** ii/iii AD *IOlbia* 52, 6 (I f. *Αὐρ. Ἰουλιανός* II)
—OLBIA-BORYSTHENES (ACHILLEIOS DR.): **(32)** ii-iii AD *IOSPE* I^{2} 330
TAURIS:
—CHERSONESOS: **(33)** ii-iii AD *SEG* XXIX 714 (*[Ἰου]λιανός*: s. *Μύρων*); **(34)** ?114 AD ib. XLVIII 999, 42; **(35)** c. 120-130 AD Solomonik, *NEPKh* 112, 21 (s. *Ἀκύλας*); **(36)** iii AD *VDI* 1938 (3), p. 80 no. 10. I (f. *Βασιλική*)
THRACE:
—ASOMATOI (MOD.): **(37)** ?iii AD *SEG* XVI 414 (*IThrakAig* E386) (s. *Δόλης*)
—BEROE-AUGUSTA TRAIANA: **(38)** iii AD *IGB* III 1605, 3 (f. *Αὐρ. Κρισπῖνα*)
—BYZANTION (TERRIT.): **(39)** imp. Unp. (Sayar) (s. *Βιθυνικός*)
—ISPERIH (MOD.): **(40)** iii AD *IGB* II 779 (*CCET* II (2) 612) (I f. *Ἰουλιανὸς* II); **(41)** ~ *IGB* II 779 (*CCET* II (2) 612) (II s. *Ἰουλιανὸς* I)
—KELLAI (NR.): **(42)** iii AD *IGB* III 1535 (*Εἰου*-: f. *Αὐρ. Μουκιανός*)
—MARKIANOPOLIS (NR.): **(43)** iii AD *SEG* XL 596 (*Ἰουλι[ανός]*?: f. *Ἀπολλώνιος*)
—ODESSOS: **(44)** 215 AD *IGB* I^{2} 47, 7 (f. *Αὐρ. Διονυσόδωρος*, *Αὐρ. Ἀγαθήνωρ*)
—PĂDARINO (MOD.): **(45)** ii-iii AD ib. V 5286 (s. *Ἰούλιος*)
—PAUTALIA: **(46)** s. ii AD *SEG* XLVI 864, 16 (s. *Ἡρακλείδης*)
—PAUTALIA (TERRIT.): **(47)** ii AD *IGB* IV 2214, 13 (s. *Κάσιος*); **(48)** ii-iii AD ib. 2219 (*Ἰ]ουλιανός*); **(49)** ~ ib. V 5829 (*[Ἰ]ουλιανός*: s. *Τήρης*)
—PAUTALIA:
——(Herakleis): **(50)** ?ii AD ib. IV 2077, 17 (s. *Διογενιανός*)
—PERINTHOS-HERAKLEIA: **(51)** i-ii AD *IPerinth* 89 (II s. *Γ. Ἰούλ. Ἰουλιανὸς* I); **(52)** ~ ib. 271; **(53)** c. 100-115 AD *SEG* XXVI 1288, 11 (f. *Ἀσκλᾶς*)
—PERINTHOS-HERAKLEIA?: **(54)** ii-iii AD *IGB* V 5128
—PHILIPPOPOLIS-TRIMONTIUM: **(55)** iv-v AD Beševliev 209, 1-2 (f. *Ἡλιόδωρος*)
——(Eumolpis): **(56)** ii AD *IGB* III 1023, 7 (*GVI* 726)
—SERDICA: **(57)** 117-138 AD *IGB* IV 1925 d, 17 (f. *—α*); **(58)** iii AD ib. 1974; **(59)** iii-iv AD ib. 1964 (*GVI* 396); **(60)** 261-268 AD *IGB* IV 1911, 5
—SERDICA (NR.): **(61)** imp. *SEG* XVII 336 (*Ἰου[λ]ιανό[ς]*)
—SPINOPARA: **(62)** ii AD *IGB* IV 2192, 11
—TRAIANOPOLIS: **(63)** ii AD *SEG* XXIV 643, 7 (*IThrakAig* E438)
—VRACA (MOD.): **(64)** ii-iii AD *IGB* II 487 (s. *Δαμόστρατος*)

Ἰούλιος
MACEDONIA (BOTTIAIA):
—BEROIA: **(1)** 177 AD *IBer* 135 A, 19 (s. *Κοΐντα*); **(2)** iii AD ib. 364 (Tataki 592)
—EDESSA: **(3)** 180 AD *SEG* XXIV 531, 8 (Tataki, *Edessa* 86) (*Εἰ*-: s. *Μαρκία*); **(4)** ~ *SEG* XXIV 531, 16 (Tataki, *Edessa* 135) (f. *Παράμονος*, *Ἰούλις*, *Ἀκύλας*); **(5)** v-vi AD Feissel, *RICM* 19
MACEDONIA (DERRIOPOS):
—STUBERRA: **(6)** 116 AD *IG* X (2) (2) 327, 29 (f. *Φίλων*); **(7)** ~ ib. l. 31 (f. *Μάξιμος*)
MACEDONIA (LYNKESTIS):
—HERAKLEIA: **(8)** i AD ib. 75, 41-42 (s. *Οὔηρος*)
MACEDONIA (ORESTIS):
—SISANI (MOD.): **(9)** 146 AD *EAM* 187, 11 (f. *Πρόκλος*)
MACEDONIA (PAIONIA):
—KAVADARCI (MOD.): **(10)** ii-iii AD *Sp.* 71 (1931) p. 63 no. 136, 2 (*Εἰ*-: s. *Λούκιος*, *Σεκοῦνδα*)
—NEGOTINO (MOD.): **(11)** ii-iii AD ib. 98 (1941-8) p. 53 no. 107 (f. *Καλλικράτης*)
MACEDONIA (PAIONIA)?:
—KASARSENOI: **(12)** ii-iii AD ib. 75 (1933) p. 46 no. 153; Papazoglou, *Villes* p. 343 n. 32 (locn.) (s. *Ἕσπερος*, f. *Ἰουλιανός*)
TAURIS:
—CHERSONESOS: **(13)** f. ii AD Solomonik, *NEPKh* 111, 10 (*Ἰούλι[ος]*, *Ἰουλι[ανός]*?) ?= (*14*); **(14)** c. 120-130 AD ib. 112, 18; cf. *VDI* 1993 (4), p. 63 ?= (*13*)
THRACE:
—AQUAE CALIDAE*: **(15)** iii AD *IGB* I^{2} 380 (f. *Ζωπᾶς*)
—BEROE-AUGUSTA TRAIANA: **(16)** 222-235 AD ib. III 1590, 11 (*Eastern cults* pp. 232-3 no. 23); cf. *SEG* XL 568 (*Ἄστεος ὁ καὶ Ἰ.*)
—DIONYSOPOLIS: **(17)** iii AD *IGB* I^{2} 14 b, 10 (f. *Αὐρ. Μουκιανός*)
—GLAVA PANEGA (MOD.): **(18)** i-ii AD ib. II 510 (s. *Κένσος*)
—KABYLE: **(19)** 144 AD ib. V 5636, 20
—KELLAI: **(20)** 241-244 AD ib. III 1517, 9 (f. *Αὐρ. Ἡλιόδωρος*)
—MARKIANOPOLIS (TERRIT.): **(21)** f. iii AD ib. II 856 (*CCET* II (1) 256) (f. *Δυζάτραλις*)
—ODESSOS?: **(22)** ii AD *IGB* I^{2} 51 bis a, 5 (s. *Ἐπισᾶς*)
—PĂDARINO (MOD.): **(23)** ii-iii AD ib. V 5286 (f. *Ἰουλιανός*)
—PAUTALIA: **(24)** ii-iii AD ib. II 544 (f. *Πρίσκος*)
—SERDICA: **(25)** ii-iii AD ib. V 5683 (f. *Ῥοδόπη*)

Ἰούλις
MACEDONIA (BOTTIAIA):
—EDESSA: **(1)** 180 AD *SEG* XXIV 531, 16 (Tataki, *Edessa* 137) (s. *Ἰούλιος*)
MACEDONIA (ELIMEIA):
—AIANE (TERRIT.): **(2)** ?iii AD *EAM* 24 a (*Ἀντίγονος [ὁ] [καὶ] Ἰ.*: s. *—λιναιος*)
MACEDONIA (MYGDONIA):
—THESSALONIKE?: **(3)** ii-iii AD *IG* X (2) (1) 872 (f. *Ἰουλία*)
SCYTHIA MINOR:
—TOMIS: **(4)** ii-iii AD *ISM* II 369, 10 (s. *Διονυσόδωρος*, *Ἰουλία*)
THRACE:
—STROUNEILOS: **(5)** 202 AD *IGB* III 1690 d, 63 (and Thrace Pizos: s. *Δαλήτραλις*)

Ἰούλιττα
MACEDONIA (MYGDONIA):
—THESSALONIKE?: **(1)** ii AD *IG* X (2) (1) 706 (m. *Ἀντωνία*)

Ἰουνία
Macedonia (Mygdonia):
—thessalonike: **(1)** 209 ad ib. 506, 3 (d. Ἰσίδωρος, Ἀρτέμιν)
—thessalonike?: **(2)** ii ad ib. 863 (Ἰουν(ί)α: d. Τυραννίς)

Ἰούνιλλα
Thrace:
—beroe-augusta traiana: **(1)** c. 320-324 ad *Anal. Boll.* 31 (1912) p. 198; p. 208 (Ἰουλιάνα—p. 208)

Ἰούνιος
Thrace:
—nicopolis ad istrum: **(1)** ii-iii ad *IGB* ii 684 (Χρηστίων ὁ καὶ Ἰ.)

Ἰοῦστα
Thrace:
—beroe-augusta traiana: **(1)** c. 320-324 ad *Anal. Boll.* 31 (1912) p. 198; p. 208
—bizye: **(2)** imp. Dumont–Homolle 62a 1 (d. Ἰοῦστος)

Ἰουστῖνος
Macedonia (Bottiaia):
—beroia: **(1)** iv ad *SEG* xlix 688 (-στῆ-: ?s. Γοργόνις: Jew)
Macedonia (Mygdonia):
—thessalonike: **(2)** ?v-vi ad *AD* 4 (1918) Parart. p. 31
Thrace:
—nicopolis ad istrum: **(3)** ii-iii ad *IGB* ii 662 (f. Βαλέριος Θεόδοτος)

Ἰοῦστος
Macedonia (Edonis):
—amphipolis: **(1)** ii ad Dimitsas 874; **(2)** ii-iii ad *Thrakika* 13 (1940) p. 26 *Θ*; cf. *Epigraphica* 37 (1975) p. 28 (-στους)
Scythia Minor:
—tomis: **(3)** ii-iii ad *ISM* ii 19 b, 4
—tomis?: **(4)** ii ad ib. v 78, 3 (*CCET* iv 106) (s. Ἄττας)
Thrace:
—bizye: **(5)** imp. Dumont–Homolle 62a 1 (f. Ἰοῦστα)
Thrace?: **(6)** s. iii ad Dain, *IGLouvre* 27; *Dacia* 19 (1975) p. 200 no. 6 (locn., date) (or Macedonia?: s. Διονύσιος)

Ἱππαγόρας
Thrace:
—odessos: **(1)** 12-19 ad *IGB* v 5011, 11 (f. Λεόκριτος)

Ἵππαλος
Macedonia: **(1)** 164-153 bc *UPZ* 9; 61; 67; 74; 85; 100 + p. 113 (s. Γλαυκίας)

Ἱππαρῖνος
Cimmerian Bosporos:
—gorgippia: **(1)** s. ii ad *CIRB* 1177, 2 ([Ἱπ]παρῖνος); **(2)** ii/iii ad ib. 1179, 23 (-ρεῖ-: f. —λατας); **(3)** ~ ib. l. 52 (-ρεῖ-: s. Χάρδεις)
—pantikapaion: **(4)** ii/iii ad ib. 839, 3 (Ἱππαρεῖνο[ς]—Tokhtas'ev)

Ἱππαρχία
Thrace:
—maroneia: **(1)** s. iv bc *RE* (1) (m. Πασικλῆς (Boiotia, Thebes))

Ἵππαρχος
Cimmerian Bosporos:
—hermonassa: **(1)** i ad *CIRB* 1082 (s. Μενέστρατος, Χρήστη); **(2)** ~ ib. (f. Χρήστη)
Macedonia (Chalkidike):
—olynthos: **(3)** ?355 bc *TAPA* 69 (1938) p. 51 no. 5, 6, 10; Hatzopoulos, *Actes Chalc.* p. 80 (date) (f. Ζώπυρος)
—olynthos?: **(4)** ?350 bc *SEG* xxxvii 570, 3; Hatzopoulos, *Actes Chalc.* p. 80 (date)
—stageiros: **(5)** iv bc *RE* (17) (Tataki, *Macedonians* p. 175 no. 4)
Macedonia (Edonis):
—amphipolis?: **(6)** 359-336 bc Procl., *in R.* ii 116 (fict.?)
Scythia Minor:
—tomis*: **(7)** ii ad *ISM* ii 327, 5 (Ἱπ(π)αρχος)
Thrace:
—mesambria: **(8)** v/iv bc *IGB* I^2 330 (PM 63); cf. *IGB* v 5105 (f. Καλλικρίτα)

Ἱππᾶς
Macedonia (Chalkidike):
—olynthos: **(1)** v/iv bc *Olynthus* 10 pp. 143-5 no. 464 (ring)

Ἱππῆς
Thrace:
—abdera: **(1)** c. 475-450 bc *Horos* 14-16 (2000-2003) p. 246 no. 1 (*IThrakAig* E33) (Ἵππεω (gen.): s. Καλλιάναξ)

Ἱππίας
Macedonia: **(1)** hell. *IG* xii (5) 434 (Tataki, *Macedonians* p. 332 no. 13) (I f. Ἱππίας II); **(2)** ~ *IG* xii (5) 434 (Tataki, *Macedonians* p. 332 no. 12) (II s. Ἱππίας I)
Macedonia (Bottiaia):
—beroia: **(3)** f. ii bc *RE* (4) (Tataki 632; Tataki, *Macedonians* p. 78 no. 28)
—mieza: **(4)** s. ii bc *SEG* xliii 420
—skydra: **(5)** iii ad ib. xlix 793, 6
Macedonia (Derriopos):
—stuberra: **(6)** 74 ad *IG* x (2) (2) 326, 41 (s. Πρῖμος); **(7)** 116 ad ib. 327, 20 (f. Λῦσις)
Macedonia (Mygdonia):
—kalindoia: **(8)** a. 98 ad *SEG* xlii 582, 55 (s. Δημήτριος)
—thessalonike: **(9)** c. 230 bc *IG* xi (4) 1053, 11 = x (2) (1) 1028 (*RE* Supplbd. 4 (9a); Tataki, *Macedonians* p. 183 no. 35)
Macedonia (Pieria):
—phila?: **(10)** ?iii bc *RPh* 1911, pp. 133-4 no. 36, 93; cf. Helly, *L'État thessalien* pp. 319-20 (locn.) (Ἱππί[ας]: f. Κλεαρχίδης)
—pydna: **(11)** iv bc *GRBS* 43 (2002-3) p. 111 no. 2, 5; **(12)** ~ ib. p. 119 no. 5, 1
Skythia:
—olbia-borysthenes?: **(13)** iv bc Dubois, *IGDOlbia* 35 (vase)
Thrace:
—philippopolis-trimontium (territ.): **(14)** ii-iii ad *IGB* iii 1320, 2 (s. Κοκκήϊος)
Thrace?: **(15)** 316-309 bc *IG* II^2 1956, 9 (*FRA* 2542); *Ancient Macedonia* 5 p. 445 with n. 10 (date) ([Ἱπ]πίας)

Ἱππίης
Macedonia (Chalkidike):
—stolos?: **(1)** ?350 bc *SEG* xxxviii 671, 8 (Ἱππίω (gen.): f. Στράτων)

Ἱππόδημος
Thrace:
—apollonia-sozopolis: **(1)** iv bc *BMNBurgas* 4 (2002) p. 123 no. 14 (Ἱππόδ[ημος]?)

Ἱππόθοος
Thrace:
—perinthos-herakleia: **(1)** ii ad X. Eph. ii. 11 etc. (fict.)
—perinthos-herakleia?: **(2)** iv bc Hp., *Epid.* vi 8. 10

Ἱπποθῶν
Scythia Minor:
—kallatis: **(1)** s. iii bc *ISM* iii 9, 1 (s. Στράτων)

Ἱπποκλέα
Macedonia (Pieris):
—oisyme-emathia: **(1)** i-ii ad *SEG* xxxii 844 (Tataki, *Macedonians* p. 106 no. 3); cf. Hatzopoulos, *MI* 1 pp. 186-7 (d. Διονύσιος)

Ἱπποκλῆς
Macedonia (Bottiaia):
—beroia: **(1)** iii bc *IBer* 37, 3
Skythia:
—olbia-borysthenes: **(2)** f. iv bc Dubois, *IGDOlbia* 103, 8 (lead)

Ἱπποκράτη
Cimmerian Bosporos:
—pantikapaion: **(1)** f. iv bc *CIRB* 190; cf. KW pl. 6 no. 110 (d. Ἡρακλείδης)

Ἱπποκράτης
Cimmerian Bosporos:
—gorgippia: **(1)** f. iii bc *CIRB* 1137 A I, 16 (s. Εὔτιμος); **(2)** ~ ib. 1137 A II, 6 (s. Δημήτριος); **(3)** ~ ib. l. 20 (s. Θεόκριτος); **(4)** ~ ib. 1137 B I, 15 (Ἱπποκρά[τ]ης: f. Θεόκριτος); **(5)** ~ ib. l. 22 (f. —δης)
—hermonassa: **(6)** iv bc ib. 1056 II, 8 (s. Δημήτριος)
—pantikapaion: **(7)** iv bc *IGAIMK* 104 (1935) p. 304 nos. 35-8 (tile) (Ἱπποκρά(της))
Macedonia (Bottiaia):
—beroia: **(8)** b. 167 bc *IBer* 1 A, 1 (Tataki 633) (s. Νικοκράτης); **(9)** ii bc *IBer* 159 (Tataki 634) (f. Γλαυκιννώ)
Tauris:
—chersonesos: **(10)** iii bc Solomonik, *NEPKh* 145 (*SEG* xxx 964) (f. Πολυκάστα)

Ἱπποκρατίδης
Macedonia (Mygdonia):
—thessalonike: **(1)** ii ad *IG* x (2) (1) 303

Ἱππόκριτος
Thrace:
—stryme: **(1)** c. 425-400 bc *IThrakAig* E118 ([Ἱπ]πόκριτος: f. Ἡρόνεστος)

Ἱππολοχίδης
Thrace:
—perinthos-herakleia:
——(Geleuntes): **(1)** iii-ii bc *IPerinth* 61, 35 (s. Ἱππόλοχος)

Ἱππόλοχος
Macedonia: **(1)** iv/iii bc Ath. 126 d; 127 e; 128 a-b; 129 a; 402 a; 614 d (Tataki, *Macedonians* p. 332 no. 15)
Scythia Minor:
—istros: **(2)** v/iv bc *ISM* i 144; 169 (s. Ἡγησαγόρης, f. Ξενοκλῆς, Θεόξενος) ?= (*4*); **(3)** ~ ib.; [170] (s. Θεόδοτος); **(4)** iv bc ib. 236 ([Ἱπ]πόλοχος: s. Ἡγησαγόρης) ?= (*2*); **(5)** ii ad ib. 137, 11 ([Ἱ]ππόλοχος: s. Πυθίων); **(6)** 138 ad ib. 193 I, 37 (s. Φλ. Εὐξενίδης); **(7)** ~ ib. l. 62 (s. Χα—); **(8)** ii/iii ad ib. 227, 11 (Ἱππόλ<λ>οχ[ος])
Thrace:
—perinthos-herakleia:
——(Geleuntes): **(9)** iii-ii bc *IPerinth* 61, 35 (f. Ἱππολοχίδης)

Ἱππόλυτος
Macedonia (Mygdonia):
—thessalonike*: **(1)** ii-iii ad *IG* x (2) (1) 443 ([Ἱππό]λυτος?: slave?)
Macedonia (Paionia):
—stoboi: **(2)** s. iii ad *JÖAI* 32 (1940) Beibl. col. 19 no. 9. 113

Ἱππομάχα
Macedonia (Bottiaia):
—edessa: **(1)** f. iii bc *SEG* xxxviii 606 (vase); xli 569 (date) (Tataki, *Edessa* 138)

Ἱππόμαχος
CIMMERIAN BOSPOROS:
—NYMPHAION: (1) iii BC *CIRB* 912 II, 11 (s. *Διόδωρος*)
THRACE:
—DUVANLI (MOD.): (2) s. v BC Filow, *Duvanlij* p. 58 (vase) (*Ἱππόμαχ(ο)ς*)

Ἱππομέδων
THRACE:
—ODESSOS: (1) 2 BC *IGB* I² 46, 45 (f. *Νουμήνιος*); (2) m. ii AD ib. 176 ter (PM 1693); *IGB* I² 272 (PM 1676); *Dacia* 21 (1977) p. 161 (date) (f. *Ἀρτεμίδωρος*)
—PERINTHOS-HERAKLEIA: (3) ii-i BC *ISmyrna* 689 III, 36 (*Ἱππο[μέ]δων*: f. *Εὐγένεια*)

Ἱππόνικος
MACEDONIA: (1) m. iv BC *RE* (6); *Olynthus* 10 pp. 424-6 nos. 2186-2201; *BCH* 106 (1982) p. 83 no. 35 (bullets) (Tataki, *Macedonians* p. 332 no. 16); (2) 218 BC *PEnt* 15, 1 and verso (Tataki, *Macedonians* p. 333 no. 18); cf. La'da E1766 (I f. *Ἑρμίας*, *Ἱππόνικος* II); (3) ~ *PEnt* 15, 1 and verso (Tataki, *Macedonians* p. 332 no. 17; La'da E1766) (II s. *Ἱππόνικος* I: t.e.); (4) 106-105 BC *PDion* 19, 11, 15, 22, [36], 40, 42; 20, [11], [18]; 24, 2, [13]; 30, 2, [10], 13, 18 (Tataki, *Macedonians* p. 487 no. 142; La'da E1515) (s. *Πτολεμαῖος*)
MACEDONIA (CHALKIDIKE):
—ANTHEMOUS: (5) ii BC *Anthémonte–Kalindoia* 1 p. 56 no. A10 (*SEG* II 411) (f. *Πολέμων*)
MACEDONIA (DERRIOPOS):
—STUBERRA: (6) c. 41-48 AD *IG* X (2) (2) 323, 15 (-νει-: s. *Μενεκράτης*); (7) 50 AD ib. 324, 18 (-νει-: s. *Τιμέας*)
MACEDONIA (PIERIA):
—DION: (8) ii-iii AD Oikonomos 42 (-νει-)
SKYTHIA:
—OLBIA-BORYSTHENES: (9) f. iv BC Dubois, *IGDOlbia* 105 (s. *Τελεσικράτης*)
THRACE:
—LYSIMACHEIA: (10) m. ii BC *ISestos* 38 b, 2 (s. *Ἀλέξανδρος*)

Ἱπποσθένης
CIMMERIAN BOSPOROS:
—HERMONASSA: (1) 344-311 BC *CIRB* 1039 (f. *Μήστωρ*)
SCYTHIA MINOR:
—ISTROS: (2) 138 AD *ISM* I 193 I, 43 (s. *Ἡρόδωρος*); (3) ~ ib. l. 75 (s. *Σαραπίων*)

Ἱππόστρατος
CIMMERIAN BOSPOROS:
—PANTIKAPAION: (1) iii-ii BC *CIRB* 254 (f. *Μύρον*)
MACEDONIA: (2) iv BC Arr., *An.* iii 11. 8 (f. *Ἡγέλοχος*) ?= (4); (3) m. iv BC *RE* Supplbd. 3 (8); Berve 390 (Tataki, *Macedonians* p. 333 no. 19) ?= (4); (4) 344 BC *RE* Supplbd. 3 (10) (Tataki, *Macedonians* p. 333 no. 20) (s. *Ἀμύντας*) ?= (2) (3); (5) ?i BC Bernand, *El-Kanaïs* 23 (Tataki, *Macedonians* p. 487 no. 143); cf. La'da E1508 (f. *Θεόφιλος*)
MACEDONIA (BOTTIAIA):
—BEROIA: (6) 223 BC *IBer* 4, 11 (s. *Κάλλιππος*); (7) b. 167 BC ib. 1 A, 5, 18 (Tataki 636) (f. *Κάλλιππος*); (8) ii-i BC *IBer* 204 (Tataki 635) (s. *Ἀλέξανδρος*)
—PELLA: (9) iii BC Akamatis, *Amph. Pellas* p. 37 no. PAR31 (amph.) (*SEG* L 613); (10) iii-ii BC Dimitsas 134
MACEDONIA (CHALKIDIKE):
—POTIDAIA-KASSANDREIA: (11) ii BC *IG* XII (8) 178, 6; cf. Stephanis 1669 (Tataki, *Macedonians* p. 91 no. 53) (f. *Μένυλλα*)
MACEDONIA (ELIMEIA):
—AIANE: (12) s. ii AD *EAM* 14 (f. *Κλεονίκη*)
MACEDONIA (MYGDONIA):
—LETE: (13) m. i BC *SEG* XVII 318, 2; *KGAM Thess.* 1 56 (date) (f. *Διονυσοφῶν*)
MACEDONIA (ORESTIS):
—AGIA ANNA (MOD.): (14) ii-i BC *EAM* 192 (f. *Φιλωτέρα*)
MACEDONIA (PIERIA):
—KASTANIA (MOD.): (15) ii/i BC *SEG* L 593 (s. *Παράμονος*)
—KOLINDROS (MOD.): (16) imp. Dimitsas 204 (*[Ἱπ]πόστρα[τ]ος*: I f. *Ἱππόστρατος* II); (17) ~ ib. (II s. *Ἱππόστρατος* I, *Ἀντιγόνα*)

Ἱππότας
MACEDONIA (BOTTIAIA):
—BEROIA: (1) s. iii BC *IBer* 46, 15
MACEDONIA (EDONIS):
—AMPHIPOLIS: (2) a. 357 BC Hatzopoulos, *Actes Amphipolis* pp. 38-9 no. 7, 12
MACEDONIA (MYGDONIA):
—HERAKLEIA: (3) hell. Hatzopoulos, *MI* 1 p. 211 (f. *Νικάνωρ*)
—LETE: (4) f. ii BC *SEG* XLVI 764, 18 (f. *Σιμίας*)
MACEDONIA (PIERIA):
—KOLINDROS (MOD.): (5) ii/i BC ib. XXXIV 639 (f. *Φίλιππος*)

Ἱππώ
MACEDONIA (BOTTIAIA):
—ALLANTE? (PARTHENION (MOD.)): (1) imp. *AM* 27 (1902) p. 309 no. 12
MACEDONIA (MYGDONIA):
—THESSALONIKE (TERRIT.): (2) ii AD *IG* X (2) (1) 1016

Ἵππων
CIMMERIAN BOSPOROS:
—GORGIPPIA: (1) f. iii BC *CIRB* 1137 B II, 43 (f. *Μηνόφιλος*)
—PANTIKAPAION: (2) v BC Tolstoi 190 (vase) (*Ἱππῶνα[ξ]*—ed.); (3) iv/iii BC *KSIA* 109 (1967) p. 21 no. 6 (tile) (*Ἱππω(ν)*?)
MACEDONIA (DERRIOPOS):
—STUBERRA: (4) 74 AD *IG* X (2) (2) 325, 34 (f. *Φίλιππος*)
MACEDONIA (PIERIA):
—PHILA?: (5) ?iii BC *RPh* 1911, pp. 133-4 no. 36, 78; cf. Helly, *L'État thessalien* pp. 319-20 (locn.) (f. *Λυσικλῆς*)
THRACE:
—ABDERA: (6) c. 450-425 BC May, *Abdera* pp. 131-2 nos. 156-8 (coin)
—BYZANTION: (7) ii-i BC *IByz* 218 (Fıratlı–Robert p. 78 no. 87) (I f. *Ἵππων* II); (8) ~ *IByz* 218 (Fıratlı–Robert p. 78 no. 87) (II s. *Ἵππων* I)
—PERINTHOS-HERAKLEIA (NR.): (9) v BC *IPerinth* 288 (f. *Διῆς*)

Ἱππῶναξ
MACEDONIA (BISALTIA):
—TERPNI (MOD.): (1) iii BC *SEG* XXV 719 (XLVIII 846) (s. *Ἀπολλόδωρος*)
MACEDONIA?: (2) f. ii BC *PHels* 3, 29 (*[Ἱπ]πῶναξ*)
THRACE:
—ABDERA: (3) c. 336-311 BC May, *Abdera* pp. 292-3 nos. 543-4 (coin)
—ODESSOS: (4) v/iv BC *IGB* I² 101 bis (*[Ἱ]ππῶν[αξ]*?: s. *Ἀρίστων*)
—PERINTHOS-HERAKLEIA?: (5) iv BC Hp., *Epid.* iv 33

Ἰράμβουστος
SKYTHIA:
—TANAIS: (1) 188 AD *CIRB* 1242, 18, 20 (f. *Σιαύακος*, *Ἴρβις*)

Ἰράσταμος
SKYTHIA:
—TYRAS: (1) ii-iii AD *ISM* II 313 (*SEG* XXIV 1080) (s. *Ἄττας*)

Ἰραύαδις
SKYTHIA:
—TANAIS: (1) 225 AD *CIRB* 1279, 13 (s. *Δημήτριος*)

Ἴρβις
SKYTHIA:
—TANAIS: (1) 188 AD ib. 1242, 20 (s. *Ἰράμβουστος*)

Ἴργανος
SKYTHIA:
—TANAIS: (1) 224 AD ib. 1287, 25 (s. *X*—)

Ἶρις
MACEDONIA (PAIONIA):
—STOBOI: (1) ii AD Šašel, *IL* 457 (Lat. Iris)

Ἴρκιος
CIMMERIAN BOSPOROS:
—PANTIKAPAION: (1) imp. *CIRB* 787

Ἱρομνήμων
THRACE:
—ABDERA: (1) c. 360-350 BC May, *Abdera* pp. 258-9 nos. 439-46 (coin); Masson, *OGS* p. 431

Ἰσαάκ
THRACE:
—BISANTHE-PANION: (1) iv-vi AD *JÖAI* 23 (1926) Beibl. cols. 152-3 no. 88, 4 (*Ἡσάκ*: Jew)
—PHILIPPOPOLIS-TRIMONTIUM: (2) iii/iv AD *SEG* XXXIX 663 C (mosaic) (*Ἑλλ[ιος] [ὁ] [καὶ] Ἰ.*: Jew)

Ἰσαάκιος
THRACE:
—MARONEIA: (1) iv-v AD ib. XLVII 1073 (*IThrakAig* E354) (*Ἡσάκ*-: f. *Θαλάσσιος*)

Ἰσαγόρας
MACEDONIA (BOTTIAIA):
—BEROIA: (1) ii-iii AD *IBer* 317, 3-4 (Tataki 416) (*Δομίτιος Ἰσαγ(ό)ρας*: threptos)
SCYTHIA MINOR:
—KALLATIS: (2) iii/ii BC *ISM* III 161 (*Εἰ*-: s. *Ὀλύμπιχος*); (3) s. i AD ib. 32, 8 (s. *Ἰατροκλῆς*); (4) iii AD ib. 186 (f. *Ἡρακλέων*)
THRACE:
—ABDERA: (5) f. iii BC *AMNG* II (1) 239 (coin)

Ἰσαγόρης
SCYTHIA MINOR:
—ISTROS: (1) iv BC Unp. (Avram, defixio) 1, 7 (*[Ἰ]σαγόρης*)

Ἰσάζελμις
THRACE: (1) 231 or 206 BC *CPR* XVIII 3, 46, 53, 55, 59 (La'da E761)

Ἰσάνθης
THRACE:
—KROBYZOI: (1) iii BC *FGrH* 81 F 20 (king)

Ἰσᾶς
MACEDONIA (ODOMANTIKE):
—SIRRHA (TERRIT.): (1) ii-iii AD Kaphtantzis 474 (f. *Διονύσιος*)

Ἰσαυρικός
THRACE:
—BYZANTION: (1) c. 252-253 AD Schönert-Geiss, *Byzantion* 1808-11; 1836-9; 1850 (coin)

Ἰσιάδης
THRACE: (1) 130 BC *PBad* II 2, 36, 46 (Velkov 158; La'da E762)

Ἰσιάς
MACEDONIA (CHALKIDIKE):
—MONI LAVRAS (MOD.): (1) imp. Dimitsas 776; cf. Robert, *OMS* 2 pp. 1288-9 (*Σερβιλία Ἰ.*)

Macedonia (Mygdonia):
—thessalonike: (2) 48 ad *IG* x (2) (1) 623 C-D (*Εἰ-*); (3) ii ad ib. 357
—thessalonike?: (4) ii ad ib. 867 (*Κασσία Εἰσιάς*)
Macedonia (Odomantike):
—sirrha (nr.): (5) ii-iii ad *Tekmeria* 6 (2001) p. 10 (*SEG* xlix 743) (*Εἰ-*: d. *Παίβης*)
Macedonia (Pelagonia):
—mariovo (mod.): (6) 132 ad *IG* x (2) (2) 164 (*Εἰ-*: d. *Ζαικα*)
Thrace: (7) hell. *Historia* (Milan) 7 (1933) p. 581 no. 3
—perinthos-herakleia: (8) ii bc *ISmyrna* 145 (PM 925) (*Εἰ-*: d. *Διονύσιος*)

Ἰσιγένης
Macedonia (Odomantike):
—skotoussa?: (1) ii-iii ad Dimitsas 843 (*Εἰ-*: s. *Ἀλέξανδρος, Σελήνη*)

Ἰσιγόνη
Cimmerian Bosporos:
—pantikapaion: (1) i bc/i ad *CIRB* 311 (*Ἰσι[γ]όνη*: m. *Διογένης*); (2) f. ii ad ib. 684; cf. KW pl. 52 no. 711 (m. *Ἡρακλείδης*); (3) m. ii ad *CIRB* 678 (m. *Θαβεις*)
Macedonia (Mygdonia):
—thessalonike: (4) i ad *IG* x (2) (1) 388 (*Καιρελλία Ἰ.*); (5) ii-iii ad ib. 485 (*Καλαουιανὴ Εἰσιγόνη*: d. *Ἰουν. Νοτίς*)

Ἰσίγονος
Macedonia (Mygdonia):
—thessalonike?: (1) ii-iii ad *AEpThess* p. 12 no. 9 (f. *Φιλόλογος*)

Ἰσιδογένης
Cimmerian Bosporos:
—akra: (1) imp. *ZOOID* 31 (1913) Prot. p. 36 no. 1 (ring) (*Ἰσιδογ(έ)νης*)

Ἰσίδοτος
Macedonia (Odomantike):
—sirrha: (1) f. iii ad *SEG* xxx 590, 31 (*Αὐρ. Ἰ.*: s. *Γάϊος*)
Macedonia (Orestis):
—sisani (mod.): (2) 146 ad *EAM* 187, 14 (*Φλ. Εἰσίδοτος*)
Thrace:
—byzantion: (3) i bc-i ad *IByz* 19, 12 (*Μάρκελλος Εἰσίδοτος*)

Ἰσιδώρα
Macedonia (Bottiaia):
—beroia: (1) iii-iv ad *IBer* 446, 3 (Feissel, *RICM* 58; Tataki 638); (2) f. iii ad *IBer* 94, 7 (Tataki 1303) (*Φλ. Ἰ.*: m. *Τιβ. Κλ. Κοϊντιανή*)
Macedonia (Krestonia):
—ioron?: (3) s. ii ad *IBer* 87, 4 (Tataki 639) (or Macedonia (Bottiaia) Beroia: d. *Ἀντίγονος*)
Macedonia (Mygdonia):
—thessalonike: (4) ii-iii ad *SEG* xxxviii 709 c (*Π. Φοντεῖα Εἰσιδώρα*: d. *Σιθόνιος Ἰσίδωρος, Π. Φοντεῖα Κλεοπάτρα*); (5) m. iii ad *IG* x (2) (1) 158, 11; 207, 12 (*Αὐρ. Ἰ.*: m. *Τ. Στατίλιος Θεόδωρος, Αὐρ. Στατίλιος Θεόδωρος ὁ καὶ Ἀψιμάχις*)
—thessalonike (territ.): (6) 208 ad ib. 1014
—thessalonike?: (7) ii-iii ad ib. 887 (*Ἰσιδώ[ρα]*)
Macedonia (Pelagonia):
—keramiai (nr.): (8) 193-211 ad ib. x (2) (2) 218, 5 (*Οὐλπία Εἰσιδώρα ἡ καὶ Σαραπιάς*)
Macedonia (Pieria):
—dion?: (9) i-ii ad *AEMTh* 15 (2001) p. 343 (*Ἰουλ. Ἰ.*)
Thrace:
—salymbria: (10) v-vi ad *BCH* 36 (1912) p. 638 no. 96 (*AD* 53 (1998) Mel. p. 475 no. 216) (*Εἰσι[δώ]ρα*: d. *Παῦλος*)

Ἰσιδωριανός
Macedonia (Mygdonia):
—thessalonike: (1) 238 ad *IG* x (2) (1) 157, 3 (*Ἰσιδωριανὸς Αὐρ. Ἰσίδωρος*: II s. *Ἰσιδωριανὸς* I *Αὐρ. Ἰοῦστος*); (2) ~ ib. l. 5 (*Ἰσιδωριανὸς Αὐρ. Ἰοῦστος*: I f. *Ἰσιδωριανὸς* II *Αὐρ. Ἰσίδωρος*)
Macedonia (Sintike):
—parthikopolis: (3) f. iii ad *IGB* v 5910 (*Ἰσιδωριανὸς Ζωΐλος*)

Ἰσίδωρος
Macedonia: (1) 74 bc *SB* 7532, 26 (Tataki, *Macedonians* p. 487 no. 144); cf. La'da E1473 (f. *Διονύσιος*); (2) 41 ad *PMich* 267-8, 1 (*Ἡρωΐδης ὁ καὶ Ἰ.*: f. *Ἡρωΐδης*)
Macedonia (Bisaltia):
—euporia?: (3) iii ad *SEG* xxx 592 (*Eastern cults* p. 202 no. 20) (*Τόκης ὁ καὶ Ἰ.*)
—terpni (mod.): (4) i-ii ad *SEG* i 283 (s. *Ἀπολλᾶς*)
Macedonia (Bottiaia):
—beroia: (5) ii-iii ad *IBer* 488, 11 (*[Ἰ]σίδωρος*) ?= (*6*); (6) s. ii ad ib. 88, 7 (Tataki 75) (*Αἰλ. Ἰ.*: f. *Αἰλ. Λυκομήδης*) ?= (*5*)
—beroia?: (7) 102-117 ad *IBer* 64, 3 (*Εἰσίδωρ[ος]*)
Macedonia (Edonis):
—amphipolis: (8) ?iii ad *SEG* xxviii 539 (s. *Τελεσφόρος*)
Macedonia (Krestonia):
—ioron: (9) i bc-i ad ib. xlviii 816. 3 (sherd) (*Ἰσίδω[ρος]?*)
Macedonia (Mygdonia):
—lete: (10) ii ad *Makedonika* 2 (1951) p. 619 no. 42 θ, 5 (*Εἰ-*: s. *Γλαυκίας*)
—thessalonike: (11) f. i ad *IG* x (2) (1) 133, 10; Robert, *OMS* 5 pp. 295-302 (date) (*Εἰ-*: f. *Σωσίπατρος*); (12) ?ii ad *IG* x (2) (1) 655; (13) ii-iii ad ib. 473 (s. *Γ. Ἰούλ. Ζήνων*); (14) ~ ib. 599 (*Μ. Ἀουιάνιος Ἰ.*: s. *Μᾶρκος, Ἀνδριανή*); (15) ~ *SEG* xxxviii 709 a (*Σιθόνιος Ἰ.*: s. *Π. Φοντεῖα Κλεοπάτρα*, f. *Π. Φοντεῖα Ἰσιδώρα*); (16) 209 ad *IG* x (2) (1) 506, 2 (II s. *Ἰσίδωρος* I, *Ἀρτέμιν*); (17) ~ ib. l. 3, 4 (I s. *Σαβῖνος*, f. *Ἰσίδωρος* II, *Ἰουνία*); (18) m. iii ad ib. 149, 10; 176, 8 (*Αὐρ. Ἰ.*) ?= (*20*); (19) 238 ad ib. 157, 4 (*Ἰσιδωριανὸς Αὐρ. Ἰ.*: s. *Ἰσιδωριανὸς Αὐρ. Ἰοῦστος*); (20) 248 ad ib. 163, 24 (*Αὐρ. Ἰ.*) ?= (*18*)
—thessalonike?: (21) ii ad ib. 251, 4 (*Τ. Αἰλ. Ἰσίδωρ[ος]*); (22) ~ ib. 807 (*Μ. Οὐλπ. Εἰσίδωρος*); (23) s. ii ad ib. 252, 2 (*Εἰ-*: s. *Σκευᾶς*); (24) s. iii ad *AEpThess* p. 10 no. 8 A (*Εἰσίδω[ρος]*)
Macedonia (Odomantike):
—sirrha: (25) 105 or 221 ad *SEG* xxx 595 (s. *Ποσειδώνιος*); (26) s. ii ad Dimitsas 812, 12 (Kaphtantzis 16) (*Εἰ-*: f. *Πέλοψ*); (27) ~ Dimitsas 812, 13 (Kaphtantzis 16) (*Εἰ-*: s. *Οὐαλέριος*); (28) 155 ad Dimitsas 821, 15 (Kaphtantzis 1) (s. *Γάϊος*); (29) f. iii ad *SEG* xxx 590, 14 (f. *Αὐρ. Γαλάτης*)
Sarmatia:
—maiotai: (30) ii/i bc *EAD* xxx 418, 1 (slave)
Scythia Minor:
—tomis: (31) ii ad *ISM* ii 96, 5 (*Αὐρ. Πρείσκιος Ἰ.*)
Thrace: (32) 274 bc *PCZ* 59001, 5, 9, 14, etc. (Velkov 159; La'da E763)
—byzantion: (33) i bc-i ad? *IByz* 117 A (*Εἰ-*: s. *Ἀπολλώνιος*)
—dionysopolis: (34) 241-244 ad *IGB* i² 22 bis, 12 (*Ἰσίδω[ρος]?*)
—maroneia: (35) ii ad *IThrakAig* E279 (*Ἰσίδω[ρος]*: f. *Μηνόδοτος*)
—perinthos-herakleia: (36) imp. *IG* xii (8) 197 a + xii Suppl. p. 149 (f. *Μνησικλῆς*)
—salymbria: (37) v-vi ad *IPerinth* 224 (*AD* 53 (1998) Mel. p. 471 no. 209) (*Εἰσήδ[ω]ρος*: s. *Ἀλεξάνδρα*)

Ἰσίερος
Macedonia (Bottiaia):
—beroia: (1) ii-iii ad *IBer* 28 (Tataki 849) (*Τ. Μάλλιος Εἰσίερος*)

Ἰσίων
Cimmerian Bosporos:
—pantikapaion: (1) f. ii ad *CIRB* 685; cf. KW pl. 45 no. 639 (s. *Παπίας*)
Macedonia (Mygdonia):
—thessalonike: (2) ?ii ad *IG* x (2) (1) 127, 8 (*Τι. Κλ. Εἰσίων*)
Macedonia (Orestis):
—sisani (mod.): (3) 146 ad *EAM* 187, 12 (*Κλ. Εἰσίων*)
Thrace: (4) 46-54 ad *SEG* xvi 415 II, 17 (*IThrakAig* E84) (*Τιβ. Κλ. Εἰσίων*); (5) ~ *SEG* xvi 415 III, 36 (*IThrakAig* E84) (*Εἰ-*: s. *Φίλων*)
—abdera: (6) ii ad *BCH* 37 (1913) p. 138 no. 42, 4 (*IThrakAig* E21) (*—ισίων?*)
—kallipolis: (7) imp. *ISestos* 19 (s. *Ἡρακλείδης*, f. *Δημήτριος*)
—mesambria: (8) ii/i bc *IGB* v 5102 ?= (*9*); (9) ~ ib. 5104 I (s. *Δαμάτριος*) ?= (*8*)

Ἰσόδημος
Cimmerian Bosporos:
—bosporos?: (1) f. iv bc *CVA* Zurich 1 pl. 29, 12 (vase) (*Arch. Class.* 25-6 (1973-4) p. 350 no. 19); cf. *SEG* xxix 715 (?f. *Εὐτύχη*)
Macedonia (Bottiaia):
—beroia: (2) ii-iii ad *IBer* 89, 3 (Tataki 996) (*Μ. Οὐλπ. Ἰ.*)
Thrace:
—ainos: (3) ii bc *SEG* xxvii 251 (f. *Ἀπολλοφάνης*)

Ἰσοκράτης
Cimmerian Bosporos:
—achilleion: (1) v-iv bc *CIRB* 1059
Macedonia (Bisaltia):
—tragilos: (2) s. iv bc *AD* 22 (1967) Chron. p. 424 (23 (1968) Chron. p. 358; Kaphtantzis 528)
Macedonia (Bottiaia):
—pella: (3) c. 320 bc *CEG* ii 877 iv (Tataki, *Macedonians* p. 155 no. 51) (s. *Κλεῖνος, Σύνεσις*); (4) iii bc *IOrop* 230 (Tataki, *Macedonians* p. 155 no. 50)
Macedonia (Edonis):
—amphipolis: (5) iv bc *SEG* xxiv 587 (*Ἰσοκράτ[ης]*: f. *Εὐρύλοχος*)
Skythia:
—olbia-borysthenes: (6) f. iv bc *CEG* ii 734 (Dubois, *IGDOlbia* 45) (f. *Ἐπικράτης*)
Tauris:
—chersonesos: (7) ii-i bc Solomonik, *NEPKh* 2, 6 (*[Ἰ]σοκράτης*)

Ἴσορμος
Thrace:
—pautalia: (1) 135 ad *IGB* iv 2057, 10 (f. *Λου—*)

Ἶσος
Macedonia (Edonis):
—amphipolis: (1) ii-iii ad *SEG* xxxix 572 (*Εἶ-*: f. *Δημοσθένης*)
Thrace:
—bessoi: (2) 158 ad *CIL* xvi 108 (*IDR* i p. 118 no. 16) (Lat. Isi (gen.): f. *Ἐπτάπορις*)

Ἰσόχρυσος
Macedonia (Derriopos):
—stuberra: (1) 87 ad *IG* x (2) (2) 325, 77 (s. *Παράμονος*)
Thrace:
—odessos: (2) i bc-i ad *IGB* i² 151 (PM 713) (f. *Ἕλλην*)

Ἱστιαῖος

CIMMERIAN BOSPOROS:

—HERMONASSA: **(1)** f. v BC *SEG* XLIV 659 (vase) (Ἱστια(ῖος)?)

—PANTIKAPAION: **(2)** iv BC *CIRB* 157 (f. Ἀναξίστρατος); **(3)** ~ ib. 191 (s. Ἀπολλώνιος); **(4)** f. iv BC ib. 218; cf. KW pl. 2 no. 38 (f. Παρμένων); **(5)** s. iv BC *MIA* 56 (1957) p. 224 (tile) (Ἱστ(ιαῖος)?); **(6)** ~ *CIRB* 192, 1; cf. KW pl. 5 no. 88 (s. Δημήτριος)

MACEDONIA: **(7)** ?209 BC *PTeb* 821, 1 (Tataki, *Macedonians* p. 333 no. 23); cf. La'da E1807; E2786 (-τιή-: f. Ἱστίεια)

MACEDONIA (EDONIS):

—PHILIPPOI: **(8)** hell. Hatzopoulos, *MI* 1 p. 188 n. 1

MACEDONIA (MYGDONIA):

—THESSALONIKE: **(9)** iii BC *IG* X (2) (1) 302; cf. *AEMTh* 15 (2001) p. 215 (s. Σωσικράτης)

MACEDONIA?: **(10)** 168 BC *RE* Supplbd. 4 (-) (Tataki, *Macedonians* p. 333 no. 21) (Lat. Histiaeus)

SCYTHIA MINOR:

—TOMIS: **(11)** ii-iii AD *ISM* II 468, 10 (*Aἰ*-: f. Ποντικός)

SKYTHIA:

—NIKONION (NR.): **(12)** ?iv BC *North Pontic Archaeology* p. 104 fig. 6 no. 24 (sherd) (Ἱσ(τ)ιαῖο(ς)?)

—OLBIA-BORYSTHENES: **(13)** s. ii AD *IOlbia* 81, 7 (*IOSPE* I² 94); cf. Zgusta, *PNS* 1035 (Ἱστ(ι)αῖος: s. Σαδαῖος)

—OLBIA-BORYSTHENES*: **(14)** ?v-iv BC *ZOOID* 23 (1900) p. 18 no. 1 (vase)

THRACE:

—APOLLONIA-SOZOPOLIS: **(15)** v/iv BC *Greek Colonisation* p. 100 (Ἱστιαῖο (gen.))

—PERINTHOS-HERAKLEIA?: **(16)** iv BC Hp., *Epid.* iv 49

—ZONE?: **(17)** iv/iii BC *IG* XII (8) 267, 6; *IThrakAig* E400, 5 (f. Πολυάρατος); **(18)** ~ *IG* XII (8) 267, 7; cf. *IThrakAig* E400 (locn.) (I s. Πολυάρατος, f. Πολυάρατος, Ἀντιγένης, Ἱστιαῖος II, Παρμένουσα, Νίκα); **(19)** ~ *IG* XII (8) 267, 8; cf. *IThrakAig* E400 (locn.) (II s. Ἱστιαῖος I)

Ἱστίεια

MACEDONIA: **(1)** 209 BC *PTeb* 821, 1, 20 (Tataki, *Macedonians* p. 333 no. 22; La'da E1807) (Ἱστίεα—l. 1: d. Ἱστιαῖος)

Ἱστιειός

SCYTHIA MINOR:

—KALLATIS: **(1)** iii BC *ISM* III 126, 10 (Ἱστιει[ός]: f. ...οίτας)

TAURIS:

—CHERSONESOS: **(2)** iv/iii BC Solomonik, *GAKh* 986 (vase); **(3)** c. 320-310 BC Anokhin p. 138 no. 74 (coin)

Ἱστικῶν

CIMMERIAN BOSPOROS:

—GORGIPPIA: **(1)** ii-iii AD *NE* 9 (1971) p. 9 no. 6 A, 11 ([Ἱσ]τικῶν?)

—PANTIKAPAION: **(2)** v/iv BC Tolstoi 207 (vase) (Ἱστιχ(ῶν)?)

SKYTHIA:

—OLBIA-BORYSTHENES: **(3)** iii BC *Arkheologiia* (Kiev) 39 (1982) p. 35 (Vinogradov–Kryžickij pl. 91. 6 (vase)) ([Ἱσ]τικῶντ[ος]); **(4)** s. iii BC *IOSPE* I² 76, 8 (Sokolowski II 88; Dubois, *IGDOlbia* 88) (s. Μητρόδωρος)

Ἵστιος

SCYTHIA MINOR:

—TOMIS: **(1)** 201 AD *ISM* II 83 II, 29 (Αὐρ. Ἰούλ. Ἵ.); **(2)** ~ ib. l. 30 (Φλ. Ἵ.)

Ἱστορία

CIMMERIAN BOSPOROS:

—MYRMEKION (NR.): **(1)** ii AD *CIRB* 894; cf. KW pl. 4 no. 77

MACEDONIA (LYNKESTIS):

—HERAKLEIA?: **(2)** ii AD *IG* X (2) (2) 125 (d. Γράπτος, Κάλη)

Ἱσ-ρόδωρος

SCYTHIA MINOR:

—ISTROS?: **(1)** iii BC *IGB* II 877; cf. V 5393 (locn.) (f. Ἄρτις)

Ἵστρων

TAURIS:

—CHERSONESOS: **(1)** c. 300-285 BC Kats p. 100 no. 63 (amph.) ?= (*4*); **(2)** f. iii BC ib. p. 88 no. 18 (amph.) (s. Ἀπολλωνίδας); **(3)** ~ ib. p. 92 no. 37 (amph.) (f. Δελφός); **(4)** c. 290-280 BC Anokhin p. 139 no. 86 (coin) ?= (*5*) (*1*); **(5)** ~ ib. p. 140 no. 89 (coin) ?= (*4*); **(6)** c. 272-262 BC Kats p. 100 no. 64 (amph.) (s. Ἀπολλωνίδας); **(7)** c. 250-230 BC Anokhin p. 141 no. 106 (coin)

Ἰσχόλαος

MACEDONIA (LOWER PAIONIA):

—IDOMENE?: **(1)** s. ii BC *BCH* 98 (1974) p. 279 (f. Ζωΐλος)

THRACE:

—LYSIMACHEIA: **(2)** m. ii BC *ISestos* 38 b, 6 (f. Τιμόλαος)

Ἰσχόμαχος

MACEDONIA (CHALKIDIKE):

—OLYNTHOS: **(1)** s. iv BC *IG* XII (8) 435 (Tataki, *Macedonians* p. 138 no. 69) (f. Δήμαρχος)

Ἰσχυρίων

MACEDONIA: **(1)** 102 BC *PWürzb* 6, 29 (Tataki, *Macedonians* p. 487 no. 146); cf. La'da 1422 (f. Ἀπολλώνιος); **(2)** 88-81 BC *BGU* 2374, 2 (Tataki, *Macedonians* p. 487 no. 145); cf. La'da E1679; **(3)** 12 AD *PKöln* 227 B, 23 (s. Ἀφροδίσιος)

Ἰταλία

CIMMERIAN BOSPOROS:

—PANTIKAPAION: **(1)** s. i AD *CIRB* 546; cf. KW pl. 30 no. 439a (d. Μόνιμος); **(2)** i/ii AD *CIRB* 595; **(3)** ~ ib. 613

MACEDONIA (PIERIA):

—DION: **(4)** s. ii AD Oikonomos 17; cf. Spiliopoulou-Donderer, *KGN* p. 196 no. D14 (date) (d. Ἰουλία)

THRACE:

—CHERSONESOS (KÖY DERESI (MOD.)): **(5)** imp. *SEG* XXIV 654 (—ια Ἰ.)

—PERINTHOS-HERAKLEIA: **(6)** i-ii AD *IPerinth* 90 (Αἰμιλία Ἰ.)

Ἰταλικός

SCYTHIA MINOR:

—KALLATIS: **(1)** 241-244 AD *ISM* III 74, 10 (f. Ἡραίων) ?= (*2*); **(2)** ~ ib. 74 A, 23 (f. Διονυσόδωρος) ?= (*1*)

SKYTHIA:

—OLBIA-BORYSTHENES: **(3)** 149 AD *SEG* XXX 1534 (and Bithynia Prousias: *Eἰ*-: s. Ἑρμόδωρος)

THRACE:

—BYZANTION: **(4)** s. i AD *IByz* 34, 6 (Γ. Ἰούλ. Ἰ.)

—RHAIDESTOS*: **(5)** imp. *CIL* III 729 (Lat. Italicus: f. Περίνθιος: slave?)

Ἰταλός

MACEDONIA (DERRIOPOS):

—STUBERRA: **(1)** 74 AD *IG* X (2) (2) 325, 38 (f. Τιβέριος)

THRACE:

—ALOPEKONNESOS: **(2)** i-ii AD *ISestos* 10 (Γ. Ἰούλ. Ἰ.)

Ἴταμος

MACEDONIA (MYGDONIA):

—THESSALONIKE: **(1)** ii-iii AD *IG* X (2) (1) 544, 1 (Γορδιανὸς Ἴ.: ?f. Λ. Ἀτέλλιος Ἐπίκτητος, Λ. Ἀτέλλιος Θάλλος)

Ἴτης

CIMMERIAN BOSPOROS:

—GORGIPPIA: **(1)** f. iii BC *CIRB* 1137 B II, 31 (s. Ἐπικράτης)

—PANTIKAPAION: **(2)** v-iv BC *AA* 1907, p. 139 (vase)

Ἰτίη

CIMMERIAN BOSPOROS:

—PANTIKAPAION: **(1)** f. iv BC *CIRB* 193, 1; cf. KW pl. 5 no. 104 (m. Σῖμος, Βόλας); **(2)** 344-311 BC *CIRB* 11, 2

Ἰφιάδας

SCYTHIA MINOR:

—KALLATIS: **(1)** s. iii BC *ISM* III 13, 1 ([Ἰ]φιάδας)

Ἰφιάδης

CIMMERIAN BOSPOROS:

—PANTIKAPAION: **(1)** iii-ii BC Chuistova, *AIB* p. 77 n. 11 (weight) (Ἰσιάδης—ed., Ἰφιάδης—Vinogradov)

THRACE:

—DIONYSOPOLIS: **(2)** iii-ii BC *SNG Stancomb* 115-16 (coin) (Ἰφιά(δης))

Ἰφικράτης

MACEDONIA (PIERIA):

—DION: **(1)** iv BC *SEG* XXXVI 610 ([Ἰ]φικράτης: s. Σάθων)

Ἴχεις

CIMMERIAN BOSPOROS:

—PANTIKAPAION: **(1)** i BC/i AD *CIRB* 306; cf. KW pl. 20 no. 297; Zgusta, *PNS* 657 (Ἴχειος (gen.))

Ἰχναῖος

MACEDONIA (EDONIS):

—AMPHIPOLIS: **(1)** m. iii BC Hatzopoulos, *Actes Amphipolis* p. 52 no 12, 10; *SEG* XLI 566 (date) (f. Νέων)

Ἰωάννα

MACEDONIA (BOTTIAIA):

—EDESSA: **(1)** v-vi AD Feissel, *RICM* 45 (Ἰοάνα)

MACEDONIA (MYGDONIA):

—THESSALONIKE: **(2)** 535 AD *IG* X (2) (1) 403 (*SEG* XXIX 644; Feissel, *RICM* 135)

THRACE:

—ODESSOS: **(3)** vi AD Beševliev 87 (-άνα)

Ἰωάννης

MACEDONIA (BOTTIAIA):

—BEROIA: **(1)** v-vi AD *IBer* 439 (Feissel, *RICM* 71) (s. Ζηνόβιος); **(2)** vi AD *IBer* 437, 3 (Feissel, *RICM* 72)

—EDESSA: **(3)** v-vi AD ib. 15, 8; **(4)** ~ ib. 16; **(5)** ~ ib. 33; **(6)** ~ ib. 38 (s. Ἀλέξανδρος, Σαμβάτα)

MACEDONIA (CHALKIDIKE):

—MONI PROKOPIOU (MOD.): **(7)** iv-vi AD *SEG* XXXVII 543 b (*Eἰ*-)

MACEDONIA (EDONIS):

—AMPHIPOLIS: **(8)** v AD ib. XLVIII 724

—PHILIPPOI: **(9)** iv/v AD Feissel, *RICM* 229 (Pilhofer 247); **(10)** ?v AD *AAA* 13 (1980) p. 95 (Pilhofer 115)

MACEDONIA (ELIMEIA):

—AIANE: **(11)** iv-vi AD *RQ* 1931, p. 326 no. 167 (Ἰ. [Σα]βᾶ[ς])

MACEDONIA (MYGDONIA):

—THESSALONIKE: **(12)** ?iv AD *AEMTh* 15 (2001) p. 326; **(13)** v-vi AD *IG* X (2) (1) 334 (Feissel, *RICM* 167); **(14)** ~ *IG* X (2) (1) 632 (Feissel, *RICM* 143) (Ἰωάνν(η)ς)

—THESSALONIKE?: **(15)** v-vi AD *IG* X (2) (1) 365, 2 (Feissel, *RICM* 141)

—THESSALONIKE*: (**16**) ?v-vi AD *AD* 4 (1918) Parart. p. 31

MACEDONIA (PAIONIA):

—STOBOI: (**17**) iv-v AD Feissel, *RICM* 279 (mosaic); (**18**) v AD *RE* (18); *PLRE* II (9) ('I. *Στοβαῖος*)

MACEDONIA (PIERIA):

—PYDNA (LOULOUDIES (MOD.)): (**19**) s. vi AD *SEG* XLIX 728 B, 11 (Lat. Iohannes)

MACEDONIA (SINTIKE):

—PARTHIKOPOLIS*: (**20**) vi AD ib. XXXV 763 (bp.)

SCYTHIA MINOR:

—KALLATIS: (**21**) v-vi AD Barnea 53 (Popescu, *IGL* 98) (*'Ιωάν(νης)*: s. *Κυρᾶς*)

—TOMIS: (**22**) v-vi AD Barnea 14, 6 (Popescu, *IGL* 32) (f. *Μαρού*); (**23**) ~ Barnea 18, 3 (Popescu, *IGL* 37) (s. *Φωκᾶς*, f. *Ῥωμανά*); (**24**) m. v AD ib. 14

—TOMIS?: (**25**) c. 490-500 AD Barnea 40 (d) (Popescu, *IGL* 64. 3)

SKYTHIA:

—SKYTHAI: (**26**) s. v AD *PLRE* II (34) ('I. *ὁ Σκύθης*)

THRACE: (**27**) 460-463 AD ib. (24) (s. *Σέργιος*); (**28**) s. vi AD ib. III (101) ('I. *ὁ Μυστάκων*)

—BEROE-AUGUSTA TRAIANA: (**29**) v-vi AD Beševliev 193

—BISANTHE-PANION: (**30**) v-vi AD *AD* 49-50 (1994-5) Mel. p. 320 no. 146

—DIOKLETIANOPOLIS: (**31**) v-vi AD *PLRE* II (90); Beševliev 224, 11 (s. *Θεόδωρος*)

—MARKIANOPOLIS: (**32**) v-vi AD ib. 82 (Lat. Ioannis)

—MARONEIA: (**33**) iv-vi AD *SEG* XXX 696 (bronze) (*'Ηοάνης*); (**34**) v AD Meïmaris–Bakirtzis 7 (*SEG* XLIV 594; *IThrakAig* E353) (*Εἰο-*)

—MESAMBRIA: (**35**) v-vi AD *Nessebre* I p. 220 no. 45 (*'Ιωάνν[ης]*)

—ODESSOS: (**36**) v-vi AD Beševliev 115, 6; (**37**) vi AD ib. 106, 6

—PERINTHOS-HERAKLEIA: (**38**) v-vi AD *IPerinth* 229 (*AD* 51-2 (1996-7) Mel. p. 375 no. 190)

—RHAIDESTOS: (**39**) iv AD ib. 49-50 (1994-5) Mel. p. 298 no. 124 (*'Ιω(ά)νν[ης]?*)

—SALYMBRIA: (**40**) iv-vi AD ib. 53 (1998) Mel. p. 464 no. 204; (**41**) v-vi AD *IPerinth* 224 (*AD* 53 (1998) Mel. p. 471 no. 209) (*Εἰω-*: s. *Ἀλεξάνδρα*); (**42**) 492-499 AD *PLRE* II (93) ('I. *τὸ ἐπίκλην Κυρτός*)

—SERDICA: (**43**) v-vi AD Beševliev 5 (Lat. Ioannes: s. *Γεώργιος*)

—TZOUROULON: (**44**) v-vi AD *AD* 49-50 (1994-5) Mel. p. 341 no. 164 + 51-2 (1996-7) Mel. p. 386 (*'Ηοάνης*)

'Ιώδας

CIMMERIAN BOSPOROS:

—PANTIKAPAION: (**1**) ii AD *CIRB* 706; Zgusta, *PNS* 121 (I f. *'Ιώδας* II); (**2**) ~ *CIRB* 706 (*'Ιώ[δας]*?: II s. *'Ιώδας* I); (**3**) 275-278 AD ib. 36, 35 (s. *Βαρδάνης*)

'Ιωδέσμαγος

SKYTHIA:

—OLBIA-BORYSTHENES: (**1**) iii AD *IOSPE* I² 103, 4; Zgusta, *PNS* 116; 122 (s. *Νεῖλος*)

'Ιων

MACEDONIA (MYGDONIA):

—THESSALONIKE: (**1**) 171-168 BC *RE* (9) (Tataki, *Macedonians* p. 183 no. 36)

THRACE:

—APOLLONIA-SOZOPOLIS: (**2**) iv BC *IGB* I² 424 (s. *Εὔφημος*)

'Ιωνία

THRACE:

—AINOS: (**1**) ii AD *SEG* XXXVI 657, 9 (*'Ιο-*: m. *Ξενοκλῆς*, *Θεόξενος*, *Διόσκορος*)

—BYZANTION: (**2**) ii-i BC *IByz* 81 (Fıratlı–Robert p. 51 no. 23) (*Εἰ-*: d. *Καλλίστρατος*)

'Ιωνίη

CIMMERIAN BOSPOROS:

—PANTIKAPAION: (**1**) iii BC *CIRB* 244 (m. *Εὐπορία*)

'Ιωνικός

THRACE:

—SALYMBRIA: (**1**) hell.? *IByz* S 30 (PM 745) (dub.)

'Ιωσάρας

CIMMERIAN BOSPOROS:

—PANTIKAPAION: (**1**) i BC *CIRB* 280

'Ιωσήφ

THRACE:

—PHILIPPOPOLIS-TRIMONTIUM: (**1**) f. iii AD *SEG* XXXIX 663 A-B (mosaic) (*Κοσμιανὸς ὁ καὶ 'I.*: Jew)

—SALYMBRIA: (**2**) v AD *AD* 53 (1998) Mel. p. 469 no. 208 (*Κόμης ὁ κὲ Εἰωσήφ*: s. *Συμεών*: Jew)

K

Καβαθάξης

CIMMERIAN BOSPOROS:

—HERMONASSA: (**1**) iv BC *CIRB* 1056 I, 20 (f. *—λας*)

—KEPOI?: (**2**) iv/iii BC ib. 1113 (*GVI* 1445; *CEG* II 739) (f. *Κπηεθύρης*)

Καβιρίς

THRACE:

—APOLLONIA-SOZOPOLIS: (**1**) ?iv-iii BC *SEG* III 557 (vase)

Καδάνακος

SKYTHIA:

—TANAIS: (**1**) 220 AD *CIRB* 1278, 11 (s. *Ναύαγος*)

Κάδδινος

SKYTHIA:

—OLBIA-BORYSTHENES: (**1**) ii-iii AD *IOSPE* I² 46, 2; (**2**) ii/iii AD *IOlbia* 52, 3 (f. *Ἀχιλλεύς*)

Κάδμος

MACEDONIA (EDONIS):

—PHILIPPOI*: (**1**) 37 AD *BCH* 58 (1934) p. 450 no. 1 A (Pilhofer 287) (Lat. Cadmus: imp. freed.)

Καεινόχα

THRACE:

—BOURDAPA: (**1**) ii-iii AD *IGB* III 1359

Καζίζης

MACEDONIA (PIERIS):

—GALEPSOS: (**1**) 63 BC or 53 AD *SEG* XXVII 285 (s. *Διοσκουρίδης*)

Καζίνας

SKYTHIA:

—OLBIA-BORYSTHENES: (**1**) ii AD *IOSPE* I² 96, 7; Zgusta, *PNS* 299 (s. *Φάρναγος*) ?= (*2*)

—OLBIA-BORYSTHENES (BEREZAN (MOD.)): (**2**) ?ii AD *VDI* 1993 (1), p. 90 = *SEG* XLIX 1028 B, 6 (s. *Φάρναγος*) ?= (*1*)

Κάθαις

SKYTHIA:

—OLBIA-BORYSTHENES: (**1**) ii AD *IOSPE* I² 686, 6 (*VDI* 1975 (1), p. 69) (s. *Πάρνουγος*) ?= (*Κάσαις* (*1*))

Καθαρά

SCYTHIA MINOR:

—KALLATIS: (**1**) f. iii BC *ISM* III 78 (d. *Διονύσιος*)

THRACE:

—BYZANTION: (**2**) ii-i BC *IByz* 254 (Fıratlı–Robert p. 117 no. 197) (*[Κα]θαρά*: d. *Σωτήριχος*)

—BYZANTION (TERRIT.): (**3**) ii BC *IByz* 169 (Fıratlı–Robert p. 109 no. 176) (d. *Φείδων*)

Καθαρίς

TAURIS:

—CHERSONESOS: (**1**) iv BC Solomonik, *GAKh* 1032-3 (vases) (*Καθάρει*—1032, *Καθάρι*—1033)

Κάθιος?

SCYTHIA MINOR:

—TOMIS: (**1**) ii AD *ISM* II 17, 3 (*Κά̣θιος*?, *Κλοῖος*?: f. *Κρήσκης*)

Καιγεις

THRACE:

—MARKIANOPOLIS (TERRIT.): (**1**) f. iii AD *IGB* V 5385 = *CCET* II (1) 359 (s. *Δρίζενις*)

Καιγεισος

THRACE:

—DUROSTORUM (TERRIT.)?: (**1**) ii-iii AD *IGB* II 874; cf. V 5392 (f. *Πεισσουσος*)

—GLAVA PANEGA (MOD.): (**2**) ii-iii AD ib. II 561; cf. V 5191 (*Τιβ. Κλ. Κ.*)

Καικίλις

MACEDONIA (BOTTIAIA):

—BEROIA: (**1**) iii AD *IBer* 398, 1 (Tataki 647)

Καικιλλία

MACEDONIA (MYGDONIA):

—THESSALONIKE: (**1**) iv-vi AD *SEG* XLVI 818 (*[Κ]αικιλλία*)

Καινάξαρθος

SKYTHIA:

—OLBIA-BORYSTHENES: (**1**) ii AD *IOSPE* I² 91, 3; Zgusta, *PNS* 123 (s. *Ἀργουάναγος*)

Καινίς
THRACE:
—PHILIPPOPOLIS-TRIMONTIUM: (**1**) ii-iii AD *IGB* III 1022, 3 (*GVI* 1338) (d. *Μιθριδάτης, Χρήστη*)

Καίπριζος
MACEDONIA (EDONIS):
—AMPHIPOLIS: (**1**) ?ii AD *FGrH* 257 F 37, 54 (Tataki, *Macedonians* p. 54 no. 68) (f. *Μάντις*)

Καῖσαρ
SKYTHIA:
—TYRAS: (**1**) 181 AD *IOSPE* I² 2, 23 (s. *Ζούρης*)

Καισία
MACEDONIA (BOTTIAIA):
—BEROIA: (**1**) i AD *IBer* 125, 3 (Tataki 653) (d. *Σέξ. Καίσιος*, m. *Τορπιλία Οὐέτυλλα*)
MACEDONIA (MYGDONIA):
—THESSALONIKE: (**2**) ii-iii AD *IG* X (2) (1) 437 (*Κε-*: d. *Μαντώ*)

Κακοῦς
THRACE:
—BEROE-AUGUSTA TRAIANA (TERRIT.): (**1**) ii-iii AD *IGB* III 1760 (*Κακοῦδος* (gen.): f. *Αὐλούζενις*)

Κάλα
THRACE:
—BYZANTION: (**1**) i-ii AD *IByz* 315 a (Fıratlı–Robert pp. 122-3 no. 205) (d. *Ἡρακλέων*)

Κάλαμος
THRACE:
—BYZANTION (TERRIT.): (**1**) imp. Unp. (Sayar) (?f. *Ἀσκληπιάς*)

Καλανδία
MACEDONIA (MYGDONIA):
—THESSALONIKE: (**1**) m. iii AD *IG* X (2) (1) 195, 7; 196, 8 (*Αὐρ. Κ.*)

Καλανδίων
MACEDONIA (BOTTIAIA):
—BEROIA: (**1**) f. iii AD *IBer* 236, 1 (Tataki 655) (s. *Ἑρμιόνη*)
MACEDONIA (MYGDONIA):
—THESSALONIKE: (**2**) ii-iii AD *AD* 26 (1971) Chron. p. 377 no. 2 (threptos)
—THESSALONIKE (NR.): (**3**) ii-iii AD *IG* X (2) (1) 1007
SCYTHIA MINOR:
—ISTROS: (**4**) ii AD *ISM* I 197 II, 3 (s. *Γλύκων*)
—KALLATIS: (**5**) 241-244 AD ib. III 74 B, 19
SKYTHIA:
—OLBIA-BORYSTHENES: (**6**) ii AD *IOlbia* 82; *IOSPE* I² 90; 100, 6; 175, 9 (f. *Εὔπλους*); (**7**) ~ ib. 83, 10 (f. *Στέφανος*); (**8**) f. ii AD *Drev. Prichern.* 3 pp. 27-8, 4 (*Καλαν[δί]ων*: f. *Ἀχιλλεύς*)
THRACE:
—AQUAE CALIDAE: (**9**) ?iii AD *IGB* I² 383, 2 (*Αὐρ. Καλ[α]νδίων*: s. *Ἐλπιδηφόρος*)
—BIZYE: (**10**) ii-iii AD *SEG* XXXII 660, 7 (*Μ. Αὐρ. Κ.*: s. *Διονύσιος*)
—KELLAI: (**11**) 241-244 AD *IGB* III 1517, 43 (*Αὐρ. Κ.*: s. *Κάνδιδος*); (**12**) ~ ib. l. 54 (f. *Αὐρ. Τάταρος*)
—PERINTHOS-HERAKLEIA:
——(*φυλ. τετάρτ.*): (**13**) iii-iv AD *IPerinth* 186, 1 (*AD* 51-2 (1996-7) Mel. p. 341 no. 171) (*Φλ. Κ.*)
—PHILIPPOPOLIS-TRIMONTIUM:
——Parembole: (**14**) ?ii AD *IGB* III 1512, 1 (*Ἰούλιος Κ.*)
—SERDICA: (**15**) 261-268 AD ib. IV 1912 (*Φλ. Κ.*)
—SPINOPARA: (**16**) ii AD ib. 2192, 9 (*Καλα(ν)δίων*)

Κάλας
MACEDONIA: (**1**) 336-328 BC *RE* Supplbd. 4 (1); Berve 397 (Tataki, *Macedonians* p. 195 no. 11) (*Κάλλας*—D.S. xvii: s. *Ἅρπαλος*); (**2**) 331 BC Arr., *An.* iii 5. 6 + Hoffmann, *Makedonen* p. 196; cf. *RE* Supplbd. 4 (2); Berve 395; Tataki, *Macedonians* p. 334 no. 5 (*Κάλανος*—Arr. mss.); (**3**) 317 BC *RE* Supplbd. 4 (3) (Tataki, *Macedonians* p. 335 no. 8); (**4**) 236 BC *PPetr*² 16, 73 (Tataki, *Macedonians* p. 334 no. 3; La'da E1516) (?f. *Δημητρία*); (**5**) iii-ii BC *Athena* 20 (1908) pp. 214-6 no. 13 II, 1 (Tataki, *Macedonians* p. 334 no. 2); (**6**) c. 223 BC *PTeb* 815 fr. 3 verso I, 25 (Tataki, *Macedonians* p. 335 no. 6; La'da E1767) (s. *Φιλίσκος*: t.e.)
MACEDONIA (PELAGONIA): (**7**) ii-i BC *IG* X (2) (2) 159, 7 (f. *Ἀττίδως*?)

Καλατύχα
MACEDONIA (BOTTIAIA):
—EDESSA: (**1**) ii AD *BSA* 58 (1963) p. 23 no. 5 (Tataki, *Edessa* 281) (*Σερβειλία Κ.*)

Καλάτυχος
MACEDONIA (MYGDONIA):
—THESSALONIKE: (**1**) s. ii AD *IG* X (2) (1) 244 II, 13 (*Μ. Αἴλ. Καλάτυ(χ)ος*?)

Καλδένθης
MACEDONIA (SINTIKE):
—NEINE: (**1**) 77 AD *IGB* V 5883, 8 (s. *Ἄσος*)

Κάλη
CIMMERIAN BOSPOROS:
—PANTIKAPAION: (**1**) m. i AD *CIRB* 515 (m. *Μοίριμος*)
MACEDONIA (BOTTIAIA):
—BEROIA: (**2**) ii-iii AD *IBer* 91, 9; 92, 10 (Tataki 627) (*Ἰουν. Κ.*: m. *Ἰούν. Ἀντίγονος ὁ καὶ Ἀνακτόριος, Ἰούν. Διοσκουρίδης ὁ καὶ Δουλκίτιος*); (**3**) 2[illegible]0 AD *ILeukopetra* 56, 10
MACEDONIA (LYNKESTIS):
—HERAKLEIA?: (**4**) ii AD *IG* X (2) (2) 125 (m. *Ἱστορία*)
SCYTHIA MINOR:
—TOMIS*: (**5**) i-ii AD *ISM* II 177 (Lat. Maria Cale: freed.)

Καλημέρα
MACEDONIA (BOTTIAIA):
—EDESSA: (**1**) v-vi AD Feissel, *RICM* 23 (-λι-)

Καλημερία
MACEDONIA (BOTTIAIA):
—BEROIA: (**1**) ii-iii AD *IBer* 251 (Tataki 656)

Κάλης
MACEDONIA (PAIONIA):
—BYLAZORA: (**1**) m. ii AD *Sp.* 98 (1941-8) p. 30 no. 74 (s. *Μέστριος*)

Καλησικράτης
THRACE:
—ABDERA: (**1**) c. 450-425 BC May, *Abdera* pp. 137-8 nos. 177-81 (coin); Masson, *OGS* p. 431

Καλητύχη
CIMMERIAN BOSPOROS:
—PANTIKAPAION: (**1**) f. i AD *CIRB* 435

Κάλις?
MACEDONIA: (**1**) 330 BC *RE* Supplbd. 4 (-); Berve 398 (Tataki, *Macedonians* p. 334 no. 4) (Lat. Calis—mss., Calas—em. Hedicke)

Κάλλαισχρος
SKYTHIA:
—OLBIA-BORYSTHENES: (**1**) iii BC *IOSPE* I² 201 I, 7 (*Κάλλα[ισχρος]*?—ed.: f. *Φιλωνίδης*)

Κάλλας
MACEDONIA (EDONIS):
—AMPHIPOLIS: (**1**) a. 332 BC *CEG* II 879 (*SEG* XLVIII 716 bis) (f. *Ἀντίγονος*)

Καλλέας
MACEDONIA (BOTTIAIA):
—BEROIA: (**1**) ii AD *IBer* 345 (Tataki 657)
MACEDONIA (DERRIOPOS):
—STUBERRA: (**2**) 74 AD *IG* X (2) (2) 326, 44 (s. *Διονύσιος*)
SCYTHIA MINOR:
—ISTROS: (**3**) ii AD *ISM* I 196, 13; 201 I, 14 (s. *Δορυφόρος*)
—TOMIS: (**4**) ii-iii AD ib. II 468, 9 (f. *—λις*)
TAURIS:
—CHERSONESOS: (**5**) i BC-i AD *IOSPE* I² 454 (s. *Γάϊος*)

Κάλλη
CIMMERIAN BOSPOROS:
—PANTIKAPAION: (**1**) i AD *CIRB* 444

Κάλλης
MACEDONIA (BOTTIAIA):
—SKYDRA: (**1**) iii AD *SEG* XLIX 793, 23 (*Αὐρ. Κ.*)

Καλλιάδας
TAURIS:
—CHERSONESOS: (**1**) iv-iii BC *Drev. Bosp.* 1 pp. 98-99 fig. 3 (s. *Συρίσκος*); (**2**) ~ Solomonik, *NEPKh* 29 (s. *Ἀρτεμίδωρος*); (**3**) iii BC ib. 33 (*Καλλι[ά]δ[ας]*: f. *Διονύσιος*); (**4**) f. iii BC Kats p. 96 no. 53 (amph.) (f. *Ἡρόγειτος*); (**5**) c. 237-230 BC ib. pp. 100-1 no. 65 (amph.) (s. *Διονύσιος*); (**6**) ii-i BC *IOSPE* I² 709 (*Καλ[λιά]δας*)
—KERKINITIS: (**7**) f. iii BC *SNG BM Black Sea* 700 (coin) (*Καλλιά(δας)*?, *Καλλία(ς)*?)
THRACE:
—BYZANTION: (**8**) iii-ii BC *FGrH* 390 F 1. 34 (-δης)

Καλλιάδης
SCYTHIA MINOR:
—ISTROS: (**1**) iii BC *ISM* I 70 (I f. *Καλλιάδης* II); (**2**) ~ ib. (II s. *Καλλιάδης* I)

Καλλιάναξ
THRACE:
—ABDERA: (**1**) c. 475-450 BC *Horos* 14-16 (2000-2003) p. 246 no. 1 (*IThrakAig* E33) (f. *Ἱππῆς*); (**2**) c. 360-350 BC May, *Abdera* pp. 260-1 nos. 449-51 (coin)

Καλλιάνασσα
THRACE:
—APOLLONIA-SOZOPOLIS: (**1**) ?iii BC *IGB* I² 458 bis, 3 (d. *Εὐκλέων*, m. *Νικοῦς*)

Καλλίαρος
CIMMERIAN BOSPOROS:
—THEODOSIA: (**1**) iii-ii BC *CIRB* 950 (*[Κ]αλλίαρο[ς]*: s. *Δάμων*)

Καλλίας
CIMMERIAN BOSPOROS:
—PANTIKAPAION: (**1**) s. iv BC ib. 201; cf. KW pl. 7 no. 120a
MACEDONIA: (**2**) ?417-413 BC *IG* I³ 89, 65 (Tataki, *Macedonians* p. 335 no. 9); (**3**) c. 235-200 BC *TCam* 35, 28; *IG* XII (1) 104 c, 7 (Tataki, *Macedonians* p. 335 no. 11) (f. *Εὐθυκράτης*); (**4**) ?150 BC *PBad* II 11, 5 (Tataki, *Macedonians* p. 335 no. 10; La'da E1517) (s. *Ἀπολλόδωρος*, f. *Ἀπολλόδωρος*)
MACEDONIA (BOTTIAIA):
—AIGAI: (**5**) s. iv BC *SEG* XXXV 773 (?s. *Ἀρτεμίδωρος*, f. *Ἀρτεμίδωρος, Δημητρία*)
—PELLA: (**6**) s. iv BC ib. XLI 575, 1-2 (s. *Δημήτριος*, f. *Δημήτριος*)
MACEDONIA (CHALKIDIKE):
—SKIONE: (**7**) f. iv BC *IG* II² 10366 (Tataki, *Macedonians* p. 173 no. 7; *FRA* 6906) (f. *Ἰσήρατος, Εὐγένης*)

Macedonia (Edonis):
—amphipolis: **(8)** s. iv bc *Mous. Kavalas* pp. 117-18 no. *Λ*. 202 (f. *Δωρόθεος*)
Macedonia (Mygdonia):
—kalindoia: **(9)** c. 333 bc Hatzopoulos, *MI* 2 p. 84 no. 62, 12 (s. *Ἀπολλώνιος*)
—thessalonike (territ.): **(10)** hell. *SEG* xlix 812
Macedonia (Pieria):
—pydna: **(11)** iv bc *GRBS* 47 (2002-3) p. 116 no. 4, 3 with fig. 3 (s. *Πολεμοκράτης*)
Skythia:
—olbia-borysthenes: **(12)** iv bc *SEG* xxx 919 (vase) (*Καλλία[ς]*?)
Tauris:
—chersonesos: **(13)** iv bc *In. Fil.* 85 (1987) p. 112 no. 2 (f. *Συρίσκος*)
Thrace:
—apollonia-sozopolis: **(14)** v/iv bc *IGB* I^2 408 (s. *Κράτιππος*)
—byzantion: **(15)** s. iv bc *RPh* 1937, p. 325 no. 6 A, 18 (s. *Μάτρων*)
—madytos: **(16)** ?464 bc *IG* I^3 1144, 35
—maroneia: **(17)** 311-306 bc Maier, *Mauerbauinschr.* 69 II, 145 (s. *Ἀπολλωνοφάνης*)

Καλλίβιος
Macedonia (Edonis):
—amphipolis: **(1)** hell.? *SEG* xxxiv 609 (s. *Στράτων*)

Καλλιβούλη
Macedonia (Chalkidike):
—polichne?: **(1)** ?353 bc ib. xxxvii 576, 13

Καλλίγειτος
Cimmerian Bosporos:
—theodosia: **(1)** iv bc *CIRB* 948 (f. *Ἀρεσίας*)
Macedonia (Chalkidike):
—olynthos: **(2)** ?350 bc *TAPA* 65 (1934) p. 125 no. 3, 10; Hatzopoulos, *Actes Chalc.* p. 80 (date) (*Καλλίγειτ[ος]*?: f. *Τεδέσιος*)

Καλλιγείτων
Thrace:
—byzantion: **(1)** c. 220 bc Plb. iv 52. 4; cf. Robert, *OMS* 2 p. 1093 (f. *Κόθων*); **(2)** i bc/i ad *IByz* 285 (Fıratlı–Robert pp. 56-7 no. 36) (f. *Ματρόδωρος*); **(3)** ~ *IByz* 285 (Fıratlı–Robert pp. 56-7 no. 36) (s. *Ματρόδωρος*)
—mesambria: **(4)** s. iv bc *IGB* I^2 334 bis (s. *Σώσανδρος*); **(5)** i bc ib. 324 (f. *Ἀντίφιλος*)

Καλλιγένης
Cimmerian Bosporos:
—gorgippia: **(1)** f. iii bc *CIRB* 1137 A I, 52 (f. *Μαίσης*); **(2)** ~ ib. 1137 B I, 44 (*[Κ]αλλιγένης*: s. *Κράτερος*); **(3)** ~ ib. 1137 B II, 19 (s. *Ἀ—α—*)
—nymphaion: **(4)** iii bc ib. 912 II, 15 (s. *Πρωταγόρας*)
—pantikapaion: **(5)** iii-ii bc ib. 251; cf. KW pl. 20 no. 294; **(6)** i-ii ad *CIRB* 614 (*Κα[λλι]γένης*); **(7)** f. i ad ib. 350 (f. *Ἀπολλώνιος*); **(8)** m. i ad ib. 430 (f. *Θεόφιλος*); **(9)** ~ ib. (s. *Διονύσιος*)
Macedonia (Bottiaia):
—edessa: **(10)** ii-iii ad *Arch. Pap.* 22 (1973) p. 205 no. 5 (Tataki, *Edessa* 139) (*Καλι-*: s. *Κουσπίδιος Παριανός, Κοκκεία Ἐπιγόνη*)
Macedonia (Chalkidike):
—olynthos: **(11)** c. 100 bc *GP* 253 (Tataki, *Macedonians* p. 138 no. 70) (f. *Διόδωρος*: fict.?)
Skythia:
—tanais: **(12)** 104 ad *CIRB* 1259, 15 (*[Κ]αλλιγένης*: s. *Θεόνικος*); **(13)** 228 ad ib. 1282, 23 (f. *—ους*); **(14)** ~ ib. 1283, 9 (*Καλλιγ[ένη]ς*: s. *Μύρων*)
Thrace:
—lysimacheia: **(15)** m. ii bc *ISestos* 38 a, 1 (f. *Κάλλιππος*)
—maroneia: **(16)** ii-i bc *IThrakAig* E212, 40 (f. *Διοσκουρίδης*)

Καλλιγόνα
Thrace:
—byzantion?: **(1)** i bc-i ad *IByz* 375 (Fıratlı–Robert p. 126 no. 211) (*Καλλιγόνα*: d. *Ἀπολλώνιος*)

Καλλιδάμας
Thrace:
—abdera: **(1)** c. 450-425 bc May, *Abdera* pp. 127-30 nos. 142-50 (coin)

Καλλίδρομος
Macedonia (Chalkidike):
—potidaia-kassandreia: **(1)** ?iv/iii bc *BCH* 17 (1893) p. 633 (Tataki, *Macedonians* p. 91 no. 54) (f. *Ἄνδρων*)

Καλλίης
Cimmerian Bosporos:
—hermonassa: **(1)** c. 475-450 bc *SEG* xliv 659 (vase)

Καλλικλέα
Thrace:
—mesambria: **(1)** c. 150-89 bc *Milet* I (3) 48, 6 (and Caria Miletos: d. *Διονύσιος*)

Καλλίκλεια
Cimmerian Bosporos:
—pantikapaion: **(1)** ii ad *CIRB* 687 (*Καλλίκλε[ια]*: m. *Ἑρμογένεια*)

Καλλικλείδης
Macedonia (Chalkidike):
—torone: **(1)** c. 450-420 bc *IG* I^3 1378 (Tataki, *Macedonians* p. 191 no. 8; *FRA* 7142) (f. *Μίκκος*)

Καλλικλῆς
Cimmerian Bosporos:
—pantikapaion: **(1)** f. i ad *CIRB* 392 (s. *Ἐπαφρᾶς*); **(2)** ~ ib. 412
Macedonia: **(3)** 340 bc *CID* II 43, 17 (Tataki, *Macedonians* p. 336 no. 13)
Macedonia (Bottiaia):
—mieza: **(4)** iii/ii bc *SEG* xliii 406; 411; 412; 413; 416; 418 (s. *Ἀριστοφάνης*, f. *Ἀριστοφάνης, Ἀριστέας, Εὔιππος*)
Macedonia (Mygdonia):
—kalindoia: **(5)** i bc/i ad ib. xlii 597
Scythia Minor:
—istros: **(6)** c. 140-160 ad *ISM* I 207, 21; cf. *SEG* xlviii 970 (f. *Αἴμ.λις*)
Skythia:
—olbia-borysthenes: **(7)** ?s. iv bc *IOSPE* I^2 178, 3 (*Καλλικλ[ῆ]ς*: f. *Νι—ος*); **(8)** ii-iii ad *IOlbia* 102, 5 (f. *Ἀχιλλεύς*)
Tauris:
—chersonesos: **(9)** 130 ad *VDI* 1960 (3), pp. 154-5, 28 (s. *Ἡδύλος*)
Thrace:
—byzantion: **(10)** s. iv bc *SEG* xviii 180, 1 (*[Καλ]λικλῆς*: s. *Ἡρακλείδας*)

Καλλικόμας
Thrace:
—odessos: **(1)** ii-iii ad *IGB* I^2 127 (s. *Μητρόδωρος*)

Καλλικράτεια
Thrace:
—nicopolis ad istrum: **(1)** iii ad ib. II 691 (*Καλει-*: d. *Μαρκιανός*)

Καλλικράτης
Cimmerian Bosporos:
—gorgippia: **(1)** f. iii bc *CIRB* 1137 B II, 50 (s. *Ἀγαθοκλῆς*)
Macedonia: **(2)** iv/iii bc *PP* 14606; cf. *RE* Supplbd. 4 (7d) (Tataki, *Macedonians* p. 336 no. 14)
Macedonia (Bottiaia):
—beroia: **(3)** 41-44 ad *IBer* 60, 5 (Tataki 658)
—edessa*: **(4)** v-vi ad Feissel, *RICM* 28
Macedonia (Chalkidike):
—chalkideis: **(5)** ?352 bc *TAPA* 65 (1934) p. 128 no. 4, 3; *SEG* xxxviii 637, 6; xlvi 804, 2 (f. *Ἀριστόβουλος*)
—potidaia-kassandreia: **(6)** 360 bc *IG* IV (1)^2 94 b, 12 (Perlman, *City and Sanctuary* E.1 with p. 69 f. (date); Tataki, *Macedonians* p. 169 no. 6)
Macedonia (Edonis):
—amphipolis (territ.)?: **(7)** 26 or 142 ad *SEG* xxxiv 637 (or Macedonia (Pieris) Phagres: s. *Μελάνωπος*)
Macedonia (Mygdonia):
—charakoma?: **(8)** hell.? Dimitsas 684 (*Καλικράτη[ς]*)
—thessalonike: **(9)** ii ad *IG* x (2) (1) 588 (*Καλι-*: s. *Νικάνωρ*)
—thessalonike?: **(10)** ii ad ib. 251, 10 (*Καλλικράτ[ης]*: f. *Φίλητος*)
Macedonia (Paionia):
—negotino (mod.): **(11)** ii-iii ad *Sp.* 98 (1941-8) p. 53 no. 107 (s. *Ἰούλιος*)
Macedonia (Pieria):
—pydna: **(12)** hell. *Essays Laourdas* p. 111 no. 2; **(13)** imp. *SEG* xlvii 907 (*-λλει-*: s. *Ἀντίγονος*)
Macedonia?: **(14)** 182 bc *IG* II^2 2314, 3, 7 (s. *Ἡγέστρατος*)
Scythia Minor:
—istros: **(15)** iii/ii bc *ISM* I 112 (I f. *Καλλικράτης* II); **(16)** ~ ib. (*[Καλλικ]ράτης*?: II s. *Καλλικράτης* I); **(17)** ii bc *Histria* 9 pp. 143-4 no. 204 (*[Κ]αλλικράτης*: s. *Ἀπολλόδωρος*)
—tomis: **(18)** f. i ad *RPC* I 1817 (coin) (*Καλλικρά(της)*); **(19)** ii-iii ad *ISM* II 468, 16 (f. *Κουθίας*); **(20)** ~ ib. l. 17 (f. *Διονύσις*)
Skythia:
—olbia-borysthenes: **(21)** iii bc *IOSPE* I^2 201 II, 7 (s. *Νικήρατος*); **(22)** imp. ib. 261
Tauris:
—chersonesos: **(23)** s. iv bc *CIRB* 194 (s. *Εὔκριτος*)
Thrace:
—ainos: **(24)** i-ii ad *IG* xii (8) 218, 5 (f. *—ία*)
—byzantion?: **(25)** c. 225-200 bc *PMich* 781 II, 25; cf. La'da E343 (f. *Δωρόθεος*)
—dionysopolis: **(26)** iii/ii bc *IGB* I^2 21 (s. *Ταῦρις, Γυκέρα*); **(27)** iii ad ib. 14 c, 18 (f. *Αὐρ. Ἰκέσιος*)
—maroneia: **(28)** c. 365-336 bc Schönert-Geiss, *Maroneia* 487-91 (coin)
—odessos: **(29)** m. ii ad *IGB* I^2 177 ter; *Dacia* 21 (1977) p. 161 (date) (f. *Αὐτοκράτης*)
Thrace?: **(30)** 184 bc *BGU* 1968, 3, 7, 10 (La'da E764)

Καλλικρατίδης
Thrace:
—maroneia: **(1)** c. 230-200 bc *BCH* 45 (1921) p. 18 III, 91 (s. *Διονυσᾶς*)

Καλλικρίτα
Macedonia (Paionia):
—kavadarci (mod.): **(1)** ii-iii ad *Sp.* 71 (1931) p. 71 no. 161 + *Arch. Karte Kavadarci* p. 15 (*Καλικρ[ί]τα*: ?d. *Μάξιμος*, m. *Μέλλιος*)
Thrace:
—mesambria: **(2)** v/iv bc *IGB* I^2 330 (PM 63); cf. *IGB* v 5105 (*[Καλ]λικρίτα*: d. *Ἵππαρχος*)

Καλλίκριτος
Thrace:
—maroneia: **(1)** ?ii bc Dumont–Homolle 110b 5, 2 (Wilhelm, *Beitr.* p. 199 no. 171) + *IThrakAig* E175 (f. *—ος*)

Καλλίλεως
CIMMERIAN BOSPOROS:
—BOSPOROS: (**1**) s. iv BC *IG* II^2 8429 (*FRA* 1374) (s. *Θρασυμήδης*)

Καλλίμαχος
CIMMERIAN BOSPOROS:
—GORGIPPIA: (**1**) f. iii BC *CIRB* 1137 A II, 24 (f. *Εὔβουλος*); (**2**) ~ ib. 1137 B I, 47; 1137 B II, 33 (f. *Διονύσιος*)
—MYRMEKION: (**3**) f. iv BC ib. 874 (s. *Ἀριστόμαχος*)
—NYMPHAION: (**4**) iii BC ib. 912 II, 4 (f. *—νος*)
—PANTIKAPAION: (**5**) i AD ib. 550
—TYRITAKE (NR.): (**6**) f. i AD ib. 969 (f. *Μασατίς*)
MACEDONIA: (**7**) ?417-413 BC *IG* I^3 89, 68 (Tataki, *Macedonians* p. 336 no. 15) (*Καλλίμα[χος]*); (**8**) m. ii BC *BGU* 1938 B, 7 (Tataki, *Macedonians* p. 487 no. 147); cf. La'da E1680
MACEDONIA (BOTTIAIA):
—PELLA: (**9**) f. iii BC Akamatis, *Amph. Pellas* pp. 37-8 nos. PAR32-5 (amph.); p. 20 (date) (*SEG* L 613)
MACEDONIA (PIERIA):
—DION: (**10**) imp. ib. XLVIII 788
SCYTHIA MINOR:
—TOMIS: (**11**) ii-i BC *ISM* II 36 (s. *Κα—*); (**12**) f. i AD *RPC* I 1815-16 (coin) (*Καλλί-μ(αχος)*?); (**13**) ii-iii AD *ISM* II 104, 17-18 (*Καλλ<λ>ίμαχ[ος]*—l.18: f. *—ος*)
THRACE:
—ODESSOS: (**14**) s. iii BC *IGB* I^2 36, 7 (s. *Φανερός*)
—PERINTHOS-HERAKLEIA: (**15**) i-ii AD *IPerinth* 48 (*Οὐ[α]τίνιος Καλίμαχος*)

Καλλιμέδουσα
CIMMERIAN BOSPOROS:
—PANTIKAPAION: (**1**) i AD *CIRB* 436, 1 (m. *Σωκλῆς*, *Παρθενοκλῆς*)

Καλλιμέδων
MACEDONIA (BOTTIAIA):
—BEROIA: (**1**) 122 BC *IBer* 134, 6 (s. *Ἀμύντας*)
THRACE:
—PERINTHOS-HERAKLEIA:
——(Podargoi): (**2**) iii-ii BC *IPerinth* 61, 26 (s. *Ἀπολλώνιος*)

Καλλιμέλης
MACEDONIA (CHALKIDIKE):
—POTIDAIA-KASSANDREIA: (**1**) c. 300-275 BC Polyaen. vi 7. 2 (Tataki, *Macedonians* p. 91 no. 55) (*Καλλιμένης*—Roth)

Καλλίμορφος
MACEDONIA (PIERIA):
—PYDNA: (**1**) 250 AD *SEG* XLVI 800 A, 38 (*Κορνιφ. Κ.*)
THRACE:
—NICOPOLIS AD ISTRUM (TERRIT.): (**2**) ii-iii AD *IGB* II 696 (*-μορπος*)

Καλλιναῖος
MACEDONIA (ELIMEIA):
—AIANE (TERRIT.): (**1**) ?iii AD *EAM* 24 a (*[Καλ]λιναῖος*?: f. *Ἀντίγονος ὁ καὶ Ἰούλις*)

Καλλίνας
MACEDONIA: (**1**) 324 BC *RE* Supplbd. 4 (-); Berve 405 (Tataki, *Macedonians* p. 337 no. 16) (*Καλλίνης*—Arr.)
MACEDONIA (BOTTIAIA):
—BEROIA: (**2**) ii-i BC *IBer* 183 (Tataki 660) (s. *Μόλυκκος*, f. *Καλλίχη*, *Θεμίσων*)

Καλλινίκη
THRACE:
—BEROE-AUGUSTA TRAIANA: (**1**) c. 320-324 AD *Anal. Boll.* 31 (1912) p. 198; p. 208

Καλλίνικος
MACEDONIA: (**1**) ?17 BC *SB* 12524, 2 (Tataki, *Macedonians* p. 487 no. 149); cf. La'da E1637 (I f. *Σωσίνικος*, *Καλλίνικος* II); (**2**) ~ *SB* 12524, 3, 7 (Tataki, *Macedonians* p. 487 no. 148) (II s. *Καλλίνικος* I)
MACEDONIA (EDONIS):
—PHILIPPOI: (**3**) i BC-i AD *SIRIS* 115-16 (Pilhofer 190-1); cf. *AD* 42 (1987) Chron. p. 442 (*-νει-*: I f. *Καλλίνικος* II); (**4**) ~ *SIRIS* 115-16 (Pilhofer 190-1); cf. *AD* 42 (1987) Chron. p. 442 (*-νει-*: II s. *Καλλίνικος* I)
MACEDONIA (PELAGONIA): (**5**) ?ii AD *IG* X (2) (2) 284
SCYTHIA MINOR:
—ISTROS: (**6**) 222-225 AD *ISM* I 100 A, 19 (*[Κα]λλίνεικος*: s. *Ἡρακλιανός*)
—KALLATIS: (**7**) 241-244 AD ib. III 74 B, 24 (*-νει-*)
—TOMIS: (**8**) ii-iii AD ib. II 28, 2 (*[Καλ]λίνεικος*, *[Πο]λίνεικος*—ed.); (**9**) ~ ib. 256, 19 (*Καλεί-*: s. *Στροφῆς*)
—ULMETUM: (**10**) 216 AD ib. V 76, 5 = II 130 (*CCET* IV 202) (Lat. Valerius Callinicus)
SKYTHIA:
—OLBIA-BORYSTHENES: (**11**) s. iv BC *SEG* XXXII 794, 1, 13; cf. Vinogradov, *Pont. Stud.* pp. 276-322 (s. *Εὔξενος*); (**12**) iv/iii BC Dubois, *IGDOlbia* 95 (vase); cf. *SEG* XLII 709 I a (s. *Φιλόξενος*); (**13**) iii BC *IOSPE* I^2 201 I, 16 (*[Κ]αλλίνικ[ος]*: f. *Κάλλιππος*); (**14**) ~ ib. l. 28 (s. *Φιλόξενος*); (**15**) ii-i BC *SEG* XXX 950 (vase) (f. *Ἀρίστων*)
—TANAIS: (**16**) 225 AD *CIRB* 1280, 22 (*Κα[λ]λίνει[κος]*: f. *—κις*)
THRACE:
—SALYMBRIA: (**17**) v-vi AD *AD* 53 (1998) Mel. p. 472 no. 210 (*Καλί-*)

Κάλλιον
THRACE:
—MESAMBRIA: (**1**) iii BC *IGB* I^2 335 ter (PM 1014)

Καλλιόπη
MACEDONIA (EDONIS):
—AMPHIPOLIS?: (**1**) ii-iii AD Dimitsas 906 (Kaphtantzis 543) (d. *Ἡνλιζις*)
SCYTHIA MINOR:
—TOMIS: (**2**) v-vi AD Barnea 8 (Popescu, *IGL* 44) (*-λ ηώ-*: ?d. *Σουλιφέρα*)
SKYTHIA:
—SKYTHAI: (**3**) ii-i BC *IG* XII (1) 527 (slave?)
THRACE:
—ODESSOS: (**4**) ii/i BC *EAD* XXX 418, 3 (slave)
—TOPEIROS?: (**5**) iii AD *SEG* XXXV 770 (*IThrakAig* E89) (or Macedonia (Lynkestis) Nikaia: *Αὐρ. Κ.*)

Καλλιοτέρα
SCYTHIA MINOR:
—ISTROS*: (**1**) iii AD *ISM* I 292, 3 (*Ἰουλ. Κ.*: m. *Ἰουλ. Γλύκαινα*)

Καλλιότερος
CIMMERIAN BOSPOROS:
—PANTIKAPAION: (**1**) 227 AD *CIRB* 147, 7 (s. *Βασιλείδης*) ?= (*2*); (**2**) ~ ib. l. 8 (*Καλ(λ)ιότερος*: f. *Μυρομένη*) ?= (*1*)

Καλλίπολις
CIMMERIAN BOSPOROS:
—PANTIKAPAION: (**1**) ii BC ib. 273 (s./d. *Θεόμνηστος*)

Καλλιππίδης
CIMMERIAN BOSPOROS:
—GORGIPPIA: (**1**) f. iii BC ib. 1137 A II, 44 (f. *Κλέανδρος*)
MACEDONIA (CHALKIDIKE):
—CHALKIDEIS: (**2**) ?351 BC *SEG* XXXVII 575, 2; XXXVIII 672, 2; 673, 2; *A' Panell. Synedr. Epigr.* pp. 80-1, 2; Hatzopoulos, *Actes Chalc.* p. 28, [2]; p. 80 (date) (s. *Μενεκλῆς*)

Κάλλιππος
MACEDONIA (BISALTIA):
—ARGILOS?: (**1**) 364-357 BC Hatzopoulos, *Actes Amphipolis* p. 15 no. 1, 2; pp. 73-4 (locn., date) (or Macedonia (Edonis) Amphipolis: *[Κά]λλιπος*)
MACEDONIA (BOTTIAIA):
—BEROIA: (**2**) 223 BC *IBer* 4, 11-12 (f. *Ἱππόστρατος*, *Τιμοκλῆς*) ?= (*3*); (**3**) b. 167 BC ib. 1 A, 4, 18; *BE* 1997, no. 370 (ident.) (Tataki 661) (s. *Ἱππόστρατος*) ?= (*2*)
MACEDONIA (DERRIOPOS):
—STUBERRA: (**4**) 50 AD *IG* X (2) (2) 324, 20 (*-ιπος*: f. *Σωτᾶς*)
MACEDONIA (EDONIS):
—AMPHIPOLIS: (**5**) c. 200-170 BC Hatzopoulos, *MI* 2 p. 87 no. 65, 3 (*SEG* XLVI 720) (*[Κά]λλιππος*: s. *Μένανδρος*)
MACEDONIA?: (**6**) 168 BC *RE* (16) (Tataki, *Macedonians* p. 337 no. 17) (Lat. Callippus)
SKYTHIA:
—OLBIA-BORYSTHENES: (**7**) iii BC *IOSPE* I^2 201 I, 16 (s. *Καλλίνικος*)
—OLBIA-BORYSTHENES?: (**8**) iv/iii BC *SEG* XXXVII 681; XLII 728 (locn.)
TAURIS:
—KERKINITIS: (**9**) f. iii BC *SNG BM Black Sea* 701 (coin) (*Κάλλιππο(ς)*)
THRACE: (**10**) c. 100-75 BC *SB* 8974 fr. 3 II, 43 (Velkov 162; La'da E765) (s. *Φιλώτας*: katoikos)
—AINOS?: (**11**) c. 230-200 BC *BCH* 45 (1921) p. 19 III, 93 (or Thrace Maroneia: f. *Κράτιππος*: reading—Oulhen)
—LYSIMACHEIA: (**12**) m. ii BC *ISestos* 38 a, 1 (*-ιπος*: s. *Καλλιγένης*)
—MARONEIA: (**13**) iii/ii BC Unp. (Teos) (s. *Παντοκρατίδης*) ?= (*14*)
—MARONEIA?: (**14**) c. 209-190 BC *IG* XI (4) 705 a-b, 3; 705 c, 7 (f. *Παντοκρατίδης*) ?= (*13*)

Καλλιρρόη
MACEDONIA (BOTTIAIA):
—EDESSA: (**1**) ii AD Dimitsas 24 (*Makedonika* 15 (1975) p. 202; Tataki, *Edessa* 140) (*-ιρόη*)

Κάλλις
MACEDONIA: (**1**) 78 BC *BGU* 1736, 8; *PBingen* 48, 9 (Tataki, *Macedonians* p. 487 no. 150); cf. La'da 1423 (*Κάλλιδος* (gen.): f. *Ἀπολλώνιος*: katoikos)

Καλλισθένεια
CIMMERIAN BOSPOROS:
—PANTIKAPAION: (**1**) m. i AD *CIRB* 437; cf. KW pl. 17 no. 249 (*-νια*); (**2**) 106 AD *CIRB* 697, 3 (*Οὐλπ. Κ.*)

Καλλισθένης
CIMMERIAN BOSPOROS:
—GORGIPPIA: (**1**) i-ii AD *NE* 9 (1971) p. 5 no. 2, 5 (*[Κα]λλισθε(ν)είη[ς]*?); (**2**) s. ii AD *CIRB* 1129 B, 2 (*[Κ]αλλισθ[έν]η[ς]*)
—HERMONASSA: (**3**) 116 AD ib. 1087; cf. KW pl. 19 no. 281
—NYMPHAION: (**4**) s. ii AD *CIRB* 934 (f. *Χρύσιον*)
—PANTIKAPAION: (**5**) imp. ib. 719 (*Γ. Κ(α)λλισθένης*); (**6**) i AD ib. 468 (s. *Μενέλαος*); (**7**) f. i AD ib. 561 (f. *Γάστεις*); (**8**) i/ii AD ib. 647 (f. *Χρηστίων*); (**9**) 82 AD ib. 76, 22 (*SEG* XVIII 310) (f. *Ἀριστόδημος*); (**10**) f. ii AD *CIRB* 83, 2 (*Καλι-*: f. *Μάης*: reading—Yailenko and Tokhtas'ev); (**11**) s. ii AD ib. 686 (*Καλι-*: s. *Στέφανος*); (**12**) 214 AD ib. 98, 2 (I f. *Καλλισθένης* II); (**13**) ~ ib. l. 2 (II s. *Καλλισθένης* I); (**14**) 275-278 AD ib. 36, 59 (*Καλλισθ(ένης)*); (**15**) ~ ib. l. 69 (*Καλλισθ(ένης)*: s. *.ικ—*)

—PATRAEUS: (16) i/ii AD ib. 1018 (*Καλλι-σ<σ>θένης*: f. *Ἄττας*); (17) ~ ib. 1019 (s. *Κόλλεις*)
—TAMAN PENINSULA: (18) f. ii AD ib. 1224
MACEDONIA: (19) 228-221 BC *PTeb* 815 fr. 2 recto III, 52 (Tataki, *Macedonians* p. 337 no. 18; La'da E1519) (s. *Πολέμων*); (20) c. 223 BC *PTeb* 815 fr. 3 verso I, 21 (Tataki, *Macedonians* p. 337 no. 19); cf. La'da E1660 (*Καλι-*: f. *—ζηνι* (dat.))
MACEDONIA (CHALKIDIKE):
—OLYNTHOS: (21) c. 370-327 BC *RE* (2); *FGrH* 124; *FD* III (1) 400, [4], 7; *CR* 8 (1958) p. 108 (date); cf. *SEG* XXXVIII 410 (s. *Δαμότιμος*)
SKYTHIA:
—OLBIA-BORYSTHENES: (22) i BC-i AD *IOSPE* I² 221; *SEG* XXXVI 720 (f. *Εὐρησίβιος*); (23) f. i AD *IOSPE* I² 181, 6 (f. *Ἄβαβος*); (24) ii AD *IOlbia* 86, 4 (II s. *Καλλισθένης* I); (25) ~ ib. l. 5 (I f. *Καλλισθένης* II); (26) ii-iii AD *IOSPE* I² 137, 4 (s. *Σάτυρος*); (27) c. 193-211 AD ib. 42, 3; 43, 6; 174, 10 (s. *Δάδος*); (28) ~ ib. 42, 4 (II s. *Καλλισθένης* I); (29) ~ ib. l. 5 (I f. *Καλλισθένης* II); (30) ~ ib. 174, 9 (s. *Κρ—*); (31) iii AD ib. 98, 8 (f. *Ἄνθος*); (32) f. iii AD ib. 185, 3 (f. *Αὐρ. Βασιλεύς*)
—TANAIS: (33) 225 AD *CIRB* 1279, 13 (f. *Σύμφορος*); (34) ~ ib. 1280, 4 (*Κ. ὁ καὶ Θυλόγανος*: s. *Πάππος*)
THRACE:
—BYZANTION: (35) ii AD Ach. Tat. ii 13 and passim (fict.)
—BYZANTION?: (36) imp. *IByz* 350 (f. *Κλεοπάτρα*)
—MESAMBRIA: (37) iii BC *IGB* I² 307 bis, 2 + V 5087 (*Καλλισθένειος* (gen.): f. *Τυνδάριχος*)
—ODESSOS: (38) i-ii AD ib. I² 51 b, 8 (f. *—ταγόρας*); (39) f. ii AD ib. 78 ter, 6 (*CCET* I 30) (s. *Ἀρτεμίδωρος*)
—ODESSOS (NR.): (40) i-ii AD *IGB* I² 261 bis (*CCET* I 78) (*[Κ]αλλισθ[ένης]*)
—PERINTHOS-HERAKLEIA: (41) vi/v BC *IPerinth* 71 (s. *Σινωπίων*)

Καλλίστα
MACEDONIA (EDONIS):
—AMPHIPOLIS: (1) hell.? Dimitsas 854 = 890 (*Καλλιστα—?*)

Καλλίστη
CIMMERIAN BOSPOROS:
—PANTIKAPAION: (1) i AD *CIRB* 388 (*Καλ(λ)ίστη*: ?m. *Πάμφιλος*); (2) f. i AD ib. 372; cf. KW pl. 29 no. 412 (*Καλλίσστ[η]*)
MACEDONIA (BOTTIAIA):
—EDESSA: (3) 180 AD *SEG* XXIV 531, 13 (Tataki, *Edessa* 141) (m. *Σοῦδις*)
MACEDONIA (EDONIS):
—PHILIPPOI: (4) iii AD *BCH* 61 (1937) p. 418 no. 12 (Pilhofer 136) (Lat. Aur. Calliste: m. Aur. Lucilla)
MACEDONIA (MYGDONIA):
—THESSALONIKE: (5) iii AD *IG* X (2) (1) 622 (*[Κ]αλλίστη*)
SCYTHIA MINOR:
—TOMIS: (6) ii AD *ISM* II 187 (d. *Κάλλιστος*, *Μαρκία*)
THRACE:
—PERINTHOS-HERAKLEIA: (7) iii-iv AD *IPerinth* 188 (*AD* 51-2 (1996-7) Mel. p. 350 no. 175)

Καλλιστιανή
MACEDONIA (MYGDONIA):
—THESSALONIKE: (1) f. iii AD *IG* X (2) (1) 174, 2; 194, 8 (*Ποντία Κ.*)

Καλλιστιανός
MACEDONIA (MYGDONIA):
—THESSALONIKE: (1) ii AD ib. 241 A II, 9 (*Του[ρ]πίλι. Καλλιστιανό[ς]*)

Καλλίστιον
THRACE:
—BYZANTION: (1) f. iii BC *SEG* XXIII 679 (d. *Ὀνομακλῆς*)
—PERINTHOS-HERAKLEIA: (2) iii AD *IPerinth* 161 (*[Αὐ]ρ. Καλλίστιον*: d. *Θεόδοτος*)

Καλλιστίων
MACEDONIA (BOTTIAIA):
—BEROIA: (1) 188 AD *ILeukopetra* 21, 10 (*Καλλισ[τίωνο]ς* (gen.), *Καλλισ[θένου]ς?*)
MACEDONIA (MYGDONIA):
—THESSALONIKE: (2) ii-iii AD *IG* X (2) (1) 498
SKYTHIA:
—TANAIS: (3) ii AD *CIRB* 1268, 8; (4) 224 AD ib. 1287, 6 (*[Κα]λλιστί(ω)ν*: f. *Φαζίναμος*) ?= (*5*); (5) c. 225-250 AD ib. 1288, 9 (*Καλλιστί[ων]*: f. *Φαδίναμος*) ?= (*4*)

Κάλλιστος
CIMMERIAN BOSPOROS:
—GORGIPPIA: (1) s. ii AD ib. 1145, 4 (s. *Δασ—*)
—PANTIKAPAION: (2) f. iii AD ib. 104, 10; 105, 6 (I f. *Κάλλιστος* II); (3) ~ ib. 104, 10; 105, 6 (II s. *Κάλλιστος* I); (4) 214 AD ib. 98, 13 (s. *Βάθυλλος*)
MACEDONIA (BOTTIAIA):
—BEROIA: (5) 177 AD *IBer* 135 A, 17 (Tataki 1191) (*Σουλπίκιος Κ.*); (6) c. 190 AD *ILeukopetra* 53, 7 (*Βετούριος Κ.*)
MACEDONIA (DERRIOPOS):
—STUBERRA: (7) f. ii AD *IG* X (2) (2) 329 (s. *Ποσειδιππος*)
MACEDONIA (EDONIS):
—PHILIPPOI: (8) ii/iii AD *CIL* III 633 II b, 16 (Pilhofer 163); *CRAI* 1923, p. 277 (date); Collart, *Philippes* pls. 64-5 (Lat. L. Domitius Callistus)
MACEDONIA (MYGDONIA):
—THESSALONIKE: (9) ii-iii AD *IG* X (2) (1) 435; p. 160 (stemma) (*Γν. Δομίτιος Κ.*: s. *Δομίτιος Ὑγῖνος*); (10) ii/iii AD ib. 262, 5 (*Κ. Καικίλιος Κ.*)
—THESSALONIKE*: (11) f. iv AD ib. 351, 1 (Feissel, *RICM* 120; *PLRE* I (4)) (*Φλ. Κ.*)
MACEDONIA (PIERIA):
—DION: (12) ii AD *Essays Laourdas* p. 109 no. 8
SCYTHIA MINOR:
—ISTROS: (13) ii-iii AD *ISM* I 195, 12 (*[Κάλ]λιστος?*)
—TOMIS: (14) ii AD ib. II 187 (s. *Μίδας*, f. *Καλλίστη*)
THRACE:
—GLAVA PANEGA (MOD.): (15) ii-iii AD *IGB* II 522
—KALLIPOLIS (NR.): (16) imp. Dumont–Homolle 100g (*Καμισλος*—lap., *Κά[λλ]ισ[τ]ος*—*CIG* 2017, *Καμίσαος*—Mordtmann: f. *Ἀλέξανδρος*)
—PHILIPPOPOLIS-TRIMONTIUM (TERRIT.): (17) iii AD *IGB* III 1191 (I f. *Κάλλιστος* II); (18) ~ ib. (*Κάλ(λ)ιστος*: II s. *Κάλλιστος* I, f. *Αὐρ. Ἑρμίας*)

Καλλιστράτεια
CIMMERIAN BOSPOROS:
—PANTIKAPAION: (1) i AD *CIRB* 438; cf. KW pl. 48 no. 671 (-τια); (2) ?i AD *CIRB* 488; (3) ii AD ib. 709, 4 (or Cimmerian Bosporos Pantikapaion: d. *Ἀχαιμένης*, m. *Τιμόθεος*)

Καλλίστρατος
CIMMERIAN BOSPOROS:
—GORGIPPIA: (1) f. iii BC ib. 1137 A II, 36 (s. *Νικόβουλος*)
—ILOURATON*: (2) iii AD *MIA* 85 (1958) p. 60 (vase-stamp)
—KOROKONDAME: (3) ii-iii AD *CIRB* 1109 B (*Καλ(λ)ίστρατος*: f. *Μόκκος*)
—PANTIKAPAION: (4) iii BC ib. 110, 5 (*Καλλίστρ[ατος]*: f. *Στράτιος*); (5) ii AD ib. 86, 3
MACEDONIA (BOTTIAIA):
—BEROIA?: (6) 178 BC *SGDI* 2071, 9 (f. *Παράμονος*)
MACEDONIA (EDONIS):
—AMPHIPOLIS: (7) m. iii BC Hatzopoulos, *Actes Amphipolis* p. 52 no 12, 8; *SEG* XLI 566 (date) (s. *Δάδας*)
—PHILIPPOI: (8) 262-254 BC Nachtergael, *Les Galates* 5, 26; 9, 28 (Tataki, *Macedonians* p. 165 no. 18); cf. Stephanis 809 (f. *Δωρόθεος*)
MACEDONIA (MYGDONIA):
—THESSALONIKE: (9) i BC/i AD *IG* X (2) (1) 58, 18; cf. *SEG* XLVII 971; *KGAM Thess.* I 111 (date) (*Καλ(λ)ίστρατος ὁ καὶ Ἄρχων*)
—THESSALONIKE?: (10) ii AD *IG* X (2) (1) 883, 2 (*Γ. Ἰούλ. Κ.*: I f. *Γ. Ἰούλ. Καλλίστρατος* II); (11) ~ ib. l. 5 (*Γ. Ἰούλ. Κ.*: II s. *Γ. Ἰούλ. Καλλίστρατος* I, *Ἀφροδισία*)
MACEDONIA?: (12) ?ii AD *PFreib* 2 a I, 2, 11, 22 (*Καλί-*: fict.)
SCYTHIA MINOR:
—ISTROS: (13) c. 48-52 AD *ISM* I 67, 38; 68 [40] (s. *Δημήτριος*); (14) ii AD ib. 137, 13 (*[Κ]αλλίστρατος*: s. *Ἀπολλόδωρος*); (15) ~ ib. 201 I, 6; (16) ~ ib. 212, 9 (f. *Ἀρτεμίδωρος*); (17) ~ ib. l. 13 (f. *Νουμήνιος*); (18) 138 AD ib. 193, 8 (s. *Δημήτριος*); (19) c. 138-160 AD ib. 193 II, 45; 207, 10 (s. *Κάρπος*); (20) ~ ib. 193 II, 63; 207, 5 (*Μ. Οὖλπ. Κ.*)
—KALLATIS: (21) 241-244 AD ib. III 74, 13 (f. *Φρόντων*, *Διονύσιος*)
SKYTHIA:
—OLBIA-BORYSTHENES: (22) iii BC *IOSPE* I² 201 I, 19 (*Καλλίστρα[τος]*: f. *Εὔξενος*); (23) i/ii AD *SEG* XLIII 505, 8 (s. *Ἡρακλείδης*) ?= (*24*); (24) ii AD *IOSPE* I² 140, 3 (s. *Ἡρακλείδης*) ?= (*23*); (25) iii AD *IOlbia* 83, 7 (*IOSPE* I² 97) (f. *Ναύτιμος*)
—TYRAS: (26) ?i/ii AD ib. 9 (s. *Σίλιος*, f. *Φλ. Ἰουλιανός*)
TAURIS:
—CHERSONESOS: (27) f. iii BC Kats p. 101 no. 66 (amph.) (I f. *Καλλίστρατος* II); (28) c. 262-237 BC ib. (amph.) (II s. *Καλλίστρατος* I); (29) s. i BC *SEG* XXXII 786 (*Καλλίστρ[ατος]?*); (30) f. ii AD Solomonik, *NEPKh* 111, 12 (-σστρα-: s. *Ν—*) ?= (*31*); (31) c. 120-130 AD ib. 112, 20 (f. *Νάνων*) ?= (*30*)
THRACE:
—APOLLONIA-SOZOPOLIS: (32) f. iii BC *Arkheologiia* (Sofia) 1976 (4), pp. 58-61 (*Stud. Fol* p. 408 no. 28 (coin))
—BYZANTION: (33) hell. Unp. (Sayar) (-σστρα-: f. *Ἁρπάλη*); (34) ii-i BC *IByz* 81 (Fıratlı–Robert p. 51 no. 23) (f. *Ἰωνία*); (35) i-ii AD *IByz* 281 (Fıratlı–Robert pp. 87-8 no. 110) (*Διόδωρος ὁ καὶ Κ.*: f. *Τατίς*, *Πῶλλα*, *Παῦλα*, *Διόδωρος*)
—LYSIMACHEIA?: (36) c. 208 BC *FD* III (4) 135 II, 18 (s. [.....]αιος)
—MARONEIA: (37) ii-i BC *IThrakAig* E269 (*[Κ]αλλίστ[ρα]τος*: s. *Μενεκλῆς*)
—MESAMBRIA: (38) iv BC *IGB* I² 333 ter (*[Καλ]λίστρατος*: I f. *Καλλίστρατος* II); (39) ~ ib. (*[Κ]αλλίστρατος*: II s. *Καλλίστρατος* I)
—PERINTHOS-HERAKLEIA:
——(Podargoi): (40) iii-ii BC *IPerinth* 61, 17 (s. *Ἡγῖνος*)
THRACE?: (41) 316-309 BC *IG* II² 1956, 44; *Ancient Macedonia* 5 p. 445 with n. 10 (date) (*FRA* 2543)

Καλλιστώ
CIMMERIAN BOSPOROS:
—PANTIKAPAION: (1) m. i AD *CIRB* 439
MACEDONIA (BOTTIAIA):
—MIEZA: (2) m. ii BC *SEG* XLIII 422 (d. *Δημήτριος*, m. *Στρατονίκη*)
MACEDONIA (MYGDONIA):
—THESSALONIKE?: (3) ii AD *IG* X (2) (1) 713 (*Τουρπιλλία Κ.*)

THRACE:
—AINOS: (4) hell. *SEG* XXIV 243 (*FRA* 255) (*Καλλισ[τ]ώ*)

Καλλιστώνασσα
SCYTHIA MINOR:
—KALLATIS: (1) iv BC *ISM* III 130, 2 (*CEG* II 731) ([*Καλλι*]*στώνασσα*?)

Καλλιτέλης
MACEDONIA (CHALKIDIKE):
—TORONE: (1) ?353 BC *SEG* XXIV 574, 14; Hatzopoulos, *Actes Chalc.* p. 80 (date) (s. *Ἀριστοκλῆς*)
MACEDONIA (PIERIA):
—PHYLAKAI?: (2) ?i BC Oikonomos 59 = *IG* IX (2) 231 (f. *Οὐαδέα*)

Καλλιτύχη
CIMMERIAN BOSPOROS:
—PANTIKAPAION: (1) i AD *CIRB* 428 (?m. *Θεόνικος*)
MACEDONIA: (2) 230 AD *ILeukopetra* 76, 5 (slave/freed.)
MACEDONIA (BOTTIAIA):
—KYRRHOS?: (3) 199 AD ib. 45, 17
MACEDONIA (MYGDONIA):
—THESSALONIKE: (4) i/ii AD *IG* X (2) (1) 417, 5 (*Ποππία Κ.*: m. *Λ. Πόππιος Αὔκτος*)
PENESTAI?: (5) c. 200 AD *SEG* XXXIX 593, 1-2 (m. —*a*)

Καλλίτυχος
MACEDONIA (MYGDONIA):
—THESSALONIKE: (1) ii AD *IG* X (2) (1) 1039, 1 (Tataki, *Macedonians* p. 183 no. 37) (*Καλί-*)

Καλλιφάνης
CIMMERIAN BOSPOROS:
—PANTIKAPAION: (1) iv BC *KSIA* 109 (1967) p. 21 no. 7 (tile) (*Καλλιφ(άνης)*?, *Καλλιφ(ῶν)*?)
SKYTHIA:
—OLBIA-BORYSTHENES: (2) 149 AD *SEG* XXX 1334 (f. *Ἑρμόδωρος*)
THRACE:
—AINOS: (3) 236-232 or 206 BC *PPetr*² 16, 90; *CPR* XVIII 30, 130; cf. La'da E90 (f. *Ἀττίνας*)

Καλλιφυτίων
MACEDONIA (PIERIA):
—DION (TERRIT.): (1) ?i AD Dimitsas 158

Καλλιφῶν
THRACE:
—PERINTHOS-HERAKLEIA:
——(Podargoi): (1) iii-ii BC *IPerinth* 61, 25 (s. *Σῶσις*)

Καλλίχη
MACEDONIA (BOTTIAIA):
—BEROIA: (1) ii-i BC *IBer* 183 (Tataki 664) (d. *Καλλίνας*)

Καλλίχορος
SKYTHIA:
—TYRAS: (1) v-iv BC *SEG* XLV 1026. 1 (vase) = *KSOGAM* 1961, p. 111 no. 4 (*Κάλλιχρος*—*KSOGAM*)

Καλλίχρυσος
THRACE:
—BYZANTION: (1) i AD *Mus. Arch. di Bari* p. 163 no. 13 (*IG* XIV 687) (f. *Νέπως*)

Καλλώ
KOLCHIS: (1) 139 BC *SGDI* 2218, 7, 11, 17, 24 (slave/freed.)
MACEDONIA (MYGDONIA):
—KALINDOIA: (2) 254 AD *SEG* XLII 604, 1 (*Αὐρ. Κ.*: m. *Αὐρ. Τρόπος*)
THRACE:
—BYZANTION: (3) i BC *IByz* 231 (Firatlı–Robert p. 84 no. 103) (d. *Διονύσιος*)

Κάλλων
CIMMERIAN BOSPOROS:
—HERMONASSA: (1) s. ii BC *CIRB* 1044 (I f. *Κάλλων* II); (2) ~ ib. (II s. *Κάλλων* I)
—PANTIKAPAION: (3) s. ii AD ib. 688 (s. *Ἄδας*)
SCYTHIA MINOR:
—TOMIS: (4) iii-ii BC *AMNG* I (2) 2415 (coin) (*Κάλλω(ν)*?)
THRACE: (5) 46-54 AD *SEG* XVI 415 II, 26 (*IThrakAig* E84) (*Τιβ. Κλ. Κ.*)
—LYSIMACHEIA: (6) c. 208 BC *FD* III (4) 135 I, 16 (f. *Θεόδωρος*) ?= (7); (7) ~ ib. 135 III, 17-18 (f. *Ἀριστοκλῆς, Τίμαρχος*) ?= (6)

Καλογέννητος
MACEDONIA (BOTTIAIA):
—BEROIA: (1) iii AD *IBer* 278 (Tataki 687) (*Κεσστρωνιανὸς Κ.*: s. *Αὐρ. Ῥοδογύνη*)

Καλόκαιρος
MACEDONIA: (1) 254 AD *ILeukopetra* 107, 4 (*Κ. ὁ καὶ Ὀλύμπις*: slave/freed.)
MACEDONIA (BOTTIAIA):
—BEROIA*: (2) ii/iii AD *IBer* 144 B, 16 (Tataki 1320) (*Φλ. Κ.*: freed.)
MACEDONIA (MYGDONIA):
—THESSALONIKE: (3) ii-iii AD *IG* X (2) (1) 440, 1 (Feissel, *RICM* 119) (-*κε*-: s. *Μακεδών, Σωσιγένεια*)
THRACE:
—BESSOI?: (4) imp. *CIL* X 3573 (Lat. Dinnius Calocaerus: s. C. Dinnius Valens)
—DIONYSOPOLIS: (5) 241-244 AD *IGB* I² 22 bis, 13 (*Καλόκα(ι)ρος*: s. *Σπε*—)

Κάλος
SCYTHIA MINOR:
—TOMIS: (1) ii-iii AD *ISM* II 31 II, 8 with pl. (*Κάλλος*—ed.: f. *Θεόδοτος*)

Καλοῦς
CIMMERIAN BOSPOROS:
—GORGIPPIA: (1) iii AD *NE* 9 (1971) p. 10 no. 6 B, 17 (*Καλο[ῦς]*: f. *Πάππος*)
—HERMONASSA: (2) i AD *CIRB* 495 (*Καλοῦνος* (gen.): f. *Πολεμοκράτης*); (3) 123-132 AD ib. 1054, 16 (s. *Μυρῖνος*)
—PANTIKAPAION: (4) i BC ib. 123, 1, 3 (*GVI* 1467) (s. *Διόδωρος*); (5) ~ *CIRB* 296; (6) i AD ib. 440 (s. *Ἀπολλώνιος*); (7) i-ii AD ib. 592 (f. *Γάστιν*); (8) 82 AD ib. 76, 15 (*SEG* XVIII 310) (f. *Ἀρίστων*); (9) ~ *CIRB* 76, 17 (*SEG* XVIII 310) (*Καλ[οῦς]*: s. *Ἀθήναιος*); (10) f. ii AD *CIRB* 81, 2; cf. KW pl. 33 no. 455; (11) 275-278 AD *CIRB* 36, 68 (f. *Νι*—)
—PANTIKAPAION?: (12) i AD *SEG* XLV 1011 (s. *Δαμόφιλος*, f. *Χρύσιον*)
SKYTHIA:
—TANAIS: (13) c. 200-210 AD *CIRB* 1277, 18 (s. *Ἀθήνιος*)
TAURIS:
—CHERSONESOS: (14) ii AD Solomonik, *NEPKh* 126 (f. *Βασιλείδης*)

Καλοφρόνιος
MACEDONIA (PIERIA):
—PYDNA: (1) 250 AD *SEG* XLVI 800 A, 46 (*Αἴλ. Κ.*)

Κάλπη
THRACE:
—NICOPOLIS AD NESTUM: (1) ii AD *IGB* IV 2346 (m. *Πυρούλας*)

Καλπουρνία
MACEDONIA (PIERIA):
—DION: (1) ii AD *Klio* 52 (1970) p. 59 no. 12
THRACE:
—SERDICA?: (2) ii AD *IGB* IV 1955, 7

Καλπουρνιανός
MACEDONIA (PAIONIA):
—NEAPOLIS? (SMILOVCI (MOD.)): (1) iii/iv AD *ZA* 23 (1973) p. 150 no. 4 (s. *Ἐπιγένης*)
SCYTHIA MINOR:
—TOMIS: (2) ii AD *ISM* II 12, 4 (*Καρπ-*)

Καλπούρνιος
SCYTHIA MINOR:
—ISTROS: (1) c. 140-160 AD ib. I 207, 9 (s. *Κάρπος*)

Καλπούρνις
SCYTHIA MINOR:
—ISTROS: (1) f. iii AD *Stud. Fischer* p. 32 no. 4, 4 (s. *Ἡροφ*—)

Καλύβη
MACEDONIA (MYGDONIA):
—THESSALONIKE: (1) ii-iii AD *IG* X (2) (1) 665, 9 (*SEG* XLIII 460)

Καλχάδων
SCYTHIA MINOR:
—KALLATIS: (1) s. iii BC *ISM* III 35 A, 25 ([*Καλ*]*χάδων*: f. *Διονύσιος*)

Κάλχας
MACEDONIA (CHALKIDIKE):
—MENDE: (1) ?v BC *BE* 1998, no. 270 (*AEMTh* 7 (1993) p. 404); cf. *SEG* XLVII 939 (s. *Λύσος*)
THRACE:
—HERAION TEICHOS?: (2) f. iv BC Taşlıklıoğlu 1 p. 10 no. 3 (*Κάλχαντος* (gen.))

Κάλων
MACEDONIA (BOTTIAIA):
—BEROIA: (1) ii-iii AD *IBer* 265 (Tataki 667) (*Κάλωνει* (dat.))

Καμασαρύη
CIMMERIAN BOSPOROS:
—BOSPOROS: (1) c. 200-160 BC *RE* Supplbd. 6 (-); *CIRB* 75, 1, 5, 8; *IDidyma* 463, 29; *SEG* XXIII 314, 5; cf. *Historia* 4 (1955) pp. 424 ff.; Vinogradov, *Pont. Stud.* pp. 531-7; Zgusta, *PNS* 564 (d. *Σπάρτοκος*, m. *Παιρισάδης*: queen)

Κάμασις
SCYTHIA MINOR:
—NOVIODUNUM (NR.): (1) iii-iv AD Barnea 63 b (Popescu, *IGL* 267 b)

Κάμμις
TAURIS:
—CHERSONESOS: (1) iv BC Solomonik, *NEPKh* 177 (s. *Ἀντίφιλος*)

Καμορσάζης
CIMMERIAN BOSPOROS:
—PANTIKAPAION: (1) ii AD *CIRB* 689; Zgusta, *PNS* 124 (f. *Ξαιορσάζης*)

Κάμρυς
MACEDONIA (MYGDONIA):
—THESSALONIKE: (1) iii/ii BC *Tekmeria* 6 (2001) p. 2 no. 1 (*Κάμρυος* (gen.): f. *Πελειγένης*)

Κανδιδέα
THRACE:
—BEROE-AUGUSTA TRAIANA:
——Karasoura: (1) ii-iii AD *IGB* III 1632, 6 (m. *Οὐαλεντῖνος*)

Κανδιδιανός
THRACE:
—DUROSTORUM: (1) s. v AD *SEG* XLV 890 (bronze)

Κάνδιδος
MACEDONIA (MYGDONIA):
—THESSALONIKE?: (1) ii-iii AD *IG* X (2) (1) 818 (f. *Λύκος*)

THRACE:
—KELLAI: (2) 241-244 AD *IGB* III 1517, 43 (f. *Αὐρ. Καλανδίων*)

Κανδιτζις
CIMMERIAN BOSPOROS:
—HERMONASSA: (1) s. V AD *CIRB* 1099, 11 + *SEG* XXXIX 697 (*Κ̣ανδιτζις*)

Κανθάρα
TAURIS:
—CHERSONESOS: (1) iv BC *IOSPE* I^2 406, 2 ([*Καν*]*θάρα*?: d. *Δαμοκλῆς*)

Κανθαρίων
THRACE:
—MARONEIA: (1) f. iii BC *IThrakAig* E229 (f. *Σωσιπάτρα*)

Κάνθαρος
SCYTHIA MINOR:
—TOMIS: (1) ii AD *ISM* II 285, 7 (*Κάνθα*[*ρος*])
THRACE:
—BEROE-AUGUSTA TRAIANA?: (2) inc. *CIL* VI 32627, 12 (Lat. M. Priscinius Cantarus)

Κανίτας
SCYTHIA MINOR: (1) f. ii BC *IGB* I^2 41, 5; *SNG Stancomb* 306 (coin) (king)

Κάνουν
MACEDONIA (MYGDONIA):
—KALINDOIA: (1) c. 323 BC Hatzopoulos, *MI* 2 p. 84 no. 62, 22; cf. *Anthémonte–Kalindoia* 2 p. 268 (name) (s. *Ἀσσα..μικος*)

Κάντιος
THRACE:
—DIONYSOPOLIS: (1) iii AD *IGB* I^2 14 a, 7 (s. *Αὐρ. Θεαγένης*)

Κάνωβος
SKYTHIA:
—OLBIA-BORYSTHENES: (1) f. iv BC *IOSPE* I^2 24, 3 (*IKalch* 16; Dubois, *IGDOlbia* 14) (s. *Θρασυδάμας*)

Κάνωπος
MACEDONIA (BOTTIAIA):
—BEROIA: (1) ii/iii AD *IBer* 145, 9 (Tataki 1103) (*Ποπίλλιος Κ.*)

Καπένα?
MACEDONIA (MYGDONIA):
—KALINDOIA: (1) a. 98 AD *SEG* XLII 582, 38; cf. *Anthémonte–Kalindoia* 2 pp. 268-9 (name) (*Καπένας*? (gen.), *Καπενᾶς*? (nom.): ?m. *Ἡρακλείδης*)

Καπιτίων
THRACE:
—NICOPOLIS AD ISTRUM (TERRIT.): (1) iii AD *IGB* II 723

Καπιτωλῖνα
THRACE:
—BISANTHE-PANION (NR.): (1) iii AD *AD* 49-50 (1994-5) Mel. p. 328 no. 153 (d. *Αὐγουστῖνος*, *Πατροφίλα*)

Καπιτωλῖνος
THRACE:
—BEROE-AUGUSTA TRAIANA (TERRIT.): (1) iii AD *IGB* III 1664 (-*πετωλεῖ*-)

Καπίτων
MACEDONIA (DERRIOPOS):
—STUBERRA: (1) 74 AD *IG* X (2) (2) 326, 26 (s. *Φίλιππος*)
MACEDONIA (MYGDONIA):
—THESSALONIKE: (2) 132 AD ib. X (2) (1) 35, 4 (s. *Διονυσογένης*)
MACEDONIA (ODOMANTIKE):
—SIRRHA (TERRIT.): (3) ii-iii AD *SEG* XXX 593 + Kaphtantzis 478 (s. *Δέκιμος*)
MACEDONIA (PELAGONIA): (4) 94 or 211 AD *IG* X (2) (2) 278 (*Δημήτριος ὁ καὶ Κ.*: s. *Φίλιππος*)
MACEDONIA (SINTIKE):
—NEINE: (5) 158 AD *IGB* IV 2241 (f. *Πύρρος*)
THRACE: (6) imp. ib. III 1882 (s. *Σαβῖνος*); (7) 149 AD Dumont–Homolle 110b, 7 (sculptor)
—GLAVA PANEGA (MOD.): (8) ii-iii AD *IGB* II 537 (s. *Σαβῖνος*)
—PAUTALIA (TERRIT.): (9) ii AD ib. IV 2124 (f. *Δράκων*)
—SERDICA: (10) ii-iii AD ib. 1922, 4 (*Ἐπτέκενθος ὁ Κ.*)

Καπρούβηβος?
THRACE:
—DYME (MOD.): (1) i AD *AD* 26 (1971) Chron. pl. 422 γ (*Belomorski Pregled* 1 (1941) p. 335 no. 40; *IThrakAig* E387); cf. Bakalakis, *Oinos Ismarikos* p. 1015; *Epigraphica* 37 (1975) p. 33 (*Καπρουβήβου* (gen.), *Κάπρου Βήβου*?—Robert)

Κάπυλλος
MACEDONIA (ELIMEIA):
—AIANE: (1) i-ii AD *EAM* 7 (f. *Ἀτρείδης*)

Καραΐχος
THRACE:
—BYZANTION: (1) ?352 BC Rhodes–Osborne 57, 24 (*Καράτιχος*—lap, *Καρα*(*ί*)*ϊχος*?—edd.: f. *Σῶσις*)

Καραΐκας
MACEDONIA (MYGDONIA):
—PERISTERA (MOD.): (1) f. v BC *AEMTh* 15 (2001) p. 190 (sherd) (*Καραΐκδας*—sherd, *Καραΐκ*<*δ*>*ας*?)

Καραΐκης
MACEDONIA (MYGDONIA):
—LETE: (1) f. ii BC *SEG* XLVI 764, 16 (s. *Φίλιππος*)

Καράνδας
THRACE:
—BYZANTION: (1) inc. Dion. Byz. 42 (fict.)

Κάρανος
MACEDONIA: (1) her. *RE* (-); cf. Hoffmann, *Makedonen* pp. 122 ff. (Tataki, *Macedonians* p. 337 no. 20) (f. *Κοῖνος*: king/fict.?); (2) 336 BC Berve 411 (Tataki, *Macedonians* p. 338 no. 22) (Lat. Caranus: ?s. *Φίλιππος* II, *Φίλα*); (3) 331-329 BC *RE* Supplbd. 4 (2); Berve 412 (Tataki, *Macedonians* p. 337 no. 21); (4) iv/iii BC Ath. 128 b-c; 129 c, f; 130 c-d
MACEDONIA (CHALKIDIKE):
—STAGEIROS: (5) v BC *AEMTh* 10 (1996) p. 283 (*AD* 51 (1996) Chron. p. 454) (*Κάρ*[*ανος*]?—*AEMTh*)

Κάραξτος
SKYTHIA:
—OLBIA-BORYSTHENES: (1) ii AD *IOSPE* I^2 92, 3; Zgusta, *PNS* 125 (-*στος*: s. *Σάρατος*); (2) ~ *IOSPE* I^2 686, 3 (*VDI* 1975 (1), p. 69) (-*στος*: f. *Ἀργουάναγος*) ?= (*5*); (3) ii-iii AD *IOlbia* 102, 2 (-*στος*: f. *Ἀσφώρουγος*); (4) ~ *IOSPE* I^2 138, 6 (-*ξστος*: s. *Ἀργουάναγος*); (5) c. 150-175 AD ib. 82, 4; 132, 11; cf. *SEG* XLII 713 (f. *Ἀργουάναγος*) ?= (*2*)

Κάρβανος
CIMMERIAN BOSPOROS:
—PANTIKAPAION: (1) f. iv AD *IAK* 45 (1912) p. 19 no. 9

Καρβερένθης
MACEDONIA (MYGDONIA):
—KALINDOIA: (1) 68-98 AD *SEG* XLII 580, 26; cf. *Anthémonte–Kalindoia* 2 p. 269 (name) (f. *Παράμονος*); (2) ~ *SEG* XLII 580, 93 (f. *Κότυς*); (3) ~ ib. l. 94 (s. *Σόφη*); (4) a. 98 AD ib. 582, 11 (I s. *Παράμονος*, f. *Καρβερένθης* II); (5) ~ ib. l. 11 (II s. *Καρβερένθης* I); (6) ~ ib. l. 43 (f. *Βοδύλος*); (7) ~ ib. l. 56 (f. *Τήλεφος*)

Καρδένθης
THRACE: (1) 46-54 AD ib. XVI 415 I, 16 (*IThrakAig* E84) (*Τιβ. Κλ. Κ.*)
—BEROE-AUGUSTA TRAIANA: (2) 241-244 AD *IGB* III 1707, 14 (*Αὐρ. Καρ*[*δέν*]*θης*) ?= (*3*)
—KELLAI: (3) 241-244 AD ib. 1517, 42 (*Αὐρ. Κ.*: s. *Μουκιανός*) ?= (*2*)
—NICOPOLIS AD ISTRUM (TERRIT.): (4) f. iii AD *CCET* II (2) 675, 9 (*ILB* 349) (Lat. Cardentis (gen.): f. Carcenus)
—ODESSOS: (5) i-ii AD *IGB* I^2 53, 7 ([*Κ*]*αρδένθης*)
—PAUTALIA: (6) 135 AD ib. IV 2057, 7
—PHILIPPOPOLIS-TRIMONTIUM (TERRIT.): (7) ?ii AD ib. III 1420, 3; cf. V 5523 (s. *Μενέμαχος*, f. *M. Ἀσσύριος Κλαυδιανός*); (8) ii-iii AD ib. III 1312 (*Καρδ̣ένθης*)
—PHILIPPOPOLIS-TRIMONTIUM:
——(Hebreis): (9) 222-235 AD ib. 1473, 11 (*Αὐρ. Κ.*: s. *Βιθυνικός*)
THRACE?: (10) 243 BC *PEnt* 12, 1 (*PP* 1923; Velkov 164); cf. Robert, *EEP* p. 185 (name) (-*δένδ*-)

Καρδίους
CIMMERIAN BOSPOROS:
—PANTIKAPAION: (1) ii AD Greifenhagen, *Schmuckarb.* 2 p. 81 (ring)
—THEODOSIA: (2) iii AD *CIRB* 947 A, 5 (*Καρδίο*[*υς*]: f. *Δημήτριος*)
SKYTHIA:
—TANAIS: (3) 228 AD ib. 1282, 19; Zgusta, *PNS* 1047 (f. *Παρθενοκλῆς*); (4) ~ *CIRB* 1282, 22 (f. —*τονε.κος*); (5) ~ ib. 1283, 13 (s. *Δάδας*)

Καρδοῦς
MACEDONIA (MYGDONIA):
—KALINDOIA: (1) 68-98 AD *SEG* XLII 580, 67; cf. *Anthémonte–Kalindoia* 2 pp. 269-70 (name) (s. *Κέτρηζις*)

Καρζᾶς
MACEDONIA (EDONIS):
—AMPHIPOLIS: (1) ii-iii AD *Thrakika* 13 (1940) p. 27 *M* + *Epigraphica* 37 (1975) p. 29 (*Καρζᾶνος* (gen.))

Κάρζεις
SKYTHIA:
—OLBIA-BORYSTHENES: (1) ?ii AD *IOSPE* I^2 99, 7; Zgusta, *PNS* 590 (f. *Κάσαγος*); (2) ii AD *IOSPE* I^2 101, 9 (s. *Βωρόψαζος*)

Καρζόαζος
SKYTHIA:
—OLBIA-BORYSTHENES: (1) i/ii AD ib. 39, 3, 35, 40; 169; Zgusta, *PNS* 126 (s. *Ἄτταλος*); (2) ii AD *IOSPE* I^2 83, 5, 8 (-*ζού*-: f. *Ξάρταμος ὁ καὶ Ἴλβιος*, *Χάλαις*)

Καριάς
MACEDONIA (ELIMEIA): (1) 168 BC *SGDI* 1797, 4-5 (slave/freed.)

Καριδάβα
THRACE:
—ODESSOS?: (1) ii AD *IGB* I^2 172 (PM 1700); *Dacia* 21 (1977) p. 161 (date)

Καριδεύς
CIMMERIAN BOSPOROS:
—PANTIKAPAION: (1) iv BC *CIRB* 216; Zgusta, *PNS* 776 (f. *Πάρμα*)

Καριέλας
THRACE:
—PAUTALIA (TERRIT.): (1) ii AD *IGB* IV 2147, 7 (*Καριέλ*[*ου*] (gen.), *Καρίελος*—ed.: f. *Δόλης*)

Κάρκος
THRACE:
—TYRODIZA-TIRISTASIS: (**1**) imp. Dumont–Homolle 89b (s. *Δόλης*, *Ἡρυλλα*)

Καρμίνιος
MACEDONIA (MYGDONIA):
—THESSALONIKE: (**1**) s. ii AD *SEG* XXXIII 850 (Stephanis 1381a; Tataki, *Macedonians* p. 183 no. 38)

Καρνεάδης
THRACE:
—APOLLONIA-SOZOPOLIS: (**1**) i-ii AD *IGB* I^2 401, 1 (s. *Ἡρα—*)

Καρνίτης
CIMMERIAN BOSPOROS:
—GORGIPPIA: (**1**) i BC-i AD *CIRB* 1195

Κάρος
THRACE:
—ELAIOUS: (**1**) iii BC *AD* 49 (1994) Chron. p. 299 no. β with pl. 96 β (f. *Ἀρτεμώ*)
THRACE?: (**2**) m. iii BC *SEG* XLI 963, 4 (f. *Δάρσης*)

Κᾶρος
THRACE:
—DIOKLETIANOPOLIS: (**1**) v-vi AD Beševliev 226, 2

Καρπίμη
MACEDONIA (MYGDONIA):
—THESSALONIKE?: (**1**) ii AD *IG* X (2) (1) 850; (**2**) ii-iii AD ib. 731
MACEDONIA (PELAGONIA):
—DOSTONEIS: (**3**) iii AD ib. X (2) (2) 201, 9
MACEDONIA (PIERIA):
—DION: (**4**) s. ii AD Oikonomos 11; cf. Spiliopoulou-Donderer, *KGN* p. 203 no. D20 (date) (m. *Ἑρμαδίων*); (**5**) ii/iii AD Oikonomos 29 (*Οὔλπ. Κ.*)

Κάρπος
CIMMERIAN BOSPOROS:
—PANTIKAPAION: (**1**) iii-iv AD *CIRB* 737 (s. *Βάσσαρος*)
MACEDONIA (DERRIOPOS):
—STUBERRA: (**2**) c. 41-48 AD *IG* X (2) (2) 323, 26 (f. *Ποσείδιππος*); (**3**) 74 AD ib. 325, 35 (f. *Παράμονος*)
SCYTHIA MINOR:
—ISTROS: (**4**) i BC-i AD *ISM* I 186 (f. *Εὐξενίδης*); (**5**) ii AD ib. 180, 1 (s. *Ἀρτεμίδωρος*) ?= (*11*); (**6**) ~ ib. 214, 8 + 226, 6 (s. *Εὐ—*); (**7**) 138 AD ib. 193 I, 11 (I f. *Κάρπος* II); (**8**) ~ ib. l. 11 (II s. *Κάρπος* I); (**9**) ~ ib. l. 28 (f. *Γρήγορος*); (**10**) ~ ib. l. 40 (s. *Ἀρτεμίδωρος*) ?= (*11*) (*14*); (**11**) ~ ib. 193 II, 8, 16 (s. *Ἀρτεμίδωρος*) ?= (*5*) (*10*); (**12**) ~ ib. l. 52 (f. *Θεόδωρος*); (**13**) c. 138-160 AD ib. 137, 12; 193 II, 34 (s. *Ἀπολλόδωρος*) ?= (*15*); (**14**) ~ ib. 193 I, 77; 193 II, 44-5, 60; 207, 8-10 (f. *Ἀρτεμίδωρος*, *Διογένης*, *Ἡρόδωρος*, *Καλλίστρατος*, *Καλπούρνιος*) ?= (*10*); (**15**) c. 140-160 AD ib. l. 11 (s. *Ἀπολλόδωρος*) ?= (*13*); (**16**) iii AD ib. 222, 4
—KALLATIS: (**17**) ii AD ib. III 84 (*Ἰούλ. Κ.*); (**18**) 241-244 AD ib. 74 B, 21 (s. *Σύντροφος*)
SKYTHIA:
—OLBIA-BORYSTHENES: (**19**) ii AD *IOSPE* I^2 128, 7 (f. *Σόσσιος*)
—OLBIA-BORYSTHENES (BEREZAN (MOD.)): (**20**) f. ii AD *SEG* XLIX 1028 A, 3 (s. *Αἰλ. Ἐπικράτης*)
THRACE:
—APOLLONIA-SOZOPOLIS: (**21**) i-ii AD *IGB* I^2 401, 12 ([*Κ*]*άρπος*: s. *Ἀλέξανδρος*)
—KALLIPOLIS: (**22**) iii AD *Araşt. Sonuçları Topl.* 2001 (2), p. 103 (*Αὐρ. Κ.*)
—NICOPOLIS AD ISTRUM:
——(Apollonias): (**23**) ii-iii AD *IGB* II 692 (*Καλπούρνιος Γάϊος ὁ καὶ Κ.*: f. *Εὐτυχίς*)
—TRAIANOPOLIS: (**24**) iii AD *AWE* 2 (2003) pp. 325-47 (*IThrakAig* E435) (*Αὐρ. Κ.*)

Καρποφόρος
MACEDONIA (BOTTIAIA):
—BEROIA: (**1**) ii AD *IBer* 169, 6 (Tataki 671) (*Καρποφό*[*ρ*]*ος*: s. *Τέρπνη*)
MACEDONIA (EDONIS):
—PHILIPPOI: (**2**) ii-iii AD *BCH* 59 (1935) p. 156 no. 52 (Pilhofer 266) (*Οὐαρίνιος Κ.*: s. *Βασίλεια*)
MACEDONIA (MYGDONIA):
—THESSALONIKE: (**3**) ii-iii AD *IG* X (2) (1) 475 (*Καρποφ*[*ό*]*ρος*)
SCYTHIA MINOR:
—TOMIS: (**4**) ii AD *ISM* II 11, 7 (*Καρποφόρ*[*ος*])

Κάρπων
MACEDONIA (BOTTIAIA):
—BEROIA: (**1**) ii-iii AD *IBer* 28 (Tataki 672)
THRACE:
—HADRIANOPOLIS (TERRIT.): (**2**) iii AD *IGB* III 1820

Κάρρος
THRACE:
—PAUTALIA (TERRIT.): (**1**) ii-iii AD ib. V 5856 (f. *Αἰλ. Μουκιανός*)

Καρσας
CIMMERIAN BOSPOROS:
—GORGIPPIA: (**1**) ii/iii AD *CIRB* 1179, 43; Zgusta, *PNS* 127 (f. *Ἀταμάζας*)

Κάρσις
THRACE: (**1**) 327 BC Arr., *An.* iv 13. 4 (f. *Φιλώτας*)
THRACE?: (**2**) 316-309 BC *IG* II^2 1956, 27; *Ancient Macedonia* 5 p. 445 with n. 10 (date) (*FRA* 2544)

Καρσούπης
MACEDONIA (MYGDONIA):
—KALINDOIA: (**1**) a. 98 AD *SEG* XLII 582, 46; cf. *Anthémonte–Kalindoia* 2 p. 270 (name) (I f. *Καρσούπης* II); (**2**) ~ *SEG* XLII 582, 46 (II s. *Καρσούπης* I)

Καρτέα
THRACE:
—BYZANTION: (**1**) i BC-i AD *Türk Tarih Kongresi XI* (6) p. 2703 with pl. 493. 2 (*Ḳαρτέα̣*: freed.)

Καρτέρις
THRACE:
—BEROE-AUGUSTA TRAIANA: (**1**) ii-iii AD *SEG* XXXIX 649, 4 (s. *Ναννᾶς*)

Καρτερόμαχος?
SCYTHIA MINOR:
—ISTROS: (**1**) ii-i BC *ISM* I 37, 2 ([*Καρ*]*τ*[*ε*]*ρόμαχος?*)

Κάρτουζα
THRACE:
—MARONEIA: (**1**) iii AD Dumont–Homolle 110b 10 (*IThrakAig* E328) (*—νος ἡ καὶ Κ.*)
—TRAIANOPOLIS (TERRIT.): (**2**) imp. ib. E450 (*Κ̣άρτ̣ο̣υ̣ζα̣*)

Καρτοῦς
THRACE:
—MARONEIA: (**1**) ii/iii AD *AD* 26 (1971) Chron. pp. 428-9 no. η (*IThrakAig* E295) (s. *Γάϊος*)

Καρύστιος
THRACE:
—MARONEIA: (**1**) ii-i BC ib. E212, 46 (I f. *Καρύστιος* II); (**2**) ~ ib. l. 46 (II s. *Καρύστιος* I)

Καρώσης
MACEDONIA (EDONIS):
—PHILIPPOI: (**1**) ii-iii AD *BIAB* 16 (1950) p. 9 no. 2 (Pilhofer 50); Collart, *Philippes* pl. 36. 1 (*Κ. ὁ καὶ Ἀ*[...]*λας*: s. *Αὐλούπορις*)
THRACE: (**2**) 46-54 AD *SEG* XVI 415 III, 30 (*IThrakAig* E84) (s. *Αὐλούπορις*)

Καρωσσός
THRACE:
—STRATOPARA: (**1**) 202 AD *IGB* III 1690 b, 36 (and Thrace Pizos: f. *Κότυς*)

Κάσαγος
SKYTHIA:
—OLBIA-BORYSTHENES: (**1**) i/ii AD *IOlbia* 79, 13 (*IOSPE* I^2 116); *IOSPE* I^2 141, 5; Zgusta, *PNS* 128 (f. *Κάσκηνος*); (**2**) ii AD *IOSPE* I^2 82, 9 (f. *Ἀρσηούαχος*); (**3**) ?ii AD ib. 99, 7 (-*κος*: s. *Κάρζεις*); (**4**) f. ii AD ib. 85, 8 (f. *Γάϊος*)

Κάσαις
SKYTHIA:
—OLBIA-BORYSTHENES: (**1**) ii AD ib. 92, 8 with Add. p. 518; Zgusta, *PNS* 129 (s. *Πάρνουγος*) ?= (*Κάθαις* (*1*))

Κασείπορις
THRACE:
—HADRIANOPOLIS (TERRIT.): (**1**) ii-iii AD *IGB* III 1806 (*Κασείπορ*(*ις*): f. *Τάρσας*)

Κασεύς
MACEDONIA (CHALKIDIKE):
—AKANTHOS: (**1**) v/iv BC *SEG* XLI 554 (vase)

Κασιγνάκις
THRACE:
—MARONEIA: (**1**) c. 359-341 BC *HN*^{2} p. 283 (coin); *BMC Tauric Chersonese* p. 202; Peter, *MTD* p. 135 n. 728; p. 141 n. 766; cf. Masson, *OGS* p. 438 (name) (*Κασιγνάκιος* (gen.))

Κάσιος
SCYTHIA MINOR:
—TOMIS: (**1**) ii-iii AD *ISM* II 468, 11 (f. *Κυρώνας*)
THRACE:
—APOLLONIA-SOZOPOLIS: (**2**) i-ii AD *IGB* I^2 401, 7 (f. *Διονύσις*); (**3**) v-vi AD Beševliev 178
—BYZANTION: (**4**) ii AD *IByz* 282 (f. *Παπύλος*)
—NICOPOLIS AD ISTRUM: (**5**) ii-iii AD *IGB* V 5235 (f. *Μάξιμος*)
—PAUTALIA (TERRIT.): (**6**) ii AD ib. IV 2214, 13 (*Κά*[*σ*]*ιος*: f. *Ἰουλιανός*)
—PHILIPPOPOLIS-TRIMONTIUM (TERRIT.): (**7**) ii-iii AD ib. III 1194 (s. *Βρῖλος*)

Κάσις
TAURIS:
—CHERSONESOS: (**1**) iv BC Solomonik, *GAKh* 1039 (vase) (*Κάσιος* (gen.))

Κάσκηνος
SKYTHIA:
—OLBIA-BORYSTHENES: (**1**) i/ii AD *IOlbia* 79, 13 (*IOSPE* I^2 116); *IOSPE* I^2 141, 4; Zgusta, *PNS* 300 (s. *Κάσαγος*)

Κασσαλία
CIMMERIAN BOSPOROS:
—PHANAGOREIA: (**1**) 344-311 BC *CIRB* 972 (Rhodes–Osborne 65 E); Zgusta, *PNS* 1048 (d. *Πόσις*)

Κασσάνδρα
MACEDONIA (ALMOPIA):
—NEROMYLOI (MOD.): (**1**) imp. *SEG* XLVII 918 (*Κασά-*: d. *Ἀλέξανδρος*)
MACEDONIA (BOTTIAIA):
—AIGAI: (**2**) 229 AD *ILeukopetra* 73, 6 (*Κασά-*)
—EDESSA: (**3**) iii AD Feissel, *RICM* 10 (Tataki, *Edessa* 142) (d. *Ὀλύμπιος*, *Χαριδημία*)

Macedonia (Elimeia):
—velvendos (mod.): **(4)** s. ii ad *EAM* 57 (m. *Ἁρμονία*)
Macedonia (Lower Paionia):
—idomene?: **(5)** ii/iii ad Sokolovska, *Isar-Marvinci* p. 130
Macedonia (Lynkestis):
—herakleia (area): **(6)** imp. *IG* x (2) (2) 28 (*Κ[ασ]σάνδρα*: m. *Εὔτυχος, Ζωσίμη*)
Macedonia (Mygdonia):
—thessalonike: **(7)** s. i ad ib. x (2) (1) 593 (d. *Ἰουκοῦνδος*); **(8)** ii-iii ad ib. 453, 3 (*Φλ. Κ.*: m. *Λύκα*); **(9)** v-vi ad ib. 353, 3 (Feissel, *RICM* 170)
Macedonia (Pelagonia): **(10)** iii ad *IG* x (2) (2) 188, 3 (d. *Κάσσανδρος*, m. *Ἀλεξάνδρα*)

Κασσανδριανή
Macedonia (Bottiaia):
—beroia: **(1)** 229 ad *ILeukopetra* 73, 8 (*Φερωνία Κασανδριανὴ Ἰουλία*)

Κάσσανδρος
Macedonia: **(1)** f. iv bc *RE* (1) (Tataki, *Macedonians* p. 338 no. 25) (f. *Ἀντιγόνη*); **(2)** c. 355-297 bc *RE* (2); Berve 414 (Tataki, *Macedonians* p. 338 no. 27) (s. *Ἀντίπατρος*, f. *Φίλιππος* IV, *Ἀλέξανδρος*, *Ἀντίπατρος*: king); **(3)** hell.? *CIA* iii 3623 (fals.?); cf. *Mus. Helv.* 1993, p. 52 (Tataki, *Macedonians* p. 338 no. 26) (s. *Ἀμύντας*); **(4)** c. 260-240 bc *IG* iv (1)² 96, 67 (Perlman, *City and Sanctuary* E.3); cf. *Ancient Macedonia* 2 pp. 515-16 (ident., stemma) (Tataki, *Macedonians* p. 202 no. 11) (s. *Ἀρραβαῖος*) ?= (*50*); **(5)** 232 or 207 bc *CPR* xviii 19, 400, 406 (Tataki, *Macedonians* p. 339 no. 28; La'da E1768) (s. *Νίκων*: t.e.); **(6)** 184 bc *RE* (6) (Tataki, *Macedonians* p. 338 no. 24) (Lat. Casander); **(7)** ~ *PHeid* viii 414, 45 (La'da E1520); **(8)** ~ *PHeid* viii 414, 46 (La'da E1521); **(9)** 138 ad *SEG* xxxvii 593, 15 (*Ἰούλ. Κ.*)
Macedonia?:
—bistyros: **(10)** 244 ad *ILeukopetra* 100, 3 (*Αὐρ. Κ.*: II s. *Κάσσανδρος* I); **(11)** ~ ib. l. 4 (I f. *Αὐρ. Κάσσανδρος* II)
Macedonia (Bisaltia):
—sitochori (mod.): **(12)** ii-iii ad Kaphtantzis 524
Macedonia (Bottiaia):
—aigai: **(13)** i bc *SEG* xlix 841
—beroia: **(14)** iii bc *IBer* 391 (Tataki 676) (f. *Ἀδέα*); **(15)** 112 bc *IBer* 134, 43 (s. *Ἀντίγονος*); **(16)** i ad ib. 189 (s. *Παράμονος*); **(17)** ii ad ib. 84, 5 (Tataki 673); cf. *Chiron* 31 (2001) pp. 446-50; **(18)** ~ *IBer* 106, 2 (Tataki 1321) (*Τ. Φλ. Κ.*); **(19)** ~ *IBer* 300 (Tataki 678) (f. *Διονύσιος*); **(20)** ~ *IBer* 375 (Tataki 674) (*Κάσσα(ν)δρος*); **(21)** 173 ad *IBer* 505 (*[Κάσ]σανδρος*: s. *Κλεο*—); **(22)** ii/iii ad *ILeukopetra* 54, 3; **(23)** 220 ad ib. 70, 3 (Tataki 287) (*Αὐρ. Κ.*: II s. *Κάσσανδρος* I); **(24)** ~ *ILeukopetra* 70, 4 (Tataki 677) (I f. *Αὐρ. Κάσσανδρος* II)
—edessa: **(25)** iii bc *IG* xii (9) 1135 (Tataki, *Edessa* 145; Tataki, *Macedonians* p. 103 no. 9) (f. *Κλεοπάτρα*); **(26)** c. 200-175 bc *SEG* xliv 409, 4 (Tataki, *Macedonians* p. 103 no. 8) (s. *Νίκαρχος*); **(27)** 229 ad *Ancient Macedonia* 1 p. 200 no. 12, 4 (Tataki, *Edessa* 88) (*Ἔλιος Πεδουκαῖος Κ.*); **(28)** ~ ib. 55 (*Αὐρ. Κάσανδρος*)
Macedonia (Derriopos):
—stuberra: **(29)** 74 ad *IG* x (2) (2) 325, 48 (s. *Ἀντίγονος*); **(30)** ~ ib. l. 51 (f. *Ἀντίγονος*); **(31)** ~ ib. 326, 36 (f. *Φίλαγρος*); **(32)** ~ ib. l. 39 (s. *Νικάνωρ*)
Macedonia (Derriopos)?:
—dolenestai: **(33)** 87 ad ib. 325, 80; Hatzopoulos, *MI* 1 p. 87 (ethn.) (s. *Ζώπυρος*)
Macedonia (Edonis):
—amphipolis: **(34)** ?ii ad *BCH* 22 (1898) p. 350 (f. *Ζωΐλος*); **(35)** ii-iii ad Dimitsas 856 (Kaphtantzis 612) (*Κάσσαν[δρος]*: f. —ος)
Macedonia (Elimeia):
—velvendos (mod.): **(36)** ii ad *SEG* xlvii 1001, 1 (s. *Ἀγοραῖος*); **(37)** ~ ib. l. 3 (f. *Κασσίας*); **(38)** ~ ib. l. 4 (*Κάσσ[ανδρος]*?)
Macedonia (Eordaia):
—ermakia (mod.): **(39)** 75 bc ib. 943 (*Κάσσαν[δρος]*: f. *Περδίκκας*)
—kelle?: **(40)** m. ii ad *EAM* 124, 4 (*Κασ<α>σάνδ[ρ]ο̣υ* (gen.))
Macedonia (Krestonia):
—bragylai: **(41)** c. 230-200 bc *BCH* 45 (1921) p. 18 III, 70 (Tataki, *Macedonians* p. 84 no. 3) (f. *Ἀνδρόνικος*)
Macedonia (Lynkestis):
—aetos (mod.): **(42)** iv/iii bc *EAM* 151 (s. *Νίκων*)
Macedonia (Mygdonia):
—thessalonike: **(43)** s. i ad *IG* x (2) (1) 68, 40; 69, 26 (s. *Ἀξίωμα*)
—thessalonike?: **(44)** 109 ad ib. 849, 1 (s. *Τόρκος*, f. *Παράμονος*, *Τόρκος*)
—thessalonike*: **(45)** c. 303 ad Musurillo, *Acts Christian Martyrs* pp. 281 ff.
Macedonia (Odomantike):
—sirrha: **(46)** ii ad Dimitsas 811, 11 (Kaphtantzis 15) (*Κάσα-*: I f. *Κάσσανδρος* II); **(47)** ~ Dimitsas 811, 11 (Kaphtantzis 15) (*Κάσα-*: II s. *Κάσσανδρος* I)
Macedonia (Orestis):
—apidia (mod.): **(48)** f. iii bc *SEG* xlix 678 (pithoi)
—battynaioi: **(49)** 192 ad *EAM* 186 I, 51 (*Κάσα-*: f. *Ἀντίγονος*)
—pentavryso (mod.): **(50)** ?f. iii bc ib. 190 + *SEG* xxxix 563 (*[Κ]άσσανδρο[ς]*: s. *Ἀρραβαῖος*) ?= (*4*)
Macedonia (Paionia): **(51)** 201 bc *PTeb* 820, 6 (Tataki, *Macedonians* p. 209 no. 11) (f. *Θεόδοτος*)
—neapolis? (smilovci (mod.)): **(52)** ii-iii ad *Sp.* 98 (1941-8) p. 32 no. 77 (*Τίτιος Αὐρ. Κ.*)
Macedonia (Pelagonia): **(53)** iii ad *IG* x (2) (2) 188, 4 (f. *Κασσάνδρα*); **(54)** ~ ib. 266 (s. *Οὐάλης*, *Αὐρ. Κασσία*)
—keramiai (nr.): **(55)** ii-iii ad ib. 210 (s. *Λυσᾶς*, *Ἀμμία*)
—mariovo (mod.): **(56)** ii-iii ad ib. 161 (*[Κ]ά̣σσανδρος*: s. *Κασσία*)
Skythia:
—tanais: **(57)** ii ad *CIRB* 1262, 4 (*Κάσανδ[ρος]*: f. *Θεαγένης*)

Κασσία
Macedonia (Eordaia):
—arnisa?: **(1)** m. ii ad *EAM* 122; Hatzopoulos, *MI* 1 p. 94 n. 4 (locn.) (d. *Βλάστη*)
Macedonia (Mygdonia):
—thessalonike: **(2)** c. 303 ad Musurillo, *Acts Christian Martyrs* pp. 281 ff.
—thessalonike?: **(3)** ii ad *IG* x (2) (1) 868 (m. *Νουμέριος*)
Macedonia (Pelagonia):
—mariovo (mod.): **(4)** ii-iii ad ib. x (2) (2) 161 (*[Κ]α̣σσία*: m. *Κάσσανδρος*)
Macedonia (Pieria):
—dion: **(5)** imp. *Klio* 52 (1970) p. 54 no. 5 = *SEG* xlviii 882

Κασσιανός
Macedonia (Mygdonia):
—thessalonike: **(1)** v-vi ad *IG* x (2) (1) 360 (Feissel, *RICM* 144) (*Κασι-*)
Thrace:
—nicopolis ad istrum (territ.): **(2)** ii ad *IGB* v 5244 b, 14

Κασσίας
Macedonia (Elimeia):
—velvendos (mod.): **(1)** ii ad *SEG* xlvii 1001, 3 (s. *Κάσσανδρος*)

Κάσσιος
Macedonia (Derriopos):
—stuberra: **(1)** 50 ad *IG* x (2) (2) 324, 19 (s. *Κόϊντος*); **(2)** 107 ad ib. 325, 100 (f. *Νικόλαος*, *Παράμονος*)

Κάσσις
Macedonia (Bottiaia):
—pella: **(1)** f. i bc *AEMTh* 8 (1994) p. 56 (s. *Μυρτίλος*)

Κάστος
Scythia Minor:
—istros: **(1)** ii ad *ISM* i 197 I, 1 (f. *Βαλεντῖνος*); **(2)** ~ ib. l. 4 (s. *Πομπήϊος*); **(3)** ~ ib. l. 6 (s. *Τέρτιος*); **(4)** ~ ib. l. 13 (f. *Σουλπικιανός*); **(5)** ~ ib. l. 17 (s. *Νυμφιδιανός*); **(6)** 138 ad ib. 193 II, 69 (s. *Ἀλέξανδρος*); **(7)** 218 ad ib. 99, 10 (f. *Αὐρ. Βίκτωρ*)

Καστρήσιος
Scythia Minor:
—tomis*: **(1)** ii ad ib. ii 289

Κάστωρ
Cimmerian Bosporos:
—phanagoreia: **(1)** f. i bc App., *Mithr.* 114
Macedonia: **(2)** 77 bc *PMerton* 6, 2, 9, 19 (Tataki, *Macedonians* p. 488 no. 152; La'da E1522) (s. *Μιθροδάτης*)
Macedonia (Bottiaia):
—beroia?: **(3)** f. iii ad *IBer* 399, 1 (Tataki 682)
—beroia (territ.)*: **(4)** ii ad *IBer* 500 (Tataki 681) (freed.)
Macedonia (Edonis):
—philippoi: **(5)** ii-i bc *SEG* iii 504 (*SIRIS* 118; Pilhofer 193) (s. *Ἀρτεμίδωρος*)
Macedonia (Elimeia):
—aiane: **(6)** s. ii ad *EAM* 56 (f. *Ἔρως*, *Προκόπη*, *Ἀγαθοκλέα*, *Δημοκράτης*)
Macedonia (Mygdonia):
—thessalonike: **(7)** 90 ad *SEG* xlii 625, 8 (*Κ. Πούπιος Κ.*); **(8)** f. iii ad *IG* x (2) (1) 182, 7; 628 B, 5 (*GVI* 1275) (*Ἰούλ. Κ.*: f. *Ἰούλ. Εἰρηναῖος*, *Ἰούλ. Γαϊανός*, *Ἰούλ. Ὄλυμπος*, *Μεγέθιν*)
Macedonia (Pieria):
—dion: **(9)** ?ii-iii ad Oikonomos 26 (*Γ. Ἰούλ. Κάσστωρ*)
Scythia Minor:
—capidava (nr.): **(10)** ii-iii ad *ISM* v 3 (Lat. Castoris (gen.): f. Veneria)
—carsium: **(11)** iii ad ib. 101, 6 (Lat. Aurel. Castor)
Thrace:
—bazopara: **(12)** 202 ad *IGB* iii 1690 d, 23 (and Thrace Pizos: s. *Αὐλούζενις*)
—dragoevo (mod.): **(13)** 238-244 ad *BIAB* 11 (1937) pp. 193-5 (*Eastern cults* p. 220 no. 3) (Lat. Castor)
—kellai: **(14)** ii-iii ad *IGB* iii 1527 (*Eastern cults* p. 235 no. 26); **(15)** ~ *IGB* iii 1527 (*Eastern cults* p. 235 no. 26)
—serdica (territ.): **(16)** ii-iii ad *IGB* v 5734 (*[Κά]στωρ*: s. *Αἴλιος*)

Κάσων
Macedonia (Edonis):
—amphipolis: **(1)** b. 357 bc Hatzopoulos, *Actes Amphipolis* p. 20 no. 2, 5 (*SEG* xli 556)

Κατάνικος
Macedonia (Bottiaia):
—aigai: **(1)** s. iv bc ib. xxxv 802 (f. *Ἄλκιμος*)

Κατάστασις
Macedonia (Chalkidike):
—aphytis: **(1)** ?351 bc *Α΄ Panell. Synedr. Epigr.* pp. 80-1, 7 (*Καταστάσιδος* (gen.): f. *Διονύσιος*, *Ἀντιπατρίδης*, *Σώσων*)

Κατίων
TAURIS:
—CHERSONESOS: (1) ?ii AD *IOSPE* I^2 451, 4-5; Zgusta, *PNS* 130 (f. —δησσα)

Κάτλος
THRACE:
—ODESSOS: (1) 215 AD *IGB* I^2 47 c, 26 (*Κλ. Κ.*: f. *Αὐρ. Γερμανός*); (2) 221 AD ib. 47 bis b, 36 (*Οὐαλέριος Κ. νεώτ.*)

Κατόκας
CIMMERIAN BOSPOROS:
—GORGIPPIA: (1) ii/iii AD *CIRB* 1179, 53; Zgusta, *PNS* 130 (s. *Δάδος*)

Κάτος
MACEDONIA (SINTIKE):
—PARTHIKOPOLIS (NR.): (1) ii-iii AD *IGB* IV 2289; cf. V 5913 (f. *Πύρουλα*)

Κατρουβήα
THRACE:
—MARONEIA: (1) ii-iii AD Dumont–Homolle 110b 19 (*IThrakAig* E290) (d. *Πλουτογένης*)

Κάττας
CIMMERIAN BOSPOROS:
—GORGIPPIA: (1) ii AD *CIRB* 1140, 5; Zgusta, *PNS* 130

Κάτυλλα
SCYTHIA MINOR:
—TOMIS: (1) iii AD *ISM* II 379 (*Κάτυλλα*: d. *Φλ. Κάτυλλος*)

Κατυλλῖνος
THRACE:
—TIŠEVICA (MOD.): (1) ii-iii AD *IGB* V 5164 (-λλεῖ-)

Κάτων
MACEDONIA (DERRIOPOS)?: (1) ii-iii AD *IG* X (2) (2) 44 (*Λυσίμαχος ὁ καὶ Κάτων*: s. *Αὐρηλιανή*)

Καύαρος
THRACE: (1) 278-213 BC Youroukova p. 82 nos. 107-9; Draganov, *Kabile* 862-73; *Nom. Chron.* 16 (1997) pp. 21-24 (coin) (king)

Καύκασος
MACEDONIA (PAIONIA):
—STOBOI: (1) s. iii AD *SEG* XLVII 954; cf. L 635 (*Κ. ὁ πρὶν Στράτηγος*: glad.?)

Καφάκης
SKYTHIA:
—OLBIA-BORYSTHENES: (1) m. iv BC Dubois, *IGDOlbia* 106, 10 (*SEG* XLIV 669); (2) s. iv BC Dubois, *IGDOlbia* 104; cf. Vinogradov, *Pont. Stud.* p. 159 no. 12 quinquies (-κες)

Καφάναγος
SKYTHIA:
—OLBIA-BORYSTHENES: (1) ii-iii AD *IOSPE* I^2 138, 9; Zgusta, *PNS* 301 (f. *Μούρδαγος*)

Κάχιον
CIMMERIAN BOSPOROS:
—PANTIKAPAION: (1) i/ii AD *CIRB* 645 (d. *Βοστάκων, Χοίδρα*)

Κεβαλῖνος
MACEDONIA: (1) 330 BC Berve 418 (Tataki, *Macedonians* p. 339 nos. 30-31)

Κέβαλος
MACEDONIA?: (1) 317 BC D.S. xix 44. 1 (Tataki, *Macedonians* p. 339 no. 32) (*Κελβανός*—mss. RX, *Κ.*—ms. F and Wesseling)

Κέββας
MACEDONIA (BOTTIAIA):
—AIGAI: (1) c. 300-275 BC *SEG* XXXV 804 (f. *Ἀμείνανδρος*)

Κέβων
MACEDONIA (EDONIS):
—AMPHIPOLIS: (1) hell.? ib. XXXIII 504 (tile) (*Κέβων*: s. *Ἐπίξενος*)

Κεδρήπολις
THRACE?: (1) 316-309 BC *IG* II^2 1956, 37; *Ancient Macedonia* 5 p. 445 with n. 10 (date) (*FRA* 2545)

Κειλαίβιθυς
MACEDONIA (SINTIKE):
—NEINE: (1) 77 AD *IGB* V 5883, 9 (-βει-: f. *Μύκασος*); (2) ii AD ib. IV 2253 (-βει-: f. *Βίθυς*)
—NEINE (NR.): (3) ii-iii AD ib. V 5890 (-βει-: f. *Πύρρος*)

Κειμήλιον
MACEDONIA (CHALKIDIKE):
—AKANTHOS: (1) s. vi BC *SEG* XLI 550 (vase) (*Κεμέλιον* (n. pr.?))

Κέκροψ
THRACE:
—PERINTHOS-HERAKLEIA?: (1) iv BC Hp., *Epid.* iv 25

Κέλαδος
MACEDONIA (PAIONIA):
—STOBOI: (1) 132 AD *IG* X (2) (2) 164 (*Π. Ἰούλ. Κ.*)

Κελαίδοσα
THRACE:
—KELLAI: (1) 241-244 AD *IGB* III 1517, 51 (*Αὐρ. Κελαίδοσα*: d. *Τολμεάριος*)

Κελέπυρις
THRACE:
—MARKIANOPOLIS (TERRIT.): (1) iii AD ib. V 5329, 4 (f. *Δαλήτραλις*)

Κέλερ
MACEDONIA (LYNKESTIS):
—HERAKLEIA: (1) i AD *IG* X (2) (2) 75, 23 (s. *Τίτος*)
MACEDONIA (MYGDONIA):
—KALINDOIA: (2) 68-98 AD *SEG* XLII 580, 25 (f. *Λ. Ἰούλ. Κέλερ, Γ. Ἰούλ. Πρόκλος*)
THRACE:
—BEROE-AUGUSTA TRAIANA: (3) 222-235 AD *IGB* III 1562, 6 (f. *Αὐρ. Ἰνγένοος*)
—KELLAI: (4) 241-244 AD ib. 1517, 23 (f. *Αὐρ. Ἀσκληπιάδης*)

Κελεριανός
TAURIS:
—CHERSONESOS: (1) 174 AD *SEG* XLV 985 A, 35 (s. *Στρατόφιλος*)

Κελερῖνα
MACEDONIA (BOTTIAIA):
—BEROIA*: (1) 492 AD *IBer* 441, 2 (Feissel, *RICM* 64)
THRACE:
—NOVAE: (2) m. vi AD *IGLNovae* 180 (*SEG* XLV 945)
—TYRODIZA-TIRISTASIS: (3) imp. Dumont–Homolle 89d (threpte)

Κελήκενθος
THRACE: (1) f. ii BC *IC* 2 p. 30 no. 15 (-γεν-: f. *Βίθυς*)

Κελσῖνα
THRACE:
—BEROE-AUGUSTA TRAIANA: (1) iii AD *IGB* III 1605, 5 (-σεῖ-: d. *Αὐρ. Κρισπῖνα*); (2) c. 320-324 AD *Anal. Boll.* 31 (1912) pp. 195 ff.; p. 207
—PHILIPPOPOLIS-TRIMONTIUM (TERRIT.): (3) ii-iii AD *IGB* III 1062 + V 5470 (*Κελσῖνα*)

Κελσῖνος
THRACE:
—SERDICA:
——Scretisca*: (1) iii AD ib. IV 2017 (*Αὐρ. Κ.*)

Κέλσος
THRACE:
—BAZOPARA: (1) 202 AD ib. III 1690 d, 24 (and Thrace Pizos: s. *Δρινγίστας*); (2) ~ ib. l. 26 (and Thrace Pizos: s. *Σάλας*); (3) ~ ib. l. 54 (and Thrace Pizos: f. *Τήρης*); (4) ~ ib. l. 60 (and Thrace Pizos: f. *Σκέλης*); (5) ~ ib. 1690 c, 50 (and Thrace Pizos: s. *Μουκάπορις*); (6) ~ ib. l. 60 (and Thrace Pizos: f. *Σάλας*)
—BEROE-AUGUSTA TRAIANA (TERRIT.): (7) ii AD ib. 1741 bis (biling.) (*Κ. Μάριος*); (8) 222-230 AD ib. 1666, 4 (f. *Βίθυς*)
—ERGISSENOI: (9) ii AD ib. 1593, 19 (f. *Μουκάτραλις*)
—HADRIANOPOLIS (TERRIT.): (10) ii-iii AD ib. 1819 (*Ἰοῦστος Κ.*: f. *Λαβείων*)
—KELLAI: (11) 241-244 AD ib. 1517, 6 (s. *Σώσανδρος*)
—MARONEIA: (12) ii AD *SEG* XLVII 1069 (*IThrakAig* E189) (s. *Μᾶρκος*)
—PAUTALIA: (13) ii AD *IGB* IV 2074, 11; (14) ~ ib. l. 16 (f. *Τάρσας*); (15) 135 AD ib. 2057, 9 (f. *Λοῦππος*)
—PHILIPPOPOLIS-TRIMONTIUM (TERRIT.): (16) ii-iii AD ib. III 1478, 1, 5 (or Thrace Diokletianopolis: *Κέλσσος*—l. 1)
—SKEDABRIA: (17) 202 AD ib. 1690 b, 16 (and Thrace Pizos: f. *Δύδης*)
—SKEPTA: (18) 202 AD ib. 1690 c, 13 (and Thrace Pizos: s. *Δαλήπορις*)

Κενδεβαῖος
THRACE?: (1) 139-129 BC *IMacc* 15, 38 ff.; J., *AJ* xiii 225 f.

Κενθίαρος
THRACE:
—KELLAI: (1) 241-244 AD *IGB* III 1517, 40 (*Αὐρ. Κ.*: s. *Πείσων*); (2) ~ ib. l. 44 (*Αὐρ. Κ.*: s. *Ἡραΐς*)

Κένθος
THRACE?: (1) 316-309 BC *IG* II^2 1956, 40; *Ancient Macedonia* 5 p. 445 with n. 10 (date) (*FRA* 2546)

Κένσος
THRACE:
—GLAVA PANEGA (MOD.): (1) i-ii AD *IGB* II 510 (f. *Ἰούλιος*)

Κεράστης
MACEDONIA (ORESTIS): (1) v/iv BC J., *AJ* xi 304; cf. Tataki, *Macedonians* p. 206 s.v. no. 11 (f. *Παυσανίας*)

Κερβίων
MACEDONIA (BOTTIAIA):
—EDESSA: (1) iii AD Feissel, *RICM* 9, 6 (Tataki, *Edessa* 147) (s. *Στερκόριος, Παραμόνα*)

Κέρδηζος
THRACE:
—KABYLE*: (1) iii-ii BC *Act. IX Ep. Congr.* p. 237 (coin)

Κερδίμμας
MACEDONIA: (1) iv BC Arr., *An.* ii 13. 7 (Tataki, *Macedonians* p. 340 no. 33) (f. *Μένων*)

Κερδώλας
MACEDONIA (EDONIS):
—PHILIPPOI?: (1) ?i-ii AD *AE* 1950-1, p. 64 no. 7 (Pilhofer 722) (or Macedonia (Mygdonia) Thessalonike: Lat. Annius Cerdola: s. Annia Prima)

Macedonia (Odomantike):
—sirrha?: (2) iii ad *IGB* v 5932 (*Γάϊος ὁ καὶ Κ.*: f. *Βῆρος*)

Κέρδων
Cimmerian Bosporos:
—gorgippia?: (1) s. ii ad *CIRB* 1231 A, 13 (s. *Φ—*)
Kolchis: (2) ii bc *IG* ii² 9050 (*FRA* 2937) (s. *Ἕρμων*)
Macedonia (Edonis):
—philippoi: (3) imp. *BSA* 23 (1918-19) p. 97 no. 24 (Pilhofer 152) (Lat. Cerdo); (4) ~ *BCH* 56 (1932) p. 225 no. 15 (Pilhofer 78) (Lat. Cerdo: s. Cassius); (5) ~ ib. 310 (Lat. N. Caesius Cerdo); (6) ~ *CIL* iii 688 (Pilhofer 358) (Lat. [C]erdo)
Macedonia (Mygdonia):
—thessalonike: (7) s. i ad *IG* x (2) (1) 68, 44; 69, 29 (*Τι. Κλ. Κ.*)
Macedonia (Odomantike):
—sirrha: (8) f. iii ad *SEG* xxx 590, 10 (f. *Αὐρ. Ἑρμοῦς*)
Sarmatia:
—maiotai: (9) ii bc *IG* ii² 9254 (*FRA* 3452) (slave?)
Scythia Minor:
—tomis: (10) ii-iii ad *ISM* ii 138 (Lat. Cerdo)
Skythia:
—olbia-borysthenes: (11) v-iii bc *SEG* xxx 958 (vase); (12) m. iv bc Dubois, *IGDOlbia* 25 b, 3 (*Κέρδω[ν]*)
—skythai: (13) m. ii bc *IIasos* 408, 15 (s. *Ἕρμων*: metic)
Thrace:
—bizone: (14) i-ii ad *IGB* i² 8 ter (*Κ̣έρδων*)
—komotini (mod.): (15) imp. *Belomorski Pregled* i (1942) p. 337 no. 44 (*IThrakAig* E488); cf. *BE* 1948, no. 148 (f. *Ζωσαροῦς*)
—maroneia: (16) imp. *BCH* 37 (1913) p. 143 no. 47 (*IThrakAig* E274)
—nicopolis ad istrum (territ.): (17) s. ii ad *ILB* 355 (Lat. M. Lucius Cerdo)
—perinthos-herakleia: (18) i-ii ad *IPerinth* 53

Κερδωνᾶς
Skythia:
—tyras*: (1) ii-iii ad *SEG* xxxv 870 (vase)

Κέρζα
Thrace:
—philippopolis-trimontium (territ.): (1) ii-iii ad *IGB* iii 1408 + v 5519 (d. *Γαρούλας*)

Κερζέας
Thrace:
—apollonia-sozopolis: (1) iv bc *BMNBurgas* 4 (2002) pp. 124-5 no. 20 (*Κερζέατος* (gen.): f. *Φανίχη*)

Κερζετραυς
Thrace:
—markianopolis (nr.): (1) f. iii ad *IGB* v 5365 (*CCET* ii (1) 226) (s. *Αὐλούζενις*)

Κέρζος
Macedonia (Edonis):
—philippoi (territ.): (1) ?ii ad *BCH* 47 (1923) pp. 64-5 no. 24, 7 (Pilhofer 519) (Lat. Cerzus: s. Dininithus)

Κερζούλας
Macedonia (Edonis):
—philippoi (territ.): (1) ?ii ad *CIL* iii 703, 5 (Pilhofer 524); Collart, *Philippes* pl. 84. 2 (Lat. Cerzula: f. *Βιθύκενθος*)
Macedonia (Odomantike):
—gazoros: (2) 215 or 174 bc *SEG* xxx 1892, 28 (Hatzopoulos, *MI* 2 pp. 57-8 no. 39) (f. *Μάντας*)

Κερίσκης?
Thrace:
—kellai: (1) 241-244 ad *IGB* iii 1517, 46 (*Αὐρ. Κ.*, *Κ<ε>ρ(έ)σκης?*—ed.: s. *Στράτων*)

Κερκᾶς
Scythia Minor:
—istros: (1) ii ad *ISM* i 211, 8 (*Κ̣ερκᾶς*: s. *Εὔνοστος*)
Thrace:
—philippopolis-trimontium: (2) c. 303 ad *Anal. Boll.* 31 (1912) p. 192

Κερκῆς
Thrace:
—philippopolis-trimontium (territ.): (1) ii-iii ad *IGB* iii 1465 (s. *Βίθυς*)

Κερκίδας
Macedonia (Odomantike):
—sirrha: (1) f. iii ad *SEG* xxx 590, 21 ([*Αὐρ.*] [*Κ*]*ερκίδας*: s. *Βε̣—*)

Κερκιθίων
Scythia Minor:
—tomis: (1) iii ad *ISM* ii 24, 6

Κερκίνος
Scythia Minor:
—kallatis: (1) iii bc ib. iii 126, 4 (f. ...*σων*); (2) ~ ib. l. 7 (s. *Εὐχείας*)
Thrace:
—byzantion: (3) ?354 bc Rhodes–Osborne 57, 12 (s. *Ἡρότιμος*); (4) i bc-i ad *IByz* 270 (Fıratlı–Robert pp. 86-7 no. 108a) (f. *Μενεκράτης*)

Κερκίων
Macedonia (Bottiaia):
—pella: (1) iii-ii bc Dimitsas 136
Scythia Minor:
—istros: (2) ii ad *ISM* i 211, 10 (s. *Κόρινθος*)
—tomis: (3) ii bc ib. ii 167; Robert, *Noms indigènes* p. 187 ff. (name) (*Κερκίο[νι]* (dat.)—ed.)
——(Argadeis): (4) iii-ii bc *ISM* ii 35; *BE* 1962, no. 231 (s. *Τιμόμαχος*)

Κερσεβλέπτης
Thrace:
—odrysai: (1) c. 380-342 bc *RE* s.v. Kersobleptes (-); Rhodes–Osborne 47, [5], [9], 10, etc.; *FD* iii (1) 392, 4; *Rogozen Treasure* p. 47 no. 15; Peter, *MTD* pp. 125-32 (coin); Osborne, *Naturalization* T54 (*Κερσοβλέπτης*—lit. test.: s. *Κότυς*, f. *Ἰόλαος*, *Ποσειδώνιος*, *Μηδίστας*, *Τήρης*: king)

Κερσίβαυλος
Thrace?: (1) iii bc Peter, *MTD* p. 250; *Nom. Chron.* 16 (1997) pp. 21-24 (coin) (king)

Κερτίμμας
Macedonia (Bottiaia):
—beroia: (1) ii bc *IBer* 141, 2 ([*Κ*]*ερτίμμου* (gen.)); (2) ~ ib. l. 12 ([*Κερ*]*τίμμου* (gen.))
—tyrissa? (asvestari (mod.)): (3) f. ii bc *SEG* xlvii 999, 21 (*Κερ*[*τίμμας*]?)
Macedonia (Mygdonia):
—kalindoia: (4) c. 322 bc Hatzopoulos, *MI* 2 p. 84 no. 62, 23 (s. *Κρίθων*); (5) i ad *SEG* xxxv 744, 7 (f. *Ἀπολλώνιος*); (6) 68-98 ad ib. xlii 580, 20 + *BE* 1999, no. 362 (*Κερτίμ(μ)ου* (gen.): f. *Ἡράκων*)
—thessalonike: (7) s. i ad *IG* x (2) (1) 68, 35 (f. (nat.) *Παράμονος*)
Macedonia (Orestis):
—koressos (mod.): (8) iii bc *EAM* 191 (*Κερτίμμα*[*ς*]?, *Κερτίμμα*—ed.)

Κέστιος
Cimmerian Bosporos:
—pantikapaion: (1) i/ii ad *CIRB* 79 A, 3 (*Κέσσ-*: s. *Βάκχιος*)

Scythia Minor:
—tomis: (2) s. ii ad *SEG* xxxiii 586 (f. *Ἑρμογένης*)

Κετρέζερις
Thrace:
—odessos: (1) ?ii ad *IGB* i² 94 + v 5037 (*Κετρέζερ*[*ις*])

Κέτρηζις
Macedonia (Edonis):
—philippoi (drama (mod.)): (1) i bc-i ad *GVI* 429 (Pilhofer 509) (*Κετρήζειδος* (gen.): f. *Ἀλλούπορις*)
Macedonia (Mygdonia):
—kalindoia: (2) 68-98 ad *SEG* xlii 580, 67; cf. *Anthémonte–Kalindoia* 2 pp. 271-2 (name) (f. *Καρδοῦς*)

Κέτριζις
Macedonia (Odomantike):
—sirrha (territ.): (1) 26 ad *SEG* xlvi 708 (Pilhofer 557a) (s. *Μεστίκενθος*)
—sirrha (nr.): (2) i-ii ad *Poikila* p. 185 (Pilhofer 563) (Lat. C. Sertorius sive Cetrizis: s. Besideltus)

Κετρίλας
Macedonia (Edonis):
—philippoi (territ.): (1) ?ii ad *BCH* 47 (1923) pp. 64-5 no. 24, 5 (Pilhofer 519, 5) (Lat. Cetrila[s]); (2) ~ *BCH* 47 (1923) pp. 64-5 no. 24, 8 (Pilhofer 519, 8) (Lat. Cetrilas)
—philippoi (drama (mod.)): (3) i-ii ad *Drama* p. 75 (Pilhofer 501c) (Lat. Cetrillas: s. *Διούλας*, f. *Διούλας*, *Δίνις*)

Κετρίπολις
Macedonia (Derriopos):
—stuberra: (1) 74 ad *IG* x (2) (2) 326, 49 (-*τρεί*-: f. *Δούλης*)

Κετρίπορις
Macedonia (Derriopos):
—stuberra: (1) 74 ad ib. l. 56 (-*τρει*-: f. *Μέστυς*); (2) 75 ad ib. l. 57 (f. *Μέστυς*)
Thrace: (3) f. iv bc *RE* (-); Rhodes–Osborne 53, 2, [9], 11, 15, etc.; Peter, *MTD* pp. 143-6 (coin) (?s. *Βηρισάδης*: king)

Κέτρις
Macedonia (Mygdonia):
—kalindoia: (1) a. 98 ad *SEG* xlii 582, 52; cf. *Anthémonte–Kalindoia* 2 p. 272 (name) (f. *Ἱέρων*)

Κεφάλις
Thrace:
—spinopara: (1) ii ad *IGB* iv 2192, 16

Κεφαλίων
Macedonia (Chalkidike):
—olynthos: (1) ii/i bc *IG* ii² 10021 (Tataki, *Macedonians* p. 139 no. 72; *FRA* 5899) ([*Κ*]*εφαλίω*[*ν*]: s. *Δωρόθεος*)
Tauris:
—chersonesos: (2) f. iv bc *CIRB* 195 (f. *Κέφαλος*)
Thrace:
—byzantion: (3) iv/iii bc *IByz* 58 (Fıratlı–Robert p. 47 no. 2) (f. *Θράσων*)

Κέφαλος
Cimmerian Bosporos:
—pantikapaion: (1) iv bc Tolstoi 245 (vase)
Skythia:
—olbia-borysthenes*: (2) ?v bc *AA* 1909, p. 174 (vase) (*Κέφ*[*α*]*λος*: kalos)
Tauris:
—chersonesos: (3) f. iv bc *CIRB* 195 (s. *Κεφαλίων*)
Thrace:
—byzantion: (4) c. 500-480 bc *SEG* xlvi 474, 6 (f. *Πυθίων*)

—ZONE: (5) s. iv BC ib. XXXIV 710 = XLVIII 904 bis = XLIX 894 (*IThrakAig* E402) (f. Ἀρχήνασσα)

Κεφάλων

CIMMERIAN BOSPOROS:

—BOSPOROS: (1) imp. *NS* 166

MACEDONIA: (2) ?243 BC *PPetr* III 82, 8 (Tataki, *Macedonians* p. 340 no. 35; La'da E1523) (s. Ἀδαῖος) ?= (3); (3) 236 BC *PPetr*² 16, 85 (Tataki, *Macedonians* p. 340 no. 34; La'da E1525) ?= (2); (4) 227 BC *SB* 7631, [5], 29 (Tataki, *Macedonians* p. 340 no. 36; La'da E1769) (s. Θεόδωρος: t.e.); (5) c. 150-125 BC *SB* 15369, 4 (La'da E1524) (s. Ἡρακλείδης: katoikos)

MACEDONIA (DERRIOPOS):

—STUBERRA: (6) 74 AD *IG* X (2) (2) 326, 44 (s. Διονύσιος)

MACEDONIA (KRESTONIA):

—BRAGYLAI: (7) c. 230-200 BC *BCH* 45 (1921) p. 18 III, 71 (Tataki, *Macedonians* p. 84 no. 4) (s. Ἀντίοχος)

Κέφθος

CIMMERIAN BOSPOROS:

—GORGIPPIA: (1) ii/iii AD *CIRB* 1179, 30; Zgusta, *PNS* 660 (f. Ἀγαθοῦς)

Κήζεβις

MACEDONIA (MYGDONIA):

—KALINDOIA: (1) a. 98 AD *SEG* XLII 582, 66; cf. *Anthémonte–Kalindoia* 2 p. 272 (name) (s. Βίθυς); (2) ~ *SEG* XLII 583, 12 (Κ. Ῥοδιανός)

Κηνέξαρθος

SKYTHIA:

—OLBIA-BORYSTHENES: (1) ?ii AD *IOSPE* I² 133, 4; Zgusta, *PNS* 123

Κηπίων

MACEDONIA (PIERIA):

—PYDNA: (1) 250 AD *SEG* XLVI 800 A, 13; 800 B, 13 (Αὐρ. Κ.: s. Πιερίων)

Κηράτων

MACEDONIA (DERRIOPOS):

—STUBERRA: (1) 90 AD *IG* X (2) (2) 326, 77 (s. Φίλων)

Κησέρνιος

SCYTHIA MINOR:

—ISTROS: (1) ii AD *ISM* I 197 I, 8 (s. Ῥωμανός)

Κήσης

MACEDONIA (PAIONIA):

—NEGOTINO (MOD.): (1) 153 AD *SEG* XXXVIII 712 (Κήσῃ (dat.): f. Μακεδών, Ποσειδώνιος, Φίλιππος)

Κῆσος

MACEDONIA (PELAGONIA):

—DOSTONEIS?: (1) ii-iii AD *IG* X (2) (2) 204 (Κῆσος: s. Μέστος)

Κήτων

THRACE:

—NAULOCHOS?: (1) s. iii BC *IGB* V 5085 (PM 1104 Add) (or Thrace Mesambria: Κήτων: I s. Θεότιμος, f. Ἐράτων, Κήτων II, Θεαίνετος); (2) ~ *IGB* V 5085 (PM 1104 Add) (or Thrace Mesambria: Κήτων: II s. Κήτων I, Μίκκα)

Κηφισόδοτος

CIMMERIAN BOSPOROS:

—PANTIKAPAION: (1) iii BC *CIRB* 110, 1 (s. Κ—)

TAURIS:

—CHERSONESOS: (2) m. ii AD *IOSPE* I² 423 (sculptor)

Κηφισόδωρος

MACEDONIA (BOTTIAIA):

—PELLA: (1) iii BC Akamatis, *Amph. Pellas* p. 38 no. PAR36 (amph.) (*SEG* L 613)

MACEDONIA (CHALKIDIKE):

—OLYNTHOS: (2) ?iv BC *IG* II² 10022 (Tataki, *Macedonians* p. 139 no. 73; *FRA* 5900) (s. —δας); (3) f. iv BC *SEG* XXIX 624 (s. Θευγέτων)

MACEDONIA (MYGDONIA):

—DIKAIA: (4) c. 365-359 BC Unp. (Voutyras–Sismanidis) l. 63 (s. Ἀγαθοκλῆς)

THRACE:

—SESTOS: (5) iv BC *IG* II² 10264 (*FRA* 6638) (f. Ναυσικρίτη)

Κήφισος

CIMMERIAN BOSPOROS:

—GORGIPPIA: (1) f. iii BC *CIRB* 1137 A I, 40; II, 35 (f. Πανταχλῆς)

Κιβᾶς

MACEDONIA (ODOMANTIKE):

—SKOTOUSSA?: (1) iv-iii BC *SEG* XLIII 402 + *Makedonika* 28 (1991-2) p. 103 with pl. 4 (Κιβᾶ (gen.): f. Ναννίς)

Κικέρων

SKYTHIA:

—TANAIS: (1) f. ii AD *CIRB* 1294 (Κικέρω[ν]?: ?f. —λας)

Κίλας

MACEDONIA (CHALKIDIKE):

—ANTHEMOUS: (1) 106 BC *SEG* XLII 561; cf. *Anthémonte–Kalindoia* pp. 273-4 (name) (Κίλα (gen.): f. Διοσκουρίδης)

Κιληβυζος

THRACE:

—ZONE: (1) f. iv BC *SEG* XXIV 640 (*IThrakAig* E415) (f. Ὀρφεύς)

Κιλία

TAURIS:

—CHERSONESOS: (1) ii AD *IOSPE* I² 455; Zgusta, *PNS* 1049 (d. Ἀπολλώνιος, m. Κυράθεων)

Κιλικᾶς

SKYTHIA:

—OLBIA-BORYSTHENES: (1) ii AD *IOSPE* I² 128, 6; Zgusta, *PNS* 777 (s. Μύροτος)

Κιλλαῖος

THRACE:

—SESTOS: (1) a. 129 BC *ISestos* 1, 1 (f. Γλαυκίας)

Κιλλεύς

MACEDONIA (ELIMEIA):

—DIPORO (MOD.): (1) ii BC *EAM* 44 (Κιλλεῖ (dat.))

Κίλλης

MACEDONIA: (1) 311 BC *RE* Supplbd. 4 (-); *PP* 2164; 14609 (Tataki, *Macedonians* p. 340 no. 37); (2) 236 BC *PPetr*² 16, 4 (Tataki, *Macedonians* p. 340 no. 38; La'da E1770) (s. Ἀντίγονος: t.e.)

MACEDONIA (ORESTIS):

—KORESSOS (MOD.): (3) iii BC *EAM* 191 (Κ. (fem. gen.?)—ed.)

Κιμᾶς

MACEDONIA (ODOMANTIKE):

—BERGE (TERRIT.): (1) iv BC *SEG* XXXII 641 (Pillhofer 569); cf. *SEG* L 608 (Κιμᾶ (gen.)—n. pr.?: ?f. Κόλπος)

Κίμβρος

MACEDONIA (SINTIKE):

—NEINE: (1) 77 AD *IGB* V 5883, 5 (s. Βίθυς)

SKYTHIA:

—TANAIS: (2) ii AD *CIRB* 1262, 21 (Κίμβρος—Tokhtas'ev: s. Δῖος); (3) 225 AD ib. 1279, 15 (f. Νάβαζος); (4) 225-236 AD ib. 1250, 13, 15; 1280, 28 (f. Ἀντίμαχος, Φιδάνους)

Κίνναμος

MACEDONIA (BOTTIAIA):

—BEROIA: (1) ii/iii AD *IBer* 27 A, 11 (slave?)

Κίνωλις

CIMMERIAN BOSPOROS:

—PANTIKAPAION: (1) i BC/i AD *CIRB* 306; cf. KW pl. 20 no. 297; Zgusta, *PNS* 778 (Κινώλιος (gen.): f. Δασχάς)

—PANTIKAPAION (NR.): (2) i AD *CIRB* 961; cf. KW pl. 35 no. 511 (Κινώλεως (gen.): f. Ἔρως)

TAURIS:

—CHERSONESOS: (3) s. iv BC Solomonik, *NEPKh* 143; *Hellenismus* p. 450 no. 17 (s. Πάσιχος)

Κίνωλος

SKYTHIA:

—TANAIS: (1) ii AD *CIRB* 1268, 5; Zgusta, *PNS* 778

Κίρβεις

SKYTHIA:

—OLBIA-BORYSTHENES?: (1) ?ii BC *JDAI* 23 (1908) pp. 59-60 nos. 13-14; 62-4 nos. 20-1; 68 no. 28; Courby, *Les vases grecs* p. 412; *MIA* 103 (1962) pp. 201-3 (vase) (potter)

Κιροάδας

THRACE:

—ODRYSAI: (1) 204 or 183 BC *HE* 3920 (king)

Κισσίς

MACEDONIA (MYGDONIA):

—THESSALONIKE: (1) ii-iii AD *SEG* XXX 641 (Κισσεῖδι (dat.): m. Κλ. Σίμων, Τιβ. Κλ. Λογγινιανός)

Κίσσος

MACEDONIA (BOTTIAIA):

—BEROIA: (1) ii-iii AD *IBer* 252 (Tataki 689) (f. Ἑρμόφιλος)

MACEDONIA (EDONIS):

—AMPHIPOLIS: (2) m. iii BC Hatzopoulos, *Actes Amphipolis* p. 52 no 12, 2; *SEG* XLI 566 (date) (s. Ἑκαταῖος)

THRACE:

—PHILIPPOPOLIS-TRIMONTIUM (TERRIT.): (3) ii-iii AD *IGB* III 1394; cf. V 5514 (Ἀπούσιος Κ.: s. Δίπορις)

Κίτρος

SKYTHIA:

—OLBIA-BORYSTHENES: (1) iv BC *SEG* XXX 958 (vase) (Κίτρο (gen.?), Κιτρό? (fem. nom.)—n. pr.?)

Κλαδαῖος

SCYTHIA MINOR:

—TOMIS: (1) ii-iii AD *GVI* 1632, 6

Κλάδεος

THRACE:

—PHILIPPOPOLIS-TRIMONTIUM: (1) m. iii AD *IGB* III 884 b, 21; cf. V 5400 (Ἰούλ. Κλάδ(ε)ος)

Κλᾶρα

MACEDONIA (PIERIA):

—DION?: (1) i-ii AD *AEMTh* 15 (2001) p. 343 (Ἰουλία ἡ καὶ Κ.)

Κλαρόνικος

MACEDONIA (MYGDONIA):

—KALINDOIA: (1) a. 98 AD *SEG* XLII 582, 26 (-νει-: f. Βίθυς); (2) ~ ib. l. 40 (-νει-: s. Ἀρχέλαος)

Κλᾶρος

MACEDONIA (EDONIS):

—AMPHIPOLIS: (1) ii/iii AD *Anal. Boll.* 31 (1912) p. 170 (f. Λαμπάδιος)

Κλαυδία
MACEDONIA (ODOMANTIKE):
—SIRRHA: (1) 155 AD Dimitsas 821, 4 (Kaphtantzis 1) (m. *Τορκοῦς*)
—SKOTOUSSA?: (2) 156 AD *SEG* XXIV 612, 6 (?d. *Λουκιλιανός*: freed.?)
MACEDONIA (PIERIA):
—DION: (3) ii-iii AD Oikonomos 20 ([*Κ*]*λαυδί*[*α*])

Κλαυδιανή
MACEDONIA (BOTTIAIA):
—EDESSA: (1) 207 AD *Arch. Pap.* 22 (1973) p. 209 no. 16 (Tataki, *Edessa* 153) (*Κλαυδιο*—— ed., *Κλαυδια*[*ν*]*ή*—Tataki)
MACEDONIA (PAIONIA): (2) ii-iii AD *Sp.* 71 (1931) p. 229 no. 608 (d. *Οὐαλέριος, Παραμόνα*)
—NEGOTINO (MOD.): (3) ii-iii AD ib. 77 (1934) p. 43 no. 25

Κλαυδιανός
MACEDONIA (BOTTIAIA):
—BEROIA (TERRIT.): (1) ii-iii AD *IBer* 512, 3 (Tataki 704)
—BEROIA?: (2) f. iii AD *IBer* 399, 1 (*GVI* 672; Tataki 703) (?f. *Κύριλλα*)
MACEDONIA (MYGDONIA):
—THESSALONIKE: (3) ?ii AD *IG* X (2) (1) 567; (4) ii-iii AD ib. 667 (*Κ*(*λα*)*υ*(*δι*)*ανός*)
—THESSALONIKE (NR.): (5) ?iii AD ib. 1004, 1 (*Κλα*(*υ*)*διανός*)
MACEDONIA (SINTIKE):
—PARTHIKOPOLIS (TERRIT.): (6) 215 AD *IGB* IV 2319
THRACE: (7) 149 AD Dumont–Homolle 110b, 4, 10
—BEROE-AUGUSTA TRAIANA: (8) c. 320-324 AD *Anal. Boll.* 31 (1912) p. 194
—EMPORION THOUIDAI: (9) ii-iii AD *IGB* III 1767; cf. V 5634 (locn.) (s. *Δορζίζενις*)

Κλαύδιος
MACEDONIA (BOTTIAIA):
—BEROIA: (1) iii AD *IBer* 275 (Tataki 705)
—EDESSA: (2) 247 AD *Athena* 12 (1900) p. 71 no. 5, 2 (Tataki, *Edessa* 155) ([*Κλαύδ*]*ιος*?)
MACEDONIA (MYGDONIA):
—THESSALONIKE: (3) i AD *SEG* XLVIII 848; (4) ii-iii AD ib. XXX 641 (f. *Κλ. Σίμων, Τιβ. Κλ. Λογγινιανός*)
MACEDONIA (ODOMANTIKE):
—GAZOROS: (5) ii-iii AD Kaphtantzis 553 (Pilhofer 550)
THRACE:
—PERINTHOS-HERAKLEIA: (6) 196-198 AD *IPerinth* 56, 17 (f. *Μάξιμος*)
—PHILIPPOPOLIS-TRIMONTIUM (TERRIT.): (7) iii AD *IGB* III 1304 (—*ος ὁ καὶ Κλαύδι*[*ος*])
—TÂRGOVIŠTE (MOD.): (8) ii AD *CCET* II (2) 535

Κλαῦδις
THRACE:
—NICOPOLIS AD ISTRUM: (1) ii-iii AD *IGB* II 663 (s. *Ἀπολλώνιος*)

Κλέα
MACEDONIA (BOTTIAIA):
—BEROIA: (1) ii-iii AD *IBer* 93, 5 (Tataki 577) (*Ἰουλ. Κ.*)
MACEDONIA (LYNKESTIS):
—HERAKLEIA?: (2) ii-iii AD *IG* X (2) (2) 132 ([*Δ*]*ομιτία Κλέ*[*α*])

Κλεαγόρα
MACEDONIA (BOTTIAIA):
—BEROIA: (1) ii-iii AD *IBer* 357 (Tataki 736) (m. *Βότρυς*)
MACEDONIA (EORDAIA):
—EXOCHI (MOD.): (2) 265 AD *EAM* 116, 3 (m. *Ζωΐχη*)

Κλεαγόρας
MACEDONIA (BOTTIAIA):
—AIGAI: (1) iv/iii BC *SEG* XXXV 785 (f. *Λύδα*)

Κλεαινετίδης
THRACE:
—ABDERA: (1) c. 395-360 BC *Studii Cercetări Numismatică* 11 (1995) p. 19 no. 1 (coin) (*Κλεαινετίδεω* (gen.))

Κλεαίνετος
MACEDONIA (CHALKIDIKE):
—OLYNTHOS: (1) ?350 BC *TAPA* 69 (1938) p. 50 no. 4, 8; Hatzopoulos, *Actes Chalc.* p. 80 (date) (*Κλεαίν*[*ε*]*τος*)

Κλεαίνιτος
SKYTHIA:
—OLBIA-BORYSTHENES: (1) v BC Dubois, *IGD-Olbia* 87 (vase)

Κλέανδρος
CIMMERIAN BOSPOROS:
—GORGIPPIA: (1) f. iii BC *CIRB* 1137 A II, 44 (s. *Καλλιππίδης*)
MACEDONIA: (2) ?417-413 BC *IG* I³ 89, 63 (Tataki, *Macedonians* p. 341 no. 41); (3) 343 BC *CID* II 36 I, 24 (Tataki, *Macedonians* p. 341 no. 40); (4) 334 BC *RE* (5); Berve 423 (Tataki, *Macedonians* p. 341 no. 42); (5) c. 225-200 BC *ICos* ED 56, 5 (Tataki, *Macedonians* p. 341 no. 43) (*Κλέ*[*ανδ*]*ρ*[*ος*]— ed., *Κλε*[*άνω*]*ρ*?, *Κλε*[*αγό*]*ρ*[*ας*]?: f. *Ἀριστέας*)
—LEUGA: (6) iv BC Arr., *An.* ii 9. 3 (Tataki, *Macedonians* p. 119 no. 1); cf. *Historia* 47 (1998) pp. 414-16 (locn.) (f. *Παντόρδανος*)
MACEDONIA (BOTTIAIA):
—AIGAI: (7) s. iv BC *SEG* XXXV 782 (f. *Δυμμινώ*)
—BEROIA: (8) 122 BC *IBer* 134, 5 (*Κλέανδρ*[*ος*]: s. *Νίκων*); (9) f. i AD ib. 103, 6 (s. *Ζώπυρος*)
MACEDONIA (CHALKIDIKE):
—CHALKIDEIS: (10) ?354 BC *TAPA* 69 (1938) pp. 52-3 no. 6, 3; Hatzopoulos, *Actes Chalc.* p. 80 (date) (s. *Σώσων*)
MACEDONIA (EDONIS):
—AMPHIPOLIS: (11) m. iii BC Hatzopoulos, *Actes Amphipolis* p. 50 no. 11, 12 (*SEG* XLI 565) ([*Κ*]*λέανδρος, Λέανδρος*—ed.: f. *Ἀγ*—); (12) ~ Hatzopoulos, *Actes Amphipolis* p. 52 no 12, 2; *SEG* XLI 566 (date); (13) 238 BC *PPetr*² 3, 3 (Tataki, *Macedonians* p. 54 no. 70; La'da E133)
MACEDONIA (ELIMEIA)?: (14) 334-324 BC *RE* (6); Berve 422 (Tataki, *Macedonians* p. 195 no. 12) (s. *Πολεμοκράτης*)
MACEDONIA (PAIONIA):
—STOBOI: (15) v-vi AD Unp. (Stobi excav.) inv. I-73-3 (*Κλέ*[*ανδ*]*ρος*)
MACEDONIA (PIERIA):
—PYDNA: (16) iv BC *GRBS* 47 (2002-3) p. 116 no. 4, 6
THRACE:
—PERINTHOS-HERAKLEIA: (17) iv-iii BC *IPerinth* 4, 3 (f. *Ἡγήσανδρος*)

Κλεάνθης
MACEDONIA (BOTTIAIA):
—BEROIA: (1) ii-iii AD *IBer* 93, 3 (Tataki 608) (*Ἰούλ. Κ.*)

Κλεαντίδης
THRACE:
—ABDERA: (1) c. 395-360 BC May, *Abdera* pp. 215-19 nos. 297-312 (coin); Masson, *OGS* p. 431

Κλεάνωρ
MACEDONIA (MYGDONIA):
—KALINDOIA: (1) a. 98 AD *SEG* XLII 582, 15 (s. *Ζωΐλος*)

THRACE:
—ODESSOS: (2) c. 225-200 BC Price, *Alexander* 1173; *AMNG* I (2) 2133 (coin) (*Κλεάν*(*ωρ*)?); (3) i BC-i AD *IGB* V 5061 (f. *Ἀπελλᾶς*); (4) ii AD ib. I² 50, 3 (*Κλεάν*[*ωρ*]?: ?f. (ad.) *Ἡφαιστίων*)
—ODESSOS (NR.): (5) ii AD ib. 292 (PM 1413; *CCET* I 102) (f. *Ἀγαθήνωρ*)

Κλεαρχίδης
MACEDONIA (PIERIA):
—PHILA?: (1) ?iii BC *RPh* 1911, pp. 133-4 no. 36, 93; cf. Helly, *L'État thessalien* pp. 319-20 (locn.) (s. *Ἱππίας*)

Κλέαρχος
MACEDONIA: (1) 338 BC *FGrH* 135-6 F 20 (Tataki, *Macedonians* p. 341 no. 44); (2) 334 BC *RE* Supplbd. 4 (6a); Berve 424 (Tataki, *Macedonians* p. 342 no. 45)
MACEDONIA (BOTTIAIA):
—BEROIA: (3) ii/iii AD *IBer* 143 B, 23 (Tataki 1104) (*Πο. Κ.*)
MACEDONIA (CHALKIDIKE):
—ANTIGONEIA?: (4) hell.? Hatzopoulos, *MI* 1 p. 203 n. 8 (s. *Ἀμύντας*)
MACEDONIA (DERRIOPOS):
—STUBERRA: (5) 50 AD *IG* X (2) (2) 324, 21 (s. *Σωσίας*); (6) ?54 AD ib. l. 5 (s. *Στρατίας*); (7) 74 AD ib. 325, 19 (f. *Ἀπολλόδωρος*); (8) ~ ib. l. 26 (s. *Ἐπιτέλης*); (9) ~ ib. 326, 56 (s. *Παράμονος*); (10) 90 AD ib. l. 82 (f. *Εὔτυχος*); (11) 116 AD ib. 327, 35 (f. *Παράμονος*); (12) ~ ib. l. 40 (s. *Γάϊος*)
MACEDONIA?: (13) 331 BC *RE* Supplbd. 4 (7a); Berve 425
SCYTHIA MINOR:
—ISTROS: (14) iii BC *ISM* I 8, 4 (s. *Ἀριστόμαχος*)
THRACE:
—APOLLONIA-SOZOPOLIS: (15) iv BC *IGB* V 5148 (f. *Αἶα*)

Κλειγένης
MACEDONIA (CHALKIDIKE):
—AKANTHOS: (1) 382 BC X., *HG* V 2. 12

Κλείδημος
SKYTHIA:
—OLBIA-BORYSTHENES: (1) iv BC *IOSPE* I² 214 (*Κλε*[*ί*]*δημος*: f. *Σπάρτοκος*)

Κλεινίας
MACEDONIA (EDONIS):
—AMPHIPOLIS: (1) a. 357 BC Hatzopoulos, *Actes Amphipolis* pp. 38-9 no. 7, 4 (*ΠΛΙΕΝΙΑ*—lap, (*Κ*)*λ*(*ει*)*νία*? (gen.)—Hatzopoulos: f. *Ἀντίπατρος*)
MACEDONIA (MYGDONIA):
—THESSALONIKE: (2) ii-i BC *IG* X (2) (1) 78, 3 (s. *Μενίσκος*)
SCYTHIA MINOR:
—ISTROS: (3) ii AD *ISM* I 212, 27 (f. *Ἀσκληπιάδης*)
THRACE:
—APOLLONIA-SOZOPOLIS: (4) iv BC *SNG Cop. Thrace* 455; Unp. (Hermitage) inv. 4524-5
—HADRIANOPOLIS (TERRIT.): (5) ii AD *IGB* III 1799, 2 (*GVI* 1108) (f. *Σίτος*)

Κλεῖνος
MACEDONIA (BOTTIAIA):
—PELLA: (1) b. 333 BC *CEG* II 877 (Tataki, *Macedonians* p. 155 no. 52) (f. *Ἄρχων, Ἰσοκράτης*)
THRACE:
—LYSIMACHEIA: (2) hell. *SEG* XL 226 (*FRA* 3397) (*Κλε*(*ῖ*)*νος*?, *ΚΛΕΝΟΥ* (gen.)—lap.: f. *Διονύσιος*)

Κλειόνα
MACEDONIA (ELIMEIA):
—AIANE: (1) s. v BC *SEG* XLIII 363 B; cf. *Epigr. Makedonias* pp. 149-50 n. 37 no. 32 (name) (*Κλειόνα*—Panagiotou)

Κλέϊππος
Macedonia (Edonis):
—amphipolis: **(1)** s. iv bc Hatzopoulos, *Actes Amphipolis* p. 45 no. 9, 7 (*SEG* xli 563); cf. *SEG* xliv 504 (s. *Ζωΐλος*)

Κλεισθένης
Thrace:
—abdera: **(1)** iv bc Hp., *Epid.* vi 8. 30
—apollonia-sozopolis?: **(2)** ?iv bc *IGB* I^2 477 (*Κλεισ(θ)ένης*: f. *Λεοντομένης*)

Κλεισίμαχος
Macedonia (Bottiaia):
—beroia: **(1)** 223 bc *IBer* 4, 23 (*Κλι-*: f. *Λυσίπολις*)
Thrace:
—byzantion?: **(2)** iv/iii bc *IByz* 326 (f. *Κλειτόμαχος*)

Κλείσοφος
Thrace:
—salymbria: **(1)** ?iv bc Wehrli, *Schule Arist.* ii fr. 26

Κλείτα
Macedonia (Mygdonia):
—lete: **(1)** s. iv bc *AD* 18 (1963) Chron. p. 194 (ring)
Thrace: **(2)** f. iii bc *HE* 3423 (slave)

Κλειτîνος
Macedonia (Eordaia?):
—euia: **(1)** 181 bc *EAM* 87, 12 (Hatzopoulos, *MI* 2 pp. 41-2 no. 17) (*Κ̣λειτίνου* (gen.): f. *Θεόξενος*)

Κλειτόδωρος
Macedonia: **(1)** m. ii bc *BGU* 2423, 27 (Tataki, *Macedonians* p. 488 no. 153; La'da E1527) (s. *Κλεῖτος*)

Κλειτόμαχος
Cimmerian Bosporos:
—brannoie polie (mod.): **(1)** iv bc *VDI* 1969 (3), p. 155 (vase)
Macedonia (Chalkidike):
—potidaia-kassandreia: **(2)** c. 200-175 bc *IG* II^2 9002 (Tataki, *Macedonians* p. 92 no. 56; *FRA* 2789) (f. *Φιλαινώ*)
Macedonia (Mygdonia):
—thessalonike: **(3)** 95 bc *IG* x (2) (1) 4, 2 (f. *Πύρρος*); **(4)** 27 bc-14 ad *SEG* xlvi 812, 6 (*Νικόλαος ὁ καὶ Κλιτόμαχος*: s. *Δημήτριος*)
Thrace:
—byzantion?: **(5)** iv/iii bc *IByz* 326 (s. *Κλεισίμαχος*)

Κλεῖτος
Macedonia: **(1)** c. 380-318 bc *RE* (10); Berve 428 (Tataki, *Macedonians* p. 342 no. 47) (*Κ. ὁ Λευκός*); **(2)** c. 375-328 bc *RE* (9); Berve 427 (Tataki, *Macedonians* p. 342 no. 48) (*Κ. ὁ Μέλας*: s. *Δρωπίδας*); **(3)** m. ii bc *BGU* 2423, 27 (Tataki, *Macedonians* p. 488 no. 154); cf. La'da E1527 (f. *Κλειτόδωρος*)
Macedonia (Bottiaia):
—aigai: **(4)** s. iv bc *SEG* xxxv 807
—beroia: **(5)** 114 bc *IBer* 134, 36 (s. *Βακχίδης*); **(6)** i-ii ad ib. 320 (Tataki 738); **(7)** ii/iii ad *IBer* 143 C, 24 (Tataki 609) (*'Ιού. Κ.*)
Macedonia (Orestis): **(8)** 192 ad *EAM* 186, 33 (s. *Πτολεμαῖος*)
—battynaioi: **(9)** 192 ad ib. 186 I, 45 (f. *Παρμενίων*); **(10)** ~ ib. 186 IV, 47 (*Κλί-*: f. *Ἀντίγονος*); **(11)** ~ ib. l. 48 (s. *Ἀντίγονος*)
—platania (mod.): **(12)** ii ad ib. 205 (s. *Πύρρος*)
Macedonia (Orestis)?: **(13)** s. iv bc *Syll*³ 268 H, 3 (Tataki, *Macedonians* p. 205 no. 8) (*Κλεί[του]*? (gen.), *Κλει[νία]*?—Pomtow: f. ......ιος)

Κλειτόμαχος — see above

Tauris:
—chersonesos: **(14)** iii bc Solomonik, *NEPKh* 167 (f. *Δάλις*)

Κλειτόστρατος
Thrace:
—perinthos-herakleia: **(1)** iv-iii bc *IPerinth* 4, 16 (*[Κ]λ̣ειτόστρατος*: ?s. *Τρυ—*)

Κλειτοφῶν
Scythia Minor:
—istros: **(1)** i bc-i ad *ISM* i 191 II, 8-10 (f. *Διονύσιος, Ἀπολλόδωρος, Ἀχιλλόδωρος*); **(2)** ii ad ib. 212, 17 (f. *Ἑρρένιος*); **(3)** ~ ib. l. 25 (f. *Ἀναξιμένης*); **(4)** f. ii ad *SEG* l 683 B, 7 (s. *Διονύσιος*); **(5)** 138 ad *ISM* i 193 II, 77 (s. *Ἑρμόδωρος*)
Thrace?: **(6)** ii bc ib. 36, 6 + *Pontica* 33-4 (2000-1) pp. 346-7 no. 3 (*Κλειτ[οφῶν]*?: f. *Βιάνωρ*)

Κλειτώ
Thrace:
—maroneia: **(1)** f. iii bc *IThrakAig* E228

Κλειώ
Macedonia (Bottiaia):
—aigai: **(1)** c. 300-275 bc *SEG* xxxv 788 (d. *Φιλώτας*)

Κλεμυτάδας
Tauris:
—chersonesos: **(1)** c. 300-290 bc Anokhin p. 139 no. 80 (coin) ?= (*2*); **(2)** c. 300-275 bc *SEG* xlvii 1168, 2 (*Κλε[μυ]τ̣ά̣δ̣α̣?* (gen.): f. *Πολύστρατος*) ?= (*1*)

Κλεόβουλος
Macedonia: **(1)** m. iv bc *Olynthus* 10 pp. 427-8 nos. 2202-16; *SEG* xlvii 952; *Torone* 1 p. 726 no. 18.3 (bullet); **(2)** f. iii bc *IEph* 1405, 4, 6 (Tataki, *Macedonians* p. 343 no. 49) (*[Κ]λε[ό]βουλος*: s. *Φίλων*)
Macedonia (Bottiaia):
—aigai: **(3)** f. iv bc *SEG* xxvii 316 = xxxv 795
Macedonia (Pieria):
—pydna: **(4)** c. 169 bc ib. xliii 451, 8 (s. *Ἀντικράτης*)
Thrace:
—byzantion: **(5)** ii bc *IByz* 78 (f. *Νέα*)

Κλεογένης
Scythia Minor:
—istros: **(1)** ii ad *ISM* i 131 (*CCET* iv 63) (f. *Βιάνωρ*); **(2)** 138 ad *ISM* i 193 I, 48 (s. *Νουμήνιος*)
Thrace:
—lysimacheia: **(3)** m. ii bc *ISestos* 38 a, 1 (s. *Ἀγαθοκλῆς*)

Κλεόδαμος
Macedonia (Edonis):
—amphipolis: **(1)** c. 357 bc Hatzopoulos, *Actes Amphipolis* p. 30 no. 4, 3 (*SEG* xli 558) (*Κ̣λ̣εό̣δ̣αμος*) ?= (*Κλεόδημος* (*1*))
Thrace:
—byzantion: **(2)** c. 267 ad *RE* (1)

Κλεόδημος
Macedonia (Edonis):
—amphipolis: **(1)** a. 357 bc Hatzopoulos, *Actes Amphipolis* p. 34 no. 6, 5; cf. p. 30 n. 5 (ident.) (*Κλεό̣[δ]ημος*) ?= (*Κλεόδαμος* (*1*))
Macedonia (Tymphaia):
—sydendro (mod.): **(2)** s. ii ad *EAM* 53 (f. *Ἀνδρόνικος*)

Κλεοδίκη
Macedonia: **(1)** 323 bc Ps.-Call. iii 33; Berve 429 (Tataki, *Macedonians* p. 343 no. 50) (Lat. Cleonice—Epit. Mett.: fict.?)

Κλεοκράτης
Thrace:
—apollonia-sozopolis: **(1)** v/iv bc *Stud. Fol* p. 405 no. 2; Naville sale (18.vi.1925) 1580 (coin)

Κλεόμαχος
Macedonia (Chalkidike):
—torone: **(1)** ?353 bc *SEG* xxiv 574, 19; Hatzopoulos, *Actes Chalc.* p. 80 (date) (f. *Ἀρχεπτόλεμος*)
Macedonia (Mygdonia):
—kalindoia: **(2)** 68-98 ad *SEG* xlii 580, 90 (s. *Σουλπᾶς*)

Κλεόμβροτος
Scythia Minor:
—istros: **(1)** s. iii bc *ISM* i 15, 2 (f. *Ἀπολλώνιος*); **(2)** i bc-i ad ib. 191 I, 47 (*Κ(λ)εόμβροτος*)
Skythia:
—olbia-borysthenes: **(3)** iii bc *IOSPE* I^2 179, [1], 5 with comm. (ident.); 180, 1; 201 I, 40; 201 II, 5 (s. *Παντακλῆς*); **(4)** ~ ib. 188 (f. *Παντακλῆς*); **(5)** iii-ii bc *IOlbia* 125 (*[Κλεό]μβροτ̣[ος]?*)

Κλεομέδων
Macedonia?: **(1)** 198 bc *RE* Supplbd. 12 (3) (Lat. Cleomedon)
Scythia Minor:
—istros: **(2)** f. ii bc *ISM* i 26, 4 (f. *Εὐπόλεμος*)

Κλεομήδης
Scythia Minor:
—kallatis: **(1)** iii/ii bc ib. iii 161 (f. *Φαίκων*)

Κλεομοιρίς
Macedonia (Edonis):
—philippoi: **(1)** s. iv bc *SEG* xxxviii 660 (xliii 450; Pilhofer 387) (d. *Ἕρμιππος*)

Κλεονίκα
Thrace:
—byzantion: **(1)** f. v bc Plu., *Mor.* 555 C; *Cimon* 6; Paus. iii 17. 8-9 (*-κη*: d. *Κορωνίδας*: fict.?)

Κλεονίκη
Cimmerian Bosporos:
—pantikapaion: **(1)** s. i ad *CIRB* 546; cf. KW pl. 30 no. 439a (*-νεί-*: d. *Μόνιμος*)
Macedonia: **(2)** her.? *POxy* 2465 fr. 1 II, 20; cf. *FGrH* 631 (m. *Περδίκκας* I)
Macedonia (Derriopos):
—stuberra?: **(3)** f. iii ad *AJA* 88 (1984) pp. 567 ff.; cf. *SEG* xxxiv 678 II, 7-8; *IG* x (2) (2) 333 (stemma) (*Σιλβανὴ Κ.*: d. *Σεπτίμιος Σιλβανὸς Νικόλαος*, m. *Π. Σέντιος Νικόλαος Σεπτίμιος* (Stoboi))
Macedonia (Elimeia):
—aiane: **(4)** s. ii ad *EAM* 14 (*Κλεο̣ν̣ίκη*: d. *Ἱππόστρατος*)
Macedonia (Eordaia):
—agios demetrios (mod.): **(5)** ii-iii ad ib. 103 (*Κ̣λεο(ν)είκη*)
—mavropigi (mod.): **(6)** iii/ii bc ib. 120; cf. *SEG* xli 578 b
Macedonia (Mygdonia):
—thessalonike: **(7)** c. 23 bc *IG* x (2) (1) 97, 5 (*Ἰουλ. Κλεονε̣[ί]κη*: d. *Φιλόδημος*); **(8)** ii ad ib. 299, 3 (*Κ. (ἡ) καὶ Κύριλλα*)
—thessalonike?: **(9)** ii ad ib. 828; **(10)** ii-iii ad ib. 919 (*Κλεω-*: ?m. *Μωμώ*)
Macedonia (Paionia):
—negotino (mod.): **(11)** ii ad *Sp.* 98 (1941-8) p. 58 no. 120 (*Κ̣λ̣[εο]νείκη*: d. *Ζωΐλος*); **(12)** ii-iii ad ib. 71 (1931) p. 65 no. 144, 3 (*-νεί-*: d. *Θεογένης*, m. *Θεογένης*)
Macedonia (Pieria):
—pydna: **(13)** iii bc *SEG* l 625 (d. *Δημοκλῆς*)

—PYDNA (TERRIT.): (**14**) iii BC *Klio* 52 (1970) p. 61 no. 13 (d. *Στράτων, Ἀμμένα*); (**15**) m. iii AD *SEG* XXXI 636 (m. *Ἀφροδίσιος*)
THRACE:
—ABDERA: (**16**) iii-ii BC *IThrakAig* E52

Κλεόνικος
CIMMERIAN BOSPOROS:
—PANTIKAPAION: (**1**) i-ii AD *CIRB* 637
MACEDONIA: (**2**) m. iv BC *BCH* 106 (1982) p. 83 no. 36 (bullet)
MACEDONIA (BOTTIAIA):
—BEROIA: (**3**) ii BC *Α΄ Panell. Synedr. Epigr.* p. 59 no. 6 (*SEG* XLIX 845) (s. *Λαμπρόμαχος*)
MACEDONIA (CHALKIDIKE):
—TORONE: (**4**) ?353 BC ib. XXIV 574, 19; Hatzopoulos, *Actes Chalc.* p. 80 (date) (s. *Ἀγαθοκλῆς*)
THRACE:
—BYZANTION: (**5**) i BC-i AD *IByz* 153 (Firatlı–Robert pp. 103-4 no. 160) (-*νεικος*)

Κλεοντίδας
THRACE:
—LYSIMACHEIA: (**1**) c. 208 BC *FD* III (4) 135 III, 12 (s. *Ἀπολλ*—)

Κλεόξενος
MACEDONIA (EDONIS):
—AMPHIPOLIS: (**1**) iii BC *SEG* XXIV 592 (f. *Στέφανος*)

Κλεοπᾶς
MACEDONIA (BOTTIAIA):
—BEROIA: (**1**) i AD *IBer* 403, 21 (*Κλεοπᾶ*—lap., *Κλέοπας*—index)

Κλεοπάτρα
CIMMERIAN BOSPOROS:
—ACHILLEION (NR.): (**1**) i/ii AD *SEG* XLV 979 (*Κλεοπ*<*ρ*>*άτ*(*ρ*)*α*)
—PANTIKAPAION?: (**2**) i/ii AD *CIRB* 144, 4
MACEDONIA: (**3**) m. vii BC *POxy* 2465 fr. 1 II, 21; cf. *FGrH* 631 (m. *Ἀργαῖος*: fict.?); (**4**) s. v BC Pl., *Gorg.* 471 c (Tataki, *Macedonians* p. 343 no. 53); cf. *RE* (11); Beloch, *GG* III (2) p. 64 ?= (*5*); (**5**) ~ Arist., *Pol.* 1311 b, 15 (?m. *Ὀρέστης*) ?= (*4*); (**6**) c. 355-309 BC *RE* (13); Berve 433 (Tataki, *Macedonians* p. 343 no. 51) (d. *Φίλιππος* II, *Ὀλυμπιάς* (Molossoi), m. *Νεοπτόλεμος* (Molossoi), *Κάδμεια* (Molossoi)); (**7**) c. 353-335 BC *RE* (12); Berve 434 (Tataki, *Macedonians* p. 343 no. 52) (m. *Εὐρώπη*: queen); (**8**) c. 215-176 BC *RE* (14) (*PP* 14515); cf. Grainger, *SPG* p. 45 (*K.* I: d. *Ἀντίοχος* III *Μέγας*, ?d. *Λαοδίκη* (Pontos), m. *Πτολεμαῖος* VI *Φιλομήτωρ*, *Πτολεμαῖος* VII *Εὐεργέτης*, *Κλεοπάτρα* II: queen); (**9**) c. 185-115 BC *RE* (15) (*PP* 14516) (*K.* II: d. *Πτολεμαῖος* V *Ἐπιφάνης*, *Κλεοπάτρα* I, m. *Πτολεμαῖος Εὐπάτωρ*, *Πτολεμαῖος* VII *νέος Φιλοπάτωρ*, *Πτολεμαῖος Μεμφίτης*, *Κλεοπάτρα* III, *Κλεοπάτρα Θεά*: queen); (**10**) m. ii BC *BGU* 1939 A, 12 (Tataki, *Macedonians* p. 488 no. 155; La'da E1808) (d. *Διογένης*); (**11**) c. 165-121 BC *RE* (24) (*PP* 14518) (*K. Θεά*: d. *Πτολεμαῖος* VI *Φιλομήτωρ*, *Κλεοπάτρα* II, m. *Ἀντίοχος* VI *Ἐπιφάνης*, *Σέλευκος* V, *Ἀντίοχος* VIII *Γρυπός*, *Ἀντίοχος* IX *Κυζικηνός*, *Λαοδίκη*, *Λαοδίκη*, *Λαοδίκη* (sic), *Ἀντίοχος*, *Σέλευκος*: queen); (**12**) c. 160-101 BC ib. (16) (*PP* 14517) (*K.* III: d. *Πτολεμαῖος* VI *Φιλομήτωρ*, *Κλεοπάτρα* II, m. *Πτολεμαῖος* IX *Λάθυρος*, *Πτολεμαῖος* X *Ἀλέξανδρος*, *Κλεοπάτρα* IV, *Τρύφαινα*, *Κλεοπάτρα Σελήνη*: queen); (**13**) c. 140-112 BC *RE* (17) (*PP* 14519) (*K.* IV: d. *Πτολεμαῖος* VIII *Εὐεργέτης*, *Κλεοπάτρα* III, ?m. *Κλεοπάτρα Βερενίκη*: queen); (**14**) c. 135-69 BC *RE* (22) (*PP* 14520); Grainger, *SPG* p. 45 (*K. Σελήνη*: d. *Πτολεμαῖος* VIII *Εὐεργέτης*, *Κλεοπάτρα* III, ?m. *Πτολεμαῖος* XII *Αὐλητής*, *Ἀντίοχος* XIII *Ἀσιατικός*: queen); (**15**) c. 120-80 BC *RE* (21) (*PP* 14522) (*K. Βερενίκη*: d. *Πτολεμαῖος* IX *Λάθυρος*, ?d. *Κλεοπάτρα* IV); (**16**) c. 110-69 BC *RE* (18) (*PP* 14523) (*K.* V *Τρύφαινα*: d. *Πτολεμαῖος* IX *Λάθυρος*, m. *Κλεοπάτρα* VI *Τρύφαινα*: queen); (**17**) c. 75-57 BC *RE* (19) (*PP* 14524) (*K.* VI *Τρύφαινα*: d. *Πτολεμαῖος* XII *Αὐλητής*, *Κλεοπάτρα* V *Τρύφαινα*: queen); (**18**) 69-30 BC *RE* (20) (*PP* 14525) (*K.* VII *Φιλοπάτωρ*: d. *Πτολεμαῖος* XII *Αὐλητής*, m. *Πτολεμαῖος* XV *Καῖσαρ* (*Καισαρίων*), *Ἀλέξανδρος Ἥλιος*, *Κλεοπάτρα Σελήνη*, *Πτολεμαῖος Φιλάδελφος*: queen); (**19**) c. 40 BC-15 AD *RE* (23) (*PP* 14526) (*K. Σελήνη*: d. *Κλεοπάτρα* VII *Φιλοπάτωρ*, M. Antonius (Rome), m. *Πτολεμαῖος* (Numidia), Drusilla (Numidia): queen)
MACEDONIA (BOTTIAIA):
—BEROIA: (**20**) 177 AD *IBer* 81, 9 (Tataki 583) (*Ἰουλιανὴ K.*); (**21**) 225 AD *ILeukopetra* 71, 14 (Tataki 50) (*Αἰλ. K.*); (**22**) 254 AD *ILeukopetra* 110, 4 (*Αὐρ. Κλ*<*λ*>*εοπάτρα*)
——Blaganoi*: (**23**) 189 AD *SEG* XXXVII 590, 7, 14 (Tataki 740) (d. *Διονυσᾶς*)
—EDESSA: (**24**) iii BC *IG* XII (9) 1135 (Tataki, *Macedonians* p. 103 no. 10) (d. *Κάσσανδρος*); (**25**) 224 AD *Athena* 12 (1900) p. 70 no. 1, 3; *BCH* 102 (1978) p. 622-3 (name, date) (Tataki, *Edessa* 73) (*Γ. Γλευπάτρα*: d. *Πετρώνιος*)
—MIEZA: (**26**) i AD Mendel, *Cat.* 1036 (Tataki 741) (d. *Φίλιππος*)
—MIEZA (TERRIT.)?: (**27**) i BC *SEG* XXIV 505 (Tataki 739); cf. Hatzopoulos, *MI* I p. 116 (locn.) (or Macedonia (Bottiaia) Beroia: d. *—τίας*, *Κλευάτα*)
—PELLA: (**28**) iii-ii BC *IG* IX (2) 369, 1 (Tataki, *Macedonians* p. 156 no. 53) (d. *Στησιμένης*)
MACEDONIA (CHALKIDIKE):
—ANTHEMOUS: (**29**) ii-iii AD *SEG* XLII 570 (*Αὐρ. K.*: m. *Οὐεντουληνὸς Ἀμμιανός*)
—POTIDAIA-KASSANDREIA: (**30**) 2 BC or 115 AD *Essays Laourdas* p. 97 (d. *Παράμονος*)
MACEDONIA (EDONIS):
—AMPHIPOLIS: (**31**) 37 BC Robert, *Coll. Froehner* 44, 11 (Tataki, *Macedonians* p. 54 no. 71) (d. *Θεόδοτος*, ?m. *Γλαυκίας*, *Βίθυς*, *Κότυς*, *Ἀπολλώνιος*)
—AMPHIPOLIS (TERRIT.): (**32**) i BC-i AD? Kaphtantzis 584 (m. *Ἡλιόδωρος*); (**33**) 212 AD ib. 592 (m. *Φίλιππος*)
—PHILIPPOI: (**34**) imp. *BCH* 58 (1934) p. 478 no. 20 (Pilhofer 269) (Lat. [Ma]rronia Cleopatr[a]); (**35**) ~ *BCH* 58 (1934) pp. 474-5 no. 13 (Pilhofer 289) (Lat. Claudia Cleo[patra]?)
—PHILIPPOI (NR.): (**36**) ii-iii AD *BCH* 24 (1900) pp. 313-14 (Pilhofer 22) (freed.?)
—PHILIPPOI (TERRIT.)?: (**37**) imp. *CIL* III 7379 (Lat. Uttiedia Cleopatra: m. *Ἀριστόκριτος*: locn.—Loukopoulou)
MACEDONIA (ELIMEIA):
—AGALAIA (MOD.): (**38**) s. ii AD *EAM* 55 (d. *Ἀντίγονος*)
—KOZANI (MOD.)?: (**39**) ii AD ib. 54 a (m. *Κρισπῖνα*)
MACEDONIA (EORDAIA):
—AGIOS CHRISTOPHOROS (MOD.): (**40**) f. iii AD ib. 136
MACEDONIA (MYGDONIA):
—APOLLONIA: (**41**) iii-iv AD *AD* 24 (1969) Chron. pl. 316
—KALINDOIA: (**42**) ii/i BC *SEG* XLII 593 (d. *Μενίδας*)
—THESSALONIKE: (**43**) i-ii AD *IG* X (2) (1) 243 II, 6 (m. *Ἀντώνιος*); (**44**) f. i AD ib. 126, 1; Robert, *OMS* 5 pp. 295-302 (date) (m. *Σωσίπατρος*); (**45**) s. i AD *IG* X (2) (1) 68, 23; 69, 17 (m. *Διονύσιος ὁ καὶ Γέμινος*); (**46**) ii-iii AD *SEG* XXXVIII 709 a (*Π. Φοντεΐα K.*: m. *Σιβόνιος Ἰσίδωρος*); (**47**) ~ ib. 709 b (*Π. Φοντεΐα K.*: m. *Π. Φοντεΐα Ἰσιδώρα*); (**48**) 125 AD *IG* X (2) (1) 624 (?m. *Στρατονίκη*); (**49**) f. iii AD ib. 193, 7 (*Κορνηλία K.*)
—THESSALONIKE?: (**50**) ii AD ib. 696; (**51**) ~ ib. 715 (?m. *Εὐμένης*)
MACEDONIA (PAIONIA):
—EUDARISTOS?: (**52**) ii-iii AD *Sp.* 98 (1941-8) p. 62 no. 128 (m. *Παράμονος*)
—KAVADARCI (MOD.): (**53**) ii-iii AD ib. 71 (1931) p. 237 no. 631 = 75 (1933) p. 41 no. 140 (m. *Διονύσιος*, *Ἀλέξανδρος*)
MACEDONIA (SINTIKE):
—PARTHIKOPOLIS (TERRIT.): (**54**) ii AD *Arkheologiia* (Sofia) 1987 (1), p. 24 no. 1, 1 (d. *Πύρρος*, m. *Ἀλέξανδρος*, *Πύρρος*)
MACEDONIA?: (**55**) 274 BC *IG* II^2 1534 A, 19; Aleshire, *Asklepieion* pp. 205-16 (Tataki, *Macedonians* p. 344 no. 61)
THRACE:
—BISANTHE-PANION: (**56**) imp. Unp. (Sayar)
—BYZANTION?: (**57**) imp. *IByz* 350 (d. *Καλλισθένης*)
—MARONEIA: (**58**) f. ii BC *BCH* 66-7 (1942-3) p. 197 no. 1 (*IThrakAig* E258) (m. *Αἰαντίδης*, *Διονυσία*)
—PERINTHOS-HERAKLEIA: (**59**) i AD *IPerinth* 88 (*Οὐαλερία Λουκία ἡ καὶ K.*)
—PERINTHOS-HERAKLEIA (NR.): (**60**) i-ii AD ib. 305 (*Ἰουλ. K.*)
—PHILIPPOPOLIS-TRIMONTIUM: (**61**) imp. *IGB* III 992 (d. *Ἀθηνόδωρος*); (**62**) ~ ib. 1026, 2 ([*K*]*λεοπάτρα*)
—PLOTINOPOLIS: (**63**) ii-iii AD Dumont–Homolle 106b (*IThrakAig* E467) (d. *Κλ. Ποτάμων*, *Φλαβία*)
—ZONE: (**64**) m. iv BC ib. E420 (d. *Πολυκράτης*)

Κλεοπάτρη
THRACE:
—STRYME?: (**1**) m. iv BC *SEG* XLIX 986 (*IThrakAig* E154)

Κλεόπατρος
MACEDONIA (MYGDONIA):
—SARAKINA (MOD.): (**1**) s. ii AD *SEG* XLVIII 838
THRACE:
—NICOPOLIS AD ISTRUM (TERRIT.): (**2**) iii AD *ILB* 393 (Lat. Spur. Cleopater)

Κλεόπολις
THRACE:
—MARONEIA: (**1**) c. 365-336 BC Schönert-Geiss, *Maroneia* 399-402 (coin) (*Κλεοπόλιος* (gen.))

Κλεόστρατος
THRACE:
—BISANTHE-PANION: (**1**) ii-i BC *BCH* 24 (1900) p. 165 no. 7 (*K*[*λεό*]*στρατος*?, *K*[*αλλί*]*στρατος*?—ed: s. *Δημόφιλος*)
—ZONE: (**2**) s. v BC *SEG* XIII 412 (*IThrakAig* E408) (s. *Δαναός*)

Κλεότιμος
MACEDONIA: (**1**) ii AD *IBer* 74, 10 (Tataki 1322) (*Φλ. Κλεότειμος*)
MACEDONIA (EDONIS):
—AMPHIPOLIS: (**2**) ?v/iv BC *RE* Supplbd. II (2)

Κλεοχάρης
MACEDONIA (EDONIS):
—AMPHIPOLIS: (**1**) ?304-301 BC *Eretria* XI p. 142 no. 10, 2, 10 (*IG* XII (9) 199) + *IG* XII (9) 230 (Tataki, *Macedonians* p. 54 no. 72); *Eretria* XI pp. 145-6 (date) (s. *Πυθέας*)
MACEDONIA?: (**2**) 326 BC Berve 436 (Lat. Cleochares)

Κλεύας
MACEDONIA (BOTTIAIA):
—BEROIA: (**1**) m. ii BC *IBer* 177 (f. *Μοσχίνη*)
MACEDONIA?: (**2**) 169 BC *RE* (-) (Tataki, *Macedonians* p. 344 no. 62) (Lat. Cleuas)

Κλευάτα
Macedonia (Bottiaia):
—mieza (territ.)?: (1) i bc *SEG* xxiv 505 (Tataki 742); cf. Hatzopoulos, *MI* 1 p. 116 (locn.) (or Macedonia (Bottiaia) Beroia: m. *Κλεοπάτρα*)

Κλευμέδης
Scythia Minor:
—istros: (1) iii-ii bc Unp. (Avram, defixio) 4, 2

Κλευπάτρα
Cimmerian Bosporos:
—myrmekion: (1) ii ad *CIRB* 886
Macedonia (Bottiaia):
—beroia: (2) 184-186 ad *ILeukopetra* 16, 6; 17, 5; 18, 4; 19, 7 (Tataki 51) (*Αἰλ. Κ.*)
Macedonia (Mygdonia):
—lete: (3) hell.-imp. Dimitsas 680 (*Κλ[ε]υπάτρα*: d. *Νικάνωρ*)
—peristera (mod.): (4) ii-iii ad *AD* 40 (1985) Chron. pp. 238-9 with pl. 101 α (d. *Παράμονος, Νίκη*)
—thessalonike: (5) s. ii ad *SEG* xlv 817 (xlviii 853) (m. *Παραμόνα*)
—thessalonike?: (6) ii ad *IG* x (2) (1) 707 (d. *Χρυσίς*)
Thrace?: (7) ?iii bc *SEG* ii 854 (Velkov 169; La'da E858)

Κλευπώ
Macedonia (Mygdonia):
—thessalonike?: (1) ?iii ad *IG* x (2) (1) 911, 2 (m. *Μακέτα, Μᾶρκος*)

Κλεώ
Cimmerian Bosporos:
—pantikapaion: (1) iv bc *CIRB* 196
Macedonia: (2) f. ii bc *IG* xii (1) 322 (Tataki, *Macedonians* p. 344 no. 63) (d. *Παυσανίας*); (3) i bc *ASAA* 2 (1916) p. 135 no. 1, 23 (*Λεωνακετις*—apogr., *[Κ]λεὼ (Μ)ακετίς*: metic)
Macedonia (Bottiaia):
—pella?: (4) iv/iii bc *IG* x (2) (1) 676 (*Pella* p. 143 no. 242); cf. Robert, *OMS* 5 p. 310 (d. *Γλαυκίας*)
Macedonia (Edonis):
—philippoi (territ.): (5) ii-iii ad Pikoulas, *Chora* p. 158 no. 65, 4 (Pilhofer 598) (*Κλέουδι* (dat.)); (6) s. ii ad Pikoulas, *Chora* p. 158 no. 64 (Pilhofer 597); cf. *Dacia* 19 (1975) p. 198 no. 2 (date); Collart, *Philippes* pl. 38. 2 (*Κλεῦδι* (dat.))
Macedonia (Odomantike):
—gazoros (territ.): (7) 132 ad *SEG* xxx 597, 4 (Pilhofer 539) (m. *Διούλας*); (8) ~ *SEG* xxx 597, 4 (Pilhofer 539) (d. *Διούλας*)
—sirrha (territ.): (9) ii-iii ad *SEG* xxx 607 (Pilhofer 556) (*Κλιό*: d. *Δούλης*)
Tauris:
—chersonesos: (10) iv/iii bc Solomonik, *GAKh* 1046 (vase) (*Κλεοῦς* (gen.)); (11) ii bc *SEG* xxviii 637 (d. *Νικαγόρας*)
Thrace: (12) i bc *IG* ii^2 8912 (*FRA* 2547)
—abdera?: (13) s. iv bc *IThrakAig* E42
—byzantion: (14) iii bc *IByz* 60 (Fıratlı-Robert p. 47 no. 3) (d. *Διονύσιος*); (15) ii-i bc *IByz* 148 (d. *Λυκοῦργος*)

Κλέων
Cimmerian Bosporos:
—pantikapaion: (1) i bc *CIRB* 278; cf. KW pl. 41 no. 599 (I f. *Κλέων* II); (2) ~ *CIRB* 278; cf. KW pl. 41 no. 599 (II s. *Κλέων* I)
—tyritake: (3) f. ii ad *CIRB* 909 (s. *Ποθίαινα*)
Macedonia: (4) 69-84 ad *IBer* 61, 5 (f. —αιρος)
Macedonia (Bottiaia):
—beroia: (5) 116 bc ib. 134, 28 (s. ....ο...νιος); (6) 113 bc ib. l. 39 (f. *Δημήτριος*); (7) i bc-i ad ib. 142, 6 (Tataki 744) (f. *Ὑγῖνος*)
Macedonia (Chalkidike):
—mende: (8) s. v bc *IG* ii^2 9335 (Tataki, *Macedonians* p. 121 no. 13; *FRA* 3680)
—olynthos: (9) ?c. 355-349 bc *TAPA* 69 (1938) p. 55 no. 7, 4
—polichne?: (10) ?353 bc *SEG* xxxvii 576, 8 (s. *Πολέμων*); (11) ~ ib. l. 18 (*[Κ]λέ]ων*: s. *Πόλυς*)
—potidaia-kassandreia: (12) ?m. iii bc *FD* iii (4) 351, 4 (Tataki, *Macedonians* p. 92 no. 57) (f. *Πραξικλῆς*)
Macedonia (Mygdonia):
—lete: (13) c. 325-300 bc *SEG* xliv 535; *KGAM Thess.* 1 30 (date) (f. *Μελίς*)
—thessalonike: (14) 27 bc-14 ad *IG* x (2) (1) 31, 15 (s. *Π*—); (15) 3 ad *SEG* xliii 353 (s. *Ἡρακλείδης*)
Thrace:
—bisanthe-panion: (16) c. 208 bc *FD* iii (4) 133 II, 28 (f. *Βίθυς*)
—byzantion?: (17) ii bc *ISamothrace* 28 c, 14; Robert, *OMS* 6 pp. 605-6 (name, locn.) (*[Κλ]έων*: s. *Βοσπόριχος*)
—lysimacheia: (18) iv/iii bc *IG* ii^2 808, 15; *SEG* xxxviii 619, 11; xlviii 817 (f. *Βίθυς*); (19) ii bc *IG* ii^2 9227 (*FRA* 3398) (f. *Θεόξενος*)
—sapai: (20) c. 230-200 bc *BCH* 45 (1921) p. 18 III, 83 (*[Κ]λέων*: f. *Ἀντιφάνης, Ἀντιγένης*)

Κλεωνυμιανός
Macedonia (Bottiaia):
—beroia: (1) 216-232 ad *ILeukopetra* 67, 1; 78, 6 + *Tyche* 16 (2001) pp. 151-2 (Tataki 745) (*Κλεωνυμιανὸς Ἀπολλόδωρος*)

Κλεώνυμος
Macedonia (Bottiaia):
—aigai: (1) s. iv bc *SEG* xxxv 787 (s. *Ἀκύλας*, f. *Ἄδυμος*)
—beroia: (2) i bc-i ad *IBer* 142, 9-10 (Tataki 746) + Tataki 747 (f. *Παρμενίων, Φίλιππος*)
Thrace:
—byzantion: (3) iv-iii bc Schönert-Geiss, *Byzantion* 962 (coin) (*Κλεώ(νυμος?)*)

Κλημέντιλλα
Macedonia (Mygdonia):
—thessalonike: (1) 215 ad *SEG* l 645

Κλημεντίνη
Macedonia (Mygdonia):
—thessalonike: (1) v-vi ad ib. xlv 821 (mosaic) (*Ἑλλὰς ἡ καὶ Κλεμεντίνη*)

Κλημεντῖνος
Thrace:
—durostorum (territ.)?: (1) iii ad *IGB* ii 869 (*CCET* ii (1) 187) (f. *Αἴλ. Κλημεντῖνος νεώτ.*)

Κλήμης
Macedonia (Edonis):
—philippoi?: (1) f. i ad *Ep. Philipp.* iv 3
Macedonia (Sintike):
—parthikopolis: (2) s. ii ad *IGB* iv 2267 (s. *Πυρρίας*)
Thrace:
—anchialos: (3) imp. *RA* 1912 (2), p. 262 no. 48 (f. *Διογένης*)
—byzantion: (4) ii ad *RE* s.v. Clemens (4); Stephanis 1469; Robert, *OMS* 5 p. 366

Κλησιθήρα
Macedonia (Bottiaia):
—aigai: (1) s. iv bc *SEG* xxxv 807 (d. *Λυκόφρων*)

Κλήτα
Macedonia (Bottiaia):
—beroia: (1) ii bc *IBer* 178 (d. *Ἀλέξανδρος*, ?d. *Ἀντιγόνα*)
Macedonia (Pieria):
—dion: (2) imp. *SEG* xlviii 788

Κλινία?
Thrace:
—ainos: (1) iv bc Hp., *Epid.* iv 48 (dub. lect.); *Index Hipp.* s.v. *Κλινία* (*οἷον κλινίαι*—cod. V, *ἡλινία*—cod. IR, *ἡ Κλινια*—Littré)

Κλιτύς
Macedonia (Eordaia): (1) imp. Dimitsas 288 (d. *Μακεδών, Φιλωτέρα*)

Κλίτων
Macedonia: (1) 328 bc Moretti, *Olymp.* 463; *FGrH* 255. 8 (Tataki, *Macedonians* p. 345 no. 64) (*Κρίτων*—*FGrH*)

Κλοιόνικος?
Thrace:
—byzantion (territ.): (1) imp. Unp. (Sayar) (s. *Παπίας*)

Κλοιωνις?
Thrace:
—byzantion (territ.): (1) imp. ib. (s. *Θεόκριτος*)

Κλόνηγος
Thrace:
—abdera: (1) iv bc Hp., *Epid.* vii 115

Κλυμένη
Macedonia (Paionia):
—stoboi (nr.): (1) ii/iii ad *SEG* xvi 406 (m. *Λύκα*)

Κλύμενος
Macedonia (Edonis):
—philippoi: (1) ii/iii ad *CIL* iii 633 II b, 15 (Pilhofer 163) (Lat. T. Flav[iu]s Clymenus)

Κλύτη
Thrace:
—odessos: (1) v/iv bc *IGB* i^2 97

Κλύτιος
Cimmerian Bosporos:
—pantikapaion: (1) c. 390-380 bc *SEG* l 710 A (vase) (fict.?)
Macedonia (Bottiaia):
—pella: (2) 202 bc Sil. xvii 429 (Tataki, *Macedonians* p. 156 no. 54) (Lat. Clytius, Clitius: dub.)

Κλύτος
Scythia Minor:
—istros: (1) i bc-i ad *ISM* i 191 II, 43 (f. *Ἀριστοκράτης*)

Κνιδία
Macedonia (Bottiaia):
—mieza (territ.)?: (1) c. 150-175 ad *SEG* xlviii 810

Κνώπων
Macedonia (Chalkidike):
—mende: (1) 360 bc *IG* iv (1)^2 94 b, 26 (Perlman, *City and Sanctuary* E.1 with p. 69 f. (date); Tataki, *Macedonians* p. 121 no. 14)

Κνῶσος
Macedonia (Edonis):
—philippoi: (1) s. i ad *BCH* 56 (1932) pp. 214-20 nos. 8-9 (Pilhofer 202-3); *BCH* 62 (1938) p. 420 no. 7 (Pilhofer 93) (Lat. L. Tatinius Cnosus)

Κοάρτα
Macedonia (Paionia):
—bylazora: (1) ii-iii ad *SEG* xvi 402, 3 (m. *Λούκασος, Σεκοῦνδος*)
Thrace:
—byzantion?: (2) imp. Robert, *OMS* 7 p. 652 (d. *Βάκχιος*)

Κόγχα
TAURIS:
—CHERSONESOS: (1) ?ii AD *IOSPE* I² 457 (-νχα); (2) ii-iii AD *SEG* XXXVII 658 (-νχα: d. *Ματρόδωρος*)

Κοδόρας
CIMMERIAN BOSPOROS:
—GORGIPPIA: (1) 173-210 AD *CIRB* 1134, 27 (f. *Σαρμάτας*)

Κοδρᾶτος
MACEDONIA (BOTTIAIA):
—BEROIA: (1) 230-232 AD *ILeukopetra* 78, 2 (*Κοδ[ρ]ᾶτος*)
MACEDONIA (ODOMANTIKE):
—SIRRHA: (2) f. iii AD *SEG* XXX 590, 29 (f. *Αὐρ. Σαυτίας*)
THRACE:
—APOLLONIA-SOZOPOLIS: (3) i-ii AD *IGB* I² 401, 10 (s. *Ἡρόφιλος*)

Κόδρος
CIMMERIAN BOSPOROS:
—GORGIPPIA: (1) f. iii BC *CIRB* 1137 A II, 31 (s. *Διονύσιος*)
SKYTHIA:
—TANAIS: (2) f. ii AD ib. 1266, 12 (*[Κ]όδρος*: f. *Εὐρήμων*)

Κοζείκενθος?
MACEDONIA (ODOMANTIKE):
—GAZOROS (TERRIT.): (1) 148 or 264 AD *BCH* 35 (1911) p. 115 (Pilhofer 540; *AD* 52 (1997) Chron. p. 847 with pl. 314 δ; *SEG* L 569) (*Κοζεί[κ]ε[ν]θος*: f. *Ζιπᾶς*)

Κοζείμασος
MACEDONIA (ODOMANTIKE):
—GAZOROS?: (1) 158 AD ib. XXIV 614, 2 (Pilhofer 544); cf. Hatzopoulos, *MI* I pp. 84-6 (s. *Πολύχαρμος*)

Κοζίβιθυς
THRACE?: (1) ii BC *Memnonion* 372 (Velkov 175) (f. *Διουκίλας*)

Κοζίλας
MACEDONIA (ODOMANTIKE):
—GAZOROS (TERRIT.): (1) 3 or 119 AD *SEG* XXXVIII 668 (Pilhofer 553) (s. *Μέστος*); (2) 148 or 264 AD *BCH* 35 (1911) p. 115 (Pilhofer 540; *AD* 52 (1997) Chron. p. 847 with pl. 314 δ; *SEG* L 569) (-ζεί-: s. *Ζιπάλας*)

Κοζισίστος
MACEDONIA (ODOMANTIKE):
—GAZOROS: (1) 215 or 174 BC ib. XXX 1892, 26 (Hatzopoulos, *MI* 2 pp. 57-8 no. 39) (s. *Βαστικίλας*)

Κοῆϊς
THRACE:
—ODESSOS: (1) s. ii AD *IGB* I² 167 with pl. (PM 1727); *Dacia* 21 (1977) p. 161 (date) (d. *Δίων*)

Κοθήλας
THRACE: (1) m. iv BC Ath. 557 d (*RE* (-)) (f. *Μήδα*: king)

Κοθίνας
CIMMERIAN BOSPOROS:
—GORGIPPIA: (1) ii AD *NE* 9 (1971) p. 6 no. 3, 3 (*Κοθίν[ας]*); (2) ~ *CIRB* 1157 B, 5 (*Κοθίνα[ς]*—Vinogradov); (3) ~ ib. 1166, 1 (*Κοθί̣ν̣[ας]*—Vinogradov); (4) s. ii AD ib. 1145, 3 (s. *Μαστοῦς*) ?= (*6*); (5) 173-210 AD ib. 1134, 23 (s. *Ἄττας*); (6) ii/iii AD ib. 1179, 55 (f. *Μαστοῦς*) ?= (*4*)

Κόθορνος
SCYTHIA MINOR:
—ISTROS: (1) iv BC Unp. (Avram, defixio) 1, 6 (*Κόθ[ο]ρνος?*)

Κόθων
THRACE:
—BYZANTION: (1) c. 220 BC Plb. iv 52. 4; Robert, *OMS* 2 p. 1093 (name) (*Κώθων*—mss.: s. *Καλλιγείτων*); (2) c. 200 BC *IG* II² 884, 6 (f. *Ἧρις*); (3) s. ii BC *BMI* 1154a B, 32 + Robert, *OMS* 2 p. 1093; *BE* 1972, no. 37 (date) (f. *Δίων*); (4) i BC *IByz* 109 (s. *Μενεκράτης*)

Κοῖδος?
CIMMERIAN BOSPOROS:
—PANTIKAPAION: (1) imp. *CIRB* 791 (*Κοίδο(υ)* (gen.)—ed., *Κο[λ]ίδο(υ)*?—Vinogradov: f. *Ἦλις*)

Κοινίδας
MACEDONIA (LOWER PAIONIA):
—EUROPOS: (1) ?iii BC *SEG* XXXVIII 614 (f. *Φίλιππος*)

Κοῖνος
MACEDONIA: (1) her. *FGrH* 631 F 1; *EM* 523, 46; D.S. vii 15. 1 (Tataki, *Macedonians* p. 345 no. 66) (*Καῖνος*—*EM*: s. *Κάρανος*, *Λανίκα*, f. *Τυρίμμας*: fict.?); (2) 324-323 BC *RE* (2); Berve 440; *FGrH* 100 F 8. 6 (Tataki, *Macedonians* p. 345 no. 65)
MACEDONIA (ELIMEIA)?: (3) c. 370-325 BC *RE* (1); Berve 439; Hatzopoulos, *Donation* p. 23, 4 (Tataki, *Macedonians* p. 196 no. 13) (s. *Πολεμοκράτης*, f. *Περδίκκας*)
MACEDONIA (MYGDONIA):
—THESSALONIKE?: (4) iii BC *IG* X (2) (1) 908, 1 (*GVI* 1709); cf. *BCH* 97 (1973) p. 597 fig. 12 (f. *Νουμήνιος*)
MACEDONIA (ORESTIS):
—BATTYNAIOI: (5) 192 AD *EAM* 186 III, 58 (f. *Ἐπιχάρης*)

Κοΐντα
MACEDONIA (BOTTIAIA):
—BEROIA: (1) 177 AD *IBer* 135 A, 19 (m. *Ἰούλιος*, *Λικίνιος*); (2) 184 AD *ILeukopetra* 16, 1 (d. *Ἰουλία*)
—EDESSA: (3) iii AD *AD* 24 (1969) Chron. p. 306 (Tataki, *Edessa* 169)
—KYRRHOS: (4) 206 AD *SEG* XLIII 435, 2 (d. *Πόρις*)
MACEDONIA (ODOMANTIKE):
—SIRRHA (NR.): (5) ii-iii AD ib. XXIX 579, 3 (Pilhofer 561)
MACEDONIA (SINTIKE):
—PARTHIKOPOLIS (NR.): (6) 165 AD *IGB* IV 2288 (d. *Δεῖδος*)

Κοϊντία
THRACE:
—AINOS: (1) i-ii AD *IG* XII (8) 218, 3 (*Κυϊ-*: d. *Μίλων*)

Κόϊντος
CIMMERIAN BOSPOROS:
—PANTIKAPAION: (1) 82 AD *CIRB* 76, 21 (*SEG* XVIII 310) (*Κόϊντ[ος]*: f. *Λούκιος*)
—PORTHMION (NR.): (2) 225 AD *CIRB* 897, 5 (*Κόϊν[τος]*: f. *Ἰούλ. Ἔρως*)
MACEDONIA (BOTTIAIA):
—BEROIA: (3) ii/iii AD *IBer* 144 B, 7 (Tataki 749) (s. *Ζωΐλος*)
MACEDONIA (CHALKIDIKE):
—POTIDAIA-KASSANDREIA (NR.): (4) imp. *SEG* XXIX 602 (Dimitsas 751)
MACEDONIA (DERRIOPOS):
—STUBERRA: (5) 50 AD *IG* X (2) (2) 324, 19 (f. *Κάσσιος*)
MACEDONIA (EDONIS):
—AMPHIPOLIS: (6) imp. Kaphtantzis 740 (terracotta)
MACEDONIA (LYNKESTIS):
—HERAKLEIA: (7) i AD *IG* X (2) (2) 75, 18 (*Κόεϊ-*: s. *Σεκοῦνδος*); (8) ~ ib. l. 29 (*Κόεϊ-*: s. *Μᾶρκος*); (9) ~ ib. l. 32 (*Κόεϊ-*: s. *Ἱέρων*); (10) ii-iii AD ib. 87 bis
MACEDONIA (MYGDONIA):
—KALINDOIA: (11) 68-98 AD *SEG* XLII 580, 42 (s. *Λυσίμαχος*); (12) ~ ib. l. 81 (s. *Δρούα*)
—LETE (NR.): (13) imp. ib. I 278 (f. *Κ. Ἰούλ. Ἀλφίδιος Σεκοῦνδος*)
—THESSALONIKE: (14) ii-iii AD *IG* X (2) (1) 437 (s. *Μαντώ*)
—THESSALONIKE?: (15) iii AD *AEpThess* p. 8 no. 6 (f. *Φίρμος*)
MACEDONIA (ODOMANTIKE):
—SIRRHA?: (16) ii-iii AD Dimitsas 826, 1, 4 (*Dodoni* 18 (1989) p. 248 no. 57) (s. *Βίθυς*)
MACEDONIA (ORESTIS):
—SISANI (MOD.): (17) 146 AD *EAM* 187, 14 (f. *Τυχικός*)
MACEDONIA (PAIONIA): (18) ii-iii AD *Sp.* 75 (1933) p. 77 no. 219 (*Κουεϊ-*: s. *Μᾶρκος*, *Ὀβουλκία*)
—KAVADARCI (MOD.): (19) ?ii AD ib. p. 33 no. 89; cf. Düll, *Götterkulte* p. 396 no. 241 (f. *Διοσκουρίδης*)
SCYTHIA MINOR:
—ISTROS: (20) ii AD *ISM* I 196, 10 (I f. *Κόϊντος* II); (21) ~ ib. l. 10 (II s. *Κόϊντος* I); (22) ~ ib. 201 I, 15; (23) ~ ib. 201 II, 15 (I f. *Κόϊντος* II); (24) ~ ib. l. 15 (*[Κό]ϊντος*: II s. *Κόϊντος* I)
—TOMIS: (25) ii-iii AD ib. II 20, 1 (*Κ̣[ό]ϊντος*: I f. *Κόϊντος* II); (26) ~ ib. l. 1 (*Κ̣όϊ̣ν̣[τ]ο̣ς̣*: II s. *Κόϊντος* I)
THRACE:
—BEROE-AUGUSTA TRAIANA: (27) 238-241 AD *IGB* III 1565, 17 (I f. *Αὐρ. Κόϊντος* II)
—BYZANTION: (28) i-ii AD *IByz* 315 c (Fıratlı-Robert pp. 122-3 no. 205) (*Κόϊν(τος)*); (29) s. i AD *IByz* 33, 3 (f. *Λολλία Κάτυλλα*); (30) ~ ib. 35, 4 (f. *Διόδωρος*); (31) ii AD *Türk Tarih Kongresi XI* (6) p. 2703 with pl. 495. 5 (f. *Ἀπφη*); (32) ~ ib. (f. *Ζωσίμη*, *Ζωσιμίων*)
—BYZANTION (TERRIT.): (33) imp. Unp. (Sayar) (f. *Νικόστρατος*)
—BYZANTION:
——(Rhegion): (34) i BC-i AD? *IByz* 172 (f. *Ζώσιμος*, ?f. *Πρώτη*)
—MAKRI (MOD.): (35) ?iii AD *Thrakika* I (1928) p. 113 (I f. *Αὐρ. Κόϊντος* II)
—SERDICA: (36) ii AD *IGB* IV 1923, 9 (f. —ς); (37) ~ ib. 1929 (f. *Φλῶρος*)

Κοιράνης
CIMMERIAN BOSPOROS:
—PANTIKAPAION: (1) s. iv BC *CIRB* 226 + *SEG* XXX 982 (*[Κ]οιράνης*: s. *Γότος*)

Κοιρανίδης
MACEDONIA (EDONIS):
—AMPHIPOLIS: (1) s. iv BC Hatzopoulos, *Actes Amphipolis* p. 48 no. 10 A, 3 (*SEG* XLI 564) (*[Κοι]ρανίδης*); (2) m. iii BC Hatzopoulos, *Actes Amphipolis* p. 50 no. 11, 1 (*SEG* XLI 565)

Κοίρανος
CIMMERIAN BOSPOROS:
—GORGIPPIA: (1) m. ii AD *Eirene* 7 (1968) p. 67, 19 (f. *Παπίας*)
—PANTIKAPAION: (2) 344-311 BC *CIRB* 11, 1 (*Κοίρ[αν]ος*); (3) iii-ii BC *MIA* 56 (1957) p. 101 (tile) (*Κοῖ(νος)*—ed., *Κοί(ρανος)*?); (4) f. iii BC *IG* XI (4) 609, 3, 8; *ID* Index I s.v. (date) (s. ...*ημις*)
—PANTIKAPAION*: (5) v BC *KSIIMK* 37 (1951) p. 221 (vase) (*Κοί(ρανος)*?, *Κοΐ* (dat.)—ed.)

MACEDONIA (BOTTIAIA):
—BEROIA: (6) m. iv BC *RE* Supplbd. 4 (10); Berve 441 (Tataki, *Macedonians* p. 79 no. 31)
MACEDONIA (MYGDONIA):
—THESSALONIKE*: (7) i AD *AD* 22 (1967) Chron. pl. 292 γ (vase)
MACEDONIA?: (8) 331 BC *RE* Supplbd. 4 (9); Berve 442 (Tataki, *Macedonians* p. 345 no. 67)
THRACE:
—APOLLONIA-SOZOPOLIS: (9) v/iv BC *IGB* I^2 409 ter (*Κοί[ρ]ανος*)
—ODESSOS: (10) c. 225-200 BC Price, *Alexander* 1161-71; *AMNG* I (2) 2119-21 (coin) (*Κοί(ρανος)*?)
—ODESSOS (NR.): (11) iii BC *IGB* I^2 253 (f. *Πόπα*)

Κοισόρμας
THRACE: (1) 46-54 AD *SEG* XVI 415 III, 38 (*IThrakAig* E84) (s. *Σπόκης*)

Κοίταρος
MACEDONIA (ODOMANTIKE):
—BERGE: (1) hell. Hatzopoulos, *MI* I p. 215 (f. *Ζωσίμη*)

Κοίτη
THRACE:
—MARKIANOPOLIS: (1) ii AD *IGB* V 5352 (m. *Σκυθικός*)

Κόκκαρος
THRACE:
—PAUTALIA: (1) ii AD ib. IV 2074, 12

Κοκκηϊανός
MACEDONIA (PELAGONIA):
—KERAMIAI (NR.): (1) ii-iii AD *IG* X (2) (2) 222

Κοκκήϊος
THRACE:
—PHILIPPOPOLIS-TRIMONTIUM (TERRIT.): (1) ii-iii AD *IGB* III 1320, 1-2 (*Κοκέ-*: f. *Ἀφφη*, *Ἱππίας*)

Κοκκίων
SKYTHIA:
—OLBIA-BORYSTHENES: (1) ?ii-i BC Dubois, *IGDOlbia* 110, 5

Κοκκωνᾶς
THRACE:
—BYZANTION: (1) s. ii AD Luc., *Alex.* 6 ff. (Stephanis 1473) (fict.)

Κοκόνακος
SKYTHIA:
—OLBIA-BORYSTHENES (NR.): (1) m. iv BC *Hyperboreus* 2002 (1), p. 73 (sherd)

Κολανδάκης
SKYTHIA:
—OLBIA-BORYSTHENES: (1) f. iv BC Tolstoi 7 (vase); cf. Vinogradov, *Pont. Stud.* p. 158 no. 12 (name) (kalos)

Κολία
CIMMERIAN BOSPOROS:
—PANTIKAPAION: (1) ii AD *CIRB* 795 (m. *Διονύσιος*)

Κολιδίων
CIMMERIAN BOSPOROS:
—PANTIKAPAION: (1) f. i AD ib. 442; cf. KW pl. 29 no. 418; Zgusta, *PNS* 1054 (f. *Δημήτριος*)

Κολκοτᾶς
MACEDONIA (MYGDONIA):
—KALINDOIA: (1) 68-98 AD *SEG* XLII 580, 21; cf. *Anthémonte–Kalindoia* 2 pp. 275-6 (name) (s. *Παράμονος*); (2) a. 98 AD *SEG* XLII 583, 17 (s. *Νικάνωρ*)

Κόλλα
CIMMERIAN BOSPOROS:
—MYRMEKION: (1) i AD *CIRB* 880 (d. *Ἔρως*)

Κολλαρίων
CIMMERIAN BOSPOROS:
—ACHILLEION: (1) i AD ib. 1024 (f. *Ὑγιαίνων*)

Κόλλεις
CIMMERIAN BOSPOROS:
—PATRAEUS: (1) i/ii AD ib. 1019 (f. *Καλλισθένης*)

Κόλλις
CIMMERIAN BOSPOROS:
—PANTIKAPAION: (1) iii BC ib. 244 (*Κολάϊος* (gen.)—ed., *Κόλλιος*—Latyshev, Yailenko and Tokhtas'ev: f. *Ἀγάθων*); (2) i AD ib. 460

Κολλίων
CIMMERIAN BOSPOROS:
—PANTIKAPAION: (1) m. i AD ib. 437; cf. KW pl. 17 no. 249

Κόλλος
THRACE:
—BYZANTION: (1) i BC *IByz* 114 (*Κόλλου* (gen.): f. *Μῆνις*)
—BYZANTION?: (2) ii BC ib. 327 (Fıratlı–Robert p. 94 no. 131) (*Κόλλου* (gen.): f. *Διονύσιος*)

Κόλλυτος
MACEDONIA (MYGDONIA):
—THESSALONIKE: (1) ii AD *IG* X (2) (1) 428 (*GVI* 428)

Κόλπος
MACEDONIA (ODOMANTIKE):
—BERGE (TERRIT.): (1) iv BC *SEG* XXXII 641 (Pilhofer 569); cf. *SEG* L 608 (n. pr.?: s. *Κιμᾶς*)
THRACE?: (2) 316-309 BC *IG* II^2 1956, 35; *Ancient Macedonia* 5 p. 445 with n. 10 (date) (*FRA* 2548)

Κόλχος
CIMMERIAN BOSPOROS:
—PANTIKAPAION: (1) vi/v BC *SGMII* 4 (1968) p. 41 (lamp); cf. *VDI* 1976 (3), p. 144 (*ρό-*); (2) iv BC *CIRB* 230 (f. *Φιλόκωμος*)
SKYTHIA:
—OLBIA-BORYSTHENES: (3) c. 150-175 AD *IOSPE* I^2 132, 8; Zgusta, *PNS* 1055; cf. *SEG* XLII 713 (f. *Ῥαοδμαῖος*); (4) s. ii AD ib. XLIII 507, 4 (*[Κ]όλχος*)
THRACE:
—BYZANTION: (5) c. 200 BC *IG* II^2 884, 12 (f. *Ἑκαταῖος*)

Κόλων
CIMMERIAN BOSPOROS:
—PANTIKAPAION: (1) m. i AD *CIRB* 433 (*Κ̣ό̣λων*: s. *Ῥόδων*, *Θεοφίλη*)
TAURIS:
—CHERSONESOS: (2) ii AD *IOSPE* I^2 364 c, 5 (s. *Παυ—*)

Κόμαρος
SCYTHIA MINOR:
—KALLATIS: (1) ?ii-i BC *IG* XII (9) 34 (s. *Νικησώ*)

Κόμης
THRACE:
—SALYMBRIA: (1) v AD *AD* 53 (1998) Mel. p. 469 no. 208 (*Κόμις ὁ κὲ Ἰωσήφ*: s. *Συμεών*)

Κομητᾶς
THRACE:
—ODESSOS: (1) vi AD Beševliev 119, 8-9 (f. *Μερκοῦρις*)

Κομινία
MACEDONIA (BOTTIAIA):
—BEROIA: (1) 234 AD *IBer* 325

Κομίνικος
CIMMERIAN BOSPOROS:
—GORGIPPIA: (1) ii AD *CIRB* 1140, 17 (*Κομίνι[κος]*: f. *Πάπας*); (2) s. ii AD ib. 1129 B, 8 (*Κομίν[ικος]*?: f. *Χρηστίων*); (3) 173-210 AD ib. 1135, 13

Κομιτούδης
THRACE:
—BISANTHE-PANION: (1) v-vi AD *AD* 49-50 (1994-5) Mel. p. 322 no. 148 (*Παρα(—) ὁ καὶ Κομιτούδ(ης)*: f. *Παῦλα*)

Κομμοῦνος
MACEDONIA (BOTTIAIA):
—BEROIA: (1) ii/iii AD *IBer* 27 A, 4 (f. *Λούκιος*)

Κομοσαρύη
CIMMERIAN BOSPOROS:
—BOSPOROS: (1) 344-311 BC *CIRB* 1015 (Rhodes–Osborne 65 D); cf. *SEG* XLV 1016; Zgusta, *PNS* 564 (d. *Γόργιππος*, m. *Σάτυρος*, *Πρύτανις*, *Εὔμηλος*)

Κόμψη
THRACE:
—BISANTHE-PANION: (1) v-iv BC Dumont–Homolle 83a (d. *Ἐπικράτης*)

Κόμων
THRACE:
—APOLLONIA-SOZOPOLIS: (1) v/iv BC *Greek Colonisation* p. 100

Κόναρος
CIMMERIAN BOSPOROS:
—PANTIKAPAION: (1) i/ii AD *CIRB* 615; cf. KW pl. 29 no. 423 (*Κόναψος*—ed., *Κόναρε* (voc.)—Tokhtas'ev: s. *Ἀλέξανδρος*)

Κόναψος
CIMMERIAN BOSPOROS:
—PANTIKAPAION: (1) i AD *CIRB* 443; Zgusta, *PNS* 661 (*Κόνακος*—KW: s. *Πάπας*)

Κονίων
CIMMERIAN BOSPOROS:
—PANTIKAPAION: (1) iv BC *CIRB* 197 (s. *Μίτος*)

Κονκόρδιος
SKYTHIA:
—OLBIA-BORYSTHENES: (1) 198-211 AD *IOSPE* I^2 174, 12 (s. *Ἄττας*)

Κονναρίων
SKYTHIA:
—OLBIA-BORYSTHENES: (1) ?iv BC *Sov. Arkh.* 28 (1958) p. 74 (vase) (*BE* 1960, no. 281)

Κοννᾶς
THRACE:
—PERINTHOS-HERAKLEIA: (1) ?iv BC *IPerinth* 259, 7 (*Κοννᾶδος* (gen.))

Κοννίων
THRACE:
—BYZANTION: (1) ii BC *IByz* 104 (Fıratlı–Robert pp. 95-6 no. 135) (f. *Βάκχιος*)

Κόνος
CIMMERIAN BOSPOROS:
—GORGIPPIA: (1) s. ii AD *CIRB* 1129 A, 8; Zgusta, *PNS* 662 (*Κόνο[ς]*); (2) ii/iii AD *CIRB* 1179, 41 (f. *Πάππος*)

Κόνων
CIMMERIAN BOSPOROS:
—GORGIPPIA: (1) f. iii BC ib. 1137 A II, 10; 1137 B II, 11 (s. *Ἀθήνιππος*)
—PANTIKAPAION: (2) iv BC ib. 156 (f. *Ἀλκίφρων*)

MACEDONIA (BOTTIAIA):
—BEROIA: (3) imp. *ILeukopetra* 155 (*M. Λόλλιος K.*)
MACEDONIA (DERRIOPOS): (4) 74-95 AD *IG* X (2) (2) 300, 7; 325, 26 (f. *Φίλων*)
SKYTHIA:
—OLBIA-BORYSTHENES: (5) iii BC *IOlbia* 72, 2 (f. *Ἀθήναιος*); (6) ~ *IOSPE* I² 32 A, 48 (Maier, *Mauerbauinschr.* 82); (7) f. iii BC *IOSPE* I² 201 II, 4; *SEG* XXXIX 702, 29 (s. *Βα—*)
—TANAIS: (8) ii/iii AD *CIRB* 1291 ([*K*]*όνων*)
THRACE:
—MESAMBRIA: (9) i BC *IGB* I² 324 (s. *Ἀθαναίων*)
—NICOPOLIS AD ISTRUM: (10) 138-161 AD ib. II 664, 7 (*Αἴ(λ). K.*)
—ODESSOS: (11) 16 BC ib. I² 46, 31 ([*K*]*όνων*: f. *Μητρόδωρος*); (12) i AD ib. 161 bis (*CCET* I 56; PM 1289) (f. *—ων*); (13) i-ii AD *IGB* I² 128, 11 (f. *Ἀρτεμίδωρος*); (14) ii AD ib. V 5063 (s. *Διονύσιος*); (15) 221 AD ib. I² 47 bis b, 20 (I f. *Αὐρ. Κόνων* II); (16) ~ ib. l. 20 (*Αὐρ. K.*: II s. *Κόνων* I); (17) ~ ib. 47 bis c, 19 (f. *Αὐρ. Σωτήρ*)
—ODESSOS (NR.): (18) ii-iii AD ib. 256 (PM 1695) (f. *Ἰαθίς*)
THRACE?: (19) 316-309 BC *IG* II² 1956, 20; *Ancient Macedonia* 5 p. 445 with n. 10 (date) (*FRA* 2549)

Κόξουρος
SKYTHIA:
—OLBIA-BORYSTHENES: (1) ii AD *IOSPE* I² 93, 9; Zgusta, *PNS* 303 (f. *Ἐπικράτης*)

Κοπρία
MACEDONIA: (1) c. 300 AD *GVI* 1948, 8 (*ISmyrna* 543; Tataki, *Macedonians* p. 345 no. 68)
MACEDONIA (BOTTIAIA):
—BEROIA: (2) 230 AD *ILeukopetra* 76, 2 (*Ἰουλ. K. Νουννία*)
MACEDONIA (CHALKIDIKE):
—SKIONE: (3) imp. *SEG* XXIX 646 (*Οὐλπ. K.*)
MACEDONIA (EORDAIA):
—ARNISA?: (4) 202 AD *EAM* 131; Hatzopoulos, *MI* I p. 94 n. 4 (locn.) (d. *Ἀλέξανδρος*)
MACEDONIA (MYGDONIA):
—LETE: (5) 179 or 296 AD Dimitsas 679 (m. *Μάξιμος*)
—THESSALONIKE: (6) i AD *IG* X (2) (1) 387; (7) ii AD ib. 396, 1 (d. *Σύμφορος*); (8) ii-iii AD Nalpantis, *Anaskaphi* p. 111 no. BE 118 (m. *Διοδώρα*)
—THESSALONIKE?: (9) ii AD *IG* X (2) (1) 867 (threpte); (10) ii-iii AD ib. 830, 3 (*Κλ. K.*)

Κοπριανή
MACEDONIA (BOTTIAIA):
—PELLA: (1) iii AD *SEG* XLIII 439

Κόπρυλλος
MACEDONIA (BOTTIAIA):
—BEROIA: (1) a. 212 AD *IBer* 136, 13 (Tataki 1171) (*Σεπτ. K.*)
MACEDONIA (MYGDONIA):
—LETE (NR.): (2) c. 220-230 AD *SEG* XLVIII 855 (f. *Παράμονος, Στρατονίκη, Παραμόνα, Σωκράτης*)
—THESSALONIKE: (3) iii AD ib. XXXVII 587
—THESSALONIKE?: (4) iv AD *IG* X (2) (1) 778 (Feissel, *RICM* 122)
MACEDONIA (ODOMANTIKE):
—SIRRHA: (5) 155 AD Dimitsas 821, 19 (Kaphtantzis 1) (s. *Ζώπυρος*)
—SIRRHA?: (6) iii AD *IGB* V 5931 (f. *Θευδᾶς*)
MACEDONIA (PIERIA):
—PYDNA: (7) 250 AD *SEG* XLVI 800 A, 37 (*Αὐρ. K.*)

Κοπρύλος
MACEDONIA (BOTTIAIA):
—BEROIA:
——Blaganoi*: (1) 216 AD ib. XXXVII 592 (Tataki 718) (*Κλ. K.*: s. *Κλ. Εὐρυδίκη*)

Κορβούλων
SCYTHIA MINOR:
—ISTROS: (1) ii AD *ISM* I 196, 15; 201 II, 11 (s. *Μᾶρκος*)

Κορδυπίων
MACEDONIA: (1) 345-325 BC *CID* II 76 II, [34]; 97, 29 (Tataki, *Macedonians* p. 346 no. 69) (f. *Τιμανορίδας*)

Κόριθος
TAURIS:
—CHERSONESOS: (1) imp. *Khers. Sbornik* 2 (1927) p. 196 (vase) (*Κόρι(ν)θος*?, *Κόρ(ρ)ιθος*?)

Κορινθία
THRACE:
—NOVAE: (1) iii AD *IGB* II 741, 11 (*-θίη*: m. *Δρακόντις, Νουνέχις, Πάκουρος, Ἑρμιόνη, Μαμάτα*)

Κορινθιάς
MACEDONIA (MYGDONIA):
—THESSALONIKE: (1) i-ii AD *AD* 49 (1994) Chron. pl. 138 γ (Lat. Vibia Corinthias)

Κόρινθος
SCYTHIA MINOR:
—ISTROS: (1) ii AD *ISM* I 196, 5 (f. *Αἰσχρίων*); (2) ~ ib. 211, 10 (f. *Κερκίων*)
THRACE:
—HADRIANOPOLIS (TERRIT.): (3) iii AD *IGB* III 1833 (s. *Βίθης*)
—OESCUS: (4) ii-iii AD *ILB* 25 (Lat. C. Valerius Corinthus)

Κορίσκος
THRACE:
—RHAIDESTOS*: (1) imp. *CIL* III 729 (Lat. Coriscus: imp. freed.)

Κορνηλία
THRACE:
—BYZANTION: (1) i AD *IByz* 141 (*Κορνηλί̣α*: d. *Μάξιμος*)

Κορνήλιος
CIMMERIAN BOSPOROS:
—PANTIKAPAION: (1) i AD *CIRB* 616; cf. KW pl. 52 no. 704 (*-νεί-*: I f. *Κορνήλιος* II); (2) ~ *CIRB* 616; cf. KW pl. 52 no. 704 (*Κορνεῖλι* (voc.): II s. *Κορνήλιος* I)
SCYTHIA MINOR:
—KALLATIS: (3) 241-244 AD *ISM* III 74 A, 32 (*Κορν(ήλιος)*: ?f. *Ἡρακλέων*)
TAURIS:
—CHERSONESOS: (4) imp. *SEG* XLVI 937 ([*Κορ*]*νήλιος*: ?f. *—κ̣ιος*)
THRACE:
—DIOSPOLIS?: (5) ii-iii AD *IGB* III 1782, 3; cf. IV 2028 (or Thrace Serdica: *Κο*[*ρν*]*ήλιος*)

Κορνοῦτος
THRACE:
—APOLLONIA-SOZOPOLIS: (1) i-ii AD ib. I² 401, 21 (I f. *Κορνοῦτος* II, *Ἀπελλῆς*); (2) ~ ib. l. 21 (II s. *Κορνοῦτος* I)
—DUROSTORUM (NR.): (3) f. iii AD ib. II 866 (*CCET* II (1) 181) (*Κορνοῦ*[*τος*]: f. *Ἰούλ. Φίρμος*)
—PERINTHOS-HERAKLEIA:
——(*φυλ. τεταρτ. Εὐανθίς*): (4) iii AD *IPerinth* 162 (I f. *Αὐρ. Κορνοῦτος* II)

Κόρος
SCYTHIA MINOR:
—ISTROS: (1) ii AD *ISM* I 196, 4 (s. *Φαρνάκης*)
THRACE:
—ABDERA: (2) iii AD *BCH* 37 (1913) p. 141 no. 44 (*IThrakAig* E70)

Κορράβων
MACEDONIA: (1) ?417-413 BC *IG* I³ 89, 66 (Tataki, *Macedonians* p. 346 no. 70) (*-βõν*)

Κόρραγος
MACEDONIA: (1) 331 BC *RE* Supplbd. 4 (1); Berve 444 (Tataki, *Macedonians* p. 346 no. 72); (2) c. 326 BC *RE* Supplbd. 4 (5); Berve 445 (Tataki, *Macedonians* p. 346 no. 73); (3) iv/iii BC *ISamothrace* 9 (Tataki, *Macedonians* p. 347 no. 77) (*Κ̣*[*ό*]*ρραγ*[*ος*]: f. *Ἀδαῖος*); (4) f. iii BC Plu., *Demetr.* 53 (Tataki, *Macedonians* p. 346 no. 71); cf. *RE* Supplbd. 4 s.v. Korrabos (-) (*Κόρραβος*—ms. Ven.: s. *Δημήτριος* I *Πολιορκητής, Εὐρυδίκη* (Athens)); (5) 263 BC *IG* IX (1)² (1) 17, 26 (Tataki, *Macedonians* p. 347 no. 81) (f. *Π.....ριχος*); (6) 189-171 BC *RE* Supplbd. 4 (3) (Tataki, *Macedonians* p. 347 no. 76) (Lat. Corragus) ?= (7); (7) a. 188 BC *IPrusa ad Olympum* 1001, 2, 29 (s. *Ἀριστόμαχος*) ?= (6)
MACEDONIA (BOTTIAIA):
—AIGAI: (8) s. iv BC *SEG* XXXV 801 (*Κό*[*ρ*]*ρα*[*γος*]?: ?f. *Φίλα*)
—BEROIA: (9) iv/iii BC *IBer* 58 (Tataki 765); cf. Tataki p. 433 (ident.) (f. *—η*) ?= (*Κορραῖος* (*1*)); (10) i BC-i AD *IBer* 142, 15 (Tataki 764) (s. *Παράμονος*); (11) i/ii AD *IBer* 35 (s. *Ἱέραξ*)
MACEDONIA (DERRIOPOS):
—STUBERRA: (12) 107 AD *IG* X (2) (2) 325, 94 (s. *Ἀντίγονος*)
MACEDONIA (EDONIS):
—AMPHIPOLIS: (13) m. iii BC Hatzopoulos, *Actes Amphipolis* p. 50 no. 11, 4 (*SEG* XLI 565)
MACEDONIA (EORDAIA?):
—GREIA*: (14) 181 BC *EAM* 87, 4 (Hatzopoulos, *MI* 2 pp. 41-2 no. 17) (*Κ̣ό*[*ρ*]*ραγος*: s. *Περδίκκας*: metic)
MACEDONIA (LYNKESTIS):
—HERAKLEIA (AREA): (15) ?ii-iii AD *IG* X (2) (2) 16 (*Κόρα-*)
MACEDONIA (MYGDONIA):
—AINEIA?: (16) ii-iii AD *SEG* XXXVIII 707 (I f. *Κόρραγος* II, *Μελίτων, Νικοῦς*); (17) ~ ib. (II s. *Κόρραγος* I, *Δαντοῦς*)
—THESSALONIKE: (18) i AD *IG* X (2) (1) 259, 25 (f. *Ἡρακλείδης*); (19) 161 AD ib. 573 bis; (20) f. iii AD ib. 188, 6; 189, 11 (*Αὐρ. Δημοκρατιανὸς K.*)
—THESSALONIKE?: (21) ii AD ib. 250 I, 6 (f. *Διονύσιος*)
MACEDONIA (PIERIA):
—DION: (22) iv-iii BC *SEG* XLVIII 787 (f. *Βερενίκη*)
MACEDONIA?: (23) iii BC *PPetr* II 30 b, 20 + III p. xix no. 103; cf. Launey I p. 311; Uebel, *Kleruchen* 828 (f. *Ἀμύντας*); (24) s. iii BC *Memnonion* 583 (*PP* 1931; Tataki, *Macedonians* p. 346 no. 75); (25) c. 220-200 BC Helly, *Gonnoi* 93 B, 29 (*Κόρρ*[*αγος*]?)

Κορραῖος
MACEDONIA: (1) iv BC Plu., *Demetr.* 2; cf. 53 (Tataki, *Macedonians* p. 347 no. 82); cf. *RE* Supplbd. 4 (-); Hoffmann, *Makedonen* pp. 144-6 (*Κόρραγος*—edd.: f. *Στρατονίκη*) ?= (*Κόρραγος* (*9*)); (2) m. iv BC *Paroem. Gr.* I p. 257; 2 p. 464

Κορράτας
MACEDONIA: (1) ?417-413 BC *IG* I³ 89, 65 (Tataki, *Macedonians* p. 348 no. 86); (2) ~ *IG* I³ 89, 66 (Tataki, *Macedonians* p. 348 no. 87)

Κόρρις
THRACE:
—BYZANTION (TERRIT.): (1) ii BC *IByz* 191 (s. *Ἡρᾶς*)

Κόρυφος
THRACE:
—NIKOPOL (MOD.): **(1)** 211-217 AD *ILB* 143, 4 (Lat. Arius Coryphus)

Κορωνίδας
THRACE:
—BYZANTION: **(1)** 478 BC *FGrH* 104 F 1. 8 (-δης: f. Κλεονίκα: fict.?)

Κοσείδης
MACEDONIA (MYGDONIA):
—KALINDOIA: **(1)** ?i-ii AD *SEG* XXIX 628, 4; cf. *Anthémonte–Kalindoia* 2 p. 276 (name) (f. *Ταρουσίνας Σκεπαρνᾶς*)

Κοσείτραλις
THRACE:
—BESSOPARA: **(1)** iii AD *IGB* III 947, 10 (s. *Κουσίτραλις*)

Κοσίγγας
THRACE: **(1)** hell.? Polyaen. vii 22

Κοσιδέλθης
MACEDONIA (MYGDONIA):
—KALINDOIA: **(1)** a. 98 AD *SEG* XLII 583, 25; cf. *Anthémonte–Kalindoia* 2 p. 277 (name) (f. *Δινείλας*)

Κοσίνα
MACEDONIA (MYGDONIA):
—THESSALONIKE (TERRIT.): **(1)** hell. *SEG* XLIX 812

Κόσις
THRACE?: **(1)** iii BC Herod. v 65 (fict.)

Κοσμᾶς
CIMMERIAN BOSPOROS:
—PANTIKAPAION: **(1)** iii/iv AD *TGE* 16 (1976) p. 160

Κοσμία
MACEDONIA (BOTTIAIA):
—BEROIA: **(1)** 208 AD *ILeukopetra* 52, 1 (*Αὐρηλιανὴ Κοσμ[ία]*)
MACEDONIA (CHALKIDIKE):
—POTIDAIA-KASSANDREIA (NR.): **(2)** ?iii AD *SEG* XLV 774 (m. *Βάσσα*)
MACEDONIA (PELAGONIA):
—MOJNO (MOD.): **(3)** ii AD *IG* X (2) (2) 169 (*Αἰλία Κ.*: d. *Αἰλ. Φιλέταιρος*)
THRACE:
—PERINTHOS-HERAKLEIA: **(4)** i-ii AD *IPerinth* 93 (d. *Ἀπολλώνιος*)

Κοσμιανή
THRACE:
—BYZANTION: **(1)** i/ii AD *SEG* L 667 VI (d. *Φλ. Κοσμίων, Παῦλα*)

Κοσμιανός
MACEDONIA (EDONIS):
—PHILIPPOI: **(1)** ii-iii AD *BCH* 47 (1923) p. 91 no. 17 (*[Κ]οσμιανό[ς]*?)
MACEDONIA (MYGDONIA):
—THESSALONIKE: **(2)** ?ii AD *IG* X (2) (1) 127, 4 (*Κ. Οὐειρίνιος Κ.*)
MACEDONIA (PIERIA):
—DION: **(3)** s. ii AD Oikonomos 17; 18; cf. Spiliopoulou-Donderer, *KGN* p. 196 no. D14 (date) (*Τιβεριανὸς Κ.*: s. *Ἰουλία*)
THRACE:
—PHILIPPOPOLIS-TRIMONTIUM: **(4)** f. iii AD *SEG* XXXIX 663 A-B (mosaic) (*Κοσμιανὸς ὁ καὶ Ἰωσήφ*: Jew)

Κοσμίων
MACEDONIA (BOTTIAIA):
—BEROIA: **(1)** ii/iii AD *IBer* 27 A, 5 (*Κοσμίω[ν]*)
MACEDONIA (MYGDONIA):
—THESSALONIKE: **(2)** 162 AD *IG* X (2) (1) 483, 8 (*Κ. Καικίλιος Ῥουστικίλιος Κ.*: s. *Κ. Καικίλιος Κόσμος, Ῥουστικιλία Πῶλλα*)
THRACE:
—BYZANTION: **(3)** i/ii AD *SEG* L 667 VI (*Φλ. Κ.*: f. *Κοσμιανή, Ἱερόκλεια, Διονύσιος*)

Κόσμος
MACEDONIA (BOTTIAIA):
—EDESSA: **(1)** ii-iii AD Dimitsas 15 (290; Tataki, *Edessa* 257) (*Πεδουκαῖος Κ.*)
MACEDONIA (MYGDONIA):
—THESSALONIKE: **(2)** ii AD *IG* X (2) (1) 241 A I, 3; **(3)** 162 AD ib. 483, 2 (*Κ. Καικίλιος Κ.*: f. *Κ. Καικίλιος Ῥουστικίλιος Κοσμίων*)
TAURIS:
—CHERSONESOS?: **(4)** imp. *SEG* XLIII 501 (amph.)
THRACE: **(5)** m. ii BC *IG* IX (1)² (3) 639. 2, 6 (slave/freed.)
—KELLAI: **(6)** 241-244 AD *IGB* III 1517, 38 (f. *Αὐρ. Θεαγένης*)
—PERINTHOS-HERAKLEIA: **(7)** iii AD *IPerinth* 105 (f. *Αὐρ. Εὐτυχία*)
——(*φυλ. πρωτ.*): **(8)** iii AD ib. (*Αὐρ. Κ.*: s. *Σοφοκλῆς*)

Κοσουμάσης
MACEDONIA (MYGDONIA):
—KALINDOIA: **(1)** a. 98 AD *SEG* XLII 582, 32; cf. *Anthémonte–Kalindoia* 2 p. 277 (name) (f. *Μέστεις*, ?f. *Διοσκουρίδης*)

Κοσούπης
MACEDONIA (EDONIS):
—PHILIPPOI (TERRIT.): **(1)** i BC/i AD Pikoulas, *Chora* p. 166 no. 73a (*Κοσούπου* (gen.): f. *Πόσα*)

Κοσοῦς
CIMMERIAN BOSPOROS:
—ACHILLEION (NR.): **(1)** inc. *SEG* XLV 983 (vase)
—KIMMERIKON: **(2)** iii AD *CIRB* 946 (f. *Παιρίσαλος*)
—MYRMEKION: **(3)** v-iv BC *SEG* XXXVII 666. 2 (vase) (*Κόσο[ῦς]*?)
—MYRMEKION (NR.): **(4)** f. ii AD *CIRB* 892 (f. *Πανέρως*)
—PANTIKAPAION: **(5)** imp. ib. 797; Zgusta, *PNS* 131; **(6)** i AD *CIRB* 444 (*[Κ]οσοῦς*: s. *Ἀριεύς*); **(7)** f. i AD ib. 393 A; cf. KW pl. 43 no. 624 (f. *Διόφαντος*); **(8)** i/ii AD *CIRB* 579 (f. *Ἀπολλώνιος*); **(9)** f. ii AD ib. 88, 4 (*Κο(σ)οῦς*?: f. *Ποθίσκος*)
SKYTHIA:
—TANAIS: **(10)** iii AD ib. 1299 (s. *Χρῆστος*)

Κοσσᾶς
CIMMERIAN BOSPOROS:
—PANTIKAPAION: **(1)** i AD ib. 445; Zgusta, *PNS* 131 (s. *Γλαῦκος*); **(2)** m. i AD *CIRB* 496; cf. KW pl. 55 no. 763 (f. *Πόπλις*); **(3)** i/ii AD *CIRB* 615; cf. KW pl. 29 no. 423 (s. *Ἀλέξανδρος*)

Κοσσοῦς
CIMMERIAN BOSPOROS:
—GORGIPPIA: **(1)** ii AD *CIRB* 1140, 12 (f. *Νουμήνιος*); **(2)** ~ ib. 1151, 9; **(3)** ~ ib. 1153; **(4)** m. ii AD *Eirene* 7 (1968) p. 67, 7 (s. *Χρηστοῦς*); **(5)** ~ ib. l. 14 (f. *Βάγης*); **(6)** s. ii AD *CIRB* 1133 B, 2 (*Κοσσ[οῦς]*—Vinogradov); **(7)** ~ ib. 1208, 5 (*Κοσσ[οῦς]*?); **(8)** 173-210 AD ib. 1134, 13; 1140, 21; *Eirene* 7 (1968) p. 67, 8 (s. *Ἄττας*); **(9)** ~ *CIRB* 1134, 13 (f. *Ἄττας*); **(10)** ~ ib. 1135, 17 (*[Κοσ]σοῦς*—Tokhtas'ev: s. *Ἔρως*); **(11)** ~ ib. l. 21 (*Κοσσ[οῦ]ς*: s. —*μαχος*); **(12)** ii/iii AD ib. 1179, 17 (*Κοσσο[ῦς]*); **(13)** ~ ib. l. 39 (f. *Νυμφαγόρας*); **(14)** ~ ib. l. 40 (s. *Βάγης*); **(15)** ~ ib. l. 51; **(16)** iii AD *NE* 9 (1971) p. 10 no. 6 B, 11 (*Κοσσ[οῦς]*?); **(17)** ~ ib. l. 18
—PANTIKAPAION: **(18)** f. ii AD *CIRB* 84, 4; cf. KW pl. 45 no. 648 (s. *Ἀπολλωνίδης*); **(19)** 173-210 AD *CIRB* 74, 5 (s. *Μένανδρος*, f. *Χρηστοῦς*)
SKYTHIA:
—TANAIS: **(20)** f. ii AD ib. 1266, 9 (s. *Γάϊος*); **(21)** c. 210-236 AD ib. 1250, 16; 1281, 19 (s. *Ἡρακλείδης*)

Κόσων
CIMMERIAN BOSPOROS:
—PANTIKAPAION: **(1)** imp. ib. 106, 6 (*Κόσ[ων]ν*—ed., *Κόσ[τω]ν*—Latyshev: f. *Τι*—)
THRACE?: **(2)** i BC *HN*² p. 289; *BCH* 35 (1911) p. 115 (coin)

Κοτιοῦς
CIMMERIAN BOSPOROS:
—PANTIKAPAION: **(1)** 275-278 AD *CIRB* 36, 76 (s. *Ἥλιος*)

Κοτίων
CIMMERIAN BOSPOROS:
—PANTIKAPAION: **(1)** f. ii AD ib. 653; cf. KW pl. 49 no. 686 (s. *Κοττίων*)

Κότος
THRACE:
—BEROE-AUGUSTA TRAIANA: **(1)** iii AD *IGB* III 1574, 10 (*Αὐρ. Μένανδρος ὁ καὶ Κότο(ς)*: s. *Μένανδρος*)

Κοττίχα
TAURIS:
—CHERSONESOS: **(1)** iv/iii BC Solomonik, *NEPKh* 156; *Hellenismus* p. 451 no. 19

Κοττίων
CIMMERIAN BOSPOROS:
—PANTIKAPAION: **(1)** f. ii AD *CIRB* 653; cf. KW pl. 49 no. 686 (f. *Κοτίων*)

Κότυς
CIMMERIAN BOSPOROS:
—BOSPOROS: **(1)** c. 10-67 AD *RE* (10); *PIR*² C 1556; *IOSPE* I² 38, [3]; *CIRB* 41, [4]; 42, [3]; 69, 3; 958; [980]; 1047, [5]; 1118, [2]; 1124, [1]; *SEG* XXXII [790]; XLIII 510, 2 (Levinskaya pp. 237-8 no. 6) (*Τιβ. Ἰούλ. Κ.*: s. *Ἀσποῦργος*, f. *Τιβ. Ἰούλ. Ῥησκούπορις*: king); **(2)** c. 100-132 AD *RE* (11); *PIR*² I 276; Frolova, *CKB A.D. 69-238* pp. 30-6 (*Τιβ. Ἰούλ. Κ.*: s. *Τιβ. Ἰούλ. Σαυρομάτης*: king); **(3)** c. 200-233 AD *RE* (12); *PIR*² I 277; *Stud. Zhebelev* p. 47, 2; Frolova, *CKB A.D. 69-238* pp. 51-2 (*Τιβ. Ἰούλ. Κ.*, *Κόττυς*—1247: s. *Τιβ. Ἰούλ. Ῥησκούπορις*: king)
MACEDONIA: **(4)** 214 BC *BGU* 2397, [4], 20 (Tataki, *Macedonians* p. 348 no. 88); cf. La'da E1415 (f. *Ἀπολλόδοτος*)
MACEDONIA (CHALKIDIKE):
—ANTHEMOUS: **(5)** ii AD *Anthémonte–Kalindoia* 1 p. 58 no. A13 (*SEG* I 281)
MACEDONIA (EDONIS):
—AMPHIPOLIS: **(6)** 37 BC Robert, *Coll. Froehner* 44, 14 (s. *Γλαυκίας*, ?s. *Κλεοπάτρα*)
—PHILIPPOI: **(7)** iii AD *CIL* VI 32624 b, 4 (Pilhofer 763) (Lat. M. Aur. Cottus)
MACEDONIA (MYGDONIA):
—KALINDOIA: **(8)** i BC *SEG* XLII 589 (s. *Σώπατρος*); **(9)** 68-98 AD ib. 580, 43 (s. *Ἀνδροσθένης*); **(10)** ~ ib. l. 66 (s. *Σίπρας*); **(11)** ~ ib. l. 93 (s. *Καρβερένθης*); **(12)** a. 98 AD ib. 582, 5 (I f. *Κότυς* II) ?= *(14)*; **(13)** ~ ib. l. 5 (II s. *Κότυς* I); **(14)** ~ ib. l. 6 (f. *Νίκων*) ?= *(12)*; **(15)** ~ ib. l. 19 (f. *Ζώσιμος*); **(16)** ~ ib. l. 22 (f. *Τάρσας*); **(17)** ~ ib. l. 36 (s. *Νικίας*); **(18)** ~ ib. l. 68 (f. *Δάλης*) ?= *(19)*; **(19)** ~ ib. l. 69 (f. *Μεστούπορις*) ?= *(18)*; **(20)** ~ ib. 583, 11 (s. *Ταρουσίνας*)
—LETE: **(21)** ii AD *Makedonika* 2 (1951) p. 619 no. 42 θ, 11 (s. *Τηρήπης*)
—THESSALONIKE: **(22)** 154-155 AD *IG* X (2) (1) 288, 4; 289, [5]; *SEG* XLIII 462, 3 (*Κώ-*: s. *Εἰρήνη*)

Macedonia (Pelagonia): **(23)** 55 or 210 AD *IG* X (2) (2) 279 (f. *Δούλης*)

Thrace: **(24)** vii/vi BC *FGrH* 90 F 71 (king/fict.); **(25)** iii BC *IGB* I² 389, 2; cf. V 5138 (f. *Ῥαισκούπορις*: king) ?= (*27*); **(26)** c. 281-277 BC ib. I² 307, 16; cf. V 5086 (king?); **(27)** ?276 or 267 BC *FD* III (4) 414, 6, 17 (s. *Ῥαίζδος*: king) ?= (*25*); **(28)** 195 BC *SGDI* 2119, 3 (s. *Μαισίρα*: slave/freed.); **(29)** ii/i BC *Syll*³ 656, 7 (Ager 169) (*Κότ[υς]*: king) ?= (*30*); **(30)** ~ *RE* (2.3); cf. *IGB* I² 43 comm. (stemma) (?f. *Σαδάλας*: king) ?= (*29*); **(31)** 57-44 BC *RE* (2.4); *SEG* XXXIV 701?; cf. *IGB* I² 43 comm. (stemma) (s. *Σαδάλας*, f. *Σαδάλας*: king); **(32)** c. 42-20 BC *RE* (2.5); *PIR*² C 1553; Dumont–Homolle 62a; cf. *PIR*² I 517 (stemma) (s. *Σαδάλας*, *Πολεμοκράτεια*, ?f. *Ῥασκούπορις*); **(33)** 46-54 AD *SEG* XVI 415 III, 31 (*IThrakAig* E84) (s. *Ὑγιηνός*)

—Abdera?: **(34)** ii-iii AD *Belomorski Pregled* I (1942) p. 336 no. 43 (*IThrakAig* E483) (*Ἀντώνιος K.*)

—Apollonia-Sozopolis: **(35)** iii/ii BC *IGB* I² 469 bis, 2-3 (s. *Ταρούλας*); **(36)** f. iii AD ib. 466 (*CCET* I 169) (*[Κό]τυς*: s. *Μαρκ—*)

—Beroe-Augusta Traiana: **(37)** ?ii-iii AD *AA* 1936, p. 71 (*Κό[τ]υς*: f. *—τραλις*)

——Karasoura: **(38)** iii AD *IGB* III 1626, 6 (s. *Δόλης*)

—Bourdapa: **(39)** ii-iii AD ib. 1353 (f. *Δεπανήτης*); **(40)** ~ ib. 1362 (f. *—ις*)

—Byzantion (nr.): **(41)** ii-i BC *IByz* 183 (Fıratlı–Robert p. 112 no. 184) (*[Κ]ότυς*)

—Markianopolis: **(42)** ii-iii AD *IGB* V 5338, 5 (*Κότυ[ς]*)

—Maroneia: **(43)** s. iv BC *IG* II² 9289 (*FRA* 3543)

—Mesambria: **(44)** iii/ii BC Karayotov, *Mesambria* I p. 90 no. 219 (Price, *Alexander* 1033 (coin))

—Odessos: **(45)** 42 BC *IGB* I² 46, 5 (s. *Δερναῖος*)

—Odessos?: **(46)** ii AD ib. 51 bis a, 9 (s. *Χρῆστος*)

—Odrysai: **(47)** c. 425-359 BC *RE* (2.1); *Rogozen Treasure* pp. 47-8 nos. 3-14; 16-22; Peter, *MTD* pp. 112-25 (coin) (s. *Σεύθης*, f. *Κερσεβλέπτης*: king) ?= (*48*); **(48)** 330 BC Tod, *GHI* II 193, 1; cf. Osborne, *Naturalization* T66 (s. *Σεύθης*) ?= (*47*); **(49)** 171-167 BC *RE* (2.2) (s. *Σεύθης*, f. *Βίθυς*: king)

—Philippopolis-Trimontium: **(50)** ii AD *IGB* III 918 (*Eastern cults* p. 264 no. 2) (f. *Βίθυς*); **(51)** ~ *IGB* V 5466 (*T. Φλ. K.*); **(52)** ii-iii AD ib. III 971 (s. *Κουθειός*); **(53)** iii AD ib. 953 (*Κοτυο<τυο>ς* (gen.): f. *Λογγῖνος*)

—Philippopolis-Trimontium (territ.): **(54)** imp. ib. 1080; **(55)** i AD ib. 1187 (f. *Σεύθης*); **(56)** i-ii AD ib. 1317, 2 (f. *—ως*); **(57)** 98-117 AD ib. 1116; cf. V 5479 (date) (f. *Διζάλας*); **(58)** ii-iii AD ib. III 1285; **(59)** ~ ib. 1303, 11 (*[Κό]τυς*: f. *Μουκάτραλις*); **(60)** ~ ib. 1895 (s. *Μουκάζενις*); **(61)** 199 AD ib. 1538, 11; **(62)** iii AD ib. 1293 (s. *Ῥοιμήζενις*)

—Salymbria: **(63)** imp. *IByz* S 44 (f. *Δάαις*)

—Sappaioi: **(64)** i BC *RE* (2.6); *IG* II² 3442 (f. *Ῥασκούπορις*, ?f. *Ῥάσκος*); **(65)** c. 42-18 BC *RE* (2.7); *PIR*² C 1552; *IG* II² 3443; *SEG* XXXIV 702; Youroukova pp. 46-53; pp. 89-90 nos. 153-7 (coin) (s. *Ῥασκούπορις*, ?f. *Ῥοιμητάλκης*, *Ῥασκούπορις*: king); **(66)** c. 12-19 AD *RE* (2.8); *PIR*² C 1554; *IGB* V 5011, 5, 31; *ISM* III 44, 1 (I s. *Ῥοιμητάλκης*, f. *Ῥοιμητάλκης*, *Πολέμων*, *Κότυς* II, *Πυθοδωρίς*: king); **(67)** 19-47 AD *RE* (2.9); *PIR*² C 1555; *SEG* XL 522 e (and Armenia Minor: *Σέξ. Ἰούλ. K.*: II s. *Κότυς* I, *Ἀντωνία Τρύφαινα* (Pontos): king)

—Serdica: **(68)** iii AD *IGB* IV 1972

—Serdica (territ.): **(69)** ii-iii AD ib. V 5741 (*Φλ. K.*)

—Sexaginta Prista: **(70)** s. ii AD *BIAB* 11 (1937) p. 285 (*Romanizmăt* II 81) (Lat. Aurelio Coto (dat.))

—Spinopara: **(71)** ii AD *IGB* IV 2192, 10

—Stratopara: **(72)** 202 AD ib. III 1690 b, 36 (and Thrace Pizos: s. *Καρωσσός*)

—Traianopolis: **(73)** v AD Meïmaris–Bakirtzis 26, 4 (*SEG* XXIV 644; *IThrakAig* E444) (*Κότεος* (gen.): ?f. *Σοφία*)

Thrace?: **(74)** hell. *SEG* XVI 864. 19 (f. *Σαδάλας*); **(75)** iii BC *POElephDAIK* 5 (ostrakon) (*Κότυι* (dat.)); **(76)** 246 BC *PPetr* II 18 I, 5, 9 (*PP* 12867; Velkov 193) (s. *Εὔηνος*); **(77)** 238 BC *PPetr*² 3, 85 (Velkov 180; La'da E2623); **(78)** ii BC *Memnonion* 82 (Velkov 185) (f. *Ἀβλούζελμις*); **(79)** ~ *Memnonion* 414 (Velkov 181); **(80)** ?ii BC *SB* 3687 (Velkov 189) (f. *Σεύθης*); **(81)** ii BC *SEG* XI 11; **(82)** 179 BC *PHeid* VIII 413, 3-4, 7, 12

Κοτυτίς

Scythia Minor:

—Kallatis: **(1)** ii-i BC *ISM* III 172 (d. *Θεαρίδας*)

Κοτυτίων

Cimmerian Bosporos:

—Gorgippia: **(1)** f. iii BC *CIRB* 1137 A I, 29; 1137 A II, 26; cf. *Etiudy* pp. 181-2 no. 1; Zgusta, *PNS* 565 (f. *Κρατῖνος*) ?= (*2*); **(2)** ~ *CIRB* 1137 A II, 30 (f. *Βλάστος*) ?= (*1*)

—Nymphaion: **(3)** f. iii BC *North Pontic Archaeology* p. 314 with fig. 7.3; cf. *Hyperboreus* 1997 (2), p. 376 (*Κοτο-*: f. *Ἡφαιστίων*)

Scythia Minor:

—Kallatis: **(4)** iii/ii BC *ISM* III 168

Tauris:

—Chersonesos: **(5)** iv BC *SEG* XXXVII 661 (sherd); *Hellenismus* p. 451 no. 20; **(6)** c. 285-272 BC Kats p. 101 no. 67 (amph., tile) (s. *Ἀρίστων*)

Κότως

Thrace: **(1)** i BC-i AD *IGB* I² 306 bis (*Κότωος* (gen.))

Κούαρτα

Macedonia (Chalkidike):

—Mende?: **(1)** ?ii AD *SEG* XXIX 614

Macedonia (Mygdonia):

—Sochos (mod.): **(2)** s. ii AD ib. XLVIII 839

—Thessalonike: **(3)** ii/iii AD ib. XLIX 814 II, 4

Κουαρτίων

Macedonia (Bottiaia):

—Beroia: **(1)** ii-iii AD *IBer* 371, 1 (Tataki 767) (s. *Γέμελλος*, *Ἀμμία*)

Κούαρτος

Macedonia (Lynkestis):

—Herakleia (area): **(1)** ?ii AD *IG* X (2) (2) 15 (s. *Θάλλος*)

Macedonia (Mygdonia):

—Thessalonike: **(2)** ii-iii AD ib. X (2) (1) 455, 3, 13 (*GVI* 318) (?f. *Ἐπίγονος*)

Macedonia (Paionia): **(3)** ii-iii AD *Sp.* 75 (1933) p. 77 no. 219 (s. *Μᾶρκος*, *Ὀβουλκία*)

—Kavadarci (mod.): **(4)** ii/iii AD Unp. (Kavadarci Mus.) inv. 10/II (f. *Γάϊος*)

Κουζαῖος

Skythia:

—Olbia-Borysthenes: **(1)** ii-iii AD *IOSPE* I² 137, 10; Zgusta, *PNS* 132 (f. *Δάδαγος*)

Κουζίλας

Macedonia (Odomantike):

—Gazoros: **(1)** ii-iii AD *SEG* XXX 571 (Pilhofer 545) (*Κουζίλα[ς]*)

Κουήτη

Thrace:

—Philippopolis-Trimontium: **(1)** ii-iii AD *IGB* V 5462 (d. *Δύδης*, m. *Αἴλ. Πολέμων*)

Κουθειός

Thrace:

—Philippopolis-Trimontium: **(1)** ii-iii AD ib. III 971 (f. *Κότυς*)

Κουθίας

Scythia Minor:

—Tomis: **(1)** ii AD *ISM* II 17, 13 (f. *Θεάδων*); **(2)** ii-iii AD ib. 468, 16 (s. *Καλλικράτης*)

Κούθιν

Macedonia (Mygdonia):

—Thessalonike?: **(1)** ii AD *IG* X (2) (1) 916 (*-θειν*: m. *Δελτίς*)

Κουθιούλας

Macedonia (Sintike):

—Parthikopolis: **(1)** s. ii AD *IGB* IV 2282 (s. *Κα—*)

Κουθιούρας

Scythia Minor:

—Istros: **(1)** iii AD *ISM* I 229, 5

Κουίζερις

Thrace:

—Anchialos (territ.): **(1)** ii/iii AD *IGB* III 1846, 3 (f. *Βρινκαζεις*, *Αὐλούζενις*, *Μουκάτραλις*)

Κουϊντιανός

Thrace:

—Perinthos-Herakleia: **(1)** iii AD *IPerinth* 170 (*Κυντ-*)

Κουϊντίων

Thrace:

—Byzantion (territ.): **(1)** imp. Unp. (Sayar) (*Κυ-*: f. *Μοσχίων*)

Κούϊντος

Thrace:

—Golemo Peštene (mod.): **(1)** ii-iii AD *IGB* V 5163 (*Κύ-*: s. *Γερου—*)

Κούκαις

Skythia:

—Olbia-Borysthenes: **(1)** imp. *IOSPE* I² 148, 4; Zgusta, *PNS* 664 (s. *Ἀρσαλίων*)

Κουκόδων

Skythia:

—Olbia-Borysthenes: **(1)** i/ii AD *IOlbia* 90, 8 (f. *Ἰνάρμαζος*)

Κουκούναγος

Skythia:

—Olbia-Borysthenes: **(1)** ii AD *IOSPE* I² 129, 9; Zgusta, *PNS* 665 (s. *Ῥηχούναγος*)

Κουλία

Cimmerian Bosporos:

—Achilleion: **(1)** i/ii AD *CIRB* 1025; cf. KW pl. 47 no. 669

—Pantikapaion: **(2)** imp. *CIRB* 758; Zgusta, *PNS* 1056; **(3)** i AD *CIRB* 446; cf. KW pl. 25 no. 367; **(4)** ~ *CIRB* 447 (*[Κο]υλία?*, *[Ἰο]υλία?*: d. *Θεοδᾶς*); **(5)** ?s. i AD ib. 526

Κούλιος

Cimmerian Bosporos:

—Pantikapaion: **(1)** i AD ib. 344; Zgusta, *PNS* 1056 (f. *Ἡλιοδώρα*); **(2)** s. i AD *CIRB* 518 (f. *Τρύφων*, *Ἀχιλλεύς*)

Skythia:

—Olbia-Borysthenes: **(3)** iii AD *IOSPE* I² 103, 8 (f. *Πίδανος*)

Tauris:

—Chersonesos: **(4)** imp.? *IAK* 20 (1906) p. 68 (vase) (f. *Σκύμνος*)

Thrace:

—Glava Panega (mod.): **(5)** ii-iii AD *IGB* II 523 (f. *Δίζας*)

Κούλις
SKYTHIA:
—OLBIA-BORYSTHENES (BEREZAN (MOD.)): **(1)** f. ii AD *SEG* XLIX 1028 A, 8 (s. *Ἄβραγος*)

Κουνθισίης?
THRACE:
—PLATANIA (MOD.): **(1)** iii AD ib. XXXII 676 (Pilhofer 510) (*Κουνθισιήους* (gen.)—Perdrizet, *Κουνοισιηους* (gen.)—Papazoglou: f. *Μάτα*)

Κοῦνος
THRACE:
—BYZANTION?: **(1)** imp. *AEMÖ* 19 (1896) p. 59 (PM 1685) (f. *Ζωσάριν*)

Κουνοῦς
SKYTHIA:
—OLBIA-BORYSTHENES: **(1)** ii AD *IOSPE* I^2 129, 7; Zgusta, *PNS* 663 (s. *Ἀθήναιος*); **(2)** f. ii AD *IOSPE* I^2 95, 10 (s. *Στέφανος*)
THRACE:
—ODESSOS: **(3)** i-ii AD *IGB* I^2 108, 8 (*Κουνοῦτος* (gen.): f. *Ἑστιαῖος*)

Κούνχακος
SKYTHIA:
—OLBIA-BORYSTHENES: **(1)** i/ii AD *SEG* XLIII 505, 8 (f. *Σάτυρος*)

Κουραγένης
SCYTHIA MINOR:
—ISTROS: **(1)** ii AD *ISM* I 212, 20 (f. *Ἀρτεμίδωρος*); **(2)** 138 AD ib. 193 I, 51 (*Κουραγένης*: f. *Θεόδωρος*)

Κούρης
THRACE:
—DIONYSOPOLIS: **(1)** 222-235 AD *IGB* I^2 23 (*M. Αὐρ. Κούρη(ς)*)
—MARKIANOPOLIS (NR.): **(2)** ii AD ib. V 5367 (*-ρεις*: s. *Μάξιμος*); **(3)** ii-iii AD ib. II 835 (*Κούρηου* (gen.))

Κουριατία
MACEDONIA (BOTTIAIA):
—EDESSA: **(1)** ii-iii AD Dimitsas 25 (Tataki, *Edessa* 173) (d. *Λ. Κουριάτιος Πατρόβιος, Κουριατία Σεκοῦνδα*)

Κουσίας
SCYTHIA MINOR:
—ISTROS: **(1)** ii AD *ISM* I 212, 12 (f. *Μενίσκος*); **(2)** 138 AD ib. 193 I, 14 (s. *Διονυσόδωρος*) ?= (*3*); **(3)** ~ ib. l. 44 (f. *Διονυσόδωρος*) ?= (*2*)

Κουσίτραλις
THRACE:
—BESSOPARA: **(1)** iii AD *IGB* III 947, 10 (*Κουσίτρα[λις]*: f. *Κοσείτραλις*)

Κουσοῦς
CIMMERIAN BOSPOROS:
—PANTIKAPAION: **(1)** i BC/i AD *CIRB* 322; cf. KW pl. 16 no. 241; Zgusta, *PNS* 131

Κούσπις
MACEDONIA (MYGDONIA):
—THESSALONIKE: **(1)** i-ii AD *IG* X (2) (1) 243 I, 7 + *Maia* 25 (1973) p. 200

Κούτζης
THRACE: **(1)** 528 AD *PLRE* III (-)

Κούτης
MACEDONIA (PAIONIA):
—KAVADARCI (MOD.): **(1)** ii AD *Sp.* 98 (1941-8) p. 77 no. 165; cf. 75 (1933) p. 40 no. 135 (*Κούτεως* (gen.), *Κούτ(σ?)εως* (gen.)—ed.: f. *Ζήνων*)
MACEDONIA (SINTIKE):
—PARTHIKOPOLIS (TERRIT.): **(2)** ii AD *Arkheologiia* (Sofia) 1987 (1), p. 25 no. 3 (*Κούτη* (gen.), *Μαμακουτη* (dat.)—ed.: f. *Μάμα*)

Κουτίλας
THRACE: **(1)** 537 AD *PLRE* III (-)

Κουτιλίη
SCYTHIA MINOR:
—ISTROS: **(1)** ii AD *ISM* I 296 + *Riv. Fil.* 111 (1983) pp. 54-5 (*Κουτίλη[ς]*?—Pippidi, *Κουτιλίη Ἀπφοῦτι* (dat.)—Moretti: ?d. *Ἀπφοῦς*)

Κούτιος
MACEDONIA (BISALTIA):
—EUPORIA?: **(1)** imp.? Kaphtantzis 512

Κουτιούλης
MACEDONIA (CHALKIDIKE):
—APHYTIS: **(1)** imp. *SEG* XXIX 573 (*[Κ]ουΐντος Οὐαλέ[ριο]ς Κ.*)
THRACE?: **(2)** ii AD *IG* X (2) (1) 910, 1 (Lat. Cutiulae (gen.))

Κόφαρνος
CIMMERIAN BOSPOROS:
—GORGIPPIA: **(1)** ii AD *CIRB* 1140, 14 (*Κόφαρ[νος]*?)
SKYTHIA:
—TANAIS: **(2)** c. 200-210 AD ib. 1277, 18

Κοωκοῦς
THRACE:
—ODESSOS (NR.): **(1)** ii-iii AD *IGB* I^2 258 (*Κοωκοῦς*: s. *Διαρζις*)

Κπηεθύρης?
CIMMERIAN BOSPOROS:
—KEPOI?: **(1)** iv/iii BC *CIRB* 1113 (*GVI* 1445; *CEG* II 739) + *Hyperboreus* 2000, pp. 138-9 (*Κ(ηπ)εθύρης*—edd.: s. *Καβαθάξης*)

Κράθων
TAURIS:
—CHERSONESOS: **(1)** c. 265-260 BC *FD* III (3) 207, 4 (f. *Σώκριτος*)

Κράσης
MACEDONIA (CHALKIDIKE):
—POLICHNE?: **(1)** ?353 BC *SEG* XXXVII 576, 20 (*Κράσεος* (gen.): f. *Νεμήνιος*)
—STOLOS?: **(2)** ?351 BC ib. XXXVIII 672, 5, 15 (*Κράσεος* (gen.): f. *Ζωΐλος*); **(3)** ?350 BC ib. 670, 6 (*Κράσεος* (gen.): f. *Πολύστρατος*)
MACEDONIA (EDONIS):
—PHILIPPOI (DRAMA (MOD.)): **(4)** ii-iii AD *AD* 52 (1997) Chron. p. 847, 2 with pl. 314 *β*

Κράστων
MACEDONIA: **(1)** ?417-413 BC *IG* I^3 89, 61 (Tataki, *Macedonians* p. 348 no. 90) (*-τõν*: f. *Βυργῖνος*); **(2)** ~ *IG* I^3 89, 64 (Tataki, *Macedonians* p. 348 no. 89) (*Κράστõ[ν]*)

Κραταῖος
MACEDONIA (CHALKIDIKE):
—APHYTIS: **(1)** s. vi BC *AAA* 4 (1971) pp. 362-3 (vase) (*SEG* L 571 C) (*—σι Κραταιος*—ed., *[Πα]σικραταῖος*?, *[Ναυ]σικραταῖος*?)

Κρατέας
SCYTHIA MINOR:
—ISTROS: **(1)** iii BC *ISM* I 5, 3 (*Eastern cults* pp. 15-16 no. 22) (*Κρατέ[ας]*?)
—KALLATIS: **(2)** iii BC *ISM* III 126, 5 (*[Κρ]ατέας*: s. *Εὐκλέων*)

Κράτεια
CIMMERIAN BOSPOROS:
—PANTIKAPAION: **(1)** s. iv BC *CIRB* 198; cf. KW pl. 4 no. 62 (*-τηα*)
MACEDONIA (BOTTIAIA):
—BEROIA: **(2)** 192 AD *ILeukopetra* 34, 1 (Tataki 52) (*(Α)ἰλ. Κρατέα*)
THRACE:
—BYZANTION: **(3)** hell. *IG* II^2 8441 (*FRA* 1395) (d. *Μάκρων*)
—BYZANTION (TERRIT.): **(4)** i BC *IByz* 134 (Fıratlı–Robert p. 99 no. 146a) (*-τηα*: d. *Ἀρτεμίδωρος*)

Κρατέννας
MACEDONIA: **(1)** ?417-413 BC *IG* I^3 89, 75 (*RE* Supplbd. 4 (-); Tataki, *Macedonians* p. 349 no. 92)

Κράτερος
CIMMERIAN BOSPOROS:
—GORGIPPIA: **(1)** f. iii BC *CIRB* 1137 B I, 44 (f. *Καλλιγένης*)
MACEDONIA: **(2)** c. 321-270 BC *RE* (1); *FGrH* 342; *CEG* II 878 (Tataki, *Macedonians* p. 349 no. 93) (II s. *Κράτερος* I (Orestis), *Φίλα*, f. *Ἀλέξανδρος*); **(3)** 130 BC *PBad* II 2, 35, 46 (Tataki, *Macedonians* p. 488 no. 156; La'da E1528)
MACEDONIA (BOTTIAIA):
—BEROIA: **(4)** s. iii BC *IBer* 46, 16; **(5)** ii/iii AD ib. 145, 10 (Tataki 770) (s. *Ἑρμῆς*)
MACEDONIA (EDONIS):
—AMPHIPOLIS: **(6)** 359-336 BC Procl., *in R.* ii 116 (fict.?); **(7)** c. 60 BC *IG* VII 420, 12 (*IOrop* 528; Stephanis 1488; Tataki, *Macedonians* p. 55 no. 74); cf. *LGPN* II s.v. (1) (s. *Ἀντίπατρος*)
MACEDONIA (MYGDONIA):
—THESSALONIKE: **(8)** ii BC *IG* X (2) (1) 327, 1 (s. *Εὐφράνωρ*, ?s. *Ἀντιγόνα*); **(9)** ii-iii AD ib. 514; **(10)** 141 AD ib. 137, 11; cf. *BCH* 97 (1973) p. 587 (*Μέμμιος Κ.*); **(11)** iii AD *IG* X (2) (1) 349, 2, 9 (*Κ. ὁ καὶ Νουνέχιος*)
MACEDONIA (ORESTIS): **(12)** c. 370-321 BC *RE* Supplbd. 4 (1a); Berve 446; *CEG* II 878; *ID* Index p. 57 (Tataki, *Macedonians* p. 205 no. 9); cf. Fraser, *Cities* pp. 224-6 (I s. *Ἀλέξανδρος*, *Ἀριστοπάτρα*, f. *Κράτερος* II)
THRACE:
—MARONEIA: **(13)** ii/iii AD *SEG* XLIX 889

Κρατεύα
THRACE:
—PERNI (MOD.): **(1)** hell. ib. XXIV 624 (d. *Ἀλκέτας*)

Κρατεύας
MACEDONIA: **(1)** c. 399 BC Arist., *Pol.* 1311 b, 8; Plu., *Mor.* 768 F; D.S. xiv 37. 6; Hoffmann, *Makedonen* p. 155 n. 56 (name) (Tataki, *Macedonians* p. 348 no. 91) (*Κραταίας*—Arist., *Κρατέας*—Plu., *Κράτερος*—D.S.); **(2)** 326 BC *Syll*^{3} 302, 7, 11 (*Chiron* 33 (2003) p. 420); Berve 447 (Tataki, *Macedonians* p. 199 no. 3) ?= (*8*); **(3)** 316 BC *RE* (1) (Tataki, *Macedonians* p. 349 no. 96); **(4)** 222 BC *PEnt* 75, 1 and verso (Tataki, *Macedonians* p. 349 no. 49; La'da E1529); **(5)** 184 BC *PHeid* VIII 414, [2], [44]?, 48 (La'da E1530)
MACEDONIA (BOTTIAIA):
—BEROIA: **(6)** f. i BC *IBer* 163 (Tataki 771) (s. *Νικάδας*); **(7)** ii-iii AD *IBer* 207 (Tataki 769) (*Κρατεύα[ς]*—Hatzopoulos, *Κράτει[α]*—Tataki)
MACEDONIA (DERRIOPOS):
—ALKOMENA: **(8)** iv BC Arr., *An.* vi 28. 4; *Ind.* xviii 5 (f. *Πείθων*, *Εὔδαμος*) ?= (*2*)
MACEDONIA (EORDAIA?):
—EUIA: **(9)** 181 BC *EAM* 87, 17 (Hatzopoulos, *MI* 2 pp. 41-2 no. 17) (f. *—μαχος*)
MACEDONIA (EORDAIA):
—RYAKI (MOD.): **(10)** ii-i BC *EAM* 121 (f. *Ἀμμία*)
MACEDONIA (PELAGONIA):
—KOLOBAISA*: **(11)** ii AD *IG* X (2) (2) 232 ?= (*12*)
MACEDONIA (PELAGONIA)?: **(12)** ii AD ib. 186, 2 (or Arabia Felix Amara?: s. (nat.) *Ἀγρίππας*, *Ἄννα*, s. (ad.) *Μένιππος*: Jew?) ?= (*11*)

MACEDONIA (PIERIA):
—PYDNA: (**13**) iv BC *GRBS* 43 (2002-3) p. 119 no. 5, 2, 8

Κράτης
CIMMERIAN BOSPOROS:
—HERMONASSA: (**1**) iv BC *CIRB* 1056 II, 14 (f. *Κτέατος*)
MACEDONIA: (**2**) m. iv BC Plu., *Mor.* 179 A (Tataki, *Macedonians* p. 350 no. 97); (**3**) f. iii BC *IG* II^2 9262; cf. *ZPE* 29 (1978) p. 68 (Tataki, *Macedonians* p. 350 no. 98; *FRA* 3473) (s. *Σατυρίων*); (**4**) 223 BC *PTeb* 815 fr. 4 recto I, 18 (Tataki, *Macedonians* p. 350 no. 99; La'da E1771) (t.e.)
THRACE:
—AINOS: (**5**) hell. PH 271 (f. *Εὐθυμία*)
—ODESSOS: (**6**) 122 BC *SEG* XXXVIII 114 V, 226 (*FRA* 5879) ([*Κρ*]*άτης*)

Κρατήσιος
THRACE:
—SALYMBRIA: (**1**) i BC *IByz* S 52 (*Κρατησίου* (gen.): f. *Μύρτα*)

Κρατησίπολις
MACEDONIA?: (**1**) 315-307 BC *RE* (2); *FD* III (4) 464, 3 (Tataki, *Macedonians* p. 350 no. 100)

Κρατήσιππος
SCYTHIA MINOR:
—ISTROS: (**1**) 138 AD *ISM* I 193 I, 17 (f. *Διονύσιος*); (**2**) ~ ib. l. 42 (s. *Θεόδωρος*)

Κρατησίς
MACEDONIA (PIERIA):
—DION (TERRIT.): (**1**) ii AD Oikonomos 48 (m. *Αὐρ. Λυκιδίων*)

Κρατησώ
MACEDONIA (MYGDONIA):
—THESSALONIKE: (**1**) ii AD *IG* X (2) (1) 57; 102, 4 (*Φλ. Κ.*: m. *Φλ. Φίλα*)

Κρατίδημος
THRACE:
—ODESSOS: (**1**) 221 AD *IGB* I^2 47 bis b, 31 (*Αὐρ. Κ.*: s. *Ἀχιλλᾶς*)

Κρατιννώ
MACEDONIA (CHALKIDIKE):
—OLYNTHOS: (**1**) f. iv BC *SEG* XXXIV 660 bis (d. *Ἡγήσαρχος*)

Κρατῖνος
CIMMERIAN BOSPOROS:
—GORGIPPIA: (**1**) f. iii BC *CIRB* 1137 A I, 29; 1137 A II, 26 (s. *Κοτυτίων*); (**2**) ~ ib. 1137 A I, 56 (f. *Εὔρυτος*); (**3**) ~ ib. 1137 B I, 31 (f. *Ἀρχέδημος*); (**4**) ~ ib. l. 42 (f. *Νικόστρατος*); (**5**) ~ ib. l. 45 (f. *Ἑστιαῖος*)
MACEDONIA (EDONIS):
—AMPHIPOLIS: (**6**) s. iv BC Hatzopoulos, *Actes Amphipolis* p. 45 no. 9, 6 (*SEG* XLI 563); cf. *SEG* XLIV 504 (f. *Πεδιεύς*)
—PHILIPPOI: (**7**) ii-i BC *BCH* 59 (1935) p. 159 no. 56 (Pilhofer 305) (s. *Νουμήνιος*)
SCYTHIA MINOR:
—KALLATIS: (**8**) s. iii BC *ISM* III 35 A, 30 ([*Κρ*]*ατῖνος*: s. *Μῖκος*)
SKYTHIA:
—OLBIA-BORYSTHENES: (**9**) i-ii AD *IOSPE* I^2 155, 5 (-*τεί*-: f. *Ἡρακλείδης*)
—TYRAS: (**10**) ii BC ib. 5 (f. —*ς*)
THRACE:
—BYZANTION: (**11**) iii BC *IByz* 292 (Fıratlı–Robert p. 114 no. 191) (f. *Νικόπολις*)
—LYSIMACHEIA: (**12**) m. ii BC *ISestos* 38 b, 5 (f. *Ἑκαταῖος*)

Κράτιππος
CIMMERIAN BOSPOROS:
—GORGIPPIA: (**1**) ii AD *CIRB* 1154, 4 (*Κράτιπ*[*πος*]: f. —*νων*)
—NYMPHAION: (**2**) iii BC ib. 912 II, 17 (I f. *Κράτιππος* II); (**3**) ~ ib. l. 17 (II s. *Κράτιππος* I)
—PANTIKAPAION: (**4**) iv BC *IGAIMK* 104 (1935) p. 306 nos. 43-4; *SEG* XXXVII 666. 5 (tile) (*Κράτιπ*(*πος*))
—PHANAGOREIA (NR.): (**5**) iii AD *CIRB* 1016, 6
—TYRITAKE: (**6**) f. ii AD ib. 908 (*Κράτιπ*[*πος*]: s. *Ἀπολλώνιος*)
MACEDONIA (CHALKIDIKE):
—OLYNTHOS: (**7**) f. iv BC *Olynthus* 5 pp. 197-8 no. 608 (vase) (*Κράτιπ*(*πος*))
—OLYNTHOS?: (**8**) c. 330 BC *IG* II^2 1496, 220 (Tataki, *Macedonians* p. 139 no. 75)
MACEDONIA (MYGDONIA):
—KALINDOIA: (**9**) c. 325 BC Hatzopoulos, *MI* 2 p. 84 no. 62, 20 (s. *Εὐρύτιος*)
THRACE:
—AINOS?: (**10**) c. 230-200 BC *BCH* 45 (1921) p. 19 III, 93 (or Thrace Maroneia: [*Κ*]*ράτιππος*: s. *Κάλλιππος*: locn.—Oulhen)
—APOLLONIA-SOZOPOLIS: (**11**) v/iv BC *IGB* I^2 408 (f. *Καλλίας*); (**12**) iv BC ib. 463 bis, 1 (f. *Μένων*)
—ODESSOS: (**13**) s. ii AD ib. 234 (*CCET* I 32)
—ODESSOS (TERRIT.): (**14**) ?i AD *IGB* I^2 276 (*Κράτιπ*[*πος*]: f. —*σιος*)

Κρατις
MACEDONIA (SINTIKE):
—PARTHIKOPOLIS (NR.): (**1**) ?ii AD ib. IV 2300 (*Κράτις*?, *Κρατίς*?)

Κρατισθένης
THRACE:
—ODESSOS: (**1**) f. ii BC ib. I^2 41, 2 (s. *Ζωΐλος*)

Κρατίστα
THRACE:
—MARONEIA: (**1**) ii BC *IThrakAig* E253 ([*Κρα*]*τίστα*?: d. *Ἡδύλος*)

Κρατίστης
THRACE:
—PERINTHOS-HERAKLEIA: (**1**) ?iv BC *IPerinth* 259, 17 (*Κρατίστεω* (gen.))

Κράτιστος
MACEDONIA (BISALTIA):
—TRAGILOS: (**1**) hell.? *SEG* XXX 617 (s. *Βίων*)

Κρατιστώ
MACEDONIA (CHALKIDIKE):
—OLYNTHOS: (**1**) iv BC *IG* II^2 10027 (Tataki, *Macedonians* p. 139 no. 77; *FRA* 5902) (d. *Πολέμων*); (**2**) s. iv BC *IG* II^2 10023 (Tataki, *Macedonians* p. 139 no. 76; *FRA* 5901) (d. *Ἄγρων*)
THRACE:
—BYZANTION: (**3**) ii BC *IByz* 216 (Fıratlı–Robert p. 75 no. 82a) (d. *Διονύσιος*)

Κράτων
MACEDONIA (BOTTIAIA):
—EDESSA: (**1**) iii AD *Makedonika* 15 (1975) p. 203 (Tataki, *Edessa* 179) (s. *Εὐπορία*)
MACEDONIA (CHALKIDRKE):
—POTIDAIA-KASSANDREIA: (**2**) iii/ii BC *IG* XII (1) 430 (Tataki, *Macedonians* p. 92 no. 58)
MACEDONIA (EDONIS):
—AMPHIPOLIS: (**3**) iv BC *AEMTh* 15 (2001) p. 119; (**4**) ?iv/iii BC Kaphtantzis 644 (s. *Ἀρτεμίδωρος*); (**5**) hell.? *AD* 22 (1967) Chron. p. 427; (**6**) ~ Kaphtantzis 645 (s. *Ἀπολλώνιος*)
MACEDONIA (MYGDONIA):
—KALINDOIA: (**7**) 68-98 AD *SEG* XLII 580, 54 (s. *Μένανδρος*)
MACEDONIA (PAIONIA):
—STOBOI: (**8**) s. iii AD *JÖAI* 32 (1940) Beibl. col. 16 no. 10. 32 (*Κρατώνου* (gen.))
TAURIS:
—CHERSONESOS: (**9**) c. 325-315 BC Kats p. 101 no. 68 (amph.)
THRACE:
—ABDERA: (**10**) ii BC *IThrakAig* E54
—MESAMBRIA: (**11**) iii BC *IGB* I^2 339 ([*Κ*]*ράτων*?, [*Στ*]*ράτων*?: f. *Ἀθαναίων*); (**12**) ii/i BC ib. V 5103, 2 (s. *Ἀριστόνικος*)

Κραυγᾶς
THRACE:
—SPINOPARA: (**1**) ii AD ib. IV 2192, 7

Κραυγάσιος
THRACE:
—BYZANTION: (**1**) iii AD *IByz* 295 (Fıratlı–Robert p. 52 no. 28) (*Αὐρ. Κ.*)

Κρέουσα
CIMMERIAN BOSPOROS:
—PANTIKAPAION: (**1**) 389-349 BC *CIRB* 8 (d. *Μέδων*)
SKYTHIA:
—OLBIA-BORYSTHENES: (**2**) ii AD *IOSPE* I^2 206, 4 (m. *Ἀχιλλεύς*)

Κρεσφόντης
THRACE:
—APOLLONIA-SOZOPOLIS: (**1**) iv/iii BC *IGB* I^2 449 (*Κρεσφόντευς* (gen.): f. *Ἡγοῦς*)

Κρέων
MACEDONIA (PAIONIA)?:
—ANTIGONEIA: (**1**) c. 168 BC Liv. xliv 32. 8; *RE* (5) (Tataki, *Macedonians* p. 65 no. 5) (Lat. Creon)

Κρηθεύς
SCYTHIA MINOR:
—KALLATIS: (**1**) s. iv BC *RE* Supplbd. 4 (-); Berve 450; (**2**) iii/ii BC *ISM* III 161 (f. *Δαμάτριος*)

Κρήθων
MACEDONIA?: (**1**) ?i BC *GP* 8 with comm. (fict.)

Κρήσκης
MACEDONIA (MYGDONIA):
—THESSALONIKE: (**1**) imp. *Tekmeria* 7 (2002) p. 92 no. 3
MACEDONIA (SINTIKE):
—PARTHIKOPOLIS: (**2**) ii AD *IGB* IV 2279, 1
SCYTHIA MINOR:
—TOMIS: (**3**) ii AD *ISM* II 17, 3 (s. *Κάθιος*); (**4**) ii-iii AD ib. 19 b, 6 (*Κρήσ*[*κης*])
——(Hopletes): (**5**) iii AD ib. 254 ([*Κρή*]*σκεντο*[*ς*] (gen.): f. *Διονύσιος*)
—TOMIS?: (**6**) ii AD ib. V 128, 4 (*CCET* IV 52) (f. *Μάμα*)
THRACE:
—STRATOPARA: (**7**) 202 AD *IGB* III 1690 b, 35 (and Thrace Pizos: f. *Ἔπτενις*)

Κρητικός
MACEDONIA (MYGDONIA):
—THESSALONIKE: (**1**) ii AD *IG* X (2) (1) 424 (s. *Διογένης*)

Κρητίνης
CIMMERIAN BOSPOROS:
—TEMRYUK (MOD.): (**1**) 284-245 BC *CIRB* 1036, 4
TAURIS:
—CHERSONESOS: (**2**) s. v BC *SEG* XL 612. 16; *DGVE* 1996-7, p. 109 fig. 1, 3b (*SEG* XLIX 1031. 2 (ostraka)) (*Κρε͂τίνε͂*[*ς*]—fig. 1: s. *Μῦς*)

Κρίθων
CIMMERIAN BOSPOROS:
—GORGIPPIA: (**1**) f. iii BC *CIRB* 1137 A II, 17 (s. *Ἡρογείτων*)
MACEDONIA (MYGDONIA):
—KALINDOIA: (**2**) c. 322 BC Hatzopoulos, *MI* 2 p. 84 no. 62, 23 (f. *Κερτίμμας*); (**3**) c. 316 BC

ib. l. 30 (f. *Γυδίας*); **(4)** c. 312 BC ib. l. 34 (*Κρ[ίθων]*?: f. *Νικάνωρ*); **(5)** f. ii BC ib. p. 88 no. 67 Index

Κρινίας
MACEDONIA (MYGDONIA):
—KALINDOIA: **(1)** 68-98 AD *SEG* XLII 580, 9 (s. *Φιλώτας*)

Κρινομένης
THRACE:
—APOLLONIA-SOZOPOLIS: **(1)** s. iv BC *IGB* I² 459 (s. *Οἰνοπίδης*)
—APOLLONIA-SOZOPOLIS?: **(2)** iv/iii BC *VDI* 2002 (4), p. 69 ([*Κρι*]*νομέ*[*νης*]?, [*Δει*]*νομέ*[*νης*]?: f. *Ἀπολ—*)

Κρινώ
MACEDONIA (BOTTIAIA):
—AIGAI: **(1)** s. iv BC *SEG* XXXV 787 (d. *Ἄδυμος*)
THRACE:
—BEROE-AUGUSTA TRAIANA: **(2)** ?i AD *IGB* III 1594 bis (*Κρει-*)

Κρίνων
MACEDONIA?: **(1)** 218 BC Plb. v 15-16; *RE* (-)

Κρισπιανός
MACEDONIA (ELIMEIA):
—AIANE: **(1)** f. iii AD *EAM* 25 (s. *Ἀδαῖος*)

Κρισπῖνα
MACEDONIA (BOTTIAIA):
—BEROIA*: **(1)** 195 AD *ILeukopetra* 43, 6 (Tataki 772) (freed.)
MACEDONIA (ELIMEIA):
—KOZANI (MOD.)?: **(2)** ii AD *EAM* 54 a (*-πεί-*: d. *Κρίσπος*, *Κλεοπάτρα*)
MACEDONIA (EORDAIA):
—KELLE?: **(3)** s. ii AD ib. 125, 1 (*-πεί-*: m. *Ἀλκιμάχη*, *Ἀντωνῖνος*)
THRACE:
—BYZANTION: **(4)** s. i AD *IByz* 33, 7 (*-πεί-*: d. *Αἰσχύλος*)

Κρισπίνιος
MACEDONIA (BOTTIAIA):
—BEROIA: **(1)** 309 or 311 AD *ILeukopetra* 116, 9 (Tataki 773) (*Κ. ὁ καὶ Ἰνάχιος*)

Κρισπῖνος
MACEDONIA (BOTTIAIA):
—BEROIA: **(1)** iii AD *IBer* 400, 1 (*GVI* 107; Tataki 774)
MACEDONIA (PAIONIA):
—KAVADARCI (MOD.): **(2)** 234 or 351 AD *Sp.* 98 (1941-8) p. 54 no. 109; cf. *SEG* XLIV s.v. 561 (date) (*-πεί-*: s. *Προ—*)
MACEDONIA (SINTIKE):
—PARTHIKOPOLIS: **(3)** vi AD Beševliev 242

Κρίσπος
MACEDONIA (EDONIS):
—PHILIPPOI: **(1)** ii-iii AD *SEG* XXXVI 632 (Pilhofer 159)
MACEDONIA (ELIMEIA):
—AIANE (TERRIT.): **(2)** ?iii AD *EAM* 24 b (*Ἀμύντας ὁ καὶ Κ.*: s. *Ἀμύντας*)
—KOZANI (MOD.)?: **(3)** ii AD ib. 54 a (f. *Κρισπῖνα*)
MACEDONIA (LYNKESTIS):
—HERAKLEIA: **(4)** i AD *IG* X (2) (2) 75, 22 (f. *Ἀλφίδιος*)
MACEDONIA (MYGDONIA):
—THESSALONIKE: **(5)** i-ii AD ib. X (2) (1) 243 I, 9 (I f. *Κρίσπος* II *ὁ καὶ Σύρος*); **(6)** ~ ib. l. 9 (*Κ. ὁ καὶ Σύρος*: II s. *Κρίσπος* I); **(7)** ii-iii AD Nalpantis, *Anaskaphi* p. 111 no. BE 117 (threptos)
—THESSALONIKE?: **(8)** ii/iii AD *IG* X (2) (1) 853, 2 (*Κρεί-*)

MACEDONIA (PAIONIA): **(9)** 227 AD *Sp.* 98 (1941-8) p. 202 no. 400
MACEDONIA (SINTIKE):
—PARTHIKOPOLIS: **(10)** ii AD *IGB* IV 2273 (f. *Πυρούσαλα*); **(11)** 158 AD ib. 2263, 15 (s. *Τόσκος*)
THRACE:
—GLAVA PANEGA (MOD.): **(12)** ii-iii AD ib. II 556 (f. *Μουκάτραλις*)
—PERINTHOS-HERAKLEIA: **(13)** ii-iii AD *IPerinth* 92 (s. *Παπίας*)

Κρίτα
THRACE:
—TYRODIZA-TIRISTASIS: **(1)** hell.? Dumont–Homolle 91b (d. *Δάϊππος*)

Κριτίας
THRACE:
—PERINTHOS-HERAKLEIA?: **(1)** iv BC Hp., *Epid.* v 57

Κριτόβουλος
MACEDONIA (CHALKIDIKE):
—TORONE: **(1)** 479 BC Hdt. viii 127; *RE* Supplbd. 6 (2) (Tataki, *Macedonians* p. 191 no. 9)
SCYTHIA MINOR:
—KALLATIS: **(2)** s. iii BC *ISM* III 35 A, 34 (s. *Πύρσος*)
SKYTHIA:
—OLBIA-BORYSTHENES: **(3)** iv-iii BC *BE* 1990, no. 508 = Chuistova, *AIB* p. 65 (weight) (*Κριτόβου(λος)*) ?= (*4*); **(4)** iii BC *Arkheologiia* (Kiev) 39 (1982) p. 31 (vase) (*Κριτόβο(υλος)*) ?= (*3*)
TAURIS:
—CHERSONESOS: **(5)** imp. *IOSPE* I² 434, 5, 7

Κριτόλαος
MACEDONIA (BOTTIAIA):
—PELLA: **(1)** c. 250-225 BC Akamatis, *Amph. Pellas* pp. 38-9 nos. PAR37-8 (amph.); pp. 19-20 (date) (*SEG* L 613)
MACEDONIA (CHALKIDIKE):
—POTIDAIA-KASSANDREIA: **(2)** 276 BC *IDidyma* 428, 7 (Tataki, *Macedonians* p. 92 no. 59)

Κρίτος
SKYTHIA:
—OLBIA-BORYSTHENES: **(1)** iii BC *IOSPE* I² 201 II, 17 (s. *Νικήρατος*)

Κριτόφημος
MACEDONIA (EDONIS):
—PHILIPPOI: **(1)** hell. *Suda M* 228 (f. *Μαρσύας*)

Κρίτων
MACEDONIA (BOTTIAIA):
—BEROIA: **(1)** ii-i BC *IBer* 31, 3 (s. *Εὐτυχίδης*); **(2)** ii AD ib. 306 (Tataki 775)
MACEDONIA (CHALKIDIKE):
—POTIDAIA-KASSANDREIA: **(3)** a. 316 BC *IG* IV (1)² 94 b, 42 (Perlman, *City and Sanctuary* E.1 with p. 78 (date); Tataki, *Macedonians* p. 92 no. 60) (f. *Τιμοσθένης*)
MACEDONIA (EDONIS):
—PHILIPPOI (TERRIT.)?: **(4)** ii BC *SEG* XLV 775 (vase) (Pilhofer 629)
MACEDONIA (MYGDONIA):
—KALINDOIA: **(5)** 68-98 AD *SEG* XLII 580, 5, 12 (f. *Χαιροφάνης*)
—ORAIOKASTRO (MOD.): **(6)** v-iv BC ib. XLIX 750 (s. *Ἕσπερος*)
MACEDONIA (PIERIA): **(7)** ?ii AD *FGrH* 277 (*RE* (5)); *Suda K* 2453 (Tataki, *Macedonians* p. 168 no. 3)
SKYTHIA:
—OLBIA-BORYSTHENES: **(8)** s. iv BC *SEG* L 702 IV, 3 (<*Σ*>*κρίτων*)

TAURIS:
—CHERSONESOS: **(9)** iv BC Solomonik, *GAKh* 495 (vase) (*Κρίτω*[*ν*])
THRACE:
—BYZANTION:
——(Rhegion?): **(10)** i BC *IByz* 151 (s. *Ἀπολλώνιος*)
—ODESSOS: **(11)** ii-iii AD *IGB* I² 107 bis (s. *Διονύσιος*); **(12)** 215 AD ib. 47 a, 11 (*Αὐρ. Κ.*: s. *Φιλῖνος*)
—PERINTHOS-HERAKLEIA:
——(Akarnanes): **(13)** iii-ii BC *IPerinth* 61, 9 (*Κρί*<*σ*>*των*, *(Ἀ)ρίστων*?: f. *Ζώπυρος*)
—STRYME?: **(14)** m. iv BC *IThrakAig* E161 (s. *Ἀντιπατρίδης*)

Κρόκος
MACEDONIA (PAIONIA):
—STOBOI: **(1)** c. 165 AD *JÖAI* 15 (1912) p. 52 no. 20 (*Studies Stobi* 1 p. 164) (*Λ. Κορν.* [*Μου*]*νδικιανὸς*? *Κ.*)

Κρονίδης
THRACE:
—PHILIPPOPOLIS-TRIMONTIUM: **(1)** ii AD *IGB* III 1005 (f. *Τιούτα*)

Κρόνιος
TAURIS:
—CHERSONESOS: **(1)** iii BC Solomonik, *NEPKh* 174 (f. *Ἱερώ*)

Κρονίων
MACEDONIA: **(1)** i AD *PMich* 303, 1 (s. *Μάρων*: katoikos)
THRACE:
—MARONEIA: **(2)** iii AD *IThrakAig* E396, 1 (*Αὐρ. Κ.*: s. *Ἔζβενις*, f. *Ῥόδη*, *Σαβῖνα*)
—PHILIPPOPOLIS-TRIMONTIUM: **(3)** c. 303 AD *Anal. Boll.* 31 (1912) p. 192

Κροῦσπις
MACEDONIA (ODOMANTIKE):
—GAZOROS (TERRIT.): **(1)** ii AD *SEG* L 568 (*Κρούσπιος* (gen.): f. *Βαστεκίλας*)

Κρωκίνας
MACEDONIA (PIERIS):
—PHAGRES: **(1)** f. iv BC Pikoulas, *Chora* p. 113 no. 1 (Tataki, *Macedonians* p. 162 no. 1); cf. *SEG* XLVIII 797 (f. *Σωσικράτης*)

Κτέατος
CIMMERIAN BOSPOROS:
—HERMONASSA: **(1)** iv BC *CIRB* 1056 II, 14 (s. *Κράτης*)

Κτημένη
THRACE:
—BYZANTION?: **(1)** i-ii AD *IByz* 341 (d. *Ματρᾶς*)

Κτησαμενός
CIMMERIAN BOSPOROS:
—PANTIKAPAION: **(1)** f. i AD *CIRB* 302 (*Ἀνθεστήριος ὁ καὶ Κ.*)

Κτησίας
CIMMERIAN BOSPOROS:
—GORGIPPIA: **(1)** f. iii BC ib. 1137 B I, 26 (f. *Δείναρχος*)
MACEDONIA (CHALKIDIKE):
—OLYNTHOS: **(2)** ?352 BC *SEG* XXXVIII 637, 9 (f. *Ἀριστοτέλης*)
TAURIS:
—CHERSONESOS: **(3)** iv-iii BC Solomonik, *GAKh* 1069 (vase) (*Κτησί*[*ας*]); **(4)** iii-ii BC *IOSPE* I² 480 (s. *Ἡράκλεος*); **(5)** f. iii BC ib. 418 (*Κτη*[*σίας*]?: f. *Ἀγασικλῆς*)
—KERKINITIS: **(6)** iii BC Solomonik, *GChKh* 462 (vase) (*Κτη(σίας)*—ed., *Κτή(σων)*?)
THRACE:
—BIZONE: **(7)** iii/ii BC *IIasos* 408, 11; cf. *RPh* 1959, p. 179 (name) ([*Κ*]*τησίου*—ed., [*Ζ*]*ησίου*—Robert: s. *Ἀπολλώνιος*)
THRACE?: **(8)** 316-309 BC *IG* II² 1956, 19; *Ancient Macedonia* 5 p. 445 with n. 10 (date) (*FRA* 2550)

Κτησίβιος
THRACE:
—MARONEIA: (1) imp. Dumont–Homolle 110b 16 (*IThrakAig* E293) (f. *Διονύσιος*)

Κτησικράτης
CIMMERIAN BOSPOROS:
—PANTIKAPAION: (1) iii BC *CIRB* 110, 6 (*Κτησικρ[άτης]*: f. —*νας*)
MACEDONIA (EDONIS):
—AMPHIPOLIS?: (2) iv BC *SEG* XLVII 887 (*Κτησικράτ[ης]*: f. *Διονυσιφάνης*)

Κτησῖνος
MACEDONIA (BOTTIAIA):
—MIEZA: (1) ii BC ib. XLIII 415

Κτησιφῶν
MACEDONIA (ODOMANTIKE):
—SIRRHA: (1) ii-iii AD Dimitsas 818 (Kaphtantzis 20)

Κτησώ
MACEDONIA (CHALKIDIKE):
—OLYNTHOS?: (1) f. iii BC *IG* XII (8) 116 (Tataki, *Macedonians* p. 139 no. 78) (d. *Ἐπιχάρης*)
THRACE: (2) iv BC *Ag.* XVII 508 (*FRA* 2551) (*[Κ]τησ[ώ]?*)

Κτήσων
MACEDONIA (CHALKIDIKE):
—STOLOS?: (1) ?351 BC *SEG* XXXVIII 672, 3, 6; 673, 5 (f. *Νίκων*) ?= (*2*); (2) ~ ib. 672, 9 (f. *Διονύσιος*) ?= (*1*); (3) ?350 BC ib. 671, 10; XL 553, 7 (f. *Στράτων*)
MACEDONIA (DERRIOPOS):
—STUBERRA: (4) 74 AD *IG* X (2) (2) 325, 23 (s. *Εὐβουλίδης*)
THRACE: (5) iv-iii BC ib. II² 8913 (*FRA* 2552) (*Κτήσω[ν]*)

Κτῆτος
THRACE:
—BYZANTION (TERRIT.): (1) imp. Unp. (Sayar) (*Φιλίσκος ὁ καὶ Κ.*: s. *Ἀπολλώνιος*)

Κτολέμμας
MACEDONIA (PIERIA):
—PYDNA: (1) iv BC *GRBS* 43 (2002-3) p. 119 no. 5, 6 (*Κτολέμμα(ς)*)

Κυδίας
MACEDONIA (CHALKIDIKE):
—POTIDAIA-KASSANDREIA: (1) c. 305-297 BC Hatzopoulos, *Donation* p. 23, 1; *SEG* XLVII 940, 1
MACEDONIA (MYGDONIA):
—KALINDOIA: (2) c. 319 BC Hatzopoulos, *MI* 2 p. 84 no. 62, 27 (*Κυδ[ίας]?*: f. *Ἀμερίας*)
THRACE:
—NOVAE*: (3) 196 AD *IGLNovae* 57 bis b II, 12 (Lat. Ael. Cydias)

Κυδρᾶς
THRACE:
—ABDERA: (1) iii BC *BCH* 37 (1913) p. 118 no. 37 (*IThrakAig* E50)

Κυδρώ
MACEDONIA (CHALKIDIKE):
—OLYNTHOS: (1) f. iv BC *SEG* XXIX 625

Κύδων
THRACE:
—BYZANTION: (1) 409-378 BC *IG* II² 41, 23; X., *HG* i 3. 18 (*FRA* 1396)

Κυζίκης
THRACE:
—BISANTHE-PANION: (1) iv-vi AD *AD* 49-50 (1994-5) Mel. p. 315 no. 140 (*Πέτρος ὁ καὶ Κ.*)

Κυζίκιος
SCYTHIA MINOR:
—TOMIS: (1) ii-iii AD *ISM* II 366 (*GVI* 1035) (*Ἑρμογένης ὁ καὶ Κ.*)
THRACE:
—NOVAE: (2) ii/iii AD *IGB* V 5262, 10 (biling.) (*SEG* XLVII 1153) (f. *Βασιλεύς*)

Κύθης?
MACEDONIA (EDONIS):
—AMPHIPOLIS: (1) ii-iii AD *Thrakika* 13 (1940) p. 27 *N* + *Epigraphica* 37 (1975) pp. 29-30 (*Κύθο(υ)* (gen.))

Κύκνος
MACEDONIA (BISALTIA):
—TRAGILOS: (1) s. iv BC *AD* 23 (1968) Chron. p. 358 with pl. 306 *a*; *BE* 1970, no. 377 (name) (*[Κ]ύκνος*: f. *Φιλιτώ*)

Κυλίανις
CIMMERIAN BOSPOROS:
—MYRMEKION: (1) iv BC *SEG* XLVIII 1005 (*Κυ(λ)ίανις*: s. *Ἄττης*)
—PANTIKAPAION: (2) iv BC *CIRB* 162; cf. KW 22 (f. *Ἀπολλώνιος*)

Κύλλις
MACEDONIA (PIERIA):
—PYDNA: (1) iv BC *GRBS* 43 (2002-3) p. 115 no. 3, 4 (*Κύλλις?*)

Κύνα
CIMMERIAN BOSPOROS:
—PANTIKAPAION: (1) inc. *AA* 1909, p. 155 (ring) (kale)

Κύναγος
MACEDONIA: (1) iii BC *OGIS* 235 II; 236 (Tataki, *Macedonians* p. 351 no. 102) (f. *Ζεῦξις*)

Κυνάριον
MACEDONIA (BOTTIAIA):
—PELLA: (1) m. ii BC Akamatis, *Pilines mitres* p. 292 (het.?/fict.)

Κύνας
MACEDONIA (EDONIS):
—AMPHIPOLIS: (1) ii-iii AD *Thrakika* 13 (1940) p. 27 *Ξ* (*Κύνα* (gen.))

Κυνδαίας
SCYTHIA MINOR:
—AXIOPOLIS*: (1) f. iv AD Barnea 71 (Popescu, *IGL* 194); *Anal. Boll.* 31 (1912) p. 259

Κυνηγίς
THRACE:
—VARIANA (NR.): (1) 161-168 AD *Romanizmăt* II 245 (Lat. Iulia Cynegis)

Κυνίσκος
MACEDONIA (CHALKIDIKE):
—POTIDAIA-KASSANDREIA: (1) iv/iii BC *PCG* 7 p. 561 nos. 1-2 (Tataki, *Macedonians* p. 92 no. 61) (f. *Ποσείδιππος*)
THRACE:
—PERINTHOS-HERAKLEIA: (2) iv BC Hp., *Epid.* iv 53; vi 7. 10

Κυννάνα
MACEDONIA: (1) c. 357-322 BC *RE* Supplbd. 6 s.v. Kynna (-); Berve 456; cf. Hoffmann, *Makedonen* p. 220; Krahe, *Altillyr. Personnamen* p. 33 (name) (Tataki, *Macedonians* p. 351 no. 103) (*Κυννάνη, Κυνάνη, Κύννα*—var.: d. *Φίλιππος* II, *Αὐδᾶτα ὕστερον Εὐρυδίκη* (Illyria), m. *Ἀδέα ὕστερον Εὐρυδίκα*)
MACEDONIA (BOTTIAIA):
—BEROIA: (2) iii BC *IBer* 23, 1 (Tataki 781) (*[Κ]υννάνα*: d. *Ἐπιγένης*); (3) ~ *IBer* 391 (Tataki 780) (m. *Ἀδέα*)

Κυννάνη
MACEDONIA (MYGDONIA):
—HERAKLEIA: (1) hell. Hatzopoulos, *MI* 1 p. 211 (unp.)

Κύπειρος
MACEDONIA (EDONIS):
—PHILIPPOI: (1) ii/iii AD *CIL* III 633 III c, 8 (Pilhofer 165); *AM* 33 (1908) p. 41 (name); *CRAI* 1923, p. 277 (date) (Lat. Cassius Cypaerus)

Κυπριανός
MACEDONIA (BOTTIAIA):
—EDESSA: (1) v-vi AD Feissel, *RICM* 15, 1
MACEDONIA (EDONIS):
—AMPHIPOLIS (TERRIT.)?: (2) ?vi AD ib. 220 (Pilhofer 591)
THRACE:
—EMPORION THOUIDAI: (3) v-vi AD Beševliev 187; *IGB* V 5634 (locn.)

Κυπρόθεμις
THRACE:
—LYSIMACHEIA: (1) hell. Kaphtantzis 629 (f. *Μητρόδωρος*)

Κυράθων
CIMMERIAN BOSPOROS:
—GORGIPPIA: (1) ii/iii AD *CIRB* 1179, 45 (*[Κ]υράθων*)
—PANTIKAPAION: (2) hell.-imp. *CIG* 8556 c (lead); (3) i-ii AD *CIRB* 618 (*[Κυρ]άθων*: I f. *Κυράθων* II); (4) ~ ib. (*Κυράθω[ν]*: II s. *Κυράθων* I); (5) i/ii AD ib. 617 (I f. *Κυράθων* II); (6) ~ ib. (II s. *Κυράθων* I); (7) ii AD ib. 690 (*[Κυρ]άθων?*: s. *Σωσθένης*, f. *Χοῖδρα*)
SKYTHIA:
—TANAIS: (8) f. ii AD ib. 1266, 9
TAURIS:
—CHERSONESOS: (9) ii AD *IOSPE* I² 455 (s. *Ἀπελλᾶς, Κιλία*); (10) ~ ib. (f. *Ἀπελλᾶς*)

Κυρᾶς
SCYTHIA MINOR:
—KALLATIS: (1) v-vi AD Barnea 53-4 (Popescu, *IGL* 98-99) (*Κυρᾶδος* (gen.): f. *Ἰωάννης*)

Κυρήνιος
MACEDONIA (BOTTIAIA):
—EDESSA: (1) ?ii AD *SEG* XII 346 (Tataki, *Edessa* 201) (*Μᾶρκος ὁ καὶ Κ.*: s. *Δημήτριος*)
SCYTHIA MINOR:
—TOMIS: (2) ii-iii AD *ISM* II 31 II, 9 (f. *Θεόδωρος*)
TAURIS:
—CHERSONESOS: (3) 174 AD *SEG* XLV 985 A, 35 (s. *Λυσίμαχος*)
THRACE:
—PERINTHOS-HERAKLEIA: (4) ii AD *IPerinth* 101 (*Ἀρτεμίδωρος ὁ καὶ Κ.*: s. *Ἀρτεμίδωρος*, f. *Νάρκισσος, Παῦλα*)

Κυρία
CIMMERIAN BOSPOROS:
—PANTIKAPAION: (1) i BC/i AD *CIRB* 315; cf. KW pl. 55 no. 747; (2) i-ii AD *MIA* 178 (1971) p. 141 (*Κυρ̣ία* (n. pr.?))
THRACE:
—BEROE-AUGUSTA TRAIANA: (3) c. 320-324 AD *Anal. Boll.* 31 (1912) p. 198; cf. p. 208
—SERDICA: (4) 117-138 AD *IGB* IV 1925 c, 9

Κυρίαινα
CIMMERIAN BOSPOROS:
—PANTIKAPAION: (1) i BC/i AD *CIRB* 310; cf. KW pl. 25 no. 368 (m. *Ἀρισταγόρας*); (2) 9 BC-7 AD *CIRB* 31, 5

Κυριακή
CIMMERIAN BOSPOROS:
—PANTIKAPAION: (1) v-vi AD *IAK* 10 (1904) p. 89 no. 104 (Κυρ(ι)ακή)
THRACE:
—BEROE-AUGUSTA TRAIANA: (2) c. 320 AD *Anal. Boll.* 31 (1912) p. 208; cf. p. 198
—HADRIANOPOLIS (NR.): (3) imp. *Thrakika* 16 (1941) p. 85
—MARONEIA: (4) v AD Meïmaris–Bakirtzis 8 (*SEG* XLIV 595; *IThrakAig* E352) (Κυρ(ι)ακή)
—PERINTHOS-HERAKLEIA: (5) iii AD *IPerinth* 173 (Αὐρ. Κ.)
—RHAIDESTOS: (6) iv-vi AD *Araşt. Sonuçları Topl.* 1996 (1), p. 108

Κυριακός
MACEDONIA (EDONIS):
—PHILIPPOI: (1) iv AD Feissel, *RICM* 231, 2 (Pilhofer 71) (Αὐρ. Κ.); (2) iv-v AD Feissel, *RICM* 243 (Pilhofer 274)
MACEDONIA (MYGDONIA):
—THESSALONIKE?: (3) v-vi AD *IG* X (2) (1) 783 (Feissel, *RICM* 174)
THRACE:
—APROI: (4) iv-v AD Unp. (Sayar) (s. Μαρκιανός)
—BISANTHE-PANION: (5) iii-v AD *AD* 49-50 (1994-5) Mel. p. 308 no. 133
—BYZANTION*: (6) s. iii AD *Anal. Boll.* 31 (1912) p. 175 (bp.)
—ODESSOS: (7) vi AD Beševliev 140
—SALYMBRIA: (8) iv-v AD *BCH* 36 (1912) p. 638 no. 95 (*AD* 53 (1998) Mel. p. 460 no. 199) (f. Δόμνα: doctor)

Κυριαμένη
THRACE:
—BOURDAPA: (1) ii-iii AD *IGB* III 1339 (Κυριαμένη)

Κυριανή
THRACE:
—BEROE-AUGUSTA TRAIANA: (1) c. 320-324 AD *Anal. Boll.* 31 (1912) p. 198; p. 208 (Κυριενή—p. 208)

Κυριλάς
THRACE:
—PERINTHOS-HERAKLEIA: (1) iii AD *IPerinth* 126 (Αὐρ. Κυριλάδι (dat.): d. Σωζομενός)

Κύριλλα
MACEDONIA (BOTTIAIA):
—BEROIA?: (1) f. iii AD *IBer* 399, 5 (*GVI* 672; Tataki 782) (?d. Κλαυδιανός)
MACEDONIA (MYGDONIA):
—THESSALONIKE: (2) ii AD *IG* X (2) (1) 299, 3 (Κλεονίκη (ἡ) καὶ Κύριλ(λ)α)
SCYTHIA MINOR:
—NOVIODUNUM (NR.): (3) iv AD *ISM* V 250, 11 (Lat. Cyrilla: d. Bona)
—TOMIS: (4) ii AD ib. II 380, 2 (*GVI* 668); (5) ii-iii AD *ISM* II 255, 6 (d. Φιλοκλῆς)
THRACE:
—BISANTHE-PANION: (6) v-vi AD *AD* 49-50 (1994-5) Mel. p. 321 no. 147
—BYZANTION: (7) 293 AD *Cod. Just.* viii 8.2; cf. *Klio* 58 (1976) p. 83 (Lat. Cyrilla)

Κύριλλος
MACEDONIA (BOTTIAIA):
—BEROIA: (1) vi AD *IBer* 429, 3 (Κύριλ[λος]?)
SCYTHIA MINOR:
—AXIOPOLIS*: (2) f. iv AD Barnea 71 (Popescu, *IGL* 194); *Anal. Boll.* 31 (1912) p. 259
—TOMIS: (3) ii-iii AD *ISM* II 364 (s. Βήσσιος Φαβιανός)
THRACE:
—PERINTHOS-HERAKLEIA: (4) iii-iv AD *IPerinth* 312 (Αὐρ. Κ.)

Κυριλλώ
THRACE:
—BYZANTION (TERRIT.)?: (1) iii AD *IByz* 383 (— ἡ καὶ Κ.: threpte)

Κυρίχα
TAURIS:
—CHERSONESOS: (1) i BC-i AD *IOSPE* I^{2} 517 (d. Μυ—)

Κυρίχη
MACEDONIA (PIERIA):
—DION: (1) f. ii AD Oikonomos 46; *Essays Laourdas* p. 112 (locn.); cf. Spiliopoulou-Donderer, *KGN* p. 192 no. D8 (date) (m. Παῦλα)

Κύρνιος
MACEDONIA (EDONIS):
—PHILIPPOI: (1) iii BC *Ét. Thas.* 3 p. 319 no. 113 bis (Tataki, *Macedonians* p. 165 no. 20) (s. Μενεκλῆς)

Κῦρος
CIMMERIAN BOSPOROS:
—PANTIKAPAION: (1) c. 390-380 BC *SEG* L 710 A (vase) (fict.?)

Κυρσᾶς
THRACE:
—APOLLONIA-SOZOPOLIS: (1) iii BC *IGB* I^{2} 458, 1, 4 (Κυρσᾶ (gen.): s. Πολυάναξ); (2) ~ ib. l. 5 (s. Πολυάναξ)
—ODESSOS: (3) c. 225-200 BC *SNG BM Black Sea* 289; Price, *Alexander* 1175-6; *AMNG* I (2) 2214-5 (coin) (Κυρσᾶ (gen.))

Κυρώνας
SCYTHIA MINOR:
—TOMIS: (1) ii-iii AD *ISM* II 468, 11 (s. Κάσιος)

Κύτων
MACEDONIA (BOTTIAIA):
—BEROIA: (1) 120 BC *IBer* 134, 19 (f. Ἰόλαος)

Κώβιος
MACEDONIA (MYGDONIA):
—THESSALONIKE*: (1) iii AD *SEG* XLIV 557

Κῶβος
THRACE:
—TRERES: (1) viii/vii BC Str. 61 (king/fict.?)

Κώδων
MACEDONIA (PIERIS):
—GALEPSOS: (1) hell. *SEG* XXXII 297 (Tataki, *Macedonians* p. 110 no. 3; *FRA* 1435) (f. Ἀπολλωνικέτης)

Κῶκος
THRACE?: (1) ?ii AD Beševliev, *EP* 25 (*SEG* XV 472) (f. Αὐλούζενις)

Κωλούμβας
SCYTHIA MINOR:
—TOMIS: (1) ?vi AD Barnea 25 (Popescu, *IGL* 51) (-υβας)

Κωλώτης
THRACE:
—APOLLONIA-SOZOPOLIS: (1) v/iv BC Lanz sale (20th Nov. 1995) 115 (Gorny–Mosch sale (17.x.2001) 4051 (coin)) ([Κ]ωλώτης); (2) ~ *IGB* I^{2} 442 (s. Λεωδάμας); (3) iv BC *BM-NBurgas* 4 (2002) p. 123 no. 16 (Κωλώτεω (gen.): s. Ἀθηναγόρης)

Κωμαῖος
SKYTHIA:
—OLBIA-BORYSTHENES: (1) iii BC Dubois, *IGDOlbia* 109, 4 (*SEG* XXXVII 673) ([Κ]ωμαῖος)
THRACE:
—ABDERA: (2) ?375 BC *IG* II^{2} 77, 5, 11 + Add. p. 658 (s. Θεόδωρος)
—STRYME?: (3) f. iv BC *IThrakAig* E134 (f. Ἀρίστας)

Κωμικός
THRACE:
—PERINTHOS-HERAKLEIA: (1) i AD *IPerinth* 49 A, 3 (Μ. Πομπή[ιος] [Κ]ωμικός: s. Κω—)

Κωμύλος
THRACE:
—APOLLONIA-SOZOPOLIS: (1) iv BC *SNG BM Black Sea* 173; *Rev. Suisse num.* 14 (1908) pp. 141-2 (coin) (Κωμύ(λος)?)

Κωνσταντία
SCYTHIA MINOR:
—TOMIS: (1) v-vi AD Barnea 18, 9 (Popescu, *IGL* 37) (Κοσταντζία: m. Ῥωμανά)
THRACE:
—MESAMBRIA: (2) vi AD Beševliev 162 (Κοσστα[ντί]α)
—PHILIPPOPOLIS-TRIMONTIUM (TERRIT.): (3) v-vi AD ib. 219 (Κωσταζία)

Κωνσταντῖνος
MACEDONIA (MYGDONIA):
—THESSALONIKE: (1) v-vi AD *IG* X (2) (1) 336, 6 (Feissel, *RICM* 154) (Κοσ-)
THRACE: (2) 531-538 AD *PLRE* III (3)
—APOLLONIA-SOZOPOLIS: (3) v-vi AD Beševliev 178 (Κοσταν-)
—ODESSOS: (4) vi AD ib. 98, 4 (s. Εὐγένιος)

Κωνστάντιος
CIMMERIAN BOSPOROS:
—PANTIKAPAION: (1) iii-iv AD *CIRB* 738 (Κ(ω)νστ[άντι]ος?)
MACEDONIA (EDONIS):
—PHILIPPOI: (2) iv-vi AD Feissel, *RICM* 236 (Pilhofer 102)

Κωνστάντις
MACEDONIA (MYGDONIA):
—THESSALONIKE*: (1) f. iii AD *IG* X (2) (1) 190, 8; 191, 10 (Αὐρηλιανὸς Κωστάντις: freed.?)

Κώνωψ
MACEDONIA (BOTTIAIA):
—BEROIA: (1) ii-iii AD *IBer* 129, 3 (Κό-: ?s. Ἀντιγόνα)

Κώραβος
MACEDONIA (EDONIS):
—AMPHIPOLIS (TERRIT.): (1) iv BC *SEG* I 291 (f. Ἑκαταίη)

Κώρυκος
SCYTHIA MINOR:
—ISTROS: (1) vi AD Popescu, *IGL* 151 (amph.)

Κωτίς
MACEDONIA (BOTTIAIA):
—SKYDRA*: (1) 105 AD *SEG* XVII 317, 17 (slave?)

Λ

Λάαγος
MACEDONIA (EORDAIA): **(1)** iv BC *RE* (1); Call. fr. 734 with n.; *Milet* VI (1) 244; *Suppl. Hell.* 922, 9; Austin–Bastianini, *Posidipp.* 88 (locn.); cf. Masson, *OGS* 3 p. 151 (Tataki, *Macedonians* p. 199 no. 4) (*Λᾶγος*—var.: f. *Πτολεμαῖος* I *Σωτήρ*, *Μενέλαος*)
MACEDONIA?: **(2)** 244 BC *PSI* 388, 27 (s. *Εὐχάρης*)

Λαάνδριχος
MACEDONIA (EDONIS):
—AMPHIPOLIS: **(1)** a. 357 BC Hatzopoulos, *Actes Amphipolis* pp. 38-9 no. 7, 5, 12

Λάανδρος
MACEDONIA (BOTTIAIA):
—AIGAI: **(1)** s. iv BC *SEG* XXXV 780 (f. *Πάτων*)
—BEROIA: **(2)** ii BC *IBer* 179 (*Λάανδ[ρος]*: f. *Ὠφελίων*); **(3)** s. ii BC ib. 24, 5 (Tataki 783) (s. *Ὀλυμπιόδωρος*)
MACEDONIA (EDONIS):
—AMPHIPOLIS: **(4)** m. iv BC *SEG* XXXVI 589 (vase) (*Amphipolis* p. 118 fig. 90)
MACEDONIA (ELIMEIA):
—AIANE (TERRIT.): **(5)** c. 225-200 BC *SEG* XL 526, 1-2; cf. *BE* 1993, no. 361 (s. *Πάτυλλος*, f. *Σατύρα*)

Λάβαζος
SKYTHIA:
—OLBIA-BORYSTHENES: **(1)** f. ii AD *SEG* XLIII 506, 13 (s. *Ταόρδουνος*)

Λαβείων
THRACE:
—HADRIANOPOLIS (TERRIT.): **(1)** ii-iii AD *IGB* III 1819 (s. *Ἰοῦστος Κέλσος*)

Λάγγαρος
THRACE:
—AGRIANES: **(1)** s. iv BC *RE* (-); Berve 460 (king)

Λάγιος
TAURIS:
—CHERSONESOS: **(1)** inc. Solomonik, *GAKh* 1107 (vase) (*Λαγίωι* (dat.))

Λαγοῖος
TAURIS:
—CHERSONESOS: **(1)** iii BC *IOSPE* I^2 481 (s. *Παρμένων*)

Λαγόρας
THRACE:
—SALYMBRIA: **(1)** i BC-i AD Unp. (Sayar) (s. *Βοσπόριχος*)

Λαγορῖνος
TAURIS:
—CHERSONESOS: **(1)** iii BC Kats p. 101 no. 69 (amph.) (I f. *Λαγορῖνος* II); **(2)** c. 230-215 BC ib. pp. 101-2 no. 70 (amph.) (s. *Παρθενοκλῆς*); **(3)** c. 230-200 BC ib. p. 122 no. 23 (amph.); **(4)** c. 200-185 BC ib. p. 101 no. 69 (amph.) (II s. *Λαγορῖνος* I); **(5)** c. 120-88 BC *IOSPE* I^2 352, 56; 353, 7 (f. *Ἀγέλας*); **(6)** i AD ib. 482, 2 (*GVI* 767); cf. KW pl. 2 no. 49 (-*ρεῖ*-: f. *Ξάνθος*); **(7)** ii-iii AD *IOSPE* I^2 452 (-*ρεῖ*-: s. *Δαμοκλῆς*); **(8)** f. ii AD *SEG* XXVIII 631, 3 (*Λα[γορ]εῖνος*: f. —*ης*) ?= *(9)*; **(9)** 129 AD *IOSPE* I^2 359, 34 (-*ρεῖ*-: f. *Δαμοκλῆς*) ?= *(8)*

Λᾶγος
MACEDONIA: **(1)** iv/iii BC *RE* (2) (*PP* 14527) (s. *Πτολεμαῖος* I *Σωτήρ* (Eordaia), *Θαΐς* (Athens))
MACEDONIA (EDONIS):
—AMPHIPOLIS: **(2)** ii/iii AD *SEG* XXXV 713, 1, 4; cf. *BE* 1999, no. 377 (s. *Διονυσοφάνης*, *Φιλού*)
—AMPHIPOLIS?: **(3)** hell. *SEG* XLIII 373; Hatzopoulos, *MI* 1 p. 192 n. 9 (name) (*[Λ]ᾶγος*: f. *Γαιτέας*)

Λάγων
MACEDONIA (BOTTIAIA):
—EDESSA: **(1)** ii-iii AD Dimitsas 27 (Tataki, *Edessa* 180) (f. *Μακεδονία*)

Λαδόμα
MACEDONIA (BOTTIAIA):
—BEROIA: **(1)** ?ii/iii AD *ILeukopetra* 153, 1 (?m. (ad.) *Ἀρτεμισία*); **(2)** 203 AD ib. 47, 2 (Tataki 784) (d. *Ἀμύντας*, m. *Παράμονος*)

Λάδων
THRACE:
—PAUTALIA (TERRIT.): **(1)** ii-iii AD *IGB* IV 2126 (s. *Λοῦππος*)

Λάζαρος
TAURIS:
—CHERSONESOS: **(1)** v-vi AD *Arkheologiia* (Kiev) 1997 (1) p. 71

Λάζενος
CIMMERIAN BOSPOROS:
—PANTIKAPAION: **(1)** 275-278 AD *CIRB* 36, 25 (s. *Ἐν*—)

Λάζερις
THRACE:
—BEROE-AUGUSTA TRAIANA (NR.): **(1)** ii-iii AD *IGB* III 1621 (f. *Μουκάτραλις*)

Λαίνιλλα
THRACE:
—SALYMBRIA: **(1)** ii-iii AD *IByz* S 63 (*GVI* 910)

Λαιόνακος
CIMMERIAN BOSPOROS:
—PANTIKAPAION*: **(1)** 143 AD *CIRB* 710, 1 (*Φιλόφημος ὁ καὶ Λ.*: freed.)

Λάϊος
THRACE:
—BISANTHE-PANION: **(1)** i AD PM 1876 (s. *Σέξτος*)
—MESAMBRIA: **(2)** iii/ii BC *IGB* I^2 322 bis (s. *Βοιωτός*)

Λαΐς
MACEDONIA (BOTTIAIA):
—BEROIA: **(1)** 192 AD *ILeukopetra* 30, 1 (Tataki 53) (*Αἰλ. Λ.*)

Λαϊσθένης
SKYTHIA:
—TYRAS: **(1)** 181 AD *IOSPE* I^2 2, 23 (s. *Μοκκᾶς*)
—TYRAS (NR.): **(2)** iii AD *SEG* XL 641 (s. *Μοκκᾶς*)

Λαΐσμος
THRACE:
—BOURDAPA: **(1)** hell. ib. XXXIX 661 = XLI 608. 1 = XLVII 1094. 1 (*Ἄδημος*—1094: s. *Δηδηγνος*)

Λάϊχος
MACEDONIA: **(1)** iii BC *IG* II^2 9263 (Tataki, *Macedonians* p. 352 no. 4; *FRA* 3474) (s. *Φίλιππος*)

Λάκαινα
MACEDONIA (MYGDONIA):
—THESSALONIKE: **(1)** ii AD *IG* X (2) (1) 356, 1 (-*κε*-)

Λάκριτος
THRACE:
—PERINTHOS-HERAKLEIA:
——(Makedones): **(1)** iii-ii BC *IPerinth* 61, 3 (f. *Λαμέδων*)

Λάκων
MACEDONIA (MYGDONIA):
—KALINDOIA: **(1)** a. 98 AD *SEG* XLII 582, 17 (f. *Ἐρέννιος*)
—THESSALONIKE: **(2)** ii-iii AD *IG* X (2) (1) 361, 2 (*M. Ἐρένιος Λ.*: s. *M. Ἐρενία Θεοδότη*)
THRACE:
—LYSIMACHEIA: **(3)** iii-ii BC *PAE* 1912, p. 188 no. 126 = *Polemon* 4 (1949-50) pp. 89-90 no. 269 (f. *Σεύθης*)
—ODESSOS: **(4)** c. 100-72 BC Price, *Alexander* 1193-4 (coin) (*Λάκω(ν)*)

Λάλα
THRACE:
—BYZANTION: **(1)** ii BC *IByz* 262 (Fıratlı–Robert p. 74 no. 80) (d. *Τρύφων*)
—RHAIDESTOS: **(2)** i BC-i AD PM 182 d (d. *Παπίας*)

Λαλζόα
THRACE:
—PHILIPPOPOLIS-TRIMONTIUM (TERRIT.): **(1)** ii-iii AD *IGB* III 1326 (*Λ̣αλζόα*)

Λαλκία
MACEDONIA (LYNKESTIS):
—HERAKLEIA: **(1)** ii-iii AD *IG* X (2) (2) 60 (d. *Παράμονος*)

Λάλος
MACEDONIA (BOTTIAIA):
—BEROIA: **(1)** 133 AD *IBer* 326 (Tataki 786) (doctor); **(2)** ii/iii AD *IBer* 143 C, 21 (Tataki 1105) (*Πο. Λ.*)
MACEDONIA (PAIONIA):
—STOBOI*: **(3)** s. i AD *Arheološki Vestnik* 41 (1990) p. 579 (*AEp* 1990, no. 885); cf. Zgusta, *KP* 790.3 (name) (Lat. Lalo (dat.): slave?)

Λαμάγα
MACEDONIA (PIERIA):
—PYDNA: **(1)** f. ii BC *SEG* L 629 (d. *Εὔλαιος*, m. *Ὀλύμπιχος*)

Λάμαχος
CIMMERIAN BOSPOROS:
—PANTIKAPAION: **(1)** imp. *CIRB* 765 (*(Λ)άμαχος*: f. *Χόσιον*); **(2)** i AD ib. 390; cf. KW pl. 24 no. 349 (f. *Διονύσιος*); **(3)** ~ *CIRB* 522; cf. KW pl. 40 no. 594 (f. *Ὑψικράτης*); **(4)** ?i AD *CIRB* 557; **(5)** 82 AD ib. 76, 17 (*SEG* XVIII 310) (f. *Ἡδύβιος*)
MACEDONIA (PAIONIA): **(6)** f. iv BC *IG* II^2 10039 (*FRA* 5943)
TAURIS:
—CHERSONESOS: **(7)** m. i BC *IOSPE* I^2 347, 1 with Add. p. 519; 691, [2]? (*Λάμαχ[ος]*: s. *Δαμάτριος*); **(8)** s. i BC Const. Porph., *De admin. imp.* 53, 234 ff.; *Sov. Arkh.* 1987 (1) p. 48 (f. *Γυκία*); **(9)** ?114 AD *SEG* XLVIII 999, 40 (*M. Οὔλπ. Λ.*)

Λαμέδων
MACEDONIA (BOTTIAIA):
—BEROIA: **(1)** 223 BC *IBer* 4, 37 (f. *Βάλακρος*)
THRACE:
—PERINTHOS-HERAKLEIA:
——(Makedones): **(2)** iii-ii BC *IPerinth* 61, 3 (s. *Λάκριτος*)

Λαμίδιον
THRACE:
—AINOS: (1) imp. *IG* II^2 7979 a (*FRA* 256) (d. Μενεκράτης)

Λάμις
MACEDONIA (BOTTIAIA):
—BEROIA: (1) s. ii AD *IBer* 253 (Tataki 787)

Λαμπαδία
THRACE:
—BEROE-AUGUSTA TRAIANA: (1) c. 320-324 AD *Anal. Boll.* 31 (1912) p. 198; p. 208

Λαμπάδιος
MACEDONIA (EDONIS):
—AMPHIPOLIS: (1) f. iii AD ib. p. 170 (s. Κλᾶρος, f. Εὐσταθία)

Λαμπαδίων
SCYTHIA MINOR:
—KALLATIS: (1) 241-244 AD *ISM* III 74

Λάμπις
SCYTHIA MINOR:
—KALLATIS: (1) iii-ii BC ib. 162 (f. Ἀπολλώνιος)

Λαμπιτώ
THRACE:
—APOLLONIA-SOZOPOLIS: (1) iv BC *IGB* I^2 451 (d. Ἀπολλωνίδης)

Λάμπος
MACEDONIA (EDONIS):
—PHILIPPOI: (1) ?s. iv BC Moretti, *Olymp.* 498
THRACE:
—PAUTALIA: (2) ii AD *Syringes* 403 (*SB* 1808); Velkov 441 (Λάν-: f. Μουκιανός)

Λάμπρη
THRACE:
—APOLLONIA-SOZOPOLIS: (1) s. v BC *IGB* I^2 411

Λαμπρόμαχος
MACEDONIA (BOTTIAIA):
—BEROIA: (1) ii BC *Α΄ Panell. Synedr. Epigr.* p. 59 no. 6 (*SEG* XLIX 845) (f. Κλεόνικος)

Λάμπρος
MACEDONIA (LYNKESTIS)?: (1) s. ii AD *EAM* 156 ([Λάμ]προς?: s. Παράμονος)
MACEDONIA (PAIONIA): (2) c. 240 BC *PP* 2255 Add. (f. Πολέμων)

Λαμπροτάτη
THRACE:
—BEROE-AUGUSTA TRAIANA: (1) c. 320-324 AD *Anal. Boll.* 31 (1912) p. 198; p. 207

Λαμπρώ
MACEDONIA (EDONIS):
—AMPHIPOLIS: (1) i BC-i AD *SEG* XXVIII 536 (d. Θεόχαρις)

Λαμπυρίς
THRACE:
—STRYME (NR.): (1) m. iv BC ib. XXVII 336 (*IThrakAig* E155) (d. Πάγχαρμος)

Λάμπων
CIMMERIAN BOSPOROS:
—NYMPHAION: (1) f. iv BC *CIRB* 920
MACEDONIA (CHALKIDIKE):
—OLYNTHOS: (2) f. iii BC Austin–Bastianini, *Posidipp.* 95, 5; cf. *ZPE* 140 (2002) pp. 297-300 (ident.) (f. Μήδειος)
SKYTHIA:
—OLBIA-BORYSTHENES: (3) m. iv BC Dubois, *IGDOlbia* 13, 3 (s. Πεδιεύς)

Λαμύρα
MACEDONIA (MYGDONIA):
—THESSALONIKE: (1) ii-iii AD *IG* X (2) (1) 346

Λαμυρίδης
MACEDONIA (BOTTIAIA):
—BEROIA:
——Kyneoi: (1) 192 AD *ILeukopetra* 31, 4 (f. Νέπων)

Λάμυρος
THRACE:
—DIONYSOPOLIS: (1) 241-244 AD *IGB* I^2 22 bis, 18 ([Λ]άμυρος?: s. Παράμυθος); (2) ~ ib. l. 20 (Λάμυρ[ος]?, Λαμυτ——ed.: f. —θις)

Λάμψις
THRACE:
—PERINTHOS-HERAKLEIA: (1) hell.? *IPerinth* 63, 2 (f. Διόδωρος)

Λᾶνδρος
MACEDONIA (MYGDONIA):
—LETE: (1) ii AD *Makedonika* 2 (1951) p. 619 no. 42 θ, 4 (s. Διονύσιος)
MACEDONIA (SINTIKE):
—PARTHIKOPOLIS (TERRIT.): (2) 215 AD *IGB* IV 2319 (f. Πύρρος)

Λανθάνουσα
MACEDONIA (EDONIS):
—PHILIPPOI: (1) imp. *BSA* 23 (1918-19) p. 97 no. 23 (Pilhofer 151) (Lat. [Lan]thanusa?)

Λανίκα
MACEDONIA: (1) her. *POxy* 2465 fr. 1 II, 18; cf. *FGrH* 631 (Λαν——pap.: m. Κοῖνος); (2) c. 380-328 BC *RE* (-); Berve 462 (Tataki, *Macedonians* p. 352 no. 5) (-κη: d. Δρωπίδας, m. Πρωτέας, ?m. Θεόδωρος)
MACEDONIA (BOTTIAIA):
—BEROIA: (3) i BC *IBer* 195 (Tataki 788) ([Λ]ανείκα: d. Νικάνωρ, ?m. Ὄκκος)

Λαοδίκη
CIMMERIAN BOSPOROS:
—PANTIKAPAION: (1) i AD *CIRB* 427 (d. Σάσας, Θεονίκη); (2) ?s. i AD ib. 448
MACEDONIA: (3) iv/iii BC *RE* (12); cf. Beloch, *GG* IV (2) p. 198; Grainger, *SPG* p. 50 (d. Σέλευκος I Νικάτωρ, Ἀπάμη (Sogdiane)); (4) c. 285-235 BC *RE* (13); Grainger, *SPG* pp. 47-8; cf. Beloch, *GG* IV (2) pp. 200-1 (I d. Ἀχαιός, m. Σέλευκος II Καλλίνικος, Ἀντίοχος Ἱέραξ, Στρατονίκη, Λαοδίκη II: queen); (5) m. iii BC *RE* (14); Grainger, *SPG* p. 48; cf. Beloch, *GG* IV (2) pp. 201; 216 (II d. Ἀντίοχος II Θεός, Λαοδίκη I, m. Λαοδίκη III (Pontos), Λαοδίκη IV (Pontos): queen); (6) ~ *RE* (15); Grainger, *SPG* p. 48; cf. Beloch, *GG* IV (2) pp. 202; 205-6 (?d. Ἀχαιός, Ἀνδρόμαχος, m. Ἀλέξανδρος ὕστερον Σέλευκος III Σωτήρ, Ἀντίοχος III Μέγας, Ἀντιοχίς: queen); (7) iii/ii BC *RE* (18); *OGIS* 771, 31; Grainger, *SPG* p. 48 (V d. Ἀντίοχος III Μέγας, Λαοδίκη IV (Pontos)) ?= (8); (8) f. ii BC *RE* (19); *OGIS* 251, [2]; 252; Grainger, *SPG* p. 50 (I m. Δημήτριος I Σωτήρ, Λαοδίκη II, Ἀντίοχος, Ἀντίοχος V Εὐπάτωρ, Νῦσα: queen) ?= (7); (9) ~ *RE* (20); *IG* XI (4) 1074; *ZPE* 131 (2000) pp. 106-8; *SEG* L 652; Grainger, *SPG* pp. 49-50; cf. Beloch, *GG* IV (2) pp. 141-2 (II d. Σέλευκος IV Φιλοπάτωρ, Λαοδίκη I, m. Φίλιππος, Ἀλέξανδρος, Ἀντίοχος VII Σιδήτης, Δημήτριος II Νικάτωρ, Ἀντίγονος: queen); (10) 153 BC *RE* (23); cf. Grainger, *SPG* pp. 50-1 (d. Ἀντίοχος IV Ἐπιφάνης); (11) s. ii BC *RE* (24); Grainger, *SPG* pp. 48-9 (d. Δημήτριος II Νικάτωρ, Κλεοπάτρα Θεά); (12) ~ *RE* (25); Grainger, *SPG* p. 48 (d. Ἀντίοχος VII Σιδήτης, Κλεοπάτρα Θεά); (13) ~ *FGrH* 260 F 32. 20; Grainger, *SPG* p. 48 (d. Ἀντίοχος VII Σιδήτης, Κλεοπάτρα Θεά); (14) ii/i BC *RE* (26); Grainger, *SPG* p. 48 (Λ. Θεά: d. Ἀντίοχος VIII Γρυπός, Τρύφαινα, m. Ἀντίοχος (Kommagene): queen); (15) 31 BC-14 AD *BGU* 1059, 3, 5, 11, 18 (Tataki, *Macedonians* p. 488 no. 157) (d. Λυσίας)
MACEDONIA (EORDAIA):
—MAVROPIGI (MOD.): (16) ii-i BC *EAM* 119; cf. *SEG* XLI 578 a (d. Ὀρέστης)
MACEDONIA (LOWER PAIONIA):
—EUROPOS: (17) m. iv BC *RE* (11); Berve 463 (Tataki, *Macedonians* p. 352 no. 6) (I m. Σέλευκος I Νικάτωρ, Λαοδίκη II, ?m. Διδύμεια); (18) s. iv BC Eust. 916; Grainger, *SPG* p. 48 (II d. Ἀντίοχος, Λαοδίκη I)
TAURIS:
—CHERSONESOS: (19) ii AD *IOSPE* I^2 431, 2 (Λαο[δ]ί[κ]η: d. Ἡρόξενος); (20) ~ ib. 432, 1 (d. T. Φλ. Ἀπολλώνιος); (21) ~ *SEG* XXXVII 656 (lead) (Αἰλ. Λ.: d. Ζῆθος)

Λαοίτας
MACEDONIA (BOTTIAIA):
—GENDERRHOS? (ANYDRON (MOD.)): (1) 132 or 135 AD ib. XLIII 394 (f. Εὔλαιος)

Λαομάγα
MACEDONIA (BOTTIAIA):
—BEROIA: (1) s. ii BC *IBer* 203 (Tataki 789) (d. Περίτας)

Λαομέδων
MACEDONIA (EDONIS):
—AMPHIPOLIS: (1) s. iv BC *PP* 16149; *RE* (7); Berve 464 (Tataki, *Macedonians* p. 55 no. 75); cf. *LGPN* I s.v. (2) (and Lesbos Mytilene: s. Λάριχος)
THRACE:
—PAUTALIA: (2) ii-iii AD *IGB* V 5779 (s. Στράτων)

Λαόμμας
MACEDONIA (PIERIA):
—PYDNA: (1) f. ii BC *SEG* L 629 (f. Ὀλύμπιχος)

Λᾶος
MACEDONIA (BOTTIAIA):
—BEROIA: (1) i BC *IBer* 506 (Tataki 790) (f. Περδίκκας)

Λαπέπωρ
THRACE:
—DUROSTORUM (TERRIT.)?: (1) iii AD *IGB* II 868, 5 (*CCET* II (1) 186) (s. Αὐλούπορις)

Λαρέτα
MACEDONIA (BOTTIAIA):
—BEROIA: (1) 239-229 BC *IBer* 45, 15; cf. Tataki 794 (?d. Ἀττίνας)

Λασθένης
MACEDONIA (CHALKIDIKE):
—OLYNTHOS: (1) 348 BC *RE* (1) (Tataki, *Macedonians* p. 139 no. 79)

Λάσιος
THRACE:
—BYZANTION: (1) imp. *IByz* 22, 6 (f. Μητρόδωρος); (2) c. 120 AD *FD* III (4) 85, 1 (s. Ἀγαθήμερος)

Λάστρατος
THRACE:
—LYSIMACHEIA: (1) c. 244-242 BC *PPetr* III 54 b fr. 3, 6 (La'da E1368)

Λᾶτος
MACEDONIA (BOTTIAIA):
—BEROIA?: (1) 178 BC *SGDI* 2071, 8; cf. *Syll*^{2} 848 (f. Ἀμύντας)

Λαυδίκη
CIMMERIAN BOSPOROS:
—PANTIKAPAION: (1) i AD *CIRB* 369 (Λαυδί[κη]); (2) 130 AD ib. 656, 3; cf. KW pl. 18 no. 272 (m. Ἀριστείδης, Παντόνικος)

Thrace:
—BYZANTION: (3) i BC-i AD *IByz* 239; cf. *BE* 2001, no. 308 (d. *Λούκιος*)
—BYZANTION?: (4) ii-i BC *IByz* 363 (Fıratlı-Robert pp. 124-5 no. 207) ([*Λ*]*αυδίκη*: d. *Ἑρμαγένης*)

Λαυδικιανός
Thrace:
—NICOPOLIS AD ISTRUM (TERRIT.): (1) ii AD *IGB* V 5244 a, 10 (*Αἴ. Λαυδικια[νός]*)

Λαυνίκας
Cimmerian Bosporos:
—PANTIKAPAION: (1) iv AD *CIRB* 741

Λαυρεντία
Thrace:
—BEROE-AUGUSTA TRAIANA: (1) c. 320-324 AD *Anal. Boll.* 31 (1912) pp. 198 ff.; p. 207 (*Λαβρεντία*—p. 207)

Λαφάεια
Skythia:
—TYRAS: (1) ii AD *IG* II^2 9580a (*FRA* 7188) (*Λαφ(ά)εια*)

Λαχητᾶς
Thrace:
—MESAMBRIA: (1) c. 55 BC *IGB* I^2 323, 2 (*Λαχητᾶ* (gen.): f. *Ξενοκλῆς*)

Λέαγρος
Skythia:
—OLBIA-BORYSTHENES (BEREZAN (MOD.)): (1) v BC *SEG* XXXII 784 (vase)

Λεάδης
Macedonia (Chalkidike):
—CHALKIDEIS: (1) c. 367-364 BC *Olynthus* 9 pp. 62-4 nos. 94-6 (coin); *Ancient Macedonia* I p. 254 (date) (*Λεάδεος* (gen.))

Λεάμβιος?
Thrace:
—PERINTHOS-HERAKLEIA?: (1) iv BC Hp., *Epid.* iv 41; *Index Hipp.* s.v.

Λεάναξ
Skythia:
—OLBIA-BORYSTHENES: (1) vi/v BC *SEG* XLVIII 1012

Λείλοος
Thrace:
—BESSOPARA: (1) iii AD *IGB* III 947, 7 (f. *Δείδης*)

Λειμανός
Cimmerian Bosporos:
—PANTIKAPAION: (1) 204 AD *CIRB* 96, 5 (*SEG* II 485); (2) 275-278 AD *CIRB* 36, 20 (s. *Φίδας*)
Skythia:
—TANAIS: (3) c. 200-210 AD ib. 1277, 11 (s. *Φίδας*); (4) 220 AD ib. 1278, 25 (f. —*βραεδος*: reading—Tokhtas'ev); (5) 225 AD ib. 1279, 14 (f. *Ἀσπάνδανος*)

Λειμείη
Cimmerian Bosporos:
—HERMONASSA: (1) 345 AD ib. 1091, 6; Zgusta, *PNS* 241

Λείμων
Macedonia?: (1) c. 265-257 BC *Cl. Rh.* 9 (1938) p. 183, 8; Robert, *Documents* p. 55 n. 4 (ethn.) (Tataki, *Macedonians* p. 354 no. 18) (or Thasos?: s. *Ἀντίπατρος*)

Λειχίας
Macedonia (Chalkidike):
—OLYNTHOS: (1) f. iv BC *Olynthus* 10 p. 479 no. 2527 (*Λειχίας*: f. *Παρμένων*)

Λεόκριτος
Macedonia (Mygdonia):
—KALINDOIA: (1) i BC/i AD *SEG* XLII 598; cf. *Anthémonte–Kalindoia* 2 p. 280 (ident.) (f. *Ἀνδροσθένης*); (2) 68-98 AD *SEG* XLII 580, 13 + *BE* 1999, no. 362 (f. *Ἀπολλώνιος*); (3) a. 98 AD *SEG* XLII 582, 7 + *BE* 1999, no. 362 (f. *Ἀνδροσθένης*)
Thrace:
—ODESSOS: (4) 12-19 AD *IGB* V 5011, 11 (s. *Ἱππαγόρας*)

Λεόννατος
Macedonia: (1) 280 BC *RE* (3) (Tataki, *Macedonians* p. 354 no. 20) (s. *Λεόφαντος*); (2) c. 148 BC *PTeb* 79, 1 (Tataki, *Macedonians* p. 488 no. 158); cf. La'da E1665 (f. —*νος*)
Macedonia (Bottiaia):
—AIGAI: (3) 327-326 BC *RE* (2); Berve 467 (Tataki, *Macedonians* p. 40 no. 10) (s. *Ἀντίπατρος*)
—PELLA: (4) c. 356-322 BC *RE* (1); Berve 466; *SEG* XLVI 787 A, 7, [10], [13] (Tataki, *Macedonians* p. 156 no. 55) (?s. *Ἀντέας*, *Ὄνασος*, *Εὔνους*)
Macedonia (Eordaia?):
—EUIA?: (5) 171 BC *RE* (4) (Tataki, *Macedonians* p. 106 no. 2) (Lat. Leonnatus)
Macedonia (Pieria):
—DION?: (6) ?c. 220-200 BC Helly, *Gonnoi* 94, 4 (or Thessaly?)
—MT. OLYMPOS*: (7) ?iii BC *SEG* XXIV 409 + *BE* 1968, no. 323 ([*Λε*]*όννατος*: s. *Ἀνδρο*—)
Scythia Minor:
—TROESMIS*: (8) 134 AD *ISM* V 137 VII, 24 (Lat. Leonatus)
Thrace: (9) ii BC *SEG* XLI 1635, 3 (La'da E766) (s. *Σαδάλας*)

Λεοντᾶς
Macedonia (Bottiaia):
—BEROIA: (1) ii/iii AD *IBer* 143 A, 2 (Tataki 611) (*Ἰούλ. Λεοντᾶς*); (2) ~ *IBer* 143 B, 5 (Tataki 1070) (*Πε. Λεοντᾶς*); (3) iii AD *ILeukopetra* 129, 1 (*Αὐρ. Λ.*: s. *Παράμονος*)

Λεοντία
Scythia Minor:
—TOMIS: (1) ?v AD Barnea 33 (Popescu, *IGL* 35)
Thrace:
—BESSOI: (2) c. 455-480 AD *PLRE* II (1) (d. *Λέων*)
—BISANTHE-PANION: (3) iv-v AD *AD* 49-50 (1994-5) Mel. p. 311 no. 136 (d. *Εὐγένιος*)

Λεοντιάδης
Thrace:
—PERINTHOS-HERAKLEIA:
——(Geleuntes): (1) iii-ii BC *IPerinth* 61, 34 (s. *Ἀριστοκλῆς*)

Λεοντιανός
Macedonia (Mygdonia):
—THESSALONIKE*: (1) v-vi AD Feissel, *RICM* 205 (Lat. Leontianus)
Scythia Minor:
—TOMIS: (2) ii-iii AD *ISM* II 369, 11 (s. *Διονυσόδωρος*, *Ἰουλία*)

Λεόντιος
Kolchis:
—LAZOI: (1) 539-540 AD *PLRE* III (2) (s. *Ζαύνας*)
Macedonia: (2) 224-218 BC *RE* (2) (Tataki, *Macedonians* p. 354 no. 21)
Macedonia (Bottiaia):
—BEROIA: (3) iii AD *IBer* 401, 7 (Tataki 796); (4) iv-v AD *IBer* 455, 4 (Feissel, *RICM* 295) (f. *Μαρία*: Jew)
Macedonia (Mygdonia):
—THESSALONIKE?: (5) iv-v AD *IG* X (2) (1) 788, 2, 5 (Feissel, *RICM* 177) (s. *Εὐάγγελος*)
Scythia Minor:
—TROESMIS: (6) 117-139 AD *ISM* V 154, 7 (Lat. M. Ulp. Leontius)
Thrace:
—NICOPOLIS AD ISTRUM: (7) iv/v AD Beševliev 48 (*ILB* 146) (Lat. L. Turranius Leontius)
—PAUTALIA: (8) s. ii AD *SEG* XLVI 864, 3
—ZONE?: (9) 582-602 AD ib. XXXVII 616

Λέοντις
Cimmerian Bosporos:
—PANTIKAPAION: (1) s. iv BC *CIRB* 192, 3; cf. KW pl. 5 no. 88 (f. *Φωκρίτη*)

Λεόντις
Macedonia (Mygdonia):
—THESSALONIKE: (1) iii AD *IG* X (2) (1) 546, 2 (*Αὐρ. Λ.*: s. *Φλ. Πάκτωλος ὁ καὶ Ἀκάκιος*)
Thrace:
—NICOPOLIS AD ISTRUM (TERRIT.): (2) 227 AD *ILB* 438 I, 19 (Lat. Leontis: s. Cocceius Super)

Λεοντίς
Macedonia (Mygdonia):
—THESSALONIKE: (1) ?i AD *IG* X (2) (1) 432; cf. *JDAI* 84 (1969) pp. 153-4 no. R18; (2) iii AD *IG* X (2) (1) 487, 2; 488 A-B (*Δομιτία Λ.*: d. *Δομίτιος Ὁμοῖος*, *Δομιτία Ὑγίνη*, m. *M. Ἐρένν. Ὀρεστῖνος*, *Ἐρεννία Ὀρεστίνη*)
Macedonia (Pieria):
—DION (TERRIT.): (3) ?i AD Dimitsas 158
Thrace:
—BIZONE: (4) iv/v AD Beševliev 247; cf. *BE* 1962, no. 223 (*Λεόντις*—*BE*)

Λεοντίσκος
Macedonia: (1) iv/iii BC *RE* (1) (*PP* 14528) (s. *Πτολεμαῖος Ι Σωτήρ* (Eordaia), *Θαΐς* (Athens))
Macedonia (Bottiaia):
—BEROIA: (2) 177 AD *IBer* 135 B, 28 (Tataki 797) (s. *Ἀντιγένης*); (3) f. iii AD *IBer* 342, 4 (Tataki 1384) ([*Λεον*]*τίσκος*: s. *Αὐρ. Λεοντογένης*, *Αὐρ. Γραφίς*)
Macedonia (Mygdonia):
—THESSALONIKE: (4) ii-iii AD Nalpantis, *Anaskaphi* p. 111 no. BE 117
Macedonia (Pieria):
—PYDNA: (5) 250 AD *SEG* XLVI 800 A, 47 (*Αὐρ. Λεοντίσκ[ος]*)
Scythia Minor:
—CIUS*: (6) 244-246 AD *ISM* V 124, 13 (Lat. Aur. Leontiscus)
—KALLATIS: (7) f. iii BC ib. III 6, 3 (s. *Ἀθαναίων*)
Skythia:
—OLBIA-BORYSTHENES: (8) ?ii-i BC Dubois, *IGDOlbia* 110, 3
Thrace:
—BYZANTION: (9) m. iii BC *IG* XI (4) 530, 8 (*Λεοντίσ[κος]*: f. *Φώκριτος*, *Ἀγασικλῆς*)
—DIONYSOPOLIS: (10) c. 225-200 BC Price, *Alexander* 960 (coin)
—PERINTHOS-HERAKLEIA:
——(Makedones): (11) iii-ii BC *IPerinth* 61, 4 (s. *Λέων*)
—PHILIPPOPOLIS-TRIMONTIUM (TERRIT.): (12) ii AD *IGB* III 1186 (*Αἰλ. Λεοντίσκ[ος]*)

Λεοντογένης
Macedonia (Bottiaia):
—BEROIA: (1) f. iii AD *IBer* 342, 1 (Tataki 1361) (*Αὐρ. Λ.*: f. *Λεοντίσκος*, *Φιλίππα*)
Macedonia (Eordaia):
—ARNISA?: (2) m. ii AD *EAM* 123, 4 + *SEG* XXXVII 534; Hatzopoulos, *MI* I p. 94 n. 4 (locn.) (*Λεοντογέν[ης]*: s. *Ὀλυμπιάς*)

Λεοντόλυκος
Macedonia (Bottiaia):
—BEROIA: (1) ii/iii AD *IBer* 143 B, 7 (Tataki 1106) (*Πο. Λ.*)

Λεοντομένης
MACEDONIA (BOTTIAIA):
—BEROIA: (1) 122 BC *IBer* 134, 4 (f. *Νικόλαος*)
MACEDONIA (CHALKIDIKE):
—POTIDAIA-KASSANDREIA: (2) c. 300-275 BC Polyaen. vi 7. 2
SKYTHIA:
—OLBIA-BORYSTHENES: (3) iii BC *IOSPE* I² 201 I, 18 (s. *Ἰκέσιος*); (4) s. iii BC ib. 76, 9 (Sokolowski II 88; Dubois, *IGDOlbia* 88) (s. *Ἡροσῶν*)
THRACE:
—APOLLONIA-SOZOPOLIS?: (5) ?iv BC *IGB* I² 477 (s. *Κλεισθένης*)
—MARONEIA: (6) ii-i BC *IThrakAig* E212, 27 (f. *Παρμενίων*)

Λεοντώ
MACEDONIA (BOTTIAIA):
—BEROIA: (1) ii-iii AD *IBer* 263, 3; (2) 191 AD *ILeukopetra* 27, 1 (Tataki 5) (*Ἀβιλία Λ.*)
MACEDONIA (MYGDONIA):
—THESSALONIKE?: (3) ii-iii AD *IG* X (2) (1) 814, 3 (*Οὐλπ. Λ.*: m. *Αἰλ. Ἐπιγόνη*)

Λεοντώι
THRACE:
—BIZYE?: (1) f. i AD *IGB* I² 378, 9; 402, 1 (d. *Αὐλουζένης*)

Λεόφαντος
MACEDONIA: (1) c. 280 BC D.H. xviii. 2 (Tataki, *Macedonians* p. 354 no. 23) (f. *Λεόννατος*)

Λέπιδος
SCYTHIA MINOR:
—ISTROS: (1) ii-iii AD *ISM* I 195, 14 (f. *—ας*)

Λέπουλα
MACEDONIA (LOWER PAIONIA):
—GORTYNIA (TERRIT.)?: (1) iii AD *SEG* L 632 + *Tekmeria* 6 (2001) p. 160; cf. *BE* 2003, no. 364 (locn.) (*Αὐρ. Λέπουλα*: m. *Αὐρ. Πάτερνος*)

Λεπτίνας
SKYTHIA:
—OLBIA-BORYSTHENES: (1) iii BC Dubois, *IGDOlbia* 109, 6 (*SEG* XXXVII 673)

Λεπτίνης
MACEDONIA: (1) III BC *POxy* 831 (Tataki, *Macedonians* p. 489 no. 159; La'da E1532) (*Λεπτίν[ης]*: s. ..*μῶναξ*)
THRACE:
—MARONEIA: (2) iii BC *SEG* XXVII 342 (*IThrakAig* E237)

Λέσβιος
MACEDONIA (MYGDONIA):
—THESSALONIKE: (1) ii AD *IG* X (2) (1) 362

Λεστόρμη?
THRACE:
—DIONYSOPOLIS: (1) ii AD *IGB* I² 27 bis (d. *Δίζδων*)

Λεττίνης
SARMATIA:
—MAIOTAI: (1) i/ii AD *IG* II² 9255 (*FRA* 3453); Zgusta, *PNS* 667 (*Λε(π)τίνης*?: slave?)

Λευκαδία
THRACE:
—APROI: (1) v-vi AD Unp. (Sayar) (m. *Τζιτας*)

Λευκάνωρ
CIMMERIAN BOSPOROS:
—BOSPOROS: (1) ii AD Luc., *Tox.* 44-51 (f. *Μαζαία, Βαρκέτις*: king/fict.)

Λεύκαρος
MACEDONIA (BOTTIAIA):
—PELLA: (1) ?263-261 BC Nachtergael, *Les Galates* 3, 21 (Tataki, *Macedonians* p. 156 no. 56) (f. *—αῖος*)

Λεύκη
MACEDONIA (BOTTIAIA):
—BEROIA: (1) ii AD *IBer* 395 (Tataki 798)
MACEDONIA (MYGDONIA):
—THESSALONIKE: (2) ii-iii AD *IG* X (2) (1) 627 (*Τυλλία Λ.*)

Λευκία
MACEDONIA (PAIONIA):
—KAVADARCI (MOD.): (1) ii-iii AD *AM* 27 (1902) p. 318 no. 46 (m. *Λευκιανή*)

Λευκιανή
MACEDONIA (PAIONIA):
—KAVADARCI (MOD.): (1) ii-iii AD ib. (d. *Λευκία, Μακέτας*)

Λεύκιος
CIMMERIAN BOSPOROS:
—PANTIKAPAION: (1) i BC *CIRB* 128, 2 (*GVI* 845) (s. *Φιλέταιρος, Τρυφωνίς*); (2) ~ *CIRB* 279; cf. KW pl. 35 no. 501 (s. *Φαρνάκης*) ?= (3); (3) i BC/i AD *CIRB* 300 (s. *Φαρνάκης*) ?= (2); (4) i AD ib. 136 (*GVI* 1521); (5) ~ *CIRB* 449; cf. KW pl. 17 no. 254 (f. *Μᾶρκος*)
MACEDONIA (MYGDONIA):
—THESSALONIKE: (6) s. i AD *IG* X (2) (1) 593 (f. *Ἰουκοῦνδος*)
—THESSALONIKE?: (7) iii AD ib. 995
MACEDONIA (PAIONIA):
—STOBOI: (8) ii-iii AD *Sp.* 75 (1933) p. 26 no. 62
THRACE: (9) 203 BC *BGU* 1266 A, 40, 45; 2386, 6 (Velkov 195; La'da E767)
—BYZANTION?: (10) i BC-i AD *IByz* 373 (Firatlı–Robert p. 125 no. 209) (f. *Πάπας*); (11) s. i BC PM 433 (f. *Κορνηλία Βρισαΐς*)
—HADRIANOPOLIS: (12) imp. *Syllogos* 27 (1900) p. 389 no. 4
—PERINTHOS-HERAKLEIA: (13) hell.? *IPerinth* 63, 4 (f. *Δίφιλος*)

Λευκίππη
MACEDONIA (MYGDONIA):
—THESSALONIKE: (1) ii AD *IG* X (2) (1) 326, 2 (d. *Σαραπιακός, Λύκα*)
THRACE:
—BYZANTION: (2) ii AD Ach. Tat. i 3. 6 and passim (d. *Σώστρατος*: fict.)

Λεύκιππος
MACEDONIA (CHALKIDIKE):
—OLYNTHOS: (1) c. 300 BC *IEph* 1454, 2, 4 (Tataki, *Macedonians* p. 140 no. 80) (s. *Ἑρμογένης*)
MACEDONIA (ELIMEIA):
—VELVENDOS (MOD.): (2) s. ii AD *EAM* 57; *Ling. Balk.* 30 (1987) p. 61 (name) (*Λε(ύ)κιππος*: s. *Ἀπολλόδωρος, Ἁρμονία*)
THRACE:
—ABDERA?: (3) v BC *RE* (13); *FVS* 67 (or S. Italy (Lucania) Hyele-Velia or Caria Miletos)
—MARONEIA: (4) iii BC *IThrakAig* E236 (*[Λ]εύκιππος*: f. *Πυρρίας*)

Λευκώ
MACEDONIA (BISALTIA):
—SITOCHORI (MOD.): (1) ii-iii AD Kaphtantzis 524 (d. *Λύκος*)

Λεύκων
CIMMERIAN BOSPOROS:
—BOSPOROS: (1) c. 420-349 BC *RE* (3); *CIRB* 6; 6a; 7; 8; 37; 1014; 1037; 1038; 1111; *SEG* XLIII 515, 1 + XLVIII 1027; XLV 1000, 9; Rhodes–Osborne 64, 2, 21, 29, etc.; *Hyperboreus* 2002 (1), p. 101; *VDI* 1967 (1), p. 64 (*Λεόκων*—*Hyperboreus* 2002: s. *Σάτυρος*, f. *Σπάρτοκος, Παιρισάδης, Ἀπολλώνιος*: king); (2) m. iii BC *RE* (4); *CIRB* 25; Shelov, *CB* pp. 133 ff. (s. *Παιρισάδης*: king)
—GORGIPPIA: (3) f. iii BC *CIRB* 1137 B II, 6 (f. *Θεώνιχος*)
MACEDONIA (BOTTIAIA):
—BEROIA: (4) ii/iii AD *IBer* 143 A, 5 (Tataki 801) (f. *Ἀλέξανδρος*); (5) 192 AD *ILeukopetra* 32, 1 (Tataki 802) (I f. *Λεύκων* II); (6) ~ *ILeukopetra* 32, 1 (Tataki 800) (II s. *Λεύκων* I)
MACEDONIA (CHALKIDIKE):
—STOLOS: (7) 360 BC *IG* IV (1)² 94 b, 23 (Perlman, *City and Sanctuary* E.1 with p. 69 f. (date); Tataki, *Macedonians* p. 177 no. 2)
TAURIS:
—CHERSONESOS: (8) f. iii BC *SEG* XL 615 B, 16 (*Λεύκω[ν]*)
—KERKINITIS: (9) iv BC Solomonik, *GChKh* 128 (vase) (*Λεύ(κων)*?)

Λεφαοσας?
CIMMERIAN BOSPOROS:
—GORGIPPIA: (1) ii/iii AD *CIRB* 1179, 26; Zgusta, *PNS* 304 (*Λεφαοσα* (gen.): f. *—τόδωρος*)

Λεωδάμας
KOLCHIS:
—PICHVNARI (MOD.): (1) f. iv BC *Anat. Stud.* 51 (2001) p. 78 (vase) (f. *Διονύσιος*)
MACEDONIA (ODOMANTIKE):
—SIRRHA: (2) ii-iii AD Dimitsas 818 (Kaphtantzis 20) (*Λεωδ̣άμας*)
SKYTHIA:
—OLBIA-BORYSTHENES: (3) v-iv BC *IOSPE* I² 211 (s. *Ἡρακλείδης*); (4) iii BC ib. 201 II, 14 (f. *Πανταλκλῆς*); (5) ~ ib. l. 23, 25 (f. *Φιλτῆς, Ἰκέσιος*); (6) ~ ib. l. 37 (*Λεωδά[μας]*)
—OLBIA-BORYSTHENES?: (7) iv/iii BC *SEG* XXXVII 681; XLII 728 (locn.)
THRACE:
—APOLLONIA-SOZOPOLIS: (8) v/iv BC *IGB* I² 442 (f. *Κωλώτης*)

Λεώδικος
CIMMERIAN BOSPOROS:
—PANTIKAPAION: (1) v BC *CIRB* 152 (f. *Εὐαλκίδης*)

Λεώκιν?
MACEDONIA (MYGDONIA):
—THESSALONIKE?: (1) i AD *IG* X (2) (1) 848 (*GVI* 365) (*Βασίλεια Λ.*)

Λεωκράτης
CIMMERIAN BOSPOROS:
—NYMPHAION: (1) iv BC *CIRB* 921 (s. *Ἀναθεμενός*)
SKYTHIA:
—OLBIA-BORYSTHENES: (2) s. iv BC *IOlbia* 65 (s. *—ος*); (3) iv/iii BC ib. 71 I, 4-10 (Dubois, *IGDOlbia* 11) (f. *Εὐρησίβιος, Πολυκράτης, Πολυμήδης, Πολύστρατος, Πολύχαρμος, Πολύδημος, Πολυμέδων*); (4) ~ *IOlbia* 71 II, 3 (Dubois, *IGDOlbia* 11) (s. *Π—*); (5) iii BC *IOSPE* I² 201 I, 1 (*Λεωκρά[της]*: f. *Εὐρησίβιος*); (6) ~ ib. l. 39 (f. *Πολυμέδων*); (7) ~ ib. l. 62 (s. *Πολυμέδων*)
TAURIS:
—KALOS LIMEN (NR.): (8) f. iv BC *SEG* XXXVIII 755 (vase); Vinogradov, *Pont. Stud.* p. 484 n. 7

Λεωμέδων
CIMMERIAN BOSPOROS:
—PANTIKAPAION: (1) iv BC Tolstoi 222 (vase) (*Λεωμέ[δων]*)

Λέων
MACEDONIA: (1) 327 BC *CID* II 97, 30; 99 A, [0] (Tataki, *Macedonians* p. 355 no. 26) (*[Λ]έων*: s. *Ἡγήσανδρος*); (2) 197 BC *RE* (16) (Tataki, *Macedonians* p. 355 no. 24)

MACEDONIA (BISALTIA):
—ARGILOS?: (3) 364-357 BC Hatzopoulos, *Actes Amphipolis* p. 15 no. 1, 12; pp. 73-4 (locn., date) (or Macedonia (Edonis) Amphipolis: *Λέων*)
MACEDONIA (BOTTIAIA):
—BEROIA: (4) ii-iii AD *IBer* 254 (Tataki 803); (5) ~ *IBer* 307 (Tataki 1323) (*Τι. Φλ. Λ.*); (6) 177 AD *IBer* 135 A, 22 (Tataki 78) (*Αἰλ. Λ.*)
—BEROIA?: (7) 38 BC Robert, *Coll. Froehner* 44, 20-1 (*IG* XII Suppl. p. 149); cf. Tataki, *Macedonians* p. 79 no. 32 (f. *Ῥουφίων, Ἄλυπος*)
—PELLA: (8) iv/iii BC *RE* (25); *FGrH* 659 (Tataki, *Macedonians* p. 156 no. 57)
—PELLA*: (9) iii BC *AEMTh* 6 (1992) p. 139 (amph.)
MACEDONIA (DERRIOPOS):
—STUBERRA: (10) c. 41-48 AD *IG* X (2) (2) 323, 23 (f. *Μενέλαος*, ?f. *Γάϊος, Ἄπερ*); (11) 74 AD ib. 326, 38 (f. *Λυσίμαχος*); (12) ~ ib. l. 43 (f. *Μένιππος*); (13) 116 AD ib. 327, 25 (f. *Λυσίμαχος*)
MACEDONIA (EORDAIA):
—KOMANOS (MOD.): (14) s. ii AD *EAM* 100 (s. *Ἀντίγονος*)
MACEDONIA (MYGDONIA):
—LETE: (15) i-ii AD Dimitsas 676 = *IG* II^2 11958; cf. *Myrtos* pp. 269-70; cf. *LGPN* II s.v. (82) (s. *Νικόλαος, Στρατονίκη*)
—THESSALONIKE: (16) 154-166 AD *IG* X (2) (1) 472 A-B (*Κλ. Λ.*: f. *Κλ. Ἀφαρεύς, Κλ. Νεβρίς*); (17) f. iii AD ib. 201, 5 (*Λ. Κατίνιος Λ.*: I f. *Αἰλ. Κατίνιος Λέων* II); (18) ~ ib. 202, 6 (*Αἰλ. Κατίνιος Λ. νέος*: III s. *Αἰλ. Κατίνιος Λέων* II); (19) ~ ib. 202 with p. 85 (stemma) (*Αἰλ. Κατίνιος Λ.*: II s. *Λ. Κατίνιος Λέων* I, f. *Αἰλ. Κατίνιος Λέων* III *νέος*, *Αἰλ. Ἀλεξάνδρα*)
—THESSALONIKE?: (20) s. i AD ib. 905; cf. *BCH* 97 (1973) p. 599 (s. *Τιβ. Νεοπτόλεμος, Κ. Πρόκλα*)
MACEDONIA (PAIONIA): (21) m. iii BC Paus. X 13. 1; *Syll*^{3} 394; *SEG* XII 263; *AMNG* III (2) p. 206 no. 1 (coin) (f. *Δρωπίων*)
—STOBOI: (22) s. iii AD *JÖAI* 32 (1940) Beibl. col. 18 no. 14. 55 (?s. *Ἄκυιος* [—] *Σε*—)
MACEDONIA (PIERIA):
—DION: (23) f. ii AD *SEG* XXXIX 580, 2 (slave?)
—PYDNA: (24) v-iv BC *BE* 1998, no. 245 (*Epigr. arch. Mak.* 56)
SCYTHIA MINOR:
—ISTROS: (25) iii BC *ISM* I 258 (f. *Ναυσικλῆς*); (26) f. iii AD ib. 143, 6 (*ἱρριος Λ.*)
—TOMIS: (27) ii AD ib. II 17, 7 (s. *Ἐπίστρατος*); (28) ii-iii AD ib. 19 b, 3 (s. *Ἐ*—); (29) ii/iii AD ib. 85, 13 (— *ὁ καὶ Λ.*)
SKYTHIA:
—OLBIA-BORYSTHENES: (30) iv/iii BC *SEG* XLII 715 (s. *Ἡρακλείδης*, f. *Ἡρακλείδης*); (31) ii AD *IOSPE* I^2 225
THRACE: (32) 137 BC *PSI* 1311, [2], 21; cf. La'da E750 (f. *Ἡρακλεόδωρος*)
—BESSOI: (33) c. 400-474 AD *PLRE* II (6); *DCB* III 645-6 (1) (f. *Ἀριάδνη, Λεοντία*: emp.)
—BYZANTION: (34) f. iv BC *Suda Λ* 265 (I f. *Λέων* II); (35) c. 375-338 BC *RE* (23); Berve 468 (II s. *Λέων* I); (36) hell.-imp. *RE* (24); *FGrH* 132
—BYZANTION?: (37) ii BC *ISamothrace* 28 c, 17; Robert, *OMS* 6 pp. 605-6 (locn.) ([*Λέο*]*ντος*? (gen.): f. *Γλαυκίας*)
—LYSIMACHEIA: (38) iii BC *ITrall* 33 B, 13, 15 (f. *Ἀρτέμων, Διογένης*)
—NICOPOLIS AD ISTRUM (TERRIT.): (39) 227 AD *ILB* 438 I, 12 (Lat. Leo: s. Val. Fronto)
—PERINTHOS-HERAKLEIA: (40) v-vi AD *IPerinth* 265; cf. *PLRE* II (8)
——(Makedones): (41) iii-ii BC *IPerinth* 61, 4 (f. *Λεοντίσκος*)
—PHILIPPOPOLIS-TRIMONTIUM: (42) V AD Beševliev 217

Λεωνᾶς
MACEDONIA (ELIMEIA):
—AIANE: (1) s. ii AD *EAM* 15 a (*Τ. Φλ. Λ.*)
MACEDONIA (MYGDONIA):
—THESSALONIKE: (2) m. ii AD *SEG* XLIII 462, 5
THRACE:
—BIZONE: (3) iii AD *IGB* I^2 8 (*Eastern cults* p. 83 no. 22)
—PERINTHOS-HERAKLEIA: (4) iii AD *IPerinth* 159, 3 (*Αὐρ. Λ.*)

Λεωνιανός
THRACE:
—SERDICA: (1) v-vi AD Beševliev 11 (Lat. Leonianus)

Λεωνίδας
MACEDONIA: (1) s. iv BC *SEG* XXXVIII 641 (s. *Δέρδας*); (2) c. 330 BC Berve 470 (Tataki, *Macedonians* p. 355 no. 28) ?= (*3*); (3) 320 BC *RE* (5) ?= (*2*)
MACEDONIA (BOTTIAIA):
—BEROIA: (4) 237-241 AD *ILeukopetra* 86, 5; 95, 3 (Tataki 1107) (*Ποπίλλιος Λ.*: II s. *Λεωνίδας* I); (5) 241 AD *ILeukopetra* 95, 4 (Tataki 807) (I f. *Ποπίλλιος Λεωνίδας* II)
MACEDONIA (ELIMEIA):
—AIANE (TERRIT.): (6) c. 225-200 BC *SEG* XL 526, 4 (f. *Ἀλέξαρχος*)
MACEDONIA (MYGDONIA):
—KALINDOIA: (7) c. 321 BC Hatzopoulos, *MI* 2 p. 84 no. 62, 24 (*Λεων*[*ίδας*]: f. *Φιλώτας*)
—THESSALONIKE: (8) 66 AD *IG* X (2) (1) 70, 11 (*Λεω*<*ι*>*νίδ*[*ας*]: s. *Λυσανίας*)
—THESSALONIKE?: (9) iii AD ib. 21, 1 (Lat. Long. Leonidas)
MACEDONIA (ORESTIS):
—BATTYNAIOI: (10) 192 AD *EAM* 186, 2, 42 (f. *Ἀλέξανδρος*)
MACEDONIA (PAIONIA):
—STOBOI: (11) s. iii AD *JÖAI* 32 (1940) Beibl. col. 18 no. 12. 46 (*Λεωνί*(*δου*?) (gen.))
THRACE:
—BYZANTION: (12) ?iv-iii BC *FGrH* 389 F 1 (*RE* (7)) (-*δης*); (13) ii-i BC ib. (16) (s. *Ματρόδωρος*)

Λεωνίδης
MACEDONIA: (1) 141 or 88 BC *SEG* II 864 (Tataki, *Macedonians* p. 489 no. 161; La'da E1533) (I s. *Φιλώτας*, f. *Λεωνίδης* II); (2) ~ *SEG* II 864 (Tataki, *Macedonians* p. 489 no. 160); cf. La'da E1533 (II s. *Λεωνίδης* I); (3) 12 AD *PKöln* 227 B, 4 (s. *Εἰρηναῖος*)
MACEDONIA (DERRIOPOS):
—STUBERRA: (4) 74 AD *IG* X (2) (2) 325, 20 (f. *Νίκαρχος*)
MACEDONIA (EDONIS):
—AMPHIPOLIS: (5) m. iii BC Hatzopoulos, *Actes Amphipolis* p. 52 no 12, 6; *SEG* XLI 566 (date) (f. *Νίκανδρος*); (6) ii-iii AD Dimitsas 922; cf. *BCH* 19 (1895) p. 110 no. 3 (s. *Τιμοκλῆς*)
—PHILIPPOI (TERRIT.): (7) 206 AD Pikoulas, *Chora* p. 164 no. 73, 4 (Pilhofer 607) (*Λεω*[*ν*]*ίδης*: f. *Σατορνῖνος*); (8) ?212 AD Pikoulas, *Chora* p. 164 no. 73, 10 (Pilhofer 607) ([*Λ*]*εωνίδης*: s. *Διοσκουρίδης*)
SKYTHIA:
—OLBIA-BORYSTHENES: (9) iii BC *IOSPE* I^2 201 I, 20 (f. *Φιλτῆς*); (10) ii-iii AD ib. 138, 3, 13 (s. *Ἀχιλλεύς*)
THRACE: (11) 180-145 BC *BGU* 1271, 18 (Velkov 196; La'da E769) (*Λεωνίδ*<*ιδ*>*ης*—pap.); (12) 150 BC *IFayoum* 103-4 (Velkov 197; La'da E768) (s. *Πτολεμαῖος*)
—NICOPOLIS AD NESTUM?: (13) 221 AD *IGB* IV 2305, 2 (f. *Ἡραΐς*)

Λέωξος
SKYTHIA:
—OLBIA-BORYSTHENES: (1) f. v BC *IOSPE* I^2 270 (*CEG* I 173; Dubois, *IGDOlbia* 44) (s. *Μολπαγόρης*)

Λεωπρέπης
SKYTHIA:
—OLBIA-BORYSTHENES: (1) iv/iii BC *IOlbia* 71 II, 8 (Dubois, *IGDOlbia* 11) (s. *Εὐ*—)

Λεωσθένης
THRACE:
—MARONEIA: (1) ii-i BC *IThrakAig* E212, 20 (f. *Φανόπολις*); (2) 102 BC *IG* II^2 1028 III, 149 (*FRA* 3544) (s. *Ὄλυμπος*)

Λεώστρατος
CIMMERIAN BOSPOROS:
—PANTIKAPAION: (1) 284-245 BC *CIRB* 23 (s. *Π*—)

Λεώφαντος
CIMMERIAN BOSPOROS:
—PANTIKAPAION: (1) v/iv BC Tolstoi 208 (vase) (*Λεώφα*(*ντος*)?, *Λεωφά*(*νης*)?)
SKYTHIA:
—OLBIA-BORYSTHENES: (2) f. iii BC *SEG* XLII 718 (s. *Ναννίων*)

Λεωχάρης
MACEDONIA (BOTTIAIA):
—TYRISSA? (ASVESTARI (MOD.)): (1) f. ii BC ib. XLVII 999, 10 ([*Λ*]*εωχάρης*)

Λήδα
THRACE:
—BOURDAPA: (1) ii AD *IGB* III 1360 (d. *Φίλιππος*)

Λήναιος
CIMMERIAN BOSPOROS:
—HERMONASSA: (1) iv BC *CIRB* 1056 I, 16
—PANTIKAPAION: (2) iv/iii BC ib. 117 (*CEG* II 737) ([*Λ*]*ήναιος*: f. *Ἑκαταῖος*)
SKYTHIA:
—OLBIA-BORYSTHENES: (3) vi/v BC Dubois, *IGDOlbia* 92 (bronze) (s. *Δημοκλῆς*, f. *Δημώνασσα*); (4) V BC *SEG* XXX 958 (vase) (*Λήνα*[*ιος*]); (5) s. v BC *IOlbia* 58, 3 (Dubois, *IGDOlbia* 2) (*Λήναιος*: f. *Διονυσόδωρος*); (6) iii BC *IOSPE* I^2 201 I, 56 (s. *Ἡρόδωρος*); (7) ~ Vinogradov–Kryžickij pl. 91. 7; (8) iii-ii BC *IOSPE* I^2 33, 1
—OLBIA-BORYSTHENES (BEREZAN (MOD.)): (9) v/iv BC Dubois, *IGDOlbia* 70 (vase)

Λῆνις
THRACE:
—PERINTHOS-HERAKLEIA (NR.): (1) V BC *IPerinth* 286 (*Λήνιος* (gen.): f. *Περίνθιος*)

Λητόδωρος
CIMMERIAN BOSPOROS:
—PHANAGOREIA: (1) 151 AD *CIRB* 976, 4
THRACE:
—APOLLONIA-SOZOPOLIS: (2) iv BC *BMNBurgas* 4 (2002) p. 120 no. 2 ([*Λ*]*ητόδ*[*ωρος*]?: f. *Ἀλπάλης*)

Λιβάνις
MACEDONIA (SINTIKE):
—PARTHIKOPOLIS: (1) 243 AD *IGB* V 5904 (*Καπιτωνιανὸς Φίλιππος ὁ καὶ Λ.*)

Λίβανος
SKYTHIA:
—TANAIS: (1) ii AD *CIRB* 1262, 22 (f. *Παντάγαθος*)

Λίβιος
MACEDONIA (PAIONIA):
—BYLAZORA: (1) ii-iii AD *SEG* XVI 402, 4 (*Λεί*-: f. *Μᾶρκος*)

Λίβυς
CIMMERIAN BOSPOROS:
—PANTIKAPAION: **(1)** iv BC *CIRB* 206

Λικίνιος
MACEDONIA (BOTTIAIA):
—BEROIA: **(1)** 177 AD *IBer* 135 A, 19 (-κίνν-: s. *Κοΐντα*)
THRACE:
—ANCHIALOS (TERRIT.): **(2)** ii-iii AD *IGB* I^2 385, 1 (-κίνν-: s. *Χρησ—*)
—APOLLONIA-SOZOPOLIS: **(3)** s. i BC ib. 395 quater, 2 (s. *Λούκιος*)

Λίκκων
MACEDONIA (EDONIS):
—AMPHIPOLIS: **(1)** v-vi AD Feissel, *RICM* 215, 5

Λιλλᾶς
SCYTHIA MINOR:
—TOMIS: **(1)** iii-iv AD *ISM* II 384, 12 (Barnea 1; Popescu, *IGL* 18); cf. *SEG* XLVIII 980 (s. *Βασσιανός*, *Ἰανουαρία*)

Λίλλεις
SCYTHIA MINOR:
—ISTROS: **(1)** f. iii AD *ISM* I 218, 5; cf. Robert, *Hell.* 11-12 (1960) pp. 373-5 (name) (s. *Ἄνδρων*)
THRACE:
—ODESSOS?: **(2)** ii AD *IGB* I^2 51 bis a, 7 (s. *Πάπας*)

Λίλλις
TAURIS:
—CHERSONESOS: **(1)** ii/iii AD *IOSPE* I^2 491; cf. KW pl. 34 no. 482; Zgusta, *PNS* 1063 (*Σεβηρᾶς ὁ καὶ Λ.*: s. *Λίλλων*)

Λίλλων
SCYTHIA MINOR:
—TOMIS: **(1)** ii-iii AD *ISM* II 20, 4 (s. *Μάρκελλος*)
TAURIS:
—CHERSONESOS: **(2)** ii/iii AD *IOSPE* I^2 491; cf. KW pl. 34 no. 482; Zgusta, *PNS* 1063 (f. *Σεβηρᾶς ὁ καὶ Λίλλις*)

Λιμναῖος
CIMMERIAN BOSPOROS:
—GORGIPPIA: **(1)** f. iii BC *CIRB* 1137 A I, 15 (s. *Πύρρος*)
MACEDONIA: **(2)** ?417-413 BC *IG* I^3 89, 68 (Tataki, *Macedonians* p. 356 no. 32) (*[Λ]ιμναῖος*); **(3)** 326 BC Berve 474 (Tataki, *Macedonians* p. 356 no. 29); **(4)** c. 285 BC *SEG* XXXVIII 619, 4 (s. *Ἅρπαλος*); **(5)** 197 BC *RE* (3) (Tataki, *Macedonians* p. 356 no. 31); **(6)** 171 BC *PTeb* 819, 43 (Tataki, *Macedonians* p. 356 no. 33; La'da E1663) (*[Λι]μṿạῖọṣ?*: s. *Ἐργεύς*); **(7)** 168 BC *RE* (4) (Tataki, *Macedonians* p. 356 no. 34) (s. *Πολεμοκράτης*)
MACEDONIA (ALMOPIA):
—MONASTIRAKI (MOD.): **(8)** iii AD *SEG* XXVIII 546 (s. *Βίθυς*)
MACEDONIA (BOTTIAIA):
—BEROIA: **(9)** i BC-i AD *IBer* 142, 3 (*Λιμ[ναῖος]?*: I f. *Λιμναῖος* II); **(10)** ~ ib. l. 3 (Tataki 812) (II s. *Λιμναῖος* I); **(11)** i AD *IBer* 188 (Tataki 814) (f. *Ἀφροδίσις*); **(12)** f. ii AD *IBer* 130 (Tataki 813) (s. *Ξενο—*)
MACEDONIA (DERRIOPOS):
—STUBERRA: **(13)** 50 AD *IG* X (2) (2) 324, 17 (*Λ̣ιμναῖος*: f. *Μενέλαος*); **(14)** 74 AD ib. 325, 29 (s. *Μενέλαος*); **(15)** ~ ib. l. 33 (I f. *Λιμναῖος* II); **(16)** ~ ib. l. 33 (II s. *Λιμναῖος* I)
MACEDONIA (ELIMEIA):
—KOZANI (MOD.): **(17)** ii BC *EAM* 3 (f. *Ὀρέστης*)
MACEDONIA (EORDAIA):
—DREPANO (MOD.): **(18)** ii-i BC ib. 95 (*Λιμ[ναῖος]*: f. *Λυσίστρατος*)
—EXOCHI (MOD.)?: **(19)** ii-i BC ib. 94 (s. *Ὀρέστης*, f. *Οὐαδήα*)
MACEDONIA (PIERIA):
—PYDNA: **(20)** iv BC *GRBS* 43 (2002-3) p. 119 no. 5, 4
MACEDONIA (TYMPHAIA):
—AGIOS GEORGIOS (MOD.): **(21)** iii-ii BC *EAM* 74 (*[Λ]ιμναῖος*: s. *Γου—*)
MACEDONIA?: **(22)** 226 BC Plb. v 90. 1 (Tataki, *Macedonians* p. 356 no. 30)

Λίμνακος
CIMMERIAN BOSPOROS:
—FRONTOVOE (MOD.): **(1)** ii/iii AD *SEG* XXXV 869, 6; cf. *BE* 1990, no. 592 (*Λιμṿạ[ῖος]*—ed., *Λίμṿạ[κος]?*: s. *Σοῦσος*)
—GORGIPPIA: **(2)** ii/iii AD *CIRB* 1179, 55 (f. *Μοιρόδωρος*)
SKYTHIA:
—TANAIS: **(3)** 244 AD ib. 1287, 21 (*Λί̣μ̣ν̣ακος*: s. *Πόπλιος*)

Λίτας
MACEDONIA (EDONIS):
—EDONOI: **(1)** c. 510 BC *Macedonia* 2 p. 130 (coin) (king)

Λίχης
THRACE:
—APOLLONIA-SOZOPOLIS: **(1)** v/iv BC Lanz sale (6th Jun. 1994) 80 (coin)

Λογγῖνα
MACEDONIA (MYGDONIA):
—THESSALONIKE: **(1)** i/ii AD *AD* 24 (1969) Chron. p. 300 (-νγεῖ-)
MACEDONIA (PIERIA):
—DION: **(2)** ii-iii AD Dimitsas 175 (-νγεῖ-: ?m. *Πολύχαρμος*)
SCYTHIA MINOR:
—TOMIS: **(3)** ii-iii AD *ISM* II 326 (*GVI* 956) (-γεῖ-)

Λογγῖνος
MACEDONIA (BOTTIAIA):
—BEROIA: **(1)** iii AD *IBer* 255 (Tataki 815) (*Λογῖ-*: I f. *Λογγῖνος* II); **(2)** ~ *IBer* 255 (Tataki 816) (*Λογῖ(νος)*: II s. *Λογγῖνος* I)
—PELLA: **(3)** ii/iii AD *SEG* XLVIII 826 (-νγεῖ-)
MACEDONIA (EDONIS):
—AMPHIPOLIS: **(4)** ii-iii AD *TAPA* 69 (1938) p. 75 no. 34
MACEDONIA (MYGDONIA):
—THESSALONIKE: **(5)** i/ii AD *SEG* XXXVIII 710 (-νγεῖ-); **(6)** ii AD *IG* X (2) (1) 241 A I, 6 (-νγεῖ-); **(7)** ~ *SEG* XXXVI 645; *KGAM Thess.* I 59 (date) (*Διονύσιος ὁ καὶ Λογγεῖνος*: s. *Διονύσιος*)
SCYTHIA MINOR:
—ISTROS: **(8)** ii AD *ISM* I 197 II, 6 (-γεῖ-: f. *Ἄνδρων*)
—TOMIS: **(9)** ii AD ib. II 17, 6 (-νγεῖ-: s. *Οὐάλης*); **(10)** ii-iii AD ib. 16 (*Λονγεῖṿ[ος]*); **(11)** ~ ib. 18, 6 (-νγεῖ-); **(12)** ~ ib. 31 III, 2 (*Λονγεῖṿ[ος]*); **(13)** 201 AD ib. 83 I, 22 (*Λονγεῖνος*—apogr.: f. *Ἄνδρων*)
THRACE: **(14)** 46-54 AD *SEG* XVI 415 III, 29 (*IThrakAig* E84) (-νγεῖ-: s. *Δορζίνθης*)
—BARGALA: **(15)** ii-iii AD *SEG* XLIV 516 (-νγῖ-)
—BEROE-AUGUSTA TRAIANA: **(16)** f. iii AD *IGB* V 5577, 6 (-νγεῖ-: f. *Φλ. Δίνις*)
—BOURDAPA: **(17)** ii-iii AD ib. III 1340 (*Ἀπολλώνις ὁ καὶ Λονγεῖνος*: s. *Ἀπολλωνίδης*)
—PHILIPPOPOLIS-TRIMONTIUM: **(18)** ii-iii AD ib. 1015 (-νγεῖ-: f. *Χαρίτων*); **(19)** iii AD ib. 953 (*Λον(γ)εῖνος*: s. *Κότυς*); **(20)** ~ ib. V 5463 (-γγει-: f. *Αὐρ. Τατία Λογγῖνα*)
—PHILIPPOPOLIS-TRIMONTIUM (TERRIT.): **(21)** ii-iii AD ib. III 1404 (-νγῖ-: f. *Αὐλούζενις*)
—SERDICA (TERRIT.): **(22)** ii-iii AD ib. IV 1988, 3; V 5688 (-νγεῖ-: f. *Νάνα*)

Λογγίων
CIMMERIAN BOSPOROS:
—PHANAGOREIA*: **(1)** 16 AD *CIRB* 985, 8 + Levinskaya pp. 236-7 no. 5 (*Διονύσιος ὁ κ̣[α]ὶ Λογ̣[γ]ίων*: threptos)

Λόγγος
THRACE:
—MESAMBRIA: **(1)** vi AD Beševliev 154 (*Λόνγ-*)
—PHILIPPOPOLIS-TRIMONTIUM: **(2)** ii-iii AD *IGB* III 1003 (*Λόνγ-*)

Λογική
MACEDONIA (ELIMEIA):
—AIANE (TERRIT.): **(1)** ?ii AD *EAM* 31

Λογισμός
MACEDONIA (BOTTIAIA):
—BEROIA: **(1)** i BC-i AD *IBer* 142, 7 (Tataki 817) (*Λογισμ[ός]*)
MACEDONIA (DERRIOPOS):
—STUBERRA: **(2)** 107 AD *IG* X (2) (2) 325, 102 (s. *Διονύσιος*)
MACEDONIA (MYGDONIA):
—THESSALONIKE: **(3)** ii-iii AD *AD* 26 (1971) Chron. p. 377 no. 2

Λόγος
SKYTHIA:
—TANAIS: **(1)** 228 AD *CIRB* 1282, 22 (s. *Χοδιάκιος*)
THRACE: **(2)** ii-i BC *IG* II^2 8914 (*FRA* 2553) (s. *Ἀλέξανδρος*)

Λογχάτης
SKYTHIA:
—SKYTHAI: **(1)** ii AD Luc., *Tox.* 44-51; 55 (fict.)

Λόγωζις?
SKYTHIA:
—TANAIS: **(1)** 225 AD *CIRB* 1280, 30 (*Λογῶζις?—CIRB*, *—λογωζις*—Tokhtas'ev, *—ιώζις*—Latyshev: s. *Ἀρδάρακος*)

Λόγων
CIMMERIAN BOSPOROS:
—PANTIKAPAION: **(1)** i/ii AD ib. 79 A, 1 (*[Λ]όγων*: s. *Ῥόδων*)

Λοκρίων
THRACE:
—MARONEIA: **(1)** ii-i BC *IThrakAig* E212, 44 (f. *Γάϊος*)

Λοκρός
MACEDONIA (PIERIA):
—PYDNA: **(1)** iv BC *GRBS* 43 (2002-3) p. 119 no. 5, 6

Λόλα
MACEDONIA (PELAGONIA): **(1)** ii-i BC *IG* X (2) (2) 158 (d. *Βαδοῦς*)

Λόλησον
CIMMERIAN BOSPOROS:
—PANTIKAPAION: **(1)** i AD *CIRB* 450 (m. *Ὑγιαίνων*)

Λολλαῖος
CIMMERIAN BOSPOROS:
—PANTIKAPAION*: **(1)** 249 AD ib. 58, 6 (f. *Αὐρ. Ῥόδων*)

Λολλία
THRACE:
—SALYMBRIA: **(1)** ii-i BC *IByz* S 45 (d. *Ῥαδινός*)

Λόλλις
MACEDONIA (PIERIA):
—DION: **(1)** ?i AD Oikonomos 7

Λολοῦς
SKYTHIA?: **(1)** iii AD Greifenhagen, *Schmuckarb.* 2 p. 81 (ring)

Λοπικῖνα
SCYTHIA MINOR:
—TOMIS: (1) v-vi AD Barnea 20 (Popescu, *IGL* 46)

Λουκᾶς
MACEDONIA (EDONIS):
—AMPHIPOLIS*: (1) ii-i BC *Ant. terakoti Bulg.* 108 (terracotta) (*Λουκᾶ* (gen.))

Λούκασος
MACEDONIA (PAIONIA):
—BYLAZORA: (1) ii-iii AD *SEG* XVI 402, 1 (s. *Βαβύλος, Κοάρτα*)

Λουκία
MACEDONIA (BOTTIAIA):
—EDESSA: (1) 211 AD ib. XLV 750 A

Λουκιανή
MACEDONIA (MYGDONIA):
—THESSALONIKE: (1) f. iii AD ib. XLIV 555 + *AEMTh* 5 (1991) p. 233 fig. 11 (*Αὐρ. Λ.*)
MACEDONIA (PAIONIA):
—KAVADARCI (MOD.): (2) ii-iii AD *Sp.* 98 (1941-8) p. 66 no. 137 (*Λουκαίνη*—ed. per err.)
THRACE:
—PERINTHOS-HERAKLEIA: (3) iii-iv AD *IPerinth* 185 (*AD* 51-2 (1996-7) Mel. p. 347 no. 174); (4) iv AD *IPerinth* 219, 5 (*AD* 49-50 (1994-5) Mel. p. 343 no. 165) (d. *Λούκις, Ἀσκληπιοδότη*)

Λουκιανός
THRACE:
—BEROE-AUGUSTA TRAIANA (TERRIT.): (1) ii-iii AD *IGB* III 1718 (s. *Ἄλκιμος*)
—PHILIPPOPOLIS-TRIMONTIUM (TERRIT.): (2) ii-iii AD ib. 1458-9 (s. *Γάϊος*)
—SKAPTOPARA: (3) ii-iii AD ib. IV 2237 (s. *Λούκιος*)

Λουκιλία
MACEDONIA (MYGDONIA):
—THESSALONIKE: (1) 154 AD *IG* X (2) (1) 288, 9 (-*κει*-: m. *Πύθων*)
—THESSALONIKE?: (2) ii AD ib. 875
MACEDONIA (PAIONIA):
—KAVADARCI (MOD.): (3) ii-iii AD *Sp.* 98 (1941-8) p. 66 no. 138 (*Λουκιδία*—Vulic, *Λ.*—Proeva)

Λουκιλιανός
MACEDONIA (ODOMANTIKE):
—SKOTOUSSA?: (1) 156 AD *SEG* XXIV 612, 6 (-*κει*-: ?f. *Κλαυδία*)

Λούκιλλα
MACEDONIA (BOTTIAIA):
—EDESSA: (1) imp. *Tekmeria* 7 (2002) p. 104 no. 8 (-*κιλα*)
MACEDONIA (PIERIA):
—DION: (2) ?iii AD Dimitsas 178 (-*κιλα*: d. *Αὐρ. Λύκος*)
SCYTHIA MINOR:
—KALLATIS (NR.): (3) ii-iii AD *ISM* III 243, 5 (*IGB* I² 2) (*Λού[κ]ιλλα*: d. *Σαβῖνα*)
THRACE:
—ABDERA: (4) iii AD *SEG* XXIV 628 (*IThrakAig* E71) (d. *Καισώνιος Σωκράτης, Αὐρ. Ἀλεξάνδρα*)

Λουκῖνος
SCYTHIA MINOR:
—CAPIDAVA: (1) iii-iv AD Popescu, *IGL* 225 ([*Λ*]*ουκεῖνος*?)

Λούκιος
CIMMERIAN BOSPOROS:
—PANTIKAPAION: (1) m. i AD *CIRB* 532 (f. *Φιλόμουσος*); (2) 82 AD ib. 76, 21 (*SEG* XVIII 310) (s. *Κόϊντος*)
MACEDONIA (BOTTIAIA):
—BEROIA: (3) ii-iii AD *IBer* 28 (Tataki 799) ([*Λο*]*ύκιος*); (4) ii/iii AD *IBer* 27 A, 3 (s. *Κομμοῦνος*)
MACEDONIA (CHALKIDIKE):
—ANTHEMOUS: (5) s. ii AD *ZPE* 140 (2002) p. 127 (I f. *Λούκιος* II); (6) ~ ib. (II s. *Λούκιος* I)
MACEDONIA (DERRIOPOS):
—STUBERRA: (7) c. 41-48 AD *IG* X (2) (2) 323, 18 (f. *Γάϊος*); (8) 50 AD ib. 324, 17 (s. *Παράμονος*); (9) ~ ib. l. 22 (*Λούκι[ος]*: f. *Αἰμίλιος*); (10) 74 AD ib. 326, 25 (s. *Λουκρήτιος*); (11) ~ ib. l. 60 (s. *Παράμονος*); (12) 87 AD ib. 325, 76 (s. *Ἔλβιος*)
MACEDONIA (ELIMEIA):
—OBLOSTAI: (13) 200 AD *EAM* 37, 6 (f. *Ἀπολλόδωρος*)
MACEDONIA (EORDAIA): (14) s. ii AD *ILeukopetra* 134, 1 (Tataki, *Macedonians* p. 199 no. 5) (*Λ(ο)ύκιος*: f. *Γλαύκα*)
MACEDONIA (KRESTONIA):
—MANDRES (MOD.): (15) 36 or 153 AD *SEG* XLIII 426
MACEDONIA (LYNKESTIS):
—HERAKLEIA: (16) i AD *IG* X (2) (2) 75, 7 (f. *Σευῆρος*); (17) ~ ib. l. 21 (f. *Τ. Σωτᾶς*); (18) ~ ib. l. 45 (I f. *Λούκιος* II); (19) ~ ib. l. 45 (II s. *Λούκιος* I)
MACEDONIA (MYGDONIA):
—KALINDOIA: (20) 68-98 AD *SEG* XLII 580, 48 (s. *Διονύσιος*); (21) a. 98 AD ib. 582, 47 (s. *Δυτύλος*)
—THESSALONIKE: (22) i-ii AD *IG* X (2) (1) 243 II, 2 (*Νικέας ὁ καὶ Λ.*: s. *Νικέας*); (23) ii AD ib. 456, 1 (s. *Εὐτυχία*); (24) 125 AD ib. 624 (s. *Στρατονίκη*); (25) ii/iii AD ib. 262 I, 7
—THESSALONIKE?: (26) ii AD ib. 875; (27) ii-iii AD ib. 856, 1 (s. *Μέστριος, Φίλα*)
MACEDONIA (ODOMANTIKE):
—SIRRHA: (28) 155 AD Dimitsas 821, 18 (Kaphtantzis 1) (s. *Λοῦππος*); (29) f. iii AD *SEG* XXX 590, 4 (f. *Αὐρ. Διοσκοῦς*)
MACEDONIA (ORESTIS):
—SISANI (MOD.): (30) 146 AD *EAM* 187, 15 (f. *Λύκος*)
MACEDONIA (PAIONIA): (31) imp. *Sp.* 98 (1941-8) p. 202 no. 401 (s. *Σελήνη*); (32) 249 AD ib. p. 202 no. 404, 1 (s. *Δ.ογ*—)
—BYLAZORA: (33) ii-iii AD ib. 75 (1933) p. 19 no. 37, 1 (s. *Ἀλέξανδρος*, f. *Φιλόξενος, Μᾶρκος*)
—BYLAZORA (NR.): (34) ii-iii AD *SEG* XVI 403b (s. *Ἀλέξανδρος, Δημάρχη*, f. *Ἀλέξανδρος*)
—KAVADARCI (MOD.): (35) ii-iii AD *Sp.* 71 (1931) p. 63 no. 136, 1 (f. *Ἰούλιος*); (36) ~ ib. p. 67 no. 149, 2 + 77 (1934) p. 81 (f. *Μᾶρκος, Σεκοῦνδος*); (37) ~ ib. 98 (1941-8) p. 66 no. 138; (38) ii/iii AD Unp. (Papazoglu archive) (s. *Γαΐα*)
—NEAPOLIS? (IZVOR (MOD.): (39) ii-iii AD Dimitsas 301, 3 (s. *Ἡρακλέων, Παυλῖνα*)
—NEAPOLIS? (VLADILOVCI (MOD.)): (40) ii-iii AD *Sp.* 71 (1931) p. 31 no. 62 (s. *Γάϊος*: sculptor)
MACEDONIA (SINTIKE):
—PARTHIKOPOLIS (TERRIT.): (41) ii AD *IGB* IV 2302, 5 (s. *Ἀρτεμίδωρος, Σωσίπολις*)
SCYTHIA MINOR:
—DINOGETIA (NR.): (42) ii-iv AD *ISM* V 309 (tile)
—ISTROS: (43) ii AD ib. I 196, 19 (f. *Δομέτις*) ?= (*46*); (44) ~ ib. 197 I, 12 (f. *Ἀλέξανδρος*); (45) ~ ib. l. 14 (s. *Ἡρακλείδης*); (46) ~ ib. 201 I, 11 (*Λού[κιος]*: f. *Δομίτιος*) ?= (*43*); (47) f. iii AD ib. 199, 7; (48) ~ ib. 218, 3 (f. *Ἱλαρίων*)
—TOMIS: (49) ii AD ib. II 125, 6 (f. *Ἄττας*); (50) ii-iii AD ib. 337 (s. *Εὐάριστος*); (51) 201 AD ib. 83 II, 27 (f. *Ἱλαρίων*)
SKYTHIA:
—OLBIA-BORYSTHENES: (52) ii AD *IOSPE* I² 89, 15 (I f. *Λούκιος* II); (53) ~ ib. l. 15 (II s. *Λούκιος* I)
—TYRAS: (54) 181 AD ib. 2, 30 (s. *Σατορνῖλος*)
TAURIS:
—CHERSONESOS: (55) ?ii AD ib. 451, 3; (56) 130 AD *VDI* 1960 (3), pp. 154-5, 25 (s. *Ἱλαρος*)
THRACE:
—APOLLONIA-SOZOPOLIS: (57) s. i BC *IGB* I² 395 quater, 3 (II s. *Λούκιος* I); (58) ~ ib. l. 2-3 (I f. *Λικίνιος, Λούκιος* II)
—BYZANTION: (59) i BC-i AD *IByz* 239; cf. *BE* 2001, no. 308 (f. *Λαυδίκη*)
—DIONYSOPOLIS: (60) iii AD *IGB* I² 14 c, 21 (f. *Αὐρ. Ἑρμόδωρος*)
—MARKIANOPOLIS: (61) iii AD ib. II 804, 4 (*CCET* II (1) 201) (*Εἰσάτραλις ὁ καὶ Λ.*: s. *Σκάρις*); (62) f. iii AD *IGB* V 5344 (*CCET* II (1) 209) (f. *Πίος*)
—MARONEIA: (63) iii AD *IThrakAig* E308
—NICOPOLIS AD ISTRUM: (64) iii AD *IGB* II 682 (*Eastern cults* p. 75 no. 7) (s. *Ἀνδρόνικος*)
—NICOPOLIS AD NESTUM (TERRIT.): (65) ii AD *IGB* IV 2349 (I f. *Λούκιος* II); (66) ~ ib. (II s. *Λούκιος* I, f. *Σέξτος*)
—ODESSOS: (67) ii-iii AD ib. I² 198 ([*Λ*]*ούκιος*: s. *Εὐάριστος*); (68) m. ii AD ib. 174 bis (PM 1703); *Dacia* 21 (1977) p. 161 (date) (s. *Διονύσιος*)
—PHILIPPOPOLIS-TRIMONTIUM (TERRIT.): (69) iii AD *IGB* III 1200 (f. *Λούκις*)
—SERDICA: (70) ii-iii AD ib. V 5816 (f. *Ἥρανος*); (71) iii AD ib. IV 1927 (*Eastern cults* p. 166 no. 8) (f. *Αὐρ. Δίζας*)
—SKAPTOPARA: (72) ii-iii AD *IGB* IV 2237 (f. *Λουκιανός*)
—SPORTELA: (73) ii-iii AD ib. 2233, 6 (*Eastern cults* p. 170 no. 16)

Λούκις
MACEDONIA (BOTTIAIA):
—BEROIA: (1) ii-iii AD *IBer* 321 (Tataki 820)
MACEDONIA (PELAGONIA):
—KERAMIAI (NR.): (2) ii AD *IG* X (2) (2) 209
THRACE:
—BYZANTION: (3) ii AD *SEG* L 667 VII (s. *Ἀγαθόπους, Φῆστα*)
—NICOPOLIS AD ISTRUM (TERRIT.): (4) ii AD *IGB* V 5244 b, 13 (?s. *Ἀ*—); (5) ii-iii AD ib. II 700
—PERINTHOS-HERAKLEIA: (6) iii AD *IPerinth* 45 (s. *Μενέλαος*); (7) iv AD ib. 219, 2 (*AD* 49-50 (1994-5) Mel. p. 343 no. 165) (II s. *Λούκις* I, *Ἀσκληπιοδότη*); (8) ~ *IPerinth* 219, 13 (*AD* 49-50 (1994-5) Mel. p. 343 no. 165) (I f. *Λούκις* II, *Θεόδοτος, Δόμνα, Λουκιανή, Ζώη, Θεοδούλη*)
—PHILIPPOPOLIS-TRIMONTIUM (TERRIT.): (9) iii AD *IGB* III 1200 (s. *Λούκιος*)

Λουκίσανδρος
THRACE:
—APOLLONIA-SOZOPOLIS: (1) i-ii AD ib. I² 401, 18 (s. *Ἀπολλώνιος*)

Λούκουλλος
THRACE:
—BYZANTION?: (1) ?ii AD *IByz* 120, 11 (Stephanis 1557) (*Λουκουμος*—lap.)

Λουκρήτιος
MACEDONIA (DERRIOPOS):
—STUBERRA: (1) 74 AD *IG* X (2) (2) 326, 26 (f. *Λούκιος*)

Λοῦος
CIMMERIAN BOSPOROS:
—PANTIKAPAION: (1) iv AD *ZOOID* 21 (1898) p. 209 no. 19 (f. *Ἀγόραστος*)

Λούπερκος
MACEDONIA (BOTTIAIA):
—BEROIA: (1) ii-iii AD *IBer* 256 (Tataki 821)

Λουπῖνα
MACEDONIA (BOTTIAIA):
—BEROIA: (1) ii-iii AD *IBer* 256 (Tataki 819) (*Λοπεῖ-, Λογγεῖνα*?—Woodward)

Λοῦππος
MACEDONIA (BOTTIAIA):
—BEROIA: **(1)** ii AD *IBer* 343 (Tataki 566) (s. *Λ.* Ἰαυλῆνος Μάξιμος, Φλ. Σαμβατίς); **(2)** ii/iii AD *IBer* 27 A, 7 (s. Παπίας)
MACEDONIA (ODOMANTIKE):
—SIRRHA: **(3)** 155 AD Dimitsas 821, 18 (Kaphtantzis 1) (f. Λούκιος)
MACEDONIA (PAIONIA):
—KAVADARCI (MOD.): **(4)** ii AD Unp. (Kavadarci)
THRACE: **(5)** iii-iv AD *IG* II² 4826, 5 (*FRA* 2554)
—KELLAI: **(6)** 241-244 AD *IGB* III 1517, 8 (I f. Αὐρ. Λοῦππος II)
—MONTANA: **(7)** iii AD *Arkheologiia* (Sofia) 1970 (3), p. 46 no. 8, 9 (*Montana* II 117) (Lat. Lupus)
—PAUTALIA: **(8)** 135 AD *IGB* IV 2057, 9 ([Λο]ῦπ(π)ος: s. Κέλσος)
—PAUTALIA (TERRIT.): **(9)** ii-iii AD ib. 2126 (f. Λάδων); **(10)** ~ ib. 2139 (Λοῦπ(π)ος: f. Παρδαλᾶς); **(11)** ~ ib. V 5812 ([Λο]ῦππο[ς]); **(12)** ~ ib. 5822 (Λο[ῦ]ππος: s. Ἀλέξανδρος)
—PHILIPPOPOLIS-TRIMONTIUM (TERRIT.): **(13)** ii-iii AD ib. III 1112 (Λο(ῦ)ππος); **(14)** ~ ib. 1217 (s. —κενθος); **(15)** iii AD ib. 1430 (f. Βίθυς)
—PLOTINOPOLIS: **(16)** imp. *Thrakika* 2 (1929) p. 89 (*IThrakAig* E468) (Λοῦπος); **(17)** 160 AD *SEG* XXXVII 970, 4 (f. Στίλας)
—SERDICA: **(18)** ii-iii AD *IGB* IV 1931; **(19)** 117-138 AD ib. 1925 d, 16 (f. —δώρα); **(20)** iii AD ib. 1941 (*Eastern cults* p. 193 no. 4) (Λόπος: f. Πομπώνιος Θεόδουλος); **(21)** ~ *IGB* IV 1950, 3 (Λό-: f. Αὐρ. Σολώνιος)
—SPORTELA: **(22)** ii-iii AD ib. 2233, 5 (*Eastern cults* p. 170 no. 16) (s. Πιεισειsος)

Λούσαλα
MACEDONIA (ODOMANTIKE):
—SIRRHA (TERRIT.): **(1)** ii-iii AD *SEG* XXX 607 (Pilhofer 556)

Λουσάτιος
MACEDONIA (BOTTIAIA):
—BEROIA: **(1)** ii/iii AD *IBer* 143 B, 22 (Tataki 1160) (I f. Λουσάτιος II); **(2)** ~ *IBer* 143 B, 22 (Tataki 1161) (II s. Λουσάτιος I)

Λούστας
THRACE:
—PERINTHOS-HERAKLEIA: **(1)** iv-v AD *IPerinth* 179 (*AD* 51-2 (1996-7) Mel. p. 371 no. 188) (Αὐρ. Λ.)

Λόχος
SKYTHIA:
—SOLOKHA (MOD.): **(1)** f. iv BC *Kurgan Solokha* p. 80 no. 55 (Rostovtsev, *SB* I p. 373) (—λοχος?)

Λύγγιον
CIMMERIAN BOSPOROS:
—PANTIKAPAION: **(1)** i AD *CIRB* 451 (Λύνγι-: m. Σαδάλας)

Λύγδαμις
MACEDONIA (BISALTIA):
—TRAGILOS: **(1)** 361 BC *CID* II 4 I, 35 (Tataki, *Macedonians* p. 192 no. 2)
SKYTHIA:
—KIMMERIOI: **(2)** vii BC *RE* (1) (king)
THRACE:
—APOLLONIA-SOZOPOLIS: **(3)** ?253 BC *ISM* III 7, 21 (Λύγ[δα]μις: f. Στρατῶναξ)

Λυγκεύς
MACEDONIA (BOTTIAIA):
—BEROIA: **(1)** 223 BC *IBer* 4, 16 (f. Ἀγάθων); **(2)** a. 212 AD ib. 136, 20 (Tataki 720) (Κλ. Λυνκεύς); **(3)** ~ *IBer* 136, 21 (Tataki 895) (Μέστρ. Λυνκεύς)

Λυγκωρίτας
MACEDONIA (PIERIA):
—PYDNA: **(1)** iv BC *GRBS* 43 (2002-3) p. 119 no. 5, 1 (Λυγκωρίτα(s))

Λύγχη
THRACE:
—NIKOPOL (MOD.): **(1)** m. i AD *ILB* 138 (Lat. Avillia Lynche)

Λύδα
MACEDONIA (BOTTIAIA):
—AIGAI: **(1)** iv/iii BC *SEG* XXXV 785 (Λυλα—ed. pr.: d. Κλεαγόρας)

Λύδη
MACEDONIA (MYGDONIA):
—THESSALONIKE: **(1)** ii AD *IG* X (2) (1) 294
—THESSALONIKE?: **(2)** ii-iii AD ib. II² 11978a (Tataki, *Macedonians* p. 183 no. 40) (Κοκ. Λ.)

Λύδιος
THRACE:
—BYZANTION: **(1)** i BC-i AD *IByz* 215 (Fıratlı–Robert p. 73 no. 78) (f. Αὖλος)

Λύδος
THRACE:
—APOLLONIA-SOZOPOLIS: **(1)** v BC *IGB* I² 432 (f. Ἀπατούριος)
—MESAMBRIA: **(2)** ii BC ib. 322 ter, 4 (*Eastern cults* p. 25 no. 42)

Λύκα
MACEDONIA (BOTTIAIA):
—BEROIA: **(1)** ii-iii AD *IBer* 341 (m. Οὐαλέρις); **(2)** ii/iii AD *ILeukopetra* 54, 1 (d. Ἄδυμος); **(3)** 190 AD ib. 23, 1 (Tataki 1056) (Πετρωνία (Λ)ύκα)
—EDESSA: **(4)** ii-iii AD Dimitsas 15 (290; Tataki, *Edessa* 183); **(5)** 256 AD *Athena* 12 (1900) p. 72 no. 6, 4 (Tataki, *Edessa* 46) (Αὐρ. Λ.: d. Λύκος)
MACEDONIA (DERRIOPOS):
—STUBERRA: **(6)** 209 AD *IG* X (2) (2) 320 (Φλαουία Λ.)
MACEDONIA (EDONIS):
—AMPHIPOLIS: **(7)** m. ii AD *SEG* XXXV 712 (d. Ζώσιμος, Χρησίμα)
MACEDONIA (MYGDONIA):
—THESSALONIKE: **(8)** ii AD *IG* X (2) (1) 326, 2 (m. Ἀθηνόδωρος, Λευκίππη); **(9)** ii-iii AD ib. 453, 1, 4 (d. Φλ. Κασσάνδρα); **(10)** ~ ib. 511 (Κασσία Λ.); **(11)** iii AD ib. 562, 1 (Ἰουλ. Ἀρρία Λ.)
MACEDONIA (ORESTIS):
—SISANI (MOD.): **(12)** 146 AD *EAM* 187, 11 (m. Τίτος)
MACEDONIA (PAIONIA):
—KAVADARCI (MOD.): **(13)** 210 AD *Sp.* 98 (1941-8) p. 57 no. 115 (?m. (nat.) Χιόνη)
—STOBOI: **(14)** ii AD *Municipium Stobensium* p. 67 no. 377 (Ὀφιλλία Λ.)
—STOBOI (NR.): **(15)** ii/iii AD *SEG* XVI 406 (d. Πούπλιος, Κλυμένη)

Λυκαγόρας
MACEDONIA: **(1)** iv BC Arr., *An.* i 12. 7 (Tataki, *Macedonians* p. 357 no. 37) (f. Πανήγορος)

Λυκαῖος
MACEDONIA: **(1)** ?417-413 BC *IG* I³ 89, 64 (Tataki, *Macedonians* p. 357 no. 38)
MACEDONIA (LOWER PAIONIA):
—GORTYNIA?: **(2)** imp. *Sp.* 98 (1941-8) p. 48 no. 101 (Sokolovska, *Isar-Marvinci* p. 131) ([Λ]υκαῖος)

Λυκαρίων
MACEDONIA (BOTTIAIA):
—BEROIA: **(1)** ii/iii AD *IBer* 143 B, 21 (Tataki 1324) (Φλ. Λ.); **(2)** 177 AD *IBer* 135 A, 13 (Tataki 614) (Ἰούλ. Λ.)
—BEROIA*: **(3)** ii/iii AD *IBer* 144 B, 15 (Tataki 66) (Αἰλιανὸς Λ.: freed.)
MACEDONIA (EORDAIA):
—PYRGOI (MOD.): **(4)** ii-iii AD *EAM* 129 (I f. Λυκαρίων II, Λυσίμαχος, Εὐτυχία); **(5)** ~ ib. (II s. Λυκαρίων I, Σελήνη)
MACEDONIA (MYGDONIA):
—THESSALONIKE: **(6)** i-ii AD *IG* X (2) (1) 243 II, 3 (*T.* Σερρήνιος Λ.); **(7)** 155 AD ib. 289, 7

Λύκαρος
MACEDONIA (DERRIOPOS):
—STUBERRA: **(1)** 116 AD ib. X (2) (2) 327, 27 (f. Ζωΐλος)

Λυκαρώ
MACEDONIA (PIERIA):
—DION*: **(1)** ?iii AD *ILGR* 191 (Lat. Aur. Lycaro)

Λυκᾶς
THRACE:
—SERDICA (TERRIT.): **(1)** ii-iii AD *IGB* V 5746

Λυκειός
SCYTHIA MINOR:
—KALLATIS: **(1)** f. iii BC *ISM* III 66, 5 (Λυκει[ός]?)

Λυκεῖς?
THRACE:
—APOLLONIA-SOZOPOLIS: **(1)** iv BC *BMNBurgas* 4 (2002) p. 120 no. 4 (d. Εὐρησίβιος)

Λυκῆς
SCYTHIA MINOR:
—ISTROS: **(1)** v BC Unp. (Avram, defixio) 2, 3 (Λύκεω (gen.): f. Ἱέρηξ, Ἄρητος)

Λυκιανή
MACEDONIA (PIERIA):
—DION: **(1)** ii-iii AD Dimitsas 165, 3 (-κει-)

Λυκιανός
THRACE:
—PHILIPPOPOLIS-TRIMONTIUM: **(1)** imp. *JÖAI* 44 (1959) Beibl. cols. 381-4 (Lat. Fl. Lycianus)

Λυκίας
TAURIS:
—CHERSONESOS*: **(1)** hell. *Khers. Sbornik* 5 (1959) p. 20 (stamp) (masc. nom.?)

Λυκιδίων
MACEDONIA (EORDAIA): **(1)** ii-iii AD *EAM* 104
MACEDONIA (PIERIA):
—DION (TERRIT.): **(2)** ii AD Oikonomos 48 + *Essays Laourdas* p. 112 (name) (Αὐ[ρή]λιος Λ.: s. Ἄμυκος, Κρατησίς)

Λυκῖνος
MACEDONIA (BOTTIAIA):
—BEROIA: **(1)** 181 AD *IBer* 49, 36 (Tataki 1108) (Σέξστος Ποπίλλιος Λ.)
—EDESSA: **(2)** 169 AD *Arch. Pap.* 22 (1973) p. 208 no. 12 (Tataki, *Edessa* 184) (-κεῖ-: s. Οὐλπ. Ἀπολλώνιος, Οὐλπ. Ῥεκέπτα)
SCYTHIA MINOR:
—KALLATIS: **(3)** iii BC *ISM* III 159
THRACE:
—BYZANTION: **(4)** hell.-imp. *IByz* 304 (s. Ἀριστείδης)

Λύκιος
MACEDONIA (MYGDONIA):
—DIKAIA: **(1)** c. 365-359 BC Unp. (Voutyras–Sismanidis) ll. 2-3, 8
—THESSALONIKE?: **(2)** ii AD *IG* X (2) (1) 249, 4

Λυκίσκος
CIMMERIAN BOSPOROS:
—GORGIPPIA: **(1)** s. ii AD *CIRB* 1129 B, 7 ([*Λυ*]*κίσκος*: s. *Πόθος*); **(2)** 173-210 AD *SEG* XXXVI 700, 5 (s. *Φαρ*—); **(3)** ii/iii AD *CIRB* 1179, 20 ([*Λυ*]*κίσκος*?)
MACEDONIA (CHALKIDIKE):
—GIGONOS?: **(4)** 204 or 320 AD *SEG* XXIX 583, 5 (*Κλαυδια*[*νὸς*] [*Λ*]*υκίσκος*: s. *Αὐρ. Κλαυδιανή, Κλαυδι— —ος*)
MACEDONIA?: **(5)** 317-312 BC *RE* (6) (Tataki, *Macedonians* p. 357 no. 40)
SKYTHIA:
—TANAIS: **(6)** c. 200-210 AD *CIRB* 1277, 13 (*Λυκίσ*[*κο*]*ς*: f. *Μενέστρατος*)

Λυκίων
MACEDONIA (BOTTIAIA):
—BEROIA: **(1)** 177 AD *IBer* 135 B, 27 (Tataki 351) (*Γεμίνιος Λ.*)

Λυκκειός
MACEDONIA (PAIONIA): **(1)** c. 356 BC *IG* II^2 127, 3, 12-13 etc. (*Syll*^{3} 196); *AMNG* III (2) pp. 199-201 nos. 1-13 (coin) (*Λύππειος*—*IG*: king)

Λυκκηΐα
MACEDONIA (BOTTIAIA):
—BEROIA: **(1)** m. i AD *IBer* 187 (Tataki 824)

Λυκόλας
MACEDONIA (BOTTIAIA):
—EDESSA: **(1)** iii AD *AD* 8 (1923) p. 267, 2 with fig. 6; cf. Tataki, *Edessa* 185 (*Λυκόλαṿ*?—lap., *Λυκομη*——ed., *Λυκομή*[*δης*]—Tataki)

Λυκολέων
MACEDONIA: **(1)** 237 AD *ILeukopetra* 86, 9 (slave/freed.)
MACEDONIA (BOTTIAIA):
—BEROIA: **(2)** ii/iii AD *IBer* 143 B, 30 (Tataki 827) (s. *Ἀλέξανδρος*); **(3)** 193-217 AD *ILeukopetra* 128, 1 (f. *Ζώσιμος*)
MACEDONIA (PIERIA):
—DION: **(4)** 213 AD *Essays Laourdas* p. 108 no. 6; *Stud. Edson* p. 294 (date)

Λυκομήδης
MACEDONIA (BOTTIAIA):
—BEROIA: **(1)** s. ii AD *IBer* 88, 4 (Tataki 79) (*Αἴλ. Λ.*: s. *Αἴλ. Ἰσίδωρος*)
THRACE:
—BIZYE (TERRIT.): **(2)** ii-iii AD *IGB* III 1865 (s. *Χρῆστος*)
—BYZANTION: **(3)** i BC *IByz* 211 (Fıratlı–Robert p. 70 no. 70) (*Λυκομήδειος* (gen.): f. *Χῆμα*)
—MARKIANOPOLIS (NR.): **(4)** iii AD *IGB* V 5366 ([*M.*] *Οὔλπ. Λ.*)

Λύκος
CIMMERIAN BOSPOROS:
—BOSPOROS: **(1)** imp. *TAM* IV (1) 239, 2 (s. *Ἀριστόδημος*)
—KUL' OBA (MOD.): **(2)** v/iv BC *Sov. Arkh.* 13 (1950) p. 231; *RA* 1914, p. 183 (Rostovtsev, *SB* I p. 373)
MACEDONIA: **(3)** c. 80-30 BC *BGU* 1733, 4, 17 (Tataki, *Macedonians* p. 489 no. 162); cf. La'da E1648 (f. *Ἡρακλείδης, Φίλων*); **(4)** ii AD *RE* (52) (Tataki, *Macedonians* p. 357 no. 41) (doctor)
MACEDONIA (BISALTIA):
—SITOCHORI (MOD.): **(5)** ii-iii AD Kaphtantzis 524 (f. *Λευκώ*)
MACEDONIA (BOTTIAIA):
—BEROIA: **(6)** ii-iii AD *IBer* 257; 288 (Tataki 80) (*Αἴλ. Λ.*: f. *Φοιβιανή*); **(7)** ii/iii AD *IBer* 143 B, 9 (Tataki 1109) (*Πο. Λ.*); **(8)** ~ *IBer* 143 B, 10 (Tataki 1071) (*Πε. Λ.*); **(9)** ~ *IBer* 143 C, 9 (Tataki 615) (*Ἰού. Λ.*); **(10)** a. 212 AD *IBer* 136, 15 (Tataki 289) (*Αὐρ. Λ.*)
—BEROIA (TERRIT.): **(11)** ii-iii AD *IBer* 508 (Tataki 1243) (*Τορπίλιος Λ.*)
—EDESSA: **(12)** 128 AD *SEG* XII 342, 4 (Tataki, *Edessa* 186) (s. *Ξενώ*); **(13)** 256 AD *Athena* 12 (1900) p. 72 no. 6, 4-5 (Tataki, *Edessa* 187) (f. *Λύκα*)
—PELLA? (GIANNITSA (MOD.)): **(14)** ?s. ii AD *JDAI* 84 (1969) p. 152 no. R14 (*Φαβρίκιος Βετουληνὸς Λύκ*[*ο*]*ς*)
—SKYDRA: **(15)** iii AD *SEG* XLIX 793, 3, 16 (f. *Τίτος*) ?= (*16*); **(16)** ~ ib. l. 22 (*Αὐρ. Λ.*) ?= (*15*)
MACEDONIA (DERRIOPOS):
—STUBERRA: **(17)** 74 AD *IG* X (2) (2) 326, 47 (s. *Παράμονος*); **(18)** 87 AD ib. 325, 75 (s. *Ἀλέξανδρος*)
MACEDONIA (ELIMEIA):
—AIANE (TERRIT.): **(19)** ii AD *EAM* 49 a (s. *Ἀριστόλαος*)
—KENTRO (MOD.): **(20)** f. iii AD ib. 60 d (slave?)
MACEDONIA (LYNKESTIS):
—HERAKLEIA (NR.): **(21)** ii-iii AD *IG* X (2) (2) 6 (f. *Ὀλυμπιάδης*)
MACEDONIA (MYGDONIA):
—THESSALONIKE: **(22)** ii AD ib. X (2) (1) 1023, 2 (*CIL* III 10500) (Lat. P. Ael. Lucus: I ?f. *Λύκος* II); **(23)** ~ *IG* X (2) (1) 1023, 5 (*CIL* III 10500) (Lat. P. Ael. Lucus: II ?s. *Λύκος* I); **(24)** s. ii AD *IG* X (2) (1) 244 I, 11; 461, 11; 484, 9; 608, 1; 609, 3 (*Τιβ. Κλ. Λ.*: f. *Κλ. Ῥόδα, Κλ. Θεοπρεπίς*); **(25)** ~ ib. 244 II, 6 (*Τ. Φλ. Γράνιος Λ.*); **(26)** iii AD ib. 561, 2 (*Αἴλ. Πετρωνιανὸς Λ. Ἀδόλις*: II ?s. *Πετρώνιος Λύκος* I, *Πετιλία Βικτωρία*); **(27)** ~ ib. l. 3 (*Πετρώνιος Λ.*: I ?f. *Αἴλ. Πετρωνιανὸς Λύκος* II *Ἀδόλις, Αἴλ. Πετρωνιανὸς Εὔτυχος Δαιδάλις*); **(28)** f. iv AD *BCH* 79 (1955) p. 272; **(29)** ~ *IG* X (2) (1) 551 (Feissel, *RICM* 116) (*Αἴλ. Λ.*)
—THESSALONIKE?: **(30)** ii-iii AD *IG* X (2) (1) 818 (*Λύ*[*κος*]: s. *Κάνδιδος, Ἑρμιόνη*)
MACEDONIA (ORESTIS):
—SISANI (MOD.): **(31)** 146 AD *EAM* 187, 15 (s. *Λούκιος*)
MACEDONIA (PAIONIA):
—NEGOTINO (MOD.): **(32)** ii AD *Sp.* 98 (1941-8) p. 56 no. 113 (*Αἴλιος Λύκ*[*ος*]: f. *Φίλιππος*: reading—Papazoglu)
MACEDONIA (PIERIA):
—DION: **(33)** imp. *Klio* 52 (1970) p. 54 no. 5 = *SEG* XLVIII 882; **(34)** 132 AD *IG* II^2 3289, 8 (*CIL* III 7281; Tataki, *Macedonians* p. 100 no. 6) (Lat. C. Memmius Lycus); **(35)** ?iii AD Dimitsas 178 (*Αὐρ. Λ.*: f. *Δῖα, Λούκιλλα, Οὐαλεριανός*)
—DION?: **(36)** ii/iii AD Spiliopoulou-Donderer, *KGN* p. 199 no. D17 (s. *Ἐπικτᾶς*, f. *Ἄδυμος*)
—PYDNA: **(37)** c. 330 BC *IG* II^2 339 b, 2 (Tataki, *Macedonians* p. 170 no. 10) (*Λύκο*[*ς*]: s. *Ἀριστοκλείδης*)
PENESTAI:
—USCANA?: **(38)** ?ii AD *SEG* XXXIX 578, 5 (?s. *Εὐβία*)
SKYTHIA:
—SKYTHAI: **(39)** vii/vi BC Hdt. iv 76 (s. *Σπαργαπείθης*, f. *Γνοῦρος*: king)
TAURIS:
—CHERSONESOS: **(40)** iii AD *IOSPE* I^2 557 (Solomonik, *LNKhT* 41) (Lat. P. Lucos)
THRACE:
—APOLLONIA-SOZOPOLIS: **(41)** v/iv BC Sotheby sale (1st Feb. 1909) 645 (ANS 1967.152.223 (coin))
—BEROE-AUGUSTA TRAIANA (TERRIT.): **(42)** ii-iii AD *IGB* III 1725 (f. *Μουκατρας*)
—BYZANTION: **(43)** s. iii BC Schönert-Geiss, *Byzantion* 1205 (coin)
—SESTOS?: **(44)** 355 BC *IG* II^2 133, 2 (f. *Φιλίσκος*)

Λυκοῦργος
MACEDONIA (MYGDONIA):
—KALINDOIA: **(1)** c. 330 BC Hatzopoulos, *MI* 2 p. 84 no. 62, 15 (s. *Νικάνωρ*)
—THESSALONIKE: **(2)** iii/iv AD *Makedonika* 14 (1974) p. 369 with pl. 71 β (*Λυκοῦ*(*ρ*)*γος*)
THRACE:
—BYZANTION: **(3)** 409 BC *RE* (15) (*FRA* 1397); **(4)** ii-i BC *IByz* 148 (f. *Ἀναξώ, Κλεώ*)

Λυκόφρων
MACEDONIA (BOTTIAIA):
—AIGAI: **(1)** s. iv BC *SEG* XXXV 807 (f. *Κλησιθήρα*)
—BEROIA: **(2)** c. 120-140 AD *IBer* 349 A (Tataki 831) (f. *Φαῦστα*); **(3)** ?ii/iii AD *ILeukopetra* 153, 1 (?f. (ad.) *Ἀρτεμισία*)
MACEDONIA (CHALKIDIKE):
—OLYNTHOS: **(4)** ?c. 355-350 BC *SEG* XXXVIII 640, 2; XXXIX 617 (s. *Θεόδωρος*)
MACEDONIA (EDONIS):
—AMPHIPOLIS: **(5)** b. 357 BC Hatzopoulos, *Actes Amphipolis* p. 20 no. 2, 1 (*SEG* XLI 556)
THRACE:
—BARGALA (AREA): **(6)** iii AD *Sp.* 98 (1941-8) p. 95 no. 209 (*Αὐρ. Λ.*: s. *Ἑρμογένης*)

Λυκώι
THRACE:
—BYZANTION: **(1)** ii BC *IByz* 279 (Fıratlı–Robert p. 64 no. 56) (d. *Μενεκράτης*)

Λύκων
CIMMERIAN BOSPOROS:
—PANTIKAPAION: **(1)** iv-iii BC *MIA* 56 (1957) p. 224 (tile) (*Λύκω*(*ν*))
TAURIS:
—CHERSONESOS: **(2)** iii BC Kats pp. 115-16 no. 126 (amph.) (f. *Χορειός*); **(3)** c. 272-262 BC ib. p. 102 no. 71 (amph.) (s. *Ἀπολλώνιος*); **(4)** c. 215-200 BC ib. p. 102 no. 72 (amph.) (s. *Χορειός*)
THRACE:
—BYZANTION: **(5)** iv-iii BC *IG* XII (5) 540, 2, 9 (s. *Πυθέας*); **(6)** i BC-i AD *IByz* 207 (Fıratlı–Robert p. 67 no. 63) (I f. *Λύκων* II); **(7)** ~ *IByz* 207 (Fıratlı–Robert p. 67 no. 63) (II s. *Λύκων* I)

Λύκωπος
MACEDONIA (ORESTIS):
—BATTYNAIOI: **(1)** 192 AD *EAM* 186 I, 54 (f. *Μενέλαος*)

Λυραγία
MACEDONIA (BOTTIAIA):
—EDESSA: **(1)** ii-iii AD Dimitsas 21; cf. Tataki, *Edessa* 188

Λυράγιος
MACEDONIA (BOTTIAIA):
—EDESSA: **(1)** ii-iii AD Dimitsas 21; cf. Tataki, *Edessa* 189

Λυρίς
MACEDONIA (MYGDONIA):
—THESSALONIKE?: **(1)** ii AD *IG* X (2) (1) 717, 5 (Lat. Lucilia Lyris)

Λυσάνδρα
MACEDONIA: **(1)** iv/iii BC *RE* (1) (*PP* 14529) (d. *Πτολεμαῖος* I *Σωτήρ* (Eordaia), *Εὐρυδίκα*)
THRACE:
—BYZANTION?: **(2)** i AD *IByz* 368 (d. *Δούλης*)

Λύσανδρος
CIMMERIAN BOSPOROS:
—GORGIPPIA: **(1)** f. iii BC *CIRB* 1137 A I, 6 ([*Λ*]*ύσανδρος*: s. *Νουμήνιος*); **(2)** ~ ib. l. 34 (f. *Ἆγις*); **(3)** ~ ib. 1137 A II, 38 (f. *Διονύσιος*); **(4)** ~ ib. 1137 B I, 4 (*Λ*[*ύ*]*σανδρος*: s. *Ἑλλανίδης*)
—PANTIKAPAION: **(5)** i AD ib. 369 (f. *Βερενίκη*); **(6)** ~ ib. 452 (s. *Δέσχας*)

Macedonia (Bottiaia):
—pella: **(7)** ii bc *Α' Panell. Synedr. Epigr.* p. 193 no. 14 (*Pella* p. 144 no. 248) (s. *Φιλόδημος*)
Macedonia (Chalkidike):
—olynthos: **(8)** 226 bc *Milet* 1 (3) 41 III, 5 (Tataki, *Macedonians* p. 140 no. 81) (and Caria Miletos: s. *Στίχος*)
Macedonia (Edonis):
—amphipolis: **(9)** b. 213 bc Hatzopoulos, *MI* 2 p. 83 no. 61, 8 (*SEG* xlvi 715) (s. *Πεδιεύς*)
Macedonia (Mygdonia):
—lete: **(10)** s. iv bc Hatzopoulos, *MI* 2 pp. 93-4 no. 79, 2 (s. *Ἀμύντας*); **(11)** 323 bc *SEG* xxxvi 331 B, 20 (Tataki, *Macedonians* p. 118 no. 7) (f. *Μένανδρος*)
Tauris:
—chersonesos: **(12)** iii bc *IOSPE* I² 507 (f. *Ἀρχεσώ*)
Thrace:
—lysimacheia?: **(13)** ?255 bc Nachtergael, *Les Galates* 8, 48 (Stephanis 1574) (s. *Δεξίθεος*)
Thrace?: **(14)** 386 bc *IG* II² 31, 25

Λυσανίας
Macedonia: **(1)** 335 bc Berve 479 (Tataki, *Macedonians* p. 358 no. 44); **(2)** ?318 bc *IG* xii (9) 196, 2 (Tataki, *Macedonians* p. 358 no. 45); *Eretria* xi pp. 181-4 (date) (f. *Τιμόθεος*); **(3)** iii/ii bc *IG* xi (4) 784, 3, 15 (Tataki, *Macedonians* p. 358 no. 46) (f. *Χαιρέας*)
Macedonia (Bottiaia):
—aigai: **(4)** s. iv bc *SEG* xxxv 789 (s. *Ἀμάδωκος*)
—beroia: **(5)** s. ii bc *IBer* 24, 2 (Tataki 833) (I f. *Λυσανίας* II); **(6)** ~ *IBer* 24, 2 (Tataki 832) (II s. *Λυσανίας* I)
—edessa: **(7)** iii-ii bc *Arch. Pap.* 22 (1973) p. 208 no. 13 (Tataki, *Edessa* 190) (f. *Λύσων*)
—mieza: **(8)** iii bc *SEG* xxiv 524 I, 15, 25 (Hatzopoulos, *MI* 2 p. 106 no. 92)
Macedonia (Edonis):
—amphipolis: **(9)** b. 213 bc ib. p. 83 no. 61, 6 (*SEG* xlvi 715) ([*Λυ*]*σανίας*—ed., [*Παυ*]*σανίας*?)
Macedonia (Elimeia):
—aiane (territ.): **(10)** ii-iii ad *EAM* 18 (*SEG* xxxiv 647) (s. *Σεύθης*)
Macedonia (Mygdonia):
—kalindoia: **(11)** i/i bc ib. xlii 578, 1 (s. *Ὀλύμπιχος*); **(12)** 68-98 ad ib. 580, 39 (s. *Ζωΐλος*); **(13)** ~ ib. l. 40 (f. *Ζωΐλος*); **(14)** ~ ib. l. 87 (f. *Ἀρχέλαος*)
—lete: **(15)** s. iv bc Hatzopoulos, *MI* 2 pp. 93-4 no. 79, 9; **(16)** iv/iii bc *IMM* 2, 11 (Tataki, *Macedonians* p. 118 no. 8) ((*Λ*)*υσανίας*: f. *Ἀπολλωνοφάνης*)
—thessalonike: **(17)** 66 ad *IG* x (2) (1) 70, 12 (f. *Λεωνίδας*)
—thessalonike?: **(18)** i ad ib. 847, 1, 2, 5
Macedonia (Pelagonia): **(19)** ii-i bc ib. x (2) (2) 159, 7 (f. *Ματελίς*)
Macedonia (Pieris):
—phagres (territ.)?: **(20)** ii-iii ad Pikoulas, *Chora* p. 168 no. 78 (s. *Διδᾶς*)
Macedonia?: **(21)** 226 bc Plb. v 90. 1 (Tataki, *Macedonians* p. 358 no. 43)
Scythia Minor:
—kallatis: **(22)** iii-ii bc *Numismatica* 13 (1947) p. 6 nos. 11; 13 (coin) (*Λυσαν*(*ίας*)?, *Λύσαν*(*δρος*)?)
Thrace:
—maroneia: **(23)** ii-i bc *IThrakAig* E212, 19 (f. *Φιλόξενος*); **(24)** i ad *BCH* 66-7 (1942-3) p. 198 no. 2 + *IThrakAig* E297 (f. *Πυθογένης*)
—salymbria: **(25)** imp. *AEMÖ* 17 (1894) p. 57 no. 4 (*Λ*(*υ*)*σανίας*?: s. *Διονύσιος*)

Λυσᾶς
Macedonia (Pelagonia):
—keramiai (nr.): **(1)** ii-iii ad *IG* x (2) (2) 210 (s. *Ἀντιχάρης*, f. *Κάσσανδρος*, *Γάϊος*)

Λυσῆς
Macedonia (Derriopos):
—stuberra: **(1)** c. 41-48 ad ib. 323, 15 (*Λυσέως* (gen.): f. *Νίκων*); **(2)** 74 ad ib. 325, 33 (*Λυσέως* (gen.): f. *Παράμονος*)

Λυσιανή
Macedonia (Bottiaia):
—beroia: **(1)** ii ad *IBer* 258 (d. *Χαρμοσύνη*)

Λυσίας
Cimmerian Bosporos:
—gorgippia: **(1)** f. iii bc *CIRB* 1137 B II, 5 (s. *Πρόμηθος*)
Macedonia: **(2)** 246-223 bc *FD* iii (4) 156, 2; *OGIS* 272, 277; *RE* (8); Holleaux, *Études* 3 pp. 357-63 (ident., stemma) (Tataki, *Macedonians* p. 359 no. 49) (s. *Φιλόμηλος*); **(3)** 31 bc-14 ad *BGU* 1059, 3 (Tataki, *Macedonians* p. 489 no. 163) (f. *Λαοδίκη*, *M. Σολπίκιος Πρώταρχος*)
Macedonia (Bottiaia):
—beroia: **(4)** ii/iii ad *IBer* 143 C, 8 (Tataki 616) (*Ἰού. Λ.*)
Macedonia (Chalkidike):
—polichne?: **(5)** ?353 bc *SEG* xxxvii 576, 14
Macedonia (Derriopos):
—stuberra: **(6)** 74 ad *IG* x (2) (2) 325, 26 (f. *Νικόμαχος*) ?= (*8*); **(7)** ~ ib. l. 33 (s. *Ζωΐλος*); **(8)** ~ ib. l. 40 (f. *Σωσίας*) ?= (*6*)
Macedonia (Odomantike):
—sirrha: **(9)** hell. *SEG* xxx 616 (f. *Ἀπολλόδωρος*)
Macedonia (Paionia):
—stoboi (nr.): **(10)** ii/iii ad ib. xl 1797 (xlvii 949)
Macedonia?: **(11)** 285 bc *RE* (11) (Tataki, *Macedonians* p. 358 no. 47); **(12)** s. ii bc *IDidyma* 458; Holleaux, *Études* 3 pp. 357-63 (ident., stemma) (Tataki, *Macedonians* p. 359 no. 50) (f. *Φιλόμηλος*)
Thrace:
—byzantion: **(13)** c. 200 bc *IG* II² 884, 13 (*Λυσί*[*ας*]: f. *Γλαῦκος*)
—maroneia: **(14)** iii bc *SEG* xxiv 1181 a (vase); cf. La'da E1821 (*Λυσίου*—Neroutsos: f. *Ἀπολλόδωρος*)
—pautalia (territ.): **(15)** ii-iii ad *IGB* iv 2119 (s. *Μάξιμος*)

Λυσίδαμος
Macedonia (Pieria):
—pydna: **(1)** iv bc *GRBS* 43 (2002-3) p. 110 no. 1 a, 8

Λυσιδίκα
Macedonia (Mygdonia):
—lete: **(1)** c. 325-300 bc *SEG* xliv 535; *KGAM Thess.* 1 30 (date) (d. *Ἀντίγονος*)

Λυσιδίκη
Thrace:
—byzantion: **(1)** i bc-i ad *IByz* 227 (Fıratlı–Robert pp. 81-2 no. 97) (d. *Ἀπολλόδωρος*)

Λυσικλῆς
Macedonia (Bottiaia):
—beroia: **(1)** iii/ii bc *IBer* 39 (Tataki 834)
Macedonia (Derriopos): **(2)** ii-iii ad *IG* x (2) (2) 317 (s. *Ἰουλιανός*, *Ζωσίμα*)
Macedonia (Pieria):
—phila?: **(3)** ?iii bc *RPh* 1911, pp. 133-4 no. 36, 77; cf. Helly, *L'État thessalien* pp. 319-20 (locn.) (*Λυσικλ*[*ῆς*]: s. *Ἵππων*); **(4)** ~ *RPh* 1911, pp. 133-4 no. 36, 112; cf. Helly, *L'État thessalien* pp. 319-20 (locn.) (s. *Εὐ*—)

Λυσικράτης
Cimmerian Bosporos:
—pantikapaion: **(1)** 275-278 ad *CIRB* 36, 48 (*Λ*[*υσ*]*ικρά*[*της*])

Macedonia (Chalkidike):
—potidaia-kassandreia: **(2)** s. iv bc *TAPA* 69 (1938) p. 64 n. 45; cf. *Ancient Macedonia* 1 p. 132 n. 19 (f. *Φιλόκλεια*)
Thrace:
—lysimacheia: **(3)** m. ii bc *ISestos* 38 a, 2 (f. *Δημοσθένης*)

Λυσιμάχεια
Cimmerian Bosporos:
—hermonassa: **(1)** m. i bc *SEG* xlv 987, 6 (m. *Πάραλος* (Crete))
—pantikapaion: **(2)** ?i ad *CIRB* 454

Λυσιμάχη
Cimmerian Bosporos:
—pantikapaion: **(1)** i ad ib. 455 (*Λυσιμάχη*<ι>)
Macedonia (Bottiaia):
—beroia: **(2)** ii ad *IBer* 20, 4 (Tataki 835); **(3)** ~ *IBer* 259 (Tataki 836); **(4)** f. iii ad *IBer* 78, 9 (Tataki 579) (*Ἰου*(*λ*). *Λ.*: m. *Κυϊντιανὴ Ἀλεξάνδρα*, *Κυϊντιανὸς Καπίτων*); **(5)** 229 ad *ILeukopetra* 73, 1 (*Αὐρ. Λ.*)
—ichnai: **(6)** ?ii ad *SEG* xii 351 ([*Λυ*]*σιμάχη*)
Macedonia (Mygdonia):
—thessalonike: **(7)** iii ad ib. xxxv 768 (d. *Λυσίμαχος*)
Macedonia (Pelagonia): **(8)** ii-iii ad *IG* x (2) (2) 256

Λυσιμαχίδης
Macedonia (Bottiaia):
—pella: **(1)** iv bc *SEG* xxiv 555 (terracotta) (f. *Ἀθήνη*)

Λυσίμαχος
Cimmerian Bosporos:
—gorgippia: **(1)** imp. *CIRB* 1189, 7 (*Λυσίμ*[*αχος*]?); **(2)** ii/iii ad ib. 1179, 33 (I f. *Λυσίμαχος* II); **(3)** ~ ib. l. 33 (II s. *Λυσίμαχος* I)
—myrmekion: **(4)** f. ii ad ib. 885 (s. *Γοζιοῦς*)
—pantikapaion: **(5)** i bc ib. 120, 1, 4 (*GVI* 843) (s. *Ψυχαρίων*); **(6)** i ad *CIRB* 137, 1, 5 (*GVI* 1316) (s. *Γάστεις*); **(7)** ?i ad *CIRB* 453; cf. KW pl. 46 no. 651 (I s. *Διονύσιος*, f. *Λυσίμαχος* II); **(8)** ~ *CIRB* 453; cf. KW pl. 46 no. 651 (II s. *Λυσίμαχος* I); **(9)** f. ii ad *CIRB* 699 (f. *Πασίων*); **(10)** ?s. ii ad ib. 90, 11 (s. *Χαρίτων*)
Macedonia: **(11)** iii bc *IG* xi (4) 1276, 3 (Tataki, *Macedonians* p. 359 no. 51); **(12)** f. iii bc Just. xxiv 3. 5; cf. Beloch, *GG* iv (2) p. 130 (Tataki, *Macedonians* p. 359 no. 53) (II s. *Λυσίμαχος* I, *Ἀρσινόη*); **(13)** c. 285-221 bc Plb. xv 25. 2; Schol. Theoc. xvii 128 (*PP* 14531) (s. *Πτολεμαῖος* II *Φιλάδελφος*, *Ἀρσινόη*); **(14)** s. iii bc *ICos* ED 56, 2; Robert, *Hell.* 7 pp. 9-10, 5, 30; *ID* Index p. 16 (and Lycia Telmessos: s. *Πτολεμαῖος*, f. *Πτολεμαῖος*); **(15)** c. 235-200 bc La'da E1756 (f. *Εὐμήδης*); **(16)** iii/ii bc *RE* (16) (Tataki, *Macedonians* p. 359 no. 52) (Lat. Lysimachus); **(17)** m. ii bc *BGU* 2423, 34 (Tataki, *Macedonians* p. 489 no. 165); cf. La'da E1450 (f. *Ἀσκληπ*—); **(18)** 118-116 bc *PTeb* 62, 63; 63, 57; 64 a, 28 (*PP* 2581; Tataki, *Macedonians* p. 489 no. 164) (s. *Πύρρος*)
Macedonia (Almopia):
—milia (mod.): **(19)** ii-i bc *SEG* xii 347 ([*Λυ*]*σίμαχος*: s. *Φιλητίων*)
Macedonia (Bottiaia):
—beroia: **(20)** ii bc *IBer* 199 (Tataki 839) (s. *Σωσίπατρος*); **(21)** 115 bc *IBer* 134, 32 (s. *Πατερῖνος*); **(22)** 114 bc ib. l. 35 (s. *Ἀσκληπιόδωρος*); **(23)** i bc-i ad ib. 142, 11 (Tataki 837) (s. *Δέρδας*); **(24)** f. i bc *IBer* 32 (f. *Νικάνωρ*); **(25)** c. 10 bc Helly, *Gonnoi* 117, 9 (Tataki, *Macedonians* p. 79 no. 33) (s. *Πτολεμαῖος*); **(26)** s. ii ad *IBer* 75, 3 (Tataki 721) (*Κλ. Λ.*); **(27)** 248 ad *IBer* 54, 3 (f. *Αὐρ. Ἀλέξανδρος*)

—EDESSA: (28) 180 AD *SEG* XXIV 531, 4 (Tataki, *Edessa* 191) (s. *Σαβιδιανός*); (29) iii AD Tataki, *Macedonians* p. 103 no. 11 (f. *Αὐρήλιος*)
—PELLA: (30) c. 360-281 BC *RE* (1); Berve 480; *SEG* XXXVIII 619, 1, 3, 9 (Tataki, *Macedonians* p. 156 no. 58); cf. Beloch, *GG* IV (2) pp. 129-30 (I s. *Ἀγαθοκλῆς*, f. *Ἀγαθοκλῆς*, *Εὐρυδίκη*, *Ἀρσινόη*, *Φίλιππος*, *Λυσίμαχος* II, *Πτολεμαῖος*: king); (31) f. iii BC *AD* 16 (1960) Mel. p. 82; *SEG* XXXIX 623; XLIII 444; *AEMTh* 10 (1996) p. 116 (tiles)
MACEDONIA (DERRIOPOS):
—STUBERRA: (32) 50 AD *IG* X (2) (2) 324, 21 (f. *Ἐπίκαδος*); (33) 74 AD ib. 325, 38 (f. *Ἔλβιος*); (34) ~ ib. 326, 37 (f. *Ἀντίγονος*); (35) ~ ib. l. 37-8 (s. *Λέων*); (36) ~ ib. l. 49-50 (f. *Ἀρτεμᾶς*); (37) 87 AD ib. 325, 83 (s. *Πύρρος*); (38) 116 AD ib. 327, 15 (s. *Παράμονος*); (39) ~ ib. l. 25 (s. *Λέων*)
MACEDONIA (DERRIOPOS)?: (40) ii-iii AD ib. 44 (*Λ. ὁ καὶ Κάτων*: s. *Αὐρηλιανή*)
MACEDONIA (EDONIS):
—AMPHIPOLIS: (41) 242 BC *SEG* XII 373, 20 (Tataki, *Macedonians* p. 55 no. 77); (42) 213 BC Hatzopoulos, *MI* 2 p. 83 no. 61, 3 (*SEG* XLVI 715); (43) ii-iii AD *PAE* 1979, p. 77 with pl. 54 *β*
MACEDONIA (ELIMEIA):
—DOUREOI: (44) 214 AD *ILeukopetra* 65, 3 (Tataki 290) (*Αὐρ. Λ.*)
MACEDONIA (EORDAIA):
—ARNISA?: (45) f. iii AD *EAM* 134; Hatzopoulos, *MI* 1 p. 94 n. 4 (locn.)
—PYRGOI (MOD.): (46) ii-iii AD *EAM* 129 (s. *Λυκαρίων*, *Σελήνη*)
MACEDONIA (KRESTONIA):
—IORON: (47) s. ii AD *IBer* 87, 4 (Tataki, *Macedonians* p. 114 no. 1) (f. *Τορκουᾶτος*)
MACEDONIA (LYNKESTIS):
—ACHLADA (MOD.): (48) m. iii AD *EAM* 148 (s. *Αὐρ. Ἰουλιανός*)
—HERAKLEIA: (49) i AD *IG* X (2) (2) 75, 54 (s. *Ἀντίγονος*); (50) iii AD ib. 97 (s. *Αὐρ. Ἀνδρέας*, *Αὐρ. Ὀλυμπία*)
MACEDONIA (MYGDONIA):
—GERAKAROU (MOD.): (51) iii AD *SEG* XLII 576 (s. *Παράμονος*, *Ἁγνή*)
—KALINDOIA: (52) 68-98 AD ib. 580, 42 (f. *Κόϊντος*)
—LETE: (53) f. ii BC ib. XLVI 764, 10 (*Λυσίμα[χος]*: f. *Φιλώτας*); (54) ~ ib. l. 15 (*Λυσίμα[χος]*: f. *Σωμένης*); (55) ii AD *Makedonika* 2 (1951) p. 619 no. 42 *θ*, 13 (f. *Ζώπυρος*)
—THESSALONIKE: (56) s. ii BC *IG* X (2) (1) 27, 2 (f. —*ων*); (57) c. 23 BC ib. 97, 4; 113, 2 (f. *Διογένης*); (58) i AD ib. 635 (f. —*ιδία*); (59) i-ii AD ib. 243 I, 13 (f. *Ἀπολλώνιος*); (60) ii AD ib. 1022 (*CIL* III 3528) (Lat. P. Aelius Lusimacus); (61) iii AD *SEG* XXXV 768 (f. *Λυσιμάχη*); (62) m. iii AD *IG* X (2) (1) 205, 8 (*T. Ἰούλ. Λ.*: I f. *T. Ἰούλ. Λυσίμαχος* II); (63) ~ ib. l. 14 (*T. Ἰούλ. Λ.*: II s. *T. Ἰούλ. Λυσίμαχος* I)
—THESSALONIKE?: (64) ii AD ib. 248 II, 3 (f. *Νικάνωρ*)
MACEDONIA (ODOMANTIKE):
—GAZOROS: (65) ?ii AD *SEG* XXIV 616 (Pilhofer 549) (f. *Πρωτέας*)
—SIRRHA: (66) s. ii AD Dimitsas 812, 5 (Kaphtantzis 16) (*Τι(β). Κλ. Φλαουϊανὸς Λ.*: s. *Τιβ. Κλ. Διογένης*)
MACEDONIA (ORESTIS):
—BATTYNAIOI: (67) 192 AD *EAM* 186 IV, 45
—LYKE: (68) ?i-ii AD ib. 147, 2 (s. *Διογένης*)
MACEDONIA (PAIONIA): (69) ?ii AD *AM* 27 (1902) p. 318 no. 45 (*[Λ]υσίμαχος*: s. *Φιλήμων*)
—KAVADARCI (MOD.): (70) ?ii AD Unp. (Skopje); (71) 116 AD ib. (s. *Ποσειδώνιος*, f. *Πείσων*)
MACEDONIA (PELAGONIA): (72) ii-iii AD *IG* X (2) (2) 175; (73) ~ ib. 290 (s. *Ἰουλία*); (74) iii AD ib. 297 (*Αὐρ. Λυσίμα[χο]ς*)
—DOSTONEIS: (75) iii AD ib. 201, 1, 10 (*[Αὐ]ρήλιος Λ.*: f. *Ὄρεινος*, *Διομήδης*, *Νικομήδης*, *Ὀρείνη*); (76) ~ ib. l. 4-5 (s. *Εὔπορος*, *Ὀρείνη*)
MACEDONIA?: (77) 406 BC *Suda E* 3695 (slave)
SARMATIA:
—MAIOTAI: (78) hell. *Cl. Rh.* 2 p. 232 no. 122
SCYTHIA MINOR:
—ISTROS: (79) ii BC *ISM* I 27, 3; (80) i BC-i AD ib. 191 II, 5 (f. *Χρύσιππος*); (81) ~ ib. l. 23 (f. *Ἀπολλωνίδης*); (82) ~ ib. l. 28 (f. *Ἀπελλᾶς*); (83) ii AD ib. 197 II, 2 (s. *Θεόδωρος*); (84) ~ ib. 204, 12 (*Λυσίμαχ[ος]*: f. *Ζω*—); (85) ~ ib. 212, 29
—TOMIS: (86) ii AD ib. II 125, 5 (f. *Νουμήνιος*) ?= (*88*); (87) ~ ib. l. 14 (f. *Ἀκορνίων*) ?= (*88*); (88) ~ ib. l. 22-3 (f. *Δαμᾶς*, *Τιμόθεος*) ?= (*86*) (*87*); (89) ii-iii AD ib. 28, 7 (*[Λ]υσίμαχος*)
SKYTHIA:
—OLBIA-BORYSTHENES (BEREZAN (MOD.)): (90) f. ii AD *SEG* XLIX 1028 A, 9 (f. *Μαρικίων*)
TAURIS:
—CHERSONESOS: (91) 174 AD ib. XLV 985 A, 36 (f. *Κυρήνιος*)
THRACE: (92) 172-169 BC *OGIS* 734, 3 (Velkov 200; La'da E770) (s. *Βαστακίλας*, f. *Βαστακίλας*, —*ωμος*)
—APOLLONIA-SOZOPOLIS: (93) ?iv BC *IGB* I² 463 (*Λυσ[ίμ]αχος*)
—HERAION TEICHOS: (94) hell. Unp. (Sayar) (s. *Θεόδωρος*)
—MARONEIA: (95) ii-i BC *IThrakAig* E212, 18 (s. *Μητροφάνης*)
—PAUTALIA: (96) ii AD *IGB* IV 2074, 9

Λυσίπολις

MACEDONIA (BOTTIAIA):
—BEROIA: (1) 223 BC *IBer* 4, 23 (s. *Κλεισίμαχος*)

Λυσίπονος

MACEDONIA (BOTTIAIA):
—PELLA: (1) iii BC Akamatis, *Amph. Pellas* p. 39 no. PAR39 (amph.) (*SEG* L 613)
MACEDONIA (MYGDONIA):
—KALINDOIA: (2) 68-98 AD ib. XLII 580, 30 (s. *Ἀλέξανδρος*) ?= (*3*); (3) a. 98 AD ib. 583, 26 (f. *Ἀλέξανδρος*) ?= (*2*)
—THESSALONIKE: (4) f. i AD *IG* X (2) (1) 133, 11; Robert, *OMS* 5 pp. 295-302 (date) (f. *Ζωΐλος*)

Λύσιππος

CIMMERIAN BOSPOROS:
—PANTIKAPAION: (1) f. iii BC *CIRB* 245 (s. *Μιτραβάτης*)
MACEDONIA: (2) s. iv BC *IG* XII (5) 1001, 8 (Tataki, *Macedonians* p. 360 no. 54) (*Λύ[σιπ]πος*: s. *Ἀλκίμαχος*)
MACEDONIA (MYGDONIA):
—THESSALONIKE: (3) ii AD *IG* X (2) (1) 315, 5 (s. *Διοσκουρίδης*)
TAURIS:
—CHERSONESOS: (4) iv/iii BC Kats p. 104 no. 78 (amph.) (f. *Μητρόδωρος*)

Λῦσις

MACEDONIA (CHALKIDIKE):
—OLYNTHOS: (1) ?355 BC *TAPA* 69 (1938) p. 51 no. 5, 2; Hatzopoulos, *Actes Chalc.* p. 80 (date) (s. *Σι*—)
MACEDONIA (DERRIOPOS):
—STUBERRA: (2) 116 AD *IG* X (2) (2) 327, 20 (s. *Ἱππίας*); (3) 121 AD ib. 328, 14 (s. *Σωσίστρατος*)
THRACE:
—ODESSOS: (4) ?iv BC Hp., *Prorrh.* i 72

Λυσιστράτη

MACEDONIA (BOTTIAIA):
—PELLA: (1) s. iv BC *SEG* XXXVIII 651 (d. *Ζώπυρος*)

Λυσίστρατος

MACEDONIA (CHALKIDIKE):
—ANTIGONEIA?: (1) m. iii BC ib. XXIX 568 (f. *Εὐαλκίδης*)
—OLYNTHOS: (2) 424 BC Th. iv 110. 2; *RE* (5) (Tataki, *Macedonians* p. 140 no. 82)
MACEDONIA (EDONIS):
—AMPHIPOLIS: (3) i BC-i AD *SEG* XXVII 247; cf. *PAE* 1977, p. 52 fig. 3 (s. *Ἀπολλόδωρος*)
MACEDONIA (EORDAIA):
—DREPANO (MOD.): (4) ii-i BC *EAM* 95 (*Λυσ(ί)στρατος*, *[Πο]λύσστρατος*?: s. *Λιμναῖος*)
TAURIS:
—CHERSONESOS: (5) f. iii BC *SEG* XL 615 A, 9-10 (s. *Εὔδρομος*)

Λῦσος

MACEDONIA: (1) ?iii BC *RE* Supplbd. 11 (-); Overbeck 2062 (sculptor)
MACEDONIA (CHALKIDIKE):
—MENDE: (2) ?v BC *AEMTh* 7 (1993) p. 404 (f. *Κάλχας*)

Λύσων

MACEDONIA (BOTTIAIA):
—EDESSA: (1) iii-ii BC *Arch. Pap.* 22 (1973) p. 208 no. 13 (Tataki, *Edessa* 193) (s. *Λυσανίας*)
—MIEZA: (2) iii/ii BC *SEG* XLIII 406; 408; 409; 410; 423 (s. *Ἀριστοφάνης*, f. *Ἀριστοφάνης*, *Σπάρτη*); (3) m. ii BC ib. 420; 421; 422 (s. *Ἀριστοφάνης*, *Θεσσαλονίκη*, f. *Στρατονίκη*)
—PELLA: (4) f. iii BC ib. XXIV 547 (f. *Εὐβούλα*)
MACEDONIA (EDONIS):
—AMPHIPOLIS: (5) iii/ii BC *CCCA* VI 263 (*Mous. Kavalas* pp. 137-8 no. *Λ*. 201) (s. *Ξέναρχος*)
MACEDONIA (LYNKESTIS):
—HERAKLEIA: (6) ii-iii AD *IG* X (2) (2) 61 (f. *Ἀλέξανδρος*)
MACEDONIA (MYGDONIA):
—LETE: (7) s. iv BC Hatzopoulos, *MI* 2 pp. 93-4 no. 79, 3 (s. *Πλειστιάδης*); (8) 117 BC *Syll*³ 700, 51 (s. *Φιλώτας*)
MACEDONIA (PIERIS):
—PHAGRES: (9) s. v BC *SEG* XLIX 766 (f. *Νίκων*)

Λυχνᾶς

MACEDONIA (BOTTIAIA):
—BEROIA: (1) ii-iii AD *IBer* 305 (*Ἀμέριμνος ὁ καὶ Λ.*)

Λώβεις

SKYTHIA:
—TANAIS: (1) 244 AD *CIRB* 1287, 31 (s. —*τόνικος*)

M

Μᾶ
CIMMERIAN BOSPOROS:
—PANTIKAPAION: (**1**) i BC *CIRB* 280; Zgusta, *PNS* 1068; (**2**) imp. *CIRB* 796; (**3**) i AD ib. 132, 4 (*GVI* 679) (m. Ἀντίπατρος); (**4**) ~ *CIRB* 135, 3 (*GVI* 1362); cf. KW pl. 29 no. 406 (m. Θεόδωρος); (**5**) ~ *CIRB* 525; cf. KW pl. 27 no. 399; (**6**) i/ii AD *CIRB* 619; (**7**) ii AD ib. 692 (m. Ταρσοῦς, Ἡραῖος, Θεονίκα)

Μάγας
MACEDONIA: (**1**) iv BC *RE* (1) (Tataki, *Macedonians* p. 360 no. 1) (f. Βερενίκη); (**2**) c. 320-258 BC *RE* (2); *IG* IX (1)² (1) 56 c; *SEG* XVII 817; XVIII 743, 4 (*PP* 14533); Beloch, *GG* III (2) pp. 186-90; cf. *LGPN* I s.v. (1) (and Cyrenaica Cyrene: s. Φίλιππος, Βερενίκη, f. Βερενίκη: king); (**3**) c. 241-221 BC *RE* (3); *IG* IX (1)² (1) 56 h; *PHaun* I 6, 28 ff; cf. *ZPE* 138 (2002) p. 145 (date) (*PP* 14534) (s. Πτολεμαῖος III Εὐεργέτης, Βερενίκη)
MACEDONIA (ORESTIS):
—BATTYNAIOI: (**4**) 192 AD *EAM* 186 II, 48 (s. Στράτων)

Μάγδις
THRACE: (**1**) iii BC *FGrH* 76 F 28 (fict.)

Μαγεάτης?
MACEDONIA (BOTTIAIA):
—PELLA: (**1**) iii/ii BC *SEG* XXXVIII 653 + *Makedonika* 26 (1987-8) p. 61 no. 7 with pl. 4 (Μαγελ[ί]του (gen.)—ed., Μαγεάτου?: f. Γενθήνα)

Μάγνα
MACEDONIA (BOTTIAIA):
—EDESSA: (**1**) f. ii AD *SEG* XXXIX 589 (Tataki, *Edessa* 194) (d. Βήριμος, Ἑρμιόνη)
MACEDONIA (MYGDONIA):
—THESSALONIKE: (**2**) ?iii AD *IG* X (2) (1) 477 (Μάγ[ν]α: d. Ζωΐλος, Μανθάρα)
—THESSALONIKE?: (**3**) ii AD ib. 710
MACEDONIA (PIERIA):
—DION: (**4**) iv-v AD *SEG* XXXIV 634 = XLIX 701
THRACE:
—MONTANA: (**5**) s. ii AD *IGB* II 480 (*Montana* II 69)

Μαγνῆτις
TAURIS:
—CHERSONESOS: (**1**) s. iv BC Solomonik, *GAKh* 1209 (vase) (n. pr.?)

Μαγνίων
SCYTHIA MINOR:
—TOMIS: (**1**) ii AD *ISM* II 125 II, 19 (s. Ἀοταῖος)
THRACE:
—NICOPOLIS AD NESTUM: (**2**) ii AD *IGB* IV 2336, 12 (f. Ποσειδώνιος)

Μάγνος
MACEDONIA (KRESTONIA):
—IORON: (**1**) i AD *SEG* XLVIII 814
MACEDONIA (MYGDONIA):
—THESSALONIKE: (**2**) ii AD *IG* X (2) (1) 368, 3, 10 (*SEG* XXVI 777); (**3**) ii-iii AD ib. XLVII 975
SCYTHIA MINOR:
—ISTROS: (**4**) ii AD *ISM* I 211, 12 (f. Μαρκιανός)
—TOMIS: (**5**) ii-iii AD ib. II 23, 10 (Μάγνος: s. Μεσσαλῖνος); (**6**) ~ ib. 31 II, 10 (f. Θεόδοτος)
THRACE:
—PERINTHOS-HERAKLEIA: (**7**) i BC-i AD? *IPerinth* 57, 7 (f. Ἡρόξενος)
—PHILIPPOPOLIS-TRIMONTIUM (TERRIT.): (**8**) ii-iii AD *IGB* III 1178 (s. Ἀπο—ος)

Μάδα
CIMMERIAN BOSPOROS:
—ILOURATON: (**1**) iii AD *KSIA* 159 (1979) p. 91 (bronze)
—PANTIKAPAION: (**2**) i/ii AD *CIRB* 456; Zgusta, *PNS* 137

Μαδαγάβα
SCYTHIA MINOR:
—TOMIS: (**1**) iii AD *SBBayerAk* 1875, p. 84 no. 9

Μαδαγαύα
SKYTHIA:
—TYRAS: (**1**) iii AD *IGB* I² 229, 5 (m. Δομνῖνος)

Μάδακος
CIMMERIAN BOSPOROS:
—GORGIPPIA: (**1**) ii/iii AD *SEG* XXXVI 714, 3 (Μάδα[κος]?: f. —ν)
SKYTHIA:
—TANAIS: (**2**) 228 AD *CIRB* 1282, 14 (s. Μενέστρατος)

Μαδινι
SKYTHIA:
—TYRAS: (**1**) iii AD *IGB* I² 228 bis, 7 (d. Ἀρτεμίδωρος, m. Αὐρ. Ἀβρινία)

Μαδύης
SKYTHIA:
—SKYTHAI: (**1**) vii BC Hdt. i 103 (s. Προτοθύης: king)

Μάδωις
SKYTHIA:
—TANAIS: (**1**) 225 AD *CIRB* 1279, 15 (s. Σαμβατίων)

Μαζαία
CIMMERIAN BOSPOROS:
—BOSPOROS: (**1**) ii AD Luc., *Tox.* 44-55 (d. Λευκάνωρ: fict.)

Μαζαῖος
THRACE:
—KOILA: (**1**) i AD *ISestos* 34; PM 1004 (date) (*T. Κλ. M.*)

Μάζαρος
MACEDONIA: (**1**) 331 BC *RE* (-); Berve 486; cf. *CQ* 26 (1976) pp. 121-3

Μάζης
CIMMERIAN BOSPOROS:
—PANTIKAPAION: (**1**) f. iv BC *CIRB* 200; cf. KW pl. 1 no. 37; Zgusta, *PNS* 138 (s. Χόλκος)

Μαζοῦς
CIMMERIAN BOSPOROS:
—PANTIKAPAION: (**1**) iv BC *CIRB* 196; cf. *Hyperboreus* 1994 (1), p. 161; Zgusta, *PNS* 138 (Μαζōτος (gen.), Μαζότōς? (gen.), Μαζότης—Tokhtas'ev)

Μάης
CIMMERIAN BOSPOROS:
—PANTIKAPAION: (**1**) ?i AD *CIRB* 457; (**2**) s. i AD ib. 546; cf. KW pl. 30 no. 439a (s. Μόνιμος); (**3**) i/ii AD *CIRB* 620; cf. KW pl. 36 no. 530 (s. Ἀνόπτηνις); (**4**) ~ *CIRB* 623; cf. KW pl 37 no. 543 (f. Μάσας); (**5**) ii AD *CIRB* 621 (I f. Μάης II); (**6**) ~ ib. (II s. Μάης I); (**7**) ~ ib 750 (f. Βατάκης); (**8**) f. ii AD ib. 83, 2 (s. Καλλισθένης)
MACEDONIA: (**9**) ?ii AD *RE* Supplbd. 6 (-) + Supplbd. 11 (Tataki, *Macedonians* p. 360 no. 4) (*M. ὁ καὶ Τιτιανός*)

SKYTHIA:
—OLBIA-BORYSTHENES: (**10**) s. i AD *IOlbia* 85, 8 (*IOSPE* I² 104); Zgusta, *KP* 844 (f. .ούσκης)
—TANAIS: (**11**) 188 AD *CIRB* 1242, 13 (s. Εὐδήμων); (**12**) 228 AD ib. 1283, 12 (s. Σάλας)

Μάθανος
SKYTHIA:
—OLBIA-BORYSTHENES: (**1**) imp. *IOSPE* I² 152, 4; Zgusta, *PNS* 306 (Μάθα[νος]?); (**2**) ii AD *IOSPE* I² 82, 8 (f. Ἀδόης); (**3**) ~ ib. 100, 8 (s. Ἄβραγος)

Μαθιάνης
CIMMERIAN BOSPOROS:
—GORGIPPIA: (**1**) m. ii AD *Eirene* 7 (1968) p. 67, 24 (s. Δροῦσος)
—PANTIKAPAION: (**2**) 275-278 AD *CIRB* 36, 50 (Μαθιάγγ[ης]—Vinogradov)
—TAMAN PENINSULA: (**3**) i BC/i AD *SEG* XLV 1018 (s. Ζαίδαρος)
SKYTHIA:
—TANAIS: (**4**) i/ii AD ib. 1023, 5

Μαῖα
CIMMERIAN BOSPOROS:
—PANTIKAPAION: (**1**) s. iv BC *CIRB* 201; cf. KW pl. 7 no. 120a

Μαίακος
SKYTHIA:
—OLBIA-BORYSTHENES: (**1**) f. ii AD *SEG* XLIII 506, 5; Zgusta, *PNS* 139 (f. Ἐπικράτης); (**2**) c. 150-175 AD *IOSPE* I² 132, 4; cf. *SEG* XLII 713 (f. Ἱκέσιος)

Μαιανδρία
THRACE:
—ZONE: (**1**) s. iv BC *AA* 1918, col. 11 + Robert, *Hell.* I p. 94 (*IThrakAig* E422) (Μαιανδρία: d. Σάτυρος)

Μαιάνδριος
CIMMERIAN BOSPOROS:
—PANTIKAPAION: (**1**) c. 200-180 BC *CIRB* 26, 3 ([Μ]αιάνδριος)
THRACE:
—ABDERA: (**2**) v BC *FGrH* 244 F 70; 690 F 6 (?f. Πρωταγόρης)

Μαιδάτης
TAURIS:
—KALOS LIMEN*: (**1**) ii BC Solomonik, *GChKh* 456 (vase); cf. *SEG* XXXVIII 749. 9; *Hellenismus* p. 452 no. 21 (or Pontos Sinope: s. Θῦς)

Μαικήνας
MACEDONIA (TYMPHAIA):
—SYDENDRO (MOD.): (**1**) imp. *EAM* 27

Μαισάδης
THRACE:
—ODRYSAI: (**1**) s. v BC X., *An.* vii 2. 32; vii 5. 1 (f. Σεύθης: king)

Μαίσης
CIMMERIAN BOSPOROS:
—GORGIPPIA: (**1**) f. iii BC *CIRB* 1137 A I, 52; Zgusta, *PNS* 140 (s. Καλλιγένης)

Μαισίρα
THRACE: (**1**) 195 BC *SGDI* 2119, 3 (m. Κότυς: slave/freed.)

Μαίσωος
CIMMERIAN BOSPOROS:
—ACHILLEION (NR.): (**1**) 105 AD *CIRB* 1021, 10-11 (?s. Ἀπολλώνιος, Γλυκαρία)

Μαίφαρνος
SKYTHIA:
—OLBIA-BORYSTHENES: **(1)** imp. *IOSPE* I^2 148, 1; Zgusta, *PNS* 141 (s. Θεότιμος)

Μαίων
THRACE:
—RHAIDESTOS: **(1)** ii-iii AD *IG* X (2) (1) 273 (Μέ-: s. Ἡρακλέων: locn.—Loukopoulou)

Μαίωρ
SCYTHIA MINOR:
—ISTROS: **(1)** f. iii AD *Stud. Fischer* p. 32 no. 4, 8 ([Μ]αίωρ?: s. Βαλέριος)

Μάκαγος
SKYTHIA:
—OLBIA-BORYSTHENES: **(1)** s. ii AD *IOlbia* 81, 13 (*IOSPE* I^2 94); Zgusta, *PNS* 307 (f. Θεόδουλος)

Μακαλωνε?
SCYTHIA MINOR:
—KALLATIS: **(1)** v-vi AD Unp. (Avram)

Μακαρεύς
SKYTHIA:
—OLBIA-BORYSTHENES: **(1)** iii BC Dubois, *IGDOlbia* 109, 3 (*SEG* XXXVII 673)

Μακαρία
CIMMERIAN BOSPOROS:
—PANTIKAPAION: **(1)** i BC/i AD *CIRB* 311; **(2)** i AD ib. 459; cf. KW pl. 22 no. 307; **(3)** i/ii AD *CIRB* 582; cf. KW pl. 13 no. 195 (d. Ἀριαράθη); **(4)** ?ii AD *CIRB* 693; cf. KW pl. 14 no. 203 (-ρεία: d. Πάπας); **(5)** f. ii AD *CIRB* 661 (d. Βασιλείδης)
—PARTHENION: **(6)** i AD ib. 896 + *Hyperboreus* 2000, p. 140 (Μα[κ]αρία)
—TYRITAKE (NR.): **(7)** f. i AD *CIRB* 969 (m. Μάσατις)
TAURIS:
—CHERSONESOS: **(8)** ii AD *IOSPE* I^2 453; cf. KW pl. 24 no. 355 (Οὐλπ. Μ.)
THRACE:
—DUROSTORUM: **(9)** ii-iii AD *CIL* III 7477 (Lat. Valeria Macaria: d. Valerius Marcus)

Μακάριος
CIMMERIAN BOSPOROS:
—BOSPOROS: **(1)** i AD *IGUR* 763 (s. Φάννας)
—GORGIPPIA: **(2)** ?93-123 AD *CIRB* 1125, 9, 14 (f. Νυμφαγόρας); **(3)** ii AD ib. 1140, 15 (f. —ορας); **(4)** m. ii AD *Eirene* 7 (1968) p. 67, 16 (f. Ποτηγοῦς); **(5)** 173-210 AD *CIRB* 1134, 16 (s. Ἀθη—); **(6)** ii/iii AD ib. 1179, 34 (s. Φαρνακίων)
—PANTIKAPAION: **(7)** imp. ib. 784; **(8)** i AD ib. 458 (s. Ἀπολλώνιος); **(9)** ~ ib. 544; **(10)** ~ ib. 552; **(11)** 82 AD ib. 76, 15 (*SEG* XVIII 310) (s. Τιμόλαος); **(12)** f. ii AD *CIRB* 87, 5 (s. Ἑρμογένης); **(13)** 275-278 AD ib. 36, 37 (Μακάρ(ιος): f. Διαγόρας); **(14)** iv-v AD *SEG* XLV 1015 g (amph.) (Μακάρ(ιος)?)
—PANTIKAPAION (NR.): **(15)** ii AD *CIRB* 963 (Μακάρης (nom.), Μακαρίου (gen.): s. Μόστιος, f. Διονυσίδωρος)
SKYTHIA:
—TANAIS: **(16)** ii AD ib. 1262, 11 (s. Βαστάκας); **(17)** 104 AD ib. 1259, 11; *LF* 75 (1950) p. 302 (name) (Μάκα[ρ]ος—ed., Μακά[ρι]ος—*LF*: f. Εὔπορος); **(18)** 220 AD *CIRB* 1278, 7 (f. Χαρίτων); **(19)** ~ ib. l. 17 (Μακάρ[ιος]: s. —ος); **(20)** c. 225-250 AD ib. 1287, 9; 1288, 12 (s. Νέρων); **(21)** ~ ib. l. 8 (Μακάρι[ος]); **(22)** 228 AD ib. 1282, 16 (f. Θεαγένης); **(23)** ~ ib. l. 31 ([Μα]κάριος: s. Ἀχαιμένης); **(24)** 244 AD ib. 1287, 6 (s. Μαστοῦς); **(25)** ~ ib. l. 23 (f. Χόμενος)
—TYRAS: **(26)** 181 AD *IOSPE* I^2 2, 28 (s. Ἀρτεμίδωρος)

Μάκαρις
THRACE:
—SALYMBRIA: **(1)** hell. *IByz* S 48; *BE* 1959, no. 251 (name) (Μακάριος (gen.): f. Νουμήνιος)

Μακάρτατος
MACEDONIA: **(1)** iv BC Arr., *An.* iii 5. 5 (Tataki, *Macedonians* p. 360 no. 6) (f. Πευκέστας)

Μακεδίων
MACEDONIA (LYNKESTIS):
—HERAKLEIA: **(1)** i AD *IG* X (2) (2) 75, 28 (Π. Κούτιος Μ.)

Μακεδονία
MACEDONIA (BOTTIAIA):
—BEROIA: **(1)** vi AD *IBer* 448, 9 (Feissel, *RICM* 61) (Μακεδο[νία])
—EDESSA: **(2)** ii/iii AD Dimitsas 27 (Tataki, *Edessa* 195) (d. Λάγων, Φλ. Προσδόχη); **(3)** 246 AD *SEG* XXXVI 617, 2 (Tataki, *Edessa* 151) (Κλ. Μ.)
MACEDONIA (EDONIS):
—PHILIPPOI: **(4)** imp. *BCH* 61 (1937) p. 413 no. 6 (Pilhofer 253) (Lat. Vari[nia] [M]acedonia: d. Μακεδών)
MACEDONIA (MYGDONIA):
—KALINDOIA: **(5)** ii-iii AD *SEG* XLII 599 (m. Ἀλέξανδρος, Στράτων); **(6)** ii/iii AD *Tekmeria* 6 (2001) p. 63 no. 2
—THESSALONIKE?: **(7)** ?iii AD *IG* X (2) (1) 749
MACEDONIA (PAIONIA):
—BYLAZORA: **(8)** iii AD *JÖAI* 6 (1903) Beibl. col. 3 no. 2 (*Sp.* 71 (1931) p. 25 no. 48, 4) ([Ποβλ]ειλεία Μακαιδονία: ?m. Αὐρ. Διονυσία)

Μακεδονιανός
THRACE:
—PAUTALIA: **(1)** s. ii AD *CIL* VI 37184 c, 15 (Lat. M. Aur. Macedonian(us))

Μακεδονικός
MACEDONIA (BOTTIAIA):
—EDESSA: **(1)** 180 AD *SEG* XXIV 531, 10 (Tataki, *Edessa* 196) (-χός: f. Εὐτυχίων)
MACEDONIA (EDONIS):
—AMPHIPOLIS: **(2)** i BC *SEG* XXIII 126, 1 (Tataki, *Macedonians* p. 55 no. 78; *FRA* 512)
—PHILIPPOI: **(3)** ?ii AD *BCH* 47 (1923) p. 71 no. 26 (Pilhofer 502) (Lat. T. Flavius Macedonicus: s. Ἀλέξανδρος) ?= (*4*)
—PHILIPPOI (DRAMA (MOD.)): **(4)** ii-iii AD *AD* 30 (1975) Chron. p. 287 (Pilhofer 485) (Lat. Flavius Macedonicus) ?= (*3*)
MACEDONIA (PAIONIA):
—STOBOI?: **(5)** ii BC *Stobi Hell. Rom. Pottery* p. 42 no. 207 (vase)

Μακεδόνιος
MACEDONIA (ELIMEIA)*: **(1)** v-vi AD *EAM* 66, 6; cf. *SEG* L 592 (bp.)
MACEDONIA (MYGDONIA):
—THESSALONIKE: **(2)** ii AD *IG* X (2) (1) 429 + *BCH* 99 (1975) pp. 175-7 (Μακεδόνιος: s. Ἀμύνανδρος)
—THESSALONIKE?: **(3)** ?i BC *RE* (1); *GP* 2544-55 (Tataki, *Macedonians* p. 184 no. 41); **(4)** ?iv AD Feissel, *RICM* 193 ([Μα]κε[δ]όνιος)
MACEDONIA (PAIONIA):
—STOBOI: **(5)** s. iii AD *JÖAI* 32 (1940) Beibl. col. 22 no. 15. 156 (Μακε[δόνι]ος)
THRACE:
—NICOPOLIS AD ISTRUM: **(6)** iv AD *IGB* II 656, 6; cf. V 5212 (Βασιλιανὸς Μακηδόνιος—metr. c.)
—PERINTHOS-HERAKLEIA: **(7)** iii AD *IPerinth* 173 (Αὐρ. Μ.)

Μακεδονίς
MACEDONIA (PIERIA):
—DION: **(1)** iv AD *SEG* XXXV 736 (masc./fem.?)

Μακεδών
MACEDONIA (BOTTIAIA):
—BEROIA: **(1)** i BC-i AD *IBer* 142, 14 (Tataki 845) (s. Ἀδαῖος); **(2)** ii AD *IBer* 120 (Tataki 778) (Π. Μ. Κυϊντιανὸς Μ.); **(3)** a. 212 AD *IBer* 136, 25 (Tataki 82) (Αἰλ. Μ.: I f. Αἰλ. Μακεδών II νέος); **(4)** ~ *IBer* 136, 25 (Tataki 81) (Αἰλ. Μ. νέος: II s. Αἰλ. Μακεδών I)
MACEDONIA (CHALKIDIKE):
—POTIDAIA-KASSANDREIA*: **(5)** imp. *CIL* III 7333 (*BCH* 103 (1979) p. 302 no. 39) (Lat. Macedo: freed.)
MACEDONIA (EDONIS):
—AMPHIPOLIS: **(6)** m. ii BC *IG* IX (1)^2 (3) 639. 6, 9, 14 (Tataki, *Macedonians* p. 55 no. 79) (slave/freed.)
—AMPHIPOLIS?: **(7)** ii-iii AD *CIL* III 632 (Lat. Libucius Macedo)
—PHILIPPOI: **(8)** imp. *BCH* 61 (1937) p. 413 no. 6 (Pilhofer 253) (Lat. [Varin]ius [M]acedo: f. Μακεδονία, Varinia Pro–)
MACEDONIA (ELIMEIA):
—PALAIOKASTRO (MOD.): **(9)** imp. *EAM* 29; cf. *SEG* XXXIX 563 (f. Μαμία)
MACEDONIA (EORDAIA): **(10)** imp. Dimitsas 288 (f. Κλιτύς, Διονύσιος)
MACEDONIA (MYGDONIA):
—LETE: **(11)** s. ii AD *SEG* XXXVIII 633 (Λ. Ἄννιος Μ.: s. Ἀττική)
—THESSALONIKE: **(12)** imp. *AD* 24 (1969) Chron. p. 303; **(13)** i AD *IG* X (2) (1) 259, 27 (Μ. Ὄμβρειος Μ.); **(14)** ii AD ib. 456, 7; **(15)** ii-iii AD ib. 309, 1; **(16)** ~ ib. 440, 1 (Feissel, *RICM* 119) (f. Καλόκαιρος); **(17)** s. ii AD *SEG* XLVIII 852 (s. Μαντώ); **(18)** ii/iii AD *IG* X (2) (1) 181, 1; 187, 8; *SEG* XLVI 815, 4; cf. *IApoll* 325; cf. *Roman Onomastics* pp. 130-4 (Τ. Αἰλ. Γεμείνιος Μ. (ὁ) (καὶ) Ὀλυμπος: f. Γεμινία Ὀλυμπιάς)
—THESSALONIKE?: **(19)** i-ii AD *IG* X (2) (1) 688, 5 (Lat. T. Minucius Macedo); **(20)** ii AD ib. 890; **(21)** ii-iii AD ib. 208, 8 (Μ. Οὐαρείνιος Μ.); **(22)** iii AD ib. 931 (Feissel, *RICM* 118)
MACEDONIA (ORESTIS):
—SISANI (MOD.): **(23)** 146 AD *EAM* 187, 19 (f. Φίλιππος)
MACEDONIA (PAIONIA):
—ANTIGONEIA? (TREMNIK (MOD.)): **(24)** ii-iii AD *SEG* II 441; 440?
—KAVADARCI (MOD.): **(25)** ?ii AD *Sp.* 71 (1931) p. 75 no. 176, 5; cf. Düll, *Götterkulte* p. 340 no. 131 (II s. Μακεδών I); **(26)** ~ *Sp.* 71 (1931) p. 75 no. 176, 5-6; cf. Düll, *Götterkulte* p. 340 no. 131 (I f. Μακεδών II, Ἑρμογένης); **(27)** ~ *Sp.* 75 (1933) p. 39 no. 128 (s. Ἀριστοφῶν, f. Ἀριστοφῶν); **(28)** ?f. iii AD *SEG* XLIV 560 (Αὐρήλιος Μακαιδών)
—NEGOTINO (MOD.): **(29)** ii AD *Sp.* 98 (1941-8) p. 58 no. 120; **(30)** ii-iii AD ib. 75 (1933) p. 36 no. 108; **(31)** 153 AD *SEG* XXXVIII 712 (s. Κήσης, Μάντα); **(32)** iii AD ib. 714 (s. Διονυσία)
—STOBOI: **(33)** ii-iii AD *AJA* 88 (1984) p. 578 n. 60
MACEDONIA (PELAGONIA):
—KERAMIAI (NR.): **(34)** iii AD *IG* X (2) (2) 214 (-και-)
—MOJNO (MOD.): **(35)** 253-259 AD ib. 173 (I f. Μακεδών II); **(36)** ~ ib. (II s. Μακεδών I)
MACEDONIA?: **(37)** f. ii AD *JDAI* 84 (1969) p. 156 no. R24 + *BCH* 99 (1975) pp. 178-9 (s. Μαντώ)
SCYTHIA MINOR:
—ISTROS (NR.): **(38)** ii AD *ISM* I 374 (Φλ. Μ.)
SKYTHIA:
—OLBIA-BORYSTHENES: **(39)** ii AD *IOSPE* I^2 128, 5 (f. Διογένης)
THRACE:
—ABRYTTOS (TERRIT.): **(40)** 212-217 AD *Romanizmăt* II 84 (Lat. Macedo)
—BYZANTION (TERRIT.): **(41)** imp. Unp. (Sayar) (s. Προμαθίων)

—DIONYSOPOLIS: **(42)** iii AD *IGB* I^2 14 b, 17 (f. *Αὐρ. Βιάτωρ*)
—MONTANA: **(43)** 159 AD *Montana* II 49 (Lat. L. Iul. Macedo)
—ODESSOS: **(44)** 221 AD *IGB* I^2 47 bis c, 11 (*Αὐρ. M.*: s. *Ἀπελλᾶς*)
—ODESSOS (NR.): **(45)** ii AD ib. 273 (PM 1322; *CCET* I 15) (I f. *Μακεδών* II); **(46)** ~ *IGB* I^2 273 (PM 1323; *CCET* I 15) (II s. *Μακεδών* I)

Μακέντης
SKYTHIA:
—SKYTHAI: **(1)** ii AD Luc., *Tox.* 44-8; 51 (fict.)

Μακέσαλα
THRACE:
—KOMOTINI (MOD.): **(1)** imp. *Belomorski Pregled* 1 (1942) p. 336 no. 41 (*BE* 1948, no. 148; *IThrakAig* E482) (d. *Βίθυς*)

Μακεσατος
THRACE:
—BEROE-AUGUSTA TRAIANA:
——Karasoura: **(1)** iii AD *IGB* III 1628, 5 (*Αὐρ. Μακεσατ[ος]*: s. *Ἀδριάνιος Μουκιανός*)
—PHILIPPOPOLIS-TRIMONTIUM (TERRIT.): **(2)** ii-iii AD ib. 1478, 2 (or Thrace Diokletianopolis: *Μακεσατ[ος]* (nom./gen.?))

Μακέτα
MACEDONIA (MYGDONIA):
—THESSALONIKE?: **(1)** ?iii AD *IG* X (2) (1) 911, 3 (d. *Τίτος, Κλευπώ*)

Μακέτας
MACEDONIA (PAIONIA):
—KAVADARCI (MOD.): **(1)** ii-iii AD *AM* 27 (1902) p. 318 no. 46 (f. *Λευκιανή*)

Μακέτη
MACEDONIA (PAIONIA):
—BYLAZORA: **(1)** ii-iii AD *Sp.* 75 (1933) p. 19 no. 37, 2-3 (m. *Μᾶρκος, Φιλόξενος*)
—KAVADARCI (MOD.): **(2)** ii AD ib. 71 (1931) p. 66 no. 148 + *SEG* XXXII 648 (d. *Ἐπικράτης*, m. *Γαΐα Γρανωνία*)

Μακετιανός
MACEDONIA (PAIONIA):
—DEMIR KAPIJA (MOD.): **(1)** ii AD *ZA* 24 (1974) p. 268 no. 2

Μάκκις
MACEDONIA (BOTTIAIA):
—EDESSA: **(1)** ii AD *SEG* L 599

Μάκλας
MACEDONIA (EDONIS):
—AMPHIPOLIS?: **(1)** imp. Dimitsas 923 (Kaphtantzis 544) (*M. Λευκείλιο[ς] M.*)

Μακος
THRACE:
—LIPNICA (MOD.): **(1)** iii AD *IGB* II 501 (*M. ὁ καὶ Γόλης*: f. *Γάϊος*)

Μακού
THRACE:
—ODESSOS: **(1)** i-ii AD ib. I^2 108, 7 (d. *Ἀμύντωρ, Ἀννώ*); **(2)** ~ ib. 190 (d. *Ἀπολλώνιος*); **(3)** ii-iii AD ib. 127 (d. *Ἀμύντωρ*)

Μακρίνη
THRACE:
—PHILIPPOPOLIS-TRIMONTIUM: **(1)** ii AD ib. III 995 (*Οὐλπ. Μακρείνη*)

Μακρῖνος
MACEDONIA (MYGDONIA):
—THESSALONIKE: **(1)** 137-161 AD *Makedonika* 9 (1969) pp. 143-4 (*T. Νουμισηνὸς M. ὁ καὶ Πριμιγένης*)

SCYTHIA MINOR:
—ISTROS: **(2)** ii AD *ISM* I 196, 8 (*-κρεῖ-*: s. *Ἀλέξανδρος*); **(3)** ~ ib. 197 I, 7; 201 I, 16 (*-κρεῖ-*: s. *Γαῦκος*)
—TOMIS: **(4)** ii-iii AD ib. II 31 III, 8 (*-κρεῖ-*: s. *Προ—*)
THRACE:
—NICOPOLIS AD ISTRUM (TERRIT.): **(5)** ii-iii AD *IGB* V 5250, 2 (*T. Αὐρ. Μαῦρος (ὁ) καὶ M.*)

Μακρόβις
MACEDONIA (BOTTIAIA):
—BEROIA*: **(1)** ii AD *IBer* 260, 1 (Tataki 846) (*-βεις*)

Μάκρος
MACEDONIA (EDONIS):
—PHILIPPOI (DRAMA (MOD.)): **(1)** ii-iii AD *AD* 52 (1997) Chron. p. 847, 6 with pl. 314 *β*

Μάκρων
MACEDONIA (BOTTIAIA):
—PELLA: **(1)** c. 380-350 BC *SEG* XLIII 434, 2; cf. XLVI 776
MACEDONIA (CHALKIDIKE):
—AKANTHOS: **(2)** iv/iii BC ib. XLVII 870, 4 (*Μάκρ[ω]ν*)
THRACE:
—BYZANTION: **(3)** hell. *IG* II^2 8441 (*FRA* 1398) (f. *Κράτεια*)

Μαλάκα
TAURIS:
—CHERSONESOS: **(1)** iv/iii BC Solomonik, *NEPKh* 158

Μάλακος
MACEDONIA: **(1)** 366-338 BC *IOrop* 520, 10 (Tataki, *Macedonians* p. 361 no. 7)
TAURIS:
—CHERSONESOS: **(2)** inc. Solomonik, *GAKh* 1371 (vase) (*[M]άλακος*)
—CHERSONESOS (NR.): **(3)** hell.? *AZ* 1857, p. 75 (vase)

Μαλάσσας
KOLCHIS:
—LAZOI: **(1)** ii AD Arr., *Peripl.* 11. 2; *PIR*^{2} M 107 (king)

Μάλθας
MACEDONIA (EDONIS):
—PHILIPPOI (TERRIT.): **(1)** ?ii AD *BIAB* 16 (1950) pp. 14-15 no. 11, 1 (Pilhofer 649) (Lat. Malthae (gen.): f. *Ζιπᾶς*)

Μάλχος
TAURIS:
—CHERSONESOS: **(1)** iv-vi AD Latyshev, *Sbornik* 13

Μάμα
MACEDONIA (SINTIKE):
—PARTHIKOPOLIS (TERRIT.): **(1)** ii AD *Arkheologiia* (Sofia) 1987 (1), p. 25 no. 3 (*Μαμακουτη*—ed.: d. *Κούτης*, m. *Πυρούλας, Σκάρκεζα*)
SCYTHIA MINOR:
—TOMIS: **(2)** ii-iii AD *ISM* II 295 (Lat. Mama: m. *Ἀπολλώνιος*)
—TOMIS?: **(3)** ii AD ib. V 128, 3 (*CCET* IV 52) (d. *Κρήσκης*)
THRACE:
—BYZANTION: **(4)** ii-i BC *IByz* 222 (Fıratlı–Robert p. 79 no. 91) (*[M]άμα?*: d. *Ἄγης*); **(5)** i BC-i AD *IByz* 240 (d. *Ἀπφοῦς*); **(6)** ~ ib. 277 (d. *Ἡρόξενος*)
—ODESSOS: **(7)** i-ii AD *IGB* I^2 116, 1 (d. *Ἀρτέμων*); **(8)** ~ ib. l. 5 (d. *Ξένων*); **(9)** ~ ib. 205 (*Μάμ̣α*); **(10)** ii-iii AD ib. 173 (PM 1731); *Dacia* 21 (1977) p. 161 (date) (*Μάμας*—lap.: d. *Ζώπυρος*); **(11)** ~ *IGB* I^2 191 (d. *Μητρόδωρος*); **(12)** s. ii AD ib. 166 (PM 1404); *Dacia* 21 (1977) p. 161 (date) (d. *Ἀντίπατρος*, m. *Ἀννι*)
—ODESSOS?: **(13)** ii AD *IGB* I^2 110 bis (?d. *Ποσ—*)

Μάμαλα
MACEDONIA (BOTTIAIA):
—PELLA: **(1)** iii BC *SEG* XLIII 437 (d. *Εὐκολῖνος*)

Μαμάλιος
THRACE:
—BYZANTION: **(1)** iii AD *IByz* 294 (Fıratlı–Robert pp. 51-2 no. 27) (s. *Αὐρ. Μάρθα*)

Μαμαρίς
MACEDONIA (BOTTIAIA):
—BEROIA: **(1)** 179 AD *ILeukopetra* 14, 3 (Tataki 866) (*Μαρσιδία M.*)

Μαμάτα
THRACE:
—NOVAE: **(1)** iii AD *IGB* II 741, 8 (d. *Σαβινιανός, Κορινθία*)

Μαμία
CIMMERIAN BOSPOROS:
—PANTIKAPAION: **(1)** i BC *CIRB* 281; Zgusta, *PNS* 600 (m. *Μήνιος*); **(2)** imp. *CIRB* 797; **(3)** i AD ib. 427 (*Μαμί̣α*: d. *Σάσας, Θεονίκη*); **(4)** ~ ib. 460
MACEDONIA (ELIMEIA):
—PALAIOKASTRO (MOD.): **(5)** imp. *EAM* 29 + *SEG* XXXIX 563 (d. *Μακεδών*)
—XEROLIMNI (MOD.): **(6)** ii AD *Α΄ Panell. Synedr. Epigr.* p. 65 no. 12 (*SEG* XLIX 851)
MACEDONIA (EORDAIA):
—PYRGOI (MOD.): **(7)** ii-iii AD *EAM* 130 (*M. Οὐαλαιρία*)

Μάμιος
CIMMERIAN BOSPOROS:
—PANTIKAPAION: **(1)** i/ii AD *CIRB* 622 (s. *Ἀχαιμένης*)

Μαμμία
CIMMERIAN BOSPOROS:
—KEPOI?: **(1)** ii BC Guarducci, *Ep. Gr.* 3 pp. 356-7 (ring) (Higgins, *GRJ* p. 174)
THRACE:
—BYZANTION:
——(Rhegion): **(2)** i BC-i AD *IByz* 249 (Fıratlı–Robert p. 80 no. 93) (d. *Διονύσιος*)

Μάμοξις
THRACE?: **(1)** 316-309 BC *IG* II^2 1956, 38; *Ancient Macedonia* 5 p. 445 with n. 10 (date) (*FRA* 2555)

Μάνας
CIMMERIAN BOSPOROS:
—GORGIPPIA: **(1)** m. ii AD *Eirene* 7 (1968) p. 67, 6 (f. *Πάπας*)

Μάνδασος
SKYTHIA:
—TANAIS: **(1)** 244 AD *CIRB* 1287, 12; Zgusta, *PNS* 751 (f. *Σιαγοῦς*)

Μανδρογένης
MACEDONIA (EDONIS):
—AMPHIPOLIS?: **(1)** hell. *SEG* L 562, 10 (s. *Ἀλέξανδρος*)

Μανδρόστρατος
THRACE:
—APOLLONIA-SOZOPOLIS: **(1)** iv BC *BMNBurgas* 4 (2002) p. 124 no. 17 (*Μανδρόσ[τ]ρατος*: f. *Ἀσπασίη*)

Μάνδρων
THRACE:
—ABDERA: **(1)** c. 395-360 BC May, *Abdera* p. 211 nos. 281-2 (coin); Masson, *OGS* p. 431
—STRYME?: **(2)** c. 400-375 BC *IThrakAig* E164 (f. *Ἀρτέμων*)

Μανδρῶναξ
THRACE:
—ABDERA: (1) c. 450-425 BC May, *Abdera* p. 138 nos. 182-3 (coin); Masson, *OGS* p. 431

Μάνης
CIMMERIAN BOSPOROS:
—PANTIKAPAION: (1) iv BC *CIRB* 222; Zgusta, *KP* 858. 1 (f. *Νᾶ*)
MACEDONIA (BOTTIAIA):
—PELLA: (2) iii BC *A' Panell. Synedr. Epigr.* p. 173 no. 1 (*Pella* p. 140 no. 223)
SKYTHIA:
—OLBIA-BORYSTHENES: (3) v/iv BC Vinogradov, *Pont. Stud.* p. 157 no. 10 (vase) (s. *Ματρόλης*)
THRACE:
—BYZANTION: (4) i AD *SEG* L 667 IV

Μανθάρα?
MACEDONIA (MYGDONIA):
—THESSALONIKE: (1) ?iii AD *IG* X (2) (1) 477 (*Μανθάρα?*: m. *Νικήτας, Μάγνα*)

Μανίαγος
SKYTHIA:
—OLBIA-BORYSTHENES: (1) imp. *IOSPE* I² 117, 3; Zgusta, *PNS* 143 (*[Μ]ανίαγο[ς]*); (2) ii AD *IOSPE* I² 86, 8 (f. *Πουρθάκης*); (3) ~ ib. 96, 8 (s. *Ποσείδηος*)

Μάνικκος
TAURIS:
—CHERSONESOS: (1) c. 300-285 BC Kats p. 100 no. 63 (amph.)

Μάνιος
MACEDONIA (DERRIOPOS):
—STUBERRA: (1) 116 AD *IG* X (2) (2) 327, 26 (f. *Πόσις*)
MACEDONIA (PAIONIA):
—STOBOI: (2) ii-iii AD *Sp.* 71 (1931) p. 46 no. 105 (f. *Σεκοῦνδα*)

Μᾶνις
CIMMERIAN BOSPOROS:
—PANTIKAPAION: (1) iv BC *CIRB* 16

Μανίτης
THRACE: (1) iii BC *IG* XII (9) 813 (f. *Μάτα*)

Μάνιχχος
MACEDONIA (PIERIA):
—LEIBETHRA (NR.): (1) iv/iii BC *Essays Laourdas* p. 112 no. 4 (s. *Εὔνοστος*)

Μαννίας
MACEDONIA (BOTTIAIA):
—SKYDRA: (1) iii BC *SEG* XXIV 524 I, 2 (Hatzopoulos, *MI* 2 p. 106 no. 92; Tataki, *Macedonians* p. 174 no. 2) (f. *Ἕκτωρ*)

Μάντα
MACEDONIA (BOTTIAIA):
—BEROIA: (1) i BC-i AD *IBer* 142, 11 (Tataki 850) (m. *Ἀπολλόδωρος*)
—PELLA? (GIANNITSA (MOD.)): (2) s. ii AD *JDAI* 84 (1969) p. 152 no. R15 (*Μαντᾶνι* (dat.))
MACEDONIA (EDONIS):
—AMPHIPOLIS (TERRIT.): (3) 20 BC or 96 AD *SEG* XXXV 710 (d. *Διοσκουρίδης*)
—AMPHIPOLIS (TERRIT.)?: (4) 82 AD Pikoulas, *Chora* p. 169 no. 80 (or Macedonia (Pieris) Phagres: d. *Ῥύμυσος*)
—AMPHIPOLIS*: (5) 37 BC Robert, *Coll. Froehner* 44, 12; *Ancient Macedonia* 5 p. 1471 (name) (Tataki, *Macedonians* p. 55 no. 80) (freed.)
—PHILIPPOI: (6) imp. *BIAB* 16 (1950) p. 9 no. 3 (Pilhofer 51) (Lat. Manta: m. *Ζιπᾶς*, L. Valerius)
—PHILIPPOI (TERRIT.): (7) ?ii AD *BCH* 24 (1900) p. 307 (Pilhofer 517) (Lat. Manta); (8) ~ *BCH* 47 (1923) pp. 64-5 no. 24, 9 (Pilhofer 519) (Lat. Manta: d. Zerkedis); (9) ~ Pikoulas, *Chora* p. 170 no. 83 (Pilhofer 643) (d. *Ῥ—βιτος*); (10) ii-iii AD Pikoulas, *Chora* p. 158 no. 65, 3 (Pilhofer 598) (m. *Μᾶρκος*); (11) 167 AD Pikoulas, *Chora* p. 159 no. 66 (Pilhofer 599) (d. *Δάγουσις*)
—PHILIPPOI (NR.): (12) ii AD *BCH* 24 (1900) p. 306 no. 2 (Pilhofer 29) (m. *Σούδιος*)
—PHILIPPOI?: (13) ii-iii AD *AEpThess* p. 19 no. 11 (Pilhofer 738); cf. *BE* 1948, no. 102 (locn.)
MACEDONIA (LYNKESTIS):
—KATO KLEINES (MOD.): (14) s. ii AD *EAM* 153 (*Κοῖντα Σηόεια Μ.*)
MACEDONIA (MYGDONIA):
—KALINDOIA: (15) 68-98 AD *SEG* XLII 580, 92; cf. *Anthémonte–Kalindoia* 2 p. 285 (name) (m. *Σύρος*, ?m. *Διοσκουρίδης*)
—THESSALONIKE: (16) ii AD *IG* X (2) (1) 357; (17) iii AD ib. 307 (*Αὐρ. Μ.*); (18) f. iii AD ib. 441 (m. *Αὐρ. Δούλης, Αὐρ. Πυρούλας*)
—THESSALONIKE?: (19) imp. *AE* 1950-1, p. 75 no. 21 (Pilhofer 738); (20) i AD *IG* X (2) (1) 846 (d. *Ἀγάθων*, m. *Ἀγάθων*); (21) ii AD ib. 920 (threpte); (22) 109 AD ib. 849, 3 (m. *Παράμονος, Τόρκος*)
MACEDONIA (ODOMANTIKE):
—SIRRHA (TERRIT.): (23) 26 AD *SEG* XLVI 708 (Pilhofer 557a)
MACEDONIA (PAIONIA):
—EUDARISTOS?: (24) ii-iii AD *Sp.* 98 (1941-8) p. 62 no. 128 (*[Μ]άντα*)
—KAVADARCI (MOD.): (25) ii-iii AD ib. 71 (1931) p. 68 no. 151 (m. *Ἀλέξανδρος*)
—NEGOTINO (MOD.): (26) ii-iii AD ib. 75 (1933) p. 37 no. 114 (m. *Ἀρτεμιδώρα*); (27) 153 AD *SEG* XXXVIII 712 (m. *Μακεδών, Ποσειδώνιος, Φίλιππος*)
MACEDONIA (PIERIS):
—PHAGRES (TERRIT.)?: (28) ii-iii AD Pikoulas, *Chora* p. 168 no. 77 (d. *Ζιπύρων*)
MACEDONIA (SINTIKE):
—PARTHIKOPOLIS (TERRIT.): (29) 152 AD *Melnik* 1 p. 166 no. 6 (m. *Μουκάσης*)
THRACE:
—LUKOVIT (MOD.): (30) imp. *ILB* 189; cf. *Ét. Balk.* 1987, p. 93 no. 22 (name) (Lat. Manta: d. *Πυρούλας*)
THRACE?: (31) ii AD *IG* X (2) (1) 910, 5 (Lat. Manta: d. *Δίζας*)

Μαντανα
THRACE:
—BEROE-AUGUSTA TRAIANA (TERRIT.): (1) ii AD *IGB* III 1714 + V 5607 (*Κλ. Μ[α]ντανα, Κλ. Μ[ο]ντᾶνα*—1714)

Μάντας
MACEDONIA (EDONIS):
—AMPHIPOLIS (TERRIT.)?: (1) 185 AD *BCH* 24 (1900) p. 308 (Pilhofer 592) (s. *Μέστος*); (2) 223 AD *BCH* 24 (1900) p. 308 (Pilhofer 593) (*Μάντα[ς]*: s. *Διονύσιος*)
MACEDONIA (ODOMANTIKE):
—GAZOROS: (3) 215 or 174 BC *SEG* XXX 1892, 27 (Hatzopoulos, *MI* 2 pp. 57-8 no. 39) (*Μάντ[ας]*: s. *Κερζούλας*)

Μαντίθεος
THRACE:
—MESAMBRIA: (1) ii BC *IGB* I² 312, 2 (f. *—ων*)

Μάντις
MACEDONIA (EDONIS):
—AMPHIPOLIS: (1) ?ii AD *FGrH* 257 F 37, 54 (Tataki, *Macedonians* p. 55 no. 81) (s. *Καίπριζος*)

Μαντοῦς
MACEDONIA (EDONIS):
—PHILIPPOI (TERRIT.): (1) ii-iii AD Pikoulas, *Chora* p. 123 no. 13, 1 (*[Μ]αντοῦς?*: d. *..ανος* (gen.))
MACEDONIA (MYGDONIA):
—THESSALONIKE: (2) ii AD *IG* X (2) (1) 357; (3) m. iii AD *SEG* XXXV 767 (d. *Σεμοῦς*)
—THESSALONIKE?: (4) s. ii AD *IG* X (2) (1) 904; *JDAI* 84 (1969) p. 154 no. R20 (date) (*Μαντοῦνι* (dat.): m. *Μύστα*)

Μαντύης
MACEDONIA (PAIONIA): (1) s. vi BC Hdt. v 12 (Tataki, *Macedonians* p. 209 no. 15)

Μαντώ
MACEDONIA (BISALTIA):
—TERPNI (MOD.): (1) ii-iii AD *SEG* XLIX 810
MACEDONIA (BOTTIAIA):
—BEROIA: (2) ii-iii AD *IBer* 90, 6 (Tataki 370) (*Δειδιανὴ Μ.*: m. *Οὐαριανὸς Διδιανὸς Δημήτριος*)
MACEDONIA (EDONIS):
—AMPHIPOLIS (TERRIT.): (3) 56 or 172 AD *SEG* XXX 600 (d. *Διοσκουρίδης*)
MACEDONIA (MYGDONIA):
—THESSALONIKE: (4) ii-iii AD *IG* X (2) (1) 437 (m. *Σοῦμμος, Κόϊντος, Καισία*); (5) ~ ib. 489; (6) s. ii AD *SEG* XLVIII 852 (m. *Μακεδών*)
—THESSALONIKE?: (7) ii AD *IG* X (2) (1) 898 (threpte); (8) ii-iii AD ib. 869 (*Μεστρία Μ.*)
MACEDONIA (ODOMANTIKE):
—SIRRHA: (9) ii-iii AD *SEG* XXX 605 (d. *Βύτις*); (10) ~ ib. 606 (*Μαντῷ*); (11) ~ ib. 613, 3 (m. *Μητρόδωρος*)
—SIRRHA (TERRIT.): (12) 55 or 171 AD ib. XXXIV 676 (m. *Διοσκουρίδης*)
—SIRRHA (NR.): (13) ii-iii AD ib. XXIV 579, 2 (Pilhofer 561)
MACEDONIA (SINTIKE):
—PARTHIKOPOLIS: (14) ii-iii AD *IGB* IV 2268 (*Πομπεία Μ.*)
MACEDONIA?: (15) f. ii AD *JDAI* 84 (1969) p. 156 no. R24 + *BCH* 99 (1975) pp. 178-9 (m. *Μακεδών*)
THRACE:
—PHILIPPOPOLIS-TRIMONTIUM: (16) iii AD *IGB* III 1024, 8 (*GVI* 695)

Μάξιμα
MACEDONIA (BOTTIAIA):
—ALLANTE? (PARTHENION (MOD.)): (1) iii-iv AD Feissel, *RICM* 80
—BEROIA: (2) ii AD *IBer* 232, 2, 5 (Tataki 852) (m. *Διοδώρα*); (3) ~ *IBer* 261 (Tataki 853) (d. *Μαξιμώ*); (4) ~ *IBer* 338, 2 (Tataki 851) (d. *Γ. Οὐα. Ἑρμᾶς, Τερτία*)
—EDESSA: (5) v-vi AD Feissel, *RICM* 39
MACEDONIA (CHALKIDIKE):
—OLYNTHOS (NR.): (6) imp. *SEG* XXIX 610
MACEDONIA (DERRIOPOS):
—STUBERRA: (7) ii/iii AD *IG* X (2) (2) 334
MACEDONIA (KRESTONIA):
—IORON: (8) iii AD *SEG* XLVIII 815
MACEDONIA (MYGDONIA):
—THESSALONIKE: (9) ?ii AD *IG* X (2) (1) 458; (10) ii-iii AD ib. 438 (d. *Δημητρία*); (11) iv AD *AEMTh* 15 (2001) p. 325 (d. *Ἀγαθάγγελος*); (12) v-vi AD *IG* X (2) (1) 352 (Feissel, *RICM* 175) (-ξη-)
—THESSALONIKE (TERRIT.): (13) iii-v AD *IG* X (2) (1) 1017
—THESSALONIKE?: (14) ii-iii AD ib. 208, 5
—THESSALONIKE*: (15) ii-iii AD ib. 306
THRACE:
—PERINTHOS-HERAKLEIA: (16) i-ii AD *IPerinth* 98 (d. *Τυραννίς*, m. *Τρόφιμος*); (17) ii AD ib. 106 (m. *Σερβίλιος Μάξιμος*)
—SESTOS: (18) ii AD *ISestos* 3 (*Τατία ἡ καὶ Μ.*)

Μαξιμιανός
MACEDONIA: (1) 239 AD *ILeukopetra* 93, 13 (slave/freed.); (2) ?iv AD *Syringes* 1558
MACEDONIA (ELIMEIA):
—AIANE (TERRIT.): (3) m. iii AD *EAM* 64

Macedonia (Mygdonia):
—thessalonike*: (4) ?v ad *IG* x (2) (1) 359, 3 (Feissel, *RICM* 153)
Thrace:
—pautalia: (5) s. ii ad *SEG* xlvi 864, 5

Μαξιμῖνα
Macedonia (Mygdonia):
—thessalonike?: (1) ii ad *IG* x (2) (1) 250 I, 7 (*Μαξιμ[εῖ]να*: m. *—της*)
Scythia Minor:
—istros: (2) iii ad *ISM* i 229, 6 (*Μ. Σισι*—ed.: ?d. *Σίσης*)

Μάξιμος
Cimmerian Bosporos:
—pantikapaion: (1) i-ii ad *MIA* 178 (1971) p. 143
Macedonia (Bottiaia):
—beroia: (2) ii/iii ad *IBer* 27 A, 7 (f. *Ζωσᾶς*) ?= (*4*); (3) ~ ib. l. 14 (f. *Ἐπάγαθος*) ?= (*4*); (4) ~ ib. l. 16 (f. *Ἐπίκτητος*) ?= (*3*) (*2*); (5) iii-iv ad ib. 446, 2 (Feissel, *RICM* 58; Tataki 856)
—beroia*: (6) s. ii ad *IBer* 402, 6 (Tataki 857)
—edessa: (7) 204 ad *Arch. Pap.* 22 (1973) p. 206 no. 8 (Tataki, *Edessa* 197)
Macedonia (Chalkidike):
—potidaia-kassandreia (nr.): (8) imp. Dimitsas 750 (s. *Ἐπίξενος, Βάσα*)
Macedonia (Derriopos):
—stuberra: (9) 116 ad *IG* x (2) (2) 327, 5 (s. *Διονύσιος*); (10) ~ ib. l. 31 (s. *Ἰούλιος*)
Macedonia (Edonis):
—amphipolis: (11) imp. Kaphtantzis 657, 4 (?s. *Ἀπολλωνᾶς*)
Macedonia (Lower Paionia):
—europos: (12) ?ii ad *SEG* xxxviii 612
Macedonia (Lynkestis):
—herakleia: (13) i ad *IG* x (2) (2) 75, 50 (f. *Γάϊος*); (14) ~ ib. l. 53 (s. *Μάρυλλος*)
Macedonia (Mygdonia):
—kalindoia: (15) 68-98 ad *SEG* xlii 580, 31 (*Θεόδοτος ὁ καὶ Μ.*: s. *Θεοδότη*)
—lete: (16) 179 or 296 ad Dimitsas 679 (I f. *Μάξιμος* II); (17) ~ ib. (II s. *Μάξιμος* I, *Κοπρία*)
—thessalonike: (18) i-ii ad *IG* x (2) (1) 243 I, 4 (s. *Χρύσανθος*); (19) ii ad ib. 362; (20) 132 ad ib. 503, 2 (*Ἀπολλώνιος ὁ καὶ Μ.*: s. *Ἀρτεμᾶς*); (21) ii/iii ad ib. 262 II, 7; (22) 206 ad ib. 236, 10
—thessalonike?: (23) ii ad ib. 906; (24) ii-iii ad ib. 750 (*-ξει-*); (25) ~ ib. 860
Macedonia (Odomantike):
—sirrha: (26) ii-iii ad *SEG* xxx 606 (f. *Ἀσκληπιόδωρος*)
Macedonia (Orestis):
—sisani (mod.): (27) 146 ad *EAM* 187, 16 (s. *Ἀφροδιτώ*)
Macedonia (Paionia):
—kavadarci (mod.): (28) ii-iii ad *Sp.* 71 (1931) p. 71 no. 161; cf. *Arch. Karte Kavadarci* p. 15 (?f. *Καλλικρίτα*: name—Papazoglu)
—stoboi: (29) ii-iii ad *Sp.* 75 (1933) p. 26 no. 60 (*-ζι-*)
Macedonia (Pelagonia): (30) imp. *IG* x (2) (2) 241; (31) ii ad ib. 288
Macedonia (Pieria):
—dion: (32) ii-iii ad *Dion* p. 64
Scythia Minor:
—istros: (33) ii ad *ISM* i 211, 3 (s. *Μόνιμος*)
—kallatis: (34) ii/iii ad ib. iii 181, 3, 9 (f. *Διοσκουρίδης, Πολυδεύκης*); (35) iii-iv ad *SEG* xxv 746, 4 (Popescu, *IGL* 85) (f. *Γ. Κρίσπος*); (36) 241-244 ad *ISM* iii 74 A, 25 (f. *Ἀλέξανδρος*)
—tomis: (37) ii-iii ad ib. ii 20, 5 (*Μάξι[μος]*: f. *Ἑρμῆς*); (38) ~ ib. 31 III, 10 (s. *Μα—*)
Thrace:
—abryttos: (39) iii ad *IGB* ii 744, 10 (s. *Ἑπτάπορις, Δρει—ούζερις*)
—bazitenoi: (40) ii-iii ad ib. 524
—bourdapa: (41) ii-iii ad ib. iii 1361 (s. *Συνέκδημος*)
—byzantion: (42) i ad *IByz* 141 (f. *Κορνηλία*); (43) m. iv ad *PLRE* i (22) (f. *Εὐκλείδης*)
—dionysopolis: (44) iii ad *IGB* I^2 14 c, 19 (f. *Αὐρ. Σουλπίκιος*)
—draganovec (mod.): (45) f. iii ad ib. v 5287 (*CCET* ii (2) 457) (s. *Ζουράζερις*)
—madytos: (46) imp. *ISestos* 57
—markianopolis: (47) ii ad *IGB* v 5339, 3; (48) c. 303-305 ad Latyshev, *Menolog. anon.* pp. 106-10; cf. *Anal. Boll.* 31 (1912) p. 244
—markianopolis (nr.): (49) ii-iii ad *IGB* v 5367 (f. *Κούρης*)
—maroneia: (50) i ad *IThrakAig* E306
—nicopolis ad istrum: (51) ii ad *IGB* ii 674, 3 (or Bithynia Nikomedeia: s. *—σιος*); (52) ii-iii ad ib. v 5235 (s. *Κάσιος*)
—odessos: (53) 221 ad ib. I^2 47 bis b, 16 (f. *Αὐρ. Διονύσιος*); (54) ~ ib. 47 bis c, 28 (f. *Αὐρ. Καστελιανός*)
—odessos (territ.): (55) iii ad ib. 282 (*CCET* i 103)
—pautalia: (56) ii-iii ad *IGB* iv 2055 (*Μάξιμ[ος]*)
—pautalia (territ.): (57) ii-iii ad ib. 2119 (I f. *Μάξιμος* II); (58) ~ ib. (II s. *Μάξιμος* I, f. *Λυσίας*)
—perinthos-herakleia: (59) ii ad *IPerinth* 142; (60) 196-198 ad ib. 56, 17 (s. *Κλαύδιος*)
—perinthos-herakleia*: (61) ii ad ib. 74
—philippopolis-trimontium: (62) ii-iii ad *IGB* iii 912, 1 (s. *Σουσίων*); (63) iii ad ib. 1024, 14 (*GVI* 695); (64) c. 303 ad *Anal. Boll.* 31 (1912) p. 192
—philippopolis-trimontium (territ.): (65) ii-iii ad *IGB* iii 1467 (doctor)
—philippopolis-trimontium:
——(Artemisias): (66) c. 163-164 ad ib. 903; v 5433 (f. *Ἄκτιος*)
—serdica: (67) s. ii ad *Sp.* 77 (1934) p. 53 no. 5? (s. *Δρόλης*)

Μαξιμώ
Macedonia (Bottiaia):
—beroia: (1) ii ad *IBer* 261 (Tataki 855) (m. *Μάξιμα*)

Μαράθωνις
Macedonia (Mygdonia):
—thessalonike: (1) i-ii ad *IG* x (2) (1) 625 (*GVI* 319)

Μαρᾶς
Macedonia (Mygdonia):
—kalindoia: (1) 68-98 ad *SEG* xlii 580, 95 (*Γ. Ἰούλιος Μ.*)

Μαργαρίτα
Thrace:
—nicopolis ad istrum (territ.): (1) ii ad *ILB* 410 (Lat. Fl. Margarita)

Μάργος
Thrace:
—nicopolis ad istrum (territ.): (1) 227 ad ib. 438 I, 47 (Lat. Margus: f. *Τρωΐλος*)

Μάρδαυος
Skythia:
—tanais: (1) 228 ad *CIRB* 1282, 15 (s. *Ζάρανδος*)

Μαρδόνιος
Scythia Minor:
—istros: (1) iv bc Unp. (Avram, defixio) 1, 4

Μαρζάκης
Cimmerian Bosporos:
—pantikapaion: (1) ii ad *CIRB* 679 A

Μάρθα
Thrace:
—byzantion: (1) iii ad *IByz* 294 (Fıratlı–Robert pp. 51-2 no. 27) (*Αὐρ. Μ.*: m. *Μαμάλιος*)

Μαρία
Cimmerian Bosporos:
—pantikapaion: (1) iv ad *CIRB* 759
Macedonia (Bottiaia):
—beroia: (2) iv-v ad *IBer* 455, 2 (Feissel, *RICM* 295) (*-ρέα*: d. *Λεόντιος, Τερτία*: Jew)
—beroia*: (3) 193 ad *ILeukopetra* 39, 1 (freed.?)
—edessa?: (4) iii-iv ad *GVI* 2036, 5, 12 (*IDyrrh* 527 bis) (*Ἡδεῖα ἡ καὶ Μ.*: d. *Εὔκλεια*, m. *Τίτος*)
Macedonia (Mygdonia):
—thessalonike: (5) ?ii-iii ad *SEG* xxx 643; (6) iv-vi ad Feissel, *RICM* 107; (7) v-vi ad ib. 194; (8) 507 ad ib. 131, 4 (*Φλ. Μ.*: m. *Φίλιππος*)
—thessalonike?: (9) ii ad *IG* x (2) (1) 697
Tauris:
—chersonesos: (10) iv ad *SEG* xlii 701. 1
Thrace:
—beroe-augusta traiana: (11) c. 320-324 ad *Anal. Boll.* 31 (1912) p. 198; p. 207
—bisanthe-panion: (12) iv-vi ad *AD* 49-50 (1994-5) Mel. p. 316 no. 142 (d. *Γεώργιος*)
—maroneia: (13) v-vi ad *SEG* xlix 892, 9 (*IThrakAig* E357)
—odessos: (14) v-vi ad Beševliev 114, 4; (15) vi ad ib. 124, 5
—perinthos-herakleia: (16) v-vi ad *IPerinth* 226 (*AD* 51-2 (1996-7) Mel. p. 369 no. 187) (m. *Ἄννα*)
—serdica: (17) v-vi ad Beševliev 16

Μαριανή
Macedonia: (1) 229 ad *ILeukopetra* 75, 8 (slave/freed.)

Μαριανός
Macedonia: (1) 229 ad ib. l. 10 (slave/freed.)
Thrace:
—perinthos-herakleia: (2) c. 320 ad *Anal. Boll.* 31 (1912) p. 205

Μαριάντας
Skythia:
—skythai: (1) ii ad Luc., *Tox.* 50 (f. *Ἀρσακόμας*: fict.)

Μαρικίων
Skythia:
—olbia-borysthenes (berezan (mod.)): (1) f. ii ad *SEG* xlix 1028 A, 9 (s. *Λυσίμαχος*)

Μαρῖνος
Macedonia (Mygdonia):
—thessalonike: (1) iii ad *IG* x (2) (1) 565, 4 (*-ρεῖ-*: s. *Ἰούλ. Σέμνος, Ἰουλ. Βιθυνία*)
—thessalonike*: (2) ii-iii ad *AD* 22 (1967) Chron. p. 391 (*-ρεῖ-*: freed.)
Thrace: (3) 386 ad *RE* (3); *DCB* (2) (bp.)
—bisanthe-panion: (4) v-vi ad *ISestos* 16 A, 1 (*AD* 49-50 (1994-5) Mel. p. 333 no. 158 A); cf. *SEG* xlviii 898 ter
—bisanthe-panion*: (5) iv-vi ad *AD* 49-50 (1994-5) Mel. p. 313 no. 138 (s. *B—*)

Μάριος
Cimmerian Bosporos:
—gorgippia: (1) ii/iii ad *CIRB* 1179, 31 (f. *Πόθος*)

Μάρις
Macedonia (Mygdonia):
—thessalonike: (1) ii-iii ad *SEG* xxxi 647 (*Μάρι* (voc.))

Μάρκελλα

Macedonia (Mygdonia):
—thessalonike: (1) v-vi ad ib. xlii 627 (m. *Φωκᾶς*)
Scythia Minor:
—tomis: (2) v-vi ad Barnea 12, 5 (Popescu, *IGL* 31) (m. *Μάρκελλος*)

Μαρκελλιανός

Macedonia (Mygdonia):
—thessalonike: (1) ii ad *IG* x (2) (1) 241 B, 9 (s. *Μαρκελλῖνος*)

Μαρκελλῖνα

Macedonia (Bottiaia):
—beroia: (1) 189 ad *ILeukopetra* 22, 1, 5 (-λλεῖ-: d. *Μᾶρκος*)
Macedonia (Mygdonia):
—peristera (mod.): (2) iii ad *SEG* xxix 590 (m. *Ζώσιμος, Σύρος*)
—thessalonike: (3) i/ii ad *AD* 22 (1967) Chron. p. 393 (*Μαρκελλ[εῖ]να*); (4) ii ad *IG* x (2) (1) 330 (-λλεῖ-); (5) ?v-vi ad *AD* 4 (1918) Parart. p. 31 (-καιλῖ-)
Macedonia (Paionia):
—kavadarci (mod.): (6) ii-iii ad *Sp.* 98 (1941-8) p. 67 no. 139 (*[Μ]αρκελλεῖνα*)
Macedonia (Pieria):
—dion: (7) ii-iii ad Oikonomos 21 (d. *Ἰούλ. Πρῶτος*)

Μαρκελλῖνος

Macedonia (Bottiaia):
—genderrhos? (mandalon (mod.)): (1) v-vi ad *SEG* xliii 397 (-κελῖ-)
Macedonia (Mygdonia):
—thessalonike: (2) ii ad *IG* x (2) (1) 241 B, 9 (*Μαρκελλεῖν[ος]*: f. *Μαρκελλιανός*)
Thrace:
—salymbria: (3) vi ad *BCH* 36 (1912) pp. 635-6 no. 92 (*AD* 53 (1998) Mel. p. 477 no. 219) (-κελῖ-: s. *Θωμᾶς, Ἀμυώ*)

Μάρκελλος

Macedonia (Bottiaia):
—skydra: (1) imp. *SEG* ii 397
Macedonia (Mygdonia):
—thessalonike: (2) ii ad *IG* x (2) (1) 392 (s. *Ἀρέτη*); (3) ~ ib. 1034 A-B (*GVI* 1972; Tataki, *Macedonians* p. 184 no. 42); (4) 215 ad *SEG* l 645
Macedonia (Odomantike):
—sirrha: (5) ii-iii ad *Belomorski Pregled* 1 (1942) p. 321 no. 9 (Kaphtantzis 30) (*Μ[άρ]κελλος*: s. *Μεσκήνις*)
Macedonia (Sintike):
—herakleia: (6) ii/iii ad *IGB* iv 2324
Scythia Minor:
—tomis: (7) ii-iii ad *ISM* ii 20, 4 (*Μάρκε[λλος]*: f. *Αἴλλων*); (8) v-vi ad Barnea 12, 2 (Popescu, *IGL* 31) (s. *Ὀρέντης, Μάρκελλα*)
Thrace:
—anchialos (territ.): (9) ii ad *IGB* iii 1841, 6
—bazopara: (10) 202 ad ib. 1690 c, 57 (and Thrace Pizos: f. *Μουκιανός*)
—odessos: (11) vi ad *PLRE* iii (8); Beševliev 89, 2 (Popescu, *IGL* 47, 5)
—pautalia:
——Karistoron: (12) ii-iii ad *IGB* iv 2178
—perinthos-herakleia: (13) i ad *IPerinth* 88 (s. *Μᾶρκος*); (14) ii ad ib. 100 (-κελος: s. *Μᾶρκος*)
—vicus trullensium: (15) ii-iii ad *IGB* ii 504

Μαρκία

Macedonia (Bisaltia):
—tragilos: (1) 164 or 280 ad *GVI* 1317, 5 = Kaphtantzis 531
Macedonia (Bottiaia):
—beroia: (2) ii ad *IBer* 262
—edessa: (3) 180 ad *SEG* xxiv 531, 8 (Tataki, *Edessa* 200) (m. *Ἀλέξανδρος, Ἰούλιος*)
—pella: (4) ?i ad *ILGR* 202 (biling.)
Macedonia (Eordaia): (5) s. ii ad *ILeukopetra* 134, 8 (d. *Ὀρέστης, Γλαύκα*)
Macedonia (Mygdonia):
—thessalonike: (6) v-vi ad *SEG* xlv 821 (mosaic)
Macedonia (Pelagonia): (7) ?ii ad *IG* x (2) (2) 284; (8) ii-iii ad ib. 262
Scythia Minor:
—kallatis: (9) v-vi ad Barnea 47 (Popescu, *IGL* 93)
—tomis: (10) ii ad *ISM* ii 187 (d. *Μᾶρκος*, m. *Καλλίστη*)
Thrace:
—bizye?: (11) imp. Unp. (Sayar)
—byzantion: (12) ii-iii ad *IByz* 140 (d. *Διονύσιος*)
—markianopolis: (13) iii ad *IGB* ii 815, 7 (m. *Ἀλέξανδρος*)

Μαρκιανή

Macedonia (Lower Paionia):
—idomene?: (1) 239 ad *SEG* xviii 273
Macedonia (Mygdonia):
—thessalonike: (2) ii-iii ad *IG* x (2) (1) 433 (Feissel, *RICM* 115); (3) ~ *IG* x (2) (1) 598; (4) ~ *SEG* xliv 554
Macedonia (Paionia):
—stoboi: (5) v-vi ad Unp. (Stobi excav.) inv. I-73-2 (*Μαρκιαν[ή]*)
Thrace:
—byzantion: (6) i-ii ad *GVI* 1083 (d. *Δαδοῦχος, Σεβῆρα*)
—perinthos-herakleia: (7) i-ii ad *IPerinth* 134; (8) ii ad ib. 141 (m. *Ματρώνα*)
—serdica: (9) ii-iii ad *IGB* iv 1960, 1

Μαρκιανός

Cimmerian Bosporos:
—pantikapaion: (1) 275-278 ad *CIRB* 36, 43 (*Μαρκιαν(ός)*: s. *Πατέριος*)
Macedonia (Chalkidike):
—potidaia-kassandreia: (2) ii-iii ad *SEG* xxix 597 (s. *Μέννυς*)
Macedonia (Orestis):
—agia anna (mod.): (3) s. ii ad *EAM* 195 (s. *Πρευρᾶδος*)
Scythia Minor:
—istros: (4) ii ad *ISM* i 211, 12 (s. *Μάγνος*); (5) 222-225 ad ib. 100 A, 23 (*Μαρ[κιαν]ός*: f. *—ωρος*)
—tomis: (6) ii-iii ad ib. ii 31 III, 11 (*Μαρκιαν[ός]*)
——(Argadeis): (7) f. ii ad ib. 179 (I f. *Μαρκιανός* II); (8) ~ ib. (II s. *Μαρκιανός* I)
Skythia:
—olbia-borysthenes: (9) ii ad *IOSPE* I^2 57, 7 (*Μαρκιαν[ός]*); (10) ~ ib. 263, 4; (11) 198-211 ad ib. 174, 11 (s. *Δομνίων*)
—tanais: (12) 225 ad *CIRB* 1279, 17 (-κε-: f. *Ἡρακλείδης*)
Tauris:
—chersonesos: (13) imp. *IOSPE* I^2 435, 10 (?s. *Φιλο—*); (14) ii-iii ad ib. 486, 3 (*[Μαρ]κιανός*?: s. *Ἀλε—*)
Thrace:
—aproi: (15) iv-v ad Unp. (Sayar) (f. *Κυριακός*)
—beroe-augusta traiana: (16) 260-268 ad *IGB* iii 1567, 7
—byzantion (territ.): (17) ii-iii ad *IByz* 181 (*[Μ]αρκιανός*: s. *Θεόφαντος*)
—hadrianopolis: (18) iv-v ad *SEG* viii 45, 7 (f. *Ῥεβοκᾶτα*)
—mesambria (territ.): (19) iv ad *IGB* v 5129, 21 (s. *Φλ. Ζῆνις, Αὐρ. Μαρτῖνα*)
—nicopolis ad istrum: (20) iii ad ib. ii 691 (-κει-: f. *Καλλικράτεια*)
—odessos: (21) 221 ad ib. I^2 47 bis a, 28 (f. *Αὐρ. Θεόδοτος*); (22) ~ ib. 47 bis b, 28 (f. *Αὐρ. Θεόφιλος*)
—pautalia: (23) ii-iii ad ib. ii 540 (s. *Διονύσιος*); (24) s. ii ad *SEG* xlvi 864 II, 20
—philippopolis-trimontium (territ.): (25) ii-iii ad *IGB* iii 1055 (-κει-)
—serdica: (26) iii ad ib. iv 1906 (f. *Αὐρ. Ἀπολλωνίδης*)

Μαρκίων

Macedonia (Mygdonia):
—thessalonike: (1) ii ad *IG* x (2) (1) 392 (s. *Ἀρέτη*)
Macedonia (Orestis):
—lyke: (2) 236 ad *SEG* xlvii 911 (f. *Νικάνωρ*)
Scythia Minor:
—istros: (3) 138 ad *ISM* i 193 II, 79 (*Μαρκίων*: s. *Μᾶρκος*)
Thrace:
—salymbria: (4) imp. *Archives Stamoulis* d. 35 (Loukopoulou, *Thrace Propontique* p. 272) (s. *Φανέτας*)

Μᾶρκος

Cimmerian Bosporos:
—gorgippia: (1) s. ii ad *CIRB* 1142, 7 (s. *Μυστικός*); (2) ~ ib. l. 16 (f. *Ἰουλιανός*)
—gorgippia*: (3) ii-iii ad Alekseeva, *Gorgippiia* pl. 89 (amph.)
—pantikapaion: (4) i bc *CIRB* 309; cf. KW pl. 15 no. 219 (f. *Θεοφίλη*); (5) i ad *CIRB* 449; cf. KW pl. 17 no. 254 (s. *Λεύκιος, Μητροφίλα*)
Macedonia (Bisaltia):
—tragilos: (6) 164 or 280 ad *GVI* 1317, 2 = Kaphtantzis 531
Macedonia (Bottiaia):
—beroia: (7) ii/iii ad *IBer* 27 A, 18 (slave?); (8) 189 ad *ILeukopetra* 22, 1 (f. *Μαρκελλῖνα*)
—edessa: (9) ?ii ad *SEG* xii 346 (Tataki, *Edessa* 201) (*Μ. ὁ καὶ Κυρήνιος*: s. *Δημήτριος*)
Macedonia (Derriopos):
—stuberra: (10) 87 ad *IG* x (2) (2) 325, 78 (s. *Ῥοῦφος*); (11) 116 ad ib. 327, 33 (f. *Πόσις*)
Macedonia (Edonis):
—amphipolis: (12) imp. Kaphtantzis 662 (terracotta) (?s. *Βετος*)
—amphipolis (territ.): (13) 157 or 273 ad *SEG* xxxiv 605
—amphipolis?: (14) imp. ib. xxiv 608 (f. *Ἀκκόλεια*)
—philippoi (territ.): (15) i-ii ad Pikoulas, *Chora* p. 163 no. 72, 4 (Pilhofer 606) (*[Μ]ᾶρκος*: s. *Ἡρόδοτος, Δομιτία*); (16) ii-iii ad Pikoulas, *Chora* p. 135 no. 38 (Pilhofer 614); Collart, *Philippes* pl. 37. 2 (*Μάρκι* (gen.): f. *Γάϊος*); (17) ~ Pikoulas, *Chora* p. 158 no. 65, 1 (Pilhofer 598) (s. *Δυνούζης, Μάντα*); (18) v-vi ad Feissel, *RICM* 219 (Pilhofer 634; Pikoulas, *Chora* p. 118 no. 9)
Macedonia (Elimeia):
—oblostai: (19) 200 ad *EAM* 37, 7 (f. *Ἀπολλόδωρος*)
Macedonia (Lower Paionia):
—europos: (20) ?ii ad *SEG* xxxviii 612 (*Μᾶρκ[ος]*: s. *Ἀντιγόνα*, ?s. *Ἀντι—*)
Macedonia (Lynkestis):
—herakleia: (21) i ad *IG* x (2) (2) 75, 29 (f. *Κόϊντος*); (22) ~ ib. l. 41-42 (s. *Οὔηρος*)
Macedonia (Mygdonia):
—thessalonike: (23) i-ii ad ib. x (2) (1) 243 I, 10 (s. *Ἄππιος*); (24) s. i ad ib. 68, 27; 69, 19 (s. *Ἑρμέρως*); (25) ii ad ib. 241 A II, 26; (26) ii-iii ad ib. II^2 12518; *Myrtos* p. 274 n. 24 (locn.); cf. *LGPN* II s.v. (51); (27) ~ *IG* x (2) (1) 599 (f. *Μ. Ἀονιάνιος Ἰσίδωρος*); (28) ~ ib. 642, 1 (s. *Μεγίστη*, f. *Μεττία Ἀνατολή*); (29) ~ ib. 670 (s. *Σωσιπάτρα*); (30) 141 ad ib. 137, 12; cf. *BCH* 97 (1973) p. 587 (s. *Διομήδης*); (31) ii/iii ad *IG* x (2) (1) 262 II, 7; (32) 209 ad ib. 506, 1 (f. *Ἀρτέμιν*)
—thessalonike?: (33) ?iii ad ib. 911, 4 (s. *Τίτος, Κλευπώ*)

Macedonia (Odomantike):
—gazoros (territ.): **(34)** ii-iii ad *SEG* xxx 610 (Pilhofer 538) (s. *Μέστος*); **(35)** 156 ad Kaphtantzis 737 (Pilhofer 539a) (*Μâρ[κος]*?)
—gazoros (nr.): **(36)** i ad *SEG* xxxviii 2038 (Pilhofer 539b)
—sirrha: **(37)** 155 ad Dimitsas 821, 6 (Kaphtantzis 1) (f. *Γάϊος*)
Macedonia (Paionia): **(38)** ii-iii ad *Sp.* 75 (1933) p. 77 no. 219 (f. *Κούαρτος, Κούϊντος*)
—bylazora: **(39)** ii-iii ad ib. p. 19 no. 37, 5 (s. *Λούκιος, Μακέτη*); **(40)** ~ *SEG* xvi 402, 4 (s. *Λίβιος*)
—kavadarci (mod.): **(41)** ii-iii ad *Sp.* 71 (1931) p. 67 no. 149 + 77 (1934) p. 81 (s. *Λούκιος*)
Macedonia (Pelagonia): **(42)** imp. *IG* x (2) (2) 272 (s. *Γάϊος, Ὦπις*); **(43)** ii ad ib. 242
Macedonia (Sintike):
—herakleia: **(44)** 230 ad *IGB* v 5922, 3 (f. *Παράμονος*)
Macedonia?: **(45)** iii ad *AD* 38 (1983) Chron. p. 411
Scythia Minor:
—istros: **(46)** ii ad *ISM* i 196, 15; 201 II, 11 (f. *Κορβούλων*); **(47)** 138 ad ib. 193 II, 79 (f. *Μαρκίων*); **(48)** f. iii ad ib. 218, 11 (*Νικίας ὁ καὶ Μ.*: s. *Οὐαλέριος*)
—tomis: **(49)** i ad *SEG* xxxiii 585 (s. *Σεκοῦνδα*); **(50)** i-ii ad *ISM* ii 150, 3, 9 (I s. *Ῥοῦφος*, f. *Μâρκος* II); **(51)** ~ ib. l. 9 (*M. νεώτ.*: II s. *Μâρκος* I); **(52)** ii ad ib. 187 (f. *Μαρκία*); **(53)** ii-iii ad ib. 18, 9; **(54)** ~ ib. 20, 3 (s. *Τερέντιος*); **(55)** ~ ib. 26, 5 (f. *Διονύσιος*); **(56)** ~ ib. 31 III, 3 (I f. *Μâρκος* II); **(57)** ~ ib. l. 3 (II s. *Μâρκος* I); **(58)** ~ ib. 104, 8 (f. *Χρῆστος*); **(59)** ~ ib. 319 with pl. (*[Μ]âρκος*); **(60)** ~ ib. 325 (*Μâρκ[ος]*?); **(61)** ~ ib. 468, 11 (s. *Νέστωρ*); **(62)** s. ii ad ib. 131 (*IGB* iii 1874; *CCET* iv 26 (locn., date)) (s. *Γραφικός*, f. *Δημοσθένης, Δημήτριος*); **(63)** 201 ad *ISM* ii 83 I, 30 (f. *Νικόστρατος*)
Skythia:
—olbia-borysthenes: **(64)** ?ii ad *IOSPE* I^2 99, 5 (s. *Ἀχιλλεύς*)
—olbia-borysthenes (berezan (mod.)): **(65)** f. ii ad *SEG* xlix 1028 A, 7 (s. *Νεοπτόλεμος*)
Tauris:
—chersonesos: **(66)** ii ad ib. xlvi 931, 3
Thrace:
—beroe-augusta traiana: **(67)** ii-iii ad *IGB* iii 1602 (?s. *Μα—*)
—beroe-augusta traiana (territ.): **(68)** ii ad ib. 1741 bis (biling.) (s. *Τραΐδακος*)
—byzantion: **(69)** ii ad *IByz* 317 a (Fıratlı–Robert p. 120 no. 201) (*Μâ[ρκ]ος*: I f. *Μâρκος* II); **(70)** ~ *IByz* 317 a (Fıratlı–Robert p. 120 no. 201) (II s. *Μâρκος* I)
—byzantion?: **(71)** imp. *IByz* 332 (f. *Διονύσιος*); **(72)** ~ ib. 382 (f. *Μητρόδωρος*)
—glava panega (mod.): **(73)** ii-iii ad *IGB* ii 525 (f. *Διογένης*)
—koila: **(74)** imp. *Olynthus* 14 p. 26 no. 5 (terracotta)
—markianopolis (nr.): **(75)** f. iii ad *IGB* ii 851 (*CCET* ii (1) 246)
—maroneia: **(76)** ii ad *SEG* xlvii 1069 (*IThrakAig* E189) (f. *Κέλσος*); **(77)** iii ad Meïmaris–Bakirtzis 3 (*SEG* xliv 592) + *IThrakAig* E329 B
—nicopolis ad istrum: **(78)** ii-iii ad *IGB* v 5229
—odessos: **(79)** i bc-i ad ib. I^2 51 c, 10 (s. *Πωλλίων*); **(80)** 215 ad ib. 47 a, 23 (f. *Αὐρ. Ἀπελλâς*); **(81)** ~ ib. 47 b, 12 (f. *Αὐρ. Ἕλλην*); **(82)** ~ ib. l. 17 (I f. *Αὐρ. Μâρκος* II); **(83)** ~ ib. l. 23 (I f. *Αὐρ. Μâρκος* II); **(84)** ~ ib. l. 28 (f. *Αὐρ. Σωτήρ*); **(85)** ~ ib. 47 c, 14 (f. *Αὐρ. Διοκλῆς*)
—pautalia: **(86)** ii ad ib. iv 2074, 9; **(87)** s. ii ad *SEG* xlvi 864, 4 (f. *Φαυστîνος*)
—pautalia (territ.): **(88)** ii-iii ad *IGB* iv 2110 (*M. ὁ καὶ Βονωλας*: s. *Ἐπιγένης*); **(89)** ~ ib. 2136 (s. *Γάϊος*); **(90)** ~ ib. 2215 (f. *Παῦλος*); **(91)** ~ ib. v 5832 (*Μâρ(κος)*: s. *Φίλιος*)
—pautalia:
——(Herakleis): **(92)** ?ii ad ib. iv 2077, 15
——Karistoron: **(93)** ii ad ib. 2152 (s. *Μη—*)
—perinthos-herakleia: **(94)** i ad *IPerinth* 88 (f. *Μάρκελλος*); **(95)** ii ad ib. 100 (f. *Μάρκελλος, Πρόκλα*); **(96)** 196-198 ad ib. 56, 10 (s. *Ὧρος*)
—philippopolis-trimontium (territ.): **(97)** ii-iii ad *IGB* iii 1185 (s. *Τάρσας*); **(98)** ~ ib. 1435
—philippopolis-trimontium:
——(Artemisias): **(99)** 163-164 ad ib. 902, 6 (f. *Φιλίσκος, Γάϊος*)
—serdica (territ.): **(100)** ii-iii ad *Sp.* 98 (1941-48) p. 127 no. 280, 5 (f. *Μούκκος*); **(101)** ~ *IGB* v 5745; **(102)** f. iii ad ib. 5701, 5 (f. *Αὐρ. Ἡρακλείδης*)
—sportela: **(103)** ii-iii ad ib. iv 2232, 4 (I f. *Μâρκος* II); **(104)** ~ ib. l. 4 (II s. *Μâρκος* I); **(105)** ~ ib. 2233, 5 (*Eastern cults* p. 170 no. 15)

Μαρκώ
Tauris:
—chersonesos: **(1)** iii bc Solomonik, *NEPKh* 30; *Hellenismus* p. 452 no. 22 (d. *Ἀριστοκλῆς*)

Μαρος
Thrace:
—nicopolis ad istrum (territ.): **(1)** ii-iii ad *IGB* ii 713

Μαρού
Scythia Minor:
—tomis: **(1)** v-vi ad Barnea 14, 2 (Popescu, *IGL* 32) (d. *Ἰωάννης*)

Μαρσîνος
Thrace: **(1)** imp.? Alex. Trall. i 15

Μαρσύας
Macedonia: **(1)** m. ii bc *IOrop* 326, 11 (Tataki, *Macedonians* p. 361 no. 8)
Macedonia (Bottiaia):
—beroia: **(2)** s. ii bc *IBer* 18, 2; 24, 1 (Tataki 868) (s. *Δημήτριος*)
—pella: **(3)** c. 360-300 bc *RE* (8); Berve 489; *FGrH* 135-6 (Tataki, *Macedonians* p. 157 no. 59) (s. *Περίανδρος*)
Macedonia (Edonis):
—philippoi: **(4)** hell. *RE* (9); *FGrH* 135-6 (Tataki, *Macedonians* p. 165 no. 21) (s. *Κριτόφημος*)

Μαρτιάλης
Thrace:
—abryttos (territ.): **(1)** iii ad *IGB* ii 750 (*CCET* ii (2) 550) (f. *Αὐρ. Ῥοιμητάλκης*)
—bizye (territ.)?: **(2)** ii-iii ad *IGB* iii 1853 (s. *Αὐλούπορις*)
—draganovec (mod.): **(3)** iii ad ib. v 5305 (*CCET* ii (2) 491) (?s. *—λος*)
—karaš (mod.): **(4)** ii-iii ad *IGB* ii 498-9 (s. *Βêθυς*)
—markianopolis (territ.): **(5)** iii ad ib. v 5383 (*CCET* ii (1) 305) (*Μαρτι[άλης]*)
—markianopolis (nr.): **(6)** iii ad *IGB* v 5364
—odessos: **(7)** 215 ad ib. I^2 47 b, 21 (f. *Αὐρ. Γλύκων*)

Μαρτîνος
Macedonia (Mygdonia):
—thessalonike?: **(1)** 525 ad *IG* x (2) (1) 804, 2 (Feissel, *RICM* 134)
Thrace: **(2)** 531-556 ad *PLRE* iii (2); *RE* (6)
—glava panega (mod.): **(3)** ii-iii ad *IGB* ii 515 (-τεῖ-)
—mesambria: **(4)** ii ad ib. I^2 346, 5 (-τεῖ-)

Μαρτύριος
Macedonia (Bottiaia):
—beroia: **(1)** v-vi ad *IBer* 425
—edessa: **(2)** v-vi ad Feissel, *RICM* 17
Macedonia (Mygdonia):
—thessalonike*: **(3)** v-vi ad *IG* x (2) (1) 791 (Feissel, *RICM* 150)
Tauris:
—chersonesos: **(4)** iv-vi ad Latyshev, *Sbornik* 15
Thrace:
—abryttos (territ.)?: **(5)** v ad *Klio* 59 (1977) p. 265 no. 1 (Lat. Marturius: f. Sperentes)

Μαρυλλîνα
Thrace:
—oescus: **(1)** i ad *ILB* 77, 6 (Lat. Maria Maryllina: d. *Ἀγαθόπους*)

Μάρυλλος
Macedonia (Lynkestis):
—herakleia: **(1)** i ad *IG* x (2) (2) 75, 53 (f. *Μάξιμος*)

Μάρων
Cimmerian Bosporos:
—bosporos?: **(1)** ?ii bc *AA* 1912, p. 341; Courby, *Les vases grecs* p. 412 (vase) (*Μάρω(ν)*: potter)
Macedonia: **(2)** 117-101 bc *PTeb* 106, 6 (Tataki, *Macedonians* p. 489 no. 166; La'da E1534) (*M. ὁ καὶ Νέκσαφθις*: s. *Διονύσιος ὁ καὶ Πετοσîρις*); **(3)** 51-20 bc *PTeb* 382, 36; *PSI* 1098, 40 (Tataki, *Macedonians* p. 490 no. 167); cf. La'da E1394 (f. *Ἀκουσίλαος*); **(4)** i ad *PMich* 303, 1 (f. *Κρονίων, Ἀπολλώνιος*)
Tauris:
—chersonesos: **(5)** c. 237-230 bc Kats pp. 102-3 no. 73 (amph.) (s. *Βάβων*)
Thrace:
—hadrianopolis (territ.): **(6)** imp. *IGB* iii 1812 (f. *Σάλας*) ?= (7); **(7)** ii-iii ad ib. 1821 ?= (6)
—mesambria: **(8)** v/iv bc *Num. Sfrag.* 1993, pp. 40-46 (vase) (s. *Μαστίας*)
—odessos: **(9)** i-ii ad *IGB* I^2 137 (?s. *Ζ—*); **(10)** 215 ad ib. 47 a, 10 (*Αὐρ. M.*: s. *Νουμήνιος*)
—perinthos-herakleia: **(11)** i-ii ad *IPerinth* 223 (*GVI* 1303)

Μαρωνίς
Macedonia (Edonis):
—philippoi?: **(1)** ?i-ii ad *AE* 1950-1, p. 68 no. 11, 5 (Pilhofer 726) (or Macedonia (Mygdonia) Thessalonike: Lat. Laelia Maronis: freed.)
Thrace:
—abdera (territ.)?: **(2)** ii-iii ad Kazarow 283 (*IThrakAig* E82) (*Γαία M.*)

Μασάρτας
Thrace: **(1)** 231 or 206 bc *CPR* xviii 3, 47, 53, 61 (La'da E833) (*Μασάρτας*: s. *Μήδοκος*: t.e.)

Μάσαρτος
Thrace: **(1)** 160 bc *BGU* 2390, 39 (La'da E773) (*Μ[.]σαρτος*)

Μάσας
Cimmerian Bosporos:
—achilleion: **(1)** s. ii ad *CIRB* 1033; Zgusta, *PNS* 145 (s. *Ἀγαθοῦς*)
—pantikapaion: **(2)** i bc-i ad *CIRB* 521; cf. KW pl. 17 no. 243; **(3)** i ad *KSIA* 116 (1969) p. 49 no. 1 ?= (5); **(4)** ~ *CIRB* 461; cf. KW pl. 18 no. 270 (s. *Μύρμηξ*); **(5)** ~ *CIRB* 462 (s. *Στρατόνικος*) ?= (3); **(6)** i/ii ad ib. 623; cf. KW pl. 37 no. 543 (s. *Μάης*)

Μασατίς
CIMMERIAN BOSPOROS:
—PANTIKAPAION: (1) s. i BC *CIRB* 282; Zgusta, *PNS* 145 (m. Μαστοῦς)
—TYRITAKE (NR.): (2) f. i AD *CIRB* 969 (d. Καλλίμαχος, Μακαρία)

Μάσθιον
CIMMERIAN BOSPOROS:
—PANTIKAPAION: (1) i BC/i AD ib. 312; cf. KW pl. 18 no. 263; Zgusta, *PNS* 1072 (Μάσφιον—*CIRB*: name—Latyshev)

Μασκελλίς
MACEDONIA (BOTTIAIA):
—BEROIA: (1) iii AD *IBer* 172 (Tataki 870)

Μάσκλος
THRACE:
—VICUS TRULLENSIUM: (1) iii AD *IGB* II 506, 6 (s. Μοῦσα, Αὐρ. Ν—)

Μάστα
CIMMERIAN BOSPOROS:
—NYMPHAION: (1) i AD Davydova, *Bosp. nadgrob.* pp. 43-4 no. 31 + *Hyperboreus* 2000, pp. 140 ff. (Μάστα)
—TAMAN PENINSULA: (2) ii-iii AD Tolstoi 250 + *KSIA* 95 (1963) p. 31 n. 18 (vase) (Μάγγα—Tolstoi)

Μάστακος
CIMMERIAN BOSPOROS:
—GORGIPPIA: (1) m. ii AD *Eirene* 7 (1968) p. 67, 5 (s. Ζαζζοῦς); (2) 173-210 AD *CIRB* 1135, 19 (s. —χος)
—PANTIKAPAION: (3) f. ii AD ib. 87, 1 (Μάστα[κο]ς?—Tokhtas'ev, Μάστ[αρος]?—*CIRB*)

Μασταρίων
CIMMERIAN BOSPOROS:
—TYRITAKE: (1) i/ii AD ib. 907 (s. Γαγανος)

Μάσταρος
SKYTHIA:
—TANAIS: (1) f. ii AD ib. 1266, 7 (s. Ἀριστόνικος)

Μασταροῦς
CIMMERIAN BOSPOROS:
—NYMPHAION: (1) i AD ib. 929 (f. Εὖνος)
—PANTIKAPAION: (2) i AD ib. 463; Zgusta, *PNS* 146 (s. Μαστοῦς); (3) m. i AD *CIRB* 465; cf. KW pl. 36 no. 529 (s. Φιλωνίδης); (4) i/ii AD *CIRB* 464; cf. KW pl. 41 no. 604 (s. Φαρνάκης); (5) ~ *CIRB* 624 (s. Μαστοῦς); (6) 275-278 AD ib. 36, 40 (Μασταρ(οῦς)?—Vinogradov: s. Σαμβίων)

Μάστας
CIMMERIAN BOSPOROS:
—PANTIKAPAION: (1) ii AD ib. 795; Zgusta, *PNS* 146 (s. Ἰάμβλοχος)

Μαστίας
THRACE:
—MESAMBRIA: (1) v/iv BC *Num. Sfrag.* 1993, pp. 40-46 (vase) (f. Μάρων)

Μαστοῦς
CIMMERIAN BOSPOROS:
—BOSPOROS: (1) ii AD *IOSPE* I² 203, 4 ([Μ.] Οὔλπ. Παρθενοκλῆς ὁ καὶ Μαστο[ῦ]ς)
—GORGIPPIA: (2) s. ii AD *CIRB* 1145, 3 (f. Κοθίνας); (3) ii/iii AD ib. 1179, 55 (s. Κοθίνας)
—HERMONASSA: (4) imp. ib. 1093
—NYMPHAION: (5) i AD ib. 930; cf. KW pl. 46 no. 655 (Μαστοῦνο[ς] (gen.): f. Φαρνάκης); (6) i/ii AD *CIRB* 932; cf. KW pl. 42 no. 668
—PANTIKAPAION: (7) ii-i BC *CIRB* 276; cf. KW pl. 23 no. 276; Zgusta, *PNS* 146 (s. Ἡδόνιν); (8) s. i BC *CIRB* 282 (s. Ἀνόπτηνις, Μασατίς); (9) i AD ib. 400 B; cf. KW pl. 50 no. 693 (s. Ἑρμῆς, ?s. Θεοφίλη); (10) ?i AD *CIRB* 417 ([Μ]ασθοῦς: f. Ἡλιόδωρος); (11) i AD ib. 463 (f. Μασταροῦς); (12) ~ ib. 467 (s. Μοιρόδωρος); (13) ~ ib. 562 (s. Μητρόδωρος, Ψύχη); (14) f. i AD ib. 138 (*GVI* 504) (s. Χρυσιαρία); (15) ~ *CIRB* 466 (s. Ἀρητφιλος); (16) i/ii AD ib. 80, 8; cf. KW pl. 33 no. 454 (II s. Μαστοῦς I); (17) ~ *CIRB* 80, 9; cf. KW pl. 33 no. 454 (I f. Μαστοῦς II); (18) ~ *CIRB* 624 (f. Μασταροῦς); (19) f. ii AD ib. 81, 8; cf. KW pl. 33 no. 455 (I f. Μαστοῦς II); (20) ~ *CIRB* 81, 8; cf. KW pl. 33 no. 455 (II s. Μαστοῦς I); (21) 106 AD *CIRB* 697 (f. Οὔλπ. Ἀντίμαχος); (22) 127 AD ib. 61, 5 ([Μ]αστοῦς: s. Βασιλείδης); (23) s. ii AD ib. 688 (s. Ἄδας); (24) 221 AD ib. 99, 8 (s. Ἀντίμαχος); (25) 275-278 AD ib. 36, 47 (f. Φιη.αγους: reading—Vinogradov)
—PANTIKAPAION (NR.): (26) i-ii AD ib. 962
SKYTHIA:
—TANAIS: (27) ii AD ib. 1269, 5; (28) ~ ib. 1272 (Μαστο[ῦς]); (29) f. ii AD ib. 1266, 4 (s. Πόπλιος); (30) 104 AD ib. 1259, 23 (s. Παπίας); (31) c. 200-210 AD ib. 1277, 28; (32) 224 AD ib. 1287, 7 (f. Μακάριος); (33) 225 AD ib. 1280, 13 (f. Ἄρδαρος); (34) 228 AD ib. 1282, 33; (35) ~ ib. 1283, 16 (f. Μυρῖνος); (36) 236 AD ib. 1250, 13 (f. Ἔρως)

Μάστωρ?
SKYTHIA:
—OLBIA-BORYSTHENES (BEREZAN (MOD.)): (1) m. vi BC Dubois, *IGDOlbia* 43

Μάσχλος
THRACE:
—KELLAI: (1) 241-244 AD *IGB* III 1517, 10 (Κλ. Μ.: s. Αὐρηλιανός); (2) ~ ib. l. 28 ([Μάσ]χλος: s. Τήρης)

Μάτα
MACEDONIA (ODOMANTIKE):
—SIRRHA (TERRIT.): (1) ii-iii AD *SEG* XXXV 764, 6 (Pilhofer 565) ([Μ]άτα: m. —ιλης)
TAURIS:
—CHERSONESOS: (2) ii/iii AD *SEG* XXXIII 603 (m. —νοος)
THRACE: (3) iii BC *IG* XII (9) 813; cf. *AJA* 64 (1960) p. 54 (Ματ[ί]α—ed.: d. Μανίτης)
—PLATANIA (MOD.): (4) iii AD *SEG* XXXII 676 (Pilhofer 510) (Ματα—lap., Μά(ν)τα?: d. Κουνθισίης, m. Οὐάλης)

Μάτασυς
SKYTHIA:
—OLBIA-BORYSTHENES: (1) s. vi BC Dubois, *IGDOlbia* 23, 2, 7, 9; cf. Vinogradov, *Pont. Stud.* p. 153 no. 2

Ματάττης
CIMMERIAN BOSPOROS:
—KOROKONDAME: (1) v BC *CIRB* 1104 + *Hyperboreus* 1994 (1), pp. 158-9 (Ματάττōς (gen.): f. Χαρσενάκης)

Μάτελα?
MACEDONIA (EORDAIA):
—EXOCHI (MOD.): (1) ii-iii AD *EAM* 102 (Μάτελ(α)?: d. Μένανδρος)

Ματελίς
MACEDONIA (PELAGONIA): (1) ii-i BC *IG* X (2) (2) 159, 7 (d. Λυσανίας)

Ματερίνας
CIMMERIAN BOSPOROS:
—PANTIKAPAION: (1) f. iv BC *CIRB* 185 (f. Θαγοῦς)

Ματερίνη
CIMMERIAN BOSPOROS:
—MYRMEKION: (1) iii BC ib. 876 (d. Διονύσιος)
MACEDONIA (BOTTIAIA):
—EDESSA: (2) i/ii AD *SEG* XLIII 390 (Tataki, *Edessa* 202) (d. Σεύθης)

Ματερώ
MACEDONIA: (1) hell. *IG* IX (2) 1186 (Tataki, *Macedonians* p. 361 no. 9) (d. Ἀλέξανδρος)
MACEDONIA (BISALTIA):
—TERPNI (MOD.): (2) ii-iii AD *SEG* XLIX 810
MACEDONIA (BOTTIAIA):
—BEROIA: (3) ii BC *IBer* 179 (d. Γλύκερος)
—EDESSA: (4) ii AD *BSA* 58 (1963) p. 24 no. 6 (Tataki, *Edessa* 203)
MACEDONIA (EDONIS):
—AMPHIPOLIS?: (5) hell. Dimitsas 902
MACEDONIA (LYNKESTIS):
—MELITI (MOD.): (6) f. iii AD *EAM* 166, 3
THRACE:
—PAUTALIA (TERRIT.): (7) 241 AD *IGB* V 5786, 6 (Α[ὐρ]. Ματερῶ (dat.))

Ματιννώ
MACEDONIA (BOTTIAIA):
—AIGAI: (1) s. iv BC *SEG* XXXV 802

Μάτιος
TAURIS:
—CHERSONESOS: (1) iv-iii BC Solomonik, *GAKh* 1171 (vase) (Μάτ(ρ)ιος? (gen.))

Ματρᾶς
THRACE:
—BYZANTION?: (1) i AD *IByz* 328 (PM 220) (Ματρᾶ (gen.): f. Ματρόδωρος); (2) i-ii AD *IByz* 341 (f. Κτημένη)

Ματρίδωρος
CIMMERIAN BOSPOROS:
—ILOURATON: (1) ii AD *CIRB* 967

Ματρικῶν
THRACE:
—BYZANTION: (1) s. iii BC Schönert-Geiss, *Byzantion* 1200-4; 1229-32; 1242-3 (coin)
—SALYMBRIA: (2) hell. *Archives Stamoulis* d. 35 (Loukopoulou, *Thrace Propontique* p. 272) (f. Στρατονίκη)

Μᾶτρις
CIMMERIAN BOSPOROS:
—GORGIPPIA: (1) f. iii BC *CIRB* 1137 A II, 9 (s. Στρατόνικος); (2) ~ ib. 1137 B II, 10 (s. Εὔμηλος)
SCYTHIA MINOR:
—KALLATIS: (3) iv/iii BC *ISM* III 125, 11 (s. Ἐπα—); (4) iii BC ib. 1 9, [4], 19 (Migeotte, *L'emprunt* 41) (f. Ἡφαιστίων); (5) ~ *ISM* III 126, 8 (f. Σάτυρος); (6) f. iii BC ib. 66, 6
—KALLATIS?: (7) ii/i BC *IGB* II 867 a, 3 = *ISM* I 219 (v 87); cf. *ISM* III p. 140 (locn.)
TAURIS:
—CHERSONESOS: (8) iv BC Solomonik, *NEPKh* 166 (f. Ἀμφίας, Γοργίππα); (9) c. 315-300 BC Kats p. 103 no. 74 (amph.); (10) c. 272-262 BC ib. p. 103 no. 75 (amph.) (s. Ἀγασικλῆς); (11) c. 230-215 BC ib. p. 104 no. 77 (amph.) (s. Ἡρόξενος); (12) c. 215-200 BC ib. p. 104 no. 76 (amph.) (s. Ἀπολλωνίδας); (13) 179 BC *IOSPE* I² 402, 11
THRACE:
—BYZANTION: (14) iii BC *IByz* 68 (Fıratlı-Robert p. 48 no. 6) (s. Ἀρχίας); (15) ~ *IG* II² 8444 (*FRA* 1399) (f. Πυθίων); (16) c. 250-220 BC Schönert-Geiss, *Byzantion* 997-1000; 1244-8 (coin); (17) i BC *IByz* 204 (Fıratlı-Robert p. 63 no. 53) (Μάτρει (gen.): s. Μοσχίων, f. Διονυσία)
——(Rhegion?): (18) hell.? *SGDI* 3074 (*IByz* 297) (Μάτριδος (gen.): s. Μηλόβιος, f. Γλυκεῖα)
—MESAMBRIA: (19) i BC-i AD *IGB* I² 340 (s. Παγχάρης)
—MESAMBRIA?: (20) hell. ib. V 5096 (s. Βύριχος)

Ματρίχα
THRACE:
—MESAMBRIA: (1) iii/ii BC ib. I² 330 ter (PM 1098) (m. *Πολυαίνετος, Ματρόδωρος*); (2) f. ii BC *IGB* I² 343 septies, 5; cf. v 5117 (m. *Ναυσίστρατος*)

Ματρόβιος
THRACE:
—MESAMBRIA: (1) ii BC ib. I² 325, 3

Ματροδώρα
THRACE:
—BYZANTION: (1) i-ii AD *IByz* 315 b (Fıratlı–Robert pp. 122-3 no. 205) (d. *Ἡρακλέων*)

Ματρόδωρος
CIMMERIAN BOSPOROS:
—PANTIKAPAION: (1) imp. *CIRB* 764 (f. *Σάκτας*); (2) ~ ib. 801 (s. *Ἀπολλώνιος, Πανταγάθη*)
TAURIS:
—CHERSONESOS: (3) iv BC *SEG* XXVIII 635 (*Ματρόδωρ[ος]?, Ματροδώρ[α]?*: s. *Δαμάτριος*); (4) c. 285-262 BC Kats p. 122 no. 26 (vase); (5) c. 272-262 BC ib. p. 104 no. 78 (amph.) (s. *Λύσιππος*); (6) ii AD *IOSPE* I² 701, 5 ([*Μα*]*τρόδωρος*: s. *Ἡρωΐδας*); (7) ii-iii AD *SEG* XXXVII 658 (f. *Κόγχα*)
THRACE:
—BYZANTION: (8) iii BC *IByz* 70 (Fıratlı–Robert p. 49 no. 11) (f. *Μόνιμος*); (9) ii BC *IByz* 262 (Fıratlı–Robert p. 74 no. 80) (f. *Τρύφων*); (10) ii-i BC *IByz* 359 (Fıratlı–Robert p. 65 no. 58) (f. *Χαρικλῆς*); (11) ~ *RE* (25a) (*Μη-*: f. *Λεωνίδας*); (12) i BC/i AD *IByz* 285 (Fıratlı–Robert pp. 56-7 no. 36) (s. *Καλλιγείτων*, f. *Καλλιγείτων*); (13) s. i AD *IByz* 35, 2 (*Π. Μέμμιος Πλαυτιανὸς Μ.*)
—BYZANTION?: (14) iii/ii BC *SEG* XXIX 666 (s. *Μένιππος*); (15) i AD *IByz* 328 (PM 220) (s. *Ματρᾶς*)
—MESAMBRIA: (16) iii BC *IGB* I² 335 sexies (*Ματρόδωρος*: f. *—ρος*); (17) s. iii BC ib. 339 ter ([*Μ*]*ατρόδω*[*ρος*]: s. *Ἡρώνυμος*); (18) iii/ii BC ib. 330 ter (PM 1098) (s. *Βοσπόριχος, Ματρίχα*); (19) ~ *IGB* I² 330 ter (PM 1098) (f. *Βοσπόριχος*); (20) i BC *IGB* I² 326, 5 (f. *Ἀθαναίων*)
—SALYMBRIA: (21) imp. *IByz* S 12 ([*Μ*]*ατρόδωρο*[*ς*]: s. *Ἀπολλόδωρος*)

Ματρόλης
SKYTHIA:
—OLBIA-BORYSTHENES: (1) v/iv BC Vinogradov, *Pont. Stud.* p. 157 no. 10 (vase) (*Ματρόλο̄ς* (gen.): f. *Μάνης*)

Ματρώ
THRACE:
—BYZANTION: (1) iii BC *IByz* 61 (Fıratlı–Robert pp. 47-8 no. 4) (d. *Σῖμος*); (2) ~ *IByz* 65 (d. *Εὐφάνης*); (3) i BC-i AD ib. 230 (Fıratlı–Robert p. 83 no. 101) (d. *Ἑρμόδωρος*)

Ματρώι
THRACE:
—MESAMBRIA: (1) iv BC *IGB* I² 330 bis (PM 997)

Μάτρων
THRACE:
—BYZANTION: (1) s. iv BC *RPh* 1937, p. 325 no. 6 A, 18 (f. *Καλλίας*); (2) ii BC *IByz* 125 (Fıratlı–Robert p. 101 no. 153) (s. *Ἀπολλώνιος*)
—HERAION TEICHOS?: (3) ii-i BC Taşlıklıoğlu 2 p. 93 no. 1
—MESAMBRIA: (4) iii BC *IGB* I² 308 septies, 11

Ματρώνα
MACEDONIA (BOTTIAIA):
—EDESSA: (1) v-vi AD Feissel, *RICM* 29 ([*Μα*]*τρούνα*)

MACEDONIA (CHALKIDIKE):
—GIGONOS?: (2) imp. *SEG* XLV 756
MACEDONIA (MYGDONIA):
—THESSALONIKE: (3) iii AD *IG* X (2) (1) 547 (*Αὐρ. Δημητριανὴ ἡ καὶ Μ.*); (4) a. 212 AD ib. 609, 1, 4, 6 (*Αὐρ. Μ.*: m. *Αὐρ. Ἀλεξάνδρα*)
MACEDONIA (ODOMANTIKE):
—SIRRHA: (5) v-vi AD Feissel, *RICM* 210
SCYTHIA MINOR:
—TOMIS: (6) ii-iii AD *ISM* II 372 (*GVI* 987; *CCET* IV 32) (m. *Ἑρμογένης, Πανθήρα*); (7) ?iii AD *ISM* II 377, 16 (*GVI* 312) (m. *Ποντιανός, Ποντιανή*); (8) iii AD *ISM* II 461
THRACE:
—BEROE-AUGUSTA TRAIANA: (9) c. 320-324 AD *Anal. Boll.* 31 (1912) p. 198
—MARONEIA: (10) iv-v AD Meïmaris–Bakirtzis 9 (*SEG* XLIV 596; *IThrakAig* E350) (*-τρό-*)
—NICOPOLIS AD NESTUM: (11) iii AD *IGB* V 5930, 12 (m. *Θέκλα, Δημοσθένης*)
—PERINTHOS-HERAKLEIA: (12) ii AD *IPerinth* 141 (d. *Μαρκιανή*)

Ματρώνη
THRACE:
—PHILIPPOPOLIS-TRIMONTIUM (TERRIT.): (1) ii-iii AD *IGB* III 1389 + V 5512 ((*Μ*)*ατρώνη*)

Ματτία
MACEDONIA (EDONIS):
—AMPHIPOLIS: (1) imp. *SEG* XXXIX 571 (d. *Γησενίδης*)

Μαῦρα
THRACE:
—BEROE-AUGUSTA TRAIANA: (1) c. 320-324 AD *Anal. Boll.* 31 (1912) p. 198; p. 207 (*Μάβρα*— p. 207)
—NOVAE: (2) ii AD *IGLNovae* 92 (*ILB* 319) (Lat. Antonia Optala quae Maura)

Μαυρέντιος
MACEDONIA (EDONIS):
—PHILIPPOI (TERRIT.): (1) v-vi AD Feissel, *RICM* 224 (Pilhofer 528)

Μαῦρος
MACEDONIA (BOTTIAIA):
—EDESSA: (1) v-vi AD Feissel, *RICM* 25, 6; (2) ~ ib. 48
MACEDONIA (EDONIS):
—AMPHIPOLIS: (3) ii-iii AD *Thracia* 2 p. 279 + *Epigraphica* 37 (1935) p. 30
THRACE:
—PAUTALIA: (4) s. ii AD *CIL* VI 37184 c, 16 (Lat. M. Aur. Maurus)

Μαχάτας
MACEDONIA: (1) iv BC Arr., *An.* iii 6. 4 (Tataki, *Macedonians* p. 196 no. 14); cf. *RE* (1) (f. *Ἅρπαλος*) ?= (2) (19); (2) ~ Arr., *An.* v 8. 3; cf. *RE* (1) (f. *Φίλιππος*) ?= (4) (1); (3) m. iv BC Plu., *Mor.* 178 F-179 A (*Μαχαίτας*—codd.) ?= (8) (4); (4) s. iv BC *IG* XII (9) 197, 4 (Tataki, *Macedonians* p. 362 no. 13); cf. *RE* (1); *Eretria* XI p. 173 (f. *Ταύρων*) ?= (3) (2); (5) ?186 BC *PHeid* VIII 412, 11; cf. La'da E1787 (*Μαχάτας*); (6) 186-182 BC *IFayoum* 150, 7 (Tataki, *Macedonians* p. 361 no. 11; La'da 1535) (*Μαχάτ*[*ας*]: II s. *Μαχάτας* I); (7) ~ *IFayoum* 150, 8 (Tataki, *Macedonians* p. 361 no. 10); cf. La'da 1424; 1535 (I f. *Ἀπολλώνιος, Μαχάτας* II)
MACEDONIA (BOTTIAIA):
—AIGAI*: (8) iv BC Andronikos, *Vergina* p. 148 ph. 108; cf. *SEG* L 654 bis. 1 ?= (3)
—BEROIA: (9) 239-229 BC *IBer* 45, 28 (s. *Θεογένης*); (10) ~ ib. l. 32 (s. *Φίλιππος*); (11) 223 BC ib. 4, 17 (f. *Εὐδημίδης*); (12) ~ ib. l. 28 (f. *Μελέαγρος*); (13) ~ ib. l. 38 (f. *Ἀλκίμαχος*); (14) ii BC ib. 201 (s. *Ἀντίγονος*)

—PELLA: (15) m. iv BC *FGrH* 257 F 36. 1; Procl., *in R.* ii 116 (*-της*: fict.?)
MACEDONIA (EDONIS):
—AMPHIPOLIS: (16) m. iii BC Hatzopoulos, *Actes Amphipolis* p. 52 no 12, 5; *SEG* XLI 566 (date) (f. *Ἀντίγονος*); (17) ~ Hatzopoulos, *Actes Amphipolis* p. 52 no 12, 7; *SEG* XLI 566 (date) (s. *Ἀνδρόνικος*)
MACEDONIA (ELIMEIA)?: (18) ?417-413 BC *IG* I³ 89, 76 (Tataki, *Macedonians* p. 196 no. 15) (*Μαχέτο̄* (gen.): f. *Παυσανίας*); (19) iv BC Satyr. ap. Ath. 557 c; cf. *RE* (1) ?= (1)
MACEDONIA (EORDAIA):
—PONTOKOMI (MOD.): (20) vi/v BC *SEG* XLIX 776; cf. *AEMTh* 14 (2000) p. 616 (vase)
MACEDONIA (LOWER PAIONIA):
—EUROPOS: (21) ?315-300 BC *FD* III (4) 405, 2 (Tataki, *Macedonians* p. 108 no. 8) (s. *Σαββατάρας*)
MACEDONIA (MYGDONIA):
—THESSALONIKE: (22) iii/ii BC *IG* X (2) (1) 1032 (Tataki, *Macedonians* p. 184 no. 44) (s. *Μελάνθιος*)
MACEDONIA (PIERIA):
—PHILA?: (23) ?iii BC *RPh* 1911, pp. 133-4 no. 36, 131; cf. Helly, *L'État thessalien* pp. 319-20 (locn.) (f. *Σιμμίας*)

Μάχη?
TAURIS:
—KERKINITIS (NR.): (1) iii BC Solomonik, *GChKh* 211 (vase) (*—μάχη?* (n. pr.?))

Μαχήτης
MACEDONIA (EDONIS):
—AMPHIPOLIS: (1) b. 213 BC Hatzopoulos, *MI* 2 p. 83 no. 61, 11 (*SEG* XLVI 715) (s. *Ἀσκληπιο—*)

Μαχορδίκη
CIMMERIAN BOSPOROS:
—PANTIKAPAION: (1) iv BC *CIRB* 202 (d. *Μητρόβιος*)

Μάχων
MACEDONIA (CHALKIDIKE):
—SERMYLIA: (1) vi/v BC *Nom. Chron.* 20 (2001) pp. 13-44 (coin) (*-χο̄ν*)
MACEDONIA (EDONIS):
—AMPHIPOLIS: (2) s. iv BC *PAE* 1981, p. 25 with pl. 43 *β*, 6

Μεγακλῆς
CIMMERIAN BOSPOROS:
—NYMPHAION: (1) 389-349 BC *Hyperboreus* 2002 (1), p. 101 (f. *Θεοπροπίδης*)
MACEDONIA: (2) 182 BC *PMich* 182, 4 (Tataki, *Macedonians* p. 362 no. 14); cf. La'da E1765 (f. *Θῦμος*)
MACEDONIA (BOTTIAIA):
—PELLA: (3) iv BC *BSA* 41 (1940-45) p. 114 no. 26 (f. *Διονύσιος*); (4) 332 BC Arr., *An.* iii 5. 3 (Tataki, *Macedonians* p. 157 no. 60) (f. *Πολέμων*)
TAURIS:
—CHERSONESOS: (5) iii BC Solomonik, *NEPKh* 146 (f. *Σαννίων*); (6) ~ ib. 148 (s. *Σαννίων*)
THRACE:
—APOLLONIA-SOZOPOLIS: (7) iv BC *IGB* I² 429 (f. *Πάρμις, Εὐκλείδης*); (8) f. iv BC ib. 419 (I f. *Μεγακλῆς* II); (9) ~ ib. (II s. *Μεγακλῆς* I)
—MARONEIA: (10) c. 365-336 BC Schönert-Geiss, *Maroneia* 404 (coin)
—MESAMBRIA: (11) iii BC *IGB* I² 337 (PM 2260) (f. *Μείδων*)
—PERINTHOS-HERAKLEIA: (12) 316-309 BC *IG* II² 1956, 197 (*FRA* 6042); *Ancient Macedonia* 5 p. 445 with n. 10 (date)

Μεγακρέων
THRACE:
—ABDERA: (1) 480 BC Hdt. vii 120

Μεγαλέας
Macedonia: **(1)** 221-218 BC *RE* (-) (Tataki, *Macedonians* p. 362 no. 15)

Μεγαλίων
Tauris:
—chersonesos: **(1)** s. v BC *DGVE* 1996-7, pp. 111 fig. 2, 7; 114 (sherd) (*Μεγ[αλ]ίων*?, *Μεγ[αρ]ίων*—ed.)

Μεγαλοκλῆς
Macedonia (Bottiaia):
—pella: **(1)** iii BC *AD* 16 (1960) Mel. p. 82; *SEG* xxxix 623 (tiles)

Μεγάνωρ
Cimmerian Bosporos:
—gorgippia: **(1)** f. iii BC *CIRB* 1137 A II, 51 (s. *Δημήτριος*)

Μεγαρέτα
Macedonia (Pieria):
—pydna: **(1)** s. iv BC *Eulimeni* 4 (2003) p. 146 no. 4

Μεγάρτας
Macedonia (Orestis):
—battynaioi: **(1)** 192 AD *EAM* 186 II, 47 (*Μ̣ε̣γάρτ̣ας*: s. *—υμονος*)

Μέγας
Cimmerian Bosporos:
—taman peninsula: **(1)** v BC Tolstoi 246 (vase)
Thrace:
—abdera: **(2)** f. iv BC *SEG* xlvii 1029 (*IThrakAig* E39) (*Μέγαδο[ς]*? (gen.))
—kardia: **(3)** 232 or 207 BC *CPR* xviii 14, 287 (La'da E983) (*Μέγας*: s. *Μοσχίων*: t.e.)

Μεγέθιν
Macedonia (Mygdonia):
—thessalonike: **(1)** f. iii AD *IG* x (2) (1) 628 B, 5 (*GVI* 1275) (d. *Ἰούλ. Κάστωρ, Γεμινία Ὀλυμπιάς*)

Μεγέθιος
Macedonia (Bottiaia):
—beroia: **(1)** ii-iii AD *IBer* 263, 1 (*Μ̣εγέθι̣[ος]*: s. *Δημήτριος*)

Μέγης
Cimmerian Bosporos:
—hermonassa: **(1)** 123-132 AD *CIRB* 1054, 17 (s. *Μηνᾶς*)
—pantikapaion: **(2)** i/ii AD ib. 696; cf. KW pl. 14 no. 205
—phanagoreia: **(3)** s. i BC *SEG* xxvii 449 (*Μ̣έ̣γης*)
Macedonia: **(4)** c. 223 BC *PTeb* 815 fr. 3 verso I, 13 (Tataki, *Macedonians* p. 362 no. 16); cf. La'da E1790 (f. *—ων*)

Μέγις
Skythia:
—tanais: **(1)** 225 AD *CIRB* 1279, 12 (I f. *Μέγις* II); **(2)** ~ ib. l. 12 (II s. *Μέγις* I)

Μεγιστεύς
Macedonia: **(1)** ?186 BC *PHeid* viii 412, 4 (La'da E1536)

Μεγίστη
Cimmerian Bosporos:
—pantikapaion: **(1)** i BC *CIRB* 283
—phanagoreia: **(2)** i AD ib. 995 (m. *Χρηστοῦς*)
Macedonia (Chalkidike):
—olynthos (nr.): **(3)** ii-iii AD *SEG* xxix 626 (*-γίσστη*)
Macedonia (Mygdonia):
—thessalonike: **(4)** ii-iii AD *IG* x (2) (1) 642, 2 (m. *Μᾶρκος*)

Μεγιστῆς
Thrace:
—apollonia-sozopolis: **(1)** v/iv BC *IGB* 1^2 435 (s. *Ἄλκανδρος*)

Μεγιστίων
Scythia Minor:
—istros: **(1)** 138 AD *ISM* i 193 I, 12 (*Δεγιστίων*—lap., *(Μ)εγιστίων*—edd.: s. *Νουμήνιος*)

Μεγιστώ
Scythia Minor:
—kallatis: **(1)** iv BC ib. iii 76 (d. *Ἐπικύδης*)

Μέγων
Macedonia (Bisaltia):
—tragilos: **(1)** hell.? Dimitsas 907 (s. *Ἀντιφάνης*)

Μεδαρία
Thrace:
—mesambria: **(1)** iii BC *IGB* v 5121

Μεδία
Macedonia (Bottiaia):
—beroia*: **(1)** f. iii AD *IBer* 387

Μέδων
Cimmerian Bosporos:
—pantikapaion: **(1)** iv BC *IGAIMK* 104 (1935) p. 306 nos. 52-4 (tile); **(2)** 389-349 BC *CIRB* 8 (f. *Κρέουσα*)
Macedonia (Edonis):
—philippoi: **(3)** s. iii BC *IG* vii 2433 II, 2 (Tataki, *Macedonians* p. 165 no. 22) (s. *Πυθίας*)

Μεζηνλις?
Thrace:
—duvanli (mod.): **(1)** v/iv BC Filow, *Duvanlij* p. 130 (Boardman, *Gems* p. 296 pl. 794 (ring)); cf. *Glossa kai mageia* pp. 133-4 (n. pr.?)

Μεθωνάδης
Macedonia (Bottiaia):
—edessa: **(1)** ii BC *BSA* 58 (1963) p. 22 no. 3 (Tataki, *Edessa* 204) (s. *Μένανδρος, Ἀννίκα*); **(2)** ~ *BSA* 58 (1963) p. 22 no. 3 (Tataki, *Edessa* 205) (f. *Ἀννίκα*)

Μειδίας
Macedonia (Chalkidike):
—potidaia-kassandreia?: **(1)** iv BC *TAPA* 69 (1938) p. 60 no. 13 (or Macedonia (Chalkidike) Olynthos: s. *Δημήτριος*)
Macedonia (Derriopos):
—stuberra: **(2)** 121 AD *IG* x (2) (2) 328, 19 (*Τ. Φλαούϊος Μ.*)
Scythia Minor:
—istros: **(3)** iii BC *ISM* i 256 (*Μει[δ]ίας*: f. *Μικ—*); **(4)** i BC ib. 267, 5 (*GVI* 1519) (s. *Ἀρισταῖος*); **(5)** c. 48-52 AD *ISM* i 67, 38, 53; 68, 41 (s. *Ἀρτεμίδωρος*) ?= *(6)*; **(6)** ~ ib. l. 53 (*[Με]ιδίας*?) ?= *(5)*; **(7)** ii AD ib. 216, 2 (*Μειδ[ίας]*); **(8)** 138 AD ib. 193 I, 30 (s. *Φανοκλῆς*) ?= *(10)*; **(9)** ~ ib. l. 46 (s. *Θεοκλῆς*); **(10)** ~ ib. l. 69 (f. *Φανοκλῆς*) ?= *(8)*
Thrace:
—abdera: **(11)** c. 475-450 BC May, *Abdera* p. 109 nos. 102-3 (coin) (*Μειδί(ας)*?)
—byzantion: **(12)** ii BC *Türk Tarih Kongresi XI* (6) p. 2705 with pl. 500. 15 (f. *Ἀρχέλαος*)
—byzantion?: **(13)** ii-i BC *IByz* 370 (Fıratlı-Robert p. 125 no. 208) (f. *Πυθίων*)

Μείδων
Macedonia (Bottiaia):
—beroia: **(1)** 223 BC *IBer* 4, 24 (s. *Με—*); **(2)** f. ii BC *RE* Supplbd. 12 s.v. Medon (13) (Tataki, *Macedonians* p. 80 no. 37) (*Μήδων*—ms., *Μίδων*—Dindorf)

Thrace:
—mesambria: **(3)** iii BC *IGB* 1^2 337 (PM 2260) (s. *Μεγακλῆς*, f. *Σικελία*)

Μείζελμις
Thrace?: **(1)** iii BC *CPR* xiii 4 XV, 257 (*Μειζέλμιος* (gen.))

Μειλάνιος
Cimmerian Bosporos:
—pantikapaion: **(1)** f. ii AD *CIRB* 654 (*Μειλάνιο[ς]*—lap., *Με<ι>λα(ί)νιος*?—Tokhtas'ev)

Μελαγκόμας
Macedonia (Pieria):
—dion: **(1)** ?ii-iii AD *SEG* xxxiii 515 (*Μελ[αγκ]όμας*)

Μελαμνίδας
Macedonia: **(1)** 330-329 BC *RE* (-); Berve 493 (Tataki, *Macedonians* p. 363 no. 19) (*Μελαννίδας*?—Hoffmann)

Μελάμπους
Thrace:
—sostis (mod.): **(1)** iii AD *IThrakAig* E394 (*Αὐ̣ρ̣. Με̣λάμπους*: s. *Αὐρ. Διονύσιος*)

Μέλανδρος
Macedonia (Mygdonia):
—thessalonike?: **(1)** i-ii AD *IG* x (2) (1) 686; cf. *CPh.* 70 (1975) p. 50 (name) (s. *Δία*)

Μελάνθιος
Macedonia (Bottiaia):
—mieza: **(1)** hell.-imp. *AD* 22 (1967) Chron. p. 412 (s. *Εὐρυμέδων*)
Macedonia (Chalkidike):
—potidaia-kassandreia: **(2)** v/iv BC *SEG* xlv 798 (s. *Διοσκουρίδης*)
Macedonia (Edonis):
—amphipolis: **(3)** ii-iii AD *Thrakika* 13 (1940) p. 26 *I* (*Μελάνθ[ιος]*?)
Macedonia (Mygdonia):
—kalindoia: **(4)** 68-98 AD *SEG* xlii 581, 9 (*Μελάν[θιος]*: f. *Θεόφιλος*)
—lete: **(5)** c. 230-200 BC *BCH* 45 (1921) p. 18 III, 73 (Tataki, *Macedonians* p. 118 no. 9) (f. *Ἀργεῖος*)
—thessalonike: **(6)** iii/ii BC *IG* x (2) (1) 1032 (Tataki, *Macedonians* p. 184 no. 45) (f. *Μαχάτας*)
Tauris:
—chersonesos: **(7)** f. v BC *SEG* xl 612. 1-2 (ostraka) (*[Μελ]άν[θιος]*—no. 2: f. *Παρμένιχος*)
Thrace:
—lysimacheia: **(8)** m. ii BC *ISestos* 38 a, 3 (s. *Ἡγησιφῶν*)

Μελανιππίδης
Thrace:
—maroneia: **(1)** i AD *SEG* xxvii 343, 3 (*IThrakAig* E302) (f. *Διονυσία*)

Μελάνιππος
Macedonia (Derriopos):
—stuberra: **(1)** 74 AD *IG* x (2) (2) 325, 41 (s. *Αἰνείας*)
Macedonia (Edonis):
—amphipolis: **(2)** m. iii BC *Polemon* 5 (1952-3) p. 10 no. 327 (Tataki, *Macedonians* p. 56 no. 82 (date)) (f. *Ὀνομακλῆς*)
Scythia Minor:
—tomis?: **(3)** hell. *Syringes* 764 d (*Με̣λ̣ά̣νιππος*?)
Thrace:
—abdera: **(4)** c. 450-425 BC May, *Abdera* pp. 133-4 nos. 161-3 (coin); **(5)** c. 415-395 BC ib. p. 167 no. 217 (coin)

Μελανίων
Macedonia (Pieria):
—sykia (mod.): **(1)** i BC-i AD *SEG* xxv 709 (s. *Ἀντίπατρος*)

Μελαντάδης
MACEDONIA (EDONIS):
—AMPHIPOLIS: (1) a. 357 BC Hatzopoulos, *Actes Amphipolis* p. 34 no. 6, 2; *SEG* XLI 560 (date) (f. *Νικόλαος*)

Μελάντιος
CIMMERIAN BOSPOROS:
—PANTIKAPAION: (1) i AD *CIRB* 503 (f. *Πύθων*)

Μελάνωπος
MACEDONIA (EDONIS):
—AMPHIPOLIS (TERRIT.)?: (1) 26 or 142 AD *SEG* XXXIV 637 (or Macedonia (Pieris) Phagres: f. *Καλλικράτης*)

Μέλας
SKYTHIA:
—OLBIA-BORYSTHENES (BEREZAN (MOD.)): (1) m. vi BC ib. XLVIII 988, 6 (*Μέλανος* (gen.))

Μελγίς
MACEDONIA (EDONIS):
—PROUPTOSOURENOI: (1) ii-iii AD Dimitsas 1051, 6 = 1082 (Pilhofer 456); cf. *BCH* 47 (1923) p. 75 no. 34 (*Μελγίδ[ι]* (dat.): m. *Βύζος*, *Βίθυς*, *Τάρσας*)

Μελέαγρος
MACEDONIA: (1) v/iv BC *FGrH* 631 F 1 (Tataki, *Macedonians* p. 364 no. 25) (?s. *Βόκρος*, ?f. *Ἀρσινόη*: fict.?); (2) ?417-413 BC *IG* I^3 89, 67 (Tataki, *Macedonians* p. 363 no. 20) ([*Με*]*λέαγρος*); (3) c. 370-323 BC *RE* (2); Berve 494 (Tataki, *Macedonians* p. 364 no. 26) (s. *Νεοπτόλεμος*); (4) 331 BC *RE* (5); Berve 495 (Tataki, *Macedonians* p. 364 no. 22) ?= (5); (5) 316 BC *RE* (6) (Tataki, *Macedonians* p. 364 no. 23) ?= (4); (6) c. 315-279 BC *RE* (3) (*PP* 14535) (s. *Πτολεμαῖος* I *Σωτήρ* (Eordaia), *Εὐρυδίκα*)
MACEDONIA (BOTTIAIA):
—BEROIA: (7) 223 BC *IBer* 4, 26 (s. *Φίλιππος*); (8) ~ ib. l. 28 (s. *Μαχάτας*)
MACEDONIA (PAIONIA):
—KAVADARCI (MOD.): (9) ?ii AD *Sp.* 71 (1931) p. 75 no. 176, 1, 7; cf. Düll, *Götterkulte* p. 340 no. 131 (s. *Μένανδρος*, f. *Γάϊος*)
MACEDONIA?: (10) ?iii-ii BC *IPerg* 201 (Tataki, *Macedonians* p. 364 no. 27) (f. *Βάλακρος*); (11) c. 157 BC *PTeb* 742, 18 (*PP* 3491); *PP* 8684 (Tataki, *Macedonians* p. 363 no. 21) (*Μελέαγρος*)

Μελεσικράτης
THRACE:
—HERAION TEICHOS: (1) c. 265-260 BC *FD* III (3) 207, 3 (?s. *Ἀριστομένης*)

Μελέτη
MACEDONIA (BOTTIAIA):
—EDESSA: (1) 51 AD *SEG* XLVI 744, 12 (Tataki, *Edessa* 206) (d. *Ἀπολλόδωρος*)

Μελέτιος
MACEDONIA (MYGDONIA):
—THESSALONIKE: (1) v-vi AD Feissel, *RICM* 96 (monogram) (*SEG* XLVII 965)

Μέλημα
CIMMERIAN BOSPOROS:
—PANTIKAPAION: (1) imp. *CIRB* 798

Μελησαγόρης
THRACE:
—ABDERA: (1) hell.? Hp., *Ep.* 11 (*Ἀμελησαγόρης*—var. lect.: fict.)

Μέλητος
MACEDONIA (PELAGONIA):
—DOSTONEIS: (1) ii AD *IG* X (2) (2) 196, 6 (s. *Διονύσιος*)

Μελίας
THRACE: (1) her. *FGrH* 390 F 1. 11 (king/her.)

Μελικέρτης
THRACE:
—PERINTHOS-HERAKLEIA: (1) i-ii AD *IPerinth* 136 (*Λούσιος Μ.*: ?f. *Βασσία Φαυστîνα*)

Μελιννίχη
MACEDONIA (BOTTIAIA):
—PELLA: (1) iv BC *Pella* p. 138 no. 206 (d. *Εὐφραῖος*)

Μελίς
MACEDONIA (MYGDONIA):
—LETE: (1) c. 325-300 BC *SEG* XLIV 535; *KGAM Thess.* 1 30 (date) (d. *Κλέων*)
—THESSALONIKE: (2) i AD *IG* X (2) (1) 402; cf. *BCH* 97 (1973) p. 589 (*-λείς*: d. *Βιλκεύς*, m. *Ἑρμογένης*)

Μέλισσα
MACEDONIA (CHALKIDIKE):
—AKANTHOS: (1) iv/iii BC *SEG* XLVII 871 B, 1; cf. XLIX 672 (d. *Ἀπολλωνίς*)
MACEDONIA (EDONIS):
—AMPHIPOLIS: (2) iii/ii BC Kaphtantzis 642 (d. *Μενεκλῆς*)
MACEDONIA (ODOMANTIKE):
—SIRRHA: (3) iii BC *A' Panell. Synedr. Epigr.* p. 173 no. 1 (*Pella* p. 140 no. 223; Tataki, *Macedonians* p. 172 no. 5) (d. *Ἐπικράτης*)

Μελισσίς
SARMATIA:
—SARMATAI: (1) f. iii BC *IG* II^2 12064 + *SEG* XXVIII 338 (*FRA* 6598) ([*Μ*]*ελισσίς*: slave?)

Μελίτα
MACEDONIA (BOTTIAIA):
—BEROIA: (1) ii-i BC *IBer* 182 (Tataki 874); (2) ?ii/iii AD *ILeukopetra* 132, [1]?, 2 (?d. *Ζωσᾶς*); (3) f. iii AD *IBer* 212 (Tataki 875) (m. *Ἀμμιανός*)
——Blaganoi*: (4) 189 AD *SEG* XXXVII 590, 5 (Tataki 876) (m. *Φοῦσκος*)

Μελίτεια
MACEDONIA (BOTTIAIA):
—AIGAI: (1) f. iv BC *SEG* XXVII 316 = XXXV 795
MACEDONIA (ELIMEIA):
—KALAMITSI (MOD.): (2) m. ii AD *EAM* 51 (-τεα: d. —βιλας)

Μελίτη
SCYTHIA MINOR:
—CAPIDAVA: (1) iii AD *ISM* V 42, 4 (Lat. Aur. Meliti)

Μελιτίνη
THRACE:
—BYZANTION: (1) ii AD *IByz* 289 (Firatlı–Robert p. 114 no. 190) (m. *Πρωτο*—)
—OESCUS?: (2) 106-162 AD *ISM* V 188, 9 (Lat. Scribonia Melitine)

Μέλιττα
THRACE:
—MONTANA: (1) iii AD *Arkheologiia* (Sofia) 1970 (3), p. 46 no. 8, 8 (*Montana* II 117) (Lat. Melitta: ?d. Aurelius Seneca, Ael. Gemella)

Μελιτώ
MACEDONIA (CHALKIDIKE):
—OLYNTHOS: (1) m. iv BC *IG* II^2 10024 (Tataki, *Macedonians* p. 140 no. 83; *FRA* 5903) (d. *Ἀθηνοκλῆς*)
THRACE:
—BYZANTION: (2) 293 AD *Cod. Just.* viii 47.6; cf. *Klio* 58 (1976) p. 84 (Lat. Melitoni (dat.))

Μελίτων
MACEDONIA (CHALKIDIKE):
—STAGEIROS: (1) v-iv BC *SEG* XXIX 633; cf. XLVIII 841 (?s. *Ἥδων*: kalos)
MACEDONIA (MYGDONIA):
—AINEIA?: (2) ii-iii AD ib. XXXVIII 707 (s. *Κόρραγος*, *Δαντοῦς*)

Μελίφθογγος
THRACE:
—BYZANTION (TERRIT.): (1) imp. *IByz* 20 (-*νγος*: f. *Ἧρις*)

Μέλλιος
MACEDONIA (PAIONIA):
—KAVADARCI (MOD.): (1) ii-iii AD *Sp.* 71 (1931) p. 71 no. 161 + *Arch. Karte Kavadarci* p. 15 (*Μέλλιος*: s. *Καλλικρίτα*)

Μελπώ
MACEDONIA (PIERIS):
—PHAGRES: (1) inc. *AEMTh* 10 (1996) pp. 835 ff.

Μελσέων
THRACE:
—MESAMBRIA: (1) iii/ii BC *IGB* I^2 308 sexies, 1 (s. *Ἡρόδωρος*); (2) ii/i BC ib. V 5103, 3 (f. *Πολύξενος*)
—SEUTHOPOLIS*: (3) hell. *Sevtopolis* I p. 152 no. 63 (amph.)

Μελτίνη
MACEDONIA (EDONIS):
—PHILIPPOI (NR.): (1) ii-iii AD Dimitsas 931 (*CCCA* VI 304; Pilhofer 468) (*Οὔλπ. Μ.*)
MACEDONIA (MYGDONIA):
—THESSALONIKE?: (2) ii-iii AD *IG* X (2) (1) 742 (?d. *Κελερία Πρίμιλλα*)

Μελτόκουζος
THRACE?: (1) iii BC *PPetr* III 29 (f), 1-3 (Velkov 202)

Μέλων
THRACE:
—ABDERA: (1) i BC *IThrakAig* E63 (f. *Νικίας*)

Μέμα
MACEDONIA (MYGDONIA):
—THESSALONIKE: (1) ii-iii AD *SEG* XLIII 353

Μέμη
MACEDONIA (LYNKESTIS):
—ACHLADA (MOD.): (1) f. iii AD *EAM* 169, 1 (*Αὐρ. Μ.*: m. *Αὐρ. Ἀρτεμισία*, *Διονύσις*)

Μεμμία
MACEDONIA (MYGDONIA):
—THESSALONIKE: (1) ii AD *IG* X (2) (1) 454 A (*Μεμία-*: m. *Δρόσος*)
MACEDONIA (PELAGONIA):
—KOLOBAISA?: (2) ii AD ib. X (2) (2) 234, 8 (m. *Ἀλέξανδρος*)

Μέμμιος
MACEDONIA (MYGDONIA):
—THESSALONIKE?: (1) iii AD ib. X (2) (1) 859, 5 (s. *Θράσων*, *Διονυσία*)

Μέμνων
CIMMERIAN BOSPOROS:
—PANTIKAPAION?: (1) 129 AD *CIRB* 705, 4 (s. *Ἀμεινίας*)
—TAMAN PENINSULA: (2) iv-v AD ib. 1225 (*Μέμν*[*ων*]?: Jew)
MACEDONIA: (3) 335-326 BC *RE* (4); Berve 499 (Tataki, *Macedonians* p. 365 no. 29)
MACEDONIA (MYGDONIA):
—THESSALONIKE: (4) ii-iii AD *IG* X (2) (1) 480, 2, 6
SCYTHIA MINOR:
—ISTROS: (5) ii AD *ISM* I 202, 5 (s. *Ἀ*—); (6) ii-iii AD ib. 195, 13; (7) c. 140-160 AD ib. 207, 13 (f. *Πωλλίων*)

—TOMIS: (8) 200-201 AD ib. II 82 B, 18 (Μέμ[ν]ων)
THRACE:
—ABDERA: (9) iii-ii BC *IThrakAig* E52
—MESAMBRIA: (10) ii/i BC *IGB* V 5103, 3 (f. Εὔμαχος)
—ODESSOS: (11) i-ii AD ib. I^2 114 ([Μ]έμνων: s. Ἀλέξανδρος)
—OESCUS: (12) ii-iii AD *Romanizmăt* II 341 (Lat. Memnon)
—PHILIPPOPOLIS-TRIMONTIUM: (13) c. 303 AD *Anal. Boll.* 31 (1912) p. 193
—SALYMBRIA: (14) imp. *Archives Stamoulis* d. 35 (Loukopoulou, *Thrace Propontique* p. 274)

Μέναιχμος
CIMMERIAN BOSPOROS:
—PANTIKAPAION: (1) i AD *CIRB* 469 (Μένεχμαι (voc.): s. Ἀπολλώνιος)

Μενάλκης
SCYTHIA MINOR:
—KALLATIS: (1) iii BC *ISM* III 126, 2 (f. ....ρων)
THRACE:
—APOLLONIA-SOZOPOLIS: (2) s. v BC *IGB* I^2 414 (s. Διοσκουρίδης)

Μένανδρος
CIMMERIAN BOSPOROS:
—GORGIPPIA: (1) f. iii BC *CIRB* 1137 A II, 45; 1137 B II, 49 (s. Ἡράκλειτος); (2) ~ ib. l. 48 (Μέναν[δρος]: I f. Μένανδρος II); (3) ~ ib. l. 48 (II s. Μένανδρος I)
—NYMPHAION: (4) iii BC ib. 912 III, 4 (Μέν-ανδ[ρος])
—PANTIKAPAION: (5) f. i AD ib. 395; cf. KW pl. 25 no. 378 (s. Ποσείδιππος); (6) 173-210 AD *CIRB* 74, 5 (f. Κοσσοῦς)
MACEDONIA: (7) c. 365-321 BC *RE* (5); Berve 501; *Syll*^{3} 302, 4 (*Chiron* 33 (2003) p. 420; Tataki, *Macedonians* p. 365 no. 31) (f. Χαρι-κλῆς); (8) c. 327 BC *RE* (6); Berve 502 (Tataki, *Macedonians* p. 366 no. 32); (9) hell.? *IG* II^2 9264 (Tataki, *Macedonians* p. 366 no. 33; *FRA* 3475) (s. Ἄτταλος); (10) 232 or 207 BC *CPR* XVIII 13, 259, 264, 271 (Tataki, *Macedonians* p. 366 no. 36); cf. La'da E1774 (f. Νικόλαος); (11) 231 BC *SB* 9258, 7 (Tataki, *Macedonians* p. 366 no. 35) (s. Φίλιππος); (12) ?219 BC *PUG* III 104, 2 (La'da E1537) (s. Δημήτριος); (13) ~ *PUG* III 105, 10 (Tataki, *Macedonians* p. 366 no. 34; La'da E1538) (s. Π—); (14) c. 210 BC *ZPE* 132 (2000) p. 228 no. 1, 9
MACEDONIA (BISALTIA):
—EUPORIA?: (15) ii-iii AD *SEG* XXX 615 (XXXIX 591) (*T. Ἄρριος M.*)
MACEDONIA (BOTTIAIA):
—AIGAI: (16) s. iv BC ib. XXXV 778 (f. Παρά-μονος); (17) ~ ib. 792 (f. Σωκλῆς); (18) iii BC ib. II 394 (f. Εὐρύλοχος)
—BEROIA: (19) iv-iii BC *IBer* 148 (Tataki 885) (Μένα[νδρος]: f. Ἀττύλος); (20) s. iii BC *IBer* 16 B, 8 (s. Πολύγνωτος); (21) c. 230-200 BC *BCH* 45 (1921) p. 17 III, 58 (Tataki 882) (s. Φιλώ-τας); (22) 223 BC *IBer* 4, 20 (s. Ἀντίγονος); (23) ~ ib. l. 26 (f. Ἐπιτέλης); (24) ~ ib. l. 29 (s. Παυ-σανίας); (25) ~ ib. l. 29 (s. Πύρρος); (26) ~ ib. l. 32 (f. Παράμονος); (27) ~ ib. l. 36 (f. Παρ-μενίων); (28) 178 BC *SGDI* 2071, 2 (Tataki, *Macedonians* p. 80 no. 35) (f. Ἀσανδρος); (29) 38 BC Robert, *Coll. Froehner* 44, 18 (*IG* XII Suppl. p. 149); cf. Tataki, *Macedonians* p. 80 no. 36 (f. Περίτας); (30) i AD *IBer* 344 (Tataki 880) (s. Ἄδυμος); (31) 41-44 AD *IBer* 60, 8 (Tataki 883); (32) ii-iii AD *IBer* 28 (Tataki 881) (s. Παμφίλα); (33) f. ii AD *IBer* 7 A, 35; (34) ~ *SEG* L 623 (s. Ἑλλάς); (35) iii AD *IBer* 499, 13 (Tataki 589) (Ἰουλιανὸς M.)
—BEROIA?: (36) 178 BC *SGDI* 2071, 8 (s. Εὐ-φρόνιος)
—EDESSA: (37) c. 200-175 BC *SEG* XLIV 409, 2 (Tataki, *Macedonians* p. 103 no. 12); (38) ii BC *BSA* 58 (1963) p. 22 no. 3 (Tataki, *Edessa* 209) (s. Παρμενίων, f. Μεθωνάδης); (39) ii/i BC *Ancient Macedonia* I p. 202 no. 16 (Tataki, *Edessa* 208) (s. Ἐπικράτης, ?s. Φίλα); (40) ~ *Ancient Macedonia* I p. 202 no. 16 (Tataki, *Edessa* 210) (f. Ἐπικράτης)
—MIEZA: (41) hell. *AM* 27 (1902) p. 314 no. 28, 6 ([Μέ]νανδρος)
—TYRISSA? (ASVESTARI (MOD.)): (42) f. ii BC *SEG* XLVII 999, 20 ([Μ]ένανδρος)
MACEDONIA (CHALKIDIKE):
—APHYTIS: (43) ii AD *AAA* 4 (1971) p. 361
—POTIDAIA-KASSANDREIA: (44) 2 BC or 115 AD *Essays Laourdas* p. 97 (s. Φιλόξενος)
MACEDONIA (DERRIOPOS):
—STUBERRA: (45) 74 AD *IG* X (2) (2) 325, 59 (s. Παράμονος); (46) ~ ib. 326, 31 (s. Ζωΐλος); (47) ~ ib. l. 64 (f. Ἀντίγονος); (48) 107 AD ib. 325, 103 (s. Ἀντίγονος)
MACEDONIA (EDONIS):
—AMPHIPOLIS: (49) b. 357 BC Hatzopoulos, *Actes Amphipolis* p. 20 no. 2, 2 (*SEG* XLI 556) (Μέναν<ν>δρ<ρ>ος); (50) 311-306 BC Maier, *Mauerbauinschr.* 69 II, 143 (Tataki, *Macedonians* p. 56 no. 84) (f. Στέφανος); (51) s. iii BC *SEG* XXIV 593, 1 (f. Νικονόα); (52) ~ ib. l. 2 (Μέναν[δρος]: s. Νικόλαος); (53) 236 BC *PPetr*^{2} 17, 20 (Tataki, *Macedonians* p. 56 no. 83; La'da E134) (Μέναν[δρ]ος); (54) c. 200-170 BC Hatzopoulos, *MI* 2 p. 87 no. 65, 3 (*SEG* XLVI 720) (f. Κάλλιππος); (55) 76 or 192 AD ib. XXXIII 501, 2 (II s. (nat.) Μένανδρος I, s. (ad.) Νικόλαος); (56) ~ ib. l. 3 (I f. (nat.) Μένανδρος II)
MACEDONIA (EORDAIA):
—EXOCHI (MOD.): (57) ii-iii AD *EAM* 102 (f. Μάτελα)
—KELLE?: (58) ii-iii AD ib. 127 (f. Παράμονος)
MACEDONIA (KRESTONIA):
—IORON?: (59) i AD *SEG* XXVII 287 a (f. Ἀμμία)
—MORRYLOS: (60) c. 185-180 BC ib. XXXIX 606, 1 (s. Ὀλώϊχος)
MACEDONIA (LYNKESTIS):
—HERAKLEIA (AREA): (61) imp. *Sp.* 98 (1941-8) p. 23 no. 56 (monogram)
MACEDONIA (MYGDONIA):
—HERAKLEIA?: (62) s. iv BC *SEG* XLIX 856; cf. *BE* 2003, no. 365 (locn.) (f. Νικάνωρ); (63) iv/iii BC *SEG* XLIX 857; cf. *BE* 2003, no. 365 (locn.) (s. Νικάνωρ)
—KALINDOIA: (64) c. 328-326 BC Hatzopoulos, *MI* 2 p. 84 no. 62, 17-19 (Μένανδ[ρος]: f. Μενέλαος, Ἀντίγονος, Ἀντιμένων); (65) c. 317 BC ib. l. 29 (Μένα[νδρος]?: f. Φίλαγρος); (66) 68-98 AD *SEG* XLII 580, 7, 35 (s. Ἔρως); (67) ~ ib. l. 14 (f. Ζώπυρος); (68) ~ ib. l. 45 (s. Βακχίας); (69) ~ ib. l. 51 (f. Εὐμένης); (70) ~ ib. l. 54 (f. Κράτων); (71) ~ ib. 581, 11 (f. Ἡρακλείδης); (72) ~ ib. l. 12 ([Μένα]νδρος?: s. Ἡρακλείδης); (73) a. 98 AD ib. 582, 39 (f. Διοσκουρίδης)
—LETE: (74) s. iv BC Hatzopoulos, *MI* 2 pp. 93-4 no. 79, 6; (75) ~ ib. l. 16; (76) 323 BC *SEG* XXXVI 331 B, 20 (Tataki, *Macedonians* p. 118 no. 10) (s. Λύσανδρος); (77) f. ii BC *SEG* XLVI 764, 2 ([Μ]ένανδρο[ς]: f. Ἡρακλείδης); (78) ~ ib. l. 8 (f. Σώστρατος); (79) ~ ib. l. 9 (f. Ἄρατος)
—LETE (NR.): (80) iii BC ib. XXXI 633 a (s. Σώ-στρατος)
—LETE?: (81) 22 or 139 AD Dimitsas 678, 5 (f. Ἑρμόλαος)
—THESSALONIKE: (82) c. 230 BC *IG* XI (4) 1053, 10 = X (2) (1) 1028 (*RE* (14); Tataki, *Macedonians* p. 184 no. 46); (83) imp. *Makedonika* 14 (1974) p. 334; (84) i BC/i AD *IG* X (2) (1) 58, 16; *KGAM Thess.* I 111 (date) (s. Νίκανδρος); (85) ?i AD *IG* X (2) (1) 53 (f. Δημοκράτης, Ζωβία)
—THESSALONIKE?: (86) 46 AD Dimitsas 366, 11 (*Epigr. arch. Mak.* 36); cf. *Essays Laourdas* pp. 98-100; *Tekmeria* 6 (2001) p. 126 n. 2 (locn.) (s. Πελειγένης); (87) a. 212 AD *IG* X (2) (1) 768, 3 (f. Ἑκαταία)
MACEDONIA (ODOMANTIKE):
—SIRRHA: (88) ii-iii AD Dimitsas 817 (Kaphtantzis 26) (s. Πυρούλας); (89) 155 AD Dimitsas 821, 36 (Kaphtantzis 1)
MACEDONIA (ORESTIS):
—NESTORION (MOD.): (90) iii BC *SEG* XLVII 921 (s. —ν)
MACEDONIA (PAIONIA):
—KAVADARCI (MOD.): (91) ?ii AD *Sp.* 71 (1931) p. 75 no. 176, 3; cf. Düll, *Götterkulte* p. 340 no. 131 (Μένα(ν)δρ[ος]: f. Μελέαγρος)
MACEDONIA (PIERIA):
—HERAKLEION: (92) hell.? *SEG* XLIX 769 (Μέν-ανδ[ρος]?)
—PHILA?: (93) ?iii BC *RPh* 1911, pp. 133-4 no. 36, 121; cf. Helly, *L'État thessalien* pp. 319-20 (locn.) (s. Σικ—)
—PYDNA: (94) ii-i BC *SEG* XXXIII 541 + *AD* 30 (1975) Chron. pl. 162 *α* (Μένανδ[ρος]: f. Θεό-δωρος)
MACEDONIA (PIERIS):
—GALEPSOS: (95) hell.? Dimitsas 916; Hatzopoulos, *MI* 1 p. 187 n. 3 (locn.)
SCYTHIA MINOR:
—KALLATIS: (96) ii BC *IG* II^2 8947 (*FRA* 2647) (s. Δῶρος)
SKYTHIA:
—OLBIA-BORYSTHENES: (97) iii BC *IOSPE* I^2 201 II, 11 (s. Ἑκατώνυμος); (98) iii-ii BC *Arkheologiia* (Kiev) 39 (1982) p. 34 (vase) (Μέναν(δρος))
—OLBIA-BORYSTHENES*: (99) iii BC Dubois, *IGDOlbia* 26, 4 (ostrakon) ([Μ]ένανδρος)
TAURIS:
—CHERSONESOS: (100) ii AD *IOSPE* I^2 464; cf. KW pl. 33 no. 468 (f. Ἀπολλωνίδας)
THRACE:
—ABDERA: (101) c. 311-280 BC *AMNG* II (1) 221 (coin) (Μέναν(δρος)); (102) iii BC *BCH* 37 (1913) p. 137 no. 41 (*IThrakAig* E48) (s. Σώ-στρατος)
—BEROE-AUGUSTA TRAIANA: (103) iii AD *IGB* III 1574, 9 (Αὐρ. Μ. ὁ καὶ Κότος: II s. Μέν-ανδρος I); (104) ~ ib. l. 10 (I f. Αὐρ. Μένανδρος II ὁ καὶ Κότος)
—BYZANTION: (105) ii-i BC *IG* II^2 8442 (*FRA* 1400) (s. Εὔβιος); (106) ii/i BC *IByz* 119 (Fıratlı–Robert pp. 115-16 no. 192) (s. Ἀφρο-δίσιος); (107) ~ *IByz* 187 (Fıratlı–Robert pp. 53-4 no. 32) (f. Δέξιος); (108) i BC-i AD *IByz* 149 (Fıratlı–Robert pp. 102-3 no. 157) (I f. Γούκουσα, Μένανδρος II); (109) ~ *IByz* 149 (Fıratlı–Robert pp. 102-3 no. 157) (II s. Μέν-ανδρος I); (110) ~ *IByz* 209 (Fıratlı–Robert p. 69 no. 67) (f. Εὐκτήμων)
—LYSIMACHEIA: (111) m. ii BC *ISestos* 38 b, 7 (f. Γέρων)
—MARKIANOPOLIS (NR.): (112) f. iii AD *IGB* II 837 (*CCET* II (1) 331) (f. Διονύσις)
—MESAMBRIA: (113) m. iv BC *IG* II^2 9338 (*FRA* 3687) (f. Ἡρότιμος)
—ODESSOS: (114) ii BC *IGB* I^2 206 ter (PM 1795) (f. Διογένης); (115) ~ *IGB* I^2 206 ter (PM 1795) (s. Διογένης); (116) i BC-i AD *IGB* I^2 107, 5, 8 (f. Αἰαντίδης); (117) i-ii AD ib. 200 (Μέναν̣δρος: s. Ἀρτεμίδωρος); (118) 12-19 AD ib. V 5011, 10 (s. Προμαθίων); (119) f. ii AD ib. I^2 78 ter, 3 (*CCET* I 30) (f. Ἀπελλᾶς); (120) ~ *IGB* I^2 78 ter, 9 (*CCET* I 30) (f. Αἰαντίδης) ?= (*126*); (121) s. ii AD *IGB* I^2 79 bis, 3 (*CCET* I 34) (Μέν̣α̣νδρος: s. Ἀπολλώνιος); (122) 215 AD *IGB* I^2 47 c, 19 (I f. Αὐρ. Μένανδρος II); (123) ~ ib. l. 19 (Αὐρ. Μ.: II s. Μένανδρος I); (124) ~ ib. l. 21 (f. Αὐρ. Βασιλεύς)
—ODESSOS (NR.): (125) i BC-i AD ib. 283 bis (*CCET* I 97) (s. Ἀμύντωρ); (126) i-ii AD *IGB* I^2 284 (f. Αἰαντίδης) ?= (*120*); (127) ii-iii AD ib. 256 (PM 1695) (s. Διονύσιος)

—SESTOS: **(128)** a. 129 BC *ISestos* 1, 2 (s. Ἀπολλᾶς)
—ZONE: **(129)** s. iv BC *SEG* XLIII 480 (*IThrakAig* E421) (s. Ἀντίπατρος)

Μένας
THRACE?: **(1)** her. Str. 319 b (fict.)

Μενδᾶς
THRACE:
—BYZANTION: **(1)** iii AD *IByz* 296 (*Αὐρ. Μ.*: s. Φίλων)

Μενδίδωρος
THRACE:
—BYZANTION: **(1)** ?iii BC ib. 11 (f. Ὀλυμπιόδωρος)

Μενδικώ
TAURIS:
—CHERSONESOS: **(1)** iii BC Solomonik, *NEPKh* 147; *Hellenismus* p. 453 no. 23 (d. Νίκαιος)

Μενδίς
MACEDONIA (MYGDONIA):
—THESSALONIKE: **(1)** ii AD *IG* X (2) (1) 446 (m. Τόρκος)

Μένδρα
THRACE:
—PAUTALIA (TERRIT.): **(1)** ii AD *IGB* IV 2141 + V 5863 (d. Μουκάτραλις)

Μενέα
MACEDONIA (LOWER PAIONIA):
—EUROPOS: **(1)** ?ii-iii AD *SEG* XXXVIII 610 (Ἐρεννία Μ.: m. Μ. Ἐρέννιος Σαβῖνος νέος)

Μενέας
MACEDONIA (MYGDONIA):
—HERAKLEIA: **(1)** iii BC ib. XLVII 901 (s. Πρίαμος)

Μενέδαμος
THRACE:
—BYZANTION: **(1)** c. 315-280 BC *FD* III (4) 152, 1 (f. Παρμενίσκος)

Μενέδημος
MACEDONIA: **(1)** iii-ii BC *TAM* V (2) 1109 (Tataki, *Macedonians* p. 367 no. 41) (s. Νεοπτόλεμος); **(2)** 102 BC *IG* II² 1335, 36 (Tataki, *Macedonians* p. 367 no. 40; *FRA* 3476); **(3)** 48-44 BC *RE* (6) (Tataki, *Macedonians* p. 367 no. 39) (Lat. Menedemus)
MACEDONIA (BOTTIAIA):
—BEROIA: **(4)** iii/ii BC *IBer* 39 ([Μεν]έδημος)
—PELLA: **(5)** iv BC *CEG* II 725 (f. —ος); **(6)** s. iii BC *SEG* XXIV 551 a ([Μ]ενέδημος)
MACEDONIA (DERRIOPOS):
—STUBERRA: **(7)** 74 AD *IG* X (2) (2) 326, 58 (f. Μέστρις); **(8)** 74-121 AD ib. 325, 37; 328, 12 (f. Παράμονος)
MACEDONIA (EDONIS):
—PHILIPPOI: **(9)** s. iii BC ib. VII 2433 II, 14 (Tataki, *Macedonians* p. 165 no. 23) ([Με]νέδ[αμος]?: f. Εὐπόλεμος)
MACEDONIA (ELIMEIA):
—AIANE: **(10)** ii BC *GVI* 871, 1 (*EAM* 47) (f. Φίλιππος)
MACEDONIA (MYGDONIA):
—THESSALONIKE: **(11)** i BC-i AD *IG* X (2) (1) 86, 4 (Μενέδη[μος]); **(12)** 42-32 BC ib. 124, 9 (Μενέδ[ημος]: f. Δαμᾶς)
MACEDONIA?: **(13)** 329 BC *RE* (2); Berve 504 (Tataki, *Macedonians* p. 367 no. 37)
THRACE:
—LYSIMACHEIA: **(14)** m. ii BC *ISestos* 38 a, 4 (f. Σώστρατος)
—SALYMBRIA (NR.): **(15)** hell. *IByz* S 54 (Μηνακῶν ὁ καὶ Μ.: s. Μήτοκος)

Μενέδωρος
CIMMERIAN BOSPOROS:
—PANTIKAPAION: **(1)** ii-i BC Tolstoi 156 (vase)

Μενεκλῆς
CIMMERIAN BOSPOROS:
—GORGIPPIA: **(1)** f. iii BC *CIRB* 1137 A II, 52 (f. Ἀρτεμίδωρος)
—PANTIKAPAION: **(2)** ii-i BC ib. 264 (f. Γλυκαρίων)
MACEDONIA (CHALKIDIKE):
—CHALKIDEIS: **(3)** ?351 BC *SEG* XXXVII 575, 3; XXXVIII 672, 2; 673, 3; *A΄ Panell. Synedr. Epigr.* pp. 80-1, 2; Hatzopoulos, *Actes Chalc.* p. 28, [2]; p. 80 (date) (Μενεκλέω (gen.): f. Καλλιππίδης)
MACEDONIA (EDONIS):
—AMPHIPOLIS: **(4)** iii/ii BC Kaphtantzis 642 (f. Μέλισσα)
—PHILIPPOI: **(5)** iii BC *Ét. Thas.* 3 p. 319 no. 113 bis (Tataki, *Macedonians* p. 165 no. 24) (f. Ἀπελλις, Κύπριος); **(6)** imp. *SEG* XXXVIII 659 (Pilhofer 96) (Μενεκλῆδος (gen.))
MACEDONIA (MYGDONIA):
—THESSALONIKE: **(7)** ii AD Luc., *Asin.* 49 (fict.)
SCYTHIA MINOR:
—KALLATIS?: **(8)** ii/i BC *IGB* II 867 a, 9 = *ISM* I 219 (V 87); cf. *ISM* III p. 140 (locn.) (s. Πασικλῆς)
—TOMIS: **(9)** ii-iii AD ib. II 307, 7 (f. Σοζίμιος)
THRACE:
—AINOS: **(10)** ii BC *SEG* XXXIV 1253 (Μενεκλείους (gen.): f. Διονύσιος)
—BISANTHE-PANION: **(11)** ii-i BC *JÖAI* 23 (1926) Beibl. cols. 155-6 no. 93 (*SIRIS* 127; *Eastern cults* p. 28 no. 48) (s. Πύρρος)
—MARONEIA: **(12)** ii-i BC *IThrakAig* E269 (Μενεκλήους (gen.): f. Καλλίστρατος)

Μενεκράτη
THRACE:
—PERINTHOS-HERAKLEIA: **(1)** i-ii AD *IPerinth* 189 ([Με]νεκράτη?)

Μενεκράτης
CIMMERIAN BOSPOROS:
—GORGIPPIA: **(1)** f. iii BC *CIRB* 1137 B II, 15
MACEDONIA (BOTTIAIA):
—BEROIA: **(2)** 223 BC *IBer* 4, 36 (Μενεκ[ρά]της: f. Ἀντίγονος); **(3)** 113 BC ib. 134, 38 ([Μ]ε[ν]εκράτης: f. Ποσειδώνιος)
MACEDONIA (CHALKIDIKE):
—OLYNTHOS: **(4)** ?v-iv BC Schol. Dion. Thr. p. 184, 20; **(5)** iv BC *SEG* XXXIV 822 (Tataki, *Macedonians* p. 140 no. 84) (Μενεκρατεῦς (gen.): f. Φιλοκράτης)
MACEDONIA (DERRIOPOS):
—STUBERRA: **(6)** c. 41-48 AD *IG* X (2) (2) 323, 16 (f. Ἱππόνικος); **(7)** 74 AD ib. 326, 20 (f. Εὐβουλίδης); **(8)** 107 AD ib. 325, 97 (s. Ἄνδρων); **(9)** ii/iii AD ib. 334
MACEDONIA (PIERIA):
—PHILA?: **(10)** ?iii BC *RPh* 1911, pp. 133-4 no. 36, 79; cf. Helly, *L'État thessalien* pp. 319-20 (locn.) ([Με]νεκράτης: s. Μένων)
MACEDONIA?: **(11)** 169 BC *RE* (8) (Tataki, *Macedonians* p. 367 no. 42)
SCYTHIA MINOR:
—ISTROS: **(12)** c. 140-160 AD *ISM* I 207, 21 (Μενεκράτ[ης])
—KALLATIS: **(13)** ii-i BC ib. III 135, 6 (f. Ἀπολλώνιος); **(14)** ~ ib. l. 9 (s. Ἀπολλώνιος)
—TOMIS: **(15)** ii AD ib. II 77, 7 (f. Βάσσος)
SKYTHIA:
—OLBIA-BORYSTHENES: **(16)** iii BC *Arkheologiia* (Kiev) 39 (1982) p. 35 (Vinogradov–Kryžickij pl. 91. 6 (vase)); **(17)** ~ *IOSPE* I² 201 I, 43 (s. Θεοκλῆς)
THRACE:
—AINOS: **(18)** f. iii BC *HE* 1233; **(19)** imp. *IG* II² 7979 a (*FRA* 257) (f. Λαμίδιον)
—APROI: **(20)** iv-v AD Unp. (Sayar) (Μενεκρ[άτης])
—BISANTHE-PANION: **(21)** hell. Dumont–Homolle 83h (I f. Μενεκράτης II); **(22)** ~ ib. (II s. Μενεκράτης I)
—BYZANTION: **(23)** s. iii BC Schönert-Geiss, *Byzantion* 1167-78; 1226-8 (coin) (Μενεκρ(άτης)); **(24)** ii BC *IByz* 279 (Fıratlı–Robert p. 64 no. 56) ((Μ)ενεκράτης, ΦΛΙΕΝΕΚΡΑΤΗ (gen.)—lap.: f. Λυκώι); **(25)** i BC *IByz* 109 (Μενεκράτη (gen.): f. Κόθων); **(26)** i BC-i AD ib. 270 (Fıratlı–Robert pp. 86-7 no. 108a) (s. Κερκίνος, f. Γλυκεῖα, Ἀπολλοφάνης); **(27)** i-ii AD *IG* II² 8447 (*FRA* 1401) (f. Σωτηρίς)
—BYZANTION?: **(28)** i BC-i AD *IByz* 337 (Fıratlı–Robert p. 129 no. 219) (s. Μήνιος); **(29)** i AD *IByz* 372 (s. Διονύσις ὁ καὶ Πόπλιος)
—MARONEIA: **(30)** ii-i BC *IThrakAig* E212, 53 (s. Θράσων)
—ODESSOS: **(31)** s. ii AD *IGB* I² 80 (*CCET* I 47) (Μενεκρά[της]); **(32)** 221 AD *IGB* I² 47 bis a, 10 (Μ. Αὐρ. Μ.: s. Ἀρτεμίδωρος)
—ODESSOS (NR.): **(33)** ii-i BC ib. V 5078 ([Μεν]εκράτης?)
—PERINTHOS-HERAKLEIA: **(34)** i-ii AD *IPerinth* 97 (f. Ἡρόξενος)
——(Podargoi): **(35)** iii-ii BC ib. 61, 22 (Μεν(ε)κράτευς (gen.): f. Σωσικλῆς)

Μενεκρίτη
MACEDONIA (PIERIA):
—DION: **(1)** iii BC *SEG* XXVII 280 (d. Θεόδωρος)

Μενέλαος
CIMMERIAN BOSPOROS:
—PANTIKAPAION: **(1)** i AD *CIRB* 468 (I f. Μενέλαος II, Καλλισθένης); **(2)** ~ ib. (II s. Μενέλαος I)
MACEDONIA: **(3)** v BC *RE* (3) (Tataki, *Macedonians* p. 368 no. 46); *IG* I³ 89, 61 (s. Ἀλέξανδρος I) ?= (*4*); **(4)** ~ Ael., *VH* xii 43 (f. Ἀμύντας) ?= (*3*); **(5)** c. 400-348 BC *RE* (4) (Tataki, *Macedonians* p. 368 no. 47); cf. Beloch, *GG* III (2) pp. 66-7 (s. Ἀμύντας III, Γυγαία); **(6)** s. iv BC *RE* (14); Berve 505 (Tataki, *Macedonians* p. 368 no. 43); **(7)** 334-330 BC Arr., *An.* i 14. 3; iii 11. 10; iii 25. 4 (f. Φίλιππος) ?= (*8*); **(8)** c. 307-301 BC *IG* II² 561, [5] + *SEG* XXXI 80; *IG* II² Add. p. 662 no. 559, 6 + *SEG* XXXII 101 (Tataki, *Macedonians* p. 369 no. 52) ([Μ]ενέλ[αος]—no. 559: f. Φίλιππος) ?= (*7*); **(9)** 243 BC *PSI* 389, 9 (Tataki, *Macedonians* p. 369 no. 50); cf. La'da E1742 (f. Ἀμύντας); **(10)** c. 235-200 BC ib. E1750 (f. Διονύσιος); **(11)** 231 or 206 BC *CPR* XVIII 2, 26, 33, 36, 39 (Tataki, *Macedonians* p. 368 no. 45; La'da E1539); **(12)** 223 BC *PHamb* 24, 22 (Tataki, *Macedonians* p. 369 no. 51); cf. La'da E1776 (f. Πολέμων); **(13)** 173 BC *PAmh* 43, 6-7, 13 (Tataki, *Macedonians* p. 369 no. 49; La'da E1772) (s. Παρίγετος: t.e.)
MACEDONIA (BOTTIAIA):
—BEROIA: **(14)** ii BC *IBer* 141, 47; **(15)** ii AD ib. 79, 2 (Tataki 888) (I s. Ἀντίγονος, f. Ἰούλ. Μενέλαος II); **(16)** ~ *IBer* 420, 8 (Lat. Gn. Domitius Menelaus: f. Δομιτία Ἀμμία); **(17)** f. ii AD ib. 79, 6; 83 (Tataki 617) (Γ. Ἰούλ. Μ.: II s. Μενέλαος I, f. Ἰουλ. Πρίσκιλλα)
MACEDONIA (DERRIOPOS):
—STUBERRA: **(18)** c. 41-48 AD *IG* X (2) (2) 323, 17 (f. Παράμονος); **(19)** ~ ib. l. 23-4 (s. Λέων); **(20)** 50-74 AD ib. 324, 17; 325, 29 (s. Λιμναῖος, f. Λιμναῖος)
MACEDONIA (EDONIS):
—AMPHIPOLIS: **(21)** a. 357 BC Hatzopoulos, *Actes Amphipolis* p. 34 no. 6, 6; *SEG* XLI 560 (date); **(22)** iii BC *Polemon* 5 (1952-3) p. 57 no. 3 (Tataki, *Macedonians* p. 56 no. 85) (s. Ἡγησίδημος)
—AMPHIPOLIS?: **(23)** ii-i BC *BCH* 55 (1931) p. 191 no. 12 (f. Ἀντιγόνα)

Macedonia (Eordaia): **(24)** c. 360-285 bc *RE* (6) (*PP* 5196; 14537) (s. *Λάαγος, Ἀρσινόη*); **(25)** a. 316 bc *IG* iv (1)² 94 b, 37 (Perlman, *City and Sanctuary* E.1 with p. 78 f. (date); Tataki, *Macedonians* p. 199 no. 6) (s. *Νικάνωρ*)
—drosia (mod.): **(26)** 203 ad *EAM* 132, 6 (*Ἀντώνιος Μ.*: f. *Ποτάμων*)
Macedonia (Mygdonia):
—kalindoia: **(27)** c. 328 bc Hatzopoulos, *MI* 2 p. 84 no. 62, 17 (s. *Μένανδρος*); **(28)** ii/i bc *SEG* xlii 594 (f. *Ἀριστίππα*); **(29)** ~ ib. (s. *Φίλιππος, Ἀριστίππα*)
—thessalonike: **(30)** inc. *AD* 23 (1968) Chron. p. 330; **(31)** f. i ad *IG* x (2) (1) 133, 12; Robert, *OMS* 5 pp. 295-302 (date) (s. *Ἀντίγονος*)
Macedonia (Orestis):
—battynaioi: **(32)** 192 ad *EAM* 186 I, 53 (f. *Νικόλαος*); **(33)** ~ ib. l. 54 (s. *Λύκωπος*); **(34)** ~ ib. 186 II, 52 (f. *Φίλιππος*)
—keletron (nr.): **(35)** hell.? *SEG* xlix 723
Macedonia (Pelagonia): **(36)** c. 360 bc Rhodes–Osborne 38; Tod, *GHI* ii 148 (*Ilion* 23); Osborne, *Naturalization* T56; Papazoglou, *Villes* p. 278 (Tataki, *Macedonians* p. 211 no. 1) (and Athens: s. *Ἀρραβαῖος*)
—dostoneis: **(37)** ii ad *IG* x (2) (2) 194 (*Π. Αἴλ. Μ.*)
—mariovo (mod.): **(38)** iii ad ib. 166 (*Αὐρ. Οὐαλέριος Μ.*: s. *Παράμονος*)
Macedonia (Pieria):
—phila?: **(39)** ?iii bc *RPh* 1911, pp. 133-4 no. 36, 66; cf. Helly, *L'État thessalien* pp. 319-20 (locn.) (f. *Φίλων*)
Macedonia?: **(40)** c. 306-302 bc *RE* (8); *FGrH* 81 F 12 (Tataki, *Macedonians* p. 368 no. 44)
Thrace: **(41)** iii bc *ZPE* 140 (2002) p. 204, 6 (s. *Ἐβρύζελμις, Δα....ς*)
—perinthos-herakleia: **(42)** c. 208 bc *FD* iii (4) 134 I, 19 (f. *—ώνιος*); **(43)** iii ad *IPerinth* 45 (f. *Λούκις*)

Μενέλας
Macedonia (Orestis):
—battynaioi: **(1)** 192 ad *EAM* 186 II, 54 (s. *Τήρης*)

Μενέμαχος
Cimmerian Bosporos:
—pantikapaion: **(1)** i ad *CIRB* 523 (f. *Φάννης, —ναιος*); **(2)** i-ii ad ib. 601
Macedonia (Edonis):
—amphipolis*: **(3)** iii-ii bc *Mous. Kavalas* p. 123 (terracotta) ?= (*4*)
Macedonia (Mygdonia):
—thessalonike*: **(4)** iii-ii bc *AD* 23 (1968) Chron. p. 332 with pl. 279 β (terracotta); cf. *SEG* xlvi 822 (*Μονόμαχος*—ed.) ?= (*3*)
Macedonia?: **(5)** a. 316 bc ib. xi 1084, 22 (Perlman, *City and Sanctuary* A.3)
Thrace: **(6)** 214 bc *BGU* 1944, 6, 9, [12], etc. (La'da E834) (s. *Ζωπυρίων*: t.e.)
—byzantion: **(7)** i bc/i ad *IG* xii (8) 206, 7 (s. *Μητρόδωρος*)
—philippopolis-trimontium (territ.): **(8)** ?ii ad *IGB* iii 1420, 4 (f. *Καρδένθης*)

Μενέσαιχμος
Thrace:
—lysimacheia: **(1)** m. ii bc *ISestos* 38 a, 7

Μενεσθεύς
Macedonia (Chalkidike):
—anthemous: **(1)** iv bc Arr., *An.* ii 9. 3 (Tataki, *Macedonians* p. 64 no. 1) (f. *Περοίδας*)
—torone: **(2)** a. 322 bc *IG* xii (6) 46, 1, 6 (Tataki, *Macedonians* p. 191 no. 10) (f. *Γύγης*)
Thrace:
—bizye: **(3)** i bc *SEG* xxxiv 701 (*[Μεν]εσθέω[ς]*? (gen.): f. *Ἡγε—*)
—byzantion: **(4)** ii-i bc *IApameia* 140 (f. *Ἀστήρ*)
—mesambria: **(5)** ii-i bc *IGB* i² 338 (PM 1660) (s. *Χαιρέας*)
—odessos: **(6)** i-ii ad *IGB* i² 128, 4 (s. *Ἀρτεμίδωρος*); **(7)** 221 ad ib. 47 bis a, 15 (*Μ. Αὐρ. Μενεσθεύ(ς)*: s. *Ἰούλ. Ῥουστικός*)
—pautalia: **(8)** ii ad ib. iv 2074, 8

Μενεστράτα
Thrace:
—perinthos-herakleia: **(1)** iii ad *IPerinth* 165 (m. *Αὐρ. Νικηφόρος*)

Μενέστρατος
Cimmerian Bosporos:
—gorgippia: **(1)** ii ad *NE* 9 (1971) p. 6 no. 3, 6 (*Μενέστ[ρατος]*); **(2)** s. ii ad *CIRB* 1129 A, 10 (*Μενέσ[τρατος]*?); **(3)** ~ ib. 1145, 8 (f. *Ἔρως*)
—hermonassa: **(4)** i ad ib. 1082 (f. *Ἵππαρχος*); **(5)** 173-210 ad ib. 1049 (*Ἰούλ. Μ.*) ?= (*34*)
—pantikapaion: **(6)** i bc/i ad ib. 321 (s. *Φιλότεχνος*); **(7)** 10-38 ad ib. 40, 4 (I f. *Μενέστρατος* II); **(8)** ~ ib. l. 4 (II s. *Μενέστρατος* I); **(9)** i/ii ad ib. 613; **(10)** 221 ad ib. 100, 5 (s. ..*δας*); **(11)** 275-278 ad ib. 36, 14 (s. *Γοσαμφλίας*); **(12)** ~ ib. l. 21 (f. *Εὔιος*); **(13)** ~ ib. l. 26 (*Μενέστρ(ατος)*: f. *Βαδάκης*); **(14)** ~ ib. l. 29 (*Μενέσ(τρατος)*: f. *Θαίβας*); **(15)** ~ ib. l. 32 (*Μενέστ(ρατος)*: s. *Ζήνων*) ?= (*18*); **(16)** ~ ib. l. 34 (I f. *Μενέστρατος* II); **(17)** ~ ib. l. 34 (II s. *Μενέστρατος* I); **(18)** ~ ib. l. 64 (*Μενέστ(ρατος)*: f. *Ζήνων*) ?= (*15*); **(19)** iv ad ib. 745 (f. *Φάρνης*)
—pantikapaion (nr.): **(20)** ii ad ib. 957 (f. *Στρατόδημος*)
—phanagoreia (nr.): **(21)** iii ad ib. 1016, 2 (s. *Ἀρδάρακος*)
Macedonia: **(22)** iii/ii bc *IG* xi (4) 785, 2, 8 (Tataki, *Macedonians* p. 369 no. 53) (s. *Παπύλος*)
Skythia:
—olbia-borysthenes: **(23)** ii ad *IOSPE* i² 100, 5 (s. *Δημήτριος*); **(24)** ~ ib. 686, 4 (*VDI* 1975 (1), p. 69) (f. *Δημήτριος*)
—olbia-borysthenes?: **(25)** iv/iii bc *SEG* xxxvii 681; xlii 728 (locn.) (-*σστρα*-)
—tanais: **(26)** ii ad *CIRB* 1262, 3 (*[Μ]ενέστρατος*: f. *Ἡγησ—*); **(27)** ~ ib. 1263, 19 (*Μενέστρα[τος]*); **(28)** ~ ib. l. 20; **(29)** ~ ib. 1264 A, 3 (*Μενέστρα[τος]*: f. *Εὐνώνας*); **(30)** f. ii ad ib. l. 12 (f. *—θους*); **(31)** 154-170 ad ib. 1260a, 17 (*[Με]νέστρατος*); **(32)** ~ ib. l. 19 (*Μενέστ[ρατ]ος*); **(33)** 188 ad ib. 1242, 16 (f. *Πολύκαρπος*); **(34)** 192 ad ib. 1243, 6 (*Ἰούλ. Μ.*) ?= (*5*); **(35)** c. 200-210 ad ib. 1277, 13 (*[Μ]ενέστρατος*: s. *Λυκίσκος*); **(36)** 224 ad ib. 1287, 9 (s. *Ἑρμῆς*); **(37)** 225 ad ib. 1279, 23 (f. *Ἀμαρδίακος*); **(38)** ~ ib. 1280, 20 (s. *Ζω—*); **(39)** 228 ad ib. 1282, 14 (f. *Μάδακος*); **(40)** ~ ib. 1283, 9 (f. *Ἀρίστων*); **(41)** 236 ad ib. 1250, 14 (s. *Φαδίναμος*)
Tauris:
—chersonesos: **(42)** s. iv bc Kats p. 123 no. 28 (amph.) (f. *Νεύπολις*) ?= (*43*); **(43)** f. iii bc ib. p. 105 no. 82 (amph.) (f. *Νεύπολις*) ?= (*42*); **(44)** c. 210-200 bc Anokhin p. 143 nos. 136; 141-2 (coins)
Thrace:
—byzantion: **(45)** 378 bc *IG* ii² 41, 23; **(46)** ii-i bc *Türk Tarih Kongresi XI* (6) p. 2703 with pl. 494. 3 (s. *Ἀρ..σης*)
——(Athyras): **(47)** i bc *IByz* 224 (Fıratlı–Robert p. 80 no. 94) (f. *Φιλήτα*)
—lysimacheia: **(48)** m. ii bc *ISestos* 38 a, 4 (s. *Ἀπολλωνίδης*)

Μενέφιλος
Macedonia (Orestis):
—battynaioi: **(1)** 192 ad *EAM* 186 III, 44 (s. *Ἀλέξανδρος*)
Scythia Minor:
—tomis: **(2)** ii-iii ad *ISM* ii 307, 1 (-*φη*-: f. *Ὀνεράτμις, Ἄττας*)
Thrace:
—apollonia-sozopolis: **(3)** hell.? *IGB* i² 462 (*Μενέφι[λος]*)

Μενέφρων
Thrace:
—byzantion: **(1)** ii bc *IByz* 284 (Fıratlı–Robert pp. 54-5 no. 32) (f. *Θεόδοτος*)
—nicopolis ad nestum: **(2)** ii ad *IGB* iv 2336, 7 (f. *—ων*)
—philippopolis-trimontium: **(3)** ii-iii ad ib. iii 894, 14 (f. *Ἀσκλ—*)

Μενέχαρμος
Scythia Minor:
—istros: **(1)** iv bc *ISM* i 171 (*CEG* ii 882) (s. *Εὐσθένης*); **(2)** ii bc *ISM* i 123 (*Μενέχαρ[μος]*); **(3)** i bc-i ad ib. 189, 6 (*[Μ]ενέχαρ[μος]*); **(4)** ii ad ib. 204, 10 (f. *Ἀπολλωνίδης*); **(5)** 138 ad ib. 193 II, 58 (s. *Σωσίας*)
Skythia:
—tanais: **(6)** iii ad *CIRB* 1253 (*Μενέχαρ(μ)[ος]*)
Thrace:
—isperih (mod.): **(7)** iv/iii bc *Chiron* 24 (1994) p. 262 n. 71 (s. *Ποσειδώνιος*)

Μένης
Macedonia (Bottiaia):
—pella: **(1)** 333-331 bc *RE* (2); Berve 507 (Tataki, *Macedonians* p. 157 no. 61) (s. *Διονύσιος*)
Thrace:
—lysimacheia: **(2)** m. ii bc *ISestos* 38 a, 6 (f. *Δημήτριος*)
—sestos: **(3)** m. ii bc ib. 1, [2], 93, 97 (f. *Μηνᾶς*)
—stryme?: **(4)** m. v bc *IThrakAig* E163 (*Μένεω* (gen.): f. *Ἡρόδωρος*)

Μενίδας
Macedonia: **(1)** 331-323 bc Berve 508 (Tataki, *Macedonians* p. 369 no. 54)
Macedonia (Mygdonia):
—kalindoia: **(2)** ii/i bc *SEG* xlii 593 (*(Μ)ενί<ι>δου* (gen.): f. *Κλεοπάτρα*)

Μενίδωρος
Skythia:
—tanais: **(1)** 228 ad *CIRB* 1282, 24 (f. *Ἡρακλείδης*)

Μένιππος
Cimmerian Bosporos:
—gorgippia: **(1)** f. iii bc ib. 1137 B II, 16 (s. *Βάττας*)
—pantikapaion: **(2)** f. ii ad ib. 716; cf. KW pl. 26 no. 384
Macedonia: **(3)** 208 bc *RE* (5) (Tataki, *Macedonians* p. 370 no. 55); **(4)** 193-191 bc *RE* (6); *IG* xi (4) 1111, 8; *SEG* xlviii 811; Sherk 34, 4 (Tataki, *Macedonians* p. 370 no. 56) (s. *Φανίας*)
Macedonia (Chalkidike):
—stolos?: **(5)** ?351 bc *SEG* xxxviii 673, 4 (s. *Θάμων*)
Macedonia (Derriopos):
—stuberra: **(6)** 74 ad *IG* x (2) (2) 325, 49 (f. *Σωσίας, Στρατόνικος*); **(7)** ~ ib. 326, 43 (s. *Λέων*)
Macedonia (Edonis):
—amphipolis: **(8)** c. 230-200 bc *BCH* 45 (1921) p. 18 III, 79 (Tataki, *Macedonians* p. 56 no. 86) (f. *Πυθίων*)
Macedonia (Mygdonia):
—thessalonike: **(9)** c. 230-200 bc *BCH* 45 (1921) p. 17 III, 67 (Tataki, *Macedonians* p. 185 no. 47) (s. *Πυθίων*)
—thessalonike?: **(10)** iii bc *IG* x (2) (1) 26, 6; cf. *Tyche* 10 (1995) pl. 4 no. 2 (*[Μ]ένιππος*: s. *Μηνοκράτης*)

Macedonia (Pelagonia)?: (11) ii ad *IG* x (2) (2) 186, 1, 3, 5 (or Arabia Felix Amara?: f. (ad.) *Κρατεύας, Παρμενίδης*)
Macedonia (Pieria):
—Dion: (12) iii bc *SEG* xlix 698; cf. Pandermalis, *Dion* p. 278 (f. *Παυσανίας*)
Scythia Minor:
—Istros: (13) ii bc *ISM* i 176 (f. *Φιλόθεος*)
Thrace:
—Byzantion?: (14) iii/ii bc *SEG* xxix 666 (f. *Ματρόδωρος*)
—Odessos: (15) i-ii ad *IGB* I² 194; (16) ii ad ib. 203 (*Μένιππ[ος]*); (17) f. ii ad ib. 78 ter, 4 (*CCET* i 30) (s. *Ἕλλην*); (18) iii ad *IGB* I² 141 bis (*[Μ]ένιπος*: f. *Χαρίδημος*); (19) 215 ad ib. 47 a, 25 (*Αὐρ. Μένιπος*: s. *Διονύσιος*); (20) ~ ib. 47 c, 12 (f. *Αὐρ. Θεόφιλος*)

Μενίσκος
Macedonia (Derriopos):
—Stuberra: (1) 74 ad *IG* x (2) (2) 326, 57 (f. *Φίλιππος*)
Macedonia (Mygdonia):
—Thessalonike: (2) ii-i bc ib. x (2) (1) 78, 3 (f. *Κλεινίας*); (3) f. i ad ib. 126, 5; Robert, *OMS* 5 pp. 295-302 (date) (*Ζωΐλος ὁ καὶ Μ.*: s. *Παρμενίων*)
—Thessalonike?: (4) f. i ad *IG* x (2) (1) 263, 3
Macedonia (Pieria):
—Phila?: (5) ?iii bc *RPh* 1911, pp. 133-4 no. 36, 95; cf. Helly, *L'État thessalien* pp. 319-20 (locn.) (*παρὰ Μενίσκου, παρ' Ἀμενίσκου*—*RPh*: s. *Σωσιγένης*)
Scythia Minor:
—Istros: (6) ii bc *ISM* i 58, 11 (*Μενίσ[κος]*); (7) ii-i bc ib. 125 (f. *Διονύσιος*); (8) ~ ib. 268 (f. *Ἱερώνυμος*); (9) i bc-i ad ib. 191 II, 52 (f. *Ἀπτηλᾶς*); (10) c. 90-89 bc *SEG* xlvii 1125, 28; (11) ii ad *ISM* i 137, 9 (*Μ[εν]ίσκος*: s. *Νουμήνιος*); (12) ~ ib. 212, 12 (s. *Κουσίας*); (13) ~ ib. l. 19 (s. *Ἀθηνάδης*); (14) 138 ad ib. 193 I, 24 (s. *Δημήτριος*); (15) ~ ib. l. 31 (*Φλ. Μ.*); (16) ~ ib. l. 68 (s. *Μοιρόδωρος*); (17) ~ ib. l. 70 (f. *Μόνιμος*); (18) ~ ib. l. 97 (f. *Φαιδρίας*); (19) ~ ib. 193 II, 49 (f. *Θεάδων*)
—Istros?: (20) iii/ii bc *Stud. Tacheva* pp. 280-1, 3, 46 (s. *Θεόδωρος*)
—Kallatis: (21) s. iii bc *ISM* iii 35 A, 27 (s. *Ἡρακλείδας*)
—Tomis: (22) hell. *Studii Cercetări Numismatică* i (1957) p. 280 no. 37 (weight) (*NZ* 10 (1917) p. 77 no. 9); (23) ii bc *SNG Stancomb* 284-5 (coin) (*Μενί(σκος)*?); (24) i bc *ISM* ii 2 B, 46 (s. *Σκύμνος*)
Thrace:
—Byzantion: (25) c. 350-325 bc *IOlbia* 9, 3 (Dubois, *IGDOlbia* 18) (*Μενίσκ[ος]*: f. *Δηλόπτιχος*); (26) c. 250-220 bc Schönert-Geiss, *Byzantion* 979-95; 1154-66; 1234 (coin); (27) c. 200-175 bc *IG* xi (4) 779, 8; 780, 3, 8 (f. *Θέων*); (28) ii bc *Türk Tarih Kongresi XI* (6) p. 2703 with pl. 494. 4 (f. *Ξένων*); (29) ~ *IByz* 74 (Fıratlı–Robert p. 50 no. 18) (f. *Εὐκλέων*); (30) ~ *IByz* 77 (Fıratlı–Robert p. 51 no. 24) (f. *Γαύκιον*); (31) ~ *IByz* 206 (Fıratlı–Robert pp. 66-7 no. 62) (I f. *Μενίσκος* II); (32) ~ *IByz* 206 (Fıratlı–Robert pp. 66-7 no. 62) (*Μενίσ[κος]*: II s. *Μενίσκος* I); (33) ~ *IByz* 216 (Fıratlı–Robert p. 75 no. 82a) (s. *Διονύσιος*); (34) ~ *IByz* 287 (Fıratlı–Robert pp. 55-6 no. 35) (s. *Βακίων*, f. *Βακίων*); (35) i-ii ad *IByz* 232 (*Με(ν)ί(σ)κος*?: f. *Τρακηλία*)
—Byzantion (territ.): (36) i bc ib. 179 (Fıratlı–Robert pp. 114-15 no. 191a) (f. *Ξένων*); (37) ~ *IByz* 179 (Fıratlı–Robert pp. 114-15 no. 191a) (s. *Ξένων*)
—Byzantion?: (38) i ad *IByz* 372 (f. *Διονύσις ὁ καὶ Πόπλιος*); (39) ii-iii ad ib. 367 (s. *Παυσᾶς*, f. *Ὑμνίς*)
—Perinthos-Herakleia: (40) c. 580-570 bc *IG* xii (6) 577, 1 (*[Με]νίσκος, [Κυ]νίσκος, [Φα]νίσκος*?: s. *Ξενόδοκος*); (41) i bc-i ad *IPerinth* 59 (f. *Σωκράτης*)
—Salymbria (nr.): (42) ?i bc *IByz* S 47 (PM 1737) (s. *Διόδωρος*)

Μεννέας
Macedonia (Bottiaia):
—Beroia: (1) a. 212 ad *IBer* 136, 18 (Tataki 998) (*Οὐλπ. Μ.*)
Macedonia (Edonis):
—Amphipolis (nr.): (2) a. 357 bc Hatzopoulos, *Actes Amphipolis* p. 43 no. 8, 3 (*SEG* xli 562) (s. *Ἄσανδρος*)
Macedonia (Mygdonia):
—Thessalonike: (3) s. ii bc *IG* x (2) (1) 27, 3 (f. —*έας*)
Thrace:
—Byzantion (territ.): (4) ii-i bc *IByz* 263 (f. *Διονύσιος*)

Μεννείας
Macedonia: (1) iii bc *IG* ix (2) 174 (Tataki, *Macedonians* p. 370 no. 57) (f. *Βούπλαγος*)

Μεννῆς
Macedonia (Bottiaia):
—Beroia?: (1) 105 ad *SEG* xvii 317, 8 (*Ἰουλ. Μ.*)

Μέννης
Scythia Minor:
—Tomis: (1) ii-iii ad *ISM* ii 277 (?f. *Ὑψίγονος*)
Thrace:
—Bizye (territ.): (2) ii ad *IGB* iii 1861, 4 (*Μεννήους* (gen.): f. *Γάϊος*)
—Bizye?: (3) imp. Unp. (Sayar)

Μεννίδας
Macedonia (Mygdonia):
—Kalindoia: (1) ii/i bc *SEG* xlii 595 (*Μεν[ν]ίδας*: s. *Δημήτριος*)
—Lete?: (2) 22 or 139 ad Dimitsas 678, 3 (s. *Δημήτριος*)

Μεννίδης
Macedonia (Bottiaia):
—Beroia: (1) ii bc *IBer* 141, 5
Macedonia (Mygdonia):
—Kalindoia: (2) 68-98 ad *SEG* xlii 580, 19 (s. *Ἡρακλείδης*)

Μεννύλος
Scythia Minor:
—Istros: (1) ii ad *ISM* i 196, 6; 201 I, 8 (s. *Χρυσίων*)

Μέννυς
Macedonia (Chalkidike):
—Potidaia-Kassandreia: (1) ii-iii ad *SEG* xxix 597 (f. *Μαρκιανός*)

Μενοίτας
Macedonia: (1) 332-316 bc *RE* (9); Berve 510 (Tataki, *Macedonians* p. 371 nos. 58-9) (s. *Ἡγήσανδρος*); (2) 267 bc *SEG* xxvii 1114, 10 b, 16 b (Tataki, *Macedonians* p. 371 no. 61) (f. *Στράτιππος*); (3) 171 bc *PTeb* 819, 43 (Tataki, *Macedonians* p. 371 no. 60; La'da E1540) (*Μενοίτ[ας], Μενοίτ[ιος]*?)
Tauris:
—Chersonesos: (4) iv/iii bc Solomonik, *NEPKh* 175 (f. *Εὔκριτος*)

Μενοίτης
Cimmerian Bosporos:
—Pantikapaion: (1) iv bc *IGAIMK* 104 (1935) p. 306 no. 55 (tile) (*Μενοί(της)*?, *Μενοί(τιος)*?)
Macedonia: (2) 144-141 bc *PBingen* 35, 6; cf. La'da E1566 (f. *Ὀλυμπιόδωρος*)

Μέντης
Thrace:
—Odessos: (1) i ad *IGB* I² 227, 1 (I f. *Μέντης* II); (2) ~ ib. l. 1, 5 (II s. *Μέντης* I); (3) ii ad ib. 183 (PM 1738) (s. *Νικίας*); (4) 215 ad *IGB* I² 47 a, 28 (f. *Αὐρ. Ἀπολλόδωρος*); (5) ~ ib. 47 b, 10 (f. *Αὐρ. Διονύσιος*); (6) 221 ad ib. 47 bis c, 21 (*Αὐρ. Μ.*: s. *Ἀγαθήνωρ*)

Μεντούτραλις
Thrace:
—Pautalia:
——Karistoron: (1) ii-iii ad ib. iv 2177

Μέντωρ
Macedonia (Pieria):
—Dion: (1) iv/iii bc *AE* 1910, p. 342 no. 2, 4 (Tataki, *Macedonians* p. 101 no. 8) (f. *Ἀγασικλῆς*); (2) iii bc *SEG* xxxiv 629 (f. *Ἀριστιώ*); (3) c. 230-200 bc *BCH* 45 (1921) p. 17 III, 54 (Tataki, *Macedonians* p. 100 no. 7) (s. *Ἀγαθοκλῆς*)

Μένυλλα
Macedonia (Chalkidike):
—Potidaia-Kassandreia: (1) ii bc *IG* xii (8) 178, 5 (Stephanis 1669; Tataki, *Macedonians* p. 92 no. 63) (d. *Ἱππόστρατος*)

Μένυλλος
Macedonia: (1) 322-319 bc *RE* (1); Berve 513 (Tataki, *Macedonians* p. 371 no. 62)
Macedonia (Edonis):
—Amphipolis: (2) hell. Dimitsas 853 (s. *Πυθόδωρος*)
Macedonia (Mygdonia):
—Kalindoia: (3) 68-98 ad *SEG* xlii 580, 46 (s. *Δημήτριος*)
Macedonia (Pieria):
—Pydna: (4) iv bc *GRBS* 43 (2002-3) p. 119 no. 5, 5
Skythia:
—Tanais: (5) 220 ad *CIRB* 1278, 26 (*[Μ]ένυλλο[ς]*—Tokhtas'ev: s. —*ος*)

Μένων
Cimmerian Bosporos:
—Nymphaion: (1) iii bc ib. 912 I, 9 (s. *Ἀντιφάνης*); (2) ~ ib. 912 III, 8 (s. *Π*—)
Macedonia: (3) 333 bc *RE* (10); Berve 514 (Tataki, *Macedonians* p. 372 no. 65) (s. *Κερδίμμας*); (4) 330-325 bc Berve 515 (Tataki, *Macedonians* p. 371 no. 63)
Macedonia (Bottiaia):
—Aigai: (5) c. 266 bc *IG* xii (9) 1187, 30; Robert, *Ét. num. gr.* pp. 179 ff. (date) (Tataki, *Macedonians* p. 41 no. 12) (f. *Ἀμύντας*)
—Beroia: (6) ii bc *IBer* 141, 3; (7) ii-i bc ib. 182 (Tataki 892) (f. *Ἀντίγονος*)
—Edessa: (8) ii/i bc *Ancient Macedonia* i p. 202 no. 16 (Tataki, *Edessa* 212) (f. *Φίλα*); (9) imp. Dimitsas 42 (Tataki, *Edessa* 211)
—Mieza?: (10) iii bc *SEG* xxiv 524 I, 7 (Hatzopoulos, *MI* 2 p. 106 no. 92)
Macedonia (Chalkidike):
—Antigoneia?: (11) ii ad *SEG* xxix 570, 2 (*Κλ. Μ.*: f. *Κλ. Θεαγένης, Κλ.* —*ωνος*)
—Olynthos: (12) m. v bc *Olynthus* 8 p. 117 (tile) (*-νōν*: kalos)
—Potidaia-Kassandreia?: (13) v/iv bc *SEG* xlvi 793 (?s. *Τι*—); (14) 285 bc ib. xxxviii 619, 15 (s. *Σωσικλῆς*)
Macedonia (Edonis):
—Amphipolis: (15) m. iii bc Hatzopoulos, *Actes Amphipolis* p. 50 no. 11, 10 (*SEG* xli 565) (f. *Ἐ*—)
Macedonia (Mygdonia):
—Kalindoia: (16) ii/i bc ib. xlii 593 (f. *Νικάνωρ*)
—Oraiokastro (mod.): (17) v-iv bc ib. xlix 750 (s. *Ἕσπερος*)
—Thessalonike: (18) ii ad *IG* x (2) (1) 57; 102, 11 (*[Μα]ξιμιανὸς Μ.*); (19) f. iii ad ib. 142, 12; 143, 11; 173, 6; 183, 3; 184, 3; 185,

3; *SEG* XLVI 815, 8; *Roman Onomastics* pp. 334-41 (*Κλ. Μ.*: I f. *Κλ. Ῥούφριος Πλωτῖνος, Κλ. Μένων* II *νέος, Ῥουφρία Κλ. Εὐβούλη, Ἰοῦστος*); (**20**) c. 225-230 AD *IG* X (2) (1) 144, 9; 183, 6; 184, 6; 185, 6; 209, 6; *Roman Onomastics* pp. 334-41 (*Κλ. Μ. νέος*: II s. *Κλ. Μένων* I); (**21**) 252-260 AD *SEG* XLIX 815, 6; 816, [6]; 817, 6 (*Τιβ. Κλ. Ῥούφριος Μ.*); (**22**) 258 AD *IG* X (2) (1) 168, 3 (*Φλ. Κλ. Μ. ὁ καὶ Στρυμόνις*); (**23**) iii/iv AD ib. 591 B, 1
MACEDONIA (PAIONIA):
—KAVADARCI (MOD.): (**24**) ii-iii AD *Sp.* 71 (1931) p. 70 no. 160 ([*Μ*]*ένων*: f. *Σεκοῦνδα, Πρίσκος*)
MACEDONIA (PAIONIA)?:
—ANTIGONEIA: (**25**) c. 171 BC Liv. xlii 58. 7 (Tataki, *Macedonians* p. 65 no. 6) (Lat. Meno)
MACEDONIA (PIERIA):
—PHILA?: (**26**) ?iii BC *RPh* 1911, pp. 133-4 no. 36, 80; cf. Helly, *L'État thessalien* pp. 319-20 (locn.) (*Μένῳ*[*ν*]: f. *Μενεκράτης*)
SCYTHIA MINOR:
—KALLATIS: (**27**) s. i AD *ISM* III 69, 5 (s. *Ἀρι*[*σ*]*τ*—)
SKYTHIA:
—OLBIA-BORYSTHENES: (**28**) vi/v BC *SEG* XLVIII 1012; (**29**) iii BC *IOSPE* I² 201 I, 27 (f. *Πολύμνηστος*)
THRACE: (**30**) hell. *Syringes* 1959 (Velkov 203; La'da E771); (**31**) 282-274 BC *PHib* 30, 22 (Velkov 336); cf. La'da E850 (f. —*λαος*)
—APOLLONIA-SOZOPOLIS: (**32**) iv BC *IGB* I² 463 bis, 1 (s. *Κράτιππος*)
—BYZANTION: (**33**) s. iv BC *IByz* 57 (Firatlı–Robert p. 47 no. 1) (f. *Δαμοφῶν*)
—ODESSOS: (**34**) ?ii AD *IGB* I² 94 (—*μένων*?: s. *Αὐλ*—)

Μερκούρις
THRACE:
—ODESSOS: (**1**) vi AD Beševliev 119, 6-7 (-*ρης*: s. *Κομητᾶς*)
—PAUTALIA: (**2**) ii AD *IGB* IV 2074, 13
—PAUTALIA (TERRIT.): (**3**) ii-iii AD ib. 2200

Μεσκήνις
MACEDONIA (ODOMANTIKE):
—SIRRHA: (**1**) ii-iii AD *Belomorski Pregled* 1 (1942) p. 321 no. 9 (Kaphtantzis 30) (f. *Μάρκελλος*)

Μεσσαλῖνος
SCYTHIA MINOR:
—TOMIS: (**1**) ii-iii AD *ISM* II 23, 4 (-*λεῖ*-) ?= (*2*); (**2**) ~ ib. l. 10 (-*λεῖ*-: f. *Μάγνος*) ?= (*1*)

Μεσσήνιος
SCYTHIA MINOR:
—ISTROS: (**1**) iv BC Unp. (Avram, defixio) 1, 1

Μέσσιος
CIMMERIAN BOSPOROS:
—PANTIKAPAION: (**1**) i-ii AD *CIRB* 672; cf. KW pl. 44 no. 634 (f. *Δροῦσος*)

Μέστα
MACEDONIA (EDONIS):
—PHILIPPOI: (**1**) ii AD *BCH* 56 (1932) pp. 230-1 no. 21 (Pilhofer 355) (*Φλ. Μέστ*[*α*]: m. *Δημοσθένης*)
MACEDONIA (LYNKESTIS):
—MELITI (MOD.): (**2**) f. iii AD *EAM* 166, 1 (m. *Ὀλυμπία, Ἀπολλόδωρος*)
MACEDONIA (PELAGONIA):
—DOSTONEIS: (**3**) ii AD *IG* X (2) (2) 199 (d. *Δημάρχη*)

Μέστας
MACEDONIA (SINTIKE):
—PARTHIKOPOLIS: (**1**) ii AD *IGB* IV 2284
—PARTHIKOPOLIS (NR.): (**2**) ii-iii AD ib. 2297 (*Αὐρ. Μαίστας*)

Μέστεις
MACEDONIA (MYGDONIA):
—KALINDOIA: (**1**) a. 98 AD *SEG* XLII 582, 29; cf. *Anthémonte–Kalindoia* 2 pp. 289-90 (name) (?s. *Πάρις*); (**2**) ~ *SEG* XLII 582, 32 (s. *Κοσουμάσης*); (**3**) ~ ib. l. 34 (s. *Δούλης*)

Μέστης
MACEDONIA (PIERIA):
—DION: (**1**) ii-iii AD Dimitsas 164 (*Μέξτεως* (gen.)—Dimitsas, *Μέστεως*?: f. *Ζαίπυρος*)

Μεστίκενα
MACEDONIA (PELAGONIA): (**1**) 67 AD *IG* X (2) (2) 250 (d. *Δούλης*)

Μεστίκενθος
MACEDONIA (ODOMANTIKE):
—SIRRHA (TERRIT.): (**1**) 26 AD *SEG* XLVI 708 (Pilhofer 557a) (f. *Κέτριζις*)
THRACE:
—NICOPOLIS AD NESTUM: (**2**) ii-iii AD *IGB* IV 2337, 9 ([*Μ*]*εστίκενθος*); (**3**) ~ ib. l. 11 ([*Μ*]*εστίκενθος*); (**4**) iii AD ib. 2343 (Kaphtantzis 480); cf. Pilhofer 527 (*Αὐρ. Μ.*: s. *Ἔζβενις*)
—NICOPOLIS AD NESTUM (TERRIT.): (**5**) ii AD *IGB* IV 2350 (s. *Βαστακείλας*)
—PAUTALIA (TERRIT.): (**6**) ii AD ib. 2214, 9 (f. *Τάρσας*); (**7**) ~ ib. l. 18; (**8**) ii-iii AD ib. V 5828 (*Μεστείκενθ*[*ος*])

Μεστικέντιος
THRACE: (**1**) iii AD *BIAB* 14 (1940-42) p. 231 no. 3 (bronze)

Μέστις
MACEDONIA (MYGDONIA):
—KALINDOIA: (**1**) iii AD *SEG* XLII 607 (f. —*ης*)

Μεστόης
THRACE:
—GOLJAMA BRESTNICA (MOD.): (**1**) iii AD *IGB* II 589 (*Μεστόη* (gen.): f. *Αὐρήλις*)

Μέστος
MACEDONIA (EDONIS):
—AMPHIPOLIS (TERRIT.)?: (**1**) 185 AD *BCH* 24 (1900) p. 308 (Pilhofer 592) (f. *Μάντας*)
—PHILIPPOI (TERRIT.): (**2**) ?ii AD *BCH* 47 (1923) p. 69 no. 25 (Pilhofer 514) (Lat. Mestus); (**3**) ?iii AD *SEG* XXX 594 B, 4 (Pilhofer 580) (s. *Βρ*(—))
—SKAPORENOI?: (**4**) ?ii AD *BCH* 24 (1900) p. 310 no. 3 (Pilhofer 512) (Lat. Mestus: f. *Ζιπᾶς*)
MACEDONIA (MYGDONIA):
—THESSALONIKE: (**5**) ii-iii AD *IG* X (2) (1) 468 (*Κ. Φούριος Μ.*: f. *Κ. Φούριος Ἑρμείας*)
MACEDONIA (ODOMANTIKE):
—GAZOROS: (**6**) 144 AD *SEG* XXX 599, 1 (Pilhofer 552); cf. *SEG* XXXVII 579 (f. *Μωμώ*)
—GAZOROS (TERRIT.): (**7**) 3 or 119 AD ib. XXXVIII 668 (Pilhofer 553) (f. *Κοζίλας*); (**8**) ii-iii AD *SEG* XXX 610 (Pilhofer 538) (f. *Δούλης, Μᾶρκος*)
—SIRRHA: (**9**) f. iii AD *SEG* XXX 590, 16 (f. *Αὐρ. Παίβης*)
MACEDONIA (PAIONIA):
—NEAPOLIS (AREA): (**10**) i AD ib. XVI 405
MACEDONIA (PELAGONIA): (**11**) ii-iii AD *IG* X (2) (2) 268 (f. *Ὀλυμπιάς*)
—DOSTONEIS?: (**12**) ii-iii AD ib. 204 (f. *Κῆσος*)
THRACE:
—NICOPOLIS AD NESTUM: (**13**) ii-iii AD *IGB* IV 2337, 5
—ODESSOS: (**14**) 215 AD ib. I² 47 b, 19 (*Ἰούλ. Μ.*: f. *Αὐρ. Ἡρακλιανός*)
—PHILIPPOPOLIS-TRIMONTIUM: (**15**) c. 303 AD *Anal. Boll.* 31 (1912) p. 192

Μεστούπορις
MACEDONIA (MYGDONIA):
—KALINDOIA: (**1**) a. 98 AD *SEG* XLII 582, 69; cf. *Anthémonte–Kalindoia* 2 p. 290 (name) (s. *Κότυς*)

Μεστριανός
MACEDONIA (MYGDONIA):
—THESSALONIKE?: (**1**) ii-iii AD *IG* X (2) (1) 754 ([*Μ*]*εστριανός*)
THRACE:
—GLAVA PANEGA (MOD.): (**2**) ii-iii AD *IGB* II 518 (*Αἴλ. Μ.*)
—GOLJAMA BRESTNICA (MOD.): (**3**) ii AD *Arkheologiia* (Sofia) 1960 (1), pp. 26-28 nos. 1 and 3 (*Φλ. Μ.*) ?= (*4*); (**4**) ii-iii AD *IGB* II 587 (*Φλ. Μ.*) ?= (*3*)
—NICOPOLIS AD NESTUM: (**5**) ii-iii AD ib. IV 2342, 2 (*Μεσστριαν*[*ός*]: s. —*λος*)
—PHILIPPOPOLIS-TRIMONTIUM: (**6**) iii AD *CIL* VI 32625 a, 13 (Lat. Aur. Mestrian(us))
—SERDICA (TERRIT.): (**7**) iii AD *IGB* IV 2034 (*Eastern cults* p. 168 no. 12); *IGB* IV 2036 (*Αὐρ. Μ.*)

Μέστριος
MACEDONIA (BOTTIAIA):
—BEROIA: (**1**) ii-iii AD *IBer* 282 (Tataki 894)
MACEDONIA (DERRIOPOS):
—ALKOMENA: (**2**) ii-iii AD *IG* X (2) (2) 351 (s. *Μεστύλας, Μώμα*)
MACEDONIA (MYGDONIA):
—THESSALONIKE?: (**3**) ii-iii AD ib. X (2) (1) 856, 3 (f. *Λούκιος, Ἀλέξανδρος, Δελοῦς, Αἴλ. Μέστριος*)
MACEDONIA (PAIONIA):
—BYLAZORA: (**4**) ii AD *Sp.* 98 (1941-8) p. 29 no. 73 (f. *Ἀμμία*) ?= (*5*); (**5**) ~ ib. p. 30 no. 74, 1, 3? (f. *Κάλης*) ?= (*4*)
—KAVADARCI (MOD.): (**6**) ii/iii AD Unp. (Kavadarci Mus.) inv. 13/II (s. *Ποντιανός*)
THRACE:
—PAUTALIA (TERRIT.): (**7**) iii AD *IGB* IV 2147, 11 (s. *Χαρίτιος*)

Μέστρις
MACEDONIA (DERRIOPOS):
—STUBERRA: (**1**) 74 AD *IG* X (2) (2) 326, 57-8 (s. *Μενέδημος*)
TAURIS:
—CHERSONESOS: (**2**) imp. *IOSPE* I² 435, 5

Μεστύλας
MACEDONIA (DERRIOPOS):
—ALKOMENA: (**1**) ii-iii AD *IG* X (2) (2) 351 (s. *Δούλης*, f. *Μέστριος*)
MACEDONIA (EDONIS):
—PHILIPPOI: (**2**) i-ii AD *AD* 30 (1975) Chron. p. 286 (Pilhofer 391) (Lat. Marronius Mestula: f. Postumius Firmus)
MACEDONIA (PAIONIA):
—NEAPOLIS (AREA): (**3**) ii-iii AD *Sp.* 71 (1931) p. 36 no. 76
THRACE:
—NICOPOLIS AD NESTUM: (**4**) ii-iii AD *IGB* IV 2337, 17 ([*Με*]*στύλας*)

Μεστύλης
MACEDONIA (PAIONIA):
—KAVADARCI (MOD.): (**1**) ii-iii AD *Sp.* 71 (1931) p. 67 no. 150 (*Μεστύλεος* (gen.): f. *Ἀλέξανδρος*)

Μεστύλος
MACEDONIA (BISALTIA):
—EUPORIA?: (**1**) imp.? *BCH* 24 (1900) p. 309 (Kaphtantzis 510)
MACEDONIA (EDONIS):
—AMPHIPOLIS: (**2**) 179 BC *SEG* XXXI 614, 8 + Hatzopoulos, *MI* 2 pp. 49-50 no. 29 (*Μεστ*[*ύλος*]?: s. *Μητρόδωρος*)
MACEDONIA (MYGDONIA):
—LETE: (**3**) ii AD *Makedonika* 2 (1951) p. 619 no. 42 *θ*, 18 (f. *Παράμονος*)

MACEDONIA (PELAGONIA):
—DOSTONEIS?: **(4)** ii-iii AD *IG* X (2) (2) 203 (*Μεσστύ<υ>λος*: f. *Ἐπιγένης*)
THRACE:
—BARGALA (AREA): **(5)** iii AD *Sp.* 98 (1941-8) p. 95 no. 209 (f. *Αὐρ. Ἐπταίκενθος*)

Μεστυπαίβης
MACEDONIA (EDONIS):
—SKIAZERENOI: **(1)** i-ii AD *SEG* XLVII 936 (Pilhofer 509a) (s. *Αὐλούζενις*)
THRACE:
—TĂMNO CAVE (MOD.): **(2)** ii-iii AD *IGB* II 751 a

Μέστυς
MACEDONIA (BOTTIAIA):
—BEROIA: **(1)** ?iii AD *IBer* 213 (Tataki 897) (f. *Ἀπολλωνία*); **(2)** 212 AD *ILeukopetra* 63, 6 (Tataki 898) (f. *Αὐρ. Ποσειδώνιος ὁ καὶ Παντακιανός*)
MACEDONIA (DERRIOPOS):
—STUBERRA: **(3)** 74 AD *IG* X (2) (2) 325, 62 (s. *Βίθυς*); **(4)** ~ ib. 326, 42 (s. *Παράμονος*); **(5)** ~ ib. l. 55 (*Μέ[σ]τυς*: s. *Κετρίπορις*); **(6)** 75 AD ib. l. 56 (f. *Κετρίπορις*)

Μετοέρασος?
MACEDONIA (BOTTIAIA):
—SKYDRA: **(1)** a. 212 AD *SEG* XXIV 530, 4

Μέτρα
MACEDONIA (PAIONIA):
—KAVADARCI (MOD.): **(1)** ii/iii AD Unp. (Papazoglu archive) (d. *Σεκοῦνδα*)

Μέτριος
THRACE:
—ZONE: **(1)** s. iv BC *PAE* 1970, p. 75 (vase) (n. pr.?)

Μέτρων
MACEDONIA: **(1)** 330 BC *RE* (2); Berve 520 (Tataki, *Macedonians* p. 373 no. 74)
MACEDONIA (PIERIA):
—PYDNA: **(2)** c. 326 BC *RE* (1); Berve 519 (Tataki, *Macedonians* p. 171 no. 11) (s. *Ἐπίχαρμος*)

Μετώ
MACEDONIA (EDONIS):
—AMPHIPOLIS?: **(1)** iii BC *SEG* XXIV 609 = XLIII 372 (d. *Πρόξενος*)

Μέτων
MACEDONIA (PIERIA):
—PHILA?: **(1)** ?iii BC *RPh* 1911, pp. 133-4 no. 36, 32; cf. Helly, *L'État thessalien* pp. 319-20 (locn.) (*Μέτω[ν]*)

Μεύακος
SKYTHIA:
—TANAIS: **(1)** 220 AD *CIRB* 1245, 19 (f. *Ναύακος*); **(2)** 225 AD ib. 1280, 14 (f. *Ἀντισθένης*); **(3)** ~ ib. l. 18 (f. *Να—ς*)

Μευαος
THRACE:
—ODESSOS: **(1)** f. iii AD *IGB* V 5070, 6 (?s. *Σάρδαυγος*, f. *Αὐρ. Γαειν*)

Μήδα
THRACE: **(1)** m. iv BC Satyr. ap. Ath. 557 d (d. *Κοθήλας*: queen)

Μήδειος
MACEDONIA (CHALKIDIKE):
—OLYNTHOS: **(1)** f. iii BC Austin–Bastianini, *Posidipp.* 95, 5; cf. *ZPE* 140 (2002) pp. 297-300 (ident.) (s. *Λάμπων*: doctor)

Μήδης
MACEDONIA (KRESTONIA):
—IOEON?: **(1)** i AD *SEG* XXVII 287 b (s. *Πάτραος*)

Μηδισαρσα
THRACE: **(1)** iii-ii BC Breccia, *Iscriz.* 250 (Velkov 206; La'da E859) (slave?)

Μηδίστας
THRACE: **(1)** c. 281-277 BC *IGB* I^2 307, 15; cf. V 5086 (*Μηδίστᾳ* (gen.): king?)
—ODRYSAI: **(2)** 356 BC *FD* III (1) 392, 3 (s. *Κερσεβλέπτης*)
—SEUTHOPOLIS: **(3)** iii BC *IGB* III 1732 (f. *Ἀμαίστας*)

Μήδοκος
THRACE: **(1)** 231 or 206 BC *CPR* XVIII 3, 47; cf. La'da E833 (f. *Μασάρτας*)

Μηδοσάδης
THRACE: **(1)** 400 BC X., *An.* vii 1. 5; vii 2. 10; vii 2. 24; **(2)** iv BC Hp., *Epid.* iv 45; Erot. p. 59, 20; cf. *Index Hipp.* s.v. *κατωμοσαδεω* (*κατομηδασαδέω* (n. pr.?)—cod. M)

Μηδοσακκος
SARMATIA:
—SARMATAI: **(1)** ?iii BC Polyaen. viii 56 (king)

Μήζακος
THRACE?: **(1)** iii BC *PPetr* II 19, 4 (Velkov 208)

Μήθακος
CIMMERIAN BOSPOROS:
—PANTIKAPAION: **(1)** f. iii AD *CIRB* 105, 7 (s. —*φ.ν*)
SKYTHIA:
—TANAIS: **(2)** 228 AD ib. 1282, 10 (s. *Στρατόνικος*)

Μηλίσκος
SCYTHIA MINOR:
—KALLATIS: **(1)** iii BC *ISM* III 15, 1 (*Μηδίσκος*?: s. *Ἀ—*)

Μηλόβιος
THRACE:
—BYZANTION:
——(Rhegion?): **(1)** hell.? *SGDI* 3074 (*IByz* 297) (*Μηλ(όβ)ιος?*—*SGDI*, *ΜΗΛΘΕΙΟΥ* (gen.)—apogr.: f. *Μᾶτρις*)

Μηνακῶν
THRACE:
—BYZANTION: **(1)** ii BC ib. 76 (Fıratlı–Robert p. 50 no. 21) (*Μηνακῶντος* (gen.): f. *Μηνοθέα*)
—BYZANTION?: **(2)** i AD *IByz* 329 (f. *Γόκων*)
—SALYMBRIA: **(3)** ?ii-i BC ib. S 32 (f. *Ὀζήα*)
—SALYMBRIA (NR.): **(4)** hell. ib. S 54 (s. *Τότης*, f. *Γλυκεία*); **(5)** ~ ib. (*Μ. ὁ καὶ Μενέδημος*: s. *Τότης*)

Μηνᾶς
CIMMERIAN BOSPOROS:
—HERMONASSA: **(1)** 123-132 AD *CIRB* 1054, 17 (f. *Μέγης*)
—PANTIKAPAION: **(2)** i AD ib. 332; cf. KW pl. 46 no. 650 (f. *Ἀθήνιος*); **(3)** i/ii AD *CIRB* 580; cf. KW pl. 18 no. 258 (f. *Ἀπολλώνιος*); **(4)** 275-278 AD *CIRB* 36, 32 (f. *Πόθος*)
MACEDONIA: **(5)** i AD *IG* II^2 9260 (Tataki, *Macedonians* p. 372 no. 66; *FRA* 3477) (f. *Εὐάδεια*)
MACEDONIA (ORESTIS): **(6)** iii-iv AD *EAM* 183 (*Μηνᾶ[ς]*)
SCYTHIA MINOR:
—ISTROS: **(7)** v-vi AD *SEG* XLIV 623 (vase)
—TOMIS?: **(8)** c. 490-500 AD Barnea 40 (c) (Popescu, *IGL* 64. 2) (*Μηννᾶ* (gen.))
SKYTHIA:
—TANAIS: **(9)** 244 AD *CIRB* 1287, 9 (s. *Νεοκλῆς*)

THRACE:
—BESSOI: **(10)** iv-vi AD *MAMA* III 592; cf. *SEG* XXXVII 1309 (ethn.)
—BISANTHE-PANION: **(11)** imp. Unp. (Sayar) (?s. *Μίδας*)
—BYZANTION: **(12)** ii BC *IByz* 126 (Fıratlı–Robert p. 101 no. 154) (s. *Μηνόθεμις*)
—BYZANTION (TERRIT.): **(13)** ii-i BC *IByz* 110 (f. *Ἀπφοῦς*)
—SESTOS: **(14)** m. ii BC *ISestos* 1, [2], 18, 47, 59, 92, 97 (s. *Μένης*)

Μηνιανός
THRACE:
—NICOPOLIS AD ISTRUM: **(1)** 238-241 AD *IGB* II 642, 10 (*Π. Αἰλ. Μ.*)
—PERINTHOS-HERAKLEIA:
——(φυλ. πρωτ.): **(2)** iii AD *IPerinth* 164 (*Αὐρ. Μ.*: s. *Ἀσκληπιάδης*)

Μηνίας
MACEDONIA (EDONIS):
—AMPHIPOLIS: **(1)** s. iv BC *PAE* 1981, p. 25 with pl. 43 *β*, 13

Μήνιος
CIMMERIAN BOSPOROS:
—PANTIKAPAION: **(1)** i BC *CIRB* 281 (s. *Μαμία*); **(2)** i AD ib. 332; cf. KW pl. 46 no. 650 (s. *Ἀθήνιος*, *Ἀρέτη*); **(3)** f. i AD *CIRB* 366 (f. *Βασιλείδης*); **(4)** 82 AD ib. 76, 9 (*SEG* XVIII 310) (s. *Βράδακος*); **(5)** ii AD *CIRB* 695 (f. *Μῆνις*); **(6)** f. ii AD ib. 84, 2; cf. KW pl. 45 no. 648 (I f. *Μήνιος* II); **(7)** ~ *CIRB* 84, 2; cf. KW pl. 45 no. 648 (II s. *Μήνιος* I); **(8)** ~ *CIRB* 88, 2 (f. *Χαρίτων*)
—THEODOSIA: **(9)** iii AD ib. 947 B, 12 (*Μήν[ιο]ς*: s. *Τόκων*)
SCYTHIA MINOR:
—ISTROS: **(10)** i BC-i AD *ISM* I 191 II, 48 (f. *Ἀριστομένης*); **(11)** 138 AD ib. 193 I, 26 (f. *Διονύσιος*); **(12)** ~ ib. 193 II, 26 (f. *Δάδας*); **(13)** ~ ib. l. 32 (*Αἰλ. Μ.*); **(14)** ~ ib. l. 42 (f. *Ἡρόφαντος*)
—KALLATIS: **(15)** ii/iii AD ib. III 183, 1 (II 362) (-νει-: f. *Παπίας*)
SKYTHIA:
—TANAIS: **(16)** ii AD *CIRB* 1263, 14 (*Μήνιο[ς]*); **(17)** 210-226 AD ib. 1285, 14 (s. *Ἑρμ—*); **(18)** 225-230 AD ib. 1280, 31; 1284, 19 (f. *Δαναράζμακος*); **(19)** 227-233 AD ib. 1247, 7 (s. *Χαρίτων*)
THRACE:
—BYZANTION: **(20)** c. 250-230 BC *IG* VII 339, 1 (*IOrop* 115) (s. *Ζωΐλος*); **(21)** s. iii BC *IByz* 305 (f. *Ἀπολλᾶς*); **(22)** ii BC ib. 75 (Fıratlı–Robert p. 50 no. 19) (s. *Δαμᾶς*); **(23)** ~ *IByz* 291 (Fıratlı–Robert pp. 113-14 no. 189) (f. *Ἧρις*); **(24)** ii-i BC *IByz* 256 (Fıratlı–Robert p. 71 no. 74) (s. *Ἀπολλόδωρος*); **(25)** ii/i BC *IByz* 168 (Fıratlı–Robert p. 109 no. 175) (f. *Μοσχίων*); **(26)** hell.-imp. *IByz* 302 (f. *Διόνυσος*); **(27)** c. 90 BC *SEG* XLVII 1125, 10 (*[Μή]νιος*?); **(28)** ii AD *IByz* 18 (I f. *Μήνιος* II); **(29)** ~ ib. (II s. *Μήνιος* I); **(30)** 117-138 AD ib. 37, 5 (s. *Ἀλέξανδρος*) ?= (*31*); **(31)** ~ ib. l. 9 (f. *Χρυσίων*) ?= (*30*)
—BYZANTION (TERRIT.): **(32)** ii-i BC ib. 162 (Fıratlı–Robert p. 107 no. 170)
—BYZANTION:
——(Rhegion): **(33)** ii BC *IByz* 99 (Fıratlı–Robert p. 94 no. 129) (f. *Ἀπολλωνίδας*)
—BYZANTION?: **(34)** ?iii BC *IByz* 347 (PM 844; *IKalch* 52) (or Bithynia Kalchedon: f. *Δαμάτριος*); **(35)** ii-i BC *IByz* 343 (f. *Ζώα*); **(36)** i BC ib. 364 (s. *Ἑρμάφιλος*); **(37)** ~ ib. 369 (PM 1663) (s. *Διλίπορις*); **(38)** i BC-i AD *IByz* 337 (Fıratlı–Robert p. 129 no. 219) (f. *Μενεκράτης*); **(39)** ii AD *IByz* 360 = *ISestos* 6; cf. Fıratlı–Robert p. 173 (f. *Δαμᾶς*)
—BYZANTION (TERRIT.)?: **(40)** imp. *BCH* 36 (1912) p. 598 no. 57 (f. *Παπίας*)

—ODESSOS: **(41)** 215 AD *IGB* I^2 47 a, 17 (f. *Αὐρ. Διονύσιος*); **(42)** 221 AD ib. 47 bis a, 37 (f. *Αὐρ. Ἀσκληπιάδης*)
—SALYMBRIA: **(43)** ?i BC *IByz* S 49 (PM 1753) (f. *Φιλήτα*)
—SALYMBRIA (NR.): **(44)** hell. *IByz* S 55 (s. *Μήτοκος*)

Μῆνις
CIMMERIAN BOSPOROS:
—PANTIKAPAION: **(1)** ii AD *CIRB* 695 (s. *Μήνιος*)
SCYTHIA MINOR:
—ISTROS: **(2)** f. iii AD *Stud. Fischer* p. 32 no. 4, 2 (s. *Ἀρτεμ—*)
—KALLATIS: **(3)** s. iii BC *ISM* III 35 B, 22 (s. *Ἱκέσιος*); **(4)** iii/ii BC ib. 161 (s. *Σάτυρος*)
—TOMIS: **(5)** i BC ib. II 2 A, 52 (s. *Ἀρτεμίδωρος*); **(6)** ~ ib. l. 58 (s. *Ἀπολλόδωρος*)
TAURIS:
—CHERSONESOS: **(7)** c. 285-262 BC Kats p. 104 no. 79; p. 123 no. 27 (amph.) (s. *Δαμοκλῆς*); **(8)** s. iii BC ib. p. 108 no. 94 (amph.) (f. *Πολύκτωρ*); **(9)** c. 120-88 BC *IOSPE* I^2 352, 57 (s. *Ἡράκλειος*)
THRACE:
—BYZANTION: **(10)** ii-i BC *ASAA* 2 (1916) p. 164 no. 106; **(11)** i BC *IByz* 114 (*[Μῆ]νις*?: s. *Κόλλος*)
—BYZANTION (TERRIT.): **(12)** ii-iii AD ib. 28 (*IGB* I^2 474) (f. *Ἀριστόβουλος*)
—LYSIMACHEIA: **(13)** m. ii BC *ISestos* 38 b, 1 (f. *Μοῖρις*)
—MESAMBRIA: **(14)** iii BC *IGB* I^2 335 (PM 842); cf. *IGB* V 5107 (s. *Ἀθαναίων*)
—NICOPOLIS AD ISTRUM (TERRIT.): **(15)** 227 AD *ILB* 438 II, 14 (Lat. Menis (gen.): f. *Μουκάπορις*)

Μηνογένης
MACEDONIA: **(1)** hell. *SEG* XXIX 230 (Tataki, *Macedonians* p. 372 no. 67; *FRA* 3478); **(2)** f. iii BC *Dritte Reise* 47, 3 (Tataki, *Macedonians* p. 372 no. 68) (s. *Ἀριστοκλῆς*)
MACEDONIA (MYGDONIA):
—LETE: **(3)** c. 160-180 AD *SEG* XLVII 974; *KGAM Thess.* I 123 (date) (*Αἰλ. Μ.*)
THRACE:
—HERAION TEICHOS: **(4)** c. 45-42 BC *IGB* I^2 43, 3, 26 (s. *Ἀσκληπίδης*)

Μηνόδοτος
CIMMERIAN BOSPOROS:
—PANTIKAPAION: **(1)** i AD *CIRB* 410; cf. KW pl. 56 no. 757
THRACE:
—BYZANTION: **(2)** 117-138 AD *IByz* 37, 3 (f. *Ποτάμων*); **(3)** ~ ib. l. 7 (s. *Τιμογένης*)
—MARONEIA: **(4)** ii AD *IThrakAig* E279 (s. *Ἰσίδωρος*)
—TOPEIROS: **(5)** iii AD *AD* 24 (1969) Chron. p. 348 (*IThrakAig* E90) (f. *Φίλων*)

Μηνοδώρα
MACEDONIA (CHALKIDIKE):
—POLICHNE (NR.)?: **(1)** i AD *TAPA* 69 (1938) p. 70 no. 26 (d. *Φιλόξενος*)

Μηνόδωρος
CIMMERIAN BOSPOROS:
—GORGIPPIA: **(1)** ii/iii AD *CIRB* 1179, 40 (s. *Βώρακος*)
—HERMONASSA: **(2)** i-ii AD ib. 1083 (*Μηνόδ(ω)ρος*: s. *Φιλοξενίδης*)
—PANTIKAPAION: **(3)** 284-245 BC ib. 21 (f. *Ἑστιαία*); **(4)** i BC ib. 285 (s. *Νάνα*); **(5)** s. i BC ib. 125, 1, 7 (*GVI* 710) (*Μηνεόδωρος*—l.7: s. *Ἡλιόδωρος*); **(6)** i AD *CIRB* 398; cf. KW pl. 13 no. 202; **(7)** s. i AD *CIRB* 374 (f. *Γάϊος*); **(8)** 133 AD ib. 675, 6 (f. *Μηνόκριτος*)

MACEDONIA (CHALKIDIKE):
—POTIDAIA-KASSANDREIA: **(9)** 209 or 208 BC *IRhamnous* 51, 23 (*FRA* 2791) (*Μηνόδωρος*)
MACEDONIA (EDONIS):
—PHILIPPOI (TERRIT.): **(10)** hell.? Dimitsas 1080 (fals.?) (Pilhofer 663) (*Μινόδωρος*—apogr.: s. *Σωσθένης*)
MACEDONIA?: **(11)** f. ii BC Bernand, *Inscr. métr.* 4 (*GVI* 1149; Tataki, *Macedonians* p. 490 no. 168) (*Μηνόοδωρος*—metr. c.: s. *Πτολεμαῖος*)
SCYTHIA MINOR:
—ISTROS: **(12)** i BC-i AD *ISM* I 186 (s. *Βιάνωρ*)
SKYTHIA:
—OLBIA-BORYSTHENES: **(13)** i/ii AD *IOlbia* 88, 6 (f. *Ῥαμάναγος*); **(14)** ii-iii AD *IOSPE* I^2 137, 6 (s. *Ποντικός*)
THRACE:
—ABDERA: **(15)** ii-i BC *SEG* XXIV 627 (*IThrakAig* E62) (s. *Ἀριστοκλῆς*)
—APOLLONIA-SOZOPOLIS: **(16)** iv BC *IGB* I^2 423 (f. *Ἑκατόδωρος*)
—BYZANTION: **(17)** hell.-imp. *IByz* 301 (I f. *Μηνόδωρος* II); **(18)** ~ ib. (II s. *Μηνόδωρος* I)
——(Athyras): **(19)** hell.-imp. ib. 250 (*Μηνόδω[ρος]*)
—ODESSOS: **(20)** c. 45-42 BC *IGB* I^2 43, 2 (f. *Ζωΐλος*); **(21)** s. ii AD ib. 182 (PM 1611); *Dacia* 21 (1977) p. 161 (date) (f. *Ἀνθεστήριος*); **(22)** 221 AD *IGB* I^2 47 bis a, 30 (f. *Αὐρ. Ἀνθεστήριος*)
—PERINTHOS-HERAKLEIA: **(23)** ii-i BC *IPerinth* 50 (f. *Ἀρτεμίδωρος*)
—SALYMBRIA (NR.): **(24)** hell. *IByz* S 53 (f. *Διοδώρα*)
—SALYMBRIA?: **(25)** iii AD *AEMÖ* 17 (1894) p. 57 no. 3, 8 (or Thrace Perinthos-Herakleia: *Αὐρ. Μη[ν]όδωρος*: s. *Αὐρ. Νέων Νεοκοριανός, Αὐρ. Δημητρία*)

Μηνοθέα
THRACE:
—BYZANTION: **(1)** ii BC *IByz* 76 (Fıratlı–Robert p. 50 no. 21) (d. *Μηνακῶν*)

Μηνόθεμις
THRACE:
—BYZANTION: **(1)** ii BC *IByz* 126 (Fıratlı–Robert p. 101 no. 154) (f. *Μηνᾶς*)

Μηνοκράτης
MACEDONIA (MYGDONIA):
—THESSALONIKE?: **(1)** iii BC *IG* X (2) (1) 26, 6; cf. *Tyche* 10 (1995) pl. 4 no. 2 (*Μην[οκ]ράτεως* (gen.): f. *Μένιππος*)

Μηνόκριτος
CIMMERIAN BOSPOROS:
—PANTIKAPAION: **(1)** 133 AD *CIRB* 675, 8 (s. *Μηνόδωρος*)

Μηνοφάνης
THRACE:
—BYZANTION: **(1)** c. 200 BC *IG* II^2 884, 11, 16 (s. *Ἀσκλαπιάδας*)
—PERINTHOS-HERAKLEIA:
——(Basileidai): **(2)** s. iii BC *IPerinth* 62, 5 (f. *Σώστρατος*)

Μηνοφίλα
THRACE: **(1)** imp. *IG* II^2 8915 (*FRA* 2556) (*Μηνοφ[ίλα]*: d. *Ἀθηνίων*)

Μηνόφιλος
CIMMERIAN BOSPOROS:
—GORGIPPIA: **(1)** f. iii BC *CIRB* 1137 B II, 43 (s. *Ἵππων*)
—PANTIKAPAION: **(2)** i BC/i AD ib. 313; cf. KW pl. 40 no. 593 (s. *Δημόστρατος*); **(3)** 143 AD *CIRB* 710, 3
MACEDONIA: **(4)** 173 BC *PGiss* 2 II, 9 (Tataki, *Macedonians* p. 372 no. 70; La'da E1541)

MACEDONIA (KRESTONIA):
—IORON: **(5)** i BC-i AD *SEG* XLVIII 816. 5 (sherd) (*Μηνόφι[λος]*)
MACEDONIA (PAIONIA): **(6)** 177 BC *SGDI* 2027, 5, 6 (slave/freed.)
SKYTHIA:
—TANAIS: **(7)** ii AD *CIRB* 1262, 13 (f. *Ἔρως*); **(8)** ~ ib. l. 16 (*[Μ]ηνόφιλος*: s. *Ἀγαθοδ—*); **(9)** f. ii AD ib. 1264 A, 5 (*[Μ]ηνόφιλος*: s. *Χρηστίων*); **(10)** c. 220-230 AD ib. 1282, 6; 1286, 7 (f. *Εὐσχήμων*); **(11)** 225 AD ib. 1279, 9 (s. *Μοσχᾶς*)
TAURIS:
—CHERSONESOS: **(12)** imp.? *IAK* 20 (1906) p. 68 (vase) (f. *Σκύμνος*) ?= (*13*); **(13)** ~ ib. (vase) ?= (*12*)
THRACE:
—BYZANTION: **(14)** ?ii-i BC *IByz* 374 (f. *Θεοδᾶς*); **(15)** ~ ib. (s. *Θεοδᾶς*); **(16)** i BC-i AD ib. 230 (Fıratlı–Robert p. 83 no. 101) (f. *Ἑρμόδωρος*); **(17)** i-ii AD *IByz* 106 (Fıratlı–Robert p. 96 no. 137) (s. *Γαῦρος*); **(18)** ii AD *IByz* 321 (f. *Ἀπολλώνιος*)
—LYSIMACHEIA: **(19)** ii-i BC *ISmyrna* 689 III, 31 (f. *Ἀρχίας*)
—MARKIANOPOLIS (TERRIT.): **(20)** f. iii AD *Romanizmăt* II 579 (Lat. Menophilus)
—MARONEIA: **(21)** ii-i BC *IThrakAig* E212, 12 (I f. *Μηνόφιλος* II); **(22)** ~ ib. l. 12 (II s. *Μηνόφιλος* I)
—PERINTHOS-HERAKLEIA: **(23)** i BC-i AD? *IPerinth* 57, 9 (I f. *Μηνόφιλος* II); **(24)** ~ ib. l. 9 (II s. *Μηνόφιλος* I)
—SALYMBRIA: **(25)** imp. *Archives Stamoulis* d. 35 (Loukopoulou, *Thrace Propontique* p. 278)

Μηνοφῶν
THRACE:
—PERINTHOS-HERAKLEIA:
——(Geleuntes): **(1)** iii-ii BC *IPerinth* 61, 32 (f. *Σῖμος*)

Μηριγένης
MACEDONIA (EORDAIA):
—RYAKI (MOD.): **(1)** 5 AD *EAM* 97 (f. *Σταδμέας*)

Μηριόνης
CIMMERIAN BOSPOROS:
—PANTIKAPAION: **(1)** s. i AD *CIRB* 342; cf. KW pl. 19 no. 274

Μηρύλος
MACEDONIA (BOTTIAIA):
—BEROIA: **(1)** 177 AD *IBer* 135 A, 18 (Tataki 899) (*Μηρύλου* (gen.): f. *Νίκανδρος*)

Μήσακος
SKYTHIA:
—TANAIS: **(1)** 210-226 AD *CIRB* 1281, 19 (f. *—σάρακος*)

Μήστωρ
CIMMERIAN BOSPOROS:
—HERMONASSA: **(1)** 344-311 BC ib. 1039 (s. *Ἱπποσθένης*)
—PANTIKAPAION: **(2)** iv/iii BC *MIA* 56 (1957) p. 101 (tile) (*Sov. Arkh.* 28 (1958) pp. 129-30 no. 8) (*Μήστο(ρος)* (gen.))

Μήτακος
SKYTHIA:
—OLBIA-BORYSTHENES: **(1)** ii AD *IOSPE* I^2 101, 10; Zgusta, *PNS* 310 (-*ταγος*: s. *Πουρθάκης*); **(2)** ?ii-iii AD *IOSPE* I^2 108; **(3)** ~ ib. I^2 110, 3 (*Μήτα[κος]*?: ?f. *—ν*); **(4)** f. ii AD ib. I^2 85, 3; 106, 11 (*[Μήτ]ακος*—85: f. *Ἀτάδων*); **(5)** f. iii AD ib. 185, 2 (*Μήτα[γ]ος, Μήτα[κ]ος*?)

Μήτοκος
MACEDONIA (SINTIKE):
—PARTHIKOPOLIS (NR.): **(1)** 165 AD *IGB* IV 2288 (f. *Πυρέτης*)
MACEDONIA?: **(2)** f. i BC *Xenia antiqua* 10 (2001) p. 19 nos. A-B (or Thrace: s. *Βαστικίλας, Ζαικίς*)

THRACE:
—APOLLONIA-SOZOPOLIS: **(3)** i-ii AD *IGB* I^2 400 (s. (nat.) *Δέκμος*, s. (ad.) *Ταρούλας*)
—KABYLE*: **(4)** iii-ii BC *Act. IX Ep. Congr.* p. 237 (coin) (*Μήτ(οκος)*)
—ODRYSAI: **(5)** c. 450-389 BC *RE* s.v. Medokos (-); *IG* II^2 22 a, 2, 4; Peter, *MTD* pp. 89-99 (coin); cf. *RE* s.v. Amadokos (2) (*Μητόκō* (gen.)—coins, *Μήδοκος*—*IG* & lit. test., *Ἀμάδοκος*—var. lect.: f. *Ἀμάτοκος*: king)
—SALYMBRIA (NR.): **(6)** hell. *IByz* S 54 (f. *Μηνακῶν ὁ καὶ Μενέδημος*); **(7)** ~ ib. S 55 (f. *Μήνιος*)
THRACE?: **(8)** hell. *PStrassb* 114, 1; **(9)** ~ *Memnonion* 607 (Velkov 209)

Μητος
KOLCHIS:
—ITHKHVISI (MOD.): **(1)** m. v BC *Archeologia* (Warsaw) 17 (1966) p. 52 with fig. 2 (vase) + Braund, *Georgia* p. 101 (*Μετος*—*Archeologia*)

Μητρᾶς
MACEDONIA (MYGDONIA):
—KALINDOIA: **(1)** a. 98 AD *SEG* XLII 582, 51 (s. *Διονύσιος*)

Μητρικέτης
THRACE:
—PERINTHOS-HERAKLEIA: **(1)** c. 265-260 BC *FD* III (3) 207, 3 (*Μα*-: s. *Παντέας*)

Μῆτρις
CIMMERIAN BOSPOROS:
—NYMPHAION: **(1)** f. iv BC *CIRB* 922 (s. *Ἡγήτωρ*)

Μητρίχη
SCYTHIA MINOR:
—ISTROS (NR.): **(1)** f. vi BC *ISM* I 361 (vase)

Μήτριχος
MACEDONIA (CHALKIDIKE):
—OLYNTHOS: **(1)** ?350 BC *TAPA* 62 (1931) p. 43 no. 2, 3; Hatzopoulos, *Actes Chalc.* p. 80 (date) (f. *Ἀρχίδαμος*)
MACEDONIA (EDONIS):
—AMPHIPOLIS?: **(2)** hell. *SEG* L 562, 8 (s. *Ἀλέξανδρος*)

Μητροβία
SKYTHIA:
—OLBIA-BORYSTHENES: **(1)** ii BC *IOSPE* I^2 220 a; cf. KW pl. 26 no. 381 (d. *Ποσίδεος*, m. *Δημήτριος*)

Μητροβίη
CIMMERIAN BOSPOROS:
—PANTIKAPAION: **(1)** m. iv BC *CIRB* 204 (*Μητροβ[ί]η*)
THRACE:
—APOLLONIA-SOZOPOLIS: **(2)** s. v BC *IGB* I^2 417 (d. *Διόμανδρος*)

Μητρόβιος
CIMMERIAN BOSPOROS:
—PANTIKAPAION: **(1)** iv BC *CIRB* 202 (f. *Μαχορδίκη*); **(2)** ~ ib. 205 (s. *Βούλιος*)
MACEDONIA (EDONIS):
—AMPHIPOLIS: **(3)** ?iii BC *IG* II^2 8084 (*FRA* 515) (s. *Ἑρμίας*); **(4)** ii BC *IG* II^2 8084 bis (Tataki, *Macedonians* p. 56 no. 87; *FRA* 513) (*Μητρό[βιος]*: s. *Ἑρμίας*); **(5)** ii-i BC *IG* II^2 8085 (Tataki, *Macedonians* p. 56 no. 88; *FRA* 514) (s. *Ἑρμίας*)
MACEDONIA (PAIONIA):
—DEMIR KAPIJA (MOD.): **(6)** iii BC *BCH* 98 (1974) p. 279 (s. *Ἀγαθοκλῆς*)
SCYTHIA MINOR:
—ISTROS: **(7)** ii BC *ISM* I 173 (f. *Ἀπολλώνιος*)
SKYTHIA:
—OLBIA-BORYSTHENES: **(8)** iv BC *IOSPE* I^2 165 ([*Μητ*]*ρόβιος*)
THRACE:
—PERINTHOS-HERAKLEIA:
——(Geleuntes): **(9)** iii-ii BC *IPerinth* 61, 29 (f. *Πυθίων*)

Μητρόδοτος
THRACE:
—MARONEIA: **(1)** c. 432-423 BC Schönert-Geiss, *Maroneia* 93-132 (coin); **(2)** hell. *IThrakAig* E245 (*Μητρόδοτος*: ?s. —*ανα*—); **(3)** ii-i BC ib. E212, 21 (I f. *Μητρόδοτος* II); **(4)** ~ ib. l. 21 (II s. *Μητρόδοτος* I); **(5)** f. ii BC *SEG* XXXIV 709 (*IThrakAig* E278) (f. *Νουμήνιος*); **(6)** s. ii BC *IG* XII (8) 170 c, 41 + XII Suppl. p. 148 (f. *Δόρκος*)
—STRYME?: **(7)** s. v BC *SEG* XXVII 337 (*IThrakAig* E115) (*Μητρόδοτος*: f. *Μητροφῶν*); **(8)** c. 400-375 BC ib. E164 (s. *Ἀρτέμων*); **(9)** c. 375-350 BC ib. E140 (f. *Ἀσπώ*)
—STRYME? (NR.): **(10)** v/iv BC *BCH* 79 (1955) p. 283 = Bakalakis, *Oinos Ismarikos* p. 552 (*IThrakAig* E128) (s. *Ἥρανδρος*)
—ZONE: **(11)** f. iv BC *AA* 1918, col. 11 (*IThrakAig* E416) (f. *Ῥόδη*)

Μητροδώρα
MACEDONIA (EDONIS):
—AMPHIPOLIS: **(1)** i BC *IG* II^2 8086 (Tataki, *Macedonians* p. 56 no. 89; *FRA* 516)
THRACE:
—ABDERA: **(2)** ii BC *SEG* XLVII 1033, 3 (*IThrakAig* E59)

Μητροδώρη
CIMMERIAN BOSPOROS:
—PANTIKAPAION: **(1)** iv BC *CIRB* 206 (*Μητροδώ[ρη]*: d. *Αἰσχρίων*)

Μητρόδωρος
CIMMERIAN BOSPOROS:
—BOSPOROS: **(1)** iv BC Polyaen. viii 55 (s. *Σάτυρος*)
—PANTIKAPAION: **(2)** iv-iii BC *CIRB* 747 (s. *Ἀρτέμων*); **(3)** f. iv BC ib. 207; cf. KW pl. 1 no. 4 (s. *Ἀπολλόδωρος*); **(4)** iii-ii BC *CIRB* 254 (s. *Νίκανδρος*); **(5)** imp. ib. 799; **(6)** i AD ib. 135, 2 (*GVI* 1362); cf. KW pl. 29 no. 406 (f. *Θεόδωρος*); **(7)** ~ *CIRB* 562 (*Μητρά*-: f. *Μαστοῦς*)
MACEDONIA: **(8)** 228 BC *Milet* I (3) 99, 3 (s. *Στράτων*) ?= (*9*); **(9)** 202 BC *RE* (2) (Tataki, *Macedonians* p. 373 no. 72); cf. Walbank 2 p. 479 ?= (*8*); **(10)** 168 BC *RE* (3) (Tataki, *Macedonians* p. 373 no. 71)
MACEDONIA (BOTTIAIA):
—BEROIA: **(11)** ii AD *IBer* 363, 3 (Tataki 900) ([*Μ*]*ητρόδωρος*: s. *Αἰλιανός*); **(12)** ii/iii AD *IBer* 27 B, 10 (slave?)
MACEDONIA (EDONIS):
—AMPHIPOLIS: **(13)** f. iii BC *OGIS* 220, 4, 10 (*IIlion* 34); *ICos* ED 190, [5]; *RE* (28) (Tataki, *Macedonians* p. 57 no. 91) (s. *Τιμοκλῆς*: doctor); **(14)** b. 213 BC Hatzopoulos, *MI* 2 p. 83 no. 61, 10 (*SEG* XLVI 715) ([*Μ*]*ητρόδωρος*); **(15)** 179 BC ib. XXXI 614, 9 (Hatzopoulos, *MI* 2 pp. 49-50 no. 29) (f. *Μεστύλος*); **(16)** 37 BC Robert, *Coll. Froehner* 44, 16 (Tataki, *Macedonians* p. 57 no. 90) (s. *Βίθυς*)
—PHILIPPOI: **(17)** ii/iii AD *CIL* III 633 II a, 3 (Pilhofer 163); *CRAI* 1923, p. 277 (date); Collart, *Philippes* pls. 64-5 (Lat. Metrodorus: f. *Ἑρμέρως*)
MACEDONIA (MYGDONIA):
—APOLLONIA: **(18)** f. ii BC *SEG* XLIV 508 (Hatzopoulos, *MI* 2 p. 87 no. 66) (f. *Ἑρμογένης*)
—KALINDOIA: **(19)** i BC *SEG* XLII 589 (s. *Ἀπολλώνιος*)
MACEDONIA (ODOMANTIKE):
—SIRRHA: **(20)** ii-iii AD ib. XXX 613, 4 (s. *Τορκουᾶτος*, *Μαντώ*)
MACEDONIA (PIERIS):
—AKONTISMA: **(21)** imp. *AD* 22 (1967) Chron. p. 421 (s. *Πόπλιος*); **(22)** ~ ib. (f. *Δ*—)
SCYTHIA MINOR:
—ISTROS: **(23)** ?iv-iii BC *ISM* I 249 (s. *Ἀρχέλοχος*)
—TOMIS: **(24)** ?ii AD *AMNG* I (2) 2524 (coin); **(25)** ii-iii AD *ISM* II 468, 5 (f. *Διονύσις*); **(26)** ~ ib. l. 8 (I f. *Μητρόδωρος* II); **(27)** ~ ib. l. 8 (II s. *Μητρόδωρος* I); **(28)** ~ ib. l. 13 (I f. *Μητρόδωρος* II); **(29)** ~ ib. l. 13 (II s. *Μητρόδωρος* I)
—TOMIS*: **(30)** ii AD ib. 261, 5 (biling.) (*Μητρόδω[ρος]*: freed.)
SKYTHIA:
—OLBIA-BORYSTHENES: **(31)** s. vi BC *SEG* XXXII 729 (vase); **(32)** f. iv BC Dubois, *IGDOlbia* 104 (s. *Δημήτριος*); **(33)** iii BC *IOSPE* I^2 201 I, 3 (*Μητρόδ[ωρος]*: f. *Ἡρόδοτος*); **(34)** ~ ib. l. 34 (f. *Εὐφρόνιμος*); **(35)** ~ ib. 201 II, 19 (f. *Εὐβίοτος*); **(36)** s. iii BC ib. 76, 8 (Sokolowski II 88; Dubois, *IGDOlbia* 88) (f. *Ἰστικῶν*)
TAURIS:
—CHERSONESOS: **(37)** i-ii AD *IOSPE* I^2 458 (*Μητρόδ[ωρος]*); **(38)** ~ ib. 471 (f. *Γαζούριος*); **(39)** ii AD *VDI* 1996 (4), p. 50 no. 10, 5 (*SEG* XLVI 931 (om. per err.)) (*Μητρ[όδωρος]*?: f. *Θεόδοτος*); **(40)** ~ *IOSPE* I^2 385, 4 (*Μητρόδω[ρος]*); **(41)** ~ ib. 513 (-*δο*-); **(42)** ~ *SEG* XLVI 932 ([*Μ*]*ητρόδωρος*); **(43)** f. ii AD Solomonik, *NEPKh* 113, 11 (*Μητρόδω[ρος]*) ?= (*45*); **(44)** ~ *IOSPE* I^2 412; *SEG* XXXV 859; *KSIIMK* 15 (1947) p. 59, 7 (Solomonik, *NEPKh* 112 d); cf. *VDI* 1993 (4), p. 63 (f. *Γαζούριος*, *Δαΐσκος*); **(45)** 129-130 AD *IOSPE* I^2 359, 34; *VDI* 1960 (3), pp. 154-5, 27 (s. *Διοσκουρίδης*) ?= (*43*)
THRACE: **(46)** 230 BC *SB* 6278, 27 (Velkov 210; La'da E772)
—APOLLONIA-SOZOPOLIS: **(47)** s. v BC *IGB* I^2 406 (f. *Πάρμις*)
—BIZYE (TERRIT.)?: **(48)** ii-iii AD ib. III 1851, 7 (*Κλ. Μητρόδω[ρ]ο[ς]*)
—BYZANTION: **(49)** i BC-i AD *IByz* 132 (Fıratlı-Robert p. 98 no. 145) (f. *Τύχη*); **(50)** ~ *IByz* 177 (Fıratlı-Robert p. 111 no. 182) (f. *Τίτθα*, *Φιλῖνος*, *Δημήτριος*); **(51)** imp. *IByz* 22, 5 (s. *Λάσιος*); **(52)** i BC/i AD *IG* XII (8) 206, 7 (f. *Μενέμαχος*)
—BYZANTION (NR.): **(53)** ii BC *SEG* XXIX 667 (f. *Ἄτταλος*)
—BYZANTION?: **(54)** imp. *IByz* 382 (s. *Μᾶρκος*)
—KARDIA: **(55)** iv BC Hp., *Epid.* v 100; vii 113; **(56)** m. iii BC *TCal* 34, 3, 11 (s. *Ἄτταλος*)
—LYSIMACHEIA: **(57)** hell. Kaphtantzis 629 (s. *Κυπρόθεμις*); **(58)** ~ *SEG* XLIII 774 ([*Μ*]*ητρόδωρος*: s. *Δημήτριος*); **(59)** c. 208 BC *FD* III (4) 135 I, 24 (*Μητρ[ό]δω[ρος]*: f. *Ἀριστοκλῆς*); **(60)** c. 200-175 BC *IG* II^2 9231 (*FRA* 3399) (f. *Παρμενίσκος*)
—MARONEIA: **(61)** c. 365-336 BC Schönert-Geiss, *Maroneia* 403; 407-9; 507-8 (coin); **(62)** s. iv BC *IThrakAig* E230 B ([*Μ*]*ητρόδωρο[ς]*); **(63)** ii BC *AD* 26 (1971) Chron. p. 428 no. δ (*IThrakAig* E267) (f. *Εὔβιος*); **(64)** hell.-imp. *Syringes* 999 (*Μητρόδορος*—Champoll., *Μητρόδιος*—Baillet, *Μητρόβιος*?); **(65)** ii-iii AD Dumont-Homolle 110b 19 (*IThrakAig* E290) (s. *Φιλόμουσος*)
—MESAMBRIA: **(66)** c. 375-350 BC *IOSPE* I^2 20, 4 (Dubois, *IGDOlbia* 15) (f. *Χαιριγένης*)
—NICOPOLIS AD ISTRUM?: **(67)** 196 AD *IMS* II 53 I b, 37 (*CIL* III 14507); cf. *ZPE* 146 (2004) pp. 216-20 (Lat. T. Aur. Metrod(orus)?)
—ODESSOS: **(68)** iii BC *IGB* I^2 106 (f. *Σιμάκων*); **(69)** 41 BC ib. 46, 6 (I f. *Μητρόδωρος* II); **(70)** ~ ib. l. 6 (II s. *Μητρόδωρος* I); **(71)** 16 BC ib. l.

31 (s. *Κόνων*); **(72)** ii-iii AD ib. 127 (f. *Καλλικόμας*); **(73)** ~ ib. 191 (f. *Μάμα*); **(74)** ~ ib. V 5040 (s. *Ἕλλην*); **(75)** f. ii AD ib. I^2 78 ter, 4 (*CCET* I 30) (f. *Ἀγαθήνωρ*); **(76)** 215 AD *IGB* I^2 47 a, 18 (f. *Αὐρ. Φαρσουλέϊος*); **(77)** ~ ib. 47 c, 23 (*Αὐρ. Μ.*: s. *Ἀσκληπιάδης*)
—PERINTHOS-HERAKLEIA: **(78)** iv-iii BC *IPerinth* 4, 15 (?f. *—τατος*); **(79)** ii-iii AD ib. 65, 6
——(Aigikoreis): **(80)** iii-ii BC ib. 61, 51 (s. *—κράτης*)
——(Boreis): **(81)** iii-ii BC ib. l. 39 (s. *Ζωΐλος*)
——(Makedones): **(82)** iii-ii BC ib. l. 2 (s. *Φιλιστίων*)
——(Theseidai): **(83)** s. iii BC ib. 62, 7 (f. *Ὀλυμπιόδωρος*)
—SERDICA: **(84)** iii AD *IGB* IV 1906 (*Αὐρ. Σαβῖνος ὁ καὶ Μ.*: s. *Σαβῖνος*)

Μητροκλῆς
THRACE:
—MARONEIA: **(1)** s. iv BC *RE* (-)

Μητρόπολις
THRACE:
—PAUTALIA (TERRIT.): **(1)** ii-iii AD *IGB* IV 2229 (I m. *Μητρόπολις* II); **(2)** ~ ib. (*[Μ]ητρόπολις*: II d. *Φλ. Ἔζβενις, Μητρόπολις* I)

Μητρόπυθος
THRACE:
—PERINTHOS-HERAKLEIA:
——(Boreis): **(1)** iii-ii BC *IPerinth* 61, 42 (f. *Ἑκατόδωρος*)

Μῆτρος
SKYTHIA:
—OLBIA-BORYSTHENES: **(1)** v BC *ZOOID* 20 (1897) p. 181 no. 45 (vase) (*Μῆτρο(ς)*—*ZOOID*, *Μητρο*—?)

Μητρότιμος
CIMMERIAN BOSPOROS:
—GORGIPPIA: **(1)** f. i AD *SEG* XXXII 790, 5 (*Μητρότε̣[μος]*)

Μητροφάνης
CIMMERIAN BOSPOROS:
—NYMPHAION: **(1)** f. iii BC ib. XXXIX 701. 4; cf. XLV 997. 12
SKYTHIA:
—OLBIA-BORYSTHENES: **(2)** v/iv BC Dubois, *IGDOlbia* 24, 10
—TANAIS: **(3)** 104 AD *CIRB* 1259, 13 (s. *Ἀλέξανδρος*); **(4)** ~ ib. l. 24 (f. *Θεαγένης*)
THRACE:
—BYZANTION*: **(5)** 313 AD *Chron. Pasch.* P281b (bp.)
—MARONEIA: **(6)** c. 400-378 BC Schönert-Geiss, *Maroneia* 165 (coin); **(7)** iv BC *IGB* I^2 104 (s. *Βάκχιος*); **(8)** c. 365-336 BC Schönert-Geiss, *Maroneia* 389-93 (coin); **(9)** s. iv BC *SEG* XLIX 888 (*IThrakAig* E225) (s. *Ἡρογείτων*); **(10)** s. iii BC ib. E252 (*[Μη]τ̣ροφάν[ης]*); **(11)** ii-i BC Meïmaris–Bakirtzis 18 (*SEG* XLIV 601) + *IThrakAig* E268 (*Μητ[ρο]φάνη[ς]*: f. *Βενδίς*); **(12)** ~ ib. E199 (s. *Ἡρόδοτος*); **(13)** ~ ib. E212, 18 (f. *Λυσίμαχος*); **(14)** 167 BC *SEG* XXXV 823, 4 (*IThrakAig* E168)

Μητροφάντη
THRACE:
—STRYME?: **(1)** s. v BC *SEG* XLIX 987 + *IThrakAig* E114 (d. *Νέστις*)

Μητρόφαντος
MACEDONIA (CHALKIDIKE):
—POTIDAIA-KASSANDREIA: **(1)** ?iii BC *IG* IX (1)^2 (4) 1533 II (Tataki, *Macedonians* p. 92 no. 64) (s. *Παρμενίων*)

Μητροφίλα
CIMMERIAN BOSPOROS:
—PANTIKAPAION: **(1)** i AD *CIRB* 449; cf. KW pl. 17 no. 254 (m. *Μᾶρκος*); **(2)** ~ *CIRB* 470; cf. KW pl. 15 no. 215; **(3)** ?f. i AD *CIRB* 527, 2; cf. KW pl. 30 no. 440 (m. *Ὑψίγονος, Φαρνάκης, Παρθένα*)

Μητρόφιλος
CIMMERIAN BOSPOROS:
—PANTIKAPAION: **(1)** i AD *CIRB* 471 (s. *Θεότιμος*); **(2)** f. ii AD ib. 651 (f. *Ἀνθεστήριος*)

Μητροφῶν
THRACE:
—MARONEIA: **(1)** c. 432-423 BC Schönert-Geiss, *Maroneia* 133-44 (coin); **(2)** c. 400-378 BC ib. 154 (coin)
—PISTIROS: **(3)** iv BC *Archeologia* (Warsaw) 44 (1993) p. 56 no. 4 (*Μητρο[φ]ῶν*)
—STRYME?: **(4)** s. v BC *SEG* XXVII 337 (*IThrakAig* E115) (*Μ̣η̣τροφῶν*: s. *Μητρόδοτος*); **(5)** c. 375-350 BC ib. E144 (s. *Ἡρόφιλος*)

Μητρώ
MACEDONIA (BOTTIAIA):
—BEROIA: **(1)** 195 AD *ILeukopetra* 43, 3 (Tataki 54) (*Αἰλ. Μ.*)
SKYTHIA:
—OLBIA-BORYSTHENES: **(2)** v BC Dubois, *IGDOlbia* 73 (vase); **(3)** iii BC *SEG* XXX 958 (vase); cf. Dubois, *IGDOlbia* 73 (*Μητρό*—ed. pr., *Μήτρο̄* (gen.)—*SEG*, *Μητρο(—)*?)

Μήτρων
THRACE:
—ABDERA: **(1)** f. iii BC Unp. (Chryssanthaki diss.) pp. 395-6 (coin) (*[Μ]ήτρων*)
—ABDERA?: **(2)** v-iv BC *IThrakAig* E486 (f. *Θρασυμήδης*)
—APOLLONIA-SOZOPOLIS: **(3)** iv BC *IGB* I^2 463 bis, 2 (f. *Ἀντιμένης*)
—MARONEIA: **(4)** c. 365-336 BC Schönert-Geiss, *Maroneia* 504-6 (coin)

Μητρώνασσα
THRACE:
—ABDERA: **(1)** iii-ii BC *IThrakAig* E53 (*[Μητ]ρώνασσα*)
—MARONEIA: **(2)** s. iv BC *SEG* XXX 691 (*IThrakAig* E226); **(3)** iii BC ib. E234 (*Μ̣ητρώνα̣σ̣σ[α]*: d. *Ἀθηνοκλῆς*)
—STRYME?: **(4)** m. iv BC *SEG* XLIX 1000 (*IThrakAig* E381) (d. *Ἑρμόφαντος*)

Μηφάζουλα
THRACE:
—BOURDAPA: **(1)** ii-iii AD *IGB* III 1349 (d. *Σάλας*)

Μίδαος
CIMMERIAN BOSPOROS:
—PANTIKAPAION: **(1)** f. iv BC *CIRB* 228; *Hyperboreus* 1994 (1), pp. 163-4 (name) (f. *Τέττευος*)

Μίδας
CIMMERIAN BOSPOROS:
—PANTIKAPAION: **(1)** v/iv BC *CIRB* 154 + *Hyperboreus* 1994 (1), p. 165; Zgusta, *PNS* 1081 (*Μιδατος* (gen.): s. *Ἰαδαάκης*)
SCYTHIA MINOR:
—TOMIS: **(2)** ii AD *ISM* II 187 (f. *Κάλλιστος*)
THRACE:
—BISANTHE-PANION: **(3)** imp. Unp. (Sayar) (?f. *Μηνᾶς*)

Μίδαχος
CIMMERIAN BOSPOROS:
—HERMONASSA: **(1)** s. v AD *CIRB* 1099, 9 (*SEG* XXXIX 697) (*Μίδαχ(ος)*)

SKYTHIA:
—TANAIS: **(2)** 220 AD *CIRB* 1278, 21 (s. *Θιάγαρος*); **(3)** 225 AD ib. 1279, 15 (f. *Ἄρδαρος*)

Μιῆζεις
MACEDONIA (MYGDONIA):
—KALINDOIA: **(1)** 68-98 AD *SEG* XLII 580, 74; cf. *Anthémonte–Kalindoia* 2 p. 291 (name) (s. *Ταρουσίνας*); **(2)** a. 98 AD *SEG* XLII 582, 63 (s. *Διοσκουρίδης*)

Μιθριδάτης
MACEDONIA: **(1)** c. 218-164 BC Ma, *Antiochos* p. 340 no. 31 A I, 3; *Chiron* 18 (1988) pp. 451-4 (name); cf. *RE* (27); Grainger, *SPG* pp. 22-7 (*Μ.* (ὕστερον) *Ἀντίοχος* IV *Ἐπιφάνης*: s. *Ἀντίοχος* III *Μέγας*, *Λαοδίκη* (Pontos), f. *Ἀντίοχος* V *Εὐπάτωρ*, *Νῦσα*: king)
THRACE:
—PHILIPPOPOLIS-TRIMONTIUM: **(2)** ii-iii AD *IGB* III 1022, 3 (*GVI* 1338) (f. *Καινίς*)
—SERDICA: **(3)** 117-138 AD *IGB* IV 1925 c, 10 (*Μιθραδ(άτης)*)

Μιθροδάτης
MACEDONIA: **(1)** 77 BC *PMerton* 6, 2, 9 (Tataki, *Macedonians* p. 490 no. 169); cf. La'da E1522 (f. *Κάστωρ*)
MACEDONIA (EDONIS):
—AMPHIPOLIS: **(2)** iii BC *SEG* XXVII 250 (f. *Ἴδας*)

Μίκα
SKYTHIA:
—OLBIA-BORYSTHENES (BEREZAN (MOD.)): **(1)** v BC ib. XXXII 783 (vase) (*Μικα*—?)
TAURIS:
—CHERSONESOS: **(2)** inc. Solomonik, *GAKh* 1223 (vase)
THRACE:
—ABRYTTOS (TERRIT.): **(3)** f. iii AD *Romanizmǎt* II 88 (Lat. Mica)

Μικαλίνη
CIMMERIAN BOSPOROS:
—PANTIKAPAION: **(1)** i BC *CIRB* 284 + *St. Clas.* 8 (1966) p. 337; cf. KW pl. 24 no. 347 (*Μικλαίνη*—lap., *Μικ(αλ)ίνη*—Russu: m. *Μοκκοῦς*)

Μικαλῖνος
MACEDONIA (PIERIA):
—PYDNA: **(1)** iv BC *GRBS* 47 (2002-3) p. 116 no. 4, 7 (*Μ̣ικαλῖνος*)

Μικαλίων
CIMMERIAN BOSPOROS:
—PANTIKAPAION: **(1)** ?i AD *CIRB* 472 (I f. *Μικαλίων* II); **(2)** ~ ib. (II s. *Μικαλίων* I)

Μίκαλος
THRACE:
—SERDICA: **(1)** ii-iii AD *IGB* IV 1959, 12 (*[Μ]ίκαλος?*: sculptor)

Μίκας
CIMMERIAN BOSPOROS:
—PANTIKAPAION: **(1)** i/ii AD *CIRB* 80, 4; cf. KW pl. 33 no. 454 (*Μ[ί]κας*)

Μίκη
CIMMERIAN BOSPOROS:
—MYRMEKION: **(1)** c. 510-500 BC *Hyperboreus* 1998 (1), pp. 29 ff. no. 2 (vase); cf. *SEG* XLVIII 1006 (*Μίκης* (gen.))
SKYTHIA:
—OLBIA-BORYSTHENES (BEREZAN (MOD.)): **(2)** s. vi BC Dubois, *IGDOlbia* 32 (vase) (*Σμίκη*—ed. pr., *—ις Μίκης*—Yailenko)
THRACE:
—APOLLONIA-SOZOPOLIS: **(3)** v-iv BC *IGB* V 5150
—BYZANTION: **(4)** ii-i BC *IByz* 362 (Fıratlı–Robert p. 66 no. 61) (d. *Δαμοκράτης*)

Μικίνας
MACEDONIA?: (1) m. iv BC *Torone* I p. 726 no. 18.2 (bullet)

Μικίνης
MACEDONIA (DERRIOPOS): (1) 95 AD *IG* X (2) (2) 300, 2 (f. *Παράμονος*)
—STUBERRA: (2) 74 AD ib. 326, 38 (*Μει-*: s. *Φοῖβος*)

Μικίων
MACEDONIA (BOTTIAIA):
—BEROIA: (1) 223 BC *IBer* 4, 34 (f. *Ἀριστοκλῆς*)
—PELLA: (2) m. iii BC Akamatis, *Amph. Pellas* pp. 39-40 nos. PAR40-7 (amph.); pp. 18-19 (date) (*SEG* L 613)
MACEDONIA?: (3) 322 BC *RE* (1); Berve 529 (Tataki, *Macedonians* p. 374 no. 76); (4) ?218 BC Helly, *Gonnoi* 98, 3; cf. Hatzopoulos, *MI* I pp. 241-2
SKYTHIA:
—OLBIA-BORYSTHENES: (5) s. i AD *IOlbia* 85, 9 (*IOSPE* I^2 104) (s. *Εὔκαιρος*); (6) ii AD *IOlbia* 80, 8 (*M. Αὐρ. M. ὁ καὶ Μουρόψαζος*)
THRACE:
—PERINTHOS-HERAKLEIA:
——(Boreis): (7) iii-ii BC *IPerinth* 61, 41 (s. *Ἀλκαῖος*)

Μίκκα
THRACE:
—NAULOCHOS?: (1) s. iii BC *IGB* V 5085 (PM 1104 Add) (or Thrace Mesambria: d. *Ἐράτων*, m. *Ἐράτων, Κήτων, Θεαίνετος*)

Μικκαλίων
CIMMERIAN BOSPOROS:
—PHANAGOREIA: (1) v/iv BC *SEG* XXVII 448 (s. *Δημήτριος*)
SCYTHIA MINOR:
—ISTROS: (2) f. ii BC *ISM* I 26, 1 (f. *Ἑστιαῖος*)

Μίκκαλος
THRACE:
—AQUAE CALIDAE*: (1) i-ii AD *IGB* I^2 381 (*M. Ἰούλ. M.*)
—PERINTHOS-HERAKLEIA: (2) 70-75 AD *IPerinth* 72; *AJA* 69 (1965) p. 149 (date) (I f. *T. Φλ. Μίκκαλος* II); (3) ~ *IPerinth* 72; *AJA* 69 (1965) p. 149 (date) (*T. Φλ. Μίκκ[αλος]*: II s. *Μίκκαλος* I); (4) c. 100-115 AD *SEG* XXVI 1288, 10 (s. *Διογένης*)
—PHILIPPOPOLIS-TRIMONTIUM (TERRIT.): (5) ii/iii AD *IGB* III 1452, 8 (*Eastern cults* p. 121 no. 104) (s. *Παπίας*)
—SALYMBRIA: (6) imp. *Archives Stamoulis* d. 35 (Loukopoulou, *Thrace Propontique* p. 278) (*Μίκα-*)

Μίκκος
MACEDONIA (CHALKIDIKE):
—TORONE: (1) c. 450-420 BC *IG* I^3 1378 (Tataki, *Macedonians* p. 191 no. 11; *FRA* 7143) (s. *Καλλικλείδης*)
SCYTHIA MINOR:
—ISTROS:
——Chora Dagei: (2) c. 159-161 AD *ISM* I 378 C, 24 (s. *Γάϊος*)
—TOMIS: (3) 41-54 AD *RPC* I 1830-1 (coin)
THRACE:
—BYZANTION: (4) ii-i BC *IByz* 213 (Firatlı–Robert p. 72 no. 75) (f. *Ἀπολλώνιος*)
—PHILIPPOPOLIS-TRIMONTIUM: (5) ii-iii AD *IGB* III 1021 (*GVI* 614) (*M. Μυρσινίων*: s. *Μύρσινος*)
—SKAPTOPARA: (6) 238-244 AD *IGB* V 5872 (s. *Γάϊος*)

Μῖκος
SCYTHIA MINOR:
—KALLATIS: (1) s. iii BC *ISM* III 35 A, 30 (f. *Κρατῖνος*)
SKYTHIA:
—OLBIA-BORYSTHENES?: (2) iii BC *SEG* XXXVII 671 (bronze) (s. *Ἀρτεμίδωρος*)
THRACE:
—ODESSOS?: (3) i-ii AD ib. I 315 (or Thrace Byzantion?: I f. *Μῖκος* II); (4) ~ ib. (or Thrace Byzantion?: II s. *Μῖκος* I)
—SALYMBRIA: (5) imp. *IByz* S 36 (PM 1152) (I f. *Μῖκος* II); (6) ~ *IByz* S 36 (PM 1152) (II s. *Μῖκος* I)

Μίκυθος
THRACE:
—STRYME?: (1) m. iv BC *IThrakAig* E380 (*Μίκυθος*: f. *Σωκλῆς*)

Μικυλίς
MACEDONIA (PIERIA):
—DION: (1) hell. *SEG* L 589 (d. *Σάμος*)

Μικυλίων
MACEDONIA (CHALKIDIKE):
—MENDE: (1) iii AD *TAPA* 69 (1938) p. 69 no. 24 (*Λικίννιος M.*: I f. *Μικυλίων* II); (2) ~ ib. (II s. *Λικίννιος Μικυλίων* I, *Μυράνθιν*)

Μικύλος
MACEDONIA: (1) hell. *Memnonion* 534 (Tataki, *Macedonians* p. 374 no. 79); cf. La'da E1542 (I f. *Μικύλος* II); (2) ~ *Memnonion* 534 (Tataki, *Macedonians* p. 374 no. 78; La'da E1542) (II s. *Μικύλος* I)
MACEDONIA (BOTTIAIA):
—PELLA?: (3) iv/iii BC *Arch. Pap.* 22 (1973) p. 205 no. 1 (f. *Φιλοπάτρα*)

Μιλησία
MACEDONIA (BOTTIAIA):
—BEROIA: (1) f. ii AD *IBer* 36, 8 (Tataki 872) (*Μει-*: d. *Λ. Βρούττιος Ἀγαθοφόρος, Ἐλευθέριον*)

Μιλήσιος
CIMMERIAN BOSPOROS:
—PANTIKAPAION: (1) i AD *CIRB* 519
MACEDONIA: (2) 366 AD *RE* s.v. Milesius (-) (bp.)
TAURIS:
—CHERSONESOS: (3) iii BC Solomonik, *NEPKh* 74 (*Μιλή[σιος]*: s. *Νικαγόρας*)

Μιλητία
THRACE:
—DUVANLI (MOD.): (1) vi BC *SEG* XLIII 484

Μίλιος
TAURIS:
—CHERSONESOS: (1) imp. *IOSPE* I^2 461; cf. Zgusta, *PNS* 1085 (*Λαίλιος*?)

Μίλος
TAURIS:
—CHERSONESOS: (1) iv-iii BC Solomonik, *GAKh* 1227 (vase) (*Μίλου* (gen.))

Μιλτίας
THRACE:
—BYZANTION: (1) c. 250-220 BC Schönert-Geiss, *Byzantion* 1014; 1190 (coin) (*Μιλτία* (gen.))

Μιλτοκύθης
THRACE: (1) 401 BC *RE* (1); X., *An.* ii 2. 7; (2) 363-359 BC *RE* (2)

Μίλων
MACEDONIA: (1) 168 BC ib. (1)
THRACE:
—AINOS: (2) i-ii AD *IG* XII (8) 218, 3 (f. *Κοϊντία*)
—BYZANTION (TERRIT.): (3) i-ii AD *IByz* 268 (Firatlı–Robert pp. 83-4 no. 102) (f. *Ζώτιχος*)
—PAUTALIA (TERRIT.): (4) ii-iii AD *IGB* V 5805-9 (*Π. Καλπούρνιος M.*)

Μινικέων
THRACE:
—MESAMBRIA: (1) ii/i BC ib. 5104 II (*Μι[ν]ικέονος*? (gen.): f. *Πρόδικος*)

Μινίων
MACEDONIA (EDONIS):
—AMPHIPOLIS: (1) hell. *IG* XII (8) 438 (Tataki, *Macedonians* p. 57 no. 92) (s. *Ἡρόδοτος*)

Μιννίων
MACEDONIA (EDONIS):
—PHILIPPOI: (1) s. iii BC *IG* VII 2433 II, 6 (Tataki, *Macedonians* p. 166 no. 25) (f. *Ἰατροκλῆς, Ἀρτεμίδωρος*)

Μιννώ
MACEDONIA (BOTTIAIA):
—PELLA: (1) s. iv BC *Stud. Siganidou* p. 364 no. 3 (lamp) (*SEG* XLVII 932)
MACEDONIA (CHALKIDIKE):
—OLYNTHOS: (2) m. iv BC *IG* II^2 10025 (Tataki, *Macedonians* p. 140 no. 85; *FRA* 5904) (d. *Διόφαντος*)

Μινουκιανός
MACEDONIA (PIERIA):
—PYDNA*: (1) s. iii AD *Hellenika* 29 (1976) p. 274

Μίνως
THRACE:
—PERINTHOS-HERAKLEIA?: (1) iv BC Hp., *Epid.* iv 39 (*Μίνωος* (gen.))

Μίσγων
MACEDONIA: (1) ?417-413 BC *IG* I^3 89, 78 (Tataki, *Macedonians* p. 374 no. 80) (*-γõν*)

Μιτακᾶς?
KOLCHIS:
—PICHVNARI (MOD.): (1) s. v BC *DHA* 20 (1994) p. 137 (vase) (*Gr. Rom. Settlements in Black Sea* p. 31) (*Μίτα κάδος*—ed., *Μιτακᾶδος* (gen.?))

Μίτος
CIMMERIAN BOSPOROS:
—PANTIKAPAION: (1) iv BC *CIRB* 197; Zgusta, *PNS* 1086 (f. *Κονίων*)

Μιτραβάτης
CIMMERIAN BOSPOROS:
—PANTIKAPAION: (1) f. iii BC *CIRB* 245; Zgusta, *PNS* 549 (f. *Λύσιππος, Ἀναίη*)

Μιχαήλ
MACEDONIA (BOTTIAIA):
—EDESSA: (1) v-vi AD Feissel, *RICM* 32 (*Μηχαεί[λ]*)

Μνασέας
MACEDONIA (BOTTIAIA):
—BEROIA: (1) hell. *IBer* 175 (Tataki 902) (*[Μ]νασέας*)
MACEDONIA (PELAGONIA): (2) ii-i BC *IG* X (2) (2) 159, 8 (f. *Παράμονος*)
THRACE:
—VICUS TRULLENSIUM: (3) 161-169 or 198-209 AD *ILB* 180, 7 (Lat. Mnaseas)

Μνασιγένης
MACEDONIA (BOTTIAIA):
—MIEZA: (1) c. 230-200 BC *BCH* 45 (1921) p. 17 III, 59 (Tataki, *Macedonians* p. 123 no. 3) (f. *Νικωνίδας, Νικάνωρ*)

Μνασίμαχος
MACEDONIA (PIERIA):
—PHILA?: (1) ?iii BC *RPh* 1911, p. 132 no. 36, 129; cf. *Polemon* 2 (1934-40) Parart. p. 13 no. 17; cf. Helly, *L'État thessalien* pp. 319-20 (locn.) (s. *Λυσι—*)

Μνασινίκα
MACEDONIA (BOTTIAIA):
—PELLA: (1) s. iv BC *SEG* XLVIII 823 B (d. Ἀντίγονος)

Μνάσων
THRACE: (1) 264 BC *PHib* 92, 10 (Velkov 211; La'da E835) (s. Σῖμος: t.e.)
—PHILIPPOPOLIS-TRIMONTIUM: (2) ii AD *IGB* III 997, 1 (s. Θεο—, f. Μουκιανός)

Μνησαγόρης
MACEDONIA (BISALTIA):
—ARGILOS?: (1) f. iv BC *SEG* XXX 547 ([Μν]ησαγόρης?: s. Ἡγήσιππος)

Μνησιγένης
MACEDONIA (CHALKIDIKE):
—POTIDAIA-KASSANDREIA: (1) ?iii BC *IG* IX (2) 1180 (Tataki, *Macedonians* p. 92 no. 65) (f. Ζώπυρος)

Μνησίκλεια
MACEDONIA (BOTTIAIA):
—PELLA: (1) i BC-i AD? *IG* IX (1)² (4) 1271 (Tataki, *Macedonians* p. 157 no. 62)

Μνησικλῆς
THRACE:
—PERINTHOS-HERAKLEIA: (1) imp. *IG* XII (8) 197 a + XII Suppl. p. 149 (s. Ἰσίδωρος)

Μνησῖνος
THRACE:
—APOLLONIA-SOZOPOLIS: (1) v/iv BC *IGB* I² 410 (f. Ἀρκεσίλεως)

Μνήσιππος
MACEDONIA: (1) ?ii AD *PFreib* 2 a I, 1, 12, 19, 21 (fict.)

Μνησιστράτη
MACEDONIA (BOTTIAIA):
—PELLA: (1) iii-ii BC Dimitsas 144 (d. Σώτιμος)

Μνησίστρατος
SKYTHIA:
—OLBIA-BORYSTHENES: (1) ii AD *IOSPE* I² 263, 2 ([Μν]ησίστρατος?, [Τιμ]ησίστρατος?)

Μνησιφῶν
THRACE:
—ODESSOS: (1) iv/iii BC *CIRB* 237 (f. Δίφιλος)

Μνήσων
MACEDONIA (EDONIS):
—AMPHIPOLIS: (1) s. v BC Socr., *Ep.* iii (ἀνήσων—ms., *M.*—Hercher: fict.)

Μόδεστα
THRACE:
—BYZANTION?: (1) imp. *IByz* 379 ([Μ]όδεστα)

Μόδεστος
SCYTHIA MINOR:
—TOMIS: (1) ii-iii AD *ISM* II 31 III, 5 (s. Ποντικός)

Μοιραγένης
CIMMERIAN BOSPOROS:
—PANTIKAPAION: (1) i AD *CIRB* 377 (f. Γάστεις)
—PANTIKAPAION (NR.): (2) i BC ib. 960; cf. KW pl. 48 no. 676 (f. Παιριφάνης)
MACEDONIA (CHALKIDIKE):
—OLYNTHOS: (3) ?c. 355-349 BC *TAPA* 69 (1938) p. 56 no. 9, 3
—POTIDAIA-KASSANDREIA: (4) ?254 BC Nachtergael, *Les Galates* 9, 55 (Stephanis 1733; Tataki, *Macedonians* p. 93 no. 66) (s. Ἀναξίλας)
MACEDONIA?: (5) 205 BC Plb. XV 27. 6-7; 28. 1, 4, 7; 29. 1

THRACE:
—MESAMBRIA: (6) i BC *IGB* I² 326, 3 (Μοιραγένειος (gen.): f. Ἑκαταῖος)

Μοιραγόρης
SKYTHIA:
—OLBIA-BORYSTHENES: (1) v BC Dubois, *IGD-Olbia* 101 (f. Εὔβουλος)

Μοιρικῶν
CIMMERIAN BOSPOROS:
—PANTIKAPAION: (1) hell. *AA* 1907, p. 127 Aa, 3 (lead)

Μοίριμος
CIMMERIAN BOSPOROS:
—PANTIKAPAION: (1) m. i AD *CIRB* 515 (s. Συνίστωρ, Κάλη)

Μοίριππος
CIMMERIAN BOSPOROS:
—PANTIKAPAION: (1) ii AD ib. 680, 3 (Μοίρ-ιππος: s. Βάκχιος, Θεοτίμα)

Μοῖρις
TAURIS:
—CHERSONESOS: (1) c. 120-110 BC Anokhin p. 146 nos. 179; 182 (coins)
THRACE:
—LYSIMACHEIA: (2) m. ii BC *ISestos* 38 b, 1 (s. Μῆνις)

Μοιρόδωρος
CIMMERIAN BOSPOROS:
—GORGIPPIA: (1) ii AD *NE* 9 (1971) p. 6 no. 3, 4 ([Μοι]ρόδωρος); (2) ~ *CIRB* 1143, 6 (Μοιρόδ[ωρος]); (3) ~ ib. 1160, 4 (Μοιρόδ[ωρος]: f. —ων); (4) m. ii AD *Eirene* 7 (1968) p. 67, 9 (Μοιρό[δωρος]?: f. Φαρνάκης); (5) ~ ib. l. 16 (Μοιρό[δωρος]?: s. Ἀθηνόδωρος); (6) ?s. ii AD *CIRB* 1158, 5 ([Μο]ιρόδωρος); (7) 173-210 AD ib. 1119, 5; 1134, 12; *SEG* XXXVI 699, [1]?; 700, 4 (s. Νεοκλῆς); (8) ~ *CIRB* 1134, 15 (Μοιρόδ(ω)ρ[ος]—Vinogradov: s. —αζος); (9) ~ ib. 1135, 23 (Μοιρ[όδωρ]ος: s. Ἴαιος, f. Τιμόθεος); (10) ii/iii AD ib. 1179, 55 ([Μ]ο[ι]ρόδωρος: s. Λίμνακος); (11) ~ ib. 1181, 7 ([Μο]ιρόδωρ[ος])
—GORGIPPIA?: (12) s. ii AD ib. 1231 B, 6
—PANTIKAPAION: (13) 304-284 BC ib. 19 (s. —σκις); (14) i AD ib. 467 (f. Μαστοῦς)
SCYTHIA MINOR:
—ISTROS: (15) iii BC *ISM* I 255 (f. Ἑστιαῖος); (16) i AD ib. 200, 2 (s. Ἡγησαγόρας); (17) ii AD ib. 201 II, 14 (f. —το[γέ]νης); (18) 138 AD ib. 193 I, 68 (f. Μενίσκος); (19) ~ ib. 193 II, 28 (Αἴλ. Μ.); (20) ~ ib. l. 80 (s. Εὐξενίδης); (21) c. 140-160 AD ib. 207, 12 (f. Διονύσιος)

Μοιροφάνης
MACEDONIA (EDONIS):
—AMPHIPOLIS: (1) f. ii BC *AD* 26 (1971) Chron. p. 417 (s. Διονύσιος)

Μοιρώ
SCYTHIA MINOR:
—ISTROS: (1) ii-i BC *ISM* I 125 (d. Διονύσιος)
THRACE:
—BYZANTION: (2) iv/iii BC *RE* (-); *HE* 2675-82; *Coll. Alex.* pp. 21-3 (Μυρώ—var. lect.: m. Ὅμηρος)

Μοίρων
CIMMERIAN BOSPOROS:
—KOROKONDAME?: (1) iv BC *IAK* 56 (1914) p. 57 no. 179 (vase) (Μοιρωννου (n. pr.?))
SKYTHIA:
—OLBIA-BORYSTHENES: (2) s. vi BC *SEG* XXX 958 (vase) (Μοιρωνο (n. pr.?))

Μοκαζεις
THRACE:
—BYZANTION: (1) i BC-i AD *Türk Tarih Kongresi XI* (6) 1990, p. 497 pl. 10 (Μοκαζει (gen.): f. Πάπας)

Μοκάζελμος
THRACE?: (1) ii BC *ILAlg* II 510 (*M.* Δίλιππος)

Μοκάζενις
THRACE:
—PAUTALIA: (1) iii AD *IGB* V 5867, 7 (f. *M.* Αὐρ. Ἑρμογένης)

Μοκαζίη
THRACE:
—PAUTALIA (TERRIT.): (1) ii-iii AD ib. IV 2228 (d. *T.* Φλ. Ἑρμιανός)

Μοκαζοίρη
THRACE:
—BYZANTION?: (1) s. iii BC *IByz* 340 (Fıratlı–Robert p. 97 no. 140) (d. Δίνις)

Μοκάπορις
CIMMERIAN BOSPOROS:
—PANTIKAPAION: (1) i-ii AD *CIRB* 663; cf. KW pl. 13 no. 183 (f. Βενζεῖς)
THRACE: (2) 12-19 AD *IGB* V 5011, 8 (f. Σαδάλας); (3) 46-54 AD *SEG* XVI 415 III, 32 (*IThrakAig* E84) (s. Ῥοιμητάλκης)
—BEROE-AUGUSTA TRAIANA (TERRIT.): (4) i-ii AD *IGB* III 1773
—BYZANTION (TERRIT.): (5) ii-i BC *IByz* 214 (Fıratlı–Robert p. 72 no. 76) (s. Μόσχος)
—DYME (MOD.): (6) i AD *AD* 26 (1971) Chron. pl. 422 γ (*Belomorski Pregled* 1 (1941) p. 335 no. 40; *IThrakAig* E387); cf. Bakalakis, *Oinos Ismarikos* p. 1015 (f. Βέσουλα)
—HERAION TEICHOS?: (7) ii BC Taşlıklıoğlu 1 p. 4 no. 1 (s. Φανίων, f. Γλύκιννα)

Μοκάπορος
CIMMERIAN BOSPOROS:
—PANTIKAPAION: (1) f. ii AD *CIRB* 756; Zgusta, *PNS* 566

Μοκᾶς
THRACE:
—SERDICA (TERRIT.): (1) ii-iii AD *AEMÖ* 10 (1886) pp. 238-9 no. 2, 9; (2) ~ *IGB* IV 2015 a (*Eastern cults* p. 167 no. 10) (s. Δίζας); (3) ~ *IGB* IV 2015 b (*Eastern cults* p. 167 no. 10) (Μοκᾶ (gen.): f. —κενθος)

Μοκασοκος
THRACE:
—PAUTALIA (TERRIT.): (1) ii-iii AD *IGB* IV 2228 (d. *T.* Φλ. Ἑρμιανός)

Μόκασος
MACEDONIA (MYGDONIA):
—LETE: (1) ii AD *Makedonika* 2 (1951) p. 619 no. 42 θ, 15 (f. Σεδάλας)
MACEDONIA (SINTIKE):
—NEINE: (2) 77 AD *IGB* V 5883, 7 (s. Δρακόλας); (3) ~ ib. l. 9 (s. Κειλαίβιθυς); (4) ~ ib. l. 10 (f. Βιτούλουσος); (5) ii-iii AD ib. 5888 bis (f. Πύρρος)

Μοκάτραλις
THRACE:
—NICOPOLIS AD NESTUM: (1) ii-iii AD ib. IV 2337, 13 ([Μ]οκάτραλις)

Μοκιανός
THRACE:
—GLAVA PANEGA (MOD.): (1) ii-iii AD ib. II 542 (s. Αὐλούζενις)
—SERDICA (TERRIT.): (2) ii-iii AD *AEMÖ* 10 (1886) pp. 238-9 no. 2, 9 (Μο[κι]ανός); (3) ~ ib. l. 12

Μοκκάπορις
CIMMERIAN BOSPOROS:
—NYMPHAION: (1) imp. *CIRB* 937; Zgusta, *PNS* 566 (s. Δόριζος, f. Ἀρέσκουσα)

Μοκκᾶς
SKYTHIA:
—TYRAS: (1) 181 AD *IOSPE* I² 2, 23; Zgusta, *PNS* 566 (f. *Λαϊσθένης*)
—TYRAS (NR.): (2) iii AD *SEG* XL 641 (*Μ*[*οκ*]*κᾶς*: f. *Λαϊσθένης*)

Μοκκόθας
CIMMERIAN BOSPOROS:
—PANTIKAPAION: (1) i AD *CIRB* 473; Zgusta, *PNS* 566

Μόκκος
CIMMERIAN BOSPOROS:
—GORGIPPIA: (1) iii BC *VDI* 2001 (1), pp. 190-1, 3 (*Μόκ*(*κ*)*ος*—ed.)
—KOROKONDAME: (2) ii-iii AD *CIRB* 1109 B + *St. Clas.* 8 (1966) p. 338 (*Μοκόσπατρις*—ed., *Μόκ*(*κ*)*ος πατρί*?—Russu: s. *Καλλίστρατος*)

Μοκκοῦς
CIMMERIAN BOSPOROS:
—NYMPHAION: (1) i-ii AD *CIRB* 933; cf. KW pl. 12 no. 160; Zgusta, *PNS* 566 (*Μοκκοῦ* (gen.))
—PANTIKAPAION: (2) i BC *CIRB* 284; cf. KW pl. 24 no. 347; Zgusta, *PNS* 566 (s. *Βασιλείδης*, *Μικαλίνη*); (3) f. i AD *CIRB* 538 (*Μοκκοῦ* (gen.)); (4) s. i AD ib. 539; cf. KW pl. 41 no. 600 (*Μοκκοῦ* (gen.): f. *Χαρίτων*); (5) 275-278 AD *CIRB* 36, 66 (s. *Διονύσιος*)
SKYTHIA:
—TANAIS: (6) c. 220-230 AD ib. 1282, 21; 1286, 10 (*Μοκκοῦ* (gen.): f. *Στρατόνικος*)

Μολίας
THRACE:
—BYZANTION: (1) c. 303 AD *Anal. Boll.* 31 (1912) p. 192

Μόλογρος
TAURIS:
—CHERSONESOS: (1) s. iv BC Solomonik, *GAKh* 1231 with pl. 8 (vase); cf. *Hellenismus* p. 452 no. 24; *BE* 1996, no. 291 (*Μόλοπρος*—edd.)

Μολοσσός
MACEDONIA?: (1) ?178 BC *PKöln* 411 fr. 3 II, 5

Μολπαγόρης
CIMMERIAN BOSPOROS:
—BOSPOROS: (1) iv/iii BC *IFayoum* 193, 9 (La'da E336) (*Μο*[*λ*]*παγό*[*ρ*]*ας*)
—KEPOI: (2) 525-500 BC *SEG* XLI 1833. 1 (vase)
—PANTIKAPAION: (3) 304-284 BC *CIRB* 19 (*Μολπα*(*γ*)*όρης*: f. —*σκις*)
SKYTHIA:
—OLBIA-BORYSTHENES: (4) f. v BC *IOSPE* I² 270 (*CEG* I 173; Dubois, *IGDOlbia* 44) (f. *Λέωξος*)
THRACE:
—ABDERA: (5) c. 395-360 BC May, *Abdera* p. 219 nos. 313-15 (coin) (*Μολπαγόρεω* (gen.)); (6) c. 360-350 BC ib. pp. 252-5 nos. 405-19 (coin)

Μολπᾶς
CIMMERIAN BOSPOROS:
—PANTIKAPAION: (1) iv BC *CIRB* 210; cf. KW pl. 1 no. 3 (*Μολπᾶτος* (gen.): f. *Νεομηνίς*)
TAURIS:
—CHERSONESOS: (2) c. 480-460 BC *SEG* XL 612. 18 (ostrakon) ([*Μ*]*ολπᾶς*)
THRACE:
—ABDERA: (3) c. 450-425 BC May, *Abdera* pp. 132-3 nos. 159-60 (coin); Masson, *OGS* p. 431 (*Μολπᾶδος* (gen.))

Μόλπις
THRACE:
—PERINTHOS-HERAKLEIA:
——(Aigikoreis): (1) iii-ii BC *IPerinth* 61, 46

Μολπόθεμις
CIMMERIAN BOSPOROS:
—NYMPHAION: (1) f. v BC *SEG* XLIX 1038 (*Bosporskii fenomen* p. 187 no. 2) (s. *Ἀλέξανδρος*)
SCYTHIA MINOR:
—ISTROS: (2) v/iv BC *ISM* I 170 (*Μο*[*λποθ*]*έμιος*? (gen.)—Avram)

Μόλπος
THRACE:
—MARONEIA: (1) c. 377-362 BC Schönert-Geiss, *Maroneia* 303-30 (coin) (*Μόλπō* (gen.?))

Μόλυκκος
MACEDONIA (BOTTIAIA):
—BEROIA: (1) ii-i BC *IBer* 183 (Tataki 903) (f. *Καλλίνας*)

Μοιος
THRACE:
—NICOPOLIS AD NESTUM (TERRIT.): (1) ii AD *IG* II² 10770; *Tekmeria* 6 (2001) pp. 149 ff. (locn.); cf. *LGPN* II s.v. (1) (*Μ*(*ω*)*μος*?: s. *Μουκάσης*)

Μονίμη
CIMMERIAN BOSPOROS:
—PANTIKAPAION*: (1) i AD *CIRB* 474 (freed.)

Μένιμος
CIMMERIAN BOSPOROS:
—PANTIKAPAION: (1) s. i AD ib. 546; cf. KW pl. 30 no. 439a (f. *Μάης*, *Χρήστη*, *Ἰταλία*, *Κλεονίκη*); (2) ii AD *CIRB* 692 (f. *Ταρσοῦς*, *Ἡραΐος*, *Θεονίκα*)
MACEDONIA (BOTTIAIA):
—BEROIA: (3) ii BC *IBer* 141, 40
—PELLA?: (4) 316 BC *RE* (3); *FGrH* 81 F 21 (Tataki, *Macedonians* p. 157 no. 63) (s. *Πυθίων*)
MACEDONIA (DERRIOPOS):
—STUBERRA: (5) 50 AD *IG* X (2) (2) 324, 23 (s. *Νίκαρχος*)
MACEDONIA?: (6) hell.-imp. *RE* (9); Giannini, *Parad. Gr.* p. 380
SARMATIA:
—MAIOTAI: (7) iii-ii BC *SEG* XXIII 144 (*FRA* 3454) (slave?)
SCYTHIA MINOR:
—ISTROS: (8) iii BC *ISM* I 5, 4 (*Eastern cults* pp. 15-16 no. 22) (f. —*δης*); (9) s. iii BC Unp. (Coll. Stancomb) (*Μόνι*(*μος*)); (10) iii/ii BC *ISM* I 64, 11, 33, 35 (*IGB* I² 388 bis); cf. *SEG* L 661 (f. *Ἡγησαγόρας*); (11) ii BC *ISM* I 27, 4 ([*Μ*]*όνιμος*); (12) ~ ib. 36, 3 + *Pontica* 33-4 (2000-1) pp. 346-7 no. 3 (f. *Εὐξενίδης*); (13) i BC-i AD *ISM* I 191 I, 12; (14) ~ ib. l. 6-7; (15) ~ ib. 209, 3 = 185 (*Μένιππος*—185 per err.); (16) i AD ib. 200, 11 (s. *Πίστος*); (17) ii AD ib. 201 I, 13 (*Μόνιμ*[*ος*]); (18) ~ ib. 202, 7 ([*Μ*]*όνιμο*[*ς*]); (19) ~ ib. 211, 3 (f. *Μάξιμος*); (20) ~ ib. l. 7 (f. *Ἀθηνάδης*); (21) ~ ib. 212, 21 (f. *Εὐξενίδης*); (22) 138 AD ib. 193 I, 70 (s. *Μενίσκος*); (23) ~ ib. l. 100 (s. *Διονύσιος*); (24) ~ ib. 193 II, 41 (f. *Διονύσιος*) ?= (*25*); (25) ~ ib. l. 43 (f. *Ἡραπίδης*) ?= (*24*)
—KALLATIS: (26) 12-19 AD *IGB* V 5011, 12 (*Μόνι*[*μο*]*ς*: f. *Ἡράκλειτος*); (27) s. i AD *ISM* III 69, 8 (f. —*ίων*); (28) f. ii AD ib. III, 6 (s. *Ἡρακλείδης*)
—TOMIS: (29) i BC ib. II 2 A, 55 (f. *Νουμήνιος*)
THRACE: (30) c. 223 BC *PTeb* 815 fr. 5, 28 (Velkov 212); cf. La'da E837 (f. *Νικόστρατος*); (31) ii BC *IG* II² 8916 (*FRA* 2557)
—BYZANTION: (32) iii BC *IByz* 70 (Firatlı–Robert p. 49 no. 11) (s. *Ματρόδωρος*)
—MONTANA: (33) ii-iii AD *Romanizmăt* II 22 (Lat. A[el.] [M]onim[us])

Μονόμαχος
THRACE:
—ZONE: (1) ?iv BC *PAE* 1975, p. 143 (vase)

Μονούνιος
MACEDONIA (EDONIS):
—AMPHIPOLIS: (1) iv/iii BC *SEG* XXXV 708 (*CEG* II 724; *Amphipolis* p. 111 fig. 80) (f. *Ἀμύντας*)
THRACE: (2) 356 BC Rhodes–Osborne 53, 9, [14], [29] ([*Μονο*]*ύνιος*?: ?s. *Βηρισάδης*)

Μονόχορδος
CIMMERIAN BOSPOROS:
—PANTIKAPAION: (1) i/ii AD *CIRB* 82, 9 (f. *Δημήτριος*)

Μόντα
THRACE:
—KELLAI*: (1) iii AD *IGB* III 1516 b, 31 (m. *Μουκάτραλις*, *Μουκάπορις*)

Μοντανός
MACEDONIA (LYNKESTIS):
—HERAKLEIA: (1) i AD *IG* X (2) (2) 75, 48 (f. *Πομπώνιος*)
MACEDONIA (ODOMANTIKE):
—SIRRHA: (2) ii-iii AD *SEG* XXX 618
THRACE:
—BOURDAPA: (3) ii-iii AD *IGB* III 1346 (f. *Γηπεπυρίς*)
—GLAVA PANEGA (MOD.): (4) ii-iii AD ib. II 539 (s. *Φλῶρος*)
—PAUTALIA (TERRIT.): (5) ii-iii AD ib. IV 2121 (s. *Δινείλας*)

Μορφή
THRACE: (1) iii BC *IG* II² 8917; cf. *SEG* XXVIII 289 (*FRA* 2558) (m. *Ζωπυρίων*)

Μορφίων
SCYTHIA MINOR:
—KALLATIS: (1) i BC *ISM* III 39, 9 (*Μορ*(*φ*)*ίων*?: f. *Δημάλκας*)

Μόσκων
SCYTHIA MINOR: (1) iii-ii BC Preda, *MGD* pp. 180-2 (coin) (king)

Μόσσης
MACEDONIA:
—BISALTAI: (1) c. 480-460 BC *AMNG* III (2) pp. 145-6 nos. 8-13; *Coinage and Administration* pp. 21-8 (coin) (*Μοσσέō*, *Μοσσέω* (gen.): king?)

Μόστιος
CIMMERIAN BOSPOROS:
—PANTIKAPAION (NR.): (1) ii AD *CIRB* 963 (f. *Μακάριος*)

Μόστις
THRACE: (1) c. 133-86 BC *RE* (-); Moretti, *ISE* 116 (*SEG* XXXVII 602); *SEG* XLII 662; *SNG BM Black Sea* 309-13 (coin) (*Μόστιδος* (gen.): king)
—APOLLONIA-SOZOPOLIS: (2) iii/ii BC *IGB* I² 469 bis, 5 (*Μόστ*[*ιο*]*ς* (gen.))

Μοσχᾶς
CIMMERIAN BOSPOROS:
—PANTIKAPAION: (1) 275-278 AD *CIRB* 36, 46 (I f. *Μοσχᾶς* II); (2) ~ ib. l. 46 (II s. *Μοσχᾶς* I)
SKYTHIA:
—TANAIS: (3) 225 AD ib. 1279, 9 (f. *Μηνόφιλος*)

Μοσχιάδης
SCYTHIA MINOR:
—ISTROS: (1) hell. *Syringes* 1202

Μοσχιανός
THRACE:
—NICOPOLIS AD ISTRUM (TERRIT.): (1) ii-iii AD *IGB* II 699 (*Αἰλ. Μ.*)

Μόσχιν
THRACE:
—BYZANTION: (1) ii-i BC *IByz* 161 (Fıratlı–Robert p. 107 no. 169) (*Βιβία Μ.*); (2) ?ii-i BC *IByz* 374 (d. *Θεοδᾶς*)

Μοσχίνη
MACEDONIA (BOTTIAIA):
—BEROIA: (1) m. ii BC *IBer* 177 (d. *Κλεύας*)
THRACE:
—MARONEIA: (2) iii-ii BC *AD* 26 (1971) Chron. p. 428 no. ε (*IThrakAig* E241)

Μόσχιον
MACEDONIA (MYGDONIA):
—THESSALONIKE?: (1) i AD *IG* X (2) (1) 844 (-σσχι-: d. *Ἀνδροκλῆς*); (2) ii AD ib. 866 (-σχει-)
SCYTHIA MINOR:
—ISTROS: (3) i BC-i AD *ISM* I 29 (d. *Διογένης*)
—TOMIS: (4) s. ii AD *SEG* XXXIII 586 (m. *Ἑρμογένης*)
THRACE:
—SALYMBRIA: (5) hell. *IByz* S 41 (d. *Ἀσκλαπιάδας*)

Μοσχίς
MACEDONIA: (1) hell. *SEG* XLVI 1021
THRACE:
—PERINTHOS-HERAKLEIA: (2) i-ii AD *IPerinth* 94 (d. *Ἀλέξανδρος*)

Μοσχίων
CIMMERIAN BOSPOROS:
—GORGIPPIA: (1) iv/iii BC *VDI* 1976 (3), p. 142 (vase) (*Μοσχιώνου* (gen.)); (2) f. iii BC *CIRB* 1137 B II, 47 (f. *Στράτιος*); (3) ~ ib. l. 54 (f. *Σῶσις*)
—HERMONASSA: (4) iii BC ib. 1071 (f. *Βακυλίων*)
—NYMPHAION: (5) iii BC ib. 912 I, 7 ([*Μοσ*]*χίων*: s. *Διονύσιος*); (6) ~ ib. 912 II, 3 (f. —*έας*)
—PANTIKAPAION: (7) iii/ii BC ib. 255 (s. *Ὑμεναῖος*); (8) m. i AD ib. 414; cf. KW pl. 48 no. 662 (f. *Ἥλιος*)
MACEDONIA: (9) 226 BC *PPetr* III 21 b, 4, 11 (Tataki, *Macedonians* p. 375 no. 84); cf. La'da E1757 (f. *Ζωπυρίων*); (10) 63 BC *POxy* 1644, 7, 10-12, 18, 22, 24 and verso (Tataki, *Macedonians* p. 490 no. 170; La'da E1543) (s. *Βερενίκη*: katoikos)
MACEDONIA (BOTTIAIA):
—EDESSA: (11) c. 230-200 BC *BCH* 45 (1921) p. 17 III, 60 (Tataki, *Edessa* 215; Tataki, *Macedonians* p. 103 no. 13) (s. *Τριακαδίων*)
—PELLA: (12) iii/ii BC *Polemon* 4 (1949-50) p. 3 no. 238 (Tataki, *Macedonians* p. 157 no. 64) (f. *Ἡρακλέων*)
MACEDONIA (CHALKIDIKE):
—OLYNTHOS: (13) ?350 BC *TAPA* 59 (1928) p. 226, 3; Hatzopoulos, *Actes Chalc.* p. 80 (date) ([*Μοσ*]*χίων*: f. *Ξένων*)
MACEDONIA (EDONIS):
—AMPHIPOLIS: (14) b. 357 BC Hatzopoulos, *Actes Amphipolis* p. 25 no. 3, 19 (*SEG* XLI 557)
SCYTHIA MINOR:
—KALLATIS: (15) ii/i BC *SNG Stancomb* 99 (coin) (*Μοσχί(ων)*); (16) s. i AD *ISM* III 69, 3 (*Μοσχί*[*ων*]); (17) ii AD ib. 128; (18) 172 AD ib. 99, 6; 100, [8] (*Τ. Αἴλ. Μινίκιος Μ.*: s. *Τ. Αἴλ. Μινίκιος Ἀθαναίων*); (19) iii AD ib. 92 (*Μ. Αὐρ. Μο*[*σχ*]*ίων*)
SKYTHIA:
—OLBIA-BORYSTHENES: (20) c. 350-330 BC *SNG BM Black Sea* 443 (coin) (*Μοσχί(ων)*)
THRACE:
—BYZANTION: (21) ii-i BC *IByz* 196 (Fıratlı–Robert p. 53 no. 31) (f. *Στρατονίκη*); (22) ii/i BC *IByz* 168 (Fıratlı–Robert p. 109 no. 175) (s. *Μήνιος*); (23) i BC *IByz* 137 (Fıratlı–Robert p. 100 no. 149) (f. —*άριν*); (24) ~ *IByz* 204 (Fıratlı–Robert p. 63 no. 53) (f. *Μᾶτρις*)
—BYZANTION (TERRIT.): (25) imp. Unp. (Sayar) (s. *Κουϊντίων*)
—DIONYSOPOLIS: (26) iii AD *IGB* I² 14 b, 9 (f. *Αὐρ. Θεόδωρος*)
—KARDIA: (27) 232 or 207 BC *CPR* XVIII 12, 248; 14, 287; cf. La'da E982-3 (f. *Ἑστιαῖος*, *Μέγας*)
—MARONEIA: (28) iii BC *IThrakAig* E235 (s. *Χαρικλῆς*)
—ODESSOS: (29) i-ii AD *IGB* I² 190 (f. *Πάρμις*); (30) 2 AD ib. 46, 48 (s. *Ζωΐλος*); (31) ii AD ib. 50 a, 14 (f. *Διονύσιος*); (32) 215 AD ib. 47 a, 27 (*Αὐρ. Μ.*: s. *Νουμήνιος*); (33) ~ ib. 47 b, 9 (f. *Αὐρ. Φιλῖνος*); (34) ~ ib. l. 14 (f. *Αὐρ. Διοκλῆς*); (35) ~ ib. 47 c, 18 (I f. *Αὐρ. Μοσχίων* II); (36) ~ ib. l. 18 (*Αὐρ. Μ.*: II s. *Μοσχίων* I); (37) 221 AD ib. 47 bis a, 39 (*Αὐρ. Μ.*: s. *Ἀντίπατρος*); (38) ~ ib. 47 bis b, 14 (*Αὐρ. Μ.*: s. *Τιμοκράτης*); (39) ~ ib. 47 bis c, 33 (f. *Αὐρ. Ῥοῦφος*)
—SESTOS: (40) s. iv BC *IG* II² 10263 (*FRA* 6640)
—SINJO BARDO (MOD.): (41) ii-iii AD *IGB* II 497

Μόσχος
MACEDONIA: (1) ?219 BC *PUG* III 103, 11 (Tataki, *Macedonians* p. 376 no. 85); cf. La'da E1467 (f. *Διοκλῆς*)
MACEDONIA (BOTTIAIA):
—BEROIA: (2) ii/iii AD *IBer* 143 B, 25 (Tataki 905) (s. *Ζωΐλος*)
MACEDONIA (EDONIS):
—AMPHIPOLIS: (3) iii BC *PAE* 1985, p. 74 (*SEG* XLVIII 719) (s. *Διονύσιος*); (4) hell.-imp. ib. XL 522 a
—PHILIPPOI: (5) ?iv/iii BC ib. XLVI 358; (6) ii/iii AD *CIL* III 633 II c, 18 (Pilhofer 163); *CRAI* 1923, p. 277 (date); Collart, *Philippes* pls. 64-5 (Lat. L. Atiarius Moschos, Moschas—Fredrich)
MACEDONIA (ELIMEIA):
—AIANE (TERRIT.): (7) 138-161 AD *EAM* 35, 8 ([*Αἴ*]*λ. Μ.*)
MACEDONIA (MYGDONIA):
—THESSALONIKE: (8) s. i AD *IG* X (2) (1) 68, 22 (I f. *Μόσχος* II); (9) ~ ib. l. 22; 69, 16 (II s. *Μόσχος* I); (10) 252 AD ib. 38 B, 26-7 (*Ἄρριος Ἰούλ. Μ.*)
SCYTHIA MINOR:
—ISTROS: (11) i BC-i AD *ISM* I 191 I, 3; (12) ~ ib. l. 14; (13) ~ ib. l. 17; (14) ~ ib. l. 33 (f. —*νιος*); (15) ~ ib. 191 II, 6 (I f. *Μόσχος* II *νεώ(τερος)*); (16) ~ ib. l. 6 (*Μ. νεώ(τερος)*: II s. *Μόσχος* I); (17) ~ ib. l. 30 (f. *Φιλιστίδης*); (18) ~ ib. l. 39 (s. *Ζωΐλος*); (19) ~ ib. l. 44 (f. *Ἀνθρωπίων*); (20) 138 AD ib. 193 I, 103 (I f. *Μ. Ἰούλ. Μόσχος* II); (21) ~ ib. l. 103 (*Μ. Ἰούλ. Μ.*: II s. *Μόσχος* I)
SKYTHIA:
—OLBIA-BORYSTHENES: (22) iii BC *IOSPE* I² 201 I, 57 (f. *Ἀθηνόδωρος*)
—OLBIA-BORYSTHENES*: (23) c. 325-300 BC Gaidukevich, *Ol'viia* p. 310 nos. 1-2; cf. *SEG* XXX 705 (tile)
THRACE:
—BIZONE: (24) i/ii AD *IGB* I² 6, 16 (-σσχος: f. *Ποσειδώνιος*)
—BIZYE: (25) 12-19 AD ib. V 5011, 7 (s. *Δίντας*)
—BYZANTION: (26) i BC-i AD *IByz* 19, 9; (27) imp. ib. 247 (-σκος); (28) ii AD ib. 314 (Fıratlı–Robert pp. 120-1 no. 203) (f. *Ἐπίκτητος*)
—BYZANTION (TERRIT.): (29) ii-i BC *IByz* 214 (Fıratlı–Robert p. 72 no. 76) (f. *Μοκάπορις*)
—BYZANTION?: (30) ii AD *IByz* 333 (s. *Χρυσέρως*)
—MESAMBRIA: (31) c. 55 BC *IGB* I² 323, 1 (s. *Φιλήμων*)
—ODESSOS: (32) ii AD ib. 50 b, 22
—ODESSOS (NR.): (33) s. ii AD ib. 254 (PM 1723); *Dacia* 21 (1977) p. 161 (date) (s. *Ἀρτεμίδωρος*)

Μουγίσαγος
SKYTHIA:
—OLBIA-BORYSTHENES: (1) iii AD *IOlbia* 83, 11 (*IOSPE* I² 97); Zgusta, *PNS* 676 (s. *Ἄσανος*)

Μούκα
THRACE:
—PHILIPPOPOLIS-TRIMONTIUM (TERRIT.): (1) ii-iii AD *IGB* III 1325 (d. *Ζεράζενις*)

Μουκάβεσος
THRACE:
—PHILIPPOPOLIS-TRIMONTIUM (TERRIT.): (1) ii-iii AD ib. 1457 (s. *Διάζενις*)

Μουκαβίθυρις
THRACE:
—KRASALOPARA: (1) 202 AD ib. 1690 b, 54 (and Thrace Pizos: s. *Δίσυρος*)

Μουκαζεις
THRACE:
—BYZANTION: (1) i BC-i AD *IByz* 199 (Fıratlı–Robert p. 60 no. 44) (*Μουκαζει* (gen.): f. —*εα*)

Μουκάζενις
THRACE:
—BEROE-AUGUSTA TRAIANA (TERRIT.): (1) ii-iii AD *IGB* III 1752 (*Μουκάζ*[*ενις*])
—BRESTE (MOD.): (2) ?iii AD *ILB* 176 (Lat. Mucazenis: f. *Ζειζεις*)
—GLAVA PANEGA (MOD.): (3) ii-iii AD *IGB* II 539 (*Μουκαζένεος* (gen.): f. *Σεύθης*)
—HADRIANOPOLIS (TERRIT.): (4) iii AD ib. III 1831 (*Αὐρ. Μουκάζινις*: s. *Πυτρος*, f. *Ἐπτησυκος*)
—KELLAI*: (5) iii AD ib. 1516 b, 3 (*Μουκάζε*[*νις*])
—MONTANA: (6) f. iii AD *Montana* II 57 (Lat. Iul. Mucazenus)
—NICOPOLIS AD ISTRUM: (7) ii-iii AD *IGB* II 677 (*Eastern cults* p. 163 no. 3) (s. *Αὐλούκενθος*)
—NICOPOLIS AD NESTUM: (8) ii-iii AD *IGB* IV 2337, 4
—PAUTALIA (TERRIT.): (9) ii-iii AD ib. 2203; (10) ~ ib. 2222 (*Μουκάζε*[*νις*]); (11) ~ ib. V 5825 ([*Μο*]*υκάζενις*: s. *Διζάτραλις*)
—PHILIPPOPOLIS-TRIMONTIUM (TERRIT.): (12) ii-iii AD ib. III 1396 (*Μουκάζεν*[*ις*]); (13) ~ ib. 1895 (f. *Κότυς*); (14) iii AD ib. 1079 (s. *Ἔπταλας*)
—SERDICA: (15) ii AD ib. IV 1923, 10 ([*Μ*]*ουκάζενι*[*ς*]) ?= (*16*); (16) ~ ib. l. 11 (*Μουκάζε*[*νις*]: f. —*νης*) ?= (*17*) (*15*); (17) ~ ib. l. 12 ([*Μο*]*υκάζενι*[*ς*]) ?= (*16*)
—SPINOPARA*: (18) ii AD ib. 2194, 1 (*Μουκά*[*ζ*]*ενις*: f. —*ας*)
THRACE?: (19) 215 AD Balty–van Rengen, *Apamea* p. 23 pl. 2 (Lat. Aurelius Mucazanus)

Μουκακάκης
THRACE:
—GLAVA PANEGA (MOD.): (1) iii AD *IGB* II 538 (*Μουκακάκεους* (gen.): f. *Ἐβρύζενις*)

Μουκάκενθος
MACEDONIA (PAIONIA):
—STOBOI: (1) ii AD Šašel, *IL* 457 (Lat. Mucacenthus: s. *Δίζας*)
THRACE:
—BEROE-AUGUSTA TRAIANA (TERRIT.): (2) ii-iii AD *IGB* III 1770 (s. *Πόρις*); (3) ~ ib. 1793; cf. V 5641 ([*Μο*]*υκάκενθος*: s. —*υτος*)
—BOURDAPA: (4) ii-iii AD ib. III 1351 (s. *Διζάλας*)
—HADRIANOPOLIS (TERRIT.): (5) ii-iii AD ib. 1803, 1 (s. *Δαικώσης*, f. *Νικήτας*)
—NOVAE*: (6) 218-222 AD *ILNovae* 18 (Lat. M. Val. Mucacentus: f. M. Val. Flavianus (Cirta))

—OMURTAG (MOD.): **(7)** f. iii AD IGB II 769 (CCET II (2) 531) ([Μου]κάκενθος: s. Βίθυς)
—PAUTALIA (TERRIT.): **(8)** ii-iii AD IGB V 5805
—PHILIPPOPOLIS-TRIMONTIUM: **(9)** ii-iii AD ib. III 951 (s. Μουκάτραλις)
—PHILIPPOPOLIS-TRIMONTIUM (TERRIT.): **(10)** ii-iii AD ib. 1073 (s. Δίνις); **(11)** ~ ib. 1199 (s. Βίθυς); **(12)** iii AD ib. 1101 (f. Αὐρ. Σάλβις)
THRACE?: **(13)** imp. AEp 1930, no. 133 (Lat. Mucacentus: f. Spinus)

Μουκαπαίβης
THRACE:
—LJUBLEN (MOD.): **(1)** iii AD IGB II 754 (CCET II (2) 563); **(2)** f. iii AD ib. (2) 566 (Lat. Aurelius Mucapaibes)

Μουκάπορις
SCYTHIA MINOR:
—ISTROS [NR.]:
——Vicus Quintionis: **(1)** 167 AD ISM I 327, 6 (Lat. Mucaporo (abl.): s. Διτούκενθος)
—TROPAEUM TRAIANI: **(2)** f. iii AD CCET IV 1, 2 (Lat. Mucapori (gen.): f. Σκῶρις)
THRACE: **(3)** 90 AD CIL XVI 36 (Lat. Mucapori (dat.): s. Ἐπταίκενθος); **(4)** ii-iii AD IGB V 5394 bis (f. Αὐλούζενις)
—BAZOPARA: **(5)** 202 AD ib. III 1690 d, 38 (and Thrace Pizos: Μουκάπορις: f. —ατραλις); **(6)** ~ ib. l. 40 (and Thrace Pizos: Μο[υ]κάπ[ορ]ις: I f. Μουκάπορις II); **(7)** ~ ib. l. 40 (and Thrace Pizos: Μο[υκ]άπ[ο]ρις: II s. Μουκάπορις I); **(8)** ~ ib. l. 45 (and Thrace Pizos: I f. Μουκάπορις II); **(9)** ~ ib. l. 45 (and Thrace Pizos: II s. Μουκάπορις I); **(10)** ~ ib. l. 59 (and Thrace Pizos: f. Σάλας); **(11)** ~ ib. 1690 c, 44 (and Thrace Pizos: Μο[υ]κάπορις: f. Διασκούπορις); **(12)** ~ ib. l. 63 (and Thrace Pizos: f. Αὐλούζενις); **(13)** ~ ib. l. 50-1 (and Thrace Pizos: f. Κέλσος, Μουκάτραλις)
—BERGULA-ARKADIOPOLIS: **(14)** i BC-i AD Taşlıklıoğlu 2 p. 6 no. 1 (Μουκαπόρεως (gen.))
—BEROE-AUGUSTA TRAIANA: **(15)** ii-iii AD IGB III 1583 (f. Σεβαστιανός); **(16)** ~ ib. (s. Μ—); **(17)** iii AD CIL VI 32625 a, 9 (Lat. Aur. Mucapor)
—BEROE-AUGUSTA TRAIANA (TERRIT.): **(18)** ii-iii AD IGB III 1670 (Μουκάβουρ(ις): s. Αὐλούζενις); **(19)** ~ ib. 1736 (f. Μουκαπουις); **(20)** ~ ib. 1741, 1 (f. Δόλης); **(21)** ~ ib. V 5611 (s. Δόλης); **(22)** ~ ib. 5628 (-πουρις)
—BEROE-AUGUSTA TRAIANA:
——Karasoura: **(23)** ii-iii AD ib. III 1633 (GVI 280) (-πουρεις); **(24)** iii AD IGB III 1626, 11 (-βορις: s. Αὐλου(—)); **(25)** ~ ib. l. 12 (s. Βρι(—)); **(26)** ~ ib. l. 13 (s. Μουκα(—))
—BYZANTION: **(27)** ii-i BC IByz 103 (Firatlı-Robert p. 95 no. 134) (Μουκάπο[ρις]: f. Γλύκων)
—DRAGANOVEC (MOD.): **(28)** f. iii AD IGB V 5300 (CCET II (2) 459) (s. Αὐλούζενις)
—ERGISSENOI: **(29)** ii AD IGB III 1593, 6 (Φλ. Μ.: s. Σκέλης)
—GELOUPARA: **(30)** 202 AD ib. 1690 c, 32 (and Thrace Pizos: Μο[υ]κ[ά]πορις: s. Δρένις)
—HADRIANOPOLIS (TERRIT.): **(31)** ii-iii AD ib. 1806 (s. Αὐλούζενις); **(32)** iii AD ib. 1816 (Μουκάβ(ου)ρις: s. Μουκάτραλις)
—KELLAI*: **(33)** iii AD ib. 1516 b, 33 (s. Διάσκενθος, Μόντα)
—KOURPISOS: **(34)** 202 AD ib. 1690 c, 35 (and Thrace Pizos: s. Βίθυς)
—KRASALOPARA: **(35)** 202 AD ib. 1690 b, 50 (and Thrace Pizos: f. Αὐλούζενις); **(36)** ~ ib. l. 52 (and Thrace Pizos: s. Ἀντίοχος); **(37)** ~ ib. l. 63 (and Thrace Pizos: f. Μουκάτραλις); **(38)** ~ ib. l. 64 (s. Μουκάτραλις); **(39)** ~ ib. l. 65 (and Thrace Pizos: s. Βίθυς); **(40)** ~ ib. l. 66 (and Thrace Pizos: Μουκάπ<π>ορις: s. Δορζένθης)
—MARKIANOPOLIS: **(41)** f. iii AD ib. V 5343 (CCET II (1) 197) + CCET II 208 (f. Αὐλούζενις)
—MARKIANOPOLIS (TERRIT.): **(42)** ii-iii AD IGB II 846 (Μου[κάπο]ρις: f. Αὐλούζενις)
—NICOPOLIS AD ISTRUM: **(43)** ii AD ib. 680, 8 (Eastern cults p. 266 no. 2) (f. Φῆλιξ)
—NICOPOLIS AD ISTRUM (TERRIT.): **(44)** 227 AD ILB 438 II, 14 (Lat. Mucap(oris): s. Μῆνις)
—ODESSOS (NR.): **(45)** iii AD BMNVarna 10 (1955) p. 133 no. 19 (Lat. Mucaporis: f. Δερζίτραλις)
—PAUTALIA (TERRIT.): **(46)** ii-iii AD IGB V 5821 (Μουκάπο[ρις]: ?s. Ἀλέξανδρος)
—PERINTHOS-HERAKLEIA*: **(47)** c. 304 AD Act. Sanct. Oct. IX p. 546 with n. (Lat. Mucapor)
—PHILIPPOPOLIS-TRIMONTIUM (TERRIT.): **(48)** ii-iii AD IGB III 1106 (f. Δίζας); **(49)** ~ ib. 1197 (s. Δίνις)
—PHILIPPOPOLIS-TRIMONTIUM?: **(50)** imp. CIL VI 2954, 8 (ILS 2137) (Lat. Mucapora (gen.): f. Τάταζα)
—PIZOS: **(51)** 202 AD IGB III 1690 e, 15 (f. Μουκιανός)
—STRATOPARA: **(52)** 202 AD ib. 1690 b, 27 (and Thrace Pizos: s. Μουκάτραλις) (Lat. M. Ulpius Mucapor)
THRACE?: **(53)** 198 AD CIL VI 3314, 8 (Speidel, Denkmäler 542) (Lat. Aurel. Mucapor); **(54)** 272-275 AD PLRE I (-); PIR² M 690 (Lat. Mucapor: fict.?)

Μουκαπουιους
THRACE:
—BOURDAPA: **(1)** ii-iii AD IGB III 1354 (Μουκαπουιους (nom./gen.?): d. Βάλης)
—ČOMAKOVCI (MOD.): **(2)** ?iii AD ILB 165 (Lat. Mucapuius: d. Δίζης)

Μουκάπουις
THRACE:
—BEROE-AUGUSTA TRAIANA (TERRIT.): **(1)** ii-iii AD IGB III 1736 (Μουκάπο<ο>υις: s. Μουκάπορις)

Μούκας
MACEDONIA (MYGDONIA):
—LETE: **(1)** 180 AD SEG XLVIII 808
THRACE:
—ABRYTTOS (TERRIT.)?: **(2)** f. iii AD Romanizmăt II 88 (Lat. Aur. Muca)
—BARGALA: **(3)** ii-iii AD SEG XLIV 514 (s. Βάβος)
—GLAVA PANEGA (MOD.): **(4)** ii-iii AD IGB II 543 (Μούκου (gen.): f. Σεουῆρος)
—PHILIPPOPOLIS-TRIMONTIUM: **(5)** ii-iii AD ib. V 5438 (s. Ἀλέξανδρος)
—SERDICA: **(6)** ii-iii AD ib. IV 1922, 9
THRACE?: **(7)** iii AD Speidel, Denkmäler 567 (Lat. Aur. Mucca)

Μουκασεισος
THRACE:
—ANCHIALOS (TERRIT.)?: **(1)** imp. SEG XXIV 907 (pithos)

Μουκάσης
MACEDONIA (MYGDONIA):
—ARDROLOS: **(1)** i/ii AD ib. XLII 590; cf. Anthémonte–Kalindoia 2 pp. 292-3 (name) (s. Βίθυς)
MACEDONIA (ODOMANTIKE):
—GAZOROS (TERRIT.): **(2)** 106 AD SEG XXX 596, 5, 7 (Pilhofer 555) (Μουκάσου (gen.): f. (ad.) Διοσκουρίδης, f. Σούρα)
MACEDONIA (SINTIKE): **(3)** 158 AD IGB V 5926 (f. Ἀρτεμίδωρος)
—PARTHIKOPOLIS: **(4)** ?ii AD FGrH 257 F 37, 53 (Tataki, Macedonians p. 147 no. 7) (Μουκάσου (gen.): f. Ζαικένθης)
—PARTHIKOPOLIS (TERRIT.): **(5)** 152 AD Melnik I p. 166 no. 6 (Μουκάσου (gen.): f. Παίβης); **(6)** ~ ib. (s. Παίβης, Μάντα); **(7)** ii/iii AD IGB IV 2312 (Μουκάσου (gen.): f. Πυρούσαλα); **(8)** 235-253 AD ib. 2314; JDAI 84 (1969) p. 160 (date) (f. Ἀρτεμιδώρα)
THRACE: **(9)** i AD IGerasa 199 (biling.) ((Μ)ου(κ)άσης?, K. Οὐεάσης—Welles, Κοτελσης—CIL: s. Ἐπταίκενθος)
—MARKIANOPOLIS (TERRIT.): **(10)** iii AD IGB V 5329, 2 (Μουκασῆους (gen.): f. Αὐλούπορις)
—NICOPOLIS AD NESTUM (TERRIT.): **(11)** ii AD IG II² 10770; Tekmeria 6 (2001) pp. 149 ff. (locn.); cf. LGPN II s.v. (1) (Μουκάσου (gen.): f. Μομος); **(12)** ~ IGB IV 2349 (Μουκασῆους (gen.): f. —τειζις)
—PAUTALIA: **(13)** ii AD ib. II 511 (Μουκασῆους (gen.): f. Δίζας)
—PAUTALIA (TERRIT.): **(14)** ii-iii AD ib. IV 2142 (Αἰλ. Μ.)
—PAUTALIA:
——Karistoron: **(15)** ii-iii AD ib. 2151
—PHILIPPOPOLIS-TRIMONTIUM (TERRIT.): **(16)** i-ii AD ib. III 1317, 4 (Μουκασῆους (gen.): f. Ταταζιη)

Μουκάσιος
SCYTHIA MINOR:
—TOMIS (NR.): **(1)** ii AD ISM II 128 (biling.) (CCET IV 205) (Τι(β). Κλ. Μ.) ?= (2); **(2)** ?ii AD ISM II 227 (Lat. [C]l. Mucasius) ?= (1)

Μούκασος
MACEDONIA (ODOMANTIKE):
—SIRRHA (NR.): **(1)** ii/iii AD SEG XXX 602 (f. Ἀλέξανδρος)

Μουκάσουκον
THRACE:
—PHILIPPOPOLIS-TRIMONTIUM: **(1)** ii-iii AD IGB III 1016

Μουκάτραλις
SCYTHIA MINOR:
—ISTROS [NR.]:
——Vicus Quintionis: **(1)** 175 AD ISM I 330, 9 (Lat. Mucatralo (dat.): s. Dolus)
—ISTROS*: **(2)** 152 AD Pontica 31 (1998) p. 111 no. 1, 5 (Lat. T. Aelius Mucatral(is))
SKYTHIA:
—OLBIA-BORYSTHENES: **(3)** imp. IOSPE I² 237, 6 (Lat. Val. Mucatralis); **(4)** i-ii AD IOlbia 139 ([Μου]κάτραλις?: s. Διο—)
THRACE: **(5)** imp. AEp 1930, no. 133 (Lat. Mucatrali (gen.): f. Quintus); **(6)** f. iii AD IGB V 5665 (Μουκάτραλ[ις]); **(7)** 223 AD ZPE 127 (1999) p. 245 no. 2 (Lat. [Mu]catralis)
—ANCHIALOS (TERRIT.): **(8)** ii-iii AD IGB V 5651 ([Μο]υκάτ[ρα]λις); **(9)** ii/iii AD ib. III 1846, 3 (s. Κουίζερις, Δεντουσυκος)
—BAZOPARA: **(10)** 202 AD ib. 1690 d, 27 (and Thrace Pizos: s. Γει..κειλος); **(11)** ~ ib. l. 28 (and Thrace Pizos: s. Βρινκάζερις); **(12)** ~ ib. l. 29 (and Thrace Pizos: s. Δόλης); **(13)** ~ ib. l. 30 (and Thrace Pizos: s. Δαλήτραλις); **(14)** ~ ib. l. 32 (and Thrace Pizos: s. Διασκούπορις); **(15)** ~ ib. l. 33 (and Thrace Pizos: Μ[ου]κ[ά]τρ[α]λις: s. Βρίζενις); **(16)** ~ ib. l. 34 (and Thrace Pizos: [Μου]κάτραλις?: f. Μου—); **(17)** ~ ib. l. 36 (and Thrace Pizos: [Μου]κάτραλις: f. Διο—); **(18)** ~ ib. l. 39 (and Thrace Pizos: Μο[υκά]τραλις: s. Δι—ζ(α)λας); **(19)** ~ ib. l. 41 (and Thrace Pizos: Μουκάτ[ρ]αλις: s. Σεύθης); **(20)** ~ ib. l. 42 (and Thrace Pizos: [Μουκ]άτραλις: s. Βίθυς); **(21)** ~ ib. l. 43 (and Thrace Pizos: Μουκάτραλ(ι)ς: s. Δυτούτραλις); **(22)** ~ ib. l. 44 (and Thrace Pizos: s. Διούπορις); **(23)** ~ ib. l. 55 (and Thrace Pizos: f. Τάρσας); **(24)** ~ ib. l. 58 (and Thrace Pizos: s. Δόλης); **(25)** ~ ib. 1690 c, 51 (and Thrace Pizos: s. Μουκάπορις); **(26)** ~ ib. l. 52 (and Thrace Pizos: s. Βρίζενις); **(27)** ~ ib. l. 53 (and Thrace Pizos: s. Διασκούπορις); **(28)** ~ ib. l. 54 (and Thrace Pizos:

s. *Δαλήζαλις*); (**29**) ~ ib. l. 55 (and Thrace Pizos: *Μουκάτραλις*: s. *Σάλας*); (**30**) ~ ib. l. 56 (and Thrace Pizos: *Μουκάτραλις*: s. *Δυτότραλις*); (**31**) ~ ib. l. 64 (and Thrace Pizos: s. *Αὐλούζενις*); (**32**) ~ ib. l. 61-2 (and Thrace Pizos: f. *Τήρης*, *Αὐρήλιος*)
—BEROE-AUGUSTA TRAIANA: (**33**) f. ii AD *CIL* VIII 3198 (18312) (Lat. Mucatralis: I s. *Αὐλούζενις*, f. *Μουκάτραλις* II); (**34**) ~ ib. 3198 (18312); cf. *Dacia* 11-12 (1945-7) p. 16 no. 4 (Lat. Mucatralis Ianurius: II s. *Μουκάτραλις* I); (**35**) 154-160 AD *ZPE* 139 (2002) p. 223 no. 4 (Lat. [M]ucatralis: s. -itus)
—BEROE-AUGUSTA TRAIANA (TERRIT.): (**36**) ii-iii AD *IGB* III 1717 (*Μουκάτρ[αλις]*); (**37**) ~ ib. 1723
—BEROE-AUGUSTA TRAIANA:
——Karasoura: (**38**) ii-iii AD ib. 1630 (*[Μο]υκάτραλις*: s. *Γρᾶτος*); (**39**) ~ ib. 1631, 1 (II s. *Μουκάτραλις* I, f. *Βρινκαζις*, *Διάτραλις*); (**40**) ~ ib. l. 2 (I f. *Μουκάτραλις* II, *Βρασιτραλις*); (**41**) iii AD ib. 1626, 7 (s. *Ἐπτη(—)*); (**42**) ~ ib. l. 14 (s. *Δια(—)*)
—BEROE-AUGUSTA TRAIANA (NR.): (**43**) ii-iii AD ib. 1621 (s. *Λάζερις*)
—BESSOI?: (**44**) ii AD *ILB* 64 (Lat. Mucatral(is): s. *Σιτᾶς*)
—BOURDAPA: (**45**) ii-iii AD *IGB* III 1367 (s. *Β—*)
—BOUSIPARA: (**46**) 202 AD ib. 1690 d, 71 (and Thrace Pizos: I f. *Μουκάτραλις* II); (**47**) ~ ib. l. 71 (and Thrace Pizos: II s. *Μουκάτραλις* I)
—DIOSPOLIS?: (**48**) ii-iii AD ib. 1782, 2; cf. IV 2028 (or Thrace Serdica: f. *Δίζας*)
—ERGISSENOI: (**49**) ii AD ib. III 1593, 19 (s. *Κέλσος*)
—GELOUPARA: (**50**) 202 AD ib. 1690 c, 23 (and Thrace Pizos: I f. *Μουκάτραλις* II); (**51**) ~ ib. l. 23 (and Thrace Pizos: II s. *Μουκάτραλις* I); (**52**) ~ ib. l. 24 (and Thrace Pizos: s. *Σάθης*); (**53**) ~ ib. l. 25 (and Thrace Pizos: s. *Βίθυς*); (**54**) ~ ib. l. 26 (and Thrace Pizos: s. *Διασκούπορις*); (**55**) ~ ib. l. 27 (and Thrace Pizos: s. *Αὐλούζενις*)
—GLAVA PANEGA (MOD.): (**56**) ii-iii AD ib. II 556 (s. *Κρίσπος*)
—HADRIANOPOLIS (TERRIT.): (**57**) ii-iii AD ib. III 1805 (*Μου[κάτ]ραλις*: f. *Δύδης*); (**58**) ~ ib. 1806 (f. *Αὐλούπορις*); (**59**) iii AD ib. 1816 (f. *Μουκάπορις*)
—IATRUS: (**60**) b. 402 AD *Arch. Bulg.* 1997 (2), p. 46 (*Πούπ(λιος) Μ.*)
—KELLAI*: (**61**) iii AD *IGB* III 1516 a, 27; (**62**) ~ ib. 1516 b, 16 (f. *Σάλας*); (**63**) ~ ib. l. 29 (f. *—οιυιος*); (**64**) ~ ib. l. 32 (*Μουκάτραλ[ις]*: s. *Διάσκενθος*, *Μόντα*)
—KOURPISOS: (**65**) 202 AD ib. 1690 c, 36 (and Thrace Pizos: f. *Βρασήτραλις*); (**66**) ~ ib. l. 37 (and Thrace Pizos: s. *Βρίζενις*); (**67**) ~ ib. l. 38 (and Thrace Pizos: s. *Βίθυς*); (**68**) ~ ib. l. 39 (and Thrace Pizos: I f. *Μουκάτραλις* II); (**69**) ~ ib. l. 39 (and Thrace Pizos: II s. *Μουκάτραλις* I)
—KRASALOPARA: (**70**) 202 AD ib. 1690 b, 51 (and Thrace Pizos: f. *Ἐπτήπορις*); (**71**) ~ ib. l. 62 (and Thrace Pizos: *Μουκάτ[ρ]αλις*: f. *Ἐπταίκενθος*); (**72**) ~ ib. l. 69 (and Thrace Pizos: f. *Σεκοῦνδος*); (**73**) ~ ib. l. 63-4 (s. *Μουκάπορις*, f. *Μουκάπορις*)
—MARKIANOPOLIS (TERRIT.): (**74**) ii AD ib. II 854 (*CCET* II (1) 270) (*Μουκάτραλ[ις]*); (**75**) ii-iii AD *IGB* II 843, 1 (*Μο[υκ]άτραλ[ι]ς*: f. *Δίνις*)
—MARKIANOPOLIS (NR.): (**76**) f. iii AD ib. 836 (*CCET* II (1) 330) (-λεις: s. *Ἐπτάτραλις*)
—MEDOVINA (MOD.): (**77**) f. iii AD *IGB* V 5275 (*CCET* II (2) 543)
—MESAMBRIA (TERRIT.): (**78**) ii-iii AD *IGB* I² 363 (*[Μου]κάτραλις*); (**79**) f. iii AD ib. 354 (*CCET* I 115)
—MESAMBRIA:
——Carsaleon: (**80**) iii AD *IGB* I² 355 (*CCET* I 119)
—NICOPOLIS AD ISTRUM: (**81**) f. iii AD *IGB* II 694 (*CCET* II (2) 629) (*Μ[ουκ]άτραλ[ις]*: s. *Βίθυς*)
—NICOPOLIS AD NESTUM: (**82**) ii-iii AD *IGB* IV 2337, 15 (*[Μ]οκάτραλις*: s. *Τόνος*)
—NOVAE: (**83**) ii-iii AD *IGLNovae* 38 (Lat. [Mu]catralu[s])
—PAUTALIA: (**84**) ii AD *IGB* IV 2074, 12
—PAUTALIA (TERRIT.): (**85**) ii AD ib. 2141 + V 5863 (*[Μ]ουκάτράλις*: f. *Μένδρα*); (**86**) ii-iii AD ib. IV 2224 (f. *Σεβαζιανός*)
—PHILIPPOPOLIS-TRIMONTIUM: (**87**) ii-iii AD ib. III 951 (f. *Μουκάκενθος*)
—PHILIPPOPOLIS-TRIMONTIUM (TERRIT.): (**88**) imp. ib. 1089 (-λης: s. *Κοσωυλ—*); (**89**) ii-iii AD ib. 1093 (*Μουκάτ[ραλις]*); (**90**) ~ ib. 1097 (f. *Ἐπτέπυρις*); (**91**) ~ ib. 1107 (I f. *Μουκάτραλις* II); (**92**) ~ ib. (II s. *Μουκάτραλις* I); (**93**) ~ ib. 1133 (f. *Σεβαστιανός*); (**94**) ~ ib. 1303, 10 (*Μουκάτρα[λις]*: s. *Κότυς*); (**95**) ~ ib. 1377 (*Μουκάτρ[αλις]*); (**96**) ~ ib. 1386; (**97**) ~ ib. 1405 (f. *Βίθυς*); (**98**) ~ ib. 1438 (*Μουκάτραλ[ις]*: s. *Διο—*); (**99**) iii AD ib. 1103 (*Αὐρ. Μ.*); (**100**) ~ ib. 1430 (f. *Βρύζος*)
—SERDICA: (**101**) 237 AD *CIL* XVI 146 (Speidel, *Denkmäler* 79) (Lat. Mucatralis (gen.): f. *Ζερούλας*)
—SERDICA (TERRIT.): (**102**) ii-iii AD *IGB* V 5716 (*[Μουκ]άτραλις*)
—SEUTHOPOLIS (NR.): (**103**) ii-iii AD ib. III 1758 (s. *Σεύθης*)
—SKEDABRIA: (**104**) 202 AD ib. 1690 b, 18 (and Thrace Pizos: s. *Ἄθυς*); (**105**) ~ ib. l. 19 (and Thrace Pizos: *Μ. Βοσις*: s. *Βίθης*); (**106**) ~ ib. l. 20 (and Thrace Pizos: s. *Βίθυς*); (**107**) ~ ib. l. 21 (and Thrace Pizos: s. *Δίνις*); (**108**) ~ ib. l. 13-14 (and Thrace Pizos: *Μο[υ]κάτρα[λις]*—l. 14: f. *Βύζης*, *Δόλης*)
—SKEPTA: (**109**) 202 AD ib. 1690 c, 14 (and Thrace Pizos: s. *Βοσις*)
—SPORTELA: (**110**) ii-iii AD ib. IV 2233, 5 (*Eastern cults* p. 170 no. 16) (f. *Βίθυς*)
—STRATOPARA: (**111**) 202 AD *IGB* III 1690 b, 27 (and Thrace Pizos: f. *Μουκάπορις*); (**112**) ~ ib. l. 29 (and Thrace Pizos: s. *Αὐλούπορις*); (**113**) ~ ib. l. 30 (and Thrace Pizos: I f. *Μουκάτραλις* II); (**114**) ~ ib. l. 30 (and Thrace Pizos: II s. *Μουκάτραλις* I); (**115**) ~ ib. l. 37 (and Thrace Pizos: s. *Ῥοιμητάλκης*); (**116**) ~ ib. l. 38 (and Thrace Pizos: s. *Ἔπτενις*); (**117**) ~ ib. l. 39 (and Thrace Pizos: s. *Σπάρτοκος*); (**118**) ~ ib. l. 40 (and Thrace Pizos: s. *Βύζης*); (**119**) ~ ib. l. 41 (and Thrace Pizos: s. *Ἔβρενις*); (**120**) ~ ib. l. 43 (and Thrace Pizos: II s. *Μουκάτραλις* I); (**121**) ~ ib. l. 46 (and Thrace Pizos: f. *Ἐπτέτραλις*); (**122**) ~ ib. l. 32-3 (and Thrace Pizos: f. *Βίθυς*, *Σάλας*); (**123**) ~ ib. l. 43-4 (and Thrace Pizos: I f. *Μουκάτραλις* II, *Τάρσας*)
—STROUNEILOS: (**124**) 202 AD ib. 1690 d, 68 (and Thrace Pizos: f. *Δυτούτραλις*)
THRACE?: (**125**) imp. *CIL* XIII 11941, 7 (Lat. Mucatralis (gen.): f. *Μουκάπορις*); (**126**) 230 AD *ZPE* 137 (2001) p. 246 (Lat. M. Aurelius Mucatralis)

Μουκατρας
SCYTHIA MINOR:
—CIUS*: (**1**) 244-246 AD *ISM* V 124, 15 (Lat. Mucatra)
THRACE:
—ANCHIALOS: (**2**) ii AD *CIL* VI 32533 b, 22 (Lat. [Mu]catra); (**3**) ?ii AD ib. 32536 d, 5 (Lat. [M]ucatr(a))
—BEROE-AUGUSTA TRAIANA (TERRIT.): (**4**) ii-iii AD *IGB* III 1725 (s. *Λύκος*)
—NICOPOLIS AD ISTRUM (TERRIT.): (**5**) iii AD ib. II 711 (f. *Ζίπυς*)
—PERINTHOS-HERAKLEIA: (**6**) c. 210-215 AD *CIL* VI 32640, 24 (Lat. Iulius Mucatra)
THRACE?: (**7**) m. iv AD *PLRE* I (-) (Lat. Mucatra)

Μουκατρίων
SCYTHIA MINOR:
—ISTROS: (**1**) iii AD *ISM* I 308 (Lat. Mucatrio: s. *Σεύθων*)

Μουκιανή
THRACE:
—MADYTOS: (**1**) imp. *ISestos* 65 (d. *Μούκιος*)
—NICOPOLIS AD ISTRUM (TERRIT.): (**2**) ii/iii AD *ILB* 430 (Lat. Muciane (dat.): d. *Μουκιανός*)

Μουκιανός
MACEDONIA (EDONIS):
—PHILIPPOI: (**1**) imp. *BCH* 61 (1937) p. 416 no. 10 (Pilhofer 134) (Lat. Mucianus: s. *Βενδίς*, Rufus)
—PHILIPPOI?: (**2**) ?iii-iv AD *CIL* III 14203. 10 (*AE* 1950-1, p. 73 no. 17; Pilhofer 732) (Lat. Mucian[us])
MACEDONIA (ODOMANTIKE):
—SIRRHA: (**3**) 155 AD Dimitsas 821, 23 (Kaphtantzis 1) (f. *Τορκουᾶτος*); (**4**) ~ Dimitsas 821, 28 (Kaphtantzis 1) (f. *Εὔτυχος*)
MACEDONIA (SINTIKE):
—NEINE: (**5**) ii AD *IGB* IV 2244 (*Μουκιαν[ός]*: s. *—βαρις*)
SCYTHIA MINOR:
—KALLATIS (NR.): (**6**) ii AD *ISM* III 246 (*CCET* IV 90)
THRACE: (**7**) iii AD *BMNRuse* 1968 (3), pp. 3 ff. no. 2 (Minkova, *PNLIB* p. 216) (Lat. Aur. Mucianus); (**8**) ~ *IGB* III 1875 (f. *Αὐρ. Σαμβαθίων*)
—ABRYTTOS (TERRIT.): (**9**) ii-iii AD ib. II 748 (*Φάλβις Μου[κια]νός*); (**10**) iii AD ib. 749 (biling.) (*Αὐρ. Μ.*)
—ANCHIALOS (TERRIT.): (**11**) iii AD ib. III 1838; cf. V 5646 (*Αὐρ. Μ.*)
—APRILOVO (MOD.): (**12**) iii AD ib. II 766 (*CCET* II (2) 540) (*Μουκιαν[ός]*)
—BARGALA: (**13**) ii-iii AD *SEG* XLIV 510 (*CCET* V 38)
—BAZOPARA: (**14**) 202 AD *IGB* III 1690 c, 57 (and Thrace Pizos: *Μουκ[ια]νός*: s. *Μάρκελλος*)
—BEROE-AUGUSTA TRAIANA: (**15**) ?s. i AD ib. V 5572 (*[Τιβ.] [Κλ.] —ελι ὁ καὶ Μουκιαν(ός)*); (**16**) c. 268 AD ib. III 1568, 7; 1569, 9; *PIR*² M 692; *PLRE* I (1) ?= (*17*); (**17**) c. 270 AD *IGB* III 1570, 1; cf. V 5559; *RE* s.v. Traianus (1); *PLRE* I (5) (*Τραιανὸς Μ.*) ?= (*16*)
—BEROE-AUGUSTA TRAIANA (TERRIT.): (**18**) ii-iii AD *IGB* III 1638 (f. *Ποτάμων*); (**19**) ~ ib. 1641; (**20**) ~ ib. 1660 (*[Μ]ουκ[ι]ανός*); (**21**) ~ ib. 1712 (*Μουκι(ανός)*); (**22**) ~ ib. 1746 (s. *Σάλας*); (**23**) iii AD ib. 1685 (*Eastern cults* p. 134 no. 134) (*Αὐρ. Μ.*); (**24**) ~ *IGB* III 1756, 6 (*Μ. Αὐρ. Μ.*: s. *Ῥουστῖνος*)
—BEROE-AUGUSTA TRAIANA:
——Karasoura: (**25**) iii AD ib. 1628, 4 (*Ἀδριάνιος Μ.*: f. *Αὐρ. Μακεσατος*)
—BOURDAPA: (**26**) ii-iii AD ib. 1345 (f. *Ἡραΐς*)
—DIONYSOPOLIS: (**27**) iii AD ib. I² 14 b, 10 (*Αὐρ. Μ.*: s. *Ἰούλιος*); (**28**) ~ ib. 14 bis, 6 (*Μουκι[ανός]*)
—DUROSTORUM (TERRIT.)?: (**29**) iii AD ib. II 868, 2 (*CCET* II (1) 186)
—GLAVA PANEGA (MOD.): (**30**) ii-iii AD *IGB* II 520 (*Φλ. Μ.*)
—HADRIANOPOLIS (TERRIT.): (**31**) ii-iii AD ib. III 1808; (**32**) iii AD *CIL* III 7414 (biling.) (*Αὐρ. Μ.*)
—KELLAI: (**33**) ii-iii AD *IGB* III 1520 (*Αὐρ. Μ.*: s. *Δίνις*); (**34**) 241-244 AD ib. 1517, 7 (s. *Δόλης*); (**35**) ~ ib. l. 12 (*Αὐρ. Μ.*: s. *Διονύσιος*); (**36**) ~ ib. l. 15 (*Αὐρ. Μ.*); (**37**) ~ ib. l. 20 (*Αὐρ. Μ.*); (**38**) ~ ib. l. 24 (f. *Αὐρ. Δόρζας*) ?= (*44*); (**39**) ~ ib. l. 24 (*Αὐρ. Μ.*); (**40**) ~ ib. l. 28 (*Αὐρ. Μ.*); (**41**) ~ ib. l. 42 (f. *Αὐρ. Καρδένθης*); (**42**) ~ ib. l. 50 (f. *Αὐρ. Ἡρακλιανός*); (**43**) ~ ib. l. 56

(*Αὐρ. Μ.*: s. *Διόδωρος*); **(44)** ~ ib. l. 6-7 (*Αὐρ. Μ.*: s. *Δόρζας*) ?= *(38)*
—KELLAI (NR.): **(45)** iii AD ib. 1535-6 (*Αὐρ. Μ.*: s. *Ἰουλιανός*)
—KOVAČEVEC (MOD.): **(46)** iii AD ib. V 5274 (*Λ. Μουκι[ανός]*)
—LJUBLEN (MOD.): **(47)** iii AD ib. II 756 (*CCET* II (2) 565) (s. *Δο—*); **(48)** f. iii AD *IGB* II 755 (*CCET* II (2) 564) (*Αὐρ. Μ.*)
—MARKIANOPOLIS: **(49)** ii AD *IGB* V 5340, 4 ([*Μου*]*κιανός*?)
—NICOPOLIS AD ISTRUM?: **(50)** 225 AD *RMD* 310 (or Thrace Nicopolis ad Nestum: Lat. T. Flavius Mucianus)
—NICOPOLIS AD NESTUM: **(51)** a. 212 AD *IGB* IV 2343 (Kaphtantzis 480); cf. Pilhofer 527
—PAUTALIA: **(52)** ii AD *Syringes* 403 (Velkov 441) (*Μουκεανός*—*Syringes*: s. *Λάμπος*); **(53)** ii-iii AD *IGB* IV 2073, 3; **(54)** s. ii AD *SEG* XLVI 864, 12 (s. *Δράκων*)
—PAUTALIA (TERRIT.): **(55)** ii-iii AD *IGB* IV 2132; **(56)** ~ ib. 2210 (f. *Διογένης*); **(57)** ~ ib. V 5788 (s. *Σατορνῖλος*); **(58)** ~ ib. 5856 (*Αἴλ. Μ.*: s. *Κάρρος*); **(59)** iii AD ib. IV 2202 (s. *Δούλης*); **(60)** ~ ib. 2220 ([*Α*]*ὐρ. Μουκιανός*); **(61)** ~ ib. V 5794 (*Αὐρ. Μουκ*[*ιανός*])
—PAUTALIA:
——(Herakleis): **(62)** ?ii AD ib. IV 2077, 5 (f. *Εὐάγριος*)
—PERINTHOS-HERAKLEIA: **(63)** iv-v AD *IPerinth* 183 (*AD* 51-2 (1996-7) Mel. p. 359 no. 180) (*Μω*-: s. *Προβόλιος*)
—PHILIPPOPOLIS-TRIMONTIUM: **(64)** ii AD *IGB* III 997, 1 (s. *Μνάσων*); **(65)** ii-iii AD ib. 885, 2 (f. *Τιβ. Κλ. Πασίνους*); **(66)** iii AD ib. V 5439 (f. *Ἐπιγένης*); **(67)** m. iii AD ib. III 884 a, 19; cf. V 5400; **(68)** ~ ib. III 884 b, 22; cf. V 5400 (*Αὐρ. Μ.*)
—PHILIPPOPOLIS-TRIMONTIUM (TERRIT.): **(69)** iii AD ib. III 1141 (*Αὐρ. Μ.*: ?f. *Ἰακησινάρις*); **(70)** ~ ib. V 5525 ([*Μ*]*ουκεια*<*α*>*νός*); **(71)** f. iii AD ib. III 1075, 4, 6 (biling.) (*Αὐρ. Μ.*)
—PHILIPPOPOLIS-TRIMONTIUM (NR.): **(72)** iii AD ib. 1417 (I f. *Αὐρ. Μουκιανός* II); **(73)** ~ ib. (*Αὐρ. Μουκιανός*: II s. *Μουκιανός* I)
—PIZOS: **(74)** 202 AD ib. 1690 e, 15 (s. *Μουκάπορις*); **(75)** ~ ib. l. 16 (s. *Ἀκύλας*); **(76)** ~ ib. l. 20 (*Φλ. Μ.*)
—SPINOPARA: **(77)** ii AD ib. IV 2192, 6-7 (s. *Σούκιος*)
—STROUNEILOS: **(78)** 202 AD ib. III 1690 d, 64 (and Thrace Pizos: s. *Δ—ε̣ζρείζενις*)

Μούκινος
THRACE:
—PHILIPPOPOLIS-TRIMONTIUM: **(1)** ii-iii AD ib. 1303, 5 (*Δημήτριος ὁ κὲ Μούκινο*[*ς*]: s. *Διο—*)
—PHILIPPOPOLIS-TRIMONTIUM (TERRIT.): **(2)** iii AD ib. 1308 (*Αὐρ. Μούκ̣ινος*)

Μούκιος
THRACE:
—MADYTOS: **(1)** imp. *ISestos* 65 (s. *Σοῦσος*, f. *Μουκιανή*)

Μούκις
THRACE:
—SPINOPARA: **(1)** ii AD *IGB* IV 2192, 14

Μούκκος
THRACE:
—SERDICA (TERRIT.): **(1)** ii-iii AD *Sp.* 98 (1941-48) p. 127 no. 280, 4, 6 (*Μούκος*—l.6: s. *Μᾶρκος*, f. *Βίθυς*)

Μούκκων
MACEDONIA (ODOMANTIKE):
—SIRRHA: **(1)** 155 AD Dimitsas 821, 26 (Kaphtantzis 1) (I f. *Μούκκων* II); **(2)** ~ Dimitsas 821, 26 (Kaphtantzis 1) (II s. *Μούκκων* I); **(3)** ii/iii AD *SEG* XLVIII 877 (s. *Πυρούλας*, *Μωμώ*)
THRACE:
—MELTA:
——Vicus Pereprum: **(4)** imp. *CIL* VI 2736 (Lat. Aur. Mucconi (dat.))

Μουκούναγος
SKYTHIA:
—OLBIA-BORYSTHENES: **(1)** ii AD *IOSPE* I^2 129, 6; Zgusta, *PNS* 677 (s. *Ἀλέξανδρος*)

Μουκουνάκυρος
SKYTHIA:
—OLBIA-BORYSTHENES: **(1)** ii AD *IOSPE* I^2 134, 11; Zgusta, *PNS* 678

Μούκων
THRACE:
—MONTANA (TERRIT.): **(1)** iii AD *Montana* II 67 (Lat. Muco: s. *Ἔπτενις*)

Μουλίουργος
SKYTHIA:
—OLBIA-BORYSTHENES: **(1)** imp. *IOSPE* I^2 113, 11; Zgusta, *PNS* 679 (s. *Ποσίδηος*)

Μουνάτιος
THRACE?: **(1)** iii AD *SEG* XXXI 670 (gem) (f. *Ἰλάρα*)

Μουνδικία
MACEDONIA (CHALKIDIKE):
—ANTIGONEIA: **(1)** i/ii AD ib. XXXVIII 598 (*Μου(ν)δικεία*)

Μουνδίκιος
MACEDONIA (PAIONIA):
—KAVADARCI (MOD.): **(1)** ii/iii AD Unp. (Papazoglu archive) (s. *Ἄρτεμις*)

Μούπορις
THRACE:
—MARONEIA: **(1)** ii AD *IThrakAig* E268 (f. *Δίας*)

Μούρδαγος
SKYTHIA:
—OLBIA-BORYSTHENES: **(1)** ii-iii AD *IOSPE* I^2 138, 8; Zgusta, *PNS* 151 (s. *Καφάναγος*)

Μουρόψαζος
SKYTHIA:
—OLBIA-BORYSTHENES: **(1)** ii AD *IOlbia* 80, 8 (*Μ. Αὐρ. Μικίων ὁ καὶ Μ.*)

Μοῦσα
CIMMERIAN BOSPOROS:
—PANTIKAPAION: **(1)** ii BC *CIRB* 259; cf. KW pl. 30 no. 431; **(2)** i AD *CIRB* 139, 1 (d. *Γλύκων*); **(3)** ?i AD ib. 475; cf. KW pl. 21 no. 300 (d. *Ἡμέρα*); **(4)** i/ii AD *CIRB* 625; cf. KW pl. 56 no. 762 (d. *Ἔρως*)
MACEDONIA (EDONIS):
—PHILIPPOI: **(5)** imp. *CIL* III 672 (Pilhofer 42) (Lat. Naevia Musa)
MACEDONIA (ODOMANTIKE):
—SIRRHA: **(6)** ii-iii AD *SEG* XXXIII 549 + XXXV 1846 (*Ἀπουλεΐα Μ.*: d. *Τ. Ἀπουλέϊος Οὐάλης*, *Ἀπουλεΐα Πριβᾶτα*, m. *Φιρμία Μάξιμα*, *Φιρμία Ὀνησίμη*)
THRACE:
—BYZANTION: **(7)** ii/i BC *IByz* 128 (d. *Ἀγαθοκλῆς*)
—VICUS TRULLENSIUM: **(8)** iii AD *IGB* II 506, 3 (d. *Ἰνγένους*, m. *Μάσκλος*, *Ζειζεις*, *Ἀλέξανδρος*)

Μουσαῖος
MACEDONIA (CHALKIDIKE):
—OLYNTHOS: **(1)** iii/ii BC *NS* 520 (Tataki, *Macedonians* p. 140 no. 86) (s. *Εὔμολπος*)
THRACE:
—DEULTUM: **(2)** ii-iii AD *IGB* III 1849, 6
—DIONYSOPOLIS: **(3)** ii BC ib. I^2 22 I, 7 ([*Μου*]*σαῖος*?)

Μουσική
MACEDONIA (EDONIS):
—PHILIPPOI?: **(1)** ?i-ii AD *AE* 1950-1, p. 68 no. 11, 6 (Pilhofer 726) (or Macedonia (Mygdonia) Thessalonike: Lat. Laelia Musica: freed.)
SCYTHIA MINOR:
—KALLATIS: **(2)** iii-iv AD *ISM* III 148, 14 (*Μουσικίη* (dat.): m. *Εὐφρονίς*)

Μουσίκις
SCYTHIA MINOR:
—TOMIS: **(1)** f. iii AD ib. II 273, 6 (*Αὐρ. Μ.*: s. *Αὐρ. Εὐτυχιανός*, *Στατιλία Ἐλπιδία*)

Μουσικόν
THRACE:
—PHILIPPOPOLIS-TRIMONTIUM: **(1)** iii AD *IGB* III 1024, 7 (*GVI* 695)

Μουσικός
MACEDONIA (EDONIS):
—PHILIPPOI: **(1)** ii AD *BCH* 55 (1931) pp. 201-2 no. 16 (Pilhofer 27) (Lat. L. Licinius Soter qui et Musicus: f. L. Licinius Firmus)
TAURIS:
—KALOS LIMEN: **(2)** ii-iii AD *SEG* XXVI 802 (Solomonik, *GChKh* p. 8 no. 7)

Μουσογένης
SCYTHIA MINOR:
—ISTROS: **(1)** iv BC Unp. (Avram, defixio) 1, 3 (*Μōσογέν*[*ης*]?)

Μουστιανός
MACEDONIA (BOTTIAIA):
—BEROIA: **(1)** ii-iii AD *IBer* 249 (Tataki 908)

Μουσώνιος
THRACE:
—BARGALA: **(1)** v-vi AD Feissel, *RICM* 284 (brick)

Μουτοῖος
THRACE:
—PLOTINOPOLIS: **(1)** 160 AD *SEG* XXXVII 970, 4 (f. *Δίων*)

Μοψύηστις
THRACE: **(1)** c. 281-277 BC *IGB* I^2 307, 15; cf. V 5086 (*Μοψυήστιος* (gen.): king?)

Μύας
MACEDONIA (MYGDONIA):
—KALINDOIA: **(1)** c. 320 BC Hatzopoulos, *MI* 2 p. 84 no. 62, 26 (s. *Φιλίσκος*)

Μυγδονία
MACEDONIA (BOTTIAIA):
—BEROIA*: **(1)** v-vi AD *IBer* 447, 4 (Feissel, *RICM* 60)
THRACE:
—PHILIPPOPOLIS-TRIMONTIUM?: **(2)** c. 303 AD *Anal. Boll.* 31 (1912) p. 192 (m. *Σευῆρος*)

Μύδιον
MACEDONIA: **(1)** ii-i BC *IG* II^2 9265 (Tataki, *Macedonians* p. 378 no. 86; *FRA* 3479) (d. *Σώπατρος*)

Μυκηνεύς
THRACE:
—MARONEIA: **(1)** ii-i BC *IThrakAig* E212, 6 (s. *Θεόξενος*)

Μύκων
MACEDONIA (LYNKESTIS):
—KRATERO (MOD.): **(1)** imp. *EAM* 173

Μύλαγος
MACEDONIA (MYGDONIA):
—THESSALONIKE: **(1)** 257 AD *IG* X (2) (1) 557 (*Κλ. Μ.*: I f. *Μύλαγος* II); **(2)** c. 260 AD ib. 491 (II s. *Ζωσίμη*, *Κλ. Μύλαγος* I)

Μυλλέας
MACEDONIA (BOTTIAIA):
—BEROIA: **(1)** 326 BC *RE* (-); Berve 541 (Tataki, *Macedonians* p. 80 no. 38) (s. *Ζωΐλος*); **(2)** c. 286-262 BC *IG* II^2 710, 6 (Osborne, *Naturalization* D81) (*Μυλλ[έας]—IG*, *Μυλλ[ένας]—IG* II^2 Add.: f. *Ἀλέξανδρος*)

Μυλλένας
MACEDONIA: **(1)** s. iv BC *RE* (-); Berve 542 (Tataki, *Macedonians* p. 81 no. 39); cf. *Eretria* XI p. 172 (ident.) (s. *Ἄσανδρος*)

Μυλλίνας
THRACE:
—SALYMBRIA: **(1)** iii BC *IG* XII Suppl. p. 39 no. 127 B, 39 (*SEG* XXVI 919) (f. [...σ]τρατος)

Μυλλίων
SKYTHIA:
—OLBIA-BORYSTHENES: **(1)** m. iv BC Dubois, *IGDOlbia* 25 a, 3

Μύλλος
THRACE:
—ZONE: **(1)** s. iv BC *PAE* 1969, p. 64 with pl. 75 α (*IThrakAig* E423) (s. *Ἀπολλόδωρος*)

Μυνΐς
CIMMERIAN BOSPOROS:
—PANTIKAPAION: **(1)** f. vi BC *VDI* 1974 (4), p. 57 (vase) (Vinogradov, *Pont. Stud.* pp. 501-14) (*Μυνΐος* (gen.))

Μυννώ
MACEDONIA (BOTTIAIA):
—AIGAI: **(1)** s. iv BC *SEG* XXXV 800 (*Μ[υ]ννώ*)

Μυράνθιν
MACEDONIA (CHALKIDIKE):
—MENDE: **(1)** iii AD *TAPA* 69 (1938) p. 69 no. 24; *BE* 1939, no. 171 (name) (m. *Μικυλίων*)

Μύρης
CIMMERIAN BOSPOROS:
—GORGIPPIA: **(1)** iv BC *SEG* XXXVII 664 g (vase) (*Μύρευ* (gen.?)—n. pr.?)
—PANTIKAPAION: **(2)** i AD *CIRB* 512; Zgusta, *PNS* 1091 (*Μύρεους* (gen.))

Μυρίνα
CIMMERIAN BOSPOROS:
—PANTIKAPAION: **(1)** ?ii AD *CIRB* 673; cf. KW pl. 16 no. 235 (-ρή-)

Μυρίνη
CIMMERIAN BOSPOROS:
—PANTIKAPAION: **(1)** i/ii AD *CIRB* 696; cf. KW pl. 14 no. 205

Μυρῖνος
CIMMERIAN BOSPOROS:
—GORGIPPIA: **(1)** imp. *CIRB* 1189, 5 (*Μυρ(εῖ)νος*: s. *Μυ—*); **(2)** ii AD ib. 1140, 5 (-ρεῖ-: f. *Ἀττακόας*); **(3)** m. ii AD *Eirene* 7 (1968) p. 67, 10 (-ρεῖ-: s. *Πάπας*); **(4)** ii/iii AD *CIRB* 1179, 28 (-ρεῖ-)
—HERMONASSA: **(5)** 123-132 AD ib. 1054, 14 (-ρεῖ-: I f. *Μυρῖνος* II) ?= (7); **(6)** ~ ib. l. 14 (-ρεῖ-: II s. *Μυρῖνος* I); **(7)** ~ ib. l. 16 (-ρεῖ-: f. *Καλοῦς*) ?= (5)
—MYRMEKION: **(8)** i AD ib. 882 (-ρεῖ-: f. *Φαρνάκης*)
—PANTIKAPAION: **(9)** i BC ib. 277; cf. KW p. 31 fig. 5 (*Μυ[ρ]ῖνος*); **(10)** imp. *CIRB* 800 (-ρεῖ-: s. *Ἀπολλόδωρος*); **(11)** i AD ib. 459; cf. KW pl. 22 no. 307 (-ρεῖ-); **(12)** ii AD *CIRB* 679 B (-ρεῖ-: f. *Γοῖσκος*)
—PHANAGOREIA: **(13)** 151 AD ib. 976, 10 (-ρεῖ-: f. *Ἀλέξανδρος*)
SKYTHIA:
—TANAIS: **(14)** 155 AD ib. 1260, 21 (I f. *Μυρῖνος* II); **(15)** ~ ib. l. 21 (-ρεῖ-: II s. *Μυρῖνος* I); **(16)** 228 AD ib. 1283, 16 (-ρεῖ-: s. *Μαστοῦς*)

Μύριππος
SKYTHIA:
—TANAIS: **(1)** 236 AD ib. 1250, 16 (s. *Ἡδύκων*)

Μυρίσκος
CIMMERIAN BOSPOROS:
—GORGIPPIA: **(1)** ii AD ib. 1140, 1 (s. *Ζαζζοῦς*); **(2)** s. ii AD ib. 1129 B, 5 (f. *Χοραγοῦς*); **(3)** ~ *SEG* XXIX 706, 5 (*Μυρίσκ[ος]*); **(4)** 173-210 AD *CIRB* 1134, 25 (s. *Χρηστοῦς*) ?= (5); **(5)** ii/iii AD ib. 1179, 28 (f. *Χρηστοῦς*) ?= (4); **(6)** ~ ib. l. 37 (f. *Ἀθηνόδωρος*)

Μύρισμος
MACEDONIA (BOTTIAIA):
—BEROIA: **(1)** ii/iii AD *IBer* 394, 3 (Tataki 911)
MACEDONIA (MYGDONIA):
—THESSALONIKE: **(2)** iii AD *ISamothrace* 58, 6 (Tataki, *Macedonians* p. 184 no. 43) (*Μάρκιος Μ.*)
TAURIS:
—CHERSONESOS: **(3)** iii AD Solomonik, *NEPKh* 19, 3 (*[Μ]ύρισμος*)
THRACE:
—MARKIANOPOLIS: **(4)** imp. *CIL* III 7471 (*Romanizmăt* II 586) (Lat. Myrizmus: freed.?)

Μύρμαξ
TAURIS:
—CHERSONESOS: **(1)** s. iv BC Solomonik, *GAKh* 1235 (vase)

Μύρμηξ
CIMMERIAN BOSPOROS:
—PANTIKAPAION: **(1)** i AD *CIRB* 461; cf. KW pl. 18 no. 270 (f. *Μάσας*); **(2)** ii AD *CIRB* 680, 4 (f. *Φιλώτας*); **(3)** f. ii AD ib. 88, 5 (f. *Διονύσιος*); **(4)** iii-iv AD ib. 738 (*Μύρμ[ηξ]*)
MACEDONIA (BOTTIAIA):
—PELLA: **(5)** iii/ii BC *A΄ Panell. Synedr. Epigr.* p. 189 no. 10 (*Μύρμηκ[ος]* (gen.): f. *Ἀσκληπιόδωρος*)
SKYTHIA:
—TANAIS: **(6)** 210-226 AD *CIRB* 1281, 15 (s. *Φ—*); **(7)** c. 225-250 AD ib. 1288, 10 (s. *Φαδίναμος*)

Μυρμιδών
MACEDONIA: **(1)** b. 156 BC *ID* 2408 + *ID Index* p. 73 s.v. *Προμαθίων* (*Μυρμιδών*: f. *Προμαθίων*)

Μυρομένη
CIMMERIAN BOSPOROS:
—PANTIKAPAION: **(1)** 227 AD *CIRB* 147, 8 (*Μυρ(ο)μένη*—ed., *Μυρ(ου)μένη*—Tokhtas'ev: d. *Καλλιότερος*)

Μύρον
CIMMERIAN BOSPOROS:
—NYMPHAION: **(1)** ii-iii AD ib. 936 (m. *Χρήστη*, *Παρρησία*)
—PANTIKAPAION: **(2)** iii-ii BC ib. 254 + *Hyperboreus* 2000, p. 138 (*Μύρ(ω)ν—CIRB*: d. *Ἱππόστρατος*)

Μυροπνοῦν
CIMMERIAN BOSPOROS:
—PANTIKAPAION: **(1)** s. i AD *CIRB* 476 (*Μυροπνο[ῦ]ν*)

Μύροτος
SKYTHIA:
—OLBIA-BORYSTHENES: **(1)** ii AD *IOSPE* I^2 128, 6; Zgusta, *PNS* 1094a (f. *Κιλικᾶς*)

Μύρουσα
CIMMERIAN BOSPOROS:
—PANTIKAPAION: **(1)** i AD *CIRB* 443

Μυρρίνη
SCYTHIA MINOR:
—KALLATIS: **(1)** iii-ii BC *IG* II^2 8948 (*FRA* 2648)

Μυρσίνη
MACEDONIA (BOTTIAIA):
—PELLA*: **(1)** 106 AD *SEG* XII 350 (*Σπεδία Μ.*: m. *Π. Σπέδιος*)
MACEDONIA?: **(2)** iii/ii BC *JHS* 57 (1937) p. 30 no. 6; *BSA* 56 (1961) p. 15 no. 39 (d. *Ὑπερβάσσας*)
THRACE:
—ZONE: **(3)** m. v BC *SEG* XXVII 346 b (*IThrakAig* E405-6) (d. *Ἀλκεβιάδης*)

Μυρσινίων
THRACE:
—PHILIPPOPOLIS-TRIMONTIUM: **(1)** ii-iii AD *IGB* III 1021 (*GVI* 614) (*Μίκκος Μ.*: s. *Μύρσινος*)

Μύρσινος
THRACE:
—PHILIPPOPOLIS-TRIMONTIUM: **(1)** ii-iii AD *IGB* III 1021 (*GVI* 614) (f. *Μίκκος Μυρσινίων*)

Μύρσος
THRACE:
—ABDERA: **(1)** c. 395-360 BC May, *Abdera* pp. 208-9 nos. 269-72 (coin)

Μύρτα
THRACE:
—SALYMBRIA: **(1)** i BC *IByz* S 52 (*[Μ]ύρτα*: d. *Κρατήσιος*)

Μυρτάλη
MACEDONIA (EDONIS):
—AMPHIPOLIS: **(1)** iv BC *AEMTh* 15 (2001) p. 119 (d. *Χαρικλῆς*)

Μύρτιλλα
MACEDONIA (BOTTIAIA):
—EDESSA: **(1)** v-vi AD Feissel, *RICM* 47 (*[Μ]ύρτιλλ[α]*)

Μυρτίλος
MACEDONIA (BOTTIAIA):
—PELLA: **(1)** f. i BC *SEG* XLVII 933 (f. *Κάσσις*)

Μύρτιν
CIMMERIAN BOSPOROS:
—PANTIKAPAION: **(1)** imp. *CIRB* 760 (m. *Βίοτης*)

Μυρτίς
MACEDONIA?: **(1)** c. 200-175 BC *IG* XI (4) 1273, 5

Μυρτώ
MACEDONIA (BOTTIAIA):
—PELLA: **(1)** iv/iii BC *SEG* XLVIII 822 (d. *Τιμοκλῆς*)

Μύρων
CIMMERIAN BOSPOROS:
—AKRA: **(1)** imp. *ZOOID* 31 (1913) Prot. p. 36 no. 2
—PANTIKAPAION: **(2)** 9 BC-7 AD *CIRB* 31, 5 (I f. *Μύρων* II); **(3)** ~ ib. l. 5 (II s. *Μύρων* I); **(4)** f. ii AD ib. 91, 2; cf. KW pl. 39 no. 574; **(5)** 275-278 AD *CIRB* 36, 38 (*Μύρ(ων)*: f. *Τίτιος*)
MACEDONIA (EDONIS):
—PHILIPPOI (NR.): **(6)** ?i AD *CIL* III 665 (Pilhofer 428) (Lat. P. Ancharius Myro: f. Ancharia Iucunda)
MACEDONIA (LYNKESTIS):
—HERAKLEIA (NR.): **(7)** iii AD *IG* X (2) (2) 33 II (f. *Ζώπυρος*)
MACEDONIA (MYGDONIA):
—LETE: **(8)** f. ii BC *SEG* XLVI 764, 7 (*[Μ]ύρων*: s. *Ἡρακλείδης*)
—THESSALONIKE: **(9)** ii/iii AD *IG* X (2) (1) 262 I, 9

Scythia Minor:
—tomis: (**10**) ii-iii AD *ISM* II 31 III, 12 (s. *Χρ*—); (**11**) ~ ib. l. 13 (s. *Δ*—)
Skythia:
—tanais: (**12**) ii AD *CIRB* 1268, 6 (f. *—ατης*); (**13**) 155 AD ib. 1260, 18 (*Μύρων*—Tokhtas'ev: f. *Ἄρδαρος*); (**14**) 192 AD ib. 1243, 17 (*Μύ[ρω]ν*: s. *Οὐαρᾶς*); (**15**) 220 AD ib. 1278, 32; (**16**) 228 AD ib. 1283, 10 (f. *Καλλιγένης*)
Skythia?: (**17**) inc. *SEG* III 613 (s. *Ἡρακλείδης*)
Tauris:
—chersonesos: (**18**) ii-iii AD *IOSPE* I² 440 (f. (ad.) *Αὐρ. Ἑρμοκράτης*); (**19**) ~ *SEG* XXIX 714 (f. *Ἰουλιανός*)
Thrace:
—apollonia-sozopolis: (**20**) i-ii AD *IGB* I² 401, 17 (f. *Βακχίς*)
—maroneia: (**21**) iii AD Dumont–Homolle 110b 17 (*IThrakAig* E194) (f. *Αὐρ. Τάρσας*)

Μυρῶσα
Macedonia (Mygdonia):
—thessalonike: (**1**) ii AD *IG* X (2) (1) 312 (d. *Εὔοδος*)

Μῦς
Skythia:
—olbia-borysthenes: (**1**) iii BC *IOSPE* I² 201 II, 10 (s. *Βοσπόριχος*)
Tauris:
—chersonesos: (**2**) s. v BC *SEG* XL 612. 16; *DGVE* 1996-7, p. 109 fig. 3b (*SEG* XLIX 1031. 2 (ostraka)) (f. *Κρητίνης*)
Thrace:
—apollonia-sozopolis: (**3**) v/iv BC Hess–Leu sale (24.v.59) 130; *Coll. Waddington* 1017 (coin) ?= (*4*); (**4**) iv BC *Apoloniia* p. 337 no. 1211 (coin) ?= (*3*)

Μυσθᾶς
Macedonia: (**1**) 46 AD *PMich* 273, 1; *PSI* 906, 1 (s. *Ἀκουσίλαος*: katoikos)

Μύσιος
Macedonia (Chalkidike):
—olynthos: (**1**) ?350 BC *TAPA* 59 (1928) p. 226, 13; Hatzopoulos, *Actes Chalc.* p. 80 (date) (s. *Τιμάνθης*)

Μύστα
Macedonia: (**1**) c. 223 BC *PTeb* 815 fr. 1 recto II, 25, 29, 34 (Tataki, *Macedonians* p. 376 no. 88; La'da E1809) (d. .αμικ..)
Macedonia (Mygdonia):
—kalindoia: (**2**) i-ii AD *SEG* XLII 588 (*Φλαουία Μ.*)
—thessalonike?: (**3**) ii AD *IG* X (2) (1) 700 (*Δομιτία Μ.*); (**4**) ~ ib. 852 (*Οὐλπ. Μ.*); (**5**) s. ii AD ib. 904; *JDAI* 84 (1969) p. 154 no. R20 (date) (d. *Ἀπολλώνιος, Μαντοῦς*)

Μύστης
Tauris:
—kerkinitis (nr.): (**1**) hell. *SEG* XL 622 (vase) (n. pr.?)

Μυστίας
Cimmerian Bosporos:
—gorgippia: (**1**) f. iii BC *CIRB* 1137 A II, 27 (s. *Δημῶναξ*)

Μυστικός
Cimmerian Bosporos:
—gorgippia: (**1**) s. ii AD ib. 1142, 8 (f. *Μᾶρκος*)
Thrace:
—burdipta?: (**2**) ii-iii AD *IGB* III 1889 (*Μοιστ(ι)κός*: f. *Ἀλεξάνδρα*)
—pautalia: (**3**) ii AD ib. IV 2060 (*Π. Ἀδριάνιος Μ.*)

Μυτιλήνη
Macedonia (Mygdonia):
—thessalonike: (**1**) imp. *Tekmeria* 7 (2002) p. 91 no. 2

Μυτίνα
Tauris:
—chersonesos: (**1**) ?iv-iii BC *SEG* XLIV 657 (weight)

Μυττίνα
Tauris:
—chersonesos: (**1**) iv BC Solomonik, *NEPKh* 142

Μώκιος
Macedonia (Edonis):
—amphipolis: (**1**) 287 AD *PLRE* I (-) (s. *Εὐφράτης, Εὐσταθία*)

Μώλας
Cimmerian Bosporos:
—pantikapaion: (**1**) s. i BC *CIRB* 126, 1, 3 (*GVI* 1473) (I f. *Μώλας* II); (**2**) ~ *CIRB* 126, 1, 3 (*GVI* 1473) (II s. *Μώλας* I)

Μώμα
Macedonia (Derriopos):
—alkomena: (**1**) ii-iii AD *IG* X (2) (2) 351 (m. *Μέστριος*)
Macedonia (Paionia): (**2**) ii-iii AD *Sp.* 98 (1941-8) p. 201 no. 398; cf. Düll, *Götterkulte* p. 359 no. 170

Μωμώ
Macedonia: (**1**) m. iii AD *SEG* XLVIII 881 (*Μωμ(ώ)*)
Macedonia (Edonis):
—amphipolis: (**2**) iii AD ib. XXIV 598; cf. XXXVII 580 (*Αὐρ. Μ(ω)μ(ώ)*: ?m. *Αὐρ. Τορκᾶτος*)
Macedonia (Mygdonia):
—thessalonike: (**3**) ii AD *IG* X (2) (1) 296 (d. *Τόρκος*); (**4**) ~ ib. 298 (m. *Ἀθηναΐς*); (**5**) ~ ib. 515 (*Αἰλ. Μ.*: d. *Ζωσίμη*); (**6**) iii AD ib. 476 A-B
—thessalonike (nr.): (**7**) ?iii AD ib. 1001
—thessalonike?: (**8**) ii-iii AD ib. 919 (*[Μ]ωμώ*: ?d. *Κλεονίκη*)
Macedonia (Odomantike):
—gazoros: (**9**) 144 AD *SEG* XXX 599, 1 (Pilhofer 552); cf. *SEG* XXXVII 579 (d. *Μέστος*, m. *Οὐενερία*)
—sirrha: (**10**) 62 or 178 AD *JDAI* 84 (1969) p. 157 no. R27, 2; Robert, *OMS* 2 pp. 1302-3 (name) (d. *Διοσκουρίδης*, ?d. *Στρατονίκη*); (**11**) ii-iii AD *SEG* XXX 603; (**12**) 155 AD Dimitsas 821, 7 (Kaphtantzis 1) (*Μωμως* (gen.): m. *Τορκουᾶτος*); (**13**) ii/iii AD *SEG* XLVIII 877 (m. *Πυρούλας, Τόρκος, Μούκκων*); (**14**) ?iii AD Dimitsas 819 (Kaphtantzis 25) (*Μωμώ*)
—sirrha (territ.): (**15**) s. ii AD *Tekmeria* 6 (2001) p. 49
—sirrha (nr.): (**16**) ii/iii AD *SEG* XXX 602 (m. *Ἀλέξανδρος*)
—sirrha?: (**17**) ii-iii AD Kaphtantzis 31
Macedonia (Pieria):
—pydna: (**18**) ii-iii AD *Essays Laourdas* p. 111 no. 1 (*Μώμονι* (dat.))

N

Νᾶ
Cimmerian Bosporos:
—pantikapaion: (**1**) iv BC *CIRB* 222; Zgusta, *PNS* 601 (d. *Μάνης, —αρία*)

Νάβαζος
Skythia:
—olbia-borysthenes: (**1**) ii-iii AD *IOSPE* I² 137, 7; Zgusta, *PNS* 152 (s. *Νουμήνιος*); (**2**) ~ *IOSPE* I² 138, 4 (s. *Δωτοῦς*)
—tanais: (**3**) 225 AD *CIRB* 1279, 15 (s. *Κίμβρος*)

Ναεις
Thrace:
—odessos?: (**1**) iii BC *IGB* I² 479 ter (PM 1732); cf. *IGB* V 5156 (s. *Διονύσιος*)

Ναιέτων
Scythia Minor:
—tomis (nr.): (**1**) ii/iii AD *SEG* XL 605 = XLIII 493 (s. *Δεκέβαλος*)

Ναῖος
Skythia:
—olbia-borysthenes: (**1**) v BC *IOSPE* I² 212 (s. *Ἑρμαγόρης*)

Naΐς
Cimmerian Bosporos:
—pantikapaion: (**1**) i BC/i AD *CIRB* 314 (m. *Θεόδωρος*)
Thrace:
—koila: (**2**) 55 AD *ISestos* 29 (Lat. Claudia Nais: d. Faustus)
—nicopolis ad istrum (territ.): (**3**) ii-iii AD *IGB* V 5250, 3 (*Ἀτιλία Ν. ἡ κὲ ὮΙΖΙΗ*)

Ναϊσσός
Thrace:
—madytos: (**1**) imp. *Sp.* 71 (1931) p. 243 no. 649 (Lat. L. Artidius Naissus)

Νάμγηνος
Skythia:
—olbia-borysthenes: (**1**) ii AD *IOSPE* I² 92, 4; Zgusta, *PNS* 153 (s. *Νικόδρομος*)

Ναμέρτης
Macedonia?: (**1**) m. iv BC *Torone* 1 p. 726 no. 18.1 (bullet); cf. *BE* 2003, no. 156 (*Ναμέρ(της)?*)

Ναμοῦχος
Tauris:
—chersonesos: (**1**) ii AD *IOSPE* I² 438; Zgusta, *PNS* 154

Νάνα
Cimmerian Bosporos:
—pantikapaion: (**1**) iv BC *CIRB* 225; Zgusta, *PNS* 601 (m. *Τίβης*); (**2**) s. iv BC *CIRB* 209; cf. KW pl. 1 no. 25; (**3**) i BC *CIRB* 285 (m. *Μηνόδωρος*, ?m. *Δημοστράτεια*)

Macedonia (Lynkestis):
—Herakleia: (4) ii-iii AD *IG* x (2) (2) 96 (*Νάν[α]*: d. *Ἀλεξαν—*)
—Herakleia (area): (5) ?ii-iii AD ib. 16
Macedonia (Pelagonia): (6) ii-iii AD ib. 256; (7) ii/iii AD ib. 265
Tauris:
—Chersonesos: (8) iv/iii BC Solomonik, *NEPKh* 168 (d. *Ἡρέας*); (9) iii-ii BC *IOSPE* I^2 713 (d. *Δαμοκλῆς*)
Thrace:
—Odessos: (10) m. ii AD *IGB* I^2 174 (PM 1726); *Dacia* 21 (1977) p. 161 (date) (*[Ν]άνα*: d. *Ἕλλην*)
—Serdica (territ.): (11) ii-iii AD *IGB* iv 1988, 3; v 5688 (d. *Λογγῖνος*)

Νανάς
Scythia Minor:
—Tomis: (1) 201 AD *ISM* ii 83 II, 13 (d. *Θεάδων*)

Νανᾶς
Cimmerian Bosporos:
—Pantikapaion: (1) ?s. v BC Tolstoi 210 (*LSAG*^{2} p. 373 no. 68 (vase)) (*Ν̣α̣νᾶδος* (gen.)); (2) iv BC Tolstoi 224 (vase) (*Νανᾶτος* (gen.))
Skythia:
—Tanais*: (3) ii-iii AD *Tanais* i p. 105 (amph.)
Tauris:
—Kalos Limen (nr.): (4) s. iv BC *Hellenismus* p. 444 no. 6a (vase) (*Νανα* (gen.?))

Νάνεις
Cimmerian Bosporos:
—Pantikapaion: (1) m. i AD *CIRB* 380 (*Νάνει* (gen.): f. *Γάστεις*)

Νάνη
Thrace:
—Abdera: (1) m. iv BC *SEG* xlvii 1035 (*IThrakAig* E60) (d. *Πάρμις*)

Νανν̂ας
Skythia:
—Olbia-Borysthenes: (1) ?ii-i BC Dubois, *IGDOlbia* 110, 5
Thrace:
—Beroe-Augusta Traiana: (2) ii-iii AD *SEG* xxxix 649, 4 (f. *Καρτέρις*)

Ναννίς
Macedonia (Odomantike):
—Skotoussa?: (1) iv/iii BC ib. xliii 402 + *Makedonika* 28 (1991-2) p. 103 with pl. 4 (d. *Κιβᾶς*)

Νάννιχος
Macedonia (Edonis):
—Amphipolis?: (1) hell. *SEG* l 562, 5 (*Νάμνιχος*—ed. pr.: s. *Σιμωνίδης* (Sparta), ?s. *Διονυσία* (Magnesia))

Νοννίων
Skythia:
—Olbia-Borysthenes: (1) f. iii BC ib. xlii 718 (f. *Λεώφαντος*)
Thrace:
—Byzantion: (2) s. iii BC Schönert-Geiss, *Byzantion* 1206-8 (coin); Masson, *OGS* 3 p. 211 (name) (*Ναννί(ων)*?)

Νανοβαλαμυρος?
Cimmerian Bosporos:
—Gorgippia: (1) ?93-123 AD *CIRB* 1125, 11; Zgusta, *PNS* 682 (*Νανοβαλαμυρου* (gen.))

Νάνος
Cimmerian Bosporos:
—Myrmekion: (1) hell. Gaidukevich, *AGB Mirmekii* p. 163 (amph.)

Νανοῦς
Macedonia (Pelagonia): (1) 81 AD *IG* x (2) (2) 276 (m. *Ἀμμία, Νικόλαος*)

Νανώ
Macedonia?: (1) i BC/i AD *Xenia antiqua* 10 (2001) p. 22 no. C (or Thrace: d. *Τηρήπης*, m. *Φίλιππος*)

Νάνων
Tauris:
—Chersonesos: (1) c. 315-300 BC Kats p. 105 no. 80 (amph.) ?= (*3*); (2) f. iii BC *SEG* xl 615 B, 10 (*[Ν]άνων*); (3) c. 270-260 BC Anokhin p. 140 no. 93 (coin) ?= (*1*); (4) c. 230-220 BC ib. p. 142 nos. 124; 126 (coins) (*Νάνω(ν)*—124, *Νά(νων)*—126); (5) c. 120-130 AD Solomonik, *NEPKh* 112, 20 (s. *Καλλίστρατος*)

Νάξος
Thrace:
—Byzantion: (1) ii BC *IByz* 261 (Fıratlı–Robert pp. 76-7 no. 85) (s. *Σωσίας*)

Ναοκάσης
Cimmerian Bosporos:
—Zenonos Chersonesos*: (1) v/iv BC *SEG* xl 643 (reading—Tokhtas'ev) ?= (*2*); (2) ~ ib. (*Ναόκα[ς]*—ed., *Ναοκά[σης]*?) ?= (*1*)

Ναοσίνικος
Thrace:
—Sestos: (1) c. 320 BC *IG* xii (6) 43, 3, 16 (*[Ν]αοσίνικος*: s. *Φιλόξενος*)

Νάπορος
Cimmerian Bosporos:
—Nymphaion: (1) f. iii BC *SEG* xxxix 701. 3

Νάρδας
Tauris:
—Chersonesos: (1) hell. Solomonik, *GAKh* 1264-5 (vases); cf. Tolstoi 82

Νάρις
Macedonia:
—Bisaltai: (1) ?vi-v BC *FGrH* 262 F 1 (king?)
Macedonia (Mygdonia):
—Lete: (2) ii AD *Makedonika* 2 (1951) p. 619 no. 42 θ, 15 (*Νάρεως* (gen.): f. *Ἀγάθων*)

Νάρκισσος
Macedonia (Bottiaia):
—Edessa: (1) 51 AD *SEG* xlvi 744, 8 (Tataki, *Edessa* 235) (*Π. Οὐέττιος Ν.*)
—Kyrrhos: (2) m. iii AD *SEG* xxxv 750, 3 (*Φουλκίνιος Ν.*)
Macedonia (Edonis):
—Philippoi: (3) iii-iv AD *CIL* iii 7335 (Kaphtantzis 724; Pilhofer 714); cf. *AD* 50 (1995) Chron. p. 637 (Lat. P. Marronius Narcissus: f. Marronia Firmina)
Macedonia (Odomantike):
—Berge: (4) imp. *CIL* iii 14206. 5 (Pilhofer 566) (Lat. G. Volvius Narcissus: f. Volvia Firmina)
Macedonia (Paionia):
—Stoboi: (5) ii-iii AD *JÖAI* 6 (1903) Beibl. col. 9 no. 11 (slave?)
Scythia Minor:
—Istros [nr.]:
——Vicus Quintionis: (6) 139-161 AD *ISM* i 324, 12 (Lat. Sulpicius Narcissus)
—Noviodunum: (7) ii AD ib. v 270, 5 (Lat. C. Atulenus Narcissus)
—Tomis: (8) ii-iii AD ib. ii 206 (*[Ν]άρκισσος*)
Thrace:
—Markianopolis: (9) m. iii AD *IGB* ii 817 (*-κει-*)
—Oescus: (10) i-ii AD *ILB* 16, 11 (Lat. Narcissus)

—Perinthos-Herakleia: (11) ii AD *IPerinth* 101 (s. *Ἀρτεμίδωρος ὁ καὶ Κυρήνιος*); (12) 144 AD *IGB* v 5636, 16; *SEG* xlii 647 (s. *Ζήνων*: sculptor)
—Philippopolis-Trimontium: (13) iv AD Beševliev 208 (*-κισος*)

Νάρρης?
Macedonia (Mygdonia):
—Perdylos: (1) ?i-ii AD *SEG* xxix 581 (*NAPPIII* (dat.)—apogr.: s. *Νουμήνιος*)

Νάσων
Macedonia (Derriopos):
—Stuberra: (1) 74 AD *IG* x (2) (2) 326, 36 (f. *Διονῦς*)

Νατάλιος
Scythia Minor:
—Tomis: (1) ii AD *ISM* ii 17, 10 (s. *Ἐπίστρατος*)

Νατάλις
Scythia Minor:
—Istros: (1) ii/iii AD ib. i 225, 6 (s. *Πο[. . .]—*)

Ναύαγος
Skythia:
—Tanais: (1) 220 AD *CIRB* 1278, 11 (f. *Καδάνακος*)

Ναύακος
Skythia:
—Tanais: (1) 220 AD ib. 1245, 19; cf. 1280, 18 (s. *Μεύακος*); (2) 244 AD ib. 1287, 8 (s. *Στοσάρακος*)

Ναυκασάμας
Scythia Minor:
—Kallatis: (1) iv BC *ISM* iii 255 (vase) (*CEG* ii 901)

Ναυκλῆς
Thrace:
—Chersonesos: (1) ?c. 450-440 BC *IG* I^3 1301 (*FRA* 7305) (*Ναυκλέōς* (gen.): f. *Ἡράκλειτος*)

Ναυσικλῆς
Scythia Minor:
—Istros: (1) iii BC *ISM* i 258 (s. *Λέων*)

Ναυσικρίτη
Thrace:
—Sestos: (1) iv BC *IG* ii^2 10264 (*FRA* 6641) (d. *Κηφισόδωρος*)

Ναυσίμαχος
Macedonia (Bottiaia):
—Pella: (1) iv/iii BC *Pella* p. 76 no. 63 = *Eulimeni* 4 (2003) p. 135 no. 1

Ναυσίνικος
Macedonia (Mygdonia):
—Thessalonike: (1) ii AD *IG* x (2) (1) 226, 7; Robert, *OMS* 5 p. 298 n. 193 (*Ναυ[σε]ί̣νικος*: s. *Σωσιπ—*)

Ναυσίστρατος
Thrace:
—Mesambria: (1) f. ii BC *IGB* I^2 343 septies, 1; cf. v 5117 (s. *Ἡρακλείδας, Ματρίχα*)

Ναύτας
Macedonia (Pieria):
—Pydna: (1) iv BC *GRBS* 43 (2002-3) p. 110 no. 1 a, 11

Ναύτης
Macedonia (Chalkidike):
—Torone: (1) c. 450-420 BC *IG* I^3 1377 (Tataki, *Macedonians* p. 192 no. 12; *FRA* 7144) (s. *Εὐδημίδης*)

Ναύτιμος
Scythia Minor:
—Kallatis: (1) s. iii BC *ISM* iii 35 A, 31; *IOSPE* I^2 27, 3, 8 (s. *Πασιάδας*)

Skythia:
—olbia-borysthenes: **(2)** iii bc *IOlbia* 72, 2 (s. Ἡρόξενος); **(3)** ii ad *IOSPE* I² 89, 7 (-τει-: f. Αἴλιος); **(4)** ?ii-iii ad ib. 118 (Ναύτει[μος]); **(5)** s. ii ad *IOlbia* 81, 3 (*IOSPE* I² 94) (s. Ἀργουάναγος); **(6)** iii ad *IOlbia* 83, 7 (*IOSPE* I² 97) (s. Καλλίστρατος)

Ναύτων
Macedonia (Chalkidike):
—stolos?: **(1)** c. 350 bc *SEG* xl 553, 5 (f. Βίας)

Νέα
Thrace:
—byzantion: **(1)** ii bc *IByz* 78 (d. Κλεόβουλος); **(2)** ii ad ib. 321 (d. Ἀπολλώνιος)

Νέανδρος
Macedonia (Bottiaia):
—pella: **(1)** f. iii bc *SEG* xxiv 549 (f. Ἡδίστη)
Macedonia (Paionia):
—negotino (mod.): **(2)** ii-iii ad *Sp*. 98 (1941-8) p. 56 no. 114, 1 (f. Ἐπιχθόνιος)
Thrace:
—apollonia-sozopolis: **(3)** i-ii ad *IGB* I² 401, 14 (f. Γάϊος)
—philippopolis-trimontium (territ.): **(4)** ii-iii ad ib. iii 1478, 3 (or Thrace Diokletianopolis: Νέα[ν]δρος)

Νεάνθης
Thrace:
—apollonia-sozopolis: **(1)** iv bc ib. I² 463 bis, 2 (Νεά[νθης]?: f. Ἀθήναιος); **(2)** iii/ii bc ib. 395 bis (Νεάνθου (gen.): f. Ἀθήναιος)

Νεανίσκος
Macedonia (Paionia):
—stoboi: **(1)** ?i-ii ad Unp. (Stobi excav.) inv. I-87-3; cf. *Arheološki Vestnik* 41 (1990) p. 579 (-νεί-)

Νέαρχος
Macedonia: **(1)** m. iv bc *BCH* 106 (1982) p. 84 no. 37 (bullet); **(2)** c. 100-75 bc *SB* 8974 fr. 3, 4, 7, [9], 11 etc. (Tataki, *Macedonians* p. 490 no. 171; La'da E1544) (s. Ἀσκληπιάδης, Ἀρτεμιδώρα)
Macedonia (Bottiaia):
—edessa: **(3)** iii ad Tataki, *Edessa* 218

Νεβρίς
Macedonia (Bottiaia):
—beroia: **(1)** imp. *ILeukopetra* 157
Macedonia (Chalkidike):
—moni lavras (mod.)*: **(2)** hell.-imp. Dimitsas 780; cf. Robert, *OMS* 2 p. 1289
Macedonia (Mygdonia):
—thessalonike: **(3)** 154 ad *IG* x (2) (1) 472 B (Κλ. Ν.: d. Κλ. Λέων)
Macedonia (Paionia):
—kavadarci (mod.): **(4)** ii ad *Sp*. 75 (1933) p. 32 no. 87 ([Νε]βρίδος? (gen.))
Thrace:
—pautalia: **(5)** ii-iii ad *IGB* iv 2088 (*GVI* 210)

Νειλᾶς
Macedonia (Mygdonia):
—thessalonike?: **(1)** ii-iii ad *IG* x (2) (1) 821 (Γ. Κάσσιος Ν.)

Νειλόξενος
Macedonia: **(1)** 330-327 bc Berve 545; Arr., *An*. iii 28. 4 (Tataki, *Macedonians* p. 377 no. 2) (s. Σάτυρος)

Νεῖλος
Macedonia: **(1)** m. ii bc *PTeb* 1075 fr. 2, 20 (Tataki, *Macedonians* p. 490 no. 173; La'da E1545) (s. Ἀπολλώνιος); **(2)** 89 bc *UPZ* 125, 29 (Tataki, *Macedonians* p. 490 no. 172; La'da E1546)
Macedonia (Mygdonia):
—thessalonike: **(3)** i-ii ad Unp. (Thessaloniki Mus.) 5704 (s. Συμφέρουσα)
Scythia Minor:
—ulmetum: **(4)** iii ad *ISM* v 72, 8 (Lat. Valerius Nilus)
Skythia:
—olbia-borysthenes: **(5)** ii ad *IOlbia* 86, 8 (s. Ποσείδηος); **(6)** ~ ib. l. 10 ([Ν]εῖλος: s. Ἀργουάναγος); **(7)** iii ad *IOSPE* I² 103, 4 (f. Ἰωδέσμαγος); **(8)** f. iii ad ib. 43, 5 (s. Πουρθαῖος)
—tyras: **(9)** ii/i bc *ISM* ii 5, [2], 26 (Νεῖλ[ος]?)
Skythia?: **(10)** ii ad *SEG* xlvi 936 (Κλ. Ν.: ?f. Θάλλος)

Νείλων
Scythia Minor:
—istros: **(1)** i ad *ISM* i 200, 6 (s. Συνέκδημος); **(2)** ii ad ib. 197 I, 15 (s. Ξενοχάρης)
Skythia:
—olbia-borysthenes: **(3)** ii ad *IOSPE* I² 106, 8 (f. Ποσειδώνιος)

Νεκτάριος
Thrace:
—odessos?: **(1)** vi ad Beševliev 102, 7 (or Thrace Hadrianopolis?)

Νεμέριος
Thrace:
—byzantion: **(1)** ii/i bc *IByz* 255 (Fıratlı-Robert p. 71 no. 73) (f. Διονυσία)

Νέμεσις
Macedonia (Pieria):
—dion: **(1)** ii/iii ad *SEG* xlix 699 (Μεστρία Ν.)

Νεμήνιος
Macedonia (Chalkidike):
—polichne?: **(1)** ?353 bc ib. xxxvii 576, 19 (Νεμ[ή]νιος: s. Κράσης)
—strepsa?: **(2)** b. 348 bc ib. 583, 4 (f. Ἀρνίας)

Νεόκας
Cimmerian Bosporos:
—gorgippia: **(1)** 173-210 ad *CIRB* 1134, 25 (s. Ἀθη—)

Νεοκλῆς
Cimmerian Bosporos:
—gorgippia: **(1)** i-ii ad ib. 1138, 1; **(2)** ?68 ad ib. 1126, 5; cf. *SEG* xlix 1032 (s. Ἀθηνόδωρος); **(3)** ii ad *CIRB* 1140, 8 (f. Χαρίτων); **(4)** ~ ib. l. 15; **(5)** ~ ib. 1160, 5 ([Ν]εοκλῆς: s. Ἀθ—); **(6)** m. ii ad *Eirene* 7 (1968) p. 67, 23 (s. Ἀθηνόδωρος); **(7)** s. ii ad *CIRB* 1129 A, 3; **(8)** ~ ib. 1142, 15 (Νεοκ[λῆς]); **(9)** ~ ib. 1142 fr. F, 4 ([Ν]εοκλ[ῆς]); **(10)** ~ ib. 1145, 11 (Νεοκ[λῆς]); **(11)** 173-210 ad ib. 1119, 6; 1134, 12; *SEG* xxxvi 699, 1?; 700, 4 (f. Μοιρόδωρος); **(12)** ii/iii ad *CIRB* 1179, 20 (s. Θ—); **(13)** ~ ib. l. 29 (s. Φαρνακίων); **(14)** ~ ib. l. 31 (s. Πόθος); **(15)** ~ ib. l. 38 (Νεοκλ[ῆ]ς: s. Ἡγουμενός, f. Ἀθηνόδωρος); **(16)** ~ ib. l. 59 (f. Ἡρακλέων); **(17)** ~ *SEG* xxxvi 712 (Νεοκ[λῆς]?)
—gorgippia?: **(18)** ii/iii ad *CIRB* 1232, 8 (f. —ρος); **(19)** ~ ib. l. 11 (f. Ἄρδαρος); **(20)** 227-233 ad ib. 1230, 10 (Νεοκλ[ῆς])
—myrmekion (nr.): **(21)** ii ad ib. 893; cf. KW pl. 51 no. 703 (Νιω-: f. Εὐγένεια)
—pantikapaion: **(22)** s. i ad *CIRB* 434 (f. Φαρνάκης)
—phanagoreia: **(23)** iii bc *IGAIMK* 104 (1935) p. 308 no. 66; *MIA* 56 (1957) p. 225; 57 (1956) p. 152 (tile)
Macedonia (Orestis):
—battynaioi: **(24)** 192 ad *EAM* 186 III, 43 (s. Νικόλαος)
Skythia:
—tanais: **(25)** 224 ad *CIRB* 1287, 9 (f. Μηνᾶς)

Νεοκοριανός
Thrace:
—salymbria?: **(1)** iii ad *AEMÖ* 17 (1894) p. 57 no. 3, 6 (or Thrace Perinthos-Herakleia: Αὐρ. Νέων Ν.: f. Αὐρ. Μηνόδωρος)

Νεομήνιος
Cimmerian Bosporos:
—hermonassa: **(1)** iv bc *CIRB* 1056 I, 8 (f. —λης); **(2)** ~ ib. 1064
—pantikapaion: **(3)** iv bc ib. 211 (Νεο<υ>μήνιος: s. Ἀσπαμιθάρης); **(4)** s. iv bc ib. 163; cf. KW pl. 1 no. 21 (f. Ἀπολλώνιος)
Tauris:
—chersonesos: **(5)** m. v bc *SEG* xl 612. 4 (ostrakon) (f. Ἰασικλῆς); **(6)** iii bc *IOSPE* I² 470 (f. Βοΐσκος)
—kerkinitis: **(7)** s. v bc *SEG* xxxvii 665, 1 (sherd)
Thrace:
—maroneia: **(8)** c. 365-336 bc Schönert-Geiss, *Maroneia* 430-2 (coin)

Νεομηνίς
Cimmerian Bosporos:
—pantikapaion: **(1)** f. iv bc *CIRB* 210; cf. KW pl. 1 no. 3 (Νεομήνι(ο)ς—edd.: d. Μολπᾶς)

Νεόπολις
Tauris:
—chersonesos: **(1)** iv-iii bc *IOSPE* I² 505 ([Ν]εόπολις); **(2)** c. 220-210 bc Anokhin p. 142 no. 127 (coin)

Νεόπολος
Skythia:
—tanais: **(1)** 220 ad *CIRB* 1245, 17 (Νεοπόλου (gen.): f. Διόφαντος)

Νεοπτόλεμος
Macedonia: **(1)** ?417-413 bc *IG* I³ 89, 62 (Tataki, *Macedonians* p. 377 no. 4) (Νεοπτόλε[μος]); **(2)** iv bc Arr., *An*. i 24. 1 (Tataki, *Macedonians* p. 378 no. 8) (f. Μελέαγρος); **(3)** c. 370-321 bc *RE* (7); Berve 548 ?= (*4*); **(4)** s. iv bc *IEph* 1431 (Tataki, *Macedonians* p. 377 no. 6) (and Ionia Ephesos: s. Βιλλέας) ?= (*3*); **(5)** iii-ii bc *TAM* v (2) 1109 (Tataki, *Macedonians* p. 378 no. 9) (f. Μενέδημος); **(6)** 254 bc *PCZ* 59236, 1, 10 (Tataki, *Macedonians* p. 377 no. 7; La'da E1547) (s. Στράτιππος); **(7)** 245 bc *PHib* 32, 5 (Tataki, *Macedonians* p. 377 no. 5; La'da E1548); **(8)** 154 or 143 bc *ZPE* 146 (2004) p. 168, 4 (s. Πτολεμαῖος)
—herakleia: **(9)** 196 ad *IMS* ii 53 III a (*CIL* iii 14507); cf. *ZPE* 146 (2004) pp. 216-20 (Lat. T. Aur. Ne(o)ptolem(us))
Macedonia (Bottiaia):
—aloros (territ.)?: **(10)** hell.? Dimitsas 211 ([Νε]οπτόλεμος: s. Παράμονος)
—beroia: **(11)** s. iii bc *IBer* 151 (f. Δίφιλος); **(12)** c. 230-200 bc *BCH* 45 (1921) p. 17 III, 57 (Tataki 936; Tataki, *Macedonians* p. 81 no. 40) (f. Ἀντάνωρ); **(13)** ii bc *IBer* 141, 46; **(14)** f. ii ad ib. 7 A, 24 (I f. Νεοπτόλεμος II); **(15)** ~ ib. l. 24 (II s. Νεοπτόλεμος I)
Macedonia (Lynkestis): **(16)** 334 bc *RE* (6); Berve 547 (Tataki, *Macedonians* p. 203 no. 12) (s. Ἀρραβαῖος)
Macedonia (Mygdonia):
—kalindoia: **(17)** f. ii bc Hatzopoulos, *MI* 2 p. 88 no. 67 Index
—thessalonike?: **(18)** i-ii ad *IG* x (2) (1) 690 (Lat. C. Minucius Neoptolemus); **(19)** s. i ad ib. 905 (Τιβ. Νε(ο)πτόλεμος: f. Λέων)
Macedonia (Pieria):
—pydna: **(20)** inc. *Hesp*. 18 (1949) p. 92 no. 3 (her.?) ?= (*21*); **(21)** ii bc Oikonomos 65 + *Hesp*. 18 (1949) pp. 87-91 no. 2 ([Νεοπ]τόλεμος: ?s. —ενος) ?= (*20*); **(22)** i bc *GVI* 1063 (f. Ἀλκίμαχος)

Macedonia (Tymphaia):
—agios georgios (mod.): **(23)** 153 ad *EAM* 12, 4 (*N. ὁ καὶ Γναῖος*: s. *Δημήτριος*)
Skythia:
—olbia-borysthenes (berezan (mod.)): **(24)** f. ii ad *SEG* xlix 1028 A, 7 (f. *Μᾶρκος*)
Thrace: **(25)** 221 bc *PTeb* 815 fr. 5, 37; cf. La'da E707 (*Νεοπτόλεμος*: f. *Ἀπολλόδωρος*)

Νεότας
Macedonia (Pieris):
—neapolis: **(1)** hell. Hatzopoulos, *MI* 1 pp. 188-9 n. 1 (s. *Σιμύλος*)

Νεότης
Thrace:
—pautalia: **(1)** s. ii ad *SEG* xlvi 864 I, 25

Νεόφυτος
Thrace:
—perinthos-herakleia: **(1)** iii-iv ad *IPerinth* 167 (*AD* 51-2 (1996-7) Mel. p. 335 no. 168) (*Αὐρ. N.*: f. *Αὐρ. Φιλιππιανός*)
—philippopolis-trimontium: **(2)** c. 303 ad *Anal. Boll.* 31 (1912) p. 192

Νέπων
Macedonia (Bottiaia):
—beroia:
——Kyneoi: **(1)** 192 ad *ILeukopetra* 31, 3 (s. *Λαμυρίδης*)

Νέπως
Thrace: **(1)** m. iii ad *IG* ii² 8918 (*GVI* 1847; *FRA* 2559) (*Νέπ[ως]*)
—byzantion: **(2)** i ad *Mus. Arch. di Bari* p. 163 no. 13 (*IG* xiv 687) (s. *Καλλίχρυσος*)
—diosoura: **(3)** ii ad *IGB* v 5589, 7 (*Νέπως*: ?s. *Βίθυς*)

Νέρβιλα
Thrace:
—perinthos-herakleia: **(1)** ii ad *IPerinth* 216 (-βει-: d. *Αἰλείνη Δομετιανή*)

Νέρυλλος
Tauris:
—chersonesos: **(1)** f. ii ad Solomonik, *NEPKh* 111, 12

Νέρων
Macedonia (Derriopos):
—stuberra: **(1)** c. 41-48 ad *IG* x (2) (2) 323, 14 (s. *Ἀντίγονος*)
Skythia:
—tanais: **(2)** c. 225-250 ad *CIRB* 1287, 10; 1288, 12 (f. *Μακάριος*)

Νέστις
Thrace:
—abdera: **(1)** c. 450-425 bc May, *Abdera* p. 131 nos. 152-5 (coin); Masson, *OGS* pp. 431-2 (*Νέστιος* (gen.))
—stryme?: **(2)** s. v bc *SEG* xlix 987 + *IThrakAig* E114 (f. *Μητροφάντη*)

Νεστόριος
Macedonia (Pelagonia):
—dostoneis: **(1)** iii ad *IG* x (2) (2) 201, 6 (*Νεστόρ[ι]ος*: s. *Εὔπορος*, *Ὀρείνη*)

Νεστορίς
Thrace:
—stryme?: **(1)** v-iv bc Bakalakis, *Oinos Ismarikos* p. 552 (*IThrakAig* E133) (d. *Πρόκριτος*)
—stryme? (nr.): **(2)** c. 425-400 bc *SEG* xxxiv 708 (*IThrakAig* E122) (*Νεσ[τορίς]*?: d. *Παντακλῆς*)

Νεστορίων
Skythia:
—olbia-borysthenes: **(1)** ?ii-i bc Dubois, *IGDOlbia* 110, 5

Νέστωρ
Macedonia (Bottiaia):
—edessa: **(1)** c. 200-175 bc *SEG* xliv 409, 3 (Tataki, *Macedonians* p. 104 no. 15) (*Νέσ[τωρ]*?: f. —αστος)
Macedonia (Chalkidike):
—torone (nr.): **(2)** i bc/i ad *SEG* iii 496 + xxix 592 (f. *Ἀριστόκλεια*)
Macedonia (Mygdonia):
—thessalonike?: **(3)** ii ad *IG* x (2) (1) 251, 5 (*T. Αἴλ. N. ὁ [καὶ]* [—])
—thessalonike*: **(4)** b. 305 ad *DCB* (2)
Scythia Minor:
—istros: **(5)** ii ad *ISM* i 196, 20; 201 II, 22 (f. *Χρυσίων*)
—tomis: **(6)** ii-iii ad ib. ii 468, 11 (f. *Μᾶρκος*)
Thrace:
—novae: **(7)** ii ad *IGLNovae* 48 (Lat. Nestor: s. *Δημήτριος*)

Νετειλία
Macedonia (Edonis):
—amphipolis: **(1)** ii-iii ad *SEG* xxvii 252, 2 (m. *Εὐτυχία*)

Νευμήνιος
Cimmerian Bosporos:
—pantikapaion: **(1)** hell. *AA* 1907, p. 127 Aa, 1 (lead); **(2)** ~ ib. l. 3 (lead)
—pantikapaion?: **(3)** iv bc *SEG* xlv 1010 (f. *Νίκαινα*)
Scythia Minor:
—istros: **(4)** iii-ii bc Unp. (Avram, defixio) 4, 6 (*Νευμήνι(ο)ς*); **(5)** ~ ib. l. 10
Skythia:
—olbia-borysthenes: **(6)** ?ii-i bc Dubois, *IGDOlbia* 110, 3
—tyras: **(7)** iv bc *SEG* xlv 1026. 20 (vase) (s. *Τίμωρις*)
Tauris:
—chersonesos: **(8)** iv bc Solomonik, *GAKh* 1540 (vase); **(9)** iv/iii bc Kats pp. 97-8 no. 56 (amph., tile) (f. *Ἡροκράτης*); **(10)** f. iii bc *SEG* xl 615 B, 20 (s. *Φιλίστιος*) ?= (*11*); **(11)** c. 285-272 bc Kats p. 105 no. 81 (amph., tile) (s. *Φιλίστιος*) ?= (*10*)

Νευμηνίς
Cimmerian Bosporos:
—porthmion: **(1)** iv bc *SEG* xxxvii 678

Νευμώ
Macedonia (Chalkidike):
—olynthos: **(1)** c. 500-480 bc *TAPA* 69 (1938) pp. 43-4 no. 1; *LSAG*² p. 369 no. 13 (date) (*Νευμοῦς* (gen.))

Νεύπολις
Skythia:
—olbia-borysthenes: **(1)** ?ii-i bc Dubois, *IGDOlbia* 110, 2
Tauris:
—chersonesos: **(2)** iv bc Solomonik, *GAKh* 1269 (vase); **(3)** c. 300-285 bc Kats p. 123 no. 28 (amph.) (s. *Μενέστρατος*) ?= (*5*) (*4*); **(4)** c. 262-237 bc ib. p. 105 no. 82 (amph.) (s. *Μενέστρατος*) ?= (*3*); **(5)** c. 250-230 bc Anokhin pp. 141-2 nos. 101; 114 (coin) ?= (*3*)

Νέων
Macedonia (Edonis):
—amphipolis: **(1)** m. iii bc Hatzopoulos, *Actes Amphipolis* p. 52 no 12, 10; *SEG* xli 566 (date) (s. *Ἰχναῖος*)
Macedonia (Mygdonia):
—thessalonike*: **(2)** m. i bc ib. xlvii 970 (biling.) (*ILGR* 220); *KGAM Thess.* i 61 (date) (*Λ. Κορνήλιος N.*: freed.)
Sarmatia:
—sarmatai: **(3)** ii bc *IG* ii² 8430 (*FRA* 1375)

Thrace:
—salymbria?: **(4)** iii ad *AEMÖ* 17 (1894) p. 57 no. 3, 6, 6 (or Thrace Perinthos-Herakleia: *Αὐρ. N. Νεοκοριανός*: f. *Αὐρ. Μηνόδωρος*)

Νηγέλλων
Macedonia (Bottiaia):
—edessa: **(1)** imp. *Tekmeria* 7 (2002) p. 104 no. 8

Νήδυμος
Macedonia (Mygdonia):
—thessalonike: **(1)** s. i ad *IG* x (2) (1) 69, 40 (*K. Πομπόνιος N.*)
Thrace:
—byzantion: **(2)** i-ii ad *IByz* 265 (Fıratlı–Robert p. 86 no. 108) (f. *Πρωτίων*)

Νηνακοῦς
Macedonia (Edonis):
—amphipolis: **(1)** ii-iii ad Dimitsas 888 (*Ποπονία Πουπιλλία ἡ ἐπιλεγ. N.*: d. *Ποπωνία Πῶλλα ἡ ἐπιλεγ. Δωρίς*)

Νηνας
Macedonia (Sintike):
—parthikopolis (nr.): **(1)** 159 ad *IGB* iv 2286, 1 (s./d. *Δούλης*)

Νηνής
Thrace:
—čomakovci (mod.): **(1)** iii ad *ILB* 163, 6 (Lat. Nene)
—lysimacheia: **(2)** i bc-i ad *NS* 542
—nicopolis ad istrum: **(3)** iii ad *IGB* ii 687, 4 (*Αὐρ. Σαβῖνα ἡ καὶ N.*: d. *Αὐρ. Σαβῖνα*)

Νηνίς
Macedonia (Paionia):
—stoboi (nr.): **(1)** ii/iii ad *SEG* xl 1797 (xlvii 949) (*Νινι* (dat.)—ed. pr., *Νηνι* (dat.)—Proeva: d. *Γαΐα Μαρκία*)

Νηρεῖς
Macedonia (Bottiaia):
—beroia: **(1)** ?171 ad *ILeukopetra* 10, 1 (d. *Νικόπολις*)

Νηρωνιανός
Macedonia (Bottiaia):
—beroia: **(1)** ii/iii ad *IBer* 144 A, 3

Νησιώτης
Scythia Minor:
—istros: **(1)** iii-ii bc Unp. (Avram, defixio) 4, 6 (*Νησ[ιώτ]ης*?, *Νησ[ιάδ]ης*?)

Νητιάζη
Thrace:
—kellai: **(1)** 241-244 ad *IGB* iii 1517, 35 (*Αὐρ. N.*)

Νήφων
Macedonia (Bottiaia):
—beroia: **(1)** ii ad *IBer* 279, 4 (Tataki 937)

Νιβλόβωρος
Skythia:
—tanais: **(1)** 220-228 ad *CIRB* 1245, 7; 1251, [7]; 1282, 4 (s. *Δοσυμοξαρθος*)

Νίγερ
Macedonia (Bottiaia):
—beroia: **(1)** ii/iii ad *IBer* 145, 13 (Tataki 938) (s. *Τόρκος*)
Skythia:
—tyras: **(2)** 181 ad *IOSPE* i² 2, 28 (s. *Ἀρτεμίδωρος*)
Thrace:
—byzantion: **(3)** ii-iii ad *IByz* 322 (f. *Χαιρέας*)

Νιγοσας?
Skythia:
—tanais: **(1)** 228 ad *CIRB* 1283, 8 (*Νιγοσα* (acc.): s. *Ἡρακλείδης*)

Νίγρος
Macedonia: (**1**) hell. *IAskl* 143 (*Ν̣ίγρος*, —*νι-γρος*?—Habicht)

Νίκα
Macedonia (Mygdonia):
—thessalonike: (**1**) 165 ad *IG* x (2) (1) 461, 3, 14 (*Νεί-*); (**2**) ~ ib. l. 5 (*Ἀπολλωνία Νείκα*: m. *Ἀπολλώνιος*)
Macedonia (Paionia):
—kavadarci (mod.): (**3**) ?ii-i bc *SEG* xlvii 946 (n. pr.?)
Thrace:
—zone?: (**4**) iv/iii bc *IG* xii (8) 267, 8; cf. *IThrakAig* E400 (locn.) (d. *Ἱστιαῖος*)

Νικαγόρα
Macedonia (Lynkestis):
—vevi (mod.): (**1**) s. ii ad *EAM* 155 (*Νε̣ι̣κ̣-α̣γό̣ρ̣[α]*)
Macedonia (Mygdonia):
—thessalonike: (**2**) ii-iii ad *IG* x (2) (1) 447, 1, 3, 11 (*Νει-*)

Νικαγόρας
Cimmerian Bosporos:
—gorgippia: (**1**) f. iii bc *CIRB* 1137 A II, 28 (s. *Θεόδωρος*)
Macedonia (Chalkidike):
—potidaia-kassandreia: (**2**) iii bc *IG* ii² 8997, 5 (Tataki, *Macedonians* p. 93 no. 67; *FRA* 2792)
Macedonia (Edonis):
—amphipolis: (**3**) ?iii bc *HE* 2697 (Tataki, *Macedonians* p. 57 no. 94) (f. *Βίτων*)
Tauris:
—chersonesos: (**4**) c. 425-400 bc *SEG* xxvi 805 (sherd); xlvi 922 (date) (f. *Βάθυλλος*); (**5**) iii bc Solomonik, *NEPKh* 74 ([*Ν*]*ικαγό*[*ρας*]: f. *Μιλήσιος*); (**6**) ii bc *SEG* xxviii 637 ([*Ν*]*ικαγόρας*: f. *Κλεώ*); (**7**) 130 ad *VDI* 1960 (3), pp. 154-5, 23 (*Νε-*: s. *Δημοκράτης*)
Thrace?: (**8**) iii-ii bc *BGU* 1251, 3 (Velkov 217) (s. *Βίθυς*)

Νικάδας
Cimmerian Bosporos:
—pantikapaion: (**1**) imp. *CIRB* 862 (*Νικά-*[*δ*]*ας*)
Macedonia: (**2**) s. iii bc *Syringes* 611 (Tataki, *Macedonians* p. 378 no. 11; La'da E1549) (s. *Δημήτριος*); (**3**) 184 bc *PHeid* viii 414, 3, [6], 11, 25, etc. (La'da E1550)
Macedonia (Bottiaia):
—beroia: (**4**) i bc *IBer* 163 (f. *Κρατεύας*) ?= (*5*); (**5**) f. i bc ib. (Tataki 940) (s. *Ἀμμάδικος*) ?= (*4*)
—pella: (**6**) s. iv bc *SEG* xlix 756 (f. *Εὐρυ-φύλη*)
Macedonia (Edonis):
—amphipolis?: (**7**) ii-i bc *BCH* 55 (1931) p. 191 no. 12 (s. *Πευκέστης*)
Macedonia (Elimeia):
—aiane: (**8**) ii-i bc *SEG* xxxix 566 (f. *Νίκ-ανδρος*)

Νικαία
Macedonia: (**1**) s. iv bc *RE* (2); Berve 552 (Tataki, *Macedonians* p. 379 no. 14) (d. *Ἀντί-πατρος*, ?m. *Ἀγαθοκλῆς*, *Εὐρυδίκη*, *Ἀρσινόη*); (**2**) iv/iii bc *Thess. Mnem.* 172 (Tataki, *Macedonians* p. 379 no. 15) (d. *Ἐπίνους*); (**3**) c. 223 bc *PTeb* 815 fr. 2 recto II, 24 (Tataki, *Macedonians* p. 378 no. 13; La'da E1810) (*Ν̣ίκα̣ι̣α*: d. *Ἀμύντας*)
Macedonia (Edonis):
—amphipolis: (**4**) m. iv bc *Mous. Kavalas* p. 135 no. Λ. 125 (d. *Φιλόμηλος*); (**5**) m. iii bc *BCH* 63 (1939) p. 6 (d. *Εὐξίθεος*)
Macedonia (Eordaia):
—kelle?: (**6**) s. ii bc *EAM* 118; Hatzopoulos, *MI* 1 p. 94 n. 4 (locn.) (d. *Ἀπολλόδωρος*)

Macedonia (Lower Paionia):
—europos: (**7**) iii bc *SEG* xliii 399 A (d. *Παράμονος*)
Macedonia (Mygdonia):
—thessalonike: (**8**) iii/ii bc *IG* x (2) (1) 107; *KGAM Thess.* i 67 (date) (d. *Χαρίξενος*, m. *Δημήτριος*)
Macedonia?: (**9**) m. iii bc *RE* (3) (Tataki, *Macedonians* p. 378 no. 12)

Νίκαινα
Cimmerian Bosporos:
—pantikapaion?: (**1**) iv bc *SEG* xlv 1010 (d. *Νευμήνιος*)

Νίκαιος
Macedonia: (**1**) ?219 bc *PUG* iii 104, 16 (s. *Πολέμων*); (**2**) a. 147 bc *Arch. Pap.* 42 (1996) p. 182 no. 1, 6 (Tataki, *Macedonians* p. 491 no. 175); cf. La'da E1551 (I f. *Νίκαιος* II); (**3**) ~ *Arch. Pap.* 42 (1996) p. 182 no. 1, 6 (Tataki, *Macedonians* p. 491 no. 174; La'da E1551) (II s. *Νίκαιος* I: katoikos)
Macedonia (Edonis):
—amphipolis: (**4**) a. 357 bc Hatzopoulos, *Actes Amphipolis* p. 34 no. 6, 6; *SEG* xli 560 (date)
Macedonia (Pieria):
—phila?: (**5**) ?iii bc *RPh* 1911, pp. 133-4 no. 36, 45; cf. Helly, *L'État thessalien* pp. 319-20 (locn.)
Tauris:
—chersonesos: (**6**) iii bc Solomonik, *NEPKh* 147 (*Ν̣*[*ί*]*κ̣αιος*?, [*Ἡρ*]*αῖος*—ed.: f. *Μενδικώ*)

Νίκαιχμος
Macedonia (Bottiaia):
—beroia: (**1**) 223 bc *IBer* 4, 17 (f. *Βότριχος*)

Νικάνδρα
Macedonia (Edonis):
—philippoi: (**1**) iv-v ad Feissel, *RICM* 243 (Pilhofer 274) (*Νικ*[*ά*]*ν̣δρ̣α̣*)
Macedonia (Eordaia):
—krannestai: (**2**) ii-iii ad *IG* x (2) (2) 36, 3 (*Νει-*: d. *Νίκανδρος*, *Ἰουλία*)
Macedonia (Mygdonia):
—thessalonike: (**3**) i/ii ad ib. x (2) (1) 379 (*Νει-*)
—thessalonike (nr.): (**4**) ii-iii ad ib. 1000 (*Αἰλ. Νικάνδ*[*ρα*])
Macedonia (Pieria):
—dion: (**5**) ii/iii ad Spiliopoulou-Donderer, *KGN* pp. 197-8 no. D15 (*Νει-*)
Scythia Minor:
—ulmetum: (**6**) iii ad *ISM* v 72, 3 (Lat. Ulp. Nicandra: m. L. V. Victorinus, L. Va. Turbo, *Σωτήρ*)

Νικανδρία
Macedonia (Paionia):
—negotino (mod.): (**1**) ii-iii ad *Sp.* 75 (1933) p. 41 no. 138, 1 (*Νει-*: d. *Συρίων*, m. *Ποσει-δώνιος*)

Νίκανδρος
Cimmerian Bosporos:
—pantikapaion: (**1**) f. iv bc *CIRB* 212 (s. *Πολυχάρης*); (**2**) iii-ii bc ib. 254 (f. *Μητρό-δωρος*); (**3**) i ad ib. 391 (f. *Διονύσιος*); (**4**) ii ad ib. 667 A (*Νή-*: f. *Διονύσιος*)
Macedonia: (**5**) ?417-413 bc *IG* i³ 89, 64 (Tataki, *Macedonians* p. 379 no. 16); (**6**) hell. *Syringes* 799 (Tataki, *Macedonians* p. 379 no. 20); cf. La'da E1640 (*Ν̣*[*ίκ*]*ανδρος*: f. *Φιλήτας*); (**7**) 203 bc *BGU* 1266, 7 (Tataki, *Macedonians* p. 379 no. 19); cf. La'da E1777 (f. *Πολι-άνθης*); (**8**) m. ii bc *BGU* 2423, 30 (Tataki, *Macedonians* p. 491 no. 176; La'da E1552) (*Νίκαν*[*δρο*]*ς̣*: s. *Ἡλιόδωρος*)

Macedonia (Bisaltia):
—euporia?: (**9**) ii-iii ad *SEG* xxx 612 (*Νεί-*: s. *Τόκης*, *Οὐαδέα*)
Macedonia (Bottiaia):
—beroia: (**10**) f. iii bc *IBer* 149 (Tataki 944) (f. *Σαδάλας*); (**11**) 223 bc *IBer* 4, 27 (s. *Εὔ-δικος*); (**12**) ~ ib. l. 35 (s. *Ποίμαχος*); (**13**) i ad ib. 125, 7 (Tataki 943) (I f. *Νίκανδρος* II); (**14**) ~ *IBer* 125, 7 (Tataki 942) (II s. *Νίκ-ανδρος* I); (**15**) ii ad *IBer* 338, 5 (Tataki 916) (*Νεί-*: s. *Γ. Οὐα. Ἑρμᾶς*, *Τερτία*); (**16**) 177 ad *IBer* 135 A, 18 (Tataki 917) (*Νεί-*: s. *Μηρύ-λος*); (**17**) 237 ad *ILeukopetra* 86, 13 (*Μ. Νείκ-ανδρος*); (**18**) 255 ad *IBer* 138, 12 (Tataki 1156) (*Ῥουφινιανὸς Νείκανδρος ὁ καὶ Σχοινᾶς*)
—edessa: (**19**) iii ad Feissel, *RICM* 5 (Tataki, *Edessa* 219) (*Νεί-*); (**20**) ~ *Arch. Pap.* 22 (1973) p. 204 no. 3 (Tataki, *Edessa* 220) (*Νεί-*); (**21**) v-vi ad Feissel, *RICM* 41
—mieza: (**22**) iii bc *SEG* xxiv 524 II, 17 (Hatzopoulos, *MI* 2 p. 106 no. 92) ([*Νί*]*κανδρος*?); (**23**) ~ *SEG* xxiv 524 II, 39 + Hatzopoulos, *MI* 2 p. 106 no. 92 ([*Νί*]*κανδρο*[*ς*])
Macedonia (Chalkidike):
—olynthos: (**24**) ?352 bc *TAPA* 65 (1934) p. 128 no. 4, 5; Hatzopoulos, *Actes Chalc.* p. 80 (date) (s. *Ἀθηνίων*); (**25**) ?350 bc *TAPA* 62 (1931) p. 43 no. 2, 10; *SEG* xlvii 922; Hatzopoulos, *Actes Chalc.* p. 80 (date) (s. *Ἐπιχάρης*)
—potidaia-kassandreia: (**26**) ?257 bc Nachtergael, *Les Galates* 7, 32; cf. Stephanis 1929 (Tataki, *Macedonians* p. 93 no. 68) (f. *Οἰκι-άδης*)
Macedonia (Edonis):
—amphipolis: (**27**) b. 357 bc Hatzopoulos, *Actes Amphipolis* p. 20 no. 2, 5 (*SEG* xli 556); (**28**) s. iv bc *AD* 24 (1969) Chron. p. 355 no. 2 (f. *Ἐρατησώ*); (**29**) m. iii bc Hatzopoulos, *Actes Amphipolis* p. 52 no 12, 6; *SEG* xli 566 (date) (s. *Λεωνίδης*)
—philippoi: (**30**) iv-vi ad *AAA* 13 (1980) p. 95
Macedonia (Elimeia):
—aiane: (**31**) ii-i bc *SEG* xxxix 566 (s. *Νικά-δας*)
Macedonia (Eordaia):
—exochi (mod.): (**32**) ii ad *EAM* 98 (s. *Παρ-μενίων*)
—krannestai: (**33**) ii-iii ad *IG* x (2) (2) 36, 1 (*Νεί-*: s. *Ὠφελίων*, f. *Νικάνδρα*, *Βασσιανός*)
Macedonia (Krestonia):
—morrylos: (**34**) ii bc *SEG* xxxix 612 (f. *Ἀντίγονος*)
Macedonia (Lynkestis):
—herakleia*: (**35**) iii ad *IG* x (2) (2) 98
Macedonia (Mygdonia):
—thessalonike: (**36**) i bc/i ad ib. x (2) (1) 58, 16; *KGAM Thess.* i 111 (date) (f. *Μένανδρος*); (**37**) i ad *IG* x (2) (1) 259, 24 (*Νεί-*: I f. *Νίκ-ανδρος* II); (**38**) ~ ib. l. 24 (*Νεί-*: II s. *Νίκανδρος* I); (**39**) f. i ad ib. 133, 9; Robert, *OMS* 5 pp. 295-302 (date) ([*Ν*]*είκανδρος*: f. —*δωρος*); (**40**) ii ad *IG* x (2) (1) 1027 (Tataki, *Macedonians* p. 185 no. 48) (*Νείκανδρος ὁ καὶ Βάλας*); (**41**) ii-iii ad *IG* x (2) (1) 499 (*Ποπίλλιος Νείκανδρος*)
—thessalonike?: (**42**) i-iii ad ib. 975 (*Νίκ-α̣ν*[*δρ*]*ο̣ς*: s. *Διονύσιος*); (**43**) iii ad ib. 234, 2 (*Νεί-*); (**44**) ~ ib. 859, 2 (*Νεί-*)
Macedonia (Orestis):
—battynaioi: (**45**) 192 ad *EAM* 186 II, 50 (*Νεί-*: s. *Ἀνδρίσκος*); (**46**) ~ ib. 186 III, 53 (*Νεί-*: f. *Ἀρραβαῖος*)
Macedonia (Paionia):
—kavadarci (mod.): (**47**) iii ad *Minalo* 2 (1911) pp. 54 (*Φλάϊος Νείκανδρος*)
Macedonia (Pelagonia): (**48**) ii-iii ad *IG* x (2) (2) 175 (s. *Ἀλέξανδρος*)
—kolobaisa*: (**49**) 112 ad ib. 230 (*Νεί-*: f. *Φλ. Νίκη*)

Macedonia (Pieria):
—dion: **(50)** s. iv bc *SEG* xxxiii 511 A = xxxvi 611 (s. Ἀντιγένης)
—pydna: **(51)** iv bc *GRBS* 43 (2002-3) p. 110 no. 1 a, 2
Macedonia (Tymphaia): **(52)** 188 ad *EAM* 71 (Νξίκα(ν)δρος: s. Δημήτριος)
Macedonia?: **(53)** c. 280 bc D.H. xx 9. 1 (Tataki, *Macedonians* p. 379 no. 18); cf. *Suda* Π 3232 (f. Βάλακρος); **(54)** 236 bc *PPetr*^{2} 18, 19 (Tataki, *Macedonians* p. 379 no. 17; La'da E2644) (Νίκα[νδ]ρος)
Scythia Minor:
—aegyssus: **(55)** ii-iii ad *ISM* v 287, 2 (Lat. Cornel. Nicander)
—istros: **(56)** i ad ib. i 200, 7 (Νεί-: s. Νίκιππος); **(57)** 138 ad ib. 193 I, 71 (Νεί-: f. Ζωΐλων)
Thrace:
—ainos: **(58)** 224-218 bc *SB* 13840 (La'da E89)
—byzantion: **(59)** iv/iii bc *IByz* 63 (s. Νυμφάρατος)
—lysimacheia: **(60)** 309-307 or 301-296 bc *IG* ii^2 1957, 8 + *ZPE* 146 (2004) p. 85 (*FRA* 3400) ([Ν]ίκανδρος)
—mesambria: **(61)** ii/i bc *IGB* v 5103, 6
—nicopolis ad istrum?: **(62)** ii-iii ad ib. 5234, 2 (Νεί-)
—perinthos-herakleia:
——(Geleuntes): **(63)** iii-ii bc *IPerinth* 61, 33 (s. Δαῦνις)
—serdica (territ.): **(64)** f. iii ad *BSAB* 3 (1912) p. 12 no. 8 (Lat. Domitius Nicander)
—sportela (nr.): **(65)** ii-iii ad ib. 2 (1911) p. 185 no. 9 (brick) (Lat. M. Aur. Nicander)

Νικανός

Macedonia (Derriopos):
—stuberra: **(1)** 74 ad *IG* x (2) (2) 325, 58 (Ν[ε]ικανός: f. Ὑλαῖος); **(2)** 87 ad ib. l. 83 (Νει-: s. Παράμονος)

Νικάνωρ

Cimmerian Bosporos:
—achilleion: **(1)** ii ad *CIRB* 1030 (Νει-: f. Ἀπολλώνιος)
Macedonia: **(2)** iv bc *RE* (2) (Tataki, *Macedonians* p. 384 no. 46) (f. Βάλακρος); **(3)** m. iv bc Plu., *Mor.* 177 D-E (Tataki, *Macedonians* p. 380 no. 22); **(4)** b. 317 bc ib. p. 383 no. 42 (s. Βάλακρος, Φίλα); **(5)** c. 365-330 bc *RE* (1); Berve 554 (Tataki, *Macedonians* p. 383 no. 44) (s. Παρμενίων); **(6)** 341-332 bc *CID* ii 43, 42; 44, [5]; 74 I, [32]; 74 II, 22; 80, [7]; 82, 19; *RE* (5) (Tataki, *Macedonians* p. 380 no. 21); **(7)** 335 bc *RE* (12); Berve 561 (Tataki, *Macedonians* p. 381 no. 29) (Lat. Nicanor: fict.?); **(8)** 334 bc *RE* (9); Berve 555 (Tataki, *Macedonians* p. 380 no. 23); **(9)** 330 bc *RE* (10); Berve 558 (Tataki, *Macedonians* p. 380 no. 25) (Lat. Nicanor); **(10)** 327-326 bc *RE* (3); Berve 556 (Tataki, *Macedonians* p. 381 no. 30); **(11)** 326 bc *RE* (11); Berve 560 (Tataki, *Macedonians* p. 380 no. 24); **(12)** 321-312 bc *RE* (13) (Tataki, *Macedonians* p. 380 no. 26); **(13)** 320 bc *RE* (6); Berve 559 (Tataki, *Macedonians* p. 381 no. 28); **(14)** 317 bc *RE* (8); Berve 553 (Tataki, *Macedonians* p. 382 no. 40) (s. Ἀντίπατρος); **(15)** 301 bc *RE* (14) (Tataki, *Macedonians* p. 382 no. 36); **(16)** iii bc *HE* 3344 (Tataki, *Macedonians* p. 383 no. 43) (s. Εὐπτοίητος?, Ἡγησώ); **(17)** ~ *SEG* xiv 850 (Brown, *Ptolemaic Paintings* p. 28 no. 26; Tataki, *Macedonians* p. 381 no. 33; La'da E1556); **(18)** 282-274 bc *PHib* 30, 3 (Tataki, *Macedonians* p. 381 no. 31; La'da E1555) ([Ν]ικάνωρ); **(19)** 263 bc *IG* ix (1)^2 (1) 17, 26 (Tataki, *Macedonians* p. 384 no. 48) (f. Νίκαρχος); **(20)** 246 bc *BGU* 1463, 2, 8 (Tataki, *Macedonians* p. 384 no. 45); cf. La'da E1393 (f. Ἀκέσανδρος); **(21)** ?241 bc *POElephDAIK* 1, 8; *ZPE* 123 (1998) pp. 149-50 (date); cf. La'da E1559 (f. Νικίας); **(22)** c. 238 bc *IG* ii^2 1299, 107; *ZPE* 78 (1989) p. 241 (date) (Tataki, *Macedonians* p. 382 no. 37); **(23)** c. 236-209 bc *PPetr*^{2} 27, 3 + p. 247 (Tataki, *Macedonians* p. 381 no. 32; La'da E1554) (s. Φιλόξενος); **(24)** c. 225-200 bc *PMich* 781, 17; cf. La'da E1553 (I f. Νικάνωρ II); **(25)** ~ *PMich* 781, 17 (La'da E1553) (II s. Νικάνωρ I); **(26)** 218 bc *PEnt* 69, 1 and verso (Tataki, *Macedonians* p. 384 no. 47); cf. La'da E1804 (f. Ἡδίστη); **(27)** 200 bc *RE* (15) (Tataki, *Macedonians* p. 382 no. 38); **(28)** 197 bc *RE* (16) (Tataki, *Macedonians* p. 382 no. 39) (N. ὁ ἐπικαλ. Ἐλέφας)
Macedonia (Bottiaia):
—beroia: **(29)** iii bc *AD* 52 (1997) Chron. p. 731 (f. Φιλώτας); **(30)** iii-ii bc *IBer* 153 (Ν[ι]κά[νωρ]: f. Ἄδυμος); **(31)** 248 bc ib. 3, 2-3 (Tataki 947 and 949) (f. Χάρτας, Ἀττύλος); **(32)** 223 bc *IBer* 4, 12 (f. Παυσανίας) ?= (*33*); **(33)** ~ ib. l. 13 (I f. Νικάνωρ II) ?= (*32*); **(34)** ~ ib. l. 13 (II s. Νικάνωρ I); **(35)** ~ ib. l. 13 (s. Ἀλέξανδρος); **(36)** ~ ib. l. 22 (s. Αἴκκυρος); **(37)** ~ ib. l. 22 (s. Ἀντίγονος); **(38)** ~ ib. l. 33 (s. Ἀδαῖος); **(39)** 121 bc ib. 134, 14 (s. Ἀντίμαχος); **(40)** i bc ib. 186 (Tataki 946) ([Ν]ικάν[ω]ρ); **(41)** ~ *IBer* 195 (Tataki 948) ([Νι]κάνωρ: f. Λανίκα); **(42)** f. i bc *IBer* 32 (s. Λυσίμαχος); **(43)** s. ii ad ib. 358 (Tataki 945) ([Νι]κάνωρ: s. Ν—); **(44)** 234 ad *ILeukopetra* 84, 6 (Tataki 292) (Αὐρ. Νεικάνωρ)
—edessa: **(45)** ii/i bc *Ancient Macedonia* i p. 202 no. 16 (Tataki, *Edessa* 223) (s. Ἐπικράτης, ?s. Φίλα)
—ichnai (territ.)?: **(46)** f. iii bc *A' Panell. Synedr. Epigr.* p. 195 no. 15 (*SEG* xlix 727) (f. Σάμος)
—mieza: **(47)** iii bc ib. xxiv 524 I, 4, 14, [24], [33] (Hatzopoulos, *MI* 2 p. 106 no. 92); **(48)** ~ *SEG* xxiv 524 II, 19 (Hatzopoulos, *MI* 2 p. 106 no. 92) (s. Ἀλ—); **(49)** c. 230-200 bc *BCH* 45 (1921) p. 17 III, 59 (Tataki, *Macedonians* p. 123 no. 4) (s. Μνασιγένης)
—mieza?: **(50)** c. 355-318 bc *RE* (4); Berve 557 (Tataki, *Macedonians* p. 175 no. 5) (and Macedonia (Chalkidike) Stageiros: s. (nat.) Πρόξενος (Atarneus), s. (ad.) Ἀριστοτέλης (Stageiros))
—tyrissa? (asvestari (mod.)): **(51)** f. ii bc *SEG* xlvii 999, 19 ([Ν]ικάν[ωρ])
Macedonia (Derriopos):
—stuberra: **(52)** 74 ad *IG* x (2) (2) 326, 39 (Νει-: f. Κάσσανδρος); **(53)** f. ii ad ib. 329 (Νει-: f. —τας)
Macedonia (Edonis):
—amphipolis: **(54)** hell.? *AEMTh* 15 (2001) p. 114 (f. Ῥόδα); **(55)** m. iii bc Hatzopoulos, *Actes Amphipolis* p. 50 no. 11, 9 (*SEG* xli 565); **(56)** c. 200-170 bc Hatzopoulos, *MI* 2 p. 87 no. 65, 1 (*SEG* xlvi 720) (Ν[ικ]άνωρ?: f. —ρος); **(57)** 90 bc ib. xlviii 716 ter, 4, 7 (f. Εὐφρόσυνος); **(58)** m. i bc ib. xl 522 d
—amphipolis (nr.): **(59)** a. 357 bc Hatzopoulos, *Actes Amphipolis* p. 43 no. 8, 4 (*SEG* xli 562) (s. Ἐπικράτης)
Macedonia (Elimeia):
—aiane (territ.): **(60)** c. 225-200 bc ib. xl 526, 3 (s. Ἀλέξανδρος)
Macedonia (Eordaia?):
—euia: **(61)** 181 bc *EAM* 87, 3, 10 (Hatzopoulos, *MI* 2 pp. 41-2 no. 17) (s. Φιλώτας); **(62)** ~ *EAM* 87, 12 (Hatzopoulos, *MI* 2 pp. 41-2 no. 17) (Νι[κά]νωρ: f. Βίλος); **(63)** ~ *EAM* 87, 16 (Hatzopoulos, *MI* 2 pp. 41-2 no. 17) (s. Ἄρμεννος)
Macedonia (Eordaia): **(64)** a. 316 bc *IG* iv (1)^2 94 b, 37 (Perlman, *City and Sanctuary* E.1 with p. 78 f. (date); Tataki, *Macedonians* p. 199 no. 8) (f. Μενέλαος)
—akrini (mod.): **(65)** ii bc *EAM* 90, 3 (Νεικ[ά]νωρ: II s. Νικάνωρ I); **(66)** ~ ib. l. 4 ([Νει]κάνω[ρ]: I f. Νικάνωρ II, Ἀρτεμᾶς)
—kelle?: **(67)** iii-ii bc *AEMTh* 9 (1995) p. 20 (vase) (f. Ἀσκληπιόδωρος)
Macedonia (Krestonia): **(68)** ii ad *SEG* xxxvii 561; cf. *BE* 1989, no. 450 (s. Δαρέας)
—morrylos: **(69)** c. 185-180 bc *SEG* xxxix 606, 2 (s. Παράμονος)
Macedonia (Lynkestis):
—herakleia (nr.): **(70)** ii-iii ad *IG* x (2) (2) 7 (Νει-: s. Ῥεκέπτος)
Macedonia (Mygdonia):
—herakleia: **(71)** hell. Hatzopoulos, *MI* 1 p. 211 (Νει-: s. Ἱππότας); **(72)** ~ ib. (s. Ἡρακλείδης)
—herakleia?: **(73)** s. iv bc *SEG* xlix 856; cf. *BE* 2003, no. 365 (locn.) (s. Μένανδρος) ?= (*74*); **(74)** iv/iii bc *SEG* xlix 857; cf. *BE* 2003, no. 365 (locn.) (f. Μένανδρος) ?= (*73*)
—kalindoia: **(75)** c. 330 bc Hatzopoulos, *MI* 2 p. 84 no. 62, 15 (f. Λυκοῦργος); **(76)** c. 313 bc ib. l. 33 (Νικά[νωρ]?: I f. Νικάνωρ II); **(77)** ~ ib. l. 33 (II s. Νικάνωρ I); **(78)** c. 312 bc ib. l. 34 (s. Κρίθων); **(79)** ii/i bc *SEG* xlii 593 (s. Μένων); **(80)** 68-98 ad ib. 580, 61 (Νει-: f. Ἀπελλᾶς); **(81)** a. 98 ad ib. 583, 17 (Νει-: f. Κολκοτᾶς); **(82)** ~ ib. l. 18 (Νει-: s. Φαυστίων)
—lete: **(83)** f. ii bc ib. xlvi 764, 12 (f. Νικόμαχος); **(84)** hell.-imp. Dimitsas 680 (Νει-: f. Κλευπάτρα); **(85)** ii ad *Makedonika* 2 (1951) p. 619 no. 42 θ, 8 (Νει-: f. Ἀντιμένων)
—thessalonike: **(86)** c. 143 bc *IG* x (2) (1) 1031, 1 (*IvOl* 325; Tataki, *Macedonians* p. 185 no. 49) (f. Δάμων); **(87)** ii ad *IG* x (2) (1) 410, 1 (Νει-: f. Παράμονος); **(88)** ~ ib. 459 A (Νει-: f. Δημάρχη); **(89)** ~ ib. 588 (f. Καλλικράτης, Ἀλεξάνδρα); **(90)** f. iii ad ib. 192, 6 (Π. Αἴλ. Νεικάνωρ)
—thessalonike?: **(91)** ii ad ib. 248 II, 2 (Νει-: I f. Νικάνωρ II); **(92)** ~ ib. l. 2 (Νει-: II s. Νικάνωρ I); **(93)** ~ ib. l. 3 (Νει-: s. Λυσίμαχος)
Macedonia (Orestis):
—agia anna (mod.): **(94)** i-ii ad *EAM* 193 (I f. Νικάνωρ II); **(95)** ~ ib. (II s. Νικάνωρ I)
—battynaioi: **(96)** 192 ad ib. 186 I, 47 (Νει-: f. Εὐφάμιος); **(97)** ~ ib. 186 II, 43 (Νει-: s. Θησεύς)
—lyke: **(98)** 236 ad *SEG* xlvii 911 (Νει-: s. Μαρκίων, f. Νικόπολις)
Macedonia (Paionia):
—demir kapija (mod.): **(99)** hell. ib. xlv 807 A (sherd) ([Νι]κάνωρ: s. Φιλ—); **(100)** ~ ib. 807 B (sherd) (Νικάν[ωρ]); **(101)** ~ ib. 807 E (sherd) (s. Δημήτριος)
—eudaristos: **(102)** ?f. ii bc *AD* 23 (1968) Mel. p. 111 no. 77; Papazoglou, *Villes* p. 327 (ethn.); Tataki, *Macedonians* p. 209 no. 16 (s. Βιαῖος)
Macedonia (Pieria):
—dion: **(103)** s. iv bc Hatzopoulos, *MI* 2 p. 73 no. 56, 14 with Index
—livadi (mod.): **(104)** imp. *SEG* xxxviii 630 (f. Παράμονος)
—phylakai?: **(105)** ?i bc Oikonomos 60 = *IG* ix (2) 231 (Νει-: f. Ἄρχιππος)
Macedonia (Tymphaia):
—agios georgios (mod.): **(106)** imp. *EAM* 30 (Νεικά[νο]ρο[ς] (gen.))
Tauris:
—chersonesos: **(107)** f. iii bc *SEG* xl 615 A, 22 (f. —ος); **(108)** ~ ib. 615 B, 10 (Νικάνω[ρ]); **(109)** c. 230-215 bc Kats p. 105 no. 83 (amph.) (s. Σατυρῖνος)
Thrace: **(110)** 238 bc *PPetr*^{2} 1, 85 (La'da E774); **(111)** 221 bc *PEnt* 111, 1 (Velkov 216); cf. La'da E836 (I f. Νικάνωρ II); **(112)** ~ *PEnt* 111, 1, verso (Velkov 216; La'da E836) (II s. Νικάνωρ I: t.e.); **(113)** ii ad Apul., *Met.* iv 16 (Lat. Nicanor: fict.)

—ABDERA: **(114)** ii BC *SEG* XLVII 1033 + *IThrakAig* E59 (Ν̣ικάνωρ: s. Ἀσκληπιόδωρος, Μητροδώρα)
—AINOS: **(115)** ?iii-ii BC *IG* II^2 7980 (*FRA* 258)
—BYZANTION: **(116)** s. iv BC *IByz* 124 (Firatlı–Robert p. 100 no. 151) (f. Ἀσκλαπιάδας, Δαμοκάδης, Ἀπολλόδωρος)
THRACE?: **(117)** 241 BC *PFrankf* 5, 20 (s. Φιλουμένη)

Νικαρέτη
MACEDONIA (BOTTIAIA):
—BEROIA: **(1)** ii AD *IBer* 308 (Tataki 1249) (Τυρία Ν.)
MACEDONIA (PIERIA):
—DION: **(2)** ii AD *Essays Laourdas* p. 109 no. 10 (Νειακα-: m. Ἀντιγονίων)
THRACE:
—STRYME?: **(3)** s. v BC *IThrakAig* E116 (Ν̣ικ̣α̣ρέτη: d. Σῖμος)

Νικάριον
CIMMERIAN BOSPOROS:
—PANTIKAPAION: **(1)** i AD *CIRB* 327; cf. KW pl. 29 no. 422 (Νει-: m. Ἀγαθοῦς, Φιλοκλῆς)

Νικαρίστη
MACEDONIA (PIERIA):
—DION: **(1)** hell. *SEG* L 589 (d. Ἀντίπατρος)

Νικαρχίδης
MACEDONIA: **(1)** 331 BC Berve 563 (Tataki, *Macedonians* p. 384 no. 49)
MACEDONIA (PIERIA):
—PYDNA: **(2)** c. 326 BC Berve 562 (Tataki, *Macedonians* p. 171 no. 12) (s. Σῖμος)

Νικαρχίς
THRACE: **(1)** 121-108 BC *FD* III (2) 128, 3, 5, 9, 11 (slave/freed.)

Νίκαρχος
CIMMERIAN BOSPOROS:
—PANTIKAPAION: **(1)** i BC/i AD *CIRB* 315; cf. KW pl. 55 no. 747 (s. Σωσιγένης)
MACEDONIA: **(2)** s. iv BC *IEph* 1432 (Tataki, *Macedonians* p. 384 no. 51) (s. Γέρων); **(3)** 263 BC *IG* IX (1)^2 (1) 17, 26 (Tataki, *Macedonians* p. 385 no. 52) (s. Νικάνωρ)
MACEDONIA (BOTTIAIA):
—EDESSA: **(4)** c. 200-175 BC *SEG* XLIV 409, 4 (Tataki, *Macedonians* p. 104 no. 16) (f. Κάσσανδρος)
MACEDONIA (DERRIOPOS):
—STUBERRA: **(5)** 50 AD *IG* X (2) (2) 324, 23 (Νεί-: f. Μόνιμος); **(6)** 74 AD ib. 325, 20 (Νεί-: s. Λεωνίδης); **(7)** ~ ib. 326, 52 (Νεί-: s. Φιλώτας); **(8)** 90 AD ib. l. 78 (Νεί-: s. Φιλώτας); **(9)** 126 AD ib. 336 (Μ. Οὐέττιος Νείκαρχος)
MACEDONIA (LOWER PAIONIA):
—EUROPOS?: **(10)** hell.? Dimitsas 145 = *SEG* XXVII 288 (f. Σιμίας); **(11)** ~ Dimitsas 145 = *SEG* XXVII 288 (s. Σιμίας)
MACEDONIA (LYNKESTIS):
—HERAKLEIA (AREA): **(12)** ii-iii AD *IG* X (2) (2) 41 (s. Γλαυκίας)
MACEDONIA (ORESTIS):
—LYKE: **(13)** s. ii AD *EAM* 149, 6 (Νείχα-: s. Δημήτριος)
MACEDONIA (PELAGONIA):
—DOSTONEIS: **(14)** ii AD *IG* X (2) (2) 196, 7-8 ([Δί]καρχος—*IG*, [Νί]καρχος?: s. Διονύσιος)
MACEDONIA (PIERIA):
—DION: **(15)** ?ii-iii AD Oikonomos 32 (Νίκαρ[χος]: f. Ἀλέξανδρος, Αὐρηλ—)
MACEDONIA (PIERIS):
—PHAGRES: **(16)** 86 or 202 AD Pikoulas, *Chora* p. 169 no. 82 (*SEG* XXVII 297) (f. Εἰρήνη)
MACEDONIA (SINTIKE):
—PARTHIKOPOLIS (TERRIT.): **(17)** f. ii AD *IGB* IV 2315 (Νεί-: s. Ζωΐλος, f. Ζωΐλος)
THRACE?: **(18)** m. v BC *AMNG* III (2) pp. 146-7 no. 15 (coin)

Νικᾶς
MACEDONIA (EDONIS):
—AMPHIPOLIS: **(1)** ii-iii AD *Thrakika* 13 (1940) p. 28 Σ

Νικάσιος
MACEDONIA (BOTTIAIA):
—EDESSA: **(1)** ?iv AD Feissel, *RICM* 12
THRACE: **(2)** imp. *Syringes* 1193 (Velkov 445)

Νικάσιππος
MACEDONIA (EDONIS):
—AMPHIPOLIS: **(1)** f. iii BC *Mous. Kavalas* pp. 112-13 no. Λ. 203 (s. Δόρκων)

Νικασίτιμος
TAURIS:
—CHERSONESOS: **(1)** f. iii BC *SEG* XL 615 A, 16-17 (s. Νικα—); **(2)** c. 285-237 BC Kats pp. 123-4 no. 30 (amph.); **(3)** c. 200-185 BC ib. pp. 105-6 no. 84 (amph.) (-τει-: s. Πυ—); **(4)** ii BC *SEG* XXVIII 637 ([Νι]κασίτιμος)

Νικασίων
THRACE:
—BYZANTION (TERRIT.): **(1)** imp. Unp. (Sayar) (Τιβ. Κλ. Ν.)

Νικασώ
CIMMERIAN BOSPOROS:
—PANTIKAPAION: **(1)** ?iv/iii BC *CIRB* 238
SCYTHIA MINOR:
—KALLATIS: **(2)** iii BC *ISM* III 131, 3 (*GVI* 1392); *ISM* III 132, 2 (d. Ἡρακλείδας)
TAURIS:
—CHERSONESOS: **(3)** i BC-i AD *IOSPE* I^2 460 ([Ν]εικασώ)

Νικέα
MACEDONIA (BOTTIAIA):
—BEROIA: **(1)** ii-iii AD *IBer* 297, 1 (Νει-: m. Χρήσιμος, Χρησίμα, Ἐρωτίς, Παράμονος, Νίκων)

Νικέας
MACEDONIA (EDONIS):
—AMPHIPOLIS (NR.): **(1)** a. 357 BC Hatzopoulos, *Actes Amphipolis* p. 43 no. 8, 1 (*SEG* XLI 562) (f. Θεοχάρης)
MACEDONIA (MYGDONIA):
—THESSALONIKE: **(2)** i-ii AD *IG* X (2) (1) 243 II, 2 (I f. Νικέας II ὁ καὶ Λούκιος); **(3)** ~ ib. l. 2 (Νεικέας ὁ καὶ Λούκιος: II s. Νικέας I)
—THESSALONIKE*: **(4)** iii AD ib. 580 (Αὐρ. Νεικέας: freed.)
TAURIS:
—CHERSONESOS: **(5)** iv-iii BC Solomonik, *GAKh* 1294-5 (vases); **(6)** iv/iii BC Kats pp. 84-5 no. 6 (amph.) (f. Ἀθανόδωρος); **(7)** iii BC ib. p. 91 no. 33 (amph.) (f. Βολλίων); **(8)** f. iii BC ib. p. 106 no. 87 (amph.) (I f. Νικέας II); **(9)** c. 285-272 BC ib. p. 124 no. 31 (amph.); **(10)** c. 272-262 BC ib. p. 106 no. 86 (amph.) (s. Ἡρόγειτος); **(11)** c. 262-237 BC ib. p. 106 no. 85 (amph.) (s. Ἡράκλειος); **(12)** ~ ib. p. 106 no. 87 (amph.) (II s. Νικέας I)

Νικέρως
MACEDONIA (BOTTIAIA):
—BEROIA: **(1)** 244 AD *ILeukopetra* 99, 3, 9 (Tataki 1339) (Φουνδάνιος Νεικέρως)
MACEDONIA (LYNKESTIS):
—HERAKLEIA (AREA): **(2)** imp. *IG* X (2) (2) 38 (Lat. Niceros: freed.)
MACEDONIA (MYGDONIA):
—THESSALONIKE: **(3)** ii AD *SEG* XLIII 463 (s. Γάϊος)
—THESSALONIKE?: **(4)** ii-iii AD *IG* X (2) (1) 698 (s. Ἕλενος)
MACEDONIA (PAIONIA):
—KAVADARCI (MOD.): **(5)** i-ii AD Šašel, *IL* 1255 A (Lat. Niceroti (gen.?): ?f. Livia Tertulla); **(6)** 210 AD *Sp.* 98 (1941-8) p. 57 no. 115 (?f. (ad.) Χιόνη)

Νικερωτίς
MACEDONIA (PAIONIA):
—STOBOI: **(1)** i-ii AD ib. 77 (1934) p. 40 no. 17 (Lat. Livia Nicerotis)
THRACE:
—ODESSOS?: **(2)** s. ii AD *IGB* I^2 206 quater; *Dacia* 21 (1977) p. 161 (date) (Νεικορο-: d. Ἀβροκόμας)

Νίκη
CIMMERIAN BOSPOROS:
—HERMONASSA: **(1)** i BC *CIRB* 1074
MACEDONIA: **(2)** a. 212 AD *SEG* XXIV 530, 2, 8 + XXXVII 581 (slave)
MACEDONIA (BOTTIAIA):
—BEROIA: **(3)** ii AD *IBer* 312; **(4)** f. iii AD ib. 267, 1 (Tataki 920) (Νεί-: m. Κουσπίδιος Ὀνησᾶς, Διονύσιος)
—EDESSA: **(5)** ii-iii AD *SEG* XII 348 (Tataki, *Edessa* 8) (Αἰλ. Νείκη); **(6)** v-vi AD Feissel, *RICM* 40
MACEDONIA (DERRIOPOS): **(7)** imp. *IG* X (2) (2) 312 (Ἰουλία Αἰλία Ν.)
—STUBERRA: **(8)** c. 126 AD ib. 341 (Τειφανία Νείκη); **(9)** ii/iii AD ib. 322 (Ἰουλ. Αἰλ. Ν.)
MACEDONIA (DERRIOPOS)?: **(10)** iii AD ib. 43 (Νεί-: d. Ἀγάθων)
MACEDONIA (EDONIS):
—PHILIPPOI: **(11)** i-ii AD *AD* 30 (1975) Chron. p. 286 (Pilhofer 391) (Lat. Tatiniae Niceni (dat.): m. Postumius Firmus)
—PHILIPPOI (TERRIT.): **(12)** imp. *CIL* III 7341 (Pilhofer 463) (Lat. Burrena Nice: m. Συμφέρουσα)
MACEDONIA (EORDAIA):
—ERMAKIA (MOD.): **(13)** ii-iii AD *EAM* 128 ([Ν]ίκη?)
MACEDONIA (LYNKESTIS):
—HERAKLEIA (AREA): **(14)** imp. *IG* X (2) (2) 29 (Νί[κ]η); **(15)** ii-iii AD ib. 24 (Αἰλία Νείκη: freed.)
MACEDONIA (MYGDONIA):
—LETE (NR.)*: **(16)** c. 160-180 AD *SEG* XLVII 974; *KGAM Thess.* I 123 (date) (Νεί-: m. Ὀνησίμη: slave?)
—PERISTERA (MOD.): **(17)** ii-iii AD *AD* 40 (1985) Chron. pp. 238-9 with pl. 101 α (m. Κλευπάτρα)
—THESSALONIKE: **(18)** ii AD *IG* X (2) (1) 530, 3 (Βειψανία Νείκη: m. Σερβιλία Ὑγίνη); **(19)** ii-iii AD ib. 344, 5 (Νεί-); **(20)** ~ ib. 435; p. 160 (stemma) (Δομιτία Νείκη: d. Δομίτιος Ὑγῖνος); **(21)** ~ ib. 442 (m. Ζώσιμος); **(22)** iii AD ib. 560 (Κλ. Νείκη); **(23)** 224 AD ib. 495, 1 (Γεγανία Νείκη: m. Πετρωνία Γεγανία Μεμμιανή); **(24)** 273 AD ib. 529 (Αἰλ. Νείκη); **(25)** v AD *SEG* XLIX 828 (Νίκις (gen.))
—THESSALONIKE?: **(26)** ii-iii AD *IG* X (2) (1) 817; **(27)** iii AD ib. 859, 7
MACEDONIA (ODOMANTIKE):
—SIRRHA?: **(28)** ii-iii AD *SEG* XLVIII 884 (d. Διονύσιος)
MACEDONIA (PAIONIA):
—KAVADARCI (MOD.): **(29)** ii AD Unp. (Kavadarci Mus.) inv. 65/II (Νεί-)
—NEAPOLIS (AREA): **(30)** 83 AD *SEG* XVI 404, 3 (m. Ἀλέξανδρος, Προκράτεια, Βίττας)
—STOBOI: **(31)** iii AD *Municipium Stobensium* p. 50 no. 241 (Νεί-)
MACEDONIA (PELAGONIA): **(32)** ii-iii AD *IG* X (2) (2) 175; **(33)** ~ ib. 256 (m. Εὐφρόσυνος); **(34)** ~ ib. 258
—DOSTONEIS?: **(35)** 232 AD ib. 191 (d. Ἀπολλώνιος, m. Σευῆρος)
—KERAMIAI (NR.): **(36)** ii AD ib. 220 (Αἰλία Ν.)

—KOLOBAISA (NR.): **(37)** ii AD ib. 235 (?m. *Ἱερατική*)
—KOLOBAISA*: **(38)** 112 AD ib. 230 (*Φλαουΐα Νείκη*: d. *Νίκανδρος*)
MACEDONIA (PIERIA):
—DION: **(39)** ?ii AD Dimitsas 177 (*Νεί-*: m. *Σέρβιος Ἡρακλείδης*)
—KOLINDROS (MOD.): **(40)** imp. *Klio* 52 (1970) p. 61 no. 14 (*Τυλλία Νείκη*: I m. *Νίκη* II); **(41)** ~ ib. (*Νε[ίκη]*?: II d. *Τυλλία Νίκη* I)
SCYTHIA MINOR:
—KALLATIS: **(42)** v-vi AD Unp. (Avram) (*Νεί-*)
THRACE:
—BYZANTION (TERRIT.): **(43)** imp. *IByz* 241 (*[Ν]είκη*?: ?d. *Ἀ—μος*)
—MADYTOS: **(44)** imp. *ISestos* 59 (*Νεί-*: m. *Γερμανός*)
—NICOPOLIS AD ISTRUM: **(45)** ii/iii AD *CCET* II (2) 627 (*ILB* 382) (Lat. Cassia Nice: m. Festivos)
—SESTOS: **(46)** i-ii AD *ISestos* 7

Νικήνωρ
SCYTHIA MINOR:
—TOMIS: **(1)** f. ii BC *ISM* I 48, 2; cf. *BE* 1984, no. 268; *VDI* 1984 (3), p. 179 (*[Νι]κήνωρ*?, *[Ἀλ]κήνωρ*?: s. *—αος*)

Νικήρατος
MACEDONIA: **(1)** i/ii AD Plu., *Mor.* 677 C
MACEDONIA (MYGDONIA):
—THESSALONIKE: **(2)** 95 BC *IG* X (2) (1) 4, 4 (*Ν[ε]ικήρατος*: s. *Ἀνδροκλῆς*); **(3)** ii AD ib. 241 A II, 7 (*[Ν]εικήρατος*)
—THESSALONIKE?: **(4)** 46 AD Dimitsas 366, 9 (*Epigr. arch. Mak.* 36); cf. *Essays Laourdas* pp. 98-100; *Tekmeria* 6 (2001) p. 126 n. 2 (locn.) (*Νει-*: s. *Θεοδᾶς*)
SCYTHIA MINOR:
—ISTROS: **(5)** iv BC *SEG* XXIV 258 (*FRA* 2628) (s. *Πολύϊδος*, f. *Πολύξενος*); **(6)** i BC-i AD *ISM* I 191 II, 34 (*Νει-*: f. *Ἀρισταγόρας*); **(7)** ~ ib. l. 14-15 (*Νει-*: f. *Πολύξενος*, *Ξενοχάρης*); **(8)** ii AD ib. 196, 10; 201 II, 4 (*Νει-*: f. *Θεόδωρος*); **(9)** 138 AD ib. 193 II, 35 (*Αἴλ. Νεικήρατος*); **(10)** iii AD ib. 222, 5 (*[Νει]κήρατος*: ?s. *Π—*); **(11)** 222-225 AD ib. 100 A, 20 (*[Νεικ]ήρατος*: s. *Ἕρμιππος*)
—TOMIS: **(12)** ii BC ib. II 392 (*Νικήρατ[ος]*: f. *Ἀσκληπιάδης*); **(13)** i BC ib. 2, 26, 29; 2 A, 46 (f. *Ἀπολλοῦς*)
—TOMIS?: **(14)** iv BC ib. 456 (s. *Ἀρτεμίδωρος*)
SKYTHIA:
—OLBIA-BORYSTHENES: **(15)** iii BC *IOSPE* I^2 190 b; 191 (f. *Ἐπικράτης*); **(16)** ~ ib. 201 I, 35 (f. *Πλειστῶναξ*); **(17)** ~ ib. 201 II, 9 (f. *Ἀρίστων*); **(18)** ~ ib. l. 17 (f. *Κρίτος*); **(19)** ~ ib. l. 30 (s. *Εὐρησίβιος*); **(20)** ~ ib. l. 35 (*Νικήρατ[ος]*); **(21)** ~ ib. l. 6-7 (f. *Χαιρήμων*, *Καλλικράτης*); **(22)** ?c. 200-175 BC ib. 34, 27; *SEG* XXXVII 670 (date) (*Νει-*: s. *Παπίας*); **(23)** imp. *IOSPE* I^2 227 (*Νει-*: I f. *Νικήρατος* II *ὁ καὶ Ὀμφάλακος*); **(24)** ~ ib. (*[Νει]κήρατος ὁ καὶ Ὀμφάλακος*: II s. *Νικήρατος* I); **(25)** i/ii AD ib. 39, 39; 169, [3]; *SEG* XLIII 505, 4 (*Νεικήρατος*—39 and 505: f. *Ζώρσανος*); **(26)** ii AD *IOSPE* I^2 84, 5 (*Νει-*: f. *Ἀχίλλητος*); **(27)** ~ ib. 134, 2 (*Νει-*: II s. *Νικήρατος* I); **(28)** ~ ib. l. 3 (*Νει-*: I f. *Νικήρατος* II); **(29)** ~ ib. 183, 4 (f. *Σωσίπατρος*)
THRACE?: **(30)** iii-ii BC *PAthen* 8, 17 (f. *Σεύθης*)

Νικήσανδρος
TAURIS:
—CHERSONESOS: **(1)** m. v BC *SEG* XL 612. 17 (ostrakon) (*[Ἀρ]κήσανδρος*—ed., *[Νι]κήσανδρος*?)

Νικήσιος
THRACE:
—MARONEIA: **(1)** i BC *RE* (-); Varro, *RR* i 1. 8 (Lat. Nicesius)

Νικησίων
MACEDONIA (MYGDONIA):
—THESSALONIKE?: **(1)** ii-iii AD *IG* X (2) (1) 721 (threptos)

Νικησώ
MACEDONIA (CHALKIDIKE):
—OLYNTHOS: **(1)** f. iv BC ib. II^2 10026 (12271; Tataki, *Macedonians* p. 140 no. 87; *FRA* 5905) (d. *Σώσων*)
—POTIDAIA-KASSANDREIA: **(2)** imp. *TAPA* 69 (1938) p. 64 (*Φλαβεία Ν.*: m. *Νίκων*, *Μαρκία Σεκοῦνδα*)
MACEDONIA (EDONIS):
—AMPHIPOLIS: **(3)** s. iv BC *AD* 24 (1969) Chron. p. 355 no. 6 (d. *Βάτων*)
—AMPHIPOLIS (NR.): **(4)** iii BC *SEG* XXIV 611 (d. *Πυθίων*)
MACEDONIA (MYGDONIA):
—THESSALONIKE?: **(5)** ii AD *IG* X (2) (1) 709 (*Νει-*: m. *Ἀριστόλυκος*); **(6)** ~ ib. 898 (*Νει-*)
MACEDONIA (PAIONIA):
—KAVADARCI (MOD.): **(7)** ii AD *Sp.* 71 (1931) p. 74 no. 174, 4 (*Νει-*)
SCYTHIA MINOR:
—KALLATIS: **(8)** ?ii-i BC *IG* XII (9) 34 (*Νει-*: m. *Κόμαρος*)

Νικήσων
MACEDONIA (PELAGONIA): **(1)** iii AD ib. X (2) (2) 263 (*Νει-*)

Νικήτας
MACEDONIA: **(1)** ?254 AD *ILeukopetra* 108, 2 (*Νει-*: slave/freed.)
MACEDONIA (MYGDONIA):
—THESSALONIKE: **(2)** ?iii AD *IG* X (2) (1) 477 (*Ν̣ικήτας*: s. *Ζωΐλος*, *Μανθάρα*)
THRACE:
—HADRIANOPOLIS (TERRIT.): **(3)** ii-iii AD *IGB* III 1803, 3 (*Νει-*: s. *Μουκάκενθος*, *Ἐπτηπυρίς*)

Νικήτης
MACEDONIA (MYGDONIA):
—THESSALONIKE: **(1)** iii AD *IG* X (2) (1) 247, 11 (*—αβηνὸς Νεικήτης*)
MACEDONIA (ORESTIS):
—LYKE: **(2)** f. iii AD *EAM* 165 (*Κ. Ἰούλ. Νεικήτης*: doctor)
MACEDONIA (PELAGONIA): **(3)** imp. *IG* X (2) (2) 272 (f. *Ὦπις*)
SCYTHIA MINOR:
—ISTROS: **(4)** iv/iii BC *ISM* I 234 (s. *Σωκλῆς*)
THRACE:
—PHILIPPOPOLIS-TRIMONTIUM (TERRIT.): **(5)** ii-iii AD *IGB* III 1312 + V 5493 (*[Νι]κήτης*?, *[Ἀ]λκήτης*—Mihailov)
—SERDICA: **(6)** ii AD ib. IV 1957, 1 (*Νει-*: s. *Ἀσκληπιάδης*, *Θεοφίλη*)

Νικητία
THRACE:
—PHILIPPOPOLIS-TRIMONTIUM: **(1)** iii/iv AD *Latomus* 17 (1958) p. 529 no. 2 (Lat. [A]urelia Nicetia)

Νικηφορίς
MACEDONIA (BOTTIAIA):
—BEROIA: **(1)** ii-iii AD *IBer* 265 (Tataki 924) (*[Νε]ικηφορίς*)

Νικηφόρος
CIMMERIAN BOSPOROS:
—PANTIKAPAION: **(1)** s. iv BC *CIRB* 169 (*Νικη[φόρ]ος*?); **(2)** imp. ib. 766 (*Νει-*: f. *Σύμμαχος*); **(3)** 221 AD ib. 99, 3 (*Ἰούλ. Νεικ(η)φόρος*); **(4)** 275-278 AD ib. 36, 18 (*Νει-*: f. *Χαρίτων*); **(5)** iv AD ib. 742 (*Νει-*: f. *Οὐσταvος*)
—TYRITAKE: **(6)** i AD ib. 906 (*[Ν]ικηφόρος*: s. *Σαβάδας*); **(7)** i/ii AD ib. 907 (*Νεικι-*: s. *Γαγανος*)
MACEDONIA (BOTTIAIA):
—BEROIA: **(8)** a. 212 AD *IBer* 136, 12 (Tataki 1072) (*Πετρ. Ν.*)
—EDESSA*: **(9)** 168 AD *SEG* XII 345 (Tataki, *Edessa* 134) (*Ἰούλ. Νεικηφόρος*: freed.)
MACEDONIA (DERRIOPOS):
—STUBERRA: **(10)** 191 AD *IG* X (2) (2) 319 (*Λ. Νεικηφόρος (Κ)έλερ*)
MACEDONIA (MYGDONIA):
—THESSALONIKE: **(11)** i BC/i AD ib. X (2) (1) 58, 7; *KGAM Thess.* I 111 (date) (*Σαλάριος Ν.*); **(12)** i AD *IG* X (2) (1) 259, 30 (*Νει-*: f. *Ἀντίγονος*); **(13)** ii-iii AD ib. 444, 3 (*Γ. Φοντέϊος Νεικηφόρος*); **(14)** ~ ib. 538 (*Γ. Ἰούλ. Ν.*); **(15)** s. ii AD ib. 244 II, 4 (*Σκρειβώνιος Ν.*); **(16)** ii/iii AD ib. 262 IV, 9 (*Νε(ι)κηφόρος*)
SCYTHIA MINOR:
—AEGYSSUS (NR.): **(17)** ii-iii AD *ISM* V 243 (Lat. Nicephorus)
—CARSIUM (NR.): **(18)** 138-161 AD ib. 129, 4 (Lat. Xe[ni](u)s? Nicephorus)
THRACE: **(19)** iii AD *RDAC* 2002, p. 372 no. 11 with fig. 4 (*Νει-*: s. *Ζώσιμος*)
—ABDERA: **(20)** 311-306 BC Maier, *Mauerbauinschr.* 69 II, 142 (s. *Ἀθήναιος*)
—DIONYSOPOLIS: **(21)** 241-244 AD *IGB* I^2 22 bis, 13 (*[Ν]εικηφόρος*: s. *Μελ—*)
—PAUTALIA: **(22)** ii-iii AD ib. IV 2062 (*Νει-*) ?= (*23*)
—PAUTALIA (TERRIT.): **(23)** imp. ib. 2138 (*-κι-*) ?= (*24*) (*22*); **(24)** ii AD ib. 2195 (*Νει-*) ?= (*23*)
—PERINTHOS-HERAKLEIA:
——(*φυλ. πεμπτ. Βορεῖς*): **(25)** iii AD *IPerinth* 165 (*Αὐρ. Νεικηφόρος*: s. *Μενεστράτα*)

Νικιάδης
CIMMERIAN BOSPOROS:
—GORGIPPIA: **(1)** f. iii BC *CIRB* 1137 B II, 39 (f. *Ὀρθαγόρας*); **(2)** ~ ib. l. 45 (I f. *Νικιάδης* II); **(3)** ~ ib. l. 45 (II s. *Νικιάδης* I)

Νικιανή
CIMMERIAN BOSPOROS:
—PANTIKAPAION: **(1)** v-vi AD Latyshev, *Sbornik* 89

Νικίας
CIMMERIAN BOSPOROS:
—BOSPOROS: **(1)** c. 265-260 BC *FD* III (3) 207, 5 (s. *Ἡρακλείδης*)
—FRONTOVOE (MOD.): **(2)** ii/iii AD *SEG* XXXV 869, 2; cf. *BE* 1990, no. 592 (*Νει-*: s. *Φαδιους*)
—GORGIPPIA: **(3)** f. iii BC *CIRB* 1137 A II, 47 (f. *Νικόμαχος*); **(4)** imp. ib. 1199 (f. *Σισουλίς*)
—NYMPHAION: **(5)** iii BC ib. 912 II, 14 (f. *Νουμήνιος*)
—PANTIKAPAION: **(6)** ii-i BC ib. 127, 1, 3 (*GVI* 1263); cf. KW pl. 37 no. 542 (*Νικίεωι* (gen.)—l.3: s. *Ἀγχίαλος*); **(7)** f. i BC *CIRB* 290 (f. *Τατία*); **(8)** i-ii AD ib. 590; cf. KW pl. 54 no. 730 (*Νει-*: f. *Γάϊος*); **(9)** s. i AD *CIRB* 426; cf. KW pl. 22 no. 322 (f. *Θεονίκη*)
MACEDONIA: **(10)** ?241 BC *POElephDAIK* 1, 7 (La'da E1559); *ZPE* 123 (1998) pp. 149-50 (date) (s. *Νικάνωρ*); **(11)** 231 BC *SB* 9258, 6 (I f. *Νικίας* II); **(12)** ~ ib. l. 6 (II s. *Νικίας* I); **(13)** ii BC *IG* II^2 9259 (Tataki, *Macedonians* p. 385 no. 55; *FRA* 3481) (f. *Δημήτριος*); **(14)** 169 BC *RE* (11) (Tataki, *Macedonians* p. 385 no. 54) (*Νίκων*—D.S.); **(15)** 51 BC *PSI* 1098, 40 (Tataki, *Macedonians* p. 491 no. 177; La'da E1558) (s. *Ἀπολλώνιος*)
MACEDONIA (BOTTIAIA):
—BEROIA: **(16)** 223 BC *IBer* 4, 29 (f. *Ἐπίνικος*)
—EDESSA: **(17)** ii AD Dimitsas 39 (Tataki, *Edessa* 161) (*Κλ. Ν.*)
—PELLA: **(18)** iii BC Akamatis, *Amph. Pellas* p. 41 no. PAR48 (amph.) (*SEG* L 613)

MACEDONIA (CHALKIDIKE):
—OLYNTHOS: **(19)** c. 330-320 BC *IG* II^2 1553, 25 (Tataki, *Macedonians* p. 140 no. 88; *FRA* 5906)
MACEDONIA (EDONIS):
—AMPHIPOLIS: **(20)** ?iii BC Unp. (Volos Mus.) inv. 362 (Tataki, *Macedonians* p. 57 no. 95) (f. *Νίκιππος*); **(21)** ii-i BC *SEG* XXVI 724; XXVIII 538 (date) (f. *Σωσαρίστη*)
MACEDONIA (MYGDONIA):
—KALINDOIA: **(22)** 68-98 AD ib. XLII 580, 83 (*Νει-*: s. *Σεύθης*); **(23)** a. 98 AD ib. 582, 36 (*Νει-*: f. *Κότυς*)
—THESSALONIKE: **(24)** ?39 BC *IG* X (2) (1) 30, [2]; 50, 2; 109, 8 (s. *Θεόδωρος*); **(25)** i-ii AD ib. 115 (*Νει-*: s. *Ἀντέρως*); **(26)** ii-iii AD ib. 535 (*M. Ὀκταούϊος Νεικίας*)
—THESSALONIKE?: **(27)** m. iii AD ib. 148, 12 (*Αὐρ. Πόντιος Νεικίας*)
MACEDONIA (PAIONIA):
—STOBOI: **(28)** ii-iii AD *Sp.* 71 (1931) p. 242 no. 644, 4 (s. *Ἐπίκτησις*, ?s. *Θυόδοτος*); **(29)** s. iii AD *ÖJAI* 32 (1940) Beibl. col. 16 no. 10. 36 (*Νει-*: I f. *Νικίας* II); **(30)** ~ ib. (*Νει(κίου?)* (gen.): II s. *Νικίας* I)
MACEDONIA?: **(31)** b. 348 BC *Olynthus* 10 pp. 429-30 no. 2219 (bullet)
SARMATIA:
—MAIOTAI: **(32)** ii/i BC *EAD* XXX 418, 12 (slave)
SCYTHIA MINOR:
—ISTROS: **(33)** iii BC *ISM* I 253 (*Νικίο[υ]* (gen.): I f. *Νικίας* II); **(34)** ~ ib. (*Ν̣ι̣κ̣ί[ας]*?: II s. *Νικίας* I); **(35)** 138 AD ib. 193 I, 66 (*Νει-*: f. *Νίννος*); **(36)** ~ ib. l. 99 (*Νει-*: s. *Νίννος*); **(37)** f. iii AD ib. 218, 11 (*Νεικίας ὁ καὶ Μᾶρκος*: s. *Οὐαλέριος*)
—KALLATIS: **(38)** iii BC ib. III 131, 1 (*GVI* 1392)
—TOMIS: **(39)** ii AD *ISM* II 125, 9 (f. *Χρῆστος*)
SKYTHIA:
—OLBIA-BORYSTHENES: **(40)** ii AD *IOSPE* I^2 80, 11 (*Νει-*: s. *Ποντικός*) ?= (*41*); **(41)** ~ ib. 102, 6 (*Νει-*: s. *Ποντικός*) ?= (*40*); **(42)** ~ *ISM* II 279, 2; *IOSPE* I^2 128, 4 (*Νει-*: f. *Ποντικός*) ?= (*43*); **(43)** f. ii AD ib. 82, 5; *VDI* 1993 (1), p. 93 = *SEG* XLIX 1028 B, 5 (*Νει-*: f. *Ποντικός*) ?= (*42*)
—TANAIS: **(44)** ii AD *CIRB* 1268, 11 (*Νει-*: f. —*ωρος*); **(45)** f. ii AD ib. 1266, 5 (*Νεικ[ί]α̣ς*: f. *Ἄρδαρος*)
THRACE: **(46)** s. iii BC *CE* 76 (2001) pp. 175-6 II, 13 (La'da E775) ([*Ν*]*ικίας*); **(47)** 226 BC *PPetr* III 21 g, 34; *PGurob* 2, 33; cf. La'da E814 (f. .....*φάνης*)
—ABDERA: **(48)** i BC *IThrakAig* E63 (s. *Μέλων*)
—BEROE-AUGUSTA TRAIANA: **(49)** ii-iii AD *IGB* III 1578, 2 (*Νει-*: f. *Ἡρωδιανός*)
—BYZANTION: **(50)** s. iii BC *IG* II^2 1958, 9 (*FRA* 1403); **(51)** ii AD *IByz* 312 (Fıratlı–Robert p. 120 no. 202) (*Νει-*: f. *Διονύσις*)
—DIONYSOPOLIS: **(52)** iii BC *IGB* I^2 13 ter, 2 (f. ..*ιππος*); **(53)** ii BC ib. 22 II, 4 (f. *Ἀπήμων*)
—LYSIMACHEIA: **(54)** iii-ii BC *IG* II^2 9229 (*FRA* 3401) (s. *Νικοκράτης*)
—MARONEIA: **(55)** ii-i BC *IThrakAig* E212, 37 (*Νει-*: s. *Ἱέρων*); **(56)** i BC-i AD *BCH* 37 (1913) p. 144 no. 49, 3 (*IThrakAig* E286) (*Νει-*: I s. *Διονύσιος*, f. *Νικίας* II); **(57)** ~ *BCH* 37 (1913) p. 144 no. 49, 3 (*IThrakAig* E286) (*Νει-*: II s. *Νικίας* I, *Ἀκονία*)
—MESAMBRIA: **(58)** i-ii AD *IGB* I^2 345, 3 (PM 2088) (*Νει-*: f. *Ἰουλία*)
—ODESSOS: **(59)** iv BC *IGB* I^2 101 ter (tile); cf. V 5042 (s. *Ἀρίστων*); **(60)** ii AD ib. I^2 183 (PM 1738) (*Νει-*: f. *Μέντης*); **(61)** f. ii AD *IGB* I^2 171 bis (PM 1612); *Dacia* 21 (1977) p. 161 (date) (*Νει-*: s. *Ξένανδρος*); **(62)** s. ii AD *IGB* I^2 78 (*CCET* I 40) (*Νει-*: f. *Ἑστιαῖος*); **(63)** ~ *IGB* I^2 78 (*CCET* I 40) (*Νει-*: s. *Ἑστιαῖος*)
—ODESSOS?: **(64)** imp. *IGB* I^2 206 quinquies (*Νει-*: f. *Ἀπολλόδωρος*)
—PERINTHOS-HERAKLEIA: **(65)** c. 100-115 AD *SEG* XXVI 1288, 3 (*Νει-*: I f. *Νικίας* II); **(66)** ~ ib. l. 3, 12 (*Νει-*: II s. *Νικίας* I, f. *Ἑρμογένης*)
—SESTOS*: **(67)** i BC-i AD *ISestos* 2, 2, 9 (*T. Φορφανὸς N.*: freed.)
—VICUS TRULLENSIUM: **(68)** ii-iii AD *IGB* II 508, 1 (*Νει-*)
THRACE?: **(69)** 316-309 BC *IG* II^2 1956, 46; *Ancient Macedonia* 5 p. 445 with n. 10 (date) (*FRA* 2560)

Νίκιππος
MACEDONIA (EDONIS):
—AMPHIPOLIS: **(1)** ?iii BC Unp. (Volos Mus.) inv. 362 (Tataki, *Macedonians* p. 57 no. 96) (s. *Νικίας*)
SCYTHIA MINOR:
—ISTROS: **(2)** i AD *ISM* I 200, 7 (*Νεί-*: f. *Νίκανδρος*)
THRACE:
—PERINTHOS-HERAKLEIA?: **(3)** iv BC Hp., *Epid.* iv 57

Νῖκις
SCYTHIA MINOR:
—KALLATIS: **(1)** iii BC *ISM* III 156 (s. *Ἱέρων*)

Νικίων
THRACE:
—ODESSOS: **(1)** iii-ii BC *IGB* I^2 157

Νικοβούλη
MACEDONIA (PIERIS):
—GALEPSOS: **(1)** imp. Dimitsas 917 (d. *Φιλίσκος*)

Νικόβουλος
CIMMERIAN BOSPOROS:
—GORGIPPIA: **(1)** f. iii BC *CIRB* 1137 A II, 36 (s. *Καλλίστρατος*)
MACEDONIA (BOTTIAIA):
—BEROIA: **(2)** 234 AD *ILeukopetra* 84, 4 (Tataki 926) (*Νει-*: I f. *Αὐρ. Νικόβουλος* II)
——Auranton: **(3)** 234 AD *ILeukopetra* 84, 3 (Tataki 293) (*Αὐρ. Νεικόβουλος*: II s. *Νικόβουλος* I)
MACEDONIA (CHALKIDIKE):
—ANTHEMOUS: **(4)** iii AD *SEG* XLII 571 (*Αὐρ. Νεικόβουλος*: s. *Αὐρ. Πρόκλος*, *Αὐρ. Διονυσία*)
THRACE:
—BYZANTION: **(5)** iii BC *ISM* I 65, 26 (*Syll*^{3} 707) (f. *Ἐπικράτης*); **(6)** ii-i BC *IByz* 217 (Fıratlı–Robert pp. 75-6 no. 83) (f. —*ορις*)

Νικόδημος
MACEDONIA: **(1)** 250 BC *PColZen* 54, 4, 12, 17, 45 (Tataki, *Macedonians* p. 385 no. 56; La'da E1773) (s. *Ἡγήσαρχος*: t.e.); **(2)** 16-12 BC *BGU* 1132, 2, 5; 1151 I, 4, 19 (Tataki, *Macedonians* p. 491 no. 179) (*Νεικόδειμος*—1132, *Νεικόδημος*—1151: f. *Ἀλέξανδρος*, *Θεόδωρος*)
MACEDONIA (BOTTIAIA):
—BEROIA: **(3)** 223 BC *IBer* 4, 21 (f. *Νικόλαος*)
MACEDONIA (CHALKIDIKE):
—OLYNTHOS: **(4)** f. iii BC *IG* XI (4) 531, 4, [11] (Tataki, *Macedonians* p. 141 no. 89) (*Νικόδ[ημος]*: f. *Ἀντίδωρος*, *Ὀνομακλῆς*, *Ἀντίγονος*)
MACEDONIA (MYGDONIA):
—THESSALONIKE: **(5)** c. 230 BC *IG* XI (4) 1053, 11 = X (2) (1) 1028 (*RE* (4); Tataki, *Macedonians* p. 185 no. 50)
—THESSALONIKE?: **(6)** iii BC *IG* X (2) (1) 26, 8; cf. *Tyche* 10 (1995) pl. 4 no. 2 (f. *Ἡράκων*)
THRACE:
—ABDERA: **(7)** iv BC Hp., *Epid.* iii 17. 10; *CMG* V (10) ii 1 p. 180

Νικόδικος
MACEDONIA (MYGDONIA):
—ARETHOUSA: **(1)** s. v BC *Suda E* 3695 (Tataki, *Macedonians* p. 69 no. 10) (*Νικόδημος*—ms. I)

Νικόδρομος
SKYTHIA:
—OLBIA-BORYSTHENES: **(1)** iii-ii BC *IOSPE* I^2 186, 1, 5 (s. *Διονύσιος*, f. *Διονύσιος*); **(2)** ii AD ib. 92, 5 (*Νει-*: f. *Νάμηγνος*)
THRACE:
—APOLLONIA-SOZOPOLIS: **(3)** iv BC *IGB* I^2 454 ([*Νικ*]*όδρομος*?: f. —*ορι*—*ις*)

Νικοκλῆς
MACEDONIA (BOTTIAIA):
—PELLA*: **(1)** iii BC *AEMTh* 3 (1989) p. 81 n. 23 (amph.)
MACEDONIA (MYGDONIA):
—KALINDOIA: **(2)** 68-98 AD *SEG* XLII 580, 1 (*Νει-*: s. *Φιλώτας*); **(3)** ~ ib. l. 1 (*Νει-*: f. *Φιλώτας*)
SKYTHIA:
—OLBIA-BORYSTHENES: **(4)** m. iv BC Dubois, *IGDOlbia* 13, 5 (*Νικοκλέος* (gen.): f. *Νικόστρατος*); **(5)** iii BC *IOSPE* I^2 201 I, 9 (s. *Ἑκατεώνυμος*); **(6)** ~ ib. l. 53 (f. *Νικόστρατος*)

Νικοκράτης
MACEDONIA (BOTTIAIA):
—BEROIA: **(1)** b. 167 BC *IBer* 1 A, 2 (Tataki 951) (f. *Ἱπποκράτης*)
MACEDONIA (CHALKIDIKE):
—MENDE?: **(2)** hell.? Dimitsas 772 (s. *Γέρων*)
MACEDONIA (PIERIA):
—PHILA?: **(3)** ?iii BC *RPh* 1911, pp. 133-4 no. 36, 101; cf. Helly, *L'État thessalien* pp. 319-20 (locn.) (s. *Φιλ*—)
MACEDONIA?: **(4)** iii BC Tataki, *Macedonians* p. 386 no. 57 (s. —*πος*)
THRACE:
—LYSIMACHEIA: **(5)** iii-ii BC *IG* II^2 9229 (*FRA* 3402) (f. *Νικίας*)

Νικολαΐς
MACEDONIA (BOTTIAIA):
—BEROIA: **(1)** 170 AD *ILeukopetra* 3, 4 (*Νει-*: m. *Εὐάρεστος*); **(2)** f. iii AD *IBer* 122, 4 (Tataki 584) (*Ἰουλιανὴ Νεικολαΐς*)
MACEDONIA (PELAGONIA): **(3)** iii AD *IG* X (2) (2) 266 (*Αὐρ. N.*: ?d. *Οὐάλης*, *Αὐρ. Κασσία*)

Νικόλαος
MACEDONIA: **(1)** iii-ii BC Bernand, *De Thèbes* 339 (Tataki, *Macedonians* p. 386 no. 58); **(2)** 232 or 207 BC *CPR* XVIII 13, 259 (Tataki, *Macedonians* p. 386 no. 60; La'da E1774) (s. *Μένανδρος*: t.e.); **(3)** m. ii BC *RE* (3) (Tataki, *Macedonians* p. 386 no. 59; Stephanis 1847); **(4)** imp. *SEG* XXXI 1538
MACEDONIA (BOTTIAIA):
—ALOROS: **(5)** iv BC Arr., *Ind.* xviii 6 (Tataki, *Macedonians* p. 44 no. 2) (f. *Πάνταυχος*, *Ἀμύντας*)
—BEROIA: **(6)** 223 BC *IBer* 4, 21 (s. *Νικόδημος*); **(7)** ~ ib. l. 27 (s. *Περίτας*); **(8)** 122 BC ib. 134, 4 (s. *Λεοντομένης*); **(9)** 120 BC ib. l. 17 (*Νικόλαο[ς]*: f. *Ἐπικράτης*); **(10)** i BC-i AD ib. 142, 4 (Tataki 952) (f. *Δημήτριος*); **(11)** ii-iii AD *IBer* 28 (Tataki 928) (*Νει-*: f. *Ἀλέξανδρος*); **(12)** s. ii AD *IBer* 75, 6 (Tataki 927) (*Νει-*)
—EDESSA: **(13)** ?246 AD *SEG* XXXVI 620, 2 (Tataki, *Edessa* 10) (*Αἰλ. Νεικόλαος*: doctor)
—PELLA: **(14)** s. iv BC *AD* 16 (1960) Mel. p. 82; *SEG* XXXIX 623; XLIII 444 (tiles)
—TYRISSA? (ASVESTARI (MOD.)): **(15)** f. ii BC ib. XLVII 999, 22
MACEDONIA (CHALKIDIKE):
—GIGONOS?: **(16)** inc. ib. XLV 757 (*Νικόλ[αος]*)
—KOMBREIA: **(17)** 87 AD *IG* X (2) (2) 325, 79 (Tataki, *Macedonians* p. 115 no. 3) (*Νει-*: s. *Ἀμμώνις*); **(18)** ~ *IG* X (2) (2) 325, 79 (Tataki, *Macedonians* p. 116 no. 4) (*Νει-*: f. *Ἀλέξανδρος*)
MACEDONIA (DERRIOPOS):
—ALKOMENA*: **(19)** 215 or 173 BC *IG* X (2) (2) 347
—STUBERRA: **(20)** i AD ib. 344 (*Νει-*); **(21)** c. 41-48 AD ib. 323, 28 (*Νει-*: f. *Ζωΐλος*); **(22)** 74 AD ib. 325, 2; 326, 2 (*Νει-*: s. *Ἀπολλόδωρος*); **(23)**

~ ib. 325, 42-3 (*Νει-*: s. *Παράμονος*); **(24)** ~ ib. 326, 48 (*Νει-*: s. *Παράμονος*); **(25)** 107 AD ib. 325, 94 (*Νει-*: s. *Ἀντίγονος*); **(26)** ~ ib. l. 99 (*Νει-*: s. *Κάσσιος*); **(27)** 116 AD ib. 327, 23 (*Νει-*: f. *Πούβλις*)
—STUBERRA?: **(28)** f. iii AD ib. 333, 12 with stemma; *AEMTh* 12 (1998) p. 104 (*Σιλβανὸς Ν.*, *Νεικόλαος*—*AEMTh*: II s. *Σεπτίμιος Σιλβανὸς Νικόλαος* I); **(29)** ~ *IG* X (2) (2) 333 with stemma (*Σεπτίμιος Σιλβανὸς Ν.*: I f. *Σιλβανὸς Νικόλαος* II, *Σ. Σιλβανὸς Κέλερ, Σιλβανὸς Κλαυδιανός, Σιλβανὴ Κλεονίκη*)
MACEDONIA (EDONIS):
—AMPHIPOLIS: **(30)** a. 357 BC Hatzopoulos, *Actes Amphipolis* p. 34 no. 6, 1; *SEG* XLI 560 (date) (*Ν[ικό]λαος*: s. *Μελαντάδης*); **(31)** s. iv BC Hatzopoulos, *Actes Amphipolis* p. 48 no. 10 B, 2 (*SEG* XLI 564) (*[Ν]ικόλαος*); **(32)** c. 315-313 BC ib. XXXVI 331 B, 18 (Perlman, *City and Sanctuary* N.1 with pp. 149-52 (date); Tataki, *Macedonians* p. 57 no. 97) (f. *Πέρσης*); **(33)** s. iii BC *SEG* XXIV 593, 3 (f. *Μένανδρος*); **(34)** imp. ib. XXXIX 571 (I f. *Νικόλαος* II); **(35)** ~ ib. (II s. *Νικόλαος* I); **(36)** 76 or 192 AD ib. XXXIII 501, 2 (*Νει-*: f. (ad.) *Μένανδρος*)
MACEDONIA (EORDAIA):
—EUIA? (POLYMYLOS (MOD.)): **(37)** iv-vi AD *AD* 32 (1977) Chron. p. 228 (mosaic); *BE* 1999, no. 325 (locn.) (f. *Ἀρίστων*)
MACEDONIA (LYNKESTIS):
—HERAKLEIA (NR.): **(38)** ?ii AD *IG* X (2) (2) 13
MACEDONIA (MYGDONIA):
—HERAKLEIA: **(39)** hell. Hatzopoulos, *MI* 1 p. 211 (s. *Ἄδυμος*, f. *Ἄδυμος*)
—LETE: **(40)** i-ii AD Dimitsas 676 = *IG* II² 11958; cf. *Myrtos* pp. 269-70; cf. *LGPN* II s.v. (24) (f. *Λέων, Νικόπολις*)
—THESSALONIKE: **(41)** 223 BC *IG* X (2) (1) 2, 2 (s. *Παυσανίας*); **(42)** 27 BC-14 AD *SEG* XLVI 812, 5 (*Ν. ὁ καὶ Κλειτόμαχος*: s. *Δημήτριος*); **(43)** i-ii AD *IG* X (2) (1) 243 I, 8 (*Νει-*: s. *Διοσκουρίδης*); **(44)** f. i AD ib. 133, 13; Robert, *OMS* 5 pp. 295-302 (date) (*Νει-*: s. *Ἐπιμένης*); **(45)** 165 AD *IG* X (2) (1) 450 (s. *Ἑρμογένης*)
—THESSALONIKE?: **(46)** ii AD ib. 248 II, 1 (*Νει-*)
—THESSALONIKE*: **(47)** iii AD ib. 384, 1 (*Αὐρ. Νεικόλαος*)
MACEDONIA (ORESTIS):
—BATTYNAIOI: **(48)** 192 AD *EAM* 186 I, 43 (*Νει-*: f. *Θεότιμος*); **(49)** ~ ib. l. 46 (*Νεικόλ[αος]*: s. *Φίλων*); **(50)** ~ ib. l. 49 (*Νει-*: f. *Ἀμύντας*); **(51)** ~ ib. l. 53 (*Νει-*: s. *Μενέλαος*); **(52)** ~ ib. 186 II, 56 (*Νει-*: f. *Ἀνδρίσκος*); **(53)** ~ ib. 186 III, 43 (*Νει-*: f. *Νεοκλῆς*)
MACEDONIA (PAIONIA):
—BYLAZORA: **(54)** iii AD *SEG* XLVII 896, 3 (*Αὐρ. Ν.*)
—KAVADARCI (MOD.): **(55)** ii-iii AD Dimitsas 286 (f. (nat.) *Αἴλ. Σεκοῦνδος*); **(56)** ~ ib. (*Κλαύδιος Ν.*: f. (ad.) *Αἴλ. Σεκοῦνδος*)
—STOBOI: **(57)** f. iii AD *AJA* 88 (1984) pp. 567 ff.; cf. *SEG* XXXIV 678 I, 3-4; 678 II, 2-4; 678 III, 4-5; *IG* X (2) (2) 333 (stemma) (*Π. Σέντιος Σεπτίμιος Ν.*: I f. *Π. Σέντιος Νικόλαος* II *Σεπτίμιος*); **(58)** ~ *AJA* 88 (1984) pp. 567 ff.; cf. *SEG* XXXIV 678 II, 1-2; *IG* X (2) (2) 333 (stemma) (*Π. Σέντιος Ν. Σεπτίμιος*: II s. *Π. Σέντιος Σεπτίμιος Νικόλαος* I, *Γρανία Ἀλεξάνδρα*)
MACEDONIA (PELAGONIA): **(59)** imp. ib. 280 (s. *Σευῆρος*); **(60)** 81 AD ib. 276 (*Νει-*: s. *Εὔβουλος, Νανοῦς*); **(61)** ?ii AD ib. 287 (*-λεως*); **(62)** ii AD ib. 288; **(63)** iii AD ib. 285
—KERAMIAI (NR.): **(64)** iii AD ib. 213
MACEDONIA (PIERIA):
—DION: **(65)** ?iii AD *SEG* XXXVI 614; cf. Spiliopoulou-Donderer, *KGN* p. 185 no. D1 (date)
—DION (TERRIT.): **(66)** i-ii AD Oikonomos 47 (*Κορνήλιος Ν.*)
—PYDNA: **(67)** iv BC *GRBS* 43 (2002-3) p. 111 no. 2, 3
SCYTHIA MINOR:
—ISTROS: **(68)** f. iii AD *ISM* I 333, 8 (f. *Σκαπούλας*)
THRACE:
—AINOS: **(69)** ii AD *IG* XII (8) 221, 6 (*Νει-*: s. *Ὀλίος*)

Νικόλας
MACEDONIA (DERRIOPOS):
—STUBERRA: **(1)** 116 AD ib. X (2) (2) 327, 28 (*Νει-*: s. *Ἀλέξανδρος*)
MACEDONIA (ORESTIS):
—BATTYNAIOI: **(2)** 192 AD *EAM* 186 III, 51 (*Νει-*: s. *Φιλώτας*)

Νικομάχα
MACEDONIA (DERRIOPOS):
—STUBERRA?: **(1)** f. iii AD *IG* X (2) (2) 333, 6 with stemma (*Λ. Αὐρ. Τρεβωνία Ν.*: m. *Σεπτιμία Σιλβανὴ Κελερίνη, Σ. Σιλβανὸς Νικόμαχος*)
MACEDONIA (MYGDONIA):
—THESSALONIKE: **(2)** ii-iii AD ib. X (2) (1) 493 (*[Ἰο]υν. Ν.*)

Νικόμαχος
CIMMERIAN BOSPOROS:
—GORGIPPIA: **(1)** f. iii BC *CIRB* 1137 A II, 47 (s. *Νικίας*)
—PANTIKAPAION: **(2)** s. iv BC ib. 209; cf. KW pl. 1 no. 25
MACEDONIA: **(3)** 330 BC *RE* (6); Berve 569 (Tataki, *Macedonians* p. 386 no. 61); **(4)** 257 BC *PLond* 1953, 12, 27 (Tataki, *Macedonians* p. 387 no. 62; La'da E1560) (s. *Βάλακρος*)
MACEDONIA (CHALKIDIKE):
—OLYNTHOS: **(5)** c. 325-300 BC *SEG* XXI 982 (Tataki, *Macedonians* p. 141 no. 90; *FRA* 5907)
—POTIDAIA-KASSANDREIA?:
——(Mekisteis): **(6)** ?f. iii BC *SEG* XLVI 796; *BE* 1998, no. 267 (locn.); cf. *LGPN* IIIA s.v. (82) (s. *Τεισαμενός*)
—STAGEIROS: **(7)** v/iv BC *RE* (18); Düring p. 264 (stemma) (Tataki, *Macedonians* p. 175 no. 6) (f. *Ἀριστοτέλης, Ἀρίμνηστος, Ἀριμνήστη*: doctor); **(8)** m. iv BC *RE* (19) (Tataki, *Macedonians* p. 175 no. 7) (s. *Ἀριστοτέλης, Ἑρπυλλίς* (Other))
MACEDONIA (DERRIOPOS):
—STUBERRA: **(9)** 74 AD *IG* X (2) (2) 325, 26 (*Νει-*: s. *Λυσίας*); **(10)** ~ ib. l. 27 (*Νει-*: I f. *Νικόμαχος* II); **(11)** ~ ib. l. 27 (*Νει-*: II s. *Νικόμαχος* I); **(12)** ~ ib. l. 31 (s. *Ζωΐλος*); **(13)** ~ ib. l. 36 (*Νει-*: f. *Στρατόνικος*); **(14)** f. ii AD ib. 329 (*Νει-*: f. *—σιος*); **(15)** f. iii AD ib. 333, 2 with stemma (*Σ(επτίμιος) Σιλβανὸς Ν.*: s. *Σεπτίμιος Σιλβανὸς Κέλερ, Λ. Αὐρ. Τρεβωνία Νικομάχα*)
MACEDONIA (EDONIS):
—PHILIPPOI: **(16)** s. iii BC ib. VII 2433 II, 11 (Tataki, *Macedonians* p. 166 no. 26) (s. *Ἀπήμαντος*)
MACEDONIA (LYNKESTIS):
—ACHLADA (MOD.): **(17)** f. iii AD *EAM* 169, 4 (*Αὐρ. Νεικόμαχος*)
—HERAKLEIA: **(18)** ii-iii AD *IG* X (2) (2) 62 (*Ν[ι]κόμαχος*)
MACEDONIA (MYGDONIA):
—KALINDOIA: **(19)** 68-98 AD *SEG* XLII 580, 55 (*Νει-*: f. *Φίλιππος*); **(20)** ~ ib. l. 60 (*Νει-*: f. *Διοσκουρίδης*); **(21)** a. 98 AD ib. 582, 8 (*Νει-*: f. *Ἡρακλείδης*)
—LETE: **(22)** f. ii BC ib. XLVI 764, 12 (s. *Νικάνωρ*)
—THESSALONIKE: **(23)** ?214-210 BC *IG* VII 295, 4, 7 (*IOrop* 126; Tataki, *Macedonians* p. 185 no. 51); **(24)** 95 BC *IG* X (2) (1) 4, 3 (*Ν[ε]ικόμαχος*: f. *Νικόστρατος*)
MACEDONIA (ORESTIS):
—BATTYNAIOI: **(25)** 192 AD *EAM* 186 I, 52 (*Νει-*: f. *Παρμενίων*)
SKYTHIA:
—OLBIA-BORYSTHENES: **(26)** f. iv BC *IOlbia* 97 (f. *Πρῶτα*)
THRACE:
—BYZANTION: **(27)** s. iii BC *IPerinth* 62, 1 (s. *Στράτων*)
—LYSIMACHEIA: **(28)** m. ii BC *ISestos* 38 b, 4 (f. *Ἀρκέσας*)
—PERINTHOS-HERAKLEIA: **(29)** iv BC *IPerinth* 260 (*Ν[ι]κόμαχ[ος]*); **(30)** ~ Hp., *Epid.* ii 2. 19
—SESTOS: **(31)** imp. *ISestos* 5 (f. *Ἀσκληπιάδης*)

Νικομήδεια
MACEDONIA (MYGDONIA):
—THESSALONIKE: **(1)** ii AD *IG* X (2) (1) 482 (*Νει-*: d. *Χρήστη*)
SCYTHIA MINOR:
—KALLATIS: **(2)** v-vi AD Barnea 47 (Popescu, *IGL* 93) (*-δι-*)

Νικομήδης
CIMMERIAN BOSPOROS:
—HERMONASSA: **(1)** i-ii AD *CIRB* 1081 (*Νικο[μή]δη[ς]*: f. *Ἀπολλώνιος*)
—PANTIKAPAION: **(2)** i AD ib. 409; cf. KW pl. 21 no. 304 (*Νει-*)
MACEDONIA (BOTTIAIA):
—BEROIA: **(3)** m. iii AD *IBer* 108, 6 (Tataki 329) (*Βετουληνὸς Νεικομήδης*: II s. *Βετουληνὸς Νικομήδης* I); **(4)** ~ *IBer* 108, 10 (Tataki 328) (*Βετουληνὸς Νεικομήδης*: I f. *Βετουληνὸς Νικομήδης* II)
—EDESSA: **(5)** 180 AD *SEG* XXIV 531, 15 (Tataki, *Edessa* 225) (f. *Φῆλιξ*)
MACEDONIA (CHALKIDIKE):
—AKANTHOS: **(6)** iv BC *RE* (10); *FGrH* 772 (Tataki, *Macedonians* p. 42 no. 6)
MACEDONIA (PELAGONIA):
—DOSTONEIS: **(7)** iii AD *IG* X (2) (2) 201, 3 (*Νει-*: s. *Αὐρ. Λυσίμαχος, Αὐρηλία*)
SCYTHIA MINOR:
—KALLATIS: **(8)** iii BC *ISM* III 133, 3 (s. *Θεόφρων*)
SKYTHIA:
—TYRAS: **(9)** 217 AD *ILB* 18, 15 (Lat. Cl. Nicom[edes]?, Nicom[achus]?)
THRACE:
—ABDERA: **(10)** s. ii BC *IG* XII (8) 170 d, 53 (s. *Διόδωρος*)
—ABRYTTOS: **(11)** ii-iii AD *IGB* V 5265, 1 (*Αἴλ. Νεικομήδης*)
—DIONYSOPOLIS: **(12)** iii AD ib. I² 14 c, 10 (*Αὐρ. Νεικομήδης*: s. *Σιληνός*)
—ODESSOS: **(13)** m. ii AD ib. 150 (PM 859) (*Νει-*: f. *Ἀννι*); **(14)** iii AD *IGB* I² 135 (f. *Σεβῆρος*)
—TRAIANOPOLIS: **(15)** iii AD *SEG* XXIV 642 + *ZPE* 10 (1973) p. 99 (*IThrakAig* E436) (*Νει-*)

Νικονόα
MACEDONIA: **(1)** vii/vi BC *POxy* 2465 fr. 1 II, 23; cf. *FGrH* 631 (*Νικονόη*—pap.: m. *Ἀέροπος* I); **(2)** iii BC *PAE* 1912, p. 188 no. 144 (Tataki, *Macedonians* p. 387 no. 64) (d. *Πρωτέας*)
MACEDONIA (EDONIS):
—AMPHIPOLIS: **(3)** s. iii BC *SEG* XXIV 593, 1 (d. *Μένανδρος*)

Νικονόη
MACEDONIA (ELIMEIA):
—ELATI (MOD.): **(1)** 108 AD *EAM* 59 a; 59 c, 2 (*Νεικονόη*—59 c)
MACEDONIA (MYGDONIA):
—THESSALONIKE?: **(2)** ii-iii AD *IG* X (2) (1) 720, 2 (*Νει-*: m. *Σιλβανός*)

Νικοξενία
CIMMERIAN BOSPOROS:
—PANTIKAPAION: **(1)** ii AD *CIRB* 795 (*Νει-*: d. *Ἰάμβλοχος*)

Νικόξενος
Macedonia (Chalkidike):
—olynthos: **(1)** v/iv bc Hp., *Epid.* vii 80. 1 (Tataki, *Macedonians* p. 141 no. 91)
Macedonia (Mygdonia):
—kalindoia: **(2)** c. 331 bc Hatzopoulos, *MI* 2 p. 84 no. 62, 14 (f. Ἡγήσιππος)

Νικοπολιανά
Macedonia (Lynkestis)?: **(1)** ii-iii ad *EAM* 159 a + *SEG* xxxix 563 (d. Συνέκδημος)

Νικοπολιανή
Macedonia (Mygdonia):
—thessalonike: **(1)** ii-iii ad *IG* x (2) (1) 343, 2 (Νικοπολιανῆνι (dat.))

Νικοπολιανός
Macedonia (Bisaltia):
—euporia?: **(1)** iii ad *RA* 1945, p. 40 (Ἰούλ. Νεικοπολιανός: s. Ἰούλ. Μᾶρκος)
Macedonia (Bottiaia):
—beroia: **(2)** a. 212 ad *IBer* 136, 16 (Tataki 900) (Οὐείβ. Νεικοπολιανός)
Macedonia (Chalkidike):
—olynthos (nr.): **(3)** imp. *SEG* xxix 610 (Ν[ι]κ[ο]πολιανός)

Νικόπολις
Cimmerian Bosporos:
—pantikapaion: **(1)** s. iv bc *CIRB* 116 (*CEG* ii 735); **(2)** hell.-imp. *CIG* 8556 c (lead) (Νεικοπολεῖν[ος]—*CIG*); **(3)** i bc/i ad *CIRB* 477; cf. KW pl. 12 no. 157
Macedonia (Bottiaia):
—beroia: **(4)** f. ii ad *IBer* 243 (Tataki 929) (Νει-: m. Ζώσιμος); **(5)** ?171 ad *ILeukopetra* 10, 1 (Νεικοπολίου (gen.): f. Νηρεΐς); **(6)** 248 ad *IBer* 53, 2 (Αἰλ. Νεικόπο[λις])
Macedonia (Chalkidike):
—potidaia-kassandreia (territ.): **(7)** imp. *SEG* xxix 588, 5 (Λικινία Ν[ικό]πολις: d. Λικίνιος Κούαρτος, Διοδώρα)
Macedonia (Elimeia):
—doureoi: **(8)** 214 ad *ILeukopetra* 65, 5 (Tataki 264) (Αὐρ. Ν.)
Macedonia (Lower Paionia):
—europos: **(9)** i bc-i ad? *SEG* xxxviii 609 (d. Ζωΐλος, m. Ἰόλας, Ἀθηναγόρας)
Macedonia (Lynkestis):
—herakleia: **(10)** ii-iii ad *IG* x (2) (2) 57 (Ἀκυλία Ν.)
Macedonia (Mygdonia):
—lete: **(11)** i-ii ad Dimitsas 676 = *IG* ii² 11958; cf. *Myrtos* pp. 269-70; cf. *LGPN* ii s.v. (10) (Νει-: s./d. Νικόλαος, Στρατονίκη)
—thessalonike: **(12)** 38 bc Robert, *Coll. Froehner* 44, 9 (Tataki, *Macedonians* p. 185 no. 52) (f. Ἀρχέπολις); **(13)** 27 bc-14 ad *IG* x (2) (1) 31, 8 (Νεικόπολ[ις]: f. —ις); **(14)** i-ii ad ib. 625 (*GVI* 319); **(15)** f. i ad *IG* x (2) (1) 126, 4; Robert, *OMS* 5 pp. 295-302 (date) (Νει-: f. Δημήτριος); **(16)** ii-iii ad *IG* x (2) (1) 186, 6 (Λογγινιανὸς Νεικόπολις: s. Ἀρρία Προκλιανὴ Φιλίστη); **(17)** 167 ad ib. 528 (Κλ. Νεικόπολις); **(18)** ii/iii ad *SEG* xlix 814 II, 3; **(19)** iii ad *IG* x (2) (1) 583, 3 (Αἰλ. Πουπλικία Ν.)
Macedonia (Odomantike):
—sirrha (territ.): **(20)** ii-iii ad Kaphtantzis 473 (*SEG* xlviii 883) (f. Διονύσιος)
Macedonia (Orestis):
—lyke: **(21)** 236 ad ib. xlvii 911 (Ν[ικό]πολις: d. Νικάνωρ)
—sisani (mod.): **(22)** 146 ad *EAM* 187, 18 (Νει-: f./m. Τερτιανός)
Macedonia (Pelagonia):
—mojno (mod.): **(23)** 199 ad *IG* x (2) (2) 171 (Νει-: d. Παράμονος)
Scythia Minor:
—kallatis: **(24)** iii-ii bc *SEG* xiv 203 (*Ag.* xvii 510; *FRA* 2649) ([Νι]κόπολις)

Thrace:
—byzantion: **(25)** iii bc *IByz* 292 (Firatlı-Robert p. 114 no. 191) (d. Κρατῖνος)

Νικοπτολέμα
Macedonia (Chalkidike):
—stratonikeia?: **(1)** i-ii ad *SEG* xxiv 575; cf. *AD* 18 (1963) Chron. p. 209 (Νεικοπτελέμα: d. Ἐπίλυκος)

Νῖκος
Cimmerian Bosporos:
—tyritake: **(1)** iii ad *CIRB* 910 (Νεῖ-)
Tauris:
—chersonesos: **(2)** f. ii ad Solomonik, *NEP-Kh* 111, 9 (Νεῖ-: s. Ἡρακλείδης)

Νικοσθένης
Skythia:
—olbia-borysthenes (berezan (mod.)): **(1)** vi/v bc *SEG* xxx 890 (vase) (Νικοσθ[ένης])

Νικοστράτη
Macedonia (Bottiaia):
—pella: **(1)** iii bc *Α΄ Panell. Synedr. Epigr.* p. 181 no. 6 (*Pella* p. 197 no. 65) (d. Ἀπολλώνιος)
Macedonia (Edonis):
—amphipolis: **(2)** hell. *CCCA* vi 228 ([Ν]ικοσ[τρά]τη)
Macedonia (Sintike):
—parthikopolis: **(3)** ii ad *IGB* iv 2271 (Νικο-σ-ρ(ά)τ(η): d. Πύρρος)
—parthikopolis*: **(4)** vi ad Beševliev 241, 6

Νικοστρατιανός
Macedonia (Sintike):
—neine: **(1)** ii-iii ad *IGB* v 5887 (Νει-: f. Διονύσιος)

Νικόστρατος
Cimmerian Bosporos:
—gorgippia: **(1)** f. iii bc *CIRB* 1137 A I, 7 (s. Ἀναξικράτης); **(2)** ~ ib. 1137 B I, 42 (s. Κρατῖνος)
—pantikapaion: **(3)** f. iii ad ib. 104, 6; 105, 4 (Νεικόστρ[α]τος: f. Οὐαλέρις)
Macedonia: **(4)** 327 bc *RE* (9); Berve 570 (Tataki, *Macedonians* p. 387 no. 65); *LCM* 6 (1981) pp. 63 ff. (name) (Lat. Nicostratus); **(5)** c. 140-130 bc *PBingen* 36, 4 (La'da E1561); **(6)** 102 bc *PWürzb* 6, 30 (Tataki, *Macedonians* p. 491 no. 180; La'da E1562); **(7)** ii ad *RE* (27); *IG* xii (1) 83 (Tataki, *Macedonians* p. 387 no. 66) (Τ. Αὐρηλιανὸς Ν. II s. Νικόστρατος I); **(8)** ~ *IG* xii (1) 83 (Tataki, *Macedonians* p. 388 no. 67) (I f. Νικόστρατος II)
Macedonia (Bottiaia):
—aigai: **(9)** s. iv bc *SEG* xxxv 789 (s. Ἀμάδωκος)
—pella: **(10)** iii bc Akamatis, *Amph. Pellas* p. 41 no. PAR50 (amph.) (*SEG* l 613) (Νικό[σ]τρατ[ος])
Macedonia (Chalkidike):
—akanthos: **(11)** iii/ii bc *PAE* 1912, p. 189 no. 225 (Tataki, *Macedonians* p. 42 no. 7) (s. Φιλωνίδης)
—potidaia-kassandreia: **(12)** 282 bc *IG* xi (2) 106, 20 (Stephanis 1866; Tataki, *Macedonians* p. 93 no. 69)
Macedonia (Derriopos):
—stuberra: **(13)** 53 ad *IG* x (2) (2) 324, 13 (Νικόστ[ρατος]: f. Ζωΐλος)
Macedonia (Edonis):
—amphipolis: **(14)** iv/iii bc *SEG* xxxi 617; **(15)** b. 213 bc Hatzopoulos, *MI* 2 p. 83 no. 61, 7 (*SEG* xlvi 715) (s. Ἀρχανδρος)
—amphipolis?: **(16)** hell. Dimitsas 904 (s. Αἰνείας)
—philippoi: **(17)** iii-iv ad *SEG* xlviii 837, 1 (Pilhofer 387a) (Φ. Νικόστρα(τος))
—philippoi?: **(18)** 320 bc *SEG* xxi 306, [1], 9 (Tataki, *Macedonians* p. 166 no. 27) ([Νι]κόστρατο[ς]: s. —λων)
Macedonia (Mygdonia):
—kalindoia: **(19)** a. 98 ad *SEG* xlii 582, 58 (Νει-: f. Ζώσιμος)
—lete: **(20)** c. 325-300 bc ib. xliv 535: *KGAM Thess.* i 30 (date) (f. Στραττώ)
—thessalonike: **(21)** 95 bc *IG* x (2) (1) 4, 3 (Νει-: s. Νικόμαχος); **(22)** s. i ad ib. 69, 48 (Νει-: I f. Νικόστρατος II); **(23)** ~ ib. l. 48 (Νει-: II s. Νικόστρατος I); **(24)** ii ad ib. 356, 1 (Νει-); **(25)** ii-iii ad ib. 584 (—ιος Νεικό[στ]ρατος); **(26)** iii ad ib. 613 (Αἰλ. Νεικόστρατος); **(27)** m. iii ad ib. 38 A, 6; 198, 7 (Βαίβιος Τερραῖος Νεικόστρατος)
—thessalonike?: **(28)** ii ad ib. 248 I, 7 ([Νεικ]όστρατος?); **(29)** ii-iii ad ib. 836 ([Νι]κόστρατος)
Macedonia (Odomantike):
—sirrha: **(30)** 62 or 178 ad *JDAI* 84 (1969) p. 157 no. R27, 6 (Νει-: f. Στρατονίκη)
—sirrha?: **(31)** ii-i bc *SEG* xl 563, 5
Macedonia (Pelagonia): **(32)** iii ad *IG* x (2) (2) 273 (Αὐρ. Ν.: s. Αὐρ. Γαϊανός, Αὐρ. Ἰουλιανή)
Macedonia (Pieria):
—leibethra: **(33)** c. 230-200 bc *BCH* 45 (1921) p. 17 III, 53 (Tataki, *Macedonians* p. 117 no. 1) (s. Νίκων)
Scythia Minor:
—tomis: **(34)** ii-iii ad *ISM* ii 31 II, 11 (Νει-: f. Θεόδωρος); **(35)** 201 ad ib. 83 I, 30 (Νει-: s. Μᾶρκος)
Skythia:
—olbia-borysthenes: **(36)** m. iv bc Dubois, *IGDOlbia* 13, 5 (s. Νικοκλῆς); **(37)** iii bc *IOSPE* i² 201 I, 53 (s. Νικοκλῆς)
—tanais: **(38)** 104 ad *CIRB* 1259, 10 (I f. Νικόστρατος II); **(39)** ~ ib. l. 10 (Νει-: II s. Νικόστρατος I); **(40)** 228 ad ib. 1282, 7 (Νει-: s. Ἀράθης)
Thrace: **(41)** c. 223 bc *PTeb* 815 fr. 5, 28 (Velkov 218; La'da E837) (-σστρα-: s. Μόνιμος: t.e.)
—abdera: **(42)** c. 415-395 bc May, *Abdera* pp. 167-8 no. 219 (coin)
—byzantion (territ.): **(43)** imp. Unp. (Sayar) (Νει-: s. Κόϊντος); **(44)** ~ ib. (f. Ἀγαθήμερος)
—perinthos-herakleia: **(45)** ii ad *IPerinth* 101 (Νει-: f. Ἀρτεμίδωρος ὁ καὶ Κυρήνιος)
—philippopolis-trimontium: **(46)** m. iii ad *IGB* iii 884 a, 21; cf. v 5400 ([Αὐ]ρ. Νεικόστρατος)
—vicus trullensium: **(47)** 161-169 or 198-209 ad *ILB* 180, 3 (Lat. Nicostratus: s. Δημοσθένης)

Νικοτύχη
Macedonia (Pelagonia):
—keramiai (nr.): **(1)** ii-iii ad *IG* x (2) (2) 222 ([Ν]εικοτύχη)

Νικοῦς
Macedonia (Chalkidike):
—anthemous: **(1)** ii ad *Anthémonte–Kalindoia* i p. 58 no. A13 (*SEG* i 281) (Νεικοῦνος (gen.): m. Οὐαλερία)
Macedonia (Mygdonia):
—aineia?: **(2)** ii-iii ad ib. xxxviii 707; cf. *BE* 1990, no. 476 (Νικοῦ (dat.): d. Κόρραγος, Δαντοῦς)
Thrace:
—apollonia-sozopolis: **(3)** ?iii bc *IGB* i² 458 bis, 1 (d. Δημοφῶν, Καλλιάνασσα)

Νικοφάνας
Skythia:
—olbia-borysthenes: **(1)** ?331 bc *SEG* xlii 711 ([Νι]κοφάνας: s. Ἄδραστος)

Νικοφῶν
MACEDONIA (EDONIS):
—AMPHIPOLIS: **(1)** s. iv BC *PAE* 1981, p. 25 with pl. 43 β, 4 (f. *Ἐπιφάνης*)

Νίκυλλα
MACEDONIA (BOTTIAIA):
—BEROIA: **(1)** iii BC *IBer* 150 (Tataki 955) (d. *Ἱέρων*)
MACEDONIA (DERRIOPOS): **(2)** ii-iii AD *IG* X (2) (2) 316 (*Νεί[κ]υλλα*)
MACEDONIA (PIERIA):
—PYDNA: **(3)** iv BC *GRBS* 43 (2002-3) p. 111 no. 2, 1, 4 (m. *Θράσων*)

Νικύλος
MACEDONIA (MYGDONIA):
—KALINDOIA: **(1)** 68-98 AD *SEG* XLII 580, 75 + *BE* 1999, no. 362 (*Νει-*: s. *Διοσκουρίδης*)
SCYTHIA MINOR:
—TOMIS: **(2)** ii-iii AD *ISM* II 23, 3 (*Γ. Ἰούλ. Νεικύλ[ος]*)

Νικώ
MACEDONIA (BOTTIAIA):
—PELLA: **(1)** ii/i BC *SEG* XLVIII 824 (*Νει-*: d. *Σίρρας*)
MACEDONIA (CHALKIDIKE):
—OLYNTHOS: **(2)** v/iv BC *IG* XII (8) 434 (Tataki, *Macedonians* p. 141 no. 92) (d. *Διονυσιφάνης*)
—POTIDAIA-KASSANDREIA (NR.): **(3)** iv/iii BC *SEG* XXXVII 559. 2 + *AD* 22 (1967) Chron. p. 377 with pl. 284 β (*Νικώ*, *—ηκώ—SEG*)
MACEDONIA (EDONIS):
—AMPHIPOLIS: **(4)** hell.-imp. *RA* 1945, p. 48 no. 2 (d. *Διονύσιος*)
THRACE: **(5)** iii BC *IG* II^2 8919 (*FRA* 2561); **(6)** ?161 BC *SGDI* 1719, 4, 6, 10, 13 (slave/freed.)
—BYZANTION: **(7)** hell.? *SEG* XXV 273 (*FRA* 1404) (d. *Νίκων*); **(8)** ii/i BC *IByz* 166 (Fıratlı–Robert p. 108 no. 173) (*Νικοῦς* (gen.): m. *Δαμώ*); **(9)** i-ii AD *IByz* 273 (Fıratlı–Robert p. 85 no. 106) (*Νει-*: d. *Λούκιος Καισώνιος*); **(10)** ~ *IByz* 278 (*Νει-*: d. *Ἀλέξανδρος*)
—BYZANTION?: **(11)** i BC-i AD ib. 375 (Fıratlı–Robert p. 126 no. 211) (*Νει-*: d. *Ἀπολλώνιος*)

Νίκων
CIMMERIAN BOSPOROS:
—GORGIPPIA: **(1)** f. iii BC *CIRB* 1137 A I, 17 (s. *Θεοτέλης*)
—HERMONASSA: **(2)** iv BC ib. 1056 II, 15 (s. *Θίβρων*)
—PANTIKAPAION: **(3)** iv BC *KSIA* 109 (1967) p. 21 no. 8 (tile) (*Νίκω(ν)*); **(4)** 195 BC *Syll*^{3} 585, 23 (f. *Ἀπατούριος*)
MACEDONIA: **(5)** c. 300 BC *IEph* 1452, 1 (*IEK* 505; Tataki, *Macedonians* p. 388 no. 68) (f. *Ἀρχέστρατος*); **(6)** 232 or 207 BC *CPR* XVIII 19, 401 (Tataki, *Macedonians* p. 388 no. 69); cf. La'da E1768 (f. *Κάσσανδρος*); **(7)** m. ii BC Helly, *Gonnoi* 48, 12 (Tataki, *Macedonians* p. 112 no. 5) (s. *Φ—*)
MACEDONIA (BISALTIA):
—TRAGILOS: **(8)** iv BC *AD* 26 (1971) Chron. p. 418 (f. *Ἀλεξίδημος*)
MACEDONIA (BOTTIAIA):
—BEROIA: **(9)** 122 BC *IBer* 134, 5 (f. *Κλέανδρος*); **(10)** ii-iii AD ib. 297, 5 (*Νεί-*: s. *Κλ. Ἀντέρως, Νικέα*); **(11)** ii/iii AD ib. 143 C, 23 (Tataki 1110) (*Πο. Νείκων*)
—EDESSA: **(12)** ii AD *Arch. Pap.* 22 (1973) p. 206 no. 7 (Tataki, *Edessa* 175) (*Κουριάτειος Νείκων*)
—PELLA: **(13)** iii BC *SEG* XXIV 539 (s. *Ἡρακλείδης*)
MACEDONIA (CHALKIDIKE):
—OLYNTHOS: **(14)** ?350 BC *TAPA* 62 (1931) p. 43 no. 2, 7; Hatzopoulos, *Actes Chalc.* p. 80 (date) (s. *Ἡδώνης*)
—POTIDAIA-KASSANDREIA: **(15)** imp. *TAPA* 69 (1938) p. 64 (*Νεί-*: s. *Φλαβία Νικησώ*)
—POTIDAIA-KASSANDREIA (NR.): **(16)** ii AD ib. pp. 61-2 no. 15, 1 (*Αἰλιανὸς Νείκων*)
—STOLOS?: **(17)** ?351 BC *SEG* XXXVIII 672, 3, 6; 673, 4 (s. *Κτήσων*); **(18)** ~ ib. 672, 10 (s. *Ὄπωρις*)
MACEDONIA (DERRIOPOS):
—STUBERRA: **(19)** c. 41-48 AD *IG* X (2) (2) 323, 14 (*Νεί-*: s. *Λυσῆς*); **(20)** 74 AD ib. 325, 59 (*Νεί-*: s. *Παράμονος*)
MACEDONIA (EDONIS):
—AMPHIPOLIS: **(21)** ii-iii AD *Thrakika* 13 (1940) p. 28 Ψ; **(22)** ~ Dimitsas 865 (*Νεί-*)
MACEDONIA (LOWER PAIONIA):
—IDOMENE?: **(23)** 161 AD Sokolovska, *Isar-Marvinci* p. 131 (*Νεί-*: f. *Δημοκράτης*)
MACEDONIA (LYNKESTIS):
—AETOS (MOD.): **(24)** iv/iii BC *EAM* 151 (f. *Κάσσανδρος*)
MACEDONIA (MYGDONIA):
—ARETHOUSA?: **(25)** f. i BC *EAD* XXX 185 (Tataki, *Macedonians* p. 69 no. 11) (or Syria Arethousa: f. *Σάμος*)
—HERAKLEIA: **(26)** iii BC *SEG* XLVI 727 (lamp)
—KALINDOIA: **(27)** 68-98 AD ib. XLII 580, 6, 28 (*Νεί-*: s. *Δασείλας*); **(28)** ~ ib. l. 27 (*Νεί-*: I s. *Ταρουσίνας*, f. *Νίκων* II); **(29)** ~ ib. l. 27 (*Νεί-*: II s. *Νίκων* I); **(30)** ~ ib. l. 36 (*Νεί-*: s. *Διονύσιος*); **(31)** ~ ib. 581, 7 (*Νεί-*: s. *Ἱέρων*); **(32)** a. 98 AD ib. 582, 5 (*Νεί-*: s. *Κότυς*); **(33)** ~ ib. l. 53 (*Νεί-*: s. *Ζωπᾶς*); **(34)** ~ ib. 583, 16 (*Νεί-*: s. *Ἀπολλώνιος*)
—THESSALONIKE: **(35)** 42-32 BC *IG* X (2) (1) 124, 7 (*Νεί-*: s. *Νικ—*); **(36)** 249 AD ib. 542 (*Μ. Φούριος Νείκων*: f. *Μ. Φούριος Εὔοδος*); **(37)** ?iv AD *AEMTh* 15 (2001) p. 326
—THESSALONIKE?: **(38)** ii AD *IG* X (2) (1) 907 (*Νεί-*); **(39)** v-vi AD Feissel, *RICM* 185 (*SEG* XLVII 983) (*Νίκω[ν]*)
MACEDONIA (PAIONIA):
—STOBOI: **(40)** ii-iii AD *Sp.* 71 (1931) p. 242 no. 644, 5 (f. *Θυόδοτος*)
MACEDONIA (PIERIA):
—DION: **(41)** ii-iii AD Oikonomos 40 (*Γ. Νείκων*)
—LEIBETHRA: **(42)** c. 230-200 BC *BCH* 45 (1921) p. 17 III, 53 (Tataki, *Macedonians* p. 117 no. 2) (f. *Νικόστρατος*)
MACEDONIA (PIERIS):
—PHAGRES: **(43)** s. v BC *SEG* XLIX 766 (s. *Λύσων*)
MACEDONIA*: **(44)** c. 324 BC *RE* (2); Berve 571 (slave)
SCYTHIA MINOR:
—KALLATIS: **(45)** inc. *ISM* III 227; **(46)** iii BC ib. 167 (f. *Ἡρακλέων*); **(47)** ii-iii AD ib. 129 (*Νεί-*)
THRACE: **(48)** 316-309 BC *IG* II^2 1956, 186 (*FRA* 2562); *Ancient Macedonia* 5 p. 445 with n. 10 (date); **(49)** c. 223 BC *PTeb* 815 fr. 1 II, 36 (Velkov 219; La'da E838) (s. *Δημήτριος*: t.e.)
—AINOS: **(50)** i-ii AD *IG* XII (8) 218, 6 (f. *—πη*)
—BEROE-AUGUSTA TRAIANA (NR.): **(51)** iii AD *IGB* III 1622 (*Αὐρ. Νί[κ]ων*: ?s. *Μα—*)
—BYZANTION: **(52)** c. 325-300 BC *IByz* 89 (Fıratlı–Robert p. 90 no. 117) (f. *Θράσων*); **(53)** hell.? *SEG* XXV 273 (*FRA* 1405) (f. *Νικώ*); **(54)** f. iii BC *SEG* XXIII 661 (s. *Θευγένης*); **(55)** ii AD *IByz* 108 (*Νεί-*: f. *Εὐφρόνιος*); **(56)** 164-169 AD Schönert-Geiss, *Byzantion* 1398; 1418-19 (coin) (?f. *Ἄνθος*)
—BYZANTION (TERRIT.): **(57)** ii-iii AD *IByz* 25; cf. Robert, *OMS* 5 p. 225 (*Νεί-*: f. *Διονύσις*)
—DIONYSOPOLIS: **(58)** ii-iii AD *IGB* I^2 31, 6 (*Νεί-*: s. *Ἀλη—*)
—LYSIMACHEIA: **(59)** i BC-i AD *IG* II^2 9230 (*Ag.* XVII 532; *FRA* 3403) (s. *Εἰκάδιος*)
—MESAMBRIA: **(60)** i BC *IGB* I^2 326, 1 (s. *Φιλήμων*); **(61)** ~ ib. 339 quinquies (*Νεί-*)
—NICOPOLIS AD ISTRUM: **(62)** ?ii AD ib. II 674, 4 (or Bithynia Nikomedeia: *Νεί[κων]*?: s. *Θεόδωρος*); **(63)** ii-iii AD ib. 663 (*Νεί-*: s. *Ἱέρων*)
—ODESSOS: **(64)** ?ii/iii AD ib. I^2 242 bis (*[Ν]ίκων*)
—PAUTALIA: **(65)** ii-iii AD ib. IV 2085, 4 (f. *Αὐρ. Πατρίκιος*)
—PERINTHOS-HERAKLEIA: **(66)** iii AD *IPerinth* 166 (*Νε[ίκ]ω[ν]*?)
—PHILIPPOPOLIS-TRIMONTIUM: **(67)** ii-iii AD *IGB* III 912, 5; **(68)** iii AD ib. 1546; cf. V 5556 (*Αὐρ. Νείκων*); **(69)** c. 303 AD *Anal. Boll.* 31 (1912) p. 192
THRACE?: **(70)** m. iv BC Arist., *Rhet.* 1412 a, 34 + *CAG* XXI (2) p. 213, 2-7 (Stephanis 1873)

Νικωνίδας
MACEDONIA (BOTTIAIA):
—MIEZA: **(1)** c. 230-200 BC *BCH* 45 (1921) p. 17 III, 59 (Tataki, *Macedonians* p. 124 no. 5) (s. *Μνασιγένης*)
MACEDONIA (PIERIA):
—PYDNA: **(2)** iv BC *GRBS* 43 (2002-3) p. 110 no. 1 a, 6

Νινας
KOLCHIS:
—SUKHUMI (MOD.): **(1)** ii AD *Stud. Orbeli* p. 99 (gem); cf. Braund, *Georgia* p. 196 fig. 14

Νινικῆς
SKYTHIA:
—OLBIA-BORYSTHENES: **(1)** ii AD *IOSPE* I^2 83, 7; Zgusta, *PNS* 684 (*Νινικέους* (gen.): f. *Πούρθαις*)

Νίνναρος
MACEDONIA (EDONIS):
—PHILIPPOI: **(1)** imp. *BCH* 58 (1934) p. 480 no. 30 (Pilhofer 316) (Lat. Ninnarus)
MACEDONIA (ODOMANTIKE):
—SIRRHA: **(2)** f. iii AD *SEG* XXX 590, 37

Νίννος
SCYTHIA MINOR:
—ISTROS: **(1)** ii AD *ISM* I 212, 24 (f. *Βάσσος*); **(2)** 138 AD ib. 193 I, 66 (*Νίν(ν)ος*: s. *Νικίας*) ?= (*3*); **(3)** ~ ib. l. 99 (f. *Νικίας*) ?= (*2*)

Νίπανος
SKYTHIA?: **(1)** ?ii-i BC Pottier–Reinach p. 172 n. 1 (terracotta)

Νισαῖος
SCYTHIA MINOR:
—KALLATIS: **(1)** iv/iii BC *ISM* III 125, 10 (s. *Ἐπ—*)

Νισκατουρμη?
THRACE:
—PHILIPPOPOLIS-TRIMONTIUM (TERRIT.): **(1)** ii-iii AD *IGB* III 1222 (*Νισκατουρμ[η]*?)

Νίχεκος
CIMMERIAN BOSPOROS:
—GORGIPPIA?: **(1)** s. ii AD *CIRB* 1231 B, 8; Zgusta, *PNS* 685 (f. *Θχήτλεις*)

Νόημα
MACEDONIA (BOTTIAIA):
—BEROIA: **(1)** ii-iii AD *IBer* 286 (Tataki 956) (m. *Κομίνιος Εὐτυχίων*)
MACEDONIA (MYGDONIA):
—THESSALONIKE: **(2)** ii AD *AD* 26 (1971) Chron. p. 377 no. 3 (m. *Δάφνος*)
THRACE: **(3)** m. ii BC *IG* IX (1)^2 (3) 638. 5, 6 (slave/freed.)

Νοήμων
CIMMERIAN BOSPOROS:
—GORGIPPIA: **(1)** f. iii BC *CIRB* 1137 A I, 28 (f. *Τιμέας*)
THRACE:
—BYZANTION: **(2)** ii BC *IByz* 165 (Fıratlı–Robert p. 108 no. 172) (f. *Τρυφῶσα*)

Νοῖος
THRACE:
—MESAMBRIA: **(1)** f. iii BC *IGB* I^2 335 bis (PM 378); cf. *IGB* V 5108 (f. *Ἀγασίκλεια*)

Νόμη
MACEDONIA (PIERIA):
—DION: **(1)** ii-iii AD Oikonomos 27

Νομήνιος
THRACE:
—MARONEIA: **(1)** ii-i BC *IThrakAig* E199 (slave?)

Νόμος
MACEDONIA: **(1)** 215 BC *BGU* 1959, 9, 15, [17], 20, 22 (Tataki, *Macedonians* p. 388 no. 71; La'da E1563)

Νόμων
MACEDONIA (CHALKIDIKE):
—AKROTHOON: **(1)** iv BC *IG* XII (8) 2, 5 (*Νόμω[νος]* (gen.): f. *Πολύμνηστος*)

Νόνιος
SCYTHIA MINOR:
—TOMIS*: **(1)** ii-iii AD *ISM* II 195, 1, 13 (biling.) (f. *Τιμόθεος*)

Νόννα
SCYTHIA MINOR:
—TOMIS: **(1)** iv-v AD Barnea 10, 5 (Popescu, *IGL* 39) (*Νόνα*: d. *Σύμφορος, Αὐρ. Βενερία*); **(2)** v-vi AD Barnea 11, 5 (Popescu, *IGL* 38) (*Νόννας* (nom.)—lap.)
THRACE:
—APOLLONIA-SOZOPOLIS: **(3)** v-vi AD Beševliev 179

Νόννελλος
SCYTHIA MINOR:
—TOMIS: **(1)** v-vi AD Barnea 11, 8 (Popescu, *IGL* 38)

Νόνος
TAURIS:
—KERKINITIS (NR.): **(1)** iii BC Solomonik, *GChKh* 425; cf. *SEG* XXXVIII 749. 7 (vase)

Νονῶσα
THRACE:
—MARONEIA: **(1)** v AD Meïmaris–Bakirtzis 13 (*IThrakAig* E351)

Νοσσίης
THRACE:
—APOLLONIA-SOZOPOLIS: **(1)** v-iv BC *IGB* I^2 439 (*Νοσσίω* (gen.): f. *Πάρμις*)

Νοσσίων
SCYTHIA MINOR:
—KALLATIS: **(1)** s. iii BC *ISM* III 35 A, 36 (s. *Ἱεροκλῆς*)

Νοσσός
SCYTHIA MINOR:
—KALLATIS: **(1)** iii-ii BC *Numismatica* 13 (1947) p. 6 no. 12 (coin)

Νοσσοῦς?
CIMMERIAN BOSPOROS:
—FRONTOVOE (MOD.): **(1)** ii-iii AD *SEG* XXXV 868; cf. *BE* 1990, no. 592 (*Ν[η]ς Σουνι*—ed., *Ν.σσουνι* (dat.)—Vinogradov)

Νόστιμος
MACEDONIA (BOTTIAIA):
—AIGAI: **(1)** ?ii BC *SEG* XXXVIII 721 (I s. *Ἀμύντας*, f. *Νόστιμος* II: locn.—Tataki); **(2)** ~ ib. (*Νό(σ)τιμος νεώτ.*: II s. *Νόστιμος* I: locn.—Tataki)

Νοτίς
MACEDONIA (MYGDONIA):
—THESSALONIKE: **(1)** ii-iii AD *IG* X (2) (1) 485 + *BCH* 97 (1973) p. 591 (*Ἰουν. Ν.*: m. *Καλαουιανὴ Ἰσιγόνη*)

Νουμᾶς
THRACE:
—BYZANTION: **(1)** ii-i BC *IByz* 85

Νουμέριος
MACEDONIA (MYGDONIA):
—THESSALONIKE?: **(1)** ii AD *IG* X (2) (1) 868 (s. *Νουμήνιος, Κασσία*)

Νουμέσις
MACEDONIA (BISALTIA):
—TERPNI (MOD.): **(1)** ii-iii AD *SEG* XLIX 810

Νουμήνιος
CIMMERIAN BOSPOROS:
—GORGIPPIA: **(1)** f. iii BC *CIRB* 1137 A I, 6 (f. *Λύσανδρος*); **(2)** ~ ib. l. 49 (f. *Δήμαρχος*); **(3)** ~ ib. l. 57 (I f. *Νουμήνιος* II); **(4)** ~ ib. l. 57 (II s. *Νουμήνιος* I); **(5)** ii AD ib. 1140, 12 (*[Ν]ουμήνιος*: s. *Κοσσοῦς*); **(6)** ~ ib. 1159 C (*Νουμήνιος*—Vinogradov); **(7)** ~ ib. 1174, 3 (*[Ν]ουμήνι[ος]*); **(8)** f. ii AD ib. 1171, 3 (*Νουμ[ήνιος]*?); **(9)** s. ii AD ib. 1165, 1 (*[Νου]μήνιος*—Vinogradov); **(10)** 168 AD ib. 1144, 4 (*Νουμή[νιος]*); **(11)** 173-210 AD ib. 1134, 13 (f. *Φαρνάκης*); **(12)** ~ ib. l. 27; **(13)** ~ ib. 1134 E, 2 (*[Νο]υμήνιος*); **(14)** ~ ib. l. 5; **(15)** ~ ib. l. 7 (f. *—ακίων*); **(16)** ii/iii AD ib. 1134, 20; *VDI* 1970 (4), p. 149, 10 (f. *Ἔρως*); **(17)** ~ *CIRB* 1179, 10 (*Νουμ[ή]νιος*); **(18)** ~ ib. l. 44 (s. *Ποθεινός*); **(19)** ~ ib. l. 47; **(20)** ~ ib. l. 51 (s. *Ἔρως*); **(21)** ~ ib. l. 60 (f. *Ἑρμαδίων*); **(22)** ~ *VDI* 1970 (4), p. 149, 11 (*[Νο]υμήν[ιος]*?: f. *Ἄττας*); **(23)** ~ ib. l. 13 (*[Νου]μήν[ιος]*?: f. *Φαρνακίων*); **(24)** iii AD *NE* 9 (1971) p. 10 no. 6 B, 10 (*[Νου]μήνιος*); **(25)** ~ ib. l. 15 (*Νουμήνι[ος]*)
—GORGIPPIA?: **(26)** 227-233 AD *CIRB* 1230, 1 (f. *Ἀλέξανδρος*)
—NYMPHAION: **(27)** iii BC ib. 912 II, 14 (s. *Νικίας*)
—PANTIKAPAION: **(28)** iii BC Chuistova, *AIB* p. 51 n. 7 (weight); **(29)** s. iii BC *CIRB* 247 (s. *Σπαρόφοτος*)
—PARTHENION: **(30)** inc. *SEG* XLV 983 (vase) (*Νυμήνι(ος)*?)
—PHANAGOREIA (NR.): **(31)** iii AD *CIRB* 1016, 5 (*Νουμ(ή)νιος*: f. *Δάδας*)
—THEODOSIA: **(32)** iii AD ib. 947 B, 9 (*Νουμή[ν]ιος*: f. *Χρηστοῦς*)
MACEDONIA: **(33)** ?417-413 BC *IG* I^3 89, 64 (Tataki, *Macedonians* p. 388 no. 70) (*Νōμέ-*); **(34)** m. iii BC *SEG* XLVIII 783, 4, 12; *Horos* 14-16 (2000-3) p. 216, [4]; cf. *Tekmeria* 5 (2000) pp. 63-9; *Horos* 14-16 (2000-3) pp. 220-4 (locn.)
MACEDONIA (BOTTIAIA):
—KYRRHOS: **(35)** hell. *IG* II^2 9141 (Tataki, *Macedonians* p. 117 no. 9; *FRA* 3160) (s. *Εὐπόλεμος*)
MACEDONIA (CHALKIDIKE):
—ANTIGONEIA?: **(36)** i BC *SEG* XLVI 726; *BE* 1997, no. 401 (locn.) (*Κ. Μάρκιος Ν.*)
—POTIDAIA-KASSANDREIA: **(37)** iii/ii BC *IG* XI (4) 1216; 1228, 3; 1229, 3 (Tataki, *Macedonians* p. 93 no. 70) (f. *Διονύσιος*)
MACEDONIA (EDONIS):
—AMPHIPOLIS: **(38)** 119 BC *ID* 2598 I, 35 (Tataki, *Macedonians* p. 58 no. 98)
—AMPHIPOLIS?: **(39)** iii BC *SEG* XXIV 609 = XLIII 372 (f. *Ἀριστώ*)
—PHILIPPOI: **(40)** ii-i BC *BCH* 59 (1935) p. 159 no. 56 (Pilhofer 305) (f. *Κρατῖνος*)
—PHILIPPOI (DRAMA (MOD.)): **(41)** ii AD ib. 506a
MACEDONIA (KRESTONIA):
—IORON: **(42)** i BC-i AD *SEG* XLVIII 816. 1 (sherd)
MACEDONIA (LYNKESTIS):
—HERAKLEIA (NR.): **(43)** ii-iii AD *IG* X (2) (2) 10 (f. *Δέντις*); **(44)** ~ ib. (s. *Δέντις*) ?= (*45*); **(45)** ~ ib. (f. *Ἀντίγονος*) ?= (*44*)
MACEDONIA (MYGDONIA):
—KALINDOIA: **(46)** a. 98 AD *SEG* XLII 582, 67 (s. *Δάλης*)
—PERDYLOS: **(47)** ?i-ii AD ib. XXIX 581 (f. *Νάρρης*)
—THESSALONIKE: **(48)** ii AD *IG* X (2) (1) 319, 3; cf. *Tyche* 10 (1995) pl. 7 (*Μ. Κότιος Ν.*)
—THESSALONIKE?: **(49)** iii BC *IG* X (2) (1) 908, 1 (*GVI* 1709); cf. *BCH* 97 (1973) p. 597 fig. 12 (s. *Κοῖνος*); **(50)** ii AD *IG* X (2) (1) 248 II, 4 (s. *Ἀμμιανός*); **(51)** ~ ib. 868 (f. *Νουμέριος*)
MACEDONIA (ORESTIS):
—TSOTYLI (MOD.): **(52)** hell. *EAM* 212 (tile) (*Νουμ[ήν]ιος*)
MACEDONIA (PAIONIA):
—ANTIGONEIA? (BUDUR ČIFLIK (MOD.)): **(53)** imp. *SEG* XIII 405 + *BE* 1954, no. 162; cf. Papazoglou, *Villes* p. 326 with n. 127 (*Ν. ὁ καὶ Τίτος*: s. *Ἀμμία*)
—DEMIR KAPIJA (MOD.): **(54)** s. v BC *SEG* XXXVIII 602 (bronze) (*Νō-*)
MACEDONIA (PIERIA):
—DION: **(55)** ii-iii AD *Chiron* 24 (1994) p. 219 fig. 1 (unp.) (f. *Ἑρμογένης*)
SCYTHIA MINOR:
—ISTROS: **(56)** iii/ii BC *ISM* I 263 (s. *Ἑστιαῖος*); **(57)** ii BC ib. 49, 7 + *Riv. Fil.* III (1983) p. 54 (*Νουμή[νιος]*); **(58)** i BC-i AD *ISM* I 191 I, 24 (*[Ν]ουμήνιος*); **(59)** ~ ib. l. 38 (f. *—ων*); **(60)** ~ ib. 191 II, 13 (s. *Διοκλῆς*); **(61)** ~ ib. 274 (f. *Πολέμων*); **(62)** ii AD ib. 137, 9 (f. *Μενίσκος*); **(63)** ~ ib. 196, 4; 201 I, 5 (*Νουμήνις*—196: s. *Θεόδωρος*); **(64)** ~ ib. 196, 8; 201 I, 17 (f. *Ἦλις*); **(65)** ~ ib. 212, 13 (s. *Καλλίστρατος*); **(66)** 138 AD ib. 193 I, 12 (f. *Μεγιστίων*); **(67)** ~ ib. l. 39 (s. *Πολέμων*) ?= (*71*); **(68)** ~ ib. l. 93 (I f. *Νουμήνιος* II); **(69)** ~ ib. l. 93 (II s. *Νουμήνιος* I, f. *Πολέμων*); **(70)** ~ ib. l. 104 (f. *Εὐξενίδης*); **(71)** ~ ib. l. 48-9 (f. *Κλεογένης, Πολέμων*) ?= (*67*); **(72)** ~ ib. 193 II, 64 (f. *Ἀρτεμίδωρος*)
—KALLATIS: **(73)** i BC/i AD ib. III 40, 3 (I f. *Νουμήνιος* II); **(74)** ~ ib. l. 3 (II s. *Νουμήνιος* I); **(75)** 241-244 AD ib. 74, 14 (f. *Ἡραίων*)
—TOMIS: **(76)** ii-i BC ib. II 36 (f. *Ποσειδώνιος*); **(77)** i BC ib. 2, 27 (f. *Θεόφιλος*); **(78)** ~ ib. 2 A, 49 (I s. *Θεόφιλος*, f. *Νουμήνιος* II); **(79)** ~ ib. l. 49 (II s. *Νουμήνιος* I); **(80)** ~ ib. l. 55 (s. *Μόνιμος*); **(81)** ~ ib. l. 59 (s. *Εἰράνιχος*); **(82)** ~ ib. 2 B, 47 (I f. *Νουμήνιος* II); **(83)** ~ ib. l. 47 (II s. *Νουμήνιος* I); **(84)** i-ii AD ib. 150, 2 (s. *Διοσκουρίδης*); **(85)** f. i AD *RPC* I 1813-14 (coin); **(86)** ii AD *ISM* II 125, 4 (s. *Λυσίμαχος*); **(87)** ii-iii AD ib. 104, 9 (*[Νου]μήνιος*?); **(88)** ~ ib. 468, 13 (f. *—στας*)
SKYTHIA:
—OLBIA-BORYSTHENES: **(89)** c. 300-260 BC Karyshkovskii, *MO* pp. 77-85; *SNG BM Black Sea* 493 (coin) (*Νου(μήνιος)*?); **(90)** iii BC *IOlbia* 24, 2 (*SEG* XXXI 710); **(91)** ~ *IOSPE* I^2 201 II, 24 (s. *Ἰκέσιος*); **(92)** iii-ii BC *SEG* XXX 925 (vase); **(93)** imp. *IOSPE* I^2 147, 5 (s. *Πάσαρος*); **(94)** ii AD ib. 80, 9; 175, 10 (s. *Ῥαδαμψῶν*) ?= (*96*); **(95)** ii-iii AD ib. 137, 7 (f. *Νάβαζος*); **(96)** f. ii AD *SEG* XLIII 506, 8 (s. *Ῥαδαμψῶν*) ?= (*94*)
TAURIS:
—CHERSONESOS: **(97)** f. ii AD ib. XXVIII 631, 4 (*Νου[μήνι]ος*?)
THRACE: **(98)** iii BC *ZPE* 140 (2002) p. 204, 7 (s. *Ἐβρύζελμις, Δα....ς*)
—BYZANTION:
——(Delkos): **(99)** i BC-i AD *IByz* 225 (Fıratlı–Robert p. 80 no. 95) (*Νουμήνιος*?: f. *Ἀ—*)

—DIONYSOPOLIS: **(100)** iii AD *IGB* I^2 14 a, 4 (f. *Αὐρ. Δημοφῶν*); **(101)** ~ ib. 14 bis, 7 (f. *—εις*); **(102)** ~ ib. 14 c, 12 (*Αὐρ. Ν.*: s. *Σιληνός*); **(103)** 241-244 AD ib. 22 bis, 8 (*Αὐρ. Νουμ[ήνιος]*)
—LYSIMACHEIA: **(104)** f. iii BC PM 105 (s. *Σεύθης*); **(105)** 236 BC *IG* XI (2) 120, 47 (Stephanis 1890)
—MARONEIA: **(106)** c. 365-336 BC Schönert-Geiss, *Maroneia* 565-92 (coin); **(107)** f. ii BC *SEG* XXXIV 709 (*IThrakAig* E278) (*Νουμήν[ιος]*: s. *Μητρόδοτος*); **(108)** i-ii AD *IG* II^2 9292 (*FRA* 3545) (f. *Συνέτη*)
—MESAMBRIA: **(109)** ?c. 240-225 BC *IG* VII 281, 1 (*IOrop* 50); *Hyettos* p. 296 (date) (f. *Ἑκαταῖος*); **(110)** i BC *IGB* I^2 326, 2 (f. *Δεινομένης*)
—ODESSOS: **(111)** i BC-i AD ib. 65, 2 (*Νουμήνι[ος]*); **(112)** ~ ib. 110, 4 (*Νουμή[νιος]*: s. *Ἀγαθήνωρ*); **(113)** ~ ib. 206 bis (PM 1682) (s. *Ἀρτεμίδωρος*); **(114)** 43 BC *IGB* I^2 46, 4 (s. *Ἕλλην*); **(115)** 36 BC ib. l. 11 (f. *Ἕλλην*); **(116)** 25 BC ib. l. 22 (s. *Ἀπολλώνιος*); **(117)** 15 BC ib. l. 32 (f. *Ἀρτεμίδωρος*); **(118)** 10 BC ib. l. 37 (f. *Ποσειδώνιος*); **(119)** 2 BC ib. l. 45 (s. *Ἱππομέδων*); **(120)** i-ii AD ib. 106 bis (I s. *Διογένης*, f. *Νουμήνιος* II); **(121)** ~ ib. (II s. *Νουμήνιος* I); **(122)** ~ ib. 108, 2 (f. *Ἀμύντωρ*); **(123)** ~ ib. 126 (*Νου[μ]ήνιος*: f. *Ἕλλην*); **(124)** ~ ib. 188 (s. *Ἀγαθήνωρ*); **(125)** ~ ib. 202 (s. *Ἕλλην*); **(126)** ~ ib. V 5065 (*[Νουμ]ήνιος*?); **(127)** s. i AD ib. I^2 160 (*CCET* I 52; PM 1446) (f. *Ἀρτεμίδωρος*); **(128)** ii AD *IGB* I^2 187 (*[Νου]μήνιος νεώτ.*: s. *Διονύσιος, Βαθεις*); **(129)** f. ii AD ib. 78 ter, 2 (*CCET* I 30) (s. *Ζῆνις*); **(130)** ~ *IGB* I^2 187 bis (PM 1728); *Dacia* 21 (1977) p. 161 (date) (f. *Βαθεις*); **(131)** 215 AD *IGB* I^2 47 a, 10 (f. *Αὐρ. Μάρων*); **(132)** ~ ib. l. 24 (f. *Αὐρ. Ἀτανδρίων*); **(133)** ~ ib. l. 27 (f. *Αὐρ. Μοσχίων*); **(134)** 221 AD ib. 47 bis a, 24 (*Αὐρ. Ν.*: s. *Γλαυκίας*); **(135)** ~ ib. l. 26 (*Αὐρ. Ν.*: s. *Ἀγαθήνωρ*); **(136)** ~ ib. 47 bis b, 11 (*Αὐρ. Ν.*: s. *Βάλης*); **(137)** ~ ib. l. 37 (f. *Αὐρ. Ξένων*); **(138)** ~ ib. 47 bis c, 15 (*Αὐρ. Ν.*: s. *Σωκράτης*); **(139)** ~ ib. l. 29 (*Αὐρ. Ν.*: s. *Βιάτωρ*)
—ODESSOS (NR.): **(140)** ii AD ib. 272 (PM 1676); *Dacia* 21 (1977) p. 161 (date) (f. *Σεακού*)
—PERINTHOS-HERAKLEIA: **(141)** iv-vi AD *IPerinth* 231 (*AD* 51-2 (1996-7) Mel. p. 368 no. 186) (*Νουμένιος ὡ καὶ —λικλ[ῆς]*?)
—SALYMBRIA: **(142)** hell. *IByz* S 48 (s. *Μάκαρις*, f. *Φιλήτα*)
—STRYME? (NR.): **(143)** c. 425-400 BC Bakalakis, *Oinos Ismarikos* p. 553 (*IThrakAig* E120) (*Ν(ο)υμήνιος*: f. *Ἀριστόβουλος*)

Νουμήνις
MACEDONIA (MYGDONIA):
—APOLLONIA: **(1)** iii-iv AD *AD* 24 (1969) Chron. pl. 316
THRACE:
—ODESSOS?: **(2)** ii AD *IGB* I^2 51 bis b, 2 (I f. *Νουμήνις* II); **(3)** ~ ib. l. 2 (II s. *Νουμήνις* I)

Νουνέχιος
MACEDONIA (MYGDONIA):
—THESSALONIKE: **(1)** iii AD *IG* X (2) (1) 349, 3 (*Κράτερος ὁ καὶ Ν.*)

Νουνέχις
THRACE:
—NOVAE: **(1)** iii AD *IGB* II 741, 6 (s. *Σαβινιανός*, *Κορινθία*)

Νυμῆς
THRACE:
—STRYME?: **(1)** c. 425-400 BC *SEG* XLIX 990 (*IThrakAig* E123) (*Νύμεω* (gen.): f. *Σίμη*)

Νυμφαγόρας
CIMMERIAN BOSPOROS:
—GORGIPPIA: **(1)** i-ii AD *CIRB* 1138, 8 (*[Νυ]μφαγόρας*: s. *Πο—*); **(2)** ?93-123 AD ib. 1125, 8, 13 (s. *Μακάριος*, f. *Τιμόθεος*, *Ἡλίς*); **(3)** m. ii AD *Eirene* 7 (1968) p. 67, 6 (f. *Φαρνακίων*); **(4)** s. ii AD *CIRB* 1129 A, 8 (*Νυμφαγ[όρας]*); **(5)** ii/iii AD ib. 1179, 39; Zgusta, *PNS* 680 (*Μυφαγόρας*—lap.: s. *Κοσσοῦς*, f. *Πάπας*); **(6)** ~ *CIRB* 1179, 57 (s. *Σαμβίων*); **(7)** iii AD ib. 1186, 3 (*[Νυ]μφαγόρας*)
—HERMONASSA: **(8)** iii BC ib. 1072 (*Νυ(μ)φαγόρας*: s. *Ἱκέσιος*)

Νυμφαγόρης
CIMMERIAN BOSPOROS:
—PANTIKAPAION: **(1)** ?s. iv BC ib. 165 (f. *Ἀρισταγόρης*)
—ZENONOS CHERSONESOS*: **(2)** v/iv BC *SEG* XL 643 (*[Νυ]μφαγόρης*)
THRACE:
—ABDERA: **(3)** c. 395-360 BC May, *Abdera* pp. 231-4 nos. 376-90 (coin)

Νυμφαῖος
CIMMERIAN BOSPOROS:
—NYMPHAION: **(1)** f. iii BC *SEG* XLV 997. 10
THRACE:
—BYZANTION: **(2)** m. iii BC *IG* XII (5) 802, 7, 10, 27, 30 (s. *Ἀθαναίων*); **(3)** ?205 BC ib. VII 298, 13 (*IOrop* 175) (f. *Φορμίων*)

Νυμφάρατος
THRACE:
—BYZANTION: **(1)** iv/iii BC *IByz* 63 (f. *Νίκανδρος*)

Νυμφᾶς
CIMMERIAN BOSPOROS:
—PANTIKAPAION: **(1)** imp. *CIRB* 805 (f. *Σωσίπατρος*)

Νυμφέρως
SKYTHIA:
—TANAIS: **(1)** 244 AD ib. 1287, 3 (s. *Ὀχωζίακος*)

Νύμφη
MACEDONIA (EDONIS):
—PHILIPPOI: **(1)** imp. *BCH* 58 (1934) p. 477 no. 18 (Pilhofer 272) (Lat. Atilia Nymphe)
MACEDONIA (PIERIA):
—PYDNA: **(2)** ii-iii AD Dimitsas 161 (*Οὐλπ. Ν.*)

Νύμφης
CIMMERIAN BOSPOROS:
—HERMONASSA: **(1)** iv BC *CIRB* 1065 (f. *Παῦνα*)

Νυμφιδιανός
SCYTHIA MINOR:
—ISTROS: **(1)** ii AD *ISM* I 197 I, 17 (f. *Κάστος*)

Νύμφιος
THRACE:
—NOVAE: **(1)** ii AD *IGLNovae* 48 (Lat. Nymphius: f. *Ἡδόνη*)

Νύμφις
MACEDONIA (PIERIS):
—NEAPOLIS: **(1)** m. vi BC *SEG* XXIV 622 (vase) (Pilhofer 10) (*[Ν]ύνφις*)
THRACE:
—ABDERA: **(2)** c. 500-475 BC *Horos* 14-16 (2000-2003) p. 253 no. 3 (*IThrakAig* E31) (*Νύμφιδος* (gen.): f. *Ἀναξίδικος*)

Νυμφόδωρος
CIMMERIAN BOSPOROS:
—GORGIPPIA: **(1)** f. iii BC *CIRB* 1137 A I, 19 (s. *Εὔτιμος*)
—PANTIKAPAION: **(2)** f. iv BC ib. 213 (s. *Ἑρμοκράτης*); **(3)** 82 AD ib. 76, 19 (*SEG* XVIII 310) (I f. *Νυμφόδωρος* II); **(4)** ~ *CIRB* 76, 19 (*SEG* XVIII 310) (*Νυμφόδ̣ωρος*: II s. *Νυμφόδωρος* I)
MACEDONIA (EDONIS):
—AMPHIPOLIS: **(5)** iii BC *RE* (5) (Tataki, *Macedonians* p. 58 no. 99); **(6)** b. 213 BC Hatzopoulos, *MI* 2 p. 83 no. 61, 8 (*SEG* XLVI 715) (*[Νυ]μφόδωρος*)
MACEDONIA (MYGDONIA):
—DIKAIA: **(7)** 360 BC *IG* IV (1)^2 94 b, 11 (Perlman, *City and Sanctuary* E.1 with p. 69 f. (date); Tataki, *Macedonians* p. 99 no. 1) (*Νυν-*)
SKYTHIA:
—OLBIA-BORYSTHENES: **(8)** iii BC *IOSPE* I^2 201 II, 21 (f. *Σωσίστρατος*)
TAURIS:
—CHERSONESOS: **(9)** f. iii BC *SEG* XL 615 A, 9 (*Νυ[μ]φόδωρος*: f. *—ίστας*)
THRACE:
—ABDERA: **(10)** c. 500-475 BC *Horos* 14-16 (2000-2003) p. 250 no. 2 (*IThrakAig* E32) (f. *Ἀρτεμισία*); **(11)** c. 450-425 BC May, *Abdera* p. 127 nos. 140-1 (coin); **(12)** 430 BC *RE* Supplbd. 10 (6); cf. May, *Abdera* p. 150 n. 1 (s. *Πυθῆς*); **(13)** c. 230-200 BC *BCH* 45 (1921) p. 18 III, 89 (f. *Διονυσόδωρος*: reading—Oulhen)
—APOLLONIA-SOZOPOLIS: **(14)** ii BC *IGB* I^2 395 (I f. *Νυμφόδωρος* II); **(15)** ~ ib. (II s. *Νυμφόδωρος* I)

Νύμφων
MACEDONIA (EDONIS):
—AMPHIPOLIS: **(1)** m. iii BC Hatzopoulos, *Actes Amphipolis* p. 52 no 12, 8; *SEG* XLI 566 (date) (s. *Ξενοφῶν*)

Νυνφόδωρος
SKYTHIA:
—OLBIA-BORYSTHENES: **(1)** v BC Dubois, *IGD-Olbia* 101 (f. *Δωριεός*)

Νῦσα
MACEDONIA: **(1)** m. ii BC *ID* 1497 bis; *OGIS* 771; Grainger, *SPG* p. 52 (d. *Ἀντίοχος* IV *Ἐπιφάνης*, *Λαοδίκη*)

Νωμινᾶτος
THRACE:
—MESAMBRIA (TERRIT.): **(1)** iv AD *IGB* V 5129, 17 (s. *Φλ. Ζῆνις*, *Αὐρ. Μαρτῖνα*)

Νωστάτη
SCYTHIA MINOR:
—KALLATIS (NR.)?: **(1)** ?iii AD ib. I^2 12 ter, 6 (*CCET* I 1) (*Νωστάτ(η)*: m. *Ἑρμογένης*)

Ξ

Ξαιορσάζης
CIMMERIAN BOSPOROS:
—PANTIKAPAION: **(1)** ii AD *CIRB* 689; Zgusta, *PNS* 156 (s. *Καμορσάζης*)

Ξάνθας
SKYTHIA:
—OLBIA-BORYSTHENES: **(1)** f. vi BC Dubois, *IGDOlbia* 86 (vase) (*Χσά-*)

Ξανθίας
MACEDONIA (BOTTIAIA):
—EDESSA: **(1)** iii AD Feissel, *RICM* 7 (Tataki, *Edessa* 227) (s. *Ἑρμαΐς*); **(2)** ~ Feissel, *RICM* 8 (Tataki, *Edessa* 226) (f. *Ξάνθιππος*, *Ἀνθυλλα*)
TAURIS:
—CHERSONESOS: **(3)** iv BC *SEG* XXVIII 634 (f. *Ἀρτεμίδωρος*); **(4)** iii BC Solomonik, *GAKh* 1671 (vase) ([*Ξ*]*ανθία*[*ς*]?)

Ξάνθιλλα
MACEDONIA (ODOMANTIKE):
—SIRRHA: **(1)** ii-iii AD Kaphtantzis 36 (d. *Κλ. Ζωσιμᾶς*, *Κλ. Ἑρμαΐς*)

Ξάνθιππος
MACEDONIA: **(1)** iii BC *IG* II^2 9266 (Tataki, *Macedonians* p. 389 no. 1; *FRA* 3482)
MACEDONIA (BOTTIAIA):
—EDESSA: **(2)** iii AD Feissel, *RICM* 8 (Tataki, *Edessa* 228) (s. *Ξανθίας*)
MACEDONIA (CHALKIDIKE):
—OLYNTHOS: **(3)** ?352 BC *TAPA* 69 (1938) p. 48 no. 3, 16; Hatzopoulos, *Actes Chalc.* p. 80 (date) (f. *Εὐξίθεος*)
MACEDONIA (EDONIS):
—AMPHIPOLIS: **(4)** c. 265-255 BC *SGDI* 2588, 2 (Tataki, *Macedonians* p. 58 no. 100) (s. *Ἑλλάνικος*)
SKYTHIA:
—OLBIA-BORYSTHENES: **(5)** v BC Dubois, *IGDOlbia* 79 (vase) (*SEG* XLVI 955) (*-πως*)
THRACE:
—PERINTHOS-HERAKLEIA: **(6)** iii BC *IG* XII (9) 802 (f. *Εὔφαμος*)

Ξανθίων
MACEDONIA (BOTTIAIA):
—BEROIA: **(1)** iii AD *IBer* 369 (Tataki 960)
MACEDONIA (MYGDONIA):
—THESSALONIKE: **(2)** s. i AD *IG* X (2) (1) 69, 32 (s. *Ἀσιατικός*); **(3)** i/ii AD *AD* 24 (1969) Chron. p. 300

Ξάνθος
MACEDONIA (BOTTIAIA):
—PELLA: **(1)** v/iv BC *SEG* XXXII 642 (s. *Δημήτριος*, *Ἀμαδίκα*); **(2)** hell.? ib. II 400 (f. *Ἀσκληπιόδωρος*)
MACEDONIA (MYGDONIA):
—THESSALONIKE?: **(3)** ii AD *IG* X (2) (1) 248 II, 5 (s. *Ἡράκων*)
MACEDONIA (PELAGONIA):
—DOSTONEIS: **(4)** iii AD ib. X (2) (2) 201, 9
SKYTHIA:
—OLBIA-BORYSTHENES: **(5)** c. 475-450 BC Dubois, *IGDOlbia* 58 (s. *Πο*—)
TAURIS:
—CHERSONESOS: **(6)** c. 315-300 BC Kats p. 106 no. 88 (amph.); **(7)** f. iii BC *SEG* XL 615 A, 10-11, 19-20 (s. *Θεοκύδης*); **(8)** c. 230-220 BC Anokhin p. 142 nos. 121; 125 (coin); **(9)** imp. Solomonik, *NEPKh* 48; **(10)** ~ *IOSPE* I^2 448 (*Ξάν*[*θος*]?); **(11)** ?i AD Solomonik, *NEPKh* 43 (f. *Ἡρακλείδας*); **(12)** i AD *IOSPE* I^2 482, 1 (*GVI* 767); cf. KW pl. 2 no. 49 (s. *Λαγορῖνος*); **(13)** f. ii AD Solomonik, *NEPKh* 111, 11 (*Ξάν*[*θος*]: I f. *Ξάνθος* II); **(14)** ~ ib. l. 11 (II s. *Ξάνθος* I); **(15)** 130 AD *VDI* 1960 (3), pp. 154-5, 17 (*Τ. Φλ. Ξ.*: s. *Φλ. Νάσων*)
THRACE:
—MESAMBRIA: **(16)** iv BC *IGB* I^2 332 (?f. *Διώ*)
—PERINTHOS-HERAKLEIA: **(17)** iii AD *IPerinth* 83 (Lat. C. Poblicius Xanthus)

Ξάρθανος
SKYTHIA:
—TANAIS: **(1)** 244 AD *CIRB* 1287, 11; Zgusta, *PNS* 157 (s. *Ἀσκληπιάδης*)

Ξάρταμος
SKYTHIA:
—OLBIA-BORYSTHENES: **(1)** ii AD *IOSPE* I^2 83, 5; Zgusta, *PNS* 157 (*Ξ. ὁ καὶ Ὄλβιος*: s. *Καρζόαζος*)

Ξείνας
THRACE:
—BYZANTION: **(1)** iii/ii BC *IG* XI (4) 778, 3, 11 (*Ξείνα* (gen.): f. *Ἡρακλείδας*)

Ξεινόθεμις
SCYTHIA MINOR:
—ISTROS: **(1)** iii-ii BC Unp. (Avram, defixio) 4, 3
THRACE:
—PERINTHOS-HERAKLEIA:
——(Boreis): **(2)** iii-ii BC *IPerinth* 61, 43 (f. *Ἀλκίμαχος*)

Ξενεῖος
THRACE:
—MARONEIA: **(1)** iii BC *IThrakAig* E238 (s. *Γι*—)

Ξένανδρος
THRACE:
—ODESSOS: **(1)** i BC-i AD *IGB* I^2 44, 6 (s. *Ἀπατεύριος*); **(2)** ii AD ib. 185 bis (PM 1729) (f. *Βλωστι*); **(3)** ~ *IGB* I^2 187 (f. *Ἀμα*); **(4)** f. ii AD ib. 78 ter, 12 (*CCET* I 30) (f. *Αἰσχρίων*); **(5)** ~ *IGB* I^2 171 bis (PM 1612); *Dacia* 21 (1977) p. 161 (date) (f. *Νικίας*); **(6)** s. ii AD *IGB* I^2 175 (PM 1739); *Dacia* 21 (1977) p. 161 (date) (f. *Τρυφῶσα*); **(7)** 215 AD *IGB* I^2 47 a, 9 (f. *Αὐρ. Ἀρτεμίδωρος*); **(8)** 221 AD ib. 47 bis a, 14 (*Μ. Αὐρ. Ξ.*: s. *Ἀρτεμίδωρος*)
—ODESSOS (NR.): **(9)** ii AD ib. 261, 2 (*CCET* I 77) (f. *Ἀγαθήνωρ*); **(10)** ~ *IGB* I^2 261, 4 (*CCET* I 77) (s. *Ἀγαθήνωρ*); **(11)** s. ii AD *IGB* I^2 287 (*CCET* I 87) (f. *Ἀπελλᾶς*)

Ξένανθος
MACEDONIA (BOTTIAIA):
—KYRRHOS: **(1)** iii-ii BC *SEG* XXVII 258 (s. *Ἀμβίκατος*)

Ξεναρίστα
THRACE:
—MESAMBRIA: **(1)** iv/iii BC *IGB* I^2 334

Ξεναρίστη
MACEDONIA (BOTTIAIA):
—PELLA: **(1)** v/iv BC *SEG* XLVIII 820 ([*Ξ*]*εναρίστη*: d. *Βουλα*—)
MACEDONIA (PIERIA):
—DION?: **(2)** i-ii AD *AEMTh* 15 (2001) p. 343 (*Κλ. Ξ.*)
—PYDNA: **(3)** m. iv BC *SEG* XLV 803 B (coin graffito)
THRACE:
—APOLLONIA-SOZOPOLIS: **(4)** v/iv BC *Greek Colonisation* p. 100

Ξέναρχος
MACEDONIA (EDONIS):
—AMPHIPOLIS: **(1)** iii/ii BC *CCCA* VI 263 (*Mous. Kavalas* pp. 137-8 no. *Λ*. 201) (f. *Λύσων*)
THRACE:
—PERINTHOS-HERAKLEIA?: **(2)** iv BC Hp., *Epid.* vi 7. 5

Ξενίας
MACEDONIA (EDONIS):
—AMPHIPOLIS: **(1)** 242 BC *SEG* XII 373, 19 (Tataki, *Macedonians* p. 58 no. 101) (s. *Ὀργεύς*)

Ξενική
THRACE:
—PERINTHOS-HERAKLEIA: **(1)** iii-iv AD *IPerinth* 143 (*AD* 51-2 (1996-7) Mel. p. 351 no. 176) (m. *Παράμονος*)

Ξένιος
THRACE:
—BYZANTION: **(1)** c. 315-280 BC *FD* III (4) 151, 1 (f. *Σιλανός*)

Ξεννέας
MACEDONIA (MYGDONIA):
—THESSALONIKE: **(1)** ?39 BC *IG* X (2) (1) 30, 2; 50, 3; 109, 9 (s. *Σιμίας*)
MACEDONIA (PIERIA):
—METHONE: **(2)** s. iv BC *IEph* 1434, 1 (Tataki, *Macedonians* p. 123 no. 5) (f. *Ἐχεκρατίδης*)

Ξεννίας
MACEDONIA?: **(1)** 321 BC *PSI* 1284, 19 (Tataki, *Macedonians* p. 389 no. 2)

Ξέννων
MACEDONIA (ODOMANTIKE):
—SIRRHA: **(1)** f. iii AD *SEG* XXX 590, 24 ([*Αὐρ.*] [*Ξ*]*έννω*(*ν*): s. *Βεν*—); **(2)** ~ ib. l. 35 ([*Αὐρ.*] [*Ξ*]*έννω*(*ν*): s. *Β*—)

Ξενόδημος
CIMMERIAN BOSPOROS:
—PANTIKAPAION: **(1)** m. iv BC *CIRB* 214; cf. KW pl. 2 no. 34 (f. *Ξενώ*, *Ξενοπείθης*)
MACEDONIA (CHALKIDIKE):
—POTIDAIA-KASSANDREIA: **(2)** ?241 BC *BCH* 49 (1925) p. 89 no. 17, 1 (Tataki, *Macedonians* p. 93 no. 71) (II s. *Ξενόδημος* I); **(3)** ~ *BCH* 49 (1925) p. 89 no. 17, 2 (Tataki, *Macedonians* p. 93 no. 72) (I f. *Ξενόδημος* II)

Ξενοδίκη
MACEDONIA (EDONIS):
—PHILIPPOI: **(1)** ii-i BC *BCH* 59 (1935) p. 159 no. 55 (Pilhofer 304) (d. *Φίλιππος*)

Ξενόδοκος
THRACE:
—PERINTHOS-HERAKLEIA: **(1)** c. 580-570 BC *IG* XII (6) 577, 1-2 (*Ξ*[*ενό*]*δοκος*: f. *Μενίσκος*)

Ξενόδοχος
THRACE:
—KARDIA: **(1)** 329 BC *RE* (-); Berve 575

Ξενοκλείδης
CIMMERIAN BOSPOROS:
—PHANAGOREIA (NR.): **(1)** 344-311 BC *CIRB* 1014 (Rhodes–Osborne 65 C) (s. *Πόσις*)

Ξενοκλῆς
SCYTHIA MINOR:
—ISTROS: **(1)** v/iv BC *ISM* I 144 (s. *Ἱππόλοχος*)
TAURIS:
—CHERSONESOS: **(2)** iii BC Solomonik, *NEPKh* 178 (s. *Θεοχάρης*); **(3)** s. iii BC Kats p. 85 no. 8 (amph.) (f. *Αἰσχίνας*); **(4)** c. 230-215 BC ib. p. 107 no. 89 (amph.) (s. *Ἀπολλᾶς*) ?= (*5*); **(5)** c. 210-200 BC Anokhin p. 144 nos. 143; 145 (coins) ?= (*4*)
THRACE:
—AINOS: **(6)** ii AD *SEG* XXXVI 657, 6 (s. *Φιλαπόδημος*, *Ἰωνία*)
—MESAMBRIA: **(7)** c. 55 BC *IGB* I^2 323, 2 (s. *Λαχητᾶς*)

—ZONE: (**8**) c. 425-400 BC *IThrakAig* E401 ([Ξε]νοκλῆς?)

Ξενοκράτης

MACEDONIA: (**1**) b. 171 BC *SEG* XLIV 409 b, 3 (Tataki, *Macedonians* p. 215 no. 5) (f. —της)
MACEDONIA (BOTTIAIA):
—AIGAI: (**2**) c. 300-275 BC *SEG* XXXV 791 (s. Πιερίων)

Ξενόκριτος

CIMMERIAN BOSPOROS:
—GORGIPPIA: (**1**) s. iv BC *CIRB* 14 (f. Ἀριστονίκη: locn.—Vinogradov)
MACEDONIA: (**2**) ?359-357 BC *SEG* XXXVIII 662, 11; cf. Hatzopoulos, *Donation* pp. 55-61 (s. Ἀμύντας)
THRACE:
—MARONEIA: (**3**) ii-i BC *IThrakAig* E212, 2, 5 (s. Δημήτριος)

Ξενομένης

CIMMERIAN BOSPOROS:
—PANTIKAPAION: (**1**) hell. *AA* 1907, p. 127 Ba, 1-3, 9 (lead)

Ξενοπείθης

CIMMERIAN BOSPOROS:
—PANTIKAPAION: (**1**) m. iv BC *CIRB* 214 (s. Ξενόδημος)

Ξενότιμος

MACEDONIA (CHALKIDIKE):
—AKANTHOS: (**1**) iv/iii BC *SEG* XLVII 870, 3
MACEDONIA (EDONIS):
—AMPHIPOLIS: (**2**) c. 230-210 BC *BCH* 45 (1921) p. 18 III, 78; Hatzopoulos, *MI* 2 p. 83 no. 61, 5; cf. *BE* 1994, no. 432 (Tataki, *Macedonians* p. 58 no. 102) (s. Ἐπικράτης)

Ξενόφαντος

MACEDONIA (BOTTIAIA):
—PELLA: (**1**) f. iii BC *Thess. Mnem.* 16 (Tataki, *Macedonians* p. 157 no. 65) (f. Δημώ)
MACEDONIA?: (**2**) iv BC *RE* (1) (Tataki, *Macedonians* p. 389 no. 3) (f. Εὔγνωστος)
SCYTHIA MINOR:
—ISTROS: (**3**) v BC Unp. (Avram, defixio) 2, 4 (f. Πυθοκληΐδης)
THRACE:
—BYZANTION: (**4**) i BC-i AD *IByz* 205 (Firatlı–Robert p. 65 no. 59) (Ξενωφάτου (gen.): f. Ἑρμῆς)

Ξενόφιλος

MACEDONIA: (**1**) 317 BC *RE* (3); Berve 578 (Tataki, *Macedonians* p. 390 no. 4); (**2**) c. 238 BC *IG* II² 1299, 103; *ZPE* 78 (1989) p. 241 (date) (Tataki, *Macedonians* p. 390 no. 5)
MACEDONIA (CHALKIDIKE):
—CHALKIDEIS: (**3**) iv BC *RE* (6); Wehrli, *Schule Arist.* ii fr. 18
SCYTHIA MINOR:
—TOMIS?: (**4**) c. 490-500 AD Barnea 40 (e) (Popescu, *IGL* 64. 4)

Ξενοφῶν

MACEDONIA (BOTTIAIA):
—BEROIA: (**1**) m. iii BC *IG* IV (1)² (1) 96, 22 (Peek, *IAEpid* 42; Perlman, *City and Sanctuary* E.3 with p. 87 f. (date); Tataki, *Macedonians* p. 81 no. 41) (f. Ἀρ.......); (**2**) 223 BC *IBer* 4, 23 (Ξενοφ[ῶν]: s. Ποσείδιππος)
MACEDONIA (CHALKIDIKE):
—AKANTHOS: (**3**) iv-iii BC *SEG* XXIX 595 (s. Ἐράτων); (**4**) ~ ib. (f. Ἐράτων)
MACEDONIA (EDONIS):
—AMPHIPOLIS: (**5**) hell. Dimitsas 921 (f. Διότιμος); (**6**) m. iii BC Hatzopoulos, *Actes Amphipolis* p. 52 no 12, 8; *SEG* XLI 566 (date) (Ξενοφῶν: f. Νύμφων)
—PHILIPPOI?: (**7**) ii AD *IG* X (2) (1) 1034 A, 5 (*GVI* 1972; Pilhofer 98; Tataki, *Macedonians* p. 185 no. 53)
MACEDONIA (MYGDONIA):
—DIKAIA: (**8**) c. 365-359 BC Unp. (Voutyras–Sismanidis) ll. 37-8
—THESSALONIKE: (**9**) ii-iii AD *IG* X (2) (1) 592 ([Ξε]νοφῶν)
THRACE:
—STRYME?: (**10**) f. iv BC *SEG* XXXVIII 674 (*IThrakAig* E146) (f. Ἀβδηρίων)

Ξενοχάρης

SCYTHIA MINOR:
—ISTROS: (**1**) f. iii BC *ISM* I 145 (s. Ἀπολλώνιος); (**2**) i BC ib. 54, 3 (s. Ἑκαταῖος); (**3**) i BC-i AD ib. 191 II, 15 (s. Νικήρατος); (**4**) ii AD ib. 197 I, 2 (f. Χαιρέας); (**5**) ~ ib. l. 15 (f. Νείλων); (**6**) 138 AD ib. 193 II, 30 (f. Ἀρχελάϊος)

Ξένυλλα

MACEDONIA (BOTTIAIA):
—BEROIA: (**1**) ii-iii AD *IBer* 268 (Tataki 964)

Ξενώ

CIMMERIAN BOSPOROS:
—PANTIKAPAION: (**1**) m. iv BC *CIRB* 214 (d. Ξενόδημος)
MACEDONIA (BOTTIAIA):
—EDESSA: (**2**) 128 AD *SEG* XII 342, 5 (Tataki, *Edessa* 229) (m. Λύκος)
MACEDONIA (EDONIS):
—PHILIPPOI: (**3**) hell. Hatzopoulos, *MI* 1 p. 188 n. 1 (d. Προκλῆς)
TAURIS:
—CHERSONESOS: (**4**) iii BC Solomonik, *GAKh* 888 (vase)
THRACE:
—MESAMBRIA: (**5**) imp. *IGB* I² 347, 3 (*GVI* 1719)
—SALYMBRIA: (**6**) ?c. 410-400 BC *IG* I³ 1369 (*FRA* 6632)

Ξένων

CIMMERIAN BOSPOROS:
—PANTIKAPAION: (**1**) i-ii AD *CIRB* 639; cf. KW pl. 19 no. 271 (f. Φάννας, Παπίας)
MACEDONIA: (**2**) ?c. 240-220 BC *IOrop* 64, 3 (Tataki, *Macedonians* p. 390 no. 9) (f. Ἀρχέστρατος, Ποσειδώνιος); (**3**) 232 or 207 BC *CPR* XVIII 10, 201, 207 (Tataki, *Macedonians* p. 390 no. 7; La'da E1564); (**4**) 173 BC *PAmh* 43, 16 (Tataki, *Macedonians* p. 390 no. 8; La'da E1565)
MACEDONIA (BOTTIAIA):
—BEROIA: (**5**) s. iii BC *IBer* 16 A, 19
—PELLA: (**6**) v/iv BC *Egnatia* 5 (1995-2000) p. 261 (*SEG* XLIX 755) (f. Εὐγένεια)
MACEDONIA (CHALKIDIKE):
—ANTIGONEIA: (**7**) c. 230-200 BC *BCH* 45 (1921) p. 18 III, 76; cf. p. 46 (Tataki, *Macedonians* p. 65 no. 7) (f. Ἡρακλέων) ?= (*10*)
—OLYNTHOS: (**8**) ?350 BC *TAPA* 59 (1928) p. 226, 2; Hatzopoulos, *Actes Chalc.* p. 80 (date) (s. Μοσχίων)
—POLICHNE?: (**9**) ?353 BC *SEG* XXXVII 576, 17 (f. Διονύσιος)
—POTIDAIA-KASSANDREIA: (**10**) c. 230-200 BC *BCH* 45 (1921) p. 18 III, 77 (I f. Ξένων II) ?= (*7*); (**11**) ~ ib. l. 77; *Syll*³ 585, 181 (Tataki, *Macedonians* p. 93 nos. 73-4) (II s. Ξένων I)
MACEDONIA (EDONIS):
—AMPHIPOLIS: (**12**) s. iv BC *PAE* 1981, p. 25 with pl. 43 β, 12 (f. —ς)
MACEDONIA (MYGDONIA):
—THESSALONIKE: (**13**) 95 BC *IG* X (2) (1) 4, 4 (f. Στράτων)
MACEDONIA?: (**14**) 190 BC *RE* (5) (Tataki, *Macedonians* p. 390 no. 6) (Lat. Xeno)
SKYTHIA:
—OLBIA-BORYSTHENES: (**15**) f. iv BC Dubois, *IGDOlbia* 103, 2 (lead)
—TANAIS: (**16**) 104 AD *CIRB* 1259, 7 (s. Ἔρως)
TAURIS:
—CHERSONESOS: (**17**) iv BC Solomonik, *NEPKh* 137 (f. Εὔβουλος); (**18**) iv/iii BC Kats p. 126 no. 36 (amph.) (f. Πολύστρατος) ?= (*19*); (**19**) c. 300-285 BC ib. p. 107 no. 90 (amph.) ?= (*18*); (**20**) c. 250-230 BC Anokhin pp. 141-2 nos. 102; 116 (coins); (**21**) ?226 BC *IG* VII 245, 2-3 (*IOrop* 128); cf. *Chiron* 22 (1992) p. 494 no. 168 (date) (s. Πασίξενος)
THRACE:
—APOLLONIA-SOZOPOLIS: (**22**) v/iv BC *IGB* I² 444 (s. Γέλων); (**23**) iv BC *BMNBurgas* 4 (2002) p. 127 no. 26 (Ξένω[ν]?: s. Πολε—)
—BYZANTION: (**24**) s. iii BC Schönert-Geiss, *Byzantion* 1144-7 (coin); (**25**) ii BC *Türk Tarih Kongresi XI* (6) p. 2703 with pl. 494. 4 ([Ξ]ένων?: s. Μενίσκος)
—BYZANTION (TERRIT.): (**26**) i BC *IByz* 179 (Firatlı–Robert pp. 114-15 no. 191a) (s. Μενίσκος, f. Μενίσκος)
—MARONEIA: (**27**) ii-i BC *IThrakAig* E212, 47 (f. Ἀριστόβουλος)
—ODESSOS: (**28**) c. 100-72 BC Price, *Alexander* 1203 (coin) (Ξένω(ν)); (**29**) i BC-i AD *IGB* I² 189 (f. Τόμιον); (**30**) 12 BC ib. 46, 35 (f. Πόσσις); (**31**) i-ii AD ib. 111 (Ξένων: s. Ἑστιαῖος); (**32**) ~ ib. 116, 5 (f. Μάμα); (**33**) ii AD ib. 183 (PM 1738) (s. Αὐτοκράτης, f. Ἀννι); (**34**) ii-iii AD *IGB* I² 142 (f. Προμαθίων); (**35**) m. ii AD ib. 177 (PM 1749); *Dacia* 21 (1977) p. 161 (date) (s. Ἀρτεμίδωρος); (**36**) ~ *IGB* I² 179 (PM 1694); *Dacia* 21 (1977) p. 161 (date) (s. Πόσις); (**37**) s. ii AD *IGB* I² 79 bis, 5 (*CCET* I 34) (f. —ρ); (**38**) ~ *IGB* I² 181 (PM 1605); *Dacia* 21 (1977) p. 161 (date) (f. Ἀπελλᾶς); (**39**) 215 AD *IGB* I² 47 a, 12 (Αὐρ. Ξ.: s. Ἀλέξανδρος); (**40**) ~ ib. 47 b, 11 9 (f. Αὐρ. Ἀτανδρίων); (**41**) ~ ib. 47 c, 25 (Αὐρ. Ξ.: s. Ἐπαμείνων); (**42**) 221 AD ib. 47 bis a, 36 (I f. Αὐρ. Ξένων II); (**43**) ~ ib. l. 36 (Αὐρ. Ξ.: II s. Ξένων I); (**44**) ~ ib. 47 bis b, 37 (Αὐρ. Ξ.: s. Νουμήνιος)
—ODESSOS (NR.): (**45**) ii AD ib. 272 (PM 1676); *Dacia* 21 (1977) p. 161 (date) (s. Ἀρτεμίδωρος)
—SALYMBRIA: (**46**) hell. *IByz* S 2 (f. Κρα—)

Ξερμοδίγεστος?

MACEDONIA (PAIONIA)?: (**1**) iv/iii BC D.S. xxi 13; Detschev p. 334 (name) (or Thrace?: Ζερμοδίγεστος?)

Ξέρξης

THRACE:
—APOLLONIA-SOZOPOLIS: (**1**) iii BC *IGB* I² 458, 3 (f. Ὑβρεῖς)

Ξηβάνοκος

SKYTHIA:
—TANAIS (NR.): (**1**) ii-iii AD Minns, *Scythians* p. 235

Ξηγόδις

SKYTHIA:
—TANAIS: (**1**) c. 225-250 AD *CIRB* 1288, 14; Zgusta, *PNS* 158 (s. Ἀχαιμένης)

Ξησσάγαρος

SKYTHIA:
—OLBIA-BORYSTHENES: (**1**) ii AD *IOSPE* I² 93, 6; Zgusta, *PNS* 313 (f. Δημήτριος)

Ξιαμφώκανος

SKYTHIA:
—TANAIS: (**1**) 225 AD *CIRB* 1279, 28; Zgusta, *PNS* 159 (Ξιαμφόκανος—Tokhtas'ev: s. Ἀντίμαχος)

Ξοβας

CIMMERIAN BOSPOROS:
—PANTIKAPAION: (**1**) i AD *CIRB* 351; Zgusta, *PNS* 160

Ξύστος

MACEDONIA (MYGDONIA):
—THESSALONIKE: (**1**) 239 AD *IG* X (2) (1) 158, 9 (*Τ. Στατίλιος Οὐαλεντίων ὁ καὶ Ξ.*: f. *Τ. Στατίλιος Θεόδωρος*)
THRACE:
—BYZANTION (TERRIT.): (**2**) ii BC *IByz* 92 (Firatlı–Robert p. 91 no. 120) (s. Διονύσιος)

O

Ὀαδίστη
MACEDONIA (BOTTIAIA):
—PELLA: (1) f. iii BC *SEG* XLI 575, 3; cf. *BE* 1992, no. 311 (d. *Δημήτριος*)

Ὀαροζβάλακος
SKYTHIA:
—TANAIS: (1) f. ii AD *CIRB* 1264 A, 15

Ὀβουλκία
MACEDONIA (PAIONIA): (1) ii-iii AD *Sp.* 75 (1933) p. 77 no. 219 (m. *Κούαρτος, Κούϊντος*)

Ὀδέτα
MACEDONIA (BOTTIAIA):
—ALOROS: (1) i/ii AD *SEG* XXXVIII 631 + *BE* 1990, no. 457 (d. *Ἀδαῖος*)
—BEROIA: (2) i BC *IBer* 185 (Tataki 1355) ([Ὀ]δέτα: d. *Ἰόλαος*)

Ὀδίαρδος
SKYTHIA:
—TANAIS: (1) 220 AD *CIRB* 1278, 18 (Ὀ[δί]αρδος—Tokhtas'ev: f. *Δαναράζμακος*); (2) 220-225 AD ib. l. 16; 1279, 20 (Ὀ[δίαρ]δος?—1278: s. *Δημήτριος*)

Ὀζήα?
THRACE:
—SALYMBRIA: (1) ?ii-i BC *IByz* S 32 (d. *Μηνακῶν*)

Ὀηδέα?
MACEDONIA (EORDAIA):
—AKRINI (MOD.): (1) ii-i BC *EAM* 89 + *BE* 1995, no. 409 (Ὀρνέα?—*EAM*, Ὀη[δ]έα?—*BE*: d. *Ἀρχέλαος*)

Οἰκιάδης
MACEDONIA (CHALKIDIKE):
—GIGONOS?: (1) i BC *SEG* XXIX 587; Hatzopoulos, *Actes Chalc.* p. 25 (date) (s. *Παρμένων*)
—POTIDAIA-KASSANDREIA: (2) ?257 BC Nachtergael, *Les Galates* 7, 32 (Stephanis 1929; Tataki, *Macedonians* p. 94 no. 75) (Ο[ἰ]κιάδ[η]ς: s. *Νίκανδρος*)

Οἴκιος
MACEDONIA (MYGDONIA):
—THESSALONIKE: (1) c. 175-200 AD *SEG* XXXVI 646; cf. XLIII 468; *KGAM Thess.* I 140 (date) (*Λ. Σηνάτιος Ὀ.*: f. *M. Οὐαρένιος Ἀρέσκων*)

Οἰκωρσις?
SCYTHIA MINOR:
—TOMIS: (1) ii-iii AD *ISM* II 26, 6 (Οἰκωρσις?: s. *Ἑστιαῖος*)

Οἰμήδης?
THRACE:
—SERDICA (TERRIT.): (1) ii-iii AD *IGB* IV 2015 b (*Eastern cults* p. 167 no. 10) (f. —ο.καλας)

Οἰνάνθη
CIMMERIAN BOSPOROS:
—PANTIKAPAION: (1) i AD *CIRB* 479 (d. *Σωσιγένης*); (2) ii AD ib. 761 (d. *Διομήδης*)
MACEDONIA (LOWER PAIONIA):
—EUROPOS: (3) ?ii AD *SEG* XXXVIII 613 (d. *Πολέμων*)
TAURIS:
—CHERSONESOS: (4) ii-iii AD *IOSPE* I² 519, 1, 3 (*GVI* 1684); cf. KW pl. 23 no. 319 (d. *Γλαυκίας*)

Οἰνιάδης
SKYTHIA:
—TYRAS: (1) c. 300-275 BC *SEG* XLIX 1051 B, 1 (Οἰνι[άδης]?: f. *Αὐτοκλῆς*)

Οἰνίας
THRACE:
—MESAMBRIA: (1) c. 175-150 BC Karayotov, *Mesambria* I p. 91 nos. 235-48; Price, *Alexander* 1024-6 (coin); (2) ii/i BC *IGB* V 5102 (Οἰνία[ς]); (3) ~ ib. 5104 VI (f. *Διονύσιος*); (4) i BC-i AD ib. I² 340 (s. *Παγχάρης*)

Οἰνοπίδης
THRACE:
—APOLLONIA-SOZOPOLIS: (1) s. iv BC ib. 459 (Οἰνοπί(δ)ης: f. *Κρινομένης*)

Οἴριvθος
THRACE:
—BOURDAPA: (1) ii-iii AD ib. III 1352 (f. *Ἐρύθη*)

Οἰσύδρης
THRACE: (1) vii-vi BC *RE* (-); Call. fr. 104 with dieg.; cf. *Ét. Thas.* 3 pp. 30-1 (*Οἰσύδρεω* (gen.))

Ὄκκος
MACEDONIA (BOTTIAIA):
—BEROIA: (1) i BC *IBer* 195 (Tataki 966) (s. *Αἰνείας*, ?s. *Λανίκα*); (2) ~ *IBer* 195 (Tataki 967) (f. *Αἰνείας*)

Ὀκταβία
MACEDONIA (PAIONIA):
—STOBOI: (1) ii-iii AD *Sp.* 75 (1933) p. 26 no. 60 (Ὠκ-)

Ὀκτάβιος
MACEDONIA (MYGDONIA):
—THESSALONIKE: (1) ii AD *IG* X (2) (1) 389 (Ὠκ-)

Ὀκταμασάδης
CIMMERIAN BOSPOROS:
—SINDOI: (1) c. 390-380 BC *SEG* XLIII 515, 5 + XLVIII 1027 (s. *Ἑκαταῖος*)
SKYTHIA:
—SKYTHAI: (2) f. v BC *RE* (-) (s. *Ἀριαπείθης*: king)

Ὄλγασυς
CIMMERIAN BOSPOROS:
—PANTIKAPAION: (1) iv BC *CIRB* 215; cf. KW pl. 3 no. 71; Zgusta, *PNS* 162 (s. *Σάγαρις*)

Ὀλθάκης
KOLCHIS: (1) 61 BC App., *Mith.* 117

Ὀλίος
THRACE:
—AINOS: (1) ii AD *IG* XII (8) 221, 6; Threatte, *Grammar* I p. 440 (name) (f. *Νικόλαος*)

Ὀλκίας
MACEDONIA: (1) 323-322 BC *RE* Supplbd. 3 (-); Berve 580 (Tataki, *Macedonians* p. 391 no. 1); cf. *LGPN* IIIA s.v. (1)

Ὀλόκαλος
SCYTHIA MINOR:
—TOMIS:
——(Aikoreis): (1) ii-iii AD *ISM* II 252 (Φ(ι)λόκαλος—Koumanoudis and Newton: f. *Χρήστος*)

Ὄλορος
THRACE: (1) vi BC *RE* (1); Hdt. vi 39; 41; Plu., *Cim* 4 (f. *Ἡγησιπύλη*: king)

Ὀλυμπᾶς
MACEDONIA (DERRIOPOS):
—STUBERRA: (1) 116 AD *IG* X (2) (2) 327, 39 (Ὀλυμ-: f. *Παράμονος*)
THRACE:
—BYZANTION?: (2) i BC-i AD *IByz* 375 (Firatlı-Robert p. 126 no. 211) (-νπᾶς: f. *Ἀπολλώνιος*)

Ὀλυμπία
MACEDONIA (BOTTIAIA):
—TYRISSA?: (1) s. iv BC *SEG* XLIII 446 ([Ὀλυ]νπία)
MACEDONIA (LYNKESTIS):
—HERAKLEIA: (2) iii AD *IG* X (2) (2) 97 (*Αὐρ. Ὀ.*: m. *Λυσίμαχος*)
—MELITI (MOD.): (3) f. iii AD *EAM* 166, 2 (-νπί-: d. *Πρωτᾶς, Μέστα*)
SCYTHIA MINOR:
—TOMIS: (4) 201 AD *ISM* II 83 II, 15 (*Π. Αἰλία Ὀλυμπ[ία]*)
THRACE:
—NICOPOLIS AD ISTRUM (TERRIT.): (5) ii-iii AD *IGB* II 698 ([Ὀλυ]μπεία Μαρκία)

Ὀλυμπιάδης
MACEDONIA (DERRIOPOS):
—STUBERRA: (1) 74 AD *IG* X (2) (2) 325, 42 (s. *Παράμονος*); (2) ~ ib. l. 45 (s. *Σιτᾶς*); (3) ~ ib. 326, 29-30 (f. *Ἀντίγονος*)
MACEDONIA (LYNKESTIS):
—HERAKLEIA (NR.): (4) ii-iii AD ib. 6 (s. *Λύκος*)
THRACE:
—MARONEIA: (5) ii BC *Milet* I (3) 82, 10 (and Caria Miletos: s. *Διονύσιος*)

Ὀλυμπιανός
CIMMERIAN BOSPOROS:
—PANTIKAPAION: (1) 306 AD *CIRB* 64, 11 (Levinskaya p. 229 no. 1) (*Αὐρ. Οὐαλέριος Σόγους ὁ καὶ Ὀ.*: s. *Ὄλυμπος*)

Ὀλυμπιάς
CIMMERIAN BOSPOROS:
—PANTIKAPAION (NR.): (1) iv BC *CIRB* 959 (d. *Ἡροφῶν*)
MACEDONIA: (2) 232 or 206 BC *CPR* XVIII 30, 120, 125, 127, 133 (Tataki, *Macedonians* p. 391 no. 3; La'da E1812) (d. *Ὀλύμπιχος*); (3) ii-i BC *ASAA* 2 (1916) p. 130 no. 17 + *SEG* XVII 360; (4) 173 BC *PGiss* 2 I, 8, 15, 18, 20-22, 24, [26-27] (Tataki, *Macedonians* p. 391 no. 2; La'da E1811) (d. *Διονύσιος*)
MACEDONIA (BOTTIAIA):
—BEROIA: (5) ii AD *IBer* 491 (Tataki 61) ([Α]ἰλιανὴ Ὀλυμπιάς); (6) s. ii AD *IBer* 266 (Tataki 970)
—EDESSA: (7) ii-iii AD *Arch. Pap.* 22 (1973) p. 206 no. 9 (Tataki, *Edessa* 9) (*Αἰλ. Ὀ.*); (8) iii AD Feissel, *RICM* 10 (Tataki, *Edessa* 230) (d. *Ὀλύμπιος, Χαριδημία*)
—MIEZA: (9) ii-iii AD Tataki 971
MACEDONIA (CHALKIDIKE):
—POTIDAIA-KASSANDREIA (NR.): (10) ?iii AD Dimitsas 746, 4 (*Τ— Ὀ.*: m. *Αὐρηλία*)
—SINGOS (NR.): (11) 180 AD *SEG* XXIX 593, 6 (d. *Γέμελλος, Διονυσία*)
MACEDONIA (EDONIS):
—AMPHIPOLIS (TERRIT.): (12) ii-iii AD *BCH* 18 (1894) p. 430 no. 1 (*Dodoni* 18 (1989) p. 293 no. 151)
MACEDONIA (EORDAIA):
—ARNISA?: (13) m. ii AD *EAM* 123, 2; Hatzopoulos, *MI* 1 p. 94 n. 4 (locn.) (-ππι-: m. *Φιλοξένη, Λεοντογένης*)
—ERMAKIA (MOD.): (14) ii-iii AD *EAM* 128 (threpte)
MACEDONIA (MYGDONIA):
—THESSALONIKE: (15) ii/iii AD *Tekmeria* 6 (2001) p. 4 no. 2 (*Φλ. Ὀ.*: d. *Γ. Σέξτιος Σεκοῦνδος, Φλ. Εὐφροσύνη*); (16) ~ *IG* X (2) (1) 181, 16; 187, 5; 628 A, 2; 628 B, 6, 9 (*GVI* 1275);

SEG XLVI 815, 1; *Roman Onomastics* pp. 130-4 (*Αἰλ. Γεμεινία Ὀ.*: d. *Τ. Αἰλ. Γεμίνιος Μακεδὼν ὁ καὶ Ὄλυμπος, Αἰκουανὴ Ἀντιοχίς*, m. *Ἰούλ. Εἰρηναῖος, Ἰούλ. Γαϊανός, Ἰούλ. Ὄλυμπος, Μεγέθιν*); **(17)** m. iii AD *IG* X (2) (1) 206, 9 (*Γ. Ἰουλ. Ὀ.*: d. *Γ. Ἰούλ. Ἀριστέας*, m. *Κλ. Τύλλιος Ἀλέξανδρος ὁ καὶ Εὐγένιος*)
MACEDONIA (PAIONIA): **(18)** i/ii AD *SEG* XVIII 367 (Tataki, *Macedonians* p. 209 no. 17) (m. *Σάνκτος, Ποντικός*)
—KAVADARCI (MOD.): **(19)** ii AD *Sp.* 71 (1931) p. 75 no. 175 (m. *Ὄλυμπος*)
MACEDONIA (PELAGONIA): **(20)** ii-iii AD *IG* X (2) (2) 268 (-λυν-: d. *Μέστος*, m. *Διοσκουρίδης*)
MACEDONIA (PIERIA):
—DION: **(21)** ii AD *Klio* 52 (1970) p. 59 no. 11 (*Οὔλπ. Ὀ.*)
THRACE:
—BYZANTION: **(22)** ii BC *IByz* 346; cf. Robert, *OMS* 7 p. 643 (d. *Ζωΐλος*); **(23)** ii-i BC *IByz* 148 ([*Ὀ*]*λυμπιάς*: d. *Ἀπολλώνιος*)
—SALYMBRIA (NR.): **(24)** imp. Unp. (Sayar) (-λυν-: d. *Τίτος*)

Ὀλυμπιόδωρος
MACEDONIA: (1) 144-141 BC *PBingen* 35, 6, 16 (La'da E1566) (s. *Μενοίτης*)
MACEDONIA (BOTTIAIA):
—BEROIA: **(2)** s. ii BC *IBer* 24, 6 (Tataki 972) (f. *Λάανδρος*)
THRACE:
—BYZANTION: **(3)** ?iii BC *IByz* 11 (s. *Μενδίδωρος*); **(4)** c. 250-220 BC Schönert-Geiss, *Byzantion* 1015-16; 1037-42 (coin) ?= (*5*); **(5)** 220 BC Plb. iv 47 ?= (*4*)
—PERINTHOS-HERAKLEIA:
——(Theseidai): **(6)** s. iii BC *IPerinth* 62, 6 (s. *Μητρόδωρος*)
—PERINTHOS-HERAKLEIA?: **(7)** iv BC Hp., *Epid.* iv 33

Ὀλυμπιόνικος
MACEDONIA (PIERIA):
—DION: **(1)** ii-iii AD Dimitsas 181; cf. *SEG* XXXIX 584 (*Αὐρ. Ὀ.*)

Ὀλύμπιος
MACEDONIA (BOTTIAIA):
—EDESSA: **(1)** iii AD Feissel, *RICM* 10 (Tataki, *Edessa* 231) (f. *Ὀλυμπιάς, Κασσάνδρα*)
SCYTHIA MINOR:
—ISTROS: **(2)** f. iii AD *ISM* I 218, 7 (*Αὐρ. Ὀ.*: s. *Ἀσκληπιάδης*)
THRACE:
—AINOS*: **(3)** 343 AD *RE* (30) (bp.)
—BYZANTION: **(4)** 359 AD *PLRE* I (7)
—PHILIPPOPOLIS-TRIMONTIUM (TERRIT.): **(5)** ii AD *IGB* III 1132 (*Ῥοιμητάλκης ὁ καὶ Ὀ.*: s. *Κλ. Σπάρτοκος*)

Ὀλύμπις
MACEDONIA: **(1)** 254 AD *ILeukopetra* 107, 5 (*Καλόκαιρος ὁ καὶ Ὀ.*: slave/freed.)
MACEDONIA (BOTTIAIA):
—BEROIA: **(2)** a. 212 AD *IBer* 136, 22 (Tataki 896) (*Μέστρ. Ὀ.*)
MACEDONIA (CHALKIDIKE):
—MENDE: **(3)** imp.? *IG* II² 9336 (Tataki, *Macedonians* p. 121 no. 15; *FRA* 3681)
THRACE:
—SPINOPARA: **(4)** ii AD *IGB* IV 2192, 12

Ὀλύμπιχον
THRACE:
—BYZANTION: **(1)** ii-i BC *IByz* 90 (Fıratlı–Robert pp. 90-1 no. 118) ([*Ὀ*]*λύνπιχον*: d. *Βακίων*)

Ὀλύμπιχος
MACEDONIA: **(1)** iii BC *ISmyrna* 183 (Tataki, *Macedonians* p. 392 no. 5) (f. *Ἀμύντας*); **(2)** 232 or 206 BC *CPR* XVIII 30, 121 (Tataki, *Macedonians* p. 392 no. 6); cf. La'da E1812 (f. *Ὀλυμπιάς*)
MACEDONIA (BOTTIAIA):
—MIEZA: **(3)** iii BC *SEG* XXIV 524 I, 26 (Hatzopoulos, *MI* 2 p. 106 no. 92) ([*Ὀλ*]*ύμπιχος*); **(4)** ~ *SEG* XXIV 524 II, 8 + Hatzopoulos, *MI* 2 p. 106 no. 92 ([*Ὀλύμ*]*πιχος*?: ?s. *Σακ—*)
MACEDONIA (CHALKIDIKE):
—CHALKIDEIS: **(5)** c. 358-355 BC *Olynthus* 9 pp. 71-6 nos. 113-18 (coin); *Ancient Macedonia* I p. 254 (date)
MACEDONIA (MYGDONIA):
—KALINDOIA: **(6)** iii BC *SEG* XLII 592; **(7)** ii/i BC ib. 578, 1 (f. *Λυσανίας*)
MACEDONIA (PIERIA):
—PYDNA: **(8)** f. ii BC ib. L 629 (s. *Λαόμμας, Λαμάγα*)
MACEDONIA?: **(9)** iii BC *Labraunda* III (1) 8, 27; *IIasos* 35, 6 (Tataki, *Macedonians* p. 392 no. 7) (I f. *Ὀλύμπιχος* II); **(10)** c. 240-220 BC *RE* (1); *Labraunda* III (1) 1, [1]; 1B, [9]; 5, 36; 7, 1; 8, 8, 10, 27; 9, 3; pp. 86-96; *IIasos* 35, 6; 150, 42, 89; *BCH* 58 (1934) pp. 291-2 no. 1, 2; *IDidyma* 439, 5?; cf. Robert, *Amyzon* pp. 147-50 (Tataki, *Macedonians* pp. 391-2 no. 4) (*Ὀλύπιχος*—*Labraunda* 8: II s. *Ὀλύμπιχος* I)
SCYTHIA MINOR:
—KALLATIS: **(11)** iii/ii BC *ISM* III 161 (f. *Ἰσαγόρας*)
SKYTHIA:
—TYRAS*: **(12)** ii/iii AD *AEp* 1995, no. 1350 (Lat. L. Pa[piri]us Olymphicus: doctor)

Ὄλυμπος
CIMMERIAN BOSPOROS:
—PANTIKAPAION: **(1)** f. ii AD *CIRB* 659 (f. *Ἀρτέμων*); **(2)** 306 AD ib. 64, 4 (Levinskaya p. 229 no. 1) (f. *Αὐρ. Οὐαλέριος Σόγους ὁ καὶ Ὀλυμπιανός*)
MACEDONIA (BOTTIAIA):
—KYRRHOS: **(3)** ii/iii AD *Eulimeni* 4 (2003) p. 146 no. 3
MACEDONIA (MYGDONIA):
—THESSALONIKE: **(4)** ii/iii AD *IG* X (2) (1) 628 A; cf. *IApoll* 325; *Roman Onomastics* pp. 130-4 (*Τ. Αἰλ. Γεμείνιος Μακεδὼν* (*ὁ*) (*καὶ*) *Ὀ.*: f. *Γεμινία Ὀλυμπιάς*); **(5)** 191 AD *IG* X (2) (1) 407, 2 (*Π. Αἰλ. Ὄλυνπος*); **(6)** f. iii AD ib. 182, 11 (*Ἰούλ. Ὀ.*: s. *Ἰούλ. Κάστωρ, Αἰλ. Γεμινία Ὀλυμπιάς*)
MACEDONIA (PAIONIA):
—KAVADARCI (MOD.): **(7)** ii AD *Sp.* 71 (1931) p. 75 no. 175 (s. *Ὀλυμπιάς*)
MACEDONIA (PELAGONIA):
—MARIOVO (MOD.): **(8)** i AD *IG* X (2) (2) 160 (Lat. C. Iulius Olympus: freed.)
SCYTHIA MINOR:
—KALLATIS: **(9)** s. iii BC *ISM* III 35 B, 36 (s. *Σωτήριχος*)
SKYTHIA:
—OLBIA-BORYSTHENES: **(10)** f. iv BC Dubois, *IGDOlbia* 103, 1 (lead) ([*Ὀ*]*λυμπο*[*ς*])
THRACE:
—BYZANTION: **(11)** iii BC *IByz* 69 (Fıratlı–Robert p. 48 no. 7) (f. *Χοιρίνα*)
—DUROSTORUM: **(12)** ii-iii AD *Arkheologiia* (Sofia) 1981 (4), p. 42 no. 7 (Lat. C. A[nt.]Olympus); **(13)** iii AD ib. 1976 (4), p. 64 no. 5 (Lat. C. A[nt]. Olympus)
—LYSIMACHEIA: **(14)** c. 240-220 BC *IG* VII 357, 2 (*IOrop* 164) (-λυν-: s. *Ἑρμίας*)
—MARONEIA: **(15)** 102 BC *IG* II² 1028 III, 149 (*FRA* 3546) (*Ὀλυμπ*[*ος*]: f. *Λεωσθένης*)

Ὀλυνπιόδωρος
CIMMERIAN BOSPOROS:
—KOROKONDAME: **(1)** s. iv BC *North Pontic Archaeology* p. 352 no. 5 with figs. 8-9 (s. *Πρωταγόρας*)

Ὀλώϊχος
MACEDONIA (BOTTIAIA):
—TYRISSA? (ASVESTARI (MOD.)): **(1)** f. ii BC *SEG* XLVII 999, 21 ([*Ὀ*]*λώϊχ*[*ος*])
MACEDONIA (EDONIS):
—AMPHIPOLIS: **(2)** i BC-i AD ib. XXVII 248, 3 (*Ὀλώϊχος*)
—AMPHIPOLIS?: **(3)** iii BC ib. XXIV 609 = XLIII 372 (s. *Ἀμύντας*)
MACEDONIA (KRESTONIA):
—MORRYLOS: **(4)** c. 185-180 BC ib. XXXIX 606, 1 (f. *Μένανδρος*)

Ὁμηρικός
MACEDONIA (BOTTIAIA):
—BEROIA: **(1)** a. 212 AD *IBer* 136, 23 (Tataki 295) (I f. *Αὐρ. Ὁμηρικός* II *νέος*); **(2)** ~ *IBer* 136, 23 (Tataki 294) (*Αὐρ. Ὁμηρικὸς νέος*: II s. *Ὁμηρικός* I)
SCYTHIA MINOR:
—TOMIS: **(3)** ii AD *ISM* II 290, 15 (*Ὁμήριχος*—edd. per err.: s. *Ἑρμάφιλος*)

Ὅμηρος
THRACE:
—ABDERA: **(1)** c. 336-311 BC May, *Abdera* p. 293 nos. 545-6 (coin)
—BYZANTION: **(2)** iv/iii BC *RE* (3); *PP* 16708; *TrGF* I pp. 268-9 no. 98; *AP* ii 407 (s. *Ἀνδρόμαχος, Μοιρώ*)

Ὁμίλις
MACEDONIA (MYGDONIA):
—THESSALONIKE: **(1)** 102 AD *IG* X (2) (1) 266

Ὁμοῖος
MACEDONIA (MYGDONIA):
—THESSALONIKE: **(1)** iii AD ib. 487, 6; p. 160 (stemma) (*Δομίτιος Ὁ.*: f. *Δομιτία Λεοντίς*)

Ὁμόνοια
CIMMERIAN BOSPOROS:
—PANTIKAPAION: **(1)** i/ii AD *CIRB* 626
THRACE:
—AINOS: **(2)** i-ii AD *IG* II² 7981 (*FRA* 259) (d. *Σώφρων*)

Ὀμράσμακος
SKYTHIA:
—TANAIS: **(1)** 225 AD *CIRB* 1280, 8 (f. *Χάραξστος*)

Ὀμφαλίων
TAURIS:
—CHERSONESOS: **(1)** iii BC *IOSPE* I² 581, 5 (s. *Ἡ—*)
THRACE:
—MESAMBRIA: **(2)** iii/ii BC *IGB* I² 338 quater (f. *Ἐρυμενίδας*); **(3)** c. 100-71 BC Karayotov, *Mesambria* I p. 87 nos. 850-3; Price, *Alexander* 1124 (coin) (*Ὀμφα*(*λίων*))

Ὀμψάλακος
CIMMERIAN BOSPOROS:
—GORGIPPIA: **(1)** s. ii AD *SEG* XXIX 705 ([*Ὀμ*]*ψάλακο*[*ς*])
—PANTIKAPAION: **(2)** i AD *CIRB* 478; cf. KW pl. 46 no. 664 (s. *Σιδαύχας*); **(3)** ~ *CIRB* 479 (*Ὀμψάλα*[*κ*]*ος*: s. *Σωσιγένης*); **(4)** 127 AD ib. 61, 2 (f. *Τρύφων*)
—THEODOSIA: **(5)** iii AD ib. 947 A, 1 (*Ὀμψά*[*λακος*]: f. *Ἀχαιμένης*)
SKYTHIA:
—OLBIA-BORYSTHENES: **(6)** imp. *IOSPE* I² 227; Zgusta, *PNS* 315 (*Νικήρατος ὁ καὶ Ὀ.*: s. *Νικήρατος*); **(7)** i/ii AD *IOSPE* I² 39, 1; 106, 5; 175, 3 (s. *Εὐρησίβιος*)
—TANAIS: **(8)** ii AD *CIRB* 1262, 18 (s. *Οὔργιος*); **(9)** ~ ib. l. 19 (s. *Τρύφων*); **(10)** ~ ib. l. 27 (s. *Θεόφιλος*); **(11)** 155 AD ib. 1260, 20 (s. *Φίδας*); **(12)** 210-226 AD ib. 1285, 13 (*Ὀμψά*[*λακος*]: s. *Φαζίναμος*); **(13)** 228 AD ib. 1282, 13 (s. *Φαδίναμος*)

TAURIS:
—NEAPOLIS: (14) imp.? *SEG* III 605 ([Ὀμ]ψά-λακος)

Ὀνασικλῆς
TAURIS:
—CHERSONESOS: (1) iv/iii BC *IOSPE* I² 504

Ὀνάσιμος
MACEDONIA: (1) m. ii BC *IG* IX (1)² (3) 639. 3, 7 (Tataki, *Macedonians* p. 392 no. 8) (slave/freed.)
MACEDONIA (BOTTIAIA):
—PELLA: (2) 190 BC *Syll*³ 585, 103 (Tataki, *Macedonians* p. 157 no. 66) (s. Ἐπικρατίδας)

Ὀνεράτμις?
SCYTHIA MINOR:
—TOMIS: (1) ii-iii AD *ISM* II 307, 5 (Ὀνεράτμιος (gen.): s. Μενέφιλος, Θιθίς)

Ὀνήσανδρος
MACEDONIA (BISALTIA):
—ARGILOS: (1) 360 BC *IG* IV (1)² 94 b, 17 (Perlman, *City and Sanctuary* E.1 with p. 69 f. (date); Tataki, *Macedonians* p. 70 no. 1)

Ὀνησᾶς
MACEDONIA (BOTTIAIA):
—BEROIA: (1) f. iii AD *IBer* 267, 1 (Tataki 768) (Κουσπίδιος Ὀ.: s. Εὐκτήμων, Νίκη)
THRACE:
—BYZANTION: (2) i/ii AD *SEG* L 667 VI (threptos)

Ὀνησίμη
MACEDONIA (MYGDONIA):
—LETE (NR.)*: (1) c. 160-180 AD ib. XLVII 974; *KGAM Thess.* I 123 (date) (d. Ὀνήσιμος, Νίκη: slave?)
MACEDONIA (ODOMANTIKE):
—SIRRHA: (2) ii-iii AD *SEG* XXXIII 549 + XXXV 1846 (Φιρμία Ὀ.: d. Λ. Φίρμιος Κοκκιανός, Ἀπουλεΐα Μοῦσα)
THRACE:
—KOILA: (3) ii-iii AD *ISestos* 30

Ὀνήσιμος
CIMMERIAN BOSPOROS:
—HERMONASSA: (1) 116 AD *CIRB* 1087; cf. KW pl. 19 no. 281
—NYMPHAION: (2) iv BC *CIRB* 919 (f. Ἀποβαλλίς)
—PANTIKAPAION: (3) i AD ib. 432 A; cf. KW pl. 27 no. 401 (f. Θεόφιλος); (4) i/ii AD *CIRB* 627 (s. Ἔρως)
MACEDONIA: (5) f. ii BC *RE* (9) (Tataki, *Macedonians* p. 392 no. 9) (Lat. Onesimus: s. Πύθων)
MACEDONIA (BOTTIAIA):
—BEROIA: (6) ?61 AD *Ep.Col.* 4. 9; *Const. Apost.* vii 46 (Tataki 975) (s. Φιλήμων: bp.); (7) ii AD *IBer* 345 (Tataki 1326) (Τι. Φλ. Ὀ.); (8) ii-iii AD *IBer* 323 (Tataki 974); (9) s. ii AD *IBer* 310, 3 (s. —μος, ?s. Φίλα, Πιθάνη); (10) ~ ib. l. 3 (s. —μος, ?s. Φίλα, Πιθάνη); (11) ii/iii AD ib. 27 A, 3 (Ὀνήσιμ[ος]: slave?); (12) ~ ib. 27 B, 6 (Μ. Ὀπήνιος Ὀ.)
MACEDONIA (CHALKIDIKE):
—POTIDAIA-KASSANDREIA: (13) iv/iii BC *Ancient Macedonia* I p. 132 n. 20
MACEDONIA (DERRIOPOS):
—STUBERRA: (14) 107 AD *IG* X (2) (2) 325, 95 (Μ. Οὐέττιος Ὀ.)
MACEDONIA (EDONIS):
—PHILIPPOI: (15) ii/iii AD *CIL* III 633 II c, 6 (Pilhofer 163); *CRAI* 1923, p. 277 (date); Collart, *Philippes* pls. 64-5 (Lat. A. Velleius Onesimus)
MACEDONIA (LYNKESTIS):
—HERAKLEIA: (16) i AD *IG* X (2) (2) 75, 25 (Λ. Φάβιος Ὀ.)
MACEDONIA (MYGDONIA):
—LETE (NR.)*: (17) c. 160-180 AD *SEG* XLVII 974; *KGAM Thess.* I 123 (date) (s. Εὐφροσύνη, f. Ὀνησίμη: slave?)
—THESSALONIKE: (18) i BC-i AD *IG* X (2) (1) 129, 2; (19) s. i AD ib. 68, 18; 69, 14 (Μ.' Οὐιούιος Ὀν<ι>ήσιμος); (20) ii AD ib. 393 (Ὀνήσιμ[ος]: s. Ἀπολλωνία); (21) 252 AD ib. 38 B, 20 (Μ. Αὐρ. Ὀ.)
—THESSALONIKE?: (22) ii AD ib. 248 II, 6 (s. Ἀ—); (23) ii-iii AD ib. 820; (24) ~ ib. 862, 2, 4 (Δομίτιος Ὀ.); (25) iii AD ib. 841 (?s. Βαιβία Διονυσία)
—THESSALONIKE*: (26) ii AD ib. 297, 3 (Πετρώνιος Ὀ.: f. Μορρία Ὀρβᾶνα: freed.?)
MACEDONIA (ODOMANTIKE):
—SIRRHA: (27) f. iii AD *SEG* XXX 590, 34 (I f. Αὐρ. Ὀνήσιμος II); (28) ~ ib. l. 34 ([Α]ὐρ. Ὀ.: II s. Ὀνήσιμος I)
MACEDONIA (SINTIKE):
—NEINE: (29) iii AD *IGB* IV 2252; cf. V 5880 (Ὀνήσε[ιμ]ος: f. Αὐρ. Πυρούλας)
SCYTHIA MINOR:
—SACIDAVA*: (30) f. iv AD Popescu, *IGL* 189, 6 (Lat. Valerius Onesim[us])
—TOMIS: (31) ii AD *ISM* II 11, 5; (32) ~ ib. 298 + *SEG* XXXIV 740 (Ἄττιος Ὀ.)
—TOMIS*: (33) imp. *AEMÖ* 14 (1891) p. 31 no. 72 (lead)
THRACE:
—APOLLONIA-SOZOPOLIS: (34) i-ii AD *IGB* I² 401, 13 (s. Πωλίων)
—BYZANTION?: (35) i-ii AD *IByz* 354 (Fıratlı–Robert p. 126 no. 212) (s. Δημήτριος)
—ODESSOS: (36) f. ii AD *IGB* I² 168 (PM 1724); *Dacia* 21 (1977) p. 161 (date) (f. Ἑκατόδωρος)
—PERINTHOS-HERAKLEIA: (37) ii AD *IPerinth* 115; (38) ~ ib. 142 (threptos); (39) iii-iv AD ib. 169 (*AD* 51-2 (1996-7) Mel. p. 365 no. 183) ([Ὀ]νήσιμος)
—PHILIPPOPOLIS-TRIMONTIUM (TERRIT.): (40) ii-iii AD *IGB* III 1168 (Ὀνήσιμο[ς]: slave?)

Ὀνησιφόρος
CIMMERIAN BOSPOROS:
—PANTIKAPAION: (1) iii BC Rostovtsev, *ADZh* p. 143 (vase)
MACEDONIA (BOTTIAIA):
—BEROIA: (2) ii AD *IBer* 489 (Tataki 976); (3) ii/iii AD *IBer* 144 A, 4 (Tataki 1368) (—λιος Ὀ.)
MACEDONIA (MYGDONIA):
—THESSALONIKE: (4) s. vi AD Lemerle pp. 63-5
THRACE:
—NOVAE: (5) ii AD *IGLNovae* 103 (*ILB* 303) (Lat. C. Popillius Onesiphorus)

Ὀνησιφῶν
THRACE:
—HADRIANOPOLIS: (1) imp.? Dumont–Homolle 62 (f. Ζώσιμος); (2) ~ ib. (s. Ζώσιμος)

Ὀνησίων
THRACE:
—NICOPOLIS AD ISTRUM: (1) iii AD *IGB* II 691 (Αὐρ. Ὀ.: s. Διομήδης)

Ὄνησος
CIMMERIAN BOSPOROS:
—ZENONOS CHERSONESOS*: (1) iv BC *SEG* XL 628 (sherd)
SKYTHIA:
—OLBIA-BORYSTHENES: (2) iv BC ib. XXX 958 (vase) (Ὀν[η]σος)

Ὀνήσυλος
MACEDONIA (MYGDONIA):
—THESSALONIKE: (1) i-ii AD *IG* X (2) (1) 243 II, 13 (Μ. Κλ. Ὀ.)

Ὀνίας
MACEDONIA: (1) 111 BC *PDion* 22, 12, [16], [20], 22, [34] (Tataki, *Macedonians* p. 491 no. 181; La'da E1567) (s. Ἀμμώνιος)

Ὀνομακλῆς
MACEDONIA (CHALKIDIKE):
—OLYNTHOS: (1) f. iii BC *IG* XI (4) 531, [3], 11 (Tataki, *Macedonians* p. 141 no. 93) (s. Νικόδημος)
MACEDONIA (EDONIS):
—AMPHIPOLIS: (2) m. iii BC *Polemon* 5 (1952-3) p. 10 no. 327 (Tataki, *Macedonians* p. 58 no. 104) (s. Μελάνιππος)
THRACE:
—BYZANTION: (3) f. iii BC *SEG* XXIII 679 (f. Καλλίστιον)

Ὀνομάστη
MACEDONIA (PAIONIA):
—ARGOS (NR.): (1) ii-iii AD ib. XVI 401, 4 (d. Εὔτροπος, Ἀγάθη)

Ὀνόμαστος
MACEDONIA: (1) 184-182 BC *RE* (2) (Tataki, *Macedonians* p. 393 no. 10)
MACEDONIA (CHALKIDIKE):
—AKANTHOS: (2) f. iv BC *AMNG* III (2) 32 (coin)
MACEDONIA (EORDAIA):
—KELLE?: (3) ii-i BC *EAM* 93; Hatzopoulos, *MI* I p. 94 n. 4 (locn.) (f. Δαβρείας) ?= (4); (4) s. ii BC *EAM* 118 (f. Δαβρείας) ?= (3)
SCYTHIA MINOR:
—ISTROS: (5) v BC Unp. (Avram, defixio) 2, 1, 5 (f. Διογένης)

Ὀνουβρία
THRACE:
—MARONEIA: (1) ii AD Meïmaris–Bakirtzis 4 (*SEG* XLIV 593) + *IThrakAig* E321 (Ὀνουβρ[ία]?)

Ὀξαρδώζιος
SKYTHIA:
—TANAIS: (1) 228 AD *CIRB* 1282, 28 (f. Παπίας)

Ὀξαρδώζις
SKYTHIA:
—TANAIS: (1) 220 AD ib. 1278, 14 (s. Εὐβάρνακος)

Ὀξύμακος
SKYTHIA:
—TANAIS: (1) 225 AD ib. 1279, 21 (Ὀκξύ-)

Ὀξυμένης
MACEDONIA: (1) c. 322-313 BC *IG* VII 4256, 9 (*IOrop* 4); Tataki, *Macedonians* p. 393 no. 11 (f. Αἴσυμνος)

Ὀξύτερπος
MACEDONIA (BOTTIAIA):
—BEROIA: (1) 255 AD *IBer* 138, 8 (Tataki 1059) (Πετρωνιανὸς Θησεὺς ὁ καὶ Ὀ.)

Ὀξυχόλιος
MACEDONIA (EDONIS):
—PHILIPPOI: (1) iii-iv AD *SEG* XLVIII 837, 2 (Pilhofer 387a) (Αὐρ. Ὀ.: Jew)

Ὀπεραῖος
SCYTHIA MINOR:
—KALLATIS: (1) 241-244 AD *ISM* III 74 B, 30

Ὀπλίς
MACEDONIA (MYGDONIA):
—THESSALONIKE: (1) ii-iii AD *IG* X (2) (1) 413

Ὄπλων
CIMMERIAN BOSPOROS:
—PANTIKAPAION: (1) ?f. i AD *CIRB* 527, 1; cf. KW pl. 30 no. 440 (f. Φαρνάκης); (2) ii AD *CIRB* 657 (f. Φαρνάκης, Ἀριστονίκη)

'Οποίη
SKYTHIA:
—SKYTHAI: **(1)** vi/v BC Hdt. iv 78 (m. *'Όρικος*: queen)

'Οπώρα
MACEDONIA (CHALKIDIKE):
—AKANTHOS: **(1)** ii BC *IG* II² 7995 (Tataki, *Macedonians* p. 42 no. 8; *FRA* 287) (d. *Στάχυς*)

'Όπωρις
MACEDONIA (CHALKIDIKE):
—STOLOS?: **(1)** ?351 BC *SEG* XXXVIII 672, 11 (f. *Νίκων*) ?= *(2)*; **(2)** ?350 BC ib. 670, 4, 6 (f. *'Αρχίας*, *'Επικράτης*) ?= *(1)*
MACEDONIA (EDONIS):
—AMPHIPOLIS: **(3)** b. 357 BC Hatzopoulos, *Actes Amphipolis* p. 25 no. 3, 17 (*SEG* XLI 557) (f. *Αἰσχύλος*)

'Όραζος
KOLCHIS:
—VANI (MOD.): **(1)** hell. *MBAH* 12 (1993) p. 69 (brick)

'Οργεύς
MACEDONIA (EDONIS):
—AMPHIPOLIS: **(1)** 242 BC *SEG* XII 373, 20 (Tataki, *Macedonians* p. 59 no. 105) (*'Οργέως* (gen.): f. *Ξενίας*)
—AMPHIPOLIS (NR.): **(2)** a. 357 BC Hatzopoulos, *Actes Amphipolis* p. 43 no. 8, 6 (*SEG* XLI 562); cf. Hatzopoulos, *Actes Chalc.* p. 54 n. 1 (*'Οργέως* (gen.), *'Όργης* (nom.)—Hatzopoulos: f. *Στησίλεως*)

'Ορδάνης
MACEDONIA?: **(1)** s. iv BC *RE* (-); Berve 590; *Anthémonte–Kalindoia* 2 pp. 235-6 (name)

'Ορείνη
MACEDONIA (PELAGONIA):
—DOSTONEIS: **(1)** iii AD *IG* X (2) (2) 201, 4 (d. *Αὐρ. Λυσίμαχος*, *Αὐρηλία*, m. *Λυσίμαχος*, *Νεστόριος*)

'Όρεινος
MACEDONIA (PELAGONIA):
—DOSTONEIS: **(1)** iii AD ib. l. 2-3 (s. *Αὐρ. Λυσίμαχος*, *Αὐρηλία*)

'Ορέντης
SCYTHIA MINOR:
—TOMIS: **(1)** v-vi AD Barnea 12, 3 (Popescu, *IGL* 31) (f. *Μάρκελλος*)

'Ορέστης
KOLCHIS:
—DIOSKOURIAS-SEBASTOPOLIS*: **(1)** ?vi AD *AEp* 1995, no. 1346
MACEDONIA: **(2)** c. 412-398 BC *RE* (8) (Tataki, *Macedonians* p. 393 no. 13); cf. *Macedonia* 2 p. 168; *Historia* 44 (1995) p. 264 (?s. *'Αρχέλαος*, *Κλεοπάτρα*: king)
MACEDONIA (BOTTIAIA):
—BEROIA: **(3)** 223 BC *IBer* 4, 31 (s. *'Αμύντας*); **(4)** 118 BC ib. 134, 22 (*'Ορέςτης*: f. *'Ασκληπιάδης*); **(5)** ii AD ib. 372 (Tataki 84) (*Αἰλ. 'Ο.*); **(6)** f. iii AD *IBer* 98, 5 (Tataki 1172) (*Σεπτίμιος Πομπώνιος Προκλιανὸς 'Ο.*: s. *Προκλιανὸς 'Ορέστης*, *Πομπωνία 'Αρκαρία ἡ καὶ 'Ηγήσιλλα*); **(7)** ~ *IBer* 98, 8 (Tataki 1140) (*Προκλιανὸς 'Ο.*: f. *Σεπτίμιος Πομπώνιος Προκλιανὸς 'Ορέστης*)
MACEDONIA (DERRIOPOS): **(8)** 95 AD *IG* X (2) (2) 300, 1 (II s. *'Ορέστης* I); **(9)** ~ ib. l. 2 (I f. *'Ορέστης* II)
—STUBERRA: **(10)** 74 AD ib. 325, 55 (s. *Θράσων*); **(11)** ~ ib. 326, 19 (s. *Διονύσιος*); **(12)** ~ ib. l. 18-19 (f. *Φιλόξενος*, *Διονύσιος*); **(13)** f. ii AD ib. 73, 3; 336; 343; cf. 4 (*T. Φλάβιος 'Ο.*: f. *T. Φλ. Φιλόξενος*); **(14)** ~ ib. 329; **(15)** 116 AD ib. 327, 14 (f. *'Αλέξανδρος*); **(16)** ~ ib. l. 22 (s. *Διονύσιος*); **(17)** 121 AD ib. 328, 10-11 (*M. 'Ινστέϊος 'Ο.*: f. *M. 'Ινστέϊος Κασσιανὸς Φιλόξενος*)
MACEDONIA (ELIMEIA):
—KOZANI (MOD.): **(18)** ii BC *EAM* 3 (s. *Λιμναῖος*)
MACEDONIA (EORDAIA): **(19)** s. ii AD *ILeukopetra* 134, 8 (f. *Μαρκία*)
—EXOCHI (MOD.)?: **(20)** ii-i BC *EAM* 94 (f. *Λιμναῖος*)
—MAVROPIGI (MOD.): **(21)** ii-i BC ib. 119; cf. *SEG* XLI 578 a (f. *Λαοδίκη*)
MACEDONIA (ORESTIS):
—BATTYNAIOI: **(22)** 192 AD *EAM* 186 I, 48 (s. *'Αριστόλαος*); **(23)** ~ ib. 186 III, 55 (s. *Ζωΐλος*)
—LYKE (NR.): **(24)** f. iii AD ib. 170, 2 (?s. *Γλαῦκος*)
SCYTHIA MINOR:
—TOMIS: **(25)** ii-iii AD *ISM* II 343 (Robert, *Gladiateurs* p. 105 no. 45)
THRACE:
—PHILIPPOPOLIS-TRIMONTIUM: **(26)** c. 210-215 AD *CIL* VI 32640, 7 (Lat. Aurel. Orestes)

'Ορεστίνη
MACEDONIA (BOTTIAIA):
—BEROIA: **(1)** 193 AD *ILeukopetra* 36, 7; 37, 7; 38, 6; 39, 11; 40, 7; 42, 6; 46, 8 (Tataki 55) (*Αἰλ. 'Ορεστείνη*—37)
MACEDONIA (MYGDONIA):
—THESSALONIKE: **(2)** ii-iii AD *IG* X (2) (1) 611, 5 (*Πωλικτήτη 'Ορεστείνη*); **(3)** iii AD ib. 487, 3; p. 160 (stemma) (*'Ερεννία 'Ορεστείνη*: d. *M. 'Ερέννιος 'Ορεστῖνος*, *Δομιτία Λεοντίς*)
MACEDONIA (PIERIA):
—DION: **(4)** ii AD Oikonomos 15 (-*στεί*-, *'Ορεστείνη Ζ(ώη)*?)

'Ορεστίνιος
MACEDONIA (MYGDONIA):
—THESSALONIKE: **(1)** ?ii AD *Thessalonike* 3 (1992) p. 17 pl. 5 (-*στείνη*-)

'Ορεστῖνος
MACEDONIA (MYGDONIA):
—THESSALONIKE: **(1)** iii AD *IG* X (2) (1) 488 A-B; *SEG* XXIX 601 (*M. 'Ερέννιος 'Ορεστεῖνος*: I f. *M. 'Ερέννιος 'Ορεστῖνος* II, *'Ερεννία 'Ορεστίνη*); **(2)** ~ *IG* X (2) (1) 488 A-B; *SEG* XXIX 601 (*M. 'Ερέννιος 'Ορεστεῖνος*: II s. *M. 'Ερέννιος 'Ορεστῖνος* I, *Δομιτία Λεοντίς*)

'Ορέστιος
MACEDONIA (BOTTIAIA):
—ICHNAI: **(1)** imp. *AM* 27 (1902) p. 310 no. 16 (*'Ο. Θεοφίλης*)

'Ορθαγόρας
CIMMERIAN BOSPOROS:
—GORGIPPIA: **(1)** f. iii BC *CIRB* 1137 B II, 37 (f. *Αἶσχρος*); **(2)** ~ ib. l. 39 (s. *Νικιάδης*)
MACEDONIA (KRESTONIA):
—IORON: **(3)** i BC-i AD *SEG* XLVIII 816. 1 (sherd)
MACEDONIA (PIERIA):
—DION: **(4)** iii BC ib. XXXI 629, 5 (s. *Χαρ*—)

'Ορθαγόρης
THRACE:
—APOLLONIA-SOZOPOLIS: **(1)** iv BC *BMNBurgas* 4 (2002) p. 126 no. 23 (*'Ορ[θαγ]όρεω* (gen.): f. *'Αθηναΐς*)

'Ορθόβιος
SCYTHIA MINOR:
—KALLATIS?: **(1)** ii/i BC *IGB* II 867 a, 10 = *ISM* I 219 (v 87); cf. *ISM* III p. 140 (locn.) (f. *Διονύσιος*)

'Ορθόβουλος
SKYTHIA:
—OLBIA-BORYSTHENES: **(1)** iii BC *IOSPE* I² 201 I, 49-50 (s. *Εὐβίοτος*, f. *Δηΐμαχος*); **(2)** ~ ib. 201 II, 22 (f. *Διονύσιος*)

'Όρθρος
MACEDONIA (MYGDONIA):
—THESSALONIKE: **(1)** 179 AD *IG* X (2) (1) 595 + *SEG* XXXVIII 697 (*'Ιούλ. 'Ο.*)

'Όρικος
SKYTHIA:
—SKYTHAI: **(1)** f. v BC Hdt. iv 78 (s. *'Αριαπείθης*, *'Οποίη*)

'Ορνίας
THRACE:
—APOLLONIA-SOZOPOLIS: **(1)** v BC *BMNBurgas* 2 (1965) p. 38 fig. 45 (vase)

'Ορνυμενός
MACEDONIA (CHALKIDIKE):
—APHYTIS: **(1)** ?351 BC *A´ Panell. Synedr. Epigr.* pp. 80-1, 4, 10 (s. *Τιμησιάναξ*)

'Ορόντης
CIMMERIAN BOSPOROS:
—PANTIKAPAION: **(1)** ii/i BC *CIRB* 265; cf. KW pl. 29 no. 417 (s. *Τίλλης*, f. *Τίλλης*, *'Αμμιον*, *'Αλεξάνδρεια*)
MACEDONIA (ORESTIS): **(2)** iv BC Arr., *An.* i 14. 2; *Ind.* xviii 5; *FGrH* 139 F 50. 4; 156 F 1. 2 (Tataki, *Macedonians* p. 206 no. 10) (f. *Περδίκκας*, *'Αλκέτας*, *'Αταλάντη*)
SKYTHIA:
—OLBIA-BORYSTHENES: **(3)** imp. *IOSPE* I² 147, 4 (s. *Σπάδακος*); **(4)** m. i AD ib. 79, 3, 25 (*IByz* 3); *IOSPE* I² 182 (*'Ορόντας*—79: s. *'Αβαβος*); **(5)** ii AD ib. 92, 5 (II s. *'Ορόντης* I); **(6)** ~ ib. l. 6 (I f. *'Ορόντης* II)

'Οροφέρνης
CIMMERIAN BOSPOROS:
—PANTIKAPAION: **(1)** i BC/i AD *CIRB* 320; cf. KW pl. 30 no. 427 (*'Οροφ[έρ]νης*: f. *Φάννας*)

'Ορσίλεως
THRACE:
—APOLLONIA-SOZOPOLIS: **(1)** iv BC *IGB* I² 463 bis, 1 (s. *Δημοῦχος*)

'Ορσοάλτιος
THRACE: **(1)** iii BC Peter, *MTD* p. 249; *Nom. Chron.* 16 (1997) pp. 21-24 (coin) (*'Ορσοαλτίου* (gen.): king)

'Ορστόμηχος
SKYTHIA:
—TANAIS: **(1)** 244 AD *CIRB* 1287, 15 (s. *'Αβδάρακος*)

'Ορτᾶς
MACEDONIA (MYGDONIA):
—KALINDOIA: **(1)** 68-98 AD *SEG* XLII 580, 22; cf. *Anthémonte–Kalindoia* 2 pp. 234-6 (name) (*'Ορτᾶ* (gen.): f. *Πολεμοκράτης*); **(2)** a. 98 AD *SEG* XLII 582, 10 (*'Ορτᾶ* (gen.): f. *Διονύσιος*)

'Ορτήσιος
MACEDONIA (PIERIA):
—DION: **(1)** i BC-i AD ib. XXXVIII 618 = XLVIII 789 (s. *Δ. Σέργιος Μᾶρκος*, *Σεξτία Μάξιμα*)

'Ορτυγᾶς
SKYTHIA:
—TANAIS: **(1)** f. ii AD *CIRB* 1264 A, 11 (f. —*ττας*)

'Ορτυκᾶς
CIMMERIAN BOSPOROS:
—GORGIPPIA: **(1)** 168 AD ib. 1144, 3 (s. *Πάβας*)
—PHANAGOREIA: **(2)** i AD ib. 987, 4; Zgusta, *PNS* 687; **(3)** 179 AD *CIRB* 1000, 2 (*'Ο[ρ]τ[υ]κ[ᾶς]*?: f. *Σακλῆς*)

Ὀρύγιος
CIMMERIAN BOSPOROS:
—ACHILLEION: **(1)** ii AD ib. 1032 (f. *Ἡράκων*)

Ὀρφεύς
MACEDONIA: **(1)** 182-178 BC *PMich* 182, 8; 183 verso, 1; 193 I, 1 (Tataki, *Macedonians* p. 394 no. 15); cf. La'da E1802 (f. *Εἰρήνη*)
MACEDONIA (ELIMEIA):
—KENTRO (MOD.): **(2)** f. iii AD *EAM* 60 c (slave?)
—OBLOSTAI?: **(3)** ?iii AD ib. 65 I b; **(4)** ~ ib. 65 II a
THRACE:
—ODESSOS: **(5)** ii-iii AD *ZPE* 137 (2001) p. 175 (bronze) (s. *Ἄττας*)
—ODESSOS?: **(6)** ii AD *IGB* I^2 51 bis b, 9 (f. *Διονύσιος*)
—PAUTALIA (TERRIT.): **(7)** ii AD ib. IV 2214, 16
—ZONE: **(8)** f. iv BC *SEG* XXIV 640 (*IThrakAig* E415) (s. *Κιλήβυζος*)

Ὄρχαμος
CIMMERIAN BOSPOROS:
—BOSPOROS: **(1)** ?iv BC *CIG* 8566 b (ring) (s. *Γόργιππος*)
—GORGIPPIA: **(2)** f. iii BC *CIRB* 1137 A I, 33 (f. *Δημόχαρις*); **(3)** ~ ib. 1137 B II, 40 (s. *Εὐάνθης*)
—PHANAGOREIA?: **(4)** iii BC *IGAIMK* 104 (1935) p. 308 no. 65 (tile)
THRACE:
—ABDERA: **(5)** c. 395-360 BC May, *Abdera* pp. 205-7 nos. 253-67 (coin); Masson, *OGS* p. 432

Ὀρωΐδυος?
MACEDONIA (PIERIA):
—PYDNA: **(1)** iv BC *GRBS* 43 (2002-3) p. 119 no. 5, 3

Ὁσία
THRACE:
—NICOPOLIS AD ISTRUM (TERRIT.): **(1)** ii/iii AD *SEG* XLIV 640, 2 (biling.) (*Atti XI Congr. Epig.* 1 p. 770) (d. *Φλ. Ἀβάσκαντος, Πριμιγένεια*)

Ὅσιος
CIMMERIAN BOSPOROS:
—PANTIKAPAION: **(1)** i AD *CIRB* 356; cf. KW pl. 43 no. 630

Ὀσμάρακος
SKYTHIA:
—TANAIS: **(1)** 225 AD *CIRB* 1279, 19 (s. *Ἀμαίακος*)

Ὄσπος
SCYTHIA MINOR:
—ISTROS: **(1)** i BC-i AD *ISM* I 191 II, 32 (f. *Πολέμων*) ?= (*2*); **(2)** ~ ib. l. 42 (f. *Σαραπίων*) ?= (*3*) (*1*); **(3)** ~ ib. l. 47 (f. *Ἀριστόνικος*) ?= (*2*)

Ὀστρακίων
CIMMERIAN BOSPOROS:
—KOROKONDAME: **(1)** imp.? *CIRB* 1110 (*Ὀστρακ[ίων]*: s. *Ἀπολλώνιος*)

Ὀτωιος?
KOLCHIS:
—PICHVNARI (MOD.): **(1)** iv BC *DHA* 20 (1994) p. 138 (*Gr. Rom. Settlements in Black Sea* p. 31 (vase)) (gen.?)

Οὐαδέα
MACEDONIA (BISALTIA):
—EUPORIA?: **(1)** ii-iii AD *SEG* XXX 612 (m. *Νίκανδρος*)
MACEDONIA (MYGDONIA):
—THESSALONIKE?: **(2)** ii/iii AD *AEpThess* p. 35 no. 13, 8 (m. *Ἕσπερος, Δείδας*)
MACEDONIA (PIERIA):
—PHYLAKAI?: **(3)** ?i BC Oikonomos 59 = *IG* IX (2) 231 (d. *Καλλιτέλης*)

Οὐαδῆα
MACEDONIA (BOTTIAIA):
—BEROIA: **(1)** ii-i BC *IBer* 184 (*Οὐδδῆα*—lap., *Οὐ(α)δῆα*—ed.: d. *Εὔλαιος*)
MACEDONIA (EORDAIA):
—EXOCHI (MOD.)?: **(2)** ii-i BC *EAM* 94 (d. *Λιμναῖος*)

Οὐαδύρα
MACEDONIA (PIERIA):
—PHYLAKAI?: **(1)** ?i BC Oikonomos 58 = *IG* IX (2) 230 (m. *Ἀμμία*)

Οὐαλεντῖνα
THRACE:
—MEZDRA (MOD.): **(1)** imp. *IGB* II 491; **(2)** ii-iii AD *BIAB* 30 (1967) p. 228 no. 26
—ODESSOS*: **(3)** ii AD *IGB* I^2 175 bis (-τεῖ-: d. *Οὐάλης*)

Οὐαλεντῖνος
THRACE:
—BEROE-AUGUSTA TRAIANA:
——Karasoura: **(1)** ii-iii AD ib. III 1632, 7 (-τεῖ-: s. *Διοφάνης, Κανδίδεα*)

Οὐαλερία
MACEDONIA (BOTTIAIA):
—BEROIA*: **(1)** iii AD *SEG* L 583 B
MACEDONIA (CHALKIDIKE):
—ANTHEMOUS: **(2)** ii AD *Anthémonte–Kalindoia* 1 p. 58 no. A13 (*SEG* L 281) (*Οὐαλ(ε)ρία*: d. *Νικοῦς*)
—POTIDAIA-KASSANDREIA (NR.): **(3)** ?ii AD ib. XLV 773 (d. *Διωνᾶς, Σαβῖνα*)
MACEDONIA (MYGDONIA):
—THESSALONIKE: **(4)** i/ii AD *IG* X (2) (1) 117 (*[Ο]ὐαλερία*)
—THESSALONIKE (NR.): **(5)** imp. *SEG* XXXVIII 687
MACEDONIA (ODOMANTIKE):
—SIRRHA?: **(6)** 157 AD *Belomorski Pregled* 1 (1942) p. 318 no. 1 (Kaphtantzis 10)
MACEDONIA (PAIONIA):
—KAVADARCI (MOD.): **(7)** ii-iii AD *Arheološki Pregled* 2 (1960) p. 108 with pl. XVIII.3 (m. *Ἑρμῆς*); **(8)** ~ *Sp.* 75 (1933) p. 35 no. 104
—STOBOI: **(9)** imp. ib. 71 (1931) p. 46 no. 103
THRACE:
—BISANTHE-PANION: **(10)** iii-v AD *AD* 49-50 (1994-5) Mel. p. 307 no. 132
—NICOPOLIS AD ISTRUM: **(11)** ii-iii AD *IGB* II 689 (d. *Ἀσκληπιάδης*)
—SERDICA: **(12)** 117-138 AD ib. IV 1925 c, 2 (*[Οὐ]αλερία*)

Οὐαλεριανός
MACEDONIA (PIERIA):
—DION: **(1)** ?iii AD Dimitsas 178 (s. *Αὐρ. Λύκος*)
SCYTHIA MINOR:
—TOMIS: **(2)** ii-iii AD *ISM* II 34, 4 (*Οὐαλε[ρ]ιαν[ός]*)
SKYTHIA:
—TYRAS: **(3)** 181 AD *IOSPE* I^2 2, 24 (s. *Ποντικός*)
TAURIS:
—CHERSONESOS: **(4)** imp. ib. 446 (*[Οὐ]αλεριανός*: s. ..ιος); **(5)** ii AD ib. 501 (*Οὐαλεριαν[ός]*)

Οὐαλέριος
MACEDONIA:
—RESEN (MOD.): **(1)** s. iii AD *IG* X (2) (2) 50 (s. *Ἀλέξανδρος, Ἀντιγόνα*)
MACEDONIA (BOTTIAIA):
—EDESSA: **(2)** 180 AD *SEG* XXIV 531, 12 (Tataki, *Edessa* 234) (f. *Ζώπυρος*); **(3)** 196 AD *Arch. Pap.* 22 (1973) p. 209 no. 16 (Tataki, *Edessa* 232) (*[Ο]ὐα[λέ]ριος*); **(4)** iii AD *BSA* 58 (1963) p. 23 no. 4 (Tataki, *Edessa* 233) (s. *Αὐρ. Ζώσιμος, Αὐρ. Βενερία*)
MACEDONIA (DERRIOPOS):
—STUBERRA: **(5)** 74 AD *IG* X (2) (2) 325, 52 (s. *Παράμονος*)
MACEDONIA (MYGDONIA):
—THESSALONIKE*: **(6)** ii AD *SEG* XLVI 821 (terracotta) (-λαί-); **(7)** ii-iv AD *PAE* 1951, p. 172
MACEDONIA (ODOMANTIKE):
—SIRRHA: **(8)** s. ii AD Dimitsas 812, 13 (Kaphtantzis 16) (*Οὐαλέρι[ος]*: f. *Ἰσίδωρος*)
MACEDONIA (ORESTIS):
—BATTYNAIOI: **(9)** 192 AD *EAM* 186 I, 44 (*—ανος ὁ καὶ Ὀ.*: s. *Φίλιππος*)
MACEDONIA (PAIONIA): **(10)** ii-iii AD *Sp.* 71 (1931) p. 229 no. 608 (f. *Κλαυδιανή*)
MACEDONIA (PELAGONIA):
—KERAMIAI (NR.): **(11)** ii-iii AD *IG* X (2) (2) 223 (f. *Παράμονος, Ἄρχος*)
SCYTHIA MINOR:
—CAPIDAVA: **(12)** iii/iv AD Popescu, *IGL* 222 (*Οὐαλέρ[ιος]*)
—ISTROS: **(13)** f. iii AD *ISM* I 218, 11 (f. *Νικίας ὁ καὶ Μᾶρκος*)
—TOMIS: **(14)** ii-iii AD ib. II 238, 1 (s. *Ἀρχέλαος*)
SKYTHIA:
—TANAIS: **(15)** c. 200-225 AD *CIRB* 1277, 12; 1280, 7 (f. *Ἀσκληπιάδης*); **(16)** 228 AD ib. 1282, 13 (f. *Δάδας*)
—TANAIS*: **(17)** f. ii AD ib. 1264 A, 16
THRACE:
—BISANTHE-PANION: **(18)** iv-vi AD *JÖAI* 23 (1926) Beibl. col. 157 no. 94g, 3 (*[Οὐ]αλέριος*)
—DIONYSOPOLIS: **(19)** iii AD *IGB* I^2 14 b, 11 (f. *Αὐρ. Γέρων*) ?= (*21*); **(20)** ~ ib. l. 15 (f. *Αὐρ. Θεόδωρος*) ?= (*21*); **(21)** ~ ib. l. 20 (f. *Αὐρ. Ἀθηνόδωρος*) ?= (*19*) (*20*)
—ODESSOS?: **(22)** ii AD ib. 51 bis a, 4 (f. *Πόπλιος*) ?= (*23*); **(23)** ~ ib. 51 bis b, 5 (f. *Διονύσιος*) ?= (*22*); **(24)** ~ ib. l. 7 (f. *Οὐάλης*)

Οὐαλέρις
CIMMERIAN BOSPOROS:
—PANTIKAPAION: **(1)** f. iii AD *CIRB* 104, 4; 105, 3 (s. *Νικόστρατος*)
MACEDONIA (BOTTIAIA):
—BEROIA: **(2)** ii-iii AD *IBer* 341 (s. *Ἡλιοφῶν, Λύκα*)

Οὐάλης
CIMMERIAN BOSPOROS:
—BOSPOROS: **(1)** 211-217 AD *SEG* XLVII 1196, 3 (*Οὐαλέ<τ>ντι* (dat.): s. *Φιλόκαλος*)
MACEDONIA (BOTTIAIA):
—BEROIA: **(2)** ii/iii AD *IBer* 27 A, 1 (*Οὐάλ[ης]*: slave?)
MACEDONIA (MYGDONIA):
—THESSALONIKE: **(3)** ii/iii AD *IG* X (2) (1) 262 III, 9
—THESSALONIKE*: **(4)** iii AD *SEG* XLVI 826 (terracotta)
MACEDONIA (PAIONIA):
—KAVADARCI (MOD.): **(5)** 325 AD ib. XLIV 561 (f. *Γρανώνιος Γαϊανός*)
MACEDONIA (PELAGONIA): **(6)** ii AD *IG* X (2) (2) 242 (f. *Δαγδας*); **(7)** iii AD ib. 266 (f. *Κάσσανδρος*, ?f. *Αὐρ. Νικολαΐς, Οὐαλητία*)
SCYTHIA MINOR:
—TOMIS: **(8)** ii AD *ISM* II 17, 5 (II s. *Οὐάλης* I); **(9)** ~ ib. l. 5-6 (I f. *Οὐάλης* II, *Λογγῖνος*)
THRACE:
—ABDERA: **(10)** ii AD *BCH* 37 (1913) p. 138 no. 42, 5 (*IThrakAig* E21) (f. *Ῥοῦφος*)
—MARKIANOPOLIS (NR.): **(11)** f. iii AD *IGB* II 832 (*CCET* II (1) 216) (f. *Στατίλις*)
—MEZDRA (MOD.): **(12)** iii AD *IGB* II 493 (I f. *Οὐάλης* II, *Γαΐα*); **(13)** ~ ib. (II s. *Οὐάλης* I)
—NICOPOLIS AD ISTRUM*: **(14)** ii-iii AD *BIAB* 33 (1972) p. 174 (sherd)
—ODESSOS?: **(15)** ii AD *IGB* I^2 51 bis b, 7 (s. *Οὐαλέριος*); **(16)** ~ ib. l. 8 (f. *Ἡραίων*)
—ODESSOS*: **(17)** ii AD ib. 175 bis (f. *Οὐαλεντῖνα*)

—PAUTALIA (TERRIT.): **(18)** iii AD ib. V 5859 (s. *M—*)
—PIZOS: **(19)** 202 AD ib. III 1690 e, 17 (I f. Οὐάλης II); **(20)** ~ ib. l. 17 (II s. Οὐάλης I)
—PLATANIA (MOD.): **(21)** iii AD *SEG* XXXII 676 (Pilhofer 510) (s. Δεντούπης, Μάτα)
—SERDICA: **(22)** ii-iii AD *IGB* IV 1922, 6
—SERDICA (TERRIT.): **(23)** ii-iii AD ib. 2030 (Ο[ὐ]άλης: f. Οὐαλέριος)

Οὐαλία
MACEDONIA (PAIONIA):
—NEAPOLIS? (IZVOR (MOD.): **(1)** ii-iii AD Dimitsas 300, 5 (m. Ἀλέξανδρος, Αἰλιανός)

Οὐαμψάλαγος
SKYTHIA:
—OLBIA-BORYSTHENES: **(1)** ii/iii AD *IOlbia* 52, 4; *IOSPE* I² 103, 5; Zgusta, *PNS* 315 (s. Σωκράτης)

Οὐανουνόβαρος
SKYTHIA:
—TANAIS: **(1)** 244 AD *CIRB* 1287, 25; Zgusta, *PNS* 688 (s. —έστρατος)

Οὐαράζακος
SKYTHIA:
—TANAIS: **(1)** 228 AD *CIRB* 1282, 14; Zgusta, *PNS* 168 (s. Ἡροφάνης)

Οὐαρᾶς
SKYTHIA:
—TANAIS: **(1)** 192 AD *CIRB* 1243, 17; Zgusta, *PNS* 167 (f. Μύρων); **(2)** 228 AD *CIRB* 1282, 30 (f. —αζιο—)

Οὐαργάδακος
SKYTHIA:
—OLBIA-BORYSTHENES: **(1)** ii AD *IOSPE* I² 93, 10; Zgusta, *PNS* 689 (f. Ἀρίστων)

Οὐάρζβαλος
SKYTHIA:
—OLBIA-BORYSTHENES: **(1)** ii AD *IOSPE* I² 91, 9; Zgusta, *PNS* 169 (s. Ἄβραγος)

Οὐαρηούης
KOLCHIS:
—SUKHUMI (MOD.): **(1)** ii AD *Stud. Orbeli* p. 100 (gem); cf. Braund, *Georgia* p. 196 fig. 14 (Οὐαρηόχης?—Tokhtas'ev)

Οὐαρίνιος
MACEDONIA (MYGDONIA):
—THESSALONIKE?: **(1)** ii-iii AD *IG* X (2) (1) 261, 14 (-ρεί-)

Οὐαστόβαλος
SKYTHIA:
—TANAIS: **(1)** 228 AD *CIRB* 1282, 30; Zgusta, *PNS* 170 (s. Στρατόνικος)

Οὐαχώζακος
SKYTHIA:
—OLBIA-BORYSTHENES: **(1)** ii AD *IOSPE* I² 86, 10; Zgusta, *PNS* 178 (Οὐαχώζα[κ]ος: f. Ἀζίαγος)

Οὐειέντων
MACEDONIA (BOTTIAIA):
—BEROIA: **(1)** ii AD *IBer* 84 + *Chiron* 31 (2001) pp. 446-7

Οὐέλιος
MACEDONIA (LYNKESTIS):
—HERAKLEIA: **(1)** i AD *IG* X (2) (2) 75, 17 (Οὐεί-: f. Σεκοῦνδος)

Οὐενερία
MACEDONIA (ODOMANTIKE):
—GAZOROS: **(1)** 144 AD *SEG* XXX 599, 2 (Pilhofer 552); cf. *SEG* XXXVII 579 ([Ο]ὐ(ε)νερία: d. Μωμώ, ?d. Γάϊος)

Οὐένετος
MACEDONIA (BOTTIAIA):
—BEROIA: **(1)** ii BC *IBer* 178 (f. Ἀντιγόνα, Ἀρτεμίκλεια)

Οὐέρουλα
THRACE:
—SERDICA: **(1)** 117-138 AD *IGB* IV 1925 c, 11

Οὐεττία
MACEDONIA (BOTTIAIA):
—BEROIA: **(1)** s. i AD *IBer* 126 (Tataki 993)

Οὐέττιος
MACEDONIA (PELAGONIA):
—DOSTONEIS?: **(1)** ii-iii AD *IG* X (2) (2) 181 (f. Ἄδυμος)

Οὐζίαγος?
SKYTHIA:
—OLBIA-BORYSTHENES: **(1)** iii AD *IOSPE* I² 135, 9; Zgusta, *PNS* 171 (Οὐζία[γ]ος: f. Σηνήκας)

Οὐηράτιος
MACEDONIA (DERRIOPOS):
—STUBERRA: **(1)** 74 AD *IG* X (2) (2) 326, 42 (f. Πούδης)

Οὐῆρος
MACEDONIA (LYNKESTIS):
—HERAKLEIA: **(1)** i AD ib. 75, 41-42 (f. Μᾶρκος, Ἰούλιος)
MACEDONIA (MYGDONIA):
—THESSALONIKE: **(2)** ii AD ib. X (2) (1) 114, 7 (s. Κ. Ἄννιος Σεκοῦνδος, Φλωρία Ἀρέσκουσα)

Οὐίβιος
MACEDONIA (MYGDONIA):
—THESSALONIKE: **(1)** 129 AD ib. 521, 2 (s. Σεραπᾶς, Ῥεία Ζωσίμη)
MACEDONIA (SINTIKE):
—PARTHIKOPOLIS (TERRIT.): **(2)** ii AD *IGB* IV 2302, 2 (f. Ἀρτεμίδωρος)

Οὐίκτωρ
THRACE:
—DRAGANOVEC (MOD.): **(1)** f. iii AD ib. V 5308 (*CCET* II (2) 495) (s. Οὐ—)

Οὐιλις
CIMMERIAN BOSPOROS:
—BOSPOROS?: **(1)** ?ii BC *JDAI* 23 (1908) p. 73; Courby, *Les vases grecs* p. 412 (vase) (potter)

Οὐλπία
MACEDONIA (PIERIA):
—DION: **(1)** f. iii AD Oikonomos 35; cf. Spiliopoulou-Donderer, *KGN* p. 195 no. D12 (date)
THRACE:
—BEROE-AUGUSTA TRAIANA: **(2)** ii-iii AD *IGB* III 1604 (d. Πωλλίων)
—BISANTHE-PANION: **(3)** iii-v AD *AD* 49-50 (1994-5) Mel. p. 307 no. 132

Οὐλπιανός
THRACE:
—PAUTALIA: **(1)** s. ii AD *SEG* XLVI 864, 11 (f. Στρυμόνις)
—TAMNO CAVE (MOD.): **(2)** ii-iii AD *IGB* II 751 e (Οὐλπ[ι]ανός)

Οὐμβηούαρος
SKYTHIA:
—OLBIA-BORYSTHENES: **(1)** ii AD *IOSPE* I² 96, 2 ([Οὐμβη]ούαρος?: f. Παπίας); **(2)** ~ ib. 101, 7 (s. Οὔργβαζος); **(3)** f. ii AD ib. 95, 5; Zgusta, *PNS* 317 (-ορος: f. Οὔργβαζος)

Οὐολογαίσης
THRACE:
—BESSOI: **(1)** 11 BC D.C. liv 34. 5

Οὐράνιος
MACEDONIA (MYGDONIA):
—THESSALONIKE?: **(1)** iii/iv AD *IG* X (2) (1) 842, 1, 6

Οὔργβαζος
SKYTHIA:
—OLBIA-BORYSTHENES: **(1)** ii AD *IOSPE* I² 101, 7; Zgusta, *PNS* 172 (f. Οὐμβηούαρος); **(2)** f. ii AD *IOSPE* I² 95, 4 (s. Οὐμβηούαρος)

Οὔργιος
CIMMERIAN BOSPOROS:
—PANTIKAPAION: **(1)** i AD *CIRB* 362; cf. KW pl. 13 no. 181; Zgusta, *PNS* 173
SKYTHIA:
—TANAIS: **(2)** ii AD *CIRB* 1262, 18 (f. Ὀμψάλακος)

Οὐροάστιρος
SKYTHIA:
—TANAIS: **(1)** 228 AD ib. 1282, 20; Zgusta, *PNS* 318 (s. Σόρχακος)

Οὐρσικῖνος
SCYTHIA MINOR:
—KALLATIS: **(1)** iii-iv AD *SEG* XXIV 1044

Οὔρσουλος
THRACE:
—BEROE-AUGUSTA TRAIANA (TERRIT.): **(1)** ii-iii AD *IGB* III 1772 (f. Ἀπολλόδωρος)

Οὐσίγασος
SKYTHIA:
—OLBIA-BORYSTHENES: **(1)** ii AD *IOSPE* I² 92, 6; Zgusta, *PNS* 174 (s. Σίραχος) ?= (Οὔσιγος (*1*))

Οὔσιγος
SKYTHIA:
—OLBIA-BORYSTHENES: **(1)** ii AD *IOSPE* I² 686, 4 (*VDI* 1975 (1), p. 69); Zgusta, *PNS* 174 (Οὐσίγ(ασ)ος?: s. Σίραχος) ?= (Οὐσίγασος (*1*))

Οὔστανος
CIMMERIAN BOSPOROS:
—PANTIKAPAION: **(1)** iv AD *CIRB* 742 (s. Νικηφόρος)
SKYTHIA:
—TANAIS: **(2)** 220 AD ib. 1278, 26; Zgusta, *PNS* 176 (s. Ζη—)

Ὀφέλλας
MACEDONIA (BOTTIAIA):
—PELLA: **(1)** c. 360-309 BC *RE* (1); Berve 598 (*PP* 15062; Tataki, *Macedonians* p. 158 no. 68) (s. Σιληνός)
MACEDONIA (CHALKIDIKE):
—OLYNTHOS: **(2)** s. iv BC *RE* (2); Berve 599; Arist., *Oec.* 1353 a 5-14 (Tataki, *Macedonians* p. 141 no. 94)
MACEDONIA (EDONIS):
—AMPHIPOLIS: **(3)** 287-245 BC *IOrop* 21, 6 (Tataki, *Macedonians* p. 59 no. 106) (Ὀφέλ[α]ς: s. Φιλήμων)

Ὀχάζανος
CIMMERIAN BOSPOROS:
—TYRITAKE: **(1)** inc. *SEG* XLV 1028. 17 (?s. Φαρ(—))

Ὀχοαρζάνης
SKYTHIA:
—TANAIS: **(1)** 188 AD *CIRB* 1242, 19; Zgusta, *PNS* 177 (s. Πάτεις)

Ὀχωδίακος
SKYTHIA:
—TANAIS: **(1)** 225 AD *CIRB* 1279, 18; Zgusta, *PNS* 178 (s. Δούλας); **(2)** ~ *CIRB* 1280, 13 (f. Ἄζος); **(3)** ~ ib. l. 15 (Ὀχ[ω]δίακος: f. Στόρμαις); **(4)** ~ ib. l. 19 (Ὀχωδ[ίακ]ος: f. Ἔρως); **(5)** c. 225-250 AD ib. 1288, 6 ([Ὀχ]ωδίακος); **(6)** 228 AD ib. 1282, 23 (s. Δημήτριος)

Ὀχωζίακος
SKYTHIA:
—TANAIS: **(1)** 244 AD ib. 1287, 4; Zgusta, *PNS* 178 (f. Νυμφέρως); **(2)** ~ *CIRB* 1287, 13 (Ὀχ[ω]ζίακος: s. Πόπλιος)

Ὀψίτης
KOLCHIS:
—ABASGOI: **(1)** m. vi AD *PLRE* III (2); *RE* (2) (king)
—LAZOI: **(2)** f. vi AD *PLRE* III (1); *RE* (1) (king)

Π

Πάβας
CIMMERIAN BOSPOROS:
—GORGIPPIA: (1) m. ii AD *Eirene* 7 (1968) p. 67, 21; Zgusta, *PNS* 602 (f. *Χρηστοῦς*); (2) s. ii AD *CIRB* 1145, 6 (f. *Φαρνάκης*); (3) 168 AD ib. 1144, 3 (*Πάβας*: f. *Ὀρτυκᾶς*); (4) ii/iii AD ib. 1179, 42 (s. *Φαρνάκης*)
—GORGIPPIA?: (5) ii/iii AD ib. 1232, 12 (f. *Γλύκων*)
SKYTHIA:
—TANAIS: (6) 104 AD ib. 1259, 14 (f. *Ἡρακλείδης*) ?= (7); (7) ~ ib. l. 20 (f. *Σούσας*) ?= (6)

Παγγαῖον
THRACE: (1) iii BC *IG* II^2 8920 (*FRA* 2563)

Πάγκαλος
SKYTHIA:
—OLBIA-BORYSTHENES: (1) iv BC *SEG* XXX 958 (vase) (*Πάγκα(λος)*?)
THRACE:
—ZONE: (2) s. iv BC *PAE* 1969, p. 64 with pl. 76 β (*IThrakAig* E425) (f. *Σωκλῆς*)

Πάγκαρπος
CIMMERIAN BOSPOROS:
—PANTIKAPAION: (1) i-ii AD Vaulina–Wąsowicz pl. 124 no. 63 B, 13
SKYTHIA:
—TANAIS: (2) ii AD *CIRB* 1262, 26 (*Πάν-*: s. *Ἔρως*)

Παγκάστα
MACEDONIA (BOTTIAIA):
—AIGAI: (1) s. iv BC *SEG* XXXV 790; cf. XLVIII 873

Παγκλῆς
CIMMERIAN BOSPOROS:
—PANTIKAPAION: (1) 275-278 AD *CIRB* 36, 38 (*Πανκλ[ῆς]*: f. *Ἀριστίων*)

Παγκράτης
SCYTHIA MINOR:
—ISTROS: (1) i AD *ISM* I 200, 10 (*Παν-*: s. *Ζεισκεαγις*); (2) 138 AD ib. 193 I, 25 (*Παν-*: f. *Εὐξενίδης*)
SKYTHIA:
—OLBIA-BORYSTHENES: (3) iii BC *IOSPE* I^2 201 I, 31 (f. *Θεοκύδης*)

Παγκράτιος
THRACE:
—PERINTHOS-HERAKLEIA: (1) c. 304 AD *Act. Sanct.* Oct. IX p. 547 (Lat. Pancrati (gen.))

Παγκράτις
MACEDONIA (MYGDONIA):
—THESSALONIKE: (1) ii-iii AD *AD* 22 (1967) Chron. p. 391 (*Παν-*)

Παγουρίων
CIMMERIAN BOSPOROS:
—GORGIPPIA: (1) f. iii BC *CIRB* 1137 A I, 51 (s. *Γοργίας*); (2) ~ ib. 1137 B I, 52 (f. *Γοργίας*); (3) ~ ib. 1137 B II, 24 (*Παγο[υρίων]*?: f. *Ἀπήμαντος*)

Παγχάρεια
MACEDONIA (EDONIS):
—PHILIPPOI: (1) iv-v AD Feissel, *RICM* 241 (Pilhofer 77) (*Πανχάρια*)
THRACE:
—MARONEIA: (2) v-vi AD *SEG* XLIX 892, 2 (*IThrakAig* E357) (*Πανχάρια*)

Παγχάρης
THRACE:
—MESAMBRIA: (1) i BC-i AD *IGB* I^2 340 (*Παν-*: f. *Παρμένων*, *Μᾶτρις*, *Οἰνίας*)

Πάγχαρις
SCYTHIA MINOR:
—KALLATIS: (1) 241-244 AD *ISM* III 74 A, 31 (*Πάν-*: s. *Διονύσιος*)

Πάγχαρμος
THRACE:
—STRYME? (NR.): (1) m. iv BC *SEG* XXVII 336 (*IThrakAig* E155) (f. *Λαμπυρίς*)

Πάδαγος
SKYTHIA:
—OLBIA-BORYSTHENES: (1) f. i AD *IOlbia* 42, 4; Zgusta, *PNS* 77; cf. Vinogradov–Kryžickij p. 144 (date) (f. *Δάδαγος*)

Πάδακος
SKYTHIA:
—OLBIA-BORYSTHENES: (1) s. i AD *IOlbia* 85, 6 with pl. 42 (*IOSPE* I^2 104); Zgusta, *PNS* 77 (*Πάδα[κ]ος*?, *Πίδα[ν]ος*—*IOlbia*: s. [.]αδάκου (gen.))

Πάης
CIMMERIAN BOSPOROS:
—TYRITAKE: (1) v-vi AD *MIA* 25 (1952) p. 101 (pithos)

Παίβης
MACEDONIA (EDONIS):
—PHILIPPOI: (1) ii/iii AD *CIL* III 633 II c, 5 (Pilhofer 163); *AM* 33 (1908) p. 40 (name); *CRAI* 1923, p. 277 (date); Collart, *Philippes* pls. 64-5 (Lat. A. Velleius Paibes)
—PHILIPPOI (TERRIT.): (2) ?ii AD *BIAB* 16 (1950) pp. 14-15 no. 11, 6 (Pilhofer 649) (Lat. Faibis (gen.): f. *Βενδίς*)
MACEDONIA (ODOMANTIKE):
—GAZOROS (TERRIT.): (3) 106 AD *SEG* XXX 596, 6 (Pilhofer 555) (f. (nat.) *Διοσκουρίδης*)
—GAZOROS (TERRIT.)?: (4) hell. *BCH* 24 (1900) p. 306 (*Παίβεω* (gen.): f. *Δειγηπις*)
—SIRRHA: (5) f. iii AD *SEG* XXX 590, 16 (*Αὐρ. Π.*: s. *Μέστος*)
—SIRRHA (NR.): (6) ii-iii AD *Tekmeria* 6 (2001) p. 10 (*SEG* XLIX 743) (*Παεί-*: f. *Ἰσιάς*)
MACEDONIA (SINTIKE):
—PARTHIKOPOLIS (TERRIT.): (7) 152 AD *Melnik* I p. 166 no. 6 (s. *Μουκάσης*, f. *Μουκάσης*)
THRACE:
—BARGALA: (8) ii-iii AD *SEG* XLIV 517 (*Παιβήδου* (gen.))
—PAUTALIA (TERRIT.): (9) iv AD *Pernik* I p. 209 (pithos) (Lat. Paibi (gen.): ?f. *Χρήστος*)

Παιβίλας
MACEDONIA (EDONIS):
—PHILIPPOI (NR.): (1) ii AD *BCH* 24 (1900) p. 306 no. 2 (Pilhofer 29) (*Παιβίλα* (gen.): f. *Σούδιος*)

Παιβίνη
THRACE:
—APOLLONIA-SOZOPOLIS: (1) iv BC *IGB* I^2 430

Παιβις
MACEDONIA (EDONIS):
—AMPHIPOLIS: (1) ii-iii AD *AE* 1932, Chron. p. 1 no. 6 + *Thrakika* 13 (1940) p. 22 *Δ*; cf. *Epigraphica* 37 (1975) p. 26 (s. *Σάνθος*)
THRACE?: (2) s. ii BC *PTeb* 80, 3 (*PP* 10860; Velkov 221)

Παιδάρχη
THRACE:
—APOLLONIA-SOZOPOLIS: (1) v/iv BC *IGB* I^2 437 (d. *Πάρμυς*); (2) iv BC *BMNBurgas* 4 (2002) p. 122 no. 11 (d. *Ποσειδώνιος*)
—APOLLONIA-SOZOPOLIS?: (3) ?iv BC *IGB* I^2 379 (or Thrace Anchialos: d. *Πόσις*)
—ODESSOS: (4) v/iv BC ib. 96 (d. *Ἀνθεστήριος*)

Παιδέρως
MACEDONIA (BOTTIAIA):
—BEROIA: (1) ii/iii AD *IBer* 145, 6 (Tataki 763) (*Κορνήλιος Π.*)

Παίζιος
MACEDONIA (EDONIS):
—PHILIPPOI (DRAMA (MOD.)): (1) iv BC Dimitsas 1063 (1101; Pilhofer 499) (s. *Πηδίζας*)

Παίζουσα
THRACE:
—NICOPOLIS AD ISTRUM (TERRIT.): (1) ii AD *ILB* 422 (Lat. Sippia Paezusa)

Παΐλλος
MACEDONIA (MYGDONIA):
—THESSALONIKE: (1) 223 BC *IG* X (2) (1) 2, 5 (f. *Γαιτέας*)

Παίρακος
CIMMERIAN BOSPOROS:
—PANTIKAPAION: (1) i AD *CIRB* 480 (s. *Σπάρτοκος*)

Παιρισάδης
CIMMERIAN BOSPOROS:
—BOSPOROS: (1) c. 370-310 BC *RE* (1); Rhodes–Osborne 64, 1, 9, 12, 22, etc.; *CIRB* 1, 2; [2]; [5]; 9; 10; 11; 36 B, 36?; 113; 971; 1014; 1015; 1039; [1040]; 1041; [1042]; *VDI* 2002 (4), p. 59; *IGAIMK* 104 (1935) pp. 308-10 nos. 67-8 (tile); Zgusta, *PNS* 567 (s. *Λεύκων*, f. *Σάτυρος*, *Πρύτανις*, *Εὔμηλος*: king); (2) 310 BC *RE* (6) (s. *Σάτυρος*); (3) c. 310-245 BC ib. (2); *CIRB* 20; 21; 23; 24; 25; [26]; 822; *SEG* XXXII 788: *SB* 7263, 5 (s. *Σπάρτοκος*, f. *Λεύκων*, *Σπάρτοκος*: king); (4) f. iii BC *SEG* XXXIX 701. 5-6 (XLV 997. 4) (*Παιρισάτου* (gen.): king); (5) f. ii BC *RE* (3); *CIRB* 75, 3; 1044, 2; cf. *Historia* 4 (1955) pp. 424 ff. (*Π. Φιλομήτωρ*: I f. *Παιρισάδης* II: king); (6) m. ii BC *RE* (4); *CIRB* 75, 1, 3; 1044, 1; *SEG* XXIII 314, 4; XXXVII 674 (II s. *Παιρισάδης* I *Φιλομήτωρ*, *Καμασαρύη*, f. *Παιρισάδης* III: king); (7) c. 150-109 BC *RE* (5); *IOSPE* I^2 352, 35, 42; *SEG* XXXVII 674 (III s. *Παιρισάδης* II: king)

Παιρίσαλος
CIMMERIAN BOSPOROS:
—ACHILLEION (NR.): (1) i/ii AD *CIRB* 1022 (*-ρεί-*)
—KIMMERIKON: (2) iii AD ib. 946 (s. *Κοσοῦς*)
—PANTIKAPAION: (3) ii-i BC ib. 266; Zgusta, *PNS* 567 (s. *Ἡρακλείδης*); (4) i AD *CIRB* 347 (s. *Ἀκκᾶς*); (5) ~ ib. 481; cf. KW pl. 17 no. 253 (I f. *Παιρίσαλος* II); (6) ~ *CIRB* 481; cf. KW pl. 17 no. 253 (II s. *Παιρίσαλος* I); (7) ~ *CIRB* 509; cf. KW pl. 27 no. 404 (s. *Σαβίων*, *Χρήστη*); (8) f. i AD *CIRB* 482; cf. KW pl. 15 no. 222 (*-λοῦς*: s. *Ταρούλας*); (9) ii AD *CIRB* 698 (s. *Σαύροφος*, f. *Ῥευσίναλος*)
—TYRITAKE: (10) i AD ib. 903 (f. *Διογένης*)
SKYTHIA:
—TANAIS (NR.): (11) ii AD ib. 1314

Παιριφάνης
CIMMERIAN BOSPOROS:
—PANTIKAPAION: (1) i AD *CIRB* 510; cf. Zgusta, *PNS* 699 (*[Π]αιριφάνης*?—Latyshev, *[Σ]αιρίφανος*—*CIRB*, *Σαιρεφάνης*—KW: s. *Ἀργόδας*)

—PANTIKAPAION (NR.): **(2)** i BC *CIRB* 960; cf. KW pl. 48 no. 676 (*Παιρ(ι)φάνης*: s. *Μοιραγένης*)

Παῖσις
THRACE: **(1)** ii BC *SEG* I 556 (Velkov 222; La'da E778) (s. *Διζάπολις*)

Παῖτος
MACEDONIA (LYNKESTIS):
—HERAKLEIA?: **(1)** 235 AD *IG* X (2) (2) 136, 4 (s. *Αὐρ. Διογένης, Αὐρ. Φίλα*)
THRACE:
—PHILIPPOPOLIS-TRIMONTIUM (TERRIT.): **(2)** ii AD *IGB* III 1102 (s. *Πρόκλος*)

Παιών
MACEDONIA (CHALKIDIKE):
—POTIDAIA-KASSANDREIA?: **(1)** 575-550 BC *BCH* 95 (1971) pp. 589-97; *LSAG*^{2} p. 479 no. A (bronze) (*-hōν*)

Παιώνιος
MACEDONIA (CHALKIDIKE):
—MENDE: **(1)** c. 421 BC *RE* (8); Overbeck 825; 851-2; *IvOl* 259 (ML 74; Tataki, *Macedonians* p. 121 no. 16) (sculptor)
MACEDONIA (MYGDONIA):
—THESSALONIKE?: **(2)** iii AD *IG* X (2) (1) 889 (*Πεώνιος* (n. pr.?))
THRACE:
—APOLLONIA-SOZOPOLIS: **(3)** iii/ii BC *IGB* I^{2} 463 ter, 5 (n. pr.?)

Πάκκις
THRACE:
—PHILIPPOPOLIS-TRIMONTIUM (TERRIT.): **(1)** ii-iii AD ib. III 1447

Πάκουρος
THRACE:
—NOVAE: **(1)** iii AD ib. II 741, 7 (s. *Σαβινιανός, Κορινθία*)

Πάκτωλος
MACEDONIA (MYGDONIA):
—THESSALONIKE: **(1)** iii AD *IG* X (2) (1) 546, 2 (*Φλ. Π. ὁ καὶ Ἀκάκιος*: f. *Αὐρ. Ἀκάκις ὁ καὶ Εὐτύχις, Αὐρ. Λεόντις*)

Πάλακος
SKYTHIA:
—SKYTHAI: **(1)** s. ii BC *RE* (-); *IOSPE* I^{2} 352, 7, 21 (*Syll*^{3} 709) (s. *Σκίλουρος*: king)

Παλάμανδρος
MACEDONIA (BOTTIAIA):
—BEROIA: **(1)** f. i BC *IBer* 205 (Tataki 1005) (s. *Γαυάνης*)

Παλλάς
MACEDONIA (MYGDONIA):
—THESSALONIKE: **(1)** ii AD *IG* X (2) (1) 304, 4 (d. *Ἑρμέρως, Τορευμάτιον*)

Παλλᾶς
CIMMERIAN BOSPOROS:
—PANTIKAPAION?: **(1)** ii BC *KSIA* 83 (1961) p. 39 (amph.) (*Παλλᾶνος* (gen.): f. *Στάτιος*)

Παλμᾶτος
THRACE:
—PHILIPPOPOLIS-TRIMONTIUM: **(1)** c. 303 AD *Anal. Boll.* 31 (1912) p. 192

Παμμύριος
MACEDONIA (MYGDONIA):
—THESSALONIKE: **(1)** iii AD *IG* X (2) (1) 606 ([*Ἰού*]*λ. Π.*)

Παμφίλα
MACEDONIA (BOTTIAIA):
—BEROIA: **(1)** ii AD *IBer* 20, 3 (Tataki 1095) (*Πο. Π.*); **(2)** ii-iii AD *IBer* 28 (Tataki 1006) (m. *Μένανδρος*); **(3)** s. ii AD *IBer* 269 (Tataki 1387) ([*Παμ*]*φίλα*)
MACEDONIA (MYGDONIA):
—THESSALONIKE: **(4)** i AD *IG* X (2) (1) 310, 3 (*Λευκιλία Π.*); **(5)** ~ ib. 399 (*Οὐολκακία Π.*: ?m. *Οὐολκάκιος Νίγερ*); **(6)** ii-iii AD ib. 618 (*Φλ. Πανφί*[*λα*])

Πάμφιλος
CIMMERIAN BOSPOROS:
—PANTIKAPAION: **(1)** i AD *CIRB* 388 (?s. *Καλλίστη*); **(2)** ~ ib. 483 (I f. *Πάμφιλος* II); **(3)** ~ ib. (II s. *Πάμφιλος* I); **(4)** ~ ib. 484 ([*Πά*]*νφιλ*[*ος*]: s. *Διομήδης*); **(5)** f. i AD ib. 485 (*Πάν-*: I f. *Πάμφιλος* II); **(6)** ~ ib. (*Πάν-*: II s. *Πάμφιλος* I); **(7)** i/ii AD ib. 609 (*Πάμφιλ*[*ος*]); **(8)** 275-278 AD ib. 36, 32 (*Πάμφιλ*(*ος*): f. *Φαδιους*)
MACEDONIA (BOTTIAIA):
—BEROIA: **(9)** ii AD *IBer* 20, 3-4 (Tataki 1229) (*Τερεντιανὸς Π.*)
—PELLA: **(10)** iii BC Akamatis, *Amph. Pellas* pp. 41-2 nos. PAR51-3 (amph.) (*SEG* L 613)
MACEDONIA (CHALKIDIKE):
—TORONE: **(11)** f. iv BC *IG* II^{2} 10454 (Tataki, *Macedonians* p. 192 no. 13; *FRA* 7145)
MACEDONIA (EDONIS):
—AMPHIPOLIS: **(12)** iv BC *RE* (30); Overbeck 1746-53 (Tataki, *Macedonians* p. 59 no. 107) (painter)
MACEDONIA (MYGDONIA):
—KALINDOIA: **(13)** 68-98 AD *SEG* XLII 580, 76 (f. *Βίθυς*)
—THESSALONIKE: **(14)** c. 40-30 BC *IG* X (2) (1) 83, 2; 84 (*KGAM Thess.* I 47); *IG* X (2) (1) 109, 2 (*Π. Σαλάριος Π.*); **(15)** iii AD *SEG* XXXVIII 711 (*Αὐρ. Π.*)
THRACE:
—ABDERA: **(16)** s. v BC *IThrakAig* E13 ([*Πά*]*μφιλος*)
—SERREION?: **(17)** iv BC *AEMTh* 10 (1996) p. 903 (bullet)

Πανάρμοστος
THRACE:
—BYZANTION: **(1)** ?464 BC *IG* I^{3} 1144, 121 ([*Παν*]*άρμοστο*[*ς*]?, [*Φιλ*]*άρμοστο*[*ς*]—ed.)

Πανάστης
THRACE: **(1)** iii AD *SEG* XLVIII 1084 (s. *Δριγίσταs*)

Πάναυχος
SKYTHIA:
—TANAIS: **(1)** 225 AD *CIRB* 1279, 18 (s. *Ἀρ—ος*)

Πανδίων
SKYTHIA:
—OLBIA-BORYSTHENES: **(1)** iii BC *IOSPE* I^{2} 201 I, 45 (f. *Εὐρησίβιος*)
THRACE:
—BEROE-AUGUSTA TRAIANA: **(2)** iii AD *IGB* III 1573, 14 (*Αὐρ.* [*Π*]*ανδίων*: s. *Ἑρμόδωρος*)

Πανέρως
CIMMERIAN BOSPOROS:
—MYRMEKION (NR.): **(1)** f. ii AD *CIRB* 892 (s. *Κοσοῦς*)
—PANTIKAPAION: **(2)** i AD ib. 403 (f. *Ἔρως*)
SKYTHIA:
—OLBIA-BORYSTHENES: **(3)** f. ii AD *IOSPE* I^{2} 85, 5 ([*Π*]*ανέρως*: s. *Ἔρως*)

Πανήγορος
MACEDONIA: **(1)** 334 BC Berve 602 (Tataki, *Macedonians* p. 395 no. 4) (s. *Λυκαγόρας*)

Πάνθεια
SCYTHIA MINOR:
—TOMIS: **(1)** ii AD *ISM* II 207 (*-θια*)
THRACE:
—SERDICA: **(2)** ii-iii AD *IGB* IV 1943, 2 (*Eastern cults* p. 195 no. 7) (*-θια*)

Πάνθηρ
CIMMERIAN BOSPOROS:
—PHANAGOREIA: **(1)** iii-ii BC *IGAIMK* 104 (1935) p. 308 no. 66; *MIA* 56 (1957) p. 225; 57 (1956) p. 152 (tile)

Πανθήρα
SCYTHIA MINOR:
—TOMIS: **(1)** ii-iii AD *ISM* II 372 (*GVI* 987; *CCET* IV 32) (d. *Ὕλας, Ματρώνα*)

Πανθήριος
THRACE:
—PHILIPPOPOLIS-TRIMONTIUM: **(1)** c. 303 AD *Anal. Boll.* 31 (1912) p. 192

Πανίσκος
MACEDONIA: **(1)** 113 BC *PDion* 21, 29 (Tataki, *Macedonians* p. 491 no. 182); cf. La'da E1452 (f. *Ἀχιλλεύς*); **(2)** 5 AD *CPR* I 224, 3 (*Πα*[*ν*]*ίσκος*: f. *Ἡρακλείδης*)

Παννόνιος
SCYTHIA MINOR:
—KALLATIS: **(1)** 241-244 AD *ISM* III 74 B, 16

Παννυχίς
MACEDONIA (BOTTIAIA):
—BEROIA: **(1)** 262 AD *IBer* 52, 3 (Tataki 219) (*Ἀππία Π.*)

Πάννυχος
CIMMERIAN BOSPOROS:
—GORGIPPIA: **(1)** 173-210 AD *CIRB* 1134 E, 6 (*Πάν*(*ν*)*υχος*—Vinogradov: s. *Πόθος*); **(2)** ii/iii AD ib. 1179, 46 (*Π*[*ά*]*ννυ*[*χ*]*ος*: s. *Φαρνακίων*)
—PANTIKAPAION: **(3)** ii AD ib. 95, 4 (f. *Πάπας*)
MACEDONIA (BOTTIAIA):
—BEROIA: **(4)** ii-iii AD *IBer* 270 (Tataki 1009) (f. *—ιμα*)
MACEDONIA (SINTIKE):
—PARTHIKOPOLIS: **(5)** 98 or 215 AD *IGB* V 5915
SKYTHIA:
—TANAIS: **(6)** 192 AD *CIRB* 1243, 18 (I f. *Πάννυχος* II); **(7)** ~ ib. l. 18 (*Πάν*[*νυ*]*χος*: II s. *Πάννυχος* I)

Πανσθένης
THRACE:
—PHILIPPOPOLIS-TRIMONTIUM: **(1)** c. 303 AD *Anal. Boll.* 31 (1912) p. 192

Πάντα
THRACE:
—KALLIPOLIS: **(1)** i BC-i AD *ISestos* 15 (d. *Θεόδοτος*)

Πανταγάθη
CIMMERIAN BOSPOROS:
—PANTIKAPAION: **(1)** imp. *CIRB* 801 (m. *Ματρόδωρος*)

Πantάγαθος
CIMMERIAN BOSPOROS:
—PANTIKAPAION: **(1)** i/ii AD ib. 80, 2; cf. KW pl. 33 no. 454; **(2)** ii AD *AGSP* p. 351 pl. 160 no. 30 (ring); **(3)** f. ii AD *CIRB* 89, 3
SKYTHIA:
—TANAIS: **(4)** ii AD ib. 1262, 22 ([*Π*]*αντάγαθος*: s. *Λίβανος*); **(5)** f. ii AD ib. 1264 A, 9 (s. *Στρατόνικος*)

Παντάγνωτος
TAURIS:
—CHERSONESOS: **(1)** iv/iii BC *SEG* XXXVI 696 (f. *Διονύσιος*)

Πάνταινος
MACEDONIA (CHALKIDIKE):
—POTIDAIA-KASSANDREIA:

——(Hippolyteis): **(1)** c. 285 BC ib. XXIX 600, 3; cf. XXXVIII 621; Hatzopoulos, *Donation* pp. 17-21 (date) (s. *Σύμμαχος*)

Παντακιανός
MACEDONIA (BOTTIAIA):
—BEROIA: **(1)** 212 AD *ILeukopetra* 63, 7 (Tataki 299) (*Αὐρ. Ποσειδώνιος ὁ καὶ Π.*: s. *Μέστυς*)

Παντακλῆς
CIMMERIAN BOSPOROS:
—GORGIPPIA: **(1)** f. iii BC *CIRB* 1137 A I, 40; II, 35 (s. *Κήφισος*); **(2)** i AD ib. 1196 (s. *Γαδίκιος*); **(3)** s. ii AD ib. 1145, 11 ([*Πα*]*ντακλῆς*); **(4)** 173-210 AD ib. 1135, 11
MACEDONIA (EDONIS):
—AMPHIPOLIS: **(5)** ?s. iv BC *SEG* XXVII 254 + *PAE* 1977, p. 44 with pl. 33 β (f. *Χαίρων*)
SKYTHIA:
—OLBIA-BORYSTHENES: **(6)** iii BC *IOSPE* I^2 179, [2], 12 with comm. (ident.); 180, 2; 188; 201 I, 40; 201 II, 5 (s. *Κλεόμβροτος*, f. *Κλεόμβροτος*); **(7)** ~ ib. 201 I, 10 (s. *Ἱκέσιος*); **(8)** ~ ib. l. 37 (f. *Ἑκατέων*); **(9)** ~ ib. l. 51; 201 II, 16 (f. *Ἱκέσιος*); **(10)** ~ ib. l. 14 (s. *Λεωδάμας*); **(11)** ~ ib. l. 32 (s. *Κ—*); **(12)** s. iii BC ib. 76, 4 (Sokolowski II 88; Dubois, *IGDOlbia* 88) (f. *Ἡρόδοτος*)
THRACE:
—MARONEIA: **(13)** m. iv BC *AD* 26 (1971) Chron. p. 428 no. στ′ (*IThrakAig* E223) ([*Π*]*αντακλέος* (gen.): f. *Ἡραΐς*); **(14)** a. 316 BC *IG* IV $(1)^2$ 94 b, 52 (Perlman, *City and Sanctuary* E.1 with pp. 78-9 (date)) (*Παντα*[*κλ*]*εῦς* (gen.): f. *Πυθόγονος*)
—STRYME? (NR.): **(15)** c. 425-400 BC *SEG* XXXIV 708 (*IThrakAig* E122) (*Παντα*[*κλῆς*]?: f. *Νεστορίς*)

Πανταλέων
CIMMERIAN BOSPOROS:
—GORGIPPIA: **(1)** imp. *CIRB* 1191, 2 (*Παντα*[*λέων*]?); **(2)** i BC/i AD *Hyperboreus* 2002 (1), p. 185 (f. *Ἀντίπατρος*, *Ἀπολλώνιος*); **(3)** 16 AD *SEG* XLVI 940 I, 2; 940 II, 1 (*Παν*[*τ*]*αλέων*); **(4)** ii AD *CIRB* 1140, 2; **(5)** ~ ib. l. 4 (*Πανταλέ*[*ων*]); **(6)** ~ ib. 1151, 5 (s. *Χρη—*); **(7)** ~ ib. 1152 ([*Παν*]*ταλέων*); **(8)** ~ ib. 1160, 2 ([*Π*]*ανταλέω*[*ν*]—Vinogradov) ?= (*9*); **(9)** ~ ib. l. 3 (*Πανταλ*[*έων*]) ?= (*8*); **(10)** ~ ib. 1161, 2 ([*Π*]*ανταλέω*[*ν*]—Vinogradov); **(11)** ~ ib. l. 4; **(12)** m. ii AD *Eirene* 7 (1968) p. 67, 7 (s. *Ἀθηνόδωρος*) ?= (*15*); **(13)** ~ ib. l. 10 (*Παντα*[*λέων*]: f. *Συβλιαγους*); **(14)** ~ ib. l. 13-14 (*Παν*[*ταλέ*]*ων*: f. *Πόθος*); **(15)** s. ii AD *CIRB* 1129 A, 4 (*Π*[*αν*]*ταλέων*: f. *Ἀθηνόδωρος*) ?= (*12*); **(16)** ~ ib. 1165, 3 ([*Παντ*]*αλέων*: s. *Φαρνα—*); **(17)** 173-210 AD ib. 1134, 14 (s. *Φαρνάκης*); **(18)** ~ ib. l. 23; **(19)** ~ ib. 1135, 25 ([*Παν*]*ταλέω*[*ν*]: s. *Φαρνακίων*); **(20)** ii/iii AD *SEG* XLIX 1033 B, 3 (*CIRB* 1182 B, 1) (*Πανταλ*[*έων*])
—PANTIKAPAION*: **(21)** 47-17 BC ib. 30, 3
MACEDONIA (PIERIA):
—PYDNA: **(22)** c. 332 BC Berve 603 (Tataki, *Macedonians* p. 171 no. 13)
THRACE:
—PHILIPPOPOLIS-TRIMONTIUM: **(23)** c. 303 AD *Anal. Boll.* 31 (1912) p. 192 (-το-)

Πάντανδρος
THRACE:
—ODESSOS: **(1)** s. iv BC *IGB* I^2 103 (f. *Χαρίδημος*)

Παντάπονος
MACEDONIA: **(1)** ?417-413 BC *IG* I^3 89, 62 (Tataki, *Macedonians* p. 395 no. 5) (f. *Ἀλέξανδρος*)

Παντάρετος
MACEDONIA (EDONIS):
—AMPHIPOLIS: **(1)** iii/ii BC *SEG* XXXI 616 + *PAE* 1981, pl. 35 α; cf. *BE* 1984, no. 254 (*Παντάρε*[*τος*], *Ἀνγάρε*[*ος*]—*SEG*, *Πανγα.ε*[*ύς*]?—Robert: s. *Δάλων*)

Παντᾶς
THRACE:
—SKEPTA: **(1)** 202 AD *IGB* III 1690 c, 18 (and Thrace Pizos: *Σοῦρις Π.*)

Πανταυχίς
MACEDONIA (BOTTIAIA):
—EDESSA: **(1)** 95 AD *Arch. Pap.* 22 (1973) p. 207 no. 10 (Tataki, *Edessa* 245) (d. *Πάνταυχος*)

Πάνταυχος
MACEDONIA: **(1)** 289 BC *RE* (2) (Tataki, *Macedonians* p. 395 no. 6)
MACEDONIA (BOTTIAIA):
—ALOROS: **(2)** c. 326 BC *RE* (1); Berve 604 (Tataki, *Macedonians* p. 44 no. 3) (s. *Νικόλαος*)
—BEROIA: **(3)** s. iii BC *IBer* 16 A, 28 (*Πάνταυ*[*χος*]: s. *—ρος*); **(4)** 172-168 BC *RE* (3) (Tataki, *Macedonians* pp. 81-2 no. 43) (s. *Βάλακρος*, f. *Βάλακρος*); **(5)** s. ii BC *IBer* 203 (Tataki 1012) (f. *Διονύσιος*); **(6)** ii AD *IBer* 346, 1 (Tataki 1010) (s. *Πολύβιος*, *Δανάη*)
—EDESSA: **(7)** 95 AD *Arch. Pap.* 22 (1973) p. 207 no. 10 (Tataki, *Edessa* 246) (f. *Πανταυχίς*)
MACEDONIA (DERRIOPOS):
—STUBERRA: **(8)** 74 AD *IG* X (2) (2) 325, 55 (s. *Ζωΐλος*); **(9)** ii/iii AD ib. 334 (*Αἰλιανὸς Π.*)
MACEDONIA (MYGDONIA):
—THESSALONIKE: **(10)** 223 BC ib. X (2) (1) 2, 4 (s. *Ἀρκεσῖνος*)

Παντέας
THRACE:
—PERINTHOS-HERAKLEIA: **(1)** c. 265-260 BC *FD* III (3) 207, 3 (f. *Ματρικέτης*)

Παντιαδης
MACEDONIA (BOTTIAIA):
—PELLA: **(1)** iv BC Arr., *Ind.* xviii 3 (Tataki, *Macedonians* p. 158 no. 69) (f. *Τιμάνθης*)

Πάντιμος
MACEDONIA (PIERIS):
—OISYME-EMATHIA: **(1)** iv BC *PAE* 1938, p. 101 (amph.) (*SEG* XXXVIII 636) (*Πάντιμ*(*ος*))

Παντοκρατίδης
THRACE:
—MARONEIA: **(1)** iii/ii BC Unp. (Teos) (f. *Κάλλιππος*)
—MARONEIA?: **(2)** c. 209-190 BC *IG* XI (4) 705 a-b, 2; 705 c, 7 (s. *Κάλλιππος*: reading—Hallof)

Παντόνικος
CIMMERIAN BOSPOROS:
—PANTIKAPAION: **(1)** 130 AD *CIRB* 656, 1; cf. KW pl. 18 no. 272 (-νει-: s. *Ἀφφοῦς*, *Λαυδίκη*)
THRACE:
—PHILIPPOPOLIS-TRIMONTIUM (TERRIT.): **(2)** iii AD *IGB* III 1171 (*Αὐρ. Παντόνεικ*[*ος*])

Παντόρδανος
MACEDONIA:
—LEUGA: **(1)** 333 BC Berve 605 (Tataki, *Macedonians* p. 119 no. 2); cf. *Historia* 47 (1998) pp. 414-16 (locn.) (s. *Κλέανδρος*)

Παντρέπις
MACEDONIA (MYGDONIA):
—THESSALONIKE: **(1)** 269 AD *IG* X (2) (1) 170, 4 (*Αὐρ. Ἰούλιος νέος ὁ καὶ Π.*: s. *Ἀνθεστιανὴ Μινουκκιανὴ Προκόπη*)

Πασσίμαχος
CIMMERIAN BOSPOROS:
—HERMONASSA: **(1)** iv BC *CIRB* 1056 I, 13

Παπάδων
SKYTHIA:
—OLBIA-BORYSTHENES: **(1)** ii AD *IOSPE* I^2 131, 13; Zgusta, *PNS* 602 (s. *Ἄλκιμος*); **(2)** ~ *IOSPE* I^2 175, 6 (f. *Παπίας*)

Πάπας
CIMMERIAN BOSPOROS:
—GORGIPPIA: **(1)** ii AD *CIRB* 1140, 6 (*Πάπα* (gen.): f. *Χρηστίων*); **(2)** ~ ib. l. 17 (s. *Κομίνικος*); **(3)** ~ ib. l. 18 (*Πάπα* (gen.): f. *—υς*); **(4)** ~ ib. 1151, 8 (*Πάπα* (gen.): f. *Πόθος*) ?= (*16*); **(5)** m. ii AD *Eirene* 7 (1968) p. 67, 6 (s. *Μάνας*); **(6)** ~ ib. l. 10 (f. *Μυρῖνος*); **(7)** s. ii AD *CIRB* 1142, 3 (*Πάπα*[*ς*]); **(8)** ~ ib. 1208, 3; **(9)** ~ *SEG* XXIX 706, 6; **(10)** 173-210 AD *CIRB* 1134, 16 (*Πάπα* (gen.): f. *Χρηστίων*); **(11)** ~ ib. 1135, 9 (s. *Σιαβα—*); **(12)** ~ ib. l. 19 (s. *Φαρνάκης*); **(13)** ~ ib. l. 21 (*Πάπα* (gen.): f. *Σια—*); **(14)** ii/iii AD ib. 1179, 28 (*Πάπα* (gen.): s. *Χῶλος*, f. *—νιος*); **(15)** ~ ib. l. 32 (s. *Χρηστίων*); **(16)** ~ ib. l. 36 (*Πάπα* (gen.): f. *Πόθος*) ?= (*4*); **(17)** ~ ib. l. 39 (*Πάπου* (gen.): f. *Ἀτταμαζας*); **(18)** ~ ib. l. 39 (s. *Νυμφαγόρας*); **(19)** ~ ib. l. 56 (s. *Ἀζίας*); **(20)** iii AD *NE* 9 (1971) p. 10 no. 6 B, 2 (*Πάπα*[*ς*])
—GORGIPPIA?: **(21)** s. ii AD *CIRB* 1231 A, 11
—KYTAIA (NR.): **(22)** i-ii AD *SEG* XXXV 866 (s. *Μαιο—*)
—PANTIKAPAION: **(23)** i AD *CIRB* 361 (*Πάπου* (gen.)); **(24)** ~ ib. 438; cf. KW pl. 48 no. 671 (*Πάπου* (gen.)); **(25)** ~ *CIRB* 443 (*Πάπα* (gen.): f. *Κόναιφος*); **(26)** ~ ib. 486; cf. KW pl. 37 no. 537; **(27)** m. i AD *CIRB* 365; cf. KW pl. 52 no. 712 (*Πάπα* (gen.): f. *Βάκχιος*); **(28)** i/ii AD *CIRB* 82, 7 (s. *Δημήτριος*); **(29)** ii AD ib. 95, 3 (s. *Πάννυχος*); **(30)** ?ii AD ib. 693; cf. KW pl. 14 no. 203 (*Πάπα* (gen.): f. *Μακαρία*); **(31)** 343 or 353 AD *CIRB* 744, 2 (*Πάπου* (gen.): f. *Ἄδας*)
—PHANAGOREIA: **(32)** m. ii AD *SEG* XLIII 512, 1 ([*Π*]*άπα* (gen.))
—SUDAK (MOD.): **(33)** 174-210 AD ib. XLV 1017, 3 (*Πάπα*[*ς*])
MACEDONIA (BOTTIAIA):
—BEROIA: **(34)** 189 AD *ILeukopetra* 24, 11 (*Πάπα* (gen.): s. *Φίλιππος*)
—EDESSA: **(35)** 180 AD *SEG* XXIV 531, 11 (Tataki, *Edessa* 247) (*Πάπα* (gen.): f. *Ἀλέξανδρος*)
MACEDONIA (EDONIS):
—AMPHIPOLIS: **(36)** ?iv BC *Bronzes antiques du Louvre* 1347; **(37)** s. iv BC *AD* 24 (1969) Chron. p. 355 no. 1 (*Πάπα* (gen.): f. *Διονύσιος*)
MACEDONIA (PAIONIA):
—DEMIR KAPIJA (MOD.): **(38)** hell. *SEG* XLV 807 E (sherd) (f. *Διονύσιος*)
SCYTHIA MINOR:
—ISTROS: **(39)** 27 BC-14 AD *ISM* I 146 (s. *Θεόπομπος*); **(40)** ii AD ib. 196, 21; 201 I, 20 (s. *Πίστος*); **(41)** ii/iii AD ib. 225, 14 (s. *Λ—*)
—TOMIS: **(42)** ii AD ib. II 125, 14 (s. *Ἡρόξενος*); **(43)** ~ ib. 125 I, 20 (s. *Ἀντώνιος*); **(44)** ii-iii AD ib. 26, 4 (f. *Ποσειδώνιος*); **(45)** ~ ib. l. 7 (f. *Δημήτρις*)
SKYTHIA: **(46)** i-ii AD *VDI* 1951 (1), pp. 150-1 no. 1 (s. *Ἀ—*)
—TANAIS: **(47)** 228-244 AD *CIRB* 1250, 12; 1282, 24; 1287, 3 (*Πάπα* (gen.)—1250: s. *Χρηστοῦς*)
THRACE:
—APOLLONIA-SOZOPOLIS: **(48)** i-ii AD *IGB* I^2 401, 10 (*Πάπα* (gen.): f. *Ἡρακλείδης*)
—BIZONE: **(49)** ?iii AD ib. 8 bis (*Eastern cults* p. 264 no. 1)
—BIZYE: **(50)** imp.? PM 1950 (s. *Δορζίνθης*)

—BYZANTION: **(51)** ii-i BC *IByz* 223 (Fıratlı–Robert pp. 79-80 no. 92) (s. Ἄνδρων); **(52)** i BC-i AD *Türk Tarih Kongresi XI* (6) p. 2704 with pl. 497. 10 (Πάπα (voc.): s. Μοκαζεις); **(53)** ~ ib. pp. 2704-5 with pl. 499. 14 (f. Ἀπφοῦς)
—BYZANTION (TERRIT.): **(54)** imp. Unp. (Sayar)
—BYZANTION (NR.): **(55)** i BC *IByz* 226 (Fıratlı–Robert p. 81 no. 96) (f. Ἀνδρόνικος)
—BYZANTION?: **(56)** hell. *IByz* 331 (f. Αἰνώ); **(57)** i BC-i AD ib. 373 (Fıratlı–Robert p. 125 no. 209) (Π̣ά[π]ας: s. Λεύκιος)
—DIONYSOPOLIS: **(58)** ii-iii AD *IGB* I^2 31, 4 (s. Σεν—); **(59)** iii AD ib. 14 a, 3 (Πάπα (gen.): f. Μ. Αὐρ. Ἀντίπατρος); **(60)** ~ ib. 14 c, 17 (Πάπα (gen.): f. Αὐρ. Γουρθιθις); **(61)** ~ ib. l. 20 (Πάπα (gen.): f. Αὐρ. Λαβέρις)
—ODESSOS: **(62)** i-ii AD ib. 211 (Διονύσιος Π.: s. Ἑστιαῖος)
—ODESSOS?: **(63)** ii AD ib. 51 bis a, 7 (Πάπα (gen.): f. Αἴλλεις)
—PERINTHOS-HERAKLEIA: **(64)** i/ii AD *IPerinth* 64, 4 (s. Παπίας)
THRACE?: **(65)** iv-iii BC *SEG* XVII 337. 3 (bullet)

Παπᾶς
THRACE:
—BYZANTION: **(1)** ii AD *IByz* 282 (Παπᾶδος (gen.): f. Εἴα)

Παπέας
CIMMERIAN BOSPOROS:
—PANTIKAPAION: **(1)** iii AD *CIRB* 730. 2

Παπῆς
CIMMERIAN BOSPOROS:
—PANTIKAPAION: **(1)** i BC ib. 286; cf. KW pl. 36 no. 520 (s. Φιλοκλῆς)
MACEDONIA (MYGDONIA):
—THESSALONIKE?: **(2)** ?iii AD *IG* X (2) (1) 769 (Παπεῖνος (gen.): s. Τερτία)

Παπιανός
MACEDONIA (MYGDONIA):
—THESSALONIKE?: **(1)** f. iii AD *SEG* XXXVI 649; *KGAM Thess.* I 130 (date) (Αὐρ. Π.)
THRACE:
—ANCHIALOS (TERRIT.): **(2)** ii-iii AD *IGB* I^2 385, 5 (Παπ̣ιανός)
—DEULTUM: **(3)** ii-iii AD ib. III 1849, 3 (s. Γαῦρος)

Παπίας
CIMMERIAN BOSPOROS:
—GORGIPPIA: **(1)** f. iii BC *CIRB* 1137 B I, 37 ([Π]απίας: s. Διονυσόδωρος); **(2)** f. ii AD *SGE* 35 (1972) p. 51, 5 (*CIRB* 1132) + *CIRB* 1162 (f. —ν); **(3)** ~ ib. 1172, 2 (Παπία[ς]); **(4)** m. ii AD *Eirene* 7 (1968) p. 67, 3 (s. Χορηγίων); **(5)** ~ ib. l. 19 (s. Κοίρανος, f. —ων); **(6)** s. ii AD *CIRB* 1142 fr. F, 2 ([Π]απίας); **(7)** ~ ib. 1209, 4; **(8)** ii/iii AD ib. 1179, 33 (s. Χρῆστος); **(9)** iii AD ib. 1186, 1 ([Π]α̣πίας: s. Ἀλ—)
—GORGIPPIA?: **(10)** s. ii AD ib. 1231 B, 9 (Παπί[ας])
—HERMONASSA: **(11)** hell.-imp. ib. 1094, 4 (s. Τιμόθεος)
—KEPOI: **(12)** i-ii AD ib. 1012 (f. Γόκων)
—PANTIKAPAION: **(13)** c. 180-150 BC ib. 75, 14 (s. Πα—); **(14)** ~ ib. l. 16 (s. Θ—); **(15)** ~ ib. l. 17 ([Π]απίας); **(16)** i-ii AD ib. 639; cf. KW pl. 19 no. 271 (s. Ξένων, Φιλωτέρα); **(17)** i/ii AD *CIRB* 629 (I f. Παπίας II); **(18)** ~ ib. (II s. Παπίας I); **(19)** f. ii AD ib. 685; cf. KW pl. 45 no. 639 (f. Ἰσίων); **(20)** 275-278 AD *CIRB* 36, 29 (Παπί[α]ς: s. Χόφαρνος); **(21)** ~ ib. l. 67 (Παπ(ίας): f. Ἀντᾶς)
—THEODOSIA: **(22)** iii AD ib. 947 A, 9 (f. Φαρνακίων)
MACEDONIA (BOTTIAIA):
—BEROIA: **(23)** ii/iii AD *IBer* 27 A, 7 (f. Λοῦππος); **(24)** 250 AD *ILeukopetra* 101, 3 (Π. Θα[ύμασ]τος ὁ καὶ Εὐ[γε]νείδης)
MACEDONIA (MYGDONIA):
—THESSALONIKE: **(25)** ?ii AD *IG* X (2) (1) 452, 3 + *BCH* 98 (1974) pp. 536-8 (Μ. Κάσσιος Σεουῆρος Π. πρεσβύτ.: ?f. Κάσσιος Ἀλέξανδρος, Κασσία Δαμαλίς)
SCYTHIA MINOR:
—ISTROS: **(26)** i BC-i AD *ISM* I 191 II, 7 (f. Διογένης); **(27)** ~ ib. l. 29 (s. Διογένης); **(28)** ~ ib. l. 38 (f. Θεόγνητος) ?= *(29)*; **(29)** ~ ib. l. 40 (f. Διοσκουρίδης) ?= *(28)*; **(30)** ii AD ib. 196, 12; 201 I, 21 (s. Ἀνθᾶς); **(31)** c. 140-160 AD ib. 207, 13 (f. Χαιρήμων)
—KALLATIS: **(32)** ii/iii AD ib. III 183, 1 (II 362) (-πεί-: s. Μήνιος)
SKYTHIA:
—OLBIA-BORYSTHENES: **(33)** ?c. 200-175 BC *IOSPE* I^2 34, 27; *SEG* XXXVII 670 (date) (f. Νικήρατος); **(34)** i BC-i AD *IOSPE* I^2 221; *SEG* XXXVI 720 (f. Ἀρέτη); **(35)** imp. *IOSPE* I^2 151, 2; **(36)** ii AD ib. 86, 5 (f. Ἀχιλλεύς); **(37)** ~ ib. 96, 2 (s. Οὐμβηούαρος); **(38)** ~ ib. 175, 5 (s. Παπάδων); **(39)** f. ii AD *SEG* XLIII 506, 8 (f. Ἄλκιμος); **(40)** s. ii AD ib. 507, 4; **(41)** iii AD *IOlbia* 83, 4 (*IOSPE* I^2 97) (II s. Παπίας I); **(42)** ~ *IOlbia* 83, 5 (*IOSPE* I^2 97) (I f. Παπίας II); **(43)** ~ *IOlbia* 83, 8 (*IOSPE* I^2 97) (f. Βαιορμαῖος); **(44)** ~ ib. 98, 4 (s. Πραξιάναξ)
—TANAIS: **(45)** 104 AD *CIRB* 1259, 23 (f. Μαστοῦς); **(46)** 228 AD ib. 1282, 28 (s. Ὀξαρδώζιος)
TAURIS:
—CHERSONESOS: **(47)** iv BC Solomonik, *NEPKh* 28; Zgusta, *PNS* 602 ([Πα]πίας: f. Γόσων); **(48)** ii AD Solomonik, *NEPKh* 13; **(49)** 174 AD *SEG* XLV 985 A, 35 ([Π]απίας: f. Χρῆστος); **(50)** 284-305 AD Const. Porph., *De admin. imp.* 53, 25, 44 (f. Χρῆστος)
THRACE:
—BYZANTION: **(51)** ii BC *SEG* XVIII 446, 5; **(52)** ii-i BC *IByz* 258 (Fıratlı–Robert p. 89 no. 114) (f. —ώ); **(53)** ~ *IRhodPer* 603, 5
—BYZANTION (TERRIT.): **(54)** imp. Unp. (Sayar) (f. Προμᾶς); **(55)** ~ ib. (f. Κλοιόνικος)
—BYZANTION (TERRIT.)?: **(56)** imp. *BCH* 36 (1912) p. 598 no. 57 (s. Μήνιος)
—ODESSOS: **(57)** f. ii BC *IGB* I^2 39, 5 (Σωκράτης ὁ καὶ Π.: s. Ἐπικράτης); **(58)** ?ii AD ib. 56
—ODESSOS?: **(59)** ii/i BC ib. II 780 (*Eastern cults* p. 190 no. 1) (— ὁ καὶ Π.: s. —μος)
—PERINTHOS-HERAKLEIA: **(60)** i/ii AD *IPerinth* 64, 5-6 (f. Πάπας, Διόδοτος); **(61)** ii-iii AD ib. 92 (f. Κρίσπος, Θεοδώρα)
—PHILIPPOPOLIS-TRIMONTIUM: **(62)** iii AD *IGB* V 5464, 8 (s. Φίλιππος)
—PHILIPPOPOLIS-TRIMONTIUM (TERRIT.): **(63)** ii/iii AD ib. III 1452, 9 (*Eastern cults* p. 121 no. 104) (f. Μίκκαλος)
—RHAIDESTOS: **(64)** i BC-i AD PM 182 d (f. Λάλα, Ἐπιγένης); **(65)** ~ ib. (s. Ἐπιγένης); **(66)** ~ ib. 182 c (f. Ἐπιγένης)
—SEXAGINTA PRISTA: **(67)** iii AD *BIAB* 11 (1937) p. 285 (*Romanizmăt* II 81) (Lat. Aur. Papias)

Πάπιος
CIMMERIAN BOSPOROS:
—PANTIKAPAION: **(1)** iii BC Rostovtsev, *SB* I p. 193 (vase)

Παπίρις
THRACE:
—PAUTALIA: **(1)** ii AD *IGB* IV 2082 (-πεί-)

Πάπος
CIMMERIAN BOSPOROS:
—GORGIPPIA: **(1)** s. ii AD *SEG* XXIX 706, 3 (s. Ψ—)
MACEDONIA: **(2)** 12 AD *PKöln* 227 B, 7 ([Πά]π̣ος: s. Ἀπολλώνιος); **(3)** ~ ib. l. 8 (f. Ἀπολλώνιος)
SCYTHIA MINOR:
—ISTROS: **(4)** i BC-i AD *ISM* I 190, 4 ([Πά]πος?: s. Ἀθην—)

Παποῦς
CIMMERIAN BOSPOROS?: **(1)** iii AD Greifenhagen, *Schmuckarb.* 2 p. 81 (ring)

Παππερωτίων
THRACE:
—BYZANTION: **(1)** ?ii AD *Türk Tarih Kongresi XI* (6) 1990, p. 501 pl. 18 (Μ. Αἰλ. Π.)

Παππίας
SKYTHIA:
—OLBIA-BORYSTHENES: **(1)** imp. *IOSPE* I^2 147, 7; Zgusta, *PNS* 602 (s. Ἀρίστων)

Πάππος
CIMMERIAN BOSPOROS:
—GORGIPPIA: **(1)** ii AD *CIRB* 1159 B, 3; **(2)** ~ ib. 1159 C (Πάππ[ος]—Vinogradov); **(3)** ~ ib. 1161, 3 ([Π]άππος); **(4)** ~ ib. 1174, 4; **(5)** ii-iii AD *NE* 9 (1971) p. 9 no. 6 A, 7 (Πάππ[ος]); **(6)** ~ ib. l. 10 (f. —ων); **(7)** 173-210 AD *CIRB* 1135, 15 ([Π]ά̣ππος—Vinogradov); **(8)** ii/iii AD ib. 1179, 30 (s. Φαρνακίων); **(9)** ~ ib. l. 41 (Π[άπ]πος: s. Κόνος, f. Ἀτακούας); **(10)** ~ ib. l. 44 (f. Πόθος); **(11)** ~ ib. l. 53 (s. Θέκας); **(12)** ~ ib. l. 54 (s. Ἑρμῆς); **(13)** ~ ib. l. 57 (s. Γόζινος); **(14)** iii AD *NE* 9 (1971) p. 10 no. 6 B, 10; **(15)** ~ ib. l. 17 (s. Καλοῦς)
—GORGIPPIA?: **(16)** s. ii AD *CIRB* 1231 A, 9
—HERMONASSA*: **(17)** 307 AD ib. 1051 (f. Μ. Αὐρ. Ἀνδρόνικος)
—PANTIKAPAION: **(18)** iii AD ib. 103, 2 (s. Ἀρδάρακος); **(19)** f. iii AD ib. 105, 11 (f. Τιμόθεος); **(20)** 210 AD ib. 97, 7 (f. Ἀράθης); **(21)** 275-278 AD ib. 36, 45 (Πάππ(ος): f. —ος); **(22)** v-vi AD Latyshev, *Sbornik* 85a
—PHANAGOREIA?: **(23)** 335 AD *CIRB* 1112, 4 (s. Πόπλιος)
—THEODOSIA: **(24)** iii AD ib. 947 A, 8 (f. Εὐκράτης); **(25)** ~ ib. 947 B, 15 (Πάππ[ος]: s. —ηρομη—); **(26)** ~ ib. l. 17 (s. —τος)
SKYTHIA:
—TANAIS: **(27)** ii AD ib. 1263, 16 ([Π]άππος); **(28)** f. ii AD ib. 1266, 6 (f. Ἄρδαρος); **(29)** ~ ib. l. 11 (s. Δαΐσκος); **(30)** 155 AD ib. 1260, 26 (Πάπ[π]ος: f. —ος); **(31)** f. iii AD ib. 1286, 9 (f. Ἡρακλείδης); **(32)** 220 AD ib. 1278, 12 (f. Δάδας); **(33)** ~ ib. l. 21 ([Π]άππος); **(34)** 225 AD ib. 1280, 4 (f. Καλλισθένης ὁ καὶ Θυλόγανος); **(35)** ~ ib. l. 19 (Πάππος: f. Μο—); **(36)** 244 AD ib. 1287, 25 (f. Φαζιους); **(37)** ~ ib. l. 31
THRACE:
—ODESSOS: **(38)** ?i-ii AD *IGB* I^2 95
—PERINTHOS-HERAKLEIA: **(39)** iii AD *IPerinth* 166 ([Αὐρ.] [Πά]ππο[ς]?)
—SERDICA: **(40)** f. iii AD *IGB* IV 1910, 11 (Ἄρριος Π.)

Παπποῦς
MACEDONIA (BOTTIAIA):
—BEROIA: **(1)** f. iii AD *IBer* 230, 5 (Tataki 1305) (Φλαβιανὸς ὁ καὶ Π.: s. Ἀννία Ἐπιγόνη)

Παπύλος
CIMMERIAN BOSPOROS:
—GORGIPPIA: **(1)** f. iii BC *CIRB* 1137 B I, 20; 1137 B II, 4 (Π[α]πύλος: s. Δημήτριος)
MACEDONIA: **(2)** iii/ii BC *IG* XI (4) 785, 2, 8 (Tataki, *Macedonians* p. 395 no. 8) (f. Μενέστρατος)
SCYTHIA MINOR:
—ISTROS: **(3)** s. iv BC *IG* II^2 8940 (*FRA* 2629) (s. Σιμίας)
THRACE:
—BYZANTION: **(4)** ii AD *IByz* 282 (s. Κάσιος)
—MARONEIA: **(5)** ii-i BC *IThrakAig* E212, 24 (f. Ἡροφῶν)

Πάπων

Cimmerian Bosporos:
—Pantikapaion: **(1)** 275-278 ad *CIRB* 36, 70 (*Πάπ[ω]ν*: s. *Θεόφιλος*)
Thrace:
—Apollonia-Sozopolis: **(2)** v/iv bc *IGB* I² 434 (s. *Ἀπατούριος*)

Παραιβάτης

Thrace: **(1)** 180 bc *Essays Thomas* pp. 78, 3 (La'da E779) (s. *Ἀνδρόμαχος*)

Πάραλος

Cimmerian Bosporos:
—Nymphaion: **(1)** iii bc *CIRB* 912 II, 9 (s. *Ἀκουσίλεως*)

Παραμόνα

Macedonia: **(1)** iii ad *ILeukopetra* 119, 5 ([*Πα*]*ραμό*[*να*]: slave); **(2)** ?243 ad ib. 98, 2 (slave/freed.)
Macedonia (Bottiaia):
—Beroia: **(3)** s. i ad *IBer* 271 (Tataki 808) (*Λικινία Παραμό*[*να*]); **(4)** ii ad *IBer* 301, 3 (Tataki 1016) (m. *Πο. Δόναξ, Ἧπις*); **(5)** ~ *IBer* 322 (Tataki 642) (*Καικιλία Π.*: m. *Καικίλιος Παράμονος*); **(6)** ii-iii ad *IBer* 272 (Tataki 1015); **(7)** m. ii ad *IBer* 318 (Tataki 1013); **(8)** s. ii ad *IBer* 289 (Tataki 1014) (*Παραμόν*[*α*]: m. *Φιλόνικος*)
—Edessa: **(9)** ii-iii ad *SEG* xii 344 (Tataki, *Edessa* 40) (*Ἀττεία Π.*: m. *Σαβῖνα*); **(10)** iii ad Feissel, *RICM* 9, 1 (Tataki, *Edessa* 249) (m. *Στερκορία, Στερκόριλλα, Ἐπινικίς, Κερβίων*); **(11)** v-vi ad *SEG* xxxiv 635 (Feissel, *RICM* 50)
Macedonia (Edonis):
—Amphipolis: **(12)** ii-iii ad *SEG* xxxi 621, 8 (m. *Φαεινός*); **(13)** iv-vi ad ib. xxxiii 502 + xxxvi 588 (*Παραμό*<υ>*να*)
Macedonia (Mygdonia):
—Lete (nr.): **(14)** c. 220-230 ad ib. xlviii 855 (d. *Κόπρυλλος, Διοσκόρη*)
—Thessalonike: **(15)** ii ad *IG* x (2) (1) 241 B, 7 (m. *Εἰρηναῖος*); **(16)** ~ ib. 410, 3 (d. *Παράμονος, Εὐτυχίς*); **(17)** ~ ib. 478, 1 ([*Π*]*αραμόνα*); **(18)** ii-iii ad ib. 499; **(19)** s. ii ad *SEG* xlv 817 (xlviii 853) (d. *Ἐπίγονος, Κλευπάτρα*); **(20)** ii/iii ad ib. xlix 814 II, 14; **(21)** 221 ad *IG* x (2) (1) 492, 2 (*Κλ. Π.*: d. *Τι. Κλ. Παράμονος*, m. *Κλ. Ἑόρτη*)
—Thessalonike?: **(22)** ii-iii ad ib. 730
Macedonia (Paionia): **(23)** ii-iii ad *Sp.* 71 (1931) p. 229 no. 608 (m. *Κλαυδιανή*)
Macedonia (Pieria):
—Pydna: **(24)** ii-i bc *SEG* l 627 ([*Παρ*]*αμόν̣α̣*: d. *Πρωτογένης*)
Thrace: **(25)** 181 bc *SGDI* 2134, 4-5 (slave/freed.)

Παραμονίχη

Macedonia (Pieria):
—Dion: **(1)** iii/iv ad *SEG* xxxix 581 (*Καλπορνία Π.*)

Παραμονιχία

Macedonia (Pieria):
—Dion: **(1)** ?35 ad Oikonomos 14 (d. *Τυχαρώ*)

Παραμονίων

Macedonia (Bottiaia):
—Edessa: **(1)** v-vi ad Feissel, *RICM* 43 (-*ουν*: ?f. *Γλαῦκος*)

Παράμονος

Cimmerian Bosporos:
—Gorgippia: **(1)** f. iii bc *CIRB* 1137 A II, 23 (s. *Εὔβουλος*) ?= (*2*); **(2)** ~ ib. 1137 B I, 61 ([*Π*]*αράμονος*: s. *Εὔβουλος*) ?= (*3*) (*1*); **(3)** ~ ib. 1137 B II, 21 (s. *Εὔβουλος*) ?= (*2*)
Macedonia: **(4)** s. iii bc *FD* iii (4) 16, 1 (Tataki, *Macedonians* p. 396 no. 10) (I f. *Παράμονος* II); **(5)** ~ *FD* iii (4) 16, 1 (Tataki, *Macedonians* p. 396 no. 9) (II s. *Παράμονος* I); **(6)** 233 ad *ILeukopetra* 83, 6 (slave/freed.); **(7)** 238 ad ib. 89, 10 (slave/freed.)
Macedonia (Bottiaia):
—Aigai: **(8)** s. iv bc *SEG* xxxv 778 (s. *Μένανδρος*); **(9)** ~ ib. 789 (s. *Ἀμάδωκος*)
—Aloros (territ.)?: **(10)** hell.? Dimitsas 211 (*Παράμ*[*ονος*]: f. *Νεοπτόλεμος*)
—Beroia: **(11)** 223 bc *IBer* 4, 18 (s. *Ἀγησίστρατος*); **(12)** ~ ib. l. 19 (f. *Ἄλκιμος*); **(13)** ~ ib. l. 28 (f. *Φίλων*); **(14)** ~ ib. l. 32 (s. *Μένανδρος*); **(15)** ii bc ib. 141, 9; **(16)** 120 bc ib. 134, 18 (s. *Ἡρακλείδης*); **(17)** 115 bc ib. l. 31 (s. *Περίτας*, f. *Ἀντίγονος*); **(18)** i bc-i ad ib. 142, 2 (Tataki 1018) (*Παράμον*[*ος*]); **(19)** ~ *IBer* 142, 15 (Tataki 1032) (f. *Κόρραγος*); **(20)** ? bc *IBer* 22, 2, 6 (s. *Θεογένης*); **(21)** i ad ib. 289 (f. *Κάσσανδρος*); **(22)** ii ad ib. 296 (Tataki 1019); **(23)** ~ *IBer* 322 (Tataki 645) (*Καικίλιος Π.*: s. *Καικιλία Παραμόνα*); **(24)** ii-iii ad *IBer* 246 (Tataki 1111) (*Κ. Ποπίλλιος Π.*); **(25)** ~ *IBer* 297, 5 (s. *Κλ. Ἀντέρως, Νικέα*); **(26)** ~ ib. 332 (Tataki 1022) (s. *Ἐπιγόνη*); **(27)** f. ii ad *IBer* 7 A, 20, 71, 78 (*Φλαΐος Π.*); **(28)** ~ ib. 119, 4 (*Τ. Φλαο*[*ύ*]*ϊος Π.*: s. *Ἀμύντας*); **(29)** ~ ib. 273 (Tataki 1021); **(30)** s. ii ad *ILeukopetra* 151, 4 (Tataki 1020) (s. *Ἀριάγνη*); **(31)** ii/iii ad *IBer* 211, 1 (Tataki 1030) (f. *Ἀμμία*); **(32)** 177 ad *IBer* 135 A, 23 (Tataki 1033) (f. *Σκίλβας*); **(33)** iii ad *ILeukopetra* 129, 2 (f. *Αὐρ. Λεοντᾶς*); **(34)** 203 ad ib. 47, 5, 9 (Tataki 1024) (s. *Λαδόμα*); **(35)** 210 ad *ILeukopetra* 57, 1 (Tataki 1031) (f. *Ἀντίγονος*); **(36)** 251 ad *IBer* 137, 6 (Tataki 330) (*Βετουληνὸς Π.*)
——Kannoneai: **(37)** 313 ad *ILeukopetra* 118, 1 (Tataki 1029) (I f. *Αὐρ. Παράμονος* II); **(38)** ~ *ILeukopetra* 118, 1 (Tataki 296) (*Αὐρ. Π.*: II s. *Παράμονος* I)
—Beroia?: **(39)** 178 bc *SGDI* 2071, 9 (s. *Καλλίστρατος*)
—Edessa: **(40)** ii ad *SEG* xii 343 (Tataki, *Edessa* 154) (*Κλαυδιανὸς Π.*); **(41)** ii-iii ad *Arch. Pap.* 22 (1973) p. 205 no. 4 (Tataki, *Edessa* 253) (f. *Σεκοῦνδος*); **(42)** 180 ad *SEG* xxiv 531, 16 (Tataki, *Edessa* 251) (s. *Ἰούλιος*); **(43)** ~ *SEG* xxiv 531, 17 (Tataki, *Edessa* 250) (s. *Γάϊος*); **(44)** iii ad *Makedonika* 15 (1975) p. 203 (Tataki, *Edessa* 252) (f. *Εὐπορία*); **(45)** ~ *SEG* xliii 392 (Tataki, *Edessa* 249a); **(46)** ~ *SEG* xliii 393 (Tataki, *Edessa* 269a) (*Ῥουπίλιος Π.*); **(47)** 229 ad *Ancient Macedonia* 1 p. 200 no. 12, 31 (Tataki, *Edessa* 57) (*Αὐρ. Π.*); **(48)** ~ ib. 58 (*Αὐρ.* [*Πα*]*ράμονος*)
—Kyrrhos?: **(49)** hell.? Dimitsas 150 (f. *Πολέμων*)
—Mieza: **(50)** iii bc *SEG* xxiv 524 II, 13 (Hatzopoulos, *MI* 2 p. 106 no. 92); **(51)** ~ *SEG* xxiv 524 II, 22 (Hatzopoulos, *MI* 2 p. 106 no. 92) ([*Παρά*]*μονος*?: s. *Κηφισ*—); **(52)** ii bc *SEG* xliii 415 (f. *Ἡγησώ*)
—Pella: **(53)** iii bc Akamatis, *Amph. Pellas* p. 42 no. PAR54 (amph.) (*SEG* l 613)
Macedonia (Chalkidike):
—Mende: **(54)** ?iii ad ib. xxix 616 ([*Α*]*ὐρ.* [*Πα*]*ράμονος*)
—Potidaia-Kassandreia: **(55)** 2 bc or 115 ad *Essays Laourdas* p. 97 (f. *Κλεοπάτρα*)
Macedonia (Derriopos): **(56)** 95 ad *IG* x (2) (2) 300, 2 (*Π*(*α*)*ράμονος*: s. *Μικίνης*)
—Stuberra: **(57)** c. 41-48 ad ib. 323, 11 (II s. *Παράμονος* I); **(58)** ~ ib. l. 17 (s. *Μενέλαος*); **(59)** ~ ib. l. 11-12 (I f. *Παράμονος* II); **(60)** c. 41-50 ad ib. l. 9; 324, 13, 17 (s. *Φίλιππος*, f. *Φίλιππος, Λούκιος*); **(61)** 74 ad ib. 325, 32 (f. *Φίλιππος*); **(62)** ~ ib. l. 32 (s. *Λυσῆς*); **(63)** ~ ib. l. 35 (s. *Κάρπος*); **(64)** ~ ib. l. 42 (f. *Ὀλυμπιάδης*); **(65)** ~ ib. l. 43 (f. *Ζωΐλος, Νικόλαος*); **(66)** ~ ib. l. 46 (s. *Ὠφελίων*); **(67)** ~ ib. l. 50 (f. *Φίλιππος, Διονύσιος*); **(68)** ~ ib. l. 52 (f. *Οὐαλέριος*); **(69)** ~ ib. l. 59 (f. *Μένανδρος*); **(70)** ~ ib. l. 60 (f. *Νίκων*); **(71)** ~ ib. l. 61 (s. *Εὐβουλίδης*); **(72)** ~ ib. 326, 25 (f. *Δικαῖος*); **(73)** ~ ib. l. 43 (f. *Μέστυς*); **(74)** ~ ib. l. 48 (f. *Νικόλαος*); **(75)** ~ ib. l. 51 (f. *Διονύσιος*); **(76)** ~ ib. l. 54 (f. *Ἀντίγονος*); **(77)** ~ ib. l. 61 (f. *Λούκιος*); **(78)** ~ ib. l. 61 (s. *Ἀλέξανδρος*); **(79)** ~ ib. l. 64 (f. *Φίλιππος*); **(80)** ~ ib. l. 65 (f. *Ἡράκλειτος*); **(81)** ~ ib. l. 31-2 (s. *Σωσίστρατος*); **(82)** ~ ib. l. 46-7 (s. *Ἀλέξανδρος*); **(83)** ~ ib. l. 47-8 (f. *Λύκος*); **(84)** ~ ib. l. 54-5 (f. *Φίλιππος*); **(85)** ~ ib. l. 56-7 (f. *Κλέαρχος*); **(86)** 74-107 ad ib. 325, 43, 89, 93 (s. *Φίλων*, f. *Φίλων*); **(87)** 74-121 ad ib. l. 36; 328, 12 (s. *Μενέδημος*, f. *Ἐπιγένης*); **(88)** 87 ad ib. 325, 77 (f. *Ἰσόχρυσος*); **(89)** ~ ib. l. 83 (f. *Νικανός*); **(90)** 90 ad ib. 326, 75 (s. *Διονύσιος*); **(91)** f. ii ad ib. 329; **(92)** 107 ad ib. 325, 98 (s. *Ἀνδρόνικος*); **(93)** ~ ib. l. 100 (s. *Κάσσιος*); **(94)** 116 ad ib. 327, 13 (f. *Σωτάδης*); **(95)** ~ ib. l. 15 (f. *Λυσίμαχος*); **(96)** ~ ib. l. 32 (s. *Τιμόθεος*); **(97)** ~ ib. l. 35 (s. *Κλέαρχος*); **(98)** ~ ib. l. 38 (s. *Αἰμίλιος*); **(99)** ~ ib. l. 39 (s. *Ὀλυμπᾶς*); **(100)** 121 ad ib. 328, 13 (s. *Σωτάδης*)
Macedonia (Edonis):
—Amphipolis: **(101)** ii-iii ad *TAPA* 69 (1938) p. 75 no. 34; **(102)** iii ad *SEG* xxiv 598; cf. xxxvii 580 (?s. *Αὐρ. Τορκᾶτος, Ἀμφίπολις*)
—Philippoi (nr.): **(103)** ii-iii ad ib. ii 427 (Pilhofer 426) ([*Π*]*αράμονος*)
Macedonia (Elimeia):
—Velvendos (mod.): **(104)** ii ad *SEG* xlvii 1001, 6 (I f. *Παράμονος* II); **(105)** ~ ib. l. 6 (II s. *Παράμονος* I)
Macedonia (Eordaia):
—Agios Panteleimonas (mod.): **(106)** s. ii ad *EAM* 126 (f. *Ἀμμία*)
—Arnisa?: **(107)** f. iii ad ib. 135; Hatzopoulos, *MI* 1 p. 94 n. 4 (locn.) (s. *Ποσειδώνιος*, f. *Θεαγένης*)
—Kelle?: **(108)** ii-iii ad *EAM* 127 (*Παρ*(*ά*)*μονος*: s. *Μένανδρος*)
Macedonia (Krestonia):
—Morrylos: **(109)** c. 185-180 bc *SEG* xxxix 606, 2 (f. *Νικάνωρ*) ?= (*110*); **(110)** ~ ib. l. 3 (s. *Σαμαγόρας*) ?= (*109*)
Macedonia (Lower Paionia):
—Europos: **(111)** iii bc ib. xliii 399 A (f. *Νικαία*); **(112)** c. 230-200 bc *BCH* 45 (1921) p. 17 III, 62 (Tataki, *Macedonians* p. 109 no. 10)
Macedonia (Lynkestis):
—Achlada (mod.): **(113)** f. iii ad *EAM* 168
—Herakleia: **(114)** ii-iii ad *IG* x (2) (2) 60 (f. *Λαλκία*); **(115)** ~ ib. 95 (f. *Φιλίππα*)
Macedonia (Lynkestis)?: **(116)** s. ii ad *EAM* 156 (f. *Λάμπρος*); **(117)** ii bc ib. 178; *Florina* p. 22 (pithoi)
Macedonia (Mygdonia):
—Aineia?: **(118)** ii-iii ad *SEG* xxxviii 707 (threptos)
—Apollonia: **(119)** f. ii bc ib. xliv 508 (Hatzopoulos, *MI* 2 p. 87 no. 66) (f. *Στράτιος*); **(120)** ~ *SEG* xliv 508 (Hatzopoulos, *MI* 2 p. 87 no. 66) (f. *Ἀντίπατρος*)
—Gerakarou (mod.): **(121)** iii ad *SEG* xlii 576 (f. *Λυσίμαχος*)
—Kalindoia: **(122)** 68-98 ad ib. 580, 21 (f. *Κολκοτᾶς*); **(123)** ~ ib. l. 23 (f. *Ταρουσίνας*); **(124)** ~ ib. l. 26 (s. *Καρβερένθης*); **(125)** ~ ib. l. 53 (s. *Τρυφωνᾶς*); **(126)** ~ ib. l. 79 (s. *Δαληζένθης*); **(127)** a. 98 ad ib. 582, 11 (f. *Καρβερένθης*); **(128)** ~ ib. l. 25 (s. *Τοΐτας*)
—Lete: **(129)** ii ad *Makedonika* 2 (1951) p. 619 no. 42 θ, 8 (I f. *Παράμονος* II); **(130)** ~ ib. l. 8 (II s. *Παράμονος* I); **(131)** ~ ib. l. 17 (s. *Μεστύλος*)
—Lete (nr.): **(132)** c. 220-230 ad *SEG* xlviii 855 (s. *Κόπρυλλος, Διοσκόρη*); **(133)** iii/iv ad ib. xlvii 976 (s. *Σεραπᾶς*)
—Peristera (mod.): **(134)** ii-iii ad *AD* 40 (1985) Chron. pp. 238-9 with pl. 101 α (f. *Κλευπάτρα*)

—THESSALONIKE: **(135)** 95 BC *IG* X (2) (1) 4, 6, 21 (s. *Ἀντίγονος*); **(136)** 27 BC-14 AD ib. 31, 12 (f. *Νικ—*); **(137)** s. i AD ib. 68, 35 (I f. (ad.) *Παράμονος* II); **(138)** ~ ib. l. 35 (II s. (nat.) *Κερτίμμας*, s. (ad.) *Παράμονος* I); **(139)** ii AD ib. 410, 1 (*[Παρ]ά̣μονος*: s. *Νικάνωρ*, f. *Παραμόνα*); **(140)** ~ ib. 638 (*Παρά[μο]νος*: ?s. *Δουλ—*); **(141)** ?ii AD ib. 652 (*-μω-*); **(142)** 129 AD ib. 521, 2 (s. *Σεραπᾶς*, *Ῥεία Ζωσίμη*); **(143)** 130 AD ib. 369 (s. *Ἰουλία*); **(144)** s. ii AD ib. 244 II, 9 (*Κλ. Π.*); **(145)** 221 AD ib. 492, 4 (*Τι. Κλ. Π.*: f. *Κλ. Παραμόνα*); **(146)** 243 AD ib. 161, 7 (*Ἰούλ. Π.*: f. *Εὐτυχιανός*); **(147)** 246 AD ib. 614 (*Μ. Αἴλ. Π.*)

—THESSALONIKE?: **(148)** i AD ib. 913; **(149)** 109 AD ib. 849, 4 (s. *Κάσσανδρος*, *Μάντα*)

—THESSALONIKE*: **(150)** ?v AD ib. 784, 1 (Feissel, *RICM* 159) (slave?)

MACEDONIA (ODOMANTIKE):

—SIRRHA: **(151)** ii AD *ISamothrace* 46, 8 (Tataki, *Macedonians* p. 172 no. 6) (s. *Ζωΐλος*); **(152)** 155 AD Dimitsas 821, 29 (Kaphtantzis 1) (s. *Ζωΐλος*)

MACEDONIA (ORESTIS):

—BATTYNAIOI: **(153)** 192 AD *EAM* 186 I, 57 (s. *Στρατονίκη*); **(154)** ~ ib. 186 II, 53 (f. *Γέλων*)

MACEDONIA (PAIONIA):

—ARGOS (NR.): **(155)** ii-iii AD *Sp.* 71 (1931) p. 38 no. 83, 1-2 (f. *Γάϊος*)

—BYLAZORA: **(156)** ii-iii AD *SEG* XVI 402, 5

—EUDARISTOS?: **(157)** ii-iii AD *Sp.* 98 (1941-8) p. 62 no. 128 (s. *Κλεοπάτρα*)

—KAVADARCI (MOD.): **(158)** ii-iii AD Dimitsas 283 (s. *Χρύσανθος*); **(159)** ii/iii AD Unp. (Kavadarci Mus.) inv. 6/II (s. *Στράτων*, f. *Γάϊος*); **(160)** iii AD *Minalo* 2 (1911) pp. 54 (*Φλάϊος Π.*); **(161)** ~ *Sp.* 71 (1931) p. 65 no. 142, 6

—NEAPOLIS (AREA): **(162)** i AD *SEG* XVI 405; **(163)** 83 AD ib. 404, 1 (s. *Ἀλέξανδρος*, f. *Ἀλέξανδρος*, *Προκράτεια*, *Βίττας*)

—NEGOTINO (MOD.): **(164)** iii AD ib. XXXVIII 713 (threptos)

MACEDONIA (PELAGONIA): **(165)** ii-i BC *IG* X (2) (2) 159, 8 (s. *Μνασέας*); **(166)** iii AD ib. 259; **(167)** ~ ib. 295; **(168)** ~ ib. 299

—KERAMIAI (AREA): **(169)** ii AD ib. 184 (*Παράμον(ος)*)

—KERAMIAI (NR.): **(170)** ii AD ib. 217, 5 (*Παρά[μο]ν̣ος*: f. *Ἀλεξάνδρα*); **(171)** ii-iii AD ib. 221; **(172)** ~ ib. 223 (s. *Οὐαλέριος*); **(173)** iii AD ib. 225 (s. *Αὐρήλιος Ἀνδρόνικος*)

—KOLOBAISA?: **(174)** ii AD ib. 234, 7 (f. *Ἀλέξανδρος*)

—MARIOVO (MOD.): **(175)** iii AD ib. 166 (f. *Αὐρ. Οὐαλέριος Μενέλαος*)

—MOJNO (MOD.): **(176)** ii AD ib. 172 (*[Π]αράμον[ος]*); **(177)** 199 AD ib. 171 (f. *Νικόπολις*)

—PELAGONIA (NR.)?: **(178)** iii AD ib. 189 (*Παράμο[νος]*: f. *Φίλιππος*)

MACEDONIA (PIERIA):

—DION: **(179)** ii/iii AD Oikonomos 29 (*Μονειν̣ιανὸς Π.*); **(180)** ~ *SEG* XXXIX 583, 11 (*Κουσπίδιος Π.*: s. *Κουσπίδιος*)

—KASTANIA (MOD.): **(181)** ii/i BC ib. L 593 (f. *Ἱππόστρατος*)

—LIVADI (MOD.): **(182)** imp. ib. XXXVIII 630 (s. *Νικάνωρ*, ?f. *Ἀντίγονος*)

—PYDNA: **(183)** 250 AD ib. XLVI 800 A, 39 (*Ἀντώνιο(ς) Π.*)

MACEDONIA (SINTIKE):

—HERAKLEIA: **(184)** 230 AD *IGB* V 5922, 2 (*[Παρά]μονος*: s. *Μᾶρκος*)

—NEINE: **(185)** 173 AD ib. IV 2240 (s. *Πύρρος*); **(186)** iii AD ib. 2255 (*[Παρ]άμονος*)

—PARTHIKOPOLIS: **(187)** 158 AD ib. 2263, 15 (f. *Δημέας*); **(188)** 219 AD ib. V 5901 (*Παράμον[ος]*: s. *Δημέας*)

—PARTHIKOPOLIS (TERRIT.): **(189)** 198 AD ib. IV 2311, 1 (f. *Βίθυς*)

SCYTHIA MINOR:

—KALLATIS: **(190)** iii/ii BC *IG* XI (4) 1238 (s. *Γαῦκος*)

THRACE:

—MARONEIA: **(191)** ii BC Grandjean, *Arétalogie* p. 118 (*Eastern cults* p. 29 no. 49; *IThrakAig* E182) (s. *Ἄτταλος*)

—PERINTHOS-HERAKLEIA: **(192)** iii-iv AD *IPerinth* 143 (*AD* 51-2 (1996-7) Mel. p. 351 no. 176) (s. *Ξενική*)

Παράμυθος

THRACE:

—DIONYSOPOLIS: **(1)** 241-244 AD *IGB* I^2 22 bis, 18 (*Παράμυ[θος]*?, *Παράμυ[ρος]*—ed.: f. *Λάμυρος*)

Παρᾶς

MACEDONIA (DERRIOPOS):

—STUBERRA: **(1)** c. 41-48 AD *IG* X (2) (2) 323, 30 (I f. *Παρᾶς* II); **(2)** ~ ib. l. 30 (II s. *Παρᾶς* I); **(3)** 50 AD ib. 324, 23 (s. *Δημᾶς*)

Παρασείων

CIMMERIAN BOSPOROS:

—HERMONASSA: **(1)** ii AD *CIRB* 1086, 3; Zgusta, *PNS* 1115 (s. *Ἡ—ν*)

Παρασκευή

MACEDONIA (BOTTIAIA):

—BEROIA: **(1)** iii AD *IBer* 362, 1, 5 (Tataki 1034) (?m. *Ἀρτεμιδώρα*)

—EDESSA: **(2)** i-ii AD Touratsoglou, *Macedonia* p. 191 pl. 239

MACEDONIA (MYGDONIA):

—THESSALONIKE: **(3)** 155 AD *IG* X (2) (1) 449 (m. *Φοίβη*)

Παρᾶτος

MACEDONIA (BOTTIAIA):

—BEROIA: **(1)** ii-iii AD *IBer* 245 (Tataki 1035)

THRACE:

—RHAIDESTOS: **(2)** ii-iii AD Taşlıklıoğlu 2 p. 225 no. 1

Παρδαλᾶς

MACEDONIA (MYGDONIA):

—THESSALONIKE?: **(1)** ii-iii AD *IG* X (2) (1) 733 (*Γ. Κύντις Π.*: ?s. *Λούκις Κύντις Κυντιανός*, *Κυντία Τύχη*)

THRACE:

—NICOPOLIS AD ISTRUM: **(2)** ii-iii AD *IGB* II 661

—PAUTALIA (TERRIT.): **(3)** ii-iii AD ib. IV 2139 (s. *Λοῦππος*)

Πάρδαλις

MACEDONIA (MYGDONIA):

—NEA MESEMBRIA (MOD.): **(1)** iii AD *SEG* XLVIII 856 (f. *Σωτήριχος*)

Παρδαλίς

MACEDONIA (BOTTIAIA):

—PELLA: **(1)** m. ii BC Akamatis, *Pilines mitres* p. 292 (het.?/fict.)

MACEDONIA (PIERIA):

—DION: **(2)** i-ii AD Oikonomos 45 (m. *Ἀγαθοκλέα*)

—DION (TERRIT.): **(3)** ii AD *Klio* 52 (1970) p. 62 no. 15 (*Σαλλουστία Π.*: m. *Γ. Σαλλούστιος Πρόκλος*)

Πάρδος

THRACE:

—MARONEIA: **(1)** iii AD *IThrakAig* E308

Πάρεδρος

THRACE:

—BYZANTION: **(1)** i-ii AD *IByz* 266 (Fıratlı–Robert p. 85 no. 105) (f. *Τρόφιμος*)

Παρηγόριος

MACEDONIA (MYGDONIA):

—THESSALONIKE?: **(1)** ?iv AD Feissel, *RICM* 193 (*-ρε-*)

Παρηγόρις

THRACE:

—SERDICA (TERRIT.): **(1)** ii-iii AD *IGB* V 5697 (*Παρηγορίς*—*IGB*: s. *Ἀπολλώνιος*)

Παρθένα

CIMMERIAN BOSPOROS:

—PANTIKAPAION: **(1)** f. i AD *CIRB* 487; cf. KW pl. 16 no. 247 (d. *Χρηστίων*); **(2)** ?f. i AD *CIRB* 527, 3; cf. KW pl. 30 no. 440 (d. *Φαρνάκης*, *Μητροφίλα*); **(3)** i/ii AD *CIRB* 630

—TAMAN PENINSULA: **(4)** i AD ib. 1221 (*Παρθαίν[α]*?)

TAURIS:

—CHERSONESOS: **(5)** iv BC *IOSPE* I^2 520 (*Παρ[θ]ένα*)

Παρθενία

THRACE:

—ODESSOS: **(1)** ii AD *IGB* I^2 186 ter (PM 1641) (d. *Ἀπελλᾶς*)

Παρθενική

THRACE:

—BYZANTION: **(1)** i-ii AD *IByz* 265 (Fıratlı–Robert p. 86 no. 108) (*Δημοκρατία ἡ καὶ Π.*: d. *Δίων*)

—PHILIPPOPOLIS-TRIMONTIUM: **(2)** ii AD *Arkheologiia* (Sofia) 1968 (2), p. 44 no. 1 (Lat. Aelia Parthenice)

Παρθένιν

THRACE:

—BYZANTION: **(1)** i BC-i AD *IByz* 276 (Fıratlı–Robert pp. 64-5 no. 57) (d. *Φι—*)

Παρθένιον

THRACE: **(1)** ii/i BC *IG* XII (1) 545

—AINOS: **(2)** ii BC ib. II^2 7982 (*FRA* 260) (d. *Ἱέρων*)

Παρθένιος

CIMMERIAN BOSPOROS:

—PANTIKAPAION: **(1)** v BC *SEG* III 596 (vase)

MACEDONIA (MYGDONIA):

—THESSALONIKE: **(2)** ii-iii AD *IG* X (2) (1) 611, 2 (*Πίννιος Π.*)

—THESSALONIKE?: **(3)** ii-iii AD ib. 755

MACEDONIA (PAIONIA):

—STOBOI: **(4)** vi AD *Antička bronza u Jugoslaviji* p. 157 no. 342 (stamp)

TAURIS:

—CHERSONESOS: **(5)** iii BC Solomonik, *NEPKh* 181 (*[Παρ]θένιος*: f. *Ἀρτεμιδώρα*); **(6)** f. iii BC *SEG* XL 615 A, 15 (*[Πα]ρθένιος*: s. *Ἀριστογένης*); **(7)** f. ii AD Solomonik, *NEPKh* 111, 4

—CHERSONESOS (TERRIT.): **(8)** s. iv BC *SEG* XXXI 697 (s. *Συρίσκος*)

Παρθένις

THRACE:

—PHILIPPOPOLIS-TRIMONTIUM: **(1)** ii AD *IGB* III 1025, 3 (*GVI* 913)

Παρθενίς

SKYTHIA:

—OLBIA-BORYSTHENES: **(1)** s. iv BC Dubois, *IGDOlbia* 46 (d. *Ἀρίσταρχος*)

Παρθενοκλῆς

CIMMERIAN BOSPOROS:

—BOSPOROS: **(1)** ii AD *IOSPE* I^2 203, 3 (*[Μ.] Οὔλπ. Παρθ[εν]οκλῆς ὁ καὶ Μαστοῦς*)

—PANTIKAPAION: **(2)** i AD *CIRB* 353 (s. *Ἡζοῦς*); **(3)** ~ ib. 404 (*[Παρ]θενοκ[λῆς]*: f. *—ως*); **(4)** ~ ib. 436, 4 (s. *Σωκλῆς*, *Καλλιμέδουσα*); **(5)** i/ii AD ib. 32, 6 (*Παρθενοκ[λῆς]*); **(6)** ii AD ib. 658 (*[Κ]αλλ[ισθ]ένης*?—ed., *Πα̣[ρθε]νοκ[λ]ῆ̣*—Yailenko and Tokhtas'ev)

SKYTHIA:
—TANAIS: **(7)** 155 AD ib. 1260, 19 (*Παρ[θ]ενοκλῆ[ς]*: f. *Ἔρως*); **(8)** 228 AD ib. 1282, 18 (s. *Καρδίους*)
—TANAIS?: **(9)** 133 AD ib. 1315 (*Π[αρθ]ενοκλῆ[ς]*: s. *Ἔρως*)
TAURIS:
—CHERSONESOS: **(10)** iii BC Kats pp. 101-2 no. 70 (amph.) (f. *Λαγορῖνος*); **(11)** s. iii BC ib. p. 111 no. 105 (amph.) (f. *Σιμαῖος*); **(12)** f. ii BC *IOSPE* I^2 351, 3 (f. *Ἀπολλώνιος*); **(13)** f. ii AD *KSIIMK* 15 (1947) p. 59, 8 (Solomonik, *NEPKh* 112 d); cf. *VDI* 1993 (4), p. 63 (*Φλ. Π.*: f. —*ης*) ?= (*18*); **(14)** ~ Solomonik, *NEPKh* 113, 9 ([*T.*] *Φλ. Π.*) ?= (*16*); **(15)** ?114 AD *SEG* XLVIII 999, 35 (*Παρθεν[οκ]λῆς*: f. *Ἀπολλώνιος*); **(16)** c. 114-129 AD *IOSPE* I^2 359, 25; *SEG* XLVIII 999, 32 (*T. Φλ. Παρθενοκλ[ῆ]ς*: s. *T. Φλ. Νάσων*) ?= (*14*); **(17)** ~ *IOSPE* I^2 363, 6; 385, 2; 431, 4; Solomonik, *NEPKh* 112, 16; *SEG* XLVIII 999, 30, 34 (*T. Φλ. Π.*: II s. *T. Φλ. Παρθενοκλῆς* I); **(18)** ~ *IOSPE* I^2 431, 5; *SEG* XLVIII 999, 31 (*T. Φλ. Π.*: I f. *T. Φλ. Παρθενοκλῆς* II) ?= (*13*); **(19)** 174 AD ib. XLV 985 A, 40 (*Φλ. Π.*); **(20)** iii AD *IOSPE* I^2 485, 2 (s. *Προκλίων*)

Παρθενοπαῖος
SCYTHIA MINOR:
—ISTROS: **(1)** ii AD *ISM* I 197 I, 9 (s. *Πωλλίων*)

Παρθενόπη
MACEDONIA (BOTTIAIA):
—BEROIA: **(1)** i AD *IBer* 403, 1; **(2)** ii AD ib. 404, 1, 23, 26 (*GVI* 1594; Tataki 1036) (d. *Ἀχιλλεύς*)
MACEDONIA (PIERIA):
—PYDNA: **(3)** 250 AD *SEG* XLVI 800 A, 27 (*Αὐρ. Π.*)

Πάρθος
MACEDONIA (PELAGONIA): **(1)** ii-iii AD *IG* X (2) (2) 262

Παριανή
MACEDONIA (MYGDONIA):
—THESSALONIKE (TERRIT.): **(1)** ii-iii AD ib. X (2) (1) 1008, 1 (*Παριανῆνι* (dat.))

Παριανός
MACEDONIA (BOTTIAIA):
—EDESSA: **(1)** ii-iii AD *Arch. Pap.* 22 (1973) p. 205 no. 6 (Tataki, *Edessa* 254); **(2)** ~ *Arch. Pap.* 22 (1973) p. 205 nos. 5-6 (Tataki, *Edessa* 178) (*Κουσπίδιος Π.*: f. *Καλλιγένης*)
MACEDONIA (ORESTIS):
—SISANI (MOD.): **(3)** 146 AD *EAM* 187, 8 (*Τι. Κλ. Π.*)

Παρίγετος?
MACEDONIA: **(1)** 173 BC *PAmh* 43, 7 (Tataki, *Macedonians* p. 396 no. 12); cf. La'da E1772 (*Παρίγετος*: f. *Μενέλαος*)

Πάρις
MACEDONIA (ALMOPIA):
—NEROMYLOI (MOD.): **(1)** s. ii AD Chrysostomou, *Almopia* p. 73; cf. *BE* 1995, no. 418
MACEDONIA (EDONIS):
—PHILIPPOI: **(2)** imp. *AD* 33 (1978) Chron. p. 292 (Pilhofer 392) (Lat. Vibius Paris: s. Pirouzir)
MACEDONIA (MYGDONIA):
—KALINDOIA: **(3)** a. 98 AD *SEG* XLII 582, 29; *Anthémonte–Kalindoia* 2 p. 298 (name) (*Π.*—lap., *Πάρι(ο)ς*? (gen.)—Hatzopoulos: ?f. *Μέστεις*)
SCYTHIA MINOR:
—KALLATIS: **(4)** c. 199 AD *ISM* III 73 B, 2 (f. *Βιτράσις*)

THRACE:
—LYSIMACHEIA: **(5)** iii BC *IG* II^2 9224 (*FRA* 3204) (f. *Γλαῦκον*); **(6)** iii/ii BC *Milet* I (3) 64, 8 (f. *Σεύθης*)

Πάρμα
CIMMERIAN BOSPOROS:
—PANTIKAPAION: **(1)** iv BC *CIRB* 216; Zgusta, *PNS* 1117a (d. *Καριδεύς*)

Παρμάτα
CIMMERIAN BOSPOROS:
—PANTIKAPAION: **(1)** f. iv BC *CIRB* 218; cf. KW pl. 2 no. 38; Zgusta, *PNS* 1117a

Παρμενέα
MACEDONIA (ELIMEIA):
—KOZANI (MOD.): **(1)** ii-i BC *EAM* 46 (m. *Εὐτιχίς*)

Παρμένεια
MACEDONIA (BOTTIAIA):
—BEROIA: **(1)** iii BC *IBer* 150 (Tataki 1039) (d. *Ἀρίστυλλα*)

Παρμενίδης
MACEDONIA (BOTTIAIA):
—BEROIA: **(1)** ii/iii AD *IBer* 143 C, 13 (Tataki 618) (*Ἰού. Π.*)
MACEDONIA (PELAGONIA)?: **(2)** ii AD *IG* X (2) (2) 186, 4-5 (or Arabia Felix Amara?: s. (nat.) *Φιλόξενος*, s. (ad.) *Μένιππος*: Jew?)

Παρμενίσκα
THRACE:
—BYZANTION: **(1)** iii/ii BC *IByz* 163 (Fıratlı–Robert p. 50 no. 17) (d. *Ἀπολλώνιος*)

Παρμενίσκος
MACEDONIA (BOTTIAIA):
—PELLA: **(1)** c. 250-225 BC Akamatis, *Amph. Pellas* pp. 42-3 nos. PAR55-9 (amph.); pp. 19-20 (date) (*SEG* L 613)
MACEDONIA (CHALKIDIKE):
—OLYNTHOS: **(2)** v/iv BC Hp., *Epid.* vii 89 (Tataki, *Macedonians* p. 141 no. 95); **(3)** iv/iii BC *SEG* XXXIX 1156, 2 (f. *Ἡγίας*)
—POTIDAIA-KASSANDREIA: **(4)** ?m. iii BC *FD* III (4) 351, 5 (Tataki, *Macedonians* p. 94 no. 76) (*Παρμενίσ[κος]*: f. *Ἀρχέστρατος*)
MACEDONIA (EDONIS):
—AMPHIPOLIS: **(5)** s. iv BC *RPh* 1937, p. 325 no. 6 A, 7 (*Παρμενίσ[κος]*: f. *Στράτων*); **(6)** hell.? *SEG* L 563 (*Ἀρμενίσκος*—ed., [*Π*]*αρμενίσκος*: f. *Σύρχων*)
MACEDONIA (MYGDONIA):
—APOLLONIA: **(7)** s. iii BC *AEMTh* 14 (2000) p. 276 (s. *Σίννας*, f. *Σίννας*, *Ἄκκης*)
—KALINDOIA: **(8)** ii/i BC *SEG* XLII 578, 8 ([*Παρμ*]*ενίσκο[ς]*?)
MACEDONIA (PIERIA):
—PHYLAKAI?: **(9)** ?i BC Oikonomos 58 = *IG* IX (2) 230 (f. *Ἀντιφάνης*)
SCYTHIA MINOR:
—ISTROS: **(10)** f. ii BC *ISM* I 20, 2 (*Παρμενίσ[κος]*: f. *Ἀπατούριος*)
THRACE:
—BYZANTION: **(11)** ?352 BC Rhodes–Osborne 57, 25 (s. *Πύραμος*); **(12)** c. 315-280 BC *FD* III (4) 152, 1 (s. *Μενέδαμος*); **(13)** ii BC *IByz* 377 (Fıratlı–Robert pp. 128-9 no. 218) (s. *Ἡρόδοτος*)
—LYSIMACHEIA: **(14)** c. 200-175 BC *IG* II^2 9231 (*FRA* 3405) (s. *Μητρόδωρος*)
THRACE?: **(15)** 316-309 BC *IG* II^2 1956, 6 (*FRA* 2564); *Ancient Macedonia* 5 p. 445 with n. 10 (date)

Παρμένιχος
TAURIS:
—CHERSONESOS: **(1)** f. v BC *SEG* XL 612. 1-2 (ostraka) (s. *Μελάνθιος*)

Παρμενίων
MACEDONIA: **(1)** c. 400-330 BC *RE* (1); Berve 606 (Tataki, *Macedonians* p. 397 no. 17) (s. *Φιλώτας*, f. *Φιλώτας*, *Νικάνωρ*, *Ἕκτωρ*); **(2)** hell. *RE* (3); *GP* 2578-2627 (Tataki, *Macedonians* p. 396 no. 13); **(3)** 267 BC *SEG* XXVII 1114, 24 a (Tataki, *Macedonians* p. 397 no. 18); cf. La'da E1681; **(4)** 226 BC *PPetr*^{2} 24, 8 (Tataki, *Macedonians* p. 396 no. 14); cf. La'da E1792 ([*Παρμ*]*εν[ί]ων*?)
MACEDONIA (BOTTIAIA):
—BEROIA: **(5)** s. iii BC *IBer* 46, 8-9; **(6)** 223 BC ib. 4, 36 (s. *Μένανδρος*); **(7)** i BC-i AD ib. 142, 9 (Tataki 1041) (s. *Κλεώνυμος*); **(8)** ~ *ILeukopetra* p. 205 (s. *Ἀδαῖος*); **(9)** ii/iii AD *IBer* 143 B, 11 (Tataki 1073) (*Πε. Π.*)
—EDESSA: **(10)** ii BC *BSA* 58 (1963) p. 22 no. 3 (Tataki, *Edessa* 256) (f. *Μένανδρος*)
—PELLA: **(11)** ii BC *SEG* XXXIV 607 (Tataki, *Macedonians* p. 158 no. 70)
MACEDONIA (CHALKIDIKE):
—POTIDAIA-KASSANDREIA: **(12)** iii BC *Milet* I (3) 63, 3 (Tataki, *Macedonians* p. 94 no. 77) (and Caria Miletos: [*Πα*]*ρμενίων*: s. *Σώπατρος*); **(13)** ?iii BC *IG* IX (1)^2 (4) 1533 II (Tataki, *Macedonians* p. 94 no. 78) (f. *Μητρόφαντος*)
MACEDONIA (DERRIOPOS):
—STUBERRA: **(14)** 74 AD *IG* X (2) (2) 326, 40 (s. *Θεογείτων*); **(15)** ~ ib. l. 22-3 (f. *Ἀντίγονος*); **(16)** 87 AD ib. 325, 82 (f. *Ζωΐλος*); **(17)** 90 AD ib. 326, 80 (f. *Ἐπιγένης*)
MACEDONIA (ELIMEIA):
—SIATISTA (MOD.): **(18)** ii-iii AD *EAM* 26, 13 (s. *Πρόκλος*)
MACEDONIA (EORDAIA):
—EXOCHI (MOD.): **(19)** ii AD ib. 98 (f. *Νίκανδρος*)
MACEDONIA (MYGDONIA):
—APOLLONIA: **(20)** f. ii BC *SEG* XLIV 508 (Hatzopoulos, *MI* 2 p. 87 no. 66) (f. *Ἄδμητος*)
—KALINDOIA: **(21)** c. 309 BC ib. p. 84 no. 62, 37 (s. *Ἀ*—)
—THESSALONIKE: **(22)** ii-i BC *IG* X (2) (1) 82 (s. *Ζωΐλος*); **(23)** i BC-i AD ib. 99 (s. *Διονύσιος*); **(24)** f. i AD ib. 126, 5; Robert, *OMS* 5 pp. 295-302 (date) (f. *Ζωΐλος ὁ καὶ Μενίσκος*)
MACEDONIA (ORESTIS):
—AGIA ANNA (MOD.): **(25)** s. ii AD *EAM* 196 (f. *Φίλα*)
—BATTYNAIOI: **(26)** 192 AD ib. 186 I, 45 (s. *Κλεῖτος*); **(27)** ~ ib. l. 52 (s. *Νικόμαχος*); **(28)** ~ ib. 186 II, 55 (s. *Γέλων*); **(29)** ~ ib. 186 III, 57 (f. *Ἀλέξανδρος*)
MACEDONIA (PAIONIA):
—ASTREA: **(30)** i/ii AD *IBer* 102 A, 5 (f. *Τι. Κλ. Αἰλιανὸς Ἀλέξανδρος*)
MACEDONIA (PELAGONIA):
—KERAMIAI (NR.): **(31)** ii-iii AD *IG* X (2) (2) 211 (*Αὐρήλιος Παρμενί[ων]*)
MACEDONIA (PELAGONIA)?: **(32)** imp. ib. 185 (s. *Σωσίπατρος*)
MACEDONIA (PIERIA):
—DION: **(33)** ii-iii AD *Klio* 52 (1970) p. 64 no. 18 (*T. Τιβεριανὸς Π.*)
—PHYLAKAI: **(34)** f. ii BC *IBer* 140, 5 (Tataki 1040; Tataki, *Macedonians* p. 167 no. 2) (s. *Γλαυκίας*)
—PYDNA: **(35)** i-ii AD *SEG* XXXVIII 666 (s. *Φίλιππος*, f. *Φιλίππα*)
THRACE:
—BYZANTION: **(36)** ?i BC *RE* (4)
—MARONEIA: **(37)** ii-i BC *IThrakAig* E212, 27 (s. *Λεοντομένης*); **(38)** ~ ib. l. 58 (*Παρμενίοντος* (gen.): f. *Βίων*); **(39)** ~ ib. l. 59 (*Παρμε[νίων]*?: I f. *Παρμενίων* II); **(40)** ~ ib. l. 59 (II s. *Παρμενίων* I)
—ODESSOS: **(41)** ii-i BC *IGB* I^2 43 bis, 2 (*Παρμεν[ίων]*: II s. *Παρμενίων* I) ?= (*44*); **(42)** ~ ib. l. 3 (I f. *Παρμενίων* II) ?= (*43*); **(43)** 28 BC ib. 46, 19 (I f. *Παρμενίων* II) ?= (*42*); **(44)** ~ ib.

l. 19 (II s. *Παρμενίων* I) ?= (*41*); **(45)** i-ii AD ib. 53, 5 ([*Π*]*αρμενίων*); **(46)** s. ii AD ib. 166 (PM 1404); *Dacia* 21 (1977) p. 161 (date) (s. *Αἰαντίδης*, f. *Ἀννι*)
—ODESSOS (NR.): **(47)** i BC-i AD *IGB* I^2 294 (*Παρμενί*[*ων*]: f. *Ἀπελλᾶς*)
THRACE?: **(48)** 316-309 BC *IG* II^2 1956, 18; *Ancient Macedonia* 5 p. 445 with n. 10 (date) (*FRA* 2565)

Παρμένουσα
THRACE:
—ZONE?: **(1)** iv/iii BC *IG* XII (8) 267, 8; cf. *IThrakAig* E400 (locn.) (d. *Ἱστιαῖος*)

Παρμένων
CIMMERIAN BOSPOROS:
—NYMPHAION: **(1)** iii BC *CIRB* 912 I, 10 (f. *Ἀντιβίων*)
—PANTIKAPAION: **(2)** f. iv BC ib. 217 (s. *Ζώπυρος*); **(3)** ~ ib. 218; cf. KW pl. 2 no. 38 (s. *Ἱστιαῖος*); **(4)** s. iv BC *CIRB* 192, 6; cf. KW pl. 5 no. 88 (s. *Δημήτριος*)
—PANTIKAPAION*: **(5)** s. iv BC Dubois, *IGD-Olbia* p. 14 (ring) (Guarducci, *Ep. Gr.* 3 p. 524); cf. Vinogradov, *Pont. Stud.* pp. 625-6
MACEDONIA: **(6)** 223 BC *PTeb* 815 fr. 5, 2 (Tataki, *Macedonians* p. 397 no. 20; La'da E1568) (*Παρμένων*)
MACEDONIA (CHALKIDIKE):
—GIGONOS?: **(7)** i BC *SEG* XXIX 587; Hatzopoulos, *Actes Chalc.* p. 25 (date) (f. *Οἰκιάδης*)
—OLYNTHOS: **(8)** f. iv BC *Olynthus* 10 p. 479 no. 2527 (s. *Λειχίας*)
—TORONE: **(9)** ?353 BC *SEG* XXIV 574, 6; Hatzopoulos, *Actes Chalc.* p. 80 (date) (f. *Ἀριστοκλῆς*)
MACEDONIA (PIERIA):
—DION: **(10)** v/iv BC *SEG* XXXIII 511 B (XXXV 735); *BE* 1987, no. 677 (f. *Θεότιμος*)
SARMATIA:
—MAIOTAI: **(11)** i BC *IG* II^2 9256 (*FRA* 3455) (s. *Ἀπολλώνιος*)
SKYTHIA:
—OLBIA-BORYSTHENES: **(12)** v-iv BC *SGAIMK* 1 (1926) p. 178 fig. 4 (vase) = *SEG* XXX 958
TAURIS:
—CHERSONESOS: **(13)** s. iv BC *IOSPE* I^2 711 (f. *Πάρμις*); **(14)** c. 300-275 BC ib. 344, 1; *SEG* XLVII 1168, 1 (f. *Ἡρακλείδας*); **(15)** iii BC *IOSPE* I^2 481 (f. *Λαγοῖος*)
THRACE:
—ABDERA: **(16)** c. 395-360 BC May, *Abdera* p. 226 no. 344 (coin)
—ABDERA (TERRIT.)?: **(17)** iv BC *SEG* XXVII 350 (*IThrakAig* E80) (*Παρμέν*[*ων*]: s. *Ἀντίβιος*)
—BYZANTION: **(18)** m. iv BC D. xxxiii passim; **(19)** iii BC *RE* (1); *Coll. Alex.* pp. 237-8; *Suppl. Hell.* 604A (*PP* 16710)
—MARONEIA: **(20)** ii-i BC *IG* II^2 9290 (*Ag.* XVII 539; *FRA* 3547) ([*Παρ*]*μένων*: f. [...]*ρον*)
—MARONEIA?: **(21)** v-iv BC *IThrakAig* E487 (f. *Σωπολίδης*, *Ἀρίννας*)
—MESAMBRIA: **(22)** i BC-i AD *IGB* I^2 340 (s. *Παγχάρης*)
—ODESSOS: **(23)** iii/ii BC ib. 38, 2; **(24)** ii-i BC ib. 45, 27 (*Π*[*αρ*]*μένων*); **(25)** 35 BC ib. 46, 12 (s. *Ἀρτεμίδωρος*); **(26)** 17 BC ib. l. 30 (s. *Ζωΐλος*); **(27)** ii AD ib. 50 a, 7 (s. *Ἀρτεμίδωρος*); **(28)** ~ ib. 171 (PM 1453) ([*Παρμ*]*ένων*?: s. *Διονυσογένης*); **(29)** 215 AD *IGB* I^2 47 b, 22 (*Αὐρ. Π.*: s. *Διογένης*); **(30)** 221 AD ib. 47 bis b, 19 (f. *Αὐρ. Φίλων*); **(31)** ~ ib. 47 bis c, 40 (*Αὐρ. Π.*: s. *Ἀσκληπιάδης*)
—ODESSOS?: **(32)** ?ii-i BC *Syllogos* 19 (1891) Parart. p. 40 (f. *Φιλίστη*)

Παρμίδης
THRACE:
—LYSIMACHEIA?: **(1)** c. 100 AD *SEG* XXXVIII 735, 10

Πάρμις
SCYTHIA MINOR:
—TOMIS: **(1)** ii-i BC *ISM* II 120, 4
SKYTHIA:
—OLBIA-BORYSTHENES: **(2)** iii BC *IOSPE* I^2 201 I, 47 (s. *Τιμόθεος*)
TAURIS:
—CHERSONESOS: **(3)** s. iv BC ib. 711 (s. *Παρμένων*); **(4)** f. iii BC Kats p. 89 no. 24 (amph.) (f. *Ἀπολλώνιος*)
THRACE:
—ABDERA: **(5)** m. iv BC *SEG* XLVII 1035 (*IThrakAig* E60) (f. *Νάνη*); **(6)** c. 336-311 BC *AMNG* II (1) 192; *AEMTh* 7 (1993) p. 633 (*AD* 47 (1992) Chron. p. 488 (coin)); **(7)** ?253 BC Nachtergael, *Les Galates* 10, 14; cf. Stephanis 765 (f. *Διονυσόδωρος*)
—AINOS: **(8)** c. 100 AD *SEG* XXXVIII 727; cf. 735, 16 (*T. Φλ. Π.*)
—APOLLONIA-SOZOPOLIS: **(9)** v-iv BC *IGB* I^2 439 (s. *Νοσσίης*); **(10)** s. v BC ib. 406 (*Πάρμις*: s. *Μητρόδωρος*); **(11)** v/iv BC ib. 420 (s. *Ἀνδροκλος*); **(12)** ~ ib. 437 (f. *Παιδάρχη*); **(13)** iv BC ib. 429 (s. *Μεγακλῆς*)
—MESAMBRIA: **(14)** iii-ii BC *IG* II^2 9339 (*FRA* 3688) (s. *Ἡρακλείδης*); **(15)** s. iii BC *IGB* I^2 335 quinquies (PM 816) (f. *Ἡρόφιλος*)
—NAULOCHOS: **(16)** ii-i BC *IGB* I^2 305 quater (*Πάρμει* (gen.): f. *Πίθων*)
—ODESSOS: **(17)** ii-i BC ib. 45, 33 (s. *.α.μ.νι*—); **(18)** i-ii AD ib. 190 (s. *Μοσχίων*); **(19)** 215 AD ib. 47, 6 (I f. *M. Αὐρ. Πάρμις* II); **(20)** ~ ib. l. 6 (*M. Αὐρ. Πάρμι* (gen.): II s. *Πάρμις* I)

Παρμίων
THRACE:
—ODESSOS: **(1)** i-ii AD ib. 53, 6 ([*Π*]*αρμείοντος* (gen.)—lap., [*Π*]*αρμέ*(*ν*)*οντος*?)

Παρνάσσιος
SARMATIA:
—MAIOTAI: **(1)** 153-144 BC *SGDI* 2163, 7, 9, 14, etc. (s. *Εὐταξία*: oikogen. slave/freed.)

Παρνασσός
MACEDONIA (MYGDONIA):
—THESSALONIKE: **(1)** 61 BC *IG* X (2) (1) 5, 12; cf. *Tekmeria* 5 (2000) p. 41 (*Παρνα*[*σσός*])
—THESSALONIKE?: **(2)** iii AD *ISmyrna* 760 (Tataki, *Macedonians* p. 186 no. 59) (*Πετρώνιος Π.*)

Πάρνουγος
SKYTHIA:
—OLBIA-BORYSTHENES: **(1)** ii AD *IOSPE* I^2 92, 8 with Add. p. 518 (*Πάρνου*[*γος*]: f. *Κάσαις*) ?= (*2*); **(2)** ~ ib. 686, 7 (*VDI* 1975 (1), p. 69) (f. *Κάθαις*) ?= (*1*)

Παρρησία
CIMMERIAN BOSPOROS:
—NYMPHAION: **(1)** ii-iii AD *CIRB* 936 (*Παρ*(*ρ*)*ησία*: d. *Δημήτριος*, *Μύρον*)

Παρσπάνακος
SKYTHIA:
—OLBIA-BORYSTHENES: **(1)** ii AD *IOSPE* I^2 84, 6; Zgusta, *PNS* 180 (f. *Ἀσποῦργος*)

Παρυάδρης
SKYTHIA:
—NOVOLUGANSKOE (MOD.): **(1)** i BC/i AD *SEG* XXXIV 754 (bronze) (Vinogradov, *Pont. Stud.* pp. 641-4); cf. *SEG* XXVI 847 (f. *Σμόρζης*)

Πασα?
CIMMERIAN BOSPOROS:
—MYRMEKION: **(1)** s. iv BC *CIRB* 875; cf. Stephanis 2014 (*Πασαφιλικατος*—lap., *Πασα Φιλικᾶτος*?, *Πασ*(*ι*)*φίλ*(*η*) *Κατο*(*υ*)?—edd.: ?d. *Φιλικᾶς*)

Πάσαρος
SKYTHIA:
—OLBIA-BORYSTHENES: **(1)** imp. *IOSPE* I^2 147, 6; Zgusta, *PNS* 1119 (f. *Νουμήνιος*)

Πασέας
TAURIS:
—CHERSONESOS: **(1)** inc. Solomonik, *GAKh* 1382 (vase)

Πασιάδας
SCYTHIA MINOR:
—KALLATIS: **(1)** s. iii BC *ISM* III 35 A, 31; *IOSPE* I^2 27, 3, 9 (f. *Ναύτιμος*)
TAURIS:
—CHERSONESOS: **(2)** f. iv BC *SEG* XXVI 803 (s. *Ἀρτεμίδωρος*); **(3)** iv/iii BC Kats p. 90 no. 25 (amph., tile) (f. *Ἀπολλώνιος*); **(4)** ~ ib. p. 91 no. 29 (amph.) (f. *Ἀρτεμίδωρος*); **(5)** c. 315-272 BC ib. pp. 125-6 no. 33 (amph.) (*Πασιά*(*δας*)?); **(6)** iii BC *IOSPE* I^2 414 (s. *Ἀρτεμίδωρος*); **(7)** s. iii BC *ISM* III 13, 2, 11 (s. *Ἡρόδοτος*) ?= (*8*); **(8)** c. 230-215 BC Kats p. 107 no. 91 (amph., tile) (s. *Ἡρόδοτος*) ?= (*7*)
THRACE:
—BYZANTION: **(9)** iv BC *RE* (1) (-*δης*)

Πασιάδης
SKYTHIA:
—OLBIA-BORYSTHENES: **(1)** imp. *IOSPE* I^2 147, 9 (*Πασιά*[*δ*]*ης*: s. *Ἀπολλω*—)

Πασιθέα
MACEDONIA (BOTTIAIA):
—BEROIA: **(1)** ?171-208 AD *ILeukopetra* 130, 2 ((*Π*)*ασιθέα*: d. *Ζώσιμος*)
—BEROIA*: **(2)** 277 AD ib. 112, 1 (freed.)
MACEDONIA (PIERIA):
—DION?: **(3)** s. ii AD *SEG* XXXV 814; cf. XLVIII 876 (-*σει*-)

Πασικλῆς
CIMMERIAN BOSPOROS:
—PANTIKAPAION: **(1)** i-ii AD Vaulina–Wąsowicz pl. 124 no. 63 B, 12
SCYTHIA MINOR:
—KALLATIS?: **(2)** ii/i BC *IGB* II 867 a, 9 = *ISM* I 219 (V 87); cf. *ISM* III p. 140 (locn.) (f. *Μενεκλῆς*)

Πάσικος
SKYTHIA:
—OLBIA-BORYSTHENES (NR.): **(1)** m. iv BC *Hyperboreus* 2002 (1), p. 73 (sherd)

Πασικράτης
CIMMERIAN BOSPOROS:
—PANTIKAPAION: **(1)** ii-i BC *CIRB* 748 (s. *Εὔθυνος*); **(2)** i BC ib. 287 (I f. *Πασικράτης* II); **(3)** ~ ib. (II s. *Πασικράτης* I)

Πασίμαχος
MACEDONIA (MYGDONIA):
—THESSALONIKE: **(1)** ii/i BC *IG* X (2) (1) 1040 (Tataki, *Macedonians* p. 186 no. 57) (s. *Πιερίων*)

Πασίνικος
MACEDONIA (EORDAIA):
—PONTOKOMI (MOD.): **(1)** inc. *SEG* XLVII 937 (pithos) ([*Πα*]*σίνικ*[*ος*]?)
MACEDONIA*: **(2)** iv AD Socr., *Hist. Eccl.* iv 12 (bp.)

Πασίνους
THRACE:
—PHILIPPOPOLIS-TRIMONTIUM: **(1)** ii-iii AD *IGB* III 885, 2 (*Τιβ. Κλ. Π.*: s. *Μουκιανός*)
—PHILIPPOPOLIS-TRIMONTIUM (TERRIT.): **(2)** ii-iii AD ib. 1146 (-*σεί*-)

Πασίξενος
TAURIS:
—CHERSONESOS: **(1)** ?226 BC *IG* VII 245, 4 (*IOrop* 128); cf. *Chiron* 22 (1992) p. 494 no. 168 (date) (f. *Ξένων*)
THRACE:
—ANCHIALOS: **(2)** ii BC *IGB* V 5133 (s. *Ἀντίφιλος*)

Πάσιππος
MACEDONIA: **(1)** 173 BC *PAmh* 43, 16 (Tataki, *Macedonians* p. 398 no. 21; La'da E1569)

Πασίφιλος
MACEDONIA (PIERIA):
—DION: **(1)** ii-iii AD *SEG* XXXIV 624 (*Γετιανὸς Π., πᾶσι φίλος?*—*SEG*)
SCYTHIA MINOR:
—ISTROS: **(2)** iii AD *ISM* I 192, 1 + *VDI* 1984 (3), p. 179 ([*Π*]*ασίφι*[*λος*]?)
SKYTHIA:
—TANAIS: **(3)** f. ii AD *CIRB* 1264 A, 8 (s. *Στρατόνικος*)

Πασιχάρης
TAURIS:
—CHERSONESOS: **(1)** f. iii BC *SEG* XL 615 B, 12

Πασιχαριανός
CIMMERIAN BOSPOROS:
—PATRAEUS (NR.): **(1)** ii-iii AD ib. XLIII 509 n. (amph.) (*Ἀρριανός*—ed. pr., [*Πασι*]*χαριανός?*—Vinogradov)

Πάσιχος
TAURIS:
—CHERSONESOS: **(1)** iv-iii BC *IOSPE* I^2 505 ([*Πά*]*σιχος?*, [*Σώ*]*σιχος*—ed.: f. *Ἀπολλωνία*); **(2)** s. iv BC Solomonik, *NEPKh* 143 (f. *Κίνωλις*); **(3)** ~ Solomonik, *GAKh* 1049 (vase); **(4)** c. 200-185 BC Kats p. 107 no. 92 (amph.) (s. *Χάρμιππος*)

Πασίων
CIMMERIAN BOSPOROS:
—GORGIPPIA: **(1)** f. iii BC *CIRB* 1137 A I, 8 (s. *Σκύθας*); **(2)** ~ ib. l. 14; 1137 A II, 12 (s. *Διόφαντος*); **(3)** ~ ib. 1137 A I, 50 (s. *Ἀριστοκλῆς*); **(4)** ii AD ib. 1159 B, 1 + *SEG* XXIX 704 (*Πασί*[*ων*]?)
—PANTIKAPAION: **(5)** ?i AD *CIRB* 488; **(6)** i AD ib. 489; cf. KW pl. 46 no. 652 (s. *Χρῆστος*); **(7)** 82 AD *CIRB* 76, 12 (*SEG* XVIII 310) (I f. *Πασίων* II); **(8)** ~ *CIRB* 76, 12 (*SEG* XVIII 310) (II s. *Πασίων* I); **(9)** f. ii AD *CIRB* 699 (s. *Λυσίμαχος*); **(10)** ?s. ii AD ib. 90, 6 (I f. *Πασίων* II); **(11)** ~ ib. l. 6 (II s. *Πασίων* I)
—ZENONOS CHERSONESOS*: **(12)** ii-iii AD *SEG* XL 628 (vase)
MACEDONIA: **(13)** iii BC *IG* II^2 9272 (Tataki, *Macedonians* p. 398 no. 22; *FRA* 3484) (f. *Φίλα*); **(14)** 63 BC *POxy* 1644, 4 and verso (Tataki, *Macedonians* p. 492 no. 183; La'da E1570) (s. *Διονύσιος*, *Ἀρσινόη*: katoikos)
SKYTHIA:
—TANAIS: **(15)** ii AD *CIRB* 1262, 8 (f. *Δροῦσος*); **(16)** ~ ib. 1263, 19 ([*Π*]*ασίων*); **(17)** f. ii AD ib. 1266, 10 (s. *Πόπλιος*); **(18)** 220-225 AD ib. 1278, 8; 1279, 5 (f. *Ἀντίμαχος*)
TAURIS:
—CHERSONESOS: **(19)** c. 300-285 BC Kats p. 108 no. 93 (amph.); **(20)** iii BC *IOSPE* I^2 341, 2; **(21)** ~ ib. 473 ([*Π*]*ασίω*[*ν*]: ?f. —*ακλ*—); **(22)** f. iii BC Kats p. 113 no. 113 (amph.) ([*Πα*]*σίω*[*ν*]: f. *Σώπολις*); **(23)** ~ *SEG* XL 615 A, 14; **(24)** ii BC *IOSPE* I^2 487 (s. *Ἀπολλᾶς*)
THRACE:
—BYZANTION (TERRIT.): **(25)** iv/iii BC *IByz* 66 (s. *Φιλόξενος*)
—MESAMBRIA: **(26)** s. iii BC *IGB* I^2 339 ter ([*Π*]*ασίων*: s. *Ἡρώνυμος*); **(27)** 71 BC ib. 314 a, 1 (*Πασίω*[*ν*]: f. *Ἡραίων*)

Πασώ
SCYTHIA MINOR:
—TOMIS: **(1)** ii-i BC *ISM* II 120, 6

Πάσων
CIMMERIAN BOSPOROS:
—PANTIKAPAION: **(1)** ii AD *CIRB* 694 (s. *Βασιλίσκος*)
MACEDONIA (MYGDONIA):
—KALINDOIA: **(2)** c. 318 BC Hatzopoulos, *MI* 2 p. 84 no. 62, 28 (s. *Σκύθης*)

Πατaικία
MACEDONIA (BOTTIAIA):
—MIEZA: **(1)** 225 AD *ILeukopetra* 71, 1 (*Αἰλ. Εἰουλ. Πατεκία*)

Πά–αικος
CIMMERIAN BOSPOROS:
—GORGIPPIA: **(1)** f. iii BC *CIRB* 1137 A I, 41 (f. *Αἰσιμίδης*)
—HERMONASSA: **(2)** iv BC ib. 1056 II, 17 (s. *Ἀστύδημος*)
—PANTIKAPAION: **(3)** iv BC Blavatskii, *Pantikapei* p. 93 (vase); **(4)** 344-311 BC *CIRB* 10, 1 (Rhodes–Osborne 65 B) (f. *Σατυρίων*)
SCYTHIA MINOR:
—ISTROS: **(5)** i BC-i AD *ISM* I 191 I, 11

Πατάμουσος
THRACE: **(1)** 267 BC *SEG* XXVII 1114, 14a; cf. La'da E700 (f. *Αἰνηζις*)

Πατάσιος
CIMMERIAN BOSPOROS:
—PANTIKAPAION: **(1)** i BC *CIRB* 270; cf. *Etiudy* pp. 187-8; Zgusta, *PNS* 692 (f. *Ἀντισθένης*)

Πάτειρος
CIMMERIAN BOSPOROS:
—HERMONASSA: **(1)** 345 AD *CIRB* 1091, 4 (*Εὐφρόσυνος ὁ καὶ Π.*: s. *Σαμβίων*)
—THEODOSIA: **(2)** iii AD ib. 947 B, 6; Zgusta, *PNS* 182 (*Πάτει*[*ρος*]?: s. *Θεόφιλος*)

Πάτεις
CIMMERIAN BOSPOROS:
—ACHILLEION: **(1)** i/ii AD *CIRB* 1027; cf. KW pl. 33 no. 464 (s. *Χρῆστος*)
—PANTIKAPAION: **(2)** imp. *CIRB* 772; Zgusta, *PNS* 181 (*Πά*<*ι*>*τεις*); **(3)** ~ *CIRB* 811; **(4)** f. ii AD ib. 81, 7; cf. KW pl. 33 no. 455; **(5)** ~ *CIRB* 700 (s. *Διονύσιος*); **(6)** f. iv AD ib. 65 (*Πάτ*<*ι*>*ε*[*ις*]: f. *Θεόφιλος*: reading—Tokhtas'ev)
SCYTHIA MINOR:
—ISTROS: **(7)** i AD *ISM* I 200, 9 (*Πάτει* (gen.): f. *Σουσούλων*)
SKYTHIA:
—TANAIS: **(8)** 188 AD *CIRB* 1242, 20 ([*Π*]*άτεις*: f. *Ὀχοάρζανος*); **(9)** 220 AD ib. 1278, 11 (s. *Ἄλκιμος*); **(10)** 225 AD ib. 1280, 19 (f. *Διονύσιος*)

Πατέρας
CIMMERIAN BOSPOROS:
—GORGIPPIA: **(1)** i-ii AD ib. 1198; Zgusta, *PNS* 1121 (f. *Ἡπατίων*); **(2)** 168 AD *CIRB* 1144, 4 (f. —*s*)
—HERMONASSA: **(3)** i-ii AD ib. 1084 (s. *Ὀρ*—)

Πατερῖνος
MACEDONIA (BOTTIAIA):
—BEROIA: **(1)** ii-i BC *IBer* 392 (Tataki 1043) (s. *Ἀντίγονος*, f. *Ἀγάθα*); **(2)** 115 BC *IBer* 134, 32 (f. *Λυσίμαχος*)

Πατέριος
CIMMERIAN BOSPOROS:
—PANTIKAPAION: **(1)** 275-278 AD *CIRB* 36, 41 (*Πατέρ*(*ιος*): f. *Ψυχαρίων*) ?= **(2)**; **(2)** ~ ib. l. 43 (*Πατέρ*[*ιο*]*ς*: f. *Μαρκιανός*) ?= (*1*)

Πατερίων
TAURIS:
—CHERSONESOS: **(1)** iii AD *VDI* 1938 (3), p. 77 no. 8 (f. *Βάσσος*)

Πατερμουθίων?
MACEDONIA?: **(1)** 4 BC *SB* 11274, 3 (Tataki, *Macedonians* p. 492 no. 184) (*Πατερμουθίων*: s. *Ἀκουσίλαος*)

Πατερνιανός
MACEDONIA: **(1)** 138 AD *SEG* XXXVII 593, 14 (*Φάβιος Π.*)

Πάτερνος
MACEDONIA (PAIONIA):
—BYLAZORA*: **(1)** iii AD *Sp.* 71 (1931) p. 27 no. 53 (threptos)

Πατεροῦς
SKYTHIA:
—TANAIS: **(1)** f. ii AD *CIRB* 1266, 3 (s. *Γόκων*)

Πατέρων
TAURIS:
—CHERSONESOS: **(1)** ?114 AD *SEG* XLVIII 999, 41 ([*Πα*]*τέρων*); **(2)** 129 AD *IOSPE* I^2 359, 31 (s. *Ἀσκληπιάδης*)

Πάτης
MACEDONIA (EORDAIA):
—AGIOS CHRISTOPHOROS (MOD.): **(1)** ii BC *SEG* XXXIX 594 (*Πάτεως* (gen.): f. *Ἀλέξανδρος*)

Πατίας
CIMMERIAN BOSPOROS:
—PANTIKAPAION: **(1)** i AD *CIRB* p. 937 no. 2; cf. *St. Clas.* 8 (1966) p. 338 (*Παπίας*—Russu: f. *Δημήτριος*); **(2)** i/ii AD *CIRB* 612; cf. KW pl. 41 no. 575 (*Ἰούλ. Π.*: s. *Δημήτριος*)

Πατίκα
CIMMERIAN BOSPOROS:
—PHANAGOREIA: **(1)** v/iv BC *SEG* XXVII 448 (d. *Δημήτριος*)

Πάτοκος
CIMMERIAN BOSPOROS:
—PANTIKAPAION: **(1)** f. i AD *CIRB* 490 (f. *Πατροκλῆς*)

Πατούμας
THRACE?: **(1)** 316-309 BC *IG* II^2 1956, 25; *Ancient Macedonia* 5 p. 445 with n. 10 (date) (*FRA* 2566)

Πατουμάσης
MACEDONIA (MYGDONIA):
—KALINDOIA: **(1)** a. 98 AD *SEG* XLII 582, 16; cf. *Anthémonte–Kalindoia* 2 pp. 299-300 (name) (s. *Βάτων*); **(2)** ~ *SEG* XLII 582, 60 (s. *Φίλιππος*)
THRACE?: **(3)** 316-309 BC *IG* II^2 1956, 21; *Ancient Macedonia* 5 p. 445 with n. 10 (date) (*FRA* 2567)

Πατουμάστης
MACEDONIA (EDONIS):
—PHILIPPOI (TERRIT.): **(1)** imp. Pikoulas, *Chora* p. 152 no. 60 (Pilhofer 603) (f. *Ζιπύρων*)

Πάτραος
MACEDONIA (KRESTONIA):
—IORON?: **(1)** i AD *SEG* XXVII 287 b-d (f. *Μήδης*, *Ζωΐλος*, *Ἀλέξανδρος*)
MACEDONIA (MYGDONIA):
—THESSALONIKE?: **(2)** ii AD *IG* X (2) (1) 866
MACEDONIA (PAIONIA): **(3)** s. iv BC ib. II^2 654, 37 (*Syll*^{3} 371); *AMNG* III (2) pp. 201-3 nos. 1-12 (coin) (f. *Αὐδωλέων*: king)
—DEMIR KAPIJA (MOD.): **(4)** hell. *SEG* XLV 807 D (sherd) (f. *Βασταρεύς*)

Πατρίκιος
MACEDONIA (MYGDONIA):
—THESSALONIKE*: (1) v-vi AD *IG* X (2) (1) 338, 6 (Feissel, *RICM* 160)
MACEDONIA (ORESTIS):
—ARGOS-DIOKLETIANOPOLIS: (2) v-vi AD *IBer* 440, 2 (Feissel, *RICM* 68) (*Πατρ[ί]κειος*)

Πατρίκις
THRACE:
—APOLLONIA-SOZOPOLIS (NR.): (1) iv-vi AD *SEG* XXIX 665 (s. *T—*)

Πατρόβιος
MACEDONIA (BOTTIAIA):
—EDESSA: (1) ii-iii AD Dimitsas 25 (Tataki, *Edessa* 176) (*Λ. Κουριάτιος Π.*: f. *Κουριατία*)
MACEDONIA (MYGDONIA):
—THESSALONIKE: (2) ?ii AD *IG* X (2) (1) 463, 2 (s. *Φορτουνᾶτος, Πετρωνία*)

Πατροκλῆς
CIMMERIAN BOSPOROS:
—MYSYR' (MOD.): (1) iv BC *SEG* XLV 994 (vase)
—PANTIKAPAION: (2) f. i AD *CIRB* 490 (s. *Πάτοκος*)
MACEDONIA (MYGDONIA):
—BORMISKOS?: (3) iv/iii BC *SEG* XLIX 844. 2 (tile); *BE* 1996, no. 270 (locn.)
MACEDONIA (PAIONIA):
—ANTIGONEIA: (4) 171 BC Liv. xlii 58. 8 (Tataki, *Macedonians* p. 65 no. 8) (Lat. Patrocles)
MACEDONIA?: (5) iv/iii BC *RE* (5); *FGrH* 712; Grainger, *SPG* p. 111
THRACE:
—MARONEIA: (6) c. 365-336 BC Schönert-Geiss, *Maroneia* 492-3 (coin); (7) hell. *IThrakAig* E254 (f. *Προκλῆς*)
—STRYME?: (8) c. 400-375 BC *SEG* XLVI 859 (*IThrakAig* E138) (s. *Παυσανίας*); (9) ~ *SEG* XLVII 1106 (*IThrakAig* E137) (s. *Διονυσοφάνης*)

Πάτροκλος
MACEDONIA: (1) 275-263 BC *RE* (4) (*PP* 15063; Tataki, *Macedonians* p. 398 no. 25) (*Πατροκλῆς—ID* 1425: s. *Πάτρων*)
SKYTHIA:
—TANAIS: (2) 228 AD *CIRB* 1283, 10 (f. *Ἀλεξίων*)

Πάτρος
TAURIS:
—CHERSONESOS: (1) 174 AD *SEG* XLV 985 A, 36 (f. *Ἀττίνας*)

Πατροφίλα
CIMMERIAN BOSPOROS:
—PANTIKAPAION: (1) i BC *CIRB* 288 (d. *Ἔρως*); (2) s. i AD ib. 421
MACEDONIA: (3) 84-60 BC *FD* III (3) 364, [2], 8 etc. (Tataki, *Macedonians* p. 399 no. 27)
THRACE:
—BISANTHE-PANION (NR.): (4) iii AD *AD* 49-50 (1994-5) Mel. p. 328 no. 153 (m. *Καπιτωλῖνα*)
—BYZANTION: (5) hell. *AP* vii 221, 2 (het.)

Πατροφίλη
CIMMERIAN BOSPOROS:
—PANTIKAPAION: (1) iv BC *CIRB* 219 (d. *Ταπερεσαῖος*)
SKYTHIA:
—OLBIA-BORYSTHENES: (2) v/iv BC *IOlbia* 96 (d. *Πόσις*)

Πάτρων
CIMMERIAN BOSPOROS:
—GORGIPPIA: (1) f. iii BC *CIRB* 1137 B II, 23 (f. *Ἀρίστων*)
MACEDONIA: (2) iv/iii BC *IC* I pp. 247-8 no. 4 A, 37; 3 pp. 81-2 no. 2, 5; p. 82 no. 3, 4; *IG* XII (3) 320, [4] (Tataki, *Macedonians* p. 399 no. 30) (f. *Πάτροκλος*); (3) ?219 BC *PUG* III 103, 7 (Tataki, *Macedonians* p. 399 no. 29; La'da E1572) (s. *Πτολεμαῖος*); (4) 103 BC *PTeb* 105, 53 (Tataki, *Macedonians* p. 492 no. 185; La'da E1775) ([*Πά*]*τρων*: s. *Πτολεμαῖος*: t.e.); (5) 92 BC *PTeb* 104, 34, 53 (Tataki, *Macedonians* p. 492 no. 186); cf. La'da E1751 (f. *Διονύσιος*)
THRACE:
—PERINTHOS-HERAKLEIA: (6) iii/ii BC Schönert, *Perinthos* 65 (coin)

Πάτυλλος
MACEDONIA (ELIMEIA):
—AIANE (TERRIT.): (1) c. 225-200 BC *SEG* XL 526, 1 + *AE* 1986, pl. 42 + *BE* 1993, no. 361 (f. *Λάανδρος*)

Πάτων
MACEDONIA (BOTTIAIA):
—AIGAI: (1) s. iv BC *SEG* XXXV 780 (s. *Λάανδρος*)

Παῦλα
MACEDONIA (BOTTIAIA):
—BEROIA: (1) vi AD *IBer* 448, 6 (Feissel, *RICM* 61)
MACEDONIA (EDONIS):
—AMPHIPOLIS (TERRIT.): (2) i-ii AD *BCH* 19 (1895) p. 112 no. 3 (Kaphtantzis 585) (*Βελλεῖα Π.*)
MACEDONIA (PIERIA):
—DION: (3) f. ii AD Oikonomos 46; *Essays Laourdas* p. 112 (locn.); cf. Spiliopoulou-Donderer, *KGN* p. 192 no. D8 (date) (d. *Σερβίλιος, Κυρίχη*)
SCYTHIA MINOR:
—TOMIS*: (4) vi AD Barnea 15, 2 (Popescu, *IGL* 48)
THRACE:
—BEROE-AUGUSTA TRAIANA: (5) c. 320-324 AD *Anal. Boll.* 31 (1912) p. 198; p. 208
—BISANTHE-PANION: (6) v-vi AD *JÖAI* 23 (1926) Beibl. cols. 159-60 no. 96 (*AD* 49-50 (1994-5) Mel. p. 322 no. 148) (d. *Παρα(—) ὁ καὶ Κομιτούδης*)
—BYZANTION: (7) i-ii AD *IByz* 281 (Firatlı–Robert pp. 87-8 no. 110) (d. *Διόδωρος*); (8) i/ii AD *SEG* L 667 VI (m. *Κοσμιανή, Ἱερόκλεια, Διονύσιος*)
—BYZANTION?: (9) imp. *IByz* 379
—PERINTHOS-HERAKLEIA: (10) ii AD *IPerinth* 101 (d. *Ἀρτεμίδωρος ὁ καὶ Κυρήνιος*)

Παυλῖνα
MACEDONIA (PAIONIA):
—NEAPOLIS? (IZVOR (MOD.): (1) ii-iii AD Dimitsas 301, 2 + *AM* 50 (1925) pp. 134-5 (*Παψαεῖνα*—Dimitsas: m. *Λούκιος, Ἀλέξανδρος*)
THRACE:
—MARKIANOPOLIS: (2) ii AD *IGB* II 805 (*Eastern cults* p. 77 no. 11) (-λεῖ-)
—PHILIPPOPOLIS-TRIMONTIUM: (3) ii AD *IGB* III 1010 (-λεῖ-: m. *Ἐπάγαθος*)
—PHILIPPOPOLIS-TRIMONTIUM (TERRIT.): (4) i-ii AD ib. 1196 (-λεῖ-: d. *Ῥοῦφος*)

Παυλῖνος
CIMMERIAN BOSPOROS:
—PANTIKAPAION: (1) 221 AD *CIRB* 99, 19 (-λεῖ-: f. *Ἥλιος*)
—ZENONOS CHERSONESOS*: (2) ?iv-v AD *SEG* XL 628 (amph.)
SCYTHIA MINOR:
—TOMIS?: (3) i BC-i AD? *SCIV* 19 (1968) p. 61 (amph.) (-λεῖ-)
THRACE:
—SERDICA (TERRIT.): (4) ii-iii AD *AEMÖ* 10 (1886) pp. 238-9 no. 2, 10 (-λεῖ-)

Παῦλος
MACEDONIA (EDONIS):
—PHILIPPOI: (1) iv-v AD Feissel, *RICM* 237 (Pilhofer 100) (doctor); (2) ~ Feissel, *RICM* 238 (Pilhofer 103)
MACEDONIA (LYNKESTIS):
—HERAKLEIA: (3) i AD *IG* X (2) (2) 75, 52 (f. *Γάϊος*)
MACEDONIA (MYGDONIA):
—THESSALONIKE: (4) iv AD *DCB* (18)
—THESSALONIKE?: (5) ?v-vi AD *AD* 12 (1929) p. 151; (6) ?469 AD *IG* X (2) (1) 779 (Feissel, *RICM* 130)
—THESSALONIKE*: (7) 492 AD *PAE* 1913, p. 143 (bp.)
MACEDONIA (PIERIA):
—DION: (8) f. ii AD *SEG* XLIX 700; cf. Spiliopoulou-Donderer, *KGN* p. 195 no. D13 (date) (s. *Δομετία*)
SCYTHIA MINOR:
—ISTROS: (9) ii AD *ISM* I 197 II, 8 (I f. *Παῦλος* II); (10) ~ ib. l. 8 (II s. *Παῦλος* I)
THRACE:
—APROI: (11) v-vi AD Unp. (Sayar) (f. *Τζιτας*)
—BISANTHE-PANION: (12) iv-vi AD *AD* 49-50 (1994-5) Mel. p. 314 no. 139 (*Π. ὁ καὶ Ἀνακούβαρος*)
—HADRIANOPOLIS: (13) v-vi AD Ebersolt, *Mission* p. 52 no. 9 (f. *Βοραΐδης*)
—MARONEIA (NR.): (14) v-vi AD Meïmaris–Bakirtzis 21 (*SEG* XXXVII 613)
—NICOPOLIS AD NESTUM: (15) vi AD Beševliev 234
—PAUTALIA (TERRIT.): (16) ii-iii AD *IGB* IV 2215 (s. *Μᾶρκος*)
—RHAIDESTOS: (17) iv-vi AD Taşlıklıoğlu I p. 25 no. 2
—SALYMBRIA: (18) imp. *Archives Stamoulis* d. 35 (Loukopoulou, *Thrace Propontique* p. 286) (*Ἀθίνιος Δόλαιος Π.*: ?s. *Δόλης*); (19) v-vi AD *BCH* 36 (1912) p. 638 no. 96 (*AD* 53 (1998) Mel. p. 475 no. 216) (f. *Ἰσιδώρα*)
—TOPEIROS: (20) v-vi AD Meïmaris–Bakirtzis 22 (*SEG* XLIV 612; *IThrakAig* E96)

Παῦνα
CIMMERIAN BOSPOROS:
—HERMONASSA: (1) iv BC *CIRB* 1065 (d. *Νύμφης*)

Παυράτας
MACEDONIA (PIERIA):
—PYDNA: (1) iv BC *GRBS* 43 (2002-3) p. 115 no. 3, 3

Παυσανίας
MACEDONIA: (1) ?417-413 BC *IG* I^3 89, 76 (Tataki, *Macedonians* p. 196 no. 16) ([*Παυσ*]*ανίας*: s. *Μαχάτας*); (2) iv BC *IGB* I^2 349 ter (Tataki, *Macedonians* p. 401 no. 39) (s. *Πευκόλαος*); (3) ?394-393 BC *RE* (4); *HN*^{2} p. 221; *Kraay-Mørkholm Essays* p. 306; pp. 311-12 (coin) (Tataki, *Macedonians* p. 400 no. 37); *Macedonia* 2 pp. 170-1; *Historia* 44 (1995) p. 279 (s. *Ἀέροπος* II: king); (4) 368-360 BC *RE* (5); *Macedonia* 2 pp. 175-6, 184 (Tataki, *Macedonians* p. 400 no. 33) (?s. *Ἀρχέλαος*) ?= (*21*); (5) c. 336 BC D.S. xvi 93. 4 (Tataki, *Macedonians* p. 400 no. 34); (6) 334 BC *RE* (7); Berve 613 (Tataki, *Macedonians* p. 399 no. 31); (7) 324 BC Berve 615 (Tataki, *Macedonians* p. 399 no. 32); (8) iii BC *IG* XII (5) 571, 14 (Tataki, *Macedonians* p. 400 no. 38) (s. *Ἀνδρόνικος*); (9) f. ii BC *IG* XII (1) 322 (Tataki, *Macedonians* p. 401 no. 40) (f. *Κλεώ*)
MACEDONIA (BOTTIAIA):
—BEROIA: (10) 239-229 BC *IBer* 45, 33 (s. *Ἄσανδρος*); (11) 223 BC ib. 4, 12 (s. *Νικάνωρ*); (12) ~ ib. l. 29 (f. *Μένανδρος*)
—MIEZA: (13) hell. *AM* 27 (1902) p. 314 no. 28, 2
—PELLA: (14) iii BC *SEG* XXXIX 623 (tile)

—PELLA?: **(15)** iv/iii BC *Arch. Pap.* 22 (1973) p. 203 no. 1 (s. *Ἀνδρίσκος*, f. *Ἀντίμαχος, Σωπάτρα*)
MACEDONIA (CHALKIDIKE):
—AKANTHOS: **(16)** iv/iii BC *SEG* XLVII 871 A-B
MACEDONIA (EDONIS):
—AMPHIPOLIS: **(17)** s. iv BC Hatzopoulos, *Actes Amphipolis* p. 45 no. 9, 7 (*SEG* XLI 563); cf. *SEG* XLIV 504
—AMPHIPOLIS?: **(18)** hell. Dimitsas 900 (s. *Στρατοκλῆς*)
—PHILIPPOI: **(19)** hell. Hatzopoulos, *MI* 1 p. 188 n. 1 (*Παυσα[νίας]*?)
MACEDONIA (ELIMEIA)?: **(20)** 432 BC *RE* (3); *Macedonia* 2 p. 18 (?s. *Ἀρριδαῖος*)
MACEDONIA (MYGDONIA):
—KALINDOIA: **(21)** 360 BC *IG* IV (1)^2 94 b, 13 (Perlman, *City and Sanctuary* E.1 with p. 273 no. 239; Tataki, *Macedonians* p. 115 no. 1) ?= (*4*)
—LETE: **(22)** ii AD *Makedonika* 2 (1951) p. 619 no. 42 *θ*, 14 (s. *Ἀδαῖος*)
—LETE?: **(23)** 22 or 139 AD Dimitsas 678, 2 (s. *Διοσκουρίδης*)
—THESSALONIKE: **(24)** 223 BC *IG* X (2) (1) 2, 2 (f. *Νικόλαος*)
—ZANKLIVERI (MOD.): **(25)** ii-i BC *Makedonika* 2 (1951) p. 620 no. 43 (s. *Ἀγαθοκλῆς*)
MACEDONIA (ORESTIS): **(26)** c. 370-336 BC *RE* (6); Berve 614 (Tataki, *Macedonians* p. 206 no. 11) (s. *Κεράστης*)
MACEDONIA (PIERIA):
—DION: **(27)** iii BC *SEG* XLIX 698; cf. Pandermalis, *Dion* p. 278 (s. *Μένιππος*)
—PYDNA: **(28)** iv BC *GRBS* 43 (2002-3) p. 119 no. 5, 1, 8
SCYTHIA MINOR:
—ISTROS: **(29)** iv/iii BC *ISM* I 248 (f. *Ἀρίστων*)
SKYTHIA:
—OLBIA-BORYSTHENES: **(30)** c. 475-450 BC Karyshkovskii, *MO* p. 42; *SNG BM Black Sea* 377-8; Dubois, *IGDOlbia* pp. 8-9 (coins) (*Παυσα(νίας)*); **(31)** f. iv BC ib. 103, 5 (lead)
THRACE:
—ABDERA: **(32)** c. 346-336 BC May, *Abdera* pp. 275-9 nos. 465-93 (coin) (*Παυσανίω* (gen.))
—MESAMBRIA: **(33)** hell.? *IGB* V 5123 (f. *Θεόδωρος*); **(34)** iii BC ib. I^2 308 bis, 12 (f. *Εὔφαμος*); **(35)** iii/ii BC ib. 334 novies b (s. *Πολύξενος*); **(36)** ii/i BC ib. V 5103, 3 (*Παυσα[νίας]*: f. *Ἀπολλόδωρος*)
—MESAMBRIA (NR.): **(37)** ii AD ib. I^2 353 (*CCET* I 118)
—MESAMBRIA?: **(38)** iii BC *IGB* I^2 308 duodecies (*Παυσα[νίας]*)
—PERINTHOS-HERAKLEIA:
——(Kastaleis): **(39)** iii-ii BC *IPerinth* 61, 57 (s. *Βάκχιος*)
—STRYME?: **(40)** c. 400-375 BC *SEG* XLVI 859 (*IThrakAig* E138) (f. *Πατροκλῆς*)

Παυσᾶς
THRACE:
—BYZANTION?: **(1)** ii-iii AD *IByz* 367 (f. *Μενίσκος*)

Παύσιλλα
THRACE:
—BYZANTION (TERRIT.): **(1)** ii BC ib. 88 (d. *Ἡράκων*)

Παυσίλυπος
MACEDONIA (MYGDONIA):
—THESSALONIKE: **(1)** c. 330-345 AD *SEG* XXXVII 841; XLII 1834 (Tataki, *Macedonians* p. 190 no. 8) (-*σύ*-)

Παυσίμαχος
SCYTHIA MINOR:
—TOMIS: **(1)** i BC *ISM* II 2 A, 63 (s. *Πολύφημος*)
THRACE:
—BYZANTION: **(2)** iv BC *IG* XII (6) 1224

Παύσων
MACEDONIA (MYGDONIA):
—THESSALONIKE: **(1)** c. 230 BC ib. XI (4) 1053, 11 = X (2) (1) 1028; cf. Robert, *Documents* p. 56; Tataki, *Macedonians* p. 186 no. 58 ([*Π*]*αύσων*—*IG*, [*Θ*]*ά*[*ρ*]*σων*?—Holleaux)

Παυτάλις
THRACE: **(1)** iii AD *BSAB* 5 (1915) p. 221 (tile) (n. pr.?)

Παχαρης
MACEDONIA (CHALKIDIKE):
—POTIDAIA-KASSANDREIA: **(1)** s. vi BC *SEG* XLVII 941 (vase) (*Λαχάρης*?)

Πάων
MACEDONIA (EDONIS):
—HILL 133 (MOD.): **(1)** m. v BC Pritchett, *Topography* 1 pp. 46-7 no. 1, 7 (sherd); cf. *SEG* XLVI 723

Πεδίαρχος
MACEDONIA (CHALKIDIKE):
—AKANTHOS: **(1)** iv/iii BC *IG* XII (7) 15, 5 (Tataki, *Macedonians* p. 42 no. 9) (*Πεδίαρχ[ος]*)

Πεδιεύς
MACEDONIA (EDONIS):
—AMPHIPOLIS: **(1)** s. iv BC Hatzopoulos, *Actes Amphipolis* p. 45 no. 9, 6 (*SEG* XLI 563); cf. *SEG* XLIV 504 ([*Πεδ*]*ιεύς*?: s. *Κρατῖνος*); **(2)** b. 213 BC Hatzopoulos, *MI* 2 p. 83 no. 61, 8 (*SEG* XLVI 715) (f. *Λύσανδρος*)
SKYTHIA:
—OLBIA-BORYSTHENES: **(3)** m. iv BC Dubois, *IGDOlbia* 13, 3 (f. *Λάμπων*); **(4)** iii BC *Arkheologiia* (Kiev) 39 (1982) p. 34 (Vinogradov–Kryžickij pl. 91. 4 (vase)); **(5)** ~ *IOSPE* I^2 201 I, 21 (f. *Ζωΐλος*)
THRACE:
—DIONYSOPOLIS: **(6)** ii BC *IGB* I^2 22 II, 6 with pl. (s. *Ὑγιαίνων*)

Πεδίων
MACEDONIA (CHALKIDIKE):
—STOLOS?: **(1)** ?350 BC *SEG* XXXVIII 671, 10 (f. *Βούλαρχος*)

Πειεσουσος
THRACE:
—DUROSTORUM (TERRIT.)?: **(1)** ii-iii AD *IGB* II 874; cf. V 5392 (s. *Καιγεισος*)

Πειθαγόρας
MACEDONIA (EDONIS):
—AMPHIPOLIS: **(1)** s. iv BC *RE* (2); Berve 618 (Tataki, *Macedonians* p. 59 no. 108) (*Πυθαγόρας*—Plu.: mantis)

Πειθέρως
CIMMERIAN BOSPOROS:
—MYRMEKION (NR.): **(1)** ii AD *VDI* 1965 (2), p. 96 no. 2; cf. *Topoi* 3 (1993) p. 198 no. 2 (f. *Ἰούλ. Φίλητος*)

Πειθεσίλεως
THRACE:
—ABDERA: **(1)** c. 360-350 BC May, *Abdera* p. 255 nos. 420-2 (coin); Masson, *OGS* p. 432 (*Πειθεσιλέω* (gen.))

Πειθινώ
MACEDONIA (MYGDONIA):
—LETE (NR.): **(1)** ii AD *SEG* XXX 637

Πειθόλαος
MACEDONIA: **(1)** 130 BC *PBad* II 2, 36, 44 (Tataki, *Macedonians* p. 492 no. 187; La'da E1573)

Πείθων
MACEDONIA: **(1)** 328 BC *RE* (5); Berve 622 (Tataki, *Macedonians* p. 402 no. 45) (s. *Σωσικλῆς*) ?= (*3*); **(2)** c. 327-325 BC *RE* (3); Berve 620 (Tataki, *Macedonians* p. 402 no. 44) (s. *Ἀντιγένης*); **(3)** 326 BC *RE* (1); Berve 623 (Tataki, *Macedonians* p. 401 no. 42) ?= (*4*) (*1*); **(4)** 326-312 BC *RE* (2); Berve 619 (Tataki, *Macedonians* pp. 401-2 no. 43) (s. *Ἀγήνωρ*) ?= (*3*)
MACEDONIA (DERRIOPOS):
—ALKOMENA: **(5)** 326-316 BC *RE* (4); Berve 621 (Tataki, *Macedonians* p. 199 no. 9) (s. *Κρατεύας*)
THRACE:
—ABDERA: **(6)** m. vi BC *IThrakAig* E30 (s. *Πρωτίας*)

Πειρίθοος
MACEDONIA (BOTTIAIA):
—EDESSA: **(1)** iii AD *BSA* 58 (1963) p. 23 no. 5 (Tataki, *Edessa* 60) (*Αὐρ. Π.*)

Πεισαῖος
MACEDONIA (BOTTIAIA):
—PELLA: **(1)** iv BC Arr., *An.* vi 28. 4; *Ind.* xviii 5; *FGrH* 156 F 1. 2 (Tataki, *Macedonians* p. 158 no. 71); cf. *Eretria* XI p. 188 (or Macedonia (Eordaia): f. *Ἀριστόνους*)

Πεισίας
SCYTHIA MINOR:
—KALLATIS?: **(1)** hell.? *Dacia* 13 (1969) p. 258 no. 1085 (amph.)

Πεισίης
MACEDONIA (BISALTIA):
—TRAGILOS: **(1)** 360 BC *IG* IV (1)^2 94 b, 20 (Perlman, *City and Sanctuary* E.1 with p. 69 f. (date); Tataki, *Macedonians* p. 192 no. 3)

Πεισίθεος
SCYTHIA MINOR:
—ISTROS: **(1)** ii AD *ISM* I 201 II, 16 (f. —*ισίας*)
SKYTHIA:
—TANAIS: **(2)** 244 AD *CIRB* 1287, 14 (f. *Ἐπάγαθος*)

Πεισίστρατος
SKYTHIA:
—OLBIA-BORYSTHENES: **(1)** c. 81-96 AD *IOSPE* I^2 139, 3 + *JHS* 59 (1939) p. 86; *SEG* XLIV 666 (date) (*Π*[*ισίστρ*]*ατος*: s. *Δάδαγος*); **(2)** ii/iii AD ib. XXXIV 766, 1, 4 (f. *Σατορνῖλος*)
—OLBIA-BORYSTHENES (NR.): **(3)** m. ii AD *VDI* 1953 (4), p. 130, 4 (f. *Δάδας*)
TAURIS:
—CHERSONESOS: **(4)** s. v BC *SEG* XL 612. 8 (ostrakon) (*Πεσίσ*[*τρατος*]?: s. *Νυμφ*—)
THRACE:
—AINOS: **(5)** a. 316 BC *IG* IV (1)^2 94 b, 49 (Perlman, *City and Sanctuary* E.1 with pp. 78-9 (date)); cf. Tataki, *Macedonians* p. 177 no. 3 (f. *Δαμόκριτος*)

Πείσων
MACEDONIA (CHALKIDIKE):
—SPARTOLOS?: **(1)** ?352 BC *SEG* XLVI 804, 7 (s. *Βάσης*) ?= (*2*); **(2)** ~ ib. l. 8 (f. *Γούρας*) ?= (*1*)
MACEDONIA (EDONIS):
—PHILIPPOI: **(3)** ?ii AD *BCH* 59 (1935) p. 152 no. 46 (Pilhofer 267) (*Πείσω*[*ν*])
MACEDONIA (PAIONIA):
—KAVADARCI (MOD.): **(4)** 116 AD Unp. (Skopje) (*Πί*-: s. *Λυσίμαχος*)
TAURIS:
—CHERSONESOS: **(5)** 174 AD *SEG* XLV 985 A, 35 (s. *Γάϊος*); **(6)** ~ ib. l. 38 (*Ἰούλ. Π.*)
THRACE:
—BEROE-AUGUSTA TRAIANA: **(7)** iii AD *IGB* III 1584 (I f. *Αὐρ. Πείσων* II); **(8)** ~ ib. (*Αὐρ. Π.*: II s. *Πείσων* I)
—BYZANTION:

——(Krateinea): **(9)** i-ii AD *IByz* 319 b (Firatlı–Robert p. 123 no. 206) (s. *Ἀπολλόδωρος*)
—KELLAI: **(10)** 241-244 AD *IGB* III 1517, 37, 40 (*Πί-*: f. *Αὐρ. Μαρκιανός, Αὐρ. Κενθίαρος*)
—NICOPOLIS AD ISTRUM: **(11)** ii-iii AD ib. II 672 (s. *Ἀκύλας*)

Πελαγία
MACEDONIA (MYGDONIA):
—THESSALONIKE: **(1)** v-vi AD *IG* X (2) (1) 336, 3 (Feissel, *RICM* 154)

Πέλανος
TAURIS:
—CHERSONESOS: **(1)** iv BC *IOSPE* I^2 488 (s. *Ἡροφάνης*)

Πέλδιος
SKYTHIA:
—OLBIA-BORYSTHENES: **(1)** ii AD ib. 134, 8; Zgusta, *PNS* 694 (s. *Ὕπανις*)

Πελειγένης
MACEDONIA (BOTTIAIA):
—BEROIA: **(1)** c. 229-232 AD *ILeukopetra* 75, 17; 79, 10 (*Π. Αἰλ. Πελιγένης*)
—MIEZA: **(2)** hell. Dimitsas 121 (I f. *Πελειγένης* II); **(3)** ~ ib. (II s. *Πελειγένης* I)
MACEDONIA (ELIMEIA):
—DIPORO (MOD.): **(4)** ii BC *EAM* 44 (f. *Ἀμμία*)
MACEDONIA (MYGDONIA):
—THESSALONIKE: **(5)** iii/ii BC *Tekmeria* 6 (2001) p. 2 no. 1 (*-γίνης*: s. *Κάμπυς*)
—THESSALONIKE?: **(6)** 46 AD Dimitsas 366, 12 (*Epigr. arch. Mak.* 36); cf. *Essays Laourdas* pp. 98-100; *Tekmeria* 6 (2001) p. 126 n. 2 (locn.) (*Πεληγείνου* (gen.): f. *Μένανδρος*)

Πελήνα
MACEDONIA (LYNKESTIS):
—HERAKLEIA: **(1)** imp. *IG* X (2) (2) 99 (m. *Γάμος*)

Πελκείας?
MACEDONIA (ODOMANTIKE):
—DRABESKOS?: **(1)** iv BC Kaphtantzis 568, 6 (Pilhofer 575) (*Πελκεία* (gen.)—ed., *Πελκεί[λ]α?*: f. *Σελης*)

Πελοπίδης
MACEDONIA (PIERIA):
—PHILA?: **(1)** ?iii BC *RPh* 1911, pp. 133-4 no. 36, 42; cf. Helly, *L'État thessalien* pp. 319-20 (locn.)

Πέλοψ
MACEDONIA: **(1)** f. iii BC *IG* XII (6) 119, 2, 9; *PHib* 92, 3 (*PP* 5227; 14618; Tataki, *Macedonians* p. 402 no. 46) (I s. *Ἀλέξανδρος*, f. *Πέλοψ* II); **(2)** s. iii BC *RE* Supplbd. 12 (3a) (*PP* 15064; Tataki, *Macedonians* p. 403 no. 47) (II s. *Πέλοψ* I, f. *Πτολεμαῖος*)
MACEDONIA (BOTTIAIA):
—PELLA: **(3)** iii BC ib. p. 158 no. 72 (f. *Πυθίων*)
MACEDONIA (ODOMANTIKE):
—SIRRHA: **(4)** s. ii AD Dimitsas 812, 12 (Kaphtantzis 16) (s. *Ἰσίδωρος*)
THRACE:
—BYZANTION: **(5)** 44 BC *RE* (4)

Πεπερία
MACEDONIA (BOTTIAIA):
—AIGAI: **(1)** f. v BC *SEG* XLVI 831

Περαῖος
MACEDONIA (CHALKIDIKE):
—MENDE: **(1)** c. 410-400 BC ib. XXIX 612 + *BE* 1999, no. 368; *KGAM Thess.* I 12 (date); cf. *SEG* XLVII 913 (f. *Θεόγνητος*)

Πέργαμος
MACEDONIA (MYGDONIA):
—THESSALONIKE: **(1)** ii AD *AD* 26 (1971) Chron. p. 377 no. 3 (f. *Δάφνος*)
MACEDONIA (PIERIS):
—NEAPOLIS: **(2)** m. vi BC *SEG* XXIV 622 (vase) (Pilhofer 10)

Περδίκκας
CIMMERIAN BOSPOROS:
—GORGIPPIA: **(1)** f. iii BC *CIRB* 1137 B I, 23 ([*Π*]*ερδίκκας*: s. *Δίνδος*)
MACEDONIA: **(2)** vii BC *RE* (1) (Tataki, *Macedonians* p. 403 no. 49) (*Π.* I: s. *Τυρίμμας, Κλεονίκη*, f. *Ἀργαῖος*: king); **(3)** c. 475-413 BC *RE* (2); *IG* I^3 61, 18, 27, 47, 50; 89, 9, 15-16, 25-6, etc.; Raymond, *MRC* pp. 136-47 (coin) (*Π.* II: s. *Ἀλέξανδρος* I, f. *Ἀρχέλαος*, ?f. *Ἀέροπος* II: king); **(4)** c. 390-359 BC *RE* (3); *IG* IV (1)^2 94 b, 9 (Perlman, *City and Sanctuary* E.1); *IG* VII 3055, 7 (*SEG* XLIV 414); Rhodes–Osborne 75 A (*IOrop* 1, 4); cf. *Eretria* XI pp. 367-87; Unp. (Voutyras–Sismanidis) ll. 23, 27; *HN*^{2} p. 222; *Kraay-Mørkholm Essays* pp. 308-9; 314 (coin) (*Π.* III: s. *Ἀμύντας* III, *Εὐρυδίκα*, f. *Ἀμύντας*: king); **(5)** 320 BC *RE* (5); Berve 628 (Tataki, *Macedonians* p. 403 no. 48); **(6)** f. iii BC *PHib* 30 d, 14; *PSI* 371, 1; 378, 1 (Tataki, *Macedonians* p. 404 no. 52; La'da E1577); **(7)** ?201 BC *RE* (7) (Tataki, *Macedonians* p. 404 no. 54); **(8)** m. ii BC *BGU* 2423, 35 (Tataki, *Macedonians* p. 492 no. 188); cf. La'da E1653 (f. *Χαιρεφάνης*)
MACEDONIA (BOTTIAIA):
—BEROIA: **(9)** i BC *IBer* 506 (Tataki 1050) (*-δίκας*: s. *Λάος*)
MACEDONIA (ELIMEIA)?: **(10)** c. 333-297 BC *RE* (6); Berve 626; Hatzopoulos, *Donation* p. 23, 3 (Tataki, *Macedonians* p. 197 no. 17) (s. *Κοῖνος*)
MACEDONIA (EORDAIA?):
—GREIA*: **(11)** 181 BC *EAM* 87, 5 (Hatzopoulos, *MI* 2 pp. 41-2 no. 17) (f. *Κόρραγος*)
MACEDONIA (EORDAIA):
—AKRINI (MOD.): **(12)** f. ii BC *EAM* 92, 3 (f. *Δράκας*)
—ERMAKIA (MOD.): **(13)** 75 BC *SEG* XLVII 943 (*Περδίκ[κας]*: s. *Κάσσανδρος*)
MACEDONIA (MYGDONIA):
—KALINDOIA: **(14)** c. 314 BC Hatzopoulos, *MI* 2 p. 84 no. 62, 32 (s. *Ἀμμάδικος*); **(15)** i BC/i AD *SEG* XLII 597 (*-δίκας*: f. —*ας*)
MACEDONIA (ORESTIS): **(16)** c. 360-321 BC *RE* (4); Berve 627 (*PP* 16088; Tataki, *Macedonians* p. 206 no. 12) (s. *Ὀρόντης*)
—AVGI (MOD.): **(17)** s. iv BC *SEG* L 573 (*Περδίκκ[ας]*)
MACEDONIA?: **(18)** ?iii/ii BC Helly, *Gonnoi* 105, 5 (or Thessaly?)
THRACE:
—LYSIMACHEIA: **(19)** m. ii BC *ISestos* 38 b, 2 (s. *Γάστρων*)

Περίανδρος
MACEDONIA (BOTTIAIA):
—PELLA?: **(1)** iv BC *RE* s.v. Marsyas (8) (Tataki, *Macedonians* p. 158 no. 73) (or Macedonia (Edonis) Philippoi: f. *Μαρσύας*)

Περιγένης
CIMMERIAN BOSPOROS:
—PANTIKAPAION: **(1)** ?s. i AD *CIRB* 491; cf. KW pl. 39 no. 559 (s. *Ἀσκληπιάδης*)
MACEDONIA: **(2)** iii-ii BC *SEG* XXVI 1770; cf. Tataki, *Macedonians* p. 405 no. 60; La'da E1396 (f. *Ἀλέξανδρος*); **(3)** ?216 BC *IG* VII 313, 1 (*IOrop* 90; Tataki, *Macedonians* p. 405 no. 59) (*Περι[γέ]νης*: f. *Ἀγαθοκλῆς*); **(4)** 158 BC *SGDI* 1880, 4-5, 8 (Tataki, *Macedonians* p. 405 no. 58) (slave/freed.)

MACEDONIA (BOTTIAIA):
—BEROIA: **(5)** ii AD *IBer* 331, 1 (Tataki 85) (*Αἰλ. Π.*)
MACEDONIA (EDONIS):
—AMPHIPOLIS: **(6)** 90 BC *SEG* XLVIII 716 ter, 3, 8 (f. *Φιλόξενος*)
MACEDONIA (MYGDONIA):
—THESSALONIKE: **(7)** ii-i BC *IG* X (2) (1) 81; 95-6 (s. *Σαραπίων*)

Περιγενίς
CIMMERIAN BOSPOROS:
—PANTIKAPAION*: **(1)** ii AD *CIRB* 701

Περικλῆς
MACEDONIA (MYGDONIA)?:
—HERAKLEIA: **(1)** ii AD *IBer* 347 with comm. (*Ἰούλ. Π.*)
MACEDONIA (PAIONIA):
—NEAPOLIS? (SMILOVCI (MOD.)): **(2)** ii-iii AD *Sp.* 98 (1941-8) p. 32 no. 77 (*Τίτιος Αὐρ. Π.*)
SCYTHIA MINOR:
—ISTROS: **(3)** iv/iii BC *ISM* I 247 (*Περικλ[ῆς]?*)
THRACE:
—ABDERA: **(4)** iv BC Hp., *Epid.* iii 17. 6

Περίλαος
MACEDONIA: **(1)** s. iv BC *RE* (7); Berve 629 (Tataki, *Macedonians* p. 405 no. 61) (s. *Ἀντίπατρος*)
THRACE:
—BEROE-AUGUSTA TRAIANA (TERRIT.): **(2)** ii AD *IGB* III 1650 (*Φλ. Π.*)

Πέριλλος
MACEDONIA: **(1)** s. iv BC *RE* (-); Berve 630 (Tataki, *Macedonians* p. 405 no. 62)

Περίνθιος
THRACE:
—PERINTHOS-HERAKLEIA (NR.): **(1)** v BC *IPerinth* 286 (s. *Λῆνις*)
—RHAIDESTOS*: **(2)** imp. *CIL* III 729 (Lat. Perinthius: s. *Ἰταλικός, Θέτις*: slave?)

Πέρινθος
MACEDONIA (CHALKIDIKE):
—POTIDAIA-KASSANDREIA (NR.): **(1)** 253 AD *SEG* XXXVIII 599, 1, 4 (*Αὐρ. Π.*: f. *Αὐρ. Διονυσία*)
THRACE:
—PERINTHOS-HERAKLEIA: **(2)** i-ii AD *ISM* II 365, 1, 16, 19 (*GVI* 1161) (s. *Καικίλιος Πρίσκος*, f. *Πρίσκος, Θεοδώρα, Ἱερωνίς*)

Περιστερία
MACEDONIA (PAIONIA):
—STOBOI: **(1)** iv AD Feissel, *RICM* 276 (mosaic) (*Περιστε[ρία]*); **(2)** iv-v AD ib. 279 (mosaic); **(3)** ~ ib. (mosaic)

Περίτας
MACEDONIA: **(1)** 238 BC *PPetr*^{2} 3, 5 (Tataki, *Macedonians* p. 405 no. 64; La'da E1578)
MACEDONIA (BOTTIAIA):
—BEROIA: **(2)** 223 BC *IBer* 4, 27 (f. *Νικόλαος*); **(3)** s. ii BC ib. 203 (Tataki 1052) (f. *Λαομάγα*); **(4)** 115 BC *IBer* 134, 31 (f. *Παράμονος*); **(5)** 38 BC Robert, *Coll. Froehner* 44, 18 (*IG* XII Suppl. p. 149); cf. Tataki, *Macedonians* p. 82 no. 44 (s. *Μένανδρος*)
MACEDONIA (ELIMEIA):
—VELVENDOS (MOD.): **(6)** ii AD *SEG* XLVII 1001, 5 (*-ρεί-*: s. *Εὔτυχος*)
MACEDONIA (MYGDONIA):
—LETE: **(7)** ii AD *Makedonika* 2 (1951) p. 619 no. 42 *θ*, 1 (*BCH* 68-9 (1944-5) p. 431) (*-ρεί-*: f. *Δημήτριος*); **(8)** ~ *Makedonika* 2 (1951) p. 619 no. 42 *θ*, 12 (*-ρεί-*: s. *Πλουτιάδης*); **(9)** 121 AD *SEG* I 276, 19 (*Περείτας ὁ καὶ Βιήσιος*: s. *Φίλα*)
—THESSALONIKE: **(10)** s. i AD *IG* X (2) (1) 69, 30 (*-ρεί-*: s. *Δημήτριος*)
MACEDONIA?: **(11)** m. iii BC *PCZ* 59715, 20 (Tataki, *Macedonians* p. 405 no. 63)
THRACE:
—APOLLONIA-SOZOPOLIS?: **(12)** c. 180-150 BC *Milet* I (3) 56 (f. *Ἀρτεμισία*)

Περοίδας
MACEDONIA (CHALKIDIKE):
—ANTHEMOUS: (1) 333 BC Berve 631 (Tataki, *Macedonians* p. 64 no. 2) (s. *Μενεσθεύς*)

Περπέτουα
MACEDONIA (PAIONIA):
—STOBOI: (1) iv-v AD Feissel, *RICM* 279; 280 (mosaic)

Περσεύς
CIMMERIAN BOSPOROS:
—GORGIPPIA: (1) imp. *CIRB* 1190, 1 (*Περσε[ύς]*)
MACEDONIA: (2) c. 212-165 BC *RE* (5); Beloch, *GG* IV (2) pp. 139-42 (Tataki, *Macedonians* p. 406 no. 66) (s. *Φίλιππος* V, ?s. *Πολυκράτεια* (Sikyon), *Γναθαίνιον* (Other), f. *Φίλιππος*, *Ἀλέξανδρος*: king)
MACEDONIA (BOTTIAIA):
—BEROIA*: (3) ii/iii AD *IBer* 144 B, 18 (Tataki 1045) (*Πατερνιανὸς Π.*)
THRACE:
—PAUTALIA (TERRIT.): (4) ii-iii AD *IGB* IV 2198, 5 (f. *Ἡρακλείδης*)
—SALYMBRIA: (5) imp. *IByz* S 6 (I f. *Περσεύς* II, *K*—); (6) ~ ib. (II s. *Περσεύς* I)

Πέρσης
MACEDONIA (EDONIS):
—AMPHIPOLIS: (1) c. 315-313 BC *SEG* XXXVI 331 B, 18 (Perlman, *City and Sanctuary* N.1 with pp. 149-52 (date); Tataki, *Macedonians* p. 59 no. 109) (-*σας*: s. *Νικόλαος*); (2) 263 BC *IG* IX (1)^2 (1) 17, 17 (Tataki, *Macedonians* p. 60 no. 112) (I f. *Πέρσης* II); (3) ~ *IG* IX (1)^2 (1) 17, 17 (Tataki, *Macedonians* p. 60 no. 111) (*Πέρσης*: II s. *Πέρσης* I); (4) c. 223 BC *PTeb* 815 fr. 8 II, 3 (Tataki, *Macedonians* p. 59 no. 110; La'da E136) ([*Πέρ*]*σης*?: s. *Ἀντίγονος*: t.e.)

Περσίς
THRACE:
—BEROE-AUGUSTA TRAIANA: (1) c. 320-324 AD *Anal. Boll.* 31 (1912) p. 198; p. 208 (*Πέρσισα*—p. 198)

Περσίων
CIMMERIAN BOSPOROS:
—PANTIKAPAION: (1) 275-278 AD *CIRB* 36, 65 (I f. *Περσίων* II); (2) ~ ib. l. 65 (II s. *Περσίων* I)

Περύσης
MACEDONIA (CHALKIDIKE):
—STOLOS?: (1) ?350 BC *SEG* XXXVIII 671, 9 (*Περύσεος* (gen.): f. *Θάμων*)

Πέταλος
MACEDONIA: (1) 221 BC *PPetr* III 112h, 2 (Tataki, *Macedonians* p. 406 no. 67; La'da E1579)
THRACE: (2) iii-ii BC *Memnonion* 53 (Velkov 225; La'da E780) (s. *Ἀγαθοκλῆς*)

Πετίκιος
MACEDONIA (DERRIOPOS):
—STUBERRA: (1) 74 AD *IG* X (2) (2) 325, 17; 326, 15 (f. *Δικαῖος ὁ καὶ Ῥοῦφος*); (2) ~ ib. 325, 40 (f. *Εὔλαιος*)

Πετραῖος
MACEDONIA (BOTTIAIA):
—BEROIA: (1) ii/iii AD *IBer* 145, 4 (Tataki 646) (*Καικίλιος Π.*)

Πέτρης
MACEDONIA: (1) iii AD *SEG* XXXV 217, 1, 6, 7, 11 (*FRA* 3485) (*Πέτρης*)

Πέτρος
MACEDONIA (BOTTIAIA):
—BEROIA*: (1) v-vi AD *IBer* 432 (Feissel, *RICM* 70)
MACEDONIA (EDONIS):
—PHILIPPOI: (2) ?v-vi AD ib. 245 (Pilhofer 293); (3) ?vi AD Feissel, *RICM* 228 (Pilhofer 324)
—PHILIPPOI (TERRIT.): (4) f. vi AD Pikoulas, *Chora* p. 130 no. 31 (Pilhofer 632)
MACEDONIA (MYGDONIA):
—THESSALONIKE: (5) v-vi AD *IG* X (2) (1) 404 (Feissel, *RICM* 169) (*Πρέτου* (gen.)—lap.: f. *Ἀνδρέας*); (6) c. 500-565 AD *PLRE* III (6) (*RE* (6)) (f. *Θεόδωρος*)
—THESSALONIKE?: (7) v-vi AD *IG* X (2) (1) 792 (Feissel, *RICM* 152)
MACEDONIA (SINTIKE):
—PARTHIKOPOLIS: (8) vi AD Beševliev 244
TAURIS:
—CHERSONESOS: (9) v-vi AD *SEG* XLVII 1172
THRACE: (10) 546 AD *PLRE* III (7); *RE* (30)
—APROI: (11) iv-vi AD Taşlıklıoğlu 2 p. 80 no. 3 (*AD* 49-50 (1994-5) Mel. p. 292 no. 120)
—BISANTHE-PANION: (12) iv-vi AD ib. p. 315 no. 140 (*Π. ὁ καὶ Κυζίκης*)
—BISANTHE-PANION*: (13) iv-vi AD ib. p. 312 no. 137
—ODESSOS: (14) vi AD Beševliev 108, 3; 109, 3 (f. *Βῶνος*)
—TRAIANOPOLIS: (15) vi AD Meïmaris–Bakirtzis 27 (*IThrakAig* E442)

Πετρωνία
MACEDONIA (BOTTIAIA):
—BEROIA: (1) ii AD *IBer* 169, 4 (Tataki 1054)
MACEDONIA (ELIMEIA):
—AIANE: (2) ii-iii AD *EAM* 23 (d. *Πούπλιος*)
MACEDONIA (MYGDONIA):
—THESSALONIKE: (3) ?ii AD *IG* X (2) (1) 463, 6 (m. *Πατρόβιος*)
THRACE:
—PAUTALIA: (4) ii-iii AD *IGB* IV 2084 (*Πετρω[νία]*?: d. *Πετρώνιος Εὐτύχης, Οὐαλ. Πο*—)
—PERINTHOS-HERAKLEIA: (5) iii AD *IPerinth* 127 ([*Πετ*]*ρωνία*)

Πετρώνιος
MACEDONIA (BOTTIAIA):
—BEROIA: (1) iii AD *IBer* 274 (Tataki 1061)
—EDESSA: (2) 224 AD *Athena* 12 (1900) p. 70 no. 1, 4; *BCH* 102 (1978) p. 622-3 (name, date) (Tataki, *Edessa* 260) (f. *Γ. Κλεοπάτρα*)
MACEDONIA (ELIMEIA):
—AIANE (TERRIT.): (3) imp. *EAM* 28 (f. *Σέξτος*)
MACEDONIA (PIERIA):
—DION: (4) ii AD Dimitsas 166
THRACE:
—PAUTALIA: (5) ii-iii AD *IGB* IV 2084 (*Πετρώνι[ος]*?: s. *Πετρώνιος Εὐτύχης, Οὐαλ. Πο*—)
—PHILIPPOPOLIS-TRIMONTIUM: (6) c. 303 AD *Anal. Boll.* 31 (1912) p. 192 (f. *Σευῆρος* (Side))

Πευκέστας
MACEDONIA: (1) 331 BC *RE* (2); Berve 635; *SB* 11942 (Tataki, *Macedonians* p. 406 no. 69) (s. *Μακάρτατος*); (2) c. 306-302 BC *RE* (3) (Tataki, *Macedonians* p. 406 no. 68); *FGrH* 81 F 12; (3) b. 279 BC *IG* XI (2) 161 B, 53, 83 (s.e.); cf. *ID Index* s.v. (*Πευκέστης*—161) ?= (*4*)
MACEDONIA (BOTTIAIA):
—MIEZA: (4) s. iv BC *RE* (1); Berve 634 (Tataki, *Macedonians* p. 124 no. 6) (s. *Ἀλέξανδρος*) ?= (*3*)
MACEDONIA (EDONIS):
—AMPHIPOLIS: (5) m. iii BC Hatzopoulos, *Actes Amphipolis* p. 50 no. 11, 3 (*SEG* XLI 565)

Πευκέστης
MACEDONIA (EDONIS):
—AMPHIPOLIS?: (1) ii-i BC *BCH* 55 (1931) p. 191 no. 12 (s. *Εὐρύλοχος*, f. *Νικάδας*)
MACEDONIA (PAIONIA):
—DOBEROS: (2) hell.? *GP* 28 (Tataki, *Macedonians* p. 101 no. 1)

Πευκόλαος
MACEDONIA: (1) iv BC *IGB* I^2 349 ter (Tataki, *Macedonians* p. 407 no. 73) (f. *Παυσανίας*); (2) 330 BC *RE* (2); Berve 637 (Tataki, *Macedonians* p. 407 no. 71) (Lat. Peucolaus); (3) 329 BC *RE* (1); Berve 636 (Tataki, *Macedonians* p. 407 no. 70) (Lat. Peucolaus); (4) 323 BC *RE* (3); Berve 638 (Tataki, *Macedonians* p. 407 no. 72) (fict.?)
MACEDONIA (BOTTIAIA):
—AIGAI: (5) s. iv BC *SEG* XXVI 781 = XXXV 781 (f. *Ἄρπαλος*); (6) ~ ib. 787 (s. *Ἄδυμος*)
—BEROIA: (7) ii BC *IBer* 158 (f. *Ἀμύντας*)

Πεφιλημένη
MACEDONIA (MYGDONIA):
—THESSALONIKE: (1) iii AD *IG* X (2) (1) 637 (*Μεινία Π.*)

Πήγασος
SKYTHIA:
—OLBIA-BORYSTHENES: (1) ?ii AD *IOSPE* I^2 99, 3 (s. *Πουρθαῖος*)

Πηδίζας
MACEDONIA (EDONIS):
—PHILIPPOI (DRAMA (MOD.)): (1) iv BC Dimitsas 1063 (1101; Pilhofer 499) (*Πηδίζα* (gen.): f. *Παίζιος*)

Πήληξ
MACEDONIA (MYGDONIA):
—ARETHOUSA: (1) c. 360 BC *IG* II^2 1176, 23, 33 (Tataki, *Macedonians* p. 69 no. 12) (s. *Ἀριστόλεως*)

Πήρακος
SKYTHIA:
—OLBIA-BORYSTHENES: (1) ?ii AD *IOSPE* I^2 99, 5; Zgusta, *PNS* 183 (s. *Ἔρως*)

Πîα
THRACE:
—ODESSOS: (1) ii AD *IGB* I^2 66, 1 (*Πεî*-: d. *Ἀπολλόδωρος*)

Πίγρης
MACEDONIA (PAIONIA): (1) s. vi BC *RE* (2); Hdt. V 12 (Tataki, *Macedonians* p. 210 no. 19)

Πίδανος
SKYTHIA:
—OLBIA-BORYSTHENES: (1) iii AD *IOSPE* I^2 103, 7; Zgusta, *PNS* 240 (s. *Κούλιος*)
—TYRAS: (2) 181 AD *IOSPE* I^2 2, 26 (s. *Πιτφαρνάκης*)

Πίδεις
SKYTHIA:
—OLBIA-BORYSTHENES: (1) iii AD ib. 98, 12; Zgusta, *PNS* 240 (f. *Ἰάφαγος*)

Πίδος
SKYTHIA:
—OLBIA-BORYSTHENES: (1) iii AD *IOSPE* I^2 135, 7; Zgusta, *PNS* 240 (*Πίδου* (gen.): f. *Δουάραγος*)

Πιεζεις
THRACE:
—MARKIANOPOLIS (TERRIT.): (1) s. ii AD *IGB* II 848 (*CCET* II (1) 285) (s. *Εἰσάτραλις*)

Πιεισεισος
THRACE:
—SPORTELA: (1) ii-iii AD *IGB* IV 2233, 2 (*Eastern cults* p. 170 no. 16) (s. *Αἰσυμώης*) ?= (*2*); (2) ~ *IGB* IV 2233, 5 (*Eastern cults* p. 170 no. 16) (*Πι*[*εισ*]*εισος*: f. *Λούππος*) ?= (*1*)

Πιεπησσος
THRACE:
—MARKIANOPOLIS (NR.): **(1)** f. iii AD *IGB* II 831 (*CCET* II (1) 225)

Πιέρις
MACEDONIA (BOTTIAIA):
—BEROIA: **(1)** iii AD *IBer* 365 (Tataki 1048) (*Πειέρεις*)
MACEDONIA (MYGDONIA):
—THESSALONIKE: **(2)** iii AD *IG* X (2) (1) 220, 4 (*Κλ. Αὔξιμος ὁ καὶ Π.*: s. *Κλ. Γάϊος*); **(3)** m. iii AD ib. 214, 20

Πιερίς
THRACE:
—EMPORIUM PIRETENSIUM: **(1)** ii AD *ILB* 397 (Lat. [V]al. Pier(is): m. C. Iulius Firmus, Marcia)
—UTUS: **(2)** i AD *CIL* III 12361 (*ILB* 122) (Lat. Pieris)

Πιερίων
MACEDONIA (BOTTIAIA):
—AIGAI: **(1)** c. 300-275 BC *SEG* XXXV 791 (f. *Ξενοκράτης, Δρύκαλος*)
—BEROIA: **(2)** s. i AD *IBer* 40, 1; 115, 4; 116, [4] (Tataki 724) (*Τι. Κλ. Πειερίων*: I f. *Τι. Κλ. Πιερίων* II, *Κλ. Ἀμμία*); **(3)** ~ *IBer* 115, 4; 116, [4]; 123, 6 (Tataki 725) (*Τι. Κλ. Πειερίων*: II s. *Τι. Κλ. Πιερίων* I); **(4)** i/ii AD *IBer* 40, 3; *SEG* XVII 317, 7 (Tataki 726) (*Κλ. Πειερίων*: s. *Κλ. Ἀμμία*)
MACEDONIA (MYGDONIA):
—THESSALONIKE: **(5)** ii/i BC *IG* X (2) (1) 1040 (Tataki, *Macedonians* p. 186 no. 60) (f. *Πασίμαχος*)
—THESSALONIKE?: **(6)** ii AD *IG* X (2) (1) 250 I, 9 (*—ανὸς Πειερίων*)
MACEDONIA (PIERIA):
—PYDNA: **(7)** 250 AD *SEG* XLVI 800 A, 14, 17; 800 B, 19 (f. *Αὐρ. Κηπίων, Αὐρ. Θεόφιλος*)
MACEDONIA (SINTIKE):
—PARTHIKOPOLIS: **(8)** ii-iii AD *IGB* V 5899 (s. *Ἀπολλώνιος*)

Πιθάνη
MACEDONIA (BOTTIAIA):
—BEROIA: **(1)** s. ii AD *IBer* 310, 1 (?m. *Ἀμμία, Πρόκλος, Ὀνήσιμος, Ὀνήσιμος* (sic))
THRACE:
—BRAŠLJANICA (MOD.): **(2)** ii-iii AD *ILB* 221 (Lat. Pitane: d. Diern–)

Πίθων
MACEDONIA (BOTTIAIA):
—PELLA: **(1)** s. iv BC *SEG* XLVIII 823 A (f. *Βιαῖος*)
THRACE:
—NAULOCHOS: **(2)** ii-i BC *IGB* I² 305 quater (*Π̣ίθων*: s. *Πάρμις*)

Πίνκισος
THRACE:
—HADRIANOPOLIS (TERRIT.): **(1)** iii AD ib. III 1813 (?f. *Αὐρ. Ἀπολλόδωρος*)

Πίνμαζος
SKYTHIA:
—OLBIA-BORYSTHENES: **(1)** ii AD *IOSPE* I² 82, 7; Zgusta, *PNS* 693 (f. *Ἀρθάμμανος*)

Πίνυτος
CIMMERIAN BOSPOROS:
—PANTIKAPAION: **(1)** i-ii AD *CIRB* 631 (s. *Ἀνόπτηνις*)

Πιόθουθος
THRACE:
—MARKIANOPOLIS (TERRIT.): **(1)** iii AD *IGB* V 5329, 5 (s. *Τρι.αθιθος*)

Πῖος
SCYTHIA MINOR:
—KALLATIS (NR.): **(1)** ii-iii AD *ISM* III 243, 3 (*IGB* I² 2) (*Πεῖ-*: f. *Σαβῖνα*)
THRACE:
—APOLLONIA-SOZOPOLIS: **(2)** i-ii AD ib. 401, 15 (⟨*Π*⟩*εῖος*: s. *Ἀρποκράτης*)
—MARKIANOPOLIS: **(3)** f. iii AD ib. V 5344 (*CCET* II (1) 209) (*Πεῖ-*: s. *Λούκιος*)
—MARKIANOPOLIS (NR.): **(4)** ii-iii AD *IGB* V 5368 (f. *Αὐλούζενις*)

Πίπης
THRACE:
—ODESSOS: **(1)** ?ii AD ib. I² 115, 2 (*Διονύσιος ὁ καὶ Πείπης*: s. *Διονύσιος*)
—PERINTHOS-HERAKLEIA: **(2)** iii-iv AD *IPerinth* 315 (*Γ. Ἰούνιος Οὐάλης Π.*)

Πιπίς
MACEDONIA (EDONIS):
—AMPHIPOLIS: **(1)** f. iii BC *Ant. Kunst* 12 (1969) pp. 68-71; cf. *SEG* XLVII 879 (m. *Φανίς*)

Πίσα
TAURIS:
—CHERSONESOS: **(1)** v/iv BC Solomonik, *GAKh* 1390 (vase) (*Πίσας* (fem. gen.?), *Πισᾶς* (masc. nom.)—ed.)

Πίση
THRACE:
—PERINTHOS-HERAKLEIA?: **(1)** iii AD *IPerinth* 309 (*Αὐρ. Π.*: m. *Αὐρ. Ἀπολλινάριος*)

Πίσκας
SKYTHIA:
—TYRAS: **(1)** 181 AD *IOSPE* I² 2, 31; Zgusta, *PNS* 695 (f. *Διονύσιος*)

Πισταρέτα
MACEDONIA (MYGDONIA):
—THESSALONIKE (NR.): **(1)** f. iii BC *SEG* XLVII 967; *BE* 1998, no. 257 (date)

Πίστη
MACEDONIA (BOTTIAIA):
—PELLA: **(1)** 150 AD *SEG* XLVIII 825 (m. *Εὐπορία*, ?m. *Ζώσιμος*)
MACEDONIA (CHALKIDIKE):
—POTIDAIA-KASSANDREIA (NR.): **(2)** imp. ib. XXIX 602 (Dimitsas 751)

Πίστις
MACEDONIA (MYGDONIA):
—THESSALONIKE: **(1)** ii AD *IG* X (2) (1) 536 + *BCH* 97 (1973) p. 593; **(2)** ?ii AD *IG* X (2) (1) 539 (*Ἀντωνία Π.*: d. *Ἀντώνιος Ἀττικός, Φαβία Σαμβώ*)

Πίστος
CIMMERIAN BOSPOROS:
—PANTIKAPAION: **(1)** i AD *CIRB* 356; cf. KW pl. 43 no. 630
MACEDONIA: **(2)** ii-i BC *IG* II² 9267 (Tataki, *Macedonians* p. 407 no. 75; *FRA* 3486)
MACEDONIA (BOTTIAIA):
—BEROIA: **(3)** ii-iii AD *IBer* 251 (Tataki 1075)
MACEDONIA (MYGDONIA):
—KALINDOIA: **(4)** a. 98 AD *SEG* XLII 582, 21 (*Τ. Τεσσίδιος Π.*)
—THESSALONIKE: **(5)** ii/iii AD ib. XXXIX 637; cf. XLIII 465 (*Κειώνιος Αἰβούτιος Π.*)
MACEDONIA (ODOMANTIKE):
—SIRRHA: **(6)** f. iii AD ib. XXX 590, 12 (f. *Αὐρ. Διοσκουρίδης*)
SARMATIA:
—MAIOTAI: **(7)** imp.? *IG* II² 9257 (*FRA* 3456) (slave?)

SCYTHIA MINOR:
—ISTROS: **(8)** i AD *ISM* I 200, 11 (f. *Μόνιμος*); **(9)** ii AD ib. 196, 6; 201 I, 7 (f. *Γλύκων*); **(10)** ~ ib. 196, 11; 211, 15 (f. *Διονυττᾶς*); **(11)** ~ ib. 196, 21; 201 I, 20 (f. *Πάπας*); **(12)** 138 AD ib. 193 I, 79 (s. *Διονύσιος*)
THRACE:
—HADRIANOPOLIS (TERRIT.): **(13)** iii AD *IGB* III 1817 (*Πεί-*: s. *Ὑκονόης*)
—NICOPOLIS AD ISTRUM (TERRIT.): **(14)** 227 AD *ILB* 438 I, 41 (Lat. Aur. Apollinaris qui et Pistus); **(15)** ~ ib. l. 42 (Lat. Pistu[s]: s. Do–)
—ODESSOS?: **(16)** iii AD *IGB* I² 228 bis, 5 (*Αὐρ. Π.*)

Πιστοῦς
SKYTHIA:
—OLBIA-BORYSTHENES: **(1)** ii AD *IOSPE* I² 131, 11 (s. *Ἀντώνιος*)
THRACE:
—BEROE-AUGUSTA TRAIANA (TERRIT.): **(2)** ii-iii AD *IGB* III 1726 ([*Πι*]*στοῦς*)
—BEROE-AUGUSTA TRAIANA:
——Karasoura: **(3)** iii AD ib. 1626, 9 (s. *Σκέλης*)
—HADRIANOPOLIS (TERRIT.): **(4)** ii-iii AD ib. 1802 (s. *Βίθυς*)
—NICOPOLIS AD ISTRUM (TERRIT.): **(5)** iii AD *CCET* II (2) 651 (*ILB* 417) (Lat. Pistunis (gen.): ?f. Severus)

Πιτθάκης
SKYTHIA:
—OLBIA-BORYSTHENES: **(1)** s. iv BC *SEG* L 702 II, 2, 6

Πίτθιος
TAURIS:
—CHERSONESOS: **(1)** f. iii BC ib. XL 615 A, 21 (s. *Νικασι—*)

Πίτθις
MACEDONIA (CHALKIDIKE):
—APHYTIS: **(1)** ?351 BC *Α΄ Panell. Synedr. Epigr.* pp. 80-1, 20 (s. *Ἀρχέδημος*)

Πιτοφαρνάκης
SKYTHIA:
—TANAIS: **(1)** 220 AD *CIRB* 1278, 9; Zgusta, *PNS* 184 (f. *Θάλαμος*)

Πιττακός
MACEDONIA (EDONIS):
—EDONOI: **(1)** b. 424 BC Th. iv 107. 3 (king)

Πιτφαρνάκης
SKYTHIA:
—TYRAS: **(1)** 181 AD *IOSPE* I² 2, 26; Zgusta, *PNS* 184 (*Πιτφαρ*[*νάκ*]*ο*[*υ*] (gen.): f. *Πίδανος*)

Πλαγγών
MACEDONIA (BOTTIAIA):
—PELLA: **(1)** iii-ii BC Dimitsas 144

Πλατθίς
THRACE:
—BYZANTION: **(1)** i BC *IByz* 147 (Fıratlı–Robert pp. 100-1 no. 152) (d. *Εὔβιος*)

Πλάτων
CIMMERIAN BOSPOROS:
—PANTIKAPAION: **(1)** v-vi AD *ZOOID* 28 (1910) Prot. p. 12 no. 2 (*Πλάτ*[*ων*])
MACEDONIA (EDONIS):
—PHILIPPOI: **(2)** i-ii AD *BCH* 58 (1934) p. 472 no. 9 (Pilhofer 322) (Lat. C. Velleius Plato: I ?f. *Πλάτων* II); **(3)** ~ *BCH* 58 (1934) p. 472 no. 9 (Pilhofer 322) (Lat. C. Velleius Plato: II ?s. *Πλάτων* I: doctor)
THRACE:
—MARONEIA: **(4)** f. iv BC *IG* II² 9291 (*FRA* 3548)

Πλάτωρ
MACEDONIA (MYGDONIA):
—THESSALONIKE: **(1)** ii AD *IG* X (2) (1) 296; cf. *SEG* XXXVII 586 (*Πλάτορες* (gen.): f. *Και. Πολύκαρπος*)

MACEDONIA (ORESTIS): **(2)** 57 BC *RE* (2) (Lat. Plator)

Πλαύτιλλα
MACEDONIA (MYGDONIA):
—THESSALONIKE: **(1)** iii/iv AD *Anal. Boll.* 28 (1909) pp. 461-4

Πλεισθένης
MACEDONIA (EDONIS):
—AMPHIPOLIS: **(1)** 401 BC X., *An.* iv 6. 1, 3 (Tataki, *Macedonians* p. 60 no. 113) (Ἐπισθένης—mss. dett.) ?= (Ἐπισθένης (*2*)

Πλείστα
MACEDONIA (BISALTIA):
—TRAGILOS (NR.): **(1)** ii-iii AD *SEG* XXX 611

Πλείσταρχος
CIMMERIAN BOSPOROS:
—PANTIKAPAION: **(1)** iii BC *CIRB* 111, 4 ([Πλ]είσταρχος)
MACEDONIA: **(2)** iv/iii BC *RE* (2); Berve 641; *Historia* 44 (1995) pp. 11-28 (Tataki, *Macedonians* p. 408 no. 76) (s. Ἀντίπατρος)
MACEDONIA (BOTTIAIA):
—PELLA (TERRIT.)?: **(3)** hell.? Dimitsas 133 (s. Πύθων)
SKYTHIA:
—OLBIA-BORYSTHENES: **(4)** iii BC *IOSPE* I² 32 A, 58 (Maier, *Mauerbauinschr.* 82)
THRACE:
—ODESSOS (NR.): **(5)** i BC-i AD *IGB* I² 294 (f. —ας)

Πλειστιάδης
MACEDONIA (MYGDONIA):
—LETE: **(1)** s. iv BC Hatzopoulos, *MI* 2 pp. 93-4 no. 79, 3 (Πλειστιάδης: f. Λύσων)

Πλειστίας
MACEDONIA (CHALKIDIKE):
—POTIDAIA-KASSANDREIA: **(1)** c. 300 BC *IG* II² 1956, 115 (Tataki, *Macedonians* p. 94 no. 79; *FRA* 2793)
TAURIS:
—CHERSONESOS: **(2)** iv BC Solomonik, *GAKh* 1392 (vase) (Πλειστί[ας]?)

Πλειστῶναξ
SKYTHIA:
—OLBIA-BORYSTHENES: **(1)** iii BC *IOSPE* I² 201 I, 35 (s. Νικήρατος)
TAURIS:
—CHERSONESOS: **(2)** f. ii BC ib. 351, 2 (s. Διονύσιος)

Πλείστωρ
THRACE:
—PERINTHOS-HERAKLEIA:
——(Geleuntes): **(1)** iii-ii BC *IPerinth* 61, 30 (f. Τάκτωρ)

Πλευρᾶτος
MACEDONIA (BOTTIAIA):
—BEROIA: **(1)** ii BC *IBer* 141, 36; **(2)** ii-i BC ib. 30 (Tataki 1077) (f. Ἀσκληπιόδωρος)
MACEDONIA (ORESTIS): **(3)** 57 BC *RE* (6) (Lat. Pleuratus)
—BATTYNAIOI: **(4)** 192 AD *EAM* 186 II, 45 (Πλευρᾶ[τ]ος—Woodward, Πλεύ(ρ)αδος—*EAM*: s. —αως)

Πληιστίδης
THRACE:
—APOLLONIA-SOZOPOLIS: **(1)** v/iv BC *IGB* I² 447 bis (s. Ἑκαταῖος)

Πλῆστις
MACEDONIA (ODOMANTIKE):
—GAZOROS: **(1)** 215 or 174 BC *SEG* XXX 1892, 20 (Hatzopoulos, *MI* 2 pp. 57-8 no. 39)

Πλόκαμος
MACEDONIA (CHALKIDIKE):
—POTIDAIA-KASSANDREIA: **(1)** i-ii AD *TAPA* 69 (1938) p. 65 no. 17 (s. Φίλητος Μάρκιος)

Πλουσία
CIMMERIAN BOSPOROS:
—PANTIKAPAION: **(1)** ii BC *CIRB* 27
MACEDONIA (MYGDONIA):
—THESSALONIKE: **(2)** f. i AD *IG* X (2) (1) 133, 12; Robert, *OMS* 5 pp. 295-302 (date) (m. Ἀθηνογένης)

Πλοῦσις
CIMMERIAN BOSPOROS:
—NYMPHAION: **(1)** iii BC *CIRB* 912 II, 8 (f. Ἡρακλείδης)

Πλούταρχος
CIMMERIAN BOSPOROS:
—PANTIKAPAION: **(1)** i AD ib. 492 (f. Πλουτέρως)
MACEDONIA (ELIMEIA):
—AIANE: **(2)** ii BC *EAM* 75 ([Π]λούταρχο[ς])
THRACE: **(3)** 146 BC *PKöln* 187, 16 (La'da E781) (s. Εὔβουλος)

Πλουτέρως
CIMMERIAN BOSPOROS:
—PANTIKAPAION: **(1)** i AD *CIRB* 492 (Π[λο]υτέρω[ς]: s. Πλούταρχος)

Πλευτιάδης
MACEDONIA (MYGDONIA):
—LETE: **(1)** ii AD *Makedonika* 2 (1951) p. 619 no. 42 θ, 13 (f. Περίτας)

Πλουτίνα
MACEDONIA (MYGDONIA):
—THESSALONIKE: **(1)** v-vi AD *IG* X (2) (1) 353, 5 (Feissel, *RICM* 170)

Πλουτίς
THRACE:
—ODESSOS: **(1)** iii/ii BC *IG* XII (1) 147 (*GVI* 1257); cf. Robert, *OMS* 5 p. 216 n. 6 (locn.) (Πλουτίδα (acc.))

Πλουτίων
THRACE:
—MESAMBRIA: **(1)** hell.? *IGB* I² 342 ([Πλο]υτίων?: f. Ἀγησίλα)

Πλουτογένης
THRACE:
—MARONEIA: **(1)** i BC-i AD *BCH* 37 (1913) p. 144 no. 49, 4 (*IThrakAig* E286) (f. Ἀκονία); **(2)** ii-iii AD Dumont–Homolle 110b 19 (*IThrakAig* E290) (f. Κατρουβήα)

Πλύσος
THRACE:
—NICOPOLIS AD NESTUM: **(1)** ii-iii AD *IGB* IV 2337, 14 (f. Βίθυς)

Πλωτῖνα
SCYTHIA MINOR:
—ISTROS: **(1)** ii AD *ISM* I 217, 2 with pl. (-τεῖ-, —φεῖνα—ed.: d. Ἀχιλ—)
THRACE:
—BIZYE?: **(2)** ?ii AD Unp. (Sayar)
—PAUTALIA (TERRIT.): **(3)** ii-iii AD *IGB* V 5801 (—ία Πλωτεῖνα)
—PERINTHOS-HERAKLEIA: **(4)** i-ii AD *IPerinth* 136 (Βασσία Πλωτεῖνα: m. Βασσία Φαυστῖνα)

Πλωτινάς
THRACE:
—PERINTHOS-HERAKLEIA: **(1)** iii AD ib. 175; *BE* 1978, no. 19 (name) (Πλωτεινάδι (dat.))

Πλωτίνη
THRACE:
—PHILIPPOPOLIS-TRIMONTIUM:
——Parembole: **(1)** ii-iii AD *IGB* III 1512, 5 (Οὐαλερία Πλωτείνη)

Πλωτίων
CIMMERIAN BOSPOROS:
—PANTIKAPAION: **(1)** ii AD *CIRB* 702; cf. KW pl. 56 no. 759 (s. Πρῶτος)
SCYTHIA MINOR:
—TOMIS: **(2)** ii-iii AD *ISM* II 21, 7; cf. *BE* 1965, no. 264 ([Π]λωτίων, [Κω]λωτίων?—*BE*)

Πογάσιος?
CIMMERIAN BOSPOROS:
—PANTIKAPAION: **(1)** i AD *CIRB* 352 + KW pl. 47 no. 666; cf. Zgusta, *PNS* 696 (Ποτάσιος—*CIRB*, Πογάσιος?—KW and Vinogradov, Πελάγιος?: f. Ἀπολλώνιος)

Ποθείνη
MACEDONIA (BOTTIAIA):
—BEROIA: **(1)** ii AD *IBer* 330, 3 (Tataki 1081) (-θί-: d. Σύμφορος, Φαβία)

Ποθεινός
CIMMERIAN BOSPOROS:
—GORGIPPIA: **(1)** imp. *CIRB* 1188, 3 ([Πο]θεινό[ς]); **(2)** i/ii AD ib. 1179, 37 (s. Τεργόνιος); **(3)** ii AD ib. 1154, 5; **(4)** ii/iii AD ib. 1179, 43 (I s. Γναφίσκος, f. Ποθεινός II); **(5)** ~ ib. l. 43 (II s. Ποθεινός I); **(6)** ~ ib. l. 44 (f. Νουμήνιος)
—GORGIPPIA?: **(7)** s. ii AD ib. 1231 B, 15 (Ποθην[ός]?)

Ποθίαινα
CIMMERIAN BOSPOROS:
—TYRITAKE: **(1)** f. ii AD ib. 909 (m. Κλέων, Χρύσιν)

Πόθις
CIMMERIAN BOSPOROS:
—GORGIPPIA: **(1)** ii/iii AD ib. 1179, 59 (s. Ἀρίστων)

Ποθίσκος
CIMMERIAN BOSPOROS:
—GORGIPPIA: **(1)** imp. ib. 1189, 6 (Ποθίσκ[ος]: f. —ος); **(2)** f. i AD ib. 1197 A (f. Γλυκαρίων); **(3)** f. ii AD ib. 1172, 1 ([Π]οθίσκ[ος]—Vinogradov); **(4)** m. ii AD *Eirene* 7 (1968) p. 67, 11 (f. Ἔρως, —θ.ας); **(5)** s. ii AD *SEG* XXIX 706, 4; **(6)** 173-210 AD *CIRB* 1135, 24; **(7)** ii/iii AD ib. 1179, 59 (s. Ἀγαθοῦς)
—GORGIPPIA?: **(8)** s. ii AD ib. 1231 A, 13; **(9)** ii/iii AD ib. 1232, 8 ([Πο]θίσκος)
—PANTIKAPAION: **(10)** f. ii AD ib. 88, 3 (s. Κοσοῦς)

Ποθίων
CIMMERIAN BOSPOROS:
—PANTIKAPAION: **(1)** ii-i BC ib. 272; cf. KW pl. 25 no. 361

Πόθος
CIMMERIAN BOSPOROS:
—GORGIPPIA: **(1)** imp. *CIRB* 1187, 5; **(2)** 41 AD ib. 1123, 7 (Levinskaya pp. 239-40 no. 7) (s. Στράβων); **(3)** i/ii AD *CIRB* 1115, 7; *SEG* XL 624, [1] (f. Φαρνακίων) ?= (*5*); **(4)** 93-123 AD *CIRB* 1122, 7 (Πόθ[ος]); **(5)** ~ ib. 1129 A, 2; 1157; 1232, 6 (—θος—1129 and 1157, Πο—— 1232: f. Φαρνακίων) ?= (*3*); **(6)** ii AD ib. 1140, 9 (s. Θεοδο—); **(7)** ~ ib. l. 11; **(8)** ~ ib. l. 16 (f. Φαρνακίων); **(9)** ~ ib. 1143, 9; **(10)** ~ ib. 1151, 3 (Πόθος: f. Ἀρίστων); **(11)** ~ ib. l. 8 (s. Πάπας); **(12)** ~ ib. 1178 A (Πόθο[ς]); **(13)** ii-iii AD *NE* 9 (1971) p. 9 no. 6 A, 4 (Πόθο[ς]); **(14)** m. ii AD *Eirene* 7 (1968) p. 67, 9 (f. Ἀθηνόδωρος) ?= (*33*); **(15)** ~ ib. l. 13 (s. Πανταλέων); **(16)** s. ii AD *CIRB* 1129 A, 7 (f. —ανδρος); **(17)** ~ ib. 1129 B, 1 (Πόθ[ος]); **(18)** ~ ib. l. 7 (f. Λυκίσκος); **(19)** ~ ib. 1142, 8 (f. —ος); **(20)** ~ ib. l. 9 (s. Πο—); **(21)** ~ ib. l. 14 (s. Ἀτίνας, f. Ἔρως); **(22)** 168 AD ib. 1144, 2 (I f. Πόθος II); **(23)**

~ ib. l. 2 (II s. *Πόθος* I, f. *—ιων*); **(24)** 173-210 AD ib. 1134, 24 (*[Π]όθος*: s. *Ἄττας*); **(25)** ~ ib. 1134 E, 6 (f. *Πάννυχος*); **(26)** ~ ib. 1135, 15 (s. *Σ—*); **(27)** ~ ib. l. 18 (s. *Τιμόθεος*, f. *Χρηστίων*); **(28)** ~ ib. l. 24 (*Πόθ[ος]*?: f. *—ων*); **(29)** ~ ib. l. 26 (*[Π]όθος*: s. *Διονύσιος*); **(30)** ~ ib. l. 30 (s. *Φαρ—*); **(31)** ii/iii AD ib. 1179, 4; **(32)** ~ ib. l. 9 (s. *Χρηστίων*); **(33)** ~ ib. l. 27 (f. *Ἀθηνόδωρος*) ?= (*14*); **(34)** ~ ib. l. 31 (s. *Μάριος*); **(35)** ~ ib. l. 31 (s. *Θεότιμος*, f. *Νεοκλῆς*); **(36)** ~ ib. l. 35 (?s. *Χρυσόχοος*); **(37)** ~ ib. l. 36 (s. *Πάπας*); **(38)** ~ ib. l. 44 (s. *Πάππος*) ?= (*41*); **(39)** ~ ib. l. 55 (s. *Ἀν—*); **(40)** ~ ib. 1180, 3 (s. *Ἑρμῆς*); **(41)** ~ *SEG* XXXVI 705, 1 (*[Π]όθος*: s. *Πα—*) ?= (*38*); **(42)** ~ ib. l. 4 (*Πόθο[ς]*); **(43)** ~ ib. 714, 2 (f. *—ν*); **(44)** ~ ib. XLIX 1033 A, 5 (*CIRB* 1182 A, 4) (*Πόθο[ς]*); **(45)** ~ *SEG* XLIX 1033 B, 7 (*CIRB* 1182 B, 5) (*[Π]όθος*); **(46)** iii AD *NE* 9 (1971) p. 10 no. 6 B, 16 (s. *Γάστεις*)
—GORGIPPIA?: **(47)** s. ii AD *CIRB* 1231 B, 9 (*[Π]όθος*: s. *Φαρνάκης*)
—PANTIKAPAION: **(48)** imp. ib. 774 (f. *Ἀβαζίων*); **(49)** i AD ib. 339 (*[Π]όθος*); **(50)** ~ ib. 354 (f. *Ἀπολλώνιος*, *Σωκράτης*); **(51)** ~ ib. 363; cf. KW pl. 33 no. 460 (f. *Ἀχιλλεύς*); **(52)** ~ *CIRB* 396 (f. *Ἕλενος*, *Πολύβιος*); **(53)** ~ ib. 493 (s. *Ἕλενος*); **(54)** i/ii AD ib. 632 (s. *Φαρνακίων*); **(55)** ii-iii AD ib. 763 (s. *Σκίλουρος*); **(56)** f. ii AD ib. 83, 7 (*Πόθος*—Yailenko and Tokhtas'ev, *Νόθος*—Marti: f. *Θεαγένης*); **(57)** 275-278 AD ib. 36, 32 (s. *Μηνᾶς*); **(58)** ~ ib. l. 44 (*Π[ό]θος*: f. *Ἀριστ(—)*)
—PHANAGOREIA: **(59)** i AD ib. 987, 4; **(60)** m. ii AD *SEG* XLIII 512, 4 (*[Π]όθος*)
MACEDONIA (DERRIOPOS):
—STUBERRA: **(61)** 121 AD *IG* X (2) (2) 328, 18 (*Τ. Φλαούϊος Π.*)
SKYTHIA:
—OLBIA-BORYSTHENES: **(62)** ii-i BC ib. II^2 8423 (*FRA* 1364) (s. *Δημήτριος*)
—TANAIS: **(63)** f. ii AD *CIRB* 1294 (*[Π]όθος*)

Ποθουμενός
MACEDONIA (MYGDONIA):
—THESSALONIKE: **(1)** ii AD *IG* X (2) (1) 394 (*Ποθου[με]νός*)

Ποθοῦς
CIMMERIAN BOSPOROS:
—PANTIKAPAION: **(1)** i-ii AD *CIRB* 598 (*Ποθοῦ[ν]ος* (gen.))

Ποθοῦσα
CIMMERIAN BOSPOROS:
—PANTIKAPAION: **(1)** f. i AD ib. 494 (d. *Ἀπολλώνιος*)

Πόθων
CIMMERIAN BOSPOROS:
—ACHILLEION: **(1)** ii AD ib. 1034 (f. *Γάϊς*)
—PANTIKAPAION: **(2)** i BC-i AD ib. 299 (f. *Ἀγαθοῦς*)
—PHANAGOREIA: **(3)** 16 AD ib. 985, 5 (Levinskaya pp. 236-7 no. 5) (f. *Φόδακος*)
—TAMAN PENINSULA: **(4)** i AD *CIRB* 1220 A (f. *Ἀ—χας*)

Ποίανθος
MACEDONIA (EDONIS):
—AMPHIPOLIS: **(1)** b. 357 BC Hatzopoulos, *Actes Amphipolis* p. 20 no. 2, 9 (*SEG* XLI 556)

Ποίμαχος
MACEDONIA (BOTTIAIA):
—BEROIA: **(1)** 223 BC *IBer* 4, 35 (f. *Νίκανδρος*)

Ποιμένιος
THRACE:
—SALYMBRIA (NR.): **(1)** v-vi AD Fıratlı, *Sculpture byzantine* pp. 65-6 no. 113

Ποῖνος
MACEDONIA: **(1)** m. ii BC *IGUR* 1540 (Tataki, *Macedonians* p. 409 no. 77) (*Ποῖνος*)

Ποκεύς
MACEDONIA?: **(1)** 216 BC *BGU* 2394, [6], 10-12, 14 (Tataki, *Macedonians* p. 409 no. 78) (*(Σ)ποκεύς*?)

Πολεμαῖος
MACEDONIA: **(1)** 334 BC *RE* s.v. Ptolemaios (5); Berve 671; *IIasos* 2, 10 (Tataki, *Macedonians* p. 409 no. 82) (*Πτολεμαῖος*—lit. test.: I s. *Φίλιππος*, f. *Πολεμαῖος* II, ?f. *Διοσκουρίδης*); **(2)** 320-309 BC *RE* (-); cf. s.v. Ptolemaios (11); Berve 643; *IG* II^2 469, 3; *IIasos* 2, 6, 10-11 (Tataki, *Macedonians* p. 409 no. 81); cf. *Epigr. Anat.* 9 (1987) pp. 31-2 (*Πτολεμαῖος*—lit. test.: II s. *Πολεμαῖος* I); **(3)** 222 BC *PEnt* 55, 1 and verso (Tataki, *Macedonians* p. 409 no. 79; La'da E1603) (*Πτολεμαῖος*—verso)
MACEDONIA (BOTTIAIA):
—BEROIA: **(4)** 223-178 BC *IBer* 4, 11; *Syll*^{3} 636, 6 (Tataki, *Macedonians* p. 82 no. 45) (s. *Ἅρπαλος*, f. *Ἅρπαλος*)
MACEDONIA?: **(5)** 163 BC *TAM* V (1) 221 (Tataki, *Macedonians* p. 469 no. 7) (f. *Φιλο—*)

Πολεμαρχίδης
MACEDONIA (CHALKIDIKE):
—OLYNTHOS: **(1)** ?352 BC *TAPA* 69 (1938) p. 48 no. 3, 13 with pl. 3; Hatzopoulos, *Actes Chalc.* p. 80 (date) (*Πολεμαρχί[δης]*, *Πολεμάρχη[ς]*—ed.: s. *Στράτων*)
MACEDONIA (PIERIS):
—GALEPSOS: **(2)** hell. Dimitsas 918; Hatzopoulos, *MI* 1 p. 187 n. 3 (locn.) (f. *Ἡγησίπολις*, *Ἐπικράτης*)

Πολέμαρχος
CIMMERIAN BOSPOROS:
—HERMONASSA: **(1)** v-iv BC *CIRB* 1059 (*Πολέμ[αρχ]ος*)
MACEDONIA (CHALKIDIKE):
—OLYNTHOS: **(2)** f. iv BC *Olynthus* 10 p. 502 no. 2567
—STOLOS?: **(3)** ?351 BC *SEG* XXXVIII 673, 9 (s. *Ἀντιφάνης*)
MACEDONIA (EDONIS):
—AMPHIPOLIS: **(4)** hell. ib. XXIV 596 (s. *Ἀριστόνικος*)
THRACE:
—BEROE-AUGUSTA TRAIANA (TERRIT.): **(5)** ii AD *IGB* III 1762 (*Φλ. Π.*)
—BIZONE: **(6)** ii-ii AD ib. I^2 6, 6 (*Πολέμ[αρ]χος*: s. *Ποσείδηος*)
—ODESSOS: **(7)** i-ii AD ib. 199
—ODESSOS (NR.): **(8)** iii/ii BC ib. 283 (*CCET* I 96) (s. *Θεόξενος*)
—PERINTHOS-HERAKLEIA?: **(9)** iv BC Hp., *Epid.* ii 3. 4
—PHILIPPOPOLIS-TRIMONTIUM: **(10)** 103-116 AD *IGB* III 880 (*Τι(β). Κλ. Π.*)

Πολεμοκράτεια
THRACE: **(1)** m. i BC Dumont–Homolle 62a; App., *BC* iv 75 (m. *Κότυς*: queen)

Πολεμοκράτης
CIMMERIAN BOSPOROS:
—HERMONASSA: **(1)** i AD *CIRB* 495 (s. *Καλοῦς*); **(2)** 123-132 AD ib. 1054, 13 (f. *Ἀγαθοῦς*)
MACEDONIA: **(3)** 169 BC Plb. xxix 4. 6 (Tataki, *Macedonians* p. 410 no. 83) (f. *Λιμναῖος*) ?= (*4*); **(4)** ~ Plb. xxix 8. 7 ?= (*3*)
MACEDONIA (CHALKIDIKE):
—OLYNTHOS: **(5)** ?iv BC *SEG* XXXVIII 642; cf. XLVII 923 (f. *Ἀριστόνικος*)
—SPARTOLOS?: **(6)** ?352 BC ib. XLVI 804, 5, 8 (s. *Τράλις*)

MACEDONIA (ELIMEIA):
—VELVENDOS (MOD.): **(7)** ii AD ib. XLVII 1001, 4 (s. *Εὔτυχος*)
MACEDONIA (ELIMEIA)?: **(8)** iv BC Arr., *An.* i 24. 1-2; ii 20. 5; v 27. 1; Hatzopoulos, *Donation* p. 23, 7 (Tataki, *Macedonians* p. 197 no. 18) (f. *Κλέανδρος*, *Κοῖνος*)
MACEDONIA (LOWER PAIONIA):
—EUROPOS: **(9)** f. iii BC *Thess. Mnem.* 127 (Tataki, *Macedonians* p. 109 no. 11) (*[Πο]λεμοκρά[της]*: f. *Πολέμων*)
MACEDONIA (MYGDONIA):
—KALINDOIA: **(10)** 68-98 AD *SEG* XLII 580, 22 (s. *Ὀρτᾶς*); **(11)** ~ ib. l. 38 (s. *Βάστος*)
MACEDONIA (PIERIA):
—PYDNA: **(12)** iv BC *GRBS* 43 (2002-3) p. 111 no. 2, 2; **(13)** ~ ib. 47 (2002-3) p. 116 no. 4, 4 with fig. 4 (f. *Καλλίας*)

Πολέμων
MACEDONIA: **(1)** iii BC *IG* XII (9) 294 (*GVI* 1191; Tataki, *Macedonians* p. 410 no. 84) (date—Knoepfler); **(2)** 259 BC *PCZ* 59003, 7, 18 (Tataki, *Macedonians* p. 411 no. 88; La'da E1582) (s. *Στράτων*); **(3)** 228-221 BC *PTeb* 815 fr. 2 recto III, 52 (Tataki, *Macedonians* p. 411 no. 89); cf. La'da E1519 (f. *Καλλισθένης*); **(4)** 223 BC *PHamb* 24, 22 and verso (Tataki, *Macedonians* p. 410 no. 87; La'da E1776) (s. *Μενέλαος*: t.e.); **(5)** 222 BC *PEnt* 55, 2, 5 and verso (Tataki, *Macedonians* p. 410 no. 85; La'da E1583); **(6)** ?219 BC *PUG* III 104, 16 (f. *Νίκαιος*); **(7)** 72 BC *ZÄS* 93 (1966) pp. 94-5 (Tataki, *Macedonians* p. 492 no. 190; La'da E1581) (s. *Εὔμηλος*)
MACEDONIA (BOTTIAIA):
—KYRRHOS?: **(8)** hell.? Dimitsas 150 (*[Π]ολέμω[ν]*: s. *Παράμονος*)
—PELLA: **(9)** 332 BC Berve 645 (Tataki, *Macedonians* p. 158 no. 74) (s. *Μεγακλῆς*)
MACEDONIA (CHALKIDIKE):
—ANTHEMOUS: **(10)** ii BC *Anthémonte-Kalindoia* 1 p. 56 no. A10 (*SEG* II 411) (*[Πο]λέμων*: s. *Ἱππόνικος*)
—OLYNTHOS: **(11)** iv BC *IG* II^2 10027 (Tataki, *Macedonians* p. 141 no. 96; *FRA* 5908) (f. *Κρατιστώ*)
—POLICHNE?: **(12)** ?353 BC *SEG* XXXVII 576, 9 (*[Πο]λέμων*: f. *Κλέων*)
—POTIDAIA-KASSANDREIA: **(13)** iii BC *IG* XII (9) 828 (Tataki, *Macedonians* p. 94 no. 80) (*[Πο]λέμων*: s. *Ὑπέρτατος*)
MACEDONIA (EDONIS):
—AMPHIPOLIS: **(14)** ?iv/iii BC Kaphtantzis 644 (s. *Ἀρτεμίδωρος*)
—AMPHIPOLIS (NR.): **(15)** a. 357 BC Hatzopoulos, *Actes Amphipolis* p. 43 no. 8, 2 (*SEG* XLI 562) (f. *Θεόδωρος*)
MACEDONIA (LOWER PAIONIA):
—EUROPOS: **(16)** f. iii BC *Thess. Mnem.* 127 (Tataki, *Macedonians* p. 109 no. 12) (s. *Πολεμοκράτης*); **(17)** ?ii AD *SEG* XXXVIII 613 (f. *Οἰνάνθη*, ?f. *Ἐπίγονος*)
MACEDONIA (MYGDONIA):
—LETE: **(18)** s. iv BC Hatzopoulos, *MI* 2 pp. 93-4 no. 79, 7
MACEDONIA (PAIONIA): **(19)** c. 240 BC *PP* 2255 with Add. (Tataki, *Macedonians* p. 210 no. 20) (s. *Λάμπρος*)
MACEDONIA (PELAGONIA):
—KERAMIAI (NR.): **(20)** 193-211 AD *IG* X (2) (2) 218, 7 (*Αὐρήλιος Ἀντίγονος ὁ καὶ Π.*)
MACEDONIA (TYMPHAIA): **(21)** c. 350-317 BC Berve 644 (Tataki, *Macedonians* p. 212 no. 5) (s. *Ἀνδρομένης*)
MACEDONIA?: **(22)** 332 BC Berve 646 (Tataki, *Macedonians* p. 410 no. 86) (s. *Θηραμένης*); **(23)** c. 319-317 BC D.S. xix 16. 1
SCYTHIA MINOR:
—ISTROS: **(24)** i BC-i AD *ISM* I 191 II, 32 (s. *Ὄσπος*); **(25)** ~ ib. 274 (s. *Νουμήνιος*); **(26)** 138 AD ib. 193 I, 39 (f. *Νουμήνιος*); **(27)** ~ ib.

l. 49 (s. *Νουμήνιος*); **(28)** ~ ib. l. 93 (s. *Νουμήνιος*); **(29)** ~ ib. 193 II, 51 (*M. Κοκκήϊος Π.*)
THRACE: **(30)** c. 100-75 BC *SB* 8974 fr. 3 II, 42; cf. La'da E804 (f. *Φιλώτας*)
—HADRIANOPOLIS (TERRIT.): **(31)** ii-iii AD *IGB* III 1818 (f. *Ζήνων*)
—PERINTHOS-HERAKLEIA: **(32)** iii BC *ITrall* 33 B, 3 (f. *Βάκχιος*)
—PHILIPPOPOLIS-TRIMONTIUM: **(33)** ii-iii AD *IGB* V 5462 (*Αἰλ. Π.*: s. *Βιθύτραλις, Κουήτη*)
—SAPPAIOI: **(34)** c. 10-67 AD *RE* (3); *PIR*^{2} I 472 (and Pontos: *Ἰούλ. Π.*: s. *Κότυς, Ἀντωνία Τρύφαινα* (Pontos))
—SPINOPARA: **(35)** ii AD *IGB* IV 2192, 10

Πολεμωνιανή
MACEDONIA (LYNKESTIS):
—HERAKLEIA?: **(1)** ii-iii AD *IG* X (2) (2) 134 (*Πολεμωνιανὴ Ἡράκλεια*)

Πολιάνθης
MACEDONIA: **(1)** 203 BC *BGU* 1266, 7, 11, 18, etc. (Tataki, *Macedonians* p. 411 no. 90; La'da E1777) (s. *Νίκανδρος*: t.e.)

Πολίτης
MACEDONIA (BOTTIAIA):
—EDESSA: **(1)** 229 AD Tataki, *Edessa* 244 (*Οὔλπ. Πολείτης*)
MACEDONIA (MYGDONIA):
—THESSALONIKE?: **(2)** ii AD *IG* X (2) (1) 881 (*-τις*)

Πολιτικός
THRACE:
—PAUTALIA (TERRIT.): **(1)** ii-iii AD *IGB* IV 2225 (*-λει-*: s. *Βίθυς*)

Πόλλα
CIMMERIAN BOSPOROS:
—PANTIKAPAION: **(1)** f. ii AD *CIRB* 703 (m. *Ἀπολλῶς*)

Πολλῆς
MACEDONIA (ODOMANTIKE):
—ODOMANTOI: **(1)** 422 BC *RE* (3); Th. V 6. 2 (king)

Πόλλις
SKYTHIA:
—OLBIA-BORYSTHENES: **(1)** ?ii-i BC Dubois, *IGDOlbia* 110, 6
THRACE:
—ZONE: **(2)** c. 425-400 BC *IThrakAig* E403 (?s. *Δε—*)

Πολυαίνετος
SCYTHIA MINOR:
—ISTROS: **(1)** f. iii BC *ISM* I 257; cf. *BE* 1955, no. 163 (*[Πολ]υαίνετ[ος]*, *[Ε]ὐαίνετ[ος]?*—*BE*: s. *Φαῖδρος*); **(2)** iii/ii BC *ISM* I 46, 2 (s. *Ἡφαιστόδωρος*); **(3)** i BC-i AD ib. 191 I, 8; **(4)** ~ ib. 191 II, 53 (f. *Ἄττας*); **(5)** ~ ib. l. 45-6 (f. *Ἀπολλώνιος, Ἀριστοκράτης*); **(6)** i AD ib. 200, 12 (s. *Γρήγορος*); **(7)** 138 AD ib. 193 I, 57 (f. *Εὐξενίδης*); **(8)** ~ ib. 193 II, 40 (I f. *Πολυαίνετος* II); **(9)** ~ ib. l. 40 (II s. *Πολυαίνετος* I)
THRACE:
—MESAMBRIA: **(10)** iii/ii BC *IGB* I^2 330 ter (PM 1098) (s. *Βοσπόριχος, Ματρίχα*)

Πολύαινος
MACEDONIA: **(1)** ii AD *RE* (8); *FGrH* 639 (Tataki, *Macedonians* p. 411 no. 91)
MACEDONIA (BOTTIAIA):
—TYRISSA? (ASVESTARI (MOD.)): **(2)** f. ii BC *SEG* XLVII 999, 1 (*[Πολ]ύαινος*)
MACEDONIA (EDONIS):
—AMPHIPOLIS: **(3)** a. 357 BC Hatzopoulos, *Actes Amphipolis* pp. 38-9 no. 7, 18 (*Πο(λ)ύαινος*)

THRACE?: **(4)** m. iii BC *SB* 12221, 7 (s. *Σάτοκος*)

Πολυάναξ
THRACE:
—APOLLONIA-SOZOPOLIS: **(1)** v/iv BC *Stud. Fol* p. 398; *Coll. McClean* 4431 (coin); **(2)** iii BC *IGB* I^2 458, 1 (f. *Κυρσᾶς*); **(3)** ~ ib. l. 5 (f. *Κυρσᾶς*)

Πολυάρατος
MACEDONIA (BOTTIAIA):
—PELLA*: **(1)** iv BC *SEG* XLVII 931 (bullet)
MACEDONIA?: **(2)** 130 BC *PBad* II 2, 36, 46 (*PP* 2574; Tataki, *Macedonians* p. 492 no. 191)
THRACE:
—ZONE?: **(3)** iv/iii BC *IG* XII (8) 267, 7 (s.e.); cf. *IThrakAig* E400 (locn.) (*-ρη-*: s. *Ἱστιαῖος*); **(4)** ~ *IG* XII (8) 267, 6-7; *IThrakAig* E400, 4 (*Πολυάρητος*—*IG*: s. *Ἱστιαῖος*, f. *Ἱστιαῖος*)

Πολυάρητος
THRACE:
—ABDERA: **(1)** c. 415-395 BC May, *Abdera* p. 172 no. 233 (coin)
—MARONEIA: **(2)** c. 365-336 BC Schönert-Geiss, *Maroneia* 494-8 (coin)
—STRYME?: **(3)** c. 375-350 BC *SEG* XXIV 639 (*IThrakAig* E141) (f. *Ἕρμων*)

Πολύαρος
MACEDONIA (CHALKIDIKE):
—MENDE: **(1)** f. v BC *SEG* XLIII 429 (vase)
—POTIDAIA-KASSANDREIA (TERRIT.)?: **(2)** ii BC *TAPA* 69 (1938) p. 69 no. 25 (s. *Θρασύλαος*)

Πολύαρχος
TAURIS:
—CHERSONESOS: **(1)** iv/iii BC *IOSPE* I^2 467 (f. *Ἀπολλώνιος*); **(2)** f. iii BC *SEG* XL 615 A, 7 (*[Π]ολύαρ[χο]ς*: s. *Γέρων*)
THRACE:
—APOLLONIA-SOZOPOLIS: **(3)** iv BC *IGB* I^2 427 (f. *Φανίχη*)

Πολύας
CIMMERIAN BOSPOROS:
—PANTIKAPAION: **(1)** iv BC Tolstoi 227 (vase) (*Πολύα* (gen.?), *Πολυα(—)?*)

Πολύβιος
CIMMERIAN BOSPOROS:
—PANTIKAPAION: **(1)** i AD *CIRB* 396 (s. *Πόθος*)
MACEDONIA (BOTTIAIA):
—BEROIA: **(2)** ii AD *IBer* 346, 4 (Tataki 1084) (f. *Πάνταυχος*)

Πολύβουλος
MACEDONIA (EDONIS):
—AMPHIPOLIS: **(1)** b. 357 BC Hatzopoulos, *Actes Amphipolis* p. 20 no. 2, 8 (*SEG* XLI 556)

Πολύγνωτος
CIMMERIAN BOSPOROS:
—PANTIKAPAION: **(1)** iii-ii BC *CIRB* 256, 1, 4-5 (s. *—ρόμιος*, f. *Ἀπολλώνιος, —ς*)
MACEDONIA (BOTTIAIA):
—BEROIA: **(2)** s. iii BC *IBer* 16 B, 10 (f. *Μένανδρος*)
THRACE:
—RHAIDESTOS: **(3)** imp. Unp. (Thessaloniki Mus.) inv. 943b (s. *Ἡρακλείδης*)

Πολυδάμας
MACEDONIA: **(1)** ?c. 390-324 BC *RE* (7); Berve 648 ?= (*Πουλυδάμας (1)*)
MACEDONIA (BOTTIAIA):
—BEROIA: **(2)** iii AD *IBer* 275

Πολυδεύκης
MACEDONIA: **(1)** 74 BC *SB* 7532, 25, 37 (Tataki, *Macedonians* p. 493 no. 192; La'da E1584) (s. *Ἡρακλᾶς*)

SCYTHIA MINOR:
—KALLATIS: **(2)** ii/iii AD *ISM* III 181, 7 (s. *Μάξιμος*)
—NOVIODUNUM (NR.): **(3)** 212-217 AD ib. V 249, 9 (*Eastern cults* p. 224 no. 9) (Lat. Polydeuces: s. *Θεόφιλος*)
THRACE:
—DUROSTORUM: **(4)** 198-209 AD *SCIV* 11 (1960) p. 148 no. 3 (*Eastern cults* p. 222 no. 5) (Lat. [Poly]deuces: f. *Σέλευκος*)
—KELLAI: **(5)** ii-iii AD *IGB* III 1527 (*Eastern cults* p. 235 no. 26)

Πολύδημος
MACEDONIA (CHALKIDIKE):
—OLYNTHOS: **(1)** iii/ii BC *SEG* XVIII 254 (Tataki, *Macedonians* p. 142 no. 97) (*[Πο]λύδη[μος]*: f. *—ικρατ—*)
SKYTHIA:
—OLBIA-BORYSTHENES: **(2)** iv/iii BC *IOlbia* 71 I, 9 (Dubois, *IGDOlbia* 11) (*[Πολύδ]ημος?*: s. *Λεωκράτης*)

Πολύδιγγος
THRACE:
—BISANTHE-PANION: **(1)** iv BC Unp. (Sayar) (f. *Διονυσοφάνης, Ποσείδιππος*)

Πολύδοξος
MACEDONIA (MYGDONIA):
—THESSALONIKE: **(1)** 155 AD *IG* X (2) (1) 321, 2 (f. *Θεοτίμα*)
TAURIS:
—CHERSONESOS: **(2)** f. iii BC *CIRB* 243; cf. KW pl. 4 no. 84 (f. *Βάττας*)

Πολύδωρος
MACEDONIA (EDONIS):
—AMPHIPOLIS: **(1)** i BC-i AD *SEG* XXVII 248, 5 (*[Π]ολύδ[ωρος]?*)
MACEDONIA (PIERIS):
—GALEPSOS: **(2)** hell.? Dimitsas 914; Hatzopoulos, *MI* 1 p. 187 n. 3 (locn.) (f. *Ἀριστόκλεια*)
SKYTHIA:
—OLBIA-BORYSTHENES: **(3)** i/ii AD *IOlbia* 88, 5 (s. *Γάδεις*)

Πολυείδης
MACEDONIA: **(1)** iv BC Arr., *An.* iii 19. 6 (Tataki, *Macedonians* p. 411 no. 92) (f. *Ἐπόκιλλος*)
SKYTHIA:
—TANAIS: **(2)** ii AD *CIRB* 1263, 17 (*Πολυείδ[ης]*: f. *—ος*)

Πολύευκτος
MACEDONIA (BOTTIAIA):
—SKYDRA: **(1)** iii BC *SEG* XXIV 524 I, 7 (Hatzopoulos, *MI* 2 p. 106 no. 92; Tataki, *Macedonians* p. 174 no. 5) (*[Πολύε]υκτος?*)
MACEDONIA (ORESTIS): **(2)** ii AD *EAM* 189 (*[Π.] Αἰλ. Π.*)

Πολύζηλος
MACEDONIA (CHALKIDIKE):
—POTIDAIA-KASSANDREIA: **(1)** ?m. iii BC *FD* III (4) 351, 6 (Tataki, *Macedonians* p. 94 no. 81) (f. *Τιμάνθης*)
MACEDONIA (MYGDONIA):
—DIKAIA: **(2)** c. 365-359 BC Unp. (Voutyras–Sismanidis) l. 63 (f. *Δάφνων*)

Πολυήρατος
THRACE: **(1)** 160 BC *BGU* 2390, [4], 7-8, 15, etc. (La'da E782) (s. *Πτολεμαῖος*)

Πολύϊδος
SCYTHIA MINOR:
—ISTROS: **(1)** iv BC *SEG* XXIV 258 (*FRA* 2630) (f. *Νικήρατος*)
—KALLATIS: **(2)** iii-ii BC Mushmov 240; *AMNG* I (1) 221 (coin) (*Πολυΐ(δος)?*)

Thrace:
—bizye: **(3)** imp. Unp. (Sayar) (-εἶδος: s. Ἑρμάφιλος)
—salymbria: **(4)** v/iv BC *RE* (9); *FGrH* 239 A 68; *TrGF* I p. 248 no. 78

Πολύκαιρος
Cimmerian Bosporos:
—bosporos: **(1)** imp. *CIRB* 1235 (s. Διονύσιος)

Πολυκαρπία
Macedonia (Mygdonia):
—kalindoia: **(1)** 254 AD *SEG* XLII 604, 3; cf. *Anthémonte–Kalindoia* 2 p. 372 (?m. Ἀλεξάνδρα)

Πολύκαρπος
Macedonia (Bottiaia):
—beroia: **(1)** v-vi AD *IBer* 426 (Πολύκ[αρπος]?)
Macedonia (Mygdonia):
—thessalonike: **(2)** i/ii AD *IG* X (2) (1) 379; **(3)** ii AD ib. 296 + *SEG* XXXVII 586 (Και. Π.: s. Πλάτωρ)
Macedonia (Odomantike):
—sirrha: **(4)** 155 AD Dimitsas 821, 16 (Kaphtantzis 1) (f. Ἆγις)
Scythia Minor:
—troesmis: **(5)** ii AD *ISM* V 161 (Lat. M. Ulp. P[o]lycarpus)
Skythia:
—tanais: **(6)** 188 AD *CIRB* 1242, 16 (s. Μενέστρατος)
Thrace:
—odessos: **(7)** i AD *IGB* I^2 195 (f. —σου)
—perinthos-herakleia: **(8)** v-vi AD *IPerinth* 232 (*AD* 51-2 (1996-7) Mel. p. 376 no. 191) (Πολύκα[ρ]πος)

Πολυκάστα
Macedonia (Pieria):
—pydna: **(1)** iv BC *GRBS* 43 (2002-3) p. 111 no. 2, 10 (Πολυκάστ[α]?)
Tauris:
—chersonesos: **(2)** iii BC Solomonik, *NEPKh* 145 (*SEG* XXX 964) (d. Ἱπποκράτης)

Πολύκλειτος
Macedonia (Mygdonia):
—thessalonike: **(1)** i AD *IG* X (2) (1) 88, 1

Πολυκλῆς
Macedonia: **(1)** 320 BC *RE* (4); Berve 652 (Tataki, *Macedonians* p. 411 no. 93)
Macedonia (Chalkidike):
—chalkideis: **(2)** f. iv BC *TAPA* 59 (1928) p. 226, 10; 62 (1931) p. 43 no. 2, 2; 65 (1934) p. 125 no. 3, 8; 69 (1938) p. 50 no. 4, 2; *SEG* XXXVIII 670, 2; 671, 3; XXXIX 617; XLVII 922 (f. Ἀντίδοτος)
—stolos?: **(3)** ?351 BC ib. XXXVIII 672, 14; 673, 9 (Πολυκλέης—673: s. Ζωΐλος)
Macedonia (Derriopos):
—stuberra: **(4)** 74 AD *IG* X (2) (2) 326, 62 (f. Ἐπαφρᾶς)
Macedonia (Pieria):
—dion: **(5)** c. 230-200 BC *BCH* 45 (1921) p. 17 III, 54 (Tataki, *Macedonians* p. 101 no. 9)
Thrace: **(6)** 258 BC *PHib* 94, 13, 17 (Velkov 226; La'da E783) (Πο[λ]υκλῆς)

Πολυκράτης
Macedonia: **(1)** m. ii BC *BGU* 1939 A, 6 (Tataki, *Macedonians* p. 493 no. 193); cf. La'da E1474 (f. Διονύσιος)
Macedonia (Chalkidike):
—potidaia-kassandreia (territ.)?: **(2)** ii BC *TAPA* 69 (1938) p. 69 no. 25 (f. Σωστράτη)
Macedonia (Edonis):
—amphipolis: **(3)** b. 357 BC Hatzopoulos, *Actes Amphipolis* p. 25 no. 3, 1 (*SEG* XLI 557) (Π̣ο̣[λυκ]ρ̣[άτης]?); **(4)** s. iv BC Hatzopoulos, *Actes Amphipolis* p. 45 no. 9, 1 (*SEG* XLI 563); cf. *SEG* XLIV 504 ([Π]ο̣λυκράτης)
Macedonia (Mygdonia):
—thessalonike: **(5)** i AD *IG* X (2) (1) 242, 5 (s. Σύντροφος)
—thessalonike?: **(6)** ii-iii AD ib. 938 (Πολυκρά[της])
Macedonia (Pieria):
—phila?: **(7)** ?iii BC *RPh* 1911, pp. 133-4 no. 36, 61; cf. Helly, *L'État thessalien* pp. 319-20 (locn.) (s. —ας); **(8)** ~ *RPh* 1911, pp. 133-4 no. 36, 69; cf. Helly, *L'État thessalien* pp. 319-20 (locn.)
Scythia Minor:
—kallatis?: **(9)** ii/i BC *IGB* II 867 a, 8 = *ISM* I 219 (v 87); cf. *ISM* III p. 140 (locn.) (s. Ἕρμων)
Skythia:
—olbia-borysthenes: **(10)** v BC Tolstoi 15 (vase) (Πολυκρά[της]); **(11)** iv/iii BC *IOlbia* 71 I, 5 (Dubois, *IGDOlbia* 11) ([Πο]λυκράτης: s. Λεωκράτης)
Tauris:
—chersonesos: **(12)** ii AD *IOSPE* I^2 364 c, 1 (Πολυ[κ]ρά[τ]ης)
Thrace:
—abdera: **(13)** c. 415-395 BC May, *Abdera* pp. 169-70 no. 225 (coin); **(14)** c. 360-350 BC ib. pp. 262-3 nos. 458-61 (coin)
—philippopolis-trimontium: **(15)** m. iii AD *IGB* III 884 a, 25; cf. V 5400 (Πολυκρά(της): f. Σεβαστιανός)
—zone: **(16)** m. iv BC *IThrakAig* E420 (f. Κλεοπάτρα)

Πολύκριτος
Cimmerian Bosporos:
—nymphaion: **(1)** iii BC *CIRB* 912 II, 2; **(2)** ~ ib. l. 10 (f. Χαλκιδεύς)
Macedonia (Chalkidike):
—mende: **(3)** 399 BC Plu., *Art.* 21 (doctor) ?= (*4*); **(4)** m. iv BC *RE* (7); *FGrH* 559 (Tataki, *Macedonians* p. 122 no. 17) ?= (*3*)
—potidaia-kassandreia: **(5)** 259 BC *IG* XI (2) 115, 16 (Stephanis 2104; Tataki, *Macedonians* p. 95 no. 82) (Πο[λύ]κ̣ρ̣ιτος)
Thrace:
—perinthos-herakleia: **(6)** i BC-i AD *IPerinth* 25 (s. Χαβρίας)

Πολύκτωρ
Macedonia: **(1)** 135 BC *PPolitJud* 5, 2 (La'da E1585) (Π̣ο̣λ̣ύ̣κτωρ: II s. Πολύκτωρ I); **(2)** ~ *PPolitJud* 5, 3; cf. La'da E1585 (I f. Πολύκτωρ II)
Tauris:
—chersonesos: **(3)** c. 200-185 BC Kats p. 108 no. 94 (amph.) (s. Μῆνις)

Πολύλας
Macedonia (Edonis):
—skaporenoi: **(1)** ?ii AD *BCH* 24 (1900) p. 310 no. 3 (Pilhofer 512) (Lat. Polulae (gen.): f. Cintis)

Πολυμέδων
Skythia:
—olbia-borysthenes: **(1)** iv/iii BC *IOlbia* 71 I, 10 with pl. 36 (Dubois, *IGDOlbia* 11) ([Πολυμέ]δων: s. Λεωκράτης); **(2)** iii BC *IOSPE* I^2 201 I, 39 (s. Λεωκράτης); **(3)** ~ ib. l. 62 (f. Λεωκράτης)

Πολυμήδης
Skythia:
—olbia-borysthenes: **(1)** iv/iii BC *IOlbia* 71 I, 6 (Dubois, *IGDOlbia* 11) ([Πο]λυμήδης: s. Λεωκράτης); **(2)** ii BC *IOlbia* 76 (?s. Κα—)

Πολυμίτας
Thrace:
—beroe-augusta traiana?: **(1)** 109 AD *RMD* 148 (Lat. M. Herennius Polymitas: f. Ianuarius, Marcellus, Lucana)

Πολύμνεια
Thrace:
—perinthos-herakleia: **(1)** iii-iv AD *IPerinth* 169 (*AD* 51-2 (1996-7) Mel. p. 365 no. 183) (Αὐρ. Πολύμνεα)

Πολύμνηστος
Macedonia (Chalkidike):
—akrothoon: **(1)** iv BC *IG* XII (8) 2, 5 (s. Νόμων)
Skythia:
—olbia-borysthenes: **(2)** iii BC *IOSPE* I^2 201 I, 27 (s. Μένων)

Πολύνδικος
Macedonia: **(1)** c. 286-226 BC *PPetr*² 27, 11 (Tataki, *Macedonians* p. 412 no. 94; La'da E1586) (Πολύ<ν>δικος?)

Πολυνείκης
Macedonia (Bottiaia):
—pella: **(1)** m. iv BC Berve 653 (Tataki, *Macedonians* p. 159 no. 76) (fict.?)
Macedonia (Chalkidike):
—gigonos?: **(2)** i BC *SEG* XXIX 587; Hatzopoulos, *Actes Chalc.* p. 25 (date) (s. Πόρις)
Macedonia (Mygdonia):
—thessalonike: **(3)** i AD *IG* X (2) (1) 387
—thessalonike (nr.): **(4)** iii AD ib. 1006, 6 (s. Αὐρ. Μεστριανός, Αὐρ. Ἀρτεμιδώρα)
Thrace:
—markianopolis: **(5)** ii AD *IGB* V 5339, 4

Πολυνίκη
Macedonia (Mygdonia):
—thessalonike: **(1)** ii-iii AD *SEG* XXX 642 (Μεστρωνία Πολυνείκη)
Macedonia (Pieria):
—dion: **(2)** iv AD ib. XXXIX 586, 1 (Πολυνείκη (dat.), Πολυνείκη (masc. dat.)—*SEG*: d. Θήσκεια)
Thrace:
—beroe-augusta traiana: **(3)** c. 320-324 AD *Anal. Boll.* 31 (1912) p. 198; p. 208
—dionysopolis: **(4)** iv/iii BC *IGB* I^2 26 (PM 1047)

Πολύνικος
Macedonia (Mygdonia):
—thessalonike: **(1)** ii-iii AD *IG* X (2) (1) 582, 1 (Κλώδιος Π.)
Thrace:
—maroneia: **(2)** c. 365-336 BC Schönert-Geiss, *Maroneia* 454-9 (coin)
—mesambria: **(3)** i BC *IGB* I^2 326, 4 (f. Πυθίων)

Πολυξένα
Macedonia (Chalkidike):
—olynthos: **(1)** c. 500-480 BC *TAPA* 62 (1931) p. 41 no. 1; *LSAG*² p. 369 no. 12 (date)

Πολυξένη
Macedonia: **(1)** 414 BC *IG* I^3 422, 79; cf. Tataki, *Macedonians* p. 413 no. 98 (Πολυχσ[έ]νε̄: slave)
Macedonia (Chalkidike):
—potidaia-kassandreia: **(2)** ii BC *Tekmeria* 6 (2001) pp. 54-5 no. 1, 4 (d. Εὔδαμος, m. Ἀριστεύς)

Πολυξενίδης
Skythia:
—olbia-borysthenes: **(1)** hell. *Arkheologiia* (Kiev) 39 (1982) p. 39 (stamp)

Πολύξενος
Macedonia (Chalkidike):
—chalkideis: **(1)** c. 361-358 BC *Olynthus* 9 pp. 66-8 nos. 100-3 (coin); *Ancient Macedonia* I p. 254 (date)

—OLYNTHOS: **(2)** ?352-350 BC *TAPA* 62 (1931) p. 43 no. 2, 5, 9; *SEG* XXXVIII 637, 8; Hatzopoulos, *Actes Chalc.* p. 80 (date) (s. Τήλαγρος); **(3)** c. 350 BC *SEG* XLVII 922
MACEDONIA (PIERIA):
—PYDNA: **(4)** 250 AD ib. XLVI 800 A, 40 (Αὐρ. Π.)
SCYTHIA MINOR:
—ISTROS: **(5)** iv BC ib. XXIV 258 (*FRA* 2631) (s. Νικήρατος); **(6)** i BC-i AD *ISM* I 191 II, 14 (s. Νικήρατος)
SKYTHIA:
—OLBIA-BORYSTHENES: **(7)** iii BC *IOSPE* I² 201 I, 48 (f. Ἀθήναιος); **(8)** ~ ib. 201 II, 13 (f. Ἱκέσιος); **(9)** ii AD ib. 206, 2 (f. Ποσειδώνιος)
THRACE:
—ANCHIALOS (TERRIT.): **(10)** ii AD *IGB* III 1841, 4 (Πολύξε[νος]: f. Ἡρακλείδης)
—APOLLONIA-SOZOPOLIS: **(11)** i-ii AD ib. I² 401, 8 (s. Ἀπολλώνιος); **(12)** ii-iii AD ib. 319, 4 (s. Μ—)
—MESAMBRIA: **(13)** iii/ii BC ib. 334 novies b (f. Παυσανίας); **(14)** ii/i BC ib. V 5103, 2 (s. Μελσέων)

Πολυπέρχων
MACEDONIA (TYMPHAIA): **(1)** c. 385-301 BC *RE* (1); Berve 654; *SEG* XI 1084, 18, 22 (Perlman, *City and Sanctuary* A.3); *SEG* XLV 473, [1]?; Hoffmann, *Makedonen* p. 156 (name) (Tataki, *Macedonians* p. 213 no. 6) (Πολυσπέρχων—lit. test.: s. Σιμμίας, f. Ἀλέξανδρος)

Πόλυς
MACEDONIA (CHALKIDIKE):
—OLYNTHOS: **(1)** ?355 BC *TAPA* 69 (1938) p. 51 no. 5, 4; Hatzopoulos, *Actes Chalc.* p. 80 (date) (Πόλ[υος] (gen.): f. Βάκχων)
—POLICHNE?: **(2)** ?353 BC *SEG* XXXVII 576, 11 (Πόλυδος (gen.)) ?= (3); **(3)** ~ ib. l. 18 (Πόλυδος (gen.): s. Διονυσίδωρος, f. Κλέων) ?= (2)
THRACE:
—ABDERA: **(4)** f. iv BC *BCH* 37 (1913) p. 118 no. 36 + *AM* 51 (1926) p. 19 no. 7 (*IThrakAig* E37) (Πόλυδος (gen.): s. Ἑκατόμβιος)

Πολυσθένης
CIMMERIAN BOSPOROS:
—BOSPOROS: **(1)** s. iv BC *SEG* XXI 298, 11 + *ZPE* 136 (2001) p. 67 no. 2 (Osborne, *Naturalization* D25) (Πολ[υ]σθέν[ης])
—PANTIKAPAION: **(2)** ii-i BC *CIRB* 264; cf. KW pl. 37 no. 550 (s. Ἀπολλώνιος); **(3)** i BC *CIRB* 283

Πολύστρατος
CIMMERIAN BOSPOROS:
—PANTIKAPAION: **(1)** i AD ib. 139, 2
MACEDONIA: **(2)** 330 BC *RE* (6); Berve 655 (Tataki, *Macedonians* p. 412 no. 96)
MACEDONIA (CHALKIDIKE):
—APHYTIS: **(3)** ?351 BC *A´ Panell. Synedr. Epigr.* pp. 80-1, 22 (f. Ἀλκισθένης)
—STOLOS?: **(4)** ?350 BC *SEG* XXXVIII 670, 6 (s. Κράσης)
MACEDONIA (EDONIS):
—AMPHIPOLIS: **(5)** ii BC ib. XXV 716; cf. *AD* 26 (1971) Chron. pl. 412 β (f. Ἀργαῖος)
MACEDONIA (ELIMEIA?):
—ERDARRIOI: **(6)** m. ii BC *EAM* 4 (s. Ἄτταλος)
SCYTHIA MINOR:
—ISTROS: **(7)** ii AD *ISM* I 196, 17; 201 II, 5 (s. Διόδοτος)
SKYTHIA:
—OLBIA-BORYSTHENES: **(8)** iv/iii BC *IOlbia* 71 I, 7 (Dubois, *IGDOlbia* 11) ([Πολ]ύστρατος: s. Λεωκράτης)
TAURIS:
—CHERSONESOS: **(9)** c. 300-285 BC Kats p. 108 no. 95 (amph.); **(10)** c. 300-275 BC *SEG* XLVII 1168, 2 (s. Κλεμυτάδας); **(11)** c. 285-272 BC Kats p. 126 no. 36 (amph.) (s. Ξένων)

Πολύτιμος
MACEDONIA (MYGDONIA):
—THESSALONIKE: **(1)** s. ii AD *IG* X (2) (1) 244 I, 13 (Σουλπίκιος Π.)
MACEDONIA (PIERIA):
—DION?: **(2)** s. ii AD Spiliopoulou-Donderer, *KGN* pp. 200-1 no. D18 (Ἔλβιος Πολύτειμος)
SCYTHIA MINOR:
—ISTROS: **(3)** ii AD *ISM* I 196, 14 (-τει-: s. Ἀρτεμίδωρος); **(4)** ~ ib. 201 I, 19 (Οὔλπ. Πολύτ[ειμος])
THRACE:
—BYZANTION: **(5)** iii AD *IByz* 296 (Αὐρ. Πολύτειμος ὁ καὶ Πρεστάντιος)

Πολυφάντας
MACEDONIA: **(1)** 208 BC *RE* (-) (Tataki, *Macedonians* p. 412 no. 97)

Πολύφαντος
MACEDONIA (PIERIA):
—METHONE: **(1)** 360 BC *IG* IV (1)² 94 b, 8 (Perlman, *City and Sanctuary* E.1 with p. 69 (date); Tataki, *Macedonians* p. 123 no. 6)
THRACE:
—ABDERA: **(2)** iv BC Hp., *Epid.* vii 112; **(3)** c. 336-311 BC May, *Abdera* p. 293 nos. 547-8 (coin)

Πολύφημος
SCYTHIA MINOR:
—ISTROS: **(1)** iii BC *ISM* I 12, 2 (f. Γλαυκίας); **(2)** ii AD ib. 214, 3 + 226, 2 (Π[ο]λύφημ[ος]); **(3)** 138 AD ib. 193 I, 16 (s. Ἑστιαῖος); **(4)** iii AD ib. 181, 2 ([Πολύ]φημος: I f. Πολύφημος II); **(5)** ~ ib. l. 2 (II s. Πολύφημος I)
—TOMIS: **(6)** i BC ib. II 2 A, 63 (f. Παυσίμαχος)

Πολυχάρης
CIMMERIAN BOSPOROS:
—PANTIKAPAION: **(1)** f. iv BC *CIRB* 212 (f. Νίκανδρος)
THRACE:
—BYZANTION: **(2)** s. ii BC *SEG* XXXIX 1124, 8 (*IMylasa* 103) (f. Ποσειδώνιος)
—ZONE: **(3)** f. iv BC *PAE* 1969, p. 67 with pl. 83 α (*IThrakAig* E414) (f. Εὐκράτης)

Πολυχαρμίς
MACEDONIA (MYGDONIA):
—THESSALONIKE: **(1)** 233 AD *IG* X (2) (1) 155, 15 (Κορνηλία Π.: m. Μ. Οὐαλέριος Ἰοῦστος)

Πολύχαρμος
MACEDONIA (BOTTIAIA):
—BEROIA: **(1)** f. iii AD *IBer* 99, 3 (Tataki 977) (Ὀνωρατιανὸς Π.: s. Αἰλ. Ποτάμων); **(2)** a. 212 AD *IBer* 136, 14 (Tataki 297) (Αὐρ. Π.)
MACEDONIA (MYGDONIA):
—THESSALONIKE: **(3)** ?ii AD *IG* X (2) (1) 517; **(4)** ii-iii AD ib. 37, 4
MACEDONIA (ODOMANTIKE):
—GAZOROS?: **(5)** 158 AD *SEG* XXIV 614, 3 (Pilhofer 544); cf. Hatzopoulos, *MI* I pp. 84-6 (f. Κοζείμασος)
MACEDONIA (ORESTIS):
—BATTYNAIOI: **(6)** 192 AD *EAM* 186 II, 58 (I f. Πολύχαρμος II); **(7)** ~ ib. l. 58 (II s. Πολύχαρμος I)
MACEDONIA (PAIONIA):
—STOBOI: **(8)** ii-iii AD *SEG* XXXIV 679 (Jew) ?= (9); **(9)** 281 AD *Sp.* 71 (1931) p. 238 no. 636, 2-3, 21 (*CIJ* I 694) (Κλ. Τιβ. Π. ὁ καὶ Ἀχύριος: Jew) ?= (8)
MACEDONIA (PIERIA):
—DION: **(10)** ii-iii AD Dimitsas 175 (?s. Ἔρως, Λογγῖνα)
SKYTHIA:
—OLBIA-BORYSTHENES: **(11)** iv/iii BC *IOlbia* 71 I, 8 with pl. 36 (Dubois, *IGDOlbia* 11) ([Πολ]ύχαρμος: s. Λεωκράτης); **(12)** hell. *Arkheologiia* (Kiev) 39 (1982) p. 39 (stamp); **(13)** iii BC *IOSPE* I² 32 A, 15 (Maier, *Mauerbauinschr.* 82)
—OLBIA-BORYSTHENES?: **(14)** iii BC *SEG* XXXVII 671 (bronze) (f. Ἀρτεμίδωρος)
TAURIS:
—KERKINITIS: **(15)** s. iv BC *Arkheologiia* (Kiev) 1995 (3) p. 152 (coin) (Πολυχ(άρης)—ed. pr., Πολύχ(αρμος))
THRACE:
—PERINTHOS-HERAKLEIA: **(16)** ii-iii AD *IPerinth* 65, 2 (Π̣ο̣λύχαρμος)

Πολυχρόνιος
THRACE:
—ANCHIALOS: **(1)** iii AD *IGB* I² 373, 2 (Αὐρ. Π.)

Πομπηϊανός
SCYTHIA MINOR:
—KALLATIS: **(1)** 241-244 AD *ISM* III 74 A, 27 (Πομ(π)ηϊανός: s. Ἡρακλείδης)

Πομπήϊος
MACEDONIA (DERRIOPOS):
—STUBERRA: **(1)** 74 AD *IG* X (2) (2) 325, 53 (-έϊος: f. Πούβλιος)
SCYTHIA MINOR:
—ISTROS: **(2)** ii AD *ISM* I 197 I, 4 (Πονπ-: f. Κάστος)

Πομπώνιος
MACEDONIA (LYNKESTIS):
—HERAKLEIA: **(1)** i AD *IG* X (2) (2) 75, 48 (s. Μοντανός)
THRACE:
—PHILIPPOPOLIS-TRIMONTIUM: **(2)** ii-iii AD *IGB* III 912, 5 (Πων-)

Πονσία
MACEDONIA (BOTTIAIA):
—PELLA: **(1)** ?iii AD Dimitsas 143

Ποντιανή
SCYTHIA MINOR:
—TOMIS: **(1)** ?iii AD *ISM* II 377, 14 (*GVI* 312) (d. Χρυσόδωρος, Ματρώνα)
THRACE:
—SERDICA: **(2)** 117-138 AD *IGB* IV 1925 c, 15 (Αὐρ. Π.)

Ποντιανός
MACEDONIA (MYGDONIA):
—THESSALONIKE: **(1)** 182 AD *IG* X (2) (1) 61
MACEDONIA (PAIONIA):
—KAVADARCI (MOD.): **(2)** ii/iii AD Unp. (Kavadarci Mus.) inv. 13/II (f. Μέστριος)
SCYTHIA MINOR:
—TOMIS: **(3)** ii-iii AD *ISM* II 31 II, 13 (f. Θεόδωρος); **(4)** ?iii AD ib. 377, 13 (*GVI* 312) (s. Χρυσόδωρος, Ματρώνα)
——(Aikoreis): **(5)** imp. *ISM* II 253 (Ποντια[νός])

Ποντικίων
CIMMERIAN BOSPOROS:
—PANTIKAPAION*: **(1)** 143 AD *CIRB* 710, 4 (Πο[ν]τικίων: freed.)

Ποντικός
CIMMERIAN BOSPOROS:
—HERMONASSA: **(1)** 208 AD ib. 1053 (f. Ἡρακᾶς)
MACEDONIA (DERRIOPOS):
—STUBERRA: **(2)** 87 AD *IG* X (2) (2) 325, 71 (Μ. Ἰνστέϊος Π.)
MACEDONIA (PAIONIA): **(3)** i/ii AD *SEG* XVIII 367 (Tataki, *Macedonians* p. 210 no. 21) (s. Σεκοῦνδος, Ὀλυμπιάς)
SCYTHIA MINOR:
—ISTROS: **(4)** ii AD *ISM* I 197 I, 3 (s. Ἑρμόδωρος); **(5)** ~ ib. 212, 18 (s. Δημήτριος); **(6)** f. iii AD *Stud. Fischer* p. 32 no. 4, 7 (s. Ἧλις);

(**7**) 222-225 AD *ISM* I 100 B, 22 (*Αὐρ. Π.*: s. *Ἑ—*)
—TOMIS: (**8**) ii AD ib. II 125 II, 21 (s. *Ἀλέξανδρος*); (**9**) ~ ib. 293; (**10**) ii-iii AD ib. 13, 2 (*Ποντικό[ς]*); (**11**) ~ ib. 31 III, 5 (*Ποντ[κός]*?: f. *Μόδεστος*); (**12**) ~ ib. 468, 10 (s. *Ἱστιαῖος*); (**13**) 201 AD ib. 83 I, 31 (s. *Ἑρμόδωρος*); (**14**) ~ ib. l. 34 (I f. *Σκιπίων ὁ καὶ Ποντικός* II); (**15**) ~ ib. l. 35 (*Σκιπίων ὁ καὶ Π.*: II s. *Ποντικός* I)
SKYTHIA:
—OLBIA-BORYSTHENES: (**16**) imp. *IOSPE* I² 117, 2 (*[Π]οντικ[ός]*); (**17**) ii AD ib. 80, 12 (f. *Νικίας*) ?= (*18*); (**18**) ~ ib. 102, 6 (f. *Νικίας*) ?= (*17*); (**19**) ~ *ISM* II 279, 1; *IOSPE* I² 128, 3 (s. *Νικίας*, f. *Σάτυρος*) ?= (*21*); (**20**) ii-iii AD ib. 137, 6 (f. *Μηνόδωρος*); (**21**) f. ii AD ib. 82, 5; *VDI* 1993 (1), p. 93 = *SEG* XLIX 1028 B, 4 (s. *Νικίας*) ?= (*19*)
—TANAIS: (**22**) ii AD *CIRB* 1263, 18; (**23**) f. ii AD ib. 1298, 3 (*Ποντικ[ός]*)
—TYRAS: (**24**) 181 AD *IOSPE* I² 2, 24 (f. *Οὐαλεριανός*)
TAURIS:
—CHERSONESOS: (**25**) imp. ib. 641 (*Ποντ[ικός]*?: ?f. *—ος*); (**26**) 129-130 AD ib. 359, 29; *VDI* 1960 (3), pp. 154-5, 29 (s. *Ἴλαρος*); (**27**) 174 AD *SEG* XLV 985 A, 37 (f. *Ἐπίγονος*)
THRACE:
—BYZANTION: (**28**) c. 178 AD Schönert-Geiss, *Byzantion* 1410-11; 1430-2; 1444-61; 2059-71 (coin) (*Αἰλ. Π.*) ?= (*29*); (**29**) c. 212-217 AD ib. 1503-5; 1553-73 (coin) (*Αἰλ. Π.*) ?= (*28*)
—DUROSTORUM: (**30**) 169-176 AD *SCIV* 11 (1960) p. 145 no. 2 (*Riv. Fil.* NS 2 (1924) p. 318) (Lat. L. Nume[ri]us Ponticus)
—PAUTALIA:
——Karistoron: (**31**) ii AD *IGB* IV 2175 (*[Πο]ντικὸς ὁ καὶ Ζειζε[ις]*)
—SERDICA (TERRIT.): (**32**) ?ii AD ib. 2048 (*Φλ. Ποντικὸς ὁ κα(ὶ) Ζειζοδύνων*)

Πόντιος
MACEDONIA (BOTTIAIA):
—BEROIA: (**1**) i BC-i AD *IBer* 142, 10 (Tataki 1091) (s. *Ῥεκέπτος*)
MACEDONIA (LYNKESTIS):
—HERAKLEIA (AREA): (**2**) ii AD *IG* X (2) (2) 20 (f. *Ἄδυμος*)

Πόπα
THRACE:
—ODESSOS (NR.): (**1**) iii BC *IGB* I² 253 (d. *Κοίρανος*)

Ποπιλλία
MACEDONIA (BISALTIA):
—EUPORIA?: (**1**) ii-iii AD *SEG* XXX 615 (XXXIX 591) (*Ἀμμία ἡ καὶ Π.*: d. *Ζωΐλος*)
MACEDONIA (CHALKIDIKE):
—POTIDAIA-KASSANDREIA (NR.): (**2**) imp. *TAPA* 69 (1938) p. 57 no. 10 a

Πόπλιος
CIMMERIAN BOSPOROS:
—MYRMEKION: (**1**) ii AD *KSIA* 95 (1963) p. 30 with fig. 10, 1 (vase)
—PHANAGOREIA: (**2**) m. ii AD *SEG* XLIII 512, 6
—PHANAGOREIA?: (**3**) 335 AD *CIRB* 1112, 4 (f. *Πάππος*)
MACEDONIA (EDONIS):
—AMPHIPOLIS: (**4**) hell.-imp. *SEG* XL 522 a
MACEDONIA (LYNKESTIS):
—HERAKLEIA: (**5**) i AD *IG* X (2) (2) 75, 37 (s. *Σουκκεσσός*)
MACEDONIA (MYGDONIA):
—THESSALONIKE: (**6**) c. 38 BC ib. X (2) (1) 83, 5; 109, 3 (*[Π]όπλιος*: f. *Μάνιος Σαλάριος*); (**7**) i AD ib. 242, 4 (f. *Ἀριστόνους*)
—THESSALONIKE?: (**8**) ii AD ib. 851 (f. *Πρόκλος*)
MACEDONIA (PIERIA):
—DION: (**9**) imp. *SEG* XXXIV 630; 631; 632 (f. *Ἀνθεστία Μάξιμα*)

MACEDONIA (PIERIS):
—AKONTISMA: (**10**) imp. *AD* 22 (1967) Chron. p. 421 (f. *Μητρόδωρος*)
SKYTHIA:
—TANAIS: (**11**) ii AD *CIRB* 1263, 13 (*[Π]όπλιος*); (**12**) f. ii AD ib. 1266, 4 (f. *Μαστοῦς*); (**13**) ~ ib. l. 10 (*Πό[πλ]ιος*: f. *Πασίων*); (**14**) 131-154 AD ib. 1261, 6 (s. *Χαρ—*); (**15**) c. 200-210 AD ib. 1277, 14 (*Πόπλ[ιο]ς*); (**16**) 225 AD ib. 1279, 14 (f. *Ἀρδάγδακος*); (**17**) 225-228 AD ib. l. 10; 1282, 11-12 (f. *Σωτήριχος*, *Φαῦχος*, *Φαδιαρόαζος*) ?= (*18*); (**18**) 228 AD ib. l. 11 (s. *Δημήτριος*) ?= (*17*); (**19**) ~ ib. 1283, 19 (f. *Ἀγαθήμερος*); (**20**) 244 AD ib. 1287, 13 (f. *Ὀχωζίακος*); (**21**) ~ ib. l. 22 (f. *Λίμνακος*)
THRACE:
—BYZANTION?: (**22**) i AD *IByz* 372 (*Διονύσις ὁ καὶ Π.*: s. *Μενίσκος*, f. *Πῶλλα*, *Μενεκράτης*)
—NICOPOLIS AD ISTRUM (TERRIT.): (**23**) s. ii AD *IGB* II 722 (*Eastern cults* p. 75 no. 6) (f. *Ἀκυλῖνος*)
—ODESSOS?: (**24**) ii AD *IGB* I² 51 bis a, 4 (s. *Οὐαλέριος*)
—PERINTHOS-HERAKLEIA: (**25**) c. 100-115 AD *SEG* XXVI 1288, 4 (f. *Ἀπολλόδωρος*)

Πόπλις
CIMMERIAN BOSPOROS:
—PANTIKAPAION: (**1**) m. i AD *CIRB* 496; cf. KW pl. 55 no. 763 (*Πόπλι* (voc.): s. *Κοσσᾶς*)

Ποππαῖος
THRACE:
—BYZANTION (TERRIT.): (**1**) imp. *IByz* 237 (*Ποπέου* (gen.): f. *Ζώτιχος*)

Ποππίας
TAURIS:
—CHERSONESOS: (**1**) iii BC Solomonik, *NEPKh* 35; *Hellenismus* p. 454 no. 25

Πόρθμος
THRACE:
—SESTOS: (**1**) 132 AD *IG* II² 3304, 5 (*T. Ῥαγώνιος Π.*)

Πόρις
MACEDONIA (BOTTIAIA):
—KYRRHOS: (**1**) 206 AD *SEG* XLIII 435, 3 (*Πορίου* (gen.): f. *Κοΐντα*)
MACEDONIA (CHALKIDIKE):
—GIGONOS?: (**2**) i BC ib. XXIX 587; Hatzopoulos, *Actes Chalc.* p. 25 (date) (f. *Πολυνείκης*)
—SPARTOLOS?: (**3**) ?352 BC *SEG* XLVI 804, 4 (s. *Ταυριάδης*)
—STOLOS?: (**4**) ?350 BC ib. XXXVIII 671, 4 (f. *Ἀπολλόδωρος*)
MACEDONIA (MYGDONIA):
—AINEIA: (**5**) b. 182 BC Liv. xl 4. 4 (Lat. Poris)
THRACE:
—BEROE-AUGUSTA TRAIANA (TERRIT.): (**6**) ii-iii AD *IGB* III 1770 (f. *Μουκάκενθος*)
—NICOPOLIS AD ISTRUM (TERRIT.): (**7**) f. iii AD *CCET* II (2) 675, 6 (*ILB* 349) (Lat. Porinis (gen.): f. *Δυτούβορις*)

Πόρκης
THRACE:
—MARONEIA: (**1**) ii BC Dumont–Homolle 110b 6 (*IThrakAig* E184) (*Πόρκεω* (gen.): I f. *Πόρκης* II); (**2**) ~ Dumont–Homolle 110b 6 (*IThrakAig* E184) (*Πόρκης*: II s. *Πόρκης* I)

Πορκία
MACEDONIA (CHALKIDIKE):
—POTIDAIA-KASSANDREIA (NR.): (**1**) imp. Dimitsas 744, 3

Πόρναχος
CIMMERIAN BOSPOROS:
—KUL' OBA (MOD.): (**1**) iv BC Minns, *Scythians* p. 267 (*Sov. Arkh.* 13 (1950) p. 231)

Πορφανός
THRACE:
—SESTOS: (**1**) ii AD *ISestos* 3 (*T. Π.*)

Πορφύρα
MACEDONIA (EDONIS):
—AMPHIPOLIS: (**1**) imp. *SEG* XXIV 603

Πορφύριος
MACEDONIA (EDONIS):
—PHILIPPOI*: (**1**) m. iv AD *RE* (11); Feissel, *RICM* 226 (Pilhofer 329) (*Πο[ρφύ]ριος*: bp.)
SCYTHIA MINOR:
—ISTROS: (**2**) 152 AD *ISM* I 130, 3 (*CCET* IV 64) (Lat. Sicinius Porphyrio)

Πορφυρίς
MACEDONIA (MYGDONIA):
—THESSALONIKE?: (**1**) iii/iv AD *IG* X (2) (1) 842, 2 (*Αὐρ. Π.*)

Πόρφυρος
MACEDONIA (MYGDONIA):
—THESSALONIKE: (**1**) f. iii AD *Α΄ Panell. Synedr. Epigr.* p. 20 no. 3 (*Κορνήλιος Π.*: s. *Αὐρ. Συντυχίων*)

Πόσα
MACEDONIA (EDONIS):
—PHILIPPOI (TERRIT.): (**1**) i BC/i AD Pikoulas, *Chora* p. 166 no. 73a (d. *Κοσσούπης*)

Ποσείδεος
CIMMERIAN BOSPOROS:
—PANTIKAPAION: (**1**) 275-278 AD *CIRB* 36, 31 (*Ποσείδ(εος)*: f. *Ἀντισθένης*)
SCYTHIA MINOR:
—KALLATIS: (**2**) iii BC *ISM* III 157 (s. *Φιλοκράτης*)

Ποσειδεώνιος
CIMMERIAN BOSPOROS:
—NYMPHAION: (**1**) f. v BC *SEG* XLIX 1037 (*Bosporskii fenomen* p. 187 no. 1) (s. *Θεόμνηστος*)
—PANTIKAPAION: (**2**) iv BC *CIRB* 172 (f. *Βάττας*); (**3**) ~ ib. 220 (*[Π]οσειδεών[ιο]ς*: s. *Εὔδημος*)
SCYTHIA MINOR:
—ISTROS: (**4**) iii BC *ISM* I 362, 2 + *VDI* 1984 (3), p. 180 (*[Πο]σειδ̣ε̣ώνι[ος]*—Vinogradov)
SKYTHIA:
—OLBIA-BORYSTHENES: (**5**) v-iv BC *IOSPE* I² 213 (s. *Θεόβιος*)

Ποσείδηος
SKYTHIA:
—OLBIA-BORYSTHENES: (**1**) ii AD *IOlbia* 86, 6 (*Ποσε(ί)δηος*: s. *Δάδος*); (**2**) ~ ib. l. 9 (f. *Νεῖλος*); (**3**) ~ *IOSPE* I² 96, 8 (f. *Μανίαγος*); (**4**) ~ ib. 102, 4 (f. *Σαράξαζος*) ?= (7); (**5**) ~ ib. l. 9 (f. *Ἀχιλλεύς*); (**6**) f. ii AD ib. 95, 13 (f. *Σώρωζος*); (**7**) ~ *SEG* XLIII 506, 12 (f. *Σαράξαζος*) ?= (*4*)
THRACE:
—BIZONE: (**8**) i-ii AD *IGB* I² 6, 7 (f. *Πολέμαρχος*)
—ODESSOS: (**9**) 27 BC ib. 46, 20 (-*σί*-: s. *Ἀπολλᾶς*); (**10**) i-ii AD ib. 51 b, 6 (f. *—λος*)

Ποσειδῆς
SKYTHIA:
—OLBIA-BORYSTHENES: (**1**) ii AD *IOSPE* I² 51, 16; 100, 3 (s. *Σάτυρος*); (**2**) ~ ib. 129, 4 (s. *Ζῆθος*)

Ποσείδιππος
CIMMERIAN BOSPOROS:
—PANTIKAPAION: (**1**) iv BC *CIRB* 176 (*[Π]ο̣σ̣είδιππος*: f. *Δημητρίη*); (**2**) f. i AD ib. 395; cf. KW pl. 25 no. 378 (f. *Δωρομέδων*, *Μένανδρος*)

Macedonia (Bottiaia):
—beroia: **(3)** 223 bc IBer 4, 23 (Ποσεί̣δ̣[ιππος]?: f. Ξενοφῶν); **(4)** f. iii ad ib. 97, 1 (Tataki 1124) (s. Ἰουλία)
—pella: **(5)** s. iv bc SEG xlii 619 b; **(6)** iii bc Akamatis, Amph. Pellas p. 43 nos. PAR60-1 (amph.) (SEG l 613); **(7)** f. iii bc RE (3); HE 3054 ff.; Suppl. Hell. 698 ff.; Austin–Bastianini, Posidipp. 1 ff.; cf. Fraser, Ptol. Alex. 2 p. 796 nn. 44-5 (Tataki, Macedonians p. 159 no. 77)
Macedonia (Chalkidike):
—potidaia-kassandreia: **(8)** iv/iii bc RE (1); PCG 7 pp. 561-81 (Tataki, Macedonians p. 95 no. 83; FRA 2794) (s. Κυνίσκος)
—torone: **(9)** ?353 bc SEG xxiv 574, 8; Hatzopoulos, Actes Chalc. p. 80 (date) (s. Διόδωρος)
Macedonia (Derriopos): **(10)** 95 ad IG x (2) (2) 300, 1 (-σί-: f. Φίλιππος)
—stuberra: **(11)** c. 41-48 ad ib. 323, 26 (s. Κάρπος); **(12)** 74 ad ib. 325, 25 (s. Ἀριστοκράτης); **(13)** ~ ib. l. 34 (s. Ἀγοραῖος); **(14)** ~ ib. l. 64-5; 326, 67 (f. Ἀπολλώνιος); **(15)** ~ ib. l. 34 (f. Φίλων); **(16)** ~ ib. l. 50 (s. Δρωπίων); **(17)** ~ ib. l. 53 (s. Θευδίας); **(18)** f. ii ad ib. 329 (-σί-); **(19)** f. iii ad ib. 335 (-σί-: s. Θεσσαλός); **(20)** 224 ad ib. 331; cf. 332 (-σί-: I f. Ποσείδιππος II); **(21)** ~ ib. 331; cf. 332 (-σί-: II s. Ποσείδιππος I)
Macedonia (Mygdonia):
—thessalonike: **(22)** ii ad ib. x (2) (1) 469 (Σουλπίκιος Π.)
Macedonia (Odomantike):
—sirrha: **(23)** s. ii ad Dimitsas 812, 13 (Kaphtantzis 16) (f. Διοσκουρίδης)
Scythia Minor:
—istros: **(24)** ii bc ISM i 36, 2, 22 + Pontica 33-4 (2000-1) pp. 346-7 no. 3 (I f. Ποσείδιππος II); **(25)** ~ ISM i 36, 2, [22] + Pontica 33-4 (2000-1) pp. 346-7 no. 3 (II s. Ποσείδιππος I)
Skythia:
—olbia-borysthenes: **(26)** m. iv bc Dubois, IGDOlbia 13, 7 (f. Διονύσιος)
Thrace:
—apollonia-sozopolis: **(27)** ii/i bc IGB i^2 390, 3 (f. Αἰσχρίων)
—bisanthe-panion: **(28)** iv bc Unp. (Sayar) (s. Πολύδιγγος)
—byzantion: **(29)** iii/ii bc IByz 170 (Fıratlı–Robert p. 109 no. 177) (f. Διονύσιος)
—maroneia: **(30)** ?c. 432 bc Schönert-Geiss, Maroneia 83-4 (coin)
—odessos: **(31)** ii ad IGB i^2 50 a, 8 (-σί-: s. Ἀπολλώνιος)

Ποσειδωνία

Macedonia: **(1)** iii ad SEG xlvii 1006 (-σι-); **(2)** 253 ad ILeukopetra 103, 9 (-σι-: slave/freed.)
Macedonia (Edonis):
—philippoi: **(3)** iv-v ad Feissel, RICM 241 (Pilhofer 77) (-σι-)
Macedonia (Mygdonia):
—thessalonike: **(4)** iii ad SEG xxvii 311 (-σι-)
Macedonia (Paionia):
—neapolis? (smilovci (mod.)): **(5)** ii-iii ad Sp. 98 (1941-8) p. 32 no. 78
—stoboi: **(6)** ?iii ad AJA 75 (1971) p. 410; BE 1972, no. 256 e (bronze) (-σιδο-: Jew); **(7)** iii ad SEG xlvii 1006

Ποσειδώνιος

Cimmerian Bosporos:
—pantikapaion: **(1)** imp. CIRB 760 (-σι-: f. Βίστης); **(2)** i ad ib. 497; cf. KW pl. 36 no. 522 (-σι-: I f. Ποσειδώνιος II); **(3)** ~ CIRB 497; cf. KW pl. 36 no. 522 (II s. Ποσειδώνιος I)
Macedonia: **(4)** s. iv bc Berve 656 (Tataki, Macedonians p. 413 no. 99); **(5)** iii bc Milet vi (2) 793, 5; cf. Stephanis 1423 (Tataki, Macedonians p. 413 no. 101) (f. Ἀμεινίας); **(6)** ?c. 240-220 bc IOrop 64, 2 (Tataki, Macedonians p. 413 no. 100) (s. Ξένων)
Macedonia (Bottiaia):
—aigai?: **(7)** 253 ad ILeukopetra 103, 3 (Tataki 298) (Αὐρ. Ποσιδώνιος)
—beroia: **(8)** 113 bc IBer 134, 38 (-σι-: s. Μενεκράτης); **(9)** s. i ad ib. 276 (Tataki 1177) ([Πο]σιδώνιος); **(10)** f. iii ad IBer 221 (Tataki 1125) (Ποσιδώνειος); **(11)** 212 ad ILeukopetra 63, 5 (Tataki 299) (Αὐρ. Ποσιδώνιος ὁ καὶ Παντακιανός: s. Μέστυς)
—beroia?:
——Drogeatai: **(12)** 239 ad ILeukopetra 93, 5 (-σι-: f. Αὐρ. Οὐαλέριος)
—edessa: **(13)** 51 ad SEG xlvi 744, 5 (Tataki, Edessa 263) (-σι-: s. Ταρούλας)
—pella: **(14)** f. i bc SEG xlvii 933
Macedonia (Chalkidike):
—anthemous: **(15)** 106 bc ib. xlii 561 (s. Ἀσκληπιόδωρος)
—aphytis: **(16)** imp. ib. xxix 606 (Κορ. Ποσιδώνιος: s. Κορ. Τρύφαινα)
Macedonia (Edonis):
—amphipolis: **(17)** c. 265-255 bc SGDI 2588, 2 (Tataki, Macedonians p. 60 no. 114) (s. Ἑλλάνικος); **(18)** v-vi ad SEG xlviii 726 (Πωσιδού-)
—philippoi: **(19)** i-ii ad Dimitsas 973 + BSA 23 (1918-19) p. 81 (Pilhofer 86) (-σι-: s. Βασιέλας)
Macedonia (Elimeia):
—velvendos (mod.): **(20)** ii ad SEG xlvii 1001, 2 (f. Εὔδημος)
Macedonia (Eordaia):
—arnisa?: **(21)** f. iii ad EAM 135; Hatzopoulos, MI i p. 94 n. 4 (locn.) (-σι-: f. Παράμονος)
Macedonia (Lynkestis):
—sitaria (mod.): **(22)** f. iii ad EAM 167 a (Π. Τερέντιος Ποσιδώνιος)
Macedonia (Mygdonia):
—thessalonike: **(23)** ?105 bc IG x (2) (1) 135, 4 (f. Δωσίθεος); **(24)** i bc-i ad ib. 129, 6 (-σι-); **(25)** i-ii ad ib. 243 II, 5 (f. Ἰουκοῦνδος)
Macedonia (Odomantike):
—sirrha: **(26)** 105 or 221 ad SEG xxx 595 (-σι-: f. Ἰσίδωρος)
Macedonia (Orestis):
—sisani (mod.): **(27)** 146 ad EAM 187, 20 (Φουνδανὸς Π.)
Macedonia (Paionia):
—demir kapija (mod.): **(28)** hell. SEG xlv 807 C (sherd) (-σι-: f. —εισων)
—kavadarci (mod.): **(29)** ii ad Sp. 98 (1941-8) p. 67 no. 140 (-σι-: s. Τόρκος, ?f. Ἀμμία); **(30)** ii-iii ad Minalo 2 (1911) pp. 54 f. (Ποσειδών<ων>ιος: f. Ἡρακλείδης); **(31)** 116 ad Unp. (Skopje) (-σι-: f. Λυσίμαχος); **(32)** ii/iii ad Sp. 75 (1933) p. 39 no. 122 ([Πο]σειδώνιος)
—neapolis? (izvor (mod.)): **(33)** ii-iii ad ib. 98 (1941-8) p. 28 no. 68 (I f. Ποσειδώνιος II, Ἀμμία); **(34)** ~ ib. (II s. Ποσειδώνιος I, Γαΐα); **(35)** ~ Dimitsas 303
—negotino (mod.): **(36)** ii-iii ad Sp. 75 (1933) p. 41 no. 138, 5 (-σι-: s. Οὐαλεριανὸς ΚΟΥΝΟΣ, Νικανδρία); **(37)** ~ SEG xxxviii 713 n. a (-σι-: f. Ἀμμακώ); **(38)** ~ ib. (-σι-: s. Ἀμμακώ); **(39)** 153 ad ib. 712 (s. Κήσης, Μάντα)
—stoboi: **(40)** s. iii ad JÖAI 32 (1940) Beibl. col. 18 no. 12. 46 (Ποσιδω(νίου) (gen.))
Macedonia (Pieria):
—herakleion: **(41)** c. 230-200 bc BCH 45 (1921) p. 17 III, 52 (Tataki, Macedonians p. 112 no. 7) (f. Γλαυκίας, Ἀντίγονος)
Macedonia (Sintike):
—parthikopolis: **(42)** ii-iii ad IGB v 5894 (Τιβεριανὸς Ποσιδώνιος)
Macedonia?: **(43)** i bc/i ad Xenia antiqua 10 (2001) p. 22 no. C (or Thrace: -σι-: f. Φίλιππος)
Scythia Minor:
—istros: **(44)** i bc-i ad ISM i 191 II, 41 (-σι-: f. Δημόχαρις); **(45)** ii ad ib. 204, 7 (s. Θεόπομπος); **(46)** 138 ad ib. 193 I, 94 (s. Ἀπολλώνιος); **(47)** ~ ib. 193 II, 29 (s. Διοσκουρίδης); **(48)** ii/iii ad ib. 225, 8
—kallatis: **(49)** iii-ii bc ib. iii 138, 1 (GVI 1279 with Add. p. 693) (Ποσειδών[ιος]: f. Διονύσιος)
—tomis: **(50)** hell. Unp. (Avram) ([Πο]σειδώνιος: s. Ἄκεσις); **(51)** iii-ii bc AMNG i (2) 2439; 2450; 2459-60 (coin) (Ποσει(δώνιος)?); **(52)** ii bc ISM ii 4, 14 (Ποσειδών[ιος]); **(53)** ii-i bc ib. 36 (s. Νουμήνιος); **(54)** i bc ib. 2, 26, 30; 2 A, 47 (s. Γέρων); **(55)** ii ad ib. 125 I, 19 (-σι-: s. Δάης); **(56)** ~ ib. 151; **(57)** ii-iii ad ib. 19 b, 5 (Ποσιδώ[νιος]); **(58)** ~ ib. 26, 3 (s. Πάπας); **(59)** ~ ib. 31 II, 27 (Ἰούλ. Ποσει[δώνιος]); **(60)** ~ ib. 104, 16; **(61)** ~ ib. 164 ([Ποσει]δ̣ώνιος?); **(62)** ~ ib. 404; **(63)** ~ ib. 468, 19 (-σι-); **(64)** 201 ad ib. 83 I, 20 (s. Πωπω.τος (gen.)); **(65)** ~ ib. l. 36 (s. Π—); **(66)** ~ ib. 83 II, 24 (-νει-: f. Αὐρ. Σεραπόδωρος)
——(Argadeis): **(67)** 130-138 ad ib. 52, 7 (Τ. Φλ. Π.: s. Φαῖδρος)
——(Hopletes): **(68)** ii ad ib. 123 (f. Εὐέλπιστος)
—tomis (nr.): **(69)** 142 ad ib. 161 (Lat. Posidoni (gen.))
Skythia:
—olbia-borysthenes: **(70)** iv/iii bc Dubois, IGDOlbia 95 (vase) ([Ποσε]ιδώνιος: s. Σωκράτης); **(71)** iii bc IOSPE i^2 201 I, 11 (f. Ἀριστόκριτος); **(72)** ~ ib. l. 15 (f. Ἀλφῖνος); **(73)** ~ ib. l. 22 (f. Σωκράτης); **(74)** ~ ib. l. 25 (s. Ἐπικράτης); **(75)** ~ ib. l. 36 (s. Ἀριστόκριτος); **(76)** s. iii bc ib. 76, 6 (Sokolowski ii 88; Dubois, IGDOlbia 88) (s. Εὐκράτης); **(77)** ?ii-i bc ib. 110, 1; **(78)** ~ ib. l. 3; **(79)** ii ad IOSPE i^2 106, 7 (s. Νεῖλων); **(80)** ~ ib. 206, 1 (s. Πολύξενος, f. Ἀχιλλεύς)
—tyras: **(81)** s. iii bc VDI 1966 (2), p. 152, 4 (Ποσειδώνι[ος])
Tauris:
—chersonesos: **(82)** c. 262-237 bc Kats p. 109 no. 96 (amph.) (s. Διοσκουρίδας)
Thrace: **(83)** 274 bc PCZ 59001, 22, [50], verso (Velkov 227; La'da E784); **(84)** 231 or 206 bc CPR xviii 6, 109; cf. La'da E832 (Ποσειδώ[νιος]: f. Θεόδωρος)
—abdera (territ.)?: **(85)** i ad IThrakAig E81 (f. —ως)
—ainos: **(86)** 156 bc ID 1416 B I, 108 (f. Ἐπικράτης)
—apollonia-sozopolis: **(87)** iv bc BMN-Burgas 4 (2002) p. 119 no. 1; **(88)** ~ ib. p. 122 no. 11 (-σε-: f. Παιδάρχη)
—bargala (area): **(89)** ?iii ad SEG xxxviii 664
—beroe-augusta traiana: **(90)** 231 ad RMD 315 (Lat. M. Aurelius Posidonius)
—bisanthe-panion: **(91)** 188-159 bc OGIS 302 (Tekmeria 6 (2001) p. 156 no. 1) (f. Δημήτριος)
—bizone: **(92)** i/ii ad IGB i^2 6, 15 (-σι-: s. Μόσχος)
—byzantion: **(93)** ii-i bc IByz 190 (Fıratlı–Robert p. 59 no. 41) (s. Ἀρτεμίδωρος); **(94)** s. ii bc SEG xxxix 1124, 8 (IMylasa 103) (s. Πολυχάρης); **(95)** i-ii ad IByz 269 (Fıratlı–Robert pp. 84-5 no. 104) (-σι-: f. Ἆδυς)
—dionysopolis: **(96)** iii ad IGB i^2 14 b, 12 (Αὐρ. Π. νεώτ.: s. Ἄττας); **(97)** ~ ib. l. 14 (Αὐρ. Π.)
—isperih (mod.): **(98)** iv/iii bc Chiron 24 (1994) p. 262 n. 71 (f. Μενέχαρμος)

—LYSIMACHEIA: **(99)** 213 BC *BGU* 2396, 6 (f. *Διότιμος*)
—MARONEIA: **(100)** s. iii BC *IThrakAig* E239 (*Ποσειδών[ιος]*); **(101)** ii-i BC ib. E212, 25 (-σιδό-: f. *Διογένης*); **(102)** i AD *IG* XII (8) 215, 14 (-σι-)
—NICOPOLIS AD NESTUM: **(103)** ii AD *IGB* IV 2336, 10 ([*Πο*]*σειδώνιος*: s. *Φίλιππος*); **(104)** ~ ib. l. 12 ([*Πο*]*σειδώνιος*: s. *Μαγνίων*); **(105)** ~ ib. l. 14 (*Ἀντώνιος Π.*)
—ODESSOS: **(106)** 10 BC ib. I^2 46, 37 (-σι-: s. *Νουμήνιος*); **(107)** i-ii AD ib. 124 (*Ποσειδών[ιος]*); **(108)** ii AD ib. 50 a, 25; **(109)** f. ii AD ib. 77, 4 (*CCET* I 31) (-σι-: f. *Ζῆνις*); **(110)** s. ii AD *IGB* I^2 163 bis (*CCET* I 55; PM 1537) (f. *Προμαθίων, Ἀπατούριος*)
—ODRYSAI: **(111)** 356 BC *FD* III (1) 392, 2 (s. *Κερσεβλέπτης*)
—PAUTALIA: **(112)** 161-169 or 244-249 AD *IGB* IV 2052 (-σι-: f. *Αὐρ. Ἡρωΐδης*)
—PERINTHOS-HERAKLEIA: **(113)** iii BC *IPerinth* 2, 2 (s. *Διοσκουρίδης*)
—PHILIPPOPOLIS-TRIMONTIUM: **(114)** 163-164 AD *IGB* III 902, 8; 903; V [5433] (*Γ. Ἄλφιος Π.*); **(115)** iii AD ib. III 1007, 3 (*Αὐρ. Π.*)
—PHILIPPOPOLIS-TRIMONTIUM (TERRIT.): **(116)** ii AD ib. 1142 (*Ποσειδῶνι[ος]*)
—TĂMNO CAVE (MOD.): **(117)** ii-iii AD ib. II 751 f (-σι-)

Ποσειδώνις
MACEDONIA (BOTTIAIA):
—BEROIA: **(1)** ii-iii AD *IBer* 371, 5 (Tataki 1129) (-σι-)
MACEDONIA (EDONIS):
—PHILIPPOI: **(2)** iii AD *BCH* 60 (1936) p. 57 no. 6 (Pilhofer 337) (*Αὐρ. Ποσιδώνις*)
MACEDONIA (PAIONIA):
—NEAPOLIS? (VLADILOVCI (MOD.)): **(3)** ii-iii AD *Sp.* 71 (1931) p. 32 no. 64 (-σι-)
SCYTHIA MINOR:
—TOMIS: **(4)** ii-iii AD *ISM* II 26, 7 (s. *Βαλέριος*)
THRACE:
—APOLLONIA-SOZOPOLIS: **(5)** i-ii AD *IGB* I^2 401, 4 (s. *Ἑστιαῖος*)
—KABYLE: **(6)** iii AD *SEG* XLII 650 (*Αὐρ. Π.*)
—NICOPOLIS AD NESTUM: **(7)** ii-iii AD *IGB* IV 2337, 16 ([*Π*]*οσιδώνις*)
—SALYMBRIA: **(8)** imp. *IByz* S 17 (-σι-: s. *Γλύκων*)

Ποσθίων
MACEDONIA (EDONIS):
—AMPHIPOLIS: **(1)** b. 357 BC Hatzopoulos, *Actes Amphipolis* p. 25 no. 3, 18 (*SEG* XLI 557) (*Ποσθίων*: s. *Σύαγρος*)

Ποσίδειος
THRACE:
—APOLLONIA-SOZOPOLIS: **(1)** iv BC *IGB* I^2 433 (s. *Ἀμπέλοργος*)
—MARONEIA: **(2)** c. 365-336 BC Schönert-Geiss, *Maroneia* 414-18; 511-13 (coin)
—PERINTHOS-HERAKLEIA:
——(Aigikoreis): **(3)** iii-ii BC *IPerinth* 61, 49

Ποσίδεος
CIMMERIAN BOSPOROS:
—GORGIPPIA: **(1)** f. iii BC *CIRB* 1137 A II, 15 (f. *Ἀπολλώνιος*); **(2)** ~ ib. l. 32; 1137 B II, 36 (s. *Ἑλλανίδης*)
—THEODOSIA: **(3)** iii AD ib. 947 A, 3 (*Ποσίδ[εος]*: f. *Ἥλιος*)
SKYTHIA:
—OLBIA-BORYSTHENES: **(4)** iii BC *Arkheologiia* (Kiev) 39 (1982) p. 35 (Vinogradov–Kryžickij pl. 91. 3a (vase)) (*Ποσίδε(ος)*) ?= (7); **(5)** ~ *IOSPE* I^2 77 (*Ποσίδε[ος]*); **(6)** ~ ib. 189 (s. *Διονύσιος*) ?= (13) (8); **(7)** ~ Vinogradov–Kryžickij pl. 91. 7 ?= (4); **(8)** c. 200-175 BC *IG* XI (4) 813, 2, 9 (s. *Διονύσιος*) ?= (6); **(9)** ii BC *IOSPE* I^2 78, 4 ([*Ποσί*]*δεος*?); **(10)** ~ ib. 168; 670-2; *BE* 1965, no. 272; cf. *Archaiognosia* 2 (1981) pp. 224-33 (*Ποσίδειος*—168: I f. *Ποσίδεος* II); **(11)** ~ *IOSPE* I^2 168; 670-2; *BE* 1965, no. 272; cf. *Archaiognosia* 2 (1981) pp. 224-33 (II s. *Ποσίδεος* I); **(12)** ~ *IOSPE* I^2 220 a; cf. KW pl. 26 no. 381 (f. *Μητροβία*); **(13)** ~ *SEG* XL 633 (s. *Διονύσιος*) ?= (6); **(14)** c. 70 BC *IOSPE* I^2 35, 1, [4] (s. *Ἀναξαγόρας*)
THRACE:
—MARONEIA: **(15)** c. 400-378 BC Schönert-Geiss, *Maroneia* 164 (coin)

Ποσιδήϊος
THRACE:
—MARONEIA: **(1)** c. 432-423 BC ib. 144-51 (coin)
—STRYME?: **(2)** s. v BC *IThrakAig* E113 (f. *Ζήνων*)

Ποσίδηος
SKYTHIA:
—OLBIA-BORYSTHENES: **(1)** imp. *IOSPE* I^2 113, 6 (f. *Ἀσκληπιάδης*); **(2)** ~ ib. l. 12 (f. *Μουλίουργος*); **(3)** ii AD ib. 183, 6 (f. *Ἀναξιμένης*); **(4)** ?ii-iii AD ib. 111, 5 (f. *Ἀλέξανδρος*)
—OLBIA-BORYSTHENES (LEUKE)*: **(5)** f. v BC Dubois, *IGDOlbia* 48 (vase) (f. *Γλαῦκος*)

Πόσις
CIMMERIAN BOSPOROS:
—GORGIPPIA: **(1)** ii AD *CIRB* 1140, 3 (*Ποσίου* (gen.): f. *Ἰᾶς*); **(2)** ii/iii AD ib. 1179, 52 ([*Π*]*όσις*: s. *Φαρνακίων*, f. *Ἀνδραλέων*); **(3)** ~ *SEG* XXXVI 710, 2 (s. *Κο*—)
—PHANAGOREIA: **(4)** 344-311 BC *CIRB* 972 (Rhodes–Osborne 65 E) (f. *Κασσαλία*) ?= (5)
—PHANAGOREIA (NR.): **(5)** 344-311 BC *CIRB* 1014 (Rhodes–Osborne 65 C) (f. *Ξενοκλείδης*) ?= (4)
MACEDONIA (DERRIOPOS):
—STUBERRA: **(6)** 116 AD *IG* X (2) (2) 327, 26 (s. *Μάνιος*); **(7)** ~ ib. l. 33 (s. *Μᾶρκος*)
SKYTHIA:
—OLBIA-BORYSTHENES: **(8)** v/iv BC *IOlbia* 96 (f. *Πατροφίλη*); **(9)** iii BC *IOSPE* I^2 32 B, 59 (Maier, *Mauerbauinschr.* 82); **(10)** ?ii-i BC Dubois, *IGDOlbia* 110, 1
—OLBIA-BORYSTHENES (BEREZAN (MOD.)): **(11)** v BC ib. 33 (vase) (*Πόσιος* (gen.))
TAURIS:
—CHERSONESOS: **(12)** iv BC *IOSPE* I^2 407
THRACE:
—APOLLONIA-SOZOPOLIS?: **(13)** ?iv BC *IGB* I^2 379 (or Thrace Anchialos: f. *Παιδάρχη*)
—MARONEIA: **(14)** c. 325-300 BC *IThrakAig* E224 (*Πόσιδος* (gen.): f. *Ἡρόβουλος*)
—ODESSOS: **(15)** ii-i BC *IGB* I^2 78 bis (*CCET* I 28) (*Πόσεως* (gen.): f. *Ἑστιαῖος*); **(16)** I BC *IGB* I^2 46, 46 (*Π*[*όσ*]*σει*[*ς*]: f. *Διονύσιος*); **(17)** f. ii AD ib. 168 (PM 1724); *Dacia* 21 (1977) p. 161 (date) (f. *Δουσπιερίς*); **(18)** m. ii AD *IGB* I^2 179 (PM 1694); *Dacia* 21 (1977) p. 161 (date) (f. *Ξένων*)

Ποσιστις
THRACE: **(1)** 257 BC *PSorb* 17b, 20, 23; cf. La'da E847 (f. *Τήρης*)

Πόσσης
SCYTHIA MINOR:
—TOMIS?: **(1)** ii AD *ISM* V 78, 1 (*CCET* IV 106); *ISM* V 128, 1 (*CCET* IV 52) (*Πόσσει* (gen.): f. *Ἄττας*)
THRACE:
—HADRIANOPOLIS (TERRIT.): **(2)** iii AD *IGB* III 1804 (s. *Βίθυς*)

Πόσσις
THRACE:
—ODESSOS: **(1)** 12 BC ib. I^2 46, 35 (-σσεις: s. *Ξένων*); **(2)** 3 BC ib. l. 44 (-σσεις: s. *Διογένης*); **(3)** i-ii AD ib. 120 (*Πόσσιο*[*ς*] (gen.): f. *Σωκράτης*); **(4)** ii AD ib. 50 a, 5 (*Πόσσειος* (gen.): f. *Ἀρτέμων*)
—ODESSOS (NR.): **(5)** i-ii AD ib. 286 (*CCET* I 83) (*Πόσσειος* (gen.): f. *Ἀγαθήνωρ ὁ καὶ Δάδας*)

Ποτάμιλλα
MACEDONIA (MYGDONIA):
—THESSALONIKE*: **(1)** 145 or 261 AD *IG* X (2) (1) 451, 5 (*Κανουλεΐα Ποτάμιλα*: freed.)
THRACE:
—KELLAI: **(2)** 241-244 AD *IGB* III 1517, 14 (*Αὐρ. Π.*: d. *Ποτάμων*)

Πόταμις
MACEDONIA?: **(1)** b. 348 BC *Olynthus* 10 p. 433 nos. 2242-3 (bullets)

Ποτάμων
MACEDONIA (BOTTIAIA):
—BEROIA: **(1)** s. i AD *IBer* 276 (Tataki 1130); **(2)** f. iii AD *IBer* 99, 4 (Tataki 86) (*Αἰλ. Π.*: f. *Ὀνωρατιανὸς Πολύχαρμος*)
—PELLA: **(3)** iv/iii BC *Pella* p. 139 no. 213 (s. *Ἀγαθοκλῆς*)
MACEDONIA (EORDAIA):
—DROSIA (MOD.): **(4)** 203 AD *EAM* 132, 7 (*Π*[*ο*]*τάμων*: s. *Ἀντώνιος Μενέλαος*)
—EXOCHI (MOD.): **(5)** 275 AD ib. 117, a 25
MACEDONIA (MYGDONIA):
—THESSALONIKE: **(6)** s. ii AD *IG* X (2) (1) 245 I, 10 (*Ποτ*[*ά*]*μων*)
MACEDONIA (ORESTIS):
—SISANI (MOD.): **(7)** 146 AD *EAM* 187, 15 (*Μάριος Π.*)
SCYTHIA MINOR:
—KALLATIS: **(8)** s. iii BC *ISM* III 11, 2 (f. *Διονύσιος*)
THRACE:
—APOLLONIA-SOZOPOLIS?: **(9)** iv BC *IGB* I^2 478 (f. —*ος*)
—BEROE-AUGUSTA TRAIANA (TERRIT.): **(10)** ii-iii AD ib. III 1638 (s. *Μουκιανός*)
—BYZANTION: **(11)** 117-138 AD *IByz* 37, 3, 10 (I s. *Μηνόδοτος*, f. *Ποτάμων* II); **(12)** ~ ib. l. 9 (II s. *Ποτάμων* I)
—GLAVA PANEGA (MOD.): **(13)** ii-iii AD *IGB* II 517 (f. *Δεινίας*)
—HERAION TEICHOS: **(14)** c. 133-86 BC *SEG* XLII 662 (f. *Ἡγέστρατος*)
—KELLAI: **(15)** 241-244 AD *IGB* III 1517, 14 (f. *Αὐρ. Ποτάμιλλα*)
—NICOPOLIS AD ISTRUM (TERRIT.): **(16)** ii AD ib. II 714 (*Αἰλ. Π.*)
—ODESSOS: **(17)** m. ii AD ib. I^2 177 ter; *Dacia* 21 (1977) p. 161 (date) (f. *Βλωστι*)
—PAUTALIA (TERRIT.): **(18)** ii-iii AD *IGB* IV 2231 (f. *Δέκεντος*)
—PLOTINOPOLIS: **(19)** ii-iii AD Dumont–Homolle 106b (*IThrakAig* E467) (*Κλ. Π.*: f. *Φλαβία, Κλεοπάτρα*)

Ποταμωνιανός
MACEDONIA (BOTTIAIA):
—BEROIA: **(1)** a. 212 AD *IBer* 136, 7 (Tataki 1155) (*Ῥουτίλιος Π.*: I f. *Ῥουτίλιος Ποταμωνιανὸς νέος* II); **(2)** ~ *IBer* 136, 7 (Tataki 1154) (*Ῥουτίλιος Ποταμωνιανὸς νέος*: II s. *Ῥουτίλιος Ποταμωνιανός* I)

Ποτηγοῦς
CIMMERIAN BOSPOROS:
—GORGIPPIA: **(1)** ii AD *CIRB* 1152 (*Ποτη*[*γοῦς*]); **(2)** ~ ib. 1159 A, 5 + *SEG* XXIX 704 (*Π*(*ό*)*τηγο*[*ς*]—edd., *Π*(*ο*)*τηγο*[*ῦς*]?); **(3)** m. ii AD *Eirene* 7 (1968) p. 67, 16; Zgusta, *PNS* 697 ([*Πο*]*τηγοῦς*: s. *Μακάριος*); **(4)** s. ii AD *CIRB* 1142, 10 (f. —*ίων*); **(5)** ~ ib. l. 17 (f. —*ας*); **(6)** ii/iii AD *SEG* XXXVI 715, 2 (*Π*[*ο*]*τη*[*γοῦς*], *Π*[*ό*]*τη*[*γος*]—*SEG*)

Πότος
MACEDONIA (EDONIS):
—HILL 133 (MOD.): **(1)** m. v BC Pritchett, *Topography* I pp. 46-7 no. 1, 2 (sherd); cf. *SEG* XLVI 723 (n. pr.?)

Ποτού
THRACE:
—ODESSOS: (1) i BC-i AD *IGB* I^2 159 (*CCET* I 50; PM 1312) (d. *Πρωταγόρας*)

Πόττης
MACEDONIA (CHALKIDIKE):
—STOLOS?: (1) ?351 BC *SEG* XXXVIII 672, 3, 10 (f. *Δύννυς*)

Πούβλιος
MACEDONIA (DERRIOPOS):
—STUBERRA: **(1)** 50 AD *IG* X (2) (2) 324, 22 (*Πόβ-*: f. *Ζωΐλος*); **(2)** 74 AD ib. 325, 53 (s. *Πομπήϊος*)
MACEDONIA (PAIONIA): **(3)** ii-iii AD *Sp.* 98 (1941-8) p. 201 no. 398; cf. Düll, *Götterkulte* p. 359 no. 170
—KAVADARCI (MOD.): **(4)** imp. *Sp.* 98 (1941-8) p. 77 no. 163; **(5)** ii-iii AD ib. 75 (1933) p. 37 no. 110; **(6)** iii AD ib. 98 (1941-8) p. 68 no. 141 (-ως)

Πούβλις
MACEDONIA (DERRIOPOS):
—STUBERRA: **(1)** 116 AD *IG* X (2) (2) 327, 23 (s. *Νικόλαος*)

Πούδης
MACEDONIA (DERRIOPOS):
—STUBERRA: **(1)** c. 74 AD ib. 326, 42 (s. *Οὐηράτιος*)
THRACE:
—PAUTALIA: **(2)** ii-iii AD *IGB* IV 2072, 17 (f. *—βωης*)

Πουλέας?
SCYTHIA MINOR:
—KALLATIS: **(1)** iii-ii BC *AMNG* I (1) 251; *SNG Stancomb* 75 (coin) (*Πουλέ(ας)?*)

Πουλυδάμας
MACEDONIA (MYGDONIA):
—ARETHOUSA: **(1)** c. 315-280 BC *FD* III (1) 186, 2 + p. 105 n. 1 (*Syll*^{3} 269 K; Tataki, *Macedonians* p. 70 no. 13) (s. *Ἀνταῖος*) ?= (*Πολυδάμας* (*1*))

Πουπλᾶς
MACEDONIA (MYGDONIA):
—THESSALONIKE: **(1)** ii AD *A΄ Panell. Synedr. Epigr.* p. 18 no. 2 (*Ῥέφριος Π.*)
MACEDONIA (ODOMANTIKE):
—SIRRHA: **(2)** 155 AD Dimitsas 821, 10 (Kaphtantzis I) (f. *Ἡρόδοτος*)

Πουπλικία
MACEDONIA (CHALKIDIKE):
—ANTHEMOUS: **(1)** iii AD *SEG* XLII 569 (II 413) (d. *Ἐλπίδιος*, m. *—ομις*)

Πούπλιος
MACEDONIA: **(1)** ii-iii AD *IGUR* 1312 (Tataki, *Macedonians* p. 413 no. 102)
MACEDONIA (ELIMEIA):
—AIANE: **(2)** ii-iii AD *EAM* 23 (f. *Πετρωνία*)
MACEDONIA (PAIONIA):
—KAVADARCI (MOD.): **(3)** ii/iii AD *Sp.* 75 (1933) p. 40 no. 131 (s. *Διοσκοῦς*)
—STOBOI (NR.): **(4)** ii/iii AD *SEG* XVI 406 (f. *Λύκα*)
THRACE:
—ODESSOS: **(5)** ?i-ii AD *IGB* I^2 95

Πουρθαῖος
SKYTHIA:
—OLBIA-BORYSTHENES: **(1)** ?ii AD *IOSPE* I^2 99, 3 (f. *Πήγασος*); **(2)** ii AD ib. 130, 6, 16; Zgusta, *PNS* 185 (*Πο[υρ]θαῖος*: I f. *Πουρθαῖος* II); **(3)** ~ *IOSPE* I^2 130, 6, 16 (II s. *Πουρθαῖος* I); **(4)** ~ ib. 176, 3 (*Πουρθαί[ος]*); **(5)** f. iii AD ib. 43, 5 (f. *Νεῖλος*)

Πούρθαις
SKYTHIA:
—OLBIA-BORYSTHENES: **(1)** i/ii AD *SEG* XLIII 505, 6; Zgusta, *PNS* 185 (s. *Ἄβνακος*); **(2)** ii AD *IOSPE* I^2 83, 7 (s. *Νινικῆς*)

Πουρθάκης
SKYTHIA:
—OLBIA-BORYSTHENES: **(1)** ii AD ib. 86, 7; Zgusta, *PNS* 185 (s. *Μανίαγος*); **(2)** ~ *IOSPE* I^2 101, 11 (*Πουρθάκητος* (gen.): s. *Μήτακος*); **(3)** ~ ib. 102, 7 (s. *Ζουρόζιος*)

Πού-η
THRACE:
—DODOPARON: **(1)** ii AD *IGB* III 1796, 3 (*Οὐλπ. Π.*: m. *Ἀπολλωνία*)

Πραιτωριανός
THRACE:
—KALLIPOLIS: **(1)** imp. *ISestos* 27 (*[Π]ραιτωρ[ι-α]νός*)

Πραξέας
CIMMERIAN BOSPOROS:
—NYMPHAION: **(1)** f. iii BC *SEG* XXXIX 701. 4 + XLV 997. 12

Πραξιάναξ
SKYTHIA:
—OLBIA-BORYSTHENES: **(1)** imp. *IOSPE* I^2 113, 4; **(2)** ii AD ib. 89, 4 (f. *Δημήτριος*); **(3)** iii AD ib. 98, 5 (f. *Παπίας*)

Πραξίας
CIMMERIAN BOSPOROS:
—GORGIPPIA: **(1)** ii/iii AD *CIRB* 1179, 36 (*Πραξ[ία]ς*: s. *Χρυσώτης*)
MACEDONIA: **(2)** 221 BC *PPetr* III 112d II, 8 (Tataki, *Macedonians* p. 413 no. 103; La'da E1587)
MACEDONIA (DERRIOPOS):
—STUBERRA: **(3)** 74 AD *IG* X (2) (2) 325, 24 (f. *Ζωΐλος*)

Πραξικλῆς
MACEDONIA (CHALKIDIKE):
—POTIDAIA-KASSANDREIA: **(1)** ?m. iii BC *FD* III (4) 351, 4 (Tataki, *Macedonians* p. 95 no. 84) (s. *Κλέων*)

Πράξιλλα
THRACE:
—PHILIPPOPOLIS-TRIMONTIUM (TERRIT.): **(1)** i-ii AD *IGB* III 1328; cf. V 5499 (*Παξίλλα*—lap.)

Πραξιμένης
SCYTHIA MINOR:
—KALLATIS: **(1)** ii AD *ISM* III 110 (*[Π]ραξιμένης*)

Πραξίνικος
MACEDONIA (PIERIA):
—DION: **(1)** iii/ii BC Oikonomos 3 (*[Π]ραξίνικ[ος]?*: ?s. *Ἀρχέδημος*)

Πραξινόη
MACEDONIA (EORDAIA):
—KELLE?: **(1)** s. ii BC *EAM* 118; Hatzopoulos, *MI* I p. 94 n. 4 (locn.) (d. *Δαβρείας*)

Πράξων
MACEDONIA (EDONIS):
—PHILIPPOI: **(1)** ii AD *IG* XII (8) 209, 1 (Tataki, *Macedonians* p. 166 no. 28) (*[Πρ]άξων?*)

Πρασίδας
THRACE:
—BYZANTION: **(1)** c. 240-220 BC *IOrop* 83 (f. *Ἀπολλόθεμις*)

Πρασιλᾶς
SKYTHIA:
—OLBIA-BORYSTHENES (NR.): **(1)** f. iv BC *Hyperboreus* 2000, pp. 124 ff. (vase) (*Πρασιλᾶτος* (gen.))

Πράσιμος
CIMMERIAN BOSPOROS:
—GORGIPPIA: **(1)** ?iii AD *SEG* XXVII 433 (*Πράσειμος* (n. pr.?))

Πρασσίδης
MACEDONIA (ELIMEIA):
—AIANE: **(1)** ii BC *EAM* 43 + *SEG* XXXIX 565 (*Πιασσίδης*—edd., *Πρασσίδης*—*SEG*: f. *Ἀντίγονος*)

Πρευς?
MACEDONIA (PAIONIA):
—KAVADARCI (MOD.): **(1)** 325 AD ib. XLIV 561

Πρεπέλαος
MACEDONIA: **(1)** 246-221 BC *PStrassb* 642, 7 (La'da E1588)
MACEDONIA?: **(2)** c. 315-280 BC *RE* (-); Welles, *RC* 1, 11, 28; *IEph* 1449, 4; *FD* III (4) 409, 1; *Claros* I pp. 77-85 (Tataki, *Macedonians* p. 414 no. 106) (s. *N—*)

Πρέπις
MACEDONIA (CHALKIDIKE):
—AKANTHOS: **(1)** v/iv BC *SEG* XLI 554 (vase)

Πρέπουσα
MACEDONIA (MYGDONIA):
—THESSALONIKE: **(1)** ii AD *AD* 21 (1966) Chron. pl. 352 (*—υαρνία Π.*)

Πρέπων
CIMMERIAN BOSPOROS:
—PANTIKAPAION: **(1)** i AD *CIRB* 388 (*Πρέπωτος*—lap., *Πρέπ(ο)(ν)τος?* (gen.): f. *Διοδότη*)
MACEDONIA (PAIONIA):
—STOBOI: **(2)** ii-iii AD *Sp.* 75 (1933) p. 25 no. 55 + *BE* 1979, no. 265 + *SEG* XXX 620 (name) (date—Papazoglu)
THRACE:
—BYZANTION: **(3)** ii/iii AD *ITrall* 114 (*M. Οὐαλέριος Σεπτίμιος Π.*)

Πρεστάντιος
THRACE:
—BYZANTION: **(1)** iii AD *IByz* 296 (*Αὐρ. Πολύτιμος ὁ καὶ Π.*)

Πρευρᾶδος
MACEDONIA (ORESTIS):
—AGIA ANNA (MOD.): **(1)** s. ii AD *EAM* 195 (f. *Μαρκιανός*)

Πρευρᾶτος
MACEDONIA (ORESTIS):
—LYKE*: **(1)** hell. ib. 179 ε-ζ (tile); cf. *AD* 17 (1961-2) Chron. pl. 269-70

Πρίαμος
MACEDONIA (MYGDONIA):
—HERAKLEIA: **(1)** iii BC *SEG* XLVII 901 (f. *Μενέας*)
—THESSALONIKE: **(2)** i BC/i AD *IG* X (2) (1) 58, 9; 318, 1; *KGAM Thess.* I 111 (date) (s. *Ἀπολλώνιος*, f. *Ἀπολλώνιος*)

Πριβᾶτος
THRACE:
—KOILA: **(1)** imp. *ISestos* 35 (f. *Βάκων*)

Πρικλος
THRACE:
—PHILIPPOPOLIS-TRIMONTIUM: (**1**) imp. *IGB* III 1004 (*Πρ(ό)κλος?*)

Πρîμα
MACEDONIA (MYGDONIA):
—APOLLONIA: (**1**) ii AD *AEMTh* 14 (2000) p. 285 (*Πρεî-*: d. *Τάρσας*)
—THESSALONIKE?: (**2**) ii-iii AD *IG* X (2) (1) 746 (*[Π]ρεîμα*)
THRACE:
—ODESSOS: (**3**) i/ii AD *IGB* I² 177 bis (PM 1736); *Dacia* 21 (1977) p. 161 (date) (*Πρεî-*: d. *Δημήτριος*); (**4**) m. ii AD *IGB* I² 174 bis (PM 1703); *Dacia* 21 (1977) p. 161 (date) (*Πρεί-*: d. *Ταταρίων*)

Πριμιγᾶς
MACEDONIA (MYGDONIA):
—THESSALONIKE: (**1**) s. ii AD *IG* X (2) (1) 244 I, 7 (*Φούριος Π.*) ?= (*3*); (**2**) 154 AD ib. 288, 7; (**3**) c. 155 AD ib. 60 C (*Φο[ύ]ρ[ι]ος Πρειμιγᾶς*) ?= (*1*)

Πριμιγένεια
MACEDONIA (EDONIS):
—PHILIPPOI: (**1**) i-ii AD *BCH* 58 (1934) p. 466 no. 7 (Pilhofer 377) (Lat. [V]elleia Primigenia)
—PHILIPPOI (DRAMA (MOD.))*: (**2**) ii AD ib. 506a (*-νια*: freed.?)
THRACE:
—NICOPOLIS AD ISTRUM (TERRIT.): (**3**) ii/iii AD *SEG* XLIV 640, 5 (biling.) (*Atti XI Congr. Epig.* I p. 770) (*-νια*: m. *Ὁσία*)
—PHILIPPOPOLIS-TRIMONTIUM: (**4**) ii AD *IGB* III 1006, [5], 9 (biling.) (*Σιλουία Πρειμιγένι[α]*: m. *Τιβ. Κλ. Μαρτιᾶλις*)

Πριμιγένης
MACEDONIA (BOTTIAIA):
—BEROIA: (**1**) ii/iii AD *IBer* 27 A, 5 (*Πρει-*)
MACEDONIA (EDONIS):
—AMPHIPOLIS (NR.): (**2**) ii AD *IG* X (2) (1) 864; cf. *BE* 1959, no. 338; Robert, *OMS* 5 p. 269 n. 11 (*Γ. Αὐφούστιος Πρειμιγένης*: s. *Αὐφωνία Εὐπορία*)
MACEDONIA (MYGDONIA):
—THESSALONIKE: (**3**) s. i AD *IG* X (2) (1) 68, 31 (*Λ. Τρέβιος Πρειμ(ι)γένης*); (**4**) ?ii AD ib. 519 (*Πρει-*); (**5**) ii AD ib. 615 (*Μ. Ἀούιος Πρειμιγένης*); (**6**) ii-iii AD ib. 329, 2 (*Σέξ. Ὀτακίλιος Πρειμιγένης*: s. *Πρόκλα*); (**7**) ~ ib. 1021 (*GVI* 1614; Tataki, *Macedonians* p. 186 no. 61) (*Πρειμο-*); (**8**) 137-161 AD *Makedonika* 9 (1969) pp. 143-4 (*Τ. Νουμισηνὸς Μακρîνος ὁ καὶ Πρειμιγένης*)
MACEDONIA (PAIONIA):
—STOBOI: (**9**) i AD *AJA* 77 (1973) p. 403 no. 7 (Lat. C. Atilius Primigenes)

Πριμιγενιανός
THRACE:
—PHILIPPOPOLIS-TRIMONTIUM: (**1**) ii AD *IGB* III 1006, 4, [9] (biling.) (*Τιβ. Κλ. [Πριμιγενιανός]*: f. *Τιβ. Κλ. Μαρτιᾶλις*)

Πριμιγένιος
MACEDONIA (EDONIS):
—PHILIPPOI (DRAMA (MOD.))*: (**1**) ii AD Pilhofer 506a (freed.)

Πριμιτîβος
MACEDONIA (MYGDONIA):
—THESSALONIKE: (**1**) ii-iii AD *IG* X (2) (1) 666, 4, 10 (biling.) (*CIL* III 7331; *IG* II² 13226; *SEG* XLIII 461) (*Πρειμιτεîβος*: f. *Σπῆνις*)

Πριμίων
MACEDONIA (PIERIA):
—DION: (**1**) i BC-i AD *AE* 1948-9, Chron. p. 36 no. 4 (s. *Φουλβία*)
THRACE:
—BIZYE (TERRIT.): (**2**) i-ii AD *IGB* V 5653 (*Τι(β). Κλ. Πρειμίων*)

Πρîμος
CIMMERIAN BOSPOROS:
—PANTIKAPAION: (**1**) i AD *CIRB* 498 (s. *Διοκλείδης*)
MACEDONIA (DERRIOPOS):
—STUBERRA: (**2**) c. 41-48 AD *IG* X (2) (2) 323, 22 (*Πρεî-*: s. *Ζωΐλος*); (**3**) 74 AD ib. 326, 41-2 (*Πρεί-*: f. *Ἀμύντας, Ἱππίας*)
MACEDONIA (MYGDONIA):
—THESSALONIKE: (**4**) i BC/i AD ib. X (2) (1) 58, 10; *KGAM Thess.* I 111 (date) (s. *Ἀρχέπολις*); (**5**) ii AD *IG* X (2) (1) 313 (*Πρεî-*); (**6**) ii-iii AD ib. 290 (s. *Γ. Ἰούλ. Σεκοῦνδος*); (**7**) s. ii AD ib. 244 I, 17 (f. *Σώσιππος*)
—THESSALONIKE?: (**8**) ii-iii AD ib. 741 (*Πρεîμ[ος]*)
MACEDONIA (ORESTIS):
—LYKE: (**9**) ?i-ii AD *EAM* 147, 2 (*Πρεî-*)
MACEDONIA (PAIONIA):
—EUDARISTOS?: (**10**) 102 AD *SEG* XXXII 655, 4 (*Πρεî-*: s. *Σεκοῦνδος, Σεκοῦνδα*)
MACEDONIA (PIERIA):
—DION*: (**11**) ii AD *Essays Laourdas* p. 108 no. 7 (*Πρεîμους*: freed.)
TAURIS:
—CHERSONESOS: (**12**) imp. *IOSPE* I² 489 (s. *Διόφαντος*)

Πρίσκα
MACEDONIA (PAIONIA):
—KAVADARCI (MOD.): (**1**) ii-iii AD *Sp.* 75 (1933) p. 37 no. 111
THRACE:
—BISANTHE-PANION: (**2**) iii-v AD *AD* 49-50 (1994-5) Mel. p. 307 no. 132; (**3**) iv-vi AD ib. p. 329 no. 154

Πρίσκος
MACEDONIA (BOTTIAIA):
—BEROIA: (**1**) s. ii AD *IBer* 75, 6 (*Πρεί-*)
—EDESSA: (**2**) iii AD Feissel, *RICM* 6, 5 (Tataki, *Edessa* 264) (s. *Ἐπαφρόδιτος, Ῥοδόπη*)
MACEDONIA (EDONIS):
—PHILIPPOI: (**3**) iv AD Feissel, *RICM* 227 (mosaic) (Pilhofer 328)
—PHILIPPOI (DRAMA (MOD.)): (**4**) ii-iii AD *AD* 52 (1997) Chron. p. 847, 10 with pl. 314 β (*Πρεί-*)
MACEDONIA (ODOMANTIKE):
—SIRRHA: (**5**) ?157 AD Kaphtantzis II, 2 (*Dodoni* 18 (1989) p. 245 no. 53) (*Πρεί-*: s. *Πρόκλος*, f. *Διδιανός*)
MACEDONIA (ORESTIS):
—BATTYNAIOI: (**6**) 192 AD *EAM* 186 I, 58 (*[Πρ]ε̣ίσκος*: s. *Φίλιππος*)
MACEDONIA (PAIONIA):
—KAVADARCI (MOD.): (**7**) ii-iii AD *Sp.* 71 (1931) p. 70 no. 160 (s. *Μένων*)
SCYTHIA MINOR:
—TOMIS: (**8**) ii-iii AD *ISM* II 18, 4 (f. *Ἀννιανός*); (**9**) ~ ib. 292 (*Eastern cults* p. 227 no. 13) (*Πρεί-*: f. *Ῥοῦφος*)
SKYTHIA:
—TYRAS: (**10**) ii AD *IOSPE* I² 7 (*-Πρεί-*: ?s. *Φ—*)
TAURIS:
—CHERSONESOS: (**11**) ii AD ib. 443 (*Πρεί-*: f. *Αὐρ. Διονύσιος*)
THRACE:
—BISANTHE-PANION: (**12**) iv-v AD *AD* 49-50 (1994-5) Mel. p. 309 no. 134; (**13**) m. v AD *RE* (35); *PLRE* II (1)
—MARONEIA: (**14**) iii AD *AD* 26 (1971) Chron. p. 428 no. ζ with pl. 425 δ (*IThrakAig* E196) (*Πρεί-*: f. *—δης*)
—PAUTALIA: (**15**) ii-iii AD *IGB* II 544 (*Πρεί-*: s. *Ἰούλιος*)
—PERINTHOS-HERAKLEIA: (**16**) i-ii AD *ISM* II 365, 17 (*GVI* 1161) (*Πρεί-*: s. *Πέρινθος, Καικιλία Ἀρτεμισία*)
THRACE?: (**17**) ii AD *SEG* XXXIV 775 (bronze); cf. *IGB* V 5645 (*Πρεί-*: f. *Ἀπολλινάριος*)

Προβόλιος
THRACE:
—PERINTHOS-HERAKLEIA: (**1**) iv-v AD *IPerinth* 183 (*AD* 51-2 (1996-7) Mel. p. 359 no. 180) (f. *Μουκιανός*)

Πρόβος
MACEDONIA (BOTTIAIA):
—BEROIA: (**1**) ii/iii AD *IBer* 27 A, 1 (*Πρώ-*: f. *Σώστρατος*)

Πρόδικος
TAURIS:
—CHERSONESOS: (**1**) f. ii AD *SEG* XXVIII 631, 5
THRACE:
—MESAMBRIA: (**2**) ii/i BC *IGB* V 5104 II (s. *Μινικέων*)

Προθόη
MACEDONIA: (**1**) s. vii BC *POxy* 2465 fr. 1 II, 22; cf. *FGrH* 631 (m. *Φίλιππος* I: fict.?)

Προθοήνωρ
MACEDONIA (BOTTIAIA):
—BEROIA: (**1**) ii-iii AD *IBer* 250 (Tataki 1139)

Προθώ
MACEDONIA (CHALKIDIKE):
—TORONE: (**1**) f. iv BC *IG* II² 10454 (Tataki, *Macedonians* p. 192 no. 14; *FRA* 7146)

Προîτος
MACEDONIA (CHALKIDIKE):
—POTIDAIA-KASSANDREIA: (**1**) ii-i BC *IG* VII 2482; Pelekidis, *Thessaloniki* p. 3 n. 4 (locn.) (Tataki, *Macedonians* p. 95 no. 85) (s. *Χαιρήμων*)
MACEDONIA (EORDAIA?):
—EUIA: (**2**) 181 BC *EAM* 87, 15 (Hatzopoulos, *MI* 2 pp. 41-2 no. 17) (f. *Ἀλέξανδρος*)

Προκελλîνα
SCYTHIA MINOR:
—KALLATIS (NR.): (**1**) ii-iii AD *ISM* III 243, 6 (*IGB* I² 2) (*-λλεî-*: d. *Σαβîνα*)

Προκίλιος
THRACE:
—DUROSTORUM (TERRIT.)?: (**1**) iii AD ib. II 868, 6 (*CCET* II (1) 186) (s. *Αὐλούπορις*)

Πρόκλα
MACEDONIA (BOTTIAIA):
—BEROIA: (**1**) 145-191 AD *ILeukopetra* 2; 26, 3 (Tataki 701) (*Τιβ. Κλ. Π.*)
—BEROIA*: (**2**) iii AD *SEG* L 581
MACEDONIA (MYGDONIA):
—THESSALONIKE: (**3**) 66 AD *IG* X (2) (1) 70, 2 (*Ἐρεννία Π.*: d. *Μ. Ἐρέννιος Πρόκλος*); (**4**) ii AD ib. 270 (*Ἀννία Π.*: ?d. *Ἄννιος Φ— Κασσιανός*); (**5**) ~ ib. 320, 3 (*Σερβειλία Π.*); (**6**) ?ii AD ib. 581 (*[Π]ρόκλα*); (**7**) ii-iii AD ib. II² 12518; *Myrtos* p. 274 n. 24 (locn.); cf. *LGPN* II s.v. (2) (*Αὐρ. Π.*); (**8**) ~ *IG* X (2) (1) 329, 3 (m. *Σέξ. Ὀτακίλιος Πριμιγένης*); (**9**) ~ ib. 516; *Ancient Macedonia* 2 pp. 328-30 (*Τιτινία Π.*); (**10**) ~ *IG* X (2) (1) 669, 4 (*Φλ. Π.*); (**11**) iii AD *SEG* L 639 (*Αἰλία Π.*); (**12**) m. iii AD *IG* X (2) (1) 558, 1, 4; p. 86 (stemma) (*Ἰουλ. Π.*); (**13**) ?iv AD Feissel, *RICM* 125 (*Αὐρ. Π.*)
—THESSALONIKE?: (**14**) s. i AD *IG* X (2) (1) 905 + *BCH* 97 (1973) p. 599 (*Κ. Π.*: m. *Λέων*); (**15**) ii-iii AD *IG* X (2) (1) 737 (*Πρώ-*); (**16**) ?iii AD ib. 743 (d. *Χαρίτιν*); (**17**) iii AD ib. 893 (*Αὐρ. Π.*)
MACEDONIA (PAIONIA):
—KAVADARCI (MOD.): (**18**) iii AD *Sp.* 75 (1933) p. 40 no. 132 (*Αἰλία Π.*)

MACEDONIA (PELAGONIA): (**19**) i AD *IG* X (2) (2) 236, 6 (*Αἰλία Π.*: I m. *Τι. Κλαύδιος Πρόκλος, Τι. Κλαύδιος Μάξιμος, Τι. Κλαύδιος Κλαύδιος* (sic), *Κλαυδία Πρόκλα* II, *Κλαυδία Δημονίκη*); (**20**) ~ ib. l. 10 (*Κλαυδία Π.*: II d. *Τι. Κλαύδιος Φόρτιος, Αἰλία Πρόκλα* I)
MACEDONIA (SINTIKE):
—NEINE: (**21**) ii-iii AD *IGB* V 5887
THRACE:
—MARONEIA: (**22**) iii AD *BCH* 37 (1913) p. 146 (Meïmaris–Bakirtzis 1; *IThrakAig* E219) (*Τυλλία Π.*)
—PAUTALIA (TERRIT.): (**23**) ii-iii AD *IGB* IV 2140 (*Σαλ. Π.*)
—PERINTHOS-HERAKLEIA: (**24**) ii AD *IPerinth* 100 (d. *Μᾶρκος*, m. *Ῥουφῖνα*)
—PHILIPPOPOLIS-TRIMONTIUM: (**25**) ii AD *IGB* III 993 ([*Πρ*]*όκλα ἡ καὶ Δι*—: d. *Ἀγχίαλος*)
—SERDICA: (**26**) ii AD ib. IV 1913 (*Οὐολκεῖα Π.*)

Προκλᾶς
MACEDONIA (PAIONIA):
—KAVADARCI (MOD.): (**1**) ii-iii AD *AM* 27 (1902) p. 318 no. 46 (*Προκλα* (dat.)—lap., *Προκλᾶ*—Proeva, *Πρόκλ(ω)*—*AM*)

Προκλῆς
MACEDONIA (EDONIS):
—PHILIPPOI: (**1**) hell. Hatzopoulos, *MI* 1 p. 188 n. 1 (f. *Ξενώ*)
MACEDONIA (PAIONIA): (**2**) ii-iii AD *Sp.* 75 (1933) p. 77 no. 218
THRACE:
—MARONEIA: (**3**) hell. *EEBS* 42 (1975-6) p. 226 (*IThrakAig* E251) (f. (nat.) *Γλυκέρα*, f. (ad.) *Διογένης*); (**4**) ~ ib. E254 ([*Π*]*ροκλῆς*: s. *Πατροκλῆς*)
—PERINTHOS-HERAKLEIA: (**5**) iv-iii BC *IPerinth* 4, 2 (s. *Ἑρμόδοτος*); (**6**) ?357-338 BC *Annot. num.* 20 (1995) pp. 437-8 (coin) (*Προκλ(ῆς)*?)
—STRYME?: (**7**) c. 400-375 BC *Pratiques funéraires* p. 88 no. 4 (*SEG* XLIX 991; *IThrakAig* E135) (f. *Ἀθηναΐς*)
—ZONE: (**8**) s. iv BC *SEG* XXXIII 566 (*IThrakAig* E425) (s. *Ἀπολλόδωρος*)

Προκλιανή
MACEDONIA (MYGDONIA):
—THESSALONIKE?: (**1**) ?182 AD *IG* X (2) (1) 692

Προκλιανός
MACEDONIA: (**1**) 366 AD *PLRE* I (3)

Προκλίων
CIMMERIAN BOSPOROS:
—KYTAIA (NR.): (**1**) imp.? *SEG* XLV 991. 4 (amulet)
TAURIS:
—CHERSONESOS: (**2**) iii AD *IOSPE* I² 485, 3 (f. *Παρθενοκλῆς*)

Πρόκλος
MACEDONIA (BOTTIAIA):
—BEROIA: (**1**) ii-iii AD *ILeukopetra* 137 (—*ος Π.*); (**2**) s. ii AD *IBer* 310, 3 (s. —*μος*, ?s. *Φίλα, Πιθάνη*)
—EDESSA: (**3**) 225 AD *Athena* 12 (1900) p. 72 no. 8, 4-5 (*Τιβ. Κλ. Π.*)
MACEDONIA (CHALKIDIKE):
—ANTHEMOUS: (**4**) iii AD *SEG* XLII 571 (*Αὐρ. Π.*: f. *Αὐρ. Διονύσιος, Αὐρ. Ἀθηνόδωρος, Αὐρ. Νικόβουλος*)
—POTIDAIA-KASSANDREIA (NR.): (**5**) imp. ib. XXXVII 559. 3
MACEDONIA (DERRIOPOS):
—STUBERRA: (**6**) 87 AD *IG* X (2) (2) 325, 75 (*Γ. Σκίρτιος Π.*); (**7**) 116 AD ib. 327, 41 (s. *Γάϊος*)
MACEDONIA (EDONIS):
—PHILIPPOI: (**8**) ii/iii AD *BCH* 60 (1936) p. 43 no. 2 (Pilhofer 248); Collart, *Philippes* pl. 40. 1 (*Ἰούν. Πόντιος Π.*); (**9**) ~ *CIL* III 633 IV, 3 (Pilhofer 166) (Lat. Q. Sedius Proclus)
MACEDONIA (ELIMEIA):
—SIATISTA (MOD.): (**10**) ii-iii AD *EAM* 26, 10 (*Πρόκ*[*λος*]: s. *Ἀλέξανδρος*, f. *Παρμενίων*)
MACEDONIA (MYGDONIA):
—CHARAKOMA?: (**11**) 149 AD Papazoglou, *Villes* pp. 215-16 (Tataki, *Macedonians* p. 98 no. 1) (*Ἀριστόδημος ὁ καὶ Π.*: s. *Ἀριστόδημος*)
—KALINDOIA: (**12**) 68-98 AD *SEG* XLII 580, 25 (*Γ. Ἰούλιος Π.*: s. *Κέλερ*); (**13**) ~ ib. l. 63 (f. *Σκάνιος*); (**14**) ~ ib. l. 97 (*Σέξ. Ἰούλιος Π.*)
—THESSALONIKE: (**15**) i-ii AD *IG* X (2) (1) 243 II, 7 (*Μ. Τάδιος Π.*); (**16**) 66 AD ib. 70, 4 (*Μ. Ἐρέννιος Π.*: f. *Ἐρεννία Πρόκλα*); (**17**) 71 or 188 AD *SEG* XXXI 644 = XLV 818 (*Πόντιος Π.*: s. *Πόντιος Βίταλος, Ποντία Εὐτυχίς*); (**18**) 74 AD *IG* X (2) (1) 67, 10 (*Μ. Οὐήτιος Π.*); (**19**) ii-iii AD ib. 386; (**20**) s. ii AD ib. 244 I, 2 (*Ἄρριος Π.*); (**21**) ~ ib. l. 18 (*Σπέδιος Π.*); (**22**) 170-180 AD *SEG* XXXV 766; (**23**) f. iii AD *IG* IX (2) (1) 175, 8 (*Πόντιος Π.*: f. *Ἀ. Πόντιος Ἀγρίππας*) ?= (*24*); (**24**) ~ ib. X (2) (1) 174, 8; 194, 10 (*Κασσιανὸς Π.*) ?= (*23*)
—THESSALONIKE?: (**25**) ii AD ib. 828; (**26**) ~ ib. 851 (s. *Πόπλιος*); (**27**) ii-iii AD ib. 208, 2, 4 (*Κ. Φούριος Π.*); (**28**) ~ ib. 737 (*Γ. Πλώτιος Πρώκλος*)
—THESSALONIKE*: (**29**) ii AD ib. 705 (*Μ. Ἄρριος Π.*)
MACEDONIA (ODOMANTIKE):
—SIRRHA: (**30**) 155 AD Dimitsas 821, 21 (Kaphtantzis 1) (s. *Τορκουᾶτος*); (**31**) ?157 AD ib. 11, 2 (*Dodoni* 18 (1989) p. 245 no. 53) (*Πρό*[*κλος*]—Kaphtantzis, *Πρείσκος*—Cousinery: f. *Πρίσκος*)
—SIRRHA (NR.): (**32**) ii-iii AD *SEG* XXIV 579, 4 (Pilhofer 561) (*Φλ. Π.*)
MACEDONIA (ORESTIS):
—SISANI (MOD.): (**33**) 146 AD *EAM* 187, 11 (s. *Ἰούλιος*)
MACEDONIA (PELAGONIA): (**34**) 167 AD *IG* X (2) (2) 252 (*Π. Αἰλ. Φηστιανὸς Π.*)
MACEDONIA (PIERIA):
—DION: (**35**) i-ii AD *Essays Laourdas* p. 104 (I f. *Αἰλ. Ῥιανὸς Πρόκλος* II); (**36**) ~ ib. (*Αἴ(λ). Ῥιανὸς Π.*: II s. *Πρόκλος* I)
—DION (TERRIT.): (**37**) ii AD *Klio* 52 (1970) p. 62 no. 15 (*Γ. Σαλλούστις Π.*: I f. *Γ. Σαλλούστιος Πρόκλος* II); (**38**) ~ ib. (*Γ. Σαλλούστιος Π.*: II s. *Γ. Σαλλούστις Πρόκλος* I, *Σαλλουστία Παρδαλίς*)
SCYTHIA MINOR:
—ISTROS: (**39**) ii AD *ISM* I 196, 7 (f. *Γαῦκος*); (**40**) c. 140-160 AD ib. 207, 19 (*Γ. Οὐαλέριος Πρόκλ*[*ος*])
—TOMIS: (**41**) ii-iii AD ib. II 30, 6 ([*Π*]*ρόκλος*?)
THRACE:
—BEROE-AUGUSTA TRAIANA (TERRIT.): (**42**) iii AD *IGB* III 1763 (*Αὐρ. Πρόκ*[*λο*]*ς*)
—BIZONE: (**43**) i-ii AD ib. I² 6, 10 (s. *Σκύθης*)
—BIZYE*: (**44**) 21 AD *JÖAI* 23 (1926) p. 127 no. 22, 9 (*Eastern cults* p. 201 no. 18) (*Γ. Ἰούλ. Π.*)
—BYZANTION: (**45**) ii-iii AD *IByz* 283
—BYZANTION (TERRIT.): (**46**) imp. Unp. (Sayar)
—DIONYSOPOLIS: (**47**) ii-iii AD *IGB* I² 31, 1 ([*Π*]*ρόκλο*[*ς*]); (**48**) iii AD ib. 14 a, 8 (I f. *Αὐρ. Πρόκλος* II); (**49**) ~ ib. l. 8 (*Αὐρ. Π.*: II s. *Πρόκλος* I); (**50**) ~ ib. 14 c, 9 (*Αὐρ. Π.*: s. *Θεαγένης*)
—DODOPARON: (**51**) ii-iii AD ib. III 1795 (*Πρόκλ*[*ος*]: f. *Ἀπολλόδωρος*)
—KELLAI: (**52**) ii-iii AD ib. 1519
—MADYTOS: (**53**) imp. *ISestos* 64 (*Γ. Ἰούλ. Π.*: s. *Πώλλα*)
—MARONEIA: (**54**) ii-i BC *IThrakAig* E212, 52 (*Γ. Ἀρρόντιος Π.*)
—NICOPOLIS AD ISTRUM (TERRIT.): (**55**) i/ii AD *ILB* 432, 2 (Lat. L. Val. Proclus); (**56**) 227 AD ib. 438 I, 45 (Lat. Proclus: s. Sinusis)
—PAISOULAI-MAXIMIANOPOLIS: (**57**) iii AD *Thrakika* 6 (1935) p. 316 no. 3 (*IThrakAig* E389) (f. *Τήρης*)
—PAKTYE: (**58**) imp. Taşlıklıoğlu 2 p. 169 no. 1
—PAUTALIA (TERRIT.): (**59**) ii-iii AD *IGB* V 5813 (*Φλ. Π.*: f. *Ἀμφίων*)
—PERINTHOS-HERAKLEIA: (**60**) i-ii AD *IPerinth* 220; (**61**) ii AD ib. 27 (*Π. Αἰλ. Ἁρποκρατίων ὁ καὶ Π.*)
—PHILIPPOPOLIS-TRIMONTIUM: (**62**) ii-iii AD *IGB* III 912, 6; (**63**) iii AD ib. 1007, 3 (f. *Αὐρ. Χρυσηΐς*)
—PHILIPPOPOLIS-TRIMONTIUM (TERRIT.): (**64**) ii AD ib. 1102 (f. *Παῖτος*)
—SERDICA: (**65**) ii-iii AD *AEMÖ* 10 (1886) p. 238 no. 1 (*Μ. Αὐρ. Ἡρώδης καὶ Π.*); (**66**) iii AD *IGB* IV 1950, 4 (*Αὐρ.* [*Πρ*]*όκλος*: s. *Αὐρ. Σολώνιος*)
—SERDICA (TERRIT.): (**67**) ii-iii AD *Starinar* 15-16 (1964-5) p. 250 no. 6 (f. *Γάϊος*)

Προκόπη
MACEDONIA (ELIMEIA):
—AIANE: (**1**) s. ii AD *EAM* 56 (d. *Κάστωρ, Δημοκρατέα*)
MACEDONIA (MYGDONIA):
—THESSALONIKE: (**2**) 269 AD *IG* X (2) (1) 170, 17 (*Ἀνθεστιανὴ Μινουκκιανὴ Π.*: m. *Αὐρ. Ἰούλιος ὁ καὶ Παντρόπις*)

Προκοπία
MACEDONIA (BOTTIAIA):
—EDESSA: (**1**) v-vi AD Feissel, *RICM* 36
THRACE:
—BEROE-AUGUSTA TRAIANA: (**2**) c. 320-324 AD *Anal. Boll.* 31 (1912) p. 198; p. 208

Προκράτεια
MACEDONIA (PAIONIA):
—NEAPOLIS (AREA): (**1**) 83 AD *SEG* XVI 404, 5 (-*τια*: d. *Παράμονος, Νίκη*)

Πρόκριτος
SCYTHIA MINOR:
—ISTROS: (**1**) iii BC *ISM* I 8, 4 (s. *Φερεκλῆς*)
THRACE:
—STRYME?: (**2**) v-iv BC Bakalakis, *Oinos Ismarikos* p. 552 (*IThrakAig* E133) (f. *Νεστορίς*)

Προκωνᾶς
TAURIS:
—CHERSONESOS: (**1**) ?iv-iii BC *SEG* XLIV 657 (weight)

Προμαθίδας
TAURIS:
—CHERSONESOS: (**1**) f. iii BC ib. XL 615 A, 11 ([*Πρ*]*ομαθίδας*: f. —*οφιλ*—)

Προμαθίων
CIMMERIAN BOSPOROS:
—GORGIPPIA: (**1**) f. iii BC *CIRB* 1137 A I, 35 (s. *Χρύσιππος*); (**2**) ~ ib. l. 37 (s. *Θόας*)
—NYMPHAION: (**3**) iii BC ib. 912 II, 12 (f. *Στράτιος*) ?= (*4*); (**4**) ~ ib. l. 19 (f. *Ἀντιφάνης*) ?= (*3*)
MACEDONIA: (**5**) b. 156 BC *ID* 1412 a, 30; 1417 a II, 6; 2408 + *ID Index* s.v. (s. *Μυρμιδών*)
SCYTHIA MINOR:
—KALLATIS: (**6**) iii-ii BC *Numismatica* 13 (1947) p. 6 no. 9 (coin) (*Προμα(θίων)*); (**7**) s. iii BC *ISM* III 35 A, 29 (f. *Σῖμος*); (**8**) ~ ib. 35 B, 32 (I f. *Προμαθίων* II); (**9**) ~ ib. l. 32 (II s. *Προμαθίων* I)
TAURIS:
—CHERSONESOS: (**10**) iv/iii BC *IOSPE* I² 463 (f. *Ἀνδροκλῆς*); (**11**) f. iii BC *SEG* XL 615 B, 9-11 (s. *Διονύσιος*); (**12**) c. 285-272 BC Kats p. 127 no. 39 (amph.); (**13**) c. 262-237 BC ib. p. 109 no. 98 (amph.) (s. *Θάσιος*); (**14**) c. 200-185 BC ib. p. 109 no. 97 (amph.) (s. *Ἐξεκράτης*); (**15**) c. 140-130 BC Anokhin p. 146 no. 174 (coin); (**16**) ii AD *IOSPE* I² 513 (*Ἀπελλᾶς ὁ καὶ Προμα*[*θίων*]: s. *Ἀπελλᾶς*)
THRACE:
—BYZANTION: (**17**) ii BC *IByz* 287 (Fıratlı–Robert pp. 55-6 no. 35) (f. *Ἀριστοβούλα*)

—BYZANTION (TERRIT.): **(18)** imp. Unp. (Sayar) (f. *Μακεδών*)
—MESAMBRIA: **(19)** ii BC *IGB* I^2 325, 2 (s. *Ἀ—*)
—ODESSOS: **(20)** 23 BC ib. 46, 24 (f. *Ἀπολλώνιος*) ?= *(23)*; **(21)** 6 BC ib. l. 41 (s. *Ἀπολλώνιος*); **(22)** 12-19 AD ib. V 5011, 11 (f. *Μένανδρος*); **(23)** 14-37 AD ib. I^2 57, 6 (f. *Ἀπολλώνιος*) ?= *(20)*; **(24)** ii-iii AD ib. 142 (s. *Ξένων*); **(25)** s. ii AD ib. 79, 2 (*CCET* I 33) (s. *Ἀ—*); **(26)** ~ *IGB* I^2 163 bis (*CCET* I 55; PM 1537) (*[Πρ]ομαθίων*: s. *Ποσειδώνιος*)
—ODESSOS (NR.): **(27)** s. ii AD *IGB* I^2 281 (*CCET* I 25) (s. *Ἀπολλώνιος*)

Προμᾶς
THRACE:
—BYZANTION (TERRIT.): **(1)** imp. Unp. (Sayar) (s. *Παπίας*)

Πρόμαχος
MACEDONIA: **(1)** 324 BC *RE* (17); Berve 660 (Tataki, *Macedonians* p. 414 no. 107)
SKYTHIA:
—OLBIA-BORYSTHENES: **(2)** m. iv BC Dubois, *IGDOlbia* 13, 6 (f. *Ἀλκιμέδων*)

Πρόμερος
MACEDONIA*: **(1)** 406 BC *Paroem. Gr.* I p. 295 no. 52 (Tataki, *Macedonians* p. 415 no. 108) (slave?)

Προμηθίδης
THRACE:
—ABDERA: **(1)** c. 395-360 BC May, *Abdera* pp. 225-6 no. 343 (coin); Masson, *OGS* p. 432

Προμηθίων
SKYTHIA:
—OLBIA-BORYSTHENES: **(1)** ?ii-i BC Dubois, *IGDOlbia* 110, 4

Πρόμηθος
CIMMERIAN BOSPOROS:
—GORGIPPIA: **(1)** f. iii BC *CIRB* 1137 B II, 5 (*[Π]ρόμη[θο]ς*: f. *Λυσίας*)
—MYRMEKION: **(2)** iii-ii BC *MIA* 4 (1941) p. 193 no. 190 (vase)
—NYMPHAION: **(3)** iii BC *CIRB* 912 II, 18 (f. *Ἀπολλώνιος*)
—PANTIKAPAION: **(4)** f. iv BC ib. 221 (s. *Πρωταγόρης*); **(5)** i AD ib. 499 (s. *Ἀγαθοῦς*)

Πρόνους
TAURIS:
—CHERSONESOS: **(1)** iii BC *IOSPE* I^2 340, 3 (s. *Αὐτέας*, f. *Ἀντίγονος*)

Πρόξενος
MACEDONIA: **(1)** 329 BC *RE* (9); Berve 662 (Tataki, *Macedonians* p. 415 no. 109)
MACEDONIA (BOTTIAIA):
—AIGAI: **(2)** s. iv BC *SEG* XXXV 786 (s. *Εὔξενος*)
MACEDONIA (EDONIS):
—AMPHIPOLIS?: **(3)** iii BC ib. XXIV 609 = XLIII 372 (f. *Μετώ*)
MACEDONIA (MYGDONIA):
—BORMISKOS?: **(4)** iv/iii BC ib. XLIX 844. 2 (tile); *BE* 1996, no. 270 (locn.)
SKYTHIA: **(5)** ?iv BC *ZOOID* 20 (1897) p. 181 no. 47 (vase)
THRACE: **(6)** ?ii BC *ZPE* 136 (2001) p. 130 no. 14, 9, [10]; cf. La'da E785 (I f. *Πρόξενος* II); **(7)** ~ *ZPE* 136 (2001) p. 130 no. 14, 9-10, 14 (La'da E785) (II s. *Πρόξενος* I)
—BYZANTION: **(8)** ?464 BC *IG* I^3 1144, 124 (*[Πρ]όχσενος*?, *[Θε]όχσενος*?)
—SERDICA: **(9)** imp. Kalinka, *Denkmäler* p. 339 no. 448 (tile) (*Πρόξε[ν]ος*)

Πρόσδεκτος
MACEDONIA (BOTTIAIA):
—BEROIA: **(1)** ii/iii AD *IBer* 143 B, 8 (Tataki 1113) (*Πο. Π.*)

Πρόσδεξις
MACEDONIA (MYGDONIA):
—THESSALONIKE?: **(1)** iii AD *IG* X (2) (1) 479 + *SEG* XXXVIII 693 (*Πρόσδ[εξις]*)
MACEDONIA (PIERIA):
—DION: **(2)** s. ii AD Oikonomos 30; cf. Spiliopoulou-Donderer, *KGN* p. 188 no. D5 (date) (*Πομπεΐα Π.*)

Προσδοκίων
CIMMERIAN BOSPOROS:
—GORGIPPIA: **(1)** ii/iii AD *CIRB* 1179, 43

Προσδόχη
MACEDONIA (BOTTIAIA):
—EDESSA: **(1)** ii/iii AD Dimitsas 27 + Oikonomos 30 comm. (Tataki, *Edessa* 309) (*Φλ. Π.*, *Προσδοχήλα*—Dimitsas: m. *Μακεδονία*)

Πρόσοδος
THRACE:
—ODESSOS: **(1)** i-ii AD *IGB* I^2 197 (*Πρόσοδος*); **(2)** ii AD ib. 64, 2 (*(Π)ρόσοδος*: s. *Φάρναγος*)

Προστασία
THRACE:
—LYSIMACHEIA: **(1)** i BC *IG* II^2 9232 (*Ag.* XVII 533; *FRA* 3406) (*-σστα-*: d. *Τάλουρος*)

Πρότιμος
THRACE:
—APOLLONIA-SOZOPOLIS: **(1)** i-ii AD *IGB* I^2 401, 9 (*-τει-*: f. *Δημήτρις*)

Προτοθύης
SKYTHIA:
—SKYTHAI: **(1)** vii BC Hdt. i 103 (f. *Μαδύης*: king)

Προύνικος
MACEDONIA (MYGDONIA):
—THESSALONIKE?: **(1)** s. ii AD *IG* X (2) (1) 252, 3 (*Π. Κερρήνιος Προύνεικος*)

Προφάνιος
MACEDONIA (MYGDONIA):
—THESSALONIKE: **(1)** ii/iii AD *SEG* XLIX 814 I, 1 (*Τιβ. Π.*)

Πρόφασις
MACEDONIA (PIERIA):
—DION: **(1)** ?i-ii AD Dimitsas 168 (*Μαΐα Π.*)

Πρύτανις
CIMMERIAN BOSPOROS:
—BOSPOROS: **(1)** 310 BC *RE* (4); *IGAIMK* 104 (1935) pp. 308 no. 68; 310 no. 72 (tile) (s. *Παιρισάδης*, *Κομοσαρύη*)
TAURIS:
—CHERSONESOS: **(2)** iii BC Kats pp. 99-100 no. 62 (amph.) (f. *Θεόδωρος*); **(3)** f. iii BC *SEG* XL 615 A, 5; **(4)** c. 285-272 BC Kats pp. 109-10 no. 99 (amph., tile) (s. *Ἀρίστων*); **(5)** m. iii BC *SEG* L 691 (f. *Χάρμιππος*); **(6)** c. 262-237 BC Kats p. 110 no. 100 (amph.) (s. *Θεόδωρος*) ?= *(7)*; **(7)** c. 250-230 BC Anokhin p. 141 nos. 100; 113 (coins) ?= *(6)*; **(8)** f. ii BC *IOSPE* I^2 351, 1 (f. *Εὐκράτης*)

Πρώτα
SKYTHIA:
—OLBIA-BORYSTHENES: **(1)** f. iv BC *IOlbia* 97 (d. *Νικόμαχος*)

Πρωταγόρας
CIMMERIAN BOSPOROS:
—KOROKONDAME: **(1)** s. iv BC *North Pontic Archaeology* p. 352 no. 5 with figs. 8-9 (s. *Ἀνοχάρης*, f. *Ὀλυνπιόδωρος*)
—NYMPHAION: **(2)** iii BC *CIRB* 912 II, 15 (f. *Καλλιγένης*)

THRACE:
—ODESSOS: **(3)** ii-i BC *IGB* I^2 192 (PM 1752) (s. *Ἱερώνυμος*); **(4)** i BC-i AD *IGB* I^2 159 (*CCET* I 50; PM 1312) (*Προ-*: f. *Ποτού*); **(5)** ~ *IGB* I^2 159 (*CCET* I 50; PM 1312) (f. *Διονύσιος*); **(6)** 215 AD *IGB* I^2 47 a, 21 (*Αὐρ. Π.*: s. *Ἀρτέμων*)

Πρωταγόρης
CIMMERIAN BOSPOROS:
—PANTIKAPAION: **(1)** f. iv BC *CIRB* 221 (f. *Πρόμηθος*)
SKYTHIA:
—OLBIA-BORYSTHENES: **(2)** s. vi BC Dubois, *IGDOlbia* 23, 1 (s. *Ἀχιλλόδωρος*); **(3)** ?v BC *Sov. Arkh.* 28 (1958) p. 78 (vase) (*BE* 1960, no. 281)
—OLBIA-BORYSTHENES (TERRIT.)?: **(4)** s. v BC *SEG* XLVIII 1029, 1
THRACE:
—ABDERA: **(5)** c. 490-420 BC *RE* s.v. Protagoras (1); *FVS* 80 (*FRA* 4) (*Π.*—Timon fr. 47 D, *Πρωταγόρας*—lit. test.: ?s. *Ἀρτέμων*, *Μαιάνδριος*)
—ODESSOS: **(6)** v/iv BC *IGB* I^2 101 (*[Π]ρωταγόρης*: s. *Ἀκάμας*)

Πρώταρχος
MACEDONIA: **(1)** 78 BC *PRyl* 588, 7, 11; cf. La'da E1589; E1635 (*Π. ὁ καὶ Ἁρμάϊς*: I f. *Σωσίβιος ὁ καὶ Ψελλός*, *Πτολεμαῖος ὁ καὶ Πετεσοῦχος*, *Πρώταρχος* II *ὁ καὶ Ἁρμάϊς*); **(2)** ~ *PRyl* 588, 10 (*Π. ὁ καὶ Ἁρμάϊς*: II s. *Πρώταρχος* I *ὁ καὶ Ἁρμάϊς*); **(3)** 31 BC-14 AD *BGU* 1059, 4 (Tataki, *Macedonians* p. 497 no. 229) (*Μ. Σολπίκιος Π.*: s. *Λυσίας*)

Πρωτᾶς
MACEDONIA (LYNKESTIS):
—MELITI (MOD.): **(1)** f. iii AD *EAM* 166, 1 (f. *Ὀλυμπία*, *Ἀπολλόδωρος*)
MACEDONIA (MYGDONIA):
—THESSALONIKE: **(2)** s. i AD *IG* X (2) (1) 68, 28; 69, 20 (f. *Θεοδῆς*); **(3)** ii/iii AD ib. 262 IV, 7
SCYTHIA MINOR:
—ISTROS: **(4)** 138 AD *ISM* I 193 I, 89 (f. *Χρῆστος*); **(5)** ~ ib. 193 II, 33 (s. *Χρῆστος*)

Πρωτάσις
MACEDONIA (PAIONIA):
—STOBOI: **(1)** iv-v AD Feissel, *RICM* 279; 280? (mosaic)

Πρωτέας
MACEDONIA: **(1)** iv-iii BC *IEph* 2009, 1 (Tataki, *Macedonians* p. 416 no. 114) (f. ....*κος*); **(2)** s. iv BC *RE* (3); Berve 665 (Tataki, *Macedonians* p. 415 no. 112) (s. *Λανίκα*, ?s. *Ἀνδρόνικος*); **(3)** 334-332 BC *RE* (2); Berve 664 (Tataki, *Macedonians* p. 415 no. 111) (s. *Ἀνδρόνικος*); **(4)** iii BC *PAE* 1912, p. 188 no. 144 (Tataki, *Macedonians* p. 415 no. 113) (f. *Νικονόα*)
MACEDONIA (MYGDONIA):
—THESSALONIKE: **(5)** imp. *AD* 25 (1970) Chron. p. 349 (?s. *Μεσ—*)
MACEDONIA (ODOMANTIKE):
—GAZOROS: **(6)** ?ii AD *SEG* XXIV 616 (Pilhofer 549) (s. *Λυσίμαχος*); **(7)** 118 AD *SEG* XXIV 615, 6 (Pilhofer 548) (s. *Ἄλκιμος*); **(8)** 119 AD *SEG* XXIV 615, 2 (Pilhofer 548) (f. *Ἄλκιμος*)
MACEDONIA (PIERIA):
—PYDNA: **(9)** c. 169 BC *SEG* XLIII 451, 2 (Hatzopoulos, *MI* 2 p. 72 no. 55) (s. *Φίλιππος*)
MACEDONIA?: **(10)** c. 260-250 BC *Eretria* XI p. 273 no. 15, 1, 8; pp. 279-84 (ident.) (s. *Θεοκλείδης*)
SKYTHIA:
—OLBIA-BORYSTHENES: **(11)** s. iv BC *SEG* XLVIII 1016 (sherd)

Πρώτη
CIMMERIAN BOSPOROS:
—MYRMEKION (NR.): **(1)** imp. *CIRB* 895 (*Πρό-*: d. *Ἀπολλωνίδης*)

—PANTIKAPAION: **(2)** i/ii AD ib. 649; cf. KW pl. 19 no. 276 (d. *Ἀλέξανδρος*, *Ψύχη*)
THRACE:
—BYZANTION:
——(Rhegion): **(3)** i BC-i AD? *IByz* 172 (?d. *Κόϊντος*)

Πρωτῆς
THRACE:
—ABDERA: **(1)** c. 395-360 BC May, *Abdera* p. 209 no. 274 (coin); Masson, *OGS* p. 432; **(2)** ~ May, *Abdera* pp. 221-5 nos. 324-42 (coin); **(3)** ~ ib. pp. 228-31 nos. 352-75 (coin) (*Πρωτέω* (gen.))

Πρωτίας
THRACE:
—ABDERA: **(1)** m. vi BC *IThrakAig* E30 (*Πρωτίō* (gen.): f. *Πείθων*)

Πρώτιππος
TAURIS:
—CHERSONESOS: **(1)** c. 250-230 BC Anokhin pp. 140-1 nos. 95; 107 (coins)

Πρωτίς
THRACE:
—STRYME?: **(1)** c. 375-350 BC *BCH* 79 (1955) p. 283 = Bakalakis, *Oinos Ismarikos* p. 552 (*IThrakAig* E133) (d. *Ἡρόνεστος*)

Πρωτίων
CIMMERIAN BOSPOROS:
—HERMONASSA: **(1)** ii AD *CIRB* 1088 ([*Πρ*]*ω-τ*[*ί*]*ων*?: s. *Καμαρ.ατης*—Tokhtas'ev)
—PANTIKAPAION: **(2)** iv BC *SEG* XXVIII 663 (vase); **(3)** i-ii AD *CIRB* 589 (*Πρωτί*[*ων*])
MACEDONIA (CHALKIDIKE):
—POTIDAIA-KASSANDREIA (NR.): **(4)** ?iii BC *SEG* XXIX 632 ([*Πρ*]*ωτίων*?, [*Σ*]*ωτίων*?)
MACEDONIA (EDONIS):
—AMPHIPOLIS: **(5)** s. iv BC Hatzopoulos, *Actes Amphipolis* p. 48 no. 10 A, 6 (*SEG* XLI 564) (*Πρωτί*[*ων*]?)
THRACE:
—BYZANTION: **(6)** i-ii AD *IByz* 265 (Fıratlı-Robert p. 86 no. 108) (s. *Νήδυμος*)
——(Athyras): **(7)** ii-i BC *IByz* 96 (Fıratlı-Robert p. 93 no. 126) (s. *Αἰνείας*)
—KARDIA: **(8)** 225 BC *PPetr* III 21 (f), 3, 10; cf. La'da E984 (f. —*αρζος*)
THRACE?: **(9)** 316-309 BC *IG* II² 1956, 31; *Ancient Macedonia* 5 p. 445 with n. 10 (date) (*FRA* 2568)

Πρωτογένης
CIMMERIAN BOSPOROS:
—GORGIPPIA: **(1)** i-ii AD *SEG* XXVII 432 (f. *Ἀγαθοῦς*)
—PANTIKAPAION: **(2)** i AD *KSIA* 116 (1969) p. 50 no. 2; **(3)** ~ *CIRB* 500 (s. *Ἑρμῆς*)
MACEDONIA: **(4)** f. ii BC *BGU* 1256, 5 (s. *Ἕρμων*)
MACEDONIA (BOTTIAIA):
—BEROIA: **(5)** ii/iii AD *IBer* 143 B, 27 (Tataki 620) (*Ἰού. Προτογένης*)
MACEDONIA (CHALKIDIKE):
—SKIONE: **(6)** imp. *SEG* XXIX 646
MACEDONIA (EORDAIA):
—KELLE?: **(7)** ii BC *EAM* 91; Hatzopoulos, *MI* I p. 94 n. 4 (locn.) (*Πρωτογέ*[*ης*]: s. *Εὔλανδρος*)
MACEDONIA (LYNKESTIS):
—HERAKLEIA: **(8)** imp. *IG* X (2) (2) 104 (f. *Φίλιππος*)
MACEDONIA (MYGDONIA):
—THESSALONIKE: **(9)** 223 BC ib. X (2) (1) 2, 6 (*Πρωτογέ*[*ης*]); **(10)** 27 BC-14 AD ib. 31, 18
MACEDONIA (PAIONIA):
—STOBOI: **(11)** s. iii AD *JÖAI* 32 (1940) Beibl. col. 22 no. 16. 162
MACEDONIA (PIERIA):
—PYDNA: **(12)** ii-i BC *SEG* L 627 ([*Πρ*]*ωτογέν*[*ς*]: f. *Παραμόνα*)
SCYTHIA MINOR:
—ISTROS: **(13)** s. v BC *ISM* I 380 + *Stud. Šćeglov* pp. 87-9 ([*Πρ*]*ωτογεν*[*ης*])
—TROPAEUM TRAIANI (NR.): **(14)** iii AD *SCIV* 20 (1969) p. 599 f.; cf. *BE* 1970, 398
SKYTHIA:
—OLBIA-BORYSTHENES: **(15)** f. iv BC Dubois, *IGDOlbia* 104 (*Πρωτογένευς* (gen.): f. *Εὐσθένης*, *Εὔδωρος*); **(16)** iii BC *IOSPE* I² 32 A passim (Maier, *Mauerbauinschr.* 82) (s. *Ἡροσῶν*) ?= (*21*); **(17)** ~ *IOSPE* I² 201 I, 17 (*Πρω*[*τ*]*ογέν*[*ης*]: f. *Εὔδωρος*) ?= (*22*) (*21*); **(18)** ~ ib. l. 33 (s. *Εὔδωρος*); **(19)** ~ ib. l. 63 (f. *Ἡροσῶν*); **(20)** iii-ii BC *Arkheologiia* (Kiev) 39 (1982) p. 34 (vase) (*Πρωτογέν*(*ης*)); **(21)** s. iii BC *SEG* XLII 716 (f. *Εὔδωρος*) ?= (*17*) (*16*); **(22)** iii/ii BC *BE* 1990, no. 519 (coin) (*Πρωτ*(*ογένης*): s. *Ἡροσῶν*) ?= (*17*)
THRACE:
—APROI: **(23)** ii-iii AD Taşlıklıoğlu 2 pp. 75-6 no. 4
—BEROE-AUGUSTA TRAIANA (TERRIT.): **(24)** ii-iii AD *IGB* III 1642

Πρωτόμαχος
MACEDONIA: **(1)** 333 BC *RE* (4); Berve 667 (Tataki, *Macedonians* p. 416 no. 115)
MACEDONIA (EDONIS):
—AMPHIPOLIS: **(2)** a. 357 BC Hatzopoulos, *Actes Amphipolis* pp. 38-9 no. 7, 17; cf. *BE* 1992, no. 321 ((*Π*)*ρω*(*τ*)*όμαχος*?—ed., *Ἀρω*(*γ*)*όμαχος*?—*BE*: f. *Φιλώτας*)
SCYTHIA MINOR:
—KALLATIS: **(3)** s. iii BC *ISM* III 35 B, 23 (f. *Σωσίβιος*)
SKYTHIA:
—OLBIA-BORYSTHENES: **(4)** ii BC *IOSPE* I² 229; cf. KW pl. 49 no. 668 (f. *Στράτων*)
THRACE:
—PHILIPPOPOLIS-TRIMONTIUM: **(5)** iii AD *IGB* III 935 (f. *Θεοφάνης*)

Πρω-όπολις
SCYTHIA MINOR:
—KALLATIS: **(1)** s. iii BC *ISM* III 35 A, 32 (f. *Ζώπυρος*)

Πρῶ-ος
CIMMERIAN BOSPOROS:
—PANTIKAPAION: **(1)** ii AD *CIRB* 702; cf. KW pl. 56 no. 759 (f. *Πλωτίων*)
MACEDONIA (PIERIA):
—DION: **(2)** ii-iii AD Oikonomos 21 (*Ἰούλ. Π.*: I f. *Πρῶτος* II, *Μαρκελλῖνα*: freed.); **(3)** ~ ib. (II s. *Ἰούλ. Πρῶτος* I)
SCYTHIA MINOR:
—TOMIS: **(4)** ii-iii AD *ISM* II 394, 5 ([*Π*]*ρῶτος*? (n. pr.?))
THRACE:
—BYZANTION: **(5)** ii-i BC *IByz* 83 (Fıratlı-Robert p. 51 no. 26) (f. *Εὐφρόσυνος*)
—PERINTHOS-HERAKLEIA: **(6)** i BC *NS* 40

Πρωτοφάνης
MACEDONIA (PIERIA):
—DION: **(1)** iii BC *SEG* XXXIV 628 (s. *Δωριεύς*)

Πρωτόφαος
THRACE:
—STRYME?: **(1)** v/iv BC *IThrakAig* E130 (s. *Ἡγέστρατος*)

Πρωτοχάρης
MACEDONIA (PIERIA):
—PYDNA: **(1)** iv BC *GRBS* 47 (2002-3) p. 122 no. 6, 5

Πρῶτυς
MACEDONIA (MYGDONIA):
—THESSALONIKE?: **(1)** i-ii AD *IG* X (2) (1) 865

Πτολέμα
MACEDONIA: **(1)** m. ii BC *BGU* 1939 A, 3 (Tataki, *Macedonians* p. 493 no. 194; La'da E1813) (d. *Ἡρακλείδης*)

Πτολεμαῖος
CIMMERIAN BOSPOROS:
—PANTIKAPAION: **(1)** i BC *CIRB* 270 (s. *Ἀπολλώνιος*)
MACEDONIA: **(2)** c. 370-334 BC *RE* (6); Berve 672; Hatzopoulos, *Donation* p. 23, 25 (Tataki, *Macedonians* p. 418 no. 134) (I f. *Πτολεμαῖος* II); **(3)** s. iv BC *RE* (9); Berve 669; Hatzopoulos, *Donation* p. 23, 16, 26 (II s. *Πτολεμαῖος* I); **(4)** 334-333 BC *RE* (10); Berve 674; **(5)** 331-329 BC *RE* (8); Berve 673 (Tataki, *Macedonians* p. 418 no. 133); **(6)** c. 320-279 BC *RE* (15) (*PP* 14539) (*Π. Κεραυνός*: s. *Πτολεμαῖος* I *Σωτήρ* (Eordaia), *Εὐρυδίκα*: king); **(7)** 308-246 BC *RE* (19) (*PP* 14540); cf. Beloch, *GG* IV (2) pp. 182-4 (*Π.* II *Φιλάδελφος*: s. *Πτολεμαῖος* I *Σωτήρ* (Eordaia), *Βερενίκη*, f. *Πτολεμαῖος* III *Εὐεργέτης*, *Πτολεμαῖος ὁ υἱός*, *Λυσίμαχος*, *Βερενίκη*: king); **(8)** c. 298-230 BC *RE* (13); *TAM* II (1) 1, 7, 22 (*OGIS* 55); *ID* Index p. 16; *Cl. Rh.* 9 (1938) pp. 183 ff.; cf. *Chiron* 8 (1978) pp. 218 ff. (date) (and Lycia Telmessos: s. *Λυσίμαχος*, *Ἀρσινόη*, f. *Λυσίμαχος*); **(9)** 288 or 280-221 BC *RE* (21); *IG* IX (1)² (1) 56 (*PP* 14543) (*Π.* III *Εὐεργέτης*: s. *Πτολεμαῖος* II *Φιλάδελφος*, *Ἀρσινόη*, f. *Πτολεμαῖος* IV *Φιλοπάτωρ*, *Μάγας*, *Ἀλέξανδρος*, *Ἀρσινόη*, *Βερενίκη*: king); **(10)** c. 285-259 BC *RE* (20) (*PP* 14542) (*Π. ὁ υἱός*: s. *Πτολεμαῖος* II *Φιλάδελφος*, *Ἀρσινόη*) ?= (*101*); **(11)** 267 BC *SEG* XXVII 1114, 16 a (Tataki, *Macedonians* p. 420 no. 149; La'da E1593) (s. *Βούβαρος*); **(12)** ~ *SEG* XXVII 1114, 18 b (Tataki, *Macedonians* p. 419 no. 146; La'da E1591) (s. *Ἄδυμος*); **(13)** s. iii BC *BGU* 1905, 7 (Tataki, *Macedonians* p. 419 no. 140; La'da E1606) ?= (*25*); **(14)** c. 244-204 BC *RE* (22) (*PP* 14545) (*Π.* IV *Φιλοπάτωρ*: s. *Πτολεμαῖος* III *Εὐεργέτης*, *Βερενίκη*, f. *Πτολεμαῖος* V *Ἐπιφάνης*: king); **(15)** 238 BC *PPetr²* 2, 15 (Tataki, *Macedonians* p. 418 no. 136; La'da E1601) ([*Π*]*τολεμαῖος*); **(16)** 236 BC *PPetr²* 16, 88 (Tataki, *Macedonians* p. 420 no. 152; La'da E1778) (s. *Διόφαντος*: t.e.); **(17)** 232 or 207 BC *CPR* XVIII 15, [298], 312, 314, 316, 318, [321] (Tataki, *Macedonians* p. 418 no. 137; La'da E1602); **(18)** iii/ii BC *RE* (14); *ID* Index p. 16; *Cl. Rh.* 9 (1938) pp. 190 ff.; Grainger, *SPG* p. 115 (and Lycia Telmessos: s. *Λυσίμαχος*, f. *Βερενίκη*); **(19)** ~ La'da E1607; **(20)** 221 BC *PEnt* 70, 1 and verso (Tataki, *Macedonians* p. 418 no. 138; La'da E1604); **(21)** ?219 BC *PUG* III 103, 7 (Tataki, *Macedonians* p. 422 no. 165); cf. La'da E1572 (f. *Πάτρων*); **(22)** ~ *PUG* III 103, 8 (Tataki, *Macedonians* p. 420 no. 151; La'da E1594) (s. *Δημέας*); **(23)** ~ *PUG* III 103, 9 (Tataki, *Macedonians* p. 423 no. 169); cf. La'da E1622 (f. *Σπάρτακος*); **(24)** 218 BC *RE* (12) (Tataki, *Macedonians* p. 418 no. 135); **(25)** ~ *BGU* 1274, 15 (Tataki, *Macedonians* p. 419 no. 139; La'da E1605) ?= (*13*); **(26)** 213 BC *BGU* 2396, 5, 8, 10 (Tataki, *Macedonians* p. 422 no. 161; La'da E1780) (s. ...*άκριτος*: t.e.); **(27)** 210-180 BC *RE* (23) (*PP* 14546) (*Π.* V *Ἐπιφάνης*: s. *Πτολεμαῖος* IV *Φιλοπάτωρ*, *Ἀρσινόη*, f. *Πτολεμαῖος* VI *Φιλομήτωρ*, *Πτολεμαῖος* VIII *Εὐεργέτης*, *Κλεοπάτρα* II: king); **(28)** ii-i BC Bernand, *El-Kanaïs* 83 (Tataki, *Macedonians* p. 493 no. 195; La'da E1612); **(29)** 192 BC *PTeb* 816, 44 (Tataki, *Macedonians* p. 420 no. 148; La'da E1592) (s. *Ἀμύντας*); **(30)**

c. 186-145 BC *RE* (24) (*PP* 14548) (*Π.* VI *Φιλομήτωρ*: s. *Πτολεμαῖος* V *Ἐπιφάνης*, *Κλεοπάτρα* I, f. *Πτολεμαῖος Εὐπάτωρ*, *Πτολεμαῖος* VII *νέος Φιλοπάτωρ*, *Κλεοπάτρα Θεά*, *Κλεοπάτρα* III: king); **(31)** 184 BC *PHeid* VIII 414, [3], 7, [11], 26, etc. (La'da E1608); **(32)** 182 BC *IG* II² 2314, 56 (Tataki, *Macedonians* p. 422 no. 162); **(33)** c. 182-116 BC *RE* (27) (*PP* 14551) (*Π.* VIII *Εὐεργέτης*: s. *Πτολεμαῖος* V *Ἐπιφάνης*, *Κλεοπάτρα* I, f. *Πτολεμαῖος Μεμφίτης*, *Πτολεμαῖος Ἀπίων*, *Πτολεμαῖος* IX *Λάθυρος*, *Πτολεμαῖος* X, *Τρύφαινα*, *Κλεοπάτρα* IV, *Κλεοπάτρα Σελήνη*: king); **(34)** 178 BC *PFreib* 21, 5, 8-9 (Tataki, *Macedonians* p. 419 no. 142; La'da E1609) ([*Πτο*]*λεμαῖος*); **(35)** m. ii BC *PTeb* 1075 fr. 1, 5 (Tataki, *Macedonians* p. 494 no. 203); cf. La'da E1683 ([*Πτ*]*ολεμαῖος*) ?= (*36*); **(36)** ~ *PTeb* 1075 fr. 1, 6 (Tataki, *Macedonians* p. 494 no. 204); cf. La'da E1684 ?= (*37*) (*35*); **(37)** ~ *PTeb* 1075 fr. 1, 7 (Tataki, *Macedonians* p. 494 no. 205); cf. La'da E1685 ([*Πτ*]*ολεμαῖος*) ?= (*38*) (*36*); **(38)** ~ *PTeb* 1075 fr. 1, 8 (Tataki, *Macedonians* p. 494 no. 206); cf. La'da E1686 ?= (*37*); **(39)** ~ *BGU* 1938 B, 11 (Tataki, *Macedonians* p. 493 no. 198); cf. La'da E1682; **(40)** ~ *BGU* 2423, 32 (Tataki, *Macedonians* p. 495 no. 209); cf. La'da E1443 (f. *Ἀρχίβιος*); **(41)** 173 BC *PAmh* 43, 16 (Tataki, *Macedonians* p. 419 no. 143; La'da E1610) (*Πτολεμαῖος*); **(42)** 172-152 BC *UPZ* 3; 5-8; 9; 10-11 etc. + pp. 105-13 and Index s.v (La'da E464); Thompson, *Memphis* pp. 213 ff. (s. *Γλαυκίας*: t.e.); **(43)** 165 BC *SB* 12101, 1 (Tataki, *Macedonians* p. 419 no. 144; La'da E1613) (*Πτολεμαῖ(ο)ς*); **(44)** 163-150 BC *RE* (25) (*PP* 14549) (*Π. Εὐπάτωρ*: s. *Πτολεμαῖος* VI *Φιλομήτωρ*, *Κλεοπάτρα* II); **(45)** c. 162-144 BC *RE* (26) (*PP* 14550) (*Π.* VII *νέος Φιλοπάτωρ*: s. *Πτολεμαῖος* VI *Φιλομήτωρ*, *Κλεοπάτρα* II: king); **(46)** 159 BC *SB* 11893, 2 (Tataki, *Macedonians* p. 422 no. 164); cf. La'da E1458 (f. *Δημήτριος*); **(47)** 154 or 143 BC *ZPE* 146 (2004) p. 168, 4 (*Πτολεμαῖ(ος)*: f. *Νεοπτόλεμος*); **(48)** 152 BC *PErasm* II 39, 19 (Tataki, *Macedonians* p. 423 no. 167); cf. La'da E1597 (I f. *Πτολεμαῖος* II); **(49)** ~ *PErasm* II 39, 19 (Tataki, *Macedonians* p. 422 no. 160; La'da E1597) (II s. *Πτολεμαῖος* I); **(50)** c. 150-96 BC *RE* (29) (*PP* 14553) (*Π. Ἀπίων*: s. *Πτολεμαῖος* VIII *Εὐεργέτης*, *Εἰρήνη*); **(51)** 145 BC *PTeb* 32, 18 (Tataki, *Macedonians* p. 495 no. 210); cf. La'da E1448 (f. *Ἀσκληπιάδης*); **(52)** ?144-131 BC *RE* (28) (*PP* 14552) (*Π. Μεμφίτης*: s. *Πτολεμαῖος* VIII *Εὐεργέτης*, *Κλεοπάτρα* II); **(53)** 142 BC *SB* 12721 I, 2; 12722, 3 (Tataki, *Macedonians* p. 496 no. 219); cf. La'da E1598 (*Πτολεμαῖος*: I f. *Πτολεμαῖος* II); **(54)** ~ *SB* 12721 I, 2; 12722, [3] (Tataki, *Macedonians* p. 494 no. 200; La'da E1598) (II s. *Πτολεμαῖος* I) ?= (*55*); **(55)** ~ *SB* 13095, 2; 13096, 2 (La'da E1611) ?= (*54*); **(56)** c. 141-80 BC *RE* (30) (*PP* 14554) (*Π.* IX *Λάθυρος*: s. *Πτολεμαῖος* VIII *Εὐεργέτης*, *Κλεοπάτρα* III, f. *Πτολεμαῖος* XII *Αὐλητής*, *Πτολεμαῖος*, *Κλεοπάτρα* V *Τρύφαινα*: king); **(57)** c. 140-88 BC *RE* (31) (*PP* 14555) (*Π.* X *Ἀλέξανδρος*: s. *Πτολεμαῖος* VIII *Εὐεργέτης*, *Κλεοπάτρα* III, f. *Πτολεμαῖος* XI *Ἀλέξανδρος*: king); **(58)** ii/i BC *SB* 11860, 4 (Tataki, *Macedonians* p. 493 no. 199; La'da E1779) (II s. *Πτολεμαῖος* I: t.e.); **(59)** ~ *SB* 11860, 5 (Tataki, *Macedonians* p. 496 no. 218); cf. La'da E1779 (I f. *Πτολεμαῖος* II); **(60)** 118-116 BC *PTeb* 61 b, 78; 64 a, 27 (Tataki, *Macedonians* p. 423 no. 168) (f. *Πύρρος*); **(61)** c. 115-58 BC *RE* (34) (*PP* 14559) (s. *Πτολεμαῖος* IX *Λάθυρος*, ?s. *Κλεοπάτρα Σελήνη*); **(62)** c. 115-51 BC *RE* (33) (*PP* 14558) (*Π.* XII *Αὐλητής*: s. *Πτολεμαῖος* IX *Λάθυρος*, ?s. *Κλεοπάτρα Σελήνη*, f. *Πτολεμαῖος* XIII, *Πτολεμαῖος* XIV, *Βερενίκη*, *Κλεοπάτρα* VI *Τρύφαινα*, *Κλεοπάτρα* VII *Φιλοπάτωρ*, *Ἀρσινόη*: king); **(63)** 110-107 BC *PDion* 14, 31; 15, 29; 18, [29] (Tataki, *Macedonians* p. 495 no. 212); cf. La'da E1475 (f. *Διονύσιος*); **(64)** 108 BC *PDion* 17, 33 (Tataki, *Macedonians* p. 496 no. 224); cf. La'da E1658 (f. *Πυθάγγελος*); **(65)** ~ *PDion* 23, 3 (Tataki, *Macedonians* p. 494 no. 207); cf. La'da E1391 (f. *Ἄδυμος*); **(66)** 107-101 BC *SEG* XXXIII 1359, 3 (Tataki, *Macedonians* p. 495 no. 213); cf. La'da E1495 (*Πτολεμαῖος*: f. *Ἡλιόδωρος*); **(67)** 106-105 BC *PDion* 19, [11], [26]; 20, 11; 24, [2]; 30, 2 (Tataki, *Macedonians* p. 495 no. 215); cf. La'da E1515 (f. *Ἱππόνικος*); **(68)** c. 105-80 BC *RE* (32) (*PP* 14557) (*Π.* XI *Ἀλέξανδρος*: s. *Πτολεμαῖος* X *Ἀλέξανδρος*: king); **(69)** 103 BC *PTeb* 105, 52 (Tataki, *Macedonians* p. 496 no. 223); cf. La'da E1785 (f. *Τήρης*); **(70)** ~ *PTeb* 105, 53 (Tataki, *Macedonians* p. 495 no. 217); cf. La'da E1775 (f. *Πάτρων*); **(71)** c. 100 BC *ILind* 277, 3 (Tataki, *Macedonians* p. 419 no. 145); **(72)** c. 100-75 BC *SB* 8974 fr. 3, 44 (Tataki, *Macedonians* p. 494 no. 208); cf. La'da E1397 (*Πτο*[*λεμ*]*αῖος*: f. *Ἀλέξανδρος*); **(73)** 92 BC *PTeb* 104, 34, 53 (Tataki, *Macedonians* p. 495 no. 214); cf. La'da E1763 (f. *Θέων*) ?= (*74*); **(74)** ~ *PTeb* 104, 35 (Tataki, *Macedonians* p. 495 no. 211); cf. La'da E1746 (f. *Δίδυμος*) ?= (*73*); **(75)** 78 BC *PRyl* 588, 7 and verso (La'da E1589) (*Π. ὁ καὶ Πετεσοῦχος*: s. *Πρώταρχος ὁ καὶ Ἁρμάϊς*); **(76)** 74 BC *SB* 7532, 25, 37 (Tataki, *Macedonians* p. 493 no. 197; La'da E1596) (s. *Ἡλιόδωρος*); **(77)** 68-58 or 55-51 BC *SB* 12569, 2, 13, 18, [21] (Tataki, *Macedonians* p. 496 no. 220); cf. La'da E1599 (I f. *Πτολεμαῖος* II) ?= (*82*); **(78)** 66-58 or 55-51 BC *SB* 12569, 2, 13, 18, [21] (Tataki, *Macedonians* p. 494 no. 201; La'da E1599) (II s. *Πτολεμαῖος* I) ?= (*83*); **(79)** 63 BC *POxy* 1644, 4 (Tataki, *Macedonians* p. 493 no. 196; La'da E1595) (s. *Διονύσιος*, *Ἀρσινόη*: katoikos); **(80)** 61-47 BC *RE* (35) (*PP* 14560) (*Π.* XIII: s. *Πτολεμαῖος* XII *Αὐλητής*: king); **(81)** 59-44 BC *RE* (36) (*PP* 14561) (*Π.* XIV: s. *Πτολεμαῖος* XII *Αὐλητής*: king); **(82)** 51 BC *PSI* 1098, 39; cf. La'da E1600 (I f. *Πτολεμαῖος* II) ?= (*77*); **(83)** ~ *PSI* 1098, 39 (La'da E1600) (II s. *Πτολεμαῖος* I) ?= (*78*); **(84)** 47-30 BC *RE* (37) (*PP* 14562) (*Π.* XV *Καῖσαρ* (*Καισαρίων*): s. *Κλεοπάτρα* VII *Φιλοπάτωρ*, ?s. G. Iulius Caesar (Rome): king); **(85)** 36-29 BC ib. (38) (*PP* 14563) (*Π. Φιλάδελφος*: s. M. Antonius (Rome), *Κλεοπάτρα* VII *Φιλοπάτωρ*); **(86)** 14 BC *BGU* 1052, 36 (Tataki, *Macedonians* p. 496 no. 221) (I f. *Πτολεμαῖος* II); **(87)** ~ *BGU* 1052, 36 (Tataki, *Macedonians* p. 494 no. 202) (II s. *Πτολεμαῖος* I)

MACEDONIA (BOTTIAIA):

—ALOROS: **(88)** c. 420-365 BC *RE* (4); *IG* II² 102, 7 (Tod, *GHI* II 129; Tataki, *Macedonians* p. 45 no. 4) (f. *Φιλόξενος*: regent)

—BEROIA: **(89)** ii BC *IBer* 141, 1; **(90)** c. 10 BC Helly, *Gonnoi* 117, 10 (Tataki 1142) (f. *Λυσίμαχος*); **(91)** i AD *IBer* 104 (Tataki 728) (*Τι. Κλ. Π.*)

MACEDONIA (EORDAIA): **(92)** c. 360-282 BC *RE* (18); Berve 668 (*PP* 14538); Austin–Bastianini, *Posidipp.* 88 (locn.); cf. Beloch, *GG* IV (2) pp. 176-82 (*Π.* I *Σωτήρ*: s. *Λάαγος*, *Ἀρσινόη*, f. *Πτολεμαῖος Κεραυνός*, *Μελέαγρος*, *Πτολεμαῖος* II *Φιλάδελφος*, *Λεοντίσκος*, *Λᾶγος*, *Ἀργαῖος*, *Λυσάνδρα*, *Πτολεμαΐς*, *Ἀρσινόη*, *Φιλωτέρα*, *Εἰρήνη*: king)

MACEDONIA (MYGDONIA):

—LETE: **(93)** s. iv BC Hatzopoulos, *MI* 2 pp. 93-4 no. 79, 5; **(94)** ~ ib. l. 10

—THESSALONIKE: **(95)** 155 AD *IG* X (2) (1) 321, 1 (f. *Ἥρων*)

MACEDONIA (ORESTIS): **(96)** 192 AD *EAM* 186, 34 (f. *Κλεῖτος*, *Φίλαγρος*)

—BATTYNAIOI: **(97)** 192 AD ib. 186 III, 45 (*Πτολ*[*ε*]*μ*[*αῖος*]); **(98)** ~ ib. 186 IV, 49 (-*με*-)

MACEDONIA (TYMPHAIA)?: **(99)** 334-333 BC *RE* (7); Berve 670 (Tataki, *Macedonians* p. 213 no. 7) (s. *Σέλευκος*)

MACEDONIA?: **(100)** 263 BC *PHib* 209, 7 (Tataki, *Macedonians* p. 422 no. 163); cf. La'da E2652 ([*Π*]*τολ*[*ε*]*μαῖος*: f. *Δημήτριος*); **(101)** ?c. 258 BC *RE* (39); *PHaun* I 6, 4; *PP* 14544; *CQ* 44 (1950) pp. 107-18 (*Π. ἐπίκλησιν Ἀνδρομάχου*) ?= (*10*); **(102)** s. iii BC *RE* (46) (Tataki, *Macedonians* p. 420 no. 147) (s. *Ἀέροπος*); **(103)** ~ *ILind* 139; cf. *JEA* 46 (1960) pp. 109-11 (*PP* 15769; Tataki, *Macedonians* p. 421 no. 157) (s. *Πέλοψ*); **(104)** 246-219 BC *PP* 1985 with Add. (s. *Ἐτεωνεύς*); **(105)** f. ii BC Bernand, *Inscr. métr.* 4 (Tataki, *Macedonians* p. 495 no. 216) (f. *Μηνόδωρος*); **(106)** 198 BC *ID* 380, [77]; 442 B, 45; cf. *ID Index* p. 84 (Tataki, *Macedonians* p. 423 no. 170) (f. *Φίλιππος*); **(107)** 144-141 BC *PBingen* 35, 11 (La'da E2646) (s. *Ὀρδ*—); **(108)** 63 BC *POxy* 1644, 13 (f. *Ἀρσινόη*); **(109)** 44-37 BC ib. 1635, 3 (Tataki, *Macedonians* p. 496 no. 222); cf. La'da E1623 (f. *Σπάρτακος*)

THRACE: **(110)** 267 BC *SEG* XXVII 1114, 10a, 18a, 22b (La'da E787) (s. *Ἀμάδοκος*); **(111)** 241 BC *PFrankf* 5, 21 (f. *Διγένης*); **(112)** 232 or 207 BC *CPR* XVIII 24, 29, 34, 40 (La'da E839) (t.e.); **(113)** 228-221 BC *PTeb* 815 r 2, 3; Velkov 332; **(114)** c. 223 BC *PTeb* 815 fr. 2 II, 3 (Velkov 297); cf. La'da E846 (f. *Ταῦρος*); **(115)** 221 BC *PPetr* III 112 f, 3 (Velkov 331); cf. La'da E817; **(116)** 179 BC *PHeid* VIII 413, 2; cf. La'da E841 ([*Πτολ*]*εμαῖος*: f. *Σίλας*); **(117)** 173 BC *BGU* 1272, 5, 20 (La'da E789); **(118)** 160 BC *BGU* 2390, [5], 15; cf. La'da E782 (f. *Πολύηρατος*); **(119)** ~ *BGU* 2390, 39 (La'da E790); **(120)** ~ *BGU* 2390, 40-1 (La'da E788) (s. *Ἀριστόδημος*); **(121)** 157 BC *UPZ* 123, 3 (Velkov 228; La'da E786) (s. *Ἀμάδοκος*, *Ἀσκληπιάς*); **(122)** 150 BC *IFayoum* 103-4; cf. La'da E768 (f. *Λεωνίδης*)

—AGRIANES: **(123)** 236 BC *PPetr*² 16, 46 (La'da E2) (s. *Ἡρακλείδης*)

—NICOPOLIS AD ISTRUM (TERRIT.): **(124)** ii AD *IGB* V 5244 b, 6 (*Πτολεμα*[*ῖος*])

Πτολεμαῒς

CIMMERIAN BOSPOROS:

—PANTIKAPAION: **(1)** i AD *CIRB* 502; cf. KW pl. 47 no. 661 (-*μαεῖς*)

MACEDONIA: **(2)** iv/iii BC *RE* (2) (*PP* 14565) (d. *Πτολεμαῖος* I *Σωτήρ* (Eordaia), *Εὐρυδίκα*, m. *Δημήτριος ὁ Καλός*)

MACEDONIA (MYGDONIA):

—THESSALONIKE: **(3)** ii AD *IG* X (2) (1) 314 (*Πτο*[*λε*]*μαΐς*: m. *Γ. Ῥέφριος* —*βος*)

Πτολέμαρχος

MACEDONIA: **(1)** 173 BC *PFreib* 34, 6 (Tataki, *Macedonians* p. 423 no. 172; La'da E1614)

Πτολέμας

MACEDONIA (BOTTIAIA):

—BEROIA: **(1)** 184 AD *ILeukopetra* 17, 1 (Tataki 1143)

MACEDONIA (EDONIS):

—PHILIPPOI: **(2)** s. iii BC *IThrakAig* E264 ([*Π*]*τολέμα*[*ς*]: s. *Φίλιππος*)

Πτολεμμᾶς

MACEDONIA (MYGDONIA):

—KALINDOIA: **(1)** c. 320 BC Hatzopoulos, *MI* 2 p. 84 no. 62, 25 (s. *M*—)

Πτολλᾶς

CIMMERIAN BOSPOROS:

—PANTIKAPAION: **(1)** m. i AD *CIRB* 501, 1, 5 (s. *Δημήτριος*, f. *Ἀρίστων*, *Ἀρίστων* (sic)); **(2)** ?s. ii AD ib. 90, 5 (*Πε*——ed., *Πτ*[*ο*]*λλᾶς*— Yailenko: f. *Ἀρίστων*)

Πτούδαγος
SKYTHIA:
—OLBIA-BORYSTHENES: (1) f. ii AD *Drev. Prichern.* 3 pp. 27-8, 9 (f. Ἔβενος)

Πυθάγγελος
MACEDONIA: (1) 108 BC *PDion* 17, 33 (La'da E1658) ([Πυθάγ]γελος?: s. Πτολεμαῖος)
THRACE:
—MESAMBRIA: (2) ii/i BC *IGB* V 5103, 2, 7 (s. Ἐπικράτης, f. Ἐπικράτης)

Πυθαγόρας
THRACE:
—SALYMBRIA: (1) c. 460-450 BC *IG* I^3 1154 (*FRA* 6633) (-ρης: s. Διονύσιος)

Πυθαγόρης
MACEDONIA (BOTTIAIA):
—PELLA: (1) f. v BC *SEG* XXXVIII 647; *BE* 1990, no. 464 (date); *Epigr. Makedonias* p. 150 n. 38 (name) ([Πυ]θαγόρης—*SEG*, [Ὀρ]θαγόρης?—*BE*: s. Ἀριστοκράτης)
SKYTHIA:
—OLBIA-BORYSTHENES: (2) ?s. vi BC *Sov. Arkh.* 28 (1958) p. 78 (vase) (*BE* 1960, no. 281)
THRACE:
—ABDERA: (3) c. 415-395 BC May, *Abdera* p. 167 no. 218; p. 176 no. 218/1 (coin)
—ABDERA?: (4) v-iv BC *IThrakAig* E35 (Πυθαγ[όρης]?: s. Σημαγόρης)
—APOLLONIA-SOZOPOLIS: (5) v/iv BC *IGB* I^2 413 (f. Βριθαγόρη)
—PERINTHOS-HERAKLEIA:
——(Boreis): (6) iii-ii BC *IPerinth* 61, 38 (*ΠΥΓΟΡΕΩ*—apogr., Πυ(θα)γόρεω? (gen.): f. Ἀχελώϊος)

Πυθᾶς
THRACE:
—BYZANTION (TERRIT.): (1) imp. Unp. (Sayar) (s. Γλυκίων)

Πυθέας
MACEDONIA (CHALKIDIKE):
—OLYNTHOS: (1) ?350 BC *TAPA* 59 (1928) p. 226, 8; Hatzopoulos, *Actes Chalc.* p. 80 (date) (s. Πυθίων)
MACEDONIA (EDONIS):
—AMPHIPOLIS: (2) ?304-301 BC *Eretria* XI p. 142 no. 10, 3 (*IG* XII (9) 199) + *IG* XII (9) 230 (Tataki, *Macedonians* p. 60 no. 115); *Eretria* XI pp. 145-6 (date) (f. Κλεοχάρης)
—PHILIPPOI: (3) iv/iii BC Collart, *Philippes* pp. 179-80 n. 5 with pl. 27. 3 (Pilhofer 285) ([Π]υθέα (gen.))
THRACE:
—ABDERA: (4) c. 450-425 BC May, *Abdera* p. 123 nos. 130-1 (coin) (Πυθέō (gen.)); (5) iv BC Hp., *Epid.* vi 8. 32
—BYZANTION: (6) iv-iii BC *IG* XII (5) 540, 2 (f. Λύκων)
—LIMNAI: (7) ii-i BC *IKyz* I 507, 2 (f. Διονυσόδωρος)

Πυθῆς
MACEDONIA (CHALKIDIKE):
—OLYNTHOS: (1) f. iv BC *Olynthus* 5 pp. 281-2 no. 121 (lamp); cf. Masson, *OGS* 2 p. 432 (Πυθέω (gen.))
THRACE:
—ABDERA: (2) v BC *RE* (4); *FGrH* 264 (f. Νυμφόδωρος); (3) iv BC *RE* (5) (s. Ἀνδρόμαχος); (4) c. 336-311 BC May, *Abdera* p. 293 no. 549 (coin); cf. Masson, *OGS* 2 p. 432 (Πυθέω (gen.))
—SESTOS*: (5) i BC-i AD *ISestos* 2, 5 (Τ. Φορφανὸς Π.: freed.)

Πυθία
MACEDONIA (PELAGONIA):
—DOSTONEIS?: (1) ii-iii AD *IG* X (2) (2) 207

Πυθιάδας
SCYTHIA MINOR:
—KALLATIS: (1) iv BC *ISM* III 256 (vase)

Πυθιανός
MACEDONIA (EDONIS):
—PHILIPPOI*: (1) ii/iii AD *BCH* 60 (1936) p. 43 no. 2 (Pilhofer 248); Collart, *Philippes* pl. 40. 1 (freed.?)

Πυθίας
MACEDONIA (EDONIS):
—PHILIPPOI: (1) s. iii BC *IG* VII 2433 II, 2 (Tataki, *Macedonians* p. 166 no. 29) (f. Μέδων)
MACEDONIA (PAIONIA):
—KAVADARCI (MOD.): (2) ii-iii AD *Sp.* 71 (1931) p. 237 no. 631 = 75 (1933) p. 41 no. 140 (Πι-: f. Διοσκουρίδης)

Πυθιάς
MACEDONIA (CHALKIDIKE):
—STAGEIROS: (1) c. 335-275 BC *RE* (2); Arist. fr. 663 (Tataki, *Macedonians* p. 175 no. 8) (II d. Ἀριστοτέλης, Πυθιάς I (Atarneus), m. Προκλῆς (Sparta), Δαμάρατος (Sparta), Ἀριστοτέλης (Other))

Πυθίδης
MACEDONIA (LYNKESTIS):
—HERAKLEIA?: (1) iii AD *IG* X (2) (2) 138 (s. Αὐρ. Κλημεντῖνος, Αἰλ. Ἀτιλία)

Πυθίννης
THRACE:
—ABDERA: (1) c. 450-425 BC May, *Abdera* p. 126 no. 139; p. 130 no. 151 (coin); Masson, *OGS* p. 433 (Πυθιννέω (gen.))

Πύθιος
MACEDONIA (SINTIKE):
—HERAKLEIA: (1) ii AD *IGB* IV 2325 (f. Ἀρτεμιδώρα, Ἀσκληπιόδωρος)

Πῦθις
THRACE:
—ABDERA: (1) a. 316 BC *IG* IV (1)^2 94 b, 51 (Perlman, *City and Sanctuary* E.1 with pp. 78-9 (date)) (f. Ζηνέας)

Πυθίς
THRACE:
—RHAIDESTOS: (1) i BC-i AD PM 182 b (d. Γόκων)

Πυθίων
MACEDONIA (BOTTIAIA):
—PELLA: (1) iii BC Tataki, *Macedonians* p. 159 no. 79 (s. Πέλοψ)
—PELLA?: (2) iv BC *FGrH* 81 F 21 (Tataki, *Macedonians* p. 159 no. 80) (f. Μόνιμος)
MACEDONIA (CHALKIDIKE):
—OLYNTHOS: (3) ?350 BC *TAPA* 59 (1928) p. 226, 8; Hatzopoulos, *Actes Chalc.* p. 80 (date) (f. Πυθέας); (4) ~ *TAPA* 62 (1931) p. 43 no. 2, 6, 10; Hatzopoulos, *Actes Chalc.* p. 80 (date) (s. Διόδωρος)
MACEDONIA (EDONIS):
—AMPHIPOLIS: (5) c. 230-200 BC *BCH* 45 (1921) p. 18 III, 79 (Tataki, *Macedonians* p. 60 no. 116) (s. Μένιππος)
—AMPHIPOLIS (NR.): (6) iii BC *SEG* XXIV 611 (f. Νικησώ)
—PHILIPPOI (TERRIT.): (7) f. ii AD Pikoulas, *Chora* pp. 125-6 no. 18 (Pilhofer 619) (Μ. Οὔλπ. Μεσσάλας Π.: freed.?)
MACEDONIA (MYGDONIA):
—THESSALONIKE: (8) c. 230-200 BC *BCH* 45 (1921) p. 17 III, 67 (Tataki, *Macedonians* p. 187 no. 62) (f. Μένιππος)

SCYTHIA MINOR:
—ISTROS: (9) ii AD *ISM* I 137, 11 (f. Ἱππόλοχος); (10) ~ ib. 202, 3 (s. Ἀπολ—)
—KALLATIS: (11) s. iii BC ib. III 35, 3; 35 B, 34 (f. Ἀγήμων)
TAURIS:
—CHERSONESOS: (12) iii BC Kats p. 115 no. 124 (amph., vase) (f. Φορμίων) ?= (*13*); (13) 192 BC *Syll*^{3} 585, 56 (f. Φορμίων) ?= (*12*); (14) c. 140-130 BC Anokhin p. 146 no. 173 (coin)
THRACE:
—AINOS: (15) 194 BC *Milet* I (3) 54, 4 (and Caria Miletos: s. Διονύσιος)
—BYZANTION: (16) c. 500-480 BC *SEG* XLVI 474, 4 (-ōν: s. Κέφαλος); (17) iv BC *ICos* ED 40, 6 (Πυθίω[ν]: s. —ν); (18) iii BC *IG* II^2 8444 (*FRA* 1406) (s. Μᾶτρις); (19) ~ *IG* XII Suppl. p. 39 no. 127 A, 10 + *SEG* XXVI 919
—BYZANTION?: (20) ii-i BC *IByz* 370 (Fıratlı-Robert p. 125 no. 208) (s. Μειδίας); (21) ii AD *SEG* XLI 1706 (f. Θάλλις)
—MARONEIA: (22) 167 BC ib. XXXV 823, 6 (*IThrakAig* E168) (s. Ἡραγόρας)
—MESAMBRIA: (23) f. iii BC *IGB* I^2 335 quater (PM 2104); (24) i BC *IGB* I^2 326, 4 (s. Πολύνικος)
—PERINTHOS-HERAKLEIA:
——(Geleuntes): (25) iii-ii BC *IPerinth* 61, 29 (s. Μητρόβιος)

Πυθογείτων
CIMMERIAN BOSPOROS:
—HERMONASSA: (1) f. iv BC Unp. (Taman Arch. Mus.) (s. Ἡρακλείδης)

Πυθογένης
MACEDONIA (BOTTIAIA):
—MIEZA?: (1) iii BC *SEG* XXIV 524 I, 6 (Hatzopoulos, *MI* 2 p. 106 no. 92) (f. Διογένης)
MACEDONIA (CHALKIDIKE):
—STAGEIROS: (2) v BC *SEG* XLVIII 841 (Πυθογέν[ης]: ?f. Καρ—)
THRACE:
—MARONEIA: (3) i AD *BCH* 66-7 (1942-3) p. 198 no. 2 + *IThrakAig* E297 (s. Λυσανίας)
—SALYMBRIA: (4) hell. *IByz* S 43 (Πυθογένη (gen.): f. Ἐπίχαρμος)

Πυθόγονος
THRACE:
—MARONEIA: (1) a. 316 BC *IG* IV (1)^2 94 b, 52 (Perlman, *City and Sanctuary* E.1 with pp. 78-9 (date)) (s. Παντακλῆς)

Πυθόδοτος
TAURIS:
—CHERSONESOS: (1) c. 230-185 BC Kats p. 127 no. 40 (amph.) (s. Δαμοκλῆς) ?= (*2*); (2) c. 200-185 BC ib. p. 110 no. 101 (amph.) (s. Δαμοκλῆς) ?= (*1*); (3) ii AD *IOSPE* I^2 364 c, 4; (4) f. ii AD ib. 359, 23; *SEG* XXVIII 633, 4?; Solomonik, *NEPKh* III, 9; *Mezhd. Kongr. Frakologii V* p. 193 no. 2, 5?; *SEG* XLVIII 999, 41 (Τ. Φλ. Π.: s. Τ. Φλ. Ἀγέπολις); (5) 129-130 AD *IOSPE* I^2 359, 30; *VDI* 1960 (3), pp. 154-5, 26 (f. Ζῆθος)

Πυθοδωρίς
TAURIS:
—CHERSONESOS: (1) imp. *IOSPE* I^2 490 + *SEG* XXXIII 604 (Πυθοδ[ωρίς]?, Πυθοδ[ώρα]?: d. Πυθόδωρος)
THRACE: (2) f. i AD *RE* (2); *PIR*^{2} P 1115; cf. P 531 (stemma) (d. Κότυς, Ἀντωνία Τρύφαινα (Pontos))

Πυθόδωρος
CIMMERIAN BOSPOROS:
—MYRMEKION: (1) imp.? *ZOOID* 31 (1913) Prot. p. 37 no. 3
MACEDONIA (BOTTIAIA):
—ALLANTE: (2) 323 BC *SEG* XXXVI 331 B, 22 (Tataki, *Macedonians* p. 44 no. 4) (f. Ἀφθόνητος)

MACEDONIA (EDONIS):
—AMPHIPOLIS: **(3)** hell. Dimitsas 853 (f. *Μένυλλος*)
MACEDONIA (MYGDONIA):
—THESSALONIKE*: **(4)** iii AD *IG* X (2) (1) 384, 5 (*Αὐρ. Π.*)
MACEDONIA (PIERIS):
—NEAPOLIS: **(5)** 360 BC ib. IV (1)² 94 b, 27 (Perlman, *City and Sanctuary* E.1 with pp. 69-70 (date); Tataki, *Macedonians* p. 126 no. 15)
SCYTHIA MINOR:
—ISTROS: **(6)** i BC-i AD *ISM* I 191 II, 17-19 (f. *Ἀρτεμίδωρος, Ἀρισταγόρας, Ἀρχέλαος*)
TAURIS:
—CHERSONESOS: **(7)** iii BC Kats pp. 93-4 no. 43 (amph.) (*Πυθόδ[ωρος]*: f. *Διοσκουρίδας*); **(8)** imp. *IOSPE* I² 490; cf. *SEG* XXXIII 604 (*Πυθόδ[ωρος]*—ed., *Πυθόδ[οτος]*?: f. *Πυθοδωρίς*); **(9)** m. ii AD ib. XLVI 930, 5 (*Φ. Πυθόδορος*) ?= (*10*); **(10)** 129 AD *IOSPE* I² 359, 33 (-δο-: s. *Χρηστίων*) ?= (*9*)
THRACE:
—ABDERA: **(11)** f. iv BC *SEG* XLVII 1031 (*IThrakAig* E40) (*Πυθόδω[ρος]*: f. *Δημήτριος*); **(12)** c. 336-311 BC May, *Abdera* p. 293 nos. 551-3 (coin)
—AINOS: **(13)** iii BC *IG* II² 7983 (*FRA* 261) (s. *Διονύσιος*)
—BYZANTION?: **(14)** i BC/i AD *SEG* XXIX 1706 (*Πυ[θόδω]ρος*: ?s. *Ἀνίκατος*)
—MARONEIA: **(15)** c. 432-423 BC Schönert-Geiss, *Maroneia* 153 (coin)
—MESAMBRIA: **(16)** iv/iii BC *IGB* I² 308 quater, 6 (*Πυθόδω[ρος]*); **(17)** iii BC ib. 308 septies, 3 (*Πυθόδω[ρος]*); **(18)** ~ ib. 337 bis (PM 2262) (f. *Βότρυς*); **(19)** ~ *IGB* I² 337 bis (PM 2262) (s. *Βότρυς, Φίλα*); **(20)** i BC *IGB* I² 324 (f. *Ἀντίανδρος*)
—MESAMBRIA?: **(21)** iii/ii BC ib. 102 (PM 923); cf. Robert, *OMS* 5 p. 259 (locn.) (f. *Σάττιον*)
—ZONE: **(22)** s. v BC *PAE* 1969, p. 67 with pl. 83 β (*IThrakAig* E409) (s. *Θεογένης*)

Πυθοκληίδης
SCYTHIA MINOR:
—ISTROS: **(1)** v BC Unp. (Avram, defixio) 2, 3 (*Πυθοκληίδεω* (gen.): s. *Ξενόφαντος*)

Πυθοκλῆς
MACEDONIA (CHALKIDIKE):
—POTIDAIA-KASSANDREIA: **(1)** c. 500-475 BC Marcadé I 29; *LSAG*² p. 369 no. 10 (date) (Tataki, *Macedonians* p. 169 no. 7) (f. *Θευγένης*)
THRACE:
—ABDERA: **(2)** c. 336-311 BC May, *Abdera* p. 293 no. 550 (coin)
—DIONYSOPOLIS: **(3)** iii AD *IGB* I² 14 a, 6 (f. *Αὐρ. Θεόμνηστος*); **(4)** ~ ib. 14 b, 13 (*Αὐρ. Π.*: s. *Ἑστιαῖος*)
—PERINTHOS-HERAKLEIA: **(5)** c. 580-570 BC *IG* XII (6) 577, 3 (*[Π]υθοκλῆς*: f. *Δῆμις*)

Πυθόλαος
MACEDONIA (MYGDONIA):
—THESSALONIKE?: **(1)** ii AD ib. X (2) (1) 886, 3

Πυθόνικος
CIMMERIAN BOSPOROS:
—HERMONASSA: **(1)** iv BC *CIRB* 1056 II, 3 (s. *Ἀπο—*)
THRACE:
—MARONEIA: **(2)** ?c. 240-200 BC Schönert-Geiss, *Maroneia* 944-51 (coin)

Πυθοτέλης
SCYTHIA MINOR:
—ISTROS: **(1)** iii BC *ISM* I 8, 2 (s. *Ἀρχέλοχος*)

Πυθοφάνης
MACEDONIA: **(1)** iv BC Arr., *An.* iii 22. 1; vi 27. 1 (Tataki, *Macedonians* p. 424 no. 174) (f. *Τληπόλεμος*)

Πύθων
CIMMERIAN BOSPOROS:
—PANTIKAPAION: **(1)** i AD *CIRB* 503 (s. *Μελάντιος*)
MACEDONIA: **(2)** 341 BC *CID* II 36 II, 14, 35 (Tataki, *Macedonians* p. 424 no. 175) (*Πύθων*); **(3)** iii/ii BC Liv. xliv 16. 4 (Lat. Pytho: f. *Ὀνήσιμος*); **(4)** 221 BC *PPetr* III 112 g, 7 (Tataki, *Macedonians* p. 424 no. 177); cf. La'da E1514 (*[Π]ύθων*: f. *Ἱππο*κ—); **(5)** 169 BC *RE* (7) (Lat. Pytho); **(6)** ii AD Luc., *Demon.* 15 (fict.)
MACEDONIA (BOTTIAIA):
—BEROIA: **(7)** s. ii BC *IBer* 202 (*Πύθ[ων]*?: f. *Ἅρπαλος*); **(8)** s. i AD ib. 117, 3; 121, 7 (Tataki 1114) (*K. Ποπίλλιος Π.*); **(9)** ii-iii AD *IBer* 114 (Tataki 1112) (*K. Ποπίλλιος Πρόκλος Ἰουνιανὸς Π.*)
—PELLA: **(10)** iv BC Hp., *Epid.* vii 118 (Tataki, *Macedonians* p. 160 no. 81)
—PELLA (TERRIT.)?: **(11)** hell.? Dimitsas 133 (f. *Πλείσταρχος*)
MACEDONIA (CHALKIDIKE):
—AKANTHOS: **(12)** 189 BC *BCH* 37 (1913) p. 122 no. 39, [1], 14, 26 (Tataki, *Macedonians* p. 42 no. 10) (f. *Φίλων*)
MACEDONIA (MYGDONIA):
—THESSALONIKE: **(13)** 154 AD *IG* X (2) (1) 288, 8 (s. *Λουκιλία*)
—THESSALONIKE?: **(14)** ii BC ib. 961 (f. *—τιμος*)
THRACE: **(15)** 231 or 206 BC *CPR* XVIII 18, 369, 372, 386 (La'da E840) (s. *Ἀπολλώνιος*: t.e.)
—ABDERA: **(16)** ?475-450 BC *IG* I³ 1018 (*CEG* I 316; *FRA* 5) (s. *Ἑρμόστρατος*); **(17)** c. 395-360 BC May, *Abdera* pp. 226-7 nos. 345-8 (coin); **(18)** 170 BC *RE* (6)
—AINOS: **(19)** f. iv BC ib. (3); Osborne, *Naturalization* T52 (and Athens)
—BYZANTION: **(20)** m. iv BC *RE* (4); *CID* II 36 II, 14, 35; cf. *RE* (5); *LGPN* III A (13) (*Πύθων—CID*)

Πυθῶναξ
MACEDONIA?: **(1)** iv BC Arr., *An.* iv 12. 5 (Tataki, *Macedonians* p. 424 no. 178) (f. *Δημήτριος*)

Πυθώνυμος
THRACE:
—STRYME? (NR.): **(1)** c. 450-425 BC *SEG* XXXIII 564 (*IThrakAig* E111) (f. *Ἀρίσταρχος*)

Πυλάδης
MACEDONIA: **(1)** 232 or 207 BC *CPR* XVIII 14, 279, 284, 289 (Tataki, *Macedonians* p. 424 no. 179; La'da E1781) (t.e.); **(2)** 171 BC *PTeb* 819, 4, 8-9, 11, 13 etc. (Tataki, *Macedonians* p. 425 no. 180; La'da E1615)
MACEDONIA (BOTTIAIA):
—PELLA: **(3)** ii AD *SEG* XXIV 554
MACEDONIA (MYGDONIA):
—THESSALONIKE: **(4)** ?i-ii AD ib. XXVII 310

Πυλάμαχος
MACEDONIA (BOTTIAIA):
—PELLA: **(1)** 324 BC Berve 679; Hoffmann, *Makedonen* pp. 212-13 (name) (Tataki, *Macedonians* p. 159 no. 75) (*Πουλάμαχος, Πολάμαχος, Πολύμαχος*—mss.)

Πύλης
MACEDONIA (ODOMANTIKE):
—SIRRHA (NR.): **(1)** ii-iii AD *SEG* XXIV 579, 6 (Pilhofer 561) (*Πύλη* (gen.): f. *Διοσκουρίδης*)

Πύλλος
MACEDONIA: **(1)** c. 139 BC Sherk 9, 28 (*IG* IX (2) 89; Tataki, *Macedonians* p. 425 no. 181)

Πυλοφάγος?
THRACE:
—PLOTINOPOLIS: **(1)** iii-iv AD *BE* 1994, no. 166 (pithos)

Πύλων
MACEDONIA (CHALKIDIKE):
—POTIDAIA-KASSANDREIA?: **(1)** 285 BC *SEG* XXXVIII 619, 16 (s. *Ἐπιτέλης*)

Πύλωρος
CIMMERIAN BOSPOROS:
—GORGIPPIA: **(1)** ii/iii AD *CIRB* 1179, 50

Πυραλλίς
MACEDONIA (EDONIS):
—PHILIPPOI (NR.): **(1)** i AD *BIAB* 16 (1950) pp. 8-9 no. 1, 5 (Pilhofer 440) (Lat. Pyrallidi (dat.): d. M. Varinius Celer, Varinia Marita)

Πυραμίς
MACEDONIA (MYGDONIA):
—THESSALONIKE: **(1)** ?i-ii AD *AD* 26 (1971) Chron. p. 376 no. 1 (*Κλ. Π.*)

Πύραμος
MACEDONIA (PIERIA):
—DION: **(1)** ii-iii AD *Klio* 52 (1970) p. 51 no. 2 (*Λ. Παπείνιος Π.*)
THRACE:
—BYZANTION: **(2)** ?352 BC Rhodes–Osborne 57, 25 (f. *Παρμενίσκος*)

Πυρέτης
MACEDONIA (SINTIKE):
—PARTHIKOPOLIS (NR.): **(1)** 165 AD *IGB* IV 2288 (s. *Μήτοκος*)
THRACE: **(2)** f. iii AD ib. V 5667 (*Πυρέ[τ]ης*?: s. *Τήρης*)

Πυριλάμπης
MACEDONIA?: **(1)** i/ii AD *SEG* XLIV 525, 2, 6, 8 (biling.) (or Bithynia?: *M. Δομίτιος Π.*)

Πύριχος
MACEDONIA: **(1)** ?246-241 BC ib. XXVII 973 bis, 20 (Tataki, *Macedonians* p. 425 no. 184)
MACEDONIA (BOTTIAIA):
—BEROIA: **(2)** 254 AD *ILeukopetra* 110, 3 (*Αὐρ. Π.*)

Πύρος
MACEDONIA (MYGDONIA):
—THERME?: **(1)** vi/v BC *SEG* XLVI 809 (vase) (Touratsoglou, *Macedonia* p. 15 pl. 10) (*Πύρ(ρ)ος*?, *Πῦρος*?)
—THESSALONIKE: **(2)** ii AD *IG* X (2) (1) 357
—THESSALONIKE?: **(3)** 63 AD ib. 925; **(4)** iii AD ib. 896 + *BE* 1999, no. 354 (*Α(ὐ)ρη. Π., Ἀρήπυρος*—ed.: s. *Γαλάτης*, f. *Διονύσιος*)
—THESSALONIKE*: **(5)** ii AD *IG* X (2) (1) 284, 1 + Robert, *OMS* 5 p. 332 (?f. *Ἀλέξανδρος*: slave?)
MACEDONIA (ODOMANTIKE):
—SIRRHA (NR.): **(6)** 25 or 141 AD *SEG* XXXII 647 (Pilhofer 560) (*Πύρου* (gen.)—ed., *Κελεπύρου*?, *Πυρού[λα]*?: f. *Δούσκελος*)
THRACE:
—PAUTALIA (TERRIT.): **(7)** ii-iii AD *IGB* V 5826 (s. *Διζάλας*)
—SERDICA (TERRIT.): **(8)** ii-iii AD *AEMÖ* 10 (1886) pp. 238-9 no. 2, 11

Πυρούβρης
MACEDONIA (ODOMANTIKE):
—SIRRHA (TERRIT.): **(1)** ii-iii AD *SEG* XXXV 764, 1, 3 (Pilhofer 565) (*Π[υρ]ουβρέους* (gen.): f. *—ιλης*)

Πύρουζα
MACEDONIA (SINTIKE):
—PARTHIKOPOLIS: **(1)** 121 AD *IGB* IV 2270, 7 (*Ἐρεννία Π.*: m. *M. Ἐρέννιος Παυλῖνος*)

Πύρουλα

Macedonia (Sintike):

—Parthikopolis (nr.): **(1)** ii-iii ad ib. 2289 + v 5913 (d. *Κάτος*)

Πυρούλας

Macedonia (Bisaltia):

—Tragilos (nr.): **(1)** ii-iii ad *SEG* xxx 611 (s. *Δεινίας*)

Macedonia (Edonis):

—Philippoi: **(2)** ii-iii ad ib. xv 417 (*JDAI* 84 (1969) p. 161 no. R39; Pilhofer 397)

Macedonia (Mygdonia):

—Thessalonike: **(3)** ii ad *IG* x (2) (1) 509; **(4)** f. iii ad ib. 441 (*Αὐρ. Π.*: s. *Αὐρ. Ἀλκιδάμας, Αὐρ. Μάντα*); **(5)** ~ ib. 564, 1 (*Αὐρ. Π.*: s. *Πύρρος Ἀλκιδάμας*); **(6)** ~ ib. l. 5 (*Αὐρ. Π.*: s. *Ζετιτίς*)

—Thessalonike?: **(7)** ?ii ad ib. 1020

Macedonia (Odomantike):

—Sirrha: **(8)** ii-iii ad Dimitsas 817 (Kaphtantzis 26) (f. *Μένανδρος*); **(9)** ii/iii ad *SEG* xlviii 877 (I f. *Πυρούλας* II, *Τόρκος, Μούκκων*); **(10)** ~ ib. (II s. *Πυρούλας* I, *Μωμώ*)

Macedonia (Sintike):

—Herakleia: **(11)** s. ii ad *IGB* v 5921 + *Melnik* 1 p. 164 no. 2 (f. *Σκαιδένθης*)

—Neine: **(12)** iii ad *IGB* iv 2252; cf. v 5880 (*Αὐρ. Π.*: s. *Ὀνήσιμος*)

—Parthikopolis: **(13)** ii ad ib. iv 2278 (f. *Ἀλέξανδρος*); **(14)** ii/iii ad ib. 2281 ([*Πυ*]*ρούλας*)

—Parthikopolis (territ.): **(15)** ii ad *Arkheologiia* (Sofia) 1987 (1), p. 25 no. 2 (f. *Ζεκαιδένθη*); **(16)** ~ ib. I p. 25 no. 3 (s. *Διονύσιος, Μάμα*); **(17)** ii/iii ad *IGB* iv 2312

—Parthikopolis (nr.): **(18)** ?ii ad ib. 2298; **(19)** ii-iii ad ib. v 5918 (f. *Δεῖδος*); **(20)** ~ ib. (s. *Δεῖδος*, ?s. *Ζαιβαλώ*); **(21)** ~ ib. (*Π. ὁ μικρός*: s. *Δεῖδος*, ?s. *Ζαιβαλώ*); **(22)** 159 ad ib. iv 2286, 1 ([*Π*]*υ*[*ρ*]*ούλας*: s. *Σεδάλας*); **(23)** ~ ib. l. 3

Thrace:

—Čomakovci (mod.): **(24)** ?iii ad *ILB* 171, 8 (Lat. Pyrulas: f. *Σούρα*)

—Lukovit (mod.): **(25)** imp. ib. 189; cf. *Ét. Balk.* 1987, p. 93 no. 22 (name) (Lat. Puru(l)a(e) (gen.): f. *Μάντα*)

—Nicopolis ad Nestum: **(26)** ii ad *IGB* iv 2346 (s. *Σεύθης, Κάλπη*); **(27)** ii-iii ad ib. 2337, 6

—Pautalia: **(28)** ii-iii ad ib. 2078 b

—Sekinenoi: **(29)** ii-iii ad ib. 2230 (f. *Βίθυς*)

Πυρουρρήδης

Thrace?: **(1)** 316-309 bc *IG* II^2 1956, 28; *Ancient Macedonia* 5 p. 445 with n. 10 (date) (*FRA* 2569)

Πυρούσαλα

Macedonia (Mygdonia):

—Thessalonike?: **(1)** ii-iii ad *SEG* xxvii 313 (*Μεινοκεία Πουρόσαλλα*)

Macedonia (Odomantike)?: **(2)** ii-iii ad *IGB* v 5927 (m. *Τίτος*)

Macedonia (Sintike):

—Herakleia (territ.): **(3)** ii-iii ad ib. iv 2329 (m. *Φίλιππος, Τιβέριος*)

—Neine: **(4)** iii ad ib. 2254; cf. v 5881 (*Αὐρ. Π.*); **(5)** 222 ad ib. 5886, 3 (m. *Αὐρ. Πύρρος, Αὐρ. Ἀρτεμίδωρος*)

—Parthikopolis: **(6)** ii ad ib. iv 2273 (d. *Κρίσπος*); **(7)** ~ ib. 2275 (*M. Οὐαλερία Π.*: m. *Ἰουλία*)

—Parthikopolis (territ.): **(8)** ii/iii ad ib. 2312 (d. *Μουκάσης*, m. *Δεντούσκαιλα*); **(9)** 198 ad ib. 2311, 3 (d. *Βίθυς, Ζαικα*); **(10)** ?242 ad ib. 2322 (*Πι-*: d. *Σαῖγος*)

—Parthikopolis (nr.): **(11)** ?ii ad ib. 2293

Πύρρα

Macedonia: **(1)** ii-i bc *IG* II^2 9268 (Tataki, *Macedonians* p. 425 no. 182; *FRA* 3488)

Πυρραλίων

Tauris:

—Chersonesos: **(1)** f. iv bc *IOlbia* 3, 2 (Dubois, *IGDOlbia* 16); cf. *SEG* xxxiii 616 (*Πυρραλίω*[*ν*])

Πυρρειός

Thrace:

—Bargala (area): **(1)** ii ad *Sp.* 77 (1934) p. 72 no. 2 (f. *Πυρρίας*)

Πυρρίας

Cimmerian Bosporos:

—Nymphaion: **(1)** v bc Tolstoi 135 (vase)

Macedonia: **(2)** iii bc *PGurob* 18, 4 (Tataki, *Macedonians* p. 425 no. 183) (f. *Δημήτριος*)

Macedonia (Mygdonia):

—Thessalonike: **(3)** 160 ad *IG* x (2) (1) 573 bis

Macedonia (Odomantike):

—Sirrha (territ.): **(4)** 203 ad *SEG* xxx 601 (f. *Συντύχη*)

Macedonia (Pieria):

—Phila?: **(5)** ?iii bc *RPh* 1911, pp. 133-4 no. 36, 99; cf. Helly, *L'État thessalien* pp. 319-20 (locn.) (f. *Σωσίβιος*)

Macedonia (Sintike):

—Neine: **(6)** 180 ad *IGB* v 5884 (*Π. ὁ καὶ Μα..ος*)

—Parthikopolis: **(7)** ii ad ib. iv 2280 (*Πυρ*(*ρ*)*ίας*); **(8)** s. ii ad ib. 2267 (f. *Κλήμης*)

Thrace: **(9)** iii bc *IG* II^2 8921 (*FRA* 2573)

—Bargala: **(10)** ii-iii ad *SEG* xliv 515

—Bargala (area): **(11)** ii ad *Sp.* 77 (1934) p. 72 no. 2 (s. *Πυρρειός*)

—Maroneia: **(12)** iii bc *IThrakAig* E236 ([*Πυ*]*ρρίας*?: s. *Λεύκιππος*)

Thrace?: **(13)** 316-309 bc *IG* II^2 1956, 7 (*FRA* 2570); *Ancient Macedonia* 5 p. 445 with n. 10 (date); **(14)** ~ *IG* II^2 1956, 33; *Ancient Macedonia* 5 p. 445 with n. 10 (date) (*FRA* 2571); **(15)** ~ *IG* II^2 1956, 36; *Ancient Macedonia* 5 p. 445 with n. 10 (date) (*FRA* 2572)

Πυρρῖνος

Tauris:

—Chersonesos: **(1)** iv/iii bc Solomonik, *NEPKh* 141 (f. *Ἀπολλώνιος*); **(2)** c. 250-230 bc Anokhin p. 142 no. 119 (coin)

Πύρριχος

Macedonia (Bottiaia):

—Edessa: **(1)** b. 183 bc *RE* (4) (Tataki, *Macedonians* p. 104 no. 17) (s. *Χρυσόγονος*); **(2)** 220-210 bc *SEG* xxvii 202, 9 (Tataki, *Macedonians* p. 104 no. 18) (*Πυρρίχειος* (patr. adj.): f. *Χρυσόγονος*)

Πύρρος

Cimmerian Bosporos:

—Gorgippia: **(1)** f. iii bc *CIRB* 1137 A I, 15 (f. *Λιμναῖος*)

—Pantikapaion: **(2)** i ad ib. 504 (s. *Ἡρακλέων*)

Macedonia: **(3)** 311-306 bc Maier, *Mauerbauinschr.* 69 II, 149 (Tataki, *Macedonians* p. 426 no. 188) (f. *Εὔδημος*); **(4)** 238 bc *PPetr*^{2} 6, 37 (La'da E1815) ([*Π*]*ύρρος*) ?= (*5*); **(5)** 215-214 bc *BGU* 1943, 4, 7-8, [9], 11-12, 14-16, 18, 25, 29, [30], [32]; 1945 A, 3; 1945 [B] (Tataki, *Macedonians* p. 425 no. 186; La'da E1617) ?= (*4*); **(6)** 162-117 bc *PTeb* 61 b, 78; 64 a, 27 (Tataki, *Macedonians* p. 425 no. 187; La'da E1616) (s. *Πτολεμαῖος*, f. *Λυσίμαχος*: katoikos); **(7)** ii/i bc *IOrop* 700 (Tataki, *Macedonians* p. 426 no. 189) ([*Π*]*ύρρο*[*ς*]: f. *Τάναος*)

Macedonia (Bottiaia):

—Beroia: **(8)** 223 bc *IBer* 4, 30 (f. *Μένανδρος*); **(9)** ii-iii ad ib. 277 (f. *Ἀρέτη*); **(10)** a. 212 ad ib. 136, 3 (Tataki 418) (*Δομίτιος Π.*)

—Beroia?: **(11)** m. i ad *Act. Ap.* 20. 4 (Tataki 1144; Tataki, *Macedonians* p. 82 no. 47) (f. *Σώπατρος*: Jew?)

Macedonia (Derriopos):

—Stuberra: **(12)** 87 ad *IG* x (2) (2) 325, 83 (f. *Λυσίμαχος*)

Macedonia (Mygdonia):

—Thessalonike: **(13)** 95 bc ib. x (2) (1) 4, 2 (s. *Κλειτόμαχος*); **(14)** 118 ad ib. 524, 4 (f. *Ἰούλ. Ἑρμῆς*); **(15)** f. iii ad ib. 564, 1; *BCH* 97 (1973) pp. 242-5 (name) (*Π. Ἀλκιδάμας*: f. *Αὐρ. Ἀλκιδάμας, Αὐρ. Δούλης, Αὐρ. Πυρούλας*)

—Thessalonike?: **(16)** ii ad *IG* x (2) (1) 703 (?f. *Δανάη*)

Macedonia (Orestis):

—Platania (mod.): **(17)** ii ad *EAM* 205 (f. *Κλεῖτος*)

Macedonia (Sintike):

—Herakleia: **(18)** ii-iii ad *IGB* iv 2328 (f. *—α*)

—Herakleia (territ.): **(19)** ii-iii ad ib. 2330 (*Πυρρουτηρης*—ed.: f. *Σκαρκαιζες*)

—Neine: **(20)** ii ad ib. 2245 (*Eastern cults* p. 258 no. 12) (f. *Ἑρμογένης*); **(21)** ii-iii ad *IGB* v 5888 bis (s. *Μόκασος*); **(22)** ~ ib. 5888 ter (s. *Πυρρ—*); **(23)** 158 ad ib. iv 2241 (*Πύρ*[*ρο*]*ς*: s. *Καπίτων*); **(24)** 173 ad ib. 2240 (s. *Γάϊος*, f. *Παράμονος*); **(25)** 180 ad ib. v 5884 (s. *Πυρρίας*); **(26)** 222 ad ib. 5886, 1 (*Αὐρ. Π.*: s. *Πυρούσαλα, Διονύσιος*)

—Neine (nr.): **(27)** ii-iii ad ib. 5890 (s. *Κειλαίβιθυς*)

—Parthikopolis: **(28)** ii ad ib. iv 2271 (f. *Νικοστράτη*); **(29)** ~ ib. 2272 (f. *Ἀρτεμιδώρα*); **(30)** 158 ad ib. 2263, 18 (*Οὐαλέριος Π.*)

—Parthikopolis (territ.): **(31)** ii ad *Arkheologiia* (Sofia) 1987 (1), p. 24 no. 1, 1 (f. *Κλεοπάτρα*); **(32)** ~ ib. l. 2 (I s. *Τόνος*, f. *Ἀλέξανδρος, Πύρρος* II); **(33)** ~ ib. l. 5 (II s. *Πύρρος* I, *Κλεοπάτρα*); **(34)** 146 ad *IGB* iv 2303 (s. *Ἀγάθων*); **(35)** 215 ad ib. 2319; **(36)** ~ ib. (s. *Λᾶνδρος*)

—Parthikopolis (nr.): **(37)** ii-iii ad ib. 2291, 2

Skythia:

—Olbia-Borysthenes: **(38)** ii ad *IOSPE* I^2 93, 4; 129, 3 (*M. Οὔλπ. Π.*: s. *Ἀρσηούαχος*)

—Olbia-Borysthenes*: **(39)** 248 ad ib. 167, 8 (Lat. Pyrrus Bithus)

Thrace:

—Bisanthe-Panion: **(40)** ii-i bc *JÖAI* 23 (1926) Beibl. cols. 155-6 no. 93 (*SIRIS* 127; *Eastern cults* p. 28 no. 48) (f. *Μενεκλῆς*)

—Nicopolis ad Nestum: **(41)** ii ad *IGB* iv 2348 (f. *Ἀπολλόδωρος*); **(42)** ii-iii ad ib. 2347 (s. *Βράσος*, ?f. *Δαμαρίων, Ἀκούτας*)

—Pautalia: **(43)** iii ad *CIL* vi 2671 (Lat. Aur. Pyrrhus: I f. *Αὐρ. Πύρρος* II, Aur. Marcellina); **(44)** ~ ib. (Lat. Aur. Pyrrhus: II s. *Αὐρ. Πύρρος* I)

—Philippopolis-Trimontium: **(45)** iii ad *IGB* iii 1007, 1 (*Αὐρ. Π. ὁ καὶ Ταῦρος*); **(46)** 267-268 ad ib. v 5409, 13

—Serdica: **(47)** 222 ad *RMD* 308 (Lat. M. Aurelius Purrus)

—Skaptopara*: **(48)** f. iii ad *SEG* xliv 610 (*Chiron* 26 (1996) pp. 183-93 (ring)) (*Αὐρ. Π.*) ?= (*49*); **(49)** 238-244 ad *IGB* iv 2236 a, 6; 2236 b, 108 + *SEG* xliv 610 with comm. (*Αὐρ. Π.*) ?= (*48*)

Πυρρούλας

Macedonia (Bottiaia):

—Kyrrhos?: **(1)** 199 ad *ILeukopetra* 45, 14 (f. *Ἀλέξανδρος*)

Πύρσος

Macedonia (Sintike):

—Parthikopolis: **(1)** ii ad *IGB* iv 2277 (s. *Ὑαῖος*, f. *Ἀρτεμίδωρος*)

Scythia Minor:

—Kallatis: **(2)** s. iii bc *ISM* iii 35 A, 34 (f. *Κριτόβουλος*); **(3)** ii/i bc *SNG Stancomb* 96 (coin); **(4)** s. i ad *ISM* iii 68 (f. *Ἡρακλέων*)

Πυτρος?
THRACE:
—HADRIANOPOLIS (TERRIT.): **(1)** iii AD *IGB* III 1831 (f. *Αὐρ. Μουκάζενις*)

Πωλίων
THRACE:
—APOLLONIA-SOZOPOLIS: **(1)** i-ii AD ib. I^{2} 401, 13 (*Πω(λί)ων*?: f. *Ὀνήσιμος*)

Πῶλλα
MACEDONIA (BOTTIAIA):
—BEROIA (TERRIT.): **(1)** ii-iii AD *IBer* 511 (Tataki 1146)
THRACE:
—BYZANTION: **(2)** i AD *IByz* 280; **(3)** i-ii AD ib. 281 (Fıratlı–Robert pp. 87-8 no. 110) (d. *Διόδωρος*)
——(Rhegion): **(4)** i-ii AD *IByz* 271 ([*Π*]*ῶλλα*: ?m. *Διότιμος*)
—BYZANTION?: **(5)** i AD ib. 372 (d. *Διονύσιις ὁ καὶ Πόπλιος*)

Πωλλίων
MACEDONIA (LYNKESTIS):
—HERAKLEIA: **(1)** i AD *IG* X (2) (2) 75, 49 (s. *Σιλουανός*)
MACEDONIA (MYGDONIA):
—THESSALONIKE: **(2)** s. i BC ib. X (2) (1) 222; **(3)** i-ii AD ib. 243 I, 15 ([*Π*]*ωλλίων*)
—THESSALONIKE?: **(4)** ?i AD ib. 55 (*Μ. Ἐρέννιος Π.*: s. *Μᾶρκος*, *Ἀρίστεια*)
SCYTHIA MINOR:
—ISTROS: **(5)** ii AD *ISM* I 197 I, 9 (f. *Παρθενοπαῖος*); **(6)** c. 140-160 AD ib. 207, 13 (s. *Μέμνων*)
—TOMIS: **(7)** ii-iii AD ib. II 197 (*GVI* 1043a) + *SEG* XXV 760 (f. *Σωτᾶς*); **(8)** 201 AD *ISM* II 83 I, 15 (I f. *Πωλλίων* II); **(9)** ~ ib. l. 15 (II s. *Πωλλίων* I); **(10)** ~ ib. l. 24 (*Πωλ*[*λίων*]: s. —*ιος*)
THRACE:
—BEROE-AUGUSTA TRAIANA: **(11)** ii-iii AD *IGB* III 1604 (*Πωλ(λ)ίων*: f. *Οὐλπία*)
—ODESSOS: **(12)** i BC-i AD ib. I^{2} 51 c, 10 (*Πωλ(λ)ίων*: f. *Μᾶρκος*)
—PHILIPPOPOLIS-TRIMONTIUM: **(13)** ii-iii AD ib. III 887; **(14)** ~ ib. 912, 6 (*Πωλ(λ)ίων*)
—VICUS TRULLENSIUM: **(15)** imp. ib. II 505

Πώμη?
SCYTHIA MINOR:
—ISTROS: **(1)** iii AD *ISM* I 303, 4 (d. *Ἀρίστων*, m. *Ἀρίστων*, *Ζούθης*, *Σίδηρος*, *Ἀρτεμίδωρος*)

Πώνθαρος
THRACE?: **(1)** iv-iii BC *SEG* XVII 337. 1 (bullet)

Πωριανή
MACEDONIA (MYGDONIA):
—THESSALONIKE: **(1)** iii AD *IG* X (2) (1) 476 C (*Ἄκυλα ἡ καὶ Π.*: d. *Ἀσκληπιάδης*)

Πώταλος
MACEDONIA: **(1)** s. iv BC *Iasos* 32, 5 (Tataki, *Macedonians* p. 426 no. 190) (f. *Εὐπόλεμος*) ?= *(2)*
MACEDONIA?: **(2)** m. iv BC *Olynthus* 10 p. 434 nos. 2244-8; *SEG* XLVII 952 (bullet) ?= *(1)*

P

Ῥαβόκενθος
THRACE:
—BESSOI: **(1)** 57 BC Cic., *In Pis.* 84 (*RE* s.v. Rabocentus (-)) (Lat. Rabocentus)

Ῥαδάμασις
CIMMERIAN BOSPOROS:
—PANTIKAPAION: **(1)** 275-278 AD *CIRB* 36, 22; Zgusta, *PNS* 186 (f. *Ἔρως*); **(2)** ~ *CIRB* 36, 64 (*Ῥαδάμασ(ις)*—Vinogradov, *Ῥαδάμιος?*—*CIRB*: s. *Σαμβίων*)

Ῥαδάμειστος
CIMMERIAN BOSPOROS:
—THEODOSIA: **(1)** iii AD ib. 947 A, 6 ([*Ῥ*]*αδάμειστος*: s. *Δα*—)
SKYTHIA:
—TANAIS: **(2)** ii AD ib. 1262, 17; Zgusta, *PNS* 187 ([*Ῥ*]*αδάμειστος*: s. *Φίλων*)

Ῥαδαμόφουρτος
SKYTHIA:
—TANAIS: **(1)** 220 AD *CIRB* 1278, 3; Zgusta, *PNS* 188 (s. *Τρύφων*)

Ῥαδαμψάδιος
CIMMERIAN BOSPOROS:
—BOSPOROS: **(1)** c. 280-322 AD *CIRB* 65; 66; Frolova, *CKB A.D. 242-341/342* pp. 54-8; Zgusta, *PNS* 189 (*Ῥαδαμσάδιος*—65, *Ῥαδαμψάδης*—coins: king)

Ῥαδαμψῶν
SKYTHIA:
—OLBIA-BORYSTHENES: **(1)** ii AD *IOSPE* I^{2} 80, 10; 175, 10; Zgusta, *PNS* 190 (f. *Νουμήνιος*) ?= *(4)*; **(2)** ~ *IOSPE* I^{2} 93, 8 (f. *Βαδάκης*); **(3)** ~ ib. 105, 5 (f. *Βώρνων*); **(4)** f. ii AD *SEG* XLIII 506, 9 (f. *Νουμήνιος*) ?= *(1)*; **(5)** iii AD *IOSPE* I^{2} 103, 7; cf. Zgusta, *PNS* 191 (*Ῥαδαμ(ψ)ῶν*: f. *Ἀγίλλας*)

Ῥαδινός
THRACE:
—SALYMBRIA: **(1)** ii-i BC *IByz* S 45 (f. *Λολλία*)

Ῥάδιος
MACEDONIA (ORESTIS):
—BATTYNAIOI: **(1)** 192 AD *EAM* 186 III, 52 (*Ῥάδ̣ιος*: f. ..*σίλας*)

Ῥάδις
MACEDONIA (CHALKIDIKE):
—OLYNTHOS: **(1)** ii BC *NS* 536 + *AM* 51 (1926) p. 6 (Tataki, *Macedonians* p. 142 no. 98) (f. *Δαμώ*)

Ῥάζδος
THRACE:
—BIZYE: **(1)** c. 153 AD Taşlıklıoğlu 2 p. 67 no. 1, 12 + *BE* 1972, no. 292 (s. *Ὑάκινθος*)

Ῥαθάγωσος
SKYTHIA:
—OLBIA-BORYSTHENES: **(1)** ii AD *IOlbia* 88, 4; *IOSPE* I^{2} 91, 7; Zgusta, *PNS* 192 (f. *Ἄβνωζος*); **(2)** ~ *IOSPE* I^{2} 101, 3; Zgusta, *PNS* 192 (s. *Ἄβναγος*)

Ῥαίζδος
THRACE: **(1)** ?276 or 267 BC *FD* III (4) 414, 6, 17 (f. *Κότυς*)

Ῥαισκήπορις
THRACE:
—PAUTALIA (TERRIT.): **(1)** ii AD *IGB* IV 2214, 14

Ῥαισκούπορις
THRACE: **(1)** iii BC ib. I^{2} 389, 2; cf. V 5138 (s. *Κότυς*)

Ῥαισκουτούρμη
THRACE:
—GERMANIA: **(1)** ii-iii AD ib. IV 2207

Ῥάλχαδος?
SKYTHIA:
—TANAIS: **(1)** c. 200-210 AD *CIRB* 1277, 4 (*Ῥ̣αλχάδου* (gen.)—*CIRB*, *Σ̣α.χάδου*—Latyshev: f. —*λ̣ιο̣ς*—Vinogradov)

Ῥαμάναγος
SKYTHIA:
—OLBIA-BORYSTHENES: **(1)** i/ii AD *IOlbia* 88, 6 (s. *Μηνόδωρος*)

Ῥαοδμαῖος
SKYTHIA:
—OLBIA-BORYSTHENES: **(1)** c. 150-175 AD *IOSPE* I^{2} 132, 8; Zgusta, *PNS* 193; cf. *SEG* XLII 713 (-*μῆος*: s. *Κόλχος*); **(2)** ii/iii AD *IOlbia* 52, 8; cf. Zgusta, *PNS* 193

Ῥαπάκης
SKYTHIA:
—OLBIA-BORYSTHENES: **(1)** ii AD *IOSPE* I^{2} 80, 14; Zgusta, *PNS* 194 (f. *Ἀρειβαλις*)

Ῥάσκος
THRACE:
—SAPPAIOI: **(1)** 42 BC *RE* (-) (?s. *Κότυς*: dynast)

Ῥασκούπορις
THRACE:
—SAPPAIOI: **(1)** 48-42 BC ib. (1); *PIR*^{2} R 58; *IG* II^{2} 3442-3; *SEG* XXXIV 665; 702; Youroukova pp. 46-53; pp. 89-90 nos. 153-7 (coin) (*Ῥησκούπορις*—*SEG*: s. *Κότυς*, f. *Κότυς*: king); **(2)** 16-11 BC *RE* (2); *PIR*^{2} R 59 (?s. *Κότυς*: dynast); **(3)** 6-19 AD *RE* (3); *PIR*^{2} R 60 (stemma); *IPerinth* 5 (?s. *Κότυς*, f. *Γ. Ἰούλ. Ῥοιμητάλκης*: king)

Ῥάσσογος
SKYTHIA:
—TANAIS: **(1)** 225 AD *CIRB* 1279, 16; Zgusta, *PNS* 195 (*Ῥάσσ*[*ο*]*γο̣ς*: f. *Ῥαχοίσακος*)

Ῥαχοίσακος
SKYTHIA:
—TANAIS: **(1)** 225 AD *CIRB* 1279, 11; Zgusta, *PNS* 321 (s. *Εὐνόϊκος*); **(2)** ~ *CIRB* 1279, 16 (*Ῥαχοίσ*[*ακο*]*ς̣*: s. *Ῥάσσογος*)

Ῥεβέκα
THRACE:
—BIZYE: **(1)** iv-v AD *CIJ* II 692 (*AD* 49-50 (1994-5) Mel. p. 339 no. 161) (Jew)

Ῥεβοκᾶτα
THRACE:
—HADRIANOPOLIS: **(1)** iv-v AD *SEG* VIII 45, 6 (d. *Μαρκιανός*)

Ῥειλαζεις
THRACE:
—BOURDAPA: (1) hell.? ib. XXXIX 659 (?s. *Δορ—*)

Ῥεκέπτος
MACEDONIA (BOTTIAIA):
—BEROIA: (1) i BC-i AD *IBer* 142, 10 (Tataki 1148) (f. *Πόντιος*); (2) ii-iii AD *IBer* 311 A (threptos)
MACEDONIA (LYNKESTIS):
—HERAKLEIA (NR.): (3) ii-iii AD *IG* X (2) (2) 7 (f. *Νικάνωρ*)

Ῥεκίθαγγος
THRACE: (1) 541-552 AD *PLRE* III (-)

Ῥεπτάτερκος
THRACE: (1) i AD *IGB* IV 2338, 8, 14; cf. V 5928 (d. *Ἡρακλείδης*, m. *Αἰδεζυρίς*)

Ῥεσπεκτιανός
THRACE:
—DUROSTORUM: (1) ii AD ib. II 863 (I f. *Π. Φλ. Ῥεσπεκτιανὸς* II *Σαβῖνος*: threptos)

Ῥευρόμανος
SKYTHIA:
—OLBIA-BORYSTHENES: (1) iii AD *IOSPE* I^2 103, 6; Zgusta, *PNS* 322 (s. *Ἥλμανος*)

Ῥευρόμαρος
SKYTHIA:
—OLBIA-BORYSTHENES: (1) i/ii AD *IOlbia* 90, 10, 16 (*Ῥοιρόμαρος*—l. 16: s. *Σιπέλαγος*)

Ῥευσίναλος
CIMMERIAN BOSPOROS:
—PANTIKAPAION: (1) ii AD *CIRB* 698; Zgusta, *PNS* 765 (s. *Παιρίσαλος*)

Ῥηβάδας
THRACE:
—MESAMBRIA*: (1) hell. *SEG* XXX 705 (tile)

Ῥηβούκενθος
MACEDONIA (EDONIS):
—PHILIPPOI (TERRIT.): (1) imp. *CIL* III 14206. 20 (Pilhofer 526) (Lat. Raebuc[ent]us: f. *Βίθυς*)
—POLGENOI: (2) 43 BC *SEG* XXXIV 665 (Pilhofer 390) (f. *Δριωζίγης*)
THRACE:
—SERDICA (TERRIT.): (3) ii-iii AD *IGB* IV 2025 (I f. *Ῥηβούκενθος* II); (4) ~ ib. (II s. *Ῥηβούκενθος* I)

Ῥηβούλας
THRACE:
—ODRYSAI: (1) 330 BC Tod, *GHI* II 193, 1; Osborne, *Naturalization* T66 (*FRA* 2574) (and Athens: s. *Σεύθης*)

Ῥηγιλλιανός
SCYTHIA MINOR:
—KALLATIS: (1) 241-244 AD *ISM* III 74 B, 23

Ῥήγιλλος
SCYTHIA MINOR:
—KALLATIS*: (1) s. i AD ib. 33, 5

Ῥηγῖνα
MACEDONIA (MYGDONIA):
—THESSALONIKE: (1) ii-iii AD *IG* X (2) (1) 419 (m. *Ἀρτέμιν*)
SCYTHIA MINOR:
—TOMIS: (2) ii AD *ISM* II 189, 2 (*GVI* 1026) (-γεί-: m. *Ἀγάθανδρος*)
THRACE:
—BEROE-AUGUSTA TRAIANA: (3) ii-iii AD *IGB* III 1766, 7 (-γεῖ-)

Ῥηγῖνος
SCYTHIA MINOR:
—KALLATIS: (1) 241-244 AD *ISM* III 74 B, 23 (-γεῖ-)

Ῥῆγλος
MACEDONIA (ELIMEIA)?: (1) f. ii AD *EAM* 10 (*Ἀλέξανδρος ὁ καὶ Ῥ.*: s. *Ῥοιμητάλκης*)
MACEDONIA (MYGDONIA):
—THESSALONIKE: (2) f. i AD *IG* X (2) (1) 126, 7-8; Robert, *OMS* 5 pp. 295-302 (date) (*Ταῦρος ὁ καὶ Ῥ.*: s. *Ἀμμία*, f. *Ταῦρος*)

Ῥησκούπορις
CIMMERIAN BOSPOROS:
—BOSPOROS: (1) i BC/i AD *RE* (1); *PIR*^{2} R 51 (king); (2) c. 40-93 AD *RE* (2); *PIR*^{2} I 512; *CIRB* [42]; [45]; 980; *SEG* XXVII [445]; XXXVIII 757?; Frolova, *CKB A.D. 69-238* pp. 14-17; Zgusta, *PNS* 568 (*Τιβ. Ἰούλ. Ῥ.*: s. *Τιβ. Ἰούλ. Κότυς*, *Εὐνίκη*, f. *Τιβ. Ἰούλ. Σαυρομάτης*: king); (3) c. 180-226 AD *RE* (3); *PIR*^{2} I 513; *CIRB* 897, 3; 953, 4; *SEG* XXXVI 701; XLV 1027 A; *Stud. Zhebelev* p. 47, 4; Frolova, *CKB A.D. 69-238* pp. 47-51 (*Τιβ. Ἰούλ. Ῥ.*: s. *Τιβ. Ἰούλ. Σαυρομάτης*, f. *Τιβ. Ἰούλ. Κότυς*: king); (4) c. 220-276 AD *RE* (5) + (6); *PIR*^{2} I 514; Frolova, *CKB A.D. 242-341/342* pp. 3-12; 27-9 (*Τιβ. Ἰούλ. Ῥ.*: king); (5) 233-234 AD *RE* (4); *PIR*^{2} R 62; *CIRB* 1285, 4?; Frolova, *CKB A.D. 69-238* p. 53 (*Τιβ. Ἰούλ. Ῥ.*: king); (6) c. 290-342 AD *RE* (7); *CIRB* 66; 1112, 2; Frolova, *CKB A.D. 242-341/342* pp. 58-80 (*Τιβ. Ἰούλ. Ῥ.*: king)
THRACE:
—BOSAGYRA: (7) iii AD *IGB* III 1829 (f. *Ἀπολλόδωρος*)
—MARKIANOPOLIS (TERRIT.): (8) iii AD ib. II 796, 1 (f. *Δίνις*)
—NICOPOLIS AD ISTRUM: (9) ii AD *ILB* 406 (Lat. Rescupori (gen.): f. Iustus)
—PHILIPPOPOLIS-TRIMONTIUM (TERRIT.): (10) ii-iii AD *IGB* III 1321 (*Ῥε-*: f. *Τάρσας*)
THRACE?: (11) imp. *CIL* X 3390, 3; cf. *AEp* 1990, no. 150 (name) (Lat. Cice[ro] [qui] [et] [R]escupo[ris]); (12) 196 AD *IMS* II 53 II B a, 95 (*CIL* III 14507) (Lat. Aur. Rescupor)

Ῥησκουτούρμη
THRACE:
—BEROE-AUGUSTA TRAIANA (TERRIT.): (1) iii AD *SEG* XLI 587 (*Αὐρ. Ῥησκοτύρμη*)
—PHILIPPOPOLIS-TRIMONTIUM (TERRIT.): (2) ii-iii AD *IGB* III 1198 (-τόρμη)
THRACE?: (3) imp. *CIL* III 1195 (Lat. Rescuturme)

Ῥησμάγας
KOLCHIS:
—ABASGOI: (1) ii AD Arr., *Peripl.* 11. 3; *PIR*^{2} R 64 (king)

Ῥῆσος
THRACE:
—BESSOI: (1) i AD *Nicholson Mus.*^{2} p. 436 no. 10 (Lat. C. Iulius Resus)

Ῥησπινδίαλος
SKYTHIA:
—OLBIA-BORYSTHENES: (1) ?ii-iii AD *IOSPE* I^2 107, 2; Zgusta, *PNS* 697a

Ῥητορική
MACEDONIA (MYGDONIA):
—THESSALONIKE: (1) ii-iii AD *IG* X (2) (1) 634 (m. *Γ. Κουσώνιος Τιτιανός*)

Ῥηχούναγος
SKYTHIA:
—OLBIA-BORYSTHENES: (1) ii AD *IOSPE* I^2 129, 9; Zgusta, *PNS* 698 (f. *Κουκούναγος*)

Ῥιανός
MACEDONIA (PIERIA):
—DION: (1) i-ii AD *Essays Laourdas* p. 104 (*Αἴ(λ). Ῥειανὸς Πρόκλος*: f. *Πρόκλος*)

Ῥινίας
TAURIS:
—CHERSONESOS: (1) f. iii BC *SEG* XL 615 A, 18; Zgusta, *PNS* 1142 (f. *Βάκις*)

Ῥίχνος
MACEDONIA (EDONIS):
—AMPHIPOLIS (NR.): (1) a. 357 BC Hatzopoulos, *Actes Amphipolis* p. 43 no. 8, 5 (*SEG* XLI 562) (f. *Δημόνικος*)

Ῥιψίμη
THRACE:
—APROI?: (1) iii AD Unp. (Sayar) (*Ῥη-*)

Ῥόδα
MACEDONIA (EDONIS):
—AMPHIPOLIS: (1) hell.? *AEMTh* 15 (2001) p. 114 (d. *Νικάνωρ*)
MACEDONIA (MYGDONIA):
—THESSALONIKE: (2) 147 AD *IG* X (2) (1) 608, 2 (*Κλ. Ῥ.*: d. *Τι. Κλ. Λύκος*, *Μινουκία Θεοπρεπίς*)
SARMATIA:
—SARMATAI: (3) 153-144 BC *BCH* 65-7 (1942-3) p. 74 no. 4, 8, 12 (slave/freed.)

Ῥοδανός
MACEDONIA (MYGDONIA):
—THESSALONIKE: (1) i AD *IG* X (2) (1) 242, 11 (s. *Χρυσέρως*)

Ῥόδη
MACEDONIA (BOTTIAIA):
—BEROIA: (1) ii AD *IBer* 224 (Tataki 1151)
—MIEZA: (2) f. iii BC *SEG* XLVII 914 (d. *Εὔδωρος*)
MACEDONIA (EDONIS):
—AMPHIPOLIS: (3) hell.-imp. Kaphtantzis 738 (?d. *Βῆλος*)
THRACE:
—BYZANTION: (4) i/ii AD *SEG* L 667 V (*Αἰλ. Ῥ.*)
—MARONEIA: (5) iii AD *IThrakAig* E396, 14 (d. *Αὐρ. Κρονίων*, ?d. *Διογένεια*, *Αὐρ. Εὐχάρεια*)
—ZONE: (6) f. iv BC *AA* 1918, col. 11 (*IThrakAig* E416) (d. *Μητρόδοτος*)

Ῥοδία
MACEDONIA (PAIONIA):
—KAVADARCI (MOD.): (1) i-ii AD Šašel, *IL* 4 (Lat. Secunda Rodia: d. Secundus, m. Secunda Iulia)
THRACE: (2) iii-ii BC *Polemon* 5 (1952-3) pp. 9-10 no. 325

Ῥοδιανός
MACEDONIA (MYGDONIA):
—KALINDOIA: (1) a. 98 AD *SEG* XLII 583, 12 (*Κήζεβις Ῥ.*)

Ῥόδινος
MACEDONIA (MYGDONIA):
—THESSALONIKE: (1) ii AD *IG* X (2) (1) 241 A II, 16 (*Κ. Ἀστρ[ίκ]ιος Ῥ.*)

Ῥόδιον
THRACE: (1) iii BC ib. II^2 8922 (*FRA* 2575)

Ῥόδιος
TAURIS:
—CHERSONESOS: (1) s. iv BC Solomonik, *GAKh* 1468 (vase)

Ῥοδογύνη
MACEDONIA (BOTTIAIA):
—BEROIA: (1) iii AD *IBer* 278 (Tataki 266) (*Αὐρ. Ῥ.*: m. *Κεστρωνιανὸς Καλογέννητος*)

Ῥοδόκλεια
THRACE:
—DIONYSOPOLIS: (1) iii-ii BC *IGB* I^2 27 (d. *Δημοχάρης*)

Ῥοδοκλῆς
Cimmerian Bosporos:
—pantikapaion: **(1)** i bc/i ad *CIRB* 312; cf. KW pl. 18 no. 263

Ῥοδόπη
Macedonia (Bottiaia):
—beroia: **(1)** iv ad *IBer* 442
—edessa: **(2)** iii ad Feissel, *RICM* 6, 1 (Tataki, *Edessa* 268) (m. Ἀγροίκιος, Πρίσκος, Ἀδέλφιος)
Scythia Minor:
—capidava: **(3)** ii ad *ISM* v 25, 7 (Lat. Iul. Rhodope: m. Iulius Valens, Iul. Vitalis)
Thrace:
—beroe-augusta traiana (territ.): **(4)** ii-iii ad *IGB* iii 1649 (Ῥοδόδη—lap.: d. Βίθυς)
—gorna bešovica (mod.): **(5)** iii ad ib. v 5180, 8
—serdica: **(6)** ii-iii ad ib. 5683 (d. Ἰούλιος)

Ῥοδοπιανός
Thrace:
—glava panega (mod.): **(1)** ii ad ib. ii 531 (Φλ. Ῥ.)

Ῥόδων
Cimmerian Bosporos:
—gorgippia: **(1)** ii ad *CIRB* 1143, 1 ([Ῥ]όδων: s. Ἀτακούας); **(2)** ii/iii ad ib. 1179, 50
—korokondame: **(3)** ii ad ib. 1107 (f. Δημόχαρις)
—pantikapaion: **(4)** i ad ib. 506 (s. Χρηστίων); **(5)** ~ ib. 507 (s. Τιμοκράτης); **(6)** f. i ad ib. 505; cf. KW pl. 27 no. 400 (s. Ἥλιος); **(7)** m. i ad *CIRB* 433 (f. Κόλων); **(8)** i/ii ad ib. 79 A, 1 (f. Λόγων); **(9)** 275-278 ad ib. 36, 39 (Ῥό[δ]ων: s. Λυσι(—))
—pantikapaion*: **(10)** 249 ad ib. 58, 6 (Αὐρ. Ῥ.: s. Λολλαῖος)
Macedonia: **(11)** 190 or 189 bc *PHeid* viii 417, 37 (La'da E1783) (s. Ἀγαθοκλῆς: t.e.)
Macedonia (Bottiaia):
—edessa: **(12)** s. ii bc *SEG* xxviii 678 (Tataki, *Edessa* 269; Tataki, *Macedonians* p. 104 no. 19) (f. Εὐπορία)
Skythia:
—tanais: **(13)** 188 ad *CIRB* 1242, 14 (f. Θαύμαστος) ?= *(14)*; **(14)** 188-192 ad ib. l. 7; 1243, 12 (s. Φαζίναμος) ?= *(13)*; **(15)** 193 ad ib. 1237, 11, 19; 1243, 14 (Ἰούλ. Ῥ.: s. Χαρίτων); **(16)** c. 200-220 ad ib. 1277, 21; 1278, 5 (f. Εὔιος); **(17)** 225-229 ad ib. 1280, 21; *Stud. Zhebelev* p. 47, 18 (s. Θαύμαστος); **(18)** 244 ad *CIRB* 1287, 13 (f. Αὐράζακος)

Ῥοδῶπις
Thrace: **(1)** vii/vi bc *RE* (-); cf. *PLF* p. 106 no. 202 (Δωρίχα ἤ καὶ Ῥ.: slave/het.); **(2)** iii ad Hld. ii 25. 1, 4 (fict.)

Ῥόθος
Thrace: **(1)** ?159 bc *SGDI* 1733, 2-3, 5 (slave/freed.)

Ῥοῖγος
Thrace:
—seuthopolis*: **(1)** f. iii bc Peter, *MTD* pp. 215-17 (coin) (Ῥοίγου (gen.))

Ῥοιμήζενις
Thrace:
—philippopolis-trimontium (territ.): **(1)** iii ad *IGB* iii 1293 (f. Κότυς)

Ῥοιμητάλκας
Thrace: **(1)** 46-54 ad *SEG* xvi 415 I, 10 (*IThrakAig* E84) (Τιβ. Κλ. Ῥ.: s. Βιθύκενθος); **(2)** ~ *SEG* xvi 415 I, 12 (*IThrakAig* E84) (Τιβ. Κλ. Ῥ.: s. Ἀπολλώνιος)
—sappaioi: **(3)** 31 bc-12 ad *RE* (1); *PIR*^{2} R 67; *IByz* 324, 2; *ISM* iii 44, 1; Youroukova pp. 54-9; pp. 90-7 nos. 158-93 (coin); cf. *PIR*^{2} P 531 (stemma) (?s. Κότυς, f. Κότυς: king); **(4)** c. 5-46 ad *RE* (3); *PIR*^{2} R 68; Youroukova pp. 63-5; p. 100 nos. 209-13 (coin) (s. Κότυς, Ἀντωνία Τρύφαινα: king); **(5)** 18-38 ad *RE* (2); *PIR*^{2} I 517 + R s.v. C. Iulius Rhoemetalces; *BCH* 56 (1932) p. 203; cf. Youroukova pp. 59-63; pp. 97-100 nos. 194-208 (coin) (Lat. C. Iulius Roeme[talce]s—*BCH*: s. Ῥασκούπορις: king)
Thrace?: **(6)** hell.? *Syringes* 292 (Velkov 231); **(7)** 324-337 ad *PLRE* i (-) (Lat. Val. Rometalca)

Ῥοιμητάλκης
Cimmerian Bosporos:
—bosporos: **(1)** c. 100-154 ad *RE* (4); *PIR*^{2} I 516; *CIRB* 1256, 2; *SEG* xlv 1017, 2; Frolova, *CKB A.D. 69-238* pp. 37-8 (Τιβ. Ἰούλ. Ῥ.: f. Τιβ. Ἰούλ. Σαυρομάτης: king)
Macedonia (Elimeia)?: **(2)** f. ii ad *EAM* 10 (Ῥυμε-: f. Ἀλέξανδρος ὁ καὶ Ῥῆγλος)
Macedonia (Lynkestis):
—ano vevi (mod.): **(3)** ii ad ib. 164 (Ῥυ-: f. Ἀντίπατρος)
Macedonia (Mygdonia):
—kalindoia: **(4)** 68-98 ad *SEG* xlii 580, 15; cf. *Anthémonte–Kalindoia* 2 p. 304 (name) (Ῥυ-: s. Δατείτας)
Thrace: **(5)** 46-54 ad *SEG* xvi 415 III, 32 (*IThrakAig* E84) (f. Μοκάπορις)
—abryttos (territ.): **(6)** iii ad *IGB* ii 750 (*CCET* ii (2) 550) (Αὐρ. Ῥ.: s. Μαρτιάλης)
—durostorum (territ.)?: **(7)** iii ad *IGB* ii 868, 4 (*CCET* ii (1) 186) (Ῥυ-: s. Δούδης)
—dyme (mod.): **(8)** i ad *AD* 26 (1971) Chron. pl. 422 γ (*Belomorski Pregled* 1 (1941) p. 335 no. 40; *IThrakAig* E387); cf. Bakalakis, *Oinos Ismarikos* p. 1015 (s. Διάσενις)
—markianopolis: **(9)** iii ad *BMNVarna* 23 (1987) p. 72 (stamp) (Ῥυμε-)
—markianopolis?: **(10)** ii-iii ad *IGB* v 5394 (or Thrace Pautalia?: f. Ἀπολλώνιος)
—pautalia (territ.): **(11)** ii-iii ad ib. 5830 ([Ῥοιμ]ητάλκης?)
—philippopolis-trimontium: **(12)** ?i-ii ad ib. iii 933 (Ῥοιμητάλ[κης]); **(13)** ii-iii ad ib. 1039 (f. Μ. Αὐρ. —ης); **(14)** m. iii ad ib. 884 b, 20; cf. v 5400 (Αὐρ. Ῥ.)
—philippopolis-trimontium (territ.): **(15)** ii ad ib. iii 1132 (Ῥυμετάλκης ὁ καὶ Ὀλύμπιος: s. Κλ. Σπάρτοκος); **(16)** iii ad ib. 1318 (Αὐρ. Ῥυμετάλκης: s. Βάσσος)
—slavjanovo (mod.): **(17)** ii ad ib. v 5276 (Π. Αἰλ. Ῥοιμητά[λκης])
—stratopara: **(18)** 202 ad ib. iii 1690 b, 37 (and Thrace Pizos: Ῥυ-: f. Μουκάτραλις)

Ῥοιμηώτης
Thrace: **(1)** 245 bc *PHib* 33, 4, 12 (Velkov 232; La'da E791)

Ῥοίμισος
Macedonia (Bottiaia):
—pella: **(1)** iii bc Akamatis, *Amph. Pellas* p. 44 no. PAR62 (amph.)

Ῥοῖμος
Macedonia (Mygdonia):
—kalindoia: **(1)** a. 98 ad *SEG* xlii 582, 41; cf. *Anthémonte–Kalindoia* 2 pp. 303-4 (name) (f. Ἀρχέλαος)
Thrace:
—pautalia (territ.): **(2)** ii-iii ad *IGB* iv 2112, 1 (s. Τάρσας)
—serdica (territ.): **(3)** ii-iii ad ib. 2015 b (*Eastern cults* p. 167 no. 10) (f. Τάρσας)

Ῥομανός
Thrace:
—pautalia: **(1)** s. ii ad *SEG* xlvi 864 II, 22

Ῥόνοικος
Scythia Minor:
—kallatis: **(1)** 241-244 ad *ISM* iii 74 B, 28 (s. Διόδωρος)

Ῥοσηζις
Thrace?: **(1)** 316-309 bc *IG* ii^2 1956, 23; *Ancient Macedonia* 5 p. 445 with n. 10 (date) (*FRA* 2576)

Ῥοτίλιος
Macedonia (Derriopos):
—stuberra: **(1)** 74 ad *IG* x (2) (2) 325, 44 (-τεί-: s. Ἀρριδαῖος)

Ῥουμανός
Thrace:
—perinthos-herakleia:
——(φυλ. ἐνατ.): **(1)** iv-v ad *IPerinth* 187 (*AD* 51-2 (1996-7) Mel. p. 354 no. 178) (Φλ. Ῥ.)

Ῥούπιος
Macedonia (Mygdonia):
—thessalonike: **(1)** ?v-vi ad ib. 4 (1918) Parart. p. 31

Ῥουστικός
Thrace:
—bazopara: **(1)** 202 ad *IGB* iii 1690 d, 46 (and Thrace Pizos: s. Βίθυς)
—draganovec (mod.): **(2)** ii-iii ad ib. v 5288 (I f. Ῥουστικός II); **(3)** ~ ib. (II s. Ῥουστικός I)

Ῥουστῖνος
Thrace:
—beroe-augusta traiana (territ.): **(1)** iii ad ib. iii 1756, 7 (f. Μ. Αὐρ. Βιβιανός, Μ. Αὐρ. Μουκιανός)

Ῥουφᾶς
Thrace:
—pizos: **(1)** 202 ad ib. 1690 e, 19 (s. Στ—ος)

Ῥουφῖνα
Scythia Minor:
—tomis: **(1)** ii ad *ISM* ii 186 (-φεῖ-: d. Ἰάσων, ?m. Θεόκριτος)
Thrace:
—perinthos-herakleia: **(2)** ii ad *IPerinth* 100 (-φεῖ-: d. Πρόκλα)

Ῥουφῖνος
Kolchis:
—lazoi: **(1)** 539-540 ad *PLRE* iii (2); *RE* (35) (s. Ζαύνας)
Macedonia (Paionia):
—stoboi: **(2)** iv-v ad Feissel, *RICM* 279 (mosaic)
Skythia:
—olbia-borysthenes: **(3)** 198-211 ad *IOSPE* i^2 174, 11 (Ῥουφεῖ[νος]: s. Φιλάδελφος)
Tauris:
—chersonesos: **(4)** iii ad Solomonik, *NEPKh* 19, 2 (Ῥουφῖ[νος]: f. Ἡρακλείδης)
Thrace: **(5)** 533-534 ad *PLRE* iii (1); *RE* (34)
—beroe-augusta traiana: **(6)** c. 320-324 ad *Anal. Boll.* 31 (1912) p. 201
—kellai: **(7)** 241-244 ad *IGB* iii 1517, 52 (f. Αὐρ. Τάτης)

Ῥουφίων
Macedonia (Bottiaia):
—beroia?: **(1)** 38 bc Robert, *Coll. Froehner* 44, 20 (*IG* xii Suppl. p. 149); cf. Tataki, *Macedonians* p. 82 no. 48 (s. Λέων)

Ῥοῦφος
Cimmerian Bosporos:
—pantikapaion: **(1)** 82 ad *CIRB* 76, 24 (*SEG* xviii 310) (s. Ἔρως)
—theodosia: **(2)** iii ad *CIRB* 947 A, 2 (I f. Ῥοῦφος II); **(3)** ~ ib. l. 2 (II s. Ῥοῦφος I)
Macedonia (Bottiaia):
—beroia: **(4)** ii/iii ad *IBer* 27 B, 7 (slave?)

MACEDONIA (DERRIOPOS):
—STUBERRA: **(5)** c. 41-48 AD *IG* X (2) (2) 323, 11 (s. *Ἀπολλόδωρος*); **(6)** 74 AD ib. 326, 55 (f. *Ἡρακλέων*); **(7)** 87 AD ib. 325, 78 (f. *Μᾶρκος*)
MACEDONIA (EDONIS):
—PHILIPPOI: **(8)** f. ii AD Eus., *HE* iii 36. 13; cf. *RE* s.v. Polykarpos (1) col. 1682
—PHILIPPOI (TERRIT.): **(9)** ii-iii AD *BCH* 24 (1900) p. 317 (Pilhofer 535); cf. Collart, *Philippes* pl. 37. 3 (s. *Ζιπᾶς*)
MACEDONIA (LOWER PAIONIA):
—EUROPOS: **(10)** 205 AD *SEG* XXXVIII 615 = XLV 760 (?s. *Ἰουβέντιος Ἐ—*, *Ἰουβεντία —α*)
MACEDONIA (MYGDONIA):
—THESSALONIKE: **(11)** 141 AD *IG* X (2) (1) 137, 11; cf. *BCH* 97 (1973) p. 587 (II s. *Ῥοῦφος* I); **(12)** ~ *IG* X (2) (1) 137, 12; cf. *BCH* 97 (1973) p. 587 ([*Ῥοῦ*]*φος*: I f. *Ῥοῦφος* II)
SCYTHIA MINOR:
—ISTROS: **(13)** ii AD *ISM* I 196, 5 (s. *Φοῖβος*); **(14)** 138 AD ib. 193 I, 98 (s. *Ἀνδρόνικος*); **(15)** 222-225 AD ib. 100 A, 22
—KALLATIS: **(16)** ii-iii AD ib. III 90, 4
—KALLATIS (NR.): **(17)** ii AD ib. 239 (I f. *Ῥοῦφος* II); **(18)** ~ ib. (II s. *Ῥοῦφος* I)
—TOMIS: **(19)** i-ii AD ib. II 150, 4 (f. *Μᾶρκος*); **(20)** ii AD ib. 17, 1 (f. *Ἀντίγονος*); **(21)** ii-iii AD ib. 31 II, 15 (f. *Θεόδωρος*); **(22)** ~ ib. 292 (*Eastern cults* p. 227 no. 13) (s. *Πρίσκος*)
SKYTHIA:
—KRASNY MAIAK (MOD.)*: **(23)** i-ii AD *SEG* XXXI 699 (terracotta)
TAURIS:
—CHERSONESOS: **(24)** i-ii AD *IOSPE* I² 606 ([*Ῥο*]*ῦφος*?); **(25)** ii AD ib. 395 ([*Ῥ*]*οῦφος*); **(26)** c. 120-130 AD Solomonik, *NEPKh* 112, 20 (I f. *Ῥοῦφος* II); **(27)** ~ ib. l. 20 (II s. *Ῥοῦφος* I)
THRACE:
—ABDERA: **(28)** ii AD *BCH* 37 (1913) p. 138 no. 42, 5 (*IThrakAig* E21) (s. *Οὐάλης*)
—BYZANTION: **(29)** ii BC *IByz* 167 (Fıratlı–Robert pp. 108-9 no. 174) (*-πος*: f. *Φιλουμένη*); **(30)** i BC-i AD *IByz* 276 (Fıratlı–Robert pp. 64-5 no. 57) (f. *Φιλήτα*)
—BYZANTION (TERRIT.): **(31)** imp. Unp. (Sayar) (s. *Ἀπολλωνίδης*)
—BYZANTION:
——(Bathonea): **(32)** i-ii AD *IByz* 315 c-d (Fıratlı–Robert pp. 122-3 no. 205) (I s. *Στράτων*, f. *Ῥοῦφος* II, *Δαμᾶς*); **(33)** ~ *IByz* 315 d (II s. *Ῥοῦφος* I)
——(Philokterea): **(34)** i-ii AD ib. 319 a (Fıratlı–Robert p. 123 no. 206) (s. *Ἀπολλώνιος*); **(35)** 85-96 AD *IByz* 30, 9 (s. *Διόδωρος*)
—HADRIANOPOLIS: **(36)** ?iii AD Taşlıklıoğlu 2 p. 35 no. 5
—MARKIANOPOLIS: **(37)** iii AD *IGB* II 808 (*CCET* II (1) 202)
—MARONEIA (TERRIT.): **(38)** iii AD Bakalakis, *Oinos Ismarikos* p. 555 (*IThrakAig* E379) (f. *Βένδιον*)
—ODESSOS: **(39)** i-ii AD *IGB* I² 140 bis, 1 (f. *Διονύσιος*)
—ODESSOS?: **(40)** i-ii AD ib. 112, 5 (f. *Χρύσιν*)
—PERINTHOS-HERAKLEIA: **(41)** ii AD *RE* s.v. Rufus (16); *PIR*² R 203
—PHILIPPOPOLIS-TRIMONTIUM: **(42)** ?s. ii AD *IGB* III 915 (I f. *Λ. Αὐρ. Ῥοῦφος* II)
—PHILIPPOPOLIS-TRIMONTIUM (TERRIT.): **(43)** i-ii AD ib. 1196 (s. *Εἰδιανός*, f. *Παυλῖνα*); **(44)** ii AD ib. 1399

Ῥυμησυκις
THRACE:
—BOURDAPA: **(1)** i-ii AD ib. 1350 (d. *Βίθυς*)

Ῥύμυσος?
MACEDONIA (EDONIS):
—AMPHIPOLIS (TERRIT.)?: **(1)** 82 AD Pikoulas, *Chora* p. 169 no. 80 (or Macedonia (Pieris) Phagres: *Ῥυμύσου* (gen.): f. *Μάντα*)

Ῥυνδακίων
SCYTHIA MINOR:
—DINOGETIA (NR.): **(1)** m. ii AD *ISM* V 296, 6 (Lat. L. Iul. Iulianus qui et Rundacio)

Ῥύνδαξ
SKYTHIA:
—OLBIA-BORYSTHENES (BEREZAN (MOD.)): **(1)** s. vi BC *SEG* XLIV 653 (vase) (*Ῥύνδα*[*ξ*])
SKYTHIA?: **(2)** s. vi BC ib. (*Ῥύν*[*δαξ*]?)

Ῥωδίγασος
SKYTHIA:
—TANAIS: **(1)** 225 AD *CIRB* 1279, 27 (s. *Σύμφορος*)

Ῥώλης
THRACE:
—DIONYSOPOLIS: **(1)** iii AD *IGB* I² 14 c, 15 (*Ῥώλη* (gen.): f. *Αὐρ. Μερκούριος*)
—GETAI: **(2)** 29 BC *RE* (-) (king)

Ῥωμανά
SCYTHIA MINOR:
—TOMIS: **(1)** v-vi AD Barnea 18, 12 (Popescu, *IGL* 37) (d. *Ἰωάννης*, *Κωνσταντία*)

Ῥωμανός
SCYTHIA MINOR:
—ISTROS: **(1)** ii AD *ISM* I 197 I, 8 (f. *Κησέρνιος*)
THRACE:
—MARONEIA: **(2)** v-vi AD *SEG* XLIX 892, 7 (*IThrakAig* E357)
—PHILIPPOPOLIS-TRIMONTIUM: **(3)** iii AD *IGB* III 925

Ῥώμη
CIMMERIAN BOSPOROS:
—PANTIKAPAION: **(1)** imp. *CIRB* 803
—PHANAGOREIA: **(2)** i AD ib. 998 (*Ῥώμηι* (nom.))
MACEDONIA (BOTTIAIA):
—EDESSA*: **(3)** 168 AD *SEG* XII 345 (Tataki, *Edessa* 127) (*Ἰουλ. Ῥ.*: freed.)
MACEDONIA (PIERIA):
—DION: **(4)** ?iii AD Oikonomos 44; *Klio* 52 (1970) p. 53 no. 4; cf. *SEG* XLIV 526 (m. *Θερίνη*)

Ῥῶμις
MACEDONIA (CHALKIDIKE):
—POTIDAIA-KASSANDREIA?: **(1)** c. 500-475 BC Marcadé I 29 + *LSAG*² p. 369 no. 10 + *SEG* XXX 496 (ident.) (or Phokis?: *Ῥō̄μις*—Johnston, *Δόμις*—Marcadé: sculptor)

Ῥωμίων
THRACE:
—BYZANTION (TERRIT.): **(1)** imp. Unp. (Sayar)

Ῥωμύλος
MACEDONIA (ORESTIS):
—NESTORION (MOD.): **(1)** v-vi AD *SEG* XXXVII 475 (*EAM* 203)

Ῥώμων
THRACE:
—BYZANTION (TERRIT.): **(1)** imp. Unp. (Sayar) (f. *Ἡρόξενος*)

Ῥωνάκης
THRACE:
—MAIDOI: **(1)** her.? Ath. 184 a

Ῥωξάνη
CIMMERIAN BOSPOROS:
—PANTIKAPAION: **(1)** i AD *CIRB* 507 (*Ῥο-*)

Σ

Σαβάδας
CIMMERIAN BOSPOROS:
—TYRITAKE: **(1)** i AD *CIRB* 906 (f. *Νικηφόρος*)

Σαβάρα
MACEDONIA (MYGDONIA):
—THESSALONIKE: **(1)** ii-iii AD *IG* X (2) (1) 382 (*Κοϊντία Λικετία Σ.*: d. *Κορνήλιος Κ. Φαρνάκιος*)

Σαββαΐς
THRACE:
—ABDERA: **(1)** iv AD *IThrakAig* E19 (*Σαβ*(*β*)*αΐς*)

Σαββατάρας
MACEDONIA (LOWER PAIONIA):
—EUROPOS: **(1)** ?315-300 BC *FD* III (4) 405, 3 (Tataki, *Macedonians* p. 109 no. 13) (f. *Μαχάτας*)

Σαββάτιος
THRACE:
—PERINTHOS-HERAKLEIA*: **(1)** v-vi AD *IPerinth* 236 (*AD* 51-2 (1996-7) Mel. p. 378 no. 193)

Σαββατίς
MACEDONIA (MYGDONIA):
—THESSALONIKE?: **(1)** v-vi AD *IG* X (2) (1) 785 (Feissel, *RICM* 168) (m. *Γλυκερία*)

Σαββίων
CIMMERIAN BOSPOROS:
—PANTIKAPAION: **(1)** imp. *CIRB* 107; Zgusta, *PNS* 740; 758 (*Σαβ*[*βί*]*ων*); **(2)** i AD *CIRB* 408; cf. KW pl. 49 no. 680 (f. *Αἰσχίνης*, *Ἀρχίας*); **(3)** ii AD *CIRB* 146, 1, 10 (*GVI* 1468); cf. KW p. 92 fig. 12 (s. *Στέφανος*); **(4)** ~ *CIRB* 704; cf. KW pl. 25 no. 371 (*Σαββί*[*ω*]*ν*)

Σαβιδιανός
MACEDONIA (BOTTIAIA):
—EDESSA: **(1)** 180 AD *SEG* XXIV 531, 4 (Tataki, *Edessa* 272) (f. *Λυσίμαχος*)

Σαβίθη?
SCYTHIA MINOR:
—TOMIS: **(1)** imp. *ISM* II 314 (*Σαβείθ*[*η*]?)

Σάβιν
CIMMERIAN BOSPOROS:
—PANTIKAPAION*: **(1)** i AD *CIRB* 407; Zgusta, *PNS* 740 (*-βειν*)

Σαβῖνα
MACEDONIA (BOTTIAIA):
—BEROIA: **(1)** vi AD *IBer* 428 (-βή-)
—EDESSA: **(2)** ii-iii AD *SEG* XII 344 (Tataki, *Edessa* 271) (-βεῖ-: d. *Γ. Πεδουκαῖος Τριακαδίων, Ἀττία Παραμόνα*)
MACEDONIA (CHALKIDIKE):
—POTIDAIA-KASSANDREIA (NR.): **(3)** ?ii AD *SEG* XLV 773 (-βεῖ-: m. *Οὐαλερία*)
MACEDONIA (LOWER PAIONIA):
—EUROPOS: **(4)** 205 AD ib. XXXVIII 615 = XLV 760 (?d. *Ἰουβέντιος Ἐ—, Ἰουβεντία —α*)
MACEDONIA (MYGDONIA):
—THESSALONIKE: **(5)** i AD ib. XLVII 991 = XLVIII 860; **(6)** f. iii AD ib. 854 (-βεῖ-: d. *Εὐτύχης, Ἀλεξάνδρα*)
—THESSALONIKE?: **(7)** ii-iii AD *IG* X (2) (1) 921 (*Σ[αβ]εῖνα?*)
SCYTHIA MINOR:
—KALLATIS (NR.): **(8)** ii-iii AD *ISM* III 243, 3 (*IGB* I² 2) (*Σα[β]εῖνα*: d. *Πῖος*, m. *Λούκιλλα, Βασία, Προκελλῖνα, Ἀκύλας, Βικτωρῖνος*)
—TOMIS: **(9)** ?v AD Barnea 33 (Popescu, *IGL* 35)
THRACE:
—BEROE-AUGUSTA TRAIANA: **(10)** i-ii AD *IGB* III 1609 (*GVI* 91) (-βεῖ-); **(11)** vi AD Beševliev 194 (*Σαβίν[η]*)
—BEROE-AUGUSTA TRAIANA (TERRIT.): **(12)** ii AD *IGB* V 5590 (-βεῖ-); **(13)** ~ *SEG* XLI 588 (-βεῖ-)
—BEROE-AUGUSTA TRAIANA:
——Karasoura: **(14)** ii-iii AD *IGB* III 1633 (*GVI* 280) (-βεῖ-)
—MARONEIA: **(15)** iii AD *IThrakAig* E396, 14 (*Σαβ(ί)να*: d. *Αὐρ. Κρονίων*, ?d. *Διογένεια, Αὐρ. Εὐχάρεια*)
—PERINTHOS-HERAKLEIA: **(16)** imp. *IPerinth* 47 (-βεῖ-)

Σαβινιανός
SCYTHIA MINOR:
—ISTROS: **(1)** ii AD *ISM* I 135; 136 (-βει-)
THRACE:
—NOVAE: **(2)** iii AD *IGB* II 741, 10 (f. *Δρακόντις, Νουνέχις, Πάκουρος, Ἑρμιόνη, Μαμάτα*)

Σαβῖνος
MACEDONIA (MYGDONIA):
—THESSALONIKE: **(1)** 209 AD *IG* X (2) (1) 506, 5 (-βεῖ-: f. *Ἰσίδωρος*); **(2)** m. iii AD ib. 64 (-βεῖ-)
MACEDONIA (PAIONIA):
—STOBOI: **(3)** s. iii AD *JÖAI* 32 (1940) Beibl. col. 16 no. 3. 7 (*Γ.? Σαβεῖνος*: ?f. *Ἐπιθύμητος*)
MACEDONIA (PIERIA):
—DION: **(4)** ii/iii AD Spiliopoulou-Donderer, *KGN* pp. 197-8 no. D15 (-βεῖ-)
MACEDONIA (SINTIKE):
—NEINE: **(5)** ii-iii AD *IGB* V 5888 (-βεῖ-)
SKYTHIA:
—OLBIA-BORYSTHENES: **(6)** i/ii AD *IOlbia* 79, 8 (*IOSPE* I² 116) (-βεῖ-: s. *Ἀπολλοῦς*)
TAURIS:
—CHERSONESOS: **(7)** f. ii AD Solomonik, *NEPKh* III, 11 (-βεῖ-: f. *Αἰμιλιανός*)
THRACE: **(8)** imp. *IGB* III 1882 (*Σαβε[ῖνος]*: f. *Καπίτων*)
—BEROE-AUGUSTA TRAIANA: **(9)** ii-iii AD ib. 1583 (-βεῖ-: s. *Χρῆστος*)
——Emporion Diskodouraterai: **(10)** iii AD ib. II 737, 8 (-βεῖ-: s. *Αὐρ. Δίνδας*)
—BYZANTION: **(11)** c. 303 AD *Anal. Boll.* 31 (1912) p. 192
—DRAGANOVEC (MOD.): **(12)** f. iii AD *IGB* V 5302 (*CCET* II (2) 479) (-βεῖ-)
—GLAVA PANEGA (MOD.): **(13)** ii-iii AD *IGB* II 537 (-βεῖ-: f. *Καπίτων*)
—KRASALOPARA: **(14)** 202 AD ib. III 1690 b, 67 (and Thrace Pizos: -βεῖ-: I f. *Σαβῖνος* II); **(15)** ~ ib. l. 67 (and Thrace Pizos: -βεῖ-: II s. *Σαβῖνος* I)
—NICOPOLIS AD ISTRUM: **(16)** ii-iii AD ib. II 686, 3 (*[Σ]αβεῖνος*)
—ODESSOS (NR.): **(17)** ii-iii AD ib. I² 263
—PAUTALIA: **(18)** ii-iii AD ib. IV 2072, 7 (s. *Ἑρμογένης*)
—PHILIPPOPOLIS-TRIMONTIUM: **(19)** ii AD ib. III 1020, 3 (*GVI* 2088) (-βε̣ί̣-)
—SERDICA: **(20)** iii AD *IGB* IV 1906 (-βεῖ-: I f. *Αὐρ. Σαβῖνος* II *ὁ καὶ Μητρόδωρος*); **(21)** ~ ib. (*Αὐρ. Σαβεῖνος ὁ καὶ Μητρόδωρος*: II s. *Σαβῖνος* I)

Σαβίων
CIMMERIAN BOSPOROS:
—PANTIKAPAION: **(1)** i BC/i AD *CIRB* 316 (s. *Στέφανος*); **(2)** ~ ib. 416; cf. KW pl. 52 no. 714; Zgusta, *PNS* 740; **(3)** i AD *CIRB* 509; cf. KW pl. 27 no. 404 (f. *Ἀπολλωνίδης, Παιρίσαλος*)

Σαβύθη
MACEDONIA (PIERIA):
—DION: **(1)** hell. *SEG* L 589 (d. *Θεόξενος*)

Σαβύττιος
MACEDONIA (ELIMEIA):
—XEROLIMNI (MOD.): **(1)** ii BC *Α΄ Panell. Synedr. Epigr.* p. 61 no. 7 (*SEG* XLIX 846) (f. *Ἀμύντας*)

Σαβώδακος
SKYTHIA:
—TANAIS: **(1)** 228 AD *CIRB* 1282, 17 (s. *Ψυχαρίων*)

Σάγαρις
CIMMERIAN BOSPOROS:
—PANTIKAPAION: **(1)** iv BC ib. 215; cf. KW pl. 3 no. 71; Zgusta, *PNS* 741 (f. *Ὀλγασυς*)
SCYTHIA MINOR:
—ISTROS: **(2)** iv BC Unp. (Avram, defixio) 1, 5 (*Σάγ[αρ]ις*)
SKYTHIA:
—OLBIA-BORYSTHENES: **(3)** v/iv BC Vinogradov, *Pont. Stud.* pp. 157-8 no. 11 (vase)

Σαγγάριος
MACEDONIA (EDONIS):
—AMPHIPOLIS (TERRIT.): **(1)** iv BC *SEG* I 291

Σαγόδας
CIMMERIAN BOSPOROS:
—KYTAIA (NR.): **(1)** ii AD *CIRB* 945 (s. *Ἰβάδα*)

Σαδαῖος
SKYTHIA:
—OLBIA-BORYSTHENES: **(1)** s. ii AD *IOlbia* 81, 8 (*IOSPE* I² 94); Zgusta, *PNS* 324 (f. *Ἱστιαῖος*)

Σαδάλας
CIMMERIAN BOSPOROS:
—PANTIKAPAION: **(1)** i BC *CIRB* 295; cf. KW pl. 22 no. 312; Zgusta, *PNS* 570 (f. *Ψυχάριον*); **(2)** imp. *CIRB* 804 (I f. *Σαδάλας* II); **(3)** ~ ib. (II s. *Σαδάλας* I); **(4)** i BC/i AD ib. 317; cf. KW pl. 40 no. 584 (I f. *Σαδάλας* II); **(5)** ~ *CIRB* 317; cf. KW pl. 40 no. 584 (II s. *Σαδάλας* I); **(6)** i AD *CIRB* 451 (s. *Λύγγιον*); **(7)** ?i AD ib. 454
MACEDONIA (BOTTIAIA):
—BEROIA: **(8)** f. iii BC *IBer* 149 (Tataki 1158) (s. *Νίκανδρος*, f. *Στράτων*)
THRACE: **(9)** c. 281-277 BC *IGB* I² 307, 2, 17, 19; cf. V 5086 (king?) ?= (*20*); **(10)** ii BC *SEG* XLI 1635, 3; cf. La'da E766 (f. *Λεόννατος*); **(11)** 160 BC *BGU* 2390, 39 (La'da E792); **(12)** c. 125 BC *SNG BM Black Sea* 309 (coin); **(13)** 87-75 BC *REG* 32 (1919) pp. 321-2, 26; *SEG* XXXIV 701?; Cic., *In Verr.* II i. 63; cf. *IGB* I² 43 comm. (f. *Κότυς*: king); **(14)** 48-42 BC ib. 43, 5; Dumont–Homolle 62a; D.C. xli 51. 3; xlvii 21. 5; Caes., *BC* iii 4. 3; Youroukova pp. 40-5; p. 89 nos. 149-51 (coin) (s. *Κότυς*, f. *Κότυς*: king); **(15)** 31 BC Plu., *Ant.* 61 (king); **(16)** imp. *IG* II² 8900 (*FRA* 2577) (*Σαδά[λας]*: f. *Ἀφροδισία*); **(17)** 12-19 AD *IGB* V 5011, 7 (s. *Μοκάπορις*)
—KABYLE: **(18)** iii-ii BC ib. 5638 bis (amph.) (s. *Τήρης*)
—PHILIPPOPOLIS-TRIMONTIUM (TERRIT.): **(19)** iii AD ib. III 1090
—SEUTHOPOLIS: **(20)** c. 300-280 BC *SEG* XLII 661, 9 (s. *Σεύθης, Βερενίκη*) ?= (*9*)
THRACE?: **(21)** hell. ib. XVI 864. 19 (s. *Κότυς*); **(22)** 360 AD ib. VII 1170 (-λλας: s. *Σαρέδαθος*)

Σαδίμανος
SKYTHIA:
—OLBIA-BORYSTHENES: **(1)** ii-iii AD *IOSPE* I² 136, 9; Zgusta, *PNS* 196 (s. *Σαμβατίων*)

Σάδοκος
MACEDONIA (BOTTIAIA):
—PELLA: **(1)** iii-ii BC Dimitsas 135

Σάθης
THRACE:
—GELOUPARA: **(1)** 202 AD *IGB* III 1690 c, 24 (and Thrace Pizos: *Σαθήους* (gen.): f. *Μουκάτραλις*)

Σάθων
MACEDONIA (MYGDONIA):
—APOLLONIA: **(1)** iv BC Arr., *An.* i 12. 7 (Tataki, *Macedonians* p. 67 no. 8) (f. *Σωκράτης*)
MACEDONIA (PIERIA):
—DION: **(2)** iv BC *SEG* XXXVI 610 (*Σ̣άθων*: f. *Ἰφικράτης*)

Σαῖγος
MACEDONIA (SINTIKE):
—PARTHIKOPOLIS (TERRIT.): **(1)** ?242 AD *IGB* IV 2322 (f. *Πυρούσαλα*)

Σαιδείλας
MACEDONIA (EDONIS):
—AMPHIPOLIS (TERRIT.)?: **(1)** 121 AD *BCH* 24 (1900) p. 309 (Pilhofer 585) (s. *Διοσκουρίδης*)

Σαικέλης
THRACE:
—SERDICA (TERRIT.): **(1)** ii-iii AD *Sp.* 98 (1941-48) p. 127 no. 280, 6 (*Σαικελήους* (gen.): s. *Αὐλούπορις*)

Σαικίθης
THRACE:
—APRILOVO (MOD.): **(1)** f. iii AD *IGB* II 765 (*CCET* II (2) 539); cf. *IGB* V 5277 (s. *Ζούρης*)

Σαίνη
SCYTHIA MINOR:
—ISTROS: **(1)** iv/iii BC *ISM* I 242

Σαῖος
CIMMERIAN BOSPOROS:
—PANTIKAPAION: **(1)** f. ii AD *CIRB* 88, 1; Zgusta, *PNS* 766

Σαιταφάρνης
SKYTHIA:
—SAIOI: **(1)** iii BC *IOSPE* I² 32 A, 10, 84 (Maier, *Mauerbauinschr.* 82); Zgusta, *PNS* 197 (king)

Σαΐτυλος
SKYTHIA:
—OLBIA-BORYSTHENES: **(1)** v BC Vinogradov, *Pont. Stud.* p. 155 no. 4 bis (vase) + *Hyperboreus* 2000, pp. 131 ff.

Σάκας
CIMMERIAN BOSPOROS:
—KYTAIA: **(1)** iv BC *SEG* XL 629. 3 (sherd)

Σάκδεος
SKYTHIA:
—TANAIS: (**1**) 228 AD *CIRB* 1282, 19; Zgusta, *PNS* 325 (*Σακδέου* (gen.): f. *Σαμβατίων*)

Σάκερ
THRACE:
—BEROE-AUGUSTA TRAIANA (TERRIT.): (**1**) ii-iii AD *IGB* III 1793; cf. V 5641 (s. *—υτος*)

Σακλῆς
CIMMERIAN BOSPOROS:
—PANTIKAPAION: (**1**) 275-278 AD *CIRB* 36, 16 (*Σάκλεως* (gen.): f. *Φάννης*)
—PHANAGOREIA: (**2**) 179 AD ib. 1000, 2 (s. *Ὀρτυκᾶς*, f. *Ἀγαθοῦς*)

Σάκτας
CIMMERIAN BOSPOROS:
—MISOVKA (MOD.): (**1**) iii AD *Sov. Arkh.* 25 (1956) p. 255 with fig. 11, 1 (vase) (Kruglikova, *Bospor* p. 53 with fig. 11)
—PANTIKAPAION: (**2**) imp. *CIRB* 764; cf. *St. Clas.* 8 (1966) p. 338 (*Σάκτα* (voc.)—*CIRB*, *Σά(ν)κτα*—Russu: s. *Ματρόδωρος*, f. *Ψύχη*)

Σαλάζων
THRACE:
—PHILIPPOPOLIS-TRIMONTIUM (TERRIT.): (**1**) ii-iii AD *IGB* III 1460 (*Τι. Κλ. Σ.*, *Σαλα ζῶν*—ed. pr.)

Σάλας
CIMMERIAN BOSPOROS:
—PANTIKAPAION: (**1**) 243 AD *CIRB* 35; Zgusta, *PNS* 571 (f. *Χρηστίων*)
MACEDONIA (EDONIS):
—PHILIPPOI (TERRIT.): (**2**) ii-iii AD Pikoulas, *Chora* p. 127 no. 22 (Pilhofer 623)
SKYTHIA:
—TANAIS: (**3**) 228 AD *CIRB* 1283, 12 (f. *Μάης*)
THRACE:
—BAZOPARA: (**4**) 202 AD *IGB* III 1690 d, 18 (and Thrace Pizos: f. *Διόσπορις*); (**5**) ~ ib. l. 26 (and Thrace Pizos: f. *Κέλσος*); (**6**) ~ ib. l. 47 (and Thrace Pizos: s. *Δόλης*); (**7**) ~ ib. l. 59 (and Thrace Pizos: s. *Μουκάπορις*); (**8**) ~ ib. 1690 c, 49 (and Thrace Pizos: f. *Δυτούτραλις*); (**9**) ~ ib. l. 55 (and Thrace Pizos: f. *Μουκάτραλις*); (**10**) ~ ib. l. 59 (and Thrace Pizos: s. *—εροδένθης*); (**11**) ~ ib. l. 60 (and Thrace Pizos: s. *Κέλσος*)
—BEROE-AUGUSTA TRAIANA (TERRIT.): (**12**) i BC-i AD ib. 1657; (**13**) ii-iii AD ib. 1746 (f. *Μουκιανός*)
—BESSOPARA: (**14**) iii AD ib. 947, 11 (f. *Δίζας*)
—BOURDAPA: (**15**) ii-iii AD ib. 1349 (f. *Μηφάζουλα*)
—HADRIANOPOLIS (TERRIT.): (**16**) imp. ib. 1812 (s. *Μάρων*)
—KELLAI*: (**17**) iii AD ib. 1516 b, 16 (s. *Μουκάτραλις*, f. *Βρίζενις*, *Τάρσας*, *Γύζη*, *Βλώστα*)
—PHILIPPOPOLIS-TRIMONTIUM (TERRIT.): (**18**) ii-iii AD ib. 1439 (f. *—τραλις*, ?f. *Βίθυς*); (**19**) ~ ib. 1441 ([*Σάλ*]*ας*?: s. *Βίθυς*)
—SERDICA: (**20**) ii-iii AD ib. IV 1963, 2, 7 (*GVI* 386) (f. *Δέξτερ*)
—STRATOPARA: (**21**) 202 AD *IGB* III 1690 b, 33 (and Thrace Pizos: s. *Μουκάτραλις*)

Σαλβία
THRACE:
—AINOS: (**1**) imp. *Thrakika* 2 (1929) p. 63 (d. *Χαρίσιος*)

Σαλβιδηνός
THRACE:
—PAUTALIA: (**1**) ii-iii AD *IGB* IV 2088 (*GVI* 210)

Σάλλας
THRACE:
—ROGOZEN (MOD.): (**1**) iv BC *Rogozen Treasure* p. 48 no. 26

Σάλλιος
SKYTHIA:
—OLBIA-BORYSTHENES: (**1**) i-ii AD *IOSPE* I² 155, 7 (s. *Ἀντιφῶν*)

Σάλλος
THRACE:
—NICOPOLIS AD NESTUM: (**1**) ii AD *IGB* IV 2348

Σαλλουστία
MACEDONIA (PAIONIA): (**1**) imp. *Sp.* 98 (1941-8) p. 201 no. 396 (*Σαλου-*)

Σαλλούστιος
THRACE:
—GERMANIA: (**1**) ii-iii AD *IGB* IV 2206 (f. *—ος*)

Σάλμος
THRACE:
—TYRODIZA-TIRISTASIS?: (**1**) ii-i BC *Stephanos nomismatikos* p. 586 (s. *Βεισταβάκης*)

Σάλος
THRACE:
—PAUTALIA: (**1**) ii-iii AD *IGB* IV 2104, 1 (f. *Ἐζβενις*)

Σαμαγόρας
MACEDONIA (KRESTONIA):
—MORRYLOS: (**1**) c. 185-180 BC *SEG* XXXIX 606, 3 (f. *Παράμονος*)
THRACE:
—PERINTHOS-HERAKLEIA: (**2**) iv-iii BC *IPerinth* 4, 5 (*Σαματορου*—apogr., *Σαμα(γ)όρου*—Wilhelm: f. *Ἄρχος*)

Σάμας
THRACE:
—APOLLONIA-SOZOPOLIS: (**1**) v-iv BC *IGB* I² 441 (*Σάμαντος* (gen.): f. *Σιληνός*)

Σαμβαθίων
MACEDONIA (ORESTIS):
—SISANI (MOD.): (**1**) 146 AD *EAM* 187, 22 (*Φλ. Σ.*)
THRACE: (**2**) iii AD *IGB* III 1875 (*Αὐρ. Σ.*: s. *Μουκιανός*)

Σαμβάτα
MACEDONIA (BOTTIAIA):
—EDESSA: (**1**) v-vi AD Feissel, *RICM* 38 (*Σαν-*: m. *Ἰωάννης*, *Ἀλεξάνδρα*)

Σαμβάτις
CIMMERIAN BOSPOROS:
—PANTIKAPAION: (**1**) vi AD *IAK* 3 (1902) pp. 48-50 no. 15; Zgusta, *PNS* 740
MACEDONIA (MYGDONIA):
—THESSALONIKE: (**2**) v-vi AD *IG* X (2) (1) 352 (Feissel, *RICM* 175) (*Σαμβά*[*τ*]*ις*)

Σαμβατίς
MACEDONIA (BOTTIAIA):
—BEROIA: (**1**) ii AD *IBer* 343 (Tataki 1304) (*Φλ. Σ.*: m. *Λοῦππος*); (**2**) ?254 AD *ILeukopetra* 108, 1 (*Ποπιλλία Σ.*: d. *Καρπ—*)
MACEDONIA (PAIONIA):
—ARGOS (NR.): (**3**) ii-iii AD *SEG* XVI 401, 5 (*Σαν-*: d. *Εὔτροπος*, *Ἀγάθη*)
SCYTHIA MINOR:
—TOMIS: (**4**) iii AD *ISM* II 367 (Popescu, *IGL* 17) (Lat. Aur. Sambatis)

Σαμβατίων
CIMMERIAN BOSPOROS:
—GORGIPPIA: (**1**) ii-iii AD *NE* 9 (1971) p. 9 no. 6 A, 14; Zgusta, *PNS* 740 (s. *Γαδίκιος*); (**2**) m. ii AD *Eirene* 7 (1968) p. 67, 17 (*Σαμ*[*βατίω*]*ν*: f. *Ἀόσας*); (**3**) s. ii AD *CIRB* 1142, 15 ([*Σ*]*αμβατίω*[*ν*])
—GORGIPPIA?: (**4**) s. ii AD ib. 1231 B, 12 (s. *Ἀγαθοῦς*)
MACEDONIA (BOTTIAIA):
—BEROIA: (**5**) ii/iii AD *IBer* 144 A, 6 (Tataki 621) (*Ἰούλ. Σ.*)
SKYTHIA:
—OLBIA-BORYSTHENES: (**6**) ii-iii AD *IOSPE* I² 136, 11 (*Σαν-*: f. *Σαδίμανος*)
—TANAIS: (**7**) 220 AD *CIRB* 1278, 16 (s. *Γοργίας*); (**8**) ~ ib. l. 24 (s. *—ακος*); (**9**) ~ ib. l. 29 ([*Σαμ*]*βατίων*: s. *Ἀταχ—*); (**10**) 225 AD ib. 1279, 15 (f. *Μάδωις*); (**11**) ~ ib. 1280, 28 (*Σαμβα*[*τί*]*ων*: s. *Ἀσμα—*: reading—Tokhtas'ev); (**12**) 228 AD ib. 1282, 19 (s. *Σάκδεος*); (**13**) 236 AD ib. 1250, 13 (s. *Σίρανος*)
THRACE:
—OESCUS: (**14**) ii-iii AD *ILB* 119 (Lat. Sanbatio)
—SERDICA: (**15**) v AD Beševliev 7, 12 (Lat. Sambatione (acc.?))

Σαμβίων
CIMMERIAN BOSPOROS:
—BOSPOROS: (**1**) imp. *TAM* IV (1) 239, 5 (s. *Ἀριστόδημος*); (**2**) ~ ib. l. 6 (s. *Ταυρέας*)
—GORGIPPIA: (**3**) ii/iii AD *CIRB* 1179, 57; Zgusta, *PNS* 740 (*Σαμβίω*[*ν*]: f. *Νυμφαγόρας*)
—HERMONASSA: (**4**) 345 AD *CIRB* 1091, 3 (f. *Εὐφρόσυνος ὁ καὶ Πάτειρος*)
—PANTIKAPAION: (**5**) i-ii AD ib. 633 (s. *Ταρούλας*); (**6**) ii AD *KSIA* 109 (1967) p. 36, 6; (**7**) 204 AD *CIRB* 96, 11 (*SEG* II 485) ([*Σαμ*]*βίων*: s. *—ης*); (**8**) 214 AD *CIRB* 98, 6 (*Ἰούλ. Σ.*); (**9**) s. iii AD ib. 36, 61 (*Σαμβ*[*ίω*]*ν*: f. *—λειος*); (**10**) 275-278 AD ib. l. 40 (f. *Μασταροῦς*); (**11**) ~ ib. l. 64 (*Σαμβ*(*ίων*): f. *Ῥαδάμασις*); (**12**) ~ ib. l. 45-6 (f. *Ἀρδάρακος*)
SKYTHIA:
—OLBIA-BORYSTHENES: (**13**) ii AD *IOSPE* I² 86, 9 (f. *Ἀνθέστιος*) ?= (*15*); (**14**) ?ii AD ib. 99, 6 (s. *Γαγγαῖος*); (**15**) ii AD ib. 129, 8 (f. *Ἀνθέστιος*) ?= (*13*)
—TANAIS: (**16**) 228 AD *CIRB* 1283, 15, 18 (s. *Ἐλπιδίων*)

Σαμβοῦς
SKYTHIA:
—OLBIA-BORYSTHENES: (**1**) ii AD *IOSPE* I² 80, 15; Zgusta, *PNS* 740 (*Σαμ*[*β*]*οῦς*?: f. *Ἄβραγος*)

Σαμβώ
MACEDONIA (MYGDONIA):
—THESSALONIKE: (**1**) ?ii AD *IG* X (2) (1) 539; 540? (*Φαβία Σ.*: m. *Γ. Ἀντώνιος Ἀττικός*, *Ἀντωνία Ἀττικίς*, *Ἀντωνία Πίστις*)

Σάμμας
CIMMERIAN BOSPOROS:
—NYMPHAION: (**1**) m. V BC *Hyperboreus* 2002 (1), pp. 13-42 (coin) (*Σάμμα* (gen.))

Σαμοκλῆς
THRACE:
—AINOS?: (**1**) s. iv BC Peek, *NIEpid* 16, 28 + Perlman, *City and Sanctuary* E.6 (or Korinthia Korinth: *Σαμο(κ)λεῦς* (gen.)—Peek, *Σαμόλα* (gen.)—Perlman: f. *Δαμέας*)

Σάμος
MACEDONIA (BOTTIAIA):
—EDESSA: (**1**) b. 183 BC *RE* (2) (Tataki, *Macedonians* p. 105 no. 20) (s. *Χρυσόγονος*); (**2**) ii BC Dimitsas 557 = *SEG* XLIX 827; cf. *ZPE* 132 (2000) pp. 161-2 (locn.) (Tataki, *Edessa* 274) (or Macedonia (Mygdonia) Thessalonike: f. *Ἀδεία*)
—ICHNAI (TERRIT.)?: (**3**) f. iii BC *Α΄ Panell. Synedr. Epigr.* p. 195 no. 15 (*SEG* XLIX 727) (s. *Νικάνωρ*)
MACEDONIA (KRESTONIA):
—MORRYLOS: (**4**) c. 185-180 BC ib. XXXIX 606, 1 (f. *Εὔξενος*)

Macedonia (Mygdonia):
—arethousa?: **(5)** f. i bc *EAD* xxx 185 (Tataki, *Macedonians* p. 70 no. 14) (or Syria Arethousa: s. *Νίκων*, f. *Βόηθος*, *Ζωΐλος*)
Macedonia (Pieria):
—dion: **(6)** hell. *SEG* l 589 (f. *Μικυλίς*)
Thrace:
—chersonesos: **(7)** 183 bc *IG* ii^2 2332 II, 162 (*FRA* 7306)

Σαμουήλ
Cimmerian Bosporos:
—pantikapaion: **(1)** iv ad *CIRB* 743 (*Σαμο(υ)ήλ*: s. *Σεβῆρος*: Jew)

Σαμύλος
Thrace:
—salymbria: **(1)** ?iv-iii bc *IByz* S 22 (*SGDI* 3071) (f. *Ἀντίφιλος*)

Σάναγος
Skythia:
—olbia-borysthenes: **(1)** ii ad *IOSPE* i^2 128, 8; Zgusta, *PNS* 198 (f. *Σώμαχος*)

Σάνβος
Macedonia (Edonis):
—amphipolis: **(1)** ii-iii ad *Thrakika* 13 (1940) pp. 19-20 *A* + *Epigraphica* 37 (1975) p. 26 (f. *Ζιπᾶς*); **(2)** ~ *AE* 1932, Chron. p. 1 no. 6 + *Thrakika* 13 (1940) p. 22; cf. *Epigraphica* 37 (1975) p. 26 (f. *Παιβις*); **(3)** ~ *AE* 1932, Chron. p. 1 no. 12 + *Thrakika* 13 (1940) p. 20 *A*; cf. *Epigraphica* 37 (1975) p. 26 (f. *Θεόδωρος*); **(4)** ~ *Thracia* 2 p. 279 + *Epigraphica* 37 (1935) p. 26 (f. *Τάρσις*)
Macedonia (Odomantike):
—drabeskos?: **(5)** ii-iii ad *SEG* xxx 619, 5 (Pilhofer 572) (s. *Δίζας*)

Σανδάρζιος
Skythia:
—tanais: **(1)** 220 ad *CIRB* 1245, 6, 8; 1251, 5; Zgusta, *PNS* 326 (f. *Χόφαρνος*, *Χορόαθος*)

Σάνεια
Cimmerian Bosporos:
—pantikapaion: **(1)** i-ii ad *CIRB* 634; Zgusta, *PNS* 1144 (m. *Ζεκυνθείς*)

Σάνκτος
Macedonia (Paionia): **(1)** i/ii ad *SEG* xviii 367 (Tataki, *Macedonians* p. 210 no. 22) (s. *Σεκοῦνδος*, *Ὀλυμπιάς*)
Thrace:
—emporion thouidai: **(2)** ii-iii ad *IGB* iii 1768; cf. v 5634 (locn.) (s. *Ἀγαθοκλῆς*)

Σαννίων
Tauris:
—chersonesos: **(1)** iii bc Solomonik, *NEPKh* 146 (s. *Μεγακλῆς*); **(2)** ~ ib. 147; **(3)** ~ ib. 148 (f. *Μεγακλῆς*); **(4)** ~ ib. 149 (f. *Ἀπολλώνιος*); **(5)** ~ ib. 150 (f. *Διονύσιος*)

Σανόκας
Cimmerian Bosporos:
—gorgippia: **(1)** ii/iii ad *CIRB* 1180, 2 (*[Σ]ανόκας*?: s. *Ἄττας*)

Σανόχας
Cimmerian Bosporos:
—taman peninsula: **(1)** i/ii ad ib. 1220 B; Zgusta, *PNS* 700

Σάνχος
Cimmerian Bosporos:
—phanagoreia: **(1)** 304-284 bc *CIRB* 974; Zgusta, *PNS* 701 (f. *Θεόφιλος*)

Σάνων
Cimmerian Bosporos:
—pantikapaion: **(1)** v/iv bc *CIRB* 115 (*CEG* i 176); Zgusta, *PNS* 1145 (s. *Γλαυκίων*)

Σάος
Skythia:
—olbia-borysthenes: **(1)** f. ii ad *Drev. Prichern.* 3 pp. 27-8, 7 (f. (nat.) *Ἀργουάναγος*)

Σαουαίνων
Cimmerian Bosporos:
—phanagoreia (nr.): **(1)** iii ad *CIRB* 1016, 7; cf. Zgusta, *PNS* 905a (*Ἀουαίνων*—ed.: name—Vinogradov)

Σαπας?
Macedonia (Edonis):
—amphipolis: **(1)** ii-iii ad *Thrakika* 13 (1940) p. 27 *Π*; cf. *Epigraphica* 37 (1975) p. 30 (*Σαπα* (gen.))

Σαπίς
Sarmatia:
—maiotai: **(1)** hell. *Cl. Rh.* 2 p. 232 no. 122

Σαπρίκιος
Scythia Minor:
—istros*: **(1)** ?vi ad Barnea 60 (Popescu, *IGL* 149 (amph.))

Σαπφώ
Macedonia (Bottiaia):
—beroia: **(1)** c. 197-203 ad *ILeukopetra* 45, 24; 46, 9; 47, 14; 48 (Tataki 268 a) (*Αὐρ. Σ.*, *Σαφφώ*—46 and 48); **(2)** 233-234 ad *ILeukopetra* 82, 8; 83, 17; 84, 19; 85, 16 (Tataki 268 b) (*Αὐρ. Σ.*, *Σαφφώ*—82 and 84-5)

Σάρακος
Skythia:
—tanais: **(1)** 244 ad *CIRB* 1287, 11; Zgusta, *PNS* 199 (s. *Δάδας*)

Σαράξαζος
Skythia:
—olbia-borysthenes: **(1)** ii ad *IOSPE* i^2 102, 3; Zgusta, *PNS* 200 (s. *Ποσείδηος*) ?= (*2*); **(2)** f. ii ad *SEG* xliii 506, 11 (s. *Ποσείδηος*) ?= (*1*)

Σαραπιάς
Macedonia (Pelagonia):
—keramiai (nr.): **(1)** 193-211 ad *IG* x (2) (2) 218, 5 (*Οὐλπία Ἰσιδώρα ἡ καὶ Σ.*); **(2)** ~ ib. l. 8 (*Αὐρηλία Ἀντιγόνη ἡ καὶ Σ.*)

Σαραπίων
Cimmerian Bosporos:
—pantikapaion: **(1)** i bc-i ad *CIRB* 511; cf. KW pl. 54 no. 739 (s. *Ἀπολλωνίδης*); **(2)** ~ *CIRB* 581; cf. KW pl. 13 no. 185 (f. *Ἀρέτη*); **(3)** i ad *CIRB* 358
Macedonia: **(4)** 231 bc *SB* 9258, 5 (Tataki, *Macedonians* p. 427 no. 1) (s. *Εὔβουλος*); **(5)** m. ii bc *PTeb* 1075 fr. 2, 17 (Tataki, *Macedonians* p. 496 no. 226; La'da E1620) (*[Σ]αραπίων*: s. *Δημήτριος*); **(6)** 164-152 bc *UPZ* 9; 64; 66; 73-4; 80; 93; cf. p. 113 and Index s.v. (s. *Γλαυκίας*); **(7)** 103 bc *PTeb* 105, 52 (Tataki, *Macedonians* p. 496 no. 227); cf. La'da E1760 (f. *Ἡράκλειος*); **(8)** ~ *PTeb* 105, 52 (Tataki, *Macedonians* p. 497 no. 228); cf. La'da E1639 (f. *Τιμόστρατος*); **(9)** 73 bc *POxy* 1628, 5, 15, 22 (Tataki, *Macedonians* p. 496 no. 225; La'da E1619) (s. *Ἀπολλώνιος*: katoikos)
Macedonia (Edonis):
—amphipolis: **(10)** ?c. 167 bc *SEG* xxiv 580, 9; cf. Hatzopoulos, *MI* 1 p. 136 (I f. *Σαραπίων* II); **(11)** ~ *SEG* xxiv 580, 9; cf. Hatzopoulos, *MI* 1 p. 136 (II s. *Σαραπίων* I)
Macedonia (Mygdonia):
—thessalonike: **(12)** ii-i bc *IG* x (2) (1) 81; 95-6 (f. *Περιγένης*)
Scythia Minor:
—istros: **(13)** i bc-i ad *ISM* i 191 II, 4 (s. *Ἀθηνόδωρος*); **(14)** ~ ib. l. 42 (s. *Ὄσπος*); **(15)** 138 ad ib. 193 I, 61 (I f. *Σαραπίων* II); **(16)** ~ ib. l. 61 (II s. *Σαραπίων* I); **(17)** ~ ib. l. 75 (f. *Ἱπποσθένης*); **(18)** ~ ib. l. 81 (f. *Φιλόδημος*)
—kallatis: **(19)** iii/ii bc *Suda H* 462; cf. Fraser, *Ptol. Alex.* 2 p. 741 n. 172 (f. *Ἡρακλείδης ὁ ἐπικαλ. ὁ Λέμβος*)
—tomis: **(20)** i bc *ISM* ii 2, 1, 29 (s. *Διοσκουρίδης*); **(21)** ii ad *AMNG* i (2) 2546 (coin)
Thrace: **(22)** 241 bc *PFrankf* 5, 19
—markianopolis: **(23)** ii ad *IGB* ii 799 with pl. (*[Σ]αραπίων*)
—rhaidestos: **(24)** ?ii-i bc PM 1405 (f. *Ἀντίοχος*)

Σαράτοκος
Thrace: **(1)** v/iv bc Peter, *MTD* pp. 99-104 (coin) (king?)

Σάρατος
Skythia:
—olbia-borysthenes: **(1)** ii ad *IOSPE* i^2 92, 3; Zgusta, *PNS* 201 (f. *Κάραξτος*)

Σαργόνιος
Cimmerian Bosporos:
—pantikapaion: **(1)** ii ad *CIRB* 92, 4 (*Σαργονία[ς]*—*CIRB*: reading—Vinogradov)

Σάρδαυγος
Thrace:
—odessos: **(1)** f. iii ad *IGB* v 5070, 6 (?f. *Μευαος*)

Σαρέδαθος
Thrace?: **(1)** 360 ad *SEG* vii 1170 (f. *Σαδάλας*)

Σαρίακος
Scythia Minor: **(1)** f. ii bc *IGB* v 5003; *SNG Stancomb* 322-8 (coin) (king)

Σάρκη
Macedonia (Edonis):
—amphipolis: **(1)** ?ii ad *FGrH* 257 F 37, 50 (Tataki, *Macedonians* p. 60 no. 117) (d. *Σκίλας*)

Σαρκοῦς
Thrace:
—odessos: **(1)** i bc *IGB* i^2 154 (PM 922) (*Σαρκοῦς*: d. *Ἕλλην*)

Σαρμάτας
Cimmerian Bosporos:
—gorgippia: **(1)** ii ad *CIRB* 1140, 7; Zgusta, *PNS* 767 (s. *Χοδέκιος*); **(2)** 173-210 ad *CIRB* 1134, 27 (s. *Κοδόρας*); **(3)** ii/iii ad ib. 1179, 60 (f. *Σιαγοῦς*)

Σαρματίων
Thrace:
—philippopolis-trimontium: **(1)** imp. *CIL* vi 2785 (Lat. Val. Sarmatio)

Σάρορργος
Skythia:
—tanais: **(1)** 225 ad *CIRB* 1280, 23 (*Σάρορ[ρ]γ[ος]*: f. —*νος*)

Σαρύκη
Cimmerian Bosporos:
—pantikapaion: **(1)** i ad ib. 512; Zgusta, *PNS* 202

Σάσας
Cimmerian Bosporos:
—hermonassa: **(1)** hell.-imp. *CIRB* 1094, 2; *Hellenismus* p. 454 no. 26 (name) (s. *Σινδέας*)
—pantikapaion: **(2)** i bc/i ad *CIRB* 318; Zgusta, *PNS* 203; **(3)** i ad *CIRB* 427 (f. *Λαοδίκη*, *Μαμία*); **(4)** ii ad ib. 660; cf. KW pl. 44 no. 631 (f. *Δωρᾶς*)

SKYTHIA:
—TANAIS: **(5)** ii AD *CIRB* 1262, 5 (I f. *Σάσας* II); **(6)** ~ ib. l. 5 (II s. *Σάσας* I)
TAURIS:
—KERKINITIS: **(7)** iii BC Solomonik, *GChKh* 132 (vase); *Hellenismus* p. 454 no. 26 (*Σάσο* (gen.))

Σασῶν
CIMMERIAN BOSPOROS:
—GORGIPPIA: **(1)** f. iii BC *CIRB* 1137 B I, 3; Zgusta, *PNS* 203 (*Σασῶντος* (gen.): f. *Χάρων*); **(2)** i BC-i AD *CIRB* 1195

Σάτοκος
THRACE: **(1)** 267 BC *SEG* XXVII 1114, 14b; cf. La'da E702 (f. *Ἀμάδοκος*); **(2)** 231 or 206 BC *CPR* XVIII 18, 382, 388 (La'da E793) ([*Σ*]*άτοκος*); **(3)** ii-i BC *Syringes* 473 (Velkov 240; La'da E794)
—MADYTOS: **(4)** hell. *ISestos* 60 (s. *Σόλων*, f. *Ἀλέξανδρος*)
—ODRYSAI: **(5)** s. v BC *RE* s.v. Sadokos (-); *Rogozen Treasure* p. 47 no. 1; Osborne, *Naturalization* T4 (*Σάδοκος*—Thuc.: s. *Σιτάλκης*)
—PHILIPPOPOLIS-TRIMONTIUM (TERRIT.): **(6)** iii AD *IGB* III 1430 (f. *Βρούθενις*)
—SEUTHOPOLIS: **(7)** c. 300-280 BC *SEG* XLII 661, 9 (s. *Σεύθης*, *Βερενίκη*)
THRACE?: **(8)** m. iii BC *BGU* 1998, 1 (-δο-); **(9)** ~ *SB* 12221, 1 (<*Σ*>[*ά*]*τοκ*[*ο*]*ς*: I f. *Σάτοκος* II) ?= (*11*); **(10)** ~ ib. l. 1 (*Σάτοκος*: II s. *Σάτοκος* I); **(11)** ~ ib. l. 7 (f. *Πολύαινος*) ?= (*9*); **(12)** ~ ib. l. 26 (s. *Διζάπορις*); **(13)** c. 260 BC *PHib* 112, 81 (Velkov 239) (f. *Στέφανος*); **(14)** 229 BC *PHib* 36, 3, 9 (*PP* 12179; Velkov 237)

Σατορνία
THRACE:
—MADYTOS: **(1)** imp. *ISestos* 66

Σατορνῖλος
CIMMERIAN BOSPOROS:
—GORGIPPIA?: **(1)** s. ii AD *CIRB* 1231 B, 14 (I f. *Σατορνῖλος* II); **(2)** ~ ib. l. 14 (-νεῖ-: II s. *Σατορνῖλος* I)
MACEDONIA (BOTTIAIA):
—EDESSA: **(3)** 180 AD *SEG* XXIV 531, 14 (Tataki, *Edessa* 275) (s. *Ἡδεῖα*)
SKYTHIA:
—OLBIA-BORYSTHENES: **(4)** ii/iii AD *SEG* XXXIV 766, [1], 3 (-νεῖ-: s. *Πεισίστρατος*)
—TYRAS: **(5)** 181 AD *IOSPE* I^2 2, 30 (-νεῖ-: f. *Λούκιος*)
THRACE:
—PAUTALIA (TERRIT.): **(6)** ii-iii AD *IGB* V 5788 (-νεῖ-: f. *Μουκιανός*)
—PERINTHOS-HERAKLEIA?: **(7)** iii AD *IPerinth* 310 (-τρονεῖ-); **(8)** ~ *IByz* 381 (or Thrace Byzantion: *Σατυρνίδωι* (dat.)—apogr.)

Σατορνῖνα
MACEDONIA (PAIONIA):
—BYLAZORA: **(1)** iii AD *SEG* XLVII 896, 2 (m. *Αὐρ. Ἰούλιος*, *Αὐρ. Ἰουλία*)
THRACE:
—BYZANTION: **(2)** i BC-i AD *IByz* 143 (-νεῖ-: d. *Φίλων*)

Σατορνῖνος
MACEDONIA (EDONIS):
—PHILIPPOI (TERRIT.): **(1)** ?iii AD *SEG* XXX 594 B, 8 (Pilhofer 580) (-νεῖ-); **(2)** 206 AD Pikoulas, *Chora* p. 164 no. 73, 3 (Pilhofer 607) ([*Σα*]*τορνεῖνος*: s. *Λεωνίδης*, *Ἀτιδία Σεκοῦνδα*)
SKYTHIA:
—SKYTHAI: **(3)** f. vi AD *PLRE* III (1); *RE* (15) (s. *Ἑρμογένης*)

THRACE:
—MONTANA?: **(4)** s. ii AD *IGB* II 480 (*Montana* II 69) (-νεῖ-)
—PHILIPPOPOLIS-TRIMONTIUM: **(5)** c. 303 AD *Anal. Boll.* 31 (1912) p. 192

Σατραβάτης
CIMMERIAN BOSPOROS:
—HERMONASSA: **(1)** f. iv BC *CIRB* 1066; Zgusta, *PNS* 553 (s. *Σπιθάμης*)

Σατρης
THRACE:
—KELLAI*: **(1)** iii AD *IGB* III 1516 a, 29

Σατριανή
THRACE:
—BYZANTION?: **(1)** imp. *IByz* 387, 1 (m. *Χρηστίνη*)

Σάτριος
THRACE:
—MARONEIA: **(1)** i-ii AD Bakalakis, *Oinos Ismarikos* p. 1015 with fig. 17 + *IThrakAig* E288 (s. *Δημόστρατος*)

Σάττιον
THRACE:
—MESAMBRIA?: **(1)** iii/ii BC *IGB* I^2 102 (PM 923); cf. Robert, *OMS* 5 p. 259 (locn.) (d. *Πυθόδωρος*)

Σαττίων
CIMMERIAN BOSPOROS:
—PANTIKAPAION: **(1)** imp. *CIRB* 803; Zgusta, *PNS* 204 (*Σαττίονος* (gen.))

Σατίρα
MACEDONIA (ELIMEIA):
—AIANE (TERRIT.): **(1)** c. 225-200 BC *SEG* XL 526, 2 (d. *Λάανδρος*)

Σατιρία
MACEDONIA (PIERIA):
—DION: **(1)** ?ii AD Oikonomos 6 (*Σ. Σεκοῦνδα*: m. *Κασσία Σαβῖνα*)

Σατιρῖνος
TAURIS:
—CHERSONESOS: **(1)** iii BC Kats p. 105 no. 83 (amph.) (f. *Νικάνωρ*)

Σατιρίς
SCYTHIA MINOR:
—KALLATIS: **(1)** iii BC *ISM* III 158 (d. *Σάτυρος*)

Σατυρίσκος
THRACE:
—BYZANTION: **(1)** iii BC *Ilion* 62, 6 (f. *Ἡρακλείδας*)

Σατυρίων
CIMMERIAN BOSPOROS:
—PANTIKAPAION: **(1)** v BC Tolstoi 239 (vase) (*LSAG*^{2} p. 373 no. 68); **(2)** 344-311 BC *CIRB* 10, 1 (Rhodes–Osborne 65 B) ([*Σ*]*ατυρίων*: s. *Πάταικος*); **(3)** f. iii BC *IGAIMK* 104 (1935) p. 310 no. 79 (tile); *Sov. Arkh.* 28 (1958) p. 125
—TEMRYUK (MOD.): **(4)** iii-ii BC *SEG* XLV 1024 (*Σατυρί*[*ων*]?—ed. pr., *Σατύρι*[*ς*]?—Vinogradov)
MACEDONIA: **(5)** f. iii BC *IG* II^2 9262; cf. *ZPE* 29 (1978) p. 68 (Tataki, *Macedonians* p. 427 no. 3; *FRA* 3489) (f. *Κράτης*)
MACEDONIA (EDONIS):
—AMPHIPOLIS: **(6)** 285-246 BC *PP* 15737; *BCH* 95 (1971) p. 567 (Tataki, *Macedonians* p. 60 no. 118) (s. *Εὔμηλος*)
SCYTHIA MINOR:
—ISTROS: **(7)** 138 AD *ISM* I 193 I, 108 (s. *Αἰσχρίων*); **(8)** ~ ib. 193 II, 72 (f. *Ἀριστόλαος*); **(9)** ii/iii AD ib. 363, 3 (*CCET* IV 62) (f. *Διονύσιος*, *Ἡρόδωρος*); **(10)** f. iii AD *Stud. Fischer* p. 32 no. 4, 5 (*Σατυρί*[*ων*]: f. *Φίλιππος*)
—KALLATIS: **(11)** hell. *ISM* III 107
THRACE:
—LYSIMACHEIA: **(12)** hell. *ISestos* 41
—ODESSOS?: **(13)** ii AD *IGB* I^2 51 bis a, 6 (f. *Διοσκουρίδης*)

Σάτυρος
CIMMERIAN BOSPOROS:
—BOSPOROS: **(1)** c. 450-389 BC *RE* (4) + (6); *CIRB* [37]; *SEG* XLIII 515, 1 + XLVIII 1027; XLV 1000, 1, [9]; Rhodes–Osborne 64, 21, 47; *VDI* 1967 (1), p. 64; D.S. xiv 93. 1; cf. xii 36 (per err.) (*Σέλευκος*—xii 36: s. *Σπάρτακος*, f. *Λεύκων*, *Μητρόδωρος*, *Γόργιππος*: king); **(2)** c. 340-310 BC *RE* (5) (s. *Παιρισάδης*, *Κομοσαρύη*, f. *Παιρισάδης*: king); **(3)** f. iii BC *SEG* XXXIX 701. 5-6 (XLV 997. 4) (king)
—GORGIPPIA: **(4)** f. iii BC *CIRB* 1137 A I, 22; 1137 A II, 18 (s. *Εὔπολις*); **(5)** ~ ib. 1137 B I, 6 (f. *Ἀπολλᾶς*)
—NYMPHAION: **(6)** iii BC ib. 912 I, 6 (f. —*μαχος*)
—PATRAEUS: **(7)** iv BC ib. 1017 (*GVI* 338; *CEG* II 738) (s. *Εὔξενος*, f. *Φιλονοίη*)
MACEDONIA: **(8)** iv BC Arr., *An.* iii 28. 4 (Tataki, *Macedonians* p. 427 no. 5) (f. *Νειλόξενος*)
—PRASSIOI: **(9)** s. iv BC *IG* II^2 9269 (Tataki, *Macedonians* p. 169 no. 2; *FRA* 3490) (s. *Γόλυς*)
MACEDONIA (BOTTIAIA):
—BEROIA: **(10)** ii/iii AD *IBer* 27 A, 3 (f. *Δημήτρις*)
MACEDONIA (CHALKIDIKE):
—OLYNTHOS?: **(11)** iv BC *RE* (13) + Supplbd. 10 (Stephanis 2235; Tataki, *Macedonians* p. 142 no. 99)
—POTIDAIA-KASSANDREIA: **(12)** ?m. iii BC *FD* III (4) 351, 5 (Tataki, *Macedonians* p. 95 no. 86) (f. *Ζαλίας*)
MACEDONIA (EDONIS):
—AMPHIPOLIS: **(13)** iv-iii BC *AEMTh* 15 (2001) p. 118 (s. *Στρυμοκλῆς*); **(14)** s. iv BC *PAE* 1981, p. 25 with pl. 43 *β*, 10 (f. —*ης*)
MACEDONIA (MYGDONIA):
—THESSALONIKE?: **(15)** i AD *JDAI* 84 (1969) pp. 150-1 no. R12 (*Τ. Φλ. Σ.*)
MACEDONIA (PIERIA):
—PYDNA: **(16)** ?f. iv BC *AEMTh* 15 (2001) p. 365 (*Σάτυρ*[*ος*])
SCYTHIA MINOR:
—KALLATIS: **(17)** iv BC *ISM* III 154 (f. *Ἀκύλλης*); **(18)** ~ *SEG* XXXV 1356, 2 (*Σάτ*[*υρος*]: s. *Ἰασιεύς*); **(19)** iii BC *ISM* III 14, 1 (*Σάτυ*[*ρος*]: f. —*ος*); **(20)** ~ ib. 126, 8 (s. *Μᾶτρις*); **(21)** ~ ib. l. 9 (f. ..*ων*); **(22)** ~ ib. 158 (f. *Σατυρίς*); **(23)** ?s. iii BC *RE* (16); **(24)** s. iii BC *ISM* III 10, 3; **(25)** ~ ib. 35 A, 22 (f. *Ἀπολλώνυμος*); **(26)** ~ ib. 35 B, 25 (*Σ*[*άτ*]*υρος*: f. *Εὐφραῖος*); **(27)** iii/ii BC ib. 161 (s. *Βάκχος*); **(28)** ~ ib. (f. *Μῆνις*); **(29)** ii/i BC *AMNG* I (1) 265 (coin monogram) (*Σάτυ*(*ρος*)); **(30)** s. i AD *ISM* III 67, 3 ([*Σά*]*τυρος*: f. *Ἀπολλοφάνης*)
—TOMIS: **(31)** i-ii AD ib. II 150, 1
SKYTHIA:
—OLBIA-BORYSTHENES: **(32)** imp. *IOSPE* I^2 50; **(33)** ~ ib. 60 c ([*Σ*]*άτυρο*[*ς*]); **(34)** ~ ib. 153, 1 (f. —*αγος*); **(35)** i/ii AD *SEG* XLIII 505, 7 (s. *Κούνχακος*) ?= (*37*); **(36)** ii AD *IOSPE* I^2 51, 16; 100, 3 (f. *Ποσειδῆς*); **(37)** ?ii AD ib. 148, 5 (s. *Κο*—) ?= (*35*); **(38)** ii AD *ISM* II 279, 4 (s. *Ποντικός*); **(39)** ii-iii AD *IOSPE* I^2 137, 5 (f. *Καλλισθένης*); **(40)** c. 150-175 AD ib. 142, 10; 176; cf. *SEG* XLII 713 (s. *Ἀρτεμίδωρος*); **(41)** ?ii/iii AD *IOSPE* I^2 40, 1, 5, 8, 38 (f. *Θεοκλῆς*)
—TYRAS*: **(42)** hell. *SEG* III 567 (amph.) (*Σάτυρ*[*ος*]: potter?)

TAURIS:
—CHERSONESOS: (43) iv BC Solomonik, *GAKh* 1494 (vase) (*Σάτυ(ρος)*?); (44) a. 46 BC *IOSPE* I^2 691, 5 (*Γ.* [*Ιο*]*ύλ. Σ.*)
THRACE:
—APOLLONIA-SOZOPOLIS: (45) v-iv BC *IGB* V 5150; (46) i-ii AD ib. I^2 401, 16 (f. *XITH*)
—MARONEIA: (47) f. iii BC *IThrakAig* E230 A ([*Σ*]*άτυρος*: f. *Ἡρᾶς*)
—MESAMBRIA: (48) iii BC *IOSPE* I^2 688 (s. *Διονύσιος*)
—PERINTHOS-HERAKLEIA: (49) iii AD *IPerinth* 171
—PERINTHOS-HERAKLEIA?: (50) v/iv BC *IGB* V 5155 (or Thrace Apollonia-Sozopolis: f. *Ἡραγόρης*); (51) ~ ib. (or Thrace Apollonia-Sozopolis: s. *Ἡραγόρης*)
—SESTOS: (52) hell.? *RA* 1912, p. 263 no. 49 (f. *Διονύσιος*)
—ZONE: (53) s. iv BC *AA* 1918, col. 11 (*IThrakAig* E422); cf. Robert, *Hell.* 1 p. 94 (f. *Μαιανδρία*)

Σαυάγας
CIMMERIAN BOSPOROS:
—BOSPOROS*: (1) 478-491 AD *CIRB* 67, 8 (*SEG* XLVIII 993); *SEG* XXXIX 697, 7 + XLVIII 994; 995; 996 B (s. *Ἀρίστων*, ?f. *Ἀββάγαζα*, f. *—τας*)

Σαυαίωσος
SKYTHIA:
—TANAIS: (1) 228 AD *CIRB* 1282, 18; Zgusta, *PNS* 206 (f. *Βαγδόσαυος*)

Σαυάνων
SKYTHIA:
—TANAIS: (1) 225 AD *CIRB* 1279, 8; Zgusta, *PNS* 207 (s. *Χόφραζμος*)

Σαυλάκης
KOLCHIS: (1) arch. *RE* Supplbd. 7 (-); Braund, *Georgia* p. 145 (Lat. Saulaces: king/fict.?)

Σαύλιος
SKYTHIA:
—SKYTHAI: (1) m. vi BC Hdt. iv 76 (s. *Γνοῦρος*, f. *Ἰδάνθυρσος*: king)

Σαύμακος
SKYTHIA:
—SKYTHAI: (1) ii BC *RE* Supplbd. 6 (-); *IOSPE* I^2 352, 34, 42 (*Syll*^{3} 709); *SNG BM Black Sea* 352 (coin) (*Σαύ(μακος)*—coin: king)

Σαυνᾶς
CIMMERIAN BOSPOROS:
—PANTIKAPAION: (1) 275-278 AD *CIRB* 36, 56; cf. Zgusta, *PNS* 702 (*—υς Λυνδ*——*CIRB*, *Σαυνα*[*ς*]?—Vinogradov)
SKYTHIA:
—TANAIS: (2) 225 AD *CIRB* 1280, 26 (*Σαυνασ*[*ος*]?—ed., *Σαυνας*?—Tokhtas'ev) ?= (*3*); (3) 230 AD ib. 1284, 14 (*Σαυν*[*ασος*]?—ed., *Σαυν*[*ας*]?: s. *—μος*) ?= (*2*)

Σαυρομάτης
CIMMERIAN BOSPOROS:
—BOSPOROS: (1) c. 70-123 AD *PIR*^{2} I 550; *SEG* XXVII 445; XLIII [511]; XLV 1023, [1]?; Frolova, *CKB A.D. 69-238* pp. 17-30; Zgusta, *PNS* 767 (*Τιβ. Ἰούλ. Σ.*: s. *Τιβ. Ἰούλ. Ῥησκούπορις*, f. *Τιβ. Ἰούλ. Κότυς*: king); (2) c. 150-210 AD *PIR*^{2} I 551; *SEG* XXXVI 699; 700, [2]; 701, 6; XLV 1017, 1; 1027 A; Frolova, *CKB A.D. 69-238* pp. 39-46 (*Τιβ. Ἰούλ. Σ.*: s. *Τιβ. Ἰούλ. Ῥοιμητάλκης*, f. *Τιβ. Ἰούλ. Ῥησκούπορις*: king); (3) 229-231 AD *CIRB* 1230, 7; Frolova, *CKB A.D. 69-238* p. 53 (king); (4) 275 AD Frolova, *CKB A.D. 242-341/342* pp. 29-31 (coins) (king)

Σαύροφος
CIMMERIAN BOSPOROS:
—PANTIKAPAION: (1) ii AD *CIRB* 698; Zgusta, *PNS* 703 (f. *Παιρίσαλος*)

Σαυτίας
MACEDONIA (ODOMANTIKE):
—SIRRHA: (1) f. iii AD *SEG* XXX 590, 29 (*Αὐρ. Σ.*: s. *Κοδρᾶτος*)

Σαφάτας
CIMMERIAN BOSPOROS:
—GORGIPPIA: (1) ii/iii AD *CIRB* 1179, 34; Zgusta, *PNS* 756 (*Σαφά*[*τ*]*ας*: s. *Χρηστίων*)

Σαφιρώ
MACEDONIA (MYGDONIA):
—THESSALONIKE: (1) ii-iii AD *SEG* XLII 626 (*ΣΑΓΙΡΩΝΙ*—ed., *Σαφιρῶνι* (dat.)—Hatzopoulos: d. *Χρῆστος*)

Σβουβας?
MACEDONIA (ODOMANTIKE):
—DRABESKOS?: (1) iv BC Kaphtantzis 568, 4 (Pilhofer 575) (*Σβούβα* (gen.)—ed., *Βουβᾶ*?)

Σεακού
THRACE:
—ODESSOS (NR.): (1) ii AD *IGB* I^2 272 (PM 1676); *Dacia* 21 (1977) p. 161 (date) (d. *Νουμήνιος*)

Σεάσας
CIMMERIAN BOSPOROS:
—GORGIPPIA: (1) 173-210 AD *CIRB* 1135, 10 (s. *Σεαβα—*)

Σεβαζιανός
THRACE:
—BESSOPARA: (1) ii-iii AD *IGB* III 1332 (s. *Βίθυς*)
—GLAVA PANEGA (MOD.): (2) ii-iii AD ib. II 513 (s. *Ἀλέξανδρος*)
—PAUTALIA: (3) s. ii AD *SEG* XLVI 864 II, 23
—PAUTALIA (TERRIT.): (4) ii-iii AD *IGB* IV 2224 (s. *Μουκάτραλις*)
—PHILIPPOPOLIS-TRIMONTIUM (TERRIT.): (5) ii-iii AD ib. III 1499

Σεβαστιανός
THRACE: (1) 353-354 AD *PLRE* I (1)
—BEROE-AUGUSTA TRAIANA: (2) ii-iii AD *IGB* III 1583; (3) ~ ib. (s. *Μουκάπορις*); (4) 241-244 AD ib. 1707, 16 (*Μ. Αὐρ. Σεβαστ*[*ια*]*νός*)
—HADRIANOPOLIS (TERRIT.): (5) ii-iii AD ib. 1807, 6 (s. *Βρίζενις*)
—NICOPOLIS AD ISTRUM: (6) iii AD ib. II 687, 2 (*Αὐρ. Σαβαστιανός*: s. *Αὐρ. Σαβῖνα*)
—PHILIPPOPOLIS-TRIMONTIUM: (7) m. iii AD ib. III 884 a, 25; cf. V 5400 (s. *Πολυκράτης*); (8) ~ ib. III 884 c, 12; cf. V 5400 (*Αὐρ. Σ.*)
—PHILIPPOPOLIS-TRIMONTIUM (TERRIT.): (9) ii-iii AD ib. III 1133 (*Σεβαστιαν*[*ός*]: s. *Μουκάτραλις*); (10) iii AD ib. 1149 (*Αὐρ. Σεβαστια*[*νός*])

Σεβερῖνα
MACEDONIA (PIERIA):
—DION: (1) v-vi AD *SEG* XLVIII 790. 2

Σεβῆρα
MACEDONIA (MYGDONIA):
—THESSALONIKE?: (1) ii AD *IG* X (2) (1) 699
THRACE:
—BYZANTION: (2) i-ii AD *GVI* 1083 (m. *Μαρκιανή*)

Σεβηρᾶς
TAURIS:
—CHERSONESOS: (1) ii/iii AD *IOSPE* I^2 491; cf. KW pl. 34 no. 482; cf. Zgusta, *PNS* 1063 (*Σ. ὁ καὶ Λίλλις*: s. *Λίλλων*)

Σεβῆρος
CIMMERIAN BOSPOROS:
—PANTIKAPAION: (1) iv AD *CIRB* 743 (*Σεβ(ῆ)ρος*: f. *Σαμουήλ*: Jew)
THRACE:
—NICOPOLIS AD ISTRUM (NR.): (2) iii AD *IGB* II 716
—ODESSOS: (3) iii AD ib. I^2 135 (s. *Νικομήδης*)

Σεγοῦννος
MACEDONIA (BOTTIAIA):
—BEROIA: (1) iii AD *IBer* 280

Σεδάλας
MACEDONIA (MYGDONIA):
—KALINDOIA: (1) 68-98 AD *SEG* XLII 580, 41 + *BE* 1999, no. 362; cf. *Anthémonte–Kalindoia* 2 pp. 304-5 (name) (f. *Τοῖτας*)
—LETE: (2) ii AD *Makedonika* 2 (1951) p. 619 no. 42 *θ*, 15 (s. *Μόκασος*)
MACEDONIA (SINTIKE):
—PARTHIKOPOLIS (NR.): (3) 159 AD *IGB* IV 2286, 2 (f. *Πυρούλας*)

Σεδάνη
MACEDONIA (EORDAIA):
—SPILIA (MOD.): (1) ii-iii AD *EAM* 101, 2 (d. *Ἄδυμος*)

Σεδέλης?
MACEDONIA (CHALKIDIKE):
—SPARTOLOS?: (1) ?352 BC *SEG* XLVI 804, 3 (*Σεδέ*[*λης*]: f. *Τάρβης*)

Σεθείλας
THRACE:
—KRASALOPARA: (1) 202 AD *IGB* III 1690 b, 59 (and Thrace Pizos: s. *Βρίζενις*)

Σεισάμης
CIMMERIAN BOSPOROS:
—PANTIKAPAION: (1) c. 390-380 BC *SEG* L 710 A (vase) (fict.?)

Σειταούενις
THRACE:
—PAUTALIA:
——Karistoron: (1) ii AD *IGB* IV 2174 (*Σειταουένε*[*ος*] (gen.): f. *—ος*)

Σείτη
THRACE:
—BEROE-AUGUSTA TRAIANA: (1) ii/iii AD *SEG* XLVIII 894 (*Σεπτ. Σ.*)
—BEROE-AUGUSTA TRAIANA (TERRIT.): (2) ii-iii AD *IGB* III 1698 (m. *Ἰνγένους*)
—KELLAI: (3) ?ii-iii AD ib. 1532-4 (*Φλ. Σ.*: d. *Ἀσιατικός*)

Σέκουλα
MACEDONIA (PAIONIA): (1) imp. *Sp.* 98 (1941-8) p. 202 no. 399

Σεκοῦνδα
MACEDONIA (BOTTIAIA):
—BEROIA: (1) ii AD Dimitsas 212; cf. *SEG* XXVIII 551 (Tataki 1162) (d. *Δεντοῦς*); (2) ii-iii AD *IBer* 281 (Tataki 1163); (3) f. ii AD *IBer* 417 (biling.) (Tataki 1164) (*Σε*[*κοῦνδα*])
MACEDONIA (EDONIS):
—AMPHIPOLIS: (4) imp. Kaphtantzis 658
MACEDONIA (LYNKESTIS):
—HERAKLEIA (AREA): (5) ?ii AD *IG* X (2) (2) 15 (d. *Θάλλος*)
MACEDONIA (MYGDONIA):
—LETE (NR.): (6) imp. *SEG* I 278 (m. *Κ. Ἰούλ. Ἀλφίδιος Σεκοῦνδος*)
—THESSALONIKE*: (7) 132 AD *IG* X (2) (1) 503, 5 (threpte)
MACEDONIA (PAIONIA):
—EUDARISTOS?: (8) 102 AD *SEG* XXXII 655, 2-3 (m. *Διονύσιος*, *Πρῖμος*)
—KAVADARCI (MOD.): (9) ii-iii AD *Sp.* 71 (1931) p. 63 no. 136, 4 (*-νδε*: m. *Ἰούλιος*); (10) ~ ib.

p. 70 no. 160 (d. *Μένων*); (**11**) ii/iii AD Unp. (Papazoglu archive) (m. *Μέτρα*); (**12**) iii AD Unp. (Kavadarci Mus.) inv. 32/II (m. *Ζῶσα*)
—STOBOI: (**13**) ii-iii AD *Sp.* 71 (1931) p. 46 no. 105 (-*κον*-: d. *Μάνιος*, m. *Φουλκίνιος*)
SCYTHIA MINOR:
—TOMIS: (**14**) i AD *SEG* XXXIII 585 (m. *Μᾶρκος*)
THRACE:
—BEROE-AUGUSTA TRAIANA: (**15**) ii-iii AD *IGB* III 1610
—BEROE-AUGUSTA TRAIANA (TERRIT.): (**16**) ii/iii AD ib. 1673, 6 (*GVI* 1980)
—GANOS: (**17**) imp. Dumont–Homolle 88b
—NOVAE: (**18**) ii/iii AD *IGB* V 5262, 11 (biling.) (*SEG* XLVII 1153)
—PAUTALIA:
——Karistoron: (**19**) ii-iii AD *IGB* IV 2176 (-*κον*-)
—PERINTHOS-HERAKLEIA: (**20**) ii AD *IPerinth* 217 (*GVI* 1631) (d. *Εὐδαίμων*, m. *Σουσᾶς*)
—PHILIPPOPOLIS-TRIMONTIUM: (**21**) imp. *IGB* III 1026, 2
—PHILIPPOPOLIS-TRIMONTIUM*: (**22**) ii-iii AD ib. V 5465

Σεκούνδιλλα
MACEDONIA (BOTTIAIA):
—BEROIA: (**1**) ii-iii AD *IBer* 282 (Tataki 1165)

Σεκουνδῖνος
MACEDONIA (EDONIS):
—AMPHIPOLIS: (**1**) V AD *SEG* XLVIII 725
THRACE:
—BYZANTION?: (**2**) iii AD *IByz* 323 (*Σεκουνδεῖνος Διόγνητος*: f. *Αὐρ. Εὐφημία*)

Σεκουνδίων
MACEDONIA (MYGDONIA):
—THESSALONIKE: (**1**) ii AD *IG* X (2) (1) 630 B, 1; 630 C, 1 (*GVI* 1979)
MACEDONIA (PIERIA):
—DION?: (**2**) 180 or 181 AD *AEMTh* 15 (2001) p. 343 (*Οὐλπ. Σ.*: s. *Οὐλπ. Ἀρέσκουσα*)

Σεκοῦνδος
MACEDONIA (BOTTIAIA):
—EDESSA: (**1**) imp. Dimitsas 30 (Tataki, *Edessa* 276); (**2**) 51 AD *SEG* XLVI 744, 11 (Tataki, *Edessa* 278) (s. *Ἄδυμος*); (**3**) ii-iii AD *Arch. Pap.* 22 (1973) p. 205 no. 4 (Tataki, *Edessa* 279) (s. *Παράμονος*)
MACEDONIA (CHALKIDIKE):
—POTIDAIA-KASSANDREIA: (**4**) imp. *TAPA* 69 (1938) p. 63 + 70 (1939) p. 62 (*Σεκο(ῦ)νδ[ος]*)
MACEDONIA (EDONIS):
—AMPHIPOLIS: (**5**) imp. Kaphtantzis 658
MACEDONIA (LYNKESTIS):
—HERAKLEIA: (**6**) i AD *IG* X (2) (2) 75, 8 (f. *Αὐρήλιος*); (**7**) ~ ib. l. 14 (s. *Γ. Ἀδριανός*); (**8**) ~ ib. l. 17 (s. *Οὐέλιος*); (**9**) ~ ib. l. 18 (f. *Κόϊντος*) ?= (*10*); (**10**) ~ ib. l. 19 (f. *Γάϊος*) ?= (*9*); (**11**) ~ ib. l. 30 (*Σεκούνδο(υ)* (gen.): f. *Τίτος*); (**12**) ~ ib. l. 44 (s. *Γάϊος*)
—HERAKLEIA?: (**13**) ii-iii AD ib. 134
MACEDONIA (MYGDONIA):
—THESSALONIKE: (**14**) i BC/i AD ib. X (2) (1) 58, 15; *KGAM Thess.* I 111 (date) (s. *Εὔφαντος*); (**15**) i-ii AD *IG* X (2) (1) 243 I, 12 (I f. *Σεκοῦνδος* II); (**16**) ~ ib. l. 12 (II s. *Σεκοῦνδος* I); (**17**) m. i AD *Act. Ap.* 20. 4 (Tataki, *Macedonians* p. 187 no. 63); (**18**) ii AD *IG* X (2) (1) 312 (s. *Εὔοδος*); (**19**) ii/iii AD ib. 262 III, 9; (**20**) V AD *SEG* XLIX 828
—THESSALONIKE?: (**21**) ?iii AD *IG* X (2) (1) 911, 1 (f. *Τίτος*)
MACEDONIA (PAIONIA): (**22**) i/ii AD *SEG* XVIII 367 (Tataki, *Macedonians* p. 210 no. 23) (f. *Σάνκτος*, *Ποντικός*)
—BYLAZORA: (**23**) ii-iii AD *SEG* XVI 402, 2 (-*κό*-: s. *Βαβύλος*, *Κοάρτα*); (**24**) ~ ib. l. 5 (-*κό*-)
—EUDARISTOS?: (**25**) 102 AD ib. XXXII 655, 2 (f. *Διονύσιος*, *Πρῖμος*)
—KAVADARCI (MOD.): (**26**) ii-iii AD *Sp.* 71 (1931) p. 67 no. 149, 1 + 77 (1934) p. 81 (s. *Λούκιος*)
—STOBOI: (**27**) f. iii AD *Studies Stobi* 1 p. 83; *Municipium Stobensium* p. 38 no. 150 (lamp) (Tataki, *Macedonians* p. 176 no. 4) (potter); (**28**) s. iii AD *JÖAI* 32 (1940) Beibl. col. 15 no. 10. 31
SCYTHIA MINOR:
—TOMIS: (**29**) ii AD *ISM* II 125, 8 (s. *Ἐπικράτης*); (**30**) ~ ib. l. 11 (s. *Δημήτριος*)
THRACE:
—KRASALOPARA: (**31**) 202 AD *IGB* III 1690 b, 69 (and Thrace Pizos: s. *Μουκάτραλις*)
—ODESSOS (NR.): (**32**) f. iii AD ib. V 5076 (*CCET* I 9) ([*Σε*]*κοῦνδος*)

Σεκοῦς
MACEDONIA (EDONIS):
—PHILIPPOI (NR.): (**1**) ii-iii AD *BCH* 54 (1930) p. 376 (Pilhofer 48); Collart, *Philippes* pl. 36. 3 (d. *Φίρμος*)
—SKAPORENOI?: (**2**) ?ii AD *BCH* 24 (1900) p. 310 no. 3 (Pilhofer 512) (Lat. Secu (dat.): d. *Βίθυς*)
MACEDONIA (PAIONIA):
—NEAPOLIS? (IZVOR (MOD.): (**3**) imp. *Sp.* 98 (1941-8) p. 28 no. 67

Σέλευκος
CIMMERIAN BOSPOROS:
—BOSPOROS: (**1**) a. 304 BC *SEG* XL 623, 1; cf. *BE* 1990, no. 600 ([*Σέλε*]*υκος*?: s. *Εὔμηλος*: king?)
—GORGIPPIA: (**2**) 103 or 202 AD *CIRB* 1213; (**3**) m. ii AD *Eirene* 7 (1968) p. 67, 2 (f. *Φαρνάκης*, *Φαρνακίων*); (**4**) s. ii AD *CIRB* 1142, 3 (f. —*ν*); (**5**) ~ ib. l. 19 (*Σέλε*[*υκος*]); (**6**) ~ *SEG* XXXVI 708, 4 ([*Σ*]*έλευκο*[*ς*]); (**7**) 173-210 AD *CIRB* 1134, 11 (f. *Ἀθηνόδωρος*) ?= (*8*); (**8**) ~ *SEG* XXXVI 700, 3 ([*Σ*]*έλευκο*[*ς*]) ?= (*7*)
MACEDONIA: (**9**) c. 290-268 BC *RE* (3); *ILaod-Lyk* 1, 1; Grainger, *SPG* p. 66; cf. Beloch, *GG* IV (2) p. 199 (s. *Ἀντίοχος* I *Σωτήρ*, *Στρατονίκη*); (**10**) c. 265-225 BC *RE* (4); Grainger, *SPG* pp. 60-3; Beloch, *GG* IV (2) pp. 201-2 (*Σ.* II *Καλλίνικος*: s. *Ἀντίοχος* II *Θεός*, *Λαοδίκη*, f. *Σέλευκος* III *Ἀλέξανδρος*, *Ἀντίοχος* III *Μέγας*, *Ἀντιοχίς*: king); (**11**) c. 245-223 BC *RE* (5); Grainger, *SPG* p. 63; cf. Beloch, *GG* IV (2) p. 202 (*Σ.* III *Ἀλέξανδρος*: s. *Σέλευκος* II *Καλλίνικος*, *Λαοδίκη*: king); (**12**) c. 220-175 BC *RE* (6); Grainger, *SPG* pp. 63-5 (*Σ.* IV *Φιλοπάτωρ*: s. *Ἀντίοχος* III *Μέγας*, *Λαοδίκη* (Pontos), f. *Δημήτριος* I *Σωτήρ*, *Ἀντίοχος*, *Λαοδίκη*: king); (**13**) s. ii BC *RE* (8); Grainger, *SPG* p. 66 (s. *Ἀντίοχος* VII *Σιδήτης*, *Κλεοπάτρα Θεά*) ?= (*14*); (**14**) c. 145-125 BC *RE* (7); Grainger, *SPG* p. 65 (*Σ.* V: s. *Δημήτριος* II *Νικάτωρ*, *Κλεοπάτρα Θεά*: king) ?= (*13*); (**15**) c. 115-95 BC *RE* (9); Grainger, *SPG* pp. 65-6 (*Σ.* VI *Ἐπιφάνης*: s. *Ἀντίοχος* VIII *Γρυπός*, *Τρύφαινα*: king); (**16**) c. 70-56 BC *RE* (11); Grainger, *SPG* p. 66 (?s. *Ἀντίοχος*, *Κλεοπάτρα Σελήνη*)
MACEDONIA (EDONIS):
—AMPHIPOLIS: (**17**) ?ii AD *BCH* 22 (1898) p. 350 (*Π. Κλώδιος Σ.*)
MACEDONIA (KRESTONIA):
—MORRYLOS: (**18**) c. 230-200 BC ib. 45 (1921) p. 18 III, 84; cf. *SEG* XXXIX 468 (Tataki, *Macedonians* p. 125 no. 3) (s. *Ἀργαῖος*)
MACEDONIA (LOWER PAIONIA):
—EUROPOS: (**19**) c. 355-281 BC *RE* (2); Berve 700 (Grainger, *SPG* pp. 53-60); cf. Beloch, *GG* IV (2) pp. 197-8 (*Σ.* I *Νικάτωρ*: s. *Ἀντίοχος*, *Λαοδίκη*, f. *Ἀντίοχος* I *Σωτήρ*, *Ἀπάμη*, *Λαοδίκη*, *Φίλα*: king)
MACEDONIA (MYGDONIA):
—THESSALONIKE: (**20**) i-ii AD *IG* X (2) (1) 243 II, 15 + *Maia* 25 (1973) p. 200 (*Κ. Πακείνιος Σ.*); (**21**) s. ii AD *IG* X (2) (1) 244 I, 5 (*Γρεκείνιος Σ.*)
MACEDONIA (TYMPHAIA)?: (**22**) iv BC *RE* (1) (Tataki, *Macedonians* p. 214 no. 8) (f. *Πτολεμαῖος*)
SCYTHIA MINOR:
—KALLATIS: (**23**) imp. *ISM* III 127, 5 (f. —*ας*)
SKYTHIA:
—TANAIS: (**24**) ii AD *CIRB* 1262, 7 (f. *Δόμνος*); (**25**) f. ii AD ib. 1266, 2 (I f. *Σέλευκος* II); (**26**) ~ ib. l. 2 (II s. *Σέλευκος* I)
THRACE: (**27**) i BC *IG* II² 8923 (*FRA* 2578)
—DUROSTORUM: (**28**) 198-209 AD *SCIV* 11 (1960) p. 148 no. 3 with fig. 3 (*Eastern cults* p. 222 no. 5) (Lat. Ael. Selucus: s. *Πολυδεύκης*)
—MARONEIA: (**29**) i BC *IG* XII (8) 189 a, 9 (Lat. Seleycys)
—MONTANA: (**30**) f. iii AD *Montana* II 20 (Lat. [S]eleucus)

Σελήνη
MACEDONIA (EORDAIA):
—PYRGOI (MOD.): (**1**) ii-iii AD *EAM* 129 (m. *Λυκαρίων*, *Λυσίμαχος*, *Εὐτυχία*)
MACEDONIA (LOWER PAIONIA):
—GORTYNIA?: (**2**) imp. *Sp.* 98 (1941-8) p. 48 no. 100 (Sokolovska, *Isar-Marvinci* p. 130)
MACEDONIA (ODOMANTIKE):
—SKOTOUSSA?: (**3**) ii-iii AD Dimitsas 843 (m. *Τόρκος*, *Ἰσιγένης*, *Ἀλεξάνδρα*)
MACEDONIA (PAIONIA): (**4**) imp. *Sp.* 98 (1941-8) p. 202 no. 401 ([*Σ*]*ελήνη*: m. *Λούκιος*)

Σελήνιλλα
MACEDONIA (CHALKIDIKE):
—POTIDAIA-KASSANDREIA (NR.): (**1**) imp. *CIL* III 7332 (*BCH* 103 (1979) pp. 300-2 no. 36) (Lat. Seleni[l]la)

Σεληνός
THRACE:
—PAUTALIA: (**1**) s. ii AD *SEG* XLVI 864 I, 24

Σέλης
MACEDONIA (CHALKIDIKE):
—ANTHEMOUS: (**1**) i BC/i AD ib. XLII 567; cf. *Anthémonte–Kalindoia* 2 p. 305 (name) (f. *Διονυσοφάνης*, *Εὐβούλα*)
MACEDONIA (ODOMANTIKE):
—DRABESKOS?: (**2**) iv BC Kaphtantzis 568, 6 (Pilhofer 575) (s. *Πελκείας*)

Σελινώ
CIMMERIAN BOSPOROS:
—PANTIKAPAION: (**1**) iv BC *CIRB* 223 (d. —*ν*)

Σεμέλη
MACEDONIA (BOTTIAIA):
—EDESSA: (**1**) 180 AD *SEG* XXIV 531, 12 (Tataki, *Edessa* 280) (m. *Ἕσπερος*)
MACEDONIA (MYGDONIA):
—THESSALONIKE?: (**2**) 78 AD *IG* X (2) (1) 926 (d. *Τόρκος*)
MACEDONIA (PAIONIA):
—ANTIGONEIA? (BUDUR ČIFLIK (MOD.)): (**3**) imp. *Sp.* 71 (1931) p. 97 no. 228
—BYLAZORA: (**4**) ii AD ib. 98 (1941-8) p. 29 no. 73 (m. *Ἀμμία*) ?= (*5*); (**5**) ~ ib. p. 30 no. 74 ?= (*4*); (**6**) ii-iii AD ib. 71 (1931) p. 40 no. 89, 3 = 71 (1931) p. 153 no. 384 ([*Σε*]*μέλη*: m. *Διοσκουρίδης*)
—NEGOTINO (MOD.): (**7**) ii-iii AD ib. 98 (1941-8) p. 58 no. 119 (—*α Σεμέ*[*λη*])
MACEDONIA (PELAGONIA):
—DOSTONEIS: (**8**) iii AD *IG* X (2) (2) 201, 8

Σέμνη
MACEDONIA (EDONIS):
—PHILIPPOI: (**1**) i-ii AD *AE* 1950-1, pp. 62-3 no. 6 (Pilhofer 721) (Lat. Licinia Semne: m. L. Licinius Saturninus)
MACEDONIA (LYNKESTIS):
—HERAKLEIA?: (**2**) ii-iii AD *IG* X (2) (2) 131 (m. *Σέμνος*)

Macedonia (Paionia):
—stoboi: **(3)** ii ad *JÖAI* 6 (1903) Beibl. 7-9 no. 10 (*Studies Stobi* I p. 176) (*Σέμ[νη]*)
Macedonia (Pieria):
—dion: **(4)** imp. Dimitsas 169
—dion (territ.): **(5)** i-ii ad Oikonomos 47 (*Κορνηλία Σ.*)
Thrace:
—perinthos-herakleia: **(6)** iii ad *IPerinth* 171 (*Αὐρ. Σ.*)

Σέμνος
Macedonia (Lynkestis):
—herakleia?: **(1)** ii-iii ad *IG* x (2) (2) 131 (s. *Ἄριστος, Σέμνη*)
Macedonia (Mygdonia):
—thessalonike: **(2)** iii ad ib. x (2) (1) 565, 3, 7 (*Ἰούλ. Σ.*: f. *Μαρῖνος*)
Scythia Minor:
—istros*: **(3)** ?vi ad Barnea 59 (amph.) (Popescu, *IGL* 141)
Thrace:
—bizone: **(4)** iii ad *IGB* I² 10, 7 with pl. (*Σέμν[ος]?*: f. *—ος*)
—byzantion*: **(5)** s. i ad *IByz* 31, 6; 32, 5 (freed.?)
—philippopolis-trimontium (territ.): **(6)** ii-iii ad *IGB* III 1127 (*Μ. Αἴλ. Σ.*)

Σεμοῦς
Macedonia (Mygdonia):
—thessalonike: **(1)** m. iii ad *SEG* xxxv 767; cf. *BE* 1987, no. 681 (*Σεμοῦνει* (dat.), *Σε(κ)οῦς—BE*: m. *Μαντοῦς*)

Σεμπρώνιος
Thrace:
—perinthos-herakleia: **(1)** iii ad *IPerinth* 164 (*Σεν-*: f. *Αὐρ. Θεοδώρα*)

Σεναμωτίς
Skythia:
—skythai: **(1)** s. ii bc *SEG* xxxvii 674 (*Σ̣ε̣ν̣α̣μ̣ω̣τ̣ίς*: d. *Σκίλουρος*)

Σέξτος
Macedonia (Elimeia):
—aiane (territ.): **(1)** imp. *EAM* 28 (s. *Πετρώνιος*)
Scythia Minor:
—istros: **(2)** 138 ad *ISM* I 193 I, 32 with comm. (*Σηξηστος*—lap., *Σηξ<ησ>τος*?: f. *Εὐκλέων*); **(3)** f. iii ad ib. 218, 10 (f. *Κλ. Δημήτρις*)
Thrace:
—bisanthe-panion: **(4)** i ad PM 1876 (f. *Ἀλέξανδρος, Λάϊος*)
—nicopolis ad nestum (territ.): **(5)** ii ad *IGB* IV 2349 (*[Σέ]ξστος*: s. *Λούκιος*)
—pautalia: **(6)** s. ii ad *SEG* xlvi 864, 9 (*-κστος*: s. *Ζῆθος*)

Σεουῆρος
Thrace:
—glava panega (mod.): **(1)** ii-iii ad *IGB* II 543 (s. *Μούκας*)

Σεους
Macedonia (Edonis):
—philippoi (drama (mod.)): **(1)** ii-iii ad *AD* 52 (1997) Chron. p. 847, 9 with pl. 314 *β*

Σεπτούμιος
Skythia:
—tyras: **(1)** 181 ad *IOSPE* I² 2, 25 (s. *Ἱεροσῶν*)

Σεραπᾶς
Macedonia (Mygdonia):
—lete (nr.): **(1)** iii/iv ad *SEG* xlvii 976 (*Σεραπᾶνος* (gen.): I f. *Παράμονος, Σεραπᾶς* II); **(2)** ~ ib. (II s. *Σεραπᾶς* I)
—thessalonike: **(3)** 129 ad *IG* x (2) (1) 521, 1 (I f. *Παράμονος, Οὐίβιος, Σεραπᾶς* II, *Μ. Ἀλφῆνος Πρίσκος*); **(4)** ~ ib. l. 3 (II s. *Σεραπᾶς* I, *Ῥεία Ζωσίμη*)

Σεραπιακός
Macedonia (Mygdonia):
—thessalonike: **(1)** ii ad ib. 326, 1 (f. *Ἀθηνόδωρος, Λευκίππη*)

Σεραπίων
Macedonia: **(1)** ?s. i bc *ZPE* 136 (2001) pp. 134-5 no. 16, 3, 7 (La'da E1621) (s. *Διονύσιος*)
Macedonia (Chalkidike):
—anthemous: **(2)** 62 ad *SEG* xlii 559 (s. *Ἔρως*)
Macedonia (Edonis):
—philippoi (territ.): **(3)** ii-iii ad Pikoulas, *Chora* p. 123 no. 13, 3 (*[Σ]εραπίων*: f. *..ανος* (gen.))
Macedonia (Mygdonia):
—thessalonike: **(4)** ii ad *IG* x (2) (1) 324 (*Π. Σ.*)
Scythia Minor:
—istros: **(5)** ii ad *ISM* I 197 I, 10 (s. *Ἀπρωνιανός*)
—kallatis: **(6)** 241-244 ad ib. III 74 B, 25
—tomis: **(7)** ii ad ib. II 17, 17 (s. *Δάδας*); **(8)** ~ ib. 125 I, 18 (I f. *Σεραπίων* II); **(9)** ~ ib. l. 18 (II s. *Σεραπίων* I); **(10)** ii-iii ad ib. 21, 3 (*Οὐλπ. Σεραπί[ων]*)
Skythia?: **(11)** hell. Tolstoi 255 (vase)
Thrace:
—maroneia: **(12)** ii-i bc *IThrakAig* E212, 28 (f. *Φιλόξενος*); **(13)** i bc ib. E204, 3 (I f. *Σεραπίων* II); **(14)** ~ ib. l. 3 (*[Σ]εραπίων*: II s. *Σεραπίων* I)
—mesambria: **(15)** i-ii ad *IGB* I² 340 bis (f. *Ἀσιατικός*)
—odessos: **(16)** i-ii ad ib. 116, 3 (s. *Δημήτριος*); **(17)** ~ ib. 135 bis (f. *—μων*)

Σεραπόδωρος
Scythia Minor:
—tomis: **(1)** 201 ad *ISM* II 83 II, 23 (*Αὐρ. Σ.*: s. *Ποσειδώνιος*)

Σεραπόλλων
Macedonia (Mygdonia):
—thessalonike: **(1)** iii ad *IG* x (2) (1) 543, 1 (*Δομέτιος Κλ. Σεραπόλ(λ)ων*)

Σεραποῦς
Macedonia (Bottiaia):
—beroia: **(1)** ii-iii ad *IBer* 340 (Tataki 1174)

Σερβίλλιος
Macedonia (Pieria):
—dion: **(1)** f. ii ad Oikonomos 46; *Essays Laourdas* p. 112 (locn.); cf. Spiliopoulou-Donderer, *KGN* p. 192 no. D8 (date) (*-βεί-*: f. *Παῦλα*)

Σέρβυλλα
Macedonia (Mygdonia):
—thessalonike: **(1)** 129 ad *IG* x (2) (1) 502

Σέργιος
Macedonia (Mygdonia):
—thessalonike: **(1)** v-vi ad Feissel, *RICM* 111 (mosaic)
Macedonia (Pelagonia): **(2)** ii ad *IG* x (2) (2) 288
Thrace?: **(3)** 460 ad *PLRE* II (1) (f. *Ἰωάννης*)

Σέργις
Scythia Minor:
—tomis: **(1)** ?vi ad Popescu, *IGL* 12 (Barnea 38); cf. *SEG* xxvii 396 (name) (*Σέργους* (gen.))

Σεργίων
Thrace: **(1)** i bc *IG* II² 8903 (*FRA* 2579) (*Σερκγ-*: f. *Δημητρία*)

Σέρδων
Thrace:
—philippopolis-trimontium (territ.): **(1)** ii-iii ad *IGB* III 1316; cf. v 5493 bis (*Αὐλουμένης Σ.*)

Σέρειλος?
Macedonia (Edonis):
—amphipolis (territ.)?: **(1)** iii ad *SEG* xxxiii 542 (Pilhofer 595) (*Σερείλου* (gen.): ?f. *—βδελος*)

Σέρεις
Cimmerian Bosporos:
—gorgippia: **(1)** ii/iii ad *CIRB* 1179, 29; Zgusta, *PNS* 704 (s. *Φανδάραζος*)

Σέρκις
Thrace:
—serdica: **(1)** ii-iii ad *IGB* IV 1947 (*Σέρκις*: s. *Αὐλούτραλις*)

Σερούδης
Macedonia (Edonis):
—amphipolis: **(1)** imp. Kaphtantzis 663

Σευῆρα
Thrace:
—philippopolis-trimontium (territ.): **(1)** ii-iii ad *IGB* III 1477 a (*[Σε]υῆρα*)

Σευῆρος
Macedonia (Chalkidike):
—potidaia-kassandreia: **(1)** ii/iii ad *IG* x (2) (1) 262, 4 (Stephanis 2264; Tataki, *Macedonians* p. 95 no. 87) (s. *Ἱέραξ*)
Macedonia (Lynkestis):
—herakleia: **(2)** i ad *IG* x (2) (2) 75, 7 (s. *Λούκιος*)
Macedonia (Paionia):
—kavadarci (mod.): **(3)** ii-iii ad *Sp.* 75 (1933) p. 37 no. 111
Macedonia (Pelagonia): **(4)** imp. *IG* x (2) (2) 280 (f. *Νικόλαος*)
—dostoneis: **(5)** 232 ad ib. 191 (I f. *Σευῆρος* II); **(6)** ~ ib. (II s. *Σευῆρος* I, *Νίκη*)
Thrace:
—serdica: **(7)** ii-iii ad *IGB* IV 1922, 7; **(8)** iii ad ib. 1975, 7 (*[Σ]ευῆρος*)

Σευθείλας
Thrace:
—serdica (territ.): **(1)** ii-iii ad ib. 2011 (f. *Δίζας*)

Σεύθης
Cimmerian Bosporos:
—pantikapaion: **(1)** imp. *CIRB* 823, 3; Zgusta, *PNS* 573; **(2)** i ad *CIRB* 543
Macedonia (Bottiaia):
—beroia: **(3)** f. ii bc *IBer* 156 (Tataki 1176) (s. *Διονύσιος*)
—edessa: **(4)** i/ii ad *SEG* xliii 390 (Tataki, *Edessa* 282) (f. *Ματερίνη*)
Macedonia (Elimeia):
—aiane (territ.): **(5)** ii-iii ad *EAM* 18 (*SEG* xxxiv 647) (f. *Λυσανίας*)
Macedonia (Mygdonia):
—ardrolos: **(6)** i/ii ad ib. xlii 590 (s. *Βίθυς*)
—kalindoia: **(7)** 68-98 ad ib. 580, 83 (f. *Νικίας*); **(8)** a. 98 ad ib. 583, 6 (*[Σ]εύθης*)
—thessalonike: **(9)** i-ii ad *IG* x (2) (1) 243 II, 12 (f. *Ἀριστέας*); **(10)** s. i ad ib. 69, 36 (*Λ. Φήσιος Σ.*)
Scythia Minor:
—ibida: **(11)** ii ad *ISM* v 228, 2 (Lat. Seutis (gen.): f. Othi(s))
—istros: **(12)** iii ad ib. I 301 + 337, 3-4 (Lat. Seuti (gen.): f. Aur. Herculanus)
—tomis: **(13)** ii ad ib. II 165 (PM 1735); cf. *IByz* 370 A

SKYTHIA:
—OLBIA-BORYSTHENES*: **(14)** ii-iii AD *IOSPE* I^2 223 (f. *Διζάζελμις*)
—TANAIS: **(15)** 228 AD *CIRB* 1282, 25 (*Σεύ[θ]ης*: f. —*κος*)
THRACE: **(16)** iv BC *RE* (3) ?= (*58*); **(17)** c. 315-275 BC *SEG* XXX 357, 5 (Perlman, *City and Sanctuary* p. 215 no. A.9) (-*θας*: f. *Λ....*); **(18)** f. iii BC *Thess. Mnem.* 189; **(19)** 292 BC *RE* (5); Polyaen. vii 25; **(20)** 263-227 BC *PCZ* 59473, 2 (Velkov 266; La'da E796) (s. *Τήρης*); **(21)** s. iii BC *CE* 76 (2001) pp. 175-6 II, 8 (La'da E795) (s. *Ἐβρύζελμις*); **(22)** ?ii AD Unp. (Tekirdağ Mus.)
—BAZOPARA: **(23)** 202 AD *IGB* III 1690 d, 41 (and Thrace Pizos: f. *Μουκάτραλις*); **(24)** ~ ib. l. 50 (and Thrace Pizos: s. *Δαλήτραλις*)
—BEROE-AUGUSTA TRAIANA (TERRIT.): **(25)** ii-iii AD ib. 1719 bis (f. *Δω*—); **(26)** ~ ib. 1727 (s. *Ἀντιφ*—)
—BESSOI: **(27)** 88 AD *CIL* XVI 35 (*AEp* 1927, no. 44; 1928, no. 155; 1933, no. 1; 1955, no. 90) (Lat. Seuthi (gen.): f. *Βίθυς*); **(28)** m. ii AD *Germania* 16 (1932) p. 289 no. 1 (Lat. L. Val. Seutes)
—BOURDAPA: **(29)** ii-iii AD *IGB* III 1343 (s. *Βρῖλος*)
—CELALETAE?: **(30)** 86 AD *CIL* XVI 33 (*IDR* I p. 152 no. 24) (Lat. Seuthes: s. *Τραίβιθυς*)
—DIZUROI: **(31)** ii-iii AD *IOSPE* I^2 223 (f. *Διζάζελμις*)
—ERGISSENOI: **(32)** ii AD *IGB* III 1593, 18 (s. *Αὔλενις*)
—GANOS: **(33)** imp. Dumont–Homolle 88a (f. *Ἀπολλώνιος*)
—GLAVA PANEGA (MOD.): **(34)** ii-iii AD *IGB* II 539 (s. *Μουκάζενις*)
—KAINOI?: **(35)** 91 AD *RMD* 5 (Lat. Seuthes)
—LYSIMACHEIA: **(36)** iii BC *AM* 67 (1942) p. 220 no. 14 (*FRA* 3408) (f. *Φίλα*); **(37)** iii-ii BC *PAE* 1912, p. 188 no. 126 = *Polemon* 4 (1949-50) pp. 89-90 no. 269 (s. *Λάκων*); **(38)** f. iii BC PM 105 (f. *Νουμήνιος*); **(39)** m. iii BC *Thess. Mnem.* 40 = Möbius, *Die Ornamente*^{2} pl. 51c (I f. *Σεύθης* II); **(40)** ~ *Thess. Mnem.* 40 = Möbius, *Die Ornamente*^{2} pl. 51c (II s. *Σεύθης* I); **(41)** ~ *IG* II^2 9233 (*FRA* 3407); *SEG* XXXII 305 (date); **(42)** iii/ii BC *Milet* I (3) 64, 8 (and Caria Miletos: s. *Πάρις*)
—MAIDOI: **(43)** her.? Ath. 184 a (fict.?)
—MARONEIA: **(44)** i BC *IThrakAig* E271 (*[Σ]ε̣ύ̣θης*: f. *...κ̣ης*); **(45)** hell.-imp. *FRA* 3549 (f. *Ἀφροδίσιος*); **(46)** i AD *SEG* XXX 698 (*IThrakAig* E255) (?f. *Ἡδεῖα*)
—MYRTOUSSA (MOD.): **(47)** imp. *AEMTh* 4 (1990) p. 632 (*IThrakAig* E106) (*Σεύθ[ης]*)
—NICOPOLIS AD NESTUM: **(48)** ii AD *IGB* IV 2336, 8 (f. —*λης*); **(49)** ~ ib. 2346 (s. *Βίθυς*, f. *Πυρούλας*)
—ODRYSAI: **(50)** c. 450-405 BC *RE* (1); Peter, *MTD* pp. 76-83 (coin) (s. *Σπαράδοκος*: king); **(51)** c. 430-383 BC *RE* (2); *IG* II^2 21, 8, 19; Tod, *GHI* II 193, 1; cf. Osborne, *Naturalization* T66; Peter, *MTD* pp. 76-88 (coin) (s. *Μαισάδης*, f. *Κότυς*, *Ῥηβούλας*: king); **(52)** iv/iii BC *RE* (4); Berve 702; *SEG* XLII 661, 3; Peter, *MTD* pp. 172-202 (coin) (f. *Ἐβρύζελμις*, *Τήρης*, *Σάτοκος*, *Σαδάλας*: king) ?= (*58*); **(53)** iii/ii BC Liv. xlii 51. 10; *RE* (6) (Lat. Seuthes: f. *Κότυς*: king?)
—PHILIPPOPOLIS-TRIMONTIUM: **(54)** 160 AD *RMD* 105 (Mello–Voza 66) (Lat. Seuthes: f. *Βίθυς*)
—PHILIPPOPOLIS-TRIMONTIUM (TERRIT.): **(55)** i AD *IGB* III 1187 (s. *Κότυς*); **(56)** ii AD ib. 1077 (*Π. Αἴλ. Σ.*)
—PISTIROS: **(57)** iv-iii BC Archibald, *Odrysian Kingdom* p. 230 (vase) (*SEG* XLVI 874 i; XLIX 910)
—PRIANEIS: **(58)** f. iii BC ib. XXXIX 653; *Tekmeria* 4 (1998-9) pp. 101-9 (date) (f. *Ἐβρύζελμις*) ?= (*16*) (*52*)
—STROUNEILOS: **(59)** 202 AD *IGB* III 1690 d, 65 (and Thrace Pizos: f. *Σκέλης*)
THRACE?: **(60)** iv/iii BC *PCG* 7 p. 576 fr. 29 (fict.); **(61)** hell. Bernand, *Pan du Désert* 4, 6 (*PP* 4505; Velkov 244); **(62)** 316-309 BC *IG* II^2 1956, 1 (*FRA* 2580); *Ancient Macedonia* 5 p. 445 with n. 10 (date) (*[Σ]εύθης*); **(63)** iii BC *PPetr* III 30, 2 (*PP* 8733; Velkov 246); **(64)** ~ *PPetr* III 100 a, 14 (Velkov 256, 327) (f. —*ς*); **(65)** iii-ii BC *PAthen* 8, 17 (Velkov 263) (s. *Νικήρατος*); **(66)** s. iii BC *Thess. Mnem.* 47 (Velkov 252) (f. *Διονύσιος*); **(67)** ~ *BGU* 2001, 1; **(68)** 221 BC *PEnt* 46, 1 (*PP* 2943; Velkov 247); **(69)** ?ii BC *SB* 3686 (Velkov 245); **(70)** ~ *SB* 3687 (Velkov 262) (s. *Κότυς*); **(71)** ii BC *PPetr* III 95 I, 10 (Velkov 255, 325) (f. —*ης*); **(72)** m. ii BC *Tyche* 9 (1994) p. 61 no. 5, 4 (f. *Σιτάλκης*)

Σεύθων
SCYTHIA MINOR:
—ISTROS: **(1)** iii AD *ISM* I 308 (Lat. Seuto: f. *Μουκατρίων*)

Σευαυῆρος
THRACE:
—BEROE-AUGUSTA TRAIANA (TERRIT.): **(1)** ii-iii AD *IGB* III 1640

Σεύραγος
CIMMERIAN BOSPOROS:
—HERMONASSA: **(1)** s. v AD *CIRB* 1099, 12 (*SEG* XXXIX 697); Zgusta, *PNS* 328 (*Σεύραγ(ος)*)

Σημαγόρης
THRACE:
—ABDERA?: **(1)** v-iv BC *IThrakAig* E35 (*Σ̣ημαγ̣[όρης]*: f. *Πυθαγόρης*)

Σημωνίδης
THRACE:
—BISANTHE-PANION?: **(1)** s. v BC PM 58 with pl. 15 (*[Σ]ημω̄νίδης*—PM, *[Φι]λημονίδης*?: s. *Ζωρίδης*)

Σηνῆκας
SKYTHIA:
—OLBIA-BORYSTHENES: **(1)** iii AD *IOSPE* I^2 135, 8; Zgusta, *PNS* 209 (s. *Οὐζίαγος*)

Σθάζεις
SKYTHIA:
—OLBIA-BORYSTHENES: **(1)** ii AD *IOSPE* I^2 102, 10; Zgusta, *PNS* 705 (s. *Ἰνσάζαγος*)

Σθέννις
MACEDONIA (CHALKIDIKE):
—OLYNTHOS: **(1)** c. 350-280 BC *RE* (-); Overbeck 1343-9; *IGUR* 1491; cf. Osborne, *Naturalization* T62 (Tataki, *Macedonians* p. 142 no. 100; *FRA* 5909); cf. *Horos* 10-12 (1992-8) pp. 21 f.; 14-16 (2000-3) pp. 125 f. (and Athens Diomeia: s. *Ἡρόδωρος*, f. *Ἡρόδωρος* (Athens, Diomeia): sculptor)
TAURIS:
—CHERSONESOS: **(2)** s. iv BC Solomonik, *GAKh* 1499 (vase) (*Σθέ(ννις)*?)

Σιαγοῦς
CIMMERIAN BOSPOROS:
—GORGIPPIA: **(1)** ii/iii AD *CIRB* 1179, 56 (s. *Χρηστίων*); **(2)** ~ ib. l. 60 (*Σι[αγ]οῦς*: s. *Σαρμάτας*)
SKYTHIA:
—TANAIS: **(3)** 244 AD ib. 1287, 12; Zgusta, *PNS* 329 (*Σιαγ[ο]ῦ<ο>ς*: s. *Μάνδασος*)

Σιαύακος
SKYTHIA:
—TANAIS: **(1)** 188 AD *CIRB* 1242, 18; Zgusta, *PNS* 210 (s. *Ἰράμβουστος*); **(2)** 225 AD *CIRB* 1279, 18 (f. —*κος*)

Σιαύασκος
SKYTHIA:
—TANAIS: **(1)** 225-244 AD ib. l. 26; 1287, 20; Zgusta, *PNS* 211 (*Σ̣ιαῠ̣α̣σ̣κος*—1279, *Σ̣ι̣α̣ύασκι̣ς̣*—1287: s. *Ἀμαίακος*)

Σιαύνανσος
SKYTHIA:
—TANAIS: **(1)** 228 AD *CIRB* 1282, 25 (*Σ̣ι̣αύνανσος*?, *[Εὐα]ύνανσος*—Latyshev: s. *Εὐάριστος*)

Σίαυος
SKYTHIA:
—OLBIA-BORYSTHENES: **(1)** ii/iii AD *IOlbia* 52, 3; *IOSPE* I^2 103, 3; Zgusta, *PNS* 213 (s. *Ἀργουάναγος*)

Σίβρας
MACEDONIA (MYGDONIA):
—KALINDOIA: **(1)** c. 335 BC Hatzopoulos, *MI* 2 p. 84 no. 62, 10; cf. *Anthémonte–Kalindoia* 2 p. 306 (name) (s. *Ἡρόδωρος*)

Σιβύρτιος
MACEDONIA: **(1)** 325-316 BC *RE* (1); Berve 703 (Tataki, *Macedonians* p. 429 no. 15)
MACEDONIA (BOTTIAIA):
—MIEZA: **(2)** iii BC *SEG* XXIV 524 II, 12 (Hatzopoulos, *MI* 2 p. 106 no. 92)
THRACE:
—STRYME?: **(3)** s. v BC *SEG* XLVII 1105 + *IThrakAig* E117 (*Σ[ιβ]ύρτιος*: f. —*κος*)

Σιγηρός
THRACE:
—BEROE-AUGUSTA TRAIANA: **(1)** f. iii AD *IGB* V 5577, 4 (*Σει-*: slave?)
—DIONYSOPOLIS: **(2)** iii AD ib. I^2 14 b, 22 (*Σει-*: f. *Αὐρ. Διονυσόδωρος*)

Σιγος
THRACE:
—PHILIPPOPOLIS-TRIMONTIUM?: **(1)** ii-iii AD ib. V 5436 (f. *Αὐλούτραλις*)

Σιδαύχας
CIMMERIAN BOSPOROS:
—PANTIKAPAION: **(1)** i AD *CIRB* 478; cf. KW pl. 46 no. 664; Zgusta, *PNS* 706 (f. *Ὀμψάλακος*)

Σίδηρος
SCYTHIA MINOR:
—ISTROS: **(1)** 138 AD *ISM* I 193 I, 50 (I f. *Σίδηρος* II); **(2)** ~ ib. l. 50 (II s. *Σίδηρος* I); **(3)** iii AD ib. 303, 2 (*Σίδ[ηρος]*: f. *Χρύσιππος*); **(4)** ~ ib. l. 8 (s. *Χρύσιππος*, *Πώμη*)

Σιδμοῦς
THRACE:
—STRATOPARA: **(1)** 202 AD *IGB* III 1690 b, 45 (and Thrace Pizos: s. *Βύζης*)

Σικελία
MACEDONIA (PIERIA):
—DION: **(1)** hell. *SEG* L 589 (d. *Ἐπίγονος*)
THRACE:
—MESAMBRIA: **(2)** iii BC *IGB* I^2 337 (PM 2260) (d. *Μείδων*)

Σίκος?
SCYTHIA MINOR:
—ISTROS: **(1)** v-iv BC *St. Clas.* 7 (1965) p. 280 no. 11 (vase) (n. pr.?)

Σικους
THRACE: **(1)** ii-iii AD *IGB* III 1885

Σίκων
MACEDONIA (BOTTIAIA):
—AIGAI*: **(1)** iv BC *SEG* L 654 bis. 9 (bronze)

Σιλαβύλλης?
Macedonia (Pieria):
—phila?: **(1)** ?iii bc *RPh* 1911, pp. 133-4 no. 36, 87 + *Polemon* 2 (1934-40) Parart. p. 13 no. 17; cf. Helly, *L'État thessalien* pp. 319-20 (locn.) (*Σιλαρυλλεου* (gen.)—*Polemon, Σ.—RPh*: s. —*της*)

Σιλανός
Macedonia: **(1)** ?308 bc *IG* v (2) 550, 12 (Tataki, *Macedonians* p. 429 no. 16) (f. *Ἐπαίνετος*)
Macedonia (Mygdonia):
—thessalonike: **(2)** ii ad *IG* x (2) (1) 241 A I, 11 (*[Κ]λ. Σειλανός*)
Scythia Minor:
—kallatis: **(3)** f. ii ad *ISM* iii 175 (*Σει-*: f. *Ζείζα*)
Tauris:
—chersonesos: **(4)** c. 300-285 bc Kats pp. 110-11 no. 102 (amph.); **(5)** c. 220-210 bc Anokhin p. 143 no. 132 (coin)
Thrace:
—byzantion: **(6)** c. 315-280 bc *FD* iii (4) 151, 1 (s. *Ξένιος*)

Σίλας
Thrace: **(1)** 179 bc *PHeid* viii 413, 2, 11 (La'da E841) (*Σίλα[ς]*: s. *Πτολεμαῖος*: t.e.)

Σιλβάνη
Macedonia (Bottiaia):
—beroia*: **(1)** c. 180 ad *IBer* 384 (Tataki 1180)

Σιλβανός
Cimmerian Bosporos:
—semenovka (mod.): **(1)** iii ad *KSIA* 89 (1962) p. 99 (amph.) (*Συλ-*)
Macedonia (Bottiaia):
—beroia*: **(2)** 492 ad *IBer* 441, 3 (Feissel, *RICM* 64) (*Σιλβα[νός]*)
Macedonia (Mygdonia):
—thessalonike (nr.): **(3)** ?iii ad *IG* x (2) (1) 1005 (*Σει-*)
—thessalonike?: **(4)** ii-iii ad ib. 720, 3 (s. *Ἀγαθήμερος, Νικονόη*)
Macedonia (Paionia):
—stoboi: **(5)** s. iii ad *JÖAI* 32 (1940) Beibl. col. 18 no. 4. 78
Thrace:
—beroe-augusta traiana: **(6)** c. 320-324 ad *Anal. Boll.* 31 (1912) p. 200
—nicopolis ad nestum: **(7)** ii-iii ad *IGB* iv 2337, 7
—serdica (territ.): **(8)** ii-iii ad ib. v 5744

Σιλβῖνος
Macedonia (Bottiaia):
—beroia: **(1)** v-vi ad *IBer* 427 (Feissel, *RICM* 67) (*Σιλβῆνος*—Feissel)

Σιληνίς
Cimmerian Bosporos:
—hermonassa: **(1)** iv bc *CIRB* 1067

Σιληνός
Macedonia (Bottiaia):
—pella: **(1)** iv bc Arr., *Ind.* xviii 3 (Tataki, *Macedonians* p. 160 no. 82) (*Σει-*: f. *Ὀφέλλας*)
Macedonia (Chalkidike):
—olynthos: **(2)** ?350 bc *TAPA* 65 (1934) p. 125 no. 3, 6; Hatzopoulos, *Actes Chalc.* p. 80 (date) (s. *Γλαυκίας*)
Thrace:
—apollonia-sozopolis: **(3)** v-iv bc *IGB* I^{2} 441 (s. *Σάμας*)
—dionysopolis: **(4)** c. 225-200 bc Price, *Alexander* 948 (coin) (*Σιλη(νός)*); **(5)** iii ad *IGB* I^{2} 14 c, 10, 12 (*Σει-*: f. *Αὐρ. Νικομήδης, Αὐρ. Νουμήνιος*)
—odessos (nr.): **(6)** f. iii ad ib. v 5076 (*CCET* I 9) (*[Σ]ιληνός*: s. *Ἀνθρωπίων*)

Σίλιος
Skythia:
—tyras: **(1)** ?i/ii ad *IOSPE* I^{2} 9 (*Σεί-*: f. *Καλλίστρατος*)

Σίλλις
Macedonia (Bottiaia):
—aigai: **(1)** m. iv bc *SEG* xxxv 796
Scythia Minor:
—kallatis: **(2)** iv/iii bc *ISM* iii 125, 3 (s. *Πασ—*)

Σιλουανός
Macedonia (Lynkestis):
—herakleia: **(1)** i ad *IG* x (2) (2) 75, 49 (f. *Πωλλίων*)
Macedonia (Orestis):
—sisani (mod.): **(2)** 146 ad *EAM* 187, 18 (s. *Ὑγίεια*)
Thrace:
—byzantion: **(3)** c. 303 ad *Anal. Boll.* 31 (1912) p. 192

Σίλων
Macedonia (Bottiaia):
—beroia: **(1)** b. 216 ad *SEG* xxxiii 533, 5 (Tataki 1337) (*Φουλκίνιος Σείλων*: s. *Φουλκίνιος Βάσσος, Ποπιλλία Ἐλπιδία*)
Macedonia (Mygdonia):
—thessalonike: **(2)** imp. *Ancient Macedonia* 5 p. 1555 n. 69 (*Λ. Ἀτέλλιος Σείλων*); **(3)** ii ad *SEG* xxxix 635 + xliii 467 (*Τ. Φουλκίνιος Σ.*: f. *Φουλκίνιος Ἥσυχος, Φουλκινία Ἡσυχία*)
Thrace:
—abdera: **(4)** c. 336-311 bc Unp. (Chryssanthaki diss.) p. 225 (coin)
—byzantion: **(5)** c. 250-220 bc Schönert-Geiss, *Byzantion* 1003 (coin); cf. Masson, *OGS* 3 p. 212

Σιμάδας
Scythia Minor:
—istros: **(1)** i bc-i ad *ISM* i 364 (s. *Διονύσιος*)

Σίμαινα
Macedonia: **(1)** s. iii bc *Milet* i (3) 67 I, 9 (Tataki, *Macedonians* p. 429 no. 17) (and Caria Miletos: d. *Εὐκλείδης*, m. *Ταυρέας*)

Σιμαῖος
Tauris:
—chersonesos: **(1)** iii bc Kats p. 89 no. 19 (amph.) (f. *Ἀπολλωνίδας*); **(2)** c. 230-215 bc ib. p. 111 no. 103 (amph.) (s. *Ἀπολλόδωρος*); **(3)** c. 215-200 bc ib. p. 111 no. 104 (amph.) (s. *Εὐρύδαμος*); **(4)** c. 200-185 bc ib. p. 111 no. 105 (amph.) (s. *Παρθενοκλῆς*) ?= (*6*); **(5)** ii-i bc *IOSPE* I^{2} 492 (s. *Δαμάτριος*); **(6)** c. 180-150 bc Anokhin p. 145 nos. 162; 166; 168 (coins) ?= (*4*)

Σιμάκων
Macedonia (Bottiaia):
—tyrissa?: **(1)** iii bc *SEG* xliii 445
Thrace:
—odessos: **(2)** iii bc *IGB* I^{2} 106 (s. *Μητρόδωρος*)

Σίμαλος
Macedonia (Mygdonia):
—lete: **(1)** f. ii bc *SEG* xlvi 764, 11 (s. *Δημαίνετος*)
Thrace:
—abdera: **(2)** f. iii bc *AMNG* ii (1) 183 (coin)

Σιμαλῶν
Tauris:
—chersonesos: **(1)** c. 285-272 bc Kats p. 128 no. 43 (amph.)

Σίμη
Cimmerian Bosporos:
—pantikapaion*: **(1)** inc. *ZOOID* 23 (1900) p. 25 no. 21 (vase) (*Σίμης* (gen.)—*ZOOID*)
Macedonia (Chalkidike):
—akanthos: **(2)** iv/iii bc *SEG* xlvii 871 A, 1, 6 (d. *Ἀμφίτριτος*)
Scythia Minor:
—istros: **(3)** i bc-i ad *IG* II^{2} 8941 (*FRA* 2632) (d. *Ἀπατούριος*)
Thrace:
—anchialos: **(4)** i-ii ad *IGB* I^{2} 375 (PM 883) (d. *Ζῆνις*)
—odessos: **(5)** i bc-i ad *IGB* I^{2} 110, 1 (*Σείμηι* (nom.): d. *Ἀγαθήνωρ*)
—stryme?: **(6)** c. 425-400 bc *SEG* xlix 990 (*IThrakAig* E123) (d. *Νυμῆς*)

Σιμίας
Cimmerian Bosporos:
—myrmekion: **(1)** hell. Gaidukevich, *Mirmekii* p. 62 (vase) (*Σιμί[ας]*: potter)
—phanagoreia: **(2)** iv bc *AO* 1969, p. 111 (vase) (*Σμιδις*—ed.)
—taman peninsula: **(3)** f. ii ad *CIRB* 1223; cf. KW pl. 44 no. 640 (*Σει-*)
Macedonia: **(4)** f. iii bc *IG* xi (2) 203 B, 39; 287 B, 42; *ID* 1409 Ba I, 8; 1441 A I, 39; cf. *ID Index* s.v. (Tataki, *Macedonians* p. 429 no. 19) (*Σιμμίας*—nos. 1409 and 1441)
Macedonia (Bottiaia):
—pella: **(5)** 117 bc *FD* iii (2) 70 b, 7 (Tataki, *Macedonians* p. 160 no. 83) (s. *Ἀγαθοκλῆς*)
Macedonia (Lower Paionia):
—europos?: **(6)** hell.? Dimitsas 145 = *SEG* xxvii 288 (s. *Νίκαρχος*, f. *Νίκαρχος*)
Macedonia (Mygdonia):
—lete: **(7)** iv/iii bc *AD* 26 (1971) Chron. p. 395 (f. *Ἀλέξανδρος*); **(8)** f. ii bc *SEG* xlvi 764, 18 (s. *Ἱππότας*)
—thessalonike: **(9)** ?39 bc *IG* x (2) (1) 30, [2]; 50, 3; 109, 9 (f. *Ξεννέας*)
Macedonia (Odomantike):
—skotoussa?: **(10)** hell.? Dimitsas 844 (s. *Ἀλέξανδρος*)
Scythia Minor:
—istros: **(11)** s. iv bc *IG* II^{2} 8940 (*FRA* 2633) (f. *Παπύλος*)
—kallatis?: **(12)** hell.? *Dacia* 13 (1969) p. 258 no. 1090 (amph.)
Tauris:
—chersonesos: **(13)** iv/iii bc *IOSPE* I^{2} 410 (f. *Βίων*)
Thrace:
—byzantion: **(14)** ii bc *IByz* 73 (Fıratlı–Robert p. 49 no. 14) (f. *Φίλα*)
Thrace?: **(15)** 316-309 bc *IG* II^{2} 1956, 2 (*FRA* 2581); *Ancient Macedonia* 5 p. 445 with n. 10 (date)

Σίμικος
Skythia:
—tanais: **(1)** 244 ad *CIRB* 1287, 31 (*Σείμει-*: s. *Βωροβάρακος*)

Σιμίχη
Macedonia?: **(1)** v bc Ael., *VH* xii 43 (Tataki, *Macedonians* p. 430 no. 20) (m. *Ἀρχέλαος*: slave/fict.?)

Σίμιχος
Thrace:
—naulochos?: **(1)** s. iii bc *IGB* v 5085 (PM 1104 Add) (or Thrace Mesambria: f. *Ἐράτων*)

Σιμμίας
Macedonia (Pieria):
—phila?: **(1)** ?iii bc *RPh* 1911, pp. 133-4 no. 36, 131; cf. Helly, *L'État thessalien* pp. 319-20 (locn.) (s. *Μαχάτας*)
—pydna: **(2)** iv bc *GRBS* 43 (2002-3) p. 119 no. 5, 2, 7
Macedonia (Tymphaia): **(3)** f. iv bc *SEG* xlv 473, 2?; Arr., *An.* ii 12. 2 (Tataki, *Macedonians* p. 214 no. 10) (*[Σι]μμίας*—*SEG*:

f. *Πολυπέρχων*); (4) 331-330 BC Berve 704 (Tataki, *Macedonians* p. 214 no. 9) (s. *Ἀνδρομένης*)
MACEDONIA?: (5) 247-221 BC *RE* (3) (*PP* 14628; Tataki, *Macedonians* p. 429 no. 18); cf. Fraser, *Ptol. Alex.* 2 p. 789 n. 245

Σίμμιχος
MACEDONIA (BOTTIAIA):
—PELLA: (1) 263 BC *IG* IX (1)^2 (1) 17, 71 (Tataki, *Macedonians* p. 160 no. 84) (f. *Ἀγακλῆς*)

Σῖμον
CIMMERIAN BOSPOROS:
—PHANAGOREIA: (1) vi/v BC *SEG* XLIX 1048 (vase)
TAURIS:
—CHERSONESOS: (2) ii BC *MIA* 34 (1953) p. 45 (vase)

Σῖμος
CIMMERIAN BOSPOROS:
—PANTIKAPAION: (1) f. iv BC *CIRB* 193, 4; cf. KW pl. 5 no. 104 (s. *Αὔασις*, *Ἰτίη*)
MACEDONIA (CHALKIDIKE):
—OLYNTHOS: (2) iii/ii BC *IG* XII (3) 41-2 (Tataki, *Macedonians* p. 142 no. 101) (s. *Ἅρπαλος*: sculptor) ?= (*3*); (3) ii BC *IG* XII (1) 75 a, 7 (sculptor) ?= (*2*)
MACEDONIA (PIERIA):
—PYDNA: (4) iv BC Arr., *Ind.* xviii 5 (Tataki, *Macedonians* p. 171 no. 14) (f. *Νικαρχίδης*)
SCYTHIA MINOR:
—KALLATIS: (5) s. iii BC *ISM* III 11, 1; (6) ~ ib. 35, 1 (s. *Ἀσκλαπιάδας*); (7) ~ ib. 35 A, 29 (*Σῖμ[ο]ς*: s. *Προμαθίων*); (8) ~ ib. 35 B, 41 (f. *Ἀπολλώνιος*); (9) 12-19 AD *IGB* V 5011, 13 (*Σεί-*: f. *Γεροντίδας*)
SKYTHIA:
—SKYTHAI: (10) 414 BC *IG* I^3 427, 7 (*FRA* 6910) (slave)
TAURIS:
—CHERSONESOS: (11) c. 272-262 BC Kats p. 111 no. 106 (amph.) (s. *Δαμάτριος*)
THRACE: (12) 264 BC *PHib* 92, 9-10; cf. La'da E835; E848 (f. *Τιμοκλῆς*, *Μνάσων*)
—BYZANTION: (13) iii BC *IByz* 61 (Fıratlı-Robert pp. 47-8 no. 4) (f. *Ματρώ*)
—KARDIA: (14) iv BC *SEG* XXXI 767 a
—LYSIMACHEIA: (15) m. ii BC *ISestos* 38 a, 3 (s. *Σῶσος*)
—PERINTHOS-HERAKLEIA:
——(Geleuntes): (16) iii-ii BC *IPerinth* 61, 32 (s. *Μηνοφῶν*)
—RHAIDESTOS: (17) f. v BC Taşlıklıoğlu 2 p. 88 no. 1 + *BE* 1972, no. 283; *LSAG*^{2} p. 479 no. G (date) (s. *Σκύθης*)
—STRYME?: (18) s. v BC *IThrakAig* E116 (*[Σ]ίμō* (gen.): f. *Νικαρέτη*)
THRACE?: (19) 316-309 BC *IG* II^2 1956, 17; *Ancient Macedonia* 5 p. 445 with n. 10 (date) (*FRA* 2582); (20) ~ *IG* II^2 1956, 34 (*FRA* 2583); *Ancient Macedonia* 5 p. 445 with n. 10 (date)

Σιμπλίκις
THRACE:
—KELLAI: (1) 241-244 AD *IGB* III 1517, 16 (*Κλ. Εὐτυχιανὸς ὁ καὶ Συνπλίκις*)

Σιμύλος
MACEDONIA (CHALKIDIKE):
—POTIDAIA-KASSANDREIA: (1) ?c. 265-254 BC Nachtergael, *Les Galates* 2 bis, [3]; 3, 13; 9, 48; cf. Stephanis 887 (Tataki, *Macedonians* p. 96 no. 88) (f. *Ἐργῖνος*)
MACEDONIA (PIERIA):
—PHILA?: (2) ?iii BC *RPh* 1911, pp. 133-4 no. 36, 116; cf. Helly, *L'État thessalien* pp. 319-20 (locn.) (s. *Μεν—*)
MACEDONIA (PIERIS):
—NEAPOLIS: (3) hell. Hatzopoulos, *MI* 1 pp. 138-9 n. 1 (f. *Νεότας*)
SCYTHIA MINOR:
—ISTROS: (4) iii BC *ISM* I 1, 7 (Migeotte, *L'emprunt* 40) (*Σιμύλ[ος]*: f. *Ἀγαθήνωρ*)

Σίμων
CIMMERIAN BOSPOROS:
—GORGIPPIA: (1) f. iii BC *CIRB* 1137 B I, 14 (f. *Δημοσῶν*)
—GORGIPPIA*: (2) i AD Alekseeva, *Gorgippiia* pl. 143 (vase)
—PANTIKAPAION: (3) ii-iii AD *CIRB* 724 (*Σεί-*)
MACEDONIA (CHALKIDIKE):
—NIKITAS (MOD.): (4) m. v AD *SEG* XXXIII 521 (mosaic)
—OLYNTHOS*: (5) f. iv BC *Olynthus* 10 p. 178 no. 546 (bronze)
MACEDONIA (DERRIOPOS):
—STUBERRA: (6) 90 AD *IG* X (2) (2) 326, 72 (s. *Βίλιστος*)
MACEDONIA (MYGDONIA):
—APOLLONIA: (7) ?iv BC *SGDI* 5284 (s. *Φοξίης*)
—THESSALONIKE: (8) ii-iii AD *SEG* XXX 641 (*Κλ. Σ.*: s. *Κλαύδιος*, *Κισσίς*); (9) ?ii-iii AD ib. 643 (*Κορνήλιος Σ.*)
—THESSALONIKE?: (10) s. iii AD *IG* X (2) (1) 772 (*Αὐρ. Σύμων*: f. *Αὐρ. Θεόδωρος*: Jew?)
THRACE: (11) c. 359 BC *RE* (8); Osborne, *Naturalization* T57 (and Athens)
—BYZANTION (TERRIT.): (12) ii BC *IByz* 193 (f. *Ἀπολλώνιος*)
—BYZANTION?: (13) i BC-i AD ib. 371 (Fıratlı-Robert pp. 126-7 no. 213) (f. *Σωσίων*)
—ODESSOS: (14) s. iii BC *IGB* I^2 36, 6 (f. *Ἀπολλώνιος*); (15) i BC-i AD ib. 145 (PM 207) (s. *Θεοτίδης*); (16) 227 AD *IGB* I^2 70 bis, 6 (I f. *M. Αὐρ. Σίμων* II); (17) ~ ib. l. 6 (*M. Αὐρ. Σ.*: II s. *Σίμων* I)
—ODESSOS (NR.): (18) i BC-i AD ib. 257 (*CCET* I 68) (f. *Ἀρτεμίδωρος*); (19) ~ *IGB* I^2 265 (*Σίμω[ν]*: f. *Ἀπολλώνιος*); (20) s. ii AD ib. 287 (*CCET* I 87) (s. *Διονύσιος*)

Σιμωνίδης
MACEDONIA (BOTTIAIA):
—BEROIA: (1) 178 BC *Syll*^{3} 636, 6 (Tataki 1182; Tataki, *Macedonians* p. 83 no. 49) (s. *Ἀπολλωνίδης*)
MACEDONIA (EDONIS):
—AMPHIPOLIS?: (2) hell. *SEG* L 562, 7 (s. *Ἀλέξανδρος*)
THRACE:
—MARONEIA: (3) 284 BC *PEleph* 2 A, 18; 2 B, 18 (La'da E1822)

Σινβρασος?
MACEDONIA (ODOMANTIKE):
—GAZOROS (TERRIT.): (1) 156 AD Kaphtantzis 737 (Pilhofer 539a) (*Σινβρασ[ω]?* (dat.), *—σιν Βράσ[ω]?*)

Σίνδαξ
CIMMERIAN BOSPOROS:
—PANTIKAPAION: (1) ii AD *CIRB* 709, 1; Robert, *Noms indigènes* p. 511 (*Τιμόθεος Σ.* (n. pr.?): s. *Ἄττας*, f. *Τιμόθεος*)

Σινδέας
CIMMERIAN BOSPOROS:
—HERMONASSA: (1) hell.-imp. *CIRB* 1094, 2; Zgusta, *PNS* 768 (*Σινδέου* (gen.): f. *Σάσας*)

Σίνδοκος
CIMMERIAN BOSPOROS:
—GORGIPPIA: (1) f. iii BC *CIRB* 1137 A II, 29; Zgusta, *PNS* 768; Dubois, *IGDOlbia* p. 14 (name) (f. *Δημήτριος*) ?= (*2*); (2) ~ *CIRB* 1137 A II, 40; 1137 B II, 41 (f. *Ἀντάλκης*) ?= (*1*)

Σίνδος
CIMMERIAN BOSPOROS:
—GORGIPPIA: (1) f. iii BC ib. 1137 A I, 5; Zgusta, *PNS* 768 (s. *Δημήτριος*); (2) ~ *CIRB* 1137 B I, 13 (f. *Ἐπικράτης*) ?= (*3*); (3) ~ ib. l. 18 (f. *Ἀναξιάδης*) ?= (*2*); (4) ~ ib. l. 39; 1137 B II, 9 (f. *Ὑλαῖος*); (5) ~ ib. l. 29 (s. *Ἐπικράτης*); (6) ~ ib. l. 46 (s. *Ὑλαῖος*)

Σίννας
MACEDONIA (MYGDONIA):
—APOLLONIA: (1) s. iii BC *AEMTh* 14 (2000) p. 276 (f. *Παρμενίσκος*); (2) ~ ib. (s. *Παρμενίσκος*)
SCYTHIA MINOR:
—ISTROS: (3) ii AD *ISM* I 196, 10 (*Σίννου* (gen.): f. *Ἰνγένους*)

Σινώπη
THRACE: (1) s. iv BC *FGrH* 115 F 253; *PCG* 2 p. 80 fr. 109; p. 224 fr. 23 (het.)

Σινωπίων
THRACE:
—APOLLONIA-SOZOPOLIS: (1) iv BC *BMN-Burgas* 4 (2002) p. 121 no. 5 (*[Σι]νωπίων*, *[Κω]νωπίων*?: f. *—σις*)
—PERINTHOS-HERAKLEIA: (2) vi/v BC *IPerinth* 71 (f. *Καλλισθένης*)

Σιουάραγος
SKYTHIA:
—OLBIA-BORYSTHENES: (1) ii AD *IOSPE* I^2 685, 5, 11 + *VDI* 1975 (1), p. 71 (s. *Θίρθαγος*)

Σιπέλαγος
SKYTHIA:
—OLBIA-BORYSTHENES: (1) i/ii AD *IOlbia* 90, 11, 16 (*Σειπέλαγος*—l. 11: f. *Ῥευρόμαρος*)

Σίππας?
MACEDONIA: (1) 323 BC Berve 706 (Tataki, *Macedonians* p. 430 no. 21) (*Σιππας*—mss., *Σίρρας*—Hoffmann)

Σίπρας
MACEDONIA (MYGDONIA):
—KALINDOIA: (1) 68-98 AD *SEG* XLII 580, 66; cf. *Anthémonte–Kalindoia* 2 p. 306 (name) (f. *Κότυς*)

Σίρανος
SKYTHIA:
—TANAIS: (1) 236 AD *CIRB* 1250, 14; Zgusta, *PNS* 214 (f. *Σαμβατίων*)

Σίραχος
SKYTHIA:
—OLBIA-BORYSTHENES: (1) ii AD *IOSPE* I^2 92, 6; Zgusta, *PNS* 769 (f. *Οὐσίγασος*) ?= (*2*); (2) ~ *IOSPE* I^2 686, 5 (*VDI* 1975 (1), p. 69) (f. *Οὔσιγος*) ?= (*1*)

Σιρδούχανος
SKYTHIA:
—OLBIA-BORYSTHENES: (1) ii-iii AD *IOSPE* I^2 136, 11; Zgusta, *PNS* 707 (s. *Βουτουνᾶς*)

Σιρούων
THRACE:
—ODESSOS: (1) i BC-i AD *IGB* I^2 203 bis (f. *Ἑστιαῖος*)

Σίρρας
MACEDONIA (BOTTIAIA):
—PELLA: (1) ii/i BC *SEG* XLVIII 824 (f. *Νικώ*)
MACEDONIA (LYNKESTIS)?: (2) s. v BC Arist., *Pol.* 1311 b, 13; Str. 326 d; *SEG* XXXIII 556; cf. XXXVIII 720; XLIII 471; L 649; *Macedonia* 2 p. 14 f. (family); *Ancient Macedonia* 5 p. 1356 (f. *Εὐρυδίκα*)
MACEDONIA (MYGDONIA):
—LETE: (3) s. iv BC Hatzopoulos, *MI* 2 pp. 93-4 no. 79, 15

Σίσας
CIMMERIAN BOSPOROS:
—PANTIKAPAION: (1) i AD *CIRB* 542 (*Σίσου* (gen.): f. *Χοίδρα*); (2) m. i AD ib. 513

Σίσης?
SCYTHIA MINOR:
—ISTROS: (1) iii AD *ISM* I 229, 6 (*Σισι* (gen.?): ?f. *Μαξιμîνα*)

Σισίας
MACEDONIA (BOTTIAIA):
—MIEZA: (1) iii BC *SEG* XXIV 524 II, 8, 15 (Hatzopoulos, *MI* 2 p. 106 no. 92)

Σισίνις
THRACE:
—BIZYE: (1) ?vi AD *AD* 49-50 (1994-5) Mel. p. 341 no. 163

Σισίννης
SKYTHIA:
—SKYTHAI: (1) ii AD Luc., *Tox.* 57-60 (fict.)

Σισιννιανός
THRACE:
—AINOS: (1) iii AD *SEG* XXXVI 655 (*Αὐρ. Σ.*)

Σισίννιος
THRACE:
—HADRIANOPOLIS (TERRIT.): (1) vi AD Beševliev 100, 3

Σισομάρκη
THRACE:
—HERAION TEICHOS?: (1) ii BC Taşlıklıoğlu I p. 7 no. 2 (d. *Ἑβρύλος*)

Σισουλίς
CIMMERIAN BOSPOROS:
—GORGIPPIA: (1) imp. *CIRB* 1199; Zgusta, *PNS* 748 (d. *Νικίας*)

Σιτάλκας
MACEDONIA (PIERIA):
—PYDNA: (1) iv BC *GRBS* 47 (2002-3) p. 116 no. 4, 2 (*Σιτάλκα[ς]*—ed., *Σιτάλκα?* (gen.): ?f. *Εὐίππας*)
THRACE: (2) b. 238 BC *PPetr* III 54 b fr. 1, 3 (Velkov 271; La'da E797) (*Σιτά̣λ̣κ̣ας*: s. *—ιστας*)
—MARONEIA: (3) ii-i BC *IThrakAig* E212, 23 (s. *Ἀπολλώνιος*)
THRACE?: (4) hell. *PPetr* II 25 d + III 61 d (Velkov 269); (5) iii BC *CPR* XIII 5 II, 23; (6) ii BC *Memnonion* 81 (Velkov 270) (s. *Ταρούλας*)

Σιτάλκης
CIMMERIAN BOSPOROS:
—PANTIKAPAION: (1) 221 AD *CIRB* 99, 6 (*Σ̣ε̣ιτά[λκης]*: II s. *Σιτάλκης* I); (2) ~ ib. l. [7] (I f. *Σιτάλκης* II)
MACEDONIA (BOTTIAIA):
—BEROIA: (3) ii BC *IBer* 141, 43; (4) f. ii BC ib. 156 (Tataki 1184) (f. *Ἦθος*)
MACEDONIA (EDONIS):
—AMPHIPOLIS: (5) ii-i BC *IG* II^2 8078 (Tataki, *Macedonians* p. 61 no. 119; *FRA* 518) (f. *Ἀπολλώνιος*)
MACEDONIA (MYGDONIA):
—KALINDOIA: (6) a. 98 AD *SEG* XLII 582, 13; cf. *Anthémonte–Kalindoia* 2 p. 307 (name) (*Σει-*: f. *Ἀνδροσθένης*)
THRACE: (7) 334-325 BC *RE* (2); Berve 712; (8) i BC/i AD *RE* (3); *CIL* VI 26608 (Lat. Sitalces)
—ODRYSAI: (9) c. 480-424 BC *RE* (1) (s. *Τήρης*, f. *Σάτοκος*: king)
THRACE?: (10) 240 BC *WChr* 198, 5 (*PP* 9955; Velkov 273) (-*κες*); (11) m. ii BC *Tyche* 9 (1994) p. 61 no. 5, 4 (s. *Σεύθης*)

Σιτᾶς
MACEDONIA (DERRIOPOS):
—STUBERRA: (1) 74 AD *IG* X (2) (2) 325, 45 (*Σει-*: f. *Ὀλυμπιάδης*)
MACEDONIA (EDONIS):
—AMPHIPOLIS: (2) imp. *SEG* XXIV 603 (*Σει-*: s. *Ζηνόβιος*)
MACEDONIA (PAIONIA):
—KAVADARCI (MOD.): (3) ii AD *Sp.* 71 (1931) p. 74 no. 174, 2 (f. *Βυρδίων*)
THRACE:
—BESSOI?: (4) ii AD *ILB* 64 (Lat. Site (gen.): f. *Μουκάτραλις*)
—DENTHELETAI: (5) 29-28 BC *RE* (-) (king)

Σίτος
THRACE:
—HADRIANOPOLIS (TERRIT.): (1) ii AD *IGB* III 1799, 2 (*GVI* 1108) (s. *Κλεινίας*)

Σιττυρᾶς
SKYTHIA:
—OLBIA-BORYSTHENES: (1) iv/iii BC Dubois, *IGDOlbia* 108 (vase)

Σιώμαχος
SKYTHIA:
—TANAIS: (1) 244 AD *CIRB* 1287, 21 (f. *Θιάβωγος*); (2) ~ ib. l. 22 (s. *Θαύμαστος*)

Σκάβης
THRACE:
—ODESSOS: (1) ii AD *IGB* I^2 133 (*Σκάβητος* (gen.): f. *Βασσοῦς*)

Σκαιδένθης
MACEDONIA (SINTIKE):
—HERAKLEIA: (1) s. ii AD ib. V 5921 + *Melnik* I p. 164 no. 2 (f. *Πυρούλας*)

Σκάμας?
MACEDONIA (EDONIS):
—AMPHIPOLIS: (1) b. 213 BC Hatzopoulos, *MI* 2 p. 83 no. 61, 6 (*SEG* XLVI 715); cf. *PAE* 1985, pl. 25 (*Σκάμα* (gen.), *Σκαμα*—— Hatzopoulos)

Σκαμμάτις
MACEDONIA (MYGDONIA):
—THESSALONIKE: (1) ii-iii AD *IG* X (2) (1) 541, 4

Σκάνιος
MACEDONIA (MYGDONIA):
—KALINDOIA: (1) 68-98 AD *SEG* XLII 580, 63 (s. *Πρόκλος*)

Σκαπούλας
SCYTHIA MINOR:
—ISTROS: (1) f. iii AD *ISM* I 333, 8 (s. *Νικόλαος*)

Σκάρης
MACEDONIA (EDONIS):
—PHILIPPOI (TERRIT.): (1) ii-iii AD Pikoulas, *Chora* p. 123 no. 13, 6 + *BE* 2002, no. 291 (*Σκαρουθειος*—ed.: f. *Ζιπύρων*)

Σκάρις
THRACE:
—ČOMAKOVCI (MOD.): (1) ?iii AD *ILB* 171, 6 (Lat. Scarini (dat.): s. Busile (gen.), f. Aureli. Longinus)
—MARKIANOPOLIS: (2) iii AD *IGB* II 804, 4 (*CCET* II (1) 201) (f. *Εἰσάτραλις ὁ καὶ Λούκιος*)
—SERDICA: (3) ii-iii AD *IGB* IV 1930 (f. *Ἰλλυρικός*)

Σκαρκαιζες
MACEDONIA (SINTIKE):
—HERAKLEIA (TERRIT.): (1) ii-iii AD ib. 2330 (d. *Πύρρος*)

Σκάρκεζα
MACEDONIA (SINTIKE):
—PARTHIKOPOLIS (TERRIT.): (1) ii AD *Arkheologiia* (Sofia) 1987 (1), p. 25 no. 3 (d. *Διονύσιος*, *Μάμα*)

Σκαρούσης
MACEDONIA (EDONIS):
—PHILIPPOI (TERRIT.): (1) iii-iv AD Pikoulas, *Chora* p. 118 no. 9a (*SEG* XLIX 706) (s. *Βίθυς*)

Σκάρτανος
SKYTHIA:
—OLBIA-BORYSTHENES: (1) c. 150-175 AD *IOSPE* I^2 142, 3; *VDI* 1953 (4), p. 130, 12; Zgusta, *PNS* 330; cf. *SEG* XLII 713 (s. *Ἀζιαῖος*)

Σκαυριανός
THRACE:
—PHILIPPOPOLIS-TRIMONTIUM (TERRIT.): (1) iii AD *IGB* III 1318 (*Αὐρ. Σ.*: s. *Βάσσος*)
—SKEPTA: (2) 202 AD ib. 1690 c, 16 (and Thrace Pizos: *Σκα[υρ]ιανός*: I f. *Σκαυριανός* II); (3) ~ ib. l. 16 (and Thrace Pizos: II s. *Σκαυριανός* I)

Σκεδέση
MACEDONIA (SINTIKE):
—NEINE: (1) iii AD ib. IV 2252; cf. V 5880

Σκέλης
MACEDONIA (SINTIKE):
—PARTHIKOPOLIS: (1) ii/iii AD ib. IV 2281 (*Σκ̣ε̣λ̣[ης]*)
THRACE:
—BAZOPARA: (2) 202 AD ib. III 1690 d, 48 (and Thrace Pizos: s. *Διάσκενθος*); (3) ~ ib. l. 49 (and Thrace Pizos: s. *Δόλης*); (4) ~ ib. l. 60 (and Thrace Pizos: s. *Κέλσος*)
—BEROE-AUGUSTA TRAIANA: (5) ii AD ib. 1601 (*Τ. Φλ. Σ.*) ?= (*6*) (*12*); (6) ~ ib. V 5592, 2 (*Eastern cults* p. 174 no. 20) (f. *Τ. Φλ. Δίνις*) ?= (*5*); (7) iii AD *IGB* III 1572 + V 5560; 5565; 5566, 4 (f. *Αὐρ. Τήρης*)
—BEROE-AUGUSTA TRAIANA (TERRIT.): (8) ii-iii AD ib. 5595 (*Σκ[έλ]εος* (gen.): f. *—λέρις*)
—BEROE-AUGUSTA TRAIANA:
——Emporion Diskodouraterai: (9) 235-238 AD ib. II 731, 9 (*Οὐαλέριος Σ.*)
——Karasoura: (10) iii AD ib. III 1626, 8 (*Σκέληνος* (gen.): f. *Τάρσας*); (11) ~ ib. l. 9 (*Σκέλου* (gen.): f. *Πιστοῦς*)
—ERGISSENOI: (12) ii AD ib. 1593, 6, 8 (*Φλ. Σ.*: f. *Φλ. Μουκάπορις*) ?= (*5*)
—PHILIPPOPOLIS-TRIMONTIUM: (13) ii-iii AD ib. 951 (s. *Βίθυς*)
—PHILIPPOPOLIS-TRIMONTIUM (TERRIT.): (14) c. 155 AD ib. 1401, 9 (*Φλ. Σ.*)
—SERDICA (TERRIT.): (15) ii-iii AD ib. V 5717 (I f. *Σκέλης* II); (16) ~ ib. (II s. *Σκέλης* I)
—STROUNEILOS: (17) 202 AD ib. III 1690 d, 65 (and Thrace Pizos: s. *Σεύθης*)

Σκεπαρνᾶς
KOLCHIS:
—ABASGOI: (1) 550 AD *PLRE* III (-) (king)
MACEDONIA (MYGDONIA):
—KALINDOIA: (2) ?i-ii AD *SEG* XXIX 628, 5; cf. *Anthémonte–Kalindoia* 2 pp. 307-8 (*Ταρουσίνας Σ.* (n. pr.?): s. *Κοσείδης*)

Σκέπτικος
MACEDONIA (BOTTIAIA):
—BEROIA: (1) ii/iii AD *IBer* 145, 8 (Tataki 623) (*Ἰούλ. Σ.*)

Σκευᾶς
MACEDONIA (MYGDONIA):
—THESSALONIKE: (1) ii AD *IG* X (2) (1) 297, 2 (*Μ. Μόρριος Σ.*)
—THESSALONIKE?: (2) s. ii AD ib. 252, 2 (f. *Ἰσίδωρος*)

Σκηζις

MACEDONIA (EDONIS):
—PHILIPPOI (DRAMA (MOD.)): **(1)** ii-i BC *SEG* XLVIII 792 (Pilhofer 501a) (s. Ἡράκλειτος)

Σκίλας

MACEDONIA (EDONIS):
—AMPHIPOLIS: **(1)** ?ii AD *FGrH* 257 F 37, 50 (Tataki, *Macedonians* p. 61 no. 120) (f. Σάρκη)

Σκίλβας

MACEDONIA (BOTTIAIA):
—BEROIA: **(1)** 177 AD *IBer* 135 A, 23 (Tataki 1185) (s. Παράμονος); **(2)** ~ *IBer* 135 A, 24 (Tataki 1187) (I f. Σκίλβας II); **(3)** ~ *IBer* 135 A, 24 (Tataki 1186) (II s. Σκίλβας I)

Σκίλουρος

CIMMERIAN BOSPOROS:
—PANTIKAPAION: **(1)** ii-iii AD *CIRB* 763; Zgusta, *PNS* 575 (f. Πόθος)
SKYTHIA:
—SKYTHAI: **(2)** ii BC *RE* (-); *IOSPE* I^2 668; *SEG* XXXVII 674, 3; *SNG BM Black Sea* 669-72 (coins) (f. Πάλακος, Σεναμωτίς: king)

Σκίνδας

MACEDONIA (EDONIS):
—HILL 133 (MOD.): **(1)** m. v BC Pritchett, *Topography* I pp. 46-7 no. 1, 3 + *SEG* XLVI 723 (sherd) (Σκίνδας, Σκίνδαξ—Vanderpool)

Σκιπίων

SCYTHIA MINOR:
—TOMIS: **(1)** 201 AD *ISM* II 83 I, 34 (Σκειπίων ὁ καὶ Ποντικός: s. Ποντικός)

Σκιρτιανή

MACEDONIA (BOTTIAIA):
—BEROIA: **(1)** ii-iii AD *ILeukopetra* 120, 3

Σκίρτος

MACEDONIA: **(1)** ii BC *IG* II^2 9270 (Tataki, *Macedonians* p. 430 no. 22; *FRA* 3491) (s. Ἀριστόδημος)

Σκόζος

CIMMERIAN BOSPOROS:
—GORGIPPIA: **(1)** ii AD *CIRB* 1141, 6; Zgusta, *PNS* 581; **(2)** 173-210 AD *CIRB* 1135, 8 (s. Ἀτ—)

Σκόντις

THRACE:
—ODESSOS: **(1)** f. iii AD *IGB* I^2 162, 1 (*CCET* I 60; PM 1383) (Μ. Αὐρ. Σ.: f. Ζουράζεις)

Σκόπας

THRACE: **(1)** ii-i BC *IG* II^2 8924 (*FRA* 2584) (s. Ταρουσίνας)

Σκοπελιανός

THRACE:
—PHILIPPOPOLIS-TRIMONTIUM (TERRIT.): **(1)** ii AD *IGB* III 1302, 3 (Γ. Οὐαλέριος Σ.)

Σκοπιάδης

THRACE:
—BEROE-AUGUSTA TRAIANA (TERRIT.): **(1)** ii-iii AD ib. 1709 (Τράλις ὁ καὶ Σ.: s. Δόλης)

Σκόρος

MACEDONIA (ODOMANTIKE):
—BERGE: **(1)** iv BC *AE* 1936, Chron. p. 17 no. 9 (Pilhofer 567); *Epigraphica* 37 (1975) p. 65 (name) (f. Γούρας)

Σκόστοκος

THRACE: **(1)** m. iii BC Peter, *MTD* pp. 218-35 (coin) (Σκοστότου (gen.)—p. 218)

Σκουζίλας

THRACE:
—KELLAI: **(1)** ii-iii AD *IGB* III 1523 (Σκουζίλ[ας])

Σκουπῖνα

MACEDONIA (PAIONIA):
—KAVADARCI (MOD.): **(1)** 210 AD *Sp.* 98 (1941-8) p. 57 no. 115 (?m. (ad.) Χιόνη)

Σκύθας

CIMMERIAN BOSPOROS:
—GORGIPPIA: **(1)** f. iii BC *CIRB* 1137 A I, 8; Zgusta, *PNS* 770 (f. Πασίων) ?= (*2*); **(2)** ~ *CIRB* 1137 A I, 10 (f. Ἀριστοκλῆς) ?= (*5*) (*1*); **(3)** ~ ib. 1137 A II, 13 (s. Ἀριστόδημος) ?= (*7*); **(4)** ~ ib. l. 22 (s. Θεόδωρος); **(5)** ~ ib. 1137 B I, 24 (Σ[κ]ύθας: f. Ἀριστοκλῆς) ?= (*2*); **(6)** ~ ib. 1137 B II, 17 (s. Ἀριστο—); **(7)** ~ ib. l. 51 (f. Ἀριστόδημος) ?= (*3*)
SCYTHIA MINOR:
—KALLATIS: **(8)** s. iii BC *ISM* III 35 B, 38 (f. Ἀφαιστίων)
TAURIS:
—CHERSONESOS: **(9)** iii BC Solomonik, *GAKh* 1513 (vase) (Σκύ(θας)?); **(10)** ~ *IOSPE* I^2 581, 2 (Σκ[ύθας]?: f. Θεόφιλος); **(11)** f. iii BC Kats p. 114 no. 119 (amph., tile) (f. Ὕμνος) ?= (*12*); **(12)** ~ *SEG* XL 615 A, 11-13 (f. Ὕμνος) ?= (*11*); **(13)** c. 285-230 BC Kats p. 128 no. 44 (vase) (Σκύ(θας)); **(14)** c. 237-230 BC ib. p. 111 no. 107 (amph.) (s. Σώπολις); **(15)** 194 BC *Syll*^{3} 585, 20 (f. Ὕμνος); **(16)** ii AD *IOSPE* I^2 493 (s. Θεαγένης)

Σκύθης

CIMMERIAN BOSPOROS:
—PHANAGOREIA?: **(1)** 389-349 BC *CIRB* 1111 (f. Δήμαρχος)
MACEDONIA (MYGDONIA):
—KALINDOIA: **(2)** c. 318 BC Hatzopoulos, *MI* 2 p. 84 no. 62, 28 (f. Πάσων)
SCYTHIA MINOR:
—TOMIS: **(3)** iii-ii BC *AMNG* I (2) 2419 (coin) (Σκύθο(υ)? (gen.))
THRACE:
—AINOS: **(4)** iii BC *BCH* 91 (1967) p. 43 (f. Ζωΐς)
—BIZONE: **(5)** i-ii AD *IGB* I^2 6, 2 (f. Θεογένης) ?= (7); **(6)** ~ ib. l. 4 (s. Θεογένης); **(7)** ~ ib. l. 9 (f. Θεάγης) ?= (*8*) (*5*); **(8)** ~ ib. l. 10 (f. Πρόκλος) ?= (7)
—RHAIDESTOS: **(9)** f. v BC Taşlıklıoğlu 2 p. 88 no. 1 + *BE* 1972, no. 283; *LSAG*^{2} p. 479 no. G (date) (Σκύθεω (gen.): f. Σῖμος)

Σκυθικός

THRACE:
—MARKIANOPOLIS: **(1)** ii AD *IGB* V 5352 (s. Κοίτη)
—ODESSOS: **(2)** ii AD ib. I^2 50 b, 4 (s. Σωσίας)

Σκυθῖνος

SCYTHIA MINOR:
—ISTROS: **(1)** ?iii BC *ISM* I 397 + *BE* 1984, no. 268 ([Σ]κυθῖνος: ?s. Δη—)

Σκυθόδοκος

THRACE:
—DUVANLI (MOD.): **(1)** f. v BC *BIAB* 7 (1933) p. 226 (Boardman, *Gems* p. 296 pl. 672); cf. Dubois, *IGDOlbia* p. 14 (ring)

Σκυλάκιος

SCYTHIA MINOR:
—KALLATIS*: **(1)** s. iii AD *ISM* III 124, 3

Σκύλαξ

MACEDONIA (PAIONIA):
—STOBOI: (1) 232 AD *AJA* 75 (1971) p. 401; *BE* 1972, no. 256 a (slave?)

Σκύλης

SKYTHIA:
—SKYTHAI: **(1)** f. v BC Hdt. iv 76; 78-80; Dubois, *IGDOlbia* 4 (ring); p. 11 (coin) (s. Ἀριαπείθης: king)

Σκύλλη

THRACE:
—APOLLONIA-SOZOPOLIS: **(1)** v/iv BC *IGB* I^2 418 (d. Ἀρτεμίδωρος)

Σκύλλις

MACEDONIA (CHALKIDIKE):
—SKIONE: **(1)** 480 BC Hdt. viii 8; Paus. x 19. 1; *GP* 1261; *Suppl. Hell.* p. 2 sub no. 5 (Tataki, *Macedonians* p. 173 no. 8) (Σκυλλίης—Hdt., Σ.—Paus., Σκύλλος—Aeschr.: f. Ὕδνα)

Σκύμνος

MACEDONIA (BOTTIAIA):
—MIEZA: **(1)** hell. *AM* 27 (1902) p. 314 no. 28, 10 ([Σκ]ύμνος)
SCYTHIA MINOR:
—TOMIS: **(2)** i BC *ISM* II 2 B, 46 (f. Μενίσκος)
TAURIS:
—CHERSONESOS: **(3)** imp.? *IAK* 20 (1906) p. 68 (vase) (s. Κούλιος); **(4)** ~ ib. (vase) (s. Μηνόφιλος)
THRACE:
—BYZANTION: **(5)** c. 230-200 BC *BCH* 45 (1921) p. 19 III, 99 (s. Ἀπολλωνίδας)
—TYRODIZA-TIRISTASIS: **(6)** ii-iii AD PM 1623 (Βενουλέϊος Σ.: s. Βενουλέϊος Ζώσιμος, Βενουλεΐα Ἀττίκιλλα)

Σκώπασις

SKYTHIA:
—SKYTHAI: **(1)** s. vi BC Hdt. iv 120; 128 (king)

Σκωριανός

THRACE:
—PHILIPPOPOLIS-TRIMONTIUM (TERRIT.): **(1)** iii AD *IGB* III 1090 (Σκωρια[νός])

Σκῶρις

SCYTHIA MINOR:
—TOMIS: **(1)** ii-iii AD *ISM* II 258 (Σκώριτος (gen.): f. Θε..νος)
—TROPAEUM TRAIANI: **(2)** ii AD *CCET* IV 4, 5-6 (Lat. Scorinis (gen.): f. Herculanus); **(3)** f. iii AD ib. 1, 2 (Lat. Scoris: s. Μουκάπορις, f. Aurelius, Sabina, Valens, Sabinianus)
THRACE:
—MESAMBRIA (TERRIT.): **(4)** f. ii AD *IGB* I^2 354 quater (*CCET* I 111) (Ταρούλας [ὁ] [κ]αὶ Σ.: s. Βίθυς)
—ODESSOS: **(5)** s. ii AD *IGB* I^2 164 (*CCET* I 54; PM 1416) (Διονύσιος ὁ καὶ Σ.: s. Ἀντίφιλος)
—PHILIPPOPOLIS-TRIMONTIUM (TERRIT.): **(6)** ii-iii AD *IGB* III 1406 (Σκῶρις)

Σκωρισεισος

THRACE:
—ODESSOS: **(1)** ii AD ib. V 5067, 5 (f. Ζουκαιβλωστι)

Σμαράγδιν

MACEDONIA (MYGDONIA):
—THESSALONIKE?: **(1)** i-ii AD *IG* X (2) (1) 689 (Ζμα-: m. Ἁγία)

Σμάραγδος

MACEDONIA (MYGDONIA):
—THESSALONIKE: **(1)** iii AD ib. 562, 1 (Αὐρ. Σ.)
MACEDONIA (PIERIA):
—PYDNA: **(2)** ii-iii AD Dimitsas 156
SCYTHIA MINOR:
—TOMIS:
——(Oinopes): **(3)** ii-iii AD *ISM* II 255, 2 (Ζμά-: f. Ἀλέξανδρος)
THRACE: **(4)** 46-54 AD *SEG* XVI 415 III, 28 (*IThrakAig* E84) (Γ. Ἰούλ. Ζμάραγδος)
—MARONEIA: **(5)** iii AD *SEG* XLIX 891, 1 (*IThrakAig* E312) ([Σμ]άραγδος Φλ.: f. Ἐλπινίκη)

Σμερδίης
THRACE: (1) s. vi BC *PMG* 346 fr. 14; 366; 402; 503; *HE* 265; Ael., *VH* ix. 4

Σμέρτις
MACEDONIA (CHALKIDIKE):
—ANTHEMOUS: (1) ii-iii AD *SEG* XLII 570; cf. *Anthémonte–Kalindoia* 2 p. 308 (name) (*Οὐεντουληνὸς Σ., Μάρτις*—Robinson: f. *Οὐεντουληνὸς Ἀμμιανός*)

Σμέρτος
MACEDONIA (EDONIS):
—AMPHIPOLIS: (1) ii-iii AD *Thrakika* 13 (1940) pp. 25-6 *H* + *Epigraphica* 37 (1975) p. 28

Σμῖκρις
SKYTHIA:
—OLBIA-BORYSTHENES (BEREZAN (MOD.)): (1) s. vi BC *SEG* XXXII 727 (vase) (*Σμίκριος* (gen.))

Σμῖκρος
CIMMERIAN BOSPOROS:
—PANTIKAPAION: (1) iv-iii BC *CIRB* 118 (*GVI* 101)

Σμίκυθος
MACEDONIA: (1) m. iv BC Plu., *Mor.* 177 D

Σμόρδος
CIMMERIAN BOSPOROS:
—PANTIKAPAION: (1) iv BC *CIRB* 171; cf. *Etiudy* pp. 184-5 (f. *Βαστάκας*)
THRACE:
—ABDERA: (2) c. 475-450 BC May, *Abdera* pp. 110-11 nos. 108-11 (coin) (*Σμόρ(δος)*); (3) c. 450-425 BC ib. pp. 125-6 nos. 134-8 (coin); Masson, *OGS* pp. 433-4 (s. *Ἑρμοκάλλης*)

Σμόρζης
SKYTHIA:
—NOVOLUGANSKOE (MOD.): (1) i BC/i AD *SEG* XXXIV 754 (bronze) (Vinogradov, *Pont. Stud.* pp. 641-4); cf. *SEG* XXVI 847 (s. *Παρυάδρης*)

Σόαιστος
CIMMERIAN BOSPOROS:
—TYRITAKE: (1) i/ii AD *CIRB* 907 (*Σοαιστος*—lap.: s. *Γαγανος*)

Σόγαμος
CIMMERIAN BOSPOROS:
—PANTIKAPAION: (1) ii AD ib. 706 (*Σόγα[μος]*—ed., *Σόγαμ[ο]ς*—Tokhtas'ev: s. *Ἰούλ. Δημήτριος*)

Σόγος
CIMMERIAN BOSPOROS:
—GORGIPPIA: (1) ii AD ib. 1143, 8 (s. *Ἀσχο*—)
—PANTIKAPAION: (2) 275-278 AD ib. 36, 24 (f. *Ψυχαρίων*)
—PHANAGOREIA: (3) 51 AD *SEG* XLIII 510, 5 (Levinskaya pp. 237-8 no. 6) (s. *Ψυχαρίων*: Jew?)
SKYTHIA:
—TANAIS: (4) c. 225-250 AD *CIRB* 1287, 11; 1288, 13 (f. *Ἀλέξανδρος*); (5) 228 AD ib. 1283, 12 (f. *Διονύσιος*)

Σόγους
CIMMERIAN BOSPOROS:
—GORGIPPIA: (1) ii AD ib. 1159 A, 1 (s. *Οὐα*—)
—PANTIKAPAION: (2) 306 AD ib. 64, 4 (Levinskaya p. 229 no. 1) (*Αὐρ. Οὐαλέριος Σ. ὁ καὶ Ὀλυμπιανός*: s. *Ὄλυμπος*)

Σοζίμιος?
SCYTHIA MINOR:
—TOMIS: (1) ii-iii AD *ISM* II 307, 7 (*Σοζεί-*: s. *Θιθίς, Μενεκλῆς*)

Σοζίρσαυος
SKYTHIA:
—TANAIS: (1) 228 AD *CIRB* 1282, 19 (s. *Ἀσκληπιάδης*)

Σόλων
CIMMERIAN BOSPOROS:
—PANTIKAPAION: (1) iv BC *IGAIMK* 104 (1935) p. 312 no. 80 (tile) (*Σόλω(ν)*)
MACEDONIA: (2) 171-168 BC *RE* (3) (Tataki, *Macedonians* p. 430 no. 23)
MACEDONIA (BOTTIAIA):
—PELLA: (3) iii-ii BC *AJA* 77 (1973) p. 69 no. 2
MACEDONIA (MYGDONIA):
—KLITAI: (4) c. 230-200 BC *BCH* 45 (1921) p. 18 III, 85 (Tataki, *Macedonians* p. 115 no. 1) (f. *Φανέας*)
THRACE:
—MADYTOS: (5) hell. *ISestos* 60 (f. *Σάτοκος*)

Σολώνιος
THRACE:
—SERDICA: (1) iii AD *IGB* IV 1950, 2, 5 (*Αὐρ. Σ.*: s. *Λοῦππος*, f. *Αὐρ. Πρόκλος*)

Σόνκος
MACEDONIA (SINTIKE):
—PARTHIKOPOLIS (TERRIT.): (1) ii AD *Arkheologiia* (Sofia) 1987 (1), p. 25 no. 3 (f. *Διονύσιος*)

Σόρχακος
SKYTHIA:
—TANAIS: (1) 228 AD *CIRB* 1282, 20; Zgusta, *PNS* 217 (f. *Οὐροάστιρος*)

Σοσίπτας
MACEDONIA (BOTTIAIA):
—TYRISSA? (ASVESTARI (MOD.)): (1) f. ii BC *SEG* XLVII 999, 12 (*Σοσίπ(π)ας*—ed.)

Σόσσιος
MACEDONIA (BOTTIAIA):
—BEROIA: (1) ii/iii AD *IBer* 143 A, 8 (Tataki 1190) (s. *Θεαγένης*)
SKYTHIA:
—OLBIA-BORYSTHENES: (2) ii AD *IOSPE* I² 128, 7 (s. *Κάρπος*)
THRACE:
—NICOPOLIS AD NESTUM: (3) ii AD *IGB* IV 2336, 6 (f. —*λος*)

Σόσσις
THRACE:
—KRETA (MOD.): (1) ii-iii AD ib. II 594 + V 5194 (*[Μ]ᾶρκος Σίκ̣ι̣ς Σ.*)

Σουάκαβος?
MACEDONIA (EDONIS):
—AMPHIPOLIS: (1) ii-iii AD *Thracia* 2 p. 279 + *Epigraphica* 37 (1935) pp. 31-2 (*Σουακάβου* (gen.))

Σουδείκενθος
THRACE:
—ABDERA: (1) ii AD *BCH* 37 (1913) p. 138 no. 42, 3 (*IThrakAig* E21)
—MARKIANOPOLIS (TERRIT.): (2) s. iii AD *Romanizmăt* II 745 (Dimitrov p. 38 no. 58) (Lat. Var. Sudicintis: s. *Σοῦσα*)
—PHILIPPOPOLIS-TRIMONTIUM: (3) imp. *CIL* VI 2785 (Lat. Sudicentius)

Σούδιος
MACEDONIA (EDONIS):
—PHILIPPOI (NR.): (1) ii AD *BCH* 24 (1900) p. 306 no. 2 (Pilhofer 29) (s. *Παιβίλας, Μάντα*)
MACEDONIA (MYGDONIA):
—THESSALONIKE: (2) ii-iii AD *IG* X (2) (1) 489

Σούδις
MACEDONIA (BOTTIAIA):
—EDESSA: (1) 180 AD *SEG* XXIV 531, 13 (Tataki, *Edessa* 283) (s. *Καλλίστη*)
MACEDONIA (EDONIS):
—PHILIPPOI (DRAMA (MOD.)): (2) ii-iii AD *AD* 52 (1997) Chron. p. 847, 5 with pl. 314 β

Σουηριανός
MACEDONIA (MYGDONIA):
—THESSALONIKE?: (1) ii-iii AD *IG* X (2) (1) 261, 13

Σουκίας
THRACE:
—PAUTALIA (TERRIT.): (1) ii-iii AD *IGB* IV 2120
—SPINOPARA: (2) ii AD ib. 2192, 6 (f. *Μουκιανός*)

Σουκκεσσός
MACEDONIA (LYNKESTIS):
—HERAKLEIA: (1) i AD *IG* X (2) (2) 75, 37 (f. *Πόπλιος*)

Σουκους
THRACE:
—PHILIPPOPOLIS-TRIMONTIUM: (1) ii-iii AD *IGB* III 975 (s./d. *Ἰσ*—)
THRACE?: (2) ii AD *IG* X (2) (1) 910, 4 (Lat. Sucus: s. Dudix)

Σούλας?
SCYTHIA MINOR:
—CAPIDAVA: (1) ?v-vi AD Popescu, *IGL* 227

Σουλιφέρα?
SCYTHIA MINOR:
—TOMIS: (1) v-vi AD Barnea 8 (Popescu, *IGL* 44) (?m. *Καλλιόπη*)

Σοῦλος
THRACE:
—PERINTHOS-HERAKLEIA: (1) ii AD *IPerinth* 217 (*GVI* 1631) (sculptor)

Σουλπᾶς
MACEDONIA (MYGDONIA):
—KALINDOIA: (1) 68-98 AD *SEG* XLII 580, 90 (*Σουλπᾶ* (gen.): f. *Κλεόμαχος*)

Σουλπικιανός
SCYTHIA MINOR:
—ISTROS: (1) ii AD *ISM* I 197 I, 13 (s. *Κάστος*)

Σουλπίκιος
THRACE:
—PERINTHOS-HERAKLEIA: (1) iii AD *IPerinth* 147 (-*κει*-: f. *ΠΑΦΙΟΜΝΑ*)

Σουλπίκις
THRACE:
—PAUTALIA: (1) f. iii AD *IBer* 387 (glad.)

Σοῦμμος
MACEDONIA (BOTTIAIA):
—BEROIA: (1) ii-iii AD ib. 408
MACEDONIA (MYGDONIA):
—THESSALONIKE: (2) ii-iii AD *IG* X (2) (1) 437 (s. *Μαντώ*)

Σουντους
THRACE:
—GEUPASA: (1) ii-iii AD *IGB* III 1811 (s. *Γενικείλας*)

Σουπερίων
THRACE:
—DIONYSOPOLIS: (1) iii AD ib. I² 14 c, 16 (f. *Αὐρ. Ἀντίπατρος*)

Σουπόλιχος
TAURIS:
—CHERSONESOS: (1) f. iv AD Const. Porph., *De admin. imp.* 53, 168 (f. *Βύσκος*)

Σούρα
MACEDONIA (ODOMANTIKE):
—GAZOROS (TERRIT.): (**1**) 106 AD *SEG* XXX 596, 7 (Pilhofer 555) (d. *Μουκάσης*, m. *Διονύσιος*, *Τόρκος*)
MACEDONIA (SINTIKE):
—PARTHIKOPOLIS (TERRIT.): (**2**) 235-253 AD *IGB* IV 2314; *JDAI* 84 (1969) p. 160 (date) (m. *Ἀρτεμιδώρα*)
THRACE:
—ČOMAKOVCI (MOD.): (**3**) ?iii AD *ILB* 171, 8 (Lat. Sura: d. *Πυρούλας*, m. Aureli. Longinus)
—NICOPOLIS AD ISTRUM (NR.): (**4**) ii-iii AD *IGB* II 708

Σουράτραλις
THRACE:
—PHILIPPOPOLIS-TRIMONTIUM (TERRIT.): (**1**) ii-iii AD ib. III 1447

Σούριος
THRACE:
—LJUBLEN (MOD.): (**1**) s. iii AD *CCET* II (2) 567 (Lat. Aur. Surius)
THRACE?: (**2**) iii AD Beševliev, *EP* 16, 3 (*SEG* XV 469); cf. *BE* 1954, no. 168

Σοῦρις
THRACE:
—KRASALOPARA: (**1**) 202 AD *IGB* III 1690 b, 68 (and Thrace Pizos: s. *Αὐλούζενις*); (**2**) ~ ib. l. 70 (and Thrace Pizos: s. *Βρινκάζερις*)
—NICOPOLIS AD ISTRUM?: (**3**) 159 AD *Chiron* 29 (1999) p. 149 no. 1 (Lat. Suri (dat.): s. *Διάλπυρις*)
—NICOPOLIS AD NESTUM: (**4**) ii-iii AD *IGB* IV 2337, 10 ([*Σ*]*οῦρις*); (**5**) ~ ib. l. 12
—PHILIPPOPOLIS-TRIMONTIUM: (**6**) iii AD ib. III 963 (s. *Αὐλούπορις*)
—PHILIPPOPOLIS-TRIMONTIUM (TERRIT.): (**7**) imp. ib. 1392 (s. *Διvίας*)
—SKEPTA: (**8**) 202 AD ib. 1690 c, 18 (and Thrace Pizos: *Σ. Παντᾶς*: s. *Δόλης*)

Σοῦσα
MACEDONIA (EDONIS):
—PHILIPPOI: (**1**) i-ii AD Dimitsas 973 + Pilhofer 86 (m. *Ποσειδώνιος*)
THRACE:
—MARKIANOPOLIS (TERRIT.): (**2**) s. iii AD *Romanizmăt* II 745 (Dimitrov p. 38 no. 58) (Lat. Susa: m. *Σουδείκενθος*)

Σούσας
SKYTHIA:
—TANAIS: (**1**) 104 AD *CIRB* 1259, 20; Zgusta, *PNS* 743 (s. *Πάβας*)

Σουσᾶς
THRACE:
—DIONYSOPOLIS: (**1**) ii AD *IGB* I^2 27 bis (*Σουσᾶνος* (gen.))
—KOMOTINI (MOD.): (**2**) imp. *Belomorski Pregled* I (1942) p. 336 no. 41 (*BE* 1948, no. 148; *IThrakAig* E482) (*Σουσᾶ* (gen.): s. *Βίθυς*)
—ODESSOS: (**3**) s. ii AD *IGB* I^2 175 (PM 1739); *Dacia* 21 (1977) p. 161 (date) (*Σουσᾶ* (gen.): f. (ad.) *Γάϊος*)
—PERINTHOS-HERAKLEIA: (**4**) ii AD *IPerinth* 217 (*GVI* 1631) (*Σουσᾶδος* (gen.): I f. *Σουσᾶς* II); (**5**) ~ *IPerinth* 217 (*GVI* 1631) (II s. *Σουσᾶς* I, *Σεκοῦνδα*)

Σουσίων
THRACE:
—NICOPOLIS AD ISTRUM (TERRIT.): (**1**) ii AD *IGB* V 5244 a, 3 (f. *Δημητριανός*) ?= (*2*); (**2**) ~ ib. l. 9 (f. *Ἡρακλιανός*) ?= (*1*)
—PERINTHOS-HERAKLEIA: (**3**) iii AD *IPerinth* 218, 11 (f. *Θεόδοτος*)
—PHILIPPOPOLIS-TRIMONTIUM: (**4**) ii-iii AD *IGB* III 912, 1 (f. *Μάξιμος*)
—SERDICA: (**5**) ii AD ib. IV 1923, 4 (f. *—ων*)

Σοῦσος
CIMMERIAN BOSPOROS:
—FRONTOVOE (MOD.): (**1**) ii/iii AD *SEG* XXXV 869, 7; cf. *BE* 1990, no. 592 (*Σούσο*[*υ*] (gen.): f. *Λίμνακος*)
SKYTHIA:
—TYRAS: (**2**) ii AD *IOSPE* I^2 11; cf. Zgusta, *PNS* 743 (*Πιασοῦσος*?)
THRACE:
—BYZANTION: (**3**) ii BC *IByz* 112 (f. *Φιλόμουσος*)
—MADYTOS: (**4**) imp. *ISestos* 65 (f. *Μούκιος*)
—PERINTHOS-HERAKLEIA: (**5**) ii-iii AD *IPerinth* 46

Σουσούλων
SCYTHIA MINOR:
—ISTROS: (**1**) i AD *ISM* I 200, 9 (s. *Πάτεις*)
SKYTHIA:
—OLBIA-BORYSTHENES: (**2**) i/ii AD *IOlbia* 79, 10 (*IOSPE* I^2 116); Zgusta, *PNS* 709 (f. *Ἀβρόαγος*)

Σοφαίνετος
CIMMERIAN BOSPOROS:
—PANTIKAPAION: (**1**) v-vi AD *ZOOID* 21 (1898) p. 207 no. 17 (*Σοφαί*[*νετος*]?)

Σόφη
MACEDONIA (BOTTIAIA):
—BEROIA: (**1**) ?211 AD *ILeukopetra* 60, 2 (m. *Ἀττίκιλλα*)
MACEDONIA (MYGDONIA):
—KALINDOIA: (**2**) 68-98 AD *SEG* XLII 580, 94 (m. *Καρβερένθης*)

Σοφία
MACEDONIA (BOTTIAIA):
—BEROIA: (**1**) ?v AD *IBer* 434
—EDESSA: (**2**) v-vi AD Feissel, *RICM* 28 (*Σω*-); (**3**) ~ ib. 31
THRACE:
—ODESSOS*: (**4**) vi AD Beševliev 103, 3 (d. *Θεόκτιστος*)
—TRAIANOPOLIS: (**5**) v AD Meïmaris–Bakirtzis 26, 3 (*SEG* XXIV 644; *IThrakAig* E444) (*Σοφ*[*ία*]?: ?d. *Κότυς*)

Σοφῖνος
THRACE:
—SERDICA (TERRIT.): (**1**) ii-iii AD *AEMÖ* 10 (1886) pp. 238-9 no. 2, 10 (-*φεῖ*-)

Σοφοκλῆς
CIMMERIAN BOSPOROS:
—PANTIKAPAION: (**1**) i/ii AD *CIRB* 576
THRACE:
—PERINTHOS-HERAKLEIA:
——(*φυλ. πρωτ.*): (**2**) iii AD *IPerinth* 105 (f. *Αὐρ. Κόσμος*)

Σόφος
THRACE:
—PERINTHOS-HERAKLEIA: (**1**) ii-iii AD ib. 103 (f. *Ἀρτεμισία*)

Σόφων
SCYTHIA MINOR:
—TOMIS: (**1**) ii-iii AD *ISM* II 342 (*GVI* 304)

Σπαδάγας
KOLCHIS:
—SANIGAI: (**1**) f. ii AD *RE* (-) (king)

Σπάδακος
SKYTHIA:
—OLBIA-BORYSTHENES: (**1**) imp. *IOSPE* I^2 147, 4; Zgusta, *PNS* 218 (f. *Ὀρόντης*)

Σπάδινος
CIMMERIAN BOSPOROS:
—PANTIKAPAION*: (**1**) 483 AD *CIRB* 67, 6 + *SEG* XLVIII 993

Σπάκος
SKYTHIA:
—OLBIA-BORYSTHENES: (**1**) ?ii AD *IOSPE* I^2 133, 6 + Zgusta, *PNS* 219 (*Σπ*[*ά*]*κος*)

Σπάλων
SKYTHIA:
—OLBIA-BORYSTHENES: (**1**) s. iv BC *SEG* L 702 II, 3 (*Σπάλω*(*ν*))

Σπαράδοκος
THRACE:
—ODRYSAI: (**1**) m. v BC *RE* (-); Peter, *MTD* pp. 62-75 (coin) (s. *Τήρης*, f. *Σεύθης*: king?)

Σπαργαπείθης
SKYTHIA:
—AGATHYRSOI: (**1**) vi/v BC Hdt. iv 78 (king)
—SKYTHAI: (**2**) s. vii BC ib. 76 (f. *Λύκος*: king)

Σπάργης
MACEDONIA (EDONIS):
—AMPHIPOLIS: (**1**) a. 357 BC Hatzopoulos, *Actes Amphipolis* p. 20 no. 2, 7 (*SEG* XLI 556); Hatzopoulos, *Actes Amphipolis* p. 25 no. 3, 11 (*SEG* XLI 557); Hatzopoulos, *Actes Amphipolis* p. 30 no. 4, 9 (*SEG* XLI 558); Hatzopoulos, *Actes Amphipolis* p. 31 no. 5, 2; p. 34 no. 6, 8; pp. 38-9 no. 7, 15 (*Σπάργεως*, *Σπάργεος* (gen.))

Σπάρκη
MACEDONIA (ODOMANTIKE):
—SIRRHA: (**1**) ii/iii AD *SEG* XLVIII 877

Σπαρόβαϊς
CIMMERIAN BOSPOROS:
—PANTIKAPAION (NR.): (**1**) ii AD *CIRB* 965 (s. *Ἔρως*)

Σπαροπάδης
CIMMERIAN BOSPOROS:
—ZENONOS CHERSONESOS*: (**1**) v/iv BC *SEG* XL 643 ([*Σ*]*παροπάδης*)

Σπαρόφοτος
CIMMERIAN BOSPOROS:
—PANTIKAPAION: (**1**) s. iii BC *CIRB* 247; Zgusta, *PNS* 220 (f. *Νουμήνιος*)

Σπαρτακίων
CIMMERIAN BOSPOROS:
—GORGIPPIA: (**1**) f. ii AD *SGE* 35 (1972) p. 51, 6 (*CIRB* 1132) + *CIRB* 1162 (*Σπαρτακί*[*ων*]?); (**2**) 173-210 AD ib. 1135, 20 (s. *Σύμμαχος*)

Σπάρτακος
MACEDONIA: (**1**) 232 or 207 BC *CPR* XVIII 13, 261 (Tataki, *Macedonians* p. 431 no. 25; La'da E1624) ([*Σ*]*πάρτακο*[*ς*]); (**2**) ?219 BC *PUG* III 103, 9 (Tataki, *Macedonians* p. 431 no. 25; La'da E1622) (s. *Πτολεμαῖος*); (**3**) 44-37 BC *POxy* 1635, 3, 8, 10, 12 (Tataki, *Macedonians* p. 497 no. 230; La'da E1623) (s. *Πτολεμαῖος*)
THRACE: (**4**) c. 250-240 BC *PHib* 235, 1 (Velkov 280; La'da E798); (**5**) 73-71 BC *RE* (-) (slave)
—AINOS: (**6**) 194 BC *Milet* I (3) 54, 3 (f. *Διονύσιος*)

Σπάρτη
MACEDONIA (BOTTIAIA):
—MIEZA: (**1**) f. ii BC *SEG* XLIII 408 (I d. *Λύσων*, *Δημαρέτη*, ?m. *Σπάρτη* II); (**2**) ~ ib. 417 (II ?d. *Εὔιππος*, *Σπάρτη* I)

Σπαρτοκίων
CIMMERIAN BOSPOROS:
—GORGIPPIA: (**1**) f. iii BC *CIRB* 1137 A II, 53; 1137 B II, 58; cf. *Etiudy* pp. 182-3 no.

2; Zgusta, *PNS* 576 (s. *Σώστρατος*); **(2)** 173-210 AD *CIRB* 1134, 24 (s. *Ἀγαθοῦς*)

Σπάρτοκος
CIMMERIAN BOSPOROS:
—BOSPOROS: **(1)** c. 390-344 BC *RE* (2); Rhodes–Osborne 64, 1, 9, 12, 22, etc.; *IGAIMK* 104 (1935) p. 312 nos. 81-2 (tile); Zgusta, *PNS* 576 (s. *Λεύκων*: king); **(2)** c. 330-284 BC *RE* (3); *IG* II^2 653, 9-10, 18, 20, etc.; *CIRB* 18; 19; 20; 21; 23; 25; 974; 1036, 1; 1043; *IGAIMK* 104 (1935) p. 312 no. 83 (tile); *Stud. Blavatskii* pp. 70-1 (vase); *SEG* XXVIII 114; XLV 990 (*Σπάρδοκος*—vase: s. *Εὔμηλος*, f. *Παιρισάδης*: king); **(3)** c. 280-240 BC *RE* (4); *CIRB* 24; 822? (s. *Παιρισάδης*: king); **(4)** iii/ii BC ib. 26, 1?; 75, 5; *SEG* XXIII 314, 5; *IGAIMK* 104 (1935) p. 312 nos. 84-6 (tile); cf. *RE* (4); *Historia* 4 (1955) pp. 424 ff. (f. *Καμασαρύα*: king?)
—BOSPOROS*: **(5)** c. 438-431 BC *RE* (1); *SEG* XLV 1000, [1] (f. *Σάτυρος*: king)
—PANTIKAPAION: **(6)** i AD *CIRB* 480 (f. *Παίρακος*)
SKYTHIA:
—OLBIA-BORYSTHENES: **(7)** iv BC *IOSPE* I^2 214 (s. *Κλείδημος*)
THRACE:
—AINOS: **(8)** ii BC *IG* II^2 7972 (*FRA* 262) (f. *Εἰρήνη*)
—DEIZENOI?: **(9)** ii-iii AD *IGB* III 1204 (*Σπάρτ[ο]κος*: f. *Ἄθυς*: doctor?)
—KABYLE: **(10)** c. 300-275 BC *SEG* XLII 661, 4-5, 11, 14-5, 21; Peter, *MTD* pp. 203-15 (coin) (king)
—PHILIPPOPOLIS-TRIMONTIUM (TERRIT.): **(11)** ii AD *IGB* III 1132 (*Κλ. Σ.*: f. *Ῥοιμητάλκης ὁ καὶ Ὀλύμπιος*)
—SEUTHOPOLIS (NR.): **(12)** iii BC ib. 1730, 2; cf. V 5612 bis
—STRATOPARA: **(13)** 202 AD ib. III 1690 b, 39 (and Thrace Pizos: f. *Μουκάτραλις*)

Σπατάλη
MACEDONIA (EDONIS):
—PHILIPPOI: **(1)** imp. *BCH* 58 (1934) p. 478 no. 19 (Pilhofer 260) (Lat. Tatinia Spatale)

Σπάταλος
MACEDONIA (BOTTIAIA):
—BEROIA?: **(1)** m. ii AD *IBer* 383, 10 (Tataki 1194)

Σπέδις
MACEDONIA (BOTTIAIA):
—EDESSA: **(1)** 128 AD *SEG* XII 342, 3 (Tataki, *Edessa* 284)

Σπένδουσα
MACEDONIA (MYGDONIA):
—THESSALONIKE?: **(1)** ii-iii AD *IG* X (2) (1) 861 (m. *Καμερία Τριβούλλα, Κ. Φάβιος Εὐφρόσυνος*)
MACEDONIA (PIERIA):
—PHILA: **(2)** imp. Dimitsas 196 (Lat. Baebia Spen[dusa])

Σπῆνις
MACEDONIA (MYGDONIA):
—THESSALONIKE: **(1)** ii-iii AD *IG* X (2) (1) 666, 2, 8 (biling.) (*CIL* III 7331; *IG* II^2 13226; *SEG* XLIII 461) (s. *Πριμιτῖβος, Σώτειρα*)

Σπιθάμης
CIMMERIAN BOSPOROS:
—HERMONASSA: **(1)** f. iv BC *CIRB* 1066; Zgusta, *PNS* 221 (f. *Σατραβάτης*)

Σπίκλος?
SCYTHIA MINOR:
—TOMIS: **(1)** ii AD *ISM* II 207 (glad.?)

Σπίνθαρος
TAURIS:
—CHERSONESOS: **(1)** iii BC Solomonik, *GAKh* 1273 (vase) (*Σπίν(θαρος)*?)

Σπινθήρ
THRACE:
—PAUTALIA (TERRIT.): **(1)** ii-iii AD *IGB* V 5800

Σπίνθων
CIMMERIAN BOSPOROS:
—PANTIKAPAION: **(1)** f. iv BC *CIRB* 183 (*[Σ]πίνθων*)

Σπόκης
MACEDONIA: **(1)** ?219 BC *PUG* III 103, 12 (Tataki, *Macedonians* p. 431 no. 27; La'da E1626); cf. *ZPE* 117 (1997) p. 211 (s. *—ζελμις*); **(2)** 216 BC *BGU* 2394, 6 + *BO* 48 (1991) p. 844 (La'da E1627)
SKYTHIA:
—OLBIA-BORYSTHENES (BEREZAN (MOD.)): **(3)** f. v BC *SEG* XLII 684 (vase); cf. Vinogradov, *Pont. Stud.* p. 154 no. 3 ter
THRACE: **(4)** c. 360 BC Peter, *MTD* pp. 146-7 (coin) (king); **(5)** 257 BC *PSorb* 17a, 6, 9, 16; 17b, 7, 10, 17, 21, 24 (La'da E842) (s. *Βίθυς*: t.e.); **(6)** 46-54 AD *SEG* XVI 415 III, 38 (*IThrakAig* E84) (f. *Κοισόρμας*)
—BYZANTION: **(7)** ii-i BC *IByz* 188 (Fıratlı–Robert pp. 73-4 no. 79) (*Σπόκη* (gen.): I f. *Σπόκης* II); **(8)** ~ *IByz* 188 (Fıratlı–Robert pp. 73-4 no. 79) (II s. *Σπόκης* I)
—PISTIROS: **(9)** iv-iii BC Archibald, *Odrysian Kingdom* p. 230 (vase) (*SEG* XLVI 874 iv; XLIX 910)

Σπόριος
THRACE:
—BYZANTION: **(1)** ii/i BC *IByz* 192 (Fıratlı–Robert p. 57 no. 37) (f. *Πῶλλα Πακωνία Γλυκεῖα*)

Σπόρος
MACEDONIA (MYGDONIA)?:
—HERAKLEIA: **(1)** ii AD *GVI* 569; cf. *Milliaires* p. 70 n. 1 (locn.)
THRACE:
—BESSOI: **(2)** 138 AD *CIL* XVI 83 (Lat. Spor(us): s. Clagissa)
—NICOPOLIS AD ISTRUM:
——Dizerpara: **(3)** 224 AD *ZPE* 127 (1999) p. 248 + 130 (2000) p. 280 (Lat. Sporus: f. *Δρουβιος*)

Σποῦρις
THRACE:
—SERDICA (TERRIT.): **(1)** ii-iii AD *IGB* IV 1997 (*Σφοῦρις ὁ καὶ Δαλ—*)

Σπουρκίων
MACEDONIA (LYNKESTIS):
—HERAKLEIA*: **(1)** v-vi AD *IG* X (2) (2) 150

Σπωτάγανος
SKYTHIA:
—OLBIA-BORYSTHENES: **(1)** s. i AD *IOlbia* 85, 3 (*IOSPE* I^2 104); Zgusta, *PNS* 332 (s. *Ἀντιφῶν*)

Σταβιλίων
SCYTHIA MINOR:
—TOMIS: **(1)** ii-iii AD *ISM* II 195, 5, 11 (biling.)

Σταδμέας
MACEDONIA: **(1)** ?417-413 BC *IG* I^3 89, 64 (Tataki, *Macedonians* p. 431 no. 28)
MACEDONIA (EORDAIA):
—RYAKI (MOD.): **(2)** 5 AD *EAM* 97 (*Σταλμέας*—lap., *Στα(δ)μέας*?: s. *Μηριγένης*)

Στάμις
THRACE:
—ODESSOS: **(1)** i AD *IGB* V 5062 (*Στάμι* (gen.): f. *Σωσανδρίων*)

Σταπόλεμος
MACEDONIA (BOTTIAIA):
—BEROIA: **(1)** 223 BC *IBer* 4, 30 (*Σταπόλε[μ]ος*: s. *Ἀμύντας*)
MACEDONIA (CHALKIDIKE):
—NEOS MARMARAS (MOD.): **(2)** ii-i BC *SEG* XXXVIII 600 (s. *Ἄδυμος*)

Στασικράτης
MACEDONIA: **(1)** ?219 BC *PUG* III 103, 10 (Tataki, *Macedonians* p. 431 no. 29); cf. La'da E1629 (f. *Στέφανος*)

Στασίμη
MACEDONIA (MYGDONIA):
—THESSALONIKE: **(1)** 129 AD *IG* X (2) (1) 311, 3 (m. *Φοῦσκα*)

Στατίλιος
THRACE:
—GLAVA PANEGA (MOD.): **(1)** ii AD *IGB* II 562 (f. *Τίτος*)

Στατίλις
THRACE:
—MARKIANOPOLIS (NR.): **(1)** f. iii AD ib. 832 (*CCET* II (1) 216) (s. *Οὐάλης*)

Στάτιος
CIMMERIAN BOSPOROS:
—PANTIKAPAION?: **(1)** ii BC *KSIA* 83 (1961) p. 39 (amph.) (s. *Παλλᾶς*)

Σταφύλος
CIMMERIAN BOSPOROS:
—PANTIKAPAION: **(1)** ?ii BC *CIRB* 260; cf. KW pl. 32 no. 450 (s. *Γλαυκίας*)
MACEDONIA: **(2)** 102 BC *PWürzb* 6, 30 (Tataki, *Macedonians* p. 497 no. 231; La'da E1628)
SKYTHIA:
—OLBIA-BORYSTHENES: **(3)** iii BC *IOSPE* I^2 201 I, 5; 201 II, 15 (s. *Ἡρόδωρος*)
THRACE:
—BYZANTION: **(4)** iii BC *IG* II^2 8446 = 8445; cf. *AM* 67 (1942) p. 106 no. 200 (*FRA* 1407) (s. *Ἀπολλώνιος*)

Σταχέμφαξ
KOLCHIS:
—ZICHOI: **(1)** f. ii AD *RE* (-) (*Σταχέμφλας*—Peripl. Anon.: king)

Στάχυς
MACEDONIA (CHALKIDIKE):
—AKANTHOS: **(1)** ii BC *IG* II^2 7995 (Tataki, *Macedonians* p. 43 no. 12; *FRA* 288) (f. *Ὀπώρα*)
MACEDONIA (EDONIS):
—PHILIPPOI: **(2)** ?ii AD *AE* 1950-1, p. 60 no. 5, 5 (Pilhofer 721) (Lat. Publicius Stacchys)
MACEDONIA (MYGDONIA):
—THESSALONIKE: **(3)** ii AD *IG* X (2) (1) 401

Στερκορία
MACEDONIA (BOTTIAIA):
—EDESSA: **(1)** iii AD Feissel, *RICM* 9, 4 (Tataki, *Edessa* 285) (d. *Στερκόριος, Παραμόνα*)

Στερκόριλλα
MACEDONIA (BOTTIAIA):
—EDESSA: **(1)** iii AD Feissel, *RICM* 9, 4 (Tataki, *Edessa* 286) (d. *Στερκόριος, Παραμόνα*)

Στερκόριος
MACEDONIA (BOTTIAIA):
—EDESSA: **(1)** iii AD Feissel, *RICM* 9, 7 (Tataki, *Edessa* 287) (f. *Στερκορία, Στερκόριλλα, Ἐπινικίς, Κερβίων*)

Στερόπη
MACEDONIA: **(1)** m. ii BC Str. 477; cf. *RE* s.v. Strabon (3) cols. 77-8 (stemma) (Tataki,

Macedonians p. 431 no. 30) (m. *Λαγέτας*, *Στρατάρχας* (both Amaseia and Knossos))

Στεφανάκις
THRACE:
—PERINTHOS-HERAKLEIA: **(1)** v-vi AD *IPerinth* 233 (*AD* 51-2 (1996-7) Mel. p. 379 no. 194) (s. *Εὐδόξιος*)

Στέφανος
CIMMERIAN BOSPOROS:
—KOROKONDAME: **(1)** ii-iii AD *CIRB* 1109 A (f. *Γυναΐς*)
—PANTIKAPAION: **(2)** i BC/i AD ib. 316 (f. *Σαβίων*, *Ἀλέξανδρος*); **(3)** i AD ib. 514 (I f. *Στέφανος* II); **(4)** ~ ib. (II s. *Στέφανος* I); **(5)** i/ii AD *KSIA* 116 (1969) p. 51 no. 3 (s. *Ἔρως*); **(6)** ii AD *CIRB* 146, 2 (*GVI* 1468); cf. KW p. 92 fig. 12 (f. *Σαββίων*); **(7)** s. ii AD *CIRB* 686 (f. *Καλλισθένης*); **(8)** v-vi AD *ZOOID* 21 (1898) p. 208 no. 18
MACEDONIA: **(9)** ?219 BC *PUG* III 103, 10 (Tataki, *Macedonians* p. 432 no. 31; La'da E1629) (s. *Στασικράτης*)
MACEDONIA (BOTTIAIA):
—BEROIA: **(10)** vi AD *IBer* 428 (*Στέφα[νος]*)
—EDESSA: **(11)** iv-vi AD *AD* 39 (1984) Chron. p. 247
MACEDONIA (CHALKIDIKE):
—TORONE?: **(12)** iv/iii BC *Epigr. Anat.* 21 (1993) p. 15 no. 1 + *BE* 1995, no. 521 (locn.) (s. *Βάλακρος*)
MACEDONIA (EDONIS):
—AMPHIPOLIS: **(13)** 311-306 BC Maier, *Mauerbauinschr.* 69 II, 143 (Tataki, *Macedonians* p. 61 no. 121) (s. *Μένανδρος*); **(14)** iii BC *SEG* XXIV 592 (s. *Κλεόξενος*); **(15)** ii-iii AD Dimitsas 857 (Kaphtantzis 613) (*Στέφ[ανος]*: ?f. *Ζωΐλος*)
—PHILIPPOI: **(16)** ?ii AD *AD* 17 (1961-2) Chron. p. 240 with pl. 287 γ (Pilhofer 154) (Lat. M. Vesonius Steph[anus])
—PHILIPPOI (TERRIT.): **(17)** f. vi AD Pikoulas, *Chora* p. 130 no. 30 (Pilhofer 631)
MACEDONIA (MYGDONIA):
—THESSALONIKE: **(18)** s. i AD *SEG* XLIX 832. 3 (vase); **(19)** v-vi AD *IG* X (2) (1) 336, 4 (Feissel, *RICM* 154)
—THESSALONIKE?: **(20)** ii AD *IG* X (2) (1) 251, 3
SCYTHIA MINOR:
—KALLATIS: **(21)** f. iii AD *ISM* III 189 (f. *Φίλιππος*)
—KALLATIS*: **(22)** vi AD Popescu, *IGL* 91 b (Lat. Stefanus: bp.)
SKYTHIA:
—OLBIA-BORYSTHENES: **(23)** ii-i BC *IOlbia* 74 (*[Στέ]φανος*: s. *Ἀλε—*); **(24)** c. 81-96 AD *IOSPE* I^2 139, 5 + *SEG* XLIV 666 (name, date) (f. *Σωτᾶς*); **(25)** ii AD *IOSPE* I^2 83, 9 (s. *Καλανδίων*); **(26)** f. ii AD ib. 95, 11 (f. *Κουνοῦς*)
TAURIS:
—CHERSONESOS: **(27)** iii BC ib. 708 (s. *Δαμάτριος*, *Θεαγενίς*); **(28)** ~ ib. (*[Στέ]φανος*: f. *Δαμάτριος*); **(29)** imp. ib. 698, 6 (*Στέφα[νος]* (n. pr.?))
THRACE: **(30)** ii/iii AD *Starinar* 43-44 (1992-3) pp. 143-5 (vase-stamp) (Lat. Stefanus: f. *Θεότιμος*)
—AINOS: **(31)** iv BC *SEG* XXXVIII 217 (*FRA* 263) (f. *Στράτεια*)
—BIZONE: **(32)** v-vi AD Beševliev 84 (Lat. Stefanus)
—MARONEIA: **(33)** ii-i BC *IThrakAig* E212, 43 (s. *Ἀρτεμίδωρος*)
—MESAMBRIA (NR.): **(34)** f. iii AD *IGB* I^2 350 (*CCET* I 158); cf. *IGB* V 5126 (*Κ. Σ.*)
—PERINTHOS-HERAKLEIA: **(35)** ii AD *IPerinth* 124 (*Λ. Οὐαλέριος Σ.*)
—SALYMBRIA: **(36)** v-vi AD *BCH* 36 (1912) p. 634 no. 90 (*AD* 53 (1998) Mel. p. 472 no. 211)
—SERDICA: **(37)** ii AD *IGB* IV 1923, 7 (f. *Ἀσκληπιάδης*)
—VALIANA*: **(38)** i AD *Acta Antiqua* 15 (1967) p. 91 (Lat. Stephanu[s]: freed.?)
THRACE?: **(39)** c. 260 BC *PHib* 112, 81 (Velkov 282) (s. *Σάτοκος*)

Στησαγόρης
THRACE:
—PERINTHOS-HERAKLEIA:
——(Kastaleis): **(1)** iii-ii BC *IPerinth* 61, 55 (*Στ(η)σαγόρεω* (gen.): f. *Ζηνόδοτος*)

Στήσανδρος
SKYTHIA:
—OLBIA-BORYSTHENES: **(1)** ?s. iv BC *IOSPE* I^2 178, 2 (*Στή[σαν]δρος*: f. *Ἀ—νδρος*)

Στησιλεως
MACEDONIA (EDONIS):
—AMPHIPOLIS (NR.): **(1)** a. 357 BC Hatzopoulos, *Actes Amphipolis* p. 43 no. 8, 6 (*SEG* XLI 562) (s. *Ὀργεύς*)

Στησιμένης
MACEDONIA (BOTTIAIA):
—PELLA: **(1)** iii-ii BC *IG* IX (2) 369, 2 (Tataki, *Macedonians* p. 160 no. 85) (f. *Κλεοπάτρα*)
MACEDONIA (MYGDONIA):
—ZANKLIVERI (MOD.): **(2)** ii-i BC *Makedonika* 2 (1951) p. 620 no. 43 (f. *Ἀγαθοκλῆς*)

Στίλας
THRACE:
—MARKIANOPOLIS (TERRIT.): **(1)** ii-iii AD *IGB* II 857 (*Φλ. Σ.*: s. *Ἀκίνδυνος*)
—PLOTINOPOLIS: **(2)** 160 AD *SEG* XXXVII 970, 4 (s. *Λοῦππος*)

Στίλβων
MACEDONIA (MYGDONIA):
—THESSALONIKE: **(1)** ?39 BC *IG* X (2) (1) 30, [6]; 50, 6; 109, 11 (f. *Διονυσοφάνης*)

Στίχος
MACEDONIA (CHALKIDIKE):
—OLYNTHOS: **(1)** 226 BC *Milet* I (3) 41 III, 5 (Tataki, *Macedonians* p. 142 no. 102) (f. *Λύσανδρος*)

Στλάκκιος
THRACE:
—BIZYE: **(1)** imp. Dumont–Homolle 62a 1 (f. *Βιτάλις*)

Στολίς
MACEDONIA (BOTTIAIA):
—BEROIA: **(1)** s. iii BC *IBer* 152 (m. *Σύνεσις*)

Στόλος
MACEDONIA (MYGDONIA):
—THESSALONIKE?: **(1)** ii AD *IG* X (2) (1) 850

Στοράνη
CIMMERIAN BOSPOROS:
—PANTIKAPAION: **(1)** 343 or 353 AD *CIRB* 744, 1; Zgusta, *PNS* 224 (m. *—λαζικος*)

Στορέσας
MACEDONIA: **(1)** 243 BC *PSI* 389, 9 (Tataki, *Macedonians* p. 432 no. 32; La'da E1630)

Στέρμαις
SKYTHIA:
—TANAIS: **(1)** 225 AD *CIRB* 1280, 15; Zgusta, *PNS* 222 (s. *Ὀχωδίακος*)

Στοσάρακος
SKYTHIA:
—TANAIS: **(1)** 225 AD *CIRB* 1280, 11; Zgusta, *PNS* 223 (s. *Φίδας*); **(2)** 244 AD *CIRB* 1287, 8 (f. *Ναύακος*)

Στράβων
CIMMERIAN BOSPOROS:
—GORGIPPIA: **(1)** 41 AD ib. 1123, 7 (Levinskaya pp. 239-40 no. 7) (f. *Πόθος*)

Στράταρχος
MACEDONIA (EDONIS):
—PHILIPPOI: **(1)** iv/iii BC Collart, *Philippes* pp. 179-80 n. 5 with pl. 27. 3 (Pilhofer 285) (*[Στ]ράταρχος*)
THRACE:
—LYSIMACHEIA: **(2)** ?182 BC *Milet* I (3) 47, 3 (f. *Ἐπιχάρης*)

Στράτεια
THRACE:
—AINOS: **(1)** iv BC *SEG* XXXVIII 217 (*FRA* 264) (d. *Στέφανος*)

Στρατήγιος
THRACE:
—ODESSOS: **(1)** v AD Beševliev 110, 3 (*-τί-*)

Στράτηγος
MACEDONIA (PAIONIA):
—STOBOI: **(1)** s. iii AD *SEG* XLVII 954; cf. L 635 (*Καύκασος ὁ πρὶν Σ.*: glad.?)

Στρατία
THRACE:
—PHILIPPOPOLIS-TRIMONTIUM: **(1)** iii AD *IGB* III 932

Στρατίας
MACEDONIA (DERRIOPOS):
—STUBERRA: **(1)** ?54 AD *IG* X (2) (2) 324, 5 (*Στρατία* (gen.): f. *Κλέαρχος*)

Στρατῖνος
THRACE:
—ODESSOS: **(1)** v/iv BC *IGB* I^2 100 (*[Σ]τρατῖνος*: f. *Ἀρτεμίδωρος*)

Στράτιος
CIMMERIAN BOSPOROS:
—GORGIPPIA: **(1)** f. iii BC *CIRB* 1137 B II, 47 (s. *Μοσχίων*)
—HERMONASSA: **(2)** 304-284 BC ib. 1043 (*Στρά[τι]ος*)
—NYMPHAION: **(3)** iii BC ib. 912 II, 12 (s. *Προμαθίων*)
—PANTIKAPAION: **(4)** iii BC ib. 110, 5 (*Στρατί[ων]*—ed., *Στράτι[ος]*?: s. *Καλλίστρατος*); **(5)** m. iii BC Page, *FGE* 133
MACEDONIA (CHALKIDIKE):
—OLYNTHOS: **(6)** ?350 BC *TAPA* 65 (1934) p. 125 no. 3, 5, 9; Hatzopoulos, *Actes Chalc.* p. 80 (date) (f. *Δερκύλος*)
MACEDONIA (MYGDONIA):
—APOLLONIA: **(7)** f. ii BC *SEG* XLIV 508 (Hatzopoulos, *MI* 2 p. 87 no. 66) (s. *Παράμονος*)
THRACE: **(8)** 235 BC *PHib* 37, 2, 10 (Velkov 285; La'da E843) (s. *Στράτων*: t.e.); **(9)** 218 BC *SB* 11061, 7; *PHamb* 26, 12; 188, 7; 189, 6, 31; *BGU* 1944, [5], [26]; cf. La'da E827 (f. *Ἀριστόλοχος*, *Στράτων* (Macedonia))

Στράτιππος
MACEDONIA: **(1)** 267 BC *SEG* XXVII 1114, 10 b, 16 b (Tataki, *Macedonians* p. 432 no. 35; La'da E1631) (s. *Μενοίτας*); **(2)** 254-249 BC *PCZ* 59236, 1; *PSI* 976, 1, [17], 20 (Tataki, *Macedonians* p. 432 no. 34; La'da E1632) (f. *Νεοπτόλεμος*)

Στρατόδημος
CIMMERIAN BOSPOROS:
—PANTIKAPAION (NR.): **(1)** ii AD *CIRB* 957 (*Στρα[τόδη]μος*: s. *Μενέστρατος*)

Στρατόκλεια
SCYTHIA MINOR:
—TOMIS: **(1)** f. iii AD *Arkheologiia* (Sofia) 1993 (3), pp. 26-7 (Lat. Aurelia Stratoclia)

Στρατοκλῆς

Cimmerian Bosporos:

—Pantikapaion: (1) 389-349 bc *CIRB* 6, 1 (s. *Δεινόστρατος*)

Macedonia: (2) ?ii-i bc *IG* ix (2) 175 (Tataki, *Macedonians* p. 432 no. 36) (f. *Ἐτεόδωρος*)

Macedonia (Edonis):

—Amphipolis: (3) 357 bc *RE* (2); Rhodes–Osborne 49, 2 (Tataki, *Macedonians* p. 61 no. 122)

—Amphipolis?: (4) hell. Dimitsas 900 (f. *Παυσανίας*)

Tauris:

—Chersonesos: (5) 174 ad *SEG* xlv 985 A, 34 (s. *Στρατόφιλος*)

Thrace?: (6) c. 303-305 ad Latyshev, *Menolog. anon.* p. 109

Στρατονίκα

Macedonia (Chalkidike):

—Potidaia-Kassandreia: (1) ?iii bc *IG* ix (1)² (4) 1533 I (Tataki, *Macedonians* p. 96 no. 89)

Macedonia (Pieria):

—Pydna: (2) iv bc *GRBS* 43 (2002-3) p. 111 no. 2, 9 (*Στρατονίκ[α]*?)

Στρατονίκη

Cimmerian Bosporos:

—Pantikapaion: (1) i bc *CIRB* 128, 4 (*GVI* 845) (d. *Φιλέταιρος, Τρυφωνίς*); (2) f. i bc *CIRB* 289 (m. *Χαρίξενος*); (3) i bc/i ad ib. 319 (d. *Δαμᾶς*, m. *Φαρνάκης*); (4) ii ad ib. 707 (-νεί-: d. *Βερενίκη*)

Macedonia: (5) 429 bc *RE* (6) (Tataki, *Macedonians* p. 432 no. 37) (d. *Ἀλέξανδρος* I); (6) c. 355-290 bc *RE* (7); Berve 725 (Tataki, *Macedonians* p. 433 no. 42) (d. *Κορραῖος*, m. *Δημήτριος* I *Πολιορκητής, Φίλιππος*); (7) c. 319-260 bc *RE* (8); *ID* Index p. 17; *OGIS* 14; 222, 8; 229, 9; Grainger, *SPG* pp. 67-8 (d. *Δημήτριος* I *Πολιορκητής, Φίλα*, m. *Φίλα, Σέλευκος, Ἀντίοχος* II *Θεός, Ἀπάμη, Στρατονίκη*: queen); (8) c. 285-235 bc *RE* (9); Grainger, *SPG* p. 67 (d. *Ἀντίοχος* I *Σωτήρ, Στρατονίκη*, ?m. *Ἀπάμη*); (9) m. iii bc *RE* (10); Grainger, *SPG* p. 67 (d. *Ἀντίοχος* II *Θεός, Λαοδίκη*, m. *Ἀριαράθης* (Kappadokia): queen)

Macedonia (Bottiaia):

—Beroia: (10) 277 ad *ILeukopetra* 112, 2 (*Ἀγαθία Στρατονείκη*)

—Mieza: (11) iii/ii bc *SEG* xliii 424 (d. *Ἀργεῖος*); (12) s. ii bc ib. 420 (d. *Λύσων, Καλλιστώ*)

Macedonia (Edonis):

—Philippoi: (13) ?i ad Acta Apocr. Paul., *3 Cor.* 2. 2 (James, *ANT* p. 289) (fict.)

Macedonia (Mygdonia):

—Lete: (14) i-ii ad Dimitsas 676 = *IG* ii² 11958; cf. *Myrtos* pp. 269-70; cf. *LGPN* ii s.v. (18) (-νεί-: m. *Λέων, Νικόπολις*); (15) ii ad *Makedonika* 2 (1951) p. 619 no. 42 η (*BCH* 68-9 (1944-5) p. 431) (*Φλ. Σ.*)

—Lete (nr.): (16) c. 220-230 ad *SEG* xlviii 855 (d. *Κόπρυλλος, Διοσκόρη*)

—Sarakina (mod.): (17) s. ii ad ib. 838 (-νεί-)

—Thessalonike: (18) 125 ad *IG* x (2) (1) 624 (-νεί-: ?d. *Κλεοπάτρα*, m. *Λούκιος*)

Macedonia (Odomantike):

—Sirrha: (19) 62 or 178 ad *JDAI* 84 (1969) p. 157 no. R27, 6 (-νεί-: d. *Νικόστρατος*, ?m. *Μωμώ*)

Macedonia (Orestis):

—Battynaioi: (20) 192 ad *EAM* 186 I, 57 (-νεί-: m. *Παράμονος*)

Macedonia (Paionia):

—Negotino (mod.): (21) ii-iii ad *Sp.* 98 (1941-8) p. 60 no. 125 (*[Στ]ρατονείκη*)

Macedonia (Pieria):

—Dion: (22) 59 ad Dimitsas 186

Macedonia?: (23) ii-i bc *NS* 622 (Tataki, *Macedonians* p. 433 no. 41)

Thrace:

—Byzantion: (24) ii-i bc *IByz* 196 (Firatlı–Robert p. 53 no. 31) (d. *Μοσχίων*); (25) i bc-i ad *IByz* 228 (Firatlı–Robert p. 82 no. 98) (-νεί-)

—Kardia: (26) iv bc *IG* ii² 8961 (*FRA* 2672) (*[Στ]ρατονίκη*)

—Maroneia: (27) hell. *IThrakAig* E259, 3 (d. *Σωτήριχος*); (28) i ad *IG* xii (8) 215, 15 (-νεί-)

—Salymbria: (29) hell. *Archives Stamoulis* d. 35 (Loukopoulou, *Thrace Propontique* p. 290) (-νεί-: d. *Ματρικῶν*)

Στρατόνικος

Cimmerian Bosporos:

—Bosporos: (1) ?ii ad *IOSPE* i² 204 (*Σ[τ]ρατόνει[κ]ος*: f. *Ζήνων*)

—Gorgippia: (2) f. iii bc *CIRB* 1137 A I, 38; 1137 B I, 51 (f. *Δημήτριος*); (3) ~ ib. 1137 A I, 42-3 (f. *Ἀθανίων, Ἀπολλώνιος*) ?= (5); (4) ~ ib. 1137 A II, 9 (f. *Μᾶτρις*); (5) ~ ib. 1137 B I, 62 (f. *Ἀπολλώνιος*) ?= (3); (6) ~ ib. 1137 B II, 7 (*Στρ[ατό]ν[ικος]*?: f. *Δελφίνιος*); (7) ii ad ib. 1141, 19 (*[Σ]τρατόν[ικος]*)

—Kytaia: (8) 234 ad ib. 942, 3 (-νει-: f. *Ἰούλ. Σύμμαχος*)

—Pantikapaion: (9) ii-i bc ib. 267; cf. KW pl. 40 no. 585 (f. *Χρηστίων*); (10) imp. *CIRB* 771 (f. *Φίλητος*); (11) i ad ib. 462 (*[Σ]τρατόνεικος*: f. *Μάσας*); (12) s. i ad ib. 551; cf. KW pl. 15 no. 226; (13) i/ii ad *CIRB* 145 (*GVI* 1475) (-νει-: s. *Ζήνων*); (14) ~ *CIRB* 595 (-νει-: f. .λ—ιων); (15) ~ ib. 635; cf. KW pl. 35 no. 502 (s. *Ἥλιος*); (16) f. ii ad *CIRB* 714; cf. KW pl. 17 no. 257 (-νει-: s. *Ἀπολλώνιος*); (17) ?s. ii ad *CIRB* 90, 14 (*Στ[ρα]τόνεικος*: s. *Τόκων*); (18) 275-278 ad ib. 36, 39 (*[Σ]τ[ρ]ατόνει(κος)*: s. *Ἀρδαρ(—)*)

—Zenonos Chersonesos*: (19) imp. *Drev. Bosp.* 2 p. 195 no. 2 (*[Στ]ρατόν[ικος]*)

Macedonia (Bottiaia):

—Skydra: (20) f. iii bc Tataki, *Macedonians* p. 174 no. 3 (f. *Φιλώτας*)

Macedonia (Derriopos):

—Stuberra: (21) 74 ad *IG* x (2) (2) 325, 36 (-νει-: s. *Νικόμαχος*); (22) ~ ib. l. 49 (-νει-: s. *Μένιππος*); (23) ~ ib. 326, 60 (-νει-: f. *Ζωΐλος*)

Macedonia (Mygdonia):

—Thessalonike: (24) ii ad ib. x (2) (1) 241 A I, 14 (*Στρατόνικος*)

Macedonia (Pieria):

—Phila?: (25) ?iii bc *RPh* 1911, pp. 133-4 no. 36, 10; cf. Helly, *L'État thessalien* pp. 319-20 (locn.) (*[Στρα]τόνικος*)

Skythia:

—Olbia-Borysthenes: (26) ii-iii ad *IOSPE* i² 136, 4 (-νει-: f. *Ζήνων*)

—Tanais: (27) f. ii ad *CIRB* 1264 A, 13 (-νει-); (28) ~ ib. l. 8-9 (-νει-: f. *Πασίφιλος, Παντάγαθος*); (29) 155 ad ib. 1260, [9], 22 (*Στ[ρα]τόνεικος*: f. *Φάννης*); (30) c. 220-230 ad ib. 1282, 21; 1286, 10 (*Στρατ[όνε]ικος*: s. *Μοκκοῦς*); (31) 225 ad ib. 1280, 27 (*Στρατόν[εικ]ος*: f. *Χόφαρνος*); (32) ~ ib. l. 23-4 (*[Στ]ρατόνει[κος]*); (33) 228 ad ib. 1282, 10 (*Στρατόνε[ι]κος*: f. *Μήθακος*); (34) ~ ib. l. 30 (*Στρα[τόνει]κος*: f. *Οὐαστόβαλος*); (35) 244 ad ib. 1287, 18 (*Στρα[τ]όνεικος*: f. —ης)

Tauris:

—Chersonesos: (36) m. i bc *IOSPE* i² 347, 3 with Add. p. 519; 691, 4 (*Στρατό[νικος]*—347: f. *Ἀθάναιος*); (37) ii ad *VDI* 1938 (3), p. 80 no. 10. II (-νει-: f. *Δελφός*); (38) f. ii ad Solomonik, *NEPKh* 111, 7 (*[Στρα]τόνεικος*: s. *Ἡρακλείδης*)

Thrace:

—Byzantion: (39) i-ii ad *IByz* S 23; Firatlı–Robert p. 148 (locn.); cf. *IPerinth* 304 (*Στρατόνεικ[ος]*)

—Perinthos-Herakleia: (40) i-ii ad ib. 134 (-νει-: f. *Ἀντίπατρος*)

—Philippopolis-Trimontium: (41) ii-iii ad *IGB* iii 950

Στρατόφιλος

Tauris:

—Chersonesos: (1) i bc/i ad Const. Porph., *De admin. imp.* 53, 471 (s. *Φιλόμουσος*); (2) ii ad Solomonik, *NEPKh* 25 (*[Στ]ρατόφ[ιλος]*?, *[Στ]ρατοφ[ῶν]*—ed.); (3) 174 ad *SEG* xlv 985 A, 34 (f. *Στρατοκλῆς*); (4) ~ ib. l. 35 (f. *Κελεριανός*)

Στράττις

Macedonia (Chalkidike):

—Olynthos: (1) s. iv bc *RE* (2); *FGrH* 118; Berve 726 (Tataki, *Macedonians* p. 142 no. 103)

Στράττος

Macedonia (Mygdonia):

—Kalindoia: (1) 68-98 ad *SEG* xlii 580, 59 (f. *Ἀλέξανδρος*)

Στραττώ

Macedonia (Mygdonia):

—Kalindoia: (1) ii bc *AEMTh* 6 (1992) p. 399 (d. *Ἀρριδαῖος*); (2) i ad *SEG* xxxv 744, 44 (m. *Ἀπολλώνιος*)

—Lete: (3) c. 325-300 bc ib. xliv 535; *KGAM Thess.* i 30 (date) (d. *Νικόστρατος*)

Στράτυλλα

Macedonia (Bottiaia):

—Edessa: (1) ii-iii ad Dimitsas 3 (Tataki, *Edessa* 259) (*Πετρ. Σ.*: d. *Λ. Πετρ. Βάσσος*)

Στράτων

Cimmerian Bosporos:

—Hermonassa: (1) 123-132 ad *CIRB* 1054, 9 (s. *Ὀ—ωρος*)

—Pantikapaion: (2) s. iv bc ib. 198; cf. KW pl. 4 no. 62; (3) iii bc *CIRB* 111, 2 (*[Σ]τράτω[ν]*); (4) ~ Chuistova, *AIB* p. 51 n. 7 (weight); (5) c. 180-150 bc *CIRB* 75, 15 (s. *Ἀ—*); (6) 82 ad ib. 76, 13 (*SEG* xviii 310) (s. *Ἡρακλείδης*); (7) iii ad *CIRB* 727 (s. *Χόδιος*); (8) 275-278 ad ib. 36, 67 (*Στράτ(ων)*?: f. *Δάδος*)

Macedonia: (9) iii-ii bc *IG* ix (2) 1185 (Tataki, *Macedonians* p. 433 no. 44) (s. *Ἀθηνόδωρος*); (10) 259 bc *PCZ* 59003, 7, 18 (Tataki, *Macedonians* p. 434 no. 46); cf. La'da E1582 (f. *Πολέμων*); (11) 228 bc *Milet* i (3) 99, 3 (Tataki, *Macedonians* p. 434 no. 45) (f. *Μητρόδωρος*); (12) 216-214 bc *PHamb* 189, 7, 12-13, 15, 17, 21, 31 and verso (*BGU* 1958); *BGU* 1265, 7 (Tataki, *Macedonians* p. 433 no. 43; La'da E1633) (s. *Στράτιος* (Thrace)); (13) m. ii bc *PTeb* 1075 fr. 1, 3, 4 (Tataki, *Macedonians* p. 497 no. 232); cf. La'da E1687-8; (14) 74 bc *SB* 7532, 24 (Tataki, *Macedonians* p. 497 no. 233); cf. La'da E1395 (f. *Ἀκουσίλαος*)

Macedonia (Bottiaia):

—Aigai?: (15) m. i bc *RE* (16) (or Epiros)

—Beroia: (16) f. iii bc *IBer* 149 (Tataki 1201) (s. *Σαδάλας, Φιλίστα*); (17) ii bc *IBer* 173 (s. *Διόδωρος*); (18) 41-44 ad ib. 60, 11 (Tataki 1200) (*[Σ]τράτων*: s. *Θεόδοτος*)

—Beroia (territ.): (19) ?iv bc *IBer* 498 (*[Στρά]των*?: f. *Ἀμύντας*)

—Edessa: (20) 265 ad *Athena* 12 (1900) p. 73 no. 12, 2 + *AD* 8 (1923) p. 267 (Tataki, *Edessa* 308) (*Φλαβ. Κλ. Σ., Στρατώ*?)

Macedonia (Chalkidike):

—Chalkideis: (21) c. 370-367 bc *Olynthus* 9 pp. 58-62 nos. 90-3 (coin); *Ancient Macedonia* i p. 254 (date)

—Olynthos: (22) iv bc *IG* ii² 10027 (Tataki, *Macedonians* p. 143 no. 104; *FRA* 5910) (s. *Ἡρακλείδης*); (23) ?352 bc *TAPA* 62 (1931) p. 50 no. 3, 7 (*Στράτω[ν]*); (24) ~ ib. 69 (1938)

p. 48 no. 3, 13; Hatzopoulos, *Actes Chalc.* p. 80 (date) ([Στ]ράτων: f. Πολεμαρχίδης); **(25)** 350 BC *SEG* XXXIX 617 (f. Διονύσιος)
—POLICHNE?: **(26)** ?353 BC ib. XXXVII 576, 7 (f. Ζωΐλος, ?f. Γερόντιος, —χος); **(27)** ?351 BC ib. 575, 4 ([Σ]τράτων)
—POTIDAIA-KASSANDREIA: **(28)** ?359-357 BC ib. XXXVIII 662, 9; **(29)** c. 240-220 BC ib. XXXVII 558, 3; *Poikila* p. 141 (date) (f. Δερκυλίδης)
—STOLOS?: **(30)** ?350 BC *SEG* XXXVIII 671, 5 (f. Γλαυκίας); **(31)** ~ ib. l. 10; XL 553, 6 (s. Κτήσων); **(32)** ~ ib. XXXVIII 671, 7-8 (Σ[τρά]των: s. Ἱππίης)
MACEDONIA (DERRIOPOS):
—STUBERRA: **(33)** c. 41-48 AD *IG* X (2) (2) 323, 28 (s. Ζωΐλος); **(34)** 74 AD ib. 325, 51 (s. Ἄλυπος); **(35)** ~ ib. 326, 21-2 (f. Ἀντίγονος, Ζώανδρος); **(36)** 87 AD ib. 325, 75 (f. Φίλητος, Φιλόκαλος); **(37)** ~ ib. l. 77 (s. Ὠφελίων)
MACEDONIA (EDONIS):
—AMPHIPOLIS: **(38)** s. iv BC *RPh* 1937, p. 325 no. 6 A, 7 (s. Παρμενίσκος); **(39)** hell.? *SEG* XXXIV 609 (f. Καλλίβιος); **(40)** ii-iii AD Kazarow 419 (f. Ἡρακλέων)
MACEDONIA (MYGDONIA):
—KALINDOIA: **(41)** ii-iii AD *SEG* XLII 599 (s. Ἀλέξιος, Μακεδονία)
—THESSALONIKE: **(42)** 95 BC *IG* X (2) (1) 4, 4 (s. Ξένων); **(43)** i AD ib. 259, 32 (s. (nat.) Διονύσιος, s. (ad.) Ἐπικράτης); **(44)** ii-iii AD ib. 90, 2 (s. Ξαν—)
MACEDONIA (ORESTIS):
—BATTYNAIOI: **(45)** 192 AD *EAM* 186 II, 48 (f. Μάγας); **(46)** ~ ib. l. 49 (s. Ἐπίκαδος)
—SISANI (MOD.): **(47)** 146 AD ib. 187, 17
MACEDONIA (PAIONIA):
—KAVADARCI (MOD.): **(48)** ii/iii AD Unp. (Kavadarci Mus.) inv. 6/II (f. Παράμονος)
MACEDONIA (PIERIA):
—PYDNA (TERRIT.): **(49)** iii BC *Klio* 52 (1970) p. 61 no. 13 (f. Κλεονίκη)
MACEDONIA (PIERIS):
—GALEPSOS: **(50)** iv BC *AE* 1938, p. 58 (?f. —η)
—OISYME-EMATHIA: **(51)** ?254 BC *SGDI* 2600, 2 (Tataki, *Macedonians* p. 128 no. 2) (f. Τελεσίας)
—OISYME-EMATHIA?: **(52)** s. iv BC *PAE* 1938, p. 92 no. 1, 3 ([Στρ]άτων?)
SCYTHIA MINOR:
—KALLATIS: **(53)** s. iii BC *ISM* III 9, 1 (f. Ἱπποθῶν)
—TOMIS: **(54)** ii/i BC ib. II 1 b, 16 (f. Τιμ—); **(55)** i BC ib. 2 A, 61 (f. Γλαυκίας)
SKYTHIA:
—OLBIA-BORYSTHENES: **(56)** ii BC *IOSPE* I^2 229; cf. KW pl. 49 no. 668 (s. Πρωτόμαχος); **(57)** ii AD *IOSPE* I^2 96, 4 (f. Ἀγαθοκλῆς); **(58)** ~ ib. 131, 6; 134, 7 (f. Εὐρησίβιος)
—OLBIA-BORYSTHENES (NR.): **(59)** m. ii AD *VDI* 1953 (4), p. 130, 8 (s. Ἀχιλλεύς)
TAURIS:
—CHERSONESOS: **(60)** iii BC Solomonik, *NEPKh* 136 (s. Ἀγνίας); **(61)** 174 AD *SEG* XLV 985 A, 33 (f. Θέμιστος) ?= *(62)*; **(62)** iii AD *VDI* 1938 (3), p. 80 no. 10. I (f. Θέμιστος) ?= *(61)*
THRACE: **(63)** 267 BC *SEG* XXVII 1114, 6a; cf. La'da E753 (f. Θεόδωρος); **(64)** 235 BC *PHib* 37, 2, 10; cf. La'da E843 (f. Στράτιος); **(65)** 222 BC *PHib* 90, 23 (Velkov 287; La'da E845) (t.e.) ?= *(66)*; **(66)** 214 BC *BGU* 1944, [5], [9], [11], [14], [16-17], 26, 29, etc. (La'da E844) (s. Ζωπυρίων: t.e.) ?= *(65)*; **(67)** c. 181 BC *PTeb* 1002, 91 (Velkov 286) (s. Βίθυς)
—ABDERA: **(68)** hell. *PAE* 1950, p. 298 (vase)
—APOLLONIA-SOZOPOLIS: **(69)** iv BC *IGB* I^2 463 bis, 1 (s. Μην—)
—BIZYE (TERRIT.): **(70)** 155 AD ib. III 1859, 4 (I f. Στράτων II); **(71)** ~ ib. l. 4 (II s. Στράτων I)
—BYZANTION: **(72)** s. iii BC *IPerinth* 62, 2 (f. Νικόμαχος); **(73)** c. 303 AD *Anal. Boll.* 31 (1912) p. 192
——(Bathonea)?: **(74)** i-ii AD *IByz* 315 d (Fıratlı–Robert pp. 122-3 no. 205) (f. Ῥοῦφος)
—KELLAI: **(75)** 241-244 AD *IGB* III 1517, 11 (Αὐρ. Σ.); **(76)** ~ ib. l. 36 (Αὐρ. Σ.: s. Σκι—); **(77)** ~ ib. l. 46 (Στράτ(ω)νος (gen.): f. Αὐρ. Κερίσκης)
—KRETA (MOD.): **(78)** ii-iii AD ib. II 595 (I f. Στράτων II); **(79)** ~ ib. (II s. Στράτων I)
—MESOCHORI (MOD.): **(80)** f. v BC *CEG* II 727 (Bakalakis, *Oinos Ismarikos* p. 554; *IThrakAig* E388)
—ODESSOS: **(81)** v/iv BC *IGB* I^2 98 (s. Ἀπολλόδωρος); **(82)** 221 AD ib. 47 bis b, 17 (Αὐρ. Σ.: s. Θεόφιλος)
—PAUTALIA: **(83)** ii-iii AD ib. V 5779 (f. Λαομέδων, Γλαυκίας)
—SERDICA: **(84)** ii AD ib. IV 1923, 1 (Στράτ[ων]?)
THRACE?: **(85)** 316-309 BC *IG* II^2 1956, 10 (*FRA* 2585); *Ancient Macedonia* 5 p. 445 with r. 10 (date)

Στρατῶναξ
CIMMERIAN BOSPOROS:
—THEODOSIA: **(1)** f. iv BC *CIRB* 231 (f. Φιλόξενος)
THRACE:
—APOLLONIA-SOZOPOLIS: **(2)** ?253 BC *ISM* III 7, 21 (s. Λύγδαμις)

Στρήνιος
MACEDONIA (CHALKIDIKE):
—OLYNTHOS: **(1)** ?354 BC *TAPA* 69 (1938) pp. 52-3 no. 6, 4; Hatzopoulos, *Actes Chalc.* p. 80 (date) (Στρήν[ιος]?: s. Ἀσπίας) ?= *(2)*; **(2)** ~ *TAPA* 69 (1938) pp. 52-3 no. 6, 13 + 70 (1939) p. 62; Hatzopoulos, *Actes Chalc.* p. 80 (date) ?= *(1)*

Στρῆνος
MACEDONIA (BOTTIAIA):
—BEROIA: **(1)** ii AD *IBer* 312
MACEDONIA (MYGDONIA):
—THESSALONIKE (TERRIT.): **(2)** ii-iii AD *IG* X (2) (1) 1008, 4
THRACE:
—BYZANTION: **(3)** ii AD *IByz* 289 (Fıratlı–Robert p. 114 no. 190) (f. Πρωτο—)

Στροβίλος
MACEDONIA (MYGDONIA):
—THESSALONIKE: **(1)** ii/iii AD *SEG* XL 556 (-βεί-)
THRACE:
—ODESSOS*: **(2)** v-vi AD Beševliev 91 ([Στ]ροβί[λος])

Στρόμβιχος
MACEDONIA (CHALKIDIKE):
—OLYNTHOS?: **(1)** c. 330-320 BC *SEG* XVIII 36 A III, 241 (Tataki, *Macedonians* p. 143 no. 105; *FRA* 5911) ([Στρό]μβιχ(ος)?: s. Θεόμνηστος)

Στρούθιον
THRACE:
—BYZANTION: **(1)** i BC *IByz* 146 (Fıratlı–Robert p. 116 no. 193) (d. Ἧρις)

Στρουθίων
SCYTHIA MINOR:
—ISTROS: **(1)** iv/iii BC *ISM* I 19, 11 with comm. (Migeotte, *L'emprunt* 42); *IOlbia* 15, 3 (Σ[τ]ρου[θίω]ν—*IOlbia*: f. Διονύσιος) ?= *(2)*; **(2)** iii BC *ISM* I 12, 4, 15 (f. Διοσκουρίδης) ?= *(1)*; **(3)** i BC-i AD ib. 191 I, 30-1 (f. —τος, —τίης)

Στρούνιος
CIMMERIAN BOSPOROS:
—PANTIKAPAION: **(1)** m. i AD *CIRB* 423 ([Σ]τρούνιος: f. Θεόδωρος)

Στροφῆς
SCYTHIA MINOR:
—TOMIS: **(1)** ii-iii AD *ISM* II 256, 20 (Στροφῆ (gen.): f. Καλλίνικος)

Στρόφιος
MACEDONIA (PIERIA):
—PHILA?: **(1)** ?iii BC *RPh* 1911, pp. 133-4 no. 36, 108; cf. Helly, *L'État thessalien* pp. 319-20 (locn.) (Στρόφ[ιος]?: f. Σώπατρος)

Στρυμοκλῆς
MACEDONIA (EDONIS):
—AMPHIPOLIS: **(1)** iv-iii BC *AEMTh* 15 (2001) p. 118 (s. Χοιρίων, f. Σάτυρος)

Στρυμόνιος
MACEDONIA (BOTTIAIA):
—BEROIA*: **(1)** v-vi AD *IBer* 421 (Feissel, *RICM* 56; *PLRE* III (-))
THRACE:
—SERDICA: **(2)** ?f. ii AD *IGB* IV 1916 (Τάρσας Σ.)

Στρυμόνις
MACEDONIA (MYGDONIA):
—THESSALONIKE: **(1)** 258 AD *IG* X (2) (1) 168, 5 (Φλ. Κλ. Μένων ὁ καὶ Σ.)
THRACE:
—PAUTALIA: **(2)** s. ii AD *SEG* XLVI 864, 11 (s. Οὐλπιανός)

Στρύμων
MACEDONIA (EDONIS):
—AMPHIPOLIS: **(1)** iii-ii BC *Makedonika* 2 (1941-52) p. 649 (Kaphtantzis 641)

Στρωφακίδης
MACEDONIA (BOTTIAIA):
—AIGAI: **(1)** iv/iii BC *SEG* XXXV 798 (f. Ἐπικράτης, Στρώφακος, ?f. Βερνίκα)

Στρώφακος
MACEDONIA (BOTTIAIA):
—AIGAI: **(1)** iv/iii BC ib. (s. Στρωφακίδης)

Στυλιανός
THRACE:
—ABDERA: **(1)** iv AD ib. XL 567 (*IThrakAig* E73)

Στυνδήρας
MACEDONIA (MYGDONIA):
—THESSALONIKE: **(1)** iii AD *IG* X (2) (1) 307 (Αὐρ. Διονύσις ὁ καὶ Σ.)

Στύρανος
CIMMERIAN BOSPOROS:
—PANTIKAPAION: **(1)** ii AD *CIRB* 708; Zgusta, *PNS* 224 (s. Τανύσαλος)
SKYTHIA:
—TANAIS: **(2)** 228 AD *CIRB* 1282, 29 (s. Πηρισ—: reading—Tokhtas'ev); **(3)** ~ ib. l. 32; 1283, 11 (f. Σωζομενός)

Στύραξ
CIMMERIAN BOSPOROS:
—GORGIPPIA: **(1)** ii/iii AD ib. 1181, 5; cf. Zgusta, *PNS* 1148 (Στύρακος (nom.)—ed.)

Σύαγρος
MACEDONIA (EDONIS):
—AMPHIPOLIS: **(1)** b. 357 BC Hatzopoulos, *Actes Amphipolis* p. 25 no. 3, 18 (*SEG* XLI 557) (Σύαγρ[ος]: f. Ποσθίων)

Συβλιαγους
CIMMERIAN BOSPOROS:
—GORGIPPIA: **(1)** m. ii AD *Eirene* 7 (1968) p. 67, 10 (s. Πανταλέων); **(2)** s. ii AD *CIRB* 1209, 3 (Συβλη[αγος]?—Vinogradov); **(3)** 173-210 AD ib. 1134 E, 1 (Συβλε[αγος]—Vinogradov); **(4)** ii/iii AD ib. 1181, 1 (Συβλ[εαγος]?—Vinogradov)

Συγγράφη
MACEDONIA (BOTTIAIA):
—MIEZA: **(1)** ii-iii AD Dimitsas 20 (293; Tataki 1096) (*Ποπιλλία Συνγγράφη*)

Συγκλητική
MACEDONIA (MYGDONIA):
—THESSALONIKE: **(1)** ?ii AD *SEG* XXX 644 (*Λαρκία Συνκλητική*)
MACEDONIA (PAIONIA):
—NEAPOLIS (AREA): **(2)** ii-iii AD *Sp.* 71 (1931) p. 37 no. 80; cf. Düll, *Götterkulte* p. 404 no. 259 (d. *Εὐάρεστος, Ἐλσ—*)

Συμεών
THRACE:
—ODESSOS: **(1)** vi AD Beševliev 141 (*[Σ]υμεών*)
—SALYMBRIA: **(2)** v AD *AD* 53 (1998) Mel. p. 469 no. 208 (*Συμε[ών]*: f. *Κόμης ὁ καὶ Ἰωσήφ*)

Συμμαχία
MACEDONIA (CHALKIDIKE):
—MENDE: **(1)** b. 317 BC *IG* II^2 9337 (Tataki, *Macedonians* p. 122 no. 18; *FRA* 3682) (d. *Σύμμαχος*)

Σύμμαχος
CIMMERIAN BOSPOROS:
—GORGIPPIA: **(1)** ii AD *CIRB* 1166, 5 (*[Σ]ύμμαχο[ς]*); **(2)** ?s. ii AD ib. 1164 (*[Σ]ύμμα[χος]*); **(3)** s. ii AD ib. 1177, 1 (*[Σύ]μμαχ[ος]*); **(4)** 173-210 AD ib. 1135, 7 (*[Σ]ύμμαχος*: f. *Δι—*); **(5)** ~ ib. l. 9 (*[Σύ]μμ[α]χος*); **(6)** ~ ib. l. 16 (*[Σύ]μμαχος*—Vinogradov); **(7)** ~ ib. l. 20 (f. *Σπαρτακίων*)
—GORGIPPIA?: **(8)** s. ii AD ib. 1231 A, 5 (*Σύμμ[αχος]*?: f. *—κιων*)
—KYTAIA: **(9)** 234 AD ib. 942, 3 (*Ἰούλ. Σ.*: s. *Στρατόνικος*)
—PANTIKAPAION: **(10)** imp. ib. 766 (s. *Νικηφόρος*)
MACEDONIA (BOTTIAIA):
—BEROIA: **(11)** ii/iii AD *IBer* 143 C, 22 (*Αἰλ. Σ.*)
—EDESSA: **(12)** ii-iii AD *Arch. Pap.* 22 (1973) p. 206 no. 9 (Tataki, *Edessa* 11) (*Αἰλ. Σ.*)
MACEDONIA (CHALKIDIKE):
—MENDE: **(13)** b. 317 BC *IG* II^2 9337 (Tataki, *Macedonians* p. 122 no. 19; *FRA* 3683) (f. *Θεοφίλη, Συμμαχία*)
—POTIDAIA-KASSANDREIA: **(14)** c. 285 BC *SEG* XXIX 600, 3; cf. XXXVIII 621; Hatzopoulos, *Donation* pp. 17-21 (date) (f. *Πάνταινος*)
MACEDONIA (MYGDONIA):
—THESSALONIKE: **(15)** ?i BC *IG* X (2) (1) 293
SCYTHIA MINOR:
—ISTROS: **(16)** ii AD *ISM* I 212, 16 (s. *Ἀρτεμίδωρος*)
SKYTHIA:
—OLBIA-BORYSTHENES: **(17)** iii BC *IOSPE* I^2 201 I, 41 (*Σύν-*: s. *Διονύσιος*); **(18)** c. 260-250 BC Karyshkovskii, *MO* pp. 77-85; *SNG BM Black Sea* 529 (coin) (*Σύμ(μαχος)*?)
—OLBIA-BORYSTHENES?: **(19)** i BC-i AD Holwerda 429 (vase)
—TANAIS: **(20)** c. 200-210 AD *CIRB* 1277, 23 (*[Σ]ύμμαχος*: s. *Σα—*); **(21)** 225 AD ib. 1280, 17 (s. *Θαύμαστος*)
—TANAIS*: **(22)** ii-iii AD *Tanais* I p. 105 (amph.) (*Σύμαχ(ος)*)
TAURIS:
—CHERSONESOS: **(23)** iii-ii BC Solomonik, *GAKh* 1528 (vase) (*Σύμμα(χος)*); **(24)** s. iii BC Kats p. 112 no. 108 (amph.) (*Σύμ[μαχος]*: I f. *Σύμμαχος* II); **(25)** c. 200-185 BC ib. (amph.) (*Σύμμ[αχος]*: II s. *Σύμμαχος* I)
THRACE:
—ABDERA: **(26)** ii BC *IThrakAig* E55
—APOLLONIA-SOZOPOLIS: **(27)** v/iv BC *IGB* V 5149 (f. *Ἑκαταῖος*)
—PERINTHOS-HERAKLEIA: **(28)** c. 100-115 AD *SEG* XXVI 1288, 13 (f. *Ἀντωνῖνος*)

Συμφέρουσα
MACEDONIA (BOTTIAIA):
—BEROIA: **(1)** i-ii AD *IBer* 335, 5 (*Μαρία Σ.*: m. *Λ. Μάριος Μάρκελλος*)
MACEDONIA (EDONIS):
—PHILIPPOI (TERRIT.): **(2)** imp. *CIL* III 7341 (Pilhofer 463) (Lat. Naevia Sympherusa: d. *Σύμφορος, Νίκη*)
MACEDONIA (MYGDONIA):
—THESSALONIKE: **(3)** i-ii AD Unp. (Thessaloniki Mus.) 5704 (m. *Συμφέρων, Νεῖλος*)
—THESSALONIKE?: **(4)** ii AD *IG* X (2) (1) 808, 2 (*Συν-*: m. *Διοσκόρη*)
MACEDONIA (PIERIA):
—DION: **(5)** ii-iii AD *Chiron* 24 (1994) p. 219 fig. 1 (unp.) (*Συν-*: m. *Ἑρμογένης*)

Συμφέρων
MACEDONIA (MYGDONIA):
—THESSALONIKE: **(1)** i-ii AD Unp. (Thessaloniki Mus.) 5704 (s. *Συμφέρουσα*)

Συμφορίς
MACEDONIA (MYGDONIA):
—CHALASTRA: **(1)** ii-iii AD *IG* X (2) (1) 815, 2 (*-ρείς*: m. *Τελεσφόρος, Ζωϊλιανή, Ἀλέξανδρος*)

Συμφορίων
MACEDONIA (BOTTIAIA):
—BEROIA: **(1)** ii AD *IBer* 330, 3 (Tataki 1207) (*Συν-*: s. *Σύμφορος, Φαβία*)

Σύμφορος
CIMMERIAN BOSPOROS:
—PANTIKAPAION: **(1)** f. iii AD *CIRB* 104, 17 (s. *Φίλιππος*); **(2)** 227 AD ib. 147, 7 (s. *Φιλέταιρος*)
MACEDONIA (BOTTIAIA):
—BEROIA: **(3)** ii AD *IBer* 330, 1, 5 (Tataki 1208) (*Σύν-*: f. *Συμφορίων, Ποθεινή, Φάβιος*); **(4)** ii-iii AD *IBer* 408 (Tataki 1204) (*[Σ]ύμφορος*); **(5)** ii/iii AD *IBer* 143 B, 13 (Tataki 1205) (s. *Εὔκαρπος*); **(6)** 211 AD *ILeukopetra* 59, 3 (Tataki 1329) (*Φλ. Σ.*: s. *Διδύμη*); **(7)** 311 AD *ILeukopetra* 117, 2 (Tataki 1203) (*Σύν-*)
—TYRISSA? (ASVESTARI (MOD.)): **(8)** f. iii AD *SEG* XLVIII 828 (*Σ[ύμ]φορος*)
MACEDONIA (EDONIS):
—AMPHIPOLIS: **(9)** ?ii AD *AE* 1932, Chron. p. 2 no. 23 (*[Σ]ύμφορος*)
—PHILIPPOI (TERRIT.): **(10)** imp. *CIL* III 7341 (Pilhofer 463) (Lat. Naevius Symphorus: f. *Συμφέρουσα*)
—PHILIPPOI (NR.): **(11)** imp. *CIL* III 14206. 12, 5 (Pilhofer 407) (Lat. Tit[ius] Symph[orus])
MACEDONIA (MYGDONIA):
—THESSALONIKE: **(12)** ii AD *IG* X (2) (1) 396, 3 (*Σύν-*: f. *Ἀλέξανδρος, Κοπρία*); **(13)** ii/iii AD ib. 262 II, 8; **(14)** ~ *SEG* XLIX 814 I, 18; **(15)** iii AD *ISamothrace* 58, 4 (Tataki, *Macedonians* p. 183 no. 39) (*Κλ. Σ.*)
—THESSALONIKE (TERRIT.): **(16)** ii-iii AD *IG* X (2) (1) 1008, 1 (*Σύν-*)
—THESSALONIKE (NR.): **(17)** ?iii AD ib. 1001 (*Σύφο-*)
MACEDONIA (PELAGONIA): **(18)** iii AD ib. X (2) (2) 295 (*Σύνφο[ρος]*: slave?)
MACEDONIA (PIERIA):
—PHILA: **(19)** ?iii AD Dimitsas 194
SCYTHIA MINOR:
—TOMIS: **(20)** 201 AD *ISM* II 83 II, 21 (*Φλ. Σ.*); **(21)** iv-v AD Barnea 10, 2 (Popescu, *IGL* 39) (f. *Νόννα*)
SKYTHIA:
—TANAIS: **(22)** 225 AD *CIRB* 1279, 5 (f. *Εὐπρέπης*); **(23)** ~ ib. l. 6 (s. *Δημήτριος*); **(24)** ~ ib. l. 13 (s. *Καλλισθένης*); **(25)** ~ ib. l. 20 (s. *Χο—*); **(26)** ~ ib. 1280, 29; **(27)** 225-228 AD ib. 1279, 25-7; 1283, 13 (f. *Δαλόσακος, Βάγδοχος, Ῥωδίγασος*)
THRACE:
—PERINTHOS-HERAKLEIA: **(28)** iii AD *IPerinth* 131, 1 (*Σύν-*: f. *Αὐρ. Εὐτύχης*)
—PHILIPPOPOLIS-TRIMONTIUM: **(29)** ii AD *Latomus* 17 (1958) p. 529 no. 3 (Lat. Sex. Pompeius Symphorus)

Συνέκδημος
MACEDONIA (LYNKESTIS)?: **(1)** ii-iii AD *EAM* 159 a (*-έγδη-*: f. *Νικοπολιανά*)
SCYTHIA MINOR:
—ISTROS: **(2)** i AD *ISM* I 200, 6 (f. *Νείλων*)
—TOMIS: **(3)** ?ii AD *AMNG* I (2) 2525 (coin) (*Συνέγ(δημος)*?)
SKYTHIA:
—TANAIS: **(4)** 155 AD *CIRB* 1260, 21 (*[Συν]έκδημος*: s. *Ἀρ—ος*); **(5)** 188 AD ib. 1242, 12 (s. *Ἀριστόδημος*); **(6)** c. 200-210 AD ib. 1277, 6 (*[Σ]υνέγδημος*—Tokhtas'ev: f. *Ἀρδάρακος*); **(7)** 228 AD ib. 1282, 15 (f. *Εὔνων*)
THRACE:
—BOURDAPA: **(8)** ii-iii AD *IGB* III 1361 (*-έγδη-*: f. *Μάξιμος*)

Σύνεργος
THRACE:
—BYZANTION: **(1)** imp. Dimitsas 993 (Pilhofer 40) (*Σύνεργ[ος]*?)

Συνέρως
MACEDONIA (BOTTIAIA):
—BEROIA: **(1)** ii AD *IBer* 309, 3
MACEDONIA (PELAGONIA):
—KOLOBAISA (NR.): **(2)** ii AD *IG* X (2) (2) 235 (f. *Ἰουλία*)
THRACE:
—BEROE-AUGUSTA TRAIANA (TERRIT.): **(3)** ii-iii AD *IGB* III 1669

Σύνεσις
MACEDONIA (BOTTIAIA):
—BEROIA: **(1)** s. iii BC *IBer* 152 (d. *Στολίς*)
—PELLA: **(2)** m. iv BC *CEG* II 877 iii; 877 v (Tataki, *Macedonians* p. 160 no. 86) (m. *Ἄρχων, Ἰσοκράτης*)
THRACE:
—ABDERA: **(3)** f. iii BC *SEG* XXVII 323 (*IThrakAig* E47)

Συνέτα
THRACE: **(1)** 134 or 130 BC *SGDI* 2205, 3, 4, 8 (slave/freed.)

Συνέτη
THRACE:
—MARONEIA: **(1)** i-ii AD *IG* II^2 9292 (*FRA* 3550) (d. *Νουμήνιος*)

Σύνετος
MACEDONIA (BOTTIAIA):
—BEROIA: **(1)** f. ii AD *IBer* 348 (Tataki 1206) (f. *Ἀκτή, Δικαῖος*)

Συνήθεια
THRACE:
—MARONEIA: **(1)** i BC-i AD *IG* II^2 9293 (*FRA* 3551) (*-θηα*: d. *Σωσίπατρος*)

Συνίστωρ
CIMMERIAN BOSPOROS:
—PANTIKAPAION: **(1)** m. i AD *CIRB* 515 (f. *Μοίριμος*)
THRACE:
—BYZANTION?: **(2)** ?14 BC *IByz* 324 (Robert, *Hell.* 11-12 p. 578; *Eastern cults* p. 33 no. 54) (or Thrace Mesambria?: f. *Ἀρτεμίδωρος*)

Σύντροφος
MACEDONIA (EDONIS):
—PHILIPPOI (DRAMA (MOD.)): **(1)** ii-iii AD Dimitsas 1054 (Pilhofer 459)
MACEDONIA (MYGDONIA):
—THESSALONIKE: **(2)** i AD *IG* X (2) (1) 242, 6 (f. *Πολυκράτης*)

Macedonia (Sintike):
—parthikopolis: **(3)** ii ad *IGB* iv 2279, 3
Scythia Minor:
—kallatis: **(4)** 241-244 ad *ISM* iii 74 B, 21 (f. *Κάρπος*)
Skythia:
—olbia-borysthenes: **(5)** ii-iii ad *IOSPE* i^2 137, 8 (*Σύν(τ)ροφος*: f. *Ἀχιλλεύς*)

Συντύχη
Macedonia (Edonis):
—philippoi: **(1)** f. i ad *Ep. Philipp.* iv 2
Macedonia (Mygdonia):
—thessalonike?: **(2)** ii-iii ad *IG* x (2) (1) 736; **(3)** ~ ib. 855 (*Μάτ[ε]ια Κοΐντα Σ.*)
Macedonia (Odomantike):
—sirrha (territ.): **(4)** 203 ad *SEG* xxx 601 (d. *Πυρρίας*, *—θόη*)

Συντυχίων
Macedonia (Mygdonia):
—thessalonike: **(1)** f. iii ad *Α΄ Panell. Synedr. Epigr.* p. 20 no. 3 (*Αὐρ. Σ.*: f. *Κορνήλιος Πόρφυρος*)

Σύρα
Macedonia (Mygdonia):
—thessalonike: **(1)** ii ad *IG* x (2) (1) 490; **(2)** f. iv ad *SEG* xlv 816 (*Αὐρ. Σ.*)
Macedonia (Pieria):
—phila: **(3)** ?iii ad Dimitsas 194
Thrace:
—triballoi: **(4)** 291 ad *Cod. Just.* viii 47. 5; cf. *Klio* 58 (1976) p. 84 (Lat. Syra)

Συραβίθυς
Macedonia (Edonis):
—philippoi (territ.): **(1)** i-ii ad Pikoulas, *Chora* p. 134 no. 36 (s. *Ἀρτίδονις*)

Συρᾶς
Thrace:
—philippopolis-trimontium (territ.): **(1)** ii-iii ad *IGB* iii 1172 (*Συρᾶδος* (gen.))

Συριανή
Thrace:
—novae: **(1)** f. iii ad *IGLNovae* 104 bis, 8 (Lat. [S]uriane (gen.): m. *Συριανός*)

Συριανός
Thrace:
—novae: **(1)** f. iii ad ib. l. 7 (Lat. Cl. Surianus: s. *Συριανή*)

Συρίσκα
Macedonia (Mygdonia):
—thessalonike?: **(1)** ii ad *IG* x (2) (1) 901; *SEG* xlvii 972 (date) (*Ἐρεννία Σ.*: m. *M. Ἐρέννιος Ἀγαθοκλῆς*)

Συρίσκος
Skythia:
—olbia-borysthenes: **(1)** c. 400-375 bc Dubois, *IGDOlbia* 9 (f. *Εὐρησίβιος*); **(2)** iv/iii bc *IOlbia* 71 II, 9 (Dubois, *IGDOlbia* 11) (*Συρίσ̣κ̣ο̣ς*); **(3)** iii bc *IOSPE* i^2 201 II, 26 (f. *Εὐμένης*)
Tauris:
—chersonesos: **(4)** iv bc *In. Fil.* 85 (1987) p. 112 no. 2 (s. *Καλλίας*); **(5)** iv-iii bc *Drev. Bosp.* i pp. 98-99 fig. 3 (f. *Καλλιάδας*); **(6)** c. 315-300 bc Kats p. 112 no. 109 (amph.) ?= (7); **(7)** c. 300-290 bc Anokhin p. 139 no. 79 (coin) ?= *(6)* *(8)*; **(8)** iii bc *IOSPE* i^2 344, 2, 15 (s. *Ἡρακλείδας*) ?= (7)
—chersonesos (territ.): **(9)** s. iv bc *SEG* xxxi 697 (f. *Παρθένιος*)
Thrace:
—byzantion: **(10)** i bc-i ad *IByz* 228 (Firatlı–Robert p. 82 no. 98) (*Συρί(σ)κος*: f. *Ζώτιχος*)
—perinthos-herakleia:
——(Akarnanes): **(11)** iii-ii bc *IPerinth* 61, 11 (f. *Σωτηρίδας*)

Συρίων
Macedonia (Mygdonia): **(1)** imp. Dimitsas 685
—dikaia (nr.)?: **(2)** s. ii ad *SEG* l 648 (f. *Ἀρ¬εμίδωρος*)
Macedonia (Paionia):
—negotino (mod.): **(3)** ii-iii ad *Sp.* 75 (1933) p. 41 no. 138, 2 (f. *Νικανδρία*)
Tauris:
—chersonesos: **(4)** ii-iii ad *IOSPE* i^2 456 (I f. *Συρίων* II, *Σώπολις*); **(5)** ~ ib. (II s. *Συρίων* I)
Thrace:
—nicopolis ad istrum?: **(6)** f. iii ad *Britannia* 20 (1989) pp. 331-3 no. 5 (Lat. [M.] [Aur.] Syrio)

Σύρμος
Thrace:
—triballoi: **(1)** 336-334 bc Arr., *An.* i 2. 2; i 4. 6 (king)

Σύρος
Macedonia (Bottiaia):
—beroia: **(1)** 181 ad *IBer* 49, 12 (Tataki 1209) (s. *Βάστος*)
Macedonia (Mygdonia):
—kalindoia: **(2)** 68-98 ad *SEG* xlii 580, 64 (s. *Βάστος*); **(3)** ~ ib. l. 92 (s. *Μάντα*)
—peristera (mod.): **(4)** iii ad ib. xxix 590 (s. *Εὐτύχης*, *Μαρκελλῖνα*)
—thessalonike: **(5)** i-ii ad *IG* x (2) (1) 243 I, 9 (*Κρίσπος ὁ καὶ Σ.*: s. *Κρίσπος*)
Macedonia (Odomantike):
—gazoros?: **(6)** 158 ad *SEG* xxiv 614, 2 (Pilhofer 544); cf. Hatzopoulos, *MI* i pp. 84-6 (s. *Εὐάλκης*)
—oldenoi: **(7)** ii-iii ad *AE* 1936, Chron. p. 17 no. 10, 2 (Pilhofer 568; *SEG* l 605) (f. *Διοσκουρίδης*)
Macedonia (Orestis):
—lyke*: **(8)** hell. *EAM* 179 *η-ι* (tile); *SEG* xlix 739; cf. *AD* 17 (1961-2) Chron. pl. 270
Macedonia (Paionia):
—bylazora: **(9)** ii-iii ad *Sp.* 71 (1931) p. 25 no. 49 (s. *Ἀλέξανδρος*)
Tauris:
—chersonesos: **(10)** imp. Solomonik, *NEPKh* 107
Thrace: **(11)** iii ad *CIL* vi 3195, 5 (Speidel, *Denkmäler* 598) (Lat. M. Aur. Surus)
—beroe-augusta traiana: **(12)** ?s. i ad *IGB* v 5572 (*Τιβ. Κλ. Σ.*); **(13)** 237 ad *RMD* 198 (Speidel, *Denkmäler* 759) (Lat. Surus: f. M. Aurelius Valens)
—byzantion: **(14)** ii bc *IByz* 71 (Firatlı–Robert p. 50 no. 16) (s. *Ἑρμογένης*, f. *Εὐταξία*)
—dentheletai: **(15)** imp. *CIL* xiii 11870 (Lat. Surus: s. Cocae (gen.))
—nicopolis ad istrum (territ.): **(16)** ii-iii ad *ILB* 377 (Lat. L. Aur. Surus: I f. *Σύρος* II); **(17)** ~ ib. (Lat. L. Aurelius Surus: II s. *Σύρος* I, Cl. Gailla)
—pautalia: **(18)** 252 ad Balty–van Rengen, *Apamea* p. 53 pl. 27 (Lat. Aur. Surus)
—philippopolis-trimontium (territ.): **(19)** ii-iii ad *IGB* iii 1190 (*Σύρου* (gen.): f. *Δίνις*)
—serdica: **(20)** iii ad *CIL* vi 32624 c, 22 (Lat. M. Aur. Surus)

Σύρχων?
Macedonia (Edonis):
—amphipolis: **(1)** hell.? *SEG* l 563 (s. *Παρμενίσκος*)

Σφαῖρος
Macedonia (Edonis):
—philippoi: **(1)** i-ii ad *BCH* 58 (1934) p. 474 no. 10 (Pilhofer 284) (Lat. M. Varinius [S]phaerus: f. Severus)
Skythia:
—olbia-borysthenes: **(2)** iii bc *RE* (3); *SVF* i pp. 139 ff. (or Cimmerian Bosporos Bosporos)

Σφαρόβαις
Cimmerian Bosporos:
—pantikapaion (nr.): **(1)** imp. *CIRB* 956; Zgusta, *PNS* 225 (s. *Τελαμών*)

Σφοδρίας
Thrace:
—byzantion: **(1)** c. 250-220 bc Schönert-Geiss, *Byzantion* 1004-13 (coin)
—byzantion (territ.): **(2)** i-ii ad *IByz* 189 (f. *Βίθυς*)

Σφραγίς
Macedonia (Pieria):
—dion: **(1)** ii ad Oikonomos 13 (*-γείς*)

Σχινείση
Thrace:
—zone: **(1)** f. iv bc Bakalakis, *Oinos Ismarikos* p. 710 (*IThrakAig* E417) (d. *Δρόσων*)

Σχοινᾶς
Macedonia (Bottiaia):
—beroia: **(1)** 255 ad *IBer* 138, 12 (Tataki 1156) (*Ῥουφινιανὸς Νίκανδρος ὁ καὶ Σ.*)

Σώανδρος
Tauris:
—chersonesos: **(1)** inc. Solomonik, *GAKh* 1529 (vase) (*Σώαν[δρος]?*)

Σωγένης
Cimmerian Bosporos:
—pantikapaion: **(1)** iii-ii bc Audollent, *Defix. Tab.* 92, 3 (*Ζωγέν[η]ς*)
Macedonia: **(2)** 215 bc *SB* 6283, 8, etc. (Tataki, *Macedonians* p. 434 no. 50; La'da E1634)
Macedonia (Bottiaia):
—beroia: **(3)** 223 bc *IBer* 4, 21 (s. *Ἑρμο—*); **(4)** ~ ib. l. 33 (*Σωγέ[ν]ης*: s. *Ἀρίσταρχος*)

Σῶζις
Thrace:
—beroe-augusta traiana (territ.): **(1)** iv bc *IGB* iii 1639 (f. *Διότιμος*)

Σωζομένη
Macedonia (Bottiaia):
—beroia: **(1)** iii ad *IBer* 400, 6 (*GVI* 107; Tataki 1210) (*Σο-*)
Macedonia (Mygdonia):
—thessalonike: **(2)** 179 ad *IG* x (2) (1) 595 + *SEG* xxxviii 697; **(3)** iii ad *IG* x (2) (1) 471 A; cf. *BCH* 97 (1973) p. 589 (*Σεξ<ε>τιανὴ Σ.*—ed., *Σεξστιανὴ Σ.?*)
—thessalonike?: **(4)** ii ad *IG* x (2) (1) 823; cf. *BCH* 98 (1974) p. 556 n. 16 (*Γ. Κλ. Σ.*)
Macedonia (Paionia):
—kavadarci (mod.): **(5)** iii ad Unp. (Kavadarci Mus.) inv. 117/II (*Σωζω-*: m. *Δαφνίς*)
Thrace:
—perinthos-herakleia: **(6)** iii-iv ad *IPerinth* 184 (*AD* 51-2 (1996-7) Mel. p. 334 no. 167)

Σωζομενός
Macedonia (Mygdonia):
—thessalonike: **(1)** ii ad *IG* x (2) (1) 241 A II, 13 (*Κ. Οὐαλέρι. Σωζομεν[ός]*)
—thessalonike?: **(2)** v-vi ad Feissel, *RICM* 198 (*[Σ]ωζομενός*)
Skythia:
—tanais: **(3)** 228 ad *CIRB* 1282, 32; 1283, 11 (s. *Στύρανος*)
Thrace:
—apollonia-sozopolis: **(4)** i-ii ad *IGB* i^2 401, 20

—BYZANTION: (**5**) iii AD *ISM* II 257 (PM 1174) (*Αὐρ. Σ.*: s. *Ζώτιχος*)
—PERINTHOS-HERAKLEIA: (**6**) iii AD *IPerinth* 126 (f. *Αὐρ. Κυριλάς*)

Σωθεμίς
SCYTHIA MINOR:
—ISTROS: (**1**) s. v BC *ISM* I 380 + *Stud. Ščeglov* pp. 87-9 (*[Σ]ωθεμ[ίς]?*)

Σωΐδας
MACEDONIA (PIERIA):
—PHILA?: (**1**) ?iii BC *RPh* 1911, pp. 133-4 no. 36, 57; cf. Helly, *L'État thessalien* pp. 319-20 (locn.) (f. *—ανδρος*); (**2**) ~ *RPh* 1911, pp. 133-4 no. 36, 82 + *Polemon* 2 (1934-40) Parart. p. 13 no. 17; cf. Helly, *L'État thessalien* pp. 319-20 (locn.) (s. *Το—ιος*)

Σωκλῆς
CIMMERIAN BOSPOROS:
—PANTIKAPAION: (**1**) i AD *CIRB* 436, 2 (I f. *Σωκλῆς* II, *Παρθενοκλῆς*); (**2**) ~ ib. l. 3 (II s. *Σωκλῆς* I, *Καλλιμέδουσα*)
MACEDONIA (BOTTIAIA):
—AIGAI: (**3**) s. iv BC *SEG* XXXV 792 (s. *Μένανδρος*)
SCYTHIA MINOR:
—ISTROS: (**4**) iv/iii BC *ISM* I 234 (f. *Νικήτης*)
THRACE:
—MARONEIA: (**5**) ii BC Grandjean, *Arétalogie* p. 119, 8, 17 = *AD* 26 (1971) Chron. p. 429 no. ι 8, 17 (*Eastern cults* p. 31 no. 51; *IThrakAig* E183) (s. *Θεοξενίδης*)
—STRYME?: (**6**) m. iv BC ib. E380 (s. *Μίκυθος*)
—ZONE: (**7**) m. iv BC *PAE* 1969, p. 64 with pl. 76 α (*IThrakAig* E418) (f. *Ἀρχέπολις*); (**8**) s. iv BC *PAE* 1969, p. 64 with pl. 76 β (*IThrakAig* E425) (s. *Πάγκαλος*)

Σωκράτης
CIMMERIAN BOSPOROS:
—GORGIPPIA: (**1**) f. iii BC *CIRB* 1137 A I, 36 (I f. *Σωκράτης* II); (**2**) ~ ib. l. 36 (II s. *Σωκράτης* I)
—PANTIKAPAION: (**3**) i AD ib. 354 (s. *Πόθος*); (**4**) ~ ib. 519
MACEDONIA:
—DEGME: (**5**) iii/ii BC *Thess. Mnem.* 139 (Tataki, *Macedonians* p. 99 no. 4) (s. *Εὐκράτης*)
MACEDONIA (BOTTIAIA):
—BEROIA: (**6**) s. i AD *IBer* 271 (Tataki 1365) (*—ιος Σ.*); (**7**) a. 212 AD *IBer* 136, 24 (Tataki 1330) (*Φλ. Σ.*)
—PELLA?: (**8**) iii BC *SEG* L 614. 1 (amph.)
MACEDONIA (EDONIS):
—PHILIPPOI: (**9**) a. 346 BC *Syll*^{3} 267 A, 2 (Tataki, *Macedonians* p. 166 no. 30) (s. *Τίμανδρος*)
—PHILIPPOI (DRAMA (MOD.)): (**10**) ?ii AD *BCH* 47 (1923) pp. 74-5 no. 32 = *ASAA* NS 1-2 (1939-40) pp. 214 and 218 (Pilhofer 508) (Lat. Flavius Socrates)
MACEDONIA (MYGDONIA):
—APOLLONIA: (**11**) c. 334 BC Berve 732 (Tataki, *Macedonians* p. 67 no. 10) (s. *Σάθων*)
—LETE (NR.): (**12**) c. 220-230 AD *SEG* XLVIII 855 (*Σωκράτη* (dat.): s. *Κόπρυλλος*, *Διοσκόρη*)
SCYTHIA MINOR:
—KALLATIS: (**13**) 241-244 AD *ISM* III 74 B, 19
—TOMIS: (**14**) i BC ib. II 2 A, 62 (f. *Διοσκουρίδης*); (**15**) ii AD ib. 290, 5 (*Σωκράτ(ης)*: f. *Ἑρμῆς*); (**16**) ii-iii AD ib. 294 (f. *Ἀβάσκαντος*)
SKYTHIA:
—OLBIA-BORYSTHENES: (**17**) iv/iii BC Dubois, *IGDOlbia* 95 (vase) (f. *Ποσειδώνιος*, *Δημήτριος*, *Φίλων*); (**18**) hell. *Arkheologiia* (Kiev) 39 (1982) p. 39 (stamp); (**19**) iii BC *IOSPE* I^2 201 I, 22 (s. *Ποσειδώνιος*); (**20**) ~ ib. l. 38 (f. *Ἱκέσιος*); (**21**) c. 45-62 AD ib. 38, 9; cf. *SEG* XXXVIII 753 (*Σω[κ]ρά[τ]ης*: I f. *Σωκράτης* II) ?= (*23*); (**22**) ~ *IOSPE* I^2 38, 9; cf. *SEG* XXXVIII 753 (II s. *Σωκράτης* I) ?= (*24*); (**23**) i/ii AD *IOlbia* 88, 7 (I f. *Σωκράτης* II) ?= (*21*); (**24**) ~ ib. l. 7 (II s. *Σωκράτης* I) ?= (*22*); (**25**) ii AD *IOSPE* I^2 105, 3 (s. *Εὐρησίβιος*); (**26**) ~ ib. 130, 4 (*Σωκράτ[ης]*: f. *Ἀναξιμένης*); (**27**) ~ ib. 134, 6 (s. *Ἀντιφῶν*); (**28**) ~ ib. 162, 8 (f. *—ζος*); (**29**) ii/iii AD *IOlbia* 52, 5; *IOSPE* I^2 103, 5 (f. *Οὐαμψάλαγος*)
THRACE:
—ABDERA: (**30**) iii AD *SEG* XXIV 628 (*IThrakAig* E71) (*Καισώνιος Σ.*: f. *Λούκιλλα*)
—BYZANTION: (**31**) ii-iii AD *IByz* 310 a (Fıratlı-Robert pp. 118-19 no. 199) (*Δημήτριος—IByz* per err.: s. *Δημήτριος*)
—NICOPOLIS AD ISTRUM: (**32**) ii-iii AD *IGB* II 661 (f. *Ἀσιατικός*)
—ODESSOS: (**33**) iii/ii BC ib. I^2 37 bis, 18; (**34**) f. ii BC ib. 39, 4 (*Σ. ὁ καὶ Παπίας*: s. *Ἐπικράτης*); (**35**) i-ii AD ib. 120 (*Σωκρά[της]*: s. *Πόσσις*); (**36**) ii AD ib. 140, 2 (f. *Ἡρακλείδης*); (**37**) ~ ib. l. 4 (s. *Ἡρακλείδης*); (**38**) f. ii AD ib. 178 (PM 1722); *Dacia* 21 (1977) p. 161 (date) (s. *Διονύσιος*, f. *Ἀμασιακίς*); (**39**) iii AD *IGB* V 5069 (I f. *Σωκράτης* II); (**40**) ~ ib. (II s. *Σωκράτης* I); (**41**) 221 AD ib. I^2 47 bis b, 18 (f. *Αὐρ. Ἀνθεστήριος*); (**42**) ~ ib. l. 27 (f. *Αὐρ. Χρῆστος*); (**43**) ~ ib. 47 bis c, 15 (f. *Αὐρ. Νουμήνιος*)
—PERINTHOS-HERAKLEIA: (**44**) i BC-i AD *IPerinth* 59 (s. *Μενίσκος*); (**45**) iii AD ib. 172 (*Αὐρ. Σ.*)
—PERINTHOS-HERAKLEIA?: (**46**) i-ii AD ib. 145; cf. PM 1349
—PHILIPPOPOLIS-TRIMONTIUM (TERRIT.): (**47**) ii-iii AD *IGB* III 1407
—TĂMNO CAVE (MOD.): (**48**) ii-iii AD ib. II 751 d (*Σωκρά(της)*)

Σωκρατίδης
SKYTHIA:
—OLBIA-BORYSTHENES: (**1**) ii-iii AD *IOSPE* I^2 192 (s. *Φιλῖνος*)

Σωκράτις
MACEDONIA (PIERIA):
—PYDNA: (**1**) ii BC *SEG* L 626 (*[Σ]ωκράτι[ς]?*: d. *Ἀντιγένης*)

Σώκριτος
TAURIS:
—CHERSONESOS: (**1**) c. 315-300 BC Kats p. 112 no. 110 (amph.); (**2**) c. 265-260 BC *FD* III (3) 207, 4 (s. *Κράθων*); (**3**) c. 237-230 BC Kats p. 112 no. 111 (amph.) (s. *Ἀρτεμίδωρος*)

Σωμᾶς
SKYTHIA:
—TYRAS: (**1**) 181 AD *IOSPE* I^2 2, 31 (f. *Ἡρακλέων*)

Σώμαχος
SKYTHIA:
—OLBIA-BORYSTHENES: (**1**) ii AD ib. 128, 8 (s. *Σάναγος*); (**2**) ?ii-iii AD ib. 107, 4 (s. *Ἄττας*); (**3**) iii AD *IOlbia* 83, 9 (*IOSPE* I^2 97) (f. *Χαρά-ξηνος*); (**4**) ~ ib. 98, 7 (f. *Ἡρόξενος*); (**5**) ~ ib. l. 11 (f. *Εὔπλους*)
TAURIS:
—CHERSONESOS (TERRIT.): (**6**) ii-iii AD *SKhM* 3 (1963) p. 13; cf. Solomonik, *GChKh* p. 7 no. 6 (f. *Ἴαμαχος*)

Σωμένης
MACEDONIA (MYGDONIA):
—LETE: (**1**) f. ii BC *SEG* XLVI 764, 15 (s. *Λυσίμαχος*)

Σῶν
CIMMERIAN BOSPOROS:
—PANTIKAPAION: (**1**) s. vi BC *VDI* 1974 (4), p. 59 (bronze) (Vinogradov, *Pont. Stud.* pp. 505-8); cf. *SEG* XXXVI 721

SCYTHIA MINOR:
—ISTROS: (**2**) iv BC *ISM* I 254 + *St. Clas.* 34-6 (1998-2000) pp. 145-6; cf. *VDI* 1984 (3), p. 180; *SEG* XXXVIII 2037 (name) (*Σῶνος* (gen.), *—σωνος* (gen.)—Vinogradov)

Σωπαῖος
CIMMERIAN BOSPOROS:
—BOSPOROS: (**1**) 393 BC Isoc. XVII 3; cf. D.H., *Isoc.* 19

Σωπᾶς
CIMMERIAN BOSPOROS:
—PANTIKAPAION: (**1**) i-ii AD *CIRB* 634 (*Σωπᾶνος* (gen.), *Σωπάν?*: f. *Ζεκυνθείς*)

Σωπάτρα
CIMMERIAN BOSPOROS:
—PANTIKAPAION: (**1**) i AD ib. 516 (*Σωπά[τει]ρα—CIRB*, *Σωπά[τ]ρα*)
MACEDONIA: (**2**) iii BC *IG* II^2 9271 (Tataki, *Macedonians* p. 435 no. 51; *FRA* 3492)
MACEDONIA (BOTTIAIA):
—PELLA: (**3**) iii-ii BC Dimitsas 137 (d. *Ἡράκλειτος*)
—PELLA?: (**4**) iv/iii BC *Arch. Pap.* 22 (1973) p. 203 no. 1 (d. *Παυσανίας*, *Φιλοπάτρα*)
MACEDONIA (ODOMANTIKE):
—SIRRHA?: (**5**) ii-i BC *SEG* XL 563, 2 (d. *Σώστρατος*, *Τιμώ*)

Σώπατρος
CIMMERIAN BOSPOROS:
—GORGIPPIA: (**1**) ii AD *CIRB* 1143, 7 (s. *Ὀ—*)
MACEDONIA: (**2**) 203 BC *RE* (2) (Tataki, *Macedonians* p. 435 no. 53) (Lat. Sopater); (**3**) ii-i BC *IG* II^2 9265 (Tataki, *Macedonians* p. 435 no. 55; *FRA* 3493) (f. *Μύδιον*); (**4**) c. 185-180 BC *SEG* XXXIX 606, 4 (f. *Δημήτριος*)
MACEDONIA (BOTTIAIA):
—BEROIA: (**5**) m. i AD *Act. Ap.* 20. 4 (Tataki, *Macedonians* p. 83 no. 50) (*Σωσίπατρος*—var. lect.: s. *Πύρρος*: Jew?) ?= (*Σωσίπατρος* (*10*)); (**6**) 171 AD *ILeukopetra* 7, 34; 8, 2; 9, 4; 10, 8; 11, 5; 12, 18 (Tataki 301) (*Αὐρ. Σ.*, *νεώτερος*—no. 10)
—MIEZA: (**7**) iii BC *SEG* XXIV 524 II, 29, 33 (Hatzopoulos, *MI* 2 p. 106 no. 92) (*Σώπατρ[ος]*: f. *—σιος*)
—PELLA: (**8**) iii BC Akamatis, *Amph. Pellas* p. 44 no. PAR63 (amph.) (*SEG* L 613)
MACEDONIA (CHALKIDIKE):
—POTIDAIA-KASSANDREIA: (**9**) iii BC *Milet* I (3) 63, 3 (Tataki, *Macedonians* p. 96 no. 90) (f. *Παρμενίων*)
MACEDONIA (DERRIOPOS):
—STUBERRA: (**10**) 74 AD *IG* X (2) (2) 325, 53 (f. *Διονύσιος*)
MACEDONIA (KRESTONIA): (**11**) ii AD *SEG* XXXVII 561 + *BE* 1989, no. 450 (f. *Δαρέας*)
MACEDONIA (MYGDONIA):
—KALINDOIA: (**12**) i BC *SEG* XLII 589 (f. *Κότυς*); (**13**) 68-98 AD ib. 580, 71 (s. *Ζωΐλος*)
—LETE: (**14**) s. iv BC Hatzopoulos, *MI* 2 pp. 93-4 no. 79, 18
—THESSALONIKE?: (**15**) i AD *IG* X (2) (1) 680
MACEDONIA (PIERIA):
—PHILA?: (**16**) ?iii BC *RPh* 1911, pp. 133-4 no. 36, 108; cf. Helly, *L'État thessalien* pp. 319-20 (locn.) (s. *Στρόφιος*)
MACEDONIA?: (**17**) 171 BC *RE* (4) (Tataki, *Macedonians* p. 435 no. 54) (Lat. Sopater)
THRACE:
—MARONEIA: (**18**) ii-i BC *IThrakAig* E212, 33 (*Σώπατ[ρ]ος*: I f. *Σώπατρος* II); (**19**) ~ ib. l. 33 (II s. *Σώπατρος* I); (**20**) ~ ib. l. 49 (f. *Ἀπολλώνιος*)

Σωπολίδης
THRACE:
—MARONEIA: (**1**) s. iv BC *SEG* XXX 691 (*IThrakAig* E226) (*Σωπολίδου* (gen.), *Σωπόλιδο(ς)?*—Masson)

—MARONEIA?: **(2)** v-iv BC ib. E487 (s. *Παρμένων*)

Σώπολις
MACEDONIA: **(1)** c. 365-328 BC Berve 736 (Tataki, *Macedonians* p. 436 no. 56) (s. *Ἑρμόδωρος*, f. *Ἑρμόλαος*)
MACEDONIA (CHALKIDIKE):
—SKIONE: **(2)** 360 BC *IG* IV (1)^2 94 b, 25 (Perlman, *City and Sanctuary* E.1 with p. 69 f. (date); Tataki, *Macedonians* p. 173 no. 9)
MACEDONIA (EDONIS):
—AMPHIPOLIS: **(3)** c. 375-350 BC *IThrakAig* E169; **(4)** 336-334 BC Arr., *An.* i 2. 5
SARMATIA:
—SARMATAI: **(5)** 113-100 BC *SGDI* 2110, 5, 7 (slave/freed.)
TAURIS:
—CHERSONESOS: **(6)** s. iv BC *IOSPE* I^2 494 ([Σ]ώπο[λις]: s. *Ὕμνος*); **(7)** c. 325-315 BC Kats p. 113 no. 112 (amph.); **(8)** iii BC Solomonik, *NEPKh* 125 (Σώπ[ο]λις?); **(9)** f. iii BC Kats p. 90 no. 26 (amph.) (f. *Ἀπολλώνιος*); **(10)** ~ ib. p. 111 no. 107 (amph.) (f. *Σκύθας*); **(11)** c. 285-185 BC ib. p. 129 no. 49 (amph.); **(12)** c. 262-237 BC ib. p. 113 no. 113 (amph.) (Σώπ[ολις]?: s. *Πασίων*); **(13)** s. iii BC ib. p. 113 no. 114 (amph.) (I f. *Σώπολις* II); **(14)** c. 200-185 BC ib. (amph.) (II s. *Σώπολις* I); **(15)** ~ ib. p. 113 no. 115 (amph.) (s. *Ὕμνος*) ?= (*16*); **(16)** ii BC *SEG* XLVI 924, 4 (Σώπολ[ις]) ?= (*15*); **(17)** ~ ib. l. 4 (Σώπολ[ις]); **(18)** s. ii BC ib. 934 (f. *Ἡρόδοτος*); **(19)** ii-iii AD *IOSPE* I^2 456 (s. *Συρίων*); **(20)** m. ii AD Solomonik, *NEPKh* 120, 3 (Σ[ώ]πολις)

Σώρακος
CIMMERIAN BOSPOROS:
—PANTIKAPAION: **(1)** s. i AD *SEG* XXVIII 641 (Σώρ[ακος]?); **(2)** iii AD *CIRB* 731, 2; Zgusta, *PNS* 333 (I f. *Σώρακος* II); **(3)** ~ *CIRB* 731, 2 (II s. *Σώρακος* I)

Σωρίας
MACEDONIA (ELIMEIA):
—DETELA: **(1)** f. iii BC *SEG* XLIII 937, 4; cf. *BE* 1996, no. 241 (Tataki, *Macedonians* p. 197 no. 19) (Σωρία (gen.): f. *Φίλιππος*)

Σώρωζος
SKYTHIA:
—OLBIA-BORYSTHENES: **(1)** f. ii AD *IOSPE* I^2 95, 12; Zgusta, *PNS* 334 (s. *Ποσείδηος*)

Σωσαγόρας
THRACE:
—MARONEIA: **(1)** ii BC *IThrakAig* E364 ([Σ]ωσαγόρας)

Σωσάνδρα
THRACE:
—BURDIPTA?: **(1)** ii-iii AD *IGB* III 1889 (Σωσά(ν)δρα: m. *Ἀλεξάνδρα*)

Σωσανδρίων
THRACE:
—ODESSOS: **(1)** i AD ib. V 5062 (s. *Στάμις*)

Σώσανδρος
CIMMERIAN BOSPOROS:
—PANTIKAPAION: **(1)** imp. *CIRB* 812 (f. *Φάνυας*)
MACEDONIA (CHALKIDIKE):
—OLYNTHOS: **(2)** 300 BC *IG* II^2 1263, 5, 21, 4 (Tataki, *Macedonians* p. 143 no. 106; *FRA* 5912) (f. *Δημήτριος*)
—POTIDAIA-KASSANDREIA (NR.): **(3)** ?iii AD Dimitsas 746, 2 ([Σε]ουῆρος Σ.: f. *Αὐρηλία*)
MACEDONIA (PAIONIA):
—ASTREA?: **(4)** f. ii BC *BCH* 45 (1921) p. 29 V C (b), 12
MACEDONIA (PIERIA):
—DION: **(5)** ii AD *Klio* 52 (1970) p. 52 no. 3 (s. *Ἀπολλώνιος*, f. *Ἀπολλώνιος*)
THRACE:
—KELLAI: **(6)** 241-244 AD *IGB* III 1517, 6 (f. *Κέλσος*); **(7)** ~ ib. l. 49 (f. *Αὐρ. Ἡρακλιανός*)
—MESAMBRIA: **(8)** s. iv BC ib. I^2 334 bis (f. *Καλλιγείτων*)

Σωσάννα
MACEDONIA (MYGDONIA):
—THESSALONIKE?: **(1)** v-vi AD *IG* X (2) (1) 787 (Feissel, *RICM* 156) (Ἄννα—*IG*, [Σω]σάννα?—Feissel)
MACEDONIA (PAIONIA):
—STOBOI: **(2)** v-vi AD Unp. (Stobi excav.) inv. I-70-48 (Σουσάνα)
TAURIS:
—CHERSONESOS: **(3)** iii BC Solomonik, *GAKh* 1130 + *Hellenismus* p. 456 no. 28 (vase) (-άνα)

Σωσαρίστη
MACEDONIA (EDONIS):
—AMPHIPOLIS: **(1)** ii-i BC *SEG* XXVI 724; XXVIII 538 (date) (d. *Νικίας*)

Σώσαρχος
MACEDONIA (EDONIS):
—AMPHIPOLIS: **(1)** iii BC *HE* 1511 (fict.?)

Σωσᾶς
MACEDONIA (EDONIS):
—AMPHIPOLIS: **(1)** imp. *BCH* 55 (1931) p. 179 no. 8 (Kanatsoulis 663) (*Μ. Καικέλιος Σ.*)

Σωσθένης
CIMMERIAN BOSPOROS:
—PANTIKAPAION: **(1)** ii AD *CIRB* 690 (f. *Κυράθων*)
MACEDONIA: **(2)** 279-278 BC *RE* (2); Helly, *Gonnoi* 93 B, 22 (Tataki, *Macedonians* p. 436 no. 57)
MACEDONIA (BOTTIAIA):
—BEROIA: **(3)** 223 BC *IBer* 4, 23 (-σθέ-: f. —χος)
MACEDONIA (EDONIS):
—PHILIPPOI: **(4)** a. 346 BC *Syll*^{3} 267 A, 2 (Tataki, *Macedonians* p. 166 no. 31) ([Σωσθ]ένης?: s. *Τίμανδρος*)
MACEDONIA?: **(5)** i AD *1 Ep. Cor.* 1. 1; cf. Eus., *HE* i 12
SCYTHIA MINOR:
—TOMIS: **(6)** ii-iii AD *ISM* II 157
THRACE:
—PHILIPPOPOLIS-TRIMONTIUM: **(7)** m. iii AD *IGB* III 884 c, 23; cf. V 5400 (Σωσθέν[ης])

Σωσίας
CIMMERIAN BOSPOROS:
—GORGIPPIA: **(1)** ii/iii AD *CIRB* 1179, 22 (s. *Γοργίας*, f. *Γλύκων*)
—PANTIKAPAION: **(2)** f. ii AD ib. 89, 8; **(3)** ~ *SEG* XLVI 958, 4 (Σωσίας)
—PANTIKAPAION*: **(4)** i/ii AD *CIRB* 145 (*GVI* 1475) (freed.)
MACEDONIA (BOTTIAIA):
—PELLA: **(5)** s. iv BC *AD* 16 (1960) Mel. p. 82; *SEG* XXXIX 623; XLIII 444 (tiles)
MACEDONIA (CHALKIDIKE):
—OLYNTHOS*: **(6)** f. iv BC *Olynthus* 10 p. 174 no. 520 (bronze); **(7)** b. 348 BC ib. p. 431 no. 2227 (bullet)
MACEDONIA (DERRIOPOS):
—STUBERRA: **(8)** c. 41-48 AD *IG* X (2) (2) 323, 21 (s. *Εὐβουλίδης*); **(9)** 50 AD ib. 324, 21 (f. *Κλέαρχος*); **(10)** 74 AD ib. 325, 29 (f. *Ἄνδρων*); **(11)** ~ ib. l. 40 (s. *Λυσίας*); **(12)** ~ ib. l. 48 (s. *Μένιππος*); **(13)** 116 AD ib. 327, 30 (s. *Διοσκουρίδης*); **(14)** ~ ib. l. 36 (f. *Θευδᾶς*)
MACEDONIA (EDONIS):
—PHILIPPOI (NR.): **(15)** ?ii AD *BCH* 47 (1923) pp. 78-9 no. 40 (Pilhofer 411) (Lat. Varin. Sosias: s. *Ζωσᾶς*)
MACEDONIA (KRESTONIA):
—IORON: **(16)** s. i AD *SEG* XXXIX 610 (Tataki, *Macedonians* p. 114 no. 2) (s. *Σωσίπολις*)
MACEDONIA (MYGDONIA):
—LETE (NR.): **(17)** ii AD *SEG* XXX 637
—THESSALONIKE: **(18)** ii/iii AD *IG* X (2) (1) 262 I, 9
SCYTHIA MINOR:
—ISTROS: **(19)** 138 AD *ISM* I 193 II, 58 (f. *Μενέχαρμος*)
SKYTHIA:
—OLBIA-BORYSTHENES: **(20)** iii BC *IOSPE* I^2 32 B, 4 (Maier, *Mauerbauinschr.* 82) (her.)
THRACE: **(21)** c. 420 BC X., *Vect.* iv 14 (Ath. 272 c; *FRA* 2586)
—APOLLONIA-SOZOPOLIS: **(22)** iv/iii BC *IGB* I^2 308, 3 (f. *Ἀριστίων*)
—BYZANTION: **(23)** ii BC *IByz* 261 (Fıratlı–Robert pp. 76-7 no. 85) (f. *Νάξος*)
—ODESSOS: **(24)** ii AD *IGB* I^2 50 a, 25 (Σωσίας); **(25)** ~ ib. 50 b, 4 (Σωσ[ίας]?: f. *Σκυθικός*)
—ODESSOS (NR.): **(26)** i BC-i AD ib. 294 (f. —ος)

Σωσιβία
MACEDONIA (BOTTIAIA):
—BEROIA: **(1)** ii-iii AD *IBer* 368

Σωσίβιος
CIMMERIAN BOSPOROS:
—MYRMEKION: **(1)** iv BC *SEG* XLVIII 1005 (s. *Ἄττης*)
—NYMPHAION: **(2)** iii BC *CIRB* 912 II, 6 (f. —φιλος); **(3)** i AD Davydova, *Bosp. nadgrob.* pp. 43-4 no. 31 with pl.; cf. *Hyperboreus* 2000, pp. 140 ff.
—THEODOSIA: **(4)** ?v-iv BC *ZOOID* 20 (1897) p. 181 no. 48 (vase)
MACEDONIA: **(5)** 198 BC *PPetr* II 38 a, 6 (III 34 b; Tataki, *Macedonians* p. 436 no. 58; La'da E1636); **(6)** m. ii BC *BGU* 2423, 38 (Tataki, *Macedonians* p. 497 no. 234); cf. La'da E1501 ([Σ]ωσίβιος: f. *Ἡρακλείδης*); **(7)** 78 BC *PRyl* 588, 6 and verso (La'da E1635) (*Σ. ὁ καὶ Ψελλός*: s. *Πρώταρχος ὁ καὶ Ἁρμαΐς*)
MACEDONIA (CHALKIDIKE):
—POTIDAIA-KASSANDREIA: **(8)** iii BC *IG* II^2 9001 (Tataki, *Macedonians* p. 96 no. 91; *FRA* 2795) (s. *Διονύσιος*)
MACEDONIA (MYGDONIA):
—THESSALONIKE: **(9)** s. i AD *IG* X (2) (1) 68, 34; 69, 23 (*Κ. Πομπώνιος Σ.*); **(10)** m. iii AD ib. 145, 6 (II s. *Σωσίβιος* I); **(11)** ~ ib. l. 8 (I f. *Σωσίβιος* II)
MACEDONIA (PIERIA):
—PHILA?: **(12)** ?iii BC *RPh* 1911, pp. 133-4 no. 36, 99; cf. Helly, *L'État thessalien* pp. 319-20 (locn.) (s. *Πυρρίας*)
SCYTHIA MINOR:
—KALLATIS: **(13)** s. iii BC *ISM* III 35 B, 23 (s. *Πρωτόμαχος*)
SKYTHIA:
—OLBIA-BORYSTHENES: **(14)** v-iv BC *ZOOID* 20 (1897) p. 181 no. 47 (vase) (Σωσιβίō (gen.)); **(15)** hell. *Arkheologiia* (Kiev) 39 (1982) p. 39 (stamp); **(16)** i/ii AD *IOSPE* I^2 200, 2; 203, 6 (f. *Δάδος*)
THRACE:
—BIZYE (TERRIT.): **(17)** f. iii AD *IGB* V 5656, 8 (-σύ-)
—BYZANTION: **(18)** i BC-i AD *IByz* 171 (Fıratlı–Robert p. 110 no. 178) (f. *Ἀντίφιλος*, *Τερέντυλλα*)

Σωσιγένεια
MACEDONIA (MYGDONIA):
—THESSALONIKE: **(1)** ii-iii AD *IG* X (2) (1) 440, 2 (Feissel, *RICM* 119) (-νια: m. *Καλόκαιρος*)

Σωσιγένης
CIMMERIAN BOSPOROS:
—PANTIKAPAION: **(1)** i BC/i AD *CIRB* 315; cf. KW pl. 55 no. 747 (f. *Νίκαρχος, Ἐρατίων*); **(2)** i AD *CIRB* 479 (f. *Ὀμψάλακος, Οἰνάνθη*)
MACEDONIA (BOTTIAIA):
—BEROIA: **(3)** ii BC *IBer* 200 (Tataki 1213) (*Σ[ω]σιγένης*: f. *Φιλοξένα*); **(4)** imp. *IBer* 112 (Tataki 1117) (*Μ. Ποπίλλιος Σ.*)
MACEDONIA (CHALKIDIKE):
—ANTHEMOUS: **(5)** ii BC *SEG* XLII 560 (*[Σω]σιγένης*: s. *Δαμᾶς*)
MACEDONIA (MYGDONIA):
—THESSALONIKE: **(6)** 196 AD *IMS* II 53 II a, 56 (*CIL* III 14507); cf. *ZPE* 146 (2004) pp. 216-20 (Lat. [Au]r. Sosigenes)
MACEDONIA (PIERIA):
—PHILA?: **(7)** ?iii BC *RPh* 1911, pp. 133-4 no. 36, 95; cf. Helly, *L'État thessalien* pp. 319-20 (locn.) (f. *Μενίσκος*)

Σωσίδημος
MACEDONIA (LOWER PAIONIA):
—EUROPOS: **(1)** f. ii BC Helly, *Gonnoi* 31, 5 (Tataki, *Macedonians* p. 109 no. 15) (f. *Αἰσχυλῖνος*)

Σωσίκα
CIMMERIAN BOSPOROS:
—PANTIKAPAION: **(1)** iv BC *CIRB* 224 (d. *Ἀναξίων*)

Σωσικλῆς
MACEDONIA: **(1)** iv BC Arr., *An.* iv 16. 6 (Tataki, *Macedonians* p. 437 no. 59) (f. *Πείθων*)
MACEDONIA (CHALKIDIKE):
—POTIDAIA-KASSANDREIA?: **(2)** 285 BC *SEG* XXXVIII 619, 15 (f. *Μένων*)
THRACE:
—PERINTHOS-HERAKLEIA:
——(Podargoi): **(3)** iii-ii BC *IPerinth* 61, 22 (*ΣΩΕΙΣΗΣ*—apogr., *Σωσικλῆς*—ed.: s. *Μενεκράτης*)

Σωσικράτεια
MACEDONIA: **(1)** f. iii BC *Thess. Mnem.* 11 (Tataki, *Macedonians* p. 437 no. 60) (d. *Ἀρτέμων*)

Σωσικράτης
MACEDONIA: **(1)** ii-i BC *NS* 622 (Tataki, *Macedonians* p. 437 no. 61) (f. *Ἡρωΐδης*)
MACEDONIA (CHALKIDIKE):
—OLYNTHOS: **(2)** iv BC *TAPA* 62 (1931) p. 54 no. 5 (f. *Ἀντίπατρος*)
MACEDONIA (EDONIS):
—AMPHIPOLIS: **(3)** m. iii BC Hatzopoulos, *Actes Amphipolis* p. 52 no 12, 3, 9; *SEG* XLI 566 (date) (s. *Ἀνδρόνικος*)
—PHILIPPOI: **(4)** a. 346 BC *Syll*³ 267 A, 1 (Tataki, *Macedonians* p. 166 no. 32) (s. *Τίμανδρος*)
MACEDONIA (MYGDONIA):
—THESSALONIKE: **(5)** iii BC *IG* X (2) (1) 302; cf. *AEMTh* 15 (2001) p. 215 (f. *Ἱστιαῖος*)
MACEDONIA (PIERIS):
—PHAGRES: **(6)** f. iv BC Pikoulas, *Chora* p. 113 no. 1 (Tataki, *Macedonians* p. 162 no. 2); cf. *SEG* XLVIII 797 (s. *Κρωκίνας*)
MACEDONIA?: **(7)** b. 348 BC *Olynthus* 10 p. 435 no. 2249 (bullet)
SCYTHIA MINOR:
—TOMIS: **(8)** i-ii AD *ISM* II 239 (I f. *Σωσικράτης* II); **(9)** ~ ib. (II s. *Σωσικράτης* I)
THRACE:
—ABDERA: **(10)** c. 275-250 BC *IG* XII (9) 218, 2; cf. *Eretria* XI pp. 268-9 no. XXIV (s. *Ἀγάθων*) ?= (*11*); **(11)** c. 260-220 BC *SEG* XXXVIII 1198, 2 ?= (*10*)
—BYZANTION: **(12)** ii/i BC *ID* 2631, 19 (I f. *Σωσικράτης* II); **(13)** ~ ib. l. 19 (II s. *Σωσικράτης* I)

Σωσίλαος
THRACE: **(1)** ii-iii AD *RDAC* 2002, p. 373 no. 15 (*Ζωσί-*: f. *Σωτήριχος*)

Σωσίλας
MACEDONIA (CHALKIDIKE):
—OLYNTHOS: **(1)** s. ii BC *EAD* XXVII p. 311 no. E 31 (amph.)

Σωσίλεως
THRACE:
—LYSIMACHEIA: **(1)** c. 208 BC *FD* III (4) 135 II, 15 (s. *Βάκχιος*)
—PERINTHOS-HERAKLEIA?: **(2)** iv BC Hp., *Epid.* iv 30; *Index Hipp.* s.v. (*κατασωσιλέω* (n. pr.?)—cod. V)

Σωσίμαχος
MACEDONIA: **(1)** ?iii BC *IG* XII (1) 1454 (Tataki, *Macedonians* p. 437 no. 62) (*Σωσίμα[χος]*)

Σωσιμένης
MACEDONIA (BOTTIAIA):
—BEROIA: **(1)** 223 BC *IBer* 4, 13 (f. *Ἀντήνωρ*); **(2)** 122 BC ib. 134, 7 (s. ...*ων*)
MACEDONIA (PIERIS):
—OISYME-EMATHIA?: **(3)** s. iv BC *PAE* 1938, p. 92 no. 1, 3
THRACE:
—PERINTHOS-HERAKLEIA:
——(Makedones): **(4)** iii-ii BC *IPerinth* 61, 5 (f. *Ἀπολλώνιος*)

Σωσίνικος
MACEDONIA: **(1)** ?17 BC *SB* 12524, 2 (Tataki, *Macedonians* p. 497 no. 235; La'da E1637) (*Σωσί<σι>νικος*: s. *Καλλίνικος*)

Σωσιπάτρα
MACEDONIA (BOTTIAIA):
—BEROIA: **(1)** 238 AD *ILeukopetra* 87, 9 (Tataki 702) (*Κλαυδιανὴ Σ.*)
—BEROIA?: **(2)** 105 AD *SEG* XVII 317, 10 (*Ποπιλλία Σ.*)
MACEDONIA (DERRIOPOS):
—STUBERRA: **(3)** ii/iii AD *IG* X (2) (2) 334 (*Αἰλιανὴ Σ.*)
MACEDONIA (MYGDONIA):
—THESSALONIKE: **(4)** s. i AD ib. X (2) (1) 69, 11 (m. *Ζωΐλος*); **(5)** ii-iii AD ib. 670 + *Maia* 25 (1973) p. 200 (*Σωσ[ιπά]τρα*: m. *Μᾶρκος*); **(6)** 191 AD *IG* X (2) (1) 407, 1 (*Αἰλ. Σωσειπάτρα*)
—THESSALONIKE?: **(7)** iii AD ib. 65, 7 (*CCCA* VI 197) (*Αὐρ. Σ.*); **(8)** c. 202-212 AD *IG* X (2) (1) 578 (or Macedonia (Mygdonia) Lete: *Παιδιανὴ Σ.*)
MACEDONIA (PAIONIA):
—ANTIGONEIA? (TREMNIK (MOD.)): **(9)** ii-iii AD *Sp.* 71 (1931) p. 98 no. 231 (*Δαστιδία Σ.*, *Δαστιλία*—ed.)
—BYLAZORA: **(10)** iii AD *JÖAI* 6 (1903) Beibl. col. 4 no. 3 (*Αὐρ. Σ.*)
THRACE:
—MARONEIA: **(11)** f. iii BC *IThrakAig* E229 (d. *Κανθαρίων*)

Σωσίπατρος
CIMMERIAN BOSPOROS:
—GORGIPPIA: **(1)** f. iii BC *CIRB* 1137 A I, 48 (s. *Ἡρακλείδης*); **(2)** ~ ib. 1137 B I, 38 (*[Σ]ωσίπατρος*: s. *Θεόδωρος*); **(3)** ~ ib. 1137 B II, 44 (s. *Ἰασίμαχος*); **(4)** ii/iii AD *SEG* XLIX 1033 A, 1 (*[Σ]ωσίπ[ατρος]?*)
—HERMONASSA: **(5)** ii AD *CIRB* 1089; **(6)** 123-132 AD ib. 1054, 8 (f. *Βάγης*)
—PANTIKAPAION: **(7)** imp. ib. 805 (s. *Νυμφᾶς*); **(8)** iv AD ib. 740 (*(Σ)ωσίπατρος*: f. *Ἡδύφιλος*)
MACEDONIA (BOTTIAIA):
—BEROIA: **(9)** ii BC *IBer* 199 (Tataki 1214) (f. *Λυσίμαχος*)
—BEROIA?: **(10)** m. i AD *Ep. Rom.* XVI 21 ?= (*Σώπατρος* (*5*))
MACEDONIA (MYGDONIA):
—THESSALONIKE: **(11)** c. 230 BC *IG* XI (4) 1053, 10 = X (2) (1) 1028 (*RE* (1); Tataki, *Macedonians* p. 187 no. 64); **(12)** f. i AD *IG* X (2) (1) 126, 1; Robert, *OMS* 5 pp. 295-302 (date) (s. *Κλεοπάτρα*); **(13)** ~ *IG* X (2) (1) 133, 10; Robert, *OMS* 5 pp. 295-302 (date) (*[Σω]σίπατρος*: s. *Ἰσίδωρος*)
MACEDONIA (PAIONIA):
—KAVADARCI (MOD.): **(14)** ii AD *Sp.* 71 (1931) p. 237 no. 632 = 75 (1933) p. 41 no. 136 (*Γ. Κορνηλιανὸς Οὐάλης ὁ καὶ Σ.*: f. *Βούκκαλος*)
MACEDONIA (PELAGONIA)?: **(15)** imp. *IG* X (2) (2) 185 (f. *Παρμενίων*)
SKYTHIA:
—OLBIA-BORYSTHENES: **(16)** ii AD *IOSPE* I² 183, 3 (s. *Νικήρατος*)
THRACE: **(17)** 282 BC *PHib* 198 I, 3; cf. *PP* 2196 Add. (*Σωσίπατρ[ο]ς*: f. *Βαστακίλας*)
—MARONEIA: **(18)** i BC-i AD *IG* II² 9293 (*FRA* 3552) (f. *Συνήθεια*)

Σωσίπολις
MACEDONIA (EDONIS):
—PHILIPPOI: **(1)** s. iv BC *SEG* XLII 621 (Pilhofer 53) (*[Σω]σιπόλιος?* (gen.): f. *Ἡρόδοτος*)
MACEDONIA (KRESTONIA):
—IORON: **(2)** s. i AD *SEG* XXXIX 610 (Tataki, *Macedonians* p. 114 no. 3) (f. *Σωσίας*)
MACEDONIA (SINTIKE):
—PARTHIKOPOLIS (TERRIT.): **(3)** ii AD *IGB* IV 2302, 4 (m. *Λούκιος, Τερεντία*)

Σώσιππος
MACEDONIA (MYGDONIA):
—THESSALONIKE: **(1)** s. ii AD *IG* X (2) (1) 244 I, 17 (s. *Πρῖμος*)
MACEDONIA (ODOMANTIKE):
—SIRRHA: **(2)** 155 AD Dimitsas 821, 32 (Kaphtantzis 1) (*Σώσιπ(π)ος*: f. *Θεοκλῆς*)

Σῶσις
CIMMERIAN BOSPOROS:
—BOSPOROS: **(1)** 346 BC Rhodes–Osborne 64, 50
—GORGIPPIA: **(2)** f. iii BC *CIRB* 1137 B I, 8 (*[Σ]ῶσις*: s. *Ἑκαταῖος*); **(3)** ~ ib. 1137 B II, 54 (s. *Μοσχίων*)
—HERMONASSA: **(4)** iv BC ib. 1062 (f. *Δημήτριος*); **(5)** ~ ib. 1068 (s. *Δημήτριος*)
MACEDONIA: **(6)** c. 322-313 BC *IG* VII 4256, 9 (*IOrop* 4; Tataki, *Macedonians* p. 437 no. 63) (f. *Ἀντίπατρος*)
MACEDONIA (EDONIS):
—AMPHIPOLIS: **(7)** s. iv BC *PAE* 1981, p. 25 with pl. 43 β, 14 (f. —*ης*)
MACEDONIA (PIERIS):
—OISYME-EMATHIA?: **(8)** s. iv BC ib. 1938, p. 92 no. 1, 4 (*[Σ]ῶσις*)
THRACE:
—BYZANTION: **(9)** ?352 BC Rhodes–Osborne 57, 24 (s. *Καράτιχος*)
—PERINTHOS-HERAKLEIA:
——(Podargoi): **(10)** iii-ii BC *IPerinth* 61, 23 (s. *Ἀπολλόδωρος*); **(11)** ~ ib. l. 25 (f. *Καλλιφῶν*)

Σωσίς
MACEDONIA (MYGDONIA):
—KALINDOIA: **(1)** i BC/i AD *SEG* XLII 598

Σωσίστρατος
MACEDONIA (DERRIOPOS):
—STUBERRA: **(1)** c. 41-90 AD *IG* X (2) (2) 323, 20; 326, 79 (s. *Φίλων*, f. *Φίλων*); **(2)** 74 AD ib. l. 32 (f. *Παράμονος*); **(3)** f. ii AD ib. 329 (s. *Πα*—); **(4)** 121 AD ib. 328, 14 (f. *Λῦσις*)
SKYTHIA:
—OLBIA-BORYSTHENES: **(5)** iii BC *IOSPE* I² 201 II, 21 (s. *Νυμφόδωρος*)

Σωσίφιλος
MACEDONIA (MYGDONIA):
—LETE: (1) f. ii BC *SEG* XLVI 764, 5 (f. —ς)
THRACE:
—MARONEIA: (2) ii-iii AD *JHS* 16 (1896) p. 320 no. 22 = *BCH* 37 (1913) p. 143 no. 48 (*IThrakAig* E250) (s. *Διον—*)

Σωσίχα
THRACE: (1) iii BC *IG* II² 8925 (*FRA* 2578)

Σωσίων
MACEDONIA (BOTTIAIA):
—PELLA: (1) ?iii BC *SEG* II 401 (f. *Ἡραΐς*, *Ἀρχίας*)
THRACE:
—BYZANTION?: (2) i BC-i AD *IByz* 371 (Firatlı-Robert pp. 126-7 no. 213) ([*Σ*]*ωσίων*: s. *Σίμων*)
—MADYTOS: (3) imp. *ISestos* 66

Σῶσος
CIMMERIAN BOSPOROS:
—PANTIKAPAION: (1) imp. *CIRB* 767 (s. *Ἔρως*)
MACEDONIA (MYGDONIA):
—KALINDOIA: (2) 68-98 AD *SEG* XLII 580, 89 (f. *Ζωΐλος*); (3) ~ ib. l. 96 (f. *Ἀσκληπιόδωρος*)
MACEDONIA (PIERIA):
—DION: (4) v/iv BC ib. XXV 705 (f. *Ἀριστοτίμα*)
THRACE:
—LYSIMACHEIA: (5) m. ii BC *ISestos* 38 a, 3 (f. *Σῖμος*)
—MARONEIA: (6) 103 BC *IG* II² 1335, 45 (*FRA* 3553)
—PERINTHOS-HERAKLEIA:
——(Akarnanes): (7) iii-ii BC *IPerinth* 61, 13 (f. *Ἀριστίων*)

Σῶσπις
MACEDONIA (BOTTIAIA):
—BEROIA: (1) ii/iii AD *IBer* 27 A, 10 (slave?)

Σωστράτα
MACEDONIA (MYGDONIA):
—SOCHOS (MOD.): (1) 189 or 306 AD *SEG* XXXI 645
THRACE:
—BYZANTION: (2) i BC *IByz* 150 (d. *Δαμόφιλος*)
—PERINTHOS-HERAKLEIA: (3) iii AD *IPerinth* 130, 5 (*Κλ. Τιβερία Σ.*: d. *Σώστρατος*)

Σωστράτη
MACEDONIA (BOTTIAIA):
—PELLA: (1) s. iv BC *A΄ Panell. Synedr. Epigr.* p. 179 no. 4 (*SEG* XXX 583) (d. *Διονύσιος*)
MACEDONIA (CHALKIDIKE):
—POTIDAIA-KASSANDREIA (TERRIT.)?: (2) ii BC *TAPA* 69 (1938) p. 69 no. 25 (d. *Πολυκράτης*)

Σωστρατίδης
MACEDONIA (BOTTIAIA):
—BEROIA: (1) ii BC *IBer* 141, 37

Σώστρατος
CIMMERIAN BOSPOROS:
—GORGIPPIA: (1) f. iii BC *CIRB* 1137 A II, 53; 1137 B II, 58 (f. *Σπαρτοκίων*); (2) ~ ib. 1137 B I, 32 ([*Σώ*]*στρατος*: s. *Ἀναξικράτης*)
—MYRMEKION: (3) f. ii AD ib. 885 (f. *Γοζιοῦς*)
—PANTIKAPAION: (4) s. i AD ib. 421; (5) 82 AD ib. 76, 20 (*SEG* XVIII 310) (*Σώ*[*σ*]*τρατος*: f. *Διονυσόδωρος*)
—PHANAGOREIA: (6) hell.? *Suppl. Hell.* 731-5 (*Σωσικράτης*—Ath.)
MACEDONIA: (7) 328 BC Berve 738 (Tataki, *Macedonians* p. 437 no. 65) (s. *Ἀμύντας*); (8) 231 BC *SB* 9258, 6 (Tataki, *Macedonians* p. 438 no. 67) (I f. *Σώστρατος* II); (9) ~ *SB* 9258, 6 (*PP* 4108a; Tataki, *Macedonians* p. 438 no. 66) (II s. *Σώστρατος* I)

MACEDONIA (BISALTIA):
—ARGILOS?: (10) 364-357 BC Hatzopoulos, *Actes Amphipolis* p. 15 no. 1, 13; pp. 73-4 (locn., date) (or Macedonia (Edonis) Amphipolis)
MACEDONIA (BOTTIAIA):
—BEROIA: (11) ii/iii AD *IBer* 27 A, 1 (s. *Πρόβος*)
MACEDONIA (EDONIS):
—AMPHIPOLIS: (12) b. 357 BC Hatzopoulos, *Actes Amphipolis* p. 25 no. 3, 2-3, 16 (*SEG* XLI 557); (13) ii-iii AD *PAE* 1979, p. 77 with pl. 54 *β*
MACEDONIA (MYGDONIA):
—KALINDOIA: (14) 68-98 AD *SEG* XLII 580, 44 (f. *Ἀλέξανδρος*)
—LETE: (15) f. ii BC ib. XLVI 764, 8 ([*Σ*]*ώ*-*στρατος*: s. *Μένανδρος*)
—LETE (NR.): (16) iii BC ib. XXXI 633 a (f. *Μέν*-*ανδρος*)
MACEDONIA (ODOMANTIKE):
—SIRRHA?: (17) ii-i BC ib. XL 563, 1 (f. *Σω*-*πάτρα*)
MACEDONIA (PIERIS):
—NEAPOLIS?: (18) hell.? ib. XXXI 769 (Tataki, *Macedonians* p. 127 no. 18)
SCYTHIA MINOR:
—KALLATIS: (19) ?264 BC *FD* III (1) 158, 2 (s. *Ἱέρων*); (20) s. ii AD *ISM* III 259, 3 (*Σώ*-*στρα*[*τος*]: s. —*ων*)
SKYTHIA:
—OLBIA-BORYSTHENES: (21) iii BC *SNG BM Black Sea* 536 (coin) (*Σώστρα*(*τος*))
THRACE: (22) 223 BC *PHamb* 24, 20 (Velkov 289; La'da E799)
—ABDERA: (23) iii BC *BCH* 37 (1913) p. 137 no. 41 (*IThrakAig* E48) (f. *Μένανδρος*)
—BYZANTION: (24) ii AD Ach. Tat. ii 13 and passim (f. *Λευκίππη*: fict.)
—LYSIMACHEIA: (25) m. ii BC *ISestos* 38 a, 4 (s. *Μενέδημος*); (26) ~ ib. l. 5 (s. *Ἁγίας*)
—ODESSOS: (27) 44 BC *IGB* I² 46, 3 (f. *Ἡγέμων*)
—PERINTHOS-HERAKLEIA: (28) iii AD *IPerinth* 130, 5 (f. *Κλ. Τιβερία Σωστράτα*)
——(Basileidai): (29) s. iii BC ib. 62, 4 (s. *Μηνο*-*φάνης*)

Σωσώ
MACEDONIA: (1) 153-144 BC *SGDI* 1940, 6, 8, 13 (Tataki, *Macedonians* p. 438 no. 68) (slave/freed.); (2) ~ *SGDI* 2279, 3, 5 (Tataki, *Macedonians* p. 438 no. 69) (slave/freed.)
SARMATIA:
—SARMATAI?: (3) m. ii BC *IG* IX (1)² (3) 679, 4, [5], 9-11 (slave/freed.)
THRACE: (4) 166 BC *SGDI* 1847, 3, 6 (slave/freed.)

Σώσων
MACEDONIA (CHALKIDIKE):
—APHYTIS: (1) ?351 BC *A΄ Panell. Synedr. Epigr.* pp. 80-1, 7, 14, 22 (s. *Κατάστασις*)
—CHALKIDEIS: (2) ?354 BC *TAPA* 69 (1938) pp. 52-3 no. 6, 3-4; Hatzopoulos, *Actes Chalc.* p. 80 (date) (f. *Κλέανδρος*)
—OLYNTHOS: (3) f. iv BC *IG* II² 10026 (12271; Tataki, *Macedonians* p. 143 no. 107; *FRA* 5913) (f. *Νικησώ*); (4) ?350 BC *TAPA* 62 (1931) p. 43 no. 2, 3; Hatzopoulos, *Actes Chalc.* p. 80 (date) (s. *Θεόδωρος*)
MACEDONIA (MYGDONIA):
—THESSALONIKE: (5) 27 BC-14 AD *IG* X (2) (1) 31, 21

Σωτάδας
TAURIS:
—CHERSONESOS: (1) c. 325-315 BC Kats p. 113 no. 116 (amph.)
THRACE:
—BYZANTION: (2) hell.? Clem. Al., *Strom.* i 61. 3; *Suda* *Σ* 869; cf. Tz., *ad Lyc.* 1349 (*Σώτας*—Tz. per err.?)

Σωτάδης
MACEDONIA (DERRIOPOS):
—STUBERRA: (1) 87 AD *IG* X (2) (2) 325, 72 (s. *Ζωΐλος*); (2) 116 AD ib. 327, 13 (s. *Παράμονος*) ?= (*3*); (3) 121 AD ib. 328, 13 (f. *Παράμονος*) ?= (*2*)
THRACE:
—MARONEIA: (4) f. iii BC *RE* (2); *Coll. Alex.* pp. 238-45 (*PP* 16717)

Σώταιρος
MACEDONIA (BOTTIAIA):
—BEROIA: (1) ii BC *IBer* 141, 4
MACEDONIA (EDONIS):
—AMPHIPOLIS: (2) b. 318 BC *IG* II² 421, 5 (Tataki, *Macedonians* p. 61 no. 123; *FRA* 519) (f. ..*κλῆς*)

Σωτᾶς
MACEDONIA (BOTTIAIA):
—BEROIA: (1) ii/iii AD *IBer* 27 A, 8 (slave?); (2) 233 AD *ILeukopetra* 81, 3 (*Ἔλβιος Σ.*)
MACEDONIA (DERRIOPOS):
—STUBERRA: (3) 50 AD *IG* X (2) (2) 324, 20 (s. *Κάλλιππος*)
MACEDONIA (EDONIS):
—AMPHIPOLIS: (4) imp. *BCH* 19 (1895) p. 110 no. 2 (55 (1931) p. 179 no. 8) (*M. Καικέλιος Σ.*)
—PHILIPPOI: (5) ii-i BC ib. 59 (1935) p. 158 no. 54 (Pilhofer 303) (f. *Ἀρμένα*)
MACEDONIA (LOWER PAIONIA): (6) imp. *Sp.* 77 (1934) p. 42 no. 23; cf. 98 (1941-8) no. 98 ([*Σ*]*ωτᾶς*?)
MACEDONIA (LYNKESTIS):
—HERAKLEIA: (7) i AD *IG* X (2) (2) 75, 21 (*Τίτος Σ.*: s. *Λούκιος*)
SCYTHIA MINOR:
—TOMIS: (8) ii-iii AD *ISM* II 197 (*GVI* 1043a) + *SEG* XXV 760 (s. *Πωλλίων*)
SKYTHIA:
—OLBIA-BORYSTHENES: (9) c. 81-96 AD *IOSPE* I² 139, 4 + *SEG* XLIV 666 (name, date) ([*Σ*]*ωτᾶς*, [*Ζ*]*ωτᾶς*?: s. *Στέφανος*)
THRACE:
—ANCHIALOS*: (10) ii AD *DCB* (-); Eus., *HE* v 19, 3 (bp.)

Σώτειρα
MACEDONIA (MYGDONIA):
—THESSALONIKE: (1) ii-iii AD *IG* X (2) (1) 666, 5, 11 (biling.) (*CIL* III 7331; *IG* II² 13226; *SEG* XLIII 461) (m. *Σπῆνις*)

Σωτήρ
MACEDONIA (BOTTIAIA):
—BEROIA: (1) c. 180-219 AD *ILeukopetra* 15, 4; 20, 2; 69, 5 (Tataki 730) (*Κλ. Σ.*); (2) 235 AD *SEG* L 577, 5 (*Λ. Κορνήλιος Σω*[*τή*]*ρ*)
MACEDONIA (EDONIS):
—PHILIPPOI: (3) ii AD *BCH* 55 (1931) pp. 201-2 no. 16 (Pilhofer 27) (Lat. L. Licinius Soter qui et Musicus: f. L. Licinius Firmus)
SCYTHIA MINOR:
—ULMETUM: (4) iii AD *ISM* V 72, 7 (Lat. L. Va. Soter: s. L. Val. Victorinus, *Νικάνδρα*)
THRACE:
—MARKIANOPOLIS (TERRIT.): (5) s. ii AD *CCET* II (1) 361; cf. *SEG* XXXIX 643 (f. —*ρος*)
—ODESSOS: (6) m. ii AD *IGB* I² 177 (PM 1749); *Dacia* 21 (1977) p. 161 (date) (f. *Τούτα*); (7) 215 AD *IGB* I² 47 b, 8 (f. *Αὐρ. Ἀπελλᾶς*); (8) ~ ib. l. 28 (*Αὐρ. Σ.*: s. *Μᾶρκος*); (9) ~ ib. 47 c, 20 (I f. *Αὐρ. Σωτήρ* II) ?= (*11*); (10) ~ ib. l. 20 (*Αὐρ. Σ.*: II s. *Σωτήρ* I); (11) ~ ib. l. 22 (f. *Αὐρ. Φιλῖνος*) ?= (*9*); (12) 221 AD ib. 47 bis a, 23 (I f. *Αὐρ. Σωτήρ* II); (13) ~ ib. l. 23 (*Αὐρ. Σ.*: II s. *Σωτήρ* I); (14) ~ ib. l. 35 (f. *Αὐρ. Μᾶρκος*); (15) ~ ib. 47 bis c, 19 (*Αὐρ. Σ.*: s. *Κόνων*)

Σωτηρᾶς
THRACE:
—PAUTALIA: (1) ii AD ib. IV 2074, 7 (-*τι*-)

Σωτηρία
Macedonia (Bottiaia):
—beroia (territ.)?: (1) 245 ad Tataki 1218

Σωτηρίδας
Thrace:
—perinthos-herakleia:
——(Akarnanes): (1) iii-ii bc *IPerinth* 61, 11 (s. *Συρίσκος*)

Σωτηρίδης
Macedonia (Paionia):
—kavadarci (mod.): (1) ii-iii ad *Sp.* 98 (1941-8) p. 64 no. 134 (*Σωτηρίδ[ης]*—*Sp.*, *Σωτήριχ[ος]*—Papazoglu)
Thrace:
—lysimacheia: (2) ii-i bc *IG* II² 9234 (*FRA* 3409)
—perinthos-herakleia:
——(Akarnanes): (3) iii-ii bc *IPerinth* 61, 14 (*Σωτηρ(ίδ)ης*: f. *Διοκλῆς*)

Σωτήριν
Macedonia (Bottiaia):
—beroia: (1) 133 ad *IBer* 326

Σωτήριος
Sarmatia:
—maiotai: (1) ii/i bc *Ag.* xvii 536 (*SEG* xix 285; *FRA* 3457) (*Σωτήρ[ιος]*?)
Tauris:
—chersonesos: (2) c. 230-215 bc Kats p. 113 no. 117 (vase) (s. *Διονύσιος*); (3) c. 120-110 bc Anokhin p. 147 no. 186 (coin) (*Σωτήρι(ος?)*, *Σωτήρι(χος)*?)

Σωτῆρις
Cimmerian Bosporos:
—pantikapaion: (1) vi ad *IAK* 3 (1902) pp. 48-50 no. 15 (-ρεις)

Σωτηρίς
Macedonia (Bottiaia):
—beroia: (1) 208 ad *ILeukopetra* 51, 1 (Tataki 42) (*Αἰλ.* [*Σ*]*οτηρίς*)
Sarmatia:
—sarmatai: (2) ii bc *IG* II² 10243 (*FRA* 6599) (slave?)
Tauris:
—chersonesos: (3) iv/iii bc Solomonik, *NEP-Kh* 162 (d. *Ἱέρων*)
Thrace: (4) ?162 bc *FD* iii (3) 6, [3], 4-5, 8, etc. (slave/freed.); (5) 158 bc *SGDI* 1839, 3, 5, 9, 12 (slave/freed.); (6) 153-144 bc ib. 2186, 7, 9, 12, etc. (slave/freed.); (7) 84-60 bc *FD* iii (3) 358, 5, 8, 11, [12], 16 (slave/freed.)
—ainos: (8) ii bc *IG* II² 7984 (*FRA* 265)
—byzantion: (9) ii bc *IByz* 194 (Fıratlı–Robert pp. 52-3 no. 29); (10) i-ii ad *IG* II² 8447 (*FRA* 1408) (d. *Μενεκράτης*)
—rhaidestos: (11) ii-iii ad Taşlıklıoğlu 2 p. 225 no. 1

Σωτήριχος
Macedonia (Bottiaia):
—beroia: (1) ii/iii ad *IBer* 143 B, 24 (Tataki 1222) (I f. *Σωτήριχος* II); (2) ~ *IBer* 143 B, 24 (Tataki 1220) (II s. *Σωτήριχος* I); (3) ~ *IBer* 144 A, 7 (Tataki 1145) (*Π. Πωλιανὸς Σ.*); (4) a. 249 ad *IBer* 109, 9 (Tataki 272) (*Λ. Αὐρηλιανὸς Σ.*: f. *Λ. Αὐρηλιανὴ Ἀλεξάνδρα*)
Macedonia (Mygdonia):
—nea mesembria (mod.): (5) iii ad *SEG* xlviii 856 (s. *Πάρδαλις*)
—thessalonike: (6) ii ad *IG* x (2) (1) 664, 1 (*SEG* xliii 459)
—thessalonike?: (7) ii ad *IG* x (2) (1) 877
Scythia Minor:
—kallatis: (8) s. iii bc *ISM* iii 35 B, 36 (f. *Ὄλυμπος*)
Skythia:
—tanais: (9) 225-228 ad *CIRB* 1279, 10; 1282, 12 (-κος: s. *Πόπλιος*)
Tauris:
—chersonesos: (10) ?ii ad *IOSPE* I² 457
Thrace: (11) 173 bc *SGDI* 1832, 2-3, 6, 8, etc. (slave/freed.); (12) 154 bc ib. 1903, 2-3, 6 (slave/freed.); (13) ii-iii ad *RDAC* 2002, p. 373 no. 15 (s. *Σωσίλαος*)
—abdera: (14) ii bc *BCH* 37 (1913) pp. 125-6 no. 39 c, 31 (*IThrakAig* E9)
—ainos: (15) imp. Dimitsas 1007 (Pilhofer 68) (I f. *Σωτήριχος* II, *Δημήτριος*); (16) ~ Dimitsas 1007 (Pilhofer 68) (II s. *Σωτήριχος* I)
—byzantion: (17) ii-i bc *IByz* 254 (Fıratlı–Robert p. 117 no. 197) (f. *Καθαρά*); (18) i bc-i ad *IByz* 19, 14 (*Κορνήλιος Σ.*); (19) s. i ad ib. 32, 5 (s. *Ἀρίστων*); (20) c. 222-235 ad Schönert-Geiss, *Byzantion* 1689-99; 1770-1 (coin) (*M. Αὐρ. Σ.*)
—durostorum: (21) 139-161 ad *CIL* iii 7474 (Lat. Cn. Oppius Soterichus: f. Oppius Severus)
—maroneia: (22) hell. *IThrakAig* E259, 2, 4 (f. *Διογένης*, *Στρατονίκη*); (23) ii-i bc ib. E212, 30 (*Σωτήρ[ιχ]ος*: f. *Ἀκέστωρ*)
—nicopolis ad istrum*: (24) s. ii ad *ILB* 361 (Lat. [T.] [Iu]l. Sote[rich]us: freed.)
—perinthos-herakleia: (25) i bc-i ad? Dumont–Homolle 72d, 8; cf. *IPerinth* 57 (om. per err.) (s. *Δάδας*); (26) i-ii ad ib. 97 (s. *Ἡρᾶς*)

Σώτιμος
Macedonia (Bottiaia):
—pella: (1) iii-ii bc Dimitsas 144 (f. *Μνησιστράτη*)
Macedonia (Edonis):
—amphipolis (territ.): (2) f. iii bc *BCH* 55 (1931) p. 172 no. 1
Tauris:
—chersonesos: (3) f. iii bc Solomonik, *NEP-Kh* 164 (s. *Ἡροκᾶς*)
—kerkinitis: (4) iv bc Solomonik, *GChKh* 171 (vase) (*SEG* xxxiii 611); *BE* 1990, no. 567 (vase) (*Σώτι(μος)*—ed., *Ζώτι(χος)*?—*BE*)
Thrace: (5) 93-88 bc Oros., *Hist.* v 18. 30; cf. Detschev p. 405 (Lat. Sothimus: king)

Σώτιον
Thrace: (1) 190 bc *SGDI* 2006, 2, 4, 6, 8, 10 (slave/freed.)

Σωφρόνις
Thrace:
—salymbria: (1) iv-v ad *AD* 53 (1998) Mel. p. 458 no. 197 (*Σο-*)

Σωφροσύνη
Thrace:
—dionysopolis: (1) ii ad *IGB* I² 28 bis; *Dacia* 21 (1977) p. 161 (date) (d. *Φιλ—*)
—perinthos-herakleia: (2) i-ii ad *IPerinth* 146 (n. pr.?)

Σώφρων
Skythia:
—tanais: (1) 225 ad *CIRB* 1279, 26 ([*Σ*]*ώφρων*: f. *Ἀρδόναστος*)
Thrace:
—ainos: (2) i-ii ad *IG* II² 7981 (*FRA* 266) (f. *Ὁμόνοια*)

Σωχάρης
Macedonia (Mygdonia):
—apollonia: (1) 355 bc *IGLMP* 128, 1, [9] (Tataki, *Macedonians* p. 68 no. 11) (s. *Χάρης*)
Thrace:
—byzantion: (2) c. 315-280 bc *FD* iii (4) 150, 1 (s. *Θράσων*)

Σωχούβαζος
Skythia:
—olbia-borysthenes: (1) ii ad *IOSPE* I² 106, 3; Zgusta, *PNS* 226 (s. *Ἀντώνιος*)

T

Τάκτωρ
Thrace:
—perinthos-herakleia:
——(Geleuntes): (1) iii-ii bc *IPerinth* 61, 30 (s. *Πλείστωρ*)

Τάλουλος
Thrace:
—maroneia: (1) imp. *IG* II² 9286 (*FRA* 3554) (f. *Γλαυκίας*)

Ταλούρα
Thrace: (1) iii bc *IG* II² 8926 (*FRA* 2588) (d. *Τάλουρος*)

Τάλουρος
Thrace: (1) iii bc *IG* II² 8926 (*FRA* 2589) (f. *Ταλούρα*)
—lysimacheia: (2) i bc *IG* II² 9232 + *Ag.* xvii 533 (*FRA* 3410) (f. *Προστασία*)

Τάμβισος?
Cimmerian Bosporos:
—nymphaion (nr.): (1) iii ad *CIRB* 941 (*Τιάμβισος*?: f. *Φάννης*: reading—Tokhtas'ev)

Ταμύρα
Cimmerian Bosporos:
—pantikapaion: (1) i bc/i ad ib. 318; Zgusta, *PNS* 227

Τάναος?
Macedonia: (1) ii/i bc *IOrop* 700 (Tataki, *Macedonians* p. 438 no. 1) (*Τάνα[ος]*?: s. *Πύρρος*)

Τανάσισος
Skythia:
—olbia-borysthenes: (1) ii ad *IOSPE* I² 92, 7; Zgusta, *PNS* 713 (s. *Χουάρσαζος*)

Τάνης
Scythia Minor:
—tomis: (1) ii-iii ad *ISM* ii 468, 6 (s. *Διονύσιος*)

Τανουσας

SCYTHIA MINOR: **(1)** ii BC *SCIV* 1.1 (1950) p. 245 no. 26; *SNG BM Black Sea* 307 (coin) (*Τανουσα* (gen.): king)

Τανύβοτος

SCYTHIA MINOR:
—KALLATIS: **(1)** f. ii BC *Iasos* 197, 7 ([*T*]*ανύβοτος*?: f. *Διογένης*)

Τανύσαλος

CIMMERIAN BOSPOROS:
—PANTIKAPAION: **(1)** ii AD *CIRB* 708 (f. *Στύρανος*)

Τάξακις

SKYTHIA:
—SKYTHAI: **(1)** s. vi BC Hdt. iv 120 (king)

Ταόρδουνος

SKYTHIA:
—OLBIA-BORYSTHENES: **(1)** f. ii AD *SEG* XLIII 506, 14 (f. *Λάβαζος*)

Ταπερεσαῖος

CIMMERIAN BOSPOROS:
—PANTIKAPAION: **(1)** iv BC *CIRB* 219; Zgusta, *PNS* 713 (f. *Πατροφίλη*)

Τάρα?

THRACE:
—KOMOTINI (MOD.): **(1)** imp. *Belomorski Pregled* 1 (1942) p. 336 no. 41 (*BE* 1948, no. 148; *IThrakAig* E482)

Ταράλας

MACEDONIA (MYGDONIA):
—KALINDOIA: **(1)** 68-98 AD *SEG* XLII 580, 88; cf. *Anthémonte–Kalindoia* 2 pp. 312-13 (name) (f. *Διοσκουρίδης*)
MACEDONIA (ODOMANTIKE):
—GAZOROS?: **(2)** 158 AD *SEG* XXIV 614, 10 (Pilhofer 544); cf. Hatzopoulos, *MI* 1 pp. 84-6 (f. *Ἄλκιμος*)

Ταραντῖνος

MACEDONIA (CHALKIDIKE):
—POTIDAIA-KASSANDREIA: **(1)** imp. *SEG* XXXVII 559. 4 (*Α. Κορνιφίκιος Τ.*)

Τάρας

SCYTHIA MINOR:
—TOMIS*: **(1)** i-ii AD *ISM* II 177 (Lat. Marius Tara: freed.)
THRACE:
—MARKIANOPOLIS (TERRIT.): **(2)** iii-iv AD *IGB* V 5328, 4 (*CCET* II (1) 365) (f. *Θιθι*)

Τάρβης

MACEDONIA (CHALKIDIKE):
—SPARTOLOS?: **(1)** ?352 BC *SEG* XLVI 804, 3 (s. *Σεδέλης*)

Ταργήλιος

CIMMERIAN BOSPOROS:
—ZENONOS CHERSONESOS*: **(1)** v/iv BC ib. XL 643 (*Ταργ*[*ή*]*λιος*)

Τάρης

MACEDONIA (BOTTIAIA):
—MIEZA: **(1)** i AD Mendel, *Cat.* 1036 (Tataki 1224) (*Τάρεος* (gen.), *Τάρυς*—Tataki: f. *Διονυσόδοτος*)

Ταρουθίνας

THRACE: **(1)** 241 BC *PFrankf* 5, [10], 18 (Velkov 292; La'da E800)
THRACE?: **(2)** iii BC *Memnonion* 430 (Velkov 293) (*-θίννας*); **(3)** m. iii BC *PCZ* 59656, 8 (Velkov 291) ?= (*Ταρυσίνας* (*1*))

Τάρουλα

THRACE:
—XANTHI (MOD.): **(1)** iii AD *IThrakAig* E104 (*Τάρ̣ουλα*)

Ταρούλας

CIMMERIAN BOSPOROS:
—PANTIKAPAION: **(1)** i-ii AD *CIRB* 633 (f. *Σαμβίων*); **(2)** f. i AD ib. 482; cf. KW pl. 15 no. 222; Zgusta, *PNS* 577 (f. *Παιρίσαλος*)
MACEDONIA (BOTTIAIA):
—EDESSA: **(3)** 51 AD *SEG* XLVI 744, 6 (Tataki, *Edessa* 290) (f. *Ποσειδώνιος*)
MACEDONIA (MYGDONIA):
—KALINDOIA: **(4)** a. 98 AD *SEG* XLII 583, 19; cf. *Anthémonte–Kalindoia* 2 pp. 312-13 (name) (s. *Διονύσιος*)
—LETE: **(5)** ii AD *Makedonika* 2 (1951) p. 619 no. 42 *θ*, 10 (f. *Ἡλιόδωρος*)
SKYTHIA:
—TANAIS (NR.): **(6)** ii-iii AD Minns, *Scythians* p. 235
THRACE:
—APOLLONIA-SOZOPOLIS: **(7)** iii/ii BC *IGB* I² 469 bis, 2 (f. *Κότυς*); **(8)** i-ii AD ib. 400 (f. (ad.) *Μήτοκος*)
—HERAION TEICHOS?: **(9)** ii-i BC Taşlıklıoğlu 2 p. 93 no. 1 + *BE* 1972, no. 285 (f. *Αὐλουζεις*)
—MARONEIA (TERRIT.): **(10)** iii AD Bakalakis, *Oinos Ismarikos* p. 555 (*IThrakAig* E379) (f. *Ἀλέξανδρος ὁ καὶ Βέβιος, Ζώσιμος*)
—MESAMBRIA (TERRIT.): **(11)** f. ii AD *IGB* I² 354 quater (*CCET* I 111) (*Τ.* [*ὁ*] [*κ*]*αὶ Σκῶρις*: s. *Βίθυς*)
—MEZDRA (MOD.): **(12)** ii-iii AD *IGB* II 489 (f. *Δεκμιανός*)
THRACE?: **(13)** iii-ii BC *Memnonion* 93 (Velkov 294); **(14)** ii BC *Memnonion* 81 (Velkov 290) (*Ταρόλλου*—lap.: f. *Σιτάλκας*)

Ταρουσίμας

MACEDONIA (MYGDONIA):
—KALINDOIA: **(1)** ?i-ii AD *SEG* XXIX 628, 1 (*Ταρουσί*(*ν*)*ας*?: f. *Δοῦρις*)

Ταρουσίνας

MACEDONIA (BISALTIA):
—TERPNI (MOD.): **(1)** ii-iii AD ib. XLIX 810
MACEDONIA (EDONIS):
—PHILIPPOI (DRAMA (MOD.)): **(2)** i-ii AD *AD* 51 (1996) Chron. p. 577, 18 (Lat. Tarusina: s. *Διοσκουρίδης*)
MACEDONIA (MYGDONIA):
—KALINDOIA: **(3)** ?i-ii AD *SEG* XXIX 628, 3 (*Τ. Σκεπαρνᾶς*: s. *Κοσείδης*); **(4)** 68-98 AD ib. XLII 580, 17 + *BE* 1999, no. 362; cf. *Anthémonte–Kalindoia* 2 pp. 312-13 (name) (f. *Ἱέρων*); **(5)** ~ *SEG* XLII 580, 23 (s. *Παράμονος*); **(6)** ~ ib. l. 27 (f. *Νίκων*); **(7)** ~ ib. l. 72, 74-5; cf. *BE* 1999, no. 362 (f. *Διοσκουρίδης, Μιήζεις*); **(8)** a. 98 AD *SEG* XLII 582, 9 (f. *Δάλης*); **(9)** ~ ib. l. 62 (s. *Διοσκουρίδης*); **(10)** ~ ib. 583, 7 (f. *—ης*); **(11)** ~ ib. l. 11 (f. *Κότυς*)
MACEDONIA (PELAGONIA):
—MARIOVO (MOD.): **(12)** imp. *IG* X (2) (2) 167 ([*Τ*]*αρουσ̣*[*ί*]*νας*?: s. *Βότυς*)
THRACE: **(13)** ii-i BC ib. II² 8924 (*FRA* 2590) (f. *Σκόπας*)

Ταρουτίνας

THRACE: **(1)** c. 281-277 BC *IGB* I² 307, 15; cf. V 5086 (king?)

Ταρρίας

MACEDONIA: **(1)** c. 223 BC *PTeb* 815 fr. 4 recto I, 24 (Tataki, *Macedonians* p. 438 no. 2); cf. La'da E1803 (*Ταρρίου* (gen.): f. *Εὐτυχίς*)
MACEDONIA (PIERIA):
—PYDNA: **(2)** iv BC *GRBS* 43 (2002-3) p. 112 no. 2, 15

Ταρσάνιος

THRACE:
—BRESTE (MOD.): **(1)** ?iii AD *ILB* 176 (Lat. Tarsanius: s. *Ζειζεις, Βενδίνα*)

Τάρσας

CIMMERIAN BOSPOROS:
—PANTIKAPAION: **(1)** i/ii AD *CIRB* 144, 10; *St. Clas.* 8 (1966) p. 337 (name) (f. *Ζεῖλας*)
MACEDONIA (EDONIS):
—PHILIPPOI: **(2)** ?i-ii AD *BCH* 57 (1933) p. 377 no. 35 (Pilhofer 378) (Lat. Vari[nius] Tarsa)
—PHILIPPOI*: **(3)** ii/iii AD *CIL* III 633 II b, 4 (Pilhofer 163); *CRAI* 1923, p. 277 (date); Collart, *Philippes* pls. 64-5 (Lat. Tharsa: slave)
—PROUPTOSOURENOI: **(4)** ii-iii AD Dimitsas 1051, 1 = 1082 (Pilhofer 456); cf. *BCH* 47 (1923) p. 75 no. 34 (I s. *Βύζος*, f. *Βύζος, Βίθυς, Τάρσας* II); **(5)** ~ Dimitsas 1051, 5 = 1082 (Pilhofer 456); cf. *BCH* 47 (1923) p. 75 no. 34 (II s. *Τάρσας* I, *Μελγίς*)
MACEDONIA (MYGDONIA):
—APOLLONIA: **(6)** ii AD *AEMTh* 14 (2000) p. 285 (f. *Πρῖμα*)
—KALINDOIA: **(7)** a. 98 AD *SEG* XLII 582, 22; cf. *Anthémonte–Kalindoia* 2 pp. 313-14 (name) (s. *Κότυς*)
MACEDONIA (PIERIS):
—AKONTISMA: **(8)** s. ii AD *SEG* XL 572
THRACE: **(9)** 26 AD Tac., *Ann.* iv 50 (Lat. Tarsa)
—BAZOPARA: **(10)** 202 AD *IGB* III 1690 d, 51 (and Thrace Pizos: s. *Βρινκάζερις*); **(11)** ~ ib. l. 55 (and Thrace Pizos: s. *Μουκάτραλις*)
—BEROE-AUGUSTA TRAIANA (TERRIT.): **(12)** ii AD ib. 1734 (f. *Αὐλουκενθος*)
—BEROE-AUGUSTA TRAIANA:
——Karasoura: **(13)** iii AD ib. 1626, 8 (s. *Σκέλης*)
—BESSOI:
——Diniscorta: **(14)** f. ii AD *Stud. Gerov* p. 253 (Lat. Tarzas: s. *Δίνις*)
—BOURDAPA: **(15)** ii-iii AD *IGB* III 1363
—DIOSPOLIS: **(16)** imp. ib. 1786
—HADRIANOPOLIS (TERRIT.): **(17)** ii-iii AD ib. 1806 (s. *Κασείπορις*)
—KABYLE: **(18)** ii AD *Kabile* 2 p. 23 no. 18 (Lat. Aelius Tarsas)
—KELLAI*: **(19)** iii AD *IGB* III 1516 b, 19 (s. *Σάλας, Ζεῖλη*)
—MARONEIA: **(20)** s. ii AD Dumont–Homolle 110b 22 (*IThrakAig* E298) (f. *Ἡδεῖα*); **(21)** iii AD Dumont–Homolle 110b 17 (*IThrakAig* E194) (*Αὐρ. Τ.*: s. *Μύρων*)
—PAUTALIA: **(22)** ii AD *IGB* IV 2074, 15 (s. *Κέλσος*); **(23)** ii-iii AD ib. II 536 (I f. *Τάρσας* II); **(24)** ~ ib. (II s. *Τάρσας* I)
—PAUTALIA (TERRIT.): **(25)** ii AD ib. IV 2214, 9 (s. *Μεστίκενθος*); **(26)** ii-iii AD ib. 2112, 2 (f. *Ῥοῖμος*); **(27)** ~ ib. 2133
—PERINTHOS-HERAKLEIA: **(28)** ii AD *IPerinth* 67 II, 4 (*CIL* III 7398) (Lat. Aelius Tarsa)
—PHILIPPOPOLIS-TRIMONTIUM: **(29)** ii AD *IGB* III 1005 (f. *Δωρίς*)
—PHILIPPOPOLIS-TRIMONTIUM (TERRIT.): **(30)** imp. ib. 1064 bis (*Τάρσα*[*ς*]?); **(31)** ii-iii AD ib. 1185 (f. *Μᾶρκος*); **(32)** ~ ib. 1321 (s. *Ῥησκούπορις*)
—SERDICA: **(33)** ?f. ii AD ib. IV 1916 ([*Τ*]*άρσας Στρυμόνιος*); **(34)** iii AD ib. 1934, 6 (*Αὐρ. Τ.*: s. *Βάσσος*)
—SERDICA (TERRIT.): **(35)** ii-iii AD ib. 2015 b (*Eastern cults* p. 167 no. 10) (s. *Ῥοῖμος*); **(36)** ~ *IGB* IV 2022 (*Τ. Φλ. Τ.*)
—SKEDABRIA: **(37)** 202 AD ib. III 1690 b, 17 (and Thrace Pizos: f. *Βίθας*); **(38)** ~ ib. l. 22 (and Thrace Pizos: f. *Αὐλούζενις*)
—SPORTELA: **(39)** ii-iii AD ib. IV 2234, 8 (s. *Βει—*)
—STRATOPARA: **(40)** 202 AD ib. III 1690 b, 44 (and Thrace Pizos: s. *Μουκάτραλις*)

Thrace?: (41) 198-209 AD *Epigr. Anat.* 10 (1987) p. 98, 11 (Lat. Aur. Tarsa)

Τάρσις
Macedonia (Edonis):
—amphipolis: (1) ii-iii AD *Thracia* 2 p. 279 + *Epigraphica* 37 (1935) p. 26 (s. *Σάνβος*)
Thrace: (2) i AD *IGerasa* 201 (Lat. Tarsi (gen.): f. *Δωρίτσης*)

Ταρσοῦς
Cimmerian Bosporos:
—pantikapaion: (1) ii AD *CIRB* 692; cf. *St. Clas.* 8 (1966) p. 338; Zgusta, *PNS* 780 ([*Τ*]*αρσοῦς*—*CIRB*, [*Κ*]*αρσοῦς*—Russu: s. *Μόνιμος*, *Μᾶ*)

Τάρυς
Macedonia (Bisaltia):
—euporia: (1) s. i AD *IBer* 121, 8 (Tataki, *Macedonians* p. 107 no. 5) (s. *Ἀπολλόδωρος*)

Ταρυσίνας
Thrace?: (1) m. iii BC *PLond* 2098, 2 ?= (*Ταρουθίνας* (3))

Τάσης
Thrace:
—philippopolis-trimontium: (1) ii-iii AD *IGB* v 5462 (*Τασῆους* (gen.): f. *Βιθύτραλις*)

Τάσιν
Cimmerian Bosporos:
—kytaia: (1) ii AD *CIRB* 944

Τασις?
Macedonia (Edonis):
—philippoi (territ.): (1) ?iii AD *SEG* xxx 594 A, 5 (Pilhofer 580) (*Τά(ρ)σις?*—Pilhofer)

Τάσκος
Cimmerian Bosporos:
—pantikapaion: (1) iii-ii BC *MIA* 103 (1962) p. 20 (vase) (*SGMII* 4 (1968) p. 41) (*Τάσκο<ι>υ* (gen.))

Τασοίτας?
Macedonia (Bottiaia):
—beroia: (1) 41-44 AD *IBer* 60, 10 (Tataki 1225) ([*Τ*]*ασοίτα* (gen.): s. *Ἄλκιμος*)

Τάταζα
Thrace:
—philippopolis-trimontium: (1) imp. *CIL* vi 2954, 6 (*ILS* 2137) (Lat. Tataza: m. Firminius Valens)
—philippopolis-trimontium?: (2) imp. *CIL* vi 2954, 7 (*ILS* 2137) (Lat. Tataza: d. *Μουκάπορις*)

Ταταζια
Thrace:
—beroe-augusta traiana (territ.): (1) ii-iii AD *IGB* iii 1667
—bourdapa: (2) ii-iii AD ib. 1341 (s./d. *Ἐπταλας*)

Ταταζιη
Thrace:
—philippopolis-trimontium (territ.): (1) i-ii AD ib. 1317, 3 (s./d. *Μουκάσης*)

Ταταρίων
Scythia Minor:
—istros: (1) ii AD *ISM* i 134
Thrace:
—odessos: (2) m. ii AD *IGB* I² 174 bis (PM 1703); *Dacia* 21 (1977) p. 161 (date) (f. *Πρῖμα*)

Τάταρος
Thrace:
—kellai: (1) 241-244 AD *IGB* iii 1517, 54 (*Αὐρ. Τ.*: s. *Καλανδίων*)

Τάτας
Thrace:
—mesambria: (1) f. iii AD ib. I² 317, 4 (*Τάτα* (gen.): f. *Αὐρ. Δημοσθένης*)
—odessos: (2) 215 AD ib. 47 a, 14 (*Τάτα* (gen.): f. *Αὐρ. Θεόδωρος*)

Τάτης
Thrace:
—kellai: (1) 241-244 AD ib. iii 1517, 52 (*Αὐρ. Τ.*: s. *Ῥουφῖνος*)

Τατία
Cimmerian Bosporos:
—pantikapaion: (1) f. i BC *CIRB* 290; Zgusta, *PNS* 829 (d. *Νικίας*)
Thrace:
—sestos: (2) ii AD *ISestos* 3 (*Τ. ἡ καὶ Μάξιμα*)

Τατιανή
Macedonia (Mygdonia):
—thessalonike: (1) ii AD *IG* x (2) (1) 412 (d. *Τατιανός*)
Thrace:
—beroe-augusta traiana: (2) c. 320-324 AD *Anal. Boll.* 31 (1912) p. 198; p. 208

Τατιανός
Macedonia (Mygdonia):
—thessalonike: (1) ii AD *IG* x (2) (1) 412 (f. *Τατιανή*)
Thrace:
—philippopolis-trimontium*: (2) iv AD Beševliev 207, 2

Τατινία
Macedonia (Edonis):
—amphipolis: (1) ii-iii AD Dimitsas 922 (-*τεινεί*-)

Τατίς
Thrace:
—byzantion: (1) i-ii AD *IByz* 281 (Fıratlı–Robert pp. 87-8 no. 110) (d. *Διόδωρος*)

Τατούπορις
Thrace:
—draganovec (mod.): (1) ii-iii AD *IGB* v 5304 (*CCET* ii (2) 520) (-*πουρις*: s. —*ρις*)

Ταττίων
Cimmerian Bosporos:
—nymphaion: (1) iii BC *CIRB* 912 II, 5 (f. —*οκράτης*)

Τάτυς
Cimmerian Bosporos:
—pantikapaion: (1) s. iv BC ib. 209; cf. KW pl. 1 no. 25; Zgusta, *PNS* 603 (s. *Ἄττης*)

Ταυρέας
Cimmerian Bosporos:
—bosporos: (1) imp. *TAM* iv (1) 239, 1, 6 (f. *Ἀριστόδημος*, *Σαμβίων*)
—gorgippia: (2) s. ii AD *CIRB* 1145, 9 (f. *Δάδας*)
Macedonia: (3) s. iii BC *Milet* i (3) 67 I, 8 (Tataki, *Macedonians* p. 438 no. 3) (and Caria Miletos: I s. *Ἀρίστων*, f. *Ταυρέας* II); (4) ~ *Milet* i (3) 67 I, 10 (Tataki, *Macedonians* p. 439 no. 4) (and Caria Miletos: II s. *Ταυρέας* I, *Σίμαινα*)
Skythia:
—tanais: (5) 220-228 AD *CIRB* 1245, 15; 1282, 12; 1286, 8 (f. *Φαρνόξαρθος*)

Ταυριάδης
Macedonia (Chalkidike):
—spartolos?: (1) ?352 BC *SEG* xlvi 804, 4 (f. *Πόρις*)

Ταυρική
Tauris:
—chersonesos: (1) i AD *IOSPE* I² 528; cf. KW pl. 28 no. 408 (n. pr.?)

Ταυρικός
Scythia Minor:
—tomis: (1) ii-iii AD *ISM* ii 31 I, 6 ([*Τ*]*αυρεικός?*)

Ταῦρις
Thrace:
—dionysopolis: (1) iii/ii BC *IGB* I² 21 (*Ταύριος* (gen.): f. *Καλλικράτης*)

Ταυρίσκος
Cimmerian Bosporos:
—achilleion (nr.): (1) 105 AD *CIRB* 1021, 11 (?s. *Ἀπολλώνιος*, *Γλυκαρία*)
Thrace:
—nicopolis ad istrum (territ.): (2) ii-iii AD *ILB* 385 (Lat. Aur. Tau[r]iscus)
—novae: (3) ii-iii AD *IGLNovae* 88 (*ILB* 310) (Lat. Tauriscus)

Ταυρίων
Macedonia: (1) s. iii BC *RE* (-) (Tataki, *Macedonians* p. 439 no. 6)
Macedonia (Eordaia):
—brynaioi: (2) 57-55 BC *EAM* 115, 4 (Tataki, *Macedonians* p. 84 no. 2) (f. *Εὔδικος*)
Skythia:
—olbia-borysthenes: (3) v BC *SEG* xlviii 1017 B-C (sherd)

Ταῦρος
Macedonia (Mygdonia):
—thessalonike: (1) f. i AD *IG* x (2) (1) 126, 7; Robert, *OMS* 5 pp. 295-302 (date) (II s. *Ταῦρος* I *ὁ καὶ Ῥῆγλος*); (2) ~ *IG* x (2) (1) 126, 6-7; Robert, *OMS* 5 pp. 295-302 (date) (*Τ. ὁ καὶ Ῥῆγλος*: I s. *Ἀμμία*, f. *Ταῦρος* II); (3) ii AD *IG* x (2) (1) 241 A II, 23 (—*ιος Τ.*)
—thessalonike (territ.): (4) ii-iii AD ib. 1013 (*Ταῦρ*[*ος*])
Thrace: (5) c. 223 BC *PTeb* 815 fr. 2 II, 2 (Velkov 297; La'da E846) (s. *Πτολεμαῖος*: t.e.)
—nicopolis ad istrum (territ.): (6) ii-iii AD *ILB* 440 (Lat. Taur(us): f. Iulianus)
—perinthos-herakleia*: (7) 193-196 AD *IPerinth* 76 (*CIL* iii 7396) (Lat. Aur. Taurus)
—philippopolis-trimontium: (8) iii AD *IGB* iii 1007, 1 (*Αὐρ. Πύρρος ὁ καὶ Τ.*)
—philippopolis-trimontium (territ.): (9) ii-iii AD ib. 1174 (*Μ. Οὐίρδιος Τ.*)

Ταύρων
Macedonia: (1) s. iv BC Berve 741; *IG* xii (9) 197, 4 (Tataki, *Macedonians* p. 197 no. 20); cf. *Eretria* xi p. 173 (ident.) (s. *Μαχάτας*)

Ταύτακος
Cimmerian Bosporos:
—pantikapaion: (1) i AD *KSIA* 116 (1969) pp. 52-3 no. 4 (f. *Τιράνης*)

Τεγέας
Macedonia (Chalkidike):
—torone?: (1) s. iv BC *SEG* xliii 488, 1 (*Τεγέαι* (dat.))

Τεδέσιος?
Macedonia (Chalkidike):
—olynthos: (1) ?350 BC *TAPA* 65 (1934) p. 125 no. 3, 10; Hatzopoulos, *Actes Chalc.* p. 80 (date) (*Τ̣εδέσ*[*ιο*]*ς̣?*: s. *Καλλίγειτος*)

Τεισαμενός
Macedonia (Chalkidike):
—potidaia-kassandreia?:
——(Mekisteis): (1) ?f. iii BC *SEG* xlvi 796; *BE* 1998, no. 267 (locn.); cf. *LGPN* iiia s.v. (15) (f. *Νικόμαχος*)

MACEDONIA (EDONIS):
—AMPHIPOLIS: (2) hell. *SEG* XXIV 595 (*Τι-*: f. *Δήμητρα*)

Τείσανδρος
THRACE:
—BYZANTION: (1) m. iii BC *IG* XI (4) 570, 4, 8 (f. *Εὐάκης*)
THRACE?: (2) 386 BC ib. II² 31, 24

Τεισίας
THRACE:
—BYZANTION: (1) iv/iii BC *CIRB* 17 ([*Τ*]*εισίας*: s. *Δηλόπτιχος*)

Τεισικλῆς
THRACE:
—LYSIMACHEIA: (1) iii BC *IG* II² 9225 (*FRA* 3411) (*Τι-*: f. *Δημήτριος*)

Τεῖσις
THRACE:
—ABDERA: (1) iii BC *SEG* XXXIX 647 (*IThrakAig* E51) (f. *Ἀπολλώνιος*)
—SPINOPARA: (2) ii AD *IGB* IV 2192, 9 ([*Τ*]*εῖσις*)

Τείσων
MACEDONIA (EDONIS):
—AMPHIPOLIS: (1) b. 357 BC Hatzopoulos, *Actes Amphipolis* p. 25 no. 3, 12 (*SEG* XLI 557); Hatzopoulos, *Actes Amphipolis* p. 30 no. 4, 8 (*SEG* XLI 558)

Τειχεύς
SCYTHIA MINOR:
—KALLATIS?: (1) hell.? *Dacia* 13 (1969) p. 258 no. 1092 (amph.) (*Τειχέως* (gen.))

Τελαμών
CIMMERIAN BOSPOROS:
—PANTIKAPAION (NR.): (1) imp. *CIRB* 956 (f. *Σφαρόβαις*)
TAURIS:
—CHERSONESOS: (2) c. 300-285 BC Kats pp. 113-14 no. 118 (amph.) ?= (*3*); (3) c. 300-272 BC ib. p. 129 no. 50 (amph.) ?= (*2*); (4) iii BC *IOSPE* I² 495 (s. *Ἐπιφάνης*); (5) f. iii BC Kats p. 116 no. 127 (amph.) (*Τελα*[*μών*]); (6) ~ *SEG* XL 615 B, 22 (s. *Αἰσχίνας*)

Τελέδαμος
TAURIS:
—CHERSONESOS: (1) ii AD *IOSPE* I² 358, 13 (*Τελ*(*έ*)*δαμο*[*ς*]: f. *Ἡρόγειτος*)

Τελένικος
THRACE:
—BYZANTION: (1) iv BC *RE* (-); Wehrli, *Schule Arist.* ix fr. 10

Τελεσάγορος
THRACE:
—MESAMBRIA: (1) iii BC *IGB* I² 336 (f. *Διονυσόδωρος*); (2) ~ ib. (s. *Διονυσόδωρος*)

Τελεσήνωρ
THRACE:
—APOLLONIA-SOZOPOLIS: (1) s. v BC ib. 411

Τελεσίας
CIMMERIAN BOSPOROS:
—NYMPHAION: (1) f. iv BC *CIRB* 924 (s. *Θεόφιλος*)
MACEDONIA (PIERIS):
—OISYME-EMATHIA: (2) ?254 BC *SGDI* 2600, 2 (s. *Στράτων*) ?= (*3*); (3) c. 230-200 BC *BCH* 45 (1921) p. 18 III, 81 (Tataki, *Macedonians* p. 128 no. 3) (f. *Ἐπιγήθης*) ?= (*2*)

Τελεσικλῆς
THRACE:
—APOLLONIA-SOZOPOLIS: (1) iii BC *IOlbia* 99

Τελεσικράτης
SKYTHIA:
—OLBIA-BORYSTHENES: (1) f. iv BC Dubois, *IGDOlbia* 105 (f. *Ἄγρων*, *Ἀρτεμίδωρος*, *Ἀχιλλόδωρος*, *Ἱππόνικος*)

Τελέστης
SCYTHIA MINOR:
—ISTROS: (1) i AD *ISM* I 200, 1 (f. *Αἰσχρίων*)

Τελεσφόρος
MACEDONIA: (1) s. iv BC *RE* (2) (Tataki, *Macedonians* p. 439 no. 8)
MACEDONIA (EDONIS):
—AMPHIPOLIS: (2) ?iii AD *SEG* XXVIII 539 (f. *Ἰσίδωρος*)
MACEDONIA (MYGDONIA):
—CHALASTRA: (3) ii-iii AD *IG* X (2) (1) 815, 2 (Tataki, *Macedonians* p. 98 no. 2) (I f. *Τελεσφόρος* II, *Ζωϊλιανή*, *Ἀλέξανδρος*); (4) ~ *IG* X (2) (1) 815, 4 (II s. *Τελεσφόρος* I, *Συμφορίς*)
—THESSALONIKE: (5) ii AD ib. 325 (*Κ. Δηναῖος Τ.*: f. *Δηναία Ἰουλία*)
—THESSALONIKE?: (6) ii AD ib. 250 I, 6 ([*Τ*]*ε̣λ̣εσφόρος*: s. *Διονύσιος*); (7) ii-iii AD ib. 813 (*Αἴλ. Τ.*: f. *Εὐχάριον*)
MACEDONIA (PAIONIA):
—KAVADARCI (MOD.): (8) ii-iii AD *Sp.* 71 (1931) p. 73 no. 171 (*Αὐρ.*? *Τελεσφ*(*ό*)*ρος*)
SCYTHIA MINOR:
—ISTROS: (9) ii AD *ISM* I 196, 19 (*Φούλβιος Τ.*)
THRACE:
—APOLLONIA-SOZOPOLIS: (10) i-ii AD *IGB* I² 401, 11 (*Τελε*(*σ*)*φόρος*: f. *Ἀσκληπιόδοτος*); (11) ~ ib. l. 17 (*Τελε*(*σ*)*φόρος*: f. *Τρηστίσσιμος*)
—PHILIPPOPOLIS-TRIMONTIUM (TERRIT.): (12) ii-iii AD ib. III 1401 bis (f. *Χρῆστος*)
—ZONE?: (13) i-ii AD *IThrakAig* E426 ([*Τ*]*ελεσφόρος*: f. *Διονύσιος*)

Τελευτίας
MACEDONIA (BOTTIAIA):
—AIGAI: (1) s. iv BC *SEG* XXXV 786 (f. *Εὔξενος*)
MACEDONIA (PIERIA):
—PHILA?: (2) ?iii BC *RPh* 1911, pp. 133-4 no. 36, 91; cf. Helly, *L'État thessalien* pp. 319-20 (locn.) (s. *Ἐπιο̣—*)

Τέλλος
MACEDONIA (BOTTIAIA):
—AIGAI: (1) s. iv BC *SEG* XXXV 784 + *ZPE* 72 (1988) pp. 111-12; cf. *SEG* XLVIII 874 + *BE* 1999, no. 336 (*Τέλλο̣*[*ς*], *Β̣ρατεά̣δ̣*[*ης*]?—Hatzopoulos: f. *Βιλάρρα*)

Τέλων
SCYTHIA MINOR:
—ISTROS: (1) vi BC *ISM* I 102

Τεργόνιος
CIMMERIAN BOSPOROS:
—GORGIPPIA: (1) ii/iii AD *CIRB* 1179, 37; Zgusta, *PNS* 714 (f. *Ποθεινός*)

Τερδέτης
KOLCHIS:
—LAZOI: (1) 550 AD *PLRE* III (-)

Τερεντία
MACEDONIA (SINTIKE):
—PARTHIKOPOLIS (TERRIT.): (1) ii AD *IGB* IV 2302, 6 (d. *Ἀρτεμίδωρος*, *Σωσίπολις*)

Τερέντιος
SCYTHIA MINOR:
—TOMIS: (1) ii-iii AD *ISM* II 20, 3 (*Τερέντ*[*ιος*]: f. *Μᾶρκος*)

Τερέντυλλα
THRACE:
—BYZANTION: (1) i BC-i AD *IByz* 171 (Fıratlı–Robert p. 110 no. 178) (d. *Σωσίβιος*)

Τερπίδης
THRACE:
—DORISKOS?: (1) iv BC Hp., *Epid.* vii 97 (*Τερπιδέω* (gen.))

Τέρπνη
MACEDONIA (BOTTIAIA):
—BEROIA: (1) ii AD *IBer* 169, 1 (Tataki 1230) ([*Τ*]*έρπνη*: m. *Ἑρμῆς*, *Καρποφόρος*)

Τέρπνος
MACEDONIA (BOTTIAIA):
—BEROIA: (1) ii/iii AD *IBer* 122, 2; *ILeukopetra* 22, 6 (Tataki 731) (*Κλ. Τ.*: f. *Κλ. Ἄλκηστις*); (2) ~ *IBer* 143 B, 19 (Tataki 732) (*Κλ. Τ.*); (3) iii AD *IBer* 127 (Tataki 1231) (s. *Ἄλκηστις*)
—BEROIA (TERRIT.): (4) ii-iii AD *IBer* 493 (*Τ. Μάριος Αἰλιανὸς Τ.*)
THRACE: (5) s. iii BC *BCH* 20 (1896) p. 338 no. 3, 5 (*PP* 15647; Velkov 298) ([*Τέ*]*ρπνος*?)

Τερτία
MACEDONIA (BOTTIAIA):
—BEROIA: (1) ii AD *IBer* 338, 1 (Tataki 1232) (m. *Μάξιμα*, *Νίκανδρος*); (2) iv-v AD *IBer* 455, 3 (Feissel, *RICM* 295) (m. *Μαρία*: Jew)
MACEDONIA (EDONIS):
—PHILIPPOI (NR.): (3) ii-iii AD *BCH* 54 (1930) p. 376 (Pilhofer 48); Collart, *Philippes* pl. 36. 3
MACEDONIA (LYNKESTIS):
—HERAKLEIA: (4) iii AD *IG* X (2) (2) 98
MACEDONIA (MYGDONIA):
—KALINDOIA: (5) ?i-ii AD *SEG* XXIX 628, 2 (d. *Διοσκουρίδης*)
—THESSALONIKE?: (6) ?iii AD *IG* X (2) (1) 769 (m. *Παπῆς*)
MACEDONIA (PAIONIA):
—KAVADARCI (MOD.): (7) ii AD *Sp.* 71 (1931) p. 69 no. 153 (d. *Ἰουλία*); (8) ii-iii AD ib. p. 70 no. 160
THRACE:
—BYZANTION: (9) i BC-i AD *IByz* 19, 12
—BYZANTION*: (10) i-ii AD ib. 242 (d. *Θαλλίων*: slave?)
—ODESSOS: (11) ii AD *IGB* I² 186 (PM 1734) (d. *Ἡρακλέων*)
—PERINTHOS-HERAKLEIA: (12) i-ii AD *IPerinth* 96 (d. *Γαῦρος*)

Τερτιανός
MACEDONIA (ORESTIS):
—SISANI (MOD.): (1) 146 AD *EAM* 187, 18 (s. *Νικόπολις*)
THRACE:
—BIZONE (NR.): (2) iii AD *IGB* I² 11 (f. *Αὐρ. Οὐαλέριος*)
—VRACA (MOD.): (3) ?ii AD ib. II 486 (s. *Τέρτιος*)

Τέρτιος
SCYTHIA MINOR:
—ISTROS: (1) ii AD *ISM* I 197 I, 6 (f. *Κάστος*); (2) 138 AD ib. 193 I, 53 (f. *Ἡρακλέων*); (3) iii AD ib. 222, 4 (*Τέρτ*[*ιος*])
THRACE:
—APOLLONIA-SOZOPOLIS: (4) i-ii AD *IGB* I² 401, 6 (s. *Χρ—*)
—VRACA (MOD.): (5) ?ii AD ib. II 486 (f. *Τερτιανός*)

Τέρτις
MACEDONIA (MYGDONIA):
—THESSALONIKE?: (1) ii AD *IG* X (2) (1) 702 (f. *Εἰρηναῖος*)
SCYTHIA MINOR:
—ISTROS: (2) ii AD *ISM* I 196, 22 (s. *Διονύσιος*)

Τέρτυλλος
MACEDONIA (MYGDONIA):
—THESSALONIKE: (1) m. ii AD *IG* X (2) (1) 400; cf. *JDAI* 84 (1969) pp. 176-7 no. R86; *KGAM Thess.* I 122 (date)

Τερψιχόρη
Macedonia (Mygdonia):
—thessalonike*: **(1)** 147 ad *IG* x (2) (1) 691 + *BCH* 98 (1974) p. 550 (*Προκουλεῖα Τερψικόρη*: freed.)

Τετραδία
Macedonia (Mygdonia):
—thessalonike: **(1)** vi ad Feissel, *RICM* 164 A (*SEG* xlvii 979 A)

Τέττευος
Cimmerian Bosporos:
—pantikapaion: **(1)** f. iv bc *CIRB* 228; Zgusta, *PNS* 604 (s. *Μίδαος*, f. *Τυαίης*)

Τεττία
Tauris:
—chersonesos: **(1)** iii bc Solomonik, *NEPKh* 35; *Hellenismus* p. 456 no. 29 (d. *Τίμων*)

Τεῦκρος
Macedonia?: **(1)** 202 bc Sil. xvii 426 with comm. (Lat. Teucrus: dub.)

Τευτάμας
Macedonia (Sintike)?: **(1)** 144 ad *IGB* iv 2331, 2-3 (*Τευ[τά]μα*? (dat.): f. *Ἀρτεμίδωρος*, *Τηρέτιθος*)

Τεύταμος
Macedonia: **(1)** 319-317 bc *RE* (3); Berve 744 (Tataki, *Macedonians* p. 440 no. 9)

Τεύταος
Macedonia (Paionia):
—demir kapija (mod.): **(1)** s. v bc *ZA* 52 (2002) p. 215 (coin) (*Τευτάō* (gen.))

Τεύτιος
Macedonia: **(1)** 218 bc *PEnt* 32, 1 and verso; 67, 1 (Tataki, *Macedonians* p. 440 no. 10; La'da E1784) (s. *Φίλιππος*: t.e.)
Macedonia (Bottiaia):
—beroia: **(2)** 223 bc *IBer* 4, 20 (f. *Φιλόξενος*)
Macedonia (Lynkestis):
—herakleia (nr.): **(3)** iv/iii bc *Antička bronza u Jugoslaviji* p. 77 no. 54; cf. *ZA* 52 (2002) pp. 211 f.

Τέχνων
Cimmerian Bosporos:
—pantikapaion: **(1)** i bc/i ad *CIRB* 325; cf. KW pl. 38 no. 551 (f. *—ο.ίδης*)
Thrace:
—maroneia: **(2)** hell.-imp. *FRA* 3555 (s. *Διονύσιος*)

Τζάθης
Kolchis:
—lazoi: **(1)** m. vi ad *PLRE* iii (2); *RE* s.v. Tzath (2) (king)

Τζιτας
Thrace:
—aproi: **(1)** v-vi ad Unp. (Sayar) (s. *Παῦλος*, *Λευκαδία*)

Τήλαγρος
Macedonia (Chalkidike):
—olynthos: **(1)** ?352-350 bc *TAPA* 62 (1931) p. 43 no. 2, 5, 9; *SEG* xxxviii 637, 8; Hatzopoulos, *Actes Chalc.* p. 80 (date) (f. *Πολύξενος*)

Τηλεκλῆς
Macedonia (Chalkidike):
—olynthos: **(1)** ?354 bc *TAPA* 69 (1938) pp. 52-3 no. 6, 9; Hatzopoulos, *Actes Chalc.* p. 80 (date)

Τηλέμαχος
Thrace:
—abdera: **(1)** c. 360-350 bc May, *Abdera* pp. 251-2 nos. 401-4 (coin)
—apollonia-sozopolis: **(2)** i-ii ad *IGB* i² 401, 19 (s. *Πασ—*)

Τήλεφος
Macedonia (Edonis):
—amphipolis: **(1)** hell.? Dimitsas 854 = 890
Macedonia (Mygdonia):
—kalindoia: **(2)** a. 98 ad *SEG* xlii 582, 56 (s. *Καρβερένθης*)
Macedonia?: **(3)** 325 bc Berve 745 (Tataki, *Macedonians* p. 440 no. 11)

Τηλοκλῆς
Macedonia (Sintike):
—parthikopolis: **(1)** 150 ad *IGB* iv 2274 (*Τηλο[κλ]έως* (gen.): f. *—ηρηας*)

Τῆλυς
Macedonia (Chalkidike):
—potidaia-kassandreia?: **(1)** v/iv bc *SEG* xlvi 792 (s. *Ἐπι—*)

Τήραλος
Thrace:
—bourdapa: **(1)** ii-iii ad *IGB* iii 1355 (f. *Βριγκαζις*)

Τηρέτιθος
Macedonia (Sintike)?: **(1)** 144 ad ib. iv 2331, 5 (s. *Τευτάμας*, *Βουζάη*)

Τηρήπης
Macedonia (Mygdonia):
—kalindoia: **(1)** a. 98 ad *SEG* xlii 582, 70; cf. *Anthémonte–Kalindoia* 2 pp. 314-15 (name) (s. *Δάγουζις*)
—lete: **(2)** ii ad *Makedonika* 2 (1951) p. 619 no. 42 *θ*, 11 (f. *Κότυς*)
Macedonia?: **(3)** i bc/i ad *Xenia antiqua* 10 (2001) p. 22 no. C (or Thrace: f. *Νανώ*)
Thrace: **(4)** 274 bc *PCZ* 59001, 21, 48, verso (Velkov 299; La'da E801)

Τήρης
Macedonia: **(1)** 103 bc *PTeb* 105, 52 (Tataki, *Macedonians* p. 497 no. 236; La'da E1785) (s. *Πτολεμαῖος*: t.e.)
Macedonia (Edonis):
—philippoi: **(2)** m. ii ad *PIR*² s.v. Iulius 597; *CIL* iii 689 + *ASAA* NS 1-2 (1939-40) p. 217 (Pilhofer 61); *CIL* iii 7339, 8 (Pilhofer 357); *BCH* 62 (1938) p. 422 no. 8 (Pilhofer 240; Collart, *Philippes* pl. 40. 3) (Lat. C. Iulius Teres: I ?f. *Γ. Ἰούλ. Τήρης* II)
—philippoi?: **(3)** ii/iii ad *SEG* xlix 885, 2; *Chiron* 31 (2001) pp. 450-5 (ident.) (*[Γ.] Ἰούλ. Τήρης*: II ?s. *Γ. Ἰούλ. Τήρης* I)
Macedonia (Lynkestis):
—nikaia?: **(4)** ii/iii ad *IG* x (2) (2) 45 (biling.) (*Ἰούλιος Τ.*: f. *Ἰούλιος Ἰουλιανός*, *Ἰουλία Ἄρτεμις*)
Macedonia (Mygdonia):
—kalindoia: **(5)** a. 98 ad *SEG* xlii 582, 20; cf. *Anthémonte–Kalindoia* 2 pp. 314-15 (name) (*Ῥέννιος Τ.*)
Macedonia (Orestis):
—battynaioi: **(6)** 192 ad *EAM* 186 II, 54 (f. *Μενέλας*)
Macedonia (Sintike):
—parthikopolis: **(7)** 150 ad *IGB* iv 2274 (f. *Βίθυς*)
—parthikopolis (nr.): **(8)** ii-iii ad ib. 2291, 1 (f. *Ἀμύντας*)
Scythia Minor:
—ulmetum: **(9)** ii ad *ISM* v 69, 3 (Lat. Iulius Teres)
Thrace: **(10)** iii bc *Num. Bulg.* 2002 (2), pp. 2-3 (coin) (king?); **(11)** 263-227 bc *PCZ* 59473, 2 (Velkov 307); cf. La'da E796 (f. *Σεύθης*); **(12)** 257 bc *PSorb* 17b, 20, 23 (La'da E847) (s. *Ποσιστις*: t.e.); **(13)** c. 244-242 bc *PPetr* ii 35 a I, 10 (Velkov 310; La'da E802); **(14)** ii bc *Suda Δ* 1172; cf. Fraser, *Ptol. Alex.* 2 pp. 678-9 n. 207 (f. *Διονύσιος*: fict.?); **(15)** c. 149 bc *RE* (3); D.S. xxxii 15. 5-6 (king); **(16)** c. 85 bc *REG* 32 (1919) pp. 321-2, 2, 22, 30 (f. *Ἀμάτοκος*); **(17)** i ad *IGB* iv 2338, 20; cf. v 5928 (f. *Ἔζβενις*); **(18)** ii ad ib. iii 1873 (*Οὐίρδιος Τ.*); **(19)** f. iii ad ib. v 5667 (f. *Πυρέτης*)
—agiasma (mod.): **(20)** s. iii ad *Thrakika* 6 (1935) p. 310 no. 2 (*IThrakAig* E384) (f. *Ἡρακλείδης*)
—bazopara: **(21)** 202 ad *IGB* iii 1690 d, 52 (and Thrace Pizos: s. *Βεσσοδένθης*); **(22)** ~ ib. l. 54 (and Thrace Pizos: s. *Κέλσος*); **(23)** ~ ib. 1690 c, 41 (and Thrace Pizos: f. *Βίθυς*); **(24)** ~ ib. l. 46 (and Thrace Pizos: f. *Δημοσθένης*); **(25)** ~ ib. l. 61 (and Thrace Pizos: s. *Μουκάτραλις*)
—beroe-augusta traiana: **(26)** ii-iii ad ib. 1595, 2; **(27)** iii ad ib. 1572 + v 5560; 5565; 5566, 4 (*Αὐρ. Τ.*: s. *Σκέλης*)
—beroe-augusta traiana (territ.): **(28)** ii-iii ad ib. 5624 (f. *Φίλιππος*)
—beroe-augusta traiana:
——Karasoura: **(29)** ii-iii ad ib. iii 1627, 3 + *SEG* xli 589 (*[Τ]ήρης*: s. *Βίθυς*)
—bessoi: **(30)** 192-212 ad *AA* 1912, p. 563 (Lat. M. Aur. Teres)
—ergissenoi: **(31)** ii ad *IGB* iii 1593, 5 (s. *Βρινκάζερις*)
—glava panega (mod.): **(32)** ii-iii ad ib. ii 564
—kabyle: **(33)** iii-ii bc ib. v 5638 bis (amph.) (*[Τ]ήρης*: f. *Σαδάλας*)
—kellai: **(34)** 241-244 ad ib. iii 1517, 28 (f. *Μάσχλος*)
—markianopolis (territ.): **(35)** ii-iii ad ib. ii 844 (*Τήρεντος* (gen.))
—maroneia: **(36)** iii ad *IThrakAig* E396, 3 (f. *Ἔζβενις*)
—odrysai: **(37)** v bc *RE* Supplbd. 7 (1a) (f. *Σιτάλκης*, *Σπαράδοκος*: king); **(38)** 400 bc X., *An.* vii 5. 1 (*RE* Supplbd. 7 (1b)); **(39)** 356 bc *FD* iii (1) 392, 3 (s. *Κερσεβλέπτης*) ?= (*40*); **(40)** c. 350-341 bc *RE* Supplbd. 7 (1c); Osborne, *Naturalization* T65; *Rogozen Treasure* p. 48 no. 23; Peter, *MTD* pp. 140-3 (coin) (king) ?= (*39*)
—paisoulai-maximianopolis: **(41)** iii ad *Thrakika* 6 (1935) p. 316 no. 3 (*IThrakAig* E389) (s. *Πρόκλος*)
—pautalia: **(42)** ii-iii ad *IGB* iv 2053, 8
—pautalia (territ.): **(43)** ii-iii ad ib. v 5796 with pl. 116 (*[Τ]ήρου* (gen.): f. *Θεαγένης*); **(44)** ~ ib. 5829 (*Τήρ[ης]*: f. *Ἰουλιανός*)
—philippopolis-trimontium (territ.): **(45)** ii-iii ad ib. iii 1111 (s. *Ἀντίοχος*); **(46)** ~ ib. 1118 (I f. *Τήρης* II); **(47)** ~ ib. (II s. *Τήρης* I); **(48)** ~ ib. 1210 (s. *Δυλάζενις*); **(49)** ~ ib. 1463 (f. *Ἔρως*); **(50)** iii ad *BIAB* 17 (1950) p. 333 no. 1 with fig. 268a
—pistiros: **(51)** iv-iii bc *SEG* xlix 912. 17 (vase) (*Τήρ(ης)*)
—serdica (territ.): **(52)** ii-iii ad *Sp.* 98 (1941-48) p. 127 no. 280, 4 (s. *Δίζας*)
—seuthopolis: **(53)** c. 300-280 bc *SEG* xlii 661, 8 (s. *Σεύθης*, *Βερενίκη*)
—sportela: **(54)** ii-iii ad *IGB* iv 2234, 8 (s. *Βει—*)
—vicus trullensium: **(55)** ii-iii ad ib. ii 507
Thrace?: **(56)** hell. *Memnonion* 409 (Velkov 300); **(57)** iii bc *PGurob* 19, 4 (*PP* 2451; Velkov 304); **(58)** ~ *CPR* xiii 4 X, 189 (s. *Ἀρτεμίδωρος*); **(59)** m. iii bc *PCZ* 59682, 8 (Velkov 302); **(60)** 209 bc *PHeid* viii 392, 3 (s. *Λυσι—*); **(61)** 156-146 bc *PBerlZill* 2, 3; *PMünch* 50, 4; *PGen* 131, 1 (Velkov 303); **(62)** c. 125-100 bc *IHermoupolis* 4, 11 (Velkov 308) (I f. *Τήρης* II); **(63)** ~ *IHermoupolis* 4, 11

(*PP* 3593; Velkov 314) (II s. *Τήρης* I); **(64)** ~ *IHermoupolis* 4, 97 (Velkov 309) (I f. *Τήρης* II); **(65)** ~ *IHermoupolis* 4, 97 (*PP* 3594; Velkov 313) (II s. *Τήρης* I); **(66)** imp. *CIL* III 4370 (Lat. Aur. Te[r]es); **(67)** c. 303-305 AD Latyshev, *Menolog. anon.* p. 109 (*Τέρις*—ms.)

Τηρίβασις
THRACE:
—ODESSOS: **(1)** i BC-i AD *IGB* V 5066 (*Τηριβάσει* (gen.): f. *Δημήτριος*)

Τιάρα
THRACE:
—APOLLONIA-SOZOPOLIS: **(1)** iii BC *BMNBurgas* 4 (2002) p. 126 no. 24 (d. *Φιλήμων*)

Τίβειος
CIMMERIAN BOSPOROS:
—PANTIKAPAION: **(1)** iv BC *CIRB* 225; Robert, *Noms indigènes* p. 531; cf. Zgusta, *PNS* 1156 (f. *Τίβης*)
SCYTHIA MINOR:
—ISTROS: **(2)** iv/iii BC *ISM* I 242
TAURIS:
—CHERSONESOS: **(3)** iii BC Solomonik, *NEPKh* 152; *Hellenismus* p. 456 no. 30 (f. *Ἡρακλει—*)
THRACE:
—APOLLONIA-SOZOPOLIS: **(4)** iv BC *IGB* I^2 450 (s. *Ἄγλαρχος*)

Τιβέριος
MACEDONIA (DERRIOPOS):
—STUBERRA: **(1)** 74 AD *IG* X (2) (2) 325, 38 (s. *Ἰταλός*)
MACEDONIA (SINTIKE):
—HERAKLEIA (TERRIT.): **(2)** ii-iii AD *IGB* IV 2329 (s. *Πυρούσαλα*)

Τίβης
CIMMERIAN BOSPOROS:
—PANTIKAPAION: **(1)** v-iv BC *AA* 1907, p. 139 (vase); **(2)** iv BC *CIRB* 225; Robert, *Noms indigènes* p. 531; cf. Zgusta, *PNS* 228 (s. *Τίβειος*, *Νάνα*)

Τιγινάγας
CIMMERIAN BOSPOROS:
—PANTIKAPAION: **(1)** v-vi AD *ZOOID* 24 (1901) p. 70 no. 10

Τιγραπάτης
KOLCHIS:
—LAZOI: **(1)** ii AD Luc., *Tox.* 44 (king/fict.)

Τίθυτα
THRACE:
—MARONEIA: **(1)** ii AD *IG* XII (8) 220, 14 (d. *Ἔντιμος*)

Τίλλης
CIMMERIAN BOSPOROS:
—PANTIKAPAION: **(1)** ii/i BC *CIRB* 265; cf. KW pl. 29 no. 417; Zgusta, *PNS* 229 (s. *Ὀρόντης*); **(2)** ~ *CIRB* 265; cf. KW pl. 29 no. 417 (f. *Ὀρόντης*)

Τιμαγένης
SCYTHIA MINOR:
—KALLATIS: **(1)** imp. *ISM* III 127, 2 (*Τιμαγέν[ης]*: f. *—ος*)

Τιμαγόρης
SKYTHIA:
—OLBIA-BORYSTHENES: **(1)** iv BC *SEG* XXX 958 (vase)

Τιμαίνετος
MACEDONIA (BOTTIAIA):
—PELLA: **(1)** iii BC Akamatis, *Amph. Pellas* p. 44 nos. PAR64-6 (amph.) (*SEG* L 613)

Τίμαιος
MACEDONIA (EDONIS):
—PHILIPPOI: **(1)** iv/iii BC Collart, *Philippes* pp. 179-80 n. 5 with pl. 27. 3 (Pilhofer 285)
TAURIS:
—CHERSONESOS: **(2)** iii BC Solomonik, *GAKh* 1567 (vase) (*Τίμαι(ος)*?)
THRACE:
—PHILIPPOPOLIS-TRIMONTIUM: **(3)** ii-iii AD *IGB* III 912, 4 (*Τίμαι[ο]ς*)

Τίμανδρος
MACEDONIA (BOTTIAIA):
—PELLA: (1) 334 BC Berve 746 (Tataki, *Macedonians* p. 160 no. 87 (ident.)) (?f. *Ἀσκληπιόδωρος*)
MACEDONIA (EDONIS):
—DATOS: **(2)** 360 BC *IG* IV (1)^2 94 b, 32 (Perlman, *City and Sanctuary* E.1 with pp. 69-70 (date); Tataki, *Macedonians* p. 99 no. 1); cf. Hatzopoulos, *MI* I p. 188 n. 1 ?= (*3*)
—PHILIPPOI: **(3)** a. 346 BC *Syll*^{3} 267 A, 3 (Tataki, *Macedonians* p. 166 no. 33) ([*Τί*]*μανδρος*: f. *Τιμοκράτης*, *Σωσικράτης*, *Σωκράτης*, *Σωσθένης*, *Τιμοκλῆς*) ?= (*2*)

Τιμάνθης
MACEDONIA (BOTTIAIA):
—PELLA: **(1)** c. 326 BC Berve 747 (Tataki, *Macedonians* p. 160 no. 88) (s. *Παντιάδης*)
MACEDONIA (CHALKIDIKE):
—OLYNTHOS: **(2)** ?350 BC *TAPA* 59 (1928) p. 226, 13; Hatzopoulos, *Actes Chalc.* p. 80 (date) (f. *Μύσιος*)
—POTIDAIA-KASSANDREIA: **(3)** ?m. iii BC *FD* III (4) 351, 6 (Tataki, *Macedonians* p. 96 no. 92) ([*Τι*]*μάνθης*: s. *Πολύζηλος*)

Τιμανορίδας
MACEDONIA: **(1)** 345-326 BC *CID* II 31, 74; 32, 31, 40; 75 II, 42; 76 II, 34; 79 A I, 10; 97, 29 (Tataki, *Macedonians* p. 440 no. 12) (*Τιμηνορίδας*—no. 79: s. *Κορδυπίων*)

Τιμαρέτη
MACEDONIA (ODOMANTIKE):
—SIRRHA: **(1)** 33 or 133 AD *SEG* XVI 411 (*Τει-*: d. *Ἐπάγαθος*, *Χρήστη*)

Τιμαρίστα
MACEDONIA (CHALKIDIKE):
—AKANTHOS: **(1)** v BC *IG* IV (1) 162 (*EAD* XXX p. 357 no. 24; Tataki, *Macedonians* p. 43 no. 13 (date))

Τίμαρχος
KOLCHIS?: **(1)** ?s. ii BC *BSA* 87 (1992) p. 373 (amph.) (*MBAH* 12 (1993) pp. 70-1); cf. Braund, *Georgia* p. 143 n. 93
MACEDONIA (CHALKIDIKE):
—CHALKIDEIS: **(2)** c. 364-361 BC *Olynthus* 9 pp. 64-5 nos. 97-9 (coin); *Ancient Macedonia* I p. 254 (date)
THRACE:
—LYSIMACHEIA: **(3)** c. 208 BC *FD* III (4) 135 III, 17 (s. *Κάλλων*)

Τιμαφενίδας
THRACE:
—AINOS: **(1)** b. 353 BC *IG* II^2 152, 1, 11

Τιμέας
CIMMERIAN BOSPOROS:
—GORGIPPIA: **(1)** f. iii BC *CIRB* 1137 A I, 27 ([*Τ*]*ιμέας*: s. *Θεόξενος*); **(2)** ~ ib. l. 28 (s. *Νοήμων*); **(3)** ~ ib. 1137 B I, 2 ([*Τ*]*ιμέας*: f. *Δημήτριος*); **(4)** ~ ib. 1137 B II, 12 (I f. *Τιμέας* II); **(5)** ~ ib. l. 12 (II s. *Τιμέας* I)
—NYMPHAION: **(6)** iii BC *TGE* 17 (1976) p. 186 (weight); **(7)** ~ *CIRB* 912 III, 12

MACEDONIA (DERRIOPOS):
—STUBERRA: **(8)** 50 AD *IG* X (2) (2) 324, 18-19 (*Τει-*: f. *Ἀπολλόδωρος*, *Ἱππόνικος*)
SKYTHIA:
—OLBIA-BORYSTHENES: **(9)** iii BC *IOSPE* I^2 201 II, 28 (s. *Θεογείτων*)
TAURIS:
—CHERSONESOS: **(10)** ?iii BC Solomonik, *GAKh* 1568 (vase) (*Τιμέ[ας]*?)
THRACE:
—BYZANTION: **(11)** i BC *IByz* 113 (*Τειμέ[ας]*?)

Τιμένης
THRACE:
—PERINTHOS-HERAKLEIA: **(1)** iv BC Hp., *Epid.* ii 1. 7; iv 25-6; vi 2. 19; *Index Hipp.* s.v. *Τιμένης* (*Τημένης*—codd. min. & Littré)

Τιμησιάναξ
CIMMERIAN BOSPOROS:
—HERMONASSA: **(1)** iv BC *CIRB* 1056 I, 7 (f. *—αχος*)
MACEDONIA (CHALKIDIKE):
—APHYTIS: **(2)** ?351 BC *Α΄ Panell. Synedr. Epigr.* pp. 80-1, 4 (f. *Ὀρνυμενός*)

Τιμησίθεος
SKYTHIA:
—OLBIA-BORYSTHENES: **(1)** iii BC *IOSPE* I^2 201 I, 29 (f. *Εὐρήμων*)

Τιμησικράτης
MACEDONIA (ODOMANTIKE):
—BERGE?: **(1)** f. v BC *SEG* L 575, 1; cf. *Horos* 14-16 (2000-3) pp. 227-32 (*Τιμησικράτ[ης]*)

Τιμήσιος
MACEDONIA (CHALKIDIKE):
—POTIDAIA-KASSANDREIA: **(1)** c. 285 BC *SEG* XXIX 600, 2; XXXVIII 619, 2; cf. Hatzopoulos, *Donation* pp. 17-21 (date)
THRACE:
—APOLLONIA-SOZOPOLIS: **(2)** v/iv BC *IGB* I^2 453 (s. *.ονυμο—*)

Τιμογένης
CIMMERIAN BOSPOROS:
—TEMRYUK (MOD.): **(1)** 284-245 BC *CIRB* 1036, 2
THRACE:
—BYZANTION: **(2)** ii-i BC *IByz* 210 (Fıratlı–Robert p. 69 no. 68) (*Τειμογένη* (gen.): f. *Ἀναξίλα*); **(3)** 117-138 AD *IByz* 37, 6 (II s. *Τιμογένης* I); **(4)** ~ ib. l. 6-7 (I f. *Τιμογένης* II, *Μηνόδοτος*)

Τιμόδημος
MACEDONIA (EDONIS):
—PHILIPPOI: **(1)** ii-i BC *BCH* 59 (1935) p. 158 no. 54 (Pilhofer 303) (f. *Ἀντίπατρος*)

Τιμοθέα
THRACE:
—BEROE-AUGUSTA TRAIANA: **(1)** c. 320-324 AD *Anal. Boll.* 31 (1912) p. 198; p. 208

Τιμόθεος
CIMMERIAN BOSPOROS:
—GORGIPPIA: **(1)** ?93-123 AD *CIRB* 1125, 8 (*Τει-*: s. *Νυμφαγόρας*); **(2)** ii AD ib. 1140, 2 (*Τειμόθ[εος]*); **(3)** ~ ib. 1143, 3 (*Τει-*: s. *Δι—*); **(4)** ~ ib. 1154, 6 (*Τειμόθε[ος]*); **(5)** ii-iii AD *NE* 9 (1971) p. 7 no. 5, 4 (*Τειμόθ[εος]*); **(6)** s. ii AD *SEG* XXXVI 708, 1 (*Τειμόθε[ος]*); **(7)** 173-210 AD *CIRB* 1135, 18 (*Τει-*: f. *Πόθος*); **(8)** ~ ib. l. 22-23 (*Τει-*: s. *Μοιρόδωρος*); **(9)** ii/iii AD ib. 1179, 32 (*Τει-*: s. *Ψιμίθας*); **(10)** ~ ib. l. 38 (*Τει-*: f. *Ζαζζοῦς*)
—HERMONASSA: **(11)** hell.-imp. ib. 1094, 4 (f. *Παπίας*); **(12)** i/ii AD ib. 1057 (*GVI* 1477) (*Τει-*: s. *Δάσεις*)
—PANTIKAPAION: **(13)** i BC *CIRB* 268 A; 268 B (f. *Ἀθηνοκλῆς*); **(14)** hell.-imp. *CIG* 8556 c (lead) (*Τειμόθε[ο]ς*); **(15)** i/ii AD *CIRB* 636 (s. *Ἔρως*); **(16)** ii AD ib. 670; cf. KW pl. 30 no. 426 (f. *Διόφαντος*, *Φιλέρως*); **(17)** ~ *CIRB* 709,

1; cf. Robert, *Noms indigènes* p. 511 (*Τειμόθεος Σίνδαξ*: I s. *Ἄττας*, f. *Τιμόθεος* II); (**18**) ~ *CIRB* 709, 7 (*Τει-*: II s. *Τιμόθεος* I *Σίνδαξ*, *Καλλιστράτεια*); (**19**) f. iii AD ib. 105, 10 (*Τει-*: s. *Πάππος*)
MACEDONIA: (**20**) 333 BC Berve 750 (Tataki, *Macedonians* p. 441 no. 13); (**21**) ?318 BC *IG* XII (9) 196, 1, 23 (Tataki, *Macedonians* p. 441 no. 15); *Eretria* XI pp. 181-4 (date) (s. *Λυσανίας*); (**22**) c. 275-250 BC *Thess. Mnem.* 6 = Möbius, *Die Ornamente*² pl. 53a; cf. *La Thessalie* p. 99 pl. 12 (Tataki, *Macedonians* p. 441 no. 16) (f. *Διόδοτος*)
MACEDONIA (BOTTIAIA):
—BEROIA: (**23**) ii-iii AD *IBer* 283 (Tataki 1226) (*Τει-*: s. *Ἔνδημος*)
MACEDONIA (DERRIOPOS):
—STUBERRA: (**24**) 74 AD *IG* X (2) (2) 325, 44 (*Τει-*: s. *Βακχύλος*); (**25**) 116 AD ib. 327, 32 (*Τει-*: f. *Παράμονος*)
MACEDONIA (EDONIS):
—AMPHIPOLIS*: (**26**) f. i AD *SEG* XXVIII 537; XXXVI 587 (date) (*Α. Καπρείλιος Τ.*: freed.)
MACEDONIA (MYGDONIA):
—THESSALONIKE: (**27**) c. 230-200 BC *BCH* 45 (1921) p. 17 III, 66 (Tataki, *Macedonians* p. 187 no. 65) (f. *Ἀρχέδημος*); (**28**) v-vi AD *IG* X (2) (1) 675 (Feissel, *RICM* 137)
MACEDONIA (ODOMANTIKE):
—SIRRHA: (**29**) 155 AD Dimitsas 821, 24 (Kaphtantzis 1) (*Τει-*: f. *Ἀπολλώνιος*)
MACEDONIA (PAIONIA):
—STOBOI: (**30**) ii-iii AD *JÖAI* 6 (1903) Beibl. col. 6 no. 7 (*Τιμό[θε]ος*)
SCYTHIA MINOR:
—TOMIS: (**31**) ii AD *ISM* II 125 I, 23 (*Τει-*: s. *Λυσίμαχος*); (**32**) ii-iii AD ib. 195, 1, 13 (biling.) (*Τει-*: s. *Νόνιος*); (**33**) ~ ib. 468, 9 (*Θει-*: f. *Διονύσις*); (**34**) iv-v AD Barnea 5 (Popescu, *IGL* 25)
SKYTHIA:
—OLBIA-BORYSTHENES: (**35**) v BC Dubois, *IGDOlbia* 101 (f. *Ἀπολλωνίδης*); (**36**) iii BC *IOSPE* I² 201 I, 44 (f. *Βάτακος*); (**37**) ~ ib. l. 47 (s. *Πάρμις*)
—TYRAS: (**38**) s. iii BC *VDI* 1966 (2), p. 152, 3
TAURIS:
—CHERSONESOS: (**39**) ii-iii AD *IOSPE* I² 440 (*Τει-*: f. (nat.) *Αὐρ. Ἑρμοκράτης*)
—CHERSONESOS?: (**40**) m. i BC ib. 347, 4 (f. *—νων*)
THRACE:
—BEROE-AUGUSTA TRAIANA (TERRIT.): (**41**) iii AD *IGB* V 5617-5618 (Lat. Aur. Timotheu)
—DUROSTORUM: (**42**) ii-iii AD *Arkheologiia* (Sofia) 1976 (4), p. 64 no. 5 = 1981 (4), p. 42 no. 7 (Lat. Timotheus)
—NICOPOLIS AD ISTRUM?: (**43**) 196 AD *IMS* II 53 I b, 48 (*CIL* III 14507); cf. *ZPE* 146 (2004) pp. 216-20 (Lat. M. Aur. Timotheus)
—PAUTALIA: (**44**) ii-iii AD *IGB* V 5780 (*Τει-*: I f. *Ἀπολλώνιος*, *Τιμόθεος* II, *Ἀγάθων*); (**45**) ~ ib. (*Τει-*: II s. *Τιμόθεος* I)
—PERINTHOS-HERAKLEIA:
——(Kastaleis): (**46**) iii-ii BC *IPerinth* 61, 56 (s. *Διόδοτος*)
—PHILIPPOPOLIS-TRIMONTIUM: (**47**) c. 303 AD *Anal. Boll.* 31 (1912) p. 192
—PLOTINOPOLIS: (**48**) ii-iii AD *SEG* XIX 453, 3 (*IThrakAig* E459) (*[Τι]μόθεος?*)
—SERDICA: (**49**) iii AD Beševliev, *EP* 42 (*SEG* XV 470) (*Αὐρ. Τειμόθ[εος] [ὁ] [καὶ] [Νί]γερ?*)

Τιμοθῆς
SCYTHIA MINOR:
—ISTROS: (**1**) ii AD *ISM* I 196, 12 (*Αἴλ. Τειμοθῆς*)

Τιμοκλῆς
CIMMERIAN BOSPOROS:
—PANTIKAPAION: (**1**) i-ii AD *CIRB* 637
MACEDONIA (BOTTIAIA):
—BEROIA: (**2**) 223 BC *IBer* 4, 11 (s. *Κάλλιππος*)
—PELLA: (**3**) iv/iii BC *SEG* XLVIII 820 (f. *Μυρτώ*)
MACEDONIA (EDONIS):
—AMPHIPOLIS: (**4**) hell. Dimitsas 851 (f. *Ἡρόδωρος*); (**5**) f. iii BC *OGIS* 220, 10 (*IIlion* 34); *ICos* ED 190, 5 (Tataki, *Macedonians* p. 61 no. 124) (f. *Μητρόδωρος*); (**6**) ii-iii AD Dimitsas 922; cf. *BCH* 19 (1895) p. 110 no. 3 (*Τει-*: f. *Λεωνίδης*)
—PHILIPPOI: (**7**) a. 346 BC *Syll*³ 267 A, 2 (Tataki, *Macedonians* p. 167 no. 34) (*Τιμοκ[λῆς]*: s. *Τίμανδρος*)
SCYTHIA MINOR:
—ISTROS: (**8**) ii AD *ISM* I 196, 15; 201 I, 22 (*Τει-*: s. *Ἀνθᾶς*)
—KALLATIS: (**9**) iv/iii BC ib. III 153 (f. *Ἄβα*)
—TOMIS: (**10**) i BC ib. II 2 A, 54 (s. *Ἀριστόμαχος*)
SKYTHIA:
—NIKONION: (**11**) ii-i BC *MASP* 5 (1966) p. 80 no. 27 (vase)
—OLBIA-BORYSTHENES: (**12**) ii AD *IOSPE* I² 101, 8 (*Τει-*: s. *Φλίανος*)
TAURIS:
—CHERSONESOS: (**13**) ?iv-iii BC *SEG* XLIV 657 (weight) (*Τιμο(κ)λῆς*)
THRACE: (**14**) 264 BC *PHib* 92, 9 (Velkov 315; La'da E848) (s. *Σῖμος*: t.e.)

Τιμοκράτης
CIMMERIAN BOSPOROS:
—PANTIKAPAION: (**1**) ii BC *CIRB* 259; cf. KW pl. 30 no. 431; (**2**) imp. *CIRB* 768 (*Τει-*: s. *Θεοφιλίσκος*); (**3**) i AD ib. 507 (f. *Ῥόδων*); (**4**) i/ii AD ib. 593 (f. *Γλαυκία*)
—THEODOSIA: (**5**) iii AD ib. 947 A, 13 (*Τειμοκρ[άτης]*: f. *Δαδοῦς*)
MACEDONIA (BOTTIAIA):
—BEROIA: (**6**) 223 BC *IBer* 4, 31 (s. *Δεινίας*)
MACEDONIA (CHALKIDIKE):
—ANTIGONEIA?: (**7**) hell.? Robert, *OMS* 2 pp. 1296-7 (Tataki, *Macedonians* p. 65 no. 9) (s. *Ἀρχίδαμος*)
MACEDONIA (EDONIS):
—PHILIPPOI: (**8**) a. 346 BC *Syll*³ 267 A, 1 (Tataki, *Macedonians* p. 167 no. 35) (*[Τιμοκ]ράτης?*: s. *Τίμανδρος*)
MACEDONIA (MYGDONIA):
—KALINDOIA: (**9**) 68-98 AD *SEG* XLII 580, 7, 50 (*Τει-*: II s. *Τιμοκράτης* I); (**10**) ~ ib. l. 8, 50 (*Τει-*: I f. *Τιμοκράτης* II)
MACEDONIA (PIERIA):
—PYDNA: (**11**) iv BC *GRBS* 43 (2002-3) p. 112 no. 2, 14
SCYTHIA MINOR:
—ISTROS: (**12**) ii/iii AD *ISM* I 298 (Lat. Timocrates: f. Sulpicianus)
SKYTHIA:
—TANAIS: (**13**) ii AD *CIRB* 1268, 10 (*Τει-*: f. *—ατος*)
THRACE:
—ABDERA: (**14**) iii-ii BC *Recherches amph. grecques* p. 494 no. 8 (amph.) (*Τιμοκράτ[ης]*)
—BYZANTION?: (**15**) ii AD *IByz* 357 (*Τει-*: s. *Δαμάτριος*)
—KOILA: (**16**) imp. *BCH* 36 (1912) p. 288 n.2 (*Αἴλ. Τ.*)
—NICOPOLIS AD ISTRUM (NR.): (**17**) f. iii AD *IGB* II 706 (*CCET* II (2) 655) (s. *Διογένης*)
—ODESSOS: (**18**) 29 BC *IGB* I² 46, 18 (*Τει-*: s. *Ἐπιμένης*); (**19**) ii AD ib. 50 b, 23 (*Τει-*); (**20**) ~ ib. 86 (*[Τι]μοκράτης?*, *[Ἐρ]μοκράτης*—ed.); (**21**) 221 AD ib. 47 bis a, 25 (*Τει-*: f. *Αὐρ. Ζωΐλος*); (**22**) ~ ib. 47 bis b, 14 (*Τει-*: f. *Αὐρ. Μοσχίων*); (**23**) ~ ib. l. 26 (*Τει-*: I f. *Αὐρ. Τιμοκράτης* II); (**24**) ~ ib. l. 26 (*Αὐρ. Τειμοκράτης*: II s. *Τιμοκράτης* I)

Τιμόλαος
CIMMERIAN BOSPOROS:
—PANTIKAPAION: (**1**) 82 AD *CIRB* 76, 15 (*SEG* XVIII 310) (*Τει-*: f. *Μακάριος*)
MACEDONIA: (**2**) s. iv BC *RE* (6) (Tataki, *Macedonians* p. 441 no. 17) (or Thessaly (Pelasgiotis) Larisa)
THRACE:
—LYSIMACHEIA: (**3**) m. ii BC *ISestos* 38 b, 6 (s. *Ἰσχόλαος*)

Τιμόλη
CIMMERIAN BOSPOROS:
—HERMONASSA: (**1**) i AD *CIRB* 1085 (*Τει-*: ?d. *Τιμο—*)

Τιμόμαχος
SCYTHIA MINOR:
—TOMIS:
——(Argadeis): (**1**) iii-ii BC *ISM* II 35; *BE* 1962, no. 231 (f. *Κερκίων*)
THRACE:
—BYZANTION: (**2**) i BC *RE* (5); Overbeck 2119 ff. (painter)

Τιμοξένα
TAURIS:
—CHERSONESOS: (**1**) iii BC *IOSPE* I² 521 (*Τιμ[ο]ξένα*: d. *Ἀπολλοφάνης*)

Τιμοξενιανή?
MACEDONIA (ODOMANTIKE):
—SIRRHA?: (**1**) ii-iii AD Kaphtantzis 29 (*Dodoni* 18 (1989) p. 251 no. 63) (*Φλ. Τειμοξενιανή*—Mihailov)

Τιμοξενίδης
THRACE:
—MARONEIA: (**1**) i BC *IThrakAig* E213, 5 (*Τει-*: s. *Ἀνάξιππος*)

Τιμόξενος
MACEDONIA (CHALKIDIKE):
—OLYNTHOS: (**1**) ?c. 355-349 BC *TAPA* 69 (1938) p. 55 no. 7, 5 (f. *—ρος*)
—SKIONE: (**2**) 480 BC Hdt. viii 128 (Tataki, *Macedonians* p. 174 no. 10)
MACEDONIA (ODOMANTIKE):
—SIRRHA: (**3**) ii-iii AD *SEG* XXXIII 550 (*[Κου]σπίδιος Τει[μό]ξενος*: f. *Διονύσιος*)

Τιμοσθένης
CIMMERIAN BOSPOROS:
—GORGIPPIA: (**1**) f. iii BC *CIRB* 1137 B II, 22 (*Τιμοσθέ[ν]ης*: f. *Ἡραῖος*)
MACEDONIA (CHALKIDIKE):
—POTIDAIA-KASSANDREIA: (**2**) a. 316 BC *IG* IV (1)² 94 b, 42 (Perlman, *City and Sanctuary* E.1 with p. 78 (date); Tataki, *Macedonians* p. 96 no. 93) (s. *Κρίτων*)
THRACE:
—PAUTALIA: (**3**) ii-iii AD *IGB* IV 2086 (*GVI* 267) (*Τει[μ]ο[σ]θένη[ς]?*)

Τιμόστρατος
MACEDONIA: (**1**) 103 BC *PTeb* 105, 52 (Tataki, *Macedonians* p. 498 no. 237; La'da E1639) (s. *Σαραπίων*)
MACEDONIA (CHALKIDIKE):
—SANE-OURANOUPOLIS: (**2**) iv/iii BC *SEG* XLIII 432 (s. *Ἀρίδηλος*)

Τιμόφιλος
MACEDONIA (MYGDONIA):
—THESSALONIKE?: (**1**) i BC-i AD *IG* X (2) (1) 909; cf. *ISM* II 307 with comm. (*Τιμό(ζ)ηλος*—ed., *Τιμό(φ)ηλος?*: s. *Δαφναῖος*)

Τίμυλλος
MACEDONIA (CHALKIDIKE):
—AKANTHOS: (**1**) c. 480-470 BC *SEG* XXXVI 580 (vase); cf. XLV 729

Τιμύλος
Scythia Minor:
—istros: (1) ii ad *ISM* i 211, 5 (*Τει-*: f. *Βάρβαρος*)

Τιμώ
Macedonia (Edonis):
—amphipolis: (1) c. 375-350 bc *IThrakAig* E166
Macedonia (Odomantike):
—sirrha?: (2) ii-i bc *SEG* xl 563, 1 (m. *Σωπάτρα*)
Skythia:
—olbia-borysthenes: (3) iii bc *IOSPE* i² 190 b (d. *Ὑψικρέων*)
Thrace:
—byzantion: (4) imp. *IByz* 248 (*Τει-*)

Τίμων
Macedonia (Bisaltia):
—argilos?: (1) 364-357 bc Hatzopoulos, *Actes Amphipolis* p. 15 no. 1, 3, 8; pp. 73-4 (locn., date) (or Macedonia (Edonis) Amphipolis)
Sarmatia:
—maiotai: (2) hell.-imp. *IG* xii (1) 514 (slave)
Tauris:
—chersonesos: (3) iii bc Solomonik, *NEPKh* 35 (f. *Τεττία*); (4) ~ *IOSPE* i² 511 (f. *Δαματρία*)
Thrace:
—lysimacheia: (5) ?c. 214-210 bc *IOrop* 125, 9 (f. *Ἀντικράτης*)
—odessos: (6) 215 ad *IGB* i² 47 b, 24 ((*Τ*)*ίμων*: f. *Αὐρ. Ἀντώνιος*)
—serdica: (7) imp. ib. iv 1973 (*Τείμ[ω]ν*)

Τιμῶναξ
Scythia Minor:
—kallatis: (1) iv bc *ISM* iii 255 (vase) (*CEG* ii 901)
Thrace:
—tirizis akra*: (2) iii/ii bc *IGB* v 5004 bis

Τιμωνίδης
Macedonia (Bisaltia):
—argilos?: (1) 364-357 bc Hatzopoulos, *Actes Amphipolis* p. 15 no. 1, 13; pp. 73-4 (locn., date) (or Macedonia (Edonis) Amphipolis: *Τιμωνίδης*)
Macedonia (Edonis):
—amphipolis: (2) 179 bc *SEG* xxxi 614, 7 (Hatzopoulos, *MI* 2 pp. 49-50 no. 29) (s. *Ἀσκληπιάδης*)
Thrace:
—maroneia?: (3) c. 229-200 bc *IG* ii² 854, 10 (*Τιμωνί[δης]*?)

Τίμωρις
Cimmerian Bosporos:
—theodosia: (1) v/iv bc *Arch. Class.* 25-6 (1973-4) p. 350 no. 18 (vase) (f. *Βοσπόριχος*)
Skythia:
—tyras: (2) iv bc *SEG* xlv 1026. 20 (vase) (f. *Νευμήνιος*)

Τίνεια
Macedonia (Bottiaia):
—edessa: (1) 247 ad *Athena* 12 (1900) p. 71 no. 5, 3 (Tataki, *Edessa* 292) (*Τίνε[ι]α*)

Τίνειος
Thrace:
—odessos: (1) i-ii ad *IGB* i² 198 bis (*Τεί-*?)

Τιούτα
Thrace:
—beroe-augusta traiana (territ.): (1) ii-iii ad ib. iii 1653, 5 (*Φλ. Τ.*: m. *Διόδωρος*)
—bourdapa: (2) ii ad ib. 1348 (d. *Δίζας*)
—philippopolis-trimontium: (3) ii ad ib. 1005 (d. *Κρονίδης*); (4) ~ ib. 1010
—philippopolis-trimontium (territ.): (5) ii ad ib. v 5472, 6 = *SEG* iii 538 (*Eastern cults* pp. 199-200 no. 15) (*Φλ. Τ.*)

Τίπας
Thrace:
—maidoi: (1) c. 117 bc *Syll*³ 700, 22

Τιράνης
Cimmerian Bosporos:
—bosporos: (1) c. 250-278 ad *RE* s.v. Teiranes (-); *PIR*² I 602; Frolova, *CKB A.D. 242-341/342* pp. 31-3 (*Τιβ. Ἰούλ. Τειράνης*: king)
—pantikapaion: (2) imp. *CIRB* 781 (f. *Ἀνόπτηνις*); (3) i ad *KSIA* 116 (1969) pp. 52-3 no. 4 (s. *Ταύτακος*)

Τιράνιος
Cimmerian Bosporos:
—pantikapaion: (1) i/ii ad *CIRB* 638; cf. KW pl. 53 no. 724 (f. *Ἀριαράθης*)

Τιργαταώ
Sarmatia:
—maiotai: (1) iv bc Polyaen. viii 55

Τίτθα
Thrace:
—byzantion: (1) i bc-i ad *IByz* 177 (Fıratlı–Robert p. 111 no. 182) (d. *Μητρόδωρος*)
—byzantion (territ.): (2) i-ii ad *IByz* 245 (d. *Δαμᾶς*)
—mesambria: (3) i-ii ad *IGB* i² 340 bis (d. *Διονύσιος*)

Τιτθᾶς
Scythia Minor:
—istros: (1) 138 ad *ISM* i 193 I, 95 (*Βαρβαρίων Τ.*?: ?f. *Βαρβαρίων*)

Τιτιανή
Macedonia (Bottiaia):
—beroia: (1) 193 ad *ILeukopetra* 38, 1 (Tataki 1235) (d. *Ἀλέξανδρος*)

Τιτιανός
Macedonia: (1) ?ii ad Ptol., *Geog.* i 11. 6; *RE* Supplbd. 6 s.v. Maes (-) + Supplbd. 11 s.v. Maes Titianus (-) (Tataki, *Macedonians* p. 360 no. 4) (*Μάης ὁ καὶ Τ.*)
Macedonia (Bottiaia):
—beroia: (2) ii-iii ad *IBer* 284 (Tataki 1236) (f. *Ἀμυντιανή*)

Τίτιος
Cimmerian Bosporos:
—pantikapaion: (1) 275-278 ad *CIRB* 36, 38 (*-τιους*: s. *Μύρων*)
Macedonia (Mygdonia):
—thessalonike: (2) ii-iii ad *SEG* xxx 645

Τίτος
Macedonia (Bottiaia):
—beroia: (1) ii/iii ad *IBer* 27 A, 6 (slave?)
—edessa: (2) iii-iv ad *GVI* 2036, 1, 6, 11, 14 (*IDyrrh* 527 bis; Tataki, *Edessa* 293) (s. *Καστρίκιος Φίλιππος, Ἡδεῖα ἡ καὶ Μαρία*)
—skydra: (3) iii ad *SEG* xlix 793, 2, 16 (*Τίτορ*—l.16: s. *Λύκος*)
Macedonia (Chalkidike):
—gigonos?: (4) s. ii ad *AEMTh* 9 (1995) pp. 321-2 n. 3
Macedonia (Derriopos):
—stuberra: (5) 87 ad *IG* x (2) (2) 325, 76 (f. *Ζωΐλος*)
Macedonia (Lynkestis):
—herakleia: (6) i ad ib. 75, 23 (f. *Κέλερ*); (7) ~ ib. l. 30 (s. *Σεκοῦνδος*)
Macedonia (Mygdonia):
—thessalonike?: (8) ?iii ad ib. x (2) (1) 911, 1 (*-τους*: s. *Σεκοῦνδος*, f. *Μακέτα, Μᾶρκος*)
Macedonia (Odomantike)?: (9) ii-iii ad *IGB* v 5927 (s. *Πυρούσαλα*)
Macedonia (Orestis):
—sisani (mod.): (10) 146 ad *EAM* 187, 11 (s. *Λύκα*)
Macedonia (Paionia):
—antigoneia? (budur čiflik (mod.)): (11) imp. *SEG* xiii 405 (*Νουμήνιος ὁ καὶ Τ.*: s. *Ἀμμία*)
—kavadarci (mod.): (12) ii ad *Sp.* 71 (1931) p. 74 no. 174, 1, 4 (s. *Βακχᾶς*, f. *Γαΐα*)
—stoboi: (13) ii-iii ad *AJA* 88 (1984) p. 578 n. 60
Scythia Minor:
—tomis: (14) c. 138-161 ad *ISM* ii 60, 9 (*Τ. νεώτ.*: I f. *Τίτος* II); (15) ~ ib. l. 9 (II s. *Τίτος* I *νεώτ.*)
Thrace:
—aquae calidae*: (16) i-ii ad *IGB* i² 382 (f. —ν)
—glava panega (mod.): (17) ii ad ib. ii 562 (s. *Στατίλιος*)
—odessos: (18) 221 ad ib. i² 47 bis a, 32 (f. *Αὐρ. Ἡρακλείδης*)
—salymbria (nr.): (19) imp. Unp. (Sayar) (f. *Ὀλυμπιάς, Γ. Ἀνναῖος Πρόβος*)
—serdica?: (20) s. ii ad *Sp.* 77 (1934) p. 53 no. 51 (f. *Ἐπτεπυρίς*)

Τίτυρος
Cimmerian Bosporos:
—gorgippia: (1) ii ad *CIRB* 1159 A, 2 (*Τίτυρ[ος]*?)

Τλασέας
Tauris:
—chersonesos: (1) s. v bc *SEG* xl 612. 10 (ostrakon)

Τληπόλεμος
Macedonia: (1) 330-316 bc *RE* (5); Berve 757 (Tataki, *Macedonians* p. 442 no. 18) (s. *Πυθοφάνης*)
Macedonia?: (2) a. 156 bc *ID* 1426 A II, 14 (Tataki, *Macedonians* p. 442 no. 19)
Thrace:
—perinthos-herakleia:
——(Theseidai): (3) s. iii bc *IPerinth* 62, 2 (s. *Εὐκλείδης*)

Τλήσων
Skythia:
—olbia-borysthenes: (1) iv bc *CEG* ii 723, 1-2 (*SEG* xxxix 568) (*Τλή[σ]ων*)

Τλιγος?
Cimmerian Bosporos:
—gorgippia: (1) ii/iii ad ib. xxxvi 713, 3 (*Τλιγο[ς]*?)

Τοῖτας
Macedonia (Mygdonia):
—kalindoia: (1) 68-98 ad ib. xlii 580, 41 + *BE* 1999, no. 362; cf. *Anthémonte–Kalindoia* 2 p. 315 (name) (s. *Σεδάλας*); (2) a. 98 ad *SEG* xlii 582, 25 (f. *Παράμονος*)

Τόκης
Macedonia (Bisaltia):
—euporia?: (1) ii-iii ad ib. xxx 612 (f. *Νίκανδρος*); (2) iii ad ib. 592 (*Eastern cults* p. 202 no. 20) (*Τ. ὁ καὶ Ἰσίδωρος*)
Macedonia (Edonis):
—amphipolis: (3) ii-iii ad *Thrakika* 13 (1940) p. 27 *Λ*; cf. *Epigraphica* 37 (1975) pp. 28-9 (f. *Βίτθις*)
—edonoi?: (4) vi/v bc *CEG* i 155 (*LSAG*² p. 479 no. C) (*Τόκεω* (gen.))

Τόκων
Cimmerian Bosporos:
—pantikapaion: (1) ?s. ii ad *CIRB* 90, 15 (f. *Στρατόνικος*)
—theodosia: (2) iii ad ib. 947 B, 12 (*Τό[κω]ν*?: f. *Μήνιος*)

Τολμεάριος
THRACE:
—KELLAI: (**1**) 241-244 AD *IGB* III 1517, 51 (f. *Αὐρ. Κελαίδοσα*)

Τόλων
MACEDONIA (BOTTIAIA):
—MIEZA: (**1**) iii BC *SEG* XXIV 524 I, 17; 524 II, 5, 25 (Hatzopoulos, *MI* 2 p. 106 no. 92) (s. *Ἄδυμος*)

Τόμιον
THRACE:
—ODESSOS: (**1**) i BC-i AD *IGB* I^2 189 (*Τώμιων*: d. *Ξένων*); (**2**) m. ii AD ib. 169 (PM 1725); *Dacia* 21 (1977) p. 161 (date) (d. *Ἀσκληπιάδης*)

Τόμος
SCYTHIA MINOR:
—TOMIS: (**1**) ii-iii AD *ISM* II 31 II, 1 (f. *Ἡρακλᾶς*)

Τόνος
MACEDONIA (SINTIKE):
—PARTHIKOPOLIS: (**1**) ?ii AD *FGrH* 257 F 37, 48 (Tataki, *Macedonians* p. 147 no. 8) (f. *Βόνζης*)
—PARTHIKOPOLIS (TERRIT.): (**2**) ii AD *Arkheologiia* (Sofia) 1987 (1), p. 24 no. 1, 2 (f. *Πύρρος*); (**3**) ~ ib. p. 25 no. 2 (s. *Ζεκαιδένθη*)
THRACE:
—NICOPOLIS AD NESTUM: (**4**) ii-iii AD *IGB* IV 2337, 15 (f. *Μουκάτραλις*)

Τόξαρις
SKYTHIA:
—SKYTHAI: (**1**) ii AD Luc., *Tox.* passim (fict.)

Τορευμάτιον
MACEDONIA (MYGDONIA):
—THESSALONIKE: (**1**) ii AD *IG* X (2) (1) 304, 1 (m. *Παλλάς*)

Τορκᾶτος
MACEDONIA (EDONIS):
—AMPHIPOLIS: (**1**) iii AD *SEG* XXIV 598; cf. XXXVII 580 (*Αὐρ. Τ.*: ?s. *Αὐρ. Μωμώ*, ?f. *Παράμονος*)
MACEDONIA (LYNKESTIS):
—HERAKLEIA: (**2**) imp. *IG* X (2) (2) 101
MACEDONIA (ODOMANTIKE):
—GAZOROS?: (**3**) 144 AD *SEG* XXX 599, 5 (Pilhofer 552); cf. *SEG* XXXVII 579 (f. *Γάϊος*)
—SKOTOUSSA (TERRIT.)?: (**4**) 59 or 175 AD ib. XXXIV 677

Τορκίων
MACEDONIA (MYGDONIA):
—THESSALONIKE?: (**1**) ii AD *IG* X (2) (1) 891

Τόρκος
MACEDONIA (BISALTIA):
—TERPNI (MOD.): (**1**) ii-iii AD *SEG* XLIX 810
MACEDONIA (BOTTIAIA):
—BEROIA: (**2**) ii/iii AD *IBer* 145, 13 (Tataki 1238) (f. *Νίγερ*)
MACEDONIA (EDONIS):
—AMPHIPOLIS: (**3**) 157 AD Dimitsas 863 (s. *Διονύσιος*, f. *Ἀμμία*)
MACEDONIA (MYGDONIA):
—LETE: (**4**) 180 AD *SEG* XLVIII 808
—THESSALONIKE: (**5**) ii AD *IG* X (2) (1) 296 (f. *Μωμώ*); (**6**) ~ ib. 446 (s. *Μενδίς*)
—THESSALONIKE?: (**7**) 78 AD ib. 926 (f. *Σεμέλη*); (**8**) 109 AD ib. 849, 1 (f. *Κάσσανδρος*); (**9**) ~ ib. l. 5 (s. *Κάσσανδρος*, *Μάντα*)
MACEDONIA (ODOMANTIKE):
—DRABESKOS?: (**10**) ii-iii AD *SEG* XXX 619, 4 (Pilhofer 572) (*Τώ-*: s. *Βιζῆς*)
—GAZOROS (TERRIT.): (**11**) 106 AD *SEG* XXX 596, 10 (Pilhofer 555) (?s. *Διοσκουρίδης*, *Σοῦρα*, f. *Διοσκουρίδης*)
—SIRRHA: (**12**) 155 AD Dimitsas 821, 31 (Kaphtantzis 1) (s. *Ζωσᾶς*); (**13**) ~ Dimitsas 821, 32 (Kaphtantzis 1) (*Τόρκου* (gen.): f. *Διοσκοῦς*); (**14**) ii/iii AD *SEG* XLVIII 877 (s. *Πυρούλας*, *Μωμώ*); (**15**) f. iii AD ib. XXX 590, 6 (*Αὐρ. Τ.*: s. *Δούλης*); (**16**) ~ ib. l. 9 (*Αὐρ. Τ.*: s. *Βοιωτός*)
—SIRRHA (TERRIT.): (**17**) 55 or 171 AD ib. XXXIV 676 (f. *Διοσκουρίδης*); (**18**) ii-iii AD ib. XXX 593 + Kaphtantzis 478 (*Γ[άϊ]ος Τορκουᾶτος*—*SEG*: f. *Κι—ος*)
—SIRRHA?: (**19**) 157 AD *Belomorski Pregled* 1 (1942) p. 318 no. 1 (Kaphtantzis 10) (*[Τό]ρκος*)
—SKOTOUSSA?: (**20**) ii-iii AD Dimitsas 843 (s. *Ἀλέξανδρος*, *Σελήνη*); (**21**) ~ *SEG* XLVIII 801
MACEDONIA (PAIONIA):
—KAVADARCI (MOD.): (**22**) ii AD *Sp.* 98 (1941-8) p. 67 no. 140 (f. *Ποσειδώνιος*)

Τορκουᾶτος
MACEDONIA (KRESTONIA):
—IORON: (**1**) s. ii AD *IBer* 87, 3 (Tataki 1239; Tataki, *Macedonians* p. 114 no. 4) (s. *Λυσίμαχος*)
MACEDONIA (MYGDONIA):
—THESSALONIKE?: (**2**) ii-iii AD *IG* X (2) (1) 274 (—*κυρις Τ.*); (**3**) ~ ib. 756
MACEDONIA (ODOMANTIKE):
—SIRRHA: (**4**) ii-iii AD *Belomorski Pregled* 1 (1942) p. 321 no. 8 (Kaphtantzis 35) (*Αἴλ. Τ.*); (**5**) ~ *SEG* XXX 613, 1 (s. *Βίθυς*, f. *Μητρόδωρος*); (**6**) 155 AD Dimitsas 821, 1 (Kaphtantzis 1) (s. *Βίθυς*); (**7**) ~ Dimitsas 821, 7 (Kaphtantzis 1) (s. *Μωμώ*); (**8**) ~ Dimitsas 821, 17 (Kaphtantzis 1) (s. *Διοσκουρίδης*); (**9**) ~ Dimitsas 821, 21 (Kaphtantzis 1) (f. *Πρόκλος*); (**10**) ~ Dimitsas 821, 23 (Kaphtantzis 1) (s. *Μουκιανός*); (**11**) 183 AD Dimitsas 816 (Kaphtantzis 12) (f. — *ὁ καὶ Διονυσόδωρος*); (**12**) f. iii AD *SEG* XXX 590, 30 (*Αὐρ. Τ.*: s. *Δυτούλας*)
—SIRRHA (TERRIT.): (**13**) iii AD ib. 608 = Dimitsas 824 (*Αὐρ. Τ.*: I f. *Αὐρ. Τορκουᾶτος* II); (**14**) ~ *SEG* XXX 608 = Dimitsas 824 (*Αὐρ. Τ.*: II s. *Αὐρ. Τορκουᾶτος* I)
THRACE:
—SERDICA: (**15**) ii-iii AD *IGB* IV 1939 (*Αἴλ. Ἀν— ὁ κὲ Τ.*)

Τορκούλας
MACEDONIA (ODOMANTIKE):
—SIRRHA: (**1**) 155 AD Dimitsas 821, 3 (Kaphtantzis 1) (s. *Τορκοῦς*); (**2**) ~ Dimitsas 821, 13 (Kaphtantzis 1) (f. *Ἀπολλοφάνης*)

Τορκουπαίβης
MACEDONIA (ODOMANTIKE):
—SIRRHA: (**1**) 155 AD Dimitsas 821, 20, 22 (Kaphtantzis 1) (s. *Διοσκουρίδης*)

Τορκοῦς
MACEDONIA (ODOMANTIKE):
—SIRRHA: (**1**) 155 AD Dimitsas 821, 3 (Kaphtantzis 1) (*Τορκοῦ* (gen.): f. *Τορκούλας*); (**2**) ~ Dimitsas 821, 4 (Kaphtantzis 1) (s. *Κλαυδία*); (**3**) ~ Dimitsas 821, 9 (Kaphtantzis 1) (*Τορκοῦ* (gen.): I f. *Τορκοῦς* II); (**4**) ~ Dimitsas 821, 9 (Kaphtantzis 1) (II s. *Τορκοῦς* I); (**5**) f. iii AD *SEG* XXX 590, 26 (I f. *Αὐρ. Τορκοῦς* II); (**6**) ~ ib. l. 26 (*Αὐρ. Τ.*: II s. *Τορκοῦς* I)

Τορπιλία
MACEDONIA (BOTTIAIA):
—BEROIA: (**1**) i-ii AD *IBer* 168, 4 (Tataki 1240)

Τόσκος
MACEDONIA (SINTIKE):
—PARTHIKOPOLIS: (**1**) 158 AD *IGB* IV 2263, 15 (f. *Κρίσπος*)

Τότης
THRACE:
—SALYMBRIA (NR.): (**1**) hell. *IByz* S 54 (f. (nat.) *Μηνακῶν ὁ καὶ Μενέδημος*); (**2**) ~ ib. (f. *Μηνακῶν*)

Τούδρουγος
CIMMERIAN BOSPOROS:
—PANTIKAPAION: (**1**) v-vi AD *IAK* 45 (1912) p. 20 no. 10

Τοῦκος?
MACEDONIA (EDONIS):
—AMPHIPOLIS: (**1**) ii/iii AD *Thracia* 2 p. 279 + *Epigraphica* 37 (1975) p. 32 (*Τούκου* (gen.), *Τουκουδεβα*—Mihailov: s. *Δέβας*)

Τούμβαγος
SKYTHIA:
—OLBIA-BORYSTHENES: (**1**) ii AD *IOSPE* I^2 100, 4; Zgusta, *PNS* 231 (s. *Ἡρακλείδης*); (**2**) ii-iii AD *IOSPE* I^2 52, [1], 16 (f. *Δάδος*); (**3**) f. ii AD ib. 85, 7 (*Τούμ[βαγος]*: f. *Ἡρακλείδης*); (**4**) s. ii AD *IOlbia* 81, 5 (*IOSPE* I^2 94); *IOSPE* I^2 136, 8 (f. *Θεόδωρος*)

Τούρβων
SCYTHIA MINOR:
—ISTROS: (**1**) ii/iii AD *ISM* I 225, 9 (s. *Δ—*)
—TOMIS: (**2**) 201 AD ib. II 83 I, 21 (s. *Διονύσιος*)
THRACE:
—BIZONE: (**3**) ii-iii AD *IGB* I^2 10 bis
—TÂRGOVIŠTE (MOD.): (**4**) ii-iii AD ib. II 768

Τουριδάτης
THRACE:
—DRAGANOVEC (MOD.): (**1**) ii-iii AD ib. V 5288 (*Τ̣ο̣υριδάτης*: s. *Δαλήτραλις*)

Τοῦσα
SCYTHIA MINOR:
—KALLATIS: (**1**) iii BC *ISM* III 159 (d. *Ἀντίφιλος*)

Τοῦτα
THRACE:
—ODESSOS: (**1**) i BC-i AD *IGB* I^2 151 (PM 713) (d. *Δημόνικος*); (**2**) i-ii AD *IGB* I^2 140 bis, 3 (*[Το]ῦτα*?: d. *Διονύσιος*); (**3**) m. ii AD ib. 177 (PM 1749); *Dacia* 21 (1977) p. 161 (date) (*Τοῦ[τα]*: d. *Σωτήρ*)

Τουτάς
THRACE:
—ODESSOS: (**1**) ii AD *IGB* I^2 178 bis (d. *Ζώπυρος*, ?m. *Ἀγαθήνωρ*, *Ζουδιεγιπτους*)

Τοφῶς
CIMMERIAN BOSPOROS:
—HERMONASSA: (**1**) i AD *CIRB* 1079; Zgusta, *PNS* 716
—PANTIKAPAION: (**2**) i AD *CIRB* 517 (d. *Χρῦσος*)

Τράγος
CIMMERIAN BOSPOROS:
—GORGIPPIA: (**1**) ii/iii AD ib. 1179, 42 (f. *Φαρνάκης*)

Τραζυρέσης
THRACE:
—BAZOPARA: (**1**) 202 AD *IGB* III 1690 c, 71 (and Thrace Pizos: *Δυτούτραλις Τ.*: s. *Δόλης*)

Τραίβιθυς
THRACE:
—CELALETAE?: (**1**) 86 AD *CIL* XVI 33 (*IDR* I p. 152 no. 24) (Lat. Traibithus: f. *Σεύθης*)

Τραΐδακος
THRACE:
—BEROE-AUGUSTA TRAIANA (TERRIT.): (**1**) ii AD *IGB* III 1741 bis (biling.) (f. *Μᾶρκος*)

Τρακηλία
THRACE:
—BYZANTION: **(1)** i-ii AD *IByz* 232 (d. *Μενίσκος*, m. *Διονυσοφάνης*)

Τραλικεῖλας
MACEDONIA (ODOMANTIKE):
—GAZOROS (TERRIT.): **(1)** hell. *SEG* XXXIX 569 (Pilhofer 554) (-λει-: f. *Ζηκαλώγη*)

Τράλιος
MACEDONIA (BOTTIAIA):
—BEROIA: **(1)** ii/iii AD *IBer* 143 A, 7 (Tataki 1244) (*Τραλίου* (gen.): f. *Ἀλέξανδρος*)

Τραλίπορις
MACEDONIA (CHALKIDIKE):
—SKABLA?: **(1)** imp. *SEG* XXIX 619; cf. Hatzopoulos, *Actes Chalc.* p. 71 (locn.) (?s. *Θράσων*, ?f. *Τραλιπορίσκος*)

Τραλιπορίσκος
MACEDONIA (CHALKIDIKE):
—SKABLA?: **(1)** imp. *SEG* XXIX 619; cf. Hatzopoulos, *Actes Chalc.* p. 71 (locn.) (*Τραλιπορίσκι* (dat.): ?s. *Τραλίπορις*)

Τράλις
MACEDONIA (CHALKIDIKE):
—ANTHEMOUS: **(1)** ii BC *SEG* XLII 560; cf. *Anthémonte–Kalindoia* 2 p. 316 (name) (f. *Διονύσιος*)
—SPARTOLOS?: **(2)** ?352 BC *SEG* XLVI 804, 6, 9 (f. *Πολεμοκράτης*)
MACEDONIA (EDONIS):
—HILL 133 (MOD.): **(3)** m. v BC Pritchett, *Topography* I pp. 46-7 no. 1, 5 (sherd); cf. *SEG* XLVI 723 (*Τράλι[ς]*)
MACEDONIA (MYGDONIA):
—KALINDOIA: **(4)** 68-98 AD ib. XLII 580, 11; cf. *Anthémonte–Kalindoia* 2 p. 316 (name) (-λεις: s. *Ἀσκοσίδης*); **(5)** ~ *SEG* XLII 580, 32 (-λεις: s. *Βίθυς*)
MACEDONIA (SINTIKE):
—NEINE (NR.): **(6)** ii-iii AD *IGB* V 5890
THRACE:
—BEROE-AUGUSTA TRAIANA (TERRIT.): **(7)** ii-iii AD ib. III 1709 (s. *Δόλης ὁ καὶ Σκοπιάδης*)
THRACE?: **(8)** 316-309 BC *IG* II^2 1956, 43; *Ancient Macedonia* 5 p. 445 with n. 10 (date) (*FRA* 2591)

Τράλλις
THRACE:
—KALYVIA (MOD.): **(1)** imp. *SEG* XLI 596 (vase) (-λλεις: s. *Ἄπτος*)

Τρεβάτιος
MACEDONIA (ALMOPIA):
—APSALOS (MOD.): **(1)** iii AD ib. XLVII 884 (f. *Ἀθηναγόρας*) ?= (*2*)
MACEDONIA (LYNKESTIS):
—HERAKLEIA (AREA): **(2)** imp. *IG* X (2) (2) 3 (s. *Δεκίμιος*, f. *Ἀθηναγόρας*) ?= (*1*)

Τρείλας
MACEDONIA (PAIONIA):
—NEGOTINO (MOD.): **(1)** imp. *Sp.* 98 (1941-8) p. 58 no. 118 (*Διοσκουρίδης ὁ καὶ Τ.*: f. *Διοσκουρίδης*)

Τρηστίσσιμος
THRACE:
—APOLLONIA-SOZOPOLIS: **(1)** i-ii AD *IGB* I^2 401, 17 (s. *Τελεσφόρος*)

Τριακάδας
SCYTHIA MINOR:
—TOMIS: **(1)** i BC *ISM* II 2 B, 51 (s. *Δόκιμος*)

Τριακαδίων
MACEDONIA (BOTTIAIA):
—BEROIA: **(1)** s. ii AD *IBer* 244 (Tataki 1245) (*Τρει-*: f. *Ζώσιμος*)
—EDESSA: **(2)** c. 230-200 BC *BCH* 45 (1921) p. 17 III, 60 (Tataki, *Edessa* 294) (f. *Μοσχίων*: name—Oulhen); **(3)** ii-iii AD *SEG* XII 344 (Tataki, *Edessa* 258) (*Γ. Πεδουκαῖος Τ.*: f. *Σαβῖνα*)
MACEDONIA (MYGDONIA):
—THESSALONIKE?: **(4)** ii AD *IG* X (2) (1) 697 (*M. T.*)

Τρίβαλλος
THRACE?: **(1)** m. v BC *Ag.* XXI F62 with pl. 13 (vase) (*Τρίβ[α]λος?*)

Τριβούλα
MACEDONIA (MYGDONIA):
—THESSALONIKE: **(1)** ii-iii AD *IG* X (2) (1) 516; *Ancient Macedonia* 2 pp. 328-30 (*Τιτινία Τ.*: m. *Γαϊανή, Γάϊος*)

Τρίπας
MACEDONIA (EDONIS):
—HILL 133 (MOD.): **(1)** m. v BC Pritchett, *Topography* I pp. 46-7 no. 1, 5 (sherd); cf. *SEG* XLVI 723

Τριπτόλεμος
MACEDONIA (BOTTIAIA):
—EDESSA: **(1)** 251 AD ib. XXXVI 621, 1 (Tataki, *Edessa* 63) (*Αὐρ. Τ.*)

Τριτωνίς
THRACE:
—HADRIANOPOLIS: **(1)** imp.? Dumont–Homolle 62 (*Τρει-*: m. *Ὀνησιφῶν*)

Τρόπος
MACEDONIA (MYGDONIA):
—KALINDOIA: **(1)** 254 AD *SEG* XLII 604, 2 (*Αὐρ. Τ.*: s. *Αὐρ. Διοσκουρίδης, Αὐρ. Καλλώ*, ?f. *Ἀλεξάνδρα*)

Τροφιμᾶς
MACEDONIA (EDONIS):
—AMPHIPOLIS: **(1)** ii-iii AD ib. XXXIV 608

Τροφίμη
MACEDONIA (BOTTIAIA):
—BEROIA: **(1)** 186 AD *ILeukopetra* 19, 1 (Tataki 1001) (*Ὀφελλία Τ.*); **(2)** 238 AD *ILeukopetra* 89, 3 (*Αὐρ. Τ.*: d. *Φίλιππος*)
MACEDONIA (EDONIS):
—PHILIPPOI: **(3)** imp. *BCH* 47 (1923) p. 94 no. 30 (Pilhofer 89) (Lat. Valeria Trophime)
MACEDONIA (MYGDONIA):
—THESSALONIKE: **(4)** ii AD *IG* X (2) (1) 509; **(5)** c. 165 AD ib. 484, 2, 11 (*Κουσωνία Ἄλκη* (*ἡ*) *καὶ Τ.*: m. *Κουσωνία Τιβερῖνα*)

Τροφιμιανός
MACEDONIA (EDONIS):
—PHILIPPOI?: **(1)** 196 AD *IMS* II 53 III a, 114 (*CIL* III 14507); cf. *ZPE* 146 (2004) pp. 216-20 (Lat. C. Val. Trophimian(us))

Τρόφιμος
CIMMERIAN BOSPOROS:
—HERMONASSA: **(1)** s. v AD *CIRB* 1099, 8 (*SEG* XXXIX 697)
—PANTIKAPAION: **(2)** v-vi AD *ZOOID* 21 (1898) p. 205 no. 16; **(3)** ~ ib. 31 (1913) p. 72 no. 171; **(4)** vi AD *IAK* 10 (1904) p. 88 no. 102
MACEDONIA (BOTTIAIA):
—BEROIA: **(5)** a. 212 AD *IBer* 136, 9 (Tataki 419) (*Δομ. Τρόφιμ[ος]*)
—EDESSA: **(6)** ii AD *SEG* XII 343 (Tataki, *Edessa* 177) (*Κουριάτιος Τ.*)
MACEDONIA (DERRIOPOS):
—STUBERRA: **(7)** 126 AD *IG* X (2) (2) 336 (*Π. Ἀνθέστιος Τ.*)
MACEDONIA (EDONIS):
—PHILIPPOI: **(8)** imp. *BCH* 58 (1934) p. 475 no. 15 (Pilhofer 277) (Lat. C. Vibius Trophimus: II ?s. *Τρόφιμος* I); **(9)** ~ *BCH* 58 (1934) p. 475 nos. 15-16 (Pilhofer 277-8) (Lat. Vibius Trophimus: I ?f. *Τρόφιμος* II); **(10)** ii/iii AD *CIL* III 633 II b, 19 (Pilhofer 163); *CRAI* 1923, p. 277 (date); Collart, *Philippes* pls. 64-5 (Lat. C. Paccius Trophimus); **(11)** ~ *CIL* III 633 III b, 7 (Pilhofer 165 with note) (Lat. -us Trophimus)
MACEDONIA (MYGDONIA):
—THESSALONIKE: **(12)** ii AD *IG* X (2) (1) 530, 2 (*Τ. Σερβείλιος Τρόφι(μος)*: f. *Σερβιλία Ὑγίνη*); **(13)** s. ii AD ib. 244 II, 11 (*M. Οὔλπ. Τ.*)
MACEDONIA (ORESTIS):
—BATTYNAIOI: **(14)** 192 AD *EAM* 186, 42
MACEDONIA (PIERIA):
—PYDNA: **(15)** 250 AD *SEG* XLVI 800 A, 23 (*Αὐρ. Τ.*)
SCYTHIA MINOR:
—KALLATIS: **(16)** iii AD *ISM* III 185 (*Τρόφι[μος]?*)
—TOMIS: **(17)** ii-iii AD ib. II 30 ([*Τρ*]*όφιμ*[*ος*] (n.pr.?)); **(18)** ~ ib. 464 ([*Τρ*]*όφιμο*[*ς*]?)
THRACE:
—BEROE-AUGUSTA TRAIANA: **(19)** ii-iii AD *SEG* XXXIX 649, 8 (*Τ. ὁ καὶ Ἀσβόλις*: s. *Ἀπολλόδωρος*)
—BYZANTION: **(20)** i-ii AD *IByz* 266 (Firatlı–Robert p. 85 no. 105) (s. *Πάρεδρος*, f. *Ἀφφία*)
——(Delkos): **(21)** imp. *IByz* 21 (s. *Διονύσιος*)
—NICOPOLIS AD ISTRUM*: **(22)** ii AD Poulter, *Nicopolis* p. 320 no. 8 (vase-stamp) ([*Τρ*]*όφιμος*)
—ODESSOS: **(23)** ii AD *Romanizmăt* II 580 (Lat. Claudius Varius Trophimus: I f. *Τρόφιμος* II); **(24)** ~ ib. (Lat. [Cl]audius Trophimus: II s. *Τρόφιμος* I)
—PERINTHOS-HERAKLEIA: **(25)** i-ii AD *IPerinth* 98 (s. *Μάξιμα*)
—RHAIDESTOS?: **(26)** iii AD Unp. (Sayar) (*Αὐρ. Τ.*)
THRACE?: **(27)** ?ii AD Beševliev, *EP* 25 (*SEG* XV 472) ([*Τρ*]*όφιμος*); **(28)** v-vi AD Beševliev 76 (brick)

Τρόφος
SKYTHIA:
—TANAIS*: **(1)** ii-iii AD *Tanais* I p. 105 (amph.)

Τρόχας
MACEDONIA (PIERIA):
—PYDNA: **(1)** iv BC *GRBS* 43 (2002-3) p. 119 no. 5, 2, 8

Τρυγητιανός
SCYTHIA MINOR:
—CAPIDAVA: **(1)** iii-iv AD *ISM* V 43, 3 (Lat. Trygitianus: f. Acrilla)

Τρύφαινα
MACEDONIA: **(1)** c. 145-111 BC *RE* s.v. Kleopatra (25) (*PP* 14521); Grainger, *SPG* p. 47 ((*Κλεοπάτρα*)? *Τ.*: d. *Πτολεμαῖος* VIII *Εὐεργέτης, Κλεοπάτρα* III, m. *Σέλευκος* VI *Ἐπιφάνης, Ἀντίοχος* XI *Φιλάδελφος, Φίλιππος* I *Φιλάδελφος, Δημήτριος* III *Φιλοπάτωρ, Ἀντίοχος* XII *Διόνυσος, Λαοδίκη*: queen)
MACEDONIA (BOTTIAIA):
—BEROIA: **(2)** ii-iii AD *IBer* 367 (*Κεκιλία Τρύφ[αι]να*: m. *Ἀρτεμίδωρος*)
MACEDONIA (CHALKIDIKE):
—APHYTIS: **(3)** imp. *SEG* XXIX 606 (*Κορ. Τρύφενα*: m. *Κορ. Ποσειδώνιος*)
MACEDONIA (MYGDONIA):
—THESSALONIKE: **(4)** s. i AD ib. XXXVIII 702 (d. *Π. Ἔλβιος Βακχύλος*); **(5)** 134 AD *IG* X (2) (1) 573 (*Ἀννία Τ.*: d. *Ἄννιος Βάσσος*)

—THESSALONIKE?: (6) v-vi AD ib. 783 (Feissel, *RICM* 174) (-φε-)
SKYTHIA?: (7) ii AD *VDI* 1951 (1), p. 155 no. 4 (pierre errante?) (Lat. Rubria Tryphena)

Τρυφέρα
MACEDONIA (MYGDONIA):
—THESSALONIKE: (1) 141 AD *IG* X (2) (1) 448 (*Ἰουλ. Τ.*)
—THESSALONIKE*: (2) ?i-ii AD *SEG* XXVII 310 (*Ἰουλ. Τ.*: freed.)

Τρύφερος
MACEDONIA (BOTTIAIA):
—BEROIA*: (1) c. 275-280 AD *ILeukopetra* 113, 1 (freed.)

Τρυφώ
THRACE:
—ZONE: (1) s. iv BC *PAE* 1970, p. 75 (vase)

Τρύφων
CIMMERIAN BOSPOROS:
—GORGIPPIA: (1) ii-iii AD *NE* 9 (1971) p. 9 no. 6 A, 13 (*Τρύφ[ων]*)
—MYRMEKION: (2) i BC-i AD *SEG* XXVIII 643 (*Τρ̣ύ̣[φ]ων*: f. *Ἡδυν*)
—PANTIKAPAION: (3) i AD *CIRB* 351; (4) s. i AD ib. 518 (s. *Κούλιος*); (5) i/ii AD ib. 79 A, 2 (I f. *Τρύφων* II); (6) ~ ib. l. 2 (II s. *Τρύφων* I); (7) ii AD ib. 660; cf. KW pl. 44 no. 631 (f. *Ἄττας*) ?= (*9*); (8) f. ii AD *CIRB* 81, 5; cf. KW pl. 33 no. 455; (9) ~ *CIRB* 83, 9 (f. *Ἄττας*) ?= (*7*); (10) 123 AD ib. 33, 6 (*Τρύ[φω]ν*: s. *Ἀπολλώνιος*); (11) 127 AD ib. 61, 1 (s. *Ὀμψάλακος*); (12) ?s. ii AD ib. 90, 9 (f. *Ἀθη—ης*); (13) f. iv AD *IAK* 45 (1912) p. 19 no. 9 (*Τρύφων*: s. *Ἀγαθοῦς*)
—PHANAGOREIA: (14) s. i BC *CIRB* 992, 6 (*Τρ[ύ]φ[ω]ν*: s. *Γόκων*)
—THEODOSIA: (15) iii AD ib. 947 B, 11 (s. *Δαδαῖος*)
MACEDONIA: (16) m. ii BC *BGU* 2423, 37 (Tataki, *Macedonians* p. 498 no. 238); cf. La'da E1405 (f. *Ἀμμώνιος*)
MACEDONIA (BOTTIAIA):
—BEROIA: (17) ii/iii AD *IBer* 143 C, 19 (Tataki 1118) (*Πο. Τ.*); (18) ~ *IBer* 145, 2 (Tataki 986) (*Μ. Οὐαλέριος Τ.*)
MACEDONIA (EDONIS):
—AMPHIPOLIS: (19) imp. Unp. (Amphipolis) (s. *Δημήτριος*)
MACEDONIA (MYGDONIA):
—THESSALONIKE: (20) 160 AD *AD* 24 (1969) Chron. p. 300
—THESSALONIKE?: (21) ii AD *IG* X (2) (1) 713
MACEDONIA (SINTIKE):
—PARTHIKOPOLIS (NR.): (22) ii AD *IGB* IV 2295
SCYTHIA MINOR:
—ISTROS: (23) f. iii AD *ISM* I 143, 7 (f. *Αὐρ. Διογένης*)
—KALLATIS: (24) 241-244 AD ib. III 74, 11 (*Μινίκιος Τ.*)
SKYTHIA:
—OLBIA-BORYSTHENES: (25) s. ii AD *IOlbia* 81, 5 (*IOSPE* I² 94); *IOSPE* I² 143 (II s. *Τρύφων* I); (26) ~ *IOlbia* 81, 6 (*IOSPE* I² 94); *IOSPE* I² 143 (I f. *Τρύφων* II)
—TANAIS: (27) ii AD *CIRB* 1262, 19 (f. *Ὀμψάλακος*); (28) ~ ib. l. 9-10 (f. *Χαρίξενος*, *Ἀνδρομένης*); (29) f. ii AD ib. 1264 A, 14 (f. *Εὔιος*); (30) m. ii AD ib. 1238 (s. *Ἀνδρομένης*) ?= (*33*); (31) 163 AD ib. 1241, 5; (32) 188 AD ib. 1242, 18 (f. *Ἀρδάρακος*) ?= (*35*); (33) c. 200-210 AD ib. 1277, 19 (*Τρύφων*—Tokhtas'ev: s. *Ἀνδρομένης*) ?= (*30*); (34) 220 AD ib. 1278, 4 (f. *Ῥαδαμοφουρτος*); (35) ~ ib. l. 15 (f. *Ἀρδάρακος*) ?= (*32*); (36) 225 AD ib. 1279, 19 (f. *Ψυχαρίων*); (37) 228 AD ib. 1282, 16 (s. *Ψυχαρίων*); (38) 244 AD ib. 1287, 16 (f. *Δούλας*); (39) ~ ib. l. 17 (s. *Φάννης*)
THRACE:
—BYZANTION: (40) ii BC *IByz* 262 (Fıratlı–Robert p. 74 no. 80) (s. *Ματρόδωρος*, f. *Λάλα*)
—DIONYSOPOLIS: (41) ii BC *IGB* I² 22 II, 7 (s. *Διονύσιος*)

Τρυφωνᾶς
MACEDONIA (MYGDONIA):
—KALINDOIA: (1) 68-98 AD *SEG* XLII 580, 4 (s. *Ἄτταλος*); (2) ~ ib. l. 49, 52-3 (f. *Διογένης*, *Εὐήμερος*, *Παράμονος*); (3) a. 98 AD ib. 583, 15 (f. *Εὔτυχος*)

Τρυφωνιανή
MACEDONIA (MYGDONIA):
—THESSALONIKE?: (1) ?v AD *IG* X (2) (1) 784, 4 (Feissel, *RICM* 159)

Τρυφωνίς
CIMMERIAN BOSPOROS:
—PANTIKAPAION: (1) i BC *CIRB* 128, 1, 6 (*GVI* 845) (m. *Λεύκιος*, *Ἡρακλεόδωρος*, *Στρατονίκη*)

Τρυφῶσα
THRACE:
—BYZANTION: (1) ii BC *IByz* 165 (Fıratlı–Robert p. 108 no. 172) (d. *Νοήμων*); (2) ii-i BC *IByz* 221 (Fıratlı–Robert p. 79 no. 90) (d. *Ἀπολλώνιος*)
—ODESSOS: (3) i-ii AD *IGB* I² 202 ([*Τρυ*]*φῶσα*?: d. *Ἱερώνυμος*); (4) s. ii AD ib. 175 (PM 1739); *Dacia* 21 (1977) p. 161 (date) (d. *Ξένανδρος*)

Τρωάδας
THRACE:
—BYZANTION (TERRIT.): (1) imp. Unp. (Sayar) (s. *Ἀπφουτίων*)

Τρωΐλος
MACEDONIA (MYGDONIA):
—KALINDOIA: (1) c. 334 BC Hatzopoulos, *MI* 2 p. 84 no. 62, 11 (s. *Ἀντίγονος*)
THRACE:
—MONTANA: (2) f. iii AD *CIL* III 7447 (*Montana* II 56) (Lat. [V]illanius T[ro]ilus)
—NICOPOLIS AD ISTRUM (TERRIT.): (3) 227 AD *ILB* 438 I, 47 (Lat. Troil(us): s. *Μάργος*)

Τσουκολειζις?
MACEDONIA (EDONIS):
—AMPHIPOLIS: (1) ii-iii AD *Thrakika* 13 (1940) p. 28 *T* + *Epigraphica* 37 (1975) p. 30 (*Τσουκολειζι* (gen.))

Τυαίης
CIMMERIAN BOSPOROS:
—PANTIKAPAION: (1) f. iv BC *CIRB* 227; Zgusta, *PNS* 718 (s. *Ἴξις*); (2) ~ *CIRB* 228 (s. *Τέττευος*)

Τύδδα
MACEDONIA (BOTTIAIA):
—BEROIA: (1) ii AD *IBer* 84 + *Chiron* 31 (2001) pp. 446-7 (*Ἀννία Τ.*)

Τυλλῆς
CIMMERIAN BOSPOROS:
—PANTIKAPAION: (1) i BC *CIRB* 275; Zgusta, *PNS* 831 (*Τύλλεως* (gen.): f. *Ἔρως*)

Τυνδάριχος
THRACE:
—APOLLONIA-SOZOPOLIS: (1) v/iv BC *Fouilles et Recherches* (Sofia) 2 (1948) p. 40 (vase)
—MESAMBRIA: (2) iv BC *IGB* I² 330 bis (PM 997); (3) iii BC *IGB* I² 307 bis, 2 (s. *Καλλισθένης*)

Τύραννα
MACEDONIA (BOTTIAIA):
—BEROIA: (1) ii-iii AD *IBer* 219; cf. Tataki 1247 (*Κλ. Τ.*: d. *Κλ. Βακχίς*)

Τυραννίς
MACEDONIA (CHALKIDIKE):
—POTIDAIA-KASSANDREIA: (1) i-ii AD *TAPA* 69 (1938) p. 66 no. 18 (*Κορνιφικία Τ.*)
MACEDONIA (MYGDONIA):
—THESSALONIKE?: (2) ii AD *IG* X (2) (1) 863 (*Τυρ<ρ>αν(ν)ίς*: m. *Ἰουνία*)
MACEDONIA (PIERIA):
—DION: (3) i-ii AD Oikonomos 12 (*Κασσία Τυρρανίς*)
SCYTHIA MINOR:
—TROESMIS*: (4) ii AD *ISM* V 177, 5 (Lat. Antonia Tyrannis: freed.)
THRACE:
—PERINTHOS-HERAKLEIA: (5) i-ii AD *IPerinth* 98 (m. *Μάξιμα*)

Τύραννος
MACEDONIA (BOTTIAIA):
—BEROIA: (1) i AD *IBer* 125, 6 (Tataki 1248) (s. *Ἀλέξανδρος*)
MACEDONIA (EDONIS):
—PHILIPPOI: (2) imp. *BCH* 57 (1933) p. 327 no. 5 (Pilhofer 220) (Lat. Tyrannus)
MACEDONIA (MYGDONIA):
—THESSALONIKE*: (3) ii AD *Ancient Macedonia* 5 p. 1557 no. 6 (Lat. Tyrannus: imp. slave)
THRACE:
—BYZANTION: (4) i BC-i AD *IByz* 102 (Fıratlı–Robert p. 95 no. 133) (s. *Γοργίας*)
—PHILIPPOPOLIS-TRIMONTIUM: (5) c. 303 AD *Anal. Boll.* 31 (1912) p. 192
—SERDICA: (6) imp. Minkova, *PNLIB* p. 267 (Lat. [Ty]rannus)

Τυρέλσης
THRACE:
—BEROE-AUGUSTA TRAIANA:
——Emporion Diskodouraterai: (1) iii AD *IGB* II 737, 3 (*Τυρέ(λ)σης*: f. *Αὐρ. Δίνδας*)
—TOPEIROS: (2) i AD *Thrakika* 8 (1937) pp. 30-1 no. 9 (*IThrakAig* E87) (f. *Ζυκουλήσης*) ?= (*3*); (3) ~ *SEG* XXXIII 535 (*IThrakAig* E86) (f. *Ζυκουλήσης*) ?= (*2*) (*4*)
—TOPEIROS?: (4) 46-54 AD *SEG* XVI 415 III, 33 (*IThrakAig* E84) (f. *Ζυκουλήσης*) ?= (*3*)

Τύριλλος
MACEDONIA (PIERIS):
—NEAPOLIS: (1) ?276 or 267 BC *FD* III (4) 414, 13 (Tataki, *Macedonians* p. 127 no. 19)

Τυρίμμας
MACEDONIA: (1) her.? *FGrH* 631 F 1; D.S. vii 15. 1 (Tataki, *Macedonians* p. 442 no. 20) (s. *Κοῖνος*, f. *Περδίκκας* I: fict.?); (2) iv BC Arr., *An.* iii 12. 4 (Tataki, *Macedonians* p. 442 no. 21) (f. *Ἀγάθων*)

Τύριος
MACEDONIA (BOTTIAIA):
—BEROIA: (1) ii BC *IBer* 160 (Tataki 1251) (s. *Ἀνδρόμαχος*); (2) ~ *SEG* XXIV 504 a-b; 504 d; *IBer* 160 (stemma) (Tataki 1252) (s. *Ἀνδρόμαχος*, f. *Ἀνδρόμαχος*, *Γαλέστης*)

Τύρισσα
MACEDONIA (MYGDONIA):
—THESSALONIKE?: (1) ii-iii AD *IG* X (2) (1) 899 (*Φουρία Τ.*)

Τυχαροῦς
MACEDONIA (MYGDONIA):
—THESSALONIKE: (1) ii-iii AD *SEG* L 642 (*Τυχαροῦτι* (dat.): m. *Φλ. Διονύσιος*)
THRACE:
—TOPEIROS: (2) ii-iii AD *Thrakika* 8 (1937) p. 18 no. 2 + Robert, *EEP* p. 192 (*IThrakAig* E93) (*Λολλία Τυχαροῦτι* (dat.))

Τυχαρώ
MACEDONIA (PIERIA):
—DION: **(1)** ?35 AD Oikonomos 14 (m. *Παραμονιχία*)

Τύχη
MACEDONIA (MYGDONIA):
—THESSALONIKE: **(1)** ii AD *IG* x (2) (1) 383, 2, 5 (*Οὐαλερία Τ.*); **(2)** iii AD ib. 824, 1
—THESSALONIKE?: **(3)** ii AD ib. 697; **(4)** ii-iii AD ib. 733 (*Κυντία Τ.*: ?m. *Γ. Κύντις Παρδαλᾶς*)
MACEDONIA (PAIONIA):
—ARGOS (NR.): **(5)** ii-iii AD *SEG* XVI 401, 3 (d. *Εὔτροπος, Ἀγάθη*)
TAURIS:
—CHERSONESOS: **(6)** ii AD *IOSPE* I² 508 (biling.) (Solomonik, *LNKhT* 23) (Lat. Tyche)
THRACE:
—BYZANTION: **(7)** i BC-i AD *IByz* 132 (Fıratlı–Robert p. 98 no. 145) (d. *Μητρόδωρος*); **(8)** i-ii AD *IByz* 278 (d. *Ἀλέξανδρος*)
—BYZANTION (TERRIT.): **(9)** imp. ib. 237
—NOVAE: **(10)** f. ii AD *IGLNovae* 94, 4 (*ILB* 326) (Lat. Atroniae Tycheni (dat.): m. M. Atronius Valens)
—OESCUS: **(11)** f. ii AD *CIL* III 7428 (*ILB* 56) (Lat. Iulia Tyche: m. C. Iulius Crescens)

Τυχικός
MACEDONIA (MYGDONIA):
—THESSALONIKE: **(1)** ?ii AD *IG* x (2) (1) 127, 5 (*M. Ἐρένιος Τ.*)
—THESSALONIKE?: **(2)** ii AD ib. 699

MACEDONIA (ORESTIS):
—SISANI (MOD.): **(3)** 146 AD *EAM* 187, 14 (s. *Κόϊντος*)

Τύχων
MACEDONIA (EDONIS):
—DATOS*: **(1)** 357 BC Hp., *Epid.* V 95; VII 121
SKYTHIA:
—OLBIA-BORYSTHENES: **(2)** c. 525-500 BC Dubois, *IGDOlbia* 62 (vase) (s. *Ἑκατοκλῆς*) ?= (*3*); **(3)** ~ ib. 63 (vase) ?= (*2*)
—OLBIA-BORYSTHENES (BEREZAN (MOD.)): **(4)** s. vi BC *SEG* XXXII 771 (vase); cf. XLVIII 989
TAURIS:
—TAUROI: **(5)** V BC *CIRB* 114 (*CEG* I 175)

Υ

Ὑαῖος
MACEDONIA (SINTIKE):
—PARTHIKOPOLIS: **(1)** ii AD *IGB* IV 2277 ((*Γ*)*αῖος*?: f. *Πύρσος*)

Ὑάκινθος
CIMMERIAN BOSPOROS:
—PANTIKAPAION: **(1)** i AD *CIRB* 519
MACEDONIA (MYGDONIA):
—THESSALONIKE: **(2)** i AD *IG* x (2) (1) 259, 29 + *SEG* XXX 622 (*N. Τερραῖος Ὑ.*); **(3)** s. i AD *IG* x (2) (1) 68, 20; 69, 15 + *BCH* 97 (1973) p. 586 (f. *Εὐβουλίδης*)
MACEDONIA (ORESTIS): **(4)** ii/iii AD *GVI* 1033 (*EAM* 194)
—BATTYNAIOI: **(5)** 192 AD ib. 186 III, 59 (s. *Ἐπιχάρης*)
THRACE:
—BIZYE: **(6)** c. 153 AD Taşlıklıoğlu 2 p. 67 no. 1, 14 + *BE* 1972, no. 292 (f. *Ῥάζδος*)
—ODESSOS: **(7)** ii-iii AD *IGB* I² 222, 7 (*GVI* 1145)
—PHILIPPOPOLIS-TRIMONTIUM (TERRIT.): **(8)** ii-iii AD *IGB* III 1433 (f. *Εὐφράτης*)

Ὑβρεῖς
THRACE:
—APOLLONIA-SOZOPOLIS: **(1)** iii BC ib. I² 458, 3 (d. *Ξέρξης*)

Ὑβρίστας
MACEDONIA (BOTTIAIA):
—BEROIA: **(1)** 117 BC *IBer* 134, 25 (s. *—τος*)

Ὑγιαίνων
CIMMERIAN BOSPOROS:
—ACHILLEION: **(1)** i AD *CIRB* 1023 (f. *Βάκχιος*); **(2)** ~ ib. 1024 (s. *Κολλαρίων*); **(3)** ii AD ib. 1035 (*Ὑγιαί*(*ν*)*ων*)
—BOSPOROS: **(4)** iii/ii BC Shelov, *CB* pp. 157-9 (coins); Minns, *Scythians* p. 585 (tiles) (*IGAIMK* 104 (1935) p. 312 nos. 92-3); *AJNum* 10 (1998) pp. 61-70 (date); *Evraz. drevn.* p. 296
—PANTIKAPAION: **(5)** i BC *CIRB* 291; cf. KW pl. 32 no. 448 (I f. *Ὑγιαίνων* II); **(6)** ~ *CIRB* 291; cf. KW pl. 32 no. 448 (II s. *Ὑγιαίνων* I); **(7)** i BC/i AD *CIRB* 300 (f. *Ψυχαρίων*); **(8)** i AD ib. 450 (-*άνων*: s. *Ἡγουμενός, Λόλησον*); **(9)** ~ ib. 520 (s. *Φαρνάκης*); **(10)** s. i AD ib. 559 (f. *Ψυχαρίων*); **(11)** 210 AD ib. 97, 3 (-*γιέ*-)
SARMATIA:
—SARMATAI: **(12)** inc. *IG* II² 10244 (*FRA* 6600) (*Ὑγυλινων*—apogr., *Ὑγ*(*ια*)*ίνων*?: slave?)

SCYTHIA MINOR:
—KALLATIS: **(13)** 241-244 AD *ISM* III 74, 10 (f. *Ἀσκληπιάδης*); **(14)** ~ ib. 74 A, 16 (s. *Ἡραίων*)
—KALLATIS?: **(15)** ii/i BC *IGB* II 867 a, 5 = *ISM* I 219 (V 87); cf. *ISM* III p. 140 (locn.) (*Ὑγιαί*[*νων*]: f. *Ἀρτεμίδωρος*)
—TOMIS: **(16)** i BC ib. II 2 B, 52 (f. *Ἀπολλώνιος*)
THRACE:
—DIONYSOPOLIS: **(17)** ii BC *IGB* I² 22 II, 6 (f. *Πεδιεύς*)

Ὑγίεια
MACEDONIA (MYGDONIA):
—THESSALONIKE: **(1)** ii AD *IG* x (2) (1) 324 (*Φλ. Ὑγεία*); **(2)** ii-iii AD ib. 510 (d. *Ἐαρίνη*); **(3)** ~ ib. (m. *Ἐαρίνη*)
MACEDONIA (ORESTIS):
—SISANI (MOD.): **(4)** 146 AD *EAM* 187, 18 (-*γεί*-: m. *Σιλουανός*)
THRACE:
—BYZANTION: **(5)** i BC-i AD *IByz* 133 (Fıratlı–Robert pp. 98-9 no. 146) (-*γεία*: d. *Εὐκλέων*)
—BYZANTION?: **(6)** ii-i BC *IByz* 344 (Fıratlı–Robert p. 128 no. 217) (-*γία*: d. *Εὐκλέων*)

Ὑγιηνός
MACEDONIA (MYGDONIA):
—LETE: **(1)** ii AD *Makedonika* 2 (1951) p. 619 no. 42 *θ*, 5 (I f. *Ὑγιηνός* II); **(2)** ~ ib. l. 5 (II s. *Ὑγιηνός* I)
THRACE: **(3)** 46-54 AD *SEG* XVI 415 III, 31 (*IThrakAig* E84) (f. *Κότυς*)

Ὑγινέρως?
CIMMERIAN BOSPOROS:
—BOSPOROS: **(1)** iv BC *SEG* XXV 272 (*Ag.* XVII 440; *FRA* 1376) ([*Ὑ*]*γεινέρω*[*ς*]?)

Ὑγίνη
MACEDONIA (MYGDONIA):
—THESSALONIKE: **(1)** ii AD *IG* x (2) (1) 530, 1 (*Σερβειλία Ὑγείνη*: d. *Τ. Σερβίλιος Τρόφιμος, Βειφανία Νίκη*); **(2)** ii-iii AD ib. 435; 487; p. 160 (stemma) (*Δομιτία Ὑγείνη*: d. *Δομίτιος Ὑγῖνος*, m. *Δομιτία Λεοντίς*); **(3)** ~ ib. 505, 1 (*Οὐαρεινία Ὑ.*: m. *Ἀλέξανδρος, Ἐπίκτητος*)

Ὑγῖνος
MACEDONIA (BOTTIAIA):
—BEROIA: **(1)** i BC-i AD *IBer* 142, 6 (Tataki 1255) (-*γεῖ*-: s. *Κλέων*); **(2)** ii/iii AD *IBer* 143 C, 14 (Tataki 624) (*Ἰού. Ὑγεῖνος*)
MACEDONIA (DERRIOPOS): **(3)** f. ii AD *IG* x (2) (2) 305 (*Τ. Φ. Ὑγεῖνος*: f. *Φ. Τειφάνιος, Φ. Διονύσιος, Φ. Φιλόξενος*: freed.)

MACEDONIA (EDONIS):
—PHILIPPOI (NR.): **(4)** i-ii AD *BCH* 47 (1923) p. 93 no. 26 (Pilhofer 454) (Lat. Oppius Hyginus: s. *Δαφνίς*)
MACEDONIA (MYGDONIA):
—THESSALONIKE: **(5)** ii-iii AD *IG* x (2) (1) 435; p. 160 (stemma) (*Δομίτιος Ὑγεῖνος*: f. *Γν. Δομίτιος Κάλλιστος, Δομιτία Ὑγίνη, Δομιτία Νίκη*)
SCYTHIA MINOR:
—TOMIS: **(6)** 201 AD *ISM* II 83 I, 38 (*Αὐρ. Ὑγεῖνος*)
THRACE:
—MADYTOS: **(7)** imp. *ISestos* 59 (-*γεῖ*-: f. *Γερμανός*)
—SERDICA: **(8)** iii AD *IGB* IV 1954, 1 (*Αὐρ. Ὑγεῖνος*)

Ὕγιος
THRACE:
—MARKIANOPOLIS (TERRIT.): **(1)** f. iii AD *IGB* II 858 (*CCET* II (1) 251) (s. *Εἰτίζενις*)

Ὕδνα
MACEDONIA (CHALKIDIKE):
—SKIONE: **(1)** 480 BC *RE* s.v. Hydne (-); Paus. X 19. 1; *Suppl. Hell.* p. 2 sub no. 5 (d. *Σκύλλις*)

Ὑκονόης
THRACE:
—HADRIANOPOLIS (TERRIT.): **(1)** iii AD *IGB* III 1817 (*Ὑκονόηος* (gen.): f. *Πίστος*)

Ὑλαῖος
CIMMERIAN BOSPOROS:
—GORGIPPIA: **(1)** f. iii BC *CIRB* 1137 B I, 39; 1137 B II, 9 (s. *Σίνδος*) ?= (*2*); **(2)** ~ ib. l. 46 (f. *Σίνδος*) ?= (*3*) (*1*); **(3)** ~ ib. l. 52 (I f. *Ὑλαῖος* II) ?= (*2*); **(4)** ~ ib. l. 52 (II s. *Ὑλαῖος* I)
MACEDONIA (DERRIOPOS):
—STUBERRA: **(5)** 74 AD *IG* x (2) (2) 325, 58 (s. *Νικανός*)

Ὕλας
MACEDONIA (MYGDONIA):
—THESSALONIKE: **(1)** 52 AD *CIL* XVI 1 (Lat. M. Minius Hyla)
MACEDONIA (PIERIA):
—DION: **(2)** imp. *ILGR* 186 (Lat. L. Iulius Hyla)
SCYTHIA MINOR:
—TOMIS: **(3)** ii-iii AD *ISM* II 372 (*GVI* 987; *CCET* IV 32) (f. *Ἑρμογένης, Πανθήρα*)
THRACE:
—TOPEIROS (NR.): **(4)** iii AD *IThrakAig* E98

Ὕλη
MACEDONIA (MYGDONIA):
—THESSALONIKE: (1) ii-iii AD *IG* X (2) (1) 1026, 1 (*GVI* 1093; Tataki, *Macedonians* p. 187 no. 66) ([Ὕ]λη)

Ὕλλος
MACEDONIA: (1) f. iii AD *SEG* XLVIII 880 (f. *Δουλαῖος*)
MACEDONIA (EDONIS):
—AMPHIPOLIS?: (2) 359-336 BC *FGrH* 257 F 36. 1 (fict.?)

Ὑμεναῖος
CIMMERIAN BOSPOROS:
—PANTIKAPAION: (1) iii/ii BC *CIRB* 255 (f. *Μοσχίων*)

Ὑμένιος
THRACE:
—PERINTHOS-HERAKLEIA: (1) iii AD *IPerinth* 159, 1 (*Αὐρ. Ὑ.*, *Ὑμεν(α)ῖος*?)

Ὑμνίς
MACEDONIA (PIERIA):
—DION?: (1) ii/iii AD Spiliopoulou-Donderer, *KGN* p. 199 no. D17 (*Αἰλ. Ὑ.*: m. *Ἄδυμος*)
THRACE:
—BYZANTION?: (2) ii-iii AD *IByz* 367 (d. *Μενίσκος*)

Ὕμνος
MACEDONIA (DERRIOPOS):
—STUBERRA: (1) 74 AD *IG* X (2) (2) 326, 30 (s. *Ἔρως*)
MACEDONIA (MYGDONIA):
—THESSALONIKE?: (2) ii-iii AD ib. X (2) (1) 748 (*Π. Λίβιος Ὑ.*)
TAURIS:
—CHERSONESOS: (3) s. iv BC *IOSPE* I² 494 (Ὑμν[ος]: f. *Σώπολις*); (4) f. iii BC *SEG* XL 615 A, 11, [12-13] (s. *Σκύθας*); (5) s. iii BC Kats p. 113 no. 115 (amph.) (f. *Σώπολις*); (6) c. 230-220 BC Anokhin p. 142 no. 123 (coin) ?= (9) (7); (7) c. 230-215 BC Kats p. 114 no. 119 (amph., tile) (s. *Σκύθας*) ?= (6); (8) c. 215-200 BC ib. p. 114 no. 120 (amph.) ([Ὕ]μνος: s. *Εὐπάλαμος*); (9) c. 210-200 BC Anokhin p. 143 nos. 133; 138 (coins) ?= (6); (10) 194 BC *Syll*³ 585, 19 (s. *Σκύθας*)
THRACE:
—KALLIPOLIS (NR.): (11) i-ii AD *ISestos* 67 (*Γ. Ἰούλ. Ὑ.*: s. *Ἅβρος*)

Ὑμνώδης
THRACE:
—PERINTHOS-HERAKLEIA: (1) iii AD *IPerinth* 158 (f. *Δεκνία Κουκία Μαρκιανή*)

Ὕπανις
SKYTHIA:
—OLBIA-BORYSTHENES: (1) ii AD *IOSPE* I² 134, 8; Zgusta, *PNS* 782 (f. *Πέλδιος*)

Ὑπάνιχος
SKYTHIA:
—OLBIA-BORYSTHENES: (1) v BC Dubois, *IGD-Olbia* 101 (f. *Ἀπατούριος*)

Ὕπανος
SKYTHIA:
—OLBIA-BORYSTHENES (ACHILLEIOS DR.): (1) ii-iii AD *IOSPE* I² 329; Zgusta, *PNS* 782

Ὕπασις?
SKYTHIA:
—OLBIA-BORYSTHENES*: (1) m. vi BC *SEG* XLIV 668 (vase); cf. *BE* 1996, no. 301 (*Ὑπάσιος* (gen.)—edd., *Πάσιος*? (nom.)—Vinogradov: ?f. *Ἄρτεμις*)

Ὑπατία
THRACE:
—APROI: (1) iv-v AD Unp. (Sayar) (d. *Ἐλλακόμη*)
—ODESSOS: (2) v-vi AD Beševliev 115, 3

Ὑπατιανός
THRACE:
—PERINTHOS-HERAKLEIA: (1) c. 303-305 AD Latyshev, *Menolog. anon.* pp. 26; 314

Ὑπάτιος
MACEDONIA (MYGDONIA):
—THESSALONIKE?: (1) iv AD *PLRE* I (4); *RE* (1) (*Φλ. Ὑ.*: ?s. *Φλ. Εὐσέβιος*)

Ὑπεράνθης
THRACE:
—PERINTHOS-HERAKLEIA: (1) ii AD X. Eph. iii. 2 etc. (fict.)

Ὑπερβάσσας
MACEDONIA?: (1) s. iii BC *IG* XII (6) 344; cf. *PP* 15772; *ID* Index s.v. (s. *Ἐτεωνεύς*, f. *Ἰάμνεια*, *Μυρσίνη*)

Ὑπερείδης
THRACE:
—PERINTHOS-HERAKLEIA:
——(Podargoi): (1) iii-ii BC *IPerinth* 61, 24 (*Ὑπερχιδης*—apogr., *Ὑπερ(ε)ίδης*—edd., *Ὑπερ(ο)χίδης*?)

Ὑπερέχων
MACEDONIA (BOTTIAIA):
—BEROIA: (1) a. 212 AD *IBer* 136, 27 (Tataki 1331) (*Φλ. Ὑ.*)

Ὑπερήφανος
MACEDONIA (MYGDONIA):
—THESSALONIKE: (1) ii AD *IG* X (2) (1) 456, 13 (s. *Εὐτυχία*)

Ὑπέροχος
TAURIS:
—CHERSONESOS: (1) c. 500-475 BC *SEG* XL 612. 3 (ostrakon) ([Ὑπ]έροχος: f. *—ίων*)

Ὑπέρτατος
MACEDONIA (CHALKIDIKE):
—POTIDAIA-KASSANDREIA: (1) iii BC *IG* XII (9) 828 (Tataki, *Macedonians* p. 96 no. 94) ([Ὑπ]έρτατος: f. *Πολέμων*)

Ὕψα
THRACE:
—ODESSOS: (1) ii-i BC *IGB* I² 153 (d. *Ἀθηναγόρας*)

Ὑψιγόνη
CIMMERIAN BOSPOROS:
—PANTIKAPAION: (1) i BC-i AD *CIRB* 521; cf. KW pl. 17 no. 243; (2) imp. *CIRB* 769

Ὑψίγονος
CIMMERIAN BOSPOROS:
—PANTIKAPAION: (1) i AD ib. 573; cf. KW pl. 26 no. 389; (2) ?f. i AD *CIRB* 527, 5 (s. *Φαρνάκης*, *Μητροφίλα*)
MACEDONIA (ORESTIS):
—SISANI (MOD.): (3) 146 AD *EAM* 187, 17 (s. *Εὔτακτος*)
SCYTHIA MINOR:
—TOMIS: (4) ii-iii AD *ISM* II 277 (?s. *Μέννης*)

Ὑψίδης
MACEDONIA: (1) 329 BC Curt. vii 7. 36-7; *RE* Supplbd. 4 (-); Berve 764 (Tataki, *Macedonians* p. 443 no. 1) (Lat. Hypsides—Curt. 37, Hypsicles—Eberhardt)

Ὑψικλῆς
CIMMERIAN BOSPOROS:
—GORGIPPIA: (1) f. iii BC *CIRB* 1137 A II, 4 (I f. *Ὑψικλῆς* II) ?= (6); (2) ~ ib. l. 4 (II s. *Ὑψικλῆς* I) ?= (7); (3) ~ ib. l. 8 (f. *Ζώπυρος*); (4) ~ ib. l. 25; 1137 B II, 28 (s. *Φιλίσκος*); (5) ~ ib. 1137 B I, 21 (f. *—λης*); (6) ~ ib. 1137 B II, 3 ([Ὑ]ψικλῆ[ς]: I f. *Ὑψικλῆς* II) ?= (1); (7) ~ ib. l. 3 ([Ὑψ]ικλῆ[ς]?: II s. *Ὑψικλῆς* I) ?= (2)

Ὑψικράτης
CIMMERIAN BOSPOROS:
—PANTIKAPAION: (1) i AD ib. 522; cf. KW pl. 40 no. 594 (s. *Λάμαχος*)
SKYTHIA:
—TANAIS: (2) ii AD *CIRB* 1263, 13 (Ὑ[ψι]κράτης: s. *Ἐ—*)

Ὑψικρέων
SKYTHIA:
—OLBIA-BORYSTHENES: (1) iii BC *IOSPE* I² 190 b (f. *Τιμώ*)

Φ

Φαβία
MACEDONIA (BOTTIAIA):
—BEROIA: (1) ii AD *IBer* 330, 1, 5 (Tataki 1256) (m. *Συμφορίων*, *Ποθείνη*, *Φάβιος*)

Φάβιος
MACEDONIA (BOTTIAIA):
—BEROIA: (1) ii AD *IBer* 330, 2 (Tataki 1257) (s. *Σύμφορος*, *Φαβία*)
—EDESSA: (2) ii AD Dimitsas 24 (*Makedonika* 15 (1975) p. 202; Tataki, *Edessa* 296)

Φάβις
MACEDONIA (MYGDONIA):
—LETE (NR.): (1) 171 or 288 AD *SEG* XXXI 633 b; cf. XXXV 751

Φαβρικιανός
MACEDONIA (BOTTIAIA):
—BEROIA: (1) i-ii AD *IBer* 11, 6 (Tataki 1258)

Φαβρίκιος
MACEDONIA (LYNKESTIS):
—HERAKLEIA (NR.): (1) ii-iii AD *IG* X (2) (2) 8 (slave?)

Φαδιανός
THRACE:
—SERDICA: (1) ii AD *IGB* IV 1923, 8 (f. *—ος*)

Φαδιαρόαζος
SKYTHIA:
—TANAIS: (1) 228 AD *CIRB* 1282, 11; Zgusta, *PNS* 335 (s. *Πόπλιος*)

Φαδίναμος
CIMMERIAN BOSPOROS:
—PANTIKAPAION: (1) 275-278 AD *CIRB* 36, 26; Zgusta, *PNS* 233 (*Φαδίναμ[ος]*: s. *Ἄρδαρος*)
SKYTHIA:
—TANAIS: (2) ii AD *CIRB* 1263, 9 (*Φαδ(ί)ν̣α̣[μ]ος*—Tokhtas'ev: s. *Ἡ*—); (3) c. 200-210 AD ib. 1277, 27 (*Φαδίνα[μος]*); (4) c. 225-250 AD ib. 1288, 9 (s. *Καλλιστίων*) ?= (*Φαζίναμος (12)*); (5) ~ ib. l. 10 (*Φ̣α̣δίναμος*: f. *Μύρμηξ*); (6) 228 AD ib. 1282, 9 (f. *Ἀθηνόδωρος*); (7) ~ ib. l. 13 (f. *Ὀμψάλακος*); (8) 236 AD ib. 1250, 14 (f. *Μενέστρατος*)

Φαδιους
CIMMERIAN BOSPOROS:
—FRONTOVOE (MOD.): (1) ii/iii AD *SEG* XXXV 869. 2; cf. *BE* 1990, no. 592; Zgusta, *PNS* 232 (f. *Νικίας*)
—PANTIKAPAION: (2) 275-278 AD *CIRB* 36, 31 (s. *Πάμφιλος*); (3) ~ ib. l. 74 (*[Φα]διου[ς]*?)
SKYTHIA:
—TANAIS: (4) 228 AD ib. 1283, 12 (*[Φ]αδιο[υς]*: s. *Φιλήμων*)

Φαδος
THRACE:
—BYZANTION (TERRIT.): (1) imp. Unp. (Sayar) (*Φαδω* (dat.), *Φαδώ* (fem. nom.?): s. *Διονύσιος*)

Φάδσιος
CIMMERIAN BOSPOROS:
—THEODOSIA: (1) iii AD *CIRB* 947 B, 10 (f. *Φίδας*)

Φαέθουσα
THRACE:
—ABDERA: (1) iv BC Hp., *Epid.* vi 8. 32

Φαεινός
MACEDONIA (EDONIS):
—AMPHIPOLIS: (1) ii-iii AD *SEG* XXXI 621, 8 (s. *Παραμόνα*)
THRACE:
—BYZANTION: (2) 175-171 BC *IByz* 1, 51

Φαέννης
MACEDONIA (EDONIS):
—AMPHIPOLIS: (1) iii BC *AD* 26 (1971) Chron. p. 417

Φαέσαξ?
THRACE:
—PAUTALIA: (1) s. ii AD *SEG* XLVI 864, 10 (*Φαέσακος* (gen.): f. *Διογενιανός, Γάϊος*)

Φαζίναμος
SKYTHIA:
—TANAIS: (1) 188-192 AD *CIRB* 1242, 8; 1243, 12; Zgusta, *PNS* 233 (f. *Ῥόδων*); (2) f. iii AD *CIRB* 1251 a, 6 (*Φαζ[ίνα]μος*: f. *Δημήτριος*) ?= (*8*); (3) 210-226 AD ib. 1281, 12 (*Φαζ[ίν]αμος*: s. *Κα̣*—); (4) ~ ib. 1285, 14 (*[Φα]ζίναμος*: f. *Ὀμψάλακος*); (5) ~ ib. l. 15 (*Φαζίν̣[αμος]*: f. —*νόδωρος*); (6) 220 AD ib. 1278, 23 (*Φαζίναμ(ος)*: s. *Ἀρ—δαμος*); (7) 225 AD ib. 1280, 14; 1281, 17 (f. *Ἀρίστων*); (8) 225-229 AD ib. 1280, 11; *Stud. Zhebelev* p. 47, 14 (f. *Δημήτριος*) ?= (*2*); (9) 228 AD *CIRB* 1282, 8 (I f. *Φαζίναμος* II); (10) ~ ib. l. 8 (II s. *Φαζίναμος* I); (11) 244 AD ib. 1287, 4 (f. *Θέων*); (12) ~ ib. l. 5 (s. *Καλλιστίων*) ?= (*Φαδίναμος (4)*)

Φαζιους
SKYTHIA:
—TANAIS: (1) 244 AD ib. l. 25; Zgusta, *PNS* 232 (s. *Πάππος*)

Φαίδιμος
CIMMERIAN BOSPOROS:
—HERMONASSA: (1) 389-349 BC *CIRB* 1038 (s. *Φαίνιππος*); (2) 304-284 BC ib. 1043 (*[Φαί]διμος*)
MACEDONIA (MYGDONIA):
—THESSALONIKE: (3) ii-iii AD *IG* X (2) (1) 634 (f. *Γ. Κουσώνιος Τιτιανός*)
—THESSALONIKE?: (4) ii AD ib. 250 I, 4 (*Τ. Φλ. Σαβεινιανὸς Φαίδιμ̣ος̣*)
SKYTHIA:
—OLBIA-BORYSTHENES: (5) c. 350-330 BC *SNG BM Black Sea* 445 (coin) (*Φαίδι(μος)*); (6) ?ii-i BC Dubois, *IGDOlbia* 110, 1
THRACE:
—BISANTHE-PANION: (7) iii BC *RE* (9); *HE* 2901-26 with comm.; *Suppl. Hell.* 667-9 (or Paphlagonia Amastris)
—DIONYSOPOLIS: (8) iv/iii BC *IGB* I^2 26 (PM 1047)

Φαιδρίας
CIMMERIAN BOSPOROS:
—NYMPHAION: (1) v BC Tolstoi 136 (vase) (*Φαιδρί(ας)*)
SCYTHIA MINOR:
—ISTROS: (2) 138 AD *ISM* I 193 I, 74 (f. *Αἰλ. Ἀρτεμίδωρος*); (3) ~ ib. l. 97 (s. *Μενίσκος*); (4) c. 140-160 AD ib. 207, 11 (*Π. Αἰλ. Φ.*)

Φαῖδρον
MACEDONIA (PAIONIA): (1) ii BC *IG* II^2 10040 (*FRA* 5944)

Φαῖδρος
MACEDONIA (BOTTIAIA):
—BEROIA: (1) ii/iii AD *IBer* 143 C, 11 (Tataki 625) (*Ἰού. Φ.*)
SCYTHIA MINOR:
—ISTROS: (2) f. iii BC *ISM* I 257 (f. *Πολυαίνετος*); (3) ii AD ib. 211, 16 (f. *Ἀρτεμίδωρος*) ?= (*4*); (4) 138 AD ib. 193 II, 36 (f. *Ἀρτεμίδωρος*) ?= (*3*)
—TOMIS: (5) 54-59 AD *RPC* I 1835 (coin) (*Φαῖδρο(ς)*)
——(Argadeis): (6) 130-138 AD *ISM* II 52, 8 (f. *Τ. Φλ. Ποσειδώνιος*)

Φαίδων
SKYTHIA:
—OLBIA-BORYSTHENES: (1) v BC Dubois, *IGDOlbia* 34 (vase)

Φαίκων
SCYTHIA MINOR:
—KALLATIS: (1) iii/ii BC *ISM* III 161 (s. *Κλεομήδης*); (2) ii BC *IByz* 72 (Fıratlı–Robert pp. 48-9 no. 10) (s. *Ἀρτεμίδωρος*)

Φαίνιππος
CIMMERIAN BOSPOROS:
—HERMONASSA: (1) iv BC *CIRB* 1056 I, 1-2 (f. —*ων*, —*ος*); (2) c. 389-370 BC *VDI* 1967 (1), p. 64 (s. *Ἀρ—ν*); (3) 389-349 BC *CIRB* 1038 (*Φα[ίν]ιππος*: s. *Φαίδιμος*)
—PANTIKAPAION: (4) 344-311 BC ib. 9, 1 (Rhodes–Osborne 65 A); (5) c. 200-180 BC *CIRB* 26, 4 (*[Φαί]νιππος*?)
MACEDONIA (BOTTIAIA):
—MIEZA: (6) hell. *AM* 27 (1902) p. 314 no. 28, 6
THRACE:
—BISANTHE-PANION: (7) hell. Dumont–Homolle 82; (8) hell.? ib. 81b (I f. *Φαίνιππος* II); (9) ~ ib. (II s. *Φαίνιππος* I)
—ODESSOS?: (10) ii-iii AD *IGB* I^2 144, 3 (s. *Ἀπολλοφάνης*)

Φαῖσκος
THRACE:
—LYSIMACHEIA: (1) 273 BC *IG* IX (1)^2 (1) 12, 4 (f. *Φιλόνικος*)

Φαιστίς
MACEDONIA (CHALKIDIKE):
—STAGEIROS: (1) v/iv BC D.L. v 1; D.H., *Amm.* i 5; Düring pp. 82; 96; 131; 263-7 (*Φαιστιάς*—*Suda A* 3929: m. *Ἀριστοτέλης, Ἀρίμνηστος, Ἀριμνήστη*)

Φαισφάρτα
CIMMERIAN BOSPOROS:
—PANTIKAPAION: (1) 491 AD *SEG* XLVIII 996 B; *VDI* 1998 (1), p. 240 no. 5a, 7 (*Φαεισπάρτα*—*SEG*: m. *Ἀββάγαζα*)

Φαλακρίων
THRACE:
—BEROE-AUGUSTA TRAIANA: (1) iii AD *IGB* III 1592, 3 (*Αὐρ. Ἀσκληπιόδοτος ὁ καὶ Φ.*)

Φάλαρις
MACEDONIA (PIERIA):
—PHILA?: (1) ?iii BC *RPh* 1911, pp. 133-4 no. 36, 85 + *Polemon* 2 (1934-40) Parart. p. 13 no. 17; cf. Helly, *L'État thessalien* pp. 319-20 (locn.) (*Φάλαρι[ς]*: f. —*ης*)

Φαλδάρανος
SKYTHIA:
—TANAIS: (1) 220-229 AD *CIRB* 1245, 16; 1278, 17; *Stud. Zhebelev* p. 47, 16; *KSIA* 145 (1975) p. 49 (*Φαλδάρανος*—1278: s. *Ἀπολλώνιος*)

Φαναγόρης
CIMMERIAN BOSPOROS:
—PHANAGOREIA: (1) 344-311 BC *CIRB* 971 (f. *Ἀπολλόδωρος*)
THRACE:
—PERINTHOS-HERAKLEIA: (2) s. vi BC *IPerinth* 69 (*Φαναγόρεω* (gen.): f. *Ἡγησίπολις*)

Φαναῖος
THRACE:
—ABDERA: (1) c. 415-395 BC May, *Abdera* p. 166 no. 215 (coin); Masson, *OGS* p. 434 (name) (*Φανα[ῖ]ος*)

Φανδάραζος
CIMMERIAN BOSPOROS:
—GORGIPPIA: (1) ii/iii AD *CIRB* 1179, 29 (f. *Σέρεις*)

Φανέας
MACEDONIA (MYGDONIA):
—KLITAI: (1) c. 230-200 BC *BCH* 45 (1921) p. 18 III, 85 (Tataki, *Macedonians* p. 115 no. 2) (*Φανέας*: s. *Σόλων*)
THRACE:
—BYZANTION (TERRIT.): (2) imp. Unp. (Sayar) (*Φανέα* (gen.): f. *Φίλιππος*)

Φανερός
THRACE:
—DIONYSOPOLIS: (1) 241-244 AD *IGB* I^2 22 bis, 15 (f. —*ωζης*)
—ODESSOS: (2) s. iii BC ib. 36, 8 (f. *Καλλίμαχος*)

Φανέτας
THRACE:
—SALYMBRIA: (1) imp. *Archives Stamoulis* d. 35 (Loukopoulou, *Thrace Propontique* p. 294) (f. *Μαρκίων*)

Φανῆς
THRACE:
—ABDERA: (1) c. 346-336 BC May, *Abdera* pp. 280-1 nos. 495-504 (coin); Masson, *OGS* p. 434 (*Φανέω* (gen.))

Φανίας
MACEDONIA: (1) c. 205-192 BC *IG* XI (4) 1111, 8; *SEG* XLVIII 811 (Tataki, *Macedonians* p. 443 no. 1) (f. *Ἡρακλείδης, Μένιππος*)

MACEDONIA (BOTTIAIA):
—PELLA: (**2**) iii BC *SEG* XXXIX 623 (tile)

Φανικός
TAURIS:
—CHERSONESOS: (**1**) iii BC *IOSPE* I² 581, 3 (s. *Ἡρόξενος*)

Φάνιππος
THRACE:
—STRYME?: (**1**) v-iv BC *IThrakAig* E162 ([*Φ*]*άν-ιππ*[*ος*]: f. ..*αγρο̣ς̣*, ...*τα̣ς̣*)

Φάνις
CIMMERIAN BOSPOROS:
—NYMPHAION: (**1**) iv BC *CIRB* 918 (f. *Ἀναξι-πόλη*)
MACEDONIA (PIERIS):
—OISYME-EMATHIA?: (**2**) s. iv BC *PAE* 1938, p. 92 no. 1, 3 (*Φάνι*[*ς̣*])

Φανίς
MACEDONIA (EDONIS):
—AMPHIPOLIS: (**1**) f. iii BC *Ant. Kunst* 12 (1969) pp. 68-71; cf. *SEG* XLVII 879 (d. *Ἡγή-μων*, *Πιπίς*)

Φανισάλης
SKYTHIA:
—OLBIA-BORYSTHENES (NR.): (**1**) iii BC *VDI* 1985 (1), p. 41 (amph.); cf. Vinogradov, *Pont. Stud.* p. 159 no. 14 (name)

Φανίχη
THRACE:
—APOLLONIA-SOZOPOLIS: (**1**) iv BC *BMNBur-gas* 4 (2002) pp. 124-5 no. 20 (d. *Κερζέας*); (**2**) ~ *IGB* I² 427 (d. *Πολύαρχος*)

Φανίων
THRACE:
—BYZANTION: (**1**) s. iii BC Schönert-Geiss, *Byzantion* 1135-43; 1224-5 (coin)
—HERAION TEICHOS?: (**2**) ii BC Taşlıklıoğlu I p. 4 no. 1 (f. *Μοκάπορις*)

Φάννας
CIMMERIAN BOSPOROS:
—BOSPOROS: (**1**) i AD *IGUR* 763 (f. *Μακάριος*)
—PANTIKAPAION: (**2**) ii-i BC *CIRB* 292; cf. KW pl. 32 no. 449 (s. *Ἀρχέλαος*); (**3**) imp. *CIRB* 770 (s. *Γλαυκίας*); (**4**) ~ ib. 788; cf. KW p. 59 fig. 9 (f. *Ἑρμῆς*); (**5**) ~ *CIRB* 812 (s. *Σώσ-ανδρος*); (**6**) i BC/i AD ib. 320; cf. KW pl. 30 no. 427 (s. *Βίστης*); (**7**) ~ *CIRB* 320; cf. KW pl. 30 no. 427 (s. *Ὀροφέρνης*); (**8**) i-ii AD *CIRB* 639; cf. KW pl. 19 no. 271 (s. *Ξένων*, *Φιλω-τέρα*); (**9**) f. ii AD *CIRB* 682 (*Φάν̣ν̣α̣ς̣*: s. *Ἰάμ-βλοχος*); (**10**) s. ii AD *KSIA* 116 (1969) p. 53 no. 5 (s. *Ἡζοῦς*)

Φάννης
CIMMERIAN BOSPOROS:
—NYMPHAION: (**1**) i/ii AD *CIRB* 935 (*Φ*[*άν*]*νης*: s. *Ἀρίστων*)
—NYMPHAION (NR.): (**2**) iii AD ib. 941 (*Φ̣άννης*—Yailenko and Tokhtas'ev: s. *Τάμβι-σος*, f. *Ἄβας*)
—PANTIKAPAION: (**3**) i AD ib. 405; cf. KW pl. 35 no. 499 (*Φάννεως* (gen.): f. *Ἔρως*); (**4**) ~ *CIRB* 419 (f. *Ἡλίς*); (**5**) ~ ib. 523 (s. *Μενέ-μαχος*); (**6**) ~ ib. 525; cf. KW pl. 27 no. 399 (I f. *Φάννης* II); (**7**) ~ *CIRB* 525; cf. KW pl. 27 no. 399 (II s. *Φάννης* I); (**8**) ?f. i AD *CIRB* 524 (I f. *Φάννης* II); (**9**) ~ ib. (II s. *Φάννης* I); (**10**) 275-278 AD ib. 36, 16 (s. *Σακλῆς*); (**11**) ~ ib. l. 17 (*Φάν*(*ν*)*ης*: s. *Ἀγαθοῦς*); (**12**) iv-v AD *OAK* 1894, p. 89
SKYTHIA:
—TANAIS: (**13**) ii AD *CIRB* 1263, 6 (*Φ̣ά̣ν̣νης*—Tokhtas'ev: s. *Στ*—); (**14**) ~ *SEG* XXIX 719 (vase) (*Φάνηι* (dat.)—ed. pr., *Φάννη* (acc.)—Mihailov) ?= (*16*); (**15**) 155 AD *CIRB* 1260, 9, 22 (s. *Στρατόνικος*) ?= (*16*); (**16**) ~ ib. l. 28 (f. —*ν*) ?= (*14*) (*15*); (**17**) 210-226 AD ib. 1245, 4, 14; 1246, 5; 1248, [7]; 1278, 7 (f. *Ζήνων*); (**18**) ~ ib. 1285, 10 (s. *Ἀμ—ραζμος*); (**19**) 220 AD ib. 1278, 10 (s. *Δάδας*); (**20**) 224 AD ib. 1287, 17 (*Φ̣άννη*[*ς*]: f. *Τρύφων*); (**21**) 225 AD ib. 1280, 9 (I f. *Φάννης* II); (**22**) ~ ib. l. 9 (II s. *Φάννης* I); (**23**) ~ ib. l. 25 (*Φ̣ά̣ν̣ν̣η̣ς̣*: s. —*ικος*)

Φαννία
MACEDONIA (PIERIA):
—DION: (**1**) ?iii AD Oikonomos 9

Φανόδικος
SKYTHIA:
—OLBIA-BORYSTHENES: (**1**) s. vi BC *Arkheo-logiia* (Kiev) 28 (1978) p. 9 (vase)
THRACE:
—TYRODIZA-TIRISTASIS: (**2**) iii-ii BC Dumont-Homolle 90 ([*Φα*]*νόδικος*?: s. *Ἑρμόδωρος*)

Φανοκλῆς
SCYTHIA MINOR:
—ISTROS: (**1**) ii-i BC *SEG* XIX 489 a (weight) (*Φανοκλ*<*κ*>*έ*(*ους*) (gen.)); (**2**) ii AD *ISM* I 214, 5 + 226, 3; (**3**) 138 AD ib. 193 I, 30 (f. *Μει-δίας*); (**4**) ~ ib. l. 69 (s. *Μειδίας*)
THRACE:
—SALYMBRIA: (**5**) 242 BC *WChr* 335, 4; cf. La'da E2413 (f. *Θεόδωρος*)

Φανοκράτης
MACEDONIA (CHALKIDIKE):
—APHYTIS: (**1**) ?351 BC *A΄ Panell. Synedr. Epigr.* pp. 80-1, 18 (s. *Φιλώνδης*)

Φανόκριτος
MACEDONIA (BOTTIAIA):
—PELLA: (**1**) iv BC *SEG* XXIV 542 (s. *Εὔφριλλος*)

Φανόλαος
MACEDONIA (BOTTIAIA):
—PELLA: (**1**) iii BC Akamatis, *Amph. Pellas* pp. 44-5 nos. PAR67-9 (amph.) (*SEG* L 613)

Φανόλεως
MACEDONIA (CHALKIDIKE):
—OLYNTHOS: (**1**) ?352 BC *TAPA* 65 (1934) p. 128 no. 4, 8, 12; *SEG* XLVII 922; Hatzo-poulos, *Actes Chalc.* p. 80 (date) (f. *Δήμαρχος*)

Φανόμαχος
CIMMERIAN BOSPOROS:
—PANTIKAPAION: (**1**) iv BC Tolstoi 232 (vase) (*Φανόμαχ*(*ος*)); (**2**) 344-310 BC *CIRB* 113, 1 (*CEG* II 885) (f. *Ἀντίστασις*)

Φανόπολις
THRACE:
—MARONEIA: (**1**) ii-i BC *IThrakAig* E212, 20 (s. *Λεωσθένης*)

Φανόστρατος
THRACE:
—LYSIMACHEIA: (**1**) c. 208 BC *FD* III (4) 135 I, 26 ([*Φ*]*ανόσ*[*τρατος*]?, [*Φ*]*ανοσ*[*θένης*]?)

Φάνων
MACEDONIA (ODOMANTIKE):
—DRABESKOS?: (**1**) iv BC Kaphtantzis 568, 9 (Pilhofer 575) (?s. *Σκίνδας*)

Φαράδης
SKYTHIA:
—OLBIA-BORYSTHENES: (**1**) ?iv BC *IOSPE* I² 283

Φάραξ
THRACE*: (**1**) iii/ii BC *JÖAI* 23 (1926) Beibl. col. 151 no. 81 (bullet)

Φαρεσμάνης
KOLCHIS: (**1**) 503 AD Procop. i 8. 3

Φάρζηος
SKYTHIA:
—OLBIA-BORYSTHENES: (**1**) s. ii AD *IOlbia* 81, 7 (*IOSPE* I² 94); Zgusta, *PNS* 336 (f. *Χώδ-αρζος*)

Φάρζοιος
SARMATIA:
—SARMATAI: (**1**) s. i AD *RE* (-); cf. Vinogradov-Kryžickij p. 97 (coins) (king)

Φαρίων
MACEDONIA (BOTTIAIA):
—EDESSA: (**1**) 180 AD *SEG* XXIV 531, 14 (Tataki, *Edessa* 298) (f. *Φίλητος*)

Φαρνάβαζος
MACEDONIA (CHALKIDIKE):
—OLYNTHOS: (**1**) ?350 BC *TAPA* 59 (1928) p. 226, 11; Hatzopoulos, *Actes Chalc.* p. 80 (date) (s. *Εὐκλῆς*)
SKYTHIA:
—OLBIA-BORYSTHENES: (**2**) v/iv BC Dubois, *IGDOlbia* 98 (vase) (*SEG* XLVI 954); cf. Vinogradov, *Pont. Stud.* p. 157 no. 9 (name) (*Φαρνάβα*(*ζ*)*ος*)

Φάρναγος
SKYTHIA:
—OLBIA-BORYSTHENES: (**1**) i/ii AD *IOlbia* 79, 11 (*IOSPE* I² 116); Zgusta, *PNS* 236 (s. *Ζῆθος*) ?= (*Φάρνακος* (*1*)); (**2**) ii AD *IOSPE* I² 96, 7 (f. *Καζίνας*) ?= (*5*); (**3**) ~ ib. 144, 3 (*Φάρν*(*α*)*γος*: s. *Ἀχιλλεύς*); (**4**) ?ii-iii AD ib. 107, 1
—OLBIA-BORYSTHENES (BEREZAN (MOD.)): (**5**) ?ii AD *VDI* 1993 (1), p. 90 = *SEG* XLIX 1028 B, 8 (f. *Καζίνας*) ?= (*2*)
THRACE:
—ODESSOS: (**6**) ii AD *IGB* I² 64, 2 (*Φαρνά*(*κ*)*ης*—ed.: f. *Πρόσοδος*)

Φαρνάκης
CIMMERIAN BOSPOROS:
—GORGIPPIA: (**1**) imp. *CIRB* 1189, 3 (s. *Ἀθ*—) ?= (*4*); (**2**) ii AD ib. 1141, 8; Zgusta, *PNS* 236 (?s. *Φ*—); (**3**) ~ *CIRB* 1141, 13; (**4**) ~ ib. l. 15 (s. *Ἀθη*—) ?= (*1*); (**5**) ~ ib. l. 17 (*Φαρνάκη*[*ς*]); (**6**) ~ ib. l. 18 (*Φαρνάκ*[*ης*]?); (**7**) ii-iii AD *NE* 9 (1971) p. 9 no. 6 A, 8 ([*Φ*]*α̣ρνάκης*: s. *Ἀ*—); (**8**) m. ii AD *Eirene* 7 (1968) p. 67, 1 (s. *Σέλευ-κος*); (**9**) ~ ib. l. 3 (f. *Φαρνακίων*); (**10**) ~ ib. l. 9 (s. *Μοιρόδωρος*); (**11**) s. ii AD *CIRB* 1129 A, 6; *Eirene* 7 (1968) p. 67, 6 (s. *Ἔρως*) ?= (*25*); (**12**) ~ *CIRB* 1133 B, 3 ([*Φ*]*αρνάκ*[*ης*]?); (**13**) ~ ib. 1145, 5 ([*Φ*]*αρνάκης*); (**14**) ~ ib. l. 6 (s. *Πάβας*); (**15**) ~ ib. l. 6 (f. *Χρηστοῦς*); (**16**) ~ ib. l. 7 (s. *Δάσεις*); (**17**) 173-210 AD ib. 1134, 13 (s. *Νουμήνιος*); (**18**) ~ ib. l. 15 (f. *Πανταλέων*); (**19**) ~ ib. 1135, 12; (**20**) ~ ib. l. 19 (f. *Πάπας*); (**21**) ~ *SEG* XXXVI 700, 7 (f. —*ς*); (**22**) ~ ib. l. 8 ([*Φα*]*ρνάκης*: s. *Φαρνακίων*) ?= (*28*); (**23**) ii/iii AD *CIRB* 1179, 21 (f. —*ων*) ?= (*24*); (**24**) ~ ib. l. 24 (f. —*ων*) ?= (*23*); (**25**) ~ ib. l. 35 (I s. *Ἔρως*, f. *Φαρνάκης* II, *Φιλοδέσποτος*) ?= (*11*); (**26**) ~ ib. l. 35 ([*Φα*]*ρνάκης*: II s. *Φαρνάκης* I); (**27**) ~ ib. l. 42 (s. *Τράγος*, f. *Πάβας*); (**28**) ~ ib. l. 58 (s. *Φαρνακίων*) ?= (*22*)
—GORGIPPIA?: (**29**) s. ii AD ib. 1231 B, 9 (f. *Πόθος*); (**30**) ii/iii AD ib. 1232, 3
—MYRMEKION: (**31**) i AD ib. 882 (s. *Μυρῖνος*)
—NYMPHAION: (**32**) i AD ib. 930; cf. KW pl. 46 no. 655 (s. *Μαστοῦς*)
—PANTIKAPAION: (**33**) i BC *CIRB* 279; cf. KW pl. 35 no. 501 (f. *Λεύκιος*) ?= (*37*); (**34**) ~ *CIRB* 293 (I f. *Φαρνάκης* II); (**35**) ~ ib. (II s. *Φαρνάκης* I); (**36**) ~ ib. 294 (f. *Φαρνακίων*); (**37**) i BC/i AD ib. 300 (f. *Λεύκιος*) ?= (*33*); (**38**) ~ ib. 319 (s. *Ἀφράνιος*, *Στρατονίκη*); (**39**) i AD ib. 500 (s. *Ἑρμῆς*); (**40**) ~ ib. 520 (f. *Ὑγιαίνων*); (**41**) ~ ib. 528 (s. —*κλει*—); (**42**) i-ii AD ib. 648 (*Φαρν*(*ά*)*κης*); (**43**) ?f. i AD ib. 527, 1; cf. KW pl. 30 no. 440 (I s. *Ὅπλων*, f. *Φαρνάκης* II,

Ὑψίγονος, Παρθένα); (**44**) ~ *CIRB* 527, 4; cf. KW pl. 30 no. 440 (II s. Φαρνάκης I, Μητροφίλα); (**45**) s. i AD *CIRB* 434 (Φαρ[ν]άκης: s. Νεοκλῆς); (**46**) ?s. i AD ib. 526 (I f. Φαρνάκης II); (**47**) ~ ib. (II s. Φαρνάκης I); (**48**) i/ii AD ib. 80, 8; cf. KW pl. 33 no. 454; (**49**) ~ *CIRB* 464; cf. KW pl. 41 no. 604 (f. Μασταροῦς); (**50**) ~ *CIRB* 640 (s. Χηματῖνος, f. Ἀφράνιος); (**51**) ~ ib. 641 (s. Ἀθηνόδωρος); (**52**) ii AD ib. 652 (s. Ἀπατούριος); (**53**) ~ ib. 657 (s. Ὅπλων)
—PHANAGOREIA: (**54**) 123 AD ib. 975, 3 (s. Ἀπολλώνιος)
—THEODOSIA: (**55**) iv AD ib. 951 (f. Ἀλέξανδρος)
SCYTHIA MINOR:
—ISTROS: (**56**) ii AD *ISM* I 196, 5 (f. Κόρος)
—KALLATIS: (**57**) 241-244 AD ib. III 74 A, 22 (f. Ἡλιόδωρος)
SKYTHIA: (**58**) ii-i BC *VDI* 1951 (1), p. 153 no. 2
—TANAIS: (**59**) ii AD *CIRB* 1268, 15 (f. —ιφανης: reading—Tokhtas'ev); (**60**) f. ii AD ib. 1264 A, 4 (Φ[α]ρνάκης: s. Θεότιμος); (**61**) ~ ib. 1295; (**62**) c. 200-220 AD ib. 1277, 21 (Φαρνάκης—Tokhtas'ev: f. —δίβαλος); (**63**) 220 AD ib. 1278, 13 (s. Ἡρακλείδης); (**64**) ~ ib. l. 13 (f. Χάραξστος); (**65**) 225 AD ib. 1280, 12 (s. Δάδας); (**66**) 244 AD ib. 1287, 27 (f. —λος)
TAURIS:
—CHERSONESOS: (**67**) ii AD *IOSPE* I² 442 (f. Χρυσοῦς); (**68**) ii-iii AD *SEG* XXXVII 658 (I f. Φαρνάκης II); (**69**) ~ ib. (II s. Φαρνάκης I); (**70**) f. iv AD Const. Porph., *De admin. imp.* 53, 187 (I f. Φαρνάκης II: fict.?); (**71**) ~ ib. l. 187 ff. (Φάρνακος—Const. Porph.: II s. Φαρνάκης I: fict.?)

Φαρνάκιος
MACEDONIA (MYGDONIA):
—THESSALONIKE: (**1**) ii-iii AD *IG* X (2) (1) 382 (Κορνήλιος Κόϊντος Φ.: f. Κοϊντία Λικετία Σαβάρα)

Φαρνακίων
CIMMERIAN BOSPOROS:
—GORGIPPIA: (**1**) imp. *CIRB* 1187, 4; Zgusta, *PNS* 236 (Φαρνακίω[ν]); (**2**) i/ii AD *CIRB* 1115, 7; *SEG* XL 624, 1 (s. Πόθος) ?= (*4*); (**3**) ii AD *CIRB* 1140, 13 (Φαρνακί[ων]) ?= (*4*); (**4**) ~ ib. l. 16 (s. Πόθος, f. —ος) ?= (*3*) (*2*); (**5**) ~ ib. 1141, 11 (f. —ωρος); (**6**) ~ ib. 1151, 6 (s. Χρησ—); (**7**) ii-iii AD *NE* 9 (1971) p. 9 no. 6 A, 15 ([Φαρ]νακίων); (**8**) f. ii AD *SGE* 35 (1972) p. 51, 7 (*CIRB* 1132) + *CIRB* 1162 ([Φ]αρνακίων); (**9**) ~ ib. 1128; (**10**) ~ ib. 1155, 7 ([Φ]αρνακίω[ν]—Vinogradov); (**11**) m. ii AD *Eirene* 7 (1968) p. 67, 2 (s. Σέλευκος); (**12**) ~ ib. l. 2 (s. Φαρνάκης) ?= (*48*); (**13**) ~ ib. l. 4 (f. Ἀθηνόδωρος); (**14**) ~ ib. l. 4 (s. Γοργίας); (**15**) ~ ib. l. 5 (s. Νυμφαγόρας); (**16**) ~ ib. l. 18 (f. Ψυχαρίων); (**17**) ~ ib. l. 21 ([Φ]α(ρ)νακίω(ν): f. Ἀρι—); (**18**) s. ii AD *CIRB* 1129 A, 2; 1157; 1232, 6 (s. Πόθος); (**19**) ~ ib. 1142, 4 ([Φα]ρνακίων: s. Χ—); (**20**) ?s. ii AD ib. 1158, 4 ([Φα]ρνακίων: s. Γα—); (**21**) ~ ib. 1215, 3; (**22**) s. ii AD *SEG* XXXVI 708, 2; (**23**) ~ ib. l. 3 ([Φαρν]ακίων?); (**24**) ~ ib. l. 7 ([Φαρν]ακίω[ν]?); (**25**) 173-210 AD *CIRB* 1135, 25 ([Φα]ρνακίων: f. Πανταλέων); (**26**) ~ *SEG* XXXVI 700, 8 (f. Φαρνάκης) ?= (*35*); (**27**) ii/iii AD *CIRB* 1179, 25 (f. Ἰα—); (**28**) ~ ib. l. 29 (s. Χάρδεις, f. Νεοκλῆς); (**29**) ~ ib. l. 30 (f. Πάππος); (**30**) ~ ib. l. 31 (s. Ἀτίας, f. Ἀθηνόδωρος); (**31**) ~ ib. l. 34 (f. Μακάριος); (**32**) ~ ib. l. 36 (s. Ἔρως, f. Ἔρως); (**33**) ~ ib. l. 41 (s. Ἑρμαδίων); (**34**) ~ ib. l. 42 (s. Ἀγαθοῦς); (**35**) ~ ib. l. 46, 58 (s. Ἡγουμενός, f. Πάννυχος, Φαρνάκης) ?= (*26*); (**36**) ~ ib. l. 51; (**37**) ~ ib. l. 52 (f. Πόσις); (**38**) ~ ib. 1183 ([Φ]αρνακίω[ν]); (**39**) ~ *VDI* 1970 (4), p. 149, 13 (s. Νουμήνιος); (**40**) ~ *SEG* XXXVI 715, 3 ([Φ]αρνακίω[ν]); (**41**) ~ ib. l. 4 ([Φα]ρνακίω[ν]); (**42**) ~ ib. XLIX 1033 B, 6 (*CIRB* 1182 B, 4) (?s. Σ—)
—GORGIPPIA?: (**43**) s. ii AD ib. 1231 A, 10 (f. —ους); (**44**) ~ ib. l. 14 (s. Θ—); (**45**) ~ ib. l. 15 (f. —ος); (**46**) ii/iii AD ib. 1232, 5; (**47**) ~ ib. l. 9; (**48**) ~ ib. l. 10 (s. Φαρνα—) ?= (*12*)
—PANTIKAPAION: (**49**) i BC ib. 294; cf. KW pl. 40 no. 587 (s. Φαρνάκης); (**50**) i/ii AD *CIRB* 632 (f. Πόθος)
—SUDAK (MOD.): (**51**) 174-210 AD *SEG* XLV 1017, 6 ([Φαρ]νακίων)
—THEODOSIA: (**52**) iii AD *CIRB* 947 A, 9 (s. Παπίας)
SKYTHIA:
—OLBIA-BORYSTHENES: (**53**) ii/iii AD *IOlbia* 145 (Φαρνακίω[ν])
—TANAIS: (**54**) 220 AD *CIRB* 1278, 8 (Φα[ρνα]κίων: f. Γοργίας)
TAURIS:
—CHERSONESOS: (**55**) ii AD Solomonik, *NEPKh* 52 (f. Φιλοκράτης)

Φάρνακος
SKYTHIA:
—OLBIA-BORYSTHENES: (**1**) f. ii AD *SEG* XLIII 506 15 (s. Ζῆθος) ?= (Φάρναγος (*1*))

Φάρναρνος
CIMMERIAN BOSPOROS:
—GORGIPPIA: (**1**) f. iii AD *CIRB* 1121; Zgusta, *PNS* 237 (Φάρναρν[ος]?)

Φάρνης
CIMMERIAN BOSPOROS:
—PANTIKAPAION: (**1**) iv AD *CIRB* 745; Zgusta, *PNS* 238 (s. Μενέστρατος)

Φαρνόξαρθος
SKYTHIA:
—TANAIS: (**1**) 220 AD *CIRB* 1278, 19; Zgusta, *PNS* 239 (s. Ἡρακλ—); (**2**) 220-228 AD *CIRB* 1245, 15; 1282, 12; 1286, 8 (s. Ταυρέας)

Φάρος
SCYTHIA MINOR:
—KALLATIS: (**1**) s. iii AD *ISM* III 75 (Φλ. Φ.)

Φάρσαλος
THRACE:
—TIRIZIS AKRA*: (**1**) c. 16 BC-14 AD *IGB* I² 12, 1 (s. Βίθυς)

Φαρσάνζης
CIMMERIAN BOSPOROS:
—BOSPOROS: (**1**) 253 AD *PIR²* P 343; Frolova, *CKB A.D. 242-341/342* pp. 12-27 (coins) (king)
KOLCHIS: (**2**) 548-556 AD *PLRE* III (-) (-σης)

Φαρτάζης
KOLCHIS:
—LAZOI: (**1**) 555 AD ib.

Φᾶσις
THRACE:
—MARONEIA: (**1**) ii-i BC *IThrakAig* E212, 51 (Φάσιδος (gen.): f. Ἐπαφρόδιτος); (**2**) ~ ib. l. 53 (s. Διοσκουρίδης); (**3**) i AD Dumont–Homolle 110b 12 (*IThrakAig* E292) (s. Ἐπαφρόδιτος)

Φασώ
TAURIS:
—CHERSONESOS: (**1**) iv BC *Drev. Bosp.* I p. 97 fig. 2

Φατάλιος
MACEDONIA (BOTTIAIA):
—BEROIA*: (**1**) 492 AD *IBer* 441, 1 (Feissel, *RICM* 64)

Φαῦλλης
SKYTHIA:
—OLBIA-BORYSTHENES?: (**1**) s. vi BC *SEG* XLVIII 1024 (slave)

Φάϋλλος
THRACE:
—ABDERA: (**1**) ii-i BC *AMNG* II (1) 236; Unp. (Chryssanthaki diss.) p. 576 (Φάϋλ(λος)—*AMNG*, Φαΰλου (gen.)—Chryssanthaki)

Φαῦστα
MACEDONIA (BOTTIAIA):
—BEROIA: (**1**) c. 120-140 AD *IBer* 349 A (Tataki 1261) (d. Λυκόφρων, m. Ἑρμᾶς)
MACEDONIA (MYGDONIA):
—THESSALONIKE?: (**2**) ?vi AD *IG* X (2) (1) 797 (Feissel, *RICM* 182)

Φαυστῖνα
SCYTHIA MINOR:
—ISTROS: (**1**) ii AD *ISM* I 217, 3 (-στεῖ-)

Φαυστῖνος
MACEDONIA (EDONIS):
—PHILIPPOI: (**1**) s. iv AD Feissel, *RICM* 235 (Pilhofer 101)
MACEDONIA (MYGDONIA):
—THESSALONIKE: (**2**) v-vi AD Feissel, *RICM* 188 (*SEG* XLVII 989) (Φαυσ[τῖνος]?, Φαῦ[στα]—Tsigaridas)
THRACE:
—PAUTALIA: (**3**) s. ii AD ib. XLVI 864, 4 (-στεῖ-: s. Μᾶρκος)

Φαυστίων
MACEDONIA (MYGDONIA):
—KALINDOIA: (**1**) a. 98 AD ib. XLII 583, 18 (f. Νικάνωρ)

Φαῦστος
MACEDONIA (BOTTIAIA):
—BEROIA: (**1**) ii-iii AD *IBer* 286 (Tataki 1262) (f. Κομίνιος Εὐτυχίων)
MACEDONIA (MYGDONIA):
—THESSALONIKE: (**2**) f. i AD *IG* X (2) (1) 126, 4; Robert, *OMS* 5 pp. 295-302 (date) (f. Δημήτριος); (**3**) ii AD *IG* X (2) (1) 241 A II, 25 (Φαῦστ[ος]); (**4**) ii/iii AD ib. 262 III, 7
—THESSALONIKE?: (**5**) ii AD ib. 906 (f. Εὐτυχίς)
MACEDONIA (SINTIKE):
—NEINE: (**6**) imp. *IGB* IV 2246, 2; cf. V 5877 (f. Φίλιππος)

Φαῦχος
SKYTHIA:
—TANAIS: (**1**) 225 AD *CIRB* 1279, 10; Zgusta, *PNS* 719 (s. Πόπλιος)

Φειδίας
SCYTHIA MINOR:
—TOMIS: (**1**) iii-ii BC *AMNG* I (2) 2421 (coin) (Φειδί(ας)?); (**2**) ii AD *ISM* II 125 I, 21 (Φι-: s. Διονύσιος)

Φείδιππος
MACEDONIA (CHALKIDIKE):
—OLYNTHOS: (**1**) ?354 BC *TAPA* 69 (1938) pp. 52-3 no. 6, 5, 7; *SEG* XLVII 922; Hatzopoulos, *Actes Chalc.* p. 80 (date) (s. Φείδων)

Φεῖδις
MACEDONIA (PIERIA):
—PHILA?: (**1**) ?iii BC *RPh* 1911, pp. 133-4 no. 36, 97; cf. Helly, *L'État thessalien* pp. 319-20 (locn.) (s. Εὐφορβίδης)

Φειδίστη
MACEDONIA (ELIMEIA):
—AIANE: (**1**) ii BC *EAM* 41 (d. Ἀντίγονος)

Φείδων
MACEDONIA (CHALKIDIKE):
—OLYNTHOS: (**1**) ?354 BC *TAPA* 69 (1938) pp. 52-3 no. 6, 5; *SEG* XLVII 922; Hatzopoulos, *Actes Chalc.* p. 80 (date) (f. Φείδιππος)
MACEDONIA?: (**2**) 327 BC Plu., *Alex.* 54 (Δημήτριος ὁ προσονομαζ. Φ.: s. Πυθῶναξ)

THRACE:
—BYZANTION (TERRIT.): **(3)** ii BC *IByz* 169 (Fıratlı–Robert p. 109 no. 176) (*Φί-*: f. *Καθαρά*)

Φερεκλῆς
MACEDONIA (PIERIA):
—DION: **(1)** iii BC *SEG* XXXI 629, 3 (f. *Γοργίας*)
SCYTHIA MINOR:
—ISTROS: **(2)** iv/iii BC *ISM* I 246, 2 (f. *—νίας*); **(3)** iii BC ib. 8, 4 (f. *Πρόκριτος*)

Φερεκράτης
MACEDONIA (CHALKIDIKE):
—NEAPOLIS?: **(1)** vi/v BC *SEG* XXXIX 614 (XL 549 (vase)) (*Φερεκρά(της)*)

Φέρουσα
MACEDONIA (MYGDONIA):
—THESSALONIKE: **(1)** i AD *IG* X (2) (1) 405

Φέρωψ
THRACE:
—PHILIPPOPOLIS-TRIMONTIUM*: **(1)** ii-iii AD *IGB* V 5465 (glad.)

Φηδάνακος
SKYTHIA:
—TANAIS: **(1)** 244 AD *CIRB* 1287, 26; Zgusta, *PNS* 240 (s. *Εὐνώνας*)

Φηλικίτα
MACEDONIA (MYGDONIA):
—THESSALONIKE: **(1)** ii-iii AD *IG* X (2) (1) 667

Φῆλιξ
CIMMERIAN BOSPOROS:
—PANTIKAPAION: **(1)** v-vi AD *IAK* 10 (1904) p. 88 no. 103 (s. *Ἀριστόβουλος*); **(2)** ~ *ZOOID* 22 (1900) Prot. p. 60 no. 3
MACEDONIA (BOTTIAIA):
—EDESSA: **(3)** 180 AD *SEG* XXIV 531, 15 (Tataki, *Edessa* 299) (s. *Νικομήδης*)
THRACE:
—NICOPOLIS AD ISTRUM: **(4)** ii AD *IGB* II 680, 8 (*Eastern cults* p. 266 no. 2) (s. *Μουκάπορις*)
—NICOPOLIS AD ISTRUM (TERRIT.): **(5)** ii AD *IGB* V 5244 b, 10 (s. *Μνη—*)

Φῆστα
THRACE:
—BYZANTION: **(1)** ii AD *SEG* L 667 VII (m. *Λούκις*, *Εὔθετος*)

Φῆστος
THRACE:
—NICOPOLIS AD ISTRUM (TERRIT.): **(1)** ii AD *IGB* V 5244 a, 11 (s. *Ἡρακλιανός*)

Φιάτακος
CIMMERIAN BOSPOROS:
—PANTIKAPAION: **(1)** iv BC *CIRB* 229; Zgusta, *PNS* 720 (s. *Ἄλδις*)

Φιδανους
CIMMERIAN BOSPOROS:
—PANTIKAPAION: **(1)** 275-278 AD *CIRB* 36, 19; Zgusta, *PNS* 240 (s. *Θεάγγελος*); **(2)** ~ *CIRB* 36, 41 (*Φιδαν(ους)*: f. *—αρι—*)
SKYTHIA:
—TANAIS: **(3)** c. 210-236 AD ib. 1250, 10; 1280, 6; 1285, 13 (f. *Ψυχαρίων*); **(4)** 220 AD ib. 1278, 10 (f. *Ἀράθης*); **(5)** 236 AD ib. 1250, 15 (s. *Κίμβρος*)

Φίδας
CIMMERIAN BOSPOROS:
—PANTIKAPAION: **(1)** iii AD ib. 103, 3; Zgusta, *PNS* 240; **(2)** 275-278 AD *CIRB* 36, 21 (f. *Λειμανός*)
—THEODOSIA: **(3)** iii AD ib. 947 B, 10 (s. *Φάδσιος*)

SKYTHIA:
—TANAIS: **(4)** ii AD ib. 1268, 12; **(5)** 155 AD ib. 1260, 20 (f. *Ὀμψάλακος*); **(6)** c. 200-210 AD ib. 1277, 11 (f. *Λειμανός*); **(7)** 225 AD ib. 1280, 11 (f. *Στοσάρακος*)

Φίλα
MACEDONIA: **(1)** c. 355-288 BC *RE* (3); Berve 772 (Tataki, *Macedonians* p. 444 no. 5) (d. *Ἀντίπατρος*, m. *Κράτερος*, *Ἀντίγονος* II *Γονατᾶς*, *Στρατονίκη*); **(2)** iv/iii BC Ath. 577 c (d. *Δημήτριος* I *Πολιορκητής*, *Λαμία* (Athens)); **(3)** iii BC *HE* 3346 (Tataki, *Macedonians* p. 443 no. 4) (d. *Εὐποίητος*?, *Ἡγησώ*); **(4)** ~ *IG* II^2 9272 (Tataki, *Macedonians* p. 444 no. 6; *FRA* 3494) (d. *Πασίων*); **(5)** f. iii BC *RE* (4); *IG* XI (4) 1098; Grainger, *SPG* p. 52 (d. *Σέλευκος* I *Νικάτωρ*, *Στρατονίκη*, m. *Δημήτριος* II); **(6)** f. ii BC *IG* XII (1) 515 (Tataki, *Macedonians* p. 443 no. 3)
MACEDONIA (BOTTIAIA):
—AIGAI: **(7)** s. iv BC *SEG* XXXV 801 (*Φί[λ]α*: ?d. *Κόρραγος*); **(8)** ~ ib. 805 (*[Φί]λα*?: d. *Φίλων*)
—BEROIA: **(9)** imp. *IBer* 170 (Tataki 1267); **(10)** ii-iii AD *IBer* 28 (Tataki 1268); **(11)** ~ *IBer* 288 (Tataki 58) (*Αἰλ. Φ.*: ?m. *Φοιβιανή*); **(12)** ~ *IBer* 350 (Tataki 1266); **(13)** s. ii AD *IBer* 310, 3 (?m. *Ἀμμία*, *Πρόκλος*, *Ὀνήσιμος*, *Ὀνήσιμος* (sic)); **(14)** 216 AD *ILeukopetra* 68, 1 (*Αὐρ. Φ.*: d. *Ἀμμία*)
—EDESSA: **(15)** ii/i BC *Ancient Macedonia* 1 p. 202 no. 16 (Tataki, *Edessa* 300) (I d. *Ἐπικράτης*, ?m. *Μένανδρος*, *Νικάνωρ*, *Δημέας*, *Φίλα* II); **(16)** ~ *Ancient Macedonia* 1 p. 202 no. 16 (Tataki, *Edessa* 301) (II d. *Μένων*, ?d. *Φίλα* I)
—MIEZA: **(17)** iii/ii BC *SEG* XLIII 412 (d. *Ἀριστέας*, m. *Ἀριστοφάνης*, *Ἀριστέας*, *Εὔιππος*)
—PELLA: **(18)** c. 380-350 BC ib. 434; cf. XLVI 776
MACEDONIA (EDONIS):
—AMPHIPOLIS: **(19)** i BC *Ag.* XVII 409 (Tataki, *Macedonians* p. 61 no. 125; *FRA* 520)
MACEDONIA (ELIMEIA): **(20)** m. iv BC *RE* (2); *Macedonia* 2 p. 19 (Tataki, *Macedonians* p. 197 no. 21) (d. *Δέρδας*, ?m. *Κάρανος*)
MACEDONIA (LYNKESTIS):
—HERAKLEIA?: **(21)** 235 AD *IG* X (2) (2) 136, 3 (*Αὐρηλία Φ.*: m. *Παῖτος*, *Ἀλέξανδρος*)
MACEDONIA (MYGDONIA):
—KALINDOIA: **(22)** iii/ii BC *SEG* XXXI 623 (XLII 591); *KGAM Thess.* I 52 (date) (d. *Δημήτριος*)
—LETE: **(23)** 121 AD *SEG* I 276, 19 (m. *Περίτας ὁ καὶ Βιήσιος*)
—THESSALONIKE: **(24)** s. i AD *IG* X (2) (1) 68, 24; 69, 18 (m. *Ἀσιατικός*); **(25)** ii AD ib. 102, 3 (*Φλ. Φ.*: d. *Φίλιππος*, *Φλ. Κρατησώ*); **(26)** ii-iii AD ib. 468 (*Αἰλ. Φ.*: m. *Κ. Φούριος Ἑρμείας*)
—THESSALONIKE?: **(27)** i-ii AD ib. 825; **(28)** ii-iii AD ib. 856, 4 (m. *Λούκιος*, *Ἀλέξανδρος*, *Δελοῦς*, *Αἴλ. Μέστριος*)
MACEDONIA (ORESTIS):
—AGIA ANNA (MOD.): **(29)** s. ii AD *EAM* 196 (d. *Παρμενίων*)
MACEDONIA (PELAGONIA): **(30)** ii AD *IG* X (2) (2) 248 (*Φίλλα*: m. *Π. Αἰλ. Μαρκελλῖνος*)
SARMATIA:
—SARMATAI: **(31)** 168 BC *SGDI* 1724, 2, 4 (slave/freed.); **(32)** 153-144 BC ib. 2108 + *BCH* 66-7 (1942-3) p. 71 no. 2, [3], 6, 8 (slave/freed.)
TAURIS:
—CHERSONESOS: **(33)** inc. Solomonik, *GAKh* 1606 (vase)
THRACE: **(34)** 182 BC *SGDI* 2047, 3-4 (slave/freed.)
—BYZANTION: **(35)** ii BC *IByz* 73 (Fıratlı–Robert p. 49 no. 14) (d. *Σιμίας*)
—LYSIMACHEIA: **(36)** iii BC *AM* 67 (1942) p. 220 no. 14 (*FRA* 3412) (d. *Σεύθης*)
—MESAMBRIA: **(37)** iii BC *IGB* I^2 337 bis (PM 2262) (m. *Πυθόδωρος*)

Φιλάγαθος
CIMMERIAN BOSPOROS:
—PANTIKAPAION: **(1)** 275-278 AD *CIRB* 36, 69 (*Φιλάγ(αθος)*)
MACEDONIA (MYGDONIA):
—THESSALONIKE: **(2)** ii AD *IG* X (2) (1) 241 A II, 12 (*Μ. Μάνλι. Φιλάγαθο[ς]*)

Φίλαγρος
MACEDONIA (BOTTIAIA):
—MIEZA: **(1)** iii BC *SEG* XXIV 524 I, 28 (Hatzopoulos, *MI* 2 p. 106 no. 92)
—PELLA: **(2)** ii/i BC *SEG* XLVIII 824 (s. *Ἡρακλείδης*)
—TYRISSA? (ASVESTARI (MOD.)): **(3)** f. ii BC ib. XLVII 999, 3, 13 (?f. *Βουκάρτας*); **(4)** ~ ib. l. 11 (*[Φ]ίλαγρος*)
MACEDONIA (DERRIOPOS):
—STUBERRA: **(5)** 74 AD *IG* X (2) (2) 326, 35-6 (s. *Κάσσανδρος*)
MACEDONIA (EDONIS):
—AMPHIPOLIS: **(6)** ?ii/i BC *PAE* 1984, p. 38 no. 2 with pl. 45, 2 (*SEG* XLIII 371); cf. *BE* 1988, no. 356 (f. *Ἄδαῖος*)
MACEDONIA (LYNKESTIS):
—HERAKLEIA: **(7)** i-ii AD *SEG* XV 380 (Tataki, *Macedonians* p. 110 no. 1)
MACEDONIA (MYGDONIA):
—KALINDOIA: **(8)** c. 317 BC Hatzopoulos, *MI* 2 p. 84 no. 62, 29 (s. *Μένανδρος*); **(9)** 68-98 AD *SEG* XLII 580, 47 (f. *Ἀπολλώνιος*); **(10)** a. 98 AD ib. 582, 42 (f. *Ἀνδρομένης*)
MACEDONIA (ORESTIS): **(11)** 192 AD *EAM* 186, 33 (s. *Πτολεμαῖος*)
MACEDONIA (PIERIA):
—PHILA?: **(12)** ?iii BC *RPh* 1911, pp. 133-4 no. 36, 75; cf. Helly, *L'État thessalien* pp. 319-20 (locn.) (s. *Κριτο—*)
THRACE:
—PAUTALIA (TERRIT.): **(13)** iii AD *IGB* V 5833 (*Αὐρ. Ἰολος Φ.*)

Φιλαδέλφη
THRACE:
—BEROE-AUGUSTA TRAIANA: **(1)** c. 320-324 AD *Anal. Boll.* 31 (1912) p. 198; p. 207

Φιλάδελφος
CIMMERIAN BOSPOROS:
—BOSPOROS?: **(1)** ii AD *SEG* XVI 441; cf. *BCH* 103 (1979) p. 522 n. 2 (f. *Γλύκων*)
—PANTIKAPAION: **(2)** ?f. ii AD *CIRB* 85, 2 (*[Φιλά]δελφος*?: f. *Το—*)
MACEDONIA (EDONIS):
—PHILIPPOI*: **(3)** ii/iii AD *CIL* III 633 I, 1, 22 (Pilhofer 164); *CIL* III 633 II, 1; 633 II a, 13 (Pilhofer 163); *CRAI* 1923, p. 277 (date); Collart, *Philippes* pls. 64-5 (Lat. P. Hostilius Philadelphus: freed.)
MACEDONIA (MYGDONIA):
—THESSALONIKE?: **(4)** ii-iii AD *IG* X (2) (1) 738
SKYTHIA:
—OLBIA-BORYSTHENES: **(5)** 198-211 AD *IOSPE* I^2 174, 11 (*[Φιλάδε]λφος*?: f. *Ῥουφῖνος*)
TAURIS:
—CHERSONESOS: **(6)** f. ii AD Solomonik, *NEPKh* 129, 6 (*[Φ]ιλάδελφος*: f. *Διο—*)
THRACE:
—BYZANTION: **(7)** i BC *IByz* 164 (Fıratlı–Robert p. 107 no. 171) (f. *Θεοφίλα*)

Φιλαθάναιος
TAURIS:
—CHERSONESOS: **(1)** iv BC Solomonik, *NEPKh* 140 + *VDI* 1975 (1), p. 174 (*[Φιλ]αθάναιος*—Vinogradov, *Ἀθάναιος*—ed.); **(2)** f. iii BC Kats p. 94 no. 46 (amph.) (f. *Εὐφρόνιος*)

Φίλαινα
MACEDONIA (CHALKIDIKE):
—OLYNTHOS: **(1)** ?350 BC *TAPA* 59 (1928) p. 226, 8; Hatzopoulos, *Actes Chalc.* p. 80 (date) (d. *Ἥρων*)

Φιλαινίς
Cimmerian Bosporos:
—Pantikapaion: (1) i ad *CIRB* 148 (*GVI* 105) (*Φιλαινία*—lap.)

Φιλαινώ
Macedonia (Chalkidike):
—Potidaia-Kassandreia: (1) c. 200-175 bc *IG* II^{2} 9002 (Tataki, *Macedonians* p. 96 no. 95; *FRA* 2796) (d. *Κλειτόμαχος*)

Φιλαῖος
Thrace:
—Abdera: (1) c. 360-350 bc May, *Abdera* pp. 256-8 nos. 423-38 (coin); Masson, *OGS* pp. 434-5

Φιλάν
Macedonia (Pieria):
—Pydna: (1) iv bc *GRBS* 43 (2002-3) p. 112 no. 2, 13

Φίλανδρος
Macedonia (Orestis):
—Battynaioi: (1) 192 ad *EAM* 186 I, 50 (*Φίλανδρος*: f. *Εὐτυχιανός*)

Φιλαπόδημος
Thrace:
—Ainos: (1) ii ad *SEG* xxxvi 657, 1 (II s. *Φιλαπόδημος* I, f. *Ξενοκλῆς, Θεόξενος, Διόσκορος*); (2) ~ ib. l. 2 (I f. *Φιλαπόδημος* II)

Φιλαργυρίς
Macedonia (Pieria):
—Pydna (territ.): (1) i ad *Essays Laourdas* p. 111 no. 3

Φιλάργυρος
Macedonia (Edonis):
—Philippoi (nr.): (1) ?ii ad *CIL* III 14206. 14 (Pilhofer 430) (Lat. C. Aelius Philarg[yrus]: freed.)
Macedonia (Lower Paionia):
—Europos: (2) 199 ad *SEG* xxxviii 611 (s. *Μεμμία Πων*—)
Macedonia (Mygdonia):
—Thessalonike?: (3) i-ii ad *IG* x (2) (1) 873
Thrace:
—Maroneia: (4) ii-i bc *IThrakAig* E212, 56 (s. *Διονύσιος*)

Φιλαρέτα
Tauris:
—Chersonesos: (1) s. iv bc Solomonik, *GAKh* 311 (vase) (*Λαρέτα*—ed., [*Φι*]*λαρέτα*?)

Φιλάρσενος
Cimmerian Bosporos:
—Pantikapaion: (1) f. i ad *CIRB* 529; cf. *Hyperboreus* 1994-5 (2), pp. 142-3 (*Φιλ*(*ά*)*ρσενος*?: s. *Θεόδωρος*)

Φίλαρχος
Macedonia (Elimeia): (1) ?257 bc *FD* III (4) 417, 14 (Tataki, *Macedonians* p. 197 no. 22) (s. *Ἑλλανίων*)

Φιλᾶς
Thrace:
—Abdera: (1) c. 395-360 bc May, *Abdera* pp. 234-5 nos. 391-97/1 (coin); Masson, *OGS* p. 435 (*Φιλᾶδος* (gen.))

Φιλέας
Cimmerian Bosporos:
—Gorgippia: (1) f. iii bc *CIRB* 1137 B II, 53 (s. *Εὔφρων*)

Φίλεια
Tauris:
—Chersonesos: (1) ?iv-iii bc *SEG* xliv 657 (weight)

Φιλέρως
Cimmerian Bosporos:
—Myrmekion (nr.): (1) f. ii ad *VDI* 1965 (2), p. 98 no. 3; cf. *Topoi* 3 (1993) p. 198 no. 3 (*Φιλέρω*[*ς*]: f. *Χρυσέρως*)
—Pantikapaion: (2) ii ad *CIRB* 670; cf. KW pl. 30 no. 426 (s. *Τιμόθεος*)
Macedonia (Edonis):
—Amphipolis: (3) 37 bc Robert, *Coll. Froehner* 44 left side (Tataki, *Macedonians* p. 62 no. 126) (s. *Βίθυς*)
Thrace:
—Maroneia: (4) i bc-i ad *IThrakAig* E303 (f. *Βερονίκη*)

Φιλέταιρος
Cimmerian Bosporos:
—Pantikapaion: (1) i bc *CIRB* 128, 1, 8 (*GVI* 845) (*Φιλέτ*(*αι*)*ρος*—l.8: f. *Λεύκιος, Ἡρακλεόδωρος, Στρατονίκη*); (2) 227 ad *CIRB* 147, 7 (-*τε*-: f. *Σύμφορος*)
Macedonia (Pelagonia):
—Mojno (mod.): (3) ii ad *IG* x (2) (2) 169 (*Αἴλιος Φ.*: f. *Αἰλ. Κοσμία*)
Thrace: (4) ii bc *IKnid* 23, 7
—Byzantion: (5) i bc *Türk Tarih Kongresi XI* (6) pp. 2704-5 with pl. 499. 13 (-*έτε*-: f. *Ἀλέξανδρος*)

Φίλη
Macedonia (Paionia):
—Stoboi: (1) i-ii ad *Sp.* 71 (1931) p. 227 no. 600 (*Αἰβουτ. Φ.*: d. *Εὔτροπος, Αἰβουτ. Ἀρέσκουσα*)

Φίληβος
Macedonia (Bottiaia):
—Beroia: (1) ii ad Luc., *Asin.* 36 (fict.)

Φιλημάτιν
Macedonia (Mygdonia):
—Thessalonike: (1) ii ad *IG* x (2) (1) 370 (*Εἰο*(*υ*)*λία Φ.*)

Φιλημάτιον
Macedonia (Mygdonia):
—Thessalonike: (1) ii-iii ad ib. 104 ([*Κε*]*ρρηνία Φ*[*ι*]*λημά*[*τιον*])
—Thessalonike*: (2) ii ad ib. 658, 3 (*Κλωδία Φ.*: freed.)

Φιλήμων
Macedonia (Bottiaia):
—Beroia: (1) ?61 ad *Const. Apost.* vii 46 (Tataki 1270) (f. *Ὀνήσιμος*)
Macedonia (Edonis):
—Amphipolis: (2) 287-245 bc *IOrop* 21, 6 (Tataki, *Macedonians* p. 62 no. 127) (*Φιλή*[*μ*]*ων*: f. *Ὀφέλλας*)
Macedonia (Elimeia)?: (3) m. iii ad *EAM* 63
Macedonia (Mygdonia):
—Thessalonike: (4) i bc *IG* x (2) (1) 1029 (*EAD* xxx 338; Tataki, *Macedonians* p. 187 no. 67) (s. *Ἄδμητος*)
Macedonia (Paionia): (5) ?ii ad *AM* 27 (1902) p. 318 no. 45 ([*Φι*]*λήμων*: s. *Διόδωρος*, f. *Λυσίμαχος*)
Scythia Minor:
—Istros: (6) 138 ad *ISM* I 193 I, 18 (I f. *Φιλήμων* II); (7) ~ ib. l. 18 (II s. *Φιλήμων* I)
Skythia:
—Olbia-Borysthenes: (8) iv-iii bc Tolstoi 57 (vase) (*Φιλήμο*(*νος*) (gen.))
—Tanais: (9) 228 ad *CIRB* 1283, 12 ([*Φι*]*λήμων*—Tokhtas'ev: f. *Φαδιους*)
Thrace: (10) s. iv bc Peter, *MTD* pp. 148-9 (coin) (*Φιλή*(*μων*)?)
—Apollonia-Sozopolis: (11) iii bc *BMN-Burgas* 4 (2002) p. 126 no. 24 (f. *Ἀλκμέων, Τιάρα*)
—Byzantion (territ.): (12) ii bc *IByz* 129 (Fıratlı–Robert p. 97 no. 142) (f. *Ἀρέτη*)

—Mesambria: (13) i bc *IGB* I^{2} 326, 1 (f. *Νίκων*); (14) c. 55 bc ib. 323, 1 (f. *Μόσχος*)
—Oescus: (15) ii-iii ad *Romanizmăt* II 341 (Lat. Filemon)
—Perinthos-Herakleia: (16) c. 100-115 ad *SEG* xxvi 1288, 11 (s. *Ἐπιγένης*)

Φιλήρεμος
Macedonia (Bottiaia):
—Beroia: (1) iii ad *IBer* 405, 2 (Tataki 1271)

Φιλήτα
Thrace:
—Byzantion: (1) i bc *IByz* 258 with comm. (Fıratlı–Robert p. 82 no. 99); (2) i bc-i ad *IByz* 276 (Fıratlı–Robert pp. 64-5 no. 57) (d. *Ῥοῦφος*)
—(Athyras): (3) i bc *IByz* 224 (Fıratlı–Robert p. 80 no. 94) (d. *Μενέστρατος*)
—Salymbria: (4) hell. *IByz* S 48 (d. *Νουμήνιος*); (5) ?i bc ib. S 49 (PM 1753) (d. *Μήνιος*)

Φιλήτας
Macedonia: (1) hell. *Syringes* 799 (Tataki, *Macedonians* p. 444 no. 7; La'da E1640) (s. *Νίκανδρος*)

Φιλήτη
Macedonia (Bottiaia):
—Edessa: (1) v-vi ad Feissel, *RICM* 41
Macedonia (Pieria):
—Dion*: (2) imp. *AEMTh* 15 (2001) p. 349 (glass)
—Kastania (mod.): (3) imp. *SEG* L 594
Thrace:
—Anchialos: (4) ii-iii ad *IGB* I^{2} 370 bis
—Bizye (territ.): (5) ii ad ib. III 1863, 16
—Byzantion: (6) i bc-i ad *IByz* 19, 13 (*Φιλή*<*η*>*τη*)

Φιλητίων
Macedonia (Almopia):
—Milia (mod.): (1) ii-i bc *SEG* XII 347 (s. *Διόδωρος*) ?= (*2*); (2) ~ ib. ([*Φιλ*]*ητίων*: f. *Λυσίμαχος*) ?= (*1*)

Φίλητος
Cimmerian Bosporos:
—Myrmekion (nr.): (1) ii ad *VDI* 1965 (2), p. 96 no. 2; cf. *Topoi* 3 (1993) p. 198 no. 2 (*Ἰούλ. Φ.*: s. *Πειθέρως*) ?= (*2*); (2) ~ *VDI* 1965 (2), p. 96 no. 2; cf. *Topoi* 3 (1993) p. 198 no. 2 (f. *Ἰούλ. Χρυσαλλεύς*) ?= (*1*)
—Pantikapaion: (3) imp. *CIRB* 771 (-*λει*-: s. *Στρατόνικος*)
Macedonia (Bottiaia):
—Beroia: (4) f. ii ad *IBer* 353 (Tataki 735) (*Τι. Κλ. Φ.*); (5) ii/iii ad *IBer* 27 A, 5 (slave?); (6) f. iii ad ib. 236, 4 (Tataki 1272) (s. *Ζωσίμη*)
—Edessa: (7) ii-iii ad *SEG* XII 348 (Tataki, *Edessa* 302) (threptos); (8) 180 ad *SEG* xxiv 531, 14 (Tataki, *Edessa* 303) (s. *Φαρίων*)
Macedonia (Chalkidike):
—Potidaia-Kassandreia: (9) i-ii ad *TAPA* 69 (1938) p. 65 no. 17 (*Φ. Μάρκιος*: f. *Πλόκαμος*)
Macedonia (Derriopos):
—Stuberra: (10) 87 ad *IG* x (2) (2) 325, 74 (s. *Στράτων*)
Macedonia (Lynkestis):
—Herakleia (area): (11) 286 ad ib. 18 C (s. *Διονυσ*?)
Macedonia (Mygdonia):
—Thessalonike?: (12) ii ad ib. x (2) (1) 251, 10 ([*Φ*]*ίλητος*: s. *Καλλικράτης*); (13) ii-iii ad ib. 821 (*Γ. Κάσσιος Φ.*)
Macedonia (Odomantike):
—Sirrha: (14) 155 ad Dimitsas 821, 24 (Kaphtantzis 1) (s. *Ἀπολλώνιος*)

Macedonia (Paionia):
—Kavadarci (mod.): **(15)** ii AD Unp. (Kavadarci)

Φιλίαρχος
Macedonia (Mygdonia):
—Thessalonike: **(1)** ?105 BC *IG* x (2) (1) 135, 5 (s. *Διονυσ—*)

Φιλικᾶς?
Cimmerian Bosporos:
—Myrmekion: **(1)** s. iv BC *CIRB* 875; cf. Stephanis 2014 (*Πασαφιλικατος*—lap., *Πασα Φιλικᾶτος?*, *Πασ(ι)φίλ(η) Κάτο(υ)?*—edd.: ?f. *Πασα*)

Φιλίκιος
Thrace: **(1)** iii AD Beševliev, *EP* 24 (*Αὐρ. Φ.*)

Φίλινα
Macedonia: **(1)** 159 BC *PHamb* 238, 2, 37 (La'da E1814) (d. *Ἀργαῖος*)

Φιλίνη
Cimmerian Bosporos:
—Pantikapaion: **(1)** iii AD *CIRB* 730. 3

Φίλιννα
Macedonia (Bottiaia):
—Beroia: **(1)** ii BC *IBer* 197 (Tataki 1273) (*Φιλίννει* (dat.): d. *Ἄδυμος*); **(2)** ?i BC *IBer* 507 (d. *Διονύσιος*)
Macedonia (Edonis):
—Amphipolis: **(3)** iv BC *SEG* xxxv 707 (d. *Εὐθύνους*)
Macedonia (Mygdonia):
—Thessalonike: **(4)** i AD *IG* x (2) (1) 367, 2, 4 (d. *Δίων*, *Εἰρήνη*)

Φιλίννιον
Macedonia (Edonis):
—Amphipolis: **(1)** 359-336 BC *FGrH* 257 F 36. 1; Procl., *in R.* ii 116 (d. *Δημόστρατος*, *Χαριτώ*: fict.?)

Φιλῖνος
Cimmerian Bosporos:
—Gorgippia: **(1)** f. iii BC *CIRB* 1137 A I, 31; 1137 B I, 60 (I f. *Φιλῖνος* II); **(2)** ~ ib. 1137 A I, 31; 1137 B I, 60 (II s. *Φιλῖνος* I); **(3)** ~ ib. 1137 A I, 54 (s. *Ἡρόδωρος*); **(4)** ~ ib. 1137 A II, 43 (s. *Εὐκρατίδης*); **(5)** ~ ib. 1137 B I, 57 (f. *Ἀρχέδημος*)
Macedonia: **(6)** ?s. iii BC *Syringes* 222 (Tataki, *Macedonians* p. 407 no. 74; La'da E1580) (*Π̣ίλινος?*—ed., *(Φ)ι̣λῖνος?*: s. *Διονύσιος*)
Macedonia (Chalkidike):
—Anthemous: **(7)** ii BC *SEG* xlii 560 (f. *—χιος*)
—Olynthos: **(8)** iv BC *IG* ii^2 10028 (Tataki, *Macedonians* p. 143 no. 109; *FRA* 5914)
Scythia Minor:
—Istros: **(9)** iii BC *ISM* i 127 (*Eastern cults* p. 104 no. 66); **(10)** ~ *ISM* i 184 (f. *—α̣ίων*)
—Kallatis: **(11)** 15-37 AD ib. iii 46, 1, 6 (-λεῖ-: II s. *Φιλῖνος* I); **(12)** ~ ib. l. 6 (-λεῖ-: I f. *Φιλῖνος* II)
Skythia:
—Olbia-Borysthenes: **(13)** ii-iii AD *IOSPE* i^2 192 (f. *Σωκρατίδης*)
Tauris:
—Chersonesos: **(14)** ii BC Solomonik, *GChKh* 445 (vase) (*Φιλ(ῖ)νος*—ed., *Φίλ(ω)νος?* (gen.))
Thrace:
—Byzantion: **(15)** ?464 BC *IG* i^3 1144, 126; **(16)** 378 BC ib. ii^2 41, 25; 76, 1, 7; **(17)** i BC-i AD *IByz* 177 (Fıratlı–Robert p. 111 no. 182) (s. *Μητρόδωρος*); **(18)** imp. *IByz* 300 (*CIL* iii 741) (Lat. V. Cn. Pompeius Philinus: f. *Φιλουμένη*)
—Nicopolis ad Istrum (territ.): **(19)** 227 AD *ILB* 438 II, 10 (Lat. Aur. Philinus)
—Odessos: **(20)** 7 BC *IGB* i^2 46, 40 (-λεῖ-: s. *Ἀλεξίμαχος*); **(21)** 215 AD ib. 47 a, 11 (-λεῖ-: f. *Αὐρ. Κρίτων*); **(22)** ~ ib. 47 b, 9 (*Αὐρ. Φ.*: s. *Μοσχίων*); **(23)** ~ ib. 47 c, 22 (*Αὐρ. Φ.*: s. *Σωτήρ*); **(24)** 221 AD ib. 47 bis b, 29 (f. *Διονύσιος*); **(25)** ~ ib. l. 34 (f. *Αὐρ. Διονύσιος*); **(26)** ~ ib. 47 bis c, 32 (-λεῖ-: f. *Αὐρ. Εὐπρόσοδος*)
—Pautalia (territ.): **(27)** ii-iii AD ib. v 5810; 5811, [1] (-λεῖ-: s. *Καλπούρ. Λοῦππος*)

Φίλιος
Macedonia: **(1)** 173 BC *PGiss* 2 II, 4 (*PP* 2829; Tataki, *Macedonians* p. 444 no. 9; La'da E1641)
Macedonia (Bottiaia):
—Beroia: **(2)** i AD *IBer* 125, 5 (Tataki 1274) (s. *Ἄδυμος*)
Thrace:
—Pautalia (territ.): **(3)** ii-iii AD *IGB* v 5832 (f. *Μᾶρκος*)
—Serdica: **(4)** ii-iii AD ib. 5700 (*Φείλει-*: s. *Διογένης*)
—Serdica (territ.)?: **(5)** iii AD ib. iv 1985, 5 (*Eastern cults* p. 167 no. 9) (*Φεί-*)

Φιλίππα
Macedonia (Bottiaia):
—Beroia: **(1)** 177 AD *IBer* 135 B, 29 (Tataki 1275) (m. *Φίλιππος*); **(2)** iii AD *IBer* 313 (*Αὐρ. Φιλίππα*); **(3)** f. iii AD ib. 342, 4 (*Φιλ[ίππα]ν?* (acc.): d. *Αὐρ. Λεοντογένης*, *Αὐρ. Γραφίς*)
Macedonia (Eordaia):
—Arnisa?: **(4)** f. iii AD *EAM* 134; Hatzopoulos, *MI* i p. 94 n. 4 (locn.) (*Αὐρ. Φιλλίππα*)
Macedonia (Lynkestis):
—Achlada (mod.): **(5)** f. iii AD *EAM* 168 (*Αὐρ. Φ.*: d. *Φίλιππος*)
—Herakleia: **(6)** ii-iii AD *IG* x (2) (2) 95 (*Φει-*: d. *Παράμονος*); **(7)** a. 202 AD ib. 74, 11 (*Σεπτιμία Φλ. Φ.*: m. *Σεπτ. Ἰουλιανός*)
Macedonia (Mygdonia):
—Thessalonike: **(8)** c. 303 AD Musurillo, *Acts Christian Martyrs* pp. 281 ff.
Macedonia (Pieria):
—Pydna: **(9)** i-ii AD *SEG* xxxviii 666 (d. *Παρμενίων*, *Αὐρηλία*)

Φιλιππάριν
Macedonia (Bottiaia):
—Skydra: **(1)** ?iii AD ib. ii 396 + Robert, *Hell.* i pp. 70-1 (*Αὐρ. Φ.*: d. *Εὐρυδίκη*)

Φιλιππᾶς
Macedonia: **(1)** 238 AD *ILeukopetra* 89, 8 (slave/freed.)

Φιλίππη
Macedonia: **(1)** 219 BC *PEnt* 32, 3 (Tataki, *Macedonians* p. 445 no. 10) (d. *Φίλιππος*)
Macedonia (Pieria):
—Dion: **(2)** f. ii AD *SEG* xxxix 580, 4

Φιλιππιανός
Thrace:
—Perinthos-Herakleia: **(1)** iii-iv AD *IPerinth* 167 (*AD* 51-2 (1996-7) Mel. p. 335 no. 168) (*Αὐρ. Φ.*: s. *Αὐρ. Νεόφυτος*)

Φιλιππίδης
Thrace:
—Pistiros: **(1)** iv-iii BC Archibald, *Odrysian Kingdom* p. 230 (vase) (*SEG* xlvi 874 v; xlix 910)

Φιλιππική
Macedonia (Edonis):
—Philippoi: **(1)** imp. *CIL* iii 658 (*ASAA* NS 1-2 (1939-40) p. 214; Pilhofer 62) (Lat. Varinia Philippica: d. *Φιλιππικός*, Petronia Rufina)
—Philippoi (nr.): **(2)** imp. *CIL* iii 655 = 14206. 16 (Pilhofer 455) (Lat. Curretia Philippica)

Φιλιππικός
Macedonia (Bottiaia):
—Edessa: **(1)** b. 41 AD *ILB* 49 (Tataki, *Edessa* 304) (Lat. Q. Phil[i]ppicus: s. Quintus)
Macedonia (Edonis):
—Philippoi: **(2)** imp. *CIL* iii 658 (*ASAA* NS 1-2 (1939-40) p. 214; Pilhofer 62) (Lat. M. Varinius Philippicus: f. *Φιλιππική*)
Thrace:
—Oescus*: **(3)** i AD *ILB* 47 (Lat. Q. Phil[i]ppicus)

Φιλιππίς
Thrace:
—Perinthos-Herakleia (nr.): **(1)** i-ii AD *IPerinth* 289 (*Κλ. Φ.*)

Φίλιππος
Cimmerian Bosporos:
—Pantikapaion: **(1)** m. i AD *CIRB* 439; **(2)** f. iii AD ib. 104, 18 (*Φίλιπ(π)ος*: f. *Σύμφορος*); **(3)** 275-278 AD ib. 36, 54 (*Φιλι(ππος)?*: f. *Βασιλίσκος*)
Macedonia: **(4)** f. vi BC *RE* (6); *FGrH* 630 F1 + *POxy* 2465 fr. 1 col. ii, 22 (*Φ.* I: s. *Ἀργαῖος*, *Προθόη*, f. *Ἀέροπος* I: king); **(5)** c. 480-430 BC *RE* (11) (Tataki, *Macedonians* p. 445 no. 11); cf. Beloch, *GG* iii (2) p. 63 (s. *Ἀλέξανδρος* I, f. *Ἀμύντας*); **(6)** v/iv BC Tod, *GHI* ii 186, 5; *FGrH* 154 F8; Arr., *An.* i 29. 3 + Bosworth, *Commentary* i p. 174 (Tataki, *Macedonians* p. 451 no. 46) (f. *Ἀντίγονος* I *Μονόφθαλμος*, *Δημήτριος*); **(7)** ?417-413 BC *IG* i^3 89, 62 (Tataki, *Macedonians* p. 450 no. 45) (f. *Ἀγερρος*); **(8)** iv BC Arr., *An.* i 14. 6 (f. *Πτολεμαῖος*); **(9)** c. 382-336 BC *RE* (7); *Macedonia* 3 p. 749 Index s.v. Philip II (Tataki, *Macedonians* p. 445 no. 13) (*Φ.* II: s. *Ἀμύντας* III, *Εὐρυδίκα*, f. *Ἀλέξανδρος* III *Μέγας*, *Κλεοπάτρα*, *Κυννάνα*, *Θεσσαλονίκη*, *Φίλιππος* III *Ἀρριδαῖος*, *Εὐρώπη*, ?f. *Κάρανος*: king); **(10)** c. 358-317 BC *RE* (8); Berve 781; *Macedonia* 3 p. 734 Index s.v. Arrhidaeus (Tataki, *Macedonians* p. 445 no. 14) (*Φ.* III *Ἀρριδαῖος*: s. *Φίλιππος* II, *Φίλιννα* (Thessaly): king); **(11)** s. iv BC *RE* (13); Berve 777 (Tataki, *Macedonians* p. 449 no. 38) (s. *Ἀντίπατρος*, f. *Ἀντίπατρος*); **(12)** ~ *RE* (15); Berve 787; *SEG* xviii 743, 4 (Tataki, *Macedonians* p. 447 no. 26) (f. *Μάγας*, *Ἀντιγόνη*); **(13)** ~ *RE* (16); Berve 786 (Tataki, *Macedonians* p. 447 no. 25); **(14)** ~ *IG* xii (6) 61, [1], 4, 6, 16 (s. *—οιος*); **(15)** 345 BC *CID* ii 31, 74 (Tataki, *Macedonians* p. 446 no. 20); **(16)** 335-334 BC *RE* (59); Berve 775 (Tataki, *Macedonians* p. 449 no. 36) (s. *Ἀμύντας*); **(17)** 334-330 BC *RE* (61); Berve 779 (Tataki, *Macedonians* p. 450 no. 43) (s. *Μενέλαος*) ?= (*28*); **(18)** c. 332-306 BC *RE* (14); Berve 776; *OGIS* 6, 28 (Tataki, *Macedonians* p. 449 no. 37) (s. *Ἀντίγονος* I *Μονόφθαλμος*, *Στρατονίκη*); **(19)** 331 BC *RE* (60); Berve 778 (Tataki, *Macedonians* p. 449 no. 40) (s. *Βάλακρος*); **(20)** 327 BC *RE* (55); Berve 783 (Tataki, *Macedonians* p. 446 no. 22) ?= (*22*); **(21)** ~ Berve 784 (Tataki, *Macedonians* p. 446 no. 23); cf. *RE* (55); **(22)** 326-325 BC ib. (56); Berve 780 (Tataki, *Macedonians* p. 198 no. 23) (s. *Μαχάτας*) ?= (*20*); **(23)** c. 325-318 BC *RE* (62); Berve 785 (Tataki, *Macedonians* p. 446 no. 24); **(24)** 324-323 BC *RE* (67); Berve 782 (Tataki, *Macedonians* p. 446 no. 21); **(25)** hell.? *SEG* xxxviii 789 (Tataki, *Macedonians* p. 448 no. 33); **(26)** c. 322-313 BC *IOrop* 6, 11 (Tataki, *Macedonians* p. 451 no. 51) (f. ......ρος); **(27)** ?315-297 BC *RE* (9); cf. Beloch, *GG* iv (2) p. 105 (Tataki, *Macedonians* p. 445 no. 15) (*Φ.* IV: s. *Κάσσανδρος*, *Θεσσαλονίκη*: king); **(28)** 307-301 BC *IG* ii^2 561, 5 + *SEG* xxxi 80; *IG* ii^2

Add. p. 662 no. 559, [5] + *SEG* XXXII 101 (Tataki, *Macedonians* p. 449 no. 41) (s. *Μενέλαος*) ?= (*17*); **(29)** iii BC *IG* II² 9263 (Tataki, *Macedonians* p. 451 no. 49; *FRA* 3495) (f. *Λάϊχος*); **(30)** 293-280 BC *RE* (20) (Tataki, *Macedonians* p. 450 no. 42) (s. *Λυσίμαχος*, *Ἀρσινόη*); **(31)** 281 BC Robert, *Documents* p. 53, 7; pp. 57-8 (ident.) (*PP* 15084; Tataki, *Macedonians* p. 448 no. 35) (s. *Ἀλέξανδρος*) ?= (*193*); **(32)** 263 BC *IG* IX (1)² (1) 17, 19 (Tataki, *Macedonians* p. 448 no. 34) (s. *Ἄδμητος*); **(33)** 238-179 BC *RE* (10); cf. Beloch, *GG* IV (2) pp. 139-42; *Macedonia* 3 p. 749 Index s.v. (Tataki, *Macedonians* p. 445 no. 16) (*Φ.* V: s. *Δημήτριος* II, *Φθία* (Molossoi), f. *Περσεύς*, *Δημήτριος*: king); **(34)** 231 BC *SB* 9258, 7 (Tataki, *Macedonians* p. 451 no. 50) (f. *Μένανδρος*); **(35)** ?219 BC *PUG* III 103, 13 (Tataki, *Macedonians* p. 449 no. 39; La'da E1642) (s. *Ἀπολλώνιος*); **(36)** ~ *PUG* III 104, 3 (La'da E1643) (*Φί[λιπ]π[ος]*: s. *Δημήτριος*); **(37)** 218 BC *PEnt* 32, 1-4, 6; 67, 1 (Tataki, *Macedonians* p. 451 no. 48); cf. La'da E1764; E1784 (f. *Τεύτιος*, *Θέων*, *Φιλίππη*); **(38)** f. ii BC *IG* XI (4) 750, 3 (f. *Ἀλέξανδρος*); **(39)** ?178-160 BC Plb. xxxvi 10. 3; D.S. xxxi 40 a; Liv. xlii 52. 5; xliv 45. 9; xlv 6. 9; 28. 11; 39. 7; *IG* X (2) (1) 76; *SEG* XLVI 829, [1] (Tataki, *Macedonians* p. 445 no. 17) (s. *Περσεύς*, *Λαοδίκη*); **(40)** 171 BC *RE* (22) (Tataki, *Macedonians* p. 448 no. 31); **(41)** ii/i BC *RE* (68) col. 2552; Grainger, *SPG* p. 52 (*Φ.* I *Φιλάδελφος*: s. *Ἀντίοχος* VIII *Γρῦπος*, *Κλεοπάτρα Τρύφαινα*, f. *Φίλιππος* II *Βαρύπους*: king); **(42)** f. i BC *RE* (69) col. 2554; Grainger, *SPG* pp. 52-3; *MAMA* III 62, 1 (*Φ.* II *Βαρύπους*: s. *Φίλιππος* I *Φιλάδελφος*: king); **(43)** i/ii AD *SEG* XLVIII 800, [1] ([*T.*] [*Φλ.*] [*Φίλιππος*] [*ν*]*εώτ.*: II s. *T. Φλ. Φίλιππος* I); **(44)** ~ ib. l. 2 (*T. Φλ. Φίλιπ(π)ος*: I f. *T. Φλ. Φίλιππος* II *νεώτ.*); **(45)** f. iii AD *RE* (32); *GVI* 882 (Tataki, *Macedonians* p. 451 no. 47) (f. *Δομίτιος Ἀντίγονος*)

—MEGARA: **(46)** hell. *SEG* XLVI 691 (pithos) (s. *Εὐρύδικος*)

—RESEN (MOD.): **(47)** 218 AD *IG* X (2) (2) 48, 32 (*Αἴλιος Φ.*)

MACEDONIA (BOTTIAIA):

—AIGAI: **(48)** c. 315-280 BC *FD* III (1) 112, 1; *BCH* 68-9 (1944-5) p. 100 (date) (Tataki, *Macedonians* p. 41 no. 15) (f. *Ἀγέλοχος*); **(49)** ?ii BC *BSA* 39 (1938-9) p. 95 no. 5 = *SEG* XLVI 828; cf. *Myrtos* pp. 441-51 (s. *Ἀπολλώνιος*: locn.—Hatzopoulos)

—BEROIA: **(50)** s. iii BC *IBer* 16 B, 25 (f. *Ἀνδροκλείδης*); **(51)** ~ ib. 46, 20 (f. *Ἀλκέτας*); **(52)** 239-229 BC ib. 45, 32 (f. *Μαχάτας*); **(53)** 223 BC ib. 4, 26 (*Φίλιπ[πος]*: f. *Μελέαγρος*); **(54)** ~ ib. l. 34 (s. *Ζωπυρίων*); **(55)** ii BC ib. 141, 42; **(56)** ~ ib. 196 (Tataki 1283) (f. *Ἀγαθοκλῆς*); **(57)** ~ *IBer* 197 (Tataki 1284) (f. *Ἀδαῖος*); **(58)** 122 BC *IBer* 134, 9; **(59)** 117 BC ib. l. 26 (s. *Ἀπο—*); **(60)** i BC-i AD ib. 142, 10 (Tataki 1280) (s. *Κλεώνυμος*); **(61)** ~ *IBer* 142, 12 (Tataki 1286) (I f. *Φίλιππος* II); **(62)** ~ *IBer* 142, 12 (Tataki 1281) (II s. *Φίλιππος* I); **(63)** f. ii AD *IBer* 7 A, 26; **(64)** ii/iii AD ib. 27 A, 20 (slave?); **(65)** ~ ib. 144 B, 3 (Tataki 1278); **(66)** 177 AD *IBer* 135 B, 29 (Tataki 1282) (s. *Φιλίππα*); **(67)** 189 AD *ILeukopetra* 24, 3 (I f. *Φίλιππος* II); **(68)** ~ ib. l. 3 (II s. *Φίλιππος* I, f. *Φίλιππος* III, *Πάπας*, *Εὐκράτης*); **(69)** ~ ib. l. 10 (*Φ[ίλιπ]πος*: III s. *Φίλιππος* II); **(70)** 208 AD ib. 51, 5 (Tataki 810) (*Λικίνιος Φ.*); **(71)** 227 AD *ILeukopetra* 72, 2 (*Αἰλιανὸς Φ.*); **(72)** 238 AD ib. 89, 4 (f. *Αὐρ. Τροφίμη*)

—EDESSA: **(73)** ii-iii AD *Arch. Pap.* 22 (1973) p. 205 no. 4 (Tataki, *Edessa* 306) (f. *Ἰουλία*); **(74)** iii-iv AD *GVI* 2036, 1, 9, 11 (*IDyrrh* 527 bis; Tataki 146) (*Καστρίκιος Φ.*: f. *Τίτος*); **(75)** 229 AD Tataki, *Edessa* 313 (*Φλ. Φ.*)

—MIEZA: **(76)** hell. *AM* 27 (1902) p. 314 no. 28, 4 ([*Φί*]*λιππος*?); **(77)** iii BC *SEG* XXIV 524 II, 26 (Hatzopoulos, *MI* 2 p. 106 no. 92) (s. *Κι—*); **(78)** i AD Mendel, *Cat.* 1036 (Tataki 1285) (f. *Κλεοπάτρα*)

—PELLA: **(79)** c. 350-325 BC *RE* (58); Berve 774 (Tataki, *Macedonians* p. 161 no. 89) (s. *Ἀγαθοκλῆς*); **(80)** s. iii BC *SEG* XXIV 551 b (f. *Ἀντιγόνα*)

—PELLA*: **(81)** iii BC *AEMTh* 3 (1989) p. 81 n. 19 (amph.)

—SKYDRA: **(82)** ii-iii AD *Arch. Pap.* 22 (1973) p. 209 no. 15 (*Φίλ(ι)ππος*)

—TYRISSA? (ASVESTARI (MOD.)): **(83)** f. ii BC *SEG* XLVII 999, 15 ([*Φί*]*λιππος*: s. *Χιωνίδας*)

MACEDONIA (CHALKIDIKE):

—OLYNTHOS: **(84)** ?352 BC *TAPA* 62 (1931) p. 50 no. 3, 9 (s. *—ης*)

—STOLOS?: **(85)** ?350 BC *SEG* XXXVIII 670, 3 (s. *Ἀννίκας*)

MACEDONIA (DERRIOPOS): **(86)** 95 AD *IG* X (2) (2) 300, 1 (s. *Ποσείδιππος*); **(87)** ~ ib. l. 5 (f. *Βάρβαρος*)

—STUBERRA: **(88)** c. 41-48 AD ib. 323, 22 (f. *Ἀντίγονος*); **(89)** ~ ib. l. 24 (f. *Ζωΐλος*); **(90)** ~ ib. l. 24 (s. *Ἡράκλειτος*); **(91)** c. 41-50 AD ib. l. 9; 324, 13 (f. *Παράμονος*); **(92)** 50 AD ib. l. 16 (s. *Παράμονος*); **(93)** 74 AD ib. 325, 32 (s. *Παράμονος*); **(94)** ~ ib. l. 34 (s. *Ἵππων*); **(95)** ~ ib. l. 49 (s. *Παράμονος*); **(96)** ~ ib. 326, 27 (f. *Καπίτων*, *Ἀπολλόδωρος*); **(97)** ~ ib. l. 29 (f. *Εὐβουλίδης*); **(98)** ~ ib. l. 45 (s. *Ἐπίνικος*); **(99)** ~ ib. l. 54 (s. *Παράμονος*); **(100)** ~ ib. l. 57 (s. *Μενίσκος*); **(101)** ~ ib. l. 63 (s. *Παράμονος*); **(102)** 87 AD ib. 325, 81 (*Φίλιπ(π)ος*: s. *Ἐπιγένης*); **(103)** f. ii AD ib. 329

MACEDONIA (EDONIS):

—AMPHIPOLIS: **(104)** 105 BC *SEG* XXX 546, 3, 42; cf. XLIII 370; *A' Panell. Synedr. Epigr.* p. 105 (date); **(105)** hell.-imp. *PAE* 1984, p. 38 no. 4 (*SEG* XL 522 a); **(106)** ?iv AD *RE* (37); *FGrH* 280; *PLRE* I (5) (Tataki, *Macedonians* p. 62 no. 128); **(107)** vi AD *SEG* XLVIII 731 (*Φίλιπ(π)ος*)

—AMPHIPOLIS (TERRIT.): **(108)** 212 AD Kaphtantzis 592 (s. *Κλεοπάτρα*)

—AMPHIPOLIS?: **(109)** iii BC Dimitsas 897 (*Aphieroma Hammond* p. 271) (f. *Ἀδεία*)

—AMPHIPOLIS (TERRIT.)?: **(110)** v-vi AD Feissel, *RICM* 221 (Pilhofer 583)

—PHILIPPOI: **(111)** s. iii BC *IThrakAig* E264 (f. *Πτολέμας*); **(112)** ii-i BC *BCH* 59 (1935) p. 159 no. 55 (Pilhofer 304) (f. *Ξενοδίκη*); **(113)** i-ii AD *BCH* 47 (1923) pp. 57-8 no. 15 (Pilhofer 588) (Lat. L. Atiarius Philippus); **(114)** ii/iii AD *CIL* III 633 II c, 15 (Pilhofer 163); *CRAI* 1923, p. 277 (date); Collart, *Philippes* pls. 64-5 (Lat. C. Iulius Philippus)

—PHILIPPOI (DRAMA (MOD.))*: **(115)** ?ii AD *BCH* 47 (1923) pp. 74-5 no. 32 + *ASAA* NS 1-2 (1939-40) pp. 214 and 218 (Pilhofer 508) (Lat. C. Oppius Philippus: freed.)

—PHILIPPOI (TERRIT.)?: **(116)** hell.? *SEG* XXXV 746 (Pilhofer 577) (f. *Διονύσιος*)

MACEDONIA (ELIMEIA):

—AIANE: **(117)** ii BC *GVI* 871, 3 (*EAM* 47) (s. *Μενέδημος*, *Ἀδίστα* (Thessaly Pelasgiotis Kerkinion))

—DETELA: **(118)** f. iii BC *SEG* XLIII 937, 1, 4; cf. *BE* 1996, no. 241 (Tataki, *Macedonians* p. 198 no. 24) (s. *Σωρίας*, *Ἀντιγόνη*)

—DIPORO (MOD.): **(119)** ?ii BC *EAM* 45 (f. *Χαρά*)

—KOZANI (MOD.): **(120)** ii-iii AD ib. 22 (f. *Χρυσέρως*)

—KROKOS (MOD.): **(121)** ii-iii AD ib. 19

MACEDONIA (EORDAIA):

—ANATOLIKO (MOD.): **(122)** ii-iii AD *SEG* XLVII 882, 4 (*Φίλιπ[πος]*)

—ASVESTOPETRA (MOD.): **(123)** i BC-i AD? ib. XLV 735 (f. *Ἀντίγονος*)

—EXOCHI (MOD.): **(124)** ii-iii AD ib. XLVII 900 (L 591) ([*Φί*]*λιππος*)

—VOSKOCHORI (MOD.): **(125)** f. vi AD *EAM* 106 (mosaic) (Feissel, *RICM* 77)

MACEDONIA (LOWER PAIONIA):

—EUROPOS: **(126)** ?iii BC *SEG* XXXVIII 614 (s. *Κοινίδας*); **(127)** ?ii AD ib. 608 = XLV 759 (s. *Ἀλέξανδρος*)

MACEDONIA (LYNKESTIS):

—ACHLADA (MOD.): **(128)** f. iii AD *EAM* 168 (f. *Αὐρ. Φιλίππα*)

—HERAKLEIA: **(129)** imp. *IG* X (2) (2) 104 (s. *Πρωτογένης*); **(130)** ii-iii AD ib. 89

MACEDONIA (MYGDONIA):

—KALINDOIA: **(131)** ii/i BC *SEG* XLII 594 (s. *Ἄτταλος*, f. *Ἀλκυάνα*, *Ἄτταλος*, *Μενέλαος*); **(132)** 68-98 AD ib. 580, 55 (s. *Νικόμαχος*); **(133)** ~ ib. 581, 1 (f. *T. Φλαούϊος Ἀνδρόνικος*); **(134)** 70 AD ib. 587, 4; **(135)** a. 98 AD ib. 582, 60 (f. *Πατουμάσης*)

—LETE: **(136)** f. ii BC ib. XLVI 764, 13 (s. *Ἀντιμένης*); **(137)** ~ ib. l. 16 (f. *Καραΐκης*)

—THESSALONIKE: **(138)** 42-32 BC *IG* X (2) (1) 124, 8 (f. *Ἄδυμος*); **(139)** i AD ib. 242, 8 (f. *Ἐπίμαχος*); **(140)** ~ ib. l. 9 (s. *Ἐπίμαχος*); **(141)** f. i AD *RE* (36); *GP* 2628-3159 (Tataki, *Macedonians* p. 188 no. 68); **(142)** s. i AD *IG* X (2) (1) 68, 33; 69, 22 (s. *Ἐπιγένης*); **(143)** ii AD ib. 102, 3 (f. *Φλ. Φίλα*); **(144)** ~ ib. 241 A I, 5 ([*Φίλ*]*ιππος*: s. *Ἀρτεμίδωρος*) ?= (*145*); **(145)** ~ ib. 507, 1 (s. *Ἀρτεμίδωρος*) ?= (*144*); **(146)** iii AD ib. 549; **(147)** 219 AD ib. 153, 9 (*Μαρειανὸς Φ.*: I f. *Μαρινιανὸς Φίλιππος* II *νέος*); **(148)** 219-248 AD ib. l. 7; 163, 10 (*Μαρεινιανὸς Φ. νέος*: II s. *Μαρινιανὸς Φίλιππος* I, *Φλαβιανὴ Νεπωτιανή*, f. *Μαρινιανὸς Φίλιππος* III *νέος*); **(149)** m. iii AD ib. 147, 7 (Lat. M. Aur. Philippus: s. M. Aur. Cassianus); **(150)** 248-249 AD ib. 163, 1 ([*Μαρινιανὸς*] *Φ. νέος*: III s. *Μαρινιανὸς Φίλιππος* II *νέος*); **(151)** v-vi AD Feissel, *RICM* 97 (monogram) (*SEG* XLVII 966); **(152)** 507 AD Feissel, *RICM* 131, 9 (s. *Αὐρ. Γερόντιος*, *Φλ. Μαρία*)

—THESSALONIKE?: **(153)** f. i AD *IG* X (2) (1) 263, 5

MACEDONIA (ORESTIS):

—BATTYNAIOI: **(154)** 192 AD *EAM* 186 I, 44 (*-ιπος*: f. *—ανος ὁ καὶ Οὐαλέριος*); **(155)** ~ ib. l. 58 (f. *Πρίσκος*); **(156)** ~ ib. 186 II, 51 (f. *Δέγμος*); **(157)** ~ ib. l. 52 (s. *Μενέλαος*); **(158)** ~ ib. 186 III, 49 (*-ιπος*: f. *Φιλώτας*); **(159)** ~ ib. l. 54 (f. *Θεότιμος*); **(160)** ~ ib. 186 IV 43 (s. *Φιλώτας*)

—LIKNADES (MOD.): **(161)** hell. ib. 209 (*SEG* XLII 616 (pithos)) ([*Φ*]*ίλιπ[ος]*)

—LYKE: **(162)** ?i-ii AD *EAM* 147, 1

—SISANI (MOD.): **(163)** 146 AD ib. 187, 19 (s. *Μακεδών*)

MACEDONIA (PAIONIA):

—ANTIGONEIA? (BUDUR ČIFLIK (MOD.)): **(164)** imp. *Sp.* 71 (1931) p. 97 no. 228

—KAVADARCI (MOD.): **(165)** ii-iii AD ib. p. 60 no. 130, 7 (*Φ. Αἴλιος Λικινειανός*: f. *Σεκοῦνδα Αἰλία*); **(166)** ~ ib. p. 71 no. 162 (*-ιπος*); **(167)** ~ ib. 98 (1941-8) p. 67 no. 139

—NEAPOLIS? (IZVOR (MOD.)): **(168)** ii-iii AD Dimitsas 301, 1 (f. *Ἡρακλέων*)

—NEGOTINO (MOD.): **(169)** ii AD *Sp.* 98 (1941-8) p. 56 no. 113 (s. *Αἴλιος*, *Λύκος*); **(170)** 153 AD *SEG* XXXVIII 712 (s. *Κήσης*, *Μάντα*)

—STOBOI: **(171)** v-vi AD Unp. (Stobi excav.) inv. I-70-12 ([*Φίλι*]*ππος*)

—STOBOI*: **(172)** c. 500 AD Feissel, *RICM* 274 (bp.)

MACEDONIA (PELAGONIA): **(173)** 94 or 211 AD *IG* X (2) (2) 278 (f. *Δημήτριος ὁ καὶ Καπίτων*); **(174)** ii-iii AD ib. 283 (*Φίλιπ[πος]*); **(175)** iii AD ib. 273 (*Αὐρ. Φ.*: s. *Αὐρ. Γαϊανός*, *Αὐρ. Ἰουλιανή*)

—KOLOBAISA: **(176)** ii AD ib. 229 (*Π. Αἴλ[ιος] Φίλιππ[ος]*)

—MOJNO (MOD.): (**177**) iii AD ib. 174 (*Αὐρήλιος Φίλλιππος*: f. *Αὐρ. Ἀλέξανδρος*)
—PELAGONIA: (**178**) 239 AD *ILeukopetra* 93, 20 with comm.; cf. Papazoglou, *Villes* p. 283 ff. (locn.) (f. *Αὐρ. Οὐαλέριος*)
—PELAGONIA (NR.)?: (**179**) iii AD *IG* X (2) (2) 189 (*[Φί]λιππος*: s. *Παράμονος, Με—*)
MACEDONIA (PIERIA):
—KOLINDROS (MOD.): (**180**) ii/i BC *SEG* XXXIV 639 (s. *Ἱππότας*); (**181**) 122 AD ib. XXXI 632
—PHILA?: (**182**) ?iii BC *RPh* 1911, pp. 133-4 no. 36, 118; cf. Helly, *L'État thessalien* pp. 319-20 (locn.) (*Φίλιππ[ος]*: f. *Ἀγέλαος*)
—PYDNA: (**183**) iv BC *GRBS* 43 (2002-3) p. 119 no. 5, 5; (**184**) c. 230-200 BC *IG* VII 316, 2 (*IOrop* 132); *BCH* 45 (1921) p. 17 III, 55 (Tataki, *Macedonians* p. 171 no. 15) (s. *Ἀλκίμαχος*) ?= (*185*); (**185**) c. 169 BC *SEG* XLIII 451, 2 (Hatzopoulos, *MI* 2 p. 72 no. 55) (f. *Πρωτέας*) ?= (*184*); (**186**) i-ii AD *SEG* XXXVIII 666 (f. *Παρμενίων*)
MACEDONIA (SINTIKE):
—HERAKLEIA: (**187**) 230 AD *IGB* V 5922, 7 (*[Φ]ί̣λ̣ιππος*: f. *Ἀλέξανδρος*)
—HERAKLEIA (TERRIT.): (**188**) ii-iii AD ib. IV 2329 (s. *Πυρούσαλα*)
—NEINE: (**189**) imp. ib. 2246, 2; cf. V 5877 (s. *Φαῦστος*)
—PARTHIKOPOLIS: (**190**) 243 AD ib. 5904 (*Καπιτωνιανὸς Φ. ὁ καὶ Λιβάνις*)
MACEDONIA?: (**191**) ?s. iv BC *HE* 746 (f. *Ἀμύντωρ*); (**192**) 323 BC *RE* (57); Berve 789 (Tataki, *Macedonians* p. 447 no. 27); (**193**) 303 BC *RE* (19) (Tataki, *Macedonians* p. 447 no. 29) ?= (*31*); (**194**) 198 BC *ID* 380, [77]; 442 B, 45; cf. *ID Index* s.v. (Tataki, *Macedonians* p. 450 no. 44) (s. *Πτολεμαῖος*); (**195**) 169 BC *RE* (23) (Tataki, *Macedonians* p. 448 no. 32) (Lat. Philippus); (**196**) i BC/i AD *Xenia antiqua* 10 (2001) p. 22 no. C (or Thrace: *Φίλιπ(π)ος*: s. *Ποσειδώνιος, Νανώ*)
SCYTHIA MINOR:
—ISTROS: (**197**) i BC-i AD *ISM* I 191 II, 35 (s. *Θεόδωρος*); (**198**) ii AD ib. 196, 20 (I f. *Φίλιππος* II); (**199**) ~ ib. l. 20 (II s. *Φίλιππος* I); (**200**) ~ ib. 201 II, 7; (**201**) ~ ib. l. 12 (*[Φί]λιππος*: s. *Ἱερώνυμος*); (**202**) ~ ib. 217, 1 (*Φίλι[ππος]*?: I f. *Φίλιππος* II); (**203**) ~ ib. l. 1 (*[Φιλ]ιππος*?: II s. *Φίλιππος* I); (**204**) 138 AD ib. 193 I, 59 (f. *Ἀντιγένης*); (**205**) ~ ib. 193 II, 57 (f. *Βάσυλλος*); (**206**) iii AD ib. 291, 3 (f. *Ἀπφία*); (**207**) f. iii AD *Stud. Fischer* p. 32 no. 4, 5 (s. *Σατυρίων*)
—KALLATIS: (**208**) s. iii BC *ISM* III 35 A, 24 (*[Φ]ίλιππος*: s. *Ἀπολλώνιος*); (**209**) f. iii AD ib. 189 (*Φίλλ-*: s. *Στέφανος*)
—NOVIODUNUM (NR.): (**210**) iii-iv AD Barnea 63 b (Popescu, *IGL* 267 b)
—TROESMIS*: (**211**) 134 AD *ISM* V 137 II, 9 (Lat. [Iu]l. Philippus)
SKYTHIA:
—TANAIS: (**212**) c. 200-210 AD *CIRB* 1277, 18 (*Φίλιπ[πος]*)
TAURIS:
—CHERSONESOS: (**213**) c. 300-285 BC Kats p. 114 no. 121 (amph., tile); (**214**) iii BC *IAK* 65 (1918) p. 12 no. 2 (f. *Γόσα*); (**215**) iii-ii BC *IOSPE* I^2 713 (*Φί[λιπ]πος*)
THRACE:
—ABDERA: (**216**) iii AD *IG* XII (8) 561 (*GVI* 248) (*Φ.*: I f. *Αὐρ. Φίλιππος* II); (**217**) ~ *IG* XII (8) 561 (*GVI* 248) (*Αὐρ. Φ.*: II s. *Φίλιππος* I)
—AQUAE CALIDAE*: (**218**) vi AD Beševliev 171, 8
—BEROE-AUGUSTA TRAIANA: (**219**) 180-185 AD *IGB* III 1585, 9 (*[Φί]λιππος*: s. *Ἀσιατικός*)
—BEROE-AUGUSTA TRAIANA (TERRIT.): (**220**) ii-iii AD ib. 1742 (s. *Γάϊος*); (**221**) ~ ib. V 5624 (s. *Τήρης*) ?= (*223*); (**222**) ~ ib. 5627 (*Φίλιππ[ος]*) ?= (*223*); (**223**) ~ ib. 5625-6 (f. *Γάϊος*) ?= (*222*) (*221*)
—BOURDAPA: (**224**) ii AD ib. III 1360 (f. *Λήδα*)
—BYZANTION: (**225**) i BC-i AD *IByz* 19, 14
—BYZANTION (TERRIT.): (**226**) imp. Unp. (Sayar) (s. *Φανέας*)
—BYZANTION?:
——(Dionysia): (**227**) ii-i BC *IByz* 378 (s. *Ζώπυρος*)
—BYZANTION*: (**228**) s. iii AD *Anal. Boll.* 31 (1912) p. 175 (bp.)
—DIOKLETIANOPOLIS: (**229**) v-vi AD *BIAB* 11 (1937) p. 235 (bronze)
—LYSIMACHEIA: (**230**) m. ii BC *ISestos* 38 b, 8 (f. *Διονυσόδωρος*)
—NICOPOLIS AD NESTUM: (**231**) ii AD *IGB* IV 2336, 9 (*[Φίλι]ππος*?: s. *Ἀλέξανδρος*) ?= (*232*); (**232**) ~ ib. l. 10 (f. *Ποσειδώνιος*) ?= (*231*)
—PAUTALIA: (**233**) ii-iii AD ib. 2085, 2 (?s. *Αὐρ. Πατρίκιος*)
—PERINTHOS-HERAKLEIA: (**234**) i-ii AD Unp. (Sayar) (*Κλ. Φ.*)
—PERINTHOS-HERAKLEIA*: (**235**) c. 304 AD *DCB* (6) (bp.)
—PHILIPPOPOLIS-TRIMONTIUM: (**236**) ii AD *IGB* III 990 (*Μ. Οὔλπ. Φ.*: s. *Ἑρμογένης*); (**237**) ii-iii AD ib. 1000 (*Φίλιππ[ος]*: s. *Διόδοτος*); (**238**) iii AD ib. V 5464, 7 (I f. *Φίλιππος* II); (**239**) ~ ib. l. 7, 9 (II s. *Φίλιππος* I, f. *Φίλιππος* III, *Παπίας*); (**240**) ~ ib. l. 10 (III s. *Φίλιππος* II)
—PHILIPPOPOLIS-TRIMONTIUM (TERRIT.): (**241**) ii-iii AD ib. III 1464 (f. *Δραυκενθίη*); (**242**) ~ ib. 1471 (*—ριος Φ.*)
—PHILIPPOPOLIS-TRIMONTIUM (NR.): (**243**) ii-iii AD ib. 1416 (f. *Ἀλέξανδρος*)
—SERDICA (TERRIT.): (**244**) iii AD ib. V 5719 (*Αὐρ. Φίλιππ[ος]*)
—STROUNEILOS: (**245**) 202 AD ib. III 1690 d, 67 (and Thrace Pizos: I f. *Φίλιππος* II); (**246**) ~ ib. l. 67 (and Thrace Pizos: II s. *Φίλιππος* I)

Φίλις
THRACE:
—PERINTHOS-HERAKLEIA?: (**1**) iv BC Hp., *Epid.* iv 4 (*Φίλιδος* (gen.): f. *Ἀριστόδημος*)

Φιλίσκος
CIMMERIAN BOSPOROS:
—GORGIPPIA: (**1**) f. iii BC *CIRB* 1137 A II, 25; 1137 B II, 28 (f. *Ὑψικλῆς*); (**2**) ~ ib. 1137 A II, 33; 1137 B I, 53 (I f. *Φιλίσκος* II); (**3**) ~ ib. 1137 A II, 33; 1137 B I, 53 (II s. *Φιλίσκος* I); (**4**) ~ ib. l. 49; 1137 B II, 30 (f. *Θεόδωρος*)
—KOROKONDAME: (**5**) iii BC *North Pontic Archaeology* pp. 350-2 no. 4 with fig. 6 (*Ἡλίσκος*—ed.: f. *Ἑρμῶναξ*)
MACEDONIA: (**6**) iii BC La'da E1645; (**7**) c. 223 BC *PTeb* 815 fr. 3 verso I, 25 (Tataki, *Macedonians* p. 451 no. 52); cf. La'da E1767 (*Φιλί[σκος]*: f. *Κάλας*)
MACEDONIA (CHALKIDIKE):
—POTIDAIA-KASSANDREIA: (**8**) iii BC *IG* XII (5) 1062 (Tataki, *Macedonians* p. 97 no. 97) (I f. *Φιλίσκος* II); (**9**) ~ *IG* XII (5) 1062 (Tataki, *Macedonians* p. 97 no. 96) (II s. *Φιλίσκος* I)
MACEDONIA (EDONIS):
—AMPHIPOLIS: (**10**) iii BC *IG* IV (1)^2 97, 29 + Peek, *IAEpid* 43 (Tataki, *Macedonians* p. 62 no. 129) (f. *.κεος*)
MACEDONIA (MYGDONIA):
—KALINDOIA: (**11**) c. 320 BC Hatzopoulos, *MI* 2 p. 84 no. 62, 26 (*Φιλίσ[κος]*?: f. *Μύας*)
—LETE: (**12**) iv/iii BC *SEG* XXIV 544 (Tataki, *Macedonians* p. 119 no. 11) (f. *Ἄρχων*)
MACEDONIA (ODOMANTIKE):
—SIRRHA?: (**13**) ii-iii AD Kaphtantzis 39 (*Φιλίσκος*?, *Πιδίσκος*—ed., *Πιλίσκος*?: s. *Δίζας*)
MACEDONIA (PIERIS):
—GALEPSOS: (**14**) imp. Dimitsas 917 (f. *Νικοβούλη*)
SKYTHIA:
—OLBIA-BORYSTHENES: (**15**) iii BC *IOSPE* I^2 201 I, 12 (s. *Ἡρόδωρος*)
THRACE:
—ABDERA: (**16**) c. 311-280 BC *AMNG* II (1) 225; Unp. (Chryssanthaki diss.) p. 239 (coin) (*Φίλιπ(πος)*—*AMNG*, *Φιλίσκ(ος)*—Chryssanthaki)
—BEROE-AUGUSTA TRAIANA: (**17**) ii-iii AD *IGB* V 5580 (?f. *Οὐ—*)
—BYZANTION: (**18**) iii BC *IByz* 64 (f. *Ἀμφικλέα*); (**19**) ii-i BC *Istanbul Ark. Müz.* 7 (1956) p. 55 with fig. 3 (*[Φ]ιλίσκος*: s. *Ἀπολλώνιος*)
—BYZANTION (TERRIT.): (**20**) imp. Unp. (Sayar) (*Φ. ὁ καὶ Κτῆτος*: s. *Ἀπολλώνιος*)
—NICOPOLIS AD ISTRUM?: (**21**) 196 AD *IMS* II 53 I b, 49 (*CIL* III 14507); cf. *ZPE* 146 (2004) pp. 216-20 (Lat. M. Val. Filiscus)
—PHILIPPOPOLIS-TRIMONTIUM: (**22**) ii-iii AD *IGB* III 912, 6
——(Artemisias): (**23**) 163-164 AD ib. 902, 5 (s. *Μᾶρκος*)
—SALYMBRIA: (**24**) imp. *IByz* S 13 (Robert, *Hell.* 7 pp. 47-9 no. 4) (I f. *Φιλίσκος* II); (**25**) ~ *IByz* S 13 (Robert, *Hell.* 7 pp. 47-9 no. 4) (II s. *Φιλίσκος* I)
—SESTOS?: (**26**) 355 BC *IG* II^2 133, 2, [9], 20, 23 (s. *Λύκος*)

Φιλίστα
MACEDONIA (BOTTIAIA):
—BEROIA: (**1**) f. iii BC *IBer* 149 (Tataki 1287) (m. *Στράτων*)
THRACE:
—BYZANTION: (**2**) i BC-i AD *IByz* 19, 6 (d. *Λ. Λούσιος Σατορνῖνος*)

Φιλίστη
MACEDONIA (BOTTIAIA):
—BEROIA: (**1**) 192 AD *ILeukopetra* 30, 6; 31, 29; 32, 4; 33, 10; 34, 7; 35, 8 (Tataki 752) (*Κομινία Φ.*)
MACEDONIA (CHALKIDIKE):
—SERMYLIA?: (**2**) m. iii BC *Cat. lampes Mus. Istanbul* I 168 (lamp)
MACEDONIA (MYGDONIA):
—THESSALONIKE: (**3**) imp. *Makedonika* 9 (1969) p. 161 with pl. 64; (**4**) ii-iii AD *IG* X (2) (1) 186, 3 (*Ἀρρία Προκλιανὴ Φ.*: m. *Λογγινιανὸς Ἀσκληπιόδωρος, Λογγινιανὸς Νικόπολις, Λογγινιανὴ Ἀκυλῖνα*)
THRACE:
—ODESSOS: (**5**) i AD *IGB* I^2 186 bis (PM 1661); *Dacia* 21 (1977) p. 161 (date) (*Φιλ[ί]στη*: d. *Ζῆνις*); (**6**) i-ii AD *IGB* I^2 139 bis (d. *Ζῆνις*); (**7**) s. ii AD ib. 170 (PM 1701); *Dacia* 21 (1977) p. 161 (date) (d. *Ἑστιαῖος*)
—ODESSOS?: (**8**) ?ii-i BC *Syllogos* 19 (1891) Parart. p. 40 (d. *Παρμένων*)

Φιλιστῆς
MACEDONIA (PELAGONIA): (**1**) ii-iii AD *IG* X (2) (2) 282 (s. *Ζωΐλος*)

Φιλιστίδης
SCYTHIA MINOR:
—ISTROS: (**1**) i BC-i AD *ISM* I 191 I, 35 (f. *—ν*); (**2**) ~ ib. 191 II, 30 (s. *Μόσχος*)

Φιλίστιος
TAURIS:
—CHERSONESOS: (**1**) iv/iii BC Kats p. 105 no. 81 (amph., tile) (f. *Νευμήνιος*) ?= (*3*); (**2**) c. 320-310 BC Anokhin p. 138 no. 70 (coin); (**3**) f. iii BC *SEG* XL 615 B, 20 (f. *Νευμήνιος*) ?= (*1*)

Φιλιστίων
THRACE:
—PERINTHOS-HERAKLEIA:
——(Makedones): (**1**) iii-ii BC *IPerinth* 61, 2 (f. *Μητρόδωρος*)

Φίλιστος
CIMMERIAN BOSPOROS:
—PANTIKAPAION: (**1**) ii AD *CIRB* 93, 4 (*Φίλ[ισ]τος*)

Macedonia (Bottiaia):
—aigai: **(2)** m. iv bc *SEG* xxxv 775 (f. *Βερεννώ*)
Macedonia (Chalkidike):
—chalkideis: **(3)** viii/vii bc Plu., *Mor.* 761 B (fict.?)
Macedonia (Mygdonia):
—thessalonike: **(4)** m. iii ad *IG* x (2) (1) 214, 2 (*Γ. Ἀντώνιος Οὐρβανιανὸς Φ.*: s. *Γ. Ἀντώνιος Οὐρβανιανός*)
Skythia:
—olbia-borysthenes: **(5)** s. iv bc *SEG* l 702 IV, 8

Φιλιτώ
Macedonia (Bisaltia):
—tragilos: **(1)** s. iv bc *AD* 23 (1968) Chron. p. 358 with pl. 306 α (*Φιλητώ*—ed.: d. *Κύκνος*)

Φιλλέας
Macedonia (Bottiaia):
—aigai: **(1)** s. iv bc *SEG* xxxv 803 (f. *—γηνη*)

Φιλλινώ
Macedonia (Chalkidike):
—potidaia-kassandreia: **(1)** ?v/iv bc *AAA* 7 (1974) p. 198 (*SEG* xlv 799)

Φιλλίς
Cimmerian Bosporos:
—patraeus (nr.): **(1)** i-ii ad ib. 989 (*Φιλλί* (voc.))

Φίλλυς
Thrace:
—perinthos-herakleia: **(1)** ii ad *IPerinth* 49 B (*Φίλλυδ[ος]* (gen.): f. *Εὐδίων*)

Φιλογήθης
Skythia:
—olbia-borysthenes: **(1)** m. iv bc Dubois, *IGDOlbia* 106, 4 (*SEG* xliv 669) (f. *Διοσκουρίδης*)

Φιλοδέσποτος
Cimmerian Bosporos:
—achilleion (nr.): **(1)** 105 ad *CIRB* 1021, 6 (threptos)
—gorgippia: **(2)** ii/iii ad ib. 1179, 35 (s. *Φαρνάκης*)
Macedonia (Bottiaia):
—beroia: **(3)** ii-iii ad *IBer* 242 (Tataki 1288)
Macedonia (Edonis):
—philippoi: **(4)** imp. *BCH* 57 (1933) p. 327 no. 5 (Pilhofer 220) (Lat. C. Fideius Philod[espotus]?, Philod[emus]?)
Macedonia (Paionia):
—kavadarci (mod.): **(5)** 224 ad *SEG* xxxviii 716 (n. pr.?: slave?)
Scythia Minor:
—kallatis: **(6)** ii/iii ad *ISM* iii 182 (f. *Γάϊος*)

Φιλόδημος
Macedonia (Bottiaia):
—pella: **(1)** ii bc *Α΄ Panell. Synedr. Epigr.* p. 193 no. 14 (*Pella* p. 144 no. 248) (f. *Λύσανδρος*)
Macedonia (Mygdonia):
—thessalonike: **(2)** c. 230 bc *IG* xi (4) 1053, 11 = x (2) (1) 1028 (*RE* (3); Tataki, *Macedonians* p. 188 no. 69); **(3)** c. 23 bc *IG* x (2) (1) 97, 6 (f. *Ἰουλ. Κλεονίκη*)
Scythia Minor:
—istros: **(4)** i bc/i ad *ISM* i 55, 3 (*Φιλόδη[μος]*); **(5)** 138 ad ib. 193 I, 81 (s. *Σαραπίων*); **(6)** ~ ib. l. 86 (f. *Ἀρίστων*); **(7)** ~ ib. 193 II, 78 (I f. *Φιλόδημος* II *νεώτ.*); **(8)** ~ ib. l. 78 (*Φ. νε(ώτ.)*: II s. *Φιλόδημος* I, f. *Διονύσιος*)

Φιλόδοξος
Macedonia (Mygdonia):
—thessalonike?: **(1)** ii ad *IG* x (2) (1) 915; cf. *Tyche* 10 (1995) pl. 14 no. 19b

Φιλοθέα
Thrace:
—salymbria: **(1)** ii-i bc *IByz* S 35 (PM 511) (*Φιλοθέ<ι>α*: d. *Ζήνων*)

Φιλόθεος
Scythia Minor:
—istros: **(1)** ii bc *ISM* i 176 (s. *Μένιππος*)

Φιλόκαλος
Cimmerian Bosporos:
—bosporos: **(1)** 211-217 ad *SEG* xlvii 1196, 3 (f. *Οὐάλης*)
Macedonia (Derriopos):
—stuberra: **(2)** 87 ad *IG* x (2) (2) 325, 74 (s. *Στράτων*)
Macedonia (Edonis):
—amphipolis: **(3)** iii-iv ad *SEG* xxvii 253, 1 (I f. *Φιλόκαλος* II); **(4)** ~ ib. l. 3 (II s. *Φιλόκαλος* I, *Ἀντιγόνα*)
—philippoi: **(5)** i-ii ad *BCH* 62 (1938) p. 412 no. 3 (Pilhofer 206) (Lat. [Va]rinius Philocal[us])
Macedonia (Mygdonia):
—thessalonike?: **(6)** ii-iii ad *IG* x (2) (1) 981 (*M. Οὐαρίνιος Φιλώκαλος*)
Skythia:
—tyras: **(7)** 181 ad *IOSPE* i^2 2, 30 (I f. *Φιλόκαλος* II); **(8)** ~ ib. l. 30 (II s. *Φιλόκαλος* I)
Thrace:
—oescus*: **(9)** a. 195 ad *ILB* 76, 7 (Lat. [Ael.] [Ph]ilocalus: freed.)

Φιλόκας
Macedonia (Bottiaia):
—mieza: **(1)** hell. *AM* 27 (1902) p. 314 no. 28, 1 (*[Φι]λόκας?*)

Φιλόκλεια
Macedonia (Chalkidike):
—potidaia-kassandreia: **(1)** s. iv bc *TAPA* 69 (1938) p. 64 n. 45; cf. *Ancient Macedonia* 1 p. 132 n. 19 (d. *Λυσικράτης*)

Φιλοκλῆς
Cimmerian Bosporos:
—pantikapaion: **(1)** i bc *CIRB* 286; cf. KW pl. 36 no. 520 (*Φιλοκλέως* (gen.): f. *Παπῆς*); **(2)** i ad *CIRB* 327; cf. KW pl. 29 no. 422 (s. *Ἀγαθοῦς*, *Νικάριον*)
Macedonia: **(3)** 201-181 bc *RE* (5) (Tataki, *Macedonians* p. 452 no. 53)
Scythia Minor:
—tomis: **(4)** ii ad *ISM* ii 132 (s. *Χρήστος*); **(5)** ii-iii ad ib. 255, 6 + *Noi monumente* p. 48 fig. 6 (*Φιλοκλέ[ους]* (gen.): f. *Κύριλλα*)
Skythia:
—tyras: **(6)** iii bc *SEG* xxx 923 = 970 (amph.) (xlv 1026. 4) (f. *Ἄρχανδρος*)

Φιλοκράτεια
Macedonia (Sintike):
—parthikopolis: **(1)** 210 ad *IGB* iv 2265, 2 (*Φλαβιανὴ Φ.*)
Sarmatia:
—sarmatai: **(2)** 142 bc *SGDI* 2142, 6, 10 (slave/freed.)

Φιλοκράτης
Cimmerian Bosporos:
—myrmekion: **(1)** ii ad *CIRB* 886 (f. *Ἀθηνόδωρος*)
Macedonia (Bottiaia):
—beroia: **(2)** f. i ad *IBer* 103, 4 (Tataki 1289) (f. *Ἀλέξανδρος*)
Macedonia (Chalkidike):
—olynthos: **(3)** iv bc *SEG* xxxiv 822 (Tataki, *Macedonians* p. 143 no. 110) (s. *Μενεκράτης*); **(4)** ?352 bc *TAPA* 69 (1938) p. 48 no. 3, 5; Hatzopoulos, *Actes Chalc.* p. 80 (date) (f. *Ζωΐλος*); **(5)** ?350 bc *TAPA* 65 (1934) p. 125 no. 3, 6; Hatzopoulos, *Actes Chalc.* p. 80 (date) (s. *Ἀρεσίδημος*)
Macedonia (Edonis):
—amphipolis: **(6)** ?c. 167 bc *SEG* xxiv 580, 5; cf. Hatzopoulos, *MI* 1 p. 136 (*[Φιλ]οκράτους*: I f. *Φιλοκράτης* II); **(7)** ~ *SEG* xxiv 580, 5; cf. Hatzopoulos, *MI* 1 p. 136 (II s. *Φιλοκράτης* I)
Scythia Minor:
—kallatis: **(8)** iii bc *ISM* iii 157 (f. *Ποσείδεος*)
Tauris:
—chersonesos: **(9)** ii ad Solomonik, *NEPKh* 52 (s. *Φαρνακίων*)
Thrace:
—dionysopolis (nr.): **(10)** s. ii ad *IGB* i^2 34 (*CCET* i 4) (*[Φι]λοκράτ[ης]*)

Φιλοκτάτης?
Macedonia (Pieria):
—herakleion: **(1)** v bc *SEG* xlix 770 (vase) (*Φιλοκ(ρ)άτης?*, *Φιλοκτήτης?*)

Φιλοκύδης
Macedonia (Edonis):
—amphipolis: **(1)** 210-207 bc *PPetr* ii 47, 28; iii 74 (a), 1 + Masson, *OGS* p. 266 (Tataki, *Macedonians* p. 62 no. 130; La'da E135)

Φιλοκύνηγος
Macedonia: **(1)** ii ad *SEG* xxxix 1340, 6, 10 (Tataki, *Macedonians* p. 452 no. 54) (glad.)

Φιλοκύριος
Macedonia (Bottiaia):
—allante? (parthenion (mod.)): **(1)** iii-iv ad Feissel, *RICM* 80 (*IG* x (2) (1) 1017) (*-ρει-*)
Macedonia (Edonis):
—philippoi: **(2)** ?iv-v ad *SEG* xxxiv 667 (Pilhofer 123) (*Φιλοκύρι[ος]?*); **(3)** v-vi ad Feissel, *RICM* 249 (Pilhofer 308)

Φιλοκύρις
Macedonia (Pieria):
—pydna: **(1)** 250 ad *SEG* xlvi 800 A, 32 (slave?)
Thrace:
—perinthos-herakleia: **(2)** iii-iv ad *IPerinth* 168 (*AD* 51-2 (1996-7) Mel. p. 337 no. 169) (*[Αὐ]ρ. Φ.*: s. *Δίων*)

Φιλόκωμος
Cimmerian Bosporos:
—pantikapaion: **(1)** iv bc *CIRB* 230 (s. *Κόλχος*)

Φιλόλογος
Cimmerian Bosporos:
—gorgippia: **(1)** iii ad *NE* 9 (1971) p. 10 no. 6 B, 11 (*[Φι]λόλογος*)
Macedonia (Mygdonia):
—thessalonike?: **(2)** ii-iii ad *AEpThess* p. 12 no. 9 (s. *Ἰσίγονος*); **(3)** ~ *IG* x (2) (1) 983

Φιλομένης
Thrace:
—byzantion: **(1)** i-ii ad *IByz* 29 (*Φιλομένου* (gen.), *Φιλο(υ)μενός?*)

Φιλόμηλος
Cimmerian Bosporos:
—pantikapaion: **(1)** i ad *CIRB* 371 (s. *Βοτῆς*); **(2)** i/ii ad ib. 582; cf. KW pl. 13 no. 195 (f. *Ἀριαράθη*)
Macedonia: **(3)** 246-226 bc *FD* iii (4) 156, 2 (Tataki, *Macedonians* p. 452 no. 57) (f. *Λυσίας*)
Macedonia (Edonis):
—amphipolis: **(4)** m. iv bc *Mous. Kavalas* p. 135 no. *Λ*. 125 (f. *Νικαία*)
Macedonia?: **(5)** 189 bc Plb. xxi 35. 2; Holleaux, *Études* 3 pp. 357-63 (ident., stemma) (Tataki, *Macedonians* p. 452 no. 55)

?= (6); (6) s. ii BC *IDidyma* 458; Holleaux, *Études* 3 pp. 357-63 (ident., stemma) (Tataki, *Macedonians* p. 452 no. 56) (s. *Λυσίας*) ?= (5)
SCYTHIA MINOR:
—ISTROS?: (7) iii BC *ISM* I 65, 4 (f. *Εὔπολις*)
SKYTHIA:
—OLBIA-BORYSTHENES: (8) iii BC *IOSPE* I^2 201 I, 54 (s. *Διονύσιος*)

Φιλόμουσος
CIMMERIAN BOSPOROS:
—PANTIKAPAION: (1) i AD *CIRB* 406; cf. KW pl. 24 no. 341 (f. *Ἔρως*); (2) m. i AD *CIRB* 532 (*Φιλό[μου]σ[ος]*?: s. *Λούκιος*)
MACEDONIA (MYGDONIA):
—THESSALONIKE: (3) i AD *IG* X (2) (1) 418, 3 (f. *Γν. Ἰούλ. Ἀρτεμᾶς, Ἰουλ. Δύναμις*); (4) ii AD ib. 328 (*CIL* III 14406 b) (Lat. M. Oppius Philomusus: f. M. Oppius Maximus)
MACEDONIA (PAIONIA):
—BYLAZORA: (5) ii-iii AD *Sp.* 75 (1933) p. 17 no. 31, 3-4 (s. *Γλαυκίας, Ἐπιγόνη*)
TAURIS:
—CHERSONESOS: (6) i BC/i AD Const. Porph., *De admin. imp.* 53, 471 (f. *Στρατόφιλος*); (7) f. ii AD *KSIIMK* 15 (1947) p. 59, 11 (Solomonik, *NEPKh* 112 d); cf. *VDI* 1993 (4), p. 63 (f. —s); (8) ~ Solomonik, *NEPKh* 111, 10; *SEG* XLVIII 999, 38 (f. *Βοΐσκος*); (9) ~ Solomonik, *NEPKh* 113, 14 (*[Φιλ]όμουσ[ος]*); (10) 129-130 AD *IOSPE* I^2 359, 27; *VDI* 1960 (3), pp. 154-5, 23 (s. *Ἀπολλωνίδης*); (11) 174 AD *SEG* XLV 985 A, 35 (I f. *Φιλόμουσος* II); (12) ~ ib. l. 35 (*Φιλόμο[υσ]ος*: II s. *Φιλόμουσος* I)
THRACE:
—BYZANTION: (13) ii BC *IByz* 112 (s. *Σοῦσος*); (14) i BC-i AD ib. 236 (s. *Ἀγα—*)
—MARONEIA: (15) ii-iii AD Dumont–Homolle 110b 19 (*IThrakAig* E290) (f. *Μητρόδωρος*)
—SALYMBRIA: (16) iv-v AD *AD* 53 (1998) Mel. p. 461 no. 200
—ZONE (NR.): (17) ii AD *IThrakAig* E431 (*Κλ. Φιλόμο[υ]σος*)

Φιλονᾶς
THRACE:
—ODESSOS?: (1) i BC-i AD *IGB* I^2 296 (*Φιλονᾶν* (acc.): ?s. *Θ—*)

Φιλόνικος
MACEDONIA (BOTTIAIA):
—BEROIA: (1) s. ii AD *IBer* 289 (Tataki 1290) (I f. *Φιλόνικος* II); (2) ~ *IBer* 289 (Tataki 1291) (II s. *Φιλόνικος* I, *Παραμόνα*)
MACEDONIA (DERRIOPOS):
—STUBERRA: (3) 74 AD *IG* X (2) (2) 326, 59 (-νει-: f. *Εἰρηναῖος*)
MACEDONIA (EDONIS):
—AMPHIPOLIS: (4) iv BC *SEG* XLII 555 (f. *Ἱεράγων*)
MACEDONIA (MYGDONIA):
—THESSALONIKE: (5) c. 23 BC *IG* X (2) (1) 113, 4 (*Μ. Ἐρέννιος Φ.*)
THRACE: (6) iv BC ib. II^2 8927 (*FRA* 2592) (s. *Βίθυς*); (7) 153-144 BC *SGDI* 1816, 3 (slave/freed.)
—LYSIMACHEIA: (8) 273 BC *IG* IX (1)^2 (1) 12, 4 (s. *Φαΐσκος*)
—MARONEIA: (9) c. 365-336 BC Schönert-Geiss, *Maroneia* 486 (coin)

Φιλονοίη
CIMMERIAN BOSPOROS:
—PATRAEUS: (1) iv BC *CIRB* 1017 (*GVI* 338; *CEG* II 738) (d. *Σάτυρος, Ἡδείη*)

Φιλοξένα
MACEDONIA (BOTTIAIA):
—BEROIA: (1) ii BC *IBer* 200 (Tataki 1292) (d. *Σωσιγένης*)
—PELLA: (2) s. iv BC *SEG* XLII 619 a

TAURIS:
—CHERSONESOS: (3) inc. *IAK* I (1901) p. 23 (vase) (*Φιλο(ξ)ένα—IAK*)

Φιλοξένη
MACEDONIA (EORDAIA):
—ARNISA?: (1) m. ii AD *EAM* 123, 3; Hatzopoulos, *MI* I p. 94 n. 4 (locn.) (d. *Ὀλυμπιάς*)

Φιλοξενίδης
CIMMERIAN BOSPOROS:
—HERMONASSA: (1) i-ii AD *CIRB* 1083 (*Φειλοξενείδης*: f. *Μηνόδωρος*)

Φιλοξενίς
MACEDONIA (EDONIS):
—AMPHIPOLIS: (1) hell.? *SEG* XXX 549 (d. *Ἀριστοκράτης*)

Φιλόξενος
CIMMERIAN BOSPOROS:
—GORGIPPIA: (1) ii/iii AD *CIRB* 1185
—PANTIKAPAION: (2) ii AD ib. 93, 1 (*Φι[λ]όξ[ε]νο[ς]*)
—PANTIKAPAION?: (3) v-vi AD *SEG* XXXIX 699 (s. *Ἀγαπητός*)
—THEODOSIA: (4) f. iv BC *CIRB* 231 (s. *Στρατῶναξ*)
MACEDONIA: (5) s. iv BC *RE* (2); Berve 794 (Tataki, *Macedonians* p. 452 no. 58) ?= (6); (6) ~ *RE* (3); Berve 796; *IG* XII (9) 222, 2, 5; *CID* II 76 I, 18 (Tataki, *Macedonians* p. 453 no. 59); *Eretria* XI pp. 97-101 (ident., date) ?= (5) (8); (7) ~ *IEph* 1433 (Tataki, *Macedonians* p. 453 no. 63) (f. *Θεύχρηστος*); (8) 333-323 BC *RE* (1); Berve 793 (Tataki, *Macedonians* p. 453 no. 61) ?= (6); (9) c. 236-209 BC *PPetr*^{2} p. 247; cf. La'da E1554 (f. *Νικάνωρ*); (10) 190 or 189 BC *PHeid* VIII 417, 12, 32; cf. La'da E1786 (*Φιλόξενος*: f. *Φιλώτας*); (11) 98 or 65 BC *SEG* VIII 504 (Tataki, *Macedonians* p. 453 no. 62; La'da E1646) (s. *Εὐκλείδης*); (12) c. 80-30 BC *BGU* 1732, [3], 6, [8], [10], 12-13 etc. (Tataki, *Macedonians* p. 498 no. 242; La'da E1647) (s. *—νιος*: katoikos); (13) 12 AD *PKöln* 227 B, 12 (*Φιλόξ[ενος]*: f. *Ἐ.....ος*)
MACEDONIA (BOTTIAIA):
—ALOROS: (14) 368 BC *RE* (7) (Tataki, *Macedonians* p. 45 no. 5) (s. *Πτολεμαῖος*)
—BEROIA: (15) 223 BC *IBer* 4, 19 (s. *Νικ—*); (16) ~ ib. l. 20 (s. *Τεύτιος*); (17) 41-44 AD ib. 60, 6 (Tataki 1294); (18) s. ii AD *IBer* 269 (Tataki 1293) (*Φιλόξε[νος]*); (19) 229 AD *IBer* 68, 9 (Tataki 984) (*Οὐαλεριανὸς Φ.*)
MACEDONIA (CHALKIDIKE):
—OLYNTHOS: (20) ?350 BC *TAPA* 59 (1928) p. 226, 5, 12; Hatzopoulos, *Actes Chalc.* p. 80 (date) (s. *Χάβρης*)
—POLICHNE (NR.)?: (21) i AD *TAPA* 69 (1938) p. 70 no. 26 (I f. *Φιλόξενος* II); (22) ~ ib. (*Φιλόξ[ενος]*: II s. *Φιλόξενος* I)
—POTIDAIA-KASSANDREIA: (23) 2 BC or 115 AD *Essays Laourdas* p. 97 (f. *Μένανδρος*)
MACEDONIA (DERRIOPOS): (24) f. ii AD *IG* X (2) (2) 305 (*Φ. Φ.*: s. *Τ. Φ. Ὑγῖνος*)
—STUBERRA: (25) 74 AD ib. 326, 18 (s. *Ὀρέστης*); (26) 121 AD ib. 328, 6 (*Μ. Ἰνστέϊος Κασσιανὸς Φ.*: s. *Μ. Ἰνστέϊος Ὀρέστης*); (27) c. 126 AD ib. 336; 342; cf. 4 (*Τ. Φλαούϊος Φ.*: s. *Τ. Φλ. Ὀρέστης*)
MACEDONIA (EDONIS):
—AMPHIPOLIS: (28) 90 BC *SEG* XLVIII 716 ter, 3, 8 (s. *Περιγένης*)
—AMPHIPOLIS (TERRIT.)*: (29) ?ii-i BC Kaphtantzis 578; 580-3 (terracotta) ?= (34)
MACEDONIA (MYGDONIA):
—CHARAKOMA*: (30) s. ii AD Dimitsas 682, 10 + *Tekmeria* 6 (2001) pp. 135-6
—KALINDOIA: (31) c. 315 BC Hatzopoulos, *MI* 2 p. 84 no. 62, 31 (s. *Ἐ—*)
—THESSALONIKE: (32) s. ii AD *IG* X (2) (1) 245 I, 8 (*[Φιλ]όξενος*?)
—THESSALONIKE?: (33) i AD ib. 913 (*Φιλόξεν[ος]*)
—THESSALONIKE*: (34) imp. *Makedonika* 14 (1974) p. 346 (terracotta) ?= (29)
MACEDONIA (PAIONIA):
—ARGOS: (35) ii AD *ZA* 15 (1965) p. 117; cf. Papazoglou, *Villes* p. 311 (locn.) (*Αὐρ. Φ.*)
—BYLAZORA: (36) ii-iii AD *Sp.* 75 (1933) p. 19 no. 37, 4 (s. *Λούκιος, Μακέτη*)
MACEDONIA (PELAGONIA)?: (37) ii AD *IG* X (2) (2) 186, 6 (or Arabia Felix Amara?: f. (nat.) *Παρμενίδης*)
MACEDONIA?: (38) 331 BC *RE* (4); Berve 795 (Tataki, *Macedonians* p. 453 no. 60)
SKYTHIA:
—OLBIA-BORYSTHENES: (39) iv/iii BC Dubois, *IGDOlbia* 95 (vase) + *SEG* XLII 709. 1 a (*Φιλ[όξε]νος*—ed., *Φιλ[όνι]κος*—Dubois: f. *Ἡροσῶν, Καλλίνικος*); (40) iii BC *IOSPE* I^2 201 I, 28 (f. *Καλλίνικος*)
THRACE: (41) 232 or 206 BC *CPR* XVIII 4, 68; cf. La'da E830 (f. *Ἡρακλείδης*)
—AINOS: (42) a. 316 BC *IG* IV (1)^2 94 b, 47 (Perlman, *City and Sanctuary* E.1 with pp. 78-9 (date)) (f. *Δεινοκλῆς*)
—BYZANTION: (43) i BC-i AD *IByz* 153 (Fıratlı–Robert pp. 103-4 no. 160) (f. *Γυκεῖα, Ἀρ.ε—*)
—BYZANTION (TERRIT.): (44) iv/iii BC *IByz* 66 (f. *Πασίων*)
—ERGISSENOI: (45) ii AD *IGB* III 1593, 16
—MARONEIA: (46) ii-i BC *IThrakAig* E212, 15 (f. *Ἀνάξιππος*); (47) ~ ib. l. 19 (s. *Λυσανίας*); (48) ~ ib. l. 28 (s. *Σεραπίων*)
—ODESSOS: (49) i-ii AD *IGB* I^2 51 b, 5 (I f. *Φιλόξενος* II); (50) ~ ib. l. 5 (*[Φιλόξ]ενος*?: II s. *Φιλόξενος* I); (51) s. ii AD ib. 79 bis, 4 (*CCET* I 34) (I f. *Φιλόξενος* II); (52) ~ *IGB* I^2 79 bis, 4 (*CCET* I 34) (II s. *Φιλόξενος* I)
—ODESSOS?: (53) s. ii AD *IGB* I^2 206 quater; *Dacia* 21 (1977) p. 161 (date) (f. *Ἀβροκόμας*)
—PERINTHOS-HERAKLEIA: (54) 316-309 BC *IG* II^2 1956, 188 (*FRA* 6044); *Ancient Macedonia* 5 p. 445 with n. 10 (date) (*Φιλόξεν[ος]*)
—SESTOS: (55) c. 320 BC *IG* XII (6) 43, 3, 16 (f. *Ναοσίνικος*)

Φιλόπαππος
MACEDONIA (PAIONIA):
—STOBOI*: (1) c. 165 AD *JÖAI* 15 (1912) p. 52 no. 20 (*Studies Stobi* I p. 164) (*Φιλοπαππίδαι* (n. gent.))
THRACE:
—SERDICA: (2) f. iii AD *IGB* IV 1910, 7; 1992, 12 (*Ἰούλ. Φ.*)

Φιλοπάτρα
CIMMERIAN BOSPOROS:
—PANTIKAPAION: (1) 14 AD *CIRB* 335, 2 (d. *Ἀλκίας*)
MACEDONIA (BOTTIAIA):
—PELLA?: (2) iv/iii BC *Arch. Pap.* 22 (1973) p. 203 no. 1 (d. *Μικύλος*, m. *Ἀντίμαχος, Σωπάτρα*)
SKYTHIA:
—TANAIS (NR.): (3) ii AD *CIRB* 1314

Φιλοποίμην
THRACE:
—ABDERA: (1) hell.? Hp., *Ep.* 12; 15; 17 (s. *Δάμων*: fict.)

Φίλος
MACEDONIA (BOTTIAIA):
—BEROIA: (1) ii/iii AD *IBer* 143 B, 26 (I f. *Φίλος* II); (2) ~ ib. l. 26 (Tataki 1295) (*Φ. ν(εώ)τ.*: II s. *Φίλος* I, *Φιλωτέρα*)
TAURIS:
—CHERSONESOS*: (3) v-vi AD *MIA* 34 (1953) p. 118 (amph.) (n. pr.?)

Φιλοσέραπις
THRACE:
—PAUTALIA (TERRIT.): (**1**) ii AD *IGB* IV 2214, 6 (*Οὔλ(π). Φ.*)

Φιλοστράτη
MACEDONIA: (**1**) iii-ii BC *PAE* 1912, p. 189 no. 219 (Tataki, *Macedonians* p. 453 no. 64)

Φιλόστρατος
THRACE:
—BYZANTION?: (**1**) ?14 BC *IByz* 324 (Robert, *Hell.* 11-12 p. 578; *Eastern cults* p. 33 no. 54) (or Thrace Mesambria?: f. *Ἀρτεμίδωρος*)
—PERINTHOS-HERAKLEIA: (**2**) ii-i BC *ISmyrna* 689 III, 21 (*Φιλόστρατος*: f. *Ἡρακλείδης*)

Φιλότεχνος
CIMMERIAN BOSPOROS:
—PANTIKAPAION: (**1**) i BC/i AD *CIRB* 321 (f. *Μενέστρατος*)

Φιλότιμος
MACEDONIA (MYGDONIA):
—THESSALONIKE: (**1**) i AD *IG* X (2) (1) 399 (*Οὐολκάκιος Φ.*: ?f. *Οὐολκάκιος Νίγερ*)
THRACE:
—APOLLONIA-SOZOPOLIS: (**2**) i-ii AD *IGB* I² 401, 11 (-τει-)
—ODESSOS: (**3**) i-ii AD ib. 125 (*Φιλότιμ[ος]*: ?f. *Ξενα—*)

Φιλού
MACEDONIA (EDONIS):
—AMPHIPOLIS: (**1**) ii/iii AD *SEG* XXXV 713, 2 + *BE* 1999, no. 377; cf. *SEG* XLVIII 722 (d. *Δάντης*, m. *Λᾶγος*)

Φιλουμένα
MACEDONIA (BOTTIAIA):
—EDESSA: (**1**) iii AD ib. XLIII 392 (Tataki, *Edessa* 307a)

Φιλουμένη
CIMMERIAN BOSPOROS:
—TAMAN PENINSULA: (**1**) ii AD *CIRB* 1222 (*Φει-*)
MACEDONIA (BOTTIAIA):
—BEROIA: (**2**) ii-iii AD *IBer* 290 (Tataki 1297); (**3**) ~ *IBer* 323 (Tataki 59) (*Αἰλ. Φ.*)
MACEDONIA (CHALKIDIKE):
—POTIDAIA-KASSANDREIA (TERRIT.): (**4**) imp. Dimitsas 771 (*Φε(ι)λουμένη*: m. *Ἀπρουσία*)
MACEDONIA (EDONIS):
—AMPHIPOLIS?: (**5**) hell. *SEG* L 562, 6 (d. *Σιμωνίδης* (Sparta), ?d. *Διονυσία* (Ionia?, Magnesia))
—PHILIPPOI: (**6**) i-ii AD *AE* 1950-1, pp. 62-3 no. 6 (Pilhofer 722) (Lat. Veturia Philumene)
MACEDONIA (MYGDONIA):
—THESSALONIKE?: (**7**) ii AD *IG* X (2) (1) 886, 3; (**8**) ?iii AD ib. 739
MACEDONIA (ODOMANTIKE):
—SKOTOUSSA (TERRIT.)?: (**9**) 59 or 175 AD *SEG* XXXIV 677 (*Φιλουμέ[νη]*, *Φιλουμε[νός]*?)
THRACE: (**10**) 241 BC *PFrankf* 5, 20 (m. *Νικάνωρ*, *Ἀνδρόμαχος*)
—BYZANTION: (**11**) ii BC *IByz* 167 (Fıratlı–Robert pp. 108-9 no. 174) (d. *Ῥοῦφος*); (**12**) imp. *IByz* 300 (*CIL* III 741) (Lat. Pompeia Philumene: d. *Φιλῖνος*)

Φιλουμενός
MACEDONIA (BOTTIAIA):
—EDESSA: (**1**) 180 AD *SEG* XXIV 531, 13 (Tataki, *Edessa* 167) (*Κλ. Φ.*)
MACEDONIA (MYGDONIA):
—LETE: (**2**) f. ii BC *SEG* XLVI 764, 14 (s. *Δίαιτος*)
—THESSALONIKE: (**3**) ii AD *IG* X (2) (1) 241 A II, 22
MACEDONIA (PAIONIA):
—STOBOI: (**4**) ii AD *JÖAI* 24 (1929) p. 86 no. 4 (*Φιλουμ[ενός]*); (**5**) ii-iii AD *AJA* 88 (1984) p. 581 (*Σεπτ. Φ.*)
MACEDONIA (PIERIA):
—PYDNA: (**6**) 250 AD *SEG* XLVI 800 A, 24 (*Κλ. Φ.*)
SCYTHIA MINOR:
—TOMIS: (**7**) ii-iii AD *ISM* II 32, 9 (*Φι[λ]ου[μενός]*?: f. *Εὐσχήμων*)
SKYTHIA:
—OLBIA-BORYSTHENES: (**8**) ii-iii AD *IOSPE* I² 136, 5 (*Τ. Φ. Φ.*)

Φιλοῦργος
THRACE:
—BYZANTION: (**1**) ?464 BC *IG* I³ 1144, 127 (-λδ-)

Φιλοῦσα
CIMMERIAN BOSPOROS:
—PANTIKAPAION: (**1**) i AD *CIRB* 533

Φιλόφημος
CIMMERIAN BOSPOROS:
—PANTIKAPAION*: (**1**) 143 AD ib. 710, 1 (*Φ. ὁ καὶ Λαιόνακος*: freed.)

Φιλόφρων
MACEDONIA (ODOMANTIKE):
—SIRRHA: (**1**) 155 AD Dimitsas 821, 14 (Kaphtantzis 1) (s. *Ἡρόδοτος*)

Φιλτάτη
THRACE:
—APOLLONIA-SOZOPOLIS: (**1**) v/iv BC *IGB* I² 412 (d. *Ἀπολλωνίδης*)

Φιλτέας
MACEDONIA (EDONIS):
—PHILIPPOI: (**1**) hell. Hatzopoulos, *MI* I p. 188 n. 1 (f. *—λης*)

Φιλτῆς
SKYTHIA:
—OLBIA-BORYSTHENES: (**1**) s. iv BC *IOSPE* I² 195, 6 (*CEG* II 883; Dubois, *IGDOlbia* 47); (**2**) iii BC *IOSPE* I² 201 I, 20 (s. *Λεωνίδης*); (**3**) ~ ib. 201 II, 23 (s. *Λεωδάμας*); (**4**) f. ii BC *SEG* XLII 717 (s. *Ἱκέσιος*, f. *Ἱκέσιος*)

Φίλτων
MACEDONIA (CHALKIDIKE):
—MENDE: (**1**) m. iv BC *AM* 66 (1941) p. 66 no. 14 (Tataki, *Macedonians* p. 122 no. 20) (f. *Ἐπινίκη*)
MACEDONIA (PIERIS):
—NEAPOLIS: (**2**) s. iv BC *SEG* XLIII 430 (Pilhofer 6) (s. *Ἀντικράτης*); (**3**) c. 230-200 BC *BCH* 45 (1921) p. 18 III, 82 (Tataki, *Macedonians* p. 127 no. 21) (I f. *Φίλτων* II, *Ἀπολλωνίδης*); (**4**) ~ *BCH* 45 (1921) p. 18 III, 82 (Tataki, *Macedonians* p. 127 no. 20) (II s. *Φίλτων* I)

Φιλύτας
THRACE:
—LYSIMACHEIA?: (**1**) iii BC *IG* XII Suppl. p. 39 no. 127 C, 56 (*SEG* XXVI 919 C i, 58) (?f. *Ἀγησις*)

Φίλων
CIMMERIAN BOSPOROS:
—BOSPOROS?: (**1**) ?ii BC *JDAI* 23 (1908) p. 72 no. 35; Courby, *Les vases grecs* p. 412 (vase) (potter)
—PANTIKAPAION: (**2**) imp. *CIRB* 755 (*Φίλω<ι>ν*: f. *Ἔρως*); (**3**) ~ ib. 789 (f. *Ἔρως*); (**4**) ii AD *KSIA* 109 (1967) p. 36, 8 (*Φίλω[ν]*); (**5**) 140 AD *CIRB* 711 (s. *Χρήστος*); (**6**) 285 AD ib. 734 (s. *Δαλόσακος*)
MACEDONIA: (**7**) iv/iii BC Tataki, *Macedonians* p. 454 no. 68 (f. *Βιλιστίχη*); (**8**) f. iii BC *IEph* 1405, 5, 6 (Tataki, *Macedonians* p. 454 no. 69) (f. *Κλεόβουλος*); (**9**) m. ii BC *BGU* 2423, 36 (Tataki, *Macedonians* p. 498 no. 244); cf. La'da E1689; (**10**) c. 80-30 BC *BGU* 1733, 1, [4], 7-8, 11, 16-17, 20, 23 (Tataki, *Macedonians* p. 498 no. 243; La'da E1648) (s. *Λύκος*: katoikos)
MACEDONIA (BOTTIAIA):
—AIGAI: (**11**) s. iv BC *SEG* XXXV 805 (f. *Φίλα*); (**12**) iv/iii BC ib. 776 (f. *Ἡρακλείδης*)
—BEROIA: (**13**) 223 BC *IBer* 4, 27 (s. *Παράμονος*)
—PELLA: (**14**) c. 265-260 BC *FD* III (3) 207, 1 (Tataki, *Macedonians* p. 161 no. 90)
MACEDONIA (CHALKIDIKE):
—AKANTHOS: (**15**) 189 BC *BCH* 37 (1913) p. 122 no. 39, [1], 13-14, 26 (Tataki, *Macedonians* p. 43 no. 14) (s. *Πύθων*)
—OLYNTHOS: (**16**) ?352 BC *TAPA* 69 (1938) p. 48 no. 3, 17; Hatzopoulos, *Actes Chalc.* p. 80 (date) (s. *Θεόδοτος*)
MACEDONIA (DERRIOPOS): (**17**) 74-95 AD *IG* X (2) (2) 300, 7; 325, 26 (s. *Κόνων*)
—STUBERRA: (**18**) c. 41-48 AD ib. 323, 20 (f. *Σωσίστρατος*); (**19**) ~ ib. l. 25 (f. *Ζωΐλος*); (**20**) c. 41-50 AD ib. l. 26; 324, 16 (I f. *Φίλων* II) ?= (*26*); (**21**) ~ ib. 323, 26; 324, 15 (II s. *Φίλων* I); (**22**) 74 AD ib. 325, 21 (f. *Ζωΐλος*); (**23**) ~ ib. l. 44 (f. *Παράμονος*); (**24**) ~ ib. l. 46 (s. *Ἀγάθων*); (**25**) ~ ib. 326, 34 (s. *Ποσείδιππος*); (**26**) 87-121 AD ib. 300, 8, 25; 325, 67, 88; 326, 72; 327, 3; 328, 4 (*Μ. Οὐέττιος Φ.*) ?= (*20*); (**27**) 90 AD ib. 326, 78 (f. *Κηράτων*); (**28**) ~ ib. l. 79 (s. *Σωσίστρατος*); (**29**) 107 AD ib. 325, 89, 93 (s. *Παράμονος*); (**30**) 116 AD ib. 327, 29 (s. *Ἰούλιος*)
MACEDONIA (EDONIS):
—AMPHIPOLIS: (**31**) 357 BC Rhodes–Osborne 49, 1
MACEDONIA (MYGDONIA):
—CHARAKOMA?: (**32**) ?ii AD *SEG* XXIX 580 (f. *Ἀνδροσθένης*)
—KALINDOIA: (**33**) 68-98 AD ib. XLII 580, 16 (f. *Δημήτριος*)
—THESSALONIKE: (**34**) i-ii AD *IG* X (2) (1) 421, 1-2; cf. *Myrtos* p. 275 (s. *Ἑλλανίχα*); (**35**) f. i AD *IG* X (2) (1) 133, 7; Robert, *OMS* 5 pp. 295-302 (date) (*Φ[ίλ]ων*)
—THESSALONIKE?: (**36**) i-ii AD Mendel, *Cat.* 971 (f. *Εὐτυχίδας*)
MACEDONIA (ORESTIS):
—BATTYNAIOI: (**37**) 192 AD *EAM* 186 I, 46 (f. *Νικόλαος*); (**38**) ~ ib. l. 55 (s. *Ἀριστόδημος*) ?= (*39*); (**39**) ~ ib. 186 II, 57 (f. *Ἀριστόδημος*) ?= (*38*); (**40**) ~ ib. 186 III, 46 (f. *Ζωΐλος*)
MACEDONIA (PAIONIA):
—ASTREA: (**41**) i/ii AD *IBer* 102 B, 4 (f. *Ἀουιδία Ἀμμία*)
MACEDONIA (PIERIA):
—DION: (**42**) imp. *SEG* XXXIV 623 (*Γ. Ὅσιος Φ.*)
—PHILA?: (**43**) ?iii BC *RPh* 1911, pp. 133-4 no. 36, 65; cf. Helly, *L'État thessalien* pp. 319-20 (locn.) (s. *Μενέλαος*)
—PYDNA: (**44**) 250 AD *SEG* XLVI 800 A, 43 (*Αἴλ. Φ.*)
MACEDONIA?: (**45**) iv BC Arr., *An.* iii 16. 4 (Tataki, *Macedonians* p. 454 no. 67) (f. *Ἀσκληπιόδωρος*)
SCYTHIA MINOR:
—ISTROS: (**46**) iv-iii BC *St. Clas.* 7 (1965) p. 275 no. 6 (vase); (**47**) 138 AD *ISM* I 193 I, 101 (f. *Ἀρτεμᾶς*); (**48**) ~ ib. l. 105 (f. *Διονύσιος*); (**49**) ~ ib. 193 II, 39 (f. *Διονύσιος*); (**50**) ~ ib. l. 73 (s. *Ἀρτεμᾶς*)
—KALLATIS: (**51**) iii-ii BC *SNG BM Black Sea* 205; *SNG Stancomb* 94 (coin); (**52**) a. 15 AD *ISM* III 45, 3-4 (s. *Διοσκουρίδας*)
—TOMIS: (**53**) iii-ii BC *AMNG* I (2) 2435 (coin) (*Φίλω(ν)*?); (**54**) i BC *ISM* II 166, 3 (f. (nat.) *Ἡρακλείδης*, ?f. (ad.) *Ἡράκλειτος*)

—ULMETUM: (**55**) 172 AD ib. v 64, 5 (Lat. Marti(u)s Pilo)
SKYTHIA:
—OLBIA-BORYSTHENES: (**56**) v-iv BC *MIA* 50 (1956) p. 69 (vase); (**57**) iv/iii BC Dubois, *IGDOlbia* 95 (vase) (s. *Σωκράτης*); (**58**) s. i AD *IOlbia* 85, 5 (*IOSPE* I² 104) (*Φίλω[ν]*: II s. *Φίλων* I); (**59**) ~ *IOlbia* 85, 6 (*IOSPE* I² 104) (*[Φ]ίλων*: I f. *Φίλων* II)
—SKYTHAI: (**60**) i BC-i AD? *NS* 421
—TANAIS: (**61**) ii AD *CIRB* 1262, 17 (*Φίλω(ν)*?: f. *Ῥαδάμειστος*); (**62**) f. ii AD ib. 1266, 13 (f. *Ἔρως*)
TAURIS:
—CHERSONESOS: (**63**) iv BC Solomonik, *NEPKh* 165 (f. *Βισθᾶς*)
THRACE: (**64**) m. ii BC *BGU* 1939 c, 4; cf. La'da E811 (f. ..*όδωρος*); (**65**) 173 BC *PAmh* 43, 16 (Velkov 318; La'da E803); (**66**) 46-54 AD *SEG* XVI 415 III, 36 (*IThrakAig* E84) (f. *Ἰσίων*)
—APOLLONIA-SOZOPOLIS: (**67**) s. iii BC *ISM* III 11, 2 (*Φίλω[ν]*: s. *Ἑκαταῖος*)
—BISANTHE-PANION: (**68**) 158-138 BC *SEG* XLIX 877 (s. *Δημήτριος*)
—BYZANTION: (**69**) c. 230-200 BC *BCH* 45 (1921) p. 19 III, 98 (f. *Δαμάτριος*); (**70**) c. 225-200 BC *PMich* 781 II, 19; cf. La'da E339 (f. *Ἀμμώνιος*); (**71**) iii/ii BC *RE* (48) (*PP* 16561); Marsden, *Treatises* pp. 6-9; Fraser, *Ptol. Alex.* 2 pp. 619-20 nn. 425-6; (**72**) ii-i BC *IByz* 200 (Fıratlı–Robert p. 61 no. 47) (f. *Ἀπολλώνιος*); (**73**) i BC-i AD *IByz* 143 (f. *Σατορνῖνα*); (**74**) iii AD ib. 296 (f. *Αὐρ. Μενδᾶς*)
—BYZANTION (TERRIT.): (**75**) i BC-i AD ib. 264 (Fıratlı–Robert p. 86 no. 107) (s. *Διόδωρος*)
—BYZANTION:
——(Delkos): (**76**) imp. *IByz* 22, 3 (s. *Ἀπολλώνιος*)
—ODESSOS: (**77**) 221 AD *IGB* I² 47 bis b, 19 (*Αὐρ. Φ.*: s. *Παρμένων*)
—PERINTHOS-HERAKLEIA:
——(Akarnanes): (**78**) iii-ii BC *IPerinth* 61, 15 (f. *Διονύσιος*)
—TOPEIROS: (**79**) iii AD *AD* 24 (1969) Chron. p. 348 (*IThrakAig* E90) (s. *Μηνόδοτος*)
THRACE?: (**80**) 316-309 BC *IG* II² 1956, 24; *Ancient Macedonia* 5 p. 445 with n. 10 (date) (*FRA* 2593)

Φιλώνδης
MACEDONIA (CHALKIDIKE):
—APHYTIS: (**1**) ?351 BC *A' Panell. Synedr. Epigr.* pp. 80-1, 19 (f. *Φανοκράτης*)

Φιλωνίδης
CIMMERIAN BOSPOROS:
—PANTIKAPAION: (**1**) i AD *CIRB* 531; cf. Zgusta, *PNS* 1171 (*Φιλωηδης*—lap., *Φιλω(νί)δης*: s. *Φιλώτας*); (**2**) f. i AD *CIRB* 534 (I f. *Φιλωνίδης* II); (**3**) ~ ib. (II s. *Φιλωνίδης* I); (**4**) m. i AD ib. 465; cf. KW pl. 36 no. 529 (f. *Μασταροῦς*)
MACEDONIA (CHALKIDIKE):
—AKANTHOS: (**5**) iii/ii BC *PAE* 1912, p. 189 no. 225 (Tataki, *Macedonians* p. 43 no. 15) (f. *Νικόστρατος*)
SKYTHIA:
—OLBIA-BORYSTHENES: (**6**) iii BC *IOSPE* I² 201 I, 7 (s. *Κάλλαισχρος*)

Φιλώνιχος
CIMMERIAN BOSPOROS:
—BOSPOROS: (**1**) iv/iii BC *IFayoum* 193, 6 (La'da E337)
MACEDONIA (CHALKIDIKE):
—TORONE: (**2**) ?353 BC *SEG* XXIV 574, 4; Hatzopoulos, *Actes Chalc.* p. 80 (date) (s. *Ἀντιφῶν*)
MACEDONIA (PIERIA):
—PYDNA: (**3**) iv BC *GRBS* 43 (2002-3) p. 119 no. 5, 6

Φιλώτας
CIMMERIAN BOSPOROS:
—GORGIPPIA: (**1**) ii AD *CIRB* 1140, 9
—PANTIKAPAION: (**2**) i AD ib. 531; cf. Zgusta, *PNS* 1171 (*Φιλοταις*—lap., *Φιλο[κλῆ]ς*—ed.: f. *Φιλωνίδης*); (**3**) ~ *CIRB* 535; (**4**) ii AD ib. 680, 4 (s. *Μύρμηξ*); (**5**) ~ ib. 712 (*Φει-*: s. *Ἡδυλίσκος*); (**6**) ~ ib. 713; cf. KW pl. 21 no. 316 (f. *Φιλωτέρα*); (**7**) iii AD *CIRB* 103, 6
—ZENONOS CHERSONESOS*: (**8**) v/iv BC *SEG* XL 643 (*Φιạτας*—ed, *Φίλτος*—Vinogradov, *Φιλ[ί]τας*, *Φιλ[ώ]τας*—Tokhtas'ev)
MACEDONIA: (**9**) v/iv BC Arr., *An.* i 17. 7; iii 11. 10; *Essays Hersh* pp. 13-17 (coin) (Tataki, *Macedonians* p. 456 no. 81) (f. *Ἄσανδρος, Παρμενίων*); (**10**) c. 365-330 BC Berve 802; *SEG* XLVI 787 A, 7, [9], [13] (Tataki, *Macedonians* p. 456 no. 80) (s. *Παρμενίων*); (**11**) 335 BC *RE* (3); Berve 805 (Tataki, *Macedonians* p. 455 no. 71); (**12**) ~ *RE* (6); Berve 808 (Tataki, *Macedonians* p. 455 no. 72); (**13**) 332 BC *RE* (4); Berve 806 (Tataki, *Macedonians* p. 455 no. 75); (**14**) 331-327 BC *RE* (2); Berve 803 (Tataki, *Macedonians* p. 454 no. 70); (**15**) 323 BC *RE* (7) = (10); Berve 804 (Tataki, *Macedonians* p. 455 no. 73); (**16**) 318 BC *RE* (8); (**17**) iii BC *ITrall* 33 B, 20 (Tataki, *Macedonians* p. 456 no. 78) (s. *Ἡράκλειτος*); (**18**) ?219 BC *PUG* III 104, 7 (La'da E1649) (II s. *Φιλώτας* I); (**19**) ~ *PUG* III 104, 8; cf. La'da E1649 (I f. *Φιλώτας* II); (**20**) 190 or 189 BC *PHeid* VIII 417, 12, 32 (La'da E1786) (*Φιλῳ̣τα̣ς*: s. *Φιλόξενος*: t.e.); (**21**) c. 142 BC *SGDI* 2165, 6, 8, 12, 18 (Tataki, *Macedonians* p. 456 no. 77) (slave/freed.); (**22**) 141 or 88 BC *SEG* II 864 (Tataki, *Macedonians* p. 498 no. 245); cf. La'da E1533 (f. *Λεωνίδης*)
MACEDONIA (BOTTIAIA):
—AIGAI: (**23**) c. 300-275 BC *SEG* XXXV 788 (s. *Ἐρρεβαῖος*, f. *Ἀλκέτας, Κλειώ*)
—AIGAI?: (**24**) 334-331 BC *RE* (5); Berve 807; Papazoglou, *Villes* p. 133 n. 56 (locn.) (Tataki, *Macedonians* p. 72 no. 1) (Lat. Philotas Augheus—Curt. mss.)
—BEROIA: (**25**) iii BC *AD* 52 (1997) Chron. p. 731 (s. *Νικάνωρ*); (**26**) c. 230-200 BC *BCH* 45 (1921) p. 17 III, 58 (Tataki 1300; Tataki, *Macedonians* p. 83 no. 51) (f. *Μένανδρος, Ἀπελλᾶς*); (**27**) ii AD *IBer* 106, 16 (Tataki 1122) (*Δέκμος Ποπλίκιος Φ.*); (**28**) f. ii AD *IBer* 26, 4-5 (Tataki 1118a) (*Σέξ. Ποπίλλιος Φιλῶ̣τα̣ς*); (**29**) ii/iii AD *IBer* 143 B, 29 (Tataki 1299) (f. *Ἴκαρος*); (**30**) 210 AD *ILeukopetra* 56, 1 (f. *Ἐπαφρόδιτος*)
—SKYDRA: (**31**) f. iii BC Tataki, *Macedonians* p. 174 no. 4 (s. *Στρατόνικος*)
MACEDONIA (DERRIOPOS):
—STUBERRA: (**32**) 74 AD *IG* X (2) (2) 326, 51 (s. *Νίκαρχος*); (**33**) 90 AD ib. l. 78 (f. *Νίκαρχος*)
MACEDONIA (EDONIS):
—AMPHIPOLIS: (**34**) a. 357 BC Hatzopoulos, *Actes Amphipolis* pp. 38-9 no. 7, 16; cf. *BE* 1992, no. 321 (s. *Πρωτόμαχος*); (**35**) iii BC *SEG* XXIII 616 (Tataki, *Macedonians* p. 62 no. 131) (f. *Ἀπολλᾶς*)
—AMPHIPOLIS (TERRIT.): (**36**) 157 or 273 AD *SEG* XXXIV 605
MACEDONIA (EORDAIA?):
—EUIA: (**37**) 181 BC *EAM* 87, 11 (Hatzopoulos, *MI* 2 pp. 41-2 no. 17) (f. *Νικάνωρ*)
MACEDONIA (MYGDONIA):
—KALINDOIA: (**38**) c. 321 BC ib. p. 84 no. 62, 24 (s. *Λεωνίδας*); (**39**) ii-i BC *SEG* XXVIII 541, 4; *Anthémonte–Kalindoia* 1 pp. 100-1 (locn.) (s. *Ἀριστομένης*, f. *Ἀριστομένης*); (**40**) ~ *SEG* XXVIII 541, 5; *Anthémonte–Kalindoia* 1 pp. 100-1 (locn.) (s. *Ἀριστομένης*); (**41**) 68-98 AD *SEG* XLII 580, 1 (s. *Νικοκλῆς*, f. *Νικοκλῆς*); (**42**) ~ ib. l. 9 (f. *Κρινίας*); (**43**) ~ ib. l. 29 (s. *Γοργίας*)
—LETE: (**44**) f. ii BC ib. XLVI 764, 4 (f. —*ικος*); (**45**) ~ ib. l. 10 (s. *Λυσίμαχος*); (**46**) 117 BC *Syll*³ 700, 51 (f. *Λύσων*)
—THESSALONIKE: (**47**) ii AD *SEG* XXXVI 645; *KGAM Thess.* 1 59 (date) (f. *Ἡγησάνδρα*)
MACEDONIA (ORESTIS):
—BATTYNAIOI: (**48**) 192 AD *EAM* 186 III, 49 (s. *Φίλιππος*) ?= (*50*); (**49**) ~ ib. l. 51 (f. *Νικόλας*); (**50**) ~ ib. 186 IV, 43 (f. *Φίλιππος*) ?= (*48*)
MACEDONIA (PIERIA):
—PHILA?: (**51**) ?iii BC *RPh* 1911, pp. 133-4 no. 36, 63; cf. Helly, *L'État thessalien* pp. 319-20 (locn.) (s. —*ίδας*)
SCYTHIA MINOR:
—TOMIS: (**52**) ii AD *ISM* II 125, 13 (s. *Εὔβουλος*)
SKYTHIA:
—TANAIS: (**53**) 155 AD *CIRB* 1260, 25 (*Φιλ[ώ]τας*: f. —*ος*); (**54**) 244 AD ib. 1287, 27 (*Φιλῶ̣τ̣α̣[ς]*—Tokhtas'ev: s. —*χος*)
THRACE: (**55**) 327 BC Arr., *An.* iv 13. 4; Berve 801 (Tataki, *Macedonians* p. 456 no. 79) (s. *Κάρσις*); (**56**) 221 BC *PPetr* III 112 e II, 28 (Velkov 319; La'da E805); (**57**) c. 100-75 BC *SB* 8974 fr. 3 II, 42 (Velkov 320; La'da E804) (s. *Πολέμων*: katoikos); (**58**) ~ *SB* 8974 fr. 3 II, 43; cf. La'da E765 (f. *Κάλλιππος*)
—AINOS: (**59**) i AD *ISamothrace* 42, 4
—APOLLONIA-SOZOPOLIS: (**60**) v/iv BC Imhoof-Blümer, *MGr* p. 235 no. 33 (coin) (*Φιλ(ώ)τας?*)
—BYZANTION: (**61**) ii AD *IByz* 317 b (Fıratlı–Robert p. 120 no. 201) (f. *Γαῦρος ὁ καὶ Γάϊος*)
—BYZANTION?: (**62**) i BC-i AD *IByz* 356 (s. *Ἀρισταγόρας*)
—LYSIMACHEIA: (**63**) m. ii BC *ISestos* 38 b, 3 (f. *Ἀντίπατρος*)

Φιλωτέρα
CIMMERIAN BOSPOROS:
—PANTIKAPAION: (**1**) i-ii AD *CIRB* 639; cf. KW pl. 19 no. 271 (*Φ(ι)λωτέρα*: m. *Φάννας, Παπίας*); (**2**) ii AD *CIRB* 713; cf. KW pl. 21 no. 316 (d. *Φιλώτας*)
MACEDONIA: (**3**) iv/iii BC *RE* (-) (*PP* 14574) (d. *Πτολεμαῖος* I *Σωτήρ* (Eordaia), *Βερενίκη*)
MACEDONIA (BOTTIAIA):
—BEROIA: (**4**) i AD *IBer* 189 (-*λο*-: d. *Ἀλέξανδρος*); (**5**) ii-iii AD ib. 227 (Tataki 1301) (d. *Ἔλενος*); (**6**) ii/iii AD *IBer* 143 B, 26 (Tataki 1296) (-*λου*-: m. *Φίλος*)
MACEDONIA (EDONIS):
—AMPHIPOLIS: (**7**) iii BC *RA* 1935 (2), p. 67 no. 2 (Kaphtantzis 605) (d. *Ἀπολλόδωρος*)
MACEDONIA (ELIMEIA):
—AIANE (TERRIT.): (**8**) f. ii AD *EAM* 9 (d. *Ἀρριδαῖος*)
—XEROLIMNI (MOD.): (**9**) ii AD *A' Panell. Synedr. Epigr.* p. 66 no. 13 (*SEG* XLIX 852)
MACEDONIA (EORDAIA): (**10**) imp. Dimitsas 288 (m. *Διονύσιος, Κλιτύς*)
MACEDONIA (MYGDONIA):
—HERAKLEIA: (**11**) iv BC *Latreies sten Perifereia* p. 28 (-*τή*-)
—THESSALONIKE: (**12**) ii-i BC *IG* X (2) (1) 77, 5 (d. *Ἀντίγονος*, m. *Διονυσία*); (**13**) m. iii AD ib. 176, 5 (*Αὐρ. Φ.*); (**14**) ~ ib. 558, 3 (m. *Ἀρτεμιδώρα, Ἡλιοδώρα*)
—THESSALONIKE?: (**15**) ii-iii AD ib. 758 A, 1 (*Ἰουλ. Φ.*)
MACEDONIA (ORESTIS):
—AGIA ANNA (MOD.): (**16**) ii-i BC *EAM* 192 (d. *Ἱππόστρατος*)
MACEDONIA (PAIONIA):
—ANTIGONEIA? (TREMNIK (MOD.)): (**17**) ii-iii AD *SEG* II 440-1
—NEAPOLIS? (SMILOVCI (MOD.)): (**18**) ii-iii AD *Sp.* 98 (1941-8) p. 32 no. 78
—STOBOI: (**19**) i/ii AD Šašel, *IL* 1253 (Lat. Philotera)

MACEDONIA (TYMPHAIA):
—SYDENDRO (MOD.): **(20)** f. iii AD *EAM* 62, 1 (m. *Χρήστη*)

Φιλώτη
MACEDONIA (PIERIA):
—DION (TERRIT.): **(1)** ?iii AD *SEG* XXVI 728 (*Φιλωτη* (dat.)—Cormack, *Φιλῶ τῇ* (dat.)—*SEG*)

Φινίων?
SCYTHIA MINOR:
—TOMIS: **(1)** ii-iii AD *ISM* II 18, 8 (*Σφινίων*—edd. prr.)

Φίντις
KOLCHIS:
—VANI (MOD.): **(1)** i BC Braund, *Georgia* p. 147 n. 110 (vase)

Φιράδμων
THRACE:
—APOLLONIA-SOZOPOLIS: **(1)** v/iv BC *IGB* V 5147 (s. *Διοφάνης*)

Φίρμενος
THRACE:
—HADRIANOPOLIS (TERRIT.): **(1)** ii AD ib. III 1830 (*Αἰλ. Φ.*)

Φιρμῖνα
THRACE:
—PERINTHOS-HERAKLEIA: **(1)** iii AD *IPerinth* 147 (*-μεῖ-*)

Φίρμος
MACEDONIA (EDONIS):
—PHILIPPOI (NR.): **(1)** ii-iii AD *BCH* 54 (1930) p. 376 (Pilhofer 48); Collart, *Philippes* pl. 36. 3 (f. *Σεκοῦς*)
MACEDONIA (MYGDONIA):
—THESSALONIKE?: **(2)** iii AD *AEpThess* p. 8 no. 6 (I s. *Κόϊντος*, f. *Φίρμος* II); **(3)** ~ ib. (II s. *Φίρμος* I)
THRACE:
—BEROE-AUGUSTA TRAIANA:
——Emporion Diskodouraterai: **(4)** iii AD *IGB* II 739, 3
—BIZYE: **(5)** c. 153 AD Taşlıklıoğlu 2 p. 67 no. 1, 14 + *BE* 1972, no. 292 (s. *Αὐλούπορις*)
—BYZANTION (TERRIT.): **(6)** ii-i BC *IByz* 97 (Fıratlı–Robert p. 93 no. 127) (f. —ος)
—PAUTALIA: **(7)** 135 AD *IGB* IV 2057, 9 (*Φίρμ[ος]*: f. *Ἀκλάνιος*)
—SIKINUSTURENOI: **(8)** ii-iii AD ib. III 1771 (s. *Αὔλου*—)

Φίτταλος
THRACE:
—ABDERA: **(1)** c. 475-450 BC May, *Abdera* p. 112 no. 113 (coin); Masson, *OGS* p. 435 ?= (*2*); **(2)** c. 450-425 BC May, *Abdera* pp. 122-3 nos. 126-9 (coin) ?= (*1*)

Φλαβία
MACEDONIA (MYGDONIA):
—THESSALONIKE: **(1)** v-vi AD Feissel, *RICM* 181, 1 (*SEG* XLVII 1011) (*Φλαβιανή*—Tsigaridas: d. *Εὐστόργιος*, ?d. *Ἀλεξάνδρα*)
THRACE:
—BYZANTION: **(2)** i-ii AD *IByz* 144 (*Φλαβ[ία]*)
—PLOTINOPOLIS: **(3)** ii-iii AD Dumont–Homolle 106b (*IThrakAig* E467) (I m. *Φλαβία* II, *Κλεοπάτρα*); **(4)** ~ Dumont–Homolle 106b (*IThrakAig* E467) (II d. *Κλ. Ποτάμων*, *Φλαβία* I)

Φλαβιανός
MACEDONIA (BOTTIAIA):
—BEROIA: **(1)** f. iii AD *IBer* 230, 2 (Tataki 1305) (*Φλαβιανὸς ὁ καὶ Παπποῦς*: s. *Ἀννία Ἐπιγόνη*)

THRACE:
—PHILIPPOPOLIS-TRIMONTIUM: **(2)** ii-iii AD *IGB* III 912, 4
—PHRYGIA*: **(3)** v AD *SEG* XXXIX 665, 3 (*AD* 53 (1998) Mel. p. 468 no. 207) (*Φ(λ)αβιανός*)

Φλάβιος
MACEDONIA (EORDAIA):
—AGIOS PANTELEIMONAS (MOD.): **(1)** s. ii AD *EAM* 126 (*[Φ]λάβιος*)
THRACE:
—BEROE-AUGUSTA TRAIANA: **(2)** 212-217 AD *IGB* V 5600, 7 (*Eastern cults* pp. 233-4 no. 24)
—PHILIPPOPOLIS-TRIMONTIUM: **(3)** ii-iii AD *IGB* III 939

Φλάβις
THRACE:
—BEROE-AUGUSTA TRAIANA: **(1)** ii-iii AD *SEG* XXXIX 649, 6
—DRAGANOVEC (MOD.): **(2)** ii-iii AD *IGB* V 5311 (*CCET* II (2) 521)
—KELLAI*: **(3)** iii AD *IGB* III 1516 a, 30
—TODORIČENE (MOD.): **(4)** ii-iii AD ib. II 590 (s. *Βάσσος*)

Φλαουΐα
MACEDONIA (ELIMEIA):
—OBLOSTAI: **(1)** 200 AD *EAM* 37, 2 (*[Φλ]αουΐα*)
SCYTHIA MINOR:
—TOMIS: **(2)** v-vi AD Barnea 30 (Popescu, *IGL* 13)

Φλαουϊανός
THRACE:
—PHILIPPOPOLIS-TRIMONTIUM: **(1)** 163-164 AD *IGB* III 902, 11; 903; V 5433 (*Φλ. Εὐδαίμων ὁ καὶ Φ.*)

Φλέγων
CIMMERIAN BOSPOROS:
—PANTIKAPAION: **(1)** ii AD *CIRB* 86, 1 (*Καίσιος Φ.*)

Φλίενος
SKYTHIA:
—OLBIA-BORYSTHENES: **(1)** ii AD *IOSPE* I^2 101, 9; Zgusta, *PNS* 242 (f. *Τιμοκλῆς*)

Φλιμάνακος
SKYTHIA:
—OLBIA-BORYSTHENES: **(1)** ii AD *IOSPE* I^2 106, 6; Zgusta, *PNS* 241 (s. *Θεαγένης*)

Φλίμναγος
SKYTHIA:
—OLBIA-BORYSTHENES: **(1)** ii AD *IOSPE* I^2 96, 4; Zgusta, *PNS* 241 (*[Φλί]μναγος*?: s. *Θρασύβουλος*) ?= (*2*); **(2)** c. 193-211 AD *IOSPE* I^2 42, 1; 43, 2 (*Φλεί-*: f. *Θρασύβουλος*) ?= (*1*)

Φλωρέντιος
THRACE: **(1)** 530 AD *PLRE* III (1); *RE* (15)
—DIOKLETIANOPOLIS: **(2)** v AD Beševliev 223, 7 (*Φλο-*)
—ODESSOS*: **(3)** vi AD ib. 95, 7 (*[Φ]λωρέντιος*)

Φλωρῖνος
THRACE:
—ODESSOS: **(1)** v-vi AD ib. 128

Φλῶρος
MACEDONIA (BOTTIAIA):
—EDESSA?: **(1)** m. v AD *PLRE* II (3) (f. *Ἡράκλειος*)
THRACE:
—GLAVA PANEGA (MOD.): **(2)** ii-iii AD *IGB* II 539 (f. *Μοντανός*)
—SERDICA: **(3)** ii AD ib. IV 1929 (*Φλό-*: s. *Κόϊντος*)

Φόδακος
CIMMERIAN BOSPOROS:
—PHANAGOREIA: **(1)** 16 AD *CIRB* 985, 5 (Levinskaya pp. 236-7 no. 5); Zgusta, *PNS* 243 (*[Φ]όδακος*: s. *Πόθων*)
SKYTHIA:
—TANAIS: **(2)** 210-226 AD *CIRB* 1281, 13 (*Φόδακ[ος]*: s. *Σα*—)

Φοίβη
MACEDONIA (MYGDONIA):
—THESSALONIKE: **(1)** 155 AD *IG* X (2) (1) 449 (d. *Παρασκευή*)
SCYTHIA MINOR:
—TROESMIS: **(2)** ii AD *ISM* V 193, 7 (Lat. Rascania Phoebe)

Φοιβιανή
MACEDONIA (BOTTIAIA):
—BEROIA: **(1)** ii-iii AD *IBer* 257 (Tataki 60) (d. *Αἰλ. Λύκος*, *Αἰλ. Φίλα*)
MACEDONIA (MYGDONIA):
—THESSALONIKE: **(2)** ii-iii AD *SEG* L 644

Φοιβίδης
MACEDONIA (EDONIS):
—PHILIPPOI (TERRIT.): **(1)** i BC-i AD Pikoulas, *Chora* p. 128 no. 24 (Pilhofer 625) (f. *Ἱκέσιος*)

Φοιβίων
SCYTHIA MINOR:
—ULMETUM: **(1)** 216 AD *ISM* V 76, 6 = II 130 (*CCET* IV 202) (Lat. Valerius Phoebio)

Φοῖβος
MACEDONIA (DERRIOPOS):
—STUBERRA: **(1)** 74 AD *IG* X (2) (2) 326, 38 (f. *Μικίνης*)
MACEDONIA (EDONIS):
—PHILIPPOI (NEAPOLIS): **(2)** i/ii AD *ILGR* 210 (Pilhofer 28) (Lat. P. Veneteius Phoebus qui et Heronianus: s. *Ἡρωνιανός*, Licinia Valeria)
—PHILIPPOI*: **(3)** ii/iii AD *CIL* III 633 II b, 5 (Pilhofer 163); *CRAI* 1923, p. 277 (date); Collart, *Philippes* pls. 64-5 (Lat. Phoebus: slave) ?= (*4*); **(4)** ~ *CIL* III 633 II c, 7 (Pilhofer 163); *CRAI* 1923, p. 277 (date); Collart, *Philippes* pls. 64-5 (Lat. Phoebus: slave) ?= (*3*)
MACEDONIA (MYGDONIA):
—THESSALONIKE?: **(5)** ?182 AD *IG* X (2) (1) 692
SCYTHIA MINOR:
—ISTROS: **(6)** ii AD *ISM* I 196, 5 (f. *Ῥοῦφος*)
—ISTROS [NR.]:
——Vicus Quintionis: **(7)** 139-161 AD ib. 324, 15 (Lat. Cocceius Phoebus)
TAURIS:
—CHERSONESOS: **(8)** i-ii AD *OAK* 1895, p. 10 (vase)
THRACE:
—BYZANTION: **(9)** m. iv AD *PLRE* I (-) (s. *Ἀλέξανδρος*)
—ODESSOS: **(10)** ii AD *IGB* I^2 76
—TRAIANOPOLIS (TERRIT.): **(11)** ii AD *SEG* XLVI 860 (*IThrakAig* E449) (*Δ. Σεῖος Φ.*)

Φοινικίδης
MACEDONIA (BOTTIAIA):
—BEROIA: **(1)** 223 BC *IBer* 4, 15 (*Φοινικί(δ)ης*: f. *Ἀντίγονος*)

Φοινίκιον
SKYTHIA:
—OLBIA-BORYSTHENES: **(1)** iv BC *SEG* XXX 947 (vase) (—ι *Νίκιον*—ed. pr., *[Φο]ινίκιον*?—*SEG*: het.?)

Φοῖνιξ
MACEDONIA: **(1)** 306 BC *RE* (10); cf. Beloch, *GG* IV (2) p. 134 (s. *Ἀντίγονος* I *Μονόφθαλμος*); **(2)** c. 259-244 BC *PHib* 110, 61 (Tataki, *Macedonians* p. 457 no. 84; La'da E1651) (*Φ. ὁ νεώτ.*: s. *Ἡράκλειτος*); **(3)** ~ *PHib* 110, 70 (*PP* 4131); *PP* 8756 (Tataki, *Macedonians* p. 457 no. 85; La'da E1650) (*Φ. ὁ πρεσβύτ.*: s. *Ἡράκλειτος*)

Macedonia (Chalkidike):
—aphytis: **(4)** iv-iii bc *SEG* xxix 572 (s. *Ἀσκληπιόδωρος*)
Thrace: **(5)** 226 bc *PPetr* iii 21 a, 3, 10 (Velkov 321; La'da E851) ([*Φ*]*οῖνιξ*: s. *Βίθυς*)
—lysimacheia: **(6)** m. ii bc *ISestos* 38 a, 2 (f. *Θεογένης*)

Φοξίης
Macedonia (Mygdonia):
—apollonia: **(1)** ?iv bc *SGDI* 5284 (f. *Σίμων*)

Φοργάβακος
Skythia:
—tanais: **(1)** c. 200-210 ad *CIRB* 1277, 7; Zgusta, *PNS* 244 (*Φοργάβακ*[*ος*]: f. *—ιος*); **(2)** 220-236 ad *CIRB* 1245, 9; 1246, 9; 1248, 8; 1250, 9; 1252, 2; 1278, 3; 1279, 4; *Stud. Zhebelev* p. 47, 6 (f. *Χόφραζμος*)

Φορήρανος
Skythia:
—tanais: **(1)** 210-226 ad *CIRB* 1285, 11 (*Φορήρα*[*νος*]) ?= (*2*); **(2)** 225 ad ib. 1280, 11; Zgusta, *PNS* 245 (s. *Εὔιος*) ?= (*1*)

Φορίαυος
Skythia:
—tanais: **(1)** 225 ad *CIRB* 1279, 16; Zgusta, *PNS* 246 (s. *Ἀντισθένης*)

Φοριύανος
Cimmerian Bosporos:
—tyritake: **(1)** inc. *SEG* xlv 1028. 17

Φορμίων
Cimmerian Bosporos:
—nymphaion: **(1)** c. 360 bc ib. xli 618 (stamp)
—pantikapaion: **(2)** s. iv bc *CIRB* 232 (s. *Βρόταχος*); **(3)** iii bc ib. 241; cf. KW pl. 55 no. 738 (f. *Ἀριστοφῶν*)
Macedonia (Chalkidike):
—olynthos: **(4)** 350 bc *SEG* xxxix 617 (s. *Δρίμακος*)
Skythia:
—olbia-borysthenes: **(5)** f. iv bc Dubois, *IGDOlbia* 104 (s. *Ζηνόδοτος*); **(6)** s. iv bc *SEG* l 702 II, 2; **(7)** iii bc *IOSPE* i^2 32 A, 54 (Maier, *Mauerbauinschr.* 82)
Tauris:
—chersonesos: **(8)** iv bc Solomonik, *GAKh* 247 (vase) (*Φορ*(*μίων*)?); **(9)** ~ ib. 1620 (vase) ?= (*11*); **(10)** iv-iii bc *IOSPE* i^2 415 (s. *Ἧρις*); **(11)** iv/iii bc Solomonik, *GAKh* 1621 (vase) ([*Φ*]*ορμί*(*ων*)?) ?= (*9*); **(12)** iii bc Solomonik, *GChKh* 15 (vase) (*Φορ*(*μίων*)?); **(13)** ~ Kats p. 95 no. 50 (amph.) (f. *Ἡράκλειος*); **(14)** c. 285-272 bc ib. p. 114 no. 122 (amph.) (s. *Αἰσχίνας*); **(15)** ~ ib. pp. 114-15 no. 123 (amph., tile) (s. *Ἀπολλᾶς*); **(16)** c. 215-200 bc ib. p. 115 no. 124 (amph., vase) (s. *Πυθίων*) ?= (*17*); **(17)** 192 bc *Syll*^{3} 585, 56; 604, 8, 14, 16 (s. *Πυθίων*) ?= (*16*); **(18)** imp. Solomonik, *NEPKh* 45 (*Φορμ*[*ίων*]?); **(19)** ~ *IOSPE* i^2 397 ([*Φ*]*ορμίων*)
Thrace:
—byzantion: **(20)** 309-307 or 301-296 bc *IG* ii^2 1957, 18 + *ZPE* 146 (2004) p. 85 (*FRA* 1409) ([*Φ*]*ορμ*[*ί*]*ων*); **(21)** ?205 bc *IG* vii 298, 4, 13 (*IOrop* 175; *OGIS* 81); *PP* 14635 (s. *Νυμφαῖος*)

Φόρος
Skythia:
—tanais: **(1)** 220 ad *CIRB* 1278, 20 (*Φό*[*ρ*]*β*[*ας*]?—*CIRB*, *Φόρ*[*ο*]*ς*—Tokhtas'ev: s. *—όδαστος*)

Φορτίων
Thrace:
—perinthos-herakleia: **(1)** iii ad *IPerinth* 159, 6 (*Αὐρ. Φ.*)

Φορτουνᾶτα
Thrace:
—deultum: **(1)** ii ad *IGB* iii 1850, 2 (*Φορτουνᾶ*[*τα*])

Φορτουνᾶτος
Macedonia (Bottiaia):
—beroia: **(1)** m. ii ad *IBer* 239 (Tataki 1333) (*Φορ<ι>τουνᾶτος*: s. *Εὐοδία*)
Macedonia (Mygdonia):
—thessalonike: **(2)** ?ii ad *IG* x (2) (1) 463, 5 (f. *Πατρόβιος*)
—thessalonike?: **(3)** ?c. 430 ad ib. 786, 10 (Feissel, *RICM* 180); cf. *SEG* xlviii 857
Thrace:
—serdica (territ.): **(4)** ii-iii ad *IGB* iv 2006, 2

Φορτούνις
Thrace:
—perinthos-herakleia: **(1)** iii ad *IPerinth* 159, 4 (*Αὐρ. Φ.*)

Φόσακος
Skythia:
—tanais: **(1)** 210-226 ad *CIRB* 1281, 20 (f. *—ανος*); **(2)** 228 ad ib. 1283, 14 (I f. *Φόσακος* II); **(3)** ~ ib. l. 14 (II s. *Φόσακος* I)

Φούβελις
Kolchis:
—lazoi: **(1)** 548 ad *PLRE* iii (-); *RE* (-)

Φουλβία
Macedonia (Edonis):
—amphipolis: **(1)** ii ad *SEG* xxxviii 581 (d. *Φούλβιος*)
Macedonia (Pieria):
—dion: **(2)** i bc-i ad *AE* 1948-9, Chron. p. 36 no. 4 (*Φο*(*υ*)*λβία*: m. *Πριμίων*)

Φούλβιος
Macedonia (Edonis):
—amphipolis: **(1)** ii ad *SEG* xxxviii 581 (f. *Φουλβία*)

Φουλκίνιος
Macedonia (Paionia):
—stoboi: **(1)** ii-iii ad *Sp.* 71 (1931) p. 46 no. 105 (s. *Σεκοῦνδα*)

Φούρνιος
Scythia Minor:
—istros: **(1)** iii ad *ISM* i 314 B + *VDI* 1984 (3), p. 180 (*Φούρνι*[*ος*]?)

Φούρτας
Cimmerian Bosporos:
—pantikapaion: **(1)** iii ad *CIRB* 101, 4 (f. *Γάϊος*)
Skythia:
—tanais: **(2)** 228 ad ib. 1282, 26; 1283, 18 (s. *Ἀγαθοῦς*)

Φοῦσκα
Macedonia (Mygdonia):
—thessalonike: **(1)** 129 ad *IG* x (2) (1) 311, 1 (d. *Στασίμη*)
Macedonia (Paionia):
—stoboi (area): **(2)** ii-iii ad Unp. (Kavadarci Mus.) inv. 61/II (d. *Διονύσιος*, m. *Ἰουλιανός*)

Φοῦσκος
Macedonia (Bottiaia):
—beroia:
——Blaganoi*: **(1)** 189 ad *SEG* xxxvii 590, 4 (Tataki 1340) (s. *Μελίτα*, f. *Ἀλεξάνδρα*)
Macedonia (Derriopos):
—stuberra: **(2)** 90 ad *IG* x (2) (2) 326, 81 (s. *Ἀσκληπιόδωρος*)

Φουφικία
Macedonia (Mygdonia):
—thessalonike: **(1)** s. i bc ib. x (2) (1) 100; *KGAM Thess.* i 51 (date)

Φρασίδαμος
Thrace:
—byzantion: **(1)** iv/iii bc *CIRB* 17 (-*δη*-: s. *Δηλόπτιχος*)

Φρασικλείδης
Macedonia (Bottiaia):
—beroia: **(1)** iv bc *IBer* 139 (Tataki 1340a)

Φρεγάνιος
Macedonia (Mygdonia):
—thessalonike?: **(1)** ii ad *IG* x (2) (1) 914 ([*Φ*]*ρεγάνιος*?)

Φρόνιμος
Thrace:
—byzantion: **(1)** s. ii bc *BMI* 1154a B, 31; cf. Robert, *OMS* 2 p. 1093; *BE* 1972, no. 37 (date) (*Φρόν*[*ιμος*]?, *Φρόν*[*ιος*]?: s. *Χαρμίας*)
—salymbria: **(2)** imp. *Araşt. Sonuçları Topl.* 1993 (1-2), p. 63

Φροντῖνος
Macedonia (Pelagonia): **(1)** ii-iii ad *IG* x (2) (2) 257, 4 (s. *Ὠφελίων Εὔπλοκος*, *Δομετία*)

Φρόντυλλα
Macedonia (Paionia):
—bylazora: **(1)** ii ad *JÖAI* 6 (1903) Beibl. col. 4 no. 5 (d. *Κοτίνιος Φρόντων*, *Οὔφρια. Σεκοῦνδα*)

Φρόντων
Macedonia (Derriopos):
—stuberra: **(1)** 119 ad *IG* x (2) (2) 294 (s. *Διονύσιος*, f. *Διονύσιος*)
Macedonia (Edonis):
—philippoi: **(2)** ?ii ad *FGrH* 257 F 37. 49 (Tataki, *Macedonians* p. 167 no. 36) (s. *Ἀλβούτιος*)
Macedonia (Mygdonia):
—thessalonike: **(3)** ii-iii ad *IG* x (2) (1) 343, 1
Scythia Minor:
—kallatis: **(4)** 241-244 ad *ISM* iii 74, 12 (s. *Καλλίστρατος*)
Thrace:
—nicopolis ad istrum (nr.): **(5)** s. ii ad *IGB* ii 704 (*CCET* ii (2) 648)

Φροῦρος
Macedonia (Mygdonia):
—charakoma?: **(1)** iii/ii bc *AD* 22 (1967) Chron. p. 377 with pl. 284 *α* (s. *..λεύς*)

Φρυγία
Macedonia (Orestis):
—avgi (mod.): **(1)** s. iv bc *SEG* l 573

Φρυγιλλίων
Thrace:
—nicopolis ad istrum: **(1)** ?iii ad *ILB* 370 (Lat. Hermadion Phrygillio)

Φρυγίλος
Macedonia (Chalkidike):
—mende: **(1)** v bc *SEG* xlvi 769 C (vase)

Φρυνέα
Sarmatia:
—sarmatai: **(1)** a. 137 bc *IG* ix (1)^2 (3) 638. 3, 8, 11 (slave/freed.)

Φρυνίων
Macedonia?: **(1)** c. 337-334 bc *CID* ii 74 I, 44; 77 I, [5] (Tataki, *Macedonians* p. 457 no. 86)

Φυλακίδης
MACEDONIA (MYGDONIA):
—CHARAKOMA?: (1) iii/ii BC *AD* 22 (1967) Chron. p. 377 with pl. 284 α (f. *Εὐγένεια*)
—THESSALONIKE?: (2) s. ii BC *IG* X (2) (1) 108, 7; cf. *ZPE* 10 (1978) p. 45

Φυλακίων
CIMMERIAN BOSPOROS:
—PANTIKAPAION: (1) i-ii AD *CIRB* 642 (I f. *Φυλακίων* II); (2) ~ ib. (II s. *Φυλακίων* I)

Φυλλίς
MACEDONIA (MYGDONIA):
—THESSALONIKE: (1) ii AD *IG* X (2) (1) 545 (*Φλ. Φ.*: d. *Ἀννία Κούαρτα*); (2) ii/iii AD ib. 121 (*Δομετία Φ.*)
MACEDONIA (PAIONIA):
—ARGOS (NR.): (3) ii-iii AD *SEG* XVI 401, 3 (d. *Εὔτροπος, Ἀγάθη*)
THRACE:
—BYZANTION: (4) i BC-i AD *IByz* 178 (Fıratlı–Robert p. 111 no. 183) (*Φυ[λ]λίς*: d. *Ἀντίπατρος*)
THRACE?: (5) i BC/i AD *CIL* VI 26608; *PIR*² I 689 (Lat. Iulia Phyllis)

Φυλομάγα
MACEDONIA (PIERIA):
—PALAIOKATACHAS (MOD.): (1) s. iv BC *SEG* XL 541

Φύρσων
THRACE:
—APOLLONIA-SOZOPOLIS: (1) iv BC *BMNBurgas* 4 (2002) p. 125 no. 22 (s. *Ζώπυρος*)

Φύσκιον
SCYTHIA MINOR:
—KALLATIS (NR.): (1) ii-i BC *ISM* III 240 (d. *Μη—κος*)

Φωκᾶς
MACEDONIA (MYGDONIA):
—THESSALONIKE: (1) v-vi AD *SEG* XLII 627 (s. *Μάσκελλα*)
MACEDONIA (PIERIA):
—PYDNA (LOULOUDIES (MOD.)): (2) s. vi AD ib. XLVIII 809. 17 (brick) (*Φ(ω)κᾶς*)
SCYTHIA MINOR:
—TOMIS: (3) v-vi AD Barnea 11, 2 (Popescu, *IGL* 38) (*Φο-*); (4) ~ Barnea 18, 5 (Popescu, *IGL* 37) (f. *Ἰωάννης*)

Φωκρίτη
CIMMERIAN BOSPOROS:
—PANTIKAPAION: (1) s. iv BC *CIRB* 192, 3; cf. KW pl. 5 no. 88 (d. *Λέοντις*)

Φώκριτος
SKYTHIA:
—OLBIA-BORYSTHENES: (1) iii BC *IOlbia* 72, 1 (f. *Δημήτριος*)

THRACE:
—BYZANTION: (2) m. iv BC D. xxxiii 14-17; 21; (3) m. iii BC *IG* XI (4) 530, 3, 7, 13 (s. *Λεοντίσκος*); (4) s. iii BC Schönert-Geiss, *Byzantion* 1215-23 (coin) (*Φώκριτ(ος)*); (5) ii-i BC *IByz* 222 (Fıratlı–Robert p. 79 no. 91) (f. *Ἄγης*)
—HERAION TEICHOS?: (6) f. iv BC Taşlıklıoğlu I p. 10 no. 3

Φωρδίγαλος
SKYTHIA:
—TYRAS: (1) iii AD *IGB* I² 228 bis, 1-2, 9 (*Αὐρ. Φ.*: f. *Αὐρ. Ἀβρινία*)

Φωσφόρος
THRACE:
—BYZANTION?: (1) imp. *IByz* 384

Φωτῖνος
THRACE:
—MARONEIA: (1) v AD Meïmaris–Bakirtzis 8 (*SEG* XLIV 595; *IThrakAig* E352) (*Φωτῆνο[ς]*)

Φωτίς
CIMMERIAN BOSPOROS:
—PANTIKAPAION: (1) v-vi AD *ZOOID* 31 (1913) p. 72 no. 170 (*Φωτίδος* (gen.))
MACEDONIA (BOTTIAIA):
—BEROIA: (2) f. ii AD *IBer* 348 (Tataki 1341) (m. *Ἀκτή, Δικαῖος*)

X

Χάβρης
MACEDONIA (CHALKIDIKE):
—OLYNTHOS: (1) ?350 BC *TAPA* 59 (1928) p. 226, 6, 12; Hatzopoulos, *Actes Chalc.* p. 80 (date) (f. *Φιλόξενος*)

Χαβρίας
CIMMERIAN BOSPOROS:
—PANTIKAPAION: (1) iv BC Audollent, *Defix. Tab.* 90 (*IAK* 58 (1915) p. 50)
SCYTHIA MINOR:
—ISTROS: (2) c. 48-52 AD *ISM* I 67, 52
THRACE:
—HERAION TEICHOS: (3) hell. Unp. (Sayar)
—PERINTHOS-HERAKLEIA: (4) iv-iii BC *IPerinth* 4, 1 (s. *Ἀρχένους*); (5) i BC-i AD ib. 25 (f. *Πολύκριτος*)
—SALYMBRIA: (6) s. iv BC *IG* II² 10261 a (*FRA* 6634)

Χαιρέας
MACEDONIA: (1) iii/ii BC *IG* XI (4) 784, 3, 15 (Tataki, *Macedonians* p. 458 no. 1) (s. *Λυσανίας*)
MACEDONIA (EDONIS):
—AMPHIPOLIS: (2) iii/ii BC *Ét. Thas.* 3 p. 318 no. 113 (Tataki, *Macedonians* p. 62 no. 132) (?s. *Ἰκκ—*)
MACEDONIA (MYGDONIA):
—THESSALONIKE: (3) i AD *IG* X (2) (1) 402 (s. *Ἑρμογένης*, f. *Ἑρμογένης*)
SCYTHIA MINOR:
—ISTROS: (4) ii-i BC *SEG* XIX 489 b (weight); (5) i AD *ISM* I 200, 5 (s. *Ζούρης*); (6) ii AD ib. 197 I, 2 (s. *Ξενοχάρης*); (7) 138 AD ib. 193 I, 19 (s. *Ἀρισταγόρας*); (8) ~ ib. l. 21 (s. *Ἄπουλλος*); (9) ~ ib. 193 II, 53 (f. *Διογένης*)

THRACE:
—APOLLONIA-SOZOPOLIS: (10) m. iii BC ib. 23 (*[Χαι]ρέου* (gen.))
—BYZANTION: (11) ii-iii AD *IByz* 322 (s. *Νίγερ*)
——(Nikatea?): (12) imp. ib. 248 (f. *Ἀπφοῦς*)
—MESAMBRIA: (13) ii-i BC *IGB* I² 338 (PM 660) (f. *Μενεσθεύς*)
—MONTANA*: (14) 155 AD *CIL* III 7449, 14 (*Romanizmăt* II 5) (Lat. Aurel. Caireas)
—ODESSOS: (15) i-ii AD *IGB* I² 51 c, 7 (f. *Ἕλλην*); (16) f. ii AD ib. 78 ter, 10 (*CCET* I 30) (f. *Ἕλλην*); (17) s. ii AD *IGB* I² 181 (PM 1605); *Dacia* 21 (1977) p. 161 (date) (f. *Γλυκυτής*)

Χαιρείας
THRACE:
—MESAMBRIA: (1) ii BC *IGB* I² 314 b, 14 (*Χ[αι]ρείας*: f. *Ζώπυρος*)

Χαιρεκράτης
MACEDONIA (BOTTIAIA):
—BEROIA: (1) 239-229 BC *IBer* 45, 31 (f. *Γαιτέας*)

Χαιρεφάνης
MACEDONIA: (1) m. ii BC *BGU* 2423, 35 (Tataki, *Macedonians* p. 499 no. 246; La'da E1653) (s. *Περδίκκας*)
MACEDONIA (BOTTIAIA):
—BEROIA: (2) f. ii BC *IBer* 157 (Tataki 1342) (s. *Ἀρτεμίδωρος*)
MACEDONIA (CHALKIDIKE):
—OLYNTHOS: (3) m. iv BC *IG* II² 10018 (Tataki, *Macedonians* p. 144 no. 112; *FRA* 5915) (f. *Ἀριστόμαχος*)
—POTIDAIA-KASSANDREIA:
——(Hippotadeis): (4) c. 305-297 BC *SEG* XLVII 940, 4 (s. *Αἰσχύλος*)

THRACE:
—MESAMBRIA: (5) ii/i BC *IGB* V 5104 III (s. *Ἀρτεμίδωρος*)

Χαιρήμων
KOLCHIS: (1) i BC *IG* II² 9049 (*FRA* 2938) (f. *Εὐφροσύνη*)
MACEDONIA: (2) 72 BC *BGU* 1738, 1, 11, 18 and verso (Tataki, *Macedonians* p. 499 no. 247; La'da E1654) (s. *Ἡρακλείδης*, f. *Ἡρακλείδης*: katoikos); (3) 33 AD *PMich* 259, 2, 21 (*Χ. ὁ καὶ Μιεύς*: s. *Ὀννῶφρις*, f. *Ἡρακλῆς*)
MACEDONIA (CHALKIDIKE):
—POTIDAIA-KASSANDREIA: (4) ii-i BC *IG* VII 2482; Pelekidis, *Thessaloniki* p. 3 n. 4 (locn.) (Tataki, *Macedonians* p. 97 no. 98) (f. *Προῖτος*)
SCYTHIA MINOR:
—ISTROS: (5) i BC-i AD *ISM* I 191 I, 46 (I f. *Χαιρήμων* II); (6) ~ ib. l. 46 (II s. *Χαιρήμων* I); (7) c. 48-52 AD ib. 67, 52; (8) ii AD ib. 202, 1 (*Χαιρήμω[ν]*); (9) 138 AD ib. 193 II, 76 (s. *Διονυσόδωρος*); (10) c. 140-160 AD ib. 207, 12 (*Χαιρή[μων]*: s. *Παπίας*); (11) iii AD ib. 192, 4 (*[Χαι]ρήμο[νος]?* (gen.))
—TOMIS: (12) i BC ib. II 2 B, 48 (s. *Εὐκράτης*); (13) ii-iii AD ib. 468, 14 (s. *Διοσκουρίδης*)
SKYTHIA:
—OLBIA-BORYSTHENES: (14) iii BC *IOSPE* I² 201 II, 6 (s. *Νικήρατος*)
THRACE:
—BYZANTION?: (15) imp. *CIG* 2039 (*Τιβ. Κλ. Χ.*)

Χαιριγένης
THRACE:
—MESAMBRIA: (1) c. 375-350 BC *IOSPE* I² 20, 3 (Dubois, *IGDOlbia* 15) (s. *Μητρόδωρος*)

Χαιρικλῆς
MACEDONIA (CHALKIDIKE):
—OLYNTHOS: (1) ?355 BC *TAPA* 69 (1938) p. 51 no. 5, 17; Hatzopoulos, *Actes Chalc.* p. 80 (date) ([*Χαι*]*ρικλῆς*—Hatzopoulos, [*Πε*]*ρικλῆς*—ed.); (2) 350 BC *SEG* XXXIX 617 (s. *Εὐφραῖος*)

Χαιρίλος
MACEDONIA (CHALKIDIKE):
—OLYNTHOS: (1) ?352 BC *TAPA* 62 (1931) p. 50 no. 3, 5 (f. *—λης*)

Χαίριππος
THRACE:
—ABDERA: (1) c. 311-280 BC *AMNG* II (1) 223 (coin)

Χαιρίων
MACEDONIA (BOTTIAIA):
—PELLA: (1) f. iii BC *SEG* XXIV 550 (f. *Δημόκριτος*)
SCYTHIA MINOR:
—TOMIS: (2) ii-i BC *IGB* I^2 43 bis, 4 (f. *Ἀρτέμων*); (3) f. i AD *RPC* I 1805-7 (coin)

Χαιρόλας
THRACE:
—LYSIMACHEIA: (1) ii BC *IG* II^2 13045 = 9236 (*Ag.* XVII 534 with comm.; *FRA* 3414) (*Χαιρο*——*IG*, *Ag.* and *FRA*: reading? - Pittakys)

Χαιρομένης
TAURIS:
—CHERSONESOS: (1) iii BC Solomonik, *NEPKh* 174 (f. *Εὐξίθεος*)

Χαιρόξενος
SCYTHIA MINOR:
—TOMIS: (1) ?41-54 AD *RPC* I 1828 (coin)

Χαιροφάνης
MACEDONIA (MYGDONIA):
—KALINDOIA: (1) 68-98 AD *SEG* XLII 580, 5, 12 (s. *Κρίτων*)

Χαίρων
MACEDONIA (EDONIS):
—AMPHIPOLIS: (1) ?s. iv BC ib. XXVII 254 + *PAE* 1977, p. 44 with pl. 33 *β* (s. *Πανταкλῆς*)
MACEDONIA (MYGDONIA):
—THESSALONIKE?: (2) ii-iii AD *IG* X (2) (1) 814, 2 + *SEG* XXVIII 549 (*M. Λικίννιος X.*: f. *Αἰλ. Ἐπιγόνη*)
THRACE:
—MESAMBRIA: (3) ii/i BC *IGB* V 5103, 2 (s. *Χορειός*)

Χάλαις
SKYTHIA:
—OLBIA-BORYSTHENES: (1) ii AD *IOSPE* I^2 83, 8; Zgusta, *PNS* 578 (s. *Καρζόαζος*)

Χάλης
THRACE:
—TRIBALLOI: (1) c. 375 BC Schol. Aristid. iii p. 275

Χαλκιδεύς
CIMMERIAN BOSPOROS:
—NYMPHAION: (1) iii BC *CIRB* 912 II, 10 (s. *Πολύκριτος*)

Χάλκις
THRACE:
—BYZANTION: (1) hell. Dion. Byz. 42 (fict.)

Χάλκων
MACEDONIA (CHALKIDIKE):
—OLYNTHOS: (1) ?350 BC *TAPA* 65 (1934) p. 125 no. 3, 3; Hatzopoulos, *Actes Chalc.* p. 80 (date) (f. *Ἀπολλόδωρος*)

Χανάκης
CIMMERIAN BOSPOROS:
—HERMONASSA: (1) iii BC *CIRB* 1073; Zgusta, *PNS* 250 (s. *Θάτης*)
—KYTAIA: (2) iv BC *CIRB* 943 (s. *Δημήτριος*)

Χανίκα
CIMMERIAN BOSPOROS:
—PANTIKAPAION: (1) f. i AD ib. 442; cf. KW pl. 29 no. 418; Zgusta, *PNS* 337 (m. *Δημήτριος*)

Χάνουσα
CIMMERIAN BOSPOROS:
—PANTIKAPAION: (1) imp. *CIRB* 772

Χανσαβόγαζος
SKYTHIA:
—TANAIS: (1) 225-230 AD ib. 1280, 15; 1284, 12; Zgusta, *PNS* 722 (s. *Χωδόνακος*)

Χάνωσος
SKYTHIA:
—OLBIA-BORYSTHENES: (1) ii AD *IOSPE* I^2 100, 7; Zgusta, *PNS* 723 (s. *Βραίαδος*)

Χαρά
MACEDONIA (ELIMEIA):
—DIPORO (MOD.): (1) ?ii BC *EAM* 45 (d. *Φίλιππος*)

Χαράκων
THRACE:
—GELOUPARA: (1) 202 AD *IGB* III 1690 c, 30 (and Thrace Pizos *Διασκούπορις* [*Χ*]*αράκων*?: s. *Βρινκάζερις*)

Χαράξηνος
SKYTHIA:
—OLBIA-BORYSTHENES: (1) ii AD *IOSPE* I^2 91, 8; Zgusta, *PNS* 1175 (s. *Ἀβραγος*); (2) iii AD *IOlbia* 83, 9 (*IOSPE* I^2 97) (s. *Σώμαχος*)

Χάραξστος
SKYTHIA:
—TANAIS: (1) 220 AD *CIRB* 1278, 13; Zgusta, *PNS* 1175 (*Χάραξσ*[*τ*]*ος*: s. *Φαρνάκης*); (2) 225 AD *CIRB* 1280, 8 (-*ρακσ*-: s. *Ὀμράσμακος*)

Χαράσπης
SCYTHIA MINOR: (1) ii BC *SCIV* 1.1 (1950) pp. 244-5 no. 25; *SNG Stancomb* 305 (coin) (*Χαράσπου* (gen.): king)

Χάρδεις
CIMMERIAN BOSPOROS:
—GORGIPPIA: (1) ii/iii AD *CIRB* 1179, 29; Zgusta, *PNS* 251 (f. *Φαρνακίων*); (2) ~ *CIRB* 1179, 52 (f. *Ἱππαρῖνος*)

Χαρζαβόγαδος
SKYTHIA:
—TANAIS: (1) 244 AD ib. 1287, 18; Zgusta, *PNS* 338 (*Χαρσαβόγαδος*: s. *Δημ*—)

Χάρης
CIMMERIAN BOSPOROS:
—PANTIKAPAION*: (1) hell. *IAK* 9 (1904) p. 147 no. 414 (vase)
MACEDONIA (BOTTIAIA):
—EDESSA: (2) f. i AD Dimitsas 38 (Tataki, *Edessa* 314) (s. *Ἀλέξανδρος*, f. *Δημήτριος*)
—PELLA: (3) c. 230-200 BC *BCH* 45 (1921) p. 17 III, 61 (Tataki, *Macedonians* p. 161 no. 91)
MACEDONIA (MYGDONIA):
—APOLLONIA: (4) 355 BC *IGLMP* 128, I, 9 (Tataki, *Macedonians* p. 68 no. 13) (f. *Σωχάρης*)
SCYTHIA MINOR:
—KALLATIS: (5) 241-244 AD *ISM* III 74, 8 (*Π. Οὐαλέρ. X.*)

Χαριδάμα
MACEDONIA (EDONIS):
—AMPHIPOLIS: (1) iii BC *SEG* XLIX 675 (m. *Δωριάς*)

Χαρίδαμος
THRACE:
—BYZANTION?: (1) ii BC *ISamothrace* 28 c, 12; Robert, *OMS* 6 pp. 605-6 (name, locn.) ([*Χα*]*ρίδαμος*: II s. *Χαρίδαμος* I); (2) ~ *ISamothrace* 28 c, 13; Robert, *OMS* 6 pp. 605-6 (name, locn.) ([*Χα*]*ρίδαμος*: I f. *Χαρίδαμος* II)

Χαριδημία
MACEDONIA (BOTTIAIA):
—EDESSA: (1) iii AD Feissel, *RICM* 10 (Tataki, *Edessa* 315) (m. *Ὀλυμπιάς*, *Κασσάνδρα*)

Χαρίδημος
MACEDONIA: (1) 89 BC *UPZ* 125, 29 (Tataki, *Macedonians* p. 499 no. 248; La'da E1655)
THRACE: (2) c. 223 BC *PTeb* 815 fr. 5, 12 (Velkov 120); cf. La'da E829 (f. *Ζηνόδοτος*)
—BYZANTION: (3) ii-iii AD *IG* XII (2) 643 (*K. Λολ. X.*)
—ODESSOS: (4) s. iv BC *IGB* I^2 103 (s. *Πάνтανδρος*); (5) iii AD ib. 141 bis ([*Χα*]*ρίδημος*: s. *Μένιππος*)

Χαρίκλεια
MACEDONIA: (1) ?i BC *IG* XII (1) 516 (Tataki, *Macedonians* p. 458 no. 2) (-*κλῆα*: slave?)

Χαρικλῆς
CIMMERIAN BOSPOROS:
—GORGIPPIA: (1) f. iii BC *CIRB* 1137 B I, 54 (f. *Ἀγησίλας*)
—PANTIKAPAION: (2) ?i AD ib. 536 (s. *Θυαίας*)
MACEDONIA: (3) 327 BC *RE* Supplbd. 4 (4a); Berve 824 (Tataki, *Macedonians* p. 458 no. 3) (s. *Μένανδρος*)
MACEDONIA (EDONIS):
—AMPHIPOLIS: (4) iv BC *AEMTh* 15 (2001) p. 119 (f. *Μυρτάλη*)
TAURIS:
—CHERSONESOS: (5) c. 490-470 BC *SEG* XL 612. 15 (ostrakon) (*Χαρικλ*[*ῆς*]: s. *Ἑρμόδωρος*)
THRACE:
—BYZANTION: (6) ii-i BC *IByz* 359 (Firatlı–Robert p. 65 no. 58) (s. *Ματρόδωρος*)
—MARONEIA: (7) iii BC *IThrakAig* E235 (f. *Μοσχίων*)

Χαριναύτης
SKYTHIA:
—OLBIA-BORYSTHENES: (1) iii BC *Arkheologiia* (Kiev) 39 (1982) p. 31 (vase) (*Χαριναύ*(*της*))

Χαρῖνος
CIMMERIAN BOSPOROS:
—PANTIKAPAION: (1) imp. *CIRB* 807 (*Χαρεῖν*[*ος*])
MACEDONIA (BOTTIAIA):
—BEROIA: (2) iii AD *IBer* 208 (Tataki 1343) ([*Χ*]*αρ*[*ί*]*νος*: threptos)
THRACE:
—BYZANTION: (3) ?253 BC Nachtergael, *Les Galates* 10, 13 (Stephanis 2616) (s. *Γέρων*)

Χαρίξενος
CIMMERIAN BOSPOROS:
—PANTIKAPAION: (1) hell. *AA* 1907, p. 127 Aa, 2 (lead); (2) i BC-i AD *CIRB* 537; cf. KW pl. 40 no. 591 (s. *Ἀπφοῦς*); (3) f. i BC *CIRB* 289 (s. *Χρῆστος*, *Στρατονίκη*); (4) f. i AD ib. 140, 1 (*GVI* 1520) (I f. *Χαρίξενος* II); (5) ~ *CIRB* 140, 1, 5 (*GVI* 1520) (II s. *Χαρίξενος* I)
MACEDONIA (MYGDONIA):
—THESSALONIKE: (6) iii/ii BC *IG* X (2) (1) 107; *KGAM Thess.* I 67 (date) (f. *Νικαία*)
SKYTHIA:
—TANAIS: (7) ii AD *CIRB* 1262, 9 (s. *Τρύφων*)
THRACE:
—SEUTHOPOLIS: (8) f. iii BC *SEG* XXXV 833. 2 (vase) ([*Χ*]*αρίξενος*, *Ἀρίξενος*—*SEG*)

Χάρις
Macedonia (Mygdonia):
—thessalonike?: (1) ii ad *IG* x (2) (1) 880 (Lat. Servilia Charis)
Macedonia (Paionia):
—antigoneia? (tremnik (mod.)): (2) ii-iii ad *Sp.* 98 (1941-8) p. 232 (*χαριν*—ed. pr.: name—Papazoglu)

Χαρίσιος
Cimmerian Bosporos:
—nymphaion: (1) iii bc *CIRB* 912 III, 11
Thrace:
—ainos: (2) imp. *Thrakika* 2 (1929) p. 63 (-*ρεί*-: f. *Σαλβία*)

Χαρίτιν
Macedonia (Mygdonia):
—thessalonike: (1) ii-iii ad *IG* x (2) (1) 464 A (*GVI* 1865) (m. *Αἴλ. Νέπως*)
—thessalonike?: (2) ?iii ad *IG* x (2) (1) 743 (m. *Πρόκλα*)
Macedonia (Pieria):
—dion: (3) ii-iii ad *Dion* p. 64

Χαριτῖνος
Macedonia (Mygdonia):
—thessalonike?: (1) ii-iii ad *IG* x (2) (1) 819 B (*Γν. Δομίτιος Χ.*)

Χαρίτιον
Cimmerian Bosporos:
—pantikapaion: (1) f. i ad *CIRB* 538 (-*τη*-)
Macedonia (Mygdonia):
—thessalonike: (2) ii ad *SEG* xliii 463 (*Ὀππία Χ.*)

Χαρίτιος
Thrace:
—bisanthe-panion: (1) iii-iv ad *AD* 49-50 (1994-5) Mel. p. 306 no. 130 (f. *Ἀπφία*)
—pautalia (territ.): (2) iii ad *IGB* iv 2147, 1 (s. *Δόλης*, f. *Χαρίτων*, *Μέστριος*)

Χαριτώ
Macedonia (Edonis):
—amphipolis: (1) 359-336 bc *FGrH* 257 F 36. 1; Procl., *in R.* ii 116 (m. *Φιλίννιον*: fict.?)
Thrace: (2) s. vi ad *PLRE* iii (-) (d. *Τιβέριος Κωνσταντῖνος*, *Ἰνώ ἡ καὶ Ἀναστασία* (Daphnoudion))

Χαρίτων
Cimmerian Bosporos:
—gorgippia: (1) ii ad *CIRB* 1140, 8 ([*Χ*]*αρίτων*: s. *Νεοκλῆς*); (2) f. ii ad ib. 1171, 2 (*Χαρίτ*[*ων*]); (3) 173-210 ad ib. 1135, 29 (*Χαρίτω*[*ν*]: f. —*ας*); (4) ii/iii ad *SEG* xlix 1033 B, 5 (*CIRB* 1182 B, 3) (?f. —*ους*); (5) iii ad *NE* 9 (1971) p. 10 no. 6 B, 8
—pantikapaion: (6) s. i ad *CIRB* 539; cf. KW pl. 41 no. 600 (s. *Μοκκοῦς*); (7) 82 ad *CIRB* 76, 11 (*SEG* xviii 310) (f. *Ἀντίμαχος*); (8) ii ad *CIRB* 757 (f. *Ἡρακλείδης*); (9) f. ii ad ib. 88, 2 (s. *Μήνιος*); (10) ?s. ii ad ib. 90, 12 (f. *Λυσίμαχος*); (11) 275-278 ad ib. 36, 18 (s. *Νικηφόρος*)
—theodosia: (12) iii ad ib. 947 A, 12 (*Χαρίτω*[*ν*]: f. *Εὐροψάτιος*)
Macedonia (Edonis):
—amphipolis: (13) 74 ad *PAE* 1959, p. 43 (*Σέξ. Ἰούλ. Χ.*: doctor)
Macedonia (Mygdonia):
—thessalonike?: (14) ii-iii ad *IG* x (2) (1) 810 (*Δέκμιος Χ.*: s. *Δεκμία Διοσκόρη*); (15) ~ ib. 817
Scythia Minor:
—tomis: (16) i-ii ad *ISM* ii 148 (biling.) (*Γ. Ἐρέννιος Χ.*)
Skythia:
—tanais: (17) 104 ad *CIRB* 1259, 9 (f. *Γάϊος*); (18) 154-170 ad ib. 1239, 9 (f. *Ἀντίμαχος*); (19) 155 ad ib. 1260, 16 (*Χ*[*α*]*ρίτων*: f. —*ακος*); (20) 193 ad ib. 1237, 19; 1243, 14 (f. *Ῥόδων*); (21) 220 ad ib. 1278, 6 (s. *Μακάριος*); (22) ~ ib. l. 12 (*Χαρ*[*ί*]*των*: f. *Ζάβαργος*); (23) 227-233 ad ib. 1247, 7 (f. *Μήνιος*); (24) 244 ad ib. 1287, 20 (s. *Δημήτριος*)
Thrace:
—bizye: (25) ii-iii ad *SEG* xxxii 660, 9 (*M. Αὐρ. Χ.*)
—pautalia (territ.): (26) iii ad *IGB* iv 2147, 9 (*Χ*[*α*]*ρίτων*: s. *Χαρίτιος*)
—perinthos-herakleia: (27) ii-iii ad *IG* II^2 10073, 1, 3 (*FRA* 6045) (*Κλ. Χ.*)
—philippopolis-trimontium: (28) ii-iii ad *IGB* iii 1015 (s. *Λογγῖνος*)
—philippopolis-trimontium (nr.): (29) ii-iii ad ib. 1413
—storgosia: (30) iii ad *ILB* 226 (Lat. Val. Charito)

Χαρμῆς
Thrace:
—abdera: (1) 346 bc *IG* II^2 218, 16, 29 (*FRA* 5) (*Χαρμῆι* (dat.): s. *Διονυσόδωρος*)

Χαρμίας
Thrace:
—byzantion: (1) s. ii bc *BMI* 1154a B, 32 + Robert, *OMS* 2 p. 1093; *BE* 1972, no. 37 (date) (*Χαρμί*[*ας*]: f. *Φρόνιμος*)

Χαρμίδης
Macedonia: (1) f. iii bc *IG* xi (2) 161 B, 73; *ID* 1441 A I, 14; 1450 A, 20; cf. *ID Index* s.v. (Tataki, *Macedonians* p. 458 no. 4)
Scythia Minor:
—istros:
——(Rhomaioi): (2) iii ad *ISM* i 142, 5 (f. *Αὐρ. Ἀσιάρχης*)

Χάρμιππος
Tauris:
—chersonesos: (1) iii bc Kats p. 107 no. 92 (amph.) (f. *Πάσιχος*); (2) m. iii bc *SEG* l 691 (s. *Πρύτανις*); (3) ii-i bc *IOSPE* I^2 468 (f. *Ἀσκλαπιάδας*)

Χαρμίων
Thrace:
—apollonia-sozopolis: (1) iv bc *BMNBurgas* 4 (2002) pp. 121-2 no. 8 (s. *Ἡρόδωρος*)

Χάρμος
Macedonia (Mygdonia):
—thessalonike: (1) ii ad *IG* x (2) (1) 241 A II, 24 ([*Αὐ*]*φίδιος Χ.*)
Macedonia (Paionia):
—stoboi: (2) ii-iii ad *AJA* 88 (1984) p. 581 (*Σεπτ. Χ.*)
Skythia:
—olbia-borysthenes: (3) v bc *IOSPE* I^2 215 (*Χάρμ*[*ος*]?, *Χαρμίδō* (gen.)—KW: s. *Δίφιλος*)
Thrace:
—abdera: (4) c. 346-336 bc May, *Abdera* pp. 281-3 nos. 505-18 (coin)

Χαρμοσύνη
Cimmerian Bosporos:
—pantikapaion: (1) i-ii ad *CIRB* 614
Macedonia (Bottiaia):
—beroia: (2) ii ad *IBer* 258 (m. *Λυσιανή*)

Χαρμόσυνος
Macedonia (Mygdonia):
—thessalonike: (1) s. ii ad *SEG* l 640 (—*λιος* [*Χαρ*]*μόσυ*[*νος*])

Χάρος
Macedonia: (1) 327 bc Curt. viii 11. 10; *RE* Supplbd. 4 (-); Berve 826 (Tataki, *Macedonians* p. 458 no. 5) (Lat. Charus: fict.?)

Χαρσενάκης
Cimmerian Bosporos:
—korokondame: (1) v bc *CIRB* 1104 (s. *Ματάττης*)

Χάρτας
Macedonia (Bottiaia):
—beroia: (1) 248 bc *IBer* 3, 2 (Tataki 1344) (s. *Νικάνωρ*)

Χάρων
Cimmerian Bosporos:
—gorgippia: (1) f. iii bc *CIRB* 1137 B I, 3 (s. *Σασῶν*)
Macedonia (Chalkidike):
—olynthos: (2) ?352 bc *TAPA* 69 (1938) p. 48 no. 3, [9], 15; Hatzopoulos, *Actes Chalc.* p. 80 (date) (f. *Διοκλῆς*)
Thrace:
—perinthos-herakleia?: (3) iv bc Hp., *Epid.* iv 41

Χαρώνδας
Scythia Minor:
—kallatis: (1) iv bc *ISM* iii 149 (*Χαρώνδα* (gen.), *Χαρόνδα*—ed.: ?f. *Ἱέρων*)

Χαύχακος
Skythia:
—tanais: (1) 244 ad *CIRB* 1287, 19; Zgusta, *PNS* 339 (s. *Στρα*—)

Χαχας
Cimmerian Bosporos:
—gorgippia: (1) ii/iii ad *CIRB* 1179, 44; Zgusta, *PNS* 724 (s. *Γοργόσας*)

Χειμάσιος
Tauris:
—chersonesos: (1) iii ad Solomonik, *NEPKh* 19, 4 (*Χειμάσ*[*ιος*], *Χειμᾶς*?)

Χειρικράτης
Macedonia (Chalkidike):
—olynthos: (1) 216 bc *Milet* i (3) 181, 9 (Tataki, *Macedonians* p. 144 no. 113) (and Caria Miletos: s. *Γοργίας*)

Χελιδόνιν
Macedonia (Mygdonia):
—thessalonike?: (1) ii-iii ad *IG* x (2) (1) 820 (-*λει*-)

Χελώνα
Scythia Minor:
—kallatis: (1) iii bc *ISM* iii 160 (d. *Ἡρώνυμος*)

Χηδόσβιος
Cimmerian Bosporos:
—bosporos: (1) iv-v ad *CIRB* 846 (king)

Χῆμα
Thrace:
—byzantion: (1) i bc *IByz* 211 (Fıratlı–Robert p. 70 no. 70); Masson, *OGS* i p. 268 (d. *Λυκομήδης*)

Χημάτα
Cimmerian Bosporos:
—pantikapaion: (1) i ad *KSIA* 116 (1969) p. 50 no. 2; Zgusta, *PNS* 725; (2) i/ii ad *CIRB* 643; cf. KW pl. 16 no. 240; (3) 173-210 ad *CIRB* 74, 6 (*Χημ*[*άτα*]?)

Χηματῖνος
Cimmerian Bosporos:
—pantikapaion: (1) i/ii ad ib. 640; Zgusta, *PNS* 725 (f. *Φαρνάκης*)
Tauris:
—chersonesos: (2) imp. *SEG* xxxvii 657 (lead) (f. *Θαμεις*); (3) 129 ad *IOSPE* I^2 359, 31 (f. *Ἡραῖος*)

Χιλιανός
TAURIS:
—CHERSONESOS: (1) imp. *SEG* XLIV 656 + *BE* 1996, no. 303 (tile)

Χίλων
MACEDONIA (EDONIS):
—PHILIPPOI (TERRIT.): (1) imp. *CIL* III 675 (Pikoulas, *Chora* p. 116 no. 5; Pilhofer 635) (Lat. Sal. Pompullius Chilo: s. Nunnia Maxima: freed.)
MACEDONIA (MYGDONIA):
—THESSALONIKE: (2) i BC/i AD *IG* X (2) (1) 58, 2; *KGAM Thess.* I 111 (date) (*Ά. Πάπιος Χείλων*)

Χίμαρος
THRACE:
—SALYMBRIA: (1) iii BC *IByz* S 3, 5 (s. *Ἐρίσκοπος*)

Χίμιρις
CIMMERIAN BOSPOROS:
—PHANAGOREIA: (1) V AD *SEG* XXXIX 704 + XLVIII 1025 (s. *Ἀγαθοῦς*)

Χιμυνάκης
SKYTHIA:
—OLBIA-BORYSTHENES (NR.): (1) vi/v BC ib. XL 635 (vase); cf. Vinogradov, *Pont. Stud.* p. 154 no. 3

Χιόνη
MACEDONIA (MYGDONIA):
—THESSALONIKE: (1) c. 303 AD Musurillo, *Acts Christian Martyrs* pp. 281 ff.
MACEDONIA (PAIONIA):
—KAVADARCI (MOD.): (2) 210 AD *Sp.* 98 (1941-8) p. 57 no. 115, 8 (*Χιονῆνι* (dat.): ?d. (nat.) *Ἀττικός, Λύκα*, ?d. (ad.) *Νικέρως, Σκουπῖνα*)
THRACE:
—KELLAI: (3) 241-244 AD *IGB* III 1517, 32 (*Αὐρ. Χ.*); (4) ~ ib. l. 35 (*Αὐρ. Χ.*)
—PERINTHOS-HERAKLEIA: (5) iii AD *IPerinth* 175
—SERDICA: (6) ii-iii AD *IGB* IV 1949

Χίονις
MACEDONIA (PIERIA):
—PHILA?: (1) ?iii BC *RPh* 1911, pp. 133-4 no. 36, 106; cf. *Polemon* 2 (1934-40) Parart. p. 13 no. 17; cf. Helly, *L'État thessalien* pp. 319-20 (locn.) (s. *Ἀλκῖνος*)

Χιονίς
MACEDONIA (MYGDONIA):
—THESSALONIKE: (1) iv-v AD Feissel, *RICM* 179, 5 (*SEG* XLVII 981)

Χίων
MACEDONIA (CHALKIDIKE):
—OLYNTHOS: (1) v/iv BC *CEG* II 719 (f. *Χιωνίδης*)

Χιωνίδας
MACEDONIA (BOTTIAIA):
—TYRISSA? (ASVESTARI (MOD.)): (1) f. ii BC *SEG* XLVII 999, 15 (f. *Φίλιππος*)

Χιωνίδης
MACEDONIA (BOTTIAIA):
—ALLANTE: (1) c. 230-200 BC *BCH* 45 (1921) p. 17 III, 65 (Tataki, *Macedonians* p. 44 no. 5) (f. *Ἀνδρόνικος, Δικαῖος*)
MACEDONIA (CHALKIDIKE):
—OLYNTHOS: (2) v/iv BC *CEG* II 719 (s. *Χίων*)
—STREPSA?: (3) 285 BC *SEG* XXXVIII 619, 21 (?s. *Δημήτριος*)

Χλόη
MACEDONIA (PAIONIA):
—STOBOI*: (1) s. i AD *Arheološki Vestnik* 41 (1990) p. 579 (*AEp* 1990, no. 885) (Lat. Pontia Chloe: freed.)
THRACE: (2) s. i BC Hor., *Car.* iii 9. 6, 9, 19; cf. i 23. 1; iii 7. 10; iii 26. 12 (Lat. Chloe: het./fict.)

Χοάργαρος
SKYTHIA:
—TANAIS: (1) 220 AD *CIRB* 1278, 23; Zgusta, *PNS* 341 (*Χοάργαρ[ος]*: s. *—αμος*)

Χοαροφάδιος
SKYTHIA:
—TANAIS: (1) 220 AD *CIRB* 1278, 18; Zgusta, *PNS* 342

Χόδαινος
SKYTHIA:
—TANAIS: (1) 188 AD *CIRB* 1242, 6; Zgusta, *PNS* 252 (f. *Διδυμόξαρθος*)

Χοδέκιος
CIMMERIAN BOSPOROS:
—GORGIPPIA: (1) ii AD *CIRB* 1140, 7; Zgusta, *PNS* 253 (f. *Σαρμάτας*)

Χοδιάκιος
SKYTHIA:
—TANAIS: (1) 228 AD *CIRB* 1282, 22; Zgusta, *PNS* 255 (f. *Λόγος*) ?= (*2*); (2) ~ *CIRB* 1283, 15 (f. *Δάδας*) ?= (*1*)

Χόδιος
CIMMERIAN BOSPOROS:
—PANTIKAPAION: (1) iii AD ib. 727; Zgusta, *PNS* 727 (s. *Δάδας*, f. *Στράτων*)

Χοζανία
CIMMERIAN BOSPOROS:
—PANTIKAPAION: (1) i AD *CIRB* 540; Zgusta, *PNS* 726 (m. *Χρήστη*)

Χοίδρα
CIMMERIAN BOSPOROS:
—PANTIKAPAION: (1) i AD *CIRB* 541; Zgusta, *PNS* 727; (2) ~ *CIRB* 542 (d. *Σίσας*); (3) i/ii AD ib. 644; (4) ~ ib. 645 (m. *Δαμοφίλα, Κάχιον, Εἰκόνιν*); (5) ii AD ib. 690 (d. *Κυράθων*)

Χοιρίνα
THRACE:
—BYZANTION: (1) iii BC *IByz* 69 (Fıratlı-Robert p. 48 no. 7) (d. *Ὄλυμπος*)
—MESAMBRIA: (2) iv BC *IGB* I^2 333 (d. *Ἡρακλείδας*)

Χοιρίων
MACEDONIA (EDONIS):
—AMPHIPOLIS: (1) iv-iii BC *AEMTh* 15 (2001) p. 118 (f. *Στρυμοκλῆς*)

Χόλκος
CIMMERIAN BOSPOROS:
—PANTIKAPAION: (1) f. iv BC *CIRB* 200; cf. KW pl. 1 no. 37; Zgusta, *PNS* 728 (f. *Μάζις*)

Χόμευος
SKYTHIA:
—TANAIS: (1) 244 AD *CIRB* 1287, 23; Zgusta, *PNS* 729 (s. *Μακάριος*)

Χόμιος?
SKYTHIA:
—TANAIS: (1) 225-228 AD *CIRB* 1279, 27; 1282, 26 (*Χόμι[ος]*?—1279 Tokhtas'ev, *Χομ——* 1282: s. *Ἀθηνόδωρος*: reading—Tokhtas'ev)

Χόνδεις
CIMMERIAN BOSPOROS:
—PANTIKAPAION: (1) f. ii AD ib. 661; Zgusta, *PNS* 730 (*Χόνδεινος* (gen.): f. *Βασιλείδης*)

Χοραγοῦς
CIMMERIAN BOSPOROS:
—GORGIPPIA: (1) ii AD *CIRB* 1141, 5 (*Χοραγ[οῦς]*?, *Χοραγ[ίων]*?); (2) ~ ib. 1157 A, 3; Zgusta, *PNS* 1178 (s. *Γ—*); (3) s. ii AD *CIRB* 1129 B, 5 (s. *Μυρίσκος*)

Χορειός
TAURIS:
—CHERSONESOS: (1) iv/iii BC Kats p. 86 no. 11 (amph.) (f. *Ἀπολλᾶς*); (2) c. 320-310 BC Anokhin p. 138 no. 73 (coin); (3) c. 300-285 BC Kats p. 115 no. 125 (amph.); (4) iii BC ib. p. 102 no. 72 (amph.) (f. *Λύκων*); (5) s. iii BC ib. p. 90 no. 28 (amph.) (f. *Ἀρίστων*); (6) c. 230-215 BC ib. pp. 115-16 no. 126 (amph.) (s. *Λύκων*); (7) c. 210-200 BC Anokhin p. 144 nos. 144; 146 (coins)
THRACE:
—LYSIMACHEIA: (8) c. 208 BC *FD* III (4) 135 II, 7 (f. *Ἄρχων*)
—MESAMBRIA: (9) ii/i BC *IGB* V 5103, 3 (f. *Χαίρων*)

Χορηγίων
CIMMERIAN BOSPOROS:
—GORGIPPIA: (1) i AD *CIRB* 1192, 2 (*GVI* 1022); Zgusta, *PNS* 1177 (f. *Γάστεις, Ἀδε—*); (2) i-ii AD *CIRB* 1138, 6 (*[Χ]ορηγίων*); (3) ii AD ib. 1140, 4 (f. *—τας*); (4) m. ii AD *Eirene* 7 (1968) p. 67, 3 (f. *Παπίας*)

Χόρηγος
THRACE:
—MARONEIA: (1) c. 365-336 BC Schönert-Geiss, *Maroneia* 433-53 (coin); Masson, *OGS* p. 439

Χόρης
CIMMERIAN BOSPOROS:
—PANTIKAPAION: (1) imp. *CIRB* 769; Zgusta, *PNS* 731 (*Χόρητος* (gen.))

Χορόαθος
SKYTHIA:
—TANAIS: (1) c. 200-210 AD *CIRB* 1277, 20; Zgusta, *PNS* 256; (2) 220 AD *CIRB* 1245, 8 (s. *Σανδάρζιος*)

Χορόνικος
MACEDONIA (CHALKIDIKE):
—STOLOS?: (1) ?351 BC *SEG* XXXVIII 672, 12 (s. *Διονύσιος*); (2) c. 350 BC ib. XL 553, 3

Χορούαθος
SKYTHIA:
—TANAIS: (1) c. 200-210 AD *CIRB* 1277, 5; Zgusta, *PNS* 256 (*Χορούαθ[ος]*)

Χόρσιππος
KOLCHIS:
—VANI (MOD.): (1) hell. *MBAH* 12 (1993) p. 69 (brick) (*Χόρσιπ(πος)*?)

Χόσα
CIMMERIAN BOSPOROS:
—PANTIKAPAION: (1) i AD *CIRB* 543

Χοσᾶς
CIMMERIAN BOSPOROS:
—MYRMEKION: (1) i AD ib. 880; Zgusta, *PNS* 732 (f. *Ἔρως*)

Χόσιον?
CIMMERIAN BOSPOROS:
—PANTIKAPAION: (1) imp. *CIRB* 765 (*Χοσιομ*—apogr., *(Σω)σί(ων)*—Latyshev: d. *Λάμαχος*)

Χοσουμένη
CIMMERIAN BOSPOROS:
—PANTIKAPAION: (1) i AD ib. 544; Zgusta, *PNS* 734 (*Χοσουμέ(ν)η*)

Χοσοχερεφεύς?
CIMMERIAN BOSPOROS:
—NYMPHAION: (1) f. iii BC *SEG* XXXIX 701. 3

Χοσσοῦς
CIMMERIAN BOSPOROS:
—GORGIPPIA: **(1)** ii AD *CIRB* 1142, 12 (f. Ἀλα—)

Χουάρσαζος
SKYTHIA:
—OLBIA-BORYSTHENES: **(1)** ii AD *IOSPE* I² 82, 6; Zgusta, *PNS* 257 (f. Ἄβραγος) ?= (*3*); **(2)** ~ *IOSPE* I² 92, 7 (Χουραρσαζος—maj.: f. Τανάσισος); **(3)** ~ ib. 686, 6 (*VDI* 1975 (1), p. 69) (f. Ἄβραγος) ?= (*1*)

Χούναρος
SKYTHIA:
—OLBIA-BORYSTHENES: **(1)** ii AD *IOSPE* I² 91, 6; Zgusta, *PNS* 258 (s. Ἡρακλείδης)

Χόφαρνος
CIMMERIAN BOSPOROS:
—PANTIKAPAION: **(1)** 275-278 AD *CIRB* 36, 11; Zgusta, *PNS* 259 (Ἰούλ. Χόφα[ρ]νος: s. Ἀφροδίσιος); **(2)** ~ *CIRB* 36, 30 (I f. Παπίας, Χόφαρνος II); **(3)** ~ ib. l. 30 (II s. Χόφαρνος I)
SKYTHIA:
—TANAIS: **(4)** f. ii AD ib. 1266, 7 ([Χ]όφαρνος: s. Ἄττας); **(5)** 209 AD ib. 1276, 5 (s. Ἀ—); **(6)** 220 AD ib. 1245, 5; 1251, 5 (s. Σανδάρζιος); **(7)** 225 AD ib. 1280, 26 (s. Στρατόνικος); **(8)** 230 AD ib. 1284, 7 ([Χ]όφαρνο[ς])

Χόφραζμος
SKYTHIA:
—TANAIS: **(1)** 220-236 AD ib. 1245, 9; 1246, 8; 1248, 7; 1250, 9; 1252, 2; 1278, 3; 1279, 3; *Stud. Zhebelev* p. 47, 5; Zgusta, *PNS* 260 (Χόφρασμος—1250 & 1252 & 1278-9: s. Φοργάβακος); **(2)** 225 AD *CIRB* 1279, 8 (-φρασ-: f. Σαυάνων); **(3)** 230 AD ib. 1284, 18 (Χ[ό]φρασμος: f. Εὔνων)

Χρησίμα
MACEDONIA (BOTTIAIA):
—BEROIA: **(1)** ii AD *IBer* 302 (Tataki 1346); **(2)** ii-iii AD *IBer* 297, 3 (d. Κλ. Ἀντέρως, Νικέα)
MACEDONIA (EDONIS):
—AMPHIPOLIS: **(3)** m. ii AD *SEG* XXXV 712 (m. Λύκα)

Χρήσιμος
MACEDONIA (BOTTIAIA):
—BEROIA: **(1)** ii-iii AD *IBer* 297, 2 (s. Κλ. Ἀντέρως, Νικέα); **(2)** ii/iii AD ib. 27 A, 20 (Χρήσ(ι)μος: s. Εὐρυμέδων)
MACEDONIA (EDONIS):
—PHILIPPOI: **(3)** ii/iii AD *CIL* III 633 II a, 11 (Pilhofer 163); *CRAI* 1923, p. 277 (date); Collart, *Philippes* pls. 64-5 (Lat. M. Varinius Chresimus)
—PHILIPPOI?: **(4)** ?i-ii AD *AE* 1950-1, p. 68 no. 11, 4 (Pilhofer 726) (or Macedonia (Mygdonia) Thessalonike: Lat. L. Laelius Chressimus: freed.)
THRACE:
—ANCHIALOS (TERRIT.): **(5)** ii-iii AD *IGB* V 5647, 3 (*Eastern cults* p. 200 no. 17) (Χρήσ(ι)μος: s. Ἑρμογένης)
—NOVAE*: **(6)** i/ii AD *IGLNovae* 97 (*ILB* 314) (Lat. Cassius Chresimus: freed.)

Χρηστακῶν
THRACE:
—BYZANTION (TERRIT.): **(1)** i-ii AD *IByz* 245 (Χρηστακῶντος (gen.): f. Δαμᾶς)

Χρήστας
CIMMERIAN BOSPOROS:
—NYMPHAION: **(1)** f. iii BC *SEG* XXXIX 701. 3

Χρήστη
CIMMERIAN BOSPOROS:
—HERMONASSA: **(1)** i AD *CIRB* 1082 (d. Ἵππαρχος, m. Ἵππαρχος)
—MYRMEKION: **(2)** s. i AD ib. 883
—NYMPHAION: **(3)** ii-iii AD ib. 936 (d. Δημήτριος, Μύρον)
—PANTIKAPAION: **(4)** i BC/i AD ib. 141, 1, 4 (*GVI* 949); cf. KW pl. 14 no. 201 (d. Ἀλέξανδρος); **(5)** ~ *CIRB* 322; cf. KW pl. 16 no. 241; **(6)** i AD *CIRB* 509; cf. KW pl. 27 no. 404 (m. Ἀπολλωνίδης, Παιρίσαλος); **(7)** ~ *CIRB* 540 (d. Χοζανία); **(8)** ~ ib. 545; cf. KW pl. 12 no. 169; **(9)** ~ *CIRB* 548 (d. Ἐπάγαθος); **(10)** ~ ib. 550; **(11)** s. i AD ib. 546; cf. KW pl. 30 no. 439a (d. Μόνιμος); **(12)** i/ii AD *CIRB* 609; cf. *SEG* XXIX 718 (Χρήστ[η] (n. pr.?)); **(13)** 81 AD *CIRB* 70, 5 (Levinskaya p. 231 no. 1) (Jew?); **(14)** ii AD *CIRB* 704; cf. KW pl. 25 no. 371
MACEDONIA (BOTTIAIA):
—BEROIA: **(15)** s. ii AD *IBer* 244 (Tataki 1347) (threpte)
—EDESSA: **(16)** 243 AD *Athena* 12 (1900) p. 72 no. 9, 1-2 (Tataki, *Edessa* 129) (Ἰουλ. Χ.)
MACEDONIA (EDONIS):
—PHILIPPOI: **(17)** i-ii AD *BCH* 57 (1933) p. 376 no. 31 (Pilhofer 194) (Lat. Chreste: d. Χρῆστος)
MACEDONIA (MYGDONIA):
—THESSALONIKE: **(18)** ii AD *IG* X (2) (1) 371, 4; 372, 2 (d. Νέος Νουμίσιος Φῆλιξ ὁ καὶ Βάλας); **(19)** ~ ib. 482 (m. Νικομήδεια)
—THESSALONIKE?: **(20)** ii AD ib. 807; **(21)** ii-iii AD ib. 836 (Ὀβουλκία Νοβία Χρήστ[η])
MACEDONIA (ODOMANTIKE):
—SIRRHA: **(22)** 33 or 133 AD *SEG* XVI 411 (m. Τιμαρέτη)
MACEDONIA (PIERIA):
—DION: **(23)** ii AD *GVI* 456 a
MACEDONIA (TYMPHAIA):
—SYDENDRO (MOD.): **(24)** f. iii AD *EAM* 62, 3 (d. Φιλωτέρα)
THRACE:
—BIZYE (TERRIT.): **(25)** f. iii AD *IGB* V 5656, 3, 9
—BYZANTION: **(26)** i BC-i AD *IByz* 234 (d. Δάδας)
—NICOPOLIS AD ISTRUM: **(27)** ii-iii AD *IGB* II 692 (d. Χρῆστος, m. Εὐτυχίς)
—PERINTHOS-HERAKLEIA (NR.): **(28)** ii AD *IPerinth* 281 (d. Χρῆστος)
—PHILIPPOPOLIS-TRIMONTIUM: **(29)** imp. *IGB* III 1026, 3; **(30)** ii AD ib. 997, 3; **(31)** ~ ib. 1011 a ([Χ]ρήστη); **(32)** ii-iii AD ib. 1022, 3 (*GVI* 1338) (m. Καινίς)
—SERDICA: **(33)** ii-iii AD *IGB* IV 2010, 5 (d. Ἀ—μαιος)

Χρηστίνη
THRACE:
—BYZANTION?: **(1)** imp. *IByz* 387, 9 (Χριστεί-: d. Χρῆστος, Σατριανή)

Χρηστῖνος
THRACE:
—SALYMBRIA?: **(1)** iii AD *AEMÖ* 17 (1894) p. 57 no. 3, 1 (or Thrace Perinthos-Herakleia: Χρησ(τ)ῆνος?: f. Αὐρ. Δημητρία)

Χρηστίων
CIMMERIAN BOSPOROS:
—GORGIPPIA: **(1)** ii AD *CIRB* 1116 ([Χρη]στίων?); **(2)** ~ ib. 1140, 6 ([Χρη]στίων: s. Πάπας); **(3)** ~ ib. l. 6 (s. Δι—); **(4)** ii-iii AD *NE* 9 (1971) p. 9 no. 6 A, 12; **(5)** m. ii AD *Eirene* 7 (1968) p. 67, 15 (Χρηστί[ων]: f. Γλύκων); **(6)** s. ii AD *CIRB* 1129 B, 8 (s. Κομίνικος); **(7)** ~ ib. 1145, 4; **(8)** ~ ib. l. 5; **(9)** ~ ib. 1156 ([Χρ]ηστίω[ν]); **(10)** 173-210 AD ib. 1134, 16 (s. Πάπας); **(11)** ~ ib. 1135, 18 ([Χρη]στίων: s. Πόθος); **(12)** ~ ib. l. 23 (Χ[ρη]στίων: s. Γαδι—); **(13)** ii/iii AD ib. 1179, 9 (f. Πόθος); **(14)** ~ ib. l. 32 (f. Πάπας); **(15)** ~ ib. l. 33, 59 (s. Ἑρμῆς, f. Ἑρμῆς, Ἀγαθοῦς); **(16)** ~ ib. l. 34 (f. Σαφάτας); **(17)** ~ ib. l. 38 (f. Ἀρίστων); **(18)** ~ ib. l. 45 (s. Θέκας); **(19)** ~ ib. l. 52 (f. Ἔρως); **(20)** ~ ib. l. 56 (s. Φαρ—, f. Σιαγοῦς); **(21)** ~ ib. 1180, 6 ([Χ]ρηστίων)
—GORGIPPIA?: **(22)** s. ii AD ib. 1231 B, 7 (f. —αλέων)
—PANTIKAPAION: **(23)** ii-i BC ib. 267; cf. KW pl. 40 no. 585 (s. Στρατόνικος); **(24)** imp. *CIRB* 773 (s. Ἀπολλώνιος); **(25)** i AD ib. 142, 1, 6 (*GVI* 979) (s. Ἀσιατικός); **(26)** ~ *CIRB* 506 (f. Ῥόδων); **(27)** ~ ib. 547 (s. Δᾶος); **(28)** ~ ib. 549 (s. Ἥλιος); **(29)** f. i AD ib. 487; cf. KW pl. 16 no. 247 (f. Παρθένα); **(30)** s. i AD *CIRB* 551; cf. KW pl. 15 no. 226; **(31)** i/ii AD *CIRB* 647 (s. Καλλισθένης); **(32)** f. ii AD ib. 671; cf. KW pl. 16 no. 255 (f. Διόφαντος); **(33)** ~ *CIRB* 754 (f. Ἑρμοκράτης); **(34)** ?iii AD *KSIA* 116 (1969) p. 54 no. 6; **(35)** 243 AD *CIRB* 35 (I s. Σάλας, f. Χρηστίων II); **(36)** ~ ib. (II s. Χρηστίων I); **(37)** iv AD ib. 746
SKYTHIA:
—TANAIS: **(38)** ii AD ib. 1263, 14; **(39)** f. ii AD ib. 1264 A, 5 (f. Μηνόφιλος); **(40)** ~ ib. 1266, 8 ([Χ]ρηστίων)
TAURIS:
—CHERSONESOS: **(41)** ii AD Solomonik, *NEPKh* 56 (s. Ἀπολλώνιος, f. Ἀλέξανδρος); **(42)** ~ *IOSPE* I² 453; cf. KW pl. 24 no. 355 (f. Θεαγένης); **(43)** f. ii AD *KSIIMK* 15 (1947) p. 59, 10 (Solomonik, *NEPKh* 112 d); cf. *VDI* 1993 (4), p. 63 ([Χρ]ηστίων); **(44)** ~ Solomonik, *NEPKh* 111, 5 (f. Βοΐσκος); **(45)** ?114 AD *SEG* XLVIII 999, 37 (f. Ἡρόξενος); **(46)** ~ ib. l. 39 (Χρηστίω[ν]: s. Ἄππας); **(47)** ~ ib. l. 43 (f. Ἀντίλοχος); **(48)** c. 120-130 AD Solomonik, *NEPKh* 112, 13 ([Χ]ρηστίων); **(49)** 129 AD *IOSPE* I² 359, 18 (s. Βοΐσκος); **(50)** ~ ib. l. 33 (f. Πυθόδωρος); **(51)** 174 AD *SEG* XLV 985 A, 37 (s. Θεαγένης)
THRACE:
—NICOPOLIS AD ISTRUM: **(52)** ii-iii AD *IGB* II 684 (Χ. ὁ καὶ Ἰούνιος)

Χρῆστος
CIMMERIAN BOSPOROS:
—ACHILLEION: **(1)** i/ii AD *CIRB* 1027; cf. KW pl. 33 no. 464 (f. Πάτεις)
—GORGIPPIA: **(2)** ii/iii AD *CIRB* 1179, 33 (f. Παπίας)
—PANTIKAPAION: **(3)** i BC ib. 279; cf. KW pl. 35 no. 501; **(4)** f. i BC *CIRB* 289 (f. Χαρίξενος); **(5)** i AD ib. 489; cf. KW pl. 46 no. 652 (f. Πασίων, Βασιλίσκος, Ἔρως); **(6)** ~ *CIRB* 552 (f. Χρύσα); **(7)** 140 AD ib. 711 (f. Φίλων)
MACEDONIA (DERRIOPOS):
—STUBERRA: **(8)** 126 AD *IG* X (2) (2) 336 (Π. Ἀνθέστιος Χ.)
MACEDONIA (EDONIS):
—PHILIPPOI: **(9)** i-ii AD *BCH* 57 (1933) p. 376 no. 31 (Pilhofer 194) (Lat. Avincilius Chrestus: f. Χρήστη)
MACEDONIA (MYGDONIA):
—THESSALONIKE: **(10)** ii-iii AD *SEG* XLII 626 (f. Σαφιρώ); **(11)** iii AD *IG* X (2) (1) 349, 1 (Αὐρ. Χ.)
SCYTHIA MINOR:
—ISTROS: **(12)** 138 AD *ISM* I 193 I, 89 (s. Πρωτᾶς) ?= (*13*); **(13)** ~ ib. 193 II, 33 (f. Πρωτᾶς) ?= (*12*)
—ISTROS*: **(14)** iii AD ib. 292, 7 (Αὐρ. Χ. Σευῆρος)
—TOMIS: **(15)** ii AD ib. II 17, 9 (s. Ἥλιος); **(16)** ~ ib. 125, 9 (s. Νικίας); **(17)** ~ ib. 132 (f. Φιλοκλῆς); **(18)** ii-iii AD ib. 104, 8 (s. Μᾶρκος)
——(Aikoreis): **(19)** ii-iii AD ib. 252 (s. Ὁλόκαλος)
—TOMIS*: **(20)** ?iii AD *SEG* XXXIV 742 (lamp)
SKYTHIA:
—TANAIS: **(21)** f. ii AD ib. L 714 A (tile); **(22)** iii AD *CIRB* 1299 (f. Κοσοῦς)
TAURIS:
—CHERSONESOS: **(23)** f. ii BC *IGB* I² 39, 5 (Χρῆσ[τος]?, Χρήσ[ιμος]?: s. Ἀρνίας); **(24)** ii-iii AD *IOSPE* I² 515; cf. KW pl. 56 no. 766a;

(**25**) 174 AD *SEG* XLV 985 A, 35 (s. *Παπίας*); (**26**) 284-305 AD Const. Porph., *De admin. imp.* 53, 25, 44 (s. *Παπίας*)
THRACE:
—ANCHIALOS (TERRIT.): (**27**) ii-iii AD *IGB* I² 383 bis, 5
—BEROE-AUGUSTA TRAIANA: (**28**) ii-iii AD ib. III 1583 (f. *Σαβῖνος*); (**29**) ii/iii AD *SEG* XLVIII 894 (f. *Αὐρ. Δημόφιλος*)
—BIZYE (TERRIT.): (**30**) ii-iii AD *IGB* III 1865 (f. *Λυκομήδης*)
—BIZYE (TERRIT.)?: (**31**) ii-iii AD ib. 1854 (I f. *Χρῆστος* II); (**32**) ~ ib. (II s. *Χρῆστος* I)
—BYZANTION: (**33**) ii AD *RE* (5)
—BYZANTION?: (**34**) imp. *IByz* 387, 1, 6 (f. *Χρηστίνη*)
—KELLAI: (**35**) 241-244 AD *IGB* III 1517, 22 (*Αὐρ. Χ.*)
—LJUBLEN (MOD.): (**36**) f. iii AD ib. V 5271 (*CCET* II (2) 571)
—MESAMBRIA: (**37**) iii-ii BC *IGB* I² 349 sexies (n. pr.?)
—NICOPOLIS AD ISTRUM: (**38**) ii-iii AD ib. II 692 (f. *Χρήστη*); (**39**) ~ ib. 693 (f. *Ἀσκλᾶς*); (**40**) iii AD ib. 671
——(Artemisias): (**41**) ii-iii AD ib. V 5234, 4 (s. *Ζωΐλος*)
—NICOPOLIS AD ISTRUM (NR.): (**42**) f. iii AD ib. II 703 (*CCET* II (2) 649) (s. *Ἀλέξανδρος*)
—NICOPOLIS AD ISTRUM?: (**43**) ii-iii AD *IGB* V 5234, 2
—ODESSOS: (**44**) ii AD ib. I² 212 bis + V 5055; (**45**) 221 AD ib. I² 47 bis a, 13 (f. *Διονύσιος*); (**46**) ~ ib. l. 18 (*Μ. Αὐρ. Χ.*: s. *Διονύσιος*); (**47**) ~ ib. 47 bis b, 27 (*Αὐρ. Χ.*: s. *Σωκράτης*)
—ODESSOS?: (**48**) ii AD ib. 51 bis a, 9 (f. *Κότυς*)
—PAUTALIA: (**49**) ii AD ib. IV 2074, 9; (**50**) ii-iii AD ib. 2076 (*Eastern cults* p. 169 no. 13) (s. *Ζωΐλος*); (**51**) ~ *IGB* IV 2078 a, 5 (f. *Αὐρ. Βάσσος*); (**52**) ~ ib. 2079, 2 (f. *Τ. Αὐρ. Αὐλούτραλις*)
—PAUTALIA (TERRIT.): (**53**) iv AD *Pernik* I p. 209 (pithos) (Lat. Christus: ?s. *Παίβης*)
—PERINTHOS-HERAKLEIA: (**54**) i BC-i AD *IPerinth* 59 (*Χρῆστ[ος]*: I f. *Χρῆστος* II); (**55**) ~ ib. (II s. *Χρῆστος* I); (**56**) imp. ib. 275 (*Χ[ρ]ῆστος*); (**57**) i-ii AD ib. 93 (s. *Ἀγαθόδωρος*); (**58**) ~ ib. 94 (s. *Ἀγαθόδωρος*); (**59**) iii AD ib. 113 (*Αὐρ. Χρῆστο[ς]*); (**60**) ~ ib. 174 (*Αὐρ. Χ.*); (**61**) f. iii AD ib. 22, 9 (*Μ. Αὐρ. Χ.*: s. *Διονύσιος*)
——(*φυλ. πεμπτ.*): (**62**) ii AD ib. 123 (I f. *Χρῆστος* II); (**63**) ~ ib. (II s. *Χρῆστος* I)
—PERINTHOS-HERAKLEIA (NR.): (**64**) ii AD ib. 281 (*Χρ[ῆ]στος*: f. *Χρήστη*)
—PHILIPPOPOLIS-TRIMONTIUM: (**65**) ii AD *IGB* III 1011 b; (**66**) iii AD ib. V 5468, 15 (*Αὐρ. Χ.*: s. *Γλαῦκος*)
—PHILIPPOPOLIS-TRIMONTIUM (TERRIT.): (**67**) ii-iii AD ib. III 1192 (f. *Ἀπολλινάρις*); (**68**) ~ ib. 1219 (f. *—ρις*); (**69**) ~ ib. 1315 (*CCCA* VI 351) (s. *Ἀφφος*); (**70**) ~ *IGB* III 1401 bis (s. *Τελεσφόρος*); (**71**) ii/iii AD ib. 1452, 7 (*Eastern cults* p. 121 no. 104) (s. *Δίζας*)
—PHILIPPOPOLIS-TRIMONTIUM:
——Vicus Cuntiegerum: (**72**) 227 AD *CIL* VI 32543, 31 (Lat. [M.] [Au]r. Chrestus)
—PODEM (MOD.): (**73**) ?iii AD *ILB* 219 (Lat. Chrestus: f. Herculanus)
—SERDICA: (**74**) ii AD *IGB* IV 1923, 5 (f. *—ος*); (**75**) ~ ib. 1957, 6 (s. *Ἀσκληπιάδης, Θεοφίλη*)

Χρηστοῦς
CIMMERIAN BOSPOROS:
—GORGIPPIA: (**1**) ii AD *CIRB* 1151, 7; Zgusta, *PNS* 1179 (*Χρηστο[ῦς]*: f. *Ἀγαθοῦς*); (**2**) m. ii AD *Eirene* 7 (1968) p. 67, 7 (f. *Κοσσοῦς*); (**3**) ~ ib. l. 21 (s. *Πάβας*); (**4**) s. ii AD *CIRB* 1129 B, 6 (f. *Ἀθηνόδωρος*); (**5**) ~ ib. 1145, 6 (s. *Φαρνάκης*); (**6**) 173-210 AD ib. 1134, 25 (f. *Μυρίσκος*) ?= (7); (**7**) ~ *SEG* XXXVI 700, 10 (*Χρη[στοῦς]*?: f. *—ς*) ?= (6); (**8**) ii/iii AD *CIRB* 1179, 28 (s. *Μυρίσκος*); (**9**) ~ ib. l. 53; (**10**) ~ ib. l. 54 (s. *Πα—*); (**11**) ~ ib. l. 60
—GORGIPPIA?: (**12**) s. ii AD ib. 1231 A, 8
—PANTIKAPAION: (**13**) 173-210 AD ib. 74, 5 (s. *Κοσσοῦς*)
—PHANAGOREIA: (**14**) i AD ib. 995 (s. *Ἀπολλώνιος, Μεγίστη*)
—THEODOSIA: (**15**) iii AD ib. 947 B, 9 (*Χρηστοῦ[ς]*: s. *Νουμήνιος*)
SKYTHIA:
—TANAIS: (**16**) 228-244 AD ib. 1250, 12; 1282, 24; 1287, 3 (f. *Πάπας*)

Χριστόδουλος
MACEDONIA (MYGDONIA):
—THESSALONIKE: (**1**) v-vi AD Feissel, *RICM* 95 (monogram) (*SEG* XLVII 964)

Χριστοφόρος
TAURIS:
—CHERSONESOS: (**1**) v-vi AD ib. 1172

Χρόνιος
MACEDONIA (PAIONIA):
—KAVADARCI (MOD.): (**1**) ii-iii AD *Sp.* 98 (1941-8) p. 65 no. 136 (*GVI* 188) (*Χρονίου* (gen.), *Χρόνιον*? (fem. nom.): f. *Ἰουλιανός*)
THRACE:
—OESCUS*: (**2**) i AD *ILB* 47 (Lat. Resius Chronius: freed.)

Χρύσα
CIMMERIAN BOSPOROS:
—GORGIPPIA*: (**1**) 41 AD *CIRB* 1123, 11 (Levinskaya pp. 239-40 no. 7) (*Χ[ρ]ύσα*: threpte)
—PANTIKAPAION: (**2**) i AD *CIRB* 552 (d. *Χρῆστος*)
THRACE:
—BYZANTION: (**3**) ii-iii AD *IByz* 283

Χρυσαλίσκος
CIMMERIAN BOSPOROS:
—HERMONASSA: (**1**) 123-132 AD *CIRB* 1054, 11; Zgusta, *PNS* 1180 (f. *Ἀπολλώνιος*)
—TAMAN PENINSULA: (**2**) i BC Sokol'skii, *Tamanskii tolos* p. 40

Χρυσαλλεύς
CIMMERIAN BOSPOROS:
—MYRMEKION (NR.): (**1**) ii AD *VDI* 1965 (2), p. 96 no. 2; cf. *Topoi* 3 (1993) p. 198 no. 2 (*Ἰούλ. Χρυσαλλεύς*: s. *Ἰούλ. Φίλητος*)

Χρυσάμπελος
THRACE:
—AINOS: (**1**) imp. Unp. (Sayar) (-*άνπ*-)

Χρυσάνθη
THRACE:
—SERDICA: (**1**) 117-138 AD *IGB* IV 1925 c, 12

Χρύσανθος
MACEDONIA (BOTTIAIA):
—EDESSA: (**1**) 229 AD Tataki, *Edessa* 64 (*Αὐρ. Χ.*)
MACEDONIA (MYGDONIA):
—THESSALONIKE: (**2**) i-ii AD *IG* X (2) (1) 243 I, 4 (f. *Μάξιμος*)
MACEDONIA (PAIONIA):
—KAVADARCI (MOD.): (**3**) ii-iii AD Dimitsas 283 (f. *Παράμονος*)
SCYTHIA MINOR:
—ISTROS: (**4**) f. iii AD *Stud. Fischer* p. 32 no. 4, 9 (*[Χρ]<ο>ύσανθος*?: s. *Ἀκκᾶς*)
TAURIS:
—CHERSONESOS: (**5**) iii-ii BC *IOSPE* I² 350 (*[Χρύ]σανθος*?: s. *Ἡρακλείδας*)
THRACE:
—PHILIPPOPOLIS-TRIMONTIUM: (**6**) c. 303 AD *Anal. Boll.* 31 (1912) p. 192

Χρυσάριν
MACEDONIA (BOTTIAIA):
—BEROIA: (**1**) ii AD *IBer* 397, 2 (Tataki 1348) (m. *Σ—*)

Χρυσάριον
MACEDONIA (MYGDONIA):
—THESSALONIKE*: (**1**) ii AD *IG* X (2) (1) 297, 4 (m. *Μορρία Ὀρβᾶνα*: freed.?)

Χρυσαρίς
MACEDONIA (LYNKESTIS):
—HERAKLEIA?: (**1**) ii-iii AD ib. X (2) (2) 129 (Lat. Ailia Chrysaris)

Χρυσάφιος
THRACE:
—BEROE-AUGUSTA TRAIANA (TERRIT.): (**1**) 575-576 AD Beševliev 198, 13

Χρυσάων
SCYTHIA MINOR:
—TOMIS: (**1**) 201 AD *ISM* II 83 I, 32 (s. (nat.) *Γαῦκος*, s. (ad.) *Ἀχιλλᾶς*)

Χρυσέα
SCYTHIA MINOR:
—KALLATIS: (**1**) f. iii AD ib. III 94 (*Αὐρ. Χ.*: d. *Διονύσιος*)
THRACE:
—BYZANTION?: (**2**) ii AD *IByz* 360 = *ISestos* 6

Χρύσερμος
THRACE: (**1**) 267 BC *SEG* XXVII 1114, 6b (La'da E806) (s. *Ἀμάδοκος*)

Χρυσέρως
CIMMERIAN BOSPOROS:
—GORGIPPIA: (**1**) ii AD *CIRB* 1140, 11; *Eirene* 7 (1968) p. 67, 12 (s. *Ἡρακλᾶς*); (**2**) iii AD *NE* 9 (1971) p. 10 no. 6 B, 5 (*[Χρυ]σέρως*)
—MYRMEKION (NR.): (**3**) f. ii AD *VDI* 1965 (2), p. 98 no. 3; cf. *Topoi* 3 (1993) p. 198 no. 3 (*Χρυσέ[ρως]*: s. *Φιλέρως*)
MACEDONIA (EDONIS):
—PHILIPPOI: (**4**) 71 AD *CIL* XVI 12, 27 (Pilhofer 30) (Lat. Chryseros)
MACEDONIA (ELIMEIA):
—KOZANI (MOD.): (**5**) ii-iii AD *EAM* 22 (s. *Φίλιππος*)
MACEDONIA (LOWER PAIONIA):
—IDOMENE?: (**6**) ii-iii AD Sokolovska, *Isar-Marvinci* p. 127
MACEDONIA (MYGDONIA):
—THESSALONIKE: (**7**) i AD *IG* X (2) (1) 242, 12 (f. *Ῥοδανός*)
MACEDONIA (PAIONIA):
—NEGOTINO (MOD.): (**8**) imp. *Sp.* 98 (1941-8) p. 60 no. 124 (s. *Εὐφρόσυνος*)
SKYTHIA:
—TANAIS: (**9**) c. 200-210 AD *CIRB* 1277, 16 (*Χρυσέ[ρως]*: f. *Ἀφροδίσιος*)
THRACE:
—BYZANTION: (**10**) i-ii AD *BMI* 1011; cf. *IByz* p. 263 (f. *Ἀττική*); (**11**) ii-iii AD *IGB* I² 147 bis (s. *Ἀλέξανδρος*)
—BYZANTION?: (**12**) ii AD *IByz* 333 (f. *Μόσχος*)

Χρύση
THRACE:
—PHILIPPOPOLIS-TRIMONTIUM: (**1**) iii AD *IGB* III 948 b, 4 (*Χρύσῃ*)

Χρυσῆϊς
MACEDONIA (BOTTIAIA):
—BEROIA: (**1**) f. iii AD *IBer* 229, 1 (Tataki 1350) (*Χρυσεΐδι* (dat.): d. *Ἐλπίς*)
SCYTHIA MINOR:
—TOMIS: (**2**) imp. *ISM* II 168 (Lat. Lab[e]ria Chrysais: d. Ti(b). Cl. Tertullus)
THRACE:
—APOLLONIA-SOZOPOLIS?: (**3**) v/iv BC *IGB* I² 331 (or Thrace Odessos?)

—PHILIPPOPOLIS-TRIMONTIUM: **(4)** iii AD ib. III 1007, 3 (*Αὐρ. Χ.*: d. *Πρόκλος*)

Χρύσης
CIMMERIAN BOSPOROS:
—PANTIKAPAION: **(1)** f. ii AD *CIRB* 81, 4; cf. KW pl. 33 no. 455
SCYTHIA MINOR:
—TOMIS: **(2)** ii AD *ISM* II 17, 2 (s. *Διονύσιος*); **(3)** ~ ib. l. 8 (*Χρύση* (gen.): I f. *Χρύσης* II); **(4)** ~ ib. l. 8 (II s. *Χρύσης* I)

Χρυσιανή
THRACE:
—ANCHIALOS: **(1)** 294 AD *Cod. Just.* V 51. 11; cf. *Klio* 58 (1976) p. 81 (Lat. Chrysiana)

Χρυσιανός
SCYTHIA MINOR:
—ISTROS: **(1)** ii AD *ISM* I 197 I, 11 (s. *Χρῦσος*)

Χρυσιαρία
CIMMERIAN BOSPOROS:
—PANTIKAPAION: **(1)** f. i AD *CIRB* 138 (*GVI* 504); Zgusta, *PNS* 1182 (*Χρυσι[α]ρία*: m. *Μαστοῦς*)

Χρύσιν
CIMMERIAN BOSPOROS:
—TAMAN PENINSULA: **(1)** f. ii AD *CIRB* 1224; Zgusta, *PNS* 1181 (*-σειν*)
—TYRITAKE: **(2)** f. ii AD *CIRB* 909 (d. *Ποθίαινα*)
THRACE:
—ODESSOS?: **(3)** i-ii AD *IGB* I^{2} 112, 4 (d. *Ροῦφος*)

Χρύσιον
CIMMERIAN BOSPOROS:
—NYMPHAION: **(1)** s. ii AD *CIRB* 934 (*[Χρ]ύσιον*: d. *Καλλισθένης*)
—PANTIKAPAION: **(2)** ii BC ib. 273 (d. *Θεόμνηστος*); **(3)** imp. ib. 774 (m. *Ἀβαζίων*); **(4)** ?i AD ib. 417 (*Χρύσ(ι)ον*: m. *Ἡλιόδωρος*); **(5)** i AD ib. 553; cf. KW pl. 22 no. 318 (d. *Δημήτριος*); **(6)** ?i AD *CIRB* 555; cf. KW pl. 23 no. 324 (I d. *.αμ..*, m. *Χρύσιον* II); **(7)** ~ *CIRB* 555; cf. KW pl. 23 no. 324 (II d. *Χρύσιον* I); **(8)** i-ii AD *CIRB* 648; **(9)** f. i AD ib. 554; cf. KW pl. 20 no. 287 (d. *Ἡρακλείδης*); **(10)** m. i AD *CIRB* 556; **(11)** f. ii AD ib. 714; cf. KW pl. 17 no. 257
—PANTIKAPAION?: **(12)** i AD *SEG* XLV 1011 (*Χρύ[σ]ιο(ν)*: d. *Καλοῦς*)
SCYTHIA MINOR:
—TOMIS: **(13)** ii-iii AD *ISM* II 282 (d. *Δημοσθένης*)

Χρύσιππος
CIMMERIAN BOSPOROS:
—GORGIPPIA: **(1)** f. iii BC *CIRB* 1137 A I, 35 (f. *Προμαθίων*)
—THEODOSIA: **(2)** iii AD ib. 947 A, 4 (I f. *Χρύσιππος* II); **(3)** ~ ib. l. 4 (II s. *Χρύσιππος* I)
MACEDONIA: **(4)** m. ii BC *BGU* 1938 B, 4 (Tataki, *Macedonians* p. 499 no. 249); cf. La'da E1690
MACEDONIA (BOTTIAIA):
—EDESSA: **(5)** 51 AD *SEG* XLVI 744, 9 (Tataki, *Edessa* 182) (*Λ. Λιβύρνιος Χ.*)
MACEDONIA (LYNKESTIS):
—HERAKLEIA (AREA): **(6)** iii AD *IG* X (2) (2) 37
SCYTHIA MINOR:
—ISTROS: **(7)** i BC-i AD *ISM* I 191 II, 5 (s. *Λυσίμαχος*); **(8)** iii AD ib. 141, 7 (V 259) (*Χρύσιππ[ος]*: f. *Αὐρ. Βάσσος*); **(9)** ~ ib. I 303, 2 (s. *Σίδηρος*, f. *Ἀρίστων*, *Ζούθης*, *Σίδηρος*, *Ἀρτεμίδωρος*)
—TOMIS: **(10)** ii-iii AD ib. II 104, 12

SKYTHIA:
—TANAIS: **(11)** 210-226 AD *CIRB* 1280, 17; 1285, 12 (f. *Ἀρδινδιανός*); **(12)** 230 AD ib. 1284, 18 (f. *Μεν—*); **(13)** 244 AD ib. 1287, 10 (f. *Θιάρμακος*)
—TYRAS: **(14)** 181 AD *IOSPE* I^{2} 2, 28 (I f. *Χρύσιππος* II); **(15)** ~ ib. l. 28 (II s. *Χρύσιππος* I)
THRACE:
—ANCHIALOS (TERRIT.): **(16)** ii-iii AD *IGB* III 1842 (f. *Γλύκων*)
—BIZONE: **(17)** i/ii AD ib. I^{2} 6, 13 (*Χρύσιπ(π)ος*: s. *—αισιος*)
—DIONYSOPOLIS: **(18)** ii-iii AD ib. 31, 3 (s. *Ἡ—*)
—PAUTALIA: **(19)** ii-iii AD ib. IV 2072, 6 (s. *Ἐπτέκενθος*)
—PHILIPPOPOLIS-TRIMONTIUM (TERRIT.): **(20)** ii/iii AD ib. III 1452, 10 (*Eastern cults* p. 121 no. 104) (f. *Ἀντίφιλος*)

Χρυσίς
MACEDONIA (EDONIS):
—AMPHIPOLIS: **(1)** iii AD *Mous. Kavalas* p. 84 no. *Λ*. 128
MACEDONIA (MYGDONIA):
—THESSALONIKE: **(2)** ii AD *Ancient Macedonia* 5 p. 1557 no. 6 (Lat. Aelia Chrysis); **(3)** iii AD *IG* X (2) (1) 543, 2 (*Νεπωτιανὴ Χ.*)
—THESSALONIKE?: **(4)** ii AD ib. 707; cf. *CPh.* 70 (1975) p. 49 (m. *Κλευπάτρα*)
THRACE:
—NOVAE: **(5)** imp. *Archeologia* (Warsaw) 50 (1999) p. 29 no. 6 (Lat. Atilia Crysis)
—PERINTHOS-HERAKLEIA: **(6)** iii AD *IPerinth* 165 (*Αὐρ. Χρυσεῖ* (dat.))

Χρυσίων
MACEDONIA (EDONIS):
—PHILIPPOI: **(1)** ii/iii AD *CIL* III 633 II b, 22 (Pilhofer 163); *CRAI* 1923, p. 277 (date); Collart, *Philippes* pls. 64-5 (Lat. Chrysio: ?s. Paccius)
SCYTHIA MINOR:
—ISTROS: **(2)** ii AD *ISM* I 196, 6; 201 I, 8 (f. *Μένυλλος*); **(3)** ~ ib. 196, 20; 201 II, 22 (s. *Νέστωρ*); **(4)** ~ ib. l. 8 (f. *—ιος*)
SKYTHIA:
—TANAIS: **(5)** 154-170 AD *CIRB* 1260a, 20
THRACE:
—BYZANTION: **(6)** 117-138 AD *IByz* 37, 8 (s. *Μήνιος*)
—NICOPOLIS AD ISTRUM (TERRIT.): **(7)** ii AD *IGB* II 715

Χρυσογόνη
MACEDONIA (MYGDONIA):
—THESSALONIKE: **(1)** s. iii AD *IG* X (2) (1) 556 (*Αὐρ. Χ.*)

Χρυσόγονος
CIMMERIAN BOSPOROS:
—GORGIPPIA: **(1)** s. ii AD *CIRB* 1129 B, 9 (*Χρυσόγο[νος]*)
MACEDONIA (BOTTIAIA):
—EDESSA: **(2)** 220-210 BC *RE* (1); *SEG* XXVII 202, 8, 17 (Tataki, *Macedonians* p. 105 no. 22) (s. *Πύρριχος*, f. *Πύρριχος*, *Σάμος*)
SCYTHIA MINOR:
—TOMIS: **(3)** ii AD *ISM* II 90 (*Μ. Κοκκεῖος Χρυσόγο[νος]*); **(4)** 201 AD ib. 83 II, 28 (*Αὐρ. Ἰούλ. Χ.*)
THRACE:
—ODESSOS: **(5)** s. ii AD *IGB* I^{2} 163 (*CCET* I 58; PM 1327)
—PERINTHOS-HERAKLEIA:
——(φυλ. δευτ.): **(6)** iii AD *IPerinth* 156 (*Αὐρ. Χ.*: s. *Αὐρ. Διονύσιος*, *Αὐρ. Χρυσοῦς*)
—PHILIPPOPOLIS-TRIMONTIUM: **(7)** iv AD Beševliev 207, 5

Χρυσόδωρος
SCYTHIA MINOR:
—TOMIS: **(1)** ?iii AD *ISM* II 377, 15 (*GVI* 312) (f. *Ποντιανός*, *Ποντιανή*)

Χρυσόλαος
CIMMERIAN BOSPOROS:
—BOSPOROS: **(1)** ?257 BC Nachtergael, *Les Galates* 7, 41 (f. *Ἡδύλος*)

Χρυσόπολις
MACEDONIA (BOTTIAIA):
—AIGAI: **(1)** s. iv BC *SEG* XXXV 802
THRACE:
—BYZANTION: **(2)** ii AD ib. L 667 IX

Χρῦσος
CIMMERIAN BOSPOROS:
—PANTIKAPAION: **(1)** i AD *CIRB* 517 (f. *Τοφῶς*); **(2)** m. i AD ib. 425 (f. *Ἑλικωνιάς*)
SCYTHIA MINOR:
—ISTROS: **(3)** ii AD *ISM* I 197 I, 11 (f. *Χρυσιανός*)

Χρυσοῦς
SKYTHIA:
—TANAIS: **(1)** 188 AD *CIRB* 1242, 15; Zgusta, *PNS* 1183 (s. *Ψυχαρίων*)
TAURIS:
—CHERSONESOS: **(2)** ii AD *IOSPE* I^{2} 442 (s. *Φαρνάκης*); **(3)** iii-iv AD *SEG* XLVIII 1000 bis. 4-5 (lamp)
THRACE:
—PERINTHOS-HERAKLEIA: **(4)** iii AD *IPerinth* 156 (*Αὐρ. Χρυσοῦτι* (dat.): m. *Αὐρ. Χρυσόγονος*)

Χρυσόχοος
CIMMERIAN BOSPOROS:
—GORGIPPIA: **(1)** ii/iii AD *CIRB* 1179, 36 (?f. *Πόθος*)

Χρυσώτης
CIMMERIAN BOSPOROS:
—GORGIPPIA: **(1)** ii/iii AD ib. l. 37 (f. *Πραξίας*)

Χρῶμις
THRACE:
—SPINOPARA: **(1)** ii AD *IGB* IV 2192, 14

Χύρις
MACEDONIA (MYGDONIA):
—LETE: **(1)** m. iv BC *SEG* XLIV 537 (*Χύρι* (dat.))

Χώδαρζος
SKYTHIA:
—OLBIA-BORYSTHENES: **(1)** s. ii AD *IOlbia* 81, 6 (*IOSPE* I^{2} 94); Zgusta, *PNS* 261 (s. *Φάρζηος*)

Χωδόνακος
SKYTHIA:
—TANAIS: **(1)** 225-230 AD *CIRB* 1280, 16; 1284, 12; Zgusta, *PNS* 262 (*[Χωδόνα]κος*?—1284: f. *Χανσαβόγαζος*)

Χῶλος
CIMMERIAN BOSPOROS:
—GORGIPPIA: **(1)** ii/iii AD *CIRB* 1179, 28 (f. *Πάπας*)

Χωνδίακος
CIMMERIAN BOSPOROS:
—THEODOSIA: **(1)** iii AD ib. 947 A, 11; Zgusta, *PNS* 735 (s. *Ἀσκληπᾶς*)

Χωρότιμος
MACEDONIA (PIERIA):
—PYDNA: **(1)** iv BC *GRBS* 47 (2002-3) p. 122 no. 6, 2

Ψ

Ψάμμις
Thrace:
—abdera: **(1)** f. iv bc *SEG* xlvii 1028 (*IThrakAig* E38) (s. Ἑρμαγόρης)

Ψελλός
Macedonia: **(1)** 78 bc *PRyl* 588, 6 (La'da E1635) (Σωσίβιος ὁ καὶ Ψ.: s. Πρώταρχος ὁ καὶ Ἁρμάϊς)

Ψεμιθλίας
Cimmerian Bosporos:
—gorgippia: **(1)** 168 ad *CIRB* 1144, 2 (Ψεμιθλία[ς]?—Vinogradov, Ψεμιθλια[νός]?—ed.)

Ψηβακος?
Cimmerian Bosporos:
—pantikapaion: **(1)** i ad Tolstoi 237 (vase); Zgusta, *PNS* 343 (Ψηβακου—ed., Ψηβακρ—?)

Ψιμίθας
Cimmerian Bosporos:
—gorgippia: **(1)** ii/iii ad *CIRB* 1179, 32 (Ψι(μ)ίθας: f. Τιμόθεος)

Ψυχάριν
Cimmerian Bosporos:
—pantikapaion: **(1)** i ad ib. 462 ?= (Ψυχάριον *(2)*); **(2)** ?i ad ib. 557

Ψυχάριον
Cimmerian Bosporos:
—pantikapaion: **(1)** i bc ib. 295; cf. KW pl. 22 no. 312; Zgusta, *PNS* 1186 (d. Σαδάλας); **(2)** i ad *KSIA* 116 (1969) p. 49 no. 1 ?= (Ψυχάριν *(1)*); **(3)** ~ *CIRB* 484 (Ψυχάρ[ι]ον: d. Διομήδης)

Ψυχαρίων
Cimmerian Bosporos:
—gorgippia: **(1)** m. ii ad *Eirene* 7 (1968) p. 67, 8; Zgusta, *PNS* 1187 (s. Ἀπελλᾶς); **(2)** ~ *Eirene* 7 (1968) p. 67, 18 (s. Φαρνακίων); **(3)** s. ii ad *CIRB* 1142, 14 (Ψυχ[αρίων]?); **(4)** ~ ib. 1145, 7 ([Ψ]υχαρίων: s. Ἀγαθοῦς) ?= *(5)*
—gorgippia?: **(5)** s. ii ad ib. 1231 A, 7 (f. —θους) ?= *(4)*
—kytaia: **(6)** 234 ad ib. 942, 4 (Ἰούλ. Ψ.)
—pantikapaion: **(7)** i bc ib. 120, 2 (*GVI* 843) (f. Λυσίμαχος); **(8)** i bc/i ad *CIRB* 300 (s. Ὑγιαίνων, f. Ἀμμία); **(9)** f. i ad ib. 143, 1; cf. KW pl. 21 no. 315; **(10)** ?s. i ad *CIRB* 78; cf. KW pl. 42 no. 627 (f. Δάφνος); **(11)** s. i ad *CIRB* 558 (s. Γάστεις); **(12)** ~ ib. 559 (s. Ὑγιαίνων); **(13)** i/ii ad ib. 596 ([Ψ]υχαρίων: f. Γλυκαρίων); **(14)** f. ii ad ib. 716; cf. KW pl. 26 no. 384 (s. Ἔρως); **(15)** 275-278 ad *CIRB* 36, 24 (s. Σόγος); **(16)** ~ ib. l. 24 (Ψ[υχα]ρίων: s. Ἡρακλείδας); **(17)** ~ ib. l. 41 (s. Πατέριος)
—phanagoreia: **(18)** 51 ad *SEG* xliii 510, 4 (Levinskaya pp. 237-8 no. 6) (f. Σόγος, Ἄνος: Jew?)
—theodosia: **(19)** iii ad *CIRB* 947 A, 7 (Ψυχαρί[ων]: f. Δημήτριος); **(20)** ~ ib. l. 16 (f. —θος); **(21)** ~ ib. 947 B, 5 (Ψυχαρίω[ν]: s. Ἀπολλώνιος)
Skythia:
—tanais: **(22)** f. ii ad ib. 1264 A, 10 (f. Ἀρδαρίσκος); **(23)** 104 ad ib. 1259, 25 (f. —ράτης); **(24)** 188 ad ib. 1242, 15 (f. Χρυσοῦς); **(25)** c. 200-210 ad ib. 1277, 20 (f. Θεότιμος); **(26)** 210-226 ad ib. 1281, 14 (Ψυχαρί[ων]: s. Τ—) ?= *(29)* *(28)*; **(27)** c. 210-236 ad ib. 1250, 10, 1280, 5; 1285, 13 (s. Φιδανους); **(28)** 225 ad ib. 1279, 19 (s. Τρύφων) ?= *(26)*; **(29)** 228 ad ib. 1282, 16 (f. Τρύφων) ?= *(30)* *(26)*; **(30)** ~ ib. l. 17 (f. Σαβώδακος) ?= *(29)*

Ψύχη
Cimmerian Bosporos:
—pantikapaion: **(1)** i bc ib. 296; Zgusta, *PNS* 1189; **(2)** imp. *CIRB* 764 (d. Σάκτας); **(3)** i bc/i ad ib. 323, 1; **(4)** ~ ib. 324; cf. KW pl. 13 no. 186; **(5)** i ad *CIRB* 562 (m. Μασтоῦς); **(6)** f. i ad ib. 389 (d. Ἔρως); **(7)** ~ ib. 560; **(8)** ~ ib. 561 (m. Γάστεις); **(9)** i/ii ad ib. 649; cf. KW pl. 19 no. 276 (m. Πρώτη); **(10)** f. ii ad *CIRB* 715; cf. KW pl. 14 no. 210
Tauris:
—chersonesos: **(11)** iii-ii bc *IOSPE* i² 523

Ω

Ὤβειος
Thrace:
—serdica: **(1)** 117-138 ad *IGB* iv 1925 c, 5

Ὠιτα
Thrace:
—serdica (territ.): **(1)** ii-iii ad ib. 2027 (d. Δίζας)

Ὠνίας
Cimmerian Bosporos:
—hermonassa: **(1)** f. i ad *CIRB* 1076 (f. Βοθύλις)

Ὦπις
Macedonia (Pelagonia): **(1)** imp. *IG* x (2) (2) 272 (d. Νικήτης, m. Μᾶρκος)

Ὥριμος
Scythia Minor:
—istros (nr.): **(1)** ii ad *ISM* i 374; 375; 376; 377 (Φλ. Ὠ.)

Ὥριος
Macedonia (Mygdonia):
—thessalonike: **(1)** 74 ad *IG* x (2) (1) 67, 3 (Γ. Ἰούλ. Ὠ.)

Ὠρίων
Macedonia: **(1)** 103 bc *PTeb* 105, 1, 3, 11, 20, 28-9 etc. (Tataki, *Macedonians* p. 499 no. 250; La'da E1657) (s. Ἀπολλώνιος)
Thrace:
—byzantion: **(2)** c. 303 ad *Anal. Boll.* 31 (1912) p. 192

Ὧρος
Thrace:
—perinthos-herakleia: **(1)** 196-198 ad *IPerinth* 56, 10 (f. Μᾶρκος)
—philippopolis-trimontium: **(2)** c. 303 ad *Anal. Boll.* 31 (1912) p. 192

Ὠφελίμα
Macedonia (Bottiaia):
—beroia: **(1)** 177 ad *IBer* 327 (Tataki 649) (Καιπιανὴ Ὠ.: m. Καιπιανὸς Ἕλενος)
Macedonia (Mygdonia):
—thessalonike?: **(2)** ii ad *IG* x (2) (1) 884 (m. Ἱμέρα)

Ὠφελίων
Macedonia (Bottiaia):
—beroia: **(1)** ii bc *IBer* 179 (s. Λάανδρος)
—beroia (territ.): **(2)** ii-iii ad ib. 512, 4 (Tataki 1351)
Macedonia (Derriopos):
—stuberra: **(3)** 74 ad *IG* x (2) (2) 325, 46 (f. Παράμονος); **(4)** 87 ad ib. l. 77 (f. Στράτων)
Macedonia (Eordaia):
—krannestai: **(5)** ii-iii ad ib. 36, 1 (f. Νίκανδρος)
Macedonia (Lynkestis)?: **(6)** ii-iii ad *EAM* 159 b, 2 (Τερεντιανὸς Ὠ.)
Macedonia (Pelagonia): **(7)** ii-iii ad *IG* x (2) (2) 257, 1 (Ὠ. Εὔπλοκος: f. Φροντῖνος)
Macedonia (Pieria):
—dion (territ.): **(8)** i/ii ad Dimitsas 159 (I f. Ὠφελίων II); **(9)** ~ ib. (II s. Ὠφελίων I)
—pydna: **(10)** 250 ad *SEG* xlvi 800 A, 31 (Κορνήλιος Ὠ.)
Skythia:
—olbia-borysthenes: **(11)** ii ad *IOSPE* i² 106, 9 (f. Δυρπάναις)
Thrace: **(12)** iii bc *IG* ii² 8928 (*FRA* 2594)

REVERSE INDEX OF NAMES IN VOLUME IV

Νικανδρία
Ἀλεξανδρία
Αἰθερία
Γλυκερία
Βαλερία
Οὐαλερία
Καλημερία
Εὐημερία
Βενερία
Οὐενερία
Πεπερία
Δροσερία
Περιστερία
Σωτηρία
Γρηγορία
Στερκορία
Εὐπορία
Ἱστορία
Κοπρία
Δαματρία
Εὐπατρία
Δημητρία
Κυρία
Σατυρία
Βικτωρία
Ἀσία
Βασία
Ἀμασία
Ἀσπασία
Προστασία
Ἱκεσία
Μιλησία
Γνησία
Παρρησία
Καισία
Ἀφροδισία
Ἀρτεμισία
Πονσία
Θεοδοσία
Ὁσία
Εὐποσία
Ἀμβροσία
Κασσία
Διονυσία
Πλουσία
Ἀπρουσία
Ἀμβατία
Κουριατία
Ἰγνατία
Ὑπατία
Δαμοκρατία
Δημοκρατία
Στρατία
Τατία
Δομετία
Νικητία
Μιλητία
Δομιτία
Βυζαντία
Ἀπαντία
Κωνσταντία

Τερεντία
Λαυρεντία
Κοϊντία
Λεοντία
Γεροντία
Τερτία
Βαστία
Σαλλουστία
Ματτία
Τεττία
Οὐεττία
Βρουτία
Φλαουΐα
Ἀφία
Σοφία
Ἀπφία
Ἀφφία
Συμμαχία
Ἀγχία
Παραμονιχία
Ἀμπελοχία
Ἱππαρχία
Ἡσυχία
Εὐτυχία
Μαλάκα
Ῥεβέκα
Ἐπτημενηκα
Ζαικα
Ἀμαδίκα
Ἀμμαδίκα
Ἠδικα
Λυσιδίκα
Εὐρυδίκα
Μίκα
Λανίκα
Χανίκα
Βερενίκα
Μνασινίκα
Νίκα
Ἀννίκα
Θεονίκα
Κλεονίκα
Δαμονίκα
Στρατονίκα
Ἀριστονίκα
Βερνίκα
Σωσίκα
Πατίκα
Ἄκκα
Μίκκα
Βιλόκκα
Δοῦλκα
Παρμενίσκα
Ἀνδρίσκα
Πρίσκα
Συρίσκα
Ἡγησίσκα
Φοῦσκα
Γλαύκα
Λύκα
Μούκα

Κάλα
Λάλα
Μάμαλα
Μακέσαλα
Λούσαλα
Πυρούσαλα
Μάτελα
Δεντούσκαιλα
Νέρβιλα
Ζαινειλα
Ἄμμιλα
Ἀναξίλα
Ἀγησίλα
Βάσσιλα
Φίλα
Ἀντιφίλα
Παμφίλα
Θεοφίλα
Δαμοφίλα
Μηνοφίλα
Πατροφίλα
Μητροφίλα
Ζωΐλα
Θέκλα
Πρόκλα
Μάρκελλα
Σεκούνδιλλα
Ξάνθιλλα
Ἀττίκιλλα
Λούκιλλα
Ἄμιλλα
Ποτάμιλλα
Σελήνιλλα
Λαίνιλλα
Ἰούνιλλα
Πράξιλλα
Ἰκάριλλα
Στερκόριλλα
Κύριλλα
Ἡγήσιλλα
Παύσιλλα
Κλημέντιλλα
Μύρτιλλα
Πλαύτιλλα
Κόλλα
Ἀπόλλα
Πόλλα
Σέρβυλλα
Ἔθυλλα
Ἄνθυλλα
Νίκυλλα
Μένυλλα
Ξένυλλα
Ἤρυλλα
Κάτυλλα
Στράτυλλα
Ἄντυλλα
Τερέντυλλα
Φρόντυλλα
Ἀρίστυλλα
Πῶλλα

Ἰόλα
Λόλα
Παῦλα
Ἄκυλα
Βούλα
Τριβούλα
Θεοβούλα
Ἀριστοβούλα
Εὐβούλα
Μηφάζουλα
Σέκουλα
Λέπουλα
Τάρουλα
Οὐέρουλα
Πύρουλα
Βέσουλα
Ἀμα
Χαριδάμα
Μάμα
Ζουμαμα
Ἐπίτευγμα
Πτολέμα
Νικοπτολέμα
Μέμα
Μέλημα
Νόημα
Ἀγάπημα
Δώρημα
Γρατίσημα
Χῆμα
Ὠφελίμα
Μάξιμα
Πρῖμα
Δωρίμα
Χρησίμα
Ζωσίμα
Θετίμα
Θεοτίμα
Ἡροτίμα
Ἀριστοτίμα
Μᾶ
Ἄμμα
Λαδόμα
Πάρμα
Ἀξίωμα
Μώμα
Γνώμα
Ἄνα
Ἀδάνα
Νικοπολιανά
Γερμανά
Ῥωμανά
Νάνα
Κυννάνα
Εἰράνα
Μαντανα
Ἀλκυάνα
Μάγνα
Ὕδνα
Ἑρμογένα
Παρθένα

Μεστίκενα
Ἀμμένα
Ἀρμένα
Φιλουμένα
Φιλοξένα
Δαμοξένα
Τιμοξένα
Πολυξένα
Καπένα
Ἀθηνᾶ
Γενθήνα
Εὐθήνα
Πελήνα
Ποθίαινα
Κυρίαινα
Λάκαινα
Νίκαινα
Γλύκαινα
Φίλαινα
Σίμαινα
Δεντούσταινα
Τρύφαινα
Σαβῖνα
Λογγῖνα
Ῥηγῖνα
Βενδῖνα
Λοπικῖνα
Φίλινα
Προκελλῖνα
Μαρκελλῖνα
Μαρυλλῖνα
Εὐκολίνα
Παυλῖνα
Ἀκυλῖνα
Καπιτωλῖνα
Μαξιμῖνα
Φιρμῖνα
Δομνῖνα
Σατορνῖνα
Ἀντωνῖνα
Ἀγριππῖνα
Κρισπῖνα
Σκουπῖνα
Λουπῖνα
Εὐαρίνα
Σεβερῖνα
Κελερῖνα
Χοιρίνα
Μυρίνα
Κελσῖνα
Κοσίνα
Οὐαλεντῖνα
Φαυστῖνα
Μυττίνα
Μυτίνα
Πλουτῖνα
Πλωτῖνα
Ῥουφῖνα
Νᾶ
Δόμνα
Ἄννα

Τύραννα
Σωσάννα
Ἰωάννα
Ἡράϊννα
Γλύκιννα
Φίλιννα
Νόννα
Καλλιγόνα
Ἀντιγόνα
Κλειόνα
Βουλόνα
Παραμόνα
Ἀριστόνα
Παῦνα
Κύνα
Χελώνα
Ματρώνα
Λαλζόα
Νικονόα
Αὐτονόα
Εὐρυνόα
Ζαιπα
Διαζείπα
Πόπα
Γοργίππα
Φιλίππα
Ἀριστίππα
Σαβάρα
Βαρβάρα
Ζυβαρα
Καθαρά
Κανθάρα
Μανθάρα
Τιάρα
Ἰλάρα
Κλᾶρα
Τάρα
Χαρά
Χοίδρα
Νικάνδρα
Ἀλεξάνδρα
Ἡγησάνδρα
Κασσάνδρα
Λυσάνδρα
Σωσάνδρα
Μένδρα
Γυκέρα
Γλυκέρα
Ἡμέρα
Καλημέρα
Ἱμέρα
Ἀμετέρα
Καλλιοτέρα
Φιλωτέρα
Σουλιφέρα
Τρυφέρα
Σεβῆρα
Κλησιθήρα
Ἀνθηρά
Πανθήρα
Σευῆρα
Γοαζείρα
Σώτειρα
Μαισίρα
Κλεαγόρα
Νικαγόρα
Βιλάρρα
Πύρρα
Σωσιπάτρα
Ἀντιπάτρα
Κλεοπάτρα
Φιλοπάτρα
Ἀριστοπάτρα
Κλευπάτρα
Σωπάτρα
Μέτρα
Δήμητρα
Μαῦρα
Ἀδύρα
Οὐαδύρα
Λαμύρα
Ταμύρα
Ταλούρα
Σούρα
Ζωπύρα
Σύρα
Σατύρα
Πορφύρα
Αἴσχρα
Βενδιδώρα
Ἀρτεμιδώρα
Ἰσιδώρα
Θεοδώρα
Διοδώρα
Ἡλιοδώρα
Ἀσκληπιοδώρα
Ἀπολλοδώρα
Ἑρμοδώρα
Ζηνοδώρα
Ἀθηνοδώρα
Μηνοδώρα
Ματροδώρα
Μητροδώρα
Διονυσοδώρα
Ὀπώρα
Βάσα
Πασα
Εὐτυχάσα
Ἀφροδεσά
Εἶσα
Πίσα
Γόσα
Κελαίδοσα
Πόσα
Χόσα
Μηδισαρσα
Βάσσα
Ἄνασσα
Ἡγεάνασσα
Ἀγαθάνασσα
Καλλιάνασσα
Ἀρχήνασσα
Δημώνασσα
Ἡρώνασσα
Μητρώνασσα
Ἑκατώνασσα
Καλλιστώνασσα
Θρέσσα
Θρᾶισσα
Μέλισσα
Βασίλισσα
Τύρισσα
Νῦσα
Καλλιμέδουσα
Σπένδουσα
Κρέουσα
Παίζουσα
Φαέθουσα
Ἀρέθουσα
Ἀνθοῦσα
Ποθοῦσα
Γόκουσα
Ἀρέσκουσα
Φιλοῦσα
Θάλλουσα
Μοῦσα
Λανθάνουσα
Αὐξάνουσα
Χάνουσα
Παρμένουσα
Πρέπουσα
Φέρουσα
Συμφέρουσα
Μύρουσα
Σοῦσα
Τούσα
Χρύσα
Ζῶσα
Νονῶσα
Μυρῶσα
Τρυφῶσα
Σαμβάτα
Ῥεβοκᾶτα
Μαμάτα
Χημάτα
Μάτα
Παρμάτα
Φορτουνᾶτα
Μενεστράτα
Σωστράτα
Κλευάτα
Ὀδέτα
Μακέτα
Συνέτα
Μεγαρέτα
Φιλαρέτα
Λαρέτα
Θαυμαρέτα
Πισταρέτα
Βενδιζητα
Φιλήτα
Κλήτα
Ἀρήτα
Βίτα
Κλείτα
Φηλικίτα
Μελίτα
Μαργαρίτα
Καλλικρίτα
Κρίτα
Θεοκρίτα
Ὦιτα
Μάντα
Πάντα
Ἡροφάντα
Κοῖντα
Μόντα
Θεοδότα
Κοάρτα
Κούαρτα
Φαισφάρτα
Μύρτα
Παγκάστα
Πολυκάστα
Μάστα
Μόδεστα
Μέστα
Φῆστα
Ἀδίστα
Πλείστα
Βιλίστα
Φιλίστα
Καλλίστα
Τιμαρίστα
Ξεναρίστα
Κρατίστα
Φαῦστα
Μύστα
Αὐγούστα
Ἰοῦστα
Βενοῦστα
Βλώστα
Θρᾶιττα
Μέλιττα
Ἰούλιττα
Τίθυτα
Ἁρπαλοσκύτα
Τιούτα
Τούτα
Πρώτα
Μαδαγαύα
Κρατεύα
Ἰνγένουα
Δρούα
Περπέτουα
Ἄττυα
Νικομάχα
Ἱππομάχα
Ἀνδρομάχα
Κόγχα
Ἑλλανίχα
Ἠρίχα
Ματρίχα
Κυρίχα
Δωρίχα
Σωσίχα
Κοττίχα
Καεινόχα
Καλατύχα
Εὐτύχα
Ὕψα
Ζώα
Ἰακώβ
Μακαλωνε
Βουζάη
Δανάη
Φοίβη
Ζιασάλβη
Καλύβη
Ἀμάγη
Αὔγη
Ζηκαλώγη
Ἴδη
Διοσκορίδη
Ζηνδη
Ῥόδη
Λύδη
Νητιάζη
Γύζη
Ἀγάθη
Πανταγάθη
Ἀριαράθη
Σαβίθη
Οἰνάνθη
Χρυσάνθη
Ζεκαιδένθη
Σαβύθη
Ἐρύθη
Ἀναίη
Γραίη
Ἀσαίη
Ἑκαταίη
Μητροβίη
Ζωβίη
Ἰνδίη
Ἡδείη
Ἀγαθοκλείη
Λειμείη
Αἰθαζίη
Μοκαζίη
Ταταζιη
Δραυκενθίη
Κουτιλίη
Εὐθυμίη
Ἀμαζονίη
Ἰωνίη
Ἀρτινοίη
Φιλονοίη
Ὀποίη
Δημητρίη
Ἀσπασίη
Ἀφροδισίη
Ἰτίη
Ἀκή
Κυριακή

Βράκη
Ζέκη
Λογική
Λυσιδίκη
Λαοδίκη
Κλεοδίκη
Ξενοδίκη
Ἀριστοδίκη
Μαχορδίκη
Λαυδίκη
Εὐδίκη
Εὐρυδίκη
Βασιλική
Μίκη
Παρθενική
Ξενική
Βερενίκη
Καλλινίκη
Ἐπινίκη
Ἐλπινίκη
Νίκη
Θεονίκη
Κλεονίκη
Ἀγαθονίκη
Θεσσαλονίκη
Δημονίκη
Ἀνδρονίκη
Βερονίκη
Ἐρατονίκη
Στρατονίκη
Ἀριστονίκη
Εὐνίκη
Πολυνίκη
Φιλιππική
Ῥητορική
Ταυρική
Μουσική
Ἱερατική
Συγκλητική
Ἀττική
Ζωτική
Ἄλκη
Ζιαμάρκη
Σισομάρκη
Σπάρκη
Σάρκη
Ἀρτεμίσκη
Λεύκη
Ζουκη
Σαρύκη
Αἰθάλη
Κάλη
Ἀλπάλη
Ἀρπάλη
Σπατάλη
Μυρτάλη
Αἴγλη
Σεμέλη
Θυμέλη
Ζείλη
Βασίλη
Ἀρκεσίλη
Ἀρτυσίλη
Φίλη
Ἀντιφίλη
Θεοφίλη
Πατροφίλη
Κάλλη
Σκύλλη
Ἰόλη
Τιμόλη
Ἀναξιπόλη
Ἡγησιπόλη
Ἀνατολή
Ἡδύλη
Ἀρχεβούλη
Καλλιβούλη
Νικοβούλη
Ἀριστοβούλη
Εὐβούλη
Θεοδούλη
Ἡγησιπύλη
Ὕλη
Εὐρυφύλη
Θαλάμη
Ἀπάμη
Ἔμη
Μέμη
Δήμη
Δοκίμη
Μονίμη
Καρπίμη
Στασίμη
Ὀνησίμη
Σίμη
Ζωσίμη
Ἐμπεδοτίμη
Θεοτίμη
Ἀκροτίμη
Τροφίμη
Ῥιψίμη
Ἑλλακόμη
Νόμη
Λεστόρμη
Νισκατουρμη
Ῥησκουτούρμη
Ῥαισκουτούρμη
Δαρουτούρμη
Διδύμη
Πώμη
Ῥώμη
Σιλβάνη
Σεδάνη
Πιθάνη
Γαϊανή
Φοιβιανή
Εὐοδιανή
Κλαυδιανή
Νικιανή
Μαρκιανή
Λευκιανή
Λυκιανή
Λουκιανή
Μουκιανή
Αὐρηλιανή
Αἰλιανή
Αἰμιλιανή
Ζωϊλιανή
Προκλιανή
Νικοπολιανή
Ἀμπλιάνη
Ἰουλιανή
Ἀμιανή
Δαμιανή
Ζωσιμιανή
Κοσμιανή
Τιμοξενιανή
Αἰτερνιανή
Πολεμωνιανή
Τρυφωνιανή
Ἀλυπιανή
Ἀριανή
Μαριανή
Παριανή
Ἀνδριανή
Κασσανδριανή
Κοπριανή
Σατριανή
Δημητριανή
Κυριανή
Συριανή
Ἀπολλοδωριανή
Πωριανή
Λυσιανή
Χρυσιανή
Τατιανή
Τιτιανή
Δαλτιανή
Ποντιανή
Ἀμυντιανή
Σκιρτιανή
Καλλιστιανή
Βωτιανή
Εὐτυχιανή
Νάνη
Κυννάνη
Ῥωξάνη
Στοράνη
Ἄγνη
Ἀριάγνη
Ἀριάδνη
Ἑλένη
Κυριαμένη
Πεφιλημένη
Κτημένη
Σωζομένη
Μυρομένη
Κλυμένη
Φιλουμένη
Χοσουμένη
Φιλοξένη
Πολυξένη
Ἀθήνη
Σελήνη
Μυτιλήνη
Ἀττυληνή
Εἰρήνη
Σαίνη
Παιβίνη
Ὑγίνη
Ποθείνη
Αὐλείνη
Ὀρείνη
Μικαλίνη
Ἀμμαλίνη
Ἀμπελίνη
Βασιλίνη
Φιλίνη
Δεσπίνη
Ἐαρίνη
Ἀρδρίνη
Θερίνη
Ματερίνη
Μακρίνη
Μυρρίνη
Μυρίνη
Μυρσίνη
Μελιτίνη
Μελτίνη
Κλημεντίνη
Ὀρεστίνη
Χρηστίνη
Πλωτίνη
Μοσχίνη
Σέμνη
Δόμνη
Ἄννη
Ἐπιγόνη
Ἰσιγόνη
Ἀντιγόνη
Ὑψιγόνη
Χρυσογόνη
Ἡδόνη
Ἡλιόνη
Ἑρμιόνη
Χιόνη
Τέρπνη
Ῥοδογύνη
Εὔνη
Χαρμοσύνη
Ἀβροσύνη
Εὐφροσύνη
Σωφροσύνη
Δάφνη
Ματρώνη
Προθόη
Χλόη
Πραξινόη
Ἀρσινόη
Θεονόη
Νικονόη
Ἀριστονόη
Βερόη
Καλλιρρόη
Ἀγάπη
Δανήπη
Κάλπη
Ῥοδόπη
Καλλιόπη
Προκόπη
Παρθενόπη
Στερόπη
Ἐντρόπη
Λευκίππη
Φιλίππη
Εὐτέρπη
Ἀλύπη
Σινώπη
Εὐρώπη
Μοκαζοίρη
Βριθαγόρη
Ἀναξαγόρη
Θεμισταγόρη
Ἀρισταγόρη
Διοσκόρη
Τερψιχόρη
Λάμπρη
Κλεοπάτρη
Ἀπατούρη
Ἀρτεμιδώρη
Μητροδώρη
Σκεδέση
Σχινείση
Πίση
Χρύση
Ἀπριάτη
Γαλάτη
Μενεκράτη
Ἐπικράτη
Ἱπποκράτη
Μνησιστράτη
Λυσιστράτη
Νικοστράτη
Φιλοστράτη
Σωστράτη
Φιλτάτη
Λαμπροτάτη
Νωστάτη
Μακέτη
Μελέτη
Γαμέτη
Ἀρισταινέτη
Συνέτη
Ἀρέτη
Νικαρέτη
Δημαρέτη
Τιμαρέτη
Φιλήτη
Ἐπιθυμήτη
Ἀρήτη
Κουήτη
Ἀφροδίτη
Σείτη
Μελίτη
Κοίτη

Μενεκρίτη
Ναυσικρίτη
Φωκρίτη
Ἀκτή
Ἀταλάντη
Μητροφάντη
Θεοδότη
Διοδότη
Ἀσκληπιοδότη
Ἡροδότη
Θευδότη
Γράπτη
Σπάρτη
Ἑόρτη
Βλάστη
Ὀνομάστη
Ἀγοράστη
Ἀριμνήστη
Θεομνήστη
Χρήστη
Μεγίστη
Ὀαδίστη
Ἡδίστη
Φειδίστη
Φιλίστη
Καλλίστη
Ἀρτεμίστη
Πίστη
Ἀρίστη
Νικαρίστη
Ξεναρίστη
Σωσαρίστη
Θεοκτίστη
Ἀπολαύστη
Κλύτη
Θιούτη
Πούτη
Φιλώτη
Πρώτη
Παρασκευή
Καμασαρύη
Κομοσαρύη
Συγγράφη
Γράφη
Φιλαδέλφη
Νύμφη
Σόφη
Ἄπφη
Μορφή
Ἄφφη
Ἀλκιμάχη
Λυσιμάχη
Μάχη
Λύγχη
Καλλίχη
Σιμίχη
Φανίχη
Μελιννίχη
Παραμονίχη
Βοσπορίχη
Μητρίχη

Κυρίχη
Βιλιστίχη
Ζωΐχη
Προσδόχη
Ἄρχη
Παιδάρχη
Δημάρχη
Ἀγαθητύχη
Καλητύχη
Καλλιτύχη
Συντύχη
Νικοτύχη
Τύχη
Εὐτύχη
Ψύχη
Κόμψη
Ζώη
Ζεκαλώη
Ἄσσει
Θιθι
Μαδινι
Ἀννι
Βλωστι
Ζουκαιβλωστι
Λυκώι
Ἡρώι
Ματρώι
Λεοντώι
Ἰσαάκ
Μιχαήλ
Δανιήλ
Σαμουήλ
Ἰάν
Φιλάν
Ἔλλαν
Ζόβην
Ἕλλην
Φιλοποίμην
Ἐζιωπην
Σάβιν
Σμαράγδιν
Γαειν
Γάστειν
Μεγέθιν
Μυράνθιν
Κούθιν
Λεώκιν
Ἀμπέλιν
Βασίλιν
Ἄμιν
Ἀρτέμιν
Ἄμμιν
Παρθένιν
Ἄννιν
Ἡδόνιν
Χελιδόνιν
Εἰκόνιν
Γλυκάριν
Φιλιππάριν
Χρυσάριν
Ζωσάριν

Ψυχάριν
Ἐλευθέριν
Σωτήριν
Τάσιν
Χρύσιν
Φιλημάτιν
Ἀρωμάτιν
Χαρίτιν
Γερόντιν
Μύρτιν
Ἐρώτιν
Μόσχιν
Ἄγαθον
Παγγαῖον
Εὐσέβιον
Λύγγιον
Λαμίδιον
Βοΐδιον
Βένδιον
Ῥόδιον
Μύδιον
Μάσθιον
Στρούθιον
Ἀνθράκιον
Εὐμήκιον
Φοινίκιον
Δόρκιον
Φύσκιον
Γαύκιον
Κειμήλιον
Κάλλιον
Ἄμμιον
Τόμιον
Ἐγκώμιον
Ἀπολλοφάνιον
Παρθένιον
Ἄννιον
Φιλίννιον
Νικάριον
Γλυκάριον
Κυνάριον
Χρυσάριον
Ζωσάριον
Εὐχάριον
Ψυχάριον
Ἐλευθέριον
Ἀγροτέριον
Θάσιον
Γυμνάσιον
Χόσιον
Χρύσιον
Φιλημάτιον
Τορευμάτιον
Χαρίτιον
Ἀσυγκρίτιον
Γάστιον
Καλλίστιον
Σάττιον
Ἀδύτιον
Δούτιον
Σώτιον

Εὔϊον
Ἀφίον
Κάχιον
Ἄρχιον
Μόσχιον
Μουσικόν
Γλαῦκον
Μουκάσουκον
Σῖμον
Ἄγνον
Φαῖδρον
Γλύκερον
Ἄνθηρον
Μύρον
Λόλησον
Ὀλύμπιχον
Ἥδυν
Κάνουν
Μυροπνοῦν
Πάων
Χρυσάων
Βάβων
Θάβων
Κορράβων
Στράβων
Κέβων
Στίλβων
Τούρβων
Θάγων
Λάγων
Ἱεράγων
Βοστάγων
Εὐάγων
Πλαγγών
Ζορδέγων
Φλέγων
Μέγων
Λόγων
Μίσγων
Ἄδων
Θεάδων
Λάδων
Παπάδων
Ἀτάδων
Καλχάδων
Μακεδών
Λαμέδων
Ἀλκιμέδων
Καλλιμέδων
Μέδων
Λαομέδων
Κλεομέδων
Ἱππομέδων
Δωρομέδων
Πολυμέδων
Εὐρυμέδων
Λεωμέδων
Δίζδων
Ἧδων
Φαίδων
Μείδων

Φείδων
Μυρμιδών
Κουκόδων
Θερμόδων
Ῥόδων
Κέρδων
Σέρδων
Κύδων
Κώδων
Θέων
Ἀρθέων
Μινικέων
Ἀνδραλέων
Πανταλέων
Ἀντιλέων
Ἡρακλέων
Κλέων
Εὐκλέων
Λέων
Λυκολέων
Αὐδωλέων
Ἀλκμέων
Συμεών
Νέων
Μεγακρέων
Ὑψικρέων
Κρέων
Ζωκρέων
Μελσέων
Ἑκατέων
Αὐγάζων
Σαλάζων
Δίζων
Θερίζων
Δέρζων
Διήων
Ἀγάθων
Γνάθων
Κράθων
Κυράθων
Σάθων
Ζήθων
Κρήθων
Πυθογείτων
Πείθων
Πίθων
Κρίθων
Σπίνθων
Κόθων
Πόθων
Ἱπποθῶν
Σεύθων
Πύθων
Μαίων
Ἀθαναίων
Παιών
Ἡραίων
Εὐαίων
Σαβίων
Σαββίων
Βίων

Φοιβίων
Ἀντιβίων
Σαμβίων
Κερβίων
Ἀνουβίων
Λογγίων
Χορηγίων
Σεργίων
Ἐνθαδίων
Τριακαδίων
Εἰκαδίων
Ἑρμαδίων
Λαμπαδίων
Δίων
Μακεδίων
Πεδίων
Λυκιδίων
Κολιδίων
Ἐλπιδίων
Καλανδίων
Πανδίων
Σεκουνδίων
Βαρδίων
Βυρδίων
Γαυδίων
Εὐδίων
Λαβείων
Παρασείων
Ἀβαζίων
Ἰων
Σαμβαθίων
Προμαθίων
Προμηθίων
Κερκιθίων
Ξανθίων
Ποθίων
Ποσθίων
Πατερμουθίων
Στρουθίων
Πυθίων
Βακίων
Ῥυνδακίων
Φυλακίων
Φαρνακίων
Ὀστρακίων
Σπαρτακίων
Βοστακίων
Μικίων
Νικίων
Μαρικίων
Ποντικίων
Κοκκίων
Δοκίων
Προσδοκίων
Σπαρτοκίων
Μαρκίων
Ζερκίων
Κερκίων
Τορκίων
Σπουρκίων
Γλαυκίων

Γλυκίων
Λυκίων
Μεγαλίων
Μικαλίων
Μικκαλίων
Πυρραλίων
Ἀρσαλίων
Βιταλίων
Κεφαλίων
Ὀμφαλίων
Ἀμπελίων
Ὠφελίων
Ἡλίων
Ἀθλίων
Σταβιλίων
Προκλίων
Θαλλίων
Φρυγιλλίων
Βολλίων
Κολλίων
Βαθυλλίων
Μυλλίων
Πωλλίων
Βακυλίων
Μικυλίων
Δουλίων
Γρυλίων
Πωλίων
Ἀραμίων
Πριμίων
Ζωσιμίων
Παρμίων
Χαρμίων
Φορμίων
Κοσμίων
Ῥωμίων
Ἀθανίων
Μελανίων
Ἑλλανίων
Φανίων
Ἀπολλοφανίων
Ἁγνίων
Μαγνίων
Θεαγενίων
Παρμενίων
Ζηνίων
Ἀθηνίων
Μινίων
Μυρσινίων
Φινίων
Δομνίων
Ἀννίων
Ναννίων
Σαννίων
Μιννίων
Κοννίων
Ἀντιγονίων
Κονίων
Παραμονίων
Κρονίων
Ἀκορνίων

Φρυνίων
Ἀναξίων
Ἀλεξίων
Σαραπίων
Σεραπίων
Κηπίων
Ἀσκληπίων
Σκιπίων
Κορδυπίων
Ἀλυπίων
Σινωπίων
Δρωπίων
Ἀνθρωπίων
Βαρβαρίων
Ἀζαρίων
Κανθαρίων
Ἰκαρίων
Γλυκαρίων
Λυκαρίων
Ἱλαρίων
Κολλαρίων
Δουλαρίων
Δαμαρίων
Κονναρίων
Ταταρίων
Μασταρίων
Φαρίων
Εὐχαρίων
Ψυχαρίων
Διομβρίων
Εὐαγρίων
Σωσανδρίων
Ἀτανδρίων
Ἐλευθερίων
Πιερίων
Σουπερίων
Πατερίων
Ἀβδηρίων
Χαιρίων
Χοιρίων
Φαλακρίων
Λοκρίων
Νεστορίων
Συμφορίων
Ἀπρίων
Μουκατρίων
Ταυρίων
Παγουρίων
Ζωπυρίων
Συρίων
Σατυρίων
Ἰσχυρίων
Αἰσχρίων
Δωρίων
Ὠρίων
Ἐργασίων
Νικασίων
Ἑρμασίων
Πασίων
Εὐθεσίων
Νικησίων

Ὀνησίων
Ἰσίων
Περσίων
Νοσσίων
Σουσίων
Χρυσίων
Σωσίων
Ἡβατίων
Σαμβατίων
Βαρβατίων
Κατίων
Σαρματίων
Ἡπατίων
Ἀππατίων
Ἐρατίων
Ἁρποκρατίων
Ἡετίων
Φιλητίων
Βιτίων
Καπιτίων
Ἀμφιτίων
Κουϊντίων
Κοτίων
Θρεπτίων
Κουαρτίων
Φορτίων
Ἀστίων
Χρηστίων
Ἀφαιστίων
Ἡφαιστίων
Μεγιστίων
Φιλιστίων
Καλλιστίων
Ἀριστίων
Φαυστίων
Βαττίων
Γαττίων
Σαττίων
Ταττίων
Κοττίων
Θαβυττίων
Πλουτίων
Ἀπφουτίων
Κοτυτίων
Καλλιφυτίων
Πλωτίων
Παππερωτίων
Πρωτίων
Ἀμφίων
Μορφίων
Ῥουφίων
Χίων
Μοσχίων
Συντυχίων
Εὐτυχίων
Βάκων
Εὐθάκων
Αἰάκων
Λάκων
Σιμάκων
Μηνακῶν

Ἐξάκων
Ζωπάκων
Χαράκων
Δράκων
Ἡράκων
Βατακῶν
Χρηστακῶν
Βοστάκων
Βαλαίκων
Φαίκων
Βίκων
Ἑλικών
Ἀπελλικῶν
Ἀθανικῶν
Νίκων
Μοιρικῶν
Ματρικῶν
Σίκων
Βατίκων
Ἀρτικῶν
Ἡφαιστικῶν
Ἰστικῶν
Λίκκων
Μούκκων
Ἄλκων
Χάλκων
Γόκων
Δημοκῶν
Τόκων
Δόρκων
Ἀρέσκων
Μόσκων
Γύκων
Ἡδύκων
Λεύκων
Γλύκων
Λύκων
Μύκων
Μούκων
Δάλων
Κάλων
Σιμαλῶν
Σπάλων
Κεφάλων
Ἴδιβλων
Ἄγλων
Γέλων
Μέλων
Βησέλων
Τέλων
Νεῖλων
Μίλων
Σίλων
Φίλων
Χίλων
Ζωΐλων
Κάλλων
Νηγέλλων
Λίλλων
Ἀπόλλων
Σεραπόλλων

Βόλων
Δόλων
Κόλων
Σόλων
Τόλων
Ὅπλων
Βαβυλών
Γύλων
Θουθύλων
Κορβούλων
Σουσούλων
Πύλων
Δάμων
Θάμων
Τελαμών
Ποτάμων
Φιράδμων
Ἡγέμων
Πολέμων
Ἀρτέμων
Ἀγήμων
Ἡγήμων
Δήμων
Αἰδήμων
Εὐδήμων
Ἥμων
Φιλήμων
Ἱερομνήμων
Ἱρομνήμων
Νοήμων
Ἀπήμων
Χαιρήμων
Εὐρήμων
Εὐκτήμων
Εὐσχήμων
Εὐδαίμων
Λείμων
Ἀρείμων
Σίμων
Τίμων
Ἄμμων
Κόμων
Νόμων
Ἕρμων
Στρύμων
Ῥώμων
Ἄνων
Νάνων
Αὐξάνων
Σάνων
Σανάνων
Φάνων
Ἐπιτυγχάνων
Ἀντιμένων
Μένων
Παρμένων
Ξένων
Ζήνων
Ἀθήνων
Ὑγιαίνων
Εὐφραίνων
Σαουαίνων
Δείνων
Ἐπαμείνων
Κρίνων
Μέμνων
Ξέννων
Κόνων
Βώρνων
Ζειζοδύνων
Εὔνων
Θαρσύνων
Δάφνων
Τέχνων
Πράξων
Αὔξων
Βοών
Ἀσκλάπων
Πάπων
Θεράπων
Νέπων
Πρέπων
Ἀσκλήπων
Λάμπων
Ἵππων
Κάρπων
Βόσπων
Κνώπων
Μάρων
Χάρων
Θίβρων
Ἄγρων
Ἄνδρων
Μάνδρων
Γέρων
Ἱέρων
Κικέρων
Νέρων
Πατέρων
Συμφέρων
Ἥρων
Θήρων
Χαίρων
Μοίρων
Μόκρων
Μάτρων
Πάτρων
Μέτρων
Μήτρων
Γάστρων
Ἴστρων
Ταύρων
Μύρων
Ζιπύρων
Ἐπάφρων
Μενέφρων
Ἀλκίφρων
Ἀρσίφρων
Θεόφρων
Δικαιόφρων
Λυκόφρων
Φιλόφρων
Εὔφρων
Εὐθύφρων
Σώφρων
Αἴσχρων
Δώρων
Ἄσων
Ἰάσων
Κάσων
Νάσων
Μνάσων
Πάσων
Θράσων
Σασῶν
Νικήσων
Τλήσων
Μνήσων
Κτήσων
Πείσων
Τείσων
Θεμίσων
Βρίσων
Γόσων
Κόσων
Δημοσῶν
Δρόσων
Ἱεροσῶν
Ἡροσῶν
Φύρσων
Σῶν
Παύσων
Λύσων
Ζώσων
Σώσων
Βάτων
Κάτων
Πλάτων
Δυνάτων
Πάτων
Ἐράτων
Κηράτων
Κράτων
Στράτων
Θευγέτων
Ναιέτων
Μέτων
Κήτων
Βίτων
Καλλιγείτων
Θεογείτων
Διογείτων
Ἡρογείτων
Εὐγείτων
Βλίτων
Μελίτων
Κλίτων
Καπίτων
Χαρίτων
Κρίτων
Φίλτων
Ἄντων
Δέντων
Οὐειέντων
Φρόντων
Κράστων
Ἀρίστων
Ἄττων
Βίττων
Ναύτων
Κύτων
Γανύων
Σιρούων
Ἐρύων
Ἀλεκτρύων
Ἀμφικτύων
Νήφων
Καλλιφῶν
Ἡγησιφῶν
Μνησιφῶν
Ὀνησιφῶν
Κτησιφῶν
Ἀντιφῶν
Δέλφων
Νύμφων
Ἡλιοφῶν
Νικοφῶν
Δαμοφῶν
Δημοφῶν
Ξενοφῶν
Μηνοφῶν
Ἡροφῶν
Μητροφῶν
Σόφων
Διονυσοφῶν
Κλειτοφῶν
Ἀριστοφῶν
Αὐτοφῶν
Τρύφων
Εὐρυφῶν
Μάχων
Ὑπερέχων
Βάκχων
Ἄρχων
Πολυπέρχων
Σύρχων
Τύχων
Ῥαδαμφῶν
Σίνδαξ
Ῥύνδαξ
Αἶαξ
Σκύλαξ
Μύρμαξ
Λεάναξ
Ἀρχαιάναξ
Καλλιάναξ
Πραξιάναξ
Ἡγησιάναξ
Τιμησιάναξ
Ἀντιάναξ
Πολυάναξ
Ἀστυάναξ
Δόναξ
Πυθῶναξ
Δημῶναξ
Τιμῶναξ
Ἑρμῶναξ
Ἱππῶναξ
Μανδρῶναξ
Στρατῶναξ
Πλειστῶναξ
Θεμιστῶναξ
Ἀριστῶναξ
Ἴαραξ
Φάραξ
Ἱέραξ
Στύραξ
Θώραξ
Φαέσαξ
Σταχέμφαξ
Πήληξ
Μύρμηξ
Ἱέρηξ
Θρᾶιξ
Ἕλιξ
Φῆλιξ
Φοῖνιξ
Δάπυξ
Ἄσπαρ
Καῖσαρ
Δένβερ
Νίγερ
Σάκερ
Κέλερ
Ἄπερ
Ζίπερ
Δέξτερ
Πάνθηρ
Σπινθήρ
Ἀστήρ
Σωτήρ
Μαίωρ
Ἀγάνωρ
Μεγάνωρ
Κλεάνωρ
Ἀγαθάνωρ
Βιάνωρ
Νικάνωρ
Ἀλκάνωρ
Λευκάνωρ
Εὐφράνωρ
Ἀντάνωρ
Ἀγήνωρ
Ἀγαθήνωρ
Νικήνωρ
Ἀναξήνωρ
Προθοήνωρ
Ἀγαπήνωρ
Τελεσήνωρ
Ἀντήνωρ
Εὐήνωρ
Λαπέπωρ
Βιάτωρ
Πλάτωρ
Εὐπάτωρ

Ἡγήτωρ
Ἐράκτωρ
Τάκτωρ
Ἕκτωρ
Βίκτωρ
Οὐίκτωρ
Πολύκτωρ
Μέντωρ
Ἀμύντωρ
Κάστωρ
Μάστωρ
Θέστωρ
Ἀκέστωρ
Νέστωρ
Ἀντιμήστωρ
Μήστωρ
Πλείστωρ
Συνίστωρ
Ἄβας
Βάβας
Βαρναβᾶς
Πάβας
Βαρσαβᾶς
Κέββας
Ἀρύββας
Δεβας
Θαίβας
Κιβᾶς
Σκίλβας
Κωλούμβας
Ξοβας
Βοσβᾶς
Βουβᾶς
Ἴβουβας
Σβουβας
Σπαδάγας
Δουτζάγας
Ἀθιάγας
Μάγας
Ῥησμάγας
Τιγινάγας
Σαυάγας
Κοσίγγας
Μέγας
Πριμιγᾶς
Ἐπιγᾶς
Διογᾶς
Κραυγᾶς
Ὀρτυγᾶς
Ἅδας
Σαβάδας
Βαδᾶς
Ῥηβάδας
Γάδας
Δάδας
Ἀρχιβιάδας
Πυθιάδας
Καλλιάδας
Ἀσκλαπιάδας
Πασιάδας
Ἀντιάδας
Ἰφιάδας
Τριακάδας
Εἰκάδας
Νικάδας
Σιμάδας
Ἀμμάδας
Κιροάδας
Κλεμυτάδας
Σωτάδας
Τρωάδας
Δαγδας
Ἀγλαΐδας
Διδᾶς
Ἀγείδας
Δείδας
Βασιλείδας
Ἡρακλείδας
Διοκλείδας
Εὐκλείδας
Ἀριστείδας
Ἴδας
Προμαθίδας
Θρακίδας
Ἀντιαλκίδας
Κερκίδας
Εὐβουλίδας
Εὐφαμίδας
Μίδας
Μενίδας
Ἐρυμενίδας
Τιμαφενίδας
Κοινίδας
Μελαμνίδας
Μεννίδας
Λεωνίδας
Χιωνίδας
Νικωνίδας
Ἀπολλωνίδας
Κορωνίδας
Βοΐδας
Περοίδας
Εὐκαμπίδας
Ἐλασιππίδας
Δρωπίδας
Θεαρίδας
Εὐανδρίδας
Σωτηρίδας
Τιμανορίδας
Διοσκουρίδας
Εὐδωρίδας
Πρασίδας
Ἐπικρατίδας
Κλεοντίδας
Γεροντίδας
Φίδας
Εὐαρχίδας
Εὐτυχίδας
Ἡρωΐδας
Σωΐδας
Καράνδας
Μενδᾶς
Δίνδας
Ἴνδας
Σκίνδας
Χαρώνδας
Δωρώνδας
Σαγόδας
Ἀργόδας
Θεοδᾶς
Νάρδας
Δέρδας
Εὐδᾶς
Θευδᾶς
Ἰούδας
Ἰώδας
Διρβέας
Τεγέας
Σινδέας
Κερζέας
Πυθέας
Νικέας
Μεγαλέας
Ἐπιμελεάς
Φιλέας
Ἡρακλέας
Ἰθυκλέας
Καλλέας
Ἀπελλέας
Βιλλέας
Φιλλέας
Μυλλέας
Πουλέας
Δαμέας
Σταδμέας
Δημέας
Τιμέας
Φανέας
Μενέας
Ζηνέας
Ἀρεταινέας
Μεννέας
Ξεννέας
Πραξέας
Παπέας
Δαρέας
Ἀβρέας
Δαβρέας
Ἀνδρέας
Ἡρέας
Χαιρέας
Βορέας
Ταυρέας
Τλασέας
Μνασέας
Πασέας
Θρασέας
Ἀτέας
Κρατέας
Γαιτέας
Φιλτέας
Ἀντέας
Παντέας
Ἀστέας
Ἀριστέας
Αὐτέας
Πρωτέας
Ἀταμάζας
Δίζας
Πηδίζας
Καρζᾶς
Δόρζας
Ἀγαθᾶς
Βίθας
Ψιμίθας
Μάλθας
Ἀνθᾶς
Ξάνθας
Μοκκόθας
Βισθᾶς
Μυσθᾶς
Τιτθᾶς
Σκύθας
Πυθᾶς
Κυνδαίας
Ἀγλαΐας
Ἀταίας
Θυαίας
Βίας
Ἀγίας
Ἡγίας
Γοργίας
Δίας
Μειδίας
Φειδίας
Θεοδίας
Βαρδίας
Γυδίας
Θευδίας
Κυδίας
Πελκείας
Ἑρμείας
Αἰνείας
Μεννείας
Δαβρείας
Ἀνδρείας
Χαιρείας
Εὐρείας
Εὐχείας
Ἀζίας
Διζίας
Ἰάς
Ἰᾶς
Ἀγαθίας
Ξανθίας
Κορινθιάς
Θίας
Κουθίας
Πυθίας
Πυθιάς
Νικίας
Ἀλκίας
Ὀλκίας
Γλαοκίας
Γαυκίας
Γλαυκίας
Λυκίας
Σουκίας
Ζαλίας
Μελίας
Ἡλιάς
Ψεμιθλίας
Ἰλιάς
Ἡρακλίας
Καλλίας
Μολίας
Γοσαμφλίας
Θαχαμφλίας
Σιμίας
Ἀμμιάς
Σιμμίας
Χαρμίας
Ἑρμίας
Παυσανίας
Λυσανίας
Φανίας
Ἁγνίας
Ξενίας
Μηνίας
Δινίας
Δεινίας
Κλεινίας
Ἀμεινίας
Οἰνίας
Κρινίας
Ῥινίας
Μαννίας
Ξεννίας
Ὀνίας
Ἀρνίας
Δορνιας
Ὀρνίας
Ἑλικωνιάς
Ἀντωνιάς
Ὠνίας
Πραξίας
Ἀλεξίας
Δισλοιας
Παπίας
Σαραπιάς
Ἀσκληπιάς
Ἐλπίας
Ὀλυμπιάς
Παππίας
Ἱππίας
Ποππίας
Ἀσπίας
Καριάς
Χαβρίας
Φαιδρίας
Ἀνδρίας
Σφοδρίας
Ἀμερίας
Ἀταρρίας
Ταρρίας

Πυρρίας
Δημητριάς
Εὐρίας
Δωριάς
Σωρίας
Ἀσίας
Ἀγασίας
Δαμασίας
Τελεσίας
Ἀρεσίας
Ἀγησίας
Ἡγησίας
Κτησίας
Αἰσίας
Ἀφροδισιάς
Πεισίας
Τεισίας
Ἰσιάς
Σισίας
Κασσίας
Λυσίας
Διονυσιάς
Κουσίας
Σωσίας
Ἀτίας
Πατίας
Στρατίας
Κριτίας
Μιλτίας
Ἀστίας
Μαστίας
Ἑστίας
Πλειστίας
Μυστίας
Ἀττίας
Σαυτίας
Τελευτίας
Πρωτίας
Ἀμφίας
Λειχίας
Ἀρχίας
Ἀμειψίας
Δράκας
Ἡρακᾶς
Σάκας
Μιτακᾶς
Βαστάκας
Ἀμηρύγκας
Θέκας
Σηνήκας
Καραΐκας
Ἶκας
Κιλικᾶς
Φιλικᾶς
Μίκας
Νικᾶς
Ἀννίκας
Λαυνίκας
Ἀκκᾶς
Περδίκκας
Μοκκᾶς

Δημάλκας
Ῥοιμητάλκας
Σιτάλκας
Γεόκας
Νεόκας
Φιλόκας
Μοκᾶς
Σανόκας
Ἡροκᾶς
Κατόκας
Κερκᾶς
Δορκάς
Πίσκας
Λυκᾶς
Λουκᾶς
Μούκας
Ὀρτυκᾶς
Φωκᾶς
Βάλας
Σαδάλας
Δαλᾶς
Σεδάλας
Παρδαλᾶς
Διζάλας
Κάλας
Δρεπάλας
Ζιπάλας
Ταράλας
Σάλας
Ἐπταλας
Ἀγέλας
Καριέλας
Βασιέλας
Μέλας
Μενέλας
Ἀρχέλας
Κοθήλας
Ἀπτηλᾶς
Παιβίλας
Σαιδείλας
Ζείλας
Σεθείλας
Σευθείλας
Τραλικείλας
Γενικείλας
Βωσκείλας
Βιθυκείλας
Δινείλας
Νειλᾶς
Τρείλας
Βουρείλας
Δασείλας
Γεσείλας
Κοζίλας
Δορζίλας
Κουζίλας
Σκουζίλας
Ζηΐλας
Βαστακίλας
Βαστεκίλας
Βαστικίλας

Κίλας
Βαστοκίλας
Βασκίλας
Σκίλας
Διουκίλας
Ἀναξίλας
Κετρίλας
Κυριλάς
Πρασιλᾶς
Ἀρκεσίλας
Ἀγησίλας
Αἰσίλας
Σίλας
Ἀκουσίλας
Σωσίλας
Στίλας
Κουτίλας
Φιλᾶς
Μάκλας
Ἡρακλᾶς
Προκλᾶς
Ἀσκλᾶς
Κάλλας
Παλλάς
Παλλᾶς
Σάλλας
Ἑλλάς
Ἀπελλᾶς
Ὀφέλλας
Ἀγίλλας
Λιλλᾶς
Ἀχιλλᾶς
Ἰόλλας
Ἀπολλᾶς
Πτολλᾶς
Βόλας
Γόλας
Ἰόλας
Δρακόλας
Νικόλας
Λυκόλας
Χαιρόλας
Πουπλᾶς
Ἀκύλας
Πολύλας
Ῥηβούλας
Δούλας
Διζούλας
Κερζούλας
Διούλας
Κουθιούλας
Ἀλιούλας
Τορκούλας
Σκαπούλας
Γαρούλας
Ταρούλας
Ζερούλας
Πυρρούλας
Πυρούλας
Βεισούλας
Βρισούλας

Σούλας
Γετούλας
Δυτούλας
Ὕλας
Μεστύλας
Θάμφλας
Κερδώλας
Μώλας
Βονωλας
Ἀμάς
Ἀμᾶς
Ἀδάμας
Δαμᾶς
Ἀλκιδάμας
Καλλιδάμας
Πολυδάμας
Πουλυδάμας
Θρασυδάμας
Ἀστυδάμας
Λεωδάμας
Ἀθάμας
Ἰαμάς
Ἀκάμας
Σκάμας
Ναυκασάμας
Σάμας
Τευτάμας
Ἀλγεμας
Πτολέμας
Ἀρτεμᾶς
Δημᾶς
Κιμᾶς
Ταρουσίμας
Ζωσιμᾶς
Ἀρτίμας
Τροφιμᾶς
Σάμμας
Κτολέμμας
Πτολεμμᾶς
Κερδίμμας
Τυρίμμας
Κερτίμμας
Λαόμμας
Ἀρσακόμας
Μελαγκόμας
Καλλικόμας
Ἀβροκόμας
Προμᾶς
Ζοτομᾶς
Γερμᾶς
Ἑρμᾶς
Κοισόρμας
Κοσμᾶς
Νουμᾶς
Πατούμας
Ζοτουμᾶς
Θωμᾶς
Σωμᾶς
Βανας
Μάνας
Νανάς

Νανᾶς
Δορπανας
Ἀρσάνας
Νικοφάνας
Ἐπιγενᾶς
Μυλλένας
Μένας
Ζηνᾶς
Μαικήνας
Μηνᾶς
Νηνας
Ξείνας
Καζίνας
Κοθίνας
Ταρουθίνας
Μικίνας
Κρωκίνας
Καλλίνας
Μυλλίνας
Νινας
Σχοινᾶς
Ματερίνας
Ταρουσίνας
Ταρυσίνας
Ἀτίνας
Λεπτίνας
Ἀττίνας
Πλωτινάς
Αἰσχίνας
Ναννᾶς
Φάννας
Κρατέννας
Ἀρίννας
Σίννας
Κοννᾶς
Φιλονᾶς
Σκεπαρνᾶς
Βέρνας
Ζαύνας
Σαυνᾶς
Δυνας
Κύνας
Βουτουνᾶς
Λυχνᾶς
Κερδωνᾶς
Λεωνᾶς
Ἀγαθωνᾶς
Διωνᾶς
Κοκκωνᾶς
Προκωνᾶς
Ἀπολλωνᾶς
Εὐνώνας
Ἐρωνᾶς
Κυρώνας
Ἀριστωνᾶς
Τρυφωνᾶς
Ἀβράξας
Ἀλεξᾶς
Θιοδίξας
Θόας
Ἀττακόας

Πάπας
Παπᾶς
Σεραπᾶς
Σαπας
Ἀσκληπᾶς
Ζιπᾶς
Τρίπας
Ἀντιπᾶς
Τίπας
Μολπᾶς
Σουλπᾶς
Ὀλυμπᾶς
Κλεοπᾶς
Ἰοπᾶς
Σκόπας
Ἄππας
Ἀππᾶς
Ἱππᾶς
Φιλιππᾶς
Ἀγρίππας
Σίππας
Εὐίππας
Ζωπᾶς
Σωπᾶς
Μαρᾶς
Παρᾶς
Ἰωσάρας
Σαββατάρας
Τάρας
Οὐαρᾶς
Σίβρας
Ζίγρας
Κυδρᾶς
Πατέρας
Σεβηρᾶς
Στυνδήρας
Ἡρᾶς
Σωτηρᾶς
Κλεαγόρας
Πειθαγόρας
Ὀρθαγόρας
Πυθαγόρας
Διαγόρας
Νικαγόρας
Λυκαγόρας
Λαγόρας
Σαμαγόρας
Ἑρμαγόρας
Ἀθαναγόρας
Ἀθηναγόρας
Δαμναγόρας
Ἀναξαγόρας
Ἱππαγόρας
Ἡραγόρας
Ἡγησαγόρας
Ἰσαγόρας
Θερσαγόρας
Σωσαγόρας
Ἀνταγόρας
Θεμισταγόρας
Ἀρισταγόρας

Πρωταγόρας
Εὐαγόρας
Νυμφαγόρας
Ἀρχαγόρας
Κοδόρας
Σίπρας
Σίρρας
Μουκατρας
Ματρᾶς
Μητρᾶς
Ἰθύρας
Κυρᾶς
Γούρας
Κουθιούρας
Ζισυρας
Συρᾶς
Σιττυρᾶς
Ἐπαφρᾶς
Εὐφρᾶς
Δωρᾶς
Σεάσας
Ἀκάσας
Μάσας
Σάσας
Ἀτάσας
Ἀρκέσας
Στορέσας
Ἡβήσας
Ἀγησᾶς
Ὀνησᾶς
Ἰσᾶς
Ἐπισᾶς
Σίσας
Ἀόσας
Λεφαοσας
Νιγοσας
Γοργόσας
Ἀκροσας
Χοσᾶς
Κάρσας
Τάρσας
Κυρσᾶς
Ὑπερβάσσας
Μαλάσσας
Κοσσᾶς
Παυσᾶς
Λυσᾶς
Δεονυσᾶς
Διονυσᾶς
Τανουσας
Σούσας
Σουσᾶς
Ζωσᾶς
Σωσᾶς
Ἀτᾶς
Βατᾶς
Γοργάτας
Ἰδάτας
Σαρμάτας
Κορράτας
Παυράτας

Εὐφράτας
Τάτας
Σαφάτας
Μαχάτας
Γέτας
Βηδέτας
Μακέτας
Ἀλκέτας
Φανέτας
Νικήτας
Φιλήτας
Κομητᾶς
Λαχητᾶς
Δατείτας
Τζιτας
Ἠλίτας
Λίτας
Πολυμίτας
Κανίτας
Λαοίτας
Βιλοίτας
Ἑρμοίτας
Μενοίτας
Τασοίτας
Τοΐτας
Περίτας
Λυγκωρίτας
Σιτᾶς
Σάκτας
Ἐπικτᾶς
Ἀντᾶς
Ἀριάντας
Μαριάντας
Μάντας
Παντᾶς
Εὐφράντας
Πολυφάντας
Δίντας
Θίντας
Ἀπίντας
Λεοντᾶς
Ἀμύντας
Ἀργότας
Νεότας
Ἱκκότας
Κολκοτᾶς
Ἱππότας
Ἀγρότας
Ἀτοτᾶς
Σοσίπτας
Μεγάρτας
Βιάρτας
Βουκάρτας
Μασάρτας
Χάρτας
Βορτᾶς
Γορτας
Ὀρτᾶς
Φούρτας
Βάστας
Μάστας

Πευκέστας
Γαλέστας
Μέστας
Χρήστας
Ἀμαίστας
Δρινγίστας
Μηδίστας
Θεμιστᾶς
Ἀρίστας
Ἀριστᾶς
Ὑβρίστας
Βοστᾶς
Λούστας
Ἄττας
Βάττας
Κάττας
Βίττας
Βελίττας
Ἠλίττας
Διονυττᾶς
Ναύτας
Ἐακύτας
Φιλύτας
Βουτᾶς
Ἀκούτας
Ζελμούτας
Τουτάς
Ζωτᾶς
Φιλώτας
Πρωτᾶς
Σωτᾶς
Ἀτώτας
Εὔας
Σκευᾶς
Κλεύας
Κρατεύας
Βιθύας
Πολύας
Μύας
Ἀμβούας
Ἀγαθούας
Ἀτακούας
Μαρσύας
Νυμφᾶς
Ῥουφᾶς
Χαχας
Βακχᾶς
Κάλχας
Σανόχας
Τρόχας
Δασχάς
Δέσχας
Μοσχᾶς
Ἀβαύχας
Σιδαύχας
Εὐτυχᾶς
Ζαες
Δειζεζες
Σκαρκαιζες
Γαιπες
Ἀδαής

Δάης
Θαῆς
Ἀγλάης
Διλάης
Μάης
Δερνάης
Πάης
Ἀτάης
Σκάβης
Ζειδέβης
Θεοσεβής
Εὐσέβης
Μουκαπαίβης
Ζιπαίβης
Παίβης
Ἀλιουπαίβης
Τορκουπαίβης
Μεστυπαίβης
Τίβης
Ζεισαλβης
Τάρβης
Ἄγης
Βάγης
Θεάγης
Δαμάγης
Μέγης
Δρωδήγης
Δριωζίγης
Σπάργης
Γύγης
Δάδης
Λεάδης
Καρνεάδης
Ἀλκεβιάδης
Ἀλκιβιάδης
Νικιάδης
Οἰκιάδης
Ἡλιάδης
Καλλιάδης
Ἰουλιάδης
Αἰνιάδης
Οἰνιάδης
Ἀναξιάδης
Ἀσκληπιάδης
Ὀλυμπιάδης
Σκοπιάδης
Ταυριάδης
Πασιάδης
Ἰσιάδης
Ἀντιάδης
Παντιάδης
Λεοντιάδης
Ἀστιάδης
Πλειστιάδης
Πλουτιάδης
Ἰφιάδης
Μοσχιάδης
Δαμοκάδης
Δημοκάδης
Πυλάδης
Ζμάδης

Ἀρμάδης
Ἀθηνάδης
Μεθωνάδης
Σπαροπάδης
Φαράδης
Ὀκταμασάδης
Μαισάδης
Βηρισάδης
Παιρισάδης
Μηδοσάδης
Μελαντάδης
Σωτάδης
Ζεργέδης
Κλευμέδης
Οἰμήδης
Μήδης
Κλεομήδης
Διομήδης
Νικομήδης
Λυκομήδης
Ἀνδρομήδης
Ἀριστομήδης
Εὐμήδης
Πολυμήδης
Θρασυμήδης
Ἀστυμήδης
Πυρουρρήδης
Βοραΐδης
Φοιβίδης
Εὐφορβίδης
Εὐκυδίδης
Δείδης
Ἀλκείδης
Βασιλείδης
Ἡρακλείδης
Καλλικλείδης
Φρασικλείδης
Εὀκλείδης
Θεοκλείδης
Διοκλείδης
Ξενοκλείδης
Ἀνδροκλείδης
Ἀριστοκλείδης
Εὐκλείδης
Ἀρρενείδης
Ὑπερείδης
Ἀτρείδης
Κοσείδης
Ποσειδῆς
Ἀριστείδης
Πολυείδης
Πυθοκληίδης
Προμηθίδης
Πυθίδης
Φυλακίδης
Θρακίδης
Ἀστακίδης
Στρωφακίδης
Φοινικίδης
Ἀντινικίδης
Εὐαλκίδης
Εὐμηλίδης
Διφιλίδης
Ἀντιφιλίδης
Σωπολίδης
Δερκυλίδης
Εὐβουλίδης
Εὐδημίδης
Αἰσιμίδης
Θεοτιμίδης
Παρμίδης
Χαρμίδης
Εὐθυμίδης
Ἑλλανίδης
Κοιρανίδης
Θεογενίδης
Εὐγενίδης
Παρμενίδης
Θεοξενίδης
Φιλοξενίδης
Τιμοξενίδης
Εὐξενίδης
Πολυξενίδης
Γησενίδης
Μεννίδης
Ἀμφιονίδης
Κρονίδης
Λεωνίδης
Χιωνίδης
Φιλωνίδης
Ἀπολλωνίδης
Σημωνίδης
Σιμωνίδης
Τιμωνίδης
Ἡραπίδης
Ἀσκληπίδης
Εὐριπίδης
Εὐελπίδης
Πελοπίδης
Οἰνοπίδης
Θεοπροπίδης
Ἀλκιππίδης
Φιλιππίδης
Καλλιππίδης
Μελανιππίδης
Ἡγησιππίδης
Τερπίδης
Σωτηρίδης
Ἀγηνορίδης
Ἡγητορίδης
Θεστορίδης
Ἀκεστορίδης
Ἀντιπατρίδης
Ζυρίδης
Λαμυρίδης
Διοσκουρίδης
Ἀσκοσίδης
Πρασσίδης
Διονυσίδης
Ἀρατίδης
Ἐχεκρατίδης
Καλλικρατίδης
Ἀντικρατίδης
Ἑρμοκρατίδης
Ἱπποκρατίδης
Παντοκρατίδης
Εὐκρατίδης
Σωκρατίδης
Σωστρατίδης
Κλεαινετίδης
Κλεαντίδης
Αἰαντίδης
Εὐφραντίδης
Θεοτίδης
Πληιστίδης
Φιλιστίδης
Λυσιμαχίδης
Ἀνδρομαχίδης
Βακχίδης
Ἀντιοχίδης
Ἱππολοχίδης
Κλεαρχίδης
Νικαρχίδης
Πολεμαρχίδης
Δημαρχίδης
Εὐχίδης
Εὐτυχίδης
Ὑψίδης
Ἡρωΐδης
Φιλώνδης
Θεοδῆς
Βίσδης
Δύδης
Ἐπικύδης
Θεοκύδης
Φιλοκύδης
Εὐκύδης
Δούδης
Πούδης
Σερούδης
Κομιτούδης
Ὑμνώδης
Ἀριστέης
Ἀρταβάζης
Βάζης
Γουβάζης
Δαμνάζης
Ξαιορσάζης
Καμορσάζης
Φαρτάζης
Βιζῆς
Δίζης
Καζίζης
Βισίζης
Δίλζης
Φαρσάνζης
Βένζης
Βόνζης
Ἡρζῆς
Σμόρζης
Κούτζης
Βύζης
Βούζης
Δυνούζης
Ἄθης
Τζάθης
Ἀραμάθης
Ἀράθης
Ἀριαράθης
Σάθης
Ζιγέθης
Ἐπιγήθης
Φιλογήθης
Εὐήθης
Βίθης
Σπαργαπείθης
Ἀριαπείθης
Διοπείθης
Ξενοπείθης
Εὐπείθης
Σαικίθης
Κοσιδέλθης
Βίλθης
Κλεάνθης
Νεάνθης
Πολιάνθης
Δημάνθης
Τιμάνθης
Ὑπεράνθης
Ἰσάνθης
Εὐάνθης
Σκαιδένθης
Καλδένθης
Βεσσοδένθης
Καρδένθης
Αὐλουδένθης
Δαληζένθης
Δορζένθης
Ζαικένθης
Καρβερένθης
Δορζίνθης
Τιμοθῆς
Βάσθης
Σεύθης
Κύθης
Μιλτοκύθης
Διοσκύθης
Σκύθης
Ἀννύθης
Ζούθης
Βουκούθης
Πυθῆς
Ἰγδαμπαίης
Τυαίης
Ἀταχαίης
Διῆς
Σμερδίης
Διουζίης
Βρυλουζίης
Καλλίης
Φοξίης
Ἱππίης
Πεισίης
Κουνθισίης
Νοσσίης
Ἀρχίης
Ἄκης
Ἰαδαάκης
Βεισταβάκης
Βαδάκης
Κολανδάκης
Μαρζάκης
Ὀλθάκης
Πουρθάκης
Πιτθάκης
Μουκακάκης
Σαυλάκης
Χανάκης
Χαρσενάκης
Ἀρνάκης
Φαρνάκης
Πιτοφαρνάκης
Πιτφαρνάκης
Χιμυνάκης
Ῥωνάκης
Ῥαπάκης
Ἀρσάκης
Ἀτάκης
Βατάκης
Εὐάκης
Καφάκης
Καραΐκης
Πολυνείκης
Κυζίκης
Νινικῆς
Ἀγλωνίκης
Ἄκκης
Βακκης
Βούκκης
Ἄλκης
Μενάλκης
Ἐπάλκης
Ῥοιμητάλκης
Σιτάλκης
Ἀντάλκης
Εὐάλκης
Σπόκης
Τόκης
Κερκῆς
Πόρκης
Κρήσκης
Κερίσκης
Πολυδεύκης
Λυκῆς
Ἀμιζώκης
Βάλης
Δάλης
Διζάλης
Αἰθάλης
Θαλῆς
Μαρτιάλης
Κάλης
Ἀλπάλης
Ἀρπάλης
Φανισάλης

Οὐάλης
Χάλης
Ἀγγελῆς
Σεδέλης
Σαικέλης
Σκέλης
Καλλιμέλης
Ἐπιμελής
Σέλης
Καλλιτέλης
Ἐπιτέλης
Θεοτέλης
Πυθοτέλης
Δαμοτέλης
Δημοτέλης
Ἑρμοτέλης
Ἀριστοτέλης
Δημωφέλης
Ἀχέλης
Δεντοζίλης
Ζίλης
Βαστακίλης
Θεοφίλης
Ἀγακλῆς
Μεγακλῆς
Ὀνομακλῆς
Ἡρακλῆς
Σακλῆς
Παντακλῆς
Παγκλῆς
Τηλεκλῆς
Μενεκλῆς
Φερεκλῆς
Καλλικλῆς
Πραξικλῆς
Χαρικλῆς
Περικλῆς
Χαιρικλῆς
Ἀγασικλῆς
Ἰασικλῆς
Δαμασικλῆς
Ὀνασικλῆς
Πασικλῆς
Τελεσικλῆς
Μνησικλῆς
Τεισικλῆς
Θαρσικλῆς
Ναυσικλῆς
Λυσικλῆς
Διονυσικλῆς
Σωσικλῆς
Ἀντικλῆς
Ἀρχικλῆς
Ὑψικλῆς
Ἐμπεδοκλῆς
Ῥοδοκλῆς
Θεοκλῆς
Νεοκλῆς
Ἀγαθοκλῆς
Πυθοκλῆς
Διοκλῆς
Ἰοκλῆς
Νικοκλῆς
Μεγαλοκλῆς
Τηλοκλῆς
Φιλοκλῆς
Ἀπολλοκλῆς
Δαμοκλῆς
Σαμοκλῆς
Δημοκλῆς
Τιμοκλῆς
Ἑρμοκλῆς
Στρυμοκλῆς
Φανοκλῆς
Παρθενοκλῆς
Ξενοκλῆς
Ἀθηνοκλῆς
Δεινοκλῆς
Ἱπποκλῆς
Ἀνδροκλῆς
Ἱεροκλῆς
Προκλῆς
Ἰατροκλῆς
Πατροκλῆς
Μητροκλῆς
Ἑκατοκλῆς
Στρατοκλῆς
Αὀτοκλῆς
Ἡφαιστοκλῆς
Θεμιστοκλῆς
Ἀριστοκλῆς
Αὐτοκλῆς
Σοφοκλῆς
Ἀσκλῆς
Ναυκλῆς
Εὐκλῆς
Πολυκλῆς
Θρασυκλῆς
Σωκλῆς
Ἀγάλλης
Κάλλης
Ἑρμοκάλλης
Ἀπελλῆς
Κίλλης
Τίλλης
Πολλῆς
Φαΰλλης
Σιλαβύλλης
Ἀκύλλης
Τυλλῆς
Γόλης
Δόλης
Δρόλης
Ματρόλης
Θύλης
Σκύλης
Δούλης
Θούλης
Κουτιούλης
Πύλης
Δρύλης
Μεστύλης
Ῥώλης
Δαμῆς
Σπιθάμης
Βενιαμῆς
Βράμης
Σεισάμης
Ζουλεμης
Ἀρτεμῆς
Δημῆς
Κλήμης
Διμης
Ἀβροζέλμης
Δόμης
Κόμης
Χαρμῆς
Ἑρμῆς
Δεντουρμής
Νυμῆς
Γυνδάνης
Βαρδάνης
Ἰορδάνης
Ὀρδάνης
Θυηζάνης
Ὀχοαρζάνης
Μαθιάνης
Μάνης
Φαρεσμάνης
Κοιράνης
Τιράνης
Τάνης
Γαυάνης
Θυάνης
Διαφάνης
Χαιρεφάνης
Φανῆς
Βενδιφάνης
Καλλιφάνης
Ἐπιφάνης
Παιριφάνης
Διονυσιφάνης
Ἀντιφάνης
Εὀφάνης
Θεοφάνης
Πυθοφάνης
Διοφάνης
Ἀπολλοφάνης
Μηνοφάνης
Ἀπολλωνοφάνης
Ἡροφάνης
Χαιροφάνης
Μοιροφάνης
Μητροφάνης
Διονυσοφάνης
Ἀριστοφάνης
Πρωτοφάνης
Εὐφάνης
Θευφάνης
Θεαγένης
Τιμαγένης
Ἁρμαγένης
Ἑρμαγένης
Ἡραγένης
Μοιραγένης
Κουραγένης
Πελειγένης
Κλειγένης
Καλλιγένης
Πριμιγένης
Ἐπιγένης
Περιγένης
Μηριγένης
Χαιριγένης
Μνασιγένης
Μνησιγένης
Ἰσιγένης
Σωσιγένης
Ἀντιγένης
Ἀρχιγένης
Ἰνγένης
Ἰσιδογένης
Θεογένης
Κλεογένης
Πυθογένης
Διογένης
Ἡλιογένης
Τιμογένης
Ἑρμογένης
Ἀθηνογένης
Μηνογένης
Μανδρογένης
Ἡρογένης
Διονυσογένης
Μουσογένης
Λεοντογένης
Ἀριστογένης
Πλουτογένης
Πρωτογένης
Ἡδυγένης
Εὐγένης
Θευγένης
Ζωγένης
Σωγένης
Λασθένης
Λαϊσθένης
Κλεισθένης
Πλεισθένης
Ἀλκισθένης
Καλλισθένης
Ἐπισθένης
Κρατισθένης
Ἀντισθένης
Πανσθένης
Νικοσθένης
Δαμοσθένης
Δημοσθένης
Τιμοσθένης
Ἱπποσθένης
Ἀνδροσθένης
Εὐσθένης
Πολυσθένης
Λεωσθένης
Σωσθένης
Ἀλκαμένης
Θηραμένης
Δαϊμένης
Ἀλθαιμένης
Ἀχαιμένης
Ἀλκιμένης
Ἀναξιμένης
Πραξιμένης
Ἀλεξιμένης
Ἐπιμένης
Στησιμένης
Σωσιμένης
Ἀντιμένης
Τιμένης
Μένης
Ἐμμένης
Φιλομένης
Ξενομένης
Δεινομένης
Κρινομένης
Ἀνδρομένης
Ἡρομένης
Χαιρομένης
Λεοντομένης
Ἀριστομένης
Αὐτομένης
Εὐμένης
Ὀξυμένης
Αὐλουμένης
Σωμένης
Εὐηφένης
Ἀθηνῆς
Ἀνοθήνης
Ἀσαμήνης
Νηνής
Δεινῆς
Ζεινης
Γοζίνης
Ζωρθίνης
Μικίνης
Ἐλπίνης
Κρητίνης
Λεπτίνης
Λεττίνης
Αἰσχίνης
Ἀριαράμνης
Φάννης
Ἰωάννης
Φαέννης
Μέννης
Πυθίννης
Σισίννης
Διονύννης
Ἐπιγονής
Ἀρτιδόνης
Μηριόνης
Εὐφρόνης
Σαιταφάρνης
Φάρνης
Διέρνης
Ὀροφέρνης

Ἠδώνης
Βιζώνης
Καβαθάξης
Ἀχαξης
Ξέρξης
Ἀδόης
Ὑκονόης
Μεστόης
Ἀπῆς
Διζάπης
Παπῆς
Εὐπρέπης
Λεωπρέπης
Τηρήπης
Θειπης
Βιθίπης
Πίπης
Πυριλάμπης
Ἱππῆς
Χαράσπης
Δισούπης
Κοσούπης
Καρσούπης
Δεντούπης
Ἀξιδάρης
Ἀσπαμιθάρης
Δαμοθάρης
Σκάρης
Εὐμάρης
Τάρης
Εὐάρης
Παχάρης
Χάρης
Παγχάρης
Ἐπιχάρης
Πασιχάρης
Ἀντιχάρης
Θεοχάρης
Κλεοχάρης
Διοχάρης
Δαμοχάρης
Δημοχάρης
Ξενοχάρης
Πρωτοχάρης
Εὐχάρης
Πολυχάρης
Λεωχάρης
Σωχάρης
Χάβρης
Δίβρης
Πυρούβρης
Πίγρης
Παρυάδρης
Γαιδρῆς
Οἰσύδρης
Δερης
Βενέρης
Γήρης
Τήρης
Ὀρθαγόρης
Πυθαγόρης

Βουλαγόρης
Δημαγόρης
Σημαγόρης
Τιμαγόρης
Ἑρμαγόρης
Ἀναγόρης
Φαναγόρης
Ἀθηναγόρης
Ἀναξαγόρης
Μολπαγόρης
Ἡραγόρης
Μοιραγόρης
Ἡγησαγόρης
Μελησαγόρης
Μνησαγόρης
Στησαγόρης
Ἰσαγόρης
Θαρσαγόρης
Βριταγόρης
Ἀρισταγόρης
Πρωταγόρης
Εὐαγόρης
Νυμφαγόρης
Ἀρχαγόρης
Χόρης
Βεσπρης
Νάρρης
Σατρης
Πέτρης
Βότρης
Κπηεθύρης
Μύρης
Ζειβούρης
Ζούρης
Κούρης
Βάσης
Ναοκάσης
Μουκάσης
Κοσουμάσης
Πατουμάσης
Κράσης
Ἑορτάσης
Τάσης
Βρικέσης
Τραζυρέσης
Ζουλγήσης
Κήσης
Ζυκουλήσης
Οὐολογαίσης
Δαίσης
Ζυκουλαίσης
Μαίσης
Δορζείσης
Σίσης
Τυρέλσης
Βίλσης
Ἀστικόσης
Δάρσης
Θαρσῆς
Ἐπιθέρσης
Ἀκέρσης

Πέρσης
Θοθόρσης
Μόσσης
Πόσσης
Δωρίτσης
Λυσῆς
Σκαρούσης
Περύσης
Χρύσης
Δαικώσης
Καρώσης
Ἄτης
Σατραβάτης
Μιτραβάτης
Παραιβάτης
Μαιδάτης
Μιθριδάτης
Τουριδάτης
Μιθροδάτης
Μαγεάτης
Θάτης
Γαλάτης
Σαυρομάτης
Τιγραπάτης
Πάτης
Βιακράτης
Παγκράτης
Ἡγεκράτης
Μενεκράτης
Φερεκράτης
Χαιρεκράτης
Ἐχεκράτης
Δαϊκράτης
Δεϊκράτης
Καλλικράτης
Ἀναξικράτης
Δεξικράτης
Ἐπικράτης
Χειρικράτης
Πασικράτης
Στασικράτης
Μελεσικράτης
Τελεσικράτης
Ἡγησικράτης
Καλησικράτης
Τιμησικράτης
Κτησικράτης
Λυσικράτης
Σωσικράτης
Ἀντικράτης
Ἰφικράτης
Ὑψικράτης
Κράτης
Κλεοκράτης
Νικοκράτης
Φιλοκράτης
Δαμοκράτης
Πολεμοκράτης
Δημοκράτης
Τιμοκράτης
Ἑρμοκράτης

Φανοκράτης
Ξενοκράτης
Μηνοκράτης
Ἱπποκράτης
Ἁρποκράτης
Ἡροκράτης
Ἰσοκράτης
Ἀριστοκράτης
Αὐτοκράτης
Ἀλφοκράτης
Εὐκράτης
Εὐθυκράτης
Πολυκράτης
Ἀστυκράτης
Λεωκράτης
Σωκράτης
Εὐφράτης
Φιλοκτάτης
Τάτης
Λογχάτης
Τερδέτης
Ζηνικέτης
Ἀπολλωνικέτης
Μητρικέτης
Ἀλκέτης
Δαυκέτης
Ἀρέτης
Πυρέτης
Δινιζήτης
Αἰήτης
Νικήτης
Δεπανήτης
Μαχήτης
Δρομιχαίτης
Ἴτης
Πολίτης
Μανίτης
Καρνίτης
Μενοίτης
Ζιποίτης
Θερσίτης
Ὀψίτης
Θεοδέκτης
Ἐφιάλτης
Φιλτῆς
Ζόλτης
Δάντης
Μακέντης
Μέντης
Ὀρέντης
Ὀρόντης
Κρεσφόντης
Ἀμύντης
Βοτῆς
Νεότης
Ἀγιότης
Ἀρρωκότης
Ἀτότης
Τότης
Κερσεβλέπτης
Ἀνόπτης

Ζημοκάρτης
Βησάρτης
Μελικέρτης
Ναμέρτης
Γιβάστης
Διζάστης
Βουλάστης
Πατουμάστης
Πανάστης
Ἐραστής
Κεράστης
Πευκέστης
Γαλέστης
Τελέστης
Μέστης
Ὀρέστης
Βίστης
Μεγιστῆς
Φιλιστῆς
Ἀριστῆς
Κρατίστης
Μύστης
Ἄττης
Ἀττῆς
Ματάττης
Πόττης
Χαριναύτης
Ναύτης
Γλυκυτής
Κούτης
Ῥοιμηώτης
Νησιώτης
Κωλώτης
Ἀρώτης
Πρωτῆς
Χρυσώτης
Ἀτώτης
Μαδύης
Προτοθύης
Οὐαρηούης
Μαντύης
Διοτρέφης
Διστέφης
Νύμφης
Στροφῆς
Ἀβάχης
Ἐντρέχης
Λίχης
Ἀσιάρχης
Εὐτύχης
Αἰσυμώης
Δάαις
Σαββαΐς
Θηβαΐς
Σπαρόβαϊς
Σφαρόβαις
Ἀγαΐς
Γάϊς
Κάθαις
Θαΐς
Πούρθαις

Κούκαις
Χάλαις
Ἀγλαΐς
Ἀρχελαΐς
Λαΐς
Νικολαΐς
Πτολεμαΐς
Ἑρμαΐς
Στόρμαις
Ἀθαναΐς
Δυρπάναις
Ἀθηναΐς
Δικηναις
Ναΐς
Ἀργόναις
Γυναΐς
Ἡραΐς
Κάσαις
Βρισαΐς
Φλάβις
Φάβις
Κήζεβις
Δρεβις
Παιβις
Διτούπαιβις
Μακρόβις
Ἶρβις
Δρουβις
Ἆγις
Ζεισκεαγις
Σφραγίς
Μέγις
Γίς
Κυνηγίς
Μελγίς
Σέργις
Γάδις
Ἀμμαδίς
Ῥάδις
Βουράδις
Ἰραύαδις
Μάγδις
Σπέδις
Δεῖδις
Φεῖδις
Ἐλπίδις
Ἄλδις
Βενδίς
Μενδίς
Βόνδις
Ξηγόδις
Γόρδις
Κλαύδις
Σούδις
Ναεις
Δαππαεις
Ἀτταεις
Δαβεις
Θαβεις
Κίρβεις
Ζώβεις
Λώβεις
Καιγεις
Γάδεις
Πίδεις
Χόνδεις
Χάρδεις
Βούδεις
Βατουδεις
Δάζεις
Σθάζεις
Βρινκαζεις
Μοκαζεις
Μουκαζεις
Ῥειλαζεις
Ζουραζεις
Πιεζεις
Μιήζεις
Ζειζεις
Δατειζεις
Βενζείς
Κάρζεις
Αὔλουζεις
Βαθεις
Ζεκυνθείς
Γύκεις
Λυκεῖς
Δαλεις
Λίλλεις
Κόλλεις
Γοσήτλεις
Θχήτλεις
Θαμεις
Ἐμμείς
Νάνεις
Ἑρμιόνεις
Ὑβρεῖς
Σέρεις
Νηρεῖς
Ἀγόρεις
Δάσεις
Ζεισεις
Πάτεις
Γάστεις
Μέστεις
Ἴχεις
Δάζις
Δριαζις
Βρινκαζις
Μάζις
Δύβηζις
Σκηζις
Αἴνηζις
Κέτρηζις
Ῥοσηζις
Τσουκολειζις
Ἠνλιζις
Κέτριζις
Δεβαβενζίς
Ζουρόζις
Διαρζις
Κανδιτζις
Δάγουζις
Λόγωζις
Ὀξαρδώζις
Σῶζις
Μεννηΐς
Κοηΐς
Βρισηΐς
Χρυσηΐς
Ἰαθίς
Εὐήθις
Εἶθις
Ἰααθιθις
Θιθίς
Γουρθιθις
Ἄνθις
Ἀνθίς
Ζιμίκενθις
Πόθις
Πλατθίς
Βίτθις
Πίτθις
Πῦθις
Πυθίς
Ἀκρωθίς
Πρειις
Μυνιΐς
Ἀκίς
Βάκις
Ἀμασιακίς
Ἀκάκις
Στεφανάκις
Κασιγνάκις
Τάξακις
Ἀμαρακίς
Ἀρσάκις
Ζαικίς
Σιμπλίκις
Ἐπινικίς
Νίκις
Σουλπίκις
Πατρίκις
Μουσίκις
Μάκκις
Πάκκις
Χάλκις
Ἀνδοκίς
Δέρκις
Σέρκις
Αὔασκις
Λούκις
Μούκις
Ῥυμησυκις
Ἀρείβαλις
Βαζοβαλίς
Δάλις
Δαιδάλις
Πάρδαλις
Παρδαλίς
Δαλήζαλις
Ἀγχιαλίς
Κάλις
Δαμαλίς
Ἀρπαλίς
Διζάτραλις
Δυζάτραλις
Διάτραλις
Ζιακάτραλις
Μοκάτραλις
Μουκάτραλις
Σουράτραλις
Δισάτραλις
Εἰσάτραλις
Ἐπτάτραλις
Ἐπτέτραλις
Δαλήτραλις
Ζιαμήτραλις
Ἐπτήτραλις
Ἐπταίτραλις
Ζείτραλις
Κοσείτραλις
Δερζίτραλις
Βρασίτραλις
Δοσίτραλις
Κουσίτραλις
Τράλις
Διώστραλις
Βιθύτραλις
Αὐλούτραλις
Μεντούτραλις
Δυτούτραλις
Νατάλις
Βιτάλις
Παυτάλις
Κεφάλις
Πούβλις
Ἀέλις
Φούβελις
Ἀγγελίς
Μελίς
Ματελίς
Ἦλις
Ἠλίς
Αἶλις
Καικίλις
Ὁμίλις
Στατίλις
Οὔιλις
Φίλις
Ἀποβαλλίς
Θάλλις
Κάλλις
Τράλλις
Πυραλλίς
Μασκελλίς
Ἄπελλις
Λίλλις
Σίλλις
Φιλλίς
Κόλλις
Λόλλις
Πόλλις
Βυλλίς
Κύλλις
Σκύλλις
Φυλλίς
Μεζηνλις
Ἀσβόλις
Ἀδόλις
Βουκόλις
Διζάπολις
Ἀγέπολις
Ἐχέπολις
Ἀρχέπολις
Κεδρήπολις
Καλλίπολις
Ἀναξίπολις
Ἐπίπολις
Κετρίπολις
Ἡγησίπολις
Κρατησίπολις
Λυσίπολις
Σωσίπολις
Ἀμφίπολις
Θεόπολις
Κλεόπολις
Νεόπολις
Νικόπολις
Διλόπολις
Δημόπολις
Φανόπολις
Ἀκρόπολις
Μητρόπολις
Χρυσόπολις
Πρωτόπολις
Εὔπολις
Νεύπολις
Ἀβρούπολις
Δορύπολις
Σώπολις
Ἀφυκτολις
Στολίς
Ἀχολίς
Ὁπλίς
Πόπλις
Γῦλις
Διήγυλις
Βοθύλις
Μικυλίς
Βοῦλις
Ἰούλις
Κούλις
Σισουλίς
Κίνωλις
Λύγδαμις
Δάνδαμις
Λάμις
Δύναμις
Ἄτραμις
Πυραμίς
Πόταμις
Στάμις
Εὐξίθεμις
Ἰδάνθεμις

Ἀπολλόθεμις
Ἀγνόθεμις
Ζηνόθεμις
Μηνόθεμις
Ξεινόθεμις
Μολπόθεμις
Ἱερόθεμις
Ἡρόθεμις
Κυπρόθεμις
Σωθεμίς
Ἄρτεμις
Δῆμις
Διζάζελμις
Διάζελμις
Ἰσάζελμις
Ἀβέζελμις
Δολήζελμις
Δουλήζελμις
Μείζελμις
Δενδύζελμις
Ἀβλούζελμις
Αὐλούζελμις
Δεντούζελμις
Δυτούζελμις
Ἐβρύζελμις
Ζουροτελμίς
Δωρουτελμίς
Κάμμις
Ψάμμις
Βρόμις
Πάρμις
Πολυχαρμίς
Ὀνεράτμις
Ῥῶμις
Χρῶμις
Λιβάνις
Κυλίανις
Μᾶνις
Ὕπανις
Αὐλόσανις
Πρύτανις
Φάνις
Φανίς
Ἐπιφάνις
Θέογνις
Ἔζβενις
Θεαγενίς
Περιγενίς
Εὐγένις
Διζάζενις
Διάζενις
Βρινκάζενις
Μοκάζενις
Μουκάζενις
Δυλάζενις
Δουλάζενις
Ἀμάζενις
Ζεράζενις
Ἐπτάζενις
Δειζέζενις
Ἐπτέζενις
Ῥοιμήζενις
Δερζίζενις
Δορζίζενις
Βρίζενις
Δρίζενις
Εἰτίζενις
Δέρζενις
Διούζενις
Αὐλούζενις
Ἐβρύζενις
Ζένις
Παρθένις
Παρθενίς
Βρούθενις
Ἀλκενίς
Αὐλούκενις
Αὔλενις
Φιλοξενίς
Ἔβρενις
Δρένις
Διάσενις
Ἀρσένις
Ἔπτενις
Δύτενις
Σειταούενις
Ζῆνις
Ζηνίς
Μεσκῆνις
Σιληνίς
Λῆνις
Μῆνις
Νεομηνίς
Νευμηνίς
Νουμήνις
Νηνίς
Σπῆνις
Ἀνόπτηνις
Βωτῆνις
Αἶνις
Καινίς
Φιλαινίς
Δῖνις
Δινέδινις
Σισίνις
Ὑμνίς
Ναννίς
Τυραννίς
Σθέννις
Γοργόνις
Μακεδονις
Ἀρτιδονις
Χίονις
Χιονίς
Στρυμόνις
Εὐφρόνις
Εὐφρονίς
Σωφρόνις
Ἀρνίς
Καλποῦρνις
Δαῦνις
Δυνις
Φορτούνις
Δάφνις
Δαφνίς
Ποσειδώνις
Θεωνίς
Μαράθωνις
Κλοιωνις
Θαλωνίς
Ἀπολλώνις
Ἀπολλωνίς
Ἀμμώνις
Μαρωνίς
Ἱερωνίς
Τριτωνίς
Ἀντώνις
Τρυφωνίς
Γόαξις
Εὔπραξις
Εὔπραξις
Πρόσδεξις
Ἄλεξις
Ἶξις
Μάμοξις
Ζάλμοξις
Ζεῦξις
Ἀνάψυξις
Θαθοις
Φιλοσέραπις
Σαπίς
Πρέπις
Θεοπρεπίς
Δειγηπις
Ἦπις
Πιπίς
Ἐλπίς
Μόλπις
Λάμπις
Ὀλύμπις
Παντρόπις
Εὐτρόπις
Φιλιππίς
Κούσπις
Κροῦσπις
Σῶσπις
Ῥοδῶπις
Ἐλεκῶπις
Ὦπις
Δενθηβαρις
Δενθαιβαρις
Σάγαρις
Καθαρίς
Μάκαρις
Σκάρις
Φάλαρις
Μαμαρίς
Μάρις
Δολιχηνάρις
Ἀπολλινάρις
Ἰακησινάρις
Νάρις
Τόξαρις
Πάρις
Χρυσαρίς
Ζωσάρις
Χάρις
Πάγχαρις
Θεόχαρις
Δημόχαρις
Εὔχαρις
Νεβρίς
Ἀντανδρίς
Βρινκάζερις
Λάζερις
Δουράζερις
Ζουράζερις
Δαέζερις
Κετρέζερις
Κουίζερις
Ζέρις
Βουθειθερίς
Ζιέρις
Πιέρις
Πιερίς
Δουσπιερίς
Βαλέρις
Οὐαλέρις
Ἀγαθημερίς
Εὐημερίς
Ἱμέρις
Καρτέρις
Ἀστέρις
Ἦρις
Ἀντηρίς
Ἀνθεστηρίς
Σωτήρις
Σωτηρίς
Καβιρίς
Ἶρις
Χίμιρις
Μοῖρις
Κλεομοιρίς
Παπίρις
Σμῖκρις
Δυτουβορις
Παρηγόρις
Διζάπορις
Μοκκάπορις
Μοκάπορις
Μουκάπορις
Ἐπτάπορις
Δωλέπορις
Ῥαισκήπορις
Δαλήπορις
Ἐπτήπορις
Δίπορις
Κασείπορις
Τραλίπορις
Διλίπορις
Κετρίπορις
Πόρις
Ζινόπορις
Διόσπορις
Διούπορις
Διασκούπορις
Ῥασκούπορις
Ῥησκούπορις
Ῥαισκούπορις
Ἀλλούπορις
Αὐλούπορις
Μούπορις
Τατούπορις
Μεστούπορις
Δυτούπορις
Νεστορίς
Νικηφορίς
Συμφορίς
Κόρρις
Μᾶτρις
Ἀντιπατρίς
Κέτρις
Δημήτρις
Μῆτρις
Ἄμαστρις
Μέστρις
Ταῦρις
Φιλαργυρίς
Αἰδεζυρίς
Μουκαβίθυρις
Φιλοκύρις
Λυρίς
Βοῦρις
Δοῦρις
Ζιουρις
Μερκούρις
Σποῦρις
Σοῦρις
Κελέπυρις
Γηπεπυρίς
Ἐπτέπυρις
Ἐπτηπυρίς
Γηπαιπυρίς
Διάλπυρις
Γίλπυρις
Λαμπυρίς
Σατυρίς
Πορφυρίς
Χύρις
Δωρίς
Πυθοδωρίς
Ζείσκωρις
Σκῶρις
Τίμωρις
Ὄπωρις
Τηρίβασις
Κάσις
Ῥαδάμασις
Κάμασις
Ὕπασις
Σκώπασις
Βράσις
Βιτράσις
Εὐφράσις
Τασις

Κατάστασις
Ἀντίστασις
Πρωτάσις
Αὔασις
Φᾶσις
Πρόφασις
Ἄκεσις
Νέμεσις
Νουμέσις
Σύνεσις
Ἀρχεσίς
Ἄγησις
Ἥγησις
Διήγησις
Ζησίς
Κρατησίς
Ἐπίκτησις
Παῖσις
Ἀφροδίσις
Τεῖσις
Ἐπτέθισις
Ζαλσίς
Βοσις
Θεοδόσις
Κόσις
Πόσις
Ἀμβρόσις
Δροσίς
Κάρσις
Τάρσις
Ἀνάχαρσις
Περσίς
Θύρσις
Οἴκωρσις
Κάσσις
Κισσίς
Μελισσίς
Πόσσις
Σόσσις
Ἐλευσίς
Λῦσις
Δινύσις
Διονύσις
Δάγουσις
Πλοῦσις
Χρυσίς
Βῶσις
Γνῶσις
Σῶσις
Σωσίς
Σαββατίς
Σαμβάτις
Σαμβατίς
Βράματις
Δαλμάτις
Σκαμμάτις
Ἀβρατίς
Παγκράτις
Κρατις
Εὐκράτις
Σωκράτις
Μασατίς
Τατίς
Θέτις
Βαρκέτις
Δομέτις
Ἄρετις
Δομῆτις
Εὔμητις
Μαγνῆτις
Γιτις
Ζετιτίς
Δελτίς
Βραγάντις
Ἄμαντις
Μάντις
Ἀμαραντίς
Βησαντίς
Κωνστάντις
Δέντις
Φίντις
Λέοντις
Λεόντις
Λεοντίς
Δρακόντις
Δρακοντίς
Σκόντις
Νοτίς
Ἀρτίς
Σμέρτις
Τέρτις
Μυρτίς
Μέστις
Νέστις
Ἄλκηστις
Πλῆστις
Μοψύηστις
Φαιστίς
Πίστις
Ποσιστις
Μόστις
Στράττις
Βουτίς
Πλουτίς
Κοτυτίς
Κωτίς
Σεναμωτίς
Ἐρωτίς
Νικερωτίς
Πρωτίς
Εὐχρωτίς
Φωτίς
Μουκάπουις
Γραφίς
Εἰφίς
Δελφίς
Νύμφις
Ἀψιμάχις
Ἀγχίς
Νουνέχις
Διστιχις
Βακχίς
Βακχις
Ἀντιοχίς
Νικαρχίς
Ζειδυμαρχίς
Μοσχίς
Πανταυχίς
Παννυχίς
Ἡσύχις
Ἡσυχίς
Εὐτύχις
Εὐτυχίς
Εὐψύχις
Ἀνάληψις
Λάμψις
Μάδωις
Ζωΐς
Γάος
Δᾶος
Μίδαος
Ἄγλαος
Ἀγέλαος
Μενέλαος
Πρεπέλαος
Ἀρχέλαος
Ἀναξίλαος
Δεξίλαος
Περίλαος
Ἀρκεσίλαος
Ἀγησίλαος
Ἡγησίλαος
Ἀκουσίλαος
Σωσίλαος
Λᾶος
Πειθόλαος
Πυθόλαος
Ἰόλαος
Νικόλαος
Πευκόλαος
Τιμόλαος
Ἑρμόλαος
Φανόλαος
Χρυσόλαος
Κριτόλαος
Ἀριστόλαος
Ἰσχόλαος
Δορύλαος
Θρασύλαος
Δαναός
Τάναος
Πάτραος
Σάος
Τεύταος
Μεναος
Πρωτόφαος
Ἄβαβος
Βάβος
Σουάκαβος
Κώραβος
Καπρούβηβος
Φίληβος
Ἀραούηβος
Φοῖβος
Πριμιτῖβος
Σάνβος
Πρόβος
Βέρβος
Εὔφορβος
Κῶβος
Κάνωβος
Λάαγος
Ζάβαγος
Τούμβαγος
Βάδαγος
Αὐβάδαγος
Δάδαγος
Πάδαγος
Ἰέζδαγος
Μούρδαγος
Ἰέσδαγος
Πτούδαγος
Ἰνσάζαγος
Θίρθαγος
Ἀλούθαγος
Ἀδίαγος
Ἀζίαγος
Οὐζίαγος
Μανίαγος
Μάκαγος
Οὐαμψάλαγος
Σιπέλαγος
Λᾶγος
Βούπλαγος
Μύλαγος
Ἰωδέσμαγος
Ῥαμάναγος
Σάναγος
Ἀργουάναγος
Καφάναγος
Ἄβναγος
Ἄμναγος
Φλίμναγος
Φάρναγος
Κύναγος
Κουκούναγος
Μουκούναγος
Ῥηχούναγος
Βάξαγος
Ἀβρόαγος
Δουάραγος
Σιουάραγος
Ἄβραγος
Κόρραγος
Τράγος
Σεύραγος
Κάσαγος
Μουγίσαγος
Βάταγος
Ναύαγος
Ἰάφαγος
Πυλοφάγος
Ῥεκίθαγγος
Πολύδιγγος
Μελίφθογγος
Λόγγος
Κλόνηγος
Φιλοκύνηγος
Χόρηγος
Στράτηγος
Σαῖγος
Τλιγος
Ῥοῖγος
Βειτύριγος
Σιγος
Οὔσιγος
Σάρδανγος
Λόγος
Φιλόλογος
Σόγος
Ῥάσσογος
Ζάβαργος
Βάργος
Μάργος
Σύνεργος
Γόργος
Ἀμπέλοργος
Σάροργος
Μουλίουργος
Λυκοῦργος
Φιλοῦργος
Ἀσποῦργος
Πάρνουγος
Τούδρουγος
Ἀσφώρουγος
Θιάβωγος
Ἄρωγος
Χαρζαβόγαδος
Δάδος
Βραίαδος
Ἐπίκαδος
Κέλαδος
Ἀμώσπαδος
Ἰέζδραδος
Πρευρᾶδος
Φαδος
Ῥάλχαδος
Σμάραγδος
Δίκεδος
Ἔμπεδος
Ῥάζδος
Ῥαίζδος
Κάνδιδος
Δεῖδος
Κοῖδος
Λέπιδος
Πῖδος
Πολύϊδος
Ζάρανδος
Δίνδος
Σίνδος
Σεκοῦνδος
Ἰουκοῦνδος
Ἡσίοδος
Ζίποδος

Πρόσοδος
Εὐπρόσοδος
Εὔοδος
Ὀδίαρδος
Πάρδος
Σμόρδος
Μονόχορδος
Βαῦδος
Λύδος
Κλάδεος
Δέος
Ποσείδεος
Ποσίδεος
Σάκδεος
Ἀβρόζεος
Ἀπολλάθεος
Δεξίθεος
Εὐξίθεος
Τιμησίθεος
Πεισίθεος
Δωσίθεος
Ἀντίθεος
Μαντίθεος
Φιλόθεος
Τιμόθεος
Ἁγνόθεος
Δωρόθεος
Δωριεός
Ἡράκλεος
Ἄστεος
Ἄζος
Λάβαζος
Νάβαζος
Φαρνάβαζος
Οὔργβαζος
Σωχούβαζος
Χανσαβόγαζος
Πίνμαζος
Ἰνάρμαζος
Σαράξαζος
Καρζόαζος
Φαδιαρόαζος
Φανδάραζος
Ὄραζος
Χουάρσαζος
Μουρόψαζος
Βωρόψαζος
Δῆζος
Κέρδηζος
Βίζος
Δίζος
Δόριζος
Καίπριζος
Σκόζος
Χώδαρζος
Κέρζος
Βύζος
Κιλήβυζος
Δίζουζος
Μελτόκουζος
Βρύζος

Ἄβνωζος
Σώρωζος
Θαλάβηος
Ποσείδηος
Ποσίδηος
Φάρζηος
Θρασύλληος
Ἀζάμηος
Ἄρμηος
Ἀβρύμηος
Ἄγαθος
Φιλάγαθος
Ἐπάγαθος
Ἀνδράγαθος
Παντάγαθος
Σαρέδαθος
Χορόαθος
Χορούαθος
Ζείγεθος
Ζῆθος
Ἦθος
Πρόμηθος
Βόηθος
Γουρθειθος
Κόριθος
Τηρέτιθος
Ἄνθος
Ποίανθος
Ἄκανθος
Ξένανθος
Ξάνθος
Χρύσανθος
Διζάκενθος
Αὐζάκενθος
Μουκάκενθος
Ζιπάκενθος
Δεσάκενθος
Ἐπτάκενθος
Ἔκενθος
Ἀπτέκενθος
Ἐπτέκενθος
Κελήκενθος
Ζηνήκενθος
Ἐπτήκενθος
Ἐπταίκενθος
Σουδείκενθος
Κοζείκενθος
Δινίκενθος
Μεστίκενθος
Κένθος
Ῥαβόκενθος
Διάσκενθος
Βιθύκενθος
Ῥηβούκενθος
Αὐλούκενθος
Διτούκενθος
Δυτούκενθος
Ὑάκινθος
Πέρινθος
Οἴρινθος
Κόρινθος

Πόθος
Ῥόθος
Δανδάξαρθος
Ἀλλάξαρθος
Καινάξαρθος
Ἀλέξαρθος
Κηνέξαρθος
Διδυμόξαρθος
Δοσυμόξαρθος
Φαρνόξαρθος
Πάρθος
Ἄδοσθος
Δίβυθος
Γόργυθος
Μίκυθος
Σμίκυθος
Παράμυθος
Πιόθουθος
Ἡρόπυθος
Μητρόπυθος
Κέφθος
Ἀρραβαῖος
Βαῖος
Βέβαιος
Κενδεβαῖος
Ἐρρεβαῖος
Γαγγαῖος
Γάϊος
Ἀκτιγαῖος
Ἀργαῖος
Βεργαῖος
Γιργαῖος
Ἀδαῖος
Δαδαῖος
Κλαδαῖος
Σαδαῖος
Ἰδαῖος
Ἀρριδαῖος
Θρασυδαῖος
Ἀζαῖος
Δαζαῖος
Μαζαῖος
Κουζαῖος
Πουρθαῖος
Βιαῖος
Ἀζιαῖος
Ἴαιος
Ἐπιαῖος
Ἀκτιαῖος
Ἑστιαῖος
Ἱστιαῖος
Δικαῖος
Νίκαιος
Βρυκκαῖος
Ἀλκαῖος
Λυκαῖος
Ἀρχελάϊος
Φιλαῖος
Λάϊος
Ἀπελλαῖος
Κιλλαῖος

Ἀχιλλαῖος
Λολλαῖος
Γολαῖος
Ἀριστολάϊος
Εὔλαιος
Δουλαῖος
Ὑλαῖος
Δαμαῖος
Ῥαοδμαῖος
Πολεμαῖος
Πτολεμαῖος
Ἰνινθιμαῖος
Σιμαῖος
Τίμαιος
Ἀκμαῖος
Ἑρμαῖος
Βαιορμαῖος
Κωμαῖος
Ἀθάναιος
Φιλαθάναιος
Φαναῖος
Γναῖος
Ὑμεναῖος
Ξεναῖος
Ἀθήναιος
Λήναιος
Εἰρηναῖος
Καλλιναῖος
Ναῖος
Λιμναῖος
Βαρναῖος
Δερναῖος
Δαφναῖος
Ἰχναῖος
Παρθενοπαῖος
Ποππαῖος
Σωπαῖος
Ἀκέραιος
Περαῖος
Ὀπεραῖος
Ἡραῖος
Ἀγοραῖος
Κορραῖος
Πετραῖος
Ἀργυραῖος
Δυραῖος
Εὀφραῖος
Εὐφραῖος
Ἀκεσαῖος
Ταπερεσαῖος
Πεισαῖος
Νισαῖος
Ἀρσαῖος
Σαῖος
Μουσαῖος
Ἑκαταῖος
Κραταῖος
Ἀνταῖος
Ἀοταῖος
Ἑορταῖος
Ἀρισταῖος

Ἀγυαῖος
Ὑαῖος
Νυμφαῖος
Ἑρμοφαῖος
Εὔφαιος
Ἀχαιός
Ἀρχαῖος
Φλάβιος
Ὀκτάβιος
Φάβιος
Βίος
Βέβιος
Εὐσέβιος
Ἀρχέβιος
Ἀρακήβιος
Λίβιος
Καλλίβιος
Ἀναξίβιος
Εὐρησίβιος
Κτησίβιος
Σωσίβιος
Ἀντίβιος
Οὐίβιος
Ἀρχίβιος
Ἔλβιος
Ἴλβιος
Φούλβιος
Λεάμβιος
Ἑκατόμβιος
Θεόβιος
Ὀρθόβιος
Μηλόβιος
Ζηνόβιος
Ἀθηνόβιος
Ματρόβιος
Πατρόβιος
Μητρόβιος
Θεοφόβιος
Λέσβιος
Χηδόσβιος
Ἡδύβιος
Εὔβιος
Πολύβιος
Ἑρμανούβιος
Δρουβιος
Κώβιος
Ζαβάγιος
Βάγιος
Γάγιος
Λάγιος
Λυράγιος
Στρατήγιος
Σέργιος
Εὐστόργιος
Οὔργιος
Γεώργιος
Ὀρύγιος
Ὕγιος
Εἰκάδιος
Εὐκλάδιος
Γεννάδιος

Λαμπάδιος
Ῥάδιος
Χοαροφάδιος
Ῥαδαμψάδιος
Δῖος
Ἴδιος
Δαφνίδιος
Αἰφνίδιος
Ἐλπίδιος
Δαστίδιος
Ἀλφίδιος
Πέλδιος
Βένδιος
Ἁρμόδιος
Ἐνόδιος
Ῥόδιος
Χόδιος
Γόρδιος
Κονκόρδιος
Κλαύδιος
Δύδιος
Λύδιος
Εἰσγούδιος
Σούδιος
Βαλώδιος
Τίβειος
Ὤβειος
Ἀργεῖος
Μήδειος
Ποσίδειος
Αἰζειός
Κουθειός
Ἱστιειός
Λυκκειός
Λυκειός
Βασίλειος
Ἡράκλειος
Δημειός
Ἰνισμειός
Τίνειος
Ἄρειος
Δαρεῖος
Χορειός
Πυρρειός
Ἀστειός
Ζουράζιος
Παίζιος
Ζουρόζιος
Σανδάρζιος
Ὀξαρδώζιος
Ποσιδήϊος
Κοκκήϊος
Πομπήϊος
Κάθιος
Γνάθιος
Ζτάθιος
Εὐστάθιος
Ἀρχάθιος
Μεγέθιος
Μελάνθιος
Γένθιος

Περίνθιος
Ἀψίνθιος
Πίτθιος
Εὔθιος
Θιούθιος
Πύθιος
Ἰσαάκιος
Χοδιάκιος
Ἀκάκιος
Σκυλάκιος
Φαρνάκιος
Χοδέκιος
Γαδίκιος
Μουνδίκιος
Κυζίκιος
Φιλίκιος
Οἴκιος
Ἀγροίκιος
Σουλπίκιος
Δαρίκιος
Φαβρίκιος
Σαπρίκιος
Πατρίκιος
Πετίκιος
Στλάκκιος
Εὐτόκιος
Ἴρκιος
Ἄσκιος
Γαρρήσκιος
Λεύκιος
Λύκιος
Λούκιος
Μούκιος
Μώκιος
Μαμάλιος
Τράλιος
Νατάλιος
Φατάλιος
Βιτάλιος
Αὐγουστάλιος
Ἀσφάλιος
Πούβλιος
Οὐέλιος
Ταργήλιος
Δήλιος
Ἥλιος
Κορνήλιος
Αὐρήλιος
Γενέθλιος
Αἴλιος
Προκίλιος
Αἰμίλιος
Μίλιος
Σίλιος
Ἀτίλιος
Στατίλιος
Ῥοτίλιος
Φίλιος
Θάλλιος
Σάλλιος
Μέλλιος

Βιτέλλιος
Σερβίλλιος
Ἀχίλλιος
Προβόλιος
Ἀδόλιος
Δόλιος
Ἰόλιος
Ὀλίος
Ἀνατόλιος
Ὀξυχόλιος
Πόπλιος
Πούπλιος
Σαύλιος
Βούλιος
Ἰούλιος
Κούλιος
Μάμιος
Ἀβράμιος
Εὐφάμιος
Βινδέμιος
Ἀνθέμιος
Ἀποδήμιος
Ἄρθμιος
Σοζίμιος
Δεκίμιος
Ζιβέλμιος
Μέμμιος
Χόμιος
Διδύμιος
Σεπτούμιος
Φρεγάνιος
Ἀσκάνιος
Σκάνιος
Μειλάνιος
Ἀκλάνιος
Μάνιος
Αὐξάνιος
Γράνιος
Τιράνιος
Οὐράνιος
Ἀφράνιος
Ταρσάνιος
Εὐάνιος
Ἐπιφάνιος
Προφάνιος
Εὐφάνιος
Πριμιγένιος
Εὐγένιος
Παρθένιος
Ποιμένιος
Ὑμένιος
Ξένιος
Ἑρρένιος
Ἀρσένιος
Αὐχένιος
Ζήνιος
Ἀθήνιος
Νεμήνιος
Μήνιος
Νεομήνιος
Νομήνιος

Νευμήνιος
Νουμήνιος
Στρήνιος
Κυρήνιος
Μεσσήνιος
Εὐξείνιος
Λικίνιος
Φουλκίνιος
Καρμίνιος
Ἀκοίνιος
Κρισπίνιος
Οὐαρίνιος
Ἐλεοσίνιος
Ἐλευσίνιος
Ὀρεστίνιος
Δελφίνιος
Ἄννιος
Αὐτάννιος
Ἑρέννιος
Σισίννιος
Σαργόνιος
Τεργόνιος
Γοργόνιος
Μακεδόνιος
Μαρδόνιος
Ἐπιχθόνιος
Αἰμόνιος
Ἁρμόνιος
Στρυμόνιος
Νόνιος
Παννόνιος
Ἀτερόνιος
Κρόνιος
Καλοφρόνιος
Εὐφρόνιος
Χρόνιος
Πολυχρόνιος
Κησέρνιος
Κύρνιος
Καλπούρνιος
Φούρνιος
Βιθύνιος
Ἰούνιος
Μονούνιος
Στρούνιος
Ποσειδώνιος
Ποσειδεώνιος
Ζώνιος
Ἀργανθώνιος
Παιώνιος
Ἀπολλώνιος
Σολώνιος
Ἀμμώνιος
Πομπώνιος
Σεμπρώνιος
Πετρώνιος
Μουσώνιος
Ἀντώνιος
Ἄξιος
Δέξιος
Ἀλέξιος

Εὐδόξιος
Λαγοῖος
Φάρζοιος
Ὁμοῖος
Νοῖος
Μουτοῖος
Ἀθαφοῖος
Πάπιος
Θεοπρέπιος
Εὐπρέπιος
Θευπρέπιος
Ἀσκληπιός
Ἐγκόλπιος
Ὀλύμπιος
Πῖος
Εὐτρόπιος
Ἄππιος
Ῥούπιος
Γλαυκώπιος
Ἀσώπιος
Σαγγάριος
Τολμεάριος
Μακάριος
Ἱλάριος
Μάριος
Ἀπολλινάριος
Βελισάριος
Νεκτάριος
Ἰανουάριος
Εὐάγριος
Μαιάνδριος
Τιβέριος
Αἰθέριος
Ἐλευθέριος
Ἱέριος
Γλυκέριος
Βαλέριος
Οὐαλέριος
Νεμέριος
Ἱμέριος
Νουμέριος
Πατέριος
Πανθήριος
Εὐθήριος
Ἀνθεστήριος
Σωτήριος
Παρηγόριος
Γρηγόριος
Στερκόριος
Βοσπόριος
Σπόριος
Ἀνακτόριος
Νεστόριος
Ἄτριος
Δαμάτριος
Εὐπάτριος
Σάτριος
Μέτριος
Δημήτριος
Μέστριος
Φιλοκύριος

Παμμύριος
Ἀρδαβούριος
Γαζούριος
Σούριος
Ἀπατούριος
Μαρτύριος
Τύριος
Πορφύριος
Ἀχύριος
Ὥριος
Πογάσιος
Κραυγάσιος
Δάσιος
Θάσιος
Διάσιος
Νικάσιος
Κάσιος
Μουκάσιος
Δαλάσιος
Γελάσιος
Λάσιος
Χειμάσιος
Ἀθανάσιος
Ἀσπάσιος
Βράσιος
Γουράσιος
Πατάσιος
Ἀναστάσιος
Φάδσιος
Τεδέσιος
Αἰδέσιος
Ἱκέσιος
Βιήσιος
Νικήσιος
Μιλήσιος
Τιμήσιος
Καστρήσιος
Κρατήσιος
Ὀρτήσιος
Δαίσιος
Ἀφροδίσιος
Ἀρτεμίσιος
Χαρίσιος
Θεοδόσιος
Θευδόσιος
Ὅσιος
Πόσις
Κάσσιος
Θαλάσσιος
Παρνάσσιος
Μέσσιος
Σόσσιος
Ἐλεύσιος
Μύσιος
Διονύσιος
Σαββάτιος
Τρεβάτιος
Μάτιος
Μουνάτιος
Ὑπάτιος
Οὐηράτιος

Παγκράτιος
Στράτιος
Εὐστράτιος
Λουσάτιος
Στάτιος
Βονιφάτιος
Ἐσχάτιος
Εὐροψάτιος
Ἀέτιος
Μελέτιος
Δομέτιος
Λουκρήτιος
Ἀμισήτιος
Ἀκίτιος
Δουλκίτιος
Δομίτιος
Χαρίτιος
Ἀσυγκρίτιος
Δορίτιος
Τίτιος
Ἄκτιος
Ὀρσοάλτιος
Κάντιος
Μελάντιος
Πρεστάντιος
Κωνστάντιος
Μεστικέντιος
Βινκέντιος
Βουκέντιος
Βιγιλέντιος
Τερέντιος
Μαυρέντιος
Φλωρέντιος
Λεόντιος
Πόντιος
Γερόντιος
Αἰγύπτιος
Τέρτιος
Σιβόρτιος
Ἀνθέστιος
Κέστιος
Ὀρέστιος
Ἀφείστιος
Ἡφαίστιος
Ἵστιος
Φιλίστιος
Μόστιος
Σαλλούστιος
Καούστιος
Ἄττιος
Οὐέττιος
Σαβύττιος
Βύτιος
Τεύτιος
Κλύτιος
Ἀλβούτιος
Κούτιος
Εὐρύτιος
Δώτιος
Εὐΐος
Χρυσάφιος

Ἄλφιος
Ἀδέλφιος
Νύμφιος
Στρόφιος
Ἰνάχιος
Νουνέχιος
Βάκχιος
Εὐστόχιος
Ἡσύχιος
Εὐτύχιος
Ἀχελώϊος
Ὀτωιος
Φοργάβακος
Βάκος
Ψηβακος
Οὐαργάδακος
Δάδακος
Μάδακος
Πάδακος
Σπάδακος
Βράδακος
Ἀρδάγδακος
Δάκος
Τραΐδακος
Φόδακος
Σαβώδακος
Οὐαράζακος
Αὐράζακος
Μήζακος
Οὐαχώζακος
Μήθακος
Αὐάρθακος
Ἀμαίακος
Μαίακος
Χωνδίακος
Ἀμαρδίακος
Ὀχωδίακος
Ὀχωζίακος
Σεραπιακός
Ἀσκληπιακός
Σαρίακος
Κυριακός
Ὀαροζβάλακος
Μάλακος
Πάλακος
Ὀμφάλακος
Δαναράζμακος
Δήμακος
Ἀφθείμακος
Δρίμακος
Μακος
Θιάρμακος
Ὀμράσμακος
Σαύμακος
Ὀξύμακος
Καδάνακος
Φηδάνακος
Ἰασανδάνακος
Φλιμάνακος
Παρσπάνακος
Ἄβνακος

Ἐμίνακος
Λίμνακος
Χωδόνακος
Λαιόνακος
Κοκόνακος
Εὐβάρνακος
Φάρνακος
Ἀβλώνακος
Ἄπακος
Ἄσπακος
Σπάκος
Βωροβάρακος
Ἀβδάρακος
Ἀρδάρακος
Ὀσμάρακος
Στοσάρακος
Σάρακος
Ἥρακος
Πήρακος
Παίρακος
Θατόρακος
Βώρακος
Σώρακος
Μήσακος
Ῥαχοίσακος
Δαλόσακος
Φόσακος
Γώσακος
Βάτακος
Φιάτακος
Μήτακος
Σπάρτακος
Μάστακος
Βόστακος
Πιττακός
Βόττακος
Βύττακος
Ταύτακος
Ἰαύακος
Σιαύακος
Ναύακος
Ζεύακος
Μεύακος
Στρώφακος
Κούνχακος
Ἠθιόχακος
Σόρχακος
Χαύχακος
Νίχεκος
Πάταικος
Ἐφηβικός
Ἀμμάδικος
Ἀναξίδικος
Ἡγησίδικος
Βενδικός
Πολύνδικος
Νικόδικος
Δημόδικος
Φανόδικος
Ἡρόδικος
Πρόδικος

Ἀριστόδικος
Αὐτόδικος
Εὔδικος
Εὐθύδικος
Εὐρύδικος
Λεώδικος
Σκυθικός
Ἰταλικός
Βασιλικός
Βελλικός
Γαμικός
Σίμικος
Μῖκος
Κωμικός
Ἑλλάνικος
Κατάνικος
Φανικός
Τελένικος
Ἐχένικος
Εἰρηνικός
Καλλίνικος
Κομίνικος
Πραξίνικος
Ἐπίνικος
Ἐλπίνικος
Πασίνικος
Ναοσίνικος
Ναυσίνικος
Σωσίνικος
Νῖκος
Μακεδονικός
Θεόνικος
Κλεόνικος
Ἀγαθόνικος
Πυθόνικος
Δικαιόνικος
Κλοιόνικος
Ὀλυμπιόνικος
Φιλόνικος
Δαμόνικος
Δημόνικος
Ἀμεινόνικος
Ἱππόνικος
Κλαρόνικος
Ἀνδρόνικος
Ἡρόνικος
Χορόνικος
Ἰασόνικος
Στρατόνικος
Παντόνικος
Ἀριστόνικος
Εὔνικος
Βιθυνικός
Πολύνικος
Προύνικος
Δαφνικός
Ἰωνικός
Ῥόνοικος
Εὐνόϊκος
Ἀγροῖκος
Φιλιππικός

Ἀνδρικός
Ὁμηρικός
Ἐμπειρικός
Ὄρικος
Ἰσαυρικός
Ταυρικός
Ἰλλυρικός
Πάσικος
Σίκος
Μουσικός
Ἀσιατικός
Κρητικός
Πολιτικός
Εὐφραντικός
Ποντικός
Σκέπτικος
Ἀστικός
Μυστικός
Ῥουστικός
Ἀττικός
Ζωτικός
Γραφικός
Δελφικός
Τυχικός
Μηδόσακκος
Μίκκος
Μάνικκος
Μόκκος
Ὄκκος
Μόλυκκος
Μούκκος
Χόλκος
Σόνκος
Ἀμάδοκος
Σπαράδοκος
Σάδοκος
Μήδοκος
Σίνδοκος
Σκυθόδοκος
Ξενόδοκος
Εὔπλοκος
Ξηβάνοκος
Δάροκος
Κρόκος
Μοκασοκος
Ἀμάτοκος
Πάτοκος
Σαράτοκος
Σάτοκος
Μήτοκος
Σπάρτοκος
Σκόστοκος
Κάρκος
Μᾶρκος
Λούπερκος
Ῥεπτάτερκος
Δόρκος
Τόρκος
Ῥάσκος
Τάσκος
Σιαύασκος
Ἄρεσκος
Δαΐσκος
Ἑρμαΐσκος
Ἡραΐσκος
Φαΐσκος
Βαδίσκος
Ἀμμαδίσκος
Ποθίσκος
Δακίσκος
Λυκίσκος
Χρυσαλίσκος
Μηλίσκος
Βασιλίσκος
Φιλίσκος
Θεοφιλίσκος
Ἡδυλίσκος
Νεανίσκος
Πανίσκος
Μενίσκος
Παρμενίσκος
Κυνίσκος
Βοΐσκος
Γοΐσκος
Ἀρδαρίσκος
Ἀβρίσκος
Ἀνδρίσκος
Κορίσκος
Τραλιπορίσκος
Πρίσκος
Ταυρίσκος
Μυρίσκος
Συρίσκος
Σατυρίσκος
Λεοντίσκος
Γναφίσκος
Τόσκος
Ἄσσκος
Δίζασσκος
Βύσκος
Φοῦσκος
Γαῦκος
Γλαῦκος
Ἥδυκος
Σέλευκος
Βρεῦκος
Ἐπίλυκος
Λύκος
Ἑρμόλυκος
Λεοντόλυκος
Ἀριστόλυκος
Αὐτόλυκος
Ἄμυκος
Αὐλουσουκος
Τοῦκος
Κώρυκος
Ἐπτησυκος
Δεντουσυκος
Ἀμάδωκος
Αὔδωκος
Κῶκος
Δεκέβαλος
Δικέβαλος
Κέβαλος
Οὐάρζβαλος
Ἀρείβαλος
Ἀρίβαλος
Δρίβαλος
Οὐαστόβαλος
Βούβαλος
Ἀστράγαλος
Φωρδίγαλος
Ἄφδαλος
Δέζαλος
Ῥησπινδίαλος
Εἰθίαλος
Ἀγχίαλος
Πάγκαλος
Μίκαλος
Κάλος
Μίκκαλος
Βούκκαλος
Φιλόκαλος
Ὁλόκαλος
Δρύκαλος
Λάλος
Σίμαλος
Ῥευσίναλος
Ἵππαλος
Ἅρπαλος
Πάραλος
Τήραλος
Παιρίσαλος
Σάλος
Φάρσαλος
Θεσσαλός
Τανύσαλος
Γάταλος
Σπάταλος
Πέταλος
Βίταλος
Ἰταλός
Ἄτταλος
Βετταλός
Βίτταλος
Φίτταλος
Πώταλος
Εὐρύαλος
Ἀντύαλος
Κέφαλος
Βύβλος
Ῥῆγλος
Θεάγγελος
Ἀγαθάγγελος
Πυθάγγελος
Εὐάγγελος
Ἰάνγελος
Δούσκελος
Εὐτράπελος
Χρυσάμπελος
Βῆλος
Ἀρίδηλος
Ἀρίζηλος
Πολύζηλος
Φιλόμηλος
Εὔμηλος
Ἔπτηλος
Βίλος
Στροβίλος
Γίλος
Φρυγίλος
Βουργειλος
Νεῖλος
Σέρειλος
Βύσειλος
Μίλος
Βενῖλος
Σατορνῖλος
Βρῖλος
Χαιρίλος
Βασίλος
Μυρτίλος
Ἑρμάφιλος
Ἡράφιλος
Μενέφιλος
Φίλος
Δίφιλος
Ἀρεΐφιλος
Ἀρηΐφιλος
Πασίφιλος
Σωσίφιλος
Ἀντίφιλος
Πάμφιλος
Θεόφιλος
Δαμόφιλος
Δημόφιλος
Τιμόφιλος
Ἑρμόφιλος
Ξενόφιλος
Μηνόφιλος
Ἡρόφιλος
Μητρόφιλος
Στρατόφιλος
Ἀριστόφιλος
Ἡδύφιλος
Ζωΐλος
Τρωΐλος
Σπίκλος
Πρικλος
Θέοκλος
Δήμοκλος
Ἄνδροκλος
Πρόκλος
Πάτροκλος
Μάσκλος
Τρίβαλλος
Γάλλος
Θάλλος
Σάλλος
Μάρκελλος
Γέμελλος
Νόννελλος
Τέλλος
Ψελλός
Παΐλλος
Ἄγιλλος
Ῥήγιλλος
Ἐπόκιλλος
Ἄμιλλος
Πέριλλος
Κύριλλος
Τύριλλος
Εὔφριλλος
Κόλλος
Φάϋλλος
Γύλλος
Βάθυλλος
Τίμυλλος
Μύλλος
Μένυλλος
Λούκουλλος
Ἄπουλλος
Κάπυλλος
Πύλλος
Μάρυλλος
Νέρυλλος
Βήρυλλος
Κόπρυλλος
Βάσυλλος
Θράσυλλος
Ὕλλος
Πάτυλλος
Τέρτυλλος
Διζάολος
Εὔβολος
Αἴολος
Ἴολος
Νεόπολος
Στόλος
Κάτλος
Αὖλος
Κερσίβαυλος
Ἄπαυλος
Παῦλος
Βαβύλος
Ἀδύλος
Ἡδύλος
Βοδύλος
Μικύλος
Νικύλος
Δερκύλος
Σαμύλος
Δημύλος
Δριμύλος
Σιμύλος
Τιμύλος
Κωμύλος
Ῥωμύλος
Μεννύλος
Ἀρχέβουλος
Εὔβουλος
Κλεόβουλος
Ἀγαθόβουλος
Ὀρθόβουλος
Νικόβουλος

Ἡρόβουλος
Κριτόβουλος
Ἀριστόβουλος
Εὔβουλος
Πολύβουλος
Θρασύβουλος
Θεόδουλος
Χριστόδουλος
Βούκουλος
Τάλουλος
Σοῦλος
Οὔρσουλος
Παπύλος
Ἑβρύλος
Μηρύλος
Κοπρύλος
Ὀνήσυλος
Σαΐτυλος
Μεστύλος
Ἀττύλος
Βοττύλος
Δυτύλος
Σταφύλος
Βακχύλος
Αἰσχύλος
Μάσχλος
Ἄδωλος
Κίνωλος
Δρῶλος
Πάκτωλος
Χῶλος
Γάμος
Σόγαμος
Πέργαμος
Εὔγαμος
Τελέδαμος
Μενέδαμος
Ἀρχέδαμος
Ζευξίδαμος
Χαρίδαμος
Φρασίδαμος
Ἁγησίδαμος
Αἰνησίδαμος
Λυσίδαμος
Ἀρχίδαμος
Κλεόδαμος
Αὐτόδαμος
Εὔδαμος
Εὐθύδαμος
Εὐρύδαμος
Πρίαμος
Πλόκαμος
Θάλαμος
Κάλαμος
Εὐπάλαμος
Φαδίναμος
Φαζίναμος
Κίνναμος
Αὔναμος
Πύραμος
Σάμος

Ἴταμος
Ξάρταμος
Ἰράσταμος
Τεύταμος
Εὔφαμος
Ὄρχαμος
Δέγμος
Κάδμος
Σταπόλεμος
Τληπόλεμος
Εὐπόλεμος
Ἀρχεπτόλεμος
Τριπτόλεμος
Νεοπτόλεμος
Φιλήρεμος
Χόφραζμος
Μενέδημος
Ἐχέδημος
Ἀρχέδημος
Κλείδημος
Ἀλεξίδημος
Χαρίδημος
Ἀσίδημος
Ἀρεσίδημος
Ἡγησίδημος
Αἰνησίδημος
Σωσίδημος
Κρατίδημος
Ἀρχίδημος
Συνέκδημος
Ἔνδημος
Εὔδημος
Κλεόδημος
Νικόδημος
Φιλόδημος
Τιμόδημος
Ξενόδημος
Φιλαπόδημος
Ἱππόδημος
Ἰσόδημος
Στρατόδημος
Ἀριστόδημος
Εὔδημος
Πολύδημος
Ἀστύδημος
Εὔφημος
Φιλόφημος
Κριτόφημος
Εὔφημος
Πολύφημος
Πόρθμος
Αἶμος
Διδύκαιμος
Δούλαιμος
Ἄδιμος
Φαίδιμος
Ἄνθιμος
Δέκιμος
Ἄλκιμος
Δόκιμος
Ἄλιμος

Μόνιμος
Φρόνιμος
Εὐφρόνιμος
Μάξιμος
Αὔξιμος
Ῥοῖμος
Βήριμος
Μοίριμος
Πρῖμος
Ὥριμος
Ὀνάσιμος
Πράσιμος
Ζήσιμος
Ὀνήσιμος
Χρήσιμος
Σῖμος
Τρηστίσσιμος
Ζώσιμος
Νικασίτιμος
Πάντιμος
Ἔντιμος
Θεότιμος
Κλεότιμος
Διότιμος
Ἱκκότιμος
Φιλότιμος
Δαμότιμος
Δημότιμος
Ἑρμότιμος
Ξενότιμος
Ἀνδρότιμος
Ἡρότιμος
Πρότιμος
Μητρότιμος
Χωρότιμος
Ἀριστότιμος
Νόστιμος
Ναύτιμος
Εὔτιμος
Θεύτιμος
Πολύτιμος
Σώτιμος
Τρόφιμος
Δέκμος
Σάλμος
Μοκάζελμος
Δαλάζελμος
Ζώσιλμος
Σοῦμμος
Μομος
Αἰγίνομος
Νόμος
Θεόνομος
Ἀριστόνομος
Αὐτόνομος
Εὔνομος
Εὐρύνομος
Ἀστύνομος
Καλλίδρομος
Νικόδρομος
Εὔδρομος

Τόμος
Εὔστομος
Χάρμος
Πάγχαρμος
Μενέχαρμος
Ἐπίχαρμος
Πολύχαρμος
Ἕρμος
Θέρμος
Διονύσερμος
Χρύσερμος
Φίρμος
Ἴσορμος
Σύρμος
Λαῖσμος
Λογισμός
Μύρισμος
Κόσμος
Δύσμος
Ἄδυμος
Νήδυμος
Δίδυμος
Θῦμος
Θεώνυμος
Κλεώνυμος
Ἑκατεώνυμος
Πυθώνυμος
Ἀπολλώνυμος
Ἱαρώνυμος
Ἱερώνυμος
Ἡρώνυμος
Ἑκατώνυμος
Ἀριστώνυμος
Ἔτυμος
Νίκαιχμος
Μέναιχμος
Μενέσαιχμος
Φιλόκωμος
Ἄνος
Λίβανος
Σιλβανός
Κάρβανος
Γαγανος
Σπωτάγανος
Θυλόγανος
Ἴργανος
Πίδανος
Βιτιδανός
Ἀσπάνδανος
Ῥοδανός
Δάρδανος
Παντόρδανος
Εὐμενεανός
Ὀχάζανος
Μάθανος
Ξάρθανος
Γαϊανός
Φλαβιανός
Ἀραβιανός
Φαδιανός
Σαβιδιανός

Διδιανός
Κανδιδιανός
Εἰδιανός
Βασιλειδιανός
Ἐλπιδιανός
Νυμφιδιανός
Ἀρδινδιανός
Ῥοδιανός
Κλαυδιανός
Ἡρωδιανός
Σεβαζιανός
Κοκκηϊανός
Πομπηϊανός
Πυθιανός
Παντακιανός
Λαυδικιανός
Εὐρυδικιανός
Δονικιανός
Βερονικιανός
Σουλπικιανός
Φαβρικιανός
Μοκιανός
Μαρκιανός
Λυκιανός
Λουκιανός
Μουκιανός
Μινουκιανός
Βιταλιανός
Σκοπελιανός
Αὐρηλιανός
Αἰλιανός
Λουκιλιανός
Αἰμιλιανός
Βασιλιανός
Ἀτιλιανός
Χιλιανός
Ἡρακλιανός
Προκλιανός
Θαλλιανός
Μαρκελλιανός
Βιτελλιανός
Ῥηγιλλιανός
Νικοπολιανός
Ἰουλιανός
Στυλιανός
Φλίανος
Μαξιμιανός
Θεοτιμιανός
Τροφιμιανός
Δεκμιανός
Ἀμμιανός
Ἑρμιανός
Κοσμιανός
Κλεωνυμιανός
Πριμιγενιανός
Διογενιανός
Γαληνιανός
Μηνιανός
Σαβινιανός
Ἀννιανός
Ἑρεννιανός

Σισιννιανός
Μακεδονιανός
Πατερνιανός
Καλπουρνιανός
Λεωνιανός
Ἀπολλωνιανός
Ποταμωνιανός
Ἡρωνιανός
Νηρωνιανός
Ἀπρωνιανός
Παπιανός
Οὐλπιανός
Ὀλυμπιανός
Ῥοδοπιανός
Ἀππιανός
Φιλιππιανός
Κρισπιανός
Ἀλυπιανός
Βαρβαριανός
Μαριανός
Παριανός
Πασιχαριανός
Ἀδριανός
Βαλεριανός
Οὐαλεριανός
Κελεριανός
Σουηριανός
Νεοκοριανός
Ῥιανός
Κυπριανός
Ἀρριανός
Δημητριανός
Μεστριανός
Σκαυριανός
Συριανός
Ἰσιδωριανός
Θεοδωριανός
Σκωριανός
Πραιτωριανός
Ἀσιανός
Βασσιανός
Κασσιανός
Διονυσιανός
Χρυσιανός
Ὑπατιανός
Δημοκρατιανός
Νικοστρατιανός
Τατιανός
Μακετιανός
Δομετιανός
Τρυγητιανός
Δομιτιανός
Τιτιανός
Ῥεσπεκτιανός
Κουϊντιανός
Λεοντιανός
Ποντιανός
Ἀμυντιανός
Ἀσκληπιοδοτιανός
Τερτιανός
Σεβαστιανός
Καλλιστιανός
Αὐγουστιανός
Μουστιανός
Ἀττιανός
Ἐρωτιανός
Φλαουϊανός
Ἀντιοχιανός
Μοσχιανός
Εὐτυχιανός
Νικανός
Ξιαμφώκανος
Πέλανος
Σιλανός
Γενήμανος
Σαδίμανος
Λειμανός
Ἤλμανος
Ἀρθάμμανος
Ῥομανός
Ῥευρόμανος
Γερμανός
Ῥουμανός
Ῥωμανός
Νάνος
Νίπανος
Ὕπανος
Φαλδάρανος
Κάρανος
Βηρανός
Ἥρανος
Φορήρανος
Κοίρανος
Σίρανος
Στύρανος
Ἄσανος
Ζώρσανος
Μοντανός
Σκάρτανος
Οὔστανος
Φοριύανος
Σιλουανός
Στέφανος
Ὑπερήφανος
Πορφανός
Ἐπιτύγχανος
Μάγνος
Δηδηγνος
Ἔβενος
Λάζενος
Ἔλενος
Κτησαμενός
Τεισαμενός
Ἀναθεμενός
Εὐκτίμενος
Σωζομενός
Ἀλεξομενός
Φίρμενος
Κλύμενος
Ὀρνυμενός
Ἡγουμενός
Διαδουμενός
Ποθουμενός
Φιλουμενός
Ἐπίξενος
Χαρίξενος
Πασίξενος
Εὔξενος
Θεόξενος
Κλεόξενος
Διόξενος
Νικόξενος
Νειλόξενος
Φιλόξενος
Τιμόξενος
Ἡρόξενος
Χαιρόξενος
Πρόξενος
Ἀριστόξενος
Εὔξενος
Πολύξενος
Φιλάρσενος
Νάμγηνος
Σαλβιδηνός
Ὑγιηνός
Ἀνχαριηνός
Κάσκηνος
Γαληνός
Σεληνός
Σιληνός
Ἀργαμηνός
Χαράξηνος
Στρῆνος
Εὔηνος
Χόδαινος
Βρίνκαινος
Ἀγλάϊνος
Ἔπαινος
Πάνταινος
Πολύαινος
Σαβῖνος
Σιλβῖνος
Ἰουβῖνος
Ζωβῖνος
Λογγῖνος
Ἡγῖνος
Ῥηγῖνος
Ἐργῖνος
Βυργῖνος
Ὑγῖνος
Δαδῖνος
Σπάδινος
Ῥαδινός
Κάδδινος
Σεκουνδῖνος
Ῥόδινος
Βορδῖνος
Φαεινός
Ποθεινός
Κλεῖνος
Εὔξεινος
Ὄρεινος
Βριζῖνος
Ἀγαθῖνος
Ζώρθινος
Σκυθῖνος
Ἀττακῖνος
Οὐρσικῖνος
Ἀλκῖνος
Κερκίνος
Λυκῖνος
Λουκῖνος
Μούκινος
Κεβαλῖνος
Μικαλῖνος
Ἀμμαλῖνος
Εὐπαλῖνος
Μεσσαλῖνος
Φιλῖνος
Μαρκελλῖνος
Κατυλλῖνος
Εὐκολῖνος
Ἀνατολῖνος
Παυλῖνος
Ἀκυλῖνος
Αἰσχυλῖνος
Καπιτωλῖνος
Ἄμινος
Γέμινος
Δομνῖνος
Σατορνῖνος
Ἀντωνῖνος
Κοῖνος
Ποῖνος
Ἐλπῖνος
Κρισπῖνος
Ἐάρινος
Μαρῖνος
Ἰππαρῖνος
Χαρῖνος
Πατερῖνος
Μακρῖνος
Λαγορῖνος
Πυρρῖνος
Μυρῖνος
Σατυρῖνος
Φλωρῖνος
Βικτωρῖνος
Γελασῖνος
Ἐρασῖνος
Ἀρκεσῖνος
Ἡγησῖνος
Μνησῖνος
Κτησῖνος
Κελσῖνος
Μαρσῖνος
Μύρσινος
Χηματῖνος
Κρατῖνος
Στρατῖνος
Κλειτῖνος
Χαριτῖνος
Ταραντῖνος
Κωνσταντῖνος
Βαλεντῖνος
Οὐαλεντῖνος
Κλημεντῖνος
Φροντῖνος
Μαρτῖνος
Ἀστῖνος
Ὀρεστῖνος
Χρηστῖνος
Φαυστῖνος
Αὐγουστῖνος
Ἰουστῖνος
Ῥουστῖνος
Ταρουτίνας
Φωτῖνος
Ἀλφῖνος
Σοφῖνος
Ῥουφῖνος
Ἀρχῖνος
Θεότεκνος
Κύκνος
Σέμνος
Δίμνος
Ἀμέριμνος
Δόμνος
Σκύμνος
Δέκρυμνος
Αἴσυμνος
Ὕμνος
Τύραννος
Ἄρμεννος
Νίννος
Δίοννος
Σεγοῦννος
Ἐπίγονος
Ἰσίγονος
Ἀντίγονος
Ὑψίγονος
Πυθόγονος
Χρυσόγονος
Κόνος
Παράμονος
Νόνος
Παντάπονος
Λυσίπονος
Τόνος
Τέρπνος
Φάρναρνος
Μαίφαρνος
Κόφαρνος
Χόφαρνος
Πάτερνος
Κόθορνος
Θαῦνος
Ἀκίνδυνος
Εὖνος
Εὔθυνος
Ταόρδουνος
Κοῦνος
Κομμοῦνος
Δούπτουνος
Χαρμόσυνος

Εὐφρόσυνος
Δάφνος
Φιλότεχνος
Ῥίχνος
Βῶνος
Νάξος
Φιλόδοξος
Εὔδοξος
Πολύδοξος
Λέωξος
Πειρίθοος
Ἱππόθοος
Λείλοος
Ἀντίνοος
Χρυσόχοος
Ἄρκαπος
Πάπος
Κόλπος
Μόλπος
Εὔμολπος
Λάμπος
Θεόπομπος
Ὄλυμπος
Ἐρίσκοπος
Ἀέροπος
Θεόπροπος
Τρόπος
Εὔτροπος
Πάππος
Φιλόπαππος
Δάϊππος
Ἄγιππος
Γόργιππος
Ποσείδιππος
Φείδιππος
Κλέϊππος
Ξάνθιππος
Νίκιππος
Ἄλκιππος
Γλαύκιππος
Λεύκιππος
Δίλιππος
Φίλιππος
Κάλλιππος
Δάμιππος
Χάρμιππος
Ἕρμιππος
Μελάνιππος
Φάνιππος
Μένιππος
Εὐξένιππος
Ἀθήνιππος
Φαίνιππος
Ἀνάξιππος
Ἀλέξιππος
Ζεύξιππος
Χαίριππος
Μοίριππος
Μύριππος
Θούριππος
Νικάσιππος

Δαμάσιππος
Πάσιππος
Θράσιππος
Ἡγήσιππος
Μνήσιππος
Εὑρήσιππος
Κρατήσιππος
Θέρσιππος
Χόρσιππος
Λύσιππος
Χρύσιππος
Σώσιππος
Κράτιππος
Στράτιππος
Ἀρίστιππος
Πρώτιππος
Εὔιππος
Ἔφιππος
Ἄρχιππος
Λοῦππος
Πάγκαρπος
Κάρπος
Εὔκαρπος
Εὔκαρπος
Πολύκαρπος
Ὀξύτερπος
Διουσπος
Βόρασπος
Βαιόρασπος
Κρίσπος
Ὄσπος
Ἄλυπος
Παυσίλυπος
Ἄσωπος
Λύκωπος
Κάνωπος
Μελάνωπος
Αἴσωπος
Οὐανουνόβαρος
Βάρβαρος
Βούβαρος
Ἀνακούβαρος
Ἄγαρος
Θιάγαρος
Ἀρδοιάγαρος
Ξησάγαρος
Λέγγαρος
Χοάργαρος
Δάρος
Ζαΐδαρος
Ἄρδαρος
Λάζαρος
Μάζαρος
Ἔθαρος
Ἴθαρος
Κάνθαρος
Σπίνθαρος
Πώνθαρος
Κενθίαρος
Καλλίαρος
Ἀχαΐκαρος

Ἴκαρος
Κάρος
Κᾶρος
Κόκκαρος
Λεύκαρος
Λύκαρος
Ἴλαρος
Κλᾶρος
Χίμαρος
Μαρος
Κόμαρος
Ῥευρόμαρος
Ἀμωρόμαρος
Νίνναρος
Κόναρος
Χούναρος
Ζίπαρος
Ἄσαρος
Πάσαρος
Βάσσαρος
Τάταρος
Κοίταρος
Μάσταρος
Καύαρος
Πολύαρος
Οὐμβηούαρος
Φάρος
Χάρος
Ἄβρος
Ἔβρος
Κίμβρος
Μελέαγρος
Λέαγρος
Βάλαγρος
Τήλαγρος
Φίλαγρος
Σύαγρος
Νίγρος
Μόλογρος
Πάρεδρος
Φαῖδρος
Λάανδρος
Κλέανδρος
Νέανδρος
Ἀγάθανδρος
Περίανδρος
Ἀντίανδρος
Νίκανδρος
Ἄλκανδρος
Μέλανδρος
Φίλανδρος
Λᾶνδρος
Εὔλανδρος
Παλάμανδρος
Τίμανδρος
Διόμανδρος
Ἀθηνόμανδρος
Διονυσόμανδρος
Μένανδρος
Ξένανδρος
Ἀμείνανδρος

Ἀμύνανδρος
Ἀνάξανδρος
Ἀλέξανδρος
Ἔπανδρος
Ἥρανδρος
Ἄσανδρος
Ἀκέσανδρος
Ἀγήσανδρος
Ἡγήσανδρος
Νικήσανδρος
Ὀνήσανδρος
Στήσανδρος
Τείσανδρος
Λουκίσανδρος
Θέρσανδρος
Κάσσανδρος
Λύσανδρος
Σώσανδρος
Ἄντανδρος
Πάντανδρος
Ἀρίστανδρος
Εὔανδρος
Ἄρχανδρος
Ζώανδρος
Σώανδρος
Κόδρος
Ἔρος
Ἐλεύθερος
Ἰσίερος
Γλύκερος
Ἀγαθήμερος
Εὐήμερος
Ἵμερος
Βρομερός
Πρόμερος
Φανερός
Ἕσπερος
Ἑκατερός
Κράτερος
Καλλιότερος
Ἀμφοτερός
Τρύφερος
Βῆρος
Σεβῆρος
Γῆρος
Σιγηρός
Σίδηρος
Ὅμηρος
Σευῆρος
Σεουῆρος
Οὐῆρος
Σευουῆρος
Ὄρθρος
Ἐπίκαιρος
Καλόκαιρος
Εὔκαιρος
Πολύκαιρος
Φιλέταιρος
Σώταιρος
Σφαῖρος
Κύπειρος

Πάτειρος
Ἀντίμοιρος
Ἀροάστιρος
Οὐροάστιρος
Βάλακρος
Μάκρος
Σμῖκρος
Βόκρος
Λοκρός
Τεῦκρος
Βοῦκρος
Τελεσάγορος
Εὐάγορος
Πανήγορος
Ζινήγορος
Γρήγορος
Κόρος
Διόσκορος
Σκόρος
Ὄλορος
Ἀρχέμορος
Ἀγαθόμορος
Μοκάπορος
Νάπορος
Βόσπορος
Σπόρος
Εὔπορος
Ἰξύπορος
Δείσορος
Ἔφορος
Φόρος
Ἐλπιδηφόρος
Νικηφόρος
Ὀνησιφόρος
Σύμφορος
Ἀγαθοφόρος
Καρποφόρος
Δωροφόρος
Χριστοφόρος
Ζωοφόρος
Ἀνθεσφόρος
Τελεσφόρος
Φωσφόρος
Δορυφόρος
Καλλίχορος
Βόχορος
Λάμπρος
Κάρρος
Ἄγερρος
Πύρρος
Σωσίπατρος
Ἀντίπατρος
Πάτρος
Κλεόπατρος
Σώπατρος
Πέτρος
Μῆτρος
Κίτρος
Πυτρος
Γαῦρος
Μαῦρος

Ταῦρος
Φιλάργυρος
Μουκουνάκυρος
Δειδίκυρος
Αἴκκυρος
Κῦρος
Θάμυρος
Νανοβαλαμυρος
Λάμυρος
Γοῦρος
Πάκουρος
Ἐπίκουρος
Τάλουρος
Σκίλουρος
Γνοῦρος
Κόξουρος
Φροῦρος
Ζαίπυρος
Γηπαίπυρος
Ζίπυρος
Πύρος
Ζώπυρος
Δίσυρος
Σύρος
Σάτυρος
Τίτυρος
Γλάφυρος
Πόρφυρος
Αἶσχρος
Κάλλαισχρος
Νιβλόβωρος
Δῶρος
Μενέδωρος
Βενδίδωρος
Μενδίδωρος
Ἀρτεμίδωρος
Μενίδωρος
Ἀναξίδωρος
Ματρίδωρος
Ἰσίδωρος
Διονυσίδωρος
Ἀντίδωρος
Θεόδωρος
Ἡρακλεόδωρος
Ἐτεόδωρος
Ἀγαθόδωρος
Πυθόδωρος
Διόδωρος
Ἡρακλειόδωρος
Ἡλιόδωρος
Βασιλιόδωρος
Ἀσκλαπιόδωρος
Ἀσκληπιόδωρος
Ὀλυμπιόδωρος
Ὀλυνπιόδωρος
Διονυσιόδωρος
Ἀχιλλόδωρος
Ἀπολλόδωρος
Ἑρμόδωρος
Ἀθανόδωρος
Ζηνόδωρος

Ἀθηνόδωρος
Μηνόδωρος
Σεραπόδωρος
Ἡρόδωρος
Μοιρόδωρος
Ματρόδωρος
Ἰητρόδωρος
Μητρόδωρος
Ἰστρόδωρος
Αἰσχρόδωρος
Κηφισόδωρος
Διονυσόδωρος
Χρυσόδωρος
Ἑκατόδωρος
Ἐχετόδωρος
Λητόδωρος
Κλειτόδωρος
Ἀφαιστόδωρος
Ἡφαιστόδωρος
Νυμφόδωρος
Νυνφόδωρος
Εὔδωρος
Θεύδωρος
Πολύδωρος
Θέωρος
Πύλωρος
Φλῶρος
Ὦρος
Ἄσος
Πήγασος
Ῥωδίγασος
Οὐσίγασος
Μάνδασος
Μόκασος
Καύκασος
Λούκασος
Μούκασος
Δάμασος
Κοζείμασος
Βιόμασος
Βράσος
Σινβρασος
Μετοέρασος
Μουκάβεσος
Ἐπτήκησος
Κῆσος
Ὄνησος
Ῥῆσος
Τάμβισος
Καιγεισος
Μουκασεισος
Πιεισεισος
Σκωρισεισος
Ἶσος
Πίνκισος
Ῥοίμισος
Τανάσισος
Ζεισισος
Κήφισος
Δάμαλσος
Κέλσος

Σιαύνανσος
Σιρδούχανσος
Κένσος
Ζορδησιοσος
Δρόσος
Ἰδάνθυρσος
Θύρσος
Μύρσος
Πύρσος
Βάσσος
Παρνασσός
Βεσσός
Σουκκεσσός
Πιεπησσος
Ναϊσσός
Κίσσος
Νάρκισσος
Μολοσσός
Νοσσός
Καρωσσός
Λῦσος
Πλύσος
Ῥύμυσος
Διόνυσος
Βιτούλουσος
Πατάμουσος
Φιλόμουσος
Γετόμουσος
Εὔμουσος
Δροῦσος
Πειεσουσος
Σοῦσος
Ἑπτάχρυσος
Χρῦσος
Καλλίχρυσος
Ἰσόχρυσος
Ῥαθάγωσος
Σαυαίωσος
Χάνωσος
Κνῶσος
Σῶσος
Βάτος
Πριβᾶτος
Δεδατος
Ἀδευδᾶτος
Κτέατος
Ἀμβίκατος
Ἀνίκατος
Κάτος
Τορκᾶτος
Βρυκατος
Λᾶτος
Παλμᾶτος
Ζάνατος
Βενενᾶτος
Νωμινᾶτος
Λεόννατος
Φορτουνᾶτος
Δωνᾶτος
Ἄρατος
Δημάρατος

Παρᾶτος
Σάρατος
Εὐάρατος
Πολυάρατος
Νυμφάρατος
Γρᾶτος
Κοδρᾶτος
Ἰδήρατος
Νικήρατος
Ἐπήρατος
Πολυήρατος
Ἄκρατος
Λάστρατος
Ἀγέστρατος
Ἡγέστρατος
Μενέστρατος
Ἐχέστρατος
Ἀρχέστρατος
Καλλίστρατος
Ἀναξίστρατος
Ἐπίστρατος
Ἀγησίστρατος
Ἡγησίστρατος
Μνησίστρατος
Πεισίστρατος
Ναυσίστρατος
Λυσίστρατος
Σωσίστρατος
Κλεόστρατος
Νικόστρατος
Φιλόστρατος
Δαμόστρατος
Δημόστρατος
Τιμόστρατος
Ἑρμόστρατος
Φανόστρατος
Δεινόστρατος
Ἱππόστρατος
Μανδρόστρατος
Ἡρόστρατος
Κλειτόστρατος
Ἰθύστρατος
Πολύστρατος
Εὐρύστρατος
Λεώστρατος
Σώστρατος
Πλευρᾶτος
Πρευρᾶτος
Δεκουρᾶτος
Μακεσατος
Μακάρτατος
Ὑπέρτατος
Τορκουᾶτος
Βετος
Παρίγετος
Εὔθετος
Οὐένετος
Αἴνετος
Θεαίνετος
Κλεαίνετος
Δημαίνετος

Τιμαίνετος
Ἐπαίνετος
Ἀρισταίνετος
Εὐαίνετος
Πολυαίνετος
Σοφαίνετος
Σύνετος
Δαμάρετος
Δημάρετος
Παντάρετος
Εὔρετος
Ἄρχετος
Ἀγάητος
Ἀφόβητος
Δαμάγητος
Θεαίδητος
Εὐποίητος
Ἀνίκητος
Μέλητος
Φίλητος
Εὐφίλητος
Ἀνέγκλητος
Ἀχίλλητος
Ἄδμητος
Ἀτίμητος
Μητος
Ἐπιθύμητος
Θεόγνητος
Διόγνητος
Δαμόγνητος
Αἴνητος
Καλογέννητος
Ἀφθόνητος
Ἀγαπητός
Ἀλύπητος
Ἄρητος
Πολυάρητος
Ἐπίκτητος
Κτῆτος
Δίαιτος
Παῖτος
Βίτος
Ἀφρόδιτος
Ἑρμαφρόδιτος
Ἐπαφρόδιτος
Καλλίγειτος
Ἡρόγειτος
Ἡράκλειτος
Κλεῖτος
Ἡρόκλειτος
Πολύκλειτος
Μίτος
Κλεαίνιτος
Προῖτος
Ἀμφήριτος
Λάκριτος
Ἀνάκριτος
Ἀσύγκριτος
Καλλίκριτος
Κρίτος
Θεόκριτος

Λεόκριτος
Δαμόκριτος
Ἀνθεμόκριτος
Δημόκριτος
Φανόκριτος
Ἁγνόκριτος
Ξενόκριτος
Ἀθηνόκριτος
Μηνόκριτος
Ἱππόκριτος
Πρόκριτος
Ἀριστόκριτος
Εὔκριτος
Θεύκριτος
Πολύκριτος
Ἀγλώκριτος
Σώκριτος
Φώκριτος
Ἀμφίτριτος
Σίτος
Τίτος
Εὔτακτος
Πρόσδεκτος
Σάνκτος
Εὖκτος
Πολύευκτος
Ἀβάσκαντος
Ἀπήμαντος
Ἀδείμαντος
Ἀμάραντος
Ἔκφαντος
Θεόφαντος
Λεόφαντος
Διόφαντος
Ἑρμόφαντος
Ξενόφαντος
Ἡρόφαντος
Μητρόφαντος
Εὔφαντος
Πολύφαντος
Λεώφαντος
Δέντος
Δέκεντος
Θίντος
Κόϊντος
Κούϊντος
Δύντος
Κάραξτος
Σέξτος
Τανύβοτος
Γότος
Ἀναξίδοτος
Ἰσίδοτος
Ἀντίδοτος
Θεόδοτος
Πυθόδοτος
Διόδοτος
Ἀσκληπιόδοτος
Ἀπολλόδοτος
Δημόδοτος
Ἑρμόδοτος

Ζηνόδοτος
Ἀθηνόδοτος
Μηνόδοτος
Ἡρόδοτος
Μητρόδοτος
Κηφισόδοτος
Διονυσόδοτος
Θυόδοτος
Θεύδοτος
Εὐβίοτος
Κοζισίοτος
Κότος
Πότος
Φιλοδέσποτος
Ἀρχέμβροτος
Ἡγησίμβροτος
Θεόμβροτος
Κλεόμβροτος
Ἄγροτος
Μύροτος
Σπαρόφοτος
Ἄπτος
Γράπτος
Ῥεκέπτος
Θρέπτος
Θεόπεμπτος
Αἴγυπτος
Ἰζίμαρτος
Μάσαρτος
Κούαρτος
Σμέρτος
Σκίρτος
Γύρτος
Ῥαδαμόφουρτος
Ἄστος
Βάστος
Ἀμάρθαστος
Ἀμώρθαστος
Ἄκαστος
Κάστος
Βλάστος
Ὀνόμαστος
Θαύμαστος
Θεόμναστος
Ἀρδόναστος
Ἄδραστος
Ἔραστος
Ἀγόραστος
Θεόφραστος
Ξερμοδίγεστος
Μόδεστος
Ἑρμόθεστος
Ἄκεστος
Ἐξάκεστος
Ἐξήκεστος
Μέστος
Ἡρόνεστος
Ἄρεστος
Εὐάρεστος
Ἀρίμνηστος
Θεόμνηστος

Πολύμνηστος
Ἄδρηστος
Χρῆστος
Θεόχρηστος
Θεύχρηστος
Φῆστος
Σόαιστος
Ἄδιστος
Ἥδιστος
Ῥαδάμειστος
Βίλιστος
Φίλιστος
Κάλλιστος
Θέμιστος
Ζουκηπιστος
Εὐέλπιστος
Πίστος
Ἄριστος
Εὐάριστος
Εὐχάριστος
Κράτιστος
Θεόκτιστος
Χάραξστος
Πανάρμοστος
Εὔνοστος
Φαῦστος
Ξύστος
Ἄμβουστος
Ἰράμβουστος
Ἰοῦστος
Ἄγνωστος
Εὔγνωστος
Στράττος
Κλύτος
Κόλλυτος
Ἱππόλυτος
Πίνυτος
Ἀργοῦτος
Ἀκοῦτος
Κορνοῦτος
Εὔρυτος
Νεόφυτος
Βοιωτός
Παντάγνωτος
Ἀρίγνωτος
Εὔγνωτος
Πολύγνωτος
Πρῶτος
Δίδαυος
Μάρδαυος
Φορίαυος
Σίαυος
Βαγδόσαυος
Γοδόσαυος
Σοζίρσαυος
Ὀρωίδυος
Χόμευος
Τέττευος
Ἀτήθυος
Διονυος
Δομύνυος

Λοῦος
Ἐπτηπουος
Ζέφος
Τήλεφος
Φιλάδελφος
Δελφός
Εὔνυμφος
Σύντροφος
Τρόφος
Σαύροφος
Κλείσοφος
Σόφος
Καλλίμορφος
Εὔμορφος
Ῥοῦφος
Κόρυφος
Ἄφφος
Μίδαχος
Δάμαχος
Ἰάμαχος
Λάμαχος
Πυλάμαχος
Ἀγέμαχος
Τηλέμαχος
Μενέμαχος
Ἀρχέμαχος
Δαΐμαχος
Δηΐμαχος
Ἀλκίμαχος
Καλλίμαχος
Ἀλεξίμαχος
Ποίμαχος
Ἐπίμαχος
Θηρίμαχος
Ἰασίμαχος
Μνασίμαχος
Πασίμαχος
Ἡγησίμαχος
Κλεισίμαχος
Παοσίμαχος
Ναυσίμαχος
Παυσίμαχος
Λυσίμαχος
Σωσίμαχος
Ἀντίμαχος
Ἀμφίμαχος
Σύμμαχος
Κλεόμαχος
Νικόμαχος
Τιμόμαχος
Φανόμαχος
Δεινόμαχος
Μονόμαχος
Ἱππόμαχος
Ἀνδρόμαχος
Καρτερόμαχος
Λαμπρόμαχος
Πρόμαχος
Κλειτόμαχος
Ἀριστόμαχος
Πρωτόμαχος

Ἰσχόμαχος
Ἀδύρμαχος
Εὔμαχος
Δορύμαχος
Εὐρύμαχος
Θρασύμαχος
Σιώμαχος
Σώμαχος
Ἴναχος
Πόρναχος
Σίραχος
Βρόταχος
Ἀρσηούαχος
Ἄψαχος
Ἔλεγχος
Ὀρστόμηχος
Λάϊχος
Στρόμβιχος
Καραΐϊχος
Ἰάμβλιχος
Δόλιχος
Σουπόλιχος
Θάμιχος
Σίμιχος
Σίμμιχος
Ὑπάνιχος
Εἰράνιχος
Παρμένιχος
Δεκάμνιχος
Νάννιχος
Δύννιχος
Θεώνιχος
Φιλώνιχος
Ὀλύμπιχος
Ἄριχος
Τυνδάριχος
Λαάνδριχος
Σωτήριχος
Βοσπόριχος
Πύρριχος
Μήτριχος
Βότριχος
Βύριχος
Πύριχος
Πάσιχος
Ἀμύντιχος
Δηλόπτιχος
Στίχος
Ζώτιχος
Ὀλώϊχος
Ἡρώϊχος
Βάκχος
Ἴακχος
Μάλχος
Κόλχος
Σάνχος
Βάγδοχος
Ξενόδοχος
Ἀντίοχος
Ἰάμβλοχος
Ἀγέλοχος

Ἡγέλοχος
Ἀρχέλοχος
Ἡγησίλοχος
Θερσίλοχος
Ἀντίλοχος
Ἀμφίλοχος
Ἀρχίλοχος
Λόχος
Ἱππόλοχος
Ἀριστόλοχος
Εὐρύλοχος
Θρασύλοχος
Ἔξοχος
Ἔποχος
Ἀσάνδροχος
Ὑπέροχος
Ἄρχος
Ἑκάγαρχος
Κλέαρχος
Νέαρχος
Ἀγάθαρχος
Πεδίαρχος
Ἀλίαρχος
Θαλίαρχος
Φιλίαρχος
Νίκαρχος
Θεσσάλαρχος
Ἄγλαρχος
Φίλαρχος
Βούλαρχος
Πολέμαρχος
Πτολέμαρχος
Δήμαρχος
Ζήμαρχος
Τίμαρχος
Διδύμαρχος
Ξέναρχος
Δείναρχος
Ἀνάξαρχος
Ἀλέξαρχος
Ἵππαρχος
Ἡγήσαρχος
Σώσαρχος
Στράταρχος
Πλείσταρχος
Ἀρίσταρχος
Πλούταρχος
Πρώταρχος
Εὔαρχος
Πολύαρχος
Μόσχος
Πάναυχος
Πάνταυχος
Φαῦχος
Πάννυχος
Δαδοῦχος
Ναμοῦχος
Δημοῦχος
Ἥσυχος
Καλάτυχος
Καλλίτυχος

Εὔτυχος
Μάνιχχος
Κόναψος
Βλέψος
Μαίσωος
Κερζετραυς
Ἀνδράβυς
Λίβυς
Δρῶβυς
Θάγυς
Ἄδυς
ϝαδδῦς
Ἥδυς
Βραβεύς
Ἐργεύς
Ὀργεύς
Χαλκιδεύς
Καριδεύς
Κρηθεύς
Μενεσθεύς
Διεύς
Πεδιεύς
Ἀριεύς
Δωριεύς
Ἰασιεύς
Λυγκεύς
Βιλκεύς
Ποκεύς
Αἰγιαλεύς
Ἁρπαλεύς
Βασιλεύς
Χρυσαλλεύς
Κιλλεύς
Ἀχιλλεύς
Μυκηνεύς
Ἀλκυονεύς
Ἐτεωνεύς
Ἀρεύς
Βριαρεύς
Μακαρεύς
Βασταρεύς
Ἀφαρεύς
Βοσπορεύς
Κασεύς
Θησεύς
Περσεύς
Μεγιστεύς
Ἀριστεύς
Χοσοχερεφεύς
Ὀρφεύς
Τειχεύς
Ἄθυς
Συραβίθυς
Βίθυς
Κειλαίβιθυς
Τραίβιθυς
Δίβιθυς
Κοζίβιθυς
Δητούβιθυς
Θῦς
Βύθυς

Ἄλυς
Θῆλυς
Τῆλυς
Ἄσκλυς
Φίλλυς
Γόλυς
Πόλυς
Μῦς
Μέννυς
Δίννυς
Δεονῦς
Διονῦς
Θαβοῦς
Βειβους
Σαμβοῦς
Θαγοῦς
Συβλιαγους
Σιαγοῦς
Χοραγοῦς
Ἡγοῦς
Ποτηγοῦς
Σόγους
Βαδοῦς
Δαδοῦς
Ἡδοῦς
Καρδοῦς
Σεους
Μαζοῦς
Ζαζζοῦς
Ἡζοῦς
Ἀγαθοῦς
Ποθοῦς
Θουθους
Φαδιους
Καρδίους
Φαζιους
Γοζιοῦς
Θιαθιοῦς
Δημητριοῦς
Κοτιοῦς
Μουκαπουιους
Κακοῦς
Νηνακοῦς
Σεκοῦς
Νικοῦς
Σικους
Μοκκοῦς
Γοκους
Δειοκοῦς
Σαρκοῦς
Τορκοῦς
Δισκοῦς
Διοσκοῦς
Σουκους
Κοωκοῦς
Καλοῦς
Δελοῦς
Ἀπολλοῦς
Δροβολους
Λολοῦς
Εὔπλους

Θαμοῦς
Σιδμοῦς
Σεμοῦς
Ἑρμοῦς
Φιδανους
Νανοῦς
Ἰνγένους
Ἀρχένους
Ἀλκίνους
Ἐπίνους
Πασίνους
Πρόνους
Ἀριστόνους
Εὔνους
Εὐθύνους
Κουνοῦς
Παποῦς
Σεραποῦς
Ἀρτίπους
Μελάμπους
Ἀγαθόπους
Παππoῦς
Ζωσαροῦς
Μασταροῦς
Τυχαροῦς
Πατεροῦς
Ἡροῦς
Εὔχρους
Δωροῦς
Κοσοῦς
Ταρσοῦς
Βασσοῦς
Κοσσοῦς
Νοσσοῦς
Χοσσοῦς
Κουσοῦς
Χρυσοῦς
Ζωσοῦς
Ἀτοῦς
Ἐπικτοῦς
Δαντοῦς
Μαντοῦς
Δεντοῦς
Σουντους
Ζουδιεγιπτους
Καρτοῦς
Μαστοῦς
Χρηστοῦς
Πιστοῦς
Δωτοῦς
Ἀλφοῦς
Ἀπφοῦς
Ἀφφοῦς
Ἔπταπυς
Ζίπυς
Τάρυς
Ἄνδρυς
Γῆρυς
Κάμρυς
Βόρυς
Βότρυς

Ὄλγασυς
Θράσυς
Μάτασυς
Βλόσυς
Τάτυς
Κλιτύς
Βότυς
Κότυς
Μέστυς
Πρῶτυς
Στάχυς
Ἀττίδως
Ἐχέλεως
Καλλίλεως
Ἀναξίλεως
Δαμασίλεως
Πειθεσίλεως
Ἀρκεσίλεως
Ἡγησίλεως
Στησίλεως
Ὀρσίλεως
Ἀκουσίλεως
Σωσίλεως
Φανόλεως
Ἀριστόλεως
Ἄθως
Γέλως
Ἀπολλῶς
Μίνως
Νέπως
Παιδέρως
Ἔρως
Πειθέρως
Νικέρως
Φιλέρως
Ἑρμέρως
Πανέρως
Ὑγινέρως
Συνέρως
Χρυσέρως
Ἀντέρως
Πλουτέρως
Νυμφέρως
Δωρώς
Κότως
Τοφῶς
Σεακού
Μακού
Φιλού
Μαρού
Ποτού
Ἰωσήφ
Πέλοψ
Κέκροψ
Κώνωψ
Φέρωψ
Τιργαταώ
Βιβώ
Σαμβώ
Ἀγώ
Ἐπιγώ

The manufacturer's authorised representative in the EU for product safety is Oxford University Press España S.A. of El Parque Empresarial San Fernando de Henares, Avenida de Castilla, 2 – 28830 Madrid (www.oup.es/en or product.safety@oup.com). OUP España S.A. also acts as importer into Spain of products made by the manufacturer.

Printed in the USA/Agawam, MA
April 3, 2025

885274.023